The SportingNews
HOCKEY
REGISTER
2001-2002 EDITION

Editors/Hockey Register
JEFF PAUR
DAVID WALTON

ON THE COVER: Mario Lemieux of the Pittsburgh Penguins. (Photos by Albert Dickson/THE SPORTING NEWS.)

Spine photo: Patrick Roy (File photo).

ISBN: 0-89204-654-6

10 9 8 7 6 5 4 3 2 1

CONTENTS

EXPLANATION OF AWARDS

NHL AWARDS: Alka-Seltzer Plus Award: plus/minus leader. **Art Ross Trophy:** leading scorer. **Bill Masterton Memorial Trophy:** perseverance, sportsmanship and dedication to hockey. **Bud Light/NHL Man of the Year:** service to community; called Budweiser/NHL Man of the Year prior to 1990-91. **Budweiser/NHL Man of the Year:** service to community; renamed Bud Light/NHL Man of the Year in 1990-91. **Calder Memorial Trophy:** rookie of the year. **Conn Smythe Trophy:** most valuable player in playoffs. **Dodge Performance of the Year Award:** most outstanding achievement or single-game performance. **Dodge Performer of the Year Award:** most outstanding performer in regular season. **Dodge Ram Tough Award:** highest combined total of power-play, shorthanded, game-winning and game-tying goals. **Emery Edge Award:** plus/minus leader; awarded from 1982-83 through 1987-88. **Frank J. Selke Trophy:** best defensive forward. **Hart Memorial Trophy:** most valuable player. **Jack Adams Award:** coach of the year. **James Norris Memorial Trophy:** outstanding defenseman. **King Clancy Memorial Trophy:** humanitarian contributions. **Lady Byng Memorial Trophy:** most gentlemanly player. **Lester B. Pearson Award:** outstanding player as selected by NHL Players' Association. **Lester Patrick Trophy:** outstanding service to hockey in U.S. **Maurice "Rocket" Richard Trophy:** leading goal scorer. **Trico Goaltender Award:** best save percentage. **Vezina Trophy:** best goaltender; awarded to goalkeeper(s) having played minimum of 25 games for team with fewest goals scored against prior to 1981-82. **William M. Jennings Trophy:** goalkeeper(s) having played minimum of 25 games for team with fewest goals scored against.

MINOR LEAGUE AWARDS: Baz Bastien Trophy: top goaltender (AHL). **Bobby Orr Trophy:** best defenseman (CHL); awarded prior to 1984-85. **Bob Gassoff Award:** most improved defenseman (CHL); awarded prior to 1984-85. **Commissioner's Trophy:** coach of the year (IHL). **Dudley (Red) Garrett Memorial Trophy:** rookie of the year (AHL). **Eddie Shore Plaque:** outstanding defenseman (AHL). **Fred Hunt Memorial Award:** sportsmanship, determination and dedication (AHL). **Garry F. Longman Memorial Trophy:** outstanding rookie (IHL). **Governors Trophy:** outstanding defenseman (IHL). **Harry (Hap) Holmes Memorial Trophy:** goaltender(s) having played minimum of 25 games for team with fewest goals scored against (AHL); awarded to outstanding goaltender prior to 1983-84. **Jack Butterfield Trophy:** Calder Cup playoffs MVP (AHL). **Jake Milford Trophy:** coach of the year (CHL); awarded prior to 1984-85. **James Gatschene Memorial Trophy:** most valuable player (IHL). **James Norris Memorial Trophy:** outstanding goaltender (IHL). **John B. Sollenberger Trophy:** leading scorer (AHL); originally called Wally Kilrea Trophy, later changed to Carl Liscombe Trophy until summer of 1955. **Ken McKenzie Trophy:** outstanding U.S.-born rookie (IHL). **Ken McKenzie Trophy:** top rookie (CHL); awarded to scoring leader from 1992-93. **Leo P. Lamoureux Memorial Trophy:** leading scorer (IHL); originally called George H. Wilkinson Trophy from 1946-47 through 1959-60. **Les Cunningham Plaque:** most valuable player (AHL). **Louis A.R. Pieri Memorial Award:** top coach (AHL). **Max McNab Trophy:** playoff MVP (CHL); awarded prior to 1984-85. **N.R. (Bud) Poile Trophy:** playoff MVP (IHL); originally called Turner Cup Playoff MVP from 1984-85 through 1988-89. **Phil Esposito Trophy:** leading scorer (CHL); awarded prior to 1984-85. **Terry Sawchuk Trophy:** top goaltenders (CHL); awarded prior to 1984-85. **Tommy Ivan Trophy:** most valuable player (CHL); awarded prior to 1984-85. **Turner Cup Playoff MVP:** playoff MVP (IHL); renamed N.R. (Bud) Poile Trophy in 1989-90.

MAJOR JUNIOR LEAGUE AWARDS: Association of Journalists for Major Junior League Hockey Trophy: top pro prospect (QMJHL); renamed Michael Bossy Trophy in 1983-84. **Bill Hunter Trophy:** top defenseman (WHL); called Top Defenseman Trophy prior to 1987-88 season. **Bob Brownridge Memorial Trophy:** top scorer (WHL); later renamed Bob Clarke Trophy. **Bobby Smith Trophy:** scholastic player of the year (OHL). **Bob Clarke Trophy:** top scorer (WHL); originally called Bob Brownridge Memorial Trophy. **Brad Hornung Trophy:** most sportsmanlike player (WHL); called Frank Boucher Memorial Trophy for most gentlemanly player prior to 1987-88 season. **Dave Pinkney Trophy:** top team goaltending (OHL). **Del Wilson Trophy:** top goaltender (WHL); called Top Goaltender Trophy prior to 1987-88 season. **Des Instructeurs Trophy:** rookie of the year (QMJHL); awarded to top rookie forward since 1981-82 season; renamed Michel Bergeron Trophy in 1985-86. **Dunc McCallum Memorial Trophy:** coach of the year (WHL). **Eddie Powers Memorial Trophy:** scoring champion (OHL). **Emile (Butch) Bouchard Trophy:** best defenseman (QMJHL). **Emms Family Award:** rookie of the year (OHL). **Four Broncos Memorial Trophy:** most valuable player as selected by coaches (WHL); called Most Valuable Player Trophy prior to 1987-88 season. **Frank Boucher Memorial Trophy:** most gentlemanly player (WHL); renamed Brad Hornung Trophy during 1987-88 season. **Frank J. Selke Trophy:** most gentlemanly player (QMJHL). **F.W. (Dinty) Moore Trophy:** rookie goalie with best goals-against average (OHL). **George Parsons Trophy:** sportsmanship in Memorial Cup (Can.HL). **Guy Lafleur Trophy:** most valuable player during playoffs (QMJHL). **Hap Emms Memorial Trophy:** outstanding goaltender in Memorial Cup (Can.HL). **Jacques Plante Trophy:** best goaltender (QMJHL). **Jean Beliveau Trophy:** leading point scorer (QMJHL). **Jim Mahon Memorial Trophy:** top-scoring right winger (OHL). **Jim Piggott Memorial Trophy:** rookie of the year (WHL); originally called Stewart (Butch) Paul Memorial Trophy. **Leo Lalonde Memorial Trophy:** overage player of the year (OHL). **Marcel Robert Trophy:** top scholastic/athletic performer (QMJHL). **Matt Leyden Trophy:** coach of the year (OHL). **Max Kaminsky Trophy:** outstanding defenseman (OHL); awarded to most gentlemanly player prior to 1969-70. **Michael Bossy Trophy:** top pro prospect (QMJHL); originally called Association of Journalists for Major Junior League Hockey Trophy from 1980-81 through 1982-83. **Michel Bergeron Trophy:** top rookie forward (QMJHL); awarded to rookie of the year prior to 1980-81 season. **Michel Briere Trophy:** most valuable player (QMJHL). **Most Valuable Player Trophy:** most valuable player (WHL); renamed Four Broncos Memorial Trophy during 1987-88 season. **Raymond Lagace Trophy:** top rookie defenseman or goaltender (QMJHL). **Red Tilson Trophy:** outstanding player (OHL). **Shell Cup:** awarded to offensive player of the year and defensive player of the year (QMJHL). **Stafford Smythe Memorial Trophy:** most valuable player of Memorial Cup (Can.HL). **Stewart (Butch) Paul Memorial Trophy:** rookie of the year (WHL); renamed Jim Piggott Memorial Trophy during 1987-88 season. **Top Defenseman Trophy:** top defenseman (WHL); renamed Bill Hunter Trophy during 1987-88 season. **Top Goaltender Trophy:** top goaltender (WHL); renamed Del Wilson Trophy during 1987-88 season. **William Hanley Trophy:** most gentlemanly player (OHL).

COLLEGE AWARDS: Hobey Baker Memorial Award: top college hockey player in U.S. **Senator Joseph A. Sullivan Trophy:** outstanding player in Canadian Interuniversity Athletic Union.

OTHER AWARDS: Golden Puck Award: Sweden's Player of the Year. **Golden Stick Award:** Europe's top player. **Izvestia Trophy:** leading scorer (Soviet Union).

EXPLANATION OF FOOTNOTES AND ABBREVIATIONS

*   League leader.
†   Tied for league lead.
‡   Overtime loss/shootout loss.
§   Led or tied for league lead, but total figure is divided between two different teams. Actual league-leading or league-tying figure is mentioned in "Statistical Notes" section.
... Statistic unavailable, unofficial or mathematically impossible to calculate.
—   Statistic inapplicable.

POSITIONS: C: center. **D:** defenseman. **G:** goaltender. **LW:** left winger. **RW:** right winger.

STATISTICS: A: assists. **Avg.:** goals-against average. **G:** goals. **GA:** goals against. **Gms.:** games. **L:** losses. **Min.:** minutes. **PIM.:** penalties in minutes. **+/-:** plus-minus. **PP:** power-play goals. **Pts:** points. **SH:** shorthanded goals. **SO:** shutouts. **T:** ties. **W:** wins.

TEAMS: Bloom. Jefferson: Bloomington Jefferson. **Chem. Litvinov:** Chemopetrol Litvinov. **Chem. Litvinov Jrs.:** Chemopetrol Litvinov Juniors. **Culver Mil. Acad.:** Culver Military Academy. **Czech. Olympic team:** Czechoslavakian Olympic team. **Czech Rep. Oly. team:** Czech Republic Olympic team. **Czechosla. Jr. national:** Czechoslavakian Junior national team. **Det. Little Caesars:** Detroit Little Caesars. **Djur. Stockholm:** Djurgarden Stockholm. **Dynamo-Energ. Yek.:** Dynamo-Energiya Yekaterinburg. **Dyn.-Energiya 2 Yek.:** Dynamo-Energiya 2 Yekaterinburg. **Dynamo Ust-Kameno.:** Dynamo Ust-Kamenogorsk. **Fin. Olympic team:** Finnish Olympic team. **German Oly. team:** German Olympic team. **HC Ceske Bude.:** HC Ceske Budejovice. **HK 32 Lip. Mikulas:** HK 32 Liptovsky Mikulas. **IS Banska Byst.:** IS Banska Bystrica. **Kiek.-Karhut Jodusuu:** Kiekko-Karhut Jodusuu. **Krylja Sov. Moscow:** Krylja Sovetov Moscow. **Mass.-Lowell:** Massachusetts-Lowell. **Metal. Cherepovets:** Metallurg Cherepovets. **Metal. Magnitogorsk:** Metallurg Magnitogorsk. **Metallurg-2 Novok.:** Metallurg-2 Novokuznetsk. **MoDo Ornsk. Jrs.:** Modo Ornskoldsvik Jrs. **Motor Ceske Bude.:** Motor Ceske Budejovice. **N. Yarmouth Acad.:** North Yarmouth Academy. **N. Arizona Univ.:** Northern Arizona University. **N. Michigan Univ.:** Northern Michigan University. **NW Americans Jr. B:** Northwest Americans Junior B. **Poji. Pardubice Jrs.:** Pojistovna Pardubice Juniors. **Prin. Edward Island:** Prince Edward Island. **Rus. Olympic team:** Russian Olympic team. **Sault Ste. Marie:** Sault Sainte Marie. **Sever. Cherepovets:** Severstal Cherepovets. **Slovakian Oly. team:** Slovakian Olympic team. **Sov. Olympic team:** Soviet Olympic team. **Spisska N.V.:** Spisska Nova Ves. **Stad. Hradec Kralove:** Stadion Hradec Kralove. **Swed. Olympic team:** Swedish Olympic team. **Tor. Nizhny Nov.:** Torpedo Nizhny Novgorod. **Torpedo Ust-Kam.:** Torpedo Ust-Kamenogorsk. **Unif. Olympic team:** Unified Olympic team. **Univ. of New Hamp.:** University of New Hampshire. **Univ. of West. Ontario:** University of Western Ontario. **V. Frolunda Goteborg:** Vastra Frolunda Goteborg.

LEAGUES: AAHL: All American Hockey League. **ACHL:** Atlantic Coast Hockey League. **AHL:** American Hockey League. **AJHL:** Alberta Junior Hockey League. **AMHL:** Alberta Minor Hockey League. **AUAA:** Atlantic Universities Athletic Association. **BCJHL:** British Columbia Junior Hockey League. **CAHL:** Central Alberta Hockey League. **CAJHL:** Central Alberta Junior Hockey League. **Can. College:** Canadian College. **Can.HL:** Canadian Hockey League. **CCHA:** Central Collegiate Hockey Association. **CHL:** Central Hockey League. **CIS:** Commonwealth of Independent States. **CJHL:** Central Junior A Hockey League. **COJHL:** Central Ontario Junior Hockey League. **CPHL:** Central Professional Hockey League. **CWUAA:** Canada West University Athletic Association. **Conn. H.S.:** Connecticut High School. **Czech.:** Czechoslovakia. **Czech Rep.:** Czechoslovakia Republic. **ECAC:** Eastern College Athletic Conference. **ECAC-II:** Eastern College Athletic Conference, Division II. **ECHL:** East Coast Hockey League. **EEHL:** Eastern European Hockey League. **EHL:** Eastern Hockey League. **EURO:** Euroliga. **Fin.:** Finland. **Ger.:** Germany. **GWHC:** Great Western Hockey Conference. **Hoc. East:** Hockey East. **IHL:** International Hockey League. **Ill. H.S.:** Illinois High School. **Indiana H.S.:** Indiana High School. **Int'l:** International. **KIJHL:** Kootenay International Junior Hockey League. **Mass. H.S.:** Massachusetts High School. **Md. H.S.:** Maryland High School. **Met. Bos.:** Metro Boston. **Mich. H.S.:** Michigan High School. **Minn. H.S.:** Minnesota High School. **MJHL:** Manitoba Junior Hockey League. **MTHL:** Metro Toronto Hockey League. **NAHL:** North American Hockey League. **NAJHL:** North American Junior Hockey League. **N.B. H.S.:** New Brunswick High School. **NCAA-II:** National Collegiate Athletic Association, Division II. **N.D. H.S.:** North Dakota High School. **NEJHL:** New England Junior Hockey League. **NHL:** National Hockey League. **N.H. H.S.:** New Hampshire High School. **N.J. H.S.:** New Jersey High School. **Nia. D. Jr. C:** Niagara District Junior C. **NSJHL:** Nova Scotia Junior Hockey League. **N.S. Jr. A:** Nova Scotia Junior A. **N.Y. H.S.:** New York High School. **NYMJHL:** New York Major Junior Hockey League. **NYOHL:** North York Ontario Hockey League. **ODHA:** Ottawa & District Hockey Association. **OHA:** Ontario Hockey Association. **OHA Jr. A:** Ontario Hockey Association Junior A. **OHA Mjr. Jr. A:** Ontario Hockey Association Major Junior A. **OHA Senior:** Ontario Hockey Association Senior. **OHL:** Ontario Hockey League. **O.H.S.:** Ohio High School. **OJHA:** Ontario Junior Hockey Association. **OJHL:** Ontario Junior Hockey League. **OMJHL:** Ontario Major Junior Hockey League. **OPJHL:** Ontario Provincial Junior Hockey League. **OUAA:** Ontario Universities Athletic Association. **PCJHL:** Peace Caribou Junior Hockey League. **PEIHA:** Prince Edward Island Hockey Association. **PEIJHL:** Prince Edward Island Junior Hockey League. **Penn. H.S.:** Pennsylvania High School. **QMJHL:** Quebec Major Junior Hockey League. **R.I. H.S.:** Rhode Island High School. **Rus. Div II, III:** Russian Division II, III. **SAJHL:** Southern Alberta Junior Hockey League. **SJHL:** Saskatchewan Junior Hockey League. **Sask. H.S.:** Saskatchewan High School. **SOJHL:** Southern Ontario Junior Hockey League. **Swed. Jr.:** Sweden Junior. **Switz.:** Switzerland. **TBAHA:** Thunder Bay Amateur Hockey Association. **TBJHL:** Thunder Bay Junior Hockey League. **UHL:** United Hockey League. **USHL:** United States Hockey League. **USHS:** United States High School. **USSR:** Union of Soviet Socialist Republics. **V. Frolunda Goteborg:** Vastra Frolunda Goteborg. **Vt. H.S.:** Vermont High School. **W. Germany, W. Ger.:** West Germany. **WCHA:** Western Collegiate Hockey Association. **WCHL:** Western Canada Hockey League. **WHA:** World Hockey Association. **WHL:** Western Hockey League. **Wisc. H.S.:** Wisconsin High School. **Yukon Sr.:** Yukon Senior.

VETERANS AND TOP PROSPECTS

AALTO, ANTTI — C

PERSONAL: Born March 4, 1975, in Lappeenranta, Finland. ... 6-2/210. ... Shoots left. ... Name pronounced AN-tee AL-toh.
TRANSACTIONS/CAREER NOTES: Selected by Mighty Ducks of Anaheim in sixth round (sixth Mighty Ducks pick, 134th overall) of NHL entry draft (June 26, 1993). ... Injured shoulder (December 16, 1998); missed one game. ... Sprained left elbow (December 4, 1999); missed 15 games. ... Suffered illness (March 2, 2000); missed three games.

Season Team	League	REGULAR SEASON								PLAYOFFS				
		Gms.	G	A	Pts.	PIM	+/-	PP	SH	Gms.	G	A	Pts.	PIM
91-92—SaiPa Jr.	Finland	19	10	10	20	38	...	...	...	—	—	—	—	—
—SaiPa	Finland	20	6	6	12	20	...	...	...	—	—	—	—	—
92-93—SaiPa	Finland	23	6	8	14	14	...	...	...	—	—	—	—	—
—TPS Turku Jr.	Finland	14	6	8	14	18	...	...	...	—	—	—	—	—
—TPS Turku	Finland	1	0	0	0	0	...	...	...	—	—	—	—	—
93-94—TPS Turku	Finland	33	5	9	14	16	...	...	...	10	1	1	2	4
94-95—TPS Turku	Finland	44	11	7	18	18	...	...	...	5	0	1	1	2
95-96—TPS Turku	Finland	40	15	16	31	22	...	...	...	11	3	5	8	14
—Kiekko-67	Finland Div. 2	2	0	2	2	2	...	...	...	—	—	—	—	—
96-97—TPS Turku	Finland	44	15	19	34	60	...	...	...	11	5	6	11	31
97-98—Cincinnati	AHL	29	4	9	13	30	...	...	...	—	—	—	—	—
—Anaheim	NHL	3	0	0	0	0	-1	0	0	—	—	—	—	—
98-99—Anaheim	NHL	73	3	5	8	24	-12	2	0	4	0	0	0	2
99-00—Anaheim	NHL	63	7	11	18	26	-13	1	0	—	—	—	—	—
00-01—Anaheim	NHL	12	1	1	2	2	1	0	0	—	—	—	—	—
—Cincinnati	AHL	40	14	26	40	39	...	...	...	3	2	1	3	2
NHL Totals (4 years)		151	11	17	28	52	-25	3	0	4	0	0	0	2

ABID, RAMZI — LW — COYOTES

PERSONAL: Born March 24, 1980, in Montreal. ... 6-2/195. ... Shoots left.
TRANSACTIONS/CAREER NOTES: Selected by Colorado Avalanche in second round (fifth Avalanche pick, 28th overall) of NHL entry draft (June 27, 1998). ... Returned to draft pool by Avalanche and selected by Phoenix Coyotes in third round (third Coyotes pick, 86th overall) of NHL entry draft (June 24, 2000).
HONORS: Named to Can.HL All-Star second team (1997-98). ... Named to QMJHL All-Star first team (1997-98 and 1999-2000). ... Won Jean Beliveau Trophy (1997-98). ... Won Michel Briere Trophy (1997-98). ... Named to Can.HL All-Star first team (1999-2000).

Season Team	League	REGULAR SEASON								PLAYOFFS				
		Gms.	G	A	Pts.	PIM	+/-	PP	SH	Gms.	G	A	Pts.	PIM
96-97—Chicoutimi	QMJHL	65	13	24	37	151	...	...	...	—	—	—	—	—
97-98—Chicoutimi	QMJHL	68	50	*85	*135	266	...	...	...	6	3	4	7	10
98-99—Chicoutimi	QMJHL	21	11	15	26	97	...	...	...	—	—	—	—	—
—Acadie-Bathurst	QMJHL	24	14	22	36	102	...	...	...	23	14	20	34	84
99-00—Acadie-Bathurst	QMJHL	13	10	11	21	61	...	...	...	—	—	—	—	—
—Halifax	QMJHL	59	57	80	137	148	...	...	...	10	10	13	23	18
00-01—Springfield	AHL	17	6	4	10	38	...	...	...	—	—	—	—	—

ADAMS, BRYAN — LW — THRASHERS

PERSONAL: Born March 20, 1977, in Fort St. James, B.C. ... 6-0/185. ... Shoots left.
TRANSACTIONS/CAREER NOTES: Signed as a non-drafted free agent by Atlanta Thrashers (July 1, 1999).

Season Team	League	REGULAR SEASON								PLAYOFFS				
		Gms.	G	A	Pts.	PIM	+/-	PP	SH	Gms.	G	A	Pts.	PIM
95-96—Michigan State	CCHA	42	3	8	11	12	...	...	...	—	—	—	—	—
96-97—Michigan State	CCHA	29	7	7	14	51	...	...	...	—	—	—	—	—
97-98—Michigan State	CCHA	31	9	21	30	39	...	...	...	—	—	—	—	—
98-99—Michigan State	CCHA	42	21	16	37	56	...	...	...	—	—	—	—	—
99-00—Orlando	IHL	64	16	18	34	27	...	...	...	4	0	1	1	6
—Atlanta	NHL	2	0	0	0	0	-1	0	0	—	—	—	—	—
00-01—Atlanta	NHL	9	0	1	1	2	-4	0	0	—	—	—	—	—
—Orlando	IHL	61	18	28	46	43	...	...	...	16	3	4	7	20
NHL Totals (2 years)		11	0	1	1	2	-5	0	0	—	—	—	—	—

ADAMS, CRAIG — RW — HURRICANES

PERSONAL: Born April 26, 1977, in Calgary. ... 6-0/200.
TRANSACTIONS/CAREER NOTES: Selected by Hartford Whalers in the ninth round (ninth Whalers pick, 223 overall) in the 1996 Entry Draft (June 22, 1996). ... Whalers franchise moved to North Carolina and renamed Carolina Hurricanes for 1997-98 season; NHL approved move on June 25, 1997. ... Bruised chest (November 30, 2000); missed four games.
HONORS: Named to ECAC All-Rookie team (1995-96).

Season Team	League	REGULAR SEASON								PLAYOFFS				
		Gms.	G	A	Pts.	PIM	+/-	PP	SH	Gms.	G	A	Pts.	PIM
95-96—Harvard University	ECAC	34	8	9	17	56	...	...	...	—	—	—	—	—
96-97—Harvard University	ECAC	32	6	4	10	36	...	...	...	—	—	—	—	—
97-98—Harvard University	ECAC	23	6	6	12	12	...	...	...	—	—	—	—	—
98-99—Harvard University	ECAC	31	9	14	23	53	...	...	...	—	—	—	—	—
99-00—Cincinnati	IHL	73	12	12	24	124	...	...	...	8	0	1	1	14
00-01—Carolina	NHL	44	1	0	1	20	-7	0	0	3	0	0	0	0
—Cincinnati	IHL	4	0	1	1	9	...	...	...	1	0	0	0	2
NHL Totals (1 year)		44	1	0	1	20	-7	0	0	3	0	0	0	0

ADAMS, GREG   LW

PERSONAL: Born August 15, 1963, in Nelson, B.C. ... 6-4/196. ... Shoots left. ... Full Name: Greg G. Adams. ... Son-in-law of George Swarbrick, right winger with three NHL teams (1967-68 through 1970-71).

TRANSACTIONS/CAREER NOTES: Signed as non-drafted free agent by New Jersey Devils (June 25, 1984). ... Tore tendon in right wrist (April 1986). ... Traded by Devils with G Kirk McLean to Vancouver Canucks for C Patrik Sundstrom, fourth-round pick (LW Matt Ruchty) in the 1988 draft and the option to flip second-round picks in 1988 draft; Devils exercised option and selected LW Jeff Christian and Canucks selected D Leif Rohlin (September 10, 1987). ... Fractured ankle (February 1989). ... Fractured cheekbone (January 4, 1990); missed 12 games. ... Sprained left knee (October 17, 1990); missed 12 games. ... Sprained forearm, wrist and abdomen (February 27, 1991). ... Suffered concussion (October 8, 1991); missed one game. ... Suffered charley horse (January 16, 1993); missed nine games. ... Suffered charley horse (February 15, 1993); missed 22 games. ... Suffered stress fracture in hand requiring minor surgery (December 14, 1993); missed 14 games. ... Bruised foot (February 22, 1994); missed one game. ... Traded by Canucks with RW Dan Kesa and fifth-round pick (traded to Los Angeles) in 1995 draft to Dallas Stars for RW Russ Courtnall (April 7, 1995). ... Fractured hand (March 2, 1996); missed 11 games. ... Broke toe (April 7, 1996); missed final four games of season. ... Suffered herniated disc in neck (December 21, 1996); missed 30 games. ... Strained groin (April 4, 1997); missed one game. ... Bruised ribs (November 16, 1997); missed 11 games. ... Injured knee (December 23, 1997); missed 20 games. ... Injured neck (April 6, 1998); missed two games. ... Signed as free agent by Phoenix Coyotes (September 1, 1998). ... Suffered from the flu (January 26, 1999); missed one game. ... Strained groin (February 20, 1999); missed six games. ... Suffered injury (December 11, 1999); missed two games. ... Underwent sinus surgery (December 29, 1999); missed 11 games. ... Signed as free agent by Florida Panthers (November 6, 2000). ... Bruised knee (December 4, 2000); missed two games. ... Injured neck (January 10, 2001); missed three games. ... Bruised sternum (March 2, 2001); missed three games.

HONORS: Played in NHL All-Star Game (1988).

MISCELLANEOUS: Failed to score on a penalty shot (vs. Alain Chevrier, January 7, 1988; vs. Alan Bester, January 9, 1989; vs. Jacques Cloutier, December 10, 1989; vs. Bill Ranford, December 1, 1991; vs. Curtis Joseph, January 25, 1992).

STATISTICAL PLATEAUS: Three-goal games: 1991-92 (1). ... Four-goal games: 1987-88 (1). ... Total hat tricks: 2.

		REGULAR SEASON								PLAYOFFS				
Season Team	League	Gms.	G	A	Pts.	PIM	+/-	PP	SH	Gms.	G	A	Pts.	PIM
80-81—Kelowna	BCJHL	47	40	50	90	16	...	...	...	—	—	—	—	—
81-82—Kelowna	BCJHL	45	31	42	73	24	...	...	...	—	—	—	—	—
82-83—N. Arizona Univ.	Indep.	29	14	21	35	46	...	...	...	—	—	—	—	—
83-84—N. Arizona Univ.	Indep.	47	40	50	90	16	...	...	...	—	—	—	—	—
84-85—Maine	AHL	41	15	20	35	12	...	...	...	11	3	4	7	0
—New Jersey	NHL	36	12	9	21	14	-14	5	0	—	—	—	—	—
85-86—New Jersey	NHL	78	35	42	77	30	-6	10	0	—	—	—	—	—
86-87—New Jersey	NHL	72	20	27	47	19	-16	6	0	—	—	—	—	—
87-88—Vancouver	NHL	80	36	40	76	30	-24	12	0	—	—	—	—	—
88-89—Vancouver	NHL	61	19	14	33	24	-21	9	0	7	2	3	5	2
89-90—Vancouver	NHL	65	30	20	50	18	-8	13	0	—	—	—	—	—
90-91—Vancouver	NHL	55	21	24	45	10	-5	5	1	5	0	0	0	2
91-92—Vancouver	NHL	76	30	27	57	26	8	13	1	6	0	2	2	4
92-93—Vancouver	NHL	53	25	31	56	14	31	6	1	12	7	6	13	6
93-94—Vancouver	NHL	68	13	24	37	20	-1	5	1	23	6	8	14	2
94-95—Vancouver	NHL	31	5	10	15	12	1	2	2	—	—	—	—	—
—Dallas	NHL	12	3	3	6	4	-4	1	0	5	2	0	2	0
95-96—Dallas	NHL	66	22	21	43	33	-21	11	1	—	—	—	—	—
96-97—Dallas	NHL	50	21	15	36	2	27	5	0	3	0	1	1	0
97-98—Dallas	NHL	49	14	18	32	20	11	7	0	12	2	2	4	0
98-99—Phoenix	NHL	75	19	24	43	26	-1	5	0	3	1	0	1	0
99-00—Phoenix	NHL	69	19	27	46	14	-1	5	0	5	0	0	0	0
00-01—Florida	NHL	60	11	12	23	10	-3	2	0	—	—	—	—	—
NHL Totals (17 years)		1056	355	388	743	326	-47	122	7	81	20	22	42	16

ADAMS, KEVYN   C   PANTHERS

PERSONAL: Born October 8, 1974, in Washington, D.C. ... 6-1/195. ... Shoots right.

TRANSACTIONS/CAREER NOTES: Selected by Boston Bruins in first round (first Bruins pick, 25th overall) of NHL entry draft (June 26, 1993). ... Signed as free agent by Toronto Maple Leafs (August 1, 1997). ... Selected by Columbus Blue Jackets in NHL expansion draft (June 23, 2000). ... Strained gluteal muscle (December 13, 2000); missed two games. ... Traded by Blue Jackets with fourth-round pick (RW Michael Woodford) in 2001 draft to Florida Panthers for LW Ray Whitney and future considerations (March 13, 2001).

HONORS: Named to CCHA All-Star second team (1994-95).

MISCELLANEOUS: Failed to score on a penalty shot (vs. Arturs Irbe, February 14, 2000).

		REGULAR SEASON								PLAYOFFS				
Season Team	League	Gms.	G	A	Pts.	PIM	+/-	PP	SH	Gms.	G	A	Pts.	PIM
90-91—Niagara	NAJHL	55	17	20	37	24	...	...	...	—	—	—	—	—
91-92—Niagara	NAJHL	40	25	33	58	51	...	...	...	—	—	—	—	—
92-93—Miami of Ohio	CCHA	41	17	16	33	18	...	...	...	—	—	—	—	—
93-94—Miami of Ohio	CCHA	36	15	28	43	24	...	...	...	—	—	—	—	—
94-95—Miami of Ohio	CCHA	38	20	29	49	30	...	...	...	—	—	—	—	—
95-96—Miami of Ohio	CCHA	36	17	30	47	30	...	...	...	—	—	—	—	—
96-97—Grand Rapids	IHL	82	22	25	47	47	...	...	...	5	1	1	2	4
97-98—Toronto	NHL	5	0	0	0	7	0	0	0	—	—	—	—	—
—St. John's	AHL	58	17	21	38	99	...	...	...	4	0	0	0	4
98-99—St. John's	AHL	80	15	35	50	85	...	...	...	5	2	0	2	4
—Toronto	NHL	1	0	0	0	0	0	0	0	7	0	2	2	14
99-00—St. John's	AHL	23	6	11	17	24	...	...	...	—	—	—	—	—
—Toronto	NHL	52	5	8	13	39	-7	0	0	12	1	0	1	7
00-01—Columbus	NHL	66	8	12	20	52	-4	0	0	—	—	—	—	—
—Florida	NHL	12	3	6	9	2	7	0	0	—	—	—	—	—
NHL Totals (4 years)		136	16	26	42	100	-4	0	0	19	1	2	3	21

ADDUONO, JEREMY   RW   SABRES

PERSONAL: Born August 4, 1979, in Thunder Bay, Ont. ... 6-0/182. ... Shoots right.
TRANSACTIONS/CAREER NOTES: Selected by Buffalo Sabres in seventh round (eighth Sabres pick, 184th overall) of NHL entry draft (June 21, 1997).

Season Team	League	Gms.	G	A	Pts.	PIM	+/-	PP	SH	Gms.	G	A	Pts.	PIM
				REGULAR SEASON								**PLAYOFFS**		
95-96—Sudbury	OHL	66	15	22	37	14	...	...	...	—	—	—	—	—
96-97—Sudbury	OHL	66	29	40	69	24	...	...	...	—	—	—	—	—
97-98—Sudbury	OHL	66	37	69	106	40	...	...	...	10	5	5	10	10
98-99—Canadian nat'l team	Int'l	44	10	16	26	8	...	...	...	—	—	—	—	—
99-00—Rochester	AHL	51	23	22	45	20	...	...	...	21	6	11	17	2
00-01—Rochester	AHL	76	24	30	54	53	...	...	...	4	1	0	1	4

AEBISCHER, DAVID   G   AVALANCHE

PERSONAL: Born February 7, 1978, in Fribourg, Switzerland. ... 6-1/185. ... Catches left. ... Name pronounced EH-bih-shuhr.
TRANSACTIONS/CAREER NOTES: Selected by Colorado Avalanche in sixth round (seventh Avalanche pick, 161st overall) of NHL entry draft (June 21, 1997). ... Suffered from pharyngitas (November 25, 2000); missed one game.
MISCELLANEOUS: Member of Stanley Cup championship team (2001).

Season Team	League	Gms.	Min	W	L	T	GA	SO	Avg.	Gms.	Min.	W	L	GA	SO	Avg.
					REGULAR SEASON								**PLAYOFFS**			
96-97—Fribourg-Gotteron	Switzerland	10	577	...	...	...	34	...	3.54	3	184	...	...	13	...	4.24
97-98—Fribourg-Gotteron	Switzerland	1	60	...	...	...	1	0	1.00	4	240	...	...	17	...	4.25
—Hershey	AHL	2	80	0	0	1	5	0	3.75	—	—	—	—	—	—	—
—Chesapeake	ECHL	17	930	5	7	2	52	0	3.35	—	—	—	—	—	—	—
—Wheeling	ECHL	10	564	5	3	1	30	1	3.19	—	—	—	—	—	—	—
98-99—Hershey	AHL	38	1932	17	10	5	79	2	2.45	3	152	1	2	6	0	2.37
99-00—Hershey	AHL	58	3259	29	23	2	*180	1	3.31	14	788	7	6	40	2	3.05
00-01—Colorado	NHL	26	1393	12	7	3	52	3	2.24	1	1	0	0	0	0	...
NHL Totals (1 year)		26	1393	12	7	3	52	3	2.24	1	1	0	0	0	0	...

AFANASENKOV, DMITRY   LW   LIGHTNING

PERSONAL: Born May 12, 1980, in Arkhangelsk, U.S.S.R. ... 6-2/200. ... Shoots right. ... Name pronounced ah-fahn-ah-SEHN-kov.
TRANSACTIONS/CAREER NOTES: Selected by Tampa Bay Lightning in third round (third Lightning pick, 72nd overall) of NHL entry draft (June 27, 1998).

Season Team	League	Gms.	G	A	Pts.	PIM	+/-	PP	SH	Gms.	G	A	Pts.	PIM
					REGULAR SEASON							**PLAYOFFS**		
95-96—Torpedo-2 Yaroslavl	CIS Div. II	25	10	5	15	10	...	...	...	—	—	—	—	—
—Torpedo Yaroslavl	CIS Jr.	35	28	16	44	8	...	...	...	—	—	—	—	—
96-97—Torpedo-2 Yaroslavl	Rus. Div. III	45	20	15	35	14	...	...	...	—	—	—	—	—
97-98—Torpedo-Yaroslavl	Russian	45	19	11	30	28	...	...	...	—	—	—	—	—
98-99—Moncton	QMJHL	15	5	5	10	12	...	...	...	—	—	—	—	—
—Sherbrooke	QMJHL	51	23	30	53	22	...	...	...	13	10	6	16	6
99-00—Sherbrooke	QMJHL	60	56	43	99	70	...	...	...	5	3	2	5	4
00-01—Detroit	IHL	65	15	22	37	26	...	...	...	—	—	—	—	—
—Tampa Bay	NHL	9	1	1	2	4	1	0	0	—	—	—	—	—
NHL Totals (1 year)		9	1	1	2	4	1	0	0					

AFINOGENOV, MAXIM   RW   SABRES

PERSONAL: Born September 4, 1979, in Moscow, U.S.S.R. ... 5-11/176. ... Shoots left. ... Name pronounced ah-FEEN-o-gin-ov.
TRANSACTIONS/CAREER NOTES: Selected by Buffalo Sabres in third round (third Sabres pick, 69th overall) of NHL entry draft (June 21, 1997).

Season Team	League	Gms.	G	A	Pts.	PIM	+/-	PP	SH	Gms.	G	A	Pts.	PIM
					REGULAR SEASON							**PLAYOFFS**		
95-96—Dynamo Moscow	CIS	1	0	0	0	0	...	...	...	—	—	—	—	—
96-97—Dynamo Moscow	Russian	29	6	5	11	10	...	...	...	4	0	2	2	0
—Dynamo-2 Moscow	Rus. Div. III	14	9	2	11	10	...	...	...	—	—	—	—	—
97-98—Dynamo Moscow	Russian	35	10	5	15	53	...	...	...	—	—	—	—	—
98-99—Dynamo Moscow	Russian	38	8	13	21	24	...	...	...	16	*10	6	†16	14
99-00—Rochester	AHL	15	6	12	18	8	...	...	...	8	3	1	4	4
—Buffalo	NHL	65	16	18	34	41	-4	2	0	5	0	1	1	2
00-01—Buffalo	NHL	78	14	22	36	40	1	3	0	11	2	3	5	4
NHL Totals (2 years)		143	30	40	70	81	-3	5	0	16	2	4	6	6

AHONEN, ARI   G   DEVILS

PERSONAL: Born February 6, 1981, in Jyvaskyla, Finland. ... 6-2/170. ... Catches left.
TRANSACTIONS/CAREER NOTES: Selected by New Jersey Devils in first round (first Devils pick, 27th overall) of NHL entry draft (June 26, 1999).

Season Team	League	REGULAR SEASON								PLAYOFFS						
		Gms.	Min	W	L	T	GA	SO	Avg.	Gms.	Min.	W	L	GA	SO	Avg.
97-98—JyP HT Jyvaskyla	Finland Jr.	31	1853	...	...	...	64	...	2.09	—	—	—	—	—	—	—
98-99—JyP HT Jyvaskyla	Finland Jr.	24	1447	...	...	...	70	0	2.90	—	—	—	—	—	—	—
99-00—HIFK Helsinki	Finland	24	1347	11	7	1	70	1	3.12	2	119	0	2	7	0	3.53
—HIFK Helsinki	Finland Jr.	11	658	...	...	...	22	...	2.01	—	—	—	—	—	—	—
00-01—HIFK Helsinki	Finland	37	2101	18	13	4	97	2	2.77	5	395	2	3	9	1	1.37

AITKEN, JOHNATHAN   D   BRUINS

PERSONAL: Born May 24, 1978, in Edmonton. ... 6-4/210. ... Shoots left. ... Full Name: Johnathan James Aitken. ... Name pronounced AYT-kihn.
TRANSACTIONS/CAREER NOTES: Selected by Boston Bruins in first round (first Bruins pick, eighth overall) of NHL entry draft (June 22, 1996).
HONORS: Named to WHL (East) All-Star second team (1997-98).

Season Team	League	REGULAR SEASON								PLAYOFFS				
		Gms.	G	A	Pts.	PIM	+/-	PP	SH	Gms.	G	A	Pts.	PIM
94-95—Medicine Hat	WHL	53	0	5	5	71	...	...	...	—	—	—	—	—
95-96—Medicine Hat	WHL	71	6	14	20	131	...	...	...	5	1	0	1	6
96-97—Brandon	WHL	65	4	18	22	211	...	...	...	6	0	0	0	4
97-98—Brandon	WHL	69	9	25	34	183	...	...	...	18	0	8	8	67
98-99—Providence	AHL	65	2	9	11	92	...	...	...	13	0	0	0	17
99-00—Providence	AHL	70	2	12	14	121	...	...	...	11	1	0	1	26
—Boston	NHL	3	0	0	0	0	-3	0	0	—	—	—	—	—
00-01—Sparta Praha	Czech Rep.	24	0	3	3	62	...	...	...	—	—	—	—	—
NHL Totals (1 year)		3	0	0	0	0	-3	0	0					

ALATALO, MIKA   LW

PERSONAL: Born June 11, 1971, in Oulu, Finland. ... 6-0/202. ... Shoots left. ... Full Name: Mikael Alatalo.
TRANSACTIONS/CAREER NOTES: Selected by Winnipeg Jets in 10th round (11th Jets pick, 203rd overall) of NHL entry draft (June 16, 1990). ... Jets franchise moved to Phoenix and renamed Coyotes for 1996-97 season; NHL approved move on January 18, 1996.

Season Team	League	REGULAR SEASON								PLAYOFFS				
		Gms.	G	A	Pts.	PIM	+/-	PP	SH	Gms.	G	A	Pts.	PIM
88-89—KooKoo Kouvola	Finland Div. 2	34	8	6	14	10	...	...	...	—	—	—	—	—
89-90—KooKoo Kouvola	Finland Div. 2	41	3	5	8	22	...	...	...	—	—	—	—	—
90-91—Lukko	Finland	39	10	1	11	10	...	...	...	—	—	—	—	—
91-92—Lukko	Finland	43	20	17	37	32	...	...	...	2	0	0	0	0
92-93—Lukko	Finland	48	16	19	35	38	...	...	...	3	0	0	0	0
93-94—Lukko	Finland	45	19	15	34	77	...	...	...	9	2	2	4	4
94-95—TPS Turku	Finland	44	23	13	36	59	...	...	...	13	2	5	7	8
95-96—TPS Turku	Finland	49	19	18	37	44	...	...	...	13	2	5	7	8
96-97—Lulea	Sweden	50	19	18	37	54	...	...	...	10	2	3	5	22
97-98—Lulea	Sweden	45	14	10	24	22	...	...	...	2	0	0	0	0
98-99—TPS Turku	Finland	53	14	23	37	44	...	...	...	10	6	3	9	6
99-00—Phoenix	NHL	82	10	17	27	36	-3	1	0	5	0	0	0	2
00-01—Phoenix	NHL	70	7	12	19	22	1	0	0	—	—	—	—	—
NHL Totals (2 years)		152	17	29	46	58	-2	1	0	5	0	0	0	2

ALBELIN, TOMMY   D   DEVILS

PERSONAL: Born May 21, 1964, in Stockholm, Sweden. ... 6-1/194. ... Shoots left. ... Name pronounced AL-buh-leen.
TRANSACTIONS/CAREER NOTES: Selected by Quebec Nordiques in eighth round (seventh Nordiques pick, 152nd overall) of NHL entry draft (June 8, 1983). ... Traded by Nordiques to New Jersey Devils for fourth-round pick (LW Niclas Andersson) in 1989 draft (December 12, 1988). ... Injured right knee (March 2, 1990); missed four games. ... Injured groin (November 21, 1992); missed two games. ... Suffered from urinary infection (1993-94 season); missed nine games. ... Bruised thigh (December 16, 1995); missed six games. ... Traded by Devils with D Cale Hulse and RW Jocelyn Lemieux to Calgary Flames for D Phil Housley and D Dan Keczmer (February 26, 1996). ... Strained groin (November 9, 1996); missed four games. ... Reinjured groin (November 25, 1996); missed two games. ... Strained abdominal muscle (December 7, 1996); missed five games. ... Suffered concussion (November 11, 1997); missed three games. ... Pulled groin (November 27, 1997); missed three games. ... Reinjured groin (December 9, 1997); missed four games. ... Injured ribs (February 2, 1998); missed three games. ... Strained groin (November 20, 1998); missed six games. ... Injured shoulder (January 6, 2000); missed final 41 games of season. ... Suffered concussion (October 27, 2000); missed five games. ... Signed as free agent by Devils (July 5, 2001).
HONORS: Named to Swedish League All-Star team (1986-87).
MISCELLANEOUS: Member of Stanley Cup championship team (1995).

Season Team	League	REGULAR SEASON								PLAYOFFS				
		Gms.	G	A	Pts.	PIM	+/-	PP	SH	Gms.	G	A	Pts.	PIM
82-83—Djurgarden Stockholm	Sweden	17	2	5	7	4	...	...	...	6	1	0	1	2
83-84—Djurgarden Stockholm	Sweden	37	9	8	17	36	...	...	...	4	0	1	1	2
84-85—Djurgarden Stockholm	Sweden	32	9	8	17	22	...	...	...	8	2	1	3	4
85-86—Djurgarden Stockholm	Sweden	35	4	8	12	26	...	...	...	—	—	—	—	—
86-87—Djurgarden Stockholm	Sweden	33	7	5	12	49	...	...	...	2	0	0	0	0
87-88—Quebec	NHL	60	3	23	26	47	-7	0	0	—	—	—	—	—
88-89—Halifax	AHL	8	2	5	7	4	...	...	...	—	—	—	—	—
—Quebec	NHL	14	2	4	6	27	-6	1	0	—	—	—	—	—
—New Jersey	NHL	46	7	24	31	40	18	1	1	—	—	—	—	—
89-90—New Jersey	NHL	68	6	23	29	63	-1	4	0	—	—	—	—	—
90-91—Utica	AHL	14	4	2	6	10	...	...	...	—	—	—	—	—
—New Jersey	NHL	47	2	12	14	44	1	1	0	3	0	1	1	2

Season Team	League	REGULAR SEASON								PLAYOFFS				
		Gms.	G	A	Pts.	PIM	+/-	PP	SH	Gms.	G	A	Pts.	PIM
91-92—New Jersey	NHL	19	0	4	4	4	7	0	0	1	1	1	2	0
—Utica	AHL	11	4	6	10	4	...	...	...	—	—	—	—	—
92-93—New Jersey	NHL	36	1	5	6	14	0	1	0	5	2	0	2	0
93-94—Albany	AHL	4	0	2	2	17	...			—	—	—	—	—
—New Jersey	NHL	62	2	17	19	36	20	1	0	20	2	5	7	14
94-95—New Jersey	NHL	48	5	10	15	20	9	2	0	20	1	7	8	2
95-96—New Jersey	NHL	53	1	12	13	14	0	0	0	—	—	—	—	—
—Calgary	NHL	20	0	1	1	4	1	0	0	4	0	0	0	0
96-97—Calgary	NHL	72	4	11	15	14	-8	2	0	—	—	—	—	—
97-98—Calgary	NHL	69	2	17	19	32	9	1	0	—	—	—	—	—
—Swedish Oly. team	Int'l	3	0	0	0	0	...	...	...	—	—	—	—	—
98-99—Calgary	NHL	60	1	5	6	8	-11	0	0	—	—	—	—	—
99-00—Calgary	NHL	41	4	6	10	12	-3	1	1	—	—	—	—	—
00-01—Calgary	NHL	77	1	19	20	22	2	1	0	—	—	—	—	—
NHL Totals (14 years)		792	41	193	234	401	31	16	2	53	6	14	20	18

ALEXEEV, NIKITA — RW — LIGHTNING

PERSONAL: Born December 27, 1981, in Murmansk, U.S.S.R. ... 6-5/215. ... Shoots left.
TRANSACTIONS/CAREER NOTES: Selected by Tampa Bay Lightning in first round (first Lightning pick, eighth overall) of NHL entry draft (June 24, 2000).

Season Team	League	REGULAR SEASON								PLAYOFFS				
		Gms.	G	A	Pts.	PIM	+/-	PP	SH	Gms.	G	A	Pts.	PIM
97-98—Krylja Sov. Moscow	Rus. Div. III	61	11	4	15	36	...	...	...					
98-99—Erie	OHL	61	17	18	35	15	...	...	...	5	1	1	2	4
99-00—Erie	OHL	64	24	29	53	42	...	...	...	13	4	3	7	6
00-01—Erie	OHL	64	31	41	72	45	...	...	...	12	7	7	14	12

ALFREDSSON, DANIEL — RW — SENATORS

PERSONAL: Born December 11, 1972, in Partille, Sweden. ... 5-11/195. ... Shoots right.
TRANSACTIONS/CAREER NOTES: Selected by Ottawa Senators in sixth round (fifth Senators pick, 133rd overall) of NHL entry draft (June 29, 1994). ... Strained abdominal muscle (January 29, 1997); missed six games. ... Injured right ankle (November 3, 1997); missed eight games. ... Fractured right fibula (December 11, 1997); missed 13 games. ... Tore medial collateral ligament in left knee (September 16, 1998); missed first nine games of season. ... Injured right eye (November 12, 1998); missed four games. ... Suffered from the flu (December 30, 1998); missed one game. ... Sprained medial collateral ligament in left knee (January 26, 1999); missed five games. ... Strained abdominal muscle (March 17, 1999); missed five games. ... Tore medial collateral ligament in right knee (October 21, 1999); missed 20 games. ... Sprained left knee (February 15, 2000); missed three games. ... Bruised left foot (March 31, 2000); missed one game. ... Strained hip flexor (October 19, 2001); missed 13 games. ... Injured right wrist (April 6, 2001); missed final game of regular season.
HONORS: Won Calder Memorial Trophy (1995-96). ... Named to NHL All-Rookie team (1995-96). ... Played in NHL All-Star Game (1996-1998).
MISCELLANEOUS: Captain of Ottawa Senators (1999-2000 and 2000-01). ... Scored on a penalty shot (vs. Scott Langkow, March 4, 2000). ... Failed to score on a penalty shot (vs. Martin Biron, January 8, 2000; vs. Dan Cloutier, January 20, 2001).
STATISTICAL PLATEAUS: Three-goal games: 1995-96 (1), 2000-01 (1). Total: 2.

Season Team	League	REGULAR SEASON								PLAYOFFS				
		Gms.	G	A	Pts.	PIM	+/-	PP	SH	Gms.	G	A	Pts.	PIM
91-92—Molndal Hockey	Sweden Dv. 2	32	12	8	20	43	...	...	...	—	—	—	—	—
92-93—Vastra Frolunda	Sweden	20	1	5	6	8	...	...	...	—	—	—	—	—
93-94—Vastra Frolunda	Sweden	39	20	10	30	18	...	...	...	4	1	1	2	...
94-95—Vastra Frolunda	Sweden	22	7	11	18	22	...	...	...	—	—	—	—	—
95-96—Ottawa	NHL	82	26	35	61	28	-18	8	2	—	—	—	—	—
96-97—Ottawa	NHL	76	24	47	71	30	5	11	1	7	5	2	7	6
97-98—Ottawa	NHL	55	17	28	45	18	7	7	0	11	7	2	9	20
—Swedish Oly. team	Int'l	4	2	3	5	2	...	...	...	—	—	—	—	—
98-99—Ottawa	NHL	58	11	22	33	14	8	3	0	4	1	2	3	4
99-00—Ottawa	NHL	57	21	38	59	28	11	4	2	6	1	3	4	2
00-01—Ottawa	NHL	68	24	46	70	30	11	10	0	4	1	0	1	2
NHL Totals (6 years)		396	123	216	339	148	24	43	5	32	15	9	24	34

ALLEN, BOBBY — D — BRUINS

PERSONAL: Born November 14, 1978, in Braintree, Mass. ... 6-1/198. ... Shoots left.
TRANSACTIONS/CAREER NOTES: Selected by Boston Bruins in second round (second Bruins pick, 52nd overall) of NHL entry draft (June 27, 1998).
HONORS: Named to Hockey East All-Star second team (1999-2000). ... Named to Hockey East All-Star first team (2000-01). ... Named to NCAA All-America (East) first team (2000-01).

Season Team	League	REGULAR SEASON								PLAYOFFS				
		Gms.	G	A	Pts.	PIM	+/-	PP	SH	Gms.	G	A	Pts.	PIM
96-97—Cushing Academy	Mass. H.S.	36	11	33	44	28	...	...	...	—	—	—	—	—
97-98—Boston College	Hockey East	37	7	19	26	34	...	...	...	—	—	—	—	—
98-99—Boston College	Hockey East	43	9	23	32	34	...	...	...	—	—	—	—	—
99-00—Boston College	Hockey East	42	4	23	27	40	...	...	...	—	—	—	—	—
00-01—Boston College	Hockey East	42	5	18	23	30	...	...	...	—	—	—	—	—

ALLEN, BRYAN   D   CANUCKS

PERSONAL: Born August 21, 1980, in Kingston, Ont. ... 6-4/210. ... Shoots left.
TRANSACTIONS/CAREER NOTES: Selected by Vancouver Canucks in first round (first Canucks pick, fourth overall) of NHL entry draft (June 27, 1998). ... Injured knee (September 15, 1999); missed first 57 games of season.
HONORS: Named to OHL All-Star first team (1998-99).

		REGULAR SEASON								PLAYOFFS				
Season Team	League	Gms.	G	A	Pts.	PIM	+/-	PP	SH	Gms.	G	A	Pts.	PIM
95-96—Ernestown..................	Jr. C	36	1	16	17	71	...	...	...	—	—	—	—	—
96-97—Oshawa.....................	OHL	60	2	4	6	76	...	...	...	18	1	3	4	26
97-98—Oshawa.....................	OHL	48	6	13	19	126	...	...	...	5	0	5	5	18
98-99—Oshawa.....................	OHL	37	7	15	22	77	...	...	...	17	0	3	3	30
99-00—Oshawa.....................	OHL	3	0	2	2	12	...	...	...	3	0	0	0	13
—Syracuse..................	AHL	9	1	1	2	11	...	...	...	2	0	0	0	2
00-01—Kansas City..............	IHL	75	5	20	25	99	...	...	...	—	—	—	—	—
—Vancouver.................	NHL	6	0	0	0	0	0	0	0	2	0	0	0	2
NHL Totals (1 year)............		6	0	0	0	0	0	0	0	2	0	0	0	2

ALLISON, JAMIE   D   BLACKHAWKS

PERSONAL: Born May 13, 1975, in Lindsay, Ont. ... 6-1/195. ... Shoots left.
TRANSACTIONS/CAREER NOTES: Selected by Calgary Flames in second round (second Flames pick, 44th overall) of NHL entry draft (June 26, 1993). ... Suffered concussion (December 20, 1996); missed three games. ... Fractured thumb (January 9, 1998); missed 11 games. ... Suffered concussion (March 28, 1998); missed 10 games. ... Traded by Flames with C/LW Marty McInnis and RW Erik Andersson to Chicago Blackhawks for C Jeff Shantz and C/LW Steve Dubinsky (October 27, 1998). ... Sprained wrist (November 17, 1998); missed 23 games. ... Strained groin (March 31, 1999); missed three games. ... Strained groin (December 26, 1999); missed four games. ... Injured muscle in rib cage (February 23, 2000); missed eight games. ... Suffered stiff neck (March 26, 2000); missed one game. ... Bruised foot (December 21, 2000); missed one game. ... Sprained knee (February 10, 2001); missed 13 games.

		REGULAR SEASON								PLAYOFFS				
Season Team	League	Gms.	G	A	Pts.	PIM	+/-	PP	SH	Gms.	G	A	Pts.	PIM
90-91—Waterloo Jr. B............	OHA	45	3	8	11	91	...	...	...	—	—	—	—	—
91-92—Windsor......................	OHL	59	4	8	12	52	...	...	...	4	1	1	2	2
92-93—Det. Jr. Red Wings......	OHL	61	0	13	13	64	...	...	...	15	2	5	7	23
93-94—Det. Jr. Red Wings......	OHL	40	2	22	24	69	...	...	...	17	2	9	11	35
94-95—Det. Jr. Red Wings......	OHL	50	1	14	15	119	...	...	...	18	2	7	9	35
—Calgary....................	NHL	1	0	0	0	0	0	0	0	—	—	—	—	—
95-96—Saint John	AHL	71	3	16	19	223	...	...	...	14	0	2	2	16
96-97—Saint John	AHL	46	3	6	9	139	...	...	...	5	0	1	1	4
—Calgary....................	NHL	20	0	0	0	35	-4	0	0	—	—	—	—	—
97-98—Saint John	AHL	16	0	5	5	49	...	...	...	—	—	—	—	—
—Calgary....................	NHL	43	3	8	11	104	3	0	0	—	—	—	—	—
98-99—Saint John	AHL	5	0	0	0	23	...	...	...	—	—	—	—	—
—Chicago...................	NHL	39	2	2	4	62	0	0	0	—	—	—	—	—
—Indianapolis..............	IHL	3	1	0	1	10	...	...	...	—	—	—	—	—
99-00—Chicago...................	NHL	59	1	3	4	102	-5	0	0	—	—	—	—	—
00-01—Chicago...................	NHL	44	1	3	4	53	7	0	0	—	—	—	—	—
NHL Totals (6 years)...........		206	7	16	23	356	1	0	0	—	—	—	—	—

ALLISON, JASON   C   BRUINS

PERSONAL: Born May 29, 1975, in North York, Ont. ... 6-4/205. ... Shoots right.
TRANSACTIONS/CAREER NOTES: Selected by Washington Capitals in first round (second Capitals pick, 17th overall) of NHL entry draft (June 26, 1993). ... Injured ankle (February 15, 1997); missed one game. ... Traded by Capitals with G Jim Carey, C Anson Carter and third-round pick (RW Lee Goren) in 1997 draft to Boston Bruins for C Adam Oates, RW Rick Tocchet and G Bill Ranford (March 1, 1997). ... Injured hip (March 1, 1998); missed one game. ... Injured wrist (October 30, 1999); missed two games. ... Injured wrist (December 23, 1999); missed three games. ... Injured ligaments in left thumb (January 8, 2000) and underwent surgery; missed 15 games. ... Injured wrist (February 12, 2000) and underwent surgery; missed final 25 games of season.
HONORS: Won Can.HL Player of the Year Award (1993-94). ... Won Can.HL Top Scorer Award (1993-94). ... Won Red Tilson Trophy (1993-94). ... Won William Hanley Trophy (1993-94). ... Won Eddie Powers Memorial Trophy (1993-94). ... Named to Can.HL All-Star first team (1993-94). ... Named to OHL All-Star first team (1993-94). ... Played in NHL All-Star Game (2001).
MISCELLANEOUS: Captain of Boston Bruins (November 9, 2000-2001). ... Scored on a penalty shot (vs. Ron Tugnutt, March 24, 1999). ... Failed to score on a penalty shot (vs. Dominik Hasek, April 10, 1997).
STATISTICAL PLATEAUS: Three-goal games: 1997-98 (2), 1998-99 (1), 2000-01 (1). Total: 4.

		REGULAR SEASON								PLAYOFFS				
Season Team	League	Gms.	G	A	Pts.	PIM	+/-	PP	SH	Gms.	G	A	Pts.	PIM
91-92—London	OHL	65	11	18	29	15	...	...	...	7	0	0	0	0
92-93—London	OHL	66	42	76	118	50	...	...	...	12	7	13	20	8
93-94—London	OHL	56	55	87	*142	68	...	...	...	5	2	13	15	13
—Washington	NHL	2	0	1	1	0	1	0	0	—	—	—	—	—
—Portland	AHL	6	2	1	3	0	...	...	...	—	—	—	—	—
94-95—London	OHL	15	15	21	36	43	...	...	...	—	—	—	—	—
—Washington	NHL	12	2	1	3	6	-3	2	0	—	—	—	—	—
—Portland	AHL	8	5	4	9	2	...	...	...	7	3	8	11	2
95-96—Washington	NHL	19	0	3	3	2	-3	0	0	—	—	—	—	—
—Portland	AHL	57	28	41	69	42	...	...	...	6	1	6	7	9
96-97—Washington	NHL	53	5	17	22	25	-3	1	0	—	—	—	—	—
—Boston	NHL	19	3	9	12	9	-3	1	0	—	—	—	—	—
97-98—Boston	NHL	81	33	50	83	60	33	5	0	6	2	6	8	4
98-99—Boston	NHL	82	23	53	76	68	5	5	1	12	2	9	11	6
99-00—Boston	NHL	37	10	18	28	20	5	3	0	—	—	—	—	—
00-01—Boston	NHL	82	36	59	95	85	-8	11	3	—	—	—	—	—
NHL Totals (8 years)...........		387	112	211	323	275	24	28	4	18	4	15	19	10

AMONTE, TONY — RW — BLACKHAWKS

PERSONAL: Born August 2, 1970, in Hingham, Mass. ... 6-0/190. ... Shoots left. ... Full Name: Anthony Lewis Amonte. ... Name pronounced ah-MAHN-tee.

TRANSACTIONS/CAREER NOTES: Selected by New York Rangers in fourth round (third Rangers pick, 68th overall) of NHL entry draft (June 11, 1988). ... Traded by Rangers with rights to LW Matt Oates to Chicago Blackhawks for LW Stephane Matteau and RW Brian Noonan (March 21, 1994). ... Pulled groin (1993-94 season); missed three games. ... Played in Europe during 1994-95 NHL lockout.

HONORS: Named to Hockey East All-Rookie team (1989-90). ... Named to NCAA All-Tournament team (1990-91). ... Named to Hockey East All-Star second team (1990-91). ... Named NHL Rookie of the Year by THE SPORTING NEWS (1991-92). ... Named to NHL All-Rookie team (1991-92). ... Played in NHL All-Star Game (1997-2001).

MISCELLANEOUS: Captain of Chicago Blackhawks (2000-01). ... Failed to score on a penalty shot (vs. Kelly Hrudey, January 27, 1994; vs. Guy Hebert, February 1, 1998).

STATISTICAL PLATEAUS: Three-goal games: 1991-92 (1), 1995-96 (1), 1996-97 (2), 1998-99 (2), 1999-00 (1). Total: 7.

Season Team	League	REGULAR SEASON								PLAYOFFS				
		Gms.	G	A	Pts.	PIM	+/-	PP	SH	Gms.	G	A	Pts.	PIM
86-87—Thayer Academy	Mass. H.S.	25	25	32	57	...	...	...	...	—	—	—	—	—
87-88—Thayer Academy	Mass. H.S.	28	30	38	68	...	...	...	...	—	—	—	—	—
88-89—Team USA Juniors	Int'l	7	1	3	4	...	...	...	...	—	—	—	—	—
—Thayer Academy	Mass. H.S.	25	35	38	73	...	...	...	...	—	—	—	—	—
89-90—Boston University	Hockey East	41	25	33	58	52	...	...	...	—	—	—	—	—
90-91—Boston University	Hockey East	38	31	37	68	82	...	...	...	—	—	—	—	—
—New York Rangers	NHL	—	—	—	—	—	—	—	—	2	0	2	2	2
91-92—New York Rangers	NHL	79	35	34	69	55	12	9	0	13	3	6	9	2
92-93—New York Rangers	NHL	83	33	43	76	49	0	13	0	—	—	—	—	—
93-94—New York Rangers	NHL	72	16	22	38	31	5	3	0	—	—	—	—	—
—Chicago	NHL	7	1	3	4	6	-5	1	0	6	4	2	6	4
94-95—Fassa	Italy	14	22	16	38	10	...	...	...	—	—	—	—	—
—Chicago	NHL	48	15	20	35	41	7	6	1	16	3	3	6	10
95-96—Chicago	NHL	81	31	32	63	62	10	5	4	7	2	4	6	6
96-97—Chicago	NHL	81	41	36	77	64	35	9	2	6	4	2	6	8
97-98—Chicago	NHL	82	31	42	73	66	21	7	3	—	—	—	—	—
—U.S. Olympic team	Int'l	4	0	1	1	4	...	...	...	—	—	—	—	—
98-99—Chicago	NHL	82	44	31	75	60	0	14	3	—	—	—	—	—
99-00—Chicago	NHL	82	43	41	84	48	10	11	5	—	—	—	—	—
00-01—Chicago	NHL	82	35	29	64	54	-22	9	1	—	—	—	—	—
NHL Totals (11 years)		779	325	333	658	536	73	87	19	50	16	19	35	32

ANDERSSON, CRAIG — G — BLACKHAWKS

PERSONAL: Born May 21, 1981, in Park Ridge, Ill. ... 6-2/170. ... Catches left.

TRANSACTIONS/CAREER NOTES: Selected by Calgary Flames in third round (third Flames pick, 77th overall) of NHL entry draft (June 26, 1999). ... Returned to draft pool by Flames and selected by Chicago Blackhawks in third round (fourth Blackhawks pick, 73th overall) of NHL entry draft (June 23, 2001).

HONORS: Named to OHL All-Star first team (2000-01).

Season Team	League	REGULAR SEASON								PLAYOFFS						
		Gms.	Min	W	L	T	GA	SO	Avg.	Gms.	Min.	W	L	GA	SO	Avg.
98-99—Chicago	NAHL	14	821	11	3	0	35	0	2.56	—	—	—	—	—	—	—
—Guelph	OHL	21	1006	12	5	1	52	1	3.10	3	114	0	2	9	0	4.74
99-00—Guelph	OHL	38	1955	12	17	2	117	0	3.59	3	110	0	1	5	0	2.73
00-01—Guelph	OHL	59	3555	30	19	*9	156	3	2.63	4	240	0	4	17	0	4.25

ANDERSSON, NIKLAS — LW

PERSONAL: Born May 20, 1971, in Kunglav, Sweden. ... 5-9/175. ... Shoots left. ... Brother of Mikael Andersson, left winger with four NHL teams (1985-86 through 1999-2000).

TRANSACTIONS/CAREER NOTES: Selected by Quebec Nordiques in third round (fifth Nordiques pick, 68th overall) of NHL entry draft (June 17, 1989). ... Signed as free agent by New York Islanders (July 15, 1994). ... Sprained shoulder (February 5, 1997); missed two games. ... Suffered sore foot (March 29, 1997); missed two games. ... Signed as free agent by San Jose Sharks (September 10, 1997). ... Signed as free agent by Toronto Maple Leafs (September 4, 1998). ... Traded by Maple Leafs to New York Islanders for C Craig Charron (August 17, 1999). ... Claimed on waivers by Nashville Predators (January 20, 2000). ... Claimed on waivers by Islanders (February 19, 2000). ... Signed as free agent by Calgary Flames (August 29, 2000).

HONORS: Named to IHL All-Star second team (1999-2000). ... Named to IHL All-Star first team (2000-01).

STATISTICAL PLATEAUS: Three-goal games: 1995-96 (1).

Season Team	League	REGULAR SEASON								PLAYOFFS				
		Gms.	G	A	Pts.	PIM	+/-	PP	SH	Gms.	G	A	Pts.	PIM
87-88—Frolunda	Sweden	15	5	5	10	...	...	...	...	—	—	—	—	—
88-89—Frolunda	Sweden	30	13	24	37	...	...	...	...	—	—	—	—	—
89-90—Frolunda	Sweden	38	10	21	31	14	...	...	...	—	—	—	—	—
90-91—Frolunda	Sweden	22	6	10	16	16	...	...	...	—	—	—	—	—
91-92—Halifax	AHL	57	8	26	34	41	...	...	...	—	—	—	—	—
92-93—Halifax	AHL	76	32	50	82	42	...	...	...	—	—	—	—	—
—Quebec	NHL	3	0	1	1	2	0	0	0	—	—	—	—	—
93-94—Cornwall	AHL	42	18	34	52	8	...	...	...	—	—	—	—	—
94-95—Denver	IHL	66	22	39	61	28	...	...	...	15	8	13	21	10
95-96—Utah	IHL	30	13	22	35	25	...	...	...	—	—	—	—	—
—New York Islanders	NHL	47	14	12	26	12	-3	3	2	—	—	—	—	—

Season Team	League	Gms.	G	A	Pts.	PIM	+/-	PP	SH	Gms.	G	A	Pts.	PIM
96-97—New York Islanders.....	NHL	74	12	31	43	57	4	1	1	—	—	—	—	—
97-98—Kentucky.................	AHL	37	10	28	38	54	...	...	...	—	—	—	—	—
—San Jose.................	NHL	5	0	0	0	2	-1	0	0	—	—	—	—	—
—Utah........................	IHL	21	6	20	26	24	...	...	...	4	3	1	4	4
98-99—Chicago.................	IHL	65	17	47	64	49	...	...	...	10	2	2	4	10
99-00—Chicago.................	IHL	52	20	21	41	59	...	...	...	9	6	1	7	4
—New York Islanders.....	NHL	17	3	7	10	8	-3	1	0	—	—	—	—	—
—Nashville.................	NHL	7	0	1	1	0	0	0	0	—	—	—	—	—
00-01—Calgary.................	NHL	11	0	1	1	4	0	0	0	—	—	—	—	—
—Chicago.................	IHL	66	33	39	72	81	...	...	...	16	1	*14	15	14
NHL Totals (6 years)...........		164	29	53	82	85	-3	5	3					

A

ANDERSSON-JUNKKA, JONAS   D — BLUE JACKETS

PERSONAL: Born May 4, 1975, in Kiruna, Sweden. ... 6-2/165. ... Shoots right.
TRANSACTIONS/CAREER NOTES: Selected by Pittsburgh Penguins in fourth round (fourth Penguins pick, 104th overall) of NHL entry draft (June 26, 1993). ... Selected by Columbus Blue Jackets in NHL expansion draft (June 23, 2000).

Season Team	League	Gms.	G	A	Pts.	PIM	+/-	PP	SH	Gms.	G	A	Pts.	PIM
89-90—HPK Hameenlinna.......	Finland	54	13	18	31	72	...	...	...	8	1	4	5	20
92-93—Kiruna.....................	Sweden Dv. 2	30	3	7	10	32	...	...	...	—	—	—	—	—
93-94—Kiruna.....................	Sweden Dv. 2	32	6	10	16	84	...	...	...	—	—	—	—	—
94-95—Vastra Frolunda	Sweden	19	0	2	2	2	...	...	...	—	—	—	—	—
95-96—Vastra Frolunda	Sweden	31	3	1	4	20	...	...	...	13	1	0	1	6
96-97—MoDo Ornskoldsvik	Sweden	12	1	3	4	10	...	...	...	—	—	—	—	—
97-98—MoDo Ornskoldsvik	Sweden	35	5	5	10	12	...	...	...	1	0	0	0	0
98-99—HPK Hameenlinna.......	Finland	50	5	9	14	36	...	...	...	8	3	1	4	8
99-00—HPK Hameenlinna.......	Finland	54	13	18	31	72	...	...	...	—	—	—	—	—

ANDREYCHUK, DAVE   LW — LIGHTNING

PERSONAL: Born September 29, 1963, in Hamilton, Ont. ... 6-4/220. ... Shoots right. ... Full Name: David Andreychuk. ... Name pronounced AN-druh-chuhk.
TRANSACTIONS/CAREER NOTES: Selected by Buffalo Sabres in first round (third Sabres pick, 16th overall) of NHL entry draft (June 9, 1982). ... Sprained knee (March 1983). ... Fractured collarbone (March 1985). ... Twisted knee (September 1985). ... Injured right knee (September 1986). ... Strained left knee ligaments (November 27, 1988). ... Fractured left thumb (February 18, 1990). ... Suspended two off-days and fined $500 by NHL for cross-checking incident (November 16, 1992). ... Traded by Sabres with G Daren Puppa and first-round pick (D Kenny Jonsson) in 1993 draft to Toronto Maple Leafs for G Grant Fuhr and fifth-round pick (D Kevin Popp) in 1995 draft (February 2, 1993). ... Injured knee (December 27, 1993); missed one game. ... Separated shoulder (December 2, 1995); missed five games. ... Suffered from the flu (December 27, 1995); missed one game. ... Underwent thumb surgery (January 15, 1996); missed two games. ... Traded by Maple Leafs to New Jersey Devils for second-round pick (D Marek Posmyk) in 1996 draft and third-round pick (traded back to New Jersey) in 1999 draft (March 13, 1996). ... Bruised left foot (October 23, 1997); missed six games. ... Bruised sternum (November 7, 1998); missed six games. ... Fractured right ankle (January 5, 1999); missed 21 games. ... Signed as free agent by Boston Bruins (July 28, 1999). ... Injured knee (January 11, 2000); missed two games. ... Traded by Bruins with D Ray Bourque to Colorado Avalanche for LW Brian Rolston, D Martin Grenier, C Samual Pahlsson and first-round pick (LW Martin Samuelsson) in 2000 draft (March 6, 2000). ... Signed as free agent by Sabres (July 13, 2000). ... Injured knee (February 13, 2001); missed two games. ... Signed as free agent by Tampa Bay Lightning (July 13, 2001).
HONORS: Played in NHL All-Star Game (1990 and 1994). ... Named to THE SPORTING NEWS All-Star second team (1993-94).
MISCELLANEOUS: Failed to score on a penalty shot (vs. Clint Malarchuk, November 22, 1986; vs. Darcy Wakaluk, February 7, 1992; vs. Tim Cheveldae, April 8, 1995).
STATISTICAL PLATEAUS: Three-goal games: 1987-88 (3), 1988-89 (1), 1989-90 (1), 1991-92 (1), 1992-93 (1). Total: 7. ... Four-goal games: 1991-92 (1), 1992-93 (1), 1999-00 (1). Total: 3. ... Five-goal games: 1985-86 (1). ... Total hat tricks: 11.

Season Team	League	Gms.	G	A	Pts.	PIM	+/-	PP	SH	Gms.	G	A	Pts.	PIM
80-81—Oshawa.....................	OMJHL	67	22	22	44	80	...	...	...	10	3	2	5	20
81-82—Oshawa.....................	OHL	67	58	43	101	71	...	...	...	3	1	4	5	16
82-83—Oshawa.....................	OHL	14	8	24	32	6	...	...	...	—	—	—	—	—
—Buffalo.....................	NHL	43	14	23	37	16	6	3	0	4	1	0	1	4
83-84—Buffalo.....................	NHL	78	38	42	80	42	20	10	0	2	0	1	1	2
84-85—Buffalo.....................	NHL	64	31	30	61	54	-4	14	0	5	4	2	6	4
85-86—Buffalo.....................	NHL	80	36	51	87	61	3	12	0	—	—	—	—	—
86-87—Buffalo.....................	NHL	77	25	48	73	46	2	13	0	—	—	—	—	—
87-88—Buffalo.....................	NHL	80	30	48	78	112	1	15	0	6	2	4	6	0
88-89—Buffalo.....................	NHL	56	28	24	52	40	0	7	0	5	0	3	3	0
89-90—Buffalo.....................	NHL	73	40	42	82	42	6	18	0	6	2	5	7	2
90-91—Buffalo.....................	NHL	80	36	33	69	32	11	13	0	6	2	2	4	8
91-92—Buffalo.....................	NHL	80	41	50	91	71	-9	*28	0	7	1	3	4	12
92-93—Buffalo.....................	NHL	52	29	32	61	48	-8	*20	0	—	—	—	—	—
—Toronto	NHL	31	25	13	38	8	12	*12	0	21	12	7	19	35
93-94—Toronto	NHL	83	53	46	99	98	22	21	5	18	5	5	10	16
94-95—Toronto	NHL	48	22	16	38	34	-7	8	0	7	3	2	5	25
95-96—Toronto	NHL	61	20	24	44	54	-11	12	2	—	—	—	—	—
—New Jersey	NHL	15	8	5	13	10	2	2	0	—	—	—	—	—
96-97—New Jersey	NHL	82	27	34	61	48	38	4	1	1	0	0	0	0
97-98—New Jersey	NHL	75	14	34	48	26	19	4	0	6	1	0	1	4
98-99—New Jersey	NHL	52	15	13	28	20	1	4	0	4	2	0	2	4
99-00—Boston.....................	NHL	63	19	14	33	28	-11	7	0	—	—	—	—	—
—Colorado.................	NHL	14	1	2	3	2	-9	1	0	17	3	2	5	18
00-01—Buffalo.....................	NHL	74	20	13	33	32	0	8	0	13	1	2	3	4
NHL Totals (19 years).........		1361	572	637	1209	924	84	236	8	128	39	38	77	138

ANTROPOV, NIK   C   MAPLE LEAFS

PERSONAL: Born February 18, 1980, in Vost, U.S.S.R. ... 6-5/203. ... Shoots left. ... Full Name: Nikolai Antropov.

TRANSACTIONS/CAREER NOTES: Selected by Toronto Maple Leafs in first round (first Maple Leafs pick, 10th overall) of NHL entry draft (June 27, 1998). ... Suffered injury (November 27, 1999); missed seven games. ... Suffered injury (January 5, 2000); missed two games. ... Suffered injury (March 29, 2000); missed one game.

STATISTICAL PLATEAUS: Three-goal games: 1999-00 (1).

		REGULAR SEASON								PLAYOFFS				
Season Team	League	Gms.	G	A	Pts.	PIM	+/-	PP	SH	Gms.	G	A	Pts.	PIM
95-96—Torpedo Ust-Kam........	CIS Jr.	20	18	20	38	30	...	...	...	—	—	—	—	—
96-97—Torpedo Ust-Kam........	Rus. Div. II	8	2	1	3	6	...	...	...	—	—	—	—	—
97-98—Torpedo Ust-Kam........	Rus. Div. II	42	15	24	39	62	...	...	...	—	—	—	—	—
98-99—Dynamo Moscow........	Russian	30	5	9	14	30	...	...	...	11	0	1	1	4
99-00—St. John's..................	AHL	2	0	0	0	4	...	...	...	—	—	—	—	—
—Toronto	NHL	66	12	18	30	41	14	0	0	3	0	0	0	4
00-01—Toronto	NHL	52	6	11	17	30	5	0	0	9	2	1	3	12
NHL Totals (2 years)............		118	18	29	47	71	19	0	0	12	2	1	3	16

ARKHIPOV, DENIS   RW   PREDATORS

PERSONAL: Born May 19, 1979, in Kazan, U.S.S.R. ... 6-3/195. ... Shoots left.

TRANSACTIONS/CAREER NOTES: Selected by Nashville Predators in third round (second Predators pick, 60th overall) of NHL entry draft (June 27, 1998).

		REGULAR SEASON								PLAYOFFS				
Season Team	League	Gms.	G	A	Pts.	PIM	+/-	PP	SH	Gms.	G	A	Pts.	PIM
94-95—Ak Bars Kazan............	CIS Jr.	40	20	12	32	10	...	...	...	—	—	—	—	—
95-96—Ak Bars Kazan............	CIS Jr.	40	15	8	23	30	...	...	...	—	—	—	—	—
—Ak Bars-2 Kazan	CIS Div. II	15	10	8	18	10	...	...	...	—	—	—	—	—
96-97—Ak Bars-2 Kazan	Rus. Div. III	50	17	23	40	20	...	...	...	—	—	—	—	—
—Ak Bars Kazan	Russian	1	1	0	1	0	...	...	...	—	—	—	—	—
97-98—Ak Bars Kazan............	Russian	29	2	2	4	2	...	...	...	—	—	—	—	—
98-99—Ak Bars Kazan............	Russian	34	12	1	13	22	...	...	...	9	2	3	5	6
99-00—Ak Bars Kazan............	Russian	32	7	9	16	14	...	...	...	18	5	5	10	6
00-01—Milwaukee..................	IHL	40	9	8	17	11	...	...	...	—	—	—	—	—
—Nashville	NHL	40	6	7	13	4	0	0	0	—	—	—	—	—
NHL Totals (1 year)............		40	6	7	13	4	0	0	0					

ARMSTRONG, CHRIS   D

PERSONAL: Born June 26, 1975, in Regina, Sask. ... 6-0/205. ... Shoots left.

TRANSACTIONS/CAREER NOTES: Selected by Florida Panthers in third round (third Panthers pick, 57th overall) of NHL entry draft (June 26, 1993). ... Selected by Nashville Predators in NHL expansion draft (June 26, 1998). ... Signed as free agent by San Jose Sharks (August 30, 1999). ... Selected by Minnesota Wild in NHL expansion draft (June 23, 2000).

HONORS: Named to Can.HL All-Star second team (1993-94). ... Named to WHL (East) All-Star first team (1993-94). ... Named to WHL (East) All-Star second team (1994-95).

		REGULAR SEASON								PLAYOFFS				
Season Team	League	Gms.	G	A	Pts.	PIM	+/-	PP	SH	Gms.	G	A	Pts.	PIM
91-92—Moose Jaw	WHL	43	2	7	9	19	...	...	...	4	0	0	0	0
92-93—Moose Jaw	WHL	67	9	35	44	104	...	...	...	—	—	—	—	—
93-94—Moose Jaw	WHL	64	13	55	68	54	...	...	...	—	—	—	—	—
—Cincinnati....................	IHL	1	0	0	0	0	...	...	...	10	1	3	4	2
94-95—Moose Jaw	WHL	66	17	54	71	61	...	...	...	10	2	12	14	22
—Cincinnati....................	IHL	—	—	—	—	—	...	...	...	9	1	3	4	10
95-96—Carolina	AHL	78	9	33	42	65	...	...	...	—	—	—	—	—
96-97—Carolina	AHL	66	9	23	32	38	...	...	...	—	—	—	—	—
97-98—Fort Wayne	IHL	79	8	36	44	66	...	...	...	4	0	2	2	4
98-99—Milwaukee	IHL	5	0	3	3	4	...	...	...	—	—	—	—	—
—Hershey	AHL	65	12	32	44	30	...	...	...	5	0	1	1	0
99-00—Kentucky....................	AHL	78	9	48	57	77	...	...	...	9	1	5	6	4
00-01—Cleveland	IHL	77	9	32	41	42	...	...	...	4	0	2	2	2
—Minnesota....................	NHL	3	0	0	0	0	-3	0	0	—	—	—	—	—
NHL Totals (1 year)............		3	0	0	0	0	-3	0	0					

ARMSTRONG, DEREK   C   RANGERS

PERSONAL: Born April 23, 1973, in Ottawa. ... 6-0/193. ... Shoots right.

TRANSACTIONS/CAREER NOTES: Selected by New York Islanders in sixth round (fifth Islanders pick, 128th overall) of NHL entry draft (June 20, 1992). ... Suffered food poisoning (January 28, 1997); missed one game. ... Signed as free agent by Ottawa Senators (July 10, 1997). ... Signed as free agent by New York Rangers (July 20, 1998).

HONORS: Won Jack Butterfield Trophy (1999-2000). ... Named to AHL All-Star second team (1999-2000). ... Named to AHL All-Star first team (2000-01). ... Won John B. Sollenberger Trophy (2000-01). ... Won Les Cunningham Plaque (2000-01).

Season Team	League	REGULAR SEASON								PLAYOFFS				
		Gms.	G	A	Pts.	PIM	+/-	PP	SH	Gms.	G	A	Pts.	PIM
89-90—Hawkesbury	COJHL	48	8	10	18	30	...	...	...	—	—	—	—	—
90-91—Hawkesbury	COJHL	54	27	45	72	49	...	...	...	—	—	—	—	—
—Sudbury	OHL	2	0	2	2	0	...	...	...	—	—	—	—	—
91-92—Sudbury	OHL	66	31	54	85	22	...	...	...	9	2	2	4	2
92-93—Sudbury	OHL	66	44	62	106	56	...	...	...	14	9	10	19	26
93-94—Salt Lake City	IHL	76	23	35	58	61	...	...	...	—	—	—	—	—
94-95—Denver	IHL	59	13	18	31	65	...	...	...	6	0	2	2	0
95-96—Worcester	AHL	51	11	15	26	33	...	...	...	4	2	1	3	0
—New York Islanders	NHL	19	1	3	4	14	-6	0	0	—	—	—	—	—
96-97—New York Islanders	NHL	50	6	7	13	33	-8	0	0	—	—	—	—	—
—Utah	IHL	17	4	8	12	10	...	...	...	6	0	4	4	4
97-98—Detroit	IHL	10	0	1	1	2	...	...	...	—	—	—	—	—
—Hartford	AHL	54	16	30	46	40	...	...	...	15	2	6	8	22
—Ottawa	NHL	9	2	0	2	9	1	0	0	—	—	—	—	—
98-99—Hartford	AHL	59	29	51	80	73	...	...	...	7	5	4	9	10
—New York Rangers	NHL	3	0	0	0	0	0	0	0	—	—	—	—	—
99-00—Hartford	AHL	77	28	54	82	101	...	...	...	23	7	16	23	24
—New York Rangers	NHL	1	0	0	0	0	0	0	0	—	—	—	—	—
00-01—Hartford	AHL	75	32	*69	*101	73	...	...	...	5	0	6	6	6
—New York Rangers	NHL	3	0	0	0	0	0	0	0	—	—	—	—	—
NHL Totals (6 years)		85	9	10	19	56	-13	0	0					

ARNOTT, JASON — C — DEVILS

PERSONAL: Born October 11, 1974, in Collingwood, Ont. ... 6-4/225. ... Shoots right. ... Name pronounced AHR-niht.
TRANSACTIONS/CAREER NOTES: Selected by Edmonton Oilers in first round (first Oilers pick, seventh overall) of NHL entry draft (June 26, 1993). ... Suffered from tonsillitis (November 3, 1993); missed one game. ... Bruised sternum (November 27, 1993); missed one game. ... Sprained back (December 7, 1993); missed one game. ... Underwent appendectomy (December 28, 1993); missed three games. ... Suffered from the flu (February 22, 1995); missed one game. ... Suffered concussion (March 23, 1995); missed two games. ... Strained knee (April 19, 1995); missed two games. ... Suspended one game by NHL for game misconduct penalties (April 22, 1995). ... Suffered concussion and lacerated face (October 8, 1995); missed seven games. ... Sprained knee (February 11, 1996); missed nine games. ... Strained knee (March 19, 1996); missed one game. ... Suffered inner ear infection (April 8, 1996); missed one game. ... Fractured ankle (December 27, 1996); missed seven games. ... Injured ankle (January 22, 1997); missed two games. ... Suffered from the flu (February 12, 1997); missed two games. ... Strained lower back (March 23, 1997); missed four games. ... Separated right shoulder (December 10, 1997); missed five games. ... Reinjured shoulder (January 2, 1998); missed two games. ... Traded to Oilers with D Bryan Muir to New Jersey Devils for RW Bill Guerin and RW Valeri Zelepukin (January 4, 1998). ... Suffered back spasms (March 21, 1998); missed one game. ... Bruised hip (April 8, 1998); missed three games. ... Reinjured hip (April 16, 1998); missed two games. ... Underwent offseason finger surgery; missed first game of 1998-99 season. ... Bruised thigh (December 28, 1998); missed one game. ... Suffered from the flu (January 15, 1999); missed two games ... Bruised foot (January 20, 1999); missed one game ... Bruised hip (March 28, 1999); missed one game. ... Reinjured hip (April 4, 1999); missed two games. ... Suffered mouth injury (October 23, 1999); missed three games. ... Suffered from the flu (February 21, 2000); missed two games. ... Bruised ribs (March 17, 2000); missed one game. ... Missed first 18 games of 2000-01 season due to contract dispute. ... Injured back (February 16, 2001); missed six games.
HONORS: Named NHL Rookie of the Year by THE SPORTING NEWS (1993-94). ... Named to NHL All-Rookie team (1993-94). ... Played in NHL All-Star Game (1997).
MISCELLANEOUS: Member of Stanley Cup championship team (2000).
STATISTICAL PLATEAUS: Three-goal games: 1994-95 (1), 1995-96 (1). Total: 2.

Season Team	League	REGULAR SEASON								PLAYOFFS				
		Gms.	G	A	Pts.	PIM	+/-	PP	SH	Gms.	G	A	Pts.	PIM
89-90—Stayner	Jr. C	34	21	31	52	12	...	...	...	—	—	—	—	—
90-91—Lindsay Jr. B	OHA	42	17	44	61	10	...	...	...	—	—	—	—	—
91-92—Oshawa	OHL	57	9	15	24	12	...	...	...	—	—	—	—	—
92-93—Oshawa	OHL	56	41	57	98	74	...	...	...	13	9	9	18	20
93-94—Edmonton	NHL	78	33	35	68	104	1	10	0	—	—	—	—	—
94-95—Edmonton	NHL	42	15	22	37	128	-14	7	0	—	—	—	—	—
95-96—Edmonton	NHL	64	28	31	59	87	-6	8	0	—	—	—	—	—
96-97—Edmonton	NHL	67	19	38	57	92	-21	10	1	12	3	6	9	18
97-98—Edmonton	NHL	35	5	13	18	78	-16	1	0	—	—	—	—	—
—New Jersey	NHL	35	5	10	15	21	-8	3	0	5	0	2	2	2
98-99—New Jersey	NHL	74	27	27	54	79	10	8	0	7	2	2	4	4
99-00—New Jersey	NHL	76	22	34	56	51	22	7	0	23	8	12	20	18
00-01—New Jersey	NHL	54	21	34	55	75	23	8	0	23	8	7	15	16
NHL Totals (8 years)		525	175	244	419	715	-9	62	1	70	21	29	50	56

ARONSON, STEVE — RW — WILD

PERSONAL: Born July 15, 1978, in Minnetonka, Minn. ... 6-1/205. ... Shoots right.
TRANSACTIONS/CAREER NOTES: Signed as non-drafted free agent by Minnesota Wild (May 4, 2000).

Season Team	League	REGULAR SEASON								PLAYOFFS				
		Gms.	G	A	Pts.	PIM	+/-	PP	SH	Gms.	G	A	Pts.	PIM
96-97—Univ. of St. Thomas	MIAC	27	11	25	36	44	...	...	...	—	—	—	—	—
97-98—Univ. of St. Thomas	MIAC	28	32	25	57	41	...	...	...	—	—	—	—	—
98-99—Univ. of St. Thomas	MIAC	31	23	37	60	73	...	...	...	—	—	—	—	—
99-00—Univ. of St. Thomas	MIAC	33	38	53	91	72	...	...	...	—	—	—	—	—
00-01—Cleveland	IHL	64	9	17	26	23	...	...	...	4	1	0	1	0
—Jackson	ECHL	3	0	1	1	2	...	...	...	—	—	—	—	—

ARVEDSON, MAGNUS — LW — SENATORS

PERSONAL: Born November 25, 1971, in Karlstad, Sweden. ... 6-2/198. ... Shoots left. ... Name pronounced AHR-vihd-suhn.
TRANSACTIONS/CAREER NOTES: Selected by Ottawa Senators in fifth round (fourth Senators pick, 119th overall) of NHL entry draft (June 21, 1997). ... Strained groin (October 17, 1997); missed seven games. ... Strained groin (November 29, 1997); missed three games. ... Suffered concussion (December 16, 1997); missed five games. ... Strained left shoulder (January 11, 1998); missed one game. ... Strained groin (March 20, 1998); missed three games. ... Suffered back spasms (October 20, 1998); missed two games. ... Bruised hip (October 14, 1999); missed one game. ... Injured abdomen (January 20, 2000) and underwent surgery; missed 34 games. ... Strained buttocks (November 2, 2000); missed one game. ... Fractured left foot (November 16, 2000); missed 19 games. ... Sprained right knee (January 10, 2001); missed 10 games. ... Strained groin (April 6, 2001); missed final game of regular season and two playoff games.
STATISTICAL PLATEAUS: Three-goal games: 1998-99 (1).

Season Team	League	REGULAR SEASON Gms.	G	A	Pts.	PIM	+/-	PP	SH	PLAYOFFS Gms.	G	A	Pts.	PIM
91-92—Orebro	Sweden Dv. 2	32	12	21	33	30	...	...	...	7	4	4	8	4
92-93—Orebro	Sweden Dv. 2	36	11	18	29	34	...	...	...	6	2	1	3	0
93-94—Farjestad Karlstad	Sweden	16	1	7	8	10				—	—	—	—	—
94-95—Farjestad Karlstad	Sweden	36	1	7	8	45				4	0	0	0	6
95-96—Farjestad Karlstad	Sweden	39	10	14	24	42				8	0	3	3	10
96-97—Farjestad Karlstad	Sweden	48	13	11	24	36				14	4	7	11	8
97-98—Ottawa	NHL	61	11	15	26	36	2	0	1	11	0	1	1	6
98-99—Ottawa	NHL	80	21	26	47	50	33	0	4	3	0	1	1	2
99-00—Ottawa	NHL	47	15	13	28	36	4	1	1	6	0	0	0	6
00-01—Ottawa	NHL	51	17	16	33	24	23	1	2	2	0	0	0	0
NHL Totals (4 years)		239	64	70	134	146	62	2	8	22	0	2	2	14

ASHAM, ARRON — RW/C — CANADIENS

PERSONAL: Born April 13, 1978, in Portage-La-Prairie, Man. ... 5-11/195. ... Shoots right.
TRANSACTIONS/CAREER NOTES: Selected by Montreal Canadiens in third round (third Canadiens pick, 71st overall) of NHL entry draft (June 22, 1996). ... Injured back (October 23, 1999); missed one game. ... Suffered from the flu (December 27, 1999); missed one game. ... Strained groin (January 22, 2000); missed 23 games. ... Strained hip flexor (February 17, 2001); missed eight games. ... Suffered from the flu (March 19, 2001); missed one game.

Season Team	League	REGULAR SEASON Gms.	G	A	Pts.	PIM	+/-	PP	SH	PLAYOFFS Gms.	G	A	Pts.	PIM
94-95—Red Deer	WHL	62	11	16	27	126	...	...	...	—	—	—	—	—
95-96—Red Deer	WHL	70	32	45	77	174	...	...	...	10	6	3	9	20
96-97—Red Deer	WHL	67	45	51	96	149	...	...	...	16	12	14	26	36
97-98—Red Deer	WHL	67	43	49	92	153	...	...	...	5	0	2	2	8
—Fredericton	AHL	2	1	1	2	0	...	...	...	2	0	1	1	0
98-99—Fredericton	AHL	60	16	18	34	118	...	...	...	13	8	6	14	11
—Montreal	NHL	7	0	0	0	0	-4	0	0	—	—	—	—	—
99-00—Montreal	NHL	33	4	2	6	24	-7	0	1	—	—	—	—	—
—Quebec	AHL	13	4	5	9	32	...	...	...	2	0	0	0	2
00-01—Quebec	AHL	15	7	9	16	51	...	...	...	7	1	2	3	2
—Montreal	NHL	46	2	3	5	59	-9	0	0	—	—	—	—	—
NHL Totals (3 years)		86	6	5	11	83	-20	0	1					

ASTASHENKO, KASPARS — D — LIGHTNING

PERSONAL: Born February 7, 1975, in Riga, U.S.S.R. ... 6-2/183. ... Shoots left. ... Name pronounced KAHS-phar ahs-tah-SHEHN-koh.
TRANSACTIONS/CAREER NOTES: Selected by Tampa Bay Lightning in fifth round (fifth Lightning pick, 127th overall) of NHL entry draft (June 26, 1999). ... Suffered concussion (April 8, 2000); missed final game of season.

Season Team	League	REGULAR SEASON Gms.	G	A	Pts.	PIM	+/-	PP	SH	PLAYOFFS Gms.	G	A	Pts.	PIM
93-94—Pardaugava Riga	CIS	4	0	0	0	10	...	...	...	—	—	—	—	—
94-95—Pardaugava Riga	CIS	25	0	0	0	24	...	...	...	—	—	—	—	—
95-96—CSKA Moscow	CIS	26	0	1	1	10	...	...	...	—	—	—	—	—
96-97—HC CSKA Moscow	Russian	41	0	0	0	48	...	...	...	2	0	1	1	4
97-98—HC CSKA Moscow	Russian	25	1	3	4	6	...	...	...	—	—	—	—	—
98-99—Cincinnati	IHL	74	3	11	14	166	...	...	...	3	0	2	2	6
—Dayton	ECHL	2	0	1	1	4	...	...	...	—	—	—	—	—
99-00—Detroit	IHL	51	1	10	11	86	...	...	...	—	—	—	—	—
—Long Beach	IHL	14	0	3	3	10	...	...	...	—	—	—	—	—
—Tampa Bay	NHL	8	0	1	1	4	-2	0	0	—	—	—	—	—
00-01—Detroit	IHL	51	6	10	16	58	...	...	...	—	—	—	—	—
—Tampa Bay	NHL	15	1	1	2	4	-4	0	0	—	—	—	—	—
NHL Totals (2 years)		23	1	2	3	8	-6	0	0					

ATCHEYNUM, BLAIR — RW

PERSONAL: Born April 20, 1969, in Estevan, Sask. ... 6-2/198. ... Shoots right. ... Name pronounced ATCH-ih-nuhm.
TRANSACTIONS/CAREER NOTES: Selected by Hartford Whalers in third round (second Whalers pick, 52nd overall) of NHL entry draft (June 17, 1989). ... Suffered concussion (January 12, 1991). ... Selected by Ottawa Senators in NHL expansion draft (June 18, 1992). ... Signed as free agent by St. Louis Blues (August 12, 1997). ... Fractured finger (March 1, 1998); missed 17 games. ... Selected by Nashville Predators in NHL expansion draft (June 26, 1998). ... Tore anterior cruciate knee ligament (November 7, 1998); missed 15 games. ... Traded by Predators to Blues for sixth-round pick (F Zbynek Irgl) in 2000 draft (March 23, 1999). ... Signed as free agent by Chicago Blackhawks (September 30, 1999). ... Suffered sore back (November 27, 1999); missed four games.
HONORS: Won Brad Hornung Trophy (1988-89). ... Named to WHL (East) All-Star first team (1988-89). ... Named to AHL All-Star first team (1996-97).

Season Team	League	REGULAR SEASON								PLAYOFFS				
		Gms.	G	A	Pts.	PIM	+/-	PP	SH	Gms.	G	A	Pts.	PIM
85-86—North Battleford	SJHL	35	25	20	45	50	...	...	...	—	—	—	—	—
—Saskatoon	WHL	19	1	4	5	22	...	...	...	—	—	—	—	—
86-87—Saskatoon	WHL	21	0	4	4	4	...	...	...	—	—	—	—	—
—Swift Current	WHL	5	2	1	3	0	...	...	...	—	—	—	—	—
—Moose Jaw	WHL	12	3	0	3	2	...	...	...	—	—	—	—	—
87-88—Moose Jaw	WHL	60	32	16	48	52	...	...	...	—	—	—	—	—
88-89—Moose Jaw	WHL	71	70	68	138	70	...	...	...	7	2	5	7	13
89-90—Binghamton	AHL	78	20	21	41	45	...	...	...	—	—	—	—	—
90-91—Springfield	AHL	72	25	27	52	42	...	...	...	13	0	6	6	6
91-92—Springfield	AHL	62	16	21	37	64	...	...	...	6	1	1	2	2
92-93—New Haven	AHL	51	16	18	34	47	...	...	...	—	—	—	—	—
—Ottawa	NHL	4	0	1	1	0	-3	0	0	—	—	—	—	—
93-94—Portland	AHL	2	0	0	0	0	...	...	...	—	—	—	—	—
—Springfield	AHL	40	18	22	40	13	...	...	...	6	0	2	2	0
—Columbus	ECHL	16	15	12	27	10	...	...	...	—	—	—	—	—
94-95—Minnesota	IHL	17	4	6	10	7	...	...	...	—	—	—	—	—
—Worcester	AHL	55	17	29	46	26	...	...	...	—	—	—	—	—
95-96—Cape Breton	AHL	79	30	42	72	65	...	...	...	—	—	—	—	—
96-97—Hershey	AHL	77	42	45	87	57	...	...	...	13	6	11	17	6
97-98—St. Louis	NHL	61	11	15	26	10	5	0	1	10	0	0	0	2
98-99—Nashville	NHL	53	8	6	14	16	-10	2	0	—	—	—	—	—
—St. Louis	NHL	12	2	2	4	2	2	0	0	13	1	3	4	6
99-00—Chicago	NHL	47	5	7	12	6	-8	0	0	—	—	—	—	—
00-01—Chicago	NHL	19	1	2	3	2	-7	0	0	—	—	—	—	—
—Norfolk	AHL	37	12	8	20	16	...	...	...	4	0	0	0	6
—Chicago	IHL	7	1	0	1	0	...	...	...	—	—	—	—	—
NHL Totals (5 years)		196	27	33	60	36	-21	2	1	23	1	3	4	8

AUBIN, JEAN-SEBASTIEN   G   PENGUINS

PERSONAL: Born July 19, 1977, in Montreal. ... 5-11/176. ... Catches right. ... Name pronounced OH-bahn.

TRANSACTIONS/CAREER NOTES: Selected by Pittsburgh Penguins in third round (second Penguins pick, 76th overall) of NHL entry draft (July 8, 1995). ... Strained hamstring (April 3, 1999); missed six games. ... Injured shoulder (November 23, 1999); missed two games. ... Sprained ankle (April 3, 2000); missed final three games of season. ... Injured knee and underwent surgery (December 3, 2000); missed 14 games.

MISCELLANEOUS: Holds Pittsburgh Penguins all-time record for goals-against average (2.73). ... Stopped a penalty shot attempt (vs. Teemu Selanne, October 27, 1999; vs. Martin Rucinsky, February 28, 2001). ... Allowed a penalty shot goal (vs. Keith Tkachuk, January 12, 2000; vs. Tim Connolly, March 21, 2000).

Season Team	League	REGULAR SEASON								PLAYOFFS						
		Gms.	Min	W	L	T	GA	SO	Avg.	Gms.	Min.	W	L	GA	SO	Avg.
94-95—Sherbrooke	QMJHL	27	1287	13	10	1	73	1	3.40	3	185	1	2	11	0	3.57
95-96—Sherbrooke	QMJHL	40	2084	18	14	2	127	1	3.66	4	174	1	3	16	0	5.52
96-97—Sherbrooke	QMJHL	4	249	3	1	0	8	0	1.93	—	—	—	—	—	—	—
—Moncton	QMJHL	23	1311	9	13	0	72	1	3.30	—						
—Laval	QMJHL	11	532	2	6	1	41	0	4.62	2	128	0	2	10	0	4.69
97-98—Syracuse	AHL	8	380	2	4	1	26	0	4.11	—						
—Dayton	ECHL	21	1177	15	2	‡2	59	1	3.01	3	142	1	1	4	0	1.69
98-99—Kansas City	IHL	13	751	5	7	‡1	41	0	3.28	—						
—Pittsburgh	NHL	17	756	4	3	6	28	2	2.22	—						
99-00—Wilkes-Barre/Scranton	AHL	11	538	2	8	0	39	0	4.35	—						
—Pittsburgh	NHL	51	2789	23	21	3	120	2	2.58	—						
00-01—Pittsburgh	NHL	36	2050	20	14	1	107	0	3.13	1	1	0	0	0	0	...
NHL Totals (3 years)		104	5595	47	38	10	255	4	2.73	1	1	0	0	0	0	...

AUBIN, SERGE   C   BLUE JACKETS

PERSONAL: Born February 15, 1975, in Val d'Or, Que. ... 6-0/190. ... Shoots left. ... Name pronounced OH-bahn.

TRANSACTIONS/CAREER NOTES: Selected by Pittsburgh Penguins in seventh round (ninth Penguins pick, 161st overall) of NHL entry draft (June 29, 1994). ... Signed as free agent by Colorado Avalanche (December 18, 1998). ... Signed as free agent by Columbus Blue Jackets (July 11, 2000). ... Suffered from the flu (January 15, 2001); missed one game.

HONORS: Named to AHL All-Star first team (1999-2000).

MISCELLANEOUS: Shares Columbus Blue Jackets all-time record for games played (81).

Season Team	League	REGULAR SEASON								PLAYOFFS				
		Gms.	G	A	Pts.	PIM	+/-	PP	SH	Gms.	G	A	Pts.	PIM
92-93—Drummondville	QMJHL	65	16	34	50	30	...	...	...	8	0	1	1	16
93-94—Granby	QMJHL	63	42	32	74	80	...	...	...	7	2	3	5	8
94-95—Granby	QMJHL	60	37	73	110	55	...	...	...	11	8	15	23	4
95-96—Cleveland	IHL	2	0	0	0	0	...	...	...	2	0	0	0	0
—Hampton Roads	ECHL	62	24	62	86	74	...	...	...	3	1	4	5	10
96-97—Cleveland	IHL	57	9	16	25	39	...	...	...	2	0	0	0	0
97-98—Syracuse	AHL	55	6	14	20	57	...	...	...	—	—	—	—	—
—Hershey	AHL	5	2	1	3	0	...	...	...	7	1	3	4	6
98-99—Hershey	AHL	64	30	39	69	58	...	...	...	3	0	1	1	2
—Colorado	NHL	1	0	0	0	0	0	0	0	—	—	—	—	—
99-00—Hershey	AHL	58	42	38	80	56	...	...	...	—	—	—	—	—
—Colorado	NHL	15	2	1	3	6	1	0	0	17	0	1	1	6
00-01—Columbus	NHL	81	13	17	30	107	-20	0	0	—	—	—	—	—
NHL Totals (3 years)		97	15	18	33	113	-19	0	0	17	0	1	1	6

PERSONAL: Born July 3, 1973, in Ottawa. ... 6-2/210. ... Shoots right. ... Name pronounced oh-COYN.
TRANSACTIONS/CAREER NOTES: Selected by Vancouver Canucks in fifth round (seventh Canucks pick, 117th overall) of NHL entry draft (June 20, 1992). ... Sprained shoulder (January 10, 1997); missed six games. ... Strained groin (October 30, 1997); missed five games. ... Reinjured groin (November 12, 1997); missed 10 games. ... Sprained ankle (December 13, 1997); missed seven games. ... Injured groin (December 4, 1999); missed four games. ... Fractured finger (February 9, 2000); missed 20 games. ... Strained groin (November 4, 2000); missed two games. ... Reinjured groin (November 9, 2000); missed three games. ... Traded by Canucks with second-round pick (C/LW Alexander Polushin) in 2001 draft to Tampa Bay Lightning for G Dan Cloutier (February 7, 2001). ... Traded by Lightning with RW Alexander Kharitonov to New York Islanders for D Mathieu Biron and second-round pick in 2002 draft (June 22, 2001).
MISCELLANEOUS: Member of silver-medal-winning Canadian Olympic team (1994).

			REGULAR SEASON								PLAYOFFS			
Season Team	League	Gms.	G	A	Pts.	PIM	+/-	PP	SH	Gms.	G	A	Pts.	PIM
91-92—Boston University	Hockey East	33	2	10	12	62	...	...	...	—	—	—	—	—
92-93—Canadian nat'l team	Int'l	42	8	10	18	71	...	...	...	—	—	—	—	—
93-94—Canadian nat'l team	Int'l	59	5	12	17	80	...	...	...	—	—	—	—	—
—Can. Olympic team	Int'l	4	0	0	0	2	...	...	...	—	—	—	—	—
—Hamilton	AHL	13	1	2	3	19	...	...	...	4	0	2	2	6
94-95—Syracuse	AHL	71	13	18	31	52	...	...	...	—	—	—	—	—
—Vancouver	NHL	1	1	0	1	0	1	0	0	4	1	0	1	0
95-96—Syracuse	AHL	29	5	13	18	47	...	...	...	—	—	—	—	—
—Vancouver	NHL	49	4	14	18	34	8	2	0	6	0	0	0	2
96-97—Vancouver	NHL	70	5	16	21	63	0	1	0	—	—	—	—	—
97-98—Vancouver	NHL	35	3	3	6	21	-4	1	0	—	—	—	—	—
98-99—Vancouver	NHL	82	23	11	34	77	-14	18	2	—	—	—	—	—
99-00—Vancouver	NHL	57	10	14	24	30	7	4	0	—	—	—	—	—
00-01—Vancouver	NHL	47	3	13	16	20	13	1	0	—	—	—	—	—
—Tampa Bay	NHL	26	1	11	12	25	-8	1	0	—	—	—	—	—
NHL Totals (7 years)		367	50	82	132	270	3	28	2	10	1	0	1	2

PERSONAL: Born September 23, 1969, in Laval, Que. ... 5-8/184. ... Shoots right. ... Name pronounced aw-DEHT.
TRANSACTIONS/CAREER NOTES: Selected by Buffalo Sabres in ninth round (eighth Sabres pick, 183rd overall) of NHL entry draft (June 17, 1989). ... Fractured left hand (February 11, 1990); missed seven games. ... Bruised thigh (September 1990). ... Bruised thigh (October 1990); missed five games. ... Tore ligaments in left knee (November 16, 1990); and underwent surgery. ... Sprained ankle (December 14, 1991); missed eight games. ... Injured knee (March 31, 1992). ... Underwent knee surgery prior to 1992-93 season; missed first 22 games of season. ... Tore knee cartilage (September 23, 1995); missed 11 games. ... Broke tip of right thumb (November 8, 1995); missed two games. ... Injured right knee (December 1, 1995); missed seven games. ... Underwent right knee surgery (January 26, 1996); missed remainder of season. ... Strained groin (October 26, 1996); missed five games. ... Suffered concussion (October 22, 1997); missed seven games. ... Missed first 25 games of 1998-99 season due to contract dispute. ... Traded by Sabres to Los Angeles Kings for second-round pick (RW Milan Bartovic) in 1999 draft (December 18, 1998). ... Suffered back spasms (April 8, 1999); missed one game. ... Suffered from the flu (April 18, 1999); missed one game. ... Sprained left ankle (January 6, 2000); missed 15 games. ... Traded by Kings with D Frantisek Kaberle to Atlanta Thrashers for RW Kelly Buchberger and RW Nelson Emerson (March 13, 2000). ... Strained groin (December 27, 2000); missed one game. ... Suspended four games by NHL for cross-checking incident (January 16, 2001). ... Suspended two games by NHL for delivering illegal blow to the head (March 12, 2001). ... Traded by Thrashers to Sabres for C Kamil Piros and fourth-round pick (traded to St. Louis) in 2001 draft (March 13, 2001). ... Signed as free agent by Dallas Stars (July 2, 2001).
HONORS: Won Guy Lafleur Trophy (1988-89). ... Named to QMJHL All-Star first team (1988-89). ... Won Dudley (Red) Garrett Memorial Trophy (1989-90). ... Named to AHL All-Star first team (1989-90). ... Played in NHL All-Star Game (2001).
MISCELLANEOUS: Failed to score on a penalty shot (vs. Felix Potvin, November 21, 1996).
STATISTICAL PLATEAUS: Three-goal games: 1994-95 (1), 1995-96 (1), 2000-01 (2). Total: 4.

			REGULAR SEASON								PLAYOFFS			
Season Team	League	Gms.	G	A	Pts.	PIM	+/-	PP	SH	Gms.	G	A	Pts.	PIM
86-87—Laval	QMJHL	66	17	22	39	36	...	...	...	14	2	6	8	10
87-88—Laval	QMJHL	63	48	61	109	56	...	...	...	14	7	12	19	20
88-89—Laval	QMJHL	70	76	85	161	123	...	...	...	17	*17	12	29	43
89-90—Rochester	AHL	70	42	46	88	78	...	...	...	15	9	8	17	29
—Buffalo	NHL	0	0	0	0	0	0	0	0	2	0	0	0	0
90-91—Rochester	AHL	5	4	0	4	2	...	...	...	—	—	—	—	—
—Buffalo	NHL	8	4	3	7	4	-1	2	0	—	—	—	—	—
91-92—Buffalo	NHL	63	31	17	48	75	-1	5	0	—	—	—	—	—
92-93—Buffalo	NHL	44	12	7	19	51	-8	2	0	8	2	2	4	6
—Rochester	AHL	6	8	4	12	10	...	...	...	—	—	—	—	—
93-94—Buffalo	NHL	77	29	30	59	41	2	16	1	7	0	1	1	6
94-95—Buffalo	NHL	46	24	13	37	27	-3	13	0	5	1	1	2	4
95-96—Buffalo	NHL	23	12	13	25	18	0	8	0	—	—	—	—	—
96-97—Buffalo	NHL	73	28	22	50	48	-6	8	0	11	4	5	9	6
97-98—Buffalo	NHL	75	24	20	44	59	10	10	0	15	5	8	13	10
98-99—Los Angeles	NHL	49	18	18	36	51	7	6	0	—	—	—	—	—
99-00—Los Angeles	NHL	49	12	20	32	45	6	1	0	—	—	—	—	—
—Atlanta	NHL	14	7	4	11	12	-4	0	1	—	—	—	—	—
00-01—Atlanta	NHL	64	32	39	71	64	-3	13	1	—	—	—	—	—
—Buffalo	NHL	12	2	6	8	12	1	1	0	13	3	6	9	4
NHL Totals (12 years)		597	235	212	447	507	0	85	3	61	15	23	38	36

PERSONAL: Born January 7, 1981, in Cold Lake, Alta. ... 6-4/196. ... Catches left. ... Full Name: Alexander Auld.
TRANSACTIONS/CAREER NOTES: Selected by Florida Panthers in second round (second Panthers pick, 40th overall) of NHL entry draft (June 26, 1999). ... Traded by Panthers to Vancouver Canucks for second-round pick (traded to New Jersey) in 2001 draft and third-round pick in 2002 draft (May 31, 2001).

Season Team	League	REGULAR SEASON							PLAYOFFS					
		Gms.	Min	W	L	T	GA	SO	Avg.	Gms.	Min.	W	L	GA	SO	Avg.
97-98—North Bay	OHL	6	206	0	4	0	17	0	4.95	—	—	—	—	—	—	—
98-99—North Bay	OHL	37	1894	9	20	1	106	1	3.36	3	170	0	3	10	0	3.53
99-00—North Bay	OHL	55	3047	21	26	6	167	2	3.29	6	374	2	4	12	0	1.93
00-01—North Bay	OHL	40	2319	22	11	5	98	1	2.54	4	240	0	4	15	0	3.75

AULIN, JARED   C   KINGS

PERSONAL: Born March 15, 1982, in Calgary. ... 5-11/175. ... Shoots right.
TRANSACTIONS/CAREER NOTES: Selected by Colorado Avalanche in second round (second Avalanche pick, 47th overall) of NHL entry draft (June 24, 2000). ... Traded by Avalanche to Los Angeles Kings (March 22, 2001); completing deal in which Kings traded D Rob Blake and C Steve Reinprecht to Colorado Avalanche for RW Adam Deadmarsh, D Aaron Miller, first-round pick (C David Steckel) in 2001 draft, a player to be named later and first-round pick in 2002 draft (February 21, 2001).
HONORS: Named to WHL (West) All-Star first team (2000-01).

Season Team	League	REGULAR SEASON								PLAYOFFS				
		Gms.	G	A	Pts.	PIM	+/-	PP	SH	Gms.	G	A	Pts.	PIM
97-98—Kamloops	WHL	2	0	0	0	0	...	...	...	0	0	0	0	0
98-99—Kamloops	WHL	55	7	19	26	23	...	...	...	13	1	3	4	2
99-00—Kamloops	WHL	57	17	38	55	70	...	...	...	4	0	1	1	6
00-01—Kamloops	WHL	70	31	†77	108	62	...	...	...	4	0	2	2	0

AXELSSON, P.J.   RW   BRUINS

PERSONAL: Born February 26, 1975, in Kungalv, Sweden. ... 6-1/174. ... Shoots left. ... Full Name: Per-Johan Axelsson. ... Name pronounced AK-sihl-suhn.
TRANSACTIONS/CAREER NOTES: Selected by Boston Bruins in seventh round (seventh Bruins pick, 177th overall) of NHL entry draft (June 8, 1995). ... Suffered concussion (October 28, 1998); missed one game. ... Suffered concussion (November 3, 1998); missed three games. ... Suffered from the flu (April 17, 1999); missed one game. ... Suffered from charley horse (October 23, 1999); missed one game.

Season Team	League	REGULAR SEASON								PLAYOFFS				
		Gms.	G	A	Pts.	PIM	+/-	PP	SH	Gms.	G	A	Pts.	PIM
93-94—Frolunda	Sweden	11	0	0	0	4	...	...	...	4	0	0	0	0
94-95—Frolunda	Sweden	8	2	1	3	6	...	...	...	—	—	—	—	—
95-96—Frolunda	Sweden	36	15	5	20	10	...	...	...	13	3	0	3	10
96-97—Vastra Frolunda	Sweden	50	19	15	34	34	...	...	...	3	0	2	2	0
97-98—Boston	NHL	82	8	19	27	38	-14	2	0	6	1	0	1	0
98-99—Boston	NHL	77	7	10	17	18	-14	0	0	12	1	1	2	4
99-00—Boston	NHL	81	10	16	26	24	1	0	0	—	—	—	—	—
00-01—Boston	NHL	81	8	15	23	27	-12	0	0	—	—	—	—	—
NHL Totals (4 years)		321	33	60	93	107	-39	2	0	18	2	1	3	4

BABENKO, YURI   C   AVALANCHE

PERSONAL: Born January 2, 1978, in Penza, U.S.S.R. ... 6-0/185. ... Shoots left.
TRANSACTIONS/CAREER NOTES: Selected by Colorado Avalanche in second round (second Avalanche pick, 51st overall) of NHL entry draft (June 22, 1996).

Season Team	League	REGULAR SEASON								PLAYOFFS				
		Gms.	G	A	Pts.	PIM	+/-	PP	SH	Gms.	G	A	Pts.	PIM
95-96—Soviet Wings	CIS	21	0	0	0	16	...	...	...	—	—	—	—	—
96-97—Soviet Wings	USSR	4	1	0	1	4	...	...	...	—	—	—	—	—
—Soviet Wings 2	Rus. Div. III	26	8	10	18	24	...	...	...	—	—	—	—	—
—CSKA	Rus. Div. II	24	3	3	6	12	...	...	...	—	—	—	—	—
97-98—Plymouth	OHL	59	22	34	56	22	...	...	...	15	3	7	10	24
98-99—Hershey	AHL	74	11	15	26	47	...	...	...	2	0	1	1	0
99-00—Hershey	AHL	75	20	25	45	53	...	...	...	14	4	3	7	37
00-01—Hershey	AHL	71	17	18	35	80	...	...	...	12	2	1	3	6
—Colorado	NHL	3	0	0	0	0	0	0	0	—	—	—	—	—
NHL Totals (1 year)		3	0	0	0	0	0	0	0					

BALA, CHRIS   LW   SENATORS

PERSONAL: Born September 24, 1978, in Alexandria, Va. ... 6-1/180. ... Shoots left.
TRANSACTIONS/CAREER NOTES: Selected by Ottawa Senators in second round (third Senators pick, 58th overall) of NHL entry draft (June 27, 1998).

Season Team	League	REGULAR SEASON								PLAYOFFS				
		Gms.	G	A	Pts.	PIM	+/-	PP	SH	Gms.	G	A	Pts.	PIM
96-97—The Hill School	USHS (East)	23	28	33	61	36	...	...	...	—	—	—	—	—
97-98—Harvard University	ECAC	33	16	14	30	23	...	...	...	—	—	—	—	—
98-99—Harvard University	ECAC	28	5	10	15	16	...	...	...	—	—	—	—	—
99-00—Harvard University	ECAC	30	10	14	24	18	...	...	...	—	—	—	—	—
00-01—Harvard University	ECAC	32	14	16	30	24	...	...	...	—	—	—	—	—

BALEJ, JOZEF RW CANADIENS

PERSONAL: Born February 22, 1982, in Ilava, Czechoslovakia. ... 5-11/170. ... Shoots right.
TRANSACTIONS/CAREER NOTES: Selected by Montreal Canadiens in third round (third Canadiens pick, 78th overall) of NHL entry draft (June 24, 2000).

		REGULAR SEASON								PLAYOFFS				
Season Team	League	Gms.	G	A	Pts.	PIM	+/-	PP	SH	Gms.	G	A	Pts.	PIM
97-98—Dukla Trencin..............	Slovakia Jrs.	52	57	40	97	60	...	...	...	—	—	—	—	—
98-99—Thunder Bay Flyers.....	USHL	38	8	7	15	9	...	...	...	—	—	—	—	—
99-00—Portland....................	WHL	65	22	23	45	33	...	...	...	—	—	—	—	—
00-01—Portland....................	WHL	46	32	21	53	18	...	...	...	16	6	9	15	6

B

BALMOCHNYKH, MAXIM LW MIGHTY DUCKS

PERSONAL: Born March 7, 1979, in Lipetsk, U.S.S.R. ... 6-1/200. ... Shoots left. ... Name pronounced bal-MOTCH-nick.
TRANSACTIONS/CAREER NOTES: Selected by Mighty Ducks of Anaheim in second round (second Mighty Ducks pick, 45th overall) of NHL entry draft (June 21, 1997).

		REGULAR SEASON								PLAYOFFS				
Season Team	League	Gms.	G	A	Pts.	PIM	+/-	PP	SH	Gms.	G	A	Pts.	PIM
94-95—HC Lipetsk	CIS Div. II	3	0	1	1	4	...	...	...	—	—	—	—	—
95-96—HC Lipetsk	CIS Div. II	40	15	5	20	60	...	...	...	—	—	—	—	—
96-97—Lada Togliatti	Russian	18	6	1	7	22	...	...	...	—	—	—	—	—
97-98—Lada Togliatti	Russian	37	10	4	14	46	...	...	...	—	—	—	—	—
—Traktor Chelyabinsk	Russian	2	0	0	0	2	...	...	...	—	—	—	—	—
98-99—Lada Togliatti	Russian	15	2	1	3	10	...	...	...	4	0	1	1	8
99-00—Cincinnati...................	AHL	40	9	12	21	82	...	...	...	—	—	—	—	—
—Anaheim	NHL	6	0	1	1	2	2	0	0	—	—	—	—	—
00-01—Cincinnati...................	AHL	65	6	9	15	45	...	...	...	—	—	—	—	—
NHL Totals (1 year)..............		6	0	1	1	2	2	0	0					

BANNISTER, DREW D RANGERS

PERSONAL: Born September 4, 1974, in Belleville, Ont. ... 6-2/208. ... Shoots right.
TRANSACTIONS/CAREER NOTES: Selected by Tampa Bay Lightning in second round (second Lightning pick, 26th overall) of NHL entry draft (June 20, 1992). ... Injured ribs (November 27, 1996); missed one game. ... Bruised shoulder (March 15, 1997); missed one game. ... Traded by Lightning with sixth-round pick (C Peter Sarno) in 1997 draft to Edmonton Oilers for D Jeff Norton (March 18, 1997). ... Traded by Oilers to Mighty Ducks of Anaheim for D Bobby Dollas (January 9, 1998). ... Traded by Mighty Ducks to Lightning for fifth-round pick (D Peter Podhradsky) in 2000 draft (December 10, 1998). ... Fractured wrist (January 15, 1999); missed 29 games. ... Released by Lightning (October 5, 1999). ... Signed as free agent by New York Rangers (October 6, 1999).
HONORS: Named to Memorial Cup All-Star team (1991-92). ... Named to OHL All-Star second team (1993-94).

		REGULAR SEASON								PLAYOFFS				
Season Team	League	Gms.	G	A	Pts.	PIM	+/-	PP	SH	Gms.	G	A	Pts.	PIM
90-91—Sault Ste. Marie	OHL	41	2	8	10	51	...	...	...	4	0	0	0	0
91-92—Sault Ste. Marie	OHL	64	4	21	25	122	...	...	...	16	3	10	13	36
92-93—Sault Ste. Marie	OHL	59	5	28	33	114	...	...	...	18	2	7	9	12
93-94—Sault Ste. Marie	OHL	58	7	43	50	108	...	...	...	14	6	9	15	20
94-95—Atlanta	IHL	72	5	7	12	74	...	...	...	5	0	2	2	22
95-96—Atlanta	IHL	61	3	13	16	105	...	...	...	3	0	0	0	4
—Tampa Bay	NHL	13	0	1	1	4	-1	0	0	—	—	—	—	—
96-97—Tampa Bay	NHL	64	4	13	17	44	-21	1	0	—	—	—	—	—
—Edmonton	NHL	1	0	1	1	0	-2	0	0	12	0	0	0	30
97-98—Edmonton	NHL	34	0	2	2	42	-7	0	0	—	—	—	—	—
—Anaheim	NHL	27	0	6	6	47	-2	0	0	—	—	—	—	—
98-99—Las Vegas	IHL	16	2	1	3	73	...	...	...	—	—	—	—	—
—Tampa Bay	NHL	21	1	2	3	24	-4	0	0	—	—	—	—	—
99-00—Hartford	AHL	44	6	14	20	121	...	...	...	18	2	9	11	53
00-01—Hartford	AHL	73	9	30	39	143	...	...	...	5	0	2	2	6
—New York Rangers......	NHL	3	0	0	0	0	-1	0	0	—	—	—	—	—
NHL Totals (5 years)..........		163	5	25	30	161	-38	1	0	12	0	0	0	30

BARCH, KRYS LW CAPITALS

PERSONAL: Born March 26, 1980, in Guelph, Ont. ... 6-2/199. ... Shoots left. ... Full Name: Krystofer Barch.
TRANSACTIONS/CAREER NOTES: Selected by Washington Capitals in fourth round (third Capitals pick, 106th overall) of NHL entry draft (June 27, 1998).

		REGULAR SEASON								PLAYOFFS				
Season Team	League	Gms.	G	A	Pts.	PIM	+/-	PP	SH	Gms.	G	A	Pts.	PIM
96-97—Georgetown	Tier II Jr. A	51	18	26	44	58	...	...	...	—	—	—	—	—
97-98—London	OHL	65	9	27	36	62	...	...	...	16	4	3	7	16
98-99—London	OHL	66	18	20	38	66	...	...	...	25	9	17	26	15
99-00—London	OHL	56	23	26	49	78	...	...	...	—	—	—	—	—
—Portland....................	AHL	—	—	—	—	—	...	...	...	4	0	2	2	2
00-01—Portland....................	AHL	76	10	15	25	91	...	...	...	2	0	0	0	0

BARKUNOV, ALEXANDER   D   BLACKHAWKS

PERSONAL: Born May 13, 1981, in Novosibirsk, U.S.S.R. ... 6-1/190. ... Shoots right.
TRANSACTIONS/CAREER NOTES: Selected by Chicago Blackhawks in fifth round (seventh Blackhawks pick, 151st overall) of NHL entry draft (June 24, 2000).

		REGULAR SEASON							PLAYOFFS				
Season Team	League	Gms.	G	A	Pts.	PIM	+/-	PP	SH	Gms.	G	A	Pts.	PIM
99-00—Yaroslavl 2	Russ.Dv. 2	57	6	11	17	82	...	...	...	—	—	—	—	—
00-01—Lokomotiv Yaroslavl	Russian	34	5	1	6	10	...	...	...	2	0	0	0	2

BARNABY, MATTHEW   LW   LIGHTNING

B

PERSONAL: Born May 4, 1973, in Ottawa. ... 6-0/189. ... Shoots left.
TRANSACTIONS/CAREER NOTES: Selected by Buffalo Sabres in fourth round (fifth Sabres pick, 83rd overall) of NHL entry draft (June 20, 1992). ... Suffered back spasms (March 28, 1995); missed one game. ... Suspended one game by NHL for accumulating three game misconduct penalties (March 31, 1996). ... Injured groin (April 3, 1996); missed five games. ... Sprained knee ligament (April 2, 1997); missed final six games of regular season and four playoff games. ... Injured sternum (October 10, 1997); missed five games. ... Strained shoulder (February 2, 1998); missed one game. ... Suspended four games and fined $1,000 by NHL for striking another player in the head (November 5, 1998). ... Suffered back spasms (December 12, 1998); missed one game. ... Injured ankle (December 18, 1998); missed one game. ... Suffered from flu (January 11, 1999); missed one game. ... Traded by Sabres to Pittsburgh Penguins for C Stu Barnes (March 11, 1999). ... Strained knee (November 2, 1999); missed five games. ... Suffered concussion (December 15, 1999); missed seven games. ... Suffered concussion (January 13, 2000); missed one game. ... Suspended five games by NHL for fighting incident (February 13, 2000). ... Traded by Penguins to Tampa Bay Lightning for C Wayne Primeau (February 1, 2001).

		REGULAR SEASON							PLAYOFFS				
Season Team	League	Gms.	G	A	Pts.	PIM	+/-	PP	SH	Gms.	G	A	Pts.	PIM
90-91—Beauport	QMJHL	52	9	5	14	262	...	...	...	—	—	—	—	—
91-92—Beauport	QMJHL	63	29	37	66	*476	...	...	...	—	—	—	—	—
92-93—Victoriaville	QMJHL	65	44	67	111	*448	...	...	...	6	2	4	6	44
—Buffalo	NHL	2	1	0	1	10	0	1	0	1	0	1	1	4
93-94—Buffalo	NHL	35	2	4	6	106	-7	1	0	3	0	0	0	17
—Rochester	AHL	42	10	32	42	153	...	...	...	—	—	—	—	—
94-95—Rochester	AHL	56	21	29	50	274	...	...	...	—	—	—	—	—
—Buffalo	NHL	23	1	1	2	116	-2	0	0	—	—	—	—	—
95-96—Buffalo	NHL	73	15	16	31	*335	-2	0	0	—	—	—	—	—
96-97—Buffalo	NHL	68	19	24	43	249	16	2	0	8	0	4	4	36
97-98—Buffalo	NHL	72	5	20	25	289	8	0	0	15	7	6	13	22
98-99—Buffalo	NHL	44	4	14	18	143	-2	0	0	—	—	—	—	—
—Pittsburgh	NHL	18	2	2	4	34	-10	1	0	13	0	0	0	35
99-00—Pittsburgh	NHL	64	12	12	24	197	3	0	0	11	0	2	2	29
00-01—Pittsburgh	NHL	47	1	4	5	168	-7	0	0	—	—	—	—	—
—Tampa Bay	NHL	29	4	4	8	97	-3	1	0	—	—	—	—	—
NHL Totals (9 years)		475	66	101	167	1744	-6	6	0	51	7	13	20	143

BARNES, STU   C   SABRES

PERSONAL: Born December 25, 1970, in Spruce Grove, Alta. ... 5-11/186. ... Shoots right. ... Full Name: Stu D. Barnes.
TRANSACTIONS/CAREER NOTES: Selected by Winnipeg Jets in first round (first Jets pick, fourth overall) of NHL entry draft (June 17, 1989). ... Traded by Jets to Florida Panthers for C Randy Gilhen (November 26, 1993). ... Strained left calf (January 1, 1994); missed one game. ... Suffered lacerations and bruises in and around left eye (February 15, 1995); missed seven games. ... Sprained left knee (March 10, 1996); missed 10 games. ... Traded by Panthers with D Jason Woolley to Pittsburgh Penguins for C Chris Wells (November 19, 1996). ... Injured hip (April 11, 1997); missed one game. ... Suffered back spasms (October 9, 1997); missed one game. ... Strained hip flexor (April 16, 1998); missed one game. ... Traded by Penguins to Buffalo Sabres for RW Matthew Barnaby (March 11, 1999). ... Injured groin (November 3, 2000); missed seven games.
HONORS: Won Jim Piggott Memorial Trophy (1987-88). ... Named to WHL All-Star second team (1987-88). ... Won Four Broncos Memorial Trophy (1988-89). ... Named to WHL All-Star first team (1988-89).
MISCELLANEOUS: Failed to score on a penalty shot (vs. Peter Sidorkiewicz, February 23, 1993; vs. Ron Hextall, March 8, 1998).
STATISTICAL PLATEAUS: Three-goal games: 1991-92 (1), 1997-98 (1), 1998-99 (1). Total: 3.

		REGULAR SEASON							PLAYOFFS				
Season Team	League	Gms.	G	A	Pts.	PIM	+/-	PP	SH	Gms.	G	A	Pts.	PIM
86-87—St. Albert	AJHL	57	43	32	75	80	...	...	...	—	—	—	—	—
87-88—New Westminster	WHL	71	37	64	101	88	...	...	...	5	2	3	5	6
88-89—Tri-City	WHL	70	59	82	141	117	...	...	...	7	6	5	11	10
89-90—Tri-City	WHL	63	52	92	144	165	...	...	...	7	1	5	6	26
90-91—Canadian nat'l team	Int'l	53	22	27	49	68	...	...	...	—	—	—	—	—
91-92—Winnipeg	NHL	46	8	9	17	26	-2	4	0	—	—	—	—	—
—Moncton	AHL	30	13	19	32	10	...	...	...	11	3	9	12	6
92-93—Moncton	AHL	42	23	31	54	58	...	...	...	—	—	—	—	—
—Winnipeg	NHL	38	12	10	22	10	-3	3	0	6	1	3	4	2
93-94—Winnipeg	NHL	18	5	4	9	8	-1	2	0	—	—	—	—	—
—Florida	NHL	59	18	20	38	30	5	6	1	—	—	—	—	—
94-95—Florida	NHL	41	10	19	29	8	7	1	0	—	—	—	—	—
95-96—Florida	NHL	72	19	25	44	46	-12	8	0	22	6	10	16	4
96-97—Florida	NHL	19	2	8	10	10	-3	1	0	—	—	—	—	—
—Pittsburgh	NHL	62	17	22	39	16	-20	4	0	5	0	1	1	0
97-98—Pittsburgh	NHL	78	30	35	65	30	15	15	1	6	3	3	6	2
98-99—Pittsburgh	NHL	64	20	12	32	20	-12	13	0	—	—	—	—	—
—Buffalo	NHL	17	0	4	4	10	1	0	0	21	7	3	10	6
99-00—Buffalo	NHL	82	20	25	45	16	-3	8	2	5	3	0	3	2
00-01—Buffalo	NHL	75	19	24	43	26	-2	3	2	13	4	4	8	2
NHL Totals (10 years)		671	180	217	397	256	-30	68	6	78	24	24	48	18

BARON, MURRAY　　　　　　　D　　　　　　CANUCKS

PERSONAL: Born June 1, 1967, in Prince George, B.C. ... 6-3/225. ... Shoots left. ... Full Name: Murray D. Baron.

TRANSACTIONS/CAREER NOTES: Selected by Philadelphia Flyers as underage player in eighth round (seventh Flyers pick, 167th overall) of NHL entry draft (June 21, 1986). ... Separated left shoulder (October 5, 1989). ... Underwent surgery to have bone spur removed from foot (April 1990). ... Traded by Flyers with C Ron Sutter to St. Louis Blues for C Rod Brind'Amour and C Dan Quinn (September 22, 1991). ... Injured shoulder (December 3, 1991); missed seven games. ... Fractured foot (March 22, 1993); missed remainder of regular season. ... Injured groin (December 1, 1993); missed three games. ... Injured groin (December 11, 1993); missed three games. ... Injured knee (March 7, 1994); missed one game. ... Injured knee (April 18, 1995); missed last nine games of regular season. ... Traded by Blues with LW Shayne Corson and fifth-round pick (D Gennady Razin) in 1997 draft to Montreal Canadiens for C Pierre Turgeon, C Craig Conroy and D Rory Fitzpatrick (October 29, 1996). ... Bruised eye (November 21, 1996); missed one game. ... Traded by Canadiens with RW Chris Murray to Phoenix Coyotes for D Dave Manson (March 18, 1997). ... Fractured foot (April 6, 1997); missed remainder of regular season. ... Tore triceps muscle (November 17, 1997); missed 37 games. ... Signed as free agent by Vancouver Canucks (July 14, 1998).

		REGULAR SEASON							PLAYOFFS				
Season Team	League	Gms.	G	A	Pts.	PIM	+/-	PP	SH	Gms.	G	A	Pts.	PIM
84-85—Vernon	BCJHL	37	5	9	14	93	...	...	...	—	—	—	—	—
85-86—Vernon	BCJHL	49	15	32	47	176	...	...	...	7	1	2	3	13
86-87—Univ. of North Dakota	WCHA	41	4	10	14	62	...	...	...	—	—	—	—	—
87-88—Univ. of North Dakota	WCHA	41	1	10	11	95	...	...	...	—	—	—	—	—
88-89—Univ. of North Dakota	WCHA	40	2	6	8	92	...	...	...	—	—	—	—	—
—Hershey	AHL	9	0	3	3	8	...	...	...	—	—	—	—	—
89-90—Hershey	AHL	50	0	10	10	101	...	...	...	—	—	—	—	—
—Philadelphia	NHL	16	2	2	4	12	-1	0	0	—	—	—	—	—
90-91—Hershey	AHL	6	2	3	5	0	...	...	...	—	—	—	—	—
—Philadelphia	NHL	67	8	8	16	74	-3	3	0	—	—	—	—	—
91-92—St. Louis	NHL	67	3	8	11	94	-3	0	0	2	0	0	0	2
92-93—St. Louis	NHL	53	2	2	4	59	-5	0	0	11	0	0	0	12
93-94—St. Louis	NHL	77	5	9	14	123	-14	0	0	4	0	0	0	10
94-95—St. Louis	NHL	39	0	5	5	93	9	0	0	7	1	1	2	2
95-96—St. Louis	NHL	82	2	9	11	190	3	0	0	13	1	0	1	20
96-97—St. Louis	NHL	11	0	2	2	11	-4	0	0	—	—	—	—	—
—Montreal	NHL	60	1	5	6	107	-16	0	0	—	—	—	—	—
—Phoenix	NHL	8	0	0	0	4	0	0	0	1	0	0	0	0
97-98—Phoenix	NHL	45	1	5	6	106	-10	0	0	6	0	2	2	6
98-99—Vancouver	NHL	81	2	6	8	115	-23	0	0	—	—	—	—	—
99-00—Vancouver	NHL	81	2	10	12	67	8	0	0	—	—	—	—	—
00-01—Vancouver	NHL	82	3	8	11	63	-13	0	0	4	0	0	0	0
NHL Totals (12 years)		769	31	79	110	1118	-72	3	0	48	2	3	5	52

BARRIE, LEN　　　　　　　C

PERSONAL: Born June 4, 1969, in Kimberley, B.C. ... 6-0/200. ... Shoots right.

TRANSACTIONS/CAREER NOTES: Selected by Edmonton Oilers in sixth round (seventh Oilers pick, 124th overall) of NHL entry draft (June 11, 1988). ... Signed as free agent by Philadelphia Flyers (February 8, 1990). ... Signed as free agent by Florida Panthers (July 20, 1993). ... Signed as free agent by Pittsburgh Penguins (August 25, 1994). ... Signed as free agent by Los Angeles Kings (July 21, 1999). ... Claimed on waivers by Panthers (March 10, 2000). ... Bruised kidney (October 25, 2000); missed six games. ... Reinjured kidneys (December 22, 2000); missed two games. ... Suspended two games by NHL for unsportsmanlike conduct (January 2, 2001). ... Reinjured kidneys (January 5, 2001); missed 11 games.

HONORS: Won Can.HL Plus/Minus Award (1989-90). ... Won Bob Clarke Trophy (1989-90). ... Named to WHL (West) All-Star first team (1989-90). ... Named to IHL All-Star second team (1993-94).

		REGULAR SEASON							PLAYOFFS				
Season Team	League	Gms.	G	A	Pts.	PIM	+/-	PP	SH	Gms.	G	A	Pts.	PIM
85-86—Calgary Spurs	AJHL	23	7	14	21	86	...	...	...	—	—	—	—	—
—Calgary	WHL	32	3	0	3	18	...	...	...	—	—	—	—	—
86-87—Calgary	WHL	34	13	13	26	81	...	...	...	—	—	—	—	—
—Victoria	WHL	34	7	6	13	92	...	...	...	5	0	1	1	15
87-88—Victoria	WHL	70	37	49	86	192	...	...	...	8	2	0	2	29
88-89—Victoria	WHL	67	39	48	87	157	...	...	...	7	5	2	7	23
89-90—Philadelphia	NHL	1	0	0	0	0	-2	0	0	—	—	—	—	—
—Kamloops	WHL	70	*85	*100	*185	108	...	...	...	17	†14	23	†37	24
90-91—Hershey	AHL	63	26	32	58	60	...	...	...	7	4	0	4	12
91-92—Hershey	AHL	75	42	43	85	78	...	...	...	3	0	2	2	32
92-93—Hershey	AHL	61	31	45	76	162	...	...	...	—	—	—	—	—
—Philadelphia	NHL	8	2	2	4	9	2	0	0	—	—	—	—	—
93-94—Cincinnati	IHL	77	45	71	116	246	...	...	...	11	8	13	21	60
—Florida	NHL	2	0	0	0	0	-2	0	0	—	—	—	—	—
94-95—Cleveland	IHL	28	13	30	43	137	...	...	...	—	—	—	—	—
—Pittsburgh	NHL	48	3	11	14	66	-4	0	0	4	1	0	1	8
95-96—Cleveland	IHL	55	29	43	72	178	...	...	...	3	2	3	5	6
—Pittsburgh	NHL	5	0	0	0	18	-1	0	0	—	—	—	—	—
96-97—San Antonio	IHL	57	26	40	66	196	...	...	...	9	5	5	10	20
97-98—San Antonio	IHL	32	7	13	20	90	...	...	...	—	—	—	—	—
—Frankfurt	Germany	25	11	19	30	32	...	...	...	—	—	—	—	—
98-99—Frankfurt	Germany	41	24	35	59	105	...	...	...	8	2	4	6	43
99-00—Long Beach	IHL	17	10	10	20	16	...	...	...	—	—	—	—	—
—Los Angeles	NHL	46	5	8	13	56	5	0	0	—	—	—	—	—
—Florida	NHL	14	4	6	10	6	4	0	0	4	0	0	0	0
00-01—Florida	NHL	60	5	18	23	135	4	0	1	—	—	—	—	—
NHL Totals (7 years)		184	19	45	64	290	6	0	1	8	1	0	1	8

BARTECKO, LUBOS   LW   THRASHERS

PERSONAL: Born July 14, 1976, in Kezmarok, Czechoslovakia. ... 6-1/195. ... Shoots left.
TRANSACTIONS/CAREER NOTES: Signed as non-drafted free agent by St. Louis Blues (October 3, 1997). ... Sprained ankle (December 2, 2000); missed 17 games. ... Reinjured ankle (January 15, 2001); missed nine games. ... Traded by Blues to Atlanta Thrashers for fourth-round pick (C Igor Valeev) in 2001 draft (June 24, 2001).

		REGULAR SEASON								PLAYOFFS				
Season Team	League	Gms.	G	A	Pts.	PIM	+/-	PP	SH	Gms.	G	A	Pts.	PIM
95-96—Chicoutimi	QMJHL	70	32	41	73	50	...	...	...	17	8	15	23	10
96-97—Drummondville	QMJHL	58	40	51	91	49	...	...	...	8	1	8	9	4
97-98—Worcester	AHL	34	10	12	22	24	...	...	...	10	4	2	6	2
98-99—Poprad	Slovakia	1	1	0	1	0	...	...	...	—	—	—	—	—
—St. Louis	NHL	32	5	11	16	6	4	0	0	5	0	0	0	2
—Worcester	AHL	49	14	24	38	22	...	...	...	—	—	—	—	—
99-00—Worcester	AHL	12	4	7	11	4	...	...	...	—	—	—	—	—
—St. Louis	NHL	67	16	23	39	51	25	3	0	7	1	1	2	0
00-01—St. Louis	NHL	50	5	8	13	12	-1	0	0	—	—	—	—	—
NHL Totals (3 years)...........		**149**	**26**	**42**	**68**	**69**	**28**	**3**	**0**	**12**	**1**	**1**	**2**	**2**

BARTOS, PETER   LW   WILD

PERSONAL: Born September 15, 1973, in Martin, Czechoslovakia. ... 6-0/185. ... Shoots right.
TRANSACTIONS/CAREER NOTES: Selected by Minnesota Wild in seventh round (seventh Wild pick, 214th overall) of NHL entry draft (June 24, 2000).

		REGULAR SEASON								PLAYOFFS				
Season Team	League	Gms.	G	A	Pts.	PIM	+/-	PP	SH	Gms.	G	A	Pts.	PIM
91-92—HC Martin	Czech II	33	13	8	21	16	...	...	...	—	—	—	—	—
92-93—HC Martin	Czech II	22	6	5	11	4	...	...	...	—	—	—	—	—
—Dukla Trencin.............	Czech.	28	1	2	3	...	...	...	...	10	1	1	2	...
93-94—ZTS Martin	Slovakia	36	12	9	21	10	...	...	...	6	2	1	3	8
94-95—ZTS Martin	Slovakia	34	14	20	34	20	...	...	...	3	0	0	0	0
95-96—ZTS Martin	Slovakia	36	23	16	39	8	...	...	...	13	4	4	8	4
96-97—ZTS Martin	Slovakia	46	22	15	37	...	...	...	...	5	1	5	6	...
97-98—ZTS Martin	Slovakia	36	20	26	46	20	...	...	...	3	0	2	2	0
98-99—Budejovice	Czech Rep.	52	22	26	48	24	...	...	...	3	3	0	3	...
99-00—HC Ceske Budejovice ..	Czech Rep.	52	23	25	48	24	...	...	...	3	0	1	1	6
00-01—Cleveland	IHL	60	18	28	46	18	...	...	...	4	0	1	1	2
—Minnesota.................	NHL	13	4	2	6	6	2	1	0	—	—	—	—	—
NHL Totals (1 year).............		**13**	**4**	**2**	**6**	**6**	**2**	**1**	**0**					

BASHKIROV, ANDREI   LW

PERSONAL: Born June 22, 1970, in Shelekhov, U.S.S.R. ... 6-0/215. ... Shoots left.
TRANSACTIONS/CAREER NOTES: Selected by Montreal Canadiens in fifth round (fourth Canadiens pick, 132nd overall) of NHL entry draft (June 27, 1998). ... Fractured jaw (September 30, 1998); missed first 13 games of season. ... Injured knee (January 2, 2001); missed 10 games.

		REGULAR SEASON								PLAYOFFS				
Season Team	League	Gms.	G	A	Pts.	PIM	+/-	PP	SH	Gms.	G	A	Pts.	PIM
91-92—Khimik Voskresensk ...	CIS	11	2	0	2	4	...	...	...	—	—	—	—	—
92-93—Yermak Angarsk	CIS Div. III						Statistics unavailable.							
93-94—Charlotte	ECHL	62	28	42	70	25	...	...	...	3	1	0	1	...
—Providence.................	AHL	1	0	0	0	2	...	...	...	—	—	—	—	—
94-95—Charlotte	ECHL	61	19	27	46	20	...	...	...	3	0	0	0	0
95-96—Huntington...................	ECHL	55	19	39	58	35	...	...	...	—	—	—	—	—
96-97—Huntington...................	ECHL	47	29	41	70	12	...	...	...	—	—	—	—	—
—Detroit.......................	IHL	2	0	0	0	0	...	...	...	—	—	—	—	—
—Las Vegas	IHL	27	10	12	22	0	...	...	...	2	0	0	0	0
97-98—Las Vegas	IHL	15	2	3	5	5	...	...	...	—	—	—	—	—
—Fort Wayne	IHL	65	28	48	76	16	...	...	...	4	2	2	4	2
98-99—Fredericton..................	AHL	13	7	5	12	4	...	...	...	—	—	—	—	—
—Montreal	NHL	10	0	0	0	0	-3	0	0	—	—	—	—	—
—Fort Wayne	IHL	34	11	25	36	10	...	...	...	—	—	—	—	—
99-00—Quebec	AHL	78	28	33	61	17	...	...	...	3	0	3	3	0
—Montreal	NHL	2	0	0	0	0	0	0	0	—	—	—	—	—
00-01—Quebec	AHL	53	17	25	42	6	...	...	...	6	1	1	2	0
—Montreal	NHL	18	0	3	3	0	-2	0	0	—	—	—	—	—
NHL Totals (3 years)...........		**30**	**0**	**3**	**3**	**0**	**-5**	**0**	**0**					

BATES, SHAWN   C   ISLANDERS

PERSONAL: Born April 3, 1975, in Melrose, Mass. ... 5-11/190. ... Shoots right.
TRANSACTIONS/CAREER NOTES: Selected by Boston Bruins in fourth round (fourth Bruins pick, 103rd overall) of NHL entry draft (June 26, 1993). ... Involved in car accident (November 8, 1997); missed one game. ... Suffered from the flu (December 1, 1998); missed one game. ... Injured hamstring (April 15, 1999); missed two games. ... Injured shoulder (October 30, 1999); missed four games. ... Sprained wrist (December 9, 1999); missed 25 games. ... Sprained wrist (March 25, 2000); missed seven games. ... Strained groin (December 16, 2000); missed three games. ... Reinjured groin (January 10, 2001); missed 16 games. ... Signed as free agent by New York Islanders (July 8, 2001).
HONORS: Named to Hockey East All-Rookie team (1993-94).

Season Team	League	REGULAR SEASON Gms.	G	A	Pts.	PIM	+/-	PP	SH	PLAYOFFS Gms.	G	A	Pts.	PIM
90-91—Medford H.S.	Mass. H.S.	22	18	43	61	6	...	...	...	—	—	—	—	—
91-92—Medford H.S.	Mass. H.S.	22	38	41	79	10	...	...	...	—	—	—	—	—
92-93—Medford H.S.	Mass. H.S.	25	49	46	95	20	...	...	...	—	—	—	—	—
93-94—Boston University	Hockey East	41	10	19	29	24	...	...	...	—	—	—	—	—
94-95—Boston University	Hockey East	38	18	12	30	48	...	...	...	—	—	—	—	—
95-96—Boston University	Hockey East	40	28	22	50	54	...	...	...	—	—	—	—	—
96-97—Boston University	Hockey East	41	17	18	35	64	...	...	...	—	—	—	—	—
97-98—Boston	NHL	13	2	0	2	2	-3	0	0	—	—	—	—	—
—Providence.................	AHL	50	15	19	34	22	...	...	...	—	—	—	—	—
98-99—Providence.................	AHL	37	25	21	46	39	...	...	...	—	—	—	—	—
—Boston	NHL	33	5	4	9	2	3	0	0	12	0	0	0	4
99-00—Boston	NHL	44	5	7	12	14	-17	0	0	—	—	—	—	—
00-01—Boston	NHL	45	2	3	5	26	-12	0	0	—	—	—	—	—
—Providence.................	AHL	11	5	8	13	12	...	...	...	8	2	6	8	8
NHL Totals (4 years)...........		135	14	14	28	44	-29	0	0	12	0	0	0	4

BATTAGLIA, BATES   LW   HURRICANES

PERSONAL: Born December 13, 1975, in Chicago. ... 6-2/205. ... Shoots left. ... Full Name: Jon Battaglia. ... Name pronounced buh-TAG-lee-uh.
TRANSACTIONS/CAREER NOTES: Selected by Mighty Ducks of Anaheim in sixth round (sixth Mighty Ducks pick, 132nd overall) of NHL entry draft (June 29, 1994). ... Traded by Mighty Ducks with fourth-round pick (C Josef Vasicek) in 1998 draft to Hartford Whalers for C Mark Janssens (March 18, 1997). ... Whalers franchise moved to North Carolina and renamed Carolina Hurricanes for 1997-98 season; NHL approved move on June 25, 1977. ... Injured shoulder (January 20, 2000); missed three games.
STATISTICAL PLATEAUS: Three-goal games: 1999-00 (1).

Season Team	League	REGULAR SEASON Gms.	G	A	Pts.	PIM	+/-	PP	SH	PLAYOFFS Gms.	G	A	Pts.	PIM
93-94—Caledon......................	Jr. A	44	15	33	48	104	...	...	...	—	—	—	—	—
94-95—Lake Superior State	CCHA	38	6	15	21	34	...	...	...	—	—	—	—	—
95-96—Lake Superior State	CCHA	40	13	22	35	48	...	...	...	—	—	—	—	—
96-97—Lake Superior State	CCHA	38	12	27	39	80	...	...	...	—	—	—	—	—
97-98—New Haven	AHL	48	15	21	36	48	...	...	...	1	0	0	0	0
—Carolina	NHL	33	2	4	6	10	-1	0	0	—	—	—	—	—
98-99—Carolina	NHL	60	7	11	18	22	7	0	0	6	0	3	3	8
99-00—Carolina	NHL	77	16	18	34	39	20	3	0	—	—	—	—	—
00-01—Carolina	NHL	80	12	15	27	76	-14	2	0	6	0	2	2	2
NHL Totals (4 years)...........		250	37	48	85	147	12	5	0	12	0	5	5	10

BAUMGARTNER, NOLAN   D

PERSONAL: Born March 23, 1976, in Calgary. ... 6-1/195. ... Shoots right.
TRANSACTIONS/CAREER NOTES: Selected by Washington Capitals in first round (first Capitals pick, 10th overall) of NHL entry draft (June 28, 1994). ... Traded by Capitals to Chicago Blackhawks for D Remi Royer (July 21, 2000).
HONORS: Named to Memorial Cup All-Star team (1993-94 and 1994-95). ... Won Can.HL Defenseman of the Year Award (1994-95). ... Won Bill Hunter Trophy (1994-95 and 1995-96). ... Named to Can.HL All-Star first team (1994-95). ... Named to WHL (West) All-Star first team (1994-95 and 1995-96).

Season Team	League	REGULAR SEASON Gms.	G	A	Pts.	PIM	+/-	PP	SH	PLAYOFFS Gms.	G	A	Pts.	PIM
92-93—Kamloops	WHL	43	0	5	5	30	...	...	...	11	1	1	2	0
93-94—Kamloops	WHL	69	13	42	55	109	...	...	...	19	3	14	17	33
94-95—Kamloops	WHL	62	8	36	44	71	...	...	...	21	4	13	17	16
95-96—Washington	NHL	1	0	0	0	0	-1	0	0	1	0	0	0	10
—Kamloops	WHL	28	13	15	28	45	...	...	...	16	1	9	10	26
96-97—Portland	AHL	8	2	2	4	4	...	...	...	—	—	—	—	—
97-98—Portland	AHL	70	2	24	26	70	...	...	...	10	1	4	5	10
—Washington	NHL	4	0	1	1	0	0	0	0	—	—	—	—	—
98-99—Portland	AHL	38	5	14	19	62	...	...	...	—	—	—	—	—
—Washington	NHL	5	0	0	0	0	-3	0	0	—	—	—	—	—
99-00—Portland	AHL	71	5	18	23	56	...	...	...	4	1	2	3	10
—Washington	NHL	8	0	1	1	2	1	0	0	—	—	—	—	—
00-01—Norfolk......................	AHL	63	5	28	33	75	...	...	...	9	2	3	5	11
—Chicago	NHL	8	0	0	0	6	-4	0	0	—	—	—	—	—
NHL Totals (5 years)...........		26	0	2	2	8	-7	0	0	1	0	0	0	10

BEAUDOIN, ERIC   LW   PANTHERS

PERSONAL: Born May 3, 1980, in Ottawa. ... 6-2/202. ... Shoots left. ... Name pronounced boh-DWEH.
TRANSACTIONS/CAREER NOTES: Selected by Tampa Bay Lightning in fourth round (fourth Lightning pick, 92nd overall) of NHL entry draft (June 27, 1998). ... Traded by Lightning to Florida Panthers for seventh-round pick (D Marek Priechodsky) in 2000 draft (June 2, 2000).

Season Team	League	REGULAR SEASON Gms.	G	A	Pts.	PIM	+/-	PP	SH	PLAYOFFS Gms.	G	A	Pts.	PIM
96-97—Ottawa	Tier II Jr. A	54	12	19	31	55	...	...	...	—	—	—	—	—
97-98—Guelph	OHL	62	9	13	22	43	...	...	...	12	3	2	5	4
98-99—Guelph	OHL	66	28	43	71	79	...	...	...	11	5	3	8	12
99-00—Guelph	OHL	68	38	34	72	126	...	...	...	6	3	0	3	2
00-01—Louisville	AHL	71	15	10	25	78	...	...	...	—	—	—	—	—

BECKETT, JASON   D   FLYERS

PERSONAL: Born July 23, 1980, in Lethbridge, Alta. ... 6-3/203. ... Shoots right.
TRANSACTIONS/CAREER NOTES: Selected by Philadelphia Flyers in second round (second Flyers pick, 42nd overall) of NHL entry draft (June 27, 1998).

		REGULAR SEASON								PLAYOFFS				
Season Team	League	Gms.	G	A	Pts.	PIM	+/-	PP	SH	Gms.	G	A	Pts.	PIM
96-97—Lethbridge	AMHL	34	7	10	17	118	...	...	...	—	—	—	—	—
97-98—Seattle	WHL	71	1	11	12	241	...	...	...	5	0	0	0	16
98-99—Seattle	WHL	70	4	26	30	195	...	...	...	11	0	1	1	40
99-00—Seattle	WHL	70	3	15	18	183	...	...	...	7	1	1	2	12
00-01—Philadelphia	AHL	56	2	10	12	107	...	...	...	—	—	—	—	—
—Trenton	ECHL	17	2	2	4	24	...	...	...	15	0	1	1	25

BEECH, KRIS   C   PENGUINS

PERSONAL: Born February 5, 1981, in Salmon Arm, B.C. ... 6-2/178. ... Shoots left.
TRANSACTIONS/CAREER NOTES: Selected by Washington Capitals in first round (first Capitals pick, seventh overall) of NHL entry draft (June 26, 1999). ... Traded by Capitals with C Michal Sivek, D Ross Lupaschuk and future considerations to Pittsburgh Penguins for RW Jaromir Jagr and D Frantisek Kucera (July 11, 2001).

		REGULAR SEASON								PLAYOFFS				
Season Team	League	Gms.	G	A	Pts.	PIM	+/-	PP	SH	Gms.	G	A	Pts.	PIM
96-97—Sicamous	Jr. A	49	34	36	70	80	...	...	...	—	—	—	—	—
—Calgary	WHL	8	1	1	2	0	...	...	...	—	—	—	—	—
97-98—Calgary	WHL	68	26	41	67	103	...	...	...	—	—	—	—	—
98-99—Calgary	WHL	58	10	25	35	24	...	...	...	—	—	—	—	—
99-00—Calgary	WHL	66	32	54	86	99	...	...	...	5	3	5	8	16
00-01—Washington	NHL	4	0	0	0	2	-2	0	0	—	—	—	—	—
—Calgary	WHL	40	22	44	66	103	...	...	...	10	2	8	10	26
NHL Totals (1 year)		4	0	0	0	2	-2	0	0					

BEGIN, STEVE   LW   FLAMES

PERSONAL: Born June 14, 1978, in Trois-Rivieres, Que. ... 5-11/190. ... Shoots left. ... Name pronounced BAY-zhin.
TRANSACTIONS/CAREER NOTES: Selected by Calgary Flames in second round (third Flames pick, 40th overall) of NHL entry draft (June 22, 1996). ... Injured shoulder (October 10, 1997); missed six games. ... Dislocated fibula (March 18, 2000); missed final 10 games of season.
HONORS: Won Jack Butterfield Trophy (2000-01).

		REGULAR SEASON								PLAYOFFS				
Season Team	League	Gms.	G	A	Pts.	PIM	+/-	PP	SH	Gms.	G	A	Pts.	PIM
95-96—Val-d'Or	QMJHL	64	13	23	36	218	...	...	...	13	1	3	4	33
96-97—Val-d'Or	QMJHL	58	13	33	46	207	...	...	...	10	0	3	3	8
—Saint John	AHL	—	—	—	—	—	...	...	...	4	0	2	2	6
97-98—Calgary	NHL	5	0	0	0	23	0	0	0	—	—	—	—	—
—Val-d'Or	QMJHL	35	18	17	35	73	...	...	...	15	2	12	14	34
98-99—Saint John	AHL	73	11	9	20	156	...	...	...	7	2	0	2	18
99-00—Calgary	NHL	13	1	1	2	18	-3	0	0	—	—	—	—	—
—Saint John	AHL	47	13	12	25	99	...	...	...	—	—	—	—	—
00-01—Saint John	AHL	58	14	14	28	109	...	...	...	19	10	7	17	18
—Calgary	NHL	4	0	0	0	21	0	0	0	—	—	—	—	—
NHL Totals (3 years)		22	1	1	2	62	-3	0	0					

BELAK, WADE   D   MAPLE LEAFS

PERSONAL: Born March 7, 1976, in Saskatoon, Sask. ... 6-4/222. ... Shoots right. ... Brother of Graham Belak, defenseman, Colorado Avalanche organization (1997-98 and 1998-99). ... Name pronounced BEE-lak.
TRANSACTIONS/CAREER NOTES: Selected by Quebec Nordiques in first round (first Nordiques pick, 12th overall) of NHL entry draft (June 28, 1994). ... Nordiques franchise moved to Colorado and renamed Avalanche for 1995-96 season (June 21, 1995). ... Pulled abdominal muscle (March 5, 1998); missed six games. ... Strained groin (October 9, 1998); missed first two games of season. ... Strained groin (October 26, 1998); missed one game. ... Reinjured groin (November 2, 1998); missed 10 games. ... Traded by Avalanche with LW Rene Corbet and future considerations to Calgary Flames for RW Theo Fleury and LW Chris Dingman (February 28, 1999). ... Flames acquired D Robyn Regehr to complete deal (March 27, 1999). ... Suffered concussion (November 10, 1999); missed one game. ... Injured shoulder (February 10, 2000); missed 18 games. ... Injured groin (March 22, 2000); missed three games. ... Claimed on waivers by Toronto Maple Leafs (February 16, 2001). ... Suffered injury (March 29, 2001); missed final four games of regular season.

		REGULAR SEASON								PLAYOFFS				
Season Team	League	Gms.	G	A	Pts.	PIM	+/-	PP	SH	Gms.	G	A	Pts.	PIM
91-92—North Battleford	SJHL	57	6	20	26	186	...	...	...	—	—	—	—	—
92-93—North Battleford	SJHL	32	3	13	16	142	...	...	...	—	—	—	—	—
93-94—Saskatoon	WHL	69	4	13	17	226	...	...	...	16	2	2	4	43
94-95—Saskatoon	WHL	72	4	14	18	290	...	...	...	9	0	0	0	36
—Cornwall	AHL	—	—	—	—	—	...	...	...	11	1	2	3	40
95-96—Saskatoon	WHL	63	3	15	18	207	...	...	...	4	0	0	0	9
—Cornwall	AHL	5	0	0	0	18	...	...	...	2	0	0	0	2
96-97—Colorado	NHL	5	0	0	0	11	-1	0	0	—	—	—	—	—
—Hershey	AHL	65	1	7	8	320	...	...	...	16	0	1	1	61
97-98—Colorado	NHL	8	1	1	2	27	-3	0	0	—	—	—	—	—
—Hershey	AHL	11	0	0	0	30	...	...	...	—	—	—	—	—

B

– 25 –

Season Team	League	Gms.	G	A	Pts.	PIM	+/-	PP	SH	Gms.	G	A	Pts.	PIM
98-99—Colorado	NHL	22	0	0	0	71	-2	0	0	—	—	—	—	—
—Hershey	AHL	17	0	1	1	49	...	...	...	—	—	—	—	—
—Saint John	AHL	12	0	2	2	43	...	...	...	6	0	1	1	23
—Calgary	NHL	9	0	1	1	23	3	0	0	—	—	—	—	—
99-00—Calgary	NHL	40	0	2	2	122	-4	0	0	—	—	—	—	—
00-01—Calgary	NHL	23	0	0	0	79	-2	0	0	—	—	—	—	—
—Toronto	NHL	16	1	1	2	31	-4	0	0	—	—	—	—	—
NHL Totals (5 years)		**123**	**2**	**5**	**7**	**364**	**-13**	**0**	**0**					

BELANGER, ERIC — LW/C — KINGS

PERSONAL: Born December 16, 1977, in Sherbrooke, Que. ... 6-0/177. ... Shoots left. ... Name pronounced buh-LAH-zhay.

TRANSACTIONS/CAREER NOTES: Selected by Los Angeles Kings in fourth round (fifth Kings pick, 96th overall) of NHL entry draft (June 22, 1996). ... Suffered back spasms (February 25, 2001); missed two games.

		REGULAR SEASON								PLAYOFFS				
Season Team	League	Gms.	G	A	Pts.	PIM	+/-	PP	SH	Gms.	G	A	Pts.	PIM
94-95—Beauport	QMJHL	71	12	28	40	24	...	...	...	—	—	—	—	—
95-96—Beauport	QMJHL	59	35	48	83	18	...	...	...	20	13	14	27	6
96-97—Beauport	QMJHL	31	13	37	50	30	...	...	...	—	—	—	—	—
—Rimouski	QMJHL	31	26	41	67	36	...	...	...	4	2	3	5	10
97-98—Fredericton	AHL	56	17	34	51	28	...	...	...	4	2	1	3	2
98-99—Springfield	AHL	33	8	18	26	10	...	...	...	3	0	1	1	2
—Long Beach	IHL	1	0	0	0	0	...	...	...	—	—	—	—	—
99-00—Lowell	AHL	65	15	25	40	20	...	...	...	7	3	3	6	2
00-01—Los Angeles	NHL	62	9	12	21	16	14	1	2	13	1	4	5	2
—Lowell	AHL	13	8	10	18	4	...	...	...	—	—	—	—	—
NHL Totals (1 year)		**62**	**9**	**12**	**21**	**16**	**14**	**1**	**2**	**13**	**1**	**4**	**5**	**2**

BELANGER, FRANCIS — LW — CANADIENS

PERSONAL: Born January 15, 1978, in Bellefeuille, Que. ... 6-2/216. ... Shoots left. ... Name pronounced buh-LAH-zhay.

TRANSACTIONS/CAREER NOTES: Selected by Philadelphia Flyers in fifth round (fifth Flyers pick, 124th overall) of NHL entry draft (June 27, 1998). ... Signed as free agent by Montreal Canadiens (February 15, 2001).

		REGULAR SEASON								PLAYOFFS				
Season Team	League	Gms.	G	A	Pts.	PIM	+/-	PP	SH	Gms.	G	A	Pts.	PIM
96-97—Hull	QMJHL	53	13	13	26	134	...	...	...	8	2	2	4	29
97-98—Hull	QMJHL	33	22	23	45	133	...	...	...	—	—	—	—	—
—Rimouski	QMJHL	30	18	10	28	248	...	...	...	—	—	—	—	—
98-99—Chicoutimi	QMJHL	3	0	0	0	0	...	...	...	—	—	—	—	—
—Philadelphia	AHL	58	13	13	26	242	...	...	...	16	4	3	7	16
99-00—Philadelphia	AHL	35	5	6	11	112	...	...	...	—	—	—	—	—
—Trenton	ECHL	9	1	1	2	29	...	...	...	—	—	—	—	—
00-01—Philadelphia	AHL	13	1	3	4	32	...	...	...	—	—	—	—	—
—Montreal	NHL	10	0	0	0	29	-3	0	0	—	—	—	—	—
—Quebec	AHL	22	15	4	19	101	...	...	...	9	2	5	7	20
NHL Totals (1 year)		**10**	**0**	**0**	**0**	**29**	**-3**	**0**	**0**					

BELANGER, JESSE — C

PERSONAL: Born June 15, 1969, in St. Georges Beauce, Que. ... 6-1/190. ... Shoots right. ... Name pronounced buh-LAH-zhay.

TRANSACTIONS/CAREER NOTES: Signed as non-drafted free agent by Montreal Canadiens (October 3, 1990). ... Selected by Florida Panthers in NHL expansion draft (June 24, 1993). ... Strained right Achilles' tendon (October 12, 1993); missed one game. ... Fractured bone in left hand (February 13, 1994); missed 12 games. ... Suffered from illness (March 24, 1995); missed one game. ... Traded by Panthers to Vancouver Canucks for future considerations (March 20, 1996). ... Signed as free agent by Edmonton Oilers (August 28, 1996). ... Signed as free agent by Tampa Bay Lightning (July 30, 1998). ... Signed as free agent by Canadiens (July 9, 1999). ... Signed as free agent by New York Islanders (July 27, 2000).

MISCELLANEOUS: Member of Stanley Cup championship team (1993).

		REGULAR SEASON								PLAYOFFS				
Season Team	League	Gms.	G	A	Pts.	PIM	+/-	PP	SH	Gms.	G	A	Pts.	PIM
87-88—Granby	QMJHL	69	33	43	76	10	...	...	...	5	3	3	6	0
88-89—Granby	QMJHL	67	40	63	103	26	...	...	...	4	0	5	5	0
89-90—Granby	QMJHL	67	53	54	107	53	...	...	...	—	—	—	—	—
90-91—Fredericton	AHL	75	40	58	98	30	...	...	...	6	2	4	6	0
91-92—Fredericton	AHL	65	30	41	71	26	...	...	...	7	3	3	6	2
—Montreal	NHL	4	0	0	0	0	-1	0	0	—	—	—	—	—
92-93—Fredericton	AHL	39	19	32	51	24	...	...	...	—	—	—	—	—
—Montreal	NHL	19	4	2	6	4	1	0	0	9	0	1	1	0
93-94—Florida	NHL	70	17	33	50	16	-4	11	0	—	—	—	—	—
94-95—Florida	NHL	47	15	14	29	18	-5	6	0	—	—	—	—	—
95-96—Florida	NHL	63	17	21	38	10	-5	7	0	—	—	—	—	—
—Vancouver	NHL	9	3	0	3	4	0	1	0	3	0	2	2	2
96-97—Hamilton	AHL	6	4	3	7	0	...	...	...	—	—	—	—	—
—Quebec	IHL	47	34	28	62	18	...	...	...	9	3	5	8	13
—Edmonton	NHL	6	0	0	0	0	-3	0	0	—	—	—	—	—

Season Team	League	REGULAR SEASON Gms.	G	A	Pts.	PIM	+/-	PP	SH	PLAYOFFS Gms.	G	A	Pts.	PIM
97-98—SC Herisau	Switzerland	5	4	3	7	4	...	...	...	—	—	—	—	—
—Las Vegas	IHL	54	32	36	68	20	...	...	...	4	0	1	1	0
98-99—Cleveland	IHL	22	9	13	22	10	...	...	...	—	—	—	—	—
99-00—Quebec	AHL	36	15	18	33	20	...	...	...	3	0	3	3	4
—Montreal	NHL	16	3	6	9	2	2	0	0	—	—	—	—	—
00-01—Chicago	IHL	58	17	22	39	28	...	...	...	14	3	4	7	10
—New York Islanders	NHL	12	0	0	0	2	-5	0	0	—	—	—	—	—
NHL Totals (8 years)		246	59	76	135	56	-20	25	0	12	0	3	3	2

BELANGER, KEN   LW   KINGS

PERSONAL: Born May 14, 1974, in Sault Ste. Marie, Ont. ... 6-4/225. ... Shoots left. ... Name pronounced buh-LAH-zhay.

TRANSACTIONS/CAREER NOTES: Selected by Hartford Whalers in seventh round (seventh Whalers pick, 153rd overall) of NHL entry draft (June 20, 1992). ... Traded by Whalers to Toronto Maple Leafs for ninth-round pick (RW Matt Ball) in 1994 draft (March 18, 1994). ... Traded by Maple Leafs with G Damian Rhodes to New York Islanders for C Kirk Muller (January 23, 1996). ... Suffered concussion (February 6, 1996); missed two games. ... Suffered concussion (February 12, 1996); missed remainder of season. ... Suffered concussion (October 13, 1997); missed four games. ... Injured hand (November 15, 1997); missed three games. ... Suffered from the flu (November 26, 1997); missed three games. ... Reinjured hand (January 8, 1998); missed two games. ... Underwent thumb surgery (January 14, 1998); missed 22 games. ... Traded by Islanders to Boston Bruins for LW Ted Donato (November 7, 1998). ... Suffered facial laceration (November 8, 1998); missed two games. ... Strained neck (December 28, 1998); missed two games. ... Injured hand (April 3, 1999); missed one game. ... Suffered concussion (November 10, 1999); missed 34 games. ... Suffered groin injury (March 29, 2000); missed final six games of season. ... Strained hip (December 8, 2000); missed three games. ... Reinjured hip (January 10, 2001) and underwent surgery; missed 18 games. ... Signed as free agent by Los Angeles Kings (July 2, 2001).

Season Team	League	REGULAR SEASON Gms.	G	A	Pts.	PIM	+/-	PP	SH	PLAYOFFS Gms.	G	A	Pts.	PIM
91-92—Ottawa	OHL	51	4	4	8	174	...	...	...	11	0	0	0	24
92-93—Ottawa	OHL	34	6	12	18	139	...	...	...	—	—	—	—	—
—Guelph	OHL	29	10	14	24	86	...	...	...	5	2	1	3	14
93-94—Guelph	OHL	55	11	22	33	185	...	...	...	9	2	3	5	30
94-95—St. John's	AHL	47	5	5	10	246	...	...	...	4	0	0	0	30
—Toronto	NHL	3	0	0	0	9	0	0	0	—	—	—	—	—
95-96—St. John's	AHL	40	16	14	30	222	...	...	...	—	—	—	—	—
—New York Islanders	NHL	7	0	0	0	27	-2	0	0	—	—	—	—	—
96-97—Kentucky	AHL	38	10	12	22	164	...	...	...	4	0	1	1	27
—New York Islanders	NHL	18	0	2	2	102	-1	0	0	—	—	—	—	—
97-98—New York Islanders	NHL	37	3	1	4	101	1	0	0	—	—	—	—	—
98-99—New York Islanders	NHL	9	1	1	2	30	1	0	0	—	—	—	—	—
—Boston	NHL	45	1	4	5	152	-2	0	0	12	1	0	1	16
99-00—Boston	NHL	37	2	2	4	44	-4	0	0	—	—	—	—	—
00-01—Boston	NHL	40	2	2	4	121	-6	0	0	—	—	—	—	—
—Providence	AHL	10	1	4	5	47	...	...	...	2	0	0	0	4
NHL Totals (7 years)		196	9	12	21	586	-13	0	0	12	1	0	1	16

BELFOUR, ED   G   STARS

PERSONAL: Born April 21, 1965, in Carman, Man. ... 5-11/192. ... Catches left. ... Full Name: Edward Belfour.

TRANSACTIONS/CAREER NOTES: Signed as non-drafted free agent by Chicago Blackhawks (June 18, 1987). ... Strained hip muscle (1993-94 season); missed four games. ... Sprained knee (January 31, 1996); missed one game. ... Injured back (February 19, 1996); missed three games. ... Traded by Blackhawks to San Jose Sharks for G Chris Terreri, D Michal Sykora and RW Ulf Dahlen (January 25, 1997). ... Injured knee ligament (February 1, 1997); missed 13 games. ... Suffered bulging disc in back (March 1, 1997); missed seven games. ... Signed as free agent by Dallas Stars (July 2, 1997). ... Strained lower back (February 2, 1998); missed three games. ... Strained groin (November 10, 1999); missed one game. ... Injured back (March 23, 2001); missed one game.

HONORS: Named top goaltender in MJHL (1985-86). ... Named to NCAA All-America (West) second team (1986-87). ... Named to NCAA All-Tournament team (1986-87). ... Named to WCHA All-Star first team (1986-87). ... Shared Garry F. Longman Memorial Trophy with John Cullen (1987-88). ... Named to IHL All-Star first team (1987-88). ... Named Rookie of the Year by THE SPORTING NEWS (1990-91). ... Won Vezina Trophy (1990-91 and 1992-93). ... Won Calder Memorial Trophy (1990-91). ... Won William M. Jennings Trophy (1990-91, 1992-93 and 1994-95). ... Won Trico Goaltender Award (1990-91). ... Named to THE SPORTING NEWS All-Star first team (1990-91). ... Named to NHL All-Star first team (1990-91 and 1992-93). ... Named to NHL All-Rookie team (1990-91). ... Played in NHL All-Star Game (1992, 1993, 1996, 1998 and 1999). ... Named to THE SPORTING NEWS All-Star second team (1992-93 and 1994-95). ... Shared William M. Jennings Trophy with Roman Turek (1998-99).

RECORDS: Shares NHL single-season playoff record for most consecutive wins by goaltender—11 (1992); most wins by goaltender—16 (1999); and most minutes played by goaltender—1,544 (1999).

MISCELLANEOUS: Member of Stanley Cup championship team (1999). ... Holds Dallas Stars franchise all-time record for goals-against average (2.08). ... Stopped penalty shot attempt (vs. Steve Maltais, February 25, 1993; vs. Roman Oksiuta, February 4, 1994; vs. Mark Howe, March 22, 1994; vs. Alex Tanguay, December 1, 2000). ... Allowed penalty shot goal (vs. Philippe Bozon, April 3, 1993; vs. Steve Larmer, January 16, 1994).

STATISTICAL NOTES: Led NHL with .910 save percentage (1990-91). ... Led NHL with .669 winning percentage (1998-99). ... Tied for NHL lead in save percentage with .919 (1999-2000).

Season Team	League	REGULAR SEASON Gms.	Min	W	L	T	GA	SO	Avg.	PLAYOFFS Gms.	Min.	W	L	GA	SO	Avg.
85-86—Winkler	MJHL	48	2880	...	...	...	124	1	2.58	—	—	—	—	—	—	—
86-87—Univ. of North Dakota	WCHA	34	2049	29	4	0	81	3	2.37	—	—	—	—	—	—	—
87-88—Saginaw	IHL	61	*3446	32	25	‡0	183	3	3.19	9	561	4	5	33	0	3.53
88-89—Chicago	NHL	23	1148	4	12	3	74	0	3.87	—	—	—	—	—	—	—
—Saginaw	IHL	29	1760	12	10	‡0	92	0	3.14	5	298	2	3	14	0	2.82
89-90—Canadian nat'l team	Int'l	33	1808	...	...	...	93	...	3.09	—	—	—	—	—	—	—
—Chicago	NHL	—	—	...	...	...	—	—	—	9	409	4	2	17	0	2.49

Season Team	League	REGULAR SEASON								PLAYOFFS						
		Gms.	Min	W	L	T	GA	SO	Avg.	Gms.	Min.	W	L	GA	SO	Avg.
90-91—Chicago	NHL	*74	*4127	*43	19	7	170	4	*2.47	6	295	2	4	20	0	4.07
91-92—Chicago	NHL	52	2928	21	18	10	132	†5	2.70	18	949	12	4	39	1	*2.47
92-93—Chicago	NHL	*71	*4106	41	18	11	177	*7	2.59	4	249	0	4	13	0	3.13
93-94—Chicago	NHL	70	3998	37	24	6	178	†7	2.67	6	360	2	4	15	0	2.50
94-95—Chicago	NHL	42	2450	22	15	3	93	†5	2.28	16	1014	9	†7	37	1	2.19
95-96—Chicago	NHL	50	2956	22	17	10	135	1	2.74	9	666	6	3	23	1	*2.07
96-97—Chicago	NHL	33	1966	11	15	6	88	1	2.69	—	—	—	—	—	—	—
—San Jose	NHL	13	757	3	9	0	43	1	3.41	—	—	—	—	—	—	—
97-98—Dallas	NHL	61	3581	37	12	10	112	9	*1.88	17	1039	10	7	31	1	1.79
98-99—Dallas	NHL	61	3536	35	15	9	117	5	1.99	*23	*1544	*16	7	43	*3	*1.67
99-00—Dallas	NHL	62	3620	32	21	7	127	4	2.10	†23	1443	14	*9	*45	*4	1.87
00-01—Dallas	NHL	63	3687	35	20	7	144	8	2.34	10	671	4	6	25	0	2.24
NHL Totals (13 years)		675	38860	343	215	89	1590	57	2.45	141	8639	79	57	308	11	2.14

BELL, MARK   C/LW   BLACKHAWKS

PERSONAL: Born August 5, 1980, in St. Paul's, Ont. ... 6-3/198. ... Shoots left.
TRANSACTIONS/CAREER NOTES: Selected by Chicago Blackhawks in first round (first Blackhawks pick, eighth overall) of NHL entry draft (June 27, 1998).

Season Team	League	REGULAR SEASON							PLAYOFFS				
		Gms.	G	A	Pts.	PIM	+/-	PP	SH	Gms.	G	A	Pts.	PIM
95-96—Stratford Jr. B	OHA	47	8	15	23	32	...	...	...	—	—	—	—	—
96-97—Ottawa	OHL	65	8	12	20	40	...	...	...	24	4	7	11	13
97-98—Ottawa	OHL	55	34	26	60	87	...	...	...	13	6	5	11	14
98-99—Ottawa	OHL	44	29	26	55	69	...	...	...	9	6	5	11	8
99-00—Ottawa	OHL	48	34	38	72	95	...	...	...	2	0	1	1	0
00-01—Norfolk	AHL	61	15	27	42	126	...	...	...	9	4	3	7	10
—Chicago	NHL	13	0	1	1	4	0	0	0	—	—	—	—	—
NHL Totals (1 year)		13	0	1	1	4	0	0	0					

BELLEFEUILLE, BLAKE   C   BLUE JACKETS

PERSONAL: Born December 27, 1977, in Framingham, Mass. ... 5-10/208. ... Shoots right. ... Name pronounced BELL-fay.
TRANSACTIONS/CAREER NOTES: Signed as non-drafted free agent by Columbus Blue Jackets (May 31, 2000).
HONORS: Named to Hockey East All-Star second team (1999-2000).

Season Team	League	REGULAR SEASON							PLAYOFFS				
		Gms.	G	A	Pts.	PIM	+/-	PP	SH	Gms.	G	A	Pts.	PIM
94-95—Framingham	USHS (East)	20	42	50	92	...	...	...	...	—	—	—	—	—
95-96—Framingham	USHS (East)	20	31	60	91	...	...	...	...	—	—	—	—	—
96-97—Boston College	Hockey East	34	16	19	35	20	...	...	...	—	—	—	—	—
97-98—Boston College	Hockey East	41	19	20	39	35	...	...	...	—	—	—	—	—
98-99—Boston College	Hockey East	43	24	25	49	80	...	...	...	—	—	—	—	—
99-00—Boston College	Hockey East	41	19	32	51	28	...	...	...	—	—	—	—	—
00-01—Syracuse	AHL	50	5	5	10	18	...	...	...	5	0	0	0	0

BENYSEK, LADISLAV   D   WILD

PERSONAL: Born March 24, 1975, in Olomouc, Czechoslavakia. ... 6-2/190. ... Shoots left. ... Name pronounced BEHN-ih-sikh.
TRANSACTIONS/CAREER NOTES: Selected by Edmonton Oilers in 11th round (16th Oilers pick, 266th overall) of NHL entry draft (June 29, 1994). ... Claimed by Mighty Ducks of Anaheim from Oilers in NHL waiver draft (September 27, 1999). ... Selected by Minnesota Wild in NHL expansion draft (June 23, 2000). ... Fractured finger (February 7, 2001); missed one game. ... Bruised shoulder (March 4, 2001); missed one game.

Season Team	League	REGULAR SEASON							PLAYOFFS				
		Gms.	G	A	Pts.	PIM	+/-	PP	SH	Gms.	G	A	Pts.	PIM
93-94—HC Olomouc	Czech Rep.					Statistics unavailable.								
94-95—Cape Breton	AHL	58	2	7	9	54	...	...	...	—	—	—	—	—
95-96—HC Olomouc	Czech Rep.	33	1	4	5	...	...	...	...	—	—	—	—	—
96-97—HC Olomouc	Czech Rep.	14	0	1	1	8	...	...	...	—	—	—	—	—
—Sparta Praha	Czech Rep.	36	5	5	10	28	...	...	...	—	—	—	—	—
97-98—Edmonton	NHL	2	0	0	0	0	-2	0	0	—	—	—	—	—
—Hamilton	AHL	53	2	14	16	29	...	...	...	9	1	1	2	2
98-99—Sparta Praha	Czech Rep.	52	8	11	19	47	...	...	...	8	0	1	1	...
99-00—Sparta Praha	Czech Rep.	51	1	5	6	45	...	...	...	9	0	0	0	4
00-01—Minnesota	NHL	71	2	5	7	38	-11	1	0	—	—	—	—	—
NHL Totals (2 years)		73	2	5	7	38	-13	1	0					

BERANEK, JOSEF   LW

PERSONAL: Born October 25, 1969, in Litvinov, Czechoslovakia. ... 6-2/195. ... Shoots left. ... Name pronounced JOH-sehf buh-RAH-nehk.
TRANSACTIONS/CAREER NOTES: Selected by Edmonton Oilers in fourth round (third Oilers pick, 78th overall) of NHL entry draft (June 17, 1989). ... Traded by Oilers with D Greg Hawgood to Philadelphia Flyers for D Brian Benning (January 16, 1993). ... Bruised left shoulder (January 30, 1994); missed three games. ... Played in Europe during 1994-95 NHL lockout. ... Traded by Flyers to Vancouver Canucks for LW Shawn Antoski (February 15, 1995). ... Sprained thumb (February 2, 1996); missed two games. ... Injured thumb (February 17, 1996); missed one game. ... Traded by Canucks to Pittsburgh Penguins for future considerations (March 18, 1997). ... Bruised shoulder (March 24, 1997);

missed one game. ... Strained groin (April 8, 1997); missed two games. ... Traded by Penguins to Oilers for D Bobby Dollas and C Tony Hrkac (June 16, 1998). ... Bruised thigh (October 20, 1998); missed two games. ... Sprained shoulder (December 8, 1998); missed three games. ... Sprained knee (February 23, 1999); missed three games. ... Injured left knee (April 3, 1999) and underwent arthoscopic surgery; missed final six games of regular season and two playoff games. ... Traded by Oilers to Penguins for C German Titov (March 14, 2000). ... Strained hamstring (November 22, 2000); missed one game. ... Strained shoulder (December 10, 2000); missed one game. ... Injured hip (December 16, 2000); missed one game. ... Strained groin (January 21, 2001); missed six games. ... Bruised thigh (March 20, 2001); missed one game.

MISCELLANEOUS: Member of gold-medal-winning Czech Republic Olympic Team (1998).

STATISTICAL PLATEAUS: Three-goal games: 1994-95 (1).

			REGULAR SEASON								PLAYOFFS				
Season Team	League	Gms.	G	A	Pts.	PIM	+/-	PP	SH		Gms.	G	A	Pts.	PIM
87-88—CHZ Litvinov	Czech.	14	7	4	11	12	...	...	...		—	—	—	—	—
88-89—CHZ Litvinov	Czech.	32	18	10	28	47	...	...	...		—	—	—	—	—
—Czechoslovakia Jr.	Czech.	5	2	7	9	2	...	...	...		—	—	—	—	—
89-90—Dukla Trencin	Czech.	49	16	21	37	...	...	...	...		—	—	—	—	—
90-91—CHZ Litvinov	Czech.	50	27	27	54	98	...	...	...		—	—	—	—	—
91-92—Edmonton	NHL	58	12	16	28	18	-2	0	0		12	2	1	3	0
92-93—Edmonton	NHL	26	2	6	8	28	-7	0	0		—	—	—	—	—
—Cape Breton	AHL	6	1	2	3	8	...	...	...		—	—	—	—	—
—Philadelphia	NHL	40	13	12	25	50	-1	1	0		—	—	—	—	—
93-94—Philadelphia	NHL	80	28	21	49	85	-2	6	0		—	—	—	—	—
94-95—Czech Rep.	Czech Rep.	16	7	7	14	26	...	...	...		—	—	—	—	—
—Philadelphia	NHL	14	5	5	10	2	3	1	0		—	—	—	—	—
—Vancouver	NHL	37	8	13	21	28	-10	2	0		11	1	1	2	12
95-96—Vancouver	NHL	61	6	14	20	60	-11	0	0		3	2	1	3	0
96-97—Vsetin	Czech Rep.	39	19	24	43	115	...	...	...		3	3	2	5	4
—Pittsburgh	NHL	8	3	1	4	4	-1	1	0		5	0	0	0	2
97-98—Vsetin	Czech Rep.	45	24	27	51	92	...	...	...		10	2	8	10	14
—Czech Rep. Oly. team..	Int'l	6	1	0	1	4	...	...	...		—	—	—	—	—
98-99—Edmonton	NHL	66	19	30	49	23	6	7	0		2	0	0	0	4
99-00—Edmonton	NHL	58	9	8	17	39	-6	3	0		—	—	—	—	—
—Pittsburgh	NHL	13	4	4	8	18	-6	1	0		11	0	3	3	4
00-01—Pittsburgh	NHL	70	9	14	23	43	-7	2	0		13	0	2	2	2
NHL Totals (9 years)		531	118	144	262	398	-44	24	0		57	5	8	13	24

BEREHOWSKY, DRAKE D CANUCKS

PERSONAL: Born January 3, 1972, in Toronto. ... 6-2/212. ... Shoots right. ... Name pronounced BAIR-ih-HOW-skee.

TRANSACTIONS/CAREER NOTES: Selected by Toronto Maple Leafs in first round (first Maple Leafs pick, 10th overall) of NHL entry draft (June 16, 1990). ... Sprained knee (April 15, 1993); missed remainder of season. ... Underwent knee surgery prior to 1994-95 season; missed first four games of season. ... Traded by Maple Leafs to Pittsburgh Penguins for D Grant Jennings (April 7, 1995). ... Signed as free agent by Edmonton Oilers (September 29, 1997). ... Traded by Oilers with G Eric Fichaud and D Greg de Vries to Nashville Predators for F Jim Dowd and G Mikhail Shtalenkov (October 1, 1998). ... Sprained knee (February 4, 1999); missed two games. ... Injured neck (October 2, 1999); missed first game of season. ... Strained elbow (November 26, 2000); missed two games. ... Suspended one game by NHL for receiving match penalty (December 29, 2000). ... Traded by Predators to Vancouver Canucks for second-round pick (RW Timofei Shiskanov) in 2001 draft (March 9, 2001).

HONORS: Won Can.HL Defenseman of the Year Award (1991-92). ... Won Max Kaminsky Trophy (1991-92). ... Named to Can.HL All-Star first team (1991-92). ... Named to OHL All-Star first team (1991-92).

MISCELLANEOUS: Holds Nashville Predators all-time record for most penalty minutes (327).

			REGULAR SEASON								PLAYOFFS				
Season Team	League	Gms.	G	A	Pts.	PIM	+/-	PP	SH		Gms.	G	A	Pts.	PIM
87-88—Barrie Jr. B	OHA	40	10	36	46	81	...	...	...		—	—	—	—	—
88-89—Kingston	OHL	63	7	39	46	85	...	...	...		—	—	—	—	—
89-90—Kingston	OHL	9	3	11	14	28	...	...	...		—	—	—	—	—
90-91—Toronto	NHL	8	0	1	1	25	-6	0	0		—	—	—	—	—
—Kingston	OHL	13	5	13	18	28	...	...	...		—	—	—	—	—
—North Bay	OHL	26	7	23	30	51	...	...	...		10	2	7	9	21
91-92—North Bay	OHL	62	19	63	82	147	...	...	...		21	7	24	31	22
—Toronto	NHL	1	0	0	0	0	0	0	0		—	—	—	—	—
—St. John's	AHL	—	—	—	—	—	...	...	...		6	0	5	5	21
92-93—Toronto	NHL	41	4	15	19	61	1	1	0		—	—	—	—	—
—St. John's	AHL	28	10	17	27	38	...	...	...		—	—	—	—	—
93-94—Toronto	NHL	49	2	8	10	63	-3	2	0		—	—	—	—	—
—St. John's	AHL	18	3	12	15	40	...	...	...		—	—	—	—	—
94-95—Toronto	NHL	25	0	2	2	15	-10	0	0		—	—	—	—	—
—Pittsburgh	NHL	4	0	0	0	13	1	0	0		1	0	0	0	0
95-96—Cleveland	IHL	74	6	28	34	141	...	...	...		3	0	3	3	6
—Pittsburgh	NHL	1	0	0	0	0	1	0	0		—	—	—	—	—
96-97—San Antonio	IHL	16	3	4	7	36	...	...	...		—	—	—	—	—
—Carolina	AHL	49	2	15	17	55	...	...	...		—	—	—	—	—
97-98—Edmonton	NHL	67	1	6	7	169	1	1	0		12	1	2	3	14
—Hamilton	AHL	8	2	0	2	21	...	...	...		—	—	—	—	—
98-99—Nashville	NHL	74	2	15	17	140	-9	0	0		—	—	—	—	—
99-00—Nashville	NHL	79	12	20	32	87	-4	5	0		—	—	—	—	—
00-01—Nashville	NHL	66	6	18	24	100	-9	3	0		—	—	—	—	—
—Vancouver	NHL	14	1	1	2	21	0	1	0		4	0	0	0	12
NHL Totals (10 years)		429	28	86	114	694	-37	13	0		17	1	2	3	26

PERSONAL: Born August 8, 1977, in Arlington Heights, Ill. ... 6-2/218. ... Shoots left. ... Full Name: Andrew Berenzweig.

TRANSACTIONS/CAREER NOTES: Selected by New York Islanders in fifth round (fifth Islanders pick, 109th overall) of NHL entry draft (June 22, 1996). ... Traded by Islanders to Nashville Predators for fourth-round pick (D Johan Halvardsson) in 1999 draft (April 19, 1999).

HONORS: Named to NCAA All-Tournament team (1997-98). ... Named to CCHA All-Star second team (1997-98). ... Won Ken McKenzie Trophy (1999-2000). ... Named to IHL All-Star second team (2000-01).

Season Team	League	REGULAR SEASON								PLAYOFFS				
		Gms.	G	A	Pts.	PIM	+/-	PP	SH	Gms.	G	A	Pts.	PIM
92-93—Loomis-Chaffee	Conn. H.S.	22	5	13	18	...	...	...	...	—	—	—	—	—
93-94—Loomis-Chaffee	Conn. H.S.	22	12	27	39	...	...	...	...	—	—	—	—	—
94-95—Loomis-Chaffee	Conn. H.S.	23	19	23	42	24	...	...	...	—	—	—	—	—
95-96—Univ. of Michigan	CCHA	42	4	8	12	4	...	...	...	—	—	—	—	—
96-97—Univ. of Michigan	CCHA	38	7	12	19	49	...	...	...	—	—	—	—	—
97-98—Univ. of Michigan	CCHA	43	6	10	16	28	...	...	...	—	—	—	—	—
98-99—Univ. of Michigan	CCHA	42	7	24	31	38	...	...	...	—	—	—	—	—
99-00—Milwaukee	IHL	79	4	23	27	48	...	...	...	3	1	2	3	0
—Nashville	NHL	2	0	0	0	0	-1	0	0	—	—	—	—	—
00-01—Milwaukee	IHL	72	10	26	36	38	...	...	...	5	0	4	4	4
—Nashville	NHL	5	0	0	0	0	0	0	0	—	—	—	—	—
NHL Totals (2 years)		7	0	0	0	0	-1	0	0					

PERSONAL: Born November 5, 1971, in Voskresensk, U.S.S.R. ... 5-10/200. ... Shoots right. ... Name pronounced BAIR-ih-zihn.

TRANSACTIONS/CAREER NOTES: Selected by Toronto Maple Leafs in 10th round (eighth Maple Leafs pick, 256th overall) of NHL entry draft (June 29, 1994). ... Injured hand (November 19, 1996); missed one game. ... Underwent hand surgery (December 3, 1996); missed six games. ... Strained knee (December 23, 1996); missed two games. ... Suffered hip pointer (October 30, 1998); missed four games. ... Bruised foot (November 12, 1998); missed two games. ... Suffered injury (January 8, 2000); missed five games. ... Injured hamstring (January 27, 2000); missed 14 games. ... Suffered injury (April 5, 2000); missed one game. ... Suffered injury (January 10, 2001); missed one game. ... Traded by Maple Leafs to Phoenix Coyotes for RW Mikael Renberg (June 22, 2001).

HONORS: Named to NHL All-Rookie team (1996-97).

STATISTICAL PLATEAUS: Three-goal games: 1998-99 (2).

Season Team	League	REGULAR SEASON								PLAYOFFS				
		Gms.	G	A	Pts.	PIM	+/-	PP	SH	Gms.	G	A	Pts.	PIM
90-91—Khimik Voskresensk	USSR	30	6	2	8	4	...	...	...	—	—	—	—	—
91-92—Khimik Voskresensk	CIS	36	7	5	12	10	...	...	...	—	—	—	—	—
92-93—Khimik Voskresensk	CIS	38	9	3	12	12	...	...	...	2	1	0	1	0
93-94—Khimik Voskresensk	CIS	40	31	10	41	16	...	...	...	—	—	—	—	—
—Russian nat'l team	Int'l	6	2	1	3	2	...	...	...	—	—	—	—	—
—Russian Oly. team	Int'l	8	3	2	5	2	...	...	...	—	—	—	—	—
94-95—Koln	Germany	43	38	19	57	8	...	...	...	18	17	8	25	18
—Russian nat'l team	Int'l	6	7	1	8	4	...	...	...	—	—	—	—	—
95-96—Koln	Germany	45	49	31	80	8	...	...	...	14	13	9	22	4
—Russian nat'l team	Int'l	8	4	5	9	2	...	...	...	—	—	—	—	—
96-97—Toronto	NHL	73	25	16	41	2	-3	7	0	—	—	—	—	—
97-98—Toronto	NHL	68	16	15	31	10	-3	3	0	—	—	—	—	—
98-99—Toronto	NHL	76	37	22	59	12	16	9	1	17	6	6	12	4
99-00—Toronto	NHL	61	26	13	39	2	8	5	0	12	4	4	8	0
00-01—Toronto	NHL	79	22	28	50	8	2	10	0	11	2	5	7	2
NHL Totals (5 years)		357	126	94	220	34	20	34	1	40	12	15	27	6

PERSONAL: Born July 28, 1977, in Turku, Finland. ... 6-3/220. ... Shoots left. ... Full Name: Aki-Petteri Berg. ... Name pronounced AH-kee BUHRG.

TRANSACTIONS/CAREER NOTES: Selected by Los Angeles Kings in first round (first Kings pick, third overall) of NHL entry draft (July 8, 1995). ... Suffered charley horse (January 25, 1997); missed one game. ... Suffered concussion (February 3, 1997); missed two games. ... Sprained left ankle (April 9, 1997); missed final two games of regular season. ... Bruised right foot (December 4, 1997); missed one game. ... Sprained right wrist (March 10, 1998); missed two games. ... Injured ribs (December 23, 1999); missed two games. ... Suffered concussion (March 13, 2000); missed two games. ... Suffered injury (January 4, 2001); missed three games. ... Traded by Kings to Toronto Maple Leafs for C Adam Mair and second-round pick (C Mike Cammaleri) in 2001 draft (March 13, 2001).

MISCELLANEOUS: Member of bronze-medal-winning Finnish Olympic team (1998).

Season Team	League	REGULAR SEASON								PLAYOFFS				
		Gms.	G	A	Pts.	PIM	+/-	PP	SH	Gms.	G	A	Pts.	PIM
92-93—TPS Turku Jr.	Finland	39	18	24	42	59	...	...	...	—	—	—	—	—
93-94—TPS Turku Jr.	Finland	21	3	11	14	24	...	...	...	7	0	0	0	10
—TPS Turku	Finland	6	0	3	3	4	...	...	...	—	—	—	—	—
94-95—Kiekko-67	Finland Div. 2	20	3	9	12	34	...	...	...	—	—	—	—	—
—TPS Turku Jr.	Finland	8	1	0	1	30	...	...	...	—	—	—	—	—
—TPS Turku	Finland	5	0	0	0	4	...	...	...	—	—	—	—	—
95-96—Los Angeles	NHL	51	0	7	7	29	-13	0	0	—	—	—	—	—
—Phoenix	IHL	20	0	3	3	18	...	...	...	2	0	0	0	4
96-97—Los Angeles	NHL	41	2	6	8	24	-9	2	0	—	—	—	—	—
—Phoenix	IHL	23	1	3	4	21	...	...	...	—	—	—	—	—
97-98—Los Angeles	NHL	72	0	8	8	61	3	0	0	4	0	3	3	0
—Fin. Olympic team	Int'l	6	0	0	0	6	...	...	...	—	—	—	—	—

Season Team	League	REGULAR SEASON								PLAYOFFS				
		Gms.	G	A	Pts.	PIM	+/-	PP	SH	Gms.	G	A	Pts.	PIM
98-99—TPS Turku	Finland	48	8	7	15	137	...	...	...	9	1	1	2	45
99-00—Los Angeles	NHL	70	3	13	16	45	-1	0	0	2	0	0	0	2
00-01—Los Angeles	NHL	47	0	4	4	43	3	0	0	—	—	—	—	—
—Toronto	NHL	12	3	0	3	2	-6	3	0	11	0	2	2	4
NHL Totals (5 years)		293	8	38	46	204	-23	5	0	17	0	5	5	6

BERGEVIN, MARC　　D

PERSONAL: Born August 11, 1965, in Montreal. ... 6-1/214. ... Shoots left. ... Name pronounced BUHR-jih-vihn.

TRANSACTIONS/CAREER NOTES: Selected by Chicago Blackhawks in third round (third Blackhawks pick, 59th overall) of NHL entry draft (June 8, 1983). ... Sprained neck (March 18, 1987). ... Traded by Blackhawks with D Gary Nylund to New York Islanders for D Steve Konroyd and C Bob Bassen (November 25, 1988). ... Bruised ribs (November 25, 1989). ... Broke hand (May 1990). ... Traded by Islanders to Hartford Whalers for future considerations; Islanders later received fifth-round pick in 1992 draft (C Ryan Duthie) to complete deal (October 31, 1990). ... Signed as free agent by Tampa Bay Lightning (July 9, 1992). ... Injured foot (March 18, 1993); missed one game. ... Bruised back (November 19, 1993); missed one game. ... Injured elbow (March 10, 1995); missed one game. ... Suffered from sore neck (April 22, 1995); missed three games. ... Traded by Lightning with RW Ben Hankinson to Detroit Red Wings for LW Shawn Burr and third-round pick (traded to Boston) in 1996 draft (August 17, 1995). ... Suffered from the flu (November 1, 1995); missed one game. ... Injured groin (April 7, 1996); missed three games. ... Signed as free agent by St. Louis Blues (July 9, 1996). ... Injured ankle (December 13, 1997); missed one game. ... Strained abdominal muscle (January 9, 1999); missed 20 games. ... Reinjured abdominal muscle (April 3, 1999) and underwent surgery; missed remainder of season. ... Fractured thumb (September 12, 2000); missed first 18 games of season. ... Traded by Blues to Pittsburgh Penguins for D Dan Trebil (December 28, 2000). ... Strained knee (February 21, 2001); missed seven games.

Season Team	League	REGULAR SEASON								PLAYOFFS				
		Gms.	G	A	Pts.	PIM	+/-	PP	SH	Gms.	G	A	Pts.	PIM
82-83—Chicoutimi	QMJHL	64	3	27	30	113	...	...	...	—	—	—	—	—
83-84—Chicoutimi	QMJHL	70	10	35	45	125	...	...	...	—	—	—	—	—
—Springfield	AHL	7	0	1	1	2	...	...	...	—	—	—	—	—
84-85—Chicago	NHL	60	0	6	6	54	-9	0	0	6	0	3	3	2
—Springfield	AHL	—	—	—	—	—	...	...	...	4	0	0	0	0
85-86—Chicago	NHL	71	7	7	14	60	0	0	0	3	0	0	0	0
86-87—Chicago	NHL	66	4	10	14	66	4	0	0	3	1	0	1	2
87-88—Chicago	NHL	58	1	6	7	85	-19	0	0	—	—	—	—	—
—Saginaw	IHL	10	2	7	9	20	...	...	...	—	—	—	—	—
88-89—Chicago	NHL	11	0	0	0	18	-3	0	0	—	—	—	—	—
—New York Islanders	NHL	58	2	13	15	62	2	1	0	—	—	—	—	—
89-90—New York Islanders	NHL	18	0	4	4	30	-8	0	0	—	—	—	—	—
—Springfield	AHL	47	7	16	23	66	...	...	...	17	2	11	13	16
90-91—Hartford	NHL	4	0	0	0	4	-3	0	0	—	—	—	—	—
—Capital District	AHL	7	0	5	5	6	...	...	...	—	—	—	—	—
—Springfield	AHL	58	4	23	27	85	...	...	...	18	0	7	7	26
91-92—Hartford	NHL	75	7	17	24	64	-13	4	1	5	0	0	0	2
92-93—Tampa Bay	NHL	78	2	12	14	66	-16	0	0	—	—	—	—	—
93-94—Tampa Bay	NHL	83	1	15	16	87	-5	0	0	—	—	—	—	—
94-95—Tampa Bay	NHL	44	2	4	6	51	-6	0	1	—	—	—	—	—
95-96—Detroit	NHL	70	1	9	10	33	7	0	0	17	1	0	1	14
96-97—St. Louis	NHL	82	0	4	4	53	-9	0	0	6	1	0	1	8
97-98—St. Louis	NHL	81	3	7	10	90	-2	0	0	10	0	1	1	8
98-99—St. Louis	NHL	52	1	1	2	99	-14	0	0	—	—	—	—	—
99-00—St. Louis	NHL	81	1	8	9	75	27	0	0	7	0	1	1	6
00-01—St. Louis	NHL	2	0	0	0	0	1	0	0	—	—	—	—	—
—Pittsburgh	NHL	36	1	4	5	26	5	0	0	12	0	1	1	2
NHL Totals (17 years)		1030	33	127	160	1023	-61	5	2	69	3	6	9	44

BERGLUND, CHRISTIAN　　C　　DEVILS

PERSONAL: Born March 12, 1980, in Orebro, Sweden. ... 5-11/185. ... Shoots left.

TRANSACTIONS/CAREER NOTES: Selected by New Jersey Devils in second round (third Devils pick, 37th overall) of NHL entry draft (June 27, 1998).

Season Team	League	REGULAR SEASON								PLAYOFFS				
		Gms.	G	A	Pts.	PIM	+/-	PP	SH	Gms.	G	A	Pts.	PIM
94-95—Karlskoga	Sweden Dv. 4	20	14	13	27	...	...	...	...	—	—	—	—	—
95-96—Kristinehamn	Sweden Dv. 3	23	8	8	16	12	...	...	...	—	—	—	—	—
96-97—Farjestad Karlstad	Sweden Jr.	21	2	3	5	24	...	...	...	—	—	—	—	—
97-98—Farjestad Karlstad	Sweden Jr.	29	23	19	42	88	...	...	...	2	0	0	0	0
—Farjestad Karlstad	Sweden	1	0	0	0	0	...	...	...	—	—	—	—	—
98-99—Farjestad Karlstad	Sweden Jr.	5	3	4	7	22	...	...	...	—	—	—	—	—
—Farjestad Karlstad	Sweden	37	2	4	6	37	...	...	...	4	1	0	1	4
99-00—Farjestad Karlstad	Sweden	43	8	6	14	44	...	...	...	7	2	1	3	10
—Bofors	Sweden 2	6	2	0	2	12	...	...	...	—	—	—	—	—
00-01—Farjestad Karlstad	Sweden	49	17	20	37	142	...	...	...	16	7	7	14	22

BERRY, RICK　　D　　AVALANCHE

PERSONAL: Born November 4, 1978, in Brandon, Man. ... 6-1/190. ... Shoots left.

TRANSACTIONS/CAREER NOTES: Selected by Colorado Avalanche in third round (third Avalanche pick, 55th overall) of NHL entry draft (June 21, 1997).

			REGULAR SEASON								PLAYOFFS				
Season Team	League	Gms.	G	A	Pts.	PIM	+/-	PP	SH		Gms.	G	A	Pts.	PIM
95-96—Seattle......................	WHL	59	4	9	13	103	...	...	...		1	0	0	0	0
96-97—Seattle......................	WHL	72	12	21	33	125	...	...	...		15	3	7	10	23
97-98—Spokane....................	WHL	59	9	21	30	131	...	...	...		17	1	4	5	26
—Seattle......................	WHL	37	5	12	17	100	...	...	...		—	—	—	—	—
98-99—Hershey	AHL	62	2	6	8	153	...	...	...		—	—	—	—	—
99-00—Hershey	AHL	64	9	16	25	148	...	...	...		13	2	3	5	24
00-01—Hershey	AHL	48	6	17	23	87	...	...	...		12	2	2	4	18
—Colorado	NHL	19	0	4	4	38	5	0	0		—	—	—	—	—
NHL Totals (1 year)............		19	0	4	4	38	5	0	0						

B

BERTRAND, ERIC   LW

PERSONAL: Born April 16, 1975, in St. Ephrem, Que. ... 6-1/205. ... Shoots left.
TRANSACTIONS/CAREER NOTES: Selected by New Jersey Devils in eighth round (ninth Devils pick, 207th overall) of NHL entry draft (June 29, 1994). ... Traded by Devils to with RW Wes Mason and seventh-round pick (LW Ken Magowan) in 2000 draft to Atlanta Thrashers for LW Jeff Williams and C Sylvain Cloutier (November 1, 1999). ... Traded by Thrashers to Philadelphia Flyers for RW Brian Wesenberg (December 9, 1999). ... Traded by Flyers to Nashville Predators for future consideration (February 14, 2000). ... Signed as free agent by Montreal Canadiens (July 7, 2000).

			REGULAR SEASON								PLAYOFFS				
Season Team	League	Gms.	G	A	Pts.	PIM	+/-	PP	SH		Gms.	G	A	Pts.	PIM
92-93—Granby.......................	QMJHL	64	10	15	25	82	...	...	...		—	—	—	—	—
93-94—Granby.......................	QMJHL	60	11	15	26	151	...	...	...		6	1	0	1	18
94-95—Granby.......................	QMJHL	56	14	26	40	268	...	...	...		13	3	8	11	50
95-96—Albany.......................	AHL	70	16	13	29	199	...	...	...		4	0	0	0	6
96-97—Albany.......................	AHL	77	16	27	43	204	...	...	...		8	3	3	6	15
97-98—Albany.......................	AHL	76	20	29	49	256	...	...	...		13	5	5	10	4
98-99—Albany.......................	AHL	78	34	31	65	160	...	...	...		5	4	2	6	0
99-00—New Jersey	NHL	4	0	0	0	0	-1	0	0		—	—	—	—	—
—Atlanta	NHL	8	0	0	0	4	-5	0	0		—	—	—	—	—
—Philadelphia	AHL	15	3	6	9	67	...	...	...		—	—	—	—	—
—Milwaukee	IHL	27	7	9	16	56	...	...	...		3	0	0	0	2
00-01—Quebec	AHL	66	21	21	42	113	...	...	...		9	4	2	6	12
—Montreal	NHL	3	0	0	0	0	0	0	0		—	—	—	—	—
NHL Totals (2 years)...........		15	0	0	0	4	-6	0	0						

BERTUZZI, TODD   LW   CANUCKS

PERSONAL: Born February 2, 1975, in Sudbury, Ont. ... 6-3/230. ... Shoots left. ... Name pronounced buhr-TOO-zee.
TRANSACTIONS/CAREER NOTES: Selected by New York Islanders in first round (first Islanders pick, 23rd overall) of NHL entry draft (June 26, 1993). ... Injured eye (February 22, 1996); missed two games. ... Suspended three games by NHL for attempting to break free of a linesman (April 2, 1996). ... Suffered from bone chips in elbow (November 23, 1996); missed one game. ... Traded by Islanders with D Bryan McCabe and third-round pick (LW Jarkko Ruutu) in 1998 draft to Vancouver Canucks for C Trevor Linden (February 6, 1998). ... Bruised thigh (March 17, 1998); missed four games. ... Fractured tibia (November 1, 1998); missed 31 games. ... Tore anterior cruciate ligament in knee (March 5, 1999); missed remainder of season. ... Suffered concussion (October 20, 1999); missed one game. ... Injured thumb (February 23, 2000); missed one game. ... Bruised shoulder (January 28, 2001); missed three games.
HONORS: Named to OHL All-Star second team (1994-95).
STATISTICAL PLATEAUS: Three-goal games: 2000-01 (1).

			REGULAR SEASON								PLAYOFFS				
Season Team	League	Gms.	G	A	Pts.	PIM	+/-	PP	SH		Gms.	G	A	Pts.	PIM
91-92—Guelph	OHL	47	7	14	21	145	...	...	...		—	—	—	—	—
92-93—Guelph	OHL	59	27	32	59	164	...	...	...		5	2	2	4	6
93-94—Guelph	OHL	61	28	54	82	165	...	...	...		9	2	6	8	30
94-95—Guelph	OHL	62	54	65	119	58	...	...	...		14	*15	18	33	41
95-96—New York Islanders.....	NHL	76	18	21	39	83	-14	4	0		—	—	—	—	—
96-97—New York Islanders.....	NHL	64	10	13	23	68	-3	3	0		—	—	—	—	—
—Utah	IHL	13	5	5	10	16	...	...	...		—	—	—	—	—
97-98—New York Islanders.....	NHL	52	7	11	18	58	-19	1	0		—	—	—	—	—
—Vancouver..................	NHL	22	6	9	15	63	2	1	1		—	—	—	—	—
98-99—Vancouver.................	NHL	32	8	8	16	44	-6	1	0		—	—	—	—	—
99-00—Vancouver.................	NHL	80	25	25	50	126	-2	4	0		—	—	—	—	—
00-01—Vancouver.................	NHL	79	25	30	55	93	-18	14	0		4	2	2	4	8
NHL Totals (6 years).........		405	99	117	216	535	-60	28	1		4	2	2	4	8

BERUBE, CRAIG   LW

PERSONAL: Born December 17, 1965, in Calahoo, Alta. ... 6-1/205. ... Shoots left. ... Name pronounced buh-ROO-bee.
TRANSACTIONS/CAREER NOTES: Signed as non-drafted free agent by Philadelphia Flyers (March 19, 1986). ... Sprained left knee (March 1988). ... Traded by Flyers with RW Scott Mellanby and C Craig Fisher to Edmonton Oilers for RW Dave Brown, D Corey Foster and the NHL rights to RW Jari Kurri (May 30, 1991). ... Traded by Oilers with G Grant Fuhr and RW/LW Glenn Anderson to Toronto Maple Leafs for LW Vincent Damphousse, D Luke Richardson, G Peter Ing, C Scott Thornton and future considerations (September 19, 1991). ... Traded by Maple Leafs with D Alexander Godynyuk, RW Gary Leeman, D Michel Petit and G Jeff Reese to Calgary Flames for C Doug Gilmour, D Jamie Macoun, LW Kent Manderville, D Ric Nattress and G Rick Wamsley (January 2, 1992). ... Traded by Flames to Washington Capitals for fifth-round pick (C Darryl LaFrance) in 1993 draft (June 26, 1993). ... Suffered from the flu (March 31, 1995); missed three games. ... Fractured jaw (September 14, 1995); missed seven games. ... Suffered mild concussion (November 10, 1995); missed four games. ... Suspended 10 games by NHL for coming off bench to fight (December 22, 1995). ... Injured right knee (March 22, 1996); missed 11 games. ... Suspended two

games and fined $1,000 by NHL for slashing incident (January 19, 1997). ... Injured hip (October 15, 1997); missed seven games. ... Suspended one game by NHL for directing a racial slur at another player (November 25, 1997). ... Traded by Capitals for Philadelphia Flyers for future considerations (March 23, 1999). ... Suffered from the flu (January 11, 2000); missed one game. ... Signed as free agent by Capitals (July 7, 2000). ... Traded by Capitals to New York Islanders for ninth-round pick (F Robert Muller) in 2001 draft (January 11, 2001).

Season Team	League	Gms.	G	A	Pts.	PIM	+/-	PP	SH	Gms.	G	A	Pts.	PIM
82-83—Williams Lake	PCJHL	33	9	24	33	99	...	...	...	—	—	—	—	—
—Kamloops	WHL	4	0	0	0	0				—	—	—	—	—
83-84—New Westminster	WHL	70	11	20	31	104				8	1	2	3	5
84-85—New Westminster	WHL	70	25	44	69	191				10	3	2	5	4
85-86—Kamloops	WHL	32	17	14	31	119				—	—	—	—	—
—Medicine Hat	WHL	34	14	16	30	95				25	7	8	15	102
86-87—Hershey	AHL	63	7	17	24	325				—	—	—	—	—
—Philadelphia	NHL	7	0	0	0	57	2	0	0	5	0	0	0	17
87-88—Hershey	AHL	31	5	9	14	119				—	—	—	—	—
—Philadelphia	NHL	27	3	2	5	108	1	0	0	—	—	—	—	—
88-89—Hershey	AHL	7	0	2	2	19				—	—	—	—	—
—Philadelphia	NHL	53	1	1	2	199	-15	0	0	16	0	0	0	56
89-90—Philadelphia	NHL	74	4	14	18	291	-7	0	0	—	—	—	—	—
90-91—Philadelphia	NHL	74	8	9	17	293	-6	0	0	—	—	—	—	—
91-92—Toronto	NHL	40	5	7	12	109	-2	1	0	—	—	—	—	—
—Calgary	NHL	36	1	4	5	155	-3	0	0	—	—	—	—	—
92-93—Calgary	NHL	77	4	8	12	209	-6	0	0	6	0	1	1	21
93-94—Washington	NHL	84	7	7	14	305	-4	0	0	8	0	0	0	21
94-95—Washington	NHL	43	2	4	6	173	-5	0	0	7	0	0	0	29
95-96—Washington	NHL	50	2	10	12	151	1	1	0	2	0	0	0	19
96-97—Washington	NHL	80	4	3	7	218	-11	0	0	—	—	—	—	—
97-98—Washington	NHL	74	6	9	15	189	-3	0	0	21	1	0	1	21
98-99—Washington	NHL	66	5	4	9	166	-7	0	0	—	—	—	—	—
—Philadelphia	NHL	11	0	0	0	28	-3	0	0	6	1	0	1	4
99-00—Philadelphia	NHL	77	4	8	12	162	3	0	0	18	1	0	1	23
00-01—Washington	NHL	22	0	1	1	18	-3	0	0	—	—	—	—	—
—New York Islanders	NHL	38	0	2	2	54	-5	0	0	—	—	—	—	—
NHL Totals (15 years)		933	56	93	149	2885	-73	2	0	89	3	1	4	211

BETTS, BLAIR   C   FLAMES

PERSONAL: Born February 16, 1980, in Edmonton. ... 6-1/183. ... Shoots left.
TRANSACTIONS/CAREER NOTES: Selected by Calgary Flames in second round (second Flames pick, 33rd overall) of NHL entry draft (June 27, 1998).

Season Team	League	Gms.	G	A	Pts.	PIM	+/-	PP	SH	Gms.	G	A	Pts.	PIM
96-97—Prince George	WHL	58	12	18	30	19	...	...	...	15	2	2	4	6
97-98—Prince George	WHL	71	35	41	76	38				11	4	6	10	8
98-99—Prince George	WHL	42	20	22	42	39				7	3	2	5	8
99-00—Prince George	WHL	44	24	35	59	38				13	11	11	22	6
00-01—Saint John	AHL	75	13	15	28	28				19	2	3	5	4

BICANEK, RADIM   D   BLUE JACKETS

PERSONAL: Born January 18, 1975, in Uherske Hradiste, Czechoslovakia. ... 6-1/195. ... Shoots left. ... Name pronounced RA-deem bih-CHAN-ihk.
TRANSACTIONS/CAREER NOTES: Selected by Ottawa Senators in second round (second Senators pick, 27th overall) of NHL entry draft (June 26, 1993). ... Traded by Senators to Chicago Blackhawks for sixth-round pick (G Martin Prusek) in 1999 draft (March 12, 1999). ... Selected by Columbus Blue Jackets in NHL expansion draft (June 23, 2000).
HONORS: Named to AHL All-Star second team (2000-01).

Season Team	League	Gms.	G	A	Pts.	PIM	+/-	PP	SH	Gms.	G	A	Pts.	PIM
92-93—Jihlava	Czech	43	2	3	5	...	...	...	...	—	—	—	—	—
93-94—Belleville	OHL	63	16	27	43	49				12	2	8	10	21
94-95—Belleville	OHL	49	13	26	39	61				16	6	5	11	30
—Ottawa	NHL	6	0	0	0	0	3	0	0	—	—	—	—	—
—Prin. Edward Island	AHL	—	—	—	—	—				3	0	1	1	0
95-96—Prin. Edward Island	AHL	74	7	19	26	87				5	0	2	2	6
96-97—Worcester	AHL	44	1	15	16	22				—	—	—	—	—
—Ottawa	NHL	21	0	1	1	8	-4	0	0	7	0	0	0	8
97-98—Ottawa	NHL	1	0	0	0	0	0	0	0	—	—	—	—	—
—Detroit	IHL	9	1	3	4	16				—	—	—	—	—
—Manitoba	IHL	42	1	7	8	52				—	—	—	—	—
98-99—Ottawa	NHL	7	0	0	0	4	-1	0	0	—	—	—	—	—
—Grand Rapids	IHL	46	8	17	25	48				—	—	—	—	—
—Chicago	NHL	7	0	0	0	6	-3	0	0	—	—	—	—	—
99-00—Cleveland	IHL	70	5	27	32	125				9	2	2	4	8
—Chicago	NHL	11	0	3	3	4	7	0	0	—	—	—	—	—
00-01—Syracuse	AHL	68	22	43	65	124				5	4	2	6	2
—Columbus	NHL	9	0	2	2	6	1	0	0	—	—	—	—	—
NHL Totals (6 years)		62	0	6	6	28	3	0	0	7	0	0	0	8

B

BICEK, JIRI — LW — DEVILS

PERSONAL: Born December 3, 1978, in Kosice, Czechoslovakia. ... 5-10/195. ... Shoots left.
TRANSACTIONS/CAREER NOTES: Selected by New Jersey Devils in fifth round (fourth Devils pick, 131st overall) of NHL entry draft (June 21, 1997).

Season Team	League	REGULAR SEASON								PLAYOFFS				
		Gms.	G	A	Pts.	PIM	+/-	PP	SH	Gms.	G	A	Pts.	PIM
94-95—HC Kosice Jrs.	Slovakia	42	38	36	74	18	...	...	...	—	—	—	—	—
95-96—HC Kosice	Slovakia	30	10	15	25	16	...	...	...	9	2	4	6	0
96-97—HC Kosice	Slovakia	44	11	14	25	20	...	...	...	7	1	3	4	...
97-98—Albany	AHL	50	10	10	20	22	...	...	...	13	1	6	7	4
98-99—Albany	AHL	79	15	45	60	102	...	...	...	5	2	2	4	2
99-00—Albany	AHL	80	7	36	43	51	...	...	...	4	0	2	2	0
00-01—Albany	AHL	73	12	29	41	73	...	...	...	—	—	—	—	—
—New Jersey	NHL	5	1	0	1	4	0	0	0	—	—	—	—	—
NHL Totals (1 year)		**5**	**1**	**0**	**1**	**4**	**0**	**0**	**0**					

BIERK, ZAC — G

PERSONAL: Born September 17, 1976, in Peterborough, Ont. ... 6-4/205. ... Catches left. ... Name pronounced BUHRK.
TRANSACTIONS/CAREER NOTES: Selected by Tampa Bay Lightning in ninth round (eighth Lightning pick, 212th overall) of NHL entry draft (July 8, 1995). ... Injured neck (April 6, 2000); missed final two games of season. ... Selected by Minnesota Wild in NHL expansion draft (June 23, 2000).
HONORS: Won Leo Lalonde Memorial Trophy (1996-97). ... Named to Can.HL All-Star second team (1996-97). ... Named to OHL All-Star first team (1996-97).
MISCELLANEOUS: Allowed a penalty shot goal (vs. Robert Reichel, January 14, 1998).

Season Team	League	REGULAR SEASON								PLAYOFFS					
		Gms.	Min	W	L	T	GA	SO	Avg.	Gms.	Min.	W	L	GA	SO	Avg.
93-94—Peterborough	Tier II Jr. A	4	205				17	0	4.98	—	—				—	—
—Peterborough	OHL	9	423	0	4	2	37	0	5.25	1	33	0	0	7	0	12.73
94-95—Peterborough	OHL	35	1798	12	15	5	118	0	3.94	6	301	2	3	24	0	4.78
95-96—Peterborough	OHL	58	3292	31	16	6	174	2	3.17	*22	*1383	*14	†7	*83	0	3.60
96-97—Peterborough	OHL	49	2744	*28	16	0	151	2	3.30	11	666	6	5	35	0	3.15
97-98—Adirondack	AHL	12	558	1	6	1	36	0	3.87	—	—				—	—
—Tampa Bay	NHL	13	433	1	4	1	30	0	4.16	—	—				—	—
98-99—Cleveland	IHL	27	1556	11	12	‡4	79	0	3.05	—	—				—	—
—Tampa Bay	NHL	1	59	0	1	0	2	0	2.03	—	—				—	—
99-00—Detroit	IHL	15	846	6	8	2	46	1	3.26	—	—				—	—
—Tampa Bay	NHL	12	509	4	4	1	31	0	3.65	—	—				—	—
00-01—Cleveland	IHL	49	2785	24	18	‡5	134	6	2.89	4	182	0	3	10	0	3.30
—Minnesota	NHL	1	60	0	1	0	6	0	6.00	—	—				—	—
NHL Totals (4 years)		**27**	**1061**	**5**	**10**	**2**	**69**	**0**	**3.90**							

BILLINGTON, CRAIG — G — CAPITALS

PERSONAL: Born September 11, 1966, in London, Ont. ... 5-10/166. ... Catches left.
TRANSACTIONS/CAREER NOTES: Selected by New Jersey Devils in second round (second Devils pick, 23rd overall) of NHL entry draft (June 9, 1984). ... Injured hamstring (February 15, 1992); missed two games. ... Strained knee (March 11, 1992); missed six games. ... Underwent knee surgery (April 13, 1992). ... Suffered from sore throat (March 27, 1993); missed one game. ... Traded by Devils with C/LW Troy Mallette and fourth-round pick (C Cosmo Dupaul) in 1993 draft to Ottawa Senators for G Peter Sidorkiewicz and future considerations (June 20, 1993). ... Senators sent LW Mike Peluso to Devils to complete deal (June 26, 1993). ... Injured knee (January 27, 1995); missed 17 games. ... Traded by Senators to Boston Bruins for eighth-round pick (D Ray Schultz) in 1995 draft (April 7, 1995). ... Signed as free agent by Florida Panthers (September 4, 1996). ... Selected by Colorado Avalanche in NHL waiver draft for cash (September 30, 1996). ... Sprained knee ligament (November 19, 1996); missed seven games. ... Traded by Avalanche to Washington Capitals for future considerations (July 16, 1999). ... Bruised hand (March 2, 2001); missed six games.
HONORS: Won Bobby Smith Trophy (1984-85). ... Named to OHL All-Star first team (1984-85). ... Played in NHL All-Star Game (1993).
MISCELLANEOUS: Stopped penalty shot attempt (vs. Rick Tocchet, January 6, 1987).

Season Team	League	REGULAR SEASON								PLAYOFFS					
		Gms.	Min	W	L	T	GA	SO	Avg.	Gms.	Min.	W	L	GA	SO	Avg.
82-83—London Diamonds	OPJHL	23	1338	...	...	...	76	0	3.41	—	—				—	—
83-84—Belleville	OHL	44	2335	20	19	0	162	1	4.16	1	30	0	0	3	0	6.00
84-85—Belleville	OHL	47	2544	26	19	0	180	1	4.25	14	761	7	5	47	†1	3.71
85-86—Belleville	OHL	3	180	2	1	0	11	0	3.67	†20	1133	9	6	*68	0	3.60
—New Jersey	NHL	18	701	4	9	1	77	0	6.59	—	—				—	—
86-87—Maine	AHL	20	1151	9	8	2	70	0	3.65	—	—				—	—
—New Jersey	NHL	22	1114	4	13	2	89	0	4.79	—	—				—	—
87-88—Utica	AHL	*59	*3404	22	27	8	*208	1	3.67	—	—				—	—
88-89—New Jersey	NHL	3	140	1	1	0	11	0	4.71	—	—				—	—
—Utica	AHL	41	2432	17	18	6	150	2	3.70	4	219	1	3	18	0	4.93
89-90—Utica	AHL	38	2087	20	13	1	138	0	3.97	—	—				—	—
90-91—Canadian nat'l team	Int'l	34	1879	17	14	2	110	2	3.51	—	—				—	—
91-92—New Jersey	NHL	26	1363	13	7	1	69	2	3.04	—	—				—	—
92-93—New Jersey	NHL	42	2389	21	16	4	146	2	3.67	2	78	0	1	5	0	3.85
93-94—Ottawa	NHL	63	3319	11	*41	4	*254	0	4.59	—	—				—	—
94-95—Boston	NHL	8	373	5	1	0	19	0	3.06	1	25	0	0	1	0	2.40
—Ottawa	NHL	9	472	0	6	2	32	0	4.07	—	—				—	—

Season Team	League	REGULAR SEASON								PLAYOFFS					
		Gms.	Min	W	L	T	GA	SO	Avg.	Gms.	Min.	W	L	GA	SO	Avg.
95-96—Boston	NHL	27	1380	10	13	3	79	1	3.43	1	60	0	1	6	0	6.00
96-97—Colorado	NHL	23	1200	11	8	2	53	1	2.65	1	20	0	0	1	0	3.00
97-98—Colorado	NHL	23	1162	8	7	4	45	1	2.32	1	1	0	0	0	0	...
98-99—Colorado	NHL	21	1086	11	8	1	52	0	2.87	1	9	0	0	1	0	6.67
99-00—Washington	NHL	13	611	3	6	1	28	2	2.75	1	20	0	0	1	0	3.00
00-01—Washington	NHL	12	660	3	5	2	27	0	2.45	—	—	—	—	—	—
NHL Totals (13 years)		310	15970	105	141	27	981	9	3.69	8	213	0	2	15	0	4.23

BIRON, MARTIN   G   SABRES

B

PERSONAL: Born August 15, 1977, in Lac St. Charles, Que. ... 6-1/154. ... Catches left. ... Brother of Mathieu Biron, defenseman, Tampa Bay Lightning.

TRANSACTIONS/CAREER NOTES: Selected by Buffalo Sabres in first round (second Sabres pick, 16th overall) of NHL entry draft (July 8, 1995). ... Missed first 12 games of 2000-01 season due to contract dispute.

HONORS: Won Can.HL Goaltender of the Year Award (1994-95). ... Won Raymond Lagace Trophy (1994-95). ... Won Mike Bossy Trophy (1994-95). ... Won Jacques Plante Trophy (1994-95). ... Named to Can.HL All-Star first team (1994-95). ... Named to Can.HL All-Rookie team (1994-95). ... Named to AHL All-Star first team (1998-99). ... Won Baz Bastien Trophy (1998-99). ... Shared Harry (Hap) Holmes Memorial Trophy with Tom Draper (1998-99). ... Shared William M. Jennings Trophy with Dominik Hasek (2000-01).

MISCELLANEOUS: Stopped a penalty shot attempt (vs. Daniel Alfredsson, January 8, 2000; vs. Mike Johnson, February 1, 2001).

Season Team	League	REGULAR SEASON								PLAYOFFS					
		Gms.	Min	W	L	T	GA	SO	Avg.	Gms.	Min.	W	L	GA	SO	Avg.
94-95—Beauport	QMJHL	56	3193	29	16	9	132	3	2.48	16	902	8	7	37	4	2.46
95-96—Beauport	QMJHL	55	3207	29	17	7	152	1	2.84	*19	1132	*12	†8	64	0	3.39
—Buffalo	NHL	3	119	0	2	0	10	0	5.04	—	—	—	—	—	—
96-97—Beauport	QMJHL	18	935	6	10	1	62	1	3.98	—	—	—	—	—	—
—Hull	QMJHL	16	972	11	4	1	43	2	2.65	6	326	3	1	19	0	3.50
97-98—Rochester	AHL	41	2312	14	18	6	113	*5	2.93	4	239	1	3	16	0	4.02
—South Carolina	ECHL	2	86	0	1	1	3	0	2.09	—	—	—	—	—	—
98-99—Rochester	AHL	52	3129	36	13	3	108	*6	*2.07	*20	1167	12	*8	42	†1	*2.16
—Buffalo	NHL	6	281	1	2	1	10	0	2.14	—	—	—	—	—	—
99-00—Rochester	AHL	6	344	6	0	0	12	1	2.09	—	—	—	—	—	—
—Buffalo	NHL	41	2229	19	18	2	90	5	2.42	—	—	—	—	—	—
00-01—Rochester	AHL	4	239	3	1	0	4	1	1.00	—	—	—	—	—	—
—Buffalo	NHL	18	918	7	7	1	39	2	2.55	—	—	—	—	—	—
NHL Totals (4 years)		68	3547	27	29	4	149	7	2.52						

BIRON, MATHIEU   D   LIGHTNING

PERSONAL: Born April 29, 1980, in Lac St. Charles, Que. ... 6-6/212. ... Shoots right. ... Brother of Martin Biron, goaltender, Buffalo Sabres.

TRANSACTIONS/CAREER NOTES: Selected by Los Angeles Kings in first round (first Kings pick, 21st overall) of NHL entry draft (June 27, 1998). ... Traded by Kings with C Olli Jokinen, LW Josh Green and first-round pick (LW Taylor Pyatt) in 1999 draft to New York Islanders for RW Zigmund Palffy, C Bryan Smolinski, G Marcel Cousineau and fourth-round pick (C Daniel Johansson) in 1999 draft (June 20, 1999). ... Traded by Islanders with second-round pick in 2002 draft to Tampa Bay Lightning for RW Alexander Kharitonov and D Adrian Aucoin (June 22, 2001).

HONORS: Named to QMJHL All-Rookie Team (1997-98).

Season Team	League	REGULAR SEASON							PLAYOFFS				
		Gms.	G	A	Pts.	PIM	+/-	PP	SH	Gms.	G	A	Pts.	PIM
97-98—Shawinigan	QMJHL	59	8	28	36	60	...	...	...	6	0	1	1	10
98-99—Shawinigan	QMJHL	69	13	32	45	116	...	...	...	6	0	2	2	6
99-00—New York Islanders	NHL	60	4	4	8	38	-13	2	0	—	—	—	—	—
00-01—Lowell	AHL	22	1	3	4	17	...	...	...	—	—	—	—	—
—New York Islanders	NHL	14	0	1	1	12	2	0	0	—	—	—	—	—
—Springfield	AHL	34	0	6	6	18	...	...	...	—	—	—	—	—
NHL Totals (2 years)		74	4	5	9	50	-11	2	0					

BLACK, JAMES   LW

PERSONAL: Born August 15, 1969, in Regina, Sask. ... 6-0/203. ... Shoots left.

TRANSACTIONS/CAREER NOTES: Selected by Hartford Whalers in fifth round (fourth Whalers pick, 94th overall) of NHL entry draft (June 17, 1989). ... Traded by Whalers to Minnesota North Stars for C Mark Janssens (September 3, 1992). ... North Stars franchise moved from Minnesota to Dallas and renamed Stars for 1993-94 season. ... Traded by Stars with seventh-round pick (RW Steve Webb) in 1994 draft to Buffalo Sabres for RW Gord Donnelly (December 15, 1993). ... Lacerated forehead (October 27, 1993); missed five games. ... Signed as free agent by Chicago Blackhawks (August 10, 1995). ... Injured hand (October 22, 1997); missed six games. ... Sprained knee (November 8, 1997); missed three games. ... Traded by Blackhawks to Washington Capitals for future considerations (October 15, 1998). ... Fractured leg (February 3, 2000); missed final 31 games of season.

Season Team	League	REGULAR SEASON							PLAYOFFS				
		Gms.	G	A	Pts.	PIM	+/-	PP	SH	Gms.	G	A	Pts.	PIM
87-88—Portland	WHL	72	30	50	80	50	...	...	...	—	—	—	—	—
88-89—Portland	WHL	71	45	51	96	57	...	...	...	19	13	6	19	28
89-90—Hartford	NHL	1	0	0	0	0	0	0	0	—	—	—	—	—
—Binghamton	AHL	80	37	35	72	34	...	...	...	—	—	—	—	—
90-91—Hartford	NHL	1	0	0	0	0	0	0	0	—	—	—	—	—
—Springfield	AHL	79	35	61	96	34	...	...	...	18	9	9	18	6
91-92—Springfield	AHL	47	15	25	40	33	...	...	...	10	3	2	5	18
—Hartford	NHL	30	4	6	10	10	-4	1	0	—	—	—	—	—

Season Team	League	REGULAR SEASON								PLAYOFFS				
		Gms.	G	A	Pts.	PIM	+/-	PP	SH	Gms.	G	A	Pts.	PIM
92-93—Minnesota	NHL	10	2	1	3	4	0	0	0	—	—	—	—	—
—Kalamazoo	IHL	63	25	45	70	40	...	...	...	—	—	—	—	—
93-94—Dallas	NHL	13	2	3	5	2	-4	2	0	—	—	—	—	—
—Buffalo	NHL	2	0	0	0	0	0	0	0	—	—	—	—	—
—Rochester	AHL	45	19	32	51	28	...	...	...	4	2	3	5	0
94-95—Las Vegas	IHL	78	29	44	73	54	...	...	...	10	1	6	7	4
95-96—Indianapolis	IHL	67	32	50	82	56	...	...	...	—	—	—	—	—
—Chicago	NHL	13	3	3	6	16	1	0	0	8	1	0	1	2
96-97—Chicago	NHL	64	12	11	23	20	6	0	0	5	1	1	2	2
97-98—Chicago	NHL	52	10	5	15	8	-8	2	1	—	—	—	—	—
98-99—Chicago	IHL	5	6	0	6	0	...	...	...	—	—	—	—	—
—Washington	NHL	75	16	14	30	14	5	1	1	—	—	—	—	—
99-00—Washington	NHL	49	8	9	17	6	-1	1	0	—	—	—	—	—
00-01—Washington	NHL	42	1	5	6	4	-3	0	0	—	—	—	—	—
—Portland	AHL	5	2	3	5	0	...	...	...	—	—	—	—	—
NHL Totals (11 years)		352	58	57	115	84	-8	7	2	13	2	1	3	4

BLACKBURN, JOSH — G — COYOTES

PERSONAL: Born November 13, 1978, in Del Rio, Texas. ... 6-0/185. ... Catches left.
TRANSACTIONS/CAREER NOTES: Selected by Phoenix Coyotes in fifth round (sixth Coyotes pick, 116th overall) of NHL entry draft (June 27, 1998).
HONORS: Named to CCHA All-Star second team (2000-01).

Season Team	League	REGULAR SEASON								PLAYOFFS						
		Gms.	Min	W	L	T	GA	SO	Avg.	Gms.	Min.	W	L	GA	SO	Avg.
96-97—Dubuque-Lincoln	USHL	52	2979	...	...	...	185	1	3.73	—	—	—	—	—	—	—
97-98—Lincoln	USHL	45	2609	...	...	...	135	1	3.10	—	—	—	—	—	—	—
98-99—Univ. of Michigan	CCHA	*42	*2398	*25	10	6	91	3	2.28	—	—	—	—	—	—	—
99-00—Univ. of Michigan	CCHA	20	1205	13	3	4	46	1	2.29	—	—	—	—	—	—	—
00-01—Univ. of Michigan	CCHA	*45	*2647	26	13	5	101	5	2.29	—	—	—	—	—	—	—

BLAKE, JASON — C — ISLANDERS

PERSONAL: Born September 2, 1973, in Moorhead, Minn. ... 5-10/180. ... Shoots left.
TRANSACTIONS/CAREER NOTES: Signed as non-drafted free agent by Los Angeles Kings (April 17, 1999). ... Suffered concussion (December 19, 1999); missed four games. ... Bruised hip (October 19, 2000). ... Traded by Kings to New York Islanders for conditional pick in 2002 draft (January 3, 2001). ... Suffered concussion (February 9, 2001); missed one game. ... Granted personal leave for final 13 games of season.
HONORS: Named to NCAA All-America (West) second team (1997-98). ... Named to WCHA All-Star first team (1996-97 through 1998-99). ... Named to NCAA All-America (West) first team (1998-99).

Season Team	League	REGULAR SEASON								PLAYOFFS				
		Gms.	G	A	Pts.	PIM	+/-	PP	SH	Gms.	G	A	Pts.	PIM
94-95—Ferris State	CCHA	36	16	16	32	46	...	...	...	—	—	—	—	—
96-97—Univ. of North Dakota	WCHA	43	19	32	51	44	...	...	...	—	—	—	—	—
97-98—Univ. of North Dakota	WCHA	38	24	27	51	62	...	...	...	—	—	—	—	—
98-99—Univ. of North Dakota	WCHA	38	*28	†41	*69	49	...	...	...	—	—	—	—	—
—Orlando	IHL	5	3	5	8	6	...	...	...	13	3	4	7	20
—Los Angeles	NHL	1	1	0	1	0	1	0	0	—	—	—	—	—
99-00—Los Angeles	NHL	64	5	18	23	26	4	0	0	3	0	0	0	0
—Long Beach	IHL	7	3	6	9	2	...	...	...	—	—	—	—	—
00-01—Los Angeles	NHL	17	1	3	4	10	-8	0	0	—	—	—	—	—
—Lowell	AHL	2	0	1	1	2	...	...	...	—	—	—	—	—
—New York Islanders	NHL	30	4	8	12	24	-12	1	1	—	—	—	—	—
NHL Totals (3 years)		112	11	29	40	60	-15	1	1	3	0	0	0	0

BLAKE, ROB — D — AVALANCHE

PERSONAL: Born December 10, 1969, in Simcoe, Ont. ... 6-4/220. ... Shoots right. ... Full Name: Robert Bowlby Blake.
TRANSACTIONS/CAREER NOTES: Selected by Los Angeles Kings in fourth round (fourth Kings pick, 70th overall) of NHL entry draft (June 11, 1988). ... Sprained knee (April 1990). ... Injured knee (February 12, 1991); missed two games. ... Injured shoulder (October 8, 1991); missed 11 games. ... Sprained knee ligaments (November 28, 1991); missed six games. ... Suffered from the flu (January 23, 1992); missed one game. ... Suffered from the flu (February 13, 1992); missed one game. ... Strained shoulder (March 14, 1992); missed four games. ... Fractured rib (December 19, 1992); missed three games. ... Bruised lower back (April 3, 1993); missed final five games of regular season and one playoff game. ... Strained groin (January 23, 1995); missed 11 games. ... Strained groin (March 11, 1995); missed 12 games. ... Strained groin (April 7, 1995); missed one game. ... Suffered partial tear of left knee ligaments (October 20, 1995); missed 76 games. ... Fractured hand (December 26, 1996); missed 11 games. ... Suspended two games and fined $1,000 by NHL for high-sticking incident (February 5, 1997). ... Suffered tendinitis in left knee (February 22, 1997); missed seven games. ... Fractured right foot (November 6, 1998); missed 15 games. ... Suspended three games and fined $1,000 by NHL for slashing incident (December 14, 1998). ... Suspended two games by NHL for cross-checking incident (April 9, 1999); missed two games. ... Bruised knee (April 1, 2000); missed three games. ... Suffered hairline fracture of lumbar vertebrae (October 13, 2000); missed three games. ... Bruised shoulder (February 21, 2001); missed two games. ... Traded by Kings with C Steve Reinprecht to Colorado Avalanche for RW Adam Deadmarsh, D Aaron Miller, first-round pick (C David Steckel) in 2001 draft, a player to be named later and first-round pick in 2002 draft (February 21, 2001); Kings acquired C Jared Aulin to complete deal (March 22, 2001). ... Sprained knee (March 20, 2001); missed eight games.
HONORS: Named to CCHA All-Star second team (1988-89). ... Named to NCAA All-America (West) first team (1989-90). ... Named to CCHA All-Star first team (1989-90). ... Named to NHL All-Rookie team (1990-91). ... Played in NHL All-Star Game (1994, 1999, 2000 and 2001). ...

Named to play in NHL All-Star Game (1997); replaced by LW Dimitri Khristich due to injury. ... Named to THE SPORTING NEWS All-Star team (1997-98). ... Won James Norris Memorial Trophy (1997-98). ... Named to NHL All-Star first team (1997-98). ... Named to NHL All-Star second team (1999-2000 and 2000-01). ... Named to THE SPORTING NEWS All-Star first team (2000-01).
MISCELLANEOUS: Member of Stanley Cup championship team (2001). ... Captain of Los Angeles Kings (1996-97 through February 21, 2001). ... Failed to score on a penalty shot (vs. Dwayne Roloson, April 13, 1998).
STATISTICAL PLATEAUS: Three-goal games: 2000-01 (1).

		REGULAR SEASON								PLAYOFFS				
Season Team	League	Gms.	G	A	Pts.	PIM	+/-	PP	SH	Gms.	G	A	Pts.	PIM
86-87—Stratford Jr. B	OHA	31	11	20	31	115	...	...	...	—	—	—	—	—
87-88—Bowling Green	CCHA	36	5	8	13	72	...	...	...	—	—	—	—	—
88-89—Bowling Green	CCHA	46	11	21	32	140	...	...	...	—	—	—	—	—
89-90—Bowling Green	CCHA	42	23	36	59	140	...	...	...	—	—	—	—	—
—Los Angeles	NHL	4	0	0	0	4	0	0	0	8	1	3	4	4
90-91—Los Angeles	NHL	75	12	34	46	125	3	9	0	12	1	4	5	26
91-92—Los Angeles	NHL	57	7	13	20	102	-5	5	0	6	2	1	3	12
92-93—Los Angeles	NHL	76	16	43	59	152	18	10	0	23	4	6	10	46
93-94—Los Angeles	NHL	84	20	48	68	137	-7	7	0	—	—	—	—	—
94-95—Los Angeles	NHL	24	4	7	11	38	-16	4	0	—	—	—	—	—
95-96—Los Angeles	NHL	6	1	2	3	8	0	0	0	—	—	—	—	—
96-97—Los Angeles	NHL	62	8	23	31	82	-28	4	0	—	—	—	—	—
97-98—Los Angeles	NHL	81	23	27	50	94	-3	11	0	4	0	0	0	6
—Can. Olympic team	Int'l	6	1	1	2	2	...	...	...	—	—	—	—	—
98-99—Los Angeles	NHL	62	12	23	35	128	-7	5	1	—	—	—	—	—
99-00—Los Angeles	NHL	77	18	39	57	112	10	12	0	4	0	2	2	4
00-01—Los Angeles	NHL	54	17	32	49	69	-8	9	0	—	—	—	—	—
—Colorado	NHL	13	2	8	10	8	11	1	0	23	6	13	19	16
NHL Totals (12 years)		675	140	299	439	1059	-32	77	1	80	14	29	43	114

BLATNY, ZDENEK   C/LW   THRASHERS

PERSONAL: Born January 14, 1981, in Brno, Czechoslovakia. ... 6-1/187. ... Shoots left.
TRANSACTIONS/CAREER NOTES: Selected by Atlanta Thrashers in third round (third Thrashers pick, 68th overall) of NHL entry draft (June 26, 1999).
HONORS: Named to WHL (East) All-Star first team (1999-2000).

		REGULAR SEASON								PLAYOFFS				
Season Team	League	Gms.	G	A	Pts.	PIM	+/-	PP	SH	Gms.	G	A	Pts.	PIM
97-98—Kometa Brno	Czech. Jrs.	42	22	21	43	40	...	...	...	—	—	—	—	—
98-99—Seattle	WHL	44	18	15	33	25	...	...	...	11	4	0	4	24
99-00—Seattle	WHL	7	4	5	9	12	...	...	...	—	—	—	—	—
—Kootenay	WHL	61	43	39	82	119	...	...	...	21	10	*17	27	46
00-01—Kootenay	WHL	58	37	48	85	120	...	...	...	11	8	10	18	24

BLOUIN, SYLVAIN   RW   WILD

PERSONAL: Born May 21, 1974, in Montreal. ... 6-2/222. ... Shoots left. ... Name pronounced bloo-AN.
TRANSACTIONS/CAREER NOTES: Selected by New York Rangers in fourth round (fifth Rangers pick, 104th overall) of NHL entry draft (June 29, 1994). ... Bruised hand (February 19, 1997); missed two games. ... Suspended two games and fined $1,000 by NHL for illegal check (October 1, 1998). ... Suffered from the flu (March 11, 1999); missed two games. ... Traded by Rangers with sixth-round pick (traded to Phoenix) in 1999 draft to Montreal Canadiens for D Peter Popovic (June 30, 1999). ... Signed as free agent by St. Louis Blues (August 25, 1999). ... Signed as free agent by Canadiens (July 7, 2000). ... Claimed by Minnesota Wild from Canadiens in NHL waiver draft (September 29, 2000). ... Bruised shoulder (December 7, 2000); missed 14 games.

		REGULAR SEASON								PLAYOFFS				
Season Team	League	Gms.	G	A	Pts.	PIM	+/-	PP	SH	Gms.	G	A	Pts.	PIM
91-92—Laval	QMJHL	28	0	0	0	23	...	...	...	9	0	0	0	35
92-93—Laval	QMJHL	68	0	10	10	373	...	...	...	13	1	0	1	*66
93-94—Laval	QMJHL	62	18	22	40	*492	...	...	...	21	4	13	17	*177
94-95—Binghamton	AHL	10	1	0	1	46	...	...	...	2	0	0	0	24
—Chicago	IHL	1	0	0	0	2	...	...	...	—	—	—	—	—
—Charlotte	ECHL	50	5	7	12	280	...	...	...	3	0	0	0	6
95-96—Binghamton	AHL	71	5	8	13	*352	...	...	...	4	0	3	3	4
96-97—Binghamton	AHL	62	13	17	30	301	...	...	...	4	2	1	3	16
—New York Rangers	NHL	6	0	0	0	18	-1	0	0	—	—	—	—	—
97-98—Hartford	AHL	53	8	9	17	286	...	...	...	9	0	1	1	63
—New York Rangers	NHL	1	0	0	0	5	0	0	0	—	—	—	—	—
98-99—Fredericton	AHL	67	6	10	16	333	...	...	...	15	2	0	2	*87
—Montreal	NHL	5	0	0	0	19	0	0	0	—	—	—	—	—
99-00—Worcester	AHL	70	16	18	34	337	...	...	...	8	3	5	8	30
00-01—Minnesota	NHL	41	3	2	5	117	-5	0	0	—	—	—	—	—
NHL Totals (4 years)		53	3	2	5	159	-6	0	0	—	—	—	—	—

BOGUNIECKI, ERIC   C   BLUES

PERSONAL: Born May 6, 1975, in New Haven, Conn. ... 5-8/192. ... Shoots right.
TRANSACTIONS/CAREER NOTES: Selected by St. Louis Blues in eighth round (sixth Blues pick, 193rd overall) of NHL entry draft (June 29, 1993). ... Signed as free agent by Florida Panthers (July 20, 1999). ... Traded by Panthers to Blues for C Andrej Podkonicky (December 18, 2000).
HONORS: Names to Hockey East All-Star team (1996-97).

Season Team	League	REGULAR SEASON								PLAYOFFS				
		Gms.	G	A	Pts.	PIM	+/-	PP	SH	Gms.	G	A	Pts.	PIM
92-93—Westminster School ...	Conn. H.S.	24	30	24	54	55	...	...	...	—	—	—	—	—
93-94—Univ. of New Hamp.....	Hockey East	40	17	16	33	66	...	...	...	—	—	—	—	—
94-95—Univ. of New Hamp.....	Hockey East	34	12	19	31	62	...	...	...	—	—	—	—	—
95-96—Univ. of New Hamp.....	Hockey East	32	23	28	51	46	...	...	...	—	—	—	—	—
96-97—Univ. of New Hamp.....	Hockey East	36	26	31	57	58	...	...	...	—	—	—	—	—
97-98—Dayton	ECHL	26	19	18	37	36	...	...	...	—	—	—	—	—
—Fort Wayne	IHL	35	4	8	12	29	...	...	...	4	1	2	3	10
98-99—Fort Wayne	IHL	72	32	34	66	100	...	...	...	2	0	1	1	2
99-00—Louisville	AHL	57	33	42	75	148	...	...	...	4	3	2	5	20
—Florida	NHL	4	0	0	0	2	-1	0	0	—	—	—	—	—
00-01—Louisville	AHL	28	13	12	25	56	...	...	...	—	—	—	—	—
—Worcester	AHL	45	17	28	45	100	...	...	...	9	3	2	5	10
—St. Louis	NHL	1	0	0	0	0	-1	0	0	—	—	—	—	—
NHL Totals (2 years)		5	0	0	0	2	-2	0	0					

BOIKOV, ALEXANDRE   D   PREDATORS

PERSONAL: Born February 7, 1975, in Chelyabinsk, U.S.S.R. ... 6-0/198. ... Shoots left. ... Name pronounced BOY-kahf.
TRANSACTIONS/CAREER NOTES: Signed as non-drafted free agent by San Jose Sharks (August 26, 1996). ... Signed as free agent by Nashville Predators (July 26, 1999). ... Suffered injury (April 3, 2000); missed final two games of season.

Season Team	League	REGULAR SEASON								PLAYOFFS				
		Gms.	G	A	Pts.	PIM	+/-	PP	SH	Gms.	G	A	Pts.	PIM
93-94—Victoria	WHL	70	4	31	35	250	...	...	...	—	—	—	—	—
94-95—Prince George	WHL	46	5	23	28	115	...	...	...	—	—	—	—	—
—Tri-City	WHL	24	3	13	16	63	...	...	...	17	1	7	8	30
95-96—Tri-City	WHL	71	3	49	52	230	...	...	...	11	2	4	6	28
96-97—Kentucky	AHL	61	1	19	20	182	...	...	...	4	0	1	1	4
97-98—Kentucky	AHL	69	5	14	19	153	...	...	...	3	0	1	1	8
98-99—Kentucky	AHL	55	5	13	18	116	...	...	...	—	—	—	—	—
—Rochester	AHL	13	0	1	1	15	...	...	...	17	1	3	4	24
99-00—Milwaukee	IHL	58	1	6	7	120	...	...	...	—	—	—	—	—
—Nashville	NHL	2	0	0	0	2	0	0	0	—	—	—	—	—
00-01—CSKA	Russian	44	6	10	16	44	...	...	...	—	—	—	—	—
—Milwaukee	IHL	56	2	11	13	147	...	...	...	5	2	1	3	0
—Nashville	NHL	8	0	0	0	13	-1	0	0	—	—	—	—	—
NHL Totals (2 years)		10	0	0	0	15	-1	0	0					

BOMBARDIR, BRAD   D   WILD

PERSONAL: Born May 5, 1972, in Powell River, B.C. ... 6-1/205. ... Shoots left. ... Full Name: Luke Bradley Bombardir. ... Name pronounced BAHM-bahr-deer.
TRANSACTIONS/CAREER NOTES: Selected by New Jersey Devils in third round (fifth Devils pick, 56th overall) of NHL entry draft (June 16, 1990). ... Bruised left knee (November 29, 1997); missed six games. ... Suffered from the flu (April 14, 1999); missed three games. ... Suffered throat injury (October 27, 1999); missed four games. ... Bruised left hand (December 9, 1999); missed six games. ... Traded by Devils to Minnesota Wild for G Chris Terreri (June 23, 2000). ... Strained groin (October 20, 2000); missed six games. ... Suffered back spasms (March 19, 2001); missed two games.
HONORS: Named to AHL All-Star second team (1995-96).
MISCELLANEOUS: Member of Stanley Cup championship team (2000). ... Captain of Minnesota Wild (January 1-February 28, 2001).

Season Team	League	REGULAR SEASON								PLAYOFFS				
		Gms.	G	A	Pts.	PIM	+/-	PP	SH	Gms.	G	A	Pts.	PIM
88-89—Powell River	BCJHL	30	6	5	11	24	...	...	...	6	0	0	0	0
89-90—Powell River	BCJHL	60	10	35	45	93	...	...	...	8	2	3	5	4
90-91—Univ. of North Dakota .	WCHA	33	3	6	9	18	...	...	...	—	—	—	—	—
91-92—Univ. of North Dakota .	WCHA	35	3	14	17	54	...	...	...	—	—	—	—	—
92-93—Univ. of North Dakota .	WCHA	38	8	15	23	34	...	...	...	—	—	—	—	—
93-94—Univ. of North Dakota .	WCHA	38	5	17	22	38	...	...	...	—	—	—	—	—
94-95—Albany	AHL	77	5	22	27	22	...	...	...	14	0	3	3	6
95-96—Albany	AHL	80	6	25	31	63	...	...	...	3	0	1	1	4
96-97—Albany	AHL	32	0	8	8	6	...	...	...	16	1	3	4	8
97-98—New Jersey	NHL	43	1	5	6	8	11	0	0	—	—	—	—	—
—Albany	AHL	5	0	0	0	0	...	...	...	—	—	—	—	—
98-99—New Jersey	NHL	56	1	7	8	16	-4	0	0	5	0	0	0	0
99-00—New Jersey	NHL	32	3	1	4	6	-6	0	0	1	0	0	0	0
00-01—Minnesota	NHL	70	0	15	15	42	-6	0	0	—	—	—	—	—
NHL Totals (4 years)		201	5	28	33	72	-5	0	0	6	0	0	0	0

BONDRA, PETER   LW   CAPITALS

PERSONAL: Born February 7, 1968, in Luck, Ukraine. ... 6-1/205. ... Shoots left. ... Name pronounced BAHN-druh.
TRANSACTIONS/CAREER NOTES: Selected by Washington Capitals in eighth round (ninth Capitals pick, 156th overall) of NHL entry draft (June 16, 1990). ... Dislocated left shoulder (January 17, 1991). ... Suffered recurring shoulder problems (February 15, 1991); missed 13 games. ... Injured throat (April 4, 1993); missed one game. ... Fractured left hand (November 26, 1993); missed 12 games. ... Played in Europe during 1994-95 NHL lockout. ... Suffered from the flu (April 8, 1995); missed one game. ... Signed by Detroit Vipers of IHL during contract holdout (September 28, 1995); re-signed by Capitals (October 20, 1995). ... Separated shoulder (November 11, 1995); missed six games. ... Pulled groin (February 24, 1996); missed four games. ... Strained groin (December 4, 1996); missed three games. ... Suspended one game

and fined $1,000 by NHL for kneeing incident (February 4, 1997). ... Suffered back spasms (April 1, 1997); missed one game. ... Injured foot (November 29, 1997); missed three games. ... Injured knee (April 8, 1998); missed two games. ... Injured hip (November 28, 1998); missed one game. ... Fractured hand (March 15, 1999); missed remainder of season. ... Underwent knee surgery (December 5, 1999); missed eight games. ... Injured knee (January 4, 2000); missed seven games. ... Injured shoulder (March 30, 1999); missed five games.

HONORS: Played in NHL All-Star Game (1993 and 1996-1999).

MISCELLANEOUS: Scored on a penalty shot (vs. Stephane Fiset, January 29, 1999). ... Failed to score on a penalty shot (vs. Mikhail Shtalenkov, December 13, 1996; vs. Stephane Fiset, April 4, 1998).

STATISTICAL NOTES: Led NHL with 13 game-winning goals (1997-98).

STATISTICAL PLATEAUS: Three-goal games: 1993-94 (1), 1994-95 (1), 1995-96 (2), 1996-97 (1), 1997-98 (1), 1998-99 (2), 1999-00 (1), 2000-01 (2). Total: 11. ... Four-goal games: 1995-96 (2), 1996-97 (1), 1998-99 (1), 2000-01 (1). Total: 5. ... Total hat tricks: 16.

		REGULAR SEASON								PLAYOFFS				
Season Team	League	Gms.	G	A	Pts.	PIM	+/-	PP	SH	Gms.	G	A	Pts.	PIM
86-87—Kosice	Czech.	32	4	5	9	24	...	...	...	—	—	—	—	—
87-88—Kosice	Czech.	45	27	11	38	20	...	...	...	—	—	—	—	—
88-89—Kosice	Czech.	40	30	10	40	20	...	...	...	—	—	—	—	—
89-90—Kosice	Czech.	42	29	17	46	...	...	...	...	—	—	—	—	—
90-91—Washington	NHL	54	12	16	28	47	-10	4	0	4	0	1	1	2
91-92—Washington	NHL	71	28	28	56	42	16	4	0	7	6	2	8	4
92-93—Washington	NHL	83	37	48	85	70	8	10	0	6	0	6	6	0
93-94—Washington	NHL	69	24	19	43	40	22	4	0	9	2	4	6	4
94-95—HC Kosice	Slovakia	2	1	0	1	0	...	...	...	—	—	—	—	—
—Washington	NHL	47	*34	9	43	24	9	12	*6	7	5	3	8	10
95-96—Detroit	IHL	7	8	1	9	0	...	...	...	—	—	—	—	—
—Washington	NHL	67	52	28	80	40	18	11	4	6	3	2	5	8
96-97—Washington	NHL	77	46	31	77	72	7	10	4	—	—	—	—	—
97-98—Washington	NHL	76	†52	26	78	44	14	11	5	17	7	5	12	12
—Slovakian Oly. team	Int'l	2	1	0	1	25	...	...	...	—	—	—	—	—
98-99—Washington	NHL	66	31	24	55	56	-1	6	3	—	—	—	—	—
99-00—Washington	NHL	62	21	17	38	30	5	5	3	5	1	1	2	4
00-01—Washington	NHL	82	45	36	81	60	8	*22	4	6	2	0	2	2
NHL Totals (11 years)		754	382	282	664	525	96	99	29	67	26	24	50	46

BONIN, BRIAN — C

PERSONAL: Born November 28, 1973, in St. Paul, Minn. ... 5-9/187. ... Shoots left. ... Name pronounced BAH-nihn.

TRANSACTIONS/CAREER NOTES: Selected by Pittsburgh Penguins in ninth round (ninth Penguins pick, 211th overall) of NHL entry draft (June 20, 1992). ... Signed as free agent by Vancouver Canucks (August 25, 1999). ... Signed as free agent by Minnesota Wild (July 6, 2000).

HONORS: Named WCHA Player of the Year (1994-95 and 1995-96). ... Named to NCAA All-America (West) first team (1994-95 and 1995-96). ... Named to WCHA All-Star first team (1994-95 and 1995-96). ... Won Hobey Baker Memorial Award (1995-96). ... Named to IHL All-Star second team (2000-01).

		REGULAR SEASON								PLAYOFFS				
Season Team	League	Gms.	G	A	Pts.	PIM	+/-	PP	SH	Gms.	G	A	Pts.	PIM
91-92—White Bear Lake H.S.	Minn. H.S.	23	22	35	57	8	...	...	...	—	—	—	—	—
92-93—Univ. of Minnesota	WCHA	38	10	18	28	10	...	...	...	—	—	—	—	—
93-94—Univ. of Minnesota	WCHA	42	24	20	44	14	...	...	...	—	—	—	—	—
94-95—Univ. of Minnesota	WCHA	44	32	31	63	28	...	...	...	—	—	—	—	—
95-96—Univ. of Minnesota	WCHA	42	34	47	81	30	...	...	...	—	—	—	—	—
96-97—Cleveland	IHL	60	13	26	39	18	...	...	...	1	1	0	1	0
97-98—Syracuse	AHL	67	31	38	69	46	...	...	...	5	1	3	4	6
98-99—Kansas City	IHL	19	2	5	7	10	...	...	...	—	—	—	—	—
—Adirondack	AHL	54	19	16	35	31	...	...	...	2	0	0	0	0
—Pittsburgh	NHL	5	0	0	0	0	-2	0	0	3	0	0	0	0
99-00—Syracuse	AHL	67	19	28	47	20	...	...	...	4	0	1	1	0
00-01—Cleveland	IHL	75	35	42	77	45	...	...	...	4	2	0	2	0
—Minnesota	NHL	7	0	0	0	0	-3	0	0	—	—	—	—	—
NHL Totals (2 years)		12	0	0	0	0	-5	0	0	3	0	0	0	0

BONK, RADEK — C — SENATORS

PERSONAL: Born January 9, 1976, in Koprivnice, Czechoslovakia. ... 6-3/210. ... Shoots left. ... Name pronounced BAHNK.

TRANSACTIONS/CAREER NOTES: Selected by Ottawa Senators in first round (first Senators pick, third overall) of NHL entry draft (June 28, 1994). ... Injured ankle (April 26, 1995); missed last five games of season. ... Injured hand (1995-96 season); missed one game. ... Suffered abdominal strain (November 8, 1996); missed six games. ... Fractured left wrist (November 23, 1996); missed 23 games. ... Bruised knee (March 5, 1998); missed one game. ... Injured hip flexor (November 7, 1998); missed one game. ... Suffered from the flu (January 4, 2000); missed two games. ... Suffered from the flu (February 19, 2001); missed one game. ... Fractured left thumb (March 24, 2001); missed final seven games of regular season and two playoff games.

HONORS: Won Garry F. Longman Memorial Trophy (1993-94). ... Played in NHL All-Star Game (2000 and 2001).

MISCELLANEOUS: Failed to score on a penalty shot (vs. Daren Puppa, January 13, 1996).

STATISTICAL PLATEAUS: Three-goal games: 2000-01 (1).

		REGULAR SEASON								PLAYOFFS				
Season Team	League	Gms.	G	A	Pts.	PIM	+/-	PP	SH	Gms.	G	A	Pts.	PIM
90-91—Opava	Czech.	35	47	42	89	25	...	...	...	—	—	—	—	—
91-92—ZPS Zlin	Czech Dv.II	45	47	36	83	30	...	...	...	—	—	—	—	—
92-93—ZPS Zlin	Czech.	30	5	5	10	10	...	...	...	—	—	—	—	—
93-94—Las Vegas	IHL	76	42	45	87	208	...	...	...	5	1	2	3	10
94-95—Las Vegas	IHL	33	7	13	20	62	...	...	...	—	—	—	—	—
—Ottawa	NHL	42	3	8	11	28	-5	1	0	1	0	0	0	0
—Prin. Edward Island	AHL	—	—	—	—	—	...	...	...	—	—	—	—	—

Season Team	League	REGULAR SEASON								PLAYOFFS				
		Gms.	G	A	Pts.	PIM	+/-	PP	SH	Gms.	G	A	Pts.	PIM
95-96—Ottawa	NHL	76	16	19	35	36	-5	5	0	—	—	—	—	—
96-97—Ottawa	NHL	53	5	13	18	14	-4	0	1	7	0	1	1	4
97-98—Ottawa	NHL	65	7	9	16	16	-13	1	0	5	0	0	0	2
98-99—Ottawa	NHL	81	16	16	32	48	15	0	1	4	0	0	0	6
99-00—HC Pardubice	Czech Rep.	3	1	0	1	4	...	...	...	—	—	—	—	—
—Ottawa	NHL	80	23	37	60	53	-2	10	0	6	0	0	0	8
00-01—Ottawa	NHL	74	23	36	59	52	27	5	2	2	0	0	0	2
NHL Totals (7 years)		471	93	138	231	247	13	22	4	24	0	1	1	22

B

BONNI, RYAN — D — CANUCKS

PERSONAL: Born February 18, 1979, in Winnipeg. ... 6-4/190. ... Shoots left. ... Name pronounced BAH-nee.
TRANSACTIONS/CAREER NOTES: Selected by Vancouver Canucks in second round (second Canucks pick, 34th overal) of NHL entry draft (June 21, 1997).

Season Team	League	REGULAR SEASON								PLAYOFFS				
		Gms.	G	A	Pts.	PIM	+/-	PP	SH	Gms.	G	A	Pts.	PIM
95-96—Saskatoon	WHL	63	1	7	8	78	...	...	...	3	0	0	0	0
96-97—Saskatoon	WHL	69	11	19	30	219	...	...	...	—	—	—	—	—
97-98—Saskatoon	WHL	42	5	14	19	100	...	...	...	—	—	—	—	—
98-99—Saskatoon	WHL	51	6	26	32	211	...	...	...	—	—	—	—	—
—Red Deer	WHL	20	3	10	13	41	...	...	...	9	0	4	4	25
99-00—Syracuse	AHL	71	5	13	18	125	...	...	...	2	0	1	1	2
—Vancouver	NHL	3	0	0	0	0	-1	0	0	—	—	—	—	—
00-01—Kansas City	IHL	80	2	9	11	127	...	...	...	—	—	—	—	—
NHL Totals (1 year)		3	0	0	0	0	-1	0	0					

BONVIE, DENNIS — D

PERSONAL: Born July 23, 1973, in Antigonish, Nova Scotia. ... 5-11/205. ... Shoots right. ... Name pronounced BAHN-vee.
TRANSACTIONS/CAREER NOTES: Signed as free agent by Edmonton Oilers (August 26, 1994). ... Selected by Chicago Blackhawks from Oilers in NHL waiver draft (October 5, 1998). ... Traded by Blackhawks to Philadelphia Flyers for D Frank Bialowas (January 8, 1999). ... Signed as free agent by Pittsburgh Penguins (September 20, 1999).

Season Team	League	REGULAR SEASON								PLAYOFFS				
		Gms.	G	A	Pts.	PIM	+/-	PP	SH	Gms.	G	A	Pts.	PIM
90-91—Antigonish	N.S.Jr.A					Statistics unavailable.								
91-92—Kitchener	OHL	7	1	1	2	23	...	...	...	—	—	—	—	—
—North Bay	OHL	49	0	12	12	261	...	...	...	21	0	1	1	91
92-93—North Bay	OHL	64	3	21	24	316	...	...	...	5	0	0	0	34
93-94—Cape Breton	AHL	63	1	10	11	278	...	...	...	4	0	0	0	11
94-95—Cape Breton	AHL	74	5	15	20	422	...	...	...	—	—	—	—	—
—Edmonton	NHL	2	0	0	0	0	0	0	0	—	—	—	—	—
95-96—Edmonton	NHL	8	0	0	0	47	-3	0	0	—	—	—	—	—
—Cape Breton	AHL	38	13	14	27	269	...	...	...	—	—	—	—	—
96-97—Hamilton	AHL	73	9	20	29	*522	...	...	...	22	3	11	14	*91
97-98—Edmonton	NHL	4	0	0	0	27	0	0	0	—	—	—	—	—
—Hamilton	AHL	57	11	19	30	295	...	...	...	9	0	5	5	18
98-99—Chicago	NHL	11	0	0	0	44	-4	0	0	—	—	—	—	—
—Portland	AHL	3	1	0	1	16	...	...	...	—	—	—	—	—
—Philadelphia	AHL	37	4	10	14	158	...	...	...	14	3	3	6	26
99-00—Wilkes-Barre/Scranton	AHL	42	5	26	31	243	...	...	...	—	—	—	—	—
—Pittsburgh	NHL	28	0	0	0	80	-2	0	0	—	—	—	—	—
00-01—Pittsburgh	NHL	3	0	0	0	0	-1	0	0	—	—	—	—	—
—Wilkes-Barre/Scranton	AHL	65	5	18	23	221	...	...	...	21	0	4	4	35
NHL Totals (6 years)		56	0	0	0	198	-10	0	0					

BORDELEAU, SEBASTIEN — C — BLUES

PERSONAL: Born February 15, 1975, in Vancouver. ... 5-11/185. ... Shoots right. ... Son of Paulin Bordeleau, head coach with Fredericton Canadiens of AHL (1990-91 through 1996-97). ... Name pronounced BOHR-dih-loh.
TRANSACTIONS/CAREER NOTES: Selected by Montreal Canadiens in third round (third Canadiens pick, 73rd overall) of NHL entry draft (June 26, 1993). ... Pulled groin (January 13, 1997); missed one game. ... Strained hip flexor (November 17, 1997); missed two games. ... Bruised thigh (November 24, 1997); missed four games. ... Bruised testicles (January 24, 1998); missed two games. ... Strained hip flexor (Feburary 4, 1998); missed two games. ... Traded by Canadiens to Nashville Predators for future considerations (June 27, 1998). ... Sprained thumb (January 11, 1999); missed four games. ... Injured neck (April 12, 1999) and underwent surgery; missed final three games of season. ... Suffered injury (October 2, 1999); missed first seven games of season. ... Separated shoulder (November 2, 1999); missed 11 games. ... Strained muscle in abdomen (October 31, 2000); missed two games. ... Injured groin (November 18, 2000); missed 52 games. ... Claimed on waivers by St. Louis Blues (March 13, 2001).
HONORS: Named to QMJHL All-Star first team (1994-95).

Season Team	League	REGULAR SEASON								PLAYOFFS				
		Gms.	G	A	Pts.	PIM	+/-	PP	SH	Gms.	G	A	Pts.	PIM
91-92—Hull	QMJHL	62	26	32	58	91	...	...	...	5	0	3	3	23
92-93—Hull	QMJHL	60	18	39	57	95	...	...	...	10	3	8	11	20
93-94—Hull	QMJHL	60	26	57	83	147	...	...	...	17	6	14	20	26
94-95—Hull	QMJHL	68	52	76	128	142	...	...	...	18	13	19	32	25

Season Team	League	REGULAR SEASON								PLAYOFFS				
		Gms.	G	A	Pts.	PIM	+/-	PP	SH	Gms.	G	A	Pts.	PIM
95-96—Fredericton	AHL	43	17	29	46	68	...	...	...	7	0	2	2	8
—Montreal	NHL	4	0	0	0	0	-1	0	0	—	—	—	—	—
96-97—Fredericton	AHL	33	17	21	38	50	...	...	...	—	—	—	—	—
—Montreal	NHL	28	2	9	11	2	-3	0	0	—	—	—	—	—
97-98—Montreal	NHL	53	6	8	14	36	5	2	1	5	0	0	0	2
98-99—Nashville	NHL	72	16	24	40	26	-14	1	2	—	—	—	—	—
99-00—Nashville	NHL	60	10	13	23	30	-12	0	2	—	—	—	—	—
00-01—Nashville	NHL	14	2	3	5	14	-4	0	0	—	—	—	—	—
—Worcester	AHL	2	0	2	2	9	...	...	...	11	1	7	8	23
NHL Totals (6 years)		231	36	57	93	108	-29	3	5	5	0	0	0	2

BOUCHARD, JOEL   D   COYOTES   B

PERSONAL: Born January 23, 1974, in Montreal. ... 6-0/200. ... Shoots left.
TRANSACTIONS/CAREER NOTES: Selected by Calgary Flames in sixth round (sixth Flames pick, 129th overall) of NHL entry draft (June 20, 1992). ... Strained abdominal muscle (September 30, 1997); missed one game. ... Suffered concussion (January 24, 1998); missed six games. ... Selected by Nashville Predators in NHL expansion draft (June 26, 1998). ... Sprained ankle (October 27, 1998); missed 11 games. ... Sprained ankle (December 19, 1998); missed seven games. ... Suffered concussion (December 15, 1999); missed nine games. ... Claimed on waivers by Dallas Stars (March 14, 2000). ... Signed as free agent by Phoenix Coyotes (August 31, 2000). ... Suffered back spasms (December 30, 2000); missed two games.
HONORS: Named to QMJHL All-Star first team (1993-94).

Season Team	League	REGULAR SEASON								PLAYOFFS				
		Gms.	G	A	Pts.	PIM	+/-	PP	SH	Gms.	G	A	Pts.	PIM
90-91—Longueuil	QMJHL	53	3	19	22	34	...	...	...	8	0	1	1	11
91-92—Verdun	QMJHL	70	9	37	46	55	...	...	...	19	1	7	8	20
92-93—Verdun	QMJHL	60	10	49	59	126	...	...	...	4	0	2	2	4
93-94—Verdun	QMJHL	60	15	55	70	62	...	...	...	4	1	0	1	6
—Saint John	AHL	1	0	0	0	0	...	...	...	2	0	0	0	0
94-95—Saint John	AHL	77	6	25	31	63	...	...	...	5	1	0	1	4
—Calgary	NHL	2	0	0	0	0	0	0	0	—	—	—	—	—
95-96—Saint John	AHL	74	8	25	33	104	...	...	...	16	1	4	5	10
—Calgary	NHL	4	0	0	0	4	0	0	0	—	—	—	—	—
96-97—Calgary	NHL	76	4	5	9	49	-23	0	1	—	—	—	—	—
97-98—Calgary	NHL	44	5	7	12	57	0	0	1	—	—	—	—	—
—Saint John	AHL	3	2	1	3	6	...	...	...	—	—	—	—	—
98-99—Nashville	NHL	64	4	11	15	60	-10	0	0	—	—	—	—	—
99-00—Nashville	NHL	52	1	4	5	23	-11	0	0	—	—	—	—	—
—Dallas	NHL	2	0	0	0	2	1	0	0	—	—	—	—	—
00-01—Grand Rapids	IHL	19	3	9	12	8	...	...	...	—	—	—	—	—
—Phoenix	NHL	32	1	2	3	22	-8	0	0	—	—	—	—	—
NHL Totals (7 years)		276	15	29	44	217	-51	0	2	—	—	—	—	—

BOUCHER, BRIAN   G   FLYERS

PERSONAL: Born August 1, 1977, in Woonsocket, R.I. ... 6-1/190. ... Catches left. ... Name pronounced boo-SHAY.
TRANSACTIONS/CAREER NOTES: Selected by Philadelphia Flyers in first round (first Flyers pick, 22nd overall) of NHL entry draft (July 8, 1995). ... Suffered from throat infection (January 16, 2001); missed one game.
HONORS: Named to WHL (West) All-Star second team (1995-96). ... Named to WHL (West) All-Star first team (1996-97). ... Won Del Wilson Trophy (1996-97). ... Named to NHL All-Rookie team (1999-2000).

Season Team	League	REGULAR SEASON								PLAYOFFS						
		Gms.	Min	W	L	T	GA	SO	Avg.	Gms.	Min.	W	L	GA	SO	Avg.
93-94—Mt. St. Charles H.S.	R.I.H.S.	23	1170	...	...	...	23	12	1.18	—	—	—	—	—	—	—
94-95—Wexford	Tier II Jr. A	8	425	...	...	...	23	0	3.25	—	—	—	—	—	—	—
—Tri-City	WHL	35	1969	17	11	2	108	1	3.29	13	795	6	5	50	0	3.77
95-96—Tri-City	WHL	55	3183	33	19	2	181	1	3.41	11	653	6	5	37	†2	3.40
96-97—Tri-City	WHL	41	2458	10	24	†6	149	1	3.64	—	—	—	—	—	—	—
97-98—Philadelphia	AHL	34	1901	16	12	3	101	0	3.19	2	31	0	0	1	0	1.94
98-99—Philadelphia	AHL	36	2061	20	8	5	89	2	2.59	16	947	9	7	45	0	2.85
99-00—Philadelphia	NHL	35	2038	20	10	3	65	4	*1.91	18	1183	11	7	40	1	2.03
—Philadelphia	AHL	1	65	0	0	1	3	0	2.77	—	—	—	—	—	—	—
00-01—Philadelphia	NHL	27	1470	8	12	5	80	1	3.27	1	37	0	0	3	0	4.86
NHL Totals (2 years)		62	3508	28	22	8	145	5	2.48	19	1220	11	7	43	1	2.11

BOUCHER, PHILIPPE   D   KINGS

PERSONAL: Born March 24, 1973, in St. Apollnaire, Que. ... 6-3/221. ... Shoots right. ... Name pronounced fih-LEEP boo-SHAY.
TRANSACTIONS/CAREER NOTES: Selected by Buffalo Sabres in first round (first Sabres pick, 13th overall) of NHL entry draft (June 22, 1991). ... Traded by Sabres with G Grant Fuhr and D Denis Tsygurov to Los Angeles Kings for D Alexei Zhitnik, D Charlie Huddy, G Robb Stauber and fifth-round pick (D Marian Menhart) in 1995 draft (February 14, 1995). ... Sprained wrist (February 25, 1995); missed first 31 games of season. ... Suffered tendinitis in right wrist (October 6, 1995); missed first 25 games of season. ... Injured left hand (February 19, 1996); missed four games. ... Sprained right shoulder (October 4, 1996); missed 10 games. ... Suffered from the flu (December 18, 1997); missed two games. ... Suffered illness (January 10, 1998); missed 12 games. ... Suffered from the flu (March 3, 1999); missed two games. ... Underwent foot surgery (April 27, 1999); missed first 71 games of 1999-2000 season.
HONORS: Won Can.HL Rookie of the Year Award (1990-91). ... Won Raymond Lagace Trophy (1990-91). ... Won Michael Bossy Trophy (1990-91). ... Named to QMJHL All-Star second team (1990-91 and 1991-92).

Season Team	League	REGULAR SEASON								PLAYOFFS				
		Gms.	G	A	Pts.	PIM	+/-	PP	SH	Gms.	G	A	Pts.	PIM
90-91—Granby	QMJHL	69	21	46	67	92	...	...	...	—	—	—	—	—
91-92—Granby	QMJHL	49	22	37	59	47	...	...	...	—	—	—	—	—
—Laval	QMJHL	16	7	11	18	36	...	...	...	10	5	6	11	8
92-93—Laval	QMJHL	16	12	15	27	37	...	...	...	13	6	15	21	12
—Rochester	AHL	5	4	3	7	8	...	...	...	3	0	1	1	2
—Buffalo	NHL	18	0	4	4	14	1	0	0	—	—	—	—	—
93-94—Buffalo	NHL	38	6	8	14	29	-1	4	0	7	1	1	2	2
—Rochester	AHL	31	10	22	32	51	...	...	...	—	—	—	—	—
94-95—Rochester	AHL	43	14	27	41	26	...	...	...	—	—	—	—	—
—Buffalo	NHL	9	1	4	5	0	6	0	0	—	—	—	—	—
—Los Angeles	NHL	6	1	0	1	4	-3	0	0	—	—	—	—	—
95-96—Los Angeles	NHL	53	7	16	23	31	-26	5	0	—	—	—	—	—
—Phoenix	IHL	10	4	3	7	4	...	...	...	—	—	—	—	—
96-97—Los Angeles	NHL	60	7	18	25	25	0	2	0	—	—	—	—	—
97-98—Los Angeles	NHL	45	6	10	16	49	6	1	0	—	—	—	—	—
—Long Beach	IHL	2	0	1	1	4	...	...	...	—	—	—	—	—
98-99—Los Angeles	NHL	45	2	6	8	32	-12	1	0	—	—	—	—	—
99-00—Long Beach	IHL	14	4	11	15	8	...	...	...	6	0	9	9	8
—Los Angeles	NHL	1	0	0	0	0	0	0	0	—	—	—	—	—
00-01—Manitoba	IHL	45	10	22	32	99	...	...	...	—	—	—	—	—
—Los Angeles	NHL	22	2	4	6	20	4	2	0	13	0	1	1	2
NHL Totals (9 years)		297	32	70	102	204	-25	15	0	20	1	2	3	4

BOUCK, TYLER — RW — COYOTES

PERSONAL: Born January 13, 1980, in Camrose, Alta. ... 6-0/185. ... Shoots left.
TRANSACTIONS/CAREER NOTES: Selected by Dallas Stars in second round (second Stars pick, 57th overall) of NHL entry draft (June 27, 1998). ... Traded by Stars to Phoenix Coyotes for D Jyrki Lumme (June 23, 2001).
HONORS: Named to WHL (West) All-Star second team (1999-2000).

Season Team	League	REGULAR SEASON								PLAYOFFS				
		Gms.	G	A	Pts.	PIM	+/-	PP	SH	Gms.	G	A	Pts.	PIM
96-97—Prince George	WHL	12	0	2	2	11	...	...	...	—	—	—	—	—
97-98—Prince George	WHL	65	11	26	37	90	...	...	...	11	1	0	1	21
98-99—Prince George	WHL	56	22	25	47	178	...	...	...	2	0	2	2	10
99-00—Prince George	WHL	57	30	33	63	183	...	...	...	13	6	13	19	36
00-01—Dallas	NHL	48	2	5	7	29	-3	0	0	1	0	0	0	0
—Utah	IHL	24	2	6	8	39	...	...	...	—	—	—	—	—
NHL Totals (1 year)		48	2	5	7	29	-3	0	0	1	0	0	0	0

BOUGHNER, BOB — D — FLAMES

PERSONAL: Born March 8, 1971, in Windsor, Ont. ... 6-0/203. ... Shoots right. ... Name pronounced BOOG-nuhr.
TRANSACTIONS/CAREER NOTES: Selected by Detroit Red Wings in second round (second Red Wings pick, 32nd overall) of NHL entry draft (June 17, 1989). ... Signed as free agent by Florida Panthers (August 10, 1994). ... Traded by Panthers to Buffalo Sabres for third-round pick (D Chris Allen) in 1996 draft (February 1, 1996). ... Bruised left thigh (February 28, 1996); missed one game. ... Bruised shoulder (February 7, 1998); missed two games. ... Injured wrist (March 12, 1998); missed three games. ... Bruised foot (April 29, 1998); missed one game. ... Selected by Nashville Predators in NHL expansion draft (June 26, 1998). ... Suffered from the flu (October 27, 1998); missed one game. ... Suffered from the flu (January 14, 1999); missed two games. ... Suffered from the flu (November, 1999); missed two games. ... Sprained ankle (December, 1999); missed two games. ... Fractured finger (February 2, 2000); missed three games. ... Traded by Predators to Pittsburgh Penguins for D Pavel Skrbek (March 13, 2000). ... Fractured wrist (November 11, 2000); missed 23 games. ... Bruised chest (March 2, 2001); missed one game. ... Signed as free agent by Calgary Flames (July 2, 2001).

Season Team	League	REGULAR SEASON								PLAYOFFS				
		Gms.	G	A	Pts.	PIM	+/-	PP	SH	Gms.	G	A	Pts.	PIM
87-88—St. Mary's Jr. B	OHA	36	4	18	22	177	...	...	...	—	—	—	—	—
88-89—Sault Ste. Marie	OHL	64	6	15	21	182	...	...	...	—	—	—	—	—
89-90—Sault Ste. Marie	OHL	49	7	23	30	122	...	...	...	—	—	—	—	—
90-91—Sault Ste. Marie	OHL	64	13	33	46	156	...	...	...	14	2	9	11	35
91-92—Adirondack	AHL	1	0	0	0	7	...	...	...	—	—	—	—	—
—Toledo	ECHL	28	3	10	13	79	...	...	...	5	2	0	2	15
92-93—Adirondack	AHL	69	1	16	17	190	...	...	...	—	—	—	—	—
93-94—Adirondack	AHL	72	8	14	22	292	...	...	...	10	1	1	2	18
94-95—Cincinnati	IHL	81	2	14	16	192	...	...	...	10	0	0	0	18
95-96—Carolina	AHL	46	2	15	17	127	...	...	...	—	—	—	—	—
—Buffalo	NHL	31	0	1	1	104	3	0	0	—	—	—	—	—
96-97—Buffalo	NHL	77	1	7	8	225	12	0	0	11	0	1	1	9
97-98—Buffalo	NHL	69	1	3	4	165	5	0	0	14	0	4	4	15
98-99—Nashville	NHL	79	3	10	13	137	-6	0	0	—	—	—	—	—
99-00—Nashville	NHL	62	2	4	6	97	-13	0	0	—	—	—	—	—
—Pittsburgh	NHL	11	1	0	1	69	2	1	0	11	0	2	2	15
00-01—Pittsburgh	NHL	58	1	3	4	147	18	0	0	18	0	1	1	22
NHL Totals (6 years)		387	9	28	37	944	21	1	0	54	0	8	8	61

BOUILLON, FRANCIS — D — CANADIENS

PERSONAL: Born October 17, 1975, in New York. ... 5-8/189. ... Shoots left.
TRANSACTIONS/CAREER NOTES: Signed as non-drafted free agent by Montreal Canadiens (August 18, 1998). ... Fractured hand (November 14, 2000); missed 13 games. ... Sprained ankle (December 30, 2000); missed 23 games.

Season Team	League	REGULAR SEASON								PLAYOFFS				
		Gms.	G	A	Pts.	PIM	+/-	PP	SH	Gms.	G	A	Pts.	PIM
92-93—Laval	QMJHL	46	0	7	7	45	...	...	...	—	—	—	—	—
93-94—Laval	QMJHL	68	3	15	18	129	...	...	...	19	2	9	11	48
94-95—Laval	QMJHL	72	8	25	33	115	...	...	...	20	3	11	14	21
95-96—Granby	QMJHL	68	11	35	46	156	...	...	...	21	2	12	14	30
96-97—Wheeling	ECHL	69	10	32	42	77	...	...	...	3	0	2	2	10
97-98—Quebec	IHL	71	8	27	35	76	...	...	...	—	—	—	—	—
98-99—Fredericton	AHL	79	19	36	55	174	...	...	...	5	2	1	3	0
99-00—Montreal	NHL	74	3	13	16	38	-7	2	0	—	—	—	—	—
00-01—Montreal	NHL	29	0	6	6	26	3	0	0	—	—	—	—	—
—Quebec	AHL	4	0	0	0	0				—	—	—	—	—
NHL Totals (2 years)		103	3	19	22	64	-4	2	0					

BOULTON, ERIC LW SABRES B

PERSONAL: Born August 17, 1976, in Halifax, Nova Scotia. ... 6-0/201. ... Shoots left.
TRANSACTIONS/CAREER NOTES: Selected by New York Rangers in ninth round (12th Rangers pick, 234th overall) of NHL entry draft (June 29, 1994). ... Signed as free agent by Buffalo Sabres (August 20, 1999).

Season Team	League	REGULAR SEASON								PLAYOFFS				
		Gms.	G	A	Pts.	PIM	+/-	PP	SH	Gms.	G	A	Pts.	PIM
93-94—Cole Harbour	NSJHL					Statistics unavailable.								
—Oshawa	OHL	45	4	3	7	149	...	...	...	5	0	0	0	16
94-95—Oshawa	OHL	27	7	5	12	125	...	...	...	—	—	—	—	—
—Sarnia	OHL	24	3	7	10	134	...	...	...	4	0	1	1	10
95-96—Sarnia	OHL	66	14	29	43	243	...	...	...	9	0	3	3	29
96-97—Binghamton	AHL	23	2	3	5	67	...	...	...	3	0	0	0	4
—Charlotte	ECHL	44	14	11	25	325	...	...	...	3	0	1	1	6
97-98—Charlotte	ECHL	53	11	16	27	202	...	...	...	4	1	0	1	0
—Fort Wayne	IHL	8	0	2	2	42	...	...	...	—	—	—	—	—
98-99—Houston	IHL	7	1	0	1	41	...	...	...	—	—	—	—	—
—Florida	ECHL	26	9	13	22	143	...	...	...	—	—	—	—	—
—Kentucky	AHL	34	3	3	6	154	...	...	...	10	0	1	1	36
99-00—Rochester	AHL	76	2	2	4	276	...	...	...	18	2	1	3	53
00-01—Buffalo	NHL	35	1	2	3	94	-1	0	0	—	—	—	—	—
NHL Totals (1 year)		35	1	2	3	94	-1	0	0					

BOUMEDIENNE, JOSEF D DEVILS

PERSONAL: Born January 12, 1978, in Stockholm, Sweden. ... 6-1/190. ... Shoots left.
TRANSACTIONS/CAREER NOTES: Selected by New Jersey Devils in fourth round (seventh Devils pick, 91st overall) of NHL entry draft (June 22, 1996).

Season Team	League	REGULAR SEASON								PLAYOFFS				
		Gms.	G	A	Pts.	PIM	+/-	PP	SH	Gms.	G	A	Pts.	PIM
95-96—Huddinge Jrs.	Sweden	25	2	4	6	66	...	...	...	—	—	—	—	—
—Huddinge	Sweden Dv. 2	7	0	0	0	14	...	...	...	—	—	—	—	—
96-97—Sodertalje SK	Sweden	32	1	1	2	32	...	...	...	—	—	—	—	—
97-98—Sodertalje SK	Sweden	26	3	3	6	28	...	...	...	—	—	—	—	—
98-99—Tappara Tampere	Finland	51	6	8	14	119	...	...	...	—	—	—	—	—
99-00—Tappara Tampere	Finland	50	8	24	32	160	...	...	...	4	1	2	3	10
00-01—Albany	AHL	79	8	29	37	117	...	...	...	—	—	—	—	—

BOURQUE, RAY D

PERSONAL: Born December 28, 1960, in Montreal. ... 5-11/215. ... Shoots left. ... Full Name: Raymond Jean Bourque. ... Name pronounced BOHRK.
TRANSACTIONS/CAREER NOTES: Selected by Boston Bruins in first round (first Bruins pick, eighth overall) of NHL entry draft (August 9, 1979). ... Fractured jaw (November 11, 1980). ... Injured left shoulder (October 1981). ... Fractured left wrist (April 21, 1982). ... Refractured left wrist and fractured left forearm (summer 1982). ... Fractured bone over left eye (October 1982). ... Sprained left knee ligaments (December 10, 1988). ... Bruised hip (April 7, 1990). ... Bruised right shoulder (October 17, 1990); missed four games. ... Fractured finger (May 5, 1992); missed remainder of playoffs. ... Injured back (December 19, 1992); missed two games. ... Injured ankle (January 21, 1993); missed three games. ... Injured knee (March 22, 1994); missed 11 games. ... Bruised shoulder (October 20, 1996); missed nine games. ... Strained abdominal muscle (December 14, 1996); missed five games. ... Bruised ankle (March 6, 1997); missed three games. ... Injured ankle (March 17, 1997); missed three games. ... Strained hip flexor (January 7, 1999); missed one game. ... Traded by Bruins with LW Dave Andreychuk to Colorado Avalanche for LW Brian Rolston, D Martin Grenier, C Samual Pahlsson and first-round pick (LW Martin Samuelsson) in 2000 draft (March 6, 2000). ... Injured groin (March 7, 2000); missed one game. ... Announced retirement (June 26, 2001).
HONORS: Named to QMJHL All-Star first team (1977-78 and 1978-79). ... Won Frank J. Selke Trophy (1978-79). ... Won Emile (Butch) Bouchard Trophy (1978-79). ... Named NHL Rookie of the Year by THE SPORTING NEWS (1979-80). ... Won Calder Memorial Trophy (1979-80). ... Named to NHL All-Star first team (1979-80, 1981-82, 1983-84, 1984-85, 1986-87, 1987-88, and 1989-90 through 1993-94, 1995-96 and 2000-01). ... Named to THE SPORTING NEWS All-Star second team (1980-81, 1982-83, 1985-86 and 1988-89). ... Named to NHL All-Star second team (1980-81, 1982-83, 1985-86, 1988-89, 1994-95 and 1998-99). ... Played in NHL All-Star Game (1981-1986, 1988-1994 and 1996-2001). ... Named to THE SPORTING NEWS All-Star first team (1981-82, 1983-84, 1984-85, 1986-87, 1987-88 and 1989-90 through 1995-96). ... Won James Norris Memorial Trophy (1986-87, 1987-88, 1989-90, 1990-91 and 1993-94). ... Won King Clancy Memorial Trophy (1991-92). ... Named All-Star Game Most Valuable Player (1996).
RECORDS: Holds NHL career record for most goals by defenseman—410; most assists by a defenseman—1,169; and most points by a defenseman—1,579. ... Holds NHL career playoff record for most years in playoffs—21 (1979-80 through 1995-96, 1997-98, 1999-2000 and 2000-01); and most years in All-Star Game —19. ... Shares NHL career All-Star Game record for most assists—13.

STATISTICAL PLATEAUS: Three-goal games: 1982-83 (1).
MISCELLANEOUS: Member of Stanley Cup championship team (2001). ... Co-captain of Boston Bruins (1985-86 through 1987-88). ... Captain of Bruins (1988-89 through March 6, 2000). ... Holds Boston Bruins all-time records for most games played (1,518), most assists (1,111) and most points (1,506). ... Scored on a penalty shot (vs. Chris Terreri, March 19, 1994). ... Failed to score on a penalty shot (vs. John Vanbiesbrouck, November 11, 1988).

Season Team	League	Gms.	G	A	Pts.	PIM	+/-	PP	SH	Gms.	G	A	Pts.	PIM
76-77—Sorel	QMJHL	69	12	36	48	61	...	...	...	—	—	—	—	—
77-78—Verdun	QMJHL	72	22	57	79	90	...	...	...	4	2	1	3	0
78-79—Verdun	QMJHL	63	22	71	93	44	...	...	...	11	3	16	19	18
79-80—Boston	NHL	80	17	48	65	73	52	3	2	10	2	9	11	27
80-81—Boston	NHL	67	27	29	56	96	29	9	1	3	0	1	1	2
81-82—Boston	NHL	65	17	49	66	51	22	4	0	9	1	5	6	16
82-83—Boston	NHL	65	22	51	73	20	49	7	0	17	8	15	23	10
83-84—Boston	NHL	78	31	65	96	57	51	12	1	3	0	2	2	0
84-85—Boston	NHL	73	20	66	86	53	30	10	1	5	0	3	3	4
85-86—Boston	NHL	74	19	58	77	68	17	11	0	3	0	0	0	0
86-87—Boston	NHL	78	23	72	95	36	44	6	1	4	1	2	3	0
87-88—Boston	NHL	78	17	64	81	72	34	7	1	23	3	18	21	26
88-89—Boston	NHL	60	18	43	61	52	20	6	0	10	0	4	4	6
89-90—Boston	NHL	76	19	65	84	50	31	8	0	17	5	12	17	16
90-91—Boston	NHL	76	21	73	94	75	33	7	0	19	7	18	25	12
91-92—Boston	NHL	80	21	60	81	56	11	7	1	13	3	6	9	12
92-93—Boston	NHL	78	19	63	82	40	38	8	0	4	1	0	1	2
93-94—Boston	NHL	72	20	71	91	58	26	10	3	13	2	8	10	0
94-95—Boston	NHL	46	12	31	43	20	3	9	0	5	0	3	3	0
95-96—Boston	NHL	82	20	62	82	58	31	9	2	5	1	6	7	2
96-97—Boston	NHL	62	19	31	50	18	-11	8	1	—	—	—	—	—
97-98—Boston	NHL	82	13	35	48	80	2	9	0	6	1	4	5	2
—Can. Olympic team	Int'l	6	1	2	3	4	...	...	...	—	—	—	—	—
98-99—Boston	NHL	81	10	47	57	34	-7	8	0	12	1	9	10	14
99-00—Boston	NHL	65	10	28	38	20	-11	6	0	—	—	—	—	—
—Colorado	NHL	14	8	6	14	6	9	7	0	13	1	8	9	8
00-01—Colorado	NHL	80	7	52	59	48	25	2	2	21	4	6	10	12
NHL Totals (22 years)		**1612**	**410**	**1169**	**1579**	**1141**	**528**	**173**	**16**	**214**	**41**	**139**	**180**	**171**

BOWLER, BILL · C · PREDATORS

PERSONAL: Born September 25, 1974, in Toronto. ... 5-9/180. ... Shoots left.
TRANSACTIONS/CAREER NOTES: Signed as non-drafted free agent by Columbus Blue Jackets (August 3, 2000). ... Claimed on waivers by Nashville Predators (June 1, 2001).
HONORS: Named to IHL All-Star second team (1998-99).

Season Team	League	Gms.	G	A	Pts.	PIM	+/-	PP	SH	Gms.	G	A	Pts.	PIM
91-92—Windsor	OHL	66	25	63	88	28	...	...	...	—	—	—	—	—
92-93—Windsor	OHL	57	44	77	121	41	...	...	...	—	—	—	—	—
93-94—Windsor	OHL	66	47	76	123	39	...	...	...	—	—	—	—	—
94-95—Windsor	OHL	61	33	102	135	63	...	...	...	—	—	—	—	—
—Las Vegas	IHL	—	—	—	—	—	...	...	...	1	0	0	0	0
95-96—Las Vegas	IHL	75	31	55	86	26	...	...	...	14	3	5	8	22
96-97—Houston	IHL	78	22	43	65	79	...	...	...	13	2	5	7	6
97-98—Hamilton	AHL	46	7	24	31	22	...	...	...	—	—	—	—	—
—Manitoba	IHL	30	9	25	34	30	...	...	...	3	0	2	2	4
98-99—Manitoba	IHL	82	26	67	93	59	...	...	...	5	6	5	11	6
99-00—Manitoba	IHL	75	20	42	62	59	...	...	...	2	1	2	3	6
00-01—Syracuse	AHL	72	21	58	79	50	...	...	...	4	1	3	4	2
—Columbus	NHL	9	0	2	2	8	-3	0	0	—	—	—	—	—
NHL Totals (1 year)		**9**	**0**	**2**	**2**	**8**	**-3**	**0**	**0**					

BOYES, BRAD · C · MAPLE LEAFS

PERSONAL: Born April 17, 1982, in Mississauga, Ont. ... 6-0/181. ... Shoots right.
TRANSACTIONS/CAREER NOTES: Selected by Toronto Maple Leafs in first round (first Maple Leafs pick, 24th overall) of NHL entry draft (June 24, 2000).
HONORS: Won Can.HL Scholastic Player of the Year Award (1999-2000). ... Named to OHL All-Star second team (2000-01). ... Won Red Tilson Trophy (2000-01). ... Won William Hanley Trophy (2000-01).

Season Team	League	Gms.	G	A	Pts.	PIM	+/-	PP	SH	Gms.	G	A	Pts.	PIM
98-99—Erie	OHL	59	24	36	60	30	...	...	...	5	1	2	3	10
99-00—Erie	OHL	68	36	46	82	38	...	...	...	13	6	8	14	10
00-01—Erie	OHL	59	45	45	90	42	...	...	...	15	10	13	23	8

BOYLE, DAN · D · PANTHERS

PERSONAL: Born July 12, 1976, in Ottawa. ... 5-11/190. ... Shoots right.
TRANSACTIONS/CAREER NOTES: Signed as non-drafted free agent by Florida Panthers (March 30, 1998).
HONORS: Named to NCAA All-America (West) first team (1996-97 and 1997-98). ... Named to CCHA All-Star first team (1996-97 and 1997-98). ... Named to AHL All-Star second team (1998-99 and 1999-2000).

Season Team	League	Gms.	G	A	Pts.	PIM	+/-	PP	SH	Gms.	G	A	Pts.	PIM
94-95—Miami of Ohio	CCHA	35	8	18	26	24	...	...	...	—	—	—	—	—
95-96—Miami of Ohio	CCHA	36	7	20	27	70	...	...	...	—	—	—	—	—
96-97—Miami of Ohio	CCHA	40	11	43	54	52	...	...	...	—	—	—	—	—
97-98—Miami of Ohio	CCHA	37	14	26	40	58	...	...	...	—	—	—	—	—
—Cincinnati	IHL	8	0	3	3	20	...	...	...	5	0	1	1	4
98-99—Kentucky	AHL	53	8	34	42	87	...	...	...	12	3	5	8	16
—Florida	NHL	22	3	5	8	6	0	1	0	—	—	—	—	—
99-00—Louisville	AHL	58	14	38	52	75	...	...	...	4	0	2	2	8
—Florida	NHL	13	0	3	3	4	-2	0	0	—	—	—	—	—
00-01—Florida	NHL	69	4	18	22	28	-14	1	0	—	—	—	—	—
—Louisville	AHL	6	0	5	5	12	...	...	...	—	—	—	—	—
NHL Totals (3 years)		104	7	26	33	38	-16	2	0					

BOYNTON, NICK — D — BRUINS

B

PERSONAL: Born January 14, 1979, in Etobicoke, Ont. ... 6-2/210. ... Shoots right. ... Full Name: Nicholas Boynton.
TRANSACTIONS/CAREER NOTES: Selected by Washington Capitals in first round (first Capitals pick, ninth overall) of NHL entry draft (June 21, 1997). ... Returned to draft pool by Capitals and selected by Boston Bruins in first round (first Bruins pick, 21st overall) of NHL entry draft (June 26, 1999).
HONORS: Named to OHL All-Rookie team (1995-96). ... Won Can.HL Plus/Minus Award (1996-97).

Season Team	League	Gms.	G	A	Pts.	PIM	+/-	PP	SH	Gms.	G	A	Pts.	PIM
94-95—Caledon	Jr. A	44	10	35	45	139	...	...	...	—	—	—	—	—
95-96—Ottawa	OHL	64	10	14	24	90	...	...	...	4	0	3	3	10
96-97—Ottawa	OHL	63	13	51	64	143	...	...	...	24	4	24	28	38
97-98—Ottawa	OHL	40	7	31	38	94	...	...	...	13	0	4	4	24
98-99—Ottawa	OHL	51	11	48	59	83	...	...	...	9	1	9	10	18
99-00—Providence	AHL	53	5	14	19	66	...	...	...	12	1	0	1	6
—Boston	NHL	5	0	0	0	0	-5	0	0	—	—	—	—	—
00-01—Providence	AHL	78	6	27	33	105	...	...	...	17	0	2	2	35
—Boston	NHL	1	0	0	0	0	-1	0	0	—	—	—	—	—
NHL Totals (2 years)		6	0	0	0	0	-6	0	0					

BRADLEY, MATT — RW — SHARKS

PERSONAL: Born June 13, 1978, in Stittsville, Ont. ... 6-2/195. ... Shoots right.
TRANSACTIONS/CAREER NOTES: Selected by San Jose Sharks in fourth round (fourth Sharks pick, 102nd overall) of NHL entry draft (June 22, 1996). ... Injured shoulder (February 14, 2001); missed seven games.
HONORS: Won William Hanley Trophy (1997-98).

Season Team	League	Gms.	G	A	Pts.	PIM	+/-	PP	SH	Gms.	G	A	Pts.	PIM
94-95—Cumberland	CJHL	49	13	20	33	18	...	...	...	—	—	—	—	—
95-96—Kingston	OHL	55	10	14	24	17	...	...	...	6	0	1	1	6
96-97—Kingston	OHL	65	24	24	48	41	...	...	...	5	0	4	4	2
—Kentucky	AHL	1	0	1	1	0	...	...	...	—	—	—	—	—
97-98—Kingston	OHL	55	33	50	83	24	...	...	...	8	3	4	7	7
—Kentucky	AHL	1	0	1	1	0	...	...	...	—	—	—	—	—
98-99—Kentucky	AHL	79	23	20	43	57	...	...	...	10	1	4	5	4
99-00—Kentucky	AHL	80	22	19	41	81	...	...	...	9	6	3	9	9
00-01—Kentucky	AHL	22	5	8	13	16	...	...	...	1	1	0	1	5
—San Jose	NHL	21	1	1	2	19	0	0	0	—	—	—	—	—
NHL Totals (1 year)		21	1	1	2	19	0	0	0					

BRASHEAR, DONALD — LW — CANUCKS

PERSONAL: Born January 7, 1972, in Bedford, Ind. ... 6-2/230. ... Shoots left. ... Name pronounced brah-SHEER.
TRANSACTIONS/CAREER NOTES: Signed non-drafted as free agent by Montreal Canadiens (July 28, 1992). ... Bruised knee (November 23, 1993); missed one game. ... Injured shoulder (February 27, 1995); missed one game. ... Bruised hand (March 20, 1995); missed one game. ... Suffered cut to right thigh (December 30, 1995); missed seven games. ... Traded by Canadiens to Vancouver Canucks for D Jassen Cullimore (November 13, 1996). ... Strained back (February 8, 1997); missed three games. ... Suspended four games and fined $1,000 by NHL for fighting (February 25, 1997). ... Injured shoulder (March 11, 1998); missed two games. ... Suspended two games by NHL for illegal check (October 24, 1999). ... Suffered concussion (February 21, 2000); missed 20 games. ... Strained knee (October 18, 2000); missed one game. ... Strained back (November 21, 2000); missed two games.

Season Team	League	Gms.	G	A	Pts.	PIM	+/-	PP	SH	Gms.	G	A	Pts.	PIM
89-90—Longueuil	QMJHL	64	12	14	26	169	...	...	...	7	0	0	0	11
90-91—Longueuil	QMJHL	68	12	26	38	195	...	...	...	8	0	3	3	33
91-92—Verdun	QMJHL	65	18	24	42	283	...	...	...	18	4	2	6	98
92-93—Fredericton	AHL	76	11	3	14	261	...	...	...	5	0	0	0	8
93-94—Fredericton	AHL	62	38	28	66	250	...	...	...	—	—	—	—	—
—Montreal	NHL	14	2	2	4	34	0	0	0	2	0	0	0	0
94-95—Montreal	NHL	20	1	1	2	63	-5	0	0	—	—	—	—	—
—Fredericton	AHL	29	10	9	19	182	...	...	...	17	7	5	12	77
95-96—Montreal	NHL	67	0	4	4	223	-10	0	0	6	0	0	0	2

Season Team	League	REGULAR SEASON								PLAYOFFS				
		Gms.	G	A	Pts.	PIM	+/-	PP	SH	Gms.	G	A	Pts.	PIM
96-97—Montreal	NHL	10	0	0	0	38	-2	0	0	—	—	—	—	—
—Vancouver	NHL	59	8	5	13	207	-6	0	0	—	—	—	—	—
97-98—Vancouver	NHL	77	9	9	18	*372	-9	0	0	—	—	—	—	—
98-99—Vancouver	NHL	82	8	10	18	209	-25	2	0	—	—	—	—	—
99-00—Vancouver	NHL	60	11	2	13	136	-9	1	0	—	—	—	—	—
00-01—Vancouver	NHL	79	9	19	28	145	0	0	0	4	0	0	0	0
NHL Totals (8 years)		468	48	52	100	1427	-66	3	0	12	0	0	0	2

BRATHWAITE, FRED   G   BLUES

PERSONAL: Born November 24, 1972, in Ottawa. ... 5-7/175. ... Catches left. ... Name pronounced BRATH-wayt.

TRANSACTIONS/CAREER NOTES: Signed as non-drafted free agent by Edmonton Oilers (October 6, 1993). ... Signed as free agent by Calgary Flames (January 7, 1999). ... Injured groin (November 7, 2000); missed two games. ... Traded by Flames with C Daniel Tkaczuk, RW Sergei Varlamov and ninth-round pick (C Grant Jacobsen) in 2001 draft to St. Louis Blues for G Roman Turek and fourth-round pick (LW Egor Shastin) in 2001 draft (June 23, 2001).

MISCELLANEOUS: Holds Calgary Flames all-time record for goals-against average (2.54). ... Stopped a penalty shot attempt (vs. Ziggy Palffy, April 7, 2001).

STATISTICAL NOTES: Led OHL with 3.31 goals-against average and four shutouts (1991-92).

Season Team	League	REGULAR SEASON								PLAYOFFS						
		Gms.	Min	W	L	T	GA	SO	Avg.	Gms.	Min.	W	L	GA	SO	Avg.
89-90—Oshawa	OHL	20	901	11	2	1	45	1	3.00	10	451	4	2	22	0	*2.93
90-91—Oshawa	OHL	39	1986	25	6	3	112	1	3.38	13	677	*9	2	43	0	3.81
91-92—Oshawa	OHL	24	1248	12	7	2	81	§0	§3.89	—	—	—	—	—	—	—
—London	OHL	23	1325	23	10	4	61	§4	§2.76	10	615	5	5	36	0	3.51
92-93—Det. Jr. Red Wings	OHL	37	2192	23	10	4	134	0	3.67	15	858	9	6	48	1	3.36
93-94—Cape Breton	AHL	2	119	1	1	0	6	0	3.03	—	—	—	—	—	—	—
—Edmonton	NHL	19	982	3	10	3	58	0	3.54	—	—	—	—	—	—	—
94-95—Edmonton	NHL	14	601	2	5	1	40	0	3.99	—	—	—	—	—	—	—
95-96—Cape Breton	AHL	31	1699	12	16	0	110	1	3.88	—	—	—	—	—	—	—
—Edmonton	NHL	7	293	0	2	0	12	0	2.46	—	—	—	—	—	—	—
96-97—Manitoba	IHL	58	2945	22	22	‡5	167	1	3.40	—	—	—	—	—	—	—
97-98—Manitoba	IHL	51	2737	23	18	‡4	138	1	3.03	2	73	0	1	4	0	3.29
98-99—Canadian nat'l team	Int'l	24	989	6	8	3	47	...	2.85	—	—	—	—	—	—	—
—Calgary	NHL	28	1663	11	9	7	68	1	2.45	—	—	—	—	—	—	—
99-00—Calgary	NHL	61	3448	25	25	7	158	5	2.75	—	—	—	—	—	—	—
—Saint John	AHL	2	120	2	0	0	4	0	2.00	—	—	—	—	—	—	—
00-01—Calgary	NHL	49	2742	15	17	10	106	5	2.32	—	—	—	—	—	—	—
NHL Totals (6 years)		178	9729	56	68	28	442	11	2.73							

BRENDL, PAVEL   RW   RANGERS

PERSONAL: Born March 23, 1981, in Opocno, Czechoslovakia. ... 6-1/197. ... Shoots right.

TRANSACTIONS/CAREER NOTES: Selected by New York Rangers in first round (first Rangers pick, fourth overall) of NHL entry draft (June 26, 1999).

HONORS: Won Bob Clarke Trophy (1998-99). ... Won Jim Piggott Memorial Trophy (1998-99). ... Won Can.HL Rookie of the Year Award (1998-99). ... Won Can.HL Top Draft Prospect Award (1998-99). ... Named to WHL (East) All-Star first team (1998-99). ... Named to Can.HL All-Star first team (1998-99). ... Named to WHL (East) All-Star second team (1999-2000).

Season Team	League	REGULAR SEASON								PLAYOFFS				
		Gms.	G	A	Pts.	PIM	+/-	PP	SH	Gms.	G	A	Pts.	PIM
96-97—Olomouc	Czech. Jrs.	40	35	17	52	...	...	...	...	—	—	—	—	—
97-98—Olomouc	Czech. Jrs.	38	29	23	52	...	...	...	...	—	—	—	—	—
—Olomouc	Czech Dv.II	12	1	1	2	...	...	...	...	—	—	—	—	—
98-99—Calgary	WHL	68	*73	61	*134	40	...	...	...	20	*21	†25	*46	18
99-00—Calgary	WHL	61	*59	52	111	94	...	...	...	10	7	12	19	8
—Hartford	AHL	—	—	—	—	—	...	...	...	2	0	0	0	0
00-01—Calgary	WHL	49	40	35	75	66	...	...	...	10	7	6	13	6

BRENNAN, RICH   D   KINGS

PERSONAL: Born November 26, 1972, in Schenectady, N.Y. ... 6-2/205. ... Shoots right.

TRANSACTIONS/CAREER NOTES: Selected by Quebec Nordiques in third round (third Nordiques pick, 56th overall) of NHL entry draft (June 22, 1991). ... Nordiques franchise moved to Colorado and renamed Avalanche for 1995-96 season (June 21, 1995). ... Signed as free agent by San Jose Sharks (July 9, 1997). ... Traded by Sharks to New York Rangers for G Jason Muzzatti (March 24, 1998). ... Signed as free agent by Nashville Predators (September 1999). ... Claimed by Los Angeles Kings from Predators in NHL waiver draft (September 27, 1999).

HONORS: Named to Hockey East All-Star first team (1993-94).

Season Team	League	REGULAR SEASON								PLAYOFFS				
		Gms.	G	A	Pts.	PIM	+/-	PP	SH	Gms.	G	A	Pts.	PIM
88-89—Albany Academy	N.Y. H.S.	25	17	30	47	57	...	...	...	—	—	—	—	—
89-90—Tabor Academy	Mass. H.S.	33	12	14	26	68	...	...	...	—	—	—	—	—
90-91—Tabor Academy	Mass. H.S.	34	13	37	50	91	...	...	...	—	—	—	—	—
91-92—Boston University	Hockey East	31	4	13	17	54	...	...	...	—	—	—	—	—
92-93—Boston University	Hockey East	40	9	11	20	68	...	...	...	—	—	—	—	—
93-94—Boston University	Hockey East	41	8	27	35	82	...	...	...	—	—	—	—	—
94-95—Boston University	Hockey East	31	5	23	28	56	...	...	...	—	—	—	—	—
95-96—Brantford	Col.HL	5	1	2	3	2	...	...	...	—	—	—	—	—

Season Team	League	REGULAR SEASON								PLAYOFFS				
		Gms.	G	A	Pts.	PIM	+/-	PP	SH	Gms.	G	A	Pts.	PIM
96-97—Hershey	AHL	74	11	45	56	88	...	...	...	23	2	†16	18	22
—Colorado	NHL	2	0	0	0	0	0	0	0	—	—	—	—	—
97-98—Kentucky	AHL	42	11	17	28	71				—	—	—	—	—
—San Jose	NHL	11	1	2	3	2	-4	1	0	—	—	—	—	—
—Hartford	AHL	9	2	4	6	12	...	...	...	—	—	—	—	—
98-99—Hartford	AHL	47	4	24	28	42	...	...	...	—	—	—	—	—
—New York Rangers	NHL	24	1	3	4	23	-4	0	0	—	—	—	—	—
99-00—Lowell	AHL	67	15	30	45	110	...	...	...	7	1	5	6	0
00-01—Lowell	AHL	69	10	31	41	146	...	...	...	—	—	—	—	—
—Los Angeles	NHL	2	0	0	0	0	-3	0	0	—	—	—	—	—
NHL Totals (4 years)		39	2	5	7	25	-11	1	0					

BREWER, ERIC — D — OILERS — B

PERSONAL: Born April 17, 1979, in Verona, B.C. ... 6-3/220. ... Shoots left.
TRANSACTIONS/CAREER NOTES: Selected by New York Islanders in first round (second Islanders pick, fifth overall) of NHL entry draft (June 21, 1997). ... Strained Achilles' tendon (April 8, 1999); missed four games. ... Injured toe (November 19, 1999); missed six games. ... Traded by Islanders with LW Josh Green and second-round pick (LW Brad Winchester) in 2000 draft to Edmonton Oilers for D Roman Hamrlik (June 24, 2000). ... Strained buttocks (October 6, 2000); missed four games.
HONORS: Named to WHL (West) All-Star second team (1997-98).

Season Team	League	REGULAR SEASON								PLAYOFFS				
		Gms.	G	A	Pts.	PIM	+/-	PP	SH	Gms.	G	A	Pts.	PIM
95-96—Prince George	WHL	63	4	10	14	25	...	...	...	—	—	—	—	—
96-97—Prince George	WHL	71	5	24	29	81	...	...	...	15	2	4	6	16
97-98—Prince George	WHL	34	5	28	33	45	...	...	...	11	4	2	6	19
98-99—New York Islanders	NHL	63	5	6	11	32	-14	2	0	—	—	—	—	—
99-00—New York Islanders	NHL	26	0	2	2	20	-11	0	0	—	—	—	—	—
—Lowell	AHL	25	2	2	4	26	...	...	...	7	0	0	0	0
00-01—Edmonton	NHL	77	7	14	21	53	15	2	0	6	1	5	6	2
NHL Totals (3 years)		166	12	22	34	105	-10	4	0	6	1	5	6	2

BRIERE, DANIEL — C — COYOTES

PERSONAL: Born October 6, 1977, in Gatineau, Que. ... 5-10/181. ... Shoots left.
TRANSACTIONS/CAREER NOTES: Selected by Phoenix Coyotes in first round (second Coyotes pick, 24th overall) of NHL entry draft (June 22, 1996). ... Separated shoulder (March 21, 1998); missed five games. ... Suffered concussion (October 6, 1998); missed first two games of season. ... Strained groin (September 25, 2000); missed first game of season.
HONORS: Won Michel Bergeron Trophy (1994-95). ... Won Marcel Robert Trophy (1994-95). ... Won Jean Beliveau Trophy (1995-96). ... Named to QMJHL All-Star second team (1995-96). ... Won Frank J. Selke Trophy (1996-97). ... Named to Can.HL All-Star second team (1996-97). ... Named to AHL All-Star first team (1997-98). ... Won Dudley (Red) Garrett Trophy (1997-98).

Season Team	League	REGULAR SEASON								PLAYOFFS				
		Gms.	G	A	Pts.	PIM	+/-	PP	SH	Gms.	G	A	Pts.	PIM
94-95—Drummondville	QMJHL	72	51	72	123	54	...	...	...	—	—	—	—	—
95-96—Drummondville	QMJHL	67	*67	*96	*163	84	...	...	...	6	6	12	18	8
96-97—Drummondville	QMJHL	59	52	78	130	86	...	...	...	8	7	7	14	14
97-98—Springfield	AHL	68	36	56	92	42	...	...	...	4	1	2	3	4
—Phoenix	NHL	5	1	0	1	2	1	0	0	—	—	—	—	—
98-99—Las Vegas	IHL	1	1	1	2	0	...	...	...	—	—	—	—	—
—Phoenix	NHL	64	8	14	22	30	-3	2	0	—	—	—	—	—
—Springfield	AHL	13	2	6	8	20	...	...	...	3	0	1	1	2
99-00—Springfield	AHL	58	29	42	71	56	...	...	...	—	—	—	—	—
—Phoenix	NHL	13	1	1	2	0	0	0	0	1	0	0	0	0
00-01—Phoenix	NHL	30	11	4	15	12	-2	9	0	—	—	—	—	—
—Springfield	AHL	30	21	25	46	30	...	...	...	—	—	—	—	—
NHL Totals (4 years)		112	21	19	40	44	-4	11	0	1	0	0	0	0

BRIMANIS, ARIS — D

PERSONAL: Born March 14, 1972, in Cleveland. ... 6-3/195. ... Shoots right. ... Full Name: Aris Aldis Brimanis. ... Name pronounced AIR-ihz brih-MAN-ihz.
TRANSACTIONS/CAREER NOTES: Selected by Philadelphia Flyers in fourth round (third Flyers pick, 86th overall) of NHL entry draft (June 22, 1991). ... Signed as free agent by New York Islanders (August 12, 1999).

Season Team	League	REGULAR SEASON								PLAYOFFS				
		Gms.	G	A	Pts.	PIM	+/-	PP	SH	Gms.	G	A	Pts.	PIM
88-89—Culver Military	Indiana H.S.	38	10	13	23	24	...	...	...	—	—	—	—	—
89-90—Culver Military	Indiana H.S.	37	15	10	25	52	...	...	...	—	—	—	—	—
90-91—Bowling Green	CCHA	38	3	6	9	42	...	...	...	—	—	—	—	—
91-92—Bowling Green	CCHA	32	2	9	11	38	...	...	...	—	—	—	—	—
92-93—Brandon	WHL	71	8	50	58	110	...	...	...	4	2	1	3	12
93-94—Philadelphia	NHL	1	0	0	0	0	-1	0	0	—	—	—	—	—
—Hershey	AHL	75	8	15	23	65	...	...	...	11	2	3	5	12
94-95—Hershey	AHL	76	8	17	25	68	...	...	...	6	1	1	2	14
95-96—Hershey	AHL	54	9	22	31	64	...	...	...	5	1	2	3	4
—Philadelphia	NHL	17	0	2	2	12	-1	0	0	—	—	—	—	—

Season Team	League	REGULAR SEASON								PLAYOFFS				
		Gms.	G	A	Pts.	PIM	+/-	PP	SH	Gms.	G	A	Pts.	PIM
96-97—Philadelphia	AHL	65	14	18	32	69	...	...	...	10	2	2	4	13
—Philadelphia	NHL	3	0	1	1	0	0	0	0	—	—	—	—	—
97-98—Philadelphia	AHL	30	1	11	12	26	...	...	...	—	—	—	—	—
—Michigan	IHL	35	3	9	12	24	...	...	...	4	1	0	1	4
98-99—Grand Rapids	IHL	66	16	21	37	70	...	...	...	—	—	—	—	—
—Fredericton	AHL	8	2	4	6	6	...	...	...	15	3	10	13	18
99-00—Kansas City	IHL	46	5	17	22	28	...	...	...	—	—	—	—	—
—New York Islanders	NHL	18	2	1	3	6	-5	2	0	—	—	—	—	—
00-01—Chicago	IHL	20	2	2	4	14	...	...	...	16	3	1	4	8
—New York Islanders	NHL	56	0	8	8	26	-12	0	0	—	—	—	—	—
NHL Totals (5 years)		95	2	12	14	44	-19	2	0					

B

BRIND'AMOUR, ROD   C   HURRICANES

PERSONAL: Born August 9, 1970, in Ottawa. ... 6-1/200. ... Shoots left. ... Full Name: Rod Jean Brind'Amour. ... Name pronounced BRIHN-duh-MOHR.

TRANSACTIONS/CAREER NOTES: Selected by St. Louis Blues in first round (first Blues pick, ninth overall) of NHL entry draft (June 11, 1988). ... Traded by Blues with C Dan Quinn to Philadelphia Flyers for C Ron Sutter and D Murray Baron (September 22, 1991). ... Lacerated elbow (November 19, 1992); missed two games. ... Bruised right hand (February 20, 1993); missed one game. ... Fractured foot (September 25, 1999) and underwent surgery; missed first 34 games of season. ... Traded by Flyers with G Jean-Marc Pelletier and second-round pick (traded to Colorado) in 2000 draft to Carolina Hurricanes for rights to C Keith Primeau and fifth-round pick (traded to New York Islanders) in 2000 draft (January 23, 2000). ... Suffered concussion (April 3, 2000); missed one game. ... Injured groin (December 27, 2000); missed three games.

HONORS: Named CCHA Rookie of the Year (1988-89). ... Named to CCHA All-Rookie team (1988-89). ... Named to NHL All-Rookie team (1989-90). ... Played in NHL All-Star Game (1992).

STATISTICAL PLATEAUS: Three-goal games: 1992-93 (1), 2000-01 (1). Total: 2.

Season Team	League	REGULAR SEASON								PLAYOFFS				
		Gms.	G	A	Pts.	PIM	+/-	PP	SH	Gms.	G	A	Pts.	PIM
87-88—Notre Dame	SJHL	56	46	61	107	136	...	...	...	—	—	—	—	—
88-89—Michigan State	CCHA	42	27	32	59	63	...	...	...	—	—	—	—	—
—St. Louis	NHL	—	—	—	—	—	—	—	—	5	2	0	2	4
89-90—St. Louis	NHL	79	26	35	61	46	23	10	0	12	5	8	13	6
90-91—St. Louis	NHL	78	17	32	49	93	2	4	0	13	2	5	7	10
91-92—Philadelphia	NHL	80	33	44	77	100	-3	8	4	—	—	—	—	—
92-93—Philadelphia	NHL	81	37	49	86	89	-8	13	4	—	—	—	—	—
93-94—Philadelphia	NHL	84	35	62	97	85	-9	14	1	—	—	—	—	—
94-95—Philadelphia	NHL	48	12	27	39	33	-4	4	1	15	6	9	15	8
95-96—Philadelphia	NHL	82	26	61	87	110	20	4	4	12	2	5	7	6
96-97—Philadelphia	NHL	82	27	32	59	41	2	8	2	19	13	8	21	10
97-98—Philadelphia	NHL	82	36	38	74	54	-2	10	2	5	2	2	4	7
—Can. Olympic team	Int'l	6	1	2	3	0	...	...	...	—	—	—	—	—
98-99—Philadelphia	NHL	82	24	50	74	47	3	10	0	6	1	3	4	0
99-00—Philadelphia	NHL	12	5	3	8	4	-1	4	0	—	—	—	—	—
—Carolina	NHL	33	4	10	14	22	-12	0	1	—	—	—	—	—
00-01—Carolina	NHL	79	20	36	56	47	-7	5	1	6	1	3	4	6
NHL Totals (13 years)		902	302	479	781	771	4	94	20	93	34	43	77	57

BRISEBOIS, PATRICE   D   CANADIENS

PERSONAL: Born January 27, 1971, in Montreal. ... 6-1/203. ... Shoots right. ... Name pronounced pa-TREEZ BREES-bwah.

TRANSACTIONS/CAREER NOTES: Selected by Montreal Canadiens in second round (second Canadiens pick, 30th overall) of NHL entry draft (June 17, 1989). ... Sprained right ankle (October 10, 1992); missed two games. ... Suffered charley horse (December 16, 1992); missed two games. ... Injured knee (October 30, 1993); missed 10 games. ... Suffered hairline fracture of ankle (December 1, 1993); missed 14 games. ... Sprained ankle (February 21, 1994); missed seven games. ... Suffered acute herniated disc (April 3, 1995); missed 12 games. ... Injured rib cage (November 1, 1995). ... Sprained back (February 17, 1996); missed four games. ... Suffered mild disc irritation (March 25, 1996); missed last nine games of regular season. ... Separated shoulder (January 4, 1997); missed 27 games. ... Strained shoulder (March 22, 1997); missed four games. ... Injured rib (April 10, 1997); missed remainder of regular season and two playoff games. ... Sprained knee (April 15, 1998); missed three games. ... Injured back (October 2, 1998); missed first six games of season. ... Separated shoulder (December 23, 1998); missed nine games. ... Sprained knee (February 20, 1999); missed one game. ... Injured shoulder (March 11, 1999); missed 12 games. ... Injured back prior to start of 1999-2000 season; missed first 27 games of season. ... Injured back (January 28, 2001); missed five games.

HONORS: Won Michael Bossy Trophy (1988-89). ... Named to QMJHL All-Star second team (1989-90). ... Won Can.HL Defenseman of the Year Award (1990-91). ... Won Emile (Butch) Bouchard Trophy (1990-91). ... Named to QMJHL All-Star first team (1990-91). ... Named to Memorial Cup All-Star team (1990-91).

MISCELLANEOUS: Member of Stanley Cup championship team (1993).

Season Team	League	REGULAR SEASON								PLAYOFFS				
		Gms.	G	A	Pts.	PIM	+/-	PP	SH	Gms.	G	A	Pts.	PIM
87-88—Laval	QMJHL	48	10	34	44	95	...	...	...	6	0	2	2	2
88-89—Laval	QMJHL	50	20	45	65	95	...	...	...	17	8	14	22	45
89-90—Laval	QMJHL	56	18	70	88	108	...	...	...	13	7	9	16	26
90-91—Montreal	NHL	10	0	2	2	4	1	0	0	—	—	—	—	—
—Drummondville	QMJHL	54	17	44	61	72	...	...	...	14	6	18	24	49
91-92—Fredericton	AHL	53	12	27	39	51	...	...	...	—	—	—	—	—
—Montreal	NHL	26	2	8	10	20	9	0	0	11	2	4	6	6
92-93—Montreal	NHL	70	10	21	31	79	6	4	0	20	0	4	4	18
93-94—Montreal	NHL	53	2	21	23	63	5	1	0	7	0	4	4	6

Season Team	League	REGULAR SEASON								PLAYOFFS				
		Gms.	G	A	Pts.	PIM	+/-	PP	SH	Gms.	G	A	Pts.	PIM
94-95—Montreal	NHL	35	4	8	12	26	-2	0	0	—	—	—	—	—
95-96—Montreal	NHL	69	9	27	36	65	10	3	0	6	1	2	3	6
96-97—Montreal	NHL	49	2	13	15	24	-7	0	0	3	1	1	2	24
97-98—Montreal	NHL	79	10	27	37	67	16	5	0	10	1	0	1	0
98-99—Montreal	NHL	54	3	9	12	28	-8	1	0	—	—	—	—	—
99-00—Montreal	NHL	54	10	25	35	18	-1	5	0	—	—	—	—	—
00-01—Montreal	NHL	77	15	21	36	28	-31	11	0	—	—	—	—	—
NHL Totals (11 years)		576	67	182	249	422	-2	30	0	57	5	15	20	60

BROCHU, MARTIN   G   WILD

B

PERSONAL: Born March 10, 1973, in Anjou, Que. ... 6-0/199. ... Catches left. ... Name pronounced MAHR-tai broh-SHOO.
TRANSACTIONS/CAREER NOTES: Signed as free agent by Montreal Canadiens (September 22, 1992). ... Traded by Canadiens to Washington Capitals for future considerations (March 15, 1996). ... Signed as free agent by Minnesota Wild (July 9, 2001).
HONORS: Won Les Cunningham Plaque (1999-2000). ... Won Baz Bastien Trophy (1999-2000). ... Named to AHL All-Star first team (1999-2000).

Season Team	League	REGULAR SEASON								PLAYOFFS						
		Gms.	Min	W	L	T	GA	SO	Avg.	Gms.	Min.	W	L	GA	SO	Avg.
91-92—Granby	QMJHL	52	2772	15	29	2	218	0	4.72	—	—	—	—	—	—	—
92-93—Hull	QMJHL	29	1453	9	15	1	137	0	5.66	2	69	0	1	7	0	6.09
93-94—Fredericton	AHL	32	1506	10	11	3	76	2	3.03	—	—	—	—	—	—	—
94-95—Fredericton	AHL	44	2475	18	18	4	145	0	3.52	—	—	—	—	—	—	—
95-96—Fredericton	AHL	17	985	6	8	2	70	0	4.26	—	—	—	—	—	—	—
—Wheeling	ECHL	19	1060	10	6	2	51	1	2.89	—	—	—	—	—	—	—
—Portland	AHL	5	286	2	2	1	15	0	3.15	12	700	7	4	28	‡2	*2.40
96-97—Portland	AHL	55	2962	23	17	7	150	2	3.04	5	324	2	3	13	0	2.41
97-98—Portland	AHL	37	1926	16	14	1	96	2	2.99	6	297	3	2	16	0	3.23
98-99—Utah	IHL	5	298	1	3	‡1	13	0	2.62	—	—	—	—	—	—	—
—Portland	AHL	20	1164	6	10	3	57	2	2.94	—	—	—	—	—	—	—
—Washington	NHL	2	120	0	2	0	6	0	3.00	—	—	—	—	—	—	—
99-00—Portland	AHL	54	3192	32	15	6	116	4	2.18	2	80	0	2	7	0	5.25
00-01—Saint John	AHL	55	3049	27	19	5	132	2	2.60	19	1148	*14	4	39	*4	2.04
NHL Totals (1 year)		2	120	0	2	0	6	0	3.00							

BRODEUR, MARTIN   G   DEVILS

PERSONAL: Born May 6, 1972, in Montreal. ... 6-2/205. ... Catches left. ... Son of Denis Brodeur, goaltender with bronze medal-winning Canadian Olympic Team (1956). ... Name pronounced MAHR-tan broh-DOOR.
TRANSACTIONS/CAREER NOTES: Selected by New Jersey Devils in first round (first Devils pick, 20th overall) of NHL entry draft (June 16, 1990). ... Suffered from the flu (December 30, 1997); missed two games.
HONORS: Named to QMJHL All-Star second team (1991-92). ... Won Calder Memorial Trophy (1993-94). ... Named to NHL All-Rookie team (1993-94). ... Played in NHL All-Star Game (1996-2001). ... Shared William M. Jennings Trophy with Mike Dunham (1996-1997). ... Named to NHL All-Star second team (1996-97). ... Won William M. Jennings Trophy (1997-98). ... Named to THE SPORTING NEWS All-Star first team (2000-01).
RECORDS: Holds NHL single-season record for most minutes played by goaltender—4,434 (1995-96). ... Shares NHL single-season playoff record for most wins by goaltender—16 (1995 and 2000). ... Shares NHL single-season playoff record for most shutouts—4 (2000).
MISCELLANEOUS: Member of Stanley Cup championship teams (1995 and 2000). ... Holds New Jersey Devils franchise all-time records for most games played by a goalie (519), most wins (286), most shutouts (51) and goals-against average (2.21). ... Stopped a penalty shot attempt (vs. Valeri Zelepukin, October 30, 1999; vs. Dave Scatchard, February 27, 2001). ... Allowed a penalty shot goal (vs. Frederick Olausson, November 24, 1999).
STATISTICAL NOTES: Scored a goal (April 7, 1997, vs. Montreal (playoffs) and February 15, 2000, vs. Philadelphia).

Season Team	League	REGULAR SEASON								PLAYOFFS						
		Gms.	Min	W	L	T	GA	SO	Avg.	Gms.	Min.	W	L	GA	SO	Avg.
89-90—St. Hyacinthe	QMJHL	42	2333	23	13	2	156	0	4.01	12	678	5	7	46	0	4.07
90-91—St. Hyacinthe	QMJHL	52	2946	22	24	4	162	2	3.30	4	232	0	4	16	0	4.14
91-92—St. Hyacinthe	QMJHL	48	2846	27	16	4	161	2	3.39	5	317	2	3	14	0	2.65
—New Jersey	NHL	4	179	2	1	0	10	0	3.35	1	32	0	1	3	0	5.63
92-93—Utica	AHL	32	1952	14	13	5	131	0	4.03	4	258	1	3	18	0	4.19
93-94—New Jersey	NHL	47	2625	27	11	8	105	3	2.40	17	1171	8	†9	38	1	1.95
94-95—New Jersey	NHL	40	2184	19	11	6	89	3	2.45	*20	*1222	*16	4	34	*3	*1.67
95-96—New Jersey	NHL	77	*4434	34	†30	12	173	6	2.34	—	—	—	—	—	—	—
96-97—New Jersey	NHL	67	3838	37	14	13	120	*10	*1.88	10	659	5	5	19	2	1.73
97-98—New Jersey	NHL	70	4128	*43	17	8	130	10	1.89	6	366	2	4	12	0	1.97
98-99—New Jersey	NHL	*70	*4239	*39	21	10	162	4	2.29	7	425	3	4	20	0	2.82
99-00—New Jersey	NHL	72	4312	*43	20	8	161	6	2.24	†23	*1450	*16	7	39	2	*1.61
00-01—New Jersey	NHL	72	4297	*42	17	11	166	9	2.32	*25	*1505	15	*10	*52	†4	2.07
NHL Totals (9 years)		519	30236	286	142	76	1116	51	2.21	109	6830	65	44	217	12	1.91

BROUSSEAU, PAUL   RW   PANTHERS

PERSONAL: Born September 18, 1973, in Pierrefonds, Que. ... 6-2/200. ... Shoots right. ... Name pronounced broo-SOH.
TRANSACTIONS/CAREER NOTES: Selected by Quebec Nordiques in second round (second Nordiques pick, 28th overall) of NHL entry draft (June 20, 1992). ... Nordiques franchise moved to Colorado and renamed Avalanche for 1995-96 season (June 21, 1995). ... Signed as free agent by Tampa Bay Lightning (September 5, 1996). ... Selected by Nashville Predators in NHL expansion draft (June 26, 1998). ... Signed as free agent by Florida Panthers (August 3, 2000).
HONORS: Won Michael Bossy Trophy (1991-92). ... Named to AHL All-Star second team (1997-98).

Season Team	League	REGULAR SEASON								PLAYOFFS				
		Gms.	G	A	Pts.	PIM	+/-	PP	SH	Gms.	G	A	Pts.	PIM
89-90—Chicoutimi	QMJHL	57	17	24	41	32	...	...	...	7	0	3	3	0
90-91—Trois-Rivieres	QMJHL	67	30	66	96	48	...	...	...	6	3	2	5	2
91-92—Hull	QMJHL	57	35	61	96	54	...	...	...	6	3	5	8	10
92-93—Hull	QMJHL	59	27	48	75	49	...	...	...	10	7	8	15	6
93-94—Cornwall	AHL	69	18	26	44	35	...	...	...	1	0	0	0	0
94-95—Cornwall	AHL	57	19	17	36	29	...	...	...	7	2	1	3	10
95-96—Cornwall	AHL	63	21	22	43	60	...	...	...	8	4	0	4	2
—Colorado	NHL	8	1	1	2	2	1	0	0	—	—	—	—	—
96-97—Adirondack	AHL	66	35	31	66	25	...	...	...	4	1	2	3	0
—Tampa Bay	NHL	6	0	0	0	0	-4	0	0	—	—	—	—	—
97-98—Adirondack	AHL	67	45	20	65	18	...	...	...	3	1	1	2	0
—Tampa Bay	NHL	11	0	2	2	27	0	0	0	—	—	—	—	—
98-99—Milwaukee	IHL	5	1	1	2	2	...	...	...	—	—	—	—	—
—Hershey	AHL	39	11	21	32	15	...	...	...	5	1	1	2	0
99-00—Louisville	AHL	36	19	24	43	10	...	...	...	4	1	1	2	12
00-01—Louisville	AHL	73	29	39	68	21	...	...	...	—	—	—	—	—
—Florida	NHL	1	0	0	0	0	0	0	0	—	—	—	—	—
NHL Totals (4 years)		26	1	3	4	29	-3	0	0					

BROWN, BRAD   D   RANGERS

PERSONAL: Born December 27, 1975, in Baie Verte, Ont. ... 6-4/218. ... Shoots right.

TRANSACTIONS/CAREER NOTES: Selected by Montreal Canadiens in first round (first Canadiens pick, 18th overall) of NHL entry draft (June 28, 1994). ... Suffered back spasms (October 17, 1998); missed three games. ... Traded by Canadiens with G Jocelyn Thibault and D Dave Manson to Chicago Blackhawks for G Jeff Hackett, D Eric Weinrich, D Alain Nasreddine and fourth-round pick (D Chris Dyment) in 1999 draft (November 16, 1998). ... Suffered sore back (December 17, 1998); missed two games. ... Bruised foot (March 12, 1999); missed two games. ... Bruised wrist (October 4, 1999); missed three games. ... Lacerated hand (December 17, 1999); missed two games. ... Injured hand (December 26, 1999); missed 10 games. ... Bruised left hand (March 15, 2000); missed four games. ... Traded by Blackhawks with LW Michal Grosek to New York Rangers for future considerations (October 5, 2000). ... Injured shoulder (January 4, 2001); missed 10 games. ... Fractured right foot (February 23, 2001); missed remainder of season.

Season Team	League	REGULAR SEASON								PLAYOFFS				
		Gms.	G	A	Pts.	PIM	+/-	PP	SH	Gms.	G	A	Pts.	PIM
91-92—North Bay	OHL	49	2	9	11	170	...	...	...	18	0	6	6	43
92-93—North Bay	OHL	61	4	9	13	228	...	...	...	2	0	2	2	13
93-94—North Bay	OHL	66	8	24	32	196	...	...	...	18	3	12	15	33
94-95—North Bay	OHL	64	8	38	46	172	...	...	...	6	1	4	5	8
95-96—Barrie	OHL	27	3	13	16	82	...	...	...	—	—	—	—	—
—Fredericton	AHL	38	0	3	3	148	...	...	...	10	2	1	3	6
96-97—Fredericton	AHL	64	3	7	10	368	...	...	...	4	0	0	0	29
—Montreal	NHL	8	0	0	0	22	-1	0	0	—	—	—	—	—
97-98—Fredericton	AHL	64	1	8	9	297	...	...	...	—	—	—	—	—
98-99—Montreal	NHL	5	0	0	0	21	0	0	0	—	—	—	—	—
—Chicago	NHL	61	1	7	8	184	-4	0	0	—	—	—	—	—
99-00—Chicago	NHL	57	0	9	9	134	-1	0	0	—	—	—	—	—
00-01—New York Rangers	NHL	48	1	3	4	107	0	0	0	—	—	—	—	—
NHL Totals (4 years)		179	2	19	21	468	-6	0	0					

BROWN, CURTIS   C/LW   SABRES

PERSONAL: Born February 12, 1976, in Unity, Sask. ... 6-0/190. ... Shoots left.

TRANSACTIONS/CAREER NOTES: Selected by Buffalo Sabres in second round (second Sabres pick, 43rd overall) of NHL entry draft (June 28, 1994). ... Injured ankle prior to 1995-96 season; missed two games. ... Bruised knee (February 11, 1999); missed two games. ... Bruised knee (March 27, 1999); missed one game. ... Missed first game of 1999-2000 season due to contract dispute. ... Suffered concussion (October 22, 1999); missed one game. ... Suffered from the flu (February 10, 2000); missed five games. ... Injured knee (December 23, 2000); missed eight games. ... Suffered back spasms (January 30, 2001); missed four games.

HONORS: Named to Can.HL All-Star second team (1994-95). ... Named to WHL (East) All-Star first team (1994-95). ... Named to WHL (Central/East) All-Star second team (1995-96).

STATISTICAL NOTES: Tied for NHL lead in game-tying goals with 3 (1998-99).

Season Team	League	REGULAR SEASON								PLAYOFFS				
		Gms.	G	A	Pts.	PIM	+/-	PP	SH	Gms.	G	A	Pts.	PIM
92-93—Moose Jaw	WHL	71	13	16	29	30	...	...	...	—	—	—	—	—
93-94—Moose Jaw	WHL	72	27	38	65	82	...	...	...	—	—	—	—	—
94-95—Moose Jaw	WHL	70	51	53	104	63	...	...	...	10	8	7	15	20
—Buffalo	NHL	1	1	1	2	2	2	0	0	—	—	—	—	—
95-96—Buffalo	NHL	4	0	0	0	0	0	0	0	—	—	—	—	—
—Moose Jaw	WHL	25	20	18	38	30	...	...	...	—	—	—	—	—
—Prince Albert	WHL	19	12	21	33	8	...	...	...	18	10	15	25	18
—Rochester	AHL	—	—	—	—	—	...	...	...	12	0	1	1	2
96-97—Buffalo	NHL	28	4	3	7	18	4	0	0	—	—	—	—	—
—Rochester	AHL	51	22	21	43	30	...	...	...	10	4	6	10	4
97-98—Buffalo	NHL	63	12	12	24	34	11	1	1	13	1	2	3	10
98-99—Buffalo	NHL	78	16	31	47	56	23	5	1	21	7	6	13	10
99-00—Buffalo	NHL	74	22	29	51	42	19	5	0	5	1	3	4	6
00-01—Buffalo	NHL	70	10	22	32	34	15	2	1	13	5	0	5	8
NHL Totals (7 years)		318	65	98	163	186	74	13	3	52	14	11	25	34

BROWN, DOUG — RW

PERSONAL: Born June 12, 1964, in New Haven, Conn. ... 5-11/185. ... Shoots right. ... Full Name: Douglas Allen Brown. ... Brother of Greg Brown, defenseman with three NHL teams (1990-91 and 1992-93 through 1994-95).

TRANSACTIONS/CAREER NOTES: Signed as non-drafted free agent by New Jersey Devils (August 6, 1986). ... Fractured nose (October 1988). ... Injured back (November 25, 1989). ... Bruised right foot (February 13, 1991). ... Suspended by Devils for refusing to report to Utica (November 20, 1992). ... Reinstated by Devils (November 30, 1992). ... Signed as free agent by Pittsburgh Penguins (September 29, 1993). ... Injured leg (March 26, 1994); missed seven games. ... Selected by Detroit Red Wings from Penguins in waiver draft (January 18, 1995); Penguins claimed C Micah Aivazoff as compensation. ... Suffered from the flu (December 2, 1995); missed one game. ... Separated shoulder (April 18, 1998); missed 11 playoff games ... Selected by Nashville Predators in NHL expansion draft (June 26, 1998). ... Traded by Predators to Red Wings for C Petr Sykora, third- (traded to Edmonton) and fourth-round (RW Alexandre Krevsun) picks in 1999 draft (July 14, 1998). ... Fractured foot (October 30, 1999); missed 10 games. ... Reinjured foot (November 26, 1999); missed seven games. ... Strained hip flexor (January 19, 2000); missed three games.

HONORS: Named to NCAA All-America (East) second team (1984-85 and 1985-86). ... Named to Hockey East All-Star second team (1984-85 and 1985-86).

MISCELLANEOUS: Member of Stanley Cup championship team (1997 and 1998). ... Scored on a penalty shot (vs. Ken Wregget, November 23, 1991).

Season Team	League	Gms.	G	A	Pts.	PIM	+/-	PP	SH	Gms.	G	A	Pts.	PIM
82-83—Boston College	ECAC	22	9	8	17	0	...	...	...	—	—	—	—	—
83-84—Boston College	ECAC	38	11	10	21	6	...	...	...	—	—	—	—	—
84-85—Boston College	Hockey East	45	37	31	68	10	...	...	...	—	—	—	—	—
85-86—Boston College	Hockey East	38	16	40	56	16	...	...	...	—	—	—	—	—
86-87—Maine	AHL	73	24	34	58	15	...	...	...	—	—	—	—	—
—New Jersey	NHL	4	0	1	1	0	-4	0	0	—	—	—	—	—
87-88—New Jersey	NHL	70	14	11	25	20	7	1	4	19	5	1	6	6
—Utica	AHL	2	0	2	2	2	...	...	...	—	—	—	—	—
88-89—New Jersey	NHL	63	15	10	25	15	-7	4	0	—	—	—	—	—
—Utica	AHL	4	1	4	5	0	...	...	...	—	—	—	—	—
89-90—New Jersey	NHL	69	14	20	34	16	7	1	3	6	0	1	1	2
90-91—New Jersey	NHL	58	14	16	30	4	18	0	2	7	2	2	4	2
91-92—New Jersey	NHL	71	11	17	28	27	17	1	2	—	—	—	—	—
92-93—New Jersey	NHL	15	0	5	5	2	3	0	0	—	—	—	—	—
—Utica	AHL	25	11	17	28	8	...	...	...	—	—	—	—	—
93-94—Pittsburgh	NHL	77	18	37	55	18	19	2	0	6	0	0	0	2
94-95—Detroit	NHL	45	9	12	21	16	14	1	1	18	4	8	12	2
95-96—Detroit	NHL	62	12	15	27	4	10	0	1	13	3	3	6	4
96-97—Detroit	NHL	49	6	7	13	8	-3	1	0	14	3	3	6	2
97-98—Detroit	NHL	80	19	23	42	12	17	6	1	9	4	2	6	0
98-99—Detroit	NHL	80	9	19	28	42	5	3	1	10	2	2	4	4
99-00—Detroit	NHL	51	10	8	18	12	8	0	1	3	0	1	1	0
00-01—Detroit	NHL	60	9	13	22	14	0	2	1	4	0	0	0	2
NHL Totals (15 years)		854	160	214	374	210	112	22	17	109	23	23	46	26

BROWN, MIKE — LW — CANUCKS

PERSONAL: Born April 27, 1979, in Surrey, B.C. ... 6-4/205. ... Shoots left.

TRANSACTIONS/CAREER NOTES: Selected by Florida Panthers in first round (first Panthers pick, 20th overall) of NHL entry draft (June 21, 1997). ... Traded by Panthers with D Ed Jovanovski, G Kevin Weekes, C Dave Gagner and first-round pick in 2000 (C Nathan Smith) draft to Vancouver Canucks for RW Pavel Bure, D Bret Hedican, D Brad Ference and third-round pick (RW Robert Fried) in 2000 draft (January 17, 1999).

HONORS: Won Jim Piggott Memorial Trophy (1995-96).

Season Team	League	Gms.	G	A	Pts.	PIM	+/-	PP	SH	Gms.	G	A	Pts.	PIM
94-95—Merritt	BCJHL	45	3	4	7	128	...	...	...	—	—	—	—	—
95-96—Red Deer	WHL	62	4	5	9	125	...	...	...	10	0	0	0	18
96-97—Red Deer	WHL	70	19	13	32	243	...	...	...	16	1	2	3	47
97-98—Kamloops	WHL	72	23	33	56	305	...	...	...	7	2	1	3	22
98-99—Kamloops	WHL	69	28	16	44	*285	...	...	...	15	3	7	10	68
99-00—Syracuse	AHL	71	13	18	31	284	...	...	...	4	0	0	0	0
00-01—Kansas City	IHL	78	14	13	27	214	...	...	...	—	—	—	—	—
—Vancouver	NHL	1	0	0	0	5	0	0	0	—	—	—	—	—
NHL Totals (1 year)		1	0	0	0	5	0	0	0					

BROWN, SEAN — D — OILERS

PERSONAL: Born November 5, 1976, in Oshawa, Ont. ... 6-3/205. ... Shoots left.

TRANSACTIONS/CAREER NOTES: Selected by Boston Bruins in first round (second Bruins pick, 21st overall) of NHL entry draft (July 8, 1995). ... Traded by Boston Bruins with RW Mariusz Czerkawski and first-round pick (D Mattieu Descoteaux) in 1996 draft to Edmonton Oilers for G Bill Ranford (January 11, 1996). ... Suspended three games and fined $1,000 by NHL for high-sticking incident (November 13, 1998).

HONORS: Named to OHL All-Star second team (1995-96).

Season Team	League	REGULAR SEASON								PLAYOFFS				
		Gms.	G	A	Pts.	PIM	+/-	PP	SH	Gms.	G	A	Pts.	PIM
92-93—Oshawa	Tier II Jr. A	15	0	1	1	9	...	...	...	—	—	—	—	—
93-94—Wellington	OJHL	32	5	14	19	165	...	...	...	—	—	—	—	—
—Belleville	OHL	28	1	2	3	53	...	...	...	8	0	0	0	17
94-95—Belleville	OHL	58	2	16	18	200	...	...	...	16	4	2	6	67
95-96—Belleville	OHL	37	10	23	33	150	...	...	...	—	—	—	—	—
—Sarnia	OHL	26	8	17	25	112	...	...	...	10	1	0	1	38
96-97—Hamilton	AHL	61	1	7	8	238	...	...	...	19	1	0	1	47
—Edmonton	NHL	5	0	0	0	4	-1	0	0	—	—	—	—	—
97-98—Edmonton	NHL	18	0	1	1	43	-1	0	0	—	—	—	—	—
—Hamilton	AHL	43	4	6	10	166	...	...	...	6	0	2	2	38
98-99—Edmonton	NHL	51	0	7	7	188	1	0	0	1	0	0	0	10
99-00—Edmonton	NHL	72	4	8	12	192	1	0	0	3	0	0	0	23
00-01—Edmonton	NHL	62	2	3	5	110	2	0	0	—	—	—	—	—
NHL Totals (5 years)		208	6	19	25	537	2	0	0	4	0	0	0	33

BRULE, STEVE RW RED WINGS

PERSONAL: Born January 15, 1975, in Montreal. ... 6-0/200. ... Shoots right. ... Name pronounced broo-LAY.

TRANSACTIONS/CAREER NOTES: Selected by New Jersey Devils in sixth round (sixth Devils pick, 143rd overall) of NHL entry draft (June 26, 1993). ... Signed as free agent by Detroit Red Wings (July 20, 2000).

HONORS: Won Michel Bergeron Trophy (1992-93). ... Named to QMJHL All-Rookie team (1992-93). ... Named to QMJHL All-Star second team (1994-95).

MISCELLANEOUS: Member of Stanley Cup championship team (2000).

Season Team	League	REGULAR SEASON								PLAYOFFS				
		Gms.	G	A	Pts.	PIM	+/-	PP	SH	Gms.	G	A	Pts.	PIM
92-93—St. Jean	QMJHL	70	33	47	80	46	...	...	...	4	0	0	0	9
93-94—St. Jean	QMJHL	66	41	64	105	46	...	...	...	5	2	1	3	0
94-95—St. Jean	QMJHL	69	44	64	108	42	...	...	...	7	3	4	7	8
—Albany	AHL	3	1	4	5	0	...	...	...	14	9	5	14	4
95-96—Albany	AHL	80	30	21	51	37	...	...	...	4	0	0	0	17
96-97—Albany	AHL	79	28	48	76	27	...	...	...	16	7	7	14	12
97-98—Albany	AHL	80	34	43	77	34	...	...	...	13	8	3	11	4
98-99—Albany	AHL	78	32	52	84	35	...	...	...	5	3	1	4	4
99-00—Albany	AHL	75	30	46	76	18	...	...	...	5	1	2	3	0
—New Jersey	NHL	—	—	—	—	—				1	0	0	0	0
00-01—Manitoba	IHL	78	21	48	69	22	...	...		13	3	10	13	12
NHL Totals (1 year)		0	0	0	0	0	0	0	0	1	0	0	0	0

BRUNET, BENOIT LW CANADIENS

PERSONAL: Born August 24, 1968, in Montreal. ... 5-11/198. ... Shoots left. ... Name pronounced BEHN-wah broo-NAY.

TRANSACTIONS/CAREER NOTES: Selected by Montreal Canadiens in second round (second Canadiens pick, 27th overall) of NHL entry draft (June 21, 1986). ... Injured ankle (September 1987). ... Tore left knee ligaments (September 24, 1990); missed 24 games. ... Fractured ankle (December 4, 1991). ... Sprained left knee (November 21, 1992); missed 10 games. ... Fractured thumb (January 22, 1993); missed 14 games. ... Bruised knee (November 17, 1993); missed four games. ... Suffered mild concussion (February 2, 1994); missed six games. ... Suffered sore throat (April 8, 1994); missed three games. ... Pulled hamstring (March 18, 1995); missed two games. ... Bruised right knee (May 3, 1995); missed one game. ... Sprained wrist (November 11, 1995); missed five games. ... Reinjured wrist (November 25, 1995); missed 18 games. ... Sprained back (January 11, 1996); missed 28 games. ... Bruised thigh (October 24, 1996); missed one game. ... Fractured left leg (November 2, 1996); missed 21 games. ... Suffered from tonsillitis (December 21, 1996); missed one game. ... Fractured hand (January 20, 1997); missed 19 games. ... Strained shoulder (October 23, 1997); missed three games. ... Suffered concussion (November 22, 1997); missed eight games. ... Suffered from the flu (December 22, 1997); missed one game. ... Strained rib (March 19, 1998); missed two games. ... Strained rib (November 27, 1998); missed four games. ... Injured groin (February 11, 1999); missed one game. ... Injured back (March 2, 1999); missed four games. ... Reinjured back (March 22, 1999); missed 12 games. ... Injured back prior to start of 1999-2000 season; missed first 27 games of season. ... Suffered injury to face (February 14, 2000); missed three games. ... Suffered back spasms (March 18, 2000); missed two games. ... Strained groin (November 8, 2000); missed 11 games. ... Sprained medial collateral ligament in knee (December 15, 2000); missed 36 games.

HONORS: Named to QMJHL All-Star second team (1986-87). ... Named to AHL All-Star first team (1988-89).

MISCELLANEOUS: Member of Stanley Cup championship team (1993).

Season Team	League	REGULAR SEASON								PLAYOFFS				
		Gms.	G	A	Pts.	PIM	+/-	PP	SH	Gms.	G	A	Pts.	PIM
85-86—Hull	QMJHL	71	33	37	70	81	...	...	...	—	—	—	—	—
86-87—Hull	QMJHL	60	43	67	110	105	...	...	...	6	7	5	12	8
87-88—Hull	QMJHL	62	54	89	143	131	...	...	...	10	3	10	13	11
88-89—Montreal	NHL	2	0	1	1	0	0	0	0	—	—	—	—	—
—Sherbrooke	AHL	73	41	*76	117	95	...	...	...	6	2	0	2	4
89-90—Sherbrooke	AHL	72	32	35	67	82	...	...	...	12	8	7	15	20
90-91—Fredericton	AHL	24	13	18	31	16	...	...	...	6	5	6	11	2
—Montreal	NHL	17	1	3	4	0	-1	0	0	—	—	—	—	—
91-92—Fredericton	AHL	6	7	9	16	27	...	...	...	—	—	—	—	—
—Montreal	NHL	18	4	6	10	14	4	0	0	—	—	—	—	—
92-93—Montreal	NHL	47	10	15	25	19	13	0	0	20	2	8	10	8
93-94—Montreal	NHL	71	10	20	30	20	14	0	3	7	1	4	5	16
94-95—Montreal	NHL	45	7	18	25	16	7	1	1	—	—	—	—	—
95-96—Montreal	NHL	26	7	8	15	17	-4	3	1	3	0	2	2	0
—Fredericton	AHL	3	2	1	3	6	...	...	...	—	—	—	—	—
96-97—Montreal	NHL	39	10	13	23	14	6	2	0	4	1	3	4	4
97-98—Montreal	NHL	68	12	20	32	61	11	1	2	8	1	0	1	4
98-99—Montreal	NHL	60	14	17	31	31	-1	4	2	—	—	—	—	—
99-00—Montreal	NHL	50	14	15	29	13	3	6	1	—	—	—	—	—
00-01—Montreal	NHL	35	3	11	14	12	-4	0	0	—	—	—	—	—
NHL Totals (12 years)		478	92	147	239	217	48	17	10	42	5	17	22	32

BRUNETTE, ANDREW   LW   WILD

PERSONAL: Born August 24, 1973, in Sudbury, Ont. ... 6-1/210. ... Shoots left. ... Name pronounced broo-NEHT.
TRANSACTIONS/CAREER NOTES: Selected by Washington Capitals in sixth round (sixth Capitals pick, 174th overall) of NHL entry draft (June 26, 1993). ... Selected by Nashville Predators in NHL expansion draft (June 26, 1998). ... Traded by Predators to Atlanta Thrashers for fifth-round pick (C Matt Hendricks) in 2000 draft (June 21, 1999). ... Suffered concussion (January 13, 2001); missed four games. ... Bruised thigh (February 15, 2001); missed one game. ... Signed as free agent by Minnesota Wild (July 6, 2001).
HONORS: Won Eddie Powers Memorial Trophy (1992-93). ... Named to Can.HL All-Star second team (1992-93). ... Named to OHL All-Star first team (1992-93).

		REGULAR SEASON								PLAYOFFS				
Season Team	League	Gms.	G	A	Pts.	PIM	+/-	PP	SH	Gms.	G	A	Pts.	PIM
90-91—Owen Sound	OHL	63	15	20	35	15	...	...	...					
91-92—Owen Sound	OHL	66	51	47	98	42	...	...	...	5	5	0	5	8
92-93—Owen Sound	OHL	66	*62	*100	*162	91	...	...	...	8	8	6	14	16
93-94—Portland	AHL	23	9	11	20	10	...	...	...	2	0	1	1	0
—Hampton	ECHL	20	12	18	30	32	...	...	...	7	7	6	13	18
—Providence	AHL	3	0	0	0	0	...	...	...					
94-95—Portland	AHL	79	30	50	80	53	...	...	...	7	3	3	6	10
95-96—Portland	AHL	69	28	66	94	125	...	...	...	20	11	18	29	15
—Washington	NHL	11	3	3	6	5	0	0	0	6	1	3	4	0
96-97—Portland	AHL	50	22	51	73	48	...	...	...	5	1	2	3	0
—Washington	NHL	23	4	7	11	12	-3	2	0	—	—	—	—	—
97-98—Portland	AHL	43	21	46	67	64	...	...	...	10	1	11	12	12
—Washington	NHL	28	11	12	23	12	2	4	0	—	—	—	—	—
98-99—Nashville	NHL	77	11	20	31	26	-10	7	0	—	—	—	—	—
99-00—Atlanta	NHL	81	23	27	50	30	-32	9	0	—	—	—	—	—
00-01—Atlanta	NHL	77	15	44	59	26	-5	6	0	—	—	—	—	—
NHL Totals (6 years)		297	67	113	180	111	-48	28	0	6	1	3	4	0

BRYLIN, SERGEI   C   DEVILS

PERSONAL: Born January 13, 1974, in Moscow, U.S.S.R. ... 5-10/190. ... Shoots left. ... Name pronounced BREE-lihn.
TRANSACTIONS/CAREER NOTES: Selected by New Jersey Devils in second round (second Devils pick, 42nd overall) of NHL entry draft (June 20, 1992). ... Suffered from tonsillitis (May 3, 1995); missed last game of season. ... Fractured hand (November 16, 1995); missed 13 games. ... Injured knee (September 19, 1997); missed 19 games. ... Injured knee (November 28, 2000); missed one game. ... Injured knee (February 22, 2001); missed five games.
MISCELLANEOUS: Member of Stanley Cup championship team (1995 and 2000).

		REGULAR SEASON								PLAYOFFS				
Season Team	League	Gms.	G	A	Pts.	PIM	+/-	PP	SH	Gms.	G	A	Pts.	PIM
90-91—CSKA Moscow	USSR					Statistics unavailable.								
91-92—CSKA Moscow	CIS	44	1	6	7	4	...	...	...	—	—	—	—	—
92-93—CSKA Moscow	CIS	42	5	4	9	36	...	...	...	—	—	—	—	—
93-94—CSKA Moscow	CIS	39	4	6	10	36	...	...	...	3	0	1	1	0
—Russian Penguins	IHL	13	4	5	9	18	...	...	...	—	—	—	—	—
94-95—Albany	AHL	63	19	35	54	78	...	...	...	—	—	—	—	—
—New Jersey	NHL	26	6	8	14	8	12	0	0	12	1	2	3	4
95-96—New Jersey	NHL	50	4	5	9	26	-2	0	0	—	—	—	—	—
96-97—New Jersey	NHL	29	2	2	4	20	-13	0	0	—	—	—	—	—
—Albany	AHL	43	17	24	41	38	...	...	...	16	4	8	12	12
97-98—New Jersey	NHL	18	2	3	5	0	4	0	0	—	—	—	—	—
—Albany	AHL	44	21	22	43	60	...	...	...	—	—	—	—	—
98-99—New Jersey	NHL	47	5	10	15	28	8	3	0	5	3	1	4	4
99-00—New Jersey	NHL	64	9	11	20	20	0	1	0	17	3	5	8	0
00-01—New Jersey	NHL	75	23	29	52	24	25	3	1	20	3	4	7	6
NHL Totals (7 years)		309	51	68	119	126	34	7	1	54	10	12	22	14

BRYZGALOV, ILJA   G   MIGHTY DUCKS

PERSONAL: Born June 22, 1980, in Togliatti, U.S.S.R. ... 6-3/196. ... Catches left.
TRANSACTIONS/CAREER NOTES: Selected by Mighty Ducks of Anaheim in second round (second Mighty Ducks pick, 44th overall) of NHL entry draft (June 24, 2000).

		REGULAR SEASON								PLAYOFFS						
Season Team	League	Gms.	Min	W	L	T	GA	SO	Avg.	Gms.	Min.	W	L	GA	SO	Avg.
97-98—Lada-2 Togliatti	Rus. Div. III	8	480	...	...	...	28	...	3.50	—	—	—	—	—	—	—
98-99—Lada-2 Togliatti	Rus.-4	20	1200	...	...	...	43	...	2.15	—	—	—	—	—	—	—
99-00—Spartak Moscow	Russian	9	500	...	...	...	21	...	2.52	—	—	—	—	—	—	—
—Lada Togliatti	Russian	14	796	...	...	...	18	3	1.36	7	407	...	...	10	1	1.47
00-01—Lada Togliatti	Russian	34	1992	...	...	...	61	*8	1.84	5	249	...	...	8	0	1.93

BUCHBERGER, KELLY   RW   KINGS

PERSONAL: Born December 2, 1966, in Langenburg, Sask. ... 6-2/210. ... Shoots left. ... Full Name: Kelly Michael Buchberger. ... Name pronounced BUK-buhr-guhr.
TRANSACTIONS/CAREER NOTES: Selected by Edmonton Oilers in ninth round (eighth Oilers pick, 188th overall) of NHL entry draft (June 15, 1985). ... Suspended six games by AHL for leaving bench to fight (March 30, 1988). ... Fractured right ankle (March 1989). ... Dislocated left

shoulder (March 13, 1990). ... Reinjured shoulder (May 4, 1990). ... Strained shoulder (April 7, 1993); missed one game. ... Fractured right forearm (January 5, 1999); missed 30 games. ... Selected by Atlanta Thrashers in NHL expansion draft (June 25, 1999). ... Traded by Thrashers with RW Nelson Emerson to Los Angeles Kings for RW Donald Audette and D Frantisek Kaberle (March 13, 2000).

MISCELLANEOUS: Member of Stanley Cup championship team (1987 and 1990). ... Captain of Edmonton Oilers (1995-96 through 1998-99). ... Captain of Atlanta Thrashers (1999-March 13, 2000). ... Holds Edmonton Oilers all-time record for most penalty minutes (1,747).

STATISTICAL PLATEAUS: Three-goal games: 1992-93 (1).

		REGULAR SEASON								PLAYOFFS				
Season Team	League	Gms.	G	A	Pts.	PIM	+/-	PP	SH	Gms.	G	A	Pts.	PIM
83-84—Melville	SAJHL	60	14	11	25	139	...	...	...	—	—	—	—	—
84-85—Moose Jaw	WHL	51	12	17	29	114	...	...	...	—	—	—	—	—
85-86—Moose Jaw	WHL	72	14	22	36	206	...	...	...	13	11	4	15	37
86-87—Nova Scotia	AHL	70	12	20	32	257	...	...	...	5	0	1	1	23
—Edmonton	NHL	—	—	—	—	—				3	0	1	1	5
87-88—Edmonton	NHL	19	1	0	1	81	-1	0	0	—	—	—	—	—
—Nova Scotia	AHL	49	21	23	44	206	...	...	...	2	0	0	0	11
88-89—Edmonton	NHL	66	5	9	14	234	-14	1	0	—	—	—	—	—
89-90—Edmonton	NHL	55	2	6	8	168	-8	0	0	19	0	5	5	13
90-91—Edmonton	NHL	64	3	1	4	160	-6	0	0	12	2	1	3	25
91-92—Edmonton	NHL	79	20	24	44	157	9	0	4	16	1	4	5	32
92-93—Edmonton	NHL	83	12	18	30	133	-27	1	2	—	—	—	—	—
93-94—Edmonton	NHL	84	3	18	21	199	-20	0	0	—	—	—	—	—
94-95—Edmonton	NHL	48	7	17	24	82	0	2	1	—	—	—	—	—
95-96—Edmonton	NHL	82	11	14	25	184	-20	0	2	—	—	—	—	—
96-97—Edmonton	NHL	81	8	30	38	159	4	0	0	12	5	2	7	16
97-98—Edmonton	NHL	82	6	17	23	122	-10	1	1	12	1	2	3	25
98-99—Edmonton	NHL	52	4	4	8	68	-6	0	2	4	0	0	0	0
99-00—Atlanta	NHL	68	5	12	17	139	-34	0	0	—	—	—	—	—
—Los Angeles	NHL	13	2	1	3	13	-2	0	0	4	0	0	0	4
00-01—Los Angeles	NHL	82	6	14	20	75	-10	0	0	8	1	0	1	2
NHL Totals (15 years)		958	95	185	280	1974	-145	5	12	90	10	15	25	122

BULIS, JAN   C   CANADIENS

PERSONAL: Born March 18, 1978, in Pardubice, Czechoslovakia. ... 6-1/201. ... Shoots left. ... Name pronounced YAHN BOO-lihsh.

TRANSACTIONS/CAREER NOTES: Selected by Washington Capitals in second round (third Capitals pick, 43rd overall) of NHL entry draft (June 22, 1996). ... Suffered concussion (November 11, 1997); missed one game. ... Sprained ankle prior to 1998-99 season; missed first 13 games of season. ... Sprained ankle (November 21, 1998); missed 15 games. ... Suffered back spasms (November 11, 1999); missed one game. ... Bruised ribs (November 20, 1999); missed two games. ... Injured groin (December 15, 1999); missed three games. ... Separated shoulder (February 26, 2000); missed remainder of season. ... Fractured right thumb (November 22, 2000); missed 18 games. ... Traded by Capitals with RW Richard Zednik and first-round pick (C Alexander Perezhogin) in 2001 draft to Montreal Canadiens for C Trevor Linden, RW Dainius Zubrus and second-round pick (traded to Tampa Bay) in 2001 draft (March 13, 2001).

		REGULAR SEASON								PLAYOFFS				
Season Team	League	Gms.	G	A	Pts.	PIM	+/-	PP	SH	Gms.	G	A	Pts.	PIM
94-95—Kelowna	BCJHL	51	23	25	48	36	...	...	...	17	7	9	16	...
95-96—Barrie	OHL	59	29	30	59	22	...	...	...	7	2	3	5	2
96-97—Barrie	OHL	64	42	61	103	42	...	...	...	9	3	7	10	10
97-98—Washington	NHL	48	5	11	16	18	-5	0	0	—	—	—	—	—
—Portland	AHL	3	1	4	5	12	...	...	...	—	—	—	—	—
—Kingston	OHL	2	0	1	1	0	...	...	...	12	8	10	18	12
98-99—Washington	NHL	38	7	16	23	6	3	3	0	—	—	—	—	—
—Cincinnati	IHL	10	2	2	4	14	...	...	...	—	—	—	—	—
99-00—Washington	NHL	56	9	22	31	30	7	0	0	—	—	—	—	—
00-01—Washington	NHL	39	5	13	18	26	0	1	0	—	—	—	—	—
—Portland	AHL	4	0	2	2	0	...	...	...	—	—	—	—	—
—Montreal	NHL	12	0	5	5	0	-1	0	0	—	—	—	—	—
NHL Totals (4 years)		193	26	67	93	80	4	4	0					

BURE, PAVEL   RW   PANTHERS

PERSONAL: Born March 31, 1971, in Moscow, U.S.S.R. ... 5-10/189. ... Shoots left. ... Brother of Valeri Bure, right winger, Florida Panthers. ... Name pronounced PA-vihl BOOR-ay. ... Nickname: The Russian Rocket.

TRANSACTIONS/CAREER NOTES: Selected by Vancouver Canucks in sixth round (fourth Canucks pick, 113th overall) of NHL entry draft (June 17, 1989). ... Strained groin (October 24, 1993); missed eight games. ... Fined $500 by NHL for hitting another player with flagrant elbow (May 6, 1994). ... Played in Europe during 1994-95 NHL lockout. ... Suffered injury (March 17, 1995); missed two games. ... Tore knee ligament (November 9, 1995); missed remainder of season. ... Suspended one game and fined $1,000 by NHL for forearm blow (December 6, 1996). ... Suffered whiplash (March 3, 1997); missed remainder of season. ... Missed first 43 games of 1998-99 season due to contract dispute. ... Traded by Canucks with D Bret Hedican, D Brad Ference and third-round pick (Robert Fried) in 2000 draft to Florida Panthers for D Ed Jovanovski, G Kevin Weekes, C Dave Gagner, C Mike Brown and first-round pick (C Nathan Smith) in 2000 draft (January 17, 1999). ... Strained right knee (February 5, 1999); missed eight games. ... Reinjured knee (March 3, 1999); missed final 21 games of season. ... Strained groin (October 12, 1999); missed five games. ... Fractured finger (November 9, 1999); missed three games.

HONORS: Named Soviet League Rookie of the Year (1988-89). ... Won Calder Memorial Trophy (1991-92). ... Named to THE SPORTING NEWS All-Star second team (1993-94 and 2000-01). ... Played in NHL All-Star Game (1993, 1994, 1997, 1998, 2000 and 2001). ... Named to NHL All-Star first team (1993-94). ... Named to play in NHL All-Star Game (1996); replaced due to injury. ... Named All-Star Game Most Valuable Player (2000). ... Named to NHL All-Star second team (1999-2000 and 2000-01). ... Won Maurice "Rocket" Richard Trophy (1999-2000 and 2000-01).

MISCELLANEOUS: Member of silver-medal-winning Russian Olympic team (1998). ... Scored on a penalty shot (vs. Rick Tabaracci, February 28, 1992; vs. Mike Vernon, November 12, 1997; vs. Nikolai Khabibulin, January 26, 1998; vs. Damian Rhodes, February 28, 1998; vs. Chris Osgood, February 26, 1999). ... Failed to score on a penalty shot (vs. John Vanbiesbrouck, February 17, 1992; vs. Kelly Hrudey, October 6, 1993; vs. Mike Richter, June 7, 1994 (playoffs)).

STATISTICAL NOTES: Led NHL with 329 shots (1997-98), with 360 (1999-2000) and with 384 (2000-01). ... Led NHL with 14 game-winning goals (1999-2000). ... Tied for NHL lead in game-tying goals with three (2000-01).
STATISTICAL PLATEAUS: Three-goal games: 1992-93 (1), 1993-94 (3), 1994-95 (1), 1997-98 (3), 1998-99 (2), 1999-00 (3), 2000-01 (3). Total: 16. ... Four-goal games: 1992-93 (1), 1999-00 (1), 2000-01 (1). Total: 3. ... Total hat tricks: 19.

Season Team	League	REGULAR SEASON								PLAYOFFS				
		Gms.	G	A	Pts.	PIM	+/-	PP	SH	Gms.	G	A	Pts.	PIM
87-88—CSKA Moscow	USSR	5	1	1	2	0	...	...	...	—	—	—	—	—
88-89—CSKA Moscow	USSR	32	17	9	26	8	...	...	...	—	—	—	—	—
89-90—CSKA Moscow	USSR	46	14	11	25	22	...	...	...	—	—	—	—	—
90-91—CSKA Moscow	USSR	46	35	12	47	24	...	...	...	—	—	—	—	—
91-92—Vancouver	NHL	65	34	26	60	30	0	7	3	13	6	4	10	14
92-93—Vancouver	NHL	83	60	50	110	69	35	13	†7	12	5	7	12	8
93-94—Vancouver	NHL	76	*60	47	107	86	1	†25	4	24	*16	15	31	40
94-95—Landshut	Germany	1	3	0	3	2	...	...	...	—	—	—	—	—
—Spartak Moscow	CIS	1	2	0	2	2	...	...	...	—	—	—	—	—
—Vancouver	NHL	44	20	23	43	47	-8	6	2	11	7	6	13	10
95-96—Vancouver	NHL	15	6	7	13	8	-2	1	1	—	—	—	—	—
96-97—Vancouver	NHL	63	23	32	55	40	-14	4	1	—	—	—	—	—
97-98—Vancouver	NHL	82	51	39	90	48	5	13	†6	—	—	—	—	—
—Russian Oly. team	Int'l	6	9	0	9	2	...	...	...	—	—	—	—	—
98-99—Florida	NHL	11	13	3	16	4	3	5	1	—	—	—	—	—
99-00—Florida	NHL	74	*58	36	94	16	25	11	2	4	1	3	4	2
00-01—Florida	NHL	82	*59	33	92	58	-2	19	5	—	—	—	—	—
NHL Totals (10 years)		595	384	296	680	406	43	104	32	64	35	35	70	74

BURE, VALERI RW PANTHERS

PERSONAL: Born June 13, 1974, in Moscow, U.S.S.R. ... 5-10/185. ... Shoots right. ... Brother of Pavel Bure, right winger, Florida Panthers. ... Name pronounced BOOR-ay.
TRANSACTIONS/CAREER NOTES: Selected by Montreal Canadiens in second round (second Canadiens pick, 33rd overall) of NHL entry draft (June 20, 1992). ... Bruised forearm (April 3, 1995); missed two games. ... Bruised kidney (October 19, 1996); missed 11 games. ... Bruised wrist (December 28, 1996); missed two games. ... Suffered concussion (January 4, 1997); missed five games. ... Bruised cheekbone (January 8, 1998); missed three games. ... Traded by Canadiens to Calgary Flames with fourth-round pick (C Shaun Sutter) in 1998 draft for D Zarley Zalapski and RW Jonas Hoglund (February 1, 1998). ... Suffered concussion (March 3, 1998); missed five games. ... Hyperextended shoulder (April 5, 1998); missed final seven games of season. ... Suffered concussion (January 10, 1999); missed two games. ... Traded by Flames with C Jason Wiemer to Florida Panthers for Rob Niedermayer and second-round pick (G Andrei Medvedev) in 2001 draft (June 23, 2001).
HONORS: Named to WHL (West) All-Star first team (1992-93). ... Named to WHL (West) All-Star second team (1993-94). ... Played in NHL All-Star Game (2000).
MISCELLANEOUS: Member of silver-medal-winning Russian Olympic team (1998).
STATISTICAL PLATEAUS: Three-goal games: 1997-98 (1).

Season Team	League	REGULAR SEASON								PLAYOFFS				
		Gms.	G	A	Pts.	PIM	+/-	PP	SH	Gms.	G	A	Pts.	PIM
90-91—CSKA Moscow	USSR	3	0	0	0	0	...	...	...	—	—	—	—	—
91-92—Spokane	WHL	53	27	22	49	78	...	...	...	10	11	6	17	10
92-93—Spokane	WHL	66	68	79	147	49	...	...	...	9	6	11	17	14
93-94—Spokane	WHL	59	40	62	102	48	...	...	...	3	5	3	8	2
94-95—Fredericton	AHL	45	23	25	48	32	...	...	...	—	—	—	—	—
—Montreal	NHL	24	3	1	4	6	-1	0	0	—	—	—	—	—
95-96—Montreal	NHL	77	22	20	42	28	10	5	0	6	0	1	1	6
96-97—Montreal	NHL	64	14	21	35	6	4	4	0	5	0	1	1	2
97-98—Montreal	NHL	50	7	22	29	33	-5	2	0	—	—	—	—	—
—Calgary	NHL	16	5	4	9	2	0	0	0	—	—	—	—	—
—Russian Oly. team	Int'l	6	1	0	1	0	...	...	...	—	—	—	—	—
98-99—Calgary	NHL	80	26	27	53	22	0	7	0	—	—	—	—	—
99-00—Calgary	NHL	82	35	40	75	50	-7	13	0	—	—	—	—	—
00-01—Calgary	NHL	78	27	28	55	26	-21	16	0	—	—	—	—	—
NHL Totals (7 years)		471	139	163	302	173	-20	47	0	11	0	2	2	8

BURKE, SEAN G COYOTES

PERSONAL: Born January 29, 1967, in Windsor, Ont. ... 6-4/210. ... Catches left. ... Name pronounced BUHRK.
TRANSACTIONS/CAREER NOTES: Selected by New Jersey Devils in second round (second Devils pick, 24th overall) of NHL entry draft (June 15, 1985). ... Injured groin (December 1988). ... Underwent arthroscopic surgery to right knee (September 5, 1989). ... Traded by Devils with D Eric Weinrich to Hartford Whalers for RW Bobby Holik, second-round pick (LW Jay Pandolfo) in 1993 draft and future considerations (August 28, 1992). ... Sprained ankle (December 27, 1992); missed seven games. ... Suffered back spasms (March 13, 1993); missed remainder of season. ... Pulled hamstring (September 29, 1993); missed seven games. ... Reinjured hamstring (October 27, 1993); missed 14 games. ... Suffered back spasms (December 23, 1993); missed one game. ... Strained groin (February 28, 1995); missed two games. ... Suffered back spasms (November 19, 1995); missed two games. ... Suffered back spasms (February 7, 1996); missed three games. ... Dislocated thumb (November 30, 1996); missed 19 games. ... Strained hip flexor (February 26, 1997); missed one game. ... Whalers franchise moved to North Carolina and renamed Carolina Hurricanes for 1997-98 season; NHL approved move on June 25, 1997. ... Traded by Hurricanes with LW Geoff Sanderson and D Enrico Ciccone to Vancouver Canucks for LW Martin Gelinas and G Kirk McLean (January 3, 1998). ... Traded by Canucks to Philadelphia Flyers for G Garth Snow (March 4, 1998). ... Suffered lower back spasms (March 8, 1998); missed six games. ... Signed as free agent by Florida Panthers (September 11, 1998). ... Strained hip flexor (April 10, 1999); missed final three games of season. ... Traded by Panthers with fifth-round pick (D Nate Kiser) in 2000 draft to Phoenix Coyotes for G Mikhail Shtalenkov and fourth-round pick (D Chris Eade) in 2000 draft (November 19, 1999). ... Suffered partially torn thumb ligament (November 26, 1999); missed 16 games. ... Strained hip flexor (January 12, 2000); missed one game. ... Injured groin (February 1, 2000); missed one game. ... Strained groin (March 1, 2000); missed one game. ... Injured elbow (November 30, 2000); missed one game. ... Bruised knee (February 11, 2001); missed two games. ... Strained groin (March 2, 2001); missed four games.
HONORS: Played in NHL All-Star Game (1989 and 2001). ... Named to THE SPORTING NEWS All-Star second team (2000-01).

MISCELLANEOUS: Member of silver-medal-winning Canadian Olympic team (1992). ... Holds Carolina Hurricanes franchise all-time record for most games played by a goaltender (281). ... Stopped a penalty shot attempt (vs. Luc Robitaille, February 2, 1989; vs. Michal Pivonka, January 21, 1995; vs. Wayne Presley, March 8, 1996; vs. Brian Bradley, April 3, 1996; vs. Kevin Stevens, March 22, 1998; vs. Terry Yake, November 18, 1999). ... Allowed a penalty shot goal (vs. Brad Isbister, January 10, 2000).

Season Team	League	REGULAR SEASON								PLAYOFFS						
		Gms.	Min	W	L	T	GA	SO	Avg.	Gms.	Min.	W	L	GA	SO	Avg.
83-84—St. Michael's H.S.	MTHL	25	1482	...	...	...	120	0	4.86	—						
84-85—Toronto	OHL	49	2987	25	21	3	211	0	4.24	5	266	1	3	25	0	5.64
85-86—Toronto	OHL	47	2840	16	27	3	†233	0	4.92	4	238	0	4	24	0	6.05
—Canadian nat'l team	Int'l	5	284	...	...	...	22	0	4.65	—						
86-87—Canadian nat'l team	Int'l	42	2550	27	13	2	130	0	3.06	—						
87-88—Canadian nat'l team	Int'l	37	1962	19	9	2	92	1	2.81	—						
—Can. Olympic team	Int'l	4	238	1	2	1	12	0	3.03	—						
—New Jersey	NHL	13	689	10	1	0	35	1	3.05	17	1001	9	8	*57	†1	3.42
88-89—New Jersey	NHL	62	3590	22	31	9	†230	3	3.84	—						
89-90—New Jersey	NHL	52	2914	22	22	6	175	0	3.60	2	125	0	2	8	0	3.84
90-91—New Jersey	NHL	35	1870	8	12	8	112	0	3.59	—						
91-92—Canadian nat'l team	Int'l	31	1721	18	6	4	75	1	2.61	—						
—Can. Olympic team	Int'l	7	429	5	2	0	17	0	2.38	—						
—San Diego	IHL	7	424	4	2	‡1	17	0	2.41	3	160	0	3	13	0	4.88
92-93—Hartford	NHL	50	2656	16	27	3	184	0	4.16	—						
93-94—Hartford	NHL	47	2750	17	24	5	137	2	2.99	—						
94-95—Hartford	NHL	42	2418	17	19	4	108	0	2.68	—						
95-96—Hartford	NHL	66	3669	28	28	6	190	4	3.11	—						
96-97—Hartford	NHL	51	2985	22	22	6	134	4	2.69	—						
97-98—Carolina	NHL	25	1415	7	11	5	66	1	2.80	—						
—Vancouver	NHL	16	838	2	9	4	49	0	3.51	—						
—Philadelphia	NHL	11	632	7	3	0	27	1	2.56	5	283	1	4	17	0	3.60
98-99—Florida	NHL	59	3402	21	24	14	151	3	2.66	—						
99-00—Florida	NHL	7	418	2	5	0	18	0	2.58	—						
—Phoenix	NHL	35	2074	17	14	3	88	3	2.55	5	296	1	4	16	0	3.24
00-01—Phoenix	NHL	62	3644	25	22	*13	138	4	2.27	—						
NHL Totals (13 years)		633	35964	243	274	86	1842	26	3.07	29	1705	11	18	98	1	3.45

BURT, ADAM — D — THRASHERS

PERSONAL: Born January 15, 1969, in Detroit. ... 6-2/205. ... Shoots left.

TRANSACTIONS/CAREER NOTES: Selected by Hartford Whalers in second round (second Whalers pick, 39th overall) of NHL entry draft (June 13, 1987). ... Separated left shoulder (September 13, 1988). ... Bruised hip (December 1989). ... Dislocated left shoulder (January 19, 1989). ... Tore right knee ligaments (February 16, 1991); missed remainder of season. ... Sprained left wrist (January 11, 1992); missed six games. ... Fractured bone in right foot (January 25, 1993); missed 13 games. ... Sprained shoulder (February 27, 1994); missed remainder of season. ... Strained groin (February 3, 1997); missed eight games. ... Sprained shoulder (March 5, 1997); missed three games. ... Whalers franchise moved to North Carolina and renamed Carolina Hurricanes for 1997-98 season; NHL approved move on June 25, 1997. ... Strained groin (October 5, 1998); missed first five games of season. ... Suffered back spasms (November 21, 1998); missed one game. ... Bruised shoulder (December 19, 1998); missed one game. ... Strained groin (February 10, 1999); missed one game. ... Traded by Hurricanes to Philadelphia Flyers for RW Andrei Kovalenko (March 6, 1999). ... Bruised right foot (December 18, 1999); missed one game. ... Suffered concussion (January 27, 2000); missed two games. ... Signed as free agent by Atlanta Thrashers (July 14, 2000). ... Fractured cheekbone (September 23, 2000); missed first six games of season. ... Suffered herniated disk in lower back (December 30, 2000); missed remainder of season.

HONORS: Named to OHL All-Star second team (1987-88).

MISCELLANEOUS: Captain of Hartford Whalers (1994-95).

Season Team	League	REGULAR SEASON								PLAYOFFS				
		Gms.	G	A	Pts.	PIM	+/-	PP	SH	Gms.	G	A	Pts.	PIM
85-86—North Bay	OHL	49	0	11	11	81	...	...	...	10	0	0	0	24
86-87—North Bay	OHL	57	4	27	31	138	...	...	...	24	1	6	7	68
87-88—North Bay	OHL	66	17	54	71	176	...	...	...	2	0	3	3	6
—Binghamton	AHL	—	—	—	—	—	...	...	...	2	1	1	2	0
88-89—North Bay	OHL	23	4	11	15	45	...	...	...	12	2	12	14	12
—Binghamton	AHL	5	0	2	2	13	...	...	...	—				
—Hartford	NHL	5	0	0	0	6	-1	0	0	—				
89-90—Hartford	NHL	63	4	8	12	105	3	1	0	2	0	0	0	0
90-91—Springfield	AHL	9	1	3	4	22	...	...	...	—				
—Hartford	NHL	42	2	7	9	63	-4	1	0	—				
91-92—Hartford	NHL	66	9	15	24	93	-16	4	0	2	0	0	0	0
92-93—Hartford	NHL	65	6	14	20	116	-11	0	0	—				
93-94—Hartford	NHL	63	1	17	18	75	-4	0	0	—				
94-95—Hartford	NHL	46	7	11	18	65	0	3	0	—				
95-96—Hartford	NHL	78	4	9	13	121	-4	0	0	—				
96-97—Hartford	NHL	71	2	11	13	79	-13	0	0	—				
97-98—Carolina	NHL	76	1	11	12	106	-6	0	1	—				
98-99—Carolina	NHL	51	0	3	3	46	3	0	0	—				
—Philadelphia	NHL	17	0	1	1	14	1	0	0	6	0	0	0	4
99-00—Philadelphia	NHL	67	1	6	7	45	-2	0	0	11	0	1	1	4
00-01—Atlanta	NHL	27	0	2	2	27	2	0	0	—				
NHL Totals (13 years)		737	37	115	152	961	-52	9	1	21	0	1	1	8

BUTENSCHON, SVEN — D — OILERS

PERSONAL: Born March 22, 1976, in Itzehoe, West Germany. ... 6-4/215. ... Shoots left. ... Name pronounced BOO-tihn-SHAHN.

TRANSACTIONS/CAREER NOTES: Selected by Pittsburgh Penguins in third round (third Penguins pick, 57th overall) of NHL entry draft (June 29, 1994). ... Suffered from the flu (November 7, 1997); missed two games. ... Injured shoulder (March 3, 2001); missed four games. ... Traded by Penguins to Edmonton Oilers for LW Dan LaCouture (March 13, 2001).

Season Team	League	REGULAR SEASON								PLAYOFFS				
		Gms.	G	A	Pts.	PIM	+/-	PP	SH	Gms.	G	A	Pts.	PIM
93-94—Brandon	WHL	70	3	19	22	51	...	...	...	4	0	0	0	6
94-95—Brandon	WHL	21	1	5	6	44	...	...	...	18	1	2	3	11
95-96—Brandon	WHL	70	4	37	41	99	...	...	...	19	1	12	13	18
96-97—Cleveland	IHL	75	3	12	15	68	...	...	...	10	0	1	1	4
97-98—Syracuse	AHL	65	14	23	37	66	...	...	...	5	1	2	3	0
—Pittsburgh	NHL	8	0	0	0	6	-1	0	0	—	—	—	—	—
98-99—Houston	IHL	57	1	4	5	81	...	...	...	—	—	—	—	—
—Pittsburgh	NHL	17	0	0	0	6	-7	0	0	—	—	—	—	—
99-00—Wilkes-Barre/Scranton	AHL	75	19	21	40	101	...	...	...	—	—	—	—	—
—Pittsburgh	NHL	3	0	0	0	0	3	0	0	—	—	—	—	—
00-01—Wilkes-Barre/Scranton	AHL	55	7	28	35	85	...	...	...	—	—	—	—	—
—Pittsburgh	NHL	5	0	1	1	2	1	0	0	—	—	—	—	—
—Edmonton	NHL	7	1	1	2	2	2	0	0	—	—	—	—	—
NHL Totals (4 years)		40	1	2	3	16	-2	0	0					

BUTSAYEV, YURI — C — RED WINGS

PERSONAL: Born October 11, 1978, in Togliatti, U.S.S.R. ... 6-1/183. ... Shoots left. ... Brother of Slava Butsayev, center with six NHL teams (1992-93 through 1999-2000).

TRANSACTIONS/CAREER NOTES: Selected by Detroit Red Wings in second round (first Red Wings pick, 49th overall) of NHL entry draft (June 21, 1997).

Season Team	League	REGULAR SEASON								PLAYOFFS				
		Gms.	G	A	Pts.	PIM	+/-	PP	SH	Gms.	G	A	Pts.	PIM
95-96—Lada Togliatti	CIS	1	0	0	0	0	...	...	...	—	—	—	—	—
—Lada-2 Togliatti	CIS Div. II	35	19	7	26		...	...	...	—	—	—	—	—
96-97—Lada Togliatti	Russian	42	13	11	24	38	...	...	...	11	2	2	4	8
97-98—Lada Togliatti	Russian	44	8	9	17	63	...	...	...	—	—	—	—	—
98-99—Lada Togliatti	Russian	39	10	7	17	55	...	...	...	7	1	2	3	14
—Dynamo Moscow	Russian	1	0	1	1	0	...	...	...	—	—	—	—	—
99-00—Detroit	NHL	57	5	3	8	12	-6	0	0	—	—	—	—	—
—Cincinnati	AHL	9	0	1	1	0	...	...	...	—	—	—	—	—
00-01—Detroit	NHL	15	1	1	2	4	-2	0	0	—	—	—	—	—
—Cincinnati	AHL	54	29	17	46	26	...	...	...	4	0	2	2	2
NHL Totals (2 years)		72	6	4	10	16	-8	0	0					

BUTURLIN, ALEXANDER — LW — CANADIENS

PERSONAL: Born September 3, 1981, in Moscow, U.S.S.R. ... 5-11/183. ... Shoots left.

TRANSACTIONS/CAREER NOTES: Selected by Montreal Canadiens in second round (first Canadiens pick, 39th overall) of NHL entry draft (June 26, 1999).

Season Team	League	REGULAR SEASON								PLAYOFFS				
		Gms.	G	A	Pts.	PIM	+/-	PP	SH	Gms.	G	A	Pts.	PIM
97-98—CSKA Moscow	Russian	2	0	0	0	0	...	...	...	—	—	—	—	—
—CSKA-2 Moscow	Rus. Div. III	50	12	15	27	46	...	...	...	—	—	—	—	—
98-99—CSKA Moscow	Russian	16	1	0	1	6	...	...	...	3	1	0	1	2
99-00—Sarnia	OHL	57	20	27	47	46	...	...	...	7	4	2	6	12
00-01—Sarnia	OHL	57	28	37	65	27	...	...	...	4	3	1	4	0

BUZEK, PETR — D — THRASHERS

PERSONAL: Born April 26, 1977, in Jihlava, Czechoslovakia. ... 6-0/215. ... Shoots left. ... Name pronounced BOO-zihk.

TRANSACTIONS/CAREER NOTES: Selected by Dallas Stars in third round (third Stars pick, 63rd overall) of NHL entry draft (July 8, 1995). ... Selected by Atlanta Thrashers in NHL expansion draft (June 25, 1999). ... Suffered from dehydration (October 26, 1999); missed two games. ... Suffered concussion (November 13, 1999); missed six games. ... Sprained shoulder (December 17, 1999); missed one game. ... Strained groin (January 21, 2000); missed four games. ... Sprained neck (October 11, 2000); missed 76 games.

HONORS: Played in NHL All-Star Game (2000).

Season Team	League	REGULAR SEASON								PLAYOFFS				
		Gms.	G	A	Pts.	PIM	+/-	PP	SH	Gms.	G	A	Pts.	PIM
93-94—Jihlava	Czech Rep.	29	6	16	22	...	...	...	...	—	—	—	—	—
—Dukla Jihlava	Czech Rep.	3	0	0	0	...	...	...	...	—	—	—	—	—
94-95—Dukla Jihlava	Czech Rep.	43	2	5	7	...	...	...	...	2	0	0	0	...
95-96—Jihlava	Czech Rep.						Did not play.							
96-97—Michigan	IHL	67	4	6	10	48	...	...	...	—	—	—	—	—
97-98—Michigan	IHL	60	10	15	25	58	...	...	...	2	0	1	1	17
—Dallas	NHL	2	0	0	0	2	1	0	0	—	—	—	—	—
98-99—Michigan	IHL	74	5	14	19	68	...	...	...	5	0	0	0	10
—Dallas	NHL	2	0	0	0	2	0	0	0	—	—	—	—	—
99-00—Atlanta	NHL	63	5	14	19	41	-22	3	0	—	—	—	—	—
00-01—Atlanta	NHL	5	0	0	0	8	2	0	0	—	—	—	—	—
NHL Totals (4 years)		72	5	14	19	53	-19	3	0					

B

BYLSMA, DAN   RW   MIGHTY DUCKS

PERSONAL: Born September 19, 1970, in Grand Haven, Mich. ... 6-2/212. ... Shoots left. ... Full Name: Daniel Brian Bylsma. ... Name pronounced BIGHLS-muh.

TRANSACTIONS/CAREER NOTES: Selected by Winnipeg Jets in fourth round (sixth Jets pick, 69th overall) of NHL entry draft (June 17, 1989). ... Signed as free agent by Los Angeles Kings (July 14, 1994). ... Injured knee (March 19, 1997); missed one game. ... Strained groin (April 3, 1997); missed one game. ... Signed as free agent by Mighty Ducks of Anaheim (July 13, 2000).

		REGULAR SEASON								PLAYOFFS				
Season Team	League	Gms.	G	A	Pts.	PIM	+/-	PP	SH	Gms.	G	A	Pts.	PIM
87-88—St. Mary's Jr. B	OHA	40	30	39	69	33	...	...	...	—	—	—	—	—
88-89—Bowling Green	CCHA	39	4	7	11	16	...	...	...	—	—	—	—	—
89-90—Bowling Green	CCHA	44	13	17	30	32	...	...	...	—	—	—	—	—
90-91—Bowling Green	CCHA	40	9	12	21	48	...	...	...	—	—	—	—	—
91-92—Bowling Green	CCHA	34	11	14	25	24	...	...	...	—	—	—	—	—
92-93—Rochester	AHL	2	0	1	1	0	...	...	...	—	—	—	—	—
—Greensboro	ECHL	60	25	35	60	66	...	...	...	1	0	1	1	10
93-94—Albany	AHL	3	0	1	1	2	...	...	...	—	—	—	—	—
—Moncton	AHL	50	12	16	28	25	...	...	...	21	3	4	7	31
—Greensboro	ECHL	25	14	16	30	52	...	...	...	—	—	—	—	—
94-95—Phoenix	IHL	81	19	23	42	41	...	...	...	—	—	—	—	—
95-96—Phoenix	IHL	78	22	20	42	48	...	...	...	4	1	0	1	2
—Los Angeles	NHL	4	0	0	0	0	0	0	0	—	—	—	—	—
96-97—Los Angeles	NHL	79	3	6	9	32	-15	0	0	—	—	—	—	—
97-98—Long Beach	IHL	8	2	3	5	0	...	...	...	—	—	—	—	—
—Los Angeles	NHL	65	3	9	12	33	9	0	0	2	0	0	0	0
98-99—Long Beach	IHL	58	10	8	18	53	...	...	...	4	0	0	0	8
—Los Angeles	NHL	8	0	0	0	2	-1	0	0	—	—	—	—	—
—Springfield	AHL	2	0	2	2	2	...	...	...	—	—	—	—	—
99-00—Los Angeles	NHL	64	3	6	9	55	-2	0	1	3	0	0	0	0
—Long Beach	IHL	6	0	3	3	2	...	...	...	—	—	—	—	—
—Lowell	AHL	2	1	1	2	2	...	...	...	—	—	—	—	—
00-01—Anaheim	NHL	82	1	9	10	22	-12	0	0	—	—	—	—	—
NHL Totals (6 years)		302	10	30	40	144	-21	0	1	5	0	0	0	0

CAIRNS, ERIC   D   ISLANDERS

PERSONAL: Born June 27, 1974, in Oakville, Ont. ... 6-6/235. ... Shoots left. ... Name pronounced KAIR-ihns.

TRANSACTIONS/CAREER NOTES: Selected by New York Rangers in third round (third Rangers pick, 72nd overall) of NHL entry draft (June 20, 1992). ... Claimed on waivers by New York Islanders (December 22, 1998). ... Strained back (January 6, 2000); missed one game. ... Suspended four games by NHL for fighting incident (February 13, 2000). ... Fractured thumb (October 1, 2000); missed first 18 games of season. ... Underwent hand surgery (December 8, 2000); missed 17 games. ... Sprained left wrist (February 18, 2001); missed two games.

		REGULAR SEASON								PLAYOFFS				
Season Team	League	Gms.	G	A	Pts.	PIM	+/-	PP	SH	Gms.	G	A	Pts.	PIM
90-91—Burlington Jr. B	OHA	37	5	16	21	120	...	...	...	—	—	—	—	—
91-92—Det. Jr. Red Wings	OHL	64	1	11	12	237	...	...	...	7	0	0	0	31
92-93—Det. Jr. Red Wings	OHL	64	3	13	16	194	...	...	...	15	0	3	3	24
93-94—Det. Jr. Red Wings	OHL	59	7	35	42	204	...	...	...	17	0	4	4	46
94-95—Birmingham	ECHL	11	1	3	4	49	...	...	...	—	—	—	—	—
—Binghamton	AHL	27	0	3	3	134	...	...	...	9	1	1	2	28
95-96—Binghamton	AHL	46	1	13	14	192	...	...	...	4	0	0	0	37
—Charlotte	ECHL	6	0	1	1	34	...	...	...	—	—	—	—	—
96-97—New York Rangers	NHL	40	0	1	1	147	-7	0	0	3	0	0	0	0
—Binghamton	AHL	10	1	1	2	96	...	...	...	—	—	—	—	—
97-98—New York Rangers	NHL	39	0	3	3	92	-3	0	0	—	—	—	—	—
—Hartford	AHL	7	1	2	3	43	...	...	...	—	—	—	—	—
98-99—Hartford	AHL	11	0	2	2	49	...	...	...	—	—	—	—	—
—Lowell	AHL	24	0	0	0	91	...	...	...	3	1	0	1	32
—New York Islanders	NHL	9	0	3	3	23	1	0	0	—	—	—	—	—
99-00—Providence	AHL	4	1	1	2	14	...	...	...	—	—	—	—	—
—New York Islanders	NHL	67	2	7	9	196	-5	0	0	—	—	—	—	—
00-01—New York Islanders	NHL	45	2	2	4	106	-18	0	0	—	—	—	—	—
NHL Totals (5 years)		200	4	16	20	564	-32	0	0	3	0	0	0	0

CALDER, KYLE   C   BLACKHAWKS

PERSONAL: Born January 5, 1979, in Mannville, Alta. ... 5-11/180. ... Shoots left.

TRANSACTIONS/CAREER NOTES: Selected by Chicago Blackhawks in fifth round (seventh Blackhawks pick, 130th overall) of NHL entry draft (June 21, 1997).

		REGULAR SEASON								PLAYOFFS				
Season Team	League	Gms.	G	A	Pts.	PIM	+/-	PP	SH	Gms.	G	A	Pts.	PIM
95-96—Regina	WHL	27	1	8	9	10	...	...	...	11	0	0	0	0
96-97—Regina	WHL	62	25	34	59	17	...	...	...	5	3	0	3	6
97-98—Regina	WHL	62	27	50	77	58	...	...	...	2	0	1	1	0
98-99—Regina	WHL	34	23	28	51	29	...	...	...	—	—	—	—	—
—Kamloops	WHL	27	19	18	37	30	...	...	...	15	6	10	16	6
99-00—Cleveland	IHL	74	14	22	36	43	...	...	...	9	2	2	4	14
—Chicago	NHL	8	1	1	2	2	-3	0	0	—	—	—	—	—
00-01—Norfolk	AHL	37	12	15	27	21	...	...	...	9	2	6	8	2
—Chicago	NHL	43	5	10	15	14	-4	0	0	—	—	—	—	—
NHL Totals (2 years)		51	6	11	17	16	-7	0	0	—	—	—	—	—

CALOUN, JAN   RW   BLUE JACKETS

PERSONAL: Born December 20, 1972, in Usti-nad-Labem, Czechoslovakia. ... 5-10/190. ... Shoots right. ... Name pronounced YAHN shah-LOON.
TRANSACTIONS/CAREER NOTES: Selected by San Jose Sharks in fourth round (fourth Sharks pick, 75th overall) of NHL entry draft (June 20, 1992). ... Traded by Sharks with ninth-round pick (LW Martin Paroulek) in 2000 draft to Columbus Blue Jackets for future considerations (June 12, 2000).
HONORS: Named to AHL All-Star second team (1996-97).

Season Team	League	REGULAR SEASON Gms.	G	A	Pts.	PIM	+/-	PP	SH	PLAYOFFS Gms.	G	A	Pts.	PIM
90-91—CHZ Litvinov	Czech.	50	28	19	47	12	...	...	...	—	—	—	—	—
91-92—Chemopetrol Litvinov .	Czech.	46	39	13	52	...	...	...	...	—	—	—	—	—
92-93—Chemopetrol Litvinov .	Czech.	47	45	22	67	...	...	...	...	—	—	—	—	—
93-94—Chem. Litvinov	Czech Rep.	41	25	17	42	...	...	...	...	4	2	0	2	...
94-95—Kansas City	IHL	76	34	39	73	50	...	...	...	21	13	10	23	18
95-96—Kansas City	IHL	61	38	30	68	58	...	...	...	5	0	1	1	6
—San Jose	NHL	11	8	3	11	0	4	2	0	—	—	—	—	—
96-97—Kentucky	AHL	66	43	43	86	68	...	...	...	4	0	1	1	4
—San Jose	NHL	2	0	0	0	0	-2	0	0	—	—	—	—	—
97-98—Czech Rep. Oly. team..	Int'l	3	0	0	0	6	...	...	...	—	—	—	—	—
98-99—HIFK Helsinki	Finland	51	24	*57	*81	95	...	...	...	8	*8	6	*14	31
99-00—HIFK Helsinki	Finland	44	38	34	72	94	...	...	...	9	3	6	9	10
00-01—Columbus	NHL	11	0	3	3	2	-8	0	0	—	—	—	—	—
—HIFK Helsinki	Finland	24	8	14	22	42	...	...	...	—	—	—	—	—
NHL Totals (3 years)		24	8	6	14	2	-6	2	0					

CAMPBELL, BRIAN   D   SABRES

PERSONAL: Born May 23, 1979, in Strathroy, Ont. ... 5-11/185. ... Shoots left.
TRANSACTIONS/CAREER NOTES: Selected by Buffalo Sabres in sixth round (seventh Sabres pick, 156th overall) of NHL entry draft (June 21, 1997).
HONORS: Won Can.HL Player of the Year Award (1998-99). ... Named to Can.HL All-Star first team (1998-99). ... Named to OHL All-Star first team (1998-99). ... Won Red Tilson Trophy (1998-99). ... Won Max Kaminsky Trophy (1998-99). ... Won William Hanley Trophy (1998-99).

Season Team	League	REGULAR SEASON Gms.	G	A	Pts.	PIM	+/-	PP	SH	PLAYOFFS Gms.	G	A	Pts.	PIM
94-95—Petrolia	Jr. B	50	1	2	3	...	...	...	...	—	—	—	—	—
95-96—Ottawa	OHL	66	5	22	27	23	...	...	...	4	0	1	1	2
96-97—Ottawa	OHL	66	7	36	43	12	...	...	...	24	2	11	13	8
97-98—Ottawa	OHL	66	14	39	53	31	...	...	...	13	1	14	15	0
98-99—Ottawa	OHL	62	12	75	87	27	...	...	...	9	2	10	12	6
—Rochester	AHL	—	—	—	—	—	...	...	...	2	0	0	0	0
99-00—Buffalo	NHL	12	1	4	5	4	-2	0	0	—	—	—	—	—
—Rochester	AHL	67	2	24	26	22	...	...	...	21	0	3	3	0
00-01—Rochester	AHL	65	7	25	32	24	...	...	...	4	0	1	1	0
—Buffalo	NHL	8	0	0	0	2	-2	0	0	—	—	—	—	—
NHL Totals (2 years)		20	1	4	5	6	-4	0	0					

CAMPBELL, JIM   RW

PERSONAL: Born February 3, 1973, in Worcester, Mass. ... 6-2/205. ... Shoots right. ... Full Name: James Tower Campbell.
TRANSACTIONS/CAREER NOTES: Selected by Montreal Canadiens in second round (second Canadiens pick, 28th overall) of NHL entry draft (June 22, 1991). ... Traded by Canadiens to Mighty Ducks of Anaheim for D Robert Dirk (January 21, 1996). ... Signed as free agent by St. Louis Blues (July 3, 1996). ... Strained thumb (February 25, 1997); missed 10 games. ... Reinjured thumb (April 6, 1997); missed remainder of regular season. ... Strained groin (December 6, 1997); missed one game. ... Injured left heel (January 20, 1998); missed five games. ... Bruised right shoulder (October 23, 1998); missed two games. ... Injured groin (February 9, 1999); missed three games. ... Injured abdominal muscle (March 18, 1999) and underwent surgery; missed remainder of season. ... Signed as free agent by Canadiens (August 22, 2000). ... Suffered concussion (October 17, 2000); missed one game. ... Strained groin (November 14, 2000); missed nine games.
HONORS: Named to NHL All-Rookie team (1996-97).

Season Team	League	REGULAR SEASON Gms.	G	A	Pts.	PIM	+/-	PP	SH	PLAYOFFS Gms.	G	A	Pts.	PIM
88-89—Northwood School	N.Y. H.S.	12	12	8	20	6	...	...	...	—	—	—	—	—
89-90—Northwood School	N.Y. H.S.	8	14	7	21	8	...	...	...	—	—	—	—	—
90-91—Northwood School	N.Y. H.S.	26	36	47	83	36	...	...	...	—	—	—	—	—
91-92—Hull	QMJHL	64	41	44	85	51	...	...	...	6	7	3	10	8
92-93—Hull	QMJHL	50	42	29	71	66	...	...	...	8	11	4	15	43
93-94—U.S. national team	Int'l	56	24	33	57	59	...	...	...	—	—	—	—	—
—U.S. Olympic team	Int'l	8	0	0	0	6	...	...	...	—	—	—	—	—
—Fredericton	AHL	19	6	17	23	6	...	...	...	—	—	—	—	—
94-95—Fredericton	AHL	77	27	24	51	103	...	...	...	12	0	7	7	8
95-96—Fredericton	AHL	44	28	23	51	24	...	...	...	—	—	—	—	—
—Baltimore	AHL	16	13	7	20	8	...	...	...	12	7	5	12	10
—Anaheim	NHL	16	2	3	5	36	0	1	0	—	—	—	—	—
96-97—St. Louis	NHL	68	23	20	43	68	3	5	0	4	1	0	1	6
97-98—St. Louis	NHL	76	22	19	41	55	0	7	0	10	7	3	10	12
98-99—St. Louis	NHL	55	4	21	25	41	-8	1	0	—	—	—	—	—
99-00—Manitoba	IHL	10	1	3	4	10	...	...	...	—	—	—	—	—
—Worcester	AHL	66	31	34	65	88	...	...	...	9	1	2	3	6
—St. Louis	NHL	2	0	0	0	9	0	0	0	—	—	—	—	—
00-01—Montreal	NHL	57	9	11	20	53	-3	6	0	—	—	—	—	—
—Quebec	AHL	3	5	0	5	6	...	...	...	—	—	—	—	—
NHL Totals (6 years)		274	60	74	134	262	-8	20	0	14	8	3	11	18

C

CARKNER, MATT — D — SHARKS

PERSONAL: Born November 3, 1980, in Winchester, Ont. ... 6-4/222. ... Shoots right.
TRANSACTIONS/CAREER NOTES: Selected by Montreal Canadiens in second round (second Canadiens pick, 58th overall) of NHL entry draft (June 26, 1999). ... Signed as free agent by San Jose Sharks (June 12, 2001).

		REGULAR SEASON								PLAYOFFS				
Season Team	League	Gms.	G	A	Pts.	PIM	+/-	PP	SH	Gms.	G	A	Pts.	PIM
96-97—Winchester	Jr. B	29	1	18	19	...	...	...	...	—	—	—	—	—
97-98—Peterborough	OHL	57	0	6	6	121	...	...	...	4	0	0	0	2
98-99—Peterborough	OHL	60	2	16	18	173	...	...	...	5	0	0	0	20
99-00—Peterborough	OHL	62	3	13	16	177	...	...	...	5	0	1	1	6
00-01—Peterborough	OHL	53	8	8	16	128	...	...	...	7	0	3	3	25

CARNEY, KEITH — D — MIGHTY DUCKS

PERSONAL: Born February 3, 1970, in Providence, R.I. ... 6-2/211. ... Shoots left. ... Full Name: Keith Edward Carney.
TRANSACTIONS/CAREER NOTES: Selected by Buffalo Sabres in fourth round (third Sabres pick, 76th overall) of NHL entry draft (June 11, 1988). ... Traded by Sabres to Chicago Blackhawks for D Craig Muni (October 27, 1993). ... Traded by Blackhawks with RW Jim Cummins to Phoenix Coyotes for C Chad Kilger and D Jayson More (March 4, 1998). ... Traded by Coyotes to Mighty Ducks of Anaheim for second-round pick (traded to New Jersey) in 2001 draft (June 19, 2001).
HONORS: Named to Hockey East All-Rookie team (1988-89). ... Named to NCAA All-America (East) second team (1989-90). ... Named to Hockey East All-Star second team (1989-90). ... Named to NCAA All-America (East) first team (1990-91). ... Named to Hockey East All-Star first team (1990-91).

C

		REGULAR SEASON								PLAYOFFS				
Season Team	League	Gms.	G	A	Pts.	PIM	+/-	PP	SH	Gms.	G	A	Pts.	PIM
88-89—Univ. of Maine	Hockey East	40	4	22	26	24	...	...	...	—	—	—	—	—
89-90—Univ. of Maine	Hockey East	41	3	41	44	43	...	...	...	—	—	—	—	—
90-91—Univ. of Maine	Hockey East	40	7	49	56	38	...	...	...	—	—	—	—	—
91-92—U.S. national team	Int'l	49	2	17	19	16	...	...	...	—	—	—	—	—
—Rochester	AHL	24	1	10	11	2	...	...	...	2	0	2	2	0
—Buffalo	NHL	14	1	2	3	18	-3	1	0	7	0	3	3	0
92-93—Buffalo	NHL	30	2	4	6	55	3	0	0	8	0	3	3	6
—Rochester	AHL	41	5	21	26	32	...	...	...	—	—	—	—	—
93-94—Louisville	ECHL	15	1	4	5	14	...	...	...	—	—	—	—	—
—Buffalo	NHL	7	1	3	4	4	-1	0	0	—	—	—	—	—
—Indianapolis	IHL	28	0	14	14	20	...	...	...	—	—	—	—	—
—Chicago	NHL	30	3	5	8	35	15	0	0	6	0	1	1	4
94-95—Chicago	NHL	18	1	0	1	11	-1	0	0	4	0	1	1	0
95-96—Chicago	NHL	82	5	14	19	94	31	1	0	10	0	3	3	4
96-97—Chicago	NHL	81	3	15	18	62	26	0	0	6	1	1	2	2
97-98—Chicago	NHL	60	2	13	15	73	-7	0	1	—	—	—	—	—
—U.S. Olympic team	Int'l	4	0	0	0	2	...	...	...	—	—	—	—	—
—Phoenix	NHL	20	1	6	7	18	5	1	0	6	0	0	0	4
98-99—Phoenix	NHL	82	2	14	16	62	15	0	2	7	1	2	3	10
99-00—Phoenix	NHL	82	4	20	24	87	11	0	0	5	0	0	0	17
00-01—Phoenix	NHL	82	2	14	16	86	15	0	0	—	—	—	—	—
NHL Totals (10 years)		588	27	110	137	605	109	3	3	59	2	14	16	47

CARTER, ANSON — C — OILERS

PERSONAL: Born June 6, 1974, in Toronto. ... 6-1/175. ... Shoots right.
TRANSACTIONS/CAREER NOTES: Selected by Quebec Nordiques in 10th round (10th Nordiques pick, 220th overall) of NHL entry draft (June 20, 1992). ... Nordiques franchise moved to Colorado and renamed Avalanche for 1995-96 season (June 21, 1995). ... Traded by Avalanche to Washington Capitals for fourth-round pick (D Ben Storey) in 1996 entry draft (April 3, 1996). ... Sprained thumb (February 7, 1997); missed five games. ... Traded by Capitals with G Jim Carey, C Jason Allison and third-round pick in 1997 draft to Boston Bruins for C Adam Oates, RW Rick Tocchet and G Bill Ranford (March 1, 1997). ... Strained hip flexor (October 7, 1997); missed two games. ... Suffered from upper respiratory infection (November 22, 1997); missed two games. ... Missed first 12 games of 1998-99 season due to contract dispute; played with Utah of IHL. ... Sprained ankle (January 2, 1999); missed 15 games. ... Bruised shoulder (February 21, 2000); missed eight games. ... Underwent wrist surgery (March 10, 2000); missed final 15 games of season. ... Traded by Bruins with second-round pick (D Doug Lynch) in 2001 draft and swap of first-round picks in 2001 to Edmonton Oilers for RW Bill Guerin (November 15, 2000).
HONORS: Named to CCHA All-Star first team (1993-94 and 1994-95). ... Named to NCAA All-America (West) second team (1994-95). ... Named to CCHA All-Star second team (1995-96).
STATISTICAL PLATEAUS: Three-goal games: 1998-99 (1).

		REGULAR SEASON								PLAYOFFS				
Season Team	League	Gms.	G	A	Pts.	PIM	+/-	PP	SH	Gms.	G	A	Pts.	PIM
91-92—Wexford	OHA Jr. A	42	18	22	40	24	...	...	...	—	—	—	—	—
92-93—Michigan State	CCHA	36	19	11	30	20	...	...	...	—	—	—	—	—
93-94—Michigan State	CCHA	39	30	24	54	36	...	...	...	—	—	—	—	—
94-95—Michigan State	CCHA	39	34	17	51	40	...	...	...	—	—	—	—	—
95-96—Michigan State	CCHA	42	23	20	43	36	...	...	...	—	—	—	—	—
96-97—Washington	NHL	19	3	2	5	7	0	1	0	—	—	—	—	—
—Portland	AHL	27	19	19	38	11	...	...	...	—	—	—	—	—
—Boston	NHL	19	8	5	13	2	-7	1	1	—	—	—	—	—
97-98—Boston	NHL	78	16	27	43	31	7	6	0	6	1	1	2	0
98-99—Utah	IHL	6	1	1	2	0	...	...	...	—	—	—	—	—
—Boston	NHL	55	24	16	40	22	7	6	0	12	4	3	7	0
99-00—Boston	NHL	59	22	25	47	14	8	4	0	—	—	—	—	—
00-01—Edmonton	NHL	61	16	26	42	23	1	7	1	6	3	1	4	4
NHL Totals (5 years)		291	89	101	190	99	16	25	2	24	8	5	13	4

PERSONAL: Born July 23, 1969, in Bramalea, Ont. ... 6-1/185. ... Shoots left. ... Name pronounced KAS-uhls.
TRANSACTIONS/CAREER NOTES: Selected by Montreal Canadiens in first round (first Canadiens pick, 17th overall) of NHL entry draft (June 13, 1987). ... Separated right shoulder (November 22, 1989); missed 10 games. ... Traded by Canadiens to Hartford Whalers for second-round pick (RW Valeri Bure) in 1992 draft (September 17, 1991). ... Bruised kneecap (December 4, 1993); missed one game. ... Suffered facial injury (March 13, 1994); missed four games. ... Bruised forearm (December 2, 1995); missed one game. ... Suffered charley horse (March 6, 1997); missed one game. ... Whalers franchise moved to North Carolina and renamed Carolina Hurricanes for 1997-98 season; NHL approved move on June 25, 1997. ... Traded by Hurricanes with G Jean-Sebastien Giguere to Calgary Flames for LW Gary Roberts and G Trevor Kidd (August 25, 1997). ... Strained rib cage (October 9, 1997); missed one game. ... Injured groin (February 1, 1999); missed 12 games. ... Signed as free agent by Vancouver Canucks (July 13, 1999). ... Sprained thumb (October 19, 1999); missed three games. ... Fractured toe (January 20, 2001); missed 10 games. ... Sprained ankle (March 25, 2001); missed remainder of season.
HONORS: Won Emms Family Award (1986-87). ... Won Red Tilson Trophy (1987-88). ... Won Eddie Powers Memorial Trophy (1987-88). ... Won William Hanley Trophy (1987-88). ... Named to OHL All-Star first team (1987-88 and 1988-89).
MISCELLANEOUS: Captain of Hartford Whalers (1994-95). ... Scored on a penalty shot (vs. Ron Hextall, April 6, 1994). ... Failed to score on a penalty shot (vs. Patrick Roy, November 30, 1999; vs. Norm Maracle, March 18, 2001).
STATISTICAL PLATEAUS: Three-goal games: 2000-01 (1).

		REGULAR SEASON								PLAYOFFS				
Season Team	League	Gms.	G	A	Pts.	PIM	+/-	PP	SH	Gms.	G	A	Pts.	PIM
85-86—Bramalea Jr. B	OHA	33	18	25	43	26	...	...	...	—	—	—	—	—
86-87—Ottawa	OHL	66	26	66	92	28	...	...	...	11	5	9	14	7
87-88—Ottawa	OHL	61	48	*103	*151	39	...	...	...	16	8	*24	†32	13
88-89—Ottawa	OHL	56	37	97	134	66	...	...	...	12	5	10	15	10
89-90—Sherbrooke	AHL	55	22	45	67	25	...	...	...	12	2	11	13	6
—Montreal	NHL	6	2	0	2	2	1	0	0	—	—	—	—	—
90-91—Montreal	NHL	54	6	19	25	20	2	1	0	8	0	2	2	2
91-92—Hartford	NHL	67	11	30	41	18	3	2	2	7	2	4	6	6
92-93—Hartford	NHL	84	21	64	85	62	-11	8	3	—	—	—	—	—
93-94—Hartford	NHL	79	16	42	58	37	-21	8	1	—	—	—	—	—
94-95—Hartford	NHL	46	7	30	37	18	-3	1	0	—	—	—	—	—
95-96—Hartford	NHL	81	20	43	63	39	8	6	0	—	—	—	—	—
96-97—Hartford	NHL	81	22	44	66	46	-16	8	0	—	—	—	—	—
97-98—Calgary	NHL	81	17	27	44	32	-7	6	1	—	—	—	—	—
98-99—Calgary	NHL	70	12	25	37	18	-12	4	1	—	—	—	—	—
99-00—Vancouver	NHL	79	17	45	62	16	8	6	0	—	—	—	—	—
00-01—Vancouver	NHL	66	12	44	56	10	1	2	0	—	—	—	—	—
NHL Totals (12 years)		794	163	413	576	318	-47	52	8	15	2	6	8	8

PERSONAL: Born June 12, 1975, in Sorel, Que. ... 6-4/220. ... Catches left. ... Name pronounced kuh-SIH-vee.
TRANSACTIONS/CAREER NOTES: Selected by Ottawa Senators in ninth round (seventh Senators pick, 210th overall) of NHL entry draft (June 29, 1994). ... Signed as free agent by Colorado Avalanche (August 3, 1999).

		REGULAR SEASON							PLAYOFFS					
Season Team	League	Gms.	Min	W	L	T	GA	SO	Avg.	Gms.	Min.	W	L	GA	SO	Avg.
93-94—St. Hyacinthe	QMJHL	35	1751	15	13	3	127	1	4.35	0	0	0	0	0	0	—
94-95—Halifax	QMJHL	24	1362	9	12	1	105	0	4.63	—	—	—	—	—	—	—
—St. Jean	QMJHL	19	1021	12	6	0	55	1	3.23	5	258	2	3	18	0	4.19
95-96—Prin. Edward Island	AHL	41	2346	20	14	3	128	1	3.27	5	317	2	3	24	0	4.54
—Thunder Bay	Col.HL	12	714	6	4	2	51	0	4.29	—	—	—	—	—	—	—
96-97—Syracuse	AHL	55	3069	23	22	8	164	2	3.21	1	60	0	1	3	0	3.00
97-98—Worcester	AHL	45	2594	20	22	2	140	1	3.24	6	326	3	3	18	0	3.31
98-99—Cincinnati	IHL	44	2418	21	17	‡2	123	1	3.05	3	139	1	2	6	0	2.59
99-00—Hershey	AHL	31	1554	14	9	3	78	1	3.01	2	63	0	1	5	0	4.76
00-01—Hershey	AHL	49	2620	17	24	3	124	2	2.84	9	564	7	2	14	1	*1.49

PERSONAL: Born March 2, 1971, in Gottwaldov, Czechoslovakia. ... 6-3/187. ... Catches left.
TRANSACTIONS/CAREER NOTES: Selected by Philadelphia Flyers in sixth round (third Flyers pick, 171st overall) of NHL entry draft (June 24, 2000).
HONORS: Played in NHL All-Star Game (2001). ... Named to NHL All-Star second team (2000-01).

		REGULAR SEASON							PLAYOFFS					
Season Team	League	Gms.	Min	W	L	T	GA	SO	Avg.	Gms.	Min.	W	L	GA	SO	Avg.
94-95—Vsetin	Czech Rep.	52	3046	...	...	...	121	5	2.38	11	619	...	...	23	1	2.23
95-96—Vsetin	Czech Rep.	49	2925	...	...	...	94	4	1.93	13	783	...	...	17	2	1.30
96-97—Vsetin	Czech Rep.	58	3364	...	...	...	109	3	1.94	10	602	...	...	11	2	1.10
97-98—Vsetin	Czech Rep.	51	2906	...	...	...	92	...	1.90	10	600	...	...	16	1	1.60
98-99—Vsetin	Czech Rep.	46	2875	...	...	...	97	...	2.02	12	747	...	...	23	1	1.85
99-00—Vsetin	Czech Rep.	46	2875	...	...	...	97	...	2.02	9	545	...	...	15	...	1.65
00-01—Philadelphia	AHL	3	160	1	1	0	3	0	1.13	—	—	—	—	—	—	—
—Philadelphia	NHL	59	3431	35	15	6	115	10	2.01	6	347	2	4	18	0	3.11
NHL Totals (1 year)		59	3431	35	15	6	115	10	2.01	6	347	2	4	18	0	3.11

CEREDA, LUCA   C   MAPLE LEAFS

PERSONAL: Born September 7, 1981, in Lugano, Switzerland. ... 6-2/203. ... Shoots left.
TRANSACTIONS/CAREER NOTES: Selected by Toronto Maple Leafs in first round (first Maple Leafs pick, 24th overall) of NHL entry draft (June 26, 1999).

		REGULAR SEASON								PLAYOFFS				
Season Team	League	Gms.	G	A	Pts.	PIM	+/-	PP	SH	Gms.	G	A	Pts.	PIM
96-97—Ambri-Piotta	Switzerland Jr.	35	13	8	21	21	...	...	...	—	—	—	—	—
97-98—Ambri-Piotta	Switzerland Jr.	28	17	27	44	24	...	...	...	—	—	—	—	—
98-99—Ambri-Piotta	Switzerland	38	6	10	16	8	...	...	...	15	0	6	6	4
99-00—Ambri-Piotta	Switzerland	44	1	5	6	14	...	...	...	9	0	1	1	2

CHARA, ZDENO   D   SENATORS

PERSONAL: Born March 18, 1977, in Trencin, Czechoslovakia. ... 6-9/246. ... Shoots left. ... Name pronounced zuh-DAY-noh CHAH-ruh.
TRANSACTIONS/CAREER NOTES: Selected by New York Islanders in third round (third Islanders pick, 56th overall) of NHL entry draft (June 22, 1996). ... Injured left shoulder (January 10, 2000); missed 16 games. ... Suffered from the flu (April 9, 2000); missed one game. ... Traded by Islanders with RW Bill Muckalt and first-round pick (C Jason Spezza) in 2001 draft to Ottawa Senators for C Alexei Yashin (June 23, 2001).

		REGULAR SEASON								PLAYOFFS				
Season Team	League	Gms.	G	A	Pts.	PIM	+/-	PP	SH	Gms.	G	A	Pts.	PIM
94-95—Dukla Trencin..............	Slovakia Jrs.	2	0	0	0	2	...	...	...	—	—	—	—	—
95-96—Dukla Trencin..............	Slovakia Jrs.	22	1	13	14	80	...	...	...	—	—	—	—	—
—HC Piestany	Slov. Div. II	10	1	3	4	10	...	...	...	—	—	—	—	—
—Sparta Praha..............	Czech Rep. Jrs.	15	1	2	3	42	...	...	...	—	—	—	—	—
—Sparta Praha..............	Czech Rep.	1	0	0	0	0	...	...	...	—	—	—	—	—
96-97—Prince George............	WHL	49	3	19	22	120	...	...	...	15	1	7	8	45
97-98—Kentucky	AHL	48	4	9	13	125	...	...	...	1	0	0	0	4
—New York Islanders.....	NHL	25	0	1	1	50	1	0	0	—	—	—	—	—
98-99—Lowell	AHL	23	2	2	4	47	...	...	...	—	—	—	—	—
—New York Islanders.....	NHL	59	2	6	8	83	-8	0	1	—	—	—	—	—
99-00—New York Islanders.....	NHL	65	2	9	11	57	-27	0	0	—	—	—	—	—
00-01—New York Islanders.....	NHL	82	2	7	9	157	-27	0	1	—	—	—	—	—
NHL Totals (4 years)...........		231	6	23	29	347	-61	0	2					

CHARPENTIER, SEBASTIEN   G   CAPITALS

PERSONAL: Born April 18, 1977, in Drummondville, Que. ... 5-9/173. ... Catches left. ... Name pronounced SHAHR-pihnt-yay.
TRANSACTIONS/CAREER NOTES: Selected by Washington Capitals in fourth round (fourth Capitals pick, 93rd overall) of NHL entry draft (July 8, 1995).
HONORS: Won ECHL Playoff MVP Award (1997-98).

		REGULAR SEASON								PLAYOFFS						
Season Team	League	Gms.	Min	W	L	T	GA	SO	Avg.	Gms.	Min.	W	L	GA	SO	Avg.
94-95—Laval	QMJHL	41	2152	25	12	1	99	2	2.76	16	886	9	4	45	0	3.05
95-96—Laval	QMJHL	18	938	4	10	0	97	0	6.20	—	—	—	—	—	—	—
—Val-d'Or........................	QMJHL	33	1906	21	9	1	87	1	2.74	13	778	7	5	47	0	3.62
96-97—Shawinigan	QMJHL	*62	*3474	*37	17	4	176	1	3.04	4	195	2	1	13	0	4.00
97-98—Hampton Roads	ECHL	43	2388	20	16	6	114	0	2.86	18	*1183	*14	4	38	1	*1.93
—Portland	AHL	4	230	1	3	0	10	0	2.61	—	—	—	—	—	—	—
98-99—Portland	AHL	3	180	0	3	0	10	0	3.33	—	—	—	—	—	—	—
—Portland	UHL	6	4	0	0	0	0	0	...	—	—	—	—	—	—	—
99-00—Portland	AHL	18	1041	10	4	3	48	0	2.77	3	183	1	1	9	0	2.95
00-01—Portland	AHL	34	1978	16	16	1	113	1	3.43	1	102	0	1	3	0	1.76

CHARTIER, CHRISTIAN   D   MAPLE LEAFS

PERSONAL: Born October 29, 1980, in Russel, Man. ... 6-0/219. ... Shoots left.
TRANSACTIONS/CAREER NOTES: Selected by Edmonton Oilers in seventh round (eighth Oilers pick, 199th overall) of NHL entry draft (June 26, 1999). ... Signed as free agent by Toronto Maple Leafs (June 6, 2001).
HONORS: Named to WHL (West) All-Star second team (1999-2000). ... Named to WHL (West) All-Star first team (2000-01). ... Won Bill Hunter Trophy (2000-01).

		REGULAR SEASON								PLAYOFFS				
Season Team	League	Gms.	G	A	Pts.	PIM	+/-	PP	SH	Gms.	G	A	Pts.	PIM
96-97—Saskatoon	WHL	64	2	23	25	32	...	...	...	—	—	—	—	—
97-98—Saskatoon	WHL	68	8	33	41	43	...	...	...	6	0	3	3	12
98-99—Saskatoon	WHL	62	2	14	16	71	...	...	...	—	—	—	—	—
99-00—Saskatoon	WHL	11	2	2	4	4	...	...	...	—	—	—	—	—
—Prince George............	WHL	51	16	29	45	24	...	...	...	13	4	9	13	12
00-01—Prince George............	WHL	63	12	56	68	99	...	...	...	6	1	4	5	6

CHARTRAND, BRAD   RW   KINGS

PERSONAL: Born December 14, 1974, in Winnipeg. ... 5-11/191. ... Shoots left.
TRANSACTIONS/CAREER NOTES: Signed as non-drafted free agent by Los Angeles Kings (July 21, 1999).

Season Team	League	REGULAR SEASON								PLAYOFFS				
		Gms.	G	A	Pts.	PIM	+/-	PP	SH	Gms.	G	A	Pts.	PIM
88-89—Winnipeg	MAHA	24	30	50	80	40	...	...	...	—	—	—	—	—
89-90—Winnipeg	MAHA	24	26	55	81	40	...	...	...	—	—	—	—	—
90-91—Winnipeg	MAHA	34	26	45	71	40	...	...	...	—	—	—	—	—
91-92—St. James	MJHL						Statistics unavailable.			—	—	—	—	—
92-93—Cornell University	ECAC	26	10	6	16	16	...	...	...	—	—	—	—	—
93-94—Cornell University	ECAC	30	4	14	18	48	...	...	...	—	—	—	—	—
94-95—Cornell University	ECAC	28	9	9	18	10	...	...	...	—	—	—	—	—
95-96—Cornell University	ECAC	34	24	19	43	16	...	...	...	—	—	—	—	—
96-97—Canadian nat'l team	Int'l	54	10	14	24	42	...	...	...	—	—	—	—	—
97-98—Canadian nat'l team	Int'l	60	24	30	54	47	...	...	...	—	—	—	—	—
—Rapperswil	Switzerland	8	2	3	5	4	...	...	...	—	—	—	—	—
98-99—St. John's	AHL	64	16	14	30	48	...	...	...	5	0	2	2	2
99-00—Los Angeles	NHL	50	6	6	12	17	4	0	1	4	0	0	0	6
—Long Beach	IHL	1	0	0	0	0	...	...	...	3	0	0	0	0
—Lowell	AHL	16	5	10	15	8	...	...	...	—	—	—	—	—
00-01—Lowell	AHL	72	17	34	51	44	...	...	...	4	0	1	1	8
—Los Angeles	NHL	4	1	0	1	2	-2	0	0	—	—	—	—	—
NHL Totals (2 years)		54	7	6	13	19	2	0	1	4	0	0	0	6

CHEBATURKIN, VLADIMIR — D — BLUES

PERSONAL: Born April 23, 1975, in Tyumen, U.S.S.R. ... 6-2/212. ... Shoots left. ... Name pronounced VLAD-ih-meer chuh-buh-TUHR-kihn.
TRANSACTIONS/CAREER NOTES: Selected by New York Islanders in third round (third Islanders pick, 66th overall) of NHL entry draft (June 26, 1993). ... Signed as free agent by St. Louis Blues (June 12, 2000). ... Injured groin (September 27, 2000); missed first four games of season.

Season Team	League	REGULAR SEASON								PLAYOFFS				
		Gms.	G	A	Pts.	PIM	+/-	PP	SH	Gms.	G	A	Pts.	PIM
92-93—Kristall Elektrostal	CIS Div. II						Statistics unavailable.			—	—	—	—	—
93-94—Kristall Elektrostal	CIS Div. II	42	4	4	8	38	...	...	...	—	—	—	—	—
94-95—Kristall Elektrostal	CIS	52	2	6	8	90	...	...	...	—	—	—	—	—
95-96—Kristall Elektrostal	CIS	44	1	6	7	30	...	...	...	1	0	0	0	0
96-97—Utah	IHL	68	0	4	4	34	...	...	...	—	—	—	—	—
97-98—Kentucky	AHL	54	6	8	14	52	...	...	...	2	0	0	0	4
—New York Islanders	NHL	2	0	2	2	0	-1	0	0	—	—	—	—	—
98-99—Lowell	AHL	69	2	12	14	85	...	...	...	3	0	0	0	0
—New York Islanders	NHL	8	0	0	0	12	6	0	0	—	—	—	—	—
99-00—Lowell	AHL	63	1	8	9	118	...	...	...	7	0	4	4	11
—New York Islanders	NHL	17	1	1	2	8	-3	0	0	—	—	—	—	—
00-01—St. Louis	NHL	22	1	2	3	26	5	0	0	—	—	—	—	—
—Worcester	AHL	33	0	7	7	73	...	...	...	10	1	0	1	10
NHL Totals (4 years)		49	2	5	7	46	7	0	0					

CHEECHOO, JONATHAN — RW — SHARKS

PERSONAL: Born July 15, 1980, in Moose Factory, Ont. ... 6-0/205. ... Shoots right.
TRANSACTIONS/CAREER NOTES: Selected by San Jose Sharks in second round (second Sharks pick, 29th overall) of NHL entry draft (June 27, 1998).

Season Team	League	REGULAR SEASON								PLAYOFFS				
		Gms.	G	A	Pts.	PIM	+/-	PP	SH	Gms.	G	A	Pts.	PIM
96-97—Kitchener Jr. B	OHA	43	35	41	76	33	...	...	...	—	—	—	—	—
97-98—Belleville	OHL	64	31	45	76	62	...	...	...	10	4	2	6	10
98-99—Belleville	OHL	63	35	47	82	74	...	...	...	21	15	15	30	27
99-00—Belleville	OHL	66	45	46	91	102	...	...	...	16	5	12	17	16
00-01—Kentucky	AHL	75	32	34	66	63	...	...	...	3	0	0	0	0

CHELIOS, CHRIS — D — RED WINGS

PERSONAL: Born January 25, 1962, in Chicago. ... 6-1/190. ... Shoots right. ... Full Name: Christos K. Chelios. ... Cousin of Nikos Tselios, defenseman, Carolina Hurricanes organization. ... Name pronounced CHEH-lee-ohz.
TRANSACTIONS/CAREER NOTES: Selected by Montreal Canadiens in second round (fifth Canadiens pick, 40th overall) of NHL entry draft (June 10, 1981). ... Sprained right ankle (January 1985). ... Injured left knee (April 1985). ... Sprained knee (December 19, 1985). ... Reinjured knee (January 20, 1986). ... Suffered back spasms (October 1986). ... Fractured finger on left hand (December 1987). ... Bruised tailbone (February 7, 1988). ... Strained left knee ligaments (February 1990). ... Underwent surgery to repair torn abdominal muscle (April 30, 1990). ... Traded by Canadiens with second-round pick (C Michael Pomichter) in 1991 draft to Chicago Blackhawks for C Denis Savard (June 29, 1990). ... Lacerated left temple (February 9, 1991). ... Suspended four games by NHL (October 15, 1993). ... Suspended four games without pay and fined $500 by NHL for eye-scratching incident (February 5, 1994). ... Played in Europe during 1994-95 NHL lockout. ... Sprained knee (March 1, 1997); missed eight games. ... Suffered sore back (April 6, 1997); missed one game. ... Strained groin (November 12, 1998); missed five games. ... Traded by Blackhawks to Detroit Red Wings for D Anders Eriksson, first-round pick (D Steve McCarthy) in 1999 draft and first-round pick (G Adam Munro) in 2001 draft (March 23, 1999). ... Strained groin (April 7, 1999); missed two games. ... Suffered injury (April 7, 2000); missed one game. ... Injured knee and underwent surgery (October 18, 2000); missed five games. ... Underwent knee surgery (November 20, 2000); missed 44 games. ... Fractured thumb (March 17, 2001); missed final seven games of regular season.
HONORS: Named to NCAA All-Tournament team (1982-83). ... Named to WCHA All-Star second team (1982-83). ... Named to NHL All-Rookie team (1984-85). ... Played in NHL All-Star Game (1985, 1990-1994, 1996-1998 and 2000). ... Won James Norris Memorial Trophy (1988-89, 1992-93 and 1995-96). ... Named to THE SPORTING NEWS All-Star first team (1988-89, 1992-93 and 1995-96). ... Named to NHL All-Star first team (1988-89, 1992-93, 1994-95 and 1995-96). ... Named to THE SPORTING NEWS All-Star second team (1990-91 and 1991-92). ... Named to NHL All-Star second team (1990-91). ... Named to THE SPORTING NEWS All-Star team (1996-97).
MISCELLANEOUS: Member of Stanley Cup championship team (1986). ... Captain of Chicago Blackhawks (1996-97 through March 23, 1999).

Season Team	League	REGULAR SEASON								PLAYOFFS				
		Gms.	G	A	Pts.	PIM	+/-	PP	SH	Gms.	G	A	Pts.	PIM
79-80—Moose Jaw	SJHL	53	12	31	43	118	...	...	...	—	—	—	—	—
80-81—Moose Jaw	SJHL	54	23	64	87	175	...	...	...	—	—	—	—	—
81-82—Univ. of Wisconsin	WCHA	43	6	43	49	50	...	...	...	—	—	—	—	—
82-83—Univ. of Wisconsin	WCHA	45	16	32	48	62	...	...	...	—	—	—	—	—
83-84—U.S. national team	Int'l	60	14	35	49	58	...	...	...	—	—	—	—	—
—U.S. Olympic team	Int'l	6	0	3	3	8	...	...	...	—	—	—	—	—
—Montreal	NHL	12	0	2	2	12	-5	0	0	15	1	9	10	17
84-85—Montreal	NHL	74	9	55	64	87	11	2	1	9	2	8	10	17
85-86—Montreal	NHL	41	8	26	34	67	4	2	0	20	2	9	11	49
86-87—Montreal	NHL	71	11	33	44	124	-5	6	0	17	4	9	13	38
87-88—Montreal	NHL	71	20	41	61	172	15	10	1	11	3	1	4	29
88-89—Montreal	NHL	80	15	58	73	185	35	8	0	21	4	15	19	28
89-90—Montreal	NHL	53	9	22	31	136	20	1	2	5	0	1	1	8
90-91—Chicago	NHL	77	12	52	64	192	23	5	2	6	1	7	8	46
91-92—Chicago	NHL	80	9	47	56	245	24	2	2	18	6	15	21	37
92-93—Chicago	NHL	84	15	58	73	282	14	8	0	4	0	2	2	14
93-94—Chicago	NHL	76	16	44	60	212	12	7	1	6	1	1	2	8
94-95—Biel-Bienne	Switzerland	3	0	3	3	4	...	...	...	—	—	—	—	—
—Chicago	NHL	48	5	33	38	72	17	3	1	16	4	7	11	12
95-96—Chicago	NHL	81	14	58	72	140	25	7	0	9	0	3	3	8
96-97—Chicago	NHL	72	10	38	48	112	16	2	0	6	0	1	1	8
97-98—Chicago	NHL	81	3	39	42	151	-7	1	0	—	—	—	—	—
—U.S. Olympic team	Int'l	4	2	0	2	2	...	...	...	—	—	—	—	—
98-99—Chicago	NHL	65	8	26	34	89	-4	2	1	—	—	—	—	—
—Detroit	NHL	10	1	1	2	4	5	1	0	10	0	4	4	14
99-00—Detroit	NHL	81	3	31	34	103	48	0	0	9	0	1	1	8
00-01—Detroit	NHL	24	0	3	3	45	4	0	0	5	1	0	1	2
NHL Totals (18 years)		1181	168	667	835	2430	252	67	11	187	29	93	122	343

CHERNOV, MIKHAIL   D   PREDATORS

PERSONAL: Born November 11, 1978, in Prokopjevsk, U.S.S.R. ... 6-2/196. ... Shoots right.
TRANSACTIONS/CAREER NOTES: Selected by Philadelphia Flyers in fourth round (fourth Flyers pick, 103rd overall) of NHL entry draft (June 21, 1997). ... Traded by Flyers to Nashville Predators for LW/C Mike Watt (May 24, 2001).

Season Team	League	REGULAR SEASON								PLAYOFFS				
		Gms.	G	A	Pts.	PIM	+/-	PP	SH	Gms.	G	A	Pts.	PIM
94-95—Metal.-2 Novok.	CIS Div. II	12	0	3	3	0	...	...	...	—	—	—	—	—
95-96—Metal.-2 Novok.	CIS Div. II	40	2	7	9	10	...	...	...	—	—	—	—	—
96-97—Torpedo-2 Yaroslavl	Rus. Div. III	33	4	2	6	40	...	...	...	—	—	—	—	—
—Torpedo Yaroslavl	Russian	5	0	0	0	0	...	...	...	—	—	—	—	—
97-98—Torpedo Yaroslavl	Russian	7	0	0	0	4	...	...	...	—	—	—	—	—
98-99—Philadelphia	AHL	56	4	3	7	98	...	...	...	14	1	0	1	8
99-00—Philadelphia	AHL	67	10	6	16	54	...	...	...	5	1	2	3	22
00-01—Philadelphia	AHL	50	8	12	20	32	...	...	...	6	1	2	3	4

CHIMERA, JASON   C   OILERS

PERSONAL: Born May 2, 1979, in Edmonton. ... 6-0/180. ...·Shoots left. ... Name pronounced chih-MAIR-uh.
TRANSACTIONS/CAREER NOTES: Selected by Edmonton Oilers in fifth round (fifth Oilers pick, 121st overall) of NHL entry draft (June 21, 1997).

Season Team	League	REGULAR SEASON								PLAYOFFS				
		Gms.	G	A	Pts.	PIM	+/-	PP	SH	Gms.	G	A	Pts.	PIM
96-97—Medicine Hat	WHL	71	16	23	39	64	...	...	...	4	0	1	1	4
97-98—Medicine Hat	WHL	72	34	32	66	93	...	...	...	—	—	—	—	—
—Hamilton	AHL	4	0	0	0	8	...	...	...	—	—	—	—	—
98-99—Medicine Hat	WHL	37	18	22	40	84	...	...	...	—	—	—	—	—
—Brandon	WHL	21	14	12	26	32	...	...	...	5	4	1	5	8
99-00—Hamilton	AHL	78	15	13	28	77	...	...	...	10	0	2	2	12
00-01—Hamilton	AHL	78	29	25	54	93	...	...	...	—	—	—	—	—
—Edmonton	NHL	1	0	0	0	0	0	0	0	—	—	—	—	—
NHL Totals (1 year)		1	0	0	0	0	0	0	0					

CHOUINARD, ERIC   C   CANADIENS

PERSONAL: Born July 8, 1980, in Atlanta. ... 6-2/195. ... Shoots left. ... Son of Guy Chouinard, center with Atlanta/Calgary Flames (1974-75 through 1982-83) and St. Louis Blues (1983-84); and cousin of Marc Chouinard, center, Mighty Ducks of Anaheim. ... Name pronounced shwee-NAHRD.
TRANSACTIONS/CAREER NOTES: Selected by Montreal Canadiens in first round (first Canadiens pick, 16th overall) of NHL entry draft (June 27, 1998).
HONORS: Won QMJHL Frank Selke Trophy (1998-99).

Season Team	League	REGULAR SEASON								PLAYOFFS				
		Gms.	G	A	Pts.	PIM	+/-	PP	SH	Gms.	G	A	Pts.	PIM
97-98—Quebec	QMJHL	68	41	42	83	18	...	...	...	14	7	10	17	6
98-99—Quebec	QMJHL	62	50	59	109	56	...	...	...	13	8	10	18	8
99-00—Fredericton	AHL	—	—	—	—	—	...	...	...	6	3	2	5	0
—Quebec	QMJHL	50	57	47	104	105	...	...	...	11	14	4	18	8
00-01—Quebec	AHL	48	12	21	33	6	...	...	...	9	2	0	2	2
—Montreal	NHL	13	1	3	4	0	0	1	0	—	—	—	—	—
NHL Totals (1 year)		13	1	3	4	0	0	1	0					

CHOUINARD, MARC   C   MIGHTY DUCKS

PERSONAL: Born May 5, 1977, in Charlesbourg, Ont. ... 6-5/204. ... Shoots right. ... Cousin of Eric Chouinard, center, Montreal Canadiens organization; and nephew of Guy Chouinard, center with Atlanta/Calgary Flames (1974-75 through 1982-83) and St. Louis Blues (1983-84). ... Name pronounced shwee-NAHRD.

TRANSACTIONS/CAREER NOTES: Selected by Winnipeg Jets in second round (second Jets pick, 32nd overall) of NHL entry draft (July 8, 1995). ... Traded by Jets with RW Teemu Selanne and fourth-round pick (traded to Toronto) in 1996 draft to Mighty Ducks of Anaheim for C Chad Kilger, D Oleg Tverdovsky and third-round pick (D Per-Anton Lundstrom) in 1996 draft (February 7, 1996). ... Tore Achilles' tendon (October 31, 1997); missed remainder of season.

Season Team	League	REGULAR SEASON								PLAYOFFS				
		Gms.	G	A	Pts.	PIM	+/-	PP	SH	Gms.	G	A	Pts.	PIM
93-94—Beauport	QMJHL	62	11	19	30	23	...	...	...	13	2	5	7	2
94-95—Beauport	QMJHL	68	24	40	64	32	...	...	...	18	1	6	7	4
95-96—Beauport	QMJHL	30	14	21	35	19	...	...	...	—	—	—	—	—
—Halifax	QMJHL	24	6	12	18	17	...	...	...	6	2	1	3	2
96-97—Halifax	QMJHL	63	24	49	73	52	...	...	...	18	10	16	26	12
97-98—Cincinnati	AHL	8	1	2	3	4	...	...	...	—	—	—	—	—
98-99—Cincinnati	AHL	69	7	8	15	20	...	...	...	3	0	0	0	4
99-00—Cincinnati	AHL	70	17	16	33	29	...	...	...	—	—	—	—	—
00-01—Cincinnati	AHL	32	10	9	19	4	...	...	...	—	—	—	—	—
—Anaheim	NHL	44	3	4	7	12	-5	0	0	—	—	—	—	—
NHL Totals (1 year)		44	3	4	7	12	-5	0	0					

CHOUINARD, MATHIEU   G   SENATORS

PERSONAL: Born April 11, 1980, in Laval, Que. ... 6-1/209. ... Catches left.

TRANSACTIONS/CAREER NOTES: Selected by Ottawa Senators in first round (first Senators pick, 15th overall) of NHL entry draft (June 27, 1998). ... Returned to draft pool by Senators and selected by Senators in second round (second Senators pick, 45th overall) of NHL entry draft (June 24, 2000).

HONORS: Named to QMJHL All-Star first team (1998-99). ... Won Michel Briere Trophy (1998-99 and 1999-2000).

Season Team	League	REGULAR SEASON								PLAYOFFS						
		Gms.	Min.	W	L	T	GA	SO	Avg.	Gms.	Min.	W	L	GA	SO	Avg.
96-97—Shawinigan	QMJHL	17	793	4	7	1	51	0	3.86	4	264	1	3	15	0	3.41
97-98—Shawinigan	QMJHL	55	3055	*32	18	3	142	2	2.79	6	348	2	4	24	0	4.14
98-99—Shawinigan	QMJHL	56	3288	36	16	4	150	*5	2.74	6	392	2	4	27	0	4.13
99-00—Shawinigan	QMJHL	†59	*3338	32	20	5	186	4	3.34	13	769	7	6	41	0	3.20
00-01—Grand Rapids	IHL	28	1567	17	7	1	69	1	2.64	3	135	1	1	4	0	*1.78

CHUBAROV, ARTEM   C   CANUCKS

PERSONAL: Born December 12, 1979, in Gorky, U.S.S.R. ... 6-1/189. ... Shoots left.

TRANSACTIONS/CAREER NOTES: Selected by Vancouver Canucks in second round (second Canucks pick, 31st overall) of NHL entry draft (June 27, 1998). ... Injured hip (February 19, 2000); missed nine games.

Season Team	League	REGULAR SEASON								PLAYOFFS				
		Gms.	G	A	Pts.	PIM	+/-	PP	SH	Gms.	G	A	Pts.	PIM
94-95—Tor. Nizhny Nov.	CIS Jr.	60	20	30	50	20	...	...	...	—	—	—	—	—
95-96—Tor. Nizhny Nov.	CIS Jr.	60	22	25	47	20	...	...	...	—	—	—	—	—
96-97—Tor.-2 Nizhny Nov.	Rus. Div. III	40	24	5	29	16	...	...	...	—	—	—	—	—
—Tor. Nizhny Nov.	Rus. Div. II	15	1	1	2	8	...	...	...	—	—	—	—	—
97-98—Dynamo Moscow	Russian	30	1	4	5	4	...	...	...	—	—	—	—	—
98-99—Dynamo Moscow	Russian	34	8	2	10	10	...	...	...	12	0	0	0	4
99-00—Vancouver	NHL	49	1	8	9	10	-4	0	0	—	—	—	—	—
—Syracuse	AHL	14	7	6	13	4	...	...	...	1	0	0	0	0
00-01—Vancouver	NHL	1	0	0	0	0	-1	0	0	—	—	—	—	—
—Kansas City	IHL	10	7	4	11	12	...	...	...	—	—	—	—	—
NHL Totals (2 years)		50	1	8	9	10	-5	0	0					

CICCONE, ENRICO   D

PERSONAL: Born April 10, 1970, in Montreal. ... 6-5/220. ... Shoots left. ... Name pronounced en-REE-koh chih-KOH-nee.

TRANSACTIONS/CAREER NOTES: Selected by Minnesota North Stars in fifth round (fifth North Stars pick, 92nd overall) of NHL entry draft (June 16, 1990). ... North Stars franchise moved from Minnesota to Dallas and renamed Stars for 1993-94 season. ... Traded by Stars to Washington Capitals (June 25, 1993) to complete deal in which Capitals sent D Paul Cavallini to Stars for future considerations (June 20, 1993). ... Pulled groin (January 25, 1994); missed seven games. ... Traded by Capitals with third-round pick (traded to Mighty Ducks) in 1994 draft and conditional draft pick to Tampa Bay Lightning for D Joe Reekie (March 21, 1994). ... Suffered whiplash (February 5, 1995); missed one game. ... Injured neck (March 1, 1995); missed one game. ... Injured shoulder (April 26, 1995); missed two games. ... Tore ligament in right thumb (November 18, 1995); missed 10 games. ... Sprained right knee (January 30, 1996); missed one game. ... Traded by Lightning to Chicago Blackhawks for LW Patrick Poulin, D Igor Ulanov and second-round pick (traded to New Jersey) in 1996 draft (March 20, 1996). ... Bruised ribs prior to 1996-97 season; missed first six games of season. ... Strained hip flexor (March 20, 1997); missed one game. ... Traded by Blackhawks to Carolina Hurricanes for D Ryan Risidore and fifth-round pick (traded to Toronto) in 1998 draft (July 25, 1997). ... Strained groin (October 22, 1997); missed 20 games. ... Traded by Hurricanes with G Sean Burke and LW Geoff Sanderson to Vancouver Canucks for LW Martin Gelinas and G Kirk McLean (January 3, 1998). ... Fractured tibia (January 8, 1998); missed 10 games. ... Traded by Canucks to Tampa Bay Lightning for D Jamie Huscroft (March 14, 1998). ... Strained groin (March 25, 1998); missed two games. ... Suspended one game and fined $1,000 by NHL for elbowing incident (November 12, 1998). ... Traded by Lightning to Capitals for future considerations (December 28, 1998). ... Strained groin (January 1, 1999); missed one game. ... Reinjured groin (January 7, 1999); missed four games. ... Signed as free agent by Montreal Canadiens (July 7, 2000). ... Strained groin (September 26, 2000); missed first nine games of season. ... Injured back (November 8, 2000); missed 13 games. ... Announced retirement (December 8, 2000).

MISCELLANEOUS: Holds Tampa Bay Lightning all-time record for most penalty minutes (604).

Season Team	League	REGULAR SEASON								PLAYOFFS				
		Gms.	G	A	Pts.	PIM	+/-	PP	SH	Gms.	G	A	Pts.	PIM
87-88—Shawinigan	QMJHL	61	2	12	14	324	...	...	...	—	—	—	—	—
88-89—Shawinigan	QMJHL	34	7	11	18	132	...	...	...	—	—	—	—	—
—Trois-Rivieres	QMJHL	24	0	7	7	153	...	...	...	—	—	—	—	—
89-90—Trois-Rivieres	QMJHL	40	4	24	28	227	...	...	...	3	0	0	0	15
90-91—Kalamazoo	IHL	57	4	9	13	384	...	...	...	4	0	1	1	32
91-92—Kalamazoo	IHL	53	4	16	20	406	...	...	...	10	0	1	1	58
—Minnesota	NHL	11	0	0	0	48	-2	0	0	—	—	—	—	—
92-93—Minnesota	NHL	31	0	1	1	115	2	0	0	—	—	—	—	—
—Kalamazoo	IHL	13	1	3	4	50	...	...	...	—	—	—	—	—
—Hamilton	AHL	6	1	3	4	44	...	...	...	—	—	—	—	—
93-94—Washington	NHL	46	1	1	2	174	-2	0	0	—	—	—	—	—
—Portland	AHL	6	0	0	0	27	...	...	...	—	—	—	—	—
—Tampa Bay	NHL	11	0	1	1	52	-2	0	0	—	—	—	—	—
94-95—Tampa Bay	NHL	41	2	4	6	225	3	0	0	—	—	—	—	—
95-96—Tampa Bay	NHL	55	2	3	5	258	-4	0	0	—	—	—	—	—
—Chicago	NHL	11	0	1	1	48	5	0	0	9	1	0	1	30
96-97—Chicago	NHL	67	2	2	4	233	-1	0	0	4	0	0	0	18
97-98—Carolina	NHL	14	0	3	3	83	3	0	0	—	—	—	—	—
—Vancouver	NHL	13	0	1	1	47	-2	0	0	—	—	—	—	—
—Tampa Bay	NHL	12	0	0	0	45	-3	0	0	—	—	—	—	—
98-99—Tampa Bay	NHL	16	1	1	2	24	-1	0	0	—	—	—	—	—
—Cleveland	IHL	6	0	0	0	23	...	...	...	—	—	—	—	—
—Washington	NHL	43	2	0	2	103	-6	0	0	—	—	—	—	—
99-00—Essen	Germany	14	0	4	4	101	...	...	...	—	—	—	—	—
00-01—Montreal	NHL	3	0	0	0	14	-1	0	0	—	—	—	—	—
—Quebec	AHL	2	0	0	0	22	...	...	...	—	—	—	—	—
NHL Totals (9 years)		**374**	**10**	**18**	**28**	**1469**	**-11**	**0**	**0**	**13**	**1**	**0**	**1**	**48**

CIERNIK, IVAN   RW   SENATORS

PERSONAL: Born October 30, 1977, in Levice, Czechoslovakia. ... 6-1/234. ... Shoots left. ... Name pronounced SEER-nihk.

TRANSACTIONS/CAREER NOTES: Selected by Ottawa Senators in ninth round (sixth Senators pick, 216th overall) of NHL entry draft (June 22, 1996). ... Injured shoulder (January 26, 2001); missed four games.

Season Team	League	REGULAR SEASON								PLAYOFFS				
		Gms.	G	A	Pts.	PIM	+/-	PP	SH	Gms.	G	A	Pts.	PIM
94-95—HC Nitra	Slovakia Jrs.	30	22	15	37	36	...	...	...	—	—	—	—	—
—HC Nitra	Slovakia	7	1	0	1	2	...	...	...	—	—	—	—	—
95-96—HC Nitra	Slovakia	35	9	7	16	36	...	...	...	—	—	—	—	—
96-97—HC Nitra	Slovakia	41	11	19	30		...	...	...	—	—	—	—	—
97-98—Worcester	AHL	53	9	12	21	38	...	...	...	1	0	0	0	2
—Ottawa	NHL	2	0	0	0	0	0	0	0	—	—	—	—	—
98-99—Adirondack	AHL	21	1	4	5	4	...	...	...	—	—	—	—	—
—Cincinnati	AHL	32	10	3	13	10	...	...	...	2	0	0	0	2
99-00—Grand Rapids	IHL	66	13	12	25	64	...	...	...	6	0	6	6	2
00-01—Grand Rapids	IHL	66	27	38	65	53	...	...	...	—	—	—	—	—
—Ottawa	NHL	4	2	0	2	2	2	0	0	—	—	—	—	—
NHL Totals (2 years)		**6**	**2**	**0**	**2**	**2**	**2**	**0**	**0**	**—**	**—**	**—**	**—**	**—**

CIGER, ZDENO   LW   RANGERS

PERSONAL: Born October 19, 1969, in Martin, Czechoslovakia. ... 6-1/190. ... Shoots left. ... Full Name: Zdenek Ciger. ... Name pronounced zuh-DAYN-yoh SEE-guhr.

TRANSACTIONS/CAREER NOTES: Selected by New Jersey Devils in third round (third Devils pick, 54th overall) of NHL entry draft (June 11, 1988). ... Bruised left shoulder (October 6, 1990). ... Injured elbow (January 24, 1991). ... Fractured right wrist (September 24, 1991); missed first 59 games of season. ... Traded by Devils with C Kevin Todd to Edmonton Oilers for C Bernie Nicholls (January 13, 1993). ... Played in Europe during 1994-95 NHL lockout. ... Injured lower right leg (December 10, 1995); missed four games. ... Claimed by Nashville Predators from Oilers in NHL waiver draft (October 5, 1998). ... Claimed by Minnesota Wild from Predators in NHL waiver draft (September 29, 2000). ... Signed as free agent by New York Rangers (July 17, 2001).

HONORS: Named Czechoslovakian League Rookie of the Year (1988-89).

Season Team	League	REGULAR SEASON								PLAYOFFS				
		Gms.	G	A	Pts.	PIM	+/-	PP	SH	Gms.	G	A	Pts.	PIM
87-88—Dukla Trencin	Czech.	8	3	4	7	2	...	...	...	—	—	—	—	—
88-89—Dukla Trencin	Czech.	32	15	21	36	18	...	...	...	—	—	—	—	—
89-90—Dukla Trencin	Czech.	53	18	28	46		...	...	...	—	—	—	—	—
90-91—New Jersey	NHL	45	8	17	25	8	3	2	0	6	0	2	2	4
—Utica	AHL	8	5	4	9	2	...	...	...	—	—	—	—	—
91-92—New Jersey	NHL	20	6	5	11	10	-2	1	0	7	2	4	6	0
92-93—New Jersey	NHL	27	4	8	12	2	-8	2	0	—	—	—	—	—
—Edmonton	NHL	37	9	15	24	6	-5	0	0	—	—	—	—	—
93-94—Edmonton	NHL	84	22	35	57	8	-11	8	0	—	—	—	—	—
94-95—Dukla Trencin	Slovakia	34	23	26	49	10	...	...	...	9	2	9	11	2
—Edmonton	NHL	5	2	2	4	0	-1	1	0	—	—	—	—	—
95-96—Edmonton	NHL	78	31	39	70	41	-15	12	0	—	—	—	—	—
96-97—Slavia Praha	Czech Rep.	44	26	27	53		...	...	...	2	1	3	4	...
97-98—Slavia Praha	Czech Rep.	36	14	31	45	2	...	...	...	11	6	10	16	4
—Slovakian Oly. team	Int'l	4	1	1	2	4	...	...	...	—	—	—	—	—
98-99—Slovan Bratislava	Slovakia	40	26	32	*58	8	...	...	...	9	3	*10	13	2
99-00—Slovan Bratislava	Slovakia	51	23	39	62	48	...	...	...	8	1	*8	†9	0
00-01—Slovan Bratislava	Slovakia	53	17	32	49	22	...	...	...	8	6	3	9	16
NHL Totals (6 years)		**296**	**82**	**121**	**203**	**75**	**-39**	**26**	**0**	**13**	**2**	**6**	**8**	**4**

CISAR, MARIAN — RW — PREDATORS

PERSONAL: Born February 25, 1978, in Bratislava, Czechoslovakia. ... 6-0/192. ... Shoots right. ... Name pronounced say-SAHR.
TRANSACTIONS/CAREER NOTES: Selected by Los Angeles Kings in second round (second Kings pick, 37th overall) of NHL entry draft (June 22, 1996). ... Traded by Kings to Nashville Predators for future considerations (May 29, 1998).

Season Team	League	REGULAR SEASON								PLAYOFFS				
		Gms.	G	A	Pts.	PIM	+/-	PP	SH	Gms.	G	A	Pts.	PIM
94-95—Slov. Bratislava	Slovakia Jrs.	38	42	28	70	16	...	...	...	—	—	—	—	—
95-96—Slov. Bratislava	Slovakia Jrs.	16	26	17	43	2	...	...	...	—	—	—	—	—
—Slovan Bratislava	Slovakia	13	3	3	6	0	...	...	...	6	3	0	3	0
96-97—Spokane	WHL	70	31	35	66	52	...	...	...	9	6	2	8	4
97-98—Spokane	WHL	52	33	40	73	34	...	...	...	18	8	5	13	8
98-99—Milwaukee	IHL	51	11	17	28	31	...	...	...	2	0	0	0	12
99-00—Milwaukee	IHL	78	20	32	52	82	...	...	...	1	0	0	0	0
—Nashville	NHL	3	0	0	0	4	-2	0	0	—	—	—	—	—
00-01—Milwaukee	IHL	15	4	7	11	4	...	...	...	—	—	—	—	—
—Nashville	NHL	60	12	15	27	45	-7	5	0	—	—	—	—	—
NHL Totals (2 years)		63	12	15	27	49	-9	5	0					

CLARK, BRETT — D — THRASHERS

C

PERSONAL: Born December 23, 1976, in Wapella, Sask. ... 6-1/185. ... Shoots left.
TRANSACTIONS/CAREER NOTES: Selected by Montreal Canadiens in sixth round (seventh Canadiens pick, 154th overall) of NHL entry draft (June 22, 1996). ... Suffered concussion (November 19, 1998); missed four games. ... Selected by Atlanta Thrashers in NHL expansion draft (June 25, 1999).
HONORS: Named to Hockey East All-Rookie team (1995-96).

Season Team	League	REGULAR SEASON								PLAYOFFS				
		Gms.	G	A	Pts.	PIM	+/-	PP	SH	Gms.	G	A	Pts.	PIM
94-95—Melville	SJHL	62	19	32	51	77	...	...	...	—	—	—	—	—
95-96—Univ. of Maine	Hockey East	39	7	31	38	22	...	...	...	—	—	—	—	—
96-97—Canadian nat'l team	Int'l	60	12	20	32	87	...	...	...	—	—	—	—	—
97-98—Montreal	NHL	41	1	0	1	20	-3	0	0	—	—	—	—	—
—Fredericton	AHL	20	0	6	6	6	...	...	...	4	0	1	1	17
98-99—Montreal	NHL	61	2	2	4	16	-3	0	0	—	—	—	—	—
—Fredericton	AHL	3	1	0	1	0	...	...	...	—	—	—	—	—
99-00—Orlando	IHL	63	9	17	26	31	...	...	...	6	0	1	1	0
—Atlanta	NHL	14	0	1	1	4	-12	0	0	—	—	—	—	—
00-01—Atlanta	NHL	28	1	2	3	14	-12	0	0	—	—	—	—	—
—Orlando	IHL	43	2	9	11	32	...	...	...	15	1	6	7	2
NHL Totals (4 years)		144	4	5	9	54	-30	0	0					

CLARK, CHRIS — RW — FLAMES

PERSONAL: Born March 8, 1976, in South Windsor, Conn. ... 6-0/202. ... Shoots right.
TRANSACTIONS/CAREER NOTES: Selected by Calgary Flames in third round (third Flames pick, 77th overall) of NHL entry draft (June 29, 1994). ... Injured shoulder (January 15, 2000); missed one game. ... Suffered injury (March 31, 2000); missed remainder of season.
HONORS: Named to ECAC All-Star second team (1997-98).

Season Team	League	REGULAR SEASON								PLAYOFFS				
		Gms.	G	A	Pts.	PIM	+/-	PP	SH	Gms.	G	A	Pts.	PIM
93-94—Springfield Jr. B	NEJHL	35	31	26	57	185	...	...	...	—	—	—	—	—
94-95—Clarkson	ECAC	32	12	11	23	92	...	...	...	—	—	—	—	—
95-96—Clarkson	ECAC	38	10	8	18	108	...	...	...	—	—	—	—	—
96-97—Clarkson	ECAC	37	23	25	48	86	...	...	...	—	—	—	—	—
97-98—Clarkson	ECAC	35	18	21	39	*106	...	...	...	—	—	—	—	—
98-99—Saint John	AHL	73	13	27	40	123	...	...	...	7	2	4	6	15
99-00—Saint John	AHL	48	16	17	33	134	...	...	...	—	—	—	—	—
—Calgary	NHL	22	0	1	1	14	-3	0	0	—	—	—	—	—
00-01—Saint John	AHL	48	18	17	35	131	...	...	...	18	4	10	14	49
—Calgary	NHL	29	5	1	6	38	0	1	0	—	—	—	—	—
NHL Totals (2 years)		51	5	2	7	52	-3	1	0					

CLARKE, DALE — D — BLUES

PERSONAL: Born March 23, 1978, in Belleville, Ont. ... 6-1/193. ... Shoots right.
TRANSACTIONS/CAREER NOTES: Signed as non-drafted free agent by St. Louis Blues (May 15, 2000).

Season Team	League	REGULAR SEASON								PLAYOFFS				
		Gms.	G	A	Pts.	PIM	+/-	PP	SH	Gms.	G	A	Pts.	PIM
96-97—St. Lawrence	WCHA	34	1	6	7	20	...	...	...	—	—	—	—	—
97-98—St. Lawrence	WCHA	33	1	6	7	66	...	...	...	—	—	—	—	—
98-99—St. Lawrence	WCHA	39	3	13	16	44	...	...	...	—	—	—	—	—
99-00—St. Lawrence	WCHA	36	6	17	23	24	...	...	...	—	—	—	—	—
—Worcester	AHL	2	0	0	0	0	...	...	...	—	—	—	—	—
00-01—Worcester	AHL	67	7	25	32	26	...	...	...	1	0	0	0	0
—Peoria	ECHL	2	1	0	1	0	...	...	...	—	—	—	—	—
—St. Louis	NHL	3	0	0	0	0	1	0	0	—	—	—	—	—
NHL Totals (1 year)		3	0	0	0	0	1	0	0					

CLASSEN, GREG   C   PREDATORS

PERSONAL: Born August 24, 1977, in Aylsham, Sask. ... 6-1/194. ... Shoots left.
TRANSACTIONS/CAREER NOTES: Signed as non-drafted free agent by Nashville Predators (March 27, 2000). ... Sprained knee (November 28, 2000); missed 14 games. ... Suffered concussion (February 21, 2001); missed two games.

		REGULAR SEASON							PLAYOFFS				
Season Team	League	Gms.	G	A	Pts.	PIM	+/-	PP	SH	Gms.	G	A	Pts.	PIM
98-99—Merrimack College......	Hockey East	36	14	11	25	28	...	...	...	—	—	—	—	—
99-00—Merrimack College......	Hockey East	36	14	16	30	16	...	...	...	—	—	—	—	—
—Milwaukee.................	IHL	9	1	0	1	2	...	...	...	2	0	0	0	2
00-01—Nashville	NHL	27	2	4	6	14	-4	1	0	—	—	—	—	—
—Milwaukee.................	IHL	23	5	10	15	31	...	...	...	5	0	0	0	0
NHL Totals (1 year).............		27	2	4	6	14	-4	1	0					

CLEARY, DAN   LW   OILERS

PERSONAL: Born December 18, 1978, in Carbonear, Nfld. ... 6-0/203. ... Shoots left. ... Full Name: Daniel Cleary.
TRANSACTIONS/CAREER NOTES: Selected by Chicago Blackhawks in first round (first Blackhawks pick, 13th overall) of NHL entry draft (June 21, 1997). ... Traded by Blackhawks with C Chad Kilger, LW Ethan Moreau and D Christian Laflamme to Edmonton Oilers for D Boris Mironov, LW Dean McAmmond and D Jonas Elofsson (March 20, 1999).
HONORS: Named to OHL All-Star first team (1995-96 and 1996-97). ... Named to AHL All-Star second team (1999-2000).

		REGULAR SEASON							PLAYOFFS				
Season Team	League	Gms.	G	A	Pts.	PIM	+/-	PP	SH	Gms.	G	A	Pts.	PIM
93-94—Kingston	Tier II Jr. A	41	18	28	46	33	...	...	...	—	—	—	—	—
94-95—Belleville	OHL	62	26	55	81	62	...	...	...	16	7	10	17	23
95-96—Belleville	OHL	64	53	62	115	74	...	...	...	14	10	17	27	40
96-97—Belleville	OHL	64	32	48	80	88	...	...	...	6	3	4	7	6
97-98—Chicago....................	NHL	6	0	0	0	0	-2	0	0	—	—	—	—	—
—Indianapolis...............	IHL	4	2	1	3	6	...	...	...	—	—	—	—	—
—Belleville.................	OHL	30	16	31	47	14	...	...	...	10	6	*17	*23	10
98-99—Chicago....................	NHL	35	4	5	9	24	-1	0	0	—	—	—	—	—
—Portland....................	AHL	30	9	17	26	74	...	...	...	—	—	—	—	—
—Hamilton..................	AHL	9	0	1	1	7	...	...	...	3	0	0	0	0
99-00—Hamilton..................	AHL	58	22	52	74	108	...	...	...	5	2	3	5	18
—Edmonton..................	NHL	17	3	2	5	8	-1	0	0	4	0	1	1	2
00-01—Edmonton..................	NHL	81	14	21	35	37	5	2	0	6	1	1	2	8
NHL Totals (4 years)...........		139	21	28	49	69	1	2	0	10	1	2	3	10

CLOUTIER, DAN   G   CANUCKS

PERSONAL: Born April 22, 1976, in Mont-Laurier, Que. ... 6-1/182. ... Catches left. ... Brother of Sylvain Cloutier, center, New Jersey Devils organization. ... Name pronounced KLOO-tee-yay.
TRANSACTIONS/CAREER NOTES: Selected by New York Rangers in first round (first Rangers pick, 26th overall) of NHL entry draft (June 28, 1994). ... Traded by Rangers with LW Niklas Sundstrom and first-(RW Nikita Alexeev) and third-round (traded to San Jose) picks in 2000 draft to Tampa Bay Lightning for first-round pick (RW Pavel Brendl) in 1999 draft (June 26, 1999). ... Strained groin (November 18, 1999); missed two games. ... Suspended four games by NHL for kicking incident (January 14, 2000). ... Strained groin (February 21, 2000); missed three games. ... Injured neck (March 14, 2000); missed four games. ... Strained medial collateral ligament in knee (March 28, 2000); missed five games. ... Strained biceps (October 22, 2000); missed nine games. ... Suffered from the flu (December 8, 2000); missed one game. ... Traded by Lightning to Vancouver Canucks for D Adrian Aucoin and second-round pick (C/LW Alexander Polushin) in 2001 draft (February 7, 2001).
HONORS: Named to OHL All-Star second team (1995-96). ... Won Dave Pinkney Trophy (1995-96). ... Named to AHL All-Rookie team (1996-97).
MISCELLANEOUS: Stopped a penalty shot attempt (vs. Marian Hossa, January 4, 2001; vs. Daniel Alfredsson, January 20, 2001). ... Allowed a penalty shot goal (vs. Jeremy Roenick, December 2, 1999).

		REGULAR SEASON							PLAYOFFS					
Season Team	League	Gms.	Min	W	L	T	GA	SO	Avg.	Gms.	Min.	W	L	GA	SO	Avg.
91-92—St. Thomas	Jr. B	14	823	...	...	...	80	...	5.83	—	—	—	—	—	—	—
92-93—Sault Ste. Marie	OHL	12	572	4	6	0	44	0	4.62	4	231	1	2	12	0	3.12
93-94—Sault Ste. Marie	OHL	55	2934	28	14	6	174	†2	3.56	14	833	†10	4	52	0	3.75
94-95—Sault Ste. Marie	OHL	45	2517	15	25	2	184	1	4.39	—	—	—	—	—	—	—
95-96—Sault Ste. Marie	OHL	13	641	9	3	0	43	0	4.02	—	—	—	—	—	—	—
—Guelph	OHL	17	1004	12	2	2	35	2	2.09	16	993	11	5	52	*2	3.14
96-97—Binghamton	AHL	60	3367	23	†28	8	199	3	3.55	4	236	1	3	13	0	3.31
97-98—Hartford	AHL	24	1417	12	8	3	62	0	2.63	8	479	5	3	24	0	3.01
—New York Rangers	NHL	12	551	4	5	1	23	0	2.50	—	—	—	—	—	—	—
98-99—New York Rangers	NHL	22	1097	6	8	3	49	0	2.68	—	—	—	—	—	—	—
99-00—Tampa Bay	NHL	52	2492	9	30	3	145	0	3.49	—	—	—	—	—	—	—
00-01—Detroit........................	IHL	1	59	0	1	0	3	0	3.05	—	—	—	—	—	—	—
—Tampa Bay	NHL	24	1005	3	13	3	59	1	3.52	—	—	—	—	—	—	—
—Vancouver..................	NHL	16	914	4	6	5	37	0	2.43	2	117	0	2	9	0	4.62
NHL Totals (4 years).............		126	6059	26	62	15	313	1	3.10	2	117	0	2	9	0	4.62

CLOUTIER, SYLVAIN   C   DEVILS

PERSONAL: Born February 13, 1974, in Mont-Laurier, Que. ... 6-0/195. ... Shoots left. ... Brother of Dan Cloutier, goaltender, Vancouver Canucks. ... Name pronounced sihl-VAY CLOO-tee-yay.
TRANSACTIONS/CAREER NOTES: Selected by Detroit Red Wings in third round (third Red Wings pick, 70th overall) of NHL entry draft (June

20, 1992). ... Signed as free agent by Chicago Blackhawks (August 7, 1998). ... Selected by Atlanta Thrashers in NHL expansion draft (June 25, 1999). ... Traded by Thrashers with LW Jeff Williams to New Jersey Devils for LW Eric Bertrand, RW Wes Mason and seventh-round pick (LW Ken Magowan) in 2000 draft (November 1, 1999).

Season Team	League	REGULAR SEASON								PLAYOFFS				
		Gms.	G	A	Pts.	PIM	+/-	PP	SH	Gms.	G	A	Pts.	PIM
90-91—Sault Ste. Marie	OHA	34	51	40	91	92	...	...	...	—	—	—	—	—
91-92—Guelph	OHL	62	35	31	66	74	...	...	...	—	—	—	—	—
92-93—Guelph	OHL	44	26	29	55	78	...	...	...	5	0	5	5	14
93-94—Guelph	OHL	66	45	71	116	127	...	...	...	9	7	9	16	32
—Adirondack	AHL	2	0	2	2	2	...	...	...	—	—	—	—	—
94-95—Adirondack	AHL	71	7	26	33	144	...	...	...	—	—	—	—	—
95-96—Adirondack	AHL	65	11	17	28	118	...	...	...	3	0	0	0	4
—Toledo........................	ECHL	6	4	2	6	4	...	...	...	—	—	—	—	—
96-97—Adirondack	AHL	77	13	36	49	190	...	...	...	4	0	2	2	4
97-98—Adirondack	AHL	72	14	22	36	155	...	...	...	—	—	—	—	—
—Detroit.......................	IHL	8	0	1	1	18	...	...	...	21	7	5	12	31
98-99—Indianapolis	IHL	73	21	33	54	128	...	...	...	7	3	2	5	12
—Chicago......................	NHL	7	0	0	0	0	-1	0	0	—	—	—	—	—
99-00—Orlando....................	IHL	9	1	1	2	25	...	...	...	—	—	—	—	—
—Albany........................	AHL	66	15	28	43	127	...	...	...	5	0	0	0	6
00-01—Albany......................	AHL	79	16	35	51	115	...	...	...	—	—	—	—	—
NHL Totals (1 year)............		7	0	0	0	0	-1	0	0					

CLYMER, BEN — C/D — LIGHTNING — C

PERSONAL: Born April 11, 1978, in Edina, Minn. ... 6-1/195. ... Shoots right.
TRANSACTIONS/CAREER NOTES: Selected by Boston Bruins in second round (third Bruins pick, 27th overall) of NHL entry draft (June 21, 1997). ... Signed as free agent by Tampa Bay Lightning (October 2, 1999).
HONORS: Named to WCHA All-Rookie team (1996-97).

Season Team	League	REGULAR SEASON								PLAYOFFS				
		Gms.	G	A	Pts.	PIM	+/-	PP	SH	Gms.	G	A	Pts.	PIM
93-94—Thomas Jefferson.......	Minn. H.S.	23	3	7	10	6	...	...	...	—	—	—	—	—
94-95—Thomas Jefferson.......	Minn. H.S.	28	6	20	26	26	...	...	...	—	—	—	—	—
95-96—Thomas Jefferson.......	Minn. H.S.	19	12	28	40	38	...	...	...	—	—	—	—	—
96-97—Univ. of Minnesota......	WCHA	29	7	13	20	64	...	...	...	—	—	—	—	—
97-98—Univ. of Minnesota......	WCHA	1	0	0	0	2	...	...	...	—	—	—	—	—
98-99—Seattle......................	WHL	70	12	44	56	93	...	...	...	11	1	5	6	12
99-00—Detroit......................	IHL	19	1	9	10	30	...	...	...	—	—	—	—	—
—Tampa Bay..................	NHL	60	2	6	8	87	-26	2	0	—	—	—	—	—
00-01—Detroit......................	IHL	53	5	8	13	88	...	...	...	—	—	—	—	—
—Tampa Bay..................	NHL	23	5	1	6	21	-7	3	0	—	—	—	—	—
NHL Totals (2 years)............		83	7	7	14	108	-33	5	0					

COFFEY, PAUL — D

PERSONAL: Born June 1, 1961, in Weston, Ont. ... 6-0/200. ... Shoots left. ... Full Name: Paul Douglas Coffey.
TRANSACTIONS/CAREER NOTES: Selected by Edmonton Oilers in first round (first Oilers pick, sixth overall) of NHL entry draft (June 11, 1980). ... Suffered recurring back spasms (December 1986); missed 10 games. ... Traded by Oilers with LW Dave Hunter and RW Wayne Van Dorp to Pittsburgh Penguins for C Craig Simpson, C Dave Hannan, D Moe Mantha and D Chris Joseph (November 24, 1987). ... Tore knee cartilage (December 1987). ... Bruised right shoulder (November 16, 1988). ... Fractured finger (May 1990). ... Injured back (February 27, 1991). ... Injured hip muscle (March 9, 1991). ... Scratched left eye cornea (April 9, 1991). ... Fractured jaw (April 1991). ... Pulled hip muscle (February 3, 1992); missed three games. ... Traded by Penguins to Los Angeles Kings for D Brian Benning, D Jeff Chychrun and first-round pick (LW Jason Bowen) in 1992 draft (February 19, 1992). ... Suffered back spasms (March 3, 1992). ... Fractured wrist (March 17, 1992); missed five games. ... Traded by Kings with RW Jim Hiller and C/LW Sylain Couturier to Detroit Red Wings for C Jimmy Carson, RW Marc Potvin and C Gary Shuchuk (January 29, 1993). ... Injured groin (March 18, 1993); missed one game. ... Injured groin and left knee (October 18, 1993); missed four games. ... Injured back (January 28, 1995); missed two games. ... Injured back (November 4, 1995); missed two games. ... Sprained right thumb (January 6, 1996); missed two games. ... Suffered back spasms (April 7, 1996); missed one game. ... Traded by Red Wings with C Keith Primeau and first-round pick (traded to San Jose) in 1997 draft to Hartford Whalers for LW Brendan Shanahan and D Brian Glynn (October 9, 1996). ... Strained hip flexor (October 17, 1996); missed three games. ... Suffered from the flu (November 8, 1996); missed two games. ... Injured groin (November 29, 1996); missed one game. ... Injured lower back (December 14, 1996); missed one game. ... Traded by Whalers with third-round pick (D Kris Mallette) in 1997 draft to Philadelphia Flyers for D Kevin Haller and first- (traded to San Jose) and seventh-round (C Andrew Merrick) picks in 1997 draft (December 15, 1996). ... Bruised left quadricep (December 21, 1996); missed one game. ... Suffered concussion (December 31, 1996); missed five games. ... Strained hamstring (February 4, 1997); missed two games. ... Separated left shoulder (March 25, 1997); missed three games. ... Twisted knee (April 12, 1997); missed final game of regular season. ... Strained rib muscle (January 11, 1998); missed two games. ... Suffered back spasms (March 16, 1998); missed one game. ... Traded by Flyers to Chicago Blackhawks for fifth-round pick (LW Francis Belanger) in 1998 draft (June 27, 1998). ... Suffered pinched nerve in lower back (September 25, 1998); missed first 15 games of season. ... Suffered pinched nerve in back (November 22, 1998); missed nine games. ... Traded by Blackhawks to Carolina Hurricanes for RW Nelson Emerson (December 29, 1998). ... Strained hip flexor (February 20, 1999); missed one game. ... Strained neck (March 8, 1999); missed one game. ... Signed as free agent by Boston Bruins (July 13, 2000). ... Bruised shoulder (October 7, 2000); missed three games. ... Strained hip flexor (October 17, 2000); missed two games. ... Suffered concussion (November 4, 2000); missed four games.
HONORS: Named to OMJHL All-Star second team (1979-80). ... Named to NHL All-Star second team (1980-81 through 1983-84 and 1989-90). ... Named to THE SPORTING NEWS All-Star second team (1981-82 through 1983-84, 1986-87 and 1989-90). ... Played in NHL All-Star Game (1982-1986, 1988-1994 and 1996-1997). ... Won James Norris Memorial Trophy (1984-85, 1985-86 and 1994-95). ... Named to THE SPORTING NEWS All-Star first team (1984-85, 1985-86, 1988-89 and 1994-95). ... Named to NHL All-Star first team (1984-85, 1985-86, 1988-89 and 1994-95).

RECORDS: Holds NHL single-season record for most goals by a defenseman—48 (1985-86). ... Shares NHL single-game records for most points by a defenseman—8 (March 14, 1986); and most assists by a defenseman—6 (March 14, 1986). ... Holds NHL record for most consecutive games scoring points by a defenseman—28 (1985-86). ... Holds NHL single-season playoff records for most goals by a defenseman—12; assists by a defenseman—25; and points by a defenseman—37 (1985). ... Holds NHL single-game playoff record for most points by a defenseman—6 (May 14, 1985).
STATISTICAL PLATEAUS: Three-goal games: 1982-83 (1), 1984-85 (1), 1985-86 (1), 1987-88 (1). Total: 4. ... Four-goal games: 1984-85 (1). ... Total hat tricks: 5.
MISCELLANEOUS: Member of Stanley Cup championship team (1984, 1985, 1987 and 1991).

			REGULAR SEASON							PLAYOFFS				
Season Team	League	Gms.	G	A	Pts.	PIM	+/-	PP	SH	Gms.	G	A	Pts.	PIM
77-78—Kingston	OMJHL	8	2	2	4	11	...	...	...	—	—	—	—	—
—North York	MTHL	50	14	33	47	64	...	...	...	—	—	—	—	—
78-79—Sault Ste. Marie	OMJHL	68	17	72	89	99	...	...	...	—	—	—	—	—
79-80—Sault Ste. Marie	OMJHL	23	10	21	31	63	...	...	...	—	—	—	—	—
—Kitchener	OMJHL	52	19	52	71	130	...	...	...	—	—	—	—	—
80-81—Edmonton	NHL	74	9	23	32	130	4	2	0	9	4	3	7	22
81-82—Edmonton	NHL	80	29	60	89	106	35	13	0	5	1	1	2	6
82-83—Edmonton	NHL	80	29	67	96	87	52	9	1	16	7	7	14	14
83-84—Edmonton	NHL	80	40	86	126	104	52	14	1	19	8	14	22	21
84-85—Edmonton	NHL	80	37	84	121	97	55	12	2	18	12	25	37	44
85-86—Edmonton	NHL	79	48	90	138	120	61	9	*9	10	1	9	10	30
86-87—Edmonton	NHL	59	17	50	67	49	12	10	2	17	3	8	11	30
87-88—Pittsburgh	NHL	46	15	52	67	93	-1	6	2	—	—	—	—	—
88-89—Pittsburgh	NHL	75	30	83	113	195	-10	11	0	11	2	13	15	31
89-90—Pittsburgh	NHL	80	29	74	103	95	-25	10	0	—	—	—	—	—
90-91—Pittsburgh	NHL	76	24	69	93	128	-18	8	0	12	2	9	11	6
91-92—Pittsburgh	NHL	54	10	54	64	62	4	5	0	—	—	—	—	—
—Los Angeles	NHL	10	1	4	5	25	-3	0	0	6	4	3	7	2
92-93—Los Angeles	NHL	50	8	49	57	50	9	2	0	—	—	—	—	—
—Detroit	NHL	30	4	26	30	27	7	3	0	7	2	9	11	2
93-94—Detroit	NHL	80	14	63	77	106	28	5	0	7	1	6	7	8
94-95—Detroit	NHL	45	14	44	58	72	18	4	1	18	6	12	18	10
95-96—Detroit	NHL	76	14	60	74	90	19	3	1	17	5	9	14	30
96-97—Hartford	NHL	20	3	5	8	18	0	1	0	—	—	—	—	—
—Philadelphia	NHL	37	6	20	26	20	11	0	1	17	1	8	9	6
97-98—Philadelphia	NHL	57	2	27	29	30	3	1	0	—	—	—	—	—
98-99—Chicago	NHL	10	0	4	4	0	-6	0	0	—	—	—	—	—
—Carolina	NHL	44	2	8	10	28	-1	1	0	5	0	1	1	2
99-00—Carolina	NHL	69	11	29	40	40	-6	6	0	—	—	—	—	—
00-01—Boston	NHL	18	0	4	4	30	-6	0	0	—	—	—	—	—
NHL Totals (21 years)		1409	396	1135	1531	1802	294	135	20	194	59	137	196	264

COLE, ERIK   LW   HURRICANES

PERSONAL: Born November 6, 1978, in Oswego, N.Y. ... 6-0/185. ... Shoots left.
TRANSACTIONS/CAREER NOTES: Selected by Carolina Hurricanes in third round (third Hurricanes pick, 71st overall) of NHL entry draft (June 27, 1998).
HONORS: Named to NCAA All-America (East) second team (1998-99). ... Named to ECAC All-Star first team (1998-99 and 1999-2000).

			REGULAR SEASON							PLAYOFFS				
Season Team	League	Gms.	G	A	Pts.	PIM	+/-	PP	SH	Gms.	G	A	Pts.	PIM
96-97—Des Moines	USHL	48	30	34	64	185	...	...	...	—	—	—	—	—
97-98—Clarkson	ECAC	34	11	20	31	55	...	...	...	—	—	—	—	—
98-99—Clarkson	ECAC	36	†22	20	42	50	...	...	...	—	—	—	—	—
99-00—Clarkson	ECAC	33	19	11	30	46	...	...	...	—	—	—	—	—
—Cincinnati	IHL	9	4	3	7	2	...	...	...	7	1	1	2	2
00-01—Cincinnati	IHL	69	23	20	43	28	...	...	...	5	1	0	1	2

COMMODORE, MIKE   D   DEVILS

PERSONAL: Born November 4, 1979, in Fort Saskatchewan, Alta. ... 6-4/225. ... Shoots right.
TRANSACTIONS/CAREER NOTES: Selected by New Jersey Devils in second round (second Devils pick, 42nd overall) of NHL entry draft (June 26, 1999).
HONORS: Named to NCAA All-Tournament team (1999-2000).

			REGULAR SEASON							PLAYOFFS				
Season Team	League	Gms.	G	A	Pts.	PIM	+/-	PP	SH	Gms.	G	A	Pts.	PIM
96-97—Fort Saskatchewan	Tier II Jr. A	51	3	8	11	244	...	...	...	—	—	—	—	—
97-98—Univ. of North Dakota	WCHA	29	0	5	5	74	...	...	...	—	—	—	—	—
98-99—Univ. of North Dakota	WCHA	39	5	8	13	*154	...	...	...	—	—	—	—	—
99-00—Univ. of North Dakota	WCHA	38	5	7	12	*154	...	...	...	—	—	—	—	—
00-01—Albany	AHL	41	2	5	7	59	...	...	...	—	—	—	—	—
—New Jersey	NHL	20	1	4	5	14	5	0	0	—	—	—	—	—
NHL Totals (1 year)		20	1	4	5	14	5	0	0					

COMRIE, MIKE   C   OILERS

PERSONAL: Born September 11, 1980, in Edmonton. ... 5-9/172. ... Shoots left. ... Brother of Paul Comrie, center, Edmonton Oilers organization.
TRANSACTIONS/CAREER NOTES: Selected by Edmonton Oilers in third round (fifth Oilers pick, 91st overall) of NHL entry draft (June 26, 1999).
HONORS: Named to CCHA All-Star first team (1999-2000). ... Named to NCAA All-America (West) second team (1999-2000).

Season Team	League	REGULAR SEASON								PLAYOFFS				
		Gms.	G	A	Pts.	PIM	+/-	PP	SH	Gms.	G	A	Pts.	PIM
96-97—St. Albert	Jr. A	63	37	41	78	44	...	...	...	—	—	—	—	—
97-98—St. Albert	Jr. A	58	60	78	138	134	...	...	...	—	—	—	—	—
98-99—Univ. of Michigan.......	CCHA	42	19	25	44	38	...	...	...	—	—	—	—	—
99-00—Univ. of Michigan.......	CCHA	38	21	34	55	93	...	...	...	—	—	—	—	—
00-01—Kootenay....................	WHL	37	39	40	79	79	...	...	...	—	—	—	—	—
—Edmonton..................	NHL	41	8	14	22	14	6	3	0	6	1	2	3	0
NHL Totals (1 year)..............		41	8	14	22	14	6	3	0	6	1	2	3	0

CONKLIN, TY   G   OILERS

PERSONAL: Born March 30, 1976, in Anchorage, Alaska. ... 6-0/180. ... Catches left.
TRANSACTIONS/CAREER NOTES: Signed as non-drafted free agent by Edmonton Oilers (April 18, 2000).
HONORS: Named to Hockey East All-Star second team (1998-99). ... Named to Hockey East All-Star first team (1999-2000 and 2000-01). ... Named to NCAA All-America (East) second team (1999-2000). ... Named to NCAA All-America (East) first team (2000-01).

Season Team	League	REGULAR SEASON								PLAYOFFS					
		Gms.	Min	W	L	T	GA	SO	Avg.	Gms.	Min.	W	L	GA	SO	Avg.
98-99—Univ. of New Hamp.......	Hockey East	22	1338	18	3	1	41	0	*1.84	—	—	—	—	—	—	—
99-00—Univ. of New Hamp.......	Hockey East	*37	*2194	*22	8	*6	*91	1	2.49	—	—	—	—	—	—	—
00-01—Univ. of New Hamp.......	Hockey East	34	2048	17	12	*5	70	*4	*2.05	—	—	—	—	—	—	—

CONNOLLY, TIM   C   SABRES   C

PERSONAL: Born May 7, 1981, in Baldwinsville, N.Y. ... 6-0/186. ... Shoots right.
TRANSACTIONS/CAREER NOTES: Selected by New York Islanders in first round (first Islanders pick, fifth overall) of NHL entry draft (June 26, 1999). ... Traded by Islanders with LW Taylor Pyatt to Buffalo Sabres for C Michael Peca (June 24, 2001).
MISCELLANEOUS: Scored on a penalty shot (vs. Jean-Sebastien Aubin, March 21, 2000).

Season Team	League	REGULAR SEASON								PLAYOFFS				
		Gms.	G	A	Pts.	PIM	+/-	PP	SH	Gms.	G	A	Pts.	PIM
96-97—Syracuse....................	Jr. A	50	42	62	104	34	...	...	...	—	—	—	—	—
97-98—Erie	OHL	59	30	32	62	32	...	...	...	7	1	6	7	6
98-99—Erie	OHL	46	34	34	68	50	...	...	...	—	—	—	—	—
99-00—New York Islanders.....	NHL	81	14	20	34	44	-25	2	1	—	—	—	—	—
00-01—New York Islanders.....	NHL	82	10	31	41	42	-14	5	0	—	—	—	—	—
NHL Totals (2 years)...........		163	24	51	75	86	-39	7	1					

CONROY, CRAIG   C   FLAMES

PERSONAL: Born September 4, 1971, in Potsdam, N.Y. ... 6-2/193. ... Shoots right. ... Full Name: Craig Michael Conroy.
TRANSACTIONS/CAREER NOTES: Selected by Montreal Canadiens in sixth round (seventh Canadiens pick, 123rd overall) of NHL entry draft (June 16, 1990). ... Traded by Canadiens with C Pierre Turgeon and D Rory Fitzpatrick to St. Louis Blues for LW Shayne Corson, D Murray Baron and fifth-round pick (D Gennady Razin) in 1997 draft (October 29, 1996). ... Sprained ankle (March 12, 1999); missed 11 games. ... Reinjured ankle (April 7, 1999); missed two games. ... Suffered from the flu (October 2, 1999); missed one game. ... Traded by Blues with seventh-round pick (LW David Moss) in 2001 draft to Calgary Flames for LW Cory Stillman (March 13, 2001).
HONORS: Named to NCAA All-America (East) first team (1993-94). ... Named to NCAA All-Tournament team (1993-94). ... Named to ECAC All-Star first team (1993-94).
STATISTICAL PLATEAUS: Three-goal games: 1998-99 (1).

Season Team	League	REGULAR SEASON								PLAYOFFS				
		Gms.	G	A	Pts.	PIM	+/-	PP	SH	Gms.	G	A	Pts.	PIM
89-90—Northwood School......	N.Y. H.S.	31	33	43	76	...	...	...	...	—	—	—	—	—
90-91—Clarkson	ECAC	40	8	21	29	24	...	...	...	—	—	—	—	—
91-92—Clarkson	ECAC	31	19	17	36	36	...	...	...	—	—	—	—	—
92-93—Clarkson	ECAC	35	10	23	33	26	...	...	...	—	—	—	—	—
93-94—Clarkson	ECAC	34	26	40	66	66	...	...	...	—	—	—	—	—
94-95—Fredericton	AHL	55	26	18	44	29	...	...	...	11	7	3	10	6
—Montreal	NHL	6	1	0	1	0	-1	0	0	—	—	—	—	—
95-96—Fredericton	AHL	67	31	38	69	65	...	...	...	10	5	7	12	6
—Montreal	NHL	7	0	0	0	2	-4	0	0	—	—	—	—	—
96-97—Fredericton	AHL	9	10	6	16	10	...	...	...	—	—	—	—	—
—St. Louis	NHL	61	6	11	17	43	0	0	0	6	0	0	0	8
—Worcester	AHL	5	5	6	11	2	...	...	...	—	—	—	—	—
97-98—St. Louis	NHL	81	14	29	43	46	20	0	3	10	1	2	3	8
98-99—St. Louis	NHL	69	14	25	39	38	14	0	1	13	2	1	3	6
99-00—St. Louis	NHL	79	12	15	27	36	5	1	2	7	0	2	2	2
00-01—St. Louis	NHL	69	11	14	25	46	2	0	3	—	—	—	—	—
—Calgary	NHL	14	3	4	7	14	0	0	1	—	—	—	—	—
NHL Totals (7 years)...........		386	61	98	159	225	36	1	10	36	3	5	8	24

COOKE, MATT   C   CANUCKS

PERSONAL: Born September 7, 1978, in Belleville, Ont. ... 5-11/205. ... Shoots left.
TRANSACTIONS/CAREER NOTES: Selected by Vancouver Canucks in sixth round (eighth Canucks pick, 144th overall) of NHL entry draft (June 21, 1997). ... Suspended two games by AHL for attempting to injure an opponent (February 24, 1999). ... Injured knee (March 2, 2001); missed one game.

Season Team	League	REGULAR SEASON								PLAYOFFS				
		Gms.	G	A	Pts.	PIM	+/-	PP	SH	Gms.	G	A	Pts.	PIM
95-96—Windsor	OHL	61	8	11	19	102	...	...	...	7	1	3	4	6
96-97—Windsor	OHL	65	45	50	95	146	...	...	...	5	5	5	10	4
97-98—Windsor	OHL	23	14	19	33	50	...	...	...	—	—	—	—	—
—Kingston	OHL	25	8	13	21	49	...	...	...	12	8	8	16	20
98-99—Vancouver	NHL	30	0	2	2	27	-12	0	0	—	—	—	—	—
—Syracuse	AHL	37	15	18	33	119	...	...	...	—	—	—	—	—
99-00—Syracuse	AHL	18	5	8	13	27	...	...	...	—	—	—	—	—
—Vancouver	NHL	51	5	7	12	39	3	0	1	—	—	—	—	—
00-01—Vancouver	NHL	81	14	13	27	94	5	0	2	4	0	0	0	4
NHL Totals (3 years)		162	19	22	41	160	-4	0	3	4	0	0	0	4

COOPER, DAVID   D   MAPLE LEAFS

PERSONAL: Born November 2, 1973, in Ottawa. ... 6-2/204. ... Shoots left.

TRANSACTIONS/CAREER NOTES: Selected by Buffalo Sabres in first round (first Sabres pick, 11th overall) of NHL entry draft (June 20, 1992). ... Signed as free agent by Toronto Maple Leafs (September 26, 1996). ... Suffered from the flu (January 3, 1997); missed one game. ... Sprained knee (March 19, 1997); missed 11 games. ... Traded by Maple Leafs to Calgary Flames for RW Ladislov Kohn (July 2, 1998). ... Signed as free agent by Maple Leafs (October 5, 2000).

HONORS: Won WHL Top Prospect Award (1991-92). ... Named to WHL (East) All-Star first team (1991-92). ... Named to AHL All-Star second team (1997-98).

Season Team	League	REGULAR SEASON								PLAYOFFS				
		Gms.	G	A	Pts.	PIM	+/-	PP	SH	Gms.	G	A	Pts.	PIM
89-90—Medicine Hat	WHL	61	4	11	15	65	...	...	...	3	0	2	2	2
90-91—Medicine Hat	WHL	64	12	31	43	66	...	...	...	11	1	3	4	23
91-92—Medicine Hat	WHL	72	17	47	64	176	...	...	...	4	1	4	5	8
92-93—Medicine Hat	WHL	63	15	50	65	88	...	...	...	10	2	2	4	32
—Rochester	AHL	—	—	—	—	—	...	...	...	2	0	0	0	2
93-94—Rochester	AHL	68	10	25	35	82	...	...	...	4	1	1	2	2
94-95—Rochester	AHL	21	2	4	6	48	...	...	...	—	—	—	—	—
—South Carolina	ECHL	39	9	19	28	90	...	...	...	9	3	8	11	24
95-96—Rochester	AHL	67	9	18	27	79	...	...	...	8	0	1	1	12
96-97—St. John's	AHL	44	16	19	35	65	...	...	...	—	—	—	—	—
—Toronto	NHL	19	3	3	6	16	-3	2	0	—	—	—	—	—
97-98—Toronto	NHL	9	0	4	4	8	2	0	0	—	—	—	—	—
—St. John's	AHL	60	19	23	42	117	...	...	...	4	0	1	1	6
98-99—Saint John	AHL	65	18	24	42	121	...	...	...	7	1	4	5	10
99-00—Kassel	Germany	55	11	13	24	82	...	...	...	6	2	1	3	38
00-01—St. John's	AHL	71	16	26	42	117	...	...	...	4	1	1	2	10
—Toronto	NHL	2	0	0	0	0	-1	0	0	—	—	—	—	—
NHL Totals (3 years)		30	3	7	10	24	-2	2	0					

CORBET, RENE   LW

PERSONAL: Born June 25, 1973, in St. Hyacinthe, Que. ... 6-0/195. ... Shoots left. ... Name pronounced ruh-NAY kohr-BAY.

TRANSACTIONS/CAREER NOTES: Selected by Quebec Nordiques in second round (second Nordiques pick, 24th overall) of NHL entry draft (June 22, 1991). ... Nordiques franchise moved to Colorado and renamed Avalanche for 1995-96 season (June 21, 1995). ... Injured shoulder (April 3, 1996); missed five games. ... Suffered concussion (December 17, 1996); missed three games. ... Suffered from the flu (October 24, 1997); missed two games. ... Strained hip muscle (November 21, 1997); missed two games. ... Sprained wrist (January 3, 1998); missed three games. ... Injured shoulder (February 25, 1998); missed three games. ... Reinjured shoulder (March 14, 1998); missed four games. ... Bruised right foot (January 6, 1999); missed three games. ... Injured hamstring (February 22, 1999); missed three games. ... Traded by Avalanche with D Wade Belak and future considerations to Calgary Flames for RW Theo Fleury and LW Chris Dingman (February 28, 1999); Flames acquired D Robyn Regehr to complete deal (March 27, 1999). ... Injured groin (April 1, 1999); missed two games. ... Injured groin (October 2, 1999); missed two games. ... Injured foot (November 9, 1999); missed 18 games. ... Traded by Flames with G Tyler Moss to Pittsburgh Penguins for D Brad Werenka (March 14, 2000). ... Bruised shoulder (March 21, 2000); missed final 10 games of season. ... Injured shoulder (December 5, 2000); missed three games. ... Injured back (December 20, 2000); missed four games. ... Bruised foot (February 10, 2001); missed three games. ... Fractured foot (February 16, 2001); missed final 25 games of season.

HONORS: Won Michel Bergeron Trophy (1990-91). ... Named to QMJHL All-Rookie team (1990-91). ... Won Jean Beliveau Trophy (1992-93). ... Named to Can.HL All-Star first team (1992-93). ... Named to QMJHL All-Star first team (1992-93). ... Won Dudley (Red) Garrett Memorial Trophy (1993-94).

MISCELLANEOUS: Member of Stanley Cup championship team (1996).

Season Team	League	REGULAR SEASON								PLAYOFFS				
		Gms.	G	A	Pts.	PIM	+/-	PP	SH	Gms.	G	A	Pts.	PIM
90-91—Drummondville	QMJHL	45	25	40	65	34	...	...	...	14	11	6	17	15
91-92—Drummondville	QMJHL	56	46	50	96	90	...	...	...	4	1	2	3	17
92-93—Drummondville	QMJHL	63	*79	69	*148	143	...	...	...	10	7	13	20	16
93-94—Cornwall	AHL	68	37	40	77	56	...	...	...	13	7	2	9	18
—Quebec	NHL	9	1	1	2	0	1	0	0	—	—	—	—	—
94-95—Cornwall	AHL	65	33	24	57	79	...	...	...	12	2	8	10	27
—Quebec	NHL	8	0	3	3	2	3	0	0	2	0	1	1	0
95-96—Cornwall	AHL	9	5	6	11	10	...	...	...	—	—	—	—	—
—Colorado	NHL	33	3	6	9	33	10	0	0	8	3	2	5	2
96-97—Colorado	NHL	76	12	15	27	67	14	1	0	17	2	2	4	27
97-98—Colorado	NHL	68	16	12	28	133	8	4	0	2	0	0	0	2
98-99—Colorado	NHL	53	8	14	22	58	3	2	0	—	—	—	—	—
—Calgary	NHL	20	5	4	9	10	-2	1	0	—	—	—	—	—
99-00—Calgary	NHL	48	4	10	14	60	-7	0	0	—	—	—	—	—
—Pittsburgh	NHL	4	1	0	1	0	-4	1	0	7	1	1	2	9
00-01—Pittsburgh	NHL	43	8	9	17	57	-3	2	0	17	1	0	1	12
NHL Totals (8 years)		362	58	74	132	420	23	11	0	53	7	6	13	52

PERSONAL: Born December 18, 1967, in Salisbury, Mass. ... 6-0/222. ... Shoots right. ... Full Name: Robert Freeman Corkum.
TRANSACTIONS/CAREER NOTES: Selected by Buffalo Sabres in third round (third Sabres pick, 47th overall) of NHL entry draft (June 21, 1986). ... Injured hip (March 19, 1992). ... Selected by Mighty Ducks of Anaheim in NHL expansion draft (June 24, 1993). ... Ruptured ankle tendon (March 27, 1994); missed remainder of season. ... Lacerated lower lip (November 24, 1995); missed two games. ... Traded by Mighty Ducks to Philadelphia Flyers for C Chris Herperger and seventh-round pick (LW Tony Mohagen) in 1997 draft (February 6, 1996). ... Strained right shoulder (February 17, 1996); missed three games. ... Selected by Phoenix Coyotes from Flyers in NHL waiver draft for cash (September 30, 1996). ... Suffered from the flu (January 13, 1997); missed one game. ... Strained back (October 23, 1997); missed one game. ... Suffered concussion (March 16, 1998); missed five games. ... Strained hip flexor (January 19, 1999); missed one game. ... Strained groin (March 23, 1999); missed four games. ... Signed as free agent by Los Angeles Kings (December 29, 1999). ... Traded by Kings to New Jersey Devils for future considerations (February 23, 2001). ... Signed as free agent by Atlanta Thrashers (July 13, 2001).

			REGULAR SEASON								PLAYOFFS				
Season Team	League	Gms.	G	A	Pts.	PIM	+/-	PP	SH		Gms.	G	A	Pts.	PIM
84-85—Triton Regional	Mass. H.S.	18	35	36	71	...	...	...	...		—	—	—	—	—
85-86—Univ. of Maine	Hockey East	39	7	26	33	53	...	...	...		—	—	—	—	—
86-87—Univ. of Maine	Hockey East	35	18	11	29	24	...	...	...		—	—	—	—	—
87-88—Univ. of Maine	Hockey East	40	14	18	32	64	...	...	...		—	—	—	—	—
88-89—Univ. of Maine	Hockey East	45	17	31	48	64	...	...	...		—	—	—	—	—
89-90—Rochester	AHL	43	8	11	19	45	...	...	...		12	2	5	7	16
—Buffalo	NHL	8	2	0	2	4	2	0	0		5	1	0	1	4
90-91—Rochester	AHL	69	13	21	34	77	...	...	...		15	4	4	8	4
91-92—Rochester	AHL	52	16	12	28	47	...	...	...		8	0	6	6	8
—Buffalo	NHL	20	2	4	6	21	-9	0	0		4	1	0	1	0
92-93—Buffalo	NHL	68	6	4	10	38	-3	0	1		5	0	0	0	2
93-94—Anaheim	NHL	76	23	28	51	18	4	3	3		—	—	—	—	—
94-95—Anaheim	NHL	44	10	9	19	25	-7	0	0		—	—	—	—	—
95-96—Anaheim	NHL	48	5	7	12	26	0	0	0		—	—	—	—	—
—Philadelphia	NHL	28	4	3	7	8	3	0	0		12	1	2	3	6
96-97—Phoenix	NHL	80	9	11	20	40	-7	0	1		7	2	2	4	4
97-98—Phoenix	NHL	76	12	9	21	28	-7	0	5		6	1	0	1	4
98-99—Phoenix	NHL	77	9	10	19	17	-9	0	0		7	0	1	1	4
99-00—Los Angeles	NHL	45	5	6	11	14	0	0	0		4	0	0	0	0
00-01—Los Angeles	NHL	58	4	6	10	18	-12	1	0		—	—	—	—	—
—New Jersey	NHL	17	3	1	4	4	4	0	0		12	1	2	3	0
NHL Totals (11 years).........		645	94	98	192	261	-41	4	10		62	7	7	14	24

PERSONAL: Born October 29, 1978, in Derby, Conn. ... 6-3/220. ... Shoots right.
TRANSACTIONS/CAREER NOTES: Selected by Washington Capitals in fourth round (fourth Capitals pick, 107th overall) of NHL entry draft (June 27, 1998).

			REGULAR SEASON								PLAYOFFS				
Season Team	League	Gms.	G	A	Pts.	PIM	+/-	PP	SH		Gms.	G	A	Pts.	PIM
96-97—Deerfield Academy......	USHS (East)	16	6	15	21	10	...	...	...		—	—	—	—	—
97-98—Princeton University ...	ECAC	31	3	6	9	22	...	...	...		—	—	—	—	—
98-99—Princeton University ...	ECAC	32	10	6	16	38	...	...	...		—	—	—	—	—
99-00—Princeton University ...	ECAC	30	10	14	24	41	...	...	...		—	—	—	—	—
00-01—Princeton University ...	ECAC	31	13	12	25	30	...	...	...		—	—	—	—	—
—Portland.....................	AHL	6	0	1	1	4	...	...	...		2	1	0	1	0

PERSONAL: Born April 3, 1978, in St. Hubert, Que. ... 5-10/184.
TRANSACTIONS/CAREER NOTES: Selected by St. Louis Blues in seventh round (fifth Blues pick, 169th overall) of NHL entry draft (June 22, 1996).
HONORS: Won Michel Briere Trophy (1996-97). ... Named to Can.HL All-Star second team (1996-97). ... Named to QMJHL All-Star first team (1996-97).

			REGULAR SEASON								PLAYOFFS				
Season Team	League	Gms.	G	A	Pts.	PIM	+/-	PP	SH		Gms.	G	A	Pts.	PIM
94-95—Victoriaville................	QMJHL	65	27	26	53	6	...	...	...		4	2	5	7	2
95-96—Victoriaville................	QMJHL	65	49	65	114	77	...	...	...		12	6	7	13	4
96-97—Victoriaville................	QMJHL	54	51	68	119	50	...	...	...		—	—	—	—	—
97-98—Victoriaville................	QMJHL	35	24	51	75	20	...	...	...		3	1	1	2	2
98-99—Worcester	AHL	63	14	14	28	26	...	...	...		—	—	—	—	—
99-00—Worcester	AHL	71	21	34	55	19	...	...	...		9	2	3	5	10
00-01—Worcester	AHL	52	19	37	56	47	...	...	...		—	—	—	—	—
—St. Louis	NHL	28	10	3	13	14	0	5	0		12	0	1	1	0
NHL Totals (1 year)............		28	10	3	13	14	0	5	0		12	0	1	1	0

PERSONAL: Born August 13, 1966, in Barrie, Ont. ... 6-1/198. ... Shoots left.
TRANSACTIONS/CAREER NOTES: Selected by Montreal Canadiens in first round (second Canadiens pick, eighth overall) of NHL entry draft (June 9, 1984). ... Fractured jaw (January 24, 1987). ... Strained ligament in right knee (September 1987). ... Injured groin (March 1988). ... Injured knee (April 1988). ... Injured knee (April 1989). ... Bruised left shoulder (October 29, 1989). ... Fractured toe on right foot (December 1989).

... Suffered hip pointer (November 10, 1990); missed seven games. ... Pulled groin (February 11, 1991). ... Traded by Canadiens with LW Vladimir Vujtek and C Brent Gilchrist to Edmonton Oilers for LW Vincent Damphousse and fourth-round pick (D Adam Wiesel) in 1993 draft (August 27, 1992). ... Fractured fibula (February 18, 1994); missed 12 games. ... Injured leg (March 23, 1994); missed remainder of season. ... Signed by St. Louis Blues to an offer sheet (July 28, 1995); Oilers received Blues first-round picks in 1996 and 1997 drafts as compensation; Oilers then traded picks to Blues for rights to G Curtis Joseph and RW Michael Grier (August 4, 1995). ... Fractured jaw (March 26, 1996); missed five games. ... Traded by Blues with D Murray Baron and fifth-round pick (D Gennady Razin) in 1997 draft to Canadiens for C Pierre Turgeon, C Craig Conroy and D Rory Fitzpatrick (October 29, 1996). ... Injured knee (November 25, 1996) and underwent surgery; missed 10 games. ... Sprained ankle (December 26, 1996); missed 10 games. ... Strained hip flexor (February 3, 1997); missed five games. ... Strained hip flexor (January 21, 1998); missed six games. ... Strained abdominal muscle and groin (February 25, 1998); missed 13 games. ... Suffered charley horse (April 18, 1998); missed one game. ... Injured ribs (October 16, 1998); missed six games. ... Suffered nerve irritation in neck (November 19, 1998); missed four games. ... Sprained ankle (March 8, 1999); missed three games. ... Suspended six games by NHL for high-sticking incident (April 1, 1999). ... Suffered colitis (October 6, 1999); missed 10 games. ... Suffered eye injury (March 16, 2000); missed two games. ... Signed as free agent by Toronto Maple Leafs (July 4, 2000). ... Suffered injury (February 15, 2000); missed one game. ... Suffered injury (March 21, 2001); missed four games.

HONORS: Played in NHL All-Star Game (1990, 1994 and 1998).
MISCELLANEOUS: Captain of Edmonton Oilers (1994-95). ... Captain of St. Louis Blues (October 25, 1995 through February 24, 1996).
STATISTICAL PLATEAUS: Three-goal games: 1988-89 (2), 1993-94 (1). Total: 3.

Season Team	League	REGULAR SEASON Gms.	G	A	Pts.	PIM	+/-	PP	SH	PLAYOFFS Gms.	G	A	Pts.	PIM
82-83—Barrie	COJHL	23	13	29	42	87	...	...	...	—	—	—	—	—
83-84—Brantford	OHL	66	25	46	71	165	...	...	...	6	4	1	5	26
84-85—Hamilton	OHL	54	27	63	90	154	...	...	...	11	3	7	10	19
85-86—Hamilton	OHL	47	41	57	98	153	...	...	...	—	—	—	—	—
—Montreal	NHL	3	0	0	0	2	-3	0	0	—	—	—	—	—
86-87—Montreal	NHL	55	12	11	23	144	10	0	1	17	6	5	11	30
87-88—Montreal	NHL	71	12	27	39	152	22	2	0	3	1	0	1	12
88-89—Montreal	NHL	80	26	24	50	193	-1	10	0	21	4	5	9	65
89-90—Montreal	NHL	76	31	44	75	144	33	7	0	11	2	8	10	20
90-91—Montreal	NHL	71	23	24	47	138	9	7	0	13	9	6	15	36
91-92—Montreal	NHL	64	17	36	53	118	15	3	0	10	2	5	7	15
92-93—Edmonton	NHL	80	16	31	47	209	-19	9	2	—	—	—	—	—
93-94—Edmonton	NHL	64	25	29	54	118	-8	11	0	—	—	—	—	—
94-95—Edmonton	NHL	48	12	24	36	86	-17	2	0	—	—	—	—	—
95-96—St. Louis	NHL	77	18	28	46	192	3	13	0	13	8	6	14	22
96-97—St. Louis	NHL	11	2	1	3	24	-4	1	0	—	—	—	—	—
—Montreal	NHL	47	6	15	21	80	-5	2	0	5	1	0	1	4
97-98—Montreal	NHL	62	21	34	55	108	2	14	1	10	3	6	9	26
—Can. Olympic team	Int'l	6	1	1	2	2	...			—	—	—	—	—
98-99—Montreal	NHL	63	12	20	32	147	-10	7	0	—	—	—	—	—
99-00—Montreal	NHL	70	8	20	28	115	-2	2	0	—	—	—	—	—
00-01—Toronto	NHL	77	8	18	26	189	1	0	0	11	1	1	2	14
NHL Totals (16 years)		1019	249	386	635	2159	26	90	4	114	37	42	79	244

CORVO, JOE — D — KINGS

PERSONAL: Born June 20, 1977, in Oak Park, Ill. ... 6-1/205. ... Shoots right. ... Full Name: Joseph Corvo.
TRANSACTIONS/CAREER NOTES: Selected by Los Angeles Kings in fourth round (fourth Kings pick, 83rd overall) of NHL entry draft (June 21, 1997). ... Sat out entire 1999-2000 season due to contract dispute.
HONORS: Named to CCHA All-Rookie team (1995-96). ... Named to CCHA All-Star second team (1996-97).

Season Team	League	REGULAR SEASON Gms.	G	A	Pts.	PIM	+/-	PP	SH	PLAYOFFS Gms.	G	A	Pts.	PIM
95-96—Western Michigan U.	CCHA	41	5	25	30	38	...	...	...	—	—	—	—	—
96-97—Western Michigan U.	CCHA	32	12	21	33	85	...	...	...	—	—	—	—	—
97-98—Western Michigan U.	CCHA	32	5	12	17	93	...	...	...	—	—	—	—	—
98-99—Springfield	AHL	50	5	15	20	32	...	...	...	—	—	—	—	—
—Hampton Roads	ECHL	5	0	0	0	15	...	...	...	4	0	1	1	0
99-00—							Did not play.							
00-01—Lowell	AHL	77	10	23	33	31	...	...	...	4	3	1	4	0

COTE, PATRICK — LW

PERSONAL: Born January 24, 1975, in Lasalle, Que. ... 6-3/218. ... Shoots left. ... Name pronounced koh-TAY.
TRANSACTIONS/CAREER NOTES: Selected by Dallas Stars in second round (second Stars pick, 37th overall) of NHL entry draft (July 8, 1995). ... Separated shoulder (November 12, 1997); missed 69 games. ... Selected by Nashville Predators in NHL expansion draft (June 26, 1998). ... Suffered from the flu (December 19, 1998); missed one game. ... Injured shoulder (March 2, 1999); missed three games. ... Strained groin (March 18, 1999); missed one game. ... Injured hand (November 5, 1999); missed nine games. ... Injured hand (January 15, 2000); missed final 37 games of season. ... Traded by Predators to Edmonton Oilers for fifth-round pick (C Matt Koalska) in 2000 draft (June 12, 2000). ... Suffered injury (October 28, 2000); missed five games.

Season Team	League	REGULAR SEASON Gms.	G	A	Pts.	PIM	+/-	PP	SH	PLAYOFFS Gms.	G	A	Pts.	PIM
93-94—Beauport	QMJHL	48	2	4	6	230	...	...	...	12	1	0	1	61
94-95—Beauport	QMJHL	56	20	20	40	314	...	...	...	17	8	8	16	115
95-96—Michigan	IHL	57	4	6	10	239	...	...	...	3	0	0	0	2
—Dallas	NHL	2	0	0	0	5	-2	0	0	—	—	—	—	—
96-97—Michigan	IHL	58	14	10	24	237	...	...	...	4	2	0	2	6
—Dallas	NHL	3	0	0	0	27	0	0	0	—	—	—	—	—
97-98—Dallas	NHL	3	0	0	0	15	-1	0	0	—	—	—	—	—
—Michigan	IHL	4	2	0	2	4	...	...	...	—	—	—	—	—

Season Team	League	REGULAR SEASON								PLAYOFFS				
		Gms.	G	A	Pts.	PIM	+/-	PP	SH	Gms.	G	A	Pts.	PIM
98-99—Nashville	NHL	70	1	2	3	242	-7	0	0	—	—	—	—	—
99-00—Nashville	NHL	21	0	0	0	70	-7	0	0	—	—	—	—	—
00-01—Hamilton	AHL	16	0	1	1	61	...	...	...	—	—	—	—	—
—Edmonton	NHL	6	0	0	0	18	-2	0	0	—	—	—	—	—
NHL Totals (6 years)		105	1	2	3	377	-19	0	0					

COTE, SYLVAIN   D   CAPITALS

PERSONAL: Born January 19, 1966, in Quebec City. ... 6-0/190. ... Shoots right. ... Brother of Alain Cote, defenseman with five NHL teams (1985-86 through 1993-94). ... Name pronounced KOH-tay.

TRANSACTIONS/CAREER NOTES: Selected by Hartford Whalers in first round (first Whalers pick, 11th overall) of NHL entry draft (June 9, 1984). ... Fractured toe on left foot (October 28, 1989). ... Sprained left knee (December 1989). ... Fractured right foot (January 22, 1990). ... Traded by Whalers to Washington Capitals for second-round pick (LW Andrei Nikolishin) in 1992 draft (September 8, 1991). ... Fractured wrist (September 25, 1992); missed six games. ... Suffered hip pointer (January 7, 1993); missed one game. ... Injured ankle (January 16, 1996); missed one game. ... Tore medial collateral ligament in right knee (October 18, 1996); missed 19 games. ... Strained knee (December 6, 1996); missed five games. ... Traded by Capitals to Toronto Maple Leafs for D Jeff Brown (March 24, 1998). ... Sprained shoulder (March 27, 1999); missed three games. ... Traded by Maple Leafs to Chicago Blackhawks for second-round pick (D Karel Pilar) in 2001 draft and conditional pick in 2001 draft (October 8, 1999). ... Strained hamstring (December 6, 1999); missed four games. ... Traded by Blackhawks with D Dave Manson to Dallas Stars for C Derek Plante, D Kevin Dean and second-round pick (RW Matt Keith) in 2001 draft (February 8, 2000). ... Signed as free agent by Capitals (July 6, 2000).

HONORS: Named to QMJHL All-Star second team (1983-84). ... Won Emile (Butch) Bouchard Trophy (1985-86). ... Shared Guy Lafleur Trophy with Luc Robitaille (1985-86). ... Named to QMJHL All-Star first team (1985-86).

C

Season Team	League	REGULAR SEASON								PLAYOFFS				
		Gms.	G	A	Pts.	PIM	+/-	PP	SH	Gms.	G	A	Pts.	PIM
82-83—Quebec	QMJHL	66	10	24	34	50	...	...	...	—	—	—	—	—
83-84—Quebec	QMJHL	66	15	50	65	89	...	...	...	5	1	1	2	0
84-85—Hartford	NHL	67	3	9	12	17	-30	1	0	—	—	—	—	—
85-86—Hartford	NHL	2	0	0	0	0	1	0	0	—	—	—	—	—
—Hull	QMJHL	26	10	33	43	14	...	...	...	13	6	*28	34	22
—Binghamton	AHL	12	2	6	8	0	...	...	...	—	—	—	—	—
86-87—Hartford	NHL	67	2	8	10	20	10	0	0	2	0	2	2	2
87-88—Hartford	NHL	67	7	21	28	30	-8	0	1	6	1	1	2	4
88-89—Hartford	NHL	78	8	9	17	49	-7	1	0	3	0	1	1	4
89-90—Hartford	NHL	28	4	2	6	14	2	1	0	5	0	0	0	4
90-91—Hartford	NHL	73	7	12	19	17	-17	1	0	6	0	2	2	2
91-92—Washington	NHL	78	11	29	40	31	7	6	0	7	1	2	3	4
92-93—Washington	NHL	77	21	29	50	34	28	8	2	6	1	1	2	4
93-94—Washington	NHL	84	16	35	51	66	30	3	2	9	1	8	9	6
94-95—Washington	NHL	47	5	14	19	53	2	1	0	7	1	3	4	2
95-96—Washington	NHL	81	5	33	38	40	5	3	0	6	2	0	2	12
96-97—Washington	NHL	57	6	18	24	28	11	2	0	—	—	—	—	—
97-98—Washington	NHL	59	1	15	16	36	-5	0	0	—	—	—	—	—
—Toronto	NHL	12	3	6	9	6	2	1	0	—	—	—	—	—
98-99—Toronto	NHL	79	5	24	29	28	22	0	0	17	2	1	3	10
99-00—Toronto	NHL	3	0	1	1	0	1	0	0	—	—	—	—	—
—Chicago	NHL	45	6	18	24	14	-4	5	0	—	—	—	—	—
—Dallas	NHL	28	2	8	10	14	6	0	0	23	2	1	3	8
00-01—Washington	NHL	68	7	11	18	18	-3	1	1	5	0	0	0	2
NHL Totals (17 years)		1100	119	302	421	515	53	34	6	102	11	22	33	60

COUSINEAU, MARCEL   G   KINGS

PERSONAL: Born April 30, 1973, in Delson, Que. ... 5-9/180. ... Catches left. ... Name pronounced KOO-sih-noh.

TRANSACTIONS/CAREER NOTES: Selected by Boston Bruins in third round (third Bruins pick, 62nd overall) of NHL entry draft (June 22, 1991). ... Signed as free agent by Toronto Maple Leafs (November 13, 1993). ... Signed as free agent by New York Islanders (July 14, 1998). ... Traded by Islanders with RW Zigmund Palffy, C Bryan Smolinski and fourth-round pick (C Daniel Johansson) in 1999 draft to Los Angeles Kings for C Olli Jokinen, LW Josh Green, D Mathieu Biron and first-round pick (LW Taylor Pyatt) in 1999 draft (June 20, 1999). ... Suffered appendicitis (March 16, 2000); missed final 12 games of season.

HONORS: Named to QMJHL All-Rookie team (1990-91).

Season Team	League	REGULAR SEASON							PLAYOFFS						
		Gms.	Min	W	L	T	GA	SO	Avg.	Gms.	Min.	W	L	GA	SO	Avg.
90-91—Beauport	QMJHL	49	2739	13	29	3	196	1	4.29	—	—	—	—	—	—	—
91-92—Beauport	QMJHL	*67	*3673	26	*32	5	*241	0	3.94	—	—	—	—	—	—	—
92-93—Drummondville	QMJHL	60	3298	20	32	2	225	0	4.09	9	498	3	6	37	1	4.46
93-94—St. John's	AHL	37	2015	13	11	9	118	0	3.51	—	—	—	—	—	—	—
94-95—St. John's	AHL	58	3342	22	27	6	171	4	3.07	3	180	0	3	9	0	3.00
95-96—St. John's	AHL	62	3629	21	26	13	192	1	3.17	4	257	1	3	11	0	2.57
96-97—St. John's	AHL	19	1053	7	8	3	58	0	3.30	11	658	6	5	28	0	2.55
—Toronto	NHL	13	566	3	5	1	31	1	3.29	—	—	—	—	—	—	—
97-98—St. John's	AHL	57	3306	17	25	*13	167	1	3.03	4	254	1	3	10	0	2.36
—Toronto	NHL	2	17	0	0	0	0	0	...	—	—	—	—	—	—	—
98-99—Lowell	AHL	53	3034	26	17	†7	139	3	2.75	3	186	0	3	13	0	4.19
—New York Islanders	NHL	6	293	0	4	0	14	0	2.87	—	—	—	—	—	—	—
99-00—Long Beach	IHL	23	1328	18	6	1	62	0	2.80	—	—	—	—	—	—	—
—Los Angeles	NHL	5	171	1	1	0	6	0	2.11	—	—	—	—	—	—	—
00-01—Lowell	AHL	37	2135	15	20	2	101	1	2.84	1	58	0	1	4	0	4.14
NHL Totals (4 years)		26	1047	4	10	1	51	1	2.92							

COWAN, JEFF — LW — FLAMES

PERSONAL: Born September 27, 1976, in Scarborough, Ont. ... 6-2/192. ... Shoots left. ... Name pronounced KOW-ihn.
TRANSACTIONS/CAREER NOTES: Signed as non-drafted free agent by Calgary Flames (October 2, 1995). ... Suffered injury (March 3, 2000); missed one game. ... Suffered illness (March 25, 2000); missed final six games of season. ... Injured knee (February 10, 2001); missed 19 games. ... Reinjured knee (March 28, 2001); missed three games.

Season Team	League	REGULAR SEASON Gms.	G	A	Pts.	PIM	+/-	PP	SH	PLAYOFFS Gms.	G	A	Pts.	PIM
92-93—Guelph	Jr. B	45	8	8	16	22	...	...	...	—	—	—	—	—
93-94—Guelph	Jr. B	43	30	26	56	96	...	...	...	—	—	—	—	—
—Guelph	OHL	17	1	0	1	5	...	...	...	0	0	0	0	0
94-95—Guelph	OHL	51	10	7	17	14	...	...	...	14	1	1	2	0
95-96—Barrie	OHL	66	38	14	52	29	...	...	...	5	1	2	3	6
96-97—Saint John	AHL	22	5	5	10	8	...	...	...	—	—	—	—	—
—Roanoke	ECHL	47	21	13	34	42	...	...	...	—	—	—	—	—
97-98—Saint John	AHL	69	15	13	28	23	...	...	...	13	4	1	5	14
98-99—Saint John	AHL	71	7	12	19	117	...	...	...	4	0	1	1	10
99-00—Saint John	AHL	47	15	10	25	77	...	...	...	—	—	—	—	—
—Calgary	NHL	13	4	1	5	16	2	0	0	—	—	—	—	—
00-01—Calgary	NHL	51	9	4	13	74	-8	2	0	—	—	—	—	—
NHL Totals (2 years)		64	13	5	18	90	-6	2	0					

C — CROSS, CORY — D — MAPLE LEAFS

PERSONAL: Born July 31, 1975, in Lloydminster, Alta. ... 6-5/219. ... Shoots left. ... Full Name: Cory James Cross.
TRANSACTIONS/CAREER NOTES: Selected by Tampa Bay Lightning in NHL supplemental draft (June 19, 1992). ... Injured foot (November 3, 1995); missed one game. ... Bruised right foot (November 10, 1996); missed five games. ... Suffered from the flu (March 28, 1998); missed one game. ... Injured ankle (January 4, 1999); missed two games. ... Suffered hip pointer (January 30, 1999); missed 12 games. ... Traded by Lightning with seventh-round pick (F Ivan Kolozvary) in 2001 draft to Toronto Maple Leafs for RW Fredrik Modin (October 1, 1999). ... Suffered injury (November 15, 1999); missed two games. ... Suffered injury (March 29, 2000); missed two games. ... Suffered injury (November 10, 2000); missed five games. ... Injured hip (November 29, 2000); missed 14 games. ... Injured foot (February 10, 2001); missed 12 games. ... Suffered injury (March 20, 2001); missed five games.
HONORS: Named to CWUAA All-Star second team (1992-93).

Season Team	League	REGULAR SEASON Gms.	G	A	Pts.	PIM	+/-	PP	SH	PLAYOFFS Gms.	G	A	Pts.	PIM
90-91—Univ. of Alberta	CWUAA	20	2	5	7	16	...	...	...	—	—	—	—	—
91-92—Univ. of Alberta	CWUAA	39	3	10	13	76	...	...	...	—	—	—	—	—
92-93—Univ. of Alberta	CWUAA	43	11	28	39	105	...	...	...	—	—	—	—	—
—Atlanta	IHL	7	0	1	1	2	...	...	...	4	0	0	0	6
93-94—Atlanta	IHL	70	4	14	18	72	...	...	...	9	1	2	3	14
—Tampa Bay	NHL	5	0	0	0	6	-3	0	0	—	—	—	—	—
94-95—Atlanta	IHL	41	5	10	15	67	...	...	...	—	—	—	—	—
—Tampa Bay	NHL	43	1	5	6	41	-6	0	0	—	—	—	—	—
95-96—Tampa Bay	NHL	75	2	14	16	66	4	0	0	6	0	0	0	22
96-97—Tampa Bay	NHL	72	4	5	9	95	6	0	0	—	—	—	—	—
97-98—Tampa Bay	NHL	74	3	6	9	77	-24	0	1	—	—	—	—	—
98-99—Tampa Bay	NHL	67	2	16	18	92	-25	0	0	—	—	—	—	—
99-00—Toronto	NHL	71	4	11	15	64	13	0	0	12	0	2	2	2
00-01—Toronto	NHL	41	3	5	8	50	7	1	0	11	2	1	3	10
NHL Totals (8 years)		448	19	62	81	491	-28	1	1	29	2	3	5	34

CROWLEY, MIKE — D — WILD

PERSONAL: Born July 4, 1975, in Bloomington, Minn. ... 5-11/190. ... Shoots left.
TRANSACTIONS/CAREER NOTES: Selected by Philadelphia Flyers in sixth round (fifth Flyers pick, 140th overall) of NHL entry draft (June 26, 1993). ... Traded by Flyers with C Anatoli Semenov to Mighty Ducks of Anaheim for RW Brian Wesenberg (March 19, 1996). ... Signed as free agent by Minnesota Wild (July 26, 2001).
HONORS: Named WCHA Rookie of the Year (1994-95). ... Named to NCAA All-America (West) first team (1995-96 and 1996-97). ... Named to WCHA All-Star first team (1995-96 and 1996-97). ... Named WCHA Player of the Year (1996-97). ... Named to IHL All-Star first team (1999-2000).

Season Team	League	REGULAR SEASON Gms.	G	A	Pts.	PIM	+/-	PP	SH	PLAYOFFS Gms.	G	A	Pts.	PIM
90-91—Thomas Jefferson	Minn. H.S.	20	3	9	12	2	...	...	...	—	—	—	—	—
91-92—Thomas Jefferson	Minn. H.S.	28	5	18	23	8	...	...	...	—	—	—	—	—
92-93—Thomas Jefferson	Minn. H.S.	22	10	32	42	18	...	...	...	—	—	—	—	—
93-94—Thomas Jefferson	Minn. H.S.	28	23	54	77	26	...	...	...	—	—	—	—	—
94-95—Univ. of Minnesota	WCHA	41	11	27	38	60	...	...	...	—	—	—	—	—
95-96—Univ. of Minnesota	WCHA	42	17	46	63	28	...	...	...	—	—	—	—	—
96-97—Univ. of Minnesota	WCHA	42	9	47	56	24	...	...	...	—	—	—	—	—
97-98—Cincinnati	AHL	76	12	26	38	91	...	...	...	—	—	—	—	—
—Anaheim	NHL	8	2	2	4	8	0	0	0	—	—	—	—	—
98-99—Cincinnati	AHL	44	5	23	28	42	...	...	...	3	0	3	3	2
—Anaheim	NHL	20	2	3	5	16	-10	1	0	—	—	—	—	—
99-00—Long Beach	IHL	67	9	39	48	35	...	...	...	4	2	1	3	6
00-01—Grand Rapids	IHL	22	4	12	16	10	...	...	...	—	—	—	—	—
—Anaheim	NHL	39	1	10	11	20	-16	0	0	—	—	—	—	—
NHL Totals (3 years)		67	5	15	20	44	-26	1	0					

CROZIER, GREG — LW — PENGUINS

PERSONAL: Born July 6, 1976, in Williamsville, N.Y. ... 6-3/199. ... Shoots left.
TRANSACTIONS/CAREER NOTES: Selected by Pittsburgh Penguins in third round (fourth Penguins pick, 73rd overall) of NHL entry draft (June 29, 1994).

		REGULAR SEASON								PLAYOFFS				
Season Team	League	Gms.	G	A	Pts.	PIM	+/-	PP	SH	Gms.	G	A	Pts.	PIM
90-91—Amherst	Mass. H.S.	41	52	34	86	17	...	...	...	—	—	—	—	—
91-92—Amherst	Mass. H.S.	46	61	47	108	47	...	...	...	—	—	—	—	—
92-93—Lawrence Academy	Mass. H.S.	21	22	13	35	9	...	...	...	—	—	—	—	—
93-94—Lawrence Academy	Mass. H.S.	19	22	26	48	10	...	...	...	—	—	—	—	—
94-95—Lawrence Academy	Mass. H.S.	31	45	32	77	22	...	...	...	—	—	—	—	—
95-96—Univ. of Michigan	CCHA	42	14	10	24	46	...	...	...	—	—	—	—	—
96-97—Univ. of Michigan	CCHA	31	5	15	20	45	...	...	...	—	—	—	—	—
97-98—Univ. of Michigan	CCHA	43	12	9	21	24	...	...	...	—	—	—	—	—
98-99—Univ. of Michigan	CCHA	39	7	6	13	63	...	...	...	—	—	—	—	—
99-00—Wilkes-Barre/Scranton	AHL	71	22	22	44	33	...	...	...	—	—	—	—	—
00-01—Wilkes-Barre/Scranton	AHL	77	24	36	60	81	...	...	...	21	6	5	11	16
—Pittsburgh	NHL	1	0	0	0	0	0	0	0	—	—	—	—	—
NHL Totals (1 year)		1	0	0	0	0	0	0	0					

CULLEN, DAVID — D — COYOTES

PERSONAL: Born December 30, 1976, in St. Catherine's, Ont. ... 6-1/195.
TRANSACTIONS/CAREER NOTES: Signed as non-drafted free agent by Phoenix Coyotes (April 8, 1999).
HONORS: Named to NCAA All-America (East) first team (1998-99). ... Named to Hockey East first team (1998-99). ... Named to NCAA All-Tournament team (1998-99).

		REGULAR SEASON								PLAYOFFS				
Season Team	League	Gms.	G	A	Pts.	PIM	+/-	PP	SH	Gms.	G	A	Pts.	PIM
95-96—Univ. of Maine	Hockey East	34	2	4	6	22	...	...	...	—	—	—	—	—
96-97—Univ. of Maine	Hockey East	35	5	25	30	8	...	...	...	—	—	—	—	—
97-98—Univ. of Maine	Hockey East	36	10	27	37	24	...	...	...	—	—	—	—	—
98-99—Univ. of Maine	Hockey East	41	11	33	44	24	...	...	...	—	—	—	—	—
99-00—Springfield	AHL	78	10	21	31	57	...	...	...	2	0	0	0	2
00-01—Springfield	AHL	69	13	29	42	40	...	...	...	—	—	—	—	—
—Phoenix	NHL	2	0	0	0	0	1	0	0	—	—	—	—	—
NHL Totals (1 year)		2	0	0	0	0	1	0	0					

CULLEN, MATT — C — MIGHTY DUCKS

PERSONAL: Born November 2, 1976, in Virginia, Minn. ... 6-0/195. ... Shoots left.
TRANSACTIONS/CAREER NOTES: Selected by Mighty Ducks of Anaheim in second round (second Mighty Ducks pick, 35th overall) of NHL entry draft (June 22, 1996). ... Sprained ankle (December 16, 1998); missed one game.
HONORS: Named to WCHA All-Rookie team (1995-96). ... Named to WCHA All-Star second team (1996-97).

		REGULAR SEASON								PLAYOFFS				
Season Team	League	Gms.	G	A	Pts.	PIM	+/-	PP	SH	Gms.	G	A	Pts.	PIM
94-95—Moorhead Senior	Minn. H.S.	28	47	42	89	78	...	...	...	—	—	—	—	—
95-96—St. Cloud State	WCHA	39	12	29	41	28	...	...	...	—	—	—	—	—
96-97—St. Cloud State	WCHA	36	15	30	45	70	...	...	...	—	—	—	—	—
—Baltimore	AHL	6	3	3	6	7	...	...	...	3	0	2	2	0
97-98—Anaheim	NHL	61	6	21	27	23	-4	2	0	—	—	—	—	—
—Cincinnati	AHL	18	15	12	27	2	...	...	...	—	—	—	—	—
98-99—Anaheim	NHL	75	11	14	25	47	-12	5	1	4	0	0	0	0
—Cincinnati	AHL	3	1	2	3	8	...	...	...	—	—	—	—	—
99-00—Anaheim	NHL	80	13	26	39	24	5	1	0	—	—	—	—	—
00-01—Anaheim	NHL	82	10	30	40	38	-23	4	0	—	—	—	—	—
NHL Totals (4 years)		298	40	91	131	132	-34	12	1	4	0	0	0	0

CULLIMORE, JASSEN — D — LIGHTNING

PERSONAL: Born December 4, 1972, in Simcoe, Ont. ... 6-5/220. ... Shoots left. ... Name pronounced KUHL-ih-MOHR.
TRANSACTIONS/CAREER NOTES: Selected by Vancouver Canucks in second round (second Canucks pick, 29th overall) of NHL entry draft (June 22, 1991). ... Suffered knee injury (March 31, 1995); missed three games. ... Traded by Canucks to Montreal Canadiens for LW Donald Brashear (November 13, 1996). ... Bruised eye (March 1, 1997); missed one game. ... Claimed on waivers by Tampa Bay Lightning (January 22, 1998). ... Sprained knee (April 4, 1998); missed final seven games of season. ... Injured neck (October 14, 1998); missed two games. ... Injured wrist (December 11, 1998); missed one game. ... Injured knee (April 2, 2000); missed final four games of season. ... Bruised hand (November 27, 2000); missed one game. ... Injured knee (January 10, 2001); missed one game. ... Injured shin (February 10, 2001); missed one game. ... Strained muscle in abdomen (March 8, 2001); missed two games.
HONORS: Named to OHL All-Star second team (1991-92).

		REGULAR SEASON								PLAYOFFS				
Season Team	League	Gms.	G	A	Pts.	PIM	+/-	PP	SH	Gms.	G	A	Pts.	PIM
88-89—Peterborough	OHL	20	2	1	3	6	...	...	...	—	—	—	—	—
—Peterborough	Jr. B	29	11	17	28	88	...	...	...	—	—	—	—	—
89-90—Peterborough	OHL	59	2	6	8	61	...	...	...	11	0	2	2	8
90-91—Peterborough	OHL	62	8	16	24	74	...	...	...	4	1	0	1	7

Season Team	League	REGULAR SEASON									PLAYOFFS				
		Gms.	G	A	Pts.	PIM	+/-	PP	SH		Gms.	G	A	Pts.	PIM
91-92—Peterborough............	OHL	54	9	37	46	65	...	...	...		10	3	6	9	8
92-93—Hamilton...................	AHL	56	5	7	12	60	...	...	...		—	—	—	—	—
93-94—Hamilton...................	AHL	71	8	20	28	86	...	...	...		3	0	1	1	2
94-95—Syracuse..................	AHL	33	2	7	9	66	...	...	...		—	—	—	—	—
—Vancouver................	NHL	34	1	2	3	39	-2	0	0		11	0	0	0	12
95-96—Vancouver................	NHL	27	1	1	2	21	4	0	0		—	—	—	—	—
96-97—Vancouver................	NHL	3	0	0	0	2	-2	0	0		—	—	—	—	—
—Montreal..................	NHL	49	2	6	8	42	4	0	1		2	0	0	0	2
97-98—Montreal..................	NHL	3	0	0	0	4	0	0	0		—	—	—	—	—
—Fredericton	AHL	5	1	0	1	8	...	...	...		—	—	—	—	—
—Tampa Bay..............	NHL	25	1	2	3	22	-4	1	0		—	—	—	—	—
98-99—Tampa Bay..............	NHL	78	5	12	17	81	-22	1	1		—	—	—	—	—
99-00—Providence...............	AHL	16	5	10	15	31	...	...	...		—	—	—	—	—
—Tampa Bay..............	NHL	46	1	1	2	66	-12	0	0		—	—	—	—	—
00-01—Tampa Bay..................	NHL	74	1	6	7	80	-6	0	0		—	—	—	—	—
NHL Totals (7 years)...........		339	12	30	42	357	-40	2	2		13	0	0	0	14

CUMMINS, JIM   RW   MIGHTY DUCKS

PERSONAL: Born May 17, 1970, in Dearborn, Mich. ... 6-2/219. ... Shoots right. ... Full Name: James Stephen Cummins. ... Name pronounced KUH-mihns.

TRANSACTIONS/CAREER NOTES: Selected by New York Rangers in fourth round (fifth Rangers pick, 67th overall) of NHL entry draft (June 17, 1989). ... Traded by Rangers with LW Kevin Miller and D Dennis Vial to Detroit Red Wings for RW Joe Kocur and D Per Djoos (March 5, 1991). ... Suspended 11 games by NHL for leaving penalty box to join fight (January 23, 1993). ... Traded by Red Wings with fourth-round pick (traded to Boston) in 1993 draft to Philadelphia Flyers for rights to C Greg Johnson and fifth-round pick (G Frederic Deschene) in 1994 draft (June 20, 1993). ... Suffered slightly separated shoulder during 1993-94 season. ... Traded by Flyers with fourth-round pick in 1995 draft to Tampa Bay Lightning with D Jeff Buchanan and D Tom Tilley to Chicago Blackhawks for LW Paul Ysebaert and RW Rich Sutter (February 22, 1995). ... Sprained triceps (March 16, 1995); missed three games. ... Fractured thumb (November 1, 1995); missed 16 games. ... Suspended eight games and fined $1,000 by NHL for cross checking and punching another player (March 14, 1996). ... Bruised clavicle (December 9, 1996); missed 11 games. ... Suspended one game by NHL for third game misconduct of season (January 23, 1997). ... Suffered from the flu (November 11, 1997); missed three games. ... Traded by Blackhawks with D Keith Carney to Phoenix Coyotes for C Chad Kilger and D Jayson More (March 4, 1998). ... Suspended five games by NHL for elbowing incident (February 8, 1999). ... Traded by Coyotes to Montreal Canadiens for sixth-round pick (D Erik Lewerstrom) in 1999 draft (June 26, 1999). ... Suffered concussion (September 12, 1999); missed first two games of season. ... Separated shoulder (December 20, 1999); missed three games. ... Sprained ankle (January 24, 2000); missed 22 games. ... Signed as free agent by Mighty Ducks of Anaheim (July 5, 2000).

MISCELLANEOUS: Failed to score on a penalty shot (vs. Mike Vernon, April 7, 1996).

Season Team	League	REGULAR SEASON									PLAYOFFS				
		Gms.	G	A	Pts.	PIM	+/-	PP	SH		Gms.	G	A	Pts.	PIM
87-88—Detroit Compuware.....	NAJHL	31	11	15	26	146	...	...	...		—	—	—	—	—
88-89—Michigan State...........	CCHA	36	3	9	12	100	...	...	...		—	—	—	—	—
89-90—Michigan State...........	CCHA	41	8	7	15	94	...	...	...		—	—	—	—	—
90-91—Michigan State...........	CCHA	34	9	6	15	110	...	...	...		—	—	—	—	—
91-92—Adirondack	AHL	65	7	13	20	338	...	...	...		5	0	0	0	19
—Detroit......................	NHL	1	0	0	0	7	0	0	0		—	—	—	—	—
92-93—Adirondack	AHL	43	16	4	20	179	...	...	...		9	3	1	4	4
—Detroit......................	NHL	7	1	1	2	58	0	0	0		—	—	—	—	—
93-94—Philadelphia	NHL	22	1	2	3	71	0	0	0		—	—	—	—	—
—Hershey...................	AHL	17	6	6	12	70	...	...	...		—	—	—	—	—
—Atlanta	IHL	7	4	5	9	14	...	...	...		13	1	2	3	90
—Tampa Bay	NHL	4	0	0	0	13	-1	0	0		—	—	—	—	—
94-95—Tampa Bay	NHL	10	1	0	1	41	-3	0	0		—	—	—	—	—
—Chicago...................	NHL	27	3	1	4	117	-3	0	0		14	1	1	2	4
95-96—Chicago...................	NHL	52	2	4	6	180	-1	0	0		10	0	0	0	2
96-97—Chicago...................	NHL	65	6	6	12	199	4	0	0		6	0	0	0	24
97-98—Chicago...................	NHL	55	0	2	2	178	-9	0	0		—	—	—	—	—
—Phoenix..................	NHL	20	0	0	0	47	-7	0	0		3	0	0	0	4
98-99—Phoenix..................	NHL	55	1	7	8	190	3	0	0		3	0	1	1	0
99-00—Montreal	NHL	47	3	5	8	92	-5	0	0		—	—	—	—	—
00-01—Anaheim	NHL	79	5	6	11	167	-11	0	0		—	—	—	—	—
NHL Totals (10 years).........		444	23	34	57	1360	-33	0	0		36	1	2	3	34

CUTTA, JAKUB   D   CAPITALS

PERSONAL: Born December 29, 1981, in Yablonec, Czechoslovakia. ... 6-3/195. ... Shoots left.

TRANSACTIONS/CAREER NOTES: Selected by Washington Capitals in second round (third Capitals pick, 61st overall) of NHL entry draft (June 24, 2000).

Season Team	League	REGULAR SEASON									PLAYOFFS				
		Gms.	G	A	Pts.	PIM	+/-	PP	SH		Gms.	G	A	Pts.	PIM
98-99—Swift Current	WHL	59	3	3	6	63	...	...	...		—	—	—	—	—
99-00—Swift Current	WHL	71	2	12	14	114	...	...	...		12	0	2	2	24
00-01—Washington	NHL	3	0	0	0	0	-1	0	0		—	—	—	—	—
—Swift Current	WHL	47	5	8	13	102	...	...	...		16	1	3	4	32
NHL Totals (1 year).............		3	0	0	0	0	-1	0	0						

CZERKAWSKI, MARIUSZ   RW   ISLANDERS

PERSONAL: Born April 13, 1972, in Radomski, Poland. ... 6-0/199. ... Shoots right. ... Name pronounced MAIR-ee-uhz chuhr-KAW-skee.
TRANSACTIONS/CAREER NOTES: Selected by Boston Bruins (fifth Bruins pick, 106th overall) of NHL entry draft (June 22, 1991). ... Played in Europe during 1994-95 NHL lockout. ... Traded by Bruins with D Sean Brown and first-round pick (D Mathieu Descoteaux) in 1996 draft to Edmonton Oilers for G Bill Ranford (January 11, 1996). ... Injured finger (March 23, 1996); missed two games. ... Suffered hip pointer (January 11, 1997); missed two games. ... Traded by Oilers to New York Islanders for LW Dan Lacouture (August 25, 1997). ... Strained muscle in rib cage (December 15, 1999); missed three games.
HONORS: Played in NHL All-Star Game (2000).
MISCELLANEOUS: Failed to score on a penalty shot (vs. Rick Tabaracci, December 4, 1998).
STATISTICAL PLATEAUS: Three-goal games: 1996-97 (2), 1999-00 (1). Total: 3.

Season Team	League	REGULAR SEASON								PLAYOFFS				
		Gms.	G	A	Pts.	PIM	+/-	PP	SH	Gms.	G	A	Pts.	PIM
90-91—GKS Tychy	Poland	24	25	15	40	...	...	...	...	—	—	—	—	—
91-92—Djurgarden Stockholm	Sweden	39	8	5	13	4	...	...	...	3	0	0	0	2
—Polish Olympic Team..	Int'l	5	0	1	1	4	...	...	...	—	—	—	—	—
92-93—Hammarby	Sweden Dv. 2	32	39	30	69	74	...	...	...	—	—	—	—	—
93-94—Djurgarden Stockholm	Sweden	39	13	21	34	20	...	...	...	—	—	—	—	—
—Boston	NHL	4	2	1	3	0	-2	1	0	13	3	3	6	4
94-95—Kiekko-Espoo	Finland	7	9	3	12	10	...	...	...	—	—	—	—	—
—Boston	NHL	47	12	14	26	31	4	1	0	5	1	0	1	0
95-96—Boston	NHL	33	5	6	11	10	-11	1	0	—	—	—	—	—
—Edmonton	NHL	37	12	17	29	8	7	2	0	—	—	—	—	—
96-97—Edmonton	NHL	76	26	21	47	16	0	4	0	12	2	1	3	10
97-98—New York Islanders	NHL	68	12	13	25	23	11	2	0	—	—	—	—	—
98-99—New York Islanders	NHL	78	21	17	38	14	-10	4	0	—	—	—	—	—
99-00—New York Islanders	NHL	79	35	35	70	34	-16	16	0	—	—	—	—	—
00-01—New York Islanders	NHL	82	30	32	62	48	-24	10	1	—	—	—	—	—
NHL Totals (8 years)		504	155	156	311	184	-41	41	1	30	6	4	10	14

DACKELL, ANDREAS   RW   CANADIENS   C D

PERSONAL: Born December 29, 1972, in Gavle, Sweden. ... 5-10/195. ... Shoots right. ... Name pronounced AHN-dray-uhz DA-kuhl.
TRANSACTIONS/CAREER NOTES: Selected by Ottawa Senators in sixth round (third Senators pick, 136th overall) of NHL entry draft (June 22, 1996). ... Suffered concussion (October 29, 1998); missed four games. ... Injured knee (January 14, 1999); missed one game. ... Suffered from the flu (November 18, 2000); missed one game. ... Traded by Senators to Montreal Canadiens for eighth-round pick (D Neil Petruic) in 2001 draft (June 24, 2001).
STATISTICAL PLATEAUS: Three-goal games: 2000-01 (1).

Season Team	League	REGULAR SEASON								PLAYOFFS				
		Gms.	G	A	Pts.	PIM	+/-	PP	SH	Gms.	G	A	Pts.	PIM
90-91—Brynas Gavle	Sweden	3	0	1	1	2	...	...	...	—	—	—	—	—
91-92—Brynas Gavle	Sweden	4	0	0	0	2	...	...	...	2	0	1	1	4
92-93—Brynas Gavle	Sweden	40	12	15	27	12	...	...	...	10	4	5	9	2
93-94—Brynas Gavle	Sweden	38	12	17	29	47	...	...	...	7	2	2	4	8
94-95—Brynas Gavle	Sweden	39	17	16	33	34	...	...	...	14	3	3	6	14
95-96—Brynas Gavle	Sweden	22	6	6	12	8	...	...	...	—	—	—	—	—
96-97—Ottawa	NHL	79	12	19	31	8	-6	2	0	7	1	0	1	0
97-98—Ottawa	NHL	82	15	18	33	24	-11	3	2	11	1	1	2	2
98-99—Ottawa	NHL	77	15	35	50	30	9	6	0	4	0	1	1	0
99-00—Ottawa	NHL	82	10	25	35	18	5	0	0	6	2	1	3	2
00-01—Ottawa	NHL	81	13	18	31	24	7	1	0	4	0	0	0	0
NHL Totals (5 years)		401	65	115	180	104	4	12	2	32	4	3	7	4

DAFOE, BYRON   G   BRUINS

PERSONAL: Born February 25, 1971, in Sussex, England. ... 5-11/190. ... Catches left. ... Full Name: Byron Jaromir Dafoe.
TRANSACTIONS/CAREER NOTES: Selected by Washington Capitals in second round (second Capitals pick, 35th overall) of NHL entry draft (June 17, 1989). ... Traded by Capitals with RW Dimitri Khristich to Los Angeles Kings for first-(C Alexander Volchkov) and fourth-round (RW Justin Davis) picks in 1996 draft (July 8, 1995). ... Strained thumb (February 1, 1997); missed two games. ... Traded by Kings with RW Dimitri Khristich to Boston Bruins for C Jozef Stumpel, RW Sandy Moger and fourth-round pick (traded to New Jersey) in 1998 draft (August 29, 1997). ... Injured knee (February 21, 2000) and underwent surgery; missed remainder of season. ... Injured hamstring (October 13, 2000); missed 11 games. ... Injured knee (November 22, 2000); missed 11 games. ... Strained hamstring (February 10, 2001); missed 13 games.
HONORS: Shared Harry (Hap) Holmes Memorial Trophy with Olaf Kolzig (1993-94). ... Named to AHL All-Star first team (1993-94). ... Named to NHL All-Star second team (1998-99).
MISCELLANEOUS: Stopped a penalty shot attempt (vs. Martin Straka, January 9, 2001). ... Allowed penalty shot goal (vs. Steve Chiasson, December 11, 1995).

Season Team	League	REGULAR SEASON								PLAYOFFS						
		Gms.	Min	W	L	T	GA	SO	Avg.	Gms.	Min.	W	L	GA	SO	Avg.
87-88—Juan de Fuca	BCJHL	32	1716	...	...	...	129	0	4.51	—	—	—	—	—	—	—
88-89—Portland	WHL	59	3279	29	24	3	*291	1	5.32	*18	*1091	10	8	*81	*1	4.45
89-90—Portland	WHL	40	2265	14	21	3	193	0	5.11	—	—	—	—	—	—	—
90-91—Portland	WHL	8	414	1	5	1	41	0	5.94	—	—	—	—	—	—	—
—Prince Albert	WHL	32	1839	13	12	4	124	0	4.05	—	—	—	—	—	—	—
91-92—New Haven	AHL	7	364	3	2	1	22	0	3.63	—	—	—	—	—	—	—
—Baltimore	AHL	33	1847	12	16	4	119	0	3.87	—	—	—	—	—	—	—
—Hampton Roads	ECHL	10	562	6	4	‡0	26	1	2.78	—	—	—	—	—	—	—

Season Team	League	Gms.	Min	W	L	T	GA	SO	Avg.	Gms.	Min.	W	L	GA	SO	Avg.
92-93 —Baltimore	AHL	48	2617	16	*20	7	191	1	4.38	5	241	2	3	22	0	5.48
—Washington	NHL	1	1	0	0	0	0	0	...	—	—	—	—	—	—	—
93-94 —Portland	AHL	47	2662	24	16	4	148	1	3.34	1	9	0	0	1	0	6.67
—Washington	NHL	5	230	2	2	0	13	0	3.39	2	118	0	2	5	0	2.54
94-95 —Portland	AHL	6	330	5	0	0	16	0	2.91	7	417	3	4	29	0	4.17
—Phoenix	IHL	49	2744	25	16	‡6	169	2	3.70	—	—	—	—	—	—	—
—Washington	NHL	4	187	1	1	1	11	0	3.53	1	20	0	0	1	0	3.00
95-96 —Los Angeles	NHL	47	2666	14	24	8	172	1	3.87	—	—	—	—	—	—	—
96-97 —Los Angeles	NHL	40	2162	13	17	5	112	0	3.11	—	—	—	—	—	—	—
97-98 —Boston	NHL	65	3693	30	25	9	138	6	2.24	6	422	2	4	14	1	1.99
98-99 —Boston	NHL	68	4001	32	23	11	133	*10	1.99	12	768	6	6	26	2	2.03
99-00 —Boston	NHL	41	2307	13	16	10	114	3	2.96	—	—	—	—	—	—	—
00-01 —Boston	NHL	45	2536	22	14	7	101	2	2.39	—	—	—	—	—	—	—
NHL Totals (9 years)		316	17783	127	122	51	794	22	2.68	21	1328	8	12	46	3	2.08

DAGENAIS, PIERRE — LW — DEVILS

PERSONAL: Born March 4, 1978, in Blainville, Que. ... 6-4/210. ... Shoots left. ... Name pronounced da-zhih-NAY.
TRANSACTIONS/CAREER NOTES: Selected by New Jersey Devils in second round (fourth Devils pick, 47th overall) of NHL entry draft (June 22, 1996). ... Returned to draft pool by Devils and selected by Devils in fourth round (sixth Devils pick, 105th overall) of NHL entry draft (June 27, 1998).
HONORS: Named to Can.HL All-Rookie team (1995-96). ... Named to QMJHL All-Rookie team (1995-96). ... Named to QMJHL All-Star second team (1997-98). ... Named to AHL All-Star second team (2000-01).

Season Team	League	Gms.	G	A	Pts.	PIM	+/-	PP	SH	Gms.	G	A	Pts.	PIM
95-96 —Moncton	QMJHL	67	43	25	68	59	...	...	...	—	—	—	—	—
96-97 —Moncton	QMJHL	6	4	2	6	0	...	...	...	—	—	—	—	—
—Laval	QMJHL	37	16	14	30	40	...	...	...	—	—	—	—	—
—Rouyn-Noranda	QMJHL	27	21	8	29	22	...	...	...	—	—	—	—	—
97-98 —Rouyn-Noranda	QMJHL	60	*66	67	133	50	...	...	...	6	6	2	8	2
98-99 —Albany	AHL	69	17	13	30	37	...	...	...	4	0	0	0	0
99-00 —Albany	AHL	80	35	30	65	47	...	...	...	5	1	0	1	14
00-01 —Albany	AHL	69	34	28	62	52	...	...	...	—	—	—	—	—
—New Jersey	NHL	9	3	2	5	6	1	1	0	—	—	—	—	—
NHL Totals (1 year)		9	3	2	5	6	1	1	0					

DAHL, KEVIN — D

PERSONAL: Born December 30, 1968, in Regina, Sask. ... 5-11/190. ... Shoots right.
TRANSACTIONS/CAREER NOTES: Selected by Montreal Canadiens in 11th round (12th Canadiens pick, 230th overall) of NHL entry draft (June 11, 1988). ... Signed as free agent by Calgary Flames (August 1, 1991). ... Suffered charley horse (November 2, 1992); missed two games. ... Injured heel (November 28, 1992); missed one game. ... Strained left knee (December 15, 1992); missed 18 games. ... Fractured left foot (April 9, 1993); missed one game. ... Separated left shoulder (November 6, 1993); missed nine games. ... Strained left shoulder (December 7, 1993); missed 30 games. ... Separated left shoulder (February 16, 1995); missed two games. ... Injured rib cartilage (March 31, 1995); missed seven games. ... Injured knee (November 11, 1995); missed one game. ... Injured knee (December 19, 1995); missed three games. ... Signed as free agent by Phoenix Coyotes (August 26, 1996). ... Signed as free agent by Calgary Flames (August 29, 1997). ... Bruised hand (January 11, 1997); missed two games. ... Signed as free agent by St. Louis Blues (September 4, 1998). ... Selected by Toronto Maple Leafs from Blues in NHL waiver draft (October 5, 1998). ... Sprained ankle (October 17, 1998); missed 16 games. ... Signed as free agent by Columbus Blue Jackets (August 24, 2000). ... Suffered from the flu (December 18, 2000); missed one game.
MISCELLANEOUS: Member of silver-medal-winning Canadian Olympic team (1992).

Season Team	League	Gms.	G	A	Pts.	PIM	+/-	PP	SH	Gms.	G	A	Pts.	PIM
86-87 —Bowling Green	CCHA	32	2	6	8	54	...	...	...	—	—	—	—	—
87-88 —Bowling Green	CCHA	44	2	23	25	78	...	...	...	—	—	—	—	—
88-89 —Bowling Green	CCHA	46	9	26	35	51	...	...	...	—	—	—	—	—
89-90 —Bowling Green	CCHA	43	8	22	30	74	...	...	...	—	—	—	—	—
90-91 —Fredericton	AHL	32	1	15	16	45	...	...	...	9	0	1	1	11
—Winston-Salem	ECHL	36	7	17	24	58	...	...	...	—	—	—	—	—
91-92 —Canadian nat'l team	Int'l	45	2	15	17	44	...	...	...	—	—	—	—	—
—Can. Olympic team	Int'l	8	2	0	2	6	...	...	...	—	—	—	—	—
—Salt Lake City	IHL	13	0	2	2	12	...	...	...	5	0	0	0	13
92-93 —Calgary	NHL	61	2	9	11	56	9	1	0	6	0	2	2	8
93-94 —Calgary	NHL	33	0	3	3	23	-2	0	0	6	0	0	0	4
—Saint John	AHL	2	0	0	0	0	...	...	...	—	—	—	—	—
94-95 —Calgary	NHL	34	4	8	12	38	8	0	0	3	0	0	0	0
95-96 —Calgary	NHL	32	1	1	2	26	-2	0	0	1	0	0	0	0
—Saint John	AHL	23	4	11	15	37	...	...	...	—	—	—	—	—
96-97 —Las Vegas	IHL	73	10	21	31	101	...	...	...	3	0	0	0	2
—Phoenix	NHL	2	0	0	0	0	0	0	0	—	—	—	—	—
97-98 —Calgary	NHL	19	0	1	1	6	-3	0	0	—	—	—	—	—
—Chicago	IHL	45	8	9	17	61	...	...	...	20	1	8	9	32
98-99 —Toronto	NHL	3	0	0	0	2	0	0	0	—	—	—	—	—
—Chicago	IHL	34	3	6	9	61	...	...	...	10	2	3	5	8
99-00 —Chicago	IHL	27	1	2	3	44	...	...	...	3	0	1	1	2
00-01 —Chicago	IHL	72	2	6	8	63	...	...	...	16	2	2	4	16
—Columbus	NHL	4	0	0	0	2	...	...	...	—	—	—	—	—
NHL Totals (8 years)		188	7	22	29	153	11	1	0	16	0	2	2	12

PERSONAL: Born January 12, 1967, in Ostersund, Sweden. ... 6-3/191. ... Shoots left. ... Name pronounced DAH-lihn.

TRANSACTIONS/CAREER NOTES: Selected by New York Rangers in first round (first Rangers pick, seventh overall) of NHL entry draft (June 15, 1985). ... Bruised shin (November 1987). ... Bruised left shoulder (November 1988). ... Separated right shoulder (January 1989). ... Traded by Rangers with fourth-round pick (C Cal McGowan) in 1990 draft and future considerations to Minnesota North Stars for RW Mike Gartner (March 6, 1990). ... North Stars franchise moved from Minnesota to Dallas and renamed Stars for 1993-94 season. ... Traded by Stars with future considerations to San Jose Sharks for D Mike Lalor and D Doug Zmolek (March 19, 1994). ... Suffered from the flu (February 20, 1995); missed two games. ... Injured groin (October 28, 1995); missed three games. ... Fractured toe (January 11, 1996); missed 20 games. ... Traded by Sharks with G Chris Terreri and D Michal Sykora to Chicago Blackhawks for G Ed Belfour (January 25, 1997). ... Suffered back spasms (March 26, 1997); missed one game. ... Signed as free agent by Washington Capitals (July 21, 1999). ... Injured neck (March 15, 2000); missed one game. ... Injured back (December 14, 2000); missed four games. ... Suffered from the flu (February 7, 2001); missed one game. ... Injured neck (March 1, 2001); missed one game. ... Reinjured neck (March 6, 2001); missed two games. ... Bruised foot (March 30, 2001); missed one game.

MISCELLANEOUS: Failed to score on a penalty shot (vs. Daren Puppa, March 17, 1992; vs. Curtis Joseph, April 1, 2000).

STATISTICAL PLATEAUS: Three-goal games: 1987-88 (1), 1990-91 (1), 1992-93 (1), 1993-94 (2). Total: 5.

Season Team	League	REGULAR SEASON								PLAYOFFS				
		Gms.	G	A	Pts.	PIM	+/-	PP	SH	Gms.	G	A	Pts.	PIM
83-84—Ostersund	Sweden	36	15	11	26	10	...	...	...	—	—	—	—	—
84-85—Ostersund	Sweden	36	33	26	59	20	...	...	...	—	—	—	—	—
85-86—Bjorkloven	Sweden	22	4	3	7	8	...	...	...	—	—	—	—	—
86-87—Bjorkloven	Sweden	31	9	12	21	20	...	...	...	6	6	2	8	4
87-88—New York Rangers	NHL	70	29	23	52	26	5	11	0	—	—	—	—	—
—Colorado	IHL	2	2	2	4	0	...	...	...	—	—	—	—	—
88-89—New York Rangers	NHL	56	24	19	43	50	-6	8	0	4	0	0	0	0
89-90—New York Rangers	NHL	63	18	18	36	30	-4	13	0	—	—	—	—	—
—Minnesota	NHL	13	2	4	6	0	1	0	0	7	1	4	5	2
90-91—Minnesota	NHL	66	21	18	39	6	7	4	0	15	2	6	8	4
91-92—Minnesota	NHL	79	36	30	66	10	-5	16	1	7	0	3	3	2
92-93—Minnesota	NHL	83	35	39	74	6	-20	13	0	—	—	—	—	—
93-94—Dallas	NHL	65	19	38	57	10	-1	12	0	—	—	—	—	—
—San Jose	NHL	13	6	6	12	0	0	3	0	14	6	2	8	0
94-95—San Jose	NHL	46	11	23	34	11	-2	4	1	11	5	4	9	0
95-96—San Jose	NHL	59	16	12	28	27	-21	5	0	—	—	—	—	—
96-97—San Jose	NHL	43	8	11	19	8	-11	3	0	—	—	—	—	—
—Chicago	NHL	30	6	8	14	10	9	1	0	5	0	1	1	0
97-98—HV 71 Jonkoping	Sweden	29	9	22	31	16	...	...	...	—	—	—	—	—
—Swedish Oly. team	Int'l	4	1	0	1	2	...	...	...	—	—	—	—	—
98-99—HV 71 Jonkoping	Sweden	25	14	15	29	4	...	...	...	—	—	—	—	—
99-00—Washington	NHL	75	15	23	38	8	11	5	0	5	0	1	1	2
00-01—Washington	NHL	73	15	33	48	6	11	6	0	6	0	1	1	2
NHL Totals (12 years)		834	261	305	566	208	-26	104	2	74	14	22	36	12

PERSONAL: Born October 12, 1965, in Montreal. ... 5-11/192. ... Shoots left. ... Full Name: Jean-Jacques Daigneault. ... Name pronounced DAYN-yoh.

TRANSACTIONS/CAREER NOTES: Selected by Vancouver Canucks in first round (first Canucks pick, 10th overall) of NHL entry draft (June 1984). ... Fractured finger (March 19, 1986). ... Traded by Canucks with second-round pick (C Kent Hawley) in 1986 draft to Philadelphia Flyers for RW Rich Sutter, D Dave Richter and third-round pick (D Don Gibson) in 1986 draft (June 1986). ... Sprained ankle (April 12, 1987). ... Traded by Flyers to Montreal Canadiens for D Scott Sandelin (November 1988). ... Bruised shoulder (December 1990). ... Suffered hip pointer (March 16, 1991). ... Injured knee (April 7, 1991). ... Bruised left knee (November 28, 1992); missed one game. ... Injured shoulder (December 23, 1992); missed two games. ... Sprained right ankle (March 1, 1993); missed 11 games. ... Suffered injury (December 22, 1993); missed one game. ... Suspended three games and fined $500 by NHL for elbowing (January 7, 1994). ... Sprained wrist (January 10, 1994); missed six games. ... Suffered sore back (March 1, 1994); missed one game. ... Injured shoulder (February 4, 1995); missed one game. ... Suffered from cold (February 13, 1995); missed one game. ... Bruised ankle (April 12, 1995); missed one game. ... Traded by Canadiens to St. Louis Blues for G Pat Jablonski (November 7, 1995). ... Traded by Blues to Pittsburgh Penguins for sixth-round pick (G Stephen Wagner) in 1996 draft (March 20, 1996). ... Suffered back spasms (December 30, 1996); missed one game. ... Suffered back spasms (January 4, 1997); missed two games. ... Traded by Penguins to Anaheim Mighty Ducks for LW Garry Valk (February 21, 1997). ... Suspended 10 games and fined $1,000 by NHL for abusing an official (February 26, 1997). ... Traded by Mighty Ducks with C Mark Janssens and RW Joe Sacco to New York Islanders for C Travis Green, D Doug Houda and RW Tony Tuzzolino (February 6, 1998). ... Separated shoulder (March 12, 1998); missed six games. ... Reinjured shoulder (April 18, 1998); missed one game. ... Selected by Nashville Predators in NHL expansion draft (June 26, 1998). ... Traded by Predators to Phoenix Coyotes for future considerations (January 13, 1999). ... Strained shoulder (February 16, 1999); missed three games. ... Bruised hip (March 11, 1999); missed six games. ... Strained groin (October 26, 1999); missed two games. ... Strained groin (October 31, 1999); missed four games. ... Suffered lower back pain (November 20, 1999); missed one game. ... Sprained ankle (March 13, 2000); missed four games. ... Signed as free agent by Minnesota Wild (July 24, 2000).

HONORS: Won Emile (Butch) Bouchard Trophy (1982-83). ... Named to QMJHL All-Star first team (1982-83).

MISCELLANEOUS: Member of Stanley Cup championship team (1993).

Season Team	League	REGULAR SEASON								PLAYOFFS				
		Gms.	G	A	Pts.	PIM	+/-	PP	SH	Gms.	G	A	Pts.	PIM
81-82—Laval	QMJHL	64	4	25	29	41	...	...	...	18	1	3	4	2
82-83—Longueuil	QMJHL	70	26	58	84	58	...	...	...	15	4	11	15	35
83-84—Can. Olympic team	Int'l	62	6	15	21	40	...	...	...	—	—	—	—	—
—Longueuil	QMJHL	10	2	11	13	6	...	...	...	14	3	13	16	30
—Canadian nat'l team	Int'l	55	5	14	19	40	...	...	...	—	—	—	—	—
84-85—Vancouver	NHL	67	4	23	27	69	-14	2	0	—	—	—	—	—
85-86—Vancouver	NHL	64	5	23	28	45	-20	4	0	3	0	2	2	0
86-87—Philadelphia	NHL	77	6	16	22	56	12	0	0	9	1	0	1	0

Season Team	League	REGULAR SEASON								PLAYOFFS				
		Gms.	G	A	Pts.	PIM	+/-	PP	SH	Gms.	G	A	Pts.	PIM
87-88—Philadelphia	NHL	28	2	2	4	12	-8	2	0	—	—	—	—	—
—Hershey	AHL	10	1	5	6	8	...	...	...	—	—	—	—	—
88-89—Hershey	AHL	12	0	10	10	13	...	...	...	—	—	—	—	—
—Sherbrooke	AHL	63	10	33	43	48	...	...	...	6	1	3	4	2
89-90—Sherbrooke	AHL	28	8	19	27	18	...	...	...	—	—	—	—	—
—Montreal	NHL	36	2	10	12	14	11	0	0	9	0	0	0	2
90-91—Montreal	NHL	51	3	16	19	31	-2	2	0	5	0	1	1	0
91-92—Montreal	NHL	79	4	14	18	36	16	2	0	11	0	3	3	4
92-93—Montreal	NHL	66	8	10	18	57	25	0	0	20	1	3	4	22
93-94—Montreal	NHL	68	2	12	14	73	16	0	0	7	0	1	1	12
94-95—Montreal	NHL	45	3	5	8	40	2	0	0	—	—	—	—	—
95-96—Montreal	NHL	7	0	1	1	6	0	0	0	—	—	—	—	—
—St. Louis	NHL	37	1	3	4	24	-6	0	0	—	—	—	—	—
—Worcester	AHL	9	1	10	11	10	...	...	...	—	—	—	—	—
—Pittsburgh	NHL	13	3	3	6	23	0	2	0	17	1	9	10	36
96-97—Pittsburgh	NHL	53	3	14	17	36	-5	0	0	—	—	—	—	—
—Anaheim	NHL	13	2	9	11	22	5	0	0	11	2	7	9	16
97-98—Anaheim	NHL	53	2	15	17	28	-10	1	0	—	—	—	—	—
—New York Islanders	NHL	18	0	6	6	21	1	0	0	—	—	—	—	—
98-99—Nashville	NHL	35	2	2	4	38	-4	1	0	—	—	—	—	—
—Phoenix	NHL	35	0	7	7	32	-8	0	0	6	0	0	0	8
99-00—Phoenix	NHL	53	1	6	7	22	-16	0	0	1	0	0	0	0
00-01—Cleveland	IHL	44	8	9	17	18	...	...	...	—	—	—	—	—
—Minnesota	NHL	1	0	0	0	2	-1	0	0	—	—	—	—	—
NHL Totals (16 years)		899	53	197	250	687	-6	16	0	99	5	26	31	100

DAMPHOUSSE, J.F. G DEVILS

PERSONAL: Born July 21, 1979, in St. Alexis-des-Monts, Que. ... 6-0/175. ... Catches left. ... Full Name: Jean-Francois Damphousse. ... Name pronounced dahm-FOOZ.

TRANSACTIONS/CAREER NOTES: Selected by New Jersey Devils in first round (first Devils pick, 24th overall) of NHL entry draft (June 21, 1997).

D

Season Team	League	REGULAR SEASON								PLAYOFFS					
		Gms.	Min	W	L	T	GA	SO	Avg.	Gms.	Min.	W	L	GA	SO	Avg.
96-97—Moncton	QMJHL	39	2063	6	25	2	190	0	5.53	—	—	—	—	—	—	—
97-98—Moncton	QMJHL	59	3400	24	26	*6	174	1	3.07	10	595	5	5	28	0	2.82
98-99—Moncton	QMJHL	40	2163	19	17	2	121	1	3.36	4	200	0	4	12	0	3.60
—Albany	AHL	1	59	0	1	0	3	0	3.05	—	—	—	—	—	—	—
99-00—Albany	AHL	26	1326	9	11	2	62	0	2.81	2	62	0	1	4	0	3.87
—Augusta	ECHL	14	676	6	7	0	49	0	4.35	—	—	—	—	—	—	—
00-01—Albany	AHL	55	2963	24	23	3	141	1	2.86	—	—	—	—	—	—	—

DAMPHOUSSE, VINCENT C SHARKS

PERSONAL: Born December 17, 1967, in Montreal. ... 6-1/200. ... Shoots left. ... Name pronounced dahm-FOOZ.

TRANSACTIONS/CAREER NOTES: Selected by Toronto Maple Leafs in first round (first Maple Leafs pick, sixth overall) of NHL entry draft (June 21, 1986). ... Traded by Maple Leafs with D Luke Richardson, G Peter Ing, C Scott Thornton and future considerations to Edmonton Oilers for G Grant Fuhr, LW//RW Glenn Anderson and LW Craig Berube (September 19, 1991). ... Traded by Oilers with fourth-round pick (D Adam Wiesel) in 1993 draft to Montreal Canadiens for LW Shayne Corson, LW Vladimir Vujtek and C Brent Gilchrist (August 27, 1992). ... Played in Europe during 1994-95 NHL lockout. ... Suspended two games and fined $1,000 by NHL for cross-checking incident (March 30, 1996). ... Partially dislocated left shoulder (March 11, 1998); missed six games. ... Suffered back spasms (November 27, 1998); missed five games. ... Traded by Canadiens to San Jose Sharks for fifth-round pick (RW Marc-Andre Thinel) in 1999 draft and first-round pick (C Marcel Hossa) in 2000 draft (March 23, 1999). ... Injured shoulder (January 15, 2001); missed 36 games.

HONORS: Named to QMJHL All-Star second team (1985-86). ... Played in NHL All-Star Game (1991 and 1992). ... Named All-Star Game Most Valuable Player (1991). ... Named to play in NHL All-Star Game (2001); replaced by C Simon Gagne due to injury.

RECORDS: Shares NHL All-Star single-game record for most goals—4 (1991).

STATISTICAL PLATEAUS: Three-goal games: 1988-89 (1), 1989-90 (2), 1992-93 (2), 1993-94 (2), 1996-97 (1), 1997-98 (2), 1998-99 (1). Total: 11. ... Four-goal games: 1991-92 (1). ... Total hat tricks: 12.

MISCELLANEOUS: Member of Stanley Cup championship team (1993). ... Captain of Montreal Canadiens (October 29, 1996 through March 23, 1999). ... Failed to score on a penalty shot (vs. Dominik Hasek, March 8, 1997).

Season Team	League	REGULAR SEASON								PLAYOFFS				
		Gms.	G	A	Pts.	PIM	+/-	PP	SH	Gms.	G	A	Pts.	PIM
83-84—Laval	QMJHL	66	29	36	65	25	...	...	...	—	—	—	—	—
84-85—Laval	QMJHL	68	35	68	103	62	...	...	...	—	—	—	—	—
85-86—Laval	QMJHL	69	45	110	155	70	...	...	...	14	9	27	36	12
86-87—Toronto	NHL	80	21	25	46	26	-6	4	0	12	1	5	6	8
87-88—Toronto	NHL	75	12	36	48	40	2	1	0	6	0	1	1	10
88-89—Toronto	NHL	80	26	42	68	75	-8	6	0	—	—	—	—	—
89-90—Toronto	NHL	80	33	61	94	56	2	9	0	5	0	2	2	2
90-91—Toronto	NHL	79	26	47	73	65	-31	10	1	—	—	—	—	—
91-92—Edmonton	NHL	80	38	51	89	53	10	12	1	16	6	8	14	8
92-93—Montreal	NHL	84	39	58	97	98	5	9	3	20	11	12	23	16
93-94—Montreal	NHL	84	40	51	91	75	0	13	0	7	1	2	3	8
94-95—Ratingen	Germany	11	5	6	11	24	...	...	...	—	—	—	—	—
—Montreal	NHL	48	10	30	40	42	15	4	0	—	—	—	—	—
95-96—Montreal	NHL	80	38	56	94	158	5	11	4	6	4	4	8	0
96-97—Montreal	NHL	82	27	54	81	82	-6	7	2	5	0	0	0	2

Season Team	League	REGULAR SEASON								PLAYOFFS				
		Gms.	G	A	Pts.	PIM	+/-	PP	SH	Gms.	G	A	Pts.	PIM
97-98—Montreal	NHL	76	18	41	59	58	14	2	1	10	3	6	9	22
98-99—Montreal	NHL	65	12	24	36	46	-7	3	2	—	—	—	—	—
—San Jose	NHL	12	7	6	13	4	3	3	0	6	3	2	5	6
99-00—San Jose	NHL	82	21	49	70	58	4	3	1	12	1	7	8	16
00-01—San Jose	NHL	45	9	37	46	62	17	4	0	6	2	1	3	14
NHL Totals (15 years)		1132	377	668	1045	998	19	101	15	111	32	50	82	112

DANDENAULT, MATHIEU   D   RED WINGS

PERSONAL: Born February 3, 1976, in Magog, Que. ... 6-1/196. ... Shoots right. ... Cousin of Eric Dandenault, defenseman with Philadelphia Flyers organization (1991-92 through 1993-94). ... Name pronounced DAN-dih-noh.
TRANSACTIONS/CAREER NOTES: Selected by Detroit Red Wings in second round (second Red Wings pick, 49th overall) of NHL entry draft (June 28, 1994). ... Suffered from the flu (November 11, 1995); missed one game. ... Bruised ribs (March 10, 1997); missed four games. ... Injured ankle (December 15, 2000).
MISCELLANEOUS: Member of Stanley Cup championship team (1997 and 1998).

Season Team	League	REGULAR SEASON								PLAYOFFS				
		Gms.	G	A	Pts.	PIM	+/-	PP	SH	Gms.	G	A	Pts.	PIM
91-92—Gloucester	OPJHL	6	3	4	7	0	...	...	...	—	—	—	—	—
92-93—Gloucester	OPJHL	55	11	26	37	64	...	...	...	—	—	—	—	—
93-94—Sherbrooke	QMJHL	67	17	36	53	67	...	...	...	12	4	10	14	12
94-95—Sherbrooke	QMJHL	67	37	70	107	76	...	...	...	7	1	7	8	10
95-96—Detroit	NHL	34	5	7	12	6	6	1	0	—	—	—	—	—
—Adirondack	AHL	4	0	0	0	0	...	...	...	—	—	—	—	—
96-97—Detroit	NHL	65	3	9	12	28	-10	0	0	—	—	—	—	—
97-98—Detroit	NHL	68	5	12	17	43	5	0	0	3	1	0	1	0
98-99—Detroit	NHL	75	4	10	14	59	17	0	0	10	0	1	1	0
99-00—Detroit	NHL	81	6	12	18	20	-12	0	0	6	0	0	0	2
00-01—Detroit	NHL	73	10	15	25	38	11	2	0	6	0	1	1	0
NHL Totals (6 years)		396	33	65	98	194	17	3	0	25	1	2	3	2

DANEYKO, KEN   D   DEVILS

PERSONAL: Born April 17, 1964, in Windsor, Ont. ... 6-1/215. ... Shoots left. ... Full Name: Kenneth Daneyko. ... Name pronounced DAN-ih-koh.
TRANSACTIONS/CAREER NOTES: Selected by New Jersey Devils in first round (second Devils pick, 18th overall) of NHL entry draft (June 1982). ... Fractured right fibula (November 2, 1983). ... Suspended one game and fined $500 by NHL for playing in West Germany without permission (October 1985). ... Injured wrist (February 25, 1987). ... Fractured nose (February 24, 1988). ... Injured shoulder (March 29, 1994); missed six games. ... Injured knee (March 8, 1995); missed 23 games. ... Suffered from the flu (March 9, 1996); missed two games. ... Injured hip (October 12, 1996); missed one game. ... Suffered from the flu (January 31, 1997); missed one game. ... Voluntarily entered NHL/NHLPA substance abuse and behavioral health program (November 6, 1997); missed 45 games. ... Suffered injury (October 16, 1999); missed one game.
HONORS: Won Bill Masterson Memorial Trophy (1999-2000).
MISCELLANEOUS: Member of Stanley Cup championship team (1995 and 2000). ... Holds New Jersey Devils franchise all-time records for most games played (1,147) and most penalty minutes (2,426).

Season Team	League	REGULAR SEASON								PLAYOFFS				
		Gms.	G	A	Pts.	PIM	+/-	PP	SH	Gms.	G	A	Pts.	PIM
80-81—Spokane	WHL	62	6	13	19	140	...	...	...	4	0	0	0	6
—St. Albert	AJHL	1	0	0	0	4	...	...	...	—	—	—	—	—
81-82—Spokane	WHL	26	1	11	12	147	...	...	...	—	—	—	—	—
—Seattle	WHL	38	1	22	23	151	...	...	...	14	1	9	10	49
82-83—Seattle	WHL	69	17	43	60	150	...	...	...	4	1	3	4	14
83-84—Kamloops	WHL	19	6	28	34	52	...	...	...	17	4	9	13	28
—New Jersey	NHL	11	1	4	5	17	-1	0	0	—	—	—	—	—
84-85—New Jersey	NHL	1	0	0	0	10	-1	0	0	—	—	—	—	—
—Maine	AHL	80	4	9	13	206	...	...	...	11	1	3	4	36
85-86—Maine	AHL	21	3	2	5	75	...	...	...	—	—	—	—	—
—New Jersey	NHL	44	0	10	10	100	1	0	0	—	—	—	—	—
86-87—New Jersey	NHL	79	2	12	14	183	-13	0	0	—	—	—	—	—
87-88—New Jersey	NHL	80	5	7	12	239	-3	1	0	20	1	6	7	83
88-89—New Jersey	NHL	80	5	5	10	283	-22	1	0	—	—	—	—	—
89-90—New Jersey	NHL	74	6	15	21	219	15	0	1	6	2	0	2	21
90-91—New Jersey	NHL	80	4	16	20	249	-10	1	2	7	0	1	1	10
91-92—New Jersey	NHL	80	1	7	8	170	7	0	0	7	0	3	3	16
92-93—New Jersey	NHL	84	2	11	13	236	4	0	0	5	0	0	0	8
93-94—New Jersey	NHL	78	1	9	10	176	27	0	0	20	0	1	1	45
94-95—New Jersey	NHL	25	1	2	3	54	4	0	0	20	1	0	1	22
95-96—New Jersey	NHL	80	2	4	6	115	-10	0	0	—	—	—	—	—
96-97—New Jersey	NHL	77	2	7	9	70	24	0	0	10	0	0	0	28
97-98—New Jersey	NHL	37	0	1	1	57	3	0	0	6	0	1	1	10
98-99—New Jersey	NHL	82	2	9	11	63	27	0	0	7	0	0	0	8
99-00—New Jersey	NHL	78	0	6	6	98	13	0	0	23	1	2	3	14
00-01—New Jersey	NHL	77	0	4	4	87	8	0	0	25	0	3	3	21
NHL Totals (18 years)		1147	34	129	163	2426	73	3	3	156	5	17	22	286

DARBY, CRAIG   C   CANADIENS

PERSONAL: Born September 26, 1972, in Oneida, N.Y. ... 6-3/200. ... Shoots right.

TRANSACTIONS/CAREER NOTES: Selected by Montreal Canadiens in second round (third Canadiens pick, 43rd overall) of NHL entry draft (June 22, 1991). ... Traded by Canadiens with LW Kirk Muller and D Mathieu Schneider to New York Islanders for D Vladimir Malakhov and C Pierre Turgeon (April 5, 1995). ... Claimed on waivers by Philadelphia Flyers (June 4, 1996). ... Selected by Nashville Predators in NHL expansion draft (June 26, 1998). ... Signed as free agent by Canadiens (July 9, 1999). ... Separated shoulder (January 10, 2001); missed four games.

HONORS: Named Hockey East co-Rookie of the Year with Ian Moran (1991-92). ... Named to Hockey East All-Rookie team (1991-92). ... Named to AHL All-Star first team (1997-98).

Season Team	League	REGULAR SEASON								PLAYOFFS				
		Gms.	G	A	Pts.	PIM	+/-	PP	SH	Gms.	G	A	Pts.	PIM
89-90—Albany Academy	N.Y. H.S.	29	32	53	85	...	...	...	...	—	—	—	—	—
90-91—Albany Academy	N.Y. H.S.	27	33	61	94	53	...	...	...	—	—	—	—	—
91-92—Providence College	Hockey East	35	17	24	41	47	...	...	...	—	—	—	—	—
92-93—Providence College	Hockey East	35	11	21	32	62	...	...	...	—	—	—	—	—
93-94—Fredericton	AHL	66	23	33	56	51	...	...	...	—	—	—	—	—
94-95—Fredericton	AHL	64	21	47	68	82	...	...	...	—	—	—	—	—
—Montreal	NHL	10	0	2	2	0	-5	0	0	—	—	—	—	—
—New York Islanders	NHL	3	0	0	0	0	-1	0	0	—	—	—	—	—
95-96—Worcester	AHL	68	22	28	50	47	...	...	...	4	1	1	2	2
—New York Islanders	NHL	10	0	2	2	0	-1	0	0	—	—	—	—	—
96-97—Philadelphia	AHL	59	26	33	59	24	...	...	...	10	3	6	9	0
—Philadelphia	NHL	9	1	4	5	2	2	0	1	—	—	—	—	—
97-98—Philadelphia	NHL	3	1	0	1	0	0	0	0	—	—	—	—	—
—Philadelphia	AHL	77	†42	45	87	34	...	...	...	20	5	9	14	4
98-99—Milwaukee	IHL	81	32	22	54	33	...	...	...	2	3	0	3	0
99-00—Montreal	NHL	76	7	10	17	14	-14	0	1	—	—	—	—	—
00-01—Montreal	NHL	78	12	16	28	16	-17	0	1	—	—	—	—	—
NHL Totals (6 years)		189	21	34	55	32	-36	0	3					

D | DARCHE, MATHIEU   LW   BLUE JACKETS

PERSONAL: Born November 26, 1976, in St. Laurent, Que. ... 6-1/225. ... Shoots left.

TRANSACTIONS/CAREER NOTES: Signed as non-drafted free agent by Columbus Blue Jackets (May 8, 2000).

HONORS: Named to OUA (East) All-Star first team (1998-99).

Season Team	League	REGULAR SEASON								PLAYOFFS				
		Gms.	G	A	Pts.	PIM	+/-	PP	SH	Gms.	G	A	Pts.	PIM
96-97—McGill University	CIAU	23	1	2	3	27	...	...	...	—	—	—	—	—
97-98—McGill University	CIAU	40	28	17	45	69	...	...	...	—	—	—	—	—
98-99—McGill University	CIAU	32	16	24	40	60	...	...	...	—	—	—	—	—
99-00—McGill University	CIAU	38	33	49	82	54	...	...	...	—	—	—	—	—
00-01—Syracuse	AHL	66	16	24	40	21	...	...	...	5	0	1	1	4
—Columbus	NHL	9	0	0	0	0	-4	0	0	—	—	—	—	—
NHL Totals (1 year)		9	0	0	0	0	-4	0	0					

DAVIDSON, MATT   RW   BLUE JACKETS

PERSONAL: Born August 9, 1977, in Flin Flon, Man. ... 6-2/190. ... Shoots right.

TRANSACTIONS/CAREER NOTES: Selected by Buffalo Sabres in fourth round (fifth Sabres pick, 94th overall) of NHL entry draft (July 8, 1995). ... Traded by Sabres with D Jean-Luc Grand-Pierre, fifth-round pick (C Tyler Kolarik) in 2000 draft and fifth-round pick (traded to Detroit) in 2001 draft to Columbus Blue Jackets for future considerations (June 23, 2000).

Season Team	League	REGULAR SEASON								PLAYOFFS				
		Gms.	G	A	Pts.	PIM	+/-	PP	SH	Gms.	G	A	Pts.	PIM
93-94—Portland	WHL	59	4	12	16	18	...	...	...	10	0	0	0	4
94-95—Portland	WHL	72	17	20	37	51	...	...	...	9	1	3	4	0
95-96—Portland	WHL	70	24	26	50	96	...	...	...	7	2	2	4	2
96-97—Portland	WHL	72	44	27	71	47	...	...	...	6	0	1	1	2
97-98—Rochester	AHL	72	15	12	27	12	...	...	...	3	1	0	1	2
98-99—Rochester	AHL	80	26	15	41	42	...	...	...	18	2	1	3	6
99-00—Rochester	AHL	80	12	20	32	30	...	...	...	19	4	2	6	8
00-01—Syracuse	AHL	72	14	11	25	24	...	...	...	5	1	2	3	2
—Columbus	NHL	5	0	0	0	0	2	0	0	—	—	—	—	—
NHL Totals (1 year)		5	0	0	0	0	2	0	0					

DAVIDSSON, JOHAN   C/RW   CANUCKS

PERSONAL: Born January 6, 1976, in Jonkoping, Sweden. ... 6-1/181. ... Shoots left.

TRANSACTIONS/CAREER NOTES: Selected by Mighty Ducks of Anaheim in second round (second Mighty Ducks pick, 28th overall) of NHL entry draft (June 28, 1994). ... Sprained right ankle (January 1, 1999); missed five games. ... Traded by Mighty Ducks with future considerations to New York Islanders for LW Jorgen Jonsson (March 11, 2000). ... Signed as free agent by Vancouver Canucks (September 6, 2000).

Season Team	League	REGULAR SEASON								PLAYOFFS				
		Gms.	G	A	Pts.	PIM	+/-	PP	SH	Gms.	G	A	Pts.	PIM
92-93—HV 71 Jonkoping.......	Sweden	8	1	0	1	0	...	...	...	—	—	—	—	—
93-94—Swedish nat'l Jr. team	Sweden	6	1	4	5	6	...	...	...	—	—	—	—	—
—HV 71 Jonkoping.......	Sweden	38	2	5	7	4	...	...	...	—	—	—	—	—
94-95—HV 71 Jonkoping.......	Sweden	37	4	7	11	20	...	...	...	13	3	2	5	0
95-96—HV 71 Jonkoping........	Sweden	39	7	11	18	20	...	...	...	4	0	2	2	0
96-97—HV 71 Jonkoping........	Sweden	50	18	21	39	18	...	...	...	5	0	3	3	2
97-98—HIFK Helsinki	Finland	43	10	30	40	73	...	...	...	9	3	10	13	0
98-99—Anaheim	NHL	64	3	5	8	14	-9	1	0	1	0	0	0	0
—Cincinnati..................	AHL	9	1	6	7	2	...	...	...	—	—	—	—	—
99-00—Cincinnati..................	AHL	56	9	31	40	24	...	...	...	—	—	—	—	—
—Anaheim	NHL	5	1	0	1	2	0	0	0	—	—	—	—	—
—New York Islanders.....	NHL	14	2	4	6	0	0	0	0	—	—	—	—	—
00-01—Blues Espoo................	Finland	35	12	17	29	34	...	...	...	—	—	—	—	—
NHL Totals (2 years)...........		83	6	9	15	16	-9	1	0	1	0	0	0	0

DAVISON, ROB — D — SHARKS

PERSONAL: Born May 1, 1980, in St. Catharine's, Ont. ... 6-2/210. ... Shoots left.
TRANSACTIONS/CAREER NOTES: Selected by San Jose Sharks in fourth round (fourth Sharks pick, 98th overall) of NHL entry draft (June 27, 1998).

Season Team	League	REGULAR SEASON								PLAYOFFS				
		Gms.	G	A	Pts.	PIM	+/-	PP	SH	Gms.	G	A	Pts.	PIM
96-97—St. Michael's	Tier II Jr. A	45	2	6	8	93	...	...	...	—	—	—	—	—
97-98—North Bay	OHL	59	0	11	11	200	...	...	...	—	—	—	—	—
98-99—North Bay	OHL	59	2	17	19	150	...	...	...	4	0	1	1	12
99-00—North Bay	OHL	67	4	6	10	194	...	...	...	6	0	1	1	8
00-01—Kentucky....................	AHL	72	0	4	4	230	...	...	...	3	0	0	0	0

DAZE, ERIC — RW — BLACKHAWKS

PERSONAL: Born July 2, 1975, in Montreal. ... 6-6/234. ... Shoots left. ... Name pronounced dah-ZAY.
TRANSACTIONS/CAREER NOTES: Selected by Chicago Blackhawks in fourth round (fifth Blackhawks pick, 90th overall) of NHL entry draft (June 26, 1993). ... Sprained left ankle prior to 1996-97 season; missed eight games. ... Suffered from the flu (January 20, 1997); missed one game. ... Injured back (March 27, 1998); missed two games. ... Bruised ankle (October 22, 1998); missed three games. ... Suffered back spasms (October 27, 1999); missed three games. ... Suffered from the flu (January 2, 2000); missed one game. ... Suffered from migraine headache (February 16, 2000); missed one game. ... Suffered back spasms (March 3, 2000) and underwent surgery; missed final 18 games of season.
HONORS: Named to QMJHL All-Star first team (1993-94 and 1994-95). ... Won Can.HL Most Sportsmanlike Player of the Year Award (1994-95). ... Won Frank J. Selke Trophy (1994-95). ... Named NHL Rookie of the Year by THE SPORTING NEWS (1995-96). ... Named to NHL All-Rookie team (1995-96).
STATISTICAL NOTES: Tied for NHL lead in game-tying goals with three (1998-99).
STATISTICAL PLATEAUS: Three-goal games: 1996-97 (1). ... Four-goal games: 1997-98 (1). ... Total hat tricks: 2.

Season Team	League	REGULAR SEASON								PLAYOFFS				
		Gms.	G	A	Pts.	PIM	+/-	PP	SH	Gms.	G	A	Pts.	PIM
92-93—Beauport....................	QMJHL	68	19	36	55	24	...	...	...	—	—	—	—	—
93-94—Beauport....................	QMJHL	66	59	48	107	31	...	...	...	15	16	8	24	2
94-95—Beauport....................	QMJHL	57	54	45	99	20	...	...	...	16	9	12	21	23
—Chicago......................	NHL	4	1	1	2	2	2	0	0	16	0	1	1	4
95-96—Chicago......................	NHL	80	30	23	53	18	16	2	0	10	3	5	8	0
96-97—Chicago......................	NHL	71	22	19	41	16	-4	11	0	6	2	1	3	2
97-98—Chicago......................	NHL	80	31	11	42	22	4	10	0	—	—	—	—	—
98-99—Chicago......................	NHL	72	22	20	42	22	-13	8	0	—	—	—	—	—
99-00—Chicago......................	NHL	59	23	13	36	28	-16	6	0	—	—	—	—	—
00-01—Chicago......................	NHL	79	33	24	57	16	1	9	1	—	—	—	—	—
NHL Totals (7 years)...........		445	162	111	273	124	-10	46	1	32	5	7	12	6

de VRIES, GREG — D — AVALANCHE

PERSONAL: Born January 4, 1973, in Sundridge, Ont. ... 6-3/215. ... Shoots left. ... Name pronounced duh-VREES.
TRANSACTIONS/CAREER NOTES: Signed as non-drafted free agent by Edmonton Oilers (March 28, 1994). ... Sprained ankle (January 26, 1997); missed four games. ... Traded by Oilers with G Eric Fichaud and D Drake Berehowsky to Nashville Predators for C Jim Dowd and G Mikhail Shtalenkov (October 1, 1998). ... Traded by Predators to Colorado Avalanche for third-round pick (RW Branko Radivojevic) in 1999 draft (October 25, 1998). ... Suffered from the flu (December 27, 1999); missed two games. ... Separated shoulder (February 19, 2001); missed three games.
MISCELLANEOUS: Member of Stanley Cup championship team (2001).

Season Team	League	REGULAR SEASON								PLAYOFFS				
		Gms.	G	A	Pts.	PIM	+/-	PP	SH	Gms.	G	A	Pts.	PIM
91-92—Bowling Green	CCHA	24	0	3	3	20	...	...	...	—	—	—	—	—
92-93—Niagara Falls	OHL	62	3	23	26	86	...	...	...	4	0	1	1	6
93-94—Niagara Falls	OHL	64	5	40	45	135	...	...	...	—	—	—	—	—
—Cape Breton	AHL	9	0	0	0	11	...	...	...	1	0	0	0	0
94-95—Cape Breton	AHL	77	5	19	24	68	...	...	...	—	—	—	—	—
95-96—Edmonton	NHL	13	1	1	2	12	-2	0	0	—	—	—	—	—
—Cape Breton	AHL	58	9	30	39	174	...	...	...	—	—	—	—	—

Season Team	League	Gms.	G	A	Pts.	PIM	+/-	PP	SH	Gms.	G	A	Pts.	PIM
96-97—Hamilton	AHL	34	4	14	18	26	...			—	—	—	—	—
—Edmonton	NHL	37	0	4	4	52	-2	0	0	12	0	1	1	8
97-98—Edmonton	NHL	65	7	4	11	80	-17	1	0	7	0	0	0	21
98-99—Nashville	NHL	6	0	0	0	4	-4	0	0	—	—	—	—	—
—Colorado	NHL	67	1	3	4	60	-3	0	0	19	0	2	2	22
99-00—Colorado	NHL	69	2	7	9	73	-7	0	0	5	0	0	0	4
00-01—Colorado	NHL	79	5	12	17	51	23	0	0	23	0	1	1	20
NHL Totals (6 years)		336	16	31	47	332	-12	1	0	66	0	4	4	75

DEADMARSH, ADAM   RW   KINGS

PERSONAL: Born May 10, 1975, in Trail, B.C. ... 6-0/195. ... Shoots right. ... Cousin of Butch Deadmarsh, left winger with three NHL teams (1970-71 through 1974-75); and brother of Jake Deadmarsh, left winger with San Jose Sharks organization (1996-97 and 1997-98).

TRANSACTIONS/CAREER NOTES: Selected by Quebec Nordiques in first round (second Nordiques pick, 14th overall) of NHL entry draft (June 26, 1993). ... Nordiques franchise moved to Colorado and renamed Avalanche for 1995-96 season (June 21, 1995). ... Strained groin (April 3, 1996); missed four games. ... Strained shoulder (December 13, 1997); missed one game. ... Suffered from the flu (January 14, 1998); missed one game. ... Strained hip flexor (March 19, 1998); missed one game. ... Injured shoulder (April 1, 1998); missed two games. ... Bruised thigh (April 11, 1998); missed two games. ... Bruised ribs (October 9, 1998); missed first two games of season. ... Suffered infected left elbow (October 24, 1998); missed three games. ... Suffered back spasms (March 16, 1999); missed five games. ... Injured eye (April 3, 1999); missed final six games of regular season. ... Suffered hip pointer prior to start of 1999-2000 regular season; missed first two games of season. ... Bruised toe (December 12, 1999); missed one game. ... Sprained knee (January 13, 2000); missed three games. ... Injured rib (February 15, 2000); missed five games. ... Injured eye (October 18, 2000); missed one game. ... Suffered concussion (November 1, 2000); missed 14 games. ... Injured knee (January 18, 2001); missed five games. ... Traded by Avalanche with D Aaron Miller, first-round pick (C David Steckel) in 2001 draft, a player to be named later and future considerations to Los Angeles Kings for C Steve Reinprecht and D Rob Blake (February 21, 2001); Kings acquired C Jared Aulin to complete deal (March 22, 2001). ... Bruised hand (March 5, 2001); missed three games.

MISCELLANEOUS: Member of Stanley Cup championship team (1996). ... Scored on a penalty shot (vs. Jeff Hackett, March 1, 1997).

STATISTICAL NOTES: Tied for NHL lead with three game-tying goals (1997-98).

STATISTICAL PLATEAUS: Three-goal games: 1999-00 (1).

Season Team	League	Gms.	G	A	Pts.	PIM	+/-	PP	SH	Gms.	G	A	Pts.	PIM
91-92—Portland	WHL	68	30	30	60	81	...	...	...	6	3	3	6	13
92-93—Portland	WHL	58	33	36	69	126	...	...	...	16	7	8	15	29
93-94—Portland	WHL	65	43	56	99	212	...	...	...	10	9	8	17	33
94-95—Portland	WHL	29	28	20	48	129	...	...	...	—	—	—	—	—
—Quebec	NHL	48	9	8	17	56	16	0	0	6	0	1	1	0
95-96—Colorado	NHL	78	21	27	48	142	20	3	0	22	5	12	17	25
96-97—Colorado	NHL	78	33	27	60	136	8	10	3	17	3	6	9	24
97-98—Colorado	NHL	73	22	21	43	125	0	10	0	7	2	0	2	4
—U.S. Olympic team	Int'l	4	1	0	1	2	...	...	...	—	—	—	—	—
98-99—Colorado	NHL	66	22	27	49	99	-2	10	0	19	8	4	12	20
99-00—Colorado	NHL	71	18	27	45	106	-10	5	0	17	4	11	15	21
00-01—Colorado	NHL	39	13	13	26	59	-2	7	0	—	—	—	—	—
—Los Angeles	NHL	18	4	2	6	4	3	0	0	13	3	3	6	4
NHL Totals (7 years)		471	142	152	294	727	33	45	3	101	25	37	62	98

DEAN, KEVIN   D   BLACKHAWKS

PERSONAL: Born April 1, 1969, in Madison, Wis. ... 6-3/210. ... Shoots left.

TRANSACTIONS/CAREER NOTES: Selected by New Jersey Devils in fourth round (fourth Devils pick, 86th overall) of NHL entry draft (June 13, 1987). ... Suffered rib injury (September 19, 1996); missed three games. ... Strained groin (November 25, 1998); missed three games. ... Reinjured groin (December 4, 1998); missed six games. ... Suffered from the flu (January 24, 1999); missed one game. ... Suffered from irregular heartbeat (February 1, 1999); missed two games. ... Strained right knee (February 9, 1999); missed five games. ... Selected by Atlanta Thrashers in NHL expansion draft (June 25, 1999). ... Traded by Thrashers to Dallas Stars for future considerations (December 15, 1999). ... Suffered irregular heartbeat (December 23, 1999); missed three games. ... Traded by Stars with C Derek Plante and second-round pick (RW Matt Keith) in 2001 draft to Chicago Blackhawks for D Sylvain Cote and D Dave Manson (February 8, 2000).

HONORS: Named to AHL All-Star first team (1994-95).

MISCELLANEOUS: Member of Stanley Cup championship team (1995).

Season Team	League	Gms.	G	A	Pts.	PIM	+/-	PP	SH	Gms.	G	A	Pts.	PIM
85-86—Culver Military	Indiana H.S.	35	28	44	72	48	...	...	...	—	—	—	—	—
86-87—Culver Military	Indiana H.S.	25	19	25	44	30	...	...	...	—	—	—	—	—
87-88—Univ. of New Hamp.	Hockey East	27	1	6	7	34	...	...	...	—	—	—	—	—
88-89—Univ. of New Hamp.	Hockey East	34	1	12	13	28	...	...	...	—	—	—	—	—
89-90—Univ. of New Hamp.	Hockey East	39	2	6	8	42	...	...	...	—	—	—	—	—
90-91—Univ. of New Hamp.	Hockey East	31	10	12	22	22	...	...	...	—	—	—	—	—
—Utica	AHL	7	0	1	1	2	...	...	...	—	—	—	—	—
91-92—Utica	AHL	23	0	3	3	6	...	...	...	—	—	—	—	—
—Cincinnati	ECHL	30	3	22	25	43	...	...	...	9	1	6	7	8
92-93—Utica	AHL	57	2	16	18	76	...	...	...	5	1	0	1	8
—Cincinnati	IHL	13	2	1	3	15	...	...	...	—	—	—	—	—
93-94—Albany	AHL	70	9	33	42	92	...	...	...	5	0	2	2	7
94-95—Albany	AHL	68	5	37	42	66	...	...	...	8	0	4	4	4
—New Jersey	NHL	17	0	1	1	4	6	0	0	3	0	2	2	0
95-96—New Jersey	NHL	41	0	6	6	28	4	0	0	—	—	—	—	—
—Albany	AHL	1	1	0	1	2	...	...	...	—	—	—	—	—

Season Team	League	REGULAR SEASON								PLAYOFFS				
		Gms.	G	A	Pts.	PIM	+/-	PP	SH	Gms.	G	A	Pts.	PIM
96-97—New Jersey	NHL	28	2	4	6	6	2	0	0	1	1	0	1	0
—Albany	AHL	2	0	1	1	4	...	...	...	—	—	—	—	—
97-98—New Jersey	NHL	50	1	8	9	12	12	1	0	5	1	0	1	2
—Albany	AHL	2	0	1	1	2	...	...	...	—	—	—	—	—
98-99—New Jersey	NHL	62	1	10	11	22	4	1	0	7	0	0	0	0
99-00—Atlanta	NHL	23	1	0	1	14	-5	0	1	—	—	—	—	—
—Dallas	NHL	14	0	0	0	10	-1	0	0	—	—	—	—	—
—Chicago	NHL	27	2	8	10	12	9	0	0	—	—	—	—	—
00-01—Chicago	NHL	69	0	11	11	30	-16	0	0	—	—	—	—	—
NHL Totals (7 years)		331	7	48	55	138	15	2	1	16	2	2	4	2

DeBRUSK, LOUIE   LW

PERSONAL: Born March 19, 1971, in Cambridge, Ont. ... 6-2/238. ... Shoots left. ... Full Name: Dennis Louis DeBrusk. ... Name pronounced dee-BRUHSK.

TRANSACTIONS/CAREER NOTES: Selected by New York Rangers in third round (fourth Rangers pick, 49th overall) of NHL entry draft (June 17, 1989). ... Traded by Rangers with C Bernie Nicholls, RW Steven Rice and future considerations to Edmonton Oilers for C Mark Messier and future considerations (October 4, 1991); Rangers traded D David Shaw to Oilers for D Jeff Beukeboom to complete deal (November 12, 1991). ... Separated shoulder (January 28, 1992); missed four games. ... Strained groin (January 1993); missed five games. ... Strained abdominal muscle (January 1993); missed 11 games. ... Underwent blood tests (April 17, 1995); missed one game. ... Suspended two games by NHL for headbutting an opponent (October 6, 1995). ... Injured elbow (November 26, 1995); missed 14 games. ... Suspended four games and fined $1,000 by NHL for slashing (October 9, 1996). ... Signed as free agent by Tampa Bay Lightning (August 26, 1997). ... Traded by Lightning with fifth-round pick (D Jay Leach) in 1998 draft to Phoenix Coyotes for C Craig Janney (June 11, 1998). ... Suffered from the flu (April 17, 1999); missed final game of regular season. ... Strained groin (December 5, 2000); missed two games.

Season Team	League	REGULAR SEASON								PLAYOFFS				
		Gms.	G	A	Pts.	PIM	+/-	PP	SH	Gms.	G	A	Pts.	PIM
87-88—Stratford Jr. B	OHA	43	13	14	27	205	...	...	...	—	—	—	—	—
88-89—London	OHL	59	11	11	22	149	...	...	...	19	1	1	2	43
89-90—London	OHL	61	21	19	40	198	...	...	...	6	2	2	4	24
90-91—London	OHL	61	31	33	64	*223	...	...	...	7	2	2	4	14
—Binghamton	AHL	2	0	0	0	7	...	...	...	2	0	0	0	9
91-92—Edmonton	NHL	25	2	1	3	124	4	0	0	—	—	—	—	—
—Cape Breton	AHL	28	2	2	4	73	...	...	...	—	—	—	—	—
92-93—Edmonton	NHL	51	8	2	10	205	-16	0	0	—	—	—	—	—
93-94—Edmonton	NHL	48	4	6	10	185	-9	0	0	—	—	—	—	—
—Cape Breton	AHL	5	3	1	4	58	...	...	...	—	—	—	—	—
94-95—Edmonton	NHL	34	2	0	2	93	-4	0	0	—	—	—	—	—
95-96—Edmonton	NHL	38	1	3	4	96	-7	0	0	—	—	—	—	—
96-97—Edmonton	NHL	32	2	0	2	94	-6	0	0	6	0	0	0	4
97-98—Tampa Bay	NHL	54	1	2	3	166	-2	0	0	—	—	—	—	—
—San Antonio	IHL	17	7	4	11	130	...	...	...	—	—	—	—	—
98-99—Las Vegas	IHL	26	3	6	9	160	...	...	...	—	—	—	—	—
—Phoenix	NHL	15	0	0	0	34	-2	0	0	6	2	0	2	6
—Springfield	AHL	3	1	0	1	0	...	...	...	—	—	—	—	—
—Long Beach	IHL	24	5	5	10	134	...	...	...	—	—	—	—	—
99-00—Phoenix	NHL	61	4	3	7	78	1	0	0	3	0	0	0	0
00-01—Phoenix	NHL	39	0	0	0	79	-5	0	0	—	—	—	—	—
NHL Totals (10 years)		397	24	17	41	1154	-46	0	0	15	2	0	2	10

DeFAUW, BRAD   LW   HURRICANES

PERSONAL: Born November 10, 1977, in Edina, Minn. ... 6-2/210. ... Shoots left.
TRANSACTIONS/CAREER NOTES: Selected by Carolina Hurricanes in second round (second Hurricanes pick, 28th overall) of NHL entry draft (June 21, 1997).

Season Team	League	REGULAR SEASON								PLAYOFFS				
		Gms.	G	A	Pts.	PIM	+/-	PP	SH	Gms.	G	A	Pts.	PIM
95-96—Apple Valley	Minn. H.S.	28	21	34	55	14	...	...	...	—	—	—	—	—
96-97—Univ. of North Dakota	WCHA	37	7	6	13	39	...	...	...	—	—	—	—	—
97-98—Univ. of North Dakota	WCHA	36	9	11	20	34	...	...	...	—	—	—	—	—
98-99—Univ. of North Dakota	WCHA	34	11	12	23	64	...	...	...	—	—	—	—	—
99-00—Univ. of North Dakota	WCHA	43	13	9	22	52	...	...	...	—	—	—	—	—
00-01—Cincinnati	IHL	82	20	31	51	39	...	...	...	4	2	0	2	8

DeLEEUW, ADAM   LW   RED WINGS

PERSONAL: Born February 29, 1980, in Brampton, Ont. ... 6-0/206. ... Shoots left.
TRANSACTIONS/CAREER NOTES: Selected by Detroit Red Wings in sixth round (seventh Red Wings pick, 151st overall) of NHL entry draft (June 27, 1998).

Season Team	League	REGULAR SEASON								PLAYOFFS				
		Gms.	G	A	Pts.	PIM	+/-	PP	SH	Gms.	G	A	Pts.	PIM
96-97—Brampton	Tier II Jr. A	45	11	17	28	97	...	...	...	—	—	—	—	—
97-98—Barrie	OHL	56	10	6	16	224	...	...	...	—	—	—	—	—
98-99—Barrie	OHL	39	15	16	31	146	...	...	...	—	—	—	—	—
—Toronto St. Michael's	OHL	29	10	5	15	55	...	...	...	—	—	—	—	—
99-00—Toronto St. Michael's	OHL	45	11	19	30	107	...	...	...	—	—	—	—	—
—Dayton	ECHL	2	0	0	0	2	...	...	...	3	0	0	0	2
00-01—Toronto	OHL	54	11	14	25	122	...	...	...	18	1	1	2	21

D

DELISLE, XAVIER · RW · CANADIENS

PERSONAL: Born May 24, 1977, in Quebec City. ... 5-11/200. ... Shoots right. ... Name pronounced ZAYV-yoor dee-LIGHL.
TRANSACTIONS/CAREER NOTES: Selected by Tampa Bay Lightning in sixth round (fifth Lightning pick, 157th overall) of NHL entry draft (June 22, 1996). ... Signed as free agent by Montreal Canadiens (August 8, 2000).
HONORS: Named to QMJHL All-Star second team (1995-96). ... Named to Memorial Cup All-Star team (1995-96).

Season Team	League	REGULAR SEASON								PLAYOFFS				
		Gms.	G	A	Pts.	PIM	+/-	PP	SH	Gms.	G	A	Pts.	PIM
93-94—Granby	QMJHL	46	11	22	33	25	...	...	...	7	2	0	2	0
94-95—Granby	QMJHL	72	18	36	54	48	...	...	...	13	2	6	8	4
95-96—Granby	QMJHL	67	45	75	120	45	...	...	...	20	13	*27	*40	12
96-97—Granby	QMJHL	59	36	56	92	20	...	...	...	5	1	4	5	6
97-98—Adirondack	AHL	76	10	19	29	47	...	...	...	3	0	0	0	0
98-99—Cleveland	IHL	77	15	29	44	36	...	...	...	—	—	—	—	—
—Tampa Bay	NHL	2	0	0	0	0	0	0	0	—	—	—	—	—
99-00—Detroit	IHL	20	2	6	8	18	...	...	...	—	—	—	—	—
—Quebec	AHL	42	17	28	45	8	...	...	...	3	1	2	3	0
—Toledo	ECHL	2	0	1	1	0	...	...	...	—	—	—	—	—
00-01—Montreal	NHL	14	3	2	5	6	-5	1	0	—	—	—	—	—
—Quebec	AHL	62	18	29	47	34	...	...	...	9	1	5	6	2
NHL Totals (2 years)		16	3	2	5	6	-5	1	0	—	—	—	—	—

DELMORE, ANDY · D · FLYERS

PERSONAL: Born December 26, 1976, in Windsor, Ont. ... 6-1/192. ... Shoots right.
TRANSACTIONS/CAREER NOTES: Signed as non-drafted free agent by Philadelphia Flyers (July 9, 1997). ... Sprained right knee (March 5, 2000); missed nine games.
HONORS: Named to OHL All-Star first team (1996-97).

Season Team	League	REGULAR SEASON								PLAYOFFS				
		Gms.	G	A	Pts.	PIM	+/-	PP	SH	Gms.	G	A	Pts.	PIM
92-93—Chatham Jr. B	OHA	47	4	21	25	38	...	...	...	—	—	—	—	—
93-94—North Bay	OHL	45	2	7	9	33	...	...	...	17	0	0	0	2
94-95—North Bay	OHL	40	2	14	16	21	...	...	...	—	—	—	—	—
—Sarnia	OHL	27	5	13	18	27	...	...	...	3	0	0	0	2
95-96—Sarnia	OHL	64	21	38	59	45	...	...	...	10	3	7	10	2
96-97—Sarnia	OHL	63	18	60	78	39	...	...	...	12	2	10	12	10
—Fredericton	AHL	4	0	1	1	0	...	...	...	—	—	—	—	—
97-98—Philadelphia	AHL	73	9	30	39	46	...	...	...	18	4	4	8	21
98-99—Philadelphia	AHL	70	5	18	23	51	...	...	...	15	1	4	5	6
—Philadelphia	NHL	2	0	1	1	0	-1	0	0	—	—	—	—	—
99-00—Philadelphia	AHL	39	12	14	26	31	...	...	...	—	—	—	—	—
—Philadelphia	NHL	27	2	5	7	8	-1	0	0	18	5	2	7	14
00-01—Philadelphia	NHL	66	5	9	14	16	2	2	0	2	1	0	1	2
NHL Totals (3 years)		95	7	15	22	24	0	2	0	20	6	2	8	16

DEMITRA, PAVOL · RW · BLUES

PERSONAL: Born November 29, 1974, in Dubnica, Czechoslovakia. ... 6-0/190. ... Shoots left. ... Name pronounced PA-vuhl dih-MEE-truh.
TRANSACTIONS/CAREER NOTES: Selected by Ottawa Senators in ninth round (ninth Senators pick, 227th overall) of NHL entry draft (June 26, 1993). ... Fractured ankle (October 14, 1993); missed 23 games. ... Traded by Senators to St. Louis Blues for D Christer Olsson (November 27, 1996). ... Suffered back spasms and bruised tailbone (December 8, 1997); missed 10 games. ... Fractured jaw (March 7, 1998); missed 11 games. ... Injured triceps (December 26, 1999); missed three games. ... Suffered concussion (March 24, 2000); missed remainder of season. ... Suffered eye injury (December 30, 2000); missed 17 games. ... Injured hamstring (February 10, 2001); missed 14 games. ... Reinjured hamstring (March 14, 2001); missed seven games.
HONORS: Played in NHL All-Star Game (1999 and 2000). ... Won Lady Byng Memorial Trophy (1999-2000).
STATISTICAL PLATEAUS: Three-goal games: 1999-00 (1), 2000-01 (1). Total: 2.

Season Team	League	REGULAR SEASON								PLAYOFFS				
		Gms.	G	A	Pts.	PIM	+/-	PP	SH	Gms.	G	A	Pts.	PIM
91-92—Sparta Dubnica	Czech Dv.II	28	13	10	23	12	...	...	...	—	—	—	—	—
92-93—Dukla Trencin	Czech.	46	11	17	28	0	...	...	...	—	—	—	—	—
—CAPEH Dubnica	Czech Dv.II	4	3	0	3		...	...	...	—	—	—	—	—
93-94—Ottawa	NHL	12	1	1	2	4	-7	1	0	—	—	—	—	—
—Prin. Edward Island	AHL	41	18	23	41	8	...	...	...	—	—	—	—	—
94-95—Prin. Edward Island	AHL	61	26	48	74	23	...	...	...	5	0	7	7	0
—Ottawa	NHL	16	4	3	7	0	-4	1	0	—	—	—	—	—
95-96—Prin. Edward Island	AHL	48	28	53	81	44	...	...	...	—	—	—	—	—
—Ottawa	NHL	31	7	10	17	6	-3	2	0	—	—	—	—	—
96-97—Las Vegas	IHL	22	8	13	21	10	...	...	...	—	—	—	—	—
—Grand Rapids	IHL	42	20	30	50	24	...	...	...	—	—	—	—	—
—Dukla Trencin	Slovakia	1	1	1	2		...	...	...	—	—	—	—	—
—St. Louis	NHL	8	3	0	3	2	0	2	0	6	1	3	4	6
97-98—St. Louis	NHL	61	22	30	52	22	11	4	4	10	3	3	6	2
98-99—St. Louis	NHL	82	37	52	89	16	13	14	0	13	5	4	9	4
99-00—St. Louis	NHL	71	28	47	75	8	34	8	0	—	—	—	—	—
00-01—St. Louis	NHL	44	20	25	45	16	27	5	0	15	2	4	6	2
NHL Totals (8 years)		325	122	168	290	74	71	37	4	44	11	14	25	14

DEMPSEY, NATHAN — D — MAPLE LEAFS

PERSONAL: Born July 14, 1974, in Spruce Grove, Alta. ... 6-0/190. ... Shoots left.
TRANSACTIONS/CAREER NOTES: Selected by Toronto Maple Leafs in 11th round (11th Leafs pick, 245th overall) of NHL entry draft (June 20, 1992).

Season Team	League	REGULAR SEASON								PLAYOFFS				
		Gms.	G	A	Pts.	PIM	+/-	PP	SH	Gms.	G	A	Pts.	PIM
91-92—Regina	WHL	70	4	22	26	72	...	...	...	—	—	—	—	—
92-93—Regina	WHL	72	12	29	41	95	...	...	...	13	3	8	11	14
—St. John's	AHL	—	—	—	—	—	...	...	...	2	0	0	0	0
93-94—Regina	WHL	56	14	36	50	100	...	...	...	4	0	0	0	4
94-95—St. John's	AHL	74	7	30	37	91	...	...	...	5	1	0	1	11
95-96—St. John's	AHL	73	5	15	20	103	...	...	...	4	1	0	1	9
96-97—St. John's	AHL	52	8	18	26	108	...	...	...	6	1	0	1	4
—Toronto	NHL	14	1	1	2	2	-2	0	0	—	—	—	—	—
97-98—St. John's	AHL	68	12	16	28	85	...	...	...	4	0	0	0	0
98-99—St. John's	AHL	67	2	29	31	70	...	...	...	5	0	1	1	2
99-00—St. John's	AHL	44	15	12	27	40	...	...	...	—	—	—	—	—
—Toronto	NHL	6	0	2	2	2	2	0	0	—	—	—	—	—
00-01—St. John's	AHL	55	11	28	39	60	...	...	...	4	0	4	4	8
—Toronto	NHL	25	1	9	10	4	13	1	0	—	—	—	—	—
NHL Totals (3 years)		45	2	12	14	8	13	1	0					

DENIS, MARC — G — BLUE JACKETS

PERSONAL: Born August 1, 1977, in Montreal. ... 6-0/190. ... Catches left. ... Name pronounced deh-NEE.
TRANSACTIONS/CAREER NOTES: Selected by Colorado Avalanche in first round (first Avalanche pick, 25th overall) of NHL entry draft (July 8, 1995). ... Traded by Avalanche to Columbus Blue Jackets for second-round pick (traded to Carolina) in 2000 draft (June 7, 2000).
HONORS: Won Marcel Robert Trophy (1995-96). ... Won Can.HL Goaltender of the Year Award (1996-97). ... Won Jacques Plante Trophy (1996-97). ... Named to Can.HL All-Star first team (1996-97). ... Named to QMJHL All-Star first team (1996-97).
MISCELLANEOUS: Stopped a penalty shot attempt (vs. Jeremy Roenick, February 28, 2001).

Season Team	League	REGULAR SEASON								PLAYOFFS						
		Gms.	Min	W	L	T	GA	SO	Avg.	Gms.	Min.	W	L	GA	SO	Avg.
94-95—Chicoutimi	QMJHL	32	1688	9	9	7	98	0	3.48	6	374	4	2	19	1	3.05
95-96—Chicoutimi	QMJHL	51	2895	23	21	4	157	2	3.25	16	917	8	†8	66	0	4.32
96-97—Chicoutimi	QMJHL	41	2317	22	15	2	104	4	*2.69	*21	*1226	*11	*10	*70	*1	3.43
—Colorado	NHL	1	60	0	1	0	3	0	3.00	—	—	—	—	—	—	—
—Hershey	AHL	—	—	—	—	—	—	—	—	4	56	1	0	1	0	*1.07
97-98—Hershey	AHL	47	2589	17	23	4	125	1	2.90	6	347	3	3	15	0	2.59
98-99—Hershey	AHL	52	2908	20	23	5	137	4	2.83	3	143	1	1	7	0	2.94
—Colorado	NHL	4	217	1	1	1	9	0	2.49	—	—	—	—	—	—	—
99-00—Colorado	NHL	23	1203	9	8	3	51	3	2.54	—	—	—	—	—	—	—
00-01—Columbus	NHL	32	1830	6	20	4	99	0	3.25	—	—	—	—	—	—	—
NHL Totals (4 years)		60	3310	16	30	8	162	3	2.94							

DESCOTEAUX, MATHIEU — D — CANADIENS

PERSONAL: Born September 23, 1977, in Pierreville, Que. ... 6-3/220. ... Shoots left. ... Name pronounced day-koh-TOH.
TRANSACTIONS/CAREER NOTES: Selected by Edmonton Oilers in first round (second Oilers pick, 19th overall) of NHL entry draft (June 22, 1996). ... Traded by Oilers with D Christian LaFlamme to Montreal Canadiens for D Igor Ulanov and D Alain Nasreddine (March 9, 2000).

Season Team	League	REGULAR SEASON								PLAYOFFS				
		Gms.	G	A	Pts.	PIM	+/-	PP	SH	Gms.	G	A	Pts.	PIM
94-95—Shawinigan	QMJHL	50	3	2	5	28	...	...	...	—	—	—	—	—
95-96—Shawinigan	QMJHL	69	2	13	15	129	...	...	...	6	0	0	0	6
96-97—Shawinigan	QMJHL	38	6	18	24	121	...	...	...	—	—	—	—	—
—Hull	QMJHL	32	6	19	25	34	...	...	...	14	2	5	7	20
97-98—Hamilton	AHL	67	2	8	10	70	...	...	...	2	0	0	0	0
98-99—Hamilton	AHL	74	6	12	18	49	...	...	...	4	0	0	0	0
99-00—Hamilton	AHL	49	5	7	12	29	...	...	...	—	—	—	—	—
—Quebec	AHL	12	0	6	6	6	...	...	...	2	0	1	1	0
00-01—Quebec	AHL	73	16	27	43	38	...	...	...	7	0	3	3	4
—Montreal	NHL	5	1	1	2	4	-2	1	0	—	—	—	—	—
NHL Totals (1 year)		5	1	1	2	4	-2	1	0					

DESJARDINS, ERIC — D — FLYERS

PERSONAL: Born June 14, 1969, in Rouyn, Que. ... 6-1/205. ... Shoots right. ... Name pronounced day-zhar-DAN.
TRANSACTIONS/CAREER NOTES: Selected by Montreal Canadiens in second round (third Canadiens pick, 38th overall) of NHL entry draft (June 13, 1987). ... Suffered from the flu (January 1989). ... Pulled groin (November 2, 1989); missed seven games. ... Sprained left ankle (January 26, 1991); missed 16 games. ... Fractured right thumb (December 8, 1991); missed two games. ... Traded by Canadiens with LW Gilbert Dionne and C John LeClair to Philadelphia Flyers for RW Mark Recchi and third-round pick (C Martin Hohenberger) in 1995 draft (February 9, 1995). ... Slightly strained groin (March 28, 1995); missed one game. ... Reinjured groin (April 1, 1995); missed three games. ... Suffered from the flu (December 26, 1995); missed one game. ... Suffered inflamed pelvic bone (October 1, 1997); missed five games. ... Strained groin (October 27, 1998); missed four games. ... Suffered from stomach virus (March 6, 1999); missed three games. ... Sprained left knee (March 21, 1999); missed seven games. ... Suffered head injury prior to start of 1999-2000 season; missed first game of season. ... Suffered from stomach virus (December 21, 2000); missed one game. ... Suffered concussion (March 8, 2001); missed two games.

HONORS: Named to QMJHL All-Star second team (1986-87). ... Won Emile (Butch) Bouchard Trophy (1987-88). ... Named to QMJHL All-Star first team (1987-88). ... Played in NHL All-Star Game (1992, 1996 and 2000). ... Named to NHL All-Star second team (1998-99 and 1999-2000).
RECORDS: Shares NHL single-game playoff record for most goals by defensemen—3 (June 3, 1993).
MISCELLANEOUS: Member of Stanley Cup championship team (1993). ... Captain of Philadelphia Flyers (March 27, 1999-remainder of season and 2000-01). ... Failed to score on a penalty shot (vs. Dominik Hasek, April 16, 2000 (playoffs)).

| | | | | REGULAR SEASON | | | | | | | | PLAYOFFS | | | |
Season Team	League	Gms.	G	A	Pts.	PIM	+/-	PP	SH	Gms.	G	A	Pts.	PIM
86-87—Granby	QMJHL	66	14	24	38	75	...	...	...	8	3	2	5	10
87-88—Granby	QMJHL	62	18	49	67	138	...	...	...	5	0	3	3	10
—Sherbrooke	AHL	3	0	0	0	6	...	...	...	4	0	2	2	2
88-89—Montreal	NHL	36	2	12	14	26	9	1	0	14	1	1	2	6
89-90—Montreal	NHL	55	3	13	16	51	1	1	0	6	0	0	0	10
90-91—Montreal	NHL	62	7	18	25	27	7	0	0	13	1	4	5	8
91-92—Montreal	NHL	77	6	32	38	50	17	4	0	11	3	3	6	4
92-93—Montreal	NHL	82	13	32	45	98	20	7	0	20	4	10	14	23
93-94—Montreal	NHL	84	12	23	35	97	-1	6	1	7	0	2	2	4
94-95—Montreal	NHL	9	0	6	6	2	2	0	0	—	—	—	—	—
—Philadelphia	NHL	34	5	18	23	12	10	1	0	15	4	4	8	10
95-96—Philadelphia	NHL	80	7	40	47	45	19	5	0	12	0	6	6	2
96-97—Philadelphia	NHL	82	12	34	46	50	25	5	1	19	2	8	10	12
97-98—Philadelphia	NHL	77	6	27	33	36	11	2	1	5	0	1	1	0
—Can. Olympic team	Int'l	6	0	0	0	2	...	...	...	—	—	—	—	—
98-99—Philadelphia	NHL	68	15	36	51	38	18	6	0	6	2	2	4	4
99-00—Philadelphia	NHL	81	14	41	55	32	20	8	0	18	2	10	12	2
00-01—Philadelphia	NHL	79	15	33	48	50	-3	6	1	6	1	1	2	0
NHL Totals (13 years)		906	117	365	482	614	155	52	4	152	20	52	72	85

DesROCHERS, PATRICK   G   COYOTES

PERSONAL: Born October 27, 1979, in Penetang, Ont. ... 6-3/195. ... Catches left.
TRANSACTIONS/CAREER NOTES: Selected by Phoenix Coyotes in first round (first Coyotes pick, 14th overall) of NHL entry draft (June 27, 1998).

| | | | | | REGULAR SEASON | | | | | | | | PLAYOFFS | | | | |
Season Team	League	Gms.	Min	W	L	T	GA	SO	Avg.	Gms.	Min.	W	L	GA	SO	Avg.
95-96—Sarnia	OHL	29	1265	12	6	2	96	0	4.55	3	71	0	1	5	0	4.23
96-97—Sarnia	OHL	50	2667	22	17	4	154	4	3.46	11	576	6	5	42	0	4.38
97-98—Sarnia	OHL	56	3205	26	17	11	179	1	3.35	4	160	1	2	12	0	4.50
98-99—Sarnia	OHL	8	425	3	5	0	26	0	3.67	—	—	—	—	—	—	—
—Kingston	OHL	44	2389	14	22	3	177	1	4.45	5	323	1	4	21	0	3.90
—Canadian nat'l team	Int'l	6	60	1	0	0	4	...	4.00	—	—	—	—	—	—	—
99-00—Springfield	AHL	52	2710	21	17	†7	137	1	3.03	2	120	1	1	7	1	3.50
00-01—Springfield	AHL	50	2807	17	24	5	156	0	3.33	—	—	—	—	—	—	—

DESSNER, JEFF   D   THRASHERS

PERSONAL: Born April 16, 1977, in Glenview, Ill.. ... Shoots left. ... Full Name: Jeffrey Marc Dessner.
TRANSACTIONS/CAREER NOTES: Selected by New York Rangers in seventh round (sixth Rangers pick, 185th overall) of NHL entry draft (June 22, 1996). ... Traded by Rangers to Atlanta Thrashers for eighth-round pick (D Leonid Zhvachin) in 2001 draft (June 24, 2001).
HONORS: Named to WCHA All-Star first team (1999-2000). ... Named to NCAA All-America (West) first team (1999-2000).

| | | | | REGULAR SEASON | | | | | | | | PLAYOFFS | | | |
Season Team	League	Gms.	G	A	Pts.	PIM	+/-	PP	SH	Gms.	G	A	Pts.	PIM
97-98—Univ. of Wisconsin	WCHA	19	1	3	4	43	...	...	...	—	—	—	—	—
98-99—Univ. of Wisconsin	WCHA	37	7	14	21	46	...	...	...	—	—	—	—	—
99-00—Univ. of Wisconsin	WCHA	40	11	16	27	61	...	...	...	—	—	—	—	—
00-01—Univ. of Wisconsin	WCHA	39	7	12	19	58	...	...	...	—	—	—	—	—

DEVEREAUX, BOYD   C   RED WINGS

PERSONAL: Born April 16, 1978, in Seaforth, Ont. ... 6-2/195. ... Shoots left. ... Name pronounced DEH-vuh-roh.
TRANSACTIONS/CAREER NOTES: Selected by Edmonton Oilers in first round (first Oilers pick, sixth overall) of NHL entry draft (June 22, 1996). ... Suffered concussion (April 1, 2000); missed remainder of season. ... Signed as free agent by Detroit Red Wings (August 23, 2000).
HONORS: Won Can.HL Scholastic Player of the Year Award (1995-96). ... Named to OHL All-Rookie second team (1995-96). ... Won Bobby Smith Trophy (1995-96).
STATISTICAL PLATEAUS: Three-goal games: 1999-00 (1).

| | | | | REGULAR SEASON | | | | | | | | PLAYOFFS | | | |
Season Team	League	Gms.	G	A	Pts.	PIM	+/-	PP	SH	Gms.	G	A	Pts.	PIM
93-94—Stratford	OPJHL	46	12	27	39	8	...	...	...	—	—	—	—	—
94-95—Stratford	OPJHL	45	31	74	105	21	...	...	...	—	—	—	—	—
95-96—Kitchener	OHL	66	20	38	58	35	...	...	...	12	3	7	10	4
96-97—Kitchener	OHL	54	28	41	69	37	...	...	...	13	4	11	15	8
—Hamilton	AHL	—	—	—	—	—	...	...	...	1	0	1	1	0
97-98—Edmonton	NHL	38	1	4	5	6	-5	0	0	—	—	—	—	—
—Hamilton	AHL	14	5	6	11	6	...	...	...	9	1	1	2	8

Season Team	League	REGULAR SEASON								PLAYOFFS				
		Gms.	G	A	Pts.	PIM	+/-	PP	SH	Gms.	G	A	Pts.	PIM
98-99—Edmonton..................	NHL	61	6	8	14	23	2	0	1	1	0	0	0	0
—Hamilton....................	AHL	7	4	6	10	2	...	...	...	8	0	3	3	4
99-00—Edmonton..................	NHL	76	8	19	27	20	7	0	1	—	—	—	—	—
00-01—Detroit.......................	NHL	55	5	6	11	14	1	0	0	2	0	0	0	0
NHL Totals (4 years)............		230	20	37	57	63	5	0	2	3	0	0	0	0

DIDUCK, GERALD   D   STARS

PERSONAL: Born April 6, 1965, in Edmonton. ... 6-2/220. ... Shoots right. ... Name pronounced DIH-dihk.
TRANSACTIONS/CAREER NOTES: Selected by New York Islanders first round (second Islanders pick, 16th overall) of NHL entry draft (June 8, 1983). ... Fractured left foot (November 1987). ... Fractured right hand (November 1988). ... Injured knee (January 1989). ... Traded by Islanders to Montreal Canadiens for D Craig Ludwig (September 4, 1990). ... Traded by Canadiens to Vancouver Canucks for fourth-round pick (LW Vladimir Vujtek) in 1991 draft (January 12, 1991). ... Bruised knee (March 16, 1991). ... Strained groin (January 4, 1993); missed three games. ... Suffered stress fracture in ankle (January 1, 1994); missed 14 games. ... Bruised foot (February 17, 1994); missed six games. ... Suffered eye contusion (March 31, 1994); missed five games. ... Traded by Canucks to Chicago Blackhawks for RW Bogdan Savenko and third-round pick (LW Larry Courville) in 1995 draft (April 7, 1995). ... Signed as free agent by Hartford Whalers (August 1, 1995). ... Strained ham-string (November 4, 1996); missed four games. ... Suffered hernia (December 16, 1996); missed nine games. ... Traded by Whalers to Phoenix Coyotes for RW Chris Murray (March 18, 1997). ... Suffered back spasms (December 3, 1997); missed two games. ... Injured hand (February 7, 1998); missed two games. ... Bruised shoulder (November 24, 1998); missed two games. ... Suffered charley horse (December 6, 1998); missed one game. ... Sprained knee (January 8, 1999); missed 14 games. ... Fractured foot (March 2, 1999); missed 21 games. ... Signed as free agent by Toronto Maple Leafs (January 28, 2000). ... Traded by Maple Leafs to Dallas Stars for future considerations (October 29, 2000). ... Sprained ankle (December 1, 2000); missed 12 games. ... Reinjured ankle (January 17, 2001); missed remainder of season.

Season Team	League	REGULAR SEASON								PLAYOFFS				
		Gms.	G	A	Pts.	PIM	+/-	PP	SH	Gms.	G	A	Pts.	PIM
81-82—Lethbridge	WHL	71	1	15	16	81	...	...	...	12	0	3	3	27
82-83—Lethbridge	WHL	67	8	16	24	151	...	...	...	20	3	12	15	49
83-84—Lethbridge	WHL	65	10	24	34	133	...	...	...	5	1	4	5	27
—Indianapolis	IHL	—	—	—	—	—	...	...	...	10	1	6	7	19
84-85—New York Islanders.....	NHL	65	2	8	10	80	2	0	0	—	—	—	—	—
85-86—New York Islanders.....	NHL	10	1	2	3	2	5	0	0	—	—	—	—	—
—Springfield	AHL	61	6	14	20	175	...			—	—	—	—	—
86-87—Springfield	AHL	45	6	8	14	120	...			—	—	—	—	—
—New York Islanders.....	NHL	30	2	3	5	67	-3	0	0	14	0	1	1	35
87-88—New York Islanders.....	NHL	68	7	12	19	113	22	4	0	6	1	0	1	42
88-89—New York Islanders.....	NHL	65	11	21	32	155	9	6	0	—	—	—	—	—
89-90—New York Islanders.....	NHL	76	3	17	20	163	2	1	0	5	0	0	0	12
90-91—Montreal......................	NHL	32	1	2	3	39	3	0	0	—	—	—	—	—
—Vancouver..................	NHL	31	3	7	10	66	-8	0	0	6	1	0	1	11
91-92—Vancouver..................	NHL	77	6	21	27	229	-3	2	0	5	0	0	0	10
92-93—Vancouver..................	NHL	80	6	14	20	171	32	0	1	12	4	2	6	12
93-94—Vancouver..................	NHL	55	1	10	11	72	2	0	0	24	1	7	8	22
94-95—Vancouver..................	NHL	22	1	3	4	15	-8	1	0	—	—	—	—	—
—Chicago.....................	NHL	13	1	0	1	48	3	0	0	16	1	3	4	22
95-96—Hartford	NHL	79	1	9	10	88	7	0	0	—	—	—	—	—
96-97—Hartford	NHL	56	1	10	11	40	-9	0	0	—	—	—	—	—
—Phoenix.....................	NHL	11	1	2	3	23	2	1	0	7	0	0	0	10
97-98—Phoenix.......................	NHL	78	8	10	18	118	14	1	0	6	0	2	2	20
98-99—Phoenix.......................	NHL	44	0	2	2	72	9	0	0	3	0	0	0	2
99-00—Toronto	NHL	26	0	3	3	33	2	0	0	10	0	1	1	14
00-01—Dallas.........................	NHL	14	0	0	0	18	4	0	0	—	—	—	—	—
NHL Totals (17 years).........		932	56	156	212	1612	87	16	1	114	8	16	24	212

DiMAIO, ROB   RW   STARS

PERSONAL: Born February 19, 1968, in Calgary. ... 5-10/190. ... Shoots right. ... Full Name: Robert DiMaio. ... Name pronounced duh-MIGH-oh.
TRANSACTIONS/CAREER NOTES: Selected by New York Islanders in sixth round (sixth Islanders pick, 118th overall) of NHL entry draft (June 13, 1987). ... Bruised left hand (February 1989). ... Sprained clavicle (November 1989). ... Sprained wrist (February 20, 1992); missed four games. ... Reinjured wrist (February 29, 1992); missed remainder of season. ... Selected by Tampa Bay Lightning in NHL expansion draft (June 18, 1992). ... Bruised wrist (November 28, 1992); missed four games. ... Sprained ankle (February 14, 1993); missed nine games. ... Reinjured right ankle (March 20, 1993); missed three games. ... Reinjured right ankle (April 1, 1993); missed remainder of season. ... Fractured left leg (October 16, 1993); missed 27 games. ... Traded by Lightning to Philadelphia Flyers for RW Jim Cummins and fourth-round pick in 1995 draft (March 18, 1994). ... Bruised foot (February 28, 1995); missed two games. ... Suffered from the flu (April 16, 1995); missed one game. ... Suffered bone bruise in left leg (December 16, 1995); missed 14 games. ... Sprained right knee (March 29, 1996); missed final eight games of regular season. ... Selected by San Jose Sharks from Flyers in NHL waiver draft for cash (September 30, 1996). ... Traded by Sharks to Boston Bruins for fifth-round pick (RW Adam Nittel) in 1997 draft (September 30, 1996). ... Strained knee (November 6, 1996); missed five games. ... Suffered from the flu (December 17, 1996); missed one game. ... Sprained knee (March 8, 1997); missed two games. ... Injured hip (April 5, 1997); missed two games. ... Strained groin (January 12, 1998); missed one game. ... Suffered concussion (February 26, 1998); missed one game. ... Injured ankle (November 3, 1998); missed one game. ... Suffered viral meningitis (December 26, 1998); missed five games. ... Strained elbow (April 1, 1999); missed one game. ... Reinjured elbow (April 7, 1999); missed two games. ... Injured hip (October 20, 1999); missed one game. ... Bruised foot (November 10, 1999); missed two games. ... Fractured foot (November 17, 1999); missed eight games. ... Injured wrist (February 25, 2000); missed seven games. ... Traded by Bruins to New York Rangers for RW Mike Knuble (March 10, 2000). ... Suffered concussion (March 19, 2000); missed one game. ... Traded by Rangers with LW Darren Langdon to Carolina Hurricanes for RW Sandy McCarthy and fourth-round pick (D Bryce Lampman) in 2001 draft (August 4, 2000). ... Suffered back spasms (November 4, 2000); missed three games. ... Strained shoulder (March 21, 2001); missed two games. ... Bruised sternum (March 30, 2001); missed three games. ... Signed as free agent by Dallas Stars (July 1, 2001).
HONORS: Won Stafford Smythe Memorial Trophy (1987-88). ... Named to Memorial Cup All-Star team (1987-88).
MISCELLANEOUS: Failed to score on a penalty shot (vs. Andy Moog, October 4, 1997).

Season Team	League	REGULAR SEASON								PLAYOFFS				
		Gms.	G	A	Pts.	PIM	+/-	PP	SH	Gms.	G	A	Pts.	PIM
84-85—Kamloops	WHL	55	9	18	27	29	...	...	...	—	—	—	—	—
85-86—Kamloops	WHL	6	1	0	1	0	...	...	...	—	—	—	—	—
—Medicine Hat............	WHL	55	20	30	50	82	...	...	...	—	—	—	—	—
86-87—Medicine Hat............	WHL	70	27	43	70	130	...	...	...	20	7	11	18	46
87-88—Medicine Hat............	WHL	54	47	43	90	120	...	...	...	14	12	19	†31	59
88-89—New York Islanders.....	NHL	16	1	0	1	30	-6	0	0	—	—	—	—	—
—Springfield	AHL	40	13	18	31	67	...	...	...	—	—	—	—	—
89-90—New York Islanders.....	NHL	7	0	0	0	2	0	0	0	1	1	0	1	4
—Springfield	AHL	54	25	27	52	69	...	...	...	16	4	7	11	45
90-91—New York Islanders.....	NHL	1	0	0	0	0	0	0	0	—	—	—	—	—
—Capital District	AHL	12	3	4	7	22	...	...	...	—	—	—	—	—
91-92—New York Islanders.....	NHL	50	5	2	7	43	-23	0	2	—	—	—	—	—
92-93—Tampa Bay	NHL	54	9	15	24	62	0	2	0	—	—	—	—	—
93-94—Tampa Bay	NHL	39	8	7	15	40	-5	2	0	—	—	—	—	—
—Philadelphia	NHL	14	3	5	8	6	1	0	0	—	—	—	—	—
94-95—Philadelphia	NHL	36	3	1	4	53	8	0	0	15	2	4	6	4
95-96—Philadelphia	NHL	59	6	15	21	58	0	1	1	3	0	0	0	0
96-97—Boston	NHL	72	13	15	28	82	-21	0	3	—	—	—	—	—
97-98—Boston	NHL	79	10	17	27	82	-13	0	0	6	1	0	1	8
98-99—Boston	NHL	71	7	14	21	95	-14	1	0	12	2	0	2	8
99-00—Boston	NHL	50	5	16	21	42	-1	0	0	—	—	—	—	—
—New York Rangers......	NHL	12	1	3	4	8	-8	0	0	—	—	—	—	—
00-01—Carolina	NHL	74	6	18	24	54	-14	0	2	6	0	0	0	4
NHL Totals (13 years).........		634	77	128	205	657	-96	6	8	43	6	4	10	28

DINEEN, KEVIN   RW   BLUE JACKETS

PERSONAL: Born October 28, 1963, in Quebec City. ... 5-11/189. ... Shoots right. ... Full Name: Kevin W. Dineen. ... Son of Bill Dineen, right winger with Detroit Red Wings (1953-54 through 1957-58) and Chicago Blackhawks (1957-58) and head coach with Philadelphia Flyers (1992-93); brother of Gord Dineen, defenseman with four NHL teams (1982-83 through 1994-95); and brother of Peter Dineen, defenseman with Los Angeles Kings (1986-87) and Red Wings (1989-90).

TRANSACTIONS/CAREER NOTES: Selected by Hartford Whalers in third round (third Whalers pick, 56th overall) of NHL entry draft (June 9, 1982). ... Sprained left shoulder (October 24, 1985); missed nine games. ... Fractured knuckle (January 12, 1986); missed seven games. ... Sprained knee (February 14, 1986). ... Suffered shoulder tendinitis (September 1988). ... Underwent surgery to right knee cartilage (August 1, 1990). ... Suffered hip pointer (November 28, 1990). ... Hospitalized due to complications caused by Crohn's disease (January 1, 1991); missed eight games. ... Injured groin (March 1991). ... Traded by Whalers to Philadelphia Flyers for LW Murray Craven and fourth-round pick (LW Kevin Smyth) in 1992 draft (November 13, 1991). ... Sprained wrist (February 4, 1992); missed one game. ... Strained right rotator cuff (December 3, 1992); missed one game. ... Suffered injury (October 9, 1993); missed one game. ... Bruised right shoulder (November 13, 1993); missed two games. ... Suffered recurrence of Crohn's disease (February 10, 1994); missed five games. ... Separated shoulder (March 8, 1994); missed three games. ... Strained left shoulder (January 31, 1995); missed three games. ... Reinjured left shoulder (February 11, 1995); missed three games. ... Traded by Flyers to Whalers for third-round pick (D Kris Mallette) in 1997 draft (December 28, 1995). ... Fractured bone in wrist (February 9, 1996); missed 27 games. ... Strained abdominal muscle (March 13, 1997); missed one game. ... Whalers franchise moved to North Carolina and renamed Carolina Hurricanes for 1997-98 season; NHL approved move on June 25, 1997. ... Strained hamstring (October 4, 1997); missed five games. ... Reinjured hamstring (November 21, 1997); missed six games. ... Reinjured hamstring (December 26, 1997); missed seven games. ... Reinjured hamstring (January 10, 1998); missed two games. ... Suffered charley horse (February 7, 1998); missed one game. ... Injured groin (March 23, 1998); missed four games. ... Reinjured groin (April 8, 1998); missed one game. ... Strained groin (November 4, 1998); missed four games. ... Suffered back spasms (February 20, 1999); missed five games. ... Injured groin (March 6, 1999); missed six games. ... Signed as free agent by Ottawa Senators (September 2, 1999). ... Suspended one game by NHL for elbowing incident (November 1, 1999). ... Strained groin (December 11, 1999); missed three games. ... Reinjured groin (January 16, 2000); missed two games. ... Strained groin (March 25, 2000); missed three games. ... Separated left shoulder (April 6, 2000); missed final two games of season. ... Selected by Columbus Blue Jackets in NHL expansion draft (June 23, 2000). ... Strained groin (October 14, 2000); missed one game. ... Strained groin (December 13, 2000); missed one game. ... Strained groin (January 6, 2001); missed one game. ... Sprained knee (January 15, 2001); missed six games. ... Tore anterior cruciate ligament and medial collateral ligament in knee (April 5, 2001); missed remainder of season.

HONORS: Named to THE SPORTING NEWS All-Star second team (1986-87). ... Played in NHL All-Star Game (1988 and 1989). ... Named Bud Light/NHL Man of the Year (1990-91).

MISCELLANEOUS: Captain of Philadelphia Flyers (1993-94). ... Captain of Hartford Whalers (1996-97). ... Captain of Carolina Hurricanes (1997-98). ... Holds Carolina Hurricanes franchise all-time record for most penalty minutes (1,441). ... Failed to score on a penalty shot (vs. Mike Richter, October 19, 1989). ... Holds Columbus Blue Jackets all-time record for most penalty minutes (126).

STATISTICAL PLATEAUS: Three-goal games: 1985-86 (1), 1986-87 (1), 1988-89 (1), 1989-90 (2), 1992-93 (3), 1993-94 (1). Total: 9. ... Four-goal games: 1993-94 (1). ... Total hat tricks: 1.

Season Team	League	REGULAR SEASON								PLAYOFFS				
		Gms.	G	A	Pts.	PIM	+/-	PP	SH	Gms.	G	A	Pts.	PIM
80-81—St. Michael's Jr. B.......	ODHA	40	15	28	43	167	...	...	...	—	—	—	—	—
81-82—Univ. of Denver..........	WCHA	38	12	22	34	105	...	...	...	—	—	—	—	—
82-83—Univ. of Denver..........	WCHA	36	16	13	29	108	...	...	...	—	—	—	—	—
83-84—Canadian nat'l team	Int'l	52	5	11	16	2	...	...	...	—	—	—	—	—
—Can. Olympic team	Int'l	7	0	0	0	0	...	...	...	—	—	—	—	—
84-85—Binghamton	AHL	25	15	8	23	41	...	...	...	—	—	—	—	—
—Hartford	NHL	57	25	16	41	120	-6	8	4	—	—	—	—	—
85-86—Hartford	NHL	57	33	35	68	124	16	6	0	10	6	7	13	18
86-87—Hartford	NHL	78	40	39	79	110	7	11	0	6	2	1	3	31
87-88—Hartford	NHL	74	25	25	50	217	-14	5	0	6	4	4	8	8
88-89—Hartford	NHL	79	45	44	89	167	-6	20	1	4	1	0	1	10
89-90—Hartford	NHL	67	25	41	66	164	7	8	2	6	3	2	5	18
90-91—Hartford	NHL	61	17	30	47	104	-15	4	0	6	1	0	1	16
91-92—Hartford	NHL	16	4	2	6	23	-6	1	0	—	—	—	—	—
—Philadelphia	NHL	64	26	30	56	130	1	5	3	—	—	—	—	—
92-93—Philadelphia	NHL	83	35	28	63	201	14	6	3	—	—	—	—	—

Season Team	League	REGULAR SEASON								PLAYOFFS				
		Gms.	G	A	Pts.	PIM	+/-	PP	SH	Gms.	G	A	Pts.	PIM
93-94—Philadelphia	NHL	71	19	23	42	113	-9	5	1	—	—	—	—	—
94-95—Houston	IHL	17	6	4	10	42	...	...	...	—	—	—	—	—
—Philadelphia	NHL	40	8	5	13	39	-1	4	0	15	6	4	10	18
95-96—Philadelphia	NHL	26	0	2	2	50	-8	0	0	—	—	—	—	—
—Hartford	NHL	20	2	7	9	67	7	0	0	—	—	—	—	—
96-97—Hartford	NHL	78	19	29	48	141	-6	8	0	—	—	—	—	—
97-98—Carolina	NHL	54	7	16	23	105	-7	0	0	—	—	—	—	—
98-99—Carolina	NHL	67	8	10	18	97	5	0	0	6	0	0	0	8
99-00—Ottawa	NHL	67	4	8	12	57	2	0	0	—	—	—	—	—
00-01—Columbus	NHL	66	8	7	15	126	2	0	0	—	—	—	—	—
NHL Totals (17 years)		1125	350	397	747	2155	-17	91	14	59	23	18	41	127

DINGMAN, CHRIS   LW   HURRICANES

PERSONAL: Born July 6, 1976, in Edmonton. ... 6-4/245. ... Shoots left.
TRANSACTIONS/CAREER NOTES: Selected by Calgary Flames in first round (first Flames pick, 19th overall) of NHL entry draft (June 28, 1994). ... Traded by Flames with RW Theo Fleury to Colorado Avalanche for LW Rene Corbet, D Wade Belak and future considerations (February 28, 1999); Flames acquired D Robyn Regehr to complete deal (March 27, 1999). ... Partially dislocated right shoulder (November 15, 1999); missed six games. ... Sprained knee (November 13, 2000); missed 13 games. ... Traded by Avalanche to Carolina Hurricanes for fifth-round pick (D Mikko Viitanen) in 2001 draft (June 24, 2001).
MISCELLANEOUS: Member of Stanley Cup championship team (2001).

Season Team	League	REGULAR SEASON								PLAYOFFS				
		Gms.	G	A	Pts.	PIM	+/-	PP	SH	Gms.	G	A	Pts.	PIM
92-93—Brandon	WHL	50	10	17	27	64	...	...	...	4	0	0	0	0
93-94—Brandon	WHL	45	21	20	41	77	...	...	...	13	1	7	8	39
94-95—Brandon	WHL	66	40	43	83	201	...	...	...	3	1	0	1	9
95-96—Brandon	WHL	40	16	29	45	109	...	...	...	19	12	11	23	60
—Saint John	AHL	—	—	—	—	—	...	...	...	1	0	0	0	0
96-97—Saint John	AHL	71	5	6	11	195	...	...	...	—	—	—	—	—
97-98—Calgary	NHL	70	3	3	6	149	-11	1	0	—	—	—	—	—
98-99—Saint John	AHL	50	5	7	12	140	...	...	...	—	—	—	—	—
—Calgary	NHL	2	0	0	0	17	-2	0	0	—	—	—	—	—
—Hershey	AHL	17	1	3	4	102	...	...	...	5	0	2	2	6
—Colorado	NHL	1	0	0	0	7	0	0	0	—	—	—	—	—
99-00—Colorado	NHL	68	8	3	11	132	-2	2	0	—	—	—	—	—
00-01—Colorado	NHL	41	1	1	2	108	-3	0	0	16	0	4	4	14
NHL Totals (4 years)		182	12	7	19	413	-18	3	0	16	0	4	4	14

DiPENTA, JOE   D   FLYERS

PERSONAL: Born February 25, 1979, in Barrie, Ont. ... 6-2/220. ... Shoots right.
TRANSACTIONS/CAREER NOTES: Selected by Florida Panthers in third round (second Panthers pick, 61st overall) of NHL entry draft (June 27, 1998). ... Signed as free agent by Philadelphia Flyers (August 1, 2000).

Season Team	League	REGULAR SEASON								PLAYOFFS				
		Gms.	G	A	Pts.	PIM	+/-	PP	SH	Gms.	G	A	Pts.	PIM
96-97—Smith Falls	OJHL	54	13	22	35	92	...	...	...	—	—	—	—	—
97-98—Boston University	Hockey East	38	2	16	18	50	...	...	...	—	—	—	—	—
98-99—Boston University	Hockey East	36	2	15	17	72	...	...	...	—	—	—	—	—
99-00—Halifax	QMJHL	63	13	43	56	83	...	...	...	10	3	4	7	26
00-01—Philadelphia	AHL	71	3	5	8	65	...	...	...	10	1	2	3	15

DiPIETRO, RICK   G   ISLANDERS

PERSONAL: Born September 19, 1981, in Lewiston, Maine. ... 6-0/185. ... Catches right.
TRANSACTIONS/CAREER NOTES: Selected by New York Islanders in first round (first Islanders pick, first overall) of NHL entry draft (June 24, 2000).
HONORS: Named to Hockey East All-Star second team (1999-2000).

Season Team	League	REGULAR SEASON								PLAYOFFS				
		Gms.	Min	W	L	T	GA	SO	Avg.	Gms.	Min.	W	L	GA	SO	Avg.
97-98—U.S. Jr. national team	Int'l	46	2526	21	19	0	131	2	3.11	—	—	—	—	—	—	—
98-99—U.S. Jr. national team	Int'l	30	1733	22	6	2	67	3	2.32	—	—	—	—	—	—	—
99-00—Boston University	Hockey East	30	1791	18	5	5	73	2	2.45	—	—	—	—	—	—	—
00-01—Chicago	IHL	14	778	4	5	‡2	44	0	3.39	—	—	—	—	—	—	—
—New York Islanders	NHL	20	1083	3	15	1	63	0	3.49	—	—	—	—	—	—	—
NHL Totals (1 year)		20	1083	3	15	1	63	0	3.49							

DIVISEK, TOMAS   C   FLYERS

PERSONAL: Born July 17, 1979, in Most, Czechoslovakia. ... 6-2/194.
TRANSACTIONS/CAREER NOTES: Selected by Philadelphia Flyers in seventh round (ninth Flyers pick, 195th overall) of NHL entry draft (June 21, 1997).

Season Team	League	Gms.	G	A	Pts.	PIM	+/-	PP	SH	Gms.	G	A	Pts.	PIM
97-98—Slavia Praha	Czech Rep.	22	2	0	2	8	...	...	...	—	—	—	—	—
98-99—Slavia Praha	Czech Rep.	42	7	3	10	0	...	...	...	—	—	—	—	—
99-00—Philadelphia	AHL	59	18	31	49	30	...	...	...	5	0	3	3	2
00-01—Philadelphia	AHL	45	10	22	32	33	...	...	...	10	4	9	13	4
—Philadelphia	NHL	2	0	0	0	0	-1	0	0	—	—	—	—	—
NHL Totals (1 year)		2	0	0	0	0	-1	0	0					

DOAN, SHANE — RW — COYOTES

PERSONAL: Born October 10, 1976, in Halkirk, Alta. ... 6-2/218. ... Shoots right. ... Name pronounced DOHN.

TRANSACTIONS/CAREER NOTES: Selected by Winnipeg Jets in first round (first Jets pick, seventh overall) of NHL entry draft (July 8, 1995). ... Suffered from the flu (January 8, 1996); missed one game. ... Bruised ribs (January 14, 1996); missed two games. ... Strained back (February 23, 1996); missed two games. ... Jets franchise moved to Phoenix and renamed Coyotes for 1996-97 season; NHL approved move on January 18, 1996. ... Sprained ankle (October 14, 1996); missed two games. ... Strained ligament in foot (November 8, 1996); missed eight games. ... Bruised hand (February 22, 1997); missed four games. ... Injured eye (February 20, 1999); missed one game. ... Injured forearm (March 15, 1999); missed one game. ... Injured knee (December 10, 2000); missed one game. ... Strained muscle in abdomen (January 24, 2001); missed five games.

HONORS: Won Stafford Smyth Memorial Trophy (1994-95). ... Named to Memorial Cup All-Star team (1994-95).

Season Team	League	Gms.	G	A	Pts.	PIM	+/-	PP	SH	Gms.	G	A	Pts.	PIM
92-93—Kamloops	WHL	51	7	12	19	55	...	...	...	13	0	1	1	8
93-94—Kamloops	WHL	52	24	24	48	88	...	...	...	—	—	—	—	—
94-95—Kamloops	WHL	71	37	57	94	106	...	...	...	21	6	10	16	16
95-96—Winnipeg	NHL	74	7	10	17	101	-9	1	0	6	0	0	0	6
96-97—Phoenix	NHL	63	4	8	12	49	-3	0	0	4	0	0	0	2
97-98—Phoenix	NHL	33	5	6	11	35	-3	0	0	6	1	0	1	6
—Springfield	AHL	39	21	21	42	64	...	...	...	—	—	—	—	—
98-99—Phoenix	NHL	79	6	16	22	54	-5	0	0	7	2	2	4	6
99-00—Phoenix	NHL	81	26	25	51	66	6	1	1	4	1	2	3	8
00-01—Phoenix	NHL	76	26	37	63	89	0	6	1	—	—	—	—	—
NHL Totals (6 years)		406	74	102	176	394	-14	8	2	27	4	4	8	28

DOIG, JASON — D — SENATORS

PERSONAL: Born January 29, 1977, in Montreal. ... 6-3/228. ... Shoots right. ... Name pronounced DOYG.

TRANSACTIONS/CAREER NOTES: Selected by Winnipeg Jets in second round (third Jets pick, 34th overall) of NHL entry draft (July 8, 1995). ... Suffered irregular heart beat (November 17, 1995); missed four games. ... Jets franchise moved to Phoenix and renamed Coyotes for 1996-97 season; NHL approved move on January 18, 1996. ... Hyperextended elbow prior to 1996-97 season; missed first five games of season. ... Sprained knee (November 20, 1997); missed 26 games. ... Suffered torn pectoral muscle prior to the 1998-99 regular season; missed first 18 games of season. ... Traded by Coyotes with sixth-round pick (C Jay Dardis) in 1999 draft to New York Rangers for D Stan Neckar (March 23, 1999). ... Sprained knee (February 8, 2000); missed five games. ... Traded by Rangers with RW Jeff Ulmer to Ottawa Senators for D Sean Gagnon (June 29, 2001).

HONORS: Won Guy Lafleur Trophy (1995-96). ... Named to Memorial Cup All-Star team (1995-96).

Season Team	League	Gms.	G	A	Pts.	PIM	+/-	PP	SH	Gms.	G	A	Pts.	PIM
93-94—St. Jean	QMJHL	63	8	17	25	65	...	...	...	5	0	2	2	2
94-95—Laval	QMJHL	55	13	42	55	259	...	...	...	20	4	13	17	39
95-96—Winnipeg	NHL	15	1	1	2	28	-2	0	0	—	—	—	—	—
—Springfield	AHL	5	0	0	0	28	...	...	...	—	—	—	—	—
—Laval	QMJHL	2	1	1	2	6	...	...	...	—	—	—	—	—
—Granby	QMJHL	27	6	35	41	*105	...	...	...	20	10	22	32	110
96-97—Las Vegas	IHL	6	0	1	1	19	...	...	...	—	—	—	—	—
—Granby	QMJHL	39	14	33	47	197	...	...	...	5	0	4	4	27
—Springfield	AHL	5	0	3	3	2	...	...	...	17	1	4	5	37
97-98—Springfield	AHL	46	2	25	27	153	...	...	...	3	0	0	0	2
—Phoenix	NHL	4	0	1	1	12	-4	0	0	—	—	—	—	—
98-99—Phoenix	NHL	9	0	1	1	10	2	0	0	—	—	—	—	—
—Springfield	AHL	32	3	5	8	67	...	...	...	—	—	—	—	—
—Hartford	AHL	8	1	4	5	40	...	...	...	7	1	1	2	39
99-00—New York Rangers	NHL	7	0	1	1	22	-2	0	0	—	—	—	—	—
—Hartford	AHL	27	3	11	14	70	...	...	...	21	1	5	6	20
00-01—New York Rangers	NHL	3	0	0	0	0	0	0	0	—	—	—	—	—
—Hartford	AHL	52	4	20	24	178	...	...	...	5	0	1	1	4
NHL Totals (5 years)		38	1	4	5	72	-6	0	0					

DOLLAS, BOBBY — D

PERSONAL: Born January 31, 1965, in Montreal. ... 6-2/212. ... Shoots left. ... Name pronounced DAHL-ihz.

TRANSACTIONS/CAREER NOTES: Selected by Winnipeg Jets in first round (second Jets pick, 14th overall) of NHL entry draft (June 8, 1983). ... Traded by Jets to Quebec Nordiques for RW Stu Kulak (December 17, 1987). ... Signed as free agent by Detroit Red Wings (October 18, 1990). ... Suffered from the flu (December 15, 1990); missed two games. ... Injured leg (January 9, 1991). ... Strained abdominal muscle (November 7, 1991); missed 15 games. ... Selected by Mighty Ducks of Anaheim in NHL expansion draft (June 24, 1993). ... Sprained left thumb (October 1, 1993); missed five games. ... Suffered from chicken pox (March 30, 1997); missed three games. ... Tore tendon in left wrist (October 30, 1997); missed 16 games. ... Traded by Mighty Ducks to Edmonton Oilers for D Drew Bannister (January 9, 1998). ... Partially dislocated shoulder (March 9, 1998); missed seven games. ... Traded by Oilers with C Tony Hrkac to Pittsburgh Penguins for LW Josef Beranek (June 16, 1998). ... Fractured toe (December 26, 1998); missed three games. ... Signed as free agent by Ottawa Senators (November 9, 1999). ... Claimed on waivers by Calgary Flames (November 11, 1999). ... Suffered back spasms (December 26, 1999); missed two games. ... Suffered concussion (February 18, 2000); missed four games. ... Suffered concussion (March 18, 2000); missed final 10 games of season. ... Signed as free agent by San Jose Sharks (November 5, 2000). ... Injured hand (November 9, 2000); missed nine games. ... Injured hip (February 6, 2001); missed three games. ... Traded by Sharks with G Johan Hedberg to Penguins for D Jeff Norton (March 12, 2001).

HONORS: Won Raymond Lagace Trophy (1982-83). ... Named to QMJHL All-Star second team (1982-83). ... Won Eddie Shore Plaque (1992-93). ... Named to AHL All-Star first team (1992-93).

			REGULAR SEASON							PLAYOFFS				
Season Team	League	Gms.	G	A	Pts.	PIM	+/-	PP	SH	Gms.	G	A	Pts.	PIM
82-83—Laval	QMJHL	63	16	45	61	144	...	...	...	11	5	5	10	23
83-84—Laval	QMJHL	54	12	33	45	80	...	...	...	14	1	8	9	23
—Winnipeg	NHL	1	0	0	0	0	-2	0	0	—	—	—	—	—
84-85—Winnipeg	NHL	9	0	0	0	0	3	0	0	—	—	—	—	—
—Sherbrooke	AHL	8	1	3	4	4	...	...	...	17	3	6	9	17
85-86—Sherbrooke	AHL	25	4	7	11	29	...	...	...	—	—	—	—	—
—Winnipeg	NHL	46	0	5	5	66	-3	0	0	3	0	0	0	2
86-87—Sherbrooke	AHL	75	6	18	24	87	...	...	...	16	2	4	6	13
87-88—Quebec	NHL	9	0	0	0	2	-4	0	0	—	—	—	—	—
—Moncton	AHL	26	4	10	14	20	...	...	...	—	—	—	—	—
—Fredericton	AHL	33	4	8	12	27	...	...	...	15	2	2	4	24
88-89—Halifax	AHL	57	5	19	24	65	...	...	...	4	1	0	1	14
—Quebec	NHL	16	0	3	3	16	-11	0	0	—	—	—	—	—
89-90—Canadian nat'l team	Int'l	68	8	29	37	60	...	...	...	—	—	—	—	—
90-91—Detroit	NHL	56	3	5	8	20	6	0	0	7	1	0	1	13
91-92—Detroit	NHL	27	3	1	4	20	4	0	1	2	0	1	1	0
—Adirondack	AHL	19	1	6	7	33	...	...	...	18	7	4	11	22
92-93—Adirondack	AHL	64	7	36	43	54	...	...	...	11	3	8	11	8
—Detroit	NHL	6	0	0	0	2	-1	0	0	—	—	—	—	—
93-94—Anaheim	NHL	77	9	11	20	55	20	1	0	—	—	—	—	—
94-95—Anaheim	NHL	45	7	13	20	12	-3	3	1	—	—	—	—	—
95-96—Anaheim	NHL	82	8	22	30	64	9	0	1	—	—	—	—	—
96-97—Anaheim	NHL	79	4	14	18	55	17	1	0	11	0	0	0	4
97-98—Anaheim	NHL	22	0	1	1	27	-12	0	0	—	—	—	—	—
—Edmonton	NHL	30	2	5	7	22	6	0	0	11	0	0	0	16
98-99—Pittsburgh	NHL	70	2	8	10	60	-3	0	0	13	1	0	1	6
99-00—Long Beach	IHL	13	2	4	6	8	...	...	...	—	—	—	—	—
—Ottawa	NHL	1	0	0	0	0	2	0	0	—	—	—	—	—
—Calgary	NHL	49	3	7	10	28	4	1	0	—	—	—	—	—
00-01—Manitoba	IHL	8	1	2	3	2	...	...	...	—	—	—	—	—
—San Jose	NHL	16	1	1	2	14	4	0	0	—	—	—	—	—
—Pittsburgh	NHL	5	0	0	0	4	0	0	0	—	—	—	—	—
NHL Totals (16 years)		646	42	96	138	467	36	6	3	47	2	1	3	41

DOMENICHELLI, HNAT   LW   THRASHERS

PERSONAL: Born February 17, 1976, in Edmonton. ... 6-0/194. ... Shoots left. ... Name pronounced NAT dah-mih-nuh-KEHL-ee.

TRANSACTIONS/CAREER NOTES: Selected by Hartford Whalers in fourth round (second Whalers pick, 83rd overall) of NHL entry draft (June 29, 1994). ... Traded by Whalers with D Glen Featherstone, second-round pick (D Dimitri Kokorev) in 1997 draft and third-round pick (D Paul Manning) in 1998 draft to Calgary Flames for D Steve Chiasson and third-round pick (D Francis Lessard) in 1997 draft (March 5, 1997). ... Traded by Flames with LW Dmitri Vlasenkov to Atlanta Thrashers for D Darryl Shannon and LW Jason Botterill (February 11, 2000). ... Sprained ankle (September 5, 2000); missed first three games of season. ... Strained groin (January 5, 2001); missed four games. ... Reinjured groin (January 18, 2001); missed 11 games.

HONORS: Named to WHL (West) All-Star second team (1994-95). ... Won Brad Hornung Trophy (1995-96). ... Won Can.HL Most Sportsmanlike Player of the Year Award (1995-96). ... Named to Can.HL All-Star first team (1995-96). ... Named to WHL (West) All-Star first team (1995-96).

MISCELLANEOUS: Scored on a penalty shot (vs. Arturs Irbe, Febraury 27, 1998).

			REGULAR SEASON							PLAYOFFS				
Season Team	League	Gms.	G	A	Pts.	PIM	+/-	PP	SH	Gms.	G	A	Pts.	PIM
92-93—Kamloops	WHL	45	12	8	20	15	...	...	...	11	1	1	2	2
93-94—Kamloops	WHL	69	27	40	67	31	...	...	...	19	10	12	22	0
94-95—Kamloops	WHL	72	52	62	114	34	...	...	...	19	9	9	18	9
95-96—Kamloops	WHL	62	59	89	148	37	...	...	...	16	7	9	16	29
96-97—Hartford	NHL	13	2	1	3	7	-4	1	0	—	—	—	—	—
—Springfield	AHL	39	24	24	48	12	...	...	...	—	—	—	—	—
—Calgary	NHL	10	1	2	3	2	1	0	0	—	—	—	—	—
—Saint John	AHL	1	1	1	2	0	...	...	...	5	5	0	5	2
97-98—Saint John	AHL	48	33	13	46	24	...	...	...	19	7	8	15	14
—Calgary	NHL	31	9	7	16	6	4	1	0	—	—	—	—	—
98-99—Saint John	AHL	51	25	21	46	26	...	...	...	7	4	4	8	2
—Calgary	NHL	23	5	5	10	11	-4	3	0	—	—	—	—	—
99-00—Saint John	AHL	12	6	7	13	8	...	...	...	—	—	—	—	—
—Calgary	NHL	32	5	9	14	12	0	1	0	—	—	—	—	—
—Atlanta	NHL	27	6	9	15	4	-9	4	0	—	—	—	—	—
00-01—Atlanta	NHL	63	15	12	27	18	-9	4	0	—	—	—	—	—
NHL Totals (5 years)		199	43	45	88	60	-33	10	0	—	—	—	—	—

DOMI, TIE   RW   MAPLE LEAFS

PERSONAL: Born November 1, 1969, in Windsor, Ont. ... 5-10/200. ... Shoots right. ... Full Name: Tahir Domi. ... Name pronounced TIGH DOH-mee. ... Nickname: The Albanian Agressor.

TRANSACTIONS/CAREER NOTES: Selected by Toronto Maple Leafs in second round (second Maple Leafs pick, 27th overall) of NHL entry draft (June 11, 1988). ... Traded by Maple Leafs with G Mark Laforest to New York Rangers for RW Greg Johnston (June 28, 1990). ... Suspended six games by AHL for pre-game fighting (November 25, 1990). ... Sprained right knee (March 11, 1992); missed eight games. ... Traded by Rangers with LW Kris King to Winnipeg Jets for C Ed Olczyk (December 28, 1992). ... Fined $500 by NHL for premeditated fight (January 4, 1993). ... Sprained knee (January 25, 1994); missed three games. ... Traded by Jets to Maple Leafs for C Mike Eastwood and third-round pick (RW Brad Isbister) in 1995 draft (April 7, 1995). ... Strained groin (April 8, 1995); missed two games. ... Suffered from the flu (April 19, 1995); missed one game. ... Suspended eight games by NHL for fighting (October 17, 1995). ... Sprained knee (December 2, 1995); missed two games. ... Fined $1,000 by NHL for fighting (November 13, 1996). ... Sprained ankle (April 2, 1997); missed two games. ... Strained abdominal muscle (October 25, 1997); missed two games. ... Sprained knee (January 7, 1999); missed 10 games. ... Suffered injury (October 30, 1999); missed five games. ... Suffered injury (January 14, 2000); missed seven games. ... Suspended remainder of playoffs and first eight games of 2001-02 regular season game by NHL for elbowing incident (May 4, 2001).

Season Team	League	REGULAR SEASON								PLAYOFFS				
		Gms.	G	A	Pts.	PIM	+/-	PP	SH	Gms.	G	A	Pts.	PIM
85-86—Windsor Jr. B	OHA	32	8	17	25	346	...	...	...	—	—	—	—	—
86-87—Peterborough	OHL	18	1	1	2	79	...	...	...	—	—	—	—	—
87-88—Peterborough	OHL	60	22	21	43	*292	...	...	...	12	3	9	12	24
88-89—Peterborough	OHL	43	14	16	30	175	...	...	...	17	10	9	19	*70
89-90—Newmarket	AHL	57	14	11	25	285	...	...	...	—	—	—	—	—
—Toronto	NHL	2	0	0	0	42	0	0	0	—	—	—	—	—
90-91—New York Rangers	NHL	28	1	0	1	185	-5	0	0	—	—	—	—	—
—Binghamton	AHL	25	11	6	17	219	...	...	...	7	3	2	5	16
91-92—New York Rangers	NHL	42	2	4	6	246	-4	0	0	6	1	1	2	32
92-93—New York Rangers	NHL	12	2	0	2	95	-1	0	0	—	—	—	—	—
—Winnipeg	NHL	49	3	10	13	249	2	0	0	6	1	0	1	23
93-94—Winnipeg	NHL	81	8	11	19	*347	-8	0	0	—	—	—	—	—
94-95—Winnipeg	NHL	31	4	4	8	128	-6	0	0	—	—	—	—	—
—Toronto	NHL	9	0	1	1	31	1	0	0	7	1	0	1	0
95-96—Toronto	NHL	72	7	6	13	297	-3	0	0	6	0	2	2	4
96-97—Toronto	NHL	80	11	17	28	275	-17	2	0	—	—	—	—	—
97-98—Toronto	NHL	80	4	10	14	365	-5	0	0	—	—	—	—	—
98-99—Toronto	NHL	72	8	14	22	198	5	0	0	14	0	2	2	24
99-00—Toronto	NHL	70	5	9	14	198	-5	0	0	12	0	1	1	20
00-01—Toronto	NHL	82	13	7	20	214	2	1	0	8	0	1	1	20
NHL Totals (12 years)		710	68	93	161	2870	-44	3	0	59	3	7	10	123

DONATO, TED   LW

PERSONAL: Born April 28, 1968, in Boston. ... 5-10/180. ... Shoots left. ... Full Name: Edward Paul Donato. ... Brother of Dan Donato, infielder, Tampa Bay Devil Rays organization. ... Name pronounced duh-NAH-toh.

TRANSACTIONS/CAREER NOTES: Selected by Boston Bruins in sixth round (sixth Bruins pick, 98th overall) of NHL entry draft (June 13, 1987). ... Played in Europe during 1994-95 NHL lockout. ... Injured groin (November 21, 1996); missed two games. ... Fractured finger (March 9, 1997); missed 13 games. ... Suspended three games by NHL and fined $1,000 for high-sticking (December 22, 1997). ... Traded by Bruins to New York Islanders for LW Ken Belanger (November 7, 1998). ... Traded by Islanders to Ottawa Senators for fourth-round pick (traded to Phoenix) in 1999 draft (March 20, 1999). ... Traded by Senators with D Antti-Jussi Niemi to Mighty Ducks of Anaheim for G Patrick Lalime (June 18, 1999). ... Signed as free agent by Dallas Stars (August 17, 2000).

HONORS: Named NCAA Tournament Most Valuable Player (1988-89). ... Named to NCAA All-Tournament team (1988-89). ... Named to ECAC All-Star first team (1990-91).

MISCELLANEOUS: Failed to score on a penalty shot (vs. Kirk McLean, April 12, 1999).

Season Team	League	REGULAR SEASON								PLAYOFFS				
		Gms.	G	A	Pts.	PIM	+/-	PP	SH	Gms.	G	A	Pts.	PIM
86-87—Catholic Memorial	Mass. H.S.	22	29	34	63	30	...	...	...	—	—	—	—	—
87-88—Harvard University	ECAC	28	12	14	26	24	...	...	...	—	—	—	—	—
88-89—Harvard University	ECAC	34	14	37	51	30	...	...	...	—	—	—	—	—
89-90—Harvard University	ECAC	16	5	6	11	34	...	...	...	—	—	—	—	—
90-91—Harvard University	ECAC	28	19	37	56	26	...	...	...	—	—	—	—	—
91-92—U.S. national team	Int'l	52	11	22	33	24	...	...	...	—	—	—	—	—
—U.S. Olympic team	Int'l	8	4	3	7	8	...	...	...	—	—	—	—	—
—Boston	NHL	10	1	2	3	8	-1	0	0	15	3	4	7	4
92-93—Boston	NHL	82	15	20	35	61	2	3	2	4	0	1	1	0
93-94—Boston	NHL	84	22	32	54	59	0	9	2	13	4	2	6	10
94-95—TuTo Turku	Finland	14	5	5	10	47	...	...	...	—	—	—	—	—
—Boston	NHL	47	10	10	20	10	3	1	0	5	0	0	0	4
95-96—Boston	NHL	82	23	26	49	46	6	7	0	5	1	2	3	2
96-97—Boston	NHL	67	25	26	51	37	-9	6	2	—	—	—	—	—
97-98—Boston	NHL	79	16	23	39	54	6	3	0	5	0	0	0	2
98-99—Boston	NHL	14	1	3	4	4	0	0	0	—	—	—	—	—
—New York Islanders	NHL	55	7	11	18	27	-10	2	0	—	—	—	—	—
—Ottawa	NHL	13	3	2	5	10	2	1	0	1	0	0	0	0
99-00—Anaheim	NHL	81	11	19	30	26	-3	2	0	—	—	—	—	—
00-01—Dallas	NHL	65	8	17	25	26	6	1	0	8	0	1	1	0
NHL Totals (10 years)		679	142	191	333	368	2	35	6	56	8	10	18	22

DONOVAN, SHEAN   RW   THRASHERS

PERSONAL: Born January 22, 1975, in Timmins, Ont. ... 6-3/210. ... Shoots right. ... Name pronounced SHAWN DAHN-ih-vihn.

TRANSACTIONS/CAREER NOTES: Selected by San Jose Sharks in second round (second Sharks pick, 28th overall) of NHL entry draft (June 26, 1993). ... Suffered concussion (October 5, 1996); missed two games. ... Injured knee (December 21, 1996); missed two games. ... Traded by Sharks with first-round pick (C Alex Tanguay) in 1998 draft to Colorado Avalanche for C Mike Ricci and second-round pick (RW Jonathan Cheechoo) in 1998 draft (November 20, 1997). ... Bruised knee (January 3, 1998); missed one game. ... Bruised knee (January 21, 1998); missed three games. ... Suffered concussion (October 24, 1998); missed one game. ... Injured shoulder and jaw (February 5, 1999); missed one game. ... Injured hip (March 20, 1999); missed two games. ... Traded by Avalanche to Atlanta Thrashers for G Rick Tabaracci (December 8, 1999). ... Strained muscle in abdomen (January 1, 2000); missed three games. ... Fractured right foot (January 27, 2000); missed 20 games. ... Sprained medial collateral ligament in knee (December 9, 2000); missed 13 games.

STATISTICAL PLATEAUS: Three-goal games: 2000-01 (1).

Season Team	League	REGULAR SEASON								PLAYOFFS				
		Gms.	G	A	Pts.	PIM	+/-	PP	SH	Gms.	G	A	Pts.	PIM
91-92—Ottawa	OHL	58	11	8	19	14	...	...	...	11	1	0	1	5
92-93—Ottawa	OHL	66	29	23	52	33	...	...	...	—	—	—	—	—
93-94—Ottawa	OHL	62	35	49	84	63	...	...	...	17	10	11	21	14
94-95—Ottawa	OHL	29	22	19	41	41	...	...	...	—	—	—	—	—
—San Jose	NHL	14	0	0	0	6	-6	0	0	7	0	1	1	6
—Kansas City	IHL	5	0	2	2	7	...	...	...	14	5	3	8	23
95-96—Kansas City	IHL	4	0	0	0	8	...	...	...	5	0	0	0	8
—San Jose	NHL	74	13	8	21	39	-17	0	1	—	—	—	—	—
96-97—San Jose	NHL	73	9	6	15	42	-18	0	1	—	—	—	—	—
—Kentucky	AHL	3	1	3	4	18	...	...	...	—	—	—	—	—
—Canadian nat'l team	Int'l	10	0	1	1	31	...	...	...	—	—	—	—	—
97-98—San Jose	NHL	20	3	3	6	22	3	0	0	—	—	—	—	—
—Colorado	NHL	47	5	7	12	48	3	0	0	—	—	—	—	—
98-99—Colorado	NHL	68	7	12	19	37	4	1	0	5	0	0	0	2
99-00—Colorado	NHL	18	1	0	1	8	-4	0	0	—	—	—	—	—
—Atlanta	NHL	33	4	7	11	18	-13	1	0	—	—	—	—	—
00-01—Atlanta	NHL	63	12	11	23	47	-14	1	3	—	—	—	—	—
NHL Totals (7 years)		410	54	54	108	267	-62	3	5	12	0	1	1	8

DOPITA, JIRI   C   FLYERS

PERSONAL: Born December 2, 1968, in Sumperk, Czechoslovakia. ... 6-3/209. ... Shoots left.

TRANSACTIONS/CAREER NOTES: Selected by Boston Bruins in sixth round (fourth Bruins pick, 133rd overall) of NHL entry draft (June 20, 1992). ... Returned to draft pool by Bruins and selected by New York Islanders in fifth round (fourth Islanders pick, 123rd overall) of NHL entry draft (June 27, 1998). ... Rights traded by Islanders to Florida Panthers for fifth-round pick (D Adam Johnson) in 1999 draft (June 26, 1999). ... Rights traded by Panthers to Philadelphia Flyers for second-round pick (traded to Calgary) in 2001 draft (June 23, 2001).

MISCELLANEOUS: Member of gold-medal-winning Czech Republic Olympic team (1998).

Season Team	League	REGULAR SEASON								PLAYOFFS				
		Gms.	G	A	Pts.	PIM	+/-	PP	SH	Gms.	G	A	Pts.	PIM
88-89—DS Olomouc	Czech Dv.II						Statistics unavailable.							
89-90—Dukla Jihlava	Czech.	5	1	2	3	...	...	...	...	—	—	—	—	—
90-91—DS Olomouc	Czech.	42	11	13	24	...	...	...	...	—	—	—	—	—
91-92—DS Olomouc	Czech.	38	23	20	43	...	...	...	...	—	—	—	—	—
92-93—DS Olomouc	Czech.	28	12	17	29	...	...	...	...	—	—	—	—	—
—Eisbaren Berlin	Germany	11	7	8	15	49	...	...	...	4	3	5	8	5
94-95—Eisbaren Berlin	Germany	42	28	40	68	55	...	...	...	—	—	—	—	—
95-96—Petra Vsetin	Czech Rep.	38	19	20	39	20	...	...	...	13	9	11	20	10
96-97—Petra Vsetin	Czech Rep.	52	30	31	61	55	...	...	...	10	7	4	11	22
97-98—Petra Vsetin	Czech Rep.	50	21	34	55	64	...	...	...	10	*12	6	18	4
—Czech Rep. Oly. team	Int'l	6	1	2	3	0	...	...	...	—	—	—	—	—
98-99—Vsetin	Czech Rep.	50	19	32	51	43	...	...	...	12	1	6	7	...
99-00—Vsetin	Czech Rep.	49	*30	29	59	83	...	...	...	9	0	4	4	6
00-01—Vsetin	Czech Rep.	46	19	31	50	53	...	...	...	14	8	*13	*21	18

DOWD, JIM   C   WILD

PERSONAL: Born December 25, 1968, in Brick, N.J. ... 6-1/190. ... Shoots right. ... Full Name: James Thomas Dowd Jr.

TRANSACTIONS/CAREER NOTES: Selected by New Jersey Devils in eighth round (seventh Devils pick, 149th overall) of NHL entry draft (June 13, 1987). ... Injured shoulder (February 2, 1995) and underwent shoulder surgery; missed 35 games. ... Traded by Devils with second-round pick (traded to Calgary) in 1997 draft to Hartford Whalers for RW Jocelyn Lemieux and second-round pick (traded to Dallas) in 1998 draft (December 19, 1995). ... Traded by Whalers with D Frantisek Kucera and second-round pick (D Ryan Bonni) in 1997 draft to Vancouver Canucks for D Jeff Brown and fifth-round pick (traded to Dallas) in 1998 draft (December 19, 1995). ... Selected by New York Islanders from Canucks in waiver draft for cash (September 30, 1996). ... Signed as free agent by Calgary Flames (July 10, 1997). ... Traded by Flames to Nashville Predators for future considerations (June 27, 1998). ... Traded by Predators with G Mikhail Shtalenkov to Edmonton Oilers for G Eric Fichaud, D Drake Berehowsky and D Greg de Vries (October 1, 1998). ... Selected by Minnesota Wild in NHL expansion draft (June 23, 2000). ... Injured ribs (January 6, 2001); missed 10 games. ... Strained neck (March 31, 2001); missed four games.

HONORS: Named to NCAA All-America (West) second team (1989-90). ... Named to CCHA All-Star second team (1989-90). ... Named to NCAA All-America (West) first team (1990-91). ... Named CCHA Player of the Year (1990-91). ... Named to CCHA All-Star first team (1990-91).

MISCELLANEOUS: Member of Stanley Cup championship team (1995).

Season Team	League	Gms.	G	A	Pts.	PIM	+/-	PP	SH	Gms.	G	A	Pts.	PIM
		REGULAR SEASON								**PLAYOFFS**				
83-84—Brick Township	N.J. H.S.	...	19	30	49	...	...	...	...	—	—	—	—	—
84-85—Brick Township	N.J. H.S.	...	58	55	113	...	...	...	...	—	—	—	—	—
85-86—Brick Township	N.J. H.S.	...	47	51	98	...	...	...	...	—	—	—	—	—
86-87—Brick Township	N.J. H.S.	24	22	33	55	...	...	...	...	—	—	—	—	—
87-88—Lake Superior State	CCHA	45	18	27	45	16	...	...	...	—	—	—	—	—
88-89—Lake Superior State	CCHA	46	24	35	59	40	...	...	...	—	—	—	—	—
89-90—Lake Superior State	CCHA	46	25	67	92	30	...	...	...	—	—	—	—	—
90-91—Lake Superior State	CCHA	44	24	54	78	53	...	...	...	—	—	—	—	—
91-92—Utica	AHL	78	17	42	59	47	...	...	...	4	2	2	4	4
—New Jersey	NHL	1	0	0	0	0	0	0	0	—	—	—	—	—
92-93—Utica	AHL	78	27	45	72	62	...	...	...	5	1	7	8	10
—New Jersey	NHL	1	0	0	0	0	-1	0	0	—	—	—	—	—
93-94—Albany	AHL	58	26	37	63	76	...	...	...	—	—	—	—	—
—New Jersey	NHL	15	5	10	15	0	8	2	0	19	2	6	8	8
94-95—New Jersey	NHL	10	1	4	5	0	-5	1	0	11	2	1	3	8
95-96—New Jersey	NHL	28	4	9	13	17	-1	0	0	—	—	—	—	—
—Vancouver	NHL	38	1	6	7	6	-8	0	0	1	0	0	0	0
96-97—New York Islanders	NHL	3	0	0	0	0	-1	0	0	—	—	—	—	—
—Utah	IHL	48	10	21	31	27	...	...	...	—	—	—	—	—
—Saint John	AHL	24	5	11	16	18	...	...	...	5	1	2	3	0
97-98—Saint John	AHL	35	8	30	38	20	...	...	...	19	3	13	16	10
—Calgary	NHL	48	6	8	14	12	10	0	1	—	—	—	—	—
98-99—Hamilton	AHL	51	15	29	44	82	...	...	...	11	3	6	9	8
—Edmonton	NHL	1	0	0	0	0	0	0	0	—	—	—	—	—
99-00—Edmonton	NHL	69	5	18	23	45	10	2	0	5	2	1	3	4
00-01—Minnesota	NHL	68	7	22	29	80	-6	0	0	—	—	—	—	—
NHL Totals (10 years).........		282	29	77	106	160	6	5	1	36	6	8	14	20

DOWNEY, AARON — RW — BLACKHAWKS

PERSONAL: Born September 27, 1974, in Shelburne, Ont. ... 6-0/210. ... Shoots right. ... Full Name: Aaron Douglas Downey.
TRANSACTIONS/CAREER NOTES: Signed as non-drafted free agent by Boston Bruins (January 20, 1998). ... Signed as free agent by Chicago Blackhawks (August 8, 2000).

Season Team	League	Gms.	G	A	Pts.	PIM	+/-	PP	SH	Gms.	G	A	Pts.	PIM
		REGULAR SEASON								**PLAYOFFS**				
92-93—Guelph	OHL	53	3	3	6	88	...	...	...	5	1	0	1	0
93-94—Cole Harbor	MWJHL	35	8	20	28	210	...	...	...	—	—	—	—	—
94-95—Cole Harbor	MWJHL	40	10	31	41	320	...	...	...	—	—	—	—	—
95-96—Hampton	ECHL	65	12	11	23	354	...	...	...	—	—	—	—	—
96-97—Hampton	ECHL	64	8	8	16	338	...	...	...	9	0	3	3	26
—Portland	AHL	3	0	0	0	19	...	...	...	—	—	—	—	—
—Manitoba....................	IHL	2	0	0	0	17	...	...	...	—	—	—	—	—
97-98—Providence..................	AHL	78	5	10	15	*407	...	...	...	—	—	—	—	—
98-99—Providence..................	AHL	75	10	12	22	*401	...	...	...	19	1	1	2	46
99-00—Providence..................	AHL	47	6	4	10	221	...	...	...	14	1	0	1	24
—Boston	NHL	1	0	0	0	0	0	0	0	—	—	—	—	—
00-01—Norfolk....................	AHL	67	6	15	21	234	...	...	...	9	0	0	0	4
—Chicago....................	NHL	3	0	0	0	6	-1	0	0	—	—	—	—	—
NHL Totals (2 years)...........		4	0	0	0	6	-1	0	0					

DRAKE, DALLAS — RW — BLUES

PERSONAL: Born February 4, 1969, in Trail, B.C. ... 6-1/190. ... Shoots left. ... Full Name: Dallas James Drake.
TRANSACTIONS/CAREER NOTES: Selected by Detroit Red Wings in sixth round (sixth Red Wings pick, 116th overall) of NHL entry draft (June 17, 1989). ... Bruised left leg (November 27, 1992); missed three games. ... Suffered back spasms (December 28, 1992); missed one game. ... Bruised kneecap (January 23, 1993); missed three games. ... Suffered concussion (February 13, 1993); missed one game. ... Injured right wrist (October 16, 1993); missed three games. ... Injured tendon in right hand (December 14, 1993); missed 16 games. ... Traded by Detroit Red Wings with G Tim Cheveldae to Winnipeg Jets for G Bob Essensa and D Sergei Bautin (March 8, 1994). ... Suffered back spasms (March 17, 1995); missed four games. ... Bruised right shoulder (October 22, 1995); missed seven games. ... Suffered ear infection (November 21, 1995); missed two games. ... Jets franchise moved to Phoenix and renamed Coyotes for 1996-97 season; NHL approved move on January 18, 1996. ... Sprained ankle (November 16, 1996); missed eight games. ... Sprained knee (January 29, 1997); missed 10 games. ... Suffered from the flu (October 19, 1997); missed one game. ... Injured knee (December 3, 1997); missed 12 games. ... Bruised knee (March 2, 1998); missed one game. ... Injured wrist (March 18, 1998); missed five games. ... Bruised ankle (October 21, 1998); missed one game. ... Suffered concussion (November 6, 1998); missed two games. ... Bruised elbow (December 28, 1998); missed one game. ... Suspended four games by NHL for illegal hit (December 29, 1998). ... Separated shoulder (January 29, 1999); missed three games. ... Strained shoulder (March 15, 1999); missed two games. ... Bruised shoulder (March 23, 1999); missed five games. ... Sprained shoulder (October 30, 1999); missed three games. ... Selected by Columbus Blue Jackets in NHL expansion draft (June 23, 2000). ... Signed as free agent by St. Louis Blues (July 1, 2000).
HONORS: Named to NCAA All-America (West) first team (1991-92). ... Won WCHA Player of the Year Award (1991-92). ... Named to WCHA All-Star first team (1991-92).

Season Team	League	Gms.	G	A	Pts.	PIM	+/-	PP	SH	Gms.	G	A	Pts.	PIM
		REGULAR SEASON								**PLAYOFFS**				
84-85—Rossland....................	KIJHL	30	13	37	50	...	...	...	...	—	—	—	—	—
85-86—Rossland....................	KIJHL	41	53	73	126	...	...	...	...	—	—	—	—	—
86-87—Rossland....................	KIJHL	40	55	80	135	...	...	...	...	—	—	—	—	—
87-88—Vernon	BCJHL	47	39	85	124	50	...	...	...	11	9	17	26	30
88-89—N. Michigan Univ.	WCHA	45	18	24	42	26	...	...	...	—	—	—	—	—

Season Team	League	REGULAR SEASON								PLAYOFFS				
		Gms.	G	A	Pts.	PIM	+/-	PP	SH	Gms.	G	A	Pts.	PIM
89-90—N. Michigan Univ.	WCHA	36	13	24	37	42	...	...	...	—	—	—	—	—
90-91—N. Michigan Univ.	WCHA	44	22	36	58	89	...	...	...	—	—	—	—	—
91-92—N. Michigan Univ.	WCHA	40	*39	44	83	58	...	...	...	—	—	—	—	—
92-93—Detroit......................	NHL	72	18	26	44	93	15	3	2	7	3	3	6	6
93-94—Detroit......................	NHL	47	10	22	32	37	5	0	1	—	—	—	—	—
—Adirondack	AHL	1	2	0	2	0	...	...	...	—	—	—	—	—
—Winnipeg	NHL	15	3	5	8	12	-6	1	1	—	—	—	—	—
94-95—Winnipeg..................	NHL	43	8	18	26	30	-6	0	0	—	—	—	—	—
95-96—Winnipeg..................	NHL	69	19	20	39	36	-7	4	4	3	0	0	0	0
96-97—Phoenix....................	NHL	63	17	19	36	52	-11	5	1	7	0	1	1	2
97-98—Phoenix....................	NHL	60	11	29	40	71	17	3	0	4	0	1	1	2
98-99—Phoenix....................	NHL	53	9	22	31	65	17	0	0	7	4	3	7	4
99-00—Phoenix....................	NHL	79	15	30	45	62	11	0	2	5	0	1	1	4
00-01—St. Louis..................	NHL	82	12	29	41	71	18	2	0	15	4	2	6	16
NHL Totals (9 years)...........		583	122	220	342	529	53	18	11	48	11	11	22	34

DRAPER, KRIS   C   RED WINGS

PERSONAL: Born May 24, 1971, in Toronto. ... 5-10/190. ... Shoots left. ... Full Name: Kris Bruce Draper. ... Related to Kevin Grimes, defenseman, Ottawa Senators organization.

TRANSACTIONS/CAREER NOTES: Selected by Winnipeg Jets in third round (fourth Jets pick, 62nd overall) of NHL entry draft (June 17, 1989). ... Traded by Jets to Detroit Red Wings for future considerations (June 30, 1993). ... Sprained right knee ligament (February 4, 1995); missed eight games. ... Suffered from the flu (January 5, 1996); missed one game. ... Injured right knee (February 15, 1996); missed 12 games. ... Reinjured right knee (March 25, 1996); missed three games. ... Dislocated thumb (December 17, 1997) and underwent surgery; missed 18 games. ... Suspended two games by NHL for slashing incident (January 29, 1999). ... Suffered facial lacerations (November 15, 1999); missed three games. ... Fractured wrist (November 24, 1999); missed 25 games.

MISCELLANEOUS: Member of Stanley Cup championship team (1997 and 1998).

Season Team	League	REGULAR SEASON								PLAYOFFS				
		Gms.	G	A	Pts.	PIM	+/-	PP	SH	Gms.	G	A	Pts.	PIM
88-89—Canadian nat'l team	Int'l	60	11	15	26	16	...	...	...	—	—	—	—	—
89-90—Canadian nat'l team	Int'l	61	12	22	34	44	...	...	...	—	—	—	—	—
90-91—Winnipeg	NHL	3	1	0	1	5	0	0	0	—	—	—	—	—
—Moncton	AHL	7	2	1	3	2	...	...	...	—	—	—	—	—
—Ottawa	OHL	39	19	42	61	35	...	...	...	17	8	11	19	20
91-92—Moncton	AHL	61	11	18	29	113	...	...	...	4	0	1	1	6
—Winnipeg	NHL	10	2	0	2	2	0	0	0	2	0	0	0	0
92-93—Winnipeg	NHL	7	0	0	0	2	-6	0	0	—	—	—	—	—
—Moncton	AHL	67	12	23	35	40	...	...	...	5	2	2	4	18
93-94—Adirondack	AHL	46	20	23	43	49	...	...	...	—	—	—	—	—
—Detroit......................	NHL	39	5	8	13	31	11	0	1	7	2	2	4	4
94-95—Detroit......................	NHL	36	2	6	8	22	1	0	0	18	4	1	5	12
95-96—Detroit......................	NHL	52	7	9	16	32	2	0	1	18	4	2	6	18
96-97—Detroit......................	NHL	76	8	5	13	73	-11	1	0	20	2	4	6	12
97-98—Detroit......................	NHL	64	13	10	23	45	5	1	0	19	1	3	4	12
98-99—Detroit......................	NHL	80	4	14	18	79	2	0	1	10	0	1	1	6
99-00—Detroit......................	NHL	51	5	7	12	28	3	0	0	9	2	0	2	6
00-01—Detroit......................	NHL	75	8	17	25	38	17	0	1	6	0	1	1	2
NHL Totals (11 years)..........		493	55	76	131	357	24	2	4	109	15	14	29	72

DRUKEN, HAROLD   C   CANUCKS

PERSONAL: Born January 26, 1979, in St. John's, Nfld. ... 6-0/200. ... Shoots left. ... Name pronounced DROO-kihn.

TRANSACTIONS/CAREER NOTES: Selected by Vancouver Canucks in second round (third Canucks pick, 36th overall) of NHL entry draft (June 21, 1997).

HONORS: Named to OHL All-Rookie team (1996-97). ... Named to OHL All-Star second team (1998-99).

STATISTICAL PLATEAUS: Three-goal games: 2000-01 (1).

Season Team	League	REGULAR SEASON								PLAYOFFS				
		Gms.	G	A	Pts.	PIM	+/-	PP	SH	Gms.	G	A	Pts.	PIM
95-96—Noble & Greenough....	Mass. H.S.	30	37	28	65	28	...	...	...	—	—	—	—	—
96-97—Detroit......................	OHL	63	27	31	58	14	...	...	...	5	3	2	5	0
97-98—Plymouth	OHL	64	38	44	82	12	...	...	...	15	9	11	20	4
98-99—Plymouth	OHL	60	*58	45	103	34	...	...	...	11	9	12	21	14
99-00—Syracuse..................	AHL	47	20	25	45	32	...	...	...	4	1	2	3	6
—Vancouver..................	NHL	33	7	9	16	10	14	2	0	—	—	—	—	—
00-01—Kansas City	IHL	15	5	9	14	20	...	...	...	—	—	—	—	—
—Vancouver..................	NHL	55	15	15	30	14	2	6	0	4	0	1	1	0
NHL Totals (2 years)...........		88	22	24	46	24	16	8	0	4	0	1	1	0

DRULIA, STAN   RW

PERSONAL: Born January 5, 1968, in Elmira, N.Y. ... 5-11/190. ... Shoots right. ... Name pronounced DROOL-yuh.

TRANSACTIONS/CAREER NOTES: Selected by Pittsburgh Penguins in 11th round (11th Penguins pick, 214th overall) of NHL entry draft (June 21, 1986). ... Signed as free agent by Edmonton Oilers (May 1989). ... Signed as free agent by Tampa Bay Lightning (September 1, 1992). ... Signed as free agent by Lightning (September 29, 1999). ... Strained muscle in abdomen (December 10, 1999); missed one game. ... Suffered concussion (January 5, 2000); missed nine games. ... Bruised hand (March 1, 2000); missed two games. ... Strained wrist (March 17, 2000);

D

missed three games. ... Fractured hand (October 15, 2000); missed five games. ... Suffered sore ribs (November 22, 2000). ... Bruised foot (November 27, 2000); missed one game. ... Suffered from back pains (December 2, 2000); missed two games. ... Strained lower back (December 11, 2000); missed nine games. ... Suffered from back pains (February 6, 2001); missed four games. ... Suffered from back spasms (March 1, 2001); missed remainder of season.

HONORS: Won Jim Mahon Memorial Trophy (1988-89). ... Won Leo Lalonde Memorial Trophy (1988-89). ... Named to OHL All-Star first team (1988-89). ... Won ECHL Most Valuable Player Award (1990-91). ... Won ECHL Top Scorer Award (1990-91). ... Named to ECHL All-Star first team (1990-91). ... Named to AHL All-Star second team (1991-92). ... Named to IHL All-Star first team (1993-94 and 1994-95).

MISCELLANEOUS: Failed to score on a penalty shot (vs. Dominic Roussel, October 15, 1999).

Season Team	League	REGULAR SEASON								PLAYOFFS				
		Gms.	G	A	Pts.	PIM	+/-	PP	SH	Gms.	G	A	Pts.	PIM
84-85—Belleville	OHL	63	24	31	55	33	...	...	...	—	—	—	—	—
85-86—Belleville	OHL	66	43	37	80	73	...	...	...	—	—	—	—	—
86-87—Hamilton	OHL	55	27	51	78	26	...	...	...	—	—	—	—	—
87-88—Hamilton	OHL	65	52	69	121	44	...	...	...	14	8	16	24	12
88-89—Niagara Falls	OHL	47	52	93	145	59	...	...	...	17	11	*26	37	18
—Maine..........................	AHL	3	1	1	2	0	...	...	...	—	—	—	—	—
89-90—Cape Breton	AHL	31	5	7	12	2	...	...	...	—	—	—	—	—
—Phoenix......................	IHL	16	6	3	9	2	...	...	...	—	—	—	—	—
90-91—Knoxville	ECHL	64	*63	77	*140	39	...	...	...	3	3	2	5	4
91-92—New Haven	AHL	77	49	53	102	46	...	...	...	5	2	4	6	4
92-93—Tampa Bay	NHL	24	2	1	3	10	1	0	0	—	—	—	—	—
—Atlanta........................	IHL	47	28	26	54	38	...	...	...	3	2	3	5	4
93-94—Atlanta....................	IHL	79	54	60	114	70	...	...	...	14	13	12	25	8
94-95—Atlanta....................	IHL	66	41	49	90	60	...	...	...	5	1	5	6	2
95-96—Atlanta....................	IHL	75	38	56	94	80	...	...	...	3	0	2	2	18
96-97—Detroit....................	IHL	73	33	38	71	42	...	...	...	†21	5	*21	26	14
97-98—Detroit....................	IHL	58	25	35	60	50	...	...	...	15	2	4	6	16
98-99—Detroit....................	IHL	82	23	52	75	64	...	...	...	11	5	4	9	10
99-00—Tampa Bay	NHL	68	11	22	33	24	-18	1	2	—	—	—	—	—
00-01—Tampa Bay	NHL	34	2	4	6	18	-11	1	0	—	—	—	—	—
NHL Totals (3 years)............		126	15	27	42	52	-28	2	2					

D

DRURY, CHRIS   C   AVALANCHE

PERSONAL: Born August 20, 1976, in Trumbull, Conn. ... 5-10/180. ... Shoots right. ... Brother of Ted Drury, center, Columbus Blue Jackets.
TRANSACTIONS/CAREER NOTES: Selected by Quebec Nordiques in third round (fifth Nordiques pick, 72nd overall) of NHL entry draft (June 29, 1994). ... Nordiques franchise moved to Colorado and renamed Avalanche for 1995-96 season (June 21, 1995). ... Suffered hip pointer (October 29, 1998); missed two games. ... Sprained knee (November 1, 2000); missed 11 games.
HONORS: Named to NCAA All-America (East) second team (1995-96). ... Named to Hockey East All-Star team (1995-96 and 1996-97). ... Named to NCAA All-America (East) first team (1996-97 and 1997-98). ... Named Hockey East Player of the Year (1996-97 and 1997-98). ... Named to NCAA All-Tournament team (1996-97). ... Won Hobey Baker Memorial Award (1997-98). ... Named to Hockey East All-Star first team (1997-98). ... Named NHL Rookie of the Year by THE SPORTING NEWS (1998-99). ... Won Calder Memorial Trophy (1998-99). ... Named to NHL All-Rookie team (1998-99).
MISCELLANEOUS: Member of Stanley Cup championship team (2001). ... Scored on a penalty shot (vs. Ken Wregget, March 18, 2000).

Season Team	League	REGULAR SEASON								PLAYOFFS				
		Gms.	G	A	Pts.	PIM	+/-	PP	SH	Gms.	G	A	Pts.	PIM
92-93—Fairfield College Prep..	Conn. H.S.	24	25	32	57	15	...	...	...	—	—	—	—	—
93-94—Fairfield College Prep..	Conn. H.S.	24	37	18	55	...	...	...	...	—	—	—	—	—
94-95—Boston University	Hockey East	39	12	15	27	38	...	...	...	—	—	—	—	—
95-96—Boston University	Hockey East	37	35	33	68	46	...	...	...	—	—	—	—	—
96-97—Boston University	Hockey East	41	38	24	62	64	...	...	...	—	—	—	—	—
97-98—Boston University	Hockey East	38	28	29	57	88	...	...	...	—	—	—	—	—
98-99—Colorado	NHL	79	20	24	44	62	9	6	0	19	6	2	8	4
99-00—Colorado	NHL	82	20	47	67	42	8	7	0	17	4	10	14	4
00-01—Colorado	NHL	71	24	41	65	47	6	11	0	23	11	5	16	4
NHL Totals (3 years)............		232	64	112	176	151	23	24	0	59	21	17	38	12

DRURY, TED   C   BLUE JACKETS

PERSONAL: Born September 13, 1971, in Boston. ... 6-0/204. ... Shoots left. ... Full Name: Theodore Evans Drury. ... Brother of Chris Drury, center, Colorado Avalanche.
TRANSACTIONS/CAREER NOTES: Selected by Calgary Flames in second round (second Flames pick, 42nd overall) of NHL entry draft (June 17, 1989). ... Fractured kneecap (December 22, 1993); missed 15 games. ... Traded by Flames with D Gary Suter and LW Paul Ranheim to Hartford Whalers for C Mikael Nylander, D Zarley Zalapski and D James Patrick (March 10, 1994). ... Strained back (March 9, 1995); missed three games. ... Claimed by Ottawa Senators from Whalers in NHL waiver draft (October 2, 1995). ... Injured shoulder (November 4, 1995); missed three games. ... Suffered slight concussion (January 22, 1996); missed two games. ... Injured wrist (January 29, 1996). ... Traded by Senators with rights to D Marc Moro to Mighty Ducks of Anaheim for C Shaun Van Allen and D Jason York (October 1, 1996). ... Fractured wrist (January 31, 1997); missed five games. ... Traded by Mighty Ducks to New York Islanders for C Tony Hrkac and D Dean Malkoc (October 29, 1999). ... Injured back (February 15, 2000); missed one game. ... Selected by Columbus Blue Jackets in NHL expansion draft (June 23, 2000).
HONORS: Named to NCAA All-America (East) first team (1992-93). ... Named ECAC Player of the Year (1992-93). ... Named to ECAC All-Star first team (1992-93).

Season Team	League	REGULAR SEASON								PLAYOFFS				
		Gms.	G	A	Pts.	PIM	+/-	PP	SH	Gms.	G	A	Pts.	PIM
87-88—Fairfield College Prep..	Conn. H.S.	...	21	28	49	...	...	...	...	—	—	—	—	—
88-89—Fairfield College Prep..	Conn. H.S.	25	35	31	66	...	...	...	...	—	—	—	—	—
89-90—Harvard University	ECAC	17	9	13	22	10	...	...	...	—	—	—	—	—
90-91—Harvard University	ECAC	26	18	18	36	22	...	...	...	—	—	—	—	—

Season Team	League	REGULAR SEASON								PLAYOFFS				
		Gms.	G	A	Pts.	PIM	+/-	PP	SH	Gms.	G	A	Pts.	PIM
91-92—U.S. national team	Int'l	53	11	23	34	30	...	...	...	—	—	—	—	—
—U.S. Olympic team	Int'l	7	1	1	2	0	...	...	...	—	—	—	—	—
92-93—Harvard University	ECAC	31	22	41	*63	26	...	...	...	—	—	—	—	—
93-94—Calgary	NHL	34	5	7	12	26	-5	0	1	—	—	—	—	—
—U.S. national team	Int'l	11	1	4	5	11	...	...	...	—	—	—	—	—
—U.S. Olympic team	Int'l	7	1	2	3	2	...	...	...	—	—	—	—	—
—Hartford	NHL	16	1	5	6	10	-10	0	0	—	—	—	—	—
94-95—Hartford	NHL	34	3	6	9	21	-3	0	0	—	—	—	—	—
—Springfield	AHL	2	0	1	1	0	...	...	...	—	—	—	—	—
95-96—Ottawa	NHL	42	9	7	16	54	-19	1	0	—	—	—	—	—
96-97—Anaheim	NHL	73	9	9	18	54	-9	1	0	10	1	0	1	4
97-98—Anaheim	NHL	73	6	10	16	82	-10	0	1	—	—	—	—	—
98-99—Anaheim	NHL	75	5	6	11	83	2	0	0	4	0	0	0	0
99-00—Anaheim	NHL	11	1	1	2	6	-1	0	0	—	—	—	—	—
—New York Islanders	NHL	55	2	1	3	31	-8	1	0	—	—	—	—	—
00-01—Columbus	NHL	1	0	0	0	0	-3	0	0	—	—	—	—	—
—Chicago	IHL	68	21	21	42	53	...	...	...	14	5	4	9	4
NHL Totals (8 years)		414	41	52	93	367	-66	3	2	14	1	0	1	4

DUBINSKY, STEVE　　RW

PERSONAL: Born July 9, 1970, in Montreal. ... 6-0/190. ... Shoots left. ... Name pronounced doo-BIHN-skee.
TRANSACTIONS/CAREER NOTES: Selected by Chicago Blackhawks in 11th round (11th Blackhawks pick, 226th overall) of NHL entry draft (June 16, 1990). ... Traded by Blackhawks with C Jeff Shantz to Calgary Flames for D Jamie Allison, C/LW Marty McInnis and RW Erik Andersson (October 27, 1998). ... Injured knee (March 13, 1999); missed eight games. ... Injured knee (December 12, 1999); missed final 52 games of season. ... Signed as free agent by Blackhawks (August 25, 2000).

Season Team	League	REGULAR SEASON								PLAYOFFS				
		Gms.	G	A	Pts.	PIM	+/-	PP	SH	Gms.	G	A	Pts.	PIM
89-90—Clarkson	ECAC	35	7	10	17	24	...	...	...	—	—	—	—	—
90-91—Clarkson	ECAC	38	15	23	38	26	...	...	...	—	—	—	—	—
91-92—Clarkson	ECAC	33	21	34	55	40	...	...	...	—	—	—	—	—
92-93—Clarkson	ECAC	35	18	26	44	58	...	...	...	—	—	—	—	—
93-94—Chicago	NHL	27	2	6	8	16	1	0	0	6	0	0	0	10
—Indianapolis	IHL	54	15	25	40	63	...	...	...	—	—	—	—	—
94-95—Indianapolis	IHL	62	16	11	27	29	...	...	...	—	—	—	—	—
—Chicago	NHL	16	0	0	0	8	-5	0	0	—	—	—	—	—
95-96—Indianapolis	IHL	16	8	8	16	10	...	...	...	—	—	—	—	—
—Chicago	NHL	43	2	3	5	14	3	0	0	—	—	—	—	—
96-97—Indianapolis	IHL	77	32	40	72	53	...	...	...	1	3	1	4	0
—Chicago	NHL	5	0	0	0	0	2	0	0	4	1	0	1	4
97-98—Chicago	NHL	82	5	13	18	57	-6	0	1	—	—	—	—	—
98-99—Chicago	NHL	1	0	0	0	0	0	0	0	—	—	—	—	—
—Calgary	NHL	61	4	10	14	14	-7	0	2	—	—	—	—	—
99-00—Calgary	NHL	23	0	1	1	4	-12	0	0	—	—	—	—	—
00-01—Norfolk	AHL	14	6	5	11	4	...	...	...	—	—	—	—	—
—Chicago	NHL	60	6	4	10	33	-4	0	1	—	—	—	—	—
NHL Totals (8 years)		318	19	37	56	146	-28	0	4	10	1	0	1	14

DUCHESNE, STEVE　　D　　RED WINGS

PERSONAL: Born June 30, 1965, in Sept-Iles, Que. ... 5-11/195. ... Shoots left. ... Name pronounced doo-SHAYN.
TRANSACTIONS/CAREER NOTES: Signed as non-drafted free agent by Los Angeles Kings (October 1, 1984). ... Strained left knee (January 26, 1988). ... Separated left shoulder (November 1988). ... Traded by Kings with C Steve Kasper and fourth-round pick (D Aris Brimanis) in 1991 draft to Philadelphia Flyers for D Jeff Chychrun and rights to RW Jari Kurri (May 30, 1991). ... Traded by Flyers with G Ron Hextall, C Mike Ricci, C Peter Forsberg, D Kerry Huffman, first-round pick (G Jocelyn Thibault) in 1993 draft, cash and future considerations to Quebec Nordiques for C Eric Lindros (June 20, 1992); Nordiques acquired LW Chris Simon and first-round pick (traded to Toronto) in 1994 draft to complete deal (July 21, 1992). ... Suffered concussion (January 2, 1993); missed one game. ... Suffered from the flu (March 20, 1993); missed one game. ... Refused to report to Nordiques in 1993-94 due to contract dispute. ... Traded by Nordiques with RW Denis Chasse to St. Louis Blues for C Ron Sutter, C Bob Bassen and D Garth Butcher (January 23, 1994). ... Injured back (March 30, 1994); missed one game. ... Injured shoulder (March 31, 1995); missed one game. ... Traded by Blues to Ottawa Senators for second-round pick (traded to Buffalo) in 1996 draft (August 4, 1995). ... Sprained ankle (November 18, 1995); missed 20 games. ... Bruised hand (October 9, 1996); missed two games. ... Suffered sore back (March 4, 1997); missed two games. ... Traded by Senators to Blues for D Igor Kravchuk (August 25, 1997). ... Suffered sore knee (April 7, 1998); missed one game. ... Signed as free agent by Los Angeles Kings (July 2, 1998). ... Suffered back spasms (January 14, 1999); missed one game. ... Suffered an illness (February 13, 1999); missed one game. ... Traded by Kings to Flyers for D Dave Babych and fifth-round pick (G Nathan Marsters) in 2000 draft (March 23, 1999). ... Signed as free agent by Detroit Red Wings (September 3, 1999). ... Suspended two games by NHL for high-sticking incident (March 25, 2000). ... Strained knee (November 27, 2000); missed three games.
HONORS: Named to QMJHL All-Star first team (1984-85). ... Named to NHL All-Rookie team (1986-87). ... Played in NHL All-Star Game (1989, 1990 and 1993).
STATISTICAL PLATEAUS: Three-goal games: 1988-89 (1), 1991-92 (1), 1993-94 (1). Total: 3.

Season Team	League	REGULAR SEASON								PLAYOFFS				
		Gms.	G	A	Pts.	PIM	+/-	PP	SH	Gms.	G	A	Pts.	PIM
83-84—Drummondville	QMJHL	67	1	34	35	79	...	...	...	—	—	—	—	—
84-85—Drummondville	QMJHL	65	22	54	76	94	...	...	...	5	4	7	11	8
85-86—New Haven	AHL	75	14	35	49	76	...	...	...	5	0	2	2	9
86-87—Los Angeles	NHL	75	13	25	38	74	8	5	0	5	2	2	4	4
87-88—Los Angeles	NHL	71	16	39	55	109	0	5	0	5	1	3	4	14
88-89—Los Angeles	NHL	79	25	50	75	92	31	8	5	11	4	4	8	12

Season Team	League	REGULAR SEASON								PLAYOFFS				
		Gms.	G	A	Pts.	PIM	+/-	PP	SH	Gms.	G	A	Pts.	PIM
89-90—Los Angeles	NHL	79	20	42	62	36	-3	6	0	10	2	9	11	6
90-91—Los Angeles	NHL	78	21	41	62	66	19	8	0	12	4	8	12	8
91-92—Philadelphia	NHL	78	18	38	56	86	-7	7	2	—	—	—	—	—
92-93—Quebec	NHL	82	20	62	82	57	15	8	0	6	0	5	5	6
93-94—St. Louis	NHL	36	12	19	31	14	1	8	0	4	0	2	2	2
94-95—St. Louis	NHL	47	12	26	38	36	29	1	0	7	0	4	4	2
95-96—Ottawa	NHL	62	12	24	36	42	-23	7	0	—	—	—	—	—
96-97—Ottawa	NHL	78	19	28	47	38	-9	10	2	7	1	4	5	0
97-98—St. Louis	NHL	80	14	42	56	32	9	5	1	10	0	4	4	6
98-99—Los Angeles	NHL	60	4	19	23	22	-6	1	0	—	—	—	—	—
—Philadelphia	NHL	11	2	5	7	2	0	1	0	6	0	2	2	2
99-00—Detroit	NHL	79	10	31	41	42	12	1	0	9	0	4	4	10
00-01—Detroit	NHL	54	6	19	25	48	9	2	0	6	2	4	6	0
NHL Totals (15 years)		1049	224	510	734	796	85	83	10	98	16	55	71	72

DUMONT, J.P. RW SABRES

PERSONAL: Born May 1, 1978, in Montreal. ... 6-1/187. ... Shoots left. ... Full Name: Jean-Pierre Dumont.
TRANSACTIONS/CAREER NOTES: Selected by New York Islanders in first round (first Islanders pick, third overall) of NHL entry draft (June 22, 1996). ... Traded by Islanders with fifth-round pick (traded to Philadelphia) in 1998 draft to Chicago Blackhawks for C/LW Dmitri Nabokov (May 30, 1998). ... Injured back (April 8, 1999); missed two games. ... Traded by Blackhawks with C Doug Gilmour to Buffalo Sabres for LW Michal Grosek (March 10, 2000). ... Suffered rib injury (February 13, 2001); missed two games.
HONORS: Won Michael Bossy Trophy (1995-96). ... Named to QMJHL All-Star second team (1996-97). ... Won Guy Lafleur Trophy (1997-98).
STATISTICAL PLATEAUS: Three-goal games: 1998-99 (1), 2000-01 (1). Total: 2.

Season Team	League	REGULAR SEASON								PLAYOFFS				
		Gms.	G	A	Pts.	PIM	+/-	PP	SH	Gms.	G	A	Pts.	PIM
93-94—Val-d'Or	QMJHL	25	9	11	20	10	...	...	...	—	—	—	—	—
94-95—Val-d'Or	QMJHL	48	5	14	19	24	...	...	...	—	—	—	—	—
95-96—Val-d'Or	QMJHL	66	48	57	105	109	...	...	...	13	12	8	20	22
96-97—Val-d'Or	QMJHL	62	44	64	108	88	...	...	...	13	9	7	16	12
97-98—Val-d'Or	QMJHL	55	57	42	99	63	...	...	...	19	*31	15	*46	18
98-99—Portland	AHL	50	32	14	46	39	...	...	...	—	—	—	—	—
—Chicago	NHL	25	9	6	15	10	7	0	0	—	—	—	—	—
99-00—Chicago	NHL	47	10	8	18	18	-6	0	0	—	—	—	—	—
—Cleveland	IHL	7	5	2	7	8	...	...	...	—	—	—	—	—
—Rochester	AHL	13	7	10	17	18	...	...	...	21	*14	7	21	32
00-01—Buffalo	NHL	79	23	28	51	54	1	9	0	13	4	3	7	8
NHL Totals (3 years)		151	42	42	84	82	2	9	0	13	4	3	7	8

DUNHAM, MIKE G PREDATORS

PERSONAL: Born June 1, 1972, in Johnson City, N.Y. ... 6-3/200. ... Catches left. ... Full Name: Michael Francis Dunham.
TRANSACTIONS/CAREER NOTES: Selected by New Jersey Devils in third round (fourth Devils pick, 53rd overall) of NHL entry draft (June 16, 1990). ... Injured hand (January 1, 1998); missed three games. ... Injured knee and underwent surgery (March 5, 1998); missed 18 games. ... Selected by Nashville Predators in NHL expansion draft (June 26, 1998). ... Strained right groin (November 29, 1998); missed seven games. ... Reinjured groin (December 19, 1998); missed 13 games. ... Strained groin (March 27, 1999); missed six games. ... Suffered from the flu (December 26, 1999); missed one game. ... Sprained right thumb (February 3, 2000); missed four games. ... Sprained left knee (October 27, 2000); missed 15 games. ... Injured knee (December 4, 2000); missed two games. ... Strained neck (February 20, 2001); missed one game.
HONORS: Named to NCAA All-America (East) first team (1992-93). ... Named to Hockey East All-Star first team (1992-93). ... Shared Harry (Hap) Holmes Memorial Trophy with Corey Schwab (1994-95). ... Shared Jack Butterfield Trophy with Corey Schwab (1994-95). ... Named to AHL All-Star second team (1995-96). ... Shared William M. Jennings Trophy with Martin Brodeur (1996-97).
MISCELLANEOUS: Holds Nashville Predators all-time records for most games played by a goalie (144), most wins (56) and most shutouts (5). ... Stopped a penalty shot attempt (vs. John Madden, February 29, 2000; vs. Gary Roberts, December 20, 2000). ... Allowed a penalty shot goal (vs. Markus Naslund, December 19, 1998).

Season Team	League	REGULAR SEASON							PLAYOFFS					
		Gms.	Min	W	L	T	GA	SO	Avg.	Gms.	Min.	W	L	GA	SO	Avg.
87-88—Canterbury School	Conn. H.S.	29	...	...	...	...	...	4	...	—	—	—	—	—	—	—
88-89—Canterbury School	Conn. H.S.	25	...	...	...	...	63	2	...	—	—	—	—	—	—	—
89-90—Canterbury School	Conn. H.S.	32	1558	...	...	...	55	...	2.12	—	—	—	—	—	—	—
90-91—Univ. of Maine	Hockey East	23	1275	14	5	2	63	2	*2.96	—	—	—	—	—	—	—
91-92—Univ. of Maine	Hockey East	7	382	6	0	0	14	1	2.20	—	—	—	—	—	—	—
—U.S. national team	Int'l	3	157	0	1	1	10	0	3.82	—	—	—	—	—	—	—
92-93—Univ. of Maine	Hockey East	25	1429	21	1	1	63	0	2.65	—	—	—	—	—	—	—
—U.S. national team	Int'l	1	60	0	0	1	1	0	1.00	—	—	—	—	—	—	—
93-94—U.S. national team	Int'l	33	1983	22	9	2	125	2	3.78	—	—	—	—	—	—	—
—U.S. Olympic team	Int'l	3	180	0	1	2	15	0	5.00	—	—	—	—	—	—	—
—Albany	AHL	5	305	2	2	1	26	0	5.11	—	—	—	—	—	—	—
94-95—Albany	AHL	35	2120	20	7	8	99	1	2.80	7	420	6	1	20	1	2.86
95-96—Albany	AHL	44	2591	30	10	2	109	1	2.52	3	181	1	2	5	1	1.66
96-97—Albany	AHL	3	184	1	1	1	12	0	3.91	—	—	—	—	—	—	—
—New Jersey	NHL	26	1013	8	7	1	43	2	2.55	—	—	—	—	—	—	—
97-98—New Jersey	NHL	15	773	5	5	3	29	1	2.25	—	—	—	—	—	—	—
98-99—Nashville	NHL	44	2472	16	23	3	127	1	3.08	—	—	—	—	—	—	—
99-00—Milwaukee	IHL	1	60	2	0	0	1	0	1.00	—	—	—	—	—	—	—
—Nashville	NHL	52	3077	19	27	6	146	0	2.85	—	—	—	—	—	—	—
00-01—Nashville	NHL	48	2810	21	21	4	107	4	2.28	—	—	—	—	—	—	—
NHL Totals (5 years)		185	10145	69	83	17	452	8	2.67							

DUPONT, MICKI — D — FLAMES

PERSONAL: Born April 15, 1980, in Calgary. ... 5-9/180. ... Shoots right.
TRANSACTIONS/CAREER NOTES: Signed as non-drafted free agent by Calgary Flames (October 6, 2000).
HONORS: Won Bill Hunter Trophy (1999-2000). ... Named to WHL (West) All-Star first team (1999-2000). ... Named to Can.HL All-Star first team (1999-2000). ... Won Can.HL Defenseman of the Year Award (1999-2000).

		REGULAR SEASON								PLAYOFFS				
Season Team	League	Gms.	G	A	Pts.	PIM	+/-	PP	SH	Gms.	G	A	Pts.	PIM
96-97—Kamloops	WHL	59	8	27	35	...	...	...	...	5	0	4	4	8
97-98—Kamloops	WHL	71	13	41	54	93	...	...	...	7	0	1	1	10
98-99—Kamloops	WHL	59	8	27	35	110	...	...	...	15	2	8	10	22
99-00—Kamloops	WHL	70	26	62	88	159	...	...	...	4	0	2	2	17
—Long Beach	IHL	1	0	0	0	0	...	...	...	—	—	—	—	—
—San Diego	WCHL	—	—	—	—	—	...	...	...	7	2	2	4	0
00-01—Saint John	AHL	67	8	21	29	28	...	...	...	19	1	9	10	14

DUPUIS, PASCAL — LW — WILD

PERSONAL: Born April 7, 1979, in Laval Que. ... 6-0/196. ... Shoots right.
TRANSACTIONS/CAREER NOTES: Signed as non-drafted free agent by Minnesota Wild (September 18, 2000).

		REGULAR SEASON								PLAYOFFS				
Season Team	League	Gms.	G	A	Pts.	PIM	+/-	PP	SH	Gms.	G	A	Pts.	PIM
96-97—Rovyn-Noranda	QMJHL	44	9	15	24	20	...	...	...	—	—	—	—	—
97-98—Rovyn-Noranda	QMJHL	39	9	17	26	36	...	...	...	—	—	—	—	—
—Shawinigan	QMJHL	28	7	13	20	10	...	...	...	6	2	0	2	4
98-99—Shawinigan	QMJHL	57	30	42	72	118	...	...	...	6	1	8	9	18
99-00—Shawinigan	QMJHL	61	50	55	105	164	...	...	...	13	†15	7	22	4
00-01—Cleveland	IHL	70	19	24	43	37	...	...	...	4	0	0	0	0
—Minnesota	NHL	4	1	0	1	4	0	1	0	—	—	—	—	—
NHL Totals (1 year)		4	1	0	1	4	0	1	0					

DVORAK, RADEK — RW — RANGERS

PERSONAL: Born March 9, 1977, in Tabor, Czechoslovakia. ... 6-1/194. ... Shoots right. ... Name pronounced RA-dihk duh-VOHR-ak.
TRANSACTIONS/CAREER NOTES: Selected by Florida Panthers in first round (first Panthers pick, 10th overall) of NHL entry draft (July 8, 1995). ... Fractured left wrist (October 30, 1997); missed 15 games. ... Traded by Panthers to San Jose Sharks for G Mike Vernon and third-round pick (RW Sean O'Connor) in 2000 draft (December 30, 1999). ... Traded by Sharks to New York Rangers for RW Todd Harvey and fourth-round pick (G Dimitri Patzold) in 2001 draft (December 30, 1999).
MISCELLANEOUS: Failed to score on a penalty shot (vs. Manny Fernandez, March 13, 2000).
STATISTICAL PLATEAUS: Three-goal games: 1999-00 (1). ... Four-goal games: 2000-01 (1). ... Total hat tricks: 2.

		REGULAR SEASON								PLAYOFFS				
Season Team	League	Gms.	G	A	Pts.	PIM	+/-	PP	SH	Gms.	G	A	Pts.	PIM
92-93—Motor-Ceske Bude.	Czech.	35	44	46	90	...	...	...	...	—	—	—	—	—
93-94—HC Ceske Budejovice	Czech Rep.	8	0	0	0	...	...	...	...	—	—	—	—	—
—Motor-Ceske Bude.	Czech Rep.	20	17	18	35	...	...	...	...	—	—	—	—	—
94-95—HC Ceske Budejovice	Czech Rep.	10	3	5	8	...	...	...	...	9	5	1	6	...
95-96—Florida	NHL	77	13	14	27	20	5	0	0	16	1	3	4	0
96-97—Florida	NHL	78	18	21	39	30	-2	2	0	3	0	0	0	0
97-98—Florida	NHL	64	12	24	36	33	-1	2	3	—	—	—	—	—
98-99—Florida	NHL	82	19	24	43	29	7	0	4	—	—	—	—	—
99-00—Florida	NHL	35	7	10	17	6	5	0	0	—	—	—	—	—
—New York Rangers	NHL	46	11	22	33	10	0	2	1	—	—	—	—	—
00-01—New York Rangers	NHL	82	31	36	67	20	9	5	2	—	—	—	—	—
NHL Totals (6 years)		464	111	151	262	148	23	11	10	19	1	3	4	0

DWYER, GORDIE — LW — LIGHTNING

PERSONAL: Born January 25, 1978, in Dalhousie, N.B. ... 6-2/216. ... Shoots left.
TRANSACTIONS/CAREER NOTES: Selected by St. Louis Blues in third round (second Blues pick, 67th overall) of NHL entry draft (June 22, 1996). ... Returned to draft pool by Blues and selected by Montreal Canadiens in sixth round (fifth Canadiens pick, 152nd overall) of NHL entry draft (June 27, 1998). ... Traded by Canadiens to Tampa Bay Lightning for D Mike McBain (November 26, 1999). ... Injured finger (April 8, 2000); missed final game of season. ... Suspended 23 games by NHL for abuse of an official (September 28, 2000).

		REGULAR SEASON								PLAYOFFS				
Season Team	League	Gms.	G	A	Pts.	PIM	+/-	PP	SH	Gms.	G	A	Pts.	PIM
94-95—Hull	QMJHL	57	3	7	10	204	...	...	...	17	1	3	4	54
95-96—Hull	QMJHL	25	5	9	14	199	...	...	...	—	—	—	—	—
—Laval	QMJHL	22	5	17	22	72	...	...	...	—	—	—	—	—
—Beauport	QMJHL	22	4	9	13	87	...	...	...	20	3	5	8	104
96-97—Drummondville	QMJHL	66	21	48	69	391	...	...	...	8	6	1	7	39
97-98—Quebec	QMJHL	59	18	27	45	365	...	...	...	14	4	9	13	67
98-99—Fredericton	AHL	14	0	0	0	46	...	...	...	—	—	—	—	—
—New Orleans	ECHL	36	1	3	4	163	...	...	...	11	0	0	0	27
99-00—Quebec	AHL	7	0	0	0	37	...	...	...	—	—	—	—	—
—Detroit	IHL	27	0	2	2	147	...	...	...	—	—	—	—	—
—Tampa Bay	NHL	24	0	1	1	135	-6	0	0	—	—	—	—	—
00-01—Tampa Bay	NHL	28	0	1	1	96	-7	0	0	—	—	—	—	—
—Detroit	IHL	24	2	3	5	169	...	...	...	—	—	—	—	—
NHL Totals (2 years)		52	0	2	2	231	-13	0	0					

DYKHUIS, KARL   D   CANADIENS

PERSONAL: Born July 8, 1972, in Sept-Iles, Que. ... 6-3/214. ... Shoots left. ... Name pronounced DIGH-kowz.

TRANSACTIONS/CAREER NOTES: Selected by Chicago Blackhawks in first round (first Blackhawks pick, 16th overall) of NHL entry draft (June 16, 1990). ... Traded by Blackhawks to Philadelphia Flyers for D Bob Wilkie (February 16, 1995). ... Sprained knee (November 26, 1996); missed two games. ... Suffered facial lacerations (December 31, 1996); missed two games. ... Dislocated shoulder (January 28, 1997); missed 13 games. ... Traded by Flyers with RW Mikael Renberg to Tampa Bay Lightning for C Chris Gratton (August 20, 1997). ... Suffered from the flu (November 14, 1997); missed one game. ... Suffered from the flu (January 31, 1998); missed one game. ... Traded by Lightning to Flyers for D Petr Svoboda (December 28, 1998). ... Fractured cheekbone (December 29, 1998); missed one game. ... Traded by Flyers to Montreal Canadiens for future considerations (October 20, 1999). ... Injured knee (March 6, 2000); missed one game. ... Injured groin (March 18, 2000); missed five games. ... Underwent off-season abdominal surgery (October 6, 2000); missed first 11 games of season.

HONORS: Won Raymond Lagace Trophy (1988-89). ... Won Michael Bossy Trophy (1989-90). ... Named to QMJHL All-Star first team (1989-90).

		REGULAR SEASON								PLAYOFFS				
Season Team	League	Gms.	G	A	Pts.	PIM	+/-	PP	SH	Gms.	G	A	Pts.	PIM
88-89—Hull	QMJHL	63	2	29	31	59	...	...	...	9	1	9	10	6
89-90—Hull	QMJHL	69	10	45	55	119	...	...	...	11	2	5	7	2
90-91—Longueuil	QMJHL	3	1	4	5	6	...	...	...	—	—	—	—	—
—Canadian nat'l team	Int'l	37	2	9	11	16	...	...	...	—	—	—	—	—
91-92—Longueuil	QMJHL	29	5	19	24	55	...	...	...	17	0	12	12	14
—Chicago	NHL	6	1	3	4	4	-1	1	0	—	—	—	—	—
92-93—Indianapolis	IHL	59	5	18	23	76	...	...	...	5	1	1	2	8
—Chicago	NHL	12	0	5	5	0	2	0	0	—	—	—	—	—
93-94—Indianapolis	IHL	73	7	25	32	132	...	...	...	—	—	—	—	—
94-95—Indianapolis	IHL	52	2	21	23	63	...	...	...	—	—	—	—	—
—Hershey	AHL	1	0	0	0	0	...	...	...	—	—	—	—	—
—Philadelphia	NHL	33	2	6	8	37	7	1	0	15	4	4	8	14
95-96—Philadelphia	NHL	82	5	15	20	101	12	1	0	12	2	2	4	22
96-97—Philadelphia	NHL	62	4	15	19	35	6	2	0	18	0	3	3	2
97-98—Tampa Bay	NHL	78	5	9	14	110	-8	0	1	—	—	—	—	—
98-99—Tampa Bay	NHL	33	2	1	3	18	-21	0	0	—	—	—	—	—
—Philadelphia	NHL	45	2	4	6	32	-2	1	0	5	1	0	1	4
99-00—Philadelphia	NHL	5	0	1	1	6	-2	0	0	—	—	—	—	—
—Montreal	NHL	67	7	12	19	40	-3	3	1	—	—	—	—	—
00-01—Montreal	NHL	67	8	9	17	44	9	2	0	—	—	—	—	—
NHL Totals (9 years)		490	36	80	116	427	-1	11	2	50	7	9	16	42

EAKINS, DALLAS   D   FLAMES

PERSONAL: Born January 20, 1967, in Dade City, Fla. ... 6-1/198. ... Shoots left. ... Name pronounced AY-kihns.

TRANSACTIONS/CAREER NOTES: Selected by Washington Capitals in 10th round (11th Capitals pick, 208th overall) of NHL entry draft (June 15, 1985). ... Injured back (October 1988). ... Signed as free agent by Winnipeg Jets (September 1989). ... Signed as free agent by Florida Panthers (July 14, 1993). ... Traded by Panthers to St. Louis Blues for fourth-round draft pick (RW Ivan Novoseltsev) in 1997 draft (September 28, 1995). ... Fractured wrist (December 8, 1995); missed 29 games. ... Claimed on waivers by Jets (March 20, 1996). ... Jets franchise moved to Phoenix and renamed Coyotes for 1996-97 season; NHL approved move on January 18, 1996. ... Suffered back spasms (November 26, 1996); missed three games. ... Traded by Coyotes with C Mike Eastwood to New York Rangers for D Jay More (February 6, 1997). ... Signed as free agent by Florida Panthers (July 7, 1997). ... Sprained left knee prior to 1997-98 season; missed first 11 games of season. ... Signed as free agent by Toronto Maple Leafs (July 14, 1998). ... Sprained shoulder (November 14, 1998); missed three games. ... Signed as free agent by New York Islanders (August 12, 1999). ... Traded by Islanders to Chicago Blackhawks for future considerations (March 3, 2000). ... Signed as free agent by Calgary Flames (July 27, 2000).

HONORS: Named to IHL All-Star second team (1999-2000).

		REGULAR SEASON								PLAYOFFS				
Season Team	League	Gms.	G	A	Pts.	PIM	+/-	PP	SH	Gms.	G	A	Pts.	PIM
84-85—Peterborough	OHL	48	0	8	8	96	...	...	...	7	0	0	0	18
85-86—Peterborough	OHL	60	6	16	22	134	...	...	...	16	0	1	1	30
86-87—Peterborough	OHL	54	3	11	14	145	...	...	...	12	1	4	5	37
87-88—Peterborough	OHL	64	11	27	38	129	...	...	...	12	3	12	15	16
88-89—Baltimore	AHL	62	0	10	10	139	...	...	...	—	—	—	—	—
89-90—Moncton	AHL	75	2	11	13	189	...	...	...	—	—	—	—	—
90-91—Moncton	AHL	75	1	12	13	132	...	...	...	9	0	1	1	44
91-92—Moncton	AHL	67	3	13	16	136	...	...	...	11	2	1	3	16
92-93—Moncton	AHL	55	4	6	10	132	...	...	...	—	—	—	—	—
—Winnipeg	NHL	14	0	2	2	38	2	0	0	—	—	—	—	—
93-94—Cincinnati	IHL	80	1	18	19	143	...	...	...	8	0	1	1	41
—Florida	NHL	1	0	0	0	0	0	0	0	—	—	—	—	—
94-95—Cincinnati	IHL	59	6	12	18	69	...	...	...	—	—	—	—	—
—Florida	NHL	17	0	1	1	35	2	0	0	—	—	—	—	—
95-96—St. Louis	NHL	16	0	1	1	34	-2	0	0	—	—	—	—	—
—Worcester	AHL	4	0	0	0	12	...	...	...	—	—	—	—	—
—Winnipeg	NHL	2	0	0	0	0	1	0	0	—	—	—	—	—
96-97—Springfield	AHL	38	6	7	13	63	...	...	...	—	—	—	—	—
—Phoenix	NHL	4	0	0	0	10	-3	0	0	—	—	—	—	—
—Binghamton	AHL	19	1	7	8	15	...	...	...	—	—	—	—	—
—New York Rangers	NHL	3	0	0	0	6	-1	0	0	4	0	0	0	4
97-98—Florida	NHL	23	0	1	1	44	1	0	0	—	—	—	—	—
—New Haven	AHL	4	0	1	1	7	...	...	...	—	—	—	—	—
98-99—Chicago	IHL	2	0	0	0	0	...	...	...	—	—	—	—	—
—Toronto	NHL	18	0	2	2	24	3	0	0	1	0	0	0	0
—St. John's	AHL	20	3	7	10	16	...	...	...	5	0	1	1	6
99-00—Chicago	IHL	68	5	26	31	99	...	...	...	16	1	4	5	16
—New York Islanders	NHL	2	0	1	1	2	3	0	0	—	—	—	—	—
00-01—Chicago	IHL	64	3	16	19	49	...	...	...	14	0	0	0	24
—Calgary	NHL	17	0	1	1	11	-1	0	0	—	—	—	—	—
NHL Totals (9 years)		117	0	9	9	204	5	0	0	5	0	0	0	4

EASTWOOD, MIKE   C   BLUES

PERSONAL: Born July 1, 1967, in Cornwall, Ont. ... 6-3/209. ... Shoots right. ... Full Name: Michael Barry Eastwood.
TRANSACTIONS/CAREER NOTES: Selected by Toronto Maple Leafs in fifth round (fifth Maple Leafs pick, 91st overall) of NHL entry draft (June 13, 1987). ... Traded by Maple Leafs with third-round pick (RW Brad Isbister) in 1995 draft to Winnipeg Jets for RW Tie Domi (April 7, 1995). ... Jets franchise moved to Phoenix and renamed Coyotes for 1996-97 season; NHL approved move on January 18, 1996. ... Fractured wrist (October 28, 1996); missed eight games. ... Traded by Coyotes with D Dallas Eakins to New York Rangers for D Jay More (February 6, 1997). ... Traded by Rangers to St. Louis Blues for C Harry York (March 24, 1998). ... Suffered sore wrist (April 18, 1998); missed two games. ... Sprained ankle (October 8, 2000); missed three games. ... Suffered from the flu (March 10, 2001); missed one game.
HONORS: Named to CCHA All-Star second team (1990-91).
STATISTICAL NOTES: Led NHL with 22.9 shooting percentage (1999-2000).
STATISTICAL PLATEAUS: Three-goal games: 1999-00 (1).

		REGULAR SEASON								PLAYOFFS				
Season Team	League	Gms.	G	A	Pts.	PIM	+/-	PP	SH	Gms.	G	A	Pts.	PIM
86-87—Pembroke	COJHL						Statistics unavailable.							
87-88—Western Michigan	CCHA	42	5	8	13	14	...	...	...	—	—	—	—	—
88-89—Western Michigan	CCHA	40	10	13	23	87	...	...	...	—	—	—	—	—
89-90—Western Michigan	CCHA	40	25	27	52	36	...	...	...	—	—	—	—	—
90-91—Western Michigan	CCHA	42	29	32	61	84	...	...	...	—	—	—	—	—
91-92—St. John's	AHL	61	18	25	43	28	...	...	...	16	9	10	19	16
—Toronto	NHL	9	0	2	2	4	-4	0	0	—	—	—	—	—
92-93—St. John's	AHL	60	24	35	59	32	...	...	...	—	—	—	—	—
—Toronto	NHL	12	1	6	7	21	-2	0	0	10	1	2	3	8
93-94—Toronto	NHL	54	8	10	18	28	2	1	0	18	3	2	5	12
94-95—Toronto	NHL	36	5	5	10	32	-12	0	0	—	—	—	—	—
—Winnipeg	NHL	13	3	6	9	4	3	0	0					
95-96—Winnipeg	NHL	80	14	14	28	20	-14	2	0	6	0	1	1	2
96-97—Phoenix	NHL	33	1	3	4	4	-3	0	0	—	—	—	—	—
—New York Rangers	NHL	27	1	7	8	10	2	0	0	15	1	2	3	22
97-98—New York Rangers	NHL	48	5	5	10	16	-2	0	0	—	—	—	—	—
—St. Louis	NHL	10	1	0	1	6	0	0	0	3	1	0	1	0
98-99—St. Louis	NHL	82	9	21	30	36	6	0	0	13	1	1	2	6
99-00—St. Louis	NHL	79	19	15	34	32	5	1	3	7	1	1	2	6
00-01—St. Louis	NHL	77	6	17	23	28	4	0	2	15	0	2	2	2
NHL Totals (10 years)		560	73	111	184	241	-15	4	5	87	8	11	19	58

EATON, MARK   D   PREDATORS

PERSONAL: Born May 6, 1977, in Wilmington, Del. ... 6-2/205. ... Shoots left. ... Full Name: Mark Andrew Eaton.
TRANSACTIONS/CAREER NOTES: Signed as non-drafted free agent by Philadelphia Flyers (July 28, 1998). ... Suffered from stomach virus (March 26, 2000); missed one game. ... Traded by Flyers to Nashville Predators for third-round pick (C Patrick Sharp) in 2001 draft (September 29, 2000).

		REGULAR SEASON								PLAYOFFS				
Season Team	League	Gms.	G	A	Pts.	PIM	+/-	PP	SH	Gms.	G	A	Pts.	PIM
97-98—Notre Dame	CCHA	41	12	17	29	32	...	...	...	—	—	—	—	—
98-99—Philadelphia	AHL	74	9	27	36	38	...	...	...	16	4	8	12	0
99-00—Philadelphia	NHL	27	1	1	2	8	1	0	0	7	0	0	0	0
—Philadelphia	AHL	47	9	17	26	6	...	...	...	—	—	—	—	—
00-01—Milwaukee	IHL	34	3	12	15	27	...	...	...	—	—	—	—	—
—Nashville	NHL	34	3	8	11	14	7	1	0	—	—	—	—	—
NHL Totals (2 years)		61	4	9	13	22	8	1	0	7	0	0	0	0

EKMAN, NILS   LW   RANGERS

PERSONAL: Born March 11, 1976, in Stockholm, Sweden. ... 5-11/182. ... Shoots left.
TRANSACTIONS/CAREER NOTES: Selected by Calgary Flames in fifth round (sixth Flames pick, 107th overall) of NHL entry draft (June 29, 1994). ... Rights traded by Flames with fourth-round pick (traded to New York Islanders) in 2000 draft to Tampa Bay Lightning for C/LW Andreas Johansson (November 20, 1999). ... Injured hip (January 20, 2000); missed one game. ... Traded by Lightning with LW Kyle Freadrich to New York Rangers for C Tim Taylor (July 1, 2001).
HONORS: Won Garry F. Longman Memorial Trophy (1999-2000).

		REGULAR SEASON								PLAYOFFS				
Season Team	League	Gms.	G	A	Pts.	PIM	+/-	PP	SH	Gms.	G	A	Pts.	PIM
93-94—Hammarby	Sweden Dv. 2	18	7	2	9	4	...	...	...	—	—	—	—	—
94-95—Hammarby	Sweden Dv. 2	29	10	7	17	18	...	...	...	—	—	—	—	—
95-96—Hammarby	Sweden Dv. 2	22	9	7	16	20	...	...	...	—	—	—	—	—
96-97—Kiekko-Espoo	Finland	50	24	19	43	60	...	...	...	4	2	0	2	4
97-98—Kiekko-Espoo	Finland	43	14	14	28	86	...	...	...	7	2	2	4	27
—Saint John	AHL	—	—	—	—	—	...	...	...	1	0	0	0	2
98-99—Blues Espoo	Finland	52	20	14	34	96	...	...	...	3	1	1	2	6
99-00—Tampa Bay	NHL	28	2	2	4	36	-8	1	0	—	—	—	—	—
—Detroit	IHL	10	7	2	9	8	...	...	...					
—Long Beach	IHL	27	11	12	23	26	...	...	...	5	3	3	6	4
00-01—Detroit	IHL	33	22	14	36	63	...	...	...	—	—	—	—	—
—Tampa Bay	NHL	43	9	11	20	40	-15	2	1	—	—	—	—	—
NHL Totals (2 years)		71	11	13	24	76	-23	3	1	—	—	—	—	—

ELIAS, PATRIK   LW   DEVILS

PERSONAL: Born April 13, 1976, in Trebic, Czechoslovakia. ... 6-1/200. ... Shoots left. ... Name pronounced EH-lee-ahsh.
TRANSACTIONS/CAREER NOTES: Selected by New Jersey Devils in second round (second Devils pick, 51st overall) of NHL entry draft (June 28, 1994). ... Suffered from the flu (January 14, 1999); missed five games. ... Missed first nine games of 1999-2000 season due to contract dispute.
HONORS: Named to NHL All-Rookie team (1997-98). ... Played in NHL All-Star Game (2000). ... Named to NHL All-Star first team (2000-01). ... Named to THE SPORTING NEWS All-Star second team (2000-01).
MISCELLANEOUS: Member of Stanley Cup championship team (2000). ... Scored on a penalty shot (vs. Damian Rhodes, March 10, 2000). ... Failed to score on a penalty shot (vs. John Vanbiesbrouck, December 1, 2000).
STATISTICAL PLATEAUS: Three-goal games: 2000-01 (3).

		REGULAR SEASON								PLAYOFFS				
Season Team	League	Gms.	G	A	Pts.	PIM	+/-	PP	SH	Gms.	G	A	Pts.	PIM
92-93—HC Kladno	Czech.	2	0	0	0	0	...	...	...	—	—	—	—	—
93-94—HC Kladno	Czech Rep.	15	1	2	3	...	...	...	...	11	2	2	4	...
—Czech Rep. Oly. team..	Int'l	5	2	5	7	...	...	...	...	—	—	—	—	—
94-95—HC Kladno	Czech Rep.	28	4	3	7	...	...	...	...	7	1	2	3	...
95-96—Albany	AHL	74	27	36	63	83	...	...	...	4	1	1	2	2
—New Jersey	NHL	1	0	0	0	0	-1	0	0	—	—	—	—	—
96-97—Albany	AHL	57	24	43	67	76	...	...	...	6	1	2	3	8
—New Jersey	NHL	17	2	3	5	2	-4	0	0	8	2	3	5	4
97-98—New Jersey	NHL	74	18	19	37	28	18	5	0	4	0	1	1	0
—Albany	AHL	3	3	0	3	2	...	...	...	—	—	—	—	—
98-99—New Jersey	NHL	74	17	33	50	34	19	3	0	7	0	5	5	6
99-00—SK Trebic	Czech Dv.II	2	2	1	3	2	...	...	...	—	—	—	—	—
—HC Pardubice	Czech Rep.	5	1	4	5	6	...	...	...	—	—	—	—	—
—New Jersey	NHL	72	35	37	72	58	16	9	0	23	7	†13	20	9
00-01—New Jersey	NHL	82	40	56	96	51	†45	8	3	25	9	14	23	10
NHL Totals (6 years)		320	112	148	260	173	93	25	3	67	18	36	54	29

ELICH, MATT   RW   LIGHTNING

PERSONAL: Born September 22, 1979, in Detroit. ... 6-3/196. ... Shoots right. ... Name pronounced EE-lihch.
TRANSACTIONS/CAREER NOTES: Selected by Tampa Bay Lightning in third round (third Lightning pick, 61st overall) of NHL entry draft (June 21, 1997).

		REGULAR SEASON								PLAYOFFS				
Season Team	League	Gms.	G	A	Pts.	PIM	+/-	PP	SH	Gms.	G	A	Pts.	PIM
95-96—Windsor	OHL	52	10	2	12	17	...	...	...	5	1	0	1	2
96-97—Windsor	OHL	58	15	13	28	19	...	...	...	5	0	1	1	6
97-98—Windsor	OHL	20	9	12	21	8	...	...	...	—	—	—	—	—
—Kingston	OHL	34	14	4	18	2	...	...	...	12	2	4	6	2
98-99—Kingston	OHL	67	44	30	74	32	...	...	...	5	3	5	8	0
99-00—Detroit	IHL	48	12	4	16	12	...	...	...	—	—	—	—	—
—Tampa Bay	NHL	8	1	1	2	0	-1	0	0	—	—	—	—	—
00-01—Detroit	IHL	60	12	16	28	12	...	...	...	—	—	—	—	—
—Tampa Bay	NHL	8	0	0	0	0	-5	0	0	—	—	—	—	—
NHL Totals (2 years)		16	1	1	2	0	-6	0	0					

ELOMO, MIIKKA   LW   FLAMES

PERSONAL: Born April 21, 1977, in Turku, Finland. ... 6-0/198. ... Shoots left. ... Brother of Teemu Elomo, left winger, Dallas Stars organization. ... Name pronounced EHL-ih-moh.
TRANSACTIONS/CAREER NOTES: Selected by Washington Capitals in first round (second Capitals pick, 23rd overall) of NHL entry draft (July 8, 1995). ... Traded by Capitals with fourth-round pick (G Levente Szuper) in 2000 draft to Calgary Flames for second-round pick (LW Matt Pettinger) in 2000 draft (June 24, 2000).

		REGULAR SEASON								PLAYOFFS				
Season Team	League	Gms.	G	A	Pts.	PIM	+/-	PP	SH	Gms.	G	A	Pts.	PIM
91-92—London	OHL	65	11	19	30	15	...	...	...	7	0	0	0	0
93-94—TPS Turku Jr.	Finland	30	8	5	13	24	...	...	...	5	1	1	2	2
94-95—Kiekko-67	Finland Div. 2	14	9	2	11	39	...	...	...	—	—	—	—	—
—TPS Turku Jr.	Finland	14	3	8	11	24	...	...	...	—	—	—	—	—
95-96—Kiekko-67	Finland Div. 2	21	9	6	15	100	...	...	...	—	—	—	—	—
—TPS Turku Jr.	Finland	6	0	2	2	18	...	...	...	—	—	—	—	—
—TPS Turku	Finland	10	1	1	2	8	...	...	...	3	0	0	0	2
96-97—Portland	AHL	52	8	9	17	37	...	...	...	—	—	—	—	—
97-98—Portland	AHL	33	1	1	2	54	...	...	...	—	—	—	—	—
—HIFK Helsinki	Finland	16	4	1	5	6	...	...	...	9	4	3	7	6
98-99—TPS Turku	Finland	36	5	10	15	76	...	...	...	10	3	5	8	6
99-00—Portland	AHL	59	21	14	35	50	...	...	...	—	—	—	—	—
—Washington	NHL	2	0	1	1	2	1	0	0	—	—	—	—	—
00-01—Saint John	AHL	72	10	21	31	109	...	...	...	6	0	2	2	12
NHL Totals (1 year)		2	0	1	1	2	1	0	0					

ELORANTA, MIKKO   C/LW   BRUINS

PERSONAL: Born August 24, 1972, in Turku, Finland. ... 6-0/185. ... Shoots left.
TRANSACTIONS/CAREER NOTES: Selected by Boston Bruins in ninth round (ninth Bruins pick, 247th overall) of NHL entry draft (June 26, 1999). ... Fractured ankle (December 10, 1999); missed 26 games. ... Suffered from the flu (December 27, 2000); missed one game.

Season Team	League	Gms.	G	A	Pts.	PIM	+/-	PP	SH	Gms.	G	A	Pts.	PIM
				REGULAR SEASON								PLAYOFFS		
95-96—Ilves Tampere	Finland	43	18	15	33	86	...	...	...	3	0	2	2	2
96-97—TPS Turku	Finland	31	6	15	21	52	...	...	...	10	5	2	7	6
97-98—TPS Turku	Finland	46	23	14	37	82	...	...	...	2	0	0	0	8
98-99—TPS Turku	Finland	52	19	21	40	103	...	...	...	10	1	6	7	26
99-00—Boston	NHL	50	6	12	18	36	-10	1	0	—	—	—	—	—
00-01—Boston	NHL	62	12	11	23	38	2	1	1	—	—	—	—	—
NHL Totals (2 years)		112	18	23	41	74	-8	2	1					

EMERSON, NELSON   RW   KINGS

PERSONAL: Born August 17, 1967, in Hamilton, Ont. ... 5-10/180. ... Shoots right. ... Full Name: Nelson Donald Emerson.

TRANSACTIONS/CAREER NOTES: Selected by St. Louis Blues in third round (second Blues pick, 44th overall) of NHL entry draft (June 15, 1985). ... Fractured bone under eye (December 28, 1991). ... Injured leg (April 3, 1993); missed one game. ... Traded by Blues with D Stephane Quintal to Winnipeg Jets for D Phil Housley (September 24, 1993). ... Sprained neck (January 25, 1994); missed one game. ... Traded by Jets to Hartford Whalers for C Darren Turcotte (October 6, 1995). ... Suffered mild concussion (February 17, 1996); missed one game. ... Fractured ankle prior to 1996-97 season; missed five games. ... Fractured ankle (November 4, 1996); missed six games. ... Strained groin (January 1, 1997); missed three games. ... Whalers franchise moved to North Carolina and renamed Carolina Hurricanes for 1997-98 season; NHL approved move on June 25, 1997. ... Traded by Hurricanes to Chicago Blackhawks for D Paul Coffey (December 29, 1998). ... Separated shoulder (February 28, 1999); missed 18 games. ... Traded by Blackhawks to Ottawa Senators for RW Chris Murray (March 23, 1999). ... Signed as free agent by Atlanta Thrashers (July 20, 1999). ... Suspended one game by NHL for slashing incident (November 22, 1999). ... Suffered concussion (November 28, 1999); missed seven games. ... Traded by Thrashers with RW Kelly Buchberger to Los Angeles Kings for RW Donald Audette and D Frantisek Kaberle (March 13, 2000). ... Fractured finger (March 25, 2000); missed eight games.

HONORS: Named CCHA Rookie of the Year (1986-87). ... Named to NCAA All-America (West) second team (1987-88). ... Named to CCHA All-Star first team (1987-88 and 1989-90). ... Named to NCAA All-America (West) first team (1989-90). ... Named to CCHA All-Star second team (1988-89). ... Won Garry F. Longman Memorial Trophy (1990-91). ... Named to IHL All-Star first team (1990-91).

STATISTICAL PLATEAUS: Three-goal games: 1994-95 (1).

Season Team	League	Gms.	G	A	Pts.	PIM	+/-	PP	SH	Gms.	G	A	Pts.	PIM
				REGULAR SEASON								PLAYOFFS		
84-85—Stratford Jr. B	OHA	40	23	38	61	70	...	...	...	—	—	—	—	—
85-86—Stratford Jr. B	OHA	39	54	58	112	91	...	...	...	—	—	—	—	—
86-87—Bowling Green	CCHA	45	26	35	61	28	...	...	...	—	—	—	—	—
87-88—Bowling Green	CCHA	45	34	49	83	54	...	...	...	—	—	—	—	—
88-89—Bowling Green	CCHA	44	22	46	68	46	...	...	...	—	—	—	—	—
89-90—Bowling Green	CCHA	44	30	52	82	42	...	...	...	—	—	—	—	—
—Peoria	IHL	3	1	1	2	0	...	...	...	—	—	—	—	—
90-91—St. Louis	NHL	4	0	3	3	2	-2	0	0	—	—	—	—	—
—Peoria	IHL	73	36	79	115	91	...	...	...	17	9	12	21	16
91-92—St. Louis	NHL	79	23	36	59	66	-5	3	0	6	3	3	6	21
92-93—St. Louis	NHL	82	22	51	73	62	2	5	2	11	1	6	7	6
93-94—Winnipeg	NHL	83	33	41	74	80	-38	4	5	—	—	—	—	—
94-95—Winnipeg	NHL	48	14	23	37	26	-12	4	1	—	—	—	—	—
95-96—Hartford	NHL	81	29	29	58	78	-7	12	2	—	—	—	—	—
96-97—Hartford	NHL	66	9	29	38	34	-21	2	1	—	—	—	—	—
97-98—Carolina	NHL	81	21	24	45	50	-17	6	0	—	—	—	—	—
98-99—Carolina	NHL	35	8	13	21	36	1	3	0	—	—	—	—	—
—Chicago	NHL	27	4	10	14	13	8	0	0	—	—	—	—	—
—Ottawa	NHL	3	1	1	2	2	-1	0	0	4	1	3	4	0
99-00—Atlanta	NHL	58	14	19	33	47	-24	4	0	—	—	—	—	—
—Los Angeles	NHL	5	1	1	2	0	1	0	0	1	0	0	0	0
00-01—Los Angeles	NHL	78	11	11	22	54	-13	0	0	13	2	2	4	4
NHL Totals (11 years)		730	190	291	481	550	-128	43	11	35	7	14	21	31

EMMA, DAVID   C/RW

PERSONAL: Born January 14, 1969, in Cranston, R.I. ... 5-11/187. ... Shoots left. ... Full Name: David Anaclethe Emma.

TRANSACTIONS/CAREER NOTES: Selected by New Jersey Devils in sixth round (sixth Devils pick, 110th overall) of NHL entry draft (June 17, 1989). ... Signed as free agent by Boston Bruins (August 27, 1996). ... Signed as free agent by Florida Panthers (August 1, 2000). ... Traded by Panthers to Washington Capitals for D Remi Royer (March 3, 2001).

HONORS: Named to Hockey East All-Freshman team (1987-88). ... Named to Hockey East All-Star second team (1988-89). ... Named to Hockey East All-Star first team (1989-90 and 1990-91). ... Won Hobey Baker Memorial Award (1990-91). ... Named Hockey East Player of the Year (1990-91). ... Named to NCAA All-America East first team (1989-90 and 1990-91). ... Named to Hockey East All-Decade team (1994).

Season Team	League	Gms.	G	A	Pts.	PIM	+/-	PP	SH	Gms.	G	A	Pts.	PIM
				REGULAR SEASON								PLAYOFFS		
86-87—Bishop Hendricken	R.I.H.S.					Statistics unavailable.								
87-88—Boston College	Hockey East	30	19	16	35	30	...	...	...	—	—	—	—	—
88-89—Boston College	Hockey East	36	20	31	51	36	...	...	...	—	—	—	—	—
89-90—Boston College	Hockey East	42	38	34	*72	46	...	...	...	—	—	—	—	—
90-91—Boston College	Hockey East	39	35	46	81	44	...	...	...	—	—	—	—	—
91-92—U.S. national team	Int'l	55	15	16	31	32	...	...	...	—	—	—	—	—
—U.S. Olympic team	Int'l	6	0	1	1	6	...	...	...	—	—	—	—	—
—Utica	AHL	15	4	7	11	12	...	...	...	4	1	1	2	2
92-93—Utica	AHL	61	21	40	61	47	...	...	...	5	2	1	3	6
—New Jersey	NHL	2	0	0	0	0	0	0	0	—	—	—	—	—
93-94—New Jersey	NHL	15	5	5	10	2	0	1	0	—	—	—	—	—
—Albany	AHL	56	26	29	55	53	...	...	...	5	1	2	3	8
94-95—New Jersey	NHL	6	0	1	1	0	-2	0	0	—	—	—	—	—
—Albany	AHL	1	0	0	0	0	...	...	...	—	—	—	—	—

Season Team	League	Gms.	G	A	Pts.	PIM	+/-	PP	SH	Gms.	G	A	Pts.	PIM
		REGULAR SEASON								**PLAYOFFS**				
95-96—Detroit	IHL	79	30	32	62	75	...	...	...	11	5	2	7	2
96-97—Boston	NHL	5	0	0	0	0	-1	0	0	—	—	—	—	—
—Providence	AHL	53	10	18	28	24	...	...	...	—	—	—	—	—
—Phoenix	IHL	8	0	4	4	4	...	...	...	—	—	—	—	—
97-98—Klagenfurt	Austria	28	17	18	35	26	...	...	...	—	—	—	—	—
98-99—Klagenfurt	Austria	26	15	32	47	49	...	...	...	—	—	—	—	—
—Klagenfurt	Alpenliga	15	8	7	15	16	...	...	...	—	—	—	—	—
99-00—Klagenfurt	Austria	32	26	28	54	...	...	...		—	—	—	—	—
00-01—Louisville	AHL	55	22	28	50	63	...	...	...	—	—	—	—	—
—Florida	NHL	6	0	0	0	0	-1	0	0	—	—	—	—	—
—Portland	AHL	16	2	8	10	6	...	...	...	2	0	0	0	0
NHL Totals (5 years)		34	5	6	11	2	-4	1	0					

EMMONS, JOHN   C

PERSONAL: Born August 17, 1974, in San Jose, Calif. ... 6-0/185. ... Shoots left. ... Full Name: John T. Emmons.
TRANSACTIONS/CAREER NOTES: Selected by Calgary Flames in fifth round (seventh Flames pick, 122nd overall) of NHL entry draft (June 26, 1993). ... Signed as free agent by Ottawa Senators (July 28, 1998). ... Suffered concussion (February 18, 2001); missed two games. ... Traded by Senators to Tampa Bay Lightning for D Craig Millar (March 13, 2001).

Season Team	League	Gms.	G	A	Pts.	PIM	+/-	PP	SH	Gms.	G	A	Pts.	PIM
		REGULAR SEASON								**PLAYOFFS**				
90-91—New Canaan H.S.	Conn. H.S.	20	19	37	56	20	...	...	...	—	—	—	—	—
91-92—New Canaan H.S.	Conn. H.S.	22	24	49	73	24	...	...	...	—	—	—	—	—
92-93—Yale University	ECAC	28	3	5	8	66	...	...	...	—	—	—	—	—
93-94—Yale University	ECAC	25	5	12	17	66	...	...	...	—	—	—	—	—
94-95—Yale University	ECAC	28	4	16	20	57	...	...	...	—	—	—	—	—
95-96—Yale University	ECAC	31	8	20	28	124	...	...	...	—	—	—	—	—
96-97—Dayton	ECHL	69	20	37	57	62	...	...	...	4	0	1	1	2
—Fort Wayne	IHL	1	0	0	0	0	...	...	...	—	—	—	—	—
97-98—Michigan	IHL	81	9	25	34	85	...	...	...	4	1	1	2	10
98-99—Detroit	IHL	75	13	22	35	172	...	...	...	11	4	5	9	22
99-00—Grand Rapids	IHL	64	10	16	26	78	...	...	...	16	1	4	5	28
—Ottawa	NHL	10	0	0	0	6	-2	0	0	—	—	—	—	—
00-01—Grand Rapids	IHL	9	1	0	1	4	...	...	...	—	—	—	—	—
—Ottawa	NHL	41	1	1	2	20	-5	0	0	—	—	—	—	—
—Tampa Bay	NHL	12	1	1	2	22	0	0	0	—	—	—	—	—
NHL Totals (2 years)		63	2	2	4	48	-7	0	0					

ERIKSSON, ANDERS   D   MAPLE LEAFS

PERSONAL: Born January 9, 1975, in Bollnas, Sweden. ... 6-2/220. ... Shoots left.
TRANSACTIONS/CAREER NOTES: Selected by Detroit Red Wings in first round (first Red Wings pick, 22nd overall) of NHL entry draft (June 26, 1993). ... Traded by Red Wings with first-round pick (D Steve McCarthy) in 1999 draft and first-round pick (G Adam Munro) in 2001 draft to Chicago Blackhawks for D Chris Chelios (March 23, 1999). ... Traded by Blackhawks to Florida Panthers for D Jaroslav Spacek (November 6, 2000). ... Injured knee (November 10, 2000); missed one game. ... Sprained knee (February 22, 2001); missed nine games. ... Signed as free agent by Toronto Maple Leafs (July 4, 2001).
MISCELLANEOUS: Member of Stanley Cup championship team (1998).

Season Team	League	Gms.	G	A	Pts.	PIM	+/-	PP	SH	Gms.	G	A	Pts.	PIM
		REGULAR SEASON								**PLAYOFFS**				
92-93—MoDo Ornskoldsvik	Sweden	20	0	2	2	2	...	...	...	—	—	—	—	—
93-94—MoDo Ornskoldsvik	Sweden	38	2	8	10	42	...	...	...	11	0	0	0	8
94-95—MoDo Ornskoldsvik	Sweden	39	3	6	9	54	...	...	...	—	—	—	—	—
95-96—Adirondack	AHL	75	6	36	42	64	...	...	...	3	0	0	0	0
—Detroit	NHL	1	0	0	0	2	1	0	0	3	0	0	0	0
96-97—Detroit	NHL	23	0	6	6	10	5	0	0	—	—	—	—	—
—Adirondack	AHL	44	3	25	28	36	...	...	...	4	0	1	1	4
97-98—Detroit	NHL	66	7	14	21	32	21	1	0	18	0	5	5	16
98-99—Detroit	NHL	61	2	10	12	34	5	0	0	—	—	—	—	—
—Chicago	NHL	11	0	8	8	0	6	0	0	—	—	—	—	—
99-00—Chicago	NHL	73	3	25	28	20	4	0	0	—	—	—	—	—
00-01—Chicago	NHL	13	2	3	5	2	-4	1	0	—	—	←	—	—
—Florida	NHL	60	0	21	21	28	2	0	0	—	—	—	—	—
NHL Totals (6 years)		308	14	87	101	128	40	2	0	21	0	5	5	16

ERSKINE, JOHN   D   STARS

PERSONAL: Born June 26, 1980, in Kingston, Ont. ... 6-4/197. ... Shoots left.
TRANSACTIONS/CAREER NOTES: Selected by Dallas Stars in second round (first Stars pick, 39th overall) of NHL entry draft (June 27, 1998).
HONORS: Named to OHL All-Rookie second team (1997-98). ... Won Max Kaminsky Trophy (1999-2000). ... Named to OHL All-Star first team (1999-2000). ... Named to Can.HL All-Star second team (1999-2000).

Season Team	League	Gms.	G	A	Pts.	PIM	+/-	PP	SH	Gms.	G	A	Pts.	PIM
		REGULAR SEASON								**PLAYOFFS**				
96-97—Quinte	Tier II Jr. A	48	4	16	20	241	...	...	...	—	—	—	—	—
97-98—London	OHL	55	0	9	9	205	...	...	...	16	0	5	5	25
98-99—London	OHL	57	8	12	20	208	...	...	...	25	5	10	15	38
99-00—London	OHL	58	12	31	43	177	...	...	...	—	—	—	—	—
00-01—Utah	IHL	77	1	8	9	284	...	...	...	—	—	—	—	—

ESCHE, ROBERT   G   COYOTES

PERSONAL: Born January 22, 1978, in Utica, N.Y. ... 6-0/188. ... Catches left. ... Name pronounced EHSH.

TRANSACTIONS/CAREER NOTES: Selected by Phoenix Coyotes in sixth round (fifth Coyotes pick, 139th overall) of NHL entry draft (June 22, 1996).

HONORS: Named to OHL All-Star second team (1997-98).

		REGULAR SEASON								PLAYOFFS						
Season Team	League	Gms.	Min	W	L	T	GA	SO	Avg.	Gms.	Min.	W	L	GA	SO	Avg.
95-96 —Det. Jr. Red Wings........	OHL	23	1219	13	6	0	76	1	3.74	3	105	0	2	4	0	2.29
96-97 —Det. Jr. Red Wings........	OHL	58	3241	24	28	2	206	2	3.81	5	317	1	4	19	0	3.60
97-98 —Plymouth	OHL	48	2810	29	13	4	135	3	2.88	15	869	8	†7	45	0	3.11
98-99 —Springfield	AHL	55	2957	24	20	6	138	1	2.80	1	60	0	1	4	0	4.00
—Phoenix.......................	NHL	3	130	0	1	0	7	0	3.23	—	—	—	—	—	—	—
99-00 —Houston	IHL	7	419	4	2	1	16	2	2.29	—	—	—	—	—	—	—
—Phoenix.......................	NHL	8	408	2	5	0	23	0	3.38	—	—	—	—	—	—	—
—Springfield	AHL	21	1207	9	9	2	61	2	3.03	3	180	1	2	12	0	4.00
00-01 —Phoenix.......................	NHL	25	1350	10	8	4	68	2	3.02	—	—	—	—	—	—	—
NHL Totals (3 years).............		36	1888	12	14	4	98	2	3.11							

ESSENSA, BOB   G

PERSONAL: Born January 14, 1965, in Toronto. ... 6-0/188. ... Catches left. ... Full Name: Robert Earle Essensa. ... Name pronounced EH-sihn-zuh.

TRANSACTIONS/CAREER NOTES: Selected by Winnipeg Jets in fourth round (fifth Jets pick, 69th overall) of NHL entry draft (June 8, 1983). ... Injured groin (September 1990); missed three weeks. ... Sprained knee (October 12, 1991); missed four games. ... Injured left hamstring (December 8, 1991); missed four games. ... Sprained knee (March 6, 1992); missed seven games. ... Strained knee (March 6, 1993); missed two games. ... Traded by Jets with D Sergei Bautin to Detroit Red Wings for G Tim Cheveldae and LW Dallas Drake (March 8, 1994). ... Traded by Red Wings to Edmonton Oilers for future considerations (June 14, 1996). ... Signed as free agent by Phoenix Coyotes (September 5, 1999). ... Strained hamstring (January 4, 2000); missed seven games. ... Signed as free agent by Vancouver Canucks (July 26, 2000). ... Released by Canucks (June 26, 2001).

HONORS: Named to CCHA All-Star first team (1984-85). ... Named to CCHA All-Star second team (1985-86). ... Named to NHL All-Rookie team (1989-90).

MISCELLANEOUS: Holds Edmonton Oilers record for goals-against average (2.73). ... Stopped a penalty shot attempt (vs. Philippe Bozon, November 3, 1993; vs. Keith Tkachuk, January 24, 1998). ... Allowed a penalty shot goal (vs. Steve Yzerman, February 13, 1989; vs. Mike Craig, January 21, 1991; vs. Paul Ranheim, October 31, 1993). ... Holds Phoenix Coyotes franchise all-time records for games played by a goaltender (311) and wins (129).

		REGULAR SEASON								PLAYOFFS						
Season Team	League	Gms.	Min	W	L	T	GA	SO	Avg.	Gms.	Min.	W	L	GA	SO	Avg.
81-82 —Henry Carr H.S.............	MTHL	17	948	...	...	...	79	...	5.00	—	—	—	—	—	—	—
82-83 —Henry Carr H.S.............	MTHL	31	1840	...	...	...	98	2	3.20	—	—	—	—	—	—	—
83-84 —Michigan State	CCHA	17	947	11	4	0	44	2	2.79	—	—	—	—	—	—	—
84-85 —Michigan State	CCHA	18	1059	15	2	0	29	2	1.64	—	—	—	—	—	—	—
85-86 —Michigan State	CCHA	23	1333	17	4	1	74	1	3.33	—	—	—	—	—	—	—
86-87 —Michigan State	CCHA	25	1383	19	3	1	64	*2	*2.78	—	—	—	—	—	—	—
87-88 —Moncton......................	AHL	27	1287	7	11	1	100	1	4.66	—	—	—	—	—	—	—
88-89 —Winnipeg....................	NHL	20	1102	6	8	3	68	1	3.70	—	—	—	—	—	—	—
—Fort Wayne.................	IHL	22	1287	14	7	0	70	0	3.26	—	—	—	—	—	—	—
89-90 —Moncton......................	AHL	6	358	3	3	0	15	0	2.51	—	—	—	—	—	—	—
—Winnipeg...................	NHL	36	2035	18	9	5	107	1	3.15	4	206	2	1	12	0	3.50
90-91 —Moncton......................	AHL	2	125	1	0	1	6	0	2.88	—	—	—	—	—	—	—
—Winnipeg...................	NHL	55	2916	19	24	6	153	4	3.15	—	—	—	—	—	—	—
91-92 —Winnipeg....................	NHL	47	2627	21	17	6	126	†5	2.88	1	33	0	0	3	0	5.45
92-93 —Winnipeg....................	NHL	67	3855	33	26	6	227	2	3.53	6	367	2	4	20	0	3.27
93-94 —Winnipeg....................	NHL	56	3136	19	30	6	201	1	3.85	—	—	—	—	—	—	—
—Detroit.......................	NHL	13	778	4	7	2	34	1	2.62	2	109	0	2	9	0	4.95
94-95 —San Diego	IHL	16	919	6	8	‡1	52	0	3.39	1	59	0	1	3	0	3.05
95-96 —Adirondack..................	AHL	3	178	1	2	0	11	0	3.71	—	—	—	—	—	—	—
—Fort Wayne.................	IHL	45	2529	24	14	‡5	122	1	2.89	5	298	2	3	12	0	2.42
96-97 —Edmonton	NHL	19	868	4	8	0	41	1	2.83	—	—	—	—	—	—	—
97-98 —Edmonton	NHL	16	825	6	6	1	35	0	2.55	1	27	0	0	1	0	2.22
98-99 —Edmonton	NHL	39	2091	12	14	6	96	0	2.75	—	—	—	—	—	—	—
99-00 —Phoenix.......................	NHL	30	1573	13	10	3	73	1	2.78	—	—	—	—	—	—	—
00-01 —Vancouver	NHL	39	2059	18	12	3	92	1	2.68	2	122	0	2	6	0	2.95
NHL Totals (11 years)...........		437	23865	173	171	47	1253	18	3.15	16	864	4	9	51	0	3.54

FANKHOUSER, SCOTT   G   THRASHERS

PERSONAL: Born July 1, 1975, in Bismark, N.D. ... 6-2/206. ... Catches left.

TRANSACTIONS/CAREER NOTES: Selected by St. Louis Blues in 11th round (eighth Blues pick, 276th overall) of NHL entry draft (June 29, 1994). ... Signed as free agent by Atlanta Thrashers (August 24, 1999). ... Injured hand (January 31, 2000); missed two games.

HONORS: Shared James Norris Memorial Trophy with Norm Maracle (2000-01).

MISCELLANEOUS: Holds Atlanta Thrashers all-time record for goals-against average (3.31).

E

F

			REGULAR SEASON							PLAYOFFS						
Season Team	League	Gms.	Min	W	L	T	GA	SO	Avg.	Gms.	Min.	W	L	GA	SO	Avg.
95-96 —Mass.-Lowell..............	Hockey East	11	499	4	4	1	37	...	4.45	—	—	—	—	—	—	—
96-97 —Mass.-Lowell..............	Hockey East	11	518	2	4	1	38	...	4.40	—	—	—	—	—	—	—
97-98 —Mass.-Lowell..............	Hockey East	16	798	4	7	2	48	...	3.61	—	—	—	—	—	—	—
98-99 —Mass.-Lowell..............	Hockey East	32	1729	16	14	0	80	1	2.78	—	—	—	—	—	—	—
99-00 —Greenville	ECHL	8	419	7	1	0	18	0	2.58	—	—	—	—	—	—	—
—Orlando	IHL	6	320	3	2	1	14	0	2.63	—	—	—	—	—	—	—
—Atlanta........................	NHL	16	920	2	11	2	49	0	3.20	—	—	—	—	—	—	—
—Louisville.....................	AHL	1	59	0	1	0	3	0	3.05	—	—	—	—	—	—	—
00-01 —Orlando	IHL	28	1603	13	12	‡3	69	1	2.58	1	37	0	0	3	0	4.86
—Atlanta........................	NHL	7	260	2	1	0	16	0	3.69	—	—	—	—	—	—	—
NHL Totals (2 years).............		23	1180	4	12	2	65	0	3.31							

FARKAS, JEFF   C   MAPLE LEAFS

PERSONAL: Born January 24, 1978, in Amherst, Mass. ... 6-0/185. ... Shoots left.
TRANSACTIONS/CAREER NOTES: Selected by Toronto Maple Leafs in third round (first Maple Leafs pick, 57th overall) of NHL entry draft (June 21, 1997).
HONORS: Named to Hockey East All-Star first team (1999-2000). ... Named to NCAA All-America (East) first team (1999-2000). ... Named to NCAA All-Tournament team (1999-2000).

			REGULAR SEASON							PLAYOFFS				
Season Team	League	Gms.	G	A	Pts.	PIM	+/-	PP	SH	Gms.	G	A	Pts.	PIM
94-95 —Niagara	NAJHL	53	54	58	112	34	...	...	...	—	—	—	—	—
95-96 —Niagara	NAJHL	74	64	107	171	95	...	...	...	—	—	—	—	—
96-97 —Boston College	Hockey East	35	13	23	36	34	...	...	...	—	—	—	—	—
97-98 —Boston College	Hockey East	40	11	28	39	42	...	...	...	—	—	—	—	—
98-99 —Boston College	Hockey East	43	32	25	57	56	...	...	...	—	—	—	—	—
99-00 —Boston College	Hockey East	41	32	26	*58	59	...	...	...	—	—	—	—	—
—Toronto	NHL	—	—	—	—	—	—	—	—	3	1	0	1	2
00-01 —St. John's...................	AHL	77	28	40	68	62	...	...	...	4	1	2	3	4
—Toronto	NHL	2	0	0	0	2	-1	0	0	—	—	—	—	—
NHL Totals (2 years)...........		2	0	0	0	2	-1	0	0	3	1	0	1	2

FARRELL, MIKE   D   CAPITALS

PERSONAL: Born October 20, 1978, in Edina, Minn. ... 6-1/205. ... Shoots right. ... Full Name: Michael Farrell.
TRANSACTIONS/CAREER NOTES: Selected by Washington Capitals in eighth round (ninth Capitals pick, 220th overall) of NHL entry draft (June 27, 1998).

			REGULAR SEASON							PLAYOFFS				
Season Team	League	Gms.	G	A	Pts.	PIM	+/-	PP	SH	Gms.	G	A	Pts.	PIM
97-98 —Providence College	Hockey East	33	5	8	13	32	...	...	...	—	—	—	—	—
98-99 —Providence College	Hockey East	29	3	12	15	51	...	...	...	—	—	—	—	—
99-00 —Providence College	Hockey East	36	3	6	9	71	...	...	...	—	—	—	—	—
—Portland	AHL	7	2	0	2	0	...	...	...	4	0	1	1	0
00-01 —Portland	AHL	79	6	18	24	61	...	...	...	3	0	2	2	4

FATA, RICO   RW   FLAMES

PERSONAL: Born February 12, 1980, in Sault Ste. Marie, Ont. ... 5-11/197. ... Shoots left. ... Brother of Drew Fata, defenseman, Pittsburgh Penguins organization.
TRANSACTIONS/CAREER NOTES: Selected by Calgary Flames in first round (first Flames pick, sixth overall) of NHL entry draft (June 27, 1998).

			REGULAR SEASON							PLAYOFFS				
Season Team	League	Gms.	G	A	Pts.	PIM	+/-	PP	SH	Gms.	G	A	Pts.	PIM
95-96 —Sault Ste. Marie	OMJHL	62	11	15	26	52	...	...	...	—	—	—	—	—
96-97 —London	OHL	59	19	34	53	76	...	...	...	—	—	—	—	—
97-98 —London	OHL	64	43	33	76	110	...	...	...	16	9	5	14	*49
98-99 —Calgary	NHL	20	0	1	1	4	0	0	0	—	—	—	—	—
—London	OHL	23	15	18	33	41	...	...	...	25	10	12	22	42
99-00 —Calgary	NHL	2	0	0	0	0	-1	0	0	—	—	—	—	—
—Saint John	AHL	76	29	29	58	65	...	...	...	3	0	0	0	4
00-01 —Saint John	AHL	70	23	29	52	129	...	...	...	19	2	3	5	22
—Calgary	NHL	5	0	0	0	6	-3	0	0	—	—	—	—	—
NHL Totals (3 years)...........		27	0	1	1	10	-4	0	0					

FEDOROV, FEDOR   C   CANUCKS

PERSONAL: Born June 11, 1981, in Moscow, U.S.S.R. ... 6-3/187. ... Shoots left. ... Brother of Sergei Fedorov, center, Detroit Red Wings. ... Name pronounced FEH-duh FEH-duhr-rahf.
TRANSACTIONS/CAREER NOTES: Selected by Tampa Bay Lightning in sixth round (seventh Lightning pick, 182nd overall) of NHL entry draft (June 26, 1999). ... Returned to draft pool by Lightning and selected by Vancouver Canucks in third round (second Canucks pick, 66th overall) of NHL entry draft (June 23, 2001).

F

Season Team	League	REGULAR SEASON								PLAYOFFS				
		Gms.	G	A	Pts.	PIM	+/-	PP	SH	Gms.	G	A	Pts.	PIM
97-98—Detroit Little Caesars ..	MNHL	13	3	7	10	18	...	...	...	—	—	—	—	—
98-99—Port Huron	UHL	42	2	5	7	20	...	...	...	—	—	—	—	—
99-00—Windsor	OHL	60	7	10	17	115	...	...	...	12	1	0	1	4
00-01—Sudbury	OHL	37	33	45	78	88	...	...	...	12	4	6	10	36

FEDOROV, SERGEI — C — RED WINGS

PERSONAL: Born December 13, 1969, in Pskov, U.S.S.R. ... 6-2/200. ... Shoots left. ... Brother of Fedor Fedorov, center, Vancouver Canucks organization. ... Name pronounced SAIR-gay FEH-duh-rahf.

TRANSACTIONS/CAREER NOTES: Selected by Detroit Red Wings in fourth round (fourth Red Wings pick, 74th overall) of NHL entry draft (June 17, 1989). ... Bruised left shoulder (October 1990). ... Reinjured left shoulder (January 16, 1991). ... Sprained left shoulder (November 27, 1992); missed seven games. ... Suffered from the flu (January 30, 1993); missed two games. ... Suffered charley horse (February 11, 1993); missed one game. ... Suffered concussion (April 5, 1994); missed two games. ... Suspended four games without pay and fined $500 by NHL for high-sticking incident in playoff game (May 17, 1994); suspension reduced to three games due to abbreviated 1994-95 season. ... Suffered from the flu (February 7, 1995); missed one game. ... Bruised right hamstring (April 9, 1995); missed one game. ... Suffered from tonsillitis (October 6, 1995); missed three games. ... Sprained left wrist (December 15, 1995); missed one game. ... Strained groin (January 9, 1997); missed two games. ... Reinjured groin (January 20, 1997); missed six games. ... Missed first 59 games of 1997-98 season due to contract dispute. ... Tendered offer sheet by Carolina Hurricanes (February 19, 1998). ... Offer matched by Red Wings (February 26, 1998). ... Suspended two games and fined $1,000 by NHL for illegal check (March 31, 1998). ... Suspended five games by NHL for slashing incident (March 3, 1999). ... Suffered head injury (November 20, 1999); missed six games. ... Injured neck (January 16, 2000); missed three games. ... Injured wrist (February 18, 2000); missed five games. ... Fractured nose (February 23, 2001); missed six games.

HONORS: Named to NHL All-Rookie team (1990-91). ... Played in NHL All-Star Game (1992, 1994, 1996 and 2001). ... Named NHL Player of the Year by THE SPORTING NEWS (1993-94). ... Named to THE SPORTING NEWS All-Star first team (1993-94). ... Won Hart Memorial Trophy (1993-94). ... Won Frank J. Selke Trophy (1993-94 and 1995-96). ... Won Lester B. Pearson Award (1993-94). ... Named to NHL All-Star first team (1993-94).

MISCELLANEOUS: Member of Stanley Cup championship team (1997 and 1998). ... Member of silver-medal-winning Russian Olympic team (1998). ... Scored on a penalty shot (vs. Andy Moog, December 27, 1993). ... Failed to score on a penalty shot (vs. Kelly Hrudey, February 12, 1995).

STATISTICAL PLATEAUS: Three-goal games: 1993-94 (1), 2000-01 (1). Total: 2. ... Four-goal games: 1994-95 (1). ... Five-goal games: 1996-97 (1). ... Total hat tricks: 4.

Season Team	League	REGULAR SEASON								PLAYOFFS				
		Gms.	G	A	Pts.	PIM	+/-	PP	SH	Gms.	G	A	Pts.	PIM
85-86—Dynamo Minsk	USSR	15	6	1	7	10				—				
86-87—CSKA Moscow	USSR	29	6	6	12	12	...	...	...	—				
87-88—CSKA Moscow	USSR	48	7	9	16	20	...	...	...	—				
88-89—CSKA Moscow	USSR	44	9	8	17	35	...	...	...	—				
89-90—CSKA Moscow	USSR	48	19	10	29	20	...	...	...	—				
90-91—Detroit	NHL	77	31	48	79	66	11	11	3	7	1	5	6	4
91-92—Detroit	NHL	80	32	54	86	72	26	7	2	11	5	5	10	8
92-93—Detroit	NHL	73	34	53	87	72	33	13	4	7	3	6	9	23
93-94—Detroit	NHL	82	56	64	120	34	48	13	4	7	1	7	8	6
94-95—Detroit	NHL	42	20	30	50	24	6	7	3	17	7	*17	*24	6
95-96—Detroit	NHL	78	39	68	107	48	49	11	3	19	2	*18	20	10
96-97—Detroit	NHL	74	30	33	63	30	29	9	2	20	8	12	20	12
97-98—Russian Oly. team	Int'l	6	1	5	6	8	...			—				
—Detroit	NHL	21	6	11	17	25	10	2	0	22	10	10	20	12
98-99—Detroit	NHL	77	26	37	63	66	9	6	2	10	1	8	9	8
99-00—Detroit	NHL	68	27	35	62	22	8	4	4	—				
00-01—Detroit	NHL	75	32	37	69	40	12	14	2	6	2	5	7	0
NHL Totals (11 years)		747	333	470	803	499	241	97	29	126	40	93	133	89

FEDORUK, TODD — LW — FLYERS

PERSONAL: Born February 13, 1979, in Redwater, Alta. ... 6-1/205.

TRANSACTIONS/CAREER NOTES: Selected by Philadelphia Flyers in seventh round (sixth Flyers pick, 164th overall) of NHL entry draft (June 21, 1997). ... Strained elbow (January 13, 2001); missed two games. ... Lacerated eyelid (January 31, 2001); missed one game.

Season Team	League	REGULAR SEASON								PLAYOFFS				
		Gms.	G	A	Pts.	PIM	+/-	PP	SH	Gms.	G	A	Pts.	PIM
96-97—Kelowna	WHL	31	1	5	6	87	...	...	...	6	0	0	0	13
97-98—Kelowna	WHL	31	3	5	8	120	...	...	...	—				
—Regina	WHL	21	4	3	7	80	...	...	...	9	1	2	3	23
98-99—Regina	WHL	39	12	12	24	107	...	...	...	—				
—Prince Albert	WHL	28	6	4	10	75	...	...	...	—				
99-00—Philadelphia	AHL	19	1	2	3	40	...	...	...	5	0	1	1	2
—Trenton	ECHL	18	2	5	7	118	...	...	...	—				
00-01—Philadelphia	AHL	14	0	1	1	49	...	...	...	—				
—Philadelphia	NHL	53	5	5	10	109	0	0	0	2	0	0	0	20
NHL Totals (1 year)		53	5	5	10	109	0	0	0	2	0	0	0	20

FEDOTENKO, RUSLAN — RW — FLYERS

PERSONAL: Born January 18, 1979, in Kiev, U.S.S.R. ... 6-2/190.

TRANSACTIONS/CAREER NOTES: Signed as non-drafted free agent by Philadelphia Flyers (August 3, 1999).

F

Season Team	League	REGULAR SEASON								PLAYOFFS				
		Gms.	G	A	Pts.	PIM	+/-	PP	SH	Gms.	G	A	Pts.	PIM
97-98—Melfort	SJHL	68	35	31	66	...	...	...	...	—	—	—	—	—
98-99—Sioux City	USHL	55	43	34	77	139	...	...	...	5	5	1	6	9
99-00—Philadelphia	AHL	67	16	34	50	42	...	...	...	2	0	0	0	0
—Trenton	ECHL	8	5	3	8	9	...	...	...	—	—	—	—	—
00-01—Philadelphia	AHL	8	1	0	1	8	...	...	...	—	—	—	—	—
—Philadelphia	NHL	74	16	20	36	72	8	3	0	6	0	1	1	4
NHL Totals (1 year)		74	16	20	36	72	8	3	0	6	0	1	1	4

FERENCE, ANDREW   D   PENGUINS

PERSONAL: Born March 17, 1979, in Edmonton. ... 5-10/190. ... Shoots left.
TRANSACTIONS/CAREER NOTES: Selected by Pittsburgh Penguins in eighth round (eighth Penguins pick, 208th overall) of 1997 NHL entry draft. ... Suffered from the flu (December 9, 1999); missed four games.
HONORS: Named to WHL (West) All-Star first team (1997-98). ... Won Can.HL Plus/Minus Award (1997-98). ... Named to WHL (West) All-Star second team (1998-99).

Season Team	League	REGULAR SEASON								PLAYOFFS				
		Gms.	G	A	Pts.	PIM	+/-	PP	SH	Gms.	G	A	Pts.	PIM
95-96—Portland	WHL	72	9	31	40	159	...	...	...	7	1	3	4	12
96-97—Portland	WHL	72	12	32	44	163	...	...	...	—	—	—	—	—
97-98—Portland	WHL	72	11	57	68	142	...	...	...	16	2	18	20	28
98-99—Portland	WHL	40	11	21	32	104	...	...	...	4	1	4	5	10
—Kansas City	IHL	5	1	2	3	4	...	...	...	3	0	0	0	9
99-00—Pittsburgh	NHL	30	2	4	6	20	3	0	0	—	—	—	—	—
—Wilkes-Barre/Scranton	AHL	44	8	20	28	58	...	...	...	—	—	—	—	—
00-01—Wilkes-Barre/Scranton	AHL	43	6	18	24	95	...	...	...	3	1	0	1	12
—Pittsburgh	NHL	36	4	11	15	28	6	1	0	18	3	7	10	16
NHL Totals (2 years)		66	6	15	21	48	9	1	0	18	3	7	10	16

FERENCE, BRAD   D   PANTHERS

PERSONAL: Born April 2, 1979, in Calgary. ... 6-3/196. ... Shoots right.
TRANSACTIONS/CAREER NOTES: Selected by Vancouver Canucks in first round (first Canucks pick, 10th overall) of NHL entry draft (June 21, 1997). ... Traded by Canucks with RW Pavel Bure, D Bret Hedican and third-round pick (RW Robert Fried) in 2000 draft to Florida Panthers for D Ed Jovanovski, G Kevin Weekes, C Dave Gagner, C Mike Brown and first-round pick (C Nathan Smith) in 2000 draft (January 17, 1999). ... Fractured jaw (September 4, 2000); missed first nine games of season.
HONORS: Named to Can.HL All-Rookie team (1996-97).

Season Team	League	REGULAR SEASON								PLAYOFFS				
		Gms.	G	A	Pts.	PIM	+/-	PP	SH	Gms.	G	A	Pts.	PIM
95-96—Spokane	WHL	5	0	2	2	18	...	...	...	—	—	—	—	—
96-97—Spokane	WHL	67	6	20	26	324	...	...	...	9	0	4	4	21
97-98—Spokane	WHL	54	9	29	38	213	...	...	...	18	0	7	7	59
98-99—Spokane	WHL	31	3	22	25	125	...	...	...	—	—	—	—	—
—Tri-City	WHL	20	6	15	21	116	...	...	...	12	1	9	10	63
99-00—Louisville	AHL	58	2	7	9	231	...	...	...	2	0	0	0	2
—Florida	NHL	13	0	2	2	46	2	0	0	—	—	—	—	—
00-01—Florida	NHL	14	0	1	1	14	-10	0	0	—	—	—	—	—
—Louisville	AHL	52	3	21	24	200	...	...	...	—	—	—	—	—
NHL Totals (2 years)		27	0	3	3	60	-8	0	0	—	—	—	—	—

F FERGUSON, SCOTT   D   OILERS

PERSONAL: Born January 6, 1973, in Camrose, Alta. ... 6-1/202. ... Shoots left.
TRANSACTIONS/CAREER NOTES: Signed as non-drafted free agent by Edmonton Oilers (June 2, 1994). ... Traded by Oilers to Ottawa Senators for D Frank Musil (March 9, 1998). ... Signed as free agent by Mighty Ducks of Anaheim (July 22, 1998). ... Signed as free agent by Oilers (July 5, 2000).

Season Team	League	REGULAR SEASON								PLAYOFFS				
		Gms.	G	A	Pts.	PIM	+/-	PP	SH	Gms.	G	A	Pts.	PIM
90-91—Kamloops	WHL	4	0	0	0	0	...	...	...	—	—	—	—	—
91-92—Kamloops	WHL	62	4	10	14	148	...	...	...	12	0	2	2	21
92-93—Kamloops	WHL	71	4	19	23	206	...	...	...	13	0	2	2	24
93-94—Kamloops	WHL	68	5	49	54	180	...	...	...	19	5	11	16	48
94-95—Wheeling	ECHL	5	1	5	6	16	...	...	...	—	—	—	—	—
—Cape Breton	AHL	58	4	6	10	103	...	...	...	—	—	—	—	—
95-96—Cape Breton	AHL	80	5	16	21	196	...	...	...	—	—	—	—	—
96-97—Hamilton	AHL	74	6	14	20	115	...	...	...	21	5	7	12	59
97-98—Hamilton	AHL	77	7	17	24	150	...	...	...	9	0	3	3	16
—Edmonton	NHL	1	0	0	0	0	1	0	0	—	—	—	—	—
98-99—Cincinnati	AHL	78	4	31	35	144	...	...	...	3	0	0	0	4
—Anaheim	NHL	2	0	1	1	0	0	0	0	—	—	—	—	—
99-00—Cincinnati	AHL	77	7	25	32	166	...	...	...	—	—	—	—	—
00-01—Hamilton	AHL	42	3	18	21	79	...	...	...	—	—	—	—	—
—Edmonton	NHL	20	0	1	1	13	2	0	0	6	0	0	0	0
NHL Totals (3 years)		23	0	2	2	13	3	0	0	6	0	0	0	0

FERNANDEZ, MANNY   G   WILD

PERSONAL: Born August 27, 1974, in Etobicoke, Ont. ... 6-0/185. ... Catches left. ... Full Name: Emmanuel Fernandez. ... Nephew of Jacques Lemaire, head coach, Minnesota Wild; and Hall of Fame center with Montreal Canadiens (1967-68 through 1978-79).
TRANSACTIONS/CAREER NOTES: Selected by Quebec Nordiques in third round (fourth Nordiques pick, 52nd overall) of NHL entry draft (June 20, 1992). ... Traded by Nordiques to Dallas Stars for D Tommy Sjodin and third-round pick (C Chris Drury) in 1994 draft (February 13, 1994). ... Traded by Stars with D Brad Lukowich to Minnesota Wild for third-round pick (C Joel Lundqvist) in 2000 draft and fourth-round pick in 2002 draft (June 12, 2000). ... Injured right ankle (October 14, 2000); missed five games. ... Sprained right knee (March 6, 2001); missed two games. ... Sprained left ankle (March 15, 2001); missed final 11 games of season.
HONORS: Won Guy Lafleur Trophy (1992-93). ... Won Michel Briere Trophy (1993-94). ... Named to QMJHL All-Star first team (1993-94). ... Named to Can.HL All-Star second team (1993-94). ... Named to IHL All-Star second team (1994-95).
MISCELLANEOUS: Stopped a penalty shot attempt (vs. Radek Dvorak, March 13, 2000; vs. Petr Sykora, January 21, 2001). ... Holds Minnesota Wild all-time records for games played by goaltender (42), most wins (19), most shutouts (4) and for goals-against average (2.24).

			REGULAR SEASON							PLAYOFFS						
Season Team	League	Gms.	Min	W	L	T	GA	SO	Avg.	Gms.	Min.	W	L	GA	SO	Avg.
91-92—Laval	QMJHL	31	1593	14	13	2	99	1	3.73	9	468	3	5	†39	0	5.00
92-93—Laval	QMJHL	43	2348	26	14	2	141	1	3.60	13	818	12	1	42	0	3.08
93-94—Laval	QMJHL	51	2776	29	14	1	143	*5	3.09	19	1116	14	5	49	†1	*2.63
94-95—Kalamazoo	IHL	46	2470	21	10	‡9	115	2	2.79	12	655	9	1	‡30	1	2.75
—Dallas	NHL	1	59	0	1	0	3	0	3.05	—	—	—	—	—	—	—
95-96—Michigan	IHL	47	2663	22	15	‡9	133	†4	3.00	6	372	5	1	14	0	*2.26
—Dallas	NHL	5	249	0	1	1	19	0	4.58	—	—	—	—	—	—	—
96-97—Michigan	IHL	48	2721	20	24	‡2	142	2	3.13	4	277	1	3	15	0	3.25
97-98—Michigan	IHL	55	3023	27	17	5	139	5	2.76	2	89	0	2	7	0	4.72
—Dallas	NHL	2	69	1	0	0	2	0	1.74	1	2	0	0	0	0	...
98-99—Houston	IHL	50	2949	34	6	‡9	116	2	2.36	*19	*1126	*11	*8	49	1	2.61
—Dallas	NHL	1	60	0	1	0	2	0	2.00	—	—	—	—	—	—	—
99-00—Dallas	NHL	24	1353	11	8	3	48	1	2.13	1	17	0	0	1	0	3.53
00-01—Minnesota	NHL	42	2461	19	17	4	92	4	2.24	—	—	—	—	—	—	—
NHL Totals (6 years)		75	4251	31	28	8	166	5	2.34	2	19	0	0	1	0	3.16

FERRARO, RAY   C   THRASHERS

PERSONAL: Born August 23, 1964, in Trail, B.C. ... 5-9/200. ... Shoots left. ... Name pronounced fuh-RAH-roh.
TRANSACTIONS/CAREER NOTES: Selected by Hartford Whalers in fifth round (fifth Whalers pick, 88th overall) of NHL entry draft (June 9, 1982). ... Traded by Whalers to New York Islanders for D Doug Crossman (November 13, 1990). ... Fractured right fibula (December 10, 1992); missed 36 games. ... Suffered from the flu (March 25, 1993); missed one game. ... Injured knee (March 9, 1995); missed one game. ... Signed as free agent by New York Rangers (July 19, 1995). ... Traded by Rangers with C Nathan Lafayette, C Ian Laperriere, D Mattias Norstrom and fourth-round pick (D Sean Blanchard) in 1997 draft to Los Angeles Kings for RW Shane Churla, LW Jari Kurri and D Marty McSorley (March 14, 1996). ... Strained neck (February 1, 1997); missed one game. ... Tore cartilage in left knee (October 5, 1997); missed 17 games. ... Underwent knee surgery (December 9, 1997); missed eight games. ... Strained lower back (January 20, 1998); missed two games. ... Suffered from the flu (March 2, 1998); missed one game. ... Strained left knee (March 21, 1998); missed three games. ... Reinjured left knee (April 11, 1998); missed three games. ... Tore lateral meniscus in right knee (January 5, 1999); missed eight games. ... Signed as free agent by Atlanta Thrashers (August 2, 1999). ... Strained neck (November 22, 2000); missed one game.
HONORS: Won WHL Most Valuable Player Trophy (1983-84). ... Won Bob Brownridge Memorial Trophy (1983-84). ... Won WHL Player of the Year Award (1983-84). ... Named to WHL (East) All-Star first team (1983-84). ... Played in NHL All-Star Game (1992).
MISCELLANEOUS: Holds Atlanta Thrashers all-time records for most games played (162), most goals (48), most assists (72) and points (120). ... Scored on a penalty shot (vs. Arturs Irbe, February 21, 2001).
STATISTICAL PLATEAUS: Three-goal games: 1984-85 (2), 1986-87 (1), 1988-89 (1), 1989-90 (1), 1991-92 (1), 1995-96 (1), 2000-01 (2). Total: 9. ... Four-goal games: 1991-92 (1). ... Total hat tricks: 10.

			REGULAR SEASON							PLAYOFFS				
Season Team	League	Gms.	G	A	Pts.	PIM	+/-	PP	SH	Gms.	G	A	Pts.	PIM
81-82—Penticton	BCJHL	48	65	70	135	50	...	...	...	—	—	—	—	—
82-83—Portland	WHL	50	41	49	90	39	...	...	...	14	14	10	24	13
83-84—Brandon	WHL	72	*108	84	*192	84	...	...	...	11	13	15	28	20
84-85—Binghamton	AHL	37	20	13	33	29	...	...	...	—	—	—	—	—
—Hartford	NHL	44	11	17	28	40	-1	6	0	—	—	—	—	—
85-86—Hartford	NHL	76	30	47	77	57	12	14	0	10	3	6	9	4
86-87—Hartford	NHL	80	27	32	59	42	-9	14	0	6	1	1	2	8
87-88—Hartford	NHL	68	21	29	50	81	1	6	0	6	1	1	2	6
88-89—Hartford	NHL	80	41	35	76	86	1	11	0	4	2	0	2	4
89-90—Hartford	NHL	79	25	29	54	109	-15	7	0	7	0	3	3	2
90-91—Hartford	NHL	15	2	5	7	18	-1	1	0	—	—	—	—	—
—New York Islanders	NHL	61	19	16	35	52	-11	5	0	—	—	—	—	—
91-92—New York Islanders	NHL	80	40	40	80	92	25	7	0	—	—	—	—	—
92-93—New York Islanders	NHL	46	14	13	27	40	0	3	0	18	13	7	20	18
—Capital District	AHL	1	0	2	2	2	...	...	...	—	—	—	—	—
93-94—New York Islanders	NHL	82	21	32	53	83	1	5	0	4	1	0	1	6
94-95—New York Islanders	NHL	47	22	21	43	30	1	2	0	—	—	—	—	—
95-96—New York Rangers	NHL	65	25	29	54	82	13	8	0	—	—	—	—	—
—Los Angeles	NHL	11	4	2	6	10	-13	1	0	—	—	—	—	—
96-97—Los Angeles	NHL	81	25	21	46	112	-22	11	0	—	—	—	—	—
97-98—Los Angeles	NHL	40	6	9	15	42	-10	0	0	3	0	1	1	2
98-99—Los Angeles	NHL	65	13	18	31	59	0	4	0	—	—	—	—	—
99-00—Atlanta	NHL	81	19	25	44	88	-33	10	0	—	—	—	—	—
00-01—Atlanta	NHL	81	29	47	76	91	-11	11	0	—	—	—	—	—
NHL Totals (17 years)		1182	394	467	861	1214	-72	126	0	58	21	19	40	50

F

FICHAUD, ERIC   G

PERSONAL: Born November 4, 1975, in Anjou, Que. ... 5-11/171. ... Catches left. ... Name pronounced FEE-shoh.
TRANSACTIONS/CAREER NOTES: Selected by Toronto Maple Leafs in first round (first Maple Leafs pick, 16th overall) of NHL entry draft (June 28, 1994). ... Traded by Maple Leafs to New York Islanders for C Benoit Hogue, third-round pick (RW Ryan Pepperall) in 1995 draft and fifth-round pick (D Brandon Sugden) in 1996 draft (April 6, 1995). ... Strained abdominal muscle (October 12, 1996); missed two games. ... Partially dislocated left shoulder (December 2, 1997); missed seven games. ... Underwent shoulder surgery while assigned to Utah Grizzlies of IHL (January 20, 1998); missed remainder of season. ... Traded by Islanders to Edmonton Oilers for LW Mike Watt (June 18, 1998). ... Traded by Oilers with D Drake Berehowsky and D Greg de Vries to Nashville Predators for F Jim Dowd and G Mikhail Shtalenkov (October 1, 1998). ... Partially dislocated left shoulder (December 8, 1998); missed five games. ... Reinjured shoulder (January 4, 1999) and underwent surgery; missed remainder of season. ... Traded by Predators to Carolina Hurricanes for fourth-round pick (C/RW Yevgeny Pavlov) in 1999 draft and future considerations (June 26, 1999). ... Claimed on waivers by Montreal Canadiens (February 11, 2000). ... Injured shoulder (February 11, 2000); missed 14 games.
HONORS: Named to Memorial Cup All-Star team (1993-94). ... Won Hap Emms Memorial Trophy (1993-94). ... Won QMJHL Top Draft Prospect Award (1993-94). ... Won Guy Lafleur Award (1993-94). ... Named to QMJHL All-Star first team (1994-95).
MISCELLANEOUS: Stopped a penalty shot attempt (vs. Shaun Van Allen, December 1, 1998).

						REGULAR SEASON						PLAYOFFS					
Season Team	League	Gms.	Min	W	L	T	GA	SO	Avg.	Gms.	Min.	W	L	GA	SO	Avg.
92-93—Chicoutimi	QMJHL	43	2040	18	13	1	149	0	4.38	—	—	—	—	—	—	—
93-94—Chicoutimi	QMJHL	63	3493	37	21	3	192	4	3.30	26	1560	16	10	86	†1	3.31
94-95—Chicoutimi	QMJHL	46	2637	21	19	4	151	4	3.44	7	430	2	5	20	0	2.79
95-96—Worcester	AHL	34	1988	13	15	6	97	1	2.93	2	127	1	1	7	0	3.31
—New York Islanders	NHL	24	1234	7	12	2	68	1	3.31	—	—	—	—	—	—	—
96-97—New York Islanders	NHL	34	1759	9	14	4	91	0	3.10	—	—	—	—	—	—	—
97-98—New York Islanders	NHL	17	807	3	8	3	40	0	2.97	—	—	—	—	—	—	—
—Utah	IHL	1	40	0	0	0	3	0	4.50	—	—	—	—	—	—	—
98-99—Milwaukee	IHL	8	480	5	2	†1	25	0	3.13	—	—	—	—	—	—	—
—Nashville	NHL	9	447	0	6	0	24	0	3.22	—	—	—	—	—	—	—
99-00—Carolina	NHL	9	490	3	5	1	24	1	2.94	—	—	—	—	—	—	—
—Quebec	AHL	6	368	4	1	1	17	0	2.77	3	177	0	3	10	0	3.39
00-01—Quebec	AHL	42	2441	19	19	2	127	1	3.12	2	98	0	1	3	0	1.84
—Montreal	NHL	2	62	0	2	0	4	0	3.87	—	—	—	—	—	—	—
NHL Totals (6 years)		95	4799	22	47	10	251	2	3.14							

FINLEY, BRIAN   G   PREDATORS

PERSONAL: Born July 3, 1981, in Sault Ste. Marie, Ont. ... 6-2/180. ... Catches right.
TRANSACTIONS/CAREER NOTES: Selected by Nashville Predators in first round (first Predators pick, sixth overall) of NHL entry draft (June 26, 1999).
HONORS: Named to OHL All-Rookie first team (1997-98). ... Named to Can.HL All-Star second team (1998-99). ... Named to OHL All-Star first team (1998-99).

						REGULAR SEASON						PLAYOFFS					
Season Team	League	Gms.	Min	W	L	T	GA	SO	Avg.	Gms.	Min.	W	L	GA	SO	Avg.
97-98—Barrie	OHL	41	2154	23	14	1	105	3	2.92	5	260	1	3	13	0	3.00
98-99—Barrie	OHL	52	3063	*36	10	4	136	3	2.66	5	323	4	1	15	0	2.79
99-00—Barrie	OHL	47	2540	24	12	6	130	2	3.07	*23	1353	14	†8	*58	1	2.57
00-01—Barrie	OHL	16	818	5	8	0	42	0	3.08	—	—	—	—	—	—	—
—Brampton	OHL	11	631	7	3	1	31	0	2.95	9	503	5	4	26	1	3.10

FINLEY, JEFF   D   BLUES

PERSONAL: Born April 14, 1967, in Edmonton. ... 6-2/205. ... Shoots left. ... Full Name: John Jeffrey Finley.
TRANSACTIONS/CAREER NOTES: Selected by New York Islanders in third round (fourth Islanders pick, 55th overall) of NHL entry draft (June 15, 1985). ... Suffered swollen left knee (September 1988). ... Traded by Islanders to Ottawa Senators for D Chris Luongo (June 30, 1993). ... Signed as free agent by Philadelphia Flyers (August 2, 1994). ... Traded by Flyers to Winnipeg Jets for LW Russ Romaniuk (June 26, 1995). ... Separated shoulder (December 10, 1995); missed one game. ... Jets franchise moved to Phoenix and renamed Coyotes for 1996-97 season; NHL approved move on January 18, 1996. ... Suffered from the flu (December 7, 1996); missed two games. ... Strained hip flexor (December 30, 1996); missed one game. ... Sprained ankle (March 27, 1997); missed remainder of regular season and first six games of playoffs. ... Signed as free agent by New York Rangers (July 16, 1997). ... Traded by Rangers with D Geoff Smith to St. Louis Blues for future considerations (February 13, 1999); Rangers acquired RW Chris Kenady to complete deal (February 22, 1999). ... Injured back (December 21, 1999); missed two games. ... Injured groin (March 12, 2000); missed one game. ... Suffered back spasms (March 30, 2000); missed final five games of regular season. ... Suffered from the flu (November 16, 2000); missed one game. ... Suffered concussion (March 25, 2001); missed final six games of regular season.

					REGULAR SEASON					PLAYOFFS			
Season Team	League	Gms.	G	A	Pts.	PIM	+/-	PP	SH	Gms.	G	A	Pts.	PIM
83-84—Portland	WHL	5	0	0	0	0	...	...	...	5	0	1	1	4
—Summerland	BCJHL	49	0	21	21	14	...	...	...	—	—	—	—	—
84-85—Portland	WHL	69	6	44	50	57	...	...	...	6	1	2	3	2
85-86—Portland	WHL	70	11	59	70	83	...	...	...	15	1	7	8	16
86-87—Portland	WHL	72	13	53	66	113	...	...	...	20	1	†21	22	27
87-88—Springfield	AHL	52	5	18	23	50	...	...	...	—	—	—	—	—
—New York Islanders	NHL	10	0	5	5	15	5	0	0	1	0	0	0	2
88-89—New York Islanders	NHL	4	0	0	0	6	1	0	0	—	—	—	—	—
—Springfield	AHL	65	3	16	19	55	...	...	...	—	—	—	—	—
89-90—New York Islanders	NHL	11	0	1	1	0	0	0	0	5	0	2	2	4
—Springfield	AHL	57	1	15	16	41	...	...	...	13	1	4	5	23
90-91—Capital District	AHL	67	10	34	44	34	...	...	...	—	—	—	—	—
—New York Islanders	NHL	11	0	0	0	4	-1	0	0	—	—	—	—	—

Season Team	League	REGULAR SEASON								PLAYOFFS				
		Gms.	G	A	Pts.	PIM	+/-	PP	SH	Gms.	G	A	Pts.	PIM
91-92—Capital District	AHL	20	1	9	10	6	...	...	...	—	—	—	—	—
—New York Islanders.....	NHL	51	1	10	11	26	-6	0	0	—	—	—	—	—
92-93—Capital District	AHL	61	6	29	35	34	...	...	...	4	0	1	1	0
93-94—Philadelphia	NHL	55	1	8	9	24	16	0	0	—	—	—	—	—
94-95—Hershey	AHL	36	2	9	11	33	...	...	...	6	0	1	1	8
95-96—Springfield	AHL	14	3	12	15	22	...	...	...	—	—	—	—	—
—Winnipeg	NHL	65	1	5	6	81	-2	0	0	6	0	0	0	4
96-97—Phoenix	NHL	65	3	7	10	40	-8	1	0	1	0	0	0	2
97-98—New York Rangers	NHL	63	1	6	7	55	-3	0	0	—	—	—	—	—
98-99—Hartford	AHL	42	2	10	12	28	...	...	...	—	—	—	—	—
—New York Rangers	NHL	2	0	0	0	0	-1	0	0	—	—	—	—	—
—St. Louis	NHL	30	1	2	3	20	12	0	0	13	1	2	3	8
99-00—St. Louis	NHL	74	2	8	10	38	26	0	0	7	0	2	2	4
00-01—St. Louis	NHL	72	2	8	10	38	7	0	0	2	0	0	0	0
NHL Totals (12 years).........		513	12	60	72	347	46	1	0	35	1	6	7	22

FISCHER, JIRI D RED WINGS

PERSONAL: Born July 31, 1980, in Horovice, Czechoslovakia. ... 6-5/210. ... Shoots left.
TRANSACTIONS/CAREER NOTES: Selected by Detroit Red Wings in first round (first Red Wings pick, 25th overall) of NHL entry draft (June 27, 1998). ... Sprained ankle (December 2, 2000); missed eight games.
HONORS: Named to QMJHL All-Star first team (1998-99). ... Won Emile (Butch) Bouchard Trophy (1998-99). ... Named to Can.HL All-Star second team (1998-99).

Season Team	League	REGULAR SEASON								PLAYOFFS				
		Gms.	G	A	Pts.	PIM	+/-	PP	SH	Gms.	G	A	Pts.	PIM
95-96—Poldi Kladno	Czech Rep.	39	6	10	16	...	...	...	...	—	—	—	—	—
96-97—Poldi Kladno	Czech Rep.	38	11	16	27	...	...	...	...	—	—	—	—	—
97-98—Hull	QMJHL	70	3	19	22	112	...	...	...	11	1	4	5	16
98-99—Hull	QMJHL	65	22	56	78	141	...	...	...	23	6	17	23	44
99-00—Detroit........................	NHL	52	0	8	8	45	1	0	0	—	—	—	—	—
—Cincinnati...................	AHL	7	0	2	2	10	...	...	...	—	—	—	—	—
00-01—Detroit........................	NHL	55	1	8	9	59	3	0	0	5	0	0	0	9
—Cincinnati...................	AHL	18	2	6	8	22	...	...	...	—	—	—	—	—
NHL Totals (2 years)..........		107	1	16	17	104	4	0	0	5	0	0	0	9

FISET, STEPHANE G KINGS

PERSONAL: Born June 17, 1970, in Montreal. ... 6-1/198. ... Catches left. ... Name pronounced fih-SAY.
TRANSACTIONS/CAREER NOTES: Selected by Quebec Nordiques in second round (third Nordiques pick, 24th overall) of NHL entry draft (June 13, 1987). ... Underwent shoulder surgery (May 1989). ... Twisted knee (December 9, 1990). ... Sprained left knee (January 14, 1992); missed 12 games. ... Suffered slipped disc (November 4, 1993); missed 18 games. ... Injured groin (February 28, 1995); missed two games. ... Nordiques franchise moved to Colorado and renamed Avalanche for 1995-96 season (June 21, 1995). ... Traded by Avalanche with first-round pick (D Mathieu Biron) in 1998 draft to Los Angeles Kings for LW Eric Lacroix and first-round pick (D Martin Skoula) in 1998 draft (June 20, 1996). ... Strained abdominal muscle (December 3, 1996); missed one game. ... Strained groin and abdominal muscles (March 5, 1997); missed 13 games. ... Bruised thigh (January 24, 1998); missed one game. ... Strained groin (February 28, 1998); missed two games. ... Strained right groin (October 18, 1998); missed four games. ... Strained left groin (October 28, 1998); missed 12 games. ... Strained right groin (December 16, 1998); missed seven games. ... Bruised right hand (November 9, 1999); missed 14 games. ... Strained left groin (March 4, 2000); missed six games. ... Sprained left knee (September 22, 2000); missed first 25 games of season. ... Strained left knee (December 22, 2000); missed 31 games.
HONORS: Won Can.HL Goaltender of the Year Award (1988-89). ... Won Jacques Plante Trophy (1988-89). ... Named to QMJHL All-Star first team (1988-89).
MISCELLANEOUS: Member of Stanley Cup championship team (1996). ... Stopped a penalty shot attempt (vs. Craig Janney, January 9, 1992; vs. Chris Dahlquist, March 21, 1992; vs. Peter Bondra, April 4, 1998; vs. Paul Kariya, March 18, 1999; vs. Mike Ricci, October 24, 1999). ... Allowed a penalty shot goal (vs. Kevin Miller, December 5, 1995; vs. Peter Bondra, January 29, 1999; vs. Tomas Sandstrom, February 15, 1999).

Season Team	League	REGULAR SEASON							PLAYOFFS					
		Gms.	Min	W	L	T	GA	SO	Avg.	Gms.	Min.	W	L	GA	SO	Avg.
87-88—Victoriaville	QMJHL	40	2221	14	17	4	146	1	3.94	2	163	0	2	10	0	3.68
88-89—Victoriaville	QMJHL	43	2401	25	14	0	138	1	*3.45	12	711	9	2	33	0	*2.78
89-90—Victoriaville	QMJHL	24	1383	14	6	3	63	1	2.73	*14	*790	7	6	*49	0	3.72
—Quebec........................	NHL	6	342	0	5	1	34	0	5.96	—	—	—	—	—	—	—
90-91—Quebec........................	NHL	3	186	0	2	1	12	0	3.87	—	—	—	—	—	—	—
—Halifax	AHL	36	1902	10	15	8	131	0	4.13	—	—	—	—	—	—	—
91-92—Halifax	AHL	29	1675	8	14	6	110	†3	3.94	—	—	—	—	—	—	—
—Quebec........................	NHL	23	1133	7	10	2	71	1	3.76	—	—	—	—	—	—	—
92-93—Quebec........................	NHL	37	1939	18	9	4	110	0	3.40	1	21	0	0	1	0	2.86
—Halifax	AHL	3	180	2	1	0	11	0	3.67	—	—	—	—	—	—	—
93-94—Cornwall	AHL	1	60	0	1	0	4	0	4.00	—	—	—	—	—	—	—
—Quebec........................	NHL	50	2798	20	25	4	158	2	3.39	—	—	—	—	—	—	—
94-95—Quebec........................	NHL	32	1879	17	10	3	87	2	2.78	4	209	1	2	16	0	4.59
95-96—Colorado	NHL	37	2107	22	6	7	103	1	2.93	1	1	0	0	0	0	...
96-97—Los Angeles	NHL	44	2482	13	24	5	132	4	3.19	—	—	—	—	—	—	—
97-98—Los Angeles	NHL	60	3497	26	25	8	158	2	2.71	2	93	0	2	7	0	4.52
98-99—Los Angeles	NHL	42	2403	18	21	1	104	3	2.60	—	—	—	—	—	—	—
99-00—Los Angeles	NHL	47	2592	20	15	7	119	1	2.75	4	200	0	3	10	0	3.00
00-01—Los Angeles	NHL	7	318	3	0	1	19	0	3.58	1	0	0	0	0	0	...
—Lowell	AHL	3	190	1	0	2	9	0	2.84	—	—	—	—	—	—	—
NHL Totals (12 years)..........		388	21676	164	152	44	1107	16	3.06	13	524	1	7	34	0	3.89

F

PERSONAL: Born June 5, 1980, in Peterborough, Ont. ... 6-1/193. ... Shoots right.

TRANSACTIONS/CAREER NOTES: Selected by Ottawa Senators in second round (second Senators pick, 44th overall) of NHL entry draft (June 27, 1998). ... Suffered hip pointer (October 5, 1999); missed three games. ... Tore anterior cruciate ligament in right knee (December 30, 1999); missed remainder of season. ... Injured left shoulder (Novmeber 2, 2000); missed 22 games.

Season Team	League	Gms.	G	A	Pts.	PIM	+/-	PP	SH	Gms.	G	A	Pts.	PIM
96-97—Peterborough	Tier II Jr. A	51	26	30	56	33	...	...	...	—	—	—	—	—
97-98—Sudbury	OHL	66	24	25	49	65	...	...	...	9	2	2	4	13
98-99—Sudbury	OHL	68	41	65	106	55	...	...	...	4	2	1	3	4
99-00—Ottawa	NHL	32	4	5	9	15	-6	0	0	—	—	—	—	—
00-01—Ottawa	NHL	60	7	12	19	46	-1	0	0	4	0	1	1	4
NHL Totals (2 years)		92	11	17	28	61	-7	0	0	4	0	1	1	4

PERSONAL: Born August 28, 1968, in Billerica, Mass. ... 6-0/196. ... Shoots right. ... Full Name: Thomas James Fitzgerald. ... Cousin of Keith Tkachuk, left winger, St. Louis Blues.

TRANSACTIONS/CAREER NOTES: Selected by New York Islanders in first round (first Islanders pick, 17th overall) of NHL entry draft (June 21, 1986). ... Bruised left knee (November 7, 1990). ... Strained abdominal muscle (October 22, 1991); missed 16 games. ... Tore rib cage muscle (October 24, 1992); missed four games. ... Selected by Florida Panthers in NHL expansion draft (June 24, 1993). ... Suffered sore hip (March 18, 1994); missed one game. ... Bruised eye (November 13, 1996); missed one game. ... Suffered from the flu (December 29, 1996); missed one game. ... Strained abdominal muscle (January 25, 1997); missed three games. ... Reinjured abdominal muscle (February 22, 1997); missed five games. ... Traded by Panthers to Colorado Avalanche for rights to LW Mark Parrish and third-round pick (D Lance Ward) in 1998 draft (March 24, 1998). ... Signed as free agent by Nashville Predators (July 6, 1998). ... Strained neck (December 8, 1998); missed one game.

RECORDS: Shares NHL single-game playoff record for most shorthanded goals—2 (May 8, 1993).

MISCELLANEOUS: Captain of Nashville Predators (1998-99 through 2000-01). ... Holds Nashville Predators all-time record for most games played (244). ... Failed to score on a penalty shot (vs. Mark Fitzpatrick, January 31, 1998).

Season Team	League	Gms.	G	A	Pts.	PIM	+/-	PP	SH	Gms.	G	A	Pts.	PIM
84-85—Austin Prep	Mass. H.S.	18	20	21	41	...	...	...	...	—	—	—	—	—
85-86—Austin Prep	Mass. H.S.	24	35	38	73	...	...	...	...	—	—	—	—	—
86-87—Providence College	Hockey East	27	8	14	22	22	...	...	...	—	—	—	—	—
87-88—Providence College	Hockey East	36	19	15	34	50	...	...	...	—	—	—	—	—
88-89—Springfield	AHL	61	24	18	42	43	...	...	...	—	—	—	—	—
—New York Islanders	NHL	23	3	5	8	10	1	0	0	—	—	—	—	—
89-90—Springfield	AHL	53	30	23	53	32	...	...	...	14	2	9	11	13
—New York Islanders	NHL	19	2	5	7	4	-3	0	0	4	1	0	1	4
90-91—New York Islanders	NHL	41	5	5	10	24	-9	0	0	—	—	—	—	—
—Capital District	AHL	27	7	7	14	50	...	...	...	—	—	—	—	—
91-92—New York Islanders	NHL	45	6	11	17	28	-3	0	2	—	—	—	—	—
—Capital District	AHL	4	1	1	2	4	...	...	...	—	—	—	—	—
92-93—New York Islanders	NHL	77	9	18	27	34	-2	0	3	18	2	5	7	18
93-94—Florida	NHL	83	18	14	32	54	-3	0	3	—	—	—	—	—
94-95—Florida	NHL	48	3	13	16	31	-3	0	0	—	—	—	—	—
95-96—Florida	NHL	82	13	21	34	75	-3	1	6	22	4	4	8	34
96-97—Florida	NHL	71	10	14	24	64	7	0	2	5	0	1	1	0
97-98—Florida	NHL	69	10	5	15	57	-4	0	1	—	—	—	—	—
—Colorado	NHL	11	2	1	3	22	0	0	1	7	0	1	1	20
98-99—Nashville	NHL	80	13	19	32	48	-18	0	0	—	—	—	—	—
99-00—Nashville	NHL	82	13	9	22	66	-18	0	3	—	—	—	—	—
00-01—Nashville	NHL	82	9	9	18	71	-5	0	2	—	—	—	—	—
NHL Totals (13 years)		813	116	149	265	588	-63	1	23	56	7	11	18	76

PERSONAL: Born January 11, 1975, in Rochester, N.Y. ... 6-2/205. ... Shoots right.

TRANSACTIONS/CAREER NOTES: Selected by Montreal Canadiens in second round (second Canadiens pick, 47th overall) of NHL entry draft (June 26, 1993). ... Traded by Canadiens with C Pierre Turgeon and C Craig Conroy to St. Louis Blues for LW Shayne Corson, D Murray Baron and fifth-round pick (D Gennady Razin) in 1997 draft (October 29, 1996). ... Selected by Boston Bruins from Blues in NHL waiver draft (October 5, 1998). ... Claimed on waivers by Blues (October 7, 1998). ... Traded by Blues to Nashville Predators for D Dan Keczmer (February 9, 2000). ... Traded by Predators to Edmonton Oilers for future considerations (January 12, 2001).

HONORS: Named to OHL All-Rookie team (1992-93).

Season Team	League	Gms.	G	A	Pts.	PIM	+/-	PP	SH	Gms.	G	A	Pts.	PIM
90-91—Rochester Jr. B	OHA	40	0	5	5	...	...	...	...	—	—	—	—	—
91-92—Rochester Jr. B	OHA	28	8	28	36	141	...	...	...	—	—	—	—	—
92-93—Sudbury	OHL	58	4	20	24	68	...	...	...	14	0	0	0	17
93-94—Sudbury	OHL	65	12	34	46	112	...	...	...	10	2	5	7	10
94-95—Sudbury	OHL	56	12	36	48	72	...	...	...	18	3	15	18	21
—Fredericton	AHL	—	—	—	—	—	...	...	...	10	1	2	3	5
95-96—Fredericton	AHL	18	4	6	10	36	...	...	...	—	—	—	—	—
—Montreal	NHL	42	0	2	2	18	-7	0	0	6	1	1	2	0
96-97—Montreal	NHL	6	0	1	1	6	-2	0	0	—	—	—	—	—
—Worcester	AHL	49	4	13	17	78	...	...	...	5	1	2	3	0
—St. Louis	NHL	2	0	0	0	2	-2	0	0	—	—	—	—	—

F

Season Team	League	REGULAR SEASON								PLAYOFFS				
		Gms.	G	A	Pts.	PIM	+/-	PP	SH	Gms.	G	A	Pts.	PIM
97-98—Worcester	AHL	62	8	22	30	111	...	...	...	11	0	3	3	26
98-99—Worcester	AHL	53	5	16	21	82	...	...	...	4	0	1	1	17
—St. Louis	NHL	1	0	0	0	2	-3	0	0	—	—	—	—	—
99-00—Worcester	AHL	28	0	5	5	48	...	...	...	—	—	—	—	—
—Milwaukee	IHL	27	2	1	3	27	...	...	...	3	0	2	2	2
00-01—Hamilton	AHL	34	3	17	20	29	...	...	...	—	—	—	—	—
—Nashville	NHL	2	0	0	0	2	-2	0	0	—	—	—	—	—
—Milwaukee	IHL	22	0	2	2	32	...	...	...	—	—	—	—	—
NHL Totals (4 years)		53	0	3	3	30	-16	0	0	6	1	1	2	0

FLAHERTY, WADE — G

PERSONAL: Born January 11, 1968, in Terrace, B.C. ... 6-0/187. ... Catches left.
TRANSACTIONS/CAREER NOTES: Selected by Buffalo Sabres in ninth round (10th Sabres pick, 181st overall) of NHL entry draft (June 11, 1988). ... Signed as free agent by San Jose Sharks (September 3, 1991). ... Injured ribs (February 28, 1995); missed three games. ... Strained groin (February 1, 1996); missed two games. ... Suffered back spasms (March 8, 1996); missed six games. ... Suffered back spasms (March 31, 1996); missed seven games. ... Fractured collarbone (September 12, 1996); missed 23 games. ... Signed as free agent by New York Islanders (July 1, 1997). ... Sprained shoulder (November 21, 1999) and underwent surgery; missed remainder of season. ... Traded by Islanders to Tampa Bay Lightning for conditional ninth-round pick (February 16, 2001).
HONORS: Named to WHL All-Star second team (1987-88). ... Won ECHL Playoff Most Valuable Player Award (1989-90). ... Shared James Norris Memorial Trophy with Arturs Irbe (1991-92). ... Named to IHL All-Star second team (1992-93 and 1993-94).

Season Team	League	REGULAR SEASON							PLAYOFFS					
		Gms.	Min	W	L	T	GA	SO	Avg.	Gms.	Min.	W	L	GA	SO	Avg.
84-85—Kelowna	WHL	1	55	0	0	0	5	0	5.45	—	—	—	—	—	—	—
85-86—Seattle	WHL	9	271	1	3	0	36	0	7.97	—	—	—	—	—	—	—
—Spokane	WHL	5	161	0	3	0	21	0	7.83	—	—	—	—	—	—	—
86-87—Nanaimo	BCJHL	15	830	...	...	...	53	0	3.83	—	—	—	—	—	—	—
—Victoria	WHL	3	127	0	2	0	16	0	7.56	—	—	—	—	—	—	—
87-88—Victoria	WHL	36	2052	20	15	0	135	0	3.95	5	300	2	3	18	0	3.60
88-89—Victoria	WHL	42	2408	21	19	0	180	0	4.49	8	480	3	5	35	0	4.38
89-90—Kalamazoo	IHL	1	13	0	0	0	0	0	0	—	—	—	—	—	—	—
—Greensboro	ECHL	27	1308	12	10	0	96	...	4.40	†9	567	*8	1	21	0	*2.22
90-91—Kansas City	IHL	†56	2990	16	31	‡4	*224	0	4.49	1	1	0	0	0	0	...
91-92—Kansas City	IHL	43	2603	26	14	‡3	140	1	3.23	1	1	0	0	0	0	...
—San Jose	NHL	3	178	0	3	0	13	0	4.38	—	—	—	—	—	—	—
92-93—Kansas City	IHL	61	*3642	*34	19	0	*195	2	3.21	12	*733	6	*5	†34	*1	2.78
—San Jose	NHL	1	60	0	1	0	5	0	5.00	—	—	—	—	—	—	—
93-94—Kansas City	IHL	60	*3564	32	19	‡9	202	0	3.40	—	—	—	—	—	—	—
94-95—San Jose	NHL	18	852	5	6	1	44	1	3.10	7	377	2	3	31	0	4.93
95-96—San Jose	NHL	24	1137	3	12	1	92	0	4.85	—	—	—	—	—	—	—
96-97—Kentucky	AHL	19	1032	8	6	2	54	1	3.14	3	200	1	2	11	0	3.30
—San Jose	NHL	7	359	2	4	0	31	0	5.18	—	—	—	—	—	—	—
97-98—Utah	IHL	24	1341	16	5	3	40	3	1.79	—	—	—	—	—	—	—
98-99—New York Islanders	NHL	16	694	4	4	3	23	3	1.99	—	—	—	—	—	—	—
—New York Islanders	NHL	20	1048	5	11	2	53	0	3.03	—	—	—	—	—	—	—
—Lowell	AHL	5	305	1	3	1	16	0	3.15	—	—	—	—	—	—	—
99-00—New York Islanders	NHL	4	182	0	1	1	7	0	2.31	—	—	—	—	—	—	—
00-01—New York Islanders	NHL	20	1017	6	10	0	56	1	3.30	—	—	—	—	—	—	—
—Tampa Bay	NHL	2	118	0	2	0	8	0	4.07	—	—	—	—	—	—	—
NHL Totals (9 years)		115	5645	25	54	8	332	5	3.53	7	377	2	3	31	0	4.93

FLEURY, THEO — RW — RANGERS

F

PERSONAL: Born June 29, 1968, in Oxbow, Sask. ... 5-6/180. ... Shoots right. ... Full Name: Theoren Fleury. ... Name pronounced THAIR-ihn FLUH-ree.
TRANSACTIONS/CAREER NOTES: Selected by Calgary Flames in eighth round (ninth Flames pick, 166th overall) of NHL entry draft (June 13, 1987). ... Played in Europe during 1994-95 NHL lockout. ... Injured eye (April 6, 1996); missed two games. ... Injured knee (April 6, 1997); missed one game. ... Traded by Flames with LW Chris Dingman to Colorado Avalanche for LW Rene Corbet, D Wade Belak and future considerations (February 28, 1999); Flames acquired D Robyn Regehr to complete deal (March 27, 1999). ... Sprained knee (March 1, 1999); missed seven games. ... Signed as free agent by New York Rangers (July 9, 1999). ... Suffered back spasms (February 8, 2000); missed one game. ... Strained right knee (April 8, 2000); missed final game of season. ... Missed final 20 games of 2000-01 season due to personal problems.
HONORS: Named to WHL (East) All-Star first team (1986-87). ... Shared Bob Clarke Trophy with Joe Sakic (1987-88). ... Named to WHL All-Star second team (1987-88). ... Shared Alka-Seltzer Plus Award with Marty McSorley (1990-91). ... Played in NHL All-Star Game (1991, 1992, 1996-1999 and 2001). ... Named to NHL All-Star second team (1994-95).
RECORDS: Holds NHL single-game record for highest plus-minus rating—9 (February 10, 1993).
STATISTICAL PLATEAUS: Three-goal games: 1990-91 (5), 1992-93 (1), 1993-94 (1), 1995-96 (3), 1996-97 (1), 1998-99 (3), 2000-01 (1). Total: 15.
MISCELLANEOUS: Member of Stanley Cup championship team (1989). ... Captain of Calgary Flames (1995-96 and 1996-97). ... Holds Calgary Flames all-time records for most goals (364) and most points (830). ... Scored on a penalty shot (vs. Jacques Cloutier, February 23, 1991; vs. Rick Wamsley, December 11, 1992; vs. Patrick Roy, October 22, 1996).

Season Team	League	REGULAR SEASON								PLAYOFFS				
		Gms.	G	A	Pts.	PIM	+/-	PP	SH	Gms.	G	A	Pts.	PIM
84-85—Moose Jaw	WHL	71	29	46	75	82	...	...	...	—	—	—	—	—
85-86—Moose Jaw	WHL	72	43	65	108	124	...	...	...	—	—	—	—	—
86-87—Moose Jaw	WHL	66	61	68	129	110	...	...	...	9	7	9	16	34
87-88—Moose Jaw	WHL	65	68	92	†160	235	...	...	...	—	—	—	—	—
—Salt Lake City	IHL	2	3	4	7	7	...	...	...	8	11	5	16	16
88-89—Salt Lake City	IHL	40	37	37	74	81	...	...	...	—	—	—	—	—
—Calgary	NHL	36	14	20	34	46	5	5	0	22	5	6	11	24

Season Team	League	REGULAR SEASON								PLAYOFFS				
		Gms.	G	A	Pts.	PIM	+/-	PP	SH	Gms.	G	A	Pts.	PIM
89-90—Calgary	NHL	80	31	35	66	157	22	9	3	6	2	3	5	10
90-91—Calgary	NHL	79	51	53	104	136	†48	9	7	7	2	5	7	14
91-92—Calgary	NHL	80	33	40	73	133	0	11	1	—	—	—	—	—
92-93—Calgary	NHL	83	34	66	100	88	14	12	2	6	5	7	12	27
93-94—Calgary	NHL	83	40	45	85	186	30	16	1	7	6	4	10	5
94-95—Tappara	Finland	10	8	9	17	22	...	...	...	—	—	—	—	—
—Calgary	NHL	47	29	29	58	112	6	9	2	7	7	7	14	2
95-96—Calgary	NHL	80	46	50	96	112	17	17	5	4	2	1	3	14
96-97—Calgary	NHL	81	29	38	67	104	-12	9	2	—	—	—	—	—
97-98—Calgary	NHL	82	27	51	78	197	0	3	2	—	—	—	—	—
—Can. Olympic team	Int'l	6	1	3	4	2	...	...	...	—	—	—	—	—
98-99—Calgary	NHL	60	30	39	69	68	18	7	3	—	—	—	—	—
—Colorado	NHL	15	10	14	24	18	8	1	0	18	5	12	17	20
99-00—New York Rangers	NHL	80	15	49	64	68	-4	1	0	—	—	—	—	—
00-01—New York Rangers	NHL	62	30	44	74	122	0	8	7	—	—	—	—	—
NHL Totals (13 years)		948	419	573	992	1547	152	117	35	77	34	45	79	116

FOOTE, ADAM — D — AVALANCHE

PERSONAL: Born July 10, 1971, in Toronto. ... 6-1/202. ... Shoots right. ... Full Name: Adam David Vernon Foote.

TRANSACTIONS/CAREER NOTES: Selected by Quebec Nordiques in second round (second Nordiques pick, 22nd overall) of NHL entry draft (June 17, 1989). ... Fractured right thumb (February 1992); missed remainder of season. ... Injured knee (October 21, 1992); missed one game. ... Suffered from the flu (January 28, 1993); missed two games. ... Injured groin (January 18, 1994); missed eight games. ... Suffered herniated disc (February 11, 1994) and underwent surgery; missed remainder of season. ... Injured back (February 9, 1995); missed two games. ... Injured groin (February 28, 1995); missed two games. ... Injured groin (March 26, 1995); missed four games. ... Reinjured groin (April 6, 1995); missed five games. ... Nordiques franchise moved to Colorado and renamed Avalanche for 1995-96 season (June 21, 1995). ... Fractured wrist prior to 1995-96 season; missed first two games of season. ... Separated left shoulder (January 6, 1996); missed five games. ... Bruised left knee (February 8, 1997); missed two games. ... Bruised knee (January 2, 1998); missed one game. ... Bruised knee (January 10, 1998); missed three games. ... Injured elbow (October 24, 1998); missed 15 games. ... Suffered concussion (December 4, 1998); missed three games. ... Injured shoulder (October 10, 1999); missed one game. ... Reinjured shoulder (October 21, 1999); missed six games. ... Reinjured shoulder (November 17, 1999); missed eight games. ... Injured groin (January 9, 2000); missed one game. ... Injured groin (February 10, 2000); missed six games. ... Suffered stress fracture in heel (November 9, 2000); missed 12 games. ... Separated right shoulder (January 4, 2001); missed 35 games.

HONORS: Named to OHL All-Star first team (1990-91).

MISCELLANEOUS: Member of Stanley Cup championship team (1996 and 2001).

Season Team	League	REGULAR SEASON								PLAYOFFS				
		Gms.	G	A	Pts.	PIM	+/-	PP	SH	Gms.	G	A	Pts.	PIM
88-89—Sault Ste. Marie	OHL	66	7	32	39	120	...	...	...	—	—	—	—	—
89-90—Sault Ste. Marie	OHL	61	12	43	55	199	...	...	...	—	—	—	—	—
90-91—Sault Ste. Marie	OHL	59	18	51	69	93	...	...	...	14	5	12	17	28
91-92—Quebec	NHL	46	2	5	7	44	-4	0	0	—	—	—	—	—
—Halifax	AHL	6	0	1	1	2	...	...	...	—	—	—	—	—
92-93—Quebec	NHL	81	4	12	16	168	6	0	1	6	0	1	1	2
93-94—Quebec	NHL	45	2	6	8	67	3	0	0	—	—	—	—	—
94-95—Quebec	NHL	35	0	7	7	52	17	0	0	6	0	1	1	14
95-96—Colorado	NHL	73	5	11	16	88	27	1	0	22	1	3	4	36
96-97—Colorado	NHL	78	2	19	21	135	16	0	0	17	0	4	4	62
97-98—Colorado	NHL	77	3	14	17	124	-3	0	0	7	0	0	0	23
—Can. Olympic team	Int'l	6	0	1	1	4	...	...	...	—	—	—	—	—
98-99—Colorado	NHL	64	5	16	21	92	20	3	0	19	2	3	5	24
99-00—Colorado	NHL	59	5	13	18	98	5	1	0	16	0	7	7	28
00-01—Colorado	NHL	35	3	12	15	42	6	1	1	23	3	4	7	*47
NHL Totals (10 years)		593	31	115	146	910	93	6	2	116	6	23	29	236

FORBES, COLIN — LW — RANGERS

PERSONAL: Born February 16, 1976, in New Westminister, B.C. ... 6-3/205. ... Shoots left.

TRANSACTIONS/CAREER NOTES: Selected by Philadelphia Flyers in seventh round (fifth Flyers pick, 166th overall) of NHL entry draft (June 29, 1994). ... Bruised thumb (November 7, 1998); missed one game. ... Suffered from stomach virus (January 7, 1999); missed one game. ... Traded by Flyers with fifth-round pick (G Michal Lanicek) in 1999 draft to Tampa Bay Lightning for RW Mikael Andersson and RW Sandy McCarthy (March 20, 1999). ... Traded by Lightning to Ottawa Senators for C Bruce Gardiner (November 11, 1999). ... Traded by Senators to New York Rangers for LW Eric Lacroix (March 1, 2001).

Season Team	League	REGULAR SEASON								PLAYOFFS				
		Gms.	G	A	Pts.	PIM	+/-	PP	SH	Gms.	G	A	Pts.	PIM
93-94—Sherwood Park	AJHL	47	18	22	40	76	...	...	...	—	—	—	—	—
94-95—Portland	WHL	72	24	31	55	108	...	...	...	9	1	3	4	10
95-96—Portland	WHL	72	33	44	77	137	...	...	...	7	2	5	7	14
—Hershey	AHL	2	1	0	1	2	...	...	...	4	0	2	2	2
96-97—Philadelphia	AHL	74	21	28	49	108	...	...	...	10	5	5	10	33
—Philadelphia	NHL	3	1	0	1	0	0	0	0	3	0	0	0	0
97-98—Philadelphia	AHL	13	7	4	11	22	...	...	...	—	—	—	—	—
—Philadelphia	NHL	63	12	7	19	59	2	2	0	5	0	0	0	2
98-99—Philadelphia	NHL	66	9	7	16	51	0	0	0	—	—	—	—	—
—Tampa Bay	NHL	14	3	1	4	10	-5	0	1	—	—	—	—	—
99-00—Tampa Bay	NHL	8	0	0	0	18	-4	0	0	—	—	—	—	—
—Ottawa	NHL	45	2	5	7	12	-1	0	0	5	1	0	1	14
00-01—Ottawa	NHL	39	0	1	1	31	-3	0	0	—	—	—	—	—
—New York Rangers	NHL	19	1	4	5	15	-3	0	0	—	—	—	—	—
NHL Totals (5 years)		257	28	25	53	196	-14	2	1	13	1	0	1	16

FORSBERG, PETER   C   AVALANCHE

PERSONAL: Born July 20, 1973, in Ornskoldsvik, Sweden. ... 6-0/190. ... Shoots left. ... Son of Kent Forsberg, head coach Swedish Olympic team and Swedish National team (1995-98).

TRANSACTIONS/CAREER NOTES: Selected by Philadelphia Flyers in first round (first Flyers pick, sixth overall) of NHL entry draft (June 22, 1991). ... Traded by Flyers with G Ron Hextall, C Mike Ricci, D Steve Duchesne, D Kerry Huffman, first-round pick (G Jocelyn Thibault) in 1993 draft, cash and future considerations to Quebec Nordiques for C Eric Lindros (June 20, 1992); Nordiques acquired LW Chris Simon and first-round pick (traded to Toronto) in 1994 draft to complete deal (July 21, 1992). ... Played in Europe during 1994-95 NHL lockout. ... Suffered from the flu (March 1, 1995); missed one game. ... Nordiques franchise moved to Colorado and renamed Avalanche for 1995-96 season (June 21, 1995). ... Bruised thigh (December 14, 1996); missed 17 games. ... Bruised shoulder (November 8, 1997); missed three games. ... Pulled groin (March 26, 1998); missed seven games. ... Suffered concussion (May 7, 1998); missed two playoff games. ... Suffered charley horse (May 22, 1998); missed one playoff game. ... Injured groin (December 14, 1998); missed one game. ... Injured elbow (March 4, 1999); missed three games. ... Underwent shoulder surgery prior to start of 1999-2000 season; missed first 23 games of season. ... Suffered hip pointer (November 30, 1999); missed two games. ... Suffered concussion (February 1, 2000); missed five games. ... Bruised shoulder (March 26, 2000); missed two games. ... Separated shoulder (April 7, 2000); missed final game of season. ... Injured ribs (November 11, 2000); missed eight games.

HONORS: Named to Swedish League All-Star team (1991-92). ... Named Swedish League Player of the Year (1993-94). ... Named NHL Rookie of the Year by THE SPORTING NEWS (1994-95). ... Won Calder Memorial Trophy (1994-95). ... Named to NHL All-Rookie team (1994-95). ... Played in NHL All-Star Game (1996, 1998, 1999 and 2001). ... Named to play in NHL All-Star Game (1997); replaced by LW Brendan Shanahan due to injury. ... Named to THE SPORTING NEWS All-Star team (1997-98). ... Named to NHL All-Star first team (1997-98 and 1998-99). ... Named to play in NHL All-Star Game (2000); replaced by LW Patrik Elias due to injury.

MISCELLANEOUS: Member of Stanley Cup championship team (1996 and 2001). ... Member of gold-medal-winning Swedish Olympic team (1994). ... Failed to score on a penalty shot vs. Tim Cheveldae, February 1, 1996; vs. Grant Fuhr, December 6, 1996).

STATISTICAL PLATEAUS: Three-goal games: 1995-96 (2), 1996-97 (1), 1998-99 (1). Total: 4.

		REGULAR SEASON								PLAYOFFS				
Season Team	League	Gms.	G	A	Pts.	PIM	+/-	PP	SH	Gms.	G	A	Pts.	PIM
89-90—MoDo Hockey	Sweden Jr.	30	15	12	27	42	...	...	...	—	—	—	—	—
90-91—MoDo Ornskoldsvik	Sweden	23	7	10	17	22	...	...	...	—	—	—	—	—
91-92—MoDo Ornskoldsvik	Sweden	39	9	19	28	78	...	...	...	—	—	—	—	—
92-93—MoDo Ornskoldsvik	Sweden	39	23	24	47	92	...	...	...	3	4	1	5	...
93-94—MoDo Ornskoldsvik	Sweden	39	18	26	44	82	...	...	...	11	9	7	16	14
—Swedish Oly. team	Int'l	8	2	6	8	6	...	...	...	—	—	—	—	—
94-95—MoDo Ornskoldsvik	Sweden	11	5	9	14	20	...	...	...	—	—	—	—	—
—Quebec	NHL	47	15	35	50	16	17	3	0	6	2	4	6	4
95-96—Colorado	NHL	82	30	86	116	47	26	7	3	22	10	11	21	18
96-97—Colorado	NHL	65	28	58	86	73	31	5	4	14	5	12	17	10
97-98—Colorado	NHL	72	25	66	91	94	6	7	3	7	6	5	11	12
—Swedish Oly. team	Int'l	4	1	4	5	6	...	...	...	—	—	—	—	—
98-99—Colorado	NHL	78	30	67	97	108	27	9	2	19	8	16	*24	31
99-00—Colorado	NHL	49	14	37	51	52	9	3	0	16	7	8	15	12
00-01—Colorado	NHL	73	27	62	89	54	23	12	2	11	4	10	14	6
NHL Totals (7 years)		466	169	411	580	444	139	46	14	95	42	66	108	93

FOUNTAIN, MIKE   G

PERSONAL: Born January 26, 1972, in North York, Ont. ... 6-1/180. ... Catches left. ... Full Name: Michael Fountain. ... Name pronounced FOWN-tihn.

TRANSACTIONS/CAREER NOTES: Selected by Vancouver Canucks in second round (third Canucks pick, 45th overall) of NHL entry draft (June 20, 1992). ... Signed as free agent by Carolina Hurricanes (August 14, 1997). ... Signed as free agent by Ottawa Senators (July 12, 1999).

HONORS: Named to Can.HL All-Star second team (1991-92). ... Named to OHL All-Star first team (1991-92). ... Named to AHL All-Star second team (1993-94). ... Named to IHL All-Star second team (2000-01).

		REGULAR SEASON							PLAYOFFS					
Season Team	League	Gms.	Min	W	L	T	GA	SO	Avg.	Gms.	Min.	W	L	GA	SO	Avg.
88-89—Huntsville Jr. C	OHA	22	1306	...	...	...	82	0	3.77	—	—	—	—	—	—	—
89-90—Chatham Jr. B	OHA	21	1249	...	...	...	76	0	3.65	—	—	—	—	—	—	—
90-91—Sault Ste. Marie	OHL	7	380	5	2	0	19	0	3.00	—	—	—	—	—	—	—
—Oshawa	OHL	30	1483	17	5	1	84	0	3.40	8	292	1	4	26	0	5.34
91-92—Oshawa	OHL	40	2260	18	13	6	149	1	3.96	7	428	3	4	26	0	3.64
92-93—Canadian nat'l team	Int'l	13	745	7	5	1	37	1	2.98	—	—	—	—	—	—	—
—Hamilton	AHL	12	618	2	8	0	46	0	4.47	—	—	—	—	—	—	—
93-94—Hamilton	AHL	*70	*4005	*34	28	6	241	*4	3.61	3	146	0	2	12	0	4.93
94-95—Syracuse	AHL	61	*3618	25	*29	7	225	2	3.73	—	—	—	—	—	—	—
95-96—Syracuse	AHL	54	3060	21	27	3	184	1	3.61	15	915	8	*7	57	†2	3.74
96-97—Vancouver	NHL	6	245	2	2	0	14	1	3.43	—	—	—	—	—	—	—
—Syracuse	AHL	25	1462	8	14	2	78	1	3.20	2	120	0	2	12	0	6.00
97-98—New Haven	AHL	50	2923	25	19	5	139	3	2.85	—	—	—	—	—	—	—
—Carolina	NHL	3	163	0	3	0	10	0	3.68	—	—	—	—	—	—	—
98-99—New Haven	AHL	51	2989	23	24	3	150	2	3.01	—	—	—	—	—	—	—
99-00—Grand Rapids	IHL	36	1851	25	7	‡4	77	3	2.50	1	20	0	0	4	0	12.00
—Ottawa	NHL	1	16	0	0	0	1	0	3.75	—	—	—	—	—	—	—
00-01—Grand Rapids	IHL	*52	*3005	*34	10	‡6	104	6	2.08	8	522	5	1	21	1	2.41
—Ottawa	NHL	1	59	0	1	0	3	0	3.05	—	—	—	—	—	—	—
NHL Totals (4 years)		11	483	2	6	0	28	1	3.48							

FRANCIS, RON   C   HURRICANES

PERSONAL: Born March 1, 1963, in Sault Ste. Marie, Ont. ... 6-3/200. ... Shoots left. ... Full Name: Ronald Francis. ... Cousin of Mike Liut, goaltender with three NHL teams (1979-80 through 1991-92) and Cincinnati Stingers of WHA (1977-78 and 1978-79).

TRANSACTIONS/CAREER NOTES: Selected by Hartford Whalers in first round (first Whalers pick, fourth overall) of NHL entry draft (June 10, 1981). ... Injured eye (January 27, 1982); missed three weeks. ... Strained ligaments in right knee (November 30, 1983). ...

Fractured left ankle (January 18, 1986); missed 27 games. ... Fractured left index finger (January 28, 1989); missed 11 games. ... Fractured nose (November 24, 1990). ... Traded by Whalers with D Ulf Samuelsson and D Grant Jennings to Pittsburgh Penguins for C John Cullen, D Zarley Zalapski and RW Jeff Parker (March 4, 1991). ... Suffered from the flu (February 19, 1995); missed one game. ... Suffered back spasms (February 21, 1995); missed three games. ... Strained hip flexor (January 5, 1996); missed two games. ... Suspended two games and fined $1000 by NHL for checking player from behind (February 27, 1996). ... Fractured left foot (May 11, 1996); missed remainder of playoffs. ... Injured groin (February 22, 1997); missed one game. ... Pulled hamstring (April 16, 1998); missed one game. ... Signed as free agent by Carolina Hurricanes (July 13, 1998). ... Suffered from vertigo (November 26, 1999); missed two games. ... Injured back (January 27, 2000); missed two games.

HONORS: Played in NHL All-Star Game (1983, 1985, 1990 and 1996). ... Won Lady Byng Memorial Trophy (1994-95 and 1997-98). ... Won Frank J. Selke Trophy (1994-95). ... Won NHL Alka-Seltzer Plus award (1994-95).

MISCELLANEOUS: Member of Stanley Cup championship teams (1991 and 1992). ... Captain of Hartford Whalers (1984-85 through 1990-1991). ... Captain of Pittsburgh Penguins (1994-95, 1995-96 and 1997-98). ... Captain of Carolina Hurricanes (1999-2000 and 2000-01). ... Holds Carolina Hurricanes franchise all-time records for most games played (956), most goals (323), most assists (688) and most points (1,011). ... Scored on a penalty shot (vs. Richard Sevigny, January 17, 1986).

STATISTICAL PLATEAUS: Three-goal games: 1982-83 (1), 1984-85 (1), 1985-86 (2), 1987-88 (1), 1988-89 (1), 1989-90 (1), 1990-91 (1), 1995-96 (1), 1997-98 (1). Total: 10. ... Four-goal games: 1983-84 (1). ... Total hat tricks: 11.

			REGULAR SEASON							PLAYOFFS				
Season Team	League	Gms.	G	A	Pts.	PIM	+/-	PP	SH	Gms.	G	A	Pts.	PIM
80-81—Sault Ste. Marie	OMJHL	64	26	43	69	33	...	...	...	19	7	8	15	34
81-82—Sault Ste. Marie	OHL	25	18	30	48	46	...	...	...	—	—	—	—	—
—Hartford	NHL	59	25	43	68	51	-13	12	0	—	—	—	—	—
82-83—Hartford	NHL	79	31	59	90	60	-25	4	2	—	—	—	—	—
83-84—Hartford	NHL	72	23	60	83	45	-10	5	0	—	—	—	—	—
84-85—Hartford	NHL	80	24	57	81	66	-23	4	0	—	—	—	—	—
85-86—Hartford	NHL	53	24	53	77	24	8	7	1	10	1	2	3	4
86-87—Hartford	NHL	75	30	63	93	45	10	7	0	6	2	2	4	6
87-88—Hartford	NHL	80	25	50	75	87	-8	11	1	6	2	5	7	2
88-89—Hartford	NHL	69	29	48	77	36	4	8	0	4	0	2	2	0
89-90—Hartford	NHL	80	32	69	101	73	13	15	1	7	3	3	6	8
90-91—Hartford	NHL	67	21	55	76	51	-2	10	1	—	—	—	—	—
—Pittsburgh	NHL	14	2	9	11	21	0	0	0	24	7	10	17	24
91-92—Pittsburgh	NHL	70	21	33	54	30	-7	5	1	21	8	*19	27	6
92-93—Pittsburgh	NHL	84	24	76	100	68	6	9	2	12	6	11	17	19
93-94—Pittsburgh	NHL	82	27	66	93	62	-3	8	0	6	0	2	2	6
94-95—Pittsburgh	NHL	44	11	*48	59	18	*30	3	0	12	6	13	19	4
95-96—Pittsburgh	NHL	77	27	92	119	56	25	12	1	11	3	6	9	4
96-97—Pittsburgh	NHL	81	27	63	90	20	7	10	1	5	1	2	3	2
97-98—Pittsburgh	NHL	81	25	62	87	20	12	7	0	6	1	5	6	2
98-99—Carolina	NHL	82	21	31	52	34	-2	8	0	3	0	1	1	0
99-00—Carolina	NHL	78	23	50	73	18	10	7	0	—	—	—	—	—
00-01—Carolina	NHL	82	15	50	65	32	-15	7	0	3	0	0	0	0
NHL Totals (20 years)		1489	487	1137	1624	917	17	159	11	136	40	83	123	87

FREADRICH, KYLE   LW   RANGERS

PERSONAL: Born December 28, 1978, in Edmonton. ... 6-5/231. ... Shoots left. ... Name pronounced FREED-rihk.

TRANSACTIONS/CAREER NOTES: Selected by Vancouver Canucks in third round (fourth Canucks pick, 64th overall) of NHL entry draft (June 21, 1997). ... Signed as free agent by Tampa Bay Lightning (July 16, 1999). ... Suffered back spasms (March 3, 2000); missed three games. ... Traded by Lightning with LW Nils Ekman to New York Rangers for C Tim Taylor (July 1, 2001).

			REGULAR SEASON							PLAYOFFS				
Season Team	League	Gms.	G	A	Pts.	PIM	+/-	PP	SH	Gms.	G	A	Pts.	PIM
96-97—Prince George	WHL	12	0	0	0	12	...	...	...	—	—	—	—	—
—Regina	WHL	50	1	3	4	152	...	...	...	4	0	0	0	8
97-98—Regina	WHL	62	6	5	11	259	...	...	...	9	0	1	1	25
98-99—Regina	WHL	52	2	2	4	215	...	...	...	—	—	—	—	—
—Syracuse	AHL	5	0	0	0	20	...	...	...	—	—	—	—	—
—Louisiana	ECHL	5	0	0	0	17	...	...	...	4	0	0	0	2
99-00—Detroit	IHL	45	0	1	1	203	...	...	...	—	—	—	—	—
—Louisiana	ECHL	3	0	0	0	17	...	...	...	—	—	—	—	—
—Tampa Bay	NHL	10	0	0	0	39	-1	0	0	—	—	—	—	—
00-01—Detroit	IHL	29	3	3	6	120	...	...	...	—	—	—	—	—
—Tampa Bay	NHL	13	0	1	1	36	-1	0	0	—	—	—	—	—
NHL Totals (2 years)		23	0	1	1	75	-2	0	0					

FRIESEN, JEFF   LW   MIGHTY DUCKS

PERSONAL: Born August 5, 1976, in Meadow Lake, Sask. ... 6-0/205. ... Shoots left. ... Name pronounced FREE-sihn.

TRANSACTIONS/CAREER NOTES: Selected by San Jose Sharks in first round (first Sharks pick, 11th overall) of NHL entry draft (June 28, 1994). ... Injured hand (October 18, 1996); missed two games. ... Missed first two games of 1997-98 season due to contract dispute. ... Injured shoulder (December 26, 1998); missed two games. ... Traded by Sharks with G Steve Shields and conditional pick in draft to Mighty Ducks of Anaheim for RW Teemu Selanne (March 5, 2001).

HONORS: Won Can.HL Rookie of the Year Award (1992-93). ... Won Jim Piggott Memorial Trophy (1992-93). ... Named to NHL All-Rookie team (1994-95).

MISCELLANEOUS: Holds San Jose Sharks all-time records for most games played (512), most assists (201) and most points (350). ... Scored on a penalty shot (vs. Jim Carey, December 2, 1995). ... Failed to score on a penalty shot (vs. Roman Turek, December 30, 1999; vs. Dominic Roussel, January 24, 2001).

STATISTICAL PLATEAUS: Three-goal games: 1995-96 (1), 1999-00 (1). Total: 2.

F

Season Team	League	REGULAR SEASON Gms.	G	A	Pts.	PIM	+/-	PP	SH	PLAYOFFS Gms.	G	A	Pts.	PIM
91-92—Regina	WHL	4	3	1	4	2	...	...	...	—	—	—	—	—
92-93—Regina	WHL	70	45	38	83	23	...	...	...	13	7	10	17	8
93-94—Regina	WHL	66	51	67	118	48	...	...	...	4	3	2	5	2
94-95—Regina	WHL	25	21	23	44	22	...	...	...	—	—	—	—	—
—San Jose	NHL	48	15	10	25	14	-8	5	1	11	1	5	6	4
95-96—San Jose	NHL	79	15	31	46	42	-19	2	0	—	—	—	—	—
96-97—San Jose	NHL	82	28	34	62	75	-8	6	2	—	—	—	—	—
97-98—San Jose	NHL	79	31	32	63	40	8	7	†6	6	0	1	1	2
98-99—San Jose	NHL	78	22	35	57	42	3	10	1	6	2	2	4	14
99-00—San Jose	NHL	82	26	35	61	47	-2	11	3	11	2	2	4	10
00-01—San Jose	NHL	64	12	24	36	56	7	2	0	—	—	—	—	—
—Anaheim	NHL	15	2	10	12	10	-2	2	0	—	—	—	—	—
NHL Totals (7 years)		527	151	211	362	326	-21	45	13	34	5	10	15	30

GABORIK, MARIAN   LW   WILD

PERSONAL: Born February 14, 1982, in Trencin, Czechoslovakia. ... 6-1/183. ... Shoots left.
TRANSACTIONS/CAREER NOTES: Selected by Minnesota Wild in first round (first Wild pick, third overall) of NHL entry draft (June 24, 2000). ... Bruised leg (November 15, 2000); missed six games. ... Strained muscle in abdomen (March 31, 2001); missed four games.
MISCELLANEOUS: Shares Minnesota Wild all-time record for most goals (18).

Season Team	League	REGULAR SEASON Gms.	G	A	Pts.	PIM	+/-	PP	SH	PLAYOFFS Gms.	G	A	Pts.	PIM
98-99—Dukla Trencin	Slovakia	33	11	9	20	6	...	...	...	3	1	0	1	2
99-00—Dukla Trencin	Slovakia	50	25	21	46	34	...	...	...	5	1	2	3	2
00-01—Minnesota	NHL	71	18	18	36	32	-6	6	0					
NHL Totals (1 year)		71	18	18	36	32	-6	6	0					

GAFFANEY, BRIAN   D   PENGUINS

PERSONAL: Born October 4, 1977, in Alexandria, Minn. ... 6-5/205. ... Shoots left.
TRANSACTIONS/CAREER NOTES: Selected by Pittsburgh Penguins in second round (second Penguins pick, 44th overall) of NHL entry draft (June 21, 1997).

Season Team	League	REGULAR SEASON Gms.	G	A	Pts.	PIM	+/-	PP	SH	PLAYOFFS Gms.	G	A	Pts.	PIM
96-97—North Iowa	USHL	48	8	13	21	49	...	...	...	—	—	—	—	—
97-98—St. Cloud State	WCHA	26	0	2	2	37	...	...	...	—	—	—	—	—
98-99—St. Cloud State	WCHA	37	3	5	8	45	...	...	...	—	—	—	—	—
99-00—St. Cloud State	WCHA	38	1	4	5	51	...	...	...	—	—	—	—	—
00-01—St. Cloud State	WCHA	32	2	1	3	44	...	...	...	—	—	—	—	—
—Wilkes-Barre/Scranton	AHL	2	0	1	1	0	...	...	...	1	0	0	0	0

GAGE, JOAQUIN   G

PERSONAL: Born October 19, 1973, in Vancouver. ... 6-0/200. ... Catches left. ... Name pronounced wah-KEEN GAYJ.
TRANSACTIONS/CAREER NOTES: Selected by Edmonton Oilers in fifth round (sixth Oilers pick, 109th overall) of NHL entry draft (June 20, 1992).
MISCELLANEOUS: Stopped a penalty shot attempt (vs. Scott Pellerin, October 15, 2000).

Season Team	League	REGULAR SEASON Gms.	Min	W	L	T	GA	SO	Avg.	PLAYOFFS Gms.	Min.	W	L	GA	SO	Avg.
90-91—Bellingham Jr. A	BCJHL	16	751	...	...	...	64	0	5.11	—	—	—	—	—	—	—
—Portland	WHL	3	180	0	3	0	17	0	5.67	—	—	—	—	—	—	—
91-92—Portland	WHL	63	3635	27	30	4	269	2	4.44	6	366	2	4	28	0	4.59
92-93—Portland	WHL	38	2302	21	16	1	153	2	3.99	8	427	5	2	30	0	4.22
93-94—Prince Albert	WHL	53	3041	24	25	3	212	1	4.18	—	—	—	—	—	—	—
94-95—Cape Breton	AHL	54	3010	17	28	5	207	0	4.13	—	—	—	—	—	—	—
—Edmonton	NHL	2	99	0	2	0	7	0	4.24	—	—	—	—	—	—	—
95-96—Edmonton	NHL	16	717	2	8	1	45	0	3.77	—	—	—	—	—	—	—
—Cape Breton	AHL	21	1161	8	11	0	80	0	4.13	—	—	—	—	—	—	—
96-97—Hamilton	AHL	29	1558	7	14	4	91	0	3.50	—	—	—	—	—	—	—
—Wheeling	ECHL	3	120	1	0	0	8	0	4.00	—	—	—	—	—	—	—
97-98—Raleigh	ECHL	39	2173	19	14	‡3	116	1	3.20	—	—	—	—	—	—	—
—Syracuse	AHL	2	120	1	1	0	7	0	3.50	—	—	—	—	—	—	—
98-99—Portland	AHL	26	1429	8	11	3	69	2	2.90	—	—	—	—	—	—	—
—Providence	AHL	3	130	0	2	0	9	0	4.15	—	—	—	—	—	—	—
—Syracuse	AHL	12	706	2	8	2	46	0	3.91	—	—	—	—	—	—	—
—Augusta	ECHL	5	300	5	0	0	16	0	3.20	—	—	—	—	—	—	—
99-00—Hamilton	AHL	1	59	0	1	0	3	0	3.05	10	580	5	5	28	0	2.90
00-01—Edmonton	NHL	5	260	2	2	0	15	0	3.46	—	—	—	—	—	—	—
—Hamilton	AHL	37	2129	12	22	2	118	0	3.33	—	—	—	—	—	—	—
NHL Totals (3 years)		23	1076	4	12	1	67	0	3.74							

GAGNE, SIMON　　　　　C　　　　　FLYERS

PERSONAL: Born February 29, 1980, in Ste. Foy, Que. ... 6-0/175. ... Shoots left. ... Name pronounced see-MONE gahn-YAY.
TRANSACTIONS/CAREER NOTES: Selected by Philadelphia Flyers in first round (first Flyers pick, 22nd overall) of NHL entry draft (June 27, 1998). ... Suffered from the flu (January 2, 2000); missed one game. ... Suffered from the flu (March 23, 2000); missed one game. ... Strained lower back (February 19, 2001); missed one game. ... Separated shoulder (February 24, 2001); missed 12 games.
HONORS: Named to QMJHL All-Star second team (1998-99). ... Named to NHL All-Rookie team (1999-2000). ... Played in NHL All-Star Game (2001).

		REGULAR SEASON								PLAYOFFS				
Season Team	League	Gms.	G	A	Pts.	PIM	+/-	PP	SH	Gms.	G	A	Pts.	PIM
96-97—Beauport	QMJHL	51	9	22	31	39	...	...	...	—	—	—	—	—
97-98—Quebec	QMJHL	53	30	39	69	26	...	...	...	12	11	5	16	23
98-99—Quebec	QMJHL	61	50	70	120	42	...	...	...	13	9	8	17	4
99-00—Philadelphia	NHL	80	20	28	48	22	11	8	1	17	5	5	10	2
00-01—Philadelphia	NHL	69	27	32	59	18	24	6	0	6	3	0	3	0
NHL Totals (2 years)		149	47	60	107	40	35	14	1	23	8	5	13	2

GAGNON, SEAN　　　　　D　　　　　RANGERS

PERSONAL: Born September 11, 1973, in Sault Ste. Marie, Ont. ... 6-2/210. ... Shoots left.
TRANSACTIONS/CAREER NOTES: Signed as non-drafted free agent by Phoenix Coyotes (May 14, 1997). ... Bruised thigh (December 20, 1997); missed 11 games. ... Signed by Dallas Stars to offer sheet (July 15, 1998). ... Phoenix matched Dallas offer sheet (July 22, 1998). ... Suffered concussion prior to 1998-99 season; missed first game of season. ... Signed as free agent by Ottawa Senators (July 7, 2000). ... Traded by Senators to New York Rangers for RW Jeff Ulmer and D Jason Doig (June 29, 2001).

		REGULAR SEASON								PLAYOFFS				
Season Team	League	Gms.	G	A	Pts.	PIM	+/-	PP	SH	Gms.	G	A	Pts.	PIM
91-92—Sudbury	OHL	44	3	4	7	60	...	...	...	5	0	1	1	0
92-93—Sudbury	OHL	6	1	1	2	2	...	...	...	—	—	—	—	—
—Ottawa	OHL	33	2	10	12	68	...	...	...	—	—	—	—	—
—Sault Ste. Marie	OMJHL	24	1	5	6	65	...	...	...	15	2	2	4	25
93-94—Sault Ste. Marie	OMJHL	42	4	12	16	147	...	...	...	14	1	1	2	52
94-95—Dayton	ECHL	68	9	23	32	339	...	...	...	8	0	3	3	69
95-96—Dayton	ECHL	68	7	22	29	326	...	...	...	3	0	1	1	33
96-97—Fort Wayne	IHL	72	7	7	14	457	...	...	...	—	—	—	—	—
97-98—Springfield	AHL	54	4	13	17	330	...	...	...	2	0	1	1	17
—Phoenix	NHL	5	0	1	1	14	1	0	0	—	—	—	—	—
98-99—Springfield	AHL	68	8	14	22	331	...	...	...	3	0	0	0	14
—Phoenix	NHL	2	0	0	0	7	-2	0	0	—	—	—	—	—
99-00—Jokerit	Finland	42	3	5	8	183	...	...	...	11	4	1	5	22
00-01—Ottawa	NHL	5	0	0	0	13	0	0	0	—	—	—	—	—
—Grand Rapids	IHL	70	4	16	20	226	...	...	...	10	2	3	5	30
NHL Totals (3 years)		12	0	1	1	34	-1	0	0					

GAINEY, STEVE　　　　　LW　　　　　STARS

PERSONAL: Born January 26, 1979, in Montreal. ... 6-0/180. ... Shoots left. ... Son of Bob Gainey, general manager, Dallas Stars.
TRANSACTIONS/CAREER NOTES: Selected by Dallas Stars in third round (third Stars pick, 77th overall) of NHL entry draft (June 21, 1997).

		REGULAR SEASON								PLAYOFFS				
Season Team	League	Gms.	G	A	Pts.	PIM	+/-	PP	SH	Gms.	G	A	Pts.	PIM
95-96—Kamloops	WHL	49	1	4	5	40	...	...	...	3	0	0	0	0
96-97—Kamloops	WHL	60	9	18	27	60	...	...	...	2	0	0	0	9
97-98—Kamloops	WHL	68	21	34	55	93	...	...	...	7	1	7	8	15
98-99—Kamloops	WHL	68	30	34	64	155	...	...	...	15	5	4	9	38
99-00—Michigan	IHL	58	8	10	18	41	...	...	...	—	—	—	—	—
—Fort Wayne	UHL	1	0	0	0	0	...	...	...	—	—	—	—	—
00-01—Utah	IHL	61	7	7	14	167	...	...	...	—	—	—	—	—
—Dallas	NHL	1	0	0	0	0	0	0	0	—	—	—	—	—
NHL Totals (1 year)		1	0	0	0	0	0	0	0					

GALANOV, MAXIM　　　　　D　　　　　MAPLE LEAFS

PERSONAL: Born March 13, 1974, in Krasnoyarsk, U.S.S.R. ... 6-1/210. ... Shoots left. ... Name pronounced guh-LAH-nahf.
TRANSACTIONS/CAREER NOTES: Selected by New York Rangers in third round (third Rangers pick, 61st overall) of NHL entry draft (June 26, 1993). ... Selected by Pittsburgh Penguins from Rangers in NHL waiver draft (October 5, 1998). ... Injured shoulder (January 26, 1999); missed seven games. ... Separated shoulder (March 13, 1999); missed 17 games. ... Selected by Atlanta Thrashers in NHL expansion draft (June 25, 1999). ... Injured wrist prior to start of 1999-2000 season and underwent surgery; missed first 36 games of season. ... Bruised foot (February 15, 2000); missed one game. ... Signed as free agent by Florida Panthers (October 7, 2000). ... Claimed on waivers by Tampa Bay Lightning (November 3, 2000). ... Traded by Lightning to Toronto Maple Leafs for LW Konstantin Kalmikov (February 20, 2001).

		REGULAR SEASON								PLAYOFFS				
Season Team	League	Gms.	G	A	Pts.	PIM	+/-	PP	SH	Gms.	G	A	Pts.	PIM
92-93—Lada Togliatti	CIS	41	4	2	6	12	...	...	...	10	1	1	2	12
93-94—Lada Togliatti	CIS	7	1	0	1	4	...	...	...	12	1	0	1	8
94-95—Lada Togliatti	CIS	45	5	6	11	54	...	...	...	9	0	1	1	12

G

			REGULAR SEASON								PLAYOFFS				
Season Team	League	Gms.	G	A	Pts.	PIM	+/-	PP	SH		Gms.	G	A	Pts.	PIM
95-96—Binghamton	AHL	72	17	36	53	24	...	...	...		4	1	1	2	0
96-97—Binghamton	AHL	73	13	30	43	30	...	...	...		3	0	0	0	2
97-98—Hartford	AHL	61	6	24	30	22	...	...	...		13	3	6	9	2
—New York Rangers......	NHL	6	0	1	1	2	1	0	0		—	—	—	—	—
98-99—Pittsburgh................	NHL	51	4	3	7	14	-8	2	0		1	0	0	0	0
99-00—Atlanta	NHL	40	4	3	7	20	-12	0	0		—	—	—	—	—
00-01—Louisville	AHL	9	4	5	9	11	...	...	...		—	—	—	—	—
—Tampa Bay	NHL	25	0	5	5	8	-5	0	0		—	—	—	—	—
—Detroit.................	IHL	6	0	3	3	2	...	...	...		—	—	—	—	—
—St. John's..................	AHL	17	2	7	9	10	...	...	...		4	0	0	0	2
NHL Totals (4 years)...........		122	8	12	20	44	-24	2	0		1	0	0	0	0

GALLEY, GARRY   D

PERSONAL: Born April 16, 1963, in Ottawa. ... 6-0/207. ... Shoots left.
TRANSACTIONS/CAREER NOTES: Selected by Los Angeles Kings in fifth round (fourth Kings pick, 100th overall) of NHL entry draft (June 8, 1983). ... Injured knee (December 8, 1985). ... Traded by Kings to Washington Capitals for G Al Jensen (February 14, 1987). ... Signed as free agent by Boston Bruins; third-round pick in 1989 draft awarded to Capitals as compensation (July 8, 1988). ... Sprained left shoulder (September 30, 1989); missed first nine games of season. ... Suffered lacerations to cheek, both lips and part of neck (October 6, 1990). ... Dislocated right shoulder (December 22, 1990). ... Bruised left kneecap (March 23, 1991); missed two games. ... Pulled hamstring (April 17, 1991); missed three playoff games. ... Traded by Bruins with C Wes Walz and third-round pick (D Milos Holan) in 1993 draft to Philadelphia Flyers for D Gord Murphy, RW Brian Dobbin, third-round pick (LW Sergei Zholtok) in 1992 draft and fourth-round pick (D Charles Paquette) in 1993 draft (January 2, 1992). ... Bruised ribs (January 9, 1992); missed one game. ... Fractured foot (March 3, 1992); missed two games. ... Bruised jaw (February 24, 1993); missed one game. ... Strained shoulder (March 6, 1994); missed three games. ... Sprained wrist (February 13, 1995); missed three games. ... Traded by Flyers to Buffalo Sabres for D Petr Svoboda (April 7, 1995). ... Injured shoulder (November 12, 1995); missed three games. ... Injured knee (February 14, 1996); missed one game. ... Strained right shoulder (November 7, 1996); missed four games. ... Suffered concussion (December 4, 1996); missed two games. ... Tore abdominal muscle (February 9, 1997); missed one game. ... Fractured jaw (February 23, 1997); missed two games. ... Signed as free agent by Kings (July 5, 1997). ... Bruised left knee (February 24, 1998); missed three games. ... Strained abdominal muscle (April 5, 1999); missed six games. ... Suffered concussion (December 19, 1999); missed nine games. ... Signed as free agent by New York Islanders (September 13, 2000). ... Suffered concussion (November 16, 2000); missed three games. ... Strained left shoulder (February 7, 2001); missed 19 games.
HONORS: Named to CCHA All-Star first team (1982-83 and 1983-84). ... Named to NCAA All-Tournament team (1983-84). ... Played in NHL All-Star Game (1991 and 1994).

			REGULAR SEASON								PLAYOFFS				
Season Team	League	Gms.	G	A	Pts.	PIM	+/-	PP	SH		Gms.	G	A	Pts.	PIM
81-82—Bowling Green	CCHA	42	3	36	39	48	...	...	...		—	—	—	—	—
82-83—Bowling Green	CCHA	40	17	29	46	40	...	...	...		—	—	—	—	—
83-84—Bowling Green	CCHA	44	15	52	67	61	...	...	...		—	—	—	—	—
84-85—Los Angeles...............	NHL	78	8	30	38	82	3	1	1		3	1	0	1	2
85-86—Los Angeles...............	NHL	49	9	13	22	46	-9	1	0		—	—	—	—	—
—New Haven	AHL	4	2	6	8	6	...	...	...		—	—	—	—	—
86-87—Los Angeles...............	NHL	30	5	11	16	57	-9	2	0		—	—	—	—	—
—Washington..................	NHL	18	1	10	11	10	3	1	0		2	0	0	0	0
87-88—Washington	NHL	58	7	23	30	44	11	3	0		13	2	4	6	13
88-89—Boston	NHL	78	8	21	29	80	-7	2	1		9	0	1	1	33
89-90—Boston	NHL	71	8	27	35	75	2	1	0		21	3	3	6	34
90-91—Boston	NHL	70	6	21	27	84	0	1	0		16	1	5	6	17
91-92—Boston	NHL	38	2	12	14	83	-3	1	0		—	—	—	—	—
—Philadelphia...............	NHL	39	3	15	18	34	1	2	0		—	—	—	—	—
92-93—Philadelphia	NHL	83	13	49	62	115	18	4	1		—	—	—	—	—
93-94—Philadelphia	NHL	81	10	60	70	91	-11	5	1		—	—	—	—	—
94-95—Philadelphia	NHL	33	2	20	22	20	0	1	0		—	—	—	—	—
—Buffalo	NHL	14	1	9	10	10	4	1	0		5	0	3	3	4
95-96—Buffalo	NHL	78	10	44	54	81	-2	7	1		—	—	—	—	—
96-97—Buffalo	NHL	71	4	34	38	102	10	1	1		12	0	6	6	14
97-98—Los Angeles...............	NHL	74	9	28	37	63	-5	7	0		4	0	1	1	2
98-99—Los Angeles...............	NHL	60	4	12	16	30	-9	3	0		—	—	—	—	—
99-00—Los Angeles...............	NHL	70	9	21	30	52	9	2	0		4	0	0	0	0
00-01—New York Islanders.....	NHL	56	6	14	20	59	-4	4	0		—	—	—	—	—
NHL Totals (17 years).........		1149	125	474	599	1218	2	50	6		89	7	23	30	119

GARDINER, BRUCE   C   BLUE JACKETS

PERSONAL: Born February 11, 1972, in North York, Ont. ... 6-1/193. ... Shoots right.
TRANSACTIONS/CAREER NOTES: Selected by St. Louis Blues in sixth round (sixth Blues pick, 131st overall) of NHL entry draft (June 22, 1991). ... Signed as free agent by Ottawa Senators (June 14, 1994). ... Fractured leg (September 23, 1995). ... Bruised left foot (November 27, 1996); missed two games. ... Separated left shoulder (February 1, 1997); missed 10 games. ... Bruised thigh (November 6, 1997); missed two games. ... Bruised thigh (November 15, 1997); missed three games. ... Tore medial collateral ligament in knee (December 13, 1997); missed 21 games. ... Sprained thumb (October 23, 1998); missed six games. ... Bruised foot (January 1, 1999); missed one game. ... Reinjured foot (January 30, 1999); missed two games. ... Reinjured foot (February 6, 1999); missed seven games. ... Reinjured foot (March 6, 1999); missed seven games. ... Sprained medial collateral ligament in left knee (October 14, 1999); missed three games. ... Traded by Senators to Tampa Bay Lightning for LW Colin Forbes (November 11, 1999). ... Sprained knee (November 17, 1999); missed 13 games. ... Injured abdomen (February 27, 2000); missed four games. ... Selected by Columbus Blue Jackets in NHL expansion draft (June 23, 2000). ... Bruised hip (November 4, 2000); missed one game. ... Strained hip flexor (November 22, 2000); missed three games. ... Injured hip (February 20, 2001); missed four games.
HONORS: Named to ECAC All-Star second team (1993-94).

G

Season Team	League	REGULAR SEASON								PLAYOFFS				
		Gms.	G	A	Pts.	PIM	+/-	PP	SH	Gms.	G	A	Pts.	PIM
90-91—Colgate University.......	ECAC	27	4	9	13	72	...	...	...	—	—	—	—	—
91-92—Colgate University.......	ECAC	23	7	8	15	77	...	...	...	—	—	—	—	—
92-93—Colgate University.......	ECAC	33	17	12	29	64	...	...	...	—	—	—	—	—
93-94—Colgate University.......	ECAC	33	23	23	46	68	...	...	...	—	—	—	—	—
—Peoria....................	IHL	3	0	0	0	0	...	...	...	—	—	—	—	—
94-95—Prin. Edward Island	AHL	72	17	20	37	132	...	...	...	7	4	1	5	4
95-96—Prin. Edward Island	AHL	38	11	13	24	87	...	...	...	5	2	4	6	4
96-97—Ottawa................	NHL	67	11	10	21	49	4	0	1	7	0	1	1	2
97-98—Ottawa................	NHL	55	7	11	18	50	2	0	0	11	1	3	4	2
98-99—Ottawa................	NHL	59	4	8	12	43	6	0	0	3	0	0	0	4
99-00—Ottawa................	NHL	10	0	3	3	4	1	0	0	—	—	—	—	—
—Tampa Bay...............	NHL	41	3	6	9	37	-21	0	0	—	—	—	—	—
00-01—Columbus.............	NHL	73	7	15	22	78	-1	0	0	—	—	—	—	—
NHL Totals (5 years)...........		305	32	53	85	261	-9	0	1	21	1	4	5	8

GARON, MATHIEU   G   CANADIENS

PERSONAL: Born January 9, 1978, in Chandler, Que. ... 6-2/182. ... Catches right.

TRANSACTIONS/CAREER NOTES: Selected by Montreal Canadiens in second round (second Canadiens pick, 44th overall) of NHL entry draft (June 22, 1996).

HONORS: Won Raymond Lagace Trophy (1995-96). ... Named to QMJHL All-Rookie team (1995-96). ... Named to Can.HL All-Star first team (1997-98). ... Won Jacques Plante Trophy (1997-98). ... Named to QMJHL All-Star first team (1997-98). ... Won Can.HL Goaltender of the Year Award (1997-98).

Season Team	League	REGULAR SEASON								PLAYOFFS						
		Gms.	Min	W	L	T	GA	SO	Avg.	Gms.	Min.	W	L	GA	SO	Avg.
95-96—Victoriaville	QMJHL	51	2709	18	27	0	189	1	4.19	12	676	7	4	38	1	3.37
96-97—Victoriaville	QMJHL	53	3026	29	18	3	148	*6	2.93	6	330	2	4	23	0	4.18
97-98—Victoriaville	QMJHL	47	2802	27	18	2	125	5	2.68	6	345	2	4	22	0	3.83
98-99—Fredericton	AHL	40	2222	14	22	2	114	3	3.08	6	208	1	1	12	0	3.46
99-00—Quebec.....................	AHL	53	2884	17	28	3	149	2	3.10	1	20	0	0	3	0	9.00
00-01—Montreal....................	NHL	11	589	4	5	1	24	2	2.44	—	—	—	—	—	—	—
—Quebec.....................	AHL	31	1768	16	13	1	86	1	2.92	8	459	4	4	22	1	2.88
NHL Totals (1 year)...............		11	589	4	5	1	24	2	2.44							

GAUL, MIKE   D

PERSONAL: Born April 22, 1973, in Lachine, Que. ... 6-1/200. ... Shoots right. ... Full Name: Michael Gaul. ... Name pronounced GAHL.

TRANSACTIONS/CAREER NOTES: Selected by Los Angeles Kings in 12th round (10th Kings pick, 262nd overall) of NHL entry draft (June 22, 1991). ... Signed as free agent by New York Islanders (August 19, 1998). ... Traded by Islanders to Colorado Avalanche for D Ted Crowley (December 15, 1998). ... Signed as free agent by Columbus Blue Jackets (August 24, 2000). ... Strained shoulder (April 1, 2001); missed one game.

HONORS: Named to Memorial Cup All-Star team (1992-93). ... Named to AHL All-Star second team (1999-2000 and 2000-01).

Season Team	League	REGULAR SEASON								PLAYOFFS				
		Gms.	G	A	Pts.	PIM	+/-	PP	SH	Gms.	G	A	Pts.	PIM
90-91—St. Lawrence Univ.......	ECAC	31	1	3	4	46	...	...	...	—	—	—	—	—
91-92—Laval..........................	QMJHL	50	6	38	44	44	...	...	...	10	0	2	2	20
92-93—Laval..........................	QMJHL	57	16	57	73	66	...	...	...	13	3	10	13	10
93-94—Laval..........................	QMJHL	22	10	17	27	24	...	...	...	21	5	15	20	14
94-95—Knoxville	ECHL	68	13	41	54	51	...	...	...	—	—	—	—	—
—Phoenix.....................	IHL	4	0	1	1	2	...	...	...	—	—	—	—	—
95-96—Knoxville	ECHL	54	13	48	61	44	...	...	...	—	—	—	—	—
96-97—Timmendorf................	Ger. Div. II	20	40	52	92	100	...	...	...	—	—	—	—	—
97-98—Hershey	AHL	60	12	47	59	69	...	...	...	7	0	7	7	6
—Mobile.....................	ECHL	5	0	7	7	0	...	...	...	—	—	—	—	—
98-99—Lowell	AHL	18	3	5	8	14	...	...	...	—	—	—	—	—
—Hershey	AHL	43	9	31	40	22	...	...	...	5	1	1	2	6
—Colorado.....................	NHL	1	0	0	0	0	0	0	0	—	—	—	—	—
99-00—Hershey	AHL	65	12	57	69	52	...	...	...	12	0	8	8	6
00-01—Syracuse	AHL	70	16	45	61	80	...	...	...	5	1	2	3	8
—Columbus.....................	NHL	2	0	0	0	4	0	0	0	—	—	—	—	—
NHL Totals (2 years)...........		3	0	0	0	4	0	0	0					

GAUTHIER, DENIS   D   FLAMES

PERSONAL: Born October 1, 1976, in Montreal. ... 6-2/210. ... Shoots left. ... Full Name: Denis Gauthier Jr. ... Name pronounced GO-tee-ay.

TRANSACTIONS/CAREER NOTES: Selected by Calgary Flames in first round (first Flames pick, 20th overall) of NHL entry draft (July 8, 1995). ... Suffered concussion (September 27, 1997); missed two games. ... Suffered concussion (January 10, 1999); missed two games. ... Injured groin (March 25, 1999); missed two games. ... Injured shoulder (October 26, 1999); missed 11 games. ... Suspended two games by NHL for elbowing incident (December 7, 1999). ... Suffered hip pointer (February 1, 2000); missed remainder of season. ... Injured wrist (October 15, 2000); missed 17 games. ... Injured shoulder (March 16, 2001); missed two games.

HONORS: Named to Can.HL All-Star first team (1995-96). ... Won Emile Bouchard Trophy (1995-96). ... Named to QMJHL All-Star first team (1995-96).

G

Season Team	League	REGULAR SEASON								PLAYOFFS				
		Gms.	G	A	Pts.	PIM	+/-	PP	SH	Gms.	G	A	Pts.	PIM
92-93—Drummondville	QMJHL	61	1	7	8	136	...	...	...	10	0	5	5	40
93-94—Drummondville	QMJHL	60	0	7	7	176	...	...	...	9	2	0	2	41
94-95—Drummondville	QMJHL	64	9	31	40	190	...	...	...	4	0	5	5	12
95-96—Drummondville	QMJHL	53	25	49	74	140	...	...	...	6	4	4	8	32
—Saint John	AHL	5	2	0	2	8	...	...	...	16	1	6	7	20
96-97—Saint John	AHL	73	3	28	31	74	...	...	...	5	0	0	0	6
97-98—Calgary	NHL	10	0	0	0	16	-5	0	0	—	—	—	—	—
—Saint John	AHL	68	4	20	24	154	...	...	...	21	0	4	4	83
98-99—Saint John	AHL	16	0	3	3	31	...	...	...	—	—	—	—	—
—Calgary	NHL	55	3	4	7	68	3	0	0	—	—	—	—	—
99-00—Calgary	NHL	39	1	1	2	50	-4	0	0	—	—	—	—	—
00-01—Calgary	NHL	62	2	6	8	78	3	0	0	—	—	—	—	—
NHL Totals (4 years)		166	6	11	17	212	-3	0	0					

GAVEY, AARON   LW   WILD

PERSONAL: Born February 22, 1974, in Sudbury, Ont. ... 6-2/200. ... Shoots left. ... Name pronounced GAY-vee.

TRANSACTIONS/CAREER NOTES: Selected by Tampa Bay Lightning in fourth round (fourth Lightning pick, 74th overall) of NHL entry draft (June 20, 1992). ... Suffered facial laceration (February 4, 1996); missed eight games. ... Traded by Lightning to Calgary Flames for G Rick Tabaracci (November 19, 1996). ... Strained neck (February 28, 1997); missed 14 games. ... Strained abdominal muscle (January 11, 1997); missed 37 games. ... Sprained thumb (April 15, 1998); missed two games. ... Traded by Flames to Dallas Stars for C Bob Bassen (July 14, 1998). ... Fractured hand (September 22, 1998); missed first three games of 1998-99 season. ... Sprained knee (February 2, 2000); missed one game. ... Traded by Stars with C Pavel Patera, eighth-round pick (C Eric Johansson) in 2000 draft and fourth-round pick in 2002 draft to Minnesota Wild for D Brad Lukowich, third- (C Yared Hagos) and ninth-round (RW Dale Sullivan) picks in 2001 draft (June 25, 2000). ... Bruised foot (November 14, 2000); missed three games.

Season Team	League	REGULAR SEASON								PLAYOFFS				
		Gms.	G	A	Pts.	PIM	+/-	PP	SH	Gms.	G	A	Pts.	PIM
90-91—Peterborough Jr. B	OHA	42	26	30	56	68	...	...	...	—	—	—	—	—
91-92—Sault Ste. Marie	OHL	48	7	11	18	27	...	...	...	19	5	1	6	10
92-93—Sault Ste. Marie	OHL	62	45	39	84	114	...	...	...	18	5	9	14	36
93-94—Sault Ste. Marie	OHL	60	42	60	102	116	...	...	...	14	11	10	21	22
94-95—Atlanta	IHL	66	18	17	35	85	...	...	...	5	0	1	1	9
95-96—Tampa Bay	NHL	73	8	4	12	56	-6	1	1	6	0	0	0	4
96-97—Tampa Bay	NHL	16	1	2	3	12	-1	0	0	—	—	—	—	—
—Calgary	NHL	41	7	9	16	34	-11	3	0	—	—	—	—	—
97-98—Calgary	NHL	26	2	3	5	24	-5	0	0	—	—	—	—	—
—Saint John	AHL	8	4	3	7	28	...	...	...	—	—	—	—	—
98-99—Dallas	NHL	7	0	0	0	10	-1	0	0	—	—	—	—	—
—Michigan	IHL	67	24	33	57	128	...	...	...	5	2	3	5	4
99-00—Michigan	IHL	28	14	15	29	73	...	...	...	—	—	—	—	—
—Dallas	NHL	41	7	6	13	44	0	1	0	13	1	2	3	10
00-01—Minnesota	NHL	75	10	14	24	52	-8	1	0	—	—	—	—	—
NHL Totals (6 years)		279	35	38	73	232	-32	6	1	19	1	2	3	14

GELINAS, MARTIN   LW   HURRICANES

PERSONAL: Born June 5, 1970, in Shawinigan, Que. ... 5-11/195. ... Shoots left. ... Name pronounced MAHR-tahn ZHEHL-ih-nuh.

TRANSACTIONS/CAREER NOTES: Selected by Los Angeles Kings in first round (first Kings pick, seventh overall) of NHL entry draft (June 11, 1988). ... Traded by Kings with C Jimmy Carson, first-round picks in 1989 (traded to New Jersey), 1991 (LW Martin Rucinsky) and 1993 (D Nick Stajduhar) drafts and cash to Edmonton Oilers for C Wayne Gretzky, RW/D Marty McSorley and LW/C Mike Krushelnyski (August 9, 1988). ... Suspended five games by NHL (March 9, 1990). ... Underwent shoulder surgery (June 1990). ... Traded by Oilers with sixth-round pick (C Nicholas Checco) in 1993 draft to Quebec Nordiques for LW Scott Pearson (June 20, 1993). ... Injured thigh (October 20, 1993); missed one game. ... Separated left shoulder (November 25, 1993); missed 10 games. ... Claimed on waivers by Vancouver Canucks (January 15, 1994). ... Suffered charley horse (March 27, 1994); missed six games. ... Injured knee (April 30, 1995); missed last game of season and eight playoff games. ... Fractured rib (November 2, 1996); missed eight games. ... Sprained knee (October 13, 1997); missed 16 games. ... Traded by Canucks with G Kirk McLean to Carolina Hurricanes for LW Geoff Sanderson, D Enrico Ciccone and G Sean Burke (January 3, 1998). ... Strained quadriceps (October 27, 1998); missed two games. ... Bruised thigh (April 3, 1999); missed four games. ... Injured knee (February 8, 2001); missed three games.

HONORS: Won Can.HL Rookie of the Year Award (1987-88). ... Won Michel Bergeron Trophy (1987-88). ... Named to QMJHL All-Star first team (1987-88).

MISCELLANEOUS: Member of Stanley Cup championship team (1990).

STATISTICAL PLATEAUS: Three-goal games: 1989-90 (1), 1996-97 (1). Total: 2. ... Four-goal games: 1996-97 (1). ... Total hat tricks: 3.

G

Season Team	League	REGULAR SEASON								PLAYOFFS				
		Gms.	G	A	Pts.	PIM	+/-	PP	SH	Gms.	G	A	Pts.	PIM
87-88—Hull	QMJHL	65	63	68	131	74	...	...	...	17	15	18	33	32
88-89—Edmonton	NHL	6	1	2	3	0	-1	0	0	—	—	—	—	—
—Hull	QMJHL	41	38	39	77	31	...	...	...	9	5	4	9	14
89-90—Edmonton	NHL	46	17	8	25	30	0	5	0	20	2	3	5	6
90-91—Edmonton	NHL	73	20	20	40	34	-7	4	0	18	3	6	9	25
91-92—Edmonton	NHL	68	11	18	29	62	14	1	0	15	1	3	4	10
92-93—Edmonton	NHL	65	11	12	23	30	3	0	0	—	—	—	—	—
93-94—Quebec	NHL	31	6	6	12	8	-2	0	0	—	—	—	—	—
—Vancouver	NHL	33	8	8	16	26	-6	3	0	24	5	4	9	14
94-95—Vancouver	NHL	46	13	10	23	36	8	1	0	3	0	1	1	0
95-96—Vancouver	NHL	81	30	26	56	59	8	3	4	6	1	1	2	12
96-97—Vancouver	NHL	74	35	33	68	42	6	6	1	—	—	—	—	—

Season Team	League	REGULAR SEASON								PLAYOFFS				
		Gms.	G	A	Pts.	PIM	+/-	PP	SH	Gms.	G	A	Pts.	PIM
97-98—Vancouver	NHL	24	4	4	8	10	-6	1	1	—	—	—	—	—
—Carolina	NHL	40	12	14	26	30	1	2	1	—	—	—	—	—
98-99—Carolina	NHL	76	13	15	28	67	3	0	0	6	0	3	3	2
99-00—Carolina	NHL	81	14	16	30	40	-10	3	0	—	—	—	—	—
00-01—Carolina	NHL	79	23	29	52	59	-4	6	1	6	0	1	1	6
NHL Totals (13 years)		823	218	221	439	533	7	35	8	98	12	22	34	75

GIGUERE, JEAN-SEBASTIEN   G   MIGHTY DUCKS

PERSONAL: Born June 16, 1977, in Montreal. ... 6-0/185. ... Catches left. ... Name pronounced zhee-GAIR.

TRANSACTIONS/CAREER NOTES: Selected by Hartford Whalers in first round (first Whalers pick, 13th overall) of NHL entry draft (July 8, 1995). ... Whalers franchise moved to North Carolina and renamed Carolina Hurricanes for 1997-98 season; NHL approved move on June 25, 1997. ... Traded by Hurricanes with C Andrew Cassels to Calgary Flames for LW Gary Roberts and G Trevor Kidd (August 25, 1997). ... Strained hamstring (December 27, 1998); missed seven games. ... Traded by Flames to Mighty Ducks of Anaheim for second-round pick (traded to Washington) in 2000 draft (June 10, 2000).

HONORS: Named to QMJHL All-Star second team (1996-97). ... Shared Harry (Hap) Holmes Trophy with Tyler Moss (1997-98).

Season Team	League	REGULAR SEASON								PLAYOFFS						
		Gms.	Min	W	L	T	GA	SO	Avg.	Gms.	Min.	W	L	GA	SO	Avg.
93-94—Verdun	QMJHL	25	1234	13	5	2	66	0	3.21	—	—	—	—	—	—	—
94-95—Halifax	QMJHL	47	2755	14	27	5	181	2	3.94	7	417	3	4	17	1	2.45
95-96—Verdun	QMJHL	55	3228	26	23	2	185	1	3.44	6	356	1	5	24	0	4.04
96-97—Halifax	QMJHL	50	3009	28	19	3	169	2	3.37	16	954	9	7	58	0	3.65
—Hartford	NHL	8	394	1	4	0	24	0	3.65	—	—	—	—	—	—	—
97-98—Saint John	AHL	31	1758	16	10	3	72	2	2.46	10	537	5	3	27	0	3.02
98-99—Saint John	AHL	39	2145	18	16	3	123	3	3.44	7	304	3	2	21	0	4.14
—Calgary	NHL	15	860	6	7	1	46	0	3.21	—	—	—	—	—	—	—
99-00—Saint John	AHL	41	2243	17	17	3	114	0	3.05	3	178	0	3	9	0	3.03
—Calgary	NHL	7	330	1	3	1	15	0	2.73	—	—	—	—	—	—	—
00-01—Cincinnati	AHL	23	1306	12	7	2	53	0	2.43	—	—	—	—	—	—	—
—Anaheim	NHL	34	2031	11	17	5	87	4	2.57	—	—	—	—	—	—	—
NHL Totals (4 years)		64	3615	19	31	7	172	4	2.85							

GILCHRIST, BRENT   LW   RED WINGS

PERSONAL: Born April 3, 1967, in Moose Jaw, Sask. ... 5-11/180. ... Shoots left.

TRANSACTIONS/CAREER NOTES: Selected by Montreal Canadiens in sixth round (sixth Canadiens pick, 79th overall) of NHL entry draft (June 15, 1985). ... Injured knee (January 1987). ... Fractured right index finger (November 17, 1990); missed 19 games. ... Separated left shoulder (February 6, 1991); missed two games. ... Reinjured left shoulder (February 13, 1991); missed five games. ... Traded by Canadiens with LW Shayne Corson and LW Vladimir Vujtek to Edmonton Oilers for LW Vincent Damphousse and fourth-round pick (D Adam Wiesel) in 1993 draft (August 27, 1992). ... Suffered concussion (October 1992); missed two games. ... Fractured nose (December 21, 1992); missed two games. ... Traded by Oilers to Minnesota North Stars for C Todd Elik (March 5, 1993). ... Separated shoulder (March 18, 1993); missed remainder of season. ... North Stars franchise moved from Minnesota to Dallas and renamed Stars for 1993-94 season. ... Strained shoulder (October 27, 1993); missed four games. ... Pulled groin (November 21, 1993); missed four games. ... Strained groin (February 20, 1995); missed two games. ... Strained groin and sprained wrist (February 26, 1995); missed 13 games. ... Suffered from sore wrist (April 11, 1995); missed one game. ... Injured groin (October 14, 1995); missed four games. ... Strained hip flexor (November 6, 1996); missed two games. ... Strained groin (December 21, 1996); missed three games. ... Strained groin (March 5, 1997); missed two games. ... Strained groin (March 16, 1997); missed seven games. ... Signed as free agent by Detroit Red Wings (July 8, 1997). ... Injured groin (March 4, 1998); missed 20 games. ... Selected by Tampa Bay Lightning from Red Wings in NHL waiver draft (October 5, 1998). ... Traded by Lightning to Red Wings for sixth-round pick (traded back to Detroit) in 1999 draft (October 5, 1998). ... Underwent surgery for hernia (September 21, 1998); missed first 68 games of season. ... Strained lower abdominal muscle (March 21, 1999); missed eight games. ... Suffered hernia prior to start of 1999-2000 season; missed first 56 games of season. ... Injured groin (November 17, 2000); missed four games.

MISCELLANEOUS: Member of Stanley Cup championship team (1998). ... Failed to score on a penalty shot (vs. Kirk McLean, January 27, 1994).

STATISTICAL PLATEAUS: Three-goal games: 1991-92 (1).

Season Team	League	REGULAR SEASON								PLAYOFFS				
		Gms.	G	A	Pts.	PIM	+/-	PP	SH	Gms.	G	A	Pts.	PIM
83-84—Kelowna	WHL	69	16	11	27	16	...	...	...	—	—	—	—	—
84-85—Kelowna	WHL	51	35	38	73	58	...	...	...	6	5	2	7	8
85-86—Spokane	WHL	52	45	45	90	57	...	...	...	9	6	7	13	19
86-87—Spokane	WHL	46	45	55	100	71	...	...	...	5	2	7	9	6
—Sherbrooke	AHL	—	—	—	—	—	...	...	...	10	2	7	9	2
87-88—Sherbrooke	AHL	77	26	48	74	83	...	...	...	6	1	3	4	6
88-89—Montreal	NHL	49	8	16	24	16	9	0	0	9	1	1	2	10
—Sherbrooke	AHL	7	6	5	11	7	...	...	...	—	—	—	—	—
89-90—Montreal	NHL	57	9	15	24	28	3	1	0	8	2	0	2	2
90-91—Montreal	NHL	51	6	9	15	10	-3	1	0	13	5	3	8	6
91-92—Montreal	NHL	79	23	27	50	57	29	2	0	11	2	4	6	6
92-93—Edmonton	NHL	60	10	10	20	47	-10	2	0	—	—	—	—	—
—Minnesota	NHL	8	0	1	1	2	-2	0	0	—	—	—	—	—
93-94—Dallas	NHL	76	17	14	31	31	0	3	1	9	3	1	4	2
94-95—Dallas	NHL	32	9	4	13	16	-3	1	3	5	0	1	1	2
95-96—Dallas	NHL	77	20	22	42	36	-11	6	1	—	—	—	—	—
96-97—Dallas	NHL	67	10	20	30	24	6	2	0	6	2	2	4	2
97-98—Detroit	NHL	61	13	14	27	40	4	5	0	15	2	1	3	12
98-99—Detroit	NHL	5	1	0	1	0	-1	0	0	3	0	0	0	0
99-00—Detroit	NHL	24	4	2	6	24	1	0	0	6	0	0	0	6
00-01—Detroit	NHL	60	1	8	9	41	-8	0	0	5	0	1	1	0
NHL Totals (13 years)		706	131	162	293	372	14	23	5	90	17	14	31	48

G

GILL, HAL   D   BRUINS

PERSONAL: Born April 6, 1975, in Concord, Mass. ... 6-7/240. ... Shoots left.

TRANSACTIONS/CAREER NOTES: Selected by Boston Bruins in eighth round (eighth Bruins pick, 207th overall) of NHL entry draft (June 26, 1993). ... Suffered from the flu (January 21, 1998); missed one game. ... Strained hip flexor (April 7, 1999); missed two games. ... Suffered from the flu (January 11, 2000); missed one game.

		REGULAR SEASON								PLAYOFFS				
Season Team	League	Gms.	G	A	Pts.	PIM	+/-	PP	SH	Gms.	G	A	Pts.	PIM
93-94—Providence College	Hockey East	31	1	2	3	26	...	...	...	—	—	—	—	—
94-95—Providence College	Hockey East	26	1	3	4	22	...	...	...	—	—	—	—	—
95-96—Providence College	Hockey East	39	5	12	17	54	...	...	...	—	—	—	—	—
96-97—Providence College	Hockey East	35	5	16	21	52	...	...	...	—	—	—	—	—
97-98—Boston	NHL	68	2	4	6	47	4	0	0	6	0	0	0	4
—Providence	AHL	4	1	0	1	23	...	...	...	—	—	—	—	—
98-99—Boston	NHL	80	3	7	10	63	-10	0	0	12	0	0	0	14
99-00—Boston	NHL	81	3	9	12	51	0	0	0	—	—	—	—	—
00-01—Boston	NHL	80	1	10	11	71	-2	0	0	—	—	—	—	—
NHL Totals (4 years)		309	9	30	39	232	-8	0	0	18	0	0	0	18

GILL, TODD   D   AVALANCHE

PERSONAL: Born November 9, 1965, in Brockville, Ont. ... 6-2/179. ... Shoots left.

TRANSACTIONS/CAREER NOTES: Selected by Toronto Maple Leafs in second round (second Maple Leafs pick, 25th overall) of NHL entry draft (June 9, 1984). ... Fractured right foot (October 1987). ... Bruised shoulder (March 1989). ... Fractured finger (October 15, 1991); missed three games. ... Strained back (February 8, 1992); missed three games. ... Injured back prior to 1992-93 season; missed first two games of season. ... Bruised foot (November 14, 1992); missed 11 games. ... Strained groin (November 1, 1993); missed 26 games. ... Suffered back spasms (February 24, 1994); missed 13 games. ... Injured shoulder (March 17, 1995); missed one game. ... Pulled hamstring (November 10, 1995); missed four games. ... Suffered back spasms (February 7, 1996); missed four games. ... Traded by Maple Leafs to San Jose Sharks for C Jamie Baker and fifth-round pick (C Peter Cava) in 1996 draft (June 14, 1996). ... Suffered sore knee (April 9, 1997); missed three games. ... Traded by Sharks to St. Louis Blues for RW Joe Murphy (March 24, 1998). ... Bruised foot (November 23, 1998); missed three games. ... Claimed on waivers by Detroit Red Wings (December 30, 1998). ... Fractured forearm (February 1, 1999); missed 24 games. ... Signed as free agent by Phoenix Coyotes (July 15, 1999). ... Strained muscle in abdomen (November 23, 1999); missed seven games. ... Lacerated face (December 22, 1999); missed one game. ... Strained muscle in abdomen (January 8, 2000); missed 13 games. ... Traded by Coyotes to Red Wings for LW Philippe Audet (March 13, 2000). ... Signed as free agent by Colorado Avalanche (July 24, 2001).

MISCELLANEOUS: Captain of San Jose Sharks (1996-97 through March 2, 1998).

		REGULAR SEASON								PLAYOFFS				
Season Team	League	Gms.	G	A	Pts.	PIM	+/-	PP	SH	Gms.	G	A	Pts.	PIM
81-82—Brockville	OJHL	48	5	16	21	169	...	...	...	—	—	—	—	—
82-83—Windsor	OHL	70	12	24	36	108	...	...	...	3	0	0	0	11
83-84—Windsor	OHL	68	9	48	57	184	...	...	...	3	1	1	2	10
84-85—Toronto	NHL	10	1	0	1	13	-1	0	0	—	—	—	—	—
—Windsor	OHL	53	17	40	57	148	...	...	...	4	0	1	1	14
85-86—St. Catharines	AHL	58	8	25	33	90	...	...	...	10	1	6	7	17
—Toronto	NHL	15	1	2	3	28	0	0	0	1	0	0	0	0
86-87—Newmarket	AHL	11	1	8	9	33	...	...	...	—	—	—	—	—
—Toronto	NHL	61	4	27	31	92	-3	1	0	13	2	2	4	42
87-88—Newmarket	AHL	2	0	1	1	2	...	...	...	—	—	—	—	—
—Toronto	NHL	65	8	17	25	131	-20	1	0	6	1	3	4	20
88-89—Toronto	NHL	59	11	14	25	72	-3	0	0	—	—	—	—	—
89-90—Toronto	NHL	48	1	14	15	92	-8	0	0	5	0	3	3	16
90-91—Toronto	NHL	72	2	22	24	113	-4	0	0	—	—	—	—	—
91-92—Toronto	NHL	74	2	15	17	91	-22	1	0	—	—	—	—	—
92-93—Toronto	NHL	69	11	32	43	66	4	5	0	21	1	10	11	26
93-94—Toronto	NHL	45	4	24	28	44	8	2	0	18	1	5	6	37
94-95—Toronto	NHL	47	7	25	32	64	-8	3	1	7	0	3	3	6
95-96—Toronto	NHL	74	7	18	25	116	-15	1	0	6	0	0	0	24
96-97—San Jose	NHL	79	0	21	21	101	-20	0	0	—	—	—	—	—
97-98—San Jose	NHL	64	8	13	21	31	-13	4	0	—	—	—	—	—
—St. Louis	NHL	11	5	4	9	10	2	3	0	10	2	2	4	10
98-99—St. Louis	NHL	28	2	3	5	16	-6	1	0	—	—	—	—	—
—Detroit	NHL	23	2	2	4	11	-4	0	0	2	0	1	1	0
99-00—Phoenix	NHL	41	1	6	7	30	-10	0	0	—	—	—	—	—
—Detroit	NHL	13	2	0	2	15	2	0	0	9	0	1	1	4
00-01—Cincinnati	AHL	2	0	1	1	2	...	...	...	—	—	—	—	—
—Detroit	NHL	68	3	8	11	53	17	0	1	5	0	0	0	8
NHL Totals (17 years)		966	82	267	349	1189	-104	22	2	103	7	30	37	193

G

GILMOUR, DOUG   LW/C

PERSONAL: Born June 25, 1963, in Kingston, Ont. ... 5-11/185. ... Shoots left. ... Full Name: Douglas Gilmour.

TRANSACTIONS/CAREER NOTES: Selected by St. Louis Blues in seventh round (fourth Blues pick, 134th overall) of NHL entry draft (June 9, 1982). ... Sprained ankle (October 7, 1985); missed four games. ... Suffered concussion (January 1988). ... Bruised shoulder (March 1988). ... Traded by Blues with RW Mark Hunter, LW Steve Bozek and D/RW Michael Dark to Calgary Flames for C Mike Bullard, C Craig Coxe and D Tim Corkery (September 5, 1988). ... Suffered abscessed jaw (March 1989); missed six games. ... Fractured bone in right foot (August 12, 1989). ... Traded by Flames with D Ric Nattress, D Jamie Macoun, LW Kent Manderville and G Rick Wamsley to Toronto Maple Leafs for LW Craig Berube, D Alexander Godynyuk, LW Gary Leeman, D Michel Petit and G Jeff Reese (January 2, 1992). ... Suspended eight off-days and fined $500 by NHL for slashing (November 27, 1992). ... Suspended one preseason game and fined $500 by NHL for headbutting (September 26, 1993). ... Played in Europe during 1994-95 NHL lockout. ... Suffered pinched nerve in neck (February 8, 1995); missed one game. ...

Fractured nose (April 7, 1995); missed three games. ... Bruised ribs (March 19, 1996); missed one game. ... Traded by Maple Leafs with D Dave Ellett and third-round pick (D Andre Lakos) in 1999 draft to New Jersey Devils for D Jason Smith, C Steve Sullivan and C Alyn McCauley (February 25, 1997). ... Bruised eye (March 5, 1997); missed three games. ... Injured knee (March 5, 1998) and underwent surgery; missed 18 games. ... Signed as free agent by Chicago Blackhawks (July 3, 1998). ... Injured back (March 27, 1999) and underwent surgery; missed final 10 games of season. ... Bruised ribs (March 1, 2000); missed five games. ... Traded by Blackhawks with RW Jean-Pierre Dumont to Buffalo Sabres for LW Michal Grosek (March 10, 2000). ... Suffered from the flu (April 7, 2000); missed final two games of season. ... Injured hip (November 22, 2000); missed 10 games.

HONORS: Won Red Tilson Trophy (1982-83). ... Won Eddie Powers Memorial Trophy (1982-83). ... Named to OHL All-Star first team (1982-83). ... Won Frank J. Selke Trophy (1992-93). ... Named to THE SPORTING NEWS All-Star second team (1992-93). ... Played in NHL All-Star Game (1993 and 1994).

MISCELLANEOUS: Member of Stanley Cup championship team (1989). ... Captain of Toronto Maple Leafs (1994-95 through February 25, 1997). ... Captain of Chicago Blackhawks (1999-March 10, 2000). ... Failed to score on a penalty shot (vs. Gilles Meloche, February 3, 1985; vs. Pat Riggin, March 1, 1987; vs. Mark Fitzpatrick, October 27, 1989; vs. Peter Skudra, October 16, 1999).

STATISTICAL PLATEAUS: Three-goal games: 1985-86 (1), 1987-88 (1), 1993-94 (1). Total: 3.

			REGULAR SEASON								PLAYOFFS				
Season Team	League	Gms.	G	A	Pts.	PIM	+/-	PP	SH		Gms.	G	A	Pts.	PIM
80-81—Cornwall	QMJHL	51	12	23	35	35	...	...	...		—	—	—	—	—
81-82—Cornwall	OHL	67	46	73	119	42	...	...	...		5	6	9	15	2
82-83—Cornwall	OHL	68	*70	*107	*177	62	...	...	...		8	8	10	18	16
83-84—St. Louis	NHL	80	25	28	53	57	6	3	1		11	2	9	11	10
84-85—St. Louis	NHL	78	21	36	57	49	3	3	1		3	1	1	2	2
85-86—St. Louis	NHL	74	25	28	53	41	-3	2	1		19	9	12	†21	25
86-87—St. Louis	NHL	80	42	63	105	58	-2	17	1		6	2	2	4	16
87-88—St. Louis	NHL	72	36	50	86	59	-13	19	2		10	3	14	17	18
88-89—Calgary	NHL	72	26	59	85	44	45	11	0		22	11	11	22	20
89-90—Calgary	NHL	78	24	67	91	54	20	12	1		6	3	1	4	8
90-91—Calgary	NHL	78	20	61	81	144	27	2	2		7	1	1	2	0
91-92—Calgary	NHL	38	11	27	38	46	12	4	1		—	—	—	—	—
—Toronto	NHL	40	15	34	49	32	13	6	0		—	—	—	—	—
92-93—Toronto	NHL	83	32	95	127	100	32	15	3		21	10	†25	35	30
93-94—Toronto	NHL	83	27	84	111	105	25	10	1		18	6	22	28	42
94-95—Rapperswil..................	Switzerland	9	2	13	15	16	...	...	...		—	—	—	—	—
—Toronto	NHL	44	10	23	33	26	-5	3	0		7	0	6	6	6
95-96—Toronto	NHL	81	32	40	72	77	-5	10	2		6	1	7	8	12
96-97—Toronto	NHL	61	15	45	60	46	-5	2	1		—	—	—	—	—
—New Jersey	NHL	20	7	15	22	22	7	2	0		10	0	4	4	14
97-98—New Jersey	NHL	63	13	40	53	68	10	3	0		6	5	2	7	4
98-99—Chicago....................	NHL	72	16	40	56	56	-16	7	1		—	—	—	—	—
99-00—Chicago....................	NHL	63	22	34	56	51	-12	8	0		—	—	—	—	—
—Buffalo	NHL	11	3	14	17	12	3	2	0		5	0	1	1	0
00-01—Buffalo	NHL	71	7	31	38	70	3	4	0		13	2	4	6	12
NHL Totals (18 years).........		1342	429	914	1343	1217	145	145	18		170	56	122	178	219

GIONTA, BRIAN   RW   DEVILS

PERSONAL: Born January 18, 1979, in Rochester, N.Y. ... 5-7/160. ... Shoots right.

TRANSACTIONS/CAREER NOTES: Selected by New Jersey Devils in third round (fourth Devils pick, 82nd overall) of NHL entry draft (June 27, 1998).

HONORS: Named to NCAA All-America (East) second team (1997-98). ... Named to Hockey East All-Star second team (1997-98). ... Named Hockey East Rookie of the Year (1997-98). ... Named to NCAA All-America (East) first team (1998-99 through 2000-01). ... Named to Hockey East All-Star first team (1998-99 through 2000-01).

			REGULAR SEASON								PLAYOFFS				
Season Team	League	Gms.	G	A	Pts.	PIM	+/-	PP	SH		Gms.	G	A	Pts.	PIM
97-98—Boston College	Hockey East	40	30	32	62	44	...	...	...		—	—	—	—	—
98-99—Boston College	Hockey East	39	27	33	60	46	...	...	...		—	—	—	—	—
99-00—Boston College	Hockey East	42	*33	23	56	66	...	...	...		—	—	—	—	—
00-01—Boston College	Hockey East	43	*33	21	*54	47	...	...	...		—	—	—	—	—

GIRARD, JONATHAN   D   BRUINS

PERSONAL: Born May 27, 1980, in Joliette, Que. ... 5-11/192. ... Shoots right.

TRANSACTIONS/CAREER NOTES: Selected by Boston Bruins in second round (first Bruins pick, 48th overall) of NHL entry draft (June 27, 1998).

HONORS: Named to QMJHL All-Rookie team (1996-97). ... Named to QMJHL All-Star second team (1997-98). ... Named to QMJHL All-Star first team (1998-99 and 1999-2000).

			REGULAR SEASON								PLAYOFFS				
Season Team	League	Gms.	G	A	Pts.	PIM	+/-	PP	SH		Gms.	G	A	Pts.	PIM
96-97—Laval	QMJHL	38	11	21	32	23	...	...	...		3	0	3	3	0
97-98—Laval	QMJHL	64	20	47	67	44	...	...	...		16	2	16	18	13
98-99—Acadie-Bathurst	QMJHL	50	9	58	67	60	...	...	...		23	13	18	31	22
—Boston	NHL	3	0	0	0	0	1	0	0		—	—	—	—	—
99-00—Boston	NHL	23	1	2	3	2	-1	0	0		—	—	—	—	—
—Providence..................	AHL	5	0	1	1	0	...	...	...		—	—	—	—	—
—Moncton	QMJHL	26	10	25	35	36	...	...	...		16	3	15	18	36
00-01—Boston	NHL	31	3	13	16	14	2	2	0		—	—	—	—	—
—Providence..................	AHL	39	3	21	24	6	...	...	...		17	0	5	5	4
NHL Totals (3 years)..........		57	4	15	19	16	2	2	0						

G

GOC, SASCHA　　　　　D　　　　　DEVILS

PERSONAL: Born April 17, 1979, in Schwenningen, West Germany. ... 6-2/220. ... Shoots right. ... Brother of Marcel Goc, center, San Jose Sharks organization.

TRANSACTIONS/CAREER NOTES: Selected by New Jersey Devils in sixth round (fifth Devils pick, 159th overall) of NHL entry draft (June 21, 1997). ... Sprained left ankle (October 12, 2000); missed two games. ... Injured right knee (November 4, 2000); missed seven games.

Season Team	League	Gms.	G	A	Pts.	PIM	+/-	PP	SH	Gms.	G	A	Pts.	PIM
95-96—Schwenningen Jrs.	Germany	11	3	6	9	77	...	...	...	—	—	—	—	—
—Schwenningen	Germany	1	0	0	0	0	...	...	...	—	—	—	—	—
96-97—Schwenningen	Germany	41	3	1	4	28	...	...	...	5	0	0	0	0
97-98—Schwenningen	Germany	49	5	5	10	45	...	...	...	—	—	—	—	—
98-99—Albany	AHL	55	1	12	13	24	...	...	...	2	0	0	0	0
99-00—Albany	AHL	64	9	22	31	35	...	...	...	5	2	0	2	6
00-01—Albany	AHL	55	10	29	39	49	...	...	...	—	—	—	—	—
—New Jersey	NHL	11	0	0	0	4	7	0	0	—	—	—	—	—
NHL Totals (1 year)		11	0	0	0	4	7	0	0					

GOLUBOVSKY, YAN　　　　　D

PERSONAL: Born March 9, 1976, in Novosibirsk, U.S.S.R. ... 6-3/183. ... Shoots right. ... Name pronounced goh-loo-BAHV-skee.

TRANSACTIONS/CAREER NOTES: Selected by Detroit Red Wings in first round (first Red Wings pick, 23rd overall) of NHL entry draft (June 28, 1994). ... Injured rib (November 20, 1999); missed six games. ... Injured hand (February 8, 2000); missed 12 games. ... Traded by Red Wings to Florida Panthers for C Igor Larionov (December 28, 2000).

Season Team	League	Gms.	G	A	Pts.	PIM	+/-	PP	SH	Gms.	G	A	Pts.	PIM
93-94—Dynamo-2 Moscow	CIS Div. III	10	0	1	1	...	...	...	...	—	—	—	—	—
—Russian Penguins	IHL	8	0	0	0	23	...	...	...	—	—	—	—	—
94-95—Adirondack	AHL	57	4	2	6	39	...	...	...	—	—	—	—	—
95-96—Adirondack	AHL	71	5	16	21	97	...	...	...	3	0	0	0	2
96-97—Adirondack	AHL	62	2	11	13	67	...	...	...	4	0	0	0	0
97-98—Adirondack	AHL	52	1	15	16	57	...	...	...	3	0	0	0	2
—Detroit	NHL	12	0	2	2	6	1	0	0	—	—	—	—	—
98-99—Detroit	NHL	17	0	1	1	16	4	0	0	—	—	—	—	—
—Adirondack	AHL	43	2	2	4	32	...	...	...	2	0	0	0	4
99-00—Detroit	NHL	21	1	2	3	8	3	0	0	—	—	—	—	—
00-01—Cincinnati	AHL	28	4	4	8	16	...	...	...	—	—	—	—	—
—Louisville	AHL	30	1	12	13	36	...	...	...	—	—	—	—	—
—Florida	NHL	6	0	2	2	2	3	0	0	—	—	—	—	—
NHL Totals (4 years)		56	1	7	8	32	11	0	0					

GOMEZ, SCOTT　　　　　C　　　　　DEVILS

PERSONAL: Born December 23, 1979, in Anchorage, Alaska. ... 5-11/200. ... Shoots left.

TRANSACTIONS/CAREER NOTES: Selected by New Jersey Devils in first round (second Devils pick, 27th overall) of NHL entry draft (June 27, 1998). ... Injured back (February 17, 2001); missed six games.

HONORS: Named to WHL All-Rookie Team (1997-98). ... Named to WHL (West) All-Star first team (1998-99). ... Named NHL Rookie of the Year by THE SPORTING NEWS (1999-2000). ... Won Calder Memorial Trophy (1999-2000). ... Named to NHL All-Rookie Team (1999-2000). ... Played in NHL All-Star Game (2000).

MISCELLANEOUS: Member of Stanley Cup championship team (2000).

STATISTICAL PLATEAUS: Three-goal games: 1999-00 (1).

Season Team	League	Gms.	G	A	Pts.	PIM	+/-	PP	SH	Gms.	G	A	Pts.	PIM
96-97—Surrey Jr. A	BCJHL	56	48	76	124	94	...	...	...	—	—	—	—	—
97-98—Tri-City	WHL	45	12	37	49	57	...	...	...	—	—	—	—	—
98-99—Tri-City	WHL	58	30	*78	108	55	...	...	...	10	6	13	19	31
99-00—New Jersey	NHL	82	19	51	70	78	14	7	0	23	4	6	10	4
00-01—New Jersey	NHL	76	14	49	63	46	-1	2	0	25	5	9	14	24
NHL Totals (2 years)		158	33	100	133	124	13	9	0	48	9	15	24	28

GONCHAR, SERGEI　　　　　D　　　　　CAPITALS

PERSONAL: Born April 13, 1974, in Chelyabinsk, U.S.S.R. ... 6-2/208. ... Shoots left. ... Name pronounced GAHN-shahr.

TRANSACTIONS/CAREER NOTES: Selected by Washington Capitals in first round (first Capitals pick, 14th overall) of NHL entry draft (June 20, 1992). ... Injured groin (November 30, 1995); missed two games. ... Suffered from the flu (December 13, 1995); missed one game. ... Suffered from the flu (November 7, 1996); missed one game. ... Hyperextended elbow (November 18, 1996); missed one game. ... Suffered back spasms (December 28, 1996); missed eight games. ... Bruised knee (January 29, 1997); missed two games. ... Sprained knee (February 26, 1997); missed 12 games. ... Sprained knee (October 23, 1998); missed 10 games. ... Strained groin (January 1, 1999); missed one game. ... Sprained wrist (January 30, 1999); missed eight games. ... Sprained ankle (March 13, 1999); missed two games. ... Reinjured ankle (April 7, 1999); missed remainder of season. ... Suffered injury (November 11, 1999); missed five games. ... Injured neck (February 28, 2000); missed two games. ... Reinjured neck (March 5, 2000); missed two games. ... Missed first two games of 2000-01 season due to contract dispute. ... Injured neck (December 21, 2000); missed one game. ... Bruised shoulder (January 18, 2001); missed three games.

HONORS: Played in NHL All-Star Game (2001).

STATISTICAL PLATEAUS: Three-goal games: 1999-00 (1).

Season Team	League	REGULAR SEASON								PLAYOFFS				
		Gms.	G	A	Pts.	PIM	+/-	PP	SH	Gms.	G	A	Pts.	PIM
90-91—Mechel Chelyabinsk....	USSR	2	0	0	0	0	...	...	...	—	—	—	—	—
91-92—Traktor Chelyabinsk....	CIS	31	1	0	1	6	...	...	...	—	—	—	—	—
92-93—Dynamo Moscow	CIS	31	1	3	4	70	...	...	...	10	0	0	0	12
93-94—Dynamo Moscow	CIS	44	4	5	9	36	...	...	...	10	0	3	3	14
—Portland	AHL	—	—	—	—	—	...	...	...	2	0	0	0	0
94-95—Portland	AHL	61	10	32	42	67	...	...	...	—	—	—	—	—
—Washington	NHL	31	2	5	7	22	4	0	0	7	2	2	4	2
95-96—Washington	NHL	78	15	26	41	60	25	4	0	6	2	4	6	4
96-97—Washington	NHL	57	13	17	30	36	-11	3	0	—	—	—	—	—
97-98—Washington	NHL	72	5	16	21	66	2	2	0	21	7	4	11	30
—Russian Oly. team	Int'l	6	0	2	2	0	...	...	...	—	—	—	—	—
98-99—Washington	NHL	53	21	10	31	57	1	13	1	—	—	—	—	—
99-00—Washington	NHL	73	18	36	54	52	26	5	0	5	1	0	1	6
00-01—Washington	NHL	76	19	38	57	70	12	8	0	6	1	3	4	2
NHL Totals (7 years)		440	93	148	241	363	59	35	1	45	13	13	26	44

GOREN, LEE RW BRUINS

PERSONAL: Born December 26, 1977, in Winnipeg. ... 6-3/190. ... Shoots right.
TRANSACTIONS/CAREER NOTES: Selected by Boston Bruins in third round (fifth Bruins pick, 63rd overall) of NHL entry draft (June 21, 1997).
HONORS: Named to WCHA All-Star first team (1999-2000). ... Named to NCAA All-America (West) second team (1999-2000). ... Named to NCAA All-Tournament team (1999-2000). ... Named NCAA Tournament Most Valuable Player (1999-2000).

Season Team	League	REGULAR SEASON								PLAYOFFS				
		Gms.	G	A	Pts.	PIM	+/-	PP	SH	Gms.	G	A	Pts.	PIM
95-96—Minote	Jr. A	64	31	55	86	...	...	...		—	—	—	—	—
96-97—Univ. of North Dakota	WCHA							Did not play.						
97-98—Univ. of North Dakota	WCHA	29	3	13	16	26	...	...	...	—	—	—	—	—
98-99—Univ. of North Dakota	WCHA	38	26	19	45	20	...	...	...	—	—	—	—	—
99-00—Univ. of North Dakota	WCHA	44	*34	29	63	42	...	...	...	—	—	—	—	—
00-01—Providence	AHL	54	15	18	33	72	...	...	...	17	5	2	7	11
—Boston	NHL	21	2	0	2	7	-3	1	0	—	—	—	—	—
NHL Totals (1 year)		21	2	0	2	7	-3	1	0	—	—	—	—	—

GOSSELIN, CHRISTIAN D RANGERS

PERSONAL: Born August 21, 1976, in Laval, Que. ... 6-5/235. ... Shoots right.
TRANSACTIONS/CAREER NOTES: Selected by New Jersey Devils in fifth round (fifth Devils pick, 129th overall) of NHL entry draft (June 29, 1994). ... Signed as free agent by San Jose Sharks (July 22, 1998). ... Traded by Sharks with C Mikael Samuelsson to New York Rangers for LW Adam Graves (June 24, 2001).

Season Team	League	REGULAR SEASON								PLAYOFFS				
		Gms.	G	A	Pts.	PIM	+/-	PP	SH	Gms.	G	A	Pts.	PIM
92-93—Hull	QMJHL	49	1	3	4	24	...	...	...	—	—	—	—	—
93-94—St. Hyacinthe	QMJHL	12	3	2	5	16	...	...	...	—	—	—	—	—
94-95—St. Hyacinthe	QMJHL	60	5	10	15	202	...	...	...	5	0	0	0	11
95-96—Laval	QMJHL	21	1	8	9	69	...	...	...	—	—	—	—	—
96-97—Macon	CHL	63	8	10	18	229	...	...	...	5	0	0	0	29
97-98—Fredericton	AHL	6	0	0	0	17	...	...	...	—	—	—	—	—
—Pensacola	ECHL	42	6	5	11	181	...	...	...	19	0	1	1	54
98-99—Kentucky	AHL	31	1	1	2	107	...	...	...	—	—	—	—	—
99-00—Kentucky	AHL	68	0	4	4	266	...	...	...	9	0	0	0	34
00-01—Kentucky	AHL	42	2	3	5	145	...	...	...	3	0	1	1	6

GRAHAME, JOHN G BRUINS

PERSONAL: Born August 31, 1975, in Denver. ... 6-2/210. ... Catches left. ... Full Name: John Gillies Mark Grahame. ... Son of Ron Grahame, goaltender with three NHL teams (1977-78 through 1980-81). ... Name pronounced GRAY-ihm.
TRANSACTIONS/CAREER NOTES: Selected by Boston Bruins in ninth round (seventh Bruins pick, 229th overall) of NHL entry draft (June 29, 1994). ... Injured ankle (December 19, 2000) and underwent surgery; missed seven games.

Season Team	League	REGULAR SEASON								PLAYOFFS						
		Gms.	Min	W	L	T	GA	SO	Avg.	Gms.	Min.	W	L	GA	SO	Avg.
93-94—Sioux City	USHL	20	1136	...	...	...	72	0	3.80	—	—	—	—	—	—	—
94-95—Lake Superior State	CCHA	28	1616	16	7	3	75	1	2.78	—	—	—	—	—	—	—
95-96—Lake Superior State	CCHA	29	1658	21	4	2	67	2	2.42	—	—	—	—	—	—	—
96-97—Lake Superior State	CCHA	37	2197	19	13	4	134	3	3.66	—	—	—	—	—	—	—
97-98—Providence	AHL	55	3054	15	*31	4	164	3	3.22	—	—	—	—	—	—	—
98-99—Providence	AHL	48	2771	*37	9	1	134	3	2.90	19	*1209	*15	4	*48	†1	2.38
99-00—Boston	NHL	24	1344	7	10	5	55	2	2.46	—	—	—	—	—	—	—
—Providence	AHL	27	1528	11	13	2	86	1	3.38	13	839	10	3	35	0	2.50
00-01—Boston	NHL	10	471	3	4	0	28	0	3.57	—	—	—	—	—	—	—
—Providence	AHL	16	893	4	7	3	47	0	3.16	17	1043	8	*9	46	2	2.65
NHL Totals (2 years)		34	1815	10	14	5	83	2	2.74							

G

PERSONAL: Born June 25, 1964, in Downers Grove, Ill. ... 5-10/185. ... Shoots right. ... Full Name: Anthony Lewis Granato. ... Name pronounced gruh-NAH-toh.

TRANSACTIONS/CAREER NOTES: Selected by New York Rangers in sixth round (fifth Rangers pick, 120th overall) of NHL entry draft (June 9, 1982). ... Bruised foot (February 1989). ... Traded by Rangers with RW Tomas Sandstrom to Los Angeles Kings for C Bernie Nicholls (January 20, 1990). ... Strained groin (January 25, 1990); missed 12 games. ... Injured knee (March 20, 1990). ... Tore rib cartilage (December 18, 1990); missed 10 games. ... Strained back (October 6, 1992); missed three games. ... Strained back (December 4, 1993); missed nine game. ... Strained lower back (December 13, 1993); missed nine games. ... Suspended 15 games without pay and fined $500 by NHL for slashing incident (February 16, 1994). ... Strained back (April 3, 1994); missed remainder of season. ... Strained hip flexor (March 13, 1995); missed one game. ... Fractured bone in foot (April 6, 1995); missed 13 games. ... Underwent brain surgery (February 14, 1996); missed remainder of season. ... Signed as free agent by San Jose Sharks (August 15, 1996). ... Injured back (December 21, 1996); missed one game. ... Reinjured back (January 29, 1997); missed two games. ... Suspended three games and fined $1,000 by NHL for cross-checking incident (February 5, 1997). ... Injured jaw (November 1, 1997); missed 19 games. ... Suspended two games and fined $1,000 by NHL for high-sticking incident (January 24, 1998). ... Suffered injury (November 21, 1998); missed two games. ... Injured back (December 10, 1998); missed six games. ... Tore anterior cruciate ligament in knee (January 11, 1999); missed 36 games. ... Suffered head injury (January 22, 2001); missed four games.

HONORS: Named to NCAA All-America (West) second team (1984-85 and 1986-87). ... Named to WCHA All-Star second team (1986-87). ... Named to NHL All-Rookie team (1988-89). ... Played in NHL All-Star Game (1997). ... Won Bill Masterton Memorial Trophy (1996-97).

MISCELLANEOUS: Failed to score on a penalty shot (vs. Jocelyn Thibault, November 25, 1993).

STATISTICAL PLATEAUS: Three-goal games: 1988-89 (2), 1991-92 (1), 1994-95 (1), 1996-97 (2). Total: 6. ... Four-goal games: 1988-89 (1). ... Total hat tricks: 7.

Season Team	League	REGULAR SEASON								PLAYOFFS				
		Gms.	G	A	Pts.	PIM	+/-	PP	SH	Gms.	G	A	Pts.	PIM
81-82—Northwood School	N.Y. H.S.					Statistics unavailable.				—	—	—	—	—
82-83—Northwood School	N.Y. H.S.					Statistics unavailable.				—	—	—	—	—
83-84—Univ. of Wisconsin	WCHA	35	14	17	31	48	...	...	...	—	—	—	—	—
84-85—Univ. of Wisconsin	WCHA	42	33	34	67	94	...			—	—	—	—	—
85-86—Univ. of Wisconsin	WCHA	32	25	24	49	36	...			—	—	—	—	—
86-87—Univ. of Wisconsin	WCHA	42	28	45	73	64	...			—	—	—	—	—
87-88—U.S. national team	Int'l	49	40	31	71	55	...			—	—	—	—	—
—U.S. Olympic team	Int'l	6	1	7	8	4	...			—	—	—	—	—
—Denver	IHL	22	13	14	27	36	...			8	9	4	13	16
88-89—New York Rangers	NHL	78	36	27	63	140	17	4	4	4	1	1	2	21
89-90—New York Rangers	NHL	37	7	18	25	77	1	1	0	—	—	—	—	—
—Los Angeles	NHL	19	5	6	11	45	-2	1	0	10	5	4	9	12
90-91—Los Angeles	NHL	68	30	34	64	154	22	11	1	12	1	4	5	28
91-92—Los Angeles	NHL	80	39	29	68	187	4	7	2	6	1	5	6	10
92-93—Los Angeles	NHL	81	37	45	82	171	-1	14	2	24	6	11	17	50
93-94—Los Angeles	NHL	50	7	14	21	150	-2	2	0	—	—	—	—	—
94-95—Los Angeles	NHL	33	13	11	24	68	9	2	0	—	—	—	—	—
95-96—Los Angeles	NHL	49	17	18	35	46	-5	5	0	—	—	—	—	—
96-97—San Jose	NHL	76	25	15	40	159	-7	5	1	—	—	—	—	—
97-98—San Jose	NHL	59	16	9	25	70	3	3	0	1	0	0	0	0
98-99—San Jose	NHL	35	6	6	12	54	4	0	1	6	1	1	2	2
99-00—San Jose	NHL	48	6	7	13	39	2	1	0	12	0	1	1	14
00-01—San Jose	NHL	60	4	5	9	65	-1	1	0	4	1	0	1	4
NHL Totals (13 years)		773	248	244	492	1425	44	57	11	79	16	27	43	141

PERSONAL: Born February 2, 1977, in Montreal. ... 6-3/207. ... Shoots right. ... Name pronounced zhah-LOOK GRAHN-pee-AIR.

TRANSACTIONS/CAREER NOTES: Selected by St. Louis Blues in seventh round (sixth Blues pick, 179th overall) of NHL entry draft (July 8, 1995). ... Traded by Blues with second-round pick (D Cory Sarich) in 1996 draft and third-round pick (RW Maxim Afinogenov) in 1997 draft to Buffalo Sabres for LW Yuri Khmylev and eighth-round pick (C Andrei Podkonicky) in 1996 draft (March 20, 1996). ... Suspended one game by NHL for tripping incident (April 10, 1999). ... Suffered from the flu (March 12, 2000); missed one game. ... Traded by Sabres with RW Matt Davidson, fifth-round pick (C Tyler Kolarik) in 2000 draft and fifth-round pick (traded to Detroit) in 2001 draft to Columbus Blue Jackets for future considerations (June 23, 2000). ... Bruised foot (October 21, 2000); missed two games. ... Suffered concussion (December 26, 2000); missed three games. ... Bruised foot (March 7, 2001); missed six games.

Season Team	League	REGULAR SEASON								PLAYOFFS				
		Gms.	G	A	Pts.	PIM	+/-	PP	SH	Gms.	G	A	Pts.	PIM
93-94—Beauport	QMJHL	46	1	4	5	27	...	...	...	1	0	0	0	0
94-95—Val-d'Or	QMJHL	59	10	13	23	126	...			—	—	—	—	—
95-96—Val-d'Or	QMJHL	67	13	21	34	209	...			13	1	4	5	47
96-97—Val-d'Or	QMJHL	58	9	24	33	196	...			13	5	8	13	46
97-98—Rochester	AHL	75	4	6	10	211	...			4	0	0	0	2
98-99—Rochester	AHL	56	5	4	9	90	...			—	—	—	—	—
—Buffalo	NHL	16	0	1	1	17	0	0	0	—	—	—	—	—
99-00—Buffalo	NHL	11	0	0	0	15	-1	0	0	4	0	0	0	4
—Rochester	AHL	62	5	8	13	124	...			17	0	1	1	40
00-01—Columbus	NHL	64	1	4	5	73	-6	0	0	—	—	—	—	—
NHL Totals (3 years)		91	1	5	6	105	-7	0	0	4	0	0	0	4

G

PERSONAL: Born December 28, 1976, in Montreal. ... 5-11/194. ... Shoots left. ... Name pronounced gruh-TAHN.

TRANSACTIONS/CAREER NOTES: Selected by Washington Capitals in fifth round (sixth Capitals pick, 105th overall) of NHL entry draft (July 8, 1995). ... Injured groin (December 20, 1997); missed one game. ... Traded by Capitals to Calgary Flames for D Steve Shirreffs (August 18, 1999). ... Suffered head injury (February 13, 2001). ... Claimed on waivers by Montreal Canadiens (April 11, 2001).

Season Team	League	REGULAR SEASON Gms.	G	A	Pts.	PIM	+/-	PP	SH	PLAYOFFS Gms.	G	A	Pts.	PIM
93-94—Laval	QMJHL	51	9	14	23	70	...	...	...	20	2	1	3	19
94-95—Laval	QMJHL	71	30	58	88	199	...	...	...	20	8	21	29	42
95-96—Laval	QMJHL	38	21	39	60	130	...	...	...	—	—	—	—	—
—Granby	QMJHL	27	12	46	58	97	...	...	...	21	13	26	39	68
96-97—Portland	AHL	76	6	40	46	140	...	...	...	5	2	1	3	14
97-98—Portland	AHL	58	19	31	50	137	...	...	...	8	4	2	6	24
—Washington	NHL	6	0	1	1	6	1	0	0	—	—	—	—	—
98-99—Portland	AHL	64	18	42	60	135	...	...	...	—	—	—	—	—
—Washington	NHL	16	4	3	7	16	-1	0	0	—	—	—	—	—
99-00—Saint John	AHL	65	17	49	66	137	...	...	...	3	0	1	1	4
—Calgary	NHL	10	0	2	2	10	1	0	0	—	—	—	—	—
00-01—Saint John	AHL	53	10	36	46	153	...	...	...	—	—	—	—	—
—Calgary	NHL	14	1	3	4	14	0	0	0	—	—	—	—	—
NHL Totals (4 years)		46	5	9	14	46	1	0	0					

GRATTON, CHRIS   C   SABRES

PERSONAL: Born July 5, 1975, in Brantford, Ont. ... 6-4/219. ... Shoots left. ... Name pronounced GRA-tuhn.

TRANSACTIONS/CAREER NOTES: Selected by Tampa Bay Lightning in first round (first Lightning pick, third overall) of NHL entry draft (June 26, 1993). ... Bruised shoulder (April 2, 1995); missed two games. ... Traded by Lightning to Philadelphia Flyers for RW Mikael Renberg and D Karl Dykhuis (August 20, 1997). ... Traded by Flyers with C/RW Mike Sillinger to Lightning for RW Mikael Renberg and C Daymond Langkow (December 12, 1998). ... Suspended three games by NHL for spitting at referee (December 25, 1998). ... Bruised right foot (February 17, 2000); missed seven games. ... Traded by Lightning with second-round pick (C Derek Roy) in 2001 draft to Buffalo Sabres for C/RW Brian Holzinger, C Wayne Primeau, D Cory Sarich and third-round pick (RW Alexandre Kharitonov) in 2000 draft (March 9, 2000).

HONORS: Won Emms Family Award (1991-92). ... Named to OHL Rookie All-Star team (1991-92). ... Won OHL Top Draft Prospect Award (1992-93).

MISCELLANEOUS: Captain of Tampa Bay Lightning (November 10, 1999-March 9, 2000).

STATISTICAL PLATEAUS: Three-goal games: 1996-97 (1).

Season Team	League	REGULAR SEASON Gms.	G	A	Pts.	PIM	+/-	PP	SH	PLAYOFFS Gms.	G	A	Pts.	PIM
90-91—Brantford Jr. B	OHA	31	30	30	60	28	...	...	...	—	—	—	—	—
91-92—Kingston	OHL	62	27	39	66	35	...	...	...	—	—	—	—	—
92-93—Kingston	OHL	58	55	54	109	125	...	...	...	16	11	18	29	42
93-94—Tampa Bay	NHL	84	13	29	42	123	-25	5	1	—	—	—	—	—
94-95—Tampa Bay	NHL	46	7	20	27	89	-2	2	0	—	—	—	—	—
95-96—Tampa Bay	NHL	82	17	21	38	105	-13	7	0	6	0	2	2	27
96-97—Tampa Bay	NHL	82	30	32	62	201	-28	9	0	—	—	—	—	—
97-98—Philadelphia	NHL	82	22	40	62	159	11	5	0	5	2	0	2	10
98-99—Philadelphia	NHL	26	1	7	8	41	-8	0	0	—	—	—	—	—
—Tampa Bay	NHL	52	7	19	26	102	-20	1	0	—	—	—	—	—
99-00—Tampa Bay	NHL	58	14	27	41	121	-24	4	0	—	—	—	—	—
—Buffalo	NHL	14	1	7	8	15	1	0	0	5	0	1	1	4
00-01—Buffalo	NHL	82	19	21	40	102	0	5	0	13	6	4	10	14
NHL Totals (8 years)		608	131	223	354	1058	-108	38	1	29	8	7	15	55

GRAVES, ADAM   LW   SHARKS

PERSONAL: Born April 12, 1968, in Tecumseh, Ont. ... 6-0/200. ... Shoots left.

TRANSACTIONS/CAREER NOTES: Selected by Detroit Red Wings in second round (second Red Wings pick, 22nd overall) of NHL entry draft (June 21, 1986). ... Traded by Red Wings with C/RW Joe Murphy, LW Petr Klima and D Jeff Sharples to Edmonton Oilers for C Jimmy Carson, C Kevin McClelland and fifth-round pick (traded to Montreal) in 1991 draft (November 2, 1989). ... Signed as free agent by New York Rangers (September 2, 1991); Oilers received C/LW Troy Mallette as compensation (September 9, 1991). ... Suffered from infected elbow (February 11, 1995); missed one game. ... Sprained right knee (October 26, 1997); missed 10 games. ... Traded by Rangers to San Jose Sharks for C Mikael Samuelsson and D Christian Gosselin (June 24, 2001).

HONORS: Won King Clancy Memorial Trophy (1993-94). ... Named to THE SPORTING NEWS All-Star first team (1993-94). ... Named to NHL All-Star second team (1993-94). ... Played in NHL All-Star Game (1994). ... Won Bill Masterson Memorial Trophy (2000-01).

MISCELLANEOUS: Member of Stanley Cup championship team (1990 and 1994). ... Captain of New York Rangers (1995-96 and November 26, 1999-February 9, 2000).

STATISTICAL PLATEAUS: Three-goal games: 1989-90 (1), 1991-92 (1), 1992-93 (1), 1993-94 (1), 1994-95 (1), 1996-97 (1). Total: 6.

Season Team	League	REGULAR SEASON Gms.	G	A	Pts.	PIM	+/-	PP	SH	PLAYOFFS Gms.	G	A	Pts.	PIM
84-85—King City Jr. B	OHA	25	23	33	56	29	...	...	...	—	—	—	—	—
85-86—Windsor	OHL	62	27	37	64	35	...	...	...	16	5	11	16	10
86-87—Windsor	OHL	66	45	55	100	70	...	...	...	14	9	8	17	32
—Adirondack	AHL	—	—	—	—	—				5	0	1	1	0
87-88—Detroit	NHL	9	0	1	1	8	-2	0	0	—	—	—	—	—
—Windsor	OHL	37	28	32	60	107	...	...	...	12	14	18	†32	16
88-89—Detroit	NHL	56	7	5	12	60	-5	0	0	5	0	0	0	4
—Adirondack	AHL	14	10	11	21	28	...	...	...	14	11	7	18	17
89-90—Detroit	NHL	13	0	1	1	13	-5	0	0	—	—	—	—	—
—Edmonton	NHL	63	9	12	21	123	5	1	0	22	5	6	11	17
90-91—Edmonton	NHL	76	7	18	25	127	-21	2	0	18	2	4	6	22
91-92—New York Rangers	NHL	80	26	33	59	139	19	4	4	10	5	3	8	22
92-93—New York Rangers	NHL	84	36	29	65	148	-4	12	1	—	—	—	—	—
93-94—New York Rangers	NHL	84	52	27	79	127	27	20	4	23	10	7	17	24
94-95—New York Rangers	NHL	47	17	14	31	51	9	9	0	10	4	4	8	8

G

Season Team	League	REGULAR SEASON								PLAYOFFS				
		Gms.	G	A	Pts.	PIM	+/-	PP	SH	Gms.	G	A	Pts.	PIM
95-96—New York Rangers......	NHL	82	22	36	58	100	18	9	1	10	7	1	8	4
96-97—New York Rangers......	NHL	82	33	28	61	66	10	10	4	15	2	1	3	12
97-98—New York Rangers......	NHL	72	23	12	35	41	-30	10	0	—	—	—	—	—
98-99—New York Rangers......	NHL	82	38	15	53	47	-12	14	2	—	—	—	—	—
99-00—New York Rangers......	NHL	77	23	17	40	14	-15	11	0	—	—	—	—	—
00-01—New York Rangers......	NHL	82	10	16	26	77	-16	1	0	—	—	—	—	—
NHL Totals (14 years).........		989	303	264	567	1141	-22	103	16	113	35	26	61	113

GREEN, JOSH   LW   OILERS

PERSONAL: Born November 16, 1977, in Camrose, Alta. ... 6-4/213. ... Shoots left.
TRANSACTIONS/CAREER NOTES: Selected by Los Angeles Kings in second round (first Kings pick, 30th overall) of NHL entry draft (June 22, 1996). ... Strained shoulder (October 18, 1998); missed three games. ... Traded by Kings with C Olli Jokinen, D Mathieu Biron and first-round pick (LW Taylor Pyatt) in 1999 draft to New York Islanders for RW Zigmund Palffy, C Bryan Smolinski, G Marcel Cousineau and fourth-round pick (C Daniel Johansson) in 1999 draft (June 20, 1999). ... Injured shoulder (March 21, 2000); missed remainder of season. ... Traded by Islanders with D Eric Brewer and second-round pick (LW Brad Winchester) in 2000 draft to Edmonton Oilers for D Roman Hamrlik (June 24, 2000). ... Dislocated shoulder (September 11, 2000); missed first 39 games of season. ... Reinjured shoulder (December 30, 2000); missed final 42 games of season.

Season Team	League	REGULAR SEASON								PLAYOFFS				
		Gms.	G	A	Pts.	PIM	+/-	PP	SH	Gms.	G	A	Pts.	PIM
93-94—Medicine Hat..............	WHL	63	22	22	44	43	...	...	...	3	0	0	0	4
94-95—Medicine Hat..............	WHL	68	32	23	55	64	...	...	...	5	5	1	6	2
95-96—Medicine Hat..............	WHL	46	18	25	43	55	...	...	...	5	2	2	4	4
96-97—Medicine Hat..............	WHL	51	25	32	57	61	...	...	...	—	—	—	—	—
—Swift Current	WHL	23	10	15	25	33	...	...	...	10	9	7	16	19
97-98—Swift Current	WHL	5	9	1	10	9	...	...	...	—	—	—	—	—
—Portland	WHL	31	35	19	54	36	...	...	...	—	—	—	—	—
—Fredericton	AHL	43	16	15	31	14	...	...	...	4	1	3	4	6
98-99—Los Angeles................	NHL	27	1	3	4	8	-5	1	0	—	—	—	—	—
—Springfield..................	AHL	41	15	15	30	29	...	...	...	—	—	—	—	—
99-00—Lowell	AHL	17	6	2	8	19	...	...	...	—	—	—	—	—
—New York Islanders.....	NHL	49	12	14	26	41	-7	2	0	—	—	—	—	—
00-01—Hamilton	AHL	2	2	0	2	2	...	...	...	—	—	—	—	—
—Edmonton..................	NHL	—	—	—	—	—	—	—	—	3	0	0	0	0
NHL Totals (3 years)............		76	13	17	30	49	-12	3	0	3	0	0	0	0

GREEN, TRAVIS   C   MAPLE LEAFS

PERSONAL: Born December 20, 1970, in Castlegar, B.C. ... 6-2/200. ... Shoots right.
TRANSACTIONS/CAREER NOTES: Selected by New York Islanders in second round (second Islanders pick, 23rd overall) of NHL entry draft (June 17, 1989). ... Suffered sore groin (November 30, 1995); missed four games. ... Sprained knee (February 8, 1996); missed nine games. ... Traded by Islanders with D Doug Houda and RW Tony Tuzzolino to Mighty Ducks of Anaheim for D J.J. Daigneault, C Mark Janssens and RW Joe Sacco (February 6, 1998). ... Strained groin (February 7, 1998); missed five games. ... Sprained right knee (November 20, 1998); missed three games. ... Traded by Mighty Ducks with first-round pick (C Scott Kelman) in 1999 draft to Phoenix Coyotes for D Oleg Tverdovsky (June 26, 1999). ... Suffered knee infection (November 25, 1999); missed three games. ... Suffered concussion (March 21, 2000); missed one game. ... Strained knee (January 6, 2001); missed nine games. ... Bruised knee (March 4, 2001); missed three games. ... Traded by Coyotes with C Robert Reichel and RW Craig Mills to Toronto Maple Leafs for D Danny Markov (June 12, 2001).
STATISTICAL PLATEAUS: Three-goal games: 1993-94 (1).

Season Team	League	REGULAR SEASON								PLAYOFFS				
		Gms.	G	A	Pts.	PIM	+/-	PP	SH	Gms.	G	A	Pts.	PIM
85-86—Castlegar....................	KIJHL	35	30	40	70	41	...	...	...	—	—	—	—	—
86-87—Spokane.....................	WHL	64	8	17	25	27	...	...	...	3	0	0	0	0
87-88—Spokane.....................	WHL	72	33	53	86	42	...	...	...	15	10	10	20	13
88-89—Spokane.....................	WHL	72	51	51	102	79	...	...	...	—	—	—	—	—
89-90—Spokane.....................	WHL	50	45	44	89	80	...	...	...	—	—	—	—	—
—Medicine Hat..............	WHL	25	15	24	39	19	...	...	...	3	0	0	0	2
90-91—Capital District	AHL	73	21	34	55	26	...	...	...	—	—	—	—	—
91-92—Capital District	AHL	71	23	27	50	10	...	...	...	7	0	4	4	21
92-93—Capital District	AHL	20	12	11	23	39	...	...	...	—	—	—	—	—
—New York Islanders.....	NHL	61	7	18	25	43	4	1	0	12	3	1	4	6
93-94—New York Islanders.....	NHL	83	18	22	40	44	16	1	0	4	0	0	0	2
94-95—New York Islanders.....	NHL	42	5	7	12	25	-10	0	0	—	—	—	—	—
95-96—New York Islanders.....	NHL	69	25	45	70	42	-20	14	1	—	—	—	—	—
96-97—New York Islanders.....	NHL	79	23	41	64	38	-5	10	0	—	—	—	—	—
97-98—New York Islanders.....	NHL	54	14	12	26	66	-19	8	0	—	—	—	—	—
—Anaheim	NHL	22	5	11	16	16	-10	1	0	—	—	—	—	—
98-99—Anaheim	NHL	79	13	17	30	81	-7	3	1	4	0	1	1	4
99-00—Phoenix.....................	NHL	78	25	21	46	45	-4	6	0	5	2	1	3	2
00-01—Phoenix.....................	NHL	69	13	15	28	63	-11	3	0	—	—	—	—	—
NHL Totals (9 years)............		636	148	209	357	463	-66	47	2	25	5	3	8	14

GREIG, MARK   RW   FLYERS

PERSONAL: Born January 25, 1970, in High River, Alta. ... 5-11/190. ... Shoots right. ... Brother of Bruce Greig, left winger with California Golden Seals (1973-74 and 1974-75). ... Name pronounced GRAYG.
TRANSACTIONS/CAREER NOTES: Selected by Hartford Whalers in first round (first Whalers pick, 15th overall) of NHL entry draft (June 16, 1990). ... Injured right knee (April 11, 1993); missed final three games of regular season. ... Traded by Whalers with sixth-round pick (G Doug

G

Bonner) in 1995 draft to Toronto Maple Leafs for D Ted Crowley (January 25, 1994). ... Strained hip flexor (February 21, 1994); missed one game. ... Signed as free agent by Calgary Flames (August 9, 1994). ... Signed as free agent by Philadelphia Flyers (August 4, 1998).
HONORS: Named to WHL (East) All-Star first team (1989-90). ... Named to AHL All-Star first team (2000-01).

| Season Team | League | REGULAR SEASON | | | | | | | | PLAYOFFS | | | | |
		Gms.	G	A	Pts.	PIM	+/-	PP	SH	Gms.	G	A	Pts.	PIM
86-87—Calgary	WHL	5	0	0	0	0	...	...	...	—	—	—	—	—
87-88—Lethbridge	WHL	65	9	18	27	38	...	...	...	—	—	—	—	—
88-89—Lethbridge	WHL	71	36	72	108	113	...	...	...	8	5	5	10	16
89-90—Lethbridge	WHL	65	55	80	135	149	...	...	...	18	11	21	32	35
90-91—Hartford	NHL	4	0	0	0	0	-1	0	0	—	—	—	—	—
—Springfield	AHL	73	32	55	87	73	...	...	...	17	2	6	8	22
91-92—Hartford	NHL	17	0	5	5	6	7	0	0	—	—	—	—	—
—Springfield	AHL	50	20	27	47	38	...	...	...	9	1	1	2	20
92-93—Hartford	NHL	22	1	7	8	27	-11	0	0	—	—	—	—	—
—Springfield	AHL	55	20	38	58	86	...	...	...	—	—	—	—	—
93-94—Hartford	NHL	31	4	5	9	31	-6	0	0	—	—	—	—	—
—Springfield	AHL	4	0	4	4	21	...	...	...	—	—	—	—	—
—Toronto	NHL	13	2	2	4	10	1	0	0	—	—	—	—	—
—St. John's	AHL	9	4	6	10	0	...	...	...	11	4	2	6	26
94-95—Saint John	AHL	67	31	50	81	82	...	...	...	2	0	1	1	0
—Calgary	NHL	8	1	1	2	2	1	0	0	—	—	—	—	—
95-96—Atlanta	IHL	71	25	48	73	104	...	...	...	3	2	1	3	4
96-97—Quebec	IHL	5	1	2	3	0	...	...	...	—	—	—	—	—
—Houston	IHL	59	12	30	42	59	...	...	...	13	5	8	13	2
97-98—Grand Rapids	IHL	69	26	36	62	103	...	...	...	3	0	4	4	4
98-99—Philadelphia	AHL	67	23	46	69	102	...	...	...	7	1	5	6	14
—Philadelphia	NHL	7	1	3	4	2	1	0	0	2	0	1	1	0
99-00—Philadelphia	AHL	68	34	48	82	116	...	...	...	5	3	2	5	6
—Philadelphia	NHL	11	3	2	5	6	0	0	0	3	0	0	0	0
00-01—Philadelphia	AHL	74	31	57	88	98	...	...	...	10	6	5	11	4
—Philadelphia	NHL	7	1	1	2	4	-2	0	0	—	—	—	—	—
NHL Totals (8 years)		120	13	26	39	88	-10	0	0	5	0	1	1	0

GRENIER, MARTIN — D — COYOTES

PERSONAL: Born November 2, 1980, in Laval, Que. ... 6-5/230. ... Shoots left.
TRANSACTIONS/CAREER NOTES: Selected by Colorado Avalanche in second round (second Avalanche pick, 45th overall) of NHL entry draft (June 26, 1999). ... Traded by Avalanche with LW Brian Rolston, C Samual Pahlsson and first-round pick (Martin Samuelsson) in 2000 draft to Boston Bruins for D Ray Bourque and LW Dave Andreychuk (March 6, 2000). ... Signed as free agent by Phoenix Coyotes (June 5, 2001).

| Season Team | League | REGULAR SEASON | | | | | | | | PLAYOFFS | | | | |
		Gms.	G	A	Pts.	PIM	+/-	PP	SH	Gms.	G	A	Pts.	PIM
97-98—Quebec	QMJHL	61	4	11	15	202	...	...	...	14	0	2	2	36
98-99—Quebec	QMJHL	60	7	18	25	*479	...	...	...	13	0	4	4	29
99-00—Quebec	QMJHL	67	11	35	46	302	...	...	...	7	1	4	5	27
00-01—Quebec	QMJHL	26	5	16	21	82	...	...	...	—	—	—	—	—
—Victoriaville	QMJHL	28	9	19	28	108	...	...	...	13	2	8	10	51

GRIER, MIKE — RW — OILERS

PERSONAL: Born January 5, 1975, in Detroit. ... 6-1/227. ... Shoots right.
TRANSACTIONS/CAREER NOTES: Selected by St. Louis Blues in ninth round (seventh Blues pick, 219th overall) of NHL entry draft (June 26, 1993). ... Rights traded by Blues with rights to G Curtis Joseph to Edmonton Oilers for first-round picks in 1996 (C Marty Reasoner) and 1997 (traded to Los Angeles) drafts (August 4, 1995); picks had been awarded earlier to Oilers as compensation for Blues signing free agent LW Shayne Corson (July 28, 1995). ... Strained medial collateral ligament in left knee (November 19, 1997); missed 14 games. ... Fractured clavicle (November 24, 1999); missed four games. ... Suffered torn triceps (March 13, 2000) and underwent surgery; missed remainder of season. ... Dislocated right shoulder (December 3, 2000); missed eight games.
HONORS: Named to NCAA All-America (East) first team (1994-95). ... Named to Hockey East All-Star first team (1994-95).
STATISTICAL PLATEAUS: Three-goal games: 1998-99 (1).

| Season Team | League | REGULAR SEASON | | | | | | | | PLAYOFFS | | | | |
		Gms.	G	A	Pts.	PIM	+/-	PP	SH	Gms.	G	A	Pts.	PIM
92-93—St. Sebastian's	USHS (East)	22	16	27	43	32	...	...	...	—	—	—	—	—
93-94—Boston University	Hockey East	39	9	9	18	56	...	...	...	—	—	—	—	—
94-95—Boston University	Hockey East	37	29	26	55	85	...	...	...	—	—	—	—	—
95-96—Boston University	Hockey East	38	21	25	46	82	...	...	...	—	—	—	—	—
96-97—Edmonton	NHL	79	15	17	32	45	7	4	0	12	3	1	4	4
97-98—Edmonton	NHL	66	9	6	15	73	-3	1	0	12	2	2	4	13
98-99—Edmonton	NHL	82	20	24	44	54	5	3	2	4	1	1	2	6
99-00—Edmonton	NHL	65	9	22	31	68	9	0	3	—	—	—	—	—
00-01—Edmonton	NHL	74	20	16	36	20	11	2	3	6	0	0	0	8
NHL Totals (5 years)		366	73	85	158	260	29	10	8	34	6	4	10	31

GRIMSON, STU — LW — PREDATORS

PERSONAL: Born May 20, 1965, in Kamloops, B.C. ... 6-5/239. ... Shoots left. ... Full Name: Stuart Grimson. ... Nickname: The Grim Reaper.
TRANSACTIONS/CAREER NOTES: Selected by Detroit Red Wings in 10th round (11th Red Wings pick, 186th overall) of NHL entry draft (June 8, 1983). ... Returned to draft pool and selected by Calgary Flames in seventh round (eighth Flames pick, 143rd overall) of NHL entry draft (June 15, 1985). ... Fractured cheekbone (January 9, 1990). ... Claimed on waivers by Chicago Blackhawks (October 1, 1990). ... Injured eye

G

(February 3, 1993). ... Selected by Mighty Ducks of Anaheim in NHL expansion draft (June 24, 1993). ... Lacerated hand (January 16, 1994); missed one game. ... Lacerated hand (March 9, 1994); missed one game. ... Lacerated hand (March 26, 1994); missed five games. ... Traded by Mighty Ducks with D Mark Ferner and sixth-round pick (LW Magnus Nilsson) in 1996 draft to Red Wings for C/RW Mike Sillinger and D Jason York (April 4, 1995). ... Signed by New York Rangers to offer sheet (August 18, 1995); Red Wings matched offer (August 24, 1995). ... Suffered from the flu (December 12, 1995); missed two games. ... Suspended two games and fined $1,000 by NHL for striking another player with a gloved hand (January 12, 1996). ... Claimed on waivers by Hartford Whalers (October 12, 1996). ... Whalers franchise moved to North Carolina and renamed Carolina Hurricanes for 1997-98 season; NHL approved move on June 25, 1997. ... Traded by Hurricanes with D Kevin Haller to Mighty Ducks of Anaheim for D Dave Karpa and fourth-round pick (traded to Atlanta) in 2000 draft (August 11, 1998). ... Suspended one playoff game by NHL for cross-checking incident (April 26, 1999). ... Strained neck (October 2, 1999); missed one game. ... Fractured left hand (January 18, 2000); missed 14 games. ... Signed as free agent by Los Angeles Kings (July 6, 2000). ... Injured right hand (September 16, 2000); missed first three games of season. ... Signed as free agent by Nashville Predators (July 2, 2001).

				REGULAR SEASON								PLAYOFFS			
Season Team	League	Gms.	G	A	Pts.	PIM	+/-	PP	SH	Gms.	G	A	Pts.	PIM
82-83—Regina	WHL	48	0	1	1	144	...	...	...	5	0	0	0	14
83-84—Regina	WHL	63	8	8	16	131	...	...	...	21	0	1	1	29
84-85—Regina	WHL	71	24	32	56	248	...	...	...	8	1	2	3	14
85-86—Univ. of Manitoba	CWUAA	12	7	4	11	113	...	...	...	3	1	1	2	20
86-87—Univ. of Manitoba	CWUAA	29	8	8	16	67	...	...	...	14	4	2	6	28
87-88—Salt Lake City	IHL	38	9	5	14	268	...	...	...	—	—	—	—	—
88-89—Calgary	NHL	1	0	0	0	5	0	0	0	—	—	—	—	—
—Salt Lake City	IHL	72	9	18	27	*397	...	...	...	15	2	3	5	*86
89-90—Salt Lake City	IHL	62	8	8	16	319	...	...	...	4	0	0	0	8
—Calgary	NHL	3	0	0	0	17	-1	0	0	—	—	—	—	—
90-91—Chicago	NHL	35	0	1	1	183	-3	0	0	5	0	0	0	46
91-92—Chicago	NHL	54	2	2	4	234	-2	0	0	14	0	1	1	10
—Indianapolis	IHL	5	1	1	2	17	...	...	...	—	—	—	—	—
92-93—Chicago	NHL	78	1	1	2	193	2	1	0	2	0	0	0	4
93-94—Anaheim	NHL	77	1	5	6	199	-6	0	0	—	—	—	—	—
94-95—Anaheim	NHL	31	0	1	1	110	-7	0	0	—	—	—	—	—
—Detroit	NHL	11	0	0	0	37	-4	0	0	11	1	0	1	26
95-96—Detroit	NHL	56	0	1	1	128	-10	0	0	2	0	0	0	0
96-97—Detroit	NHL	1	0	0	0	0	-1	0	0	—	—	—	—	—
—Hartford	NHL	75	2	2	4	218	-7	0	0	—	—	—	—	—
97-98—Carolina	NHL	82	3	4	7	204	0	0	0	—	—	—	—	—
98-99—Anaheim	NHL	73	3	0	3	158	0	0	0	3	0	0	0	30
99-00—Anaheim	NHL	50	1	2	3	116	0	0	0	—	—	—	—	—
00-01—Los Angeles	NHL	72	3	2	5	235	-2	0	0	5	0	0	0	4
NHL Totals (13 years)		699	16	21	37	2037	-41	1	0	42	1	1	2	120

GRON, STANISLAV   C   DEVILS

PERSONAL: Born October 28, 1978, in Bratislava, Czechoslovakia. ... 6-2/210. ... Shoots left.
TRANSACTIONS/CAREER NOTES: Selected by New Jersey Devils in second round (second Devils pick, 38th overall) of NHL entry draft (June 21, 1997).

				REGULAR SEASON								PLAYOFFS			
Season Team	League	Gms.	G	A	Pts.	PIM	+/-	PP	SH	Gms.	G	A	Pts.	PIM
94-95—Slovan Bratislava	Slovakia Jrs.	40	49	26	75	20	...	...	...	—	—	—	—	—
95-96—Slovan Bratislava	Slovakia Jrs.	43	33	25	58	14	...	...	...	—	—	—	—	—
—Slovan Bratislava	Slovakia	—	—	—	—	—	...	...	...	1	0	0	0	0
96-97—Slovan Bratislava	Slovakia Jrs.	22	20	16	36	...	...	...	...	—	—	—	—	—
—Slovan Bratislava	Slovakia	7	0	0	0	0	...	...	...	—	—	—	—	—
97-98—Seattle	WHL	61	9	29	38	21	...	...	...	5	1	5	6	0
98-99—Kootenay	WHL	49	28	18	46	18	...	...	...	7	3	8	11	12
—Utah	IHL	4	0	3	3	0	...	...	...	—	—	—	—	—
99-00—Albany	AHL	65	19	10	29	17	...	...	...	5	1	1	2	2
00-01—Albany	AHL	61	16	9	25	19	...	...	...	—	—	—	—	—
—New Jersey	NHL	1	0	0	0	0	1	0	0	—	—	—	—	—
NHL Totals (1 year)		1	0	0	0	0	1	0	0					

GROSEK, MICHAL   LW   RANGERS

PERSONAL: Born June 1, 1975, in Vyskov, Czechoslovakia. ... 6-2/216. ... Shoots right. ... Name pronounced GROH-shek.
TRANSACTIONS/CAREER NOTES: Selected by Winnipeg Jets in sixth round (seventh Jets pick, 145th overall) of NHL entry draft (June 26, 1993). ... Sprained knee ligaments (February 15, 1995); missed four games. ... Fractured foot (April 5, 1995); missed remainder of season. ... Traded by Jets with D Darryl Shannon to Buffalo Sabres for D Craig Muni (February 15, 1996). ... Suffered back spasms (April 9, 1999); missed five games. ... Traded by Sabres to Chicago Blackhawks for C Doug Gilmour and RW Jean-Pierre Dumont (March 10, 2000). ... Traded by Blackhawks with D Brad Brown to New York Rangers for future considerations (October 5, 2000). ... Suffered from the flu (December 20, 2000); missed one game.
STATISTICAL PLATEAUS: Three-goal games: 1996-97 (1).

G

				REGULAR SEASON								PLAYOFFS			
Season Team	League	Gms.	G	A	Pts.	PIM	+/-	PP	SH	Gms.	G	A	Pts.	PIM
92-93—ZPS Zlin	Czech.	17	1	3	4	0	...	...	...	—	—	—	—	—
93-94—Moncton	AHL	20	1	2	3	47	...	...	...	2	0	0	0	0
—Tacoma	WHL	30	25	20	45	106	...	...	...	7	2	2	4	30
—Winnipeg	NHL	3	1	0	1	0	-1	0	0	—	—	—	—	—
94-95—Springfield	AHL	45	10	22	32	98	...	...	...	—	—	—	—	—
—Winnipeg	NHL	24	2	2	4	21	-3	0	0	—	—	—	—	—
95-96—Springfield	AHL	39	16	19	35	68	...	...	...	—	—	—	—	—
—Winnipeg	NHL	1	0	0	0	0	-1	0	0	—	—	—	—	—
—Buffalo	NHL	22	6	4	10	31	0	2	0	—	—	—	—	—

Season Team	League	Gms.	G	A	Pts.	PIM	+/-	PP	SH	Gms.	G	A	Pts.	PIM
		REGULAR SEASON								**PLAYOFFS**				
96-97—Buffalo	NHL	82	15	21	36	71	25	1	0	12	3	3	6	8
97-98—Buffalo	NHL	67	10	20	30	60	9	2	0	15	6	4	10	28
98-99—Buffalo	NHL	76	20	30	50	102	21	4	0	13	0	4	4	28
99-00—Buffalo	NHL	61	11	23	34	35	12	2	0	—	—	—	—	—
—Chicago	NHL	14	2	4	6	12	-1	1	0	—	—	—	—	—
00-01—New York Rangers	NHL	65	9	11	20	61	-10	2	0	—	—	—	—	—
—Hartford	AHL	12	8	7	15	12	...	...	...	—	—	—	—	—
NHL Totals (8 years)		415	76	115	191	393	51	14	0	40	9	11	20	64

GUERIN, BILL   RW   BRUINS

PERSONAL: Born November 9, 1970, in Wilbraham, Mass. ... 6-2/210. ... Shoots right. ... Full Name: William Robert Guerin. ... Name pronounced GAIR-ihn.

TRANSACTIONS/CAREER NOTES: Selected by New Jersey Devils in first round (first Devils pick, fifth overall) of NHL entry draft (June 17, 1989). ... Suffered from the flu (February 1992); missed three games. ... Suffered from sore leg (March 19, 1994); missed two games. ... Suffered from the flu (December 6, 1995); missed two games. ... Missed first 21 games of 1997-98 season due to contract dispute. ... Traded by Devils with RW Valeri Zelepukin to Edmonton Oilers for C Jason Arnott and D Bryan Muir (January 4, 1998). ... Sprained medial collateral ligament in left knee (April 12, 1999); missed final two games of regular season and one playoff game. ... Suffered from the flu (December 9, 1999); missed one game. ... Traded by Oilers to Boston Bruins for C Anson Carter, second-round pick (D Doug Lynch) in 2001 draft and swap of first-round picks in 2001 (November 15, 2000).

HONORS: Played in NHL All-Star Game (2001). ... Named All-Star Game Most Valuable Player (2001).

MISCELLANEOUS: Member of Stanley Cup championship team (1995).

STATISTICAL PLATEAUS: Three-goal games: 1996-97 (1).

STATISTICAL NOTES: Led NHL in games played with 85 (2000-01).

Season Team	League	Gms.	G	A	Pts.	PIM	+/-	PP	SH	Gms.	G	A	Pts.	PIM
		REGULAR SEASON								**PLAYOFFS**				
85-86—Springfield Jr. B	NEJHL	48	26	19	45	71	...	...	...	—	—	—	—	—
86-87—Springfield Jr. B	NEJHL	32	34	20	54	40	...	...	...	—	—	—	—	—
87-88—Springfield Jr. B	NEJHL	38	31	44	75	146	...	...	...	—	—	—	—	—
88-89—Springfield Jr. B	NEJHL	31	32	37	69	90	...	...	...	—	—	—	—	—
89-90—Boston College	Hockey East	39	14	11	25	64	...	...	...	—	—	—	—	—
90-91—Boston College	Hockey East	38	26	19	45	102	...	...	...	—	—	—	—	—
91-92—U.S. national team	Int'l	46	12	15	27	67	...	...	...	—	—	—	—	—
—Utica	AHL	22	13	10	23	6	...	...	...	4	1	3	4	14
—New Jersey	NHL	5	0	1	1	9	1	0	0	6	3	0	3	4
92-93—New Jersey	NHL	65	14	20	34	63	14	0	0	5	1	1	2	4
—Utica	AHL	18	10	7	17	47	...	...	...	—	—	—	—	—
93-94—New Jersey	NHL	81	25	19	44	101	14	2	0	17	2	1	3	35
94-95—New Jersey	NHL	48	12	13	25	72	6	4	0	20	3	8	11	30
95-96—New Jersey	NHL	80	23	30	53	116	7	8	0	—	—	—	—	—
96-97—New Jersey	NHL	82	29	18	47	95	-2	7	0	8	2	1	3	18
97-98—New Jersey	NHL	19	5	5	10	13	0	1	0	—	—	—	—	—
—Edmonton	NHL	40	13	16	29	80	1	8	0	12	7	1	8	17
—U.S. Olympic team	Int'l	4	0	3	3	2	...	...	...	—	—	—	—	—
98-99—Edmonton	NHL	80	30	34	64	133	7	13	0	3	0	2	2	2
99-00—Edmonton	NHL	70	24	22	46	123	4	11	0	5	3	2	5	9
00-01—Edmonton	NHL	§21	12	10	22	18	11	4	0	—	—	—	—	—
—Boston	NHL	§64	28	35	63	122	-4	7	1	—	—	—	—	—
NHL Totals (10 years)		655	215	223	438	945	59	65	1	76	21	16	37	119

GUOLLA, STEVE   C

PERSONAL: Born March 15, 1973, in Scarborough, Ont. ... 6-0/191. ... Shoots left. ... Full Name: Stephen Guolla. ... Name pronounced GWAH-luh.

TRANSACTIONS/CAREER NOTES: Selected by Ottawa Senators (first Senators pick, third overall) in NHL supplemental draft (June 28, 1994). ... Signed as free agent by San Jose Sharks (August 26, 1996). ... Traded by Sharks with D Andrei Zyuzin, D Bill Houlder and LW Shawn Burr to Tampa Bay Lightning for LW Niklas Sundstrom and third-round pick (traded to Chicago) in 2000 draft (August 4, 1999). ... Injured ankle (October 23, 1999); missed four games. ... Strained groin (January 7, 2000); missed four games. ... Claimed on waivers by Atlanta Thrashers (March 1, 2000). ... Strained buttocks (January 29, 2001); missed three games.

HONORS: Named to NCCA All-America (West) second team (1993-94). ... Named to CCHA All-Star second team (1993-94). ... Named to AHL All-Star second team (1997-98 and 1998-99). ... Won Les Cunningham Plaque (1997-98 and 1998-99).

Season Team	League	Gms.	G	A	Pts.	PIM	+/-	PP	SH	Gms.	G	A	Pts.	PIM
		REGULAR SEASON								**PLAYOFFS**				
90-91—Wexford Jr. B	MTHL	...	37	42	79	...	...	...	...	—	—	—	—	—
91-92—Michigan State	CCHA	33	4	9	13	8	...	...	...	—	—	—	—	—
92-93—Michigan State	CCHA	39	19	35	54	6	...	...	...	—	—	—	—	—
93-94—Michigan State	CCHA	41	23	46	69	16	...	...	...	—	—	—	—	—
94-95—Michigan State	CCHA	40	16	35	51	16	...	...	...	—	—	—	—	—
95-96—Prin. Edward Island	AHL	72	32	48	80	28	...	...	...	3	0	0	0	0
96-97—Kentucky	AHL	34	22	22	44	10	...	...	...	4	2	1	3	0
—San Jose	NHL	43	13	8	21	14	-10	2	0	—	—	—	—	—
97-98—Kentucky	AHL	69	37	63	100	45	...	...	...	3	0	0	0	0
—San Jose	NHL	7	1	1	2	0	-2	0	0	—	—	—	—	—
98-99—Kentucky	AHL	53	29	47	76	33	...	...	...	—	—	—	—	—
—San Jose	NHL	14	2	2	4	6	3	0	0	—	—	—	—	—
99-00—Tampa Bay	NHL	46	6	10	16	11	2	2	0	—	—	—	—	—
—Atlanta	NHL	20	4	9	13	4	-13	2	0	—	—	—	—	—
00-01—Atlanta	NHL	63	12	16	28	23	-6	2	0	—	—	—	—	—
NHL Totals (5 years)		193	38	46	84	58	-26	8	0					

G

PERSONAL: Born September 24, 1976, in Uherske Hradiste, Czechoslovakia. ... 6-2/213. ... Shoots left.
TRANSACTIONS/CAREER NOTES: Selected by Montreal Canadiens in third round (second Canadiens pick, 60th overall) of NHL entry draft (July 8, 1995).

Season Team	League	REGULAR SEASON								PLAYOFFS				
		Gms.	G	A	Pts.	PIM	+/-	PP	SH	Gms.	G	A	Pts.	PIM
93-94—ZPS Zlin	Czech Rep.	22	1	5	6	...	...	...	...	3	0	0	0	...
94-95—ZPS Zlin	Czech Rep.	32	3	7	10	...	...	...	...	12	1	0	1	...
95-96—ZPS Zlin	Czech Rep.	27	1	2	3	...	...	...	...	7	1	0	1	...
96-97—Fredericton	AHL	79	6	26	32	26	...	...	...	—	—	—	—	—
97-98—Fredericton	AHL	78	15	36	51	36	...	...	...	4	1	2	3	0
98-99—Montreal	NHL	12	0	1	1	4	-1	0	0	—	—	—	—	—
—Fredericton	AHL	63	5	16	21	24	...	...	...	15	4	7	11	10
99-00—Montreal	NHL	24	1	2	3	12	-5	1	0	—	—	—	—	—
—Quebec	AHL	29	5	12	17	16	...	...	...	3	0	0	0	2
00-01—Quebec	AHL	75	11	40	51	24	...	...	...	8	4	2	6	6
NHL Totals (2 years)		36	1	3	4	16	-6	1	0					

PERSONAL: Born July 8, 1964, in Leningrad, U.S.S.R. ... 6-3/185. ... Shoots left. ... Name pronounced GOO-sah-rahf.
TRANSACTIONS/CAREER NOTES: Selected by Quebec Nordiques in 11th round (11th Nordiques pick, 213th overall) in the NHL entry draft (June 11, 1988). ... Suffered hairline fracture of left ankle (December 15, 1990); missed seven games. ... Hyperextended right knee (February 28, 1991). ... Fractured finger (October 13, 1991); missed four games. ... Suffered from the flu (February 9, 1993); missed two games. ... Suffered concussion (March 31, 1993); missed two games. ... Bruised left thumb (November 13, 1993); missed one game. ... Suffered from the flu (January 11, 1994); missed two games. ... Suffered from inflammation of sinuses (March 30, 1994); missed two games. ... Injured foot (January 21, 1995); missed nine games. ... Reinjured foot (February 11, 1995); missed six games. ... Injured knee (March 26, 1995); missed last 17 games of season and entire playoffs. ... Nordiques franchise moved to Colorado and renamed Avalanche for 1995-96 season (June 21, 1995). ... Suffered concussion (December 13, 1995); missed two games. ... Suffered from the flu (November 11, 1996); missed three games. ... Scratched cornea (November 30, 1996); missed three games. ... Suffered concussion (December 17, 1996); missed 13 games. ... Suffered from the flu (January 28, 1998); missed one game. ... Injured finger (April 2, 1998); missed one game. ... Fractured finger (November 17, 1998); missed 25 games. ... Sprained knee (April 24, 1999); missed 14 playoff games. ... Injured shoulder (October 16, 1999) and underwent surgery; missed 12 games. ... Fractured finger (November 19, 1999); missed 11 games. ... Suffered from the flu (January 6, 2000); missed two games. ... Suspended two games by NHL for cross-checking incident (January 14, 2000). ... Suffered concussion (January 25, 2000); missed four games. ... Fractured leg (February 27, 2000); missed remainder of season. ... Bruised foot (October 1, 2000); missed five games. ... Traded by Avalanche to New York Rangers for fifth-round pick (LW Frantisek Skladany) in 2001 draft (December 28, 2000). ... Traded by Rangers to St. Louis Blues for D Peter Smrek (March 5, 2001).
MISCELLANEOUS: Member of Stanley Cup championship team (1996). ... Member of gold-medal-winning U.S.S.R. Olympic team (1988). ... Member of silver-medal-winning Russian Olympic team (1998). ... Scored on a penalty shot (vs. Grant Fuhr, March 10, 1993).

Season Team	League	REGULAR SEASON								PLAYOFFS				
		Gms.	G	A	Pts.	PIM	+/-	PP	SH	Gms.	G	A	Pts.	PIM
81-82—SKA Leningrad	USSR	20	1	2	3	16	...	...	...	—	—	—	—	—
82-83—SKA Leningrad	USSR	42	2	1	3	32	...	...	...	—	—	—	—	—
83-84—SKA Leningrad	USSR	43	2	3	5	32	...	...	...	—	—	—	—	—
84-85—CSKA Moscow	USSR	36	3	2	5	26	...	...	...	—	—	—	—	—
85-86—CSKA Moscow	USSR	40	3	5	8	30	...	...	...	—	—	—	—	—
86-87—CSKA Moscow	USSR	38	4	7	11	24	...	...	...	—	—	—	—	—
87-88—CSKA Moscow	USSR	39	3	2	5	28	...	...	...	—	—	—	—	—
88-89—CSKA Moscow	USSR	42	5	4	9	37	...	...	...	—	—	—	—	—
89-90—CSKA Moscow	USSR	42	4	7	11	42	...	...	...	—	—	—	—	—
90-91—CSKA Moscow	USSR	15	0	0	0	12	...	...	...	—	—	—	—	—
—Quebec	NHL	36	3	9	12	12	-4	1	0	—	—	—	—	—
—Halifax	AHL	2	0	3	3	2	...	...	...	—	—	—	—	—
91-92—Quebec	NHL	68	5	18	23	22	-9	3	0	—	—	—	—	—
—Halifax	AHL	3	0	0	0	0	...	...	...	—	—	—	—	—
92-93—Quebec	NHL	79	8	22	30	57	18	0	2	5	0	1	1	0
93-94—Quebec	NHL	76	5	20	25	38	3	0	1	—	—	—	—	—
94-95—Quebec	NHL	14	1	2	3	6	-1	0	0	—	—	—	—	—
95-96—Colorado	NHL	65	5	15	20	56	29	0	0	21	0	9	9	12
96-97—Colorado	NHL	58	2	12	14	28	4	0	0	17	0	3	3	14
97-98—Colorado	NHL	72	4	10	14	42	9	0	1	7	0	1	1	6
—Russian Oly. team	Int'l	6	0	1	1	8	...	...	...	—	—	—	—	—
98-99—Colorado	NHL	54	3	10	13	24	12	1	0	5	0	0	0	2
99-00—Colorado	NHL	33	2	2	4	10	-8	0	0	—	—	—	—	—
00-01—Colorado	NHL	9	0	1	1	6	2	0	0	—	—	—	—	—
—New York Rangers	NHL	26	1	3	4	6	-2	0	0	—	—	—	—	—
—St. Louis	NHL	16	0	4	4	6	-3	0	0	13	0	0	0	4
NHL Totals (11 years)		606	39	128	167	313	50	5	4	68	0	14	14	38

G

PERSONAL: Born July 31, 1975, in Nizhny Tagil, U.S.S.R. ... 6-1/205. ... Shoots left. ... Name pronounced GOO-sehf.
TRANSACTIONS/CAREER NOTES: Selected by Dallas Stars in third round (fourth Stars pick, 69th overall) of NHL entry draft (July 8, 1995). ... Bruised thigh (October 18, 1997); missed two games. ... Traded by Stars to Tampa Bay Lightning for LW Benoit Hogue and sixth-round pick (D Michal Blazek) in 2001 draft (March 21, 1999). ... Tore anterior cruciate ligament in knee (December 19, 1999); missed remainder of season. ... Sprained knee (September 9, 2000); missed three games. ... Reinjured knee (October 23, 2000); missed six games. ... Suffered concussion (January 25, 2001); missed three games.

Season Team	League	Gms.	G	A	Pts.	PIM	+/-	PP	SH	Gms.	G	A	Pts.	PIM
94-95—CSK VVS Samara	CIS	50	3	5	8	58	...	...	...	—	—	—	—	—
95-96—Michigan	IHL	73	11	17	28	76	...	...	...	—	—	—	—	—
96-97—Michigan	IHL	51	7	8	15	44	...	...	...	4	0	4	4	6
97-98—Dallas	NHL	9	0	0	0	2	-5	0	0	—	—	—	—	—
—Michigan	IHL	36	3	6	9	36	...	...	...	4	0	2	2	6
98-99—Dallas	NHL	22	1	4	5	6	5	0	0	—	—	—	—	—
—Michigan	IHL	12	0	6	6	14	...	...	...	—	—	—	—	—
—Tampa Bay	NHL	14	0	3	3	10	-8	0	0	—	—	—	—	—
99-00—Tampa Bay	NHL	28	2	3	5	6	-9	1	0	—	—	—	—	—
00-01—Tampa Bay	NHL	16	1	0	1	10	-3	0	0	—	—	—	—	—
—Detroit	IHL	13	1	4	5	10	...	...	...	—	—	—	—	—
NHL Totals (4 years)		89	4	10	14	34	-20	1	0					

GUSMANOV, RAVIL   RW   WILD

PERSONAL: Born July 22, 1972, in Naberezhnye Chelny, U.S.S.R. ... 6-3/185. ... Shoots left. ... Name pronounced RAH-vihl GOOZ-muh-nahf.
TRANSACTIONS/CAREER NOTES: Selected by Winnipeg Jets in fourth round (fifth Jets pick, 93rd overall) of NHL entry draft (June 26, 1993). ... Traded by Jets to Chicago Blackhawks for fourth-round pick (traded to Toronto) in 1996 draft (March 20, 1996); Maple Leafs then traded pick to Phoenix Coyotes (Coyotes selected LW Vladimir Antipov) for RW Mike Gartner. ... Traded by Blackhawks to Calgary Flames for D Marc Hussey (March 18, 1997). ... Signed as free agent by Minnesota Wild (May 30, 2001).

Season Team	League	Gms.	G	A	Pts.	PIM	+/-	PP	SH	Gms.	G	A	Pts.	PIM
90-91—Traktor Chelyabinsk	USSR	15	0	0	0	10	...	...	...	—	—	—	—	—
91-92—Traktor Chelyabinsk	CIS	38	4	4	8	20	...	...	...	—	—	—	—	—
92-93—Traktor Chelyabinsk	CIS	39	15	8	23	30	...	...	...	8	4	0	4	2
93-94—Traktor Chelyabinsk	CIS	43	18	9	27	51	...	...	...	6	4	3	7	10
—Russian Oly. team	Int'l	8	3	1	4	0	...	...	...	—	—	—	—	—
94-95—Springfield	AHL	72	18	15	33	14	...	...	...	—	—	—	—	—
95-96—Springfield	AHL	60	36	32	68	20	...	...	...	—	—	—	—	—
—Winnipeg	NHL	4	0	0	0	0	-3	0	0	—	—	—	—	—
—Indianapolis	IHL	11	6	10	16	4	...	...	...	5	2	3	5	4
96-97—Indianapolis	IHL	60	21	27	48	14	...	...	...	—	—	—	—	—
—Saint John	AHL	12	4	4	8	2	...	...	...	3	0	1	1	2
97-98—Chicago	IHL	56	27	28	55	26	...	...	...	11	1	3	4	19
98-99—Metal. Magnitogorsk	Russian	42	14	24	38	28	...	...	...	16	2	8	10	16
99-00—Metal. Magnitogorsk	Russian	37	12	13	25	30	...	...	...	11	3	5	8	6
00-01—Metal. Magnitogorsk	Russian	43	6	19	25	20	...	...	...	12	1	†9	10	10
NHL Totals (1 year)		4	0	0	0	0	-3	0	0					

GUSTAFSON, DEREK   G   WILD

PERSONAL: Born June 21, 1979, in Gresham, Ore. ... 5-11/210. ... Catches left.
TRANSACTIONS/CAREER NOTES: Signed as non-drafted free agent by Minnesota Wild (June 9, 2000).
HONORS: Named to ECAC All-Star second team (1999-2000).

Season Team	League	Gms.	Min	W	L	T	GA	SO	Avg.	Gms.	Min.	W	L	GA	SO	Avg.
99-00—St. Lawrence Univ.	ECAC	24	1475	17	4	2	51	2	2.07	—	—	—	—	—	—	—
00-01—Jackson	ECHL	7	404	4	3	0	15	1	2.23	—	—	—	—	—	—	—
—Cleveland	IHL	24	1293	14	7	‡1	59	2	2.74	2	53	0	1	5	0	5.66
—Minnesota	NHL	4	239	1	3	0	10	0	2.51	—	—	—	—	—	—	—
NHL Totals (1 year)		4	239	1	3	0	10	0	2.51							

HACKETT, JEFF   G   CANADIENS

PERSONAL: Born June 1, 1968, in London, Ont. ... 6-1/198. ... Catches left.
TRANSACTIONS/CAREER NOTES: Selected by New York Islanders in second round (second Islanders pick, 34th overall) of NHL entry draft (June 13, 1987). ... Strained groin (May 13, 1990). ... Selected by San Jose Sharks in NHL expansion draft (May 30, 1991). ... Injured groin and hamstring (December 3, 1991); missed nine games. ... Injured knee (March 23, 1992). ... Injured groin (October 30, 1992); missed 12 games. ... Suffered from the flu (February 20, 1993); missed five games. ... Traded by Sharks to Chicago Blackhawks for third-round pick (C Alexei Yegorov) in 1994 draft (July 13, 1993). ... Pulled groin (October 17, 1995); missed three games. ... Fractured finger (March 22, 1996); missed three games. ... Fractured finger (October 6, 1996); missed 12 games. ... Pulled groin (March 18, 1997); missed two games. ... Sprained ankle (October 9, 1997); missed 11 games. ... Traded by Blackhawks with D Eric Weinrich, D Alain Nasreddine and fourth-round pick (D Chris Dyment) in 1999 draft to Montreal Canadiens for G Jocelyn Thibault, D Dave Manson and D Brad Brown (November 16, 1998). ... Injured knee (March 27, 1999); missed one game. ... Injured hip flexor (April 1, 1999); missed five games. ... Suffered back spasms and bruised shoulder (October 18, 1999); missed one game. ... Fractured right hand (October 24, 2000); missed 21 games. ... Reinjured hand (December 31, 2000); missed 15 games. ... Reinjured hand (February 24, 2001); missed remainder of season.
HONORS: Won F.W. (Dinty) Moore Trophy (1986-87). ... Shared Dave Pinkney Trophy with Sean Evoy (1986-87). ... Won Jack Butterfield Trophy (1989-90).
MISCELLANEOUS: Stopped a penalty shot attempt (vs. Brett Hull, January 4, 1996). ... Allowed a penalty shot goal (vs. Randy Wood, January 11, 1994; vs. Geoff Courtnall, December 13, 1996; vs. Adam Deadmarsh, March 1, 1997; vs. Kimmo Timonen, November 18, 1999).

Season Team	League	Gms.	Min	W	L	T	GA	SO	Avg.	Gms.	Min.	W	L	GA	SO	Avg.
84-85—London Jr. B	OHA	18	1078	...	...	...	73	1	4.06	—	—	—	—	—	—	—
85-86—London Jr. B	OHA	19	1150	...	...	...	66	0	3.44	—	—	—	—	—	—	—
86-87—Oshawa	OHL	31	1672	18	9	2	85	2	3.05	15	895	8	7	40	0	2.68
87-88—Oshawa	OHL	53	3165	30	21	2	205	0	3.89	7	438	3	4	31	0	4.25
88-89—New York Islanders	NHL	13	662	4	7	0	39	0	3.53	—	—	—	—	—	—	—
—Springfield	AHL	29	1677	12	14	2	116	0	4.15	—	—	—	—	—	—	—
89-90—Springfield	AHL	54	3045	24	25	3	187	1	3.68	†17	934	10	5	*60	0	3.85
90-91—New York Islanders	NHL	30	1508	5	18	1	91	0	3.62	—	—	—	—	—	—	—
91-92—San Jose	NHL	42	2314	11	27	1	148	0	3.84	—	—	—	—	—	—	—
92-93—San Jose	NHL	36	2000	2	30	1	176	0	5.28	—	—	—	—	—	—	—
93-94—Chicago	NHL	22	1084	2	12	3	62	0	3.43	—	—	—	—	—	—	—
94-95—Chicago	NHL	7	328	1	3	2	13	0	2.38	2	26	0	0	1	0	2.31
95-96—Chicago	NHL	35	2000	18	11	4	80	4	2.40	1	60	0	1	5	0	5.00
96-97—Chicago	NHL	41	2473	19	18	4	89	2	2.16	6	345	2	4	25	0	4.35
97-98—Chicago	NHL	58	3441	21	25	11	126	8	2.20	—	—	—	—	—	—	—
98-99—Chicago	NHL	10	524	2	6	1	33	0	3.78	—	—	—	—	—	—	—
—Montreal	NHL	53	3091	24	20	9	117	5	2.27	—	—	—	—	—	—	—
99-00—Montreal	NHL	56	3301	23	25	7	132	3	2.40	—	—	—	—	—	—	—
00-01—Montreal	NHL	19	998	4	10	2	54	0	3.25	—	—	—	—	—	—	—
NHL Totals (12 years)		422	23724	136	212	46	1160	22	2.93	9	431	2	5	31	0	4.32

HAGGERTY, SEAN — LW

PERSONAL: Born February 11, 1976, in Rye, N.Y. ... 6-1/186. ... Shoots left. ... Brother of Ryan Haggerty, center with Edmonton Oilers organization (1991-92 through 1995-96).

TRANSACTIONS/CAREER NOTES: Selected by Toronto Maple Leafs in second round (second Maple Leafs pick, 48th overall) of NHL entry draft (June 28, 1994). ... Traded by Maple Leafs with C Darby Hendrickson, D Kenny Jonsson and first-round pick (G Roberto Luongo) in 1997 draft to New York Islanders for LW Wendel Clark, D Mathieu Schneider and D D.J. Smith (March 13, 1996). ... Claimed on waivers by Nashville Predators (May 23, 2000).

HONORS: Named to OHL All-Rookie team (1993-94). ... Named to Memorial Cup All-Star team (1994-95). ... Named to OHL All-Star second team (1995-96). ... Named to AHL All-Star second team (1997-98).

Season Team	League	Gms.	G	A	Pts.	PIM	+/-	PP	SH	Gms.	G	A	Pts.	PIM
90-91—Westminster Prep	USHS (East)	25	20	22	42	...	...	...	...	—	—	—	—	—
91-92—Westminster Prep	USHS (East)	25	24	36	60	...	...	...	...	—	—	—	—	—
92-93—Boston	NEJHL	72	70	111	181	80	...	...	...	—	—	—	—	—
93-94—Det. Jr. Red Wings	OHL	60	31	32	63	21	...	...	...	17	9	10	19	11
94-95—Det. Jr. Red Wings	OHL	61	40	49	89	37	...	...	...	21	13	24	37	18
95-96—Det. Jr. Red Wings	OHL	66	*60	51	111	78	...	...	...	17	15	9	24	30
—Toronto	NHL	1	0	0	0	0	0	0	0	—	—	—	—	—
—Worcester	AHL	—	...	...	...	...	...	...	...	1	0	0	0	2
96-97—Kentucky	AHL	77	13	22	35	60	...	...	...	4	1	0	1	4
97-98—Kentucky	AHL	63	33	20	53	64	...	...	...	3	0	2	2	4
—New York Islanders	NHL	5	0	0	0	0	-3	0	0	—	—	—	—	—
98-99—Lowell	AHL	77	19	27	46	40	...	...	...	3	0	1	1	0
99-00—Kansas City	IHL	76	27	33	60	94	...	...	...	—	—	—	—	—
—New York Islanders	NHL	5	1	1	2	4	3	0	0	—	—	—	—	—
00-01—Milwaukee	IHL	76	27	23	50	59	...	...	...	5	0	1	1	8
—Nashville	NHL	3	0	1	1	0	1	0	0	—	—	—	—	—
NHL Totals (4 years)		14	1	2	3	4	1	0	0					

HAGMAN, NIKLAS — LW — PANTHERS

PERSONAL: Born December 5, 1979, in Espoo, Finland. ... 5-11/183. ... Shoots left.

TRANSACTIONS/CAREER NOTES: Selected by Florida Panthers in third round (third Panthers pick, 70th overall) of NHL entry draft (June 26, 1999).

Season Team	League	Gms.	G	A	Pts.	PIM	+/-	PP	SH	Gms.	G	A	Pts.	PIM
96-97—HIFK Helsinki	Finland Jr.	30	13	12	25	30	...	...	...	4	1	1	2	0
97-98—HIFK Helsinki	Finland	8	1	0	1	0	...	...	...	—	—	—	—	—
—HIFK Helsinki	Finland Jr.	26	9	5	14	16	...	...	...	—	—	—	—	—
98-99—HIFK Helsinki	Finland	17	1	1	2	14	...	...	...	—	—	—	—	—
—HIFK Helsinki	Finland Jr.	14	4	9	13	43	...	...	...	—	—	—	—	—
99-00—Karpat	Finland	41	17	18	35	12	...	...	...	7	4	2	6	...
—Espoo	Finland	14	1	1	2	2	...	...	...	—	—	—	—	—
00-01—Karpat	Finland	56	28	18	46	32	...	...	...	8	3	1	4	0

HAINSEY, RON — D — CANADIENS

PERSONAL: Born March 24, 1981, in Bolton, Conn. ... 6-2/187. ... Shoots left.

TRANSACTIONS/CAREER NOTES: Selected by Montreal Canadiens in first round (first Canadiens pick, 13th overall) of NHL entry draft (June 24, 2000).

HONORS: Named to Hockey East All-Star first team (2000-01). ... Named to NCAA All-America (East) second team (2000-01).

H

Season Team	League	Gms.	G	A	Pts.	PIM	+/-	PP	SH	Gms.	G	A	Pts.	PIM
						REGULAR SEASON						**PLAYOFFS**		
98-99—U.S. National	USHL	48	5	12	17	45	...	...	...	—	—	—	—	—
99-00—Mass.-Lowell	Hockey East	30	3	8	11	20	...	...	...	—	—	—	—	—
00-01—Mass.-Lowell	Hockey East	33	10	26	36	51	...	...	...	—	—	—	—	—
—Quebec	AHL	4	1	0	1	0	...	...	...	1	0	0	0	0

HAJT, CHRIS D OILERS

PERSONAL: Born July 5, 1978, in Amherst, N.Y. ... 6-3/206. ... Shoots left. ... Son of Bill Hajt, defenseman with Buffalo Sabres (1973-74 through 1986-87). ... Name pronounced HIGHT.
TRANSACTIONS/CAREER NOTES: Selected by Edmonton Oilers in second round (third Oilers pick, 32nd overall) of NHL entry draft (June 22, 1996).
HONORS: Named to OHL All-Star second team (1997-98).

Season Team	League	Gms.	G	A	Pts.	PIM	+/-	PP	SH	Gms.	G	A	Pts.	PIM
						REGULAR SEASON						**PLAYOFFS**		
94-95—Guelph	OHL	57	1	7	8	35	...	...	...	14	0	2	2	9
95-96—Guelph	OHL	63	8	27	35	69	...	...	...	16	0	6	6	13
96-97—Guelph	OHL	58	11	15	26	62	...	...	...	18	0	8	8	25
97-98—Guelph	OHL	44	2	21	23	42	...	...	...	12	1	5	6	11
98-99—Hamilton	AHL	64	0	4	4	36	...	...	...	—	—	—	—	—
99-00—Hamilton	AHL	54	0	8	8	30	...	...	...	10	0	2	2	0
00-01—Hamilton	AHL	70	0	10	10	48	...	...	...	—	—	—	—	—
—Edmonton	NHL	1	0	0	0	0	-1	0	0	—	—	—	—	—
NHL Totals (1 year)		1	0	0	0	0	-1	0	0					

HAKANSSON, MIKAEL C MAPLE LEAFS

PERSONAL: Born March 31, 1974, in Stockholm, Sweden. ... 6-1/196. ... Shoots left. ... Name pronounced HAK-ihn-suhn.
TRANSACTIONS/CAREER NOTES: Selected by Toronto Maple Leafs in sixth round (seventh Maple Leafs pick, 125th overall) of NHL entry draft (June 20, 1992).

Season Team	League	Gms.	G	A	Pts.	PIM	+/-	PP	SH	Gms.	G	A	Pts.	PIM
						REGULAR SEASON						**PLAYOFFS**		
90-91—Nacka	Sweden	27	2	5	7	6	...	...	...	—	—	—	—	—
91-92—Nacka	Sweden	29	3	15	18	24	...	...	...	—	—	—	—	—
92-93—Djurgarden Stockholm	Sweden	40	0	1	1	6	...	...	...	6	0	0	0	...
93-94—Djurgarden Stockholm	Sweden	37	3	3	6	12	...	...	...	6	0	0	0	...
94-95—MoDo Ornskoldsvik	Sweden	37	3	7	10	16	...	...	...	—	—	—	—	—
95-96—MoDo Ornskoldsvik	Sweden	40	8	4	12	18	...	...	...	8	2	0	2	0
96-97—Djurgarden Stockholm	Sweden	48	8	12	20	12	...	...	...	4	0	0	0	0
97-98—Djurgarden Stockholm	Sweden	43	9	2	11	8	...	...	...	15	3	0	3	14
98-99—Djurgarden Stockholm	Sweden	50	13	12	25	14	...	...	...	4	1	0	1	4
99-00—Djurgarden Stockholm	Sweden	48	17	17	34	26	...	...	...	13	3	8	11	12
00-01—St. John's	AHL	64	10	40	50	46	...	...	...	4	0	0	0	0

HALKO, STEVE D HURRICANES

PERSONAL: Born March 8, 1974, in Etobicoke, Ont. ... 6-1/190. ... Shoots right. ... Full Name: Steven Halko. ... Name pronounced HAHL-koh.
TRANSACTIONS/CAREER NOTES: Selected by Hartford Whalers in 10th round (10th Whalers pick, 225th overall) of NHL entry draft (June 20, 1992). ... Whalers franchise moved to North Carolina and renamed Carolina Hurricanes for 1997-98 season; NHL approved move on June 25, 1997.
HONORS: Named to CCHA All-Star second team (1994-95 and 1995-96). ... Named to NCAA All-Tournament team (1995-96).

Season Team	League	Gms.	G	A	Pts.	PIM	+/-	PP	SH	Gms.	G	A	Pts.	PIM
						REGULAR SEASON						**PLAYOFFS**		
91-92—Thornhill	OHA Jr. A	44	15	46	61	43	...	...	...	—	—	—	—	—
92-93—Univ. of Michigan	CCHA	39	1	12	13	12	...	...	...	—	—	—	—	—
93-94—Univ. of Michigan	CCHA	41	2	13	15	32	...	...	...	—	—	—	—	—
94-95—Univ. of Michigan	CCHA	39	2	14	16	20	...	...	...	—	—	—	—	—
95-96—Univ. of Michigan	CCHA	43	4	16	20	32	...	...	...	—	—	—	—	—
96-97—Springfield	AHL	70	1	5	6	37	...	...	...	11	0	2	2	8
97-98—Carolina	NHL	18	0	2	2	10	-1	0	0	—	—	—	—	—
—New Haven	AHL	65	1	19	20	44	...	...	...	1	0	0	0	0
98-99—New Haven	AHL	42	2	7	9	58	...	...	...	—	—	—	—	—
—Carolina	NHL	20	0	3	3	24	5	0	0	4	0	0	0	2
99-00—Carolina	NHL	58	0	8	8	25	0	0	0	—	—	—	—	—
00-01—Carolina	NHL	48	0	1	1	6	-10	0	0	—	—	—	—	—
NHL Totals (4 years)		144	0	14	14	65	-6	0	0	4	0	0	0	2

HALLER, KEVIN D ISLANDERS

PERSONAL: Born December 5, 1970, in Trochu, Alta. ... 6-2/199. ... Shoots left. ... Name pronounced HAW-luhr.
TRANSACTIONS/CAREER NOTES: Selected by Buffalo Sabres in first round (first Sabres pick, 14th overall) of NHL entry draft (June 17, 1989). ... Separated shoulder (May 7, 1991); missed seven games. ... Traded by Sabres to Montreal Canadiens for D Petr Svoboda (March 10, 1992). ... Suspended four games by NHL for slashing incident (November 2, 1993). ... Traded by Canadiens to Philadelphia Flyers for D Yves Racine (June 29, 1994). ... Pulled right groin (January 26, 1995); missed four games. ... Suffered from the flu (March 2, 1995); missed two games. ... Strained groin (March 15, 1995); missed six games. ... Sprained muscle in chest (December 16, 1995); missed 13 games. ... Fractured thumb (April 27, 1996); missed remainder of playoffs. ... Traded by Flyers with first- (traded to San Jose) and seventh-round (C Andrew

Merrick) picks in 1997 draft to Hartford Whalers for D Paul Coffey and third-round pick (D Kris Mallette) in 1997 draft (December 15, 1996). ... Suffered from the flu (December 20, 1996); missed one game. ... Strained groin (January 1, 1997); missed 13 games. ... Sprained shoulder (March 5, 1997); missed six games. ... Whalers franchise moved to North Carolina and renamed Carolina Hurricanes for 1997-98 season; NHL approved move on June 25, 1997. ... Suffered infected ankle (March 15, 1998); missed one game. ... Injured groin (March 28, 1998); missed 11 games. ... Traded by Hurricanes with LW Stu Grimson to Mighty Ducks of Anaheim for D Dave Karpa and fourth-round pick (traded to Atlanta) in 2000 draft (August 11, 1998). ... Underwent knee surgery prior to start of 1999-2000 season; missed first game of season. ... Sprained knee (November 15, 1999); missed 12 games. ... Signed as free agent by New York Islanders (July 3, 2000). ... Strained hip (December 15, 2000); missed 21 games. ... Underwent hernia surgery (February 1, 2001); missed remainder of season.

HONORS: Won Bill Hunter Trophy (1989-90). ... Named to WHL (East) All-Star first team (1989-90).

MISCELLANEOUS: Member of Stanley Cup championship team (1993).

			REGULAR SEASON								PLAYOFFS			
Season Team	League	Gms.	G	A	Pts.	PIM	+/-	PP	SH	Gms.	G	A	Pts.	PIM
87-88—Olds	AJHL	54	13	31	44	58	...	...	...	—	—	—	—	—
88-89—Regina	WHL	72	10	31	41	99	...	...	...	—	—	—	—	—
89-90—Regina	WHL	58	16	37	53	93	...	...	...	11	2	9	11	16
—Buffalo	NHL	2	0	0	0	0	0	0	0	—	—	—	—	—
90-91—Rochester	AHL	52	2	8	10	53	...	...	...	10	2	1	3	6
—Buffalo	NHL	21	1	8	9	20	9	1	0	6	1	4	5	10
91-92—Buffalo	NHL	58	6	15	21	75	-13	2	0	—	—	—	—	—
—Rochester	AHL	4	0	0	0	18	...	...	...	—	—	—	—	—
—Montreal	NHL	8	2	2	4	17	4	1	0	9	0	0	0	6
92-93—Montreal	NHL	73	11	14	25	117	7	6	0	17	1	6	7	16
93-94—Montreal	NHL	68	4	9	13	118	3	0	0	7	1	1	2	19
94-95—Philadelphia	NHL	36	2	8	10	48	16	0	0	15	4	4	8	10
95-96—Philadelphia	NHL	69	5	9	14	92	18	0	2	6	0	1	1	8
96-97—Philadelphia	NHL	27	0	5	5	37	-1	0	0	—	—	—	—	—
—Hartford	NHL	35	2	6	8	48	-11	0	0	—	—	—	—	—
97-98—Carolina	NHL	65	3	5	8	94	-5	0	0	—	—	—	—	—
98-99—Anaheim	NHL	82	1	6	7	122	-1	0	0	4	0	0	0	2
99-00—Anaheim	NHL	67	3	5	8	61	-8	0	0	—	—	—	—	—
00-01—New York Islanders	NHL	30	1	5	6	56	5	0	0	—	—	—	—	—
NHL Totals (12 years)		641	41	97	138	905	23	10	2	64	7	16	23	71

HALPERN, JEFF   C   CAPITALS

PERSONAL: Born May 3, 1976, in Potomac, Md. ... 5-11/198. ... Shoots right.

TRANSACTIONS/CAREER NOTES: Signed as non-drafted free agent by Washington Capitals (March 29, 1999). ... Suffered back spasms (February 19, 2000); missed three games. ... Strained groin (January 8, 2001); missed two games.

HONORS: Named to ECAC All-Star second team (1997-98 and 1998-99).

			REGULAR SEASON								PLAYOFFS			
Season Team	League	Gms.	G	A	Pts.	PIM	+/-	PP	SH	Gms.	G	A	Pts.	PIM
95-96—Princeton University	ECAC	29	3	11	14	30	...	...	...	—	—	—	—	—
96-97—Princeton University	ECAC	33	7	24	31	35	...	...	...	—	—	—	—	—
97-98—Princeton University	ECAC	36	*28	25	*53	46	...	...	...	—	—	—	—	—
98-99—Princeton University	ECAC	33	†22	22	44	32	...	...	...	—	—	—	—	—
—Portland	AHL	6	2	1	3	4	...	...	...	—	—	—	—	—
99-00—Washington	NHL	79	18	11	29	39	21	4	4	5	2	1	3	0
00-01—Washington	NHL	80	21	21	42	60	13	2	1	6	2	3	5	17
NHL Totals (2 years)		159	39	32	71	99	34	6	5	11	4	4	8	17

HAMEL, DENIS   RW   SABRES

PERSONAL: Born May 10, 1977, in Lachute, Que. ... 6-2/200. ... Shoots left. ... Name pronounced uh-MEHL.

TRANSACTIONS/CAREER NOTES: Selected by St. Louis Blues in sixth round (fifth Blues pick, 153rd overall) of NHL entry draft (July 8, 1995). ... Traded by Blues to Buffalo Sabres for D Charlie Huddy and seventh-round pick (C Daniel Corso) in 1996 draft (March 19, 1996). ... Tore anterior cruciate ligament in knee (January 27, 2001); missed remainder of season.

			REGULAR SEASON								PLAYOFFS			
Season Team	League	Gms.	G	A	Pts.	PIM	+/-	PP	SH	Gms.	G	A	Pts.	PIM
94-95—Chicoutimi	QMJHL	66	15	12	27	155	...	...	...	13	2	0	2	29
95-96—Chicoutimi	QMJHL	65	40	49	89	199	...	...	...	17	10	14	24	64
96-97—Chicoutimi	QMJHL	70	50	50	100	339	...	...	...	20	15	10	25	65
97-98—Rochester	AHL	74	10	15	25	98	...	...	...	4	1	2	3	0
98-99—Rochester	AHL	74	16	17	33	121	...	...	...	20	3	4	7	10
99-00—Rochester	AHL	76	34	24	58	122	...	...	...	21	6	7	13	49
—Buffalo	NHL	3	1	0	1	0	-1	0	0	—	—	—	—	—
00-01—Buffalo	NHL	41	8	3	11	22	-2	1	1	—	—	—	—	—
NHL Totals (2 years)		44	9	3	12	22	-3	1	1					

HAMRLIK, ROMAN   D   ISLANDERS

PERSONAL: Born April 12, 1974, in Gottwaldov, Czechoslovakia. ... 6-2/215. ... Shoots left. ... Brother of Martin Hamrlik, defenseman with Hartford Whalers (1991-92 through 1993-94) and St. Louis Blues (1993-94 and 1994-95) organizations. ... Name pronounced ROH-muhn HAM-uhr-lihk.

TRANSACTIONS/CAREER NOTES: Selected by Tampa Bay Lightning in first round (first Lightning pick, first overall) of NHL entry draft (June 20, 1992). ... Bruised shoulder (November 3, 1993); missed six games. ... Bruised shoulder (March 1, 1994); missed seven games. ... Played in Europe during 1994-95 NHL lockout. ... Suffered back spasms (January 9, 1997); missed two games. ... Traded by Lightning with C Paul Comrie to Edmonton Oilers for C Steve Kelly, D Bryan Marchment and C Jason Bonsignore (December 30, 1997). ... Fractured toe (January

H

5, 1999); missed six games. ... Bruised finger (December 1, 1999); missed two games. ... Traded by Oilers to Islanders for D Eric Brewer, LW Josh Green and second-round pick (LW Brad Winchester) in 2000 draft (June 24, 2000). ... Strained groin (December 21, 2000); missed five games. ... Strained hip flexor (January 31, 2001); missed one game.

HONORS: Played in NHL All-Star Game (1996 and 1999).

MISCELLANEOUS: Member of gold-medal-winning Czech Republic Olympic team (1998).

Season Team	League	REGULAR SEASON								PLAYOFFS				
		Gms.	G	A	Pts.	PIM	+/-	PP	SH	Gms.	G	A	Pts.	PIM
90-91—TJ Zlin	Czech.	14	2	2	4	18	...	...	...	—	—	—	—	—
91-92—ZPS Zlin	Czech.	34	5	5	10	34	...	...	...	—	—	—	—	—
92-93—Tampa Bay	NHL	67	6	15	21	71	-21	1	0	—	—	—	—	—
—Atlanta	IHL	2	1	1	2	2	...	...	...	—	—	—	—	—
93-94—Tampa Bay	NHL	64	3	18	21	135	-14	0	0	—	—	—	—	—
94-95—ZPS Zlin	Czech Rep.	2	1	0	1	10	...	...	...	—	—	—	—	—
—Tampa Bay	NHL	48	12	11	23	86	-18	7	1	—	—	—	—	—
95-96—Tampa Bay	NHL	82	16	49	65	103	-24	12	0	5	0	1	1	4
96-97—Tampa Bay	NHL	79	12	28	40	57	-29	6	0	—	—	—	—	—
97-98—Tampa Bay	NHL	37	3	12	15	22	-18	1	0	—	—	—	—	—
—Edmonton	NHL	41	6	20	26	48	3	4	1	12	0	6	6	12
—Czech Rep. Oly. team..	Int'l	6	1	0	1	2	...	...	...	—	—	—	—	—
98-99—Edmonton	NHL	75	8	24	32	70	9	3	0	3	0	0	0	2
99-00—Edmonton	NHL	80	8	37	45	68	1	5	0	5	0	1	1	4
00-01—New York Islanders	NHL	76	16	30	46	92	-20	5	1	—	—	—	—	—
NHL Totals (9 years)		649	90	244	334	752	-131	44	3	25	0	8	8	22

HANDZUS, MICHAL   C   COYOTES

PERSONAL: Born March 11, 1977, in Banska Bystrica, Czechoslovakia. ... 6-5/210. ... Shoots left. ... Name pronounced han-ZOOZ.

TRANSACTIONS/CAREER NOTES: Selected by St. Louis Blues in fourth round (third Blues pick, 101st overall) of NHL entry draft (July 8, 1995). ... Bruised shoulder (February 26, 1999); missed five games. ... Bruised shoulder (March 25, 1999); missed final 11 games of regular season and two playoffs games. ... Injured groin (October 1, 2000); missed first five games of season. ... Strained muscle in abdomen (January 11, 2001) and underwent surgery; missed 33 games. ... Traded by Blues with RW Ladislav Nagy, C Jeff Taffe and first-round pick in 2002 draft to Phoenix Coyotes for LW Keith Tkachuk (March 13, 2001).

STATISTICAL PLATEAUS: Three-goal games: 2000-01 (1).

Season Team	League	REGULAR SEASON								PLAYOFFS				
		Gms.	G	A	Pts.	PIM	+/-	PP	SH	Gms.	G	A	Pts.	PIM
93-94—IS Banska Bystrica	Slovakia Jrs.	40	23	36	59	...	...	...	...	—	—	—	—	—
94-95—IS Banska Bystrica	Slov. Div. II	22	15	14	29	10	...	...	...	—	—	—	—	—
95-96—IS Banska Bystrica	Slov. Div. II	19	3	1	4	8	...	...	...	—	—	—	—	—
96-97—Poprad	Slovakia	44	15	18	33	...	...	...	...	—	—	—	—	—
97-98—Worcester	AHL	69	27	36	63	54	...	...	...	11	2	6	8	10
98-99—St. Louis	NHL	66	4	12	16	30	-9	0	0	11	0	2	2	8
99-00—St. Louis	NHL	81	25	28	53	44	19	3	4	7	0	3	3	6
00-01—St. Louis	NHL	36	10	14	24	12	11	3	2	—	—	—	—	—
—Phoenix	NHL	10	4	4	8	21	5	0	1	—	—	—	—	—
NHL Totals (3 years)		193	43	58	101	107	26	6	7	18	0	5	5	14

HANKINSON, CASEY   LW

PERSONAL: Born May 8, 1976, in Edina, Minn. ... 6-1/187. ... Shoots left. ... Brother of Ben Hankinson, right winger with New Jersey Devils (1992-93 through 1994-95) and Tampa Bay Lightning (1994-95); and brother of Peter Hankinson, center with Winnipeg Jets organization (1989-90 through 1991-92).

TRANSACTIONS/CAREER NOTES: Selected by Chicago Blackhawks in eighth round (ninth Blackhawks pick, 201st overall) of NHL entry draft (July 8, 1995).

Season Team	League	REGULAR SEASON								PLAYOFFS				
		Gms.	G	A	Pts.	PIM	+/-	PP	SH	Gms.	G	A	Pts.	PIM
92-93—Edina High School	Minn. H.S.	25	20	26	46	...	...	...	...	—	—	—	—	—
93-94—Edina High School	Minn. H.S.	24	21	20	41	50	...	...	...	—	—	—	—	—
94-95—Univ. of Minnesota	WCHA	33	7	1	8	86	...	...	...	—	—	—	—	—
95-96—Univ. of Minnesota	WCHA	39	16	19	35	101	...	...	...	—	—	—	—	—
96-97—Univ. of Minnesota	WCHA	42	17	24	41	79	...	...	...	—	—	—	—	—
97-98—Univ. of Minnesota	WCHA	35	10	12	22	81	...	...	...	—	—	—	—	—
98-99—Portland	AHL	72	10	13	23	106	...	...	...	—	—	—	—	—
99-00—Cleveland	IHL	82	7	22	29	140	...	...	...	2	0	0	0	2
00-01—Norfolk	AHL	69	30	21	51	74	...	...	...	9	5	4	9	2
—Chicago	NHL	11	0	1	1	9	-3	0	0	—	—	—	—	—
NHL Totals (1 year)		11	0	1	1	9	-3	0	0					

HANNAN, SCOTT   D   SHARKS

H

PERSONAL: Born January 23, 1979, in Richmond, B.C. ... 6-2/220. ... Shoots left.

TRANSACTIONS/CAREER NOTES: Selected by San Jose Sharks in first round (second Sharks pick, 23rd overall) of NHL entry draft (June 21, 1997). ... Injured ankle (October 24, 2000); missed three games.

HONORS: Name to WHL (West) All-Star first team (1998-99).

Season Team	League	REGULAR SEASON								PLAYOFFS				
		Gms.	G	A	Pts.	PIM	+/-	PP	SH	Gms.	G	A	Pts.	PIM
94-95—Tacoma	WHL	2	0	0	0	0	...	...	...	—	—	—	—	—
95-96—Kelowna	WHL	69	4	5	9	76	...	...	...	6	0	1	1	4
96-97—Kelowna	WHL	70	17	26	43	101	...	...	...	6	0	0	0	8
97-98—Kelowna	WHL	47	10	30	40	70	...	...	...	—	—	—	—	—
98-99—San Jose	NHL	5	0	2	2	6	0	0	0	—	—	—	—	—
—Kelowna	WHL	47	15	30	45	92	...	...	...	6	1	2	3	14
—Kentucky	AHL	2	0	0	0	2	...	...	...	12	0	2	2	10
99-00—Kentucky	AHL	41	5	12	17	40	...	...	...	—	—	—	—	—
—San Jose	NHL	30	1	2	3	10	7	0	0	1	0	1	1	0
00-01—San Jose	NHL	75	3	14	17	51	10	0	0	6	0	1	1	6
NHL Totals (3 years)		110	4	18	22	67	17	0	0	7	0	2	2	6

HANSEN, TAVIS   C/RW

PERSONAL: Born June 17, 1975, in Prince Albert, Sask. ... 6-1/180. ... Shoots right.
TRANSACTIONS/CAREER NOTES: Selected by Winnipeg Jets in third round (third Jets pick, 58th overall) of NHL entry draft (June 29, 1994). ... Jets franchise moved to Phoenix and renamed Coyotes for 1996-97 season; NHL approved move on January 18, 1996.

Season Team	League	REGULAR SEASON								PLAYOFFS				
		Gms.	G	A	Pts.	PIM	+/-	PP	SH	Gms.	G	A	Pts.	PIM
93-94—Tacoma	WHL	71	23	31	54	122	...	...	...	8	1	3	4	17
94-95—Tacoma	WHL	71	32	41	73	142	...	...	...	4	1	1	2	8
—Winnipeg	NHL	1	0	0	0	0	0	0	0	—	—	—	—	—
95-96—Springfield	AHL	67	6	16	22	85	...	...	...	5	1	2	3	2
96-97—Springfield	AHL	12	3	1	4	23	...	...	...	—	—	—	—	—
—Phoenix	NHL	1	0	0	0	0	0	0	0	—	—	—	—	—
97-98—Springfield	AHL	73	20	14	34	70	...	...	...	4	1	2	3	18
98-99—Springfield	AHL	63	23	11	34	85	...	...	...	3	0	1	1	5
—Phoenix	NHL	20	2	1	3	12	-4	0	0	2	0	0	0	0
99-00—Springfield	AHL	59	21	27	48	164	...	...	...	5	2	1	3	4
—Phoenix	NHL	5	0	0	0	0	0	0	0	—	—	—	—	—
00-01—Springfield	AHL	24	6	10	16	81	...	...	...	—	—	—	—	—
—Phoenix	NHL	7	0	0	0	4	-1	0	0	—	—	—	—	—
NHL Totals (5 years)		34	2	1	3	16	-5	0	0	2	0	0	0	0

HARKINS, BRETT   LW   BLUE JACKETS

PERSONAL: Born July 2, 1970, in North Ridgefield, Ohio. ... 6-1/185. ... Shoots left. ... Full Name: Brett Alan Harkins. ... Brother of Todd Harkins, right winger with Calgary Flames (1991-92 and 1992-93) and Hartford Whalers (1993-94).
TRANSACTIONS/CAREER NOTES: Selected by New York Islanders in seventh round (ninth Islanders pick, 133rd overall) of NHL entry draft (June 17, 1989). ... Signed as free agent by Adirondack Red Wings (1993). ... Signed as free agent by Boston Bruins (July 6, 1994). ... Signed as free agent by Florida Panthers (July 19, 1995). ... Signed as free agent by Boston Bruins (September 5, 1996). ... Suffered back spasms (March 27, 1997); missed five games. ... Signed as free agent by Columbus Blue Jackets (June 25, 2001).
HONORS: Named to CCHA All-Rookie team (1989-90).
MISCELLANEOUS: Failed to score on penalty shot (vs. Ron Tugnutt, March 22, 1997).

Season Team	League	REGULAR SEASON								PLAYOFFS				
		Gms.	G	A	Pts.	PIM	+/-	PP	SH	Gms.	G	A	Pts.	PIM
87-88—Brockville	COJHL	55	21	55	76	36	...	...	...	—	—	—	—	—
88-89—Detroit Compuware	NAJHL	38	23	46	69	94	...	...	...	—	—	—	—	—
89-90—Bowling Green	CCHA	41	11	43	54	45	...	...	...	—	—	—	—	—
90-91—Bowling Green	CCHA	40	22	38	60	30	...	...	...	—	—	—	—	—
91-92—Bowling Green	CCHA	34	8	39	47	32	...	...	...	—	—	—	—	—
92-93—Bowling Green	CCHA	35	19	28	47	28	...	...	...	—	—	—	—	—
93-94—Adirondack	AHL	80	22	47	69	23	...	...	...	10	1	5	6	4
94-95—Providence	AHL	80	23	†69	92	32	...	...	...	13	8	14	22	4
—Boston	NHL	1	0	1	1	0	0	0	0	—	—	—	—	—
95-96—Carolina	AHL	55	23	†71	94	44	...	...	...	—	—	—	—	—
—Florida	NHL	8	0	3	3	6	-2	0	0	—	—	—	—	—
96-97—Providence	AHL	28	9	31	40	32	...	...	...	10	2	10	12	0
—Boston	NHL	44	4	14	18	8	-3	3	0	—	—	—	—	—
97-98—Cleveland	IHL	80	32	62	94	82	...	...	...	10	4	13	17	14
98-99—Cleveland	IHL	74	20	67	87	84	...	...	...	—	—	—	—	—
99-00—Cleveland	IHL	76	20	50	70	79	...	...	...	9	2	8	10	6
00-01—Houston	IHL	81	16	*64	80	51	...	...	...	7	0	3	3	8
NHL Totals (3 years)		53	4	18	22	14	-5	3	0					

HARLOCK, DAVID   D   THRASHERS

PERSONAL: Born March 16, 1971, in Toronto. ... 6-2/220. ... Shoots left. ... Full Name: David Alan Harlock.
TRANSACTIONS/CAREER NOTES: Selected by New Jersey Devils in second round (second Devils pick, 24th overall) of NHL entry draft (June 16, 1990). ... Signed as free agent by Toronto Maple Leafs (August 20, 1993). ... Loaned by Maple Leafs to Canadian national team (October 3, 1993). ... Signed as free agent by Washington Capitals (August 31, 1997). ... Signed as free agent by New York Islanders (August 19, 1998). ... Bruised foot (October 29, 1998); missed one game. ... Selected by Atlanta Thrashers in NHL expansion draft (June 25, 1999). ... Strained shoulder (December 23, 1999) and underwent surgery; missed 36 games. ... Injured neck (December 1, 2000); missed six games.
MISCELLANEOUS: Member of silver-medal-winning Canadian Olympic team (1994).

H

Season Team	League	REGULAR SEASON Gms.	G	A	Pts.	PIM	+/-	PP	SH	PLAYOFFS Gms.	G	A	Pts.	PIM
86-87—Toronto Red Wings	MTHL	86	17	55	72	60	...	...	...	—	—	—	—	—
87-88—Toronto Red Wings	MTHL	70	16	56	72	100	...	...	...	—	—	—	—	—
88-89—St. Michael's Jr. B	ODHA	25	4	15	19	34	...	...	...	—	—	—	—	—
89-90—Univ. of Michigan	CCHA	42	2	13	15	44	...	...	...	—	—	—	—	—
90-91—Univ. of Michigan	CCHA	39	2	8	10	70	...	...	...	—	—	—	—	—
91-92—Univ. of Michigan	CCHA	44	1	6	7	80	...	...	...	—	—	—	—	—
92-93—Univ. of Michigan	CCHA	38	3	9	12	58	...	...	...	—	—	—	—	—
—Canadian nat'l team	Int'l	4	0	0	0	2	...	...	...	—	—	—	—	—
93-94—Canadian nat'l team	Int'l	41	0	3	3	28	...	...	...	—	—	—	—	—
—Can. Olympic team	Int'l	8	0	0	0	8	...	...	...	—	—	—	—	—
—Toronto	NHL	6	0	0	0	0	-2	0	0	—	—	—	—	—
—St. John's	AHL	10	0	3	3	2	...	...	...	9	0	0	0	6
94-95—St. John's	AHL	58	0	6	6	44	...	...	...	5	0	0	0	0
—Toronto	NHL	1	0	0	0	0	-1	0	0	—	—	—	—	—
95-96—St. John's	AHL	77	0	12	12	92	...	...	...	4	0	1	1	2
—Toronto	NHL	1	0	0	0	0	0	0	0	—	—	—	—	—
—Portland	AHL	1	0	0	0	0	...	...	...	—	—	—	—	—
96-97—San Antonio	IHL	69	3	10	13	82	...	...	...	9	0	0	0	10
97-98—Portland	AHL	71	3	15	18	66	...	...	...	10	2	2	4	6
—Washington	NHL	6	0	0	0	4	2	0	0	—	—	—	—	—
98-99—New York Islanders	NHL	70	2	6	8	68	-16	0	0	—	—	—	—	—
99-00—Atlanta	NHL	44	0	6	6	36	-8	0	0	—	—	—	—	—
00-01—Atlanta	NHL	65	0	1	1	62	-28	0	0	—	—	—	—	—
NHL Totals (7 years)		193	2	13	15	170	-53	0	0					

HARTNELL, SCOTT   RW   PREDATORS

PERSONAL: Born April 18, 1982, in Regina, Sask. ... 6-2/192. ... Shoots left. ... Cousin of Mark Deyell, center, Toronto Maple Leafs organization.
TRANSACTIONS/CAREER NOTES: Selected by Nashville Predators in first round (first Predators pick, sixth overall) of NHL entry draft (June 24, 2000). ... Suffered concussion (November 26, 2000); missed six games.

Season Team	League	REGULAR SEASON Gms.	G	A	Pts.	PIM	+/-	PP	SH	PLAYOFFS Gms.	G	A	Pts.	PIM
97-98—Lloydminster	Jr. A	56	9	16	25	82	...	...	...	4	2	1	3	8
—Prince Albert	WHL	1	0	1	1	2	...	...	...	—	—	—	—	—
98-99—Prince Albert	WHL	65	10	34	44	104	...	...	...	14	0	5	5	22
99-00—Prince Albert	WHL	62	27	55	82	124	...	...	...	6	3	2	5	6
00-01—Nashville	NHL	75	2	14	16	48	-8	0	0	—	—	—	—	—
NHL Totals (1 year)		75	2	14	16	48	-8	0	0					

HARVEY, TODD   RW   SHARKS

PERSONAL: Born February 17, 1975, in Hamilton, Ont. ... 6-0/205. ... Shoots right.
TRANSACTIONS/CAREER NOTES: Selected by Dallas Stars in first round (first Stars pick, ninth overall) of NHL entry draft (June 26, 1993). ... Strained back (March 13, 1995); missed one game. ... Sprained knee (October 30, 1995); missed two games. ... Strained groin (November 3, 1996); missed one game. ... Sprained knee (November 19, 1996); missed five games. ... Suffered from the flu (December 29, 1996); missed one game. ... Suspended two games and fined $1,000 by NHL for elbowing incident (February 2, 1997). ... Bruised hand (April 4, 1997); missed one game. ... Suffered concussion (November 16, 1997); missed one game. ... Strained hip flexor (December 20, 1997); missed one game. ... Sprained knee (January 7, 1998); missed five games. ... Injured hand (February 4, 1998); missed one game. ... Strained lower back (March 13, 1998); missed one game. ... Underwent right knee surgery (March 22, 1998); missed 12 games. ... Traded by Stars with LW Bob Errey and fourth-round pick (LW Boyd Kane) in 1998 draft to New York Rangers for RW Mike Keane, C Brian Skrudland and sixth-round pick (RW Pavel Patera) in 1998 draft (March 24, 1998). ... Strained hip flexor (October 9, 1998); missed first two games of season. ... Suspended one game and fined $1,000 by NHL for roughing incident (December 13, 1998). ... Bruised right thumb (December 11, 1998); missed two games. ... Sprained medial collateral ligament (January 13, 1999); missed 10 games. ... Fractured thumb (February 17, 1999); missed final 27 games of season. ... Sprained knee (November 18, 1999); missed three games. ... Traded by Rangers with fourth-round pick (G Dimitri Patzold) in 2001 draft to San Jose Sharks for RW Radek Dvorak (December 30, 1999). ... Suffered concussion and whiplash (January 1, 2001); missed 10 games.
HONORS: Named to Can.HL All-Rookie team (1991-92). ... Named to OHL Rookie All-Star team (1991-92).
STATISTICAL PLATEAUS: Three-goal games: 1994-95 (1), 2000-01 (1). Total: 2.

Season Team	League	REGULAR SEASON Gms.	G	A	Pts.	PIM	+/-	PP	SH	PLAYOFFS Gms.	G	A	Pts.	PIM
89-90—Cambridge Jr. B	OHA	41	35	27	62	213	...	...	...	—	—	—	—	—
90-91—Cambridge Jr. B	OHA	35	32	39	71	174	...	...	...	—	—	—	—	—
91-92—Det. Jr. Red Wings	OHL	58	21	43	64	141	...	...	...	7	3	5	8	32
92-93—Det. Jr. Red Wings	OHL	55	50	50	100	83	...	...	...	15	9	12	21	39
93-94—Det. Jr. Red Wings	OHL	49	34	51	85	75	...	...	...	17	10	12	22	26
94-95—Det. Jr. Red Wings	OHL	11	8	14	22	12	...	...	...	—	—	—	—	—
—Dallas	NHL	40	11	9	20	67	-3	2	0	5	0	0	0	8
95-96—Dallas	NHL	69	9	20	29	136	-13	3	0	—	—	—	—	—
—Michigan	IHL	5	1	3	4	8	...	...	...	—	—	—	—	—
96-97—Dallas	NHL	71	9	22	31	142	19	1	0	7	0	1	1	10
97-98—Dallas	NHL	59	9	10	19	104	5	0	0	—	—	—	—	—
98-99—New York Rangers	NHL	37	11	17	28	72	-1	6	0	—	—	—	—	—
99-00—New York Rangers	NHL	31	3	3	6	62	-9	0	0	—	—	—	—	—
—San Jose	NHL	40	8	4	12	78	-2	2	0	12	1	0	1	8
00-01—San Jose	NHL	69	10	11	21	72	6	1	0	6	0	0	0	8
NHL Totals (7 years)		416	70	96	166	733	2	15	0	30	1	1	2	34

H

PERSONAL: Born January 29, 1965, in Pardubice, Czechoslovakia. ... 5-11/168. ... Catches left. ... Name pronounced HA-shehk.

TRANSACTIONS/CAREER NOTES: Selected by Chicago Blackhawks in 10th round (11th Blackhawks pick, 199th overall) of NHL entry draft (June 8, 1983). ... Traded by Blackhawks to Buffalo Sabres for G Stephane Beauregard and fourth-round pick (LW Eric Daze) in 1993 draft (August 7, 1992). ... Injured groin (November 25, 1992); missed three games. ... Strained abdominal muscle (January 6, 1993); missed six games. ... Played in Europe during 1994-95 NHL lockout. ... Strained rotator cuff (March 16, 1995); missed three games. ... Injured abdominal muscle (December 15, 1995); missed 10 games. ... Sprained left knee (April 6, 1996); missed last two games of season. ... Fractured rib (March 19, 1997); missed five games. ... Sprained knee ligament (April 21, 1997); missed six playoff games. ... Suspended three playoff games and fined $10,000 by NHL for grabbing a reporter who had written a critical column (May 1, 1997). ... Suffered ear infection (April 15, 1998); missed one game. ... Strained groin (February 17, 1999); missed 12 games. ... Strained back (March 23, 1999); missed one game. ... Tore groin muscle (October 29, 1999); missed 40 games. ... Injured knee (October 5, 2000); missed one game. ... Traded by Sabres to Detroit Red Wings for LW Slava Kozlov, first-round pick in 2002 draft and future considerations (July 1, 2001).

HONORS: Named Czechoslovakian League Player of the Year (1986-87, 1988-89 and 1989-90). ... Named to Czechoslovakian League All-Star team (1988-89 and 1989-90). ... Named to IHL All-Star first team (1990-91). ... Named to NHL All-Rookie team (1991-92). ... Won Vezina Trophy (1993-94, 1994-95, 1996-97 through 1998-99 and 2000-01). ... Shared William M. Jennings Trophy with Grant Fuhr (1993-94). ... Named to THE SPORTING NEWS All-Star second team (1993-94). ... Named to NHL All-Star first team (1993-94, 1994-95, 1996-97 through 1998-99 and 2000-01). ... Named to THE SPORTING NEWS All-Star team (1994-95 and 1996-97 through 1998-99). ... Played in NHL All-Star Game (1996-1999 and 2001). ... Named NHL Player of the Year by THE SPORTING NEWS (1996-97 and 1997-98). ... Won Lester B. Pearson Award (1996-97 and 1997-98). ... Won Hart Memorial Trophy (1996-97 and 1997-98). ... Named to play in NHL All-Star Game (2000); replaced by G Roman Turek due to injury. ... Shared William M. Jennings Trophy with Martin Biron (2000-01).

MISCELLANEOUS: Member of gold-medal-winning Czech Republic Olympic team (1998). ... Holds Buffalo Sabres all-time records for most games played in by a goalie (491), most wins (234), most shutouts (55) and goals-against average (2.22). ... Stopped a penalty shot attempt (vs. Mark Recchi, March 8, 1995; vs. Mario Lemieux, March 23, 1996; vs. Vincent Damphousse, March 8, 1997; vs. Jason Allison, April 10, 1997; vs. Eric Desjardins, April 16, 2000 (playoffs); vs. Dainius Zubrus, November 3, 2000; vs. Mark Recchi, April 11, 2001 (playoffs); vs. Martin Straka, May 2, 2001 (playoffs)). ... Allowed a penalty shot goal (vs. John MacLean, February 27, 1997; vs. Jere Lehtinen, October 7, 1997; vs. Mats Sundin, May 29, 1999 (playoffs); vs Olli Jokinen, March 4, 2000).

STATISTICAL NOTES: Led NHL in save percentage with .930 in 1993-94, .930 in 1994-95, .920 in 1995-96, .930 in 1996-97, .932 in 1997-98 and .937 in 1998-99. ... Tied for NHL lead with .919 save percentage (1999-2000).

Season Team	League	REGULAR SEASON								PLAYOFFS						
		Gms.	Min	W	L	T	GA	SO	Avg.	Gms.	Min.	W	L	GA	SO	Avg.
81-82—Pardubice	Czech Rep.	12	661	...	...	...	34	0	3.09	—	—	—	—	—	—	—
82-83—Pardubice	Czech Rep.	42	2358	...	...	...	105	0	2.67	—	—	—	—	—	—	—
83-84—Pardubice	Czech Rep.	40	2304	...	...	...	108	0	2.81	—	—	—	—	—	—	—
84-85—Pardubice	Czech Rep.	42	2419	...	...	...	131	0	3.25	—	—	—	—	—	—	—
85-86—Pardubice	Czech Rep.	45	2689	...	...	...	138	0	3.08	—	—	—	—	—	—	—
86-87—Pardubice	Czech Rep.	23	2515	...	...	...	103	0	2.46	—	—	—	—	—	—	—
87-88—Pardubice	Czech Rep.	31	2265	...	...	...	98	0	2.60	—	—	—	—	—	—	—
—Czech. Olympic Team	Int'l	8	217	...	...	...	18	...	4.98	—	—	—	—	—	—	—
88-89—Pardubice	Czech Rep.	42	2507	...	...	...	114	0	2.73	—	—	—	—	—	—	—
89-90—Dukla Jihlava	Czech.	40	2251	...	...	...	80	0	2.13	—	—	—	—	—	—	—
90-91—Chicago	NHL	5	195	3	0	1	8	0	2.46	3	69	0	0	3	0	2.61
—Indianapolis	IHL	33	1903	20	11	‡4	80	*5	*2.52	1	60	1	0	3	0	3.00
91-92—Indianapolis	IHL	20	1162	7	10	‡3	69	1	3.56	—	—	—	—	—	—	—
—Chicago	NHL	20	1014	10	4	1	44	1	2.60	3	158	0	2	8	0	3.04
92-93—Buffalo	NHL	28	1429	11	10	4	75	0	3.15	1	45	1	0	1	0	1.33
93-94—Buffalo	NHL	58	3358	30	20	6	109	†7	*1.95	7	484	3	4	13	2	*1.61
94-95—HC Pardubice	Czech Rep.	2	125	...	...	...	6	...	2.88	—	—	—	—	—	—	—
—Buffalo	NHL	41	2416	19	14	7	85	†5	*2.11	5	309	1	4	18	0	3.50
95-96—Buffalo	NHL	59	3417	22	†30	6	161	2	2.83	—	—	—	—	—	—	—
96-97—Buffalo	NHL	67	4037	37	20	10	153	5	2.27	3	153	1	1	5	0	1.96
97-98—Buffalo	NHL	*72	*4220	33	23	13	147	*13	2.09	15	948	10	5	32	1	2.03
—Czech Rep. Oly. team	Int'l	6	369	5	1	0	6	2	.98	—	—	—	—	—	—	—
98-99—Buffalo	NHL	64	3817	30	18	14	119	9	1.87	19	1217	13	6	36	2	1.77
99-00—Buffalo	NHL	35	2066	15	11	6	76	3	2.21	5	301	1	4	10	0	2.39
00-01—Buffalo	NHL	67	3904	37	24	4	137	*11	2.11	13	833	7	6	29	1	2.09
NHL Totals (11 years)		516	29873	247	174	72	1114	56	2.24	74	4517	37	32	157	6	2.09

PERSONAL: Born June 4, 1972, in Sterling Heights, Mich. ... 6-5/230. ... Shoots left. ... Brother of Kevin Hatcher, defenseman with five NHL teams (1984-85 through 2000-01).

TRANSACTIONS/CAREER NOTES: Selected by Minnesota North Stars in first round (first North Stars pick, eighth overall) of NHL entry draft (June 16, 1990). ... Suspended 10 games by NHL (December 1991). ... Fractured ankle in off-ice incident (January 19, 1992); missed 21 games. ... Sprained knee (January 6, 1993); missed 14 games. ... Suspended one game by NHL for game misconduct penalties (March 9, 1993). ... North Stars franchise moved from Minnesota to Dallas and renamed Stars for 1993-94 season. ... Sprained ankle (February 2, 1995); missed one game. ... Suffered staph infection on little finger (February 14, 1995); missed four games. ... Injured right knee ligament (May 1, 1995); missed entire playoffs. ... Injured shoulder (November 14, 1995); missed three games. ... Strained knee (December 8, 1996); missed 14 games. ... Underwent knee surgery (March 19, 1997); missed five games. ... Injured knee (March 8, 1998); missed seven games. ... Suspended four pre-season games and fined $1,000 by NHL for injuring another player (September 23, 1998). ... Suspended seven games by NHL for illegal check (April 17, 1999); missed final two games of regular season and first five playoff games. ... Suffered lacerated calf (December 17, 1999); missed 24 games. ... Strained Achilles' tendon (March 8, 2000); missed one game. ... Suspended two games by NHL for elbowing incident (March 27, 2001).

HONORS: Played in NHL All-Star Game (1997).

MISCELLANEOUS: Member of Stanley Cup championship team (1999). ... Captain of Dallas Stars (1995-96 through 2000-01).

H

Season Team	League	REGULAR SEASON								PLAYOFFS				
		Gms.	G	A	Pts.	PIM	+/-	PP	SH	Gms.	G	A	Pts.	PIM
88-89—Detroit G.P.D.	MNHL	51	19	35	54	100	...	...	...	—				
89-90—North Bay	OHL	64	14	38	52	81	...	...	...	5	2	3	5	8
90-91—North Bay	OHL	64	13	50	63	163	...	...	...	10	2	10	12	28
91-92—Minnesota	NHL	43	8	4	12	88	7	0	0	5	0	2	2	8
92-93—Minnesota	NHL	67	4	15	19	178	-27	0	0	—				
—Kalamazoo	IHL	2	1	2	3	21	...	...	...					
93-94—Dallas	NHL	83	12	19	31	211	19	2	1	9	0	2	2	14
94-95—Dallas	NHL	43	5	11	16	105	3	2	0	—				
95-96—Dallas	NHL	79	8	23	31	129	-12	2	0	—				
96-97—Dallas	NHL	63	3	19	22	97	8	0	0	7	0	2	2	20
97-98—Dallas	NHL	70	6	25	31	132	9	3	0	17	3	3	6	39
—U.S. Olympic team	Int'l	4	0	0	0	0	...	...	...	—				
98-99—Dallas	NHL	80	9	21	30	102	21	3	0	18	1	6	7	24
99-00—Dallas	NHL	57	2	22	24	68	6	0	0	23	1	3	4	29
00-01—Dallas	NHL	80	2	21	23	77	5	1	0	10	0	1	1	16
NHL Totals (10 years)		665	59	180	239	1187	39	13	1	89	5	19	24	150

HATCHER, KEVIN D

PERSONAL: Born September 9, 1966, in Detroit. ... 6-3/220. ... Shoots right. ... Full Name: Kevin John Hatcher. ... Brother of Derian Hatcher, defenseman, Dallas Stars.

TRANSACTIONS/CAREER NOTES: Selected by Washington Capitals as underage junior in first round (first Capitals pick, 17th overall) of NHL entry draft (June 9, 1984). ... Tore left knee cartilage (October 1987). ... Strained groin (January 1989). ... Fractured two metatarsal bones in left foot (February 5, 1989); missed 15 games. ... Sprained left knee (April 27, 1990). ... Did not attend Capitals training camp due to contract dispute (September 1990). ... Injured right knee (November 10, 1990). ... Suspended one game by NHL for game misconduct penalties (February 2, 1993). ... Fractured right hand (December 23, 1993); missed 10 games. ... Suffered from the flu (March 29, 1994); missed one game. ... Pulled thigh (April 9, 1994); missed one game. ... Traded by Capitals to Dallas Stars for D Mark Tinordi and rights to D Rick Mrozik (January 18, 1995). ... Injured shoulder (October 17, 1995); missed three games. ... Suspended four games and fined $1,000 by NHL for slashing (December 5, 1995). ... Traded by Stars to Pittsburgh Penguins for D Sergei Zubov (June 22, 1996). ... Suffered stiff neck (February 5, 1997); missed two games. ... Bruised lower leg (November 8, 1997); missed six games. ... Suffered from the flu (April 16, 1998); missed one game. ... Fractured foot (March 4, 1999); missed 16 games. ... Traded by Penguins to New York Rangers for D Peter Popovic (September 30, 1999). ... Signed as free agent by Carolina Hurricanes (July 31, 2000). ... Bruised hand (October 18, 2000); missed eight games. ... Fractured hand (November 16, 2000); missed eight games. ... Injured knee (January 12, 2001); missed nine games.

HONORS: Named to OHL All-Star second team (1984-85). ... Played in NHL All-Star Game (1990-1992, 1996 and 1997).

STATISTICAL PLATEAUS: Three-goal games: 1992-93 (1), 1995-96 (1). Total: 2.

Season Team	League	REGULAR SEASON								PLAYOFFS				
		Gms.	G	A	Pts.	PIM	+/-	PP	SH	Gms.	G	A	Pts.	PIM
83-84—North Bay	OHL	67	10	39	49	61	...	...	...	4	2	2	4	11
84-85—North Bay	OHL	58	26	37	63	75	...	...	...	8	5	8	13	9
—Washington	NHL	2	0	1	1	0	1	0	1	1	0	0	0	0
85-86—Washington	NHL	79	9	10	19	119	6	1	0	9	1	1	2	19
86-87—Washington	NHL	78	8	16	24	144	-29	1	0	7	1	0	1	20
87-88—Washington	NHL	71	14	27	41	137	1	5	0	14	5	7	12	55
88-89—Washington	NHL	62	13	27	40	101	19	3	0	6	1	4	5	20
89-90—Washington	NHL	80	13	41	54	102	4	4	0	11	0	8	8	32
90-91—Washington	NHL	79	24	50	74	69	-10	9	2	11	3	3	6	8
91-92—Washington	NHL	79	17	37	54	105	18	8	1	7	2	4	6	19
92-93—Washington	NHL	83	34	45	79	114	-7	13	1	6	0	1	1	14
93-94—Washington	NHL	72	16	24	40	108	-13	6	0	11	3	4	7	37
94-95—Dallas	NHL	47	10	19	29	66	-4	3	0	5	2	1	3	2
95-96—Dallas	NHL	74	15	26	41	58	-24	7	0	—				
96-97—Pittsburgh	NHL	80	15	39	54	103	11	9	0	5	1	1	2	4
97-98—Pittsburgh	NHL	74	19	29	48	66	-3	13	1	6	1	0	1	12
—U.S. Olympic team	Int'l	3	0	2	2	0	...	...	...	—				
98-99—Pittsburgh	NHL	66	11	27	38	24	11	4	2	13	2	3	5	4
99-00—New York Rangers	NHL	74	4	19	23	38	-10	2	0	—				
00-01—Carolina	NHL	57	4	14	18	38	2	3	0	6	0	0	0	6
NHL Totals (17 years)		1157	227	450	677	1392	-27	91	8	118	22	37	59	252

HAUER, BRETT D KINGS

PERSONAL: Born July 11, 1971, in Richfield, Minn. ... 6-2/180. ... Shoots right. ... Full Name: Brett Timothy Hauer. ... Cousin of Don Jackson, defenseman with three NHL teams (1977-78 through 1986-87). ... Name pronounced HOW-uhr.

TRANSACTIONS/CAREER NOTES: Selected by Vancouver Canucks in fourth round (third Canucks pick, 71st overall) of NHL entry draft (June 17, 1989). ... Traded by Canucks to Edmonton Oilers for sixth-round pick (D Larry Shapley) in 1997 draft (August 24, 1995). ... Signed as free agent by Los Angeles Kings (July 2, 2001).

HONORS: Named WCHA Student-Athlete of the Year (1992-93). ... Named to NCAA All-America West first team (1992-93). ... Named to WCHA All-Star first team (1992-93). ... Named to IHL All-Star first team (1998-99 through 2000-01). ... Won Larry D. Gordon Trophy (1999-2000 and 2000-01).

H

Season Team	League	REGULAR SEASON								PLAYOFFS				
		Gms.	G	A	Pts.	PIM	+/-	PP	SH	Gms.	G	A	Pts.	PIM
87-88—Richfield H.S..............	Minn. H.S.	24	3	3	6	...	...	...	...	—	—	—	—	—
88-89—Richfield H.S..............	Minn. H.S.	24	8	15	23	70	...	...	...	—	—	—	—	—
89-90—Minnesota-Duluth......	WCHA	37	2	6	8	44	...	...	...	—	—	—	—	—
90-91—Minnesota-Duluth......	WCHA	30	1	7	8	54	...	...	...	—	—	—	—	—
91-92—Minnesota-Duluth......	WCHA	33	8	14	22	40	...	...	...	—	—	—	—	—
92-93—Minnesota-Duluth......	WCHA	40	10	46	56	54	...	...	...	—	—	—	—	—
93-94—U.S. national team	Int'l	57	6	14	20	88	...	...	...	—	—	—	—	—
—U.S. Olympic team......	Int'l	8	0	0	0	10	...	...	...	—	—	—	—	—
—Las Vegas	IHL	21	0	7	7	8	...	...	...	1	0	0	0	0
94-95—AIK............................	Sweden	37	1	3	4	38	...	...	...	—	—	—	—	—
95-96—Cape Breton	AHL	17	3	5	8	29	...	...	...	—	—	—	—	—
—Edmonton	NHL	29	4	2	6	30	-11	2	0	—	—	—	—	—
96-97—Chicago.....................	IHL	81	10	30	40	50	...	...	...	4	2	0	2	4
97-98—Manitoba...................	IHL	82	13	48	61	58	...	...	...	3	0	0	0	2
98-99—Manitoba...................	IHL	81	15	56	71	66	...	...	...	5	0	5	5	4
99-00—Manitoba...................	IHL	77	13	47	60	92	...	...	...	2	0	1	1	2
—Edmonton	NHL	5	0	2	2	2	-2	0	0	—	—	—	—	—
00-01—Manitoba...................	IHL	82	17	42	59	52	...	...	...	13	1	9	10	12
NHL Totals (2 years)...........		34	4	4	8	32	-13	2	0					

HAVELID, NICLAS   D   MIGHTY DUCKS

PERSONAL: Born April 12, 1973, in Enkoping, Sweden. ... 5-11/200. ... Shoots left.

TRANSACTIONS/CAREER NOTES: Selected by Mighty Ducks of Anaheim in third round (second Mighty Ducks pick, 83rd overall) of NHL entry draft (June 26, 1999). ... Fractured finger (January 15, 2000); missed 23 games. ... Tore anterior cruciate ligament in knee (January 15, 2001); missed remainder of season.

Season Team	League	REGULAR SEASON								PLAYOFFS				
		Gms.	G	A	Pts.	PIM	+/-	PP	SH	Gms.	G	A	Pts.	PIM
91-92—AIK Solna...................	Sweden	10	0	0	0	2	...	...	...	—	—	—	—	—
92-93—AIK Solna...................	Sweden	22	1	0	1	16	...	...	...	—	—	—	—	—
93-94—AIK Solna...................	Sweden Dv. 2				Statistics unavailable.									
94-95—AIK Solna...................	Sweden	40	3	7	10	38	...	...	...	—	—	—	—	—
95-96—AIK Solna...................	Sweden	40	5	6	11	30	...	...	...	—	—	—	—	—
96-97—AIK Solna...................	Sweden	49	3	6	9	42	...	...	...	7	1	2	3	8
97-98—AIK Solna...................	Sweden	43	8	4	12	42	...	...	...	—	—	—	—	—
98-99—Malmo	Sweden	50	10	12	22	42	...	...	...	8	0	4	4	10
99-00—Anaheim	NHL	50	2	7	9	20	0	0	0	—	—	—	—	—
—Cincinnati..................	AHL	2	0	0	0	0	...	...	...	—	—	—	—	—
00-01—Anaheim	NHL	47	4	10	14	34	-6	2	0	—	—	—	—	—
NHL Totals (2 years)...........		97	6	17	23	54	-6	2	0					

HAVLAT, MARTIN   C/LW   SENATORS

PERSONAL: Born April 19, 1981, in Brno, Czechoslovakia. ... 6-1/178. ... Shoots left.

TRANSACTIONS/CAREER NOTES: Selected by Ottawa Senators in first round (first Senators pick, 26th pick overall) of NHL entry draft (June 26, 1999). ... Injured shoulder (November 23, 2000); missed eight games. ... Strained groin (April 6, 2001); missed final game of regular season.

HONORS: Named to NHL All-Rookie team (2000-01).

STATISTICAL PLATEAUS: Three-goal games: 2000-01 (1).

Season Team	League	REGULAR SEASON								PLAYOFFS				
		Gms.	G	A	Pts.	PIM	+/-	PP	SH	Gms.	G	A	Pts.	PIM
96-97—Ytong Brno	Czech. Jrs.	34	43	27	70	...	...	...	...	—	—	—	—	—
97-98—Ytong Brno	Czech. Jrs.	32	38	29	67	...	...	...	...	—	—	—	—	—
98-99—Zelezarny Trinec.........	Czech. Jrs.	31	28	23	51	...	...	...	...	—	—	—	—	—
—Zelezarny Trinec.........	Czech Rep.	24	2	3	5	4	...	...	...	8	0	0	0	...
99-00—Zelezarny Trinec.........	Czech Rep.	46	13	29	42	42	...	...	...	4	0	2	2	8
00-01—Ottawa	NHL	73	19	23	42	20	8	7	0	4	0	0	0	2
NHL Totals (1 year)...........		73	19	23	42	20	8	7	0	4	0	0	0	2

HAWGOOD, GREG   D   STARS

PERSONAL: Born August 10, 1968, in St. Albert, Alta. ... 5-10/190. ... Shoots left. ... Full Name: Gregory William Hawgood.

TRANSACTIONS/CAREER NOTES: Selected by Boston Bruins in 10th round (ninth Bruins pick, 202nd overall) of NHL entry draft (June 21, 1986). ... Announced that he would play in Italy for 1990-91 season (July 1990). ... Traded by Bruins to Edmonton Oilers for C Vladimir Ruzicka (October 22, 1990). ... Traded by Oilers with C Josef Beranek to Philadelphia Flyers for D Brian Benning (January 16, 1993). ... Traded by Flyers to Florida Panthers for future considerations (November 28, 1993). ... Bruised left thumb (January 13, 1994); missed seven games. ... Traded by Panthers to Pittsburgh Penguins for LW Jeff Daniels (March 19, 1994). ... Dislocated left shoulder (February 14, 1995); missed eight games. ... Signed as free agent by San Jose Sharks (September 8, 1996). ... Suspended two games and fined $1,000 by NHL for slashing incident (December 31, 1996). ... Signed as free agent by Vancouver Canucks (September 30, 1999). ... Sprained knee (November 15, 1999); missed one game. ... Signed as free agent by Dallas Stars (July 17, 2001).

HONORS: Named to WHL (West) All-Star first team (1985-86 through 1987-88). ... Won Can.HL Defenseman of the Year Award (1987-88). ... Won Bill Hunter Trophy (1987-88). ... Won Eddie Shore Plaque (1991-92). ... Named to AHL All-Star first team (1991-92). ... Named to IHL All-Star first team (1995-96, 1997-98 and 1998-99). ... Won James Norris Memorial Trophy (1995-96). ... Won Governors Trophy (1995-96 and 1998-99).

H

Season Team	League	REGULAR SEASON								PLAYOFFS				
		Gms.	G	A	Pts.	PIM	+/-	PP	SH	Gms.	G	A	Pts.	PIM
83-84—Kamloops	WHL	49	10	23	33	39	...	...	...	—	—	—	—	—
84-85—Kamloops	WHL	66	25	40	65	72	...	...	...	—	—	—	—	—
85-86—Kamloops	WHL	71	34	85	119	86	...	...	...	16	9	22	31	16
86-87—Kamloops	WHL	61	30	93	123	139	...	...	...	—	—	—	—	—
87-88—Boston	NHL	1	0	0	0	0	-1	0	0	3	1	0	1	0
—Kamloops	WHL	63	48	85	133	142	...	...	...	16	10	16	26	33
88-89—Boston	NHL	56	16	24	40	84	4	5	0	10	0	2	2	2
—Maine	AHL	21	2	9	11	41	...	...	...	—	—	—	—	—
89-90—Boston	NHL	77	11	27	38	76	12	2	0	15	1	3	4	12
90-91—Asiago	Italy	2	3	0	3	9	...	...	...	—	—	—	—	—
—Maine	AHL	5	0	1	1	13	...	...	...	—	—	—	—	—
—Cape Breton	AHL	55	10	32	42	73	...	...	...	4	0	3	3	23
—Edmonton	NHL	6	0	1	1	6	-2	0	0	—	—	—	—	—
91-92—Cape Breton	AHL	56	20	55	75	26	...	...	...	3	2	2	4	0
—Edmonton	NHL	20	2	11	13	22	19	0	0	13	0	3	3	23
92-93—Edmonton	NHL	29	5	13	18	35	-1	2	0	—	—	—	—	—
—Philadelphia	NHL	40	6	22	28	39	-7	5	0	—	—	—	—	—
93-94—Philadelphia	NHL	19	3	12	15	19	2	3	0	—	—	—	—	—
—Florida	NHL	33	2	14	16	9	8	0	0	—	—	—	—	—
—Pittsburgh	NHL	12	1	2	3	8	-1	1	0	1	0	0	0	0
94-95—Cleveland	IHL	—	—	—	—	—	...	...	...	3	1	0	1	4
—Pittsburgh	NHL	21	1	4	5	25	2	1	0	—	—	—	—	—
95-96—Las Vegas	IHL	78	20	65	85	101	...	...	...	15	5	11	16	24
96-97—San Jose	NHL	63	6	12	18	69	-22	3	0	—	—	—	—	—
97-98—Houston	IHL	81	19	52	71	75	...	...	...	4	0	4	4	0
98-99—Houston	IHL	76	17	57	74	90	...	...	...	19	4	8	12	24
99-00—Vancouver	NHL	79	5	17	22	26	5	2	0	—	—	—	—	—
00-01—Vancouver	NHL	16	2	5	7	6	8	1	0	—	—	—	—	—
—Kansas City	IHL	46	6	16	22	21	...	...	...	—	—	—	—	—
NHL Totals (11 years)		472	60	164	224	424	26	25	0	42	2	8	10	37

HAY, DWAYNE — LW — FLAMES

PERSONAL: Born February 11, 1977, in London, Ont. ... 6-1/183. ... Shoots left.
TRANSACTIONS/CAREER NOTES: Selected by Washington Capitals in second round (third Capitals pick, 43rd overall) of NHL entry draft (July 8, 1995). ... Traded by Capitals with fourth-round pick (RW Morgan McCormick) in 1999 draft to Florida Panthers for F Esa Tikkanen (March 9, 1998). ... Traded by Panthers with C Ryan Johnson to Tampa Bay Lightning for C/RW Mike Sillinger (March 14, 2000). ... Claimed on waivers by Calgary Flames (October 3, 2000). ... Suffered head injury (January 23, 2001); missed five games.

Season Team	League	REGULAR SEASON								PLAYOFFS				
		Gms.	G	A	Pts.	PIM	+/-	PP	SH	Gms.	G	A	Pts.	PIM
93-94—Listowel Jr. B	OHA	48	10	24	34	56	...	...	...	—	—	—	—	—
94-95—Guelph	OHL	65	26	28	54	37	...	...	...	14	5	7	12	6
95-96—Guelph	OHL	60	28	30	58	49	...	...	...	16	4	9	13	18
96-97—Guelph	OHL	32	17	17	34	21	...	...	...	11	4	6	10	0
97-98—Portland	AHL	58	6	7	13	35	...	...	...	—	—	—	—	—
—Washington	NHL	2	0	0	0	2	0	0	0	—	—	—	—	—
—New Haven	AHL	10	3	2	5	4	...	...	...	2	0	0	0	0
98-99—Florida	NHL	9	0	0	0	0	-1	0	0	—	—	—	—	—
—New Haven	AHL	46	18	17	35	22	...	...	...	—	—	—	—	—
99-00—Louisville	AHL	41	11	20	31	18	...	...	...	—	—	—	—	—
—Florida	NHL	6	0	0	0	2	-2	0	0	—	—	—	—	—
—Tampa Bay	NHL	13	1	1	2	2	0	0	0	—	—	—	—	—
00-01—Calgary	NHL	49	1	3	4	16	-4	0	0	—	—	—	—	—
NHL Totals (4 years)		79	2	4	6	22	-7	0	0	—	—	—	—	—

HEALEY, PAUL — RW — MAPLE LEAFS

PERSONAL: Born March 20, 1975, in Edmonton. ... 6-2/200. ... Shoots right.
TRANSACTIONS/CAREER NOTES: Selected by Philadelphia Flyers in eighth round (seventh Flyers pick, 192nd overall) of NHL entry draft (June 26, 1993). ... Traded by Flyers to Nashville Predators for RW Matt Henderson (September 27, 1999). ... Signed as free agent by Edmonton Oilers (August 31, 2000). ... Signed as free agent by Toronto Maple Leafs (July 24, 2001).
HONORS: Named to WHL (East) All-Star second team (1994-95).

Season Team	League	REGULAR SEASON								PLAYOFFS				
		Gms.	G	A	Pts.	PIM	+/-	PP	SH	Gms.	G	A	Pts.	PIM
92-93—Prince Albert	WHL	72	12	20	32	66	...	...	...	—	—	—	—	—
93-94—Prince Albert	WHL	63	23	26	49	70	...	...	...	—	—	—	—	—
94-95—Prince Albert	WHL	71	43	50	93	67	...	...	...	12	3	4	7	2
95-96—Hershey	AHL	61	7	15	22	35	...	...	...	—	—	—	—	—
96-97—Philadelphia	AHL	64	21	19	40	56	...	...	...	10	4	1	5	10
—Philadelphia	NHL	2	0	0	0	0	0	0	0	—	—	—	—	—
97-98—Philadelphia	AHL	71	34	18	52	48	...	...	...	20	6	2	8	4
—Philadelphia	NHL	4	0	0	0	12	0	0	0	—	—	—	—	—
98-99—Philadelphia	AHL	72	26	20	46	39	...	...	...	15	4	6	10	11
99-00—Milwaukee	IHL	76	21	18	39	28	...	...	...	3	1	2	3	0
00-01—Hamilton	AHL	79	39	32	71	34	...	...	...	—	—	—	—	—
NHL Totals (2 years)		6	0	0	0	12	0	0	0					

H

HEALY, GLENN   G

PERSONAL: Born August 23, 1962, in Pickering, Ont. ... 5-9/190. ... Catches left. ... Full Name: Glenn M. Healy.

TRANSACTIONS/CAREER NOTES: Signed as non-drafted free agent by Los Angeles Kings (June 13, 1985). ... Signed as free agent by New York Islanders (August 16, 1989); Kings received fourth-round pick (traded to Minnesota) in 1990 draft as compensation. ... Strained left ankle ligaments (October 13, 1990); missed eight games. ... Fractured right index finger (November 10, 1991); missed five games. ... Fractured right thumb (January 3, 1992); missed 10 games. ... Severed tip of finger in practice (March 2, 1992) and underwent reconstructive surgery; missed 13 games. ... Suffered from tendinitis in right wrist (January 9, 1993); missed four games. ... Selected by Mighty Ducks of Anaheim in NHL expansion draft (June 24, 1993). ... Selected by Tampa Bay Lightning in Phase II of NHL expansion draft (June 25, 1993). ... Traded by Lightning to New York Rangers for third-round pick (traded back to Tampa Bay) in 1993 draft (June 25, 1993). ... Signed as free agent by Toronto Maple Leafs (July 8, 1997). ... Strained groin (December 4, 1997); missed 10 games. ... Sprained knee (January 10, 1999); missed 11 games. ... Released by Maple Leafs (July 1, 2001).

HONORS: Named to NCAA All-America (West) second team (1984-85). ... Named to CCHA All-Star second team (1984-85).

MISCELLANEOUS: Member of Stanley Cup championship team (1994). ... Stopped a penalty shot attempt (vs. Brad Isbister, October 11, 2000).

			REGULAR SEASON							PLAYOFFS						
Season Team	League	Gms.	Min	W	L	T	GA	SO	Avg.	Gms.	Min.	W	L	GA	SO	Avg.
81-82 —Western Michigan U.	CCHA	27	1569	7	19	1	116	0	4.44	—	—	—	—	—	—	—
82-83 —Western Michigan U.	CCHA	30	1733	8	19	2	116	0	4.02	—	—	—	—	—	—	—
83-84 —Western Michigan U.	CCHA	38	2242	19	16	3	146	0	3.91	—	—	—	—	—	—	—
84-85 —Western Michigan U.	CCHA	37	2172	21	14	2	118	0	3.26	—	—	—	—	—	—	—
85-86 —Toledo	IHL	7	402	...	...	...	28	0	4.18	—	—	—	—	—	—	—
—New Haven..................	AHL	43	2410	21	15	4	160	0	3.98	2	119	0	2	11	0	5.55
—Los Angeles	NHL	1	51	0	0	0	6	0	7.06	—	—	—	—	—	—	—
86-87 —New Haven..................	AHL	47	2828	21	15	0	173	1	3.67	7	427	3	4	19	0	2.67
87-88 —Los Angeles	NHL	34	1869	12	18	1	135	1	4.33	4	240	1	3	20	0	5.00
88-89 —Los Angeles	NHL	48	2699	25	19	2	192	0	4.27	3	97	0	1	6	0	3.71
89-90 —New York Islanders.......	NHL	39	2197	12	19	6	128	2	3.50	4	166	1	2	9	0	3.25
90-91 —New York Islanders.......	NHL	53	2999	18	24	9	166	0	3.32	—	—	—	—	—	—	—
91-92 —New York Islanders.......	NHL	37	1960	14	16	4	124	1	3.80	—	—	—	—	—	—	—
92-93 —New York Islanders.......	NHL	47	2655	22	20	2	146	1	3.30	18	1109	9	8	59	0	3.19
93-94 —New York Rangers	NHL	29	1368	10	12	2	69	2	3.03	2	68	0	0	1	0	.88
94-95 —New York Rangers	NHL	17	888	8	6	1	35	1	2.36	5	230	2	1	13	0	3.39
95-96 —New York Rangers	NHL	44	2564	17	14	11	124	2	2.90	—	—	—	—	—	—	—
96-97 —New York Rangers	NHL	23	1357	5	12	4	59	1	2.61	—	—	—	—	—	—	—
97-98 —Toronto	NHL	21	1068	4	10	2	53	0	2.98	—	—	—	—	—	—	—
98-99 —Chicago	IHL	10	597	6	3	‡1	33	0	3.32	—	—	—	—	—	—	—
—Toronto	NHL	9	546	6	3	0	27	0	2.97	1	20	0	0	0	0	...
99-00 —Toronto	NHL	20	1164	9	10	0	59	2	3.04	—	—	—	—	—	—	—
00-01 —Toronto	NHL	15	871	4	7	3	38	0	2.62	—	—	—	—	—	—	—
NHL Totals (15 years)...........		437	24256	166	190	47	1361	13	3.37	37	1930	13	15	108	0	3.36

HEATLEY, DANY   LW   THRASHERS

PERSONAL: Born January 21, 1981, in Freibourg, Germany. ... 6-1/200. ... Shoots left. ... Full Name: Daniel James Heatley.

TRANSACTIONS/CAREER NOTES: Selected by Atlanta Thrashers in first round (first Thrashers pick, second overall) of NHL entry draft (June 24, 2000).

HONORS: Named to WCHA All-Star first team (1999-2000). ... Named to NCAA All-America (West) second team (1999-2000). ... Named to WCHA All-Star second team (2000-01). ... Named to NCAA All-America (West) first team (2000-01).

			REGULAR SEASON						PLAYOFFS				
Season Team	League	Gms.	G	A	Pts.	PIM	+/-	PP	SH	Gms.	G	A	Pts.	PIM
98-99 —Calgary Royals.............	AJHL	60	*70	56	*126	91	...	...	...	13	*22	13	*35	6
99-00 —Univ. of Wisconsin......	WCHA	38	28	28	56	32	...	...	...	—	—	—	—	—
00-01 —Univ. of Wisconsin......	WCHA	39	24	33	57	74	...	...	...	—	—	—	—	—

HEBERT, GUY   G   RANGERS

PERSONAL: Born January 7, 1967, in Troy, N.Y. ... 5-11/185. ... Catches left. ... Full Name: Guy Andrew Hebert. ... Name pronounced GEE ay-BAIR.

TRANSACTIONS/CAREER NOTES: Selected by St. Louis Blues in eighth round (eighth Blues pick, 159th overall) of NHL entry draft (June 13, 1987). ... Selected by Mighty Ducks of Anaheim in NHL expansion draft (June 24, 1993). ... Suffered concussion (April 30, 1995); missed one game. ... Suffered concussion (December 9, 1996); missed two games. ... Strained right shoulder (March 8, 1998); missed remainder of season. ... Separated shoulder (October 9, 1998); missed first game of season. ... Suffered neck spasms (December 26, 1999); missed two games. ... Injured shoulder (November 22, 2000); missed four games. ... Claimed on waivers by New York Rangers (March 7, 2001). ... Strained groin (March 17, 2001); missed two games.

HONORS: Shared James Norris Memorial Trophy with Pat Jablonski (1990-91). ... Named to IHL All-Star second team (1990-91). ... Played in NHL All-Star Game (1997).

MISCELLANEOUS: Holds Mighty Ducks of Anaheim all-time records for most games played by a goaltender (441), most wins (173), most shutouts (27) and goals-against average (2.77). ... Stopped a penalty shot attempt (vs. Alexandre Daigle, December 30, 1996; vs. Tony Amonte, February 1, 1998; vs. Glen Murray, February 7, 1998). ... Allowed a penalty shot goal (vs. Ray Whitney, March 21, 1999).

			REGULAR SEASON							PLAYOFFS						
Season Team	League	Gms.	Min	W	L	T	GA	SO	Avg.	Gms.	Min.	W	L	GA	SO	Avg.
85-86 —Hamilton College..........	Div. II	18	1011	4	12	2	69	2	4.09	—	—	—	—	—	—	—
86-87 —Hamilton College..........	Div. II	18	1070	12	5	0	40	0	2.24	—	—	—	—	—	—	—
87-88 —Hamilton College..........	Div. II	8	450	5	3	0	19	0	2.53	—	—	—	—	—	—	—
88-89 —Hamilton College..........	Div. II	25	1453	18	7	0	62	0	2.56	—	—	—	—	—	—	—
89-90 —Peoria...........................	IHL	30	1706	7	13	‡7	124	1	4.36	2	76	0	1	5	0	3.95
90-91 —Peoria...........................	IHL	36	2093	24	10	‡1	100	2	*2.87	8	458	3	4	32	0	4.19

H

Season Team	League	REGULAR SEASON								PLAYOFFS						
		Gms.	Min	W	L	T	GA	SO	Avg.	Gms.	Min.	W	L	GA	SO	Avg.
91-92—Peoria	IHL	29	1731	20	9	‡0	98	0	3.40	4	239	3	1	9	0	*2.26
—St. Louis	NHL	13	738	5	5	1	36	0	2.93	—	—	—	—	—	—	—
92-93—St. Louis	NHL	24	1210	8	8	2	74	1	3.67	1	2	0	0	0	0	...
93-94—Anaheim	NHL	52	2991	20	27	3	141	2	2.83	—	—	—	—	—	—	—
94-95—Anaheim	NHL	39	2092	12	20	4	109	2	3.13	—	—	—	—	—	—	—
95-96—Anaheim	NHL	59	3326	28	23	5	157	4	2.83	—	—	—	—	—	—	—
96-97—Anaheim	NHL	67	3863	29	25	12	172	4	2.67	9	534	4	4	18	1	2.02
97-98—Anaheim	NHL	46	2660	13	24	6	130	3	2.93	—	—	—	—	—	—	—
98-99—Anaheim	NHL	69	4083	31	29	9	165	6	2.42	4	208	0	3	15	0	4.33
99-00—Anaheim	NHL	68	3976	28	†31	9	166	4	2.51	—	—	—	—	—	—	—
00-01—Anaheim	NHL	41	2215	12	23	4	115	2	3.12	—	—	—	—	—	—	—
—New York Rangers	NHL	13	735	5	7	1	42	0	3.43	—	—	—	—	—	—	—
NHL Totals (10 years)		491	27889	191	222	56	1307	28	2.81	14	744	4	7	33	1	2.66

HECHT, JOCHEN   C   OILERS

PERSONAL: Born June 21, 1977, in Mannheim, West Germany. ... 6-3/196. ... Shoots left. ... Full Name: Jochen Thomas Hecht.

TRANSACTIONS/CAREER NOTES: Selected by St. Louis Blues in second round (first Blues pick, 49th overall) of NHL entry draft (July 8, 1995). ... Sprained ankle (January 13, 2000); missed 13 games. ... Reinjured ankle (February 23, 2000); missed six games. ... Strained oblique muscle (January 27, 2001); missed one game. ... Strained oblique muscle (February 1, 2001); missed two games. ... Strained oblique muscle (March 24, 2001); missed seven games. ... Traded by Blues with C Marty Reasoner and D Jan Horacek to Edmonton Oilers for center C Doug Weight and LW Michel Riesen (July 1, 2001).

Season Team	League	REGULAR SEASON								PLAYOFFS				
		Gms.	G	A	Pts.	PIM	+/-	PP	SH	Gms.	G	A	Pts.	PIM
94-95—Mannheim	Germany	43	11	12	23	68	...	...	...	10	5	4	9	12
95-96—Mannheim	Germany	44	12	16	28	68	...	...	...	8	3	2	5	6
96-97—Mannheim	Germany	46	21	21	42	36	...	...	...	—	—	—	—	—
97-98—Mannheim	Germany	44	7	19	26	42	...	...	...	10	1	1	2	14
—German Oly. team	Int'l	4	1	0	1	6	...	...	...	—	—	—	—	—
98-99—Worcester	AHL	74	21	35	56	48	...	...	...	4	1	1	2	2
—St. Louis	NHL	3	0	0	0	0	-2	0	0	5	2	0	2	0
99-00—St. Louis	NHL	63	13	21	34	28	20	5	0	7	4	6	10	2
00-01—St. Louis	NHL	72	19	25	44	48	11	8	3	15	2	4	6	4
NHL Totals (3 years)		138	32	46	78	76	29	13	3	27	8	10	18	6

HEDBERG, JOHAN   G   PENGUINS

PERSONAL: Born May 5, 1973, in Leksand, Sweden. ... 5-11/185. ... Catches left.

TRANSACTIONS/CAREER NOTES: Selected by Philadelphia Flyers in ninth round (eighth Flyers pick, 218th overall) of NHL entry draft (June 29, 1994). ... Traded by Flyers to San Jose Sharks for seventh-round pick (C Pavel Kasparik) in 1999 draft (July 6, 1998). ... Traded by Sharks with D Bobby Dollas to Pittsburgh Penguins for D Jeff Norton (March 12, 2001).

Season Team	League	REGULAR SEASON								PLAYOFFS						
		Gms.	Min	W	L	T	GA	SO	Avg.	Gms.	Min.	W	L	GA	SO	Avg.
92-93—Leksand	Sweden	10	600	...	...	...	24	...	2.40	—	—	—	—	—	—	—
93-94—Leksand	Sweden	17	1020	...	...	...	48	0	2.82	—	—	—	—	—	—	—
94-95—Leksand	Sweden	17	986	...	...	...	58	1	3.53	—	—	—	—	—	—	—
95-96—Leksand	Sweden	34	2013	...	...	...	95	0	2.83	4	240	...	...	13	...	3.25
96-97—Leksand	Sweden	38	2260	...	...	...	95	3	2.52	4	581	...	...	18	1	1.86
97-98—Baton Rouge	ECHL	2	100	1	1	0	7	0	4.20	—	—	—	—	—	—	—
—Detroit	IHL	16	726	7	2	‡2	32	1	2.64	—	—	—	—	—	—	—
—Manitoba	IHL	14	745	8	4	‡1	32	1	2.58	2	106	0	2	6	0	3.40
98-99—Leksand	Sweden	48	2940	...	...	...	140	0	2.86	4	255	...	...	15	0	3.53
99-00—Kentucky	AHL	33	1973	18	9	5	88	3	2.68	5	311	3	2	10	1	1.93
00-01—Manitoba	IHL	46	2697	23	13	‡7	115	1	2.56	—	—	—	—	—	—	—
—Pittsburgh	NHL	9	545	7	1	1	24	0	2.64	18	1123	9	9	43	2	2.30
NHL Totals (1 year)		9	545	7	1	1	24	0	2.64	18	1123	9	9	43	2	2.30

HEDICAN, BRET   D   PANTHERS

PERSONAL: Born August 10, 1970, in St. Paul, Minn. ... 6-2/205. ... Shoots left. ... Full Name: Bret Michael Hedican. ... Name pronounced HEHD-ih-kihn.

TRANSACTIONS/CAREER NOTES: Selected by St. Louis Blues in 10th round (10th Blues pick, 198th overall) of NHL entry draft (June 11, 1988). ... Strained knee ligaments (September 27, 1992); missed first 15 games of season. ... Injured shoulder (October 24, 1993); missed three games. ... Injured groin (January 18, 1994); missed six games. ... Traded by Blues with D Jeff Brown and C Craig Janney to Vancouver Canucks for C Craig Janney (March 21, 1994). ... Strained groin (March 27, 1994); missed three games. ... Injured back (February 1, 1996); missed three games. ... Strained back (October 5, 1996); missed six games. ... Strained groin (December 4, 1996); missed five games. ... Strained groin (December 26, 1996); missed four games. ... Missed one game for personal reasons (December 13, 1997). ... Strained back (January 21, 1998); missed one game. ... Strained abdominal muscle (February 17, 1998); missed six games. ... Sprained ankle (September 23, 1998); missed first game of season. ... Traded by Canucks with RW Pavel Bure, D Brad Ference and third-round pick (RW Robert Fried) in 2000 draft to Florida Panthers for D Ed Jovanovski, G Kevin Weekes, C Dave Gagner, C Mike Brown and first-round pick (C Nathan Smith) in 2000 draft (January 17, 1999). ... Injured eye (February 11, 1999); missed eight games. ... Strained groin (March 31, 1999); missed eight games. ... Suspended three games by NHL for slashing incident (November 3, 1999). ... Strained groin (October 22, 1999); missed two games. ... Strained groin (February 26, 2000); missed one game. ... Suffered concussion (December 4, 2000); missed three games. ... Sprained left ankle (December 29, 2000); missed nine games.

HONORS: Named to WCHA All-Star first team (1990-91).

H

Season Team	League	Gms.	G	A	Pts.	PIM	+/-	PP	SH	Gms.	G	A	Pts.	PIM
				REGULAR SEASON								PLAYOFFS		
88-89—St. Cloud State	WCHA	28	5	3	8	28	...	...	...	—	—	—	—	—
89-90—St. Cloud State	WCHA	36	4	17	21	37	...	...	...	—	—	—	—	—
90-91—St. Cloud State	WCHA	41	18	30	48	52	...	...	...	—	—	—	—	—
91-92—U.S. national team	Int'l	54	1	8	9	59	...	...	...	—	—	—	—	—
—U.S. Olympic team	Int'l	8	0	0	0	4	...	...	...	—	—	—	—	—
—St. Louis	NHL	4	1	0	1	0	1	0	0	5	0	0	0	0
92-93—Peoria	IHL	19	0	8	8	10	...	...	...	—	—	—	—	—
—St. Louis	NHL	42	0	8	8	30	-2	0	0	10	0	0	0	14
93-94—St. Louis	NHL	61	0	11	11	64	-8	0	0	—	—	—	—	—
—Vancouver	NHL	8	0	1	1	0	1	0	0	24	1	6	7	16
94-95—Vancouver	NHL	45	2	11	13	34	-3	0	0	11	0	2	2	6
95-96—Vancouver	NHL	77	6	23	29	83	8	1	0	6	0	1	1	10
96-97—Vancouver	NHL	67	4	15	19	51	-3	2	0	—	—	—	—	—
97-98—Vancouver	NHL	71	3	24	27	79	3	1	0	—	—	—	—	—
98-99—Vancouver	NHL	42	2	11	13	34	7	0	2	—	—	—	—	—
—Florida	NHL	25	3	7	10	17	-2	0	0	—	—	—	—	—
99-00—Florida	NHL	76	6	19	25	68	4	2	0	4	0	0	0	0
00-01—Florida	NHL	70	5	15	20	72	-7	4	0	—	—	—	—	—
NHL Totals (10 years)		588	32	145	177	532	-1	10	2	60	1	9	10	46

HEEREMA, JEFF RW HURRICANES

PERSONAL: Born January 17, 1980, in Thunder Bay, Ont. ... 6-1/184. ... Shoots right.
TRANSACTIONS/CAREER NOTES: Selected by Carolina Hurricanes in first round (first Hurricanes pick, 11th overall) of NHL entry draft (June 27, 1998).
HONORS: Named to OHL All-Rookie Second Team (1997-98).

Season Team	League	Gms.	G	A	Pts.	PIM	+/-	PP	SH	Gms.	G	A	Pts.	PIM
				REGULAR SEASON								PLAYOFFS		
97-98—Sarnia	OHL	63	32	40	72	88	...	...	...	5	4	1	5	10
98-99—Sarnia	OHL	62	31	39	70	113	...	...	...	6	5	1	6	0
99-00—Sarnia	OHL	67	36	41	77	62	...	...	...	7	4	2	6	10
00-01—Cincinnati	IHL	73	17	16	33	42	...	...	...	4	0	0	0	0

HEINS, SHAWN D

PERSONAL: Born December 24, 1973, in Eganville, Ont. ... 6-4/210. ... Shoots left.
TRANSACTIONS/CAREER NOTES: Signed as non-drafted free agent by San Jose Sharks (January 5, 1998). ... Injured finger (February 29, 2000); missed five games.
HONORS: Named to AHL All-Star first team (1999-2000).

Season Team	League	Gms.	G	A	Pts.	PIM	+/-	PP	SH	Gms.	G	A	Pts.	PIM
				REGULAR SEASON								PLAYOFFS		
91-92—Peterborough	OHL	49	1	1	2	73	...	...	...	—	—	—	—	—
92-93—Peterborough	OHL	5	0	0	0	10	...	...	...	—	—	—	—	—
—Windsor	OHL	53	7	10	17	107	...	...	...	—	—	—	—	—
93-94—Renfrew	EOGHL	32	16	34	50	250	...	...	...	—	—	—	—	—
94-95—Renfrew	EOGHL	49	40	90	130	175	...	...	...	—	—	—	—	—
95-96—Cape Breton	AHL	1	0	0	0	0	...	...	...	—	—	—	—	—
—Mobile	ECHL	62	7	20	27	152	...	...	...	—	—	—	—	—
96-97—Mobile	ECHL	56	6	17	23	253	...	...	...	3	0	2	2	2
—Kansas City	IHL	6	0	0	0	9	...	...	...	—	—	—	—	—
97-98—Kansas City	IHL	82	22	28	50	303	...	...	...	11	1	0	1	49
98-99—Canadian nat'l team	Int'l	36	5	16	21	66	...	...	...	—	—	—	—	—
—San Jose	NHL	5	0	0	0	0	0	0	0	—	—	—	—	—
—Kentucky	AHL	18	2	2	4	108	...	...	...	12	2	7	9	10
99-00—Kentucky	AHL	69	11	52	63	238	...	...	...	9	3	3	6	44
—San Jose	NHL	1	0	0	0	2	-1	0	0	—	—	—	—	—
00-01—San Jose	NHL	38	3	4	7	57	2	2	0	2	0	0	0	0
NHL Totals (3 years)		44	3	4	7	72	1	2	0	2	0	0	0	0

HEINZE, STEVE RW KINGS

PERSONAL: Born January 30, 1970, in Lawrence, Mass. ... 5-11/193. ... Shoots right. ... Full Name: Stephen Herbert Heinze. ... Name pronounced HIGHNS.
TRANSACTIONS/CAREER NOTES: Selected by Boston Bruins in second round (second Bruins pick, 60th overall) of NHL entry draft (June 11, 1988). ... Injured shoulder (May 1, 1992). ... Injured shoulder (March 20, 1993); missed 11 games. ... Injured knee (February 18, 1994); missed five games. ... Reinjured knee (March 26, 1994); missed two games. ... Strained abdominal muscle (December 5, 1996); missed one game. ... Strained hip and groin and tore knee ligament (December 17, 1996); missed remainder of season. ... Sprained ankle (October 7, 1997); missed seven games. ... Fractured foot (October 23, 1997); missed 14 games. ... Injured finger (October 24, 1998); missed one game. ... Strained hip flexor (February 9, 1999); missed five games. ... Suffered from the flu (March 1, 1999); missed three games. ... Suffered from the flu (February 3, 2000); missed one game. ... Strained muscle in ribs (March 10, 2000); missed six games. ... Selected by Columbus Blue Jackets in NHL expansion draft (June 23, 2000). ... Suffered concussion (November 24, 2000); missed three games. ... Traded by Blue Jackets to Buffalo Sabres for third-round pick (C/RW Per Mars) in 2001 draft (March 13, 2001). ... Signed as free agent by Los Angeles Kings (July 3, 2001).
HONORS: Named to Hockey East All-Rookie team (1988-89). ... Named to NCAA All-America (East) first team (1989-90). ... Named to Hockey East All-Star first team (1989-90).
MISCELLANEOUS: Failed to score on a penalty shot (vs. Corey Schwab, December 17, 1997).
STATISTICAL PLATEAUS: Three-goal games: 1992-93 (1), 1995-96 (1), 1997-98 (2), 2000-01 (1). Total: 5.

H

Season Team	League	REGULAR SEASON								PLAYOFFS				
		Gms.	G	A	Pts.	PIM	+/-	PP	SH	Gms.	G	A	Pts.	PIM
86-87—Lawrence Academy.....	Mass. H.S.	23	26	24	50	...	...	...	...	—	—	—	—	—
87-88—Lawrence Academy.....	Mass. H.S.	23	30	25	55	...	...	...	...	—	—	—	—	—
88-89—Boston College	Hockey East	36	26	23	49	26	...	...	...	—	—	—	—	—
89-90—Boston College	Hockey East	40	27	36	63	41	...	...	...	—	—	—	—	—
90-91—Boston College	Hockey East	35	21	26	47	35	...	...	...	—	—	—	—	—
91-92—U.S. national team	Int'l	49	18	15	33	38	...	...	...	—	—	—	—	—
—U.S. Olympic team......	Int'l	8	1	3	4	8	...	...	...	—	—	—	—	—
—Boston	NHL	14	3	4	7	6	-1	0	0	7	0	3	3	17
92-93—Boston	NHL	73	18	13	31	24	20	0	2	4	1	1	2	2
93-94—Boston	NHL	77	10	11	21	32	-2	0	2	13	2	3	5	7
94-95—Boston	NHL	36	7	9	16	23	0	0	1	5	0	0	0	0
95-96—Boston	NHL	76	16	12	28	43	-3	0	1	5	1	1	2	4
96-97—Boston	NHL	30	17	8	25	27	-8	4	2	—	—	—	—	—
97-98—Boston	NHL	61	26	20	46	54	8	9	0	6	0	0	0	6
98-99—Boston	NHL	73	22	18	40	30	7	9	0	12	4	3	7	0
99-00—Boston	NHL	75	12	13	25	36	-8	2	0	—	—	—	—	—
00-01—Columbus	NHL	65	22	20	42	38	-19	14	0	—	—	—	—	—
—Buffalo	NHL	14	5	7	12	8	6	1	0	13	3	4	7	10
NHL Totals (10 years).........		594	158	135	293	321	0	39	8	65	11	15	26	46

HEISTEN, BARRETT — LW — RANGERS

PERSONAL: Born March 19, 1980, in Anchorage, Alaska. ... 6-1/189. ... Shoots left.
TRANSACTIONS/CAREER NOTES: Selected by Buffalo Sabres in first round (first Sabres pick, 20th overall) of NHL entry draft (June 26, 1999). ... Signed as free agent by New York Rangers (June 12, 2001).

Season Team	League	REGULAR SEASON								PLAYOFFS				
		Gms.	G	A	Pts.	PIM	+/-	PP	SH	Gms.	G	A	Pts.	PIM
97-98—U.S. National..............	NAHL	50	11	26	37	245	...	...	...	—	—	—	—	—
98-99—Univ. of Maine	Hockey East	34	12	16	28	72	...	...	...	—	—	—	—	—
99-00—Univ. of Maine	Hockey East	37	13	24	37	86	...	...	...	—	—	—	—	—
00-01—Seattle.......................	WHL	58	20	57	77	61	...	...	...	9	2	6	8	20

HEJDUK, MILAN — RW — AVALANCHE

PERSONAL: Born February 14, 1976, in Sstnad-Laberm, Czechoslovakia. ... 5-11/185. ... Shoots right.
TRANSACTIONS/CAREER NOTES: Selected by Quebec Nordiques in fourth round (sixth Nordiques pick, 72nd overall) of NHL entry draft (June 29, 1994). ... Nordiques franchise moved to Colorado and renamed Avalanche for 1995-96 season (June 21, 1995). ... Strained back (January 7, 2000); missed one game. ... Suffered from the flu (March 31, 2001).
HONORS: Named Czech Republic League Rookie of the Year (1993-94). ... Named to NHL All-Rookie team (1998-99). ... Played in NHL All-Star Game (2000 and 2001).
MISCELLANEOUS: Member of Stanley Cup championship team (2001). ... Member of gold-medal-winning Czech Republic Olympic Team (1998).

Season Team	League	REGULAR SEASON								PLAYOFFS				
		Gms.	G	A	Pts.	PIM	+/-	PP	SH	Gms.	G	A	Pts.	PIM
93-94—HC Pardubice..............	Czech Rep.	22	6	3	9	...	...	...	...	10	5	1	6	...
94-95—HC Pardubice..............	Czech Rep.						Did not play.							
95-96—HC Pardubice..............	Czech Rep.	37	13	7	20	...	...	...	...	—	—	—	—	—
96-97—HC Pardubice..............	Czech Rep.	51	27	11	38	10	...	...	...	10	6	0	6	27
97-98—Pojistovna Pardubice..	Czech Rep.	48	26	19	45	20	...	...	...	3	0	0	0	2
—Czech Rep. Oly. team..	Int'l	4	0	0	0	2	...	...	...	—	—	—	—	—
98-99—Colorado	NHL	82	14	34	48	26	8	4	0	16	6	6	12	4
99-00—Colorado	NHL	82	36	36	72	16	14	13	0	17	5	4	9	6
00-01—Colorado	NHL	80	41	38	79	36	32	12	1	23	7	*16	23	6
NHL Totals (3 years)............		244	91	108	199	78	54	29	1	56	18	26	44	16

HELENIUS, SAMI — D — STARS

PERSONAL: Born January 22, 1974, in Helsinki, Finland. ... 6-5/225. ... Shoots left. ... Name pronounced huh-LEH-nuhz.
TRANSACTIONS/CAREER NOTES: Selected by Calgary Flames in fifth round (fifth Flames pick, 102nd overall) of NHL entry draft (June 20, 1992). ... Traded by Flames to Tampa Bay Lightning for future considerations (January 29, 1999). ... Traded by Lightning to Colorado Avalanche for future considerations (March 23, 1999). ... Signed as free agent by Dallas Stars (July 12, 2000).

Season Team	League	REGULAR SEASON								PLAYOFFS				
		Gms.	G	A	Pts.	PIM	+/-	PP	SH	Gms.	G	A	Pts.	PIM
91-92—Jokerit Helsinki	Finland Jr.						Statistics unavailable.							
92-93—Vantaa HT	Finland Div. 2	21	3	2	5	60	...	...	...	—	—	—	—	—
—Jokerit Helsinki	Finland Jr.	1	0	0	0	0	...	...	...	—	—	—	—	—
93-94—Reipas Lahti...............	Finland	37	2	3	5	46	...	...	...	—	—	—	—	—
94-95—Saint John	AHL	69	2	5	7	217	...	...	...	—	—	—	—	—
95-96—Saint John	AHL	68	0	3	3	231	...	...	...	10	0	0	0	9
96-97—Saint John	AHL	72	5	10	15	218	...	...	...	2	0	0	0	0
—Calgary	NHL	3	0	1	1	0	1	0	0	—	—	—	—	—
97-98—Saint John	AHL	63	1	2	3	185	...	...	...	—	—	—	—	—
—Las Vegas	IHL	10	0	1	1	19	...	...	...	4	0	0	0	25

H

Season Team	League	REGULAR SEASON Gms.	G	A	Pts.	PIM	+/-	PP	SH	PLAYOFFS Gms.	G	A	Pts.	PIM
98-99—Calgary	NHL	4	0	0	0	8	-2	0	0	—	—	—	—	—
—Chicago	IHL	4	0	0	0	11	...	...	...	—	—	—	—	—
—Tampa Bay	NHL	4	1	0	1	15	-3	0	1	—	—	—	—	—
—Las Vegas	IHL	42	2	3	5	193	...	...	...	—	—	—	—	—
—Hershey	AHL	8	0	0	0	29	...	...	...	5	0	0	0	16
99-00—Colorado	NHL	33	0	0	0	46	-5	0	0	—	—	—	—	—
—Hershey	AHL	12	0	1	1	31	...	...	...	9	0	0	0	40
00-01—Dallas	NHL	57	1	2	3	99	1	0	0	1	0	0	0	0
NHL Totals (4 years)		101	2	3	5	168	-8	0	1	1	0	0	0	0

HELMER, BRYAN — D — CANUCKS

PERSONAL: Born July 15, 1972, in Sault Ste. Marie, Ont. ... 6-1/190. ... Shoots right.
TRANSACTIONS/CAREER NOTES: Signed as non-drafted free agent by New Jersey Devils (October 1, 1993). ... Signed as free agent by Phoenix Coyotes (July 22, 1998). ... Claimed on waivers by St. Louis Blues (December 19, 1998). ... Signed as free agent by Vancouver Canucks (August 21, 2000).
HONORS: Named to AHL All-Star first team (1997-98).

Season Team	League	REGULAR SEASON Gms.	G	A	Pts.	PIM	+/-	PP	SH	PLAYOFFS Gms.	G	A	Pts.	PIM
89-90—Wellington	OJHL	51	6	22	28	204	...	...	...	—	—	—	—	—
—Belleville	OHL	6	0	1	1	0	...	...	...	—	—	—	—	—
90-91—Wellington	OJHL	50	11	14	25	109	...	...	...	—	—	—	—	—
91-92—Wellington	OJHL	45	19	32	51	66	...	...	...	—	—	—	—	—
92-93—Wellington	OJHL	57	25	62	87	62	...	...	...	—	—	—	—	—
93-94—Albany	AHL	65	4	19	23	79	...	...	...	5	0	0	0	9
94-95—Albany	AHL	77	7	36	43	101	...	...	...	7	1	0	1	0
95-96—Albany	AHL	80	14	30	44	107	...	...	...	4	2	0	2	6
96-97—Albany	AHL	77	12	27	39	113	...	...	...	16	1	7	8	10
97-98—Albany	AHL	80	14	49	63	101	...	...	...	13	4	9	13	18
98-99—Phoenix	NHL	11	0	0	0	23	2	0	0	—	—	—	—	—
—Las Vegas	IHL	8	1	3	4	28	...	...	...	—	—	—	—	—
—St. Louis	NHL	29	0	4	4	19	3	0	0	—	—	—	—	—
—Worcester	AHL	16	7	8	15	18	...	...	...	4	0	0	0	12
99-00—Worcester	AHL	54	10	25	35	124	...	...	...	9	1	4	5	10
—St. Louis	NHL	15	1	1	2	10	-3	1	0	—	—	—	—	—
00-01—Kansas City	IHL	42	4	15	19	76	...	...	...	—	—	—	—	—
—Vancouver	NHL	20	2	4	6	18	0	0	0	—	—	—	—	—
NHL Totals (3 years)		75	3	9	12	70	2	1	0					

HENDERSON, JAY — LW — BRUINS

PERSONAL: Born September 17, 1978, in Edmonton. ... 5-11/188. ... Shoots left. ... Full Name: Jay Elliot Henderson.
TRANSACTIONS/CAREER NOTES: Selected by Boston Bruins in 12th round (12th Bruins pick, 246th overall) of NHL entry draft (June 21, 1997). ... Injured knee (April 4, 2000); missed final three games of season. ... Suffered concussion (September 21, 2000); missed first five games of season.

Season Team	League	REGULAR SEASON Gms.	G	A	Pts.	PIM	+/-	PP	SH	PLAYOFFS Gms.	G	A	Pts.	PIM
94-95—Red Deer	WHL	54	3	9	12	80	...	...	...	—	—	—	—	—
95-96—Red Deer	WHL	71	15	13	28	139	...	...	...	10	1	1	2	11
96-97—Edmonton	WHL	66	28	32	60	127	...	...	...	—	—	—	—	—
97-98—Edmonton	WHL	72	49	45	94	132	...	...	...	—	—	—	—	—
—Providence	AHL	11	3	1	4	11	...	...	...	—	—	—	—	—
98-99—Providence	AHL	55	7	9	16	172	...	...	...	2	0	0	0	2
—Boston	NHL	4	0	0	0	2	-1	0	0	—	—	—	—	—
99-00—Providence	AHL	60	18	27	45	200	...	...	...	14	1	2	3	16
—Boston	NHL	16	1	3	4	9	1	0	0	—	—	—	—	—
00-01—Boston	NHL	13	0	0	0	26	-1	0	0	—	—	—	—	—
—Providence	AHL	41	9	7	16	121	...	...	...	1	0	0	0	2
NHL Totals (3 years)		33	1	3	4	37	-1	0	0					

HENDRICKSON, DARBY — LW — WILD

PERSONAL: Born August 28, 1972, in Richfield, Minn. ... 6-1/195. ... Shoots left.
TRANSACTIONS/CAREER NOTES: Selected by Toronto Maple Leafs in fourth round (third Maple Leafs pick, 73rd overall) of NHL entry draft (June 16, 1990). ... Suspended three games by NHL for kneeing incident (October 26, 1995). ... Suffered from the flu (December 30, 1995); missed one game. ... Traded by Maple Leafs with LW Sean Haggerty, D Kenny Jonsson and first-round pick (G Roberto Luongo) in 1997 draft to New York Islanders for LW Wendel Clark, D Mathieu Schneider and D D.J. Smith (March 13, 1996). ... Traded by Islanders to Maple Leafs for fifth-round pick (C Jiri Dopita) in 1998 draft (October 11, 1996). ... Strained back (January 27, 1997); missed five games. ... Suffered back spasms (November 4, 1997); missed two games. ... Suffered back spasms (November 3, 1998); missed six games. ... Traded by Maple Leafs to Vancouver Canucks for D/LW Chris McAllister (February 16, 1999). ... Injured ankle (September 11, 1999); missed four games. ... Selected by Minnesota Wild in NHL expansion draft (June 23, 2000). ... Suffered concussion (November 22, 2000); missed six games. ... Suffered head injury (February 14, 2001); missed three games.
HONORS: Won WCHA Rookie of the Year Award (1991-92). ... Named to WCHA All-Rookie team (1991-92).
MISCELLANEOUS: Captain of Minnesota Wild (March 1-April 8, 2001). ... Shares Minnesota Wild all-time record for most goals (18).

H

Season Team	League	REGULAR SEASON								PLAYOFFS				
		Gms.	G	A	Pts.	PIM	+/-	PP	SH	Gms.	G	A	Pts.	PIM
87-88—Richfield H.S.	Minn. H.S.	22	12	9	21	10	...	...	...	—	—	—	—	—
88-89—Richfield H.S.	Minn. H.S.	22	22	20	42	12	...	...	...	—	—	—	—	—
89-90—Richfield H.S.	Minn. H.S.	24	23	27	50	49	...	...	...	—	—	—	—	—
90-91—Richfield H.S.	Minn. H.S.	27	32	29	61	...	...	...	...	—	—	—	—	—
91-92—Univ. of Minnesota	WCHA	41	25	28	53	61	...	...	...	—	—	—	—	—
92-93—Univ. of Minnesota	WCHA	31	12	15	27	35	...	...	...	—	—	—	—	—
93-94—U.S. national team	Int'l	59	12	16	28	30	...	...	...	—	—	—	—	—
—U.S. Olympic team	Int'l	8	0	0	0	6	...	...	...	—	—	—	—	—
—St. John's	AHL	6	4	1	5	4	...	...	...	3	1	1	2	0
—Toronto	NHL	—	—	—	—	—	—	—	—	2	0	0	0	0
94-95—St. John's	AHL	59	16	20	36	48	...	...	...	—	—	—	—	—
—Toronto	NHL	8	0	1	1	4	0	0	0	—	—	—	—	—
95-96—Toronto	NHL	46	6	6	12	47	-2	0	0	—	—	—	—	—
—New York Islanders	NHL	16	1	4	5	33	-6	0	0	—	—	—	—	—
96-97—St. John's	AHL	12	5	4	9	21	...	...	...	—	—	—	—	—
—Toronto	NHL	64	11	6	17	47	-20	0	1	—	—	—	—	—
—U.S. national team	Int'l	8	0	1	1	8	...	...	...	—	—	—	—	—
97-98—Toronto	NHL	80	8	4	12	67	-20	0	0	—	—	—	—	—
98-99—Toronto	NHL	35	2	3	5	30	-4	0	0	—	—	—	—	—
—Vancouver	NHL	27	2	2	4	22	-15	1	0	—	—	—	—	—
99-00—Vancouver	NHL	40	5	4	9	14	-3	0	1	—	—	—	—	—
—Syracuse	AHL	20	5	8	13	16	...	...	...	—	—	—	—	—
00-01—Minnesota	NHL	72	18	11	29	36	1	3	1	—	—	—	—	—
NHL Totals (8 years)		388	53	41	94	300	-69	4	3	2	0	0	0	0

HENRICH, MICHAEL — RW — OILERS

PERSONAL: Born March 3, 1980, in Thornhill, Ont. ... 6-2/206. ... Shoots right.
TRANSACTIONS/CAREER NOTES: Selected by Edmonton Oilers in first round (first Oilers pick, 13th overall) of NHL entry draft (June 27, 1998).

Season Team	League	REGULAR SEASON								PLAYOFFS				
		Gms.	G	A	Pts.	PIM	+/-	PP	SH	Gms.	G	A	Pts.	PIM
96-97—Barrie	OHL	52	9	15	24	19	...	...	...	9	0	5	5	0
97-98—Barrie	OHL	66	41	22	63	75	...	...	...	5	1	3	4	4
98-99—Barrie	OHL	62	38	33	71	42	...	...	...	12	0	2	2	4
99-00—Barrie	OHL	66	38	48	86	69	...	...	...	25	10	18	28	30
00-01—Hamilton	AHL	73	5	10	15	36	...	...	...	—	—	—	—	—
—Tallahassee	ECHL	6	1	1	2	0	...	...	...	—	—	—	—	—

HENRY, ALEX — D — OILERS

PERSONAL: Born October 18, 1979, in Elliot Lake, Ont. ... 6-5/220. ... Shoots left.
TRANSACTIONS/CAREER NOTES: Selected by Edmonton Oilers in third round (second Oilers pick, 67th overall) of NHL entry draft (June 27, 1998).

Season Team	League	REGULAR SEASON								PLAYOFFS				
		Gms.	G	A	Pts.	PIM	+/-	PP	SH	Gms.	G	A	Pts.	PIM
96-97—London	OHL	61	1	10	11	65	...	...	...	—	—	—	—	—
97-98—London	OHL	62	5	9	14	97	...	...	...	16	0	3	3	14
98-99—London	OHL	68	5	23	28	105	...	...	...	25	3	10	13	22
99-00—Hamilton	AHL	60	1	0	1	69	...	...	...	—	—	—	—	—
00-01—Hamilton	AHL	56	2	3	5	87	...	...	...	—	—	—	—	—

HENRY, FREDERIC — G — DEVILS

PERSONAL: Born August 9, 1977, in Cap Rouge, Que. ... 5-11/180. ... Catches left.
TRANSACTIONS/CAREER NOTES: Selected by New Jersey Devils in eighth round (10th Devils pick, 200th overall) of NHL entry draft (July 8, 1995).

Season Team	League	REGULAR SEASON								PLAYOFFS						
		Gms.	Min	W	L	T	GA	SO	Avg.	Gms.	Min.	W	L	GA	SO	Avg.
94-95—Granby	QMJHL	15	866	8	5	0	47	0	3.26	6	232	1	2	21	0	5.43
95-96—Granby	QMJHL	28	1533	19	5	2	69	†3	2.70	12	610	9	2	21	*2	*2.07
96-97—Granby	QMJHL	57	3330	33	16	*6	162	4	2.92	5	251	1	4	17	0	4.06
—Albany	AHL	1	60	1	0	0	3	0	3.00	—	—	—	—	—	—	—
97-98—Albany	AHL	4	199	2	0	1	8	0	2.41	—	—	—	—	—	—	—
—Raleigh	ECHL	34	1889	13	17	‡2	119	2	3.78	—	—	—	—	—	—	—
98-99—Albany	AHL	35	1690	17	10	3	84	1	2.98	—	—	—	—	—	—	—
99-00—Albany	AHL	53	2732	18	23	3	138	1	3.03	4	236	2	2	6	1	1.53
00-01—Albany	AHL	32	1651	6	17	3	99	1	3.60	—	—	—	—	—	—	—

HENTUNEN, JUKKA — LW/RW — FLAMES

PERSONAL: Born May 3, 1974, in Finland. ... 5-10/187. ... Shoots right.
TRANSACTIONS/CAREER NOTES: Selected by Calgary Flames in sixth round (seventh Flames pick, 176th overall) of NHL entry draft (June 24, 2000).

Season Team	League	REGULAR SEASON								PLAYOFFS				
		Gms.	G	A	Pts.	PIM	+/-	PP	SH	Gms.	G	A	Pts.	PIM
99-00—HPK Hameenlinna	Finland	53	17	28	45	76	...	...	...	—	—	—	—	—
00-01—Jokerit Helsinki	Finland	56	27	28	55	24	...	...	...	5	1	0	1	4

H

HERPERGER, CHRIS   LW   SENATORS

PERSONAL: Born February 24, 1974, in Esterhazy, Sask. ... 6-0/190. ... Shoots left. ... Name pronounced HUHR-puhr-guhr.
TRANSACTIONS/CAREER NOTES: Signed by Philadelphia Flyers in 10th round (10th Flyers pick, 223rd overall) of NHL entry draft (June 20, 1992). ... Traded by Flyers with seventh-round pick (LW Tony Mohagen) in 1997 draft to Mighty Ducks of Anaheim for C Bob Corkum (February 6, 1996). ... Signed as free agent by Chicago Blackhawks (September 2, 1998). ... Suffered concussion (January 21, 2001); missed three games. ... Bruised ribs (February 7, 2001); missed two games. ... Signed as free agent by Ottawa Senators (July 13, 2001).
HONORS: Named to WHL (West) All-Star second team (1994-95).

		REGULAR SEASON								PLAYOFFS				
Season Team	League	Gms.	G	A	Pts.	PIM	+/-	PP	SH	Gms.	G	A	Pts.	PIM
90-91—Swift Current	WHL	10	0	1	1	5	...	...	...	—	—	—	—	—
91-92—Swift Current	WHL	72	14	19	33	44	...	...	...	8	0	1	1	9
92-93—Swift Current	WHL	20	9	7	16	31	...	...	...	—	—	—	—	—
—Seattle	WHL	66	29	18	47	61	...	...	...	5	1	1	2	6
93-94—Seattle	WHL	71	44	51	95	110	...	...	...	9	12	10	22	12
94-95—Seattle	WHL	59	49	52	101	106	...	...	...	4	4	0	4	6
—Hershey	AHL	4	0	0	0	0	...	...	...	—	—	—	—	—
95-96—Hershey	AHL	46	8	12	20	36	...	...	...	—	—	—	—	—
—Baltimore	AHL	21	2	3	5	17	...	...	...	9	2	3	5	6
96-97—Baltimore	AHL	67	19	22	41	88	...	...	...	3	0	0	0	0
97-98—Canadian nat'l team	Int'l	62	20	30	50	102	...	...	...	—	—	—	—	—
98-99—Indianapolis	IHL	79	19	29	48	81	...	...	...	7	0	4	4	4
99-00—Chicago	NHL	9	0	0	0	5	-2	0	0	—	—	—	—	—
—Cleveland	IHL	73	22	26	48	122	...	...	...	9	3	3	6	8
00-01—Norfolk	AHL	9	1	4	5	9	...	...	...	—	—	—	—	—
—Chicago	NHL	61	10	15	25	20	0	0	1	—	—	—	—	—
NHL Totals (2 years)		70	10	15	25	25	-2	0	1					

HERR, MATT   LW   FLYERS

PERSONAL: Born May 26, 1976, in Hackensack, N.J. ... 6-2/203. ... Shoots left. ... Full Name: Matthew Herr.
TRANSACTIONS/CAREER NOTES: Selected by Washington Capitals in fourth round (fourth Capitals pick, 93rd overall) of NHL entry draft (June 29, 1994). ... Traded by Capitals to Philadelphia Flyers for D Dean Melanson (March 13, 2001).
MISCELLANEOUS: Selected by Atlanta Braves organization in 29th round of free-agent draft (June 2, 1994); did not sign.

		REGULAR SEASON								PLAYOFFS				
Season Team	League	Gms.	G	A	Pts.	PIM	+/-	PP	SH	Gms.	G	A	Pts.	PIM
90-91—Hotchkiss	Conn. H.S.	26	9	5	14	...	...	...	...	—	—	—	—	—
91-92—Hotchkiss	Conn. H.S.	25	17	16	33	...	...	...	...	—	—	—	—	—
92-93—Hotchkiss	Conn. H.S.	24	48	30	78	...	...	...	...	—	—	—	—	—
93-94—Hotchkiss	Conn. H.S.	20	28	19	47	...	...	...	...	—	—	—	—	—
94-95—Univ. of Michigan	CCHA	37	11	8	19	51	...	...	...	—	—	—	—	—
95-96—Univ. of Michigan	CCHA	40	18	13	31	55	...	...	...	—	—	—	—	—
96-97—Univ. of Michigan	CCHA	43	29	23	52	67	...	...	...	—	—	—	—	—
97-98—Univ. of Michigan	CCHA	29	13	17	30	60	...	...	...	—	—	—	—	—
98-99—Washington	NHL	30	2	2	4	8	-7	1	0	—	—	—	—	—
—Portland	AHL	46	15	14	29	29	...	...	...	—	—	—	—	—
99-00—Portland	AHL	77	22	21	43	51	...	...	...	4	1	1	2	4
00-01—Portland	AHL	40	21	13	34	58	...	...	...	—	—	—	—	—
—Washington	NHL	22	2	3	5	17	3	0	0	—	—	—	—	—
—Philadelphia	AHL	11	2	4	6	18	...	...	...	9	2	1	3	8
NHL Totals (2 years)		52	4	5	9	25	-4	1	0					

HEWARD, JAMIE   D   BLUE JACKETS

PERSONAL: Born March 30, 1971, in Regina, Sask. ... 6-2/207. ... Shoots right. ... Name pronounced HYOO-uhrd.
TRANSACTIONS/CAREER NOTES: Selected by Pittsburgh Penguins in first round (first Penguins pick, 16th overall) of NHL entry draft (June 17, 1989). ... Signed as free agent by Toronto Maple Leafs (May 4, 1995). ... Signed as free agent by Philadelphia Flyers (July 10, 1997). ... Signed as free agent by Nashville Predators (August 6, 1998). ... Sprained ankle (December 8, 1998); missed five games. ... Injured heel (March 14, 1999); missed five games. ... Signed as free agent by New York Islanders (July 7, 1999). ... Suffered concussion (October 23, 1999); missed two games. ... Strained lower back (December 9, 1999); missed two games. ... Fractured right ankle (February 17, 2000); missed remainder of season. ... Claimed on waivers by Columbus Blue Jackets (May 26, 2000). ... Sprained wrist (January 7, 2001); missed two games.
HONORS: Named to WHL (East) All-Star first team (1990-91). ... Named to AHL All-Star first team (1995-96 and 1997-98). ... Won Eddie Shore Plaque (1997-98).

		REGULAR SEASON								PLAYOFFS				
Season Team	League	Gms.	G	A	Pts.	PIM	+/-	PP	SH	Gms.	G	A	Pts.	PIM
87-88—Regina	WHL	68	10	17	27	17	...	...	...	4	1	1	2	2
88-89—Regina	WHL	52	31	28	59	29	...	...	...	—	—	—	—	—
89-90—Regina	WHL	72	14	44	58	42	...	...	...	11	2	2	4	10
90-91—Regina	WHL	71	23	61	84	41	...	...	...	8	2	9	11	6
91-92—Muskegon	IHL	54	6	21	27	37	...	...	...	14	1	4	5	4
92-93—Cleveland	IHL	58	9	18	27	64	...	...	...	—	—	—	—	—
93-94—Cleveland	IHL	73	8	16	24	72	...	...	...	—	—	—	—	—
94-95—Canadian nat'l team	Int'l	51	11	35	46	32	...	...	...	—	—	—	—	—
95-96—St. John's	AHL	73	22	34	56	33	...	...	...	3	1	1	2	6
—Toronto	NHL	5	0	0	0	0	-1	0	0	—	—	—	—	—
96-97—Toronto	NHL	20	1	4	5	6	-6	0	0	—	—	—	—	—
—St. John's	AHL	27	8	19	27	26	...	...	...	9	1	3	4	6

– 155 –

H

Season Team	League	Gms.	G	A	Pts.	PIM	+/-	PP	SH	Gms.	G	A	Pts.	PIM
					REGULAR SEASON							PLAYOFFS		
97-98—Philadelphia	AHL	72	17	48	65	54	...	...	...	20	3	16	19	10
98-99—Nashville	NHL	63	6	12	18	44	-24	4	0	—	—	—	—	—
99-00—New York Islanders	NHL	54	6	11	17	26	-9	2	0	—	—	—	—	—
00-01—Columbus	NHL	69	11	16	27	33	3	9	0	—	—	—	—	—
NHL Totals (5 years)		211	24	43	67	109	-37	15	0					

HIGGINS, MATT   C

PERSONAL: Born October 29, 1977, in Vernon, B.C. ... 6-2/190. ... Shoots left.
TRANSACTIONS/CAREER NOTES: Selected by Montreal Canadiens in first round (first Canadiens pick, 18th overall) of NHL entry draft (June 22, 1996). ... Suffered concussion (November 21, 1998); missed three games.

Season Team	League	Gms.	G	A	Pts.	PIM	+/-	PP	SH	Gms.	G	A	Pts.	PIM
					REGULAR SEASON							PLAYOFFS		
93-94—Moose Jaw	WHL	64	6	10	16	10	...	...	...	—	—	—	—	—
94-95—Moose Jaw	WHL	72	36	34	70	26	...	...	...	10	1	2	3	2
95-96—Moose Jaw	WHL	67	30	33	63	43	...	...	...	—	—	—	—	—
96-97—Moose Jaw	WHL	71	33	57	90	51	...	...	...	12	3	5	8	2
97-98—Fredericton	AHL	50	5	22	27	12	...	...	...	4	1	2	3	2
—Montreal	NHL	1	0	0	0	0	-1	0	0	—	—	—	—	—
98-99—Montreal	NHL	25	1	0	1	0	-2	0	0	—	—	—	—	—
—Fredericton	AHL	11	3	4	7	6	...	...	...	5	0	2	2	0
99-00—Montreal	NHL	25	0	2	2	4	-6	0	0	—	—	—	—	—
—Quebec	AHL	29	1	15	16	21	...	...	...	—	—	—	—	—
00-01—Quebec	AHL	66	10	18	28	18	...	...	...	8	0	1	1	4
—Montreal	NHL	6	0	0	0	2	-2	0	0	—	—	—	—	—
NHL Totals (4 years)		57	1	2	3	6	-11	0	0					

HILBERT, ANDY   C   BRUINS

PERSONAL: Born February 6, 1981, in Howell, Mich. ... 5-11/190. ... Shoots left.
TRANSACTIONS/CAREER NOTES: Selected by Boston Bruins in second round (third Bruins pick, 37th overall) of NHL entry draft (June 24, 2000).
HONORS: Named to CCHA All-Star first team (2000-01). ... Named to NCAA All-America (West) first team (2000-01).

Season Team	League	Gms.	G	A	Pts.	PIM	+/-	PP	SH	Gms.	G	A	Pts.	PIM
					REGULAR SEASON							PLAYOFFS		
98-99—U.S. National	USHL	46	23	35	58	140	...	...	...	—	—	—	—	—
99-00—Univ. of Michigan	CCHA	35	17	15	32	39	...	...	...	—	—	—	—	—
00-01—Univ. of Michigan	CCHA	42	26	38	64	72	...	...	...	—	—	—	—	—

HILL, SEAN   D   BLUES

PERSONAL: Born February 14, 1970, in Duluth, Minn. ... 6-0/203. ... Shoots right. ... Full Name: Sean Ronald Hill.
TRANSACTIONS/CAREER NOTES: Selected by Montreal Canadiens in eighth round (ninth Canadiens pick, 167th overall) of NHL entry draft (June 11, 1988). ... Strained abdominal muscle (October 13, 1992); missed 14 games. ... Selected by Mighty Ducks of Anaheim in NHL expansion draft (June 24, 1993). ... Sprained shoulder (January 6, 1994); missed nine games. ... Traded by Mighty Ducks with ninth-round pick (G Frederic Cassivi) in 1994 draft to Ottawa Senators for third-round pick (traded to Tampa Bay) in 1994 draft (June 29, 1994). ... Strained abdominal muscle during 1995-96 season; missed two games. ... Tore left knee ligament (October 18, 1996); missed remainder of season. ... Traded by Senators to Carolina Hurricanes for RW Chris Murray (November 18, 1997). ... Strained hip flexor (December 1, 1997); missed three games. ... Fractured fibula (March 26, 1998); missed final 11 games of season. ... Fractured ankle and strained abdominal muscle (December 21, 1998); missed 20 games. ... Strained abdominal muscle (February 13, 1999); missed one game. ... Sprained ankle (March 21, 1999); missed four games. ... Fractured cheekbone (April 14, 1999); missed final two games of season. ... Strained groin (December 22, 1999); missed 18 games. ... Reinjured groin (April 3, 2000); missed final two games of season. ... Signed as free agent by St. Louis Blues (July 1, 2000). ... Strained muscle in abdomen (November 29, 2000); missed 32 games.
HONORS: Named to WCHA All-Star second team (1989-90 and 1990-91). ... Named to NCAA All-America (West) second team (1990-91).
MISCELLANEOUS: Member of Stanley Cup championship team (1993).

Season Team	League	Gms.	G	A	Pts.	PIM	+/-	PP	SH	Gms.	G	A	Pts.	PIM
					REGULAR SEASON							PLAYOFFS		
88-89—Univ. of Wisconsin	WCHA	45	2	23	25	69	...	...	...	—	—	—	—	—
89-90—Univ. of Wisconsin	WCHA	42	14	39	53	78	...	...	...	—	—	—	—	—
90-91—Univ. of Wisconsin	WCHA	37	19	32	51	122	...	...	...	—	—	—	—	—
—Fredericton	AHL	—	—	—	—	—	...	...	...	3	0	2	2	2
—Montreal	NHL	—	—	—	—	—	...	...	...	1	0	0	0	0
91-92—Fredericton	AHL	42	7	20	27	65	...	...	...	7	1	3	4	6
—U.S. national team	Int'l	12	4	3	7	16	...	...	...	—	—	—	—	—
—U.S. Olympic team	Int'l	8	2	0	2	6	...	...	...	—	—	—	—	—
—Montreal	NHL	—	—	—	—	—	...	...	...	4	1	0	1	2
92-93—Montreal	NHL	31	2	6	8	54	-5	1	0	3	0	0	0	4
—Fredericton	AHL	6	1	3	4	10	...	...	...	—	—	—	—	—
93-94—Anaheim	NHL	68	7	20	27	78	-12	2	1	—	—	—	—	—
94-95—Ottawa	NHL	45	1	14	15	30	-11	0	0	—	—	—	—	—
95-96—Ottawa	NHL	80	7	14	21	94	-26	2	0	—	—	—	—	—
96-97—Ottawa	NHL	5	0	0	0	4	1	0	0	—	—	—	—	—
97-98—Ottawa	NHL	13	1	1	2	6	-3	0	0	—	—	—	—	—
—Carolina	NHL	42	0	5	5	48	-2	0	0	—	—	—	—	—
98-99—Carolina	NHL	54	0	10	10	48	9	0	0	—	—	—	—	—
99-00—Carolina	NHL	62	13	31	44	59	3	8	0	—	—	—	—	—
00-01—St. Louis	NHL	48	1	10	11	51	5	0	0	15	0	1	1	12
NHL Totals (11 years)		448	32	111	143	472	-41	13	1	23	1	1	2	18

H

HINOTE, DAN   RW   AVALANCHE

PERSONAL: Born January 30, 1977, in Leesburg, Fla. ... 6-0/190. ... Shoots right.
TRANSACTIONS/CAREER NOTES: Selected by Colorado Avalanche in seventh round (ninth Avalanche pick, 167th overall) of NHL entry draft (June 22, 1996). ... Sprained knee (February 19, 2001); missed one game.
MISCELLANEOUS: Member of Stanley Cup championship team (2001).

			REGULAR SEASON								PLAYOFFS				
Season Team	League	Gms.	G	A	Pts.	PIM	+/-	PP	SH	Gms.	G	A	Pts.	PIM
95-96—Army	Indep.	33	20	24	44	20	...	...	...	—	—	—	—	—
96-97—Oshawa	OHL	60	15	13	28	58	...	...	...	18	4	5	9	8
97-98—Hershey	AHL	24	1	4	5	25	...	...	...	—	—	—	—	—
—Oshawa	OHL	35	12	15	27	39	...	...	...	5	2	2	4	7
98-99—Hershey	AHL	65	4	16	20	95	...	...	...	5	3	1	4	6
99-00—Colorado	NHL	27	1	3	4	10	0	0	0	—	—	—	—	—
—Hershey	AHL	55	28	31	59	96	...	...	...	14	4	5	9	19
00-01—Colorado	NHL	76	5	10	15	51	1	1	0	23	2	4	6	21
NHL Totals (2 years)		103	6	13	19	61	1	1	0	23	2	4	6	21

HIRSCH, COREY   G

PERSONAL: Born July 1, 1972, in Medicine Hat, Alta. ... 5-10/168. ... Catches left.
TRANSACTIONS/CAREER NOTES: Selected by New York Rangers in eighth round (seventh Rangers pick, 169th overall) of NHL entry draft (June 22, 1991). ... Loaned by Rangers to Canadian national team (October 1, 1993). ... Returned to Rangers (March 8, 1994). ... Traded by Rangers to Vancouver Canucks for C Nathan LaFayette (April 7, 1995). ... Bruised ribs (October 6, 1996); missed five games. ... Signed as free agent by Nashville Predators (August 10, 1999). ... Traded by Predators to Mighty Ducks of Anaheim for future considerations (March 14, 2000). ... Signed as free agent by Washington Capitals (November 1, 2000).
HONORS: Named to WHL (West) All-Star second team (1989-90). ... Won Can.HL Goaltender of the Year Award (1991-92). ... Won Hap Emms Memorial Trophy (1991-92). ... Won Del Wilson Trophy (1991-92). ... Won WHL Player of the Year Award (1991-92). ... Named to Can.HL All-Star first team (1991-92). ... Named to Memorial Cup All-Star team (1991-92). ... Named to WHL (West) All-Star first team (1991-92). ... Won Aldege (Baz) Bastien Trophy (1992-93). ... Won Dudley (Red) Garrett Memorial Trophy (1992-93). ... Shared Harry (Hap) Holmes Memorial Trophy with Boris Rousson (1992-93). ... Named to AHL All-Star first team (1992-93). ... Named to NHL All-Rookie team (1995-96).
MISCELLANEOUS: Member of silver-medal-winning Canadian Olympic team (1994). ... Stopped a penalty shot attempt (vs. Martin Rucinsky, January 2, 1999). ... Allowed a penalty shot goal (vs. Paul Kariya, Februaury 20, 1999).

				REGULAR SEASON								PLAYOFFS				
Season Team	League	Gms.	Min.	W	L	T	GA	SO	Avg.	Gms.	Min.	W	L	GA	SO	Avg.
88-89—Kamloops	WHL	32	1516	11	12	2	106	2	4.20	5	245	3	2	19	0	4.65
89-90—Kamloops	WHL	63	3608	48	13	0	230	3	3.82	17	1043	14	3	60	0	3.45
90-91—Kamloops	WHL	38	1970	26	7	1	100	3	3.05	11	623	5	6	42	0	4.04
91-92—Kamloops	WHL	48	2732	35	10	2	124	*5	*2.72	*16	*954	*11	5	35	*2	*2.20
92-93—Binghamton	AHL	46	2692	*35	4	5	125	1	*2.79	14	831	7	7	46	0	3.32
—New York Rangers	NHL	4	224	1	2	1	14	0	3.75	—	—	—	—	—	—	—
93-94—Canadian nat'l team	Int'l	37	2158	19	15	2	107	0	2.97	—	—	—	—	—	—	—
—Can. Olympic team	Int'l	8	495	5	2	1	17	0	2.06	—	—	—	—	—	—	—
—Binghamton	AHL	10	611	5	4	1	38	0	3.73	—	—	—	—	—	—	—
94-95—Binghamton	AHL	57	3371	31	20	5	175	0	3.11	—	—	—	—	—	—	—
95-96—Vancouver	NHL	41	2338	17	14	6	114	1	2.93	6	338	2	3	21	0	3.73
96-97—Vancouver	NHL	39	2127	12	20	4	116	2	3.27	—	—	—	—	—	—	—
97-98—Vancouver	NHL	1	50	0	0	0	5	0	6.00	—	—	—	—	—	—	—
—Syracuse	AHL	60	3513	30	22	6	187	1	3.19	5	297	2	3	10	1	2.02
98-99—Vancouver	NHL	20	919	3	8	3	48	1	3.13	—	—	—	—	—	—	—
—Syracuse	AHL	5	300	2	3	0	14	0	2.80	—	—	—	—	—	—	—
99-00—Milwaukee	IHL	19	1098	11	8	1	49	0	2.68	—	—	—	—	—	—	—
—Utah	IHL	17	937	9	5	1	42	3	2.69	2	121	0	2	4	0	1.98
00-01—Washington	NHL	1	20	1	0	0	0	0	...	—	—	—	—	—	—	—
—Cincinnati	IHL	13	783	11	2	‡0	28	1	2.15	—	—	—	—	—	—	—
—Albany	AHL	4	199	0	4	0	19	0	5.73	—	—	—	—	—	—	—
—Portland	AHL	36	2142	17	17	2	104	1	2.91	2	118	0	2	7	0	3.56
NHL Totals (6 years)		106	5678	34	44	14	297	4	3.14	6	338	2	3	21	0	3.73

HLAVAC, JAN   LW   RANGERS

PERSONAL: Born September 20, 1976, in Prague, Czechoslovakia. ... 6-0/183. ... Shoots left. ... Name pronounced YAHN luh-VAHCH.
TRANSACTIONS/CAREER NOTES: Selected by New York Islanders in second round (second Islanders pick, 28th overall) of NHL entry draft (July 8, 1995). ... Traded by Islanders to Calgary Flames for LW Jorgen Jonsson (July 14, 1998). ... Traded by Flames with first- (C Jamie Lundmark) and third-round (D Pat Aufiero) picks in 1999 draft to New York Rangers for C Marc Savard and first-round pick (C/LW Oleg Saprykin) in 1999 draft (June 26, 1999). ... Strained hip flexor (March 15, 2000); missed two games. ... Bruised foot (April 4, 2000); missed one game. ... Injured shoulder (January 14, 2001); missed one game. ... Injured left knee (April 4, 2001); missed final two games of season.
STATISTICAL PLATEAUS: Three-goal games: 1999-00 (1), 2000-01 (1). Total: 2.

				REGULAR SEASON						PLAYOFFS				
Season Team	League	Gms.	G	A	Pts.	PIM	+/-	PP	SH	Gms.	G	A	Pts.	PIM
93-94—Sparta Prague	Czech Rep.Jrs.	27	12	15	27	...	...	...	...	—	—	—	—	—
—Sparta Prague	Czech Rep.	9	1	1	2	...	...	...	...	—	—	—	—	—
94-95—Sparta Prague	Czech Rep.	38	7	6	13	...	...	...	...	5	0	2	2	...
95-96—Sparta Prague	Czech Rep.	34	8	5	13	...	...	...	...	12	1	2	3	...
96-97—Sparta Praha	Czech Rep.	38	8	13	21	24	...	...	...	10	5	2	7	2
97-98—Sparta Praha	Czech Rep.	48	17	30	47	40	...	...	...	5	1	0	1	2
98-99—Sparta Praha	Czech Rep.	49	*33	20	53	52	...	...	...	6	1	3	4	...
99-00—New York Rangers	NHL	67	19	23	42	16	3	6	0	—	—	—	—	—
—Hartford	AHL	3	1	0	1	0	...	...	...	—	—	—	—	—
00-01—New York Rangers	NHL	79	28	36	64	20	3	5	0	—	—	—	—	—
NHL Totals (2 years)		146	47	59	106	36	6	11	0	—	—	—	—	—

H

HNIDY, SHANE　　　　　　D　　　　　　SENATORS

PERSONAL: Born November 8, 1975, in Brandon, Man. ... 6-1/200. ... Shoots right. ... Name pronounced NIGH-dee.
TRANSACTIONS/CAREER NOTES: Selected by Buffalo Sabres in seventh round (Sabres seventh pick, 173rd overall) of NHL entry draft (June 28, 1994). ... Signed as free agent by Detroit Red Wings (August 6, 1998). ... Traded by Red Wings to Ottawa Senators for eighth-round pick (RW Todd Jackson) in 2000 draft (June 25, 2000). ... Bruised left foot (December 14, 2000); missed four games. ... Strained groin (March 26, 2001); missed final six game of regular season.

		REGULAR SEASON								PLAYOFFS				
Season Team	League	Gms.	G	A	Pts.	PIM	+/-	PP	SH	Gms.	G	A	Pts.	PIM
91-92—Swift Current	WHL	56	1	3	4	11	...	...	...	—	—	—	—	—
92-93—Swift Current	WHL	72	7	22	29	105	...	...	...	—	—	—	—	—
93-94—Prince Albert	WHL	69	7	26	33	113	...	...	...	—	—	—	—	—
94-95—Prince Albert	WHL	72	5	29	34	169	...	...	...	15	4	7	11	29
95-96—Prince Albert	WHL	58	11	42	53	100	...	...	...	18	4	11	15	34
96-97—Baton Rouge	ECHL	21	3	10	13	50	...	...	...	—	—	—	—	—
—Saint John	AHL	44	2	12	14	112	...	...	...	—	—	—	—	—
97-98—Grand Rapids	IHL	77	6	12	18	210	...	...	...	3	0	2	2	23
98-99—Adirondack	AHL	68	9	20	29	121	...	...	...	3	0	1	1	0
99-00—Cincinnati	AHL	68	9	19	28	153	...	...	...	—	—	—	—	—
00-01—Ottawa	NHL	52	3	2	5	84	8	0	0	1	0	0	0	0
—Grand Rapids	IHL	2	0	0	0	2	...	...	...	—	—	—	—	—
NHL Totals (1 year).............		52	3	2	5	84	8	0	0	1	0	0	0	0

HNILICKA, MILAN　　　　　　G　　　　　　THRASHERS

PERSONAL: Born June 24, 1973, in Kladno, Czechoslovakia. ... 6-0/180. ... Catches left. ... Name pronounced MEE-lahn nun-LEECH-kuh.
TRANSACTIONS/CAREER NOTES: Selected by New York Islanders in fourth round (fourth Islanders pick, 70th overall) of NHL entry draft (June 22, 1991). ... Signed as free agent by New York Rangers (July 22, 1999). ... Signed as free agent by Atlanta Thrashers (July 28, 2000).
HONORS: Shared Harry (Hap) Holmes Memorial Trophy with Jean-Francois Labbe (1999-2000).
MISCELLANEOUS: Holds Atlanta Thrashers all-time record for shutouts (2). ... Shares Atlanta Thrashers all-time record for wins (12).

		REGULAR SEASON								PLAYOFFS						
Season Team	League	Gms.	Min	W	L	T	GA	SO	Avg.	Gms.	Min.	W	L	GA	SO	Avg.
89-90—Poldi Kladno	Czech Rep.	24	1113	...	...	...	70	...	3.77	—	—					
90-91—Poldi Kladno	Czech Rep.	35	2122	...	...	...	98	...	2.77	—	—					
91-92—Poldi Kladno	Czech Rep.	30	1788	...	...	...	107	...	3.59	—	—					
92-93—Swift Current	WHL	65	3679	*46	12	2	206	2	3.36	17	1017	12	5	54	*2	3.19
93-94—Salt Lake City	IHL	9	381	5	1	0	25	0	3.94	—	—					
—Richmond	ECHL	43	2299	18	16	‡5	155	0	4.05	—	—					
94-95—Denver	IHL	15	798	9	4	‡1	47	1	3.53	—	—					
95-96—Poldi Kladno	Czech Rep.	33	1959	...	...	...	93	1	2.85	8	493	...	...	24	...	2.92
96-97—Poldi Kladno	Czech Rep.	48	2736	...	...	...	120	4	2.63	3	151	...	...	14	0	5.56
97-98—Sparta Praha	Czech Rep.	49	2847	...	...	...	99	...	2.09	11	632	...	...	31	...	2.94
98-99—Sparta Praha	Czech Rep.	50	2877	...	...	...	109	...	2.27	8	507	...	...	13	...	1.54
99-00—New York Rangers	NHL	2	86	0	1	0	5	0	3.49	—	—					
—Hartford	AHL	36	1979	22	11	0	71	5	2.15	3	99	0	1	6	0	3.64
00-01—Atlanta.........................	NHL	36	1879	12	19	2	105	2	3.35	—	—					
NHL Totals (2 years).............		38	1965	12	20	2	110	2	3.36							

HOGLUND, JONAS　　　　　　LW　　　　　　MAPLE LEAFS

PERSONAL: Born August 29, 1972, in Karlstad, Sweden. ... 6-3/215. ... Shoots right. ... Name pronounced YOH-nuhz HOHG-luhnd.
TRANSACTIONS/CAREER NOTES: Selected by Calgary Flames in 10th round (11th Flames pick, 222nd overall) of NHL entry draft (June 20, 1992). ... Traded by Flames with D Zarley Zalapski to Montreal Canadiens for RW Valeri Bure and fourth-round pick (C Shaun Sutter) in 1998 draft (February 1, 1998). ... Signed as free agent by Toronto Maple Leafs (July 7, 1999).
STATISTICAL PLATEAUS: Three-goal games: 2000-01 (1).

		REGULAR SEASON								PLAYOFFS				
Season Team	League	Gms.	G	A	Pts.	PIM	+/-	PP	SH	Gms.	G	A	Pts.	PIM
88-89—Farjestad Karlstad	Sweden	1	0	0	0	0	...	...	...	—	—	—	—	—
89-90—Farjestad Karlstad	Sweden	1	0	0	0	0	...	...	...	—	—	—	—	—
90-91—Farjestad Karlstad	Sweden	40	5	5	10	4	...	...	...	8	1	0	1	0
91-92—Farjestad Karlstad	Sweden	40	14	11	25	6	...	...	...	6	2	4	6	2
92-93—Farjestad Karlstad	Sweden	40	13	13	26	14	...	...	...	3	1	0	1	0
93-94—Farjestad Karlstad	Sweden	22	7	2	9	10	...	...	...	—	—	—	—	—
94-95—Farjestad Karlstad	Sweden	40	14	12	26	16	...	...	...	4	3	2	5	0
95-96—Farjestad Karlstad	Sweden	40	32	11	43	18	...	...	...	8	2	1	3	6
96-97—Calgary	NHL	68	19	16	35	12	-4	3	0	—	—	—	—	—
97-98—Calgary	NHL	50	6	8	14	16	-9	0	0	—	—	—	—	—
—Montreal	NHL	28	6	5	11	6	2	4	0	10	2	0	2	0
98-99—Montreal	NHL	74	8	10	18	16	-5	1	0	—	—	—	—	—
99-00—Toronto	NHL	82	29	27	56	10	-2	9	1	12	2	4	6	2
00-01—Toronto	NHL	82	23	26	49	14	1	5	0	10	0	0	0	4
NHL Totals (5 years)...........		384	91	92	183	74	-17	22	1	32	4	4	8	6

H

HOGUE, BENOIT   C   STARS

PERSONAL: Born October 28, 1966, in Repentigny, Que. ... 5-10/194. ... Shoots left. ... Name pronounced BEHN-wah HOHG.

TRANSACTIONS/CAREER NOTES: Selected by Buffalo Sabres in second round (second Sabres pick, 35th overall) of NHL entry draft (June 15, 1985). ... Suffered sore back (March 1988). ... Fractured left cheekbone (October 11, 1989); missed 20 games. ... Sprained left ankle (March 14, 1990). ... Traded by Sabres with C Pierre Turgeon, D Uwe Krupp and C Dave McLlwain to New York Islanders for C Pat LaFontaine, LW Randy Wood, D Randy Hillier and future considerations; Sabres later received fourth-round pick (D Dean Melanson) in 1992 draft (October 25, 1991). ... Suffered stiff neck (December 7, 1992); missed five games. ... Suffered sore hand and foot (January 14, 1993); missed three games. ... Sprained knee ligament (March 14, 1993); missed six games. ... Injured shoulder (February 4, 1995); missed one game. ... Traded by Islanders with third-round pick (RW Ryan Pepperall) in 1995 draft and fifth-round pick (D Brandon Sugden) in 1996 draft to Toronto Maple Leafs for G Eric Fichaud (April 6, 1995). ... Sprained wrist (December 27, 1995); missed four games. ... Traded by Maple Leafs with LW Randy Wood to Dallas Stars for C Dave Gagner (January 28, 1996). ... Sprained neck (November 27, 1996); missed one game. ... Injured elbow (February 2, 1997); missed two games. ... Reinjured elbow (February 23, 1997); missed four games. ... Fractured ankle (December 3, 1997); missed 12 games. ... Suffered facial fracture (March 8, 1998); missed 13 games. ... Signed as free agent by Tampa Bay Lightning (July 29, 1998). ... Traded by Lightning with sixth-round pick (D Michal Blazek) in 2001 draft to Stars for D Sergey Gusev (March 21, 1999). ... Signed as free agent by Phoenix Coyotes (February 3, 2000). ... Strained neck (March 23, 2000); missed one game. ... Signed as free agent by Stars (January 5, 2001). ... Injured groin (January 26, 2001); missed three games. ... Bruised shoulder (March 25, 2001); missed three games.

MISCELLANEOUS: Member of Stanley Cup championship team (1999). ... Scored on a penalty shot (vs. Ron Tugnutt, February, 16, 1993; vs. Ron Hextall, January 24, 1995).

STATISTICAL PLATEAUS: Three-goal games: 1992-93 (1).

		REGULAR SEASON								PLAYOFFS				
Season Team	League	Gms.	G	A	Pts.	PIM	+/-	PP	SH	Gms.	G	A	Pts.	PIM
83-84—St. Jean	QMJHL	59	14	11	25	42	...	...	...	—	—	—	—	—
84-85—St. Jean	QMJHL	63	46	44	90	92	...	...	...	—	—	—	—	—
85-86—St. Jean	QMJHL	65	54	54	108	115	...	...	...	9	6	4	10	26
86-87—Rochester	AHL	52	14	20	34	52	...	...	...	12	5	4	9	8
87-88—Buffalo	NHL	3	1	1	2	0	3	0	0	—	—	—	—	—
—Rochester	AHL	62	24	31	55	141	...	...	...	7	6	1	7	46
88-89—Buffalo	NHL	69	14	30	44	120	-5	1	2	5	0	0	0	17
89-90—Buffalo	NHL	45	11	7	18	79	0	1	0	3	0	0	0	10
90-91—Buffalo	NHL	76	19	28	47	76	-8	1	0	5	3	1	4	10
91-92—Buffalo	NHL	3	0	1	1	0	0	0	0	—	—	—	—	—
—New York Islanders	NHL	72	30	45	75	67	30	8	0	—	—	—	—	—
92-93—New York Islanders	NHL	70	33	42	75	108	13	5	3	18	6	6	12	31
93-94—New York Islanders	NHL	83	36	33	69	73	-7	9	5	4	0	1	1	4
94-95—New York Islanders	NHL	33	6	4	10	34	0	1	0	—	—	—	—	—
—Toronto	NHL	12	3	3	6	0	0	1	0	7	0	0	0	6
95-96—Toronto	NHL	44	12	25	37	68	6	3	0	—	—	—	—	—
—Dallas	NHL	34	7	20	27	36	4	2	0	—	—	—	—	—
96-97—Dallas	NHL	73	19	24	43	54	8	5	0	7	2	2	4	6
97-98—Dallas	NHL	53	6	16	22	35	7	3	0	17	4	2	6	16
98-99—Tampa Bay	NHL	62	11	14	25	50	-12	2	0	—	—	—	—	—
—Dallas	NHL	12	1	3	4	4	2	0	0	14	0	2	2	16
99-00—Phoenix	NHL	27	3	10	13	10	-1	0	0	5	1	2	3	2
00-01—Dallas	NHL	34	3	7	10	26	-1	0	0	7	1	0	1	6
NHL Totals (14 years)		805	215	313	528	840	39	42	10	92	17	16	33	124

HOLDEN, JOSH   C   CANUCKS

PERSONAL: Born January 18, 1978, in Calgary. ... 6-1/190. ... Shoots left.

TRANSACTIONS/CAREER NOTES: Selected by Vancouver Canucks in first round (first Canucks pick, 12th overall) of NHL entry draft (June 22, 1996). ... Suffered hernia prior to start of 1999-2000 season; missed first 22 games of season.

HONORS: Named to WHL (East) All-Star second team (1997-98).

		REGULAR SEASON								PLAYOFFS				
Season Team	League	Gms.	G	A	Pts.	PIM	+/-	PP	SH	Gms.	G	A	Pts.	PIM
94-95—Regina	WHL	62	20	23	43	45	...	...	...	4	3	1	4	0
95-96—Regina	WHL	70	57	55	112	105	...	...	...	11	4	5	9	23
96-97—Regina	WHL	58	49	49	98	148	...	...	...	5	3	2	5	10
97-98—Regina	WHL	56	41	58	99	134	...	...	...	2	2	2	4	10
98-99—Syracuse	AHL	38	14	15	29	48	...	...	...	—	—	—	—	—
—Vancouver	NHL	30	2	4	6	10	-10	1	0	—	—	—	—	—
99-00—Syracuse	AHL	45	19	32	51	113	...	...	...	4	1	0	1	10
—Vancouver	NHL	6	1	5	6	2	2	0	0	—	—	—	—	—
00-01—Kansas City	IHL	60	27	26	53	136	...	...	...	—	—	—	—	—
—Vancouver	NHL	10	1	0	1	0	0	0	0	—	—	—	—	—
NHL Totals (3 years)		46	4	9	13	12	-8	1	0					

HOLIK, BOBBY   C   DEVILS

PERSONAL: Born January 1, 1971, in Jihlava, Czechoslovakia. ... 6-4/230. ... Shoots right. ... Full Name: Robert Holik. ... Name pronounced hoh-LEEK.

TRANSACTIONS/CAREER NOTES: Selected by Hartford Whalers in first round (first Whalers pick, 10th overall) of NHL entry draft (June 17, 1989). ... Traded by Whalers with second-round pick (LW Jay Pandolfo) in 1993 draft and future considerations to New Jersey Devils for G Sean Burke and D Eric Weinrich (August 28, 1992). ... Bruised left shoulder (December 8, 1993); missed 11 games. ... Fractured left index finger (October 7, 1995); missed 13 games. ... Sprained left ankle (February 1996); missed six games. ... Suspended two games and fined $1,000 by NHL for tripping incident (November 8, 1998). ... Suspended two games by NHL for slashing incident (March 23, 1999). ... Suspended two games by NHL for slashing incident (November 25, 1999). ... Injured knee (February 15, 2001); missed two games.

HONORS: Played in NHL All-Star Game (1998 and 1999).

MISCELLANEOUS: Member of Stanley Cup championship team (1995 and 2000).

STATISTICAL PLATEAUS: Three-goal games: 1992-93 (2), 1998-99 (1). Total: 3.

H

Season Team	League	REGULAR SEASON								PLAYOFFS				
		Gms.	G	A	Pts.	PIM	+/-	PP	SH	Gms.	G	A	Pts.	PIM
87-88—Dukla Jihlava	Czech.	31	5	9	14	...	...	...	...	—	—	—	—	—
88-89—Dukla Jihlava	Czech.	24	7	10	17	...	...	...	...	—	—	—	—	—
89-90—Dukla Jihlava	Czech.	42	15	26	41	...	...	...	...	—	—	—	—	—
—Czech. national team ..	Int'l	10	1	5	6	0	...	...	...	—	—	—	—	—
90-91—Hartford	NHL	78	21	22	43	113	-3	8	0	6	0	0	0	7
91-92—Hartford	NHL	76	21	24	45	44	4	1	0	7	0	1	1	6
92-93—Utica	AHL	1	0	0	0	2	...	...	...	—	—	—	—	—
—New Jersey	NHL	61	20	19	39	76	-6	7	0	5	1	1	2	6
93-94—New Jersey	NHL	70	13	20	33	72	28	2	0	20	0	3	3	6
94-95—New Jersey	NHL	48	10	10	20	18	9	0	0	20	4	4	8	22
95-96—New Jersey	NHL	63	13	17	30	58	9	1	0	—	—	—	—	—
96-97—New Jersey	NHL	82	23	39	62	54	24	5	0	10	2	3	5	4
97-98—New Jersey	NHL	82	29	36	65	100	23	8	0	5	0	0	0	8
98-99—New Jersey	NHL	78	27	37	64	119	16	5	0	7	0	7	7	6
99-00—New Jersey	NHL	79	23	23	46	106	7	7	0	23	3	7	10	14
00-01—New Jersey	NHL	80	15	35	50	97	19	3	0	25	6	10	16	37
NHL Totals (11 years).........		797	215	282	497	857	130	47	0	128	16	36	52	116

HOLMQVIST, JOHAN   G   RANGERS

PERSONAL: Born May 24, 1978, in Tierp, Sweden. ... 6-1/200. ... Catches left.
TRANSACTIONS/CAREER NOTES: Selected by New York Rangers in seventh round (ninth Rangers pick, 182nd overall) of NHL entry draft (June 21, 1997).

Season Team	League	REGULAR SEASON							PLAYOFFS					
		Gms.	Min	W	L	T	GA	SO	Avg.	Gms.	Min.	W	L	GA	SO	Avg.
96-97—Brynas Gavle.................	Sweden	2	80	0	0	0	4	...	3.00	—	—	—	—	—	—	—
97-98—Brynas Gavle.................	Sweden	33	1897	...	...	...	82	...	2.59	3	180	0	3	14	...	4.67
98-99—Brynas Gavle.................	Sweden	41	2383	...	...	...	111	4	2.79	14	855	9	5	34	0	2.39
99-00—Brynas Gavle.................	Sweden	41	2402	...	...	...	104	4	2.60	11	671	...	...	30	1	2.68
00-01—Hartford	AHL	43	2305	19	14	4	111	2	2.89	5	314	2	3	13	0	2.48
—New York Rangers	NHL	2	119	0	2	0	10	0	5.04	—	—	—	—	—	—	—
NHL Totals (1 year)...............		2	119	0	2	0	10	0	5.04							

HOLMSTROM, TOMAS   LW   RED WINGS

PERSONAL: Born January 23, 1973, in Pieta, Sweden. ... 6-0/198. ... Shoots left.
TRANSACTIONS/CAREER NOTES: Selected by Detroit Red Wings in 10th round (ninth Red Wings pick, 257th overall) of NHL entry draft (June 29, 1994). ... Sprained knee (October 30, 1996); missed seven games. ... Bruised shoulder (March 28, 1997); missed one game. ... Sprained knee (November 17, 1999); missed five games. ... Suffered injury (March 3, 2000); missed one game. ... Suffered facial lacerations (March 29, 2000); missed two games. ... Suffered charley horse (November 12, 2000); missed one game. ... Suffered back spasms (December 31, 2000); missed three games.
MISCELLANEOUS: Member of Stanley Cup championship team (1997 and 1998).
STATISTICAL PLATEAUS: Three-goal games: 2000-01 (1).

Season Team	League	REGULAR SEASON								PLAYOFFS				
		Gms.	G	A	Pts.	PIM	+/-	PP	SH	Gms.	G	A	Pts.	PIM
94-95—Lulea..........................	Sweden	40	14	14	28	56	...	...	...	8	1	2	3	20
95-96—Lulea..........................	Sweden	34	12	11	23	78	...	...	...	11	6	2	8	22
96-97—Detroit........................	NHL	47	6	3	9	33	-10	3	0	1	0	0	0	0
—Adirondack	AHL	6	3	1	4	7	...	...	...	—	—	—	—	—
97-98—Detroit........................	NHL	57	5	17	22	44	6	1	0	22	7	12	19	16
98-99—Detroit........................	NHL	82	13	21	34	69	-11	5	0	10	4	3	7	4
99-00—Detroit........................	NHL	72	13	22	35	43	4	4	0	9	3	1	4	16
00-01—Detroit........................	NHL	73	16	24	40	40	-12	9	0	6	1	3	4	8
NHL Totals (5 years)............		331	53	87	140	229	-23	22	0	48	15	19	34	44

HOLZINGER, BRIAN   C/RW   LIGHTNING

PERSONAL: Born October 10, 1972, in Parma, Ohio. ... 5-11/190. ... Shoots right. ... Full Name: Brian Alan Holzinger. ... Name pronounced HOHL-zihng-uhr.
TRANSACTIONS/CAREER NOTES: Selected by Buffalo Sabres in sixth round (seventh Sabres pick, 124th overall) of NHL entry draft (June 22, 1991). ... Bruised heel (November 10, 1997); missed three games. ... Sprained ankle (March 1, 1998); missed seven games. ... Suffered from the flu (January 7, 1999); missed one game. ... Injured shoulder (October 17, 1999); missed three games. ... Injured shoulder (January 6, 2000); missed three games. ... Traded by Sabres with C Wayne Primeau, D Cory Sarich and third-round pick (RW Alexandre Kharitonov) in 2000 draft to Tampa Bay Lightning for C Chris Gratton and second-round pick (C Derek Roy) in 2001 draft (March 9, 2000). ... Strained muscle in abdomen (March 12, 2000); missed three games. ... Fractured finger (December 2, 2000); missed five games. ... Injured foot (March 24, 2001); missed two games. ... Fractured right ankle (April 1, 2001); missed final two games of season.
HONORS: Named to CCHA All-Star second team (1993-94). ... Won Hobey Baker Memorial Award (1994-95). ... Named to NCAA All-America (West) first team (1994-95). ... Named CCHA Player of the Year (1994-95). ... Named to CCHA All-Star first team (1994-95).

Season Team	League	REGULAR SEASON								PLAYOFFS				
		Gms.	G	A	Pts.	PIM	+/-	PP	SH	Gms.	G	A	Pts.	PIM
90-91—Det. Jr. Red Wings.....	NAJHL	37	45	41	86	16	...	...	...	—	—	—	—	—
91-92—Bowling Green	CCHA	30	14	8	22	36	...	...	...	—	—	—	—	—
92-93—Bowling Green	CCHA	41	31	26	57	44	...	...	...	—	—	—	—	—
93-94—Bowling Green	CCHA	38	22	15	37	24	...	...	...	—	—	—	—	—
94-95—Bowling Green	CCHA	38	35	34	69	42	...	...	...	—	—	—	—	—
—Buffalo	NHL	4	0	3	3	0	2	0	0	4	2	1	3	2

H

Season Team	League	REGULAR SEASON								PLAYOFFS				
		Gms.	G	A	Pts.	PIM	+/-	PP	SH	Gms.	G	A	Pts.	PIM
95-96—Buffalo	NHL	58	10	10	20	37	-21	5	0	—	—	—	—	—
—Rochester	AHL	17	10	11	21	14	...	...	...	19	10	14	24	10
96-97—Buffalo	NHL	81	22	29	51	54	9	2	2	12	2	5	7	8
97-98—Buffalo	NHL	69	14	21	35	36	-2	4	2	15	4	7	11	18
98-99—Buffalo	NHL	81	17	17	34	45	2	5	0	21	3	5	8	33
99-00—Buffalo	NHL	59	7	17	24	30	4	0	1	—	—	—	—	—
—Tampa Bay	NHL	14	3	3	6	21	-7	1	1	—	—	—	—	—
00-01—Tampa Bay	NHL	70	11	25	36	64	-9	3	0	—	—	—	—	—
NHL Totals (7 years)		436	84	125	209	287	-22	20	6	52	11	18	29	61

HORACEK, JAN   D   OILERS

PERSONAL: Born May 22, 1979, in Benesov, Czechoslovakia. ... 6-4/206. ... Shoots right. ... Name pronounced HOHR-ih-chehk.
TRANSACTIONS/CAREER NOTES: Selected by St. Louis Blues in fourth round (third Blues pick, 98th overall) of NHL entry draft (June 21, 1997). ... Traded by Blues with C Jochen Hecht and C Marty Reasoner to Edmonton Oilers for C Doug Weight and LW Michel Riesen (July 1, 2001).

Season Team	League	REGULAR SEASON								PLAYOFFS				
		Gms.	G	A	Pts.	PIM	+/-	PP	SH	Gms.	G	A	Pts.	PIM
95-96—Slavia Praha	Czech Rep.	8	0	1	1	4	...	...	...	—	—	—	—	—
—Slavia Praha Jrs.	Czech	18	1	5	6		...	...	...	—	—	—	—	—
—HC Kralupy	Czech II	11	0	0	0		...	...	...	—	—	—	—	—
96-97—Slavia Praha Jrs.	Czech	25	4	14	18		...	...	...	—	—	—	—	—
—Slavia Praha	Czech Rep.	9	0	0	0	6	...	...	...	3	0	0	0	...
—HC Beroun	Czech II	2	0	0	0		...	...	...	—	—	—	—	—
97-98—Moncton	QMJHL	54	3	18	21	146	...	...	...	10	1	5	6	20
98-99—Slavia Praha	Czech Rep.	1	0	0	0	2	...	...	...	—	—	—	—	—
—Worcester	AHL	53	1	13	14	119	...	...	...	4	0	0	0	6
99-00—Worcester	AHL	68	1	8	9	145	...	...	...	9	0	0	0	2
00-01—Worcester	AHL	11	0	1	1	20	...	...	...	2	0	0	0	2
—Peoria	ECHL	6	0	3	3	8	...	...	...	—	—	—	—	—

HORCOFF, SHAWN   C   OILERS

PERSONAL: Born September 17, 1978, in Trail, B.C. ... 6-1/194. ... Shoots left.
TRANSACTIONS/CAREER NOTES: Selected by Edmonton Oilers in fourth round (third Oilers pick, 99th overall) of NHL entry draft (June 27, 1998).
HONORS: Named to CCHA All-Star first team (1999-2000). ... Named to NCAA All-America (West) All-Star first team (1999-2000).

Season Team	League	REGULAR SEASON								PLAYOFFS				
		Gms.	G	A	Pts.	PIM	+/-	PP	SH	Gms.	G	A	Pts.	PIM
95-96—Chilliwack	BCJHL	58	49	96	*145	44	...	...	...	—	—	—	—	—
96-97—Michigan State	CCHA	40	10	13	23	20	...	...	...	—	—	—	—	—
97-98—Michigan State	CCHA	34	14	13	27	50	...	...	...	—	—	—	—	—
98-99—Michigan State	CCHA	39	12	25	37	70	...	...	...	—	—	—	—	—
99-00—Michigan State	CCHA	41	14	*48	*62	46	...	...	...	—	—	—	—	—
00-01—Hamilton	AHL	24	10	18	28	19	...	...	...	—	—	—	—	—
—Edmonton	NHL	49	9	7	16	10	8	0	0	5	0	0	0	0
NHL Totals (1 year)		49	9	7	16	10	8	0	0	5	0	0	0	0

HORDICHUK, DARCY   LW   THRASHERS

PERSONAL: Born August 10, 1980, in Kamsack, Sask. ... 6-1/200. ... Shoots left.
TRANSACTIONS/CAREER NOTES: Selected by Atlanta Thrashers in sixth round (eighth Thrashers pick, 180th overall) of NHL entry draft (June 24, 2000).

Season Team	League	REGULAR SEASON								PLAYOFFS				
		Gms.	G	A	Pts.	PIM	+/-	PP	SH	Gms.	G	A	Pts.	PIM
96-97—Calgary	WHL	3	0	0	0	2	...	...	...	—	—	—	—	—
98-99—Saskatoon	WHL	66	3	2	5	246	...	...	...	—	—	—	—	—
99-00—Saskatoon	WHL	63	6	8	14	269	...	...	...	—	—	—	—	—
00-01—Orlando	IHL	69	7	3	10	*369	...	...	...	16	3	3	6	*41
—Atlanta	NHL	11	0	0	0	38	-3	0	0	—	—	—	—	—
NHL Totals (1 year)		11	0	0	0	38	-3	0	0	—	—	—	—	—

HOSSA, MARCEL   C   CANADIENS

PERSONAL: Born October 12, 1981, in Ilava, Czechoslovakia. ... 6-1/200. ... Shoots left. ... Brother of Marian Hossa, left winger, Ottawa Senators. ... Name pronounced HOH-suh.
TRANSACTIONS/CAREER NOTES: Selected by Montreal Canadiens in first round (second Canadiens pick, 16th overall) of NHL entry draft (June 24, 2000).
HONORS: Named to WHL (West) All-Star second team (2000-01).

Season Team	League	REGULAR SEASON								PLAYOFFS				
		Gms.	G	A	Pts.	PIM	+/-	PP	SH	Gms.	G	A	Pts.	PIM
96-97—Dukla Trencin	Slovakia Jrs.	45	30	21	51	30	...	...	...	—	—	—	—	—
97-98—Dukla Trencin	Slovakia Jrs.	39	11	38	49	44	...	...	...	—	—	—	—	—
98-99—Portland	WHL	70	7	14	21	66	...	...	...	2	0	0	0	0
99-00—Portland	WHL	60	24	29	53	58	...	...	...	—	—	—	—	—
00-01—Portland	WHL	58	34	56	90	58	...	...	...	16	5	7	12	14

H

HOSSA, MARIAN   LW   SENATORS

PERSONAL: Born January 12, 1979, in Stara Lubovna, Czechoslovakia. ... 6-1/199. ... Shoots left. ... Brother of Marcel Hossa, center, Montreal Canadiens organization. ... Name pronounced HOH-suh.

TRANSACTIONS/CAREER NOTES: Selected by Ottawa Senators in first round (first Senators pick, 12th overall) of NHL entry draft (June 21, 1997). ... Tore anterior cruciate and medial collateral ligaments in knee (May 21, 1998); missed first 22 games of season. ... Suffered concussion (November 18, 1999); missed one game. ... Bruised left wrist (January 6, 2000); missed two games. ... Suffered illness (February 1, 2000); missed one game. ... Bruised calf (February 18, 2001); missed one game.

HONORS: Won Jim Piggott Memorial Trophy (1997-98). ... Named to WHL (West) All-Star first team (1997-98). ... Named to Can.HL All-Star first team (1997-98). ... Named to NHL All-Rookie team (1998-99). ... Played in NHL All-Star Game (2001).

MISCELLANEOUS: Failed to score on a penalty shot (vs. Dan Cloutier, January 4, 2001).

STATISTICAL PLATEAUS: Three-goal games: 2000-01 (1).

		REGULAR SEASON									PLAYOFFS				
Season Team	League	Gms.	G	A	Pts.	PIM	+/-	PP	SH		Gms.	G	A	Pts.	PIM
95-96—Dukla Trencin Jrs.	Slovakia Jrs.	53	42	49	91	26	...	...	...		—	—	—	—	—
96-97—Dukla Trencin	Slovakia	46	25	19	44	33	...	...	...		7	5	5	10	...
97-98—Ottawa	NHL	7	0	1	1	0	-1	0	0		—	—	—	—	—
—Portland	WHL	53	45	40	85	50	...	...	...		16	13	6	19	6
98-99—Ottawa	NHL	60	15	15	30	37	18	1	0		4	0	2	2	4
99-00—Ottawa	NHL	78	29	27	56	32	5	5	0		6	0	0	0	2
00-01—Ottawa	NHL	81	32	43	75	44	19	11	2		4	1	1	2	4
NHL Totals (4 years)		226	76	86	162	113	41	17	2		14	1	3	4	10

HOULDER, BILL   D   PREDATORS

PERSONAL: Born March 11, 1967, in Thunder Bay, Ont. ... 6-2/211. ... Shoots left. ... Full Name: William Houlder.

TRANSACTIONS/CAREER NOTES: Selected by Washington Capitals in fourth round (fourth Capitals pick, 82nd overall) of NHL entry draft (June 15, 1985). ... Pulled groin (January 1989). ... Traded by Capitals to Buffalo Sabres for D Shawn Anderson (September 30, 1990). ... Selected by Mighty Ducks of Anaheim in NHL expansion draft (June 24, 1993). ... Traded by Mighty Ducks to St. Louis Blues for D Jason Marshall (August 29, 1994). ... Signed as free agent by Tampa Bay Lightning (August 1, 1995). ... Strained groin (October 7, 1995); missed two games. ... Injured ribs (November 8, 1995); missed four games. ... Strained groin (February 3, 1996); missed three games. ... Reinjured groin (March 5, 1996); missed six games ... Reinjured groin (March 26, 1996); missed five games. ... Bruised wrist (November 4, 1996); missed three games. ... Signed as free agent by San Jose Sharks (July 9, 1997). ... Injured knee (March 6, 1999); missed five games. ... Traded by Sharks with D Andrei Zyuzin, LW Shawn Burr and C Steve Guolla to Lightning for LW Niklas Sundstrom and third-round pick (traded to Chicago) in 2000 draft (August 4, 1999). ... Claimed on waivers by Nashville Predators (November 10, 1999). ... Suffered concussion (November 11, 1999); missed 11 games. ... Suffered from the flu (October 6, 2000); missed first game of season.

HONORS: Named to AHL All-Star first team (1990-91). ... Won Governors Trophy (1992-93). ... Named to IHL All-Star first team (1992-93).

MISCELLANEOUS: Captain of Tampa Bay Lightning (October 2, 1999-November 9, 1999).

		REGULAR SEASON									PLAYOFFS				
Season Team	League	Gms.	G	A	Pts.	PIM	+/-	PP	SH		Gms.	G	A	Pts.	PIM
83-84—Thunder Bay Beavers	TBAHA	23	4	18	22	37	...	...	...		—	—	—	—	—
84-85—North Bay	OHL	66	4	20	24	37	...	...	...		8	0	0	0	2
85-86—North Bay	OHL	59	5	30	35	97	...	...	...		10	1	6	7	12
86-87—North Bay	OHL	62	17	51	68	68	...	...	...		22	4	19	23	20
87-88—Washington	NHL	30	1	2	3	10	-2	0	0		—	—	—	—	—
—Fort Wayne	IHL	43	10	14	24	32	...	...	...		—	—	—	—	—
88-89—Baltimore	AHL	65	10	36	46	50	...	...	...		—	—	—	—	—
—Washington	NHL	8	0	3	3	4	7	0	0		—	—	—	—	—
89-90—Baltimore	AHL	26	3	7	10	12	...	...	...		7	0	2	2	4
—Washington	NHL	41	1	11	12	28	8	0	0		—	—	—	—	—
90-91—Rochester	AHL	69	13	53	66	28	...	...	...		15	5	13	18	4
—Buffalo	NHL	7	0	2	2	4	-2	0	0		—	—	—	—	—
91-92—Rochester	AHL	42	8	26	34	16	...	...	...		16	5	6	11	4
—Buffalo	NHL	10	1	0	1	8	-2	0	0		—	—	—	—	—
92-93—San Diego	IHL	64	24	48	72	39	...	...	...		—	—	—	—	—
—Buffalo	NHL	15	3	5	8	6	5	0	0		8	0	2	2	4
93-94—Anaheim	NHL	80	14	25	39	40	-18	3	0		—	—	—	—	—
94-95—St. Louis	NHL	41	5	13	18	20	16	1	0		4	1	1	2	0
95-96—Tampa Bay	NHL	61	5	23	28	22	1	3	0		6	0	1	1	4
96-97—Tampa Bay	NHL	79	4	21	25	30	16	0	0		—	—	—	—	—
97-98—San Jose	NHL	82	7	25	32	48	13	4	0		6	1	2	3	2
98-99—San Jose	NHL	76	9	23	32	40	8	7	0		6	3	0	3	4
99-00—Tampa Bay	NHL	14	1	2	3	2	-3	1	0		—	—	—	—	—
—Nashville	NHL	57	2	12	14	24	-6	1	0		—	—	—	—	—
00-01—Nashville	NHL	81	4	12	16	40	-7	0	1		—	—	—	—	—
NHL Totals (14 years)		682	57	179	236	326	34	20	1		30	5	6	11	14

HOUSE, BOBBY   RW   MAPLE LEAFS

H

PERSONAL: Born January 7, 1973, in Whitehorse, Yukon. ... 6-1/210. ... Shoots right. ... Name pronounced HOUZ.

TRANSACTIONS/CAREER NOTES: Selected by Chicago Blackhawks in third round (fourth Blackhawks pick, 66th overall) of NHL entry draft (June 22, 1991). ... Traded by Blackhawks to New Jersey Devils for cash considerations (May 21, 1996). ... Signed as free agent by Toronto Maple Leafs (July 23, 1999).

HONORS: Named to WHL (East) All-Star second team (1992-93). ... Named to AHL All-Star second team (2000-01).

Season Team	League	REGULAR SEASON								PLAYOFFS				
		Gms.	G	A	Pts.	PIM	+/-	PP	SH	Gms.	G	A	Pts.	PIM
88-89—Houjens	YUKON SR.	28	36	27	63	28	...	...	...	—	—	—	—	—
89-90—Spokane..................	WHL	64	18	16	34	74	...	...	...	5	0	0	0	6
90-91—Spokane..................	WHL	38	11	19	30	63	...	...	...	—	—	—	—	—
—Brandon..................	WHL	23	18	7	25	14	...	...	...	—	—	—	—	—
91-92—Brandon..................	WHL	71	35	42	77	133	...	...	...	—	—	—	—	—
92-93—Brandon..................	WHL	61	57	39	96	87	...	...	...	4	2	2	4	0
93-94—Indianapolis	IHL	42	10	8	18	51	...	...	...	—	—	—	—	—
—Flint............................	Col.HL	4	3	3	6	0	...	...	...	—	—	—	—	—
94-95—Indianapolis	IHL	26	2	3	5	26	...	...	...	—	—	—	—	—
—Columbus	ECHL	9	11	6	17	2	...	...	...	—	—	—	—	—
—Albany......................	AHL	26	4	7	11	12	...	...	...	8	1	1	2	0
95-96—Albany......................	AHL	77	37	49	86	57	...	...	...	4	0	0	0	4
96-97—Albany......................	AHL	68	18	16	34	65	...	...	...	16	3	2	5	23
97-98—Albany......................	AHL	19	10	10	20	10	...	...	...	—	—	—	—	—
—Quebec	IHL	24	5	7	12	12	...	...	...	—	—	—	—	—
—Hershey	AHL	20	2	6	8	8	...	...	...	—	—	—	—	—
—Syracuse	AHL	9	5	6	11	6	...	...	...	5	2	0	2	4
98-99—Augusta	ECHL	5	1	0	1	15	...	...	...	—	—	—	—	—
—Albany......................	AHL	1	0	0	0	0	...	...	...	—	—	—	—	—
—Springfield	AHL	56	11	18	29	27	...	...	...	3	1	0	1	2
99-00—St. John's.................	AHL	68	24	29	53	46	...	...	...	—	—	—	—	—
00-01—St. John's.................	AHL	65	36	33	69	49	...	...	...	—	—	—	—	—

HOUSLEY, PHIL   D   FLAMES

PERSONAL: Born March 9, 1964, in St. Paul, Minn. ... 5-10/185. ... Shoots left. ... Full Name: Phil F. Housley.

TRANSACTIONS/CAREER NOTES: Selected by Buffalo Sabres in first round (first Sabres pick, sixth overall) of NHL entry draft (June 9, 1982). ... Bruised shoulder (January 1984). ... Suspended three games by NHL (October 1984). ... Injured back (November 1987). ... Bruised back (January 12, 1989). ... Suffered hip pointer and bruised back (March 18, 1989). ... Pulled shoulder ligaments while playing at World Cup Tournament (April 1989). ... Traded by Sabres with LW Scott Arniel, RW Jeff Parker and first-round pick (C Keith Tkachuk) in 1990 draft to Winnipeg Jets for C Dale Hawerchuk and first-round pick (LW Brad May) in 1990 draft (June 16, 1990). ... Strained abdominal muscle (February 26, 1992); missed five games. ... Strained groin (October 31, 1992); missed two games. ... Sprained wrist (January 19, 1993); missed two games. ... Traded by Jets to St. Louis Blues for RW Nelson Emerson and D Stephane Quintal (September 24, 1993). ... Suffered back spasms (October 26, 1993); missed five games. ... Suffered sore back (November 18, 1993). ... Underwent back surgery (January 4, 1994); missed 53 games. ... Traded by Blues with second-round picks in 1996 (C Steve Begin) and 1997 (RW John Tripp) drafts to Calgary Flames for free-agent rights to D Al MacInnis and fourth-round pick (D Didier Tremblay) in 1997 draft (July 4, 1994). ... Played in Europe during 1994-95 NHL lockout. ... Injured right pinky (February 9, 1995); missed five games. ... Suffered from the flu (January 10, 1996); missed two games. ... Suffered from the flu (January 17, 1996); missed one game. ... Traded by Flames with D Dan Keczmer to New Jersey Devils for D Tommy Albelin, D Cale Hulse and LW Jocelyn Lemieux (February 26, 1996). ... Signed as free agent by Washington Capitals (July 22, 1996). ... Strained groin (March 16, 1997); missed five games. ... Fractured finger (March 7, 1998); missed 10 games. ... Claimed on waivers by Flames (July 21, 1998). ... Injured abdomen (February 19, 1999); missed one game. ... Injured foot (November 12, 2000); missed one game. ... Suffered concussion (November 18, 2000); missed three games. ... Suffered concussion (December 13, 2000); missed nine games.

HONORS: Named to NHL All-Rookie team (1982-83). ... Played in NHL All-Star Game (1984, 1989-1993 and 2000). ... Named to The Sporting News All-Star second team (1991-92). ... Named to NHL All-Star second team (1991-92).

MISCELLANEOUS: Failed to score on a penalty shot (vs. Curtis Joseph, December 19, 1992). ... Member of Team U.S.A. at World Junior Championships and World Cup Tournament (1982).

STATISTICAL PLATEAUS: Three-goal games: 1982-83 (1), 1987-88 (1). Total: 2.

Season Team	League	REGULAR SEASON								PLAYOFFS				
		Gms.	G	A	Pts.	PIM	+/-	PP	SH	Gms.	G	A	Pts.	PIM
80-81—St. Paul's	USHL	6	7	7	14	6	...	...	...	—	—	—	—	—
81-82—South St. Paul H.S......	Minn. H.S.	22	31	34	65	18	...	...	...	—	—	—	—	—
82-83—Buffalo	NHL	77	19	47	66	39	-4	11	0	10	3	4	7	2
83-84—Buffalo	NHL	75	31	46	77	33	4	13	2	3	0	0	0	6
84-85—Buffalo	NHL	73	16	53	69	28	15	3	0	5	3	2	5	2
85-86—Buffalo	NHL	79	15	47	62	54	-9	7	0	—	—	—	—	—
86-87—Buffalo	NHL	78	21	46	67	57	-2	8	1	—	—	—	—	—
87-88—Buffalo	NHL	74	29	37	66	96	-17	6	0	6	2	4	6	6
88-89—Buffalo	NHL	72	26	44	70	47	6	5	0	5	1	3	4	2
89-90—Buffalo	NHL	80	21	60	81	32	11	8	1	6	1	4	5	4
90-91—Winnipeg	NHL	78	23	53	76	24	-13	12	1	—	—	—	—	—
91-92—Winnipeg	NHL	74	23	63	86	92	-5	11	0	7	1	4	5	0
92-93—Winnipeg	NHL	80	18	79	97	52	-14	6	0	6	0	7	7	2
93-94—St. Louis	NHL	26	7	15	22	12	-5	4	0	4	2	1	3	4
94-95—Grasshoppers	Switz. Div. 2	10	6	8	14	34	...	...	...	—	—	—	—	—
—Calgary	NHL	43	8	35	43	18	17	3	0	7	0	9	9	0
95-96—Calgary	NHL	59	16	36	52	22	-2	6	0	—	—	—	—	—
—New Jersey	NHL	22	1	15	16	8	-4	0	0	—	—	—	—	—
96-97—Washington	NHL	77	11	29	40	24	-10	3	1	—	—	—	—	—
97-98—Washington	NHL	64	6	25	31	24	-10	4	1	18	0	4	4	4
98-99—Calgary	NHL	79	11	43	54	52	14	4	0	—	—	—	—	—
99-00—Calgary	NHL	78	11	44	55	24	-12	5	0	—	—	—	—	—
00-01—Calgary	NHL	69	4	30	34	24	-15	0	0	—	—	—	—	—
NHL Totals (19 years).........		1357	317	847	1164	762	-55	119	7	77	13	42	55	32

H

HRDINA, JAN   C   PENGUINS

PERSONAL: Born February 5, 1976, in Hradec Kralove, Czechoslovakia. ... 6-0/200. ... Shoots right. ... Name pronounced YAHN huhr-DEE-nuh.
TRANSACTIONS/CAREER NOTES: Selected by Pittsburgh Penguins in fifth round (fourth Penguins pick, 128th overall) of NHL entry draft (July 8, 1995). ... Sprained ankle (October 14, 1999); missed 12 games. ... Strained groin (December 5, 2000); missed three games. ... Bruised hip (January 12, 2001); missed one game.

		REGULAR SEASON								PLAYOFFS				
Season Team	League	Gms.	G	A	Pts.	PIM	+/-	PP	SH	Gms.	G	A	Pts.	PIM
93-94—Std.Hradec Kralove.....	Czech Rep.	21	1	5	6	...	...	...	...	—	—	—	—	—
94-95—Seattle......................	WHL	69	41	59	100	79	...	...	...	4	0	1	1	8
95-96—Seattle......................	WHL	30	19	28	47	37	...	...	...	—	—	—	—	—
—Spokane......................	WHL	18	10	16	26	25	...	...	...	18	5	14	19	49
96-97—Cleveland	IHL	68	23	31	54	82	...	...	...	13	1	2	3	8
97-98—Syracuse	AHL	72	20	24	44	82	...	...	...	5	1	3	4	10
98-99—Pittsburgh..................	NHL	82	13	29	42	40	-2	3	0	13	4	1	5	12
99-00—Pittsburgh..................	NHL	70	13	33	46	43	13	3	0	9	4	8	12	2
00-01—Pittsburgh..................	NHL	78	15	28	43	48	19	3	0	18	2	5	7	8
NHL Totals (3 years)...........		230	41	90	131	131	30	9	0	40	10	14	24	22

HRKAC, TONY   C   THRASHERS

PERSONAL: Born July 7, 1966, in Thunder Bay, Ont. ... 5-11/170. ... Shoots left. ... Full Name: Anthony J. Hrkac. ... Name pronounced HUHR-kuhz.
TRANSACTIONS/CAREER NOTES: Selected by St. Louis Blues as underage junior in second round (second Blues pick, 32nd overall) of NHL entry draft (June 9, 1984). ... Bruised left leg (January 1987). ... Sprained shoulder (January 12, 1988). ... Lacerated ankle (March 1988). ... Bruised left shoulder (November 28, 1989). ... Traded by Blues with G Greg Millen to Quebec Nordiques for D Jeff Brown (December 13, 1989). ... Traded by Nordiques to San Jose Sharks for RW Greg Paslawski (May 30, 1991). ... Injured wrist during preseason (September 1991); missed first 27 games of season. ... Traded by Sharks to Chicago Blackhawks for future considerations (February 7, 1992). ... Signed as free agent by Blues (July 30, 1993). ... Signed as free agent by Dallas Stars (July 25, 1997). ... Claimed on waivers by Edmonton Oilers (January 6, 1998). ... Traded by Oilers with D Bobby Dollas to Pittsburgh Penguins for LW Josef Beranek (June 16, 1998). ... Selected by Nashville Predators in NHL expansion draft (June 26, 1998). ... Traded by Predators to Stars for future considerations (July 9, 1998). ... Signed as free agent by New York Islanders (July 29, 1999). ... Traded by Islanders with D Dean Malkoc to Mighty Ducks of Anaheim for C/LW Ted Drury (October 29, 1999). ... Signed as free agent by Atlanta Thrashers (July 16, 2001).
HONORS: Won Hobey Baker Memorial Award (1986-87). ... Won WCHA Most Valuable Player Award (1986-87). ... Named NCAA Tournament Most Valuable Player (1986-87). ... Named to NCAA All-America (West) first team (1986-87). ... Named to WCHA All-Star first team (1986-87). ... Named to NCAA All-Tournament team (1986-87). ... Won James Gatschene Memorial Trophy (1992-93). ... Won Leo P. Lamoureux Memorial Trophy (1992-93). ... Named to IHL All-Star first team (1992-93).
MISCELLANEOUS: Member of Stanley Cup championship team (1999).

		REGULAR SEASON								PLAYOFFS				
Season Team	League	Gms.	G	A	Pts.	PIM	+/-	PP	SH	Gms.	G	A	Pts.	PIM
83-84—Orillia	OHA	42	*52	54	*106	20	...	...	...	—	—	—	—	—
84-85—Univ. of North Dakota .	WCHA	36	18	36	54	16	...	...	...	—	—	—	—	—
85-86—Canadian nat'l team	Int'l	62	19	30	49	36	...	...	...	—	—	—	—	—
86-87—Univ. of North Dakota .	WCHA	48	46	*70	*116	48	...	...	...	—	—	—	—	—
—St. Louis	NHL	—	—	—	—	—	—	—	—	3	0	0	0	0
87-88—St. Louis	NHL	67	11	37	48	22	5	2	1	10	6	1	7	4
88-89—St. Louis	NHL	70	17	28	45	8	-10	5	0	4	1	1	2	0
89-90—St. Louis	NHL	28	5	12	17	8	1	1	0	—	—	—	—	—
—Quebec	NHL	22	4	8	12	2	-5	2	0	—	—	—	—	—
—Halifax	AHL	20	12	21	33	4	...	...	...	6	5	9	14	4
90-91—Halifax	AHL	3	4	1	5	2	...	...	...	—	—	—	—	—
—Quebec	NHL	70	16	32	48	16	-22	6	0	—	—	—	—	—
91-92—San Jose	NHL	22	2	10	12	4	-2	0	0	—	—	—	—	—
—Chicago	NHL	18	1	2	3	6	4	0	0	3	0	0	0	2
92-93—Indianapolis	IHL	80	45	*87	*132	70	...	...	...	5	0	2	2	2
93-94—St. Louis	NHL	36	6	5	11	8	-11	1	1	4	0	0	0	0
—Peoria	IHL	45	30	51	81	25	...	...	...	1	1	2	3	0
94-95—Milwaukee	IHL	71	24	67	91	26	...	...	...	15	4	9	13	16
95-96—Milwaukee	IHL	43	14	28	42	18	...	...	...	5	1	3	4	4
96-97—Milwaukee	IHL	81	27	61	88	20	...	...	...	3	1	1	2	2
97-98—Michigan	IHL	20	7	15	22	6	...	...	...	—	—	—	—	—
—Dallas	NHL	13	5	3	8	0	0	3	0	—	—	—	—	—
—Edmonton	NHL	36	8	11	19	10	3	4	0	12	0	3	3	2
98-99—Dallas	NHL	69	13	14	27	26	2	2	0	5	0	2	2	4
99-00—New York Islanders.....	NHL	7	0	2	2	0	-1	0	0	—	—	—	—	—
—Anaheim	NHL	60	4	7	11	8	-2	1	0	—	—	—	—	—
00-01—Anaheim	NHL	80	13	25	38	29	0	0	0	—	—	—	—	—
NHL Totals (11 years).........		598	105	196	301	147	-38	27	2	41	7	7	14	12

H HUBACEK, PETR   C   FLYERS

PERSONAL: Born September 2, 1979, in Brno, Czechoslovakia. ... 6-2/183. ... Shoots right.
TRANSACTIONS/CAREER NOTES: Selected by Philadelphia Flyers in ninth round (11th Flyers pick, 243rd overall) of NHL entry draft (June 27, 1998).

Season Team	League	REGULAR SEASON								PLAYOFFS				
		Gms.	G	A	Pts.	PIM	+/-	PP	SH	Gms.	G	A	Pts.	PIM
97-98—Brno	Czech. Jrs.	17	9	5	14	...	...	...	...	—	—	—	—	—
—Zetor Brno	Czech. Jrs.	48	6	10	16	...	...	...	...	—	—	—	—	—
98-99—Vitkovice	Czech. Jrs.	25	0	4	4	2	...	...	...	4	0	0	0	...
99-00—Vitkovice	Czech. Jrs.	48	11	12	23	81	...	...	...	—	—	—	—	—
00-01—Philadelphia	AHL	62	3	9	12	29	...	...	...	9	0	1	1	6
—Philadelphia	NHL	6	1	0	1	2	-1	0	0	—	—	—	—	—
NHL Totals (1 year)		6	1	0	1	2	-1	0	0					

HULBIG, JOE   LW

PERSONAL: Born September 29, 1973, in Norwood, Mass. ... 6-3/215. ... Shoots left. ... Name pronounced HUHL-bihg.

TRANSACTIONS/CAREER NOTES: Selected by Edmonton Oilers in first round (first Oilers pick, 13th overall) of NHL entry draft (June 20, 1992). ... Signed as free agent by Boston Bruins (July 19, 1999). ... Strained groin (January 4, 2000); missed remainder of season. ... Suffered concussion (November 5, 2000); missed two games. ... Suffered hernia (November 15, 2000) and underwent surgey; missed 24 games.

Season Team	League	REGULAR SEASON								PLAYOFFS				
		Gms.	G	A	Pts.	PIM	+/-	PP	SH	Gms.	G	A	Pts.	PIM
89-90—St. Sebastian's	USHS (East)	30	13	12	25	...	...	...	...	—	—	—	—	—
90-91—St. Sebastian's	USHS (East)	...	23	19	42	...	...	...	...	—	—	—	—	—
91-92—St. Sebastian's	USHS (East)	17	19	24	43	30	...	...	...	—	—	—	—	—
92-93—Providence College	Hockey East	26	3	13	16	22	...	...	...	—	—	—	—	—
93-94—Providence College	Hockey East	28	6	4	10	36	...	...	...	—	—	—	—	—
94-95—Providence College	Hockey East	37	14	21	35	36	...	...	...	—	—	—	—	—
95-96—Providence College	Hockey East	31	14	22	36	56	...	...	...	—	—	—	—	—
96-97—Hamilton	AHL	73	18	28	46	59	...	...	...	16	6	10	16	6
—Edmonton	NHL	6	0	0	0	0	-1	0	0	6	0	1	1	2
97-98—Edmonton	NHL	17	2	2	4	2	-1	0	0	—	—	—	—	—
—Hamilton	AHL	46	15	16	31	52	...	...	...	3	0	1	1	2
98-99—Hamilton	AHL	76	22	24	46	68	...	...	...	11	4	2	6	18
—Edmonton	NHL	1	0	0	0	2	1	0	0	—	—	—	—	—
99-00—Providence	AHL	15	4	5	9	17	...	...	...	—	—	—	—	—
—Boston	NHL	24	2	2	4	8	-8	0	0	—	—	—	—	—
00-01—Boston	NHL	7	0	0	0	4	-3	0	0	—	—	—	—	—
—Providence	AHL	36	4	11	15	19	...	...	...	15	2	2	4	20
NHL Totals (5 years)		55	4	4	8	16	-12	0	0	6	0	1	1	2

HULL, BRETT   RW

PERSONAL: Born August 9, 1964, in Belleville, Ont. ... 5-11/203. ... Shoots right. ... Full Name: Brett A. Hull. ... Son of Bobby Hull, Hall of Fame left winger with three NHL teams (1957-58 through 1971-72 and 1979-80) and Winnipeg Jets of WHA (1972-73 through 1978-79); and nephew of Dennis Hull, left winger with Chicago Blackhawks (1964-65 through 1976-77) and Detroit Red Wings (1977-78).

TRANSACTIONS/CAREER NOTES: Selected by Calgary Flames in sixth round (sixth Flames pick, 117th overall) of NHL entry draft (June 9, 1984). ... Traded by Flames with LW Steve Bozek to St. Louis Blues for D Rob Ramage and G Rick Wamsley (March 7, 1988). ... Sprained left ankle (January 15, 1991); missed two regular-season games and All-Star Game. ... Suffered back spasms (March 12, 1992); missed seven games. ... Suffered sore wrist (March 20, 1993); missed four games. ... Injured abdominal muscle (October 7, 1993); missed three games. ... Strained groin (November 1, 1995); missed two games. ... Reinjured groin (November 10, 1995); missed five games. ... Injured hamstring (March 28, 1996); missed four games. ... Strained groin (March 30, 1997); missed four games. ... Strained buttocks (December 8, 1997); missed two games. ... Fractured left hand (December 27, 1997); missed 13 games. ... Signed as free agent by Dallas Stars (July 3, 1998). ... Bruised kidney (November 20, 1998); missed two games. ... Strained groin (November 25, 1998); missed one game. ... Reinjured groin (December 2, 1998); missed six games. ... Strained back (January 10, 1999); missed one game. ... Strained hamstring (February 24, 1999); missed 11 games. ... Injured groin (January 12, 2000); missed one game. ... Fractured nose (February 9, 2000); missed one game. ... Strained hip flexor (March 8, 2000); missed one game. ... Strained lower back (December 23, 2000); missed three games.

HONORS: Won WCHA Freshman of the Year Award (1984-85). ... Named to WCHA All-Star first team (1985-86). ... Won Dudley (Red) Garrett Memorial Trophy (1986-87). ... Named to AHL All-Star first team (1986-87). ... Won Lady Byng Memorial Trophy (1989-90). ... Won Dodge Ram Tough Award (1989-90 and 1990-91). ... Named to THE SPORTING NEWS All-Star first team (1989-90 through 1991-92). ... Named to NHL All-Star first team (1989-90 through 1991-92). ... Played in NHL All-Star Game (1989, 1990, 1992-1994, 1996, 1997 and 2001). ... Named NHL Player of the Year by THE SPORTING NEWS (1990-91). ... Won Hart Memorial Trophy (1990-91). ... Won Lester B. Pearson Award (1990-91). ... Won Pro Set NHL Player of the Year Award (1990-91). ... Named All-Star Game Most Valuable Player (1992).

RECORDS: Holds NHL single-season record for most goals by a right winger—86 (1990-91).

STATISTICAL PLATEAUS: Three-goal games: 1987-88 (1), 1989-90 (5), 1990-91 (4), 1991-92 (8), 1993-94 (3), 1994-95 (1), 1995-96 (1), 1996-97 (2), 1997-98 (1), 2000-01 (1). Total: 27. ... Four-goal games: 1994-95 (1), 1995-96 (1), 2000-01 (1). Total: 3. ... Total hat tricks: 30.

MISCELLANEOUS: Member of Stanley Cup championship team (1999). ... Captain of St. Louis Blues (1992-93 through October 22, 1995). ... Holds St. Louis Blues all-time record for most goals (527). ... Failed to score on a penalty shot (vs. Glen Healy, December 31, 1992; vs. Bill Ranford, March 26, 1995; vs. Jeff Hackett, January 4, 1996; vs. Felix Potvin, January 22, 2001). ... Shares distinction with Bobby Hull of being the first father-son duo to win the same NHL trophy (both the Lady Byng Memorial and Hart Memorial trophies).

STATISTICAL NOTES: Became the first son of an NHL 50-goal scorer to score 50 goals in one season (1989-90). ... Tied for NHL lead with 12 game-winning goals (1989-90). ... Led NHL in game-winning goals with 11 (1990-91) and 11 (1998-99).

Season Team	League	REGULAR SEASON								PLAYOFFS				
		Gms.	G	A	Pts.	PIM	+/-	PP	SH	Gms.	G	A	Pts.	PIM
82-83—Penticton	BCJHL	50	48	56	104	27	...	...	...	—	—	—	—	—
83-84—Penticton	BCJHL	56	*105	83	*188	20	...	...	...	—	—	—	—	—
84-85—Minnesota-Duluth	WCHA	48	32	28	60	24	...	...	...	—	—	—	—	—
85-86—Minnesota-Duluth	WCHA	42	*52	32	84	46	...	...	...	—	—	—	—	—
—Calgary	NHL	—	—	—	—	—	...	...	...	2	0	0	0	0
86-87—Moncton	AHL	67	50	42	92	16	...	...	...	3	2	2	4	2
—Calgary	NHL	5	1	0	1	0	-1	0	0	4	2	1	3	0

H

		REGULAR SEASON								PLAYOFFS				
Season Team	League	Gms.	G	A	Pts.	PIM	+/-	PP	SH	Gms.	G	A	Pts.	PIM
87-88—Calgary	NHL	52	26	24	50	12	10	4	0	—	—	—	—	—
—St. Louis	NHL	13	6	8	14	4	4	2	0	10	7	2	9	4
88-89—St. Louis	NHL	78	41	43	84	33	-17	16	0	10	5	5	10	6
89-90—St. Louis	NHL	80	*72	41	113	24	-1	*27	0	12	13	8	21	17
90-91—St. Louis	NHL	78	*86	45	131	22	23	*29	0	13	11	8	19	4
91-92—St. Louis	NHL	73	*70	39	109	48	-2	20	5	6	4	4	8	4
92-93—St. Louis	NHL	80	54	47	101	41	-27	29	0	11	8	5	13	2
93-94—St. Louis	NHL	81	57	40	97	38	-3	†25	3	4	2	1	3	0
94-95—St. Louis	NHL	48	29	21	50	10	13	9	3	7	6	2	8	0
95-96—St. Louis	NHL	70	43	40	83	30	4	16	5	13	6	5	11	10
96-97—St. Louis	NHL	77	42	40	82	10	-9	12	2	6	3	7	9	2
97-98—St. Louis	NHL	66	27	45	72	26	-1	10	0	10	3	3	6	2
—U.S. Olympic team	Int'l	4	2	1	3	0	...	...	...	—	—	—	—	—
98-99—Dallas	NHL	60	32	26	58	30	19	15	0	22	8	7	15	4
99-00—Dallas	NHL	79	24	35	59	43	-21	11	0	23	*11	†13	*24	4
00-01—Dallas	NHL	79	39	40	79	18	10	11	0	10	2	5	7	6
NHL Totals (16 years)		1019	649	534	1183	389	1	236	18	163	90	76	166	65

HULL, JODY — RW

PERSONAL: Born February 2, 1969, in Cambridge, Ont. ... 6-2/195. ... Shoots right.
TRANSACTIONS/CAREER NOTES: Selected by Hartford Whalers in first round (first Whalers pick, 18th overall) of NHL entry draft (June 13, 1987). ... Injured hamstring (March 1989). ... Traded by Whalers to New York Rangers for C Carey Wilson and third-round pick (C Mikael Nylander) in 1991 draft (July 9, 1990). ... Sprained muscle in right hand (October 6, 1990). ... Bruised left big toe (November 19, 1990); missed six games. ... Injured knee (March 13, 1991). ... Traded by Rangers to Ottawa Senators for future considerations (July 28, 1992). ... Injured groin (December 7, 1992); missed three games. ... Suffered concussion (January 10, 1993); missed one game. ... Sprained ankle (January 19, 1993); missed eight games. ... Sprained left ankle (April 1, 1993); missed two games. ... Signed as free agent by Florida Panthers (August 10, 1993). ... Bruised right shoulder (February 1, 1994); missed one game. ... Separated right shoulder (March 4, 1994); missed three games. ... Separated right shoulder (March 18, 1994); missed six games. ... Suffered viral illness (February 1, 1995); missed two games. ... Fractured rib (October 28, 1995); missed four games. ... Suffered back spasms (May 5, 1996); missed four playoff games. ... Fractured left wrist (December 20, 1997); missed 13 games. ... Traded by Panthers with G Mark Fitzpatrick to Tampa Bay Lightning for RW Dino Ciccarelli and D Jeff Norton (January 15, 1998). ... Injured ankle (February 2, 1998); missed two games. ... Injured knee (April 2, 1998); missed three games. ... Signed as free agent by Philadelphia Flyers (October 7, 1998). ... Strained groin (October 31, 1998); missed two games. ... Suffered concussion (December 20, 1998); missed one game. ... Suffered post-concussion syndrome (December 26, 1998); missed four games. ... Sprained left knee (April 8, 1999); missed two games. ... Selected by Atlanta Thrashers in NHL expansion draft (June 25, 1999). ... Traded by Thrashers to Flyers for future considerations (October 15, 1999). ... Sprained medial collateral ligament in left knee (January 27, 2000); missed 10 games. ... Sprained shoulder (September 27, 2000); missed first eight games of season. ... Bruised left foot (November 9, 2000); missed two games.
HONORS: Named to OHL All-Star second team (1987-88).
STATISTICAL PLATEAUS: Three-goal games: 1988-89 (1).

		REGULAR SEASON								PLAYOFFS				
Season Team	League	Gms.	G	A	Pts.	PIM	+/-	PP	SH	Gms.	G	A	Pts.	PIM
84-85—Cambridge Jr. B	OHA	38	13	17	30	39	...	...	...					
85-86—Peterborough	OHL	61	20	22	42	29	...	...	...	16	1	5	6	4
86-87—Peterborough	OHL	49	18	34	52	22	...	...	...	12	4	9	13	14
87-88—Peterborough	OHL	60	50	44	94	33	...	...	...	12	10	8	18	8
88-89—Hartford	NHL	60	16	18	34	10	6	6	0	1	0	0	0	2
89-90—Binghamton	AHL	21	7	10	17	6	...	...	...	—	—	—	—	—
—Hartford	NHL	38	7	10	17	21	-6	2	0	5	0	1	1	2
90-91—New York Rangers	NHL	47	5	8	13	10	2	0	0	—	—	—	—	—
91-92—New York Rangers	NHL	3	0	0	0	2	-4	0	0	—	—	—	—	—
—Binghamton	AHL	69	34	31	65	28	...	...	...	11	5	2	7	4
92-93—Ottawa	NHL	69	13	21	34	14	-24	5	1	—	—	—	—	—
93-94—Florida	NHL	69	13	13	26	8	6	0	1	—	—	—	—	—
94-95—Florida	NHL	46	11	8	19	8	-1	0	0	—	—	—	—	—
95-96—Florida	NHL	78	20	17	37	25	5	2	0	14	3	2	5	0
96-97—Florida	NHL	67	10	6	16	4	1	0	1	5	0	0	0	0
97-98—Florida	NHL	21	2	0	2	4	1	0	1	—	—	—	—	—
—Tampa Bay	NHL	28	2	4	6	4	2	0	0	—	—	—	—	—
98-99—Philadelphia	NHL	72	3	11	14	12	-2	0	0	6	0	0	0	4
99-00—Orlando	IHL	1	0	0	0	0	...	...	...	—	—	—	—	—
—Philadelphia	NHL	67	10	3	13	4	8	0	2	18	0	1	1	0
00-01—Philadelphia	NHL	71	7	8	15	10	-1	0	2	6	0	0	0	4
NHL Totals (13 years)		736	119	127	246	136	-7	15	8	55	3	4	7	12

HULSE, CALE — D — PREDATORS

PERSONAL: Born November 10, 1973, in Edmonton. ... 6-3/215. ... Shoots right. ... Name pronounced HUHLZ.
TRANSACTIONS/CAREER NOTES: Selected by New Jersey Devils in third round (third Devils pick, 66th overall) of NHL entry draft (June 20, 1992). ... Traded by Devils with D Tommy Albelin and RW Jocelyn Lemieux to Calgary Flames for D Phil Housley and D Dan Keczmer (February 26, 1996). ... Bruised ankle (February 28, 1997); missed four games. ... Reinjured ankle (March 7, 1997); missed one game. ... Reinjured ankle (March 21, 1997); missed one game. ... Suffered bruised ribs (April 1, 1999); missed six games. ... Fractured hand (September 18, 1999); missed first four games of season. ... Sprained ankle (February 23, 2000); missed nine games. ... Traded by Flames with third-round pick (C/LW Denis Platonov) in 2001 draft to Nashville Predators for RW Sergei Krivokrasov (March 14, 2000); missed Predators final 12 games due to sprained ankle.

H

Season Team	League	REGULAR SEASON								PLAYOFFS				
		Gms.	G	A	Pts.	PIM	+/-	PP	SH	Gms.	G	A	Pts.	PIM
90-91—Calgary Royals	AJHL	49	3	23	26	220	...	...	...	—	—	—	—	—
91-92—Portland	WHL	70	4	18	22	250	...	...	...	6	0	2	2	27
92-93—Portland	WHL	72	10	26	36	284	...	...	...	16	4	4	8	*65
93-94—Albany	AHL	79	7	14	21	186	...	...	...	5	0	3	3	11
94-95—Albany	AHL	77	5	13	18	215	...	...	...	12	1	1	2	17
95-96—Albany	AHL	42	4	23	27	107	...	...	...	—	—	—	—	—
—New Jersey	NHL	8	0	0	0	15	-2	0	0	—	—	—	—	—
—Saint John	AHL	13	2	7	9	39	...	...	...	—	—	—	—	—
—Calgary	NHL	3	0	0	0	5	3	0	0	1	0	0	0	0
96-97—Calgary	NHL	63	1	6	7	91	-2	0	1	—	—	—	—	—
97-98—Calgary	NHL	79	5	22	27	169	1	1	1	—	—	—	—	—
98-99—Calgary	NHL	73	3	9	12	117	-8	0	0	—	—	—	—	—
99-00—Calgary	NHL	47	1	6	7	47	-11	0	0	—	—	—	—	—
00-01—Nashville	NHL	82	1	7	8	128	-5	0	0	—	—	—	—	—
NHL Totals (6 years)		355	11	50	61	572	-24	1	2	1	0	0	0	0

HURLBUT, MIKE   D   SABRES

PERSONAL: Born July 10, 1966, in Massena, N.Y. ... 6-2/200. ... Shoots left. ... Full Name: Michael Ray Hurlbut.
TRANSACTIONS/CAREER NOTES: Selected by New York Rangers in NHL supplemental draft (June 10, 1988). ... Sprained left knee (January 25, 1993); missed 13 games. ... Traded by Rangers to Quebec Nordiques for D Alexander Karpovtsev (September 9, 1993). ... Nordiques franchise moved to Colorado and renamed Avalanche for 1995-96 season (June 21, 1995). ... Signed as free agent by Buffalo Sabres (August 11, 1997).
HONORS: Named to NCAA All-America (East) first team (1988-89). ... Named to ECAC All-Star first team (1988-89). ... Named to AHL All-Star second team (1994-95).

Season Team	League	REGULAR SEASON								PLAYOFFS				
		Gms.	G	A	Pts.	PIM	+/-	PP	SH	Gms.	G	A	Pts.	PIM
84-85—Northwood School	N.Y. H.S.	34	20	27	47	30	...	...	...	—	—	—	—	—
85-86—St. Lawrence Univ.	ECAC	25	2	10	12	40	...	...	...	—	—	—	—	—
86-87—St. Lawrence Univ.	ECAC	35	8	15	23	44	...	...	...	—	—	—	—	—
87-88—St. Lawrence Univ.	ECAC	38	6	12	18	18	...	...	...	—	—	—	—	—
88-89—St. Lawrence Univ.	ECAC	36	8	25	33	30	...	...	...	—	—	—	—	—
—Denver	IHL	8	0	2	2	13	...	...	...	4	1	2	3	2
89-90—Flint	IHL	74	3	34	37	38	...	...	...	3	0	1	1	2
90-91—Binghamton	AHL	33	2	11	13	27	...	...	...	3	0	1	1	0
—San Diego	IHL	2	1	0	1	0	...	...	...	—	—	—	—	—
91-92—Binghamton	AHL	79	16	39	55	64	...	...	...	11	2	7	9	8
92-93—Binghamton	AHL	46	11	25	36	46	...	...	...	14	2	5	7	12
—New York Rangers	NHL	23	1	8	9	16	4	1	0	—	—	—	—	—
93-94—Cornwall	AHL	77	13	33	46	100	...	...	...	13	3	7	10	12
—Quebec	NHL	1	0	0	0	0	-1	0	0	—	—	—	—	—
94-95—Cornwall	AHL	74	11	49	60	69	...	...	...	3	1	0	1	15
95-96—Houston	IHL	38	3	12	15	33	...	...	...	—	—	—	—	—
—Minnesota	IHL	22	1	4	5	22	...	...	...	—	—	—	—	—
96-97—Houston	IHL	70	11	24	35	62	...	...	...	13	5	8	13	12
97-98—Buffalo	NHL	3	0	0	0	2	-1	0	0	—	—	—	—	—
—Rochester	AHL	45	10	20	30	48	...	...	...	4	1	1	2	2
98-99—Rochester	AHL	72	15	39	54	46	...	...	...	20	4	5	9	12
—Buffalo	NHL	1	0	0	0	0	2	0	0	—	—	—	—	—
99-00—Rochester	AHL	74	10	29	39	83	...	...	...	21	5	6	11	14
—Buffalo	NHL	1	0	0	0	2	1	0	0	—	—	—	—	—
00-01—Rochester	AHL	53	6	26	32	36	...	...	...	4	1	0	1	6
NHL Totals (5 years)		29	1	8	9	20	5	1	0	—	—	—	—	—

HURME, JANI   G   SENATORS

PERSONAL: Born January 7, 1975, in Turku, Finland. ... 6-0/187. ... Catches left. ... Name pronounced hoor-MAY.
TRANSACTIONS/CAREER NOTES: Selected by Ottawa Senators in third round (second Senators pick, 58th overall) of NHL entry draft (June 21, 1997). ... Injured right knee (February 27, 2001); missed six games.
HONORS: Named to IHL All-Star second team (1999-2000).

Season Team	League	REGULAR SEASON								PLAYOFFS						
		Gms.	Min	W	L	T	GA	SO	Avg.	Gms.	Min.	W	L	GA	SO	Avg.
92-93—TPS Turku	Finland Jrs.	12	669	...	...	...	47	0	4.22	1	60	...	...	...	11	...
93-94—TPS Turku	Finland	1	2	...	...	...	0	0		—	—	—	—	—	—	—
—Kiekko-67 Turku	Fin. Div. 2	3	190	...	...	...	7	0	2.21	—	—	—	—	—	—	—
—Kiekko-67 Turku	Finland Jrs.	18	...	...	...	...	...	...	...							
94-95—Kiekko-67 Turku	Fin. Div. 2	19	1049	...	...	...	53	0	3.03	3	180	...	...	...	6	2.00
—TPS Turku	Finland Jrs.	2	125	...	...	...	5	0	2.40	—						
—Kiekko-67 Turku	Finland Jrs.	9	540	...	...	...	47	...	5.22	—						
95-96—TPS Turku	Finland	16	945	...	...	...	34	2	2.16	10	545	...	...	...	22	2.42
—Kiekko-67 Turku	Fin. Div. 2	16	968	...	...	...	39	1	2.42	—						
—TPS Turku.	Finland Jrs.	13	777	...	...	...	34	1	2.63	—						
96-97—TPS Turku	Finland	48	2917	31	11	6	101	6	2.08	12	722	...	...	...	39	3.24
97-98—Detroit	IHL	6	290	2	2	‡2	20	0	4.14	—						
—Indianapolis	IHL	29	1506	11	11	‡3	83	...	3.31	3	130	1	0	10	0	4.62
98-99—Detroit	IHL	12	643	7	3	‡1	26	1	2.43	—						
—Cincinnati	IHL	26	1428	14	9	‡2	81	0	3.40	—						

H

Season Team	League	REGULAR SEASON								PLAYOFFS						
		Gms.	Min	W	L	T	GA	SO	Avg.	Gms.	Min.	W	L	GA	SO	Avg.
99-00—Grand Rapids	IHL	52	2948	35	15	‡4	107	4	2.18	*17	*1028	*10	*7	*37	1	2.16
—Ottawa	NHL	1	60	1	0	0	2	0	2.00	—	—	—	—	—	—	—
00-01—Ottawa	NHL	22	1296	12	5	4	54	2	2.50	—	—	—	—	—	—	—
NHL Totals (2 years)		23	1356	13	5	4	56	2	2.48							

HUSELIUS, KRISTIAN — LW — PANTHERS

PERSONAL: Born November 10, 1978, in Stockholm, Sweden. ... 6-1/183. ... Shoots left.

TRANSACTIONS/CAREER NOTES: Selected by Florida Panthers in second round (second Panthers pick, 47th overall) of NHL entry draft (June 21, 1997).

Season Team	League	REGULAR SEASON								PLAYOFFS				
		Gms.	G	A	Pts.	PIM	+/-	PP	SH	Gms.	G	A	Pts.	PIM
94-95—Hammarby	Sweden Jr.	17	6	2	8	2	...	...	...	—	—	—	—	—
95-96—Hammarby	Sweden Jr.	25	13	8	21	14	...	...	...	—	—	—	—	—
—Hammarby	Sweden Dv. 2	6	1	0	1	0	...	...	...	—	—	—	—	—
96-97—Farjestad Karlstad	Sweden	13	2	0	2	4	...	...	...	5	1	0	1	0
97-98—Farjestad Karlstad	Sweden	34	2	1	3	2	...	...	...	11	0	0	0	0
98-99—Farjestad Karlstad	Sweden	28	4	4	8	4	...	...	...	—	—	—	—	—
—Vastra Frolunda	Sweden	20	2	2	4	2	...	...	...	4	1	0	1	0
99-00—Vastra Frolunda	Sweden	50	21	23	44	20	...	...	...	5	2	2	4	8
00-01—Vastra Frolunda	Sweden	49	*32	*35	*67	26	...	...	...	5	4	5	9	14

IGINLA, JAROME — RW — FLAMES

PERSONAL: Born July 1, 1977, in Edmonton. ... 6-1/202. ... Shoots right. ... Name pronounced ih-GIHN-luh.

TRANSACTIONS/CAREER NOTES: Selected by Dallas Stars in first round (first Stars pick, 11th overall) of NHL entry draft (July 8, 1995). ... Traded by Stars with C Corey Millen to Calgary Flames for C Joe Nieuwendyk (December 19, 1995). ... Fractured bone in right hand (January 21, 1998); missed 10 games. ... Missed first three games of 1999-2000 season due to contract dispute. ... Bruised knee (March 22, 2000); missed two games. ... Injured knee (December 13, 2000); missed one game. ... Fractured wrist (March 31, 2001); missed remainder of season.

HONORS: Won George Parsons Trophy (1994-95). ... Won Four Broncos Memorial Trophy (1995-96). ... Named to Can.HL All-Star first team (1995-96). ... Named to WHL (West) All-Star first team (1995-96). ... Named to NHL All-Rookie team (1996-97).

STATISTICAL NOTES: Tied for NHL lead in game-tying goals with three (2000-01).

Season Team	League	REGULAR SEASON								PLAYOFFS				
		Gms.	G	A	Pts.	PIM	+/-	PP	SH	Gms.	G	A	Pts.	PIM
93-94—Kamloops	WHL	48	6	23	29	33	...	...	...	19	3	6	9	10
94-95—Kamloops	WHL	72	33	38	71	111	...	...	...	21	7	11	18	34
95-96—Kamloops	WHL	63	63	73	136	120	...	...	...	16	16	13	29	44
—Calgary	NHL	—	—	—	—	—	—	—	—	2	1	1	2	0
96-97—Calgary	NHL	82	21	29	50	37	-4	8	1	—	—	—	—	—
97-98—Calgary	NHL	70	13	19	32	29	-10	0	2	—	—	—	—	—
98-99—Calgary	NHL	82	28	23	51	58	1	7	0	—	—	—	—	—
99-00—Calgary	NHL	77	29	34	63	26	0	12	0	—	—	—	—	—
00-01—Calgary	NHL	77	31	40	71	62	-2	10	0	—	—	—	—	—
NHL Totals (6 years)		388	122	145	267	212	-15	37	3	2	1	1	2	0

IRBE, ARTURS — G — HURRICANES

PERSONAL: Born February 2, 1967, in Riga, U.S.S.R. ... 5-8/190. ... Catches left. ... Name pronounced AHR-tuhrs UHR-bay.

TRANSACTIONS/CAREER NOTES: Selected by Minnesota North Stars in 10th round (11th North Stars pick, 196th overall) of NHL entry draft (June 17, 1989). ... Selected by San Jose Sharks in NHL dispersal draft (May 30, 1991). ... Sprained knee (November 27, 1992); missed 19 games. ... Injured foot (February 15, 1995); missed one game. ... Injured knee (January 17, 1996); remainder of season. ... Signed as free agent by Dallas Stars (July 22, 1996). ... Strained groin (November 8, 1996); missed six games. ... Signed as free agent by Vancouver Canucks (August 5, 1997). ... Signed as free agent by Carolina Hurricanes (September 10, 1998).

HONORS: Named Soviet League Rookie of the Year (1987-88). ... Shared James Norris Memorial Trophy with Wade Flaherty (1991-92). ... Named to IHL All-Star first team (1991-92). ... Played in NHL All-Star Game (1994 and 1999).

MISCELLANEOUS: Holds San Jose Sharks all-time records for most games played by goalie (183) and most wins (57). ... Holds Carolina Hurricanes franchise all-time records for goals-against average (2.38) and most shutouts (17). ... Holds Vancouver Canucks all-time record for goals-against average (2.73). ... Stopped a penalty shot attempt (vs. Kevyn Adams, February 14, 2000). ... Allowed a penalty shot goal (vs. Mats Sundin, March 15, 1995; vs. Igor Larionov, November 22, 1995; vs. Hnat Domenichelli, February 27, 1998; vs. Ray Ferraro, February 21, 2001; vs. Joe Sacco, March 30, 2001).

Season Team	League	REGULAR SEASON								PLAYOFFS						
		Gms.	Min	W	L	T	GA	SO	Avg.	Gms.	Min.	W	L	GA	SO	Avg.
86-87—Dynamo Riga	USSR	2	27	...	...	...	1	0	2.22	—	—	—	—	—	—	—
87-88—Dynamo Riga	USSR	34	1870	...	...	...	84	0	2.70	—	—	—	—	—	—	—
88-89—Dynamo Riga	USSR	41	2460	...	...	...	117	0	2.85	—	—	—	—	—	—	—
89-90—Dynamo Riga	USSR	48	2880	...	...	...	116	0	2.42	—	—	—	—	—	—	—
90-91—Dynamo Riga	USSR	46	2713	...	...	...	133	0	2.94	—	—	—	—	—	—	—
91-92—Kansas City	IHL	32	1955	24	7	‡1	80	0	*2.46	15	914	12	3	44	0	2.89
—San Jose	NHL	13	645	2	6	3	48	0	4.47	—	—	—	—	—	—	—
92-93—Kansas City	IHL	6	364	3	3	0	20	0	3.30	—	—	—	—	—	—	—
—San Jose	NHL	36	2074	7	26	0	142	1	4.11	—	—	—	—	—	—	—
93-94—San Jose	NHL	*74	*4412	30	28	*16	209	3	2.84	14	806	7	7	50	0	3.72
94-95—San Jose	NHL	38	2043	14	19	3	111	4	3.26	6	316	2	4	27	0	5.13

Season Team	League	REGULAR SEASON								PLAYOFFS					
		Gms.	Min	W	L	T	GA	SO	Avg.	Gms.	Min.	W	L	GA	SO	Avg.
95-96—San Jose	NHL	22	1112	4	12	4	85	0	4.59	—	—	—	—	—	—	
—Kansas City	IHL	4	226	1	2	1	16	0	4.25	—	—	—	—	—	—	
96-97—Dallas	NHL	35	1965	17	12	3	88	3	2.69	1	13	0	0	0	0	...
97-98—Vancouver	NHL	41	1999	14	11	6	91	2	2.73	—	—	—	—	—	—	
98-99—Carolina	NHL	62	3643	27	20	12	135	6	2.22	6	408	2	4	15	0	2.21
99-00—Carolina	NHL	*75	4345	34	28	9	*175	5	2.42	—	—	—	—	—	—	
00-01—Carolina	NHL	*77	*4406	37	29	9	†180	6	2.45	6	360	2	4	20	0	3.33
NHL Totals (10 years)		473	26644	186	191	65	1264	30	2.85	33	1903	13	19	112	0	3.53

ISBISTER, BRAD RW ISLANDERS

PERSONAL: Born May 7, 1977, in Edmonton. ... 6-4/228. ... Shoots right. ... Name pronounced ihs-BIH-stuhr.

TRANSACTIONS/CAREER NOTES: Selected by Winnipeg Jets in third round (fourth Jets pick, 67th overall) of NHL entry draft (July 8, 1995). ... Jets franchise moved to Phoenix and renamed Coyotes for 1996-97 season; NHL approved move on January 18, 1996. ... Strained muscle in abdomen (November 22, 1997); missed six games. ... Strained groin (January 8, 1999); missed six games. ... Suffered from hernia (January 27, 1999); missed 19 games. ... Strained groin (March 11, 1999); missed remainder of season. ... Traded by Coyotes with third-round pick (C Brian Collins) in 1999 draft to New York Islanders for C Robert Reichel and third- (C/LW Jason Jaspers) and fourth-round (C Preston Mizzi) picks in 1999 draft (March 20, 1999). ... Sprained ankle (January 26, 2000); missed 18 games. ... Fractured jaw (December 12, 2000); missed 15 games. ... Suffered from the flu (February 1, 2001); missed one game. ... Sprained medial collateral ligament in right knee (March 3, 2001); missed remainder of season.

HONORS: Named to WHL (West) All-Star second team (1996-97).

MISCELLANEOUS: Scored on a penalty shot (vs. Sean Burke, January 10, 2000). ... Failed to score on a penalty shot (vs. Damian Rhodes, March 16, 2000; vs. Glenn Healy, October 11, 2000).

Season Team	League	REGULAR SEASON							PLAYOFFS				
		Gms.	G	A	Pts.	PIM	+/-	PP	SH	Gms.	G	A	Pts.	PIM
93-94—Portland	WHL	64	7	10	17	45	...	...	...	10	0	2	2	0
94-95—Portland	WHL	67	16	20	36	123	...	...	...	—	—	—	—	—
95-96—Portland	WHL	71	45	44	89	184	...	...	...	7	2	4	6	20
96-97—Springfield	AHL	7	3	1	4	14	...	...	...	9	1	2	3	10
—Portland	WHL	24	15	18	33	45	...	...	...	6	2	1	3	16
97-98—Phoenix	NHL	66	9	8	17	102	4	1	0	5	0	0	0	2
—Springfield	AHL	9	8	2	10	36	...	...	...	—	—	—	—	—
98-99—Las Vegas	IHL	2	0	0	0	9	...	...	...	—	—	—	—	—
—Springfield	AHL	4	1	1	2	12	...	...	...	—	—	—	—	—
—Phoenix	NHL	32	4	4	8	46	1	0	0	—	—	—	—	—
99-00—New York Islanders	NHL	64	22	20	42	100	-18	9	0	—	—	—	—	—
00-01—New York Islanders	NHL	51	18	14	32	59	-19	7	1	—	—	—	—	—
NHL Totals (4 years)		213	53	46	99	307	-32	17	1	5	0	0	0	2

JACKMAN, BARRET D BLUES

PERSONAL: Born March 5, 1981, in Trail, B.C. ... 6-1/200. ... Shoots left.

TRANSACTIONS/CAREER NOTES: Selected by St. Louis Blues in first round (first Blues pick, 17th overall) of NHL entry draft (June 26, 1999).

HONORS: Named to WHL (East) All-Star second team (1999-2000).

Season Team	League	REGULAR SEASON							PLAYOFFS				
		Gms.	G	A	Pts.	PIM	+/-	PP	SH	Gms.	G	A	Pts.	PIM
97-98—Regina	WHL	68	2	11	13	224	...	...	...	9	0	3	3	32
98-99—Regina	WHL	70	8	36	44	259	...	...	...	—	—	—	—	—
99-00—Regina	WHL	53	9	37	46	175	...	...	...	6	1	1	2	19
—Worcester	AHL	—	—	—	—	—	...	...	...	2	0	0	0	13
00-01—Regina	WHL	43	9	27	36	138	...	...	...	6	0	3	3	8

JACKMAN, RICHARD D BRUINS

PERSONAL: Born June 28, 1978, in Toronto. ... 6-2/192. ... Shoots right.

TRANSACTIONS/CAREER NOTES: Selected by Dallas Stars in first round (first Stars pick, fifth overall) of NHL entry draft (June 22, 1996). ... Traded by Stars to Boston Bruins for RW Cameron Mann (June 24, 2001).

HONORS: Named to Can.HL All-Rookie team (1995-96). ... Named to OHL All-Rookie first team (1995-96). ... Named to OHL All-Star second team (1997-98).

Season Team	League	REGULAR SEASON							PLAYOFFS				
		Gms.	G	A	Pts.	PIM	+/-	PP	SH	Gms.	G	A	Pts.	PIM
95-96—Sault Ste. Marie	OHL	66	13	29	42	97	...	...	...	4	1	0	1	15
96-97—Sault Ste. Marie	OHL	53	13	34	47	116	...	...	...	10	2	6	8	24
97-98—Sault Ste. Marie	OHL	60	33	40	73	111	...	...	...	—	—	—	—	—
—Michigan	IHL	14	1	5	6	10	...	...	...	4	0	0	0	10
98-99—Michigan	IHL	71	13	17	30	106	...	...	...	5	0	4	4	6
99-00—Michigan	IHL	50	3	16	19	51	...	...	...	—	—	—	—	—
—Dallas	NHL	22	1	2	3	6	-1	1	0	—	—	—	—	—
00-01—Dallas	NHL	16	0	0	0	18	-6	0	0	—	—	—	—	—
—Utah	IHL	57	9	19	28	24	...	...	...	—	—	—	—	—
NHL Totals (2 years)		38	1	2	3	24	-7	1	0	—	—	—	—	—

PERSONAL: Born February 15, 1972, in Kladno, Czechoslovakia. ... 6-2/235. ... Shoots left. ... Name pronounced YAHR-oh-meer YAH-gihr.

TRANSACTIONS/CAREER NOTES: Selected by Pittsburgh Penguins in first round (first Penguins pick, fifth overall) of NHL entry draft (June 16, 1990). ... Separated shoulder (February 23, 1993); missed three games. ... Strained groin (January 21, 1994); missed four games. ... Played in Europe during 1994-95 NHL lockout. ... Suffered from the flu (January 11, 1997); missed one game. ... Strained groin (February 16, 1997); missed three games. ... Pulled groin (February 27, 1997); missed 13 games. ... Strained groin (April 10, 1997); missed two games. ... Strained hip flexor and groin (November 14, 1997); missed four games. ... Injured groin (April 16, 1998); missed one game. ... Injured groin (April 5, 1999); missed one game. ... Bruised thigh (November 18, 1999); missed one game. ... Strained muscle in abdomen (January 15, 2000); missed four games. ... Injured hamstring (February 21, 2000); missed 12 games. ... Bruised upper back (March 26, 2000); missed two games. ... Bruised finger (April 7, 2001); missed one game. ... Traded by Penguins with D Frantisek Kucera to Washington Capitals for C Kris Beech, C Michal Sivak, D Ross Lupaschuk and future considerations (July 11, 2001).

HONORS: Named to Czechoslovakian League All-Star team (1989-90). ... Named to NHL All-Rookie team (1990-91). ... Won Art Ross Trophy (1994-95, 1997-98 through 2000-01). ... Named to THE SPORTING NEWS All-Star team (1994-95, 1995-96, 1998-99 and 1999-2000). ... Named to NHL All-Star first team (1994-95, 1995-96, 1997-98 through 2000-01). ... Played in NHL All-Star Game (1988, 1990-1994 and 1998-2001). ... Named to play in NHL All-Star Game (1997); replaced by C Adam Oates due to injury. ... Named to NHL All-Star second team (1996-97). ... Named NHL Player of the Year by THE SPORTING NEWS (1998-99 and 1999-2000). ... Won Lester B. Pearson Award (1998-99 and 1999-2000). ... Won Hart Memorial Trophy (1998-99). ... Named to THE SPORTING NEWS All-Star first team (2000-01).

RECORDS: Holds NHL single-season records for most points by a right winger—149 (1995-96); and most assists by a right winger—87 (1995-96).

STATISTICAL PLATEAUS: Three-goal games: 1990-91 (1), 1994-95 (1), 1996-97 (2), 1999-00 (2), 2000-01 (2). Total: 8. ... Four-goal games: 2000-01 (1). ... Total hat tricks: 9.

MISCELLANEOUS: Member of Stanley Cup championship teams (1991 and 1992). ... Member of gold-medal-winning Czech Republic Olympic team (1998). ... Captain of Pittsburgh Penguins (1998-99 through 2000-01). ... Failed to score on a penalty shot (vs. Don Beaupre, January 26, 1993; vs. Mark Fitzpatrick, November 9, 1996). ... Holds Pittsburgh Penguins all-time record for games played (806).

STATISTICAL NOTES: Led NHL with 12 game-winning goals (1995-96).

Season Team	League	Gms.	G	A	Pts.	PIM	+/-	PP	SH	Gms.	G	A	Pts.	PIM
					REGULAR SEASON							PLAYOFFS		
88-89—Poldi Kladno	Czech.	39	8	10	18	...	...	...	...	—	—	—	—	—
89-90—Poldi Kladno	Czech.	51	30	30	60	...	...	...	...	—	—	—	—	—
90-91—Pittsburgh	NHL	80	27	30	57	42	-4	7	0	24	3	10	13	6
91-92—Pittsburgh	NHL	70	32	37	69	34	12	4	0	†21	11	13	24	6
92-93—Pittsburgh	NHL	81	34	60	94	61	30	10	1	12	5	4	9	23
93-94—Pittsburgh	NHL	80	32	67	99	61	15	9	0	6	2	4	6	16
94-95—HC Kladno	Czech Rep.	11	8	14	22	10	...	...	...	—	—	—	—	—
—HC Bolzano	Euro	5	8	8	16	4	...	...	...	—	—	—	—	—
—HC Bolzano	Italy	1	0	0	0	0	...	...	...	—	—	—	—	—
—Schalker Haie	Ger. Div. II	1	1	10	11	0	...	...	...	—	—	—	—	—
—Pittsburgh	NHL	48	32	38	†70	37	23	8	3	12	10	5	15	6
95-96—Pittsburgh	NHL	82	62	87	149	96	31	20	1	18	11	12	23	18
96-97—Pittsburgh	NHL	63	47	48	95	40	22	11	2	5	4	4	8	4
97-98—Pittsburgh	NHL	77	35	†67	102	64	17	7	0	6	4	5	9	2
—Czech Rep. Oly. team..	Int'l	6	1	4	5	2	...	...	...	—	—	—	—	—
98-99—Pittsburgh	NHL	81	44	*83	*127	66	17	10	1	9	5	7	12	16
99-00—Pittsburgh	NHL	63	42	54	*96	50	25	10	0	11	8	8	16	6
00-01—Pittsburgh	NHL	81	52	†69	*121	42	19	14	1	16	2	10	12	18
NHL Totals (11 years)		806	439	640	1079	593	207	110	9	140	65	82	147	121

PERSONAL: Born May 16, 1975, in Toronto. ... 6-5/239. ... Shoots left. ... Name pronounced JAK-oh-pihn.

TRANSACTIONS/CAREER NOTES: Selected by Detroit Red Wings in fourth round (fourth Red Wings pick, 97th overall) of NHL entry draft (June 26, 1993). ... Signed as free agent by Florida Panthers (June 4, 1997). ... Strained neck (November 5, 1999); missed five games. ... Injured groin (February 1, 2000); missed remainder of season.

HONORS: Named to Hockey East All-Rookie team (1993-94).

Season Team	League	Gms.	G	A	Pts.	PIM	+/-	PP	SH	Gms.	G	A	Pts.	PIM
					REGULAR SEASON							PLAYOFFS		
92-93—St. Michael's	Tier II Jr. A	45	9	21	30	42	...	...	...	—	—	—	—	—
93-94—Merrimack College	Hockey East	36	2	8	10	64	...	...	...	—	—	—	—	—
94-95—Merrimack College	Hockey East	37	4	10	14	42	...	...	...	—	—	—	—	—
95-96—Merrimack College	Hockey East	32	10	15	25	68	...	...	...	—	—	—	—	—
96-97—Merrimack College	Hockey East	31	4	12	16	68	...	...	...	—	—	—	—	—
—Adirondack	AHL	3	0	0	0	9	...	...	...	—	—	—	—	—
97-98—New Haven	AHL	60	2	18	20	151	...	...	...	3	0	0	0	0
—Florida	NHL	2	0	0	0	4	-3	0	0	—	—	—	—	—
98-99—New Haven	AHL	60	2	7	9	154	...	...	...	—	—	—	—	—
—Florida	NHL	3	0	0	0	0	-1	0	0	—	—	—	—	—
99-00—Florida	NHL	17	0	0	0	26	-2	0	0	—	—	—	—	—
—Louisville	AHL	23	4	6	10	47	...	...	...	—	—	—	—	—
00-01—Louisville	AHL	8	0	1	1	21	...	...	...	—	—	—	—	—
—Florida	NHL	60	1	2	3	62	-4	0	0	—	—	—	—	—
NHL Totals (4 years)		82	1	2	3	92	-10	0	0					

PERSONAL: Born June 15, 1981, in Windsor, Ont. ... 6-3/208. ... Shoots left.

TRANSACTIONS/CAREER NOTES: Selected by Dallas Stars in second round (second Stars pick, 66th overall) of NHL entry draft (June 22, 1999).

Season Team	League	REGULAR SEASON								PLAYOFFS				
		Gms.	G	A	Pts.	PIM	+/-	PP	SH	Gms.	G	A	Pts.	PIM
97-98—Tecumseh	Jr. B	49	3	11	14	145	...	...	...	—	—	—	—	—
98-99—London	OHL	68	2	12	14	115	...	...	...	25	1	7	8	24
99-00—London	OHL	59	8	15	23	138	...	...	...	—	—	—	—	—
00-01—London	OHL	39	4	23	27	95	...	...	...	—	—	—	—	—
—Sudbury	OHL	31	3	14	17	42	...	...	...	12	0	9	9	17

JANSSENS, MARK   C

PERSONAL: Born May 19, 1968, in Surrey, B.C. ... 6-3/216. ... Shoots left.
TRANSACTIONS/CAREER NOTES: Selected by New York Rangers in fourth round (fourth Rangers pick, 72nd overall) of NHL entry draft (June 21, 1986). ... Fractured skull and suffered cerebral concussion (December 10, 1988). ... Traded by Rangers to Minnesota North Stars for C Mario Thyer and third-round pick (D Maxim Galanov) in 1993 draft (March 10, 1992). ... Traded by North Stars to Hartford Whalers for C James Black (September 3, 1992). ... Separated shoulder (December 26, 1992); missed five games. ... Suffered slight concussion (February 4, 1995); missed two games. ... Sprained knee (January 22, 1997); missed 14 games. ... Traded by Whalers to Mighty Ducks of Anaheim for LW Bates Battaglia and fourth-round pick (C Josef Vasicek) in 1998 draft (March 18, 1997). ... Traded by Mighty Ducks with D J.J. Daigneault and RW Joe Sacco to New York Islanders for C Travis Green, D Doug Houda and RW Tony Tuzzolino (February 6, 1998). ... Traded by Islanders to Phoenix Coyotes for ninth-round pick (RW Jason Doyle) in 1998 draft (March 24, 1998). ... Signed as free agent by Chicago Blackhawks (July 3, 1998). ... Lacerated leg (November 10, 1998); missed four games. ... Injured back (March 6, 1999); missed 11 games. ... Reinjured back (April 2, 1999); missed two games. ... Suffered sore back (December 9, 1999) and underwent surgery; missed 33 games. ... Traded by Blackhawks to Philadelphia Flyers for ninth-round pick (D Arne Ramholt) in 2000 draft (June 12, 2000). ... Claimed on waivers by Blackhawks (July 6, 2000).

Season Team	League	REGULAR SEASON								PLAYOFFS				
		Gms.	G	A	Pts.	PIM	+/-	PP	SH	Gms.	G	A	Pts.	PIM
84-85—Regina	WHL	70	8	22	30	51	...	...	...	5	1	1	2	0
85-86—Regina	WHL	71	25	38	63	146	...	...	...	9	0	2	2	17
86-87—Regina	WHL	68	24	38	62	209	...	...	...	3	0	1	1	14
87-88—Regina	WHL	71	39	51	90	202	...	...	...	4	3	4	7	6
—New York Rangers	NHL	1	0	0	0	0	0	0	0	—	—	—	—	—
—Colorado	IHL	6	2	2	4	24	...	...	...	12	3	2	5	20
88-89—New York Rangers	NHL	5	0	0	0	0	-4	0	0	—	—	—	—	—
—Denver	IHL	38	19	19	38	104	...	...	...	4	3	0	3	18
89-90—New York Rangers	NHL	80	5	8	13	161	-26	0	0	9	2	1	3	10
90-91—New York Rangers	NHL	67	9	7	16	172	-1	0	0	6	3	0	3	6
91-92—New York Rangers	NHL	4	0	0	0	5	-1	0	0	—	—	—	—	—
—Binghamton	AHL	55	10	23	33	109	...	...	...	—	—	—	—	—
—Minnesota	NHL	3	0	0	0	0	-1	0	0	—	—	—	—	—
—Kalamazoo	IHL	2	0	0	0	2	...	...	...	11	1	2	3	22
92-93—Hartford	NHL	76	12	17	29	237	-15	0	0	—	—	—	—	—
93-94—Hartford	NHL	84	2	10	12	137	-13	0	0	—	—	—	—	—
94-95—Hartford	NHL	46	2	5	7	93	-8	0	0	—	—	—	—	—
95-96—Hartford	NHL	81	2	7	9	155	-13	0	0	—	—	—	—	—
96-97—Hartford	NHL	54	2	4	6	90	-10	0	0	—	—	—	—	—
—Anaheim	NHL	12	0	2	2	47	-3	0	0	11	0	0	0	15
97-98—Anaheim	NHL	55	4	5	9	116	-22	0	0	—	—	—	—	—
—New York Islanders	NHL	12	0	0	0	34	-3	0	0	—	—	—	—	—
—Phoenix	NHL	7	1	2	3	4	4	0	0	1	0	0	0	2
98-99—Chicago	NHL	60	1	0	1	65	-11	0	0	—	—	—	—	—
99-00—Chicago	NHL	36	0	6	6	73	-2	0	0	—	—	—	—	—
00-01—Houston	IHL	4	2	1	3	2	...	...	...	—	—	—	—	—
—Chicago	NHL	28	0	0	0	33	-8	0	0	—	—	—	—	—
—Norfolk	AHL	28	3	9	12	41	...	...	...	—	—	—	—	—
NHL Totals (14 years)		711	40	73	113	1422	-137	0	0	27	5	1	6	33

JARDINE, RYAN   LW   PANTHERS

PERSONAL: Born March 15, 1980, in Ottawa. ... 6-3/190. ... Shoots left.
TRANSACTIONS/CAREER NOTES: Selected by Florida Panthers in fourth round (fourth Panthers pick, 89th overall) of NHL entry draft (June 27, 1998).
HONORS: Named to OHL All-Rookie first team (1997-98).

Season Team	League	REGULAR SEASON								PLAYOFFS				
		Gms.	G	A	Pts.	PIM	+/-	PP	SH	Gms.	G	A	Pts.	PIM
96-97—Kanata Valley	Tier II Jr. A	52	30	27	57	70	...	...	...	—	—	—	—	—
97-98—Sault Ste. Marie	OHL	65	28	32	60	16	...	...	...	—	—	—	—	—
98-99—Sault Ste. Marie	OHL	68	27	34	61	56	...	...	...	5	0	1	1	6
99-00—Sault Ste. Marie	OHL	65	43	34	77	58	...	...	...	17	11	8	19	16
00-01—Louisville	AHL	77	12	14	26	38	...	...	...	—	—	—	—	—

JASPERS, JASON   C/LW   COYOTES

PERSONAL: Born April 8, 1981, in Thunder Bay, Ont. ... 6-0/185. ... Shoots left.
TRANSACTIONS/CAREER NOTES: Selected by Phoenix Coyotes in third round (fourth Coyotes pick, 71st overall) of NHL entry draft (June 26, 1999).
HONORS: Named to OHL All-Star second team (1999-2000).

Season Team	League	REGULAR SEASON								PLAYOFFS				
		Gms.	G	A	Pts.	PIM	+/-	PP	SH	Gms.	G	A	Pts.	PIM
97-98—Thunder Bay	NOHA	72	45	75	120	90	...	...	...	—	—	—	—	—
98-99—Sudbury	OHL	68	28	33	61	81	...	...	...	4	2	1	3	13
99-00—Sudbury	OHL	68	46	61	107	107	...	...	...	12	4	6	10	27
00-01—Sudbury	OHL	63	42	42	84	77	...	...	...	12	3	16	19	18

JEFFERSON, MIKE — C — DEVILS

PERSONAL: Born October 21, 1980, in Brampton, Ont. ... 5-9/190. ... Shoots right.
TRANSACTIONS/CAREER NOTES: Selected by New Jersey Devils in fifth round (ninth Devils pick, 135th overall) of NHL entry draft (June 24, 2000).

Season Team	League	REGULAR SEASON Gms.	G	A	Pts.	PIM	+/-	PP	SH	PLAYOFFS Gms.	G	A	Pts.	PIM
96-97—Quinte	Tier II Jr. A	35	10	18	28	281	...	...	...	—	—	—	—	—
97-98—Toronto	OHL	18	4	6	10	77	...	...	...	—	—	—	—	—
—Sarnia	OHL	12	6	1	7	37	...	...	...	—	—	—	—	—
98-99—Toronto	OHL	27	18	22	40	116	...	...	...	—	—	—	—	—
—Barrie	OHL	26	15	20	35	62	...	...	...	9	6	5	11	38
99-00—Barrie	OHL	58	34	53	87	203	...	...	...	25	7	16	23	*34
00-01—Albany	AHL	69	19	15	34	195	...	...	...	—	—	—	—	—
—New Jersey	NHL	2	0	0	0	6	0	0	0	—	—	—	—	—
NHL Totals (1 year)		2	0	0	0	6	0	0	0					

JILLSON, JEFF — D — SHARKS

PERSONAL: Born July 24, 1980, in North Smithfield, R.I. ... 6-3/219. ... Shoots right.
TRANSACTIONS/CAREER NOTES: Selected by San Jose Sharks in first round (first Sharks pick, 14th overall) of NHL entry draft (June 26, 1999).
HONORS: Named to CCHA All-Star first team (1999-2000 and 2000-01). ... Named to NCAA All-America (West) first team (1999-2000). ... Named to NCAA All-America (West) second team (2000-01).

Season Team	League	REGULAR SEASON Gms.	G	A	Pts.	PIM	+/-	PP	SH	PLAYOFFS Gms.	G	A	Pts.	PIM
96-97—Mount St. Charles	USHS (East)	15	16	14	30	20	...	...	...	—	—	—	—	—
97-98—Mount St. Charles	USHS (East)	15	10	13	23	32	...	...	...	—	—	—	—	—
98-99—Univ. of Michigan	CCHA	38	5	19	24	71	...	...	...	—	—	—	—	—
99-00—Univ. of Michigan	CCHA	36	8	26	34	111	...	...	...	—	—	—	—	—
00-01—Univ. of Michigan	CCHA	43	10	20	30	74	...	...	...	—	—	—	—	—

JINDRICH, ROBERT — D — SHARKS

PERSONAL: Born November 14, 1976, in Plezn, Czechoslovakia. ... 5-11/190. ... Shoots left.
TRANSACTIONS/CAREER NOTES: Selected by San Jose Sharks in seventh round (10th Sharks pick, 168th overall) of NHL entry draft (July 8, 1995).

Season Team	League	REGULAR SEASON Gms.	G	A	Pts.	PIM	+/-	PP	SH	PLAYOFFS Gms.	G	A	Pts.	PIM
94-95—HC Keramika Plzen	Czech Rep.	11	1	0	1		...	...	...	—	—	—	—	—
—Sokolov	Czech Rep.					Statistics unavailable.				—	—	—	—	—
95-96—HC Keramika Plzen	Czech Rep.	37	1	3	4		...	...	...	—	—	—	—	—
96-97—HC Keramika Plzen	Czech Rep.	49	7	9	16	44	...	...	...	—	—	—	—	—
97-98—HC Keramika Plzen	Czech Rep.	39	2	5	7		...	...	...	—	—	—	—	—
—Beroun	Czech Rep.	13	4	2	6		...	...	...	—	—	—	—	—
98-99—HC Keramika Plzen	Czech Rep.	52	6	12	18	24	...	...	...	5	1	0	1	...
99-00—Kentucky	AHL	78	2	21	23	51	...	...	...	9	0	4	4	6
00-01—Kentucky	AHL	62	4	16	20	36	...	...	...	2	0	0	0	0

JOHANSSON, ANDREAS — C/LW — RANGERS

PERSONAL: Born May 19, 1973, in Hofors, Sweden. ... 6-2/202. ... Shoots left. ... Name pronounced yoh-HAN-suhn.
TRANSACTIONS/CAREER NOTES: Selected by New York Islanders in seventh round (seventh Islanders pick, 136th overall) of NHL entry draft (June 22, 1991). ... Injured back (April 5, 1996); missed three games. ... Traded by Islanders with D Darius Kasparaitis to Pittsburgh Penguins for C Bryan Smolinski (November 17, 1996). ... Bruised shoulder (December 10, 1996); missed 12 games. ... Suffered from the flu (January 26, 1997); missed one game. ... Suffered back spasms (February 15, 1997); missed one game. ... Bruised ribs (November 15, 1997); missed six games. ... Sprained medial collateral ligament in knee (March 8, 1998); missed 10 games. ... Signed as free agent by Ottawa Senators (September 29, 1998). ... Injured left knee (January 18, 1999); missed two games. ... Reinjured left knee (February 25, 1999); missed three games. ... Strained hamstring (March 8, 1999); missed two games. ... Injured knee (April 5, 1999); missed two games. ... Suffered back spasms (April 15, 1999); missed one game. ... Traded by Senators to Tampa Bay Lightning for LW Rob Zamuner and second-round pick in 2000, 2001 or 2002 draft to complete deal that allowed Tampa Bay to sign general manager Rick Dudley (June 30, 1999). ... Suffered concussion (October 7, 1999); missed one game. ... Bruised foot (November 2, 1999); missed four games. ... Traded by Lightning to Calgary Flames for rights to LW Nils Ekman and fourth-round pick (traded to New York Islanders) in 2000 draft (November 20, 1999). ... Suffered injury (December 21, 1999); missed three games. ... Suffered from the flu (January 5, 2000); missed three games. ... Suffered back spasms (January 12, 2000); missed 15 games. ... Injured back (March 11, 2000); missed remainder of season. ... Claimed by New York Rangers from Flames in NHL waiver draft (September 29, 2000).

Season Team	League	REGULAR SEASON Gms.	G	A	Pts.	PIM	+/-	PP	SH	PLAYOFFS Gms.	G	A	Pts.	PIM
90-91—Falun	Sweden	31	12	10	22	38	...	...	...	—	—	—	—	—
91-92—Farjestad Karlstad	Sweden	30	3	1	4	4	...	...	...	6	0	0	0	4
92-93—Farjestad Karlstad	Sweden	38	4	7	11	38	...	...	...	2	0	0	0	0
93-94—Farjestad Karlstad	Sweden	20	3	6	9	6	...	...	...	—	—	—	—	—
94-95—Farjestad Karlstad	Sweden	36	9	10	19	42	...	...	...	4	0	0	0	10
95-96—Worcester	AHL	29	5	5	10	32	...	...	...	—	—	—	—	—
—Utah	IHL	22	4	13	17	28	...	...	...	12	0	5	5	6
—New York Islanders	NHL	3	0	1	1	0	1	0	0	—	—	—	—	—

Season Team	League	REGULAR SEASON								PLAYOFFS				
		Gms.	G	A	Pts.	PIM	+/-	PP	SH	Gms.	G	A	Pts.	PIM
96-97—New York Islanders.....	NHL	15	2	2	4	0	-6	1	0	—	—	—	—	—
—Pittsburgh..................	NHL	27	2	7	9	20	-6	0	0	—	—	—	—	—
—Cleveland	IHL	10	2	4	6	42	...	...	...	11	1	5	6	8
97-98—Pittsburgh..................	NHL	50	5	10	15	20	4	0	1	1	0	0	0	0
—Swedish Oly. team	Int'l	3	0	0	0	2	...	...	...	—	—	—	—	—
98-99—Ottawa	NHL	69	21	16	37	34	1	7	0	2	0	0	0	0
99-00—Tampa Bay	NHL	12	2	3	5	8	1	0	0	—	—	—	—	—
—Calgary	NHL	28	3	7	10	14	-3	1	0	—	—	—	—	—
00-01—Bern........................	Switzerland	40	15	29	44	94	...	...	...	7	5	4	9	0
NHL Totals (5 years)............		204	35	46	81	96	-8	9	1	3	0	0	0	0

JOHANSSON, CALLE   D   CAPITALS   J

PERSONAL: Born February 14, 1967, in Goteborg, Sweden. ... 5-11/203. ... Shoots left. ... Name pronounced KAL-ee yoh-HAHN-suhn.

TRANSACTIONS/CAREER NOTES: Selected by Buffalo Sabres in first round (first Sabres pick, 14th overall) of NHL entry draft (June 15, 1985). ... Dislocated thumb (October 9, 1988). ... Traded by Sabres with second-round pick (G Byron Dafoe) in 1989 draft to Washington Capitals for D Grant Ledyard, G Clint Malarchuk and sixth-round pick (C Brian Holzinger) in 1991 draft (March 6, 1989). ... Injured back (October 7, 1989); missed 10 games. ... Bruised ribs (January 9, 1993); missed seven games. ... Played in Europe during 1994-95 NHL lockout. ... Suffered from the flu (March 25, 1995); missed two games. ... Fractured hand (April 4, 1996); missed remainder of season. ... Fractured jaw (November 12, 1996); missed 16 games. ... Bruised foot (February 14, 1997); missed one game. ... Sprained knee (January 13, 1998); missed nine games. ... Sprained knee (March 15, 1999); missed remainder of season. ... Suffered sore back (November 2, 2000); missed five games.

HONORS: Named to NHL All-Rookie team (1987-88).

Season Team	League	REGULAR SEASON								PLAYOFFS				
		Gms.	G	A	Pts.	PIM	+/-	PP	SH	Gms.	G	A	Pts.	PIM
83-84—Vastra Frolunda	Sweden	34	5	10	15	20	...	...	...	—	—	—	—	—
84-85—Vastra Frolunda	Sweden	36	14	15	29	20	...	...	...	6	1	2	3	4
85-86—Bjorkloven..............	Sweden	17	1	1	2	14	...	...	...	—	—	—	—	—
86-87—Bjorkloven	Sweden	30	2	13	15	18	...	...	...	6	1	3	4	6
87-88—Buffalo	NHL	71	4	38	42	37	12	2	0	6	0	1	1	0
88-89—Buffalo	NHL	47	2	11	13	33	-7	0	0	—	—	—	—	—
—Washington	NHL	12	1	7	8	4	1	1	0	6	1	2	3	0
89-90—Washington	NHL	70	8	31	39	25	7	4	0	15	1	6	7	4
90-91—Washington	NHL	80	11	41	52	23	-2	2	1	10	2	7	9	8
91-92—Washington	NHL	80	14	42	56	49	2	5	2	7	0	5	5	4
92-93—Washington	NHL	77	7	38	45	56	3	6	0	6	0	5	5	4
93-94—Washington	NHL	84	9	33	42	59	3	4	0	6	1	3	4	4
94-95—Kloten	Switzerland	5	1	2	3	8	...	...	...	—	—	—	—	—
—Washington	NHL	46	5	26	31	35	-6	4	0	7	3	1	4	0
95-96—Washington	NHL	78	10	25	35	50	13	4	0	—	—	—	—	—
96-97—Washington	NHL	65	6	11	17	16	-2	2	0	—	—	—	—	—
97-98—Washington	NHL	73	15	20	35	30	-11	10	1	21	2	8	10	16
—Swedish Oly. team	Int'l	4	0	0	0	2	...	...	...	—	—	—	—	—
98-99—Washington	NHL	67	8	21	29	22	10	2	0	—	—	—	—	—
99-00—Washington	NHL	82	7	25	32	24	13	1	0	5	1	2	3	0
00-01—Washington	NHL	76	7	29	36	26	11	5	0	6	1	2	3	2
NHL Totals (14 years).........		1008	114	398	512	489	47	52	4	95	12	42	54	42

JOHNSON, BRENT   G   BLUES

PERSONAL: Born March 12, 1977, in Farmington, Mich. ... 6-2/200. ... Catches left. ... Full Name: Brent Spencer Johnson. ... Son of Bob Johnson, goalie with St. Louis Blues (1972-73) and Pittsburgh Penguins (1974-75).

TRANSACTIONS/CAREER NOTES: Selected by Colorado Avalanche in fifth round (fifth Avalanche pick, 129th overall) of NHL entry draft (July 8, 1995). ... Traded by Avalanche to St. Louis Blues for third-round pick (RW Ville Nieminen) in 1997 draft and conditional third-round pick in 2000 draft (May 30, 1997). ... Injured knee (January 23, 2001); missed three games.

Season Team	League	REGULAR SEASON								PLAYOFFS					
		Gms.	Min	W	L	T	GA	SO	Avg.	Gms.	Min.	W	L	GA	SO	Avg.
94-95—Owen Sound	OHL	18	904	3	9	1	75	0	4.98	4	253	0	4	24	0	5.69
95-96—Owen Sound	OHL	58	3211	24	28	1	243	1	4.54	6	371	2	4	29	0	4.69
96-97—Owen Sound	OHL	50	2798	20	28	1	201	1	4.31	4	253	0	4	24	0	5.69
97-98—Worcester	AHL	42	2241	14	15	7	119	0	3.19	6	332	3	2	19	0	3.43
98-99—Worcester	AHL	49	2925	22	22	4	146	2	2.99	4	238	1	3	12	0	3.03
—St. Louis	NHL	6	286	3	2	0	10	0	2.10	—	—	—	—	—	—
99-00—Worcester	AHL	58	3319	24	27	5	161	3	2.91	9	561	4	5	23	1	2.46
00-01—St. Louis	NHL	31	1744	19	9	2	63	4	2.17	2	62	0	1	2	0	1.94
NHL Totals (2 years)............		37	2030	22	11	2	73	4	2.16	2	62	0	1	2	0	1.94

JOHNSON, CRAIG   LW   KINGS

PERSONAL: Born March 8, 1972, in St. Paul, Minn. ... 6-2/197. ... Shoots left.

TRANSACTIONS/CAREER NOTES: Selected by St. Louis Blues in second round (first Blues pick, 33rd overall) of NHL entry draft (June 16, 1990). ... Traded by Blues with C Patrice Tardiff, C Roman Vopat, fifth-round pick (D Peter Hogan) in 1996 draft and first-round pick (LW Matt Zultek) in 1997 draft to Los Angeles Kings for C Wayne Gretzky (February 27, 1996). ... Sprained left shoulder (March 13, 1996); missed seven games. ... Strained abdominal muscle prior to 1996-97 season; missed first seven games of season. ... Strained groin (November 2, 1996); missed one game. ... Strained abdominal muscle (November 30, 1996); missed 36 games. ... Strained groin (March 29, 1997); missed six games. ... Suffered from the flu (December 18, 1997); missed two games. ... Bruised abdomen (February 2, 1998); missed three games. ... Injured ribs (January 14, 1999); missed four games. ... Lacerated finger (February 16, 2000); missed three games. ... Lacerated tendon in right leg (December 26, 2000); missed remainder of season.

HONORS: Named to WCHA All-Rookie Team (1990-91).

		REGULAR SEASON								PLAYOFFS				
Season Team	League	Gms.	G	A	Pts.	PIM	+/-	PP	SH	Gms.	G	A	Pts.	PIM
87-88—Hill-Murray H.S.	Minn. H.S.	28	14	20	34	4	...	...	...	—	—	—	—	—
88-89—Hill-Murray H.S.	Minn. H.S.	24	22	30	52	10	...	...	...	—	—	—	—	—
89-90—Hill-Murray H.S.	Minn. H.S.	23	15	36	51		...	...	...	—	—	—	—	—
90-91—Univ. of Minnesota	WCHA	33	13	18	31	34	...	...	...	—	—	—	—	—
91-92—Univ. of Minnesota	WCHA	44	19	39	58	70	...	...	...	—	—	—	—	—
92-93—Univ. of Minnesota	WCHA	42	22	24	46	70	...	...	...	—	—	—	—	—
93-94—U.S. national team	Int'l	54	25	26	51	64	...	...	...	—	—	—	—	—
—U.S. Olympic team	Int'l	8	0	4	4	4	...	...	...	—	—	—	—	—
94-95—Peoria	IHL	16	2	6	8	25	...	...	...	9	0	4	4	10
—St. Louis	NHL	15	3	3	6	6	4	0	0	1	0	0	0	2
95-96—Worcester	AHL	5	3	0	3	2	...	...	...	—	—	—	—	—
—St. Louis	NHL	49	8	7	15	30	-4	1	0	—	—	—	—	—
—Los Angeles	NHL	11	5	4	9	6	-4	3	0	—	—	—	—	—
96-97—Mobile	ECHL	4	0	0	0	74	...	...	...	—	—	—	—	—
—Los Angeles	NHL	31	4	3	7	26	-7	1	0	—	—	—	—	—
—Oklahoma City	CHL	36	6	11	17	134	...	...	...	—	—	—	—	—
—Michigan	IHL	2	0	0	0	2	...	...	...	—	—	—	—	—
—Manitoba	IHL	16	2	2	4	38	...	...	...	—	—	—	—	—
97-98—Los Angeles	NHL	74	17	21	38	42	9	6	0	4	1	0	1	4
98-99—Los Angeles	NHL	69	7	12	19	32	-12	2	0	—	—	—	—	—
—Houston	IHL	1	0	0	0	0	...	...	...	—	—	—	—	—
99-00—Los Angeles	NHL	76	9	14	23	28	-10	1	0	4	1	0	1	2
00-01—Los Angeles	NHL	26	4	5	9	16	0	0	0	—	—	—	—	—
NHL Totals (7 years)		351	57	69	126	186	-24	14	0	9	2	0	2	8

JOHNSON, GREG   C   PREDATORS

PERSONAL: Born March 16, 1971, in Thunder Bay, Ont. ... 5-10/202. ... Shoots left. ... Full Name: Gregory Johnson. ... Brother of Ryan Johnson, center, Florida Panthers.

TRANSACTIONS/CAREER NOTES: Selected by Philadelphia Flyers in second round (first Flyers pick, 33rd overall) of NHL entry draft (June 17, 1989). ... Separated right shoulder (November 24, 1990). ... Rights traded by Flyers with fifth-round pick (G Frederic Deschenes) in 1994 draft to Detroit Red Wings for RW Jim Cummins and fourth-round pick (traded to Boston) in 1993 draft (June 20, 1993). ... Loaned to Canadian Olympic Team (January 19, 1994). ... Returned to Red Wings (March 1, 1994). ... Sprained left ankle (April 14, 1995); missed final nine games of season. ... Injured left hand (October 8, 1995); missed two games. ... Injured knee (March 19, 1996); missed 12 games. ... Traded by Red Wings to Pittsburgh Penguins for RW Tomas Sandstrom (January 27, 1997). ... Bruised shoulder (April 3, 1997); missed one game. ... Strained groin (October 3, 1997); missed five games. ... Traded by Penguins to Chicago Blackhawks for D Tuomas Gronman (October 27, 1997). ... Strained groin (October 31, 1997); missed three games. ... Selected by Nashville Predators in NHL expansion draft (June 26, 1998). ... Suffered concussion (December 10, 1998); missed four games. ... Strained groin (February 20, 1999); missed five games. ... Suffered stress fracture in ankle (April 7, 1999); missed final five games of season.

HONORS: Named to USHL All-Star first team (1988-89). ... Named Canadian Junior A Player of the Year (1989). ... Named to Centennial Cup All-Star first team (1989). ... Named to NCAA All-America (West) first team (1990-91 and 1992-93). ... Named to WCHA All-Star first team (1990-91 through 1992-93). ... Named to NCAA All-America (West) second team (1991-92).

MISCELLANEOUS: Member of silver-medal-winning Canadian Olympic team (1994).

		REGULAR SEASON								PLAYOFFS				
Season Team	League	Gms.	G	A	Pts.	PIM	+/-	PP	SH	Gms.	G	A	Pts.	PIM
88-89—Thunder Bay Jrs.	USHL	47	32	64	96	4	...	...	...	12	5	13	18	...
89-90—Univ. of North Dakota	WCHA	44	17	38	55	11	...	...	...	—	—	—	—	—
90-91—Univ. of North Dakota	WCHA	38	18	*61	79	6	...	...	...	—	—	—	—	—
91-92—Univ. of North Dakota	WCHA	39	20	54	74	8	...	...	...	—	—	—	—	—
92-93—Canadian nat'l team	Int'l	23	6	14	20	2	...	...	...	—	—	—	—	—
—Univ. of North Dakota	WCHA	34	19	45	64	18	...	...	...	—	—	—	—	—
93-94—Detroit	NHL	52	6	11	17	22	-7	1	1	7	2	2	4	2
—Canadian nat'l team	Int'l	6	2	6	8	4	...	...	...	—	—	—	—	—
—Can. Olympic team	Int'l	8	0	3	3	0	...	...	...	—	—	—	—	—
—Adirondack	AHL	3	2	4	6	0	...	...	...	4	0	4	4	2
94-95—Detroit	NHL	22	3	5	8	14	1	2	0	1	0	0	0	0
95-96—Detroit	NHL	60	18	22	40	30	6	5	0	13	3	1	4	8
96-97—Detroit	NHL	43	6	10	16	12	-5	0	0	—	—	—	—	—
—Pittsburgh	NHL	32	7	9	16	14	-13	1	0	5	1	0	1	2
97-98—Pittsburgh	NHL	5	1	0	1	2	0	0	0	—	—	—	—	—
—Chicago	NHL	69	11	22	33	38	-2	4	0	—	—	—	—	—
98-99—Nashville	NHL	68	16	34	50	24	-8	2	3	—	—	—	—	—
99-00—Nashville	NHL	82	11	33	44	40	-15	2	0	—	—	—	—	—
00-01—Nashville	NHL	82	15	17	32	46	-6	1	0	—	—	—	—	—
NHL Totals (8 years)		515	94	163	257	242	-49	18	4	26	6	3	9	12

JOHNSON, MATT   LW   WILD

PERSONAL: Born November 23, 1975, in Welland, Ont. ... 6-5/235. ... Shoots left.

TRANSACTIONS/CAREER NOTES: Selected by Los Angeles Kings in second round (second Kings pick, 33rd overall) of NHL entry draft (June 28, 1994). ... Suffered from the flu (February 25, 1995); missed one game. ... Bruised right hand (April 3, 1995); missed four games. ... Strained shoulder (December 18, 1996); missed six games. ... Suffered concussion (February 1, 1997); missed one game. ... Suspended four games and fined $1,000 by NHL for elbowing incident (February 5, 1997). ... Strained back (March 10, 1997); missed final 13 games of season. ... Suspended four games and fined $1,000 by NHL for slashing incident (September 29, 1997). ... Strained groin (December 23, 1997); missed one game. ... Strained left biceps (March 21, 1998); missed three games. ... Suspended 12 games by NHL for deliberately injuring another player (November 23, 1998). ... Selected by Atlanta Thrashers in NHL expansion draft (June 25, 1999). ... Injured groin (October 7, 1999); missed two games. ... Strained hip flexor (November 25, 1999); missed two games. ... Suffered eye injury (December 13, 1999); missed nine games. ... Sprained medial collateral ligament in knee (March 28, 2000); missed two games. ... Traded by Thrashers to Minnesota

J

Wild for third-round pick (traded to Pittsburgh) in 2001 draft (September 29, 2000). ... Sprained finger (November 7, 2000); missed four games. ... Suffered concussion (November 26, 2000); missed eight games. ... Suffered concussion and bruised hand (January 14, 2001); missed seven games. ... Suffered from dizziness (March 1, 2001); missed 10 games.

MISCELLANEOUS: Holds Minnesota Wild all-time record for most penalty minutes (137).

Season Team	League	REGULAR SEASON								PLAYOFFS				
		Gms.	G	A	Pts.	PIM	+/-	PP	SH	Gms.	G	A	Pts.	PIM
91-92—Welland	Jr. B	38	6	19	25	214	...	...	...	—	—	—	—	—
92-93—Peterborough	OHL	66	8	17	25	211	...	...	...	16	1	1	2	54
93-94—Peterborough	OHL	50	13	24	37	233	...	...	...	—	—	—	—	—
94-95—Peterborough	OHL	14	1	2	3	43	...	...	...	—	—	—	—	—
—Los Angeles	NHL	14	1	0	1	102	0	0	0	—	—	—	—	—
95-96—Los Angeles	NHL	1	0	0	0	5	0	0	0	—	—	—	—	—
—Phoenix	IHL	29	4	4	8	87	...	...	...	—	—	—	—	—
96-97—Los Angeles	NHL	52	1	3	4	194	-4	0	0	—	—	—	—	—
97-98—Los Angeles	NHL	66	2	4	6	249	-8	0	0	4	0	0	0	6
98-99—Los Angeles	NHL	49	2	1	3	131	-5	0	0	—	—	—	—	—
99-00—Atlanta	NHL	64	2	5	7	144	-11	0	0	—	—	—	—	—
00-01—Minnesota	NHL	50	1	1	2	137	-6	0	0	—	—	—	—	—
NHL Totals (7 years)		296	9	14	23	962	-34	0	0	4	0	0	0	6

JOHNSON, MIKE RW COYOTES

PERSONAL: Born October 3, 1974, in Scarborough, Ont. ... 6-2/200. ... Shoots right. ... Full Name: Michael Johnson.

TRANSACTIONS/CAREER NOTES: Signed as non-drafted free agent by Toronto Maple Leafs (March 16, 1997). ... Suspended two games by NHL for elbowing incident (April 8, 1999). ... Traded by Maple Leafs with D Marek Posmyk and fifth-(F Pavel Sedov) and sixth-round (D Aaron Gionet) picks in 2000 draft to Tampa Bay Lightning for C Darcy Tucker and fourth-round pick (RW Miguel Delisle) in 2000 draft (February 9, 2000). ... Suffered injury (November 27, 1999); missed two games. ... Suffered facial fracture (March 17, 2000); missed one game. ... Injured ribs (December 2, 2000); missed two games. ... Traded by Lightning with D Paul Mara, RW Ruslan Zainullin and second-round pick (D Matthew Spiller) in 2001 draft to Phoenix Coyotes for G Nikolai Khabibulin and D Stan Neckar (March 5, 2001). ... Injured shoulder (March 8, 2001); missed four games.

HONORS: Named to NHL All-Rookie team (1997-98).

MISCELLANEOUS: Failed to score on a penalty shot (vs. Martin Biron, vs. February 1, 2001).

Season Team	League	REGULAR SEASON								PLAYOFFS				
		Gms.	G	A	Pts.	PIM	+/-	PP	SH	Gms.	G	A	Pts.	PIM
92-93—Aurora	OPJHL	48	25	40	65	18	...	...	...	—	—	—	—	—
93-94—Bowling Green	CCHA	38	6	14	20	18	...	...	...	—	—	—	—	—
94-95—Bowling Green	CCHA	37	16	33	49	35	...	...	...	—	—	—	—	—
95-96—Bowling Green	CCHA	30	12	19	31	22	...	...	...	—	—	—	—	—
96-97—Bowling Green	CCHA	38	30	32	62	46	...	...	...	—	—	—	—	—
—Toronto	NHL	13	2	2	4	4	-2	0	1	—	—	—	—	—
97-98—Toronto	NHL	82	15	32	47	24	-4	5	0	—	—	—	—	—
98-99—Toronto	NHL	79	20	24	44	35	13	5	3	17	3	2	5	4
99-00—Toronto	NHL	52	11	14	25	23	8	2	1	—	—	—	—	—
—Tampa Bay	NHL	28	10	12	22	4	-2	4	0	—	—	—	—	—
00-01—Tampa Bay	NHL	64	11	27	38	38	-10	3	1	—	—	—	—	—
—Phoenix	NHL	12	2	3	5	4	0	1	0	—	—	—	—	—
NHL Totals (5 years)		330	71	114	185	132	3	20	6	17	3	2	5	4

JOHNSON, RYAN C PANTHERS

PERSONAL: Born June 14, 1976, in Thunder Bay, Ont. ... 6-1/200. ... Shoots left. ... Brother of Greg Johnson, center, Nashville Predators.

TRANSACTIONS/CAREER NOTES: Selected by Florida Panthers in second round (fourth Panthers pick, 36th overall) of NHL entry draft (June 28, 1994). ... Loaned to Canadian national team prior to 1995-96 season. ... Bruised left ankle (October 16, 1999); missed two games. ... Suffered from the flu (January 6, 2000); missed one game. ... Traded by Panthers with LW Dwayne Hay to Tampa Bay Lightning for C/RW Mike Sillinger (March 14, 2000). ... Suffered from virus (December 2, 2000); missed two games. ... Traded by Lightning with sixth-round pick in 2003 draft to Panthers for C Vaclav Prospal (July 10, 2001).

Season Team	League	REGULAR SEASON								PLAYOFFS				
		Gms.	G	A	Pts.	PIM	+/-	PP	SH	Gms.	G	A	Pts.	PIM
93-94—Thunder Bay Jrs.	USHL	48	14	36	50	28	...	...	...	—	—	—	—	—
94-95—Univ. of North Dakota	WCHA	38	6	22	28	39	...	...	...	—	—	—	—	—
95-96—Canadian nat'l team	Int'l	28	5	12	17	14	...	...	...	—	—	—	—	—
—Univ. of North Dakota	WCHA	21	2	17	19	14	...	...	...	—	—	—	—	—
96-97—Carolina	AHL	79	18	24	42	28	...	...	...	—	—	—	—	—
97-98—New Haven	AHL	64	19	48	67	12	...	...	...	3	0	1	1	0
—Florida	NHL	10	0	2	2	0	-4	0	0	—	—	—	—	—
98-99—New Haven	AHL	37	8	19	27	18	...	...	...	—	—	—	—	—
—Florida	NHL	1	1	0	1	0	0	0	0	—	—	—	—	—
99-00—Florida	NHL	66	4	12	16	14	1	0	0	—	—	—	—	—
—Tampa Bay	NHL	14	0	2	2	2	-9	0	0	—	—	—	—	—
00-01—Tampa Bay	NHL	80	7	14	21	44	-20	1	0	—	—	—	—	—
NHL Totals (4 years)		171	12	30	42	60	-32	1	0	—	—	—	—	—

JOHNSSON, KIM D RANGERS

PERSONAL: Born March 16, 1976, in Malmo, Sweden. ... 6-2/189. ... Shoots left. ... Full Name: Kimmo Johnsson.

TRANSACTIONS/CAREER NOTES: Selected by New York Rangers in 11th round (15th Rangers pick, 286th overall) of NHL entry draft (June 29, 1994). ... Suffered eye injury (February 8, 2000); missed one game. ... Fractured hand (November 2, 2000); missed five games.

Season Team	League	REGULAR SEASON Gms.	G	A	Pts.	PIM	+/-	PP	SH	PLAYOFFS Gms.	G	A	Pts.	PIM
93-94—Malmo	Sweden						Statistics unavailable.							
94-95—Malmo	Sweden	13	0	0	0	4	...	...	...	1	0	0	0	0
95-96—Malmo	Sweden	38	2	0	2	30	...	...	...	4	0	1	1	8
96-97—Malmo	Sweden	49	4	9	13	42	...	...	...	4	0	0	0	2
97-98—Malmo	Sweden	45	5	9	14	29	...	...	...	—	—	—	—	—
98-99—Malmo	Sweden	49	9	8	17	76	...	...	...	8	2	3	5	12
99-00—New York Rangers	NHL	76	6	15	21	46	-13	1	0	—	—	—	—	—
00-01—New York Rangers	NHL	75	5	21	26	40	-3	4	0	—	—	—	—	—
NHL Totals (2 years)		151	11	36	47	86	-16	5	0					

JOKINEN, OLLI   C   PANTHERS

PERSONAL: Born December 5, 1978, in Kuopio, Finland. ... 6-3/218. ... Shoots left. ... Name pronounced OH-lee YOH-kih-nehn.

TRANSACTIONS/CAREER NOTES: Selected by Los Angeles Kings in first round (first Kings pick, third overall) of NHL entry draft (June 21, 1997). ... Traded by Kings with LW Josh Green, D Mathieu Biron and first-round pick (LW Taylor Pyatt) in 1999 draft to New York Islanders for RW Zigmund Palffy, C Bryan Smolinski, G Marcel Cousineau and fourth-round pick (C Daniel Johansson) in 1999 draft (June 20, 1999). ... Traded by Islanders with G Roberto Luongo to Florida Panthers for RW Mark Parrish and LW Oleg Kvasha (June 24, 2000).

MISCELLANEOUS: Scored on a penalty shot (vs. Dominik Hasek, March 4, 2000).

Season Team	League	REGULAR SEASON Gms.	G	A	Pts.	PIM	+/-	PP	SH	PLAYOFFS Gms.	G	A	Pts.	PIM
94-95—KalPa Kuopio	Finland Jr.	6	0	1	1	6	...	...	...	—	—	—	—	—
95-96—KalPa Kuopio	Finland Jr.	15	1	1	2	2	...	...	...	—	—	—	—	—
—KalPa Kuopio	Finland	15	1	1	2	2	...	...	...	—	—	—	—	—
96-97—HIFK Helsinki	Finland	50	14	27	41	88	...	...	...	—	—	—	—	—
97-98—Los Angeles	NHL	8	0	0	0	6	-5	0	0	—	—	—	—	—
—HIFK Helsinki	Finland	30	11	28	39	8	...	...	...	9	7	2	9	2
98-99—Springfield	AHL	9	3	6	9	6	...	...	...	—	—	—	—	—
—Los Angeles	NHL	66	9	12	21	44	-10	3	1	—	—	—	—	—
99-00—New York Islanders	NHL	82	11	10	21	80	0	1	2	—	—	—	—	—
00-01—Florida	NHL	78	6	10	16	106	-22	0	0	—	—	—	—	—
NHL Totals (4 years)		234	26	32	58	236	-37	4	3					

JONES, KEITH   RW

PERSONAL: Born November 8, 1968, in Brantford, Ont. ... 6-2/200. ... Shoots left.

TRANSACTIONS/CAREER NOTES: Selected by Washington Capitals in seventh round (seventh Capitals pick, 141st overall) of NHL entry draft (June 11, 1988). ... Suffered from the flu (January 21, 1993); missed two games. ... Sprained wrist (January 25, 1994); missed six games. ... Injured foot (March 16, 1995); missed one game. ... Separated ribs and bruised foot (March 29, 1995); missed six games. ... Injured groin (March 12, 1996); missed seven games. ... Reinjured groin (March 29, 1996); missed seven games. ... Traded by Capitals with first- (D Scott Parker) and fourth-round (traded back to Washington) picks in 1998 draft to Colorado Avalanche for D Curtis Leschyshyn and LW Chris Simon (November 2, 1996). ... Injured knee (April 26, 1997); missed remainder of playoffs. ... Injured knee (October 1, 1997) and underwent surgery; missed 58 games. ... Suspended two games and fined $1,000 by NHL for illegal check to the head (October 15, 1998). ... Traded by Avalanche to Philadelphia Flyers for LW Shjon Podein (November 12, 1998). ... Bruised left knee (November 22, 1998); missed one game. ... Underwent knee surgery (September 29, 1999); missed first 25 games of season. ... Suffered concussion (October 21, 2000); missed 12 games. ... Announced retirement (November 21, 2000).

HONORS: Named to CCHA All-Star first team (1991-92).

MISCELLANEOUS: Failed to score on a penalty shot (vs. Patrick Labrecque, November 1, 1995).

Season Team	League	REGULAR SEASON Gms.	G	A	Pts.	PIM	+/-	PP	SH	PLAYOFFS Gms.	G	A	Pts.	PIM
87-88—Niagara Falls	OHA	40	50	80	130	...	...	...	...	—	—	—	—	—
88-89—Western Michigan U.	CCHA	37	9	12	21	51	...	...	...	—	—	—	—	—
89-90—Western Michigan U.	CCHA	40	19	18	37	82	...	...	...	—	—	—	—	—
90-91—Western Michigan U.	CCHA	41	30	19	49	106	...	...	...	—	—	—	—	—
91-92—Western Michigan U.	CCHA	35	25	31	56	77	...	...	...	—	—	—	—	—
—Baltimore	AHL	6	2	4	6	0	...	...	...	—	—	—	—	—
92-93—Baltimore	AHL	8	7	3	10	4	...	...	...	—	—	—	—	—
—Washington	NHL	71	12	14	26	124	18	0	0	6	0	0	0	10
93-94—Washington	NHL	68	16	19	35	149	4	5	0	11	0	1	1	36
—Portland	AHL	6	5	7	12	4	...	...	...	—	—	—	—	—
94-95—Washington	NHL	40	14	6	20	65	-2	1	0	7	4	4	8	22
95-96—Washington	NHL	68	18	23	41	103	8	5	0	2	0	0	0	7
96-97—Washington	NHL	11	2	3	5	13	-2	1	0	—	—	—	—	—
—Colorado	NHL	67	23	20	43	105	5	13	1	6	3	3	6	4
97-98—Colorado	NHL	23	3	7	10	22	-4	1	0	7	0	0	0	13
—Hershey	AHL	4	2	1	3	2	...	...	...	—	—	—	—	—
98-99—Colorado	NHL	12	2	2	4	20	-6	1	0	—	—	—	—	—
—Philadelphia	NHL	66	18	31	49	78	29	2	0	6	2	1	3	14
99-00—Philadelphia	NHL	57	9	16	25	82	8	1	0	18	3	3	6	14
00-01—Philadelphia	NHL	8	0	0	0	4	-5	0	0	—	—	—	—	—
NHL Totals (9 years)		491	117	141	258	765	53	30	1	63	12	12	24	120

JONES, MIKE   D   LIGHTNING

PERSONAL: Born May 18, 1976, in Toledo, Ohio. ... 6-4/195. ... Full Name: Michael Jones.

TRANSACTIONS/CAREER NOTES: Signed as non-drafted free agent by Tampa Bay Lightning (April 13, 2000).

HONORS: Named to CCHA All-Star second team (1998-99).

Season Team	League	Gms.	G	A	Pts.	PIM	+/-	PP	SH	Gms.	G	A	Pts.	PIM
96-97—Bowling Green	CCHA	27	1	6	7	47	...	...	...	—	—	—	—	—
97-98—Bowling Green	CCHA	28	3	12	15	69	...	...	...	—	—	—	—	—
98-99—Bowling Green	CCHA	38	8	21	29	80	...	...	...	—	—	—	—	—
99-00—Bowling Green	CCHA	34	6	13	19	71	...	...	...	—	—	—	—	—
00-01—Detroit........................	IHL	71	9	17	26	41	...	...	...	—	—	—	—	—

JONSSON, HANS — D — PENGUINS

PERSONAL: Born August 2, 1973, in Jarved, Sweden. ... 6-1/202. ... Shoots left. ... Name pronounced YAHN-suhn.

TRANSACTIONS/CAREER NOTES: Selected by Pittsburgh Penguins in 11th round (11th Penguins pick, 286th overall) of NHL entry draft (June 29, 1993). ... Bruised hip (February 1, 2000); missed two games. ... Suffered lacerated elbow (March 19, 2000); missed one game. ... Bruised foot (September 21, 2000); missed first two games of season. ... Suffered concussion (October 13, 2000); missed four games. ... Bruised hip (January 27, 2001); missed five games. ... Strained shoulder (February 21, 2001); missed seven games. ... Suffered infected elbow (March 29, 2001); missed final five games of season.

		REGULAR SEASON								PLAYOFFS				
Season Team	League	Gms.	G	A	Pts.	PIM	+/-	PP	SH	Gms.	G	A	Pts.	PIM
91-92—MoDo Ornskoldsvik	Sweden	6	0	1	1	4	...	...	...	—	—	—	—	—
92-93—MoDo Ornskoldsvik	Sweden	40	2	2	4	24	...	...	...	3	0	1	1	2
93-94—MoDo Ornskoldsvik	Sweden	23	4	1	5	18	...	...	...	10	0	1	1	12
94-95—MoDo Ornskoldsvik	Sweden	39	4	6	10	30	...	...	...	—	—	—	—	—
95-96—MoDo Ornskoldsvik	Sweden	36	10	6	16	30	...	...	...	8	2	1	3	24
96-97—MoDo Ornskoldsvik	Sweden	27	7	5	12	18	...	...	...	—	—	—	—	—
97-98—MoDo Ornskoldsvik	Sweden	40	8	6	14	40	...	...	...	8	1	1	2	12
98-99—MoDo Ornskoldsvik	Sweden	41	3	4	7	40	...	...	...	13	2	4	6	22
99-00—Pittsburgh..................	NHL	68	3	11	14	12	-5	0	1	11	0	1	1	6
00-01—Pittsburgh..................	NHL	58	4	18	22	22	11	2	0	16	0	0	0	8
NHL Totals (2 years)...........		126	7	29	36	34	6	2	1	27	0	1	1	14

JONSSON, KENNY — D — ISLANDERS

PERSONAL: Born October 6, 1974, in Angelholm, Sweden. ... 6-3/211. ... Shoots left. ... Brother of Jorgen Jonsson, left winger with New York Islanders (1999-2000) and Mighty Ducks of Anaheim (1999-2000). ... Name pronounced YAHN-suhn.

TRANSACTIONS/CAREER NOTES: Selected by Toronto Maple Leafs in first round (first Maple Leafs pick, 12th overall) of NHL entry draft (June 26, 1993). ... Played in Europe during 1994-95 NHL lockout. ... Suffered from the flu (February 13, 1995); missed two games. ... Strained hip flexor (February 27, 1995); missed one game. ... Suffered hip pointer (April 7, 1995); missed one game. ... Suffered from the flu (April 19, 1995); missed one game. ... Strained back (December 9, 1995); missed one game. ... Separated shoulder (January 30, 1996); missed 17 games. ... Traded by Maple Leafs with C Darby Hendrickson, LW Sean Haggerty and first-round pick (G Robert Luongo) in 1997 draft to New York Islanders for LW Wendel Clark, D Mathieu Schneider and D D.J. Smith (March 13, 1996). ... Suffered from the flu (December 23, 1996); missed one game. ... Sprained knee (February 4, 1998); missed one game. ... Suffered concussion (November 17, 1998); missed eight games. ... Sprained knee (January 16, 1999); missed nine games. ... Fractured finger (April 17, 1999); missed final game of season. ... Suffered illness (December 30, 1999); missed four games. ... Suffered concussion (January 19, 2000); missed 11 games. ... Sprained left wrist (March 26, 2000); missed one game. ... Suffered headaches (April 1, 2000); missed final five games of regular season. ... Injured neck (December 3, 2000); missed one game. ... Sprained medial collateral ligament in left knee (December 19, 2000); missed 13 games. ... Injured knee (January 23, 2001); missed one game.

HONORS: Named Swedish League Rookie of the Year (1992-93). ... Named to NHL All-Rookie team (1994-95). ... Named to play in NHL All-Star Game (1999); replaced by D Mattias Norstrom due to injury.

MISCELLANEOUS: Captain of New York Islanders (1999-2000 through November 18, 2000).

		REGULAR SEASON								PLAYOFFS				
Season Team	League	Gms.	G	A	Pts.	PIM	+/-	PP	SH	Gms.	G	A	Pts.	PIM
91-92—Rogle Angelholm	Sweden	30	4	11	15	24	...	...	...	—	—	—	—	—
92-93—Rogle Angelholm	Sweden	39	3	10	13	42	...	...	...	—	—	—	—	—
93-94—Rogle Angelholm	Sweden	36	4	13	17	40	...	...	...	3	1	1	2	...
—Swedish Oly. team	Int'l	3	1	0	1	0	...	...	...	—	—	—	—	—
94-95—Rogle Angelholm	Sweden	8	3	1	4	20	...	...	...	—	—	—	—	—
—St. John's....................	AHL	10	2	5	7	2	...	...	...	—	—	—	—	—
—Toronto	NHL	39	2	7	9	16	-8	0	0	4	0	0	0	0
95-96—Toronto	NHL	50	4	22	26	22	12	3	0	—	—	—	—	—
—New York Islanders.....	NHL	16	0	4	4	10	-5	0	0	—	—	—	—	—
96-97—New York Islanders.....	NHL	81	3	18	21	24	10	1	0	—	—	—	—	—
97-98—New York Islanders.....	NHL	81	14	26	40	58	-2	6	0	—	—	—	—	—
98-99—New York Islanders.....	NHL	63	8	18	26	34	-18	6	0	—	—	—	—	—
99-00—New York Islanders.....	NHL	65	1	24	25	32	-15	1	0	—	—	—	—	—
00-01—New York Islanders.....	NHL	65	8	21	29	30	-22	5	0	—	—	—	—	—
NHL Totals (7 years).........		460	40	140	180	226	-48	22	0	4	0	0	0	0

JOSEPH, CHRIS — D

PERSONAL: Born September 10, 1969, in Burnaby, B.C. ... 6-3/212. ... Shoots left. ... Full Name: Robin Christopher Joseph.

TRANSACTIONS/CAREER NOTES: Selected by Pittsburgh Penguins in first round (first Penguins pick, fifth overall) of NHL entry draft (June 13, 1987). ... Traded by Penguins with C Craig Simpson, C Dave Hannan and D Moe Mantha to Edmonton Oilers for D Paul Coffey, LW Dave Hunter and RW Wayne Van Dorp (November 24, 1987). ... Strained knee ligaments (January 1989). ... Traded by Oilers to Tampa Bay Lightning for D Bob Beers (November 12, 1993). ... Selected by Pittsburgh Penguins from Oilers in NHL waiver draft for cash (January 18, 1995). ... Injured knee (March 2, 1995); missed 14 games. ... Injured knee (March 7, 1996); missed four games. ... Selected by Vancouver Canucks in NHL waiver draft for cash (September 30, 1996). ... Injured groin (December 18, 1996); missed seven games. ... Suffered from the flu (February 27, 1997); missed two games. ... Signed as free agent by Philadelphia Flyers (September 4, 1997). ... Signed as free agent by Ottawa Senators (July 29, 1999). ... Claimed by Canucks from Senators in NHL waiver draft (September 27, 1999). ... Injured groin (February 16, 2000); missed 11 games. ... Claimed on waivers by Phoenix Coyotes (March 14, 2000). ... Claimed on waivers by Atlanta Thrashers (February 14, 2001).

Season Team	League	REGULAR SEASON								PLAYOFFS				
		Gms.	G	A	Pts.	PIM	+/-	PP	SH	Gms.	G	A	Pts.	PIM
85-86—Seattle	WHL	72	4	8	12	50	...	...	...	5	0	3	3	12
86-87—Seattle	WHL	67	13	45	58	155	...	...	...	—	—	—	—	—
87-88—Pittsburgh	NHL	17	0	4	4	12	2	0	0	—	—	—	—	—
—Edmonton	NHL	7	0	4	4	6	-3	0	0	—	—	—	—	—
—Nova Scotia	AHL	8	0	2	2	8	...	...	...	4	0	0	0	9
—Seattle	WHL	23	5	14	19	49	...	...	...	—	—	—	—	—
88-89—Cape Breton	AHL	5	1	1	2	18	...	...	...	—	—	—	—	—
—Edmonton	NHL	44	4	5	9	54	-9	0	0	—	—	—	—	—
89-90—Edmonton	NHL	4	0	2	2	2	-2	0	0	—	—	—	—	—
—Cape Breton	AHL	61	10	20	30	69	...	...	...	6	2	1	3	4
90-91—Edmonton	NHL	49	5	17	22	59	3	2	0	—	—	—	—	—
91-92—Edmonton	NHL	7	0	0	0	8	-1	0	0	5	1	3	4	2
—Cape Breton	AHL	63	14	29	43	72	...	...	...	5	0	2	2	8
92-93—Edmonton	NHL	33	2	10	12	48	-9	1	0	—	—	—	—	—
93-94—Edmonton	NHL	10	1	1	2	28	-8	1	0	—	—	—	—	—
—Tampa Bay	NHL	66	10	19	29	108	-13	7	0	—	—	—	—	—
94-95—Pittsburgh	NHL	33	5	10	15	46	3	3	0	10	1	1	2	12
95-96—Pittsburgh	NHL	70	5	14	19	71	6	0	0	15	1	0	1	8
96-97—Vancouver	NHL	63	3	13	16	62	-21	2	0	—	—	—	—	—
97-98—Philadelphia	NHL	15	1	0	1	19	1	0	0	1	0	0	0	2
—Philadelphia	AHL	6	2	3	5	2	...	...	...	—	—	—	—	—
98-99—Cincinnati	IHL	27	11	19	30	38	...	...	...	—	—	—	—	—
—Philadelphia	NHL	2	0	0	0	2	0	0	0	—	—	—	—	—
—Philadelphia	AHL	51	9	29	38	26	...	...	...	16	3	10	13	8
99-00—Vancouver	NHL	38	2	9	11	6	-4	1	0	—	—	—	—	—
—Phoenix	NHL	9	0	0	0	0	-5	0	0	—	—	—	—	—
00-01—Phoenix	NHL	24	1	1	2	16	-4	0	1	—	—	—	—	—
—Atlanta	NHL	19	0	3	3	20	-7	0	0	—	—	—	—	—
NHL Totals (14 years)		510	39	112	151	567	-71	17	1	31	3	4	7	24

JOSEPH, CURTIS   G   MAPLE LEAFS

PERSONAL: Born April 29, 1967, in Keswick, Ont. ... 5-11/190. ... Catches left. ... Full Name: Curtis Shayne Joseph. ... Nickname: Cujo.

TRANSACTIONS/CAREER NOTES: Signed as non-drafted free agent by St. Louis Blues (June 16, 1989). ... Dislocated left shoulder (April 11, 1990). ... Underwent surgery to left shoulder (May 10, 1990). ... Sprained right knee (February 26, 1991); missed remainder of season. ... Injured ankle (March 12, 1992); missed seven games. ... Suffered sore knee (January 2, 1993); missed three games. ... Suffered from the flu (February 9, 1993); missed one game. ... Slightly strained groin (January 26, 1995); missed three games. ... Pulled hamstring (April 16, 1995); missed four games. ... Traded by Blues with rights to RW Michael Grier to Edmonton Oilers for first-round picks in 1996 (C Marty Reasoner) and 1997 (traded to Los Angeles) drafts (August 4, 1995); picks had been awarded to Oilers as compensation for Blues signing free agent LW Shayne Corson (July 28, 1995). ... Injured right knee (March 30, 1996); missed three games. ... Strained groin (December 18, 1996); missed seven games. ... Signed as free agent by Toronto Maple Leafs (July 15, 1998). ... Strained groin (January 21, 1999); missed one game.

HONORS: Named OHA Most Valuable Player (1986-87). ... Won WCHA Most Valuable Player Award (1988-89). ... Won WCHA Rookie of the Year Award (1988-89). ... Named to NCAA All-America (West) second team (1988-89). ... Named to WCHA All-Star first team (1988-89). ... Played in NHL All-Star Game (1994 and 2000). ... Named to play in NHL All-Star Game (1999); replaced by G Ron Tugnutt due to injury. ... Won King Clancy Memorial Trophy (1999-2000).

MISCELLANEOUS: Holds Edmonton Oilers all-time record for most shutouts (14). ... Stopped a penalty shot attempt (vs. Greg Adams, January 25, 1992; vs. Todd Elik, April 16, 1992; vs. Phil Housley, December 19, 1992; vs. Mike Donnelly, April 7, 1994; vs. J.F. Jomphe, April 15, 1998; vs. Landon Wilson, March 17, 1999; vs. Ulf Dahlen, April 1, 2000). ... Allowed a penalty shot goal (vs. Valeri Kamensky, October 26, 1996; vs. Adam Oates, November 18, 1998).

STATISTICAL NOTES: Led NHL with .911 save percentage (1992-93).

Season Team	League	REGULAR SEASON								PLAYOFFS						
		Gms.	Min	W	L	T	GA	SO	Avg.	Gms.	Min.	W	L	GA	SO	Avg.
86-87—Richmond Hill	OHA					Statistics unavailable.										
87-88—Notre Dame	SCMHL	36	2174	25	4	7	94	1	2.59	—						
88-89—Univ. of Wisconsin	WCHA	38	2267	21	11	5	94	1	2.49	—						
89-90—Peoria	IHL	23	1241	10	8	‡2	80	0	3.87	—						
—St. Louis	NHL	15	852	9	5	1	48	0	3.38	6	327	4	1	18	0	3.30
90-91—St. Louis	NHL	30	1710	16	10	2	89	0	3.12	—						
91-92—St. Louis	NHL	60	3494	27	20	10	175	2	3.01	6	379	2	4	23	0	3.64
92-93—St. Louis	NHL	68	3890	29	28	9	196	1	3.02	11	715	7	4	27	2	2.27
93-94—St. Louis	NHL	71	4127	36	23	11	213	1	3.10	4	246	0	4	15	0	3.66
94-95—St. Louis	NHL	36	1914	20	10	1	89	1	2.79	7	392	3	3	24	0	3.67
95-96—Las Vegas	IHL	15	873	12	2	‡1	29	1	1.99	—						
—Edmonton	NHL	34	1936	15	16	2	111	0	3.44	—						
96-97—Edmonton	NHL	72	4100	32	29	9	200	6	2.93	12	767	5	7	36	2	2.82
97-98—Edmonton	NHL	71	4132	29	31	9	181	8	2.63	12	716	5	7	23	1	1.93
98-99—Toronto	NHL	67	4001	35	24	7	†163	3	2.56	17	1011	9	†8	41	1	2.43
99-00—Toronto	NHL	63	3801	36	20	7	158	4	2.49	12	729	6	6	25	1	2.06
00-01—Toronto	NHL	68	4100	33	27	8	163	6	2.39	11	685	7	4	24	3	2.10
NHL Totals (12 years)		655	38057	317	243	76	1794	32	2.83	98	5967	48	48	256	12	2.57

JOVANOVSKI, ED   D   CANUCKS

PERSONAL: Born June 26, 1976, in Windsor, Ont. ... 6-2/210. ... Shoots left. ... Name pronounced joh-vuh-NAHV-skee.

TRANSACTIONS/CAREER NOTES: Selected by Florida Panthers in first round (first Panthers pick, first overall) of NHL entry draft (June 28, 1994). ... Fractured right index finger (September 29, 1995); missed first 11 games of season. ... Sprained knee (January 15, 1997); missed 16 games. ... Traded by Panthers with G Kevin Weekes, C Dave Gagner, C Mike Brown and first-round pick (C Nathan Smith) in 2000 draft to

Vancouver Canucks for RW Pavel Bure, D Bret Hedican, D Brad Ference and third-round pick (RW Robert Fried) in 2000 draft (January 17, 1999). ... Fractured foot (February 9, 1999); missed eight games. ... Injured groin (January 12, 2000); missed six games. ... Injured hip (March 13, 2000); missed one game. ... Strained oblique muscle (October 27, 2000); missed one game.

HONORS: Named to Can.HL All-Rookie team (1993-94). ... Named to OHL All-Star second team (1993-94). ... Named to OHL All-Rookie team (1993-94). ... Named to Can.HL All-Star second team (1994-95). ... Named to OHL All-Star first team (1994-95). ... Named to NHL All-Rookie team (1995-96). ... Played in NHL All-Star Game (2001).

			REGULAR SEASON								PLAYOFFS			
Season Team	League	Gms.	G	A	Pts.	PIM	+/-	PP	SH		Gms.	G	A	Pts.	PIM
92-93—Windsor	OHL Jr. B	48	7	46	53	88	...	...	...		—	—	—	—	—
93-94—Windsor	OHL	62	15	35	50	221	...	...	...		4	0	0	0	15
94-95—Windsor	OHL	50	23	42	65	198	...	...	...		9	2	7	9	39
95-96—Florida	NHL	70	10	11	21	137	-3	2	0		22	1	8	9	52
96-97—Florida	NHL	61	7	16	23	172	-1	3	0		5	0	0	0	4
97-98—Florida	NHL	81	9	14	23	158	-12	2	1		—	—	—	—	—
98-99—Florida	NHL	41	3	13	16	82	-4	1	0		—	—	—	—	—
—Vancouver	NHL	31	2	9	11	44	-5	0	0		—	—	—	—	—
99-00—Vancouver	NHL	75	5	21	26	54	-3	1	0		—	—	—	—	—
00-01—Vancouver	NHL	79	12	35	47	102	-1	4	0		4	1	1	2	0
NHL Totals (6 years)		438	48	119	167	749	-29	13	1		31	2	9	11	56

JUNEAU, JOE　　　　　LW　　　　　CANADIENS

PERSONAL: Born January 5, 1968, in Pont-Rouge, Que. ... 6-0/199. ... Shoots left. ... Name pronounced zhoh-AY ZHOO-noh.
TRANSACTIONS/CAREER NOTES: Selected by Boston Bruins in fourth round (third Bruins pick, 81st overall) of NHL entry draft (June 11, 1988). ... Fractured jaw (November 7, 1993); missed seven games. ... Reinjured jaw (February 18, 1994); missed two games. ... Traded by Bruins to Washington Capitals for D Al Iafrate (March 21, 1994). ... Strained hip flexor (January 29, 1995); missed one game. ... Strained back (February 15, 1995); missed one game. ... Bruised arm (April 11, 1995); missed one game. ... Injured leg (April 30, 1995); missed one game. ... Suffered from the flu (January 17, 1996); missed two games. ... Pulled hamstring (November 19, 1996); missed eight games. ... Bruised back and shoulder (January 1, 1997); missed two games. ... Sprained shoulder (February 7, 1997); missed four games. ... Sprained shoulder (February 18, 1997); missed five games. ... Strained hip (March 26, 1997); missed four games. ... Strained hip (April 12, 1997); missed one game. ... Strained groin (October 29, 1997); missed eight games. ... Strained posterior cruciate ligament in knee (December 13, 1997); missed 16 games. ... Suffered from the flu (December 17, 1998); missed one game. ... Bruised foot (February 28, 1999); missed one game. ... Suffered from headaches (March 9, 1999); missed five games. ... Traded by Capitals with third-round pick (LW Tim Preston) in 1999 draft to Buffalo Sabres for D Alexei Tezikov and future considerations (March 23, 1999). ... Suffered from the flu (March 27, 1999); missed two games. ... Suffered concussion (April 13, 1999); missed final three games of regular season. ... Signed as free agent by Ottawa Senators (October 25, 1999). ... Strained hip flexor (February 19, 2000); missed five games. ... Strained hip flexor (April 4, 2000); missed two games. ... Selected by Minnesota Wild in NHL expansion draft (June 23, 2000). ... Traded by Wild to Phoenix Coyotes for C Rickard Wallin (June 23, 2000). ... Strained shoulder (October 27, 2000); missed 10 games. ... Suffered concussion (February 14, 2001); missed two games. ... Suffered eye contusion (April 6, 2001); missed one game. ... Traded by Coyotes to Montreal Canadiens for future considerations (June 15, 2001).
HONORS: Named to NCAA All-America (East) first team (1989-90). ... Named to ECAC All-Star first team (1989-90). ... Named to NCAA All-America (East) second team (1990-91). ... Named to ECAC All-Star second team (1990-91). ... Named to NHL All-Rookie team (1992-93).
RECORDS: Holds NHL single-season record for most assists by a left winger—70 (1992-93). ... Holds NHL single-season record for most assists by a rookie—70 (1992-93).
STATISTICAL PLATEAUS: Three-goal games: 1992-93 (1), 1996-97 (1). Total: 2.
MISCELLANEOUS: Member of silver-medal-winning Canadian Olympic team (1992).

			REGULAR SEASON								PLAYOFFS			
Season Team	League	Gms.	G	A	Pts.	PIM	+/-	PP	SH		Gms.	G	A	Pts.	PIM
87-88—R.P.I.	ECAC	31	16	29	45	18	...	...	...		—	—	—	—	—
88-89—R.P.I.	ECAC	30	12	23	35	40	...	...	...		—	—	—	—	—
89-90—R.P.I.	ECAC	34	18	*52	*70	31	...	...	...		—	—	—	—	—
—Canadian nat'l team	Int'l	3	0	2	2	4	...	...	...		—	—	—	—	—
90-91—R.P.I.	ECAC	29	23	40	63	70	...	...	...		—	—	—	—	—
—Canadian nat'l team	Int'l	7	2	3	5	0	...	...	...		—	—	—	—	—
91-92—Canadian nat'l team	Int'l	60	20	49	69	35	...	...	...		—	—	—	—	—
—Can. Olympic team	Int'l	8	6	9	15	4	...	...	...		—	—	—	—	—
—Boston	NHL	14	5	14	19	4	6	2	0		15	4	8	12	21
92-93—Boston	NHL	84	32	70	102	33	23	9	0		4	2	4	6	6
93-94—Boston	NHL	63	14	58	72	35	11	4	0		—	—	—	—	—
—Washington	NHL	11	5	8	13	6	0	2	0		11	4	5	9	6
94-95—Washington	NHL	44	5	38	43	8	-1	3	0		7	2	6	8	2
95-96—Washington	NHL	80	14	50	64	30	-3	7	2		5	0	7	7	6
96-97—Washington	NHL	58	15	27	42	8	-11	9	1		—	—	—	—	—
97-98—Washington	NHL	56	9	22	31	26	-8	4	1		21	7	10	17	8
98-99—Washington	NHL	63	14	27	41	20	-3	2	1		—	—	—	—	—
—Buffalo	NHL	9	1	1	2	2	-1	0	0		20	3	8	11	10
99-00—Ottawa	NHL	65	13	24	37	22	3	2	0		6	2	1	3	0
00-01—Phoenix	NHL	69	10	23	33	28	-2	5	0		—	—	—	—	—
NHL Totals (10 years)		616	137	362	499	222	14	49	5		89	24	49	73	59

KABERLE, FRANTISEK　　　　　D　　　　　THRASHERS

PERSONAL: Born November 8, 1973, in Kladno, Czechoslovakia. ... 6-0/185. ... Shoots left. ... Brother of Tomas Kaberle, defenseman, Toronto Maple Leafs.
TRANSACTIONS/CAREER NOTES: Selected by Los Angeles Kings in third round (third Kings pick, 76th overall) of NHL entry draft (June 26, 1999). ... Traded by Kings with RW Donald Audette to Atlanta Thrashers for RW Kelly Buchberger and RW Nelson Emerson (March 13, 2000). ... Bruised foot (October 15, 2000); missed one game. ... Suffered from the flu (January 25, 2001); missed one game. ... Fractured foot (February 1, 2001); missed 25 games. ... Strained groin (April 1, 2001); missed final three games of season.

Season Team	League	Gms.	G	A	Pts.	PIM	+/-	PP	SH	Gms.	G	A	Pts.	PIM
REGULAR SEASON										PLAYOFFS				
91-92—Poldi Kladno	Czech.	37	1	4	5	8	...	...	...	8	0	1	1	0
92-93—Poldi Kladno	Czech.	49	6	9	15	...	...	...	...	—	—	—	—	—
93-94—HC Kladno	Czech Rep.	40	4	15	19	...	...	...	...	9	1	2	3	...
94-95—HC Kladno	Czech Rep.	40	7	17	24	...	...	...	...	8	0	3	3	...
95-96—MoDo Ornskoldsvik	Sweden	40	5	7	12	34	...	...	...	8	0	1	1	0
96-97—MoDo Ornskoldsvik	Sweden	50	3	11	14	28	...	...	...	—	—	—	—	—
97-98—MoDo Ornskoldsvik	Sweden	46	5	4	9	22	...	...	...	9	1	1	2	4
98-99—MoDo Ornskoldsvik	Sweden	45	15	18	33	4	...	...	...	13	2	5	7	8
99-00—Los Angeles	NHL	37	0	9	9	4	3	0	0	—	—	—	—	—
—Long Beach	IHL	18	2	8	10	8	...	...	...	—	—	—	—	—
—Lowell	AHL	4	0	2	2	0	...	...	...	—	—	—	—	—
—Atlanta	NHL	14	1	6	7	6	-13	0	1	—	—	—	—	—
00-01—Atlanta	NHL	51	4	11	15	18	11	1	0	—	—	—	—	—
NHL Totals (2 years)		102	5	26	31	28	1	1	1					

KABERLE, TOMAS — D — MAPLE LEAFS

PERSONAL: Born March 2, 1978, in Rakovnik, Czechoslovakia. ... 6-2/200. ... Shoots left. ... Brother of Frantisek Kaberle, defenseman, Atlanta Thrashers.

TRANSACTIONS/CAREER NOTES: Selected by Toronto Maple Leafs in eighth round (13th Maple Leafs pick, 204th overall) of NHL entry draft (June 22, 1996).

K

Season Team	League	Gms.	G	A	Pts.	PIM	+/-	PP	SH	Gms.	G	A	Pts.	PIM
REGULAR SEASON										PLAYOFFS				
94-95—Kladno	Czech. Jrs.	38	7	10	17	...	...	...	...	—	—	—	—	—
—Poldi Kladno	Czech Rep.	1	0	1	1	0	...	...	...	3	0	0	0	2
95-96—Poldi Kladno	Czech Jrs.	23	6	13	19	19	...	...	...	—	—	—	—	—
—Poldi Kladno	Czech Rep.	23	0	1	1	2	...	...	...	2	0	0	0	0
96-97—Poldi Kladno	Czech Rep.	49	0	5	5	26	...	...	...	3	0	0	0	0
97-98—Poldi Kladno	Czech Rep.	47	4	19	23	12	...	...	...	—	—	—	—	—
—St. John's	AHL	2	0	0	0	0	...	...	...	—	—	—	—	—
98-99—Toronto	NHL	57	4	18	22	12	3	0	0	14	0	3	3	2
99-00—Toronto	NHL	82	7	33	40	24	3	2	0	12	1	4	5	0
00-01—Toronto	NHL	82	6	39	45	24	10	0	0	11	1	3	4	0
NHL Totals (3 years)		221	17	90	107	60	16	2	0	37	2	10	12	2

KALININ, DMITRI — D — SABRES

PERSONAL: Born July 22, 1980, in Chelyabinsk, U.S.S.R. ... 6-2/198. ... Shoots left.

TRANSACTIONS/CAREER NOTES: Selected by Buffalo Sabres in first round (first Sabres pick, 18th overall) of NHL entry draft (June 27, 1998).

Season Team	League	Gms.	G	A	Pts.	PIM	+/-	PP	SH	Gms.	G	A	Pts.	PIM
REGULAR SEASON										PLAYOFFS				
95-96—Traktor Chelyabinsk	CIS Jr.	30	10	10	20	60	...	...	...	—	—	—	—	—
—Nadezhda Chelyabinsk	CIS Div. II	20	0	3	3	10	...	...	...	—	—	—	—	—
96-97—Traktor Chelyabinsk	Russian	2	0	0	0	0	...	...	...	—	—	—	—	—
—Traktor-2 Chelyabinsk	Rus. Div. III	20	0	0	0	10	...	...	...	—	—	—	—	—
97-98—Traktor Chelyabinsk	Russian	26	0	2	2	24	...	...	...	—	—	—	—	—
98-99—Moncton	QMJHL	39	7	18	25	44	...	...	...	4	1	1	2	0
—Rochester	AHL	3	0	1	1	14	...	...	...	7	0	0	0	6
99-00—Rochester	AHL	75	2	19	21	52	...	...	...	21	2	9	11	8
—Buffalo	NHL	4	0	0	0	4	0	0	0	—	—	—	—	—
00-01—Buffalo	NHL	79	4	18	22	38	-2	2	0	13	0	2	2	4
NHL Totals (2 years)		83	4	18	22	42	-2	2	0	13	0	2	2	4

KALLIO, TOMI — LW — THRASHERS

PERSONAL: Born January 27, 1977, in Turku, Finland. ... 6-1/180. ... Shoots left.

TRANSACTIONS/CAREER NOTES: Selected by Colorado Avalanche in fourth round (fourth Avalanche pick, 81st overall) of NHL entry draft (July 8, 1995). ... Selected by Atlanta Thrashers in NHL expansion draft (June 25, 1999). ... Strained groin (October 20, 2000); missed three games. ... Fractured shoulder (December 15, 2000); missed 23 games.

STATISTICAL PLATEAUS: Three-goal games: 2000-01 (1).

Season Team	League	Gms.	G	A	Pts.	PIM	+/-	PP	SH	Gms.	G	A	Pts.	PIM
REGULAR SEASON										PLAYOFFS				
93-94—TPS Turku	Finland Jr.	33	9	7	16	16	...	...	...	6	0	1	1	2
94-95—Kiekko-67	Finland Div. 2	25	8	5	13	16	...	...	...	7	3	1	4	6
—TPS Turku	Finland Jr.	14	5	12	17	24	...	...	...	—	—	—	—	—
95-96—Kiekko-67	Finland Div. 2	29	10	11	21	28	...	...	...	—	—	—	—	—
—TPS Turku	Finland	8	2	3	5	10	...	...	...	4	0	0	0	2
—TPS Turku	Finland Jr.	8	8	3	11	14	...	...	...	—	—	—	—	—
96-97—TPS Turku	Finland	47	9	10	19	18	...	...	...	8	2	0	2	2
97-98—TPS Turku	Finland	47	10	10	20	8	...	...	...	4	0	2	2	0
98-99—TPS Turku	Finland	54	15	21	36	20	...	...	...	10	3	4	7	6
99-00—TPS Turku	Finland	50	26	27	53	40	...	...	...	11	4	†9	13	4
00-01—Atlanta	NHL	56	14	13	27	22	-3	2	0	—	—	—	—	—
NHL Totals (1 year)		56	14	13	27	22	-3	2	0					

KAMENSKY, VALERI   LW   STARS

PERSONAL: Born April 18, 1966, in Voskresensk, U.S.S.R. ... 6-2/202. ... Shoots right. ... Name pronounced kuh-MEHN-skee.

TRANSACTIONS/CAREER NOTES: Selected by Quebec Nordiques in seventh round (eighth Nordiques pick, 129th overall) of NHL entry draft (June 11, 1988). ... Fractured leg (October 1991); missed 57 games. ... Fractured left thumb (October 17, 1992); missed three games. ... Fractured right ankle (October 27, 1992); missed 47 games. ... Bruised left foot (October 21, 1993); missed two games. ... Bruised right foot (December 21, 1993); missed one game. ... Played in Europe during 1994-95 NHL lockout. ... Suffered kidney infection (February 26, 1995); missed eight games. ... Nordiques franchise moved to Colorado and renamed Avalanche for 1995-96 season (June 21, 1995). ... Bruised ribs (January 3, 1996); missed one game. ... Separated shoulder (December 31, 1996); missed six games. ... Injured shoulder (February 25, 1997); missed three games. ... Bruised shoulder (December 13, 1997); missed three games. ... Suffered from the flu (December 31, 1997); missed two games. ... Bruised foot (November 8, 1998); missed two games. ... Fractured arm (March 14, 1999); missed final 15 games of regular season and first eight playoff games. ... Signed as free agent by New York Rangers (July 6, 1999). ... Suffered stress fracture in arm (October 1, 1999); missed six games. ... Fractured arm (October 24, 1999); missed ten games. ... Bruised forearm (December 3, 1999); missed seven games. ... Bruised ankle (April 4, 2000); missed one game. ... Bruised kidney (October 29, 2000); missed three games. ... Bruised kidney (December 3, 2000); missed two games. ... Injured right shoulder (January 6, 2001); missed one game. ... Bruised kidney (January 20, 2001); missed 11 games. ... Released by Rangers (June 30, 2001). ... Signed as free agent by Dallas Stars (July 5, 2001).

HONORS: Won Soviet Player of the Year Award (1990-91). ... Played in NHL All-Star Game (1998).

MISCELLANEOUS: Member of Stanley Cup championship team (1996). ... Member of gold-medal-winning U.S.S.R. Olympic team (1988). ... Member of silver-medal-winning Russian Olympic team (1998). ... Scored on penalty shot (vs. Curtis Joseph, October 26, 1996).

STATISTICAL PLATEAUS: Three-goal games: 1995-96 (2), 1996-97 (1), 1997-98 (1), 1998-99 (1). Total: 5.

				REGULAR SEASON								PLAYOFFS			
Season Team	League	Gms.	G	A	Pts.	PIM	+/-	PP	SH		Gms.	G	A	Pts.	PIM
82-83—Khimik	USSR	5	0	0	0	0	...	...	...		—	—	—	—	—
83-84—Khimik	USSR	20	2	2	4	6	...	...	...		—	—	—	—	—
84-85—Khimik	USSR	45	9	3	12	24	...	...	...		—	—	—	—	—
85-86—CSKA Moscow	USSR	40	15	9	24	8	...	...	...		—	—	—	—	—
86-87—CSKA Moscow	USSR	37	13	8	21	16	...	...	...		—	—	—	—	—
87-88—CSKA Moscow	USSR	51	26	20	46	40	...	...	...		—	—	—	—	—
—Soviet Olympic Team	Int'l	8	4	2	6	4	...	...	...		—	—	—	—	—
88-89—CSKA Moscow	USSR	40	18	10	28	30	...	...	...		—	—	—	—	—
89-90—CSKA Moscow	USSR	45	19	18	37	38	...	...	...		—	—	—	—	—
90-91—CSKA Moscow	USSR	46	20	26	46	66	...	...	...		—	—	—	—	—
91-92—Quebec	NHL	23	7	14	21	14	-1	2	0		—	—	—	—	—
92-93—Quebec	NHL	32	15	22	37	14	13	2	3		6	0	1	1	6
93-94—Quebec	NHL	76	28	37	65	42	12	6	0		—	—	—	—	—
94-95—Ambri Piotta	Switzerland	12	13	6	19	2	...	...	...		—	—	—	—	—
—Quebec	NHL	40	10	20	30	22	3	5	1		2	1	0	1	0
95-96—Colorado	NHL	81	38	47	85	85	14	18	1		22	10	12	22	28
96-97—Colorado	NHL	68	28	38	66	38	5	8	0		17	8	14	22	16
97-98—Colorado	NHL	75	26	40	66	60	-2	8	0		7	2	3	5	18
—Russian Oly. team	Int'l	6	1	2	3	0	...	...	...		—	—	—	—	—
98-99—Colorado	NHL	65	14	30	44	28	1	2	0		10	4	5	9	4
99-00—New York Rangers	NHL	58	13	19	32	24	-13	3	0		—	—	—	—	—
00-01—New York Rangers	NHL	65	14	20	34	36	-18	6	0		—	—	—	—	—
NHL Totals (10 years)		583	193	287	480	363	14	60	5		64	25	35	60	72

KAPANEN, NIKO   C   STARS

PERSONAL: Born April 29, 1978, in Hameenlinna, Finland. ... 5-9/180. ... Shoots left.

TRANSACTIONS/CAREER NOTES: Selected by Dallas Stars in sixth round (fifth Stars pick, 173rd overall) of NHL entry draft (June 27, 1998).

				REGULAR SEASON								PLAYOFFS			
Season Team	League	Gms.	G	A	Pts.	PIM	+/-	PP	SH		Gms.	G	A	Pts.	PIM
93-94—HPK Hameenlinna	Finland Jr.	31	17	33	50	34	...	...	...		—	—	—	—	—
94-95—HPK Hameenlinna	Finland Jr.	37	19	44	63	40	...	...	...		—	—	—	—	—
95-96—HPK Hameenlinna	Finland Jr.	26	15	22	37	34	...	...	...		—	—	—	—	—
—HPK Hameenlinna	Finland	7	1	0	1	0	...	...	...		—	—	—	—	—
96-97—HPK Hameenlinna	Finland	41	6	9	15	12	...	...	...		10	4	5	9	2
—HPK Hameenlinna	Finland Jr.	5	1	7	8	2	...	...	...		2	0	1	1	2
97-98—HPK Hameenlinna	Finland	48	8	18	26	44	...	...	...		—	—	—	—	—
—HPK Hameenlinna	Finland Jr.	2	1	1	2	0	...	...	...		—	—	—	—	—
98-99—HPK Hameenlinna	Finland	53	14	29	43	49	...	...	...		8	3	4	7	4
99-00—HPK Hameenlinna	Finland	53	20	28	48	40	...	...	...		8	1	†9	10	4
00-01—TPS Turku	Finland	56	11	21	32	20	...	...	...		10	2	1	3	4

KAPANEN, SAMI   RW   HURRICANES

PERSONAL: Born June 14, 1973, in Helsinki, Finland. ... 5-10/175. ... Shoots left. ... Name pronounced KAP-ih-nehn.

TRANSACTIONS/CAREER NOTES: Selected by Hartford Whalers in fourth round (fourth Whalers pick, 87th overall) of NHL entry draft (July 8, 1995). ... Suffered from the flu (October 20, 1996); missed two games. ... Sprained knee (November 30, 1996); missed 16 games. ... Sprained knee (January 10, 1997); missed nine games. ... Sprained knee (February 26, 1997); missed three games. ... Sprained knee (March 15, 1997); missed six games. ... Suffered from the flu (April 5, 1997); missed one game. ... Whalers franchise moved to North Carolina and renamed Carolina Hurricanes for 1997-98 season; NHL approved move on June 25, 1997. ... Suffered from the flu (March 12, 1998); missed one game. ... Bruised knee (October 24, 1998); missed one game. ... Bruised shoulder (February 19, 2000); missed two games. ... Suffered concussion (March 29, 2000); missed four games.

HONORS: Played in NHL All-Star Game (2000).

MISCELLANEOUS: Member of bronze-medal-winning Finnish Olympic team (1998). ... Scored on a penalty shot (vs. Jim Carey, March 12, 1997). ... Failed to score on a penalty shot (vs. Tom Barrasso, January 7, 1999).

STATISTICAL PLATEAUS: Three-goal games: 1997-98 (2).

K

Season Team	League	REGULAR SEASON								PLAYOFFS				
		Gms.	G	A	Pts.	PIM	+/-	PP	SH	Gms.	G	A	Pts.	PIM
90-91—KalPa Kuopio	Finland	14	1	2	3	2	...	...	...	8	2	1	3	2
91-92—KalPa Kuopio	Finland	42	15	10	25	8	...	...	...	—	—	—	—	—
92-93—KalPa Kuopio	Finland	37	4	17	21	12	...	...	...	—	—	—	—	—
93-94—KalPa Kuopio	Finland	48	23	32	55	16	...	...	...	—	—	—	—	—
94-95—HIFK Helsinki	Finland	49	14	28	42	42	...	...	...	3	0	0	0	0
95-96—Springfield	AHL	28	14	17	31	4	...	...	...	3	1	2	3	0
—Hartford	NHL	35	5	4	9	6	0	0	0	—	—	—	—	—
96-97—Hartford	NHL	45	13	12	25	2	6	3	0	—	—	—	—	—
97-98—Carolina	NHL	81	26	37	63	16	9	4	0	—	—	—	—	—
—Fin. Olympic team	Int'l	6	0	1	1	0	...	...	...	—	—	—	—	—
98-99—Carolina	NHL	81	24	35	59	10	-1	5	0	5	1	1	2	0
99-00—Carolina	NHL	76	24	24	48	12	10	7	0	—	—	—	—	—
00-01—Carolina	NHL	82	20	37	57	24	-12	7	0	6	2	3	5	0
NHL Totals (6 years)		400	112	149	261	70	12	26	0	11	3	4	7	0

KARALAHTI, JERE   D   KINGS

PERSONAL: Born March 25, 1975, in Helsinki, Finland. ... 6-2/210. ... Shoots right. ... Name pronounced YAIR-ee KAIR-uh-LAH-tee.
TRANSACTIONS/CAREER NOTES: Selected by Los Angeles Kings in sixth round (seventh Kings pick, 146th overall) of NHL entry draft (June 26, 1993). ... Bruised left foot (November 28, 2000); missed six games.

Season Team	League	REGULAR SEASON								PLAYOFFS				
		Gms.	G	A	Pts.	PIM	+/-	PP	SH	Gms.	G	A	Pts.	PIM
91-92—HIFK Juniors	Finland Jr.	30	12	5	17	36	...	...	...	—	—	—	—	—
92-93—HIFK Juniors	Finland Jr.	30	2	13	15	49	...	...	...	—	—	—	—	—
93-94—HIFK Helsinki	Finland	46	1	10	11	36	...	...	...	3	0	0	0	6
94-95—HIFK Helsinki	Finland	37	1	7	8	42	...	...	...	3	0	0	0	0
95-96—HIFK Helsinki	Finland	36	4	6	10	102	...	...	...	3	0	0	0	4
96-97—HIFK Helsinki	Finland	18	3	5	8	20	...	...	...	—	—	—	—	—
97-98—HIFK Helsinki	Finland	43	14	16	30	32	...	...	...	9	2	0	2	8
98-99—HIFK Helsinki	Finland	49	11	22	33	65	...	...	...	11	1	1	2	10
99-00—HIFK Helsinki	Finland	13	2	2	4	55	...	...	...	—	—	—	—	—
—Long Beach	IHL	10	0	3	3	4	...	...	...	—	—	—	—	—
—Los Angeles	NHL	48	6	10	16	18	3	4	0	4	0	1	1	2
00-01—Los Angeles	NHL	56	2	7	9	38	8	0	0	13	0	0	0	18
NHL Totals (2 years)		104	8	17	25	56	11	4	0	17	0	1	1	20

KARIYA, PAUL   LW   MIGHTY DUCKS

PERSONAL: Born October 16, 1974, in Vancouver. ... 5-10/180. ... Shoots left. ... Brother of Steve Kariya, left winger, Vancouver Canucks. ... Name pronounced kuh-REE-uh.
TRANSACTIONS/CAREER NOTES: Selected by Mighty Ducks of Anaheim in first round (first Mighty Ducks pick, fourth overall) of NHL entry draft (June 26, 1993). ... Suffered lower back spasms (February 12, 1995); missed one game. ... Strained abdominal muscle prior to 1996-97 season; missed first 11 games of season. ... Suffered mild concussion (November 13, 1996); missed two games. ... Missed first 32 games of 1997-98 season due to contract dispute. ... Suffered concussion (February 1, 1998); missed remainder of season. ... Injured hip prior to start of 1999-2000 season: missed first game of season. ... Fractured right foot (February 18, 2000); missed seven games. ... Fractured right foot (December 20, 2000); missed 16 games.
HONORS: Won Hobey Baker Memorial Award (1992-93). ... Named Hockey East Player of the Year (1992-93). ... Named Hockey East Rookie of the Year (1992-93). ... Named to NCAA All-America (East) All-Star first team (1992-93). ... Named to NCAA All-Tournament team (1992-93). ... Named to Hockey East All-Star first team (1992-93). ... Named to Hockey East All-Rookie team (1992-93). ... Named to Hockey East All-Decade team (1994). ... Named to NHL All-Rookie team (1994-95). ... Played in NHL All-Star Game (1996, 1997 and 1999-2001). ... Won Lady Byng Memorial Trophy (1995-96 and 1996-97). ... Named to NHL All-Star first team (1995-96, 1996-97 and 1998-99). ... Named to THE SPORTING NEWS All-Star team (1998-99 and 1999-2000). ... Named to NHL All-Star second team (1999-2000).
MISCELLANEOUS: Member of silver-medal-winning Canadian Olympic team (1994). ... Captain of Mighty Ducks of Anaheim (1996-97, December 11, 1997 through February 4, 1998, 1998-99, 1999-2000 and 2000-01). ... Holds Mighty Ducks of Anaheim all-time records for most games (442), most goals (243), most assists (288) and most points (531). ... Scored on a penalty shot (vs. Kevin Weekes, January 21, 1998; vs. Corey Hirsch, February 20, 1999). ... Failed to score on a penalty shot (vs. Stephane Fiset, March 18, 1999).
STATISTICAL NOTES: Led NHL in game-winning goals with 10 (1996-97). ... Led NHL in shots with 429 (1998-99).
STATISTICAL PLATEAUS: Three-goal games: 1996-97 (2), 1997-98 (1), 2000-01 (2). Total: 5.

Season Team	League	REGULAR SEASON								PLAYOFFS				
		Gms.	G	A	Pts.	PIM	+/-	PP	SH	Gms.	G	A	Pts.	PIM
90-91—Penticton	BCJHL	54	45	67	112	8	...	...	...	—	—	—	—	—
91-92—Penticton	BCJHL	40	46	86	132	16	...	...	...	—	—	—	—	—
92-93—Univ. of Maine	Hockey East	39	25	*75	*100	12	...	...	...	—	—	—	—	—
93-94—Canadian nat'l team	Int'l	23	7	34	41	2	...	...	...	—	—	—	—	—
—Can. Olympic team	Int'l	8	3	4	7	2	...	...	...	—	—	—	—	—
—Univ. of Maine	Hockey East	12	8	16	24	4	...	...	...	—	—	—	—	—
94-95—Anaheim	NHL	47	18	21	39	4	-17	7	1	—	—	—	—	—
95-96—Anaheim	NHL	82	50	58	108	20	9	20	3	—	—	—	—	—
96-97—Anaheim	NHL	69	44	55	99	6	36	15	3	11	7	6	13	4
97-98—Anaheim	NHL	22	17	14	31	23	12	3	0	—	—	—	—	—
98-99—Anaheim	NHL	82	39	62	101	40	17	11	2	3	1	3	4	0
99-00—Anaheim	NHL	74	42	44	86	24	22	11	3	—	—	—	—	—
00-01—Anaheim	NHL	66	33	34	67	20	-9	18	3	—	—	—	—	—
NHL Totals (7 years)		442	243	288	531	137	70	85	15	14	8	9	17	4

KARIYA, STEVE   LW   CANUCKS

PERSONAL: Born December 22, 1977, in Vancouver. ... 5-7/170. ... Shoots left. ... Brother of Paul Kariya, left winger, Mighty Ducks of Anaheim. ... Name pronounced kuh-REE-uh.
TRANSACTIONS/CAREER NOTES: Signed as non-drafted free agent by Vancouver Canucks (April 16, 1999).
HONORS: Named to NCAA All-America (East) first team (1998-99). ... Named to Hockey East All-Star first team (1998-99).

				REGULAR SEASON						PLAYOFFS				
Season Team	League	Gms.	G	A	Pts.	PIM	+/-	PP	SH	Gms.	G	A	Pts.	PIM
94-95—Nanaimo	BCJHL	60	39	60	99	...				—	—	—	—	—
95-96—Univ. of Maine	Hockey East	39	7	15	22	38	...	...	...	—	—	—	—	—
96-97—Univ. of Maine	Hockey East	35	19	31	50	10	...	...	...	—	—	—	—	—
97-98—Univ. of Maine	Hockey East	35	25	25	50	22	...	...	...	—	—	—	—	—
98-99—Univ. of Maine	Hockey East	41	27	38	65	24	...	...	...	—	—	—	—	—
99-00—Vancouver	NHL	45	8	11	19	22	9	0	0	—	—	—	—	—
—Syracuse	AHL	29	18	23	41	22	...	...	...	4	2	1	3	0
00-01—Vancouver	NHL	17	1	6	7	8	-1	1	0	—	—	—	—	—
—Kansas City	IHL	43	15	29	44	51	...	...	...	—	—	—	—	—
NHL Totals (2 years)		62	9	17	26	30	8	1	0					

KARLSSON, ANDREAS   C   THRASHERS

PERSONAL: Born August 19, 1975, in Leksand, Sweden. ... 6-3/195. ... Shoots left.
TRANSACTIONS/CAREER NOTES: Selected by Calgary Flames in sixth round (eighth Flames pick, 148th overall) of NHL entry draft (June 26, 1993). ... Traded by Flames to Atlanta Thrashers for future considerations (June 25, 1999). ... Strained shoulder (February 3, 2000); missed 11 games. ... Strained hip flexor (January 14, 2001); missed 15 games.

				REGULAR SEASON						PLAYOFFS				
Season Team	League	Gms.	G	A	Pts.	PIM	+/-	PP	SH	Gms.	G	A	Pts.	PIM
92-93—Leksand	Sweden	13	0	0	0	6	...	...	...	—	—	—	—	—
93-94—Leksand	Sweden	21	0	0	0	10	...	...	...	—	—	—	—	—
94-95—Leksand	Sweden	24	7	8	15	4	...	...	...	4	0	1	1	0
95-96—Leksand	Sweden	40	10	13	23	10	...	...	...	5	2	1	3	4
96-97—Leksand	Sweden	49	13	11	24	39	...	...	...	9	2	0	2	2
97-98—Leksand	Sweden	33	9	14	23	20	...	...	...	4	1	0	1	0
98-99—Leksand	Sweden	49	18	15	33	18	...	...	...	4	1	0	1	6
99-00—Orlando	IHL	18	5	5	10	6	...	...	...	—	—	—	—	—
—Atlanta	NHL	51	5	9	14	14	-17	1	0	—	—	—	—	—
00-01—Atlanta	NHL	60	5	11	16	16	-2	0	1	—	—	—	—	—
NHL Totals (2 years)		111	10	20	30	30	-19	1	1					

KARPA, DAVE   D   RANGERS

PERSONAL: Born May 7, 1971, in Regina, Sask. ... 6-1/210. ... Shoots right. ... Full Name: David James Karpa.
TRANSACTIONS/CAREER NOTES: Selected by Quebec Nordiques in fourth round (fourth Nordiques pick, 68th overall) of NHL entry draft (June 22, 1991). ... Fractured right wrist (January 26, 1994); missed 18 games. ... Traded by Nordiques to Los Angeles Kings for fourth-round pick in 1995 or 1996 draft (February 28, 1995); trade invalidated by NHL because Karpa failed his physical examination (March 3, 1995). ... Traded by Nordiques to Mighty Ducks of Anaheim for fourth-round pick (traded to St. Louis) in 1997 draft (March 8, 1995). ... Underwent right wrist surgery (May 9, 1995). ... Bruised right knee (November 24, 1995); missed eight games. ... Fractured right hand (February 4, 1997); missed 13 games. ... Traded by Mighty Ducks with fourth-round pick (traded to Atlanta) in 2000 draft to Carolina Hurricanes for LW Stu Grimson and D Kevin Haller (August 11, 1998). ... Injured hamstring (December 6, 1997); missed two games. ... Suffered torn anterior cruciate ligament and medial collateral ligament in knee (November 22, 1998); missed 41 games. ... Bruised shoulder (March 10, 1999); missed five games. ... Reinjured shoulder (March 26, 1999); missed three games. ... Injured foot (March 29, 2000); missed final five games of season. ... Bruised ribs (February 27, 2001); missed two games. ... Signed as free agent by New York Rangers (July 1, 2001).
MISCELLANEOUS: Holds Mighty Ducks of Anaheim all-time record for most penalty minutes (788).

				REGULAR SEASON						PLAYOFFS				
Season Team	League	Gms.	G	A	Pts.	PIM	+/-	PP	SH	Gms.	G	A	Pts.	PIM
88-89—Notre Dame	SCMHL	...	16	37	53	...	...	...	...	—	—	—	—	—
89-90—Notre Dame	SCMHL	43	9	19	28	271	...	...	...	—	—	—	—	—
90-91—Ferris State	CCHA	41	6	19	25	109	...	...	...	—	—	—	—	—
91-92—Ferris State	CCHA	34	7	12	19	124	...	...	...	—	—	—	—	—
—Halifax	AHL	2	0	0	0	4	...	...	...	—	—	—	—	—
—Quebec	NHL	4	0	0	0	14	2	0	0	—	—	—	—	—
92-93—Halifax	AHL	71	4	27	31	167	...	...	...	—	—	—	—	—
—Quebec	NHL	12	0	1	1	13	-6	0	0	3	0	0	0	0
93-94—Quebec	NHL	60	5	12	17	148	0	2	0	—	—	—	—	—
—Cornwall	AHL	1	0	0	0	0	...	...	...	12	2	2	4	27
94-95—Cornwall	AHL	6	0	2	2	19	...	...	...	—	—	—	—	—
—Quebec	NHL	2	0	0	0	0	-1	0	0	—	—	—	—	—
—Anaheim	NHL	26	1	5	6	91	0	0	0	—	—	—	—	—
95-96—Anaheim	NHL	72	3	16	19	270	-3	0	1	—	—	—	—	—
96-97—Anaheim	NHL	69	2	11	13	210	11	0	0	8	1	1	2	20
97-98—Anaheim	NHL	78	1	11	12	217	-3	0	0	—	—	—	—	—
98-99—Carolina	NHL	33	0	2	2	55	1	0	0	2	0	0	0	2
99-00—Cincinnati	IHL	39	1	8	9	147	...	...	...	—	—	—	—	—
—Carolina	NHL	27	1	4	5	52	9	0	0	—	—	—	—	—
00-01—Carolina	NHL	80	4	6	10	159	-19	2	0	6	0	0	0	17
NHL Totals (10 years)		463	17	68	85	1229	-9	4	1	19	1	1	2	39

KARPOVTSEV, ALEXANDER   D   BLACKHAWKS

PERSONAL: Born April 7, 1970, in Moscow, U.S.S.R. ... 6-3/215. ... Shoots right. ... Name pronounced KAHR-puht-sehf.

TRANSACTIONS/CAREER NOTES: Selected by Quebec Nordiques in seventh round (seventh Nordiques pick, 158th overall) of NHL entry draft (June 16, 1990). ... Traded by Nordiques to New York Rangers for D Mike Hurlbut (September 9, 1993). ... Bruised buttocks (October 9, 1993); missed one game. ... Bruised hip (November 3, 1993); missed six games. ... Reinjured hip (November 23, 1993); missed one game. ... Injured face (February 28, 1994); missed two games. ... Suffered injury (March 14, 1994); missed two games. ... Played in Europe during 1994-95 NHL lockout. ... Suffered sore ankle (April 14, 1995); missed one game. ... Hyperextended elbow (October 29, 1995); missed one game. ... Suffered back spasms (February 10, 1996); missed one game. ... Suffered back spasms (February 18, 1996); missed one game. ... Bruised thumb (March 13, 1996); missed two games. ... Suffered back spasms (March 27, 1996); missed six games. ... Bruised toe (April 3, 1997); missed one game. ... Hyperextended elbow (April 10, 1997); missed one game. ... Suffered throat infection (October 10, 1997); missed one game. ... Sprained right wrist (January 19, 1998); missed one game. ... Underwent wrist surgery (February 2, 1998); missed 28 games. ... Bruised knee (October 13, 1998); missed two games. ... Traded by Rangers with fourth-round pick (LW Mirko Murovic) in 1999 draft to Toronto Maple Leafs for D Mathieu Schneider (October 14, 1998). ... Fractured thumb (November 14, 1998); missed 12 games. ... Sprained wrist (January 2, 1999); missed three games. ... Strained wrist (February 2, 1999); missed three games. ... Fractured finger (March 17, 1999); missed three games. ... Strained shoulder (April 26, 1999); missed three playoff games. ... Suffered injury (November 5, 1999); missed one game. ... Sprained shoulder (November 26, 1999); missed five games. ... Fractured hand (January 11, 2000); missed four games. ... Suffered injury (March 16, 2000); missed one game. ... Suffered injury (March 23, 2000); missed one game. ... Traded by Maple Leafs with fourth-round pick (D Vladimir Gusev) in 2001 draft to Chicago Blackhawks for D Bryan McCabe (October 2, 2000). ... Bruised ankle (November 2, 2000); missed one game. ... Reinjured ankle (November 5, 2000); missed two games. ... Injured knee (December 3, 2000); missed one game. ... Underwent knee surgery (December 10, 2000); missed 11 games. ... Lacerated arm (January 7, 2001); missed one game. ... Suspended two games by NHL elbowing incident (February 10, 2001). ... Bruised knee (February 27, 2001); missed three games. ... Injured elbow (March 24, 2001); missed remainder of season.

MISCELLANEOUS: Member of Stanley Cup championship team (1994). ... Member of silver-medal-winning Russian Olympic team (1998).

STATISTICAL NOTES: Led NHL in plus/minus with plus 39 in 1998-99.

| | | REGULAR SEASON | | | | | | | | PLAYOFFS | | | | |
Season Team	League	Gms.	G	A	Pts.	PIM	+/-	PP	SH	Gms.	G	A	Pts.	PIM
89-90—Dynamo Moscow	USSR	35	1	1	2	27	...	...	...	—	—	—	—	—
90-91—Dynamo Moscow	USSR	40	0	5	5	15	...	...	...	—	—	—	—	—
91-92—Dynamo Moscow	CIS	28	3	2	5	22	...	...	...	—	—	—	—	—
92-93—Dynamo Moscow	CIS	40	3	11	14	100	...	...	...	—	—	—	—	—
93-94—New York Rangers	NHL	67	3	15	18	58	12	1	0	17	0	4	4	12
94-95—Dynamo Moscow	CIS	13	0	2	2	10	...	...	...	—	—	—	—	—
—New York Rangers	NHL	47	4	8	12	30	-4	1	0	8	1	0	1	0
95-96—New York Rangers	NHL	40	2	16	18	26	12	1	0	6	0	1	1	4
96-97—New York Rangers	NHL	77	9	29	38	59	1	6	1	13	1	3	4	20
97-98—New York Rangers	NHL	47	3	7	10	38	-1	1	0	—	—	—	—	—
98-99—New York Rangers	NHL	2	1	0	1	0	1	0	0	—	—	—	—	—
—Toronto	NHL	56	2	25	27	52	38	1	0	14	1	3	4	12
99-00—Toronto	NHL	69	3	14	17	54	9	3	0	11	0	3	3	4
00-01—Dynamo Moscow	Russian	5	0	1	1	0	...	...	...	—	—	—	—	—
—Chicago	NHL	53	2	13	15	39	-4	1	0	—	—	—	—	—
NHL Totals (8 years)		458	29	127	156	356	64	15	1	69	3	14	17	52

KASPARAITIS, DARIUS   D   PENGUINS

PERSONAL: Born October 16, 1972, in Elektrenai, U.S.S.R. ... 5-11/212. ... Shoots left. ... Name pronounced kas-puhr-IGH-tihz.

TRANSACTIONS/CAREER NOTES: Selected by New York Islanders in first round (first Islanders pick, fifth overall) of NHL entry draft (June 20, 1992). ... Suffered back spasms (February 12, 1993); missed two games. ... Strained back (April 15, 1993); missed one game. ... Strained lower back (November 10, 1993); missed two games. ... Jammed wrist (March 5, 1994); missed four games. ... Tore knee ligament (February 20, 1995); missed remainder of season and first 15 games of 1995-96 season. ... Suffered from the flu (December 2, 1995); missed two games. ... Severed two tendons in right hand (December 9, 1995); missed 16 games. ... Injured groin (February 8, 1996); missed two games. ... Traded by Islanders with C Andreas Johansson to Pittsburgh Penguins for C Bryan Smolinski (November 17, 1996). ... Suffered concussion (December 23, 1996); missed two games. ... Suffered facial laceration (January 2, 1997); missed one game. ... Twisted ankle (January 23, 1997); missed one game. ... Suffered concussion (March 18, 1997); missed three games. ... Suffered from the flu (March 29, 1998); missed one game. ... Injured knee (September 20, 1998); missed first eight games of season. ... Strained knee (December 21, 1998); missed one game. ... Strained groin (February 24, 1999); missed two games. ... Strained knee (March 5, 1999) and underwent surgery; missed remainder of season. ... Injured knee prior to start of 1999-2000 season; missed first four games of season. ... Suspended two games by NHL for elbowing incident (October 20, 1999). ... Suffered from headaches (December 30, 1999); missed two games. ... Suspended one game by NHL for second major penalty and game misconduct in season (January 19, 2000). ... Bruised foot (December 16, 2000); missed three games. ... Suffered injury (April 4, 2001); missed final two games of season.

MISCELLANEOUS: Member of gold-medal-winning Unified Olympic team (1992). ... Member of silver-medal-winning Russian Olympic team (1998).

| | | REGULAR SEASON | | | | | | | | PLAYOFFS | | | | |
Season Team	League	Gms.	G	A	Pts.	PIM	+/-	PP	SH	Gms.	G	A	Pts.	PIM
88-89—Dynamo Moscow	USSR	3	0	0	0	0	...	...	...	—	—	—	—	—
89-90—Dynamo Moscow	USSR	1	0	0	0	0	...	...	...	—	—	—	—	—
90-91—Dynamo Moscow	USSR	17	0	1	1	10	...	...	...	—	—	—	—	—
91-92—Dynamo Moscow	CIS	31	2	10	12	14	...	...	...	—	—	—	—	—
—Unif. Olympic team	Int'l	8	0	2	2	2	...	...	...	—	—	—	—	—
92-93—Dynamo Moscow	CIS	7	1	3	4	8	...	...	...	—	—	—	—	—
—New York Islanders	NHL	79	4	17	21	166	15	0	0	18	0	5	5	31
93-94—New York Islanders	NHL	76	1	10	11	142	-6	0	0	4	0	0	0	8
94-95—New York Islanders	NHL	13	0	1	1	22	-11	0	0	—	—	—	—	—
95-96—New York Islanders	NHL	46	1	7	8	93	-12	0	0	—	—	—	—	—
96-97—New York Islanders	NHL	18	0	5	5	16	-7	0	0	—	—	—	—	—
—Pittsburgh	NHL	57	2	16	18	84	24	0	0	5	0	0	0	6
97-98—Pittsburgh	NHL	81	4	8	12	127	3	0	2	5	0	0	0	8
—Russian Oly. team	Int'l	6	0	2	2	6	...	...	...	—	—	—	—	—
98-99—Pittsburgh	NHL	48	1	4	5	70	12	0	0	—	—	—	—	—
99-00—Pittsburgh	NHL	73	3	12	15	146	-12	1	0	11	1	1	2	10
00-01—Pittsburgh	NHL	77	1	16	19	111	11	1	0	17	1	1	2	26
NHL Totals (9 years)		568	19	96	115	977	17	2	2	60	2	7	9	89

PERSONAL: Born March 14, 1979, in Ottawa. ... 6-3/192. ... Shoots right.

TRANSACTIONS/CAREER NOTES: Selected by Philadelphia Flyers in second round (second Flyers pick, 50th overall) of NHL entry draft (June 21, 1997). ... Traded by Flyers to Vancouver Canucks for sixth-round pick (F Konstantin Rudenko) in 1999 draft (June 1, 1999).

Season Team	League		REGULAR SEASON								PLAYOFFS			
		Gms.	G	A	Pts.	PIM	+/-	PP	SH	Gms.	G	A	Pts.	PIM
96-97—Peterborough.............	OHL	43	6	8	14	53	...	...	...	11	1	1	2	12
97-98—Peterborough.............	OHL	66	10	16	26	85	...	...	...	4	1	0	1	6
98-99—Peterborough.............	OHL	68	26	43	69	118	...	...	...	5	0	5	5	10
99-00—Syracuse....................	AHL	68	12	8	20	56	...	...	...	4	0	0	0	0
00-01—Kansas City................	IHL	78	26	15	41	86	...	...	...	—	—	—	—	—
—Vancouver..................	NHL	—	—	—	—	—	—	—	—	3	0	0	0	2
NHL Totals (1 year).............		—	—	—	—	—	—	—	—	3	0	0	0	2

K

PERSONAL: Born May 29, 1967, in Winnipeg. ... 6-0/185. ... Shoots right. ... Name pronounced KEEN.

TRANSACTIONS/CAREER NOTES: Signed as non-drafted free agent by Montreal Canadiens (September 25, 1985). ... Separated right shoulder (December 21, 1988). ... Lacerated left kneecap (October 31, 1990); missed seven games. ... Injured neck (March 1991). ... Sprained ankle (January 16, 1992); missed four games. ... Reinjured ankle (February 1, 1992); missed 10 games. ... Bruised ankle (March 11, 1992); missed one game. ... Suspended four off-days and fined $500 by NHL for swinging stick in preseason game (October 13, 1992). ... Suffered wrist tendinitis (January 26, 1993); missed three games. ... Suffered back spasms (February 12, 1993); missed two games. ... Fractured toe (February 27, 1993); missed two games. ... Suffered back spasms (October 16, 1993); missed one game. ... Suffered back spasms (January 12, 1994); missed three games. ... Injured groin (November 1, 1995); missed one game. ... Injured neck (November 18, 1995); missed three games. ... Injured groin (November 25, 1995); missed two games. ... Traded by Canadiens with G Patrick Roy to Colorado Avalanche for G Jocelyn Thibault, LW Martin Rucinsky and RW Andrei Kovalenko (December 6, 1995). ... Signed as free agent by New York Rangers (July 7, 1997). ... Traded by Rangers with C Brian Skrudland and sixth-round pick (RW Pavel Patera) in 1998 draft to Dallas Stars for LW Bob Errey, RW Todd Harvey and fourth-round pick (LW Boyd Kane) in 1998 draft (March 24, 1998). ... Strained back (March 5, 2000); missed one game. ... Injured groin (December 13, 2000); missed five games. ... Bruised ankle (January 17, 2001); missed two games. ... Fractured ankle (January 22, 2001); missed six games. ... Bruised chest muscle (April 2, 2001); missed final two games of regular season. ... Signed as free agent by St. Louis Blues (July 5, 2001).

MISCELLANEOUS: Member of Stanley Cup championship team (1993, 1996 and 1999). ... Captain of Montreal Canadiens (1994-95 through December 6, 1995). ... Scored on a penalty shot (vs. Corey Schwab, October 24, 1997).

Season Team	League		REGULAR SEASON								PLAYOFFS			
		Gms.	G	A	Pts.	PIM	+/-	PP	SH	Gms.	G	A	Pts.	PIM
83-84—Winnipeg	WHL	1	0	0	0	0	...	...	...	—	—	—	—	—
84-85—Moose Jaw	WHL	65	17	26	43	141	...	...	...	—	—	—	—	—
85-86—Moose Jaw	WHL	67	34	49	83	162	...	...	...	13	6	8	14	9
86-87—Moose Jaw	WHL	53	25	45	70	107	...	...	...	9	3	9	12	11
—Sherbrooke	AHL	—	—	—	—	—	...	...	...	9	2	2	4	16
87-88—Sherbrooke	AHL	78	25	43	68	70	...	...	...	6	1	1	2	18
88-89—Montreal	NHL	69	16	19	35	69	9	5	0	21	4	3	7	17
89-90—Montreal	NHL	74	9	15	24	78	0	1	0	11	0	1	1	8
90-91—Montreal	NHL	73	13	23	36	50	6	2	1	12	3	2	5	6
91-92—Montreal	NHL	67	11	30	41	64	16	2	0	8	1	1	2	16
92-93—Montreal	NHL	77	15	45	60	95	29	0	0	19	2	13	15	6
93-94—Montreal	NHL	80	16	30	46	119	6	6	2	6	3	1	4	4
94-95—Montreal	NHL	48	10	10	20	15	5	1	0	—	—	—	—	—
95-96—Montreal	NHL	18	0	7	7	6	-6	0	0	—	—	—	—	—
—Colorado	NHL	55	10	10	20	40	1	0	2	22	3	2	5	16
96-97—Colorado	NHL	81	10	17	27	63	2	0	1	17	3	1	4	24
97-98—New York Rangers......	NHL	70	8	10	18	47	-12	2	0	—	—	—	—	—
—Dallas.........................	NHL	13	2	3	5	5	0	0	0	17	4	4	8	0
98-99—Dallas.........................	NHL	81	6	23	29	62	-2	1	1	23	5	2	7	6
99-00—Dallas.........................	NHL	81	13	21	34	41	9	0	4	23	2	4	6	14
00-01—Dallas.........................	NHL	67	10	14	24	35	4	1	0	10	3	2	5	4
NHL Totals (13 years).........		954	149	277	426	789	67	21	11	189	33	36	69	121

PERSONAL: Born September 17, 1980, in Brampton, Ont. ... 5-11/185. ... Shoots right.

TRANSACTIONS/CAREER NOTES: Selected by Tampa Bay Lightning in second round (first Lightning pick, 47th overall) of NHL entry draft (June 26, 1999).

HONORS: Won Emms Family Award (1998-99). ... Won Eddie Powers Memorial Trophy (1999-2000). ... Won Jim Mahon Memorial Trophy (1999-2000). ... Named to OHL All-Star second team (1999-2000). ... Named to Can.HL All-Star second team (1999-2000).

Season Team	League		REGULAR SEASON								PLAYOFFS			
		Gms.	G	A	Pts.	PIM	+/-	PP	SH	Gms.	G	A	Pts.	PIM
96-97—Quinte	Tier II Jr. A	44	21	23	44	...	...	...	...	—	—	—	—	—
97-98—Caledon......................	Jr. A	51	52	51	103	117	...	...	...	—	—	—	—	—
98-99—Toronto St. Michael's..	OHL	38	37	37	74	80	...	...	...	—	—	—	—	—
—Barrie..........................	OHL	28	14	28	42	60	...	...	...	10	5	5	10	31
99-00—Barrie	OHL	66	48	*73	*121	95	...	...	...	25	10	13	23	41
00-01—Detroit........................	IHL	13	7	5	12	23	...	...	...	—	—	—	—	—
—Tampa Bay	NHL	49	4	0	4	38	-13	0	0	—	—	—	—	—
NHL Totals (1 year).............		49	4	0	4	38	-13	0	0					

KELLY, STEVE   C   KINGS

PERSONAL: Born October 26, 1976, in Vancouver. ... 6-2/211. ... Shoots left.

TRANSACTIONS/CAREER NOTES: Selected by Edmonton Oilers in first round (first Oilers pick, sixth overall) of NHL entry draft (July 8, 1995). ... Traded by Oilers to Tampa Bay Lightning with C Jason Bonsignore and D Bryan Marchment for D Roman Hamrlik and C Paul Comrie (December 30, 1997). ... Suffered from the flu (January 21, 1998); missed two games. ... Suffered from the flu (January 31, 1998); missed one game. ... Suffered concussion (October 10, 1998); missed eight games. ... Traded by Lightning to New Jersey Devils for seventh-round pick (G Brian Eklund) in 2000 draft (October 7, 1999). ... Traded by Devils to Los Angeles Kings for future considerations (February 27, 2001). ... Strained lower back (March 19, 2001); missed two games.

MISCELLANEOUS: Member of Stanley Cup championship team (2000).

		REGULAR SEASON								PLAYOFFS				
Season Team	League	Gms.	G	A	Pts.	PIM	+/-	PP	SH	Gms.	G	A	Pts.	PIM
92-93—Prince Albert	WHL	65	11	9	20	75	...	...	...	—	—	—	—	—
93-94—Prince Albert	WHL	65	19	42	61	106	...	...	...	—	—	—	—	—
94-95—Prince Albert	WHL	68	31	41	72	153	...	...	...	15	7	9	16	35
95-96—Prince Albert	WHL	70	27	74	101	203	...	...	...	18	13	18	31	47
96-97—Hamilton	AHL	48	9	29	38	111	...	...	...	11	3	3	6	24
—Edmonton	NHL	8	1	0	1	6	-1	0	0	6	0	0	0	2
97-98—Edmonton	NHL	19	0	2	2	8	-4	0	0	—	—	—	—	—
—Hamilton	AHL	11	2	8	10	18	...	...	...	—	—	—	—	—
—Tampa Bay	NHL	24	2	1	3	15	-9	1	0	—	—	—	—	—
—Milwaukee	IHL	5	0	1	1	19	...	...	...	—	—	—	—	—
—Cleveland	IHL	5	1	1	2	29	...	...	...	1	0	1	1	0
98-99—Tampa Bay	NHL	34	1	3	4	27	-15	0	0	—	—	—	—	—
—Cleveland	IHL	18	6	7	13	36	...	...	...	—	—	—	—	—
99-00—Detroit	IHL	1	0	0	0	4	...	...	...	—	—	—	—	—
—Albany	AHL	76	21	36	57	131	...	...	...	3	1	1	2	2
—New Jersey	NHL	1	0	0	0	0	0	0	0	10	0	0	0	4
00-01—New Jersey	NHL	24	2	2	4	21	0	0	0	—	—	—	—	—
—Los Angeles	NHL	11	1	0	1	4	0	0	0	8	0	0	0	2
NHL Totals (5 years)		121	7	8	15	81	-29	1	0	24	0	0	0	8

KHABIBULIN, NIKOLAI   G   LIGHTNING

PERSONAL: Born January 13, 1973, in Sverdlovsk, U.S.S.R. ... 6-1/195. ... Catches left. ... Name pronounced hah-bee-BOO-lihn.

TRANSACTIONS/CAREER NOTES: Selected by Winnipeg Jets in ninth round (eighth Jets pick, 204th overall) of NHL entry draft (June 20, 1992). ... Sprained knee (November 30, 1995); missed 20 games. ... Jets franchise moved to Phoenix and renamed Coyotes for 1996-97 season; NHL approved move on January 18, 1996. ... Bruised hand (November 6, 1998); missed two games. ... Strained groin (March 2, 1999); missed one game. ... Traded by Coyotes with D Stan Neckar to Tampa Bay Lightning for D Paul Mara, RW Mike Johnson, RW Ruslan Zainullin and second-round pick (D Matthew Spiller) in 2001 (March 5, 2001).

HONORS: Played in NHL All-Star Game (1998 and 1999). ... Shared James Gatschene Memorial Trophy with Frederic Chabot (1999-2000).

MISCELLANEOUS: Holds Phoenix Coyotes franchise all-time records for most shutouts (21) and goals-against average (2.75). ... Stopped a penalty shot attempt (vs. Bob Errey, March 22, 1995; vs. Kevin Stevens, February 26, 1996; vs. Dino Ciccarelli, December 3, 1997). ... Allowed a penalty shot goal (vs. Pavel Bure, January 26, 1998).

		REGULAR SEASON								PLAYOFFS						
Season Team	League	Gms.	Min	W	L	T	GA	SO	Avg.	Gms.	Min.	W	L	GA	SO	Avg.
88-89—Avtomo. Sverdlovsk	USSR	1	3	0	0	0	0	0	...	—	—	—	—	—	—	—
89-90—Avtomo. Sverd. Jr.	USSR					Statistics unavailable.										
90-91—Sputnik Nizhny Tagil	USSR Dv.III					Statistics unavailable.										
91-92—CSKA Moscow	CIS	2	34	...	...	...	2	...	3.53	—	—	—	—	—	—	—
92-93—CSKA Moscow	CIS	13	491	...	...	...	27	...	3.30	—	—	—	—	—	—	—
93-94—Russian Penguins	IHL	12	639	2	7	‡2	47	0	4.41	—	—	—	—	—	—	—
—CSKA Moscow	CIS	46	2625	...	...	...	116	5	2.65	3	193	1	2	11	0	3.42
94-95—Springfield	AHL	23	1240	9	9	3	80	0	3.87	—	—	—	—	—	—	—
—Winnipeg	NHL	26	1339	8	9	4	76	0	3.41	—	—	—	—	—	—	—
95-96—Winnipeg	NHL	53	2914	26	20	3	152	2	3.13	6	359	2	4	19	0	3.18
96-97—Phoenix	NHL	72	4091	30	33	6	193	7	2.83	7	426	3	4	15	1	2.11
97-98—Phoenix	NHL	70	4026	30	28	10	†184	4	2.74	4	185	2	1	13	0	4.22
98-99—Phoenix	NHL	63	3657	32	23	7	130	8	2.13	7	449	3	4	15	0	2.41
99-00—Long Beach	IHL	33	1936	26	11	1	59	5	*1.83	5	321	2	3	15	0	2.80
00-01—Tampa Bay	NHL	2	123	1	1	0	6	0	2.93	—	—	—	—	—	—	—
NHL Totals (6 years)		286	16150	127	114	30	741	21	2.75	24	1419	10	13	65	1	2.75

KHARITONOV, ALEXANDER   RW   ISLANDERS

PERSONAL: Born March 30, 1976, in Moscow, U.S.S.R. ... 5-8/150. ... Shoots right.

TRANSACTIONS/CAREER NOTES: Selected by Tampa Bay Lightning in third round (third Lightning pick, 81st overall) of NHL entry draft (June 24, 2000). ... Suffered concussion (November 22, 2000); missed five games. ... Suffered from the flu (February 15, 2001); missed one game. ... Traded by Lightning with D Adrian Aucoin to New York Islanders for D Mathieu Biron and second-round pick in 2002 draft (June 22, 2001).

		REGULAR SEASON								PLAYOFFS				
Season Team	League	Gms.	G	A	Pts.	PIM	+/-	PP	SH	Gms.	G	A	Pts.	PIM
96-97—Dynamo-2 Moscow	Rus. Div. III	3	1	1	2	0	...	...	...	—	—	—	—	—
—Dynamo Moscow	Russian	36	11	9	20	12	...	...	...	4	2	0	2	2
97-98—Dynamo Moscow	Russian	44	19	16	35	20	...	...	...	—	—	—	—	—
98-99—Dynamo Moscow	Russian	42	8	6	14	24	...	...	...	16	4	3	7	2
99-00—Dynamo Moscow	Russian	35	14	20	34	26	...	...	...	17	*8	4	12	10
00-01—Tampa Bay	NHL	66	7	15	22	8	-9	0	0	—	—	—	—	—
NHL Totals (1 year)		66	7	15	22	8	-9	0	0					

KHAVANOV, ALEXANDER   D   BLUES

PERSONAL: Born January 30, 1972, in Dynamo, U.S.S.R. ... 6-2/190. ... Shoots left.

TRANSACTIONS/CAREER NOTES: Selected by St. Louis Blues in eighth round (eighth Blues pick, 232nd overall) of NHL entry draft (June 24, 2000).

		REGULAR SEASON								PLAYOFFS				
Season Team	League	Gms.	G	A	Pts.	PIM	+/-	PP	SH	Gms.	G	A	Pts.	PIM
92-93—Birmingham	ECHL	19	0	3	3	14	...	...	...	—	—	—	—	—
—Raleigh	ECHL	17	0	6	6	8	...	...	...	—	—	—	—	—
93-94—St. Petersburg	CIS	41	1	2	3	24	...	...	...	—	—	—	—	—
94-95—St. Petersburg	CIS	49	7	0	7	32	...	...	...	3	0	0	0	0
95-96—St. Petersburg	CIS	32	1	5	6	41	...	...	...	—	—	—	—	—
—HPK Hameenlinna	Finland	16	0	2	2	4	...	...	...	9	0	0	0	0
96-97—Cherepovets	Russian	39	3	8	11	56	...	...	...	3	1	0	1	4
97-98—Cherepovets	Russian	44	3	5	8	46	...	...	...	—	—	—	—	—
98-99—Dynamo	Russian	40	2	7	9	14	...	...	...	16	1	5	6	35
99-00—Dynamo	Russian	38	5	12	17	49	...	...	...	17	0	3	3	4
00-01—St. Louis	NHL	74	7	16	23	52	16	2	0	15	3	2	5	14
NHL Totals (1 year)		74	7	16	23	52	16	2	0	15	3	2	5	14

KHRISTICH, DMITRI   RW   CAPITALS

PERSONAL: Born July 23, 1969, in Kiev, U.S.S.R. ... 6-2/195. ... Shoots right. ... Name pronounced KHRIHZ-tihch.

TRANSACTIONS/CAREER NOTES: Selected by Washington Capitals in sixth round (sixth Capitals pick, 120th overall) of NHL entry draft (June 11, 1988). ... Injured hip (February 16, 1990); missed six games. ... Fractured foot (October 3, 1992); missed 20 games. ... Traded by Capitals with G Byron Dafoe to Los Angeles Kings for first-(C Alexander Volchkov) and fourth-round (RW Justin Davis) picks in 1996 draft (July 8, 1995). ... Suffered concussion (December 22, 1995); missed three games. ... Sprained right knee (February 23, 1996); missed three games. ... Suffered laceration near right eye (February 7, 1997); missed seven games. ... Traded by Kings with G Byron Dafoe to Boston Bruins for C Jozef Stumpel, RW Sandy Moger and fourth-round pick (traded to New Jersey) in 1998 draft (August 29, 1997). ... Strained shoulder (September 30, 1998); missed first game of season. ... Injured shoulder (March 24, 1999); missed two games. ... Rights traded by Bruins to Toronto Maple Leafs for second-round pick (RW Ivan Huml) in 2000 draft (October 21, 1999). ... Suffered injury (February 12, 2000); missed one game. ... Injured groin (February 16, 2000); missed 12 games. ... Suffered injury (March 23, 2000); missed seven games. ... Traded by Maple Leafs to Capitals for third-round pick (D Brendan Bell) in 2001 draft (December 11, 2000). ... Strained hamstring (January 3, 2001); missed five games. ... Bruised foot (March 1, 2001); missed three games. ... Reinjured foot (March 9, 2001); missed one game.

HONORS: Played in NHL All-Star Game (1997 and 1999).

MISCELLANEOUS: Scored on a penalty shot (vs. Darcy Wakaluk, January 7, 1992).

STATISTICAL NOTES: Led NHL with 20.1 shooting percentage (1998-99).

STATISTICAL PLATEAUS: Three-goal games: 1992-93 (2), 1998-99 (1). Total: 3.

		REGULAR SEASON								PLAYOFFS				
Season Team	League	Gms.	G	A	Pts.	PIM	+/-	PP	SH	Gms.	G	A	Pts.	PIM
85-86—Sokol Kiev	USSR	4	0	0	0	0	...	...	...	—	—	—	—	—
86-87—Sokol Kiev	USSR	20	3	0	3	4	...	...	...	—	—	—	—	—
87-88—Sokol Kiev	USSR	37	9	1	10	18	...	...	...	—	—	—	—	—
88-89—Sokol Kiev	USSR	42	17	8	25	15	...	...	...	—	—	—	—	—
89-90—Sokol Kiev	USSR	47	14	22	36	32	...	...	...	—	—	—	—	—
90-91—Sokol Kiev	USSR	28	10	12	22	20	...	...	...	—	—	—	—	—
—Baltimore	AHL	3	0	0	0	0	...	...	...	—	—	—	—	—
—Washington	NHL	40	13	14	27	21	-1	1	0	11	1	3	4	6
91-92—Washington	NHL	80	36	37	73	35	24	14	1	7	3	2	5	15
92-93—Washington	NHL	64	31	35	66	28	29	9	1	6	2	5	7	2
93-94—Washington	NHL	83	29	29	58	73	-2	10	0	11	2	3	5	10
94-95—Washington	NHL	48	12	14	26	41	0	8	0	7	1	4	5	0
95-96—Los Angeles	NHL	76	27	37	64	44	0	12	0	—	—	—	—	—
96-97—Los Angeles	NHL	75	19	37	56	38	8	3	0	—	—	—	—	—
97-98—Boston	NHL	82	29	37	66	42	25	13	2	6	2	2	4	2
98-99—Boston	NHL	79	29	42	71	48	11	13	1	12	3	4	7	6
99-00—Toronto	NHL	53	12	18	30	24	8	3	0	12	1	2	3	0
00-01—Toronto	NHL	27	3	6	9	8	8	2	0	—	—	—	—	—
—Washington	NHL	43	10	19	29	8	-8	4	0	3	0	0	0	0
NHL Totals (11 years)		750	250	325	575	410	102	92	5	75	15	25	40	41

KIDD, TREVOR   G   PANTHERS

PERSONAL: Born March 29, 1972, in Dugald, Man. ... 6-2/190. ... Catches left.

TRANSACTIONS/CAREER NOTES: Selected by Calgary Flames in first round (first Flames pick, 11th overall) of NHL entry draft (June 16, 1990). ... Sprained left ankle (October 18, 1993); missed one game. ... Traded by Flames with LW Gary Roberts to Carolina Hurricanes for G Jean-Sebastien Giguere and C Andrew Cassels (August 25, 1997). ... Strained groin (November 9, 1997); missed seven games. ... Fractured finger on right hand (December 20, 1997); missed seven games. ... Injured groin (April 16, 1998); missed three games. ... Selected by Atlanta Thrashers in NHL expansion draft (June 25, 1999). ... Traded by Thrashers to Florida Panthers for D Gord Murphy, C Herbert Vasiljevs, D Daniel Tjarnqvist and sixth-round pick (traded to Dallas) in 1999 draft (June 25, 1999). ... Separated shoulder (December 13, 1999); missed 29 games.

HONORS: Won Del Wilson Trophy (1989-90). ... Named to WHL (West) All-Star first team (1989-90).

MISCELLANEOUS: Member of silver-medal-winning Canadian Olympic team (1992). ... Holds Calgary Flames all-time record for most shutouts (10). ... Holds Carolina Hurricanes records for most games played by a goaltender (72) and most wins (28). ... Stopped a penalty shot attempt (vs. Teemu Selanne, February 6, 1995; vs. Brendan Shanahan, November 5, 1997). ... Allowed a penalty shot goal (vs. Wendel Clark, November 24, 1993; vs. Joe Sakic, January 14, 1996).

Season Team	League	REGULAR SEASON								PLAYOFFS						
		Gms.	Min	W	L	T	GA	SO	Avg.	Gms.	Min.	W	L	GA	SO	Avg.
88-89—Brandon	WHL	32	1509	11	13	1	102	0	4.06	—	—	—	—	—	—	—
89-90—Brandon	WHL	*63	*3676	24	32	2	254	2	4.15	—	—	—	—	—	—	—
90-91—Brandon	WHL	30	1730	10	19	1	117	0	4.06	—	—	—	—	—	—	—
—Spokane	WHL	14	749	8	3	0	44	0	3.52	15	926	*14	1	32	*2	*2.07
91-92—Canadian nat'l team	Int'l	28	1349	18	4	4	79	2	3.51	—	—	—	—	—	—	—
—Can. Olympic team	Int'l	1	60	1	0	0	0	1	...	—	—	—	—	—	—	—
—Calgary	NHL	2	120	1	1	0	8	0	4.00	—	—	—	—	—	—	—
92-93—Salt Lake City	IHL	30	1696	10	16	0	111	1	3.93	—	—	—	—	—	—	—
93-94—Calgary	NHL	31	1614	13	7	6	85	0	3.16	—	—	—	—	—	—	—
94-95—Calgary	NHL	‡43	2463	22	14	6	107	3	2.61	7	434	3	4	26	1	3.59
95-96—Calgary	NHL	47	2570	15	21	8	119	3	2.78	2	83	0	1	9	0	6.51
96-97—Calgary	NHL	55	2979	21	23	6	141	4	2.84	—	—	—	—	—	—	—
97-98—Carolina	NHL	47	2685	21	21	3	97	3	2.17	—	—	—	—	—	—	—
98-99—Carolina	NHL	25	1358	7	10	6	61	2	2.70	—	—	—	—	—	—	—
99-00—Florida	NHL	28	1574	14	11	2	69	1	2.63	—	—	—	—	—	—	—
—Louisville	AHL	1	60	0	1	0	5	0	5.00	—	—	—	—	—	—	—
00-01—Florida	NHL	42	2354	10	23	6	130	1	3.31	—	—	—	—	—	—	—
NHL Totals (9 years)		320	17717	124	131	43	817	17	2.77	9	517	3	5	35	1	4.06

KILGER, CHAD   C   CANADIENS

PERSONAL: Born November 27, 1976, in Cornwall, Ont. ... 6-4/215. ... Shoots left. ... Son of Bob Kilger, former NHL referee (1970-71 through 1979-80).

TRANSACTIONS/CAREER NOTES: Selected by Mighty Ducks of Anaheim in first round (first Mighty Ducks pick, fourth overall) of NHL entry draft (July 8, 1995). ... Traded by Mighty Ducks with D Oleg Tverdovsky and third-round pick (D Per-Anton Lundstrom) in 1996 draft to Winnipeg Jets for C Marc Chouinard, RW Teemu Selanne and fourth-round pick (traded to Toronto) in 1996 draft (February 7, 1996). ... Suffered from the flu (February 21, 1996); missed one game. ... Jets franchise moved to Phoenix and renamed Coyotes for 1996-97 season; NHL approved move on January 18, 1996. ... Bruised thigh (October 7, 1996); missed one game. ... Traded by Coyotes with D Jayson More to Chicago Blackhawks for D Keith Carney and RW Jim Cummins (March 4, 1998). ... Suffered concussion (February 19, 1999); missed three games. ... Traded by Blackhawks with LW Daniel Cleary, LW Ethan Moreau and D Christian Laflamme to Edmonton Oilers for D Boris Mironov, LW Dean McAmmond and D Jonas Elofsson (March 20, 1999). ... Suffered hip pointer (December 30, 1999); missed five games. ... Suffered hip pointer (February 23, 2000); missed two games. ... Traded by Oilers to Montreal Canadiens for C Sergei Zholtok (December 18, 2000). ... Suffered concussion (March 3, 2001); missed five games. ... Strained groin (April 2, 2001); missed one game.

Season Team	League	REGULAR SEASON							PLAYOFFS				
		Gms.	G	A	Pts.	PIM	+/-	PP	SH	Gms.	G	A	Pts.	PIM
92-93—Cornwall	CJHL	55	30	36	66	26	...	...	...	6	0	0	0	0
93-94—Kingston	OHL	66	17	35	52	23	...	...	...	6	7	2	9	8
94-95—Kingston	OHL	65	42	53	95	95	...	...	...	6	5	2	7	10
95-96—Anaheim	NHL	45	5	7	12	22	-2	0	0	—	—	—	—	—
—Winnipeg	NHL	29	2	3	5	12	-2	0	0	4	1	0	1	0
96-97—Phoenix	NHL	24	4	3	7	13	-5	1	0	—	—	—	—	—
—Springfield	AHL	52	17	28	45	36	...	...	...	16	5	7	12	56
97-98—Springfield	AHL	35	14	14	28	33	...	...	...	—	—	—	—	—
—Phoenix	NHL	10	0	1	1	4	-2	0	0	—	—	—	—	—
—Chicago	NHL	22	3	8	11	6	2	2	0	—	—	—	—	—
98-99—Chicago	NHL	64	14	11	25	30	-1	2	1	—	—	—	—	—
—Edmonton	NHL	13	1	1	2	4	-3	0	0	4	0	0	0	4
99-00—Edmonton	NHL	40	3	2	5	18	-6	0	0	3	0	0	0	0
—Hamilton	AHL	3	3	3	6	0	...	...	...	—	—	—	—	—
00-01—Edmonton	NHL	34	5	2	7	17	-7	1	0	—	—	—	—	—
—Montreal	NHL	43	9	16	25	34	-1	1	1	—	—	—	—	—
NHL Totals (6 years)		324	46	54	100	160	-27	7	2	11	1	0	1	4

KINCH, MATT   D   RANGERS

PERSONAL: Born February 17, 1980, in Red Deer, Alta. ... 5-11/189. ... Shoots left. ... Full Name: Matthew Kinch.

TRANSACTIONS/CAREER NOTES: Selected by Buffalo Sabres in fifth round (eighth Sabres pick, 146th overall) of NHL entry draft (June 26, 1999). ... Signed as free agent by New York Rangers (June 12, 2001).

HONORS: Won Brad Hornung Trophy (1998-99 and 2000-01). ... Won Can.HL Most Sportsmanlike Player of the Year Award (1998-99). ... Named to WHL (East) All-Star first team (1998-99 and 2000-01). ... Named to Can.HL All-Star second team (1998-99). ... Named to WHL (East) All-Star second team (1999-2000). ... Named to Can.HL All-Star first team (2000-01).

Season Team	League	REGULAR SEASON							PLAYOFFS				
		Gms.	G	A	Pts.	PIM	+/-	PP	SH	Gms.	G	A	Pts.	PIM
97-98—Calgary	WHL	55	7	24	31	13	...	...	...	18	3	2	5	4
98-99—Calgary	WHL	68	14	69	83	16	...	...	...	21	7	23	30	8
99-00—Calgary	WHL	62	14	61	75	24	...	...	...	13	2	12	14	8
00-01—Calgary	WHL	70	18	66	84	52	...	...	...	12	3	6	9	6

KING, KRIS   LW

PERSONAL: Born February 18, 1966, in Bracebridge, Ont. ... 5-11/205. ... Shoots left.

TRANSACTIONS/CAREER NOTES: Selected by Washington Capitals in fourth round (fourth Capitals pick, 80th overall) of NHL entry draft (June 9, 1984). ... Signed as free agent by Detroit Red Wings (June 1987). ... Traded by Red Wings to New York Rangers for LW Chris McRae and fifth-round pick (D Tony Burns) in 1990 draft (September 7, 1989). ... Sprained knee (January 7, 1991); missed six games. ... Traded by

Rangers with RW Tie Domi to Winnipeg Jets for C Ed Olczyk (December 28, 1992). ... Suffered abdominal injury (February 13, 1996); missed one game. ... Jets franchise moved to Phoenix and renamed Coyotes for 1996-97 season; NHL approved move on January 18, 1996. ... Signed as free agent by Toronto Maple Leafs (July 7, 1997). ... Fractured hand (December 7, 1998); missed eight games. ... Released by Maple Leafs (June 28, 2000). ... Signed as free agent by Chicago Blackhawks (October 9, 2000). ... Announced retirement (December 2, 2000).

HONORS: Won King Clancy Trophy (1995-96).

			REGULAR SEASON								PLAYOFFS				
Season Team	League	Gms.	G	A	Pts.	PIM	+/-	PP	SH		Gms.	G	A	Pts.	PIM
82-83—Gravenhurst..............	SOJHL	32	72	53	125	115	...	...	...		—	—	—	—	—
83-84—Peterborough.............	OHL	62	13	18	31	168	...	...	...		8	3	3	6	14
84-85—Peterborough.............	OHL	61	18	35	53	222	...	...	...		16	2	8	10	28
85-86—Peterborough.............	OHL	58	19	40	59	254	...	...	...		8	4	0	4	21
86-87—Peterborough.............	OHL	46	23	33	56	160	...	...	...		12	5	8	13	41
—Binghamton	AHL	7	0	0	0	18	...	...	...		—	—	—	—	—
87-88—Adirondack	AHL	78	21	32	53	337	...	...	...		10	4	4	8	53
—Detroit.......................	NHL	3	1	0	1	2	1	0	0		—	—	—	—	—
88-89—Detroit......................	NHL	55	2	3	5	168	-7	0	0		2	0	0	0	2
89-90—New York Rangers......	NHL	68	6	7	13	286	2	0	0		10	0	1	1	38
90-91—New York Rangers......	NHL	72	11	14	25	154	-1	0	0		6	2	0	2	36
91-92—New York Rangers......	NHL	79	10	9	19	224	13	0	0		13	4	1	5	14
92-93—New York Rangers......	NHL	30	0	3	3	67	-1	0	0		—	—	—	—	—
—Winnipeg	NHL	48	8	8	16	136	5	0	0		6	1	1	2	4
93-94—Winnipeg	NHL	83	4	8	12	205	-22	0	0		—	—	—	—	—
94-95—Winnipeg	NHL	48	4	2	6	85	0	0	0		—	—	—	—	—
95-96—Winnipeg	NHL	81	9	11	20	151	-7	0	1		5	0	1	1	4
96-97—Phoenix....................	NHL	81	3	11	14	185	-7	0	0		7	0	0	0	17
97-98—Toronto	NHL	82	3	3	6	199	-13	0	0		—	—	—	—	—
98-99—Toronto	NHL	67	2	2	4	105	-16	0	1		17	1	1	2	25
99-00—Toronto	NHL	39	2	4	6	55	4	0	0		1	0	0	0	2
—Chicago....................	IHL	15	2	4	6	19	...	...	...		—	—	—	—	—
00-01—Chicago....................	NHL	13	1	0	1	8	-3	0	0		—	—	—	—	—
NHL Totals (14 years).........		849	66	85	151	2030	-52	0	2		67	8	5	13	142

KIPRUSOFF, MARKO   D   ISLANDERS

PERSONAL: Born June 6, 1972, in Turku, Finland. ... 6-0/194. ... Shoots right. ... Brother of Mikko Kiprusoff, goaltender, San Jose Sharks. ... Name pronounced KIHP-roo-sahf.
TRANSACTIONS/CAREER NOTES: Selected by Montreal Canadiens in fourth round (fourth Canadiens pick, 70th overall) of NHL entry draft (June 29, 1994). ... Suffered concussion (December 15, 1995); missed two games. ... Signed as free agent by New York Islanders (June 16, 2001).
HONORS: Named to Finnish League All-Star team (1993-94).

			REGULAR SEASON								PLAYOFFS				
Season Team	League	Gms.	G	A	Pts.	PIM	+/-	PP	SH		Gms.	G	A	Pts.	PIM
90-91—TPS Turku	Finland	3	0	0	0	0	...	...	...		—	—	—	—	—
91-92—TPS Turku	Finland	23	0	2	2	0	...	...	...		—	—	—	—	—
—HPK Hameenlinna.......	Finland	3	0	0	0	0	...	...	...		—	—	—	—	—
92-93—TPS Turku	Finland	43	3	7	10	14	...	...	...		12	2	3	5	6
93-94—TPS Turku	Finland	48	5	19	24	8	...	...	...		11	0	6	6	4
94-95—TPS Turku	Finland	50	10	21	31	16	...	...	...		13	0	9	9	2
95-96—Montreal	NHL	24	0	4	4	8	-3	0	0		—	—	—	—	—
—Fredericton	AHL	28	4	10	14	2	...	...	...		10	2	5	7	2
96-97—Kiekko-Espoo	Finland Div. 2	21	6	2	8	98	...	...	...		6	2	2	4	6
—TPS Turku	Finland Jr.	11	5	1	6	28	...	...	...		—	—	—	—	—
98-99—TPS Turku	Finland	49	15	22	37	12	...	...	...		10	3	6	9	0
99-00—TPS Turku	Finland	53	6	27	33	10	...	...	...		11	0	3	3	0
00-01—Kloten	Switzerland	43	6	20	26	10	...	...	...		9	2	7	9	2
NHL Totals (1 year)..............		24	0	4	4	8	-3	0	0		—	—	—	—	—

KIPRUSOFF, MIIKKA   G   SHARKS

PERSONAL: Born October 26, 1976, in Turku, Finland. ... 6-2/190. ... Catches left. ... Brother of Marko Kiprusoff, defenseman, New York Islanders organization.
TRANSACTIONS/CAREER NOTES: Selected by San Jose Sharks in fifth round (fifth Sharks pick, 115th overall) of NHL entry draft (July 8, 1995).

			REGULAR SEASON								PLAYOFFS					
Season Team	League	Gms.	Min	W	L	T	GA	SO	Avg.		Gms.	Min.	W	L	GA	SO	Avg.
93-94—TPS Turku Jr.	Finland	35	...	...	...	...	...	...	...		6	...	...	...	...	...	...
94-95—TPS Turku Jr.	Finland	31	1880	...	...	...	93	...	2.97		—	—	—	—	—	—	—
—TPS Turku	Finland	4	240	...	...	...	12	0	3.00		2	120	...	...	7	...	3.50
95-96—TPS Turku	Finland	12	550	...	...	...	38	...	4.15		—	—	—	—	—	—	—
—Kiekko	Finland	5	300	...	...	...	7	...	1.40		—	—	—	—	—	—	—
96-97—AIK	Sweden	42	2466	...	...	...	104	3	2.53		7	420	...	...	23	0	3.29
97-98—AIK Solna	Sweden	42	2457	...	...	...	110	...	2.69		—	—	—	—	—	—	—
98-99—TPS Turku	Finland	39	2259	*26	6	6	70	4	1.86		10	580	*9	1	15	*3	*1.55
99-00—Kentucky	AHL	47	2759	23	19	4	114	3	2.48		5	239	1	3	13	0	3.26
00-01—Kentucky	AHL	36	2038	19	9	6	76	2	2.24		—	—	—	—	—	—	—
—San Jose	NHL	5	154	2	1	0	5	0	1.95		3	149	1	1	5	0	2.01
NHL Totals (1 year)..............		5	154	2	1	0	5	0	1.95		3	149	1	1	5	0	2.01

PERSONAL: Born June 17, 1969, in Trelleborg, Sweden. ... 6-2/208. ... Shoots left.
TRANSACTIONS/CAREER NOTES: Selected by Montreal Canadiens in fourth round (fourth Canadiens pick, 83rd overall) of NHL entry draft (June 11, 1988). ... Signed as free agent by Nashville Predators (June 26, 1998). ... Bruised hip (March 28, 1999); missed final nine games of season. ... Suffered back spasms (January 17, 2001); missed one game.
MISCELLANEOUS: Member of gold-medal-winning Swedish Olympic team (1994).

		REGULAR SEASON								PLAYOFFS				
Season Team	League	Gms.	G	A	Pts.	PIM	+/-	PP	SH	Gms.	G	A	Pts.	PIM
86-87—Falun	Sweden	27	11	13	24	14	...	...	...	—	—	—	—	—
87-88—Falun	Sweden	29	15	10	25	18	...	...	...	—	—	—	—	—
88-89—AIK Solna	Sweden	25	7	9	16	8	...	...	...	—	—	—	—	—
89-90—AIK Solna	Sweden	33	8	16	24	6	...	...	...	3	1	0	1	0
90-91—AIK Solna	Sweden	38	4	11	15	18	...	...	...	—	—	—	—	—
91-92—AIK Solna	Sweden	40	20	13	33	16	...	...	...	—	—	—	—	—
—Swedish Oly. team	Int'l	8	1	3	4	0	...	...	...	—	—	—	—	—
92-93—Montreal	NHL	7	0	0	0	2	-3	0	0	—	—	—	—	—
—Fredericton	AHL	41	10	27	37	14	...	...	...	5	2	2	4	0
93-94—HV 71 Jonkoping	Sweden	40	11	17	28	18	...	...	...	—	—	—	—	—
—Swedish Oly. team	Int'l	8	0	1	1	2	...	...	...	—	—	—	—	—
94-95—HV 71 Jonkoping	Sweden	29	5	15	20	12	...	...	...	—	—	—	—	—
95-96—Djurgarden Stockholm	Sweden	40	9	7	16	10	...	...	...	4	0	2	2	2
96-97—Djurgarden Stockholm	Sweden	49	29	11	40	18	...	...	...	4	2	3	5	2
97-98—Swedish Oly. team	Int'l	4	1	0	1	0	...	...	...	—	—	—	—	—
—Djurgarden Stockholm	Sweden	46	30	18	48	16	...	...	...	15	7	3	10	12
98-99—Nashville	NHL	71	11	20	31	24	-13	2	0	—	—	—	—	—
99-00—Nashville	NHL	82	23	23	46	14	-11	9	0	—	—	—	—	—
00-01—Nashville	NHL	81	14	31	45	12	-2	5	0	—	—	—	—	—
NHL Totals (4 years)		241	48	74	122	52	-29	16	0					

PERSONAL: Born January 30, 1971, in Minneapolis. ... 6-1/210. ... Shoots right. ... Full Name: Trent Thomas Klatt.
TRANSACTIONS/CAREER NOTES: Selected by Washington Capitals in fourth round (fifth Capitals pick, 82nd overall) of NHL entry draft (June 17, 1989). ... Rights traded by Capitals with LW Steve Maltais to Minnesota North Stars for D Sean Chambers (June 21, 1991). ... Injured finger (January 7, 1993); missed three games. ... North Stars franchise moved from Minnesota to Dallas and renamed Stars for 1993-94 season. ... Strained back (November 7, 1993); missed one game. ... Sprained knee (November 11, 1993); missed two games. ... Sprained knee (February 6, 1994); missed three games. ... Traded by Stars to Philadelphia Flyers for LW Brent Fedyk (December 13, 1995). ... Suffered concussion (March 9, 1997); missed two games. ... Traded by Flyers to Vancouver Canucks for sixth-round pick (traded to Atlanta) in 2000 draft (October 19, 1998). ... Suffered skin rash (February 14, 2001); missed five games.
MISCELLANEOUS: Failed to score on a penalty shot (vs. John Vanbiesbrouck, October 1, 1997).
STATISTICAL PLATEAUS: Three-goal games: 1996-97 (1).

		REGULAR SEASON								PLAYOFFS				
Season Team	League	Gms.	G	A	Pts.	PIM	+/-	PP	SH	Gms.	G	A	Pts.	PIM
87-88—Osseo H.S.	Minn. H.S.	22	19	17	36	...	...	...	...	—	—	—	—	—
88-89—Osseo H.S.	Minn. H.S.	22	24	39	63	...	...	...	...	—	—	—	—	—
89-90—Univ. of Minnesota	WCHA	38	22	14	36	16	...	...	...	—	—	—	—	—
90-91—Univ. of Minnesota	WCHA	39	16	28	44	58	...	...	...	—	—	—	—	—
91-92—Univ. of Minnesota	WCHA	44	30	36	66	78	...	...	...	—	—	—	—	—
—Minnesota	NHL	1	0	0	0	0	0	0	0	6	0	0	0	2
92-93—Kalamazoo	IHL	31	8	11	19	18	...	...	...	—	—	—	—	—
—Minnesota	NHL	47	4	19	23	38	2	1	0	—	—	—	—	—
93-94—Dallas	NHL	61	14	24	38	30	13	3	0	9	2	1	3	4
—Kalamazoo	IHL	6	3	2	5	4	...	...	...	—	—	—	—	—
94-95—Dallas	NHL	47	12	10	22	26	-2	5	0	5	1	0	1	0
95-96—Dallas	NHL	22	4	4	8	23	0	0	0	—	—	—	—	—
—Michigan	IHL	2	1	2	3	5	...	...	...	—	—	—	—	—
—Philadelphia	NHL	49	3	8	11	21	2	0	0	12	4	1	5	0
96-97—Philadelphia	NHL	76	24	21	45	20	9	5	5	19	4	3	7	12
97-98—Philadelphia	NHL	82	14	28	42	16	2	5	0	5	0	0	0	0
98-99—Philadelphia	NHL	2	0	0	0	0	0	0	0	—	—	—	—	—
—Vancouver	NHL	73	4	10	14	12	-3	0	0	—	—	—	—	—
99-00—Syracuse	AHL	24	13	10	23	6	...	...	...	—	—	—	—	—
—Vancouver	NHL	47	10	10	20	26	-8	8	0	—	—	—	—	—
00-01—Vancouver	NHL	77	13	20	33	31	8	3	0	4	3	0	3	0
NHL Totals (10 years)		584	102	154	256	243	23	30	5	60	14	5	19	18

PERSONAL: Born April 24, 1971, in Indianapolis. ... 6-1/211. ... Shoots right. ... Full Name: Kenneth William Klee.
TRANSACTIONS/CAREER NOTES: Selected by Washington Capitals in ninth round (11th Capitals pick, 177th overall) of NHL entry draft (June 16, 1990). ... Injured foot (January 27, 1995); missed six games. ... Pulled groin (March 12, 1996); missed 13 games. ... Sprained knee (April 10, 1997); missed two games. ... Fractured facial bone (March 28, 1998); missed eight games. ... Bruised foot (February 12, 2000); missed one game. ... Injured wrist (October 19, 2000); missed six games. ... Strained left knee (December 12, 2000); missed one game. ... Strained back (February 13, 2001); missed six games. ... Suffered concussion (March 7, 2001); missed two games.
MISCELLANEOUS: Failed to score on penalty shot (vs. Mike Richter, March 12, 1997).

K

Season Team	League	REGULAR SEASON								PLAYOFFS				
		Gms.	G	A	Pts.	PIM	+/-	PP	SH	Gms.	G	A	Pts.	PIM
89-90—Bowling Green	CCHA	39	0	5	5	52	...	...	...	—	—	—	—	—
90-91—Bowling Green	CCHA	37	7	28	35	50	...	...	...	—	—	—	—	—
91-92—Bowling Green	CCHA	10	0	1	1	14	...	...	...	—	—	—	—	—
92-93—Baltimore	AHL	77	4	14	18	68	...	...	...	7	0	1	1	15
93-94—Portland	AHL	65	2	9	11	87	...	...	...	17	1	2	3	14
94-95—Portland	AHL	49	5	7	12	89	...	...	...	—	—	—	—	—
—Washington	NHL	23	3	1	4	41	2	0	0	7	0	0	0	4
95-96—Washington	NHL	66	8	3	11	60	-1	0	1	1	0	0	0	0
96-97—Washington	NHL	80	3	8	11	115	0	0	0	—	—	—	—	—
97-98—Washington	NHL	51	4	2	6	46	-3	0	0	9	1	0	1	10
98-99—Washington	NHL	78	7	13	20	80	-9	0	0	—	—	—	—	—
99-00—Washington	NHL	80	7	13	20	79	8	0	0	5	0	1	1	10
00-01—Washington	NHL	54	2	4	6	60	-5	0	0	6	0	1	1	8
NHL Totals (7 years)		432	34	44	78	481	-13	0	1	28	1	2	3	32

KLEMM, JON　　　　　D　　　　　BLACKHAWKS

PERSONAL: Born January 8, 1970, in Cranbrook, B.C. ... 6-3/200. ... Shoots right. ... Full Name: Jonathan Darryl Klemm.
TRANSACTIONS/CAREER NOTES: Signed as non-drafted free agent by Quebec Nordiques (May 14, 1991). ... Injured abdomen (March 28, 1995); missed five games. ... Reinjured abdomen (April 8, 1995); missed remainder of season. ... Nordiques franchise moved to Colorado and renamed Avalanche for 1995-96 season (June 21, 1995). ... Injured groin (January 27, 1996); missed one game. ... Sprained left thumb (October 30, 1997) and underwent surgery; missed 11 games. ... Strained groin (December 27, 1997); missed one game. ... Tore patella tendon in knee (November 15, 1998); missed 29 games. ... Suffered from appendicitis (March 25, 1999); missed six games. ... Injured groin (October 20, 1999); missed seven games. ... Suffered back spasms (February 25, 2000); missed one game. ... Injured hamstring (December 5, 2000); missed three games. ... Signed as free agent by Chicago Blackhawks (July 1, 2001).
HONORS: Named to WHL (West) All-Star second team (1990-91).
MISCELLANEOUS: Member of Stanley Cup championship team (1996 and 2001).

Season Team	League	REGULAR SEASON								PLAYOFFS				
		Gms.	G	A	Pts.	PIM	+/-	PP	SH	Gms.	G	A	Pts.	PIM
87-88—Seattle	WHL	68	6	7	13	24	...	...	...	—	—	—	—	—
88-89—Seattle	WHL	2	1	1	2	0	...	...	...	—	—	—	—	—
—Spokane	WHL	66	6	34	40	42	...	...	...	—	—	—	—	—
89-90—Spokane	WHL	66	3	28	31	100	...	...	...	6	1	1	2	5
90-91—Spokane	WHL	72	7	58	65	65	...	...	...	15	3	6	9	8
91-92—Halifax	AHL	70	6	13	19	40	...	...	...	—	—	—	—	—
—Quebec	NHL	4	0	1	1	0	2	0	0	—	—	—	—	—
92-93—Halifax	AHL	80	3	20	23	32	...	...	...	—	—	—	—	—
93-94—Cornwall	AHL	66	4	26	30	78	...	...	...	13	1	2	3	6
—Quebec	NHL	7	0	0	0	4	-1	0	0	—	—	—	—	—
94-95—Cornwall	AHL	65	6	13	19	84	...	...	...	—	—	—	—	—
—Quebec	NHL	4	0	1	1	2	3	0	0	—	—	—	—	—
95-96—Colorado	NHL	56	3	12	15	20	12	0	1	15	2	1	3	0
96-97—Colorado	NHL	80	9	15	24	37	12	1	2	17	1	1	2	6
97-98—Colorado	NHL	67	6	8	14	30	-3	0	0	4	0	0	0	0
98-99—Colorado	NHL	39	1	2	3	31	4	0	0	19	0	1	1	10
99-00—Colorado	NHL	73	5	7	12	34	26	0	0	17	2	1	3	9
00-01—Colorado	NHL	78	4	11	15	54	22	2	0	22	1	2	3	16
NHL Totals (9 years)		408	29	56	85	212	77	3	3	94	6	6	12	41

KLESLA, ROSTISLAV　　　　　D　　　　　BLUE JACKETS

PERSONAL: Born March 21, 1982, in Novy Jicin, Czechoslovakia. ... 6-2/198. ... Shoots left.
TRANSACTIONS/CAREER NOTES: Selected by Columbus Blue Jackets in first round (first Blue Jackets pick, fourth overall) of NHL entry draft (June 24, 2000).
HONORS: Won Can.HL Top Draft Prospect Award (1999-2000). ... Named to OHL All-Star first team (2000-01).

Season Team	League	REGULAR SEASON								PLAYOFFS				
		Gms.	G	A	Pts.	PIM	+/-	PP	SH	Gms.	G	A	Pts.	PIM
97-98—Opava	Czech. Jrs.	40	11	16	27	...	...	...	...	—	—	—	—	—
98-99—Sioux City	USHL	54	4	12	16	100	...	...	...	—	—	—	—	—
99-00—Brampton	OHL	67	16	29	45	174	...	...	...	6	1	1	2	21
00-01—Columbus	NHL	8	2	0	2	6	-1	0	0	—	—	—	—	—
—Brampton	OHL	45	18	36	54	59	...	...	...	9	2	9	11	26
NHL Totals (1 year)		8	2	0	2	6	-1	0	0					

KLOUCEK, TOMAS　　　　　D　　　　　RANGERS

PERSONAL: Born March 7, 1980, in Prague, Czechoslovakia. ... 6-3/203. ... Shoots left.
TRANSACTIONS/CAREER NOTES: Selected by New York Rangers in fifth round (sixth Rangers pick, 131st overall) of NHL entry draft (June 27, 1998). ... Bruised ankle (February 19, 2001); missed one game. ... Bruised shoulder (March 10, 2001): mised two games. ... Bruised heel (March 25, 2001); missed two games. ... Injured knee (April 1, 2001); missed final three games of season.

Season Team	League	REGULAR SEASON								PLAYOFFS				
		Gms.	G	A	Pts.	PIM	+/-	PP	SH	Gms.	G	A	Pts.	PIM
95-96—Slavia Praha	Czech Jrs.	40	2	8	10	...	...	...	...	—	—	—	—	—
96-97—Slavia Praha	Czech Jrs.	43	4	14	18	44	...	...	...	—	—	—	—	—
97-98—Slavia Praha	Czech Jrs.	43	1	9	10	...	...	...	...	—	—	—	—	—
98-99—Cape Breton	QMJHL	59	4	17	21	162	...	...	...	2	0	0	0	4
99-00—Hartford	AHL	73	2	8	10	113	...	...	...	23	0	4	4	18
00-01—Hartford	AHL	21	0	2	2	44	...	...	...	—	—	—	—	—
—New York Rangers	NHL	43	1	4	5	74	-3	0	0	—	—	—	—	—
NHL Totals (1 year)		43	1	4	5	74	-3	0	0					

K

KNUBLE, MIKE — LW — BRUINS

PERSONAL: Born July 4, 1972, in Toronto. ... 6-3/222. ... Shoots right. ... Full Name: Michael Knuble. ... Name pronounced kuh-NOO-buhl.
TRANSACTIONS/CAREER NOTES: Selected by Detroit Red Wings in fourth round (fourth Red Wings pick, 76th overall) of NHL entry draft (June 22, 1991). ... Traded by Red Wings to New York Rangers for third-round pick (traded back to New York Rangers) in 2000 draft (October 1, 1998). ... Traded by Rangers to Boston Bruins for LW Rob DiMaio (March 10, 2000).
HONORS: Named to CCHA All-Star second team (1993-94 and 1994-95). ... Named to NCAA All-America (West) second team (1994-95).
MISCELLANEOUS: Member of Stanley Cup championship team (1998).

		REGULAR SEASON								PLAYOFFS				
Season Team	League	Gms.	G	A	Pts.	PIM	+/-	PP	SH	Gms.	G	A	Pts.	PIM
88-89—East Kentwood H.S.....	Mich. H.S.	28	52	37	89	60	...	...	...	—	—	—	—	—
89-90—East Kentwood H.S.....	Mich. H.S.	29	63	40	103	40	...	...	...	—	—	—	—	—
90-91—Kalamazoo	NAJHL	36	18	24	42	30	...	...	...	—	—	—	—	—
91-92—Univ. of Michigan.......	CCHA	43	7	8	15	48	...	...	...	—	—	—	—	—
92-93—Univ. of Michigan.......	CCHA	39	26	16	42	57	...	...	...	—	—	—	—	—
93-94—Univ. of Michigan.......	CCHA	41	32	26	58	71	...	...	...	—	—	—	—	—
94-95—Univ. of Michigan.......	CCHA	34	38	22	60	62	...	...	...	—	—	—	—	—
95-96—Adirondack	AHL	80	22	23	45	59	...	...	...	3	1	0	1	0
96-97—Adirondack	AHL	68	28	35	63	54	...	...	...	—	—	—	—	—
—Detroit......................	NHL	9	1	0	1	0	-1	0	0	—	—	—	—	—
97-98—Detroit..................	NHL	53	7	6	13	16	2	0	0	3	0	1	1	0
98-99—New York Rangers......	NHL	82	15	20	35	26	-7	3	0	—	—	—	—	—
99-00—New York Rangers......	NHL	59	9	5	14	18	-5	1	0	—	—	—	—	—
—Boston	NHL	14	3	3	6	8	-2	1	0	—	—	—	—	—
00-01—Boston	NHL	82	7	13	20	37	0	0	1	—	—	—	—	—
NHL Totals (5 years)...........		299	42	47	89	105	-13	5	1	3	0	1	1	0

KNUTSEN, ESPEN — C — BLUE JACKETS

PERSONAL: Born January 12, 1972, in Oslo, Norway. ... 5-11/180. ... Shoots left. ... Name pronounced kuh-NOOT-sihn.
TRANSACTIONS/CAREER NOTES: Selected by Hartford Whalers in 10th round (ninth Whalers pick, 204th overall) of NHL entry draft (June 16, 1990). ... Traded by Whalers to Mighty Ducks of Anaheim for RW Kevin Brown (October 1, 1996). ... Traded by Mighty Ducks to Columbus Blue Jackets for fourth-round pick (D Vladimir Korsunov) in 2001 draft (May 25, 2000). ... Fractured finger (September 20, 2000); missed first eight games of season. ... Suffered from the flu (December 10, 2000); missed one game. ... Suffered from the flu (January 15, 2001); missed one game. ... Strained neck (March 26, 2001); missed six games.

		REGULAR SEASON								PLAYOFFS				
Season Team	League	Gms.	G	A	Pts.	PIM	+/-	PP	SH	Gms.	G	A	Pts.	PIM
88-89—Valerengen.................	Norway Jr.	36	14	7	21	18	...	...	...	—	—	—	—	—
89-90—Valerengen.................	Norway	34	22	26	48	...	...	...	...	—	—	—	—	—
90-91—Valerengen.................	Norway	31	30	24	54	42	...	...	...	5	3	4	7	...
91-92—Valerengen.................	Norway	30	28	26	54	37	...	...	...	8	7	8	15	15
92-93—Valerengen.................	Norway	13	11	13	24	4	...	...	...	—	—	—	—	—
93-94—Valerengen.................	Norway	38	32	26	58	20	...	...	...	—	—	—	—	—
94-95—Djurgarden Stockholm	Sweden	30	6	14	20	18	...	...	...	3	0	1	1	0
95-96—Djurgarden Stockholm	Sweden	32	10	23	33	50	...	...	...	4	1	0	1	2
96-97—Djurgarden Stockholm	Sweden	39	16	33	49	20	...	...	...	4	2	4	6	6
97-98—Anaheim	NHL	19	3	0	3	6	-10	1	0	—	—	—	—	—
—Cincinnati...................	AHL	41	4	13	17	18	...	...	...	—	—	—	—	—
98-99—Djurgarden Stockholm	Sweden	39	18	24	42	32	...	...	...	4	0	1	1	2
99-00—Djurgarden Stockholm	Sweden	48	18	35	53	65	...	...	...	13	5	*16	*21	2
00-01—Columbus	NHL	66	11	42	53	30	-3	2	0	—	—	—	—	—
NHL Totals (2 years)...........		85	14	42	56	36	-13	3	0					

KOCHAN, DIETER — G — LIGHTNING

PERSONAL: Born November 5, 1974, in Saskatoon, Sask. ... 6-1/165. ... Catches left.
TRANSACTIONS/CAREER NOTES: Selected by Vancouver Canucks in fourth round (third Canucks pick, 98th overall) of NHL entry draft (June 26, 1993). ... Signed as free agent by Tampa Bay Lightning (March 27, 2000).
HONORS: Named to UHL All-Star second team (1999-2000).

		REGULAR SEASON								PLAYOFFS						
Season Team	League	Gms.	Min	W	L	T	GA	SO	Avg.	Gms.	Min.	W	L	GA	SO	Avg.
91-92—Sioux City....................	USHL	23	1131	7	10	0	100	...	5.31	—	—	—	—	—	—	—
92-93—Kelowna	BCJHL	44	2582	34	8	0	137	1	*3.18	—	—	—	—	—	—	—
93-94—N. Michigan U.	WCHA	16	984	9	7	0	57	2	3.48	—	—	—	—	—	—	—
94-95—N. Michigan U.	WCHA	29	1512	8	17	3	107	0	4.25	—	—	—	—	—	—	—
95-96—N. Michigan U.	WCHA	31	1627	7	21	2	123	0	4.54	—	—	—	—	—	—	—
96-97—N. Michigan U.	WCHA	26	1528	8	15	2	99	0	3.89	—	—	—	—	—	—	—
97-98—Louisville....................	ECHL	18	980	7	9	‡2	61	1	3.73	—	—	—	—	—	—	—
98-99—Binghamton	UHL	40	2321	18	16	‡5	115	2	2.97	4	207	1	2	9	0	2.61
99-00—Binghamton	UHL	43	2544	29	11	‡3	110	4	2.59	—	—	—	—	—	—	—
—Orlando	IHL	4	240	4	0	0	4	1	1.00	—	—	—	—	—	—	—
—Grand Rapids	IHL	2	93	1	0	‡1	1	0	.65	—	—	—	—	—	—	—
—Springfield	AHL	2	120	1	1	0	5	1	2.50	—	—	—	—	—	—	—
—Tampa Bay	NHL	5	238	1	4	0	17	0	4.29	—	—	—	—	—	—	—
00-01—Detroit......................	IHL	49	2606	13	*28	‡3	*154	0	3.55	—	—	—	—	—	—	—
—Tampa Bay	NHL	10	314	0	3	0	18	0	3.44	—	—	—	—	—	—	—
NHL Totals (2 years)...........		15	552	1	7	0	35	0	3.80							

KOEHLER, GREG — C — HURRICANES

PERSONAL: Born February 27, 1975, in Scarborough, Ont. ... 6-2/195. ... Shoots left.
TRANSACTIONS/CAREER NOTES: Signed as non-drafted free agent by Carolina Hurricanes (March 31, 1998).
HONORS: Named to IHL All-Star second team (2000-01).

Season Team	League	Gms.	G	A	Pts.	PIM	+/-	PP	SH	Gms.	G	A	Pts.	PIM
		REGULAR SEASON								PLAYOFFS				
96-97—Mass.-Lowell	Hockey East	37	16	20	36	49	...	...	...	—	—	—	—	—
97-98—Mass.-Lowell	Hockey East	33	20	17	37	62	...	...	...	—	—	—	—	—
—New Haven	AHL	3	0	0	0	2	...	...	...	—	—	—	—	—
98-99—Florida	ECHL	29	13	14	27	62	...	...	...	6	2	3	5	12
—New Haven	AHL	26	4	0	4	29	...	...	...	—	—	—	—	—
99-00—Cincinnati	IHL	74	12	13	25	157	...	...	...	8	0	3	3	14
00-01—Cincinnati	IHL	80	35	36	71	122	...	...	...	5	2	2	4	6
—Carolina	NHL	1	0	0	0	0	0	0	0	—	—	—	—	—
NHL Totals (1 year)		1	0	0	0	0	0	0	0					

KOHN, LADISLAV — RW

PERSONAL: Born March 4, 1975, in Uherske Hrada, Czechoslovakia. ... 5-10/172. ... Shoots left. ... Name pronounced KOHN.
TRANSACTIONS/CAREER NOTES: Selected by Calgary Flames in seventh round (ninth Flames pick, 175th overall) in NHL entry draft (June 29, 1994). ... Suffered concussion (November 26, 1997); missed 12 games. ... Traded by Flames to Toronto Maple Leafs for D David Cooper (July 2, 1998). ... Claimed by Atlanta Thrashers from Maple Leafs in NHL waiver draft (September 27, 1999). ... Traded by Thrashers to Mighty Ducks of Anaheim for eighth-round pick (D Evan Nielsen) in 2000 draft (September 27, 1999). ... Strained groin (November 26, 1999); missed five games. ... Traded by Mighty Ducks to Thrashers for D Sergei Vyshedkevich and G Scott Langkow (February 9, 2001).

Season Team	League	Gms.	G	A	Pts.	PIM	+/-	PP	SH	Gms.	G	A	Pts.	PIM
		REGULAR SEASON								PLAYOFFS				
93-94—Brandon	WHL	2	0	0	0	0	...	...	...	—	—	—	—	—
—Swift Current	WHL	69	33	35	68	68	...	...	...	7	5	4	9	8
94-95—Swift Current	WHL	65	32	60	92	122	...	...	...	6	2	6	8	14
—Saint John	AHL	1	0	0	0	0	...	...	...	—	—	—	—	—
95-96—Saint John	AHL	73	28	45	73	97	...	...	...	16	6	5	11	12
—Calgary	NHL	5	1	0	1	2	-1	0	0	—	—	—	—	—
96-97—Saint John	AHL	76	28	29	57	81	...	...	...	5	0	0	0	0
97-98—Saint John	AHL	65	25	31	56	90	...	...	...	21	*14	6	20	20
—Calgary	NHL	4	0	1	1	0	2	0	0	—	—	—	—	—
98-99—St. John's	AHL	61	27	42	69	90	...	...	...	2	0	0	0	5
—Toronto	NHL	16	1	3	4	4	1	0	0	2	0	0	0	5
99-00—Anaheim	NHL	77	5	16	21	27	-17	1	0	—	—	—	—	—
00-01—Anaheim	NHL	51	4	3	7	42	-15	0	1	—	—	—	—	—
—Atlanta	NHL	26	3	4	7	44	-12	0	1	—	—	—	—	—
NHL Totals (5 years)		179	14	27	41	119	-42	1	2	2	0	0	0	5

KOIVU, SAKU — C — CANADIENS

PERSONAL: Born November 23, 1974, in Turku, Finland. ... 5-10/181. ... Shoots left. ... Brother of Mikko Koivu, center, Minnesota Wild organization. ... Name pronounced SAK-oo KOY-voo.
TRANSACTIONS/CAREER NOTES: Selected by Montreal Canadiens in first round (first Canadiens pick, 21st overall) of NHL entry draft (June 26, 1993). ... Tore knee ligament (December 7, 1996); missed 26 games. ... Sprained shoulder (March 10, 1997); missed five games. ... Suffered from tonsillitis (March 29, 1997); missed one game. ... Strained ribcage (January 8, 1998); missed seven games. ... Fractured hand (April 7, 1998); missed six games. ... Strained abdominal muscle (October 24, 1998); missed 12 games. ... Suffered from elbow infection (January 18, 1999); missed three games. ... Injured knee (March 24, 1999); missed two games. ... Suffered injury (October 30, 1999); missed five games. ... Separated shoulder (November 2, 1999); missed 40 games. ... Tore medial collateral ligament in knee (March 11, 2000); missed remainder of season. ... Tore medial collateral ligament in left knee (October 11, 2000) and underwent surgery; missed 28 games.
HONORS: Played in NHL All-Star Game (1998).
MISCELLANEOUS: Captain of Montreal Canadiens (1999-2000, October 5-14, 2000 and December 15, 2000-remainder of season). ... Member of bronze-medal-winning Finnish Olympic team (1994 and 1998).

Season Team	League	Gms.	G	A	Pts.	PIM	+/-	PP	SH	Gms.	G	A	Pts.	PIM
		REGULAR SEASON								PLAYOFFS				
90-91—TPS Turku	Finland Jr.	24	20	28	48	26	...	...	...	—	—	—	—	—
91-92—TPS Turku	Finland Jr.	42	30	37	67	63	...	...	...	—	—	—	—	—
92-93—TPS Turku	Finland	46	3	7	10	28	...	...	...	—	—	—	—	—
93-94—TPS Turku	Finland	47	23	30	53	42	...	...	...	11	4	8	12	16
—Fin. Olympic team	Int'l	8	4	3	7	12	...	...	...	—	—	—	—	—
94-95—TPS Turku	Finland	45	27	47	74	73	...	...	...	13	7	10	17	16
95-96—Montreal	NHL	82	20	25	45	40	-7	8	3	6	3	1	4	8
96-97—Montreal	NHL	50	17	39	56	38	7	5	0	5	1	3	4	10
97-98—Montreal	NHL	69	14	43	57	48	8	2	2	6	2	3	5	2
—Fin. Olympic team	Int'l	6	2	8	10	4	...	...	...	—	—	—	—	—
98-99—Montreal	NHL	65	14	30	44	38	-7	4	2	—	—	—	—	—
99-00—Montreal	NHL	24	3	18	21	14	7	1	0	—	—	—	—	—
00-01—Montreal	NHL	54	17	30	47	40	2	7	0	—	—	—	—	—
NHL Totals (6 years)		344	85	185	270	218	10	27	7	17	6	7	13	20

K

KOLANOS, KRYS   C   COYOTES

PERSONAL: Born July 27, 1981, in Calgary. ... 6-2/196. ... Shoots right. ... Full Name: Krystofer Kolanos.
TRANSACTIONS/CAREER NOTES: Selected by Phoenix Coyotes in first round (first Coyotes pick, 19th overall) of NHL entry draft (June 24, 2000).
HONORS: Named to Hockey East All-Star second team (2000-01). ... Named to NCAA All-Tournament team (2000-01). ... Named to NCAA All-America (East) second team (2000-01).

		REGULAR SEASON								PLAYOFFS				
Season Team	League	Gms.	G	A	Pts.	PIM	+/-	PP	SH	Gms.	G	A	Pts.	PIM
98-99—Calgary Royals...........	AJHL	58	43	67	110	98	...	...	...	—	—	—	—	—
99-00—Boston College	Hockey East	34	14	13	27	44	...	...	...	—	—	—	—	—
00-01—Boston College	Hockey East	41	25	25	50	54	...	...	...	—	—	—	—	—

KOLARIK, PAVEL   D   BRUINS

PERSONAL: Born October 24, 1972, in Vyskov, Czechoslovakia. ... 6-1/207.
TRANSACTIONS/CAREER NOTES: Selected by Boston Bruins in ninth round (ninth Bruins pick, 268th overall) of 2000 NHL entry draft (June 24, 2000).

		REGULAR SEASON								PLAYOFFS				
Season Team	League	Gms.	G	A	Pts.	PIM	+/-	PP	SH	Gms.	G	A	Pts.	PIM
96-97—Slavia Praha...............	Czech Rep.	27	1	2	3	10	...	...	...	3	0	0	0	2
97-98—Slavia Praha...............	Czech Rep.	51	0	4	4	24	...	...	...	5	0	0	0	2
98-99—Slavia Praha...............	Czech Rep.	51	1	8	9	41	...	...	...	—	—	—	—	—
99-00—Slavia Praha...............	Czech Rep.	52	5	3	8	38	...	...	...	—	—	—	—	—
00-01—Providence.................	AHL	51	5	6	11	14	...	...	...	17	0	4	4	...
—Boston	NHL	10	0	0	0	4	-2	0	0	—	—	—	—	—
NHL Totals (1 year).............		10	0	0	0	4	-2	0	0					

KOLNIK, JURAJ   RW   ISLANDERS

PERSONAL: Born November 13, 1980, in Nitra, Czechoslovakia. ... 5-10/182. ... Shoots right.
TRANSACTIONS/CAREER NOTES: Selected by New York Islanders in fourth round (seventh Islanders pick, 101st overall) of NHL entry draft (June 26, 1999).

		REGULAR SEASON								PLAYOFFS				
Season Team	League	Gms.	G	A	Pts.	PIM	+/-	PP	SH	Gms.	G	A	Pts.	PIM
97-98—Plastika Nitra	Slovakia	28	1	3	4	6	...	...	...	—	—	—	—	—
98-99—Quebec	QMJHL	12	6	5	11	6	...	...	...	—	—	—	—	—
—Rimouski	QMJHL	50	36	37	73	34	...	...	...	11	9	6	15	6
99-00—Rimouski	QMJHL	47	53	53	106	53	...	...	...	14	10	17	27	16
00-01—Lowell.......................	AHL	25	2	6	8	18	...	...	...	—	—	—	—	—
—Springfield	AHL	29	15	20	35	20	...	...	...	—	—	—	—	—
—New York Islanders.....	NHL	29	4	3	7	12	-8	0	0	—	—	—	—	—
NHL Totals (1 year).............		29	4	3	7	12	-8	0	0					

KOLTSOV, KONSTANTIN   LW   PENGUINS

PERSONAL: Born April 17, 1981, in Minsk, U.S.S.R. ... 6-0/187. ... Shoots left.
TRANSACTIONS/CAREER NOTES: Selected by Pittsburgh Penguins in first round (first Penguins pick, 18th overall) of NHL entry draft (June 26, 1999).

		REGULAR SEASON								PLAYOFFS				
Season Team	League	Gms.	G	A	Pts.	PIM	+/-	PP	SH	Gms.	G	A	Pts.	PIM
97-98—Minsk.......................	Russian Div. 1	52	15	18	33	60	...	...	...	—	—	—	—	—
—Severstal Cherepovets	Russian	2	0	0	0	2	...	...	...	—	—	—	—	—
—Sev.-2 Cherepovets.....	Rus. Div. III	44	11	12	23	16	...	...	...	—	—	—	—	—
98-99—Severstal Cherepovets	Russian	33	3	0	3	8	...	...	...	1	0	0	0	2
99-00—Met. Novokuznetsk	Russian	30	3	4	7	28	...	...	...	14	1	1	2	8
00-01—Ak Bars Kazan............	Russian	24	7	8	15	10	...	...	...	2	0	0	0	4

KOLZIG, OLAF   G   CAPITALS

PERSONAL: Born April 6, 1970, in Johannesburg, South Africa. ... 6-3/226. ... Catches left. ... Name pronounced OH-lahf KOHL-zihg.
TRANSACTIONS/CAREER NOTES: Selected by Washington Capitals in first round (first Capitals pick, 19th overall) of NHL entry draft (June 17, 1989). ... Dislocated kneecap (October 13, 1993); missed 14 games. ... Suffered from mononucleosis (October 8, 1996); missed three games. ... Underwent knee surgery (September 26, 2000); missed first two games of regular season.
HONORS: Shared Harry (Hap) Holmes Memorial Trophy with Byron Dafoe (1993-94). ... Won Jack Butterfield Trophy (1993-94). ... Played in NHL All-Star Game (1998 and 2000). ... Named to NHL All-Star first team (1999-2000). ... Won Vezina Trophy (1999-2000).
RECORDS: Shares NHL single-season playoff record for most shutouts—4 (1998).
MISCELLANEOUS: Holds Washington Capitals all-time records in games played (344), most wins (151) and most shutouts (21). ... Stopped a penalty shot attempt (vs. Mike Hough, February 29, 1996; vs. Todd Marchant, January 26, 1997; vs. Sergei Nemchinov, March 11, 2000). ... Allowed a penalty shot goal (vs. Viktor Kozlov, February 23, 2000).

Season Team	League	REGULAR SEASON Gms.	Min	W	L	T	GA	SO	Avg.	PLAYOFFS Gms.	Min.	W	L	GA	SO	Avg.
87-88—New Westminster..........	WHL	15	650	6	5	0	48	1	4.43	3	149	0	0	11	0	4.43
88-89—Tri-City	WHL	30	1671	16	10	2	97	1	*3.48	—	—	—	—	—	—	—
89-90—Washington...............	NHL	2	120	0	2	0	12	0	6.00	—	—	—	—	—	—	—
—Tri-City	WHL	48	2504	27	27	3	187	1	4.48	6	318	4	0	27	0	5.09
90-91—Baltimore	AHL	26	1367	10	12	1	72	0	3.16	—	—	—	—	—	—	—
—Hampton Roads...........	ECHL	21	1248	11	9	‡1	71	2	3.41	3	180	1	2	14	0	4.67
91-92—Baltimore	AHL	28	1503	5	17	2	105	1	4.19	—	—	—	—	—	—	—
—Hampton Roads...........	ECHL	14	847	11	3	0	41	0	2.90	—	—	—	—	—	—	—
92-93—Rochester	AHL	49	2737	25	16	4	168	0	3.68	17	*1040	9	*8	61	0	3.52
—Washington...............	NHL	1	20	0	0	0	2	0	6.00	—	—	—	—	—	—	—
93-94—Portland	AHL	29	1726	16	8	5	88	3	3.06	17	1035	†12	5	44	0	*2.55
—Washington...............	NHL	7	224	0	3	0	20	0	5.36	—	—	—	—	—	—	—
94-95—Washington...............	NHL	14	724	2	8	2	30	0	2.49	2	44	1	0	1	0	1.36
—Portland	AHL	2	125	1	0	1	3	0	1.44	—	—	—	—	—	—	—
95-96—Washington...............	NHL	18	897	4	8	2	46	0	3.08	5	341	2	3	11	0	1.94
—Portland	AHL	5	300	5	0	0	7	1	1.40	—	—	—	—	—	—	—
96-97—Washington...............	NHL	29	1644	8	15	4	71	2	2.59	—	—	—	—	—	—	—
97-98—Washington...............	NHL	64	3788	33	18	10	139	5	2.20	21	1351	12	9	44	4	1.95
—German Oly. team	Int'l	2	120	2	0	0	2	1	1.00	—	—	—	—	—	—	—
98-99—Washington...............	NHL	64	3586	26	†31	3	154	4	2.58	—	—	—	—	—	—	—
99-00—Washington...............	NHL	73	*4371	41	20	11	163	5	2.24	5	284	1	4	16	0	3.38
00-01—Washington...............	NHL	72	4279	37	26	8	177	5	2.48	6	375	2	4	14	1	2.24
NHL Totals (10 years)..........		344	19653	151	131	40	814	21	2.49	39	2395	18	20	86	5	2.15

K

KOMARNISKI, ZENITH   D   CANUCKS

PERSONAL: Born August 13, 1978, in Edmonton. ... 6-0/200. ... Shoots left. ... Name pronounced ZEH-nihth koh-mahr-NIH-skee.
TRANSACTIONS/CAREER NOTES: Selected by Vancouver Canucks in third round (second Canucks pick, 75th overall) of NHL entry draft (June 22, 1996). ... Injured shoulder (November 26, 1999); missed four games.
HONORS: Named to WHL (West) All-Star first team (1996-97).

Season Team	League	REGULAR SEASON Gms.	G	A	Pts.	PIM	+/-	PP	SH	PLAYOFFS Gms.	G	A	Pts.	PIM
94-95—Tri-City	WHL	66	5	19	24	110	...	...	...	17	1	2	3	47
95-96—Tri-City	WHL	42	5	21	26	85	...	...	...	—	—	—	—	—
96-97—Tri-City	WHL	58	12	44	56	112	...	...	...	—	—	—	—	—
97-98—Tri-City	WHL	3	0	4	4	18	...	...	...	—	—	—	—	—
—Spokane.....................	WHL	43	7	20	27	90	...	...	...	18	4	6	10	49
98-99—Syracuse...................	AHL	58	9	19	28	89	...	...	...	—	—	—	—	—
99-00—Syracuse...................	AHL	42	4	12	16	130	...	...	...	4	2	0	2	6
—Vancouver.................	NHL	18	1	1	2	8	-1	0	0	—	—	—	—	—
00-01—Kansas City...............	IHL	70	7	22	29	191	...	...	...	—	—	—	—	—
NHL Totals (1 year).............		18	1	1	2	8	-1	0	0					

KONOWALCHUK, STEVE   RW   CAPITALS

PERSONAL: Born November 11, 1972, in Salt Lake City. ... 6-2/210. ... Shoots left. ... Full Name: Steven Reed Konowalchuk. ... Name pronounced kah-nah-WAHL-chuhk.
TRANSACTIONS/CAREER NOTES: Selected by Washington Capitals in third round (fifth Capitals pick, 58th overall) of NHL entry draft (June 22, 1991). ... Separated shoulder (October 13, 1995); missed four games. ... Injured left hand (March 26, 1996); missed eight games. ... Separated rib cartilage prior to 1996-97 season; missed four games. ... Strained groin (January 28, 1998); missed two games. ... Sprained ankle (October 10, 1998); missed 15 games. ... Suffered concussion (March 2, 1999); missed remainder of season.
HONORS: Won Four Broncos Memorial Trophy (1991-92). ... Named to Can.HL All-Star second team (1991-92). ... Named to WHL (West) All-Star first team (1991-92).
MISCELLANEOUS: Failed to score on a penalty shot (vs. Mike Richter, March 5, 1995).
STATISTICAL PLATEAUS: Three-goal games: 1995-96 (2), 2000-01 (1). Total: 3.

Season Team	League	REGULAR SEASON Gms.	G	A	Pts.	PIM	+/-	PP	SH	PLAYOFFS Gms.	G	A	Pts.	PIM
90-91—Portland	WHL	72	43	49	92	78	...	...	...	—	—	—	—	—
91-92—Portland	WHL	64	51	53	104	95	...	...	...	6	3	6	9	12
—Baltimore	AHL	3	1	1	2	0	...	...	...	—	—	—	—	—
—Washington...............	NHL	1	0	0	0	0	0	0	0	—	—	—	—	—
92-93—Baltimore	AHL	37	18	28	46	74	...	...	...	—	—	—	—	—
—Washington...............	NHL	36	4	7	11	16	4	1	0	2	0	1	1	0
93-94—Portland	AHL	8	11	4	15	4	...	...	...	—	—	—	—	—
—Washington...............	NHL	62	12	14	26	33	9	0	0	11	0	1	1	10
94-95—Washington...............	NHL	46	11	14	25	44	7	3	3	7	2	5	7	12
95-96—Washington...............	NHL	70	23	22	45	92	13	7	1	2	0	2	2	0
96-97—Washington...............	NHL	78	17	25	42	67	-3	2	1	—	—	—	—	—
97-98—Washington...............	NHL	80	10	24	34	80	9	2	0	—	—	—	—	—
98-99—Washington...............	NHL	45	12	12	24	26	0	4	1	—	—	—	—	—
99-00—Washington...............	NHL	82	16	27	43	80	19	3	0	5	1	0	1	2
00-01—Washington...............	NHL	82	24	23	47	87	8	6	0	6	2	3	5	14
NHL Totals (10 years)..........		582	129	168	297	525	66	28	6	33	5	12	17	38

KONSTANTINOV, EVGENY   G   LIGHTNING

PERSONAL: Born March 29, 1981, in Kazan, U.S.S.R. ... 6-0/167. ... Catches left. ... Name pronounced ev-GEHN-ee kohn-stahn-TEE-nanf.
TRANSACTIONS/CAREER NOTES: Selected by Tampa Bay Lightning in third round (second Lightning pick, 67th overall) of NHL entry draft (June 26, 1999).

			REGULAR SEASON									PLAYOFFS						
Season Team	League	Gms.	Min	W	L	T	GA	SO	Avg.		Gms.	Min.	W	L	GA	SO	Avg.
97-98—Ak Bars-2 Kazan...........	Rus. Div. III	34	2040	...	...	...	129	...	3.79		—	—	—	—	—	—	—
98-99—Ak Bars-2 Kazan.............	Rus. Div. III	17	1020	...	...	...	38	...	2.24		—	—	—	—	—	—	—
99-00—Ak Bars Kazan..............	Russian	2	59	...	...	...	5	0	5.08		—	—	—	—	—	—	—
00-01—Detroit........................	IHL	27	1197	4	15	‡2	85	0	4.26		—	—	—	—	—	—	—
—Tampa Bay	NHL	1	0	0	0	0	0	0	...		—	—	—	—	—	—	—
—Louisiana	ECHL	8	458	4	4	0	21	0	2.75		12	637	5	6	32	0	3.01
NHL Totals (1 year)..............		1	0	0	0	0	0	0	...								

KOPECKY, TOMAS   C/LW   RED WINGS

PERSONAL: Born February 2, 1982, in Ilava, Czechoslovakia. ... 6-3/187. ... Shoots left.
TRANSACTIONS/CAREER NOTES: Selected by Detroit Red Wings in second round (second Red Wings pick, 38th overall) of NHL entry draft (June 24, 2000).

			REGULAR SEASON								PLAYOFFS			
Season Team	League	Gms.	G	A	Pts.	PIM	+/-	PP	SH		Gms.	G	A	Pts.	PIM
98-99—Dukla Trencin Jrs........	Slovakia Jrs.	44	13	16	29	...	...	...	...		—	—	—	—	—
99-00—Dukla Trencin..............	Slovakia	52	3	4	7	24	...	...	...		5	0	0	0	0
—Dukla Trencin Jrs........	Slovakia Jrs.	12	11	13	24	10	...	...	...		—	—	—	—	—
00-01—Lethbridge	WHL	49	22	28	50	52	...	...	...		5	1	1	2	6
—Cincinnati....................	AHL	1	0	0	0	0	...	...	...		—	—	—	—	—

KOROLEV, EVGENY   D   ISLANDERS

PERSONAL: Born July 24, 1978, in Moscow, U.S.S.R. ... 6-1/186. ... Shoots left.
TRANSACTIONS/CAREER NOTES: Selected by New York Islanders in sixth round (seventh Islanders pick, 138th overall) of NHL entry draft (June 22, 1996).

			REGULAR SEASON								PLAYOFFS			
Season Team	League	Gms.	G	A	Pts.	PIM	+/-	PP	SH		Gms.	G	A	Pts.	PIM
95-96—Peterborough..............	OHL	60	2	12	14	60	...	...	...		6	0	0	0	2
96-97—Peterborough..............	OHL	64	5	17	22	60	...	...	...		11	1	1	2	8
97-98—Peterborough..............	OHL	37	5	21	26	39	...	...	...		—	—	—	—	—
—London	OHL	27	4	10	14	36	...	...	...		15	2	7	9	29
98-99—Lowell......................	AHL	54	2	6	8	48	...	...	...		2	0	1	1	0
—Roanoke	ECHL	2	0	1	1	0	...	...	...		—	—	—	—	—
99-00—Lowell......................	AHL	57	1	10	11	61	...	...	...		6	0	0	0	4
—New York Islanders.....	NHL	17	1	2	3	8	-10	0	0		—	—	—	—	—
00-01—New York Islanders.....	NHL	8	0	0	0	6	0	0	0		—	—	—	—	—
—Louisville....................	AHL	36	2	14	16	68	...	...	...		—	—	—	—	—
NHL Totals (2 years)...........		25	1	2	3	14	-10	0	0						

KOROLEV, IGOR   C   BLACKHAWKS

PERSONAL: Born September 6, 1970, in Moscow, U.S.S.R. ... 6-1/190. ... Shoots left. ... Name pronounced EE-gohr KOHR-ih-lehv.
TRANSACTIONS/CAREER NOTES: Selected by St. Louis Blues in second round (first Blues pick, 38th overall) of NHL entry draft (June 20, 1992). ... Suffered from the flu (March 3, 1994); missed one game. ... Injured hip (March 12, 1994); missed three games. ... Selected by Winnipeg Jets from Blues in NHL waiver draft for cash (January 18, 1995). ... Played in Europe during 1994-95 NHL lockout. ... Fractured wrist (December 10, 1995); missed two games. ... Suffered hip pointer (February 1, 1996); missed three games. ... Jets franchise moved to Phoenix and renamed Coyotes for 1996-97 season; NHL approved move on January 18, 1996. ... Signed as free agent by Toronto Maple Leafs (September 28, 1997). ... Sprained shoulder (October 28, 1997); missed one game. ... Strained back (January 6, 1998); missed one game. ... Suffered back spasms (January 9, 1999); missed three games. ... Fractured finger (March 20, 1999); missed 13 games. ... Fractured fibula (April 22, 1999); missed remainder of playoffs. ... Suffered injury (October 13, 1999); missed two games. ... Suffered injury (February 8, 2001); missed five games. ... Traded by Maple Leafs to Chicago Blackhawks for third-round pick (C Nicolas Corbeil) in 2001 draft (June 23, 2001).
STATISTICAL PLATEAUS: Three-goal games: 1995-96 (1).

			REGULAR SEASON								PLAYOFFS			
Season Team	League	Gms.	G	A	Pts.	PIM	+/-	PP	SH		Gms.	G	A	Pts.	PIM
88-89—Dynamo Moscow........	USSR	1	0	0	0	2	...	...	...		—	—	—	—	—
89-90—Dynamo Moscow........	USSR	17	3	2	5	2	...	...	...		—	—	—	—	—
90-91—Dynamo Moscow........	USSR	38	12	4	16	12	...	...	...		—	—	—	—	—
91-92—Dynamo Moscow........	CIS	39	15	12	27	16	...	...	...		—	—	—	—	—
92-93—Dynamo Moscow........	CIS	5	1	2	3	4	...	...	...		—	—	—	—	—
—St. Louis	NHL	74	4	23	27	20	-1	2	0		3	0	0	0	0
93-94—St. Louis	NHL	73	6	10	16	40	-12	0	0		2	0	0	0	0
94-95—Dynamo Moscow........	CIS	13	4	6	10	18	...	...	...		—	—	—	—	—
—Winnipeg	NHL	45	8	22	30	10	1	1	0		—	—	—	—	—
95-96—Winnipeg	NHL	73	22	29	51	42	1	8	0		6	0	3	3	0
96-97—Michigan	IHL	4	2	2	4	0	...	...	...		—	—	—	—	—
—Phoenix.....................	IHL	4	2	6	8	4	...	...	...		—	—	—	—	—
—Phoenix......................	NHL	41	3	7	10	28	-5	2	0		1	0	0	0	0

Season Team	League	Gms.	G	A	Pts.	PIM	+/-	PP	SH	Gms.	G	A	Pts.	PIM
		REGULAR SEASON								PLAYOFFS				
97-98—Toronto	NHL	78	17	22	39	22	-18	6	3	—	—	—	—	—
98-99—Toronto	NHL	66	13	34	47	46	11	1	0	1	0	0	0	0
99-00—Toronto	NHL	80	20	26	46	22	12	5	3	12	0	4	4	6
00-01—Toronto	NHL	73	10	19	29	28	3	2	0	11	0	0	0	0
NHL Totals (9 years)		603	103	192	295	258	-8	27	6	36	0	7	7	6

KOROLYUK, ALEX   RW   SHARKS

PERSONAL: Born January 15, 1976, in Moscow, U.S.S.R. ... 5-9/195. ... Shoots left. ... Full Name: Alexander Korolyuk. ... Name pronounced KOH-rohl-yook.

TRANSACTIONS/CAREER NOTES: Selected by San Jose Sharks in sixth round (sixth Sharks pick, 141st overall) of NHL entry draft (June 29, 1994). ... Suffered eye injury (December 2, 1999); missed three games. ... Injured back (January 19, 2000); missed eight games. ... Reinjured back (February 11, 2000); missed four games.

MISCELLANEOUS: Scored on a penalty shot (vs. Roman Turek, January 11, 2000).

Season Team	League	Gms.	G	A	Pts.	PIM	+/-	PP	SH	Gms.	G	A	Pts.	PIM
		REGULAR SEASON								PLAYOFFS				
93-94—Soviet Wings	CIS	22	4	4	8	20	...	...	...	3	1	0	1	4
94-95—Soviet Wings	CIS	52	16	13	29	62	...	...	...	4	1	2	3	4
95-96—Soviet Wings	CIS	50	30	19	49	77	...	...	...	—	—	—	—	—
96-97—Soviet Wings	CIS	17	8	5	13	46	...	...	...	—	—	—	—	—
—Manitoba	IHL	42	20	16	36	71	...	...	...	—	—	—	—	—
97-98—San Jose	NHL	19	2	3	5	6	-5	1	0	—	—	—	—	—
—Kentucky	AHL	44	16	23	39	96	...	...	...	3	0	0	0	0
98-99—Kentucky	AHL	23	9	13	22	16	...	...	...	—	—	—	—	—
—San Jose	NHL	55	12	18	30	26	3	2	0	6	1	3	4	2
99-00—San Jose	NHL	57	14	21	35	35	4	3	0	9	0	3	3	6
00-01—Ak Bars Kazan	Russian	6	0	5	5	4	...	...	...	—	—	—	—	—
—San Jose	NHL	70	12	13	25	41	2	3	0	2	0	0	0	0
NHL Totals (4 years)		201	40	55	95	108	4	9	0	17	1	6	7	8

K

KOSTOPOULOS, TOM   RW   PENGUINS

PERSONAL: Born January 24, 1979, in Mississauga, Ont. ... 6-0/205. ... Shoots right.

TRANSACTIONS/CAREER NOTES: Selected by Pittsburgh Penguins in ninth round (ninth Penguins pick, 204th overall) of NHL entry draft (June 26, 1999).

Season Team	League	Gms.	G	A	Pts.	PIM	+/-	PP	SH	Gms.	G	A	Pts.	PIM
		REGULAR SEASON								PLAYOFFS				
96-97—London	OHL	64	13	12	25	67	...	...	...	—	—	—	—	—
97-98—London	OHL	66	24	26	50	108	...	...	...	16	6	4	10	26
98-99—London	OHL	66	27	60	87	114	...	...	...	25	19	16	35	32
99-00—Wilkes-Barre/Scranton	AHL	76	26	32	58	121	...	...	...	—	—	—	—	—
00-01—Wilkes-Barre/Scranton	AHL	80	16	36	52	120	...	...	...	21	3	9	12	6

KOVALENKO, ANDREI   RW

PERSONAL: Born July 7, 1970, in Gorky, U.S.S.R. ... 5-10/215. ... Shoots right. ... Name pronounced koh-vuh-LEHN-koh.

TRANSACTIONS/CAREER NOTES: Selected by Quebec Nordiques in eighth round (sixth Nordiques pick, 148th overall) of NHL entry draft (June 16, 1990). ... Suffered from tonsillitis (December 22, 1992); missed two games. ... Suffered from the flu (March 15, 1993); missed one game. ... Suffered concussion (November 4, 1993); missed five games. ... Bruised ribs (January 11, 1994); missed two games. ... Injured shoulder (January 25, 1994); missed 14 games. ... Suffered from tonsillitis (April 3, 1994); missed two games. ... Played in Europe during 1994-95 NHL lockout. ... Pulled groin (March 9, 1995); missed one game. ... Injured back (April 5, 1995); missed one game. ... Injured thumb (April 20, 1995); missed one game. ... Nordiques franchise moved to Colorado and renamed Avalanche for 1995-96 season (June 21, 1995). ... Traded by Avalanche with G Jocelyn Thibault and LW Martin Rucinsky to Montreal Canadiens for G Patrick Roy and RW Mike Keane (December 6, 1995). ... Fractured nose (December 16, 1995); missed five games. ... Strained left rotator cuff (February 15, 1996); missed two games. ... Traded by Canadiens to Edmonton Oilers for C Scott Thornton (September 6, 1996). ... Suffered back spasms (February 17, 1997); missed two games. ... Suffered hip pointer (March 1, 1997); missed five games. ... Suffered back spasms (October 13, 1997); missed one game. ... Suffered from flu (December 30, 1997); missed one game. ... Suffered from the flu (March 4, 1998); missed one game. ... Suffered back spasms (March 11, 1998); missed three games. ... Suffered back spasms (March 30, 1998); missed final eight games of regular season and 11 playoff games. ... Traded by Oilers to Philadelphia Flyers for C/RW Alexandre Daigle (January 29, 1999). ... Traded by Flyers to Carolina Hurricanes for D Adam Burt (March 6, 1999). ... Suffered back spasms (November 17, 1999); missed three games. ... Injured knee (April 8, 2000); missed final game of season. ... Signed as free agent by Boston Bruins (July 25, 2000). ... Strained back (January 13, 2001); missed one game. ... Strained back (January 22, 2001); missed one game. ... Suffered back spasms (February 23, 2001); missed four games.

MISCELLANEOUS: Member of gold-medal-winning Unified Olympic team (1992). ... Member of silver-medal-winning Russian Olympic team (1998). ... Scored on a penalty shot (vs. Kirk McLean, December 4, 1993).

STATISTICAL PLATEAUS: Three-goal games: 1992-93 (1), 2000-01 (1). Total: 2.

Season Team	League	Gms.	G	A	Pts.	PIM	+/-	PP	SH	Gms.	G	A	Pts.	PIM
		REGULAR SEASON								PLAYOFFS				
88-89—CSKA Moscow	USSR	10	1	0	1	0	...	...	...	—	—	—	—	—
89-90—CSKA Moscow	USSR	48	8	5	13	18	...	...	...	—	—	—	—	—
90-91—CSKA Moscow	USSR	45	13	8	21	26	...	...	...	—	—	—	—	—
91-92—CSKA Moscow	CIS	44	19	13	32	32	...	...	...	—	—	—	—	—
—Unif. Olympic team	Int'l	8	1	1	2	2	...	...	...	—	—	—	—	—
92-93—CSKA Moscow	CIS	3	3	1	4	4	...	...	...	—	—	—	—	—
—Quebec	NHL	81	27	41	68	57	13	8	1	4	1	0	1	2
93-94—Quebec	NHL	58	16	17	33	46	-5	5	0	—	—	—	—	—
94-95—Lada Togliatti	CIS	11	9	2	11	14	...	...	...	—	—	—	—	—
—Quebec	NHL	45	14	10	24	31	-4	1	0	6	0	1	1	2

Season Team	League	REGULAR SEASON Gms.	G	A	Pts.	PIM	+/-	PP	SH	PLAYOFFS Gms.	G	A	Pts.	PIM
95-96—Colorado	NHL	26	11	11	22	16	11	3	0	—	—	—	—	—
—Montreal	NHL	51	17	17	34	33	9	3	0	6	0	0	0	6
96-97—Edmonton	NHL	74	32	27	59	81	-5	14	0	12	4	3	7	6
97-98—Edmonton	NHL	59	6	17	23	28	-14	1	0	1	0	0	0	2
—Russian Oly. team	Int'l	6	4	1	5	14	...	...	...	—	—	—	—	—
98-99—Edmonton	NHL	43	13	14	27	30	-4	2	0	—	—	—	—	—
—Philadelphia	NHL	13	0	1	1	2	-5	0	0	—	—	—	—	—
—Carolina	NHL	18	6	6	12	0	3	1	0	4	0	2	2	2
99-00—Carolina	NHL	76	15	24	39	38	-13	2	0	—	—	—	—	—
00-01—Boston	NHL	76	16	21	37	27	-14	7	1	—	—	—	—	—
NHL Totals (9 years)		620	173	206	379	389	-28	47	2	33	5	6	11	20

KOVALEV, ALEXEI   C   PENGUINS

PERSONAL: Born February 24, 1973, in Moscow, U.S.S.R. ... 6-1/215. ... Shoots left. ... Name pronounced KOH-vuh-lahf.

TRANSACTIONS/CAREER NOTES: Selected by New York Rangers in first round (first Rangers pick, 15th overall) of NHL entry draft (June 22, 1991). ... Suffered back spasms (January 16, 1993); missed one game. ... Suspended one game by NHL (November 10, 1993). ... Suspended five games by NHL for tripping (November 30, 1993). ... Suspended two games by NHL (February 12, 1994). ... Played in Europe during 1994-95 NHL lockout. ... Suffered from the flu (December 2, 1995); missed one game. ... Tore knee ligament (January 8, 1997); missed remainder of season. ... Sprained knee and underwent athroscopic surgery (January 22, 1998); missed eight games. ... Separated shoulder (October 27, 1998); missed five games. ... Bruised shoulder (November 21, 1998); missed one game. ... Traded by Rangers with C Harry York and future considerations to Pittsburgh Penguins for C Petr Nedved, C Sean Pronger and D Chris Tamer (November 25, 1998). ... Bruised shoulder (November 21, 1998); missed one game. ... Suspended three games by NHL for unsportsmanline conduct (March 24, 2001).

HONORS: Played in NHL All-Star Game (2001). ... Named to THE SPORTING NEWS All-Star first team (2000-01).

MISCELLANEOUS: Member of Stanley Cup championship team (1994). ... Member of gold-medal-winning Unified Olympic team (1992). ... Member of silver-medal-winning Russian Olympic team (1998). ... Failed to score on a penalty shot (vs. Jon Casey, October 5, 1993).

STATISTICAL PLATEAUS: Three-goal games: 1992-93 (1), 1996-97 (1), 2000-01 (4). Total: 6.

Season Team	League	REGULAR SEASON Gms.	G	A	Pts.	PIM	+/-	PP	SH	PLAYOFFS Gms.	G	A	Pts.	PIM
89-90—Dynamo Moscow	USSR	1	0	0	0	0	...	...	...	—	—	—	—	—
90-91—Dynamo Moscow	USSR	18	1	2	3	4	...	...	...	—	—	—	—	—
91-92—Dynamo Moscow	CIS	33	16	9	25	20	...	...	...	—	—	—	—	—
—Unif. Olympic team	Int'l	8	1	2	3	14	...	...	...	—	—	—	—	—
92-93—New York Rangers	NHL	65	20	18	38	79	-10	3	0	—	—	—	—	—
—Binghamton	AHL	13	13	11	24	35	...	...	...	9	3	5	8	14
93-94—New York Rangers	NHL	76	23	33	56	154	18	7	0	23	9	12	21	18
94-95—Lada Togliatti	CIS	12	8	8	16	49	...	...	...	—	—	—	—	—
—New York Rangers	NHL	48	13	15	28	30	-6	1	1	10	4	7	11	10
95-96—New York Rangers	NHL	81	24	34	58	98	5	8	1	11	3	4	7	14
96-97—New York Rangers	NHL	45	13	22	35	42	11	1	0	—	—	—	—	—
97-98—New York Rangers	NHL	73	23	30	53	44	-22	8	0	—	—	—	—	—
98-99—New York Rangers	NHL	14	3	4	7	12	-6	1	0	—	—	—	—	—
—Pittsburgh	NHL	63	20	26	46	37	8	5	1	10	5	7	12	14
99-00—Pittsburgh	NHL	82	26	40	66	94	-3	9	2	11	1	5	6	10
00-01—Pittsburgh	NHL	79	44	51	95	96	12	12	2	18	5	5	10	16
NHL Totals (9 years)		626	209	273	482	686	7	55	7	83	27	40	67	82

KOZLOV, SLAVA   LW   SABRES

PERSONAL: Born May 3, 1972, in Voskresensk, U.S.S.R. ... 5-10/195. ... Shoots left. ... Full Name: Vyacheslav Kozlov. ... Name pronounced VYACH-ih-slav KAHS-lahf.

TRANSACTIONS/CAREER NOTES: Selected by Detroit Red Wings in third round (second Red Wings pick, 45th overall) of NHL entry draft (June 16, 1990). ... Played in Europe during 1994-95 NHL lockout. ... Bruised left foot (April 16, 1995); missed one game. ... Sprained knee (April 15, 1998); missed two games. ... Suspended three games by NHL for elbowing incident (December 18, 1998). ... Injured ankle (December 22, 1999); missed three games. ... Reinjured ankle (January 4, 2000); missed four games. ... Suffered concussion (March 29, 2000); missed two games. ... Traded by Red Wings with first-round pick in 2002 draft and future considerations to Buffalo Sabres for G Dominik Hasek (July 1, 2001).

HONORS: Named Soviet League Rookie of the Year (1989-90).

MISCELLANEOUS: Member of Stanley Cup championship team (1997 and 1998).

STATISTICAL PLATEAUS: Three-goal games: 1993-94 (1), 1998-99 (1). Total: 2. ... Four-goal games: 1995-96 (1). ... Total hat tricks: 3.

Season Team	League	REGULAR SEASON Gms.	G	A	Pts.	PIM	+/-	PP	SH	PLAYOFFS Gms.	G	A	Pts.	PIM
87-88—Khimik	USSR	2	0	1	1	0	...	...	...	—	—	—	—	—
88-89—Khimik	USSR	13	0	1	1	2	...	...	...	—	—	—	—	—
89-90—Khimik	USSR	45	14	12	26	38	...	...	...	—	—	—	—	—
90-91—Khimik	USSR	45	11	13	24	46	...	...	...	—	—	—	—	—
91-92—Khimik	USSR	11	6	5	11	12	...	...	...	—	—	—	—	—
—Detroit	NHL	7	0	2	2	2	-2	0	0	—	—	—	—	—
92-93—Detroit	NHL	17	4	1	5	14	-1	0	0	4	0	2	2	2
—Adirondack	AHL	45	23	36	59	54	...	...	...	4	1	1	2	4
93-94—Detroit	NHL	77	34	39	73	50	27	8	2	7	2	5	7	12
—Adirondack	AHL	3	0	1	1	15	...	...	...	—	—	—	—	—
94-95—CSKA Moscow	CIS	10	3	4	7	14	...	...	...	—	—	—	—	—
—Detroit	NHL	46	13	20	33	45	12	5	0	18	9	7	16	10
95-96—Detroit	NHL	82	36	37	73	70	33	9	0	19	5	7	12	10
96-97—Detroit	NHL	75	23	22	45	46	21	3	0	20	8	5	13	14

Season Team	League	REGULAR SEASON Gms.	G	A	Pts.	PIM	+/-	PP	SH	PLAYOFFS Gms.	G	A	Pts.	PIM
97-98—Detroit	NHL	80	25	27	52	46	14	6	0	22	6	8	14	10
98-99—Detroit	NHL	79	29	29	58	45	10	6	1	10	6	1	7	4
99-00—Detroit	NHL	72	18	18	36	28	11	4	0	8	2	1	3	12
00-01—Detroit	NHL	72	20	18	38	30	9	4	0	6	4	1	5	2
NHL Totals (10 years)		607	202	213	415	376	134	45	3	114	42	37	79	76

KOZLOV, VIKTOR   C   PANTHERS

K

PERSONAL: Born February 14, 1975, in Togliatti, U.S.S.R. ... 6-5/232. ... Shoots right. ... Name pronounced KAHZ-lahf.

TRANSACTIONS/CAREER NOTES: Selected by San Jose Sharks in first round (first Sharks pick, sixth overall) of NHL entry draft (June 26, 1993). ... Suffered displaced ankle fracture (November 27, 1994); missed 13 games. ... Played in Europe during 1994-95 NHL lockout. ... Bruised ankle (March 26, 1997); missed four games. ... Traded by Sharks with fifth-round pick (D Jaroslav Spacek) in 1998 draft to Florida Panthers for LW Dave Lowry and first-round pick (traded to Tampa Bay) in 1998 draft (November 13, 1997). ... Separated right shoulder (November 18, 1997); missed 16 games. ... Suffered concussion (April 1, 1998); missed three games. ... Separated shoulder (October 30, 1998); missed six games. ... Reinjured shoulder (January 8, 1999); missed one game. ... Strained shoulder (January 20, 1999); missed three games. ... Fractured finger (April 3, 1999); missed final seven games of season. ... Sprained shoulder (March 8, 2000); missed two games. ... Injured shoulder (October 25, 2000); missed six games. ... Injured left shoulder (December 13, 2000); missed nine games. ... Injured groin (March 14, 2001); missed five games. ... Reinjured groin (March 28, 2001); missed final five games of season.

HONORS: Named to play in NHL All-Star Game (1999); missed game due to injury. ... Played in NHL All-Star Game (2000).

MISCELLANEOUS: Scored on a penalty shot (vs. Olaf Kolzig, February 23, 2000).

STATISTICAL PLATEAUS: Three-goal games: 1999-00 (1).

Season Team	League	REGULAR SEASON Gms.	G	A	Pts.	PIM	+/-	PP	SH	PLAYOFFS Gms.	G	A	Pts.	PIM
90-91—Lada Togliatti	USSR Div. II	2	2	0	2	0	...	...	...	—	—	—	—	—
91-92—Lada Togliatti	CIS	3	0	0	0	0	...	...	...	—	—	—	—	—
92-93—Dynamo Moscow	CIS	30	6	5	11	4	...	...	...	10	3	0	3	0
93-94—Dynamo Moscow	CIS	42	16	9	25	14	...	...	...	7	3	2	5	0
94-95—Dynamo Moscow	CIS	3	1	1	2	2	...	...	...	—	—	—	—	—
—San Jose	NHL	16	2	0	2	2	-5	0	0	—	—	—	—	—
—Kansas City	IHL	—	—	—	—	—	...	...	...	13	4	5	9	12
95-96—Kansas City	IHL	15	4	7	11	12	...	...	...	—	—	—	—	—
—San Jose	NHL	62	6	13	19	6	-15	1	0	—	—	—	—	—
96-97—San Jose	NHL	78	16	25	41	40	-16	4	0	—	—	—	—	—
97-98—San Jose	NHL	18	5	2	7	2	-2	2	0	—	—	—	—	—
—Florida	NHL	46	12	11	23	14	-1	3	2	—	—	—	—	—
98-99—Florida	NHL	65	16	35	51	24	13	5	1	—	—	—	—	—
99-00—Florida	NHL	80	17	53	70	16	24	6	0	4	0	1	1	0
00-01—Florida	NHL	51	14	23	37	10	-4	6	0	—	—	—	—	—
NHL Totals (7 years)		416	88	162	250	114	-6	27	3	4	0	1	1	0

KRAFT, MILAN   C   PENGUINS

PERSONAL: Born January 17, 1980, in Plzen, Czechoslovakia. ... 6-3/191. ... Shoots right.

TRANSACTIONS/CAREER NOTES: Selected by Pittsburgh Penguins in first round (first Penguins pick, 23rd overall) of NHL entry draft (June 27, 1998).

Season Team	League	REGULAR SEASON Gms.	G	A	Pts.	PIM	+/-	PP	SH	PLAYOFFS Gms.	G	A	Pts.	PIM
96-97—Plzen	Czech Jrs.	36	26	17	43	...	...	...	...	—	—	—	—	—
—ZKZ Plzen	Czech Rep.	9	0	1	1	2	...	...	...	—	—	—	—	—
97-98—Plzen	Czech Jrs.	24	22	23	45	12	...	...	...	—	—	—	—	—
—ZKZ Plzen	Czech Rep.	16	0	5	5	0	...	...	...	—	—	—	—	—
98-99—Prince Albert	WHL	68	40	46	86	32	...	...	...	14	7	13	20	6
99-00—Prince Albert	WHL	56	34	35	69	42	...	...	...	6	4	1	5	4
00-01—Pittsburgh	NHL	42	7	7	14	8	-6	1	1	8	0	0	0	2
—Wilkes-Barre/Scranton	AHL	40	21	23	44	27	...	...	...	14	12	7	19	6
NHL Totals (1 year)		42	7	7	14	8	-6	1	1	8	0	0	0	2

KRAHN, BRENT   G   FLAMES

PERSONAL: Born April 2, 1982, in Winnipeg. ... 6-4/200. ... Catches left.

TRANSACTIONS/CAREER NOTES: Selected by Calgary Flames in first round (first Flames pick, ninth overall) of NHL entry draft (June 24, 2000).

Season Team	League	REGULAR SEASON Gms.	Min.	W	L	T	GA	SO	Avg.	PLAYOFFS Gms.	Min.	W	L	GA	SO	Avg.
99-00—Calgary	WHL	39	2315	33	6	0	92	4	2.38	5	266	2	2	13	0	2.93
00-01—Calgary	WHL	37	2087	22	10	3	104	1	2.99	—	—	—	—	—	—	—

KRAVCHUK, IGOR   D   FLAMES

PERSONAL: Born September 13, 1966, in Ufa, U.S.S.R. ... 6-1/218. ... Shoots left. ... Name pronounced EE-gohr KRAV-chuhk.

TRANSACTIONS/CAREER NOTES: Selected by Chicago Blackhawks in fourth round (fifth Blackhawks pick, 71st overall) of NHL entry draft (June 22, 1991). ... Sprained knee (October 25, 1992); missed four games. ... Sprained left ankle (December 29, 1992); missed 18 games. ... Traded by Blackhawks with C Dean McAmmond to Edmonton Oilers for RW Joe Murphy (February 25, 1993). ... Sprained left knee (April 6, 1993); missed remainder of season. ... Strained groin (November 15, 1993); missed three games. ... Injured left knee (January 30, 1995) and underwent surgery (February 6, 1995); missed 12 games. ... Suffered deep bone bruise to left leg (October 21, 1995); missed six games. ... Injured knee (November 20, 1995); missed four games. ... Traded by Oilers with D Ken Sutton to St. Louis Blues for D Donald Dufresne and D Jeff Norton (January 4, 1996). ... Traded by Blues to Ottawa Senators for D Steve Duchesne (August 25, 1997). ... Bruised hip (March 20, 1998); missed one game. ... Strained hip flexor (November 26, 1998); missed one game. ... Suffered from the flu (March 30, 1999); missed one game. ... Bruised leg (April 10, 1999); missed one game. ... Suffered partially torn medial collateral ligament in left knee (October 30, 1999); missed 15 games. ... Sprained left knee (December 11, 1999); missed one game. ... Bruised right foot (January 11, 2000); missed one game. ... Claimed on waivers by Calgary Flames (November 10, 2000). ... Injured knee (Feburary 16, 2001); missed two games. ... Injured knee (February 24, 2001); missed remainder of season.

HONORS: Played in NHL All-Star Game (1998).

MISCELLANEOUS: Member of gold-medal-winning U.S.S.R. Olympic team (1988) and gold-medal-winning Unified Olympic team (1992). ... Member of silver-medal-winning Russian Olympic team (1998).

Season Team	League	REGULAR SEASON								PLAYOFFS				
		Gms.	G	A	Pts.	PIM	+/-	PP	SH	Gms.	G	A	Pts.	PIM
87-88—CSKA Moscow	USSR	47	1	8	9	12	...	...	...	—	—	—	—	—
—Unif. Olympic team	Int'l	6	1	0	1	0	...	...	...	—	—	—	—	—
88-89—CSKA Moscow	USSR	27	3	4	7	2	...	...	...	—	—	—	—	—
89-90—CSKA Moscow	USSR	48	1	3	4	16	...	...	...	—	—	—	—	—
90-91—CSKA Moscow	USSR	41	6	5	11	16	...	...	...	—	—	—	—	—
91-92—CSKA Moscow	CIS	30	3	7	10	2	...	...	...	—	—	—	—	—
—Unif. Olympic team	Int'l	8	3	2	5	6	...	...	...	—	—	—	—	—
—Chicago	NHL	18	1	8	9	4	-3	0	0	18	2	6	8	8
92-93—Chicago	NHL	38	6	9	15	30	11	3	0	—	—	—	—	—
—Edmonton	NHL	17	4	8	12	2	-8	1	0	—	—	—	—	—
93-94—Edmonton	NHL	81	12	38	50	16	-12	5	0	—	—	—	—	—
94-95—Edmonton	NHL	36	7	11	18	29	-15	3	1	—	—	—	—	—
95-96—Edmonton	NHL	26	4	4	8	10	-13	3	0	—	—	—	—	—
—St. Louis	NHL	40	3	12	15	24	-6	0	0	10	1	5	6	4
96-97—St. Louis	NHL	82	4	24	28	35	7	1	0	2	0	0	0	2
97-98—Ottawa	NHL	81	8	27	35	8	-19	3	1	11	2	3	5	4
—Russian Oly. team	Int'l	6	0	2	2	2	...	...	...	—	—	—	—	—
98-99—Ottawa	NHL	79	4	21	25	32	14	3	0	4	0	0	0	0
99-00—Ottawa	NHL	64	6	12	18	20	-5	5	0	6	1	1	2	0
00-01—Ottawa	NHL	15	1	5	6	14	4	0	0	—	—	—	—	—
—Calgary	NHL	37	0	8	8	4	-12	0	0	—	—	—	—	—
NHL Totals (10 years)		614	60	187	247	228	-57	27	2	51	6	15	21	18

KRESTANOVICH, JORDAN   LW   AVALANCHE

PERSONAL: Born June 14, 1981, in Langley, B.C. ... 6-0/170. ... Shoots left.

TRANSACTIONS/CAREER NOTES: Selected by Colorado Avalanche in fifth round (sixth Avalanche pick, 152nd overall) of NHL entry draft (June 26, 1999).

Season Team	League	REGULAR SEASON								PLAYOFFS				
		Gms.	G	A	Pts.	PIM	+/-	PP	SH	Gms.	G	A	Pts.	PIM
97-98—Calgary	WHL	22	1	0	1	0	...	...	...	13	0	0	0	0
98-99—Calgary	WHL	62	6	13	19	10	...	...	...	20	3	8	11	4
99-00—Calgary	WHL	72	19	24	43	22	...	...	...	13	7	7	14	4
—Hershey	AHL	—	—	—	—	—	...	...	...	1	0	0	0	0
00-01—Calgary	WHL	70	40	60	100	32	...	...	...	12	8	4	12	8
—Hershey	AHL	—	—	—	—	—	...	...	...	2	0	0	0	0

KRISTEK, JAROSLOV   RW   SABRES

PERSONAL: Born March 16, 1980, in Zlin, Czechoslovakia. ... 6-0/183. ... Shoots left.

TRANSACTIONS/CAREER NOTES: Selected by Buffalo Sabres in second round (fourth Sabres pick, 50th overall) of NHL entry draft (June 27, 1998).

Season Team	League	REGULAR SEASON								PLAYOFFS				
		Gms.	G	A	Pts.	PIM	+/-	PP	SH	Gms.	G	A	Pts.	PIM
95-96—ZPS Zlin	Czech Rep.Jrs.	34	33	20	53	...	...	...	...	—	—	—	—	—
96-97—ZPS Zlin	Czech Rep.Jrs.	44	28	27	55	...	...	...	...	—	—	—	—	—
97-98—ZPS Zlin	Czech Rep.Jrs.	7	8	5	13	...	...	...	...	—	—	—	—	—
—ZPS Zlin	Czech Rep.	37	2	8	10	20	...	...	...	—	—	—	—	—
—Prostejov	Czech Dv. 2	0	0	0	0	0	...	...	...	—	—	—	—	—
98-99—Tri-City	WHL	70	38	48	86	55	...	...	...	12	4	3	7	2
99-00—Tri-City	WHL	45	26	25	51	16	...	...	...	2	0	0	0	0
00-01—Rochester	AHL	35	5	3	8	20	...	...	...	—	—	—	—	—

KRIVOKRASOV, SERGEI   RW

PERSONAL: Born April 15, 1974, in Angarsk, U.S.S.R. ... 5-11/185. ... Shoots left. ... Name pronounced SAIR-gay KREE-voh-KRAS-ahf.

TRANSACTIONS/CAREER NOTES: Selected by Chicago Blackhawks in first round (first Blackhawks pick, 12th overall) of NHL entry draft (June 20, 1992). ... Sprained knee (January 31, 1996); missed 14 games. ... Sprained knee (March 14, 1996); missed 13 games. ... Sprained left knee (December 17, 1997); missed 16 games. ... Lacerated elbow (March 9, 1998); missed five games. ... Traded by Blackhawks to Nashville Predators for future considerations (June 27, 1998). ... Suspended three pre-season games and fined $1,000 by NHL for high-sticking incident (October 1, 1998). ... Injured leg (December 19, 1998); missed 10 games. ... Sprained ankle (January 28, 1999); missed two games. ... Bruised hand (November 11, 1999); missed one game. ... Traded by Predators to Calgary Flames for D Cale Hulse and third-round pick (C/LW Denis Platonov) in 2001 draft (March 14, 2000). ... Selected by Minnesota Wild in NHL expansion draft (June 23, 2000). ... Sprained knee (October 5, 2000); missed 15 games. ... Sprained left ankle (February 9, 2001); missed four games. ... Suffered from the flu (February 26, 2001); missed one game. ... Suffered from the flu (March 22, 2001); missed four games.

HONORS: Played in NHL All-Star Game (1999).

MISCELLANEOUS: Member of silver-medal-winning Russian Olympic team (1998).

Season Team	League	REGULAR SEASON								PLAYOFFS				
		Gms.	G	A	Pts.	PIM	+/-	PP	SH	Gms.	G	A	Pts.	PIM
90-91—CSKA Moscow	USSR	41	4	0	4	8	...	...	...	—	—	—	—	—
91-92—CSKA Moscow	CIS	42	10	8	18	35	...	...	...	—	—	—	—	—
92-93—Chicago	NHL	4	0	0	0	2	-2	0	0	—	—	—	—	—
—Indianapolis	IHL	78	36	33	69	157	...	...	...	5	3	1	4	2
93-94—Indianapolis	IHL	53	19	26	45	145	...	...	...	—	—	—	—	—
—Chicago	NHL	9	1	0	1	4	-2	0	0	—	—	—	—	—
94-95—Indianapolis	IHL	29	12	15	27	41	...	...	...	—	—	—	—	—
—Chicago	NHL	41	12	7	19	33	9	6	0	10	0	0	0	8
95-96—Indianapolis	IHL	9	4	5	9	28	...	...	...	—	—	—	—	—
—Chicago	NHL	46	6	10	16	32	10	0	0	5	1	0	1	2
96-97—Chicago	NHL	67	13	11	24	42	-1	2	0	6	1	0	1	4
97-98—Chicago	NHL	58	10	13	23	33	-1	1	0	—	—	—	—	—
—Russian Oly. team	Int'l	6	0	0	0	4	...	...	...	—	—	—	—	—
98-99—Nashville	NHL	70	25	23	48	42	-5	10	0	—	—	—	—	—
99-00—Nashville	NHL	63	9	17	26	40	-7	3	0	—	—	—	—	—
—Calgary	NHL	12	1	10	11	4	2	0	0	—	—	—	—	—
00-01—Minnesota	NHL	54	7	15	22	20	-1	2	0	—	—	—	—	—
NHL Totals (9 years)		424	84	106	190	252	2	24	0	21	2	0	2	14

KROG, JASON   C   ISLANDERS

PERSONAL: Born October 9, 1975, in Fernie, B.C. ... 5-11/191.
TRANSACTIONS/CAREER NOTES: Signed as non-drafted free agent by New York Islanders (April 10, 1999). ... Sprained right ankle (March 27, 2000); missed final six games of season. ... Dislocated left shoulder (December 15, 2000); missed 20 games.
HONORS: Named to NCAA All-America (East) second team (1996-97). ... Named to Hockey East All-Star first team (1996-97 through 1998-99). ... Won Hobey Baker Memorial Award (1998-99). ... Named to NCAA All-America (East) first team (1998-99). ... Named to NCAA All-Tournament team (1998-99).

Season Team	League	REGULAR SEASON								PLAYOFFS				
		Gms.	G	A	Pts.	PIM	+/-	PP	SH	Gms.	G	A	Pts.	PIM
95-96—Univ. of New Hamp.	Hockey East	34	4	16	20	20	...	...	...	—	—	—	—	—
96-97—Univ. of New Hamp.	Hockey East	39	23	44	67	28	...	...	...	—	—	—	—	—
97-98—Univ. of New Hamp.	Hockey East	38	†33	33	66	44	...	...	...	—	—	—	—	—
98-99—Univ. of New Hamp.	Hockey East	41	*34	*51	*85	38	...	...	...	—	—	—	—	—
99-00—Lowell	AHL	45	6	21	27	22	...	...	...	—	—	—	—	—
—New York Islanders	NHL	17	2	4	6	6	-1	1	0	—	—	—	—	—
—Providence	AHL	11	9	8	17	4	...	...	...	6	2	2	4	0
00-01—Lowell	AHL	26	11	16	27	6	...	...	...	—	—	—	—	—
—Springfield	AHL	24	7	23	30	4	...	...	...	—	—	—	—	—
—New York Islanders	NHL	9	0	3	3	0	4	0	0	—	—	—	—	—
NHL Totals (2 years)		26	2	7	9	6	3	1	0					

KRON, ROBERT   C   BLUE JACKETS

PERSONAL: Born February 27, 1967, in Brno, Czechoslovakia. ... 5-11/182. ... Shoots left. ... Name pronounced KRAHN.
TRANSACTIONS/CAREER NOTES: Selected by Vancouver Canucks in fourth round (fifth Canucks pick, 88th overall) of NHL entry draft (June 15, 1985). ... Underwent surgery to repair torn knee ligaments and wrist fracture (March 22, 1991). ... Fractured ankle (January 28, 1992); missed 22 games. ... Traded by Canucks with third-round pick (D Marek Malik) in 1993 draft and future considerations to Hartford Whalers for C/LW Murray Craven and fifth-round pick (D Scott Walker) in 1993 draft (March 22, 1993); Whalers aquired RW Jim Sandlak to complete deal (May 17, 1993). ... Sprained shoulder (February 26, 1994); missed seven games. ... Fractured thumb (March 29, 1995); missed 11 games. ... Injured groin (March 27, 1996); missed one game. ... Strained abdominal muscle (April 8, 1996); missed three games. ... Sprained knee (January 25, 1997); missed 12 games. ... Whalers franchise moved to North Carolina and renamed Carolina Hurricanes for 1997-98 season; NHL approved move on June 25, 1997. ... Strained groin (November 11, 1998); missed one game. ... Strained groin (February 26, 1999); missed five games. ... Selected by Columbus Blue Jackets in NHL expansion draft (June 23, 2000). ... Strained muscle in abdomen (December 10, 2000); missed 15 games. ... Fractured ankle (March 24, 2001); missed remainder of season.
MISCELLANEOUS: Failed to score on a penalty shot (vs. Steve Shields, November 9, 2000).

Season Team	League	REGULAR SEASON								PLAYOFFS				
		Gms.	G	A	Pts.	PIM	+/-	PP	SH	Gms.	G	A	Pts.	PIM
84-85—Zetor Brno	Czech.	40	6	8	14	6	...	...	...	—	—	—	—	—
85-86—Zetor Brno	Czech.	44	5	6	11		...	...	...	—	—	—	—	—
86-87—Zetor Brno	Czech.	28	14	11	25		...	...	...	—	—	—	—	—
87-88—Zetor Brno	Czech.	32	12	6	18		...	...	...	—	—	—	—	—
88-89—Dukla Trencin	Czech.	43	28	19	47	26	...	...	...	—	—	—	—	—
89-90—Dukla Trencin	Czech.	39	22	22	44		...	...	...	—	—	—	—	—
90-91—Vancouver	NHL	76	12	20	32	21	-11	2	3	—	—	—	—	—
91-92—Vancouver	NHL	36	2	2	4	2	-9	0	0	11	1	2	3	2
92-93—Vancouver	NHL	32	10	11	21	14	10	2	2	—	—	—	—	—
—Hartford	NHL	13	4	2	6	4	-5	2	0	—	—	—	—	—
93-94—Hartford	NHL	77	24	26	50	8	0	2	1	—	—	—	—	—
94-95—Hartford	NHL	37	10	8	18	10	-3	3	1	—	—	—	—	—
95-96—Hartford	NHL	77	22	28	50	6	-1	8	1	—	—	—	—	—
96-97—Hartford	NHL	68	10	12	22	10	-18	2	0	—	—	—	—	—
97-98—Carolina	NHL	81	16	20	36	12	-8	4	0	—	—	—	—	—
98-99—Carolina	NHL	75	9	16	25	10	-13	3	1	5	2	0	2	0
99-00—Carolina	NHL	81	13	27	40	8	-4	2	1	—	—	—	—	—
00-01—Columbus	NHL	59	8	11	19	10	4	0	1	—	—	—	—	—
NHL Totals (11 years)		712	140	183	323	115	-58	30	11	16	3	2	5	2

KRUSE, PAUL — LW

PERSONAL: Born March 15, 1970, in Merritt, B.C. ... 6-0/214. ... Shoots left. ... Name pronounced KROOS.

TRANSACTIONS/CAREER NOTES: Selected by Calgary Flames in fourth round (sixth Flames pick, 83rd overall) of NHL entry draft (June 16, 1990). ... Injured eye (March 8, 1992); missed four games. ... Suffered hip pointer (March 21, 1993); missed one game. ... Broke toe on right foot (September 27, 1993); missed 12 games. ... Bruised left foot (March 2, 1995); missed one game. ... Bruised left knee (April 29, 1995); missed one game. ... Bruised ribs (February 13, 1996); missed three games. ... Cut wrist (April 9, 1996); missed two games. ... Traded by Flames to New York Islanders for third-round pick (traded to Hartford) in 1997 draft (November 27, 1996). ... Strained abdominal muscle (March 16, 1997); missed 12 games. ... Traded by Islanders with LW Jason Holland to Buffalo Sabres for RW Jason Dawe (March 24, 1998). ... Strained hip flexor (February 4, 1998); missed one game. ... Bruised hand (March 6, 1998); missed one game. ... Sprained knee (April 15, 1998); missed final two games of regular season and nine playoff games. ... Strained hip flexor (November 3, 1998); missed three games. ... Reinjured hip flexor (November 14, 1998); missed three games. ... Reinjured hip flexor and strained groin (November 28, 1998); missed 12 games. ... Injured groin (November 13, 1999); missed three games. ... Signed as free agent by San Jose Sharks (September 10, 2000).

		REGULAR SEASON								PLAYOFFS				
Season Team	League	Gms.	G	A	Pts.	PIM	+/-	PP	SH	Gms.	G	A	Pts.	PIM
86-87—Merritt	BCJHL	35	8	15	23	120	...	...	...	—	—	—	—	—
87-88—Merritt	BCJHL	44	12	32	44	227	...	...	...	4	1	4	5	18
—Moose Jaw	WHL	1	0	0	0	0	...	...	...	—	—	—	—	—
88-89—Kamloops	WHL	68	8	15	23	209	...	...	...	—	—	—	—	—
89-90—Kamloops	WHL	67	22	23	45	291	...	...	...	17	3	5	8	†79
90-91—Salt Lake City	IHL	83	24	20	44	313	...	...	...	4	1	1	2	4
—Calgary	NHL	1	0	0	0	7	-1	0	0	—	—	—	—	—
91-92—Salt Lake City	IHL	57	14	15	29	267	...	...	...	5	1	2	3	19
—Calgary	NHL	16	3	1	4	65	1	0	0	—	—	—	—	—
92-93—Salt Lake City	IHL	35	1	4	5	206	...	...	...	—	—	—	—	—
—Calgary	NHL	27	2	3	5	41	2	0	0	—	—	—	—	—
93-94—Calgary	NHL	68	3	8	11	185	-6	0	0	7	0	0	0	14
94-95—Calgary	NHL	45	11	5	16	141	13	0	0	7	4	2	6	10
95-96—Calgary	NHL	75	3	12	15	145	-5	0	0	3	0	0	0	4
96-97—Calgary	NHL	14	2	0	2	30	-4	0	0	—	—	—	—	—
—New York Islanders	NHL	48	4	2	6	111	-5	0	0	—	—	—	—	—
97-98—New York Islanders	NHL	62	6	1	7	138	-12	0	0	—	—	—	—	—
—Buffalo	NHL	12	1	1	2	49	1	0	0	1	1	0	1	4
98-99—Buffalo	NHL	43	3	0	3	114	0	0	0	10	0	0	0	4
99-00—Buffalo	NHL	11	0	0	0	43	-2	0	0	—	—	—	—	—
—Utah	IHL	44	10	13	23	71	...	...	...	5	0	3	3	28
00-01—San Jose	NHL	1	0	0	0	5	0	0	0	—	—	—	—	—
—Chicago	IHL	71	8	12	20	180	...	...	...	16	2	3	5	22
NHL Totals (11 years)		423	38	33	71	1074	-18	0	0	28	5	2	7	36

KUBA, FILIP — D — WILD

PERSONAL: Born December 29, 1976, in Ostrava, Czechoslovakia. ... 6-3/205. ... Shoots left. ... Name pronounced KOO-buh.

TRANSACTIONS/CAREER NOTES: Selected by Florida Panthers in eighth round (eighth Panthers pick, 192nd overall) of NHL entry draft (July 8, 1995). ... Traded by Panthers to Calgary Flames for RW Rocky Thompson (March 16, 2000). ... Selected by Minnesota Wild in NHL expansion draft (June 23, 2000). ... Bruised ribs (November 15, 2000); missed five games. ... Bruised knee (January 19, 2001); missed one game.

		REGULAR SEASON								PLAYOFFS				
Season Team	League	Gms.	G	A	Pts.	PIM	+/-	PP	SH	Gms.	G	A	Pts.	PIM
94-95—Vitkovice	Czech. Jrs.	35	10	15	25	...	...	...	...	—	—	—	—	—
—Vitkovice	Czech Rep.	—	—	—	—	...	...	...	...	4	0	0	0	2
95-96—Vitkovice	Czech Rep.	19	0	1	1	...	...	...	...	—	—	—	—	—
96-97—Carolina	AHL	51	0	12	12	38	...	...	...	—	—	—	—	—
97-98—New Haven	AHL	77	4	13	17	58	...	...	...	3	1	1	2	0
98-99—Kentucky	AHL	45	2	8	10	33	...	...	...	10	0	1	1	4
—Florida	NHL	5	0	1	1	0	2	0	0	—	—	—	—	—
99-00—Florida	NHL	13	1	5	6	2	-3	1	0	—	—	—	—	—
—Houston	IHL	27	3	6	9	13	...	...	...	11	1	2	3	4
00-01—Minnesota	NHL	75	9	21	30	28	-6	4	0	—	—	—	—	—
NHL Totals (3 years)		93	10	27	37	30	-7	5	0					

KUBINA, PAVEL — D — LIGHTNING

PERSONAL: Born April 15, 1977, in Caledna, Czechoslovakia. ... 6-4/230. ... Shoots left. ... Name pronounced koo-BEE-nuh.

TRANSACTIONS/CAREER NOTES: Selected by Tampa Bay Lightning in seventh round (sixth Lightning pick, 179th overall) of NHL entry draft (June 22, 1996). ... Injured knee (November 8, 1998); missed two games. ... Injured shoulder (November 29, 1998); missed three games. ... Bruised rib (January 5, 2000); missed two games. ... Bruised hand (March 1, 2000); missed one game. ... Injured ankle (March 21, 2000); missed final nine games of season. ... Suffered concussion (November 3, 2000); missed two games. ... Lacerated finger (December 30, 2000); missed two games. ... Injured leg (Feburary 24, 2001); missed eight games.

		REGULAR SEASON								PLAYOFFS				
Season Team	League	Gms.	G	A	Pts.	PIM	+/-	PP	SH	Gms.	G	A	Pts.	PIM
93-94—HC Vitkovice	Czech Rep.	1	0	0	0	0	...	...	...	—	—	—	—	—
94-95—HC Vitkovice	Czech Rep.	8	2	0	2	0	...	...	...	4	0	0	0	0
95-96—HC Vitkovice	Czech Rep.	32	3	4	7	0	...	...	...	4	0	0	0	0
96-97—Moose Jaw	WHL	61	12	32	44	116	...	...	...	11	2	5	7	27
—HC Vitkovice	Czech Rep.	1	0	0	0	0	...	...	...	—	—	—	—	—
97-98—Adirondack	AHL	55	4	8	12	86	...	...	...	1	0	1	1	14
—Tampa Bay	NHL	10	1	2	3	22	-1	0	0	—	—	—	—	—
98-99—Tampa Bay	NHL	68	9	12	21	80	-33	3	1	—	—	—	—	—
—Cleveland	IHL	6	2	2	4	16	...	...	...	—	—	—	—	—
99-00—Tampa Bay	NHL	69	8	18	26	93	-19	6	0	—	—	—	—	—
00-01—Tampa Bay	NHL	70	11	19	30	103	-14	6	1	—	—	—	—	—
NHL Totals (4 years)		217	29	51	80	298	-67	15	2					

KUCERA, FRANTISEK   D   CAPITALS

PERSONAL: Born February 3, 1968, in Prague, Czechoslovakia. ... 6-2/205. ... Shoots right. ... Name pronounced koo-CHAIR-uh.

TRANSACTIONS/CAREER NOTES: Selected by Chicago Blackhawks in fourth round (third Blackhawks pick, 77th overall) of NHL entry draft (June 21, 1986). ... Pulled groin (March 20, 1993); missed 11 games. ... Pulled groin (1993-94 season); missed five games. ... Traded by Blackhawks with LW Jocelyn Lemieux to Hartford Whalers for LW Randy Cunneyworth and D Gary Suter (March 11, 1994). ... Played in Europe during 1994-95 NHL lockout. ... Injured hip flexor (November 5, 1995); missed one game. ... Traded by Whalers with C Jim Dowd and second-round pick (D Ryan Bonni) in 1997 draft to Vancouver Canucks for D Jeff Brown and fifth-round pick (traded to Dallas) in 1998 draft (December 19, 1995). ... Separated shoulder (January 8, 1996); missed 19 games. ... Traded by Canucks to Philadelphia Flyers for future considerations (March 18, 1997). ... Signed as free agent by Columbus Blue Jackets (July 7, 2000). ... Strained muscle in abdomen (November 25, 2000); missed one game. ... Injured chest (December 10, 2000); missed 14 games. ... Suffered from the flu (February 20, 2001); missed one game. ... Suffered from back spasms (March 9, 2001); missed one game. ... Traded by Blue Jackets to Pittsburgh Penguins for sixth-round pick (C Artem Vostrikov) in 2001 draft (March 13, 2001). ... Traded by Penguins with RW Jaromir Jagr to Washington Capitals for C Kris Beech, C Michael Sivek, D Ross Luparchuk and future considerations (July 11, 2001).

		REGULAR SEASON								PLAYOFFS				
Season Team	League	Gms.	G	A	Pts.	PIM	+/-	PP	SH	Gms.	G	A	Pts.	PIM
85-86—Sparta Prague	Czech.	15	0	0	0	...	...	...	...	—	—	—	—	—
86-87—Sparta Prague	Czech.	33	7	2	9	14	...	...	...	—	—	—	—	—
87-88—Sparta Prague	Czech.	34	4	2	6	30	...	...	...	—	—	—	—	—
88-89—Dukla Jihlava	Czech.	45	10	9	19	28	...	...	...	—	—	—	—	—
89-90—Dukla Jihlava	Czech.	43	9	10	19	...	...	...	...	—	—	—	—	—
90-91—Chicago	NHL	40	2	12	14	32	3	1	0	—	—	—	—	—
—Indianapolis	IHL	35	8	19	27	23	...	...	...	7	0	1	1	15
91-92—Chicago	NHL	61	3	10	13	36	3	1	0	6	0	0	0	0
—Indianapolis	IHL	7	1	2	3	4	...	...	...	—	—	—	—	—
92-93—Chicago	NHL	71	5	14	19	59	7	1	0	—	—	—	—	—
93-94—Chicago	NHL	60	4	13	17	34	9	2	0	—	—	—	—	—
—Hartford	NHL	16	1	3	4	14	-12	1	0	—	—	—	—	—
94-95—Sparta Prague	Czech.	16	1	2	3	14	...	...	...	—	—	—	—	—
—Hartford	NHL	48	3	17	20	30	3	0	0	—	—	—	—	—
95-96—Hartford	NHL	30	2	6	8	10	-3	0	0	—	—	—	—	—
—Vancouver	NHL	24	1	0	1	10	5	0	0	6	0	1	1	0
96-97—Vancouver	NHL	2	0	0	0	0	0	0	0	—	—	—	—	—
—Houston	IHL	12	0	3	3	20	...	...	...	—	—	—	—	—
—Syracuse	AHL	42	6	29	35	36	...	...	...	—	—	—	—	—
—Philadelphia	AHL	9	1	5	6	2	...	...	...	10	1	6	7	20
—Philadelphia	NHL	2	0	0	0	2	-2	0	0	—	—	—	—	—
97-98—Kloten	Switzerland	38	8	22	30	18	...	...	...	7	1	2	3	2
—Czech Rep. Oly. team..	Int'l	6	0	0	0	0	...	...	...	—	—	—	—	—
98-99—Sparta Praha	Czech Rep.	42	3	12	15	92	...	...	...	8	0	2	2	...
99-00—Sparta Praha	Czech Rep.	51	7	26	33	40	...	...	...	9	1	*9	10	4
00-01—Columbus	NHL	48	2	5	7	12	-5	0	0	—	—	—	—	—
—Pittsburgh	NHL	7	0	2	2	0	-2	0	0	—	—	—	—	—
NHL Totals (8 years)		409	23	82	105	239	6	6	0	12	0	1	1	0

KUDROC, KRISTIAN   D   LIGHTNING

PERSONAL: Born May 21, 1981, in Michalovce, Czechoslovakia. ... 6-6/229. ... Shoots right.

TRANSACTIONS/CAREER NOTES: Selected by New York Islanders in first round (fourth Islanders pick, 28th overall) of NHL entry draft (June 26, 1999). ... Traded by Islanders with G Kevin Weekes and second-round pick (traded to Phoenix) in 2001 draft to Tampa Bay Lightning for first-(LW Raffi Torres), fourth-(RW/LW Vladimir Gorbunov) and seventh-round (D Ryan Caldwell) picks in 2000 draft (June 24, 2000).

		REGULAR SEASON								PLAYOFFS				
Season Team	League	Gms.	G	A	Pts.	PIM	+/-	PP	SH	Gms.	G	A	Pts.	PIM
97-98—Michalovce	Slovakia Jrs.	47	7	4	11	...	...	...	...	—	—	—	—	—
—HK Michalovce	Slov. Div. II	4	0	0	0	0	...	...	...	—	—	—	—	—
98-99—Michalovce	Slovakia	17	0	3	3	12	...	...	...	—	—	—	—	—
99-00—Quebec	QMJHL	57	9	22	31	172	...	...	...	11	2	5	7	29
00-01—Detroit	IHL	44	4	3	7	80	...	...	...	—	—	—	—	—
—Tampa Bay	NHL	22	2	2	4	36	0	0	0	—	—	—	—	—
NHL Totals (1 year)		22	2	2	4	36	0	0	0					

KULESHOV, MIKHAIL   LW   AVALANCHE

PERSONAL: Born January 7, 1981, in Perm, U.S.S.R. ... 6-2/200. ... Shoots right.

TRANSACTIONS/CAREER NOTES: Selected by Colorado Avalanche in first round (first Avalanche pick, 25th overall) of NHL entry draft (June 26, 1999).

		REGULAR SEASON								PLAYOFFS				
Season Team	League	Gms.	G	A	Pts.	PIM	+/-	PP	SH	Gms.	G	A	Pts.	PIM
97-98—Avangard Omsk	Russian	4	1	0	1	4	...	...	...	—	—	—	—	—
—Avangard-VDV Omsk..	Rus. Div. III	12	12	3	15	12	...	...	...	—	—	—	—	—
98-99—Severstal Cherepovets	Russian	15	2	0	2	8	...	...	...	3	0	0	0	4
99-00—Severstal Cherepovets	Russian	8	0	0	0	4	...	...	...	3	0	0	0	2
00-01—SKA St. Petersburg	Russian	7	0	0	0	8	...	...	...	—	—	—	—	—
—Hershey	AHL	3	0	0	0	4	...	...	...	11	1	0	1	0

K

KULTANEN, JARNO D BRUINS

PERSONAL: Born January 8, 1973, in Luumaki, Finland. ... 6-2/198. ... Shoots left.
TRANSACTIONS/CAREER NOTES: Selected by Boston Bruins in sixth round (eighth Bruins pick, 174th overall) of NHL entry draft (June 24, 2000). ... Sprained ankle (January 1, 2001); missed nine games. ... Suffered from the flu (February 1, 2001); missed nine games.

Season Team	League	REGULAR SEASON								PLAYOFFS				
		Gms.	G	A	Pts.	PIM	+/-	PP	SH	Gms.	G	A	Pts.	PIM
91-92—KooKoo Kouvola	Fin. Jr.	22	7	17	24	28	...	...	...	—	—	—	—	—
—KooKoo Kouvola	Fin. Dv. 2	1	0	0	0	0				—	—	—	—	—
92-93—KooKoo Kouvola	Fin. Jr.	11	6	5	11	8	...	...	...	—	—	—	—	—
—KooKoo Kouvola	Fin. Dv. 2	27	1	1	2	33				—	—	—	—	—
—Centers Pietrassari	Fin. Dv. 2	1	1	0	1	0				—	—	—	—	—
93-94—KooKoo Kouvola	Fin. Jr.	3	1	0	1	2				—	—	—	—	—
—KooKoo Kouvola	Fin. Dv. 2	45	7	10	17	42	...	...	...	—	—	—	—	—
94-95—KalPa Kuopio	Finland	47	5	12	17	26	...	...	...	3	0	0	0	8
95-96—KalPa Kuopio	Finland	49	4	10	14	42	...	...	...	—	—	—	—	—
96-97—Helsinki IFK	Finland	24	1	3	4	6	...	...	...	—	—	—	—	—
97-98—Helsinki IFK	Finland	25	0	1	1	37	...	...	...	—	—	—	—	—
98-99—Helsinki IFK	Finland	51	6	6	12	53	...	...	...	—	—	—	—	—
99-00—HIFK Helsinki	Finland	46	6	8	14	51	...	...	...	—	—	—	—	—
00-01—Boston	NHL	62	2	8	10	26	-3	0	0	—	—	—	—	—
NHL Totals (1 year)		62	2	8	10	26	-3	0	0					

KURKA, TOMAS LW HURRICANES

PERSONAL: Born December 14, 1981, in Litvinov, Czechoslovakia. ... 5-11/190. ... Shoots left.
TRANSACTIONS/CAREER NOTES: Selected by Carolina Hurricanes in second round (first Hurricanes pick, 32nd overall) of NHL entry draft (June 24, 2000).

Season Team	League	REGULAR SEASON								PLAYOFFS				
		Gms.	G	A	Pts.	PIM	+/-	PP	SH	Gms.	G	A	Pts.	PIM
97-98—Litvinov	Czech. Jrs.	44	38	23	61		...	...	...	—	—	—	—	—
98-99—Litvinov	Czech. Jrs.	48	60	42	102	38	...	...	...	—	—	—	—	—
—Litvinov	Czech.	6	0	0	0	0	...	...	...	—	—	—	—	—
99-00—Plymouth	OHL	64	36	28	64	37	...	...	...	17	7	6	13	6
00-01—Plymouth	OHL	47	15	29	44	20	...	...	...	16	8	13	21	13

KUTLAK, ZDENEK D BRUINS

PERSONAL: Born February 13, 1980, in Budejovice, Czechoslavakia. ... 6-3/207. ... Shoots left.
TRANSACTIONS/CAREER NOTES: Selected by Boston Bruins in eighth round (10th Bruins pick, 237th overall) of NHL entry draft (June 24, 2000).

Season Team	League	REGULAR SEASON								PLAYOFFS				
		Gms.	G	A	Pts.	PIM	+/-	PP	SH	Gms.	G	A	Pts.	PIM
98-99—Ceske Budejovice	Czech Jrs.	2	1	3	4	4	...	...	...	3	0	0	0	0
99-00—Ceske Budejovice	Czech Jrs.	28	1	0	1	2	...	...	...	1	0	0	0	0
00-01—Providence	AHL	62	4	5	9	16	...	...	...	—	—	—	—	—
—Boston	NHL	10	0	2	2	4	-3	0	0	—	—	—	—	—
NHL Totals (1 year)		10	0	2	2	4	-3	0	0					

KUZNETSOV, MAXIM D RED WINGS

PERSONAL: Born March 24, 1977, in Pavlodar, U.S.S.R. ... 6-5/198. ... Shoots left. ... Name pronounced koos-NEHT-sahf.
TRANSACTIONS/CAREER NOTES: Selected by Detroit Red Wings in first round (first Red Wings pick, 26th overall) of NHL entry draft (July 8, 1995). ... Sprained medial collateral ligament in knee (November 22, 2000); missed nine games. ... Strained rib muscle (December 22, 2000); missed 18 games. ... Injured back (March 11, 2001); missed one game.

Season Team	League	REGULAR SEASON								PLAYOFFS				
		Gms.	G	A	Pts.	PIM	+/-	PP	SH	Gms.	G	A	Pts.	PIM
94-95—Dynamo Moscow	CIS	11	0	0	0	8	...	...	...	—	—	—	—	—
95-96—Dynamo Moscow	CIS	9	1	1	2	22	...	...	...	4	0	0	0	0
96-97—Dynamo Moscow	CIS	23	0	2	2	16	...	...	...	—	—	—	—	—
—Adirondack	AHL	2	0	1	1	6	...	...	...	2	0	0	0	0
97-98—Adirondack	AHL	51	5	5	10	43	...	...	...	3	0	1	1	4
98-99—Adirondack	AHL	60	0	4	4	30	...	...	...	3	0	0	0	0
99-00—Cincinnati	AHL	47	2	9	11	36	...	...	...	—	—	—	—	—
00-01—Detroit	NHL	25	1	2	3	23	-1	0	0	—	—	—	—	—
NHL Totals (1 year)		25	1	2	3	23	-1	0	0					

KUZNIK, GREG D HURRICANES

PERSONAL: Born June 12, 1978, in Prince George, B.C. ... 6-0/182. ... Shoots left.
TRANSACTIONS/CAREER NOTES: Selected by Hartford Whalers in seventh round (seventh Whalers pick, 171st overall) of NHL entry draft (June 22, 1996). ... Whalers franchise moved to North Carolina and renamed Carolina Hurricanes for 1997-98 season; NHL approved move on June 25, 1997.

Season Team	League	Gms.	G	A	Pts.	PIM	+/-	PP	SH		Gms.	G	A	Pts.	PIM
94-95—New Westminster	BCJHL	45	2	13	15	83	...	...	...		—	—	—	—	—
95-96—Seattle	WHL	70	2	13	15	149	...	...	...		5	0	0	0	6
96-97—Seattle	WHL	70	4	9	13	161	...	...	...		14	0	2	2	26
97-98—Seattle	WHL	72	5	12	17	197	...	...	...		5	0	0	0	4
98-99—New Haven	AHL	27	1	0	1	33	...	...	...		—	—	—	—	—
—Florida	ECHL	50	6	8	14	110	...	...	...		5	1	0	1	0
99-00—Cincinnati	IHL	46	0	3	3	53	...	...	...		4	0	0	0	4
—Dayton	ECHL	7	1	0	1	16	...	...	...		—	—	—	—	—
—Florida	ECHL	9	1	4	5	6	...	...	...		3	0	0	0	2
00-01—Cincinnati	IHL	73	0	7	7	72	...	...	...		5	0	1	1	4
—Carolina	NHL	1	0	0	0	0	0	0	0		—	—	—	—	—
NHL Totals (1 year)		1	0	0	0	0	0	0	0		—	—	—	—	—

KVASHA, OLEG C ISLANDERS

PERSONAL: Born July 26, 1978, in Moscow, U.S.S.R. ... 6-5/216. ... Shoots right. ... Name pronounced kuh-VA-shuh.
TRANSACTIONS/CAREER NOTES: Selected by Florida Panthers in third round (third Panthers pick, 65th overall) of NHL entry draft (June 22, 1996). ... Bruised right ankle (December 16, 1998); missed one game. ... Bruised shoulder (February 27, 1999); missed one game. ... Separated left shoulder (March 31, 1999); missed final nine games of season. ... Sprained knee (March 7, 2000); missed two games. ... Traded by Panthers with RW Mark Parrish to New York Islanders for C Olli Jokinen and G Roberto Luongo (June 24, 2000). ... Strained back (December 6, 2000); missed two games. ... Sprained medial collateral ligament in right knee (January 12, 2001); missed 10 games. ... Injured left knee (February 10, 2001); missed eight games.

Season Team	League	Gms.	G	A	Pts.	PIM	+/-	PP	SH		Gms.	G	A	Pts.	PIM
94-95—CSKA	CIS Jr.						Statistics unavailable.								
95-96—CSKA Moscow	CIS	38	2	3	5	14	...	...	...		2	0	0	0	0
96-97—CSKA Moscow	Russian	44	20	22	42	115	...	...	...		—	—	—	—	—
97-98—New Haven	AHL	57	13	16	29	46	...	...	...		3	2	1	3	0
98-99—Florida	NHL	68	12	13	25	45	5	4	0		—	—	—	—	—
99-00—Florida	NHL	78	5	20	25	34	3	2	0		4	0	0	0	0
00-01—New York Islanders	NHL	62	11	9	20	46	-15	0	0		—	—	—	—	—
NHL Totals (3 years)		208	28	42	70	125	-7	6	0		4	0	0	0	0

KWIATKOWSKI, JOEL D SENATORS

PERSONAL: Born March 22, 1977, in Kendersley, Sask. ... 6-2/201. ... Shoots left. ... Name pronounced kwee-iht-KOW-skee.
TRANSACTIONS/CAREER NOTES: Signed as non-drafted free agent by Mighty Ducks of Anaheim (June 18, 1998). ... Traded by Mighty Ducks to Ottawa Senators for D Patrick Traverse (June 12, 2000).
HONORS: Named to WHL (West) All-Star first team (1996-97 and 1997-98).

Season Team	League	Gms.	G	A	Pts.	PIM	+/-	PP	SH		Gms.	G	A	Pts.	PIM
94-95—Tacoma	WHL	70	4	13	17	66	...	...	...		4	0	0	0	2
95-96—Prince George	WHL	72	12	28	40	133	...	...	...		—	—	—	—	—
96-97—Prince George	WHL	72	16	36	52	94	...	...	...		4	4	2	6	24
97-98—Prince George	WHL	62	21	43	64	65	...	...	...		11	3	6	9	6
98-99—Cincinnati	AHL	80	12	21	33	48	...	...	...		3	2	0	2	0
99-00—Cincinnati	AHL	70	4	22	26	28	...	...	...		—	—	—	—	—
00-01—Grand Rapids	IHL	77	4	17	21	58	...	...	...		10	1	0	1	4
—Ottawa	NHL	4	1	0	1	0	1	0	0		—	—	—	—	—
NHL Totals (1 year)		4	1	0	1	0	1	0	0		—	—	—	—	—

LAAKSONEN, ANTTI LW WILD

PERSONAL: Born October 3, 1973, in Tammela, Finland. ... 6-0/180. ... Shoots left. ... Full Name: Antti Akseli Laaksonen.
TRANSACTIONS/CAREER NOTES: Selected by Boston Bruins in eighth round (10th Bruins pick, 191st overall) of NHL entry draft (July 21, 1997). ... Signed as free agent by Minnesota Wild (July 20, 2000).
MISCELLANEOUS: Failed to score on a penalty shot (vs. Patrick Lalime, December 20, 2000). ... Shares Minnesota Wild all-time record for games played (82).
STATISTICAL PLATEAUS: Three-goal games: 2000-01 (1).

Season Team	League	Gms.	G	A	Pts.	PIM	+/-	PP	SH		Gms.	G	A	Pts.	PIM
92-93—HPK Hameenlinna	Finland	2	0	0	0	0	...	...	...		—	—	—	—	—
93-94—Univ. of Denver	WCHA	36	12	9	21	38	...	...	...		—	—	—	—	—
94-95—Univ. of Denver	WCHA	40	17	18	35	42	...	...	...		—	—	—	—	—
95-96—Univ. of Denver	WCHA	39	25	28	53	71	...	...	...		—	—	—	—	—
96-97—Univ. of Denver	WCHA	39	21	17	38	63	...	...	...		—	—	—	—	—
97-98—Providence	AHL	38	3	2	5	14	...	...	...		—	—	—	—	—
—Charlotte	ECHL	15	4	3	7	12	...	...	...		6	0	3	3	0
98-99—Boston	NHL	11	1	2	3	2	-1	0	0		—	—	—	—	—
—Providence	AHL	66	25	33	58	52	...	...	...		19	7	2	9	28
99-00—Providence	AHL	40	10	12	22	57	...	...	...		14	5	4	9	4
—Boston	NHL	27	6	3	9	2	3	0	0		—	—	—	—	—
00-01—Minnesota	NHL	82	12	16	28	24	-7	0	2		—	—	—	—	—
NHL Totals (3 years)		120	19	21	40	28	-5	0	2		—	—	—	—	—

PERSONAL: Born January 18, 1980, in Burnaby, B.C. ... 6-2/205. ... Catches left.
TRANSACTIONS/CAREER NOTES: Selected by New York Rangers in third round (third Rangers pick, 66th overall) of NHL entry draft (June 27, 1998).

Season Team	League	REGULAR SEASON								PLAYOFFS						
		Gms.	Min	W	L	T	GA	SO	Avg.	Gms.	Min.	W	L	GA	SO	Avg.
96-97 —Tri-City	WHL	2	...	1	0	0	...	...	...	—	—	—	—	—	—	—
—Portland	WHL	9	443	5	1	1	18	0	2.44	—	—	—	—	—	—	—
97-98 —Portland	WHL	23	1305	18	4	0	72	1	3.31	—	—	—	—	—	—	—
98-99 —Portland	WHL	51	2991	18	23	9	170	4	3.41	4	252	0	4	19	0	4.52
99-00 —Portland	WHL	34	2005	8	24	2	123	1	3.68	—	—	—	—	—	—	—
—Spokane	WHL	21	1146	12	6	2	50	0	2.62	9	435	6	1	18	1	2.48
00-01 —Hartford	AHL	4	156	1	1	0	12	0	4.62	—	—	—	—	—	—	—
—New York Rangers	NHL	1	10	0	0	0	0	0	...	—	—	—	—	—	—	—
—Charlotte	ECHL	35	2100	18	10	7	112	1	3.20	2	143	1	1	5	0	2.10
NHL Totals (1 year)		1	10	0	0	0	0	0	...							

PERSONAL: Born June 15, 1972, in Sherbrooke, Que. ... 5-10/172. ... Catches left. ... Name pronounced lah-BAY.
TRANSACTIONS/CAREER NOTES: Signed as non-drafted free agent by Ottawa Senators (May 12, 1994). ... Traded by Senators to Colorado Avalanche for conditional draft pick (September 20, 1995). ... Signed as free agent by Edmonton Oilers (August 8, 1997). ... Signed as free agent by New York Rangers (July 16, 1998). ... Traded by Rangers to Columbus Blue Jackets for D Bert Robertsson (November 9, 2000).
HONORS: Won Jacques Plante Trophy (1991-92). ... Named to QMJHL All-Star first team (1991-92). ... Named Col.HL Rookie of the Year (1993-94). ... Named Col.HL Playoff Most Valuable Player (1993-94). ... Named to Col.HL All-Star first team (1993-94). ... Won Les Cunningham Award (1996-97). ... Won Baz Batien Trophy (1996-97). ... Won Harry (Hap) Holmes Memorial Trophy (1996-97). ... Named to AHL All-Star first team (1996-97). ... Shared Harry (Hap) Holmes Memorial Trophy with Milan Hnilicka (1999-2000).

Season Team	League	REGULAR SEASON								PLAYOFFS						
		Gms.	Min	W	L	T	GA	SO	Avg.	Gms.	Min.	W	L	GA	SO	Avg.
89-90 —Trois-Rivieres	QMJHL	28	1499	13	10	0	106	1	4.24	3	132	1	1	8	0	3.64
90-91 —Trois-Rivieres	QMJHL	54	2870	35	14	0	158	5	3.30	5	230	1	4	19	0	4.96
91-92 —Trois-Rivieres	QMJHL	48	2749	31	13	3	142	3	*3.10	15	791	10	3	33	†1	*2.50
92-93 —Hull	QMJHL	46	2701	25	16	2	155	2	3.44	10	518	6	3	24	†1	*2.78
93-94 —Prin. Edward Island	AHL	7	390	4	3	0	22	0	3.38	—	—	—	—	—	—	—
—Thunder Bay	Col.HL	52	*2900	*35	11	4	150	*2	*3.10	8	493	7	1	18	*2	*2.19
94-95 —Prin. Edward Island	AHL	32	1817	13	14	3	94	2	3.10	—	—	—	—	—	—	—
—Thunder Bay	Col.HL	2	...	2	0	0	...	...	...	—	—	—	—	—	—	—
95-96 —Cornwall	AHL	55	2971	25	21	5	144	3	2.91	8	470	3	5	21	1	2.68
96-97 —Hershey	AHL	66	3811	†34	22	9	160	*6	2.52	*23	*1364	*14	8	59	1	2.60
97-98 —Hamilton	AHL	52	3139	24	17	11	149	2	2.85	7	414	3	4	20	0	2.90
98-99 —Hartford	AHL	*59	*3392	28	26	3	*182	2	3.22	7	447	3	4	22	0	2.95
99-00 —Hartford	AHL	49	2853	27	13	†7	120	1	2.52	*22	*1320	*15	7	*48	3	2.18
—New York Rangers	NHL	1	60	0	1	0	3	0	3.00	—	—	—	—	—	—	—
00-01 —Hartford	AHL	8	394	4	2	1	20	0	3.05	—	—	—	—	—	—	—
—Syracuse	AHL	37	2201	15	15	5	105	2	2.86	5	323	2	3	18	0	3.34
NHL Totals (1 year)		1	60	0	1	0	3	0	3.00							

PERSONAL: Born October 22, 1972, in Charlottesville, Va. ... 6-1/212. ... Shoots left. ... Full Name: Scott Joseph Lachance. ... Brother of Bob Lachance, right winger with St. Louis Blues organization (1992-93 through 1997-98) and Atlanta Thrashers organization (1999-2000).
TRANSACTIONS/CAREER NOTES: Selected by New York Islanders in first round (first Islanders pick, fourth overall) of NHL entry draft (June 22, 1991). ... Sprained wrist (April 13, 1993); missed remainder of season. ... Underwent wrist surgery (April 30, 1993). ... Suffered mild separation of right shoulder (October 8, 1993); missed four games. ... Fractured ankle (February 25, 1995); missed 22 games. ... Injured groin (October 31, 1995); missed 27 games. ... Suffered broken finger (November 1, 1997); missed two games. ... Strained abdominal muscle (March 14, 1998); missed five games. ... Reinjured abdomen (March 28, 1998); missed 11 games. ... Suffered charley horse (November 21, 1998); missed one game. ... Suffered from the flu (December 22, 1998); missed one game. ... Sprained knee (January 5, 1999); missed one game. ... Traded by Islanders to Montreal Canadiens for third-round pick (RW Mattias Weinhandl) in 1999 draft (March 9, 1999). ... Injured back (November 23, 1999); missed 12 games. ... Signed as free agent by Vancouver Canucks (August 14, 2000). ... Suffered from the flu (December 8, 2000); missed one game. ... Sprained knee (January 28, 2001); missed five games.
HONORS: Named to Hockey East All-Rookie team (1990-91). ... Played in NHL All-Star Game (1997).

Season Team	League	REGULAR SEASON							PLAYOFFS				
		Gms.	G	A	Pts.	PIM	+/-	PP	SH	Gms.	G	A	Pts.	PIM
88-89 —Springfield Jr. B	NEJHL	36	8	28	36	20	...	...	...	—	—	—	—	—
89-90 —Springfield Jr. B	NEJHL	34	25	41	66	62	...	...	...	—	—	—	—	—
90-91 —Boston University	Hockey East	31	5	19	24	48	...	...	...	—	—	—	—	—
91-92 —U.S. national team	Int'l	36	1	10	11	34	...	...	...	—	—	—	—	—
—U.S. Olympic team	Int'l	8	0	1	1	6	...	...	...	—	—	—	—	—
—New York Islanders	NHL	17	1	4	5	9	13	0	0	—	—	—	—	—
92-93 —New York Islanders	NHL	75	7	17	24	67	-1	0	1	—	—	—	—	—
93-94 —New York Islanders	NHL	74	3	11	14	70	-5	0	0	3	0	0	0	0
94-95 —New York Islanders	NHL	26	6	7	13	26	2	3	0	—	—	—	—	—
95-96 —New York Islanders	NHL	55	3	10	13	54	-19	1	0	—	—	—	—	—
96-97 —New York Islanders	NHL	81	3	11	14	47	-7	1	0	—	—	—	—	—
97-98 —New York Islanders	NHL	63	2	11	13	45	-11	1	0	—	—	—	—	—
98-99 —New York Islanders	NHL	59	1	8	9	30	-19	1	0	—	—	—	—	—
—Montreal	NHL	17	1	1	2	11	-2	0	0	—	—	—	—	—
99-00 —Montreal	NHL	57	0	6	6	22	-4	0	0	—	—	—	—	—
00-01 —Vancouver	NHL	76	3	11	14	46	5	0	0	2	0	1	1	2
NHL Totals (10 years)		600	30	97	127	427	-48	7	1	5	0	1	1	2

LaCOUTURE, DAN   LW   PENGUINS

PERSONAL: Born April 13, 1977, in Hyannis, Mass. ... 6-1/201. ... Shoots left. ... Name pronounced LA-kuh-toor.
TRANSACTIONS/CAREER NOTES: Selected by New York Islanders in second round (second Islanders pick, 29th overall) of NHL entry draft (June 22, 1996). ... Traded by Islanders to Edmonton Oilers for RW Mariusz Czerkawski (August 25, 1997). ... Traded by Oilers to Pittsburgh Penguins for D Steve Butenschon (March 13, 2001).

Season Team	League	REGULAR SEASON								PLAYOFFS				
		Gms.	G	A	Pts.	PIM	+/-	PP	SH	Gms.	G	A	Pts.	PIM
94-95—Springfield Jr. B	EJHL	49	37	39	76	100	...	...	...	—	—	—	—	—
95-96—Jr. Whalers	EJHL	42	36	48	84	102	...	...	...	—	—	—	—	—
96-97—Boston University	Hockey East	31	13	12	25	18	...	...	...	—	—	—	—	—
97-98—Hamilton	AHL	77	15	10	25	31	...	...	...	5	1	0	1	0
98-99—Hamilton	AHL	72	17	14	31	73	...	...	...	9	2	1	3	2
—Edmonton	NHL	3	0	0	0	0	1	0	0	—	—	—	—	—
99-00—Hamilton	AHL	70	23	17	40	85	...	...	...	6	2	1	3	0
—Edmonton	NHL	5	0	0	0	10	0	0	0	1	0	0	0	0
00-01—Edmonton	NHL	37	2	4	6	29	-2	0	0	—	—	—	—	—
—Pittsburgh	NHL	11	0	0	0	14	0	0	0	5	0	0	0	2
NHL Totals (3 years)		56	2	4	6	53	-1	0	0	6	0	0	0	2

LACROIX, ERIC   LW

PERSONAL: Born July 15, 1971, in Montreal. ... 6-1/207. ... Shoots left. ... Name pronounced luh-KWAH.
TRANSACTIONS/CAREER NOTES: Selected by Toronto Maple Leafs in seventh round (sixth Maple Leafs pick, 136th overall) of NHL entry draft (June 16, 1990). ... Separated shoulder (November 27, 1993); missed eight games. ... Traded by Maple Leafs with D Chris Snell and fourth-round pick (C Eric Belanger) in 1996 draft to Los Angeles Kings for RW Dixon Ward, C Guy Leveque, RW Shayne Toporowski and C Kelly Fairchild (October 3, 1994). ... Sprained knee (February 4, 1995); missed one game. ... Sprained knee (February 23, 1995); missed two games. ... Suspended three games by NHL for unnecessary contact with an official (October 16, 1995). ... Suspended five games by NHL for checking from behind (November 22, 1995). ... Traded by Kings with first-round pick (D Martin Skoula) in 1998 draft to Colorado Avalanche for G Stephane Fiset and first-round pick (D Mathieu Biron) in 1998 draft (June 20, 1996). ... Traded by Avalanche to Kings for C Roman Vopat and sixth-round pick (traded to Chicago) in 1999 draft (October 29, 1998). ... Fractured right clavicle (December 12, 1998); missed nine games. ... Traded by Kings to New York Rangers for C Sean Pronger (February 12, 1999). ... Fractured hand (October 11, 1999); missed eight games. ... Sprained knee (November 11, 1999). ... Fractured finger (November 22, 2000); missed 11 games. ... Traded by Rangers to Ottawa Senators for LW Colin Forbes (March 1, 2001).
STATISTICAL PLATEAUS: Three-goal games: 1996-97 (1).

Season Team	League	REGULAR SEASON								PLAYOFFS				
		Gms.	G	A	Pts.	PIM	+/-	PP	SH	Gms.	G	A	Pts.	PIM
89-90—Governor Dummer	Mass. H.S.	...	23	18	41	...				—	—	—	—	—
90-91—St. Lawrence Univ.	ECAC	35	13	11	24	35	...			—	—	—	—	—
91-92—St. Lawrence Univ.	ECAC	34	11	20	31	40	...			—	—	—	—	—
92-93—St. John's	AHL	76	15	19	34	59	...			9	5	3	8	4
93-94—St. John's	AHL	59	17	22	39	69	...			11	5	3	8	6
—Toronto	NHL	3	0	0	0	2	0	0	0	2	0	0	0	0
94-95—St. John's	AHL	1	0	0	0	2	...			—	—	—	—	—
—Phoenix	IHL	25	7	1	8	31	...			—	—	—	—	—
—Los Angeles	NHL	45	9	7	16	54	2	2	1	—	—	—	—	—
95-96—Los Angeles	NHL	72	16	16	32	110	-11	3	0	—	—	—	—	—
96-97—Colorado	NHL	81	18	18	36	26	16	2	0	17	1	4	5	19
97-98—Colorado	NHL	82	16	15	31	84	0	5	0	7	0	0	0	6
98-99—Colorado	NHL	7	0	0	0	2	-2	0	0	—	—	—	—	—
—Los Angeles	NHL	27	0	1	1	12	-5	0	0	—	—	—	—	—
—New York Rangers	NHL	30	2	1	3	4	-5	0	0	—	—	—	—	—
99-00—New York Rangers	NHL	70	4	8	12	24	-12	0	0	—	—	—	—	—
00-01—New York Rangers	NHL	46	2	3	5	39	-6	0	0	—	—	—	—	—
—Ottawa	NHL	9	0	1	1	4	0	0	0	4	0	1	1	0
NHL Totals (8 years)		472	67	70	137	361	-23	12	1	30	1	5	6	25

L

LAFLAMME, CHRISTIAN   D   CANADIENS

PERSONAL: Born November 24, 1976, in St. Charles, Que. ... 6-1/210. ... Shoots right. ... Name pronounced lah-FLAHM.
TRANSACTIONS/CAREER NOTES: Selected by Chicago Blackhawks in second round (second Blackhawks pick, 45th overall) of NHL entry draft (July 8, 1995). ... Fractured left foot (October 1, 1997); missed six games. ... Fractured right cheekbone (January 24, 1998); missed four games. ... Traded by Blackhawks with C Chad Kilger, LW Daniel Cleary and LW Ethan Moreau to Edmonton Oilers for D Boris Mironov, LW Dean McAmmond and D Jonas Elofsson (March 20, 1999). ... Suffered concussion (March 28, 1999); missed one game. ... Bruised shoulder (January 11, 2000); missed one game. ... Traded by Oilers with D Mathieu Descoteaux to Montreal Canadiens for D Igor Ulanov and D Alain Nasredine (March 9, 2000). ... Suffered concussion (October 24, 2000); missed six games. ... Strained groin (December 11, 2000); missed 10 games.
HONORS: Named to QMJHL All-Rookie team (1992-93). ... Named to QMJHL All-Star second team (1994-95).

Season Team	League	REGULAR SEASON								PLAYOFFS				
		Gms.	G	A	Pts.	PIM	+/-	PP	SH	Gms.	G	A	Pts.	PIM
92-93—Verdun	QMJHL	69	2	17	19	70	...	...	...	3	0	2	2	6
93-94—Verdun	QMJHL	72	4	34	38	85	...	...	...	4	0	3	3	4
94-95—Beauport	QMJHL	67	6	41	47	82	...	...	...	8	1	4	5	6
95-96—Beauport	QMJHL	41	13	23	36	63	...	...	...	20	7	17	24	32
96-97—Indianapolis	IHL	62	5	15	20	60	...	...	...	4	1	1	2	16
—Chicago	NHL	4	0	1	1	2	3	0	0	—	—	—	—	—
97-98—Chicago	NHL	72	0	11	11	59	14	0	0	—	—	—	—	—

Season Team	League	REGULAR SEASON Gms.	G	A	Pts.	PIM	+/-	PP	SH	PLAYOFFS Gms.	G	A	Pts.	PIM
98-99—Chicago	NHL	62	2	11	13	70	0	0	0	—	—	—	—	—
—Portland	AHL	2	0	1	1	2	...	...	...	—	—	—	—	—
—Edmonton	NHL	11	0	1	1	0	-3	0	0	4	0	1	1	2
99-00—Edmonton	NHL	50	0	5	5	32	-4	0	0	—	—	—	—	—
—Montreal	NHL	15	0	2	2	8	-5	0	0	—	—	—	—	—
00-01—Montreal	NHL	39	0	3	3	42	-11	0	0	—	—	—	—	—
NHL Totals (5 years)		253	2	34	36	213	-6	0	0	4	0	1	1	2

LAKOS, ANDRE — D — DEVILS

PERSONAL: Born July 29, 1979, in Vienna, Austria. ... 6-6/230. ... Shoots right.

TRANSACTIONS/CAREER NOTES: Selected by New Jersey Devils in third round (fourth Devils pick, 95th overall) of NHL entry draft (June 26, 1999).

Season Team	League	REGULAR SEASON Gms.	G	A	Pts.	PIM	+/-	PP	SH	PLAYOFFS Gms.	G	A	Pts.	PIM
96-97—Shelburne	Jr. A	36	5	12	17	47	...	...	...	—	—	—	—	—
97-98—Toronto St. Michael's..	OHL	49	2	10	12	54	...	...	...	—	—	—	—	—
98-99—Barrie	OHL	62	4	23	27	40	...	...	...	12	3	3	6	8
99-00—Albany	AHL	65	1	7	8	41	...	...	...	5	0	2	2	4
00-01—Albany	AHL	51	1	20	21	29	...	...	...	—	—	—	—	—

LALIME, PATRICK — G — SENATORS

PERSONAL: Born July 7, 1974, in St. Bonaventure, Que. ... 6-3/185. ... Catches left. ... Name pronounced luh-LEEM.

TRANSACTIONS/CAREER NOTES: Selected by Pittsburgh Penguins in sixth round (sixth Penguins pick, 156th overall) of NHL entry draft (June 26, 1993). ... Rights traded by Penguins to Mighty Ducks of Anaheim for C Sean Pronger (March 24, 1998). ... Traded by Mighty Ducks to Ottawa Senators for LW Ted Donato and D Antti-Jussi Niemi (June 18, 1999). ... Suffered from the flu (February 1, 2000); missed one game. ... Sprained ligament in left knee (October 14, 2000); missed 10 games.

HONORS: Named to NHL All-Rookie team (1996-97). ... Named to IHL All-Star first team (1998-99).

MISCELLANEOUS: Stopped a penalty shot attempt (vs. Antti Laaksonen, December 20, 2000).

Season Team	League	REGULAR SEASON Gms.	Min	W	L	T	GA	SO	Avg.	PLAYOFFS Gms.	Min.	W	L	GA	SO	Avg.
92-93—Shawinigan	QMJHL	44	2467	10	24	4	192	0	4.67	—	—	—	—	—	—	—
93-94—Shawinigan	QMJHL	48	2733	22	20	2	192	1	4.22	5	223	1	3	25	0	6.73
94-95—Hampton Roads	ECHL	26	1471	15	7	‡3	82	2	3.34	—	—	—	—	—	—	—
—Cleveland	IHL	23	1230	7	10	‡4	91	0	4.44	—	—	—	—	—	—	—
95-96—Cleveland	IHL	41	2314	20	12	‡7	149	0	3.86	—	—	—	—	—	—	—
96-97—Cleveland	IHL	14	834	6	6	‡2	45	1	3.24	—	—	—	—	—	—	—
—Pittsburgh	NHL	39	2058	21	12	3	101	3	2.94	—	—	—	—	—	—	—
97-98—Grand Rapids	IHL	31	1749	10	10	‡9	76	2	2.61	1	77	0	1	4	0	3.12
98-99—Kansas City	IHL	*66	*3789	*39	20	‡4	*190	2	3.01	3	179	1	2	6	1	2.01
99-00—Ottawa	NHL	38	2038	19	14	3	79	3	2.33	—	—	—	—	—	—	—
00-01—Ottawa	NHL	60	3607	36	19	5	141	7	2.35	4	251	0	4	10	0	2.39
NHL Totals (3 years)		137	7703	76	45	11	321	13	2.50	4	251	0	4	10	0	2.39

LAMBERT, DENNY — LW — MIGHTY DUCKS

PERSONAL: Born January 7, 1970, in Wawa, Ont. ... 5-10/215. ... Shoots left. ... Name pronounced lam-BAIR.

TRANSACTIONS/CAREER NOTES: Signed as non-drafted free agent by Mighty Ducks of Anaheim (August 16, 1993). ... Signed as free agent by Ottawa Senators (July 8, 1996). ... Selected by Nashville Predators in NHL expansion draft (June 26, 1998). ... Suspended four games and fined $1,000 by NHL for slashing incident (October 23, 1998). ... Suffered illness (February 4, 1999); missed two games. ... Traded by Predators to Atlanta Thrashers for C Randy Robitaille (August 16, 1999). ... Injured thumb (March 31, 2000); missed four games. ... Separated shoulder (January 10, 2001); missed three games. ... Strained shoulder (February 25, 2001); missed three games. ... Bruised thumb (March 27, 2001); missed two games. ... Traded by Thrashers to Mighty Ducks for future considerations (July 2, 2001).

MISCELLANEOUS: Holds Atlanta Thrashers all-time record for most penalty minutes (434).

Season Team	League	REGULAR SEASON Gms.	G	A	Pts.	PIM	+/-	PP	SH	PLAYOFFS Gms.	G	A	Pts.	PIM
88-89—Sault Ste. Marie	OHL	61	14	15	29	203	...	...	...	—	—	—	—	—
89-90—Sault Ste. Marie	OHL	61	23	29	52	*276	...	...	...	—	—	—	—	—
90-91—Sault Ste. Marie	OHL	59	28	39	67	169	...	...	...	14	7	9	16	48
91-92—San Diego	IHL	71	17	14	31	229	...	...	...	3	0	0	0	10
92-93—St. Thomas	Jr. B	5	2	6	8	9	...	...	...	—	—	—	—	—
—San Diego	IHL	56	18	12	30	277	...	...	...	14	1	1	2	44
93-94—San Diego	IHL	79	13	14	27	314	...	...	...	6	1	0	1	45
94-95—San Diego	IHL	75	25	35	60	222	...	...	...	—	—	—	—	—
—Anaheim	NHL	13	1	3	4	4	3	0	0	—	—	—	—	—
95-96—Anaheim	NHL	33	0	8	8	55	-2	0	0	—	—	—	—	—
—Baltimore	AHL	44	14	28	42	126	...	...	...	12	3	9	12	39
96-97—Ottawa	NHL	80	4	16	20	217	-4	0	0	6	0	1	1	9
97-98—Ottawa	NHL	72	9	10	19	250	4	0	0	11	0	0	0	19
98-99—Nashville	NHL	76	5	11	16	218	-3	1	0	—	—	—	—	—
99-00—Atlanta	NHL	73	5	6	11	*219	-17	2	0	—	—	—	—	—
00-01—Atlanta	NHL	67	1	7	8	215	-5	0	0	—	—	—	—	—
NHL Totals (7 years)		414	25	61	86	1178	-24	3	0	17	0	1	1	28

PERSONAL: Born January 20, 1975, in Gatineau, Que. ... 5-11/185. ... Shoots left.

TRANSACTIONS/CAREER NOTES: Selected by San Jose Sharks in eighth round (eighth Sharks pick, 193rd overall) of NHL entry draft (June 29, 1994). ... Signed as free agent by Calgary Flames (August 6, 1997). ... Suffered concussion (November 22, 1997); missed one game. ... Traded by Flames to Sharks for D Fredrik Oduya (July 12, 1999). ... Signed as free agent by Montreal Canadiens (July 7, 2000).

		REGULAR SEASON								PLAYOFFS				
Season Team	League	Gms.	G	A	Pts.	PIM	+/-	PP	SH	Gms.	G	A	Pts.	PIM
93-94—St. Hyacinthe	QMJHL	69	42	34	76	128	...	...	...	7	4	2	6	13
94-95—St. Hyacinthe	QMJHL	68	38	36	74	249	...	...	...	5	2	1	3	10
95-96—Cape Breton	AHL	74	19	33	52	187	...	...	...	—	—	—	—	—
96-97—Hamilton	AHL	74	15	17	32	139	...	...	...	22	6	7	13	43
97-98—St. John's	AHL	61	17	21	38	194	...	...	...	20	4	6	10	58
—Calgary	NHL	12	1	0	1	4	...	...	...	—	—	—	—	—
98-99—St. John's	AHL	56	19	22	41	158	...	...	...	7	2	5	7	12
—Calgary	NHL	3	0	1	1	0	...	...	...	—	—	—	—	—
99-00—Kentucky	AHL	79	35	31	66	170	...	...	...	9	3	6	9	2
00-01—Quebec	AHL	27	14	18	32	90	...	...	...	9	4	4	8	35
—Montreal	NHL	51	4	7	11	43	-9	2	0	—	—	—	—	—
NHL Totals (3 years)		66	5	8	13	47	...	...	...					

PERSONAL: Born December 19, 1970, in Teplice, Czechoslovakia. ... 6-2/216. ... Shoots right.

TRANSACTIONS/CAREER NOTES: Selected by Los Angeles Kings in seventh round (sixth Kings pick, 133rd overall) of NHL entry draft (June 16, 1990). ... Dislocated shoulder (April 3, 1994); missed remainder of season. ... Played in Europe during 1994-95 NHL lockout. ... Strained left shoulder (March 26, 1995); missed one game. ... Strained back (November 20, 1995); missed seven games. ... Signed as free agent by Edmonton Oilers (October 19, 1996). ... Loaned by Oilers to Sparta Praha of Czech Republic League (October 19, 1996). ... Signed as free agent by Pittsburgh Penguins (September 2, 1997). ... Claimed by Boston Bruins from Penguins in NHL waiver draft (September 28, 1997). ... Claimed on waivers by Penguins (October 25, 1997). ... Fractured thumb (March 21, 1998); missed nine games. ... Bruised ankle (March 23, 1999); missed 10 games. ... Suffered back spasms (October 16, 1999); missed one game. ... Injured thumb (December 14, 1999); missed one game. ... Suffered facial injury (March 9, 2000); missed two games.

MISCELLANEOUS: Member of gold-medal-winning Czech Republic Olympic team (1998).

STATISTICAL NOTES: Tied for NHL lead in game-tying goals with three (1998-99).

L

		REGULAR SEASON								PLAYOFFS				
Season Team	League	Gms.	G	A	Pts.	PIM	+/-	PP	SH	Gms.	G	A	Pts.	PIM
88-89—Litvinov	Czech.	7	3	2	5	0	...	...	...	—	—	—	—	—
89-90—Litvinov	Czech.	39	11	10	21	20	...	...	...	—	—	—	—	—
90-91—Litvinov	Czech.	56	26	26	52	38	...	...	...	—	—	—	—	—
91-92—Litvinov	Czech.	43	12	31	43	34	...	...	...	—	—	—	—	—
—Czech. national team	Int'l	8	5	8	13	8	...	...	...	—	—	—	—	—
—Czech. Olympic Team	Int'l	8	5	8	13	8	...	...	...	—	—	—	—	—
92-93—Los Angeles	NHL	11	0	5	5	2	-3	0	0	—	—	—	—	—
—Phoenix	IHL	38	9	21	30	20	...	...	...	—	—	—	—	—
93-94—Phoenix	IHL	44	11	24	35	34	...	...	...	—	—	—	—	—
—Los Angeles	NHL	32	9	10	19	10	7	0	0	—	—	—	—	—
94-95—Chem. Litvinov	Czech Rep.	16	4	19	23	28	...	...	...	—	—	—	—	—
—Los Angeles	NHL	36	4	8	12	4	-7	0	0	—	—	—	—	—
95-96—Los Angeles	NHL	68	6	16	22	10	-15	0	2	—	—	—	—	—
96-97—Sparta Praha	Czech Rep.	38	14	27	41	30	...	...	...	5	1	2	3	4
97-98—Boston	NHL	3	0	0	0	2	1	0	0	—	—	—	—	—
—Houston	IHL	9	1	7	8	4	...	...	...	—	—	—	—	—
—Pittsburgh	NHL	51	9	13	22	14	6	1	1	6	0	3	3	2
—Czech Rep. Oly. team	Int'l	6	0	3	3	0	...	...	...	—	—	—	—	—
98-99—Pittsburgh	NHL	72	21	23	44	24	-10	7	0	12	0	2	2	0
99-00—Pittsburgh	NHL	78	23	42	65	14	-9	13	0	11	3	3	6	0
00-01—Pittsburgh	NHL	82	32	48	80	28	20	10	0	16	4	4	8	4
NHL Totals (8 years)		433	104	165	269	108	-10	31	3	45	7	12	19	6

PERSONAL: Born January 8, 1971, in Deer Lake, Nfld. ... 6-1/210. ... Shoots left.

TRANSACTIONS/CAREER NOTES: Signed as non-drafted free agent by New York Rangers (August 16, 1993). ... Suspended three games by NHL for abuse of an official in preseason game (September 23, 1995). ... Sprained right knee (December 13, 1996); missed 13 games. ... Suspended two games by NHL for initiating an altercation (March 7, 1997). ... Sprained knee (November 21, 1997); missed six games. ... Bruised sternum (March 4, 1998); missed three games. ... Strained groin (January 2, 2000); missed remainder of season. ... Traded by Rangers with RW Rob DiMaio to Carolina Hurricanes for RW Sandy McCarthy and fourth-round pick (D Bryce Lampman) in 2001 draft (August 4, 2000). ... Injured groin (February 7, 2001); missed nine games.

		REGULAR SEASON								PLAYOFFS				
Season Team	League	Gms.	G	A	Pts.	PIM	+/-	PP	SH	Gms.	G	A	Pts.	PIM
91-92—Summerside	MJHL	44	34	49	83	441	...	...	...	—	—	—	—	—
92-93—Binghamton	AHL	18	3	4	7	115	...	...	...	8	0	1	1	14
—Dayton	ECHL	54	23	22	45	429	...	...	...	3	0	1	1	40
93-94—Binghamton	AHL	54	2	7	9	327	...	...	...	—	—	—	—	—
94-95—Binghamton	AHL	55	6	14	20	296	...	...	...	11	1	3	4	84
—New York Rangers	NHL	18	1	1	2	62	0	0	0	—	—	—	—	—
95-96—New York Rangers	NHL	64	7	4	11	175	2	0	0	2	0	0	0	0
—Binghamton	AHL	1	0	0	0	12	...	...	...	—	—	—	—	—

Season Team	League	Gms.	G	A	Pts.	PIM	+/-	PP	SH	Gms.	G	A	Pts.	PIM
96-97—New York Rangers	NHL	60	3	6	9	195	-1	0	0	10	0	0	0	2
97-98—New York Rangers	NHL	70	3	3	6	197	0	0	0	—	—	—	—	—
98-99—New York Rangers	NHL	44	0	0	0	80	-3	0	0	—	—	—	—	—
99-00—New York Rangers	NHL	21	0	1	1	26	-2	0	0	—	—	—	—	—
00-01—Carolina	NHL	54	0	2	2	94	-4	0	0	4	0	0	0	12
NHL Totals (7 years)		331	14	17	31	829	-8	0	0	16	0	0	0	14

LANGENBRUNNER, JAMIE　　RW　　STARS

PERSONAL: Born July 24, 1975, in Duluth, Minn. ... 6-1/200. ... Shoots right. ... Name pronounced LANG-ihn-BRUH-nuhr.
TRANSACTIONS/CAREER NOTES: Selected by Dallas Stars in second round (second Stars pick, 35th overall) of NHL entry draft (June 26, 1993). ... Suffered back spasms (February 21, 1997); missed one game. ... Suffered whiplash (January 12, 1998); missed one game. ... Injured shoulder (January 6, 1999); missed five games. ... Strained abdominal muscle (March 26, 1999); missed one game. ... Suffered concussion (November 30, 1999); missed one game. ... Sprained shoulder (December 17, 1999); missed one game. ... Suffered pinched nerve in neck (January 7, 2000); missed 11 games. ... Strained neck (February 16, 2000); missed three games. ... Stained muscle in abdomen (December 20, 2000); missed 22 games. ... Reinjured abdominal muscle (March 4, 2001); missed five games. ... Strained back (March 31, 2001); missed one game.
MISCELLANEOUS: Member of Stanley Cup championship team (1999).

Season Team	League	Gms.	G	A	Pts.	PIM	+/-	PP	SH	Gms.	G	A	Pts.	PIM
90-91—Cloquet H.S.	Minn. H.S.	20	6	16	22	8	...	...	...	—	—	—	—	—
91-92—Cloquet H.S.	Minn. H.S.	23	16	23	39	24	...	...	...	—	—	—	—	—
92-93—Cloquet H.S.	Minn. H.S.	27	27	62	89	18	...	...	...	—	—	—	—	—
93-94—Peterborough	OHL	62	33	58	91	53	...	...	...	7	4	6	10	2
94-95—Peterborough	OHL	62	42	57	99	84	...	...	...	11	8	14	22	12
—Dallas	NHL	2	0	0	0	2	0	0	0	—	—	—	—	—
—Kalamazoo	IHL	—	—	—	—	—	...	...	...	11	1	3	4	2
95-96—Michigan	IHL	59	25	40	65	129	...	...	...	10	3	10	13	8
—Dallas	NHL	12	2	2	4	6	-2	1	0	—	—	—	—	—
96-97—Dallas	NHL	76	13	26	39	51	-2	3	0	5	1	1	2	14
97-98—Dallas	NHL	81	23	29	52	61	9	8	0	16	1	4	5	14
—U.S. Olympic team	Int'l	3	0	0	0	4	...	...	...	—	—	—	—	—
98-99—Dallas	NHL	75	12	33	45	62	10	4	0	23	10	7	17	16
99-00—Dallas	NHL	65	18	21	39	68	16	4	2	15	1	7	8	18
00-01—Dallas	NHL	53	12	18	30	57	4	3	2	10	2	2	4	6
NHL Totals (7 years)		364	80	129	209	307	35	23	4	69	15	21	36	68

LANGFELD, JOSH　　RW　　SENATORS

PERSONAL: Born July 17, 1977, in Fridley, Minn. ... 6-3/205. ... Shoots right.
TRANSACTIONS/CAREER NOTES: Selected by Ottawa Senators in third round (third Senators pick, 66th overall) of NHL entry draft (June 21, 1997).
HONORS: Named to NCAA All-Tournament team (1997-98).

Season Team	League	Gms.	G	A	Pts.	PIM	+/-	PP	SH	Gms.	G	A	Pts.	PIM
96-97—Lincoln	Jr. A	38	35	23	58	100	...	...	...	—	—	—	—	—
97-98—Univ. of Michigan	CCHA	46	19	17	36	66	...	...	...	—	—	—	—	—
98-99—Univ. of Michigan	CCHA	41	21	14	35	84	...	...	...	—	—	—	—	—
99-00—Univ. of Michigan	CCHA	37	9	20	29	56	...	...	...	—	—	—	—	—
00-01—Univ. of Michigan	CCHA	42	16	12	28	44	...	...	...	—	—	—	—	—

LANGKOW, DAYMOND　　C　　COYOTES

PERSONAL: Born September 27, 1976, in Edmonton. ... 5-11/180. ... Shoots left. ... Brother of Scott Langkow, goaltender, Mighty Ducks of Anaheim organization.
TRANSACTIONS/CAREER NOTES: Selected by Tampa Bay Lightning in first round (first Lightning pick, fifth overall) of NHL entry draft (July 8, 1995). ... Suffered from the flu (October 1, 1997); missed one game. ... Suffered from concussion (January 7, 1998); missed two games. ... Suffered from the flu (January 31, 1998); missed three games ... Traded by Lightning with RW Mikael Renberg to Philadelphia Flyers for C Chris Gratton and C/RW Mike Sillinger (December 12, 1998). ... Fractured right foot (February 25, 2001); missed 11 games. ... Traded by Flyers to Phoenix Coyotes for second-round pick in 2002 draft and first-round pick in 2003 draft or first-round pick in 2002 draft and second-round pick in 2003 draft (July 2, 2001).
HONORS: Won Bob Clarke Trophy (1994-95). ... Named to Can.HL All-Star first team (1994-95). ... Named to WHL (West) All-Star first team (1994-95). ... Named to WHL (West) All-Star second team (1995-96).
MISCELLANEOUS: Failed to score on a penalty shot (vs. Robbie Tallas, November 24, 1998).

Season Team	League	Gms.	G	A	Pts.	PIM	+/-	PP	SH	Gms.	G	A	Pts.	PIM
91-92—Tri-City	WHL	1	0	0	0	0	...	...	...	4	2	2	4	15
92-93—Tri-City	WHL	65	22	42	64	96	...	...	...	4	1	0	1	4
93-94—Tri-City	WHL	61	40	43	83	174	...	...	...	4	2	2	4	15
94-95—Tri-City	WHL	72	67	73	140	142	...	...	...	17	12	15	27	52
95-96—Tampa Bay	NHL	4	0	1	1	0	-1	0	0	—	—	—	—	—
—Tri-City	WHL	48	30	61	91	103	...	...	...	11	14	13	27	20
96-97—Adirondack	AHL	2	1	1	2	0	...	...	...	—	—	—	—	—
—Tampa Bay	NHL	79	15	13	28	35	1	3	1	—	—	—	—	—
97-98—Tampa Bay	NHL	68	8	14	22	62	-9	2	0	—	—	—	—	—
98-99—Cleveland	IHL	4	1	1	2	18	...	...	...	—	—	—	—	—
—Tampa Bay	NHL	22	4	6	10	15	0	1	0	—	—	—	—	—
—Philadelphia	NHL	56	10	13	23	24	-8	3	1	6	0	2	2	2
99-00—Philadelphia	NHL	82	18	32	50	56	1	5	0	16	5	5	10	23
00-01—Philadelphia	NHL	71	13	41	54	50	12	3	0	6	2	4	6	2
NHL Totals (6 years)		382	68	120	188	242	-4	17	2	28	7	11	18	27

LAPERRIERE, IAN   C/RW   KINGS

PERSONAL: Born January 19, 1974, in Montreal. ... 6-1/197. ... Shoots left. ... Name pronounced EE-ihn luh-PAIR-ee-AIR.

TRANSACTIONS/CAREER NOTES: Selected by St. Louis Blues in seventh round (sixth Blues pick, 158th overall) of NHL entry draft (June 20, 1992). ... Suffered concussion (March 26, 1995); missed three games. ... Traded by Blues to New York Rangers for LW Stephane Matteau (December 28, 1995). ... Traded by Rangers with C Ray Ferraro, C Nathan Lafayette, D Matis Norstrom and fourth-round pick (D Sean Blanchard) in 1997 draft to Los Angeles Kings for RW Shane Churla, LW Jari Kurri and D/RW Marty McSorley (March 14, 1996). ... Sprained left shoulder (March 16, 1996); missed two games. ... Strained shoulder (October 29, 1996); missed three games. ... Strained hip flexor (February 1, 1997); missed three games. ... Suffered concussion (February 25, 1997); missed two games. ... Underwent shoulder surgery (March 17, 1997); missed final 11 games of regular season. ... Suffered blurred vision (December 31, 1997); missed three games. ... Suffered partial tear of anterior cruciate ligament in knee (October 12, 1998); missed nine games. ... Suffered inflammation of left knee (January 2, 1999); missed one game. ... Sprained knee (December 30, 1999); missed three games. ... Strained hip flexor (October 15, 2000); missed one game. ... Suffered concussion (April 3, 2001); missed two games.

HONORS: Named to QMJHL All-Star second team (1992-93).

STATISTICAL PLATEAUS: Three-goal games: 2000-01 (1).

		REGULAR SEASON								PLAYOFFS				
Season Team	League	Gms.	G	A	Pts.	PIM	+/-	PP	SH	Gms.	G	A	Pts.	PIM
90-91—Drummondville	QMJHL	65	19	29	48	117	...	...	...	—	—	—	—	—
91-92—Drummondville	QMJHL	70	28	49	77	160	...	...	...	—	—	—	—	—
92-93—Drummondville	QMJHL	60	44	†96	140	188	...	...	...	10	6	13	19	20
93-94—Drummondville	QMJHL	62	41	72	113	150	...	...	...	9	4	6	10	35
—St. Louis	NHL	1	0	0	0	0	0	0	0	—	—	—	—	—
—Peoria	IHL	—	—	—	—	—	...	...	...	5	1	3	4	2
94-95—Peoria	IHL	51	16	32	48	111	...	...	...	—	—	—	—	—
—St. Louis	NHL	37	13	14	27	85	12	1	0	7	0	4	4	21
95-96—St. Louis	NHL	33	3	6	9	87	-4	1	0	—	—	—	—	—
—Worcester	AHL	3	2	1	3	22	...	...	...	—	—	—	—	—
—New York Rangers	NHL	28	1	2	3	53	-5	0	0	—	—	—	—	—
—Los Angeles	NHL	10	2	3	5	15	-2	0	0	—	—	—	—	—
96-97—Los Angeles	NHL	62	8	15	23	102	-25	0	1	—	—	—	—	—
97-98—Los Angeles	NHL	77	6	15	21	131	0	0	1	4	1	0	1	6
98-99—Los Angeles	NHL	72	3	10	13	138	-5	0	0	—	—	—	—	—
99-00—Los Angeles	NHL	79	9	13	22	185	-14	0	0	4	0	0	0	2
00-01—Los Angeles	NHL	79	8	10	18	141	5	0	0	13	1	2	3	12
NHL Totals (8 years)...........		478	53	88	141	937	-38	2	2	28	2	6	8	41

L

LAPLANTE, DARRYL   LW   WILD

PERSONAL: Born March 28, 1977, in Calgary. ... 6-0/198. ... Shoots right. ... Name pronounced luh-PLANT.

TRANSACTIONS/CAREER NOTES: Selected by Detroit Red Wings in third round (third Red Wings pick, 58th overall) of NHL entry draft (July 8, 1995). ... Fractured cheekbone (February 14, 2000); missed eight games. ... Selected by Minnesota Wild in NHL expansion draft (June 23, 2000).

		REGULAR SEASON								PLAYOFFS				
Season Team	League	Gms.	G	A	Pts.	PIM	+/-	PP	SH	Gms.	G	A	Pts.	PIM
94-95—Moose Jaw	WHL	71	22	24	46	66	...	...	...	10	2	2	4	7
95-96—Moose Jaw	WHL	72	42	40	82	76	...	...	...	—	—	—	—	—
96-97—Moose Jaw	WHL	69	38	42	80	79	...	...	...	12	2	4	6	15
97-98—Adirondack	AHL	77	15	10	25	51	...	...	...	3	0	1	1	4
—Detroit.........................	NHL	2	0	0	0	0	0	0	0	—	—	—	—	—
98-99—Adirondack	AHL	71	17	15	32	96	...	...	...	3	0	1	1	0
—Detroit.........................	NHL	3	0	0	0	0	0	0	0	—	—	—	—	—
99-00—Cincinnati	AHL	35	13	9	22	47	...	...	...	—	—	—	—	—
—Detroit.........................	NHL	30	0	6	6	10	-2	0	0	—	—	—	—	—
00-01—Cleveland	IHL	67	6	19	25	43	...	...	...	4	0	1	1	6
NHL Totals (3 years)...........		35	0	6	6	10	-2	0	0					

LAPOINTE, CLAUDE   C   ISLANDERS

PERSONAL: Born October 11, 1968, in Lachine, Que. ... 5-9/183. ... Shoots left. ... Name pronounced KLOHD luh-pwah.

TRANSACTIONS/CAREER NOTES: Selected by Quebec Nordiques in 12th round (12th Nordiques pick, 234th overall) of NHL entry draft (June 11, 1988). ... Tore groin muscle (February 9, 1991). ... Injured groin (October 23, 1991); missed one game. ... Injured back in training camp (September 1992); missed first five games of season. ... Bruised hip (April 6, 1993); missed two games. ... Sprained left knee (October 18, 1993); missed 13 games. ... Sprained back (February 1, 1994); missed nine games. ... Injured back (March 19, 1994); missed three games. ... Suffered lower back pain (January 21, 1995); missed 16 games. ... Suffered from the flu (April 16, 1995); missed one game. ... Injured hip (April 30, 1995); missed one game. ... Nordiques franchise moved to Colorado and renamed Avalanche for 1995-96 season (June 21, 1995). ... Traded by Avalanche to Calgary Flames for seventh-round pick (C Samuel Pahlsson) in 1996 draft (November 1, 1995). ... Injured groin (December 20, 1995). ... Reinjured groin (December 27, 1995); missed three games. ... Reinjured groin (January 5, 1996); missed three games. ... Injured hip (January 26, 1996); missed 17 games. ... Signed as free agent by New York Islanders (August 22, 1996). ... Hyperextended ankle (January 2, 1997); missed one game. ... Suffered sore ankle (January 25, 1997); missed one game. ... Bruised foot (January 22, 1998); missed one game. ... Fractured toe (February 1, 1998); missed three games. ... Injured foot (October 16, 1999); missed one game. ... Sprained medial collateral ligament in knee (October 30, 1999); missed two games. ... Suffered facial lacerations (December 29, 1999); missed one game. ... Suffered from the flu (April 6, 2000); missed two games. ... Injured toe (February 25, 2001); missed one game. ... Bruised foot (March 28, 2001); missed one game.

MISCELLANEOUS: Failed to score on a penalty shot (vs. Mike Richter, October 22, 1998; vs. Mike Vernon, January 12, 2000).

Season Team	League	REGULAR SEASON								PLAYOFFS				
		Gms.	G	A	Pts.	PIM	+/-	PP	SH	Gms.	G	A	Pts.	PIM
85-86—Trois-Rivieres	QMJHL	72	19	38	57	74	...	...	...	—	—	—	—	—
86-87—Trois-Rivieres	QMJHL	70	47	57	104	123	...	...	...	—	—	—	—	—
87-88—Laval	QMJHL	69	37	83	120	143	...	...	...	13	2	17	19	53
88-89—Laval	QMJHL	63	32	72	104	158	...	...	...	17	5	14	19	66
89-90—Halifax	AHL	63	18	19	37	51	...	...	...	6	1	1	2	34
90-91—Quebec	NHL	13	2	2	4	4	3	0	0	—	—	—	—	—
—Halifax	AHL	43	17	17	34	46	...	...	...	—	—	—	—	—
91-92—Quebec	NHL	78	13	20	33	86	-8	0	2	—	—	—	—	—
92-93—Quebec	NHL	74	10	26	36	98	5	0	0	6	2	4	6	8
93-94—Quebec	NHL	59	11	17	28	70	2	1	1	—	—	—	—	—
94-95—Quebec	NHL	29	4	8	12	41	5	0	0	5	0	0	0	8
95-96—Colorado	NHL	3	0	0	0	0	-1	0	0	—	—	—	—	—
—Calgary	NHL	32	4	5	9	20	2	0	2	2	0	0	0	0
—Saint John	AHL	12	5	3	8	10	...	...	...	—	—	—	—	—
96-97—Utah	IHL	9	7	6	13	14	...	...	...	—	—	—	—	—
—New York Islanders	NHL	73	13	5	18	49	-12	0	3	—	—	—	—	—
97-98—New York Islanders	NHL	78	10	10	20	47	-9	0	1	—	—	—	—	—
98-99—New York Islanders	NHL	82	14	23	37	62	-19	2	2	—	—	—	—	—
99-00—New York Islanders	NHL	76	15	16	31	60	-22	2	1	—	—	—	—	—
00-01—New York Islanders	NHL	80	9	23	32	56	-2	1	1	—	—	—	—	—
NHL Totals (11 years)		677	105	155	260	593	-56	6	13	13	2	4	6	16

LAPOINTE, MARTIN   RW   BRUINS

PERSONAL: Born September 12, 1973, in Lachine, Que. ... 5-11/215. ... Shoots right. ... Name pronounced MAHR-tahn luh-POYNT.

TRANSACTIONS/CAREER NOTES: Selected by Detroit Red Wings in first round (first Red Wings pick, 10th overall) of NHL entry draft (June 22, 1991). ... Fractured wrist (October 9, 1991); missed 22 games. ... Injured left knee (February 29, 1996); missed eight games. ... Injured leg (April 10, 1996); missed two games. ... Fractured finger (December 1, 1996); missed four games. ... Strained hamstring (February 25, 1998); missed one game. ... Suspended two games and fined $1,000 by NHL for cross-checking incident (March 18, 1998). ... Suffered back spasms (December 22, 1998); missed one game. ... Bruised knee (February 12, 1999); missed three games. ... Signed as free agent by Boston Bruins (July 2, 2001).

HONORS: Won Michel Bergeron Trophy (1989-90). ... Named to QMJHL All-Star first team (1989-90 and 1992-93). ... Named to QMJHL All-Star second team (1990-91).

MISCELLANEOUS: Member of Stanley Cup championship team (1997 and 1998).

STATISTICAL PLATEAUS: Three-goal games: 1999-00 (1).

Season Team	League	REGULAR SEASON								PLAYOFFS				
		Gms.	G	A	Pts.	PIM	+/-	PP	SH	Gms.	G	A	Pts.	PIM
89-90—Laval	QMJHL	65	42	54	96	77	...	...	...	14	8	17	25	54
90-91—Laval	QMJHL	64	44	54	98	66	...	...	...	13	7	14	21	26
91-92—Detroit	NHL	4	0	1	1	5	2	0	0	3	0	1	1	4
—Laval	QMJHL	31	25	30	55	84	...	...	...	10	4	10	14	32
—Adirondack	AHL	—	—	—	—	—	...	...	...	8	2	2	4	4
92-93—Adirondack	AHL	8	1	2	3	9	...	...	...	—	—	—	—	—
—Detroit	NHL	3	0	0	0	0	-2	0	0	—	—	—	—	—
—Laval	QMJHL	35	38	51	89	41	...	...	...	13	*13	*17	*30	22
93-94—Adirondack	AHL	28	25	21	46	47	...	...	...	4	1	1	2	8
—Detroit	NHL	50	8	16	24	55	7	2	0	4	0	0	0	6
94-95—Adirondack	AHL	39	29	16	45	80	...	...	...	—	—	—	—	—
—Detroit	NHL	39	4	6	10	73	1	0	0	2	0	1	1	8
95-96—Detroit	NHL	58	6	3	9	93	0	1	0	11	1	2	3	12
96-97—Detroit	NHL	78	16	17	33	167	-14	5	1	20	4	8	12	60
97-98—Detroit	NHL	79	15	19	34	106	0	4	0	21	9	6	15	20
98-99—Detroit	NHL	77	16	13	29	141	7	7	1	10	0	2	2	20
99-00—Detroit	NHL	82	16	25	41	121	17	1	1	9	3	1	4	20
00-01—Detroit	NHL	82	27	30	57	127	3	13	0	6	0	1	1	8
NHL Totals (10 years)		552	108	122	230	888	21	33	3	86	17	22	39	158

LARAQUE, GEORGES   RW   OILERS

PERSONAL: Born December 7, 1976, in Montreal. ... 6-3/240. ... Shoots right. ... Name pronounced la-RAHK.

TRANSACTIONS/CAREER NOTES: Selected by Edmonton Oilers in second round (second Oilers pick, 31st overall) of NHL entry draft (July 8, 1995). ... Fractured left foot (November 17, 1997); missed five games. ... Tore cartilage in right knee (December 5, 1997); missed seven games. ... Suspended two games by AHL for checking from behind (October 21, 1998). ... Bruised sternum (January 17, 1999); missed two games. ... Sprained ankle (March 24, 1999); missed three games. ... Suffered concussion (April 1, 1999); missed three games. ... Suffered eye injury (December 19, 1999); missed two games. ... Sprained knee (March 27, 2000); missed one game.

STATISTICAL PLATEAUS: Three-goal games: 1999-00 (1).

Season Team	League	REGULAR SEASON								PLAYOFFS				
		Gms.	G	A	Pts.	PIM	+/-	PP	SH	Gms.	G	A	Pts.	PIM
93-94—St. Jean	QMJHL	70	11	11	22	142	...	...	...	4	0	0	0	7
94-95—St. Jean	QMJHL	62	19	22	41	259	...	...	...	7	1	1	2	42
95-96—Laval	QMJHL	11	8	13	21	76	...	...	...	—	—	—	—	—
—St. Hyacinthe	QMJHL	8	3	4	7	59	...	...	...	—	—	—	—	—
—Granby	QMJHL	22	9	7	16	125	...	...	...	18	7	6	13	104
96-97—Hamilton	AHL	73	14	20	34	179	...	...	...	15	1	3	4	12
97-98—Hamilton	AHL	46	10	20	30	154	...	...	...	3	0	0	0	11
—Edmonton	NHL	11	0	0	0	59	-4	0	0	—	—	—	—	—
98-99—Hamilton	AHL	25	6	8	14	93	...	...	...	—	—	—	—	—
—Edmonton	NHL	39	3	2	5	57	-1	0	0	4	0	0	0	2
99-00—Edmonton	NHL	76	8	8	16	123	5	0	0	5	0	1	1	6
00-01—Edmonton	NHL	82	13	16	29	148	5	1	0	6	1	1	2	8
NHL Totals (4 years)		208	24	26	50	387	5	1	0	15	1	2	3	16

LARIONOV, IGOR   C   RED WINGS

PERSONAL: Born December 3, 1960, in Voskresensk, U.S.S.R. ... 5-10/170. ... Shoots left. ... Name pronounced EE-gohr LAIR-ee-AH-nahf.

TRANSACTIONS/CAREER NOTES: Selected by Vancouver Canucks in 11th round (11th Canucks pick, 214th overall) of NHL entry draft (June 15, 1985). ... Injured groin (October 25, 1990); missed four games. ... Sprained ankle (January 8, 1991). ... Reinjured ankle (January 30, 1991); missed seven games. ... Signed to play with Lugano of Switzerland (July 14, 1992). ... Selected by San Jose Sharks in NHL waiver draft (October 4, 1992). ... Injured shoulder (September 30, 1993); missed four games. ... Reinjured shoulder (October 16, 1993); missed four games. ... Suffered from the flu (November 7, 1993); missed two games. ... Sprained knee (December 12, 1993); missed 10 games. ... Suffered from respiratory infection (February 11, 1994); missed one game. ... Suffered from the flu (February 26, 1994); missed two games. ... Injured groin (February 15, 1995); missed three games. ... Injured foot (February 26, 1995); missed 12 games. ... Traded by Sharks with second-round pick (traded to St. Louis) in 1998 draft to Detroit Red Wings for RW Ray Sheppard (October 25, 1995). ... Suffered from the flu (December 29, 1995); missed two games. ... Pulled groin (October 15, 1996); missed four games. ... Bruised wrist (October 30, 1996); missed seven games. ... Suffered from the flu (March 21, 1997); missed one game. ... Bruised back (April 8, 1997); missed three games. ... Injured groin (December 5, 1997); missed two games. ... Strained groin (December 26, 1997); missed one game. ... Reinjured groin (December 29, 1997); missed one game. ... Strained groin (March 18, 1998); missed two games. ... Reinjured groin (March 26, 1998); missed three games. ... Injured elbow (April 9, 1998); missed four games. ... Injured groin (March 17, 1999); missed three games. ... Signed as free agent by Florida Panthers (July 1, 2000). ... Strained hip flexor (November 4, 2000); missed nine games. ... Traded by Panthers to Red Wings for D Yan Golubovsky (December 28, 2000).

HONORS: Named to Soviet League All-Star team (1982-83 and 1985-86 through 1987-88). ... Won Soviet Player of the Year Award (1987-88). ... Played in NHL All-Star Game (1998).

MISCELLANEOUS: Member of Stanley Cup championship team (1997 and 1998). ... Member of gold-medal-winning U.S.S.R. Olympic teams (1984 and 1988). ... Scored on a penalty shot (vs. Arturs Irbe, November 22, 1995).

STATISTICAL PLATEAUS: Three-goal games: 1991-92 (2), 1993-94 (2). Total: 4.

Season Team	League		REGULAR SEASON									PLAYOFFS			
		Gms.	G	A	Pts.	PIM	+/-	PP	SH		Gms.	G	A	Pts.	PIM
77-78—Khimik Voskresensk ...	USSR	6	3	0	3	4	...	...	...		—	—	—	—	—
78-79—Khimik Voskresensk ...	USSR	25	3	4	7	12	...	...	...		—	—	—	—	—
79-80—Khimik Voskresensk ...	USSR	42	11	7	18	24	...	...	...		—	—	—	—	—
80-81—Khimik Voskresensk ...	USSR	56	22	23	45	36	...	...	...		—	—	—	—	—
81-82—CSKA Moscow	USSR	46	31	22	53	6	...	...	...		—	—	—	—	—
82-83—CSKA Moscow	USSR	44	20	19	39	20	...	...	...		—	—	—	—	—
83-84—CSKA Moscow	USSR	43	15	26	41	30	...	...	...		—	—	—	—	—
—Soviet Olympic Team ..	Int'l	7	1	4	5	6	...	...	...		—	—	—	—	—
84-85—CSKA Moscow	USSR	40	18	28	46	20	...	...	...		—	—	—	—	—
85-86—CSKA Moscow	USSR	40	21	31	52	33	...	...	...		—	—	—	—	—
86-87—CSKA Moscow	USSR	39	20	26	46	34	...	...	...		—	—	—	—	—
87-88—CSKA Moscow	USSR	51	25	32	57	54	...	...	...		—	—	—	—	—
—Soviet Olympic Team ..	Int'l	8	4	9	13	4	...	...	...		—	—	—	—	—
88-89—CSKA Moscow	USSR	31	15	12	27	22	...	...	...		—	—	—	—	—
89-90—Vancouver	NHL	74	17	27	44	20	-5	8	0		—	—	—	—	—
90-91—Vancouver	NHL	64	13	21	34	14	-3	1	1		6	1	0	1	6
91-92—Vancouver	NHL	72	21	44	65	54	7	10	3		13	3	7	10	4
92-93—Lugano	Switzerland	24	10	19	29	44	...	...	...		—	—	—	—	—
93-94—San Jose	NHL	60	18	38	56	40	20	3	2		14	5	13	18	10
94-95—San Jose	NHL	33	4	20	24	14	-3	0	0		11	1	8	9	2
95-96—San Jose	NHL	4	1	1	2	0	-6	1	0		—	—	—	—	—
—Detroit	NHL	69	21	50	71	34	37	9	1		19	6	7	13	6
96-97—Detroit	NHL	64	12	42	54	26	31	2	1		20	4	8	12	8
97-98—Detroit	NHL	69	8	39	47	40	14	3	0		22	3	10	13	12
98-99—Detroit	NHL	75	14	49	63	48	13	4	2		7	0	2	2	0
99-00—Detroit	NHL	79	9	38	47	28	13	3	0		9	1	2	3	6
00-01—Florida	NHL	26	5	6	11	10	-11	2	0		—	—	—	—	—
—Detroit	NHL	39	4	25	29	28	6	2	0		6	1	3	4	2
NHL Totals (11 years)		728	147	400	547	356	113	48	10		127	25	60	85	56

LAROCQUE, MICHEL   G

PERSONAL: Born October 3, 1976, in Lahr, West Germany. ... 5-11/198. ... Catches left.

TRANSACTIONS/CAREER NOTES: Selected by San Jose Sharks in sixth round (fifth Sharks pick, 137th overall) of NHL entry draft (June 22, 1996). ... Traded by Sharks to Chicago Blackhawks for fifth-round pick (C/LW Michael Pinc) in 2000 draft (August 23, 1999).

HONORS: Named to Hockey East All-Rookie team (1995-96). ... Named Hockey East Tournament Most Valuable Player (1996-97). ... Named to Hockey East All-Star second team (1997-98). ... Named to NCAA All-America (East) second team (1998-99). ... Named to Hockey East All-Star first team (1998-99).

Season Team	League		REGULAR SEASON									PLAYOFFS				
		Gms.	Min	W	L	T	GA	SO	Avg.		Gms.	Min.	W	L	GA	SO	Avg.
95-96 —Boston University	Hockey East	14	735	10	1	1	42	0	3.43		—	—	—	—	—	—	—
96-97 —Boston University	Hockey East	24	1466	16	4	4	58	0	2.37		—	—	—	—	—	—	—
97-98 —Boston University	Hockey East	24	1370	17	4	1	50	1	2.19		—	—	—	—	—	—	—
98-99 —Boston University	Hockey East	35	2072	14	18	3	117	0	3.39		—	—	—	—	—	—	—
99-00 —Cleveland	IHL	1	60	0	0	‡1	2	0	2.00		—	—	—	—	—	—	—
—Wilkes-Barre/Scranton ..	AHL	13	727	5	6	1	34	0	2.81		—	—	—	—	—	—	—
—Saint John	AHL	4	243	2	1	1	8	0	1.98		—	—	—	—	—	—	—
—Greensboro	ECHL	4	229	1	3	0	20	0	5.24		—	—	—	—	—	—	—
00-01 —Norfolk	AHL	35	2087	13	17	4	96	2	2.76		5	304	2	3	13	0	2.57
—Chicago	NHL	3	152	0	2	0	9	0	3.55		—	—	—	—	—	—	—
NHL Totals (1 year)		3	152	0	2	0	9	0	3.55								

LARSEN, BRAD — LW — AVALANCHE

PERSONAL: Born June 28, 1977, in Nakusp, B.C. ... 6-0/210. ... Shoots left.
TRANSACTIONS/CAREER NOTES: Selected by Ottawa Senators in third round (third Senators pick, 53rd overall) of NHL entry draft (July 8, 1995). ... Rights traded by Senators to Colorado Avalanche for D Janne Laukkanen (January 25, 1996); did not sign. ... Returned to draft pool by Avalanche and selected by Avalanche in fourth round (fifth Avalanche pick, 87th overall) of NHL entry draft (June 21, 1997).
HONORS: Named to WHL (East) All-Star second team (1996-97).

Season Team	League	Gms.	G	A	Pts.	PIM	+/-	PP	SH	Gms.	G	A	Pts.	PIM
			REGULAR SEASON								PLAYOFFS			
92-93—Nelson	Tier II Jr. A	42	31	37	68	164	...	...	...					
93-94—Swift Current	WHL	64	15	18	33	37	...	...	...	7	1	2	3	4
94-95—Swift Current	WHL	62	24	33	57	73	...	...	...	6	0	1	1	2
95-96—Swift Current	WHL	51	30	47	77	67	...	...	...	6	3	2	5	13
96-97—Swift Current	WHL	61	36	46	82	61	...	...	...					
97-98—Hershey	AHL	65	12	10	22	80	...	...	...	7	3	2	5	2
—Colorado	NHL	1	0	0	0	0	0	0	0	—	—	—	—	—
98-99—Hershey	AHL	18	3	4	7	11	...	...	...	5	1	0	1	6
99-00—Hershey	AHL	52	13	26	39	66	...	...	...	14	5	2	7	29
00-01—Hershey	AHL	67	21	25	46	93	...	...	...	10	1	3	4	6
—Colorado	NHL	9	0	0	0	0	1	0	0	—	—	—	—	—
NHL Totals (2 years)		10	0	0	0	0	1	0	0					

LASAK, JAN — G — PREDATORS

PERSONAL: Born April 10, 1979, in Zvolen, Czechoslovakia. ... 6-0/204. ... Catches left.
TRANSACTIONS/CAREER NOTES: Selected by Nashville Predators in second round (sixth Predators pick, 65th overall) of NHL entry draft (June 26, 1999).
HONORS: Won ECHL Goaltender of the Year (1999-2000). ... Won ECHL Rookie of the Year (1999-2000). ... Named to ECHL All-Star first team (1999-2000).

Season Team	League	Gms.	Min.	W	L	T	GA	SO	Avg.	Gms.	Min.	W	L	GA	SO	Avg.
			REGULAR SEASON								PLAYOFFS					
96-97—HKM Zvolen	Slovakia Jrs.	49	2940	...	...	...	111	...	2.27	—	—	—	—	—	—	—
97-98—HKM Zvolen	Slovakia Jrs.	48	2881	...	...	...	119	...	2.49	—	—	—	—	—	—	—
98-99—Zvolen	Slovakia	8	387	...	...	...	29	...	4.50	—	—	—	—	—	—	—
—HKM Zvolen	Slovakia Jrs.	43	2580	...	...	...	91	...	2.12	—	—	—	—	—	—	—
99-00—Hampton Roads	ECHL	†59	*3409	*43	17	‡4	145	0	2.55	10	610	5	5	28	1	2.75
00-01—Milwaukee	IHL	43	2439	23	17	‡2	106	1	2.61	3	60	0	1	5	0	5.00

LAUKKANEN, JANNE — D — PENGUINS

PERSONAL: Born March 19, 1970, in Lahti, Finland. ... 6-1/194. ... Shoots left. ... Name pronounced YAH-nee LOW-kih-nihn.
TRANSACTIONS/CAREER NOTES: Selected by Quebec Nordiques in eighth round (eighth Nordiques pick, 156th overall) of NHL entry draft (June 22, 1991). ... Injured groin (April 14, 1995); missed four games. ... Reinjured groin (April 30, 1995); missed last game of season. ... Nordiques franchise moved to Colorado and renamed Avalanche for 1995-96 season (June 21, 1995). ... Traded by Avalanche to Ottawa Senators for LW Brad Larsen (January 25, 1996). ... Suffered hip flexor during 1995-96 season; missed five games. ... Sprained left knee (March 25, 1996); missed two games. ... Bruised finger (November 15, 1996); missed one game. ... Suffered from the flu (December 10, 1996); missed two games. ... Suffered from the flu (March 17, 1997); missed one game. ... Injured knee (March 25, 1997); missed two games. ... Suffered concussion (October 19, 1997); missed two games. ... Strained groin (November 20, 1997); missed five games. ... Suffered from the flu (February 2, 1998); missed one game. ... Bruised foot (March 1, 1998); missed one game. ... Strained groin (March 13, 1998); missed five games. ... Reinjured groin (March 25, 1998); missed eight games. ... Underwent offseason abdominal surgery; missed first 19 games of 1998-99 season. ... Injured groin (November 23, 1998); missed four games. ... Suffered back spasms (January 26, 1999); missed three games. ... Strained back (April 3, 1999); missed one game. ... Suffered concussion (April 7, 1999); missed five games. ... Injured left shoulder (November 30, 1999); missed three games. ... Injured right ankle (December 29, 1999); missed one game. ... Suffered from the flu (January 20, 2000); missed one game. ... Suffered illness (January 26, 2000); missed three game. ... Traded by Senators with G Ron Tugnutt to Pittsburgh Penguins for G Tom Barrasso (March 14, 2000). ... Bruised ribs (March 24, 2000); missed one game. ... Reinjured ribs (April 5, 2000); missed one game. ... Bruised knee (October 13, 2000); missed three games. ... Sprained knee (November 13, 2000); missed 18 games. ... Suffered from the flu (February 16, 2001); missed one game. ... Injured groin (February 23, 2001); missed one game. ... Sprained knee (March 10, 2001); missed six games. ... Reinjured knee (March 29, 2001); missed three games.
MISCELLANEOUS: Member of bronze-medal-winning Finnish Olympic team (1994 and 1998).

Season Team	League	Gms.	G	A	Pts.	PIM	+/-	PP	SH	Gms.	G	A	Pts.	PIM
			REGULAR SEASON								PLAYOFFS			
89-90—Ilves Tampere	Finland	39	5	6	11	10	...	...	...	—	—	—	—	—
90-91—Reipas	Finland	44	8	14	22	56	...	...	...	—	—	—	—	—
91-92—Helsinki HPK	Finland	43	5	14	19	62	...	...	...	—	—	—	—	—
—Fin. Olympic team	Int'l	8	0	1	1	6	...	...	...	—	—	—	—	—
92-93—HPK Hameenlinna	Finland	47	8	21	29	76	...	...	...	12	1	4	5	10
93-94—HPK Hameenlinna	Finland	48	5	24	29	46	...	...	...	—	—	—	—	—
—Fin. Olympic team	Int'l	8	0	2	2	12	...	...	...	—	—	—	—	—
94-95—Cornwall	AHL	55	8	26	34	41	...	...	...	—	—	—	—	—
—Quebec	NHL	11	0	3	3	4	3	0	0	6	1	0	1	2
95-96—Cornwall	AHL	35	7	20	27	60	...	...	...	—	—	—	—	—
—Colorado	NHL	3	0	1	1	0	-1	1	0	—	—	—	—	—
—Ottawa	NHL	20	0	2	2	14	0	0	0	—	—	—	—	—
96-97—Ottawa	NHL	76	3	18	21	76	-14	2	0	7	0	1	1	6
97-98—Ottawa	NHL	60	4	17	21	64	-15	2	0	11	2	2	4	8
—Fin. Olympic team	Int'l	6	0	0	0	4	...	...	...	—	—	—	—	—
98-99—Ottawa	NHL	50	1	11	12	40	18	0	0	4	0	0	0	4
99-00—Ottawa	NHL	60	1	11	12	55	14	0	0	—	—	—	—	—
—Pittsburgh	NHL	11	1	7	8	12	3	1	0	11	2	4	6	10
00-01—Pittsburgh	NHL	50	3	17	20	34	9	0	0	18	2	2	4	14
NHL Totals (7 years)		341	14	86	100	299	17	6	0	57	7	9	16	44

LAUS, PAUL D PANTHERS

PERSONAL: Born September 26, 1970, in Beamsville, Ont. ... 6-1/212. ... Shoots right. ... Name pronounced LAWS.
TRANSACTIONS/CAREER NOTES: Selected by Pittsburgh Penguins in second round (second Penguins pick, 37th overall) of NHL entry draft (June 17, 1989). ... Selected by Florida Panthers in NHL expansion draft (June 24, 1993). ... Strained groin (February 19, 1995); missed six games. ... Separated left shoulder (April 16, 1995); missed two games. ... Bruised left ankle (October 16, 1996); missed two games. ... Sprained ankle (March 5, 1997); missed one game. ... Bruised hand (March 19, 1997); missed two games. ... Suffered back spasms (March 11, 1998); missed four games. ... Suffered torn right hamstring (April 7, 1999); missed final five games of season. ... Fractured hand (March 29, 2000); missed five games. ... Suffered hernia (November 13, 2000); missed 57 games.
MISCELLANEOUS: Holds Florida Panthers all-time record for most penalty minutes (1,545). ... Played defense (1986-87 through 1998-99).

				REGULAR	SEASON						PLAYOFFS			
Season Team	League	Gms.	G	A	Pts.	PIM	+/-	PP	SH	Gms.	G	A	Pts.	PIM
86-87—St. Catharines Jr. B	OHA	40	1	8	9	56	...	...	...	—	—	—	—	—
87-88—Hamilton	OHL	56	1	9	10	171	...	...	...	14	0	0	0	28
88-89—Niagara Falls	OHL	49	1	10	11	225	...	...	...	15	0	5	5	56
89-90—Niagara Falls	OHL	60	13	35	48	231	...	...	...	16	6	16	22	71
90-91—Muskegon	IHL	35	3	4	7	103	...	...	...	4	0	0	0	13
—Albany	IHL	7	0	0	0	7	...	...	...	—	—	—	—	—
—Knoxville	ECHL	20	6	12	18	83	...	...	...	—	—	—	—	—
91-92—Muskegon	IHL	75	0	21	21	248	...	...	...	14	2	5	7	70
92-93—Cleveland	IHL	76	8	18	26	427	...	...	...	4	1	0	1	27
93-94—Florida	NHL	39	2	0	2	109	9	0	0	—	—	—	—	—
94-95—Florida	NHL	37	0	7	7	138	12	0	0	—	—	—	—	—
95-96—Florida	NHL	78	3	6	9	236	-2	0	0	21	2	6	8	*62
96-97—Florida	NHL	77	0	12	12	313	13	0	0	5	0	1	1	4
97-98—Florida	NHL	77	0	11	11	293	-5	0	0	—	—	—	—	—
98-99—Florida	NHL	75	1	9	10	218	-1	0	0	—	—	—	—	—
99-00—Florida	NHL	77	3	8	11	172	-1	0	0	4	0	0	0	8
00-01—Florida	NHL	25	1	2	3	66	5	0	0	—	—	—	—	—
NHL Totals (8 years)		485	10	55	65	1545	30	0	0	30	2	7	9	74

LAW, KIRBY RW FLYERS

PERSONAL: Born March 11, 1977, in McCreary, Man. ... 6-0/180. ... Shoots right.
TRANSACTIONS/CAREER NOTES: Signed as non-drafted free agent by Atlanta Thrashers (July 6, 1999). ... Traded by Thrashers to Philadelphia Flyers for sixth-round pick (D Jeff Dwyer) in 2000 draft and conditional sixth-round pick (G Pasi Nurminen) in 2001 draft (March 14, 2000).

				REGULAR	SEASON						PLAYOFFS			
Season Team	League	Gms.	G	A	Pts.	PIM	+/-	PP	SH	Gms.	G	A	Pts.	PIM
93-94—Saskatoon	WHL	66	9	11	20	39	...	...	...	16	0	0	0	6
94-95—Saskatoon	WHL	46	10	15	25	44	...	...	...	—	—	—	—	—
—Lethbridge	WHL	24	4	10	14	38	...	...	...	—	—	—	—	—
95-96—Lethbridge	WHL	71	17	45	62	133	...	...	...	4	0	0	0	12
96-97—Lethbridge	WHL	72	39	52	91	200	...	...	...	†19	4	14	18	60
98-99—Orlando	IHL	67	18	13	31	136	...	...	...	—	—	—	—	—
—Adirondack	AHL	11	2	3	5	40	...	...	...	3	1	0	1	2
99-00—Orlando	IHL	1	1	0	1	0	...	...	...	—	—	—	—	—
—Louisville	AHL	66	31	21	52	173	...	...	...	—	—	—	—	—
—Philadelphia	AHL	12	1	4	5	6	...	...	...	5	2	0	2	2
00-01—Philadelphia	AHL	78	27	34	61	150	...	...	...	10	1	6	7	16
—Philadelphia	NHL	1	0	0	0	0	-1	0	0	—	—	—	—	—
NHL Totals (1 year)		1	0	0	0	0	-1	0	0					

LAWRENCE, MARK RW

PERSONAL: Born January 27, 1972, in Burlington, Ont. ... 6-4/219. ... Shoots right.
TRANSACTIONS/CAREER NOTES: Selected by Dallas Stars in sixth round (fourth Stars pick, 118th overall) of NHL entry draft (June 22, 1991). ... Signed as free agent by New York Islanders (July 29, 1997).

				REGULAR	SEASON						PLAYOFFS			
Season Team	League	Gms.	G	A	Pts.	PIM	+/-	PP	SH	Gms.	G	A	Pts.	PIM
87-88—Burlington Jr. B	OHA	40	11	12	23	90	...	...	...	—	—	—	—	—
88-89—Niagara Falls	OHL	63	9	27	36	142	...	...	...	—	—	—	—	—
89-90—Niagara Falls	OHL	54	15	18	33	123	...	...	...	16	2	5	7	42
90-91—Det. Jr. Red Wings	OHL	66	27	38	65	53	...	...	...	—	—	—	—	—
91-92—Det. Jr. Red Wings	OHL	28	19	26	45	54	...	...	...	—	—	—	—	—
—North Bay	OHL	24	13	14	27	21	...	...	...	21	*23	12	35	36
92-93—Dayton	ECHL	20	8	14	22	46	...	...	...	—	—	—	—	—
—Kalamazoo	IHL	57	22	13	35	47	...	...	...	—	—	—	—	—
93-94—Kalamazoo	IHL	64	17	20	37	90	...	...	...	—	—	—	—	—
94-95—Kalamazoo	IHL	77	21	29	50	92	...	...	...	16	3	7	10	28
—Dallas	NHL	2	0	0	0	0	0	0	0	—	—	—	—	—
95-96—Michigan	IHL	55	15	14	29	92	...	...	...	10	3	4	7	30
—Dallas	NHL	13	0	1	1	17	0	0	0	—	—	—	—	—
96-97—Michigan	IHL	68	15	21	36	141	...	...	...	4	0	0	0	18
97-98—Utah	IHL	80	36	28	64	102	...	...	...	4	1	1	2	4
—New York Islanders	NHL	2	0	0	0	2	0	0	0	—	—	—	—	—
98-99—Lowell	AHL	21	10	6	16	28	...	...	...	—	—	—	—	—
—New York Islanders	NHL	60	14	16	30	38	-8	4	0	—	—	—	—	—

Season Team	League	REGULAR SEASON								PLAYOFFS				
		Gms.	G	A	Pts.	PIM	+/-	PP	SH	Gms.	G	A	Pts.	PIM
99-00—New York Islanders.....	NHL	29	1	5	6	26	-13	0	0	—	—	—	—	—
—Lowell........................	AHL	18	4	4	8	8	...	...	...	7	2	2	4	10
—Chicago.....................	IHL	16	4	6	10	32	...	...	...	—	—	—	—	—
00-01—Chicago..................	IHL	32	8	6	14	26	...	...	...	2	0	0	0	0
—New York Islanders.....	NHL	36	3	4	7	32	-9	1	0	—	—	—	—	—
NHL Totals (6 years)...........		142	18	26	44	115	-30	5	0					

LAZAREV, YEVGENY   LW   AVALANCHE

PERSONAL: Born April 25, 1980, in Kharkov, U.S.S.R. ... 6-2/215. ... Shoots left.
TRANSACTIONS/CAREER NOTES: Selected by Colorado Avalanche in third round (eighth Avalanche pick, 79th overall) of NHL entry draft (June 27, 1998).

Season Team	League	REGULAR SEASON								PLAYOFFS				
		Gms.	G	A	Pts.	PIM	+/-	PP	SH	Gms.	G	A	Pts.	PIM
96-97—Torpedo Yaroslavl.......	Russian	1	0	0	0	0	...			—	—	—	—	—
—Torpedo-2 Yaroslavl....	Rus. Div. III	44	18	15	33	38	...			—	—	—	—	—
97-98—Kitchener Jr. B............	OHA	11	9	13	22	22	...			5	5	2	7	17
98-99—Hershey	AHL	53	6	15	21	18	...			—	—	—	—	—
99-00—Hershey	AHL	46	2	11	13	44	...			8	0	1	1	2
—Pensacola	ECHL	11	3	5	8	23	...			—	—	—	—	—
00-01—Hershey	AHL	80	17	21	38	50	...			12	3	8	11	10

LECAVALIER, VINCENT   C   LIGHTNING

PERSONAL: Born April 21, 1980, in Ile-Bizard, Que. ... 6-4/205. ... Shoots left.
TRANSACTIONS/CAREER NOTES: Selected by Tampa Bay Lightning in first round (first Lightning pick, first overall) of NHL entry draft (June 27, 1998). ... Injured ankle (April 6, 2000); missed final two games of season. ... Fractured left foot (January 12, 2001); missed 14 games.
HONORS: Won Can.HL Rookie of the Year Award (1996-97). ... Won Michel Bergeron Trophy (1996-97). ... Named to Can.HL All-Rookie team (1996-97). ... Named to QMJHL All-Rookie team (1996-97). ... Won Michel Bossy Trophy (1997-98). ... Won Can.HL Top Draft Prospect Award (1997-98). ... Named to Can.HL All-Star first team (1997-98). ... Named to QMJHL All-Star first team (1997-98).
MISCELLANEOUS: Captain of Tampa Bay Lightning (March 11, 2000-remainder of season and 2000-01).

Season Team	League	REGULAR SEASON								PLAYOFFS				
		Gms.	G	A	Pts.	PIM	+/-	PP	SH	Gms.	G	A	Pts.	PIM
95-96—Notre Dame	SJHL	22	52	52	104	...	...	...	...	—	—	—	—	—
96-97—Rimouski	QMJHL	64	42	60	102	36	...	...	...	4	4	3	7	2
97-98—Rimouski	QMJHL	58	44	71	115	117	...	...	...	18	15	†26	41	46
98-99—Tampa Bay	NHL	82	13	15	28	23	-19	2	0	—	—	—	—	—
99-00—Tampa Bay	NHL	80	25	42	67	43	-25	6	0	—	—	—	—	—
00-01—Tampa Bay	NHL	68	23	28	51	66	-26	7	0	—	—	—	—	—
NHL Totals (3 years)...........		230	61	85	146	132	-70	15	0					

LeCLAIR, JOHN   LW   FLYERS

PERSONAL: Born July 5, 1969, in St. Albans, Vt. ... 6-3/226. ... Shoots left. ... Full Name: John Clark LeClair.
TRANSACTIONS/CAREER NOTES: Selected by Montreal Canadiens in second round (second Canadiens pick, 33rd overall) of NHL entry draft (June 13, 1987). ... Injured shoulder (January 15, 1992); missed four games. ... Suffered charley horse (January 20, 1993); missed four games. ... Sprained knee (October 2, 1993); missed eight games. ... Bruised sternum (March 28, 1994); missed two games. ... Traded by Canadiens with LW Gilbert Dionne and D Eric Desjardins to Philadelphia Flyers for RW Mark Recchi and third-round pick (C Martin Hohenberger) in 1995 draft (February 9, 1995). ... Strained right hip (April 18, 1995); missed one playoff game. ... Strained hip flexor (March 9, 1999); missed four games. ... Suffered back spasms (April 1, 1999); missed two games. ... Injured back (October 9, 2000); missed 20 games. ... Strained lower back (December 9, 2000); missed 46 games.
HONORS: Named to ECAC All-Star second team (1990-91). ... Named to NHL All-Star first team (1994-95 and 1997-98). ... Played in NHL All-Star Game (1996-2000). ... Named to NHL All-Star second team (1995-96, 1996-97 and 1998-99). ... Named to THE SPORTING NEWS All-Star team (1994-95, 1996-97 and 1997-98).
MISCELLANEOUS: Member of Stanley Cup championship team (1993).
STATISTICAL NOTES: Tied for NHL lead in game-tying goals with three (1998-99).
STATISTICAL PLATEAUS: Three-goal games: 1994-95 (2), 1995-96 (2), 1996-97 (1), 1997-98 (1), 1998-99 (1), 2000-01 (1). Total: 8. ... Four-goal games: 1996-97 (1), 1998-99 (1). Total: 2. ... Total hat tricks: 10.

Season Team	League	REGULAR SEASON								PLAYOFFS				
		Gms.	G	A	Pts.	PIM	+/-	PP	SH	Gms.	G	A	Pts.	PIM
85-86—Bellows Free Acad.	VT. H.S.	22	41	28	69	14	...	...	...	—	—	—	—	—
86-87—Bellows Free Acad.	VT. H.S.	23	44	40	84	25	...	...	...	—	—	—	—	—
87-88—Univ. of Vermont........	ECAC	31	12	22	34	62	...	...	...	—	—	—	—	—
88-89—Univ. of Vermont........	ECAC	19	9	12	21	40	...	...	...	—	—	—	—	—
89-90—Univ. of Vermont........	ECAC	10	10	6	16	38	...	...	...	—	—	—	—	—
90-91—Univ. of Vermont........	ECAC	33	25	20	45	58	...	...	...	—	—	—	—	—
—Montreal	NHL	10	2	5	7	2	1	0	0	3	0	0	0	0
91-92—Montreal	NHL	59	8	11	19	14	5	3	0	8	1	1	2	4
—Fredericton	AHL	8	7	7	14	10	...	...	...	2	0	0	0	4
92-93—Montreal	NHL	72	19	25	44	33	11	2	0	20	4	6	10	14
93-94—Montreal	NHL	74	19	24	43	32	17	1	0	7	2	1	3	8
94-95—Montreal	NHL	9	1	4	5	10	-1	1	0	—	—	—	—	—
—Philadelphia	NHL	37	25	24	49	20	21	5	0	15	5	7	12	4
95-96—Philadelphia	NHL	82	51	46	97	64	21	19	0	11	6	5	11	6

Season Team	League	REGULAR SEASON								PLAYOFFS				
		Gms.	G	A	Pts.	PIM	+/-	PP	SH	Gms.	G	A	Pts.	PIM
96-97—Philadelphia	NHL	82	50	47	97	58	*44	10	0	19	9	12	21	10
97-98—Philadelphia	NHL	82	51	36	87	32	30	16	0	5	1	1	2	8
—U.S. Olympic team	Int'l	4	0	1	1	0	...	...	...	—	—	—	—	—
98-99—Philadelphia	NHL	76	43	47	90	30	36	16	0	6	3	0	3	12
99-00—Philadelphia	NHL	82	40	37	77	36	8	13	0	18	6	7	13	6
00-01—Philadelphia	NHL	16	7	5	12	0	2	3	0	6	1	2	3	2
NHL Totals (11 years)		681	316	311	627	331	195	89	0	118	38	42	80	74

LECLERC, MIKE   LW   MIGHTY DUCKS

PERSONAL: Born November 10, 1976, in Winnipeg. ... 6-1/205. ... Shoots left. ... Name pronounced luh-KLAIR.
TRANSACTIONS/CAREER NOTES: Selected by Mighty Ducks of Anaheim in third round (third Mighty Ducks pick, 55th overall) of NHL entry draft (July 8, 1995). ... Underwent elbow surgery (October 29, 1999); missed 11 games. ... Injured elbow (December 17, 1999); missed two games. ... Injured knee (December 28, 2000); missed 15 games. ... Strained muscle in abdomen (March 11, 2001); missed remainder of season.
HONORS: Named to WHL (Central/East) All-Star second team (1995-96). ... Named to AHL All-Rookie team (1996-97).

Season Team	League	REGULAR SEASON								PLAYOFFS				
		Gms.	G	A	Pts.	PIM	+/-	PP	SH	Gms.	G	A	Pts.	PIM
91-92—St. Boniface	Tier II Jr. A	43	16	12	28	25	...			—	—	—	—	—
—Victoria	WHL	2	0	0	0	0	...			—	—	—	—	—
92-93—Victoria	WHL	70	4	11	15	118	...			—	—	—	—	—
93-94—Victoria	WHL	68	29	11	40	112	...			—	—	—	—	—
94-95—Prince George	WHL	43	20	36	56	78	...			—	—	—	—	—
—Brandon	WHL	23	5	8	13	50	...			18	10	6	16	33
95-96—Brandon	WHL	71	58	53	111	161	...			19	6	19	25	25
96-97—Baltimore	AHL	71	29	27	56	134	...			—	—	—	—	—
—Anaheim	NHL	5	1	1	2	0	2	0	0	1	0	0	0	0
97-98—Cincinnati	AHL	48	18	22	40	83	...			—	—	—	—	—
—Anaheim	NHL	7	0	0	0	6	-6	0	0	—	—	—	—	—
98-99—Cincinnati	AHL	65	25	28	53	153	...			3	0	1	1	19
—Anaheim	NHL	7	0	0	0	4	-2	0	0	1	0	0	0	0
99-00—Anaheim	NHL	69	8	11	19	70	-15	0	0	—	—	—	—	—
00-01—Anaheim	NHL	54	15	20	35	26	-1	3	0	—	—	—	—	—
NHL Totals (5 years)		142	24	32	56	106	-22	3	0	2	0	0	0	0

LEDYARD, GRANT   D   LIGHTNING

PERSONAL: Born November 19, 1961, in Winnipeg. ... 6-2/195. ... Shoots left.
TRANSACTIONS/CAREER NOTES: Signed as non-drafted free agent by New York Rangers (July 7, 1982). ... Traded by Rangers to Los Angeles Kings for LW Brian MacLellan and fourth-round pick (C Michael Sullivan) in 1987 draft; Rangers also sent second-round pick (D Neil Wilkinson) in 1986 draft and fourth-round pick (RW John Weisbrod) in 1987 draft to Minnesota North Stars and the North Stars sent G Roland Melanson to the Kings as part of the same deal (December 1986). ... Sprained ankle (October 1987). ... Traded by Kings to Washington Capitals for RW Craig Laughlin (February 9, 1988). ... Traded by Capitals with G Clint Malarchuk and sixth-round pick (C Brian Holzinger) in 1991 draft to Buffalo Sabres for D Calle Johansson and second-round pick (G Byron Dafoe) in 1989 draft (March 6, 1989). ... Injured knee (February 12, 1991). ... Injured shoulder (March 2, 1991). ... Bruised ankle (March 14, 1992); missed four games. ... Fractured finger (October 28, 1992); missed 25 games. ... Injured eye (March 7, 1993); missed three games. ... Signed as free agent by Dallas Stars (August 13, 1993). ... Sprained ankle (February 13, 1995); missed two games. ... Fractured ankle (April 16, 1995); missed last eight games of season and first game of play-offs. ... Suffered from the flu (May 14, 1995); missed one game. ... Fractured orbital bone prior to 1996-97 season; missed first game of season. ... Suspended two games and fined $1,000 by NHL for kneeing incident (November 26, 1996). ... Suffered from the flu (February 2, 1997); missed two games. ... Signed as free agent by Vancouver Canucks (July 14, 1997). ... Suffered concussion (October 30, 1997); missed one game. ... Traded by Canucks to Boston Bruins for eighth-round pick (LW Curtis Valentine) in 1998 draft (March 3, 1998). ... Sprained knee (November 7, 1998); missed one game. ... Sprained knee (December 21, 1998); missed 13 games. ... Injured knee (February 26, 1999); missed three games. ... Signed as free agent by Ottawa Senators (November 17, 1999). ... Signed as free agent by Tampa Bay Lightning (February 1, 2001). ... Traded by Lightning to Stars for seventh-round pick (D Jeremy Van Hoof) in 2001 draft (March 13, 2001). ... Signed as free agent by Lightning (July 13, 2001).
HONORS: Named MJHL Most Valuable Player (1981-82). ... Named to MJHL All-Star first team (1981-82). ... Won Bob Gassoff Award (1983-84). ... Won Max McNab Trophy (1983-84).

Season Team	League	REGULAR SEASON								PLAYOFFS				
		Gms.	G	A	Pts.	PIM	+/-	PP	SH	Gms.	G	A	Pts.	PIM
79-80—Fort Garry	MJHL	49	13	24	37	90	...			—	—	—	—	—
80-81—Saskatoon	WHL	71	9	28	37	148	...			—	—	—	—	—
81-82—Fort Garry	MJHL	63	25	45	70	150	...			—	—	—	—	—
82-83—Tulsa	CHL	80	13	29	42	115	...			—	—	—	—	—
83-84—Tulsa	CHL	58	9	17	26	71	...			9	5	4	9	10
84-85—New Haven	AHL	36	6	20	26	18	...			—	—	—	—	—
—New York Rangers	NHL	42	8	12	20	53	8	1	0	3	0	2	2	4
85-86—New York Rangers	NHL	27	2	9	11	20	-7	0	0	—	—	—	—	—
—Los Angeles	NHL	52	7	18	25	78	-22	4	0	—	—	—	—	—
86-87—Los Angeles	NHL	67	14	23	37	93	-40	5	0	5	0	0	0	10
87-88—New Haven	AHL	3	2	1	3	4	...			—	—	—	—	—
—Los Angeles	NHL	23	1	7	8	52	-7	1	0	—	—	—	—	—
—Washington	NHL	21	4	3	7	14	-4	1	0	14	1	0	1	30
88-89—Washington	NHL	61	3	11	14	43	1	1	0	—	—	—	—	—
—Buffalo	NHL	13	1	5	6	8	1	0	0	5	1	2	3	2
89-90—Buffalo	NHL	67	2	13	15	37	2	0	0	—	—	—	—	—
90-91—Buffalo	NHL	60	8	23	31	46	13	2	1	6	3	3	6	10
91-92—Buffalo	NHL	50	5	16	21	45	-4	0	0	—	—	—	—	—

Season Team	League	REGULAR SEASON								PLAYOFFS				
		Gms.	G	A	Pts.	PIM	+/-	PP	SH	Gms.	G	A	Pts.	PIM
92-93—Buffalo	NHL	50	2	14	16	45	-2	1	0	8	0	0	0	8
—Rochester	AHL	5	0	2	2	8	...	...	...	—	—	—	—	—
93-94—Dallas	NHL	84	9	37	46	42	7	6	0	9	1	2	3	6
94-95—Dallas	NHL	38	5	13	18	20	6	4	0	3	0	0	0	2
95-96—Dallas	NHL	73	5	19	24	20	-15	2	0	—	—	—	—	—
96-97—Dallas	NHL	67	1	15	16	61	31	0	0	7	0	2	2	0
97-98—Vancouver	NHL	49	2	13	15	14	-2	1	0	—	—	—	—	—
—Boston	NHL	22	2	7	9	6	-2	1	0	6	0	0	0	2
98-99—Boston	NHL	47	4	8	12	33	-8	1	0	2	0	0	0	2
99-00—Ottawa	NHL	40	2	4	6	8	-3	0	0	6	0	0	0	16
00-01—Tampa Bay	NHL	14	2	2	4	12	-5	0	0	—	—	—	—	—
—Dallas	NHL	8	0	1	1	4	3	0	0	9	0	1	1	4
NHL Totals (17 years)		975	89	273	362	754	-49	31	1	83	6	12	18	96

LEEB, BRAD — LW — CANUCKS

PERSONAL: Born August 27, 1979, in Red Deer, Alta. ... 5-11/180. ... Shoots right.
TRANSACTIONS/CAREER NOTES: Signed as non-drafted free agent by Vancouver Canucks (October 8, 1999).
HONORS: Named to WHL (East) All-Star second team (1998-99).

Season Team	League	REGULAR SEASON								PLAYOFFS				
		Gms.	G	A	Pts.	PIM	+/-	PP	SH	Gms.	G	A	Pts.	PIM
94-95—Red Deer	WHL	3	0	0	0	4	...	...	...	—	—	—	—	—
95-96—Red Deer	WHL	38	3	6	9	30	...	...	...	10	2	0	2	11
96-97—Red Deer	WHL	70	15	20	35	76	...	...	...	16	3	3	6	6
97-98—Red Deer	WHL	63	23	23	46	88	...	...	...	3	2	0	2	2
98-99—Red Deer	WHL	64	32	47	79	84	...	...	...	9	5	9	14	10
99-00—Syracuse	AHL	61	19	18	37	50	...	...	...	4	0	0	0	6
—Vancouver	NHL	2	0	0	0	2	-2	0	0	—	—	—	—	—
00-01—Kansas City	IHL	53	18	16	34	53	...	...	...	—	—	—	—	—
NHL Totals (1 year)		2	0	0	0	2	-2	0	0					

LEEB, GREG — C — OILERS

PERSONAL: Born May 31, 1977, in Red Deer, Alta. ... 5-9/160. ... Shoots left.
TRANSACTIONS/CAREER NOTES: Signed as non-drafted free agent by Dallas Stars (July 2, 1998). ... Signed as free agent by Edmonton Oilers (July 17, 2001).
HONORS: Named to WHL (West) All-Star second team (1997-98).

Season Team	League	REGULAR SEASON								PLAYOFFS				
		Gms.	G	A	Pts.	PIM	+/-	PP	SH	Gms.	G	A	Pts.	PIM
94-95—Spokane	WHL	72	21	34	55	48	...	...	...	11	5	10	15	10
95-96—Spokane	WHL	64	33	21	54	54	...	...	...	18	1	7	8	16
96-97—Spokane	WHL	72	27	59	86	69	...	...	...	9	3	3	6	4
97-98—Spokane	WHL	68	46	50	96	54	...	...	...	18	10	10	20	10
98-99—Michigan	IHL	77	16	27	43	18	...	...	...	5	0	3	3	4
99-00—Michigan	IHL	73	9	17	26	76	...	...	...	—	—	—	—	—
00-01—Utah	IHL	78	25	40	65	36	...	...	...	—	—	—	—	—
—Dallas	NHL	2	0	0	0	0	-1	0	0	—	—	—	—	—
NHL Totals (1 year)		2	0	0	0	0	-1	0	0					

LEETCH, BRIAN — D — RANGERS

PERSONAL: Born March 3, 1968, in Corpus Christi, Texas. ... 6-0/185. ... Shoots left. ... Full Name: Brian Joseph Leetch.
TRANSACTIONS/CAREER NOTES: Selected by New York Rangers in first round (first Rangers pick, ninth overall) of NHL entry draft (June 21, 1986). ... Fractured bone in left foot (December 1988). ... Suffered hip pointer (March 15, 1989). ... Fractured left ankle (March 14, 1990). ... Injured ankle (November 21, 1992); missed one game. ... Suffered stretched nerve in neck (December 17, 1992); missed 34 games. ... Fractured ankle (March 19, 1993) and underwent ankle surgery; missed remainder of season. ... Suffered nerve compression in right leg (January 4, 1998); missed two games. ... Suffered head injury (April 5, 1998); missed four games. ... Fractured arm (November 24, 1999); missed 32 games.
HONORS: Named Hockey East Player of the Year (1986-87). ... Named Hockey East Rookie of the Year (1986-87). ... Named Hockey East Tournament Most Valuable Player (1986-87). ... Named to NCAA All-America (East) first team (1986-87). ... Named to Hockey East All-Star first team (1986-87). ... Named to Hockey East All-Freshman team (1986-87). ... Named NHL Rookie of the Year by THE SPORTING NEWS (1988-89). ... Won Calder Memorial Trophy (1988-89). ... Named to NHL All-Rookie team (1988-89). ... Named to THE SPORTING NEWS All-Star second team (1990-91, 1993-94 and 2000-01). ... Named to NHL All-Star second team (1990-91, 1993-94 and 1995-96). ... Played in NHL All-Star Game (1990-1992, 1994, 1996-1998 and 2001). ... Won James Norris Memorial Trophy (1991-92 and 1996-97). ... Named to THE SPORTING NEWS All-Star first team (1991-92). ... Named to NHL All-Star first team (1991-92 and 1996-97). ... Won Conn Smythe Trophy (1993-94). ... Named to Hockey East All-Decade team (1994). ... Named to THE SPORTING NEWS All-Star team (1996-97).
RECORDS: Holds NHL single-season record for most goals by a rookie defenseman—23 (1988-89).
MISCELLANEOUS: Member of Stanley Cup championship team (1994). ... Captain of New York Rangers (1997-98 through November 26, 1999 and February 9, 2000-remainder of season). ... Holds New York Rangers all-time record for most assists (655).

Season Team	League	REGULAR SEASON								PLAYOFFS				
		Gms.	G	A	Pts.	PIM	+/-	PP	SH	Gms.	G	A	Pts.	PIM
84-85—Avon Old Farms H.S. ..	Conn. H.S.	26	30	46	76	15	...	...	...	—	—	—	—	—
85-86—Avon Old Farms H.S. ..	Conn. H.S.	28	40	44	84	18	...	...	...	—	—	—	—	—
86-87—Boston College	Hockey East	37	9	38	47	10	...	...	...	—	—	—	—	—
87-88—U.S. national team	Int'l	60	13	61	74	38	...	...	...	—	—	—	—	—
—U.S. Olympic team	Int'l	6	1	5	6	4	...	...	...	—	—	—	—	—
—New York Rangers	NHL	17	2	12	14	0	5	1	0	—	—	—	—	—
88-89—New York Rangers	NHL	68	23	48	71	50	8	8	3	4	3	2	5	2
89-90—New York Rangers	NHL	72	11	45	56	26	-18	5	0	—	—	—	—	—
90-91—New York Rangers	NHL	80	16	72	88	42	2	6	0	6	1	3	4	0
91-92—New York Rangers	NHL	80	22	80	102	26	25	10	1	13	4	11	15	4
92-93—New York Rangers	NHL	36	6	30	36	26	2	2	1	—	—	—	—	—
93-94—New York Rangers	NHL	84	23	56	79	67	28	17	1	23	11	*23	*34	6
94-95—New York Rangers	NHL	48	9	32	41	18	0	3	0	10	6	8	14	8
95-96—New York Rangers	NHL	82	15	70	85	30	12	7	0	11	1	6	7	4
96-97—New York Rangers	NHL	82	20	58	78	40	31	9	0	15	2	8	10	6
97-98—New York Rangers	NHL	76	17	33	50	32	-36	11	0	—	—	—	—	—
—U.S. Olympic team	Int'l	4	1	1	2	0	...	...	...	—	—	—	—	—
98-99—New York Rangers	NHL	82	13	42	55	42	-7	4	0	—	—	—	—	—
99-00—New York Rangers	NHL	50	7	19	26	20	-16	3	0	—	—	—	—	—
00-01—New York Rangers	NHL	82	21	58	79	34	-18	10	1	—	—	—	—	—
NHL Totals (14 years).........		939	205	655	860	453	18	96	7	82	28	61	89	30

LEFEBVRE, SYLVAIN D RANGERS

PERSONAL: Born October 14, 1967, in Richmond, Que. ... 6-3/205. ... Shoots left. ... Name pronounced luh-FAYV.

TRANSACTIONS/CAREER NOTES: Signed as non-drafted free agent by Montreal Canadiens (September 24, 1986). ... Traded by Canadiens to Toronto Maple Leafs for third-round pick (D Martin Belanger) in 1994 draft (August 20, 1992). ... Traded by Maple Leafs with LW Wendel Clark, RW Landon Wilson and first-round pick (D Jeffrey Kealty) in 1994 draft to Quebec Nordiques for C Mats Sundin, D Garth Butcher, LW Todd Warriner and first-round pick (traded to Washington) in 1994 draft (June 28, 1994). ... Nordiques franchise moved to Colorado and renamed Avalanche for 1995-96 season (June 21, 1995). ... Sprained right ankle (November 29, 1995); missed six games. ... Fractured forearm (December 18, 1996); missed 10 games. ... Suffered sore hip (December 12, 1997); missed one game. ... Injured eye (November 8, 1998); missed six games. ... Signed as free agent by New York Rangers (July 16, 1999). ... Sprained shoulder (March 25, 2001); missed final seven games of season.

HONORS: Named to AHL All-Star second team (1988-89).

MISCELLANEOUS: Member of Stanley Cup championship team (1996).

Season Team	League	REGULAR SEASON								PLAYOFFS				
		Gms.	G	A	Pts.	PIM	+/-	PP	SH	Gms.	G	A	Pts.	PIM
84-85—Laval	QMJHL	66	7	5	12	31	...	...	...	—	—	—	—	—
85-86—Laval	QMJHL	71	8	17	25	48	...	...	...	14	1	0	1	25
86-87—Laval	QMJHL	70	10	36	46	44	...	...	...	15	1	6	7	12
87-88—Sherbrooke	AHL	79	3	24	27	73	...	...	...	6	2	3	5	4
88-89—Sherbrooke	AHL	77	15	32	47	119	...	...	...	6	1	3	4	4
89-90—Montreal	NHL	68	3	10	13	61	18	0	0	6	0	0	0	2
90-91—Montreal	NHL	63	5	18	23	30	-11	1	0	11	1	0	1	6
91-92—Montreal	NHL	69	3	14	17	91	9	0	0	2	0	0	0	2
92-93—Toronto	NHL	81	2	12	14	90	8	0	0	21	3	3	6	20
93-94—Toronto	NHL	84	2	9	11	79	33	0	0	18	0	3	3	16
94-95—Quebec	NHL	48	2	11	13	17	13	0	0	6	0	2	2	2
95-96—Colorado	NHL	75	5	11	16	49	26	2	0	22	0	5	5	12
96-97—Colorado	NHL	71	2	11	13	30	12	1	0	17	0	0	0	25
97-98—Colorado	NHL	81	0	10	10	48	2	0	0	7	0	0	0	4
98-99—Colorado	NHL	76	2	18	20	48	18	0	0	19	0	1	1	12
99-00—New York Rangers	NHL	82	2	10	12	43	-13	0	0	—	—	—	—	—
00-01—New York Rangers	NHL	71	2	13	15	55	3	0	0	—	—	—	—	—
NHL Totals (12 years).........		869	30	147	177	641	118	4	0	129	4	14	18	101

LEGACE, MANNY G RED WINGS

PERSONAL: Born February 4, 1973, in Toronto. ... 5-9/165. ... Catches left. ... Name pronounced LEH-guh-see.

TRANSACTIONS/CAREER NOTES: Selected by Hartford Whalers in eighth round (fifth Whalers pick, 188th overall) of NHL entry draft (June 26, 1993). ... Whalers franchise moved to North Carolina and renamed Carolina Hurricanes for 1997-98 season; NHL approved move on June 25, 1997. ... Traded by Hurricanes to Los Angeles Kings for conditional pick in 1999 draft (July 31, 1998); Legace did not meet conditions for the pick and the draft choice was forfeited. ... Signed as free agent by Detroit Red Wings (July 15, 1999). ... Claimed on waivers by Vancouver Canucks (September 30, 1999). ... Claimed on waivers by Detroit Red Wings (October 13, 1999). ... Suffered injury (November 27, 2000); missed two games. ... Injured elbow (March 31, 2001); missed one game.

HONORS: Named to Can.HL All-Star second team (1992-93). ... Named to OHL All-Star first team (1992-93). ... Won Harry (Hap) Holmes Memorial Trophy (1995-96). ... Won Baz Bastien Trophy (1995-96). ... Named to AHL All-Star first team (1995-96).

MISCELLANEOUS: Member of silver-medal-winning Canadian Olympic team (1994).

Season Team	League	REGULAR SEASON								PLAYOFFS						
		Gms.	Min	W	L	T	GA	SO	Avg.	Gms.	Min.	W	L	GA	SO	Avg.
89-90—Vaughan-Thornhill Jr. B	OHA	29	1660	...	...	...	119	1	4.30	—	—			—	—	—
90-91—Niagara Falls	OHL	30	1515	13	11	2	107	0	4.24	4	119	...	...	10	0	5.04
91-92—Niagara Falls	OHL	43	2384	21	16	3	143	0	3.60	14	791	...	...	56	0	4.25
92-93—Niagara Falls	OHL	†48	*2630	22	19	3	*170	0	3.88	4	240	0	4	18	0	4.50
93-94—Canadian nat'l team	Int'l	16	859	8	6	0	36	2	2.51	—	—			—	—	—
94-95—Springfield	AHL	39	2169	12	17	6	128	2	3.54	—	—			—	—	—
95-96—Springfield	AHL	37	2196	20	12	4	83	*5	*2.27	4	220	1	3	18	0	4.91

Season Team	League				REGULAR SEASON								PLAYOFFS				
		Gms.	Min	W	L	T	GA	SO	Avg.	Gms.	Min.	W	L	GA	SO	Avg.
96-97—Springfield	AHL	36	2119	17	14	5	107	1	3.03	12	746	9	3	25	†2	2.01
—Richmond	ECHL	3	157	2	1	0	8	0	3.06	—	—	—	—	—	—	—
97-98—Las Vegas	IHL	41	2107	18	16	4	111	1	3.16	4	237	1	3	16	0	4.05
—Springfield	AHL	6	345	4	2	0	16	0	2.78	—	—	—	—	—	—	—
98-99—Long Beach	IHL	33	1796	22	8	‡1	67	2	2.24	6	338	4	2	9	0	1.60
—Los Angeles	NHL	17	899	2	9	2	39	0	2.60	—	—	—	—	—	—	—
99-00—Manitoba	IHL	42	2409	20	18	‡5	104	2	2.59	2	141	0	2	7	0	2.98
—Detroit	NHL	4	240	4	0	0	11	0	2.75	—	—	—	—	—	—	—
00-01—Detroit	NHL	39	2136	24	5	5	73	2	2.05	—	—	—	—	—	—	—
NHL Totals (3 years)		60	3275	30	14	7	123	2	2.25							

LEGWAND, DAVID   C   PREDATORS

PERSONAL: Born August 17, 1980, in Detroit. ... 6-2/185. ... Shoots left.
TRANSACTIONS/CAREER NOTES: Selected by Nashville Predators in first round (first Predators pick, second overall) of NHL entry draft (June 27, 1998). ... Fractured left foot (January 13, 2000); missed 11 games.
HONORS: Named to Can.HL All-Star second team (1997-98). ... Won Red Tilson Trophy (1997-98). ... Won Emms Family Award (1997-98). ... Won Can.HL Rookie of the Year Award (1997-98). ... Named to OHL All-Star first team (1997-98). ... Named to OHL All-Rookie first team (1997-98).
MISCELLANEOUS: Scored on a penalty shot (vs. Kirk McLean, December 23, 2000).

Season Team	League				REGULAR SEASON						PLAYOFFS			
		Gms.	G	A	Pts.	PIM	+/-	PP	SH	Gms.	G	A	Pts.	PIM
96-97—Detroit	Jr. A	44	21	41	62	58	...	...	...	—	—	—	—	—
97-98—Plymouth	OHL	59	54	51	105	56	...	...	...	15	8	12	20	24
98-99—Plymouth	OHL	55	31	49	80	65	...	...	...	11	3	8	11	8
—Nashville	NHL	1	0	0	0	0	0	0	0	—	—	—	—	—
99-00—Nashville	NHL	71	13	15	28	30	-6	4	0	—	—	—	—	—
00-01—Nashville	NHL	81	13	28	41	38	1	3	0	—	—	—	—	—
NHL Totals (3 years)		153	26	43	69	68	-5	7	0					

LEHTINEN, JERE   LW   STARS

PERSONAL: Born June 24, 1973, in Espoo, Finland. ... 6-0/192. ... Shoots right. ... Name pronounced YAIR-ee LEH-tih-nehn.
TRANSACTIONS/CAREER NOTES: Selected by Minnesota North Stars in fourth round (third North Stars pick, 88th overall) of NHL entry draft (June 20, 1992). ... North Stars franchise moved from Minnesota to Dallas and renamed Stars for 1993-94 season. ... Strained groin (December 21, 1995); missed six games. ... Reinjured groin (January 10, 1996); missed one game. ... Sprained ankle (March 20, 1996); missed remainder of season. ... Sprained knee (January 31, 1997); missed 13 games. ... Sprained knee (March 5, 1997); missed five games. ... Separated shoulder (October 19, 1997); missed 10 games. ... Fractured thumb (November 14, 1998); missed five games. ... Sprained ankle (March 25, 1999); missed two games. ... Fractured ankle (October 16, 1999); missed 30 games. ... Injured ankle (January 19, 2000); missed 35 games. ... Suffered from the flu (November 14, 2000); missed one game. ... Sprained ankle (December 6, 2000); missed five games. ... Suffered from hip flexor (February 15, 2001); missed two games.
HONORS: Played in NHL All-Star Game (1998). ... Won Frank J. Selke Trophy (1997-98 and 1998-99).
MISCELLANEOUS: Member of Stanley Cup championship team (1999). ... Member of bronze-medal-winning Finnish Olympic team (1994 and 1998). ... Scored on a penalty shot (vs. Dominik Hasek, October 7, 1997).
STATISTICAL PLATEAUS: Three-goal games: 2000-01 (1).

Season Team	League				REGULAR SEASON						PLAYOFFS			
		Gms.	G	A	Pts.	PIM	+/-	PP	SH	Gms.	G	A	Pts.	PIM
90-91—Kiekko-Espoo	Finland	32	15	9	24	12	...	...	...	—	—	—	—	—
91-92—Kiekko-Espoo	Finland	43	32	17	49	6	...	...	...	—	—	—	—	—
92-93—Kiekko-Espoo	Finland	45	13	14	27	6	...	...	...	—	—	—	—	—
93-94—TPS Turku	Finland	42	19	20	39	6	...	...	...	11	11	2	13	2
—Fin. Olympic team	Int'l	8	3	0	3	11	...	...	...	—	—	—	—	—
94-95—TPS Turku	Finland	39	19	23	42	33	...	...	...	13	8	6	14	4
95-96—Dallas	NHL	57	6	22	28	16	5	0	0	—	—	—	—	—
—Michigan	IHL	1	1	0	1	0	...	...	...	—	—	—	—	—
96-97—Dallas	NHL	63	16	27	43	2	26	3	1	7	2	2	4	0
97-98—Dallas	NHL	72	23	19	42	20	19	7	2	12	3	5	8	2
—Fin. Olympic team	Int'l	6	4	2	6	2	...	...	...	—	—	—	—	—
98-99—Dallas	NHL	74	20	32	52	18	29	7	1	23	10	3	13	2
99-00—Dallas	NHL	17	3	5	8	0	1	0	0	13	1	5	6	2
00-01—Dallas	NHL	74	20	25	45	24	14	7	0	10	1	0	1	2
NHL Totals (6 years)		357	88	130	218	80	94	24	4	65	17	15	32	8

LEMIEUX, CLAUDE   RW   COYOTES

PERSONAL: Born July 16, 1965, in Buckingham, Que. ... 6-1/215. ... Shoots right. ... Brother of Jocelyn Lemieux, right winger with seven NHL teams (1986-87 through 1997-98). ... Name pronounced luh-MYOO.
TRANSACTIONS/CAREER NOTES: Selected by Montreal Canadiens in second round (second Canadiens pick, 26th overall) of NHL entry draft (June 8, 1983). ... Tore ankle ligaments (October 1987). ... Fractured orbital bone above right eye (January 14, 1988). ... Pulled groin (March 1989). ... Underwent surgery to repair torn stomach muscle (November 1, 1989); missed 41 games. ... Traded by Canadiens to New Jersey Devils for LW Sylvain Turgeon (September 4, 1990). ... Bruised right eye retina (February 25, 1991). ... Suffered sore back (November 27, 1991); missed four games. ... Injured ankle (March 11, 1992); missed two games. ... Suffered back spasms (October 24, 1992); missed three games. ... Injured right elbow (March 21, 1993); missed one game. ... Suspended three games and fined $500 by NHL for altercation with opponent's bench (March 28, 1995). ... Traded by Devils to New York Islanders for RW Steve Thomas (October 3, 1995). ... Traded by Islanders to Colorado Avalanche for LW Wendel Clark (October 3, 1995). ... Fractured finger (December 5, 1995); missed two games. ... Suspended one

playoff game and fined $1,000 by NHL for punching another player (May 24, 1996). ... Suspended two games in Stanley Cup finals and fined $1,000 by NHL for checking from behind (June 2, 1996). ... Tore abdominal muscle (October 5, 1996); missed 37 games. ... Injured back (March 2, 1998); missed two games. ... Traded by Avalanche with second-round pick (D Matt DeMarchi) in 2000 draft and swap of first-round picks in 2000 draft to Devils for LW Brian Rolston and a conditional third-round pick in the 2001 draft (November 3, 1999). ... Signed as free agent by Phoenix Coyotes (December 2, 2000). ... Sprained ankle (March 4, 2001); missed eight games.

HONORS: Named to QMJHL All-Star second team (1983-84). ... Won Guy Lafleur Trophy (1984-85). ... Named to QMJHL All-Star first team (1984-85). ... Won Conn Smythe Trophy (1994-95).

MISCELLANEOUS: Member of Stanley Cup championship teams (1986, 1995, 1996 and 2000).

STATISTICAL NOTES: Led NHL in games played with 83 (1999-2000).

STATISTICAL PLATEAUS: Three-goal games: 1988-89 (1), 1990-91 (2), 1992-93 (1), 1995-96 (2), 1997-98 (1). Total: 7.

		REGULAR SEASON								PLAYOFFS				
Season Team	League	Gms.	G	A	Pts.	PIM	+/-	PP	SH	Gms.	G	A	Pts.	PIM
82-83—Trois-Rivieres.............	QMJHL	62	28	38	66	187	...	...	...	4	1	0	1	30
83-84—Verdun.....................	QMJHL	51	41	45	86	225	...	...	...	9	8	12	20	63
—Montreal	NHL	8	1	1	2	12	-2	0	0	—	—	—	—	—
—Nova Scotia	AHL	—	—	—	—	—	...	...	...	2	1	0	1	0
84-85—Verdun.....................	QMJHL	52	58	66	124	152	...	...	...	14	*23	17	*40	38
—Montreal	NHL	1	0	1	1	7	1	0	0	—	—	—	—	—
85-86—Sherbrooke..............	AHL	58	21	32	53	145	...	...	...	—	—	—	—	—
—Montreal	NHL	10	1	2	3	22	-6	1	0	20	10	6	16	68
86-87—Montreal.................	NHL	76	27	26	53	156	0	5	0	17	4	9	13	41
87-88—Montreal.................	NHL	78	31	30	61	137	16	6	0	11	3	2	5	20
88-89—Montreal.................	NHL	69	29	22	51	136	14	7	0	18	4	3	7	58
89-90—Montreal.................	NHL	39	8	10	18	106	-8	3	0	11	1	3	4	38
90-91—New Jersey.............	NHL	78	30	17	47	105	-8	10	0	7	4	0	4	34
91-92—New Jersey.............	NHL	74	41	27	68	109	9	13	1	7	4	3	7	26
92-93—New Jersey.............	NHL	77	30	51	81	155	3	13	0	5	2	0	2	19
93-94—New Jersey.............	NHL	79	18	26	44	86	13	5	0	20	7	11	18	44
94-95—New Jersey.............	NHL	45	6	13	19	86	2	1	0	20	*13	3	16	20
95-96—Colorado.................	NHL	79	39	32	71	117	14	9	2	19	5	7	12	55
96-97—Colorado.................	NHL	45	11	17	28	43	-4	5	0	17	13	10	23	32
97-98—Colorado.................	NHL	78	26	27	53	115	-7	11	1	7	3	3	6	8
98-99—Colorado.................	NHL	82	27	24	51	102	0	11	0	19	3	11	14	26
99-00—Colorado.................	NHL	13	3	6	9	4	0	0	0	—	—	—	—	—
—New Jersey.............	NHL	70	17	21	38	86	-3	7	0	23	4	6	10	28
00-01—Phoenix....................	NHL	46	10	16	26	58	1	2	0	—	—	—	—	—
NHL Totals (18 years).........		1047	355	369	724	1642	35	109	4	221	80	77	157	517

LEMIEUX, MARIO   C   PENGUINS

PERSONAL: Born October 5, 1965, in Montreal. ... 6-4/220. ... Shoots right. ... Brother of Alain Lemieux, center for three NHL teams (1981-82 through 1986-87). ... Name pronounced luh-MYOO.

TRANSACTIONS/CAREER NOTES: Selected by Pittsburgh Penguins in first round (first Penguins pick, first overall) of NHL entry draft (June 9, 1984). ... Sprained left knee (September 1984). ... Reinjured knee (December 2, 1984). ... Sprained right knee (December 20, 1986). ... Bruised right shoulder (November 1987). ... Sprained right wrist (November 3, 1988). ... Suffered herniated disk (February 14, 1990); missed 21 games. ... Underwent surgery to remove part of herniated disk (July 11, 1990); missed first 50 games of season. ... Suffered back spasms (October 1991); missed three games. ... Suffered back spasms (January 4, 1992); missed three games. ... Injured back (January 29, 1992); missed six games. ... Suffered from the flu (February 1992); missed one game. ... Fractured bone in hand (May 5, 1992). ... Injured heel (December 1992); missed one game. ... Injured back (January 5, 1993); missed three games. ... Diagnosed with Hodgkin's Disease (January 12, 1993) and underwent radiation treatment (February 1-March 2); missed 20 games. ... Injured back prior to 1993-94 season; missed first 10 games of season. ... Injured back (October 28, 1993); missed one game. ... Injured back (November 2, 1993); missed one game. ... Suffered from the flu (November 9, 1993); missed one game. ... Injured back (November 11, 1993); missed 38 games. ... Injured back (February 13, 1994); missed two games. ... Injured back (February 19, 1994); missed two games. ... Injured back (March 12, 1994); missed four games. ... Fined $500 by NHL for charging at a referee (April 6, 1994). ... On medical leave of absence during entire 1994-95 season. ... Suffered back spasms (November 9, 1996); missed one game. ... Suffered back spasms (January 21, 1997); missed one game. ... Suffered back spasms (February 4, 1997); missed one game. ... Suffered hip flexor (March 4, 1997); missed one game. ... Suffered hip flexor (March 14, 1997); missed two games.

HONORS: Named to QMJHL All-Star second team (1982-83). ... Won Can.HL Player of the Year Award (1983-84). ... Won Jean Beliveau Trophy (1983-84). ... Won Michael Bossy Trophy (1983-84). ... Won Guy Lafleur Trophy (1983-84). ... Named to QMJHL All-Star first team (1983-84). ... Named NHL Rookie of the Year by THE SPORTING NEWS (1984-85). ... Won Calder Memorial Trophy (1984-85). ... Named to NHL All-Rookie team (1984-85). ... Won Lester B. Pearson Award (1985-86, 1987-88, 1992-93 and 1995-96). ... Named to THE SPORTING NEWS All-Star second team (1985-86). ... Named to NHL All-Star second team (1985-86, 1986-87, 1991-92 and 2000-01). ... Played in NHL All-Star Game (1985, 1986, 1988-1990, 1992, 1996, 1997 and 2001). ... Named All-Star Game Most Valuable Player (1985, 1988 and 1990). ... Named NHL Player of the Year by THE SPORTING NEWS (1987-1988, 1988-89, 1992-93 and 1995-96). ... Won Hart Memorial Trophy (1987-88, 1992-93 and 1995-96). ... Won Art Ross Memorial Trophy (1987-88, 1988-89, 1991-92, 1992-93, 1995-96 and 1996-97). ... Won Dodge Performance of the Year Award (1987-88). ... Won Dodge Performer of the Year Award (1987-88 and 1988-89). ... Named to THE SPORTING NEWS All-Star first team (1987-88, 1988-89, 1992-93 and 1995-96). ... Named to NHL All-Star first team (1987-88, 1988-89, 1992-93, 1995-96 and 1996-97). ... Won Dodge Ram Tough Award (1988-89). ... Won Conn Smythe Trophy (1990-91 and 1991-92). ... Won Pro Set NHL Player of the Year Award (1991-92). ... Won Bill Masterton Memorial Trophy (1992-93). ... Named to THE SPORTING NEWS All-Star team (1996-97). ... Named to THE SPORTING NEWS All-Star second team (2000-01).

RECORDS: Holds NHL career records for highest goals-per-game average—.823; and most overtime points—19. ... Holds NHL single-season record for most shorthanded goals—13 (1988-89). ... Shares NHL single-game playoff records for most goals—5 (April 25, 1989); most single-season playoff game-winning goals—5 (1992); most points—8 (April 25, 1989); most goals in one period—4 (April 25, 1989); and most points in one period—4 (April 25, 1989 and April 23, 1992). ... Holds NHL All-Star single-game record for most points—6 (1988). ... Shares NHL All-Star single-game record for most goals—4 (1990).

STATISTICAL PLATEAUS: Three-goal games: 1986-87 (5), 1987-88 (3), 1988-89 (7), 1989-90 (3), 1990-91 (1), 1991-92 (1), 1992-93 (1), 1995-96 (4), 1996-97 (1), 2000-01 (1). Total: 27. ... Four-goal games: 1985-86 (1), 1986-87 (1), 1987-88 (2), 1988-89 (1), 1989-90 (1), 1992-93 (2), 1995-96 (1), 1996-97 (1). Total: 10. ... Five-goal games: 1988-89 (1), 1992-93 (1), 1995-96 (1). Total: 3. ... Total hat tricks: 40.

MISCELLANEOUS: Member of Stanley Cup championship teams (1991 and 1992). ... Captain of Pittsburgh Penguins (1987-88 through 1993-94 and 1996-97). ... Holds Pittsburgh Penguins all-time records for most goals (648), most assists (922) and most points (1,570). ...

Scored on a penalty shot (vs. Mario Gosselin, December 29, 1984; vs. Kelly Hrudey, January 19, 1988; vs. Chris Terreri, December 31, 1988; vs. Kelly Hrudey, March 7, 1989; vs. Bob Mason, November 24, 1989; vs. John Vanbiesbrouck, April 11, 1997). ... Failed to score on a penalty shot (vs. Bill Ranford, March 17, 1992; vs. Dominik Hasek, March 23, 1996).

		REGULAR SEASON							PLAYOFFS				
Season Team	League	Gms.	G	A	Pts.	PIM	+/-	PP	SH	Gms.	G	A	Pts.	PIM
81-82—Laval	QMJHL	64	30	66	96	22	...	...	...	18	5	9	14	31
82-83—Laval	QMJHL	66	84	100	184	76	...	...	...	12	†14	18	32	18
83-84—Laval	QMJHL	70	*133	*149	*282	92	...	...	...	14	*29	*23	*52	29
84-85—Pittsburgh	NHL	73	43	57	100	54	-35	11	0	—	—	—	—	—
85-86—Pittsburgh	NHL	79	48	93	141	43	-6	17	0	—	—	—	—	—
86-87—Pittsburgh	NHL	63	54	53	107	57	13	19	0	—	—	—	—	—
87-88—Pittsburgh	NHL	77	*70	98	*168	92	23	22	*10	—	—	—	—	—
88-89—Pittsburgh	NHL	76	*85	†114	*199	100	41	*31	*13	11	12	7	19	16
89-90—Pittsburgh	NHL	59	45	78	123	78	-18	14	3	—	—	—	—	—
90-91—Pittsburgh	NHL	26	19	26	45	30	8	6	1	23	16	*28	*44	16
91-92—Pittsburgh	NHL	64	44	87	*131	94	27	12	4	15	*16	18	*34	2
92-93—Pittsburgh	NHL	60	69	91	*160	38	*55	16	6	11	8	10	18	10
93-94—Pittsburgh	NHL	22	17	20	37	32	-2	7	0	6	4	3	7	2
94-95—Pittsburgh	NHL							Did not play.						
95-96—Pittsburgh	NHL	70	*69	†92	*161	54	10	*31	*8	18	11	16	27	33
96-97—Pittsburgh	NHL	76	50	†72	*122	65	27	15	3	5	3	3	6	4
97-98—								Did not play.						
98-99—								Did not play.						
99-00—								Did not play.						
00-01—Pittsburgh	NHL	43	35	41	76	18	15	16	1	18	6	11	17	4
NHL Totals (17 years)		788	648	922	1570	755	158	217	49	107	76	96	172	87

LEOPOLD, JORDAN — D — FLAMES

L

PERSONAL: Born August 3, 1980, in Golden Valley, Minn. ... 6-0/193. ... Shoots left.
TRANSACTIONS/CAREER NOTES: Selected by Mighty Ducks of Anaheim in second round (first Mighty Ducks pick, 44th overall) of NHL entry draft (June 26, 1999). ... Traded by Mighty Ducks to Calgary Flames for LW Andrei Nazarov and second-round pick (traded back to Calgary) in 2001 draft (September 26, 2000).
HONORS: Named to WCHA All-Star first team (1999-2000 and 2000-01). ... Named to NCAA All-America (West) first team (2000-01).

		REGULAR SEASON							PLAYOFFS				
Season Team	League	Gms.	G	A	Pts.	PIM	+/-	PP	SH	Gms.	G	A	Pts.	PIM
97-98—U.S. National	NAHL	60	11	12	23	16	...	...	...	—	—	—	—	—
98-99—Univ. of Minnesota	WCHA	39	7	16	23	20	...	...	...	—	—	—	—	—
99-00—Univ. of Minnesota	WCHA	39	6	18	24	20	...	...	...	—	—	—	—	—
00-01—Univ. of Minnesota	WCHA	42	12	37	49	38	...	...	...	—	—	—	—	—

LEROUX, JEAN-YVES — LW

PERSONAL: Born June 24, 1976, in Montreal. ... 6-2/211. ... Shoots left. ... Name pronounced zhahn-eev luh-ROO.
TRANSACTIONS/CAREER NOTES: Selected by Chicago Blackhawks in second round (second Blackhawks pick, 40th overall) of NHL entry draft (June 28, 1994). ... Pulled abdominal muscle (October 29, 1997); missed two games. ... Injured shoulder (November 20, 1997); missed one game. ... Injured shoulder (December 4, 1997); missed one game. ... Injured back (February 3, 1998); missed three games. ... Suffered concussion (March 29, 1998); missed four games. ... Tore abdominal muscle (September 19, 1998) and underwent surgery; missed first 42 games of season. ... Suffered from strept throat (November 27, 1999); missed one game. ... Strained groin (December 6, 1999); missed 18 games. ... Fractured finger (March 3, 2000); missed seven games. ... Sprained knee (November 11, 2000); missed 17 games.

		REGULAR SEASON							PLAYOFFS				
Season Team	League	Gms.	G	A	Pts.	PIM	+/-	PP	SH	Gms.	G	A	Pts.	PIM
92-93—Beauport	QMJHL	62	20	25	45	33	...	...	...	—	—	—	—	—
93-94—Beauport	QMJHL	45	14	25	39	43	...	...	...	15	7	6	13	33
94-95—Beauport	QMJHL	59	19	33	52	125	...	...	...	17	4	6	10	39
95-96—Beauport	QMJHL	54	41	41	82	176	...	...	...	20	5	18	23	20
96-97—Indianapolis	IHL	69	14	17	31	112	...	...	...	4	1	0	1	2
—Chicago	NHL	1	0	1	1	5	1	0	0	—	—	—	—	—
97-98—Chicago	NHL	66	6	7	13	55	-2	0	0	—	—	—	—	—
98-99—Chicago	NHL	40	3	5	8	21	-7	0	0	—	—	—	—	—
99-00—Chicago	NHL	54	3	5	8	43	-10	0	0	—	—	—	—	—
00-01—Chicago	NHL	59	4	4	8	22	-9	1	0	—	—	—	—	—
NHL Totals (5 years)		220	16	22	38	146	-27	1	0					

LESCHYSHYN, CURTIS — D — SENATORS

PERSONAL: Born September 21, 1969, in Thompson, Man. ... 6-1/205. ... Shoots left. ... Full Name: Curtis Michael Leschyshyn. ... Name pronounced luh-SIH-shhn.
TRANSACTIONS/CAREER NOTES: Selected by Quebec Nordiques in first round (first Nordiques pick, third overall) of NHL entry draft (June 11, 1988). ... Separated shoulder (January 10, 1989). ... Sprained left knee (November 1989). ... Damaged knee ligaments (February 18, 1991) and underwent surgery; missed final 19 games of 1990-91 season and first 30 games of 1991-92 season. ... Strained back (October 13, 1992); missed two games. ... Injured right collarbone (December 30, 1994); missed two games. ... Pulled thigh muscle (March 19, 1994); missed two games. ... Injured groin (March 31, 1994); missed remainder of season. ... Lacerated groin (April 22, 1995); missed last four games of season. ... Nordiques franchise moved to Colorado and renamed Avalanche for 1995-96 season (June 21, 1995). ... Injured hip flexor (January 17, 1996); missed three games. ... Traded by Avalanche with LW Chris Simon to Washington Capitals for RW Keith Jones and first- (D Scott Parker) and fourth-round (traded back to Washington) picks in 1998 draft (November 2, 1996). ... Traded by Capitals to Hartford Whalers for C Andrei Nikolishin (November 9, 1996). ... Injured abdominal muscle (March 7, 1997); missed five games. ... Whalers franchise moved to

North Carolina and renamed Carolina Hurricanes for 1997-98 season; NHL approved move on June 25, 1997. ... Strained groin (September 25, 1997); missed four games. ... Strained groin (November 13, 1997); missed one game. ... Suffered back spasms (February 28, 1998); missed one game. ... Suffered back spasms (December 5, 1998); missed three games. ... Bruised sternum (December 19, 1998); missed one game. ... Strained groin (January 4, 1999); missed six games. ... Strained groin (March 24, 1999); missed six games. ... Strained groin (January 27, 2000); missed 20 games. ... Reinjured groin (March 17, 2000); missed nine games. ... Selected by Minnesota Wild in NHL expansion draft (June 23, 2000). ... Strained groin (October 20, 2000); missed one game. ... Reinjured groin (November 3, 2000); missed three games. ... Reinjured groin (November 28, 2000); missed 10 games. ... Traded by Wild to Ottawa Senators for third-round pick (C Stephane Veilleux) in 2001 draft and future considerations (March 13, 2001). ... Suffered concussion (April 3, 2001); missed final two games of regular season.

HONORS: Named to WHL (East) All-Star first team (1987-88).

MISCELLANEOUS: Member of Stanley Cup championship team (1996).

Season Team	League	REGULAR SEASON								PLAYOFFS				
		Gms.	G	A	Pts.	PIM	+/-	PP	SH	Gms.	G	A	Pts.	PIM
85-86—Saskatoon	WHL	1	0	0	0	0	...	...	...	—	—	—	—	—
86-87—Saskatoon	WHL	70	14	26	40	107	...	...	...	11	1	5	6	14
87-88—Saskatoon	WHL	56	14	41	55	86	...	...	...	10	2	5	7	16
88-89—Quebec	NHL	71	4	9	13	71	-32	1	1	—	—	—	—	—
89-90—Quebec	NHL	68	2	6	8	44	-41	1	0	—	—	—	—	—
90-91—Quebec	NHL	55	3	7	10	49	-19	2	0	—	—	—	—	—
91-92—Quebec	NHL	42	5	12	17	42	-28	3	0	—	—	—	—	—
—Halifax	AHL	6	0	2	2	4	...	...	...	—	—	—	—	—
92-93—Quebec	NHL	82	9	23	32	61	25	4	0	6	1	1	2	6
93-94—Quebec	NHL	72	5	17	22	65	-2	3	0	—	—	—	—	—
94-95—Quebec	NHL	44	2	13	15	20	29	0	0	3	0	1	1	4
95-96—Colorado	NHL	77	4	15	19	73	32	0	0	17	1	2	3	8
96-97—Colorado	NHL	11	0	5	5	6	1	0	0	—	—	—	—	—
—Washington	NHL	2	0	0	0	2	0	0	0	—	—	—	—	—
—Hartford	NHL	64	4	13	17	30	-19	1	1	—	—	—	—	—
97-98—Carolina	NHL	73	2	10	12	45	-2	1	0	—	—	—	—	—
98-99—Carolina	NHL	65	2	7	9	50	-1	0	0	6	0	0	0	6
99-00—Carolina	NHL	53	0	2	2	14	-19	0	0	—	—	—	—	—
00-01—Minnesota	NHL	54	2	3	5	19	-2	1	0	—	—	—	—	—
—Ottawa	NHL	11	0	4	4	0	7	0	0	4	0	0	0	0
NHL Totals (13 years)		844	44	146	190	591	-71	17	2	36	2	4	6	24

LESSARD, FRANCIS D FLYERS

PERSONAL: Born May 30, 1979, in Montreal. ... 6-2/184. ... Shoots right. ... Name pronounced luh-SAHRD.

TRANSACTIONS/CAREER NOTES: Selected by Carolina Hurricanes in third round (third Hurricanes pick, 80th overall) of NHL entry draft (June 21, 1997). ... Traded by Hurricanes to Philadelphia Flyers for eighth-round pick (G Antti Jokela) in 1999 draft (May 25, 1999).

Season Team	League	REGULAR SEASON								PLAYOFFS				
		Gms.	G	A	Pts.	PIM	+/-	PP	SH	Gms.	G	A	Pts.	PIM
96-97—Val-d'Or	QMJHL	66	1	9	10	287	...	...	...	—	—	—	—	—
97-98—Val-d'Or	QMJHL	63	3	20	23	338	...	...	...	19	1	6	7	*101
98-99—Drummondville	QMJHL	53	12	36	48	295	...	...	...	—	—	—	—	—
99-00—Philadelphia	AHL	78	4	8	12	416	...	...	...	5	0	1	1	7
00-01—Philadelphia	AHL	64	3	7	10	330	...	...	...	10	0	0	0	33

LETOWSKI, TREVOR C COYOTES

PERSONAL: Born April 5, 1977, in Thunder Bay, Ont. ... 5-10/176. ... Shoots right.

TRANSACTIONS/CAREER NOTES: Selected by Phoenix Coyotes in seventh round (sixth Coyotes pick, 174th overall) of NHL entry draft (June 22, 1996).

Season Team	League	REGULAR SEASON								PLAYOFFS				
		Gms.	G	A	Pts.	PIM	+/-	PP	SH	Gms.	G	A	Pts.	PIM
94-95—Sarnia	OHL	66	22	19	41	33	...	...	...	4	0	1	1	9
95-96—Sarnia	OHL	66	36	63	99	66	...	...	...	10	9	5	14	10
96-97—Sarnia	OHL	55	35	73	108	51	...	...	...	12	9	12	21	20
97-98—Springfield	AHL	75	11	20	31	26	...	...	...	4	1	2	3	18
98-99—Springfield	AHL	67	32	35	67	46	...	...	...	3	1	0	1	2
—Phoenix	NHL	14	2	2	4	2	1	0	0	—	—	—	—	—
99-00—Phoenix	NHL	82	19	20	39	20	2	3	4	5	1	1	2	4
00-01—Phoenix	NHL	77	7	15	22	32	-2	0	1	—	—	—	—	—
NHL Totals (3 years)		173	28	37	65	54	1	3	5	5	1	1	2	4

LIDSTROM, NICKLAS D RED WINGS

PERSONAL: Born April 28, 1970, in Vasteras, Sweden. ... 6-2/190. ... Shoots left. ... Name pronounced NIHK-luhs LIHD-struhm.

TRANSACTIONS/CAREER NOTES: Selected by Detroit Red Wings in third round (third Red Wings pick, 53rd overall) of NHL entry draft (June 17, 1989). ... Played in Europe during 1994-95 NHL lockout. ... Suffered back spasms (April 9, 1995); missed five games. ... Suffered from the flu (April 14, 1996); missed one game. ... Suffered from the flu (January 20, 1997); missed one game.

HONORS: Named to Swedish League All-Star team (1990-91). ... Named to NHL All-Rookie team (1991-92). ... Played in NHL All-Star Game (1996 and 1998-2001). ... Named to THE SPORTING NEWS All-Star team (1997-98 through 1999-2000). ... Named to NHL All-Star first team (1997-98 through 2000-01). ... Named to THE SPORTING NEWS All-Star first team (2000-01). ... Won James Norris Memorial Trophy (2000-01).

MISCELLANEOUS: Member of Stanley Cup championship team (1997 and 1998).

Season Team	League	REGULAR SEASON								PLAYOFFS				
		Gms.	G	A	Pts.	PIM	+/-	PP	SH	Gms.	G	A	Pts.	PIM
87-88—Vasteras	Sweden	3	0	0	0	0	...	...	...	—	—	—	—	—
88-89—Vasteras	Sweden	19	0	2	2	4	...	...	...	—	—	—	—	—
89-90—Vasteras	Sweden	39	8	8	16	14	...	...	...	—	—	—	—	—
90-91—Vasteras	Sweden	20	2	12	14	14	...	...	...	—	—	—	—	—
91-92—Detroit	NHL	80	11	49	60	22	36	5	0	11	1	2	3	0
92-93—Detroit	NHL	84	7	34	41	28	7	3	0	7	1	0	1	0
93-94—Detroit	NHL	84	10	46	56	26	43	4	0	7	3	2	5	0
94-95—Vasteras	Sweden	13	2	10	12	4	...	...	...	—	—	—	—	—
—Detroit	NHL	43	10	16	26	6	15	7	0	18	4	12	16	8
95-96—Vasteras	Sweden	13	2	10	12	4	...	...	...	—	—	—	—	—
—Detroit	NHL	81	17	50	67	20	29	8	1	19	5	9	14	10
96-97—Detroit	NHL	79	15	42	57	30	11	8	0	20	2	6	8	2
97-98—Detroit	NHL	80	17	42	59	18	22	7	1	22	6	13	19	8
—Swedish Oly. team	Int'l	4	1	1	2	2	...	...	...	—	—	—	—	—
98-99—Detroit	NHL	81	14	43	57	14	14	6	2	10	2	9	11	4
99-00—Detroit	NHL	81	20	53	73	18	19	9	4	9	2	4	6	4
00-01—Detroit	NHL	82	15	56	71	18	9	8	0	6	1	7	8	0
NHL Totals (10 years)		775	136	431	567	200	205	65	8	129	27	64	91	36

LILJA, ANDREAS   D   KINGS

PERSONAL: Born July 13, 1975, in Landskrona, Sweden. ... 6-3/220. ... Shoots left.

TRANSACTIONS/CAREER NOTES: Selected by Los Angeles Kings in second round (second Kings pick, 54th overall) of NHL entry draft (June 24, 2000).

Season Team	League	REGULAR SEASON								PLAYOFFS				
		Gms.	G	A	Pts.	PIM	+/-	PP	SH	Gms.	G	A	Pts.	PIM
95-96—Malmo	Sweden	40	1	5	6	63	...	...	...	5	0	1	1	2
96-97—Malmo	Sweden	47	1	0	1	22	...	...	...	4	0	0	0	10
97-98—Malmo	Sweden	10	0	0	0	0	...	...	...	—	—	—	—	—
98-99—Malmo	Sweden	41	0	3	3	14	...	...	...	1	0	0	0	4
99-00—Malmo	Sweden	49	8	11	19	88	...	...	...	6	0	0	0	8
00-01—Lowell	AHL	61	7	29	36	149	...	...	...	4	0	6	6	6
—Los Angeles	NHL	2	0	0	0	4	-2	0	0	1	0	0	0	0
NHL Totals (1 year)		2	0	0	0	4	-2	0	0	1	0	0	0	0

LIND, JUHA   C/LW

PERSONAL: Born January 2, 1974, in Helsinki, Finland. ... 5-11/185. ... Shoots left. ... Name pronounced YOO-hah LIHND.

TRANSACTIONS/CAREER NOTES: Selected by Minnesota North Stars in eighth round (sixth North Stars pick, 178th overall) of NHL entry draft (June 26, 1992). ... North Stars franchise moved from Minnesota to Dallas and renamed Stars for 1993-94 season. ... Bruised thigh (March 29, 1998); missed nine games. ... Strained lower back (October 26, 1999); missed five games. ... Traded by Stars to Montreal Canadiens for C Scott Thornton (January 22, 2000). ... Injured foot (February 2, 2000); missed one game. ... Strained hip flexor (February 12, 2000); missed 17 games.

MISCELLANEOUS: Member of bronze-medal-winning Finnish Olympic team (1998).

Season Team	League	REGULAR SEASON								PLAYOFFS				
		Gms.	G	A	Pts.	PIM	+/-	PP	SH	Gms.	G	A	Pts.	PIM
91-92—Jokerit Helsinki	Finland Jr.	28	16	24	40	10	...	...	...	—	—	—	—	—
92-93—Vantaa HT	Finland Div. 2	25	8	12	20	8	...	...	...	—	—	—	—	—
—Jokerit Helsinki	Finland	6	0	0	0	2	...	...	...	1	0	0	0	0
93-94—Jokerit Helsinki	Finland	47	17	11	28	37	...	...	...	11	2	5	7	4
94-95—Jokerit Helsinki	Finland	50	10	8	18	12	...	...	...	11	1	2	3	6
95-96—Jokerit Helsinki	Finland	50	15	22	37	32	...	...	...	11	4	5	9	4
96-97—Jokerit	Finland	50	16	22	38	28	...	...	...	9	5	3	8	0
97-98—Michigan	IHL	8	2	2	4	2	...	...	...	—	—	—	—	—
—Dallas	NHL	39	2	3	5	6	4	0	0	15	2	2	4	8
—Fin. Olympic team	Int'l	6	0	1	1	6	...	...	...	—	—	—	—	—
98-99—Jokerit	Finland	50	20	19	39	22	...	...	...	3	3	1	4	2
99-00—Dallas	NHL	34	3	4	7	6	-1	0	0	—	—	—	—	—
—Montreal	NHL	13	1	2	3	4	-2	0	0	—	—	—	—	—
00-01—Quebec	AHL	3	1	1	2	0	...	...	...	—	—	—	—	—
—Montreal	NHL	47	3	4	7	4	-4	0	0	—	—	—	—	—
NHL Totals (3 years)		133	9	13	22	20	-3	0	0	15	2	2	4	8

LINDEN, TREVOR   C   CAPITALS

PERSONAL: Born April 11, 1970, in Medicine Hat, Alta. ... 6-4/211. ... Shoots right. ... Brother of Jamie Linden, right winger with Florida Panthers organization (1993-94 through 1996-97).

TRANSACTIONS/CAREER NOTES: Selected by Vancouver Canucks in first round (first Canucks pick, second overall) of NHL entry draft (June 11, 1988). ... Hyperextended elbow (October 1989). ... Separated shoulder (March 17, 1990). ... Sprained knee ligament (December 1, 1996); missed 24 games. ... Bruised ribs (March 8, 1997); missed eight games. ... Injured knee (April 5, 1997); missed one game. ... Strained groin (November 16, 1997); missed eight games. ... Sprained medial collateral ligament in knee (January 26, 1998); missed six games. ... Traded by Canucks to New York Islanders for D Bryan McCabe, LW Todd Bertuzzi and third-round pick (LW Jarkko Ruutu) in 1998 draft (February 6, 1998). ... Traded by Islanders to Montreal Canadiens for first-round pick (D Branislav Mezei) in 1999 draft (May 29, 1999). ... Sprained ankle (December 1, 1999); missed 14 games. ... Reinjured ankle (January 6, 2000); missed six games. ... Fractured ribs (March 14, 2000); missed final 12 games of regular season. ... Bruised foot (December 8, 2000); missed one game. ... Bruised foot (December 30, 2000); missed 12 games. ... Traded by Canadiens with RW Dainius Zubrus and second-round pick (traded to Tampa Bay) in 2001 draft to Washington Capitals for F Jan Bulis, F Richard Zednik and first-round pick (C Alexander Perezhogin) in 2001 draft (March 13, 2001).

HONORS: Named to WHL All-Star second team (1987-88). ... Named to Memorial Cup All-Star team (1987-88). ... Named to NHL All-Rookie team (1988-89). ... Played in NHL All-Star Game (1991 and 1992). ... Won King Clancy Memorial Trophy (1996-97).
MISCELLANEOUS: Captain of Vancouver Canucks (1990-91 through 1996-97). ... Captain of New York Islanders (March 3, 1998 through 1998-99).
STATISTICAL PLATEAUS: Three-goal games: 1988-89 (2), 1990-91 (1), 1995-96 (1), 1999-00 (1). Total: 5.

Season Team	League	REGULAR SEASON Gms.	G	A	Pts.	PIM	+/-	PP	SH	PLAYOFFS Gms.	G	A	Pts.	PIM
85-86—Medicine Hat.............	WHL	5	2	0	2	0	...	...	...	—	—	—	—	—
86-87—Medicine Hat.............	WHL	72	14	22	36	59	...	...	...	20	5	4	9	17
87-88—Medicine Hat.............	WHL	67	46	64	110	76	...	...	...	16	†13	12	25	19
88-89—Vancouver................	NHL	80	30	29	59	41	-10	10	1	7	3	4	7	8
89-90—Vancouver................	NHL	73	21	30	51	43	-17	6	2	—	—	—	—	—
90-91—Vancouver................	NHL	80	33	37	70	65	-25	16	2	6	0	7	7	2
91-92—Vancouver................	NHL	80	31	44	75	101	3	6	1	13	4	8	12	6
92-93—Vancouver................	NHL	84	33	39	72	64	19	8	0	12	5	8	13	16
93-94—Vancouver................	NHL	84	32	29	61	73	6	10	2	24	12	13	25	18
94-95—Vancouver................	NHL	48	18	22	40	40	-5	9	0	11	2	6	8	12
95-96—Vancouver................	NHL	82	33	47	80	42	6	12	1	6	4	4	8	6
96-97—Vancouver................	NHL	49	9	31	40	27	5	2	2	—	—	—	—	—
97-98—Vancouver................	NHL	42	7	14	21	49	-13	2	0	—	—	—	—	—
—New York Islanders.....	NHL	25	10	7	17	33	-1	3	2	—	—	—	—	—
—Can. Olympic team	Int'l	6	1	0	1	10	...	...	...	—	—	—	—	—
98-99—New York Islanders.....	NHL	82	18	29	47	32	-14	8	1	—	—	—	—	—
99-00—Montreal	NHL	50	13	17	30	34	-3	4	0	—	—	—	—	—
00-01—Montreal	NHL	57	12	21	33	52	-2	6	0	—	—	—	—	—
—Washington	NHL	12	3	1	4	8	2	0	0	6	0	4	4	14
NHL Totals (13 years).........		928	303	397	700	704	-49	102	14	85	30	54	84	82

LINDGREN, MATS — C — ISLANDERS

PERSONAL: Born October 1, 1974, in Skelleftea, Sweden. ... 6-2/202. ... Shoots left.
TRANSACTIONS/CAREER NOTES: Selected by Winnipeg Jets in first round (first Jets pick, 15th overall) of NHL entry draft (June 26, 1993). ... Traded by Jets with D Boris Mironov and first-(C Jason Bonsignore) and fourth-round (RW Adam Copeland) picks in 1994 draft to Edmonton Oilers for D Dave Manson and sixth-round pick (traded to New Jersey) in 1994 draft (March 15, 1994). ... Strained lower back (March 17, 1995); missed 23 games. ... Suffered dislocated (September 23, 1998); missed first seven games of season. ... Suffered from the flu (November 14, 1998); missed one game. ... Traded by Oilers with eighth-round pick (F Radek Martinek) in 1999 draft to New York Islanders for G Tommy Salo (March 20, 1999). ... Injured shoulder (January 17, 2000) and underwent surgery; missed remainder of season. ... Dislocated left shoulder (November 24, 2000) and underwent surgery; missed remainder of season.
HONORS: Named Swedish League Rookie of the Year (1993-94).

Season Team	League	REGULAR SEASON Gms.	G	A	Pts.	PIM	+/-	PP	SH	PLAYOFFS Gms.	G	A	Pts.	PIM
90-91—Skelleftea	Sweden Dv. 2	1	0	0	0	0	...	...	...	—	—	—	—	—
91-92—Skelleftea	Sweden Dv. 2	29	14	8	22	14	...	...	...	—	—	—	—	—
92-93—Skelleftea	Sweden Dv. 2	32	20	14	34	18	...	...	...	—	—	—	—	—
93-94—Farjestad Karlstad	Sweden	22	11	6	17	26	...	...	...	—	—	—	—	—
94-95—Farjestad Karlstad	Sweden	37	17	15	32	20	...	...	...	3	0	0	0	4
95-96—Cape Breton	AHL	13	7	5	12	6	...	...	...	—	—	—	—	—
96-97—Hamilton	AHL	9	6	7	13	6	...	...	...	—	—	—	—	—
—Edmonton	NHL	69	11	14	25	12	-7	2	3	12	0	4	4	0
97-98—Edmonton	NHL	82	13	13	26	42	0	1	3	12	1	1	2	10
—Swedish Oly. team	Int'l	4	0	0	0	2	...	...	...	—	—	—	—	—
98-99—Edmonton	NHL	48	5	12	17	22	4	0	1	—	—	—	—	—
—New York Islanders.....	NHL	12	5	3	8	2	2	3	0	—	—	—	—	—
99-00—New York Islanders.....	NHL	43	9	7	16	24	0	1	0	—	—	—	—	—
00-01—New York Islanders.....	NHL	20	3	4	7	10	4	0	2	—	—	—	—	—
NHL Totals (5 years)...........		274	46	53	99	112	3	7	9	24	1	5	6	10

LINDROS, ERIC — C — FLYERS

PERSONAL: Born February 28, 1973, in London, Ont. ... 6-4/236. ... Shoots right. ... Brother of Brett Lindros, right winger with New York Islanders (1994-95 and 1995-96). ... Name pronounced LIHND-rahz.
TRANSACTIONS/CAREER NOTES: Selected by Quebec Nordiques in first round (first Nordiques pick, first overall) of NHL entry draft (June 22, 1991); refused to report. ... Traded by Nordiques to Philadelphia Flyers for G Ron Hextall, C Mike Ricci, C Peter Forsberg, D Steve Duchesne, D Kerry Huffman, first-round pick (G Jocelyn Thibault) in 1993 draft, cash and future considerations (June 20, 1992); Nordiques aquired LW Chris Simon and first-round pick (traded to Toronto Maple Leafs) in 1994 draft to complete deal (July 21, 1992). ... Sprained knee ligament (November 22, 1992); missed nine games. ... Injured knee (December 29, 1992); missed two games. ... Reinjured knee (January 10, 1993); missed 12 games. ... Tore ligament in right knee (November 12, 1993); missed 14 games. ... Suffered back spasms (March 6, 1994); missed one game. ... Sprained shoulder (April 4, 1994); missed remainder of season. ... Suffered from the flu (January 29, 1995); missed one game. ... Bruised eye (April 30, 1995); missed last game of season and first three playoff games. ... Bruised left knee (November 2, 1995); missed seven games. ... Injured knee (April 5, 1996); missed two games. ... Pulled right groin (October 1, 1996); missed 23 games. ... Bruised bone in back (February 13, 1997); missed two games. ... Suffered charley horse (March 2, 1997); missed one game. ... Bruised calf (March 22, 1997); missed two games. ... Suspended two games and fined $2,000 by NHL for two high-sticking incidents (April 9, 1997). ... Bruised ribs (November 6, 1997); missed one game. ... Suffered concussion (March 8, 1998); missed 18 games. ... Fined $1,000 by NHL for slashing incident (December 5, 1998). ... Suffered concussion (December 29, 1998); missed two games. ... Suspended two games by NHL for high-sticking incident (March 28, 1999). ... Suffered collapsed lung (April 1, 1999); missed remainder of season. ... Suffered illness (October 28, 1999); missed two games. ... Bruised left hand (December 11, 1999); missed two games. ... Suffered concussion (January 14, 2000); missed four games. ... Suffered back spasms (February 20, 2000); missed five games. ... Suffered concussion (March 13, 2000); missed final 14 games of regular season and missed 16 playoff games. ... Missed entire 2000-01 season due to contract dispute.

HONORS: Named to Memorial Cup All-Star Team (1989-90). ... Won Can.HL Player of the Year Award (1990-91). ... Won Can.HL Plus/Minus Award (1990-91). ... Won Can.HL Top Draft Prospect Award (1990-91). ... Won Red Tilson Trophy (1990-91). ... Won Eddie Powers Memorial Trophy (1990-91). ... Named to OHL All-Star first team (1990-91). ... Named to NHL All-Rookie team (1992-93). ... Played in NHL All-Star Game (1994 and 1996-2000). ... Named NHL Player of the Year by THE SPORTING NEWS (1994-95). ... Won Hart Memorial Trophy (1994-95). ... Won Lester B. Pearson Award (1994-95). ... Named to THE SPORTING NEWS All-Star first team (1994-95). ... Named to NHL All-Star first team (1994-95). ... Named to NHL All-Star second team (1995-96).
MISCELLANEOUS: Member of silver-medal-winning Canadian Olympic team (1992). ... Captain of Philadelphia Flyers (1994-95 through March 27, 1999). ... Scored on a penalty shot (vs. Don Beaupre, December 26, 1992; vs. Steve Shields, May 11, 1997 (playoffs)).
STATISTICAL NOTES: Tied for NHL lead with three game-tying goals (1998-99).
STATISTICAL PLATEAUS: Three-goal games: 1992-93 (3), 1993-94 (1), 1994-95 (3), 1995-96 (1), 1997-98 (1), 1999-00 (1). Total: 10. ... Four-goal games: 1996-97 (1). ... Total hat tricks: 11.

			REGULAR SEASON							PLAYOFFS				
Season Team	League	Gms.	G	A	Pts.	PIM	+/-	PP	SH	Gms.	G	A	Pts.	PIM
88-89—St. Michaels	MTHL	37	24	43	67	193	...	...	...	—	—	—	—	—
89-90—Detroit Compuware	NAJHL	14	23	29	52	123	...	...	...	—	—	—	—	—
—Oshawa	OHL	25	17	19	36	61	...	...	...	17	*18	18	36	*76
90-91—Oshawa	OHL	57	*71	78	*149	189	...	...	...	16	*18	20	*38	*93
91-92—Oshawa	OHL	13	9	22	31	54	...	...	...	—	—	—	—	—
—Canadian nat'l team	Int'l	24	19	16	35	34	...	...	...	—	—	—	—	—
—Can. Olympic team	Int'l	8	5	6	11	6	...	...	...	—	—	—	—	—
92-93—Philadelphia	NHL	61	41	34	75	147	28	8	1	—	—	—	—	—
93-94—Philadelphia	NHL	65	44	59	103	16	13	2	—	—	—	—	—	
94-95—Philadelphia	NHL	46	29	41	†70	60	27	7	0	12	4	11	15	18
95-96—Philadelphia	NHL	73	47	68	115	163	26	15	0	12	6	6	12	43
96-97—Philadelphia	NHL	52	32	47	79	136	31	9	0	19	12	14	26	40
97-98—Philadelphia	NHL	63	30	41	71	134	14	10	1	5	1	2	3	17
—Can. Olympic team	Int'l	6	2	3	5	2	...	...	...	—	—	—	—	—
98-99—Philadelphia	NHL	71	40	53	93	120	35	10	1	—	—	—	—	—
99-00—Philadelphia	NHL	55	27	32	59	83	11	10	1	2	1	0	1	0
00-01—							Did not play.							
NHL Totals (8 years)		486	290	369	659	946	188	82	6	50	24	33	57	118

LINDSAY, BILL — LW

PERSONAL: Born May 17, 1971, in Big Fork, Mont. ... 6-0/195. ... Shoots left. ... Full Name: William Hamilton Lindsay.
TRANSACTIONS/CAREER NOTES: Selected by Quebec Nordiques in fifth round (sixth Nordiques pick, 103rd overall) of NHL entry draft (June 22, 1991). ... Separated right shoulder (December 26, 1992); missed four games. ... Selected by Florida Panthers in NHL expansion draft (June 24, 1993). ... Lacerated left hand (February 22, 1996); missed seven games. ... Strained hip flexor (April 1, 1996); missed three games. ... Sprained knee (March 26, 1999); missed one game. ... Reinjured knee (April 7, 1999); missed final six games of season. ... Traded by Panthers to Calgary Flames for D Todd Simpson (September 30, 1999). ... Suffered injury (March 7, 2000); missed one game. ... Suffered injury (March 15, 2000); missed one game. ... Suspended two games by NHL for elbowing incident (December 14, 2000). ... Traded by Flames to San Jose Sharks for eighth-round pick (D Joe Campbell) in 2001 draft (March 6, 2001).
HONORS: Named to WHL (West) All-Star second team (1991-92).

			REGULAR SEASON							PLAYOFFS				
Season Team	League	Gms.	G	A	Pts.	PIM	+/-	PP	SH	Gms.	G	A	Pts.	PIM
88-89—Vernon	BCJHL	56	24	29	53	166	...	...	...	—	—	—	—	—
89-90—Tri-City	WHL	72	40	45	85	84	...	...	...	—	—	—	—	—
90-91—Tri-City	WHL	63	46	47	93	151	...	...	...	—	—	—	—	—
91-92—Tri-City	WHL	42	34	59	93	111	...	...	...	3	2	3	5	16
—Quebec	NHL	23	2	4	6	14	-6	0	0	—	—	—	—	—
92-93—Quebec	NHL	44	4	9	13	16	0	0	0	—	—	—	—	—
—Halifax	AHL	20	11	13	24	18	...	...	...	—	—	—	—	—
93-94—Florida	NHL	84	6	6	12	97	-2	0	0	—	—	—	—	—
94-95—Florida	NHL	48	10	9	19	46	1	0	1	—	—	—	—	—
95-96—Florida	NHL	73	12	22	34	57	13	0	3	22	5	5	10	18
96-97—Florida	NHL	81	11	23	34	120	1	0	1	3	0	1	1	8
97-98—Florida	NHL	82	12	16	28	80	-2	0	2	—	—	—	—	—
98-99—Florida	NHL	75	12	15	27	92	-1	0	1	—	—	—	—	—
99-00—Calgary	NHL	80	8	12	20	86	-7	0	0	—	—	—	—	—
00-01—Calgary	NHL	52	1	9	10	97	-8	0	0	—	—	—	—	—
—San Jose	NHL	16	0	4	4	29	2	0	0	6	0	0	0	16
NHL Totals (10 years)		658	78	129	207	734	-9	0	8	31	5	6	11	42

LINTNER, RICHARD — D — PREDATORS

PERSONAL: Born November 15, 1977, in Trencin, Czechoslovakia. ... 6-3/214. ... Shoots right.
TRANSACTIONS/CAREER NOTES: Selected by Phoenix Coyotes in fifth round (fourth Coyotes pick, 119th overall) of NHL entry draft (June 22, 1996). ... Traded by Coyotes with C Cliff Ronning to Nashville Predators for future considerations (October 31, 1998). ... Injured shoulder (April 3, 2000); missed final two games of season. ... Strained groin (October 7, 2000); missed four games. ... Strained groin (November 28, 2000); missed seven games. ... Suffered concussion (December 20, 2000); missed one game.

			REGULAR SEASON							PLAYOFFS				
Season Team	League	Gms.	G	A	Pts.	PIM	+/-	PP	SH	Gms.	G	A	Pts.	PIM
94-95—Dukla Trencin	Slovakia Jrs.	42	12	13	25	25	...	...	...	—	—	—	—	—
95-96—Dukla Trencin	Slovakia Jrs.	30	15	17	32	210	...	...	...	—	—	—	—	—
—Dukla Trencin	Slovakia	2	0	0	0	0	...	...	...	—	—	—	—	—
96-97—Spisska Nova Ves	Slovakia	35	2	1	3		...	...	...	—	—	—	—	—
97-98—Springfield	AHL	71	6	9	15	61	...	...	...	3	1	1	2	4
98-99—Springfield	AHL	8	0	1	1	16	...	...	...	—	—	—	—	—
—Milwaukee	IHL	66	9	16	25	75	...	...	...	—	—	—	—	—
99-00—Nashville	NHL	33	1	5	6	22	-6	0	0	—	—	—	—	—
—Milwaukee	IHL	31	13	8	21	37	...	...	...	—	—	—	—	—
00-01—Nashville	NHL	50	3	5	8	22	2	1	0	—	—	—	—	—
NHL Totals (2 years)		83	4	10	14	44	-4	1	0					

LOW, REED   RW   BLUES

PERSONAL: Born June 26, 1976, in Moose Jaw, Sask. ... 6-5/228. ... Shoots right.
TRANSACTIONS/CAREER NOTES: Selected by St. Louis Blues in seventh round (seventh Blues pick, 177th overall) of NHL entry draft (June 22, 1996). ... Injured thumb (January 29, 2001); missed three games.

Season Team	League	REGULAR SEASON								PLAYOFFS				
		Gms.	G	A	Pts.	PIM	+/-	PP	SH	Gms.	G	A	Pts.	PIM
94-95—Regina	WHL	2	0	0	0	5	...	...	...	—	—	—	—	—
95-96—Moose Jaw	WHL	61	12	7	19	221	...	...	...	—	—	—	—	—
96-97—Moose Jaw	WHL	62	16	11	27	228	...	...	...	12	2	1	3	50
97-98—Baton Rouge	ECHL	39	4	2	6	145	...	...	...	—	—	—	—	—
—Worcester	AHL	17	1	1	2	75	...	...	...	3	0	0	0	0
98-99—Worcester	AHL	77	5	6	11	239	...	...	...	4	0	0	0	2
99-00—Worcester	AHL	80	12	16	28	203	...	...	...	9	1	3	4	16
00-01—St. Louis	NHL	56	1	5	6	159	4	0	0	—	—	—	—	—
NHL Totals (1 year)		56	1	5	6	159	4	0	0					

LOWRY, DAVE   LW   FLAMES

PERSONAL: Born February 14, 1965, in Sudbury, Ont. ... 6-1/200. ... Shoots left. ... Name pronounced LOW-ree.
TRANSACTIONS/CAREER NOTES: Selected by Vancouver Canucks in sixth round (fourth Canucks pick, 110th overall) of NHL entry draft (June 8, 1983). ... Traded by Canucks to St. Louis Blues for C Ernie Vargas (September 29, 1988). ... Injured groin (March 1990). ... Sprained shoulder (October 1991); missed two games. ... Injured knee (October 26, 1992); missed 26 games. ... Selected by Florida Panthers in NHL expansion draft (June 24, 1993). ... Fractured cheekbone (November 26, 1993); missed three games. ... Injured knee (December 12, 1993); missed one game. ... Suffered abrasion to right cornea (April 28, 1995); missed three games. ... Sprained left knee (October 24, 1995); missed 18 games. ... Sprained knee ligament (February 9, 1997); missed three games. ... Traded by Panthers with first-round pick (traded to Tampa Bay) in 1998 draft to San Jose Sharks for LW Viktor Kozlov and fifth-round pick (D Jaroslav Spacek) in 1998 draft (November 13, 1997). ... Signed as free agent by San Jose Sharks (October 5, 1998). ... Injured shoulder (October 24, 1999); missed five games. ... Reinjured shoulder (November 27, 1999); missed 12 games. ... Injured back (January 29, 2000); missed six games. ... Signed as free agent by Calgary Flames (July 25, 2000). ... Injured hip (March 14, 2001); missed three games.
HONORS: Named to OHL All-Star first team (1984-85).
MISCELLANEOUS: Captain of Calgary Flames (December 7, 2000-2001).

Season Team	League	REGULAR SEASON								PLAYOFFS				
		Gms.	G	A	Pts.	PIM	+/-	PP	SH	Gms.	G	A	Pts.	PIM
82-83—London	OHL	42	11	16	27	48	...	...	...	3	0	0	0	14
83-84—London	OHL	66	29	47	76	125	...	...	...	8	6	6	12	41
84-85—London	OHL	61	60	60	120	94	...	...	...	8	6	5	11	10
85-86—Vancouver	NHL	73	10	8	18	143	-21	1	0	3	0	0	0	0
86-87—Vancouver	NHL	70	8	10	18	176	-23	0	0	—	—	—	—	—
87-88—Fredericton	AHL	46	18	27	45	59	...	...	...	14	7	3	10	72
—Vancouver	NHL	22	1	3	4	38	-2	0	0	—	—	—	—	—
88-89—Peoria	IHL	58	31	35	66	45	...	...	...	—	—	—	—	—
—St. Louis	NHL	21	3	3	6	11	1	0	1	10	0	5	5	4
89-90—St. Louis	NHL	78	19	6	25	75	1	0	2	12	2	1	3	39
90-91—St. Louis	NHL	79	19	21	40	168	19	0	2	13	1	4	5	35
91-92—St. Louis	NHL	75	7	13	20	77	-11	0	0	6	0	1	1	20
92-93—St. Louis	NHL	58	5	8	13	101	-18	0	0	11	2	0	2	14
93-94—Florida	NHL	80	15	22	37	64	-4	3	0	—	—	—	—	—
94-95—Florida	NHL	45	10	10	20	25	-3	2	0	—	—	—	—	—
95-96—Florida	NHL	63	10	14	24	36	-2	0	0	22	10	7	17	39
96-97—Florida	NHL	77	15	14	29	51	2	2	0	5	0	0	0	0
97-98—Florida	NHL	7	0	0	0	2	-1	0	0	—	—	—	—	—
—San Jose	NHL	50	4	4	8	51	0	0	0	6	0	0	0	18
98-99—San Jose	NHL	61	6	9	15	24	-5	2	0	1	0	0	0	0
99-00—San Jose	NHL	32	1	4	5	18	1	0	0	12	1	2	3	6
00-01—Calgary	NHL	79	18	17	35	47	-2	5	0	—	—	—	—	—
NHL Totals (16 years)		970	151	166	317	1107	-68	15	5	101	16	20	36	175

LUKOWICH, BRAD   D   STARS

PERSONAL: Born August 12, 1976, in Cranbrook, B.C. ... 6-1/200. ... Shoots left. ... Name pronounced LOO-kih-wihch.
TRANSACTIONS/CAREER NOTES: Selected by New York Islanders in fourth round (fourth Islanders pick, 90th overall) of NHL entry draft (June 29, 1994). ... Traded by Islanders to Dallas Stars for third-round pick (D Robert Schnabel) in 1997 draft (June 1, 1996). ... Suffered back spasms (December 6, 1999); missed one game. ... Traded by Stars with G Manny Fernandez to Minnesota Wild for third-round pick (C Joel Lundqvist) in 2000 draft and fourth-round pick in 2002 draft (June 12, 2000). ... Traded by Wild with third- (C Yared Hugos) and ninth-round (RW Dale Sullivan) picks in 2001 draft to Stars for C Aaron Gavey, C Pavel Patera, eighth-round pick (C Eric Johansson) in 2000 draft and fourth-round pick in 2002 draft (June 25, 2000).

Season Team	League	REGULAR SEASON								PLAYOFFS				
		Gms.	G	A	Pts.	PIM	+/-	PP	SH	Gms.	G	A	Pts.	PIM
92-93—Cranbook	Tier II Jr. A	54	21	41	62	162	...	...	...	—	—	—	—	—
—Kamloops	WHL	1	0	0	0	0	...	...	...	—	—	—	—	—
93-94—Kamloops	WHL	42	5	11	16	166	...	...	...	16	0	1	1	35
94-95—Kamloops	WHL	63	10	35	45	125	...	...	...	18	0	7	7	21
95-96—Kamloops	WHL	65	14	55	69	114	...	...	...	13	2	10	12	29
96-97—Michigan	IHL	69	2	6	8	77	...	...	...	4	0	1	1	2
97-98—Michigan	IHL	60	6	27	33	104	...	...	...	4	0	4	4	14
—Dallas	NHL	4	0	1	1	2	-2	0	0	—	—	—	—	—
98-99—Michigan	IHL	67	8	21	29	95	...	...	...	—	—	—	—	—
—Dallas	NHL	14	1	2	3	19	3	0	0	8	0	1	1	4
99-00—Dallas	NHL	60	3	1	4	50	-14	0	0	—	—	—	—	—
00-01—Dallas	NHL	80	4	10	14	76	28	0	0	10	1	0	1	4
NHL Totals (4 years)		158	8	14	22	147	15	0	0	18	1	1	2	8

LUMME, JYRKI   D   STARS

PERSONAL: Born July 16, 1966, in Tampere, Finland. ... 6-1/209. ... Shoots left. ... Name pronounced YUHR-kee LOO-mee.
TRANSACTIONS/CAREER NOTES: Selected by Montreal Canadiens in third round (third Canadiens pick, 57th overall) of NHL entry draft (June 21, 1986). ... Strained left knee ligaments (December 1988). ... Stretched knee ligaments (February 21, 1989). ... Bruised right foot (November 1989). ... Traded by Canadiens to Vancouver Canucks for second-round pick (C Craig Darby) in 1991 draft (March 6, 1990). ... Cut eye (November 19, 1991); missed three games. ... Sprained knee (January 19, 1993); missed nine games. ... Played in Europe during 1994-95 NHL lockout. ... Injured knee (February 15, 1995); missed six games. ... Bruised ribs (March 1, 1995); missed five games. ... Sprained ankle (November 13, 1996); missed two games. ... Strained shoulder (December 23, 1996); missed 11 games. ... Suffered charley horse (March 13, 1997); missed three games. ... Injured groin (October 11, 1997); missed two games. ... Strained groin (October 26, 1997); missed five games. ... Signed as free agent by Phoenix Coyotes (July 3, 1998). ... Strained groin (February 8, 1999); missed four games. ... Strained shoulder (March 2, 1999); missed 16 games. ... Suffered sore shoulder (April 14, 1999); missed two games. ... Bruised shoulder (November 14, 1999); missed three games. ... Bruised hand (March 5, 2000); missed four games. ... Suffered back spasms (December 26, 2000); missed 19 games. ... Strained shoulder (February 28, 2001); missed five games. ... Traded by Coyotes to Dallas Stars for RW Tyler Bouck (June 23, 2001).
MISCELLANEOUS: Member of silver-medal-winning Finnish Olympic team (1988). ... Member of bronze-medal-winning Finnish Olympic team (1998).

			REGULAR SEASON								PLAYOFFS				
Season Team	League	Gms.	G	A	Pts.	PIM	+/-	PP	SH		Gms.	G	A	Pts.	PIM
84-85—Koo Vee	Finland	30	6	4	10	44	...	...	...		—	—	—	—	—
85-86—Ilves Tampere	Finland	31	1	5	6	4	...	...	...		—	—	—	—	—
86-87—Ilves Tampere	Finland	43	12	12	24	52	...	...	...		4	0	1	1	0
87-88—Ilves Tampere	Finland	43	8	22	30	75	...	...	...		—	—	—	—	—
—Fin. Olympic team	Int'l	6	0	1	1	2	...	...	...		—	—	—	—	—
88-89—Montreal	NHL	21	1	3	4	10	3	1	0		—	—	—	—	—
—Sherbrooke	AHL	26	4	11	15	10	...	...	...		6	1	3	4	4
89-90—Montreal	NHL	54	1	19	20	41	17	0	0		—	—	—	—	—
—Vancouver	NHL	11	3	7	10	8	0	0	0		—	—	—	—	—
90-91—Vancouver	NHL	80	5	27	32	59	-15	1	0		6	2	3	5	0
91-92—Vancouver	NHL	75	12	32	44	65	25	3	1		13	2	3	5	4
92-93—Vancouver	NHL	74	8	36	44	55	30	3	2		12	0	5	5	6
93-94—Vancouver	NHL	83	13	42	55	50	3	1	3		24	2	11	13	16
94-95—Ilves Tampere	Finland	12	4	4	8	24	...	...	...		—	—	—	—	—
—Vancouver	NHL	36	5	12	17	26	4	3	0		11	2	6	8	8
95-96—Vancouver	NHL	80	17	37	54	50	-9	8	0		6	1	3	4	2
96-97—Vancouver	NHL	66	11	24	35	32	8	5	0		—	—	—	—	—
97-98—Vancouver	NHL	74	9	21	30	34	-25	4	0		—	—	—	—	—
—Fin. Olympic team	Int'l	6	1	0	1	16	...	...	...		—	—	—	—	—
98-99—Phoenix	NHL	60	7	21	28	34	5	1	0		7	0	1	1	6
99-00—Phoenix	NHL	74	8	32	40	44	9	4	0		5	0	1	1	2
00-01—Phoenix	NHL	58	4	21	25	44	3	0	0		—	—	—	—	—
NHL Totals (13 years)		846	104	334	438	552	58	34	6		84	9	33	42	44

LUNDMARK, JAMIE   C   RANGERS

PERSONAL: Born January 16, 1981, in Edmonton. ... 6-0/174. ... Shoots right.
TRANSACTIONS/CAREER NOTES: Selected by New York Rangers in first round (second Rangers pick, ninth overall) of NHL entry draft (June 26, 1999).
HONORS: Named to WHL (East) All-Star second team (1998-99). ... Named to WHL (West) All-Star first team (2000-01).

			REGULAR SEASON								PLAYOFFS				
Season Team	League	Gms.	G	A	Pts.	PIM	+/-	PP	SH		Gms.	G	A	Pts.	PIM
97-98—St. Albert	Jr. A	53	33	58	91	176	...	...	...		—	—	—	—	—
98-99—Moose Jaw	WHL	70	40	51	91	121	...	...	...		11	5	4	9	24
99-00—Moose Jaw	WHL	37	21	27	48	33	...	...	...		—	—	—	—	—
00-01—Seattle	WHL	52	35	42	77	49	...	...	...		9	4	4	8	16

LUONGO, ROBERTO   G   PANTHERS

PERSONAL: Born April 4, 1979, in St. Leonard, Que. ... 6-3/175. ... Catches left. ... Name pronounced luh-WAHN-goh.
TRANSACTIONS/CAREER NOTES: Selected by New York Islanders in first round (first Islanders pick, fourth overall) of NHL entry draft (June 21, 1997). ... Traded by Islanders with C Olli Jokinen to Florida Panthers for RW Mark Parrish and LW Oleg Kvasha (June 24, 2000).
HONORS: Won Michael Bossy Trophy (1996-97).
MISCELLANEOUS: Stopped a penalty shot attempt (vs. Dan Kesa, January 13, 2000).

			REGULAR SEASON							PLAYOFFS					
Season Team	League	Gms.	Min	W	L	T	GA	SO	Avg.		Gms.	Min.	W	L	GA	SO	Avg.
95-96—Val-d'Or	QMJHL	23	1199	6	11	4	74	0	3.70		3	68	0	1	5	0	4.41
96-97—Val-d'Or	QMJHL	60	3305	32	21	2	171	2	3.10		13	777	8	5	44	0	3.40
97-98—Val-d'Or	QMJHL	54	3046	27	20	5	157	*7	3.09		*17	*1019	*14	3	37	*2	*2.18
98-99—Val-d'Or	QMJHL	21	1177	6	10	2	77	1	3.93		—	—	—	—	—	—	—
—Acadie-Bathurst	QMJHL	22	1341	14	7	1	74	0	3.31		*23	*1400	*16	6	64	0	2.74
99-00—Lowell	AHL	26	1517	10	12	4	74	1	2.93		6	359	3	3	18	0	3.01
—New York Islanders	NHL	24	1292	7	14	1	70	1	3.25		—	—	—	—	—	—	—
00-01—Florida	NHL	47	2628	12	24	7	107	5	2.44		—	—	—	—	—	—	—
—Louisville	AHL	3	178	1	2	0	10	0	3.37		—	—	—	—	—	—	—
NHL Totals (2 years)		71	3920	19	38	8	177	6	2.71								

LUPASCHUK, ROSS   D   PENGUINS

PERSONAL: Born January 19, 1981, in Edmonton. ... 6-1/211. ... Shoots right.
TRANSACTIONS/CAREER NOTES: Selected by Washington Capitals in second round (fourth Capitals pick, 34th overall) of NHL entry draft (June 26, 1999). ... Traded by Capitals with C Kris Beech, C Michal Sivek and future considerations to Pittsburgh Penguins for RW Jaromir Jagr and D Frantisek Kucera (July 11, 2001).
HONORS: Named to WHL (East) All-Star second team (2000-01). ... Named to Can.HL All-Star second team (2000-01).

		REGULAR SEASON								PLAYOFFS				
Season Team	League	Gms.	G	A	Pts.	PIM	+/-	PP	SH	Gms.	G	A	Pts.	PIM
97-98—Prince Albert..............	WHL	67	6	12	18	170	...	...	...	—	—	—	—	—
98-99—Prince Albert..............	WHL	67	8	19	27	127	...	...	...	14	4	9	13	16
99-00—Prince Albert..............	WHL	22	8	8	16	42	...	...	...	—	—	—	—	—
—Red Deer...................	WHL	46	13	27	40	116	...	...	...	4	0	1	1	10
00-01—Red Deer...................	WHL	65	28	37	65	135	...	...	...	22	5	10	15	54

LYASHENKO, ROMAN   C   STARS

PERSONAL: Born May 2, 1979, in Murmansk, U.S.S.R. ... 6-0/188. ... Shoots right.
TRANSACTIONS/CAREER NOTES: Selected by Dallas Stars in second round (second Stars pick, 52nd overall) of NHL entry draft (June 21, 1997). ... Separated shoulder (November 17, 1999); missed five games. ... Sprained shoulder (December 21, 1999); missed one game. ... Sprained shoulder (December 31, 1999); missed two games.

		REGULAR SEASON								PLAYOFFS				
Season Team	League	Gms.	G	A	Pts.	PIM	+/-	PP	SH	Gms.	G	A	Pts.	PIM
95-96—Torpedo-2 Yaroslavl....	CIS Div. II	60	7	10	17	12	...	...	...	—	—	—	—	—
96-97—Torpedo Yaroslavl	Russian	42	5	7	12	16	...	...	...	9	3	0	3	6
—Torpedo-2 Yaroslavl....	Rus. Div. III	2	1	1	2	8	...	...	...	—	—	—	—	—
97-98—Torpedo Yaroslavl	Russian	46	7	6	13	28	...	...	...	—	—	—	—	—
98-99—Torpedo Yaroslavl	Russian	42	10	9	19	51	...	...	...	9	0	4	4	8
99-00—Michigan.....................	IHL	9	3	2	5	8	...	...	...	—	—	—	—	—
—Dallas..........................	NHL	58	6	6	12	10	-2	0	0	16	2	1	3	0
00-01—Dallas.........................	NHL	60	6	3	9	45	-1	0	0	1	0	0	0	0
—Utah............................	IHL	6	0	1	1	2	...	...	...	—	—	—	—	—
NHL Totals (2 years)...........		118	12	9	21	55	-3	0	0	17	2	1	3	0

LYDMAN, TONI   D   FLAMES

PERSONAL: Born September 25, 1977, in Lahti, Finland. ... 6-1/183. ... Shoots left.
TRANSACTIONS/CAREER NOTES: Selected by Calgary Flames in fourth round (fifth Flames pick, 89th overall) of NHL entry draft (June 22, 1996). ... Suffered concussion (January 5, 2001); missed 12 games.

		REGULAR SEASON								PLAYOFFS				
Season Team	League	Gms.	G	A	Pts.	PIM	+/-	PP	SH	Gms.	G	A	Pts.	PIM
93-94—Reipas........................	Finland Jrs.	1	0	0	0	0	...	...	...	—	—	—	—	—
94-95—Reipas........................	Finland Jrs.	26	6	4	10	10	...	...	...	—	—	—	—	—
95-96—Reipas........................	Finland Jrs.	1	0	0	0	0	...	...	...	—	—	—	—	—
—Reipas Lahti..............	Finland	39	5	2	7	30	...	...	...	—	—	—	—	—
96-97—Tappara	Finland	49	1	2	3	65	...	...	...	3	0	0	0	6
97-98—Tappara Tampere	Finland	48	4	10	14	48	...	...	...	4	0	2	2	0
98-99—HIFK Helsinki	Finland	42	4	7	11	36	...	...	...	11	0	3	3	2
99-00—HIFK Helsinki	Finland	46	4	18	22	36	...	...	...	9	0	4	4	6
00-01—Calgary	NHL	62	3	16	19	30	-7	1	0	—	—	—	—	—
NHL Totals (1 year).............		62	3	16	19	30	-7	1	0					

MacINNIS, AL   D   BLUES

PERSONAL: Born July 11, 1963, in Inverness, Nova Scotia. ... 6-2/208. ... Shoots right. ... Full Name: Allan MacInnis. ... Name pronounced muh-KIHN-ihz.
TRANSACTIONS/CAREER NOTES: Selected by Calgary Flames in first round (first Flames pick, 15th overall) of NHL entry draft (June 10, 1981). ... Twisted knee (February 1985). ... Lacerated hand (March 23, 1986). ... Stretched ligaments of knee (April 8, 1990). ... Separated shoulder (November 22, 1991); missed eight games. ... Dislocated left hip (November 12, 1992); missed 34 games. ... Strained shoulder (December 23, 1993); missed one game. ... Strained shoulder (January 2, 1994); missed four games. ... Bruised knee (February 24, 1994); missed four games. ... Traded by Flames with fourth-round pick (D Didier Tremblay) in 1997 draft to St. Louis Blues for D Phil Housley and second-round pick in 1996 (C Steve Begin) and 1997 (RW John Tripp) drafts (July 4, 1994). ... Injured shoulder (January 31, 1995); missed eight games. ... Suffered from the flu (April 9, 1995); missed three games. ... Injured shoulder (April 25, 1995); missed final five games of season. ... Dislocated shoulder (February 4, 1997); missed nine games. ... Dislocated shoulder (December 13, 1997); missed nine games. ... Suffered laceration around left eye (April 12, 1998); missed one game. ... Fractured fibula (October 9, 1999); missed 11 games. ... Suffered rib injury (January 14, 2000); missed one game. ... Suffered collapsed lung (January 21, 2000); missed five games. ... Suffered back spasms (February 10, 2000); missed three games. ... Suffered eye injury (January 29, 2001); missed 23 games.
HONORS: Named to OHL All-Star first team (1981-82 and 1982-83). ... Named to Memorial Cup All-Star team (1981-82). ... Won Max Kaminsky Trophy (1982-83). ... Played in NHL All-Star Game (1985, 1988, 1990-1992, 1994 and 1996-2000). ... Named to NHL All-Star second team (1986-87, 1988-89 and 1993-94). ... Won Conn Smythe Trophy (1988-89). ... Named to THE SPORTING NEWS All-Star first team (1989-90 and 1990-91). ... Named to THE SPORTING NEWS All-Star second team (1993-94). ... Named to NHL All-Star first team (1989-90, 1990-91 and 1998-99). ... Named to THE SPORTING NEWS All-Star first team (1998-99). ... Won James Norris Memorial Trophy (1998-99). ... Named to play in NHL All-Star Game (2001); replaced by D Scott Niedermayer due to injury.
MISCELLANEOUS: Member of Stanley Cup championship team (1989). ... Holds Calgary Flames franchise all-time records for most games played (803) and most assists (609). ... Scored on a penalty shot (vs. Kelly Hrudey, April 4, 1990 (playoffs)).
STATISTICAL PLATEAUS: Three-goal games: 1991-92 (1), 1996-97 (1), 1998-99 (1). Total: 3.

L

M

Season Team	League	Gms.	G	A	Pts.	PIM	+/-	PP	SH	Gms.	G	A	Pts.	PIM
79-80—Regina Blues............	SJHL	59	20	28	48	110	...	...	...	—	—	—	—	—
80-81—Kitchener	OMJHL	47	11	28	39	59	...	...	...	18	4	12	16	20
81-82—Kitchener	OHL	59	25	50	75	145	...	...	...	15	5	10	15	44
—Calgary	NHL	2	0	0	0	0	0	0	0	—	—	—	—	—
82-83—Kitchener	OHL	51	38	46	84	67	...	...	...	8	3	8	11	9
—Calgary	NHL	14	1	3	4	9	0	0	0	—	—	—	—	—
83-84—Colorado	CHL	19	5	14	19	22	...	...	...	—	—	—	—	—
—Calgary	NHL	51	11	34	45	42	0	7	0	11	2	12	14	13
84-85—Calgary	NHL	67	14	52	66	75	7	8	0	4	1	2	3	8
85-86—Calgary	NHL	77	11	57	68	76	39	4	0	21	4	*15	19	30
86-87—Calgary	NHL	79	20	56	76	97	20	7	0	4	1	0	1	0
87-88—Calgary	NHL	80	25	58	83	114	13	7	2	7	3	6	9	18
88-89—Calgary	NHL	79	16	58	74	126	38	8	0	22	7	*24	*31	46
89-90—Calgary	NHL	79	28	62	90	82	20	14	1	6	2	3	5	8
90-91—Calgary	NHL	78	28	75	103	90	42	17	0	7	2	3	5	8
91-92—Calgary	NHL	72	20	57	77	83	13	11	0	—	—	—	—	—
92-93—Calgary	NHL	50	11	43	54	61	15	7	0	6	1	6	7	10
93-94—Calgary	NHL	75	28	54	82	95	35	12	1	7	2	6	8	12
94-95—St. Louis	NHL	32	8	20	28	43	19	2	0	7	1	5	6	10
95-96—St. Louis	NHL	82	17	44	61	88	5	9	1	13	3	4	7	20
96-97—St. Louis	NHL	72	13	30	43	65	2	6	1	6	1	2	3	4
97-98—St. Louis	NHL	71	19	30	49	80	6	9	1	8	2	6	8	12
—Can. Olympic team	Int'l	6	2	0	2	2	...	...	...	—	—	—	—	—
98-99—St. Louis	NHL	82	20	42	62	70	33	11	1	13	4	8	12	20
99-00—St. Louis	NHL	61	11	28	39	34	20	6	0	7	1	3	4	14
00-01—St. Louis	NHL	59	12	42	54	52	23	6	1	15	2	8	10	18
NHL Totals (20 years).........		1262	313	845	1158	1382	350	151	6	164	39	113	152	251

MacKENZIE, DEREK   C   THRASHERS

PERSONAL: Born June 11, 1981, in Sudbury, Ont. ... 5-11/169. ... Shoots left.
TRANSACTIONS/CAREER NOTES: Selected by Atlanta Thrashers in fifth round (sixth Thrashers pick, 128th overall) of NHL entry draft (June 26, 1999).

Season Team	League	Gms.	G	A	Pts.	PIM	+/-	PP	SH	Gms.	G	A	Pts.	PIM
97-98—Sudbury...............	OHL	59	9	11	20	26	...	...	...	10	0	1	1	6
98-99—Sudbury...............	OHL	68	22	65	87	74	...	...	...	4	2	4	6	2
99-00—Sudbury...............	OHL	68	24	33	57	110	...	...	...	12	5	9	14	16
00-01—Sudbury...............	OHL	62	40	49	89	89	...	...	...	12	6	8	14	16

M MacLEAN, DON   C   MAPLE LEAFS

PERSONAL: Born January 14, 1977, in Sydney, Nova Scotia. ... 6-2/199. ... Shoots left. ... Full Name: Donald MacLean.
TRANSACTIONS/CAREER NOTES: Selected by Los Angeles Kings in second round (second Kings pick, 33rd overall) of NHL entry draft (July 8, 1995). ... Traded by Kings to Toronto Maple Leafs for C Craig Charron (February 23, 2000).

Season Team	League	Gms.	G	A	Pts.	PIM	+/-	PP	SH	Gms.	G	A	Pts.	PIM
94-95—Beauport...............	QMJHL	64	15	27	42	37	...	...	...	17	4	4	8	6
95-96—Beauport...............	QMJHL	1	0	1	1	0	...	...	...	—	—	—	—	—
—Laval..........................	QMJHL	21	17	11	28	29	...	...	...	—	—	—	—	—
—Hull............................	QMJHL	39	26	34	60	44	...	...	...	17	6	7	13	14
96-97—Hull......................	QMJHL	69	34	47	81	67	...	...	...	14	11	10	21	29
97-98—Los Angeles..............	NHL	22	5	2	7	4	-1	2	0	—	—	—	—	—
—Fredericton	AHL	39	9	5	14	32	...	...	...	4	1	3	4	2
98-99—Springfield	AHL	41	5	14	19	31	...	...	...	—	—	—	—	—
—Grand Rapids..............	IHL	28	6	13	19	8	...	...	...	—	—	—	—	—
99-00—Lowell	AHL	40	11	17	28	18	...	...	...	—	—	—	—	—
—St. John's...................	AHL	21	14	12	26	8	...	...	...	—	—	—	—	—
00-01—Toronto	NHL	3	0	1	1	2	-2	0	0	—	—	—	—	—
—St. John's...................	AHL	61	26	34	60	48	...	...	...	4	2	1	3	2
NHL Totals (2 years).........		25	5	3	8	6	-3	2	0					

MacLEAN, JOHN   RW

PERSONAL: Born November 20, 1964, in Oshawa, Ont. ... 6-0/205. ... Shoots right. ... Name pronounced muh-KLAYN.
TRANSACTIONS/CAREER NOTES: Selected by New Jersey Devils in first round (first Devils pick, sixth overall) of NHL entry draft (June 8, 1983). ... Bruised shoulder (November 1984). ... Injured right knee (January 25, 1985). ... Reinjured knee and underwent surgery (January 31, 1985). ... Bruised ankle (November 2, 1986). ... Sprained right elbow (December 1988). ... Bruised ribs (March 1, 1989). ... Suffered concussion and stomach contusions (October 1990). ... Suffered concussion (December 11, 1990). ... Tore ligament in right knee (September 30, 1991); missed entire 1991-92 season. ... Underwent surgery to right knee (November 23, 1991). ... Injured forearm (November 3, 1993); missed two games. ... Lacerated eye (February 24, 1994); missed one game. ... Bruised foot (April 9, 1995); missed one game. ... Injured knee (March 10, 1996); missed six games. ... Traded by Devils with D Ken Sutton to San Jose Sharks for D Doug Bodger and LW Dody Wood (December 7, 1997). ... Signed as free agent by New York Rangers (July 9, 1998). ... Suffered eye injury (March 6, 2000); missed four games. ... Traded by Rangers to Dallas Stars for future considerations (February 5, 2001).
HONORS: Named to Memorial Cup All-Star team (1982-83). ... Played in NHL All-Star Game (1989 and 1991).

MISCELLANEOUS: Member of Stanley Cup championship team (1995). ... Holds New Jersey Devils franchise all-time records for most goals (347), most assists (354) and most points (701). ... Scored on a penalty shot (vs. Dominik Hasek, February 27, 1997; vs. Bill Ranford, January 10, 1999).

STATISTICAL PLATEAUS: Three-goal games: 1987-88 (1), 1988-89 (3), 1990-91 (2). Total: 6.

		REGULAR SEASON								PLAYOFFS				
Season Team	League	Gms.	G	A	Pts.	PIM	+/-	PP	SH	Gms.	G	A	Pts.	PIM
81-82—Oshawa	OHL	67	17	22	39	197	...	...	...	12	3	6	9	63
82-83—Oshawa	OHL	66	47	51	98	138	...	...	...	17	*18	20	†38	35
83-84—New Jersey	NHL	23	1	0	1	10	-7	0	0	—	—	—	—	—
—Oshawa	OHL	30	23	36	59	58	...	...	...	7	2	5	7	18
84-85—New Jersey	NHL	61	13	20	33	44	-11	1	0	—	—	—	—	—
85-86—New Jersey	NHL	74	21	36	57	112	-2	1	0	—	—	—	—	—
86-87—New Jersey	NHL	80	31	36	67	120	-23	9	0	—	—	—	—	—
87-88—New Jersey	NHL	76	23	16	39	147	-10	12	0	20	7	11	18	60
88-89—New Jersey	NHL	74	42	45	87	122	26	14	0	—	—	—	—	—
89-90—New Jersey	NHL	80	41	38	79	80	17	10	3	6	4	1	5	12
90-91—New Jersey	NHL	78	45	33	78	150	8	19	2	7	5	3	8	20
91-92—New Jersey	NHL					Did not play.								
92-93—New Jersey	NHL	80	24	24	48	102	-6	7	1	5	0	1	1	10
93-94—New Jersey	NHL	80	37	33	70	95	30	8	0	20	6	10	16	22
94-95—New Jersey	NHL	46	17	12	29	32	13	2	1	20	5	13	18	14
95-96—New Jersey	NHL	76	20	28	48	91	3	3	3	—	—	—	—	—
96-97—New Jersey	NHL	80	29	25	54	49	11	5	0	10	4	5	9	4
97-98—New Jersey	NHL	26	3	8	11	14	-6	1	0	—	—	—	—	—
—San Jose	NHL	51	13	19	32	28	0	5	0	6	2	3	5	4
98-99—New York Rangers	NHL	82	28	27	55	46	5	11	1	—	—	—	—	—
99-00—New York Rangers	NHL	77	18	24	42	52	-2	6	2	—	—	—	—	—
00-01—New York Rangers	NHL	2	0	0	0	0	-2	0	0	—	—	—	—	—
—Manitoba	IHL	32	6	12	18	28	...	...	...	—	—	—	—	—
—Dallas	NHL	28	4	2	6	17	0	1	0	10	2	1	3	6
NHL Totals (18 years)		1174	410	426	836	1311	44	115	13	104	35	48	83	152

MADDEN, JOHN　　　C　　　DEVILS

PERSONAL: Born May 4, 1973, in Barrie, Ont. ... 5-11/195. ... Shoots left.

TRANSACTIONS/CAREER NOTES: Signed as non-drafted free agent by New Jersey Devils (June 26, 1997). ... Injured toe (January 20, 2001); missed one game.

HONORS: Named CCHA Tournament Most Valuable Player (1995-96). ... Named to NCAA All-America (West) first team (1996-97). ... Named to CCHA All-Star first team (1996-97). ... Won Frank J. Selke Trophy (2000-01).

MISCELLANEOUS: Member of Stanley Cup championship team (2000). ... Failed to score on a penalty shot (vs. Mike Dunham, February 29, 2000).

STATISTICAL PLATEAUS: Four-goal games: 2000-01 (1).

		REGULAR SEASON								PLAYOFFS				
Season Team	League	Gms.	G	A	Pts.	PIM	+/-	PP	SH	Gms.	G	A	Pts.	PIM
92-93—Barrie	COJHL	43	49	75	124	62	...	...	...	—	—	—	—	—
93-94—Univ. of Michigan	CCHA	36	6	11	17	14	...	...	...	—	—	—	—	—
94-95—Univ. of Michigan	CCHA	39	21	22	43	8	...	...	...	—	—	—	—	—
95-96—Univ. of Michigan	CCHA	43	27	30	57	45	...	...	...	—	—	—	—	—
96-97—Univ. of Michigan	CCHA	42	26	37	63	56	...	...	...	—	—	—	—	—
97-98—Albany	AHL	74	20	36	56	40	...	...	...	13	3	13	16	14
98-99—Albany	AHL	75	38	60	98	44	...	...	...	5	2	2	4	6
—New Jersey	NHL	4	0	1	1	0	-2	0	0	—	—	—	—	—
99-00—New Jersey	NHL	74	16	9	25	6	7	0	*6	20	3	4	7	0
00-01—New Jersey	NHL	80	23	15	38	12	24	0	3	25	4	3	7	6
NHL Totals (3 years)		158	39	25	64	18	29	0	9	45	7	7	14	6

MAIR, ADAM　　　C　　　KINGS

PERSONAL: Born February 15, 1979, in Hamilton, Ont. ... 6-2/194. ... Shoots right.

TRANSACTIONS/CAREER NOTES: Selected by Toronto Maple Leafs in fourth round (second Maple Leafs pick, 84th overall) of NHL entry draft (June 21, 1997). ... Traded by Maple Leafs with second-round pick (C Mike Cammaleri) in 2001 draft to Los Angeles Kings for D Aki Berg (March 13, 2001).

		REGULAR SEASON								PLAYOFFS				
Season Team	League	Gms.	G	A	Pts.	PIM	+/-	PP	SH	Gms.	G	A	Pts.	PIM
94-95—Ohsweken	Jr. B	39	21	23	44	91	...	...	...	—	—	—	—	—
95-96—Owen Sound	OHL	62	12	15	27	63	...	...	...	6	0	0	0	2
96-97—Owen Sound	OHL	65	16	35	51	113	...	...	...	4	1	0	1	2
97-98—Owen Sound	OHL	56	25	27	52	179	...	...	...	11	6	3	9	31
98-99—Owen Sound	OHL	43	23	41	64	109	...	...	...	16	10	10	20	47
—Saint John	AHL	24	5	12	17	31	...	...	...	3	1	0	1	6
—Toronto	NHL	—	—	—	—	—	—	—	—	5	1	0	1	14
99-00—St. John's	AHL	66	22	27	49	124	...	...	...	—	—	—	—	—
—Toronto	NHL	8	1	0	1	6	-1	0	0	5	0	0	0	8
00-01—St. John's	AHL	47	18	27	45	69	...	...	...	—	—	—	—	—
—Toronto	NHL	16	0	2	2	14	3	0	0	—	—	—	—	—
—Los Angeles	NHL	10	0	0	0	6	-3	0	0	—	—	—	—	—
NHL Totals (3 years)		34	1	2	3	26	-1	0	0	10	1	0	1	22

MALAKHOV, VLADIMIR   D   RANGERS

PERSONAL: Born August 30, 1968, in Sverdlovsk, U.S.S.R. ... 6-4/230. ... Shoots left. ... Name pronounced MAL-uh-kahf.
TRANSACTIONS/CAREER NOTES: Selected by New York Islanders in 10th round (12th Islanders pick, 191st overall) of NHL entry draft (June 17, 1989). ... Suffered sore groin prior to 1992-93 season; missed first two games of season. ... Injured right shoulder (January 16, 1993); missed eight games. ... Sprained shoulder (March 14, 1993); missed five games. ... Suffered concussion (December 7, 1993); missed one game. ... Strained lower back (December 28, 1993); missed six games. ... Strained hip flexor (February 9, 1995); missed five games. ... Suffered charley horse (March 14, 1995); missed two games. ... Traded by Islanders with C Pierre Turgeon to Montreal Canadiens for LW Kirk Muller, D Mathieu Schneider and C Craig Darby (April 5, 1995). ... Strained hip flexor (April 24, 1995); missed one game. ... Suffered from stomach flu (October 25, 1995); missed two games. ... Bruised right leg (December 12, 1995); missed two games. ... Bruised ribs (October 24, 1996); missed one game. ... Fractured thumb (December 23, 1996); missed 16 games. ... Bruised lower back (October 29, 1997); missed one game. ... Sprained knee (December 10, 1997); missed four games. ... Suffered shoulder tendinitis (February 28, 1998); missed three games. ... Suffered back spasms (November 9, 1998); missed two games. ... Suffered back spasms (December 5, 1998); missed six games. ... Suffered back spasms (January 31, 1999); missed two games. ... Sprained knee (March 28, 1999); missed six games. ... Reinjured knee (April 10, 1999); missed final three games of season. ... Torn anterior cruciate ligament in knee (September 17, 1999); missed first 53 games of 1999-2000 season. ... Injured knee (February 14, 2000); missed two games. ... Traded by Canadiens to New Jersey Devils for D Sheldon Souray, D Josh DeWolf and second-round draft pick (traded to Washington) in 2001 draft (March 1, 2000). ... Signed as free agent by New York Rangers (July 10, 2000). ... Sprained anterior cruciate ligament in knee (October 7, 2000); missed 14 games. ... Reinjured knee (November 15, 2000); missed remainder of season.
HONORS: Named to NHL All-Rookie team (1992-93).
MISCELLANEOUS: Member of Stanley Cup championship team (2000). ... Member of gold-medal-winning Unified Olympic team (1992).
STATISTICAL PLATEAUS: Three-goal games: 1997-98 (1).

			REGULAR SEASON								PLAYOFFS				
Season Team	League	Gms.	G	A	Pts.	PIM	+/-	PP	SH		Gms.	G	A	Pts.	PIM
86-87—Spartak Moscow	USSR	22	0	1	1	12	...	...	...		—	—	—	—	—
87-88—Spartak Moscow	USSR	28	2	2	4	26	...	...	...		—	—	—	—	—
88-89—CSKA Moscow	USSR	34	6	2	8	16	...	...	...		—	—	—	—	—
89-90—CSKA Moscow	USSR	48	2	10	12	34	...	...	...		—	—	—	—	—
90-91—CSKA Moscow	USSR	46	5	13	18	22	...	...	...		—	—	—	—	—
91-92—CSKA Moscow	CIS	40	1	9	10	12	...	...	...		—	—	—	—	—
—Unif. Olympic team	Int'l	8	3	0	3	4	...	...	...		—	—	—	—	—
92-93—Capital District	AHL	3	2	1	3	11	...	...	...		—	—	—	—	—
—New York Islanders	NHL	64	14	38	52	59	14	7	0		17	3	6	9	12
93-94—New York Islanders	NHL	76	10	47	57	80	29	4	0		4	0	0	0	6
94-95—New York Islanders	NHL	26	3	13	16	32	-1	1	0		—	—	—	—	—
—Montreal	NHL	14	1	4	5	14	-2	0	0		—	—	—	—	—
95-96—Montreal	NHL	61	5	23	28	79	7	2	0		—	—	—	—	—
96-97—Montreal	NHL	65	10	20	30	43	3	5	0		5	0	0	0	6
97-98—Montreal	NHL	74	13	31	44	70	16	8	0		9	3	4	7	10
98-99—Montreal	NHL	62	13	21	34	77	-7	8	0		—	—	—	—	—
99-00—Montreal	NHL	7	0	0	0	4	0	0	0		—	—	—	—	—
—New Jersey	NHL	17	1	4	5	19	1	1	0		23	1	4	5	18
00-01—New York Rangers	NHL	3	0	2	2	4	0	0	0		—	—	—	—	—
NHL Totals (9 years)		469	70	203	273	481	60	36	0		58	7	14	21	52

M

MALHOTRA, MANNY   C   RANGERS

PERSONAL: Born May 18, 1980, in Mississauga, Ont. ... 6-2/210. ... Shoots left.
TRANSACTIONS/CAREER NOTES: Selected by New York Rangers in first round (first Rangers pick, seventh overall) of NHL entry draft (June 27, 1998). ... Sprained ankle (November 18, 1999); missed four games.

			REGULAR SEASON								PLAYOFFS				
Season Team	League	Gms.	G	A	Pts.	PIM	+/-	PP	SH		Gms.	G	A	Pts.	PIM
96-97—Guelph	OHL	61	16	28	44	26	...	...	...		18	7	7	14	11
97-98—Guelph	OHL	57	16	35	51	29	...	...	...		12	7	6	13	8
98-99—New York Rangers	NHL	73	8	8	16	13	-2	1	0		—	—	—	—	—
99-00—New York Rangers	NHL	27	0	0	0	4	-6	0	0		—	—	—	—	—
—Hartford	AHL	12	1	5	6	2	...	...	...		23	1	2	3	10
—Guelph	OHL	5	2	2	4	4	...	...	...		6	0	2	2	4
00-01—Hartford	AHL	28	5	6	11	69	...	...	...		5	0	0	0	0
—New York Rangers	NHL	50	4	8	12	31	-10	0	0		—	—	—	—	—
NHL Totals (3 years)		150	12	16	28	48	-18	1	0		—	—	—	—	—

MALIK, MAREK   D   HURRICANES

PERSONAL: Born June 24, 1975, in Ostrava, Czechoslovakia. ... 6-5/210. ... Shoots left. ... Name pronounced muh-REHK muh-LEEK.
TRANSACTIONS/CAREER NOTES: Selected by Hartford Whalers in third round (second Whalers pick, 72nd overall) of NHL entry draft (June 26, 1993). ... Suffered from the flu (January 20, 1997); missed three games. ... Bruised shin (March 20, 1997); missed four games. ... Whalers franchise moved to North Carolina and renamed Carolina Hurricanes for 1997-98 season; NHL approved move on June 25, 1997. ... Injured knee (April 7, 1999); missed one game. ... Suffered from whiplash (September 30, 2000); missed first six games of season.

			REGULAR SEASON								PLAYOFFS				
Season Team	League	Gms.	G	A	Pts.	PIM	+/-	PP	SH		Gms.	G	A	Pts.	PIM
91-92—TJ Vitkovice	Czech. Jrs.						Statistics unavailable.								
92-93—TJ Vitkovice	Czech.	20	5	10	15	16	...	...	...		—	—	—	—	—
93-94—HC Vitkovice	Czech Rep.	38	3	3	6	...	...	...	...		3	0	1	1	...
94-95—Springfield	AHL	58	11	30	41	91	...	...	...		—	—	—	—	—
—Hartford	NHL	1	0	1	1	0	1	0	0		—	—	—	—	—
95-96—Springfield	AHL	68	8	14	22	135	...	...	...		8	1	3	4	20
—Hartford	NHL	7	0	0	0	4	-3	0	0		—	—	—	—	—

		REGULAR SEASON								PLAYOFFS				
Season Team	League	Gms.	G	A	Pts.	PIM	+/-	PP	SH	Gms.	G	A	Pts.	PIM
96-97—Springfield	AHL	3	0	3	3	4	...			—	—	—	—	—
—Hartford	NHL	47	1	5	6	50	5	0	0	—	—	—	—	—
97-98—Malmoif	Sweden	37	1	5	6	21	...	...	...	—	—	—	—	—
98-99—HC Vitkovice	Czech Rep.	1	1	0	1	6	...	...	...	—	—	—	—	—
—New Haven	AHL	21	2	8	10	28	...	...	...	—	—	—	—	—
—Carolina	NHL	52	2	9	11	36	-6	1	0	4	0	0	0	4
99-00—Carolina	NHL	57	4	10	14	63	13	0	0	—	—	—	—	—
00-01—Carolina	NHL	61	6	14	20	34	-4	1	0	3	0	0	0	6
NHL Totals (6 years)		225	13	39	52	187	6	2	0	7	0	0	0	10

MALTAIS, STEVE   LW

PERSONAL: Born January 25, 1969, in Arvida, Ont. ... 6-1/220. ... Shoots left. ... Name pronounced MAHL-tay.
TRANSACTIONS/CAREER NOTES: Selected by Washington Capitals in third round (second Capitals pick, 57th overall) of NHL entry draft (June 13, 1987). ... Traded by Capitals with C Trent Klatt to Minnesota North Stars for D Shawn Chambers (June 21, 1991). ... Traded by North Stars to Quebec Nordiques for C Kip Miller (March 8, 1992). ... Selected by Tampa Bay Lightning in NHL expansion draft (June 18, 1992). ... Traded by Lightning to Detroit Red Wings for D Dennis Vial (June 8, 1993). ... Signed as free agent by Columbus Blue Jackets (October 7, 2000).
HONORS: Named to OHL All-Star second team (1988-89). ... Named to IHL All-Star first team (1994-95). ... Named to IHL All-Star second team (1995-96 and 1996-97). ... Named to IHL All-Star first team (1998-99 and 1999-2000). ... Won Leo P. Lamoreux Memorial Trophy (1999-2000).
MISCELLANEOUS: Failed to score on a penalty shot (vs. Ed Belfour, February 25, 1993).

		REGULAR SEASON								PLAYOFFS				
Season Team	League	Gms.	G	A	Pts.	PIM	+/-	PP	SH	Gms.	G	A	Pts.	PIM
85-86—Wexford Jr. B	MTHL	33	35	19	54	38	...	...	...	—	—	—	—	—
86-87—Cornwall	OHL	65	32	12	44	29	...	...	...	5	0	0	0	2
87-88—Cornwall	OHL	59	39	46	85	30	...	...	...	11	9	6	15	33
88-89—Cornwall	OHL	58	53	70	123	67	...	...	...	18	14	16	30	16
—Fort Wayne	IHL	—	—	—	—	—				4	2	1	3	0
89-90—Washington	NHL	8	0	0	0	2	-2	0	0	1	0	0	0	0
—Baltimore	AHL	67	29	37	66	54	...	...	...	12	6	10	16	6
90-91—Baltimore	AHL	73	36	43	79	97	...	...	...	6	1	4	5	10
—Washington	NHL	7	0	0	0	2	-1	0	0	—	—	—	—	—
91-92—Kalamazoo	IHL	48	25	31	56	51	...	...	...	—	—	—	—	—
—Minnesota	NHL	12	2	1	3	2	-1	0	0	—	—	—	—	—
—Halifax	AHL	10	3	3	6	0	...	...	...	—	—	—	—	—
92-93—Atlanta	IHL	16	14	10	24	22	...	...	...	—	—	—	—	—
—Tampa Bay	NHL	63	7	13	20	35	-20	4	0	—	—	—	—	—
93-94—Adirondack	AHL	73	35	49	84	79	...	...	...	12	5	11	16	14
—Detroit	NHL	4	0	1	1	0	-1	0	0	—	—	—	—	—
94-95—Chicago	IHL	79	*57	40	97	145	...	...	...	3	1	1	2	0
95-96—Chicago	IHL	81	56	66	122	161	...	...	...	9	7	7	14	20
96-97—Chicago	IHL	81	*60	54	114	62	...	...	...	4	2	0	2	4
97-98—Chicago	IHL	82	†46	57	103	120	...	...	...	22	8	11	19	28
98-99—Chicago	IHL	82	*56	44	100	164	...	...	...	10	4	6	10	2
99-00—Chicago	IHL	82	*44	46	*90	78	...	...	...	16	9	4	13	14
00-01—Columbus	NHL	26	0	3	3	12	-9	0	0	—	—	—	—	—
—Chicago	IHL	50	25	26	51	57	...	...	...	16	7	10	17	2
NHL Totals (6 years)		120	9	18	27	53	-24	0	0	1	0	0	0	0

MALTBY, KIRK   RW   RED WINGS

PERSONAL: Born December 22, 1972, in Guelph, Ont. ... 6-0/190. ... Shoots right.
TRANSACTIONS/CAREER NOTES: Selected by Edmonton Oilers in third round (fourth Oilers pick, 65th overall) of NHL entry draft (June 20, 1992). ... Suffered chip fracture of ankle bone (February 2, 1994); missed 13 games. ... Lacerated right eye (March 1, 1995); missed last game of season. ... Scratched left cornea (February 1, 1996); missed 16 games. ... Traded by Oilers to Detroit Red Wings for D Dan McGillis (March 20, 1996). ... Separated shoulder (September 24, 1997); missed 16 games. ... Suffered from lower abdminal pain (November 14, 1998); missed 19 games. ... Sprained knee (December 31, 1998); missed five games. ... Injured ankle (March 31, 1999); missed one game. ... Suspended four games by NHL for slashing incident (March 17, 1999). ... Suffered hernia (October 5, 1999); missed 41 games.
MISCELLANEOUS: Member of Stanley Cup championship team (1997 and 1998).

		REGULAR SEASON								PLAYOFFS				
Season Team	League	Gms.	G	A	Pts.	PIM	+/-	PP	SH	Gms.	G	A	Pts.	PIM
88-89—Cambridge Jr. B	OHA	48	28	18	46	138	...	...	...	—	—	—	—	—
89-90—Owen Sound	OHL	61	12	15	27	90	...	...	...	12	1	6	7	15
90-91—Owen Sound	OHL	66	34	32	66	100	...	...	...	—	—	—	—	—
91-92—Owen Sound	OHL	64	50	41	91	99	...	...	...	5	3	3	6	18
92-93—Cape Breton	AHL	73	22	23	45	130	...	...	...	16	3	3	6	45
93-94—Edmonton	NHL	68	11	8	19	74	-2	0	1	—	—	—	—	—
94-95—Edmonton	NHL	47	8	3	11	49	-11	0	2	—	—	—	—	—
95-96—Edmonton	NHL	49	2	6	8	61	-16	0	0	—	—	—	—	—
—Cape Breton	AHL	4	1	2	3	6	...	...	...	—	—	—	—	—
—Detroit	NHL	6	1	0	1	6	0	0	0	8	0	1	1	4
96-97—Detroit	NHL	66	3	5	8	75	3	0	0	20	5	2	7	24
97-98—Detroit	NHL	65	14	9	23	89	11	2	1	22	3	1	4	30
98-99—Detroit	NHL	53	6	8	14	34	-6	0	1	10	1	0	1	8
99-00—Detroit	NHL	41	6	8	14	24	1	0	2	8	0	1	1	4
00-01—Detroit	NHL	79	12	7	19	22	16	1	3	6	0	0	0	6
NHL Totals (8 years)		474	65	52	117	434	-4	3	10	74	9	5	14	76

PERSONAL: Born April 12, 1971, in Edmonton. ... 6-3/200. ... Shoots left. ... Full Name: Kent Stephen Manderville.

TRANSACTIONS/CAREER NOTES: Selected by Calgary Flames in second round (first Flames pick, 24th overall) of NHL entry draft (June 17, 1989). ... Traded by Flames with C Doug Gilmour, D Jamie Macoun, D Ric Nattress and G Rick Wamsley to Toronto Maple Leafs for LW Craig Berube, D Alexander Godynyuk, RW Gary Leeman, D Michel Petit and G Jeff Reese (January 2, 1992). ... Bruised hand (October 5, 1993); missed one game. ... Suffered from the flu (December 17, 1993); missed two games. ... Sprained ankle (January 30, 1995); missed one game. ... Traded by Maple Leafs to Edmonton Oilers for C Peter White and fourth-round pick (RW Jason Sessa) in 1996 draft (December 4, 1995). ... Sprained left wrist (February 18, 1996); missed nine games. ... Signed as free agent by Hartford Whalers (October 1, 1996). ... Whalers franchise moved to North Carolina and renamed Carolina Hurricanes for 1997-98 season; NHL approved move on June 25, 1997. ... Strained abdominal muscle (March 12, 1998); missed four games. ... Suffered concussion (December 15, 1999); missed 10 games. ... Traded by Hurricanes to Philadelphia Flyers for RW Sandy McCarthy (March 14, 2000).

HONORS: Named ECAC Rookie of the Year (1989-90). ... Named to ECAC All-Rookie team (1989-90).

MISCELLANEOUS: Member of silver-medal-winning Canadian Olympic team (1992).

STATISTICAL PLATEAUS: Three-goal games: 1996-97 (1).

				REGULAR SEASON								PLAYOFFS				
Season Team	League	Gms.	G	A	Pts.	PIM	+/-	PP	SH		Gms.	G	A	Pts.	PIM
88-89—Notre Dame	SJHL	58	39	36	75	165	...	...	...		—	—	—	—	—
89-90—Cornell University	ECAC	26	11	15	26	28	...	...	...		—	—	—	—	—
90-91—Cornell University	ECAC	28	17	14	31	60	...	...	...		—	—	—	—	—
—Canadian nat'l team	Int'l	3	1	2	3	0	...	...	...		—	—	—	—	—
91-92—Canadian nat'l team	Int'l	63	16	23	39	75	...	...	...		—	—	—	—	—
—Can. Olympic team	Int'l	8	1	2	3	0	...	...	...		—	—	—	—	—
—Toronto	NHL	15	0	4	4	0	1	0	0		—	—	—	—	—
—St. John's	AHL	—	—	—	—	—	...	...	...		12	5	9	14	14
92-93—Toronto	NHL	18	1	1	2	17	-9	0	0		18	1	0	1	8
—St. John's	AHL	56	19	28	47	86	...	...	...		2	0	2	2	0
93-94—Toronto	NHL	67	7	9	16	63	5	0	0		12	1	0	1	4
94-95—Toronto	NHL	36	0	1	1	22	-2	0	0		7	0	0	0	6
95-96—St. John's	AHL	27	16	12	28	26	...	...	...		—	—	—	—	—
—Edmonton	NHL	37	3	5	8	38	-5	0	2		—	—	—	—	—
96-97—Springfield	AHL	23	5	20	25	18	...	...	...		—	—	—	—	—
—Hartford	NHL	44	6	5	11	18	3	0	0		—	—	—	—	—
97-98—Carolina	NHL	77	4	4	8	31	-6	0	0		—	—	—	—	—
98-99—Carolina	NHL	81	5	11	16	38	9	0	0		6	0	0	0	2
99-00—Carolina	NHL	56	1	4	5	12	-8	0	0		—	—	—	—	—
—Philadelphia	NHL	13	0	3	3	4	2	0	0		18	0	1	1	22
00-01—Philadelphia	NHL	82	5	10	15	47	-2	0	3		6	1	2	3	2
NHL Totals (10 years)		526	32	57	89	290	-12	0	5		67	3	3	6	44

M

PERSONAL: Born October 1, 1973, in Winnipeg. ... 5-11/190. ... Shoots right. ... Name pronounced MAN-ih-luhk.

TRANSACTIONS/CAREER NOTES: Signed as non-drafted free agent by Mighty Ducks of Anaheim (January 28, 1994). ... Traded by Mighty Ducks to Ottawa Senators for RW Kevin Brown (July 1, 1996). ... Traded by Senators to Philadelphia Flyers for cash (October 21, 1997). ... Traded by Flyers to Chicago Blackhawks for C Roman Vopat (November 17, 1998). ... Bruised ribs (December 8, 1998); missed two games. ... Claimed on waivers by New York Rangers (March 4, 1999). ... Signed as free agent by Flyers (August 2, 1999). ... Signed as free agent by Columbus Blue Jackets (August 24, 2000). ... Suffered back spasms (February 28, 2001); missed two games.

HONORS: Won Jack Butterfield Trophy (1997-98). ... Named to AHL All-Star first team (1999-2000).

				REGULAR SEASON								PLAYOFFS				
Season Team	League	Gms.	G	A	Pts.	PIM	+/-	PP	SH		Gms.	G	A	Pts.	PIM
89-90—Winnipeg	MAHA	40	49	38	87	92	...	...	...		—	—	—	—	—
90-91—St. Boniface	MJHL	45	29	41	70	199	...	...	...		—	—	—	—	—
91-92—Brandon	WHL	68	23	30	53	102	...	...	...		—	—	—	—	—
92-93—Brandon	WHL	72	36	51	87	75	...	...	...		4	2	1	3	2
93-94—Brandon	WHL	63	50	47	97	112	...	...	...		13	11	3	14	23
—San Diego	IHL	—	—	—	—	—	...	...	...		1	0	0	0	0
94-95—San Diego	IHL	10	0	1	1	4	...	...	...		—	—	—	—	—
—Canadian nat'l team	Int'l	44	36	24	60	34	...	...	...		—	—	—	—	—
95-96—Baltimore	AHL	74	33	38	71	73	...	...	...		6	4	3	7	14
96-97—Worcester	AHL	70	27	27	54	89	...	...	...		5	1	2	3	14
97-98—Worcester	AHL	5	3	3	6	4	...	...	...		—	—	—	—	—
—Philadelphia	AHL	66	27	35	62	62	...	...	...		20	13	*21	*34	30
98-99—Philadelphia	NHL	13	2	6	8	4	0	0	0		—	—	—	—	—
—Chicago	NHL	28	4	3	7	8	2	1	0		—	—	—	—	—
—New York Rangers	NHL	4	0	0	0	4	-1	0	0		—	—	—	—	—
99-00—Philadelphia	AHL	73	*47	40	87	158	...	...	...		4	1	2	3	4
—Philadelphia	NHL	1	0	0	0	4	0	0	0		—	—	—	—	—
00-01—Chicago	IHL	10	2	2	4	11	...	...	...		—	—	—	—	—
—Columbus	NHL	39	5	1	6	33	-11	2	0		—	—	—	—	—
NHL Totals (3 years)		85	11	10	21	57	-6	3	0						

PERSONAL: Born April 7, 1975, in Belleville, Ont. ... 6-0/190. ... Shoots left.

TRANSACTIONS/CAREER NOTES: Selected by Chicago Blackhawks in second round (second Blackhawks pick, 50th overall) of NHL entry draft (June 26, 1993). ... Released by Blackhawks (June 18, 1998). ... Signed as free agent by Boston Bruins (July 11, 2000).

Season Team	League	Gms.	G	A	Pts.	PIM	+/-	PP	SH		Gms.	G	A	Pts.	PIM
		REGULAR SEASON									PLAYOFFS				
91-92—Kitchener	OHL	59	12	20	32	17	...	...	...		14	2	5	7	8
92-93—Kitchener	OHL	53	26	21	47	31	...	...	...		4	0	1	1	2
93-94—Kitchener	OHL	49	28	32	60	25	...	...	...		3	0	1	1	4
94-95—Kitchener	OHL	44	25	29	54	26	...	...	...		—	—	—	—	—
—Det. Jr. Red Wings	OHL	16	4	16	20	11	...	...	...		21	11	10	21	18
95-96—Indianapolis	IHL	75	6	11	17	32	...	...	...		4	0	1	1	4
96-97—Columbus	ECHL	32	18	18	36	20	...	...	...		—	—	—	—	—
—Baltimore	AHL	36	6	6	12	13	...	...	...		3	0	0	0	0
97-98—Indianapolis	IHL	60	8	11	19	25	...	...	...		3	1	0	1	0
98-99—Florida	ECHL	18	8	15	23	11	...	...	...		—	—	—	—	—
—Long Beach	IHL	51	9	19	28	30	...	...	...		8	0	0	0	8
99-00—Florida	ECHL	26	14	24	38	24	...	...	...		—	—	—	—	—
—Providence	AHL	46	17	16	33	14	...	...	...		14	6	8	14	8
00-01—Providence	AHL	60	16	51	67	18	...	...	...		17	6	7	13	6
—Boston	NHL	8	0	1	1	2	0	0	0		—	—	—	—	—
NHL Totals (1 year)		8	0	1	1	2	0	0	0						

MANN, CAMERON   RW   STARS

PERSONAL: Born April 20, 1977, in Thompson, Man. ... 6-0/194. ... Shoots right.
TRANSACTIONS/CAREER NOTES: Selected by Boston Bruins in fourth round (fifth Bruins pick, 99th overall) of NHL entry draft (July 8, 1995). ... Suffered from the flu (March 21, 1999); missed one game. ... Traded by Bruins to Dallas Stars for D Richard Jackman (June 24, 2001).
HONORS: Named to OHL All-Star first team (1995-96 and 1996-97). ... Won Jim Mahon Memorial Trophy (1995-96). ... Won Stafford Smythe Memorial Trophy (May 1996). ... Named to Memorial Cup All-Star team (1995-96).

Season Team	League	Gms.	G	A	Pts.	PIM	+/-	PP	SH		Gms.	G	A	Pts.	PIM
		REGULAR SEASON									PLAYOFFS				
93-94—Peterborough	Tier II Jr. A	16	3	14	17	23	...	...	...		—	—	—	—	—
—Peterborough	OHL	49	8	17	25	18	...	...	...		7	1	1	2	2
94-95—Peterborough	OHL	64	18	25	43	40	...	...	...		11	3	8	11	4
95-96—Peterborough	OHL	66	42	60	102	108	...	...	...		24	*27	16	*43	33
96-97—Peterborough	OHL	51	33	50	83	91	...	...	...		11	10	18	28	16
97-98—Providence	AHL	71	21	26	47	99	...	...	...		—	—	—	—	—
—Boston	NHL	9	0	1	1	4	1	0	0		—	—	—	—	—
98-99—Providence	AHL	43	21	25	46	65	...	...	...		11	7	7	14	4
—Boston	NHL	33	5	2	7	17	0	1	0		1	0	0	0	0
99-00—Boston	NHL	32	8	4	12	13	-6	1	0		—	—	—	—	—
—Providence	AHL	29	7	12	19	45	...	...	...		11	6	7	13	0
00-01—Boston	NHL	15	1	3	4	6	0	0	0		—	—	—	—	—
—Providence	AHL	39	24	23	47	59	...	...	...		—	—	—	—	—
NHL Totals (4 years)		89	14	10	24	40	-5	2	0		1	0	0	0	0

MANSON, DAVE   D   MAPLE LEAFS   M

PERSONAL: Born January 27, 1967, in Prince Albert, Sask. ... 6-2/220. ... Shoots left. ... Full Name: David Manson.
TRANSACTIONS/CAREER NOTES: Selected by Chicago Blackhawks in first round (first Blackhawks pick, 11th overall) of NHL entry draft (June 15, 1985). ... Suspended three games by NHL for pushing linesman (October 8, 1989). ... Bruised right thigh (December 8, 1989). ... Suspended 13 games by NHL for abusing linesman and returning to ice to fight (December 23, 1989). ... Suspended three games by NHL for biting (February 27, 1990). ... Suspended four games by NHL for attempting to injure another player (October 20, 1990). ... Traded by Blackhawks with third-round pick (RW Kirk Maltby) in 1992 draft to Edmonton Oilers for D Steve Smith (October 2, 1991). ... Suspended five off-days and fined $500 by NHL for spearing (October 19, 1992). ... Strained ligaments in left knee (December 7, 1992); missed one game. ... Separated shoulder (October 22, 1993); missed 13 games. ... Traded by Oilers with sixth-round pick (D Chris Kibermanis) in 1994 draft to Winnipeg Jets for C Mats Lindgren, D Boris Mironov and first-(C Jason Bonsignore) and fourth-round (RW Adam Copeland) picks in 1994 draft (March 15, 1994). ... Bruised kidneys (January 21, 1995); missed one game. ... Bruised hand (April 19, 1995); missed two games. ... Jets franchise moved to Phoenix and renamed Coyotes for 1996-97 season; NHL approved move on January 18, 1996. ... Fractured toe (November 8, 1996); missed five games. ... Traded by Coyotes to Montreal Canadiens for D Murray Baron and RW Chris Murray (March 18, 1997). ... Fined $1,000 by NHL for criticizing a referee (April 21, 1997). ... Strained hip flexor (February 7, 1998); missed one game. ... Suffered hip pointer (October 17, 1998); missed two games. ... Suspended three games and fined $1,000 by NHL for elbowing incident (October 29, 1998). ... Traded by Canadiens with G Jocelyn Thibault and D Brad Brown to Blackhawks for G Jeff Hackett, D Eric Weinrich, D Alain Nasreddine and fourth-round pick (D Chris Dyment) in 1999 draft (November 16, 1998). ... Suspended three games by NHL for fighting incident (October 6, 1999). ... Bruised foot (October 30, 1999); missed four games. ... Traded by Blackhawks with D Sylvain Cote to Dallas Stars for C Derek Plante, D Kevin Dean and second-round pick (RW Matt Keith) in 2001 draft (February 8, 2000). ... Signed as free agent by Toronto Maple Leafs (August 16, 2000). ... Suffered injury (March 10, 2001); missed four games.
HONORS: Named to WHL All-Star second team (1985-86). ... Played in NHL All-Star Game (1989 and 1993).
MISCELLANEOUS: Failed to score on a penalty shot (vs. Darcy Wakaluk, January 24, 1991).

Season Team	League	Gms.	G	A	Pts.	PIM	+/-	PP	SH		Gms.	G	A	Pts.	PIM
		REGULAR SEASON									PLAYOFFS				
82-83—Prince Albert	WHL	6	0	1	1	9	...	...	...		—	—	—	—	—
83-84—Prince Albert	WHL	70	2	7	9	233	...	...	...		5	0	0	0	4
84-85—Prince Albert	WHL	72	8	30	38	247	...	...	...		13	1	0	1	34
85-86—Prince Albert	WHL	70	14	34	48	177	...	...	...		20	1	8	9	63
86-87—Chicago	NHL	63	1	8	9	146	-2	0	0		3	0	0	0	10
87-88—Saginaw	IHL	6	0	3	3	37	...	...	...		—	—	—	—	—
—Chicago	NHL	54	1	6	7	185	-12	0	0		5	0	0	0	27
88-89—Chicago	NHL	79	18	36	54	352	5	8	1		16	0	8	8	*84
89-90—Chicago	NHL	59	5	23	28	301	4	1	0		20	2	4	6	46
90-91—Chicago	NHL	75	14	15	29	191	20	6	1		6	0	1	1	36
91-92—Edmonton	NHL	79	15	32	47	220	9	7	0		16	3	9	12	44

Season Team	League	REGULAR SEASON								PLAYOFFS				
		Gms.	G	A	Pts.	PIM	+/-	PP	SH	Gms.	G	A	Pts.	PIM
92-93—Edmonton..................	NHL	83	15	30	45	210	-28	9	1	—	—	—	—	—
93-94—Edmonton..................	NHL	57	3	13	16	140	-4	0	0	—	—	—	—	—
—Winnipeg	NHL	13	1	4	5	51	-10	1	0	—	—	—	—	—
94-95—Winnipeg	NHL	44	3	15	18	139	-20	2	0	—	—	—	—	—
95-96—Winnipeg	NHL	82	7	23	30	205	8	3	0	6	2	1	3	30
96-97—Phoenix......................	NHL	66	3	17	20	164	-25	2	0	—	—	—	—	—
—Montreal	NHL	9	1	1	2	23	-1	0	0	—	—	—	—	—
97-98—Montreal....................	NHL	81	4	30	34	122	22	2	0	10	0	1	1	14
98-99—Montreal....................	NHL	11	0	2	2	48	-3	0	0	—	—	—	—	—
—Chicago......................	NHL	64	6	15	21	107	4	2	0	—	—	—	—	—
99-00—Chicago......................	NHL	37	0	7	7	40	2	0	0	—	—	—	—	—
—Dallas......................	NHL	26	1	2	3	22	10	0	0	23	0	0	0	33
00-01—Toronto	NHL	74	4	7	11	93	13	0	0	2	0	0	0	2
NHL Totals (15 years).........		1056	102	286	388	2759	-8	43	3	107	7	24	31	326

MAPLETOFT, JUSTIN   C   ISLANDERS

PERSONAL: Born June 11, 1981, in Lloydminster, Sask. ... 6-1/180. ... Shoots left.
TRANSACTIONS/CAREER NOTES: Selected by New York Islanders in fifth round (ninth Islanders pick, 130th overall) of NHL entry draft (June 26, 1999).
HONORS: Named to WHL (East) All-Star first team (1999-2000 and 2000-01). ... Won Four Broncos Memorial Trophy (2000-01). ... Won Bob Clarke Trophy (2000-01). ... Named to Can.HL All-Star first team (2000-01).

Season Team	League	REGULAR SEASON								PLAYOFFS				
		Gms.	G	A	Pts.	PIM	+/-	PP	SH	Gms.	G	A	Pts.	PIM
97-98—Red Deer..................	WHL	65	9	4	13	41	...	...	...	5	1	0	1	0
98-99—Red Deer..................	WHL	72	24	22	46	81	...	...	...	9	2	3	5	12
99-00—Red Deer..................	WHL	72	39	57	96	135	...	...	...	4	2	1	3	28
00-01—Red Deer..................	WHL	70	43	†77	*120	111	...	...	...	22	13	21	34	59

MARA, PAUL   D   COYOTES

PERSONAL: Born September 7, 1979, in Ridgewood, N.J. ... 6-4/210. ... Shoots left.
TRANSACTIONS/CAREER NOTES: Selected by Tampa Bay Lightning in first round (first Lightning pick, seventh overall) of NHL entry draft (June 21, 1997). ... Fractured jaw (November 9, 1999); missed 13 games. ... Strained hip flexor (November 14, 2000); missed six games. ... Strained muscle in abdomen (December 2, 2000); missed four games. ... Traded by Lightning with RW Mike Johnson, RW Ruslan Zainullin and second-round pick (D Matthew Spiller) in 2001 draft to Phoenix Coyotes for G Nikolai Khabibulin and D Stan Neckar (March 5, 2001).
HONORS: Named to OHL All-Rookie team (1996-97).

M

Season Team	League	REGULAR SEASON								PLAYOFFS				
		Gms.	G	A	Pts.	PIM	+/-	PP	SH	Gms.	G	A	Pts.	PIM
94-95—Belmont Hill................	Mass. H.S.	29	19	24	43	24	...	...	...	—	—	—	—	—
95-96—Belmont Hill................	Mass. H.S.	28	18	20	38	40	...	...	...	—	—	—	—	—
96-97—Sudbury......................	OHL	44	9	34	43	61	...	...	...	—	—	—	—	—
97-98—Sudbury......................	OHL	25	8	18	26	79	...	...	...	—	—	—	—	—
—Plymouth......................	OHL	25	8	15	23	30	...	...	...	15	3	14	17	30
98-99—Plymouth......................	OHL	52	13	41	54	95	...	...	...	11	5	7	12	28
—Tampa Bay	NHL	1	1	1	2	0	-3	1	0	—	—	—	—	—
99-00—Detroit......................	IHL	15	3	5	8	22	...			—	—	—	—	—
—Tampa Bay	NHL	54	7	11	18	73	-27	4	0	—	—	—	—	—
00-01—Tampa Bay	NHL	46	6	10	16	40	-17	2	0	—	—	—	—	—
—Detroit......................	IHL	10	3	3	6	22	...			—	—	—	—	—
—Phoenix......................	NHL	16	0	4	4	14	1	0	0	—	—	—	—	—
NHL Totals (3 years)...........		117	14	26	40	127	-46	7	0					

MARACLE, NORM   G   THRASHERS

PERSONAL: Born October 2, 1974, in Belleville, Ont. ... 5-9/195. ... Catches left. ... Name pronounced MAIR-ih-kuhl.
TRANSACTIONS/CAREER NOTES: Selected by Detroit Red Wings in fifth round (sixth Red Wings pick, 126th overall) of NHL entry draft (June 26, 1993). ... Selected by Atlanta Thrashers in NHL expansion draft (June 25, 1999). ... Sprained ankle (November 1, 1999); missed 12 games.
HONORS: Named to Can.HL All-Rookie team (1991-92). ... Named to WHL (East) All-Star second team (1992-93). ... Won Can.HL Goaltender-of-the-Year Award (1993-94). ... Won Del Wilson Trophy (1993-94). ... Named to Can.HL All-Star first team (1993-94). ... Named to WHL (East) All-Star first team (1993-94). ... Named to AHL All-Star second team (1996-97 and 1997-98). ... Named to IHL All-Star first team (2000-01). ... Won James Gatschene Trophy (2000-01). ... Shared James Norris Memorial Trophy with Scott Fankhouser (2000-01). ... Won N.R. (Bud) Poile Trophy (2000-01).
MISCELLANEOUS: Stopped a penalty shot attempt (vs. Andrew Cassels, March 18, 2001).

Season Team	League	REGULAR SEASON								PLAYOFFS						
		Gms.	Min	W	L	T	GA	SO	Avg.	Gms.	Min.	W	L	GA	SO	Avg.
91-92—Saskatoon	WHL	29	1529	13	6	3	87	1	3.41	15	860	9	5	37	0	2.58
92-93—Saskatoon	WHL	53	2939	27	18	3	160	1	3.27	9	569	4	5	33	0	3.48
93-94—Saskatoon	WHL	56	3219	*41	13	1	148	2	2.76	16	939	†11	5	48	†1	3.07
94-95—Adirondack	AHL	39	1997	12	15	2	119	0	3.58	—	—	—	—	—	—	—
95-96—Adirondack	AHL	54	2949	24	18	6	135	2	2.75	1	29	0	1	4	0	8.28
96-97—Adirondack	AHL	*68	*3843	†34	22	9	*173	5	2.70	4	192	1	3	10	1	3.13
97-98—Adirondack	AHL	*66	*3710	27	29	8	*190	1	3.07	3	180	0	3	10	0	3.33
—Detroit........................	NHL	4	178	2	0	1	6	0	2.02	—	—	—	—	—	—	—

Season Team	League	REGULAR SEASON								PLAYOFFS						
		Gms.	Min	W	L	T	GA	SO	Avg.	Gms.	Min.	W	L	GA	SO	Avg.
98-99—Adirondack	AHL	6	359	3	3	0	18	0	3.01	—	—	—	—	—	—	—
—Detroit	NHL	16	821	6	5	2	31	0	2.27	2	58	0	0	3	0	3.10
99-00—Atlanta	NHL	32	1618	4	19	2	94	1	3.49	—	—	—	—	—	—	—
00-01—Atlanta	NHL	13	753	2	8	3	43	0	3.43	—	—	—	—	—	—	—
—Orlando	IHL	51	2963	33	13	‡3	100	*8	*2.02	*16	*1003	*12	4	*37	1	2.21
NHL Totals (4 years)		65	3370	14	32	8	174	1	3.10	2	58	0	0	3	0	3.10

MARCHANT, TODD   C   OILERS

PERSONAL: Born August 12, 1973, in Buffalo. ... 5-10/178. ... Shoots left. ... Brother of Terry Marchant, left winger with Edmonton Oilers organization (1994-95 through 1998-99). ... Name pronounced MAHR-shahnt.

TRANSACTIONS/CAREER NOTES: Selected by New York Rangers in seventh round (eighth Rangers pick, 164th overall) of NHL entry draft (June 26, 1993). ... Traded by Rangers to Edmonton Oilers for C Craig MacTavish (March 21, 1994). ... Suffered concussion (March 9, 1997); missed three games. ... Strained groin (November 10, 1997); missed four games. ... Scratched left eye (February 4, 1998); missed two games. ... Separated left shoulder (January 10, 2001); missed 10 games. ... Sprained right knee (February 12, 2001); missed one game.

MISCELLANEOUS: Failed to score on a penalty shot (vs. Damian Rhodes, November 13, 1996; vs. Olaf Kolzig, January 26, 1997).

Season Team	League	REGULAR SEASON								PLAYOFFS				
		Gms.	G	A	Pts.	PIM	+/-	PP	SH	Gms.	G	A	Pts.	PIM
91-92—Clarkson	ECAC	33	20	12	32	32	...	...	...	—	—	—	—	—
92-93—Clarkson	ECAC	33	18	28	46	38	...	...	...	—	—	—	—	—
93-94—U.S. national team	Int'l	59	28	39	67	48	...	...	...	—	—	—	—	—
—U.S. Olympic team	Int'l	8	1	1	2	6	...	...	...	—	—	—	—	—
—Binghamton	AHL	8	2	7	9	6	...	...	...	—	—	—	—	—
—New York Rangers	NHL	1	0	0	0	0	-1	0	0	—	—	—	—	—
—Edmonton	NHL	3	0	1	1	2	-1	0	0	—	—	—	—	—
—Cape Breton	AHL	3	1	4	5	2	...	...	...	5	1	1	2	0
94-95—Cape Breton	AHL	38	22	25	47	25	...	...	...	—	—	—	—	—
—Edmonton	NHL	45	13	14	27	32	-3	3	2	—	—	—	—	—
95-96—Edmonton	NHL	81	19	19	38	66	-19	2	3	—	—	—	—	—
96-97—Edmonton	NHL	79	14	19	33	44	11	0	4	12	4	2	6	12
97-98—Edmonton	NHL	76	14	21	35	71	9	2	1	12	1	1	2	10
98-99—Edmonton	NHL	82	14	22	36	65	3	3	1	4	1	1	2	12
99-00—Edmonton	NHL	82	17	23	40	70	7	0	1	3	1	0	1	2
00-01—Edmonton	NHL	71	13	26	39	51	1	0	4	6	0	0	0	4
NHL Totals (8 years)		520	104	145	249	401	7	10	16	37	7	4	11	40

MARCHMENT, BRYAN   D   SHARKS

PERSONAL: Born May 1, 1969, in Scarborough, Ont. ... 6-1/185. ... Shoots left.

TRANSACTIONS/CAREER NOTES: Selected by Winnipeg Jets in first round (first Jets pick, 16th overall) of NHL entry draft (June 13, 1987). ... Suspended six games by AHL for fighting (December 10, 1989). ... Sprained shoulder (March 1990). ... Suffered back spasms (March 13, 1991). ... Traded by Jets with D Chris Norton to Chicago Blackhawks for C Troy Murray and LW Warren Rychel (July 22, 1991). ... Fractured cheekbone (December 12, 1991); missed 12 games. ... Suspended one preseason game and fined $500 by NHL for headbutting (September 30, 1993). ... Traded by Blackhawks with RW Steve Larmer to Hartford Whalers for LW Patrick Poulin and D Eric Weinrich (November 2, 1993). ... Suspended two games and fined $500 by NHL for illegal check (December 21, 1993). ... Sprained ankle (January 14, 1994); missed three games. ... Sprained ankle (February 19, 1994); missed remainder of season. ... Awarded to Edmonton Oilers as compensation for Whalers signing free agent RW Steven Rice (August 30, 1994). ... Suspended one game by NHL for game misconduct penalties (March 22, 1995). ... Suspended two games by NHL for game misconduct penalties (March 27, 1995). ... Strained lower back (April 15, 1995); missed two games. ... Suspended three games and fined $500 by NHL for leaving bench to fight (April 29, 1995). ... Suspended five games by NHL for kneeing player in preseason game (September 25, 1995). ... Injured ribs (October 22, 1996); missed two games. ... Suffered from the flu (January 28, 1997); missed one game. ... Cracked ribs (February 13, 1997); missed eight games. ... Suffered concussion (April 18, 1997); missed remainder of season. ... Suspended three games and fined $1,000 by NHL for hitting another player (December 5, 1997). ... Traded by Oilers to Tampa Bay Lightning with C Steve Kelly and C Jason Bonsignore for D Roman Hamrlik and C Paul Comrie (December 30, 1997). ... Suspended three games by NHL for kneeing incident (February 6, 1998). ... Suspended eight games and fined $1,000 by NHL for kneeing incident (February 25, 1998). ... Traded by Lightning with D David Shaw and first-round pick (traded to Nashville) in 1998 draft to San Jose Sharks for LW Andrei Nazarov, first-round pick (C Vincent Lecavalier) in 1998 draft and future considerations (March 24, 1998). ... Injured shoulder (January 7, 1999); missed 20 games. ... Suspended one game by NHL for unsportsmanlike conduct (April 6, 1999). ... Injured knee (October 2, 1999); missed nine games. ... Suffered from the flu (December 8, 1999); missed one game. ... Injured ankle (January 5, 2000); missed 14 games. ... Injured groin (March 2, 2000); missed five games. ... Suspended three games by NHL for spearing incident (March 19, 2000). ... Injured neck (April 3, 2000); missed one game. ... Suspended three games by NHL for kneeing incident (March 13, 2001).

HONORS: Named to OHL All-Star second team (1988-89).

MISCELLANEOUS: Failed to score on a penalty shot (vs. Pat Jablonski, December 31, 1992).

Season Team	League	REGULAR SEASON								PLAYOFFS				
		Gms.	G	A	Pts.	PIM	+/-	PP	SH	Gms.	G	A	Pts.	PIM
84-85—Toronto Nationals	MTHL	...	14	35	49	229	...	...	...	—	—	—	—	—
85-86—Belleville	OHL	57	5	15	20	225	...	...	...	21	0	7	7	*83
86-87—Belleville	OHL	52	6	38	44	238	...	...	...	6	0	4	4	17
87-88—Belleville	OHL	56	7	51	58	200	...	...	...	6	1	3	4	19
88-89—Belleville	OHL	43	14	36	50	198	...	...	...	5	0	1	1	12
—Winnipeg	NHL	2	0	0	0	2	0	0	0	—	—	—	—	—
89-90—Winnipeg	NHL	7	0	2	2	28	0	0	0	—	—	—	—	—
—Moncton	AHL	56	4	19	23	217	...	...	...	—	—	—	—	—
90-91—Winnipeg	NHL	28	2	2	4	91	-5	0	0	—	—	—	—	—
—Moncton	AHL	33	2	11	13	101	...	...	...	—	—	—	—	—
91-92—Chicago	NHL	58	5	10	15	168	-4	2	0	16	1	0	1	36
92-93—Chicago	NHL	78	5	15	20	313	15	1	0	4	0	0	0	12

M

Season Team	League	REGULAR SEASON								PLAYOFFS				
		Gms.	G	A	Pts.	PIM	+/-	PP	SH	Gms.	G	A	Pts.	PIM
93-94—Chicago	NHL	13	1	4	5	42	-2	0	0	—	—	—	—	—
—Hartford	NHL	42	3	7	10	124	-12	0	1	—	—	—	—	—
94-95—Edmonton	NHL	40	1	5	6	184	-11	0	0	—	—	—	—	—
95-96—Edmonton	NHL	78	3	15	18	202	-7	0	0	—	—	—	—	—
96-97—Edmonton	NHL	71	3	13	16	132	13	1	0	3	0	0	0	4
97-98—Edmonton	NHL	27	0	4	4	58	-2	0	0	—	—	—	—	—
—Tampa Bay	NHL	22	2	4	6	43	-3	0	0	—	—	—	—	—
—San Jose	NHL	12	0	3	3	43	2	0	0	6	0	0	0	10
98-99—San Jose	NHL	59	2	6	8	101	-7	0	0	6	0	0	0	4
99-00—San Jose	NHL	49	0	4	4	72	3	0	0	11	2	1	3	12
00-01—San Jose	NHL	75	7	11	18	204	15	0	1	5	0	1	1	2
NHL Totals (13 years)		661	34	105	139	1807	-5	4	2	51	3	2	5	80

MARHA, JOSEF C BLACKHAWKS

PERSONAL: Born June 2, 1976, in Havlickov Brod, Czechoslovakia. ... 6-0/176. ... Shoots left. ... Name pronounced MAHR-hah.
TRANSACTIONS/CAREER NOTES: Selected by Quebec Nordiques in second round (third Nordiques pick, 35th overall) of NHL entry draft (June 28, 1994). ... Nordiques franchise moved to Colorado and renamed Avalanche for 1995-96 season (June 21, 1995). ... Traded by Avalanche to Mighty Ducks of Anaheim for LW Warren Rychel and fourth-round pick (D Sanny Lindstrom) in 1999 draft (March 24, 1998). ... Sprained ankle (October 10, 1998); missed nine games. ... Traded by Mighty Ducks to Chicago Blackhawks for fourth-round pick (C Alexander Chagodayev) in 1999 draft (January 28, 1999).

Season Team	League	REGULAR SEASON								PLAYOFFS				
		Gms.	G	A	Pts.	PIM	+/-	PP	SH	Gms.	G	A	Pts.	PIM
91-92—Jihlava	Czech.	25	12	13	25	0	...	...	...	—	—	—	—	—
92-93—Dukla Jihlava	Czech.	7	2	2	4	4	...	...	...	—	—	—	—	—
93-94—Dukla Jihlava	Czech Rep.	41	7	2	9	...	...	...	...	3	0	1	1	...
94-95—Dukla Jihlava	Czech Rep.	35	3	7	10	...	...	...	...	—	—	—	—	—
95-96—Cornwall	AHL	74	18	30	48	30	...	...	...	8	1	2	3	10
—Colorado	NHL	2	0	1	1	0	1	0	0	—	—	—	—	—
96-97—Hershey	AHL	67	23	49	72	44	...	...	...	19	6	†16	*22	10
—Colorado	NHL	6	0	1	1	0	0	0	0	—	—	—	—	—
97-98—Hershey	AHL	55	6	46	52	30	...	...	...	—	—	—	—	—
—Colorado	NHL	11	2	5	7	4	0	0	0	—	—	—	—	—
—Anaheim	NHL	12	7	4	11	0	4	3	0	—	—	—	—	—
98-99—Anaheim	NHL	10	0	1	1	0	-4	0	0	—	—	—	—	—
—Cincinnati	AHL	3	1	0	1	4	...	...	...	—	—	—	—	—
—Chicago	NHL	22	2	5	7	4	5	1	0	—	—	—	—	—
—Portland	AHL	8	0	8	8	2	...	...	...	—	—	—	—	—
99-00—Chicago	NHL	81	10	12	22	18	-10	2	1	—	—	—	—	—
00-01—Chicago	NHL	15	0	3	3	6	-4	0	0	—	—	—	—	—
—Norfolk	AHL	60	18	28	46	44	...	...	...	9	1	8	9	6
NHL Totals (6 years)		159	21	32	53	32	-8	6	1					

MARKOV, ANDREI D CANADIENS

PERSONAL: Born December 20, 1978, in Voskresensk, U.S.S.R. ... 6-0/185. ... Shoots left.
TRANSACTIONS/CAREER NOTES: Selected by Montreal Canadiens in sixth round (sixth Canadiens pick, 162nd overall) of NHL entry draft (June 27, 1998).

Season Team	League	REGULAR SEASON								PLAYOFFS				
		Gms.	G	A	Pts.	PIM	+/-	PP	SH	Gms.	G	A	Pts.	PIM
95-96—Khimik Voskresensk	CIS	36	0	0	0	14	...	...	...	—	—	—	—	—
96-97—Khimik Voskresensk	Russian	43	8	4	12	32	...	...	...	2	1	1	2	0
97-98—Khimik Voskresensk	Russian	43	10	5	15	83	...	...	...	—	—	—	—	—
98-99—Dynamo Moscow	Russian	38	10	11	21	32	...	...	...	16	3	6	9	6
99-00—Dynamo Moscow	Russian	29	11	12	23	28	...	...	...	17	4	3	7	8
00-01—Montreal	NHL	63	6	17	23	18	-6	2	0	—	—	—	—	—
—Quebec	AHL	14	0	5	5	4	...	...	...	7	1	1	2	2
NHL Totals (1 year)		63	6	17	23	18	-6	2	0					

MARKOV, DANNY D COYOTES

PERSONAL: Born July 11, 1976, in Moscow, U.S.S.R. ... 6-1/190. ... Shoots left. ... Full Name: Daniil Markov.
TRANSACTIONS/CAREER NOTES: Selected by Toronto Maple Leafs in ninth round (seventh Maple Leafs pick, 223rd overall) of NHL entry draft (July 8, 1995). ... Suffered concussion (October 16, 1998); missed one game. ... Fractured foot (November 11, 1998); missed two games. ... Suffered throat injury (November 23, 1998); missed two games. ... Suffered back spasms (December 7, 1998); missed two games. ... Separated shoulder (December 16, 1998); missed 11 games. ... Suffered injury (December 15, 1999); missed three games. ... Injured ankle (January 5, 2000); missed 10 games. ... Suffered injury (March 15, 2000); missed one game. ... Injured foot (March 23, 2000); missed final eight games of season. ... Suffered injury (January 6, 2001); missed one game. ... Injured back (January 31, 2001); missed 22 games. ... Traded by Maple Leafs to Phoenix Coyotes for C Robert Reichel, C Travis Green and RW Craig Mills (June 12, 2001).

Season Team	League	REGULAR SEASON								PLAYOFFS				
		Gms.	G	A	Pts.	PIM	+/-	PP	SH	Gms.	G	A	Pts.	PIM
93-94—Spartak Moscow	CIS	13	1	0	1	6	...	...	...	1	0	0	0	0
94-95—Spartak Moscow	CIS	39	0	1	1	36	...	...	...	—	—	—	—	—
95-96—Spartak Moscow	CIS	38	2	0	2	12	...	...	...	2	0	0	0	2

M

Season Team	League	REGULAR SEASON Gms.	G	A	Pts.	PIM	+/-	PP	SH	PLAYOFFS Gms.	G	A	Pts.	PIM
96-97—Spartak Moscow	Russian	36	3	6	9	41	...	...	...	—	—	—	—	—
—St. John's	AHL	10	2	4	6	18	...	...	...	11	2	6	8	14
97-98—St. John's	AHL	52	3	23	26	124	...	...	...	2	0	1	1	0
—Toronto	NHL	25	2	5	7	28	0	1	0	—	—	—	—	—
98-99—Toronto	NHL	57	4	8	12	47	5	0	0	17	0	6	6	18
99-00—Toronto	NHL	59	0	10	10	28	13	0	0	12	0	3	3	10
00-01—Toronto	NHL	59	3	13	16	34	6	1	0	11	1	1	2	12
NHL Totals (4 years)		200	9	36	45	137	24	2	0	40	1	10	11	40

MARLEAU, PATRICK   C   SHARKS

PERSONAL: Born September 15, 1979, in Swift Current, Sask. ... 6-2/210. ... Shoots left. ... Name pronounced MAHR-loh.
TRANSACTIONS/CAREER NOTES: Selected by San Jose Sharks in first round (first Sharks pick, second overall) of NHL entry draft (June 21, 1997).
HONORS: Named to Can.HL All-Star second team (1996-97). ... Named to WHL (West) All-Star first team (1996-97).

Season Team	League	REGULAR SEASON Gms.	G	A	Pts.	PIM	+/-	PP	SH	PLAYOFFS Gms.	G	A	Pts.	PIM
93-94—Swift Current	Jr. A	53	72	95	167	...	...	...	...	—	—	—	—	—
94-95—Swift Current	Jr. A	30	30	22	52	20	...	...	...	—	—	—	—	—
95-96—Seattle	WHL	72	32	42	74	22	...	...	...	5	3	4	7	4
96-97—Seattle	WHL	71	51	74	125	37	...	...	...	15	7	16	23	12
97-98—San Jose	NHL	74	13	19	32	14	5	1	0	6	0	1	1	0
98-99—San Jose	NHL	81	21	24	45	24	10	4	0	6	2	1	3	4
99-00—San Jose	NHL	81	17	23	40	36	-9	3	0	5	1	1	2	2
00-01—San Jose	NHL	81	25	27	52	22	7	5	0	6	2	0	2	4
NHL Totals (4 years)		317	76	93	169	96	13	13	0	22	5	3	8	10

MARSHALL, GRANT   RW   STARS

PERSONAL: Born June 9, 1973, in Mississauga, Ont. ... 6-1/193. ... Shoots right.
TRANSACTIONS/CAREER NOTES: Selected by Toronto Maple Leafs in first round (second Maple Leafs pick, 23rd overall) of NHL entry draft (June 20, 1992). ... Awarded to Dallas Stars with C Peter Zezel as compensation for Maple Leafs signing free-agent RW Mike Craig (August 10, 1994). ... Strained muscle (November 15, 1996); missed four games. ... Sprained shoulder (December 8, 1996); missed four games. ... Suffered concussion (January 4, 1997); missed two games. ... Strained groin (November 21, 1997); missed five games. ... Strained groin (April 16, 1998); missed one game. ... Fined $1,000 by NHL for elbowing incident (May 8, 1998). ... Injured groin prior to start of 1999-2000 season; missed first four games of season. ... Reinjured groin (October 13, 1999); missed 22 games. ... Reinjured groin (December 15, 1999); missed two games. ... Reinjured groin (December 27, 1999); missed five games. ... Reinjured groin (March 13, 2000); missed three games. ... Strained thigh muscle (December 17, 2000); missed five games.
MISCELLANEOUS: Member of Stanley Cup championship team (1999).

Season Team	League	REGULAR SEASON Gms.	G	A	Pts.	PIM	+/-	PP	SH	PLAYOFFS Gms.	G	A	Pts.	PIM
90-91—Ottawa	OHL	26	6	11	17	25	...	...	...	1	0	0	0	0
91-92—Ottawa	OHL	61	32	51	83	132	...	...	...	11	6	11	17	11
92-93—Newmarket	OHL	31	12	25	37	85	...	...	...	7	4	7	11	20
—Ottawa	OHL	30	14	28	42	83	...	...	...	—	—	—	—	—
—St. John's	AHL	2	0	0	0	0	...	...	...	2	0	0	0	2
93-94—St. John's	AHL	67	11	29	40	155	...	...	...	11	1	5	6	17
94-95—Kalamazoo	IHL	61	17	29	46	96	...	...	...	16	9	3	12	27
—Dallas	NHL	2	0	1	1	0	1	0	0	—	—	—	—	—
95-96—Dallas	NHL	70	9	19	28	111	0	0	0	—	—	—	—	—
96-97—Dallas	NHL	56	6	4	10	98	5	0	0	5	0	2	2	8
97-98—Dallas	NHL	72	9	10	19	96	-2	3	0	17	0	2	2	47
98-99—Dallas	NHL	82	13	18	31	85	1	2	0	14	0	3	3	20
99-00—Dallas	NHL	45	2	6	8	38	-5	1	0	14	0	1	1	4
00-01—Dallas	NHL	75	13	24	37	64	1	4	0	9	0	0	0	0
NHL Totals (7 years)		402	52	82	134	492	1	10	0	59	0	8	8	79

MARSHALL, JASON   D   WILD

PERSONAL: Born February 22, 1971, in Cranbrook, B.C. ... 6-2/200. ... Shoots right.
TRANSACTIONS/CAREER NOTES: Selected by St. Louis Blues in first round (first Blues pick, ninth overall) of NHL entry draft (June 17, 1989). ... Traded by Blues to Mighty Ducks of Anaheim for D Bill Houlder (August 29, 1994). ... Lacerated finger (November 24, 1996); missed two games. ... Bruised hand (March 19, 1997); missed four games. ... Separated right shoulder (December 19, 1997); missed eight games. ... Strained left hamstring (December 18, 1998); missed six games. ... Suffered illness (March 17, 1999); missed one game. ... Traded by Mighty Ducks to Washington Capitals for D Alexei Tezikov and fourth-round pick (D Brandon Rogers) in 2001 draft (March 13, 2001). ... Signed as free agent by Minnesota Wild (July 2, 2001).

Season Team	League	REGULAR SEASON Gms.	G	A	Pts.	PIM	+/-	PP	SH	PLAYOFFS Gms.	G	A	Pts.	PIM
87-88—Columbia Valley	KIJHL	40	4	28	32	150	...	...	...	—	—	—	—	—
88-89—Vernon	BCJHL	48	10	30	40	197	...	...	...	31	6	6	12	141
—Canadian nat'l team	Int'l	2	0	1	1	0	...	...	...	—	—	—	—	—
89-90—Canadian nat'l team	Int'l	72	1	11	12	57	...	...	...	—	—	—	—	—
90-91—Tri-City	WHL	59	10	34	44	236	...	...	...	7	1	2	3	20
—Peoria	IHL	—	—	—	—	—	...	...	...	18	0	1	1	48

Season Team	League	Gms.	G	A	Pts.	PIM	+/-	PP	SH	Gms.	G	A	Pts.	PIM
91-92—Peoria	IHL	78	4	18	22	178	...	...	...	10	0	1	1	16
—St. Louis	NHL	2	1	0	1	4	0	0	0	—	—	—	—	—
92-93—Peoria	IHL	77	4	16	20	229	...	...	...	4	0	0	0	20
93-94—Peoria	IHL	20	1	1	2	72	...	...	...	3	2	0	2	2
—Canadian nat'l team	Int'l	41	3	10	13	60	...	...	...	—	—	—	—	—
94-95—San Diego	IHL	80	7	18	25	218	...	...	...	5	0	1	1	8
—Anaheim	NHL	1	0	0	0	0	-2	0	0	—	—	—	—	—
95-96—Baltimore	AHL	57	1	13	14	150	...	...	...	—	—	—	—	—
—Anaheim	NHL	24	0	1	1	42	3	0	0	—	—	—	—	—
96-97—Anaheim	NHL	73	1	9	10	140	6	0	0	7	0	1	1	4
97-98—Anaheim	NHL	72	3	6	9	189	-8	1	0	—	—	—	—	—
98-99—Anaheim	NHL	72	1	7	8	142	-5	0	0	4	1	0	1	10
99-00—Anaheim	NHL	55	0	3	3	88	-10	0	0	—	—	—	—	—
00-01—Anaheim	NHL	50	3	4	7	105	-12	2	1	—	—	—	—	—
—Washington	NHL	5	0	0	0	17	-1	0	0	—	—	—	—	—
NHL Totals (8 years)		354	9	30	39	727	-29	3	1	11	1	1	2	14

MARTINS, STEVE   C

PERSONAL: Born April 13, 1972, in Gatineau, Que. ... 5-9/175. ... Shoots left.

TRANSACTIONS/CAREER NOTES: Selected by Hartford Whalers in first round (first Whalers pick, fifth overall) of NHL supplemental draft (June 24, 1994). ... Whalers franchise moved to North Carolina and renamed Carolina Hurricanes for 1997-98 season; NHL approved move on June 25, 1997. ... Signed as free agent by Ottawa Senators (July 22, 1998). ... Suffered back spasms (December 4, 1998); missed four games. ... Injured hip flexor (February 13, 1999); missed three games. ... Reinjured hip flexor (February 23, 1999); missed four games. ... Suffered from the flu (March 24, 1999); missed four games. ... Claimed on waivers by Tampa Bay Lightning (October 29, 1999). ... Strained groin (November 13, 1999); missed one game. ... Sprained ankle (December 4, 1999); missed 12 games. ... Strained groin (November 14, 2000); missed three games. ... Traded by Lightning to New York Islanders for conditional pick in 2001 draft (January 4, 2001). ... Sprained muscle in chest (January 16, 2001); missed one game.

HONORS: Named to NCAA All-America (East) first team (1993-94). ... Named ECAC Player of the Year (1993-94). ... Named to NCAA All-Tournament team (1993-94). ... Named to ECAC All-Star first team (1993-94).

Season Team	League	Gms.	G	A	Pts.	PIM	+/-	PP	SH	Gms.	G	A	Pts.	PIM
91-92—Harvard University	ECAC	20	13	14	27	26	...	...	...	—	—	—	—	—
92-93—Harvard University	ECAC	18	6	8	14	40	...	...	...	—	—	—	—	—
93-94—Harvard University	ECAC	32	25	35	60	93	...	...	...	—	—	—	—	—
94-95—Harvard University	ECAC	28	15	23	38	93	...	...	...	—	—	—	—	—
95-96—Springfield	AHL	30	9	20	29	10	...	...	...	—	—	—	—	—
—Hartford	NHL	23	1	3	4	8	-3	0	0	—	—	—	—	—
96-97—Springfield	AHL	63	12	31	43	78	...	...	...	17	1	3	4	26
—Hartford	NHL	2	0	1	1	0	0	0	0	—	—	—	—	—
97-98—Chicago	IHL	78	20	41	61	122	...	...	...	21	6	14	20	28
—Carolina	NHL	3	0	0	0	0	0	0	0	—	—	—	—	—
98-99—Detroit	IHL	4	1	6	7	16	...	...	...	—	—	—	—	—
—Ottawa	NHL	36	4	3	7	10	4	1	0	—	—	—	—	—
99-00—Ottawa	NHL	2	1	0	1	0	-1	0	0	—	—	—	—	—
—Tampa Bay	NHL	57	5	7	12	37	-11	0	1	—	—	—	—	—
00-01—Tampa Bay	NHL	20	1	1	2	13	-9	0	0	—	—	—	—	—
—Detroit	IHL	8	5	4	9	4	...	...	...	—	—	—	—	—
—New York Islanders	NHL	39	1	3	4	20	-7	0	1	—	—	—	—	—
—Chicago	IHL	5	1	2	3	0	...	...	...	16	1	6	7	22
NHL Totals (6 years)		182	13	18	31	88	-27	1	2					

MASON, CHRIS   G   PREDATORS

PERSONAL: Born April 20, 1976, in Red Deer, Alta. ... 6-0/189. ... Catches left.

TRANSACTIONS/CAREER NOTES: Selected by New Jersey Devils in fifth round (seventh Devils pick, 122nd overall) of NHL entry draft (July 8, 1995). ... Signed as free agent by Mighty Ducks of Anaheim (May 31, 1996). ... Traded by Mighty Ducks with D Marc Moro to Nashville Predators for G Dominic Roussel (October 5, 1998).

Season Team	League	Gms.	Min.	W	L	T	GA	SO	Avg.	Gms.	Min.	W	L	GA	SO	Avg.
93-94—Victoria	WHL	3	129	0	3	0	16	...	7.44	—	—	—	—	—	—	—
94-95—Prince George	WHL	44	2288	8	30	1	192	1	5.03	—	—	—	—	—	—	—
95-96—Prince George	WHL	59	3289	16	37	1	236	1	4.31	—	—	—	—	—	—	—
96-97—Prince George	WHL	50	2851	19	24	4	172	2	3.62	15	938	9	6	44	†1	2.81
97-98—Cincinnati	AHL	47	2368	13	19	7	136	0	3.45	—	—	—	—	—	—	—
98-99—Milwaukee	IHL	34	1901	15	12	‡6	92	1	2.90	—	—	—	—	—	—	—
—Nashville	NHL	3	69	0	0	0	6	0	5.22	—	—	—	—	—	—	—
99-00—Milwaukee	IHL	53	2952	27	21	‡8	137	2	2.78	3	252	1	2	11	0	2.62
00-01—Nashville	NHL	1	59	0	1	0	2	0	2.03	—	—	—	—	—	—	—
—Milwaukee	IHL	37	2226	17	14	‡5	87	5	2.35	4	239	1	3	12	0	3.01
NHL Totals (2 years)		4	128	0	1	0	8	0	3.75							

MASON, WES   LW   THRASHERS

PERSONAL: Born December 12, 1977, in Windsor, Ont. ... 6-2/190. ... Shoots left. ... Full Name: Wesley Mason.

TRANSACTIONS/CAREER NOTES: Selected by New Jersey Devils in second round (second Devils pick, 38th overall) of NHL entry draft (June 22, 1996). ... Traded by Devils with LW Eric Bertrand and seventh-round pick (LW Ken Magowan) in 2000 draft to Atlanta Thrashers for LW Jeff Williams and C Sylvain Cloutier (November 1, 1999).

Season Team	League	Gms.	G	A	Pts.	PIM	+/-	PP	SH	Gms.	G	A	Pts.	PIM
94-95—Sarnia	OHL	38	1	8	9	50	...	...	...	2	0	0	0	9
95-96—Sarnia	OHL	63	23	45	68	97	...	...	...	10	3	2	5	16
96-97—Sarnia	OHL	66	45	46	91	72	...	...	...	12	7	11	18	10
97-98—Sarnia	OHL	2	1	0	1	4	...	...	...	—	—	—	—	—
—Sudbury	OHL	9	3	8	11	12	...	...	...	—	—	—	—	—
—Kingston	OHL	38	10	19	29	38	...	...	...	10	0	2	2	4
98-99—Albany	AHL	27	4	4	8	36	...	...	...	—	—	—	—	—
—Augusta	ECHL	30	13	14	27	75	...	...	...	2	1	0	1	6
99-00—Augusta	ECHL	28	18	20	38	41	...	...	...	—	—	—	—	—
—Orlando	IHL	33	11	15	26	30	...	...	...	—	—	—	—	—
—Louisville	AHL	8	1	2	3	2	...	...	...	3	0	0	0	0
00-01—Orlando	IHL	45	13	14	27	52	...	...	...	16	6	7	13	24

MATHIEU, ALEXANDRE   C   PENGUINS

PERSONAL: Born February 12, 1979, in Repentigny, Que. ... 6-2/177. ... Shoots left.
TRANSACTIONS/CAREER NOTES: Selected by Pittsburgh Penguins in fourth round (fourth Penguins pick, 97th overall) of NHL entry draft (June 21, 1997).

Season Team	League	Gms.	G	A	Pts.	PIM	+/-	PP	SH	Gms.	G	A	Pts.	PIM
95-96—Laval	QMJHL	44	6	24	30	24	...	...	...	—	—	—	—	—
96-97—Halifax	QMJHL	70	12	22	34	18	...	...	...	18	2	5	7	2
97-98—Halifax	QMJHL	68	35	41	76	52	...	...	...	5	1	1	2	4
98-99—Halifax	QMJHL	69	21	27	48	90	...	...	...	5	0	1	1	4
99-00—Wilkes-Barre/Scranton	AHL	52	4	4	8	18	...	...	...	—	—	—	—	—
00-01—Wilkes-Barre/Scranton	AHL	77	11	17	28	32	...	...	...	16	4	2	6	14

MATHIEU, MARQUIS   C

PERSONAL: Born May 31, 1973, in Hartford, Conn. ... 5-11/190. ... Shoots right. ... Full Name: Marquis Johnny Mathieu.
TRANSACTIONS/CAREER NOTES: Signed as non-drafted free agent by Boston Bruins (October 27, 1998).

Season Team	League	Gms.	G	A	Pts.	PIM	+/-	PP	SH	Gms.	G	A	Pts.	PIM
91-92—St. Jean	QMJHL	70	20	36	56	166	...	...	...	—	—	—	—	—
92-93—St. Jean	QMJHL	70	31	36	67	115	...	...	...	2	1	0	1	33
93-94—Fredericton	AHL	22	4	6	10	28	...	...	...	—	—	—	—	—
—Wheeling	ECHL	42	12	11	23	75	...	...	...	9	1	3	4	23
94-95—Worcester	AHL	2	0	0	0	0	...	...	...	—	—	—	—	—
—Toledo	ECHL	33	13	22	35	168	...	...	...	—	—	—	—	—
—Raleigh	ECHL	33	15	17	32	181	...	...	...	—	—	—	—	—
95-96—Worcester	AHL	17	3	10	13	26	...	...	...	—	—	—	—	—
—Houston	IHL	2	1	0	1	9	...	...	...	—	—	—	—	—
—Birmingham	ECHL	18	5	7	12	87	...	...	...	—	—	—	—	—
—Johnstown	ECHL	25	4	17	21	89	...	...	...	—	—	—	—	—
96-97—Worcester	AHL	30	8	16	24	88	...	...	...	1	0	0	0	0
97-98—Wheeling	ECHL	58	26	29	55	276	...	...	...	15	1	10	11	38
98-99—Providence	AHL	64	15	15	30	166	...	...	...	19	4	7	11	30
—Boston	NHL	9	0	0	0	8	-1	0	0	—	—	—	—	—
99-00—Boston	NHL	6	0	2	2	4	-2	0	0	—	—	—	—	—
—Providence	AHL	18	3	3	6	45	...	...	...	—	—	—	—	—
00-01—Providence	AHL	57	10	7	17	205	...	...	...	17	3	2	5	64
—Boston	NHL	1	0	0	0	2	0	0	0	—	—	—	—	—
NHL Totals (3 years)		16	0	2	2	14	-3	0	0					

MATTE, CHRISTIAN   RW

PERSONAL: Born January 20, 1975, in Hull, Que. ... 5-11/170. ... Shoots right. ... Name pronounced MAT.
TRANSACTIONS/CAREER NOTES: Selected by Quebec Nordiques in sixth round (eighth Nordiques pick, 153rd overall) of NHL entry draft (June 26, 1993). ... Nordiques franchise moved to Colorado and renamed Avalanche for 1995-96 season (June 21, 1995). ... Fractured hand (January 2, 1997); missed six games. ... Signed as free agent by Minnesota Wild (July 10, 2000).
HONORS: Named to QMJHL All-Star second team (1993-94). ... Won John B. Sollenberger Trophy (1999-2000). ... Named to AHL All-Star first team (1999-2000).

Season Team	League	Gms.	G	A	Pts.	PIM	+/-	PP	SH	Gms.	G	A	Pts.	PIM
92-93—Granby	QMJHL	68	17	36	53	56	...	...	...	—	—	—	—	—
93-94—Granby	QMJHL	59	50	47	97	103	...	...	...	7	5	5	10	12
—Cornwall	AHL	1	0	0	0	0	...	...	...	—	—	—	—	—
94-95—Granby	QMJHL	66	50	66	116	86	...	...	...	13	11	7	18	12
—Cornwall	AHL	—	—	—	—	—	...	...	...	3	0	1	1	2
95-96—Cornwall	AHL	64	20	32	52	51	...	...	...	7	1	1	2	6
96-97—Hershey	AHL	49	18	18	36	78	...	...	...	22	8	3	11	25
—Colorado	NHL	5	1	1	2	0	1	0	0	—	—	—	—	—
97-98—Hershey	AHL	71	33	40	73	109	...	...	...	7	3	2	5	4
—Colorado	NHL	5	0	0	0	6	0	0	0	—	—	—	—	—

M

Season Team	League	REGULAR SEASON								PLAYOFFS				
		Gms.	G	A	Pts.	PIM	+/-	PP	SH	Gms.	G	A	Pts.	PIM
98-99—Hershey	AHL	60	31	47	78	48	...	...	...	5	2	1	3	8
—Colorado	NHL	7	1	1	2	0	-2	0	0	—	—	—	—	—
99-00—Hershey	AHL	73	43	*61	*104	85	...	...	...	14	8	6	14	10
—Colorado	NHL	5	0	1	1	4	-2	0	0	—	—	—	—	—
00-01—Cleveland	IHL	58	*38	29	67	59	...	...	...	4	1	1	2	0
—Minnesota	NHL	3	0	0	0	2	0	0	0	—	—	—	—	—
NHL Totals (5 years)		25	2	3	5	12	-3	0	0					

MATTEAU, STEPHANE   LW   SHARKS

PERSONAL: Born September 2, 1969, in Rouyn-Noranda, Que. ... 6-4/220. ... Shoots left. ... Name pronounced muh-TOH.

TRANSACTIONS/CAREER NOTES: Selected by Calgary Flames in second round (second Flames pick, 25th overall) of NHL entry draft (June 13, 1987). ... Bruised thigh (October 10, 1991); missed 43 games. ... Traded by Flames to Chicago Blackhawks for D Trent Yawney (December 16, 1991). ... Fractured left foot (January 27, 1992); missed 12 games. ... Suffered tonsillitis (September 1992); missed first three games of 1992-93 season. ... Pulled groin (December 17, 1993); missed three games. ... Traded by Blackhawks with RW Brian Noonan to New York Rangers for RW Tony Amonte and rights to LW Matt Oates (March 21, 1994). ... Suffered from the flu (February 1, 1995); missed one game. ... Suffered back spasms (April 24, 1995); missed two games. ... Fractured hand (September 24, 1995); missed six games. ... Traded by Rangers to St. Louis Blues for C Ian Laperriere (December 28, 1995). ... Traded by Blues to San Jose Sharks for C Darren Turcotte (July 25, 1997). ... Injured back (October 9, 1997); missed three games. ... Injured back (December 16, 1997); missed two games. ... Injured hand (March 12, 1998); missed four games. ... Injured back (October 9, 1998); missed first game of season. ... Injured neck (November 7, 1998); missed two games. ... Injured thumb (November 27, 1998); missed three games. ... Injured back (January 5, 1999); missed three games. ... Injured back (March 9, 1999); missed three games. ... Reinjured back (April 8, 1999); missed one game. ... Injured back (March 6, 2000); missed four games.

MISCELLANEOUS: Member of Stanley Cup championship team (1994).

Season Team	League	REGULAR SEASON								PLAYOFFS				
		Gms.	G	A	Pts.	PIM	+/-	PP	SH	Gms.	G	A	Pts.	PIM
85-86—Hull	QMJHL	60	6	8	14	19	...	...	...	4	0	0	0	0
86-87—Hull	QMJHL	69	27	48	75	113	...	...	...	8	3	7	10	8
87-88—Hull	QMJHL	57	17	40	57	179	...	...	...	18	5	14	19	84
88-89—Hull	QMJHL	59	44	45	89	202	...	...	...	9	8	6	14	30
—Salt Lake City	IHL	—	—	—	—	—	...	...	...	9	0	4	4	13
89-90—Salt Lake City	IHL	81	23	35	58	130	...	...	...	10	6	3	9	38
90-91—Calgary	NHL	78	15	19	34	93	17	0	1	5	0	1	1	0
91-92—Calgary	NHL	4	1	0	1	19	2	0	0	—	—	—	—	—
—Chicago	NHL	20	5	8	13	45	3	1	0	18	4	6	10	24
92-93—Chicago	NHL	79	15	18	33	98	6	2	0	3	0	1	1	2
93-94—Chicago	NHL	65	15	16	31	55	10	2	0	—	—	—	—	—
—New York Rangers	NHL	12	4	3	7	2	5	1	0	23	6	3	9	20
94-95—New York Rangers	NHL	41	3	5	8	25	-8	0	0	9	0	1	1	10
95-96—New York Rangers	NHL	32	4	2	6	22	-4	1	0	—	—	—	—	—
—St. Louis	NHL	46	7	13	20	65	-4	3	0	11	0	2	2	8
96-97—St. Louis	NHL	74	16	20	36	50	11	1	2	5	0	0	0	0
97-98—San Jose	NHL	73	15	14	29	60	4	1	0	4	0	1	1	0
98-99—San Jose	NHL	68	8	15	23	73	2	0	0	5	0	0	0	6
99-00—San Jose	NHL	69	12	12	24	61	-3	0	0	10	0	2	2	8
00-01—San Jose	NHL	80	13	19	32	32	5	1	0	6	1	3	4	0
NHL Totals (11 years)		741	133	164	297	700	46	13	3	99	11	20	31	78

MATTEUCCI, MIKE   D   WILD

PERSONAL: Born December 12, 1971, in Trail, B.C. ... 6-3/225. ... Shoots left.

TRANSACTIONS/CAREER NOTES: Signed as non-drafted free agent by Edmonton Oilers (September 10, 1998). ... Traded by Oilers to Boston Bruins for G Kay Whitmore (December 29, 1999). ... Signed as free agent by Minnesota Wild (July 20, 2000).

Season Team	League	REGULAR SEASON								PLAYOFFS				
		Gms.	G	A	Pts.	PIM	+/-	PP	SH	Gms.	G	A	Pts.	PIM
92-93—Lake Superior State	CCHA	19	1	3	4	16	...	...	...	—	—	—	—	—
93-94—Lake Superior State	CCHA	45	6	11	17	64	...	...	...	—	—	—	—	—
94-95—Lake Superior State	CCHA	38	3	11	14	52	...	...	...	—	—	—	—	—
95-96—Lake Superior State	CCHA	40	3	13	16	82	...	...	...	—	—	—	—	—
—Los Angeles	IHL	4	0	0	0	7	...	...	...	—	—	—	—	—
96-97—Long Beach	IHL	81	4	4	8	254	...	...	...	18	0	1	1	42
97-98—Long Beach	IHL	79	1	7	8	258	...	...	...	17	0	2	2	57
98-99—Long Beach	IHL	79	3	9	12	253	...	...	...	8	0	1	1	12
99-00—Long Beach	IHL	64	0	4	4	170	...	...	...	6	0	0	0	16
00-01—Cleveland	IHL	69	0	7	7	189	...	...	...	4	0	0	0	15
—Minnesota	NHL	3	0	0	0	2	-2	0	0	—	—	—	—	—
NHL Totals (1 year)		3	0	0	0	2	-2	0	0					

MATVICHUK, RICHARD   D   STARS

PERSONAL: Born February 5, 1973, in Edmonton. ... 6-2/215. ... Shoots left. ... Name pronounced MAT-vih-chuk.

TRANSACTIONS/CAREER NOTES: Selected by Minnesota North Stars in first round (first North Stars pick, eighth overall) of 1991 NHL entry draft (June 22, 1991). ... Strained lower back (November 9, 1992); missed two games. ... Sprained ankle (December 27, 1992); missed 10 games. ... North Stars franchise moved from Minnesota to Dallas and renamed Stars for 1993-94 season. ... Bruised shoulder (April 5, 1994); missed one game. ... Tore knee ligaments (September 20, 1994) and underwent surgery; missed first 16 games of season. ... Suffered concussion (March 13, 1996); missed five games. ... Bruised shoulder (October 26, 1996); missed two games. ... Strained groin (February 18,

1997); missed 19 games. ... Tore anterior cruciate ligament in knee (January 21, 1998); missed eight games. ... Bruised thigh (December 31, 1998); missed one game. ... Suffered from headaches (January 8, 1999); missed one game. ... Strained groin (March 14, 1999); missed two games. ... Reinjured groin (March 19, 1999); missed final 14 games of regular season and one playoff game. ... Injured knee (October 16, 1999); missed three games. ... Injured knee (November 10, 1999); missed three games. ... Suffered from the flu (January 23, 2000); missed one game. ... Sprained thumb (February 2, 2000); missed one game. ... Sprained knee (March 1, 2000); missed one game. ... Fractured jaw (January 24, 2001); missed four games.

HONORS: Won Bill Hunter Trophy (1991-92). ... Named to Can.HL All-Star second team (1991-92). ... Named to WHL (East) All-Star first team (1991-92).

MISCELLANEOUS: Member of Stanley Cup championship team (1999).

			REGULAR SEASON							PLAYOFFS				
Season Team	League	Gms.	G	A	Pts.	PIM	+/-	PP	SH	Gms.	G	A	Pts.	PIM
88-89—Fort Saskatchewan	AJHL	58	7	36	43	147	...	...	...	—	—	—	—	—
89-90—Saskatoon	WHL	56	8	24	32	126	...	...	...	10	2	8	10	16
90-91—Saskatoon	WHL	68	13	36	49	117	...	...	...	—	—	—	—	—
91-92—Saskatoon	WHL	58	14	40	54	126	...	...	...	22	1	9	10	61
92-93—Minnesota	NHL	53	2	3	5	26	-8	1	0	—	—	—	—	—
—Kalamazoo	IHL	3	0	1	1	6	...	...	...	—	—	—	—	—
93-94—Kalamazoo	IHL	43	8	17	25	84	...	...	...	—	—	—	—	—
—Dallas	NHL	25	0	3	3	22	1	0	0	7	1	1	2	12
94-95—Dallas	NHL	14	0	2	2	14	-7	0	0	5	0	2	2	4
—Kalamazoo	IHL	17	0	6	6	16	...	...	...	—	—	—	—	—
95-96—Dallas	NHL	73	6	16	22	71	4	0	0	—	—	—	—	—
96-97—Dallas	NHL	57	5	7	12	87	1	0	2	7	0	1	1	20
97-98—Dallas	NHL	74	3	15	18	63	7	0	0	16	1	1	2	14
98-99—Dallas	NHL	64	3	9	12	51	23	1	0	22	1	5	6	20
99-00—Dallas	NHL	70	4	21	25	42	7	0	0	23	2	5	7	14
00-01—Dallas	NHL	78	4	16	20	62	5	2	0	10	0	0	0	14
NHL Totals (9 years)...........		508	27	92	119	438	33	4	2	90	5	15	20	98

MAY, BRAD — LW — COYOTES

PERSONAL: Born November 29, 1971, in Toronto. ... 6-1/210. ... Shoots left.

TRANSACTIONS/CAREER NOTES: Selected by Buffalo Sabres in first round (first Sabres pick, 14th overall) of NHL entry draft (June 16, 1990). ... Fractured bone in hand (March 11, 1995); missed 15 games. ... Injured left arm (March 3, 1996); missed one game. ... Suspended one game for accumulating three game misconduct penalties (March 31, 1996). ... Underwent right shoulder surgery (October 14, 1996); missed 27 games. ... Broken right hand (December 20, 1996); missed nine games. ... Fractured thumb (March 1, 1997); missed four games. ... Strained shoulder (September 27, 1997); missed first six games of season. ... Sprained knee (December 29, 1997); missed 11 games. ... Traded by Sabres with third-round pick (traded to Tampa Bay) in 1999 draft to Vancouver Canucks for LW Geoff Sanderson (February 4, 1998). ... Strained groin (October 30, 1998); missed five games. ... Fractured hand (March 26, 1999); missed final 10 games of season. ... Sprained medial collateral ligament in knee (December 10, 1999); missed 13 games. ... Traded by Canucks to Phoenix Coyotes for future considerations (June 25, 2000). ... Suspended 20 games by NHL for slashing incident (November 15, 2000).

HONORS: Named to OHL All-Star second team (1989-90 and 1990-91).

MISCELLANEOUS: Scored on a penalty shot (vs. Andy Moog, November, 11, 1992).

M

			REGULAR SEASON							PLAYOFFS				
Season Team	League	Gms.	G	A	Pts.	PIM	+/-	PP	SH	Gms.	G	A	Pts.	PIM
87-88—Markham Jr. B	OHA	6	1	1	2	21	...	...	...	—	—	—	—	—
88-89—Niagara Falls	OHL	65	8	14	22	304	...	...	...	17	0	1	1	55
89-90—Niagara Falls	OHL	61	33	58	91	223	...	...	...	16	9	13	22	64
90-91—Niagara Falls	OHL	34	37	32	69	93	...	...	...	14	11	14	25	53
91-92—Buffalo	NHL	69	11	6	17	309	-12	1	0	7	1	4	5	2
92-93—Buffalo	NHL	82	13	13	26	242	3	0	0	8	1	1	2	14
93-94—Buffalo	NHL	84	18	27	45	171	-6	3	0	7	0	2	2	9
94-95—Buffalo	NHL	33	3	3	6	87	5	1	0	4	0	0	0	2
95-96—Buffalo	NHL	79	15	29	44	295	6	3	0	—	—	—	—	—
96-97—Buffalo	NHL	42	3	4	7	106	-8	1	0	10	1	1	2	32
97-98—Buffalo	NHL	36	4	7	11	113	2	0	0	—	—	—	—	—
—Vancouver	NHL	27	9	3	12	41	0	4	0	—	—	—	—	—
98-99—Vancouver	NHL	66	6	11	17	102	-14	1	0	—	—	—	—	—
99-00—Vancouver	NHL	59	9	7	16	90	-2	0	0	—	—	—	—	—
00-01—Phoenix	NHL	62	11	14	25	107	10	0	0	—	—	—	—	—
NHL Totals (10 years).........		639	102	124	226	1663	-16	14	0	36	3	8	11	59

MAYERS, JAMAL — RW — BLUES

PERSONAL: Born October 24, 1974, in Toronto. ... 6-2/212. ... Shoots right. ... Full Name: Jamal David Mayers.

TRANSACTIONS/CAREER NOTES: Selected by St. Louis Blues in fourth round (third Blues pick, 89th overall) of NHL entry draft (June 26, 1993). ... Suspended one playoff game by NHL for slashing incident (May 7, 1999). ... Suffered from the flu (March 24, 2001); missed one game.

			REGULAR SEASON							PLAYOFFS				
Season Team	League	Gms.	G	A	Pts.	PIM	+/-	PP	SH	Gms.	G	A	Pts.	PIM
90-91—Thornhill	Jr. A	44	12	24	36	78	...	...	...	—	—	—	—	—
91-92—Thornhill	Jr. A	56	38	69	107	36	...	...	...	—	—	—	—	—
92-93—Western Michigan U. ..	CCHA	38	8	17	25	26	...	...	...	—	—	—	—	—
93-94—Western Michigan U. ..	CCHA	40	17	32	49	40	...	...	...	—	—	—	—	—
94-95—Western Michigan U. ..	CCHA	39	13	33	46	40	...	...	...	—	—	—	—	—
95-96—Western Michigan U. ..	CCHA	38	17	22	39	75	...	...	...	—	—	—	—	—

Season Team	League	REGULAR SEASON								PLAYOFFS				
		Gms.	G	A	Pts.	PIM	+/-	PP	SH	Gms.	G	A	Pts.	PIM
96-97—Worcester	AHL	62	12	14	26	104	...	...	...	5	4	4	8	4
—St. Louis	NHL	6	0	1	1	2	-3	0	0	—	—	—	—	—
97-98—Worcester	AHL	61	19	24	43	117	...	...	...	11	3	4	7	10
98-99—Worcester	AHL	20	9	7	16	34	...	...	...	—	—	—	—	—
—St. Louis	NHL	34	4	5	9	40	-3	0	0	11	0	1	1	8
99-00—St. Louis	NHL	79	7	10	17	90	0	0	0	7	0	4	4	2
00-01—St. Louis	NHL	77	8	13	21	117	-3	0	0	15	2	3	5	8
NHL Totals (4 years)		196	19	29	48	249	-9	0	0	33	2	8	10	18

McALLISTER, CHRIS   D   FLYERS

PERSONAL: Born June 16, 1975, in Saskatoon, Sask. ... 6-8/225. ... Shoots left.
TRANSACTIONS/CAREER NOTES: Selected by Vancouver Canucks in second round (first Canucks pick, 40th overall) of NHL entry draft (July 8, 1995). ... Suffered from heel spur (December 13, 1997); missed three games. ... Traded by Canucks to Toronto Maple Leafs for C Darby Hendrickson (February 16, 1999). ... Suspended two games by NHL for leaving the bench during an altercation (February 26, 1999). ... Suffered injury (October 20, 1999); missed six games. ... Suffered injury (January 22, 2000); missed one game. ... Injured foot (March 30, 2000); missed final five games of season. ... Traded by Maple Leafs to Philadelphia Flyers for D Regan Kelly (September 26, 2000). ... Sprained wrist (December 21, 2000); missed two games. ... Reinjured wrist (December 30, 2000); missed five games.

Season Team	League	REGULAR SEASON								PLAYOFFS				
		Gms.	G	A	Pts.	PIM	+/-	PP	SH	Gms.	G	A	Pts.	PIM
93-94—Humboldt	SJHL	50	3	5	8	150	...	...	...	—	—	—	—	—
—Saskatoon	WHL	2	0	0	0	5	...	...	...	—	—	—	—	—
94-95—Saskatoon	WHL	65	2	8	10	134	...	...	...	10	0	0	0	28
95-96—Syracuse	AHL	68	0	2	2	142	...	...	...	16	0	0	0	34
96-97—Syracuse	AHL	43	3	1	4	108	...	...	...	3	0	0	0	6
97-98—Syracuse	AHL	23	0	1	1	71	...	...	...	5	0	0	0	21
—Vancouver	NHL	36	1	2	3	106	-12	0	0	—	—	—	—	—
98-99—Vancouver	NHL	28	1	1	2	63	-7	0	0	—	—	—	—	—
—Syracuse	AHL	5	0	0	0	24	...	...	...	—	—	—	—	—
—Toronto	NHL	20	0	2	2	39	4	0	0	6	0	1	1	4
99-00—Toronto	NHL	36	0	3	3	68	-4	0	0	—	—	—	—	—
00-01—Philadelphia	NHL	60	2	2	4	124	1	0	0	2	0	0	0	0
NHL Totals (4 years)		180	4	10	14	400	-18	0	0	8	0	1	1	4

McALPINE, CHRIS   D   BLACKHAWKS

PERSONAL: Born December 1, 1971, in Roseville, Minn. ... 6-0/210. ... Shoots right. ... Full Name: Christopher McAlpine. ... Name pronounced muh-KAL-pighn.
TRANSACTIONS/CAREER NOTES: Selected by New Jersey Devils in seventh round (seventh Devils pick, 137th overall) of NHL entry draft (June 16, 1990). ... Injured thumb (March 26, 1995); missed four games. ... Traded by Devils with ninth-round pick (C James Desmarais) in 1999 draft to St. Louis Blues for C Peter Zezel (February 11, 1997). ... Suffered from the flu (March 14, 1998); missed one game. ... Bruised thigh (December 17, 1998); missed nine games. ... Traded by Blues with G Rich Parent to Tampa Bay Lightning for RW Stephane Richer (January 13, 2000). ... Suffered concussion (January 29, 2000); missed two games. ... Traded by Lightning to Atlanta Thrashers for D Mikko Kuparinen (March 11, 2000). ... Strained groin (March 23, 2000); missed six games. ... Signed as free agent by Chicago Blackhawks (July 27, 2000). ... Separated shoulder (December 21, 2000); missed five games.
HONORS: Named to NCCA All-America (West) second team (1993-94). ... Named to WCHA All-Star first team (1993-94).
MISCELLANEOUS: Member of Stanley Cup championship team (1995).

Season Team	League	REGULAR SEASON								PLAYOFFS				
		Gms.	G	A	Pts.	PIM	+/-	PP	SH	Gms.	G	A	Pts.	PIM
89-90—Roseville H.S.	Minn. H.S.	25	15	13	28		...	...	...	—	—	—	—	—
90-91—Univ. of Minnesota	WCHA	38	7	9	16	112	...	...	...	—	—	—	—	—
91-92—Univ. of Minnesota	WCHA	39	3	9	12	126	...	...	...	—	—	—	—	—
92-93—Univ. of Minnesota	WCHA	41	14	9	23	82	...	...	...	—	—	—	—	—
93-94—Univ. of Minnesota	WCHA	36	12	18	30	121	...	...	...	—	—	—	—	—
94-95—Albany	AHL	48	4	18	22	49	...	...	...	—	—	—	—	—
—New Jersey	NHL	24	0	3	3	17	4	0	0	—	—	—	—	—
95-96—Albany	AHL	57	5	14	19	72	...	...	...	4	0	0	0	13
96-97—Albany	AHL	44	1	9	10	48	...	...	...	—	—	—	—	—
—St. Louis	NHL	15	0	0	0	24	-2	0	0	4	0	1	1	0
97-98—St. Louis	NHL	54	3	7	10	36	14	0	0	10	0	0	0	16
98-99—St. Louis	NHL	51	1	1	2	50	-10	0	0	13	0	0	0	2
99-00—St. Louis	NHL	21	1	1	2	14	1	0	0	—	—	—	—	—
—Worcester	AHL	10	1	4	5	4	...	...	...	—	—	—	—	—
—Tampa Bay	NHL	10	1	1	2	10	-5	0	0	—	—	—	—	—
—Detroit	IHL	8	0	0	0	6	...	...	...	—	—	—	—	—
—Atlanta	NHL	3	0	0	0	2	-4	0	0	—	—	—	—	—
00-01—Norfolk	AHL	13	4	7	11	6	...	...	...	—	—	—	—	—
—Chicago	NHL	50	0	6	6	32	5	0	0	—	—	—	—	—
NHL Totals (6 years)		228	6	19	25	185	3	0	0	27	0	1	1	18

McAMMOND, DEAN   LW   FLAMES

PERSONAL: Born June 15, 1973, in Grand Cache, Alta. ... 5-11/195. ... Shoots left.
TRANSACTIONS/CAREER NOTES: Selected by Chicago Blackhawks in first round (first Blackhawks pick, 22nd overall) of NHL entry draft (June 22, 1991). ... Traded by Blackhawks with D Igor Kravchuk to Edmonton Oilers for RW Joe Murphy (February 25, 1993). ... Severed left Achilles'

M

tendon (February 1, 1995); missed final 41 games of season. ... Fractured nose (November 11, 1996); missed two games. ... Suffered from the flu (January 21, 1997); missed two games. ... Suffered back spasms (March 1, 1997); missed remainder of season. ... Traded by Oilers with D Boris Mironov and D Jonas Elofsson to Blackhawks for C Chad Kilger, LW Daniel Cleary, LW Ethan Moreau and D Christian Laflamme (March 20, 1999). ... Bruised ribs (October 4, 1999); missed five games. ... Suffered sore wrist (December 9, 1999); missed one game. ... Traded by Blackhawks to Philadelphia Flyers for third-round pick (traded to Toronto) in 2001 draft (March 13, 2001). ... Traded by Flyers to Calgary Flames for fourth-round pick in 2002 draft (June 24, 2001).

HONORS: Won Can.HL Plus/Minus Award (1991-92).

MISCELLANEOUS: Failed to score on a penalty shot (vs. Mark Fitzpatrick, January 5, 1996).

			REGULAR SEASON								PLAYOFFS				
Season Team	League	Gms.	G	A	Pts.	PIM	+/-	PP	SH		Gms.	G	A	Pts.	PIM
89-90—Prince Albert..............	WHL	53	11	11	22	49	...	...	...		14	2	3	5	18
90-91—Prince Albert..............	WHL	71	33	35	68	108	...	...	...		2	0	1	1	6
91-92—Prince Albert..............	WHL	63	37	54	91	189	...	...	...		10	12	11	23	26
—Chicago....................	NHL	5	0	2	2	0	-2	0	0		3	0	0	0	2
92-93—Prince Albert..............	WHL	30	19	29	48	44	...	...	...		—	—	—	—	—
—Swift Current	WHL	18	10	13	23	29	...	...	...		17	*16	19	35	20
93-94—Edmonton	NHL	45	6	21	27	16	12	2	0		—	—	—	—	—
—Cape Breton	AHL	28	9	12	21	38	...	...	...		—	—	—	—	—
94-95—Edmonton	NHL	6	0	0	0	0	-1	0	0		—	—	—	—	—
95-96—Edmonton	NHL	53	15	15	30	23	6	4	0		—	—	—	—	—
—Cape Breton	AHL	22	9	15	24	55	...	...	...		—	—	—	—	—
96-97—Edmonton	NHL	57	12	17	29	28	-15	4	0		—	—	—	—	—
97-98—Edmonton	NHL	77	19	31	50	46	9	8	0		12	1	4	5	12
98-99—Edmonton	NHL	65	9	16	25	36	5	1	0		—	—	—	—	—
—Chicago....................	NHL	12	1	4	5	2	3	0	0		—	—	—	—	—
99-00—Chicago....................	NHL	76	14	18	32	72	11	1	0		—	—	—	—	—
00-01—Chicago....................	NHL	61	10	16	26	43	4	1	0		—	—	—	—	—
—Philadelphia	NHL	10	1	1	2	0	-1	1	0		4	0	0	0	2
NHL Totals (9 years)...........		467	87	141	228	266	31	22	0		19	1	4	5	16

McCABE, BRYAN   D   MAPLE LEAFS

PERSONAL: Born June 8, 1975, in Toronto. ... 6-1/210. ... Shoots left.

TRANSACTIONS/CAREER NOTES: Selected by New York Islanders in second round (second Islanders pick, 40th overall) of NHL entry draft (June 26, 1993). ... Traded by Islanders with LW Todd Bertuzzi and third-round pick (LW Jarkko Ruutu) in 1998 draft to Vancouver Canucks for C Trevor Linden (February 6, 1998). ... Missed first 13 games of 1998-99 season due to contract dispute. ... Traded by Canucks with first-round pick (RW Pavel Vorobiev) in 2000 draft to Chicago Blackhawks for first-round pick (traded to Tampa Bay) in 1999 draft (June 26, 1999). ... Fractured orbital bone (March 11, 2000); missed two games. ... Traded by Blackhawks to Toronto Maple Leafs for D Alexander Karpovtsev and fourth-round pick (D Vladimir Gusev) in 2001 draft (October 2, 2000).

HONORS: Named to WHL (West) All-Star second team (1992-93). ... Named to WHL (West) All-Star first team (1993-94). ... Named to WHL (East) All-Star first team (1994-95). ... Named to Memorial Cup All-Star team (1994-95).

MISCELLANEOUS: Captain of New York Islanders (1997 through February 7, 1998).

M

			REGULAR SEASON								PLAYOFFS				
Season Team	League	Gms.	G	A	Pts.	PIM	+/-	PP	SH		Gms.	G	A	Pts.	PIM
91-92—Medicine Hat..............	WHL	68	6	24	30	157	...	...	...		4	0	0	0	6
92-93—Medicine Hat..............	WHL	14	0	13	13	83	...	...	...		—	—	—	—	—
—Spokane....................	WHL	46	3	44	47	134	...	...	...		10	1	5	6	28
93-94—Spokane....................	WHL	64	22	62	84	218	...	...	...		3	0	4	4	4
94-95—Spokane....................	WHL	42	14	39	53	115	...	...	...		—	—	—	—	—
—Brandon....................	WHL	20	6	10	16	38	...	...	...		18	4	13	17	59
95-96—New York Islanders.....	NHL	82	7	16	23	156	-24	3	0		—	—	—	—	—
96-97—New York Islanders.....	NHL	82	8	20	28	165	-2	2	1		—	—	—	—	—
97-98—New York Islanders.....	NHL	56	3	9	12	145	9	1	0		—	—	—	—	—
—Vancouver..................	NHL	26	1	11	12	64	10	0	1		—	—	—	—	—
98-99—Vancouver..................	NHL	69	7	14	21	120	-11	1	2		—	—	—	—	—
99-00—Chicago....................	NHL	79	6	19	25	139	-8	2	0		—	—	—	—	—
00-01—Toronto	NHL	82	5	24	29	123	16	3	0		11	2	3	5	16
NHL Totals (6 years)...........		476	37	113	150	912	-10	12	4		11	2	3	5	16

McCARTHY, SANDY   RW   RANGERS

PERSONAL: Born June 15, 1972, in Toronto. ... 6-3/225. ... Shoots right.

TRANSACTIONS/CAREER NOTES: Selected by Calgary Flames in third round (third Flames pick, 52nd overall) of NHL entry draft (June 22, 1991). ... Strained right shoulder (December 18, 1993); missed two games. ... Strained shoulder (December 27, 1993); missed one game. ... Strained right knee (January 20, 1995); missed five games. ... Suffered hernia (February 3, 1995); missed six games. ... Injured ribs (December 16, 1995); missed seven games. ... Fractured ankle (October 9, 1996); missed 25 games. ... Reinjured left ankle (January 9, 1997) and underwent surgery; missed 23 games. ... Bruised shoulder (November 13, 1997); missed six games. ... Injured groin (December 9, 1997); missed two games. ... Suffered hip pointer (December 22, 1997); missed four games. ... Suffered charley horse (January 24, 1998); missed one game. ... Traded by Flames with third- (LW Brad Richards) and fifth-round (D Curtis Rich) picks in 1998 draft to Tampa Bay Lightning for C Jason Wiemer (March 24, 1998). ... Traded by Lightning with RW Mikael Andersson to Philadelphia Flyers for LW Colin Forbes and fifth-round pick (G Michal Lanicek) in 1999 draft (March 20, 1999). ... Sprained right knee (November 5, 1999); missed one game. ... Injured groin (February 19, 2000); missed four games. ... Traded by Flyers to Carolina Hurricanes for C Kent Manderville (March 14, 2000). ... Traded by Hurricanes with fourth-round pick (D Bryce Lampman) in 2001 draft to New York Rangers for RW Rob DiMaio and LW Darren Langdon (August 4, 2000).

Season Team	League	REGULAR SEASON								PLAYOFFS				
		Gms.	G	A	Pts.	PIM	+/-	PP	SH	Gms.	G	A	Pts.	PIM
89-90—Laval	QMJHL	65	10	11	21	269	...	...	...	—	—	—	—	—
90-91—Laval	QMJHL	68	21	19	40	297	...	...	...	—	—	—	—	—
91-92—Laval	QMJHL	62	39	51	90	326	...	...	...	8	4	5	9	81
92-93—Salt Lake City	IHL	77	18	20	38	220	...	...	...	—	—	—	—	—
93-94—Calgary	NHL	79	5	5	10	173	-3	0	0	7	0	0	0	34
94-95—Calgary	NHL	37	5	3	8	101	1	0	0	6	0	1	1	17
95-96—Calgary	NHL	75	9	7	16	173	-8	3	0	4	0	0	0	10
96-97—Calgary	NHL	33	3	5	8	113	-8	1	0	—	—	—	—	—
97-98—Calgary	NHL	52	8	5	13	170	-18	1	0	—	—	—	—	—
—Tampa Bay	NHL	14	0	5	5	71	-1	0	0	—	—	—	—	—
98-99—Tampa Bay	NHL	67	5	7	12	135	-22	1	0	—	—	—	—	—
—Philadelphia	NHL	13	0	1	1	25	-2	0	0	6	0	1	1	0
99-00—Philadelphia	NHL	58	6	5	11	111	-5	1	0	—	—	—	—	—
—Carolina	NHL	13	0	0	0	9	2	0	0	—	—	—	—	—
00-01—New York Rangers	NHL	81	11	10	21	171	3	0	0	—	—	—	—	—
NHL Totals (8 years)		522	52	53	105	1252	-61	7	0	23	0	2	2	61

McCARTHY, STEVE — D — BLACKHAWKS

PERSONAL: Born February 3, 1981, in Trail, B.C. ... 6-0/197. ... Shoots left.
TRANSACTIONS/CAREER NOTES: Selected by Chicago Blackhawks in first round (first Blackhawks pick, 23rd overall) of NHL entry draft (June 26, 1999).
HONORS: Named to WHL (East) All-Star first team (1999-2000).

Season Team	League	REGULAR SEASON								PLAYOFFS				
		Gms.	G	A	Pts.	PIM	+/-	PP	SH	Gms.	G	A	Pts.	PIM
96-97—Edmonton	WHL	2	0	0	0	0	...	...	...	—	—	—	—	—
97-98—Edmonton	WHL	58	11	29	40	59	...	...	...	—	—	—	—	—
98-99—Kootenay	WHL	57	19	33	52	79	...	...	...	6	0	5	5	8
99-00—Chicago	NHL	5	1	1	2	4	0	1	0	—	—	—	—	—
—Kootenay	WHL	37	13	23	36	36	...	...	...	—	—	—	—	—
00-01—Chicago	NHL	44	0	5	5	8	-7	0	0	—	—	—	—	—
—Norfolk	AHL	7	0	4	4	2	...	...	...	—	—	—	—	—
NHL Totals (2 years)		49	1	6	7	12	-7	1	0	—	—	—	—	—

McCARTY, DARREN — RW — RED WINGS

PERSONAL: Born April 1, 1972, in Burnaby, B.C. ... 6-1/215. ... Shoots right.
TRANSACTIONS/CAREER NOTES: Selected by Detroit Red Wings in second round (second Red Wings pick, 46th overall) of NHL entry draft (June 20, 1992). ... Injured groin (January 29, 1994); missed five games. ... Injured shoulder (March 23, 1994); missed five games. ... Separated right shoulder (February 7, 1995); missed eight games. ... Injured right hand (March 30, 1995); missed two games. ... Injured left knee (April 9, 1995); missed five games. ... Injured right heel (November 7, 1995); missed one game. ... Separated shoulder (December 2, 1995); missed six games. ... Lacerated right forearm (January 12, 1996); missed three games. ... Injured left hand (February 15, 1996); missed seven games. ... Injured hand (January 3, 1997); missed seven games. ... Bruised thigh (January 29, 1997); missed four games. ... Injured groin (April 5, 1997); missed two games. ... Fractured foot (January 11, 1998); missed eight games. ... Suffered from vertigo (April 4, 1998); missed three games. ... Strained groin (March 12, 1999); missed 10 games. ... Reinjured groin (April 5, 1999); missed three games. ... Strained groin (November 12, 1999); missed 39 games. ... Injured leg (March 5, 2000); missed final 17 games of regular season. ... Suffered back spasms (December 1, 2000); missed one game. ... Sprained ankle (March 18, 2001); missed remainder of regular season.
HONORS: Won Jim Mahon Memorial Trophy (1991-92). ... Named to Can.HL All-Star first team (1991-92). ... Named to OHL All-Star first team (1991-92).
MISCELLANEOUS: Member of Stanley Cup championship team (1997 and 1998).

Season Team	League	REGULAR SEASON								PLAYOFFS				
		Gms.	G	A	Pts.	PIM	+/-	PP	SH	Gms.	G	A	Pts.	PIM
88-89—Peterborough Jr. B	OHA	34	18	17	35	135	...	...	...	—	—	—	—	—
89-90—Belleville	OHL	63	12	15	27	142	...	...	...	11	1	1	2	21
90-91—Belleville	OHL	60	30	37	67	151	...	...	...	6	2	2	4	13
91-92—Belleville	OHL	65	*55	72	127	177	...	...	...	5	1	4	5	13
92-93—Adirondack	AHL	73	17	19	36	278	...	...	...	11	0	1	1	33
93-94—Detroit	NHL	67	9	17	26	181	12	0	0	7	2	2	4	8
94-95—Detroit	NHL	31	5	8	13	88	5	1	0	18	3	2	5	14
95-96—Detroit	NHL	63	15	14	29	158	14	8	0	19	3	2	5	20
96-97—Detroit	NHL	68	19	30	49	126	14	5	0	20	3	4	7	34
97-98—Detroit	NHL	71	15	22	37	157	0	5	1	22	3	8	11	34
98-99—Detroit	NHL	69	14	26	40	108	10	6	0	10	1	1	2	23
99-00—Detroit	NHL	24	6	6	12	48	1	0	0	9	0	1	1	12
00-01—Detroit	NHL	72	12	10	22	123	-5	1	1	6	1	0	1	2
NHL Totals (8 years)		465	95	133	228	989	51	26	2	111	16	20	36	147

McCAULEY, ALYN — C — MAPLE LEAFS

PERSONAL: Born May 29, 1977, in Brockville, Ont. ... 5-11/190. ... Shoots left.
TRANSACTIONS/CAREER NOTES: Selected by New Jersey Devils in fourth round (fifth Devils pick, 79th overall) of NHL entry draft (July 8, 1995). ... Traded by Devils with D Jason Smith and C Steve Sullivan to Toronto Maple Leafs for C Doug Gilmour, D Dave Ellett and third-round pick (D Andre Lakos) in 1999 draft (February 25, 1997). ... Fractured ankle (December 31, 1997); missed 17 games. ... Strained shoulder (February 26, 1998); missed three games. ... Sprained left knee (December 30, 1998); missed 22 games. ... Suffered concussion (March 3,

M

1999); missed remainder of season. ... Suffered injury (October 9, 1999); missed one game. ... Suffered from flu (December 4, 1999); missed six games. ... Suffered illness (January 11, 2000); missed one game. ... Sprained wrist (October 11, 2000); missed four games.
HONORS: Named to OHL All-Star first team (1995-96 and 1996-97). ... Won Red Tilson Trophy (1995-96 and 1996-97). ... Won Can.HL Player of the Year Award (1996-97). ... Won William Hanley Trophy (1996-97). ... Named to Can.HL All-Star first team (1996-97).

Season Team	League	Gms.	G	A	Pts.	PIM	+/-	PP	SH	Gms.	G	A	Pts.	PIM
			REGULAR SEASON							PLAYOFFS				
92-93—Kingston Jr. A	MTHL	38	31	29	60	18	...	...	...	—	—	—	—	—
93-94—Ottawa	OHL	38	13	23	36	10	...	...	...	13	5	14	19	4
94-95—Ottawa	OHL	65	16	38	54	20	...	...	...	—	—	—	—	—
95-96—Ottawa	OHL	55	34	48	82	24	...	...	...	2	0	0	0	0
96-97—Ottawa	OHL	50	†56	56	112	16	...	...	...	22	14	22	36	14
—St. John's	AHL	—	—	—	—	—	...	...	...	3	0	1	1	0
97-98—Toronto	NHL	60	6	10	16	6	-7	0	0	—	—	—	—	—
98-99—Toronto	NHL	39	9	15	24	2	7	1	0	—	—	—	—	—
99-00—Toronto	NHL	45	5	5	10	10	-6	1	0	5	0	0	0	6
—St. John's	AHL	5	1	1	2	0	...	...	...	—	—	—	—	—
00-01—Toronto	NHL	14	1	0	1	0	0	0	0	10	0	0	0	2
—St. John's	AHL	47	16	28	44	12	...	...	...	—	—	—	—	—
NHL Totals (4 years)		158	21	30	51	18	-6	2	0	15	0	0	0	8

McDONALD, ANDY — C — MIGHTY DUCKS

PERSONAL: Born August 25, 1977, in Strathroy, Ont. ... 5-10/192. ... Shoots left.
TRANSACTIONS/CAREER NOTES: Signed as non-drafted free agent by Mighty Ducks of Anaheim (April 3, 2000). ... Suffered concussion (January 12, 2001); missed seven games.
HONORS: Named to ECAC All-Star second team (1998-99). ... Named to NCAA All-America (East) first team (1999-2000). ... Named to ECAC All-Star first team (1999-2000).

Season Team	League	Gms.	G	A	Pts.	PIM	+/-	PP	SH	Gms.	G	A	Pts.	PIM
			REGULAR SEASON							PLAYOFFS				
96-97—Colgate University	ECAC	33	9	10	19	19	...	...	...	—	—	—	—	—
97-98—Colgate University	ECAC	35	13	19	32	26	...	...	...	—	—	—	—	—
98-99—Colgate University	ECAC	35	20	26	46	42	...	...	...	—	—	—	—	—
99-00—Colgate University	ECAC	34	25	*33	*58	49	...	...	...	—	—	—	—	—
00-01—Cincinnati	AHL	46	15	25	40	21	...	...	...	3	0	1	1	2
—Anaheim	NHL	16	1	0	1	6	0	0	0	—	—	—	—	—
NHL Totals (1 year)		16	1	0	1	6	0	0	0					

McEACHERN, SHAWN — LW — SENATORS

PERSONAL: Born February 28, 1969, in Waltham, Mass. ... 5-11/193. ... Shoots left. ... Full Name: Shawn K. McEachern. ... Name pronounced muh-KEH-kuhrn.
TRANSACTIONS/CAREER NOTES: Selected by Pittsburgh Penguins in sixth round (sixth Penguins pick, 110th overall) of NHL entry draft (June 13, 1987). ... Traded by Penguins to Los Angeles Kings for D Marty McSorley (August 27, 1993). ... Traded by Kings to Penguins for D Marty McSorley and D Jim Paek (February 15, 1994). ... Played in Europe during 1994-95 NHL lockout. ... Suspended for first three games of 1994-95 season and fined $500 by NHL for slashing incident (September 21, 1994); suspension reduced to two games due to abbreviated 1994-95 season. ... Traded by Penguins with LW Kevin Stevens to Boston Bruins for C Bryan Smolinski and RW Glen Murray (August 2, 1995). ... Traded by Bruins to Ottawa Senators for RW Trent McCleary and third-round pick (LW Eric Naud) in 1996 draft (June 22, 1996). ... Fractured jaw (December 6, 1996); missed 17 games. ... Suffered back spasms (February 7, 1998); missed one game. ... Injured wrist (April 3, 1999); missed one game. ... Injured groin (April 8, 1999); missed four games. ... Suffered illness (February 1, 2000); missed one game. ... Bruised shoulder (February 26, 2000); missed four games. ... Fractured left thumb (March 25, 2000); missed final eight games of season.
HONORS: Named to Hockey East All-Star second team (1989-90). ... Named Hockey East Tournament Most Valuable Player (1990-91). ... Named to NCAA All-America (East) first team (1990-91). ... Named to Hockey East All-Star first team (1990-91).
MISCELLANEOUS: Member of Stanley Cup championship team (1992).
STATISTICAL PLATEAUS: Three-goal games: 1997-98 (1).

Season Team	League	Gms.	G	A	Pts.	PIM	+/-	PP	SH	Gms.	G	A	Pts.	PIM
			REGULAR SEASON							PLAYOFFS				
85-86—Matignon	Mass. H.S.	20	32	20	52	...	...	...	...	—	—	—	—	—
86-87—Matignon	Mass. H.S.	16	29	28	57	...	...	...	...	—	—	—	—	—
87-88—Matignon	Mass. H.S.	22	52	40	92	...	...	...	...	—	—	—	—	—
88-89—Boston University	Hockey East	36	20	28	48	32	...	...	...	—	—	—	—	—
89-90—Boston University	Hockey East	43	25	31	56	78	...	...	...	—	—	—	—	—
90-91—Boston University	Hockey East	41	34	48	82	43	...	...	...	—	—	—	—	—
91-92—U.S. national team	Int'l	57	26	23	49	38	...	...	...	—	—	—	—	—
—U.S. Olympic team	Int'l	8	1	0	1	10	...	...	...	—	—	—	—	—
—Pittsburgh	NHL	15	0	4	4	0	1	0	0	19	2	7	9	4
92-93—Pittsburgh	NHL	84	28	33	61	46	21	7	0	12	3	2	5	10
93-94—Los Angeles	NHL	49	8	13	21	24	1	0	3	—	—	—	—	—
—Pittsburgh	NHL	27	12	9	21	10	13	0	2	6	1	0	1	2
94-95—Kiekko-Espoo	Finland	8	1	3	4	6	...	...	...	—	—	—	—	—
—Pittsburgh	NHL	44	13	13	26	22	4	1	2	11	0	2	2	8
95-96—Boston	NHL	82	24	29	53	34	-5	3	2	5	2	1	3	8
96-97—Ottawa	NHL	65	11	20	31	18	-5	0	1	7	2	0	2	8
97-98—Ottawa	NHL	81	24	24	48	42	1	8	2	11	0	4	4	8
98-99—Ottawa	NHL	77	31	25	56	46	8	7	0	4	2	0	2	6
99-00—Ottawa	NHL	69	29	22	51	24	2	10	0	6	0	3	3	4
00-01—Ottawa	NHL	82	32	40	72	62	10	9	0	4	0	2	2	2
NHL Totals (10 years)		675	212	232	444	328	51	45	12	85	12	21	33	60

M

McGILLIS, DAN   D   FLYERS

PERSONAL: Born July 1, 1972, in Hawkesbury, Ont. ... 6-2/225. ... Shoots left. ... Full Name: Daniel McGillis.
TRANSACTIONS/CAREER NOTES: Selected by Detroit Red Wings in 10th round (10th Red Wings pick, 238th overall) of NHL entry draft (June 20, 1992). ... Signed as free agent by Edmonton Oilers (September 6, 1996). ... Traded by Oilers with second-round pick (D Jason Beckett) in 1998 draft to Philadelphia Flyers for D Janne Niinimaa (March 24, 1998). ... Suffered neck spasms (February 21, 1999); missed two games. ... Injured left knee (March 30, 1999); missed one game. ... Fractured right foot (November 28, 1999); missed four games. ... Strained groin (February 22, 2000); missed 10 games.
HONORS: Named to Hockey East All-Star first team (1994-95). ... Named to NCAA All-America (East) first team (1995-96). ... Named to Hockey East All-Star team (1995-96).

Season Team	League	REGULAR SEASON								PLAYOFFS				
		Gms.	G	A	Pts.	PIM	+/-	PP	SH	Gms.	G	A	Pts.	PIM
91-92—Hawkesbury	Tier II Jr. A	36	5	19	24	106	...	...	...	—	—	—	—	—
92-93—Northeastern Univ.	Hockey East	35	5	12	17	42	...	...	...	—	—	—	—	—
93-94—Northeastern Univ.	Hockey East	38	4	25	29	82	...	...	...	—	—	—	—	—
94-95—Northeastern Univ.	Hockey East	34	9	22	31	70	...	...	...	—	—	—	—	—
95-96—Northeastern Univ.	Hockey East	34	12	24	36	50	...	...	...	—	—	—	—	—
96-97—Edmonton	NHL	73	6	16	22	52	2	2	1	12	0	5	5	24
97-98—Edmonton	NHL	67	10	15	25	74	-17	5	0	—	—	—	—	—
—Philadelphia	NHL	13	1	5	6	35	-4	1	0	5	1	2	3	10
98-99—Philadelphia	NHL	78	8	37	45	61	16	6	0	6	0	1	1	12
99-00—Philadelphia	NHL	68	4	14	18	55	16	3	0	18	2	6	8	12
00-01—Philadelphia	NHL	82	14	35	49	86	13	4	0	6	1	0	1	6
NHL Totals (5 years)		381	43	122	165	363	26	21	1	47	4	14	18	64

McINNIS, MARTY   LW   MIGHTY DUCKS

PERSONAL: Born June 2, 1970, in Weymouth, Mass. ... 5-11/190. ... Shoots right. ... Full Name: Martin Edward McInnis. ... Name pronounced muh-KIH-nihz.
TRANSACTIONS/CAREER NOTES: Selected by New York Islanders in eighth round (10th Islanders pick, 163rd overall) of NHL entry draft (June 11, 1988). ... Injured eye (March 9, 1993); missed two games. ... Fractured patella (March 27, 1993); missed remainder of regular season and 14 playoff games. ... Sprained wrist (April 18, 1995); missed one game. ... Injured ribs (March 7, 1996); missed one game. ... Injured ribs (March 16, 1996); missed six games. ... Traded by Islanders with G Tyrone Garner and sixth-round pick (D Ilja Demidov) in 1997 draft to Calgary Flames for C Robert Reichel (March 18, 1997). ... Injured shoulder (December 23, 1997); missed six games. ... Traded by Flames with D Jamie Allison and RW Erik Andersson to Chicago Blackhawks for C Jeff Shantz and C/LW Steve Dubinsky (October 27, 1998). ... Traded by Blackhawks to Mighty Ducks of Anaheim for fourth-round pick (traded to Washington) in 2000 draft (October 27, 1998). ... Strained groin (January 28, 2000); missed 11 games. ... Reinjured groin (March 8, 2000); missed nine games. ... Sprained neck (October 29, 2000); missed three games. ... Strained groin (January 21, 2001); missed three games.
MISCELLANEOUS: Failed to score on a penalty shot (vs. Tom Draper, March 8, 1992).
STATISTICAL PLATEAUS: Three-goal games: 1997-98 (1), 2000-01 (1). Total: 2.

Season Team	League	REGULAR SEASON								PLAYOFFS				
		Gms.	G	A	Pts.	PIM	+/-	PP	SH	Gms.	G	A	Pts.	PIM
86-87—Milton Academy	Mass. H.S.	...	21	19	40	...	...	...	...	—	—	—	—	—
87-88—Milton Academy	Mass. H.S.	25	26	25	51	...	...	...	...	—	—	—	—	—
88-89—Boston College	Hockey East	39	13	19	32	8	...	...	...	—	—	—	—	—
89-90—Boston College	Hockey East	41	24	29	53	43	...	...	...	—	—	—	—	—
90-91—Boston College	Hockey East	38	21	36	57	40	...	...	...	—	—	—	—	—
91-92—U.S. national team	Int'l	54	15	19	34	20	...	...	...	—	—	—	—	—
—U.S. Olympic team	Int'l	8	5	2	7	4	...	...	...	—	—	—	—	—
—New York Islanders	NHL	15	3	5	8	0	6	0	0	—	—	—	—	—
92-93—New York Islanders	NHL	56	10	20	30	24	7	0	1	3	0	1	1	0
—Capital District	AHL	10	4	12	16	2	...	...	...	—	—	—	—	—
93-94—New York Islanders	NHL	81	25	31	56	24	31	3	5	4	0	0	0	0
94-95—New York Islanders	NHL	41	9	7	16	8	-1	0	0	—	—	—	—	—
95-96—New York Islanders	NHL	74	12	34	46	39	-11	2	0	—	—	—	—	—
96-97—New York Islanders	NHL	70	20	22	42	20	-7	4	1	—	—	—	—	—
—Calgary	NHL	10	3	4	7	2	-1	1	0	—	—	—	—	—
97-98—Calgary	NHL	75	19	25	44	34	1	5	4	—	—	—	—	—
98-99—Calgary	NHL	6	1	1	2	6	-1	0	0	—	—	—	—	—
—Anaheim	NHL	75	18	34	52	36	-14	11	1	4	2	0	2	2
99-00—Anaheim	NHL	62	10	18	28	26	-4	2	1	—	—	—	—	—
00-01—Anaheim	NHL	75	20	22	42	40	-21	10	0	—	—	—	—	—
NHL Totals (10 years)		640	150	223	373	259	-15	38	13	11	2	1	3	2

McKAY, RANDY   RW   DEVILS

PERSONAL: Born January 25, 1967, in Montreal. ... 6-2/210. ... Shoots right. ... Full Name: Hugh Randall McKay.
TRANSACTIONS/CAREER NOTES: Selected by Detroit Red Wings in sixth round (sixth Red Wings pick, 113th overall) of NHL entry draft (June 15, 1985). ... Injured knee (February 1989). ... Lacerated forearm (February 23, 1991). ... Sent by Red Wings with C Dave Barr to New Jersey Devils as compensation for Red Wings signing free agent RW Troy Crowder (September 9, 1991). ... Sprained knee (January 16, 1993); missed nine games. ... Bruised shoulder (November 3, 1993); missed three games. ... Bruised shoulder (January 24, 1994); missed three games. ... Injured groin (February 24, 1995); missed nine games. ... Reinjured groin (March 18, 1995); missed six games. ... Suffered charley horse (May 26, 1995); missed one playoff game. ... Suffered concussion (December 31, 1995); missed three games. ... Bruised eye (February 27, 1997); missed five games. ... Sprained left knee (March 26, 1998); missed eight games. ... Strained groin (September 23, 1998); missed first four games of season. ... Suffered infected elbow (December 19, 1998); missed one game. ... Suffered from the flu (December 26, 1998); missed four games. ... Suffered sore back (January 20, 1999); missed one game. ... Bruised knee (April 3, 1999); missed one game. ...

Suspended three games by NHL for slashing incident (November 1, 1999). ... Suffered injury (January 3, 2000); missed one game. ... Strained hip flexor (January 17, 2000); missed two games. ... Suffered injury (January 29, 2000); missed one game. ... Suffered injury (February 3, 2000); missed one game. ... Injured ankle (March 2, 2000); missed seven games. ... Bruised tailbone (February 27, 2001); missed three games.

MISCELLANEOUS: Member of Stanley Cup championship team (1995 and 2000).

STATISTICAL PLATEAUS: Three-goal games: 1996-97 (1), 1997-98 (1). Total: 2. ... Four-goal games: 2000-01 (1). ... Total hat tricks: 3.

Season Team	League	REGULAR SEASON								PLAYOFFS				
		Gms.	G	A	Pts.	PIM	+/-	PP	SH	Gms.	G	A	Pts.	PIM
84-85—Michigan Tech	WCHA	25	4	5	9	32	...	...	...	—	—	—	—	—
85-86—Michigan Tech	WCHA	40	12	22	34	46	...	...	...	—	—	—	—	—
86-87—Michigan Tech	WCHA	39	5	11	16	46	...	...	...	—	—	—	—	—
87-88—Michigan Tech	WCHA	41	17	24	41	70	...	...	...	—	—	—	—	—
—Adirondack	AHL	10	0	3	3	12	...	...	...	6	0	4	4	0
88-89—Adirondack	AHL	58	29	34	63	170	...	...	...	14	4	7	11	60
—Detroit	NHL	3	0	0	0	0	-1	0	0	2	0	0	0	2
89-90—Detroit	NHL	33	3	6	9	51	1	0	0	—	—	—	—	—
—Adirondack	AHL	36	16	23	39	99	...	...	...	6	3	0	3	35
90-91—Detroit	NHL	47	1	7	8	183	-15	0	0	5	0	1	1	41
91-92—New Jersey	NHL	80	17	16	33	246	6	2	0	7	1	3	4	10
92-93—New Jersey	NHL	73	11	11	22	206	0	1	0	5	0	0	0	16
93-94—New Jersey	NHL	78	12	15	27	244	24	0	0	20	1	2	3	24
94-95—New Jersey	NHL	33	5	7	12	44	10	0	0	19	8	4	12	11
95-96—New Jersey	NHL	76	11	10	21	145	7	3	0	—	—	—	—	—
96-97—New Jersey	NHL	77	9	18	27	109	15	0	0	10	1	1	2	0
97-98—New Jersey	NHL	74	24	24	48	86	30	8	0	6	0	1	1	0
98-99—New Jersey	NHL	70	17	20	37	143	10	3	0	7	3	2	5	2
99-00—New Jersey	NHL	67	16	23	39	80	8	3	0	23	0	6	6	9
00-01—New Jersey	NHL	77	23	20	43	50	3	12	0	19	6	3	9	8
NHL Totals (13 years)		788	149	177	326	1587	98	32	0	123	20	23	43	123

McKEE, JAY   D   SABRES

PERSONAL: Born September 8, 1977, in Kingston, Ont. ... 6-3/205. ... Shoots left.
TRANSACTIONS/CAREER NOTES: Selected by Buffalo Sabres in first round (first Sabres pick, 14th overall) of NHL entry draft (July 8, 1995). ... Bruised stomach (March 29, 1998); missed two games. ... Bruised hand (October 30, 1998); missed one game. ... Bruised foot (February 13, 1999); missed six games. ... Suffered from the flu (March 13, 1999); missed two games. ... Suffered injury (November 25, 2000); missed five games. ... Injured hand (March 16, 2001); missed three games.
HONORS: Named to OHL All-Star second team (1995-96).

Season Team	League	REGULAR SEASON								PLAYOFFS				
		Gms.	G	A	Pts.	PIM	+/-	PP	SH	Gms.	G	A	Pts.	PIM
92-93—Ernestown	Jr. C	36	0	17	17	37	...	...	...	—	—	—	—	—
93-94—Sudbury	OHL	51	0	1	1	51	...	...	...	3	0	0	0	0
94-95—Sudbury	OHL	39	6	6	12	91	...	...	...	—	—	—	—	—
—Niagara Falls	OHL	26	3	13	16	60	...	...	...	6	2	3	5	10
95-96—Niagara Falls	OHL	64	5	41	46	129	...	...	...	10	1	5	6	16
—Rochester	AHL	4	0	1	1	15	...	...	...	—	—	—	—	—
—Buffalo	NHL	1	0	1	1	2	1	0	0	—	—	—	—	—
96-97—Buffalo	NHL	43	1	9	10	35	3	0	0	3	0	0	0	0
—Rochester	AHL	7	2	5	7	4	...	...	...	—	—	—	—	—
97-98—Buffalo	NHL	56	1	13	14	42	-1	0	0	1	0	0	0	0
—Rochester	AHL	13	1	7	8	11	...	...	...	—	—	—	—	—
98-99—Buffalo	NHL	72	0	6	6	75	20	0	0	21	0	3	3	24
99-00—Buffalo	NHL	78	5	12	17	50	5	1	0	1	0	0	0	0
00-01—Buffalo	NHL	74	1	10	11	76	9	0	0	8	1	0	1	6
NHL Totals (6 years)		324	8	51	59	280	37	1	0	34	1	3	4	30

McKENNA, STEVE   LW

PERSONAL: Born August 21, 1973, in Toronto. ... 6-8/255. ... Shoots left.
TRANSACTIONS/CAREER NOTES: Signed as non-drafted free agent by Los Angeles Kings (May 17, 1996). ... Strained abdominal muscle (November 9, 1998); missed 14 games. ... Reinjured abdominal muscle (December 9, 1998); missed 42 games. ... Lacerated eye (October 4, 1999); missed six games. ... Selected by Minnesota Wild in NHL expansion draft (June 23, 2000). ... Suffered back spasms (September 8, 2000); missed 12 games. ... Traded by Wild to Pittsburgh Penguins for C Roman Simicek (January 13, 2001).

Season Team	League	REGULAR SEASON								PLAYOFFS				
		Gms.	G	A	Pts.	PIM	+/-	PP	SH	Gms.	G	A	Pts.	PIM
93-94—Merrimack College	Hockey East	37	1	2	3	74	...	...	...	—	—	—	—	—
94-95—Merrimack College	Hockey East	37	1	9	10	74	...	...	...	—	—	—	—	—
95-96—Merrimack College	Hockey East	33	3	11	14	67	...	...	...	—	—	—	—	—
96-97—Phoenix	IHL	66	6	5	11	187	...	...	...	—	—	—	—	—
—Los Angeles	NHL	9	0	0	0	37	1	0	0	—	—	—	—	—
97-98—Fredericton	AHL	6	2	1	3	48	...	...	...	—	—	—	—	—
—Los Angeles	NHL	62	4	4	8	150	-9	1	0	3	0	1	1	8
98-99—Los Angeles	NHL	20	1	0	1	36	-3	0	0	—	—	—	—	—
99-00—Los Angeles	NHL	46	0	5	5	125	3	0	0	—	—	—	—	—
00-01—Minnesota	NHL	20	1	1	2	19	0	0	0	—	—	—	—	—
—Pittsburgh	NHL	34	0	0	0	100	-4	0	0	—	—	—	—	—
NHL Totals (5 years)		191	6	10	16	467	-12	1	0	3	0	1	1	8

M

McKENZIE, JIM   RW   DEVILS

PERSONAL: Born November 3, 1969, in Gull Lake, Sask. ... 6-4/227. ... Shoots left.

TRANSACTIONS/CAREER NOTES: Selected by Hartford Whalers in fourth round (third Whalers pick, 73rd overall) of NHL entry draft (June 17, 1989). ... Injured elbow (January 31, 1992); missed two games. ... Suffered hip flexor (November 11, 1992); missed three games. ... Suffered hip flexor (December 5, 1992); missed four games. ... Suffered back spasms (January 24, 1993); missed three games. ... Suspended two games by NHL for game misconduct penalties (April 3, 1993). ... Suspended three games by NHL for game misconduct penalties (April 10, 1993). ... Traded by Whalers to Florida Panthers for D Alexander Godynyuk (December 16, 1993). ... Traded by Panthers to Dallas Stars for fourth-round pick (LW Jamie Wright) in 1994 draft (December 16, 1993). ... Traded by Stars to Pittsburgh Penguins for RW Mike Needham (March 21, 1994). ... Fractured toe (November 24, 1993); missed four games. ... Bruised hand (March 11, 1995); missed one game. ... Sprained wrist (April 5, 1995); missed seven games. ... Signed as free agent by New York Islanders (July 31, 1995). ... Claimed by Winnipeg Jets in NHL waiver draft (October 2, 1995). ... Jets franchise moved to Phoenix and renamed Coyotes for 1996-97 season; NHL approved move on January 18, 1996. ... Fractured leg (November 8, 1996); missed five games. ... Suffered from the flu (January 27, 1997); missed one game. ... Fractured leg (December 23, 1997); missed 11 games. ... Traded by Coyotes to Mighty Ducks of Anaheim for C J.F. Jomphe (June 18, 1998). ... Suffered laceration below right eye (January 10, 1999); missed five games. ... Injured ankle (February 3, 1999); missed two games. ... Suspended four games by NHL for fighting incident (October 5, 1999). ... Fractured right hand (November 9, 1999); missed 10 games. ... Claimed on waivers by Washington Capitals (January 18, 2000). ... Signed as free agent by New Jersey Devils (July 3, 2000).

STATISTICAL PLATEAUS: Three-goal games: 1996-97 (1).

		REGULAR SEASON								PLAYOFFS				
Season Team	League	Gms.	G	A	Pts.	PIM	+/-	PP	SH	Gms.	G	A	Pts.	PIM
85-86—Moose Jaw	WHL	3	0	2	2	0	...	...	...	—	—	—	—	—
86-87—Moose Jaw	WHL	65	5	3	8	125	...	...	...	9	0	0	0	7
87-88—Moose Jaw	WHL	62	1	17	18	134	...	...	...	—	—	—	—	—
88-89—Victoria	WHL	67	15	27	42	176	...	...	...	8	1	4	5	30
89-90—Binghamton	AHL	56	4	12	16	149	...	...	...	—	—	—	—	—
—Hartford	NHL	5	0	0	0	4	0	0	0	—	—	—	—	—
90-91—Springfield	AHL	24	3	4	7	102	...	...	...	—	—	—	—	—
—Hartford	NHL	41	4	3	7	108	-7	0	0	6	0	0	0	8
91-92—Hartford	NHL	67	5	1	6	87	-6	0	0	—	—	—	—	—
92-93—Hartford	NHL	64	3	6	9	202	-10	0	0	—	—	—	—	—
93-94—Hartford	NHL	26	1	2	3	67	-6	0	0	—	—	—	—	—
—Dallas	NHL	34	2	3	5	63	4	0	0	—	—	—	—	—
—Pittsburgh	NHL	11	0	0	0	16	-5	0	0	3	0	0	0	0
94-95—Pittsburgh	NHL	39	2	1	3	63	-7	0	0	5	0	0	0	4
95-96—Winnipeg	NHL	73	4	2	6	202	-4	0	0	1	0	0	0	2
96-97—Phoenix	NHL	65	5	3	8	200	-5	0	0	7	0	0	0	2
97-98—Phoenix	NHL	64	3	4	7	146	-7	0	0	1	0	0	0	0
98-99—Anaheim	NHL	73	5	4	9	99	-18	1	0	4	0	0	0	4
99-00—Anaheim	NHL	31	3	3	6	48	-5	0	0	—	—	—	—	—
—Washington	NHL	30	1	2	3	16	0	0	0	1	0	0	0	0
00-01—New Jersey	NHL	53	2	2	4	119	0	0	0	3	0	0	0	2
NHL Totals (12 years)		676	40	36	76	1440	-76	1	0	31	0	0	0	22

McLAREN, KYLE   D   BRUINS

PERSONAL: Born June 18, 1977, in Humboldt, Sask. ... 6-4/219. ... Shoots left.

TRANSACTIONS/CAREER NOTES: Selected by Boston Bruins in first round (first Bruins pick, ninth overall) of NHL entry draft (July 8, 1995). ... Injured back (November 21, 1995); missed one game. ... Injured knee (November 25, 1995); missed five games. ... Suffered from the flu (January 3, 1996); missed one game. ... Suffered concussion (March 10, 1996); missed one game. ... Suffered charley horse (October 26, 1996); missed two games. ... Strained shoulder (February 2, 1997); missed 13 games. ... Injured foot (March 15, 1997); missed one game. ... Sprained thumb (March 27, 1997); missed remainder of season. ... Suffered hip pointer (November 1, 1997); missed five games. ... Injured knee (December 17, 1997); missed one game. ... Fractured foot (March 19, 1998); missed seven games. ... Strained groin (April 7, 1998); missed three games. ... Missed first 15 games of 1998-99 season due to contract dispute. ... Separated shoulder (January 15, 1999); missed 14 games. ... Injured foot (April 10, 1999); missed one game. ... Strained thumb (November 18, 1999); missed seven games. ... Tore knee cartilage (April 1, 2000); missed final four games of season. ... Injured knee (October 20, 2000); missed 24 games.

HONORS: Named to NHL All-Rookie team (1995-96).

		REGULAR SEASON								PLAYOFFS				
Season Team	League	Gms.	G	A	Pts.	PIM	+/-	PP	SH	Gms.	G	A	Pts.	PIM
93-94—Tacoma	WHL	62	1	9	10	53	...	...	...	6	1	4	5	6
94-95—Tacoma	WHL	47	13	19	32	68	...	...	...	4	1	1	2	4
95-96—Boston	NHL	74	5	12	17	73	16	0	0	5	0	0	0	14
96-97—Boston	NHL	58	5	9	14	54	-9	0	0	—	—	—	—	—
97-98—Boston	NHL	66	5	20	25	56	13	2	0	6	1	0	1	4
98-99—Boston	NHL	52	6	18	24	48	1	3	0	12	0	3	3	10
99-00—Boston	NHL	71	8	11	19	67	-4	2	0	—	—	—	—	—
00-01—Boston	NHL	58	5	12	17	53	-5	2	0	—	—	—	—	—
NHL Totals (6 years)		379	34	82	116	351	12	9	0	23	1	3	4	28

McLEAN, KIRK   G

PERSONAL: Born June 26, 1966, in Willowdale, Ont. ... 6-1/180. ... Catches left. ... Name pronounced muh-KLAYN.

TRANSACTIONS/CAREER NOTES: Selected by New Jersey Devils in sixth round (sixth Devils pick, 107th overall) of NHL entry draft (June 9, 1984). ... Traded by Devils with C Greg Adams and second-round pick (D Leif Rohlin) in 1988 draft to Vancouver Canucks for C Patrik Sundstrom, second- (LW Jeff Christian) and fourth-round (LW Matt Ruchty) picks in 1988 draft (September 15, 1987). ... Suffered tendinitis in left wrist (February 25, 1991). ... Injured knee (January 13, 1996); missed 18 games. ... Injured knee (November 11, 1996); missed 19 games. ... Injured finger (March 5, 1997); missed nine games. ... Traded by Canucks to Hurricanes with LW Martin Gelinas for LW Geoff

Sanderson, D Enrico Ciccone and G Sean Burke (January 3, 1998). ... Traded by Hurricanes to Florida Panthers for RW Ray Sheppard (March 24, 1998). ... Bruised ribs (February 14, 1999); missed three games. ... Signed as free agent by New York Rangers (July 13, 1999). ... Suffered from the flu (February 26, 2000); missed one game. ... Suffered back spasms (October 26, 2000); missed two games.

HONORS: Played in NHL All-Star Game (1990 and 1992). ... Named to THE SPORTING NEWS All-Star second team (1991-92). ... Named to NHL All-Star second team (1991-92).

RECORDS: Shares NHL single-season playoff record for most minutes played by a goaltender—1,544 (1994); and most shutouts—4 (1994).

MISCELLANEOUS: Holds Vancouver Canucks all-time record for most games played by goalie (516), most wins (211) and most shutouts (20). ... Stopped penalty shot attempt (vs. Brent Gilchrist, January 27, 1994; vs. Ted Donato, April 12, 1999). ... Allowed penalty shot goal (vs. Brent Ashton, December 11, 1988; vs. Mike Donnelly, November 12, 1992; vs. Andrei Kovalenko, December 4, 1993; vs. David Legwand, December 23, 2000).

| | | REGULAR SEASON | | | | | | | | PLAYOFFS | | | | | | |
Season Team	League	Gms.	Min	W	L	T	GA	SO	Avg.	Gms.	Min.	W	L	GA	SO	Avg.
83-84—Oshawa	OHL	17	940	5	9	0	67	0	4.28	—	—	—	—	—	—	—
84-85—Oshawa	OHL	47	2581	23	17	2	143	1	*3.32	5	271	1	3	21	0	4.65
85-86—Oshawa	OHL	51	2830	24	21	2	169	1	3.58	4	201	1	2	18	0	5.37
—New Jersey	NHL	2	111	1	1	0	11	0	5.95	—	—	—	—	—	—	—
86-87—New Jersey	NHL	4	160	1	1	0	10	0	3.75	—	—	—	—	—	—	—
—Maine	AHL	45	2606	15	23	4	140	1	3.22	—	—	—	—	—	—	—
87-88—Vancouver	NHL	41	2380	11	27	3	147	1	3.71	—	—	—	—	—	—	—
88-89—Vancouver	NHL	42	2477	20	17	3	127	4	3.08	5	302	2	3	18	0	3.58
89-90—Vancouver	NHL	*63	*3739	21	30	10	*216	0	3.47	—	—	—	—	—	—	—
90-91—Vancouver	NHL	41	1969	10	22	3	131	0	3.99	2	123	1	1	7	0	3.41
91-92—Vancouver	NHL	65	3852	†38	17	9	176	†5	2.74	13	785	6	7	33	†2	2.52
92-93—Vancouver	NHL	54	3261	28	21	5	184	3	3.39	12	754	6	6	42	0	3.34
93-94—Vancouver	NHL	52	3128	23	26	3	156	3	2.99	24	*1544	15	†9	59	†4	2.29
94-95—Vancouver	NHL	40	2374	18	12	10	109	1	2.75	11	660	4	†7	36	0	3.27
95-96—Vancouver	NHL	45	2645	15	21	9	156	2	3.54	1	21	0	1	3	0	8.57
96-97—Vancouver	NHL	44	2581	21	18	3	138	0	3.21	—	—	—	—	—	—	—
97-98—Vancouver	NHL	29	1583	6	17	4	97	1	3.68	—	—	—	—	—	—	—
—Carolina	NHL	8	401	4	2	0	22	0	3.29	—	—	—	—	—	—	—
—Florida	NHL	7	406	4	2	1	22	0	3.25	—	—	—	—	—	—	—
98-99—Florida	NHL	30	1597	9	10	4	73	2	2.74	—	—	—	—	—	—	—
99-00—New York Rangers	NHL	22	1206	7	8	4	58	0	2.89	—	—	—	—	—	—	—
00-01—New York Rangers	NHL	23	1220	8	10	1	71	0	3.49	—	—	—	—	—	—	—
NHL Totals (16 years)		612	35090	245	262	72	1904	22	3.26	68	4189	34	34	198	6	2.84

McLENNAN, JAMIE　　G　　WILD

PERSONAL: Born June 30, 1971, in Edmonton. ... 6-0/190. ... Catches left.

TRANSACTIONS/CAREER NOTES: Selected by New York Islanders in third round (third Islanders pick, 48th overall) of NHL entry draft (June 22, 1991). ... Signed as free agent by St. Louis Blues (July 3, 1996). ... Strained groin (October 29, 1997); missed two games. ... Strained groin (March 22, 1998); missed one game. ... Strained hip flexor (January 19, 1999); missed one game. ... Suffered from the flu (March 11, 1999); missed two games. ... Selected by Minnesota Wild in NHL expansion draft (June 23, 2000). ... Bruised forearm (November 11, 2000); missed one game. ... Suffered illness (March 5, 2001); missed four games.

HONORS: Won Del Wilson Trophy (1990-91). ... Named to WHL (East) All-Star first team (1990-91). ... Won Bill Masterton Memorial Trophy (1997-98).

| | | REGULAR SEASON | | | | | | | | PLAYOFFS | | | | | | |
Season Team	League	Gms.	Min	W	L	T	GA	SO	Avg.	Gms.	Min.	W	L	GA	SO	Avg.
88-89—Spokane	WHL	11	578	...	...	...	63	0	6.54	—	—	—	—	—	—	—
—Lethbridge	WHL	7	368	...	...	...	22	0	3.59	—	—	—	—	—	—	—
89-90—Lethbridge	WHL	34	1690	20	4	2	110	1	3.91	13	677	6	5	44	0	3.90
90-91—Lethbridge	WHL	56	3230	32	18	4	205	0	3.81	*16	*970	8	8	*56	0	3.46
91-92—Capital District	AHL	18	952	4	10	2	60	1	3.78	—	—	—	—	—	—	—
—Richmond	ECHL	32	1837	16	12	‡2	114	0	3.72	—	—	—	—	—	—	—
92-93—Capital District	AHL	38	2171	17	14	6	117	1	3.23	1	20	0	1	5	0	15.00
93-94—Salt Lake City	IHL	24	1320	8	12	‡2	80	0	3.64	—	—	—	—	—	—	—
—New York Islanders	NHL	22	1287	8	7	6	61	0	2.84	2	82	0	1	6	0	4.39
94-95—New York Islanders	NHL	21	1185	6	11	2	67	0	3.39	—	—	—	—	—	—	—
—Denver	IHL	4	240	3	0	‡1	12	0	3.00	11	641	8	2	23	1	*2.15
95-96—Utah	IHL	14	728	9	2	2	29	0	2.39	—	—	—	—	—	—	—
—New York Islanders	NHL	13	636	3	9	1	39	0	3.68	—	—	—	—	—	—	—
—Worcester	AHL	22	1215	14	7	1	57	0	2.81	2	118	0	2	8	0	4.07
96-97—Worcester	AHL	39	2152	18	13	4	100	2	2.79	4	262	2	2	16	0	3.66
97-98—St. Louis	NHL	30	1658	16	8	2	60	2	2.17	1	14	0	0	1	0	4.29
98-99—St. Louis	NHL	33	1763	13	14	4	70	3	2.38	1	37	0	1	0	0	...
99-00—St. Louis	NHL	19	1009	9	5	2	33	2	1.96	—	—	—	—	—	—	—
00-01—Minnesota	NHL	38	2230	5	23	9	98	2	2.64	—	—	—	—	—	—	—
NHL Totals (7 years)		176	9768	60	77	26	428	9	2.63	4	133	0	2	7	0	3.16

MELICHAR, JOSEF　　D　　PENGUINS

PERSONAL: Born January 20, 1979, in Ceske Budejovice, Czechoslovakia. ... 6-2/214. ... Shoots left.

TRANSACTIONS/CAREER NOTES: Selected by Pittsburgh Penguins in third round (third Penguins pick, 71st overall) of NHL entry draft (June 21, 1997).

Season Team	League	REGULAR SEASON								PLAYOFFS				
		Gms.	G	A	Pts.	PIM	+/-	PP	SH	Gms.	G	A	Pts.	PIM
95-96—HC Ceske Bude	Czech Jrs.	38	3	4	7	...	...	...	...	—	—	—	—	—
96-97—HC Ceske Bude	Czech Jrs.	41	2	3	5	10	...	...	...	—	—	—	—	—
97-98—Tri-City	WHL	67	9	24	33	152	...	...	...	—	—	—	—	—
98-99—Tri-City	WHL	65	8	28	36	125	...	...	...	11	1	0	1	15
99-00—Wilkes-Barre/Scranton	AHL	80	3	9	12	126	...	...	...	—	—	—	—	—
00-01—Wilkes-Barre/Scranton	AHL	46	2	5	7	69	...	...	...	21	0	5	5	6
—Pittsburgh	NHL	18	0	2	2	21	-5	0	0	—	—	—	—	—
NHL Totals (1 year)		18	0	2	2	21	-5	0	0					

MELLANBY, SCOTT   RW   BLUES

PERSONAL: Born June 11, 1966, in Montreal. ... 6-1/205. ... Shoots right. ... Full Name: Scott Edgar Mellanby.

TRANSACTIONS/CAREER NOTES: Selected by Philadelphia Flyers as underage junior in second round (first Flyers pick, 27th overall) of NHL entry draft (June 9, 1984). ... Lacerated right index finger (October 1987). ... Severed nerve and damaged tendon in left forearm (August 1989); missed first 20 games of season. ... Suffered viral infection (November 1989). ... Traded by Flyers with LW Craig Berube and C Craig Fisher to Edmonton Oilers for RW Dave Brown, D Corey Foster and rights to RW Jari Kurri (May 30, 1991). ... Injured shoulder (February 14, 1993); missed 15 games. ... Selected by Florida Panthers in NHL expansion draft (June 24, 1993). ... Fractured nose and lacerated face (February 1 1994); missed four games. ... Fractured finger (March 7, 1996); missed three games. ... Sprained left knee (January 9, 1998); missed three games. ... Strained groin (September 29, 1998); missed first nine games of season. ... Injured neck (January 16, 1999); missed one game. ... Reinjured neck (January 21, 1999); missed three games. ... Suspended one game by NHL for cross-checking incident (March 21, 1999). ... Suffered slight concussion (April 5, 1999); missed one game. ... Suffered concussion (October 12, 1999); missed three games. ... Suffered from the flu (March 3, 2000); missed one game. ... Strained neck (October 28, 2000). ... Strained back (November 13, 2000); missed 12 games. ... Traded by Panthers to St. Louis Blues for RW David Morisset and fifth-round pick in 2002 draft (February 9, 2001).

HONORS: Played in NHL All-Star Game (1996).

MISCELLANEOUS: Captain of Florida Panthers (1997-98 through 1999-2000). ... Holds Florida Panthers all-time records for most games (552), most goals (153) and most points (341).

STATISTICAL NOTES: Tied for NHL lead in game-tying goals with three (1998-99).

Season Team	League	REGULAR SEASON								PLAYOFFS				
		Gms.	G	A	Pts.	PIM	+/-	PP	SH	Gms.	G	A	Pts.	PIM
83-84—Henry Carr H.S.	MTHL	39	37	37	74	97	...	...	...	—	—	—	—	—
84-85—Univ. of Wisconsin	WCHA	40	14	24	38	60	...	...	...	—	—	—	—	—
85-86—Univ. of Wisconsin	WCHA	32	21	23	44	89	...	...	...	—	—	—	—	—
—Philadelphia	NHL	2	0	0	0	0	-1	0	0	—	—	—	—	—
86-87—Philadelphia	NHL	71	11	21	32	94	8	1	0	24	5	5	10	46
87-88—Philadelphia	NHL	75	25	26	51	185	-7	7	0	7	0	1	1	16
88-89—Philadelphia	NHL	76	21	29	50	183	-13	11	0	19	4	5	9	28
89-90—Philadelphia	NHL	57	6	17	23	77	-4	0	0	—	—	—	—	—
90-91—Philadelphia	NHL	74	20	21	41	155	8	5	0	—	—	—	—	—
91-92—Edmonton	NHL	80	23	27	50	197	5	7	0	16	2	1	3	29
92-93—Edmonton	NHL	69	15	17	32	147	-4	6	0	—	—	—	—	—
93-94—Florida	NHL	80	30	30	60	149	0	17	0	—	—	—	—	—
94-95—Florida	NHL	48	13	12	25	90	-16	4	0	—	—	—	—	—
95-96—Florida	NHL	79	32	38	70	160	4	19	0	22	3	6	9	44
96-97—Florida	NHL	82	27	29	56	170	7	9	1	5	0	2	2	4
97-98—Florida	NHL	79	15	24	39	127	-14	6	0	—	—	—	—	—
98-99—Florida	NHL	67	18	27	45	85	5	4	0	—	—	—	—	—
99-00—Florida	NHL	77	18	28	46	126	14	6	0	4	0	1	1	2
00-01—Florida	NHL	40	4	9	13	46	-13	1	0	—	—	—	—	—
—St. Louis	NHL	23	7	1	8	25	0	2	0	15	3	3	6	17
NHL Totals (16 years)		1079	285	356	641	2016	-21	105	1	112	17	24	41	186

MELOCHE, ERIC   RW   PENGUINS

PERSONAL: Born May 1, 1976, in Montreal. ... 5-11/195. ... Shoots right.

TRANSACTIONS/CAREER NOTES: Selected by Pittsburgh Penguins in seventh round (seventh Penguins pick, 186th overall) of NHL entry draft (June 22, 1996).

Season Team	League	REGULAR SEASON								PLAYOFFS				
		Gms.	G	A	Pts.	PIM	+/-	PP	SH	Gms.	G	A	Pts.	PIM
95-96—Cornwall	Tier II	64	68	53	121	162	...	...	...	—	—	—	—	—
96-97—Ohio State	CCHA	39	12	11	23	78	...	...	...	—	—	—	—	—
97-98—Ohio State	CCHA	42	26	22	48	86	...	...	...	—	—	—	—	—
98-99—Ohio State	CCHA	35	11	16	27	87	...	...	...	—	—	—	—	—
99-00—Ohio State	CCHA	35	20	11	31	*136	...	...	...	—	—	—	—	—
00-01—Wilkes-Barre/Scranton	AHL	79	20	20	40	72	...	...	...	21	6	10	16	17

MESSIER, ERIC   D   AVALANCHE

PERSONAL: Born October 29, 1973, in Drummondville, Que. ... 6-2/200. ... Shoots left. ... Name pronounced MEHZ-yay.

TRANSACTIONS/CAREER NOTES: Signed as non-drafted free agent by Colorado Avalanche (June 14, 1995). ... Sprained ankle (October 28, 1997); missed three games. ... Fractured left elbow (October 10, 1998); missed 27 games. ... Injured eye (December 19, 1998); missed two games. ... Suffered injury (November 26, 1999); missed one game. ... Fractured lower leg (February 19, 2001); missed 17 games.

MISCELLANEOUS: Member of Stanley Cup championship team (2001).

Season Team	League	REGULAR SEASON								PLAYOFFS				
		Gms.	G	A	Pts.	PIM	+/-	PP	SH	Gms.	G	A	Pts.	PIM
91-92—Trois-Rivieres	QMJHL	58	2	10	12	28	...	...	...	15	2	2	4	13
92-93—Sherbrooke	QMJHL	51	4	17	21	82	...	...	...	15	0	4	4	18
93-94—Sherbrooke	QMJHL	67	4	24	28	69	...	...	...	12	1	7	8	14
94-95—Univ. of Quebec	OUAA	13	8	5	13	20	...	...	...	4	0	3	3	8
95-96—Cornwall	AHL	72	5	9	14	111	...	...	...	8	1	1	2	20
96-97—Hershey	AHL	55	16	26	42	69	...	...	...	9	3	8	11	14
—Colorado	NHL	21	0	0	0	4	7	0	0	—	—	—	—	—
97-98—Colorado	NHL	62	4	12	16	20	4	0	0	—	—	—	—	—
98-99—Colorado	NHL	31	4	2	6	14	0	1	0	3	0	0	0	0
—Hershey	AHL	6	1	3	4	4	...	...	...	—	—	—	—	—
99-00—Colorado	NHL	61	3	6	9	24	0	1	0	—	—	—	—	—
00-01—Colorado	NHL	64	5	7	12	26	-3	0	0	23	2	2	4	14
NHL Totals (5 years)		239	16	27	43	88	8	2	0	26	2	2	4	14

MESSIER, MARK   C   RANGERS

PERSONAL: Born January 18, 1961, in Edmonton. ... 6-1/205. ... Shoots left. ... Full Name: Mark Douglas Messier. ... Brother of Paul Messier, center with Colorado Rockies (1978-79); cousin of Mitch Messier, center/right winger with Minnesota North Stars (1987-88 through 1990-91); cousin of Joby Messier, defenseman with New York Rangers (1992-93 through 1994-95); and brother-in-law of John Blum, defenseman with four NHL teams (1982-83 through 1989-90). ... Name pronounced MEHZ-yay.

TRANSACTIONS/CAREER NOTES: Signed as non-drafted free agent to 10-game trial by Indianapolis Racers (November 5, 1978). ... Signed as free agent by Cincinnati Stingers of WHA (December 1978). ... Selected by Edmonton Oilers in third round (second Oilers pick, 48th over-all) of NHL entry draft (August 9, 1979). ... Injured ankle (November 7, 1981). ... Fractured wrist (March 1983). ... Suspended six games by NHL for hitting another player with stick (January 18, 1984). ... Sprained knee ligaments (November 1984). ... Suspended 10 games by NHL for injuring another player (December 26, 1984). ... Bruised left foot (December 3, 1985); missed 17 games. ... Suspended six games by NHL for injuring another player with his stick (October 23, 1988). ... Twisted left knee (January 28, 1989). ... Strained right knee (February 3, 1989). ... Bruised left knee (February 12, 1989). ... Sprained left knee ligaments (October 16, 1990); missed 10 games. ... Reinjured left knee (December 12, 1990); missed three games. ... Reinjured knee (December 22, 1990); missed nine games. ... Fractured left thumb (February 11, 1991); missed eight games. ... Missed one game due to contract dispute (October 1991). ... Traded by Oilers with future considerations to New York Rangers for C Bernie Nicholls, LW Louie DeBrusk, RW Steven Rice and future considerations (October 4, 1991); Oilers traded D Jeff Beukeboom to Rangers for D David Shaw to complete deal (November 12, 1991). ... Sprained ligament in wrist (January 19, 1993); missed six games. ... Strained rib cage muscle (February 27, 1993); missed two games. ... Strained rib cage muscle (March 11, 1993); missed one game. ... Suspended three off-days and fined $500 by NHL for stick-swinging incident (March 18, 1993). ... Sprained wrist (December 22, 1993); missed six games. ... Bruised thigh (March 16, 1994); missed two games. ... Suffered back spasms (April 30, 1995); missed two games. ... Bruised shoulder (February 27, 1996); missed two games. ... Bruised ribs (April 4, 1996); missed six games. ... Suspended two games and fined $1,000 by NHL for checking opponent from behind (October 8, 1996). ... Hyperextended elbow (December 7, 1996); missed four games. ... Suffered back spasms (February 23, 1997); missed two games. ... Suffered charley horse (March 27, 1997); missed two games. ... Signed as free agent by Vancouver Canucks (July 28, 1997). ... Suffered concussion (December 22, 1998); missed one game. ... Sprained medial collateral ligament in knee (February 11, 1999); missed 18 games. ... Injured groin (March 31, 1999); missed four games. ... Sprained medial collateral ligament in knee (November 9, 1999); missed 15 games. ... Injured knee (December 29, 2000); missed one game. ... Signed as free agent by Rangers (July 13, 2000).

HONORS: Named to THE SPORTING NEWS All-Star first team (1981-82, 1982-83, 1989-90 and 1991-92). ... Named to NHL All-Star first team (1981-82, 1982-83, 1989-90 and 1991-92). ... Played in NHL All-Star Game (1982-1984, 1986, 1988-1992, 1994, 1996-1998 and 2000). ... Won Conn Smythe Trophy (1983-84). ... Named to NHL All-Star second team (1983-84). ... Named to THE SPORTING NEWS All-Star second team (1986-87). ... Named NHL Player of the Year by THE SPORTING NEWS (1989-90 and 1991-92). ... Won Hart Memorial Trophy (1989-90 and 1991-92). ... Won Lester B. Pearson Award (1989-90 and 1991-92).

RECORDS: Holds NHL career playoff record for most shorthanded goals—11; and assists—236. ... Shares NHL single-game playoff record for most shorthanded goals—2 (April 21, 1992). ... Shares NHL career All-Star Game record for most assists—13.

STATISTICAL PLATEAUS: Three-goal games: 1980-81 (1), 1981-82 (2), 1982-83 (1), 1983-84 (2), 1985-86 (1), 1987-88 (1), 1989-90 (2), 1991-92 (2), 1995-96 (1), 1996-97 (2). Total: 15. ... Four-goal games: 1982-83 (1), 1988-89 (1), 1989-90 (1), 1991-92 (1). Total: 4. ... Total hat tricks: 19.

MISCELLANEOUS: Member of Stanley Cup championship teams (1984, 1985, 1987, 1988, 1990 and 1994). ... Captain of Edmonton Oilers (1988-89 through 1990-91). ... Captain of New York Rangers (1991-92 through 1996-97 and 2000-01). ... Captain of Vancouver Canucks (1997-98 through 1999-2000).

M

Season Team	League	REGULAR SEASON								PLAYOFFS				
		Gms.	G	A	Pts.	PIM	+/-	PP	SH	Gms.	G	A	Pts.	PIM
76-77—Spruce Grove	AJHL	57	27	39	66	91	...	...	...	—	—	—	—	—
77-78—St. Albert	AJHL						Statistics unavailable.							
—Portland	WHL	—	—	—	—	—				7	4	1	5	2
78-79—Indianapolis	WHA	5	0	0	0	0	...	...	...	—	—	—	—	—
—Cincinnati	WHA	47	1	10	11	58	...	...	...	—	—	—	—	—
79-80—Houston	CHL	4	0	3	3	4	...	...	...	—	—	—	—	—
—Edmonton	NHL	75	12	21	33	120	-10	1	1	3	1	2	3	2
80-81—Edmonton	NHL	72	23	40	63	102	-12	4	0	9	2	5	7	13
81-82—Edmonton	NHL	78	50	38	88	119	21	10	0	5	1	2	3	8
82-83—Edmonton	NHL	77	48	58	106	72	19	12	1	15	15	6	21	14
83-84—Edmonton	NHL	73	37	64	101	165	40	7	4	19	8	18	26	19
84-85—Edmonton	NHL	55	23	31	54	57	8	4	5	18	12	13	25	12
85-86—Edmonton	NHL	63	35	49	84	68	36	10	5	10	4	6	10	18
86-87—Edmonton	NHL	77	37	70	107	73	21	7	4	21	12	16	28	16
87-88—Edmonton	NHL	77	37	74	111	103	21	12	3	19	11	23	34	29
88-89—Edmonton	NHL	72	33	61	94	130	-5	9	6	7	1	11	12	8
89-90—Edmonton	NHL	79	45	84	129	79	19	13	6	22	9	*22	†31	20
90-91—Edmonton	NHL	53	12	52	64	34	15	3	1	18	4	11	15	16
91-92—New York Rangers	NHL	79	35	72	107	76	31	12	4	11	7	7	14	6
92-93—New York Rangers	NHL	75	25	66	91	72	-6	7	2	—	—	—	—	—
93-94—New York Rangers	NHL	76	26	58	84	76	25	6	2	23	12	18	30	33
94-95—New York Rangers	NHL	46	14	39	53	40	8	3	3	10	3	10	13	8
95-96—New York Rangers	NHL	74	47	52	99	122	29	14	1	11	4	7	11	16

Season Team	League	REGULAR SEASON								PLAYOFFS				
		Gms.	G	A	Pts.	PIM	+/-	PP	SH	Gms.	G	A	Pts.	PIM
96-97—New York Rangers	NHL	71	36	48	84	88	12	7	5	15	3	9	12	6
97-98—Vancouver	NHL	82	22	38	60	58	-10	8	2	—	—	—	—	—
98-99—Vancouver	NHL	59	13	35	48	33	-12	4	2	—	—	—	—	—
99-00—Vancouver	NHL	66	17	37	54	30	-15	6	0	—	—	—	—	—
00-01—New York Rangers	NHL	82	24	43	67	89	-25	12	3	—	—	—	—	—
WHA Totals (1 year)		52	1	10	11	58	...	...	...					
NHL Totals (22 years)		1561	651	1130	1781	1806	210	168	60	236	109	186	295	244

METHOT, FRANCOIS   C   SABRES

PERSONAL: Born April 26, 1978, in Montreal. ... 6-0/175. ... Shoots right. ... Name pronounced meh-TOH.
TRANSACTIONS/CAREER NOTES: Selected by Buffalo Sabres in third round (fourth Sabres pick, 54th overall) of NHL entry draft (June 22, 1996).

Season Team	League	REGULAR SEASON								PLAYOFFS				
		Gms.	G	A	Pts.	PIM	+/-	PP	SH	Gms.	G	A	Pts.	PIM
94-95—St. Hyacinthe	QMJHL	60	14	38	52	22	...	...	...	5	0	1	1	0
95-96—St. Hyacinthe	QMJHL	68	32	62	94	22	...	...	...	12	6	6	12	4
96-97—Rouyn-Noranda	QMJHL	47	21	30	51	22	...	...	...	—	—	—	—	—
—Shawinigan	QMJHL	18	9	17	26	2	...	...	...	7	2	6	8	2
97-98—Shawinigan	QMJHL	36	23	42	65	10	...	...	...	6	1	3	4	5
98-99—Rochester	AHL	58	5	3	8	8	...	...	...	9	0	1	1	0
99-00—Rochester	AHL	80	14	18	32	20	...	...	...	21	2	4	6	16
00-01—Rochester	AHL	79	22	33	55	35	...	...	...	4	1	3	4	0

METROPOLIT, GLEN   C   CAPITALS

PERSONAL: Born June 25, 1974, in Toronto. ... 5-11/196. ... Shoots right.
TRANSACTIONS/CAREER NOTES: Signed as non-drafted free agent by Washington Capitals (July 20, 1999).

Season Team	League	REGULAR SEASON								PLAYOFFS				
		Gms.	G	A	Pts.	PIM	+/-	PP	SH	Gms.	G	A	Pts.	PIM
92-93—Richmond Hill	OJHL	43	27	36	63	36	...	...	...	—	—	—	—	—
93-94—Richmond Hill	OJHL	49	38	62	100	83	...	...	...	—	—	—	—	—
94-95—Vernon	BCJHL	60	43	74	117	92	...	...	...	—	—	—	—	—
95-96—Nashville	ECHL	58	30	31	61	62	...	...	...	5	3	8	11	2
—Atlanta	IHL	1	0	0	0	0	...	...	...	—	—	—	—	—
96-97—Pensacola	ECHL	54	35	47	82	45	...	...	...	12	9	16	25	28
—Quebec	IHL	22	5	4	9	14	...	...	...	5	0	0	0	2
97-98—Grand Rapids	IHL	79	20	35	55	90	...	...	...	3	1	1	2	0
98-99—Grand Rapids	IHL	77	28	53	81	92	...	...	...	—	—	—	—	—
99-00—Washington	NHL	30	6	13	19	4	5	1	0	2	0	0	0	2
—Portland	AHL	48	18	42	60	73	...	...	...	1	1	0	1	0
00-01—Washington	NHL	15	1	5	6	10	-2	0	0	1	0	0	0	0
—Portland	AHL	51	25	42	67	59	...	...	...	—	—	—	—	—
NHL Totals (2 years)		45	7	18	25	14	3	1	0	3	0	0	0	2

MEZEI, BRANISLAV   D   ISLANDERS

PERSONAL: Born October 8, 1980, in Nitra, Czechoslovakia. ... 6-5/221. ... Shoots left. ... Name pronounced MEE-zy.
TRANSACTIONS/CAREER NOTES: Selected by New York Islanders in first round (third Islanders pick, 10th overall) of NHL entry draft (June 26, 1999). ... Separated left shoulder (January 16, 2001); missed 13 games.
HONORS: Named to OHL All-Star first team (1999-2000).

Season Team	League	REGULAR SEASON								PLAYOFFS				
		Gms.	G	A	Pts.	PIM	+/-	PP	SH	Gms.	G	A	Pts.	PIM
96-97—Plastika Nitra Jrs.	Slovakia Jrs.	40	8	17	25	42	...	...	...	—	—	—	—	—
97-98—Belleville	OHL	53	3	5	8	58	...	...	...	8	0	2	2	8
98-99—Belleville	OHL	60	5	18	23	90	...	...	...	18	0	4	4	29
99-00—Belleville	OHL	58	7	21	28	99	...	...	...	6	0	3	3	10
00-01—Lowell	AHL	20	0	3	3	28	...	...	...	—	—	—	—	—
—New York Islanders	NHL	42	1	4	5	53	-5	0	0	—	—	—	—	—
NHL Totals (1 year)		42	1	4	5	53	-5	0	0					

MICHAUD, ALFIE   G   CANUCKS

PERSONAL: Born November 6, 1976, in Selkirk, Man. ... 5-10/177. ... Catches left.
TRANSACTIONS/CAREER NOTES: Signed as non-drafted free agent by Vancouver Canucks (June 17, 1999).
HONORS: Named to NCAA All-Tournament team (1998-99). ... Named NCAA Tournament Most Valuable Player (1998-99).

Season Team	League	REGULAR SEASON							PLAYOFFS					
		Gms.	Min	W	L	T	GA	SO	Avg.	Gms.	Min.	W	L	GA	SO	Avg.
96-97—Univ. of Maine	Hockey East	29	1515	17	8	1	78	1	3.09	—	—	—	—	—	—	—
97-98—Univ. of Maine	Hockey East	32	1794	15	12	†4	94	2	3.14	—	—	—	—	—	—	—
98-99—Univ. of Maine	Hockey East	37	2147	*28	6	3	83	3	2.32	—	—	—	—	—	—	—
99-00—Syracuse	AHL	38	2052	10	17	5	132	0	3.86	—	—	—	—	—	—	—
—Vancouver	NHL	2	69	0	1	0	5	0	4.35	—	—	—	—	—	—	—
00-01—Kansas City	IHL	32	1778	14	14	‡2	93	1	3.14	—	—	—	—	—	—	—
NHL Totals (1 year)		2	69	0	1	0	5	0	4.35							

MILLAR, CRAIG   D

PERSONAL: Born July 12, 1976, in Winnipeg. ... 6-2/206. ... Shoots left.
TRANSACTIONS/CAREER NOTES: Selected by Buffalo Sabres in ninth round (10th Sabres pick, 225th overall) of NHL entry draft (June 29, 1994). ... Traded by Sabres with LW Barrie Moore to Edmonton Oilers for LW/RW Miroslav Satan (March 18, 1997). ... Traded by Oilers to Nashville Predators for third-round pick (C Mike Comrie) in 1999 draft (June 26, 1999). ... Claimed on waivers by Tampa Bay Lightning (October 25, 2000). ... Strained hip flexor (November 5, 2000); missed one game. ... Injured ribs (November 11, 2000); missed seven games. ... Fractured leg (December 14, 2000); missed 18 games. ... Traded by Lightning to Ottawa Senators for F John Emmons (March 13, 2001).
HONORS: Named to WHL (Central/East) All-Star first team (1995-96). ... Named to AHL All-Rookie team (1996-97).

		REGULAR SEASON								PLAYOFFS				
Season Team	League	Gms.	G	A	Pts.	PIM	+/-	PP	SH	Gms.	G	A	Pts.	PIM
92-93—Swift Current	WHL	43	2	1	3	8	...	...	...	—	—	—	—	—
93-94—Swift Current	WHL	66	2	9	11	53	...	...	...	—	—	—	—	—
94-95—Swift Current	WHL	72	8	42	50	80	...	...	...	6	1	1	2	10
95-96—Swift Current	WHL	72	31	46	77	151	...	...	...	6	1	0	1	22
96-97—Rochester	AHL	64	7	18	25	65	...	...	...	—	—	—	—	—
—Edmonton	NHL	1	0	0	0	2	0	0	0	—	—	—	—	—
—Hamilton	AHL	10	1	3	4	10	...	...	...	22	4	4	8	21
97-98—Hamilton	AHL	60	10	22	32	113	...	...	...	9	3	1	4	22
—Edmonton	NHL	11	4	0	4	8	-3	1	0	—	—	—	—	—
98-99—Edmonton	NHL	24	0	2	2	19	-6	0	0	—	—	—	—	—
—Hamilton	AHL	43	3	17	20	38	...	...	...	11	1	5	6	18
99-00—Nashville	NHL	57	3	11	14	28	-6	0	0	—	—	—	—	—
—Milwaukee	IHL	8	1	5	6	6	...	...	...	—	—	—	—	—
00-01—Nashville	NHL	5	0	0	0	6	1	0	0	—	—	—	—	—
—Tampa Bay	NHL	16	1	1	2	10	-8	0	0	—	—	—	—	—
—Detroit	IHL	11	0	2	2	32	...	...	...	—	—	—	—	—
—Grand Rapids	IHL	12	1	2	3	2	...	...	...	—	—	—	—	—
NHL Totals (5 years)		114	8	14	22	73	-22	1	0					

MILLER, AARON   D   KINGS

PERSONAL: Born August 11, 1971, in Buffalo. ... 6-3/205. ... Shoots right. ... Full Name: Aaron Michael Miller.
TRANSACTIONS/CAREER NOTES: Selected by New York Rangers in fifth round (sixth Rangers pick, 88th overall) of NHL entry draft (June 17, 1989). ... Traded by Rangers with fifth-round pick (LW Bill Lindsay) in 1991 draft to Quebec Nordiques for D Joe Cirella (January 17, 1991). ... Nordiques franchise moved to Colorado and renamed Avalanche for 1995-96 season (June 21, 1995). ... Suffered concussion (October 24, 1998); missed one game. ... Bruised knee (November 8, 1998); missed one game. ... Suffered back spasms (March 17, 1999); missed three games. ... Bruised sternum (November 17, 1999); missed 27 games. ... Bruised right hand (November 22, 2000); missed five games. ... Traded by Avalanche with RW Adam Deadmarsh, first-round pick (C David Steckel) in 2001 draft, a player to be named later and first-round pick in 2002 draft to Los Angeles Kings for C Steve Reinprecht and D Rob Blake (February 21, 2001); Kings acquired C Jared Aulin to complete deal (March 22, 2001). ... Sprained wrist (March 19, 2001); missed final nine games of season.
HONORS: Named to ECAC All-Rookie team (1989-90). ... Named to NCAA All-America (East) second team (1992-93). ... Named to ECAC All-Star first team (1992-93).

		REGULAR SEASON								PLAYOFFS				
Season Team	League	Gms.	G	A	Pts.	PIM	+/-	PP	SH	Gms.	G	A	Pts.	PIM
87-88—Niagara	NAJHL	30	4	9	13	2	...	...	...	—	—	—	—	—
88-89—Niagara	NAJHL	59	24	38	62	60	...	...	...	—	—	—	—	—
89-90—Univ. of Vermont	ECAC	31	1	15	16	24	...	...	...	—	—	—	—	—
90-91—Univ. of Vermont	ECAC	30	3	7	10	22	...	...	...	—	—	—	—	—
91-92—Univ. of Vermont	ECAC	31	3	16	19	36	...	...	...	—	—	—	—	—
92-93—Univ. of Vermont	ECAC	30	4	13	17	16	...	...	...	—	—	—	—	—
93-94—Cornwall	AHL	64	4	10	14	49	...	...	...	13	0	2	2	10
—Quebec	NHL	1	0	0	0	0	-1	0	0	—	—	—	—	—
94-95—Cornwall	AHL	76	4	18	22	69	...	...	...	—	—	—	—	—
—Quebec	NHL	9	0	3	3	6	2	0	0	—	—	—	—	—
95-96—Cornwall	AHL	62	4	23	27	77	...	...	...	8	0	1	1	6
—Colorado	NHL	5	0	0	0	0	0	0	0	—	—	—	—	—
96-97—Colorado	NHL	56	5	12	17	15	15	0	0	17	1	2	3	10
97-98—Colorado	NHL	55	2	2	4	51	0	0	0	7	0	0	0	8
98-99—Colorado	NHL	76	5	13	18	42	3	1	0	19	1	5	6	10
99-00—Colorado	NHL	53	1	7	8	36	3	0	0	17	1	1	2	6
00-01—Colorado	NHL	56	4	9	13	29	19	0	0	—	—	—	—	—
—Los Angeles	NHL	13	0	5	5	14	3	0	0	13	0	1	1	6
NHL Totals (8 years)		324	17	51	68	193	44	1	0	73	3	9	12	40

MILLER, KIP   C

PERSONAL: Born June 11, 1969, in Lansing, Mich. ... 5-10/190. ... Shoots left. ... Full Name: Kip Charles Miller. ... Brother of Kelly Miller, right winger with New York Rangers (1984-85 through 1986-87) and Washington Capitals (1986-87 through 1998-99); and brother of Kevin Miller, left winger with nine NHL teams (1988-89 through 1999-2000).
TRANSACTIONS/CAREER NOTES: Selected by Quebec Nordiques in fourth round (fourth Nordiques pick, 72nd overall) of NHL entry draft (June 13, 1987). ... Traded by Nordiques to Minnesota North Stars for LW Steve Maltais (March 8, 1992). ... North Stars franchise moved from Minnesota to Dallas and renamed Stars for 1993-94 season. ... Signed as free agent by San Jose Sharks (August 10, 1993). ... Signed as free agent by New York Islanders (August 2, 1994). ... Signed as free agent by Chicago Blackhawks (August 10, 1995). ... Signed as free agent by Islanders (November 26, 1997). ... Selected by Pittsburgh Penguins from Islanders in NHL waiver draft (October 5, 1998). ... Injured eye (March 20, 1999); missed one game. ... Sprained knee (October 30, 1999); missed one game. ... Traded by Penguins to Mighty Ducks of Anaheim for future considerations (January 30, 2000). ... Signed as free agent by Penguins (September 24, 2000). ... Strained groin (November 28, 2000); missed four games.
HONORS: Named to NCAA All-America (West) first team (1988-89 and 1989-90). ... Named to CCHA All-Star first team (1988-89 and 1989-90). ... Won Hobey Baker Memorial Award (1989-90). ... Named CCHA Player of the Year (1989-90). ... Won N.R. (Bud) Poile Trophy (1994-95).

Season Team	League	REGULAR SEASON Gms.	G	A	Pts.	PIM	+/-	PP	SH	PLAYOFFS Gms.	G	A	Pts.	PIM
86-87—Michigan State	CCHA	41	20	19	39	92	...	...	...	—	—	—	—	—
87-88—Michigan State	CCHA	39	16	25	41	51	...	...	...	—	—	—	—	—
88-89—Michigan State	CCHA	47	32	45	77	94	...	...	...	—	—	—	—	—
89-90—Michigan State	CCHA	45	*48	53	*101	60	...	...	...	—	—	—	—	—
90-91—Quebec	NHL	13	4	3	7	7	-1	0	0	—	—	—	—	—
—Halifax	AHL	66	36	33	69	40	...	...	...	—	—	—	—	—
91-92—Quebec	NHL	36	5	10	15	12	-21	1	0	—	—	—	—	—
—Halifax	AHL	24	9	17	26	8	...	...	...	—	—	—	—	—
—Minnesota	NHL	3	1	2	3	2	-1	1	0	—	—	—	—	—
—Kalamazoo	IHL	6	1	8	9	4	...	...	...	12	3	9	12	12
92-93—Kalamazoo	IHL	61	17	39	56	59	...	...	...	—	—	—	—	—
93-94—San Jose	NHL	11	2	2	4	6	-1	0	0	—	—	—	—	—
—Kansas City	IHL	71	38	54	92	51	...	...	...	—	—	—	—	—
94-95—Denver	IHL	71	46	60	106	54	...	...	...	17	*15	14	29	8
—New York Islanders	NHL	8	0	1	1	0	1	0	0	—	—	—	—	—
95-96—Indianapolis	IHL	73	32	59	91	46	...	...	...	5	2	6	8	2
—Chicago	NHL	10	1	4	5	2	1	0	0	—	—	—	—	—
96-97—Chicago	IHL	43	11	41	52	32	...	...	...	—	—	—	—	—
—Indianapolis	IHL	37	17	24	41	18	...	...	...	4	2	2	4	2
97-98—Utah	IHL	72	38	59	97	30	...	...	...	4	3	2	5	10
—New York Islanders	NHL	9	1	3	4	2	-2	0	0	—	—	—	—	—
98-99—Pittsburgh	NHL	77	19	23	42	22	1	1	0	13	2	7	9	19
99-00—Pittsburgh	NHL	44	4	15	19	10	-1	0	0	—	—	—	—	—
—Anaheim	NHL	30	6	17	23	4	1	2	0	—	—	—	—	—
00-01—Pittsburgh	NHL	33	3	8	11	6	0	1	0	—	—	—	—	—
—Grand Rapids	IHL	34	16	19	35	12	...	...	...	10	5	8	13	2
NHL Totals (9 years)		274	46	88	134	73	-23	6	0	13	2	7	9	19

MILLER, RYAN   G   SABRES

PERSONAL: Born July 17, 1980, in East Lansing, Mich. ... 6-1/150. ... Catches left.
TRANSACTIONS/CAREER NOTES: Selected by Buffalo Sabres in fifth round (seventh Sabres pick, 138th overall) of NHL entry draft (June 26, 1999).
HONORS: Named to CCHA All-Star second team (1999-2000). ... Named to CCHA All-Star first team (2000-01). ... Named to NCAA All-America (West) first team (2000-01). ... Won Hobey Baker Memorial Award (1999-2000).

Season Team	League	REGULAR SEASON Gms.	Min	W	L	T	GA	SO	Avg.	PLAYOFFS Gms.	Min.	W	L	GA	SO	Avg.
98-99—Soo	NAHL	47	2711	31	14	1	104	8	2.30	4	218	2	2	10	1	2.75
99-00—Michigan State	CCHA	25	1453	16	4	3	33	*7	*1.36	—	—	—	—	—	—	—
00-01—Michigan State	CCHA	40	2447	*31	5	4	54	*10	*1.32	—	—	—	—	—	—	—

M   MILLEY, NORM   RW   SABRES

PERSONAL: Born February 14, 1980, in Toronto. ... 5-11/175. ... Shoots right. ... Full Name: Norman Milley.
TRANSACTIONS/CAREER NOTES: Selected by Buffalo Sabres in second round (third Sabres pick, 47th overall) of NHL entry draft (June 27, 1998).
HONORS: Named to Can.HL All-Rookie team (1996-97). ... Named to OHL All-Rookie first team (1996-97). ... Named to OHL All-Star second team (1998-99). ... Won Jim Mahon Award (1998-99). ... Named to OHL All-Star first team (1999-2000). ... Named to Can.HL All-Star first team (1999-2000).

Season Team	League	REGULAR SEASON Gms.	G	A	Pts.	PIM	+/-	PP	SH	PLAYOFFS Gms.	G	A	Pts.	PIM
95-96—Toronto Red Wings	MTHL	42	42	36	78	109	...	...	...	—	—	—	—	—
96-97—Sudbury	OHL	61	30	32	62	15	...	...	...	—	—	—	—	—
97-98—Sudbury	OHL	62	33	41	74	48	...	...	...	10	0	1	1	4
98-99—Sudbury	OHL	68	52	68	120	47	...	...	...	4	2	3	5	4
99-00—Sudbury	OHL	68	*52	60	112	47	...	...	...	12	8	11	19	6
00-01—Rochester	AHL	77	20	27	47	56	...	...	...	4	0	0	0	2

MILLS, CRAIG   RW   MAPLE LEAFS

PERSONAL: Born August 27, 1976, in Toronto. ... 6-0/195. ... Shoots right.
TRANSACTIONS/CAREER NOTES: Selected by Winnipeg Jets in fifth round (fifth Jets pick, 108th overall) of NHL entry draft (June 29, 1994). ... Jets franchise moved to Phoenix and renamed Coyotes for 1996-97 season; NHL approved move on January 18, 1996. ... Traded by Coyotes with C Alexei Zhamnov and first-round pick (RW Ty Jones) in 1997 draft to Chicago Blackhawks for C Jeremy Roenick (August 16, 1996). ... Traded by Blackhawks to Coyotes for future considerations (September 11, 1999). ... Traded by Coyotes with C Robert Reichel and C Travis Green to Toronto Maple Leafs for D Danny Markov (June 12, 2001).
HONORS: Won Can.HL Humanitarian Award (1995-96).

Season Team	League	REGULAR SEASON Gms.	G	A	Pts.	PIM	+/-	PP	SH	PLAYOFFS Gms.	G	A	Pts.	PIM
92-93—St. Michael's	Tier II Jr. A	44	8	12	20	51	...	...	...	—	—	—	—	—
93-94—Belleville	OHL	63	15	18	33	88	...	...	...	12	2	1	3	11
94-95—Belleville	OHL	62	39	41	80	104	...	...	...	13	7	9	16	8
95-96—Belleville	OHL	48	10	19	29	113	...	...	...	14	4	5	9	32
—Winnipeg	NHL	4	0	2	2	0	0	0	0	1	0	0	0	0
—Springfield	AHL	—	—	—	—	—	...	...	...	2	0	0	0	0

Season Team	League	Gms.	G	A	Pts.	PIM	+/-	PP	SH	Gms.	G	A	Pts.	PIM
		REGULAR SEASON								PLAYOFFS				
96-97—Indianapolis	IHL	80	12	7	19	199	...	...	...	4	0	0	0	4
97-98—Chicago	NHL	20	0	3	3	34	1	0	0	—	—	—	—	—
—Indianapolis	IHL	42	8	11	19	119	...	...	...	5	0	0	0	27
98-99—Chicago	NHL	7	0	0	0	2	-2	0	0	—	—	—	—	—
—Chicago	IHL	5	0	0	0	14	...	...	...	—	—	—	—	—
—Indianapolis	IHL	12	2	3	5	14	...	...	...	6	1	0	1	5
99-00—Springfield	AHL	78	10	13	23	151	...	...	...	5	2	1	3	6
00-01—Springfield	AHL	64	8	5	13	131	...	...	...	—	—	—	—	—
NHL Totals (3 years)		31	0	5	5	36	-1	0	0	1	0	0	0	0

MIRONOV, BORIS   D   BLACKHAWKS

PERSONAL: Born March 21, 1972, in Moscow, U.S.S.R. ... 6-3/223. ... Shoots right. ... Brother of Dmitri Mironov, defenseman, Washington Capitals. ... Name pronounced MIHR-ih-nahf.
TRANSACTIONS/CAREER NOTES: Selected by Winnipeg Jets in second round (second Jets pick, 27th overall) of NHL entry draft (June 20, 1992). ... Bruised back (February 2, 1994); missed three games. ... Traded by Jets with C Mats Lindgren and first- (C Jason Bonsignore) and fourth-round (RW Adam Copeland) picks in 1994 draft to Edmonton Oilers for D Dave Manson and sixth-round pick (D Chris Kibermanis) in 1994 draft (March 15, 1994). ... Bruised ankle (April 3, 1995); missed one game. ... Strained lower back (April 13, 1995); missed 10 games. ... Strained abdominal muscle (January 21, 1997); missed 12 games. ... Strained groin (February 19, 1997); missed five games. ... Strained groin (March 7, 1997); missed five games. ... Bruised right shoulder (February 3, 1999); missed two games. ... Traded by Oilers with LW Dean McAmmond and D Jonas Elofsson to Chicago Blackhawks for C Chad Kilger, LW Daniel Cleary, LW Ethan Moreau and D Christian Laflamme (March 20, 1999). ... Suffered charley horse (March 25, 1999); missed one game. ... Suffered hip pointer (December 4, 1999); missed one game. ... Sprained knee (March 26, 2000); missed final seven games of season. ... Tore ligament in wrist (January 25, 2001); missed 15 games.
HONORS: Named to NHL All-Rookie team (1993-94).
MISCELLANEOUS: Member of silver-medal-winning Russian Olympic team (1998).

Season Team	League	Gms.	G	A	Pts.	PIM	+/-	PP	SH	Gms.	G	A	Pts.	PIM
		REGULAR SEASON								PLAYOFFS				
88-89—CSKA Moscow	USSR	1	0	0	0	0	...	...	...	—	—	—	—	—
89-90—CSKA Moscow	USSR	7	0	0	0	0	...	...	...	—	—	—	—	—
90-91—CSKA Moscow	USSR	36	1	5	6	16	...	...	...	—	—	—	—	—
91-92—CSKA Moscow	CIS	36	2	1	3	22	...	...	...	—	—	—	—	—
92-93—CSKA Moscow	CIS	19	0	5	5	20	...	...	...	—	—	—	—	—
93-94—Winnipeg	NHL	65	7	22	29	96	-29	5	0	—	—	—	—	—
—Edmonton	NHL	14	0	2	2	14	-4	0	0	—	—	—	—	—
94-95—Cape Breton	AHL	4	2	5	7	23	...	...	...	—	—	—	—	—
—Edmonton	NHL	29	1	7	8	40	-9	0	0	—	—	—	—	—
95-96—Edmonton	NHL	78	8	24	32	101	-23	7	0	—	—	—	—	—
96-97—Edmonton	NHL	55	6	26	32	85	2	2	0	12	2	8	10	16
97-98—Edmonton	NHL	81	16	30	46	100	-8	10	1	12	3	3	6	27
—Russian Oly. team	Int'l	6	0	2	2	2	...	...	...	—	—	—	—	—
98-99—Edmonton	NHL	63	11	29	40	104	6	5	0	—	—	—	—	—
—Chicago	NHL	12	0	9	9	27	7	0	0	—	—	—	—	—
99-00—Chicago	NHL	58	9	28	37	72	-3	4	2	—	—	—	—	—
00-01—Chicago	NHL	66	5	17	22	42	-14	3	0	—	—	—	—	—
NHL Totals (8 years)		521	63	194	257	681	-75	36	3	24	5	11	16	43

MIRONOV, DMITRI   D   CAPITALS

PERSONAL: Born December 25, 1965, in Moscow, U.S.S.R. ... 6-4/229. ... Shoots right. ... Brother of Boris Mironov, defenseman, Chicago Blackhawks. ... Name pronounced MIHR-ih-nahf.
TRANSACTIONS/CAREER NOTES: Selected by Toronto Maple Leafs in eighth round (seventh Maple Leafs pick, 160th overall) of NHL entry draft (June 22, 1991). ... Fractured nose (March 23, 1992). ... Suffered infected tooth (March 18, 1993); missed 10 games. ... Bruised quadricep (December 28, 1993); missed one game. ... Lacerated lip (March 7, 1994); missed two games. ... Suffered rib muscle strain (April 2, 1994); missed remainder of season. ... Bruised thigh (February 18, 1995); missed one game. ... Separated shoulder (March 27, 1995); missed 14 games. ... Traded by Maple Leafs with second-round pick (traded to New Jersey) in 1996 draft to Pittsburgh Penguins for D Larry Murphy (July 8, 1995). ... Bruised shoulder (March 14, 1996); missed eight games. ... Traded by Pengiuns with LW Shawn Antoski to Mighty Ducks of Anaheim for C Alex Hicks and D Fredrik Olausson (November 19, 1996). ... Traded by Mighty Ducks to Detroit Red Wings for D Jamie Pushor and fourth-round pick (C Viktor Wallin) in 1998 draft (March 24, 1998). ... Signed as free agent by Washington Capitals (July 14, 1998). ... Strained back (February 7, 1999); missed remainder of season. ... Bruised tailbone (February 23, 2000); missed four games. ... Suffered from the flu (April 1, 2000); missed one game. ... Injured wrist (November 4, 2000); missed two games. ... Strained back (January 19, 2001) and underwent surgery; missed remainder of season.
HONORS: Played in NHL All-Star Game (1998).
MISCELLANEOUS: Member of Stanley Cup championship team (1998). ... Member of gold-medal-winning Unified Olympic team (1992). ... Member of silver-medal-winning Russian Olympic team (1998).

Season Team	League	Gms.	G	A	Pts.	PIM	+/-	PP	SH	Gms.	G	A	Pts.	PIM
		REGULAR SEASON								PLAYOFFS				
85-86—CSKA Moscow	USSR	9	0	1	1	8	...	...	...	—	—	—	—	—
86-87—CSKA Moscow	USSR	20	1	3	4	10	...	...	...	—	—	—	—	—
87-88—Soviet Wings	USSR	44	12	6	18	30	...	...	...	—	—	—	—	—
88-89—Soviet Wings	USSR	44	5	6	11	44	...	...	...	—	—	—	—	—
89-90—Soviet Wings	USSR	45	4	11	15	34	...	...	...	—	—	—	—	—
90-91—Soviet Wings	USSR	45	16	12	28	22	...	...	...	—	—	—	—	—
91-92—Soviet Wings	USSR	35	15	16	31	62	...	...	...	—	—	—	—	—
—Unif. Olympic team	Int'l	8	3	1	4	4	...	...	...	—	—	—	—	—
—Toronto	NHL	7	1	0	1	0	-4	0	0	—	—	—	—	—
92-93—Toronto	NHL	59	7	24	31	40	-1	4	0	14	1	2	3	2

M

Season Team	League	REGULAR SEASON								PLAYOFFS				
		Gms.	G	A	Pts.	PIM	+/-	PP	SH	Gms.	G	A	Pts.	PIM
93-94—Toronto	NHL	76	9	27	36	78	5	3	0	18	6	9	15	6
94-95—Toronto	NHL	33	5	12	17	28	6	2	0	6	2	1	3	2
95-96—Pittsburgh	NHL	72	3	31	34	88	19	1	0	15	0	1	1	10
96-97—Pittsburgh	NHL	15	1	5	6	24	-4	0	0	—	—	—	—	—
—Anaheim	NHL	62	12	34	46	77	20	3	1	11	1	10	11	10
97-98—Anaheim	NHL	66	6	30	36	115	-7	2	0	—	—	—	—	—
—Russian Oly. team	Int'l	6	0	3	3	0	...	...	...	—	—	—	—	—
—Detroit	NHL	11	2	5	7	4	0	1	0	7	0	3	3	14
98-99—Washington	NHL	46	2	14	16	80	-5	2	0	—	—	—	—	—
99-00—Washington	NHL	73	3	19	22	28	7	1	0	4	0	0	0	4
00-01—Washington	NHL	36	3	5	8	6	-7	1	0	—	—	—	—	—
—Houston	IHL	3	2	0	2	2	...	...	...	—	—	—	—	—
NHL Totals (10 years)		556	54	206	260	568	29	20	1	75	10	26	36	48

MITCHELL, WILLIE   D   WILD

PERSONAL: Born April 23, 1977, in Port McNeill, B.C. ... 6-3/205. ... Shoots left. ... Full Name: Willis Mitchell.
TRANSACTIONS/CAREER NOTES: Selected by New Jersey Devils in eighth round (12th Devils pick, 199th overall) of NHL entry draft (June 22, 1996). ... Traded by Devils with future considerations to Minnesota Wild for D Sean O'Donnell (March 4, 2001).
HONORS: Named to NCAA All-America (East) second team (1998-99). ... Named to ECAC All-Star first team (1998-99).

Season Team	League	REGULAR SEASON								PLAYOFFS				
		Gms.	G	A	Pts.	PIM	+/-	PP	SH	Gms.	G	A	Pts.	PIM
95-96—Melfort	Jr. A	19	2	6	8	0	...	...	...	14	0	2	2	12
96-97—Melfort	Jr. A	64	14	42	56	227	...	...	...	4	0	1	1	23
97-98—Clarkson	ECAC	34	9	17	26	105	...	...	...	—	—	—	—	—
98-99—Clarkson	ECAC	34	10	19	29	40	...	...	...	—	—	—	—	—
—Albany	AHL	6	1	3	4	29	...	...	...	—	—	—	—	—
99-00—Albany	AHL	63	5	14	19	71	...	...	...	5	1	2	3	4
—New Jersey	NHL	2	0	0	0	0	1	0	0	—	—	—	—	—
00-01—Albany	AHL	41	3	13	16	94	...	...	...	—	—	—	—	—
—New Jersey	NHL	16	0	2	2	29	0	0	0	—	—	—	—	—
—Minnesota	NHL	17	1	7	8	11	4	0	0	—	—	—	—	—
NHL Totals (2 years)		35	1	9	10	40	5	0	0	—	—	—	—	—

MODANO, MIKE   C   STARS

M

PERSONAL: Born June 7, 1970, in Livonia, Mich. ... 6-3/205. ... Shoots left. ... Full Name: Michael Modano. ... Name pronounced muh-DAH-noh.
TRANSACTIONS/CAREER NOTES: Selected by Minnesota North Stars in first round (first North Stars pick, first overall) of NHL entry draft (June 11, 1988). ... Fractured nose (March 4, 1990). ... Pulled groin (November 30, 1992); missed two games. ... North Stars franchise moved from Minnesota to Dallas and renamed Stars for 1993-94 season. ... Strained medial collateral ligament in knee (January 6, 1994); missed six games. ... Suffered concussion (February 26, 1994); missed two games. ... Bruised ankle (March 12, 1995); missed four games. ... Ruptured tendons in ankle (April 4, 1995) and underwent surgery; missed remainder of season. ... Injured stomach muscle (November 9, 1995); missed four games. ... Suffered from the flu (February 9, 1997); missed one game. ... Bruised ankle (November 12, 1997); missed one game. ... Tore medial collateral ligament in knee (December 5, 1997); missed 10 games. ... Reinjured knee (January 2, 1998); missed two games. ... Separated shoulder (March 13, 1998); missed 17 games. ... Strained groin (March 31, 1999); missed four games. ... Strained ligaments in neck, suffered concussion and fractured nose (October 2, 1999); missed three games. ... Suffered concussion (January 12, 2000); missed one game. ... Strained hip flexor (March 28, 2000); missed one game. ... Strained back (October 10, 2000); missed one game.
HONORS: Named to WHL (East) All-Star first team (1988-89). ... Named to NHL All-Rookie team (1989-90). ... Played in NHL All-Star Game (1993 and 1998-2000). ... Named to play in NHL All-Star Game (1997); replaced by LW Keith Tkachuk due to injury. ... Named to NHL All-Star second team (1999-2000).
MISCELLANEOUS: Member of Stanley Cup championship team (1999). ... Holds Dallas Stars franchise all-time record for most goals (349). ... Failed to score on a penalty shot (vs. Tyler Moss, December 7, 1998).
STATISTICAL NOTES: Tied for NHL lead with three game-tying goals (1999-2000).
STATISTICAL PLATEAUS: Three-goal games: 1989-90 (1), 1993-94 (1), 1997-98 (1), 1998-99 (3). Total: 6. ... Four-goal games: 1995-96 (1). ... Total hat tricks: 7.

Season Team	League	REGULAR SEASON								PLAYOFFS				
		Gms.	G	A	Pts.	PIM	+/-	PP	SH	Gms.	G	A	Pts.	PIM
86-87—Prince Albert	WHL	70	32	30	62	96	...	...	...	8	1	4	5	4
87-88—Prince Albert	WHL	65	47	80	127	80	...	...	...	9	7	11	18	18
88-89—Prince Albert	WHL	41	39	66	105	74	...	...	...	—	—	—	—	—
—Minnesota	NHL	—	—	—	—	—				2	0	0	0	0
89-90—Minnesota	NHL	80	29	46	75	63	-7	12	0	7	1	1	2	12
90-91—Minnesota	NHL	79	28	36	64	61	2	9	0	23	8	12	20	16
91-92—Minnesota	NHL	76	33	44	77	46	-9	5	0	7	3	2	5	4
92-93—Minnesota	NHL	82	33	60	93	83	-7	9	0	—	—	—	—	—
93-94—Dallas	NHL	76	50	43	93	54	-8	18	0	9	7	3	10	16
94-95—Dallas	NHL	30	12	17	29	8	7	4	1	—	—	—	—	—
95-96—Dallas	NHL	78	36	45	81	63	-12	8	4	—	—	—	—	—
96-97—Dallas	NHL	80	35	48	83	42	43	9	5	7	4	1	5	0
97-98—Dallas	NHL	52	21	38	59	32	25	7	5	17	4	10	14	12
—U.S. Olympic team	Int'l	4	2	0	2	0	...	...	...	—	—	—	—	—
98-99—Dallas	NHL	77	34	47	81	44	29	6	4	23	5	*18	23	16
99-00—Dallas	NHL	77	38	43	81	48	0	11	1	23	10	†13	23	10
00-01—Dallas	NHL	81	33	51	84	52	26	8	3	9	3	4	7	0
NHL Totals (13 years)		868	382	518	900	596	89	106	23	127	45	64	109	86

MODIN, FREDRIK   LW   LIGHTNING

PERSONAL: Born October 8, 1974, in Sundsvall, Sweden. ... 6-4/220. ... Shoots left. ... Name pronounced moh-DEEN.
TRANSACTIONS/CAREER NOTES: Selected by Toronto Maple Leafs in third round (third Maple Leafs pick, 64th overall) of NHL entry draft (June 29, 1994). ... Suffered concussion (October 22, 1996); missed three games. ... Suffered from the flu (March 10, 1997); missed one game. ... Strained groin (December 2, 1997); missed two games. ... Fractured collar bone (February 13, 1999); missed 15 games. ... Traded by Maple Leafs to Tampa Bay Lightning for D Cory Cross and seventh-round pick (F Ivan Kolozvary) in 2001 draft (October 1, 1999). ... Bruised thigh (December 8, 2000); missed one game. ... Suffered from the flu (January 4, 2001); missed one game. ... Bruised hip (March 4, 2001); missed two games.
HONORS: Played in NHL All-Star Game (2001).
STATISTICAL PLATEAUS: Three-goal games: 2000-01 (1).

				REGULAR SEASON							PLAYOFFS				
Season Team	League	Gms.	G	A	Pts.	PIM	+/-	PP	SH		Gms.	G	A	Pts.	PIM
91-92—Sundsvall Timra	Sweden Dv. 2	11	1	0	1	0	...	...	...		—	—	—	—	—
92-93—Sundsvall Timra	Sweden Dv. 2	30	5	7	12	12	...	...	...		—	—	—	—	—
93-94—Sundsvall Timra	Sweden Dv. 2	30	16	15	31	36	...	...	...		—	—	—	—	—
94-95—Brynas Gavle	Sweden	38	9	10	19	33	...	...	...		14	4	4	8	6
95-96—Brynas Gavle	Sweden	22	4	8	12	22	...	...	...		—	—	—	—	—
96-97—Toronto	NHL	76	6	7	13	24	-14	0	0		—	—	—	—	—
97-98—Toronto	NHL	74	16	16	32	32	-5	1	0		—	—	—	—	—
98-99—Toronto	NHL	67	16	15	31	35	14	1	0		8	0	0	0	6
99-00—Tampa Bay	NHL	80	22	26	48	18	-26	3	0		—	—	—	—	—
00-01—Tampa Bay	NHL	76	32	24	56	48	-1	8	0		—	—	—	—	—
NHL Totals (5 years)		373	92	88	180	157	-32	13	0		8	0	0	0	6

MODRY, JAROSLAV   D   KINGS

PERSONAL: Born February 27, 1971, in Ceske-Budejovice, Czechoslovakia. ... 6-2/219. ... Shoots left. ... Name pronounced MOH-dree.
TRANSACTIONS/CAREER NOTES: Selected by New Jersey Devils in ninth round (10th Devils pick, 179th overall) of NHL entry draft (June 16, 1990). ... Played in Europe during 1994-95 NHL lockout. ... Injured ankle (January 31, 1995); missed three games. ... Injured ankle (February 18, 1995); missed three games. ... Traded by Devils to Ottawa Senators for fourth-round pick (C Alyn McCauley) in 1995 draft (July 8, 1995). ... Ruptured eardrum (December 27, 1995). ... Traded by Senators to Los Angeles Kings for RW Kevin Brown (March 20, 1996). ... Sprained left knee (January 14, 1997); missed one game.

				REGULAR SEASON							PLAYOFFS				
Season Team	League	Gms.	G	A	Pts.	PIM	+/-	PP	SH		Gms.	G	A	Pts.	PIM
88-89—Budejovice	Czech.	28	0	1	1	...	...	...	...		—	—	—	—	—
89-90—Budejovice	Czech.	41	2	2	4	...	...	...	...		—	—	—	—	—
90-91—Dukla Trencin	Czech.	33	1	9	10	6	...	...	...		—	—	—	—	—
91-92—Dukla Trencin	Czech.	18	0	4	4	...	...	...	...		—	—	—	—	—
—Budejovice	Czech Dv.II	14	4	10	14	...	...	...	...		—	—	—	—	—
92-93—Utica	AHL	80	7	35	42	62	...	...	...		5	0	2	2	2
93-94—New Jersey	NHL	41	2	15	17	18	10	2	0		—	—	—	—	—
—Albany	AHL	19	1	5	6	25	...	...	...		—	—	—	—	—
94-95—HC Ceske Budejovice	Czech Rep.	19	1	3	4	30	...	...	...		—	—	—	—	—
—New Jersey	NHL	11	0	0	0	0	-1	0	0		—	—	—	—	—
—Albany	AHL	18	5	6	11	14	...	...	...		14	3	3	6	4
95-96—Ottawa	NHL	64	4	14	18	38	-17	1	0		—	—	—	—	—
—Los Angeles	NHL	9	0	3	3	6	-4	0	0		—	—	—	—	—
96-97—Los Angeles	NHL	30	3	3	6	25	-13	1	1		—	—	—	—	—
—Phoenix	IHL	23	3	12	15	17	...	...	...		—	—	—	—	—
—Utah	IHL	11	1	4	5	20	...	...	...		7	0	1	1	6
97-98—Utah	IHL	74	12	21	33	72	...	...	...		4	0	2	2	6
98-99—Long Beach	IHL	64	6	29	35	44	...	...	...		8	4	2	6	4
—Los Angeles	NHL	5	0	1	1	0	1	0	0		—	—	—	—	—
99-00—Los Angeles	NHL	26	5	4	9	18	-2	5	0		2	0	0	0	2
—Long Beach	IHL	11	2	4	6	8	...	...	...		—	—	—	—	—
00-01—Los Angeles	NHL	63	4	15	19	48	16	0	0		10	1	0	1	4
NHL Totals (7 years)		249	18	55	73	153	-10	9	1		12	1	0	1	6

MOGILNY, ALEXANDER   RW   MAPLE LEAFS

PERSONAL: Born February 18, 1969, in Khabarovsk, U.S.S.R. ... 5-11/200. ... Shoots left. ... Name pronounced moh-GIHL-nee.
TRANSACTIONS/CAREER NOTES: Selected by Buffalo Sabres in fifth round (fourth Sabres pick, 89th overall) of NHL entry draft (June 11, 1988). ... Suffered from the flu (November 26, 1989). ... Missed games due to fear of flying (January 22, 1990); spent remainder of season traveling on ground. ... Separated shoulder (February 8, 1991); missed six games. ... Suffered from the flu (November 1991); missed two games. ... Suffered from the flu (December 18, 1991); missed one game. ... Bruised shoulder (October 10, 1992); missed six games. ... Fractured fibula and tore ankle ligaments (May 6, 1993); missed remainder of 1992-93 playoffs and first nine games of 1993-94 season. ... Suffered sore ankle (February 2, 1994); missed four games. ... Suffered inflamed tendon in ankle (February 15, 1994); missed four games. ... Played in Europe during 1994-95 NHL lockout. ... Pinched nerve in neck (April 9, 1995); missed three games. ... Traded by Sabres with fifth-round pick (LW Todd Norman) in 1995 draft to Vancouver Canucks for RW Mike Peca, D Mike Wilson and first-round pick (D Jay McKee) in 1995 draft (July 8, 1995). ... Pulled hamstring (October 28, 1995); missed three games. ... Suffered from the flu (December 3, 1996); missed two games. ... Strained groin (April 4, 1997); missed remainder of season. ... Missed first 16 games of 1997-98 season due to contract dispute. ... Injured groin (December 15, 1997); missed 11 games. ... Strained back (February 24, 1998); missed four games. ... Sprained medial collateral ligament in knee (November 21, 1998); missed 17 games. ... Bruised kidney (January 4, 1999); missed two games. ... Strained abdominal muscle (February 20, 1999); missed four games. ... Injured back (November 26, 1999); missed eight games. ... Injured hip (January 12, 2000); missed seven games. ... Injured shoulder (February 12, 2000); missed eight games. ... Traded by Canucks to New Jersey Devils for C Brendan Morrison and C Denis Pederson (March 14, 2000). ... Injured neck (February 10, 2000); missed one game. ... Bruised abdomen (February 14, 2001); missed four games. ... Strained groin (April 4, 2001); missed one game. ... Signed as free agent by Toronto Maple Leafs (July 3, 2001).

HONORS: Played in NHL All-Star Game (1992-1994 and 1996). ... Named to The Sporting News All-Star second team (1992-93). ... Named to NHL All-Star second team (1992-93 and 1995-96). ... Named to play in NHL All-Star Game (2001); replaced by RW Milan Hejduk due to injury.
RECORDS: Shares NHL record for fastest goal from start of a game—5 seconds (December 21, 1991).
STATISTICAL PLATEAUS: Three-goal games: 1990-91 (1), 1991-92 (1), 1992-93 (5), 1993-94 (1), 1995-96 (3), 1996-97 (1), 2000-01 (1). Total: 13. ... Four-goal games: 1992-93 (2). ... Total hat tricks: 15.
MISCELLANEOUS: Member of Stanley Cup championship team (2000). ... Member of gold-medal-winning U.S.S.R. Olympic team (1988). ... Captain of Buffalo Sabres (1993-94 and 1994-95). ... Scored on a penalty shot (vs. Chris Osgood, December 1, 1997). ... Failed to score on a penalty shot (vs. Bill Ranford, January 10, 1992; vs. Robb Stauber, December 17, 1993).
STATISTICAL NOTES: Led NHL with 11 game-winning goals (1992-93).

		REGULAR SEASON								PLAYOFFS				
Season Team	League	Gms.	G	A	Pts.	PIM	+/-	PP	SH	Gms.	G	A	Pts.	PIM
86-87—CSKA Moscow	USSR	28	15	1	16	4	...	...	...	—	—	—	—	—
87-88—CSKA Moscow	USSR	39	12	8	20	20	...	...	...	—	—	—	—	—
88-89—CSKA Moscow	USSR	31	11	11	22	24	...	...	...	—	—	—	—	—
89-90—Buffalo	NHL	65	15	28	43	16	8	4	0	4	0	1	1	2
90-91—Buffalo	NHL	62	30	34	64	16	14	3	3	6	0	6	6	2
91-92—Buffalo	NHL	67	39	45	84	73	7	15	0	2	0	2	2	0
92-93—Buffalo	NHL	77	†76	51	127	40	7	27	0	7	7	3	10	6
93-94—Buffalo	NHL	66	32	47	79	22	8	17	0	7	4	2	6	6
94-95—Spartak Moscow	CIS	1	0	1	1	0	...	...	...	—	—	—	—	—
—Buffalo	NHL	44	19	28	47	36	0	12	0	5	3	2	5	2
95-96—Vancouver	NHL	79	55	52	107	16	14	10	5	6	1	8	9	8
96-97—Vancouver	NHL	76	31	42	73	18	9	7	1	—	—	—	—	—
97-98—Vancouver	NHL	51	18	27	45	36	-6	5	4	—	—	—	—	—
98-99—Vancouver	NHL	59	14	31	45	58	0	3	2	—	—	—	—	—
99-00—Vancouver	NHL	47	21	17	38	16	7	3	1	—	—	—	—	—
—New Jersey	NHL	12	3	3	6	4	-4	2	0	23	4	3	7	4
00-01—New Jersey	NHL	75	43	40	83	43	10	12	0	25	5	11	16	8
NHL Totals (12 years)		780	396	445	841	394	74	120	16	85	24	38	62	38

MONTGOMERY, JIM — C — STARS

PERSONAL: Born June 30, 1969, in Montreal. ... 5-9/180. ... Shoots right.
TRANSACTIONS/CAREER NOTES: Signed as non-drafted free agent by St. Louis Blues (June 2, 1993). ... Suspended four games and fined $500 by NHL for high-sticking incident (October 4, 1993). ... Traded by Blues to Montreal Canadiens for C Guy Carbonneau (August 19, 1994). ... Claimed on waivers by Philadelphia Flyers (February 10, 1995). ... Signed as free agent by San Jose Sharks (August 15, 2000). ... Signed as free agent by Dallas Stars (July 11, 2001).
HONORS: Named to NCAA All-America East second team (1990-91 and 1992-93). ... Named to Hockey East All-Star second team (1990-91 and 1991-92). ... Named NCAA Tournament Most Valuable Player (1992-93). ... Named Hockey East Tournament Most Valuable Player (1992-93). ... Named to NCAA All-Tournament team (1992-93). ... Named to Hockey East All-Star first team (1992-93). ... Named to Hockey East All-Decade team (1994). ... Named to AHL All-Star second team (1995-96).

		REGULAR SEASON								PLAYOFFS				
Season Team	League	Gms.	G	A	Pts.	PIM	+/-	PP	SH	Gms.	G	A	Pts.	PIM
89-90—Univ. of Maine	Hockey East	45	26	34	60	35	...	...	...	—	—	—	—	—
90-91—Univ. of Maine	Hockey East	43	24	57	81	44	...	...	...	—	—	—	—	—
91-92—Univ. of Maine	Hockey East	37	21	44	65	46	...	...	...	—	—	—	—	—
92-93—Univ. of Maine	Hockey East	45	32	63	95	40	...	...	...	—	—	—	—	—
93-94—St. Louis	NHL	67	6	14	20	44	-1	0	0	—	—	—	—	—
—Peoria	IHL	12	7	8	15	10	...	...	...	—	—	—	—	—
94-95—Montreal	NHL	5	0	0	0	2	-2	0	0	—	—	—	—	—
—Philadelphia	NHL	8	1	1	2	6	-2	0	0	7	1	0	1	2
—Hershey	AHL	16	8	6	14	14	...	...	...	6	3	2	5	25
95-96—Hershey	AHL	78	34	†71	105	95	...	...	...	4	3	2	5	6
—Philadelphia	NHL	5	1	2	3	9	1	0	0	1	0	0	0	0
96-97—Kolner Haie	Germany	50	12	35	47	11	...	...	...	—	—	—	—	—
97-98—Philadelphia	AHL	68	19	43	62	75	...	...	...	20	13	16	29	55
98-99—Philadelphia	AHL	78	29	58	87	89	...	...	...	16	4	11	15	20
99-00—Philadelphia	AHL	13	3	9	12	22	...	...	...	—	—	—	—	—
—Manitoba	IHL	67	18	28	46	11	...	...	...	—	—	—	—	—
00-01—Kentucky	AHL	55	22	52	74	44	...	...	...	3	1	2	3	5
—San Jose	NHL	28	1	6	7	19	-1	1	0	—	—	—	—	—
NHL Totals (4 years)		113	9	23	32	80	-5	1	0	8	1	0	1	2

MORAN, BRAD — C — BLUE JACKETS

PERSONAL: Born March 20, 1979, in Abbotsford, B.C. ... 5-11/180. ... Shoots left.
TRANSACTIONS/CAREER NOTES: Selected by Buffalo Sabres in seventh round (eighth Sabres pick, 191st pick overall) of NHL entry draft (June 27, 1998). ... Signed as free agent by Columbus Blue Jackets (June 5, 2000).
HONORS: Named to WHL (East) All-Star first team (1998-99 and 1999-2000). ... Won Four Broncos Memorial Trophy (1999-2000). ... Won Bob Clarke Trophy (1999-2000). ... Named to Can.HL All-Star second team (1999-2000).

		REGULAR SEASON								PLAYOFFS				
Season Team	League	Gms.	G	A	Pts.	PIM	+/-	PP	SH	Gms.	G	A	Pts.	PIM
95-96—Calgary	WHL	70	13	31	44	28	...	...	...	—	—	—	—	—
96-97—Calgary	WHL	72	30	36	66	61	...	...	...	—	—	—	—	—
97-98—Calgary	WHL	72	53	49	102	64	...	...	...	18	10	8	18	20
98-99—Calgary	WHL	71	60	58	118	96	...	...	...	21	17	†25	42	26
99-00—Calgary	WHL	72	48	*72	*120	84	...	...	...	13	7	15	22	18
00-01—Syracuse	AHL	71	11	19	30	30	...	...	...	5	3	4	7	3

PERSONAL: Born August 24, 1972, in Cleveland. ... 6-0/206. ... Shoots right. ... Name pronounced muh-RAN.

TRANSACTIONS/CAREER NOTES: Selected by Pittsburgh Penguins in sixth round (fifth Penguins pick, 107th overall) of NHL entry draft (June 16, 1990). ... Bruised shoulder (November 22, 1995); missed nine games. ... Injured shoulder (February 21, 1996); missed one game. ... Underwent shoulder surgery (March 21, 1996); missed remainder of season. ... Injured back and neck (April 10, 1997); missed two games. ... Bruised kneecap and underwent surgery (September 30, 1997); missed 34 games. ... Suffered concussion (February 2, 1998); missed four games. ... Injured knee (March 21, 1998); missed five games. ... Injured ankle (October 26, 1998); missed five games. ... Reinjured ankle (November 7, 1998); missed nine games. ... Bruised ankle (January 5, 1999); missed two games. ... Bruised right testicle (February 5, 1999); missed three games. ... Injured ankle (April 3, 1999); missed one game. ... Fractured foot (December 2, 1999); missed two games. ... Suffered from the flu (January 2, 2000); missed one game. ... Bruised ankle (April 7, 2000); missed final game of season. ... Injured knee (October 18, 2000); missed seven games. ... Fractured hand (November 10, 2000); missed 15 games. ... Suffered from the flu (February 16, 2001); missed one game. ... Fractured thumb (February 19, 2001); missed 18 games.

HONORS: Named Hockey East co-Rookie of the Year with Craig Darby (1991-92). ... Named to Hockey East All-Rookie team (1991-92).

		REGULAR SEASON								PLAYOFFS				
Season Team	League	Gms.	G	A	Pts.	PIM	+/-	PP	SH	Gms.	G	A	Pts.	PIM
87-88—Belmont Hill	Mass. H.S.	25	3	13	16	15	...	...	...	—	—	—	—	—
88-89—Belmont Hill	Mass. H.S.	23	7	25	32	8	...	...	...	—	—	—	—	—
89-90—Belmont Hill	Mass. H.S.	...	10	36	46	0	...	...	...	—	—	—	—	—
90-91—Belmont Hill	Mass. H.S.	23	7	44	51	12	...	...	...	—	—	—	—	—
91-92—Boston College	Hockey East	30	2	16	18	44	...	...	...	—	—	—	—	—
92-93—Boston College	Hockey East	31	8	12	20	32	...	...	...	—	—	—	—	—
93-94—U.S. national team	Int'l	50	8	15	23	69	...	...	...	—	—	—	—	—
—Cleveland	IHL	33	5	13	18	39	...	...	...	—	—	—	—	—
94-95—Cleveland	IHL	64	7	31	38	94	...	...	...	4	0	1	1	2
—Pittsburgh	NHL	—	—	—	—	—	—	—	—	8	0	0	0	0
95-96—Pittsburgh	NHL	51	1	1	2	47	-1	0	0	—	—	—	—	—
96-97—Cleveland	IHL	36	6	23	29	26	...	...	...	—	—	—	—	—
—Pittsburgh	NHL	36	4	5	9	22	-11	0	0	5	1	2	3	4
97-98—Pittsburgh	NHL	37	1	6	7	19	0	0	0	6	0	0	0	2
98-99—Pittsburgh	NHL	62	4	5	9	37	1	0	1	13	0	2	2	8
99-00—Pittsburgh	NHL	73	4	8	12	28	-10	0	0	11	0	1	1	2
00-01—Pittsburgh	NHL	40	3	4	7	28	5	0	0	18	0	1	1	4
NHL Totals (7 years)		**299**	**17**	**29**	**46**	**181**	**-16**	**0**	**1**	**61**	**1**	**6**	**7**	**20**

PERSONAL: Born September 22, 1975, in Orillia, Ont. ... 6-2/205. ... Shoots left. ... Name pronounced MOHR-oh.

TRANSACTIONS/CAREER NOTES: Selected by Chicago Blackhawks in first round (first Blackhawks pick, 14th overall) of NHL entry draft (June 28, 1994). ... Fractured knuckle (November 16, 1997); missed seven games. ... Fractured ankle (February 21, 1999); missed 20 games. ... Traded by Blackhawks with LW Daniel Cleary, C Chad Kilger and D Christian Laflamme to Edmonton Oilers for D Boris Mironov, LW Dean McAmmond and D Jonas Elofsson (March 20, 1999). ... Injured ribs (November 24, 1999); missed eight games. ... Suffered from the flu (December 27, 1999); missed one game. ... Underwent shoulder surgery (May 24, 2000); missed first 14 games of season.

HONORS: Won Bobby Smith Trophy (1993-94).

		REGULAR SEASON								PLAYOFFS				
Season Team	League	Gms.	G	A	Pts.	PIM	+/-	PP	SH	Gms.	G	A	Pts.	PIM
90-91—Orillia	OHA	42	17	22	39	26	...	...	...	—	—	—	—	—
91-92—Niagara Falls	OHL	62	20	35	55	39	...	...	...	17	4	6	10	4
92-93—Niagara Falls	OHL	65	32	41	73	69	...	...	...	4	0	3	3	4
93-94—Niagara Falls	OHL	59	44	54	98	100	...	...	...	—	—	—	—	—
94-95—Niagara Falls	OHL	39	25	41	66	69	...	...	...	—	—	—	—	—
—Sudbury	OHL	23	13	17	30	22	...	...	...	18	6	12	18	26
95-96—Indianapolis	IHL	71	21	20	41	126	...	...	...	5	4	0	4	8
—Chicago	NHL	8	0	1	1	4	1	0	0	—	—	—	—	—
96-97—Chicago	NHL	82	15	16	31	123	13	0	0	6	1	0	1	9
97-98—Chicago	NHL	54	9	9	18	73	0	2	0	—	—	—	—	—
98-99—Chicago	NHL	66	9	6	15	84	-5	0	0	—	—	—	—	—
—Edmonton	NHL	14	1	5	6	8	2	0	0	4	0	3	3	6
99-00—Edmonton	NHL	73	17	10	27	62	8	1	0	5	0	1	1	0
00-01—Edmonton	NHL	68	9	10	19	90	-6	0	1	4	0	0	0	2
NHL Totals (6 years)		**365**	**60**	**57**	**117**	**444**	**13**	**3**	**1**	**19**	**1**	**4**	**5**	**17**

M

PERSONAL: Born April 6, 1981, in Langley, B.C. ... 6-2/195. ... Shoots right.

TRANSACTIONS/CAREER NOTES: Selected by St. Louis Blues in second round (second Blues pick, 65th overall) of NHL entry draft (June 24, 2000). ... Traded by Blues with fifth-round pick in 2002 draft to Florida Panthers for RW Scott Mellanby (February 9, 2001).

		REGULAR SEASON								PLAYOFFS				
Season Team	League	Gms.	G	A	Pts.	PIM	+/-	PP	SH	Gms.	G	A	Pts.	PIM
97-98—Seattle	WHL	58	6	2	8	104	...	...	...	5	1	0	1	6
98-99—Seattle	WHL	17	4	0	4	31	...	...	...	11	1	1	2	22
99-00—Seattle	WHL	60	23	34	57	71	...	...	...	7	3	4	7	12
00-01—Seattle	WHL	61	32	36	68	95	...	...	...	9	4	2	6	12

MORO, MARC　　　　D　　　　PREDATORS

PERSONAL: Born July 17, 1977, in Toronto. ... 6-1/215. ... Shoots left. ... Name pronounced muh-ROH.
TRANSACTIONS/CAREER NOTES: Selected by Ottawa Senators in second round (second Senators pick, 27th overall) of NHL entry draft (July 8, 1995). ... Rights traded by Senators with C Ted Drury to Mighty Ducks of Anaheim for C Shaun Van Allen and D Jason York (October 1, 1996). ... Traded by Mighty Ducks with G Chris Mason to Nashville Predators for G Dominic Roussel (October 5, 1998). ... Suffered injury (March 29, 2000); missed final four games of season.

		REGULAR SEASON								PLAYOFFS				
Season Team	League	Gms.	G	A	Pts.	PIM	+/-	PP	SH	Gms.	G	A	Pts.	PIM
92-93—Mississauga	MTHL	42	9	18	27	56	...	...	...	—	—	—	—	—
—Mississauga	Jr. A	2	0	0	0	0	...	...	...	—	—	—	—	—
93-94—Kingston	Tier II Jr. A	12	0	2	2	20	...	...	...	—	—	—	—	—
—Kingston	OHL	43	0	3	3	81	...	...	...	—	—	—	—	—
94-95—Kingston	OHL	64	4	12	16	255	...	...	...	6	0	0	0	23
95-96—Kingston	OHL	66	4	17	21	261	...	...	...	6	0	0	0	12
—Prin. Edward Island	AHL	2	0	0	0	7	...	...	...	2	0	0	0	4
96-97—Kingston	OHL	37	4	8	12	97	...	...	...	—	—	—	—	—
—Sault Ste. Marie	OHL	63	4	13	17	171	...	...	...	11	1	6	7	38
97-98—Cincinnati	AHL	74	1	6	7	181	...	...	...	—	—	—	—	—
—Anaheim	NHL	1	0	0	0	0	0	0	0	—	—	—	—	—
98-99—Milwaukee	IHL	80	0	5	5	264	...	...	...	2	0	0	0	4
99-00—Milwaukee	IHL	64	5	5	10	203	...	...	...	—	—	—	—	—
—Nashville	NHL	8	0	0	0	40	-3	0	0	—	—	—	—	—
00-01—Milwaukee	IHL	68	2	9	11	190	...	...	...	5	1	0	1	10
—Nashville	NHL	6	0	0	0	12	1	0	0	—	—	—	—	—
NHL Totals (3 years)		15	0	0	0	52	-2	0	0					

MOROZOV, ALEKSEY　　　　RW　　　　PENGUINS

PERSONAL: Born February 16, 1977, in Moscow, U.S.S.R. ... 6-1/196. ... Shoots left. ... Name pronounced muh-ROH-sahf.
TRANSACTIONS/CAREER NOTES: Selected by Pittsburgh Penguins in first round (first Penguins pick, 24th overall) of NHL entry draft (July 8, 1995). ... Fractured toe (December 27, 1997); missed one game. ... Suffered concussion (November 14, 1998); missed three games. ... Suffered concussion (December 21, 1998); missed 12 games. ... Suffered charley horse (October 30, 1999); missed eight games. ... Bruised back (January 25, 2000); missed two games. ... Suffered charley horse (March 16, 2000); missed four games.
MISCELLANEOUS: Member of silver-medal-winning Russian Olympic team (1998).
STATISTICAL PLATEAUS: Three-goal games: 1999-00 (1).

		REGULAR SEASON								PLAYOFFS				
Season Team	League	Gms.	G	A	Pts.	PIM	+/-	PP	SH	Gms.	G	A	Pts.	PIM
93-94—Soviet Wings	CIS	7	0	0	0	0	...	...	...	3	0	0	0	2
94-95—Soviet Wings	CIS	48	15	12	27	53	...	...	...	4	0	3	3	0
95-96—Soviet Wings	CIS	47	12	9	21	26	...	...	...	—	—	—	—	—
96-97—Kryla Sov. Moscow	Russian	44	21	11	32	32	...	...	...	2	0	1	1	2
97-98—Pittsburgh	NHL	76	13	13	26	8	-4	2	0	6	0	1	1	2
—Russian Oly. team	Int'l	6	2	2	4	0	...	...	...	—	—	—	—	—
98-99—Pittsburgh	NHL	67	9	10	19	14	5	0	0	10	1	1	2	0
99-00—Pittsburgh	NHL	68	12	19	31	14	12	0	1	5	0	0	0	0
00-01—Pittsburgh	NHL	66	5	14	19	6	-8	0	0	18	3	3	6	6
NHL Totals (4 years)		277	39	56	95	42	5	2	1	39	4	5	9	8

MORRIS, DEREK　　　　D　　　　FLAMES

PERSONAL: Born August 24, 1978, in Edmonton. ... 5-11/200. ... Shoots right.
TRANSACTIONS/CAREER NOTES: Selected by Calgary Flames in first round (first Flames pick, 13th overall) of NHL entry draft (June 22, 1996). ... Separated shoulder (February 22, 1999); missed 10 games. ... Suffered concussion (December 14, 1999); missed three games. ... Missed first 27 games of 2000-01 season due to contract dispute.
HONORS: Named to Can.HL All-Star second team (1996-97). ... Named to WHL (East) All-Star first team (1996-97). ... Named to NHL All-Rookie team (1997-98).

		REGULAR SEASON								PLAYOFFS				
Season Team	League	Gms.	G	A	Pts.	PIM	+/-	PP	SH	Gms.	G	A	Pts.	PIM
95-96—Regina	WHL	67	8	44	52	70	...	...	...	11	1	7	8	26
96-97—Regina	WHL	67	18	57	75	180	...	...	...	5	0	3	3	9
—Saint John	AHL	7	0	3	3	7	...	...	...	5	0	3	3	7
97-98—Calgary	NHL	82	9	20	29	88	1	5	1	—	—	—	—	—
98-99—Calgary	NHL	71	7	27	34	73	4	3	0	—	—	—	—	—
99-00—Calgary	NHL	78	9	29	38	80	2	3	0	—	—	—	—	—
00-01—Saint John	AHL	3	1	2	3	2	...	...	...	—	—	—	—	—
—Calgary	NHL	51	5	23	28	56	-15	3	1	—	—	—	—	—
NHL Totals (4 years)		282	30	99	129	297	-8	14	2					

MORRISON, BRENDAN　　　　C　　　　CANUCKS

PERSONAL: Born August 12, 1975, in Pitt Meadows, B.C. ... 5-11/190. ... Shoots left.
TRANSACTIONS/CAREER NOTES: Selected by New Jersey Devils in second round (third Devils pick, 39th overall) of NHL entry draft (June 26, 1993). ... Missed first nine games of 1999-2000 season due to contract dispute. ... Suffered injury (October 29, 1999); missed two games. ... Traded by Devils with C Denis Pederson to Vancouver Canucks for RW Alexander Mogilny (March 14, 2000).
HONORS: Won CCHA Rookie of the Year Award (1993-94). ... Named to CCHA All-Rookie team (1993-94). ... Named to NCAA All-America

M

(West) first team (1994-95 through 1996-97). ... Named to CCHA All-Star first team (1994-95 through 1996-97). ... Named CCHA Player of the Year (1995-96 and 1996-97). ... Named NCAA Tournament Most Valuable Player (1995-96). ... Named to NCAA All-Tournament team (1995-96). ... Won Hobey Baker Memorial Award (1996-97). ... Named CCHA Tournament Most Valuable Player (1996-97).

STATISTICAL NOTES: Tied for NHL lead in game-tying goals with three (2000-01).

		REGULAR SEASON								PLAYOFFS				
Season Team	League	Gms.	G	A	Pts.	PIM	+/-	PP	SH	Gms.	G	A	Pts.	PIM
92-93—Penticton	BCJHL	56	35	59	94	45	...	...	...	—	—	—	—	—
93-94—Univ. of Michigan	CCHA	38	20	28	48	24	...	...	...	—	—	—	—	—
94-95—Univ. of Michigan	CCHA	39	23	53	76	42	...	...	...	—	—	—	—	—
95-96—Univ. of Michigan	CCHA	35	28	44	72	41	...	...	...	—	—	—	—	—
96-97—Univ. of Michigan	CCHA	43	31	57	88	52	...	...	...	—	—	—	—	—
97-98—Albany	AHL	72	35	49	84	44	...	...	...	8	3	4	7	19
—New Jersey	NHL	11	5	4	9	0	3	0	0	3	0	1	1	0
98-99—New Jersey	NHL	76	13	33	46	18	-4	5	0	7	0	2	2	0
99-00—HC Pardubice	Czech Rep.	6	5	2	7	2	...	...	...	—	—	—	—	—
—New Jersey	NHL	44	5	21	26	8	8	2	0	—	—	—	—	—
—Vancouver	NHL	12	2	7	9	10	4	0	0	—	—	—	—	—
00-01—Vancouver	NHL	82	16	38	54	42	2	3	2	4	1	2	3	0
NHL Totals (4 years)		225	41	103	144	78	13	10	2	14	1	5	6	0

MORROW, BRENDEN   LW   STARS

PERSONAL: Born January 16, 1979, in Carlisle, Sask. ... 5-11/200. ... Shoots left.
TRANSACTIONS/CAREER NOTES: Selected by Dallas Stars in first round (first Stars pick, 25th overall) of NHL entry draft (June 21, 1997).
HONORS: Named to WHL (West) All-Star first team (1998-99).

		REGULAR SEASON								PLAYOFFS				
Season Team	League	Gms.	G	A	Pts.	PIM	+/-	PP	SH	Gms.	G	A	Pts.	PIM
95-96—Portland	WHL	65	13	12	25	61	...	...	...	7	0	0	0	8
96-97—Portland	WHL	71	39	49	88	178	...	...	...	6	2	1	3	4
97-98—Portland	WHL	68	34	52	86	184	...	...	...	16	10	8	18	65
98-99—Portland	WHL	61	41	44	85	248	...	...	...	4	0	4	4	18
99-00—Michigan	IHL	9	2	0	2	18	...	...	...	—	—	—	—	—
—Dallas	NHL	64	14	19	33	81	8	3	0	21	2	4	6	22
00-01—Dallas	NHL	82	20	24	44	128	18	7	0	10	0	3	3	12
NHL Totals (2 years)		146	34	43	77	209	26	10	0	31	2	7	9	34

MOSS, TYLER   G   HURRICANES

PERSONAL: Born June 29, 1975, in Ottawa. ... 6-0/185. ... Catches right.
TRANSACTIONS/CAREER NOTES: Selected by Tampa Bay Lightning in second round (second Lightning pick, 29th overall) of NHL entry draft (June 26, 1993). ... Traded by Lightning to Calgary Flames for D Jamie Huscroft (March 18, 1997). ... Injured groin (December 12, 1998); missed 18 games. ... Traded by Flames with LW Rene Corbet to Pittsburgh Penguins for D Brad Werenka (March 14, 2000). ... Signed as free agent by Carolina Hurricanes (August 9, 2000).
HONORS: Named to OHL All-Rookie team (1992-93). ... Named to OHL All-Star first team (1994-95). ... Shared Happy (Hap) Holmes Trophy with Jean-Sebastien Giguere (1997-98).
MISCELLANEOUS: Stopped a penalty shot attempt (vs. Mike Modano, December 7, 1998). ... Allowed a penalty shot goal (vs. Joe Sakic, November 1, 1997).

		REGULAR SEASON								PLAYOFFS						
Season Team	League	Gms.	Min	W	L	T	GA	SO	Avg.	Gms.	Min.	W	L	GA	SO	Avg.
91-92—Nepean	COJHL	26	1335	7	12	1	109	0	4.90	—	—	—	—	—	—	—
92-93—Kingston	OHL	31	1537	13	7	5	97	0	3.79	6	228	1	2	19	0	5.00
93-94—Kingston	OHL	13	795	6	4	3	42	1	3.17	3	136	0	2	8	0	3.53
94-95—Kingston	OHL	57	3249	33	17	5	164	1	3.03	6	333	2	4	27	0	4.86
95-96—Atlanta	IHL	40	2030	11	19	‡4	138	1	4.08	3	213	0	3	11	0	3.10
96-97—Adirondack	AHL	11	507	1	5	2	42	1	4.97	—	—	—	—	—	—	—
—Grand Rapids	IHL	15	715	5	6	‡1	35	0	2.94	—	—	—	—	—	—	—
—Saint John	AHL	9	534	6	1	1	17	0	1.91	5	242	2	3	15	0	3.72
—Muskegon	Col.HL	2	119	1	1	0	5	0	2.52	—	—	—	—	—	—	—
97-98—Saint John	AHL	39	2194	19	10	7	91	0	2.49	15	762	8	‡5	37	0	2.91
—Calgary	NHL	6	367	2	3	1	20	0	3.27	—	—	—	—	—	—	—
98-99—Calgary	NHL	11	550	3	7	0	23	0	2.51	—	—	—	—	—	—	—
—Saint John	AHL	9	475	2	5	1	25	0	3.16	—	—	—	—	—	—	—
—Orlando	IHL	9	515	6	2	‡1	21	1	2.45	17	1017	10	7	*53	0	3.13
99-00—Kansas City	IHL	36	2116	21	12	‡5	105	3	2.98	—	—	—	—	—	—	—
—Wilkes-Barre/Scranton	AHL	4	188	1	1	1	11	0	3.51	—	—	—	—	—	—	—
00-01—Carolina	NHL	12	557	1	6	0	37	0	3.99	—	—	—	—	—	—	—
—Cincinnati	IHL	9	506	5	3	‡1	24	2	2.85	—	—	—	—	—	—	—
NHL Totals (3 years)		29	1474	6	16	1	80	0	3.26							

M

MOTTAU, MIKE   D   RANGERS

PERSONAL: Born March 19, 1978, in Quincy, Mass. ... 6-0/192. ... Shoots left.
TRANSACTIONS/CAREER NOTES: Selected by New York Rangers in seventh round (10th pick, 182nd overall) of 1997 NHL entry draft.
HONORS: Named to NCAA All-America East second team (1997-98). ... Named to NCAA All-Tournament team (1997-98 and 1999-2000). ... Named to Hockey East All-Star first team (1997-98 and 1999-2000). ... Named to NCAA All-America (East) first team (1998-99 and 1999-2000). ... Named to Hockey East All-Star second team (1998-99). ... Won Hobey Baker Memorial Award (1999-2000).

Season Team	League	REGULAR SEASON								PLAYOFFS				
		Gms.	G	A	Pts.	PIM	+/-	PP	SH	Gms.	G	A	Pts.	PIM
96-97—Boston College	Hockey East	38	5	18	23	77	...	...	...	—	—	—	—	—
97-98—Boston College	Hockey East	40	13	36	49	50	...	...	...	—	—	—	—	—
98-99—Boston College	Hockey East	43	3	39	42	44	...	...	...	—	—	—	—	—
99-00—Boston College	Hockey East	42	6	*37	43	57	...	...	...	—	—	—	—	—
00-01—Hartford	AHL	61	10	33	43	45	...	...	...	5	0	1	1	19
—New York Rangers......	NHL	18	0	3	3	13	-6	0	0	—	—	—	—	—
NHL Totals (1 year).............		18	0	3	3	13	-6	0	0					

MOWERS, MARK   C   PREDATORS

PERSONAL: Born February 16, 1974, in Whitesboro, N.Y. ... 5-11/184. ... Shoots right.
TRANSACTIONS/CAREER NOTES: Signed as non-drafted free agent by Nashville Predators (June 11, 1998). ... Injured knee (March 19, 2000); missed final nine games of season.
HONORS: Named to NCAA All-America (East) first team (1997-98). ... Named to Hockey East All-Star second team (1997-98). ... Won Ken McKenzie Trophy (1998-99).

Season Team	League	REGULAR SEASON								PLAYOFFS				
		Gms.	G	A	Pts.	PIM	+/-	PP	SH	Gms.	G	A	Pts.	PIM
94-95—Univ. of New Hamp.....	Hockey East	36	13	23	36	16	...	...	...	—	—	—	—	—
95-96—Univ. of New Hamp.....	Hockey East	34	21	26	47	18	...	...	...	—	—	—	—	—
96-97—Univ. of New Hamp.....	Hockey East	39	26	32	58	52	...	...	...	—	—	—	—	—
97-98—Univ. of New Hamp.....	Hockey East	35	25	31	56	32	...	...	...	—	—	—	—	—
98-99—Milwaukee..................	IHL	51	14	22	36	24	...	...	...	1	0	0	0	0
—Nashville....................	NHL	30	0	6	6	4	-4	0	0	—	—	—	—	—
99-00—Milwaukee..................	IHL	23	11	15	26	34	...	...	...	—	—	—	—	—
—Nashville....................	NHL	41	4	5	9	10	0	0	0	—	—	—	—	—
00-01—Milwaukee..................	IHL	63	25	25	50	54	...	...	...	58	1	2	3	2
NHL Totals (2 years)...........		71	4	11	15	14	-4	0	0					

MUCKALT, BILL   RW   SENATORS

M

PERSONAL: Born July 15, 1974, in Surrey, B.C. ... 6-1/200. ... Shoots right.
TRANSACTIONS/CAREER NOTES: Selected by Vancouver Canucks in ninth round (seventh Canucks pick, 221st overall) of NHL entry draft (June 29, 1994). ... Sprained ankle (March 27, 1999); missed final nine games of season. ... Traded by Canucks with G Kevin Weekes and C Dave Scatchard to New York Islanders for G Felix Potvin, second-(traded to Atlanta) and third-round (C Thatcher Bell) picks in 2000 draft (December 19, 1999). ... Separated left shoulder (January 13, 2000) and underwent surgery; missed remainder of season. ... Separated right shoulder (October 17, 2000); missed 21 games. ... Traded by Islanders with D Zdeno Chara and first-round pick (C Jason Spezza) in 2001 draft to Ottawa Senators for C Alexei Yashin (June 23, 2001).
HONORS: Named to NCAA All-America (West) first team (1997-98). ... Named to CCHA All-Star first team (1997-98).

Season Team	League	REGULAR SEASON								PLAYOFFS				
		Gms.	G	A	Pts.	PIM	+/-	PP	SH	Gms.	G	A	Pts.	PIM
91-92—Merritt........................	BCJHL	55	14	11	25	75	...	...	...	—	—	—	—	—
92-93—Merritt........................	BCJHL	59	31	43	74	80	...	...	...	5	5	2	7	11
93-94—Merritt........................	BCJHL	43	58	51	109	99	...	...	...	—	—	—	—	—
—Kelowna....................	BCJHL	15	12	10	22	20	...	...	...	28	19	19	38	25
94-95—Univ. of Michigan........	CCHA	39	19	18	37	42	...	...	...	—	—	—	—	—
95-96—Univ. of Michigan........	CCHA	41	28	30	58	34	...	...	...	—	—	—	—	—
96-97—Univ. of Michigan........	CCHA	36	26	38	64	69	...	...	...	—	—	—	—	—
97-98—Univ. of Michigan........	CCHA	44	32	*33	*65	94	...	...	...	—	—	—	—	—
98-99—Vancouver..................	NHL	73	16	20	36	98	-9	4	2	—	—	—	—	—
99-00—Vancouver..................	NHL	33	4	8	12	17	6	1	0	—	—	—	—	—
—New York Islanders.....	NHL	12	4	3	7	4	5	0	0	—	—	—	—	—
00-01—New York Islanders.....	NHL	60	11	15	26	33	-4	1	0	—	—	—	—	—
NHL Totals (3 years)...........		178	35	46	81	152	-2	6	2					

MUIR, BRYAN   D   AVALANCHE

PERSONAL: Born June 8, 1973, in Winnipeg. ... 6-4/220. ... Shoots left. ... Name pronounced MYOOR.
TRANSACTIONS/CAREER NOTES: Signed as non-drafted free agent by Edmonton Oilers (April 30, 1996). ... Traded by Oilers with C Jason Arnott to New Jersey Devils for RW Bill Guerin and RW Valeri Zelepukin (January 4, 1998). ... Traded by Devils to Chicago Blackhawks for future considerations (November 13, 1998). ... Injured back (April 5, 1999); missed three games. ... Traded by Blackhawks with LW Reid Simpson to Tampa Bay Lightning for C Michael Nylander (November 12, 1999). ... Fractured ankle (November 17, 1999); missed 18 games. ... Injured ankle (March 12, 2000); missed 11 games. ... Traded by Lightning to Colorado Avalanche for eighth-round pick (LW Dimitri Bezrukov) in 2001 draft (January 23, 2001).
MISCELLANEOUS: Member of Stanley Cup championship team (2001).

Season Team	League	REGULAR SEASON								PLAYOFFS				
		Gms.	G	A	Pts.	PIM	+/-	PP	SH	Gms.	G	A	Pts.	PIM
91-92—Wexford......................	OJHL	50	11	35	46	...	...	...	...	—	—	—	—	—
92-93—Univ. of New Hamp.....	Hockey East	26	1	2	3	24	...	...	...	—	—	—	—	—
93-94—Univ. of New Hamp.....	Hockey East	36	0	4	4	48	...	...	...	—	—	—	—	—
94-95—Univ. of New Hamp.....	Hockey East	28	9	9	18	48	...	...	...	—	—	—	—	—
95-96—Canadian nat'l team	Int'l	42	6	12	18	36	...	...	...	—	—	—	—	—
—Edmonton.................	NHL	5	0	0	0	6	-4	0	0	—	—	—	—	—
96-97—Hamilton	AHL	75	8	16	24	80	...	...	...	14	0	5	5	12
—Edmonton..................	NHL	—	—	—	—	—				5	0	0	0	4

Season Team	League	REGULAR SEASON								PLAYOFFS				
		Gms.	G	A	Pts.	PIM	+/-	PP	SH	Gms.	G	A	Pts.	PIM
97-98—Hamilton	AHL	28	3	10	13	62	...	...	...	—	—	—	—	—
—Edmonton	NHL	7	0	0	0	17	0	0	0	—	—	—	—	—
—Albany	AHL	41	3	10	13	67	...	...	...	13	3	0	3	12
98-99—New Jersey	NHL	1	0	0	0	0	0	0	0	—	—	—	—	—
—Albany	AHL	10	0	0	0	29	...	...	...	—	—	—	—	—
—Chicago	NHL	53	1	4	5	50	1	0	0	—	—	—	—	—
—Portland	AHL	2	1	1	2	2	...	...	...	—	—	—	—	—
99-00—Chicago	NHL	11	2	3	5	13	-1	0	1	—	—	—	—	—
—Tampa Bay	NHL	30	1	1	2	32	-8	0	0	—	—	—	—	—
00-01—Tampa Bay	NHL	10	0	3	3	15	-7	0	0	—	—	—	—	—
—Detroit	IHL	21	5	7	12	36	...	...	...	—	—	—	—	—
—Hershey	AHL	26	5	8	13	50	...	...	...	—	—	—	—	—
—Colorado	NHL	8	0	0	0	4	0	0	0	3	0	0	0	0
NHL Totals (6 years)		125	4	11	15	137	-19	0	1	8	0	0	0	4

MULLER, KIRK — C — STARS

PERSONAL: Born February 8, 1966, in Kingston, Ont. ... 6-0/205. ... Shoots left. ... Name pronounced MUH-luhr.

TRANSACTIONS/CAREER NOTES: Selected by New Jersey Devils in first round (first Devils pick, second overall) of NHL entry draft (June 9, 1984). ... Strained knee (January 13, 1986). ... Fractured ribs (April 1986). ... Traded by Devils with G Roland Melanson to Montreal Canadiens for RW Stephane Richer and RW Tom Chorske (September 1991). ... Injured eye (January 21, 1992); missed one game. ... Bruised ribs (November 7, 1992); missed one game. ... Sprained wrist (March 6, 1993); missed two games. ... Injured shoulder (October 11, 1993); missed eight games. ... Traded by Canadiens with D Mathieu Schneider and C Craig Darby to New York Islanders for C Pierre Turgeon and D Vladimir Malakhov (April 5, 1995). ... Traded by Islanders to Toronto Maple Leafs for LW Ken Belanger and G Damian Rhodes (January 23, 1996). ... Separated shoulder (January 3, 1997); missed two games. ... Bruised ankle (March 8, 1997); missed two games. ... Traded by Maple Leafs to Florida Panthers for RW Jason Podollan (March 18, 1997). ... Suspended two games and fined $1,000 by NHL for high-sticking incident (December 1, 1997). ... Sprained left knee (December 20, 1997); missed eight games. ... Signed as free agent by Dallas Stars (December 15, 1999). ... Suffered back spasms (March 28, 2000); missed one game. ... Bruised chest (December 27, 2000); missed 24 games. ... Injured knee (March 31, 2001); missed one game.

HONORS: Won William Hanley Trophy (1982-83). ... Played in NHL All-Star Game (1985, 1986, 1988, 1990, 1992 and 1993).

MISCELLANEOUS: Member of Stanley Cup championship team (1993). ... Captain of New Jersey Devils (1987-88 through 1990-91). ... Captain of Montreal Canadiens (1994-95). ... Scored on a penalty shot (vs. Greg Millen, March 21, 1987). ... Failed to score on a penalty shot (vs. Mike Vernon, March 14, 1989).

STATISTICAL PLATEAUS: Three-goal games: 1986-87 (1), 1987-88 (3), 1991-92 (2), 1995-96 (1). Total: 7.

Season Team	League	REGULAR SEASON								PLAYOFFS				
		Gms.	G	A	Pts.	PIM	+/-	PP	SH	Gms.	G	A	Pts.	PIM
80-81—Kingston	OMJHL	2	0	0	0	0	...	...	...	—	—	—	—	—
81-82—Kingston	OHL	67	12	39	51	27	...	...	...	4	5	1	6	4
82-83—Guelph	OHL	66	52	60	112	41	...	...	...	—	—	—	—	—
83-84—Can. Olympic team	Int'l	15	2	2	4	6	...	...	...	—	—	—	—	—
—Canadian nat'l team	Int'l	15	2	2	4	6	...	...	...	—	—	—	—	—
—Guelph	OHL	49	31	63	94	27	...	...	...	—	—	—	—	—
84-85—New Jersey	NHL	80	17	37	54	69	-31	9	1	—	—	—	—	—
85-86—New Jersey	NHL	77	25	41	66	45	-19	5	1	—	—	—	—	—
86-87—New Jersey	NHL	79	26	50	76	75	-7	10	1	—	—	—	—	—
87-88—New Jersey	NHL	80	37	57	94	114	19	17	2	20	4	8	12	37
88-89—New Jersey	NHL	80	31	43	74	119	-23	12	1	—	—	—	—	—
89-90—New Jersey	NHL	80	30	56	86	74	-1	9	0	6	1	3	4	11
90-91—New Jersey	NHL	80	19	51	70	76	1	7	0	7	0	2	2	10
91-92—Montreal	NHL	78	36	41	77	86	15	15	1	11	4	3	7	31
92-93—Montreal	NHL	80	37	57	94	77	8	12	0	20	10	7	17	18
93-94—Montreal	NHL	76	23	34	57	96	-1	9	2	7	6	2	8	4
94-95—Montreal	NHL	33	8	11	19	33	-21	3	0	—	—	—	—	—
—New York Islanders	NHL	12	3	5	8	14	3	1	1	—	—	—	—	—
95-96—New York Islanders	NHL	15	4	3	7	15	-10	0	0	—	—	—	—	—
—Toronto	NHL	36	9	16	25	42	-3	7	0	6	3	2	5	0
96-97—Toronto	NHL	66	20	17	37	85	-23	9	1	—	—	—	—	—
—Florida	NHL	10	1	2	3	4	-2	1	0	5	1	2	3	4
97-98—Florida	NHL	70	8	21	29	54	-14	1	0	—	—	—	—	—
98-99—Florida	NHL	82	4	11	15	49	-11	0	0	—	—	—	—	—
99-00—Dallas	NHL	47	7	15	22	24	-3	3	0	23	2	3	5	18
00-01—Dallas	NHL	55	1	9	10	26	-4	0	0	10	1	3	4	12
NHL Totals (17 years)		1216	346	577	923	1177	-127	130	11	115	32	35	67	145

MURLEY, MATT — LW — PENGUINS

PERSONAL: Born December 17, 1979, in Troy, N.Y. ... 6-1/192. ... Shoots left.

TRANSACTIONS/CAREER NOTES: Selected by Pittsburgh Penguins in second round (second Penguins pick, 51st overall) of NHL entry draft (June 26, 1999).

Season Team	League	REGULAR SEASON								PLAYOFFS				
		Gms.	G	A	Pts.	PIM	+/-	PP	SH	Gms.	G	A	Pts.	PIM
97-98—Syracuse	Jr. A	49	56	70	126	203	...	...	...	—	—	—	—	—
98-99—Rensselaer Poly. Inst.	ECAC	36	17	32	49	32	...	...	...	—	—	—	—	—
99-00—Rensselaer Poly. Inst.	ECAC	35	9	29	38	42	...	...	...	—	—	—	—	—
00-01—Rensselaer Poly. Inst.	ECAC	34	*24	18	42	34	...	...	...	—	—	—	—	—

M

MURPHY, GORD   D

PERSONAL: Born March 23, 1967, in Willowdale, Ont. ... 6-3/195. ... Shoots right. ... Full Name: Gordon Murphy.

TRANSACTIONS/CAREER NOTES: Selected by Philadelphia Flyers in ninth round (10th Flyers pick, 189th overall) of NHL entry draft (June 15, 1985). ... Injured left foot and suffered hip pointer (March 24, 1990). ... Traded by Flyers with RW Brian Dobbin, third-round pick (LW Sergei Zholtok) in 1992 draft and fourth-round pick (D Charles Paquette) in 1993 draft to Boston Bruins for D Garry Galley, C Wes Walz and third-round pick (D Milos Holan) in 1993 draft (January 2, 1992). ... Injured ankle (January 1993); missed 16 games. ... Traded by Bruins to Dallas Stars for future considerations (June 20, 1993); Stars acquired G Andy Moog for G Jon Casey to complete deal (June 25, 1993). ... Selected by Florida Panthers in NHL expansion draft (June 24, 1993). ... Suffered illness (March 26, 1995); missed one game. ... Sprained left ankle (April 5, 1995); missed one game. ... Sprained right ankle (January 29, 1996); missed nine games. ... Injured toe (April 8, 1996); missed three games. ... Suffered from the flu (January 27, 1998); missed three games. ... Sprained neck (February 20, 1999); missed final 25 games of season. ... Traded by Panthers with C Herbert Vasiljevs, D Daniel Tjarnqvist and sixth-round pick (traded to Dallas) in 1999 draft to Atlanta Thrashers for G Trevor Kidd (June 25, 1999). ... Strained hip flexor (November 28, 1999); missed two games. ... Injured hip (February 7, 2000); missed four games. ... Dislocated shoulder (March 4, 2000); missed remainder of season. ... Injured shoulder (October 7, 2000); missed first 42 games of season. ... Fractured thumb (February 1, 2001); missed 11 games.

HONORS: Named to Memorial Cup All-Star team (1986-87).

| | | REGULAR SEASON | | | | | | | | | PLAYOFFS | | | | |
Season Team	League	Gms.	G	A	Pts.	PIM	+/-	PP	SH		Gms.	G	A	Pts.	PIM
83-84—Don Mills Flyers	MTHL	65	24	42	66	130	...	...	...		—	—	—	—	—
84-85—Oshawa	OHL	59	3	12	15	25	...	...	...		—	—	—	—	—
85-86—Oshawa	OHL	64	7	15	22	56	...	...	...		6	1	1	2	6
86-87—Oshawa	OHL	56	7	30	37	95	...	...	...		24	6	16	22	22
87-88—Hershey	AHL	62	8	20	28	44	...	...	...		12	0	8	8	12
88-89—Philadelphia	NHL	75	4	31	35	68	-3	3	0		19	2	7	9	13
89-90—Philadelphia	NHL	75	14	27	41	95	-7	4	0		—	—	—	—	—
90-91—Philadelphia	NHL	80	11	31	42	58	-7	6	0		—	—	—	—	—
91-92—Philadelphia	NHL	31	2	8	10	33	-4	0	0		—	—	—	—	—
—Boston	NHL	42	3	6	9	51	2	0	0		15	1	0	1	12
92-93—Boston	NHL	49	5	12	17	62	-13	3	0		—	—	—	—	—
—Providence	AHL	2	1	3	4	2	...	...	...		—	—	—	—	—
93-94—Florida	NHL	84	14	29	43	71	-11	9	0		—	—	—	—	—
94-95—Florida	NHL	46	6	16	22	24	-14	5	0		—	—	—	—	—
95-96—Florida	NHL	70	8	22	30	30	5	4	0		14	0	4	4	6
96-97—Florida	NHL	80	8	15	23	51	3	2	0		5	0	5	5	4
97-98—Florida	NHL	79	6	11	17	46	-3	3	0		—	—	—	—	—
98-99—Florida	NHL	51	0	7	7	16	4	0	0		—	—	—	—	—
99-00—Atlanta	NHL	58	1	10	11	38	-26	0	0		—	—	—	—	—
00-01—Atlanta	NHL	27	3	11	14	12	-11	2	0		—	—	—	—	—
NHL Totals (13 years)		847	85	236	321	655	-85	41	0		53	3	16	19	35

MURPHY, JOE   RW

PERSONAL: Born October 17, 1967, in London, Ont. ... 6-0/190. ... Shoots left. ... Full Name: Joseph Patrick Murphy.

TRANSACTIONS/CAREER NOTES: Selected by Detroit Red Wings in first round (first Red Wings pick, first overall) of NHL entry draft (June 21, 1986). ... Sprained right ankle (January 1988). ... Traded by Red Wings with C/LW Adam Graves, LW Petr Klima and D Jeff Sharples to Edmonton Oilers for C Jimmy Carson, C Kevin McClelland and fifth-round pick (traded to Montreal Canadiens) in 1991 draft (November 2, 1989). ... Bruised both thighs (March 1990). ... Did not report to Oilers in 1992-93 season because of contract dispute; missed 63 games. ... Traded by Oilers to Chicago Blackhawks for D Igor Kravchuk and C Dean McAmmond (February 25, 1993). ... Pulled groin (February 3, 1995); missed three games. ... Reinjured groin (March 6, 1995); missed four games. ... Sprained knee (March 21, 1995); missed one game. ... Suspended 10 games by NHL for being third man in fight (September 20, 1995). ... Strained back (December 28, 1995); missed four games. ... Strained back (January 6, 1996). ... Signed as free agent by St. Louis Blues (July 3, 1996). ... Suffered from a virus (October 31, 1996); missed five games. ... Strained groin (January 30, 1997); missed one game. ... Tore ligament in left wrist (November 6, 1997); missed 42 games. ... Strained groin (March 3, 1998). ... Traded by Blues to San Jose Sharks for D Todd Gill (March 24, 1998). ... Suspended two games and fined $1,000 by NHL for slashing incident (March 31, 1998). ... Strained hamstring (October 22, 1998); missed three games. ... Reinjured hamstring (October 31, 1998); missed one game. ... Injured groin (January 15, 1999); missed two games. ... Signed as free agent by Boston Bruins (November 12, 1999). ... Injured knee (November 17, 1999); missed eight games. ... Strained abdominal muscle (January 19, 2000); missed one game. ... Claimed on waivers by Washington Capitals (February 10, 2000). ... Injured shoulder (December 1, 2000); missed one game.

HONORS: Named BCJHL Rookie of the Year (1984-85). ... Named CCHA Rookie of the Year (1985-86).

MISCELLANEOUS: Member of Stanley Cup championship team (1990).

| | | REGULAR SEASON | | | | | | | | | PLAYOFFS | | | | |
Season Team	League	Gms.	G	A	Pts.	PIM	+/-	PP	SH		Gms.	G	A	Pts.	PIM
84-85—Penticton	BCJHL	51	68	84	*152	92	...	...	...		—	—	—	—	—
85-86—Michigan State	CCHA	35	24	37	61	50	...	...	...		—	—	—	—	—
—Canadian nat'l team	Int'l	8	3	3	6	2	...	...	...		—	—	—	—	—
86-87—Adirondack	AHL	71	21	38	59	61	...	...	...		10	2	1	3	33
—Detroit	NHL	5	0	1	1	2	0	0	0		—	—	—	—	—
87-88—Adirondack	AHL	6	5	6	11	4	...	...	...		—	—	—	—	—
—Detroit	NHL	50	10	9	19	37	-4	1	0		8	0	1	1	6
88-89—Detroit	NHL	26	1	7	8	28	-7	0	0		—	—	—	—	—
—Adirondack	AHL	47	31	35	66	66	...	...	...		16	6	11	17	17
89-90—Detroit	NHL	9	3	1	4	4	4	0	0		—	—	—	—	—
—Edmonton	NHL	62	7	18	25	56	1	2	0		22	6	8	14	16
90-91—Edmonton	NHL	80	27	35	62	35	2	4	1		15	2	5	7	14
91-92—Edmonton	NHL	80	35	47	82	52	17	10	2		16	8	16	24	12
92-93—Chicago	NHL	19	7	10	17	18	-3	5	0		4	0	0	0	8
93-94—Chicago	NHL	81	31	39	70	111	1	7	4		6	1	3	4	25
94-95—Chicago	NHL	40	23	18	41	89	7	7	0		16	9	3	12	29
95-96—Chicago	NHL	70	22	29	51	86	-3	8	0		10	6	2	8	33

Season Team	League	REGULAR SEASON								PLAYOFFS				
		Gms.	G	A	Pts.	PIM	+/-	PP	SH	Gms.	G	A	Pts.	PIM
96-97—St. Louis	NHL	75	20	25	45	69	-1	4	1	6	1	1	2	10
97-98—St. Louis	NHL	27	4	9	13	22	8	2	0	—	—	—	—	—
—San Jose	NHL	10	5	4	9	14	1	2	0	6	1	1	2	20
98-99—San Jose	NHL	76	25	23	48	73	10	7	0	6	0	3	3	4
99-00—Boston	NHL	26	7	7	14	41	-7	3	0	—	—	—	—	—
—Washington	NHL	29	5	8	13	53	8	1	0	5	0	0	0	8
00-01—Washington	NHL	14	1	5	6	20	-5	1	0	—	—	—	—	—
NHL Totals (15 years).........		779	233	295	528	810	29	64	8	120	34	43	77	185

MURPHY, LARRY   D

PERSONAL: Born March 8, 1961, in Scarborough, Ont. ... 6-2/215. ... Shoots right. ... Full Name: Lawrence Thomas Murphy.

TRANSACTIONS/CAREER NOTES: Selected by Los Angeles Kings in first round (first Kings pick, fourth overall) of NHL entry draft (June 11, 1980). ... Traded by Kings to Washington Capitals for D Brian Engblom and RW Ken Houston (October 18, 1983). ... Injured foot (October 29, 1985). ... Fractured ankle (May 1988). ... Traded by Capitals with RW Mike Gartner to Minnesota North Stars for RW Dino Ciccarelli and D Bob Rouse (March 7, 1989). ... Traded by North Stars with D Peter Taglianetti to Pittsburgh Penguins for D Jim Johnson and D Chris Dahlquist (December 11, 1990). ... Fractured right foot (February 22, 1991); played until March 5 then missed five games. ... Suffered back spasms (March 28, 1993); missed one game. ... Traded by Penguins to Toronto Maple Leafs for D Dmitri Mironov and second-round pick (traded to New Jersey) in 1996 draft (July 8, 1995). ... Traded by Maple Leafs to Detroit Red Wings for future considerations (March 18, 1997). ... Suffered concussion (February 1, 1999); missed one game. ... Injured heel (February 22, 2001); missed three games.

HONORS: Won Max Kaminsky Trophy (1979-80). ... Named to OMJHL All-Star first team (1979-80). ... Named to Memorial Cup All-Star team (1979-80). ... Named to THE SPORTING NEWS All-Star second team (1986-87 and 1992-93). ... Named to NHL All-Star second team (1986-87, 1992-93 and 1994-95). ... Played in NHL All-Star Game (1994, 1996 and 1999).

RECORDS: Holds NHL rookie-season records for most points by a defenseman—76; and most assists by a defenseman—60 (1980-81).

MISCELLANEOUS: Member of Stanley Cup championship team (1991, 1992, 1997 and 1998).

Season Team	League	REGULAR SEASON								PLAYOFFS				
		Gms.	G	A	Pts.	PIM	+/-	PP	SH	Gms.	G	A	Pts.	PIM
78-79—Peterborough.............	OMJHL	66	6	21	27	82	...	...	...	19	1	9	10	42
79-80—Peterborough.............	OMJHL	68	21	68	89	88	...	...	...	14	4	13	17	20
80-81—Los Angeles...............	NHL	80	16	60	76	79	17	5	1	4	3	0	3	2
81-82—Los Angeles...............	NHL	79	22	44	66	95	-13	8	1	10	2	8	10	12
82-83—Los Angeles...............	NHL	77	14	48	62	81	2	9	0	—	—	—	—	—
83-84—Los Angeles...............	NHL	6	0	3	3	0	-4	0	0	—	—	—	—	—
—Washington	NHL	72	13	33	46	50	12	2	0	8	0	3	3	6
84-85—Washington	NHL	79	13	42	55	51	21	3	0	5	2	3	5	0
85-86—Washington	NHL	78	21	44	65	50	3	8	1	9	1	5	6	6
86-87—Washington	NHL	80	23	58	81	39	25	8	0	7	2	2	4	6
87-88—Washington	NHL	79	8	53	61	72	2	7	0	13	4	4	8	33
88-89—Washington	NHL	65	7	29	36	70	-5	3	0	—	—	—	—	—
—Minnesota................	NHL	13	4	6	10	12	5	3	0	5	0	2	2	8
89-90—Minnesota................	NHL	77	10	58	68	44	-13	4	0	7	1	2	3	31
90-91—Minnesota................	NHL	31	4	11	15	38	-8	1	0	—	—	—	—	—
—Pittsburgh................	NHL	44	5	23	28	30	2	2	0	23	5	18	23	44
91-92—Pittsburgh................	NHL	77	21	56	77	48	33	7	2	21	6	10	16	19
92-93—Pittsburgh................	NHL	83	22	63	85	73	45	6	2	12	2	11	13	10
93-94—Pittsburgh................	NHL	84	17	56	73	44	10	7	0	6	0	5	5	0
94-95—Pittsburgh................	NHL	48	13	25	38	18	12	4	0	12	2	13	15	0
95-96—Toronto	NHL	82	12	49	61	34	-2	8	0	6	0	2	2	4
96-97—Toronto	NHL	69	7	32	39	20	1	4	0	—	—	—	—	—
—Detroit....................	NHL	12	2	4	6	0	2	1	0	20	2	9	11	8
97-98—Detroit....................	NHL	82	11	41	52	37	35	2	1	22	3	12	15	2
98-99—Detroit....................	NHL	80	10	42	52	42	21	5	1	10	0	2	2	8
99-00—Detroit....................	NHL	81	10	30	40	45	4	7	0	9	2	3	5	2
00-01—Detroit....................	NHL	57	2	19	21	12	-6	0	0	6	0	1	1	0
NHL Totals (21 years).........		1615	287	929	1216	1084	201	114	9	215	37	115	152	201

MURRAY, GLEN   RW   KINGS

PERSONAL: Born November 1, 1972, in Halifax, Nova Scotia. ... 6-3/222. ... Shoots right.

TRANSACTIONS/CAREER NOTES: Selected by Boston Bruins in first round (first Bruins pick, 18th overall) of NHL entry draft (June 22, 1991). ... Injured elbow (December 15, 1993); missed two games. ... Traded by Bruins with C Bryan Smolinski to Pittsburgh Penguins for LW Kevin Stevens and LW Shawn McEachern (August 2, 1995). ... Separated shoulder (January 1, 1996); missed 10 games. ... Suffered concussion (April 11, 1996); missed one game. ... Traded by Penguins to Los Angeles Kings for C Ed Olczyk (March 18, 1997). ... Suffered from the flu (November 13, 1997); missed one game. ... Tore medial collateral ligament in right knee (January 2, 1999); missed 19 games. ... Strained groin (March 28, 1999); missed two games. ... Bruised chest (January 13, 2000); missed three games. ... Strained quadriceps (November 18, 2000); missed 18 games.

MISCELLANEOUS: Failed to score on a penalty shot (vs. Guy Hebert, February 7, 1998).

STATISTICAL PLATEAUS: Three-goal games: 1997-98 (1), 1999-00 (1). Total: 2.

Season Team	League	REGULAR SEASON								PLAYOFFS				
		Gms.	G	A	Pts.	PIM	+/-	PP	SH	Gms.	G	A	Pts.	PIM
89-90—Sudbury....................	OHL	62	8	28	36	17	...	...	...	7	0	0	0	4
90-91—Sudbury....................	OHL	66	27	38	65	82	...	...	...	5	8	4	12	10
91-92—Sudbury....................	OHL	54	37	47	84	93	...	...	...	11	7	4	11	18
—Boston	NHL	5	3	1	4	0	2	1	0	15	4	2	6	10
92-93—Providence................	AHL	48	30	26	56	42	...	...	...	6	1	4	5	4
—Boston	NHL	27	3	4	7	8	-6	2	0	—	—	—	—	—
93-94—Boston	NHL	81	18	13	31	48	-1	0	0	13	4	5	9	14

– 267 –

Season Team	League	REGULAR SEASON								PLAYOFFS				
		Gms.	G	A	Pts.	PIM	+/-	PP	SH	Gms.	G	A	Pts.	PIM
94-95—Boston	NHL	35	5	2	7	46	-11	0	0	2	0	0	0	2
95-96—Pittsburgh	NHL	69	14	15	29	57	4	0	0	18	2	6	8	10
96-97—Pittsburgh	NHL	66	11	11	22	24	-19	3	0	—	—	—	—	—
—Los Angeles	NHL	11	5	3	8	8	-2	0	0	—	—	—	—	—
97-98—Los Angeles	NHL	81	29	31	60	54	6	7	3	4	2	0	2	6
98-99—Los Angeles	NHL	61	16	15	31	36	-14	3	3	—	—	—	—	—
99-00—Los Angeles	NHL	78	29	33	62	60	13	10	1	4	0	0	0	2
00-01—Los Angeles	NHL	64	18	21	39	32	9	3	1	13	4	3	7	4
NHL Totals (10 years)		578	151	149	300	373	-19	29	8	69	16	16	32	48

MURRAY, MARTY   C   FLYERS

PERSONAL: Born February 16, 1975, in Deloraine, Man. ... 5-9/178. ... Shoots left.

TRANSACTIONS/CAREER NOTES: Selected by Calgary Flames in fourth round (fifth Flames pick, 96th overall) of NHL entry draft (June 26, 1993). ... Bruised foot (April 8, 1996); missed three games. ... Strained hip flexor (October 12, 2000); missed nine games. ... Signed as free agent by Philadelphia Flyers (July 9, 2001).

HONORS: Named to Can.HL All-Star second team (1993-94). ... Named to WHL (East) All-Star first team (1993-94 and 1994-95). ... Won Four Broncos Memorial Trophy (1994-95).

Season Team	League	REGULAR SEASON								PLAYOFFS				
		Gms.	G	A	Pts.	PIM	+/-	PP	SH	Gms.	G	A	Pts.	PIM
91-92—Brandon	WHL	68	20	36	56	12	...	...	...	—	—	—	—	—
92-93—Brandon	WHL	67	29	65	94	50	...	...	...	4	1	3	4	0
93-94—Brandon	WHL	64	43	71	114	33	...	...	...	14	6	14	20	14
94-95—Brandon	WHL	65	40	88	128	53	...	...	...	18	9	20	29	16
95-96—Calgary	NHL	15	3	3	6	0	-4	2	0	—	—	—	—	—
—Saint John	AHL	58	25	31	56	20	...	...	...	14	2	4	6	4
96-97—Saint John	AHL	67	19	39	58	40	...	...	...	5	2	3	5	4
—Calgary	NHL	2	0	0	0	4	0	0	0	—	—	—	—	—
97-98—Calgary	NHL	2	0	0	0	2	1	0	0	—	—	—	—	—
—Saint John	AHL	41	10	30	40	16	...	...	...	21	10	10	20	12
99-00—Kolner Haie	Germany	56	12	47	59	28	...	...	...	10	4	3	7	2
00-01—Calgary	NHL	7	0	0	0	0	-2	0	0	—	—	—	—	—
—Saint John	AHL	56	24	52	76	36	...	...	...	19	4	16	20	18
NHL Totals (4 years)		26	3	3	6	6	-5	2	0					

MURRAY, REM   LW   OILERS

PERSONAL: Born October 9, 1972, in Stratford, Ont. ... 6-2/195. ... Shoots left. ... Full Name: Raymond Murray.

TRANSACTIONS/CAREER NOTES: Selected by Los Angeles Kings in sixth round (fifth Kings pick, 135th overall) of NHL entry draft (June 20, 1992). ... Signed as free agent by Edmonton Oilers (August 17, 1995). ... Missed first five games of 1997-98 season recovering from wrist injury and off-season appendectomy. ... Strained neck (March 17, 1998); missed one game. ... Suffered from the flu (April 6, 1998); missed three games. ... Separated shoulder (October 7, 1999); missed seven games. ... Sprained medial collateral ligament in knee (November 3, 1999); missed 28 games.

HONORS: Named to CCHA All-Star second team (1994-95).

STATISTICAL PLATEAUS: Three-goal games: 1996-97 (1).

Season Team	League	REGULAR SEASON								PLAYOFFS				
		Gms.	G	A	Pts.	PIM	+/-	PP	SH	Gms.	G	A	Pts.	PIM
90-91—Stratford Jr. B	OHA	48	39	59	98	22	...	...	...	—	—	—	—	—
91-92—Michigan State	CCHA	44	12	36	48	16	...	...	...	—	—	—	—	—
92-93—Michigan State	CCHA	40	22	35	57	24	...	...	...	—	—	—	—	—
93-94—Michigan State	CCHA	41	16	38	54	18	...	...	...	—	—	—	—	—
94-95—Michigan State	CCHA	40	20	36	56	21	...	...	...	—	—	—	—	—
95-96—Cape Breton	AHL	79	31	59	90	40	...	...	...	—	—	—	—	—
96-97—Edmonton	NHL	82	11	20	31	16	9	1	0	12	1	2	3	4
97-98—Edmonton	NHL	61	9	9	18	39	-9	2	2	11	1	4	5	2
98-99—Edmonton	NHL	78	21	18	39	20	4	4	1	4	1	1	2	2
99-00—Edmonton	NHL	44	9	5	14	8	-2	2	0	5	0	1	1	2
00-01—Edmonton	NHL	82	15	21	36	24	5	1	3	6	2	0	2	6
NHL Totals (5 years)		347	65	73	138	107	7	10	6	38	5	8	13	16

MUSIL, FRANK   D

PERSONAL: Born December 17, 1964, in Pardubice, Czechoslovakia. ... 6-3/215. ... Shoots left. ... Full Name: Frantisek Musil. ... Name pronounced MYOO-sihl.

TRANSACTIONS/CAREER NOTES: Selected by Minnesota North Stars in second round (third North Stars pick, 38th overall) of NHL entry draft (June 8, 1983). ... Separated shoulder (December 9, 1986). ... Fractured foot (December 17, 1988). ... Suffered concussion (February 9, 1989). ... Strained lower back muscles (February 18, 1989). ... Suffered back spasms (November 2, 1989); missed 10 games. ... Separated right shoulder (April 1990). ... Traded by North Stars to Calgary Flames for D Brian Glynn (October 26, 1990). ... Suffered back spasms (November 8, 1993); missed one game. ... Strained neck (December 28, 1993); missed four games. ... Hyperextended elbow (March 22, 1994); missed four games. ... Played in Europe during 1994-95 NHL lockout. ... Bruised right knee (January 24, 1995); missed one game. ... Sprained right knee (February 9, 1995); missed three games. ... Suffered back spasms (February 28, 1995); missed one game. ... Sprained knee (April 7, 1995); missed seven games. ... Traded by Flames to Ottawa Senators for fourth-round pick (D Chris St. Croix) in 1997 draft (October 7, 1995). ... Suffered concussion during 1995-96 season; missed one game. ... Lacerated neck (January 21, 1996); missed six games. ... Bruised right foot (February 3, 1996); missed seven games. ... Traded by Senators to Edmonton Oilers for D Scott Ferguson (March 9, 1998). ... Suffered compressed vertebrae (October 1, 1999); missed remainder of season. ... Sprained ankle (December 14, 2000); missed nine games. ... Suffered from inflamed nerve in neck (January 10, 2001); missed remainder of season.

Season Team	League	REGULAR SEASON								PLAYOFFS				
		Gms.	G	A	Pts.	PIM	+/-	PP	SH	Gms.	G	A	Pts.	PIM
80-81—Pardubice	Czech.	2	...	...	...	...	...	...	...	—	—	—	—	—
81-82—Pardubice	Czech.	35	1	3	4	34	...	...	...	—	—	—	—	—
82-83—Pardubice	Czech.	33	1	2	3	44	...	...	...	—	—	—	—	—
83-84—Pardubice	Czech.	37	4	8	12	72	...	...	...	—	—	—	—	—
84-85—Pardubice	Czech.	44	4	6	10	76	...	...	...	—	—	—	—	—
85-86—Dukla Jihlava	Czech.	35	3	7	10	85	...	...	...	—	—	—	—	—
86-87—Minnesota	NHL	72	2	9	11	148	0	0	0	—	—	—	—	—
87-88—Minnesota	NHL	80	9	8	17	213	-2	1	1	—	—	—	—	—
88-89—Minnesota	NHL	55	1	19	20	54	4	0	0	5	1	1	2	4
89-90—Minnesota	NHL	56	2	8	10	109	0	0	0	4	0	0	0	14
90-91—Minnesota	NHL	8	0	2	2	23	0	0	0	—	—	—	—	—
—Calgary	NHL	67	7	14	21	160	12	2	0	7	0	0	0	10
91-92—Calgary	NHL	78	4	8	12	103	12	1	1	—	—	—	—	—
92-93—Calgary	NHL	80	6	10	16	131	28	0	0	6	1	1	2	7
93-94—Calgary	NHL	75	1	8	9	50	38	0	0	7	0	1	1	4
94-95—Sparta Prague	Czech Rep.	19	1	4	5	30	...	...	...	—	—	—	—	—
—Sachsen	Germany	1	0	0	0	2	...	...	...	—	—	—	—	—
—Calgary	NHL	35	0	5	5	61	6	0	0	5	0	1	1	0
95-96—Ottawa	NHL	65	1	3	4	85	-10	0	0	—	—	—	—	—
96-97—Ottawa	NHL	57	0	5	5	58	6	0	0	—	—	—	—	—
97-98—Detroit	IHL	9	0	0	0	6	...	...	...	—	—	—	—	—
—Indianapolis	IHL	52	5	8	13	122	...	...	...	—	—	—	—	—
—Edmonton	NHL	17	1	2	3	8	1	0	1	7	0	0	0	6
98-99—Edmonton	NHL	39	0	3	3	34	0	0	0	1	0	0	0	2
00-01—Edmonton	NHL	13	0	2	2	4	-2	0	0	—	—	—	—	—
NHL Totals (14 years)		797	34	106	140	1241	93	4	3	42	2	4	6	47

MYHRES, BRANTT   RW

PERSONAL: Born March 18, 1974, in Edmonton. ... 6-4/215. ... Shoots right. ... Name pronounced MIGH-urhs.

TRANSACTIONS/CAREER NOTES: Selected by Tampa Bay Lightning in fifth round (fifth Lightning pick, 97th overall) of NHL entry draft (June 20, 1992). ... Injured shoulder (April 11, 1995); missed one game. ... Injured hip (February 1, 1997); missed one game. ... Sprained ankle (February 23, 1997); missed three games. ... Suffered from the flu (April 4, 1997); missed three games. ... Traded by Lightning with third-round pick (D Alex Henry) in 1998 draft to Edmonton Oilers for C Vladimir Vujtek (July 16, 1997). ... Traded by Oilers to Philadelphia Flyers for F Jason Bowen (October 15, 1997). ... Bruised left hand (November 26, 1997); missed two games. ... Signed as free agent by San Jose Sharks (September 11, 1998). ... Suspended 12 games by NHL for leaving the bench to start a fight (February 12, 1999). ... Injured hand (October 28, 1999); missed seven games. ... Injured back (February 15, 2000); missed eight games. ... Signed as free agent by Nashville Predators (August 15, 2000). ... Traded by Predators to Washington Capitals for future considerations (February 1, 2001).

Season Team	League	REGULAR SEASON								PLAYOFFS				
		Gms.	G	A	Pts.	PIM	+/-	PP	SH	Gms.	G	A	Pts.	PIM
90-91—Portland	WHL	59	2	7	9	125	...	...	...	—	—	—	—	—
91-92—Portland	WHL	4	0	2	2	22	...	...	...	—	—	—	—	—
—Lethbridge	WHL	53	4	11	15	359	...	...	...	5	0	0	0	36
92-93—Lethbridge	WHL	64	13	35	48	277	...	...	...	3	0	0	0	11
93-94—Atlanta	IHL	2	0	0	0	17	...	...	...	—	—	—	—	—
—Lethbridge	WHL	34	10	21	31	103	...	...	...	—	—	—	—	—
—Spokane	WHL	27	10	22	32	139	...	...	...	3	1	4	5	7
94-95—Atlanta	IHL	40	5	5	10	213	...	...	...	—	—	—	—	—
—Tampa Bay	NHL	15	2	0	2	81	-2	0	0	—	—	—	—	—
95-96—Atlanta	IHL	12	0	2	2	58	...	...	...	—	—	—	—	—
96-97—San Antonio	IHL	12	0	0	0	98	...	...	...	—	—	—	—	—
—Tampa Bay	NHL	47	3	1	4	136	1	0	0	—	—	—	—	—
97-98—Philadelphia	AHL	18	4	4	8	67	...	...	...	—	—	—	—	—
—Philadelphia	NHL	23	0	0	0	169	-1	0	0	—	—	—	—	—
98-99—San Jose	NHL	30	1	0	1	116	-2	0	0	—	—	—	—	—
—Kentucky	AHL	4	0	0	0	16	...	...	...	—	—	—	—	—
99-00—San Jose	NHL	13	0	1	1	97	0	0	0	—	—	—	—	—
—Kentucky	AHL	10	1	5	6	18	...	...	...	7	0	1	1	21
00-01—Nashville	NHL	20	0	0	0	28	-5	0	0	—	—	—	—	—
—Milwaukee	IHL	6	0	1	1	10	...	...	...	—	—	—	—	—
—Portland	AHL	9	1	0	1	53	...	...	...	—	—	—	—	—
—Washington	NHL	5	0	0	0	29	0	0	0	—	—	—	—	—
NHL Totals (6 years)		153	6	2	8	656	-9	0	0					

MYRVOLD, ANDERS   D

PERSONAL: Born August 12, 1975, in Lorenskog, Norway. ... 6-2/200. ... Shoots left. ... Name pronounced MUHR-vohld.

TRANSACTIONS/CAREER NOTES: Selected by Quebec Nordiques in fifth round (sixth Nordiques pick, 127th overall) of NHL entry draft (June 26, 1993). ... Nordiques franchise moved to Colorado and renamed Avalanche for 1995-96 season (June 21, 1995). ... Traded by Avalanche with RW Landon Wilson to Boston Bruins for first-round pick (D Robyn Regehr) in 1998 draft (November 22, 1996). ... Signed as free agent by New York Islanders (August 28, 2000).

HONORS: Named to Can.HL All-Rookie team (1994-95).

M

Season Team	League	Gms.	G	A	Pts.	PIM	+/-	PP	SH	Gms.	G	A	Pts.	PIM
92-93—Farjestad Karlstad	Sweden	2	0	0	0	0	...	...	...	—	—	—	—	—
93-94—Grums	Sweden Dv. 2	24	1	0	1	59	...	...	...	—	—	—	—	—
94-95—Laval	QMJHL	64	14	50	64	173	...	...	...	20	4	10	14	68
—Cornwall	AHL	—	—	—	—	—				3	0	1	1	2
95-96—Colorado	NHL	4	0	1	1	6	-2	0	0	—	—	—	—	—
—Cornwall	AHL	70	5	24	29	125	...	...	...	5	1	0	1	19
96-97—Hershey	AHL	20	0	3	3	16	...	...	...	—	—	—	—	—
—Providence	AHL	53	6	15	21	107	...	...	...	10	0	1	1	6
—Boston	NHL	9	0	2	2	4	-1	0	0	—	—	—	—	—
97-98—Providence	AHL	75	4	21	25	91	...	...	...	—	—	—	—	—
98-99—AIK	Sweden	19	1	3	4	24	...	...	...	—	—	—	—	—
—Djurgarden Stockholm	Sweden	29	3	4	7	52	...	...	...	—	—	—	—	—
99-00—AIK Solna	Sweden	49	1	3	4	87	...	...	...	—	—	—	—	—
00-01—Springfield	AHL	69	5	25	30	129	...	...	...	—	—	—	—	—
—New York Islanders	NHL	12	0	1	1	0	-2	0	0	—	—	—	—	—
NHL Totals (3 years)		25	0	4	4	10	-5	0	0	—	—	—	—	—

NABOKOV, EVGENI G SHARKS

PERSONAL: Born July 25, 1975, in Ust-Kamenogorsk, U.S.S.R. ... 6-0/200. ... Catches left. ... Name pronounced nuh-BAH-kahf.
TRANSACTIONS/CAREER NOTES: Selected by San Jose Sharks in ninth round (ninth Sharks pick, 219th overall) of NHL entry draft (June 29, 1994).
HONORS: Played in NHL All-Star Game (2001). ... Named to NHL All-Rookie team (2000-01). ... Won Calder Memorial Trophy (2000-01). ... Named NHL Rookie of the Year by THE SPORTING NEWS (2000-01).
MISCELLANEOUS: Holds San Jose Sharks all-time record for goals-against average (2.19). ... Stopped a penalty shot attempt (vs.Martin Straka, November 1, 2000). ... Allowed a penalty shot goal (vs. Marty Reasoner, February 26, 2001).

Season Team	League	Gms.	Min	W	L	T	GA	SO	Avg.	Gms.	Min.	W	L	GA	SO	Avg.
92-93—Torpedo Ust-Kam.	CIS	4	109	...	...	...	5	...	2.75	—	—	—	—	—	—	—
93-94—Torpedo Ust-Kam.	CIS	11	539	...	...	...	29	0	3.23	—	—	—	—	—	—	—
94-95—Dynamo Moscow	CIS	37	2075	...	...	...	70	...	2.02	—	—	—	—	—	—	—
95-96—Dynamo Moscow	CIS	37	1948	...	...	...	70	...	2.16	6	298	...	...	7	...	1.41
96-97—Dynamo Moscow	Russian	27	1588	...	...	...	56	2	2.12	4	255	...	...	12	0	2.82
97-98—Kentucky	AHL	33	1867	10	21	2	122	0	3.92	1	23	0	0	1	0	2.61
98-99—Kentucky	AHL	43	2429	26	14	1	106	5	2.62	11	599	6	5	30	2	3.01
99-00—Cleveland	IHL	20	1164	16	4	3	52	0	2.68	—	—	—	—	—	—	—
—San Jose	NHL	11	414	2	2	1	15	1	2.17	1	20	0	0	0	...	...
—Kentucky	AHL	2	120	1	1	0	3	1	1.50	—	—	—	—	—	—	—
00-01—San Jose	NHL	66	3700	32	21	7	135	6	2.19	4	218	1	3	10	1	2.75
NHL Totals (2 years)		77	4114	34	23	8	150	7	2.19	5	238	1	3	10	1	2.52

NAGY, LADISLAV C COYOTES

M
N

PERSONAL: Born June 1, 1979, in Presov, Yugoslavia. ... 5-11/183. ... Shoots left.
TRANSACTIONS/CAREER NOTES: Selected by St. Louis Blues in seventh round (sixth Blues pick, 177th overall) of NHL entry draft (June 21, 1997). ... Traded by Blues with C Michal Handzus, C Jeff Taffe and first-round pick in 2002 draft to Phoenix Coyotes for LW Keith Tkachuk (March 13, 2001).
HONORS: Won Michel Bergeron Trophy (1998-99).

Season Team	League	Gms.	G	A	Pts.	PIM	+/-	PP	SH	Gms.	G	A	Pts.	PIM
96-97—Dragon Presov	Slov. Div. II	11	6	5	11	...	...	...	...	—	—	—	—	—
97-98—HC Kosice	Slovakia	29	19	15	34	41	...	...	...	—	—	—	—	—
98-99—Halifax	QMJHL	63	*71	55	126	148	...	...	...	5	3	3	6	18
—Worcester	AHL	—	—	—	—	—		...	...	3	2	2	4	0
99-00—Worcester	AHL	69	23	28	51	67	...	...	...	2	1	0	1	0
—St. Louis	NHL	11	2	4	6	2	2	1	0	6	1	1	2	0
00-01—St. Louis	NHL	40	8	8	16	20	-2	2	0	—	—	—	—	—
—Worcester	AHL	20	6	14	20	36	...	...	...	—	—	—	—	—
—Phoenix	NHL	6	0	1	1	2	0	0	0	—	—	—	—	—
NHL Totals (2 years)		57	10	13	23	24	0	3	0	6	1	1	2	0

NASH, TYSON LW BLUES

PERSONAL: Born March 11, 1975, in Edmonton. ... 5-11/195. ... Shoots left. ... Full Name: Tyson Scott Nash.
TRANSACTIONS/CAREER NOTES: Selected by Vancouver Canucks in 10th round (eighth Canucks pick, 247th overall) of NHL entry draft (June 29, 1994). ... Signed as free agent by St. Louis Blues (July 24, 1998). ... Suffered concussion (December 5, 1999); missed three games. ... Injured shoulder (March 11, 2000); missed final 13 games of regular season. ... Injured shoulder (December 5, 2000); missed one game. ... Torn anterior cruciate ligament in knee (February 11, 2001); missed 16 games. ... Reinjured knee (March 22, 2001); missed remainder of season.

Season Team	League	REGULAR SEASON								PLAYOFFS				
		Gms.	G	A	Pts.	PIM	+/-	PP	SH	Gms.	G	A	Pts.	PIM
90-91—Kamloops	WHL	3	0	0	0	0	...	...	...	—	—	—	—	—
91-92—Kamloops	WHL	33	1	6	7	32	...	...	...	4	0	0	0	0
92-93—Kamloops	WHL	61	10	16	26	78	...	...	...	13	3	2	5	32
93-94—Kamloops	WHL	65	20	36	56	137	...	...	...	16	3	3	6	12
94-95—Kamloops	WHL	63	34	41	75	70	...	...	...	21	10	7	17	30
95-96—Syracuse	AHL	50	4	7	11	58	...	...	...	4	0	0	0	11
—Raleigh	ECHL	6	1	1	2	8	...	...	...	—	—	—	—	—
96-97—Syracuse	AHL	77	17	17	34	105	...	...	...	3	0	2	2	0
97-98—Syracuse	AHL	74	20	20	40	184	...	...	...	5	0	2	2	28
98-99—Worcester	AHL	55	14	22	36	143	...	...	...	4	4	1	5	27
—St. Louis	NHL	2	0	0	0	5	-1	0	0	1	0	0	0	2
99-00—St. Louis	NHL	66	4	9	13	150	6	0	1	6	1	0	1	24
00-01—St. Louis	NHL	57	8	7	15	110	8	0	1	—	—	—	—	—
NHL Totals (3 years)		125	12	16	28	265	13	0	2	7	1	0	1	26

NASLUND, MARKUS — LW — CANUCKS

PERSONAL: Born July 30, 1973, in Ornskoldsvik, Sweden. ... 6-0/186. ... Shoots left. ... Name pronounced NAZ-luhnd.
TRANSACTIONS/CAREER NOTES: Selected by Pittsburgh Penguins in first round (first Penguins pick, 16th overall) of NHL entry draft (June 22, 1991). ... Traded by Penguins to Vancouver Canucks for LW Alex Stojanov (March 20, 1996). ... Suffered from flu (November 26, 1996); missed one game. ... Fractured leg (March 16, 2001); missed remainder of season.
HONORS: Played in NHL All-Star Game (1999 and 2001).
MISCELLANEOUS: Captain of Vancouver Canucks (2000-01). ... Scored on a penalty shot (vs. Mike Dunham, December 19, 1998).
STATISTICAL PLATEAUS: Three-goal games: 1995-96 (1), 1995-96 (1), 1998-99 (1), 2000-01 (1). Total: 4.

Season Team	League	REGULAR SEASON								PLAYOFFS				
		Gms.	G	A	Pts.	PIM	+/-	PP	SH	Gms.	G	A	Pts.	PIM
89-90—MoDo Hockey Jrs.	Sweden Jr.	33	43	35	78	20	...	...	...	—	—	—	—	—
90-91—MoDo Ornskoldsvik	Sweden	32	10	9	19	14	...	...	...	—	—	—	—	—
91-92—MoDo Ornskoldsvik	Sweden	39	22	18	40	54	...	...	...	—	—	—	—	—
92-93—MoDo Ornskoldsvik	Sweden	39	22	17	39	67	...	...	...	3	3	2	5	...
93-94—Pittsburgh	NHL	71	4	7	11	27	-3	1	0	—	—	—	—	—
—Cleveland	IHL	5	1	6	7	4	...	...	...	—	—	—	—	—
94-95—Pittsburgh	NHL	14	2	2	4	2	0	0	0	—	—	—	—	—
—Cleveland	IHL	7	3	4	7	6	...	...	...	4	1	3	4	8
95-96—Pittsburgh	NHL	66	19	33	52	36	17	3	0	—	—	—	—	—
—Vancouver	NHL	10	3	0	3	6	3	1	0	6	1	2	3	8
96-97—Vancouver	NHL	78	21	20	41	30	-15	4	0	—	—	—	—	—
97-98—Vancouver	NHL	76	14	20	34	56	5	2	1	—	—	—	—	—
98-99—Vancouver	NHL	80	36	30	66	74	-13	15	2	—	—	—	—	—
99-00—Vancouver	NHL	82	27	38	65	64	-5	6	2	—	—	—	—	—
00-01—Vancouver	NHL	72	41	34	75	58	-2	18	1	—	—	—	—	—
NHL Totals (8 years)		549	167	184	351	353	-13	50	6	6	1	2	3	8

NASREDDINE, ALAIN — D — OILERS

PERSONAL: Born July 10, 1975, in Montreal. ... 6-1/203. ... Shoots left. ... Name pronounced AL-ai NAS-rih-DEEN.
TRANSACTIONS/CAREER NOTES: Selected by Florida Panthers in sixth round (eighth Panthers pick, 135th overall) of NHL entry draft (June 26, 1993). ... Traded by Panthers with conditional pick in 1999 draft to Chicago Blackhawks for D Ivan Droppa (December 8, 1996). ... Traded by Blackhawks with G Jeff Hackett, D Eric Weinrich and fourth-round pick (D Chris Dyment) in 1999 draft to Montreal Canadiens for G Jocelyn Thibault, D Dave Manson and D Brad Brown (November 16, 1998). ... Suspended two games and fined $1,000 by NHL for physically demeaning a linesman (December 11, 1998). ... Traded by Canadiens with D Igor Ulanov to Edmonton Oilers for D Christian LaFlamme and D Mathieu Descoteaux (March 9, 2000).
HONORS: Named to QMJHL All-Star second team (1994-95).

N

Season Team	League	REGULAR SEASON								PLAYOFFS				
		Gms.	G	A	Pts.	PIM	+/-	PP	SH	Gms.	G	A	Pts.	PIM
91-92—Drummondville	QMJHL	61	1	9	10	78	...	...	...	4	0	0	0	17
92-93—Drummondville	QMJHL	64	0	14	14	137	...	...	...	10	0	1	1	36
93-94—Chicoutimi	QMJHL	60	3	24	27	218	...	...	...	26	2	10	12	118
94-95—Chicoutimi	QMJHL	67	8	31	39	342	...	...	...	13	3	5	8	40
95-96—Carolina	AHL	63	0	5	5	245	...	...	...	—	—	—	—	—
96-97—Carolina	AHL	26	0	4	4	109	...	...	...	—	—	—	—	—
—Indianapolis	IHL	49	0	2	2	248	...	...	...	4	1	1	2	27
97-98—Indianapolis	IHL	75	1	12	13	258	...	...	...	5	0	2	2	12
98-99—Chicago	NHL	7	0	0	0	19	-2	0	0	—	—	—	—	—
—Portland	AHL	7	0	1	1	36	...	...	...	—	—	—	—	—
—Fredericton	AHL	38	0	10	10	108	...	...	...	15	0	3	3	39
—Montreal	NHL	8	0	0	0	33	1	0	0	—	—	—	—	—
99-00—Quebec	AHL	59	1	6	7	178	...	...	...	—	—	—	—	—
—Hamilton	AHL	11	0	0	0	12	...	...	...	10	1	1	2	14
00-01—Hamilton	AHL	74	4	14	18	164	...	...	...	—	—	—	—	—
NHL Totals (1 year)		15	0	0	0	52	-1	0	0					

NAUMENKO, GREGG   G   MIGHTY DUCKS

PERSONAL: Born March 30, 1977, in Chicago. ... 6-1/201. ... Catches left.
TRANSACTIONS/CAREER NOTES: Signed as non-drafted free agent by Mighty Ducks of Anaheim (March 31, 1999).
HONORS: Named to WCHA All-Star first team (1998-99).

			REGULAR SEASON								PLAYOFFS						
Season Team	League	Gms.	Min	W	L	T	GA	SO	Avg.	Gms.	Min.	W	L	GA	SO	Avg.
95-96—North Iowa	USHL	27	1649	15	12	0	103	1	3.75	4	239	1	3	15	0	3.77
96-97—North Iowa	USHL	25	1342	11	11	1	85	1	3.80	6	284	3	2	19	0	4.01
97-98—North Iowa	USHL	38	2171	23	11	3	80	—	2.21	5	299	4	1	11	0	2.21
98-99—Alaska-Anchorage	WCHA	29	1692	11	13	5	65	1	*2.30	—	—	—	—	—	—	—
99-00—Cincinnati	AHL	50	2877	17	25	†7	143	2	2.98	—	—	—	—	—	—	—
00-01—Cincinnati	AHL	39	2079	20	12	3	101	2	2.91	2	123	0	2	10	0	4.88
—Anaheim	NHL	2	70	0	1	0	7	0	6.00	—	—	—	—	—	—	—
NHL Totals (1 year)		2	70	0	1	0	7	0	6.00							

NAZAROV, ANDREI   LW   BRUINS

PERSONAL: Born April 22, 1974, in Chelyabinsk, U.S.S.R. ... 6-5/234. ... Shoots right. ... Name pronounced nuh-ZAH-rahf.
TRANSACTIONS/CAREER NOTES: Selected by San Jose Sharks in first round (second Sharks pick, 10th overall) of NHL entry draft (June 20, 1992). ... Suspended four games and fined $500 by NHL for head-butting (March 8, 1995). ... Suffered facial fracture (February 5, 1997); missed 14 games. ... Suspended 13 games by NHL for physical abuse of officials (March 25, 1997). ... Injured knee (October 13, 1997); missed seven games. ... Traded by Sharks with first-round pick (C Vincent Lecavalier) in 1998 draft and future considerations to Tampa Bay Lightning for D Bryan Marchment, D David Shaw and first-round pick (traded to Nashville) in 1998 draft (March 24, 1998). ... Injured finger (November 8, 1998); missed one game. ... Suspended seven games and fined $1,000 by NHL for cross-checking incident (November 19, 1998). ... Traded by Lightning to Calgary Flames for C Michael Nylander (January 19, 1999). ... Traded by Flames with second-round pick (traded back to Calgary) in 2001 draft to Mighty Ducks of Anaheim for D Jordan Leopold (September 26, 2000). ... Traded by Mighty Ducks with D Patrick Traverse to Boston Bruins for C Samuel Pahlsson (November 18, 2000).

			REGULAR SEASON							PLAYOFFS				
Season Team	League	Gms.	G	A	Pts.	PIM	+/-	PP	SH	Gms.	G	A	Pts.	PIM
90-91—Mechel Chelyabinsk	USSR	2	0	0	0	0	...	...	...	—	—	—	—	—
91-92—Dynamo Moscow	CIS	2	1	0	1	2	...	...	...	—	—	—	—	—
92-93—Dynamo Moscow	CIS	42	8	2	10	79	...	...	...	10	1	1	2	8
93-94—Kansas City	IHL	71	15	18	33	64	...	...	...	—	—	—	—	—
—San Jose	NHL	1	0	0	0	0	0	0	0	—	—	—	—	—
94-95—Kansas City	IHL	43	15	10	25	55	...	...	...	—	—	—	—	—
—San Jose	NHL	26	3	5	8	94	-1	0	0	6	0	0	0	9
95-96—San Jose	NHL	42	7	7	14	62	-15	2	0	—	—	—	—	—
—Kansas City	IHL	27	4	6	10	118	...	...	...	2	0	0	0	2
96-97—San Jose	NHL	60	12	15	27	222	-4	1	0	—	—	—	—	—
—Kentucky	AHL	3	1	2	3	4	...	...	...	—	—	—	—	—
97-98—San Jose	NHL	40	1	1	2	112	-4	0	0	—	—	—	—	—
—Tampa Bay	NHL	14	1	1	2	58	-9	0	0	—	—	—	—	—
98-99—Tampa Bay	NHL	26	2	0	2	43	-5	0	0	—	—	—	—	—
—Calgary	NHL	36	5	9	14	30	1	0	0	—	—	—	—	—
99-00—Calgary	NHL	76	10	22	32	78	3	1	0	—	—	—	—	—
00-01—Anaheim	NHL	16	0	1	1	29	-9	0	0	—	—	—	—	—
—Boston	NHL	63	1	4	5	200	-14	0	0	—	—	—	—	—
NHL Totals (8 years)		400	43	64	107	928	-57	4	0	6	0	0	0	9

NECKAR, STAN   D   LIGHTNING

N

PERSONAL: Born December 22, 1975, in Ceske-Budejovice, Czechoslovakia. ... 6-1/207. ... Shoots left. ... Full Name: Stanislav Neckar. ... Name pronounced NEHTS-kash.
TRANSACTIONS/CAREER NOTES: Selected by Ottawa Senators in second round (second Senators pick, 29th overall) of NHL entry draft (June 28, 1994). ... Suffered partially torn knee ligament (October 18, 1996); missed remainder of the season. ... Injured right knee (January 24, 1998); missed two games. ... Reinjured knee (April 3, 1998) and underwent surgery; missed final nine games of season. ... Fractured right foot (October 22, 1998); missed 16 games. ... Traded by Senators to New York Rangers for LW Bill Berg and second-round pick (traded to Anaheim) in 1999 draft (November 27, 1998). ... Traded by Rangers to Phoenix Coyotes for D Jason Doig and sixth-round pick (C Jay Dardis) in 1999 draft (March 23, 1999). ... Strained knee (October 18, 1999); missed 13 games. ... Injured ankle (November 21, 2000); missed 12 games. ... Traded by Coyotes with G Nikolai Khabibulin to Tampa Bay Lightning for D Paul Mara, RW Mike Johnson, RW Ruslan Zainullin and second-round pick (D Matthew Spiller) in 2001 (March 5, 2001).

			REGULAR SEASON							PLAYOFFS				
Season Team	League	Gms.	G	A	Pts.	PIM	+/-	PP	SH	Gms.	G	A	Pts.	PIM
91-92—Budejovice	Czech Dv.II	18	1	3	4	...	...	...	...	—	—	—	—	—
92-93—Motor-Ceske Bude.	Czech.	42	2	9	11	12	...	...	...	—	—	—	—	—
93-94—HC Ceske Budejovice	Czech Rep.	12	3	2	5	2	...	...	...	3	0	0	0	0
94-95—Detroit	IHL	15	2	2	4	15	...	...	...	—	—	—	—	—
—Ottawa	NHL	48	1	3	4	37	-20	0	0	—	—	—	—	—
95-96—Ottawa	NHL	82	3	9	12	54	-16	1	0	—	—	—	—	—
96-97—Ottawa	NHL	5	0	0	0	2	2	0	0	—	—	—	—	—
97-98—Ottawa	NHL	60	2	2	4	31	-14	0	0	9	0	0	0	2
98-99—Ottawa	NHL	3	0	2	2	0	-1	0	0	—	—	—	—	—
—New York Rangers	NHL	18	0	0	0	8	-1	0	0	—	—	—	—	—
—Phoenix	NHL	11	0	1	1	10	3	0	0	6	0	1	1	4
99-00—Phoenix	NHL	66	2	8	10	36	1	0	0	5	0	0	0	0
00-01—Phoenix	NHL	53	2	2	4	63	-2	0	0	—	—	—	—	—
—Tampa Bay	NHL	16	0	2	2	8	-1	0	0	—	—	—	—	—
NHL Totals (7 years)		362	10	29	39	249	-49	1	0	20	0	1	1	6

NEDOROST, ANDREJ C BLUE JACKETS

PERSONAL: Born April 30, 1980, in Trencin, Czechoslovakia. ... 6-1/198. ... Shoots left.

TRANSACTIONS/CAREER NOTES: Selected by Columbus Blue Jackets in ninth round (10th Blue Jackets pick, 286th overall) of NHL entry draft (June 24, 2000).

		REGULAR SEASON								PLAYOFFS				
Season Team	League	Gms.	G	A	Pts.	PIM	+/-	PP	SH	Gms.	G	A	Pts.	PIM
98-99—Essen	Germany	30	3	5	8	22	...	...	...	—	—	—	—	—
99-00—Essen	Germany	66	7	5	12	44	...	...	...	—	—	—	—	—
00-01—HC Keramika Plzen	Czech Rep.	33	10	8	18	22	...	...	...	—	—	—	—	—

NEDOROST, VACLAV C AVALANCHE

PERSONAL: Born March 16, 1982, in Budejovice, Czechoslovakia. ... 6-1/187. ... Shoots left.

TRANSACTIONS/CAREER NOTES: Selected by Colorado Avalanche in first round (first Avalanche pick, 14th overall) of NHL entry draft (June 24, 2000).

		REGULAR SEASON								PLAYOFFS				
Season Team	League	Gms.	G	A	Pts.	PIM	+/-	PP	SH	Gms.	G	A	Pts.	PIM
98-99—Budejovice	Czech. Jrs.	35	5	13	18	10	...	...	...	—	—	—	—	—
99-00—Budejovice	Czech Rep.	38	8	6	14	6	...	...	...	3	0	0	0	0
—Budejovice	Czech. Jrs.	7	2	5	7	6	...	...	...	—	—	—	—	—
00-01—HC Ceske Budejovice	Czech Rep.	36	3	12	15	22	...	...	...	—	—	—	—	—

NEDVED, PETR C RANGERS

PERSONAL: Born December 9, 1971, in Liberec, Czechoslovakia. ... 6-3/195. ... Shoots left. ... Name pronounced NEHD-VEHD.

TRANSACTIONS/CAREER NOTES: Selected by Vancouver Canucks in first round (first Canucks pick, second overall) of NHL entry draft (June 16, 1990). ... Signed to offer sheet by St. Louis Blues (March 4, 1994); C Craig Janney and second-round pick (C Dave Scatchard) in 1994 draft awarded to Canucks as compensation (March 14, 1994). ... Traded by Blues to New York Rangers for LW Esa Tikkanen and D Doug Lidster (July 24, 1994); trade arranged as compensation for Blues signing coach Mike Keenan. ... Strained abdomen (February 27, 1995); missed two games. ... Traded by Rangers with D Sergei Zubov to Pittsburgh Penguins for LW Luc Robitaille and D Ulf Samuelsson (August 31, 1995). ... Bruised thigh (November 18, 1995); missed two games. ... Bruised tailbone (December 19, 1996); missed two games. ... Sprained wrist (January 14, 1997); missed two games. ... Suffered charley horse (February 8, 1997); missed one game. ... Sprained wrist (March 20, 1997); missed three games. ... Missed all of 1997-98 season and first 18 games of 1998-99 season due to contract dispute; played for Las Vegas of IHL. ... Traded by Penguins with C Sean Pronger and D Chris Tamer to Rangers for RW Alexei Kovalev, C Harry York and future considerations (November 25, 1998). ... Strained muscle in ribcage (April 2, 1999); missed final seven games of season. ... Strained groin (December 2, 1999); missed four games. ... Bruised ribs (March 15, 2000); missed two games. ... Suspended three games by NHL for high-sticking incident (December 12, 2000).

HONORS: Won Can.HL Rookie of the Year Award (1989-90). ... Won Jim Piggott Memorial Trophy (1989-90).

MISCELLANEOUS: Member of silver-medal-winning Canadian Olympic team (1994).

STATISTICAL PLATEAUS: Three-goal games: 1998-99 (1), 1999-00 (3), 2000-01 (1). Total: 5. ... Four-goal games: 1995-96 (1). ... Total hat tricks: 6.

		REGULAR SEASON								PLAYOFFS				
Season Team	League	Gms.	G	A	Pts.	PIM	+/-	PP	SH	Gms.	G	A	Pts.	PIM
88-89—Litvinov Jrs.	Czech Rep.	20	32	19	51	12	...	...	...	—	—	—	—	—
89-90—Seattle	WHL	71	65	80	145	80	...	...	...	11	4	9	13	2
90-91—Vancouver	NHL	61	10	6	16	20	-21	1	0	6	0	1	1	0
91-92—Vancouver	NHL	77	15	22	37	36	-3	5	0	10	1	4	5	16
92-93—Vancouver	NHL	84	38	33	71	96	20	2	1	12	2	3	5	2
93-94—Canadian nat'l team	Int'l	17	19	12	31	16	...	...	...	—	—	—	—	—
—Can. Olympic team	Int'l	8	5	1	6	6	...	...	...	—	—	—	—	—
—St. Louis	NHL	19	6	14	20	8	2	2	0	4	0	1	1	4
94-95—New York Rangers	NHL	46	11	12	23	26	-1	1	0	10	3	2	5	6
95-96—Pittsburgh	NHL	80	45	54	99	68	37	8	1	18	10	10	20	16
96-97—Pittsburgh	NHL	74	33	38	71	66	-2	12	3	5	1	2	3	12
97-98—Sparta Praha	Czech Rep.	5	2	3	5	8	...	...	...	6	0	2	2	52
—Las Vegas	IHL	3	3	3	6	4	...	...	...	—	—	—	—	—
98-99—Las Vegas	IHL	13	8	10	18	32	...	...	...	—	—	—	—	—
—New York Rangers	NHL	56	20	27	47	50	-6	9	1	—	—	—	—	—
99-00—New York Rangers	NHL	76	24	44	68	40	2	6	2	—	—	—	—	—
00-01—New York Rangers	NHL	79	32	46	78	54	10	9	1	—	—	—	—	—
NHL Totals (10 years)		652	234	296	530	464	38	55	9	65	17	23	40	56

NEIL, CHRIS RW SENATORS

PERSONAL: Born June 18, 1979, in Markdale, Ont. ... 6-0/210. ... Shoots right. ... Full Name: Christopher Neil.

TRANSACTIONS/CAREER NOTES: Selected by Ottawa Senators in sixth round (seventh Senators pick, 161st overall) of NHL entry draft (June 27, 1998).

		REGULAR SEASON								PLAYOFFS				
Season Team	League	Gms.	G	A	Pts.	PIM	+/-	PP	SH	Gms.	G	A	Pts.	PIM
96-97—North Bay	OHL	65	13	16	29	150	...	...	...	—	—	—	—	—
97-98—North Bay	OHL	59	26	29	55	231	...	...	...	—	—	—	—	—
98-99—North Bay	OHL	66	26	46	72	215	...	...	...	4	1	0	1	15
99-00—Grand Rapids	IHL	51	9	10	19	*301	...	...	...	8	0	2	2	24
—Mobile	ECHL	4	0	2	2	39	...	...	...	—	—	—	—	—
00-01—Grand Rapids	IHL	78	15	21	36	354	...	...	...	10	2	2	4	22

NEMCHINOV, SERGEI   C   DEVILS

PERSONAL: Born January 14, 1964, in Moscow, U.S.S.R. ... 6-0/205. ... Shoots left. ... Name pronounced SAIR-gay nehm-CHEE-nahf.

TRANSACTIONS/CAREER NOTES: Selected by New York Rangers in 12th round (14th Rangers pick, 244th overall) of NHL entry draft (June 16, 1990). ... Sprained knee (November 4, 1991); missed seven games. ... Strained buttocks (April 4, 1993); missed three games. ... Suspended eight games and fined $500 by NHL for hitting another player (March 16, 1994). ... Bruised Achilles' tendon (January 30, 1995); missed one game. ... Suffered mild concussion (December 13, 1995); missed one game. ... Bruised elbow (April 7, 1996); missed two games. ... Traded by Rangers with RW Brian Noonan to Vancouver Canucks for LW Esa Tikkanen and RW Russ Courtnall (March 8, 1997). ... Strained rib muscle (February 28, 1997); missed 11 games. ... Injured foot (April 4, 1997); missed three games. ... Signed as free agent by New York Islanders (July 2, 1997). ... Suffered back spasms (November 28, 1997); missed two games. ... Suffered back spasms (December 17, 1997); missed one game. ... Injured back (April 6, 1998); missed one game. ... Suffered concussion (April 11, 1998); missed two games. ... Strained neck (April 16, 1998); missed final two games of season. ... Bruised hip (December 22, 1998); missed two games. ... Injured knee (February 7, 1999); missed one game. ... Reinjured knee (February 12, 1999); missed one game. ... Traded by Islanders to New Jersey Devils for fourth-round pick (traded to Los Angeles) in 1999 draft (March 22, 1999). ... Injured hip (April 8, 1999); missed two games ... Reinjured hip (April 14, 1999); missed final two games of regular season and three playoff games. ... Strained muscle in abdomen (December 26, 1999); missed 16 games. ... Suffered stiff neck (March 2, 2000); missed one game. ... Suffered pinched nerve in neck (March 19, 2000); missed one game. ... Bruised knee (March 2, 2001); missed six games. ... Reinjured knee (March 17, 2001); missed three games.

MISCELLANEOUS: Member of Stanley Cup championship team (1994 and 2000). ... Member of silver-medal-winning Russian Olympic team (1998). ... Failed to score on a penalty shot (vs. Olaf Kolzig, March 11, 2000).

STATISTICAL PLATEAUS: Three-goal games: 1992-93 (1).

			REGULAR SEASON							PLAYOFFS				
Season Team	League	Gms.	G	A	Pts.	PIM	+/-	PP	SH	Gms.	G	A	Pts.	PIM
81-82—Soviet Wings	USSR	15	1	0	1	0	...	...	...	—	—	—	—	—
82-83—CSKA Moscow	USSR	11	0	0	0	2	...	...	...	—	—	—	—	—
83-84—CSKA Moscow	USSR	20	6	5	11	4	...	...	...	—	—	—	—	—
84-85—CSKA Moscow	USSR	31	2	4	6	4	...	...	...	—	—	—	—	—
85-86—Soviet Wings	USSR	39	7	12	19	28	...	...	...	—	—	—	—	—
86-87—Soviet Wings	USSR	40	13	9	22	24	...	...	...	—	—	—	—	—
87-88—Soviet Wings	USSR	48	17	11	28	26	...	...	...	—	—	—	—	—
88-89—Soviet Wings	USSR	43	15	14	29	28	...	...	...	—	—	—	—	—
89-90—Soviet Wings	USSR	48	17	16	33	34	...	...	...	—	—	—	—	—
90-91—Soviet Wings	USSR	46	21	24	45	30	...	...	...	—	—	—	—	—
91-92—New York Rangers	NHL	73	30	28	58	15	19	2	0	13	1	4	5	8
92-93—New York Rangers	NHL	81	23	31	54	34	15	0	1	—	—	—	—	—
93-94—New York Rangers	NHL	76	22	27	49	36	13	4	0	23	2	5	7	6
94-95—New York Rangers	NHL	47	7	6	13	16	-6	0	0	10	4	5	9	2
95-96—New York Rangers	NHL	78	17	15	32	38	9	0	0	6	0	1	1	2
96-97—New York Rangers	NHL	63	6	13	19	12	5	1	0	—	—	—	—	—
—Vancouver	NHL	6	2	3	5	4	4	0	0	—	—	—	—	—
97-98—New York Islanders	NHL	74	10	19	29	24	3	2	1	—	—	—	—	—
—Russian Oly. team	Int'l	6	1	0	1	0	...	...	...	—	—	—	—	—
98-99—New York Islanders	NHL	67	8	8	16	22	-17	1	0	—	—	—	—	—
—New Jersey	NHL	10	4	0	4	6	4	1	0	4	0	0	0	0
99-00—New Jersey	NHL	53	10	16	26	18	1	0	1	21	3	2	5	2
00-01—New Jersey	NHL	65	8	22	30	16	11	1	0	25	1	3	4	4
NHL Totals (10 years)		693	147	188	335	241	61	12	3	102	11	20	31	24

NICKULAS, ERIC   RW

PERSONAL: Born March 25, 1975, in Cape Cod, Mass. ... 5-11/190. ... Shoots right.

TRANSACTIONS/CAREER NOTES: Selected by Boston Bruins in fourth round (third Bruins pick, 99th overall) of NHL entry draft (June 29, 1994). ... Suffered from charley horse (September 22, 2000); missed first three games of season. ... Bruised ribs (October 14, 2000); missed two games.

HONORS: Won Ken McKenzie Trophy (1997-98).

STATISTICAL PLATEAUS: Three-goal games: 1996-97 (1).

			REGULAR SEASON							PLAYOFFS				
Season Team	League	Gms.	G	A	Pts.	PIM	+/-	PP	SH	Gms.	G	A	Pts.	PIM
91-92—Barnstable H.S.	Mass. Jr. A	24	30	25	55	...	...	...	...	—	—	—	—	—
92-93—Tabor Academy	Mass. H.S.	28	25	25	50	...	...	...	...	—	—	—	—	—
93-94—Cushing Academy	Mass. H.S.	25	46	36	82	...	...	...	...	—	—	—	—	—
94-95—Univ. of New Hamp.	Hockey East	33	15	9	24	32	...	...	...	—	—	—	—	—
95-96—Univ. of New Hamp.	Hockey East	34	26	12	38	66	...	...	...	—	—	—	—	—
96-97—Univ. of New Hamp.	Hockey East	39	29	22	51	80	...	...	...	—	—	—	—	—
97-98—Orlando	IHL	76	22	9	31	77	...	...	...	6	0	0	0	10
98-99—Providence	AHL	75	31	27	58	83	...	...	...	18	8	12	20	33
—Boston	NHL	2	0	0	0	0	0	0	0	1	0	0	0	0
99-00—Providence	AHL	40	6	6	12	37	...	...	...	12	2	3	5	20
—Boston	NHL	20	5	6	11	12	-1	1	0	—	—	—	—	—
00-01—Boston	NHL	7	0	0	0	4	-2	0	0	—	—	—	—	—
—Providence	AHL	62	20	23	43	100	...	...	...	12	4	4	8	24
NHL Totals (3 years)		29	5	6	11	16	-3	1	0	1	0	0	0	2

NIEDERMAYER, ROB   C   FLAMES

PERSONAL: Born December 28, 1974, in Cassiar, B.C. ... 6-2/204. ... Shoots left. ... Brother of Scott Niedermayer, defenseman, New Jersey Devils. ... Name pronounced NEE-duhr-MIGH-uhr.

TRANSACTIONS/CAREER NOTES: Selected by Florida Panthers in first round (first Panthers pick, fifth overall) of NHL entry draft (June 26, 1993). ... Separated right shoulder (November 18, 1993); missed 17 games. ... Sprained knee ligament (November 22, 1996); missed 17 games. ... Strained groin (March 5, 1997); missed two games. ... Sprained wrist (March 20, 1997); missed three games. ... Suffered concussion (October 1, 1997); missed 10 games. ... Dislocated right thumb (November 18, 1997); missed 15 games. ... Underwent knee surgery during 1997-98 All-Star break; missed eight games. ... Suffered post-concussion syndrome (March 19, 1998); missed remainder of season. ... Suffered head injury (March 3, 2000); missed one game. ... Suffered concussion (February 21, 2001); missed 15 games. ... Traded by Panthers with second-round pick (G Andrei Medvedev) in 2001 draft to Calgary Flames for RW Valeri Bure and C Jason Wiemer (June 23, 2001).

HONORS: Won WHL Top Draft Prospect Award (1992-93). ... Named to WHL (East) All-Star first team (1992-93).

MISCELLANEOUS: Failed to score on a penalty shot (vs. Corey Hirsch, March 13, 1997).

Season Team	League	REGULAR SEASON								PLAYOFFS				
		Gms.	G	A	Pts.	PIM	+/-	PP	SH	Gms.	G	A	Pts.	PIM
90-91—Medicine Hat..............	WHL	71	24	26	50	8	...	...	...	12	3	7	10	2
91-92—Medicine Hat..............	WHL	71	32	46	78	77	...	...	...	4	2	3	5	2
92-93—Medicine Hat..............	WHL	52	43	34	77	67	...	...	...	—	—	—	—	—
93-94—Florida......................	NHL	65	9	17	26	51	-11	3	0	—	—	—	—	—
94-95—Medicine Hat..............	WHL	13	9	15	24	14	...	...	...	—	—	—	—	—
—Florida......................	NHL	48	4	6	10	36	-13	1	0	—	—	—	—	—
95-96—Florida......................	NHL	82	26	35	61	107	1	11	0	22	5	3	8	12
96-97—Florida......................	NHL	60	14	24	38	54	4	3	0	5	2	1	3	6
97-98—Florida......................	NHL	33	8	7	15	41	-9	5	0	—	—	—	—	—
98-99—Florida......................	NHL	82	18	33	51	50	-13	6	1	—	—	—	—	—
99-00—Florida......................	NHL	81	10	23	33	46	-5	1	0	4	1	0	1	6
00-01—Florida......................	NHL	67	12	20	32	50	-12	3	1	—	—	—	—	—
NHL Totals (8 years)..........		518	101	165	266	435	-58	33	2	31	8	4	12	24

NIEDERMAYER, SCOTT   D   DEVILS

PERSONAL: Born August 31, 1973, in Edmonton. ... 6-1/200. ... Shoots left. ... Brother of Rob Niedermayer, center, Calgary Flames. ... Name pronounced NEE-duhr-MIGH-uhr.

TRANSACTIONS/CAREER NOTES: Selected by New Jersey Devils in first round (first Devils pick, third overall) of NHL entry draft (June 22, 1991). ... Suffered sore back (December 9, 1992); missed four games. ... Injured knee (December 19, 1995); missed three games. ... Strained groin (February 12, 1997); missed one game. ... Suffered from the flu (February 4, 1998); missed one game. ... Missed first nine games of 1998-99 season due to contact dispute; played for Utah of IHL. ... Strained hip flexor (January 15, 2000); missed one game. ... Suffered illness (January 26, 2000); missed one game. ... Suspended final nine games of regular season and one playoff game by NHL for high-sticking incident (March 21, 2000). ... Missed first 19 games of 2000-01 season due to contract dispute. ... Injured knee (January 20, 2001); missed one game. ... Injured knee (February 8, 2001); missed five games.

HONORS: Won Can.HL Scholastic Player of the Year Award (1990-91). ... Named WHL Scholastic Player of the Year (1990-91). ... Named to WHL (West) All-Star first team (1990-91 and 1991-92). ... Won Stafford Smythe Memorial Trophy (1991-92). ... Named to Can.HL All-Star first team (1991-92). ... Named to Memorial Cup All-Star team (1991-92). ... Named to NHL All-Rookie team (1992-93). ... Played in NHL All-Star Game (1998 and 2001). ... Named to NHL All-Star second team (1997-98).

MISCELLANEOUS: Member of Stanley Cup championship team (1995 and 2000). ... Scored on a penalty shot (vs. Jose Theodore, November 11, 1998). ... Failed to score on a penalty shot (vs. Ken Wregget, February 7, 1996).

Season Team	League	REGULAR SEASON								PLAYOFFS				
		Gms.	G	A	Pts.	PIM	+/-	PP	SH	Gms.	G	A	Pts.	PIM
89-90—Kamloops	WHL	64	14	55	69	64	...	...	...	17	2	14	16	35
90-91—Kamloops	WHL	57	26	56	82	52	...	...	...	—	—	—	—	—
91-92—New Jersey	NHL	4	0	1	1	2	1	0	0	—	—	—	—	—
—Kamloops	WHL	35	7	32	39	61	...	...	...	17	9	14	23	28
92-93—New Jersey	NHL	80	11	29	40	47	8	5	0	5	0	3	3	2
93-94—New Jersey	NHL	81	10	36	46	42	34	5	0	20	2	2	4	8
94-95—New Jersey	NHL	48	4	15	19	18	19	4	0	20	4	7	11	10
95-96—New Jersey	NHL	79	8	25	33	46	5	6	0	—	—	—	—	—
96-97—New Jersey	NHL	81	5	30	35	64	-4	3	0	10	2	4	6	6
97-98—New Jersey	NHL	81	14	43	57	27	5	11	0	6	0	2	2	4
98-99—Utah	IHL	5	0	2	2	0	...	...	...	—	—	—	—	—
—New Jersey	NHL	72	11	35	46	26	16	1	1	7	1	3	4	18
99-00—New Jersey	NHL	71	7	31	38	48	19	1	0	22	5	2	7	10
00-01—New Jersey	NHL	57	6	29	35	22	14	1	0	21	0	6	6	14
NHL Totals (10 years)..........		654	76	274	350	342	117	37	1	111	14	29	43	72

NIELSEN, CHRIS   RW   BLUE JACKETS

PERSONAL: Born February 16, 1980, in Moshi, Tanzania. ... 6-1/190. ... Shoots right.

TRANSACTIONS/CAREER NOTES: Selected by New York Islanders in second round (second Islanders pick, 36th overall) of NHL entry draft (June 27, 1998). ... Traded by Islanders to Columbus Blue Jackets for fourth-(traded to Anaheim) and ninth-round (F Dmitri Altarev) picks in 2000 draft (May 11, 2000).

Season Team	League	REGULAR SEASON								PLAYOFFS				
		Gms.	G	A	Pts.	PIM	+/-	PP	SH	Gms.	G	A	Pts.	PIM
95-96—Calgary	WHL	6	0	0	0	0	...	...	...	—	—	—	—	—
—Southwest..................	MAHA	39	37	35	72	59	...	...	...	—	—	—	—	—
96-97—Calgary	WHL	62	11	19	30	39	...	...	...	18	2	4	6	10
97-98—Calgary	WHL	68	22	29	51	31	...	...	...	—	—	—	—	—
98-99—Calgary	WHL	70	22	24	46	45	...	...	...	21	11	5	16	28
99-00—Calgary	WHL	62	38	31	69	86	...	...	...	13	14	9	23	20
00-01—Syracuse....................	AHL	47	10	11	21	24	...	...	...	5	2	2	4	4
—Columbus	NHL	29	4	5	9	4	4	0	0	—	—	—	—	—
NHL Totals (1 year)..............		29	4	5	9	4	4	0	0					

N

NIELSEN, JEFF — RW

PERSONAL: Born September 20, 1971, in Grand Rapids, Minn. ... 6-0/200. ... Shoots left. ... Full Name: Jeffrey Michael Nielsen.
TRANSACTIONS/CAREER NOTES: Selected by New York Rangers in fourth round (fourth Rangers pick, 69th overall) of NHL entry draft (June 16, 1990). ... Signed as free agent by Mighty Ducks of Anaheim (August 11, 1997). ... Fractured left fibula (January 27, 1998); missed 15 games. ... Suffered injury (January 31, 2000); missed one game. ... Selected by Minnesota Wild in NHL expansion draft (June 23, 2000). ... Suffered concussion and bruised shoulder (November 8, 2000); missed four games. ... Injured shoulder (February 7, 2001); missed 18 games.
HONORS: Named to WCHA All-Star second team (1993-94).

		REGULAR SEASON								PLAYOFFS				
Season Team	League	Gms.	G	A	Pts.	PIM	+/-	PP	SH	Gms.	G	A	Pts.	PIM
87-88—Grand Rapids H.S.	Minn. H.S.	21	9	11	20	14	...	...	...	—	—	—	—	—
88-89—Grand Rapids H.S.	Minn. H.S.	25	13	17	30	26	...	...	...	—	—	—	—	—
89-90—Grand Rapids H.S.	Minn. H.S.	28	32	25	57	...	...	...	...	—	—	—	—	—
90-91—Univ. of Minnesota	WCHA	45	11	14	25	50	...	...	...	—	—	—	—	—
91-92—Univ. of Minnesota	WCHA	41	14	14	28	70	...	...	...	—	—	—	—	—
92-93—Univ. of Minnesota	WCHA	42	21	20	41	80	...	...	...	—	—	—	—	—
93-94—Univ. of Minnesota	WCHA	41	29	16	45	94	...	...	...	—	—	—	—	—
94-95—Binghamton	AHL	76	24	13	37	139	...	...	...	7	0	0	0	22
95-96—Binghamton	AHL	64	22	20	42	56	...	...	...	4	1	1	2	4
96-97—Binghamton	AHL	76	27	26	53	71	...	...	...	4	0	0	0	7
—New York Rangers	NHL	2	0	0	0	2	-1	0	0	—	—	—	—	—
97-98—Cincinnati	AHL	18	4	8	12	37	...	...	...	—	—	—	—	—
—Anaheim	NHL	32	4	5	9	16	-1	0	0	—	—	—	—	—
98-99—Anaheim	NHL	80	5	4	9	34	-12	0	0	4	0	0	0	2
99-00—Anaheim	NHL	79	8	10	18	14	4	1	0	—	—	—	—	—
00-01—Minnesota	NHL	59	3	8	11	4	-16	1	0	—	—	—	—	—
NHL Totals (5 years)		252	20	27	47	70	-26	2	0	4	0	0	0	2

NIEMI, ANTTI-JUSSI — D — MIGHTY DUCKS

PERSONAL: Born September 22, 1977, in Vantaa, Finland. ... 6-1/183. ... Shoots left.
TRANSACTIONS/CAREER NOTES: Selected by Ottawa Senators in fourth round (second Senators pick, 81st overall) of NHL entry draft (June 22, 1996). ... Traded by Senators with LW Ted Donato to Mighty Ducks of Anaheim for G Patrick Lalime (June 18, 1999).

		REGULAR SEASON								PLAYOFFS				
Season Team	League	Gms.	G	A	Pts.	PIM	+/-	PP	SH	Gms.	G	A	Pts.	PIM
93-94—Jokerit Helsinki	Finland Jr.	33	0	3	3	26	...	...	...	—	—	—	—	—
94-95—Jokerit Helsinki	Finland Jr.	24	4	8	12	74	...	...	...	—	—	—	—	—
95-96—Jokerit Helsinki	Finland Jr.	34	11	18	29	56	...	...	...	6	0	4	4	33
—Jarvenpaa	Finland Div. 2	4	0	2	2	8	...	...	...	—	—	—	—	—
—Jokerit Helsinki	Finland	6	0	2	2	6	...	...	...	3	0	1	1	0
96-97—Jokerit Helsinki	Finland	44	2	9	11	38	...	...	...	9	0	2	2	2
97-98—Jokerit Helsinki	Finland	46	2	6	8	24	...	...	...	8	0	1	1	...
98-99—Jokerit Helsinki	Finland	53	3	7	10	107	...	...	...	3	0	0	0	2
99-00—Jokerit Helsinki	Finland	53	8	8	16	79	...	...	...	11	0	3	3	6
00-01—Cincinnati	AHL	36	3	8	11	26	...	...	...	—	—	—	—	—
—Anaheim	NHL	28	1	1	2	22	-6	0	0	—	—	—	—	—
NHL Totals (1 year)		28	1	1	2	22	-6	0	0					

NIEMINEN, VILLE — LW — AVALANCHE

N

PERSONAL: Born April 6, 1977, in Tampere, Finland. ... 5-11/205. ... Shoots left.
TRANSACTIONS/CAREER NOTES: Selected by Colorado Avalanche in third round (fourth Avalanche pick, 78th overall) of NHL entry draft (June 21, 1997).
MISCELLANEOUS: Member of Stanley Cup championship team (2001).

		REGULAR SEASON								PLAYOFFS				
Season Team	League	Gms.	G	A	Pts.	PIM	+/-	PP	SH	Gms.	G	A	Pts.	PIM
94-95—Tappara Tampere	Finland Jrs.	16	11	21	32	47	...	...	...	—	—	—	—	—
—Tappara Tampere	Finland	16	0	0	0	0	...	...	...	—	—	—	—	—
95-96—Tappara Tampere	Finland Jrs.	20	20	23	43	63	...	...	...	—	—	—	—	—
—Tappara Tampere	Finland	4	0	1	1	8	...	...	...	—	—	—	—	—
—KooVee Tampere	Finland	7	2	1	3	4	...	...	...	—	—	—	—	—
96-97—Tappara Tampere	Finland	49	10	13	23	120	...	...	...	3	1	0	1	8
97-98—Hershey	AHL	74	14	22	36	85	...	...	...	—	—	—	—	—
98-99—Hershey	AHL	67	24	19	43	127	...	...	...	3	0	1	1	0
99-00—Hershey	AHL	74	21	30	51	54	...	...	...	9	2	4	6	6
—Colorado	NHL	1	0	0	0	0	0	0	0	—	—	—	—	—
00-01—Hershey	AHL	28	10	11	21	48	...	...	...	—	—	—	—	—
—Colorado	NHL	50	14	8	22	38	8	2	0	23	4	6	10	20
NHL Totals (2 years)		51	14	8	22	38	8	2	0	23	4	6	10	20

NIEUWENDYK, JOE — C — STARS

PERSONAL: Born September 10, 1966, in Oshawa, Ont. ... 6-1/205. ... Shoots left. ... Full Name: Joe T. Nieuwendyk. ... Nephew of Ed Kea, defenseman with Atlanta Flames (1973-74 through 1978-79) and St. Louis Blues (1979-80 through 1982-83); and cousin of Jeff Beukeboom, defenseman with Edmonton Oilers (1985-86 through 1991-92) and New York Rangers (1991-92 through 1998-99). ... Name pronounced NOO-ihn-dighk.

TRANSACTIONS/CAREER NOTES: Selected by Calgary Flames in second round (second Flames pick, 27th overall) of NHL entry draft (June 15, 1985). ... Suffered concussion (November 1987). ... Bruised ribs (May 25, 1989). ... Tore left knee ligament (April 17, 1990). ... Underwent arthroscopic knee surgery (September 28, 1991); missed 12 games. ... Suffered from the flu (November 19, 1992); missed one game. ... Strained right knee (March 26, 1993); missed four games. ... Suffered charley horse (November 13, 1993); missed three games. ... Strained right knee ligaments (February 24, 1994); missed 17 games. ... Strained back (April 29, 1995); missed two games. ... Traded by Flames to Dallas Stars for C Corey Millen and rights to C/RW Jarome Iginla (December 19, 1995). ... Bruised chest (October 5, 1996); missed 12 games. ... Sprained knee (December 18, 1997); missed eight games. ... Reinjured knee (January 9, 1998); missed one game. ... Suffered inflammed knee (January 10, 1999); missed five games. ... Sprained ankle (February 23, 1999); missed one game. ... Suffered back spasms (March 16, 1999); missed one game. ... Injured knee (March 31, 1999); missed one game. ... Suffered back spasms (October 20, 1999); missed three games. ... Bruised chest (December 17, 1999); missed 10 games. ... Separated shoulder (January 19, 2000); missed 21 games. ... Suffered from the flu (January 4, 2001); missed two games. ... Strained groin (February 28, 2001); missed 11 games.

HONORS: Won Ivy League Rookie of the Year Trophy (1984-85). ... Named to NCAA All-America (East) first team (1985-86 and 1986-87). ... Named to ECAC All-Star first team (1985-86 and 1986-87). ... Named ECAC Player of the Year (1986-87). ... Named NHL Rookie of the Year by THE SPORTING NEWS (1987-88). ... Won Calder Memorial Trophy (1987-88). ... Won Dodge Ram Tough Award (1987-88). ... Named to NHL All-Rookie team (1987-88). ... Played in NHL All-Star Game (1988-1990 and 1994). ... Won King Clancy Trophy (1994-95). ... Won Conn Smythe Trophy (1988-99).

RECORDS: Shares NHL single-game record for most goals in one period—4 (January 11, 1989). ... Shares NHL single-season playoff record for most game-winning goals—6 (1999).

STATISTICAL PLATEAUS: Three-goal games: 1987-88 (2), 1988-89 (1), 1989-90 (1), 1992-93 (1), 1993-94 (1), 1994-95 (1), 1997-98 (1), 2000-01 (1). Total: 9. ... Four-goal games: 1987-88 (2), 1997-98 (1). Total: 3. ... Five-goal games: 1988-89 (1). ... Total hat tricks: 13.

MISCELLANEOUS: Member of Stanley Cup championship team (1989 and 1999). ... Captain of Calgary Flames (1991-92 through 1994-95). ... Scored on a penalty shot (vs. Steve Weeks, December 16, 1988; vs. Chris Osgood, February 18, 2001). ... Failed to score on a penalty shot (vs. Jeff Reese, December 12, 1988; vs. Ken Wregget, January 23, 1993).

STATISTICAL NOTES: Third player in NHL history to score 50 goals in each of his first two seasons. ... Led NHL in game-winning goals with 11 (1988-89).

		REGULAR SEASON								PLAYOFFS				
Season Team	**League**	**Gms.**	**G**	**A**	**Pts.**	**PIM**	**+/-**	**PP**	**SH**	**Gms.**	**G**	**A**	**Pts.**	**PIM**
83-84—Pickering Jr. B	MTHL	38	30	28	58	35	...	...	...	—	—	—	—	—
84-85—Cornell University	ECAC	23	18	21	39	20	...	...	...	—	—	—	—	—
85-86—Cornell University	ECAC	21	21	21	42	45	...	...	...	—	—	—	—	—
86-87—Cornell University	ECAC	23	26	26	52	26	...	...	...	—	—	—	—	—
—Canadian nat'l team	Int'l	5	2	0	2	0	...	...	...	—	—	—	—	—
—Calgary	NHL	9	5	1	6	0	0	2	0	6	2	2	4	0
87-88—Calgary	NHL	75	51	41	92	23	20	*31	3	8	3	4	7	2
88-89—Calgary	NHL	77	51	31	82	40	26	19	3	22	10	4	14	10
89-90—Calgary	NHL	79	45	50	95	40	32	18	0	6	4	6	10	4
90-91—Calgary	NHL	79	45	40	85	36	19	22	4	7	4	1	5	10
91-92—Calgary	NHL	69	22	34	56	55	-1	7	0	—	—	—	—	—
92-93—Calgary	NHL	79	38	37	75	52	9	14	0	6	3	6	9	10
93-94—Calgary	NHL	64	36	39	75	51	19	14	1	6	2	2	4	0
94-95—Calgary	NHL	46	21	29	50	33	11	3	0	5	4	3	7	0
95-96—Dallas....................	NHL	52	14	18	32	41	-17	8	0	—	—	—	—	—
96-97—Dallas....................	NHL	66	30	21	51	32	-5	8	0	7	2	2	4	6
97-98—Dallas....................	NHL	73	39	30	69	30	16	14	0	1	1	0	1	0
—Can. Olympic team	Int'l	6	2	3	5	2	...	...	...	—	—	—	—	—
98-99—Dallas....................	NHL	67	28	27	55	34	11	8	0	23	*11	10	21	19
99-00—Dallas....................	NHL	48	15	19	34	26	-1	7	0	23	7	3	10	18
00-01—Dallas....................	NHL	69	29	23	52	30	5	12	0	7	4	0	4	4
NHL Totals (15 years).........		952	469	440	909	523	144	187	11	127	57	43	100	83

NIINIMAA, JANNE   D   OILERS

PERSONAL: Born May 22, 1975, in Raahe, Finland. ... 6-2/220. ... Shoots left. ... Name pronounced YAH-nee NEE-nuh-muh.

TRANSACTIONS/CAREER NOTES: Selected by Philadelphia Flyers in second round (first Flyers pick, 36th overall) of NHL entry draft (June 26, 1993). ... Traded by Flyers to Edmonton Oilers for D Dan McGillis and second-round pick (D Jason Beckett) in 1998 draft (March 24, 1998). ... Suffered back spasms (November 4, 1998); missed one game. ... Suffered back spasms (November 24, 1999); missed one game.

HONORS: Named to NHL All-Rookie team (1996-97). ... Played in NHL All-Star Game (2001).

MISCELLANEOUS: Member of bronze-medal-winning Finnish Olympic team (1998).

		REGULAR SEASON								PLAYOFFS				
Season Team	**League**	**Gms.**	**G**	**A**	**Pts.**	**PIM**	**+/-**	**PP**	**SH**	**Gms.**	**G**	**A**	**Pts.**	**PIM**
91-92—Karpat Oulu................	Finland Div. 2	41	2	11	13	49	...	...	...	—	—	—	—	—
92-93—Karpat Oulu................	Finland Div. 2	29	2	3	5	14	...	...	...	—	—	—	—	—
—Karpat Jr.	Finland	10	3	9	12	16	...	...	...	—	—	—	—	—
93-94—Jokerit Helsinki	Finland	45	3	8	11	24	...	...	...	12	1	1	2	4
94-95—Jokerit Helsinki	Finland	42	7	10	17	36	...	...	...	10	1	4	5	35
95-96—Jokerit Helsinki	Finland	49	5	15	20	79	...	...	...	11	0	2	2	12
96-97—Philadelphia	NHL	77	4	40	44	58	12	1	0	19	1	12	13	16
97-98—Philadelphia	NHL	66	3	31	34	56	6	2	0	—	—	—	—	—
—Fin. Olympic team......	Int'l	6	0	3	3	8	...	...	...	—	—	—	—	—
—Edmonton	NHL	11	1	8	9	6	7	1	0	11	1	1	2	12
98-99—Edmonton	NHL	81	4	24	28	88	7	2	0	4	0	0	0	2
99-00—Edmonton	NHL	81	8	25	33	89	14	2	2	5	0	2	2	2
00-01—Edmonton	NHL	82	12	34	46	90	6	8	0	6	0	2	2	6
NHL Totals (5 years)............		398	32	162	194	387	52	16	2	45	2	17	19	38

NIKOLISHIN, ANDREI   C   CAPITALS

PERSONAL: Born March 25, 1973, in Vorkuta, U.S.S.R. ... 6-0/214. ... Shoots left. ... Name pronounced nih-koh-LEE-shihn.
TRANSACTIONS/CAREER NOTES: Selected by Hartford Whalers in second round (second Whalers pick, 47th overall) of NHL entry draft (June 20, 1992). ... Played in Europe during 1994-95 NHL lockout. ... Sprained ankle (October 21, 1995); missed one game. ... Injured back (November 15, 1995); missed five games. ... Strained back (December 2, 1995); missed 15 games. ... Traded by Whalers to Washington Capitals for D Curtis Leschyshyn (November 9, 1996). ... Suffered bulging disc in back (February 2, 1997); missed eight games. ... Injured knee prior to 1997-98 season; missed first 42 games. ... Missed first nine games of 1998-99 season due to contract dispute; played in Russia. ... Strained abdominal muscle (March 28, 2000); missed four games.
HONORS: Named to CIS All-Star team (1993-94). ... Named CIS Player of the Year (1993-94).
MISCELLANEOUS: Member of gold-medal-winning Russian Olympic team (1994).

			REGULAR SEASON								PLAYOFFS				
Season Team	League	Gms.	G	A	Pts.	PIM	+/-	PP	SH		Gms.	G	A	Pts.	PIM
90-91—Dynamo Moscow	USSR	2	0	0	0	0	...	...	...		—	—	—	—	—
91-92—Dynamo Moscow	CIS	18	1	0	1	4	...	...	...		—	—	—	—	—
92-93—Dynamo Moscow	CIS	42	5	7	12	30	...	...	...		10	2	1	3	8
93-94—Dynamo Moscow	CIS	41	8	12	20	30	...	...	...		9	1	3	4	4
—Russian Oly. team	Int'l	8	2	5	7	6	...	...	...		—	—	—	—	—
94-95—Dynamo Moscow	CIS	12	7	2	9	6	...	...	...		—	—	—	—	—
—Hartford	NHL	39	8	10	18	10	7	1	1		—	—	—	—	—
95-96—Hartford	NHL	61	14	37	51	34	-2	4	1		—	—	—	—	—
96-97—Hartford	NHL	12	2	5	7	2	-2	0	0		—	—	—	—	—
—Washington	NHL	59	7	14	21	30	5	1	0		—	—	—	—	—
97-98—Portland	AHL	2	0	0	0	2	...	...	...		—	—	—	—	—
—Washington	NHL	38	6	10	16	14	1	1	0		21	1	13	14	12
98-99—Dynamo Moscow	Russian	4	0	0	0	0	...	...	...		—	—	—	—	—
—Washington	NHL	73	8	27	35	28	0	0	1		—	—	—	—	—
99-00—Washington	NHL	76	11	14	25	28	6	0	2		5	0	2	2	4
00-01—Washington	NHL	81	13	25	38	34	9	4	0		6	0	0	0	2
NHL Totals (7 years)		439	69	142	211	180	24	11	5		32	1	15	16	18

NILSON, MARCUS   C   PANTHERS

PERSONAL: Born March 1, 1978, in Balsta, Sweden. ... 6-2/193. ... Shoots right.
TRANSACTIONS/CAREER NOTES: Selected by Florida Panthers in first round (first Panthers pick, 20th overall) of NHL entry draft (June 22, 1996).

			REGULAR SEASON								PLAYOFFS				
Season Team	League	Gms.	G	A	Pts.	PIM	+/-	PP	SH		Gms.	G	A	Pts.	PIM
94-95—Djurgarden	Sweden Jrs.	24	7	8	15	22	...	...	...		—	—	—	—	—
95-96—Djurgarden	Sweden Jrs.	25	19	17	36	46	...	...	...		2	1	1	2	12
—Djurgarden Stockholm	Sweden	12	0	0	0	0	...	...	...		1	0	0	0	0
96-97—Djurgarden Stockholm	Sweden	37	0	3	3	33	...	...	...		4	0	0	0	0
97-98—Djurgarden Stockholm	Sweden	41	4	7	11	18	...	...	...		15	2	1	3	16
98-99—New Haven	AHL	69	8	25	33	10	...	...	...		—	—	—	—	—
—Florida	NHL	8	1	1	2	5	2	0	0		—	—	—	—	—
99-00—Louisville	AHL	64	9	23	32	52	...	...	...		4	0	0	0	2
—Florida	NHL	9	0	2	2	2	2	0	0		—	—	—	—	—
00-01—Florida	NHL	78	12	24	36	74	-3	0	0		—	—	—	—	—
NHL Totals (3 years)		95	13	27	40	81	1	0	0						

NOLAN, OWEN   RW   SHARKS

PERSONAL: Born February 12, 1972, in Belfast, Northern Ireland. ... 6-1/210. ... Shoots right.
TRANSACTIONS/CAREER NOTES: Selected by Quebec Nordiques in first round (first Nordiques pick, first overall) of NHL entry draft (June 16, 1990). ... Suffered concussion, sore knee and sore back (October 1990). ... Suspended four off-days by NHL for cross-checking incident (December 7, 1992). ... Bruised hand (March 2, 1993); missed three games. ... Bruised shoulder (March 15, 1993); eight games. ... Injured right shoulder (October 19, 1993); missed 11 games. ... Dislocated left shoulder (November 12, 1993); missed remainder of season. ... Bruised shoulder (April 16, 1995); missed four games. ... Nordiques franchise moved to Colorado and renamed Avalanche for 1995-96 season (June 21, 1995). ... Traded by Avalanche to San Jose Sharks for D Sandis Ozolinsh (October 26, 1995). ... Suffered from the flu (March 5, 1996); missed two games. ... Suffered from an illness (November 27, 1996); missed one game. ... Bruised shoulder (January 9, 1997); missed two games. ... Suffered sore ankle (March 20, 1997); missed four games. ... Strained groin (April 7, 1997); missed three games. ... Strained shoulder (March 26, 1998); missed six games. ... Missed first two games of 1998-99 season due to contract dispute. ... Injured back (January 26, 1999); missed one game. ... Reinjured back (February 4, 1999); missed one game. ... Injured shoulder (March 29, 2000); missed four games. ... Underwent hernia surgery (August 19, 2000); missed first four games of season. ... Strained muscle in abdomen (October 24, 2000); missed 10 games. ... Suspended 11 games by NHL for illegal check (February 2, 2001).
HONORS: Won Emms Family Award (1988-89). ... Won Jim Mahon Memorial Trophy (1989-90). ... Named to OHL All-Star first team (1989-90). ... Played in NHL All-Star Game (1992, 1996, 1997 and 2000).
MISCELLANEOUS: Captain of San Jose Sharks (1998-99 through 2000-01). ... Failed to score on a penalty shot (vs. Garth Snow, December 26, 1998). ... Holds San Jose Sharks all-time record for most goals (161).
STATISTICAL NOTES: Led NHL in game-winning goals with eight (1994-95).
STATISTICAL PLATEAUS: Three-goal games: 1991-92 (2), 1992-93 (2), 1994-95 (3), 1996-97 (1), 1999-00 (1). Total: 9. ... Four-goal games: 1995-96 (1). ... Total hat tricks: 10.

Season Team	League	REGULAR SEASON								PLAYOFFS				
		Gms.	G	A	Pts.	PIM	+/-	PP	SH	Gms.	G	A	Pts.	PIM
88-89—Cornwall	OHL	62	34	25	59	213	...	...	...	18	5	11	16	41
89-90—Cornwall	OHL	58	51	59	110	240	...	...	...	6	7	5	12	26
90-91—Quebec	NHL	59	3	10	13	109	-19	0	0	—	—	—	—	—
—Halifax	AHL	6	4	4	8	11	...	...	...	—	—	—	—	—
91-92—Quebec	NHL	75	42	31	73	183	-9	17	0	—	—	—	—	—
92-93—Quebec	NHL	73	36	41	77	185	-1	15	0	5	1	0	1	2
93-94—Quebec	NHL	6	2	2	4	8	2	0	0	—	—	—	—	—
94-95—Quebec	NHL	46	30	19	49	46	21	13	2	6	2	3	5	6
95-96—Colorado	NHL	9	4	4	8	9	-3	4	0	—	—	—	—	—
—San Jose	NHL	72	29	32	61	137	-30	12	1	—	—	—	—	—
96-97—San Jose	NHL	72	31	32	63	155	-19	10	0	—	—	—	—	—
97-98—San Jose	NHL	75	14	27	41	144	-2	3	1	6	2	2	4	26
98-99—San Jose	NHL	78	19	26	45	129	16	6	2	6	1	1	2	6
99-00—San Jose	NHL	78	44	40	84	110	-1	*18	4	10	8	2	10	6
00-01—San Jose	NHL	57	24	25	49	75	0	10	1	6	1	1	2	8
NHL Totals (11 years)		700	278	289	567	1290	-45	108	11	39	15	9	24	54

NORDQVIST, JONAS C BLACKHAWKS

PERSONAL: Born April 26, 1982, in Leksand, Sweden. ... 6-2/191. ... Shoots left.
TRANSACTIONS/CAREER NOTES: Selected by Chicago Blackhawks in second round (third Blackhawks pick, 49th overall) of NHL entry draft (June 24, 2000).

Season Team	League	REGULAR SEASON								PLAYOFFS				
		Gms.	G	A	Pts.	PIM	+/-	PP	SH	Gms.	G	A	Pts.	PIM
98-99—Leksand	Sweden Jr.	32	14	25	39	...	...	...	...	—	—	—	—	—
99-00—Leksand	Sweden Jr.	34	15	24	39	32	...	...	...	—	—	—	—	—
—Leksand	Sweden	3	0	0	0	0	...	...	...	—	—	—	—	—
00-01—Leksand	Sweden	35	2	2	4	4	...	...	...	—	—	—	—	—

NORONEN, MIKA G SABRES

PERSONAL: Born June 17, 1979, in Tampere, Finland. ... 6-1/191. ... Catches left.
TRANSACTIONS/CAREER NOTES: Selected by Buffalo Sabres in first round (first Sabres pick, 21st overall) of NHL entry draft (June 21, 1997).
HONORS: Won Dudley (Red) Garrett Memorial Trophy (1999-2000). ... Named to AHL All-Star second team (1999-2000 and 2000-01). ... Won Harry (Hap) Holmes Memorial Trophy (2000-01).

Season Team	League	REGULAR SEASON							PLAYOFFS					
		Gms.	Min	W	L	T	GA	SO	Avg.	Gms.	Min.	W	L	GA	SO	Avg.
95-96—Tappara Tampere	Finland Jrs.	16	962	...	...	...	37	2	2.31	—	—	—	—	—	—	—
96-97—Tappara Tampere	Finland	5	215	...	...	...	17	0	4.74	—	—	—	—	—	—	—
97-98—Tappara Tampere	Finland	47	1703	14	12	3	83	1	2.92	4	196	1	2	12	0	3.67
98-99—Tappara Tampere	Finland	43	2494	18	20	5	*135	2	3.25	—	—	—	—	—	—	—
99-00—Rochester	AHL	54	3089	*33	13	4	112	†6	*2.18	21	1235	13	*8	37	*6	*1.80
00-01—Buffalo	NHL	2	108	2	0	0	5	0	2.78	—	—	—	—	—	—	—
—Rochester	AHL	47	2753	26	15	5	100	4	2.18	4	250	1	3	11	0	2.64
NHL Totals (1 year)		2	108	2	0	0	5	0	2.78							

NORSTROM, MATTIAS D KINGS

N

PERSONAL: Born January 2, 1972, in Stockholm, Sweden. ... 6-2/201. ... Shoots left. ... Name pronounced muh-TEE-uhz NOHR-struhm.
TRANSACTIONS/CAREER NOTES: Selected by New York Rangers in second round (second Rangers pick, 48th overall) of NHL entry draft (June 20, 1992). ... Suffered from the flu (April 28, 1995); missed two games. ... Separated shoulder (December 30, 1995); missed six games. ... Traded by Rangers with C Ray Ferraro, C Ian Laperriere, C Nathan Lafayette and fourth-round pick (D Sean Blanchard) in 1997 draft to Los Angeles Kings for RW Shane Churla, LW Jari Kurri and D Marty McSorley (March 14, 1996). ... Bruised left wrist (November 7, 1996); missed one game. ... Suspended one game by NHL for illegal check (January 12, 1998). ... Bruised ribs (April 11, 1999); missed four games.
HONORS: Played in NHL All-Star Game (1999).

Season Team	League	REGULAR SEASON								PLAYOFFS				
		Gms.	G	A	Pts.	PIM	+/-	PP	SH	Gms.	G	A	Pts.	PIM
91-92—AIK Solna	Sweden	39	4	4	8	28	...	...	...	—	—	—	—	—
92-93—AIK Solna	Sweden	22	0	1	1	16	...	...	...	—	—	—	—	—
93-94—New York Rangers	NHL	9	0	2	2	6	0	0	0	—	—	—	—	—
—Binghamton	AHL	55	1	9	10	70	...	...	...	—	—	—	—	—
94-95—Binghamton	AHL	63	9	10	19	91	...	...	...	—	—	—	—	—
—New York Rangers	NHL	9	0	3	3	2	2	0	0	3	0	0	0	0
95-96—New York Rangers	NHL	25	2	1	3	22	5	0	0	—	—	—	—	—
—Los Angeles	NHL	11	0	1	1	18	-8	0	0	—	—	—	—	—
96-97—Los Angeles	NHL	80	1	21	22	84	-4	0	0	—	—	—	—	—
97-98—Los Angeles	NHL	73	1	12	13	90	14	0	0	4	0	0	0	2
—Swedish Oly. team	Int'l	4	0	1	1	2	...	...	...	—	—	—	—	—
98-99—Los Angeles	NHL	78	2	5	7	36	-10	0	1	—	—	—	—	—
99-00—Los Angeles	NHL	82	1	13	14	66	22	0	0	4	0	0	0	6
00-01—Los Angeles	NHL	82	0	18	18	60	10	0	0	13	0	2	2	18
NHL Totals (8 years)		449	7	76	83	384	31	0	1	24	0	2	2	26

PERSONAL: Born November 25, 1965, in Acton, Mass. ... 6-2/195. ... Shoots left. ... Full Name: Jeffrey Zaccari Norton. ... Brother of Brad Norton, defenseman, Edmonton Oilers organization (1993-94 through 2000-01).

TRANSACTIONS/CAREER NOTES: Selected by New York Islanders in third round (third Islanders pick, 62nd overall) of NHL entry draft (June 9, 1984). ... Bruised ribs (November 16, 1988). ... Injured groin (February 1990). ... Strained groin and abdominal muscles (March 2, 1990); missed games. ... Suffered concussion (April 9, 1990). ... Suspended eight games by NHL for intentionally injuring another player in preseason game (September 30, 1990). ... Dislocated right shoulder (November 3, 1990); missed four games. ... Reinjured shoulder (December 27, 1990); missed five games. ... Reinjured shoulder and underwent surgery (February 23, 1991); missed remainder of season. ... Suffered concussion (October 26, 1991); missed one game. ... Tore ligaments in left wrist (January 3, 1992); missed remainder of season. ... Underwent surgery to left wrist (January 8, 1992). ... Suffered hip flexor (October 23, 1992); missed five games. ... Suffered sore shoulder (December 31, 1992); missed one game. ... Pulled groin (February 25, 1993); missed two games. ... Traded by Islanders to San Jose Sharks for third-round pick (D Jason Strudwick) in 1994 draft (June 20, 1993). ... Sprained ankle (December 11, 1993); missed nine games. ... Reinjured ankle (January 4, 1994); missed five games. ... Sprained ankle (February 19, 1994); missed five games. ... Suffered from the flu (January 28, 1995); missed one game. ... Traded by Sharks with third-round pick (traded to Colorado) in 1997 draft and future considerations to St. Louis Blues for C Craig Janney (March 6, 1995). ... Injured hand (March 7, 1995); missed one game. ... Traded by Blues with D Donald Dufresne to Edmonton Oilers for D Igor Kravchuck and D Ken Sutton (January 4, 1996). ... Fractured thumb (February 9, 1996); missed two games. ... Suffered back spasms (March 17, 1996); missed one game. ... Sprained left knee (March 24, 1996); missed nine games. ... Sprained ankle (October 15, 1996); missed six games. ... Injured right ankle (November 7, 1996); missed one game. ... Strained groin (January 7, 1997); missed one game. ... Traded by Oilers to Tampa Bay Lightning for D Drew Bannister and sixth-round pick (C Peter Sarno) in 1997 (March 18, 1997). ... Strained groin (October 5, 1997); missed three games. ... Traded by Lightning with RW Dino Ciccarelli to Florida Panthers for G Mark Fitzpatrick and RW Jody Hull (January 15, 1998). ... Suffered cracked sternum and bruised chest (March 21, 1998); missed remainder of season. ... Traded by Panthers to Sharks for LW Alex Hicks and fifth-round pick (traded to New York Islanders) in 1999 draft (November 11, 1998). ... Suffered back spasms (October 7, 1999); missed 10 games. ... Injured shoulder (January 11, 2000); missed two games. ... Suspended four games by NHL for stick-swinging incident (February 14, 2000). ... Signed as free agent by Pittsburgh Penguins (November 14, 2000). ... Bruised knee (January 9, 2001); missed eight games. ... Injured back (February 16, 2001); missed four games. ... Traded by Penguins to Sharks for D Bobby Dollas and G Johan Hedberg (March 12, 2001). ... Signed as free agent by Panthers (July 11, 2001).

HONORS: Named to CCHA All-Star second team (1986-87).

		REGULAR SEASON								PLAYOFFS				
Season Team	League	Gms.	G	A	Pts.	PIM	+/-	PP	SH	Gms.	G	A	Pts.	PIM
83-84—Cushing Academy.......	Mass. H.S.	21	22	33	55	...	...	...	...	—	—	—	—	—
84-85—Univ. of Michigan........	CCHA	37	8	16	24	103	...	...	...	—	—	—	—	—
85-86—Univ. of Michigan........	CCHA	37	15	30	45	99	...	...	...	—	—	—	—	—
86-87—Univ. of Michigan........	CCHA	39	12	37	49	92	...	...	...	—	—	—	—	—
87-88—U.S. national team	Int'l	57	7	25	32	...	...	...	...	—	—	—	—	—
—U.S. Olympic team.......	Int'l	6	0	4	4	4	...	...	...	—	—	—	—	—
—New York Islanders.....	NHL	15	1	6	7	14	3	1	0	3	0	2	2	13
88-89—New York Islanders.....	NHL	69	1	30	31	74	-24	1	0	—	—	—	—	—
89-90—New York Islanders.....	NHL	60	4	49	53	65	-9	4	0	4	1	3	4	17
90-91—New York Islanders.....	NHL	44	3	25	28	16	-13	2	1	—	—	—	—	—
91-92—New York Islanders.....	NHL	28	1	18	19	18	2	0	1	—	—	—	—	—
92-93—New York Islanders.....	NHL	66	12	38	50	45	-3	5	0	10	1	1	2	4
93-94—San Jose....................	NHL	64	7	33	40	36	16	1	0	14	1	5	6	20
94-95—San Jose....................	NHL	20	1	9	10	39	1	0	0	—	—	—	—	—
—St. Louis........................	NHL	28	2	18	20	33	21	0	0	7	1	1	2	11
95-96—St. Louis...................	NHL	36	4	7	11	26	4	0	0	—	—	—	—	—
—Edmonton..................	NHL	30	4	16	20	16	5	1	0	—	—	—	—	—
96-97—Edmonton..................	NHL	62	2	11	13	42	-7	0	0	—	—	—	—	—
—Tampa Bay..................	NHL	13	0	5	5	16	0	0	0	—	—	—	—	—
97-98—Tampa Bay................	NHL	37	4	6	10	26	-25	4	0	—	—	—	—	—
—Florida........................	NHL	19	0	7	7	18	-7	0	0	—	—	—	—	—
98-99—Florida.....................	NHL	3	0	0	0	2	0	0	0	—	—	—	—	—
—San Jose....................	NHL	69	4	18	22	42	2	2	0	6	0	7	7	10
99-00—San Jose..................	NHL	62	0	20	20	49	-2	0	0	12	0	1	1	7
00-01—Pittsburgh..................	NHL	32	2	10	12	20	8	1	0	—	—	—	—	—
—San Jose....................	NHL	10	0	1	1	8	4	0	0	6	0	1	1	2
NHL Totals (14 years).........		767	52	327	379	605	-24	22	2	62	4	21	25	84

PERSONAL: Born May 7, 1982, in Ceske Budejovice, Czechoslovakia. ... 6-0/174. ... Shoots left.

TRANSACTIONS/CAREER NOTES: Selected by New York Rangers in second round (first Rangers pick, 64th overall) of NHL entry draft (June 24, 2000).

HONORS: Named to WHL (East) All-Star second team (2000-01).

		REGULAR SEASON								PLAYOFFS				
Season Team	League	Gms.	G	A	Pts.	PIM	+/-	PP	SH	Gms.	G	A	Pts.	PIM
98-99—Budejovice	Czech. Jrs.	68	8	10	18	34	...	...	...	—	—	—	—	—
99-00—Regina	WHL	47	7	32	39	70	...	...	...	7	1	4	5	5
00-01—Regina	WHL	64	17	50	67	75	...	...	...	6	1	4	5	6

PERSONAL: Born January 23, 1979, in Golitsino, U.S.S.R. ... 6-1/183. ... Shoots left. ... Name pronounced noh-vuh-SEHLT-sehf.

TRANSACTIONS/CAREER NOTES: Selected by Florida Panthers in fourth round (fifth Panthers pick, 95th overall) of NHL entry draft (June 21, 1997).

HONORS: Named to OHL All-Star first team (1998-99).

Season Team	League	REGULAR SEASON								PLAYOFFS				
		Gms.	G	A	Pts.	PIM	+/-	PP	SH	Gms.	G	A	Pts.	PIM
95-96—Krylja Sov. Moscow....	CIS	1	0	0	0	0	...	...	...	—	—	—	—	—
96-97—Krylja Sov. Moscow....	Russian	30	0	3	3	18	...	...	...	2	0	0	0	4
—Krylja Sov. Moscow....	Rus. Div. III	19	5	3	8	39	...	...	...	—	—	—	—	—
97-98—Sarnia	OHL	53	26	22	48	41	...	...	...	5	1	1	2	8
98-99—Sarnia	OHL	68	57	39	96	45	...	...	...	5	2	4	6	6
99-00—Louisville	AHL	47	14	21	35	22	...	...	...	4	1	0	1	6
—Florida	NHL	14	2	1	3	8	-3	2	0	—	—	—	—	—
00-01—Louisville	AHL	34	2	10	12	8	...	...	...	—	—	—	—	—
—Florida	NHL	38	3	6	9	16	-5	0	0	—	—	—	—	—
NHL Totals (2 years)...........		52	5	7	12	24	-8	2	0					

NUMMELIN, PETTERI — D — BLUE JACKETS

PERSONAL: Born November 25, 1972, in Turku, Finland. ... 5-10/183. ... Shoots left.
TRANSACTIONS/CAREER NOTES: Selected by Columbus Blue Jackets in fifth round (third Blue Jackets pick, 133rd overall) of NHL entry draft (June 24, 2000). ... Strained groin (December 8, 2000); missed four games. ... Suffered from the flu (January 10, 2001); missed one game. ... Bruised foot (March 14, 2001); missed one game.

Season Team	League	REGULAR SEASON								PLAYOFFS				
		Gms.	G	A	Pts.	PIM	+/-	PP	SH	Gms.	G	A	Pts.	PIM
92-93—Reipas Lahti	Finland	14	3	4	7	18	...	...	...	—	—	—	—	—
—TPS Turku	Finland	3	0	0	0	8	...	...	...	—	—	—	—	—
93-94—TPS Turku	Finland	44	14	24	38	20	...	...	...	—	—	—	—	—
94-95—TPS Turku	Finland	48	10	17	27	32	...	...	...	—	—	—	—	—
95-96—Vastra Frolunda	Sweden	32	7	11	18	26	...	...	...	—	—	—	—	—
96-97—Vastra Frolunda	Sweden	44	20	14	34	39	...	...	...	—	—	—	—	—
97-98—Davos HC	Switzerland	33	13	17	30	24	...	...	...	—	—	—	—	—
98-99—Davos HC	Switzerland	44	11	42	53	27	...	...	...	—	—	—	—	—
99-00—Davos	Switzerland	40	15	23	38	20	...	...	...	—	—	—	—	—
00-01—Columbus	NHL	61	4	12	16	10	-11	2	0	—	—	—	—	—
NHL Totals (1 year).............		61	4	12	16	10	-11	2	0					

NUMMINEN, TEPPO — D — COYOTES

PERSONAL: Born July 3, 1968, in Tampere, Finland. ... 6-2/199. ... Shoots right. ... Full Name: Teppo Kalevi Numminen. ... Name pronounced TEH-poh NOO-mih-nehn.
TRANSACTIONS/CAREER NOTES: Selected by Winnipeg Jets in second round (second Jets pick, 29th overall) of NHL entry draft (June 21, 1986). ... Separated shoulder (March 5, 1989). ... Fractured thumb (April 14, 1990). ... Fractured foot (January 28, 1993); missed 17 games. ... Dislocated thumb (February 9, 1994); missed remainder of season. ... Played in Europe during 1994-95 NHL lockout. ... Suffered from stomach flu (January 23, 1995); missed one game. ... Suffered stress fracture in right knee (February 22, 1995); missed five games. ... Separated shoulder (November 28, 1995); missed eight games. ... Jets franchise moved to Phoenix and renamed Coyotes for 1996-97 season; NHL approved move on January 18, 1996. ... Strained hip flexor (March 1, 2000); missed two games. ... Sprained ankle (December 30, 2000); missed one game. ... Bruised foot (November 14, 2000); missed two games. ... Bruised foot (November 29, 2000); missed three games. ... Brused foot (March 6, 2001); missed one game. ... Strained hip flexor (March 15, 2001); missed two games. ... Bruised foot (April 6, 2001); missed one game.
HONORS: Played in NHL All-Star Game (1999-2001).
MISCELLANEOUS: Member of silver-medal-winning Finnish Olympic team (1988). ... Member of bronze-medal-winning Finnish Olympic team (1998).

Season Team	League	REGULAR SEASON								PLAYOFFS				
		Gms.	G	A	Pts.	PIM	+/-	PP	SH	Gms.	G	A	Pts.	PIM
84-85—Tappara	Finland	30	14	17	31	10	...	...	...	—	—	—	—	—
85-86—Tappara	Finland	39	2	4	6	6	...	...	...	8	0	0	0	0
86-87—Tappara	Finland	44	9	9	18	16	...	...	...	9	4	1	5	4
87-88—Tappara	Finland	44	10	10	20	29	...	...	...	10	6	6	12	6
—Fin. Olympic team	Int'l	6	1	4	5	0	...	...	...	—	—	—	—	—
88-89—Winnipeg	NHL	69	1	14	15	36	-11	0	1	—	—	—	—	—
89-90—Winnipeg	NHL	79	11	32	43	20	-4	1	0	7	1	2	3	10
90-91—Winnipeg	NHL	80	8	25	33	28	-15	3	0	—	—	—	—	—
91-92—Winnipeg	NHL	80	5	34	39	32	15	4	0	7	0	0	0	0
92-93—Winnipeg	NHL	66	7	30	37	33	4	3	1	6	1	1	2	2
93-94—Winnipeg	NHL	57	5	18	23	28	-23	4	0	—	—	—	—	—
94-95—TuTo Turku	Finland	12	3	8	11	4	...	...	...	—	—	—	—	—
—Winnipeg	NHL	42	5	16	21	16	12	2	0	—	—	—	—	—
95-96—Winnipeg	NHL	74	11	43	54	22	-4	6	0	6	0	0	0	2
96-97—Phoenix	NHL	82	2	25	27	28	-3	0	0	7	3	3	6	0
97-98—Phoenix	NHL	82	11	40	51	30	25	6	0	1	0	0	0	0
—Fin. Olympic team	Int'l	6	1	1	2	2	...	...	...	—	—	—	—	—
98-99—Phoenix	NHL	82	10	30	40	30	3	1	0	7	2	1	3	4
99-00—Phoenix	NHL	79	8	34	42	16	21	2	0	5	1	1	2	0
00-01—Phoenix	NHL	72	5	26	31	36	9	1	0	—	—	—	—	—
NHL Totals (13 years).........		944	89	367	456	355	29	33	2	46	8	8	16	18

NURMINEN, KAI — LW

PERSONAL: Born March 29, 1969, in Turku, Finland. ... 6-1/198. ... Shoots left. ... Name pronounced KIGH NUHR-mih-nehn.
TRANSACTIONS/CAREER NOTES: Selected by Los Angeles Kings in eighth round (ninth Kings pick, 193rd overall) in NHL entry draft (June 22, 1996). ... Bruised thigh (January 15, 1997); missed two games. ... Bruised thigh (February 5, 1997); missed two games. ... Signed as free agent by Minnesota Wild (May 17, 2000).

PLAYOFFS

Season Team	League	Gms.	G	A	Pts.	PIM	+/-	PP	SH	Gms.	G	A	Pts.	PIM
88-89—Lethbridge	WHL	63	29	75	104	32	...	...	...	8	1	5	6	6
89-90—TPS Turku Jr.	Finland	35	28	17	45	32	...	...	...	—	—	—	—	—
90-91—TuTo Turku	Finland	33	26	20	46	14	...	...	...	—	—	—	—	—
91-92—Kiekko-67	Finland Div. 2	44	44	19	63	34	...	...	...	—	—	—	—	—
92-93—Kiekko-67	Finland Div. 2	8	6	4	10	2	...	...	...	—	—	—	—	—
—TPS Turku	Finland	31	4	6	10	13	...	...	...	7	1	2	3	0
93-94—TPS Turku	Finland	45	23	12	35	20	...	...	...	11	0	3	3	4
94-95—HPK Hameenlinna	Finland	49	30	25	55	40	...	...	...	—	—	—	—	—
95-96—HV 71 Jonkoping	Sweden	40	31	24	55	32	...	...	...	4	3	1	4	8
96-97—Los Angeles	NHL	67	16	11	27	22	-3	4	0	—	—	—	—	—
97-98—Vastra Frolunda	Sweden	23	9	7	16	24	...	...	...	—	—	—	—	—
—Jokerit....................	Finland	20	7	9	16	30	...	...	...	—	—	—	—	—
98-99—Davos HC..................	Switzerland	42	26	14	40	26	...	...	...	—	—	—	—	—
99-00—TPS Turku..................	Finland	54	*41	37	*78	40	...	...	...	10	5	†9	*14	0
00-01—Cleveland	IHL	74	28	46	74	34	...	...	...	1	0	0	0	0
—Minnesota..................	NHL	2	1	0	1	2	-1	0	0	—	—	—	—	—
NHL Totals (2 years)...........		69	17	11	28	24	-4	4	0					

NYLANDER, MICHAEL   C   BLACKHAWKS

PERSONAL: Born October 3, 1972, in Stockholm, Sweden. ... 6-1/195. ... Shoots left. ... Full Name: Mikael Nylander. ... Name pronounced NEE-lan-duhr.

TRANSACTIONS/CAREER NOTES: Selected by Hartford Whalers in third round (fourth Whalers pick, 59th overall) of NHL entry draft (June 22, 1991). ... Fractured jaw (January 23, 1993); missed 15 games. ... Traded by Whalers with D Zarley Zalapski and D James Patrick to Calgary Flames for D Gary Suter, LW Paul Ranheim and C Ted Drury (March 10, 1994). ... Played in Europe during 1994-95 NHL lockout. ... Fractured left wrist and forearm (January 24, 1995); missed 42 games. ... Injured wrist (January 16, 1996); missed three games. ... Injured left knee (March 26, 1998); missed final 11 games of season and first 23 games of 1998-99 season. ... Traded by Flames to Tampa Bay Lightning for RW Andrei Nazarov (January 19, 1999). ... Suffered concussion (April 8, 1999); missed final five games of season. ... Traded by Lightning to Chicago Blackhawks for D Bryan Muir and LW Reid Simpson (November 12, 1999).

HONORS: Named Swedish League Rookie of the Year (1991-92).

STATISTICAL PLATEAUS: Three-goal games: 1992-93 (1). ... Four-goal games: 1999-00 (1). ... Total hat tricks: 2.

		REGULAR SEASON								PLAYOFFS				
Season Team	League	Gms.	G	A	Pts.	PIM	+/-	PP	SH	Gms.	G	A	Pts.	PIM
89-90—Huddinge	Sweden	31	7	15	22	4	...	...	...	—	—	—	—	—
90-91—Huddinge	Sweden	33	14	20	34	10	...	...	...	—	—	—	—	—
91-92—AIK Solna	Sweden	40	11	17	28	30	...	...	...	—	—	—	—	—
—Swedish Oly. team	Int'l	6	0	1	1	0	...	...	...	—	—	—	—	—
92-93—Hartford	NHL	59	11	22	33	36	-7	3	0	—	—	—	—	—
—Springfield	AHL	59	11	22	33	36	...	...	...	—	—	—	—	—
93-94—Hartford	NHL	58	11	33	44	24	-2	4	0	—	—	—	—	—
—Springfield	AHL	4	0	9	9	0	...	...	...	—	—	—	—	—
—Calgary	NHL	15	2	9	11	6	10	0	0	3	0	0	0	0
94-95—JyP HT	Finland	16	11	19	30	63	...	...	...	—	—	—	—	—
—Calgary	NHL	6	0	1	1	2	1	0	0	6	0	6	6	2
95-96—Calgary	NHL	73	17	38	55	20	0	4	0	4	0	0	0	0
96-97—Lugano	Switzerland	36	12	43	55	...	...	...	...	—	—	—	—	—
97-98—Calgary	NHL	65	13	23	36	24	10	0	0	—	—	—	—	—
—Swedish Oly. team	Int'l	4	0	0	0	6	...	...	...	—	—	—	—	—
98-99—Calgary	NHL	9	2	3	5	2	1	1	0	—	—	—	—	—
—Tampa Bay	NHL	24	2	7	9	6	-10	0	0	—	—	—	—	—
99-00—Tampa Bay	NHL	11	1	2	3	4	-3	1	0	—	—	—	—	—
—Chicago......................	NHL	66	23	28	51	26	9	4	0	—	—	—	—	—
00-01—Chicago......................	NHL	82	25	39	64	32	7	4	0	—	—	—	—	—
NHL Totals (8 years)...........		468	107	205	312	182	16	21	0	13	0	6	6	2

OATES, ADAM   C   CAPITALS

N O

PERSONAL: Born August 27, 1962, in Weston, Ont. ... 5-10/180. ... Shoots right. ... Full Name: Adam R. Oates. ... Name pronounced OHTS.

TRANSACTIONS/CAREER NOTES: Signed as non-drafted free agent by Detroit Red Wings (June 28, 1985). ... Pulled abdominal muscle (October 1987). ... Suffered from chicken pox (November 1988). ... Bruised thigh (December 1988). ... Traded by Red Wings with RW Paul MacLean to St. Louis Blues for LW Tony McKegney and C Bernie Federko (June 15, 1989). ... Tore rib and abdominal muscles (November 5, 1990); missed 18 games. ... Traded by Blues to Boston Bruins for C Craig Janney and D Stephane Quintal (February 7, 1992). ... Injured groin (January 6, 1994); missed seven games. ... Injured knee (October 28, 1995); missed 12 games. ... Traded by Bruins with RW Rick Tocchet and G Bill Ranford to Washington Capitals for G Jim Carey, C Jason Allison, C Anson Carter and third-round pick (RW Lee Goren) in 1997 draft (March 1, 1997). ... Injured back (April 10, 1997); missed two games. ... Strained groin (November 27, 1998); missed 23 games.

HONORS: Named to ECAC All-Star second team (1983-84). ... Named to NCAA All-America (East) first team (1984-85). ... Named to NCAA All-Tournament team (1984-85). ... Named to ECAC All-Star first team (1984-85). ... Named to THE SPORTING NEWS All-Star second team (1990-91). ... Named to NHL All-Star second team (1990-91). ... Played in NHL All-Star Game (1991-1994 and 1997).

RECORDS: Holds NHL All-Star Game record for most assists in one period—4 (first period, 1993).

STATISTICAL PLATEAUS: Three-goal games: 1992-93 (3), 1993-94 (2), 1997-98 (1). Total: 6. ... Four-goal games: 1995-96 (1). ... Total hat tricks: 7.

MISCELLANEOUS: Captain of Washington Capitals (1999-2000 and 2000-01). ... Scored on a penalty shot (vs. Curtis Joseph, November 18, 1998).

STATISTICAL NOTES: Tied for NHL lead in game-winning goals with 11 (1992-93).

Season Team	League	REGULAR SEASON								PLAYOFFS				
		Gms.	G	A	Pts.	PIM	+/-	PP	SH	Gms.	G	A	Pts.	PIM
82-83—R.P.I.	ECAC	22	9	33	42	8	...	...	...	—	—	—	—	—
83-84—R.P.I.	ECAC	38	26	57	83	15	...	...	...	—	—	—	—	—
84-85—R.P.I.	ECAC	38	31	60	91	29	...	...	...	—	—	—	—	—
85-86—Adirondack	AHL	34	18	28	46	4	...	...	...	17	7	14	21	4
—Detroit	NHL	38	9	11	20	10	1	0	0	—	—	—	—	—
86-87—Detroit	NHL	76	15	32	47	21	0	4	0	16	4	7	11	6
87-88—Detroit	NHL	63	14	40	54	20	16	3	0	16	8	12	20	6
88-89—Detroit	NHL	69	16	62	78	14	-1	2	0	6	0	8	8	2
89-90—St. Louis	NHL	80	23	79	102	30	9	6	2	12	2	12	14	4
90-91—St. Louis	NHL	61	25	90	115	29	15	3	1	13	7	13	20	10
91-92—St. Louis	NHL	54	10	59	69	12	-4	3	0	—	—	—	—	—
—Boston	NHL	26	10	20	30	10	-5	3	0	15	5	14	19	4
92-93—Boston	NHL	84	45	*97	142	32	15	24	1	4	0	9	9	4
93-94—Boston	NHL	77	32	80	112	45	10	16	2	13	3	9	12	8
94-95—Boston	NHL	48	12	41	53	8	-11	4	1	5	1	0	1	2
95-96—Boston	NHL	70	25	67	92	18	16	7	1	5	2	5	7	2
96-97—Boston	NHL	63	18	52	70	10	-3	2	2	—	—	—	—	—
—Washington	NHL	17	4	8	12	4	-2	1	0	—	—	—	—	—
97-98—Washington	NHL	82	18	58	76	36	6	3	2	21	6	11	17	8
98-99—Washington	NHL	59	12	42	54	22	-1	3	0	—	—	—	—	—
99-00—Washington	NHL	82	15	56	71	14	13	5	0	5	0	3	3	4
00-01—Washington	NHL	81	13	†69	82	28	-9	5	0	6	0	0	0	0
NHL Totals (16 years)		1130	316	963	1279	363	65	94	12	137	38	103	141	60

OBSUT, JAROSLAV   D

PERSONAL: Born September 3, 1976, in Presov, Czechoslovakia. ... 6-1/185. ... Shoots left. ... Name pronounced ahb-SOOT.
TRANSACTIONS/CAREER NOTES: Selected by Winnipeg Jets in eighth round (ninth Jets pick, 188th overall) of NHL entry draft (July 8, 1995). ... Jets franchise moved to Phoenix and renamed Coyotes for 1996-97 season; NHL approved move on January 18, 1996. ... Signed as free agent by St. Louis Blues (May 25, 1999). ... Suffered from headaches (March 17, 2001); missed one game.

Season Team	League	REGULAR SEASON								PLAYOFFS				
		Gms.	G	A	Pts.	PIM	+/-	PP	SH	Gms.	G	A	Pts.	PIM
94-95—North Battleford	SJHL	55	21	30	51	126	...	...	...	—	—	—	—	—
95-96—Swift Current	WHL	72	10	11	21	57	...	...	...	6	0	0	0	2
96-97—Edmonton	WHL	13	2	9	11	4	...	...	...	—	—	—	—	—
—Medicine Hat	WHL	50	8	26	34	42	...	...	...	—	—	—	—	—
—Toledo	ECHL	3	1	0	1	0	...	...	...	5	0	1	1	6
97-98—Raleigh	ECHL	60	6	26	32	46	...	...	...	—	—	—	—	—
—Syracuse	AHL	4	0	1	1	4	...	...	...	—	—	—	—	—
98-99—Manitoba	IHL	2	0	0	0	0	...	...	...	—	—	—	—	—
—Augusta	ECHL	41	11	25	36	42	...	...	...	—	—	—	—	—
—Worcester	AHL	31	2	8	10	14	...	...	...	4	0	1	1	2
99-00—Worcester	AHL	7	0	2	2	4	...	...	...	—	—	—	—	—
00-01—Peoria	ECHL	3	0	4	4	2	...	...	...	—	—	—	—	—
—Worcester	AHL	47	9	12	21	20	...	...	...	7	0	1	1	4
—St. Louis	NHL	4	0	0	0	2	1	0	0	—	—	—	—	—
NHL Totals (1 year)		4	0	0	0	2	1	0	0					

ODELEIN, LYLE   D   BLUE JACKETS

PERSONAL: Born July 21, 1968, in Quill Lake, Sask. ... 6-0/210. ... Shoots right. ... Brother of Selmar Odelein, defenseman with Edmonton Oilers (1985-86 through 1988-89). ... Name pronounced OH-duh-lighn.
TRANSACTIONS/CAREER NOTES: Selected by Montreal Canadiens in seventh round (eighth Canadiens pick, 141st overall) of NHL entry draft (June 21, 1986). ... Bruised right ankle (January 22, 1991); missed five games. ... Twisted right ankle (February 9, 1991). ... Suspended one game by NHL for game misconduct penalties (March 1, 1993). ... Bruised shoulder (January 24, 1994); missed three games. ... Suspended two games without pay and fined $1,000 by NHL for shooting puck into the opposing team's bench (April 3, 1996). ... Traded by Canadiens to New Jersey Devils for RW Stephane Richer (August 22, 1996). ... Bruised knee (January 21, 1997); missed three games. ... Bruised shoulder (November 12, 1997); missed one game. ... Suffered from the flu (January 11, 1999); missed two games. ... Bruised right knee (March 22, 1999); missed nine games. ... Injured back (November 5, 1999); missed three games. ... Suffered from the flu (January 14, 2000); missed three games. ... Traded by Devils to Phoenix Coyotes for D Deron Quint and third-round pick (traded back to Phoenix) in 2001 draft (March 7, 2000). ... Selected by Columbus Blue Jackets in NHL expansion draft (June 23, 2000). ... Bruised knee (March 15, 2001); missed one game.
MISCELLANEOUS: Member of Stanley Cup championship team (1993). ... Captain of Columbus Blue Jackets (2000-01). ... Shares Columbus Blue Jackets all-time record for games played (81).
STATISTICAL PLATEAUS: Three-goal games: 1993-94 (1).

Season Team	League	REGULAR SEASON								PLAYOFFS				
		Gms.	G	A	Pts.	PIM	+/-	PP	SH	Gms.	G	A	Pts.	PIM
85-86—Moose Jaw	WHL	67	9	37	46	117	...	...	...	13	1	6	7	34
86-87—Moose Jaw	WHL	59	9	50	59	70	...	...	...	9	2	5	7	26
87-88—Moose Jaw	WHL	63	15	43	58	166	...	...	...	—	—	—	—	—
88-89—Sherbrooke	AHL	33	3	4	7	120	...	...	...	3	0	2	2	5
—Peoria	IHL	36	2	8	10	116	...	...	...	—	—	—	—	—
89-90—Sherbrooke	AHL	68	7	24	31	265	...	...	...	12	6	5	11	79
—Montreal	NHL	8	0	2	2	33	...	0	0	—	—	—	—	—
90-91—Montreal	NHL	52	0	2	2	259	7	0	0	12	0	0	0	54
91-92—Montreal	NHL	71	1	7	8	212	15	0	0	7	0	0	0	11
92-93—Montreal	NHL	83	2	14	16	205	35	0	0	20	1	5	6	30
93-94—Montreal	NHL	79	11	29	40	276	8	6	0	7	0	0	0	17

		REGULAR SEASON								PLAYOFFS				
Season Team	League	Gms.	G	A	Pts.	PIM	+/-	PP	SH	Gms.	G	A	Pts.	PIM
94-95—Montreal	NHL	48	3	7	10	152	-13	0	0	—	—	—	—	—
95-96—Montreal	NHL	79	3	14	17	230	8	0	1	6	1	1	2	6
96-97—New Jersey	NHL	79	3	13	16	110	16	1	0	10	2	2	4	19
97-98—New Jersey	NHL	79	4	19	23	171	11	1	0	6	1	1	2	21
98-99—New Jersey	NHL	70	5	26	31	114	6	1	0	7	0	3	3	10
99-00—New Jersey	NHL	57	1	15	16	104	-10	0	0	—	—	—	—	—
—Phoenix	NHL	16	1	7	8	19	1	1	0	5	0	0	0	16
00-01—Columbus	NHL	81	3	14	17	118	-16	1	0	—	—	—	—	—
NHL Totals (12 years)		802	37	169	206	2003	...	11	1	80	5	12	17	184

ODGERS, JEFF   RW   THRASHERS

PERSONAL: Born May 31, 1969, in Spy Hill, Sask. ... 6-0/200. ... Shoots right. ... Name pronounced AH-juhrs.

TRANSACTIONS/CAREER NOTES: Signed as non-drafted free agent by San Jose Sharks (September 3, 1991). ... Injured hand (December 21, 1991); missed four games. ... Fractured hand (November 5, 1992); missed 15 games. ... Suspended one game by NHL for accumulating three game-misconduct penalties (January 29, 1993). ... Suspended two games by NHL for accumulating four game-misconduct penalties (February 19, 1993). ... Traded by Sharks with fifth-round pick (D Elias Abrahamsson) in 1996 draft to Boston Bruins for D Al Iafrate (June 21, 1996). ... Injured neck (January 9, 1997); missed one game. ... Signed as free agent by Colorado Avalanche (October 24, 1997). ... Suffered from the flu (January 26, 1998); missed one game. ... Suffered from appendicitis (January 31, 1999); missed seven games. ... Selected by Minnesota Wild in NHL expansion draft (June 23, 2000). ... Claimed by Atlanta Thrashers from Wild in NHL waiver draft (September 29, 2000).

MISCELLANEOUS: Captain of San Jose Sharks (1994-95 and 1995-96). ... Holds San Jose Sharks all-time record for most penalty minutes (1,001).

		REGULAR SEASON								PLAYOFFS				
Season Team	League	Gms.	G	A	Pts.	PIM	+/-	PP	SH	Gms.	G	A	Pts.	PIM
86-87—Brandon	WHL	70	7	14	21	150	...	...	...	—	—	—	—	—
87-88—Brandon	WHL	70	17	18	35	202	...	...	...	4	1	1	2	14
88-89—Brandon	WHL	71	31	29	60	277	...	...	...	—	—	—	—	—
89-90—Brandon	WHL	64	37	28	65	209	...	...	...	—	—	—	—	—
90-91—Kansas City	IHL	77	12	19	31	*318	...	...	...	—	—	—	—	—
91-92—Kansas City	IHL	12	2	2	4	56	...	...	...	9	3	0	3	13
—San Jose	NHL	61	7	4	11	217	-21	0	0	—	—	—	—	—
92-93—San Jose	NHL	66	12	15	27	253	-26	6	0	—	—	—	—	—
93-94—San Jose	NHL	81	13	8	21	222	-13	7	0	11	0	0	0	11
94-95—San Jose	NHL	48	4	3	7	117	-8	0	0	11	1	1	2	23
95-96—San Jose	NHL	78	12	4	16	192	-4	0	0	—	—	—	—	—
96-97—Boston	NHL	80	7	8	15	197	-15	1	0	—	—	—	—	—
97-98—Providence	AHL	4	0	0	0	31	...	...	...	—	—	—	—	—
—Colorado	NHL	68	5	8	13	213	5	0	0	6	0	0	0	25
98-99—Colorado	NHL	75	2	3	5	259	-3	1	0	15	1	0	1	14
99-00—Colorado	NHL	62	1	2	3	162	-7	0	0	4	0	0	0	0
00-01—Atlanta	NHL	82	6	7	13	226	-8	0	0	—	—	—	—	—
NHL Totals (10 years)		701	69	62	131	2058	-100	15	0	47	2	1	3	73

ODJICK, GINO   LW   CANADIENS

PERSONAL: Born September 7, 1970, in Maniwaki, Que. ... 6-3/227. ... Shoots left. ... Name pronounced OH-jihk.

TRANSACTIONS/CAREER NOTES: Selected by Vancouver Canucks in fifth round (fifth Canucks pick, 86th overall) of NHL entry draft (June 16, 1990). ... Fractured cheekbone (February 27, 1991). ... Suspended six games by NHL for stick foul (November 26, 1991). ... Underwent knee surgery (February 11, 1993); missed five games. ... Suspended one game by NHL for accumulating three game misconduct penalties (January 27, 1993). ... Suspended one game by NHL for accumulating four game misconduct penalties (March 26, 1993). ... Suspended two games by NHL for stick incident (April 8, 1993). ... Separated shoulder (November 27, 1993); missed two games. ... Suspended by NHL for 10 games (September 1994); NHL reduced suspension to six games due to abbreviated 1994-95 season (January 19, 1995). ... Strained groin (March 10, 1995); missed six games. ... Strained abdomen (April 7, 1995); missed last 13 games of season. ... Injured knee (October 10, 1995); missed one game. ... Strained abdominal muscle (November 22, 1995); missed 24 games. ... Suspended four games and fined $1,000 by NHL for striking opposing player (November 29, 1995). ... Strained groin (January 20, 1997); missed five games. ... Fractured finger (April 4, 1997); missed remainder of season. ... Strained groin (November 8, 1997); missed nine games. ... Injured knee (January 24, 1998); missed seven games. ... Traded by Canucks to New York Islanders for D Jason Strudwick (March 23, 1998). ... Strained groin (October 24, 1998); missed two games. ... Strained abdominal muscle (December 2, 1998); missed three games. ... Reinjured abdominal muscle (December 12, 1998); missed remainder of season. ... Suspended nine games by NHL for striking opposing player (December 31, 1999). ... Traded by Islanders to Philadelphia Flyers for LW Mikael Andersson and fifth-round pick (F Kristofer Ottoson) in 2000 draft (February 15, 2000). ... Injured groin (February 19, 2000); missed five games. ... Traded by Flyers to Montreal Canadiens for C P.J. Stock and sixth-round pick (D Dennis Seidenberg) in 2001 draft (December 7, 2000). ... Suspended one game by NHL for elbowing incident (December 14, 2000). ... Injured groin (December 27, 2000); missed one game. ... Injured wrist (January 2, 2001) and underwent surgery; missed remainder of season.

MISCELLANEOUS: Scored on a penalty shot (vs. Mike Vernon, October 19, 1991). ... Holds Vancouver Canucks all-time record for most penalty minutes (2,127).

		REGULAR SEASON								PLAYOFFS				
Season Team	League	Gms.	G	A	Pts.	PIM	+/-	PP	SH	Gms.	G	A	Pts.	PIM
88-89—Laval	QMJHL	50	9	15	24	278	...	...	...	16	0	9	9	*129
89-90—Laval	QMJHL	51	12	26	38	280	...	...	...	13	6	5	11	*110
90-91—Milwaukee	IHL	17	7	3	10	102	...	...	...	—	—	—	—	—
—Vancouver	NHL	45	7	1	8	296	-6	0	0	6	0	0	0	18
91-92—Vancouver	NHL	65	4	6	10	348	-1	0	0	4	0	0	0	6
92-93—Vancouver	NHL	75	4	13	17	370	3	0	0	1	0	0	0	0
93-94—Vancouver	NHL	76	16	13	29	271	13	4	0	10	0	0	0	18
94-95—Vancouver	NHL	23	4	5	9	109	-3	0	0	5	0	0	0	47
95-96—Vancouver	NHL	55	3	4	7	181	-16	0	0	6	3	1	4	6
96-97—Vancouver	NHL	70	5	8	13	371	-5	1	0	—	—	—	—	—

Season Team	League	REGULAR SEASON								PLAYOFFS				
		Gms.	G	A	Pts.	PIM	+/-	PP	SH	Gms.	G	A	Pts.	PIM
97-98—Vancouver...................	NHL	35	3	2	5	181	-3	0	0	—	—	—	—	—
—New York Islanders.....	NHL	13	0	0	0	31	1	0	0	—	—	—	—	—
98-99—New York Islanders.....	NHL	23	4	3	7	133	-2	1	0	—	—	—	—	—
99-00—New York Islanders.....	NHL	46	5	10	15	90	-7	0	0	—	—	—	—	—
—Philadelphia..............	NHL	13	3	1	4	10	2	0	0	—	—	—	—	—
00-01—Philadelphia..............	NHL	17	1	3	4	28	0	0	0	—	—	—	—	—
—Montreal....................	NHL	13	1	0	1	44	0	0	0	—	—	—	—	—
NHL Totals (11 years).........		569	60	69	129	2463	-24	6	0	32	3	1	4	95

O'DONNELL, SEAN · D · BRUINS

PERSONAL: Born September 13, 1971, in Ottawa. ... 6-3/230. ... Shoots left.

TRANSACTIONS/CAREER NOTES: Selected by Buffalo Sabres in sixth round (sixth Sabres pick, 123rd overall) of NHL entry draft (June 22, 1991). ... Traded by Sabres to Los Angeles Kings for D Doug Houda (July 26, 1994). ... Bruised sternum (February 4, 1995); missed two games. ... Sprained left wrist (January 27, 1996); missed eight games. ... Sprained wrist (December 26, 1996); missed nine games. ... Suspended one game by NHL for an altercation while on the bench (January 30, 1997). ... Strained back (March 1, 1997); missed two games. ... Suspended two games by NHL for cross-checking and spearing incidents (April 14, 1999). ... Selected by Minnesota Wild in NHL expansion draft (June 23, 2000). ... Suffered from the flu (February 11, 2001); missed one game. ... Traded by Wild to New Jersey Devils for D Willie Mitchell and future considerations (March 4, 2001). ... Signed as free agent by Boston Bruins (July 2, 2001).

MISCELLANEOUS: Captain of Minnesota Wild (October 6-31, 2000).

Season Team	League	REGULAR SEASON								PLAYOFFS				
		Gms.	G	A	Pts.	PIM	+/-	PP	SH	Gms.	G	A	Pts.	PIM
88-89—Sudbury.....................	OHL	56	1	9	10	49	...	...	...	—	—	—	—	—
89-90—Sudbury.....................	OHL	64	7	19	26	84	...	...	...	—	—	—	—	—
90-91—Sudbury.....................	OHL	66	8	23	31	114	...	...	...	5	1	4	5	10
91-92—Rochester	AHL	73	4	9	13	193	...	...	...	16	1	2	3	21
92-93—Rochester	AHL	74	3	18	21	203	...	...	...	17	1	6	7	38
93-94—Rochester	AHL	64	2	10	12	242	...	...	...	4	0	1	1	21
94-95—Phoenix.....................	IHL	61	2	18	20	132	...	...	...	9	0	1	1	21
—Los Angeles...............	NHL	15	0	2	2	49	-2	0	0	—	—	—	—	—
95-96—Los Angeles...............	NHL	71	2	5	7	127	3	0	0	—	—	—	—	—
96-97—Los Angeles...............	NHL	55	5	12	17	144	-13	2	0	—	—	—	—	—
97-98—Los Angeles...............	NHL	80	2	15	17	179	7	0	0	4	1	0	1	36
98-99—Los Angeles...............	NHL	80	1	13	14	186	1	0	0	—	—	—	—	—
99-00—Los Angeles...............	NHL	80	2	12	14	114	4	0	0	4	1	0	1	4
00-01—Minnesota	NHL	63	4	12	16	128	-2	1	0	—	—	—	—	—
—New Jersey	NHL	17	0	1	1	33	2	0	0	23	1	2	3	41
NHL Totals (7 years)...........		461	16	72	88	960	0	3	0	31	3	2	5	81

OHLUND, MATTIAS · D · CANUCKS

PERSONAL: Born September 9, 1976, in Pitea, Sweden. ... 6-3/210. ... Shoots left. ... Name pronounced muh-TEE-uhz OH-luhnd.

TRANSACTIONS/CAREER NOTES: Selected by Vancouver Canucks in first round (first Canucks pick, 13th overall) of NHL entry draft (June 28, 1994). ... Suffered concussion (March 26, 1998); missed four games. ... Sprained shoulder (February 23, 1999); missed three games. ... Suffered concussion (April 3, 1999); missed final five games of season. ... Injured eye (September 12, 1999); missed first 38 games of season. ... Injured groin (March 8, 2000); missed two games. ... Underwent eye surgery (October 20, 2000); missed 17 games.

HONORS: Named to NHL All-Rookie team (1997-98). ... Played in NHL All-Star Game (1999).

Season Team	League	REGULAR SEASON								PLAYOFFS				
		Gms.	G	A	Pts.	PIM	+/-	PP	SH	Gms.	G	A	Pts.	PIM
92-93—Pitea	Sweden Dv. 2	22	0	6	6	16	...	...	...	—	—	—	—	—
93-94—Pitea	Sweden Dv. 2	28	7	10	17	62	...	...	...	—	—	—	—	—
94-95—Lulea	Sweden	34	6	10	16	34	...	...	...	9	4	0	4	16
95-96—Lulea	Sweden	38	4	10	14	26	...	...	...	13	0	1	1	47
96-97—Lulea	Sweden	47	7	9	16	38	...	...	...	10	1	2	3	8
97-98—Vancouver...................	NHL	77	7	23	30	76	3	1	0	—	—	—	—	—
—Swedish Oly. team	Int'l	4	0	1	1	4	...	...	...	—	—	—	—	—
98-99—Vancouver...................	NHL	74	9	26	35	83	-19	2	1	—	—	—	—	—
99-00—Vancouver...................	NHL	42	4	16	20	24	6	2	1	—	—	—	—	—
00-01—Vancouver...................	NHL	65	8	20	28	46	-16	1	1	4	1	3	4	6
NHL Totals (4 years)...........		258	28	85	113	229	-26	6	3	4	1	3	4	6

OLAUSSON, FREDRIK · D · RED WINGS

O

PERSONAL: Born October 5, 1966, in Dadesjo, Sweden. ... 6-0/199. ... Shoots right. ... Name pronounced OHL-ih-suhn.

TRANSACTIONS/CAREER NOTES: Selected by Winnipeg Jets in fourth round (fourth Jets pick, 81st overall) of NHL entry draft (June 15, 1985). ... Dislocated shoulder (August 1987). ... Underwent shoulder surgery (November 1987). ... Signed five-year contract with Farjestad, Sweden (June 19, 1989); Farjestad agreed to allow Olausson to remain in Winnipeg. ... Sprained knee (January 22, 1993); missed 11 games. ... Lacerated ankle (November 8, 1993); missed two games. ... Suffered from the flu (January 18, 1993); missed one game. ... Sprained knee (January 23, 1993); missed 11 games. ... Suffered from the flu (March 4, 1993); missed one game. ... Traded by Jets with seventh-round pick (LW Curtis Sheptak) in 1994 draft to Edmonton Oilers for third-round pick (C Tavis Hansen) in 1994 draft (December 5, 1993). ... Strained knee (January 11, 1994). ... Played in Europe during 1994-95 NHL lockout. ... Suffered from the flu (February 17, 1995); missed one game. ... Suffered colitis (March 3, 1995); missed 10 games. ... Cracked ribs (November 4, 1995); missed 14 games. ... Suffered irregular heartbeat (December 6, 1995); missed five games. ... Claimed on waivers by Mighty Ducks of Anaheim (January 16, 1996) ... Traded by Mighty Ducks with C Alex Hicks to Pittsburgh Penguins for LW Shawn Antoski and D Dmitri Mironov (November 19, 1996). ... Fractured cheekbone (January 26, 1997); missed nine games. ... Strained groin (February 27, 1997); missed three games. ... Bruised foot (November 2, 1997); missed three games.

... Bruised wrist (December 9, 1997); missed two games. ... Signed as free agent by Mighty Ducks (August 29, 1998). ... Injured ribs (March 17, 1999); missed two games. ... Sprained ankle (October 15, 1999); missed two games. ... Suffered injury (November 13, 1999); missed one game. ... Suffered illness (December 15, 1999); missed two games. ... Suffered illness (April 3, 2000); missed one game. ... Announced retirement (April 10, 2000). ... Signed as free agent by Detroit Red Wings (May 24, 2001).

HONORS: Named to Swedish League All-Star team (1985-86).

MISCELLANEOUS: Scored on a penalty shot (vs. Martin Brodeur, November 24, 1999).

Season Team	League	REGULAR SEASON								PLAYOFFS				
		Gms.	G	A	Pts.	PIM	+/-	PP	SH	Gms.	G	A	Pts.	PIM
82-83—Nybro	Sweden	31	4	4	8	12	...	...	...	—	—	—	—	—
83-84—Nybro	Sweden	28	8	14	22	32	...	...	...	—	—	—	—	—
84-85—Farjestad Karlstad	Sweden	34	6	12	18	24	...	...	...	3	1	0	1	0
85-86—Farjestad Karlstad	Sweden	33	5	12	17	14	...	...	...	8	3	2	5	6
86-87—Winnipeg	NHL	72	7	29	36	24	-3	1	0	10	2	3	5	4
87-88—Winnipeg	NHL	38	5	10	15	18	3	2	0	5	1	1	2	0
88-89—Winnipeg	NHL	75	15	47	62	32	6	4	0	—	—	—	—	—
89-90—Winnipeg	NHL	77	9	46	55	32	-1	3	0	7	0	2	2	2
90-91—Winnipeg	NHL	71	12	29	41	24	-22	5	0	—	—	—	—	—
91-92—Winnipeg	NHL	77	20	42	62	34	-31	13	1	7	1	5	6	4
92-93—Winnipeg	NHL	68	16	41	57	22	-4	11	0	6	0	2	2	2
93-94—Winnipeg	NHL	18	2	5	7	10	-3	1	0	—	—	—	—	—
—Edmonton	NHL	55	9	19	28	20	-4	6	0	—	—	—	—	—
94-95—Ehrwald	Austria	10	4	3	7	8	...	...	...	—	—	—	—	—
—Edmonton	NHL	33	0	10	10	20	-4	0	0	—	—	—	—	—
95-96—Edmonton	NHL	20	0	6	6	14	-14	0	0	—	—	—	—	—
—Anaheim	NHL	36	2	16	18	24	7	1	0	—	—	—	—	—
96-97—Anaheim	NHL	20	2	9	11	8	-5	1	0	—	—	—	—	—
—Pittsburgh	NHL	51	7	20	27	24	21	2	0	4	0	1	1	0
97-98—Pittsburgh	NHL	76	6	27	33	42	13	2	0	6	0	3	3	2
98-99—Anaheim	NHL	74	16	40	56	30	17	10	0	4	0	2	2	4
99-00—Anaheim	NHL	70	15	19	34	28	-13	8	0	—	—	—	—	—
00-01—Bern	Switzerland	43	12	15	27	28	...	...	...	4	1	4	5	0
NHL Totals (14 years)		931	143	415	558	406	-37	70	1	49	4	19	23	18

OLIVER, DAVID   RW

PERSONAL: Born April 17, 1971, in Sechelt, B.C. ... 5-11/190. ... Shoots right.

TRANSACTIONS/CAREER NOTES: Selected by Edmonton Oilers in seventh round (seventh Oilers pick, 144th overall) of NHL entry draft (June 22, 1991). ... Suffered hip pointer (January 24, 1997); missed one game. ... Claimed on waivers by New York Rangers (February 22, 1997). ... Signed as free agent by Ottawa Senators (July 2, 1998). ... Signed as free agent by Phoenix Coyotes (July 16, 1999). ... Signed as free agent by Ottawa Senators (August 2, 2000). ... Suffered hip pointer (November 11, 2000); missed two games. ... Strained groin (November 19, 2000); missed five games.

HONORS: Named to CCHA All-Star second team (1992-93). ... Named to NCAA All-America (West) first team (1993-94). ... Named CCHA Player of the Year (1993-94). ... Named to CCHA All-Star first team (1993-94).

STATISTICAL PLATEAUS: Three-goal games: 1994-95 (1).

Season Team	League	REGULAR SEASON								PLAYOFFS				
		Gms.	G	A	Pts.	PIM	+/-	PP	SH	Gms.	G	A	Pts.	PIM
90-91—Univ. of Michigan	CCHA	27	13	11	24	34	...	...	...	—	—	—	—	—
91-92—Univ. of Michigan	CCHA	44	31	27	58	32	...	...	...	—	—	—	—	—
92-93—Univ. of Michigan	CCHA	40	35	20	55	18	...	...	...	—	—	—	—	—
93-94—Univ. of Michigan	CCHA	41	28	40	68	16	...	...	...	—	—	—	—	—
94-95—Cape Breton	AHL	32	11	18	29	8	...	...	...	—	—	—	—	—
—Edmonton	NHL	44	16	14	30	20	-11	10	0	—	—	—	—	—
95-96—Edmonton	NHL	80	20	19	39	34	-22	14	0	—	—	—	—	—
96-97—Edmonton	NHL	17	1	2	3	4	-8	0	0	—	—	—	—	—
—New York Rangers	NHL	14	2	1	3	4	3	0	0	3	0	0	0	0
97-98—Houston	IHL	78	38	27	65	60	...	...	...	4	3	0	3	4
98-99—Ottawa	NHL	17	2	5	7	4	1	0	0	—	—	—	—	—
—Houston	IHL	37	18	17	35	30	...	...	...	19	10	6	16	22
99-00—Hartford	AHL	9	0	0	0	19	...	...	...	—	—	—	—	—
—Huntington	ECHL	26	6	9	15	151	...	...	...	5	0	1	1	17
—Phoenix	NHL	9	1	0	1	2	0	1	0	—	—	—	—	—
00-01—Grand Rapids	IHL	51	14	17	31	35	...	...	...	10	6	2	8	8
—Ottawa	NHL	7	0	0	0	2	0	0	0	—	—	—	—	—
NHL Totals (6 years)		188	42	41	83	70	-37	25	0	3	0	0	0	0

OLIWA, KRZYSZTOF   RW   PENGUINS

PERSONAL: Born April 12, 1973, in Tychy, Poland. ... 6-5/235. ... Shoots left. ... Name pronounced KRIH-stahf OH-lee-vuh.

TRANSACTIONS/CAREER NOTES: Selected by New Jersey Devils in third round (fourth Devils pick, 65th overall) of NHL entry draft (June 26, 1993). ... Injured foot (November 10, 1997); missed two games. ... Strained groin (November 28, 1998); missed one game. ... Sprained left knee (October 30, 1999); missed six games. ... Suffered from the flu (January 11, 2000); missed one game. ... Injured left knee (April 2, 2000); missed final three games of season. ... Traded by Devils to Columbus Blue Jackets for third-round pick (C/LW Brandon Nolan) in 2001 draft and future considerations (June 12, 2000); Devils acquired RW Turner Stevenson to complete deal (June 23, 2000). ... Fractured arm (October 28, 2000); missed 23 games. ... Traded by Blue Jackets to Pittsburgh Penguins for third-round pick (D Aaron Johnson) in 2001 draft (January 14, 2001). ... Injured hamstring (March 20, 2001); missed five games.

MISCELLANEOUS: Member of Stanley Cup championship team (2000).

Season Team	League	REGULAR SEASON								PLAYOFFS				
		Gms.	G	A	Pts.	PIM	+/-	PP	SH	Gms.	G	A	Pts.	PIM
90-91—GKS Katowice	Poland Jrs.	5	4	4	8	10	...	...	...	—	—	—	—	—
91-92—GKS Tychy	Poland	10	3	7	10	6	...	...	...	—	—	—	—	—
92-93—Welland Jr. B	OHA	30	13	21	34	127	...	...	...	—	—	—	—	—
93-94—Albany	AHL	33	2	4	6	151	...	...	...	—	—	—	—	—
—Raleigh	ECHL	15	0	2	2	65	...	...	...	9	0	0	0	35
94-95—Albany	AHL	20	1	1	2	77	...	...	...	—	—	—	—	—
—Detroit	IHL	4	0	1	1	24	...	...	...	—	—	—	—	—
—Saint John	AHL	14	1	4	5	79	...	...	...	—	—	—	—	—
—Raleigh	ECHL	5	0	2	2	32	...	...	...	—	—	—	—	—
95-96—Albany	AHL	51	5	11	16	217	...	...	...	—	—	—	—	—
—Raleigh	ECHL	9	1	0	1	53	...	...	...	—	—	—	—	—
96-97—Albany	AHL	60	13	14	27	322	...	...	...	15	7	1	8	49
—New Jersey	NHL	1	0	0	0	5	-1	0	0	—	—	—	—	—
97-98—New Jersey	NHL	73	2	3	5	295	3	0	0	6	0	0	0	23
98-99—New Jersey	NHL	64	5	7	12	240	4	0	0	1	0	0	0	2
99-00—New Jersey	NHL	69	6	10	16	184	-2	1	0	—	—	—	—	—
00-01—Columbus	NHL	10	0	2	2	34	1	0	0	—	—	—	—	—
—Pittsburgh	NHL	26	1	2	3	131	-4	0	0	5	0	0	0	16
NHL Totals (5 years)		243	14	24	38	889	1	1	0	12	0	0	0	41

OLVESTAD, JIMMIE — LW — LIGHTNING

PERSONAL: Born February 16, 1980, in Stockholm, Sweden. ... 6-1/194. ... Shoots left.
TRANSACTIONS/CAREER NOTES: Selected by Tampa Bay Lightning in third round (fourth Lightning pick, 88th overall) of NHL entry draft (June 26, 1999).

Season Team	League	REGULAR SEASON								PLAYOFFS				
		Gms.	G	A	Pts.	PIM	+/-	PP	SH	Gms.	G	A	Pts.	PIM
96-97—Huddinge	Sweden	40	15	16	31		...	...	...	—	—	—	—	—
97-98—Huddinge	Sweden Dv. 2	11	0	0	0	6	...	...	...	—	—	—	—	—
—Djurgarden Stockholm	Sweden Jrs.	15	6	4	10		...	...	...	—	—	—	—	—
98-99—Djurgarden Stockholm	Sweden	44	2	4	6	18	...	...	...	4	0	0	0	8
99-00—Djurgarden Stockholm	Sweden	50	6	3	9	34	...	...	...	13	1	2	3	12
00-01—Djurgarden Stockholm	Sweden	50	7	8	15	79	...	...	...	16	7	2	9	14

O'NEILL, JEFF — C — HURRICANES

PERSONAL: Born February 23, 1976, in King City, Ont. ... 6-0/195. ... Shoots right.
TRANSACTIONS/CAREER NOTES: Selected by Hartford Whalers in first round (first Whalers pick, fifth overall) of NHL entry draft (June 28, 1994). ... Bruised foot (December 30, 1995); missed four games. ... Reinjured foot (January 10, 1996); missed four games. ... Injured shoulder (February 17, 1996); missed four games. ... Injured groin (January 2, 1997); missed one game. ... Sprained wrist (April 2, 1997); missed four games. ... Whalers franchise moved to North Carolina and renamed Carolina Hurricanes for 1997-98 season; NHL approved move on June 25, 1997. ... Suffered concussion (December 20, 1997); missed one game. ... Fractured kneecap (April 13, 1998); missed three games. ... Strained neck (February 3, 1999); missed seven games. ... Suffered back spasms (November 24, 1999); missed two games.
HONORS: Won Emms Family Award (1992-93). ... Named to Can.HL All-Rookie team (1992-93). ... Named to OHL All-Rookie team (1992-93). ... Won Can.HL Top Draft Prospect Award (1993-94). ... Named to Can.HL All-Star second team (1994-95). ... Named to OHL All-Star first team (1994-95).
STATISTICAL PLATEAUS: Three-goal games: 1996-97 (1).

Season Team	League	REGULAR SEASON								PLAYOFFS				
		Gms.	G	A	Pts.	PIM	+/-	PP	SH	Gms.	G	A	Pts.	PIM
91-92—Thornhill	Tier II Jr. A	43	27	53	80	48	...	...	...	—	—	—	—	—
92-93—Guelph	OHL	65	32	47	79	88	...	...	...	5	2	2	4	6
93-94—Guelph	OHL	66	45	81	126	95	...	...	...	9	2	11	13	31
94-95—Guelph	OHL	57	43	81	124	56	...	...	...	14	8	18	26	34
95-96—Hartford	NHL	65	8	19	27	40	-3	1	0	—	—	—	—	—
96-97—Hartford	NHL	72	14	16	30	40	-24	2	1	—	—	—	—	—
—Springfield	AHL	1	0	0	0	0	...	...	...	—	—	—	—	—
97-98—Carolina	NHL	74	19	20	39	67	-8	7	1	—	—	—	—	—
98-99—Carolina	NHL	75	16	15	31	66	3	4	0	6	0	1	1	0
99-00—Carolina	NHL	80	25	38	63	72	-9	4	0	—	—	—	—	—
00-01—Carolina	NHL	82	41	26	67	106	-18	17	0	6	1	2	3	10
NHL Totals (6 years)		448	123	134	257	391	-59	35	2	12	1	3	4	10

ORPIK, BROOKS — D — PENGUINS

PERSONAL: Born September 26, 1980, in Amherst, N.Y. ... 6-3/217. ... Shoots left.
TRANSACTIONS/CAREER NOTES: Selected by Pittsburgh Penguins in first round (first Penguins pick, 18th overall) of NHL entry draft (June 24, 2000).

Season Team	League	REGULAR SEASON								PLAYOFFS				
		Gms.	G	A	Pts.	PIM	+/-	PP	SH	Gms.	G	A	Pts.	PIM
97-98—Thayer Academy	Mass. H.S.	22	0	7	7		...	...	...	—	—	—	—	—
98-99—Boston College	Hockey East	41	1	10	11	96	...	...	...	—	—	—	—	—
99-00—Boston College	Hockey East	38	1	9	10	100	...	...	...	—	—	—	—	—
00-01—Boston College	Hockey East	40	0	20	20	*124	...	...	...	—	—	—	—	—

O

ORSZAGH, VLADIMIR — RW — PREDATORS

PERSONAL: Born May 24, 1977, in Banska Bystrica, Czechoslovakia. ... 5-11/173. ... Shoots left. ... Name pronounced OHR-sahg.
TRANSACTIONS/CAREER NOTES: Selected by New York Islanders in fifth round (fourth Islanders pick, 106th overall) of NHL entry draft (July 8, 1995). ... Suffered tendinitis (December 14, 1999); missed one game. ... Signed as free agent by Nashville Predators (June 1, 2001).

Season Team	League			REGULAR SEASON							PLAYOFFS			
		Gms.	G	A	Pts.	PIM	+/-	PP	SH	Gms.	G	A	Pts.	PIM
93-94—IS Banska Byst. Jrs. ...	Slovakia	...	38	27	65	...	...	...	...	—	—	—	—	—
94-95—Banska Bystrica	Slov. Div. II	38	18	12	30	...	...	...	...	—	—	—	—	—
—Martimex ZTS Martin..	Slovakia	1	0	0	0	0	...	...	...	—	—	—	—	—
95-96—Banska Bystrica	Slovakia	31	9	5	14	22	...	...	...	—	—	—	—	—
96-97—Utah	IHL	68	12	15	27	30	...	...	...	3	0	1	1	4
97-98—Utah	IHL	62	13	10	23	60	...	...	...	4	2	0	2	0
—New York Islanders	NHL	11	0	1	1	2	-3	0	0	—	—	—	—	—
98-99—Lowell	AHL	68	18	23	41	57	...	...	...	3	2	2	4	2
—New York Islanders	NHL	12	1	0	1	6	2	0	0	—	—	—	—	—
99-00—Lowell	AHL	55	8	12	20	22	...	...	...	7	3	3	6	2
—New York Islanders	NHL	11	2	1	3	4	1	0	0	—	—	—	—	—
00-01—Djurgarden Stockholm	Sweden	50	23	13	36	62	...	...	...	16	7	3	10	20
NHL Totals (3 years)		34	3	2	5	12	0	0	0					

OSGOOD, CHRIS — G — RED WINGS

PERSONAL: Born November 26, 1972, in Peace River, Alta. ... 5-10/181. ... Catches left.
TRANSACTIONS/CAREER NOTES: Selected by Detroit Red Wings in third round (third Red Wings pick, 54th overall) of NHL entry draft (June 22, 1991). ... Strained hamstring (January 14, 1997); missed five games. ... Strained groin (March 14, 1998); missed four games. ... Strained hip flexor (November 19, 1998); missed six games. ... Injured right knee (April 27, 1999); missed four playoff games. ... Injured hand (November 24, 1999); missed 15 games.
HONORS: Named to WHL (East) All-Star second team (1990-91). ... Played in NHL All-Star Game (1996). ... Named to THE SPORTING NEWS All-Star first team (1995-96). ... Shared William M. Jennings Trophy with Mike Vernon (1995-96). ... Named to NHL All-Star second team (1995-96). ... Named to play in NHL All-Star Game (1997); replaced by G Guy Hebert due to injury.
RECORDS: Shares NHL single-season playoff record for most wins by goaltender—16 (1998).
MISCELLANEOUS: Member of Stanley Cup championship team (1997 and 1998). ... Holds Detroit Red Wings all-time record for goals-against average (2.40). ... Stopped a penalty shot attempt (vs. Peter Zezel, March 4, 1994; vs. Dave Gagner, April 1, 1995; vs. Mike Hudson, November 18, 1996). ... Allowed a penalty shot goal (vs. Alexander Mogilny, December 1, 1997; vs. Geoff Courtnall, October 29, 1998; vs. Pavel Bure, February 26, 1999; vs. Joe Nieuwendyk, February 18, 2001).
STATISTICAL NOTES: Scored goal (March 6, 1996, vs. Hartford Whalers).

Season Team	League				REGULAR SEASON								PLAYOFFS				
		Gms.	Min	W	L	T	GA	SO	Avg.	Gms.	Min.	W	L	GA	SO	Avg.
89-90—Medicine Hat	WHL	57	3094	24	28	2	228	0	4.42	3	173	3	4	17	0	5.90
90-91—Medicine Hat	WHL	46	2630	23	18	3	173	2	3.95	12	714	7	5	42	0	3.53
91-92—Medicine Hat	WHL	15	819	10	3	0	44	0	3.22	—	—	—	—	—	—	—
—Brandon	WHL	16	890	3	10	1	60	1	4.04	—	—	—	—	—	—	—
—Seattle	WHL	21	1217	12	7	1	65	1	3.20	15	904	9	6	51	0	3.38
92-93—Adirondack	AHL	45	2438	19	19	2	159	0	3.91	1	59	0	1	2	0	2.03
93-94—Adirondack	AHL	4	240	3	1	0	13	0	3.25	—	—	—	—	—	—	—
—Detroit	NHL	41	2286	23	8	5	105	2	2.76	6	307	3	2	12	1	2.35
94-95—Adirondack	AHL	2	120	1	1	0	6	0	3.00	—	—	—	—	—	—	—
—Detroit	NHL	19	1087	14	5	0	41	1	2.26	2	68	0	0	2	0	1.76
95-96—Detroit	NHL	50	2933	*39	6	5	106	5	2.17	15	936	8	7	33	2	2.12
96-97—Detroit	NHL	47	2769	23	13	9	106	6	2.30	2	47	0	0	2	0	2.55
97-98—Detroit	NHL	64	3807	33	20	11	140	6	2.21	22	1361	16	6	48	2	2.12
98-99—Detroit	NHL	63	3691	34	25	4	149	3	2.42	6	358	4	2	14	1	2.35
99-00—Detroit	NHL	53	3148	30	14	8	126	6	2.40	9	547	5	4	18	2	1.97
00-01—Detroit	NHL	52	2834	25	19	4	127	1	2.69	6	365	2	4	15	1	2.47
NHL Totals (8 years)		389	22555	221	110	46	900	30	2.39	68	3989	38	25	144	9	2.17

O'SULLIVAN, CHRIS — D — MIGHTY DUCKS

PERSONAL: Born May 15, 1974, in Dorchester, Mass. ... 6-2/205. ... Shoots left.
TRANSACTIONS/CAREER NOTES: Selected by Calgary Flames in second round (second Flames pick, 30th overall) of NHL entry draft (June 20, 1992). ... Suffered concussion (December 20, 1997); missed three games. ... Traded by Flames to New York Rangers for D Lee Sorochan (March 23, 1999). ... Signed as free agent by Vancouver Canucks (August 11, 1999). ... Signed as free agent by Mighty Ducks of Anaheim (July 20, 2000).
HONORS: Named NCAA Tournament Most Valuable Player (1994-95). ... Named to NCAA All-Tournament team (1994-95). ... Named to NCAA All-America (East) second team (1994-95).

Season Team	League			REGULAR SEASON							PLAYOFFS			
		Gms.	G	A	Pts.	PIM	+/-	PP	SH	Gms.	G	A	Pts.	PIM
91-92—Catholic Memorial	Mass. H.S.	26	26	23	49	65	...	...	...	—	—	—	—	—
92-93—Boston University	Hockey East	5	0	2	2	4	...	...	...	—	—	—	—	—
93-94—Boston University	Hockey East	32	5	18	23	25	...	...	...	—	—	—	—	—
94-95—Boston University	Hockey East	40	23	33	56	48	...	...	...	—	—	—	—	—
95-96—Boston University	Hockey East	37	12	35	47	50	...	...	...	—	—	—	—	—
96-97—Calgary	NHL	27	2	8	10	2	0	1	0	—	—	—	—	—
—Saint John	AHL	29	3	8	11	17	...	...	...	5	0	4	4	0
97-98—Saint John	AHL	32	4	10	14	2	...	...	...	21	2	17	19	18
—Calgary	NHL	12	0	2	2	10	4	0	0	—	—	—	—	—

Season Team	League	REGULAR SEASON								PLAYOFFS				
		Gms.	G	A	Pts.	PIM	+/-	PP	SH	Gms.	G	A	Pts.	PIM
98-99—Saint John	AHL	41	7	29	36	24	...	...	...	—	—	—	—	—
—Calgary	NHL	10	0	1	1	2	-1	0	0	—	—	—	—	—
—Hartford	AHL	10	1	4	5	0	...	...	...	7	1	3	4	11
99-00—Syracuse	AHL	59	18	47	65	24	...	...	...	4	0	1	1	0
—Vancouver	NHL	11	0	5	5	2	2	0	0	—	—	—	—	—
00-01—Cincinnati	AHL	60	9	40	49	31	...	...	...	4	0	3	3	0
NHL Totals (4 years)		60	2	16	18	16	5	1	0					

OTT, STEVE   C/LW   STARS

PERSONAL: Born August 19, 1982, in Stoney Point, Ont. ... 5-11/160. ... Shoots left.
TRANSACTIONS/CAREER NOTES: Selected by Dallas Stars in first round (first Stars pick, 25th overall) of NHL entry draft (June 24, 2000).
HONORS: Named to Can.HL All-Star second team (2000-01).

Season Team	League	REGULAR SEASON								PLAYOFFS				
		Gms.	G	A	Pts.	PIM	+/-	PP	SH	Gms.	G	A	Pts.	PIM
98-99—Leamington	Jr. B	48	14	30	44	110	...	...	...	—	—	—	—	—
99-00—Windsor	OHL	66	23	39	62	131	...	...	...	12	3	5	8	21
00-01—Windsor	OHL	55	50	37	87	164	...	...	...	9	3	8	11	27

OUELLET, MAXIME   G   FLYERS

PERSONAL: Born June 17, 1981, in Beauport, Que. ... 6-0/180. ... Catches left.
TRANSACTIONS/CAREER NOTES: Selected by Philadelphia Flyers in first round (first Flyers pick, 22nd overall) of NHL entry draft (June 26, 1999).
HONORS: Named to QMJHL All-Star second team (1998-99 through 2000-01). ... Won Mike Bossy Trophy (1998-99). ... Won Jacques Plante Trophy (1998-99).

Season Team	League	REGULAR SEASON								PLAYOFFS						
		Gms.	Min.	W	L	T	GA	SO	Avg.	Gms.	Min.	W	L	GA	SO	Avg.
97-98—Quebec	QMJHL	24	1199	12	7	1	66	0	3.30	7	305	3	1	16	0	3.15
98-99—Quebec	QMJHL	*58	*3447	*40	12	*6	155	3	*2.70	13	803	6	7	41	†1	3.06
99-00—Quebec	QMJHL	53	2984	31	16	4	133	2	2.67	11	638	7	4	28	*2	*2.63
00-01—Philadelphia	NHL	2	76	0	1	0	3	0	2.37	—	—	—	—	—	—	—
—Philadelphia	AHL	2	86	1	0	0	4	0	2.79	—	—	—	—	—	—	—
—Rouyn-Noranda	QMJHL	25	1471	18	6	1	65	3	2.65	8	490	4	4	25	0	3.06
NHL Totals (1 year)		2	76	0	1	0	3	0	2.37							

OZOLINSH, SANDIS   D   HURRICANES

PERSONAL: Born August 3, 1972, in Riga, U.S.S.R. ... 6-3/205. ... Shoots left. ... Name pronounced SAN-diz OH-zoh-lihnsh.
TRANSACTIONS/CAREER NOTES: Selected by San Jose Sharks in second round (third Sharks pick, 30th overall) of NHL entry draft (June 22, 1991). ... Strained back (November 7, 1992); missed one game. ... Tore anterior cruciate ligament in knee (December 30, 1992); missed remainder of season. ... Injured knee (December 11, 1993); missed one game. ... Traded by Sharks to Colorado Avalanche for RW Owen Nolan (October 26, 1995). ... Separated left shoulder (December 7, 1995); missed four games. ... Fractured finger (February 23, 1996); missed two games. ... Suffered back spasms (March 9, 1997); missed two games. ... Separated shoulder (October 7, 1997); missed two games. ... Injured knee (October 17, 1997) and underwent arthroscopic surgery; missed 13 games. ... Missed first 38 games of 1998-99 season due to contract dispute. ... Bruised sternum (February 9, 1999); missed two games. ... Traded by Avalanche with second-round pick (LW Tomas Kurka) in 2000 draft to Carolina Hurricanes for D Nolan Pratt, first-(C Vaclav Nedorost) and two second-round (C Jared Aulin and D Argis Saviels) picks in 2000 draft (June 24, 2000). ... Injured knee (December 29, 2000) and underwent surgery; missed 10 games.
HONORS: Played in NHL All-Star Game (1994, 1997, 1998, 2000 and 2001). ... Named to NHL All-Star first team (1996-97).
MISCELLANEOUS: Member of Stanley Cup championship team (1996).
STATISTICAL PLATEAUS: Three-goal games: 1999-00 (1), 2000-01 (1). Total: 2.

Season Team	League	REGULAR SEASON								PLAYOFFS				
		Gms.	G	A	Pts.	PIM	+/-	PP	SH	Gms.	G	A	Pts.	PIM
90-91—Dynamo Riga	USSR	44	0	3	3	49	...	...	...	—	—	—	—	—
91-92—HC Riga	CIS	30	5	0	5	42	...	...	...	—	—	—	—	—
—Kansas City	IHL	34	6	9	15	20	...	...	...	15	2	5	7	22
92-93—San Jose	NHL	37	7	16	23	40	-9	2	0	—	—	—	—	—
93-94—San Jose	NHL	81	26	38	64	24	16	4	0	14	0	10	10	8
94-95—San Jose	NHL	48	9	16	25	30	-6	3	1	11	3	2	5	6
95-96—San Francisco	IHL	2	1	0	1	0	...	...	...	—	—	—	—	—
—San Jose	NHL	7	1	3	4	4	2	1	0	—	—	—	—	—
—Colorado	NHL	66	13	37	50	50	0	7	1	22	5	14	19	16
96-97—Colorado	NHL	80	23	45	68	88	4	13	0	17	4	13	17	24
97-98—Colorado	NHL	66	13	38	51	65	-12	9	0	7	0	7	7	14
98-99—Colorado	NHL	39	7	25	32	22	10	4	0	19	4	8	12	22
99-00—Colorado	NHL	82	16	36	52	46	7	6	0	17	5	5	10	20
00-01—Carolina	NHL	72	12	32	44	71	-25	4	2	6	0	2	2	5
NHL Totals (9 years)		578	127	286	413	440	-3	53	4	113	21	61	82	115

O

PERSONAL: Born December 17, 1977, in Ornskoldsvik, Sweden. ... 5-11/190. ... Shoots left.

TRANSACTIONS/CAREER NOTES: Selected by Colorado Avalanche in seventh round (10th Avalanche pick, 176th overall) of NHL entry draft (June 22, 1996). ... Traded by Avalanche with LW Brian Rolston, D Martin Grenier and first-round pick (LW Martin Samuelsson) in 2000 draft to Boston Bruins for D Ray Bourque and LW Dave Andreychuk (March 6, 2000). ... Traded by Bruins to Mighty Ducks for Anaheim for LW Andrei Nazarov and D Patrick Traverse (November 18, 2000).

		REGULAR SEASON								PLAYOFFS				
Season Team	League	Gms.	G	A	Pts.	PIM	+/-	PP	SH	Gms.	G	A	Pts.	PIM
94-95—MoDo Ornsk.	Swed. Jrs.	30	10	11	21	26	...	...	...	—	—	—	—	—
—MoDo Ornskoldsvik	Sweden	1	0	0	0	0	...	...	...	—	—	—	—	—
95-96—MoDo Ornskoldsvik	Sweden	36	1	3	4	8	...	...	...	—	—	—	—	—
—MoDo Ornsk.	Swed. Jrs.	5	2	6	8	2	...	...	...	—	—	—	—	—
96-97—MoDo Ornskoldsvik	Sweden	49	8	9	17	83	...	...	...	—	—	—	—	—
97-98—MoDo Ornskoldsvik	Sweden	23	6	11	17	24	...	...	...	9	3	0	3	6
98-99—MoDo Ornskoldsvik	Sweden	50	17	17	34	44	...	...	...	13	3	3	6	10
99-00—MoDo Ornskoldsvik	Sweden	47	16	11	27	67	...	...	...	13	3	3	6	8
00-01—Boston	NHL	17	1	1	2	6	-5	0	0	—	—	—	—	—
—Anaheim	NHL	59	3	4	7	14	-9	1	1	—	—	—	—	—
NHL Totals (1 year).............		76	4	5	9	20	-14	1	1					

PERSONAL: Born May 5, 1972, in Skalica, Czechoslovakia. ... 5-10/180. ... Shoots left. ... Full Name: Zigmund Palffy. ... Name pronounced PAL-fee.

TRANSACTIONS/CAREER NOTES: Selected by New York Islanders in second round (second Islanders pick, 26th overall) of NHL entry draft (June 22, 1991). ... Suffered concussion (February 17, 1996); missed one game. ... Sprained shoulder (January 13, 1997); missed two games. ... Missed first 32 games of 1998-99 season due to contract dispute; played in Europe. ... Traded by Islanders with C Bryan Smolinski, G Marcel Cousineau and fourth-round pick (C Daniel Johansson) in 1999 draft to Los Angeles Kings for C Olli Jokinen, LW Josh Green, D Mathieu Biron and first-round pick (LW Taylor Pyatt) in 1999 draft (June 20, 1999). ... Suffered back spasms (December 4, 1999); missed four games. ... Suffered back spasms (January 4, 2000); missed one game. ... Strained right shoulder (March 15, 2000); missed final 12 games of regular season. ... Strained hamstring (December 16, 2000); missed eight games. ... Suffered from the flu (January 8, 2001); missed one game.

HONORS: Named Czechoslovakian League Rookie of the Year (1990-91). ... Named to Czechoslovakian League All-Star team (1991-92). ... Named to play in NHL All-Star Game (1997); replaced by D Scott Lachance due to injury. ... Played in NHL All-Star Game (1998 and 2001).

MISCELLANEOUS: Failed to score on a penalty shot (vs. Fred Brathwaite, April 7, 2001).

STATISTICAL PLATEAUS: Three-goal games: 1995-96 (2), 1996-97 (1), 1997-98 (1), 1998-99 (1), 2000-01 (1). Total: 7.

		REGULAR SEASON								PLAYOFFS				
Season Team	League	Gms.	G	A	Pts.	PIM	+/-	PP	SH	Gms.	G	A	Pts.	PIM
90-91—Nitra...........................	Czech.	50	34	16	50	18	...	...	...	—	—	—	—	—
91-92—Dukla Trencin..............	Czech.	32	23	25	*48		...	...	...	—	—	—	—	—
92-93—Dukla Trencin..............	Czech.	43	38	41	79		...	...	...	—	—	—	—	—
93-94—Salt Lake City..............	IHL	57	25	32	57	83	...	...	...	—	—	—	—	—
—Slovakian Oly. team	Int'l	8	3	7	10	8	...	...	...	—	—	—	—	—
—New York Islanders.....	NHL	5	0	0	0	0	-6	0	0	—	—	—	—	—
94-95—Denver	IHL	33	20	23	43	40	...	...	...	—	—	—	—	—
—New York Islanders.....	NHL	33	10	7	17	6	3	1	0	—	—	—	—	—
95-96—New York Islanders.....	NHL	81	43	44	87	56	-17	17	1	—	—	—	—	—
96-97—New York Islanders.....	NHL	80	48	42	90	43	21	6	4	—	—	—	—	—
97-98—New York Islanders.....	NHL	82	45	42	87	34	-2	*17	2	—	—	—	—	—
98-99—HK 36 Skalica	Slovakia	9	11	8	19	6	...	...	...	—	—	—	—	—
—New York Islanders.....	NHL	50	22	28	50	34	-6	5	2	—	—	—	—	—
99-00—Los Angeles...............	NHL	64	27	39	66	32	18	4	0	4	2	0	2	0
00-01—Los Angeles...............	NHL	73	38	51	89	20	22	12	4	13	3	5	8	8
NHL Totals (8 years)...........		468	233	253	486	225	33	62	13	17	5	5	10	8

PERSONAL: Born December 27, 1974, in Winchester, Mass. ... 6-1/190. ... Shoots left.

TRANSACTIONS/CAREER NOTES: Selected by New Jersey Devils in second round (second Devils pick, 32nd overall) of NHL entry draft (June 26, 1993). ... Suffered from the flu (January 14, 1999); missed two games. ... Bruised shoulder (March 17, 1999); missed 10 games. ... Suffered facial lacerations (January 29, 2000); missed three games. ... Bruised shoulder (October 14, 2000); missed 13 games.

HONORS: Named to NCAA All-America (East) first team (1995-96). ... Named Hockey East Player of the Year (1995-96). ... Named to Hockey East All-Star team (1995-96).

MISCELLANEOUS: Member of Stanley Cup championship team (2000). ... Failed to score on a penalty shot (vs. Rick Tabaracci, December 30, 1998).

		REGULAR SEASON								PLAYOFFS				
Season Team	League	Gms.	G	A	Pts.	PIM	+/-	PP	SH	Gms.	G	A	Pts.	PIM
89-90—Burlington H.S.	Mass. H.S.	23	33	30	63	18	...	...	...	—	—	—	—	—
90-91—Burlington H.S.	Mass. H.S.	20	19	27	46	10	...	...	...	—	—	—	—	—
91-92—Burlington H.S.	Mass. H.S.	20	35	34	69	14	...	...	...	—	—	—	—	—
92-93—Boston University	Hockey East	37	16	22	38	16	...	...	...	—	—	—	—	—
93-94—Boston University	Hockey East	37	17	25	42	27	...	...	...	—	—	—	—	—
94-95—Boston University	Hockey East	20	7	13	20	6	...	...	...	—	—	—	—	—
95-96—Boston University	Hockey East	39	38	29	67	6	...	...	...	—	—	—	—	—
—Albany.........................	AHL	5	3	1	4	0	...	...	...	3	0	0	0	0
96-97—Albany......................	AHL	12	3	9	12	0	...	...	...	—	—	—	—	—
—New Jersey	NHL	46	6	8	14	6	-1	0	0	6	0	1	1	0

P

Season Team	League	REGULAR SEASON								PLAYOFFS				
		Gms.	G	A	Pts.	PIM	+/-	PP	SH	Gms.	G	A	Pts.	PIM
97-98—New Jersey	NHL	23	1	3	4	4	-4	0	0	3	0	2	2	0
—Albany	AHL	51	18	19	37	24	...	...	...	—	—	—	—	—
98-99—New Jersey	NHL	70	14	13	27	10	3	1	1	7	1	0	1	0
99-00—New Jersey	NHL	71	7	8	15	4	0	0	0	23	0	5	5	0
00-01—New Jersey	NHL	63	4	12	16	16	3	0	0	25	1	4	5	4
NHL Totals (5 years)		273	32	44	76	40	1	1	1	64	2	12	14	4

PANZER, JEFF　　　　C　　　　BLUES

PERSONAL: Born April 7, 1978, in Grand Forks, N.D. ... 5-10/160. ... Shoots left.
TRANSACTIONS/CAREER NOTES: Signed as non-drafted free agent by St. Louis Blues (May 7, 2001).
HONORS: Named to WCHA All-Star second team (1998-99). ... Named to WCHA All-Star first team (1999-2000 and 2000-01). ... Named to NCAA All-America (West) first team (1999-2000 and 2000-01).

Season Team	League	REGULAR SEASON								PLAYOFFS				
		Gms.	G	A	Pts.	PIM	+/-	PP	SH	Gms.	G	A	Pts.	PIM
97-98—Univ. of North Dakota	WCHA	37	14	23	37	18	...	...	...	—	—	—	—	—
98-99—Univ. of North Dakota	WCHA	39	21	26	47	14	...	...	...	—	—	—	—	—
99-00—Univ. of North Dakota	WCHA	44	19	*44	63	16	...	...	...	—	—	—	—	—
00-01—Univ. of North Dakota	WCHA	46	26	*55	*81	28	...	...	...	—	—	—	—	—
—Worcester	AHL	—	—	—	—	—	...	...	...	5	1	2	3	0

PARENT, RICH　　　　G

PERSONAL: Born January 12, 1973, in Montreal. ... 6-3/215. ... Catches left.
TRANSACTIONS/CAREER NOTES: Signed as non-drafted free agent by St. Louis Blues (July 17, 1997). ... Strained groin (October 1, 1997); missed three games. ... Suffered scrotal contusion and ruptured testicle (February 13, 1999); missed 11 games. ... Traded by Blues with D Chris McAlpine to Tampa Bay Lightning for RW Stephane Richer (January 13, 2000). ... Suffered from tendinitis (March 28, 2000); missed final seven games of season. ... Traded by Lightning to Ottawa Senators for seventh-round pick (traded to Buffalo) in 2000 draft (June 4, 2000). ... Signed as free agent by Pittsburgh Penguins (September 19, 2000).
HONORS: Won Norris Trophy (1996-97). ... Named Colonial Hockey League Goaltender of the year (1994-95 and 1995-96).

Season Team	League	REGULAR SEASON								PLAYOFFS						
		Gms.	Min	W	L	T	GA	SO	Avg.	Gms.	Min.	W	L	GA	SO	Avg.
91-92—Fort McMurray	AJHL	23	1363	...	...	...	90	0	3.96	—	—	—	—	—	—	—
—Vernon	BCJHL	2	52	0	1	0	5	0	5.77	—	—	—	—	—	—	—
92-93—Spokane	WHL	36	1767	12	14	2	129	2	4.38	1	5	0	0	0	0	0.00
93-94—Fort McMurray	AJHL	29	1712	...	...	...	91	1	3.19	—	—	—	—	—	—	—
94-95—Muskegon	Col.HL	35	1867	17	11	3	112	1	3.60	13	725	7	3	47	1	3.89
95-96—Muskegon	Col.HL	36	2086	23	7	4	85	2	2.44	—	—	—	—	—	—	—
—Detroit	IHL	19	1040	16	0	‡1	48	2	2.77	7	362	3	3	22	0	3.65
96-97—Detroit	IHL	53	2815	31	13	‡4	104	4	2.22	15	786	8	3	21	1	*1.60
97-98—Manitoba	IHL	26	1334	8	12	‡2	69	3	3.10	—	—	—	—	—	—	—
—St. Louis	NHL	1	12	0	0	0	0	0	...	—	—	—	—	—	—	—
—Detroit	IHL	7	418	4	0	‡3	15	0	2.15	5	157	1	0	6	0	2.29
98-99—Worcester	AHL	20	1100	8	8	2	56	1	3.05	—	—	—	—	—	—	—
—St. Louis	NHL	10	519	4	3	1	22	1	2.54	—	—	—	—	—	—	—
99-00—Utah	IHL	27	1571	21	7	‡3	58	1	2.22	—	—	—	—	—	—	—
—Tampa Bay	NHL	14	698	2	7	1	43	0	3.70	—	—	—	—	—	—	—
—Detroit	IHL	10	539	3	5	‡1	23	1	2.56	—	—	—	—	—	—	—
00-01—Pittsburgh	NHL	7	332	1	1	3	17	0	3.07	—	—	—	—	—	—	—
—Wilkes-Barre/Scranton	AHL	35	2043	17	12	5	80	2	2.35	*21	*1347	13	8	*58	1	2.58
NHL Totals (4 years)		32	1561	7	11	5	82	1	3.15							

PARKER, SCOTT　　　　RW　　　　AVALANCHE

PERSONAL: Born January 29, 1978, in Hanford, Calif. ... 6-4/220. ... Shoots right.
TRANSACTIONS/CAREER NOTES: Selected by New Jersey Devils in third round (sixth Devils pick, 63rd overall) of NHL entry draft (June 22, 1996). ... Returned to draft pool by Devils and selected by Colorado Avalanche in first round (fourth Avalanche pick, 20th overall) of NHL entry draft (June 27, 1998). ... Bruised shoulder (December 11, 2000); missed four games. ... Bruised foot (February 17, 2001); missed three games.
MISCELLANEOUS: Member of Stanley Cup championship team (2001).

Season Team	League	REGULAR SEASON								PLAYOFFS				
		Gms.	G	A	Pts.	PIM	+/-	PP	SH	Gms.	G	A	Pts.	PIM
94-95—Spokane	KIJHL	43	7	21	28	128	...	...	...	—	—	—	—	—
95-96—Kelowna	WHL	64	3	4	7	159	...	...	...	6	0	0	0	12
96-97—Kelowna	WHL	68	18	8	26	*330	...	...	...	6	0	2	2	4
97-98—Kelowna	WHL	71	30	22	52	243	...	...	...	7	6	0	6	23
98-99—Hershey	AHL	32	4	3	7	143	...	...	...	4	0	0	0	6
—Colorado	NHL	27	0	0	0	71	-3	0	0	—	—	—	—	—
99-00—Hershey	AHL	68	12	7	19	206	...	...	...	11	1	1	2	56
00-01—Colorado	NHL	69	2	3	5	155	-2	0	0	4	0	0	0	2
NHL Totals (2 years)		96	2	3	5	226	-5	0	0	4	0	0	0	2

P

PAROULEK, MARTIN — LW — BLUE JACKETS

PERSONAL: Born November 4, 1979, in Uherske Hradisti, Czechoslovakia. ... 5-11/187. ... Shoots left.
TRANSACTIONS/CAREER NOTES: Selected by Columbus Blue Jackets in ninth round (ninth Blue Jackets pick, 278th overall) of NHL entry draft (June 24, 2000).

		REGULAR SEASON								PLAYOFFS				
Season Team	League	Gms.	G	A	Pts.	PIM	+/-	PP	SH	Gms.	G	A	Pts.	PIM
98-99—HC Vsetin	Czech. Jrs.	45	25	19	44	...	...	...	...	7	0	1	1	...
—Vsetin	Czech Rep.	11	1	1	2	...	...	...	...	—	—	—	—	—
99-00—Vsetin	Czech Rep.	48	11	14	25	26	...	...	...	—	—	—	—	—
00-01—Vsetin	Czech Rep.	24	9	3	12	...	...	...	...	—	—	—	—	—

PARRISH, MARK — RW — ISLANDERS

PERSONAL: Born February 2, 1977, in Edina, Minn. ... 5-11/191. ... Shoots right.
TRANSACTIONS/CAREER NOTES: Selected by Colorado Avalanche in third round (third Avalanche pick, 79th overall) of NHL entry draft (June 22, 1996). ... Rights traded by Avalanche with third-round pick (D Lance Ward) in 1998 draft to Florida Panthers for RW/C Tom Fitzgerald (March 24, 1998). ... Strained back (February 14, 2000); missed one game. ... Traded by Panthers with LW Oleg Kvasha to New York Islanders for C Olli Jokinen and G Roberto Luongo (June 24, 2000). ... Sprained medial collateral ligament in right knee (February 9, 2001); missed 12 games.
HONORS: Named to NCAA All-America (West) second team (1996-97). ... Named to Can.HL All-Star second team (1997-98). ... Named to WHL (West) All-Star first team (1997-98).
STATISTICAL PLATEAUS: Four-goal games: 1998-99 (1).

		REGULAR SEASON								PLAYOFFS				
Season Team	League	Gms.	G	A	Pts.	PIM	+/-	PP	SH	Gms.	G	A	Pts.	PIM
94-95—Thomas Jefferson	Minn. H.S.	27	40	20	60	42	...	...	...	—	—	—	—	—
95-96—St. Cloud State	WCHA	38	15	14	29	28	...	...	...	—	—	—	—	—
96-97—St. Cloud State	WCHA	35	27	15	42	60	...	...	...	—	—	—	—	—
97-98—Seattle	WHL	54	54	38	92	29	...	...	...	5	2	3	5	2
—New Haven	AHL	1	1	0	1	2	...	...	...	—	—	—	—	—
98-99—Florida	NHL	73	24	13	37	25	-6	5	0	—	—	—	—	—
—New Haven	AHL	2	1	0	1	0	...	...	...	—	—	—	—	—
99-00—Florida	NHL	81	26	18	44	39	1	6	0	4	0	1	1	0
00-01—New York Islanders	NHL	70	17	13	30	28	-27	6	0	—	—	—	—	—
NHL Totals (3 years)		224	67	44	111	92	-32	17	0	4	0	1	1	0

PASSMORE, STEVE — G — BLACKHAWKS

PERSONAL: Born January 29, 1973, in Thunder Bay, Ont. ... 5-9/165. ... Catches left.
TRANSACTIONS/CAREER NOTES: Selected by Quebec Nordiques in ninth round (10th Nordiques pick, 196th overall) of NHL entry draft (June 20, 1992). ... Traded by Nordiques to Edmonton Oilers for D Brad Werenka (March 21, 1994). ... Signed as free agent by Chicago Blackhawks (July 7, 1999). ... Traded by Blackhawks to Los Angeles Kings for fourth-round pick (D Olli Malmivaura) in 2000 draft (May 1, 2000). ... Traded by Kings to Blackhawks for eighth-round pick (D Mike Gabinet) in 2001 draft (February 28, 2001).
HONORS: Named to WHL (West) All-Star first team (1992-93 and 1993-94). ... Won Fred Hunt Memorial Award (1996-97). ... Named to AHL All-Star second team (1998-99).

		REGULAR SEASON								PLAYOFFS						
Season Team	League	Gms.	Min	W	L	T	GA	SO	Avg.	Gms.	Min.	W	L	GA	SO	Avg.
88-89—Tri-City	WHL	1	60	0	1	0	6	0	6.00	—	—	—	—	—	—	—
89-90—Tri-City	WHL	4	215	...	...	...	17	0	4.74	—	—	—	—	—	—	—
90-91—Victoria	WHL	35	1838	3	25	1	190	0	6.20	—	—	—	—	—	—	—
91-92—Victoria	WHL	*71	*4228	15	50	7	347	0	4.92	—	—	—	—	—	—	—
92-93—Victoria	WHL	43	2402	14	24	2	150	1	3.75	—	—	—	—	—	—	—
—Kamloops	WHL	25	1479	19	6	0	69	1	2.80	7	401	4	2	22	1	3.29
93-94—Kamloops	WHL	36	1927	22	9	2	88	1	*2.74	18	1099	†11	7	60	0	3.28
94-95—Cape Breton	AHL	25	1455	8	13	3	93	0	3.84	—	—	—	—	—	—	—
95-96—Cape Breton	AHL	2	90	1	0	0	2	0	1.33	—	—	—	—	—	—	—
96-97—Raleigh	ECHL	2	118	1	1	‡0	13	0	6.61	—	—	—	—	—	—	—
—Hamilton	AHL	27	1568	12	12	3	70	1	2.68	22	1325	12	*10	*61	†2	2.76
97-98—Hamilton	AHL	27	1656	11	10	6	87	2	3.15	3	133	0	2	14	0	6.32
—San Antonio	IHL	14	737	3	8	2	56	0	4.56	—	—	—	—	—	—	—
98-99—Hamilton	AHL	54	3148	24	21	†7	117	4	2.23	11	680	5	6	31	0	2.74
—Edmonton	NHL	6	362	1	4	1	17	0	2.82	—	—	—	—	—	—	—
99-00—Chicago	NHL	24	1388	7	12	3	63	1	2.72	—	—	—	—	—	—	—
—Cleveland	IHL	2	120	1	0	1	3	1	1.50	—	—	—	—	—	—	—
00-01—Lowell	AHL	6	333	2	4	0	24	0	4.32	—	—	—	—	—	—	—
—Los Angeles	NHL	14	718	3	8	1	37	1	3.09	—	—	—	—	—	—	—
—Chicago	IHL	6	340	2	2	‡2	22	0	3.88	—	—	—	—	—	—	—
—Chicago	NHL	6	340	0	4	1	14	0	2.47	—	—	—	—	—	—	—
NHL Totals (3 years)		50	2808	11	28	6	131	2	2.80							

PATERA, PAVEL — C — WILD

PERSONAL: Born September 6, 1971, in Kladno, Czechoslovakia. ... 6-1/172. ... Shoots left.
TRANSACTIONS/CAREER NOTES: Selected by Dallas Stars in sixth round (fourth Stars pick, 153rd overall) of NHL entry draft (June 27, 1998). ... Traded by Stars with C Aaron Gavey, eighth-round pick (C Eric Johansson) in 2000 draft and fourth-round pick in 2002 draft to Minnesota Wild for D Brad Lukowich, third- (C Yared Hagos) and ninth-round (RW Dale Sullivan) picks in 2001 draft (June 25, 2000).

Season Team	League	REGULAR SEASON								PLAYOFFS				
		Gms.	G	A	Pts.	PIM	+/-	PP	SH	Gms.	G	A	Pts.	PIM
90-91—Poldi Kladno	Czech.	3	0	0	0	...	...	...	...	—	—	—	—	—
91-92—Poldi Kladno	Czech.	38	12	13	25	26	...	...	...	8	8	4	12	0
92-93—Poldi Kladno	Czech.	42	9	23	32	...	...	...	...	—	—	—	—	—
93-94—HC Kladno	Czech Rep.	43	21	39	60	...	...	...	...	11	5	10	15	...
94-95—HC Kladno	Czech Rep.	43	26	49	75	24	...	...	...	11	5	7	12	6
95-96—Poldi Kladno	Czech Rep.	40	24	31	55	38	...	...	...	8	3	1	4	34
96-97—AIK Solna	Sweden	50	19	24	43	44	...	...	...	7	2	3	5	6
97-98—AIK Solna	Sweden	46	8	17	25	50	...	...	...	—	—	—	—	—
98-99—Vsetin	Czech Rep.	52	16	37	53	58	...	...	...	12	5	*10	*15	...
99-00—Dallas	NHL	12	1	4	5	4	-1	0	0	—	—	—	—	—
—Vsetin	Czech Rep.	29	8	14	22	36	...	...	...	9	3	4	7	8
00-01—Cleveland	IHL	54	8	44	52	22	...	...	...	—	—	—	—	—
—Minnesota	NHL	20	1	3	4	4	-8	0	0	—	—	—	—	—
NHL Totals (2 years)		**32**	**2**	**7**	**9**	**8**	**-9**	**0**	**0**					

PATRICK, JAMES   D   SABRES

PERSONAL: Born June 14, 1963, in Winnipeg. ... 6-2/200. ... Shoots right. ... Full Name: James A. Patrick. ... Brother of Steve Patrick, right winger with three NHL teams (1980-81 through 1985-86).

TRANSACTIONS/CAREER NOTES: Selected by New York Rangers in first round (first Rangers pick, ninth overall) of NHL entry draft (June 10, 1981). ... Injured groin (October 1984). ... Pinched nerve (December 15, 1985). ... Strained left knee ligaments (March 1988). ... Bruised shoulder and chest (December 1988). ... Pulled groin (March 13, 1989). ... Sprained shoulder (November 4, 1992); missed three games. ... Bruised right shoulder (November 27, 1992); missed three games. ... Sprained left knee (January 27, 1993); missed four games. ... Suffered herniated disc (February 24, 1993); missed two games. ... Suffered herniated disc (March 28, 1993); missed remainder of season. ... Traded by Rangers with C Darren Turcotte to Hartford Whalers for RW Steve Larmer, LW Nick Kypreos and sixth-round pick (C Yuri Litvinov) in 1994 draft (November 2, 1993). ... Suffered herniated disc (December 7, 1993); missed five games. ... Traded by Whalers with C Michael Nylander and D Zarley Zalapski to Calgary Flames for D Gary Suter, LW Paul Ranheim and C Ted Drury (March 10, 1994). ... Strained left hip (March 10, 1995); missed five games. ... Suffered concussion (April 9, 1996); missed two games. ... Injured back (October 16, 1996); missed one game. ... Strained knee (October 24, 1996); missed five games. ... Suffered concussion (November 20, 1996); missed two games. ... Underwent knee surgery (December 12, 1996); missed remainder of season. ... Strained neck (October 22, 1997); missed six games. ... Reinjured neck (November 13, 1997); missed nine games. ... Suffered charley horse (January 5, 1998); missed one game. ... Signed as free agent by Buffalo Sabres (October 7, 1998). ... Suffered pinched nerve in neck (October 10, 1998); missed three games. ... Suffered concussion (February 24, 1999); missed one game. ... Suffered back spasms (February 17, 2000); missed two games. ... Injured shoulder (September 23, 2000); missed first five games of season.

HONORS: Named SJHL Player of the Year (1980-81). ... Named to SJHL All-Star first team (1980-81). ... Won WCHA Rookie of the Year Award (1981-82). ... Named to WCHA All-Star second team (1981-82). ... Named to NCAA All-Tournament team (1981-82). ... Named to NCAA All-America (West) team (1982-83). ... Named to WCHA All-Star first team (1982-83).

Season Team	League	REGULAR SEASON								PLAYOFFS				
		Gms.	G	A	Pts.	PIM	+/-	PP	SH	Gms.	G	A	Pts.	PIM
80-81—Prince Albert	SJHL	59	21	61	82	162	...	...	...	4	1	6	7	0
81-82—Univ. of North Dakota	WCHA	42	5	24	29	26	...	...	...	—	—	—	—	—
82-83—Univ. of North Dakota	WCHA	36	12	36	48	29	...	...	...	—	—	—	—	—
83-84—Can. Olympic team	Int'l	63	7	24	31	52	...	...	...	—	—	—	—	—
—New York Rangers	NHL	12	1	7	8	2	6	0	0	5	0	3	3	2
84-85—New York Rangers	NHL	75	8	28	36	71	-17	4	1	3	0	0	0	4
85-86—New York Rangers	NHL	75	14	29	43	88	14	2	1	16	1	5	6	34
86-87—New York Rangers	NHL	78	10	45	55	62	13	5	0	6	1	2	3	2
87-88—New York Rangers	NHL	70	17	45	62	52	16	9	0	—	—	—	—	—
88-89—New York Rangers	NHL	68	11	36	47	41	3	6	0	4	0	1	1	2
89-90—New York Rangers	NHL	73	14	43	57	50	4	9	0	10	3	8	11	0
90-91—New York Rangers	NHL	74	10	49	59	58	-5	6	0	6	0	0	0	6
91-92—New York Rangers	NHL	80	14	57	71	54	34	6	0	13	0	7	7	12
92-93—New York Rangers	NHL	60	5	21	26	61	1	3	0	—	—	—	—	—
93-94—New York Rangers	NHL	6	0	3	3	2	1	0	0	—	—	—	—	—
—Hartford	NHL	47	8	20	28	32	-12	4	1	—	—	—	—	—
—Calgary	NHL	15	2	2	4	6	6	1	0	7	0	1	1	6
94-95—Calgary	NHL	43	0	10	10	14	-3	0	0	5	0	1	1	0
95-96—Calgary	NHL	80	3	32	35	30	3	1	0	4	0	0	0	2
96-97—Calgary	NHL	19	3	1	4	6	2	1	0	—	—	—	—	—
97-98—Calgary	NHL	60	6	11	17	26	-2	1	0	—	—	—	—	—
98-99—Buffalo	NHL	45	1	7	8	16	12	0	0	20	0	1	1	12
99-00—Buffalo	NHL	66	5	8	13	22	8	0	0	5	0	1	1	2
00-01—Buffalo	NHL	54	4	9	13	12	9	1	0	13	1	2	3	2
NHL Totals (18 years)		**1100**	**136**	**463**	**599**	**705**	**93**	**59**	**3**	**117**	**6**	**32**	**38**	**86**

PAYER, SERGE   C   PANTHERS

PERSONAL: Born May 7, 1979, in Rockland, Ont. ... 5-11/175. ... Shoots left.
TRANSACTIONS/CAREER NOTES: Signed as non-drafted free agent by Florida Panthers (October 2, 1997).

Season Team	League	REGULAR SEASON								PLAYOFFS				
		Gms.	G	A	Pts.	PIM	+/-	PP	SH	Gms.	G	A	Pts.	PIM
95-96—Kitchener	OHL	66	8	16	24	18	...	...	...	12	0	2	2	2
96-97—Kitchener	OHL	63	7	16	23	27	...	...	...	13	1	3	4	2
97-98—Kitchener	OHL	44	20	21	41	51	...	...	...	6	3	0	3	7
98-99—Kitchener	OHL	40	18	19	37	22	...	...	...	—	—	—	—	—
99-00—Kitchener	OHL	44	10	26	36	53	...	...	...	5	0	3	3	6
00-01—Louisville	AHL	32	6	6	12	15	...	...	...	—	—	—	—	—
—Florida	NHL	43	5	1	6	21	0	0	1	—	—	—	—	—
NHL Totals (1 year)		**43**	**5**	**1**	**6**	**21**	**0**	**0**	**1**					

P

PERSONAL: Born March 26, 1974, in Toronto. ... 5-11/181. ... Shoots right. ... Name pronounced PEH-kuh.

TRANSACTIONS/CAREER NOTES: Selected by Vancouver Canucks in second round (second Canucks pick, 40th overall) of NHL entry draft (June 20, 1992). ... Fractured cheek bone (February 9, 1995); missed 12 games. ... Injured wrist (April 26, 1995); missed one game. ... Traded by Canucks with D Mike Wilson and first-round pick (D Jay McKee) in 1995 draft to Buffalo Sabres for RW Alexander Mogilny and fifth-round pick (LW Todd Norman) in 1995 draft (July 8, 1995). ... Strained back (October 29, 1995); missed six games. ... Bruised sternum (December 2, 1995); missed one game. ... Sprained right knee (March 18, 1996); missed seven games. ... Injured shoulder (November 27, 1996); missed three games. ... Missed first 11 games of 1997-98 season due to contract dispute. ... Injured hip (November 6, 1997); missed three games. ... Suspended three games and fined $1,000 by NHL for elbowing incident (March 27, 1998). ... Reinjured hip (April 8, 1998); missed two games. ... Sprained knee (April 15, 1998); missed final two games of regular season and two playoff games. ... Dislocated shoulder (March 5, 2000); missed seven games. ... Suspended two games by NHL for elbowing incident (March 25, 2000). ... Missed entire 2000-01 season due to contract dispute. ... Traded by Sabres to New York Islanders for C Tim Connolly and LW Taylor Pyatt (June 24, 2001).

HONORS: Won Frank J. Selke Trophy (1996-97).

MISCELLANEOUS: Captain of Buffalo Sabres (1997-98 through 1999-2000).

STATISTICAL PLATEAUS: Three-goal games: 1999-00 (1).

		REGULAR SEASON								PLAYOFFS				
Season Team	League	Gms.	G	A	Pts.	PIM	+/-	PP	SH	Gms.	G	A	Pts.	PIM
90-91—Sudbury	OHL	62	14	27	41	24	...	...	...	5	1	0	1	7
91-92—Sudbury	OHL	39	16	34	50	61	...	...	...	—	—	—	—	—
—Ottawa	OHL	27	8	17	25	32	...	...	...	11	6	10	16	6
92-93—Ottawa	OHL	55	38	64	102	80	...	...	...	—	—	—	—	—
—Hamilton	AHL	9	6	3	9	11	...	...	...	—	—	—	—	—
93-94—Ottawa	OHL	55	50	63	113	101	...	...	...	17	7	22	29	30
—Vancouver	NHL	4	0	0	0	2	-1	0	0	—	—	—	—	—
94-95—Syracuse	AHL	35	10	24	34	75	...	...	...	—	—	—	—	—
—Vancouver	NHL	33	6	6	12	30	-6	2	0	5	0	1	1	8
95-96—Buffalo	NHL	68	11	20	31	67	-1	4	3	—	—	—	—	—
96-97—Buffalo	NHL	79	20	29	49	80	26	5	*6	10	0	2	2	8
97-98—Buffalo	NHL	61	18	22	40	57	12	6	5	13	3	2	5	8
98-99—Buffalo	NHL	82	27	29	56	81	7	10	0	21	5	8	13	18
99-00—Buffalo	NHL	73	20	21	41	67	6	2	0	5	0	1	1	4
00-01—								Did not play.						
NHL Totals (7 years)		400	102	127	229	384	43	29	14	54	8	14	22	46

PERSONAL: Born September 10, 1975, in Prince Albert, Sask. ... 6-2/205. ... Shoots right. ... Name pronounced PEE-duhr-suhn.

TRANSACTIONS/CAREER NOTES: Selected by New Jersey Devils in first round (first Devils pick, 13th overall) of NHL entry draft (June 26, 1993). ... Bruised thigh (December 31, 1996); missed one game. ... Suffered head injury (February 19, 1997); missed one game. ... Suffered from the flu (March 11, 1997); missed one game. ... Injured back (January 21, 1999); missed one game. ... Reinjured back (March 28, 1999); missed three games. ... Reinjured back (April 10, 1999); missed two games. ... Injured groin (October 5, 1999); missed eight games. ... Reinjured groin (November 6, 1999); missed 14 games. ... Suffered illness (March 10, 2000); missed two games. ... Traded by Devils with C Brendan Morrison to Vancouver Canucks for RW Alexander Mogilny (March 14, 2000). ... Injured hand (November 24, 2000); missed three games. ... Sprained wrist (December 23, 2000); missed 18 games.

HONORS: Named to WHL All-Rookie team (1992-93). ... Named to WHL (East) All-Star second team (1993-94).

		REGULAR SEASON								PLAYOFFS				
Season Team	League	Gms.	G	A	Pts.	PIM	+/-	PP	SH	Gms.	G	A	Pts.	PIM
91-92—Prince Albert	WHL	10	0	0	0	6	...	...	...	7	0	1	1	13
92-93—Prince Albert	WHL	72	33	40	73	134	...	...	...	—	—	—	—	—
93-94—Prince Albert	WHL	71	53	45	98	157	...	...	...	—	—	—	—	—
94-95—Prince Albert	WHL	63	30	38	68	122	...	...	...	15	11	14	25	14
—Albany	AHL	—	—	—	—	—	...	...	...	3	0	0	0	2
95-96—Albany	AHL	68	28	43	71	104	...	...	...	4	1	2	3	0
—New Jersey	NHL	10	3	1	4	0	-1	1	0	—	—	—	—	—
96-97—Albany	AHL	3	1	3	4	7	...	...	...	—	—	—	—	—
—New Jersey	NHL	70	12	20	32	62	7	3	0	9	0	0	0	2
97-98—New Jersey	NHL	80	15	13	28	97	-6	7	0	6	1	1	2	2
98-99—New Jersey	NHL	76	11	12	23	66	-10	3	0	3	0	1	1	0
99-00—New Jersey	NHL	35	3	3	6	16	-7	0	0	—	—	—	—	—
—Vancouver	NHL	12	3	2	5	2	1	0	0	—	—	—	—	—
00-01—Vancouver	NHL	61	4	8	12	65	0	0	1	4	0	1	1	4
NHL Totals (6 years)		344	51	59	110	308	-16	14	1	22	1	3	4	8

P

PERSONAL: Born January 9, 1970, in Shediac, N.B. ... 5-11/190. ... Shoots left. ... Full Name: Jaque-Frederick Scott Pellerin. ... Name pronounced PEHL-ih-rihn.

TRANSACTIONS/CAREER NOTES: Selected by New Jersey Devils in third round (fourth Devils pick, 47th overall) of NHL entry draft (June 17, 1989). ... Signed as free agent by St. Louis Blues (July 3, 1996). ... Suffered sore ankle (March 9, 1998); missed one game. ... Suffered concussion (November 28, 1998); missed one game. ... Suffered from the flu (February 3, 2000); missed one game. ... Selected by Minnesota Wild in NHL expansion draft (June 23, 2000). ... Bruised shoulder (November 10, 2000); missed three games. ... Suffered from the flu (January 14, 2001); missed one game. ... Traded by Wild to Carolina Hurricanes for LW Askhat Rakhmatullin, third-round pick (traded to New York Rangers) in 2001 draft and future considerations (March 1, 2001). ... Signed as free agent by Boston Bruins (July 26, 2001).

HONORS: Named Hockey East co-Rookie of the Year with Rob Gaudreau (1988-89). ... Named to Hockey East All-Rookie team (1988-89). ... Won Hobey Baker Memorial Award (1991-92). ... Named to NCAA All-America (East) first team (1991-92). ... Named Hockey East Player of the Year (1991-92). ... Named Hockey East Tournament Most Valuable Player (1991-92). ... Named to Hockey East All-Star first team (1991-92). ... Named to Hockey East All-Decade team (1994).

MISCELLANEOUS: Captain of Minnesota Wild (November 1-30, 2000). ... Holds Minnesota Wild all-time records for most assists (28) and most points (39). ... Failed to score on a penalty shot (vs. Joaquin Gage, October 15, 2000).

		REGULAR SEASON								PLAYOFFS				
Season Team	League	Gms.	G	A	Pts.	PIM	+/-	PP	SH	Gms.	G	A	Pts.	PIM
86-87—Notre Dame H.S.........	SASK. H.S.	72	62	68	130	98	...	...	...	—	—	—	—	—
87-88—Notre Dame	SJHL	57	37	49	86	139	...	...	...	—	—	—	—	—
88-89—Univ. of Maine	Hockey East	45	29	33	62	92	...	...	...	—	—	—	—	—
89-90—Univ. of Maine	Hockey East	42	22	34	56	68	...	...	...	—	—	—	—	—
90-91—Univ. of Maine	Hockey East	43	23	25	48	60	...	...	...	—	—	—	—	—
91-92—Univ. of Maine	Hockey East	37	32	25	57	54	...	...	...	—	—	—	—	—
—Utica	AHL	—	—	—	—	—	...	...	...	3	1	0	1	0
92-93—Utica	AHL	27	15	18	33	33	...	...	...	2	0	1	1	0
—New Jersey	NHL	45	10	11	21	41	-1	1	2	—	—	—	—	—
93-94—Albany......................	IHL	73	28	46	74	84	...	...	...	5	2	1	3	11
—New Jersey	NHL	1	0	0	0	2	0	0	0	—	—	—	—	—
94-95—Albany......................	AHL	74	23	33	56	95	...	...	...	14	6	4	10	8
95-96—Albany......................	AHL	75	35	47	82	142	...	...	...	4	0	3	3	10
—New Jersey	NHL	6	2	1	3	0	1	0	0	—	—	—	—	—
96-97—Worcester	AHL	24	10	16	26	37	...	...	...	—	—	—	—	—
—St. Louis	NHL	54	8	10	18	35	12	0	2	6	0	0	0	6
97-98—St. Louis	NHL	80	8	21	29	62	14	1	1	10	0	2	2	10
98-99—St. Louis	NHL	80	20	21	41	42	1	0	†5	8	1	0	1	4
99-00—St. Louis	NHL	80	8	15	23	48	8	0	2	7	0	0	0	2
00-01—Minnesota.................	NHL	58	11	28	39	45	6	2	2	—	—	—	—	—
—Carolina	NHL	19	0	5	5	6	-4	0	0	6	0	0	0	4
NHL Totals (8 years)...........		423	67	112	179	281	37	4	14	37	1	2	3	26

PELLETIER, JEAN-MARC   G   HURRICANES

PERSONAL: Born March 4, 1978, in Atlanta. ... 6-3/195. ... Catches left.

TRANSACTIONS/CAREER NOTES: Selected by Philadelphia Flyers in second round (first Flyers pick, 30th overall) of NHL entry draft (June 21, 1997). ... Traded by Flyers with C Rod Brind'Amour and second-round pick (traded to Colorado) in 2000 draft to Carolina Hurricanes for rights to C Keith Primeau and fifth-round pick (traded to New York Islanders) in 2000 draft (January 23, 2000).

HONORS: Named to QMJHL All-Rookie Team (1997-98).

		REGULAR SEASON								PLAYOFFS					
Season Team	League	Gms.	Min	W	L	T	GA	SO	Avg.	Gms.	Min.	W	L	GA	SO	Avg.
95-96—Cornell University.........	ECAC	5	179	1	2	0	15	0	5.03	—	—	—	—	—	—	—
96-97—Cornell University.........	ECAC	11	678	5	2	3	28	1	2.48	—	—	—	—	—	—	—
97-98—Rimouski......................	QMJHL	34	1913	17	11	3	118	0	3.70	16	895	11	3	†51	1	3.42
98-99—Philadelphia	AHL	47	2636	25	16	4	122	2	2.78	1	27	0	0	0	0	...
—Philadelphia	NHL	1	60	0	1	0	5	0	5.00	—	—	—	—	—	—	—
99-00—Philadelphia	AHL	24	1405	14	10	0	58	3	2.48	—	—	—	—	—	—	—
—Cincinnati	IHL	22	1278	16	4	‡2	52	2	2.44	3	160	1	1	8	1	3.00
00-01—Cincinnati	IHL	39	2261	18	14	‡5	119	2	3.16	5	518	1	3	15	0	1.74
NHL Totals (1 year)...............		1	60	0	1	0	5	0	5.00							

PELTONEN, VILLE   LW

PERSONAL: Born May 24, 1973, in Vantaa, Finland. ... 5-10/181. ... Shoots left. ... Name pronounced VIHL-lay PEHL-tuh-nehn.

TRANSACTIONS/CAREER NOTES: Selected by San Jose Sharks in third round (fourth Sharks pick, 58th overall) of NHL entry draft (June 26, 1993). ... Injured knee (October 15, 1996); missed 10 games. ... Signed as free agent by Nashville Predators (June 29, 1998). ... Separated shoulder (October 6, 1998); missed 10 games. ... Reinjured shoulder (December 5, 1998) and underwent surgery; missed remainder of season. ... Strained left shoulder (October 27, 2000); missed three games.

HONORS: Named to IHL All-Star second team (2000-01).

MISCELLANEOUS: Member of bronze-medal-winning Finnish Olympic team (1994 and 1998). ... Failed to score on a penalty shot (vs. Patrick Roy, March 5, 1996).

		REGULAR SEASON								PLAYOFFS				
Season Team	League	Gms.	G	A	Pts.	PIM	+/-	PP	SH	Gms.	G	A	Pts.	PIM
91-92—HIFK Helsinki	Finland	6	0	0	0	0	...	...	...	—	—	—	—	—
92-93—HIFK Helsinki	Finland	46	13	24	37	16	...	...	...	4	0	2	2	2
93-94—HIFK Helsinki	Finland	43	16	22	38	14	...	...	...	3	0	0	0	2
—Fin. Olympic team.......	Int'l	8	4	3	7	0	...	...	...	—	—	—	—	—
94-95—HIFK Helsinki	Finland	45	20	16	36	16	...	...	...	3	0	0	0	0
95-96—Kansas City................	IHL	29	5	13	18	8	...	...	...	—	—	—	—	—
—San Jose....................	NHL	31	2	11	13	14	-7	0	0	—	—	—	—	—
96-97—San Jose....................	NHL	28	2	3	5	0	-8	1	0	—	—	—	—	—
—Kentucky....................	AHL	40	22	30	52	21	...	...	...	—	—	—	—	—
97-98—Vastra Frolunda..........	Sweden	44	22	29	*51	44	...	...	...	7	4	2	6	0
—Fin. Olympic team.......	Int'l	6	2	1	3	6	...	...	...	—	—	—	—	—
98-99—Nashville	NHL	14	5	5	10	2	-1	1	0	—	—	—	—	—
99-00—Nashville	NHL	79	6	22	28	22	-1	2	0	—	—	—	—	—
00-01—Milwaukee	IHL	53	27	33	60	26	...	...	...	5	2	1	3	6
—Nashville	NHL	23	3	1	4	2	-7	0	0	—	—	—	—	—
NHL Totals (5 years)...........		175	18	42	60	40	-22	4	0					

P

PELUSO, MIKE   C   BLUES

PERSONAL: Born September 2, 1974, in Denver. ... 6-1/208. ... Shoots right. ... Full Name: Michael James Peluso. ... Cousin of Mike Peluso, left winger for six NHL teams (1989-90 through 1997-98).
TRANSACTIONS/CAREER NOTES: Selected by Calgary Flames in 10th round (11th Flames pick, 253rd overall) of NHL entry draft (June 29, 1994). ... Signed as free agent by Washington Capitals (February 10, 1999). ... Traded by Capitals to St. Louis Blues for LW/C Derek Bekar (November 29, 2000).
HONORS: Named to WCHA All-Rookie team (1994-95). ... Named to WCHA All-Star second team (1996-97).

		REGULAR SEASON								PLAYOFFS				
Season Team	League	Gms.	G	A	Pts.	PIM	+/-	PP	SH	Gms.	G	A	Pts.	PIM
91-92—Bismarck H.S.	N.D. H.S.	23	50	49	99	...	...	...	...	—	—	—	—	—
92-93—Omaha	USHL				Statistics unavailable.					—	—	—	—	—
93-94—Omaha	USHL	48	36	29	65	77	...	...	...	—	—	—	—	—
94-95—Minnesota-Duluth	WCHA	38	11	23	34	38	...	...	...	—	—	—	—	—
95-96—Minnesota-Duluth	WCHA	38	25	19	44	64	...	...	...	—	—	—	—	—
96-97—Minnesota-Duluth	WCHA	37	20	20	40	53	...	...	...	—	—	—	—	—
97-98—Minnesota-Duluth	WCHA	40	24	21	45	100	...	...	...	—	—	—	—	—
98-99—Portland	AHL	26	7	6	13	6	...	...	...	—	—	—	—	—
99-00—Portland	AHL	71	25	29	54	86	...	...	...	4	2	0	2	0
00-01—Portland	AHL	19	12	10	22	17	...	...	...	—	—	—	—	—
—Worcester	AHL	44	17	23	40	22	...	...	...	11	3	3	6	4

PERREAULT, YANIC   C   CANADIENS

PERSONAL: Born April 4, 1971, in Sherbrooke, Que. ... 5-10/185. ... Shoots left. ... Name pronounced YAH-nihk puh-ROH.
TRANSACTIONS/CAREER NOTES: Selected by Toronto Maple Leafs in third round (first Maple Leafs pick, 47th overall) of NHL entry draft (June 22, 1991). ... Signed as free agent by Los Angeles Kings (July 14, 1994). ... Strained abdominal muscle (December 13, 1996); missed 11 games. ... Underwent kidney surgery (February 3, 1997); missed remainder of season. ... Traded by Kings to Maple Leafs for C/RW Jason Podollan and third-round pick (G Cory Campbell) in 1999 draft (March 23, 1999). ... Fractured arm (December 4, 1999); missed 23 games. ... Signed as free agent by Montreal Canadiens (July 4, 2001).
HONORS: Won Can.HL Rookie of the Year Award (1988-89). ... Won Michel Bergeron Trophy (1988-89). ... Won Marcel Robert Trophy (1989-90). ... Won Michel Briere Trophy (1990-91). ... Won Jean Beliveau Trophy (1990-91). ... Won Frank J. Selke Trophy (1990-91). ... Won Shell Cup (1990-91). ... Named to QMJHL All-Star first team (1990-91).
STATISTICAL PLATEAUS: Three-goal games: 1997-98 (2). ... Four-goal games: 1998-99 (1). ... Total hat tricks: 3.

		REGULAR SEASON								PLAYOFFS				
Season Team	League	Gms.	G	A	Pts.	PIM	+/-	PP	SH	Gms.	G	A	Pts.	PIM
88-89—Trois-Rivieres	QMJHL	70	53	55	108	48	...	...	...	—	—	—	—	—
89-90—Trois-Rivieres	QMJHL	63	51	63	114	75	...	...	...	7	6	5	11	19
90-91—Trois-Rivieres	QMJHL	67	*87	98	*185	103	...	...	...	6	4	7	11	6
91-92—St. John's	AHL	62	38	38	76	19	...	...	...	16	7	8	15	4
92-93—St. John's	AHL	79	49	46	95	56	...	...	...	9	4	5	9	2
93-94—St. John's	AHL	62	45	60	105	38	...	...	...	11	*12	6	18	14
—Toronto	NHL	13	3	3	6	0	1	2	0	—	—	—	—	—
94-95—Phoenix	IHL	68	51	48	99	52	...	...	...	—	—	—	—	—
—Los Angeles	NHL	26	2	5	7	20	3	0	0	—	—	—	—	—
95-96—Los Angeles	NHL	78	25	24	49	16	-11	8	3	—	—	—	—	—
96-97—Los Angeles	NHL	41	11	14	25	20	0	1	1	—	—	—	—	—
97-98—Los Angeles	NHL	79	28	20	48	32	6	3	2	4	1	2	3	6
98-99—Los Angeles	NHL	64	10	17	27	30	-3	2	2	—	—	—	—	—
—Toronto	NHL	12	7	8	15	12	10	2	1	17	3	6	9	6
99-00—Toronto	NHL	58	18	27	45	22	3	5	0	1	0	1	1	0
00-01—Toronto	NHL	76	24	28	52	52	0	5	0	11	2	3	5	4
NHL Totals (8 years)		447	128	146	274	204	9	28	9	33	6	12	18	16

PERSSON, RICARD   D   SENATORS

PERSONAL: Born August 24, 1969, in Ostersund, Sweden. ... 6-1/201. ... Shoots left. ... Full Name: Ricard Lars Persson. ... Name pronounced RIH-kahrd PEER-suhn.
TRANSACTIONS/CAREER NOTES: Selected by New Jersey Devils in second round (second Devils pick, 23rd overall) of NHL entry draft (June 13, 1987). ... Traded by Devils with LW Mike Peluso to St. Louis Blues for D Ken Sutton and second-round pick (LW Brett Clouthier) in 1999 draft (November 26, 1996). ... Sprained knee (October 9, 1999); missed 17 games. ... Injured shoulder (March 11, 2000); missed final 14 games of regular season. ... Signed as free agent by Ottawa Senators (July 12, 2000). ... Fractured right ankle (October 21, 2000); missed 22 games. ... Reinjured right foot (December 21, 2000); missed 18 games. ... Suffered concussion (April 6, 2001); missed final game of regular season.

		REGULAR SEASON								PLAYOFFS				
Season Team	League	Gms.	G	A	Pts.	PIM	+/-	PP	SH	Gms.	G	A	Pts.	PIM
85-86—Ostersund	Sweden Dv. 2	24	2	2	4	16	...	...	...	—	—	—	—	—
86-87—Ostersund	Sweden Dv. 2	31	10	11	21	28	...	...	...	—	—	—	—	—
87-88—Leksand	Sweden	31	2	0	2	8	...	...	...	2	0	1	1	2
88-89—Leksand	Sweden	33	2	4	6	28	...	...	...	9	0	1	1	6
89-90—Leksand	Sweden	43	9	10	19	62	...	...	...	3	0	0	0	6
90-91—Leksand	Sweden	37	6	9	15	42	...	...	...	—	—	—	—	—
91-92—Leksand	Sweden	21	0	7	7	28	...	...	...	—	—	—	—	—
92-93—Leksand	Sweden	36	7	15	22	63	...	...	...	2	0	2	2	0
93-94—Malmo	Sweden	40	11	9	20	38	...	...	...	11	2	0	2	12
94-95—Malmo	Sweden	31	3	13	16	38	...	...	...	9	0	2	2	8
—Albany	AHL	—	—	—	—	—	...	...	...	9	3	5	8	7

P

Season Team	League	REGULAR SEASON								PLAYOFFS				
		Gms.	G	A	Pts.	PIM	+/-	PP	SH	Gms.	G	A	Pts.	PIM
95-96—New Jersey	NHL	12	2	1	3	8	5	1	0	—	—	—	—	—
—Albany	AHL	67	15	31	46	59	...	...	...	4	0	0	0	7
96-97—New Jersey	NHL	1	0	0	0	0	0	0	0	—	—	—	—	—
—Albany	AHL	13	1	4	5	8	...	...	...	—	—	—	—	—
—St. Louis	NHL	54	4	8	12	45	-2	1	0	6	0	0	0	27
97-98—Worcester	AHL	32	2	16	18	58	...	...	...	10	3	7	10	24
—St. Louis	NHL	1	0	0	0	0	0	0	0	—	—	—	—	—
98-99—Worcester	AHL	19	6	4	10	42	...	...	...	—	—	—	—	—
—St. Louis	NHL	54	1	12	13	94	4	0	0	13	0	3	3	17
99-00—St. Louis	NHL	41	0	8	8	38	-2	0	0	3	1	0	1	0
—Worcester	AHL	2	0	1	1	0	...	...	...	—	—	—	—	—
00-01—Ottawa	NHL	33	1	8	9	35	8	0	0	2	0	0	0	0
NHL Totals (6 years)		196	8	37	45	220	13	2	0	24	1	3	4	44

PETERS, ANDREW   LW   SABRES

PERSONAL: Born May 5, 1980, in St. Catharines, Ont. ... 6-4/195. ... Shoots left.
TRANSACTIONS/CAREER NOTES: Selected by Buffalo Sabres in second round (second Sabres pick, 34th overall) of NHL entry draft (June 27, 1998).

Season Team	League	REGULAR SEASON								PLAYOFFS				
		Gms.	G	A	Pts.	PIM	+/-	PP	SH	Gms.	G	A	Pts.	PIM
96-97—Georgetown	Tier II Jr. A	46	11	16	27	105	...	...	...	—	—	—	—	—
97-98—Oshawa	OHL	60	11	7	18	220	...	...	...	7	2	0	2	19
98-99—Oshawa	OHL	54	14	10	24	137	...	...	...	15	2	7	9	36
99-00—Kitchener	OHL	42	6	13	19	95	...	...	...	4	0	1	1	14
00-01—Rochester	AHL	49	0	4	4	118	...	...	...	—	—	—	—	—

PETERSEN, TOBY   C   PENGUINS

PERSONAL: Born October 27, 1978, in Minneapolis. ... 5-10/196. ... Shoots left.
TRANSACTIONS/CAREER NOTES: Selected by Pittsburgh Penguins in ninth round (ninth Penguins pick, 244th overall) of NHL entry draft (June 27, 1998).
HONORS: Named to WCHA All-Rookie first team (1996-97).

Season Team	League	REGULAR SEASON								PLAYOFFS				
		Gms.	G	A	Pts.	PIM	+/-	PP	SH	Gms.	G	A	Pts.	PIM
95-96—Thomas Jefferson	Minn. H.S.	25	29	30	59	...	...	...	...	—	—	—	—	—
96-97—Colorado College	WCHA	40	17	21	38	18	...	...	...	—	—	—	—	—
97-98—Colorado College	WCHA	34	13	15	28	30	...	...	...	—	—	—	—	—
98-99—Colorado College	WCHA	21	12	12	24	2	...	...	...	—	—	—	—	—
99-00—Colorado College	WCHA	37	14	19	33	8	...	...	...	—	—	—	—	—
00-01—Wilkes-Barre/Scranton	AHL	73	26	41	67	22	...	...	...	21	7	6	13	4
—Pittsburgh	NHL	12	2	6	8	4	3	0	0	—	—	—	—	—
NHL Totals (1 year)		12	2	6	8	4	3	0	0					

PETROV, OLEG   RW   CANADIENS

PERSONAL: Born April 18, 1971, in Moscow, U.S.S.R. ... 5-8/175. ... Shoots left.
TRANSACTIONS/CAREER NOTES: Selected by Montreal Canadiens in sixth round (ninth Canadiens pick, 127th overall) of NHL entry draft (June 22, 1991). ... Suffered injury (January 5, 1994); missed one game. ... Sprained ankle (April 6, 1994); missed three games. ... Torn medial collateral ligament in knee (December 11, 1999); missed 22 games. ... Injured right knee (April 5, 2001); missed final game of season.
HONORS: Named to NHL All-Rookie team (1993-94).
STATISTICAL PLATEAUS: Three-goal games: 1993-94 (1).

Season Team	League	REGULAR SEASON								PLAYOFFS				
		Gms.	G	A	Pts.	PIM	+/-	PP	SH	Gms.	G	A	Pts.	PIM
89-90—CSKA Moscow	USSR	30	4	7	11	4	...	...	...	—	—	—	—	—
90-91—CSKA Moscow	USSR	43	7	4	11	8	...	...	...	—	—	—	—	—
91-92—CSKA Moscow	CIS	34	8	13	21	6	...	...	...	—	—	—	—	—
92-93—Montreal	NHL	9	2	1	3	10	2	0	0	1	0	0	0	0
—Fredericton	AHL	55	26	29	55	36	...	...	...	5	4	1	5	0
93-94—Fredericton	AHL	23	8	20	28	18	...	...	...	—	—	—	—	—
—Montreal	NHL	55	12	15	27	2	7	1	0	2	0	0	0	0
94-95—Montreal	NHL	12	2	3	5	4	-7	0	0	—	—	—	—	—
—Fredericton	AHL	17	7	11	18	12	...	...	...	17	5	6	11	10
95-96—Montreal	NHL	36	4	7	11	23	-9	0	0	5	0	1	1	0
—Fredericton	AHL	22	12	18	30	71	...	...	...	6	2	6	8	0
96-97—Ambri Piotta	Switzerland	45	24	28	52	44	...	...	...	—	—	—	—	—
—HC Meran	Italy	12	5	12	17	4	...	...	...	—	—	—	—	—
97-98—Ambri Piotta	Switzerland	40	30	*63	*93	60	...	...	...	14	11	11	22	40
98-99—Ambri Piotta	Switzerland	45	35	52	87	52	...	...	...	15	9	11	20	32
99-00—Quebec	AHL	16	7	7	14	4	...	...	...	—	—	—	—	—
—Montreal	NHL	44	2	24	26	8	10	1	0	—	—	—	—	—
00-01—Montreal	NHL	81	17	30	47	24	-11	4	2	—	—	—	—	—
NHL Totals (6 years)		237	39	80	119	71	-8	6	2	8	0	1	1	0

P

PETROVICKY, ROBERT   C

PERSONAL: Born October 16, 1973, in Kosice, Czechoslovakia. ... 5-10/183. ... Shoots left. ... Name pronounced peht-roh-VIH-kee.

TRANSACTIONS/CAREER NOTES: Selected by Hartford Whalers in first round (first Whalers pick, ninth overall) of NHL entry draft (June 20, 1992). ... Sprained left ankle (February 28, 1993); missed five games. ... Loaned to Slovakian Olympic team (February 11, 1994). ... Returned to Whalers (February 28, 1994). ... Traded by Whalers to Dallas Stars for RW Dan Kesa (November 29, 1995). ... Signed as free agent by St. Louis Blues (September 6, 1996). ... Signed as free agent by Tampa Bay Lightning (February 14, 1999). ... Injured groin (October 28, 1999); missed two games. ... Strained neck (February 8, 2000); missed six games. ... Signed as free agent by New York Islanders (July 27, 2000).

HONORS: Named to Czechoslovakian League All-Star team (1991-92).

Season Team	League	REGULAR SEASON								PLAYOFFS				
		Gms.	G	A	Pts.	PIM	+/-	PP	SH	Gms.	G	A	Pts.	PIM
90-91—Dukla Trencin	Czech.	33	9	14	23	12	...	...	...	—	—	—	—	—
91-92—Dukla Trencin	Czech.	46	25	36	61	...	...	...	...	—	—	—	—	—
92-93—Hartford	NHL	42	3	6	9	45	-10	0	0	—	—	—	—	—
—Springfield	AHL	16	5	3	8	39	...	...	...	15	5	6	11	14
93-94—Hartford	NHL	33	6	5	11	39	-1	1	0	—	—	—	—	—
—Springfield	AHL	30	16	8	24	39	...	...	...	4	0	2	2	4
—Slovakian Oly. team	Int'l	8	1	6	7	18	...	...	...	—	—	—	—	—
94-95—Springfield	AHL	74	30	52	82	121	...	...	...	—	—	—	—	—
—Hartford	NHL	2	0	0	0	0	0	0	0	—	—	—	—	—
95-96—Springfield	AHL	9	4	8	12	18	...	...	...	—	—	—	—	—
—Detroit	IHL	12	5	3	8	16	...	...	...	—	—	—	—	—
—Michigan	IHL	50	23	23	46	63	...	...	...	7	3	1	4	16
—Dallas	NHL	5	1	1	2	0	1	1	0	—	—	—	—	—
96-97—Worcester	AHL	12	5	4	9	19	...	...	...	—	—	—	—	—
—St. Louis	NHL	44	7	12	19	10	2	0	0	2	0	0	0	0
97-98—Worcester	AHL	65	27	34	61	97	...	...	...	10	3	4	7	12
—Slovakian Oly. team	Int'l	4	2	1	3	0	...	...	...	—	—	—	—	—
98-99—Grand Rapids	IHL	49	26	32	58	87	...	...	...	—	—	—	—	—
—Tampa Bay	NHL	28	3	4	7	6	-8	0	0	—	—	—	—	—
99-00—Grand Rapids	IHL	7	5	3	8	4	...	...	...	—	—	—	—	—
—Tampa Bay	NHL	43	7	10	17	14	2	1	0	—	—	—	—	—
00-01—MoDo Ornskoldsvik	Sweden	7	3	2	5	10	...	...	...	7	1	1	2	6
—Chicago	IHL	23	13	10	23	22	...	...	...	—	—	—	—	—
—New York Islanders	NHL	11	0	0	0	4	-1	0	0	—	—	—	—	—
NHL Totals (8 years)		208	27	38	65	118	-15	3	0	2	0	0	0	0

PETROVICKY, RONALD   RW   FLAMES

PERSONAL: Born February 15, 1977, in Zlina, Czechoslovakia. ... 5-11/188. ... Shoots right.

TRANSACTIONS/CAREER NOTES: Signed as non-drafted free agent by Calgary Flames (June 1, 1998). ... Injured wrist (October 5, 2000); missed 49 games.

HONORS: Names to WHL (East) All-Star second team (1997-98).

Season Team	League	REGULAR SEASON								PLAYOFFS				
		Gms.	G	A	Pts.	PIM	+/-	PP	SH	Gms.	G	A	Pts.	PIM
93-94—Dukla Trencin	Slovakia	36	28	27	55	42	...	...	...	—	—	—	—	—
94-95—Tri-City	WHL	39	4	11	15	86	...	...	...	—	—	—	—	—
—Prince George	WHL	21	4	6	10	37	...	...	...	—	—	—	—	—
95-96—Prince George	WHL	39	19	21	40	61	...	...	...	—	—	—	—	—
96-97—Prince George	WHL	72	32	37	69	119	...	...	...	15	4	9	13	31
97-98—Regina	WHL	71	64	49	113	45	...	...	...	9	2	4	6	11
98-99—Saint John	AHL	78	12	21	33	114	...	...	...	7	1	2	3	19
99-00—Saint John	AHL	67	23	33	56	131	...	...	...	3	1	1	2	6
00-01—Calgary	NHL	30	4	5	9	54	0	1	0	—	—	—	—	—
NHL Totals (1 year)		30	4	5	9	54	0	1	0					

PETTINGER, MATT   LW   CAPITALS

PERSONAL: Born October 22, 1980, in Victoria, B.C. ... 6-0/205. ... Shoots left. ... Nephew of Gord Pettinger, center with three NHL teams (1932-33 through 1939-40).

TRANSACTIONS/CAREER NOTES: Selected by Washington Capitals in second round (second Capitals pick, 43rd overall) of NHL entry draft (June 24, 2000).

Season Team	League	REGULAR SEASON								PLAYOFFS				
		Gms.	G	A	Pts.	PIM	+/-	PP	SH	Gms.	G	A	Pts.	PIM
98-99—Univ. of Denver	WCHA	38	14	6	20	52	...	...	...	—	—	—	—	—
99-00—Univ. of Denver	WCHA	19	2	6	8	...	...	...	...	—	—	—	—	—
—Calgary	WHL	27	14	6	20	41	...	...	...	11	2	6	8	30
00-01—Portland	AHL	64	19	17	36	92	...	...	...	2	0	0	0	4
—Washington	NHL	10	0	0	0	2	-1	0	0	—	—	—	—	—
NHL Totals (1 year)		10	0	0	0	2	-1	0	0					

P

PHILLIPS, CHRIS   D   SENATORS

PERSONAL: Born March 9, 1978, in Fort McMurray, Alta. ... 6-3/215. ... Shoots left. ... Nephew of Rod Phillips, Edmonton Oilers play-by-play announcer.

TRANSACTIONS/CAREER NOTES: Selected by Ottawa Senators in first round (first Senators pick, first overall) of NHL entry draft (June 22,

1996). ... Bruised knee (November 13, 1997); missed two games. ... Bruised eye (February 25, 1998); missed five games. ... Suffered back spasms (November 18, 1998); missed three games. ... Sprained right ankle (January 1, 1999); missed 21 games. ... Reinjured right ankle (February 20, 1999); missed 23 games. ... Injured right ankle (December 9, 1999) and underwent surgery; missed 17 games. ... Suffered back spasms (November 2, 2000); missed three games. ... Suffered back spasms (December 2, 2000); missed two games. ... Injured left shoulder (April 1, 2001); missed final three games of regular season.

HONORS: Won Can.HL Top Draft Prospect Award (1995-96). ... Won Jim Piggott Memorial Trophy (1995-96). ... Named to Can.HL All-Rookie team (1995-96). ... Named to Memorial Cup All-Star Team (1996-97). ... Named to Can.HL All-Star first team (1996-97). ... Named to WHL (East) All-Star first team (1996-97). ... Won Bill Hunter Trophy (1996-97).

				REGULAR SEASON							PLAYOFFS			
Season Team	League	Gms.	G	A	Pts.	PIM	+/-	PP	SH	Gms.	G	A	Pts.	PIM
93-94—Fort McMurray............	AJHL	56	6	16	22	72	...	...	...	—	—	—	—	—
94-95—Fort McMurray............	AJHL	48	16	32	48	127	...	...	...	—	—	—	—	—
95-96—Prince Albert..............	WHL	61	10	30	40	97	...	...	...	18	2	12	14	30
96-97—Prince Albert..............	WHL	32	3	23	26	58	...	...	...	—	—	—	—	—
—Lethbridge............	WHL	26	4	18	22	28	...	...	...	19	4	*21	25	20
97-98—Ottawa	NHL	72	5	11	16	38	2	2	0	11	0	2	2	2
98-99—Ottawa	NHL	34	3	3	6	32	-5	2	0	3	0	0	0	0
99-00—Ottawa	NHL	65	5	14	19	39	12	0	0	6	0	1	1	4
00-01—Ottawa	NHL	73	2	12	14	31	8	2	0	1	1	0	1	0
NHL Totals (4 years)............		244	15	40	55	140	17	6	0	21	1	3	4	6

PICARD, MICHEL   LW

PERSONAL: Born November 7, 1969, in Beauport, Que. ... 5-11/202. ... Shoots left. ... Name pronounced pih-KAHRD.

TRANSACTIONS/CAREER NOTES: Selected by Hartford Whalers in ninth round (eighth Whalers pick, 178th overall) of NHL entry draft (June 17, 1989). ... Separated shoulder (November 14, 1991); missed seven games. ... Traded by Whalers to San Jose Sharks for future considerations (October 9, 1992); Whalers acquired LW Yvon Corriveau to complete deal (January 21, 1993). ... Signed as free agent by Ottawa Senators (June 23, 1994). ... Suspended two games and fined $1,000 by NHL for cross-checking (March 16, 1996). ... Traded by Senators to Washington Capitals for cash (May 21, 1996). ... Signed as free agent by St. Louis Blues (January 30, 1998). ... Signed as free agent by Edmonton Oilers (December 2, 1999). ... Signed as free agent by Philadelphia Flyers (August 14, 2000).

HONORS: Named to QMJHL All-Star second team (1988-89). ... Named to AHL All-Star first team (1990-91 and 1994-95). ... Named to AHL All-Star second team (1993-94). ... Named to IHL All-Star first team (1996-97).

				REGULAR SEASON							PLAYOFFS			
Season Team	League	Gms.	G	A	Pts.	PIM	+/-	PP	SH	Gms.	G	A	Pts.	PIM
86-87—Trois-Rivieres..............	QMJHL	66	33	35	68	53	...	...	...	—	—	—	—	—
87-88—Trois-Rivieres..............	QMJHL	69	40	55	95	71	...	...	...	—	—	—	—	—
88-89—Trois-Rivieres..............	QMJHL	66	59	81	140	107	...	...	...	4	1	3	4	2
89-90—Binghamton	AHL	67	16	24	40	98	...	...	...	—	—	—	—	—
90-91—Hartford	NHL	5	1	0	1	2	-2	0	0	—	—	—	—	—
—Springfield	AHL	77	*56	40	96	61	...	...	...	18	8	13	21	18
91-92—Hartford	NHL	25	3	5	8	6	-2	1	0	—	—	—	—	—
—Springfield	AHL	40	21	17	38	44	...	...	...	11	2	0	2	34
92-93—Kansas City..............	IHL	33	7	10	17	51	...	...	...	12	3	2	5	20
—San Jose................	NHL	25	4	0	4	24	-17	2	0	—	—	—	—	—
93-94—Portland	AHL	61	41	44	85	99	...	...	...	17	11	10	21	22
94-95—Prin. Edward Island	AHL	57	32	57	89	58	...	...	...	8	4	4	8	6
—Ottawa	NHL	24	5	8	13	14	-1	1	0	—	—	—	—	—
95-96—Prin. Edward Island	AHL	55	37	45	82	79	...	...	...	5	5	1	6	2
—Ottawa	NHL	17	2	6	8	10	-1	0	0	—	—	—	—	—
96-97—Grand Rapids..............	IHL	82	46	55	101	58	...	...	...	5	2	0	2	10
—Vastra Frolunda	Sweden	3	0	1	1	0	...	...	...	—	—	—	—	—
97-98—Grand Rapids..............	IHL	58	28	41	69	42	...	...	...	—	—	—	—	—
—St. Louis................	NHL	16	1	8	9	29	3	0	0	—	—	—	—	—
98-99—St. Louis....................	NHL	45	11	11	22	16	5	0	0	5	0	0	0	2
—Grand Rapids..............	IHL	6	2	2	4	2	...	...	...	—	—	—	—	—
99-00—Edmonton	NHL	2	0	0	0	2	0	0	0	—	—	—	—	—
—Grand Rapids..............	IHL	65	33	35	68	50	...	...	...	17	8	10	†18	4
00-01—Philadelphia	AHL	72	31	39	70	22	...	...	...	10	4	5	9	4
—Philadelphia	NHL	7	1	4	5	0	6	1	0	—	—	—	—	—
NHL Totals (9 years)............		166	28	42	70	103	-9	5	0	5	0	0	0	2

PILON, RICH   D   BLUES

PERSONAL: Born April 30, 1968, in Saskatoon, Sask. ... 6-2/220. ... Shoots left. ... Full Name: Richard Pilon. ... Name pronounced PEE-lahn.

TRANSACTIONS/CAREER NOTES: Selected by New York Islanders in seventh round (ninth Islanders pick, 143rd overall) of NHL entry draft (June 21, 1986). ... Injured right leg (December 1988). ... Injured right eye (November 4, 1989); missed remainder of season. ... Injured left knee ligament (February 23, 1991). ... Suffered sore left shoulder (January 9, 1992); missed three games. ... Lacerated finger (January 30, 1992); missed four games. ... Bruised hand (October 31, 1992); missed two games. ... Bruised hand (November 22, 1992); missed four games. ... Sprained left knee (December 10, 1992); missed eight games. ... Injured lower back (January 10, 1993); missed 11 games. ... Injured left shoulder (November 13, 1993); missed seven games. ... Reinjured left shoulder (December 3, 1993); missed 32 games. ... Reinjured left shoulder (March 17, 1994); missed 14 games. ... Suffered sore groin (February 22, 1995); missed four games. ... Sprained ankle (March 5, 1995); missed 17 games. ... Fractured wrist (April 18, 1995); missed remainder of season. ... Injured wrist prior to 1995-96 season; missed first 26 games of season. ... Injured groin (December 12, 1995); missed four games. ... Injured wrist (January 9, 1996); missed one game. ... Strained hip flexor (February 4, 1996); missed four games. ... Strained hip flexor (March 3, 1996); missed last 18 games of regular season. ... Strained groin (October 9, 1996); missed 20 games. ... Suspended two games and fined $1,000 by NHL for slashing incident (January 11, 1997). ... Sprained knee ligament (February 11, 1997); missed three games. ... Injured foot (March 26, 1997); missed four games. ... Bruised knee (April 2, 1997); missed one game. ... Injured groin (October 19, 1997); missed one game. ... Injured foot (November 14, 1997); missed four games. ... Strained triceps (March 6, 1998); missed one game. ... Strained groin (October 10, 1998); missed two games. ... Reinjured groin (October 17, 1998); missed two games. ... Sprained wrist (December 2, 1998); missed two games. ... Sprained

P

knee (January 5, 1999); missed seven games. ... Injured back (January 29, 1999); missed one game. ... Suffered sore back (March 6, 1999); missed one game. ... Suffered inflamed disk in back (March 14, 1999); missed final 14 games of season. ... Sprained medial collateral ligament in left knee (October 18, 1999); missed nine games. ... Sprained knee (November 23, 1999); missed two games. ... Claimed on waivers by New York Rangers (December 1, 1999). ... Strained left shoulder (February 9, 2000); missed two games. ... Reinjured left shoulder (February 15, 2000); missed six games. ... Reinjured left shoulder (March 1, 2000); missed five games. ... Reinjured left shoulder (April 3, 2000); missed one game. ... Suffered from the flu (January 6, 2001); missed two games. ... Bruised foot (January 26, 2001); missed two games. ... Suffered concussion (February 6, 2001); missed four games. ... Injured hamstring (February 26, 2001); missed three games. ... Injured hamstring (March 29, 2001); missed two games. ... Signed as free agent by St. Louis Blues (July 6, 2001).

HONORS: Named to WHL All-Star second team (1987-88).

		REGULAR SEASON							PLAYOFFS				
Season Team	League	Gms.	G	A	Pts.	PIM	+/-	PP	SH	Gms.	G	A	Pts.	PIM
85-86—Prince Albert..............	WHL	6	0	0	0	0	...	...	...	—	—	—	—	—
86-87—Prince Albert..............	WHL	68	4	21	25	192	...	...	...	7	1	6	7	17
87-88—Prince Albert..............	WHL	65	13	34	47	177	...	...	...	9	0	6	6	38
88-89—New York Islanders.....	NHL	62	0	14	14	242	-9	0	0	—	—	—	—	—
89-90—New York Islanders.....	NHL	14	0	2	2	31	2	0	0	—	—	—	—	—
90-91—New York Islanders.....	NHL	60	1	4	5	126	-12	0	0	—	—	—	—	—
91-92—New York Islanders.....	NHL	65	1	6	7	183	-1	0	0	—	—	—	—	—
92-93—New York Islanders.....	NHL	44	1	3	4	164	-4	0	0	15	0	0	0	50
—Capital District............	AHL	6	0	1	1	8	...	...	...	—	—	—	—	—
93-94—New York Islanders.....	NHL	28	1	4	5	75	-4	0	0	—	—	—	—	—
—Salt Lake City.............	IHL	2	0	0	0	8	...	...	...	—	—	—	—	—
94-95—New York Islanders.....	NHL	20	1	1	2	40	-3	0	0	—	—	—	—	—
—Chicago....................	IHL	2	0	0	0	0	...	...	...	—	—	—	—	—
95-96—New York Islanders.....	NHL	27	0	3	3	72	-9	0	0	—	—	—	—	—
96-97—New York Islanders.....	NHL	52	1	4	5	179	4	0	0	—	—	—	—	—
97-98—New York Islanders.....	NHL	76	0	7	7	291	1	0	0	—	—	—	—	—
98-99—New York Islanders.....	NHL	52	0	4	4	88	-8	0	0	—	—	—	—	—
99-00—New York Islanders.....	NHL	9	0	2	2	34	-2	0	0	—	—	—	—	—
—New York Rangers.....	NHL	45	0	4	4	36	0	0	0	—	—	—	—	—
00-01—New York Rangers.....	NHL	69	2	9	11	175	-2	0	0	—	—	—	—	—
NHL Totals (13 years).........		623	8	67	75	1736	-47	0	0	15	0	0	0	50

PISANI, FERNANDO   C/LW   OILERS

PERSONAL: Born December 27, 1976, in Edmonton. ... 6-1/185. ... Shoots left.
TRANSACTIONS/CAREER NOTES: Selected by Edmonton Oilers in eighth round (ninth Oilers pick, 195th overall) of NHL entry draft (June 22, 1996).

		REGULAR SEASON							PLAYOFFS				
Season Team	League	Gms.	G	A	Pts.	PIM	+/-	PP	SH	Gms.	G	A	Pts.	PIM
95-96—St. Albert	AJHL	58	40	63	103	134	...	...	...	18	7	22	29	28
96-97—Providence College	Hockey East	35	12	18	30	36	...	...	...	—	—	—	—	—
97-98—Providence College	Hockey East	36	16	18	34	20	...	...	...	—	—	—	—	—
98-99—Providence College	Hockey East	38	14	37	51	42	...	...	...	—	—	—	—	—
99-00—Providence College	Hockey East	38	14	24	38	56	...	...	...	—	—	—	—	—
00-01—Hamilton	AHL	52	12	13	25	28	...	...	...	—	—	—	—	—

PITLICK, LANCE   D   PANTHERS

PERSONAL: Born November 5, 1967, in Fridley, Minn. ... 5-11/211. ... Shoots right.
TRANSACTIONS/CAREER NOTES: Selected by Minnesota North Stars in ninth round (10th North Stars pick, 180th overall) of NHL entry draft (June 21, 1986). ... Signed as free agent by Philadelphia Flyers (September 5, 1990). ... Signed as free agent by Ottawa Senators (June 22, 1994). ... Bruised ribs (March 27, 1995); missed two games. ... Injured groin (January 5, 1996); missed one game. ... Injured groin during 1995-96 season; missed four games. ... Strained abdominal muscle (April 1, 1996); missed four games. ... Injured left knee (January 9, 1997); missed nine games. ... Strained groin (February 16, 1997); missed one game. ... Strained groin (December 2, 1997); missed one game. ... Bruised hip (December 12, 1998); missed 32 games. ... Signed as free agent by Florida Panthers (July 13, 1999). ... Fractured hand (October 24, 1999); missed five games. ... Fractured ankle (March 3, 2000); missed 14 games. ... Injured hand (October 20, 2000); missed eight games. ... Injured back (January 31, 2001); missed two games.

		REGULAR SEASON							PLAYOFFS				
Season Team	League	Gms.	G	A	Pts.	PIM	+/-	PP	SH	Gms.	G	A	Pts.	PIM
84-85—Cooper H.S.	Minn. H.S.	23	8	4	12	...	...	...	...	—	—	—	—	—
85-86—Cooper H.S.	Minn. H.S.	21	17	8	25	...	...	...	...	—	—	—	—	—
86-87—Univ. of Minnesota......	WCHA	45	0	9	9	88	...	...	...	10	0	2	2	4
87-88—Univ. of Minnesota......	WCHA	38	3	9	12	76	...	...	...	8	1	1	2	14
88-89—Univ. of Minnesota......	WCHA	47	4	9	13	95	...	...	...	8	2	1	3	95
89-90—Univ. of Minnesota......	WCHA	14	3	2	5	26	...	...	...	—	—	—	—	—
90-91—Hershey	AHL	64	6	15	21	75	...	...	...	3	0	0	0	9
91-92—U.S. national team	Int'l	19	0	1	1	38	...	...	...	—	—	—	—	—
—Hershey	AHL	4	0	0	0	6	...	...	...	3	0	0	0	4
92-93—Hershey	AHL	53	5	10	15	77	...	...	...	—	—	—	—	—
93-94—Hershey	AHL	58	4	13	17	93	...	...	...	11	1	0	1	11
94-95—Prin. Edward Island	AHL	61	8	19	27	55	...	...	...	11	1	4	5	10
—Ottawa	NHL	15	0	1	1	6	-5	0	0	—	—	—	—	—
95-96—Prin. Edward Island	AHL	29	4	10	14	39	...	...	...	5	0	0	0	0
—Ottawa	NHL	28	1	6	7	20	-8	0	0	—	—	—	—	—
96-97—Ottawa	NHL	66	5	5	10	91	2	0	0	7	0	0	0	4
97-98—Ottawa	NHL	69	2	7	9	50	8	0	0	11	0	1	1	17
98-99—Ottawa	NHL	50	3	6	9	33	7	0	0	2	0	0	0	0
99-00—Florida........................	NHL	62	3	5	8	44	7	0	0	4	0	1	1	0
00-01—Florida........................	NHL	68	1	2	3	42	-5	0	0	—	—	—	—	—
NHL Totals (7 years)...........		358	15	32	47	286	6	0	0	24	0	2	2	21

P

PERSONAL: Born October 1, 1974, in Calgary. ... 5-11/190. ... Shoots left. ... Name pronounced PIHT-ihz.

TRANSACTIONS/CAREER NOTES: Selected by Pittsburgh Penguins in second round (second Penguins pick, 52nd overall) of NHL entry draft (June 26, 1993). ... Signed as free agent by Buffalo Sabres (July 30, 1998). ... Suffered from the flu (October 27, 1999); missed one game. ... Injured ankle (November 9, 1999); missed three games. ... Signed as free agent by Edmonton Oilers (July 26, 2000).

HONORS: Named to WHL (East) All-Star second team (1993-94). ... Won John B. Sollenberger Trophy (1998-99).

		REGULAR SEASON								PLAYOFFS				
Season Team	League	Gms.	G	A	Pts.	PIM	+/-	PP	SH	Gms.	G	A	Pts.	PIM
91-92—Lethbridge	WHL	65	6	17	23	48	...	...	...	5	0	2	2	4
92-93—Lethbridge	WHL	66	46	73	119	69	...	...	...	4	3	3	6	8
93-94—Lethbridge	WHL	72	58	69	127	93	...	...	...	8	4	11	15	16
94-95—Cleveland	IHL	62	18	32	50	66	...	...	...	3	0	2	2	2
95-96—Cleveland	IHL	74	10	28	38	100	...	...	...	3	0	0	0	2
96-97—Pittsburgh	NHL	1	0	0	0	0	-1	0	0	—	—	—	—	—
—Long Beach	IHL	65	23	43	66	91	...	...	...	18	5	9	14	26
97-98—Syracuse	AHL	75	23	41	64	90	...	...	...	5	1	3	4	4
98-99—Rochester	AHL	76	38	66	*104	108	...	...	...	20	7	†14	*21	40
—Buffalo	NHL	3	0	0	0	2	0	0	0	—	—	—	—	—
99-00—Buffalo	NHL	7	1	0	1	6	1	0	0	—	—	—	—	—
—Rochester	AHL	53	17	48	65	85	...	...	...	21	4	*26	*30	28
00-01—Edmonton	NHL	47	4	5	9	49	-5	0	0	3	0	0	0	2
NHL Totals (4 years)		58	5	5	10	57	-5	0	0	3	0	0	0	2

PERSONAL: Born January 17, 1971, in Cloquet, Minn. ... 5-11/181. ... Shoots left. ... Full Name: Derek John Plante. ... Name pronounced PLANT.

TRANSACTIONS/CAREER NOTES: Selected by Buffalo Sabres in eighth round (seventh Sabres pick, 161st overall) of NHL entry draft (June 17, 1989). ... Bruised left shoulder (March 8, 1994); missed two games. ... Strained back (December 15, 1995); missed three games. ... Suffered back spasms (October 7, 1997); missed three games. ... Suffered back spasms (March 1, 1998); missed four games. ... Suffered back spasms and suffered from the flu (December 8, 1998); missed three games. ... Traded by Sabres to Dallas Stars for second-round pick (C Michael Zigomanis) in 1999 draft (March 23, 1999). ... Traded by Stars with D Kevin Dean and second-round pick (RW Matt Keith) in 2001 draft to Chicago Blackhawks for D Sylvain Cote and D Dave Manson (February 8, 2000). ... Signed as free agent by Philadelphia Flyers (July 26, 2000).

HONORS: Named to NCAA All-America (West) first team (1992-93). ... Named WCHA Player of the Year (1992-93). ... Named to WCHA All-Star first team (1992-93).

MISCELLANEOUS: Member of Stanley Cup championship team (1999).

STATISTICAL PLATEAUS: Three-goal games: 1993-94 (1).

		REGULAR SEASON								PLAYOFFS				
Season Team	League	Gms.	G	A	Pts.	PIM	+/-	PP	SH	Gms.	G	A	Pts.	PIM
87-88—Cloquet H.S.	Minn. H.S.	23	16	25	41	...	...	...	...	—	—	—	—	—
88-89—Cloquet H.S.	Minn. H.S.	24	30	33	63	...	...	...	...	—	—	—	—	—
89-90—Minnesota-Duluth	WCHA	28	10	11	21	12	...	...	...	—	—	—	—	—
90-91—Minnesota-Duluth	WCHA	36	23	20	43	6	...	...	...	—	—	—	—	—
91-92—Minnesota-Duluth	WCHA	37	27	36	63	28	...	...	...	—	—	—	—	—
92-93—Minnesota-Duluth	WCHA	37	*36	*56	*92	30	...	...	...	—	—	—	—	—
93-94—U.S. national team	Int'l	2	0	1	1	0	...	...	...	—	—	—	—	—
—Buffalo	NHL	77	21	35	56	24	4	8	1	7	1	0	1	0
94-95—Buffalo	NHL	47	3	19	22	12	-4	2	0	—	—	—	—	—
95-96—Buffalo	NHL	76	23	33	56	28	-4	4	0	—	—	—	—	—
96-97—Buffalo	NHL	82	27	26	53	24	14	5	0	12	4	6	10	4
97-98—Buffalo	NHL	72	13	21	34	26	8	5	0	11	0	3	3	10
98-99—Buffalo	NHL	41	4	11	15	12	3	0	0	—	—	—	—	—
—Dallas	NHL	10	2	3	5	4	1	1	0	6	1	0	1	4
99-00—Dallas	NHL	16	1	1	2	2	-4	1	0	—	—	—	—	—
—Michigan	IHL	13	0	4	4	2	...	...	...	—	—	—	—	—
—Chicago	IHL	4	2	1	3	2	...	...	...	8	3	1	4	6
—Chicago	NHL	17	1	1	2	2	-1	0	0	—	—	—	—	—
00-01—Philadelphia	AHL	57	18	35	53	19	...	...	...	—	—	—	—	—
—Philadelphia	NHL	12	1	2	3	4	0	0	0	5	0	1	1	0
NHL Totals (8 years)		450	96	152	248	138	17	26	1	41	6	10	16	18

PERSONAL: Born January 3, 1969, in Cornwall, Ont. ... 5-11/199. ... Shoots left. ... Name pronounced PAHPS.

TRANSACTIONS/CAREER NOTES: Signed as non-drafted free agent by Washington Capitals (February 4, 1995). ... Signed as free agent by Chicago Blackhawks (July 27, 2000). ... Strained groin (April 1, 2001); missed three games.

		REGULAR SEASON								PLAYOFFS				
Season Team	League	Gms.	G	A	Pts.	PIM	+/-	PP	SH	Gms.	G	A	Pts.	PIM
86-87—Smith Falls	OJHL	54	10	27	37	94	...	...	...	—	—	—	—	—
87-88—Colgate University	ECAC	32	3	13	16	22	...	...	...	—	—	—	—	—
88-89—Colgate University	ECAC	30	0	5	5	38	...	...	...	—	—	—	—	—
89-90—Colgate University	ECAC	38	4	15	19	54	...	...	...	—	—	—	—	—
90-91—Colgate University	ECAC	32	6	15	21	43	...	...	...	—	—	—	—	—
91-92—Hampton Roads	ECHL	55	8	20	28	29	...	...	...	14	1	4	5	12
92-93—Hampton Roads	ECHL	63	10	35	45	57	...	...	...	4	0	1	1	4
—Baltimore	AHL	7	0	1	1	4	...	...	...	7	0	3	3	6

P

Season Team	League	REGULAR SEASON								PLAYOFFS				
		Gms.	G	A	Pts.	PIM	+/-	PP	SH	Gms.	G	A	Pts.	PIM
93-94—Portland	AHL	78	14	21	35	47	...	...	...	12	0	3	3	8
94-95—Portland	AHL	71	8	22	30	60	...	...	...	7	0	1	1	16
95-96—Portland	AHL	70	10	24	34	79	...	...	...	20	2	6	8	16
—Washington	NHL	3	1	0	1	0	-1	0	0	6	0	0	0	0
96-97—Portland	AHL	47	1	20	21	34	...	...	...	5	0	1	1	6
97-98—Portland	AHL	76	8	29	37	46	...	...	...	10	2	3	5	8
98-99—Portland	AHL	54	3	21	24	36	...	...	...	—	—	—	—	—
—Washington	NHL	22	0	0	0	8	-8	0	0	—	—	—	—	—
99-00—Portland	AHL	56	0	14	14	20	...	...	...	3	1	0	1	2
00-01—Norfolk	AHL	37	1	8	9	14	...	...	...	—	—	—	—	—
—Chicago	NHL	36	2	3	5	12	3	0	0	—	—	—	—	—
NHL Totals (3 years)		61	3	3	6	20	-6	0	0	6	0	0	0	0

PODEIN, SHJON — LW — AVALANCHE

PERSONAL: Born March 5, 1968, in Eden Prairie, Minn. ... 6-2/200. ... Shoots left. ... Name pronounced SHAWN poh-DEEN.

TRANSACTIONS/CAREER NOTES: Selected by Edmonton Oilers in eighth round (ninth Oilers pick, 166th overall) of NHL entry draft (June 11, 1988). ... Injured knee (March 9, 1994); missed five games. ... Signed as free agent by Philadelphia Flyers (July 27, 1994). ... Bruised right foot (February 22, 1996); missed three games. ... Traded by Flyers to Colorado Avalanche for RW Keith Jones (November 12, 1998). ... Fractured lower right leg (December 4, 1998); missed 25 games. ... Bruised foot (March 30, 1999); missed one game. ... Injured knee prior to start of 1999-2000 season; missed first five games of season. ... Fractured foot (January 7, 2000); missed two games.

HONORS: Won King Clancy Memorial Trophy (2000-01).

MISCELLANEOUS: Member of Stanley Cup championship team (2001).

STATISTICAL PLATEAUS: Three-goal games: 1999-00 (1).

Season Team	League	REGULAR SEASON								PLAYOFFS				
		Gms.	G	A	Pts.	PIM	+/-	PP	SH	Gms.	G	A	Pts.	PIM
87-88—Minnesota-Duluth	WCHA	30	4	4	8	48	...	...	...	—	—	—	—	—
88-89—Minnesota-Duluth	WCHA	36	7	5	12	46	...	...	...	—	—	—	—	—
89-90—Minnesota-Duluth	WCHA	35	21	18	39	36	...	...	...	—	—	—	—	—
90-91—Cape Breton	AHL	63	14	15	29	65	...	...	...	4	0	0	0	5
91-92—Cape Breton	AHL	80	30	24	54	46	...	...	...	5	3	1	4	2
92-93—Cape Breton	AHL	38	18	21	39	32	...	...	...	9	2	2	4	29
—Edmonton	NHL	40	13	6	19	25	-2	2	1	—	—	—	—	—
93-94—Edmonton	NHL	28	3	5	8	8	3	0	0	—	—	—	—	—
—Cape Breton	AHL	5	4	4	8	4	...	...	...	—	—	—	—	—
94-95—Philadelphia	NHL	44	3	7	10	33	-2	0	0	15	1	3	4	10
95-96—Philadelphia	NHL	79	15	10	25	89	25	0	4	12	1	2	3	50
96-97—Philadelphia	NHL	82	14	18	32	41	7	0	0	19	4	3	7	16
97-98—Philadelphia	NHL	82	11	13	24	53	8	1	1	5	0	0	0	10
98-99—Philadelphia	NHL	14	1	0	1	0	-2	0	0	—	—	—	—	—
—Colorado	NHL	41	2	6	8	24	-3	0	0	19	1	1	2	12
99-00—Colorado	NHL	75	11	8	19	29	12	0	1	17	5	0	5	8
00-01—Colorado	NHL	82	15	17	32	68	7	0	0	23	2	3	5	14
NHL Totals (9 years)		567	88	90	178	370	53	3	7	110	14	12	26	120

PODHRADSKY, PETER — D — MIGHTY DUCKS

PERSONAL: Born December 10, 1979, in Bratislava, Czechoslovakia. ... 6-1/185. ... Shoots right.

TRANSACTIONS/CAREER NOTES: Selected by Mighty Ducks of Anaheim in fifth round (fourth Mighty Ducks pick, 134th overall) of NHL entry draft (June 24, 2000).

Season Team	League	REGULAR SEASON								PLAYOFFS				
		Gms.	G	A	Pts.	PIM	+/-	PP	SH	Gms.	G	A	Pts.	PIM
98-99—Bratislava	Slovakia	23	1	4	5	37	...	...	...	4	0	0	0	0
99-00—Bratislava	Slovakia	25	1	4	5	2	...	...	...	—	—	—	—	—
00-01—Cincinnati	AHL	59	4	5	9	27	...	...	...	2	0	0	0	0

PODKONICKY, ANDREJ — C

PERSONAL: Born May 9, 1978, in Zvolen, Czechoslovakia. ... 6-2/195. ... Shoots left. ... Name pronounced pahd-kah-NIH-kee.

TRANSACTIONS/CAREER NOTES: Selected by St. Louis Blues in eighth round (eighth Blues pick, 196th overall) of NHL entry draft (June 22, 1996). ... Traded by Blues to Florida Panthers for C Eric Boguniecki (December 18, 2000).

Season Team	League	REGULAR SEASON								PLAYOFFS				
		Gms.	G	A	Pts.	PIM	+/-	PP	SH	Gms.	G	A	Pts.	PIM
94-95—Zvolen	Czech Rep.	17	0	4	4	6	...	...	...	—	—	—	—	—
95-96—ZTK Zvolen	Slov. Div. II	38	18	12	30	18	...	...	...	—	—	—	—	—
96-97—Portland	WHL	71	25	46	71	127	...	...	...	6	1	1	2	8
97-98—Portland	WHL	64	30	44	74	81	...	...	...	16	4	12	16	20
98-99—Worcester	AHL	61	19	24	43	52	...	...	...	4	0	0	0	4
99-00—Worcester	AHL	77	16	25	41	68	...	...	...	9	2	5	7	6
00-01—Worcester	AHL	16	2	3	5	15	...	...	...	—	—	—	—	—
—Louisville	AHL	41	6	10	16	31	...	...	...	—	—	—	—	—
—Florida	NHL	6	1	0	1	2	0	0	0	—	—	—	—	—
NHL Totals (1 year)		6	1	0	1	2	0	0	0	—	—	—	—	—

P

PONIKAROVKSY, ALEXEI   RW   MAPLE LEAFS

PERSONAL: Born April 9, 1980, in Kiev, U.S.S.R. ... 6-4/196. ... Shoots left.
TRANSACTIONS/CAREER NOTES: Selected by Toronto Maple Leafs in fourth round (fourth Maple Leafs pick, 87th overall) of NHL entry draft (June 27, 1998).

Season Team	League	REGULAR SEASON								PLAYOFFS				
		Gms.	G	A	Pts.	PIM	+/-	PP	SH	Gms.	G	A	Pts.	PIM
95-96—Dynamo Moscow	CIS Jr.	70	14	10	24	20	...	...	...	—	—	—	—	—
96-97—Dynamo Moscow	Russian Jr.	60	12	15	27	30	...	...	...	—	—	—	—	—
—Dynamo-2 Moscow	Rus. Div. III	2	0	0	0	2	...	...	...	—	—	—	—	—
97-98—Dynamo-2 Moscow	Rus. Div. II	24	1	2	3	30	...	...	...	—	—	—	—	—
98-99—Dynamo Moscow	Russian	—	—	—	—	—	...	...	...	3	0	0	0	2
99-00—Dynamo Moscow	Russian	19	1	0	1	8	...	...	...	1	0	0	0	0
00-01—St. John's	AHL	49	12	24	36	44	...	...	...	4	0	0	0	4
—Toronto	NHL	22	1	3	4	14	-1	0	0	—	—	—	—	—
NHL Totals (1 year)		22	1	3	4	14	-1	0	0					

POPOVIC, PETER   D

PERSONAL: Born February 10, 1968, in Koping, Sweden. ... 6-6/239. ... Shoots right. ... Name pronounced PAH-poh-vihk.
TRANSACTIONS/CAREER NOTES: Selected by Montreal Canadiens in fifth round (fifth Canadiens pick, 93rd overall) of NHL entry draft (June 11, 1988). ... Injured knee (November 20, 1993); missed six games. ... Bruised shoulder (December 22, 1993); missed seven games. ... Played in Europe during 1994-95 NHL lockout. ... Suffered facial lacerations (March 11, 1995); missed six games. ... Fractured finger on right hand (December 23, 1995); missed six games. ... Bruised foot (February 17, 1997); missed one game. ... Injured rib (April 7, 1997); missed remainder of regular season and two playoff games. ... Suffered ankle infection (October 1, 1997); missed eight games. ... Traded by Canadiens to New York Rangers for LW Sylvain Blouin and sixth-round pick (traded to Phoenix) in 1999 draft (June 30, 1998). ... Bruised right eye (October 17, 1998); missed two games. ... Injured eye (February 14, 1999); missed 12 games. ... Traded by Rangers to Pittsburgh Penguins for D Kevin Hatcher (September 30, 1999). ... Injured groin (January 5, 2000); missed three games. ... Reinjured groin (January 23, 2000); missed four games. ... Fractured finger (February 1, 2000); missed 21 games. ... Signed as free agent by Boston Bruins (July 2, 2000). ... Injured foot (November 11, 2000); missed 14 games. ... Suffered concussion (January 18, 2001); missed seven games.

Season Team	League	REGULAR SEASON								PLAYOFFS				
		Gms.	G	A	Pts.	PIM	+/-	PP	SH	Gms.	G	A	Pts.	PIM
86-87—Vasteras	Sweden	24	1	2	3	10	...	...	...	—	—	—	—	—
87-88—Vasteras	Sweden	28	3	17	20	16	...	...	...	—	—	—	—	—
88-89—Vasteras	Sweden	22	1	4	5	32	...	...	...	—	—	—	—	—
89-90—Vasteras	Sweden	30	2	10	12	24	...	...	...	2	0	1	1	2
90-91—Vasteras	Sweden	40	3	2	5	62	...	...	...	4	0	0	0	4
91-92—Vasteras	Sweden	34	7	10	17	30	...	...	...	—	—	—	—	—
92-93—Vasteras	Sweden	39	6	12	18	46	...	...	...	3	0	1	1	0
93-94—Montreal	NHL	47	2	12	14	26	10	1	0	6	0	1	1	0
94-95—Vasteras	Sweden	11	0	3	3	10	...	...	...	—	—	—	—	—
—Montreal	NHL	33	0	5	5	8	-10	0	0	—	—	—	—	—
95-96—Montreal	NHL	76	2	12	14	69	21	0	0	6	0	2	2	4
96-97—Montreal	NHL	78	1	13	14	32	9	0	0	3	0	0	0	2
97-98—Montreal	NHL	69	2	6	8	38	-6	0	0	10	1	1	2	2
98-99—New York Rangers	NHL	68	1	4	5	40	-12	0	0	—	—	—	—	—
99-00—Pittsburgh	NHL	54	1	5	6	30	-8	0	0	10	0	0	0	10
00-01—Boston	NHL	60	1	6	7	48	-5	0	0	—	—	—	—	—
NHL Totals (8 years)		485	10	63	73	291	-1	1	0	35	1	4	5	18

POSMYK, MAREK   D   LIGHTNING

PERSONAL: Born September 15, 1978, in Jihlava, Czechoslovakia. ... 6-5/209. ... Shoots right.
TRANSACTIONS/CAREER NOTES: Selected by Toronto Maple Leafs in second round (first Maple Leafs pick, 36th overall) of NHL entry draft (June 22, 1996). ... Traded by Maple Leafs with RW Mike Johnson and fifth-(RW Pavel Sedov) and sixth-round (D Aaron Gionet) picks in 2000 draft to Tampa Bay Lightning for C Darcy Tucker and fourth-round pick (RW Miguel Delisle) in 2000 draft (February 9, 2000). ... Strained medial collateral ligament in knee (March 19, 2000); missed three games. ... Injured neck (April 6, 2000); missed final two games of season.

Season Team	League	REGULAR SEASON								PLAYOFFS				
		Gms.	G	A	Pts.	PIM	+/-	PP	SH	Gms.	G	A	Pts.	PIM
94-95—Czech Rep.	Czech Rep.	16	1	3	4	...	...	...	...	—	—	—	—	—
95-96—Czech Rep.	Czech Rep.	16	6	5	11	...	...	...	...	—	—	—	—	—
—Dukla Jihlava	Czech Rep.	18	1	2	3	...	...	...	...	1	0	0	0	...
—Jihlava Jrs.	Czech Rep.	16	6	5	11	...	...	...	...	—	—	—	—	—
96-97—Dukla Jihlava	Czech Rep.	24	1	7	8	44	...	...	...	—	—	—	—	—
—St. John's	AHL	2	0	0	0	2	...	...	...	—	—	—	—	—
97-98—St. John's	AHL	3	0	0	0	4	...	...	...	—	—	—	—	—
—Sarnia	OHL	48	8	16	24	94	...	...	...	5	0	2	2	6
98-99—St. John's	AHL	41	1	0	1	36	...	...	...	—	—	—	—	—
99-00—St. John's	AHL	38	1	6	7	57	...	...	...	—	—	—	—	—
—Detroit	IHL	1	0	1	1	0	...	...	...	—	—	—	—	—
—Tampa Bay	NHL	18	1	2	3	20	1	0	0	—	—	—	—	—
00-01—Tampa Bay	NHL	1	0	0	0	0	-1	0	0	—	—	—	—	—
—Detroit	IHL	49	7	14	21	58	...	...	...	—	—	—	—	—
NHL Totals (2 years)		19	1	2	3	20	0	0	0					

P

POTHIER, BRIAN　　　　　D　　　　　THRASHERS

PERSONAL: Born April 15, 1977, in New Bedford, Mass. ... 6-1/195. ... Shoots right.
TRANSACTIONS/CAREER NOTES: Signed as non-drafted free agent by Atlanta Thrashers (April 8, 2000).
HONORS: Named to ECAC All-Star second team (1999-2000). ... Named to NCAA (East) All-America second team (1999-2000). ... Won Garry F. Longman Memorial Trophy (2000-01). ... Won Ken McKenzie Trophy (2000-01).

Season Team	League		REGULAR SEASON								PLAYOFFS			
		Gms.	G	A	Pts.	PIM	+/-	PP	SH	Gms.	G	A	Pts.	PIM
96-97—R.P.I.	ECAC	34	1	11	12	42	...	...	...	—	—	—	—	—
97-98—R.P.I.	ECAC	35	2	9	11	28	...	...	...	—	—	—	—	—
98-99—R.P.I.	ECAC	37	5	13	18	36	...	...	...	—	—	—	—	—
99-00—R.P.I.	ECAC	36	9	24	33	44	...	...	...	—	—	—	—	—
00-01—Orlando	IHL	76	12	29	41	69	...	...	...	16	3	5	8	11
—Atlanta	NHL	3	0	0	0	2	4	0	0	—	—	—	—	—
NHL Totals (1 year)		3	0	0	0	2	4	0	0					

POTI, TOM　　　　　D　　　　　OILERS

PERSONAL: Born March 22, 1977, in Worcester, Mass. ... 6-3/215. ... Shoots left.
TRANSACTIONS/CAREER NOTES: Selected by Edmonton Oilers in third round (fourth Oilers pick, 59th overall) of NHL entry draft (June 22, 1996). ... Bruised right knee (November 10, 1999); missed one game. ... Strained neck (December 4, 1999); missed two games. ... Bruised thumb (January 14, 2000); missed one game. ... Bruised ankle (February 13, 2000); missed one game. ... Reinjured ankle (February 29, 2000); missed one game.
HONORS: Named to NCAA All-Tournament team (1996-97). ... Named to Hockey East All-Rookie team (1996-97). ... Named to NCAA All-America (East) first team (1997-98). ... Named to Hockey East All-Star first team (1997-98). ... Named to NHL All-Rookie team (1998-99).

Season Team	League		REGULAR SEASON								PLAYOFFS			
		Gms.	G	A	Pts.	PIM	+/-	PP	SH	Gms.	G	A	Pts.	PIM
94-95—Cushing Academy	Mass. H.S.	36	16	47	63	35	...	...	...	—	—	—	—	—
95-96—Cushing Academy	Mass. H.S.	29	14	59	73	18	...	...	...	—	—	—	—	—
96-97—Boston University	Hockey East	38	4	17	21	54	...	...	...	—	—	—	—	—
97-98—Boston University	Hockey East	38	13	29	42	60	...	...	...	—	—	—	—	—
98-99—Edmonton	NHL	73	5	16	21	42	10	2	0	4	0	1	1	2
99-00—Edmonton	NHL	76	9	26	35	65	8	2	1	5	0	1	1	0
00-01—Edmonton	NHL	81	12	20	32	60	-4	6	0	6	0	2	2	2
NHL Totals (3 years)		230	26	62	88	167	14	10	1	15	0	4	4	4

POTVIN, FELIX　　　　　G　　　　　KINGS

PERSONAL: Born June 23, 1971, in Anjou, Que. ... 6-1/190. ... Catches left. ... Name pronounced PAHT-vihn. ... Nickname: The Cat.
TRANSACTIONS/CAREER NOTES: Selected by Toronto Maple Leafs in second round (second Maple Leafs pick, 31st overall) of NHL entry draft (June 16, 1990). ... Traded by Maple Leafs with sixth-round pick (traded to Tampa Bay) in 1999 draft to New York Islanders for D Bryan Berard and sixth-round pick (RW Jan Sochor) in 1999 draft (January 9, 1999). ... Strained groin (February 13, 1999); missed 22 games. ... Traded by Islanders with second-(traded to Atlanta) and third-round (C Thatcher Bell) picks in 2000 draft to Vancouver Canucks for G Kevin Weekes, C Dave Scatchard and RW Bill Muckalt (December 19, 1999). ... Injured knee (January 23, 2000); missed five games. ... Traded by Canucks to Los Angeles Kings for future considerations (February 15, 2001).
HONORS: Named to QMJHL All-Star second team (1989-90). ... Won Can.HL Goaltender of the Year Award (1990-91). ... Won Hap Emms Memorial Trophy (1990-91). ... Won Jacques Plante Trophy (1990-91). ... Won Shell Cup (1990-91). ... Won Guy Lafleur Trophy (1990-91). ... Named to Memorial Cup All-Star team (1990-91). ... Named to QMJHL All-Star first team (1990-91). ... Won Aldege (Baz) Bastien Trophy (1991-92). ... Won Dudley (Red) Garrett Memorial Trophy (1991-92). ... Named to AHL All-Star first team (1991-92). ... Named to NHL All-Rookie team (1992-93). ... Played in NHL All-Star Game (1994 and 1996).
MISCELLANEOUS: Stopped penalty shot attempt (vs. Brian Bradley, October 22, 1992; vs. Donald Audette, November 21, 1996; vs. Maxim Sushinsky, November 26, 2000; vs. Brett Hull, January 22, 2001).

Season Team	League		REGULAR SEASON								PLAYOFFS					
		Gms.	Min	W	L	T	GA	SO	Avg.	Gms.	Min.	W	L	GA	SO	Avg.
88-89—Chicoutimi	QMJHL	*65	*3489	25	31	1	*271	†2	4.66	—	—	—	—	—	—	—
89-90—Chicoutimi	QMJHL	*62	*3478	31	26	2	231	†2	3.99	—	—	—	—	—	—	—
90-91—Chicoutimi	QMJHL	54	3216	33	15	4	145	*6	†2.71	*16	*992	*11	5	46	0	*2.78
91-92—St. John's	AHL	35	2070	18	10	6	101	2	2.93	11	642	7	4	41	0	3.83
—Toronto	NHL	4	210	0	2	1	8	0	2.29	—	—	—	—	—	—	—
92-93—Toronto	NHL	48	2781	25	15	7	116	2	*2.50	21	1308	11	10	62	1	2.84
—St. John's	AHL	5	309	3	0	2	18	0	3.50	—	—	—	—	—	—	—
93-94—Toronto	NHL	66	3883	34	22	9	187	3	2.89	18	1124	9	†9	46	3	2.46
94-95—Toronto	NHL	36	2144	15	13	7	104	0	2.91	7	424	3	4	20	1	2.83
95-96—Toronto	NHL	69	4009	30	26	11	192	2	2.87	6	350	2	4	19	0	3.26
96-97—Toronto	NHL	*74	*4271	27	*36	7	*224	2	3.15	—	—	—	—	—	—	—
97-98—Toronto	NHL	67	3864	26	*33	7	176	5	2.73	—	—	—	—	—	—	—
98-99—Toronto	NHL	5	299	3	2	0	19	0	3.81	—	—	—	—	—	—	—
—New York Islanders	NHL	11	606	2	7	1	37	0	3.66	—	—	—	—	—	—	—
99-00—New York Islanders	NHL	22	1273	5	14	3	68	1	3.21	—	—	—	—	—	—	—
—Vancouver	NHL	34	1966	12	13	7	85	0	2.59	—	—	—	—	—	—	—
00-01—Vancouver	NHL	35	2006	14	17	3	103	1	3.08	—	—	—	—	—	—	—
—Los Angeles	NHL	23	1410	13	5	5	46	5	1.96	13	812	7	6	33	2	2.44
NHL Totals (10 years)		494	28722	206	205	68	1365	19	2.85	65	4018	32	33	180	7	2.69

P

PERSONAL: Born April 23, 1973, in Vanier, Que. ... 6-1/216. ... Shoots left. ... Name pronounced POO-lahn.
TRANSACTIONS/CAREER NOTES: Selected by Hartford Whalers in first round (first Whalers pick, ninth overall) of NHL entry draft (June 22, 1991). ... Traded by Whalers with D Eric Weinrich to Chicago Blackhawks for RW Steve Larmer and D Bryan Marchment (November 2, 1993). ... Sprained ankle (December 28, 1995); missed 19 games. ... Suffered back spasms (March 5, 1996); missed two games. ... Traded by Blackhawks with D Igor Ulanov and second-round pick (traded to New Jersey) to Tampa Bay Lightning for D Enrico Ciccone (March 20, 1996). ... Injured knee (January 13, 1997); missed one game. ... Injured knee (March 6, 1997); missed six games. ... Traded by Lightning with F Mick Vukota and D Igor Ulanov to Montreal Canadiens for F Stephane Richer, F Darcy Tucker and D David Wilkie (January 15, 1998). ... Sprained knee (November 19, 1998); missed one game. ... Injured groin (October 28, 2000); missed six games. ... Reinjured groin (November 14, 2000); missed four games. ... Fractured right ankle (February 24, 2001); missed remainder of season.
HONORS: Won Jean Beliveau Trophy (1991-92). ... Named to Can.HL All-Star first team (1991-92). ... Named to QMJHL All-Star first team (1991-92).

Season Team	League	Gms.	G	A	Pts.	PIM	+/-	PP	SH	Gms.	G	A	Pts.	PIM
89-90—St. Hyacinthe	QMJHL	60	25	26	51	55	...	...	...	12	1	9	10	5
90-91—St. Hyacinthe	QMJHL	56	32	38	70	82	...	...	...	4	0	2	2	23
91-92—St. Hyacinthe	QMJHL	56	52	86	*138	58	...	...	...	5	2	2	4	4
—Springfield	AHL	—	—	—	—	...	...	...	...	1	0	0	0	0
—Hartford	NHL	1	0	0	0	2	-1	0	0	7	2	1	3	0
92-93—Hartford	NHL	81	20	31	51	37	-19	4	0	—				
93-94—Hartford	NHL	9	2	1	3	11	-8	1	0	—				
—Chicago	NHL	58	12	13	25	40	0	1	0	4	0	0	0	0
94-95—Chicago	NHL	45	15	15	30	53	13	4	0	16	4	1	5	8
95-96—Chicago	NHL	38	7	8	15	16	7	1	0	—				
—Indianapolis	IHL	1	0	1	1	0	...	...	...	—				
—Tampa Bay	NHL	8	0	1	1	0	0	0	0	2	0	0	0	0
96-97—Tampa Bay	NHL	73	12	14	26	56	-16	2	3	—				
97-98—Tampa Bay	NHL	44	2	7	9	19	-3	0	0	—				
—Montreal	NHL	34	4	6	10	8	-1	0	1	3	0	0	0	0
98-99—Montreal	NHL	81	8	17	25	21	6	0	1	—				
99-00—Montreal	NHL	82	10	5	15	17	-15	0	1	—				
00-01—Montreal	NHL	52	9	11	20	13	1	0	0	—				
NHL Totals (10 years)		606	101	129	230	293	-36	13	6	32	6	2	8	8

PERSONAL: Born December 10, 1978, in Fort McMurray, Alta. ... 6-2/191. ... Shoots right. ... Brother of Nolan Pratt, defenseman, Tampa Bay Lightning.
TRANSACTIONS/CAREER NOTES: Selected by Pittsburgh Penguins in fifth round (fifth Penguins pick, 124th overall) of NHL entry draft (June 21, 1997). ... Released by Penguins (September 17, 1999). ... Signed as free agent by Carolina Hurricanes (August 21, 2000).

Season Team	League	Gms.	G	A	Pts.	PIM	+/-	PP	SH	Gms.	G	A	Pts.	PIM
94-95—Seattle	WHL	33	1	0	1	17	...	...	...	1	0	0	0	0
95-96—Red Deer	WHL	60	2	3	5	22	...	...	...	10	0	0	0	4
96-97—Red Deer	WHL	2	0	0	0	2	...	...	...	—				
—Prince Albert	WHL	65	7	26	33	49	...	...	...	1	1	1	2	4
97-98—Prince Albert	WHL	37	6	14	20	12	...	...	...	—				
—Regina	WHL	24	2	6	8	23	...	...	...	9	2	2	4	2
98-99—Toledo	ECHL	61	4	35	39	32	...	...	...	3	0	0	0	0
—Portland	WHL	10	1	3	4	10	...	...	...	—				
99-00—Florida	ECHL	68	4	29	33	38	...	...	...	5	0	1	1	2
00-01—Cincinnati	IHL	73	6	23	29	45	...	...	...	2	0	1	1	2

PERSONAL: Born August 14, 1975, in Fort McMurray, Alta. ... 6-2/208. ... Shoots left. ... Brother of Harlan Pratt, defenseman, Carolina Hurricanes organization.
TRANSACTIONS/CAREER NOTES: Selected by Hartford Whalers in fifth round (fourth Whalers pick, 115th overall) of NHL entry draft (June 26, 1993). ... Whalers franchise moved to North Carolina and renamed Carolina Hurricanes for 1997-98 season; NHL approved move on June 25, 1997. ... Suffered back spasms (December 21, 1998); missed eight games. ... Injured hip (December 20, 1999); missed two games. ... Injured hand (April 3, 2000); missed one game. ... Traded by Hurricanes with first-(C Vaclav Nedorost) and two second-round (C Jared Aulin and D Argis Saviels) picks in 2000 draft to Colorado Avalanche for D Sandis Ozolinsh and second-round pick (LW Tomas Kurka) in 2000 draft (June 24, 2000). ... Injured wrist (October 4, 2000); missed two games. ... Traded by Avalanche to Tampa Bay Lightning for sixth-round pick (RW Scott Horvath) in 2001 draft (June 24, 2001).
MISCELLANEOUS: Member of Stanley Cup championship team (2001).

Season Team	League	Gms.	G	A	Pts.	PIM	+/-	PP	SH	Gms.	G	A	Pts.	PIM
91-92—Portland	WHL	22	2	9	11	13	...	...	...	6	1	3	4	12
92-93—Portland	WHL	70	4	19	23	97	...	...	...	16	2	7	9	31
93-94—Portland	WHL	72	4	32	36	105	...	...	...	10	1	2	3	14
94-95—Portland	WHL	72	6	37	43	196	...	...	...	9	1	6	7	10
95-96—Richmond	ECHL	4	1	0	1	2	...	...	...	—				
—Springfield	AHL	62	2	6	8	72	...	...	...	2	0	0	0	0
96-97—Hartford	NHL	9	0	2	2	6	0	0	0	—				
—Springfield	AHL	66	1	18	19	127	...	...	...	17	0	3	3	18
97-98—New Haven	AHL	54	3	15	18	135	...	...	...	—				
—Carolina	NHL	23	0	2	2	44	-2	0	0	—				
98-99—Carolina	NHL	61	1	14	15	95	15	0	0	3	0	0	0	2
99-00—Carolina	NHL	64	3	1	4	90	-22	0	0	—				
00-01—Colorado	NHL	46	1	2	3	40	2	0	0	—				
NHL Totals (5 years)		203	5	21	26	275	-7	0	0	3	0	0	0	2

P

PERSONAL: Born November 24, 1971, in Toronto. ... 6-5/220. ... Shoots left. ... Brother of Wayne Primeau, center, Pittsburgh Penguins. ... Name pronounced PREE-moh.

TRANSACTIONS/CAREER NOTES: Selected by Detroit Red Wings in first round (first Red Wings pick, third overall) of NHL entry draft (June 16, 1990). ... Suffered from the flu (January 13, 1993); missed two games. ... Sprained right shoulder (February 9, 1993); missed one game. ... Sprained right knee (March 2, 1993); missed two games. ... Sprained right knee (April 1, 1993); missed four games. ... Injured right thumb (February 10, 1995); missed one game. ... Suffered from the flu (February 25, 1995); missed one game. ... Reinjured thumb (March 2, 1995); missed one game. ... Injured ribs (November 1, 1995); missed eight games. ... Injured left knee (January 13, 1996); missed one game. ... Traded by Red Wings with D Paul Coffey and first-round pick (traded to San Jose) in 1997 draft to Hartford Whalers for LW Brendan Shanahan and D Brian Glynn (October 9, 1996). ... Suffered from the flu (December 3, 1996); missed one game. ... Suffered concussion (December 21, 1996); missed one game. ... Suspended two games by NHL for slashing incident (January 3, 1997). ... Suffered from asthma (February 12, 1997); missed one game. ... Whalers franchise moved to North Carolina and renamed Carolina Hurricanes for 1997-98 season; NHL approved move on June 25, 1997. ... Strained hip flexor (November 13, 1997); missed one game. ... Injured wrist (February 13, 1999); missed one game. ... Strained lower back (April 10, 1999); missed three games. ... Missed first 47 games of 1999-2000 season due to contract dispute. ... Rights traded by Hurricanes with fifth-round pick (traded to New York Islanders) in 2000 draft to Philadelphia Flyers for C Rod Brind'Amour, G Jean-Marc Pelletier and second-round pick (traded to Colorado) in 2000 draft (January 23, 2000). ... Fractured rib (February 12, 2000); missed nine games. ... Reinjured ribs (March 4, 2000); missed three games. ... Suffered headaches (October 29, 2000); missed two games. ... Bruised shoulder (December 27, 2000); missed three games. ... Sprained medial collateral ligament in left knee (March 26, 2001); missed final six games of regular season and two playoff games.

HONORS: Won Eddie Powers Memorial Trophy (1989-90). ... Named to OHL All-Star second team (1989-90). ... Played in NHL All-Star Game (1999).

MISCELLANEOUS: Captain of Carolina Hurricanes (1998-99).

STATISTICAL PLATEAUS: Three-goal games: 2000-01 (1).

Season Team	League	REGULAR SEASON								PLAYOFFS				
		Gms.	G	A	Pts.	PIM	+/-	PP	SH	Gms.	G	A	Pts.	PIM
87-88—Hamilton	OHL	47	6	6	12	69	...	...	...	11	0	2	2	2
88-89—Niagara Falls	OHL	48	20	35	55	56	...	...	...	17	9	6	15	12
89-90—Niagara Falls	OHL	65	*57	70	*127	97	...	...	...	16	*16	17	*33	49
90-91—Detroit	NHL	58	3	12	15	106	-12	0	0	5	1	1	2	25
—Adirondack	AHL	6	3	5	8	8	...	...	...	—	—	—	—	—
91-92—Detroit	NHL	35	6	10	16	83	9	0	0	11	0	0	0	14
—Adirondack	AHL	42	21	24	45	89	...	...	...	9	1	7	8	27
92-93—Detroit	NHL	73	15	17	32	152	-6	4	1	7	0	2	2	26
93-94—Detroit	NHL	78	31	42	73	173	34	7	3	7	0	2	2	6
94-95—Detroit	NHL	45	15	27	42	99	17	1	0	17	4	5	9	45
95-96—Detroit	NHL	74	27	25	52	168	19	6	2	17	1	4	5	28
96-97—Hartford	NHL	75	26	25	51	161	-3	6	3	—	—	—	—	—
97-98—Carolina	NHL	81	26	37	63	110	19	7	3	—	—	—	—	—
—Can. Olympic team	Int'l	6	2	1	3	4	...	...	...	—	—	—	—	—
98-99—Carolina	NHL	78	30	32	62	75	8	9	1	6	0	3	3	6
99-00—Philadelphia	NHL	23	7	10	17	31	10	1	0	18	2	11	13	13
00-01—Philadelphia	NHL	71	34	39	73	76	17	11	0	4	0	3	3	8
NHL Totals (11 years)		691	220	276	496	1234	112	52	13	92	8	31	39	171

PERSONAL: Born June 4, 1976, in Scarborough, Ont. ... 6-3/225. ... Shoots left. ... Brother of Keith Primeau, center, Philadelphia Flyers. ... Name pronounced PREE-moh.

TRANSACTIONS/CAREER NOTES: Selected by Buffalo Sabres in first round (first Sabres pick, 17th overall) of NHL entry draft (June 28, 1994). ... Bruised shoulder (November 4, 1998); missed four games. ... Reinjured shoulder (December 5, 1998); missed four games. ... Reinjured shoulder (January 11, 1999); missed one game. ... Strained groin (March 7, 1999); missed one game. ... Injured hip (January 1, 2000); missed 20 games. ... Traded by Sabres with C/RW Brian Holzinger, D Cory Sarich and third-round pick (RW Alexandre Kharitonov) in 2000 draft to Tampa Bay Lightning for C Chris Gratton and second-round pick (C Derek Roy) in 2001 draft (March 9, 2000). ... Suspended by NHL two games for slashing incident (January 23, 2001). ... Traded by Lightning to Pittsburgh Penguins for LW Matthew Barnaby (February 1, 2001). ... Injured neck (Feburary 14, 2001); missed one game. ... Suffered injury (March 14, 2001); missed one game.

Season Team	League	REGULAR SEASON								PLAYOFFS				
		Gms.	G	A	Pts.	PIM	+/-	PP	SH	Gms.	G	A	Pts.	PIM
92-93—Owen Sound	OHL	66	10	27	37	110	...	...	...	8	1	4	5	0
93-94—Owen Sound	OHL	65	25	50	75	75	...	...	...	9	1	6	7	8
94-95—Owen Sound	OHL	66	34	62	96	84	...	...	...	10	4	9	13	15
—Buffalo	NHL	1	1	0	1	0	-2	0	0	—	—	—	—	—
95-96—Buffalo	NHL	2	0	0	0	0	0	0	0	—	—	—	—	—
—Owen Sound	OHL	28	15	29	44	52	...	...	...	—	—	—	—	—
—Oshawa	OHL	24	12	13	25	33	...	...	...	3	2	3	5	2
—Rochester	AHL	8	2	3	5	6	...	...	...	17	3	1	4	11
96-97—Rochester	AHL	24	9	5	14	27	...	...	...	1	0	0	0	0
—Buffalo	NHL	45	2	4	6	64	-2	1	0	9	0	0	0	6
97-98—Buffalo	NHL	69	6	6	12	87	9	2	0	14	1	3	4	6
98-99—Buffalo	NHL	67	5	8	13	38	-6	0	0	19	3	4	7	6
99-00—Buffalo	NHL	41	5	7	12	38	-8	2	0	—	—	—	—	—
—Tampa Bay	NHL	17	2	3	5	25	-4	0	0	—	—	—	—	—
00-01—Tampa Bay	NHL	47	2	13	15	77	-17	0	0	—	—	—	—	—
—Pittsburgh	NHL	28	1	6	7	54	0	0	0	18	1	3	4	2
NHL Totals (7 years)		317	24	47	71	383	-30	5	0	60	5	10	15	20

P

PROBERT, BOB   LW   BLACKHAWKS

PERSONAL: Born June 5, 1965, in Windsor, Ont. ... 6-3/225. ... Shoots left. ... Full Name: Robert Probert. ... Name pronounced PROH-buhrt.

TRANSACTIONS/CAREER NOTES: Selected by Detroit Red Wings as underage junior in third round (third Red Wings pick, 46th overall) of NHL entry draft (June 8, 1983). ... Entered in-patient alcohol abuse treatment center (July 22, 1986). ... Suspended six games by NHL during the 1987-88 season for game misconduct penalties. ... Suspended without pay by Red Wings for skipping practice and missing team buses, flights and curfews (September 23, 1988). ... Reactivated by Red Wings (November 23, 1988). ... Suspended three games by NHL for hitting another player (December 10, 1988). ... Removed from team after showing up late for a game (January 26, 1989). ... Reactivated by Red Wings (February 15, 1989). ... Charged with smuggling cocaine into the United States (March 2, 1989). ... Expelled from the NHL (March 4, 1989). ... Reinstated by NHL (March 14, 1990). ... Unable to play any games in Canada while appealing deportation order by U.S. Immigration Department during 1990-91 and 1991-92 seasons. ... Fractured left wrist (December 1, 1990); missed 12 games. ... Suspended one game by NHL for game misconduct penalties (February 9, 1993). ... Bruised tailbone (November 20, 1993); missed eight games. ... Suspended four games by NHL for stick-swinging incident (October 16, 1993). ... Suspended two games and fined $500 by NHL for head-butting (April 7, 1994). ... Signed as free agent by Chicago Blackhawks (July 23, 1994). ... Placed on inactive status by NHL for violating substance abuse policies (September 2, 1994). ... Reinstated by NHL and declared eligible for 1995-96 season (April 28, 1995). ... Sprained knee (December 26, 1995); missed three games. ... Suspended one game by NHL for elbowing (February 10, 1996). ... Tore cartilage/sprained medial collateral ligament in right knee (October 9, 1997) and underwent surgery; missed 14 games. ... Tore rotator cuff (November 19, 1997); missed 54 games. ... Suspended four games by NHL for fighting incident (October 4, 1999). ... Strained elbow (November 27, 1999); missed one game. ... Suffered from the flu (February 23, 2000); missed one game.

HONORS: Played in NHL All-Star Game (1988).

MISCELLANEOUS: Holds Detroit Red Wings all-time record for most penalty minutes (2,090). ... Scored on a penalty shot (vs. Kari Takko, March 5, 1987).

STATISTICAL PLATEAUS: Three-goal games: 1987-88 (1).

		REGULAR SEASON								PLAYOFFS				
Season Team	League	Gms.	G	A	Pts.	PIM	+/-	PP	SH	Gms.	G	A	Pts.	PIM
82-83—Brantford	OHL	51	12	16	28	133	...	...	...	8	2	2	4	23
83-84—Brantford	OHL	65	35	38	73	189	...	...	...	6	0	3	3	16
84-85—Hamilton	OHL	4	0	1	1	21				—	—	—	—	—
—Sault Ste. Marie	OHL	44	20	52	72	172	...	...	...	15	6	11	17	*60
85-86—Adirondack	AHL	32	12	15	27	152	...	...	...	10	2	3	5	68
—Detroit	NHL	44	8	13	21	186	-14	3	0	—	—	—	—	—
86-87—Detroit	NHL	63	13	11	24	221	-6	2	0	16	3	4	7	63
—Adirondack	AHL	7	1	4	5	15				—	—	—	—	—
87-88—Detroit	NHL	74	29	33	62	*398	16	15	0	16	8	13	21	51
88-89—Detroit	NHL	25	4	2	6	106	-11	1	0	—	—	—	—	—
89-90—Detroit	NHL	4	3	0	3	21	0	0	0	—	—	—	—	—
90-91—Detroit	NHL	55	16	23	39	315	-3	4	0	6	1	2	3	50
91-92—Detroit	NHL	63	20	24	44	276	16	8	0	11	1	6	7	28
92-93—Detroit	NHL	80	14	29	43	292	-9	6	0	7	0	3	3	10
93-94—Detroit	NHL	66	7	10	17	275	-1	1	0	7	1	1	2	8
94-95—Chicago	NHL					Did not play.								
95-96—Chicago	NHL	78	19	21	40	237	15	1	0	10	0	2	2	23
96-97—Chicago	NHL	82	9	14	23	326	-3	1	0	6	2	1	3	41
97-98—Chicago	NHL	14	2	1	3	48	-7	2	0	—	—	—	—	—
98-99—Chicago	NHL	78	7	14	21	206	-11	0	0	—	—	—	—	—
99-00—Chicago	NHL	69	4	11	15	114	10	0	0	—	—	—	—	—
00-01—Chicago	NHL	79	7	12	19	103	-13	1	0	—	—	—	—	—
NHL Totals (16 years)		874	162	218	380	3124	-21	45	0	79	16	32	48	274

PRONGER, CHRIS   D   BLUES

PERSONAL: Born October 10, 1974, in Dryden, Ont. ... 6-6/220. ... Shoots left. ... Full Name: Christopher Robert Pronger. ... Brother of Sean Pronger, center, Columbus Blue Jackets.

TRANSACTIONS/CAREER NOTES: Selected by Hartford Whalers in first round (first Whalers pick, second overall) of NHL entry draft (June 26, 1993). ... Bruised left wrist (March 29, 1994); missed three games. ... Injured left shoulder (January 21, 1995); missed five games. ... Traded by Whalers to St. Louis Blues for LW Brendan Shanahan (July 27, 1995). ... Suspended four games by NHL for slashing incident (November 1, 1995). ... Injured hand (February 15, 1997); missed one game. ... Suspended four games by NHL for slashing incident (December 19, 1998). ... Bruised ankle (February 11, 1999); missed 11 games. ... Suffered back spasms (March 12, 2000); missed one game. ... Suspended one game by NHL for fighting incident (October 13, 2000). ... Underwent knee surgery (January 21, 2001); missed 15 games. ... Fractured forearm (February 26, 2001); missed 15 games.

HONORS: Named to Can.HL All-Rookie team (1991-92). ... Named to OHL Rookie All-Star team (1991-92). ... Won Can.HL Plus/Minus Award (1992-93). ... Won Can.HL Top Defenseman Award (1992-93). ... Won Max Kaminsky Award (1992-93). ... Named to Can.HL All-Star first team (1992-93). ... Named to OHL All-Star first team (1992-93). ... Named to NHL All-Rookie team (1993-94). ... Named to NHL All-Star second team (1997-98). ... Played in NHL All-Star Game (1999 and 2000). ... Named to THE SPORTING NEWS All-Star team (1999-2000). ... Named to NHL All-Star first team (1999-2000). ... Won Hart Memorial Trophy (1999-2000). ... Won James Norris Memorial Trophy (1999-2000). ... Named to THE SPORTING NEWS All-Star second team (2000-01). ... Named to play in NHL All-Star Game (2001); replaced by D Ed Jovanovski due to injury.

MISCELLANEOUS: Captain of St. Louis Blues (1997-98 through 2000-01).

		REGULAR SEASON								PLAYOFFS				
Season Team	League	Gms.	G	A	Pts.	PIM	+/-	PP	SH	Gms.	G	A	Pts.	PIM
90-91—Stratford	OPJHL	48	15	37	52	132	...	...	...	—	—	—	—	—
91-92—Peterborough	OHL	63	17	45	62	90	...	...	...	10	1	8	9	28
92-93—Peterborough	OHL	61	15	62	77	108	...	...	...	21	15	25	40	51
93-94—Hartford	NHL	81	5	25	30	113	-3	2	0	—	—	—	—	—
94-95—Hartford	NHL	43	5	9	14	54	-12	3	0	—	—	—	—	—
95-96—St. Louis	NHL	78	7	18	25	110	-18	3	1	13	1	5	6	16
96-97—St. Louis	NHL	79	11	24	35	143	15	4	0	6	1	1	2	22
97-98—St. Louis	NHL	81	9	27	36	180	*47	1	0	10	1	9	10	26
—Can. Olympic team	Int'l	6	0	0	0	4	...	...	...	—	—	—	—	—
98-99—St. Louis	NHL	67	13	33	46	113	3	8	0	13	1	4	5	28
99-00—St. Louis	NHL	79	14	48	62	92	*52	8	0	7	3	4	7	32
00-01—St. Louis	NHL	51	8	39	47	75	21	4	0	15	1	7	8	32
NHL Totals (8 years)		559	72	223	295	880	105	33	1	64	8	30	38	156

P

PRONGER, SEAN   C   BLUE JACKETS

PERSONAL: Born November 30, 1972, in Dryden, Ont. ... 6-3/210. ... Shoots left. ... Full Name: Sean James Pronger. ... Brother of Chris Pronger, defenseman, St. Louis Blues.

TRANSACTIONS/CAREER NOTES: Selected by Vancouver Canucks in third round (third Canucks pick, 51st overall) of NHL entry draft (June 22, 1991). ... Signed as free agent by Mighty Ducks of Anaheim (February 14, 1995). ... Strained abdominal muscle (February 17, 1997); missed two games. ... Traded by Mighty Ducks to Pittsburgh Penguins for rights to G Patrick Lalime (March 24, 1998). ... Fractured foot (April 4, 1998); missed seven games. ... Traded by Penguins with C Petr Nedved and D Chris Tamer to New York Rangers for RW Alexei Kovalev, C Harry York and future considerations (November 25, 1998). ... Traded by Rangers to Los Angeles Kings for LW Eric Lacroix (February 12, 1999). ... Tore medial collateral ligament in left knee (March 18, 1999); missed final 14 games of season. ... Signed as free agent by Boston Bruins (August 25, 1999). ... Claimed on waivers by Columbus Blue Jackets (May 18, 2001).

Season Team	League	REGULAR SEASON Gms.	G	A	Pts.	PIM	+/-	PP	SH	PLAYOFFS Gms.	G	A	Pts.	PIM
89-90—Thunder Bay Flyers	USHL	48	18	34	52	61	...	...	...	—	—	—	—	—
90-91—Bowling Green	CCHA	40	3	7	10	30	...	...	...	—	—	—	—	—
91-92—Bowling Green	CCHA	34	9	7	16	28	...	...	...	—	—	—	—	—
92-93—Bowling Green	CCHA	39	23	23	46	35	...	...	...	—	—	—	—	—
93-94—Bowling Green	CCHA	38	17	17	34	38	...	...	...	—	—	—	—	—
94-95—Knoxville	ECHL	34	18	23	41	55	...	...	...	—	—	—	—	—
—Greensboro	ECHL	2	0	2	2	0	...	...	...	—	—	—	—	—
—San Diego	IHL	8	0	0	0	2	...	...	...	—	—	—	—	—
95-96—Baltimore	AHL	72	16	17	33	61	...	...	...	12	3	7	10	16
—Anaheim	NHL	7	0	1	1	6	0	0	0	—	—	—	—	—
96-97—Baltimore	AHL	41	26	17	43	17	...	...	...	—	—	—	—	—
—Anaheim	NHL	39	7	7	14	20	6	1	0	9	0	2	2	4
97-98—Anaheim	NHL	62	5	15	20	30	-9	1	0	—	—	—	—	—
—Pittsburgh	NHL	5	1	0	1	2	-1	0	0	5	0	0	0	4
98-99—Houston	IHL	16	11	7	18	32	...	...	...	—	—	—	—	—
—Pittsburgh	NHL	2	0	0	0	0	0	0	0	—	—	—	—	—
—New York Rangers	NHL	14	0	3	3	4	-3	0	0	—	—	—	—	—
—Los Angeles	NHL	13	0	1	1	4	2	0	0	—	—	—	—	—
99-00—Providence	AHL	51	11	18	29	26	...	...	...	—	—	—	—	—
—Boston	NHL	11	0	1	1	13	-4	0	0	—	—	—	—	—
—Manitoba	IHL	14	3	5	8	21	...	...	...	2	0	1	1	2
00-01—Manitoba	IHL	82	18	21	39	85	...	...	...	13	3	6	9	2
NHL Totals (5 years)		**153**	**13**	**28**	**41**	**79**	**-9**	**2**	**0**	**14**	**0**	**2**	**2**	**8**

PROSPAL, VACLAV   C   LIGHTNING

PERSONAL: Born February 17, 1975, in Ceske-Budejovice, Czechoslovakia. ... 6-2/195. ... Shoots left. ... Name pronounced PRAHS-puhl.

TRANSACTIONS/CAREER NOTES: Selected by Philadelphia Flyers in third round (second Flyers pick, 71st overall) of NHL entry draft (June 26, 1993). ... Fractured left fibula (January 3, 1998); missed 18 games. ... Traded by Flyers with RW Pat Falloon and second round draft pick (LW Chris Bala) in 1998 draft to Ottawa Senators for RW Alexandre Daigle (January 17, 1998). ... Bruised thumb (April 2, 1998); missed two games. ... Bruised mouth (April 7, 1998); missed four games. ... Suffered from the flu (November 29, 1998); missed one game. ... Traded by Senators to Florida Panthers for fourth-round pick (G Ray Emery) in 2001 draft and third-round pick in 2002 draft (January 21, 2001). ... Traded by Panthers to Tampa Bay Lightning for C Ryan Johnson and sixth-round pick in 2003 draft (July 10, 2001).

HONORS: Named to AHL All-Star first team (1996-97).

Season Team	League	REGULAR SEASON Gms.	G	A	Pts.	PIM	+/-	PP	SH	PLAYOFFS Gms.	G	A	Pts.	PIM
91-92—Motor-Ceske Bude.	Czech. Jrs.	36	16	16	32	12	...	...	...	—	—	—	—	—
92-93—Motor-Ceske Bude.	Czech. Jrs.	36	26	31	57	24	...	...	...	—	—	—	—	—
93-94—Hershey	AHL	55	14	21	35	38	...	...	...	2	0	0	0	2
94-95—Hershey	AHL	69	13	32	45	36	...	...	...	2	1	0	1	4
95-96—Hershey	AHL	68	15	36	51	59	...	...	...	5	2	4	6	2
96-97—Philadelphia	AHL	63	32	63	95	70	...	...	...	—	—	—	—	—
—Philadelphia	NHL	18	5	10	15	4	3	0	0	5	1	3	4	4
97-98—Philadelphia	NHL	41	5	13	18	17	-10	4	0	—	—	—	—	—
—Ottawa	NHL	15	1	6	7	4	-1	0	0	6	0	0	0	0
98-99—Ottawa	NHL	79	10	26	36	58	8	2	0	4	0	0	0	0
99-00—Ottawa	NHL	79	22	33	55	40	-2	5	0	6	0	4	4	4
00-01—Ottawa	NHL	40	1	12	13	12	1	0	0	—	—	—	—	—
—Florida	NHL	34	4	12	16	10	-2	1	0	—	—	—	—	—
NHL Totals (5 years)		**306**	**48**	**112**	**160**	**145**	**-3**	**12**	**0**	**21**	**1**	**7**	**8**	**8**

PRPIC, JOEL   C

PERSONAL: Born September 25, 1974, in Sudbury, Ont. ... 6-7/225. ... Shoots left. ... Full Name: Joel Melvin Prpic. ... Name pronounced PUHR-pihk.

TRANSACTIONS/CAREER NOTES: Selected by Boston Bruins in ninth round (ninth Bruins pick, 233rd overall) of NHL entry draft (June 26, 1993). ... Signed as free agent by Colorado Avalanche (August 29, 2000).

Season Team	League	REGULAR SEASON Gms.	G	A	Pts.	PIM	+/-	PP	SH	PLAYOFFS Gms.	G	A	Pts.	PIM
92-93—Waterloo Jr. B	OHA	45	17	43	60	160	...	...	...	—	—	—	—	—
93-94—St. Lawrence Univ.	ECAC	31	2	4	6	90	...	...	...	—	—	—	—	—
94-95—St. Lawrence Univ.	ECAC	32	7	10	17	62	...	...	...	—	—	—	—	—
95-96—St. Lawrence Univ.	ECAC	32	3	10	13	77	...	...	...	—	—	—	—	—
96-97—St. Lawrence Univ.	ECAC	34	10	8	18	57	...	...	...	—	—	—	—	—

P

Season Team	League	Gms.	G	A	Pts.	PIM	+/-	PP	SH	Gms.	G	A	Pts.	PIM
97-98—Providence	AHL	73	17	18	35	53	...	...	...	—	—	—	—	—
—Boston	NHL	1	0	0	0	2	0	0	0	—	—	—	—	—
98-99—Providence	AHL	75	14	16	30	163	...	...	...	18	4	6	10	48
99-00—Providence	AHL	70	9	20	29	143	...	...	...	14	3	4	7	58
—Boston	NHL	14	0	3	3	0	-6	0	0	—	—	—	—	—
00-01—Hershey	AHL	74	16	23	39	128	...	...	...	12	1	1	2	26
—Colorado	NHL	3	0	0	0	2	0	0	0	—	—	—	—	—
NHL Totals (3 years)		18	0	3	3	4	-6	0	0					

PURINTON, DALE · D · RANGERS

PERSONAL: Born October 11, 1976, in Fort Wayne, Ind. ... 6-3/214. ... Shoots left.
TRANSACTIONS/CAREER NOTES: Selected by New York Rangers in fifth round (fourth Ranger pick, 117th overall) of NHL entry draft (July 8, 1995). ... Injured ribs (December 15, 2000); missed five games. ... Injured arm (January 16, 2001); missed four games.

		REGULAR SEASON								PLAYOFFS				
Season Team	League	Gms.	G	A	Pts.	PIM	+/-	PP	SH	Gms.	G	A	Pts.	PIM
93-94—Vernon	Tier II Jr. A	42	1	6	7	194	...	...	...	—	—	—	—	—
94-95—Tacoma	WHL	65	0	8	8	291	...	...	...	3	0	0	0	13
95-96—Kelowna	WHL	22	1	4	5	88	...	...	...	—	—	—	—	—
—Lethbridge	WHL	37	3	6	9	144	...	...	...	4	1	1	2	25
96-97—Lethbridge	WHL	51	6	26	32	254	...	...	...	18	3	5	8	*88
97-98—Charlotte	ECHL	34	3	5	8	186	...	...	...	—	—	—	—	—
—Hartford	AHL	17	0	0	0	95	...	...	...	—	—	—	—	—
98-99—Hartford	AHL	45	1	3	4	306	...	...	...	7	0	2	2	24
99-00—Hartford	AHL	62	4	4	8	415	...	...	...	23	0	3	3	*87
—New York Rangers	NHL	1	0	0	0	7	-1	0	0	—	—	—	—	—
00-01—Hartford	AHL	11	0	1	1	75	...	...	...	—	—	—	—	—
—New York Rangers	NHL	42	0	2	2	180	5	0	0	—	—	—	—	—
NHL Totals (2 years)		43	0	2	2	187	4	0	0					

PUSHOR, JAMIE · D · BLUE JACKETS

PERSONAL: Born February 11, 1973, in Lethbridge, Alta. ... 6-3/220. ... Shoots right. ... Full Name: James Pushor. ... Name pronounced PUSH-uhr.
TRANSACTIONS/CAREER NOTES: Selected by Detroit Red Wings in second round (second Wings pick, 32nd overall) of NHL entry draft (June 22, 1991). ... Strained groin (November 21, 1997); missed three games. ... Traded by Red Wings with fourth-round pick (C Viktor Wallin) in 1998 draft to Mighty Ducks of Anaheim for D Dmitri Mironov (March 24, 1998). ... Fractured right finger (April 15, 1998); missed remainder of season. ... Suffered eye injury (January 6, 1999); missed two games. ... Bruised left shoulder and chest (February 14, 1999); missed four games. ... Selected by Atlanta Thrashers in NHL expansion draft (June 25, 1999). ... Traded by Thrashers to Dallas Stars for LW Jason Botterill (July 15, 1999). ... Selected by Columbus Blue Jackets in NHL expansion draft (June 23, 2000). ... Sprained knee (March 26, 2001); missed seven games.
MISCELLANEOUS: Member of Stanley Cup championship team (1997).

		REGULAR SEASON								PLAYOFFS				
Season Team	League	Gms.	G	A	Pts.	PIM	+/-	PP	SH	Gms.	G	A	Pts.	PIM
88-89—Lethbridge	WHL	2	0	0	0	0	...	...	...	—	—	—	—	—
89-90—Lethbridge	WHL	10	0	2	2	2	...	...	...	—	—	—	—	—
90-91—Lethbridge	WHL	71	1	13	14	193	...	...	...	—	—	—	—	—
91-92—Lethbridge	WHL	49	2	15	17	232	...	...	...	5	0	0	0	33
92-93—Lethbridge	WHL	72	6	22	28	200	...	...	...	4	0	1	1	9
93-94—Adirondack	AHL	73	1	17	18	124	...	...	...	12	0	0	0	22
94-95—Adirondack	AHL	58	2	11	13	129	...	...	...	4	0	1	1	0
95-96—Detroit	NHL	5	0	1	1	17	2	0	0	—	—	—	—	—
—Adirondack	AHL	65	2	16	18	126	...	...	...	3	0	0	0	5
96-97—Detroit	NHL	75	4	7	11	129	1	0	0	5	0	1	1	5
97-98—Detroit	NHL	54	2	5	7	71	2	0	0	—	—	—	—	—
—Anaheim	NHL	10	0	2	2	10	1	0	0	—	—	—	—	—
98-99—Anaheim	NHL	70	1	2	3	112	-20	0	0	4	0	0	0	6
99-00—Dallas	NHL	62	0	8	8	53	0	0	0	5	0	0	0	5
00-01—Columbus	NHL	75	3	10	13	94	7	0	1	—	—	—	—	—
NHL Totals (6 years)		351	10	35	45	486	-7	0	1	14	0	1	1	16

PYATT, TAYLOR · LW · SABRES

PERSONAL: Born August 19, 1981, in Thunder Bay, Ont. ... 6-4/220. ... Shoots left. ... Son of Nelson Pyatt, center/left winger with three NHL teams (1973-74 through 1979-80).
TRANSACTIONS/CAREER NOTES: Selected by New York Islanders in first round (second Islanders pick, eighth overall) of NHL entry draft (June 26, 1999). ... Traded by Islanders with C Tim Connolly to Buffalo Sabres for C Michael Peca (June 24, 2001).
HONORS: Named to OHL All-Rookie second team (1997-98). ... Named to OHL All-Star first team (1999-2000).

		REGULAR SEASON								PLAYOFFS				
Season Team	League	Gms.	G	A	Pts.	PIM	+/-	PP	SH	Gms.	G	A	Pts.	PIM
97-98—Sudbury	OHL	58	14	17	31	104	...	...	...	10	3	1	4	6
98-99—Sudbury	OHL	68	37	38	75	95	...	...	...	4	0	4	4	6
99-00—Sudbury	OHL	68	40	49	89	98	...	...	...	12	8	7	15	25
00-01—New York Islanders	NHL	78	4	14	18	39	-17	1	0	—	—	—	—	—
NHL Totals (1 year)		78	4	14	18	39	-17	1	0					

P

PERSONAL: Born March 12, 1976, in Durham, N.H. ... 6-2/209. ... Shoots left.

TRANSACTIONS/CAREER NOTES: Selected by Winnipeg Jets in second round (first Jets pick, 30th overall) of NHL entry draft (June 28, 1994). ... Suffered from the flu (January 29, 1996); missed two games. ... Jets franchise moved to Phoenix and renamed Coyotes for 1996-97 season; NHL approved move on January 18, 1996. ... Separated shoulder (November 27, 1997); missed six games. ... Suffered concussion (January 30, 1998); missed one game. ... Underwent hernia surgery (March 8, 1998); missed 11 games. ... Suffered concussion (October 6, 1998); missed first nine games of season. ... Separated shoulder (January 31, 1999); missed three games. ... Suffered concussion (March 30, 1999); missed final seven games of season. ... Traded by Coyotes with third-round pick (traded back to Phoenix) in 2001 draft to New Jersey Devils for D Lyle Odelein (March 7, 2000). ... Traded by Devils to Columbus Blue Jackets for past considerations (June 25, 2000). ... Suffered from the flu (January 3, 2001); missed one game.

HONORS: Won WHL Top Draft Choice Award (1993-94). ... Named to Can.HL All-Rookie team (1993-94). ... Named to WHL (West) All-Star first team (1994-95).

STATISTICAL PLATEAUS: Three-goal games: 2000-01 (1).

Season Team	League	REGULAR SEASON								PLAYOFFS				
		Gms.	G	A	Pts.	PIM	+/-	PP	SH	Gms.	G	A	Pts.	PIM
90-91—Cardigan Prep School.	USHS (East)	31	67	54	121	...	...	...	...	—	—	—	—	—
91-92—Cardigan Prep School.	USHS (East)	32	111	68	179	...	...	...	...	—	—	—	—	—
92-93—Tabor Academy	Mass. H.S.	28	15	26	41	30	...	...	...	1	0	2	2	0
93-94—Seattle	WHL	63	15	29	44	47	...	...	...	9	4	12	16	8
94-95—Seattle	WHL	65	29	60	89	82	...	...	...	3	1	2	3	6
95-96—Winnipeg	NHL	51	5	13	18	22	-2	2	0	—	—	—	—	—
—Springfield	AHL	11	2	3	5	4	...	...	...	10	2	3	5	6
—Seattle	WHL	—	—	—	—	—	...	...	...	5	4	1	5	6
96-97—Springfield	AHL	43	6	18	24	20	...	...	...	12	2	7	9	4
—Phoenix	NHL	27	3	11	14	4	-4	1	0	7	0	2	2	0
97-98—Phoenix	NHL	32	4	7	11	16	-6	1	0	—	—	—	—	—
—Springfield	AHL	8	1	7	8	10	...	...	...	1	0	0	0	0
98-99—Phoenix	NHL	60	5	8	13	20	-10	2	0	—	—	—	—	—
99-00—Phoenix	NHL	50	3	7	10	22	0	0	0	—	—	—	—	—
—New Jersey	NHL	4	1	0	1	2	-2	0	0	—	—	—	—	—
00-01—Syracuse	AHL	21	5	15	20	30	...	...	...	—	—	—	—	—
—Columbus	NHL	57	7	16	23	16	-19	3	0	—	—	—	—	—
NHL Totals (6 years)		281	28	62	90	102	-43	9	0	7	0	2	2	0

PERSONAL: Born October 22, 1968, in Boucherville, Que. ... 6-3/234. ... Shoots right. ... Name pronounced steh-FAN kahn-TAHL.

TRANSACTIONS/CAREER NOTES: Selected by Boston Bruins in first round (second Bruins pick, 14th overall) of NHL entry draft (June 13, 1987). ... Fractured bone near eye (October 1988). ... Injured knee (January 1989). ... Sprained right knee (October 17, 1989); missed eight games. ... Fractured left ankle (April 9, 1991); missed remainder of playoffs. ... Traded by Bruins with C Craig Janney to St. Louis Blues for C Adam Oates (February 7, 1992). ... Traded by Blues with RW Nelson Emerson to Winnipeg Jets for D Phil Housley (September 24, 1993). ... Sprained wrist (January 16, 1994); missed two games. ... Sprained neck (April 6, 1994); missed one game. ... Sprained ankle (February 6, 1995); missed five games. ... Traded by Jets to Montreal Canadiens for second-round pick (D Jason Doig) in 1995 draft (July 8, 1995). ... Suffered concussion (November 11, 1995); missed one game. ... Sprained right Knee (February 7, 1996); missed seven games. ... Underwent knee surgery (March 19, 1996); missed five games. ... Bruised foot (December 21, 1996); missed two games. ... Injured collarbone (January 1, 1997); missed two games. ... Sprained left knee (February 6, 1997); missed seven games. ... Suffered concussion (November 8, 1997); missed one game. ... Strained hip flexor (February 7, 1998); missed one game. ... Sprained ankle (April 1, 1998); missed nine games. ... Signed as free agent by New York Rangers (July 6, 1999). ... Suffered concussion (November 24, 1999); missed one game. ... Suffered neck spasms (January 4, 2000); missed one game. ... Claimed on waivers by Chicago Blackhawks (October 5, 2000). ... Strained groin (January 21, 2001); missed two games. ... Suffered sinus infection (April 4, 2001); missed three games. ... Traded by Blackhawks to Canadiens for fourth-round pick (D Brent MacLellan) in 2001 draft (June 23, 2001).

HONORS: Named to QMJHL All-Star first team (1986-87).

Season Team	League	REGULAR SEASON								PLAYOFFS				
		Gms.	G	A	Pts.	PIM	+/-	PP	SH	Gms.	G	A	Pts.	PIM
85-86—Granby	QMJHL	67	2	17	19	144	...	...	...	—	—	—	—	—
86-87—Granby	QMJHL	67	13	41	54	178	...	...	...	8	0	9	9	10
87-88—Hull	QMJHL	38	13	23	36	138	...	...	...	19	7	12	19	30
88-89—Maine	AHL	16	4	10	14	28	...	...	...	—	—	—	—	—
—Boston	NHL	26	0	1	1	29	-5	0	0	—	—	—	—	—
89-90—Boston	NHL	38	2	2	4	22	-11	0	0	—	—	—	—	—
—Maine	AHL	37	4	16	20	27	...	...	...	—	—	—	—	—
90-91—Maine	AHL	23	1	5	6	30	...	...	...	—	—	—	—	—
—Boston	NHL	45	2	6	8	89	2	1	0	3	0	1	1	7
91-92—Boston	NHL	49	4	10	14	77	-8	0	0	4	1	2	3	6
—St. Louis	NHL	26	0	6	6	32	-3	0	0	9	0	0	0	8
92-93—St. Louis	NHL	75	1	10	11	100	-6	0	1	9	0	0	0	8
93-94—Winnipeg	NHL	81	8	18	26	119	-25	1	1	—	—	—	—	—
94-95—Winnipeg	NHL	43	6	17	23	78	0	3	0	—	—	—	—	—
95-96—Montreal	NHL	68	2	14	16	117	-4	0	1	6	0	1	1	6
96-97—Montreal	NHL	71	7	15	22	100	1	1	0	5	0	1	1	6
97-98—Montreal	NHL	71	6	10	16	97	13	0	0	9	0	2	2	4
98-99—Montreal	NHL	82	8	19	27	84	-23	1	1	—	—	—	—	—
99-00—New York Rangers	NHL	75	2	14	16	77	-10	0	0	—	—	—	—	—
00-01—Chicago	NHL	72	1	18	19	60	-9	0	0	—	—	—	—	—
NHL Totals (13 years)		822	49	160	209	1081	-88	7	4	36	1	7	8	37

RACHUNEK, KAREL   D   SENATORS

PERSONAL: Born August 27, 1979, in Gottwaldov, Czechoslovakia. ... 6-1/191. ... Shoots right.
TRANSACTIONS/CAREER NOTES: Selected by Ottawa Senators in ninth round (eighth Senators pick, 229th overall) of NHL entry draft (June 21, 1997). ... Suffered partially torn medial collateral ligament in right knee (November 17, 1999); missed 12 games. ... Sprained medial collateral ligament in left knee (November 25, 2000); missed seven games. ... Bruised left knee (April 1, 2001); missed one game.

		REGULAR SEASON								PLAYOFFS				
Season Team	League	Gms.	G	A	Pts.	PIM	+/-	PP	SH	Gms.	G	A	Pts.	PIM
95-96—ZPS Zlin Jrs.	Czech Rep.	38	8	11	19	...	...	...	...	—	—	—	—	—
96-97—ZPS Zlin Jrs.	Czech Rep.	27	2	11	13	...	...	...	...	—	—	—	—	—
97-98—ZPS Zlin	Czech Rep.	27	1	2	3	16	...	...	...	—	—	—	—	—
98-99—ZPS Zlin	Czech Rep.	39	3	9	12	88	...	...	...	6	0	0	0	...
99-00—Grand Rapids	IHL	62	6	20	26	64	...	...	...	9	0	5	5	6
—Ottawa	NHL	6	0	0	0	2	0	0	0	—	—	—	—	—
00-01—Ottawa	NHL	71	3	30	33	60	17	3	0	3	0	0	0	0
NHL Totals (2 years)		77	3	30	33	62	17	3	0	3	0	0	0	0

RADIVOJEVIC, BRANKO   RW   COYOTES

PERSONAL: Born November 24, 1980, in Piestany, Czechoslovakia. ... 6-1/185. ... Shoots right.
TRANSACTIONS/CAREER NOTES: Selected by Colorado Avalanche in third round (third Avalanche pick, 93rd overall) of NHL entry draft (June 26, 1999). ... Signed as free agent by Phoenix Coyotes (June 19, 2001).
HONORS: Named to OHL All-Star first team (2000-01). ... Won Jim Mahon Memorial Trophy (2000-01).

		REGULAR SEASON								PLAYOFFS				
Season Team	League	Gms.	G	A	Pts.	PIM	+/-	PP	SH	Gms.	G	A	Pts.	PIM
97-98—Dukla Trencin	Slovakia Jrs.	52	30	33	63	50	...	...	...	—	—	—	—	—
98-99—Belleville	OHL	68	20	38	58	61	...	...	...	21	7	17	24	18
99-00—Belleville	OHL	59	23	49	72	86	...	...	...	16	5	8	13	32
00-01—Belleville	OHL	61	34	70	104	77	...	...	...	10	6	10	16	18

RAFALSKI, BRIAN   D   DEVILS

PERSONAL: Born September 28, 1973, in Dearborn, Mich. ... 5-9/200. ... Shoots right.
TRANSACTIONS/CAREER NOTES: Signed as non-drafted free agent by New Jersey Devils (June 18, 1999). ... Suffered illness (January 3, 2000); missed one game. ... Bruised ribs (March 17, 2000); missed five games. ... Bruised left shoulder (February 8, 2001); missed three games.
HONORS: Named to NCAA All-America (West) first team (1994-95). ... Named to WCHA All-Star first team (1994-95). ... Named to NHL All-Rookie team (1999-2000).
MISCELLANEOUS: Member of Stanley Cup championship team (2000).

		REGULAR SEASON								PLAYOFFS				
Season Team	League	Gms.	G	A	Pts.	PIM	+/-	PP	SH	Gms.	G	A	Pts.	PIM
91-92—Univ. of Wisconsin	WCHA	34	3	14	17	34	...	...	...	—	—	—	—	—
92-93—Univ. of Wisconsin	WCHA	32	0	13	13	10	...	...	...	—	—	—	—	—
93-94—Univ. of Wisconsin	WCHA	37	6	17	23	26	...	...	...	—	—	—	—	—
94-95—Univ. of Wisconsin	WCHA	43	11	34	45	48	...	...	...	—	—	—	—	—
95-96—Brynas Gavle	Sweden Dv. 2	18	3	6	9	12	...	...	...	9	0	1	1	2
—Brynas Gavle	Sweden	22	1	8	9	14	...	...	...	—	—	—	—	—
96-97—HPK Hameenlinna	Finland	49	11	24	35	26	...	...	...	10	6	5	11	4
97-98—HIFK Helsinki	Finland	40	13	10	23	24	...	...	...	9	5	6	11	0
98-99—HIFK Helsinki	Finland	53	19	34	53	18	...	...	...	11	5	†9	14	4
99-00—New Jersey	NHL	75	5	27	32	28	21	1	0	23	2	6	8	8
00-01—New Jersey	NHL	78	9	43	52	26	36	6	0	25	7	11	18	7
NHL Totals (2 years)		153	14	70	84	54	57	7	0	48	9	17	26	15

RAGNARSSON, MARCUS   D   SHARKS

PERSONAL: Born August 13, 1971, in Ostervala, Sweden. ... 6-1/215. ... Shoots left. ... Name pronounced RAG-nuhr-suhn.
TRANSACTIONS/CAREER NOTES: Selected by San Jose Sharks in fifth round (fifth Sharks pick, 99th overall) of NHL entry draft (June 20, 1992). ... Injured foot (November 8, 1995); missed two games. ... Injured head (December 5, 1995); missed two games. ... Injured knee (January 10, 1996); missed one game. ... Suffered from the flu (January 16, 1996); missed one game. ... Injured hamstring (February 10, 1996); missed four games. ... Injured back (March 22, 1996); missed one game. ... Injured leg (November 1, 1996); missed two games. ... Fractured toe (December 9, 1996); missed two games. ... Suspended one game by NHL for high-sticking incident (November 3, 1997). ... Injured thumb (October 3, 1998); missed first eight games of season. ... Injured foot (October 19, 1999); missed 16 games. ... Suffered concussion (February 22, 2000); missed three games. ... Injured knee (November 1, 2000); missed seven games. ... Injured shoulder (February 16, 2001); missed five games.
HONORS: Played in NHL All-Star Game (2001).

		REGULAR SEASON								PLAYOFFS				
Season Team	League	Gms.	G	A	Pts.	PIM	+/-	PP	SH	Gms.	G	A	Pts.	PIM
89-90—Djurgarden Stockholm	Sweden	13	0	2	2	0	...	...	...	1	0	0	0	0
90-91—Djurgarden Stockholm	Sweden	35	4	1	5	12	...	...	...	7	0	0	0	6
91-92—Djurgarden Stockholm	Sweden	40	8	5	13	14	...	...	...	—	—	—	—	—
92-93—Djurgarden Stockholm	Sweden	35	3	3	6	53	...	...	...	6	0	2	2	...
93-94—Djurgarden Stockholm	Sweden	19	0	4	4	24	...	...	...	—	—	—	—	—
94-95—Djurgarden Stockholm	Sweden	38	7	9	16	20	...	...	...	3	0	0	0	4
95-96—San Jose	NHL	71	8	31	39	42	-24	4	0	—	—	—	—	—

			REGULAR SEASON							PLAYOFFS				
Season Team	League	Gms.	G	A	Pts.	PIM	+/-	PP	SH	Gms.	G	A	Pts.	PIM
96-97—San Jose....................	NHL	69	3	14	17	63	-18	2	0	—	—	—	—	—
97-98—San Jose....................	NHL	79	5	20	25	65	-11	3	0	6	0	0	0	4
—Swedish Oly. team......	Int'l	3	0	1	1	0	...	...	...	—	—	—	—	—
98-99—San Jose....................	NHL	74	0	13	13	66	7	0	0	6	0	1	1	6
99-00—San Jose....................	NHL	63	3	13	16	38	13	0	0	12	0	3	3	10
00-01—San Jose....................	NHL	68	3	12	15	44	2	1	0	5	0	1	1	8
NHL Totals (6 years)..........		424	22	103	125	318	-31	10	0	29	0	5	5	28

RALPH, BRAD LW COYOTES

R

PERSONAL: Born October 17, 1980, in Ottawa. ... 6-2/198. ... Shoots left.

TRANSACTIONS/CAREER NOTES: Selected by Phoenix Coyotes in second round (third Coyotes pick, 53rd overall) of NHL entry draft (June 26, 1999).

			REGULAR SEASON							PLAYOFFS				
Season Team	League	Gms.	G	A	Pts.	PIM	+/-	PP	SH	Gms.	G	A	Pts.	PIM
96-97—Kanata........................	OJHL	44	13	13	26	63	...	...	...	—	—	—	—	—
97-98—Oshawa......................	OHL	59	20	17	37	45	...	...	...	7	2	1	3	8
98-99—Oshawa......................	OHL	67	31	44	75	93	...	...	...	14	7	7	14	10
99-00—Oshawa......................	OHL	56	28	35	63	68	...	...	...	5	1	1	2	4
00-01—Phoenix......................	NHL	1	0	0	0	0	0	0	0	—	—	—	—	—
—Springfield	AHL	50	5	13	18	23	...	...	...	—	—	—	—	—
NHL Totals (1 year).............		1	0	0	0	0	0	0	0					

RANHEIM, PAUL LW FLYERS

PERSONAL: Born January 25, 1966, in St. Louis. ... 6-1/210. ... Shoots right. ... Full Name: Paul Stephen Ranheim. ... Name pronounced RAN-highm.

TRANSACTIONS/CAREER NOTES: Selected by Calgary Flames in second round (third Flames pick, 38th overall) of NHL entry draft (June 8, 1983). ... Fractured right ankle (December 11, 1990); missed 41 games. ... Traded by Flames with D Gary Suter and C Ted Drury to Hartford Whalers for C Michael Nylander, D Zarley Zalapski and D James Patrick (March 10, 1994). ... Suffered finger infection on left hand (November 28, 1995); missed six games. ... Suffered abdominal strain (October 27, 1996); missed five games. ... Suffered sore groin (November 11, 1996); missed one game. ... Whalers franchise moved to North Carolina and renamed Carolina Hurricanes for 1997-98 season; NHL approved move on June 25, 1997. ... Injured back (March 22, 2000); missed two games. ... Traded by Hurricanes to Philadelphia Flyers for eigth-round pick in 2002 draft (May 31, 2000).

HONORS: Named to WCHA All-Star second team (1986-87). ... Named to NCAA All-America (West) first team (1987-88). ... Named to WCHA All-Star first team (1987-88). ... Won Garry F. Longman Memorial Trophy (1988-89). ... Won Ken McKenzie Trophy (1988-89). ... Named to IHL All-Star second team (1988-89).

MISCELLANEOUS: Scored on a penalty shot (vs. Bob Essensa, October 31, 1993).

STATISTICAL PLATEAUS: Three-goal games: 1991-92 (1).

			REGULAR SEASON							PLAYOFFS				
Season Team	League	Gms.	G	A	Pts.	PIM	+/-	PP	SH	Gms.	G	A	Pts.	PIM
82-83—Edina High School	Minn. H.S.	26	12	25	37	4	...	...	...	—	—	—	—	—
83-84—Edina High School	Minn. H.S.	26	16	24	40	6	...	...	...	—	—	—	—	—
84-85—Univ. of Wisconsin......	WCHA	42	11	11	22	40	...	...	...	—	—	—	—	—
85-86—Univ. of Wisconsin......	WCHA	33	17	17	34	34	...	...	...	—	—	—	—	—
86-87—Univ. of Wisconsin......	WCHA	42	24	35	59	54	...	...	...	—	—	—	—	—
87-88—Univ. of Wisconsin......	WCHA	44	36	26	62	63	...	...	...	—	—	—	—	—
88-89—Calgary	NHL	5	0	0	0	0	-3	0	0	—	—	—	—	—
—Salt Lake City..............	IHL	75	*68	29	97	16	...	...	...	14	5	5	10	8
89-90—Calgary	NHL	80	26	28	54	23	27	1	3	6	1	3	4	2
90-91—Calgary	NHL	39	14	16	30	4	20	2	0	7	2	2	4	0
91-92—Calgary	NHL	80	23	20	43	32	16	1	3	—	—	—	—	—
92-93—Calgary	NHL	83	21	22	43	26	-4	3	4	6	0	1	1	0
93-94—Calgary	NHL	67	10	14	24	20	-7	0	2	—	—	—	—	—
—Hartford	NHL	15	0	3	3	2	-11	0	0	—	—	—	—	—
94-95—Hartford	NHL	47	6	14	20	10	-3	0	0	—	—	—	—	—
95-96—Hartford	NHL	73	10	20	30	14	-2	0	1	—	—	—	—	—
96-97—Hartford	NHL	67	10	11	21	18	-13	0	3	—	—	—	—	—
97-98—Carolina	NHL	73	5	9	14	28	-11	0	1	—	—	—	—	—
98-99—Carolina	NHL	78	9	10	19	39	4	0	2	6	0	0	0	2
99-00—Carolina	NHL	79	9	13	22	6	-14	0	0	—	—	—	—	—
00-01—Philadelphia	NHL	80	10	7	17	14	2	0	2	6	0	2	2	0
NHL Totals (13 years)..........		866	153	187	340	236	1	7	21	31	3	8	11	6

RASMUSSEN, ERIK LW/C SABRES

PERSONAL: Born March 28, 1977, in Minneapolis. ... 6-2/205. ... Shoots left. ... Name pronounced RAS-muh-suhn.

TRANSACTIONS/CAREER NOTES: Selected by Buffalo Sabres in first round (first Sabres pick, seventh overall) of NHL entry draft (June 22, 1996). ... Injured shoulder (October 26, 1997); missed one game. ... Injured foot (April 13, 1999); missed one game. ... Bruised hand (December 4, 1999); missed five games. ... Suffered back spasms (March 23, 2000); missed one game.

HONORS: Named to WCHA All-Rookie team (1995-96).

Season Team	League	REGULAR SEASON								PLAYOFFS				
		Gms.	G	A	Pts.	PIM	+/-	PP	SH	Gms.	G	A	Pts.	PIM
92-93—Saint Louis Park	Minn. H.S.	23	16	24	40	50	...	...	...	—	—	—	—	—
93-94—Saint Louis Park	Minn. H.S.	18	25	18	43	60	...	...	...	—	—	—	—	—
94-95—Saint Louis Park	Minn. H.S.	23	19	33	52	80	...	...	...	—	—	—	—	—
95-96—Univ. of Minnesota	WCHA	40	16	32	48	55	...	...	...	—	—	—	—	—
96-97—Univ. of Minnesota	WCHA	34	15	12	27	123	...	...	...	—	—	—	—	—
97-98—Buffalo	NHL	21	2	3	5	14	2	0	0	—	—	—	—	—
—Rochester	AHL	53	9	14	23	83	...	...	...	1	0	0	0	5
98-99—Rochester	AHL	37	12	14	26	47	...	...	...	—	—	—	—	—
—Buffalo	NHL	42	3	7	10	37	6	0	0	21	2	4	6	18
99-00—Buffalo	NHL	67	8	6	14	43	1	0	0	3	0	0	0	4
00-01—Buffalo	NHL	82	12	19	31	51	0	1	0	3	0	1	1	0
NHL Totals (4 years)		212	25	35	60	145	9	1	0	27	2	5	7	22

RATCHUK, PETER   D

PERSONAL: Born September 10, 1977, in Buffalo. ... 6-1/185. ... Shoots left.

TRANSACTIONS/CAREER NOTES: Selected by Colorado Avalanche in first round (first Avalanche pick, 25th overall) of NHL entry draft (June 22, 1996). ... Signed as free agent by Florida Panthers (June 17, 1998).

Season Team	League	REGULAR SEASON								PLAYOFFS				
		Gms.	G	A	Pts.	PIM	+/-	PP	SH	Gms.	G	A	Pts.	PIM
94-95—Lawrence Academy	Mass. H.S.	31	8	15	23	18	...	...	...	—	—	—	—	—
95-96—Shattuck-Saint Mary's	Minn. H.S.	32	16	27	43	30	...	...	...	—	—	—	—	—
96-97—Bowling Green	CCHA	35	9	12	21	14	...	...	...	—	—	—	—	—
97-98—Hull	QMJHL	60	23	31	54	34	...	...	...	11	3	6	9	8
98-99—New Haven	AHL	53	7	20	27	44	...	...	...	—	—	—	—	—
—Florida	NHL	24	1	1	2	10	-1	0	0	—	—	—	—	—
99-00—Louisville	AHL	76	9	17	26	64	...	...	...	4	1	2	3	0
00-01—Louisville	AHL	64	5	13	18	85	...	...	...	—	—	—	—	—
—Florida	NHL	8	0	0	0	0	-1	0	0	—	—	—	—	—
NHL Totals (2 years)		32	1	1	2	10	-2	0	0	—	—	—	—	—

RATHJE, MIKE   D   SHARKS

PERSONAL: Born May 11, 1974, in Mannville, Alta. ... 6-5/235. ... Shoots left. ... Full Name: Michael Rathje. ... Name pronounced RATH-jee.

TRANSACTIONS/CAREER NOTES: Selected by San Jose Sharks in first round (first Sharks pick, third overall) of NHL entry draft (June 20, 1992). ... Strained abdominal muscle (February 19, 1994); missed three games. ... Sprained knee (February 26, 1994); missed four games. ... Sprained knee (February 2, 1995); missed three games. ... Injured foot (February 15, 1995); missed one game. ... Injured hip flexor (April 25, 1995); missed two games. ... Strained abdominal muscle (October 6, 1995); missed first two games of season. ... Injured shoulder (November 14, 1995); missed 12 games. ... Strained groin (November 8, 1996); missed 50 games. ... Injured groin (November 12, 1999); missed 16 games.

HONORS: Named to Can.HL All-Star second team (1992-93). ... Named to WHL (East) All-Star second team (1991-92 and 1992-93).

Season Team	League	REGULAR SEASON								PLAYOFFS				
		Gms.	G	A	Pts.	PIM	+/-	PP	SH	Gms.	G	A	Pts.	PIM
90-91—Medicine Hat	WHL	64	1	16	17	28	...	...	...	12	0	4	4	2
91-92—Medicine Hat	WHL	67	11	23	34	109	...	...	...	4	0	1	1	2
92-93—Medicine Hat	WHL	57	12	37	49	103	...	...	...	10	3	3	6	12
—Kansas City	IHL	—	—	—	—	—	...	...	...	5	0	0	0	12
93-94—San Jose	NHL	47	1	9	10	59	-9	1	0	1	0	0	0	0
—Kansas City	IHL	6	0	2	2	0	...	...	...	—	—	—	—	—
94-95—Kansas City	IHL	6	0	1	1	7	...	...	...	—	—	—	—	—
—San Jose	NHL	42	2	7	9	29	-1	0	0	11	5	2	7	4
95-96—Kansas City	IHL	36	6	11	17	34	...	...	...	—	—	—	—	—
—San Jose	NHL	27	0	7	7	14	-16	0	0	—	—	—	—	—
96-97—San Jose	NHL	31	0	8	8	21	-1	0	0	—	—	—	—	—
97-98—San Jose	NHL	81	3	12	15	59	-4	1	0	6	1	0	1	6
98-99—San Jose	NHL	82	5	9	14	36	15	2	0	6	0	0	0	4
99-00—San Jose	NHL	66	2	14	16	31	-2	0	0	12	1	3	4	8
00-01—San Jose	NHL	81	0	11	11	48	7	0	0	6	0	1	1	4
NHL Totals (8 years)		457	13	77	90	297	-11	4	0	42	7	6	13	26

RAY, ROB   RW   SABRES

PERSONAL: Born June 8, 1968, in Stirling, Ont. ... 6-0/215. ... Shoots left.

TRANSACTIONS/CAREER NOTES: Selected by Buffalo Sabres in fifth round (fifth Sabres pick, 97th overall) of NHL entry draft (June 11, 1988). ... Tore right knee ligament (April 11, 1993); missed remainder of season. ... Suffered from the flu (March 11, 1995); missed one game. ... Fractured right cheekbone (November 27, 1995); missed eight games. ... Fractured thumb (November 22, 1997); missed 19 games. ... Suspended one playoff game by NHL for verbally abusing officials (April 26, 1998). ... Suspended four games by NHL for slew-footing incident (November 29, 1998). ... Bruised knee (February 6, 1999); missed one game. ... Injured shoulder (November 13, 2000); missed seven games. ... Suspended seven games by NHL for abusing an official (January 11, 2001).

HONORS: Won King Clancy Memorial Trophy (1998-99).

MISCELLANEOUS: Holds Buffalo Sabres all-time record for most penalty minutes (2,897).

Season Team	League	Gms.	G	A	Pts.	PIM	+/-	PP	SH	Gms.	G	A	Pts.	PIM
84-85—Whitby Lawmen	OPJHL	35	5	10	15	318	...			—	—	—	—	—
85-86—Cornwall	OHL	53	6	13	19	253	...			6	0	0	0	26
86-87—Cornwall	OHL	46	17	20	37	158	...			5	1	1	2	16
87-88—Cornwall	OHL	61	11	41	52	179	...			11	2	3	5	33
88-89—Rochester	AHL	74	11	18	29	*446	...			—	—	—	—	—
89-90—Buffalo	NHL	27	2	1	3	99	-2	0	0	—	—	—	—	—
—Rochester	AHL	43	2	13	15	335	...			17	1	3	4	*115
90-91—Rochester	AHL	8	1	1	2	15	...			—	—	—	—	—
—Buffalo	NHL	66	8	8	16	*350	-11	0	0	6	1	1	2	56
91-92—Buffalo	NHL	63	5	3	8	354	-9	0	0	7	0	0	0	2
92-93—Buffalo	NHL	68	3	2	5	211	-3	1	0	—	—	—	—	—
93-94—Buffalo	NHL	82	3	4	7	274	2	0	0	7	1	0	1	43
94-95—Buffalo	NHL	47	0	3	3	173	-4	0	0	5	0	0	0	14
95-96—Buffalo	NHL	71	3	6	9	287	-8	0	0	—	—	—	—	—
96-97—Buffalo	NHL	82	7	3	10	286	3	0	0	12	0	1	1	28
97-98—Buffalo	NHL	63	2	4	6	234	2	1	0	10	0	0	0	24
98-99—Buffalo	NHL	76	0	4	4	*261	-2	0	0	5	1	0	1	0
99-00—Buffalo	NHL	69	1	3	4	158	0	0	0	—	—	—	—	—
00-01—Buffalo	NHL	63	4	6	10	210	2	0	0	3	0	0	0	2
NHL Totals (12 years)		**777**	**38**	**47**	**85**	**2897**	**-30**	**2**	**0**	**55**	**3**	**2**	**5**	**169**

RAYCROFT, ANDREW   G   BRUINS

PERSONAL: Born May 4, 1980, in Belleville, Ont. ... 6-0/150. ... Catches left.
TRANSACTIONS/CAREER NOTES: Selected by Boston Bruins in fifth round (fourth Bruins pick, 135th overall) of NHL entry draft (June 27 1998).
HONORS: Named to OHL All-Star first team (1999-2000). ... Named to Can.HL All-Star first team (1999-2000). ... Won Can.HL Goaltender of the Year Award (1999-2000). ... Won Red Tilson Trophy (1999-2000).

		REGULAR SEASON								PLAYOFFS					
Season Team	League	Gms.	Min	W	L	T	GA	SO	Avg.	Gms.	Min.	W	L	GA	SO	Avg.
96-97—Wellington	Tier II Jr. A	27	1402	...	...	...	92	0	3.94	—	—	—	—	—	—	—
97-98—Sudbury	OHL	33	1802	8	16	5	125	0	4.16	2	89	0	1	8	0	5.39
98-99—Sudbury	OHL	45	2528	17	22	†5	173	1	4.11	3	96	0	2	13	0	8.13
99-00—Kingston	OHL	*61	3340	33	20	5	191	0	3.43	5	300	1	4	21	0	4.20
00-01—Boston	NHL	15	649	4	6	0	32	0	2.96	—	—	—	—	—	—	—
—Providence	AHL	26	1459	8	14	4	82	1	3.37	—	—	—	—	—	—	—
NHL Totals (1 year)		**15**	**649**	**4**	**6**	**0**	**32**	**0**	**2.96**							

RAZIN, GENNADY   D   CANADIENS

PERSONAL: Born February 3, 1978, in Kharkov, U.S.S.R. ... 6-4/200. ... Shoots left.
TRANSACTIONS/CAREER NOTES: Selected by Montreal Canadiens in fifth round (sixth Canadiens pick, 122nd overall) of NHL entry draft (June 21, 1997).

		REGULAR SEASON								PLAYOFFS				
Season Team	League	Gms.	G	A	Pts.	PIM	+/-	PP	SH	Gms.	G	A	Pts.	PIM
95-96—St. Albert	AJHL	52	3	16	19	113	...	...	...	18	1	10	11	8
96-97—Kamloops	WHL	63	7	19	26	56	...	...	...	3	0	0	0	4
97-98—Kamloops	WHL	70	2	11	13	64	...	...	...	7	0	0	0	4
98-99—Fredericton	AHL	48	0	3	3	16	...	...	...	4	0	0	0	2
99-00—Quebec	AHL	66	2	9	11	29	...	...	...	3	0	0	0	0
00-01—Quebec	AHL	69	3	19	22	25	...	...	...	9	0	0	0	4

READY, RYAN   LW   CANUCKS

PERSONAL: Born November 7, 1978, in Peterborough, Ont. ... 6-0/195. ... Shoots left.
TRANSACTIONS/CAREER NOTES: Selected by Calgary Flames in fourth round (eighth Flames pick, 100th overall) of NHL entry draft (June 21 1997). ... Signed as free agent by Vancouver Canucks (June 16, 1999).
HONORS: Named to OHL All-Star first team (1998-99). ... Named to Can.HL All-Star second team (1998-99). ... Won Leo Lalonde Memorial Trophy (1998-99).

		REGULAR SEASON								PLAYOFFS				
Season Team	League	Gms.	G	A	Pts.	PIM	+/-	PP	SH	Gms.	G	A	Pts.	PIM
94-95—Trentway	Jr. A	48	20	33	53	56	...	...	...					
95-96—Belleville	OHL	63	5	13	18	54	...	...	...	10	0	2	2	2
96-97—Belleville	OHL	66	23	24	47	102	...	...	...	6	1	3	4	4
97-98—Belleville	OHL	66	33	39	72	80	...	...	...	10	5	2	7	12
98-99—Belleville	OHL	63	33	59	92	73	...	...	...	21	10	28	38	22
99-00—Syracuse	AHL	70	4	12	16	59	...	...	...	2	0	0	0	0
00-01—Kansas City	IHL	67	10	15	25	75	...	...	...					

REASONER, MARTY   C   OILERS

PERSONAL: Born February 26, 1977, in Rochester, N.Y. ... 6-0/203. ... Shoots left.
TRANSACTIONS/CAREER NOTES: Selected by St. Louis Blues in first round (first Blues pick, 14th overall) of NHL entry draft (June 22, 1996) ... Traded by Blues with C Jochen Hecht and D Jan Horacek to Edmonton Oilers for C Doug Weight and LW Michel Riesen (July 1, 2001).

HONORS: Named to Hockey East All-Rookie team (1995-96). ... Named Hockey East Rookie of the Year (1995-96). ... Named to Hockey East All-Star team (1996-97). ... Named to NCAA All-America (East) first team (1997-98). ... Named to NCAA All-Tournament team (1997-98). ... Named Hockey East Tournament Most Valuable Player (1997-98). ... Named to Hockey East All-Star first team (1997-98).

MISCELLANEOUS: Scored on a penalty shot (vs. Evgeni Nabokov, February 26, 2001).

		REGULAR SEASON								PLAYOFFS				
Season Team	League	Gms.	G	A	Pts.	PIM	+/-	PP	SH	Gms.	G	A	Pts.	PIM
93-94—Deerfield Academy......	Mass. H.S.	22	27	24	51	...	...	...	...	—	—	—	—	—
94-95—Deerfield Academy......	Mass. H.S.	26	25	32	57	14	...	...	...	—	—	—	—	—
95-96—Boston College	Hockey East	34	16	29	45	32	...	...	...	—	—	—	—	—
96-97—Boston College	Hockey East	35	20	24	44	31	...	...	...	—	—	—	—	—
97-98—Boston College	Hockey East	42	†33	40	*73	56	...	...	...	—	—	—	—	—
98-99—St. Louis	NHL	22	3	7	10	8	2	1	0	—	—	—	—	—
—Worcester	AHL	44	17	22	39	24	...	...	...	4	2	1	3	6
99-00—Worcester	AHL	44	23	28	51	39	...	...	...	—	—	—	—	—
—St. Louis	NHL	32	10	14	24	20	9	3	0	7	2	1	3	4
00-01—St. Louis	NHL	41	4	9	13	14	-5	0	0	10	3	1	4	0
—Worcester	AHL	34	17	18	35	25	...	...	...	—	—	—	—	—
NHL Totals (3 years)..........		95	17	30	47	42	6	4	0	17	5	2	7	4

RECCHI, MARK   RW   FLYERS

PERSONAL: Born February 1, 1968, in Kamloops, B.C. ... 5-10/185. ... Shoots left. ... Name pronounced REH-kee.

TRANSACTIONS/CAREER NOTES: Selected by Pittsburgh Penguins in fourth round (fourth Penguins pick, 67th overall) of NHL entry draft (June 11, 1988). ... Injured left shoulder (December 23, 1990). ... Sprained right knee (March 30, 1991). ... Traded by Penguins with D Brian Benning and first-round pick (LW Jason Bowen) in 1992 draft to Philadelphia Flyers for RW Rick Tocchet, D Kjell Samuelsson, G Ken Wregget and third-round pick (C Dave Roche) in 1993 draft (February 19, 1992). ... Traded by Flyers with third-round pick (C Martin Hohenberger) in 1995 draft to Montreal Canadiens for D Eric Desjardins, LW Gilbert Dionne and LW John LeClair (February 9, 1995). ... Suffered from pneumonia (December 12, 1998); missed four games. ... Traded by Canadiens to Flyers for RW Dainius Zubrus and second-round pick (D Matt Carkner) in 1999 draft (March 10, 1999). ... Suffered concussion (March 22, 1999); missed three games. ... Suffered from headaches (April 1, 1999); missed two games. ... Suffered mild concussion (April 13, 1999); missed two games. ... Suffered from headaches (October 11, 2000); missed four games. ... Suffered from fatigue (October 24, 2000); missed nine games.

HONORS: Named to WHL (West) All-Star team (1987-88). ... Named to IHL All-Star second team (1988-89). ... Named to NHL All-Star second team (1991-92). ... Played in NHL All-Star Game (1991, 1993, 1994 and 1997-2000). ... Named All-Star Game Most Valuable Player (1997).

MISCELLANEOUS: Member of Stanley Cup championship team (1991). ... Failed to score on a penalty shot (vs. Don Beaupre, February 6, 1995; vs. Dominik Hasek, March 8, 1995; vs. Dominik Hasek, April 11, 2001 (playoffs)).

STATISTICAL PLATEAUS: Three-goal games: 1991-92 (1), 1996-97 (1), 1997-98 (1). Total: 3.

		REGULAR SEASON								PLAYOFFS				
Season Team	League	Gms.	G	A	Pts.	PIM	+/-	PP	SH	Gms.	G	A	Pts.	PIM
84-85—Langley Eagles............	BCJHL	51	26	39	65	39	...	...	...	—	—	—	—	—
85-86—New Westminster	WHL	72	21	40	61	55	...	...	...	—	—	—	—	—
86-87—Kamloops	WHL	40	26	50	76	63	...	...	...	13	3	16	19	17
87-88—Kamloops	WHL	62	61	*93	154	75	...	...	...	17	10	*21	†31	18
88-89—Pittsburgh	NHL	15	1	1	2	0	-2	0	0	—	—	—	—	—
—Muskegon	IHL	63	50	49	99	86	...	...	...	14	7	*14	†21	28
89-90—Muskegon	IHL	4	7	4	11	2	...	...	...	—	—	—	—	—
—Pittsburgh	NHL	74	30	37	67	44	6	6	2	—	—	—	—	—
90-91—Pittsburgh	NHL	78	40	73	113	48	0	12	0	24	10	24	34	33
91-92—Pittsburgh	NHL	58	33	37	70	78	-16	16	1	—	—	—	—	—
—Philadelphia	NHL	22	10	17	27	18	-5	4	0	—	—	—	—	—
92-93—Philadelphia	NHL	84	53	70	123	95	1	15	4	—	—	—	—	—
93-94—Philadelphia	NHL	84	40	67	107	46	-2	11	0	—	—	—	—	—
94-95—Philadelphia	NHL	10	2	3	5	12	-6	1	0	—	—	—	—	—
—Montreal	NHL	39	14	29	43	16	-3	8	0	—	—	—	—	—
95-96—Montreal	NHL	82	28	50	78	69	20	11	2	6	3	3	6	0
96-97—Montreal	NHL	82	34	46	80	58	-1	7	2	5	4	2	6	2
97-98—Montreal	NHL	82	32	42	74	51	11	9	1	10	4	8	12	6
—Can. Olympic team	Int'l	5	0	2	2	0	...	...	...	—	—	—	—	—
98-99—Montreal	NHL	61	12	35	47	28	-4	3	0	—	—	—	—	—
—Philadelphia	NHL	10	4	2	6	6	-3	0	0	6	0	1	1	2
99-00—Philadelphia	NHL	82	28	*63	91	50	20	7	1	18	6	12	18	6
00-01—Philadelphia	NHL	69	27	50	77	33	15	7	1	6	2	2	4	2
NHL Totals (13 years).........		932	388	622	1010	652	31	117	14	75	29	52	81	51

REDDEN, WADE   D   SENATORS

PERSONAL: Born June 12, 1977, in Lloydminster, Sask. ... 6-2/205. ... Shoots left.

TRANSACTIONS/CAREER NOTES: Selected by New York Islanders in first round (first Islanders pick, second overall) of NHL entry draft (July 8, 1995). ... Traded by Islanders with G Damian Rhodes to Ottawa Senators for G Don Beaupre, D Bryan Berard and C Martin Straka (January 23, 1996). ... Bruised left foot (January 29, 1998); missed one game. ... Suffered back spasms (December 22, 1998); missed two games. ... Injured shoulder (March 4, 1999); missed eight games. ... Suffered illness (February 1, 2000); missed one game. ... Bruised hand (September 25, 2000); missed first four games of regular season.

HONORS: Won Jim Piggott Memorial Trophy (1993-94). ... Won WHL Top Draft Prospect Award (1994-95). ... Named to Can.HL All-Star second team (1994-95 and 1995-96). ... Named to WHL (East) All-Star second team (1994-95). ... Named to WHL (Central/East) All-Star first team (1995-96). ... Named to Memorial Cup All-Star team (1995-96).

Season Team	League	REGULAR SEASON Gms.	G	A	Pts.	PIM	+/-	PP	SH	PLAYOFFS Gms.	G	A	Pts.	PIM
92-93—Lloydminster	SJHL	34	4	11	15	64	...	...	...	—	—	—	—	—
93-94—Brandon	WHL	64	4	35	39	98	...	...	...	14	2	4	6	10
94-95—Brandon	WHL	64	14	46	60	83	...	...	...	18	5	10	15	8
95-96—Brandon	WHL	51	9	45	54	55	...	...	...	19	5	10	15	19
96-97—Ottawa	NHL	82	6	24	30	41	1	2	0	7	1	3	4	2
97-98—Ottawa	NHL	80	8	14	22	27	17	3	0	9	0	2	2	2
98-99—Ottawa	NHL	72	8	21	29	54	7	3	0	4	1	2	3	2
99-00—Ottawa	NHL	81	10	26	36	49	-1	3	0	—	—	—	—	—
00-01—Ottawa	NHL	78	10	37	47	49	22	4	0	4	0	0	0	0
NHL Totals (5 years)		393	42	122	164	220	46	15	0	24	2	7	9	6

R

REEKIE, JOE — D — CAPITALS

PERSONAL: Born February 22, 1965, in Victoria, B.C. ... 6-3/225. ... Shoots left. ... Full Name: Joseph James Reekie.

TRANSACTIONS/CAREER NOTES: Selected by Hartford Whalers in seventh round (eighth Whalers pick, 124th overall) of NHL entry draft (June 8, 1983). ... Returned to draft pool and selected by Buffalo Sabres in sixth round (sixth Sabres pick, 119th overall) of NHL entry draft (June 15, 1985). ... Injured ankle (March 14, 1987). ... Injured shoulder (October 1987). ... Fractured kneecap (November 15, 1987). ... Underwent surgery to left knee (September 1988). ... Traded by Sabres to New York Islanders for sixth-round pick (G Bill Pye) in 1989 draft (June 17, 1989). ... Sprained right knee (November 1989). ... Fractured two bones in left hand and suffered facial cuts in automobile accident and underwent surgery (December 7, 1989). ... Fractured left middle finger (March 21, 1990). ... Injured eye (January 12, 1991); missed six games. ... Fractured knuckle on left hand (January 3, 1992); missed 22 games. ... Selected by Tampa Bay Lightning in NHL expansion draft (June 18, 1992). ... Fractured left leg (January 16, 1993); missed remainder of season. ... Traded by Lightning to Washington Capitals for D Enrico Ciccone, third-round pick (RW Craig Reichert) in 1994 draft and conditional draft pick (March 21, 1994). ... Bruised foot (April 4, 1996); missed four games. ... Fractured heel (February 14, 1997); missed 17 games. ... Injured back (October 9, 1997); missed four games. ... Strained hip flexor (April 4, 1998); missed five games. ... Fractured foot (October 18, 1998); missed nine games. ... Lacerated finger (October 8, 1999); missed two games. ... Bruised foot (October 31, 1999); missed six games. ... Bruised foot (November 19, 1999); missed 10 games. ... Bruised foot (March 3, 2000); missed two games. ... Bruised foot (March 17, 2000); missed three games. ... Suspeded two games by NHL for elbowing incident (November 16, 2000). ... Injured foot (December 20, 2000); missed one game. ... Suffered injury (February 24, 2001); missed one game.

Season Team	League	REGULAR SEASON Gms.	G	A	Pts.	PIM	+/-	PP	SH	PLAYOFFS Gms.	G	A	Pts.	PIM
81-82—Nepean	COJHL	16	2	5	7	4	...	...	...	—	—	—	—	—
82-83—North Bay	OHL	59	2	9	11	49	...	...	...	8	0	1	1	11
83-84—North Bay	OHL	9	1	0	1	18	...	...	...	—	—	—	—	—
—Cornwall	OHL	53	6	27	33	166	...	...	...	3	0	0	0	4
84-85—Cornwall	OHL	65	19	63	82	134	...	...	...	9	4	13	17	18
85-86—Rochester	AHL	77	3	25	28	178	...	...	...	—	—	—	—	—
—Buffalo	NHL	3	0	0	0	14	-2	0	0	—	—	—	—	—
86-87—Buffalo	NHL	56	1	8	9	82	6	0	0	—	—	—	—	—
—Rochester	AHL	22	0	6	6	52	...	...	...	—	—	—	—	—
87-88—Buffalo	NHL	30	1	4	5	68	-3	0	0	2	0	0	0	4
88-89—Rochester	AHL	21	1	2	3	56	...	...	...	—	—	—	—	—
—Buffalo	NHL	15	1	3	4	26	6	1	0	—	—	—	—	—
89-90—New York Islanders	NHL	31	1	8	9	43	13	0	0	—	—	—	—	—
—Springfield	AHL	15	1	4	5	24	...	...	...	—	—	—	—	—
90-91—Capital District	AHL	2	1	0	1	0	...	...	...	—	—	—	—	—
—New York Islanders	NHL	66	3	16	19	96	17	0	0	—	—	—	—	—
91-92—New York Islanders	NHL	54	4	12	16	85	15	0	0	—	—	—	—	—
—Capital District	AHL	3	2	2	4	2	...	...	...	—	—	—	—	—
92-93—Tampa Bay	NHL	42	2	11	13	69	2	0	0	—	—	—	—	—
93-94—Tampa Bay	NHL	73	1	11	12	127	8	0	0	—	—	—	—	—
—Washington	NHL	12	0	5	5	29	7	0	0	11	2	1	3	29
94-95—Washington	NHL	48	1	6	7	97	10	0	0	7	0	0	0	2
95-96—Washington	NHL	78	3	7	10	149	7	0	0	—	—	—	—	—
96-97—Washington	NHL	65	1	8	9	107	8	0	0	—	—	—	—	—
97-98—Washington	NHL	68	2	8	10	70	15	0	0	21	1	2	3	20
98-99—Washington	NHL	73	0	10	10	68	11	0	0	—	—	—	—	—
99-00—Washington	NHL	59	0	7	7	50	21	0	0	5	0	1	1	2
00-01—Washington	NHL	74	2	9	11	77	14	0	0	4	0	0	0	4
NHL Totals (16 years)		847	23	133	156	1257	155	1	0	50	3	4	7	61

REGEHR, ROBYN — D — FLAMES

PERSONAL: Born April 19, 1980, in Recife, Brazil. ... 6-2/225. ... Shoots left. ... Name pronounced ruh-ZHEER.

TRANSACTIONS/CAREER NOTES: Selected by Colorado Avalanche in first round (third Avalanche pick, 19th overall) of NHL entry draft (June 27, 1998). ... Traded by Avalanche to Calgary Flames (March 27, 1999); completing deal in which Flames traded RW Theo Fleury and LW Chris Dingman to Avalanche for LW Rene Corbet, D Wade Belak and future considerations (February 28, 1999). ... Fractured legs prior to start of 1999-2000 season; missed first five games of season. ... Suffered concussion (January 11, 2000); missed 11 games. ... Injured knee (November 4, 2000); missed six games. ... Injured knee (December 22, 2000); missed two games.

HONORS: Named to WHL (West) All-Star first team (1998-99).

Season Team	League	REGULAR SEASON Gms.	G	A	Pts.	PIM	+/-	PP	SH	PLAYOFFS Gms.	G	A	Pts.	PIM
96-97—Kamloops	WHL	64	4	19	23	96	...	...	...	5	0	1	1	18
97-98—Kamloops	WHL	65	4	10	14	120	...	...	...	5	0	3	3	8
98-99—Kamloops	WHL	54	12	20	32	130	...	...	...	12	1	4	5	21
99-00—Saint John	AHL	5	0	0	0	0	...	...	...	—	—	—	—	—
—Calgary	NHL	57	5	7	12	46	-2	2	0	—	—	—	—	—
00-01—Calgary	NHL	71	1	3	4	70	-7	0	0	—	—	—	—	—
NHL Totals (2 years)		128	6	10	16	116	-9	2	0	—	—	—	—	—

REHNBERG, HENRIK — D — DEVILS

PERSONAL: Born July 20, 1977, in Grava, Sweden. ... 6-2/195. ... Shoots left.
TRANSACTIONS/CAREER NOTES: Selected by New Jersey Devils in fourth round (sixth Devils pick, 96th overall) of NHL entry draft (July 8, 1995).

Season Team	League	REGULAR SEASON								PLAYOFFS				
		Gms.	G	A	Pts.	PIM	+/-	PP	SH	Gms.	G	A	Pts.	PIM
94-95—Farjestad Jrs.	Sweden	24	1	2	3	...	...	...	...	—	—	—	—	—
95-96—Farjestad Jrs.	Sweden	21	1	4	5	38	...	...	...	—	—	—	—	—
—Farjestad Karlstad	Sweden	4	0	0	0	0	...	...	...	—	—	—	—	—
96-97—Farjestad Karlstad	Sweden	42	2	3	5	38	...	...	...	14	1	1	2	16
97-98—Farjestad Karlstad	Sweden	32	0	1	1	24	...	...	...	10	0	0	0	12
98-99—Albany	AHL	55	1	4	5	49	...	...	...	2	0	0	0	0
99-00—Farjestad Karlstad	Sweden	46	1	3	4	66	...	...	...	7	0	1	1	18
00-01—Albany	AHL	80	1	8	9	78	...	...	...	—	—	—	—	—

REICHEL, ROBERT — C — MAPLE LEAFS

PERSONAL: Born June 25, 1971, in Litvinov, Czechoslovakia. ... 5-10/186. ... Shoots right. ... Brother of Martin Reichel, right winger, Edmonton Oilers organization. ... Name pronounced RIGH-kuhl.
TRANSACTIONS/CAREER NOTES: Selected by Calgary Flames in fourth round (fifth Flames pick, 70th overall) of NHL entry draft (June 17, 1989). ... Strained right knee (March 16, 1993); missed three games. ... Played in Europe during 1994-95 NHL lockout. ... Traded by Flames to New York Islanders for LW Marty McInnis, G Tyrone Garner and sixth-round pick (D Ilja Demidov) in 1997 draft (March 18, 1997). ... Traded by Islanders with third- (C/LW Jason Jaspers) and fourth-round (C Preston Mizzi) picks in 1999 draft to Phoenix Coyotes for RW Brad Isbister and third-round pick (C Brian Collins) in 1999 draft (March 20, 1999). ... Missed entire 1999-2000 and 2000-01 seasons due to contract dispute; played in Europe. ... Traded by Coyotes with C Travis Green and RW Craig Mills to Toronto Maple Leafs for D Danny Markov (June 12, 2001).
HONORS: Named to Czechoslovakian League All-Star team (1989-90).
MISCELLANEOUS: Member of gold-medal-winning Czech Republic Olympic team (1998). ... Scored on a penalty shot (vs. Bill Ranford, February 7, 1994; vs. Tom Barrasso, October 24, 1996; vs. Zac Bierk, January 14, 1998). ... Failed to score on a penalty shot (vs. Rick Tabaracci, March 25, 1999).
STATISTICAL NOTES: Led NHL in games played with 83 (1998-99).
STATISTICAL PLATEAUS: Three-goal games: 1992-93 (2), 1993-94 (2), 1997-98 (1). Total: 5.

Season Team	League	REGULAR SEASON								PLAYOFFS				
		Gms.	G	A	Pts.	PIM	+/-	PP	SH	Gms.	G	A	Pts.	PIM
87-88—Litvinov	Czech.	36	17	10	27	8	...	...	...	—	—	—	—	—
88-89—Litvinov	Czech.	44	23	25	48	32	...	...	...	—	—	—	—	—
89-90—Litvinov	Czech.	52	49	34	83	...	...	...	...	—	—	—	—	—
90-91—Calgary	NHL	66	19	22	41	22	17	3	0	6	1	1	2	0
91-92—Calgary	NHL	77	20	34	54	32	1	8	0	—	—	—	—	—
92-93—Calgary	NHL	80	40	48	88	54	25	12	0	6	2	4	6	2
93-94—Calgary	NHL	84	40	53	93	58	20	14	0	7	0	5	5	0
94-95—Frankfurt	Germany	21	19	24	43	41	...	...	...	—	—	—	—	—
—Calgary	NHL	48	18	17	35	28	-2	5	0	7	2	4	6	4
95-96—Frankfurt	Germany	46	47	54	101	84	...	...	...	3	1	3	4	0
96-97—Calgary	NHL	70	16	27	43	22	-2	6	0	—	—	—	—	—
—New York Islanders	NHL	12	5	14	19	4	7	0	1	—	—	—	—	—
97-98—New York Islanders	NHL	82	25	40	65	32	-11	8	0	—	—	—	—	—
—Czech Rep. Oly. team	Int'l	6	3	0	3	0	...	...	...	—	—	—	—	—
98-99—New York Islanders	NHL	§70	19	37	56	50	-15	5	1	—	—	—	—	—
—Phoenix	NHL	§13	7	6	13	4	2	3	0	7	1	3	4	2
99-00—Litvinov	Czech Rep.	45	25	32	57	24	...	...	...	7	3	4	7	2
00-01—Litvinov	Czech Rep.	49	23	33	56	72	...	...	...	5	1	2	3	4
NHL Totals (8 years)		602	209	298	507	306	42	64	2	33	6	17	23	8

REICHERT, CRAIG — RW — OILERS

PERSONAL: Born May 11, 1974, in Winnipeg. ... 6-1/200. ... Shoots right. ... Name pronounced RIGH-kuhrt.
TRANSACTIONS/CAREER NOTES: Selected by Mighty Ducks of Anaheim in third round (third Mighty Ducks pick, 67th overall) of NHL entry draft (June 29, 1994). ... Signed as free agent by Florida Panthers (July 8, 1999). ... Signed as free agent by Edmonton Oilers (May 29, 2001).

Season Team	League	REGULAR SEASON								PLAYOFFS				
		Gms.	G	A	Pts.	PIM	+/-	PP	SH	Gms.	G	A	Pts.	PIM
91-92—Spokane	WHL	68	14	30	44	86	...	...	...	4	1	0	1	4
92-93—Red Deer	WHL	66	32	33	65	62	...	...	...	4	3	1	4	2
93-94—Red Deer	WHL	72	52	67	119	153	...	...	...	4	2	2	4	8
94-95—San Diego	IHL	49	4	12	16	28	...	...	...	—	—	—	—	—
95-96—Baltimore	AHL	68	10	17	27	50	...	...	...	1	0	0	0	0
96-97—Baltimore	AHL	77	22	53	75	54	...	...	...	3	0	2	2	0
—Anaheim	NHL	3	0	0	0	0	-2	0	0	—	—	—	—	—
97-98—Cincinnati	AHL	78	28	59	87	28	...	...	...	—	—	—	—	—
98-99—Cincinnati	AHL	72	28	41	69	56	...	...	...	3	2	0	2	0
99-00—Louisville	AHL	72	16	42	58	41	...	...	...	4	1	1	2	2
00-01—Dusseldorf	Germany	60	12	23	35	76	...	...	...	—	—	—	—	—
NHL Totals (1 year)		3	0	0	0	0	-2	0	0					

REID, DAVE — LW

PERSONAL: Born May 15, 1964, in Toronto. ... 6-1/217. ... Shoots left. ... Full Name: David Reid.

TRANSACTIONS/CAREER NOTES: Selected by Boston Bruins as underage junior in third round (fourth Bruins pick, 60th overall) of NHL entry draft (June 9, 1982). ... Underwent knee surgery (December 1986). ... Separated shoulder (November 1987); missed 10 games. ... Signed as free agent by Toronto Maple Leafs (August 1988). ... Suffered from pneumonia (March 1992); missed 10 games. ... Injured knee (March 25, 1993); missed remainder of season. ... Signed as free agent by Bruins (November 22, 1991). ... Injured hip (April 1995); missed two games. ... Fractured finger (February 1, 1996); missed 16 games. ... Signed as free agent by Dallas Stars (July 3, 1996). ... Strained lower back (January 29, 1998); missed three games. ... Strained lower back (February 7, 1998); missed 13 games. ... Suffered back spasms (February 21, 1999); missed one game. ... Strained lower back (March 25, 1999); missed three games. ... Signed as free agent by Colorado Avalanche (October 6, 1999). ... Bruised ankle (December 8, 1999); missed nine games. ... Injured knee (January 25, 2000); missed two games.

MISCELLANEOUS: Member of Stanley Cup championship team (1999 and 2001).

STATISTICAL PLATEAUS: Three-goal games: 1995-96 (1), 1996-97 (1). Total: 2.

Season Team	League	REGULAR SEASON								PLAYOFFS				
		Gms.	G	A	Pts.	PIM	+/-	PP	SH	Gms.	G	A	Pts.	PIM
80-81—Mississauga	MTHL	39	21	28	49	...	...	...	...	—	—	—	—	—
81-82—Peterborough	OHL	68	10	32	42	41	...	...	...	9	2	3	5	11
82-83—Peterborough	OHL	70	23	34	57	33	...	...	...	4	3	1	4	0
83-84—Peterborough	OHL	60	33	64	97	12	...	...	...	—	—	—	—	—
—Boston	NHL	8	1	0	1	2	1	0	0	—	—	—	—	—
84-85—Hershey	AHL	43	10	14	24	6	...	...	...	—	—	—	—	—
—Boston	NHL	35	14	13	27	27	-1	2	0	5	1	0	1	0
85-86—Moncton	AHL	26	14	18	32	4	...	...	...	—	—	—	—	—
—Boston	NHL	37	10	10	20	10	2	4	0	—	—	—	—	—
86-87—Boston	NHL	12	3	3	6	0	-1	0	0	2	0	0	0	0
—Moncton	AHL	40	12	22	34	23	...	...	...	5	0	1	1	0
87-88—Maine	AHL	63	21	37	58	40	...	...	...	10	6	7	13	6
—Boston	NHL	3	0	0	0	0	0	0	0	—	—	—	—	—
88-89—Toronto	NHL	77	9	21	30	22	12	1	1	—	—	—	—	—
89-90—Toronto	NHL	70	9	19	28	9	-8	0	4	3	0	0	0	0
90-91—Toronto	NHL	69	15	13	28	18	-10	1	*8	—	—	—	—	—
91-92—Maine	AHL	12	1	5	6	4	...	...	...	—	—	—	—	—
—Boston	NHL	43	7	7	14	27	5	2	1	15	2	5	7	4
92-93—Boston	NHL	65	20	16	36	10	12	1	5	—	—	—	—	—
93-94—Boston	NHL	83	6	17	23	25	10	0	2	13	2	1	3	2
94-95—Boston	NHL	38	5	5	10	10	8	0	0	5	0	0	0	0
—Providence	AHL	7	3	0	3	0	...	...	...	—	—	—	—	—
95-96—Boston	NHL	63	23	21	44	4	14	1	6	5	0	2	2	2
96-97—Dallas	NHL	82	19	20	39	10	12	1	1	7	1	0	1	4
97-98—Dallas	NHL	65	6	12	18	14	-15	3	0	5	0	3	3	2
98-99—Dallas	NHL	73	6	11	17	16	0	1	0	23	2	8	10	14
99-00—Colorado	NHL	65	11	7	18	28	12	0	0	17	1	3	4	0
00-01—Colorado	NHL	73	1	9	10	21	1	0	0	18	0	4	4	6
NHL Totals (18 years)		961	165	204	369	253	54	17	28	118	9	26	35	34

REINPRECHT, STEVE — C — AVALANCHE

PERSONAL: Born May 7, 1976, in Edmonton. ... 6-1/195. ... Shoots left.

TRANSACTIONS/CAREER NOTES: Signed as non-drafted free agent by Los Angeles Kings (March 31, 2000). ... Traded by Kings with D Rob Blake to Colorado Avalanche for RW Adam Deadmarsh, D Aaron Miller, first-round pick (C David Steckel) in 2001 draft, a player to be named later and future considerations (February 21, 2001); Kings acquired C Jared Aulin to complete deal (March 22, 2001).

HONORS: Named to WCHA All-Star first team (1999-2000). ... Named to NCAA All-America (West) first team (1999-2000).

MISCELLANEOUS: Member of Stanley Cup championship team (2001).

Season Team	League	REGULAR SEASON								PLAYOFFS				
		Gms.	G	A	Pts.	PIM	+/-	PP	SH	Gms.	G	A	Pts.	PIM
96-97—Univ. of Wisconsin	WCHA	38	11	9	20	12	...	...	...	—	—	—	—	—
97-98—Univ. of Wisconsin	WCHA	41	19	24	43	18	...	...	...	—	—	—	—	—
98-99—Univ. of Wisconsin	WCHA	38	16	17	33	14	...	...	...	—	—	—	—	—
99-00—Univ. of Wisconsin	WCHA	37	26	40	*66	14	...	...	...	—	—	—	—	—
—Los Angeles	NHL	1	0	0	0	2	0	0	0	—	—	—	—	—
00-01—Los Angeles	NHL	59	12	17	29	12	11	3	2	—	—	—	—	—
—Colorado	NHL	21	3	4	7	2	-1	0	0	22	2	3	5	2
NHL Totals (2 years)		81	15	21	36	16	10	3	2	22	2	3	5	2

REIRDEN, TODD — D — THRASHERS

PERSONAL: Born June 25, 1971, in Deerfield, Ill. ... 6-5/220. ... Shoots left. ... Full Name: Todd Raymond Reirden.

TRANSACTIONS/CAREER NOTES: Selected by New Jersey Devils in 12th round (14th Devils pick, 242nd overall) of NHL entry draft (June 16, 1990). ... Signed as free agent by Edmonton Oilers (May 31, 1998). ... Claimed on waivers by St. Louis Blues (September 30, 1999). ... Strained shoulder (December 4, 1999); missed three games. ... Fractured foot (January 28, 2000); missed 18 games. ... Underwent foot surgery (July 2000); missed first 25 games of season. ... Strained oblique muscle (January 23, 2001); missed one game. ... Signed as free agent by Atlanta Thrashers (July 16, 2001).

Season Team	League	REGULAR SEASON								PLAYOFFS				
		Gms.	G	A	Pts.	PIM	+/-	PP	SH	Gms.	G	A	Pts.	PIM
90-91—Bowling Green	CCHA	28	1	5	6	22	...	...	...	—	—	—	—	—
91-92—Bowling Green	CCHA	33	8	7	15	34	...	...	...	—	—	—	—	—
92-93—Bowling Green	CCHA	41	8	17	25	48	...	...	...	—	—	—	—	—
93-94—Bowling Green	CCHA	38	7	23	30	56	...	...	...	—	—	—	—	—

Season Team	League	REGULAR SEASON								PLAYOFFS				
		Gms.	G	A	Pts.	PIM	+/-	PP	SH	Gms.	G	A	Pts.	PIM
94-95—Albany	AHL	2	0	1	1	2	...	...	...	—	—	—	—	—
—Raleigh	ECHL	26	2	13	15	33	...	...	...	—	—	—	—	—
—Tallahassee	ECHL	43	5	25	30	61	...	...	...	13	2	5	7	10
95-96—Chicago	IHL	31	0	2	2	39	...	...	...	9	0	2	2	16
—Tallahassee	ECHL	7	1	3	4	10	...	...	...	—	—	—	—	—
—Jacksonville	ECHL	15	1	10	11	41	...	...	...	1	0	2	2	4
96-97—Chicago	IHL	57	3	10	13	108	...	...	...	—	—	—	—	—
—San Antonio	IHL	23	2	5	7	51	...	...	...	9	0	1	1	17
97-98—San Antonio	IHL	70	5	14	19	132	...	...	...	4	0	2	2	4
—Fort Wayne	IHL	11	2	2	4	16	...	...	...	—	—	—	—	—
98-99—Hamilton	AHL	58	9	25	34	84	...	...	...	11	0	5	5	6
—Edmonton	NHL	17	2	3	5	20	-1	0	0	—	—	—	—	—
99-00—St. Louis	NHL	56	4	21	25	32	18	0	0	4	0	1	1	0
00-01—Worcester	AHL	7	2	6	8	20	...	...	...	—	—	—	—	—
—St. Louis	NHL	38	2	4	6	43	-2	1	0	1	0	0	0	0
NHL Totals (3 years)		111	8	28	36	95	15	1	0	5	0	1	1	0

RENBERG, MIKAEL   RW   MAPLE LEAFS

PERSONAL: Born May 5, 1972, in Pitea, Sweden. ... 6-2/218. ... Shoots left.

TRANSACTIONS/CAREER NOTES: Selected by Philadelphia Flyers in second round (third Flyers pick, 40th overall) of NHL entry draft (June 16, 1990). ... Played in Europe during 1994-95 NHL lockout. ... Suffered sore shoulder (March 25, 1995); missed one game. ... Strained abdominal muscles (December 30, 1995); missed one game. ... Strained lower abdominal muscles (January 22, 1996); missed 17 games. ... Reinjured lower abdominal muscles (March 12, 1996); missed one game. ... Reinjured lower abdominal muscles (March 16, 1996); missed one game. ... Reinjured lower abdominal muscles (March 19, 1996); missed 11 games. ... Underwent abdominal surgery (May 1996). ... Strained groin (March 8, 1997); missed one game. ... Cut face (April 6, 1997); missed remainder of regular season. ... Traded by Flyers with D Karl Dykhuis to Tampa Bay Lightning for C Chris Gratton (August 20, 1997). ... Suffered from the flu (October 15, 1997); missed one game. ... Fractured wrist (December 13, 1997); missed 13 games. ... Fractured left thumb (November 10, 1998); missed seven games. ... Traded by Lightning with C Daymond Langkow to Flyers for C Chris Gratton and C/RW Mike Sillinger (December 12, 1998). ... Separated shoulder (December 23, 1998); missed nine games. ... Suffered from the flu (February 9, 2000); missed two games. ... Traded by Flyers to Phoenix Coyotes for RW Rick Tocchet (March 8, 2000). ... Strained hip flexor (March 15, 2000); missed six games. ... Suffered from the flu (February 9, 2000); missed two games. ... Signed by Lulea, Swedish Elite League (June 13, 2000). ... Traded by Coyotes to Toronto Maple Leafs for LW Sergei Berezin (June 22, 2001).

HONORS: Named to NHL All-Rookie team (1993-94).

MISCELLANEOUS: Captain of Tampa Bay Lightning (1997-98).

STATISTICAL PLATEAUS: Three-goal games: 1993-94 (1), 1997-98 (1). Total: 2.

Season Team	League	REGULAR SEASON								PLAYOFFS				
		Gms.	G	A	Pts.	PIM	+/-	PP	SH	Gms.	G	A	Pts.	PIM
88-89—Pitea	Sweden	12	6	3	9	...	...	...	...	—	—	—	—	—
89-90—Pitea	Sweden	29	15	19	34	...	...	...	...	—	—	—	—	—
90-91—Lulea	Sweden	29	11	6	17	12	...	...	...	5	1	1	2	4
91-92—Lulea	Sweden	38	8	15	23	20	...	...	...	2	0	0	0	0
92-93—Lulea	Sweden	39	19	13	32	61	...	...	...	11	4	4	8	...
93-94—Philadelphia	NHL	83	38	44	82	36	8	9	0	—	—	—	—	—
94-95—Lulea	Sweden	10	9	4	13	16	...	...	...	—	—	—	—	—
—Philadelphia	NHL	47	26	31	57	20	20	8	0	15	6	7	13	6
95-96—Philadelphia	NHL	51	23	20	43	45	8	9	0	11	3	6	9	14
96-97—Philadelphia	NHL	77	22	37	59	65	36	1	0	18	5	6	11	4
97-98—Tampa Bay	NHL	68	16	22	38	34	-37	6	3	—	—	—	—	—
—Swedish Oly. team	Int'l	4	1	2	3	4	...	...	...	—	—	—	—	—
98-99—Tampa Bay	NHL	20	4	8	12	4	-2	2	0	—	—	—	—	—
—Philadelphia	NHL	46	11	15	26	14	7	4	0	6	0	1	1	0
99-00—Philadelphia	NHL	62	8	21	29	30	-1	3	0	—	—	—	—	—
—Phoenix	NHL	10	2	4	6	2	0	0	0	5	1	2	3	4
00-01—Lulea	Sweden	48	22	32	54	36	...	...	...	11	6	5	11	35
NHL Totals (7 years)		464	150	202	352	250	39	42	3	55	15	22	37	28

RHEAUME, PASCAL   LW

PERSONAL: Born June 21, 1973, in Quebec City. ... 6-1/209. ... Shoots left. ... Name pronounced ray-OHM.

TRANSACTIONS/CAREER NOTES: Signed as non-drafted free agent by New Jersey Devils (October 1, 1992). ... Claimed by St. Louis Blues from Devils in NHL waiver draft (September 28, 1997). ... Suffered concussion (February 28, 1999); missed 10 games. ... Underwent shoulder surgery prior to 1999-2000 season; missed first 62 games of season.

Season Team	League	REGULAR SEASON								PLAYOFFS				
		Gms.	G	A	Pts.	PIM	+/-	PP	SH	Gms.	G	A	Pts.	PIM
91-92—Trois-Rivieres	QMJHL	65	17	20	37	84	...	...	...	14	5	4	9	23
92-93—Sherbrooke	QMJHL	65	28	34	62	88	...	...	...	14	6	5	11	31
93-94—Albany	AHL	55	17	18	35	43	...	...	...	5	0	1	1	0
94-95—Albany	AHL	78	19	25	44	46	...	...	...	14	3	6	9	19
95-96—Albany	AHL	68	26	42	68	50	...	...	...	4	1	2	3	2
96-97—Albany	AHL	51	22	23	45	40	...	...	...	16	2	8	10	16
—New Jersey	NHL	2	1	0	1	0	-1	0	0	—	—	—	—	—
97-98—St. Louis	NHL	48	6	9	15	35	4	1	0	10	1	3	4	8
98-99—St. Louis	NHL	60	9	18	27	24	10	2	0	5	1	0	1	4
99-00—St. Louis	NHL	7	1	1	2	6	-2	0	0	—	—	—	—	—
—Worcester	AHL	7	1	1	2	4	...	...	...	—	—	—	—	—
00-01—Worcester	AHL	56	23	36	59	63	...	...	...	11	2	4	6	2
—St. Louis	NHL	8	2	0	2	5	-1	2	0	3	0	1	1	0
NHL Totals (5 years)		125	19	28	47	70	12	5	0	18	2	4	6	12

PERSONAL: Born May 28, 1969, in St. Paul, Minn. ... 6-0/180. ... Catches left. ... Full Name: Damian G. Rhodes.
TRANSACTIONS/CAREER NOTES: Selected by Toronto Maple Leafs in sixth round (sixth Maple Leafs pick, 112th overall) of NHL entry draft (June 13, 1987). ... Traded by Maple Leafs with LW Ken Belanger to New York Islanders for LW Kirk Muller (January 23, 1996). ... Traded by Islanders with D Wade Redden to Ottawa Senators for D Bryan Berard and C Martin Straka (January 23, 1996). ... Bruised calf (February 23, 1997); missed 10 games. ... Suffered from the flu (December 22, 1998); missed one game. ... Traded by Senators to Atlanta Thrashers for future considerations (June 18, 1999). ... Sprained ankle (November 17, 1999); missed 49 games. ... Sprained knee (October 30, 2000); missed one game. ... Sprained right knee (November 4, 2000); missed 18 games. ... Strained groin (February 25, 2001); missed 16 games.
MISCELLANEOUS: Holds Atlanta Thrashers all-time record for most games (56). ... Holds Ottawa Senators all-time record for most games played by goaltender (181). ... Shares Atlanta Thrashers all-time record for most wins (12). ... Stopped a penalty shot attempt (vs. Scott Pearson, November 20, 1993; vs. Geoff Courtnall, March 21, 1995; vs. Martin Straka, April 3, 1996; vs. Todd Marchant, November 13, 1996; vs. Brad Isbister, March 16, 2000). ... Allowed a penalty shot goal (vs. Pavel Bure, February 28, 1998; vs. Dixon Ward, April 11, 1998; vs. Miroslav Satan, October 9, 1999; vs. Patrick Elias, March 10, 2000; vs. Martin Straka, January 30, 2001).

R

						REGULAR SEASON						PLAYOFFS					
Season Team	League	Gms.	Min	W	L	T	GA	SO	Avg.	Gms.	Min.	W	L	GA	SO	Avg.
85-86—Richfield H.S.	Minn. H.S.	16	720	...	...	...	56	0	4.67	—	—	—	—	—	—	—
86-87—Richfield H.S.	Minn. H.S.	19	673	...	...	...	51	1	4.55	—	—	—	—	—	—	—
87-88—Michigan Tech	WCHA	29	1623	16	10	1	114	0	4.21	—	—	—	—	—	—	—
88-89—Michigan Tech	WCHA	37	2216	15	22	0	163	0	4.41	—	—	—	—	—	—	—
89-90—Michigan Tech	WCHA	25	1358	6	17	0	119	0	5.26	—	—	—	—	—	—	—
90-91—Toronto	NHL	1	60	1	0	0	1	0	1.00	—	—	—	—	—	—	—
—Newmarket	AHL	38	2154	8	24	3	144	1	4.01	—	—	—	—	—	—	—
91-92—St. John's	AHL	43	2454	20	16	5	148	1	3.62	6	331	4	1	16	0	2.90
92-93—St. John's	AHL	52	*3074	27	16	8	184	1	3.59	9	538	4	5	37	0	4.13
93-94—Toronto	NHL	22	1213	9	7	3	53	0	2.62	1	0	0	0	0	0	...
94-95—Toronto	NHL	13	760	6	6	1	34	0	2.68	—	—	—	—	—	—	—
95-96—Toronto	NHL	11	624	4	5	1	29	0	2.79	—	—	—	—	—	—	—
—Ottawa	NHL	36	2123	10	22	4	98	2	2.77	—	—	—	—	—	—	—
96-97—Ottawa	NHL	50	2934	14	20	*14	133	1	2.72	—	—	—	—	—	—	—
97-98—Ottawa	NHL	50	2743	19	19	7	107	5	2.34	10	590	5	5	21	0	2.14
98-99—Ottawa	NHL	45	2480	22	13	7	101	3	2.44	2	150	0	2	6	0	2.40
99-00—Atlanta	NHL	28	1561	5	19	3	101	1	3.88	—	—	—	—	—	—	—
00-01—Atlanta	NHL	38	2072	7	19	7	116	0	3.36	—	—	—	—	—	—	—
NHL Totals (9 years)		294	16570	97	130	47	773	12	2.80	13	740	5	7	27	0	2.19

PERSONAL: Born March 15, 1980, in Moscow, U.S.S.R. ... 5-11/200. ... Shoots right. ... Full Name: Alexander Riazantsev.
TRANSACTIONS/CAREER NOTES: Selected by Colorado Avalanche in sixth round (10th Avalanche pick, 167th overall) of NHL entry draft (June 27, 1998).

					REGULAR SEASON					PLAYOFFS			
Season Team	League	Gms.	G	A	Pts.	PIM	+/-	PP	SH	Gms.	G	A	Pts.	PIM
96-97—Spartak Moscow	Russian	20	1	2	3	4	...	...	...	—	—	—	—	—
—SAK Moscow	Rus. Div. III	18	0	0	0	8	...	...	...	—	—	—	—	—
97-98—Spartak-2 Moscow	Rus. Div. III	31	3	8	11	26	...	...	...	—	—	—	—	—
—Victoriaville	QMJHL	22	6	9	15	14	...	...	...	4	0	0	0	0
98-99—Victoriaville	QMJHL	64	17	40	57	57	...	...	...	6	0	3	3	10
—Hershey	AHL	2	0	0	0	0	...	...	...	—	—	—	—	—
99-00—Victoriaville	QMJHL	48	17	45	62	45	...	...	...	6	2	5	7	20
—Hershey	AHL	2	0	1	1	2	...	...	...	6	1	1	2	0
00-01—Hershey	AHL	66	5	18	23	26	...	...	...	11	0	0	0	2

PERSONAL: Born February 10, 1980, in Montreal. ... 5-11/150. ... Shoots left.
TRANSACTIONS/CAREER NOTES: Selected by Montreal Canadiens in second round (second Canadiens pick, 45th overall) of NHL entry draft (June 27, 1998).
HONORS: Won Michel Bergeron Trophy (1997-98). ... Named to QMJHL All-Star second team (1997-98). ... Named to QMJHL All-Rookie Team (1997-98). ... Named to QMJHL All-Star first team (1998-99). ... Won Jean Beliveau Trophy (1998-99). ... Named to Can.HL All-Star first team (1998-99).

					REGULAR SEASON					PLAYOFFS			
Season Team	League	Gms.	G	A	Pts.	PIM	+/-	PP	SH	Gms.	G	A	Pts.	PIM
97-98—Rouyn-Noranda	QMJHL	67	40	85	125	55	...	...	...	—	—	—	—	—
98-99—Rouyn-Noranda	QMJHL	69	67	*100	*167	137	...	...	...	11	5	11	16	12
—Fredericton	AHL	—	—	—	—	—	...	...	...	5	0	1	1	2
99-00—Montreal	NHL	19	1	1	2	2	-6	1	0	—	—	—	—	—
—Quebec	AHL	3	0	0	0	2	...	...	...	—	—	—	—	—
—Rouyn-Noranda	QMJHL	2	1	3	4	0	...	...	...	—	—	—	—	—
—Quebec	QMJHL	21	17	28	45	30	...	...	...	11	3	20	23	38
00-01—Quebec	AHL	74	26	40	66	44	...	...	...	9	1	5	6	23
—Montreal	NHL	2	0	0	0	2	0	0	0	—	—	—	—	—
NHL Totals (2 years)		21	1	1	2	4	-6	1	0					

RICCI, MIKE   C   SHARKS

PERSONAL: Born October 27, 1971, in Scarborough, Ont. ... 6-0/190. ... Shoots left. ... Name pronounced REE-chee.
TRANSACTIONS/CAREER NOTES: Selected by Philadelphia Flyers in first round (first Flyers pick, fourth overall) of NHL entry draft (June 16, 1990). ... Fractured right index finger and thumb (October 4, 1990); missed nine games. ... Traded by Flyers with G Ron Hextall, C Peter Forsberg, D Steve Duchesne, D Kerry Huffman, first-round pick (G Jocelyn Thibault) in 1993 draft, cash and future considerations to Quebec Nordiques for C Eric Lindros (June 20, 1992); Nordiques acquired RW Chris Simon and first-round pick (traded to Toronto) in 1994 draft to complete deal (July 21, 1992). ... Sprained left wrist (November 3, 1992); missed four games. ... Suffered from the flu (January 5, 1993); missed two games. ... Nordiques franchise moved to Colorado and renamed Avalanche for 1995-96 season (July 21, 1995). ... Underwent sinus surgery (October 15, 1995); missed one game. ... Injured ankle (November 5, 1995); missed one game. ... Sprained left ankle (December 11, 1995); missed two games. ... Suffered back spasms (January 4, 1996); missed 16 games. ... Strained shoulder (October 30, 1996); missed 11 games. ... Fractured thumb (January 6, 1997); missed four games. ... Underwent shoulder surgery prior to 1997-98 season; missed first 16 games of season. ... Traded by Avalanche with second-round pick (RW Jonathan Cheechoo) in 1998 draft to San Jose Sharks for RW Shean Donovan and first-round pick (C Alex Tanguay) in 1998 draft (November 20, 1997).
HONORS: Named to OHL All-Star second team (1988-89). ... Won Can.HL Player of the Year Award (1989-90). ... Won Red Tilson Trophy (1989-90). ... Won William Hanley Trophy (1989-90). ... Named to OHL All-Star first team (1989-90).
MISCELLANEOUS: Member of Stanley Cup championship team (1996). ... Failed to score on a penalty shot (vs. Chris Terreri, November 17, 1990; vs. Stephane Fiset, October 24, 1999).
STATISTICAL PLATEAUS: Three-goal games: 2000-01 (1). ... Five-goal games: 1993-94 (1). ... Total hat tricks: 2.

		REGULAR SEASON								PLAYOFFS				
Season Team	League	Gms.	G	A	Pts.	PIM	+/-	PP	SH	Gms.	G	A	Pts.	PIM
87-88—Peterborough	OHL	41	24	37	61	20	...	...	...	8	5	5	10	4
88-89—Peterborough	OHL	60	54	52	106	43	...	...	...	17	19	16	35	18
89-90—Peterborough	OHL	60	52	64	116	39	...	...	...	12	5	7	12	26
90-91—Philadelphia	NHL	68	21	20	41	64	-8	9	0	—	—	—	—	—
91-92—Philadelphia	NHL	78	20	36	56	93	-10	11	2	—	—	—	—	—
92-93—Quebec	NHL	77	27	51	78	123	8	12	1	6	0	6	6	8
93-94—Quebec	NHL	83	30	21	51	113	-9	13	3	—	—	—	—	—
94-95—Quebec	NHL	48	15	21	36	40	5	9	0	6	1	3	4	8
95-96—Colorado	NHL	62	6	21	27	52	1	3	0	22	6	11	17	18
96-97—Colorado	NHL	63	13	19	32	59	-3	5	0	17	2	4	6	17
97-98—Colorado	NHL	6	0	4	4	2	0	0	0	—	—	—	—	—
—San Jose	NHL	59	9	14	23	30	-4	5	0	6	1	3	4	6
98-99—San Jose	NHL	82	13	26	39	68	1	2	1	6	2	3	5	10
99-00—San Jose	NHL	82	20	24	44	60	14	10	0	12	5	1	6	2
00-01—San Jose	NHL	81	22	22	44	60	3	9	2	6	0	3	3	0
NHL Totals (11 years)		789	196	279	475	764	-2	88	9	81	17	34	51	69

RICHARDS, BRAD   LW   LIGHTNING

PERSONAL: Born May 2, 1980, in Montague, P.E.I. ... 6-1/187. ... Shoots left.
TRANSACTIONS/CAREER NOTES: Selected by Tampa Bay Lightning in third round (second Lightning pick, 64th overall) of NHL entry draft (June 27, 1998).
HONORS: Named to QMJHL All-Rookie Team (1997-98). ... Named to QMJHL All-Star first team (1999-2000). ... Won Jean Beliveau Trophy (1999-2000). ... Won Michel Briere trophy (1999-2000). ... Won Guy Lafleur Trophy (1999-2000). ... Named to Can.HL All-Star first team (1999-2000). ... Won Can.HL Player of the Year Award (1999-2000). ... Won Can.HL Plus/Minus Award (1999-2000).

		REGULAR SEASON								PLAYOFFS				
Season Team	League	Gms.	G	A	Pts.	PIM	+/-	PP	SH	Gms.	G	A	Pts.	PIM
96-97—Notre Dame	SJHL	63	39	48	87	73	...	...	...	—	—	—	—	—
97-98—Rimouski	QMJHL	68	33	82	115	44	...	...	...	19	8	24	32	2
98-99—Rimouski	QMJHL	59	39	92	131	55	...	...	...	11	9	12	21	6
99-00—Rimouski	QMJHL	63	*71	*115	*186	69	...	...	...	12	13	*24	*37	16
00-01—Tampa Bay	NHL	82	21	41	62	14	-10	7	0	—	—	—	—	—
NHL Totals (1 year)		82	21	41	62	14	-10	7	0					

RICHARDSON, LUKE   D   FLYERS

PERSONAL: Born March 26, 1969, in Kanata, Ont. ... 6-3/210. ... Shoots left. ... Full Name: Luke Glen Richardson.
TRANSACTIONS/CAREER NOTES: Selected by Toronto Maple Leafs in first round (first Maple Leafs pick, seventh overall) of NHL entry draft (June 13, 1987). ... Traded by Maple Leafs with LW Vincent Damphousse, G Peter Ing, C Scott Thornton and future considerations to Edmonton Oilers for G Grant Fuhr, LW Glenn Anderson and LW Craig Berube (September 19, 1991). ... Strained clavicular joint (February 11, 1992); missed three games. ... Suffered from the flu (March 1993); missed one game. ... Fractured cheekbone (January 7, 1994); missed 15 games. ... Suffered from the flu (February 28, 1995); missed two games. ... Signed as free agent by Philadelphia Flyers (July 14, 1997). ... Suspended two games by NHL for fighting (January 30, 2000). ... Bruised shoulder (February 24, 2000); missed five games.

		REGULAR SEASON								PLAYOFFS				
Season Team	League	Gms.	G	A	Pts.	PIM	+/-	PP	SH	Gms.	G	A	Pts.	PIM
84-85—Ottawa Jr. B	ODHA	35	5	26	31	72	...	...	...	—	—	—	—	—
85-86—Peterborough	OHL	63	6	18	24	57	...	...	...	16	2	1	3	50
86-87—Peterborough	OHL	59	13	32	45	70	...	...	...	12	0	5	5	24
87-88—Toronto	NHL	78	4	6	10	90	-25	0	0	2	0	0	0	0
88-89—Toronto	NHL	55	2	7	9	106	-15	0	0	—	—	—	—	—
89-90—Toronto	NHL	67	4	14	18	122	-1	0	0	5	0	0	0	22
90-91—Toronto	NHL	78	1	9	10	238	-28	0	0	—	—	—	—	—
91-92—Edmonton	NHL	75	2	19	21	118	-9	0	0	16	0	5	5	45
92-93—Edmonton	NHL	82	3	10	13	142	-18	0	2	—	—	—	—	—
93-94—Edmonton	NHL	69	2	6	8	131	-13	0	0	—	—	—	—	—
94-95—Edmonton	NHL	46	3	10	13	40	-6	1	1					

Season Team	League	REGULAR SEASON								PLAYOFFS				
		Gms.	G	A	Pts.	PIM	+/-	PP	SH	Gms.	G	A	Pts.	PIM
95-96—Edmonton	NHL	82	2	9	11	108	-27	0	0	—	—	—	—	—
96-97—Edmonton	NHL	82	1	11	12	91	9	0	0	12	0	2	2	14
97-98—Philadelphia	NHL	81	2	3	5	139	7	2	0	5	0	0	0	0
98-99—Philadelphia	NHL	78	0	6	6	106	-3	0	0	—	—	—	—	—
99-00—Philadelphia	NHL	74	2	5	7	140	14	0	0	18	0	1	1	41
00-01—Philadelphia	NHL	82	2	6	8	131	23	0	1	6	0	0	0	4
NHL Totals (14 years)		1029	30	121	151	1702	-92	3	4	64	0	8	8	126

RICHTER, BARRY　　　D

PERSONAL: Born September 11, 1970, in Madison, Wis. ... 6-2/200. ... Shoots left. ... Full Name: Barron Patrick Richter. ... Son of Pat Richter, tight end with Washington Redskins (1963-70). ... Name pronounced RIHK-tuhr.

TRANSACTIONS/CAREER NOTES: Selected by Hartford Whalers in second round (second Whalers pick, 32nd overall) of NHL entry draft (June 11, 1988). ... Traded by Whalers with RW Steve Larmer, LW Nick Kypreos and sixth-round pick (C Yuri Litvinov) in 1994 draft to New York Rangers for D James Patrick and C Darren Turcotte (November 2, 1993). ... Signed as free agent by Boston Bruins (July 17, 1996). ... Strained groin (November 4, 1996); missed four games. ... Signed as free agent by New York Islanders (August 19, 1998). ... Sprained shoulder (February 3, 1999); missed three games. ... Signed as free agent by Montreal Canadiens (August 6, 1999). ... Strained hip flexor (December 29, 1999); missed 19 games.

HONORS: Named to NCAA All-Tournament team (1991-92). ... Named to NCAA All-America (West) first team (1992-93). ... Named to WCHA All-Star first team (1992-93). ... Named to AHL All-Star first team (1995-96). ... Won Eddie Shore Plaque (1995-96).

Season Team	League	REGULAR SEASON								PLAYOFFS				
		Gms.	G	A	Pts.	PIM	+/-	PP	SH	Gms.	G	A	Pts.	PIM
86-87—Culver Military	Indiana H.S.	35	19	26	45	...	...	...	...	—	—	—	—	—
87-88—Culver Military	Indiana H.S.	35	24	29	53	18	...	...	...	—	—	—	—	—
88-89—Culver Military	Indiana H.S.	19	21	29	50	16	...	...	...	—	—	—	—	—
89-90—Univ. of Wisconsin	WCHA	42	13	23	36	26	...	...	...	—	—	—	—	—
90-91—Univ. of Wisconsin	WCHA	43	15	20	35	42	...	...	...	—	—	—	—	—
91-92—Univ. of Wisconsin	WCHA	39	10	25	35	62	...	...	...	—	—	—	—	—
92-93—Univ. of Wisconsin	WCHA	42	14	32	46	74	...	...	...	—	—	—	—	—
93-94—U.S. national team	Int'l	56	7	16	23	50	...	...	...	—	—	—	—	—
—U.S. Olympic team	Int'l	8	0	3	3	4	...	...	...	—	—	—	—	—
—Binghamton	AHL	21	0	9	9	12	...	...	...	—	—	—	—	—
94-95—Binghamton	AHL	73	15	41	56	54	...	...	...	11	4	5	9	12
95-96—Binghamton	AHL	69	20	61	81	64	...	...	...	3	0	3	3	0
—New York Rangers	NHL	4	0	1	1	0	2	0	0	—	—	—	—	—
96-97—Boston	NHL	50	5	13	18	32	-7	1	0	—	—	—	—	—
—Providence	AHL	19	2	6	8	4	...	...	...	10	4	4	8	4
97-98—Providence	AHL	75	16	29	45	47	...	...	...	—	—	—	—	—
98-99—New York Islanders	NHL	72	6	18	24	34	-4	0	0	—	—	—	—	—
99-00—Montreal	NHL	23	0	2	2	8	-5	0	0	—	—	—	—	—
—Quebec	AHL	2	0	0	0	0	...	...	...	—	—	—	—	—
—Manitoba	IHL	19	5	4	9	6	...	...	...	2	1	1	2	0
00-01—Quebec	AHL	68	4	47	51	45	...	...	...	6	0	3	3	2
—Montreal	NHL	2	0	0	0	2	-1	0	0	—	—	—	—	—
NHL Totals (5 years)		151	11	34	45	76	-15	1	0					

RICHTER, MIKE　　　G　　　RANGERS

PERSONAL: Born September 22, 1966, in Philadelphia. ... 5-11/185. ... Catches left. ... Full Name: Michael Thomas Richter. ... Name pronounced RIHK-tuhr.

TRANSACTIONS/CAREER NOTES: Selected by New York Rangers in second round (second Rangers pick, 28th overall) of NHL entry draft (June 15, 1985). ... Bruised thigh (January 30, 1992); missed 12 games. ... Injured groin (December 30, 1995); missed 15 games. ... Injured groin (February 18, 1996); missed eight games. ... Separated left shoulder (January 19, 1997); missed two games. ... Selected by Nashville Predators in NHL expansion draft (June 26, 1998). ... Signed as free agent by Rangers (July 14, 1998). ... Injured back (October 2, 1999); missed five games. ... Sprained left knee (February 5, 2000); missed two games. ... Reinjured left knee (February 18, 2000); missed two games. ... Reinjured left knee (March 13, 2000); missed one game. ... Reinjured left knee (March 27, 2000); missed four games. ... Underwent knee surgery (April 5, 2000); missed first five games of season. ... Tore anterior cruciate ligament in right knee (February 19, 2001); missed remainder of season.

HONORS: Won WCHA Rookie of the Year Award (1985-86). ... Named to WCHA All-Star second team (1985-86 and 1986-87). ... Played in NHL All-Star Game (1992, 1994 and 2000). ... Named All-Star Game Most Valuable Player (1994).

RECORDS: Shares NHL single-season playoff record for most wins by goaltender—16 (1994). ... Shares NHL single-season playoff record for most shutouts—4 (1994).

MISCELLANEOUS: Member of Stanley Cup championship team (1994). ... Stopped a penalty shot attempt (vs. Kevin Dineen, October 19, 1989; vs. Pelle Eklund, January 14, 1990; vs. Troy Murray, November 27, 1991; vs. Pavel Bure, June 7, 1994 (playoffs); vs. Steve Konowalchuk, March 5, 1995; vs. Ken Klee, March 12, 1997; vs. Marc Bureau, January 10, 1998; vs. Claude Lapointe, October 22, 1998; vs. Richard Zednik, November 16, 1999; vs. Randy Robitaille, January 31, 2000). ... Allowed a penalty shot goal (vs. Doug Weight, October 8, 1997). ... Holds New York Rangers all-time record for most wins (272).

Season Team	League	REGULAR SEASON								PLAYOFFS						
		Gms.	Min	W	L	T	GA	SO	Avg.	Gms.	Min.	W	L	GA	SO	Avg.
84-85—Northwood School	N.Y. H.S.	24	1374	...	...	...	52	2	2.27	—	—	—	—	—	—	—
85-86—Univ. of Wisconsin	WCHA	24	1394	14	9	0	92	1	3.96	—	—	—	—	—	—	—
86-87—Univ. of Wisconsin	WCHA	36	2136	19	16	1	126	0	3.54	—	—	—	—	—	—	—
87-88—U.S. national team	Int'l	29	1559	17	7	2	86	0	3.31	—	—	—	—	—	—	—
—U.S. Olympic team	Int'l	4	230	2	2	0	15	0	3.91	—	—	—	—	—	—	—
—Colorado	IHL	22	1298	16	5	0	68	1	3.14	10	536	5	3	35	0	3.92
88-89—Denver	IHL	*57	3031	23	26	0	*217	1	4.30	4	210	0	4	21	0	6.00
—New York Rangers	NHL	—	—	—	—	—	—	—	—	1	58	0	1	4	0	4.14

Season Team	League	REGULAR SEASON								PLAYOFFS					
		Gms.	Min	W	L	T	GA	SO	Avg.	Gms.	Min.	W	L	GA	SO	Avg.
89-90—New York Rangers	NHL	23	1320	12	5	5	66	0	3.00	6	330	3	2	19	0	3.45
—Flint	IHL	13	782	7	4	‡2	49	0	3.76	—	—	—	—	—	—	—
90-91—New York Rangers	NHL	45	2596	21	13	7	135	0	3.12	6	313	2	4	14	†1	2.68
91-92—New York Rangers	NHL	41	2298	23	12	2	119	3	3.11	7	412	4	2	24	1	3.50
92-93—New York Rangers	NHL	38	2105	13	19	3	134	1	3.82	—	—	—	—	—	—	—
—Binghamton	AHL	5	305	4	0	1	6	0	1.18	—	—	—	—	—	—	—
93-94—New York Rangers	NHL	68	3710	*42	12	6	159	5	2.57	23	1417	*16	7	49	†4	2.07
94-95—New York Rangers	NHL	35	1993	14	17	2	97	2	2.92	7	384	2	5	23	0	3.59
95-96—New York Rangers	NHL	41	2396	24	13	3	107	3	2.68	11	661	5	6	36	0	3.27
96-97—New York Rangers	NHL	61	3598	33	22	6	161	4	2.68	15	939	9	6	33	3	2.11
97-98—New York Rangers	NHL	72	4143	21	31	*15	†184	0	2.66	—	—	—	—	—	—	—
—U.S. Olympic team	Int'l	4	237	1	3	0	14	0	3.54	—	—	—	—	—	—	—
98-99—New York Rangers	NHL	68	3878	27	30	8	170	4	2.63	—	—	—	—	—	—	—
99-00—New York Rangers	NHL	61	3622	22	†31	8	173	0	2.87	—	—	—	—	—	—	—
00-01—New York Rangers	NHL	45	2635	20	21	3	144	0	3.28	—	—	—	—	—	—	—
NHL Totals (13 years)		598	34294	272	226	68	1649	22	2.89	76	4514	41	33	202	9	2.68

RIESEN, MICHEL — LW — BLUES

PERSONAL: Born April 11, 1979, in Oberbalm, Switzerland. ... 6-2/190. ... Shoots right. ... Name pronounced REE-sihn.

TRANSACTIONS/CAREER NOTES: Selected by Edmonton Oilers in first round (first Oilers pick, 14th overall) of NHL entry draft (June 21, 1997). ... Traded by Oilers with C Doug Weight to St. Louis Blues for C Marty Reasoner, C Jochen Hecht and D Jan Horacek (July 1, 2001).

Season Team	League	REGULAR SEASON								PLAYOFFS				
		Gms.	G	A	Pts.	PIM	+/-	PP	SH	Gms.	G	A	Pts.	PIM
94-95—Biel-Bienne	Switzerland	12	0	2	2	0	...	...	...	6	2	0	2	0
95-96—Biel-Bienne	Switz. Div. 2	34	9	6	15	2	...	...	...	3	1	0	1	0
96-97—Biel-Bienne	Switz. Div. 2	38	16	16	32	49	...	...	...	—	—	—	—	—
97-98—Davos HC	Switzerland	32	16	9	25	8	...	...	...	18	5	5	10	4
98-99—Hamilton	AHL	60	6	17	23	6	...	...	...	3	0	0	0	0
99-00—Hamilton	AHL	73	29	31	60	20	...	...	...	10	3	5	8	4
00-01—Edmonton	NHL	12	0	1	1	4	2	0	0	—	—	—	—	—
—Hamilton	AHL	69	26	28	54	14	...	...	...	—	—	—	—	—
NHL Totals (1 year)		12	0	1	1	4	2	0	0					

RITA, JANI — LW/RW — OILERS

PERSONAL: Born July 25, 1981, in Helsinki, Finland. ... 6-1/206. ... Shoots right.

TRANSACTIONS/CAREER NOTES: Selected by Edmonton Oilers in first round (first Oilers pick, 13th overall) of NHL entry draft (June 26, 1999).

Season Team	League	REGULAR SEASON								PLAYOFFS				
		Gms.	G	A	Pts.	PIM	+/-	PP	SH	Gms.	G	A	Pts.	PIM
96-97—Jokerit Helsinki	Finland Jr.	3	0	0	0	0	...	...	...	—	—	—	—	—
97-98—Jokerit Helsinki	Finland Jr.	36	15	9	24	2	...	...	...	8	4	1	5	0
—Jokerit Helsinki	Finland	—	—	—	—	—	...	...	...	1	0	0	0	0
98-99—Jokerit Helsinki	Finland	41	3	2	5	39	...	...	...	—	—	—	—	—
—Jokerit Helsinki	Finland Jr.	20	9	13	22	8	...	...	...	—	—	—	—	—
99-00—Jokerit Helsinki	Finland	49	6	3	9	10	...	...	...	11	1	0	1	0
00-01—Jokerit Helsinki	Finland	50	5	10	15	18	...	...	...	5	0	0	0	2

RITCHIE, BYRON — C — HURRICANES

PERSONAL: Born April 24, 1977, in Burnaby, B.C. ... 5-10/185. ... Shoots left.

TRANSACTIONS/CAREER NOTES: Selected by Hartford Whalers in seventh round (sixth Whalers pick, 165th overall) of NHL entry draft (July 8, 1995). ... Whalers franchise moved to North Carolina and renamed Carolina Hurricanes for 1997-98 season; NHL approved move on June 25, 1997.

HONORS: Named to WHL (East) All-Star second team (1995-96 and 1996-97). ... Named to Memorial Cup All-Star Team (1996-97).

Season Team	League	REGULAR SEASON								PLAYOFFS				
		Gms.	G	A	Pts.	PIM	+/-	PP	SH	Gms.	G	A	Pts.	PIM
93-94—Lethbridge	WHL	44	4	11	15	44	...	...	...	6	0	0	0	14
94-95—Lethbridge	WHL	58	22	28	50	132	...	...	...	—	—	—	—	—
95-96—Lethbridge	WHL	66	55	51	106	163	...	...	...	4	0	2	2	4
—Springfield	AHL	6	2	1	3	4	...	...	...	8	0	3	3	0
96-97—Lethbridge	WHL	63	50	76	126	115	...	...	...	18	16	12	*28	28
97-98—New Haven	AHL	65	13	18	31	97	...	...	...	—	—	—	—	—
98-99—New Haven	AHL	66	24	33	57	139	...	...	...	—	—	—	—	—
—Carolina	NHL	3	0	0	0	0	0	0	0	—	—	—	—	—
99-00—Carolina	NHL	26	0	2	2	17	-10	0	0	—	—	—	—	—
—Cincinnati	IHL	34	8	13	21	81	...	...	...	10	1	6	7	32
00-01—Cincinnati	IHL	77	31	35	66	166	...	...	...	5	3	2	5	10
NHL Totals (2 years)		29	0	2	2	17	-10	0	0					

RIVERS, JAMIE D SENATORS

PERSONAL: Born March 16, 1975, in Ottawa. ... 6-0/197. ... Shoots left. ... Brother of Shawn Rivers, defenseman with Tampa Bay Lightning (1992-93).
TRANSACTIONS/CAREER NOTES: Selected by St. Louis Blues in third round (second Blues pick, 63rd overall) of NHL entry draft (June 26, 1993). ... Claimed by New York Islanders from Blues in NHL waiver draft (September 27, 1999). ... Bruised ankle (February 26, 2000); missed three games. ... Signed as free agent by Ottawa Senators (November 10, 2000).
HONORS: Won Max Kaminsky Award (1993-94). ... Named to OHL All-Star first team (1993-94). ... Named to Can.HL All-Star second team (1993-94). ... Named to OHL All-Star second team (1994-95). ... Named to AHL All-Star second team (1996-97).

		REGULAR SEASON								PLAYOFFS				
Season Team	League	Gms.	G	A	Pts.	PIM	+/-	PP	SH	Gms.	G	A	Pts.	PIM
90-91—Ottawa	OHA Jr. A	55	4	30	34	74	...	...	...	—	—	—	—	—
91-92—Sudbury	OHL	55	3	13	16	20	...	...	...	8	0	0	0	0
92-93—Sudbury	OHL	62	12	43	55	20	...	...	...	14	7	19	26	4
93-94—Sudbury	OHL	65	32	*89	121	58	...	...	...	10	1	9	10	14
94-95—Sudbury	OHL	46	9	56	65	30	...	...	...	18	7	26	33	22
95-96—St. Louis	NHL	3	0	0	0	2	-1	0	0	—	—	—	—	—
—Worcester	AHL	75	7	45	52	130	...	...	...	4	0	1	1	4
96-97—Worcester	AHL	63	8	35	43	83	...	...	...	5	1	2	3	14
—St. Louis	NHL	15	2	5	7	6	-4	1	0	—	—	—	—	—
97-98—St. Louis	NHL	59	2	4	6	36	5	1	0	—	—	—	—	—
98-99—St. Louis	NHL	76	2	5	7	47	-3	1	0	9	1	1	2	2
99-00—New York Islanders	NHL	75	1	16	17	84	-4	1	0	—	—	—	—	—
00-01—Grand Rapids	IHL	2	0	0	0	2	...	...	...	—	—	—	—	—
—Ottawa	NHL	45	2	4	6	44	6	0	0	1	0	0	0	4
NHL Totals (6 years)		273	9	34	43	219	-1	4	0	10	1	1	2	6

RIVET, CRAIG D CANADIENS

PERSONAL: Born September 13, 1974, in North Bay, Ont. ... 6-2/207. ... Shoots right. ... Name pronounced REE-vay.
TRANSACTIONS/CAREER NOTES: Selected by Montreal Canadiens in third round (fourth Canadiens pick, 68th overall) of NHL entry draft (June 20, 1992). ... Separated shoulder (January 20, 1997); missed six games. ... Bruised back (November 1, 1997); missed one game. ... Suffered concussion (December 19, 1997); missed seven games. ... Sprained shoulder (November 9, 1998); missed five games. ... Suffered back spasms and suffered from the flu (January 18, 1999); missed three games. ... Strained groin (March 13, 1999); missed three games. ... Reinjured groin (March 24, 1999); missed five games. ... Fractured cheekbone (October 8, 1999); missed nine games. ... Suffered illness (November 3, 1999); missed four games. ... Strained groin (January 4, 2000); missed eight games. ... Injured shoulder (November 29, 2000); missed five games. ... Reinjured shoulder (December 15, 2000) and underwent surgery; missed remainder of season.

		REGULAR SEASON								PLAYOFFS				
Season Team	League	Gms.	G	A	Pts.	PIM	+/-	PP	SH	Gms.	G	A	Pts.	PIM
90-91—Barrie Jr. B	OHA	42	9	17	26	55	...	...	...	—	—	—	—	—
91-92—Kingston	OHL	66	5	21	26	97	...	...	...	—	—	—	—	—
92-93—Kingston	OHL	64	19	55	74	117	...	...	...	16	5	7	12	39
93-94—Fredericton	AHL	4	0	2	2	2	...	...	...	—	—	—	—	—
—Kingston	OHL	61	12	52	64	100	...	...	...	6	0	3	3	6
94-95—Fredericton	AHL	78	5	27	32	126	...	...	...	12	0	4	4	17
—Montreal	NHL	5	0	1	1	5	2	0	0	—	—	—	—	—
95-96—Fredericton	AHL	49	5	18	23	189	...	...	...	6	0	0	0	12
—Montreal	NHL	19	1	4	5	54	4	0	0	—	—	—	—	—
96-97—Montreal	NHL	35	0	4	4	54	7	0	0	5	0	1	1	14
—Fredericton	AHL	23	3	12	15	99	...	...	...	—	—	—	—	—
97-98—Montreal	NHL	61	0	2	2	93	-3	0	0	5	0	0	0	2
98-99—Montreal	NHL	66	2	8	10	66	-3	0	0	—	—	—	—	—
99-00—Montreal	NHL	61	3	14	17	76	11	0	0	—	—	—	—	—
00-01—Montreal	NHL	26	1	2	3	36	-8	0	0	—	—	—	—	—
NHL Totals (7 years)		273	7	35	42	384	10	0	0	10	0	1	1	16

ROBERTS, GARY LW MAPLE LEAFS

PERSONAL: Born May 23, 1966, in North York, Ont. ... 6-1/190. ... Shoots left.
TRANSACTIONS/CAREER NOTES: Selected by Calgary Flames in first round (first Flames pick, 12th overall) of NHL entry draft (June 9, 1984). ... Injured back (January 1989). ... Suffered whiplash (November 9, 1991); missed one game. ... Suffered from the flu (January 19, 1993); missed one game. ... Suffered left quadricep hematoma (February 16, 1993); missed 25 games. ... Suspended one game by NHL for high-sticking (November 19, 1993). ... Suspended four games and fined $500 by NHL for two slashing incidents and fined $500 for high-sticking (January 7, 1994). ... Fractured thumb (March 20, 1994); missed one game. ... Fractured thumb (April 3, 1994); missed last five games of season. ... Suffered neck and spinal injury (February 4, 1995); underwent surgery and missed last 40 games of 1994-95 season and first 42 games of 1995-96 season. ... Injured neck (April 3, 1996); missed five games. ... Announced retirement (June 17, 1996); did not play during 1996-97 season. ... Traded by Flames with G Trevor Kidd to Carolina Hurricanes for G Jean-Sebastion Giguere and C Andrew Cassels (August 25, 1997). ... Strained abdominal muscle (November 12, 1997); missed six games. ... Strained rib muscle (January 11, 1998); missed 10 games. ... Suffered from the flu (March 31, 1998); missed one game. ... Injured groin (April 13, 1998); missed final three games of season. ... Sprained wrist (December 2, 1998); missed four games. ... Strained neck (April 14, 1999); missed one game. ... Strained shoulder (October 7, 1999); missed one game. ... Injured groin (October 23, 1999); missed four games. ... Suffered from the flu (January 18, 2000); missed one game. ... Injured groin (February 12, 2000); missed seven games. ... Signed as free agent by Toronto Maple Leafs (July 4, 2000).
HONORS: Named to OHL All-Star second team (1984-85 and 1985-86). ... Played in NHL All-Star Game (1992 and 1993). ... Won Bill Masterton Memorial Trophy (1995-96).
MISCELLANEOUS: Member of Stanley Cup championship team (1989). ... Holds Carolina Hurricanes record for most penalty minutes (281). ... Failed to score on a penalty shot (vs. Mike Dunham, December 20, 2000).
STATISTICAL NOTES: Led NHL in shooting percentage with 21.0 (2000-01).
STATISTICAL PLATEAUS: Three-goal games: 1989-90 (1), 1991-92 (2), 1992-93 (2), 1993-94 (1), 1995-96 (3), 1997-98 (1). Total: 10. ... Four-goal games: 1993-94 (1). ... Total hat tricks: 11.

Season Team	League	REGULAR SEASON								PLAYOFFS				
		Gms.	G	A	Pts.	PIM	+/-	PP	SH	Gms.	G	A	Pts.	PIM
82-83—Ottawa	OHL	53	12	8	20	83	...	...	...	5	1	0	1	19
83-84—Ottawa	OHL	48	27	30	57	144	...	...	...	13	10	7	17	*62
84-85—Ottawa	OHL	59	44	62	106	186	...	...	...	5	2	8	10	10
—Moncton	AHL	7	4	2	6	7	...	...	...	—	—	—	—	—
85-86—Ottawa	OHL	24	26	25	51	83	...	...	...	—	—	—	—	—
—Guelph	OHL	23	18	15	33	65	...	...	...	20	18	13	31	43
86-87—Moncton	AHL	38	20	18	38	72	...	...	...	—	—	—	—	—
—Calgary	NHL	32	5	10	15	85	6	0	0	2	0	0	0	4
87-88—Calgary	NHL	74	13	15	28	282	24	0	0	9	2	3	5	29
88-89—Calgary	NHL	71	22	16	38	250	32	0	1	22	5	7	12	57
89-90—Calgary	NHL	78	39	33	72	222	31	5	0	6	2	5	7	41
90-91—Calgary	NHL	80	22	31	53	252	15	0	0	7	1	3	4	18
91-92—Calgary	NHL	76	53	37	90	207	32	15	0	—	—	—	—	—
92-93—Calgary	NHL	58	38	41	79	172	32	8	3	5	1	6	7	43
93-94—Calgary	NHL	73	41	43	84	145	37	12	3	7	2	6	8	24
94-95—Calgary	NHL	8	2	2	4	43	1	2	0	—	—	—	—	—
95-96—Calgary	NHL	35	22	20	42	78	15	9	0	—	—	—	—	—
96-97—								Did not play.						
97-98—Carolina	NHL	61	20	29	49	103	3	4	0	—	—	—	—	—
98-99—Carolina	NHL	77	14	28	42	178	2	1	1	6	1	1	2	8
99-00—Carolina	NHL	69	23	30	53	62	-10	12	0	—	—	—	—	—
00-01—Toronto	NHL	82	29	24	53	109	16	8	2	11	2	9	11	0
NHL Totals (15 years)		874	343	359	702	2188	236	76	10	75	16	40	56	224

ROBERTSSON, BERT — D — PREDATORS

PERSONAL: Born June 30, 1974, in Sodertalje, Sweden. ... 6-3/210. ... Shoots left. ... Name pronounced ROH-behrt-suhn.
TRANSACTIONS/CAREER NOTES: Selected by Vancouver Canucks in 10th round (eighth Canucks pick, 254th overall) of NHL entry draft (June 29, 1993). ... Injured groin (April 1, 1999); missed four games. ... Signed as free agent by Edmonton Oilers (August 19, 1999). ... Selected by Columbus Blue Jackets in NHL expansion draft (June 23, 2000). ... Traded by Blue Jackets to New York Rangers for G Jean-Francois Labbe (November 9, 2000). ... Traded by Rangers to Nashville Predators for LW Ryan Tobler (March 7, 2001).

Season Team	League	REGULAR SEASON								PLAYOFFS				
		Gms.	G	A	Pts.	PIM	+/-	PP	SH	Gms.	G	A	Pts.	PIM
92-93—Sodertalje	Sweden Dv. 2	23	1	2	3	24	...	...	...	—	—	—	—	—
93-94—Sodertalje	Sweden Dv. 2	28	0	1	1	12	...	...	...	—	—	—	—	—
94-95—Sodertalje	Sweden Dv. 2	23	1	2	3	24	...	...	...	—	—	—	—	—
95-96—Syracuse	AHL	65	1	7	8	109	...	...	...	16	0	1	1	26
96-97—Syracuse	AHL	80	4	9	13	132	...	...	...	3	1	0	1	4
97-98—Syracuse	AHL	42	5	9	14	87	...	...	...	3	0	0	0	6
—Vancouver	NHL	30	2	4	6	24	2	0	0	—	—	—	—	—
98-99—Vancouver	NHL	39	2	2	4	13	-7	0	0	—	—	—	—	—
—Syracuse	AHL	8	1	0	1	21	...	...	...	—	—	—	—	—
99-00—Hamilton	AHL	6	0	3	3	12	...	...	...	—	—	—	—	—
—Edmonton	NHL	52	0	4	4	34	-3	0	0	5	0	0	0	0
00-01—Houston	IHL	14	0	0	0	26	...	...	...	—	—	—	—	—
—New York Rangers	NHL	2	0	0	0	4	-1	0	0	—	—	—	—	—
—Hartford	AHL	27	7	5	12	27	...	...	...	—	—	—	—	—
—Milwaukee	IHL	10	0	0	0	0	...	...	...	5	0	1	1	2
NHL Totals (4 years)		123	4	10	14	75	-9	0	0	5	0	0	0	0

ROBIDAS, STEPHANE — D — CANADIENS

PERSONAL: Born March 3, 1973, in Sherbrooke, Que. ... 5-11/180. ... Shoots right.
TRANSACTIONS/CAREER NOTES: Selected by Montreal Canadiens in seventh round (seventh Canadiens pick, 164th overall) of NHL entry draft (June 26, 1995). ... Bruised shoulder (December 16, 2000); missed two games.
HONORS: Won Emile Bouchard Trophy (1996-97). ... Named to Can.HL All-Star second team (1996-97). ... Named to QMJHL All-Star first team (1996-97).

Season Team	League	REGULAR SEASON								PLAYOFFS				
		Gms.	G	A	Pts.	PIM	+/-	PP	SH	Gms.	G	A	Pts.	PIM
93-94—Shawinigan	QMJHL	67	3	18	21	33	...	...	...	1	0	0	0	0
94-95—Shawinigan	QMJHL	71	13	56	69	44	...	...	...	15	7	12	19	4
95-96—Shawinigan	QMJHL	67	23	56	79	53	...	...	...	6	1	5	6	10
96-97—Shawinigan	QMJHL	67	24	51	75	59	...	...	...	7	4	6	10	14
97-98—Fredericton	AHL	79	10	21	31	50	...	...	...	4	0	2	2	0
98-99—Fredericton	AHL	79	8	33	41	59	...	...	...	15	1	5	6	10
99-00—Quebec	AHL	76	14	31	45	36	...	...	...	3	0	1	1	0
—Montreal	NHL	1	0	0	0	0	0	0	0	—	—	—	—	—
00-01—Montreal	NHL	65	6	6	12	14	0	1	0	—	—	—	—	—
NHL Totals (2 years)		66	6	6	12	14	0	1	0					

ROBITAILLE, LUC — LW — RED WINGS

PERSONAL: Born February 17, 1966, in Montreal. ... 6-1/205. ... Shoots left. ... Name pronounced ROH-bih-tigh.
TRANSACTIONS/CAREER NOTES: Selected by Los Angeles Kings in ninth round (ninth Kings pick, 171st overall) of NHL entry draft (June 9, 1984). ... Suspended four games by NHL for crosschecking from behind (November 10, 1990). ... Underwent surgery to repair slight fracture of right ankle (June 15, 1994). ... Traded by Kings to Pittsburgh Penguins for RW Rick Tocchet and second-round pick (RW Pavel Rosa) in

1995 draft (July 29, 1994). ... Suspended by NHL for two games for high-sticking (February 7, 1995). ... Traded by Penguins with D Ulf Samuelsson to New York Rangers for D Sergei Zubov and C Petr Nedved (August 31, 1995). ... Suffered stress fracture in ankle (December 15, 1995); missed five games. ... Fractured foot (March 12, 1997); missed final 13 games of regular season. ... Traded by Rangers to Kings for LW Kevin Stevens (August 28, 1997). ... Injured right groin and abdomen (February 25, 1998) and underwent surgery; missed final 25 games of regular season. ... Fractured foot (November 3, 1999); missed 10 games. ... Signed as free agent by Detroit Red Wings (July 2, 2001).

HONORS: Named to QMJHL All-Star second team (1984-85). ... Won Can.HL Player of the Year Award (1985-86). ... Shared Guy Lafleur Trophy with Sylvain Cote (1985-86). ... Named to QMJHL All-Star first team (1985-86). ... Named to Memorial Cup All-Star team (1985-86). ... Won Calder Memorial Trophy (1986-87). ... Named to THE SPORTING NEWS All-Star second team (1986-87 and 1991-92). ... Named to NHL All-Star second team (1986-87, 1991-92 and 2000-01). ... Named to NHL All-Rookie team (1986-87). ... Named to THE SPORTING NEWS All-Star first team (1987-88 through 1990-91 and 1992-93). ... Played in NHL All-Star Game (1988-1993, 1999 and 2001). ... Named to NHL All-Star first team (1987-88 through 1990-91 and 1992-93).

RECORDS: Holds NHL single-season records for most points by a left-winger—125 (1992-93); and most goals by a left-winger—63 (1992-93).

STATISTICAL PLATEAUS: Three-goal games: 1986-87 (1), 1987-88 (3), 1988-89 (1), 1989-90 (2), 1992-93 (2), 1998-99 (1), 1999-00 (1). Total: 11. ... Four-goal games: 1991-92 (1), 1993-94 (1), 1994-95 (1). Total: 3. ... Total hat tricks: 14.

MISCELLANEOUS: Scored on a penalty shot (vs. Eldon Reddick, October 25, 1987; vs. Kay Whitmore, February 6, 1992). ... Failed to score on a penalty shot (vs. Sean Burke, February 2, 1989; vs. Jon Casey, April 3, 1993).

		REGULAR SEASON								PLAYOFFS				
Season Team	League	Gms.	G	A	Pts.	PIM	+/-	PP	SH	Gms.	G	A	Pts.	PIM
83-84—Hull	QMJHL	70	32	53	85	48	...	...	...	—	—	—	—	—
84-85—Hull	QMJHL	64	55	94	149	115	...	...	...	5	4	2	6	27
85-86—Hull	QMJHL	63	68	*123	†191	93	...	...	...	15	17	27	*44	28
86-87—Los Angeles	NHL	79	45	39	84	28	-18	18	0	5	1	4	5	2
87-88—Los Angeles	NHL	80	53	58	111	82	-9	17	0	5	2	5	7	18
88-89—Los Angeles	NHL	78	46	52	98	65	5	10	0	11	2	6	8	10
89-90—Los Angeles	NHL	80	52	49	101	38	8	20	0	10	5	5	10	10
90-91—Los Angeles	NHL	76	45	46	91	68	28	11	0	12	12	4	16	22
91-92—Los Angeles	NHL	80	44	63	107	95	-4	26	0	6	3	4	7	12
92-93—Los Angeles	NHL	84	63	62	125	100	18	24	2	24	9	13	22	28
93-94—Los Angeles	NHL	83	44	42	86	86	-20	24	0	—	—	—	—	—
94-95—Pittsburgh	NHL	46	23	19	42	37	10	5	0	12	7	4	11	26
95-96—New York Rangers	NHL	77	23	46	69	80	13	11	0	11	1	5	6	8
96-97—New York Rangers	NHL	69	24	24	48	48	16	5	0	15	4	7	11	4
97-98—Los Angeles	NHL	57	16	24	40	66	5	5	0	4	1	2	3	6
98-99—Los Angeles	NHL	82	39	35	74	54	-1	11	0	—	—	—	—	—
99-00—Los Angeles	NHL	71	36	38	74	68	11	13	0	4	2	2	4	6
00-01—Los Angeles	NHL	82	37	51	88	66	10	16	1	13	4	3	7	10
NHL Totals (15 years)		1124	590	648	1238	981	72	216	3	132	53	64	117	162

ROBITAILLE, RANDY C KINGS

PERSONAL: Born October 12, 1975, in Ottawa. ... 5-11/198. ... Shoots left. ... Name pronounced ROH-bih-tigh.

TRANSACTIONS/CAREER NOTES: Signed as free agent by Boston Bruins (March 27, 1997). ... Injured shoulder (March 27, 1997); missed remainder of season. ... Traded by Bruins to Atlanta Thrashers for RW Peter Ferraro (June 25, 1999). ... Traded by Thrashers to Nashville Predators for LW Denny Lambert (August 16, 1999). ... Signed as free agent by Los Angeles Kings (July 7, 2001).

HONORS: Named to CCHA All-Rookie team (1995-96). ... Named to CCHA All-Star first team (1996-97). ... Named to NCAA All-America (West) first team (1996-97). ... Named to AHL All-Star first team (1998-99). ... Won Les Cunningham Plaque (1998-99).

MISCELLANEOUS: Failed to score on a penalty shot (vs. Mike Richter, January 31, 2000).

		REGULAR SEASON								PLAYOFFS				
Season Team	League	Gms.	G	A	Pts.	PIM	+/-	PP	SH	Gms.	G	A	Pts.	PIM
94-95—Ottawa	CJHL	54	48	77	125	111	...	...	...	—	—	—	—	—
95-96—Miami of Ohio	CCHA	36	14	31	45	26	...	...	...	—	—	—	—	—
96-97—Miami of Ohio	CCHA	39	27	34	61	44	...	...	...	—	—	—	—	—
—Boston	NHL	1	0	0	0	0	0	0	0	—	—	—	—	—
97-98—Providence	AHL	48	15	29	44	16	...	...	...	—	—	—	—	—
—Boston	NHL	4	0	0	0	0	-2	0	0	—	—	—	—	—
98-99—Providence	AHL	74	28	*74	102	34	...	...	...	19	6	†14	20	20
—Boston	NHL	4	0	2	2	0	-1	0	0	1	0	0	0	0
99-00—Nashville	NHL	69	11	14	25	10	-13	2	0	—	—	—	—	—
00-01—Milwaukee	IHL	19	10	23	33	4	...	...	...	—	—	—	—	—
—Nashville	NHL	62	9	17	26	12	-11	5	0	—	—	—	—	—
NHL Totals (5 years)		140	20	33	53	22	-27	7	0	1	0	0	0	0

ROCHE, TRAVIS D WILD

PERSONAL: Born June 17, 1978, in Whitecourt, Alta. ... 6-1/190. ... Shoots right.

TRANSACTIONS/CAREER NOTES: Signed as non-drafted free agent by Minnesota Wild (April 8, 2001).

HONORS: Named to NCAA All-America (West) first team (2000-01). ... Named to NCAA All-Tournament team (2000-01).

		REGULAR SEASON								PLAYOFFS				
Season Team	League	Gms.	G	A	Pts.	PIM	+/-	PP	SH	Gms.	G	A	Pts.	PIM
99-00—Univ. of North Dakota	WCHA	42	6	22	28	60	...	...	...	—	—	—	—	—
00-01—Univ. of North Dakota	WCHA	41	10	35	45	40	...	...	...	—	—	—	—	—
—Minnesota	NHL	1	0	0	0	0	0	0	0	—	—	—	—	—
NHL Totals (1 year)		1	0	0	0	0	0	0	0					

ROENICK, JEREMY C FLYERS

PERSONAL: Born January 17, 1970, in Boston. ... 6-0/207. ... Shoots right. ... Brother of Trevor Roenick, center with Hartford Whalers/Carolina Hurricanes organization (1993-94 through 1996-97). ... Name pronounced ROH-nihk.

TRANSACTIONS/CAREER NOTES: Selected by Chicago Blackhawks in first round (first Blackhawks pick, eighth overall) of NHL entry draft (June 11, 1988). ... Sprained knee ligaments (January 9, 1989); missed one month. ... Played in Europe during 1994-95 NHL lockout. ... Sprained knee ligament (April 2, 1995); missed remainder of regular season and first eight games of playoffs. ... Pulled thigh muscle (March 4, 1996); missed three games. ... Sprained ankle (March 17, 1996); missed 12 games. ... Traded by Blackhawks to Phoenix Coyotes for C Alexei Zhamnov, RW Craig Mills and first-round pick (RW Ty Jones) in 1997 draft (August 16, 1996). ... Missed first four games of 1996-97 season due to contract dispute. ... Sprained knee (November 23, 1996); missed six games. ... Suffered mild concussion (December 5, 1997); missed one game. ... Suffered concussion (December 28, 1998); missed two games. ... Fractured jaw (April 14, 1999); missed final two games of regular season and six playoff games. ... Suspended five games by NHL for slashing incident (October 11, 1999). ... Suffered injury (March 3, 2001); missed one game. ... Suffered concussion (November 14, 2000); missed one game. ... Signed as free agent by Philadelphia Flyers (July 2, 2001).

HONORS: Named to QMJHL All-Star second team (1988-89). ... Named NHL Rookie of the Year by THE SPORTING NEWS (1989-90). ... Played in NHL All-Star Game (1991-1994, 1999 and 2000).

MISCELLANEOUS: Scored on a penalty shot (vs. Dan Cloutier, December 2, 1999; vs. Tomas Vokoun, March 17, 2000). ... Failed to score on a penalty shot (vs. Andrei Trefilov, March 7, 1995; vs. Marc Denis, February 28, 2001).

STATISTICAL NOTES: Led NHL in game-winning goals with 13 (1991-92).

STATISTICAL PLATEAUS: Three-goal games: 1989-90 (1), 1990-91 (2), 1992-93 (1), 1999-00 (2), 2000-01 (1). Total: 7. ... Four-goal games: 1991-92 (1), 1993-94 (1). Total: 2. ... Total hat tricks: 9.

Season Team	League	REGULAR SEASON								PLAYOFFS				
		Gms.	G	A	Pts.	PIM	+/-	PP	SH	Gms.	G	A	Pts.	PIM
86-87—Thayer Academy	Mass. H.S.	24	31	34	65	...	...	...	...	—	—	—	—	—
87-88—Thayer Academy	Mass. H.S.	24	34	50	84	...	...	...	...	—	—	—	—	—
88-89—U.S. national team	Int'l	11	8	8	16	0	...	...	...	—	—	—	—	—
—Chicago	NHL	20	9	9	18	4	4	2	0	10	1	3	4	7
—Hull	QMJHL	28	34	36	70	14	...	...	...	—	—	—	—	—
89-90—Chicago	NHL	78	26	40	66	54	2	6	0	20	11	7	18	8
90-91—Chicago	NHL	79	41	53	94	80	38	15	4	6	3	5	8	4
91-92—Chicago	NHL	80	53	50	103	98	23	22	3	18	12	10	22	12
92-93—Chicago	NHL	84	50	57	107	86	15	22	3	4	1	2	3	2
93-94—Chicago	NHL	84	46	61	107	125	21	24	5	6	1	6	7	2
94-95—Koln	Germany	3	3	1	4	2	...	...	...	—	—	—	—	—
—Chicago	NHL	33	10	24	34	14	5	5	0	8	1	2	3	16
95-96—Chicago	NHL	66	32	35	67	109	9	12	4	10	5	7	12	2
96-97—Phoenix	NHL	72	29	40	69	115	-7	10	3	6	2	4	6	4
97-98—Phoenix	NHL	79	24	32	56	103	5	6	1	6	5	3	8	4
—U.S. Olympic team	Int'l	4	0	1	1	6	...	...	...	—	—	—	—	—
98-99—Phoenix	NHL	78	24	48	72	130	7	4	0	1	0	0	0	0
99-00—Phoenix	NHL	75	34	44	78	102	11	6	3	5	2	2	4	10
00-01—Phoenix	NHL	80	30	46	76	114	-1	13	0	—	—	—	—	—
NHL Totals (13 years)		908	408	539	947	1134	132	147	26	100	44	51	95	71

ROEST, STACY C WILD

PERSONAL: Born March 15, 1974, in Lethbridge, Alta. ... 5-9/185. ... Shoots right. ... Name pronounced ROHST.

TRANSACTIONS/CAREER NOTES: Signed as non-drafted free agent by Detroit Red Wings (June 9, 1997). ... Selected by Minnesota Wild in NHL expansion draft (June 23, 2000).

HONORS: Named to WHL All-Star (East) first team (1993-94). ... Named to WHL All-Star (East) second team (1994-95).

Season Team	League	REGULAR SEASON								PLAYOFFS				
		Gms.	G	A	Pts.	PIM	+/-	PP	SH	Gms.	G	A	Pts.	PIM
92-93—Medicine Hat	WHL	72	33	73	106	30	...	...	...	10	3	10	13	6
93-94—Medicine Hat	WHL	72	48	72	120	48	...	...	...	3	1	0	1	4
94-95—Medicine Hat	WHL	69	37	78	115	32	...	...	...	5	2	7	9	2
—Adirondack	AHL	3	0	0	0	0	...	...	...	—	—	—	—	—
95-96—Adirondack	AHL	76	16	39	55	40	...	...	...	3	0	0	0	0
96-97—Adirondack	AHL	78	25	41	66	30	...	...	...	4	1	1	2	0
97-98—Adirondack	AHL	80	34	58	92	30	...	...	...	3	2	1	3	6
98-99—Detroit	NHL	59	4	8	12	14	-7	0	0	—	—	—	—	—
—Adirondack	AHL	2	0	1	1	0	...	...	...	—	—	—	—	—
99-00—Detroit	NHL	49	7	9	16	12	-1	1	0	3	0	0	0	0
00-01—Minnesota	NHL	76	7	20	27	20	3	1	0	—	—	—	—	—
NHL Totals (3 years)		184	18	37	55	46	-5	2	0	3	0	0	0	0

ROLOSON, DWAYNE G WILD

PERSONAL: Born October 12, 1969, in Simcoe, Ont. ... 6-1/190. ... Catches left. ... Full Name: Dwayne A. Roloson. ... Name pronounced ROH-luh-suhn.

TRANSACTIONS/CAREER NOTES: Signed as non-drafted free agent by Calgary Flames (July 4, 1994). ... Signed as free agent by Buffalo Sabres (July 9, 1998). ... Selected by Columbus Blue Jackets in NHL expansion draft (June 23, 2000). ... Signed as free agent by St. Louis Blues (July 14, 2000). ... Signed as free agent by Minnesota Wild (July 2, 2001).

HONORS: Named Hockey East Tournament Most Valuable Player (1993-94). ... Named to AHL All-Star first team (2000-01). ... Won Baz Bastien Trophy (2000-01).

MISCELLANEOUS: Stopped a penalty shot attempt (vs. Rob Blake, April 13, 1998). ... Allowed a penalty shot goal (vs. Petr Sykora, January 6, 2000).

R

		REGULAR SEASON								PLAYOFFS						
Season Team	League	Gms.	Min	W	L	T	GA	SO	Avg.	Gms.	Min.	W	L	GA	SO	Avg.
90-91—Mass.-Lowell...............	Hockey East	15	823	5	9	0	63	0	4.59	—	—	—	—	—	—	—
91-92—Mass.-Lowell...............	Hockey East	12	660	3	8	0	52	0	4.73	—	—	—	—	—	—	—
92-93—Mass.-Lowell...............	Hockey East	39	2342	20	17	2	150	0	3.84	—	—	—	—	—	—	—
93-94—Mass.-Lowell...............	Hockey East	40	2305	23	10	7	106	0	2.76	—	—	—	—	—	—	—
94-95—Saint John....................	AHL	46	2734	16	21	8	156	1	3.42	5	299	1	4	13	0	2.61
95-96—Saint John....................	AHL	67	4026	33	22	11	190	1	2.83	16	1027	10	6	49	1	2.86
96-97—Calgary........................	NHL	31	1618	9	14	3	78	1	2.89	—	—	—	—	—	—	—
—Saint John....................	AHL	8	481	6	2	0	22	1	2.74	—	—	—	—	—	—	—
97-98—Saint John....................	AHL	4	245	3	0	1	8	0	1.96	—	—	—	—	—	—	—
—Calgary........................	NHL	39	2205	11	16	8	110	0	2.99	—	—	—	—	—	—	—
98-99—Buffalo	NHL	18	911	6	8	2	42	1	2.77	4	139	1	1	10	0	4.32
—Rochester....................	AHL	2	120	2	0	0	4	0	2.00	—	—	—	—	—	—	—
99-00—Buffalo	NHL	14	677	1	7	3	32	0	2.84	—	—	—	—	—	—	—
00-01—Worcester	AHL	52	3127	*32	15	5	113	*6	*2.17	11	697	6	5	23	1	1.98
NHL Totals (4 years).............		102	5411	27	45	16	262	2	2.91	4	139	1	1	10	0	4.32

ROLSTON, BRIAN C/LW BRUINS

PERSONAL: Born February 21, 1973, in Flint, Mich. ... 6-2/205. ... Shoots left.
TRANSACTIONS/CAREER NOTES: Selected by New Jersey Devils in first round (second Devils pick, 11th overall) of NHL entry draft (June 22, 1991). ... Loaned by Devils to U.S. Olympic Team (November 2, 1993). ... Fractured foot (October 17, 1995); missed 11 games. ... Injured hamstring (January 12, 1998); missed one game. ... Suffered from the flu (January 28, 1998); missed one game. ... Traded by Devils with a conditional third-round pick in the 2001 draft to Colorado Avalanche for RW Claude Lemieux, second-round pick (D Matt DeMarchi) in 2000 draft and swap of first-round picks in 2000 draft (November 3, 1999). ... Bruised ankle (January 27, 2000); missed three games. ... Traded by Avalanche with D Martin Grenier, C Samual Pahlsson and first-round pick (LW Martin Samuelsson) in 2000 draft to Boston Bruins for D Ray Bourque and LW Dave Andreychuk (March 6, 2000). ... Injured ribs (October 28, 2000); missed five games.
HONORS: Named to NCAA All-Tournament team (1991-92 and 1992-93). ... Named to NCAA All-America (West) second team (1992-93). ... Named to CCHA All-Star first team (1992-93).
MISCELLANEOUS: Member of Stanley Cup championship team (1995).
STATISTICAL PLATEAUS: Three-goal games: 1996-97 (1).

		REGULAR SEASON								PLAYOFFS				
Season Team	League	Gms.	G	A	Pts.	PIM	+/-	PP	SH	Gms.	G	A	Pts.	PIM
89-90—Detroit Compuware.....	NAJHL	40	36	37	73	57	...	...	...	—	—	—	—	—
90-91—Detroit Compuware.....	NAJHL	36	49	46	95	14	...	...	...	—	—	—	—	—
91-92—Lake Superior State	CCHA	41	18	28	46	16	...	...	...	—	—	—	—	—
92-93—Lake Superior State	CCHA	39	33	31	64	20	...	...	...	—	—	—	—	—
—U.S. Jr. national team .	Int'l	7	6	2	8	2	...	...	...	—	—	—	—	—
93-94—U.S. national team	Int'l	41	20	28	48	36	...	...	...	—	—	—	—	—
—U.S. Olympic team......	Int'l	8	7	0	7	8	...	...	...	—	—	—	—	—
—Albany........................	AHL	17	5	5	10	8	...	...	...	5	1	2	3	0
94-95—Albany........................	AHL	18	9	11	20	10	...	...	...	—	—	—	—	—
—New Jersey...............	NHL	40	7	11	18	17	5	2	0	6	2	1	3	4
95-96—New Jersey...............	NHL	58	13	11	24	8	9	3	1	—	—	—	—	—
96-97—New Jersey...............	NHL	81	18	27	45	20	6	2	2	10	4	1	5	6
97-98—New Jersey...............	NHL	76	16	14	30	16	7	0	2	6	1	0	1	2
98-99—New Jersey...............	NHL	82	24	33	57	14	11	5	†5	7	1	0	1	2
99-00—New Jersey...............	NHL	11	3	1	4	0	-2	1	0	—	—	—	—	—
—Colorado	NHL	50	8	10	18	12	-6	1	0	—	—	—	—	—
—Boston	NHL	16	5	4	9	6	-4	3	0	—	—	—	—	—
00-01—Boston	NHL	77	19	39	58	28	6	5	0	—	—	—	—	—
NHL Totals (7 years)...........		491	113	150	263	121	32	22	10	29	8	2	10	14

RONNING, CLIFF C PREDATORS

PERSONAL: Born October 1, 1965, in Vancouver. ... 5-8/165. ... Shoots left.
TRANSACTIONS/CAREER NOTES: Selected by St. Louis Blues in seventh round (ninth Blues pick, 134th overall) of NHL entry draft (June 9, 1984). ... Injured groin (November 1988). ... Agreed to play in Italy for 1989-90 season (August 1989). ... Fractured right index finger (November 12, 1990); missed 12 games. ... Traded by Blues with LW Geoff Courtnall, D Robert Dirk, LW Sergio Momesso and fifth-round pick (RW Brian Loney) in 1992 draft to Vancouver Canucks for C Dan Quinn and D Garth Butcher (March 5, 1991). ... Sprained hand (January 4, 1993); missed five games. ... Separated shoulder (January 8, 1994); missed eight games. ... Strained groin (February 9, 1995); missed four games. ... Injured groin (October 8, 1995); missed two games. ... Signed as free agent by Phoenix Coyotes (July 2, 1996). ... Fractured hand (October 10, 1996); missed 12 games. ... Suffered from the flu (December 17, 1996); missed one game. ... Traded by Coyotes with D Richard Lintner to Nashville Predators for future considerations (October 31, 1998). ... Bruised knee (April 14, 1999); missed one game. ... Injured hamstring (January 7, 2001); missed two games.
HONORS: Won Stewart (Butch) Paul Memorial Trophy (1983-84). ... Named to WHL All-Star second team (1983-84). ... Won WHL Most Valuable Player Trophy (1984-85). ... Won Bob Brownridge Memorial Trophy (1984-85). ... Won Frank Boucher Memorial Trophy (1984-85). ... Named to WHL (West) All-Star first team (1984-85).
MISCELLANEOUS: Holds Nashville Predators all-time records for most goals (63), most assists (114) and most points (177).
STATISTICAL PLATEAUS: Three-goal games: 1986-87 (1), 1992-93 (1), 1995-96 (1). Total: 3.

		REGULAR SEASON								PLAYOFFS				
Season Team	League	Gms.	G	A	Pts.	PIM	+/-	PP	SH	Gms.	G	A	Pts.	PIM
82-83—New Westminster	BCJHL	52	82	68	150	42	...	...	...	—	—	—	—	—
83-84—New Westminster	WHL	71	69	67	136	10	...	...	...	9	8	13	21	10
84-85—New Westminster	WHL	70	*89	108	*197	20	...	...	...	11	10	14	24	4
85-86—Canadian nat'l team	Int'l	71	55	63	118	53	...	...	...	—	—	—	—	—
—St. Louis	NHL	—	—	—	—	—				5	1	1	2	2

Season Team	League	REGULAR SEASON								PLAYOFFS				
		Gms.	G	A	Pts.	PIM	+/-	PP	SH	Gms.	G	A	Pts.	PIM
86-87—Canadian nat'l team	Int'l	26	16	16	32	12	...	...	...	—	—	—	—	—
—St. Louis	NHL	42	11	14	25	6	-1	2	0	4	0	1	1	0
87-88—St. Louis	NHL	26	5	8	13	12	6	1	0	—	—	—	—	—
88-89—St. Louis	NHL	64	24	31	55	18	3	16	0	7	1	3	4	0
—Peoria	IHL	12	11	20	31	8	...	...	...	—	—	—	—	—
89-90—Asiago	Italy	42	76	60	136	30	...	...	...	6	7	12	19	4
90-91—St. Louis	NHL	48	14	18	32	10	2	5	0	—	—	—	—	—
—Vancouver	NHL	11	6	6	12	0	-2	2	0	6	6	3	9	12
91-92—Vancouver	NHL	80	24	47	71	42	18	6	0	13	8	5	13	6
92-93—Vancouver	NHL	79	29	56	85	30	19	10	0	12	2	9	11	6
93-94—Vancouver	NHL	76	25	43	68	42	7	10	0	24	5	10	15	16
94-95—Vancouver	NHL	41	6	19	25	27	-4	3	0	11	3	5	8	2
95-96—Vancouver	NHL	79	22	45	67	42	16	5	0	6	0	2	2	6
96-97—Phoenix	NHL	69	19	32	51	26	-9	8	0	7	0	7	7	12
97-98—Phoenix	NHL	80	11	44	55	36	5	3	0	6	1	3	4	4
98-99—Phoenix	NHL	7	2	5	7	2	3	2	0	—	—	—	—	—
—Nashville	NHL	72	18	35	53	40	-6	8	0	—	—	—	—	—
99-00—Nashville	NHL	82	26	36	62	34	-13	7	0	—	—	—	—	—
00-01—Nashville	NHL	80	19	43	62	28	4	6	0	—	—	—	—	—
NHL Totals (15 years)		936	261	482	743	395	48	94	0	101	27	49	76	66

RONNQVIST, JONAS   RW   MIGHTY DUCKS

PERSONAL: Born August 22, 1973, in Sweden. ... 6-1/200. ... Shoots left.
TRANSACTIONS/CAREER NOTES: Selected by Mighty Ducks of Anaheim in fourth round (third Mighty Ducks pick, 98th overall) of NHL entry draft (June 24, 2000). ... Strained knee (October 8, 2000); missed two games. ... Strained muscle in abdomen (March 24, 2001); missed final six games of season.

Season Team	League	REGULAR SEASON								PLAYOFFS				
		Gms.	G	A	Pts.	PIM	+/-	PP	SH	Gms.	G	A	Pts.	PIM
97-98—Lulea	Sweden	40	6	8	14	18	...	...	...	3	0	0	0	2
98-99—Lulea	Sweden	41	5	8	13	30	...	...	...	3	0	2	2	29
99-00—Lulea	Sweden	49	15	24	39	42	...	...	...	—	—	—	—	—
00-01—Anaheim	NHL	38	0	4	4	14	-7	0	0	—	—	—	—	—
—Cincinnati	AHL	13	3	2	5	6	...	...	...	—	—	—	—	—
NHL Totals (1 year)		38	0	4	4	14	-7	0	0					

ROSSITER, KYLE   D   PANTHERS

PERSONAL: Born June 9, 1980, in Edmonton. ... 6-3/218. ... Shoots left.
TRANSACTIONS/CAREER NOTES: Selected by Florida Panthers in second round (first Panthers pick, 30th overall) of NHL entry draft (June 27, 1998).
HONORS: Won Can.HL Scholastic Player of the Year Award (1997-98).

Season Team	League	REGULAR SEASON								PLAYOFFS				
		Gms.	G	A	Pts.	PIM	+/-	PP	SH	Gms.	G	A	Pts.	PIM
96-97—Spokane	WHL	50	0	2	2	65	...	...	...	9	0	0	0	6
97-98—Spokane	WHL	61	6	16	22	190	...	...	...	15	0	3	3	28
98-99—Spokane	WHL	71	4	17	21	206	...	...	...	—	—	—	—	—
99-00—Spokane	WHL	63	11	22	33	155	...	...	...	14	1	4	5	21
00-01—Louisville	AHL	78	2	5	7	110	...	...	...	—	—	—	—	—

ROUSSEL, DOMINIC   G

PERSONAL: Born February 22, 1970, in Hull, Que. ... 6-1/191. ... Catches left. ... Name pronounced roo-SEHL.
TRANSACTIONS/CAREER NOTES: Selected by Philadelphia Flyers in third round (fourth Flyers pick, 63rd overall) of NHL entry draft (June 11, 1988). ... Pulled groin (November 29, 1992); missed three games. ... Reinjured groin (December 11, 1992); missed 11 games. ... Suffered from the flu (March 24, 1994); missed three games. ... Suffered inner ear infection (March 2, 1995); missed five games. ... Traded by Flyers to Winnipeg Jets for G Tim Cheveldae and third-round pick (RW Chester Gallant) in 1996 draft (February 27, 1996). ... Signed as free agent by Flyers (July 10, 1996). ... Traded by Flyers with D Jeff Staples to Nashville Predators for seventh-round pick (G Cam Ondrik) in 1998 draft (June 27, 1998). ... Traded by Predators to Mighty Ducks of Anaheim for G Chris Mason and D Marc Moro (October 5, 1998). ... Suffered back spasms (April 7, 1999); missed two games. ... Claimed on waivers by Edmonton Oilers (January 10, 2001).
MISCELLANEOUS: Stopped a penalty shot attempt (vs. Stan Drulia, October 15, 1999; vs. Jeff Friesen, January 24, 2001).

Season Team	League	REGULAR SEASON							PLAYOFFS					
		Gms.	Min.	W	L	T	GA	SO	Avg.	Gms.	Min.	W	L	GA	SO	Avg.
87-88—Trois-Rivieres	QMJHL	51	2905	18	25	4	251	0	5.18	—	—	—	—	—	—	—
88-89—Shawinigan	QMJHL	46	2555	24	15	2	171	0	4.02	10	638	6	4	36	0	3.39
89-90—Shawinigan	QMJHL	37	1985	20	14	1	133	0	4.02	2	120	1	1	12	0	6.00
90-91—Hershey	AHL	45	2507	20	14	7	151	1	3.61	7	366	3	4	21	0	3.44
91-92—Hershey	AHL	35	2040	15	11	6	121	1	3.56	—	—	—	—	—	—	—
—Philadelphia	NHL	17	922	7	8	2	40	1	2.60	—	—	—	—	—	—	—
92-93—Philadelphia	NHL	34	1769	13	11	5	111	1	3.76	—	—	—	—	—	—	—
—Hershey	AHL	6	372	0	3	3	23	0	3.71	—	—	—	—	—	—	—
93-94—Philadelphia	NHL	60	3285	29	20	5	183	1	3.34	—	—	—	—	—	—	—
94-95—Philadelphia	NHL	19	1075	11	7	0	42	1	2.34	1	23	0	0	0	0	...
—Hershey	AHL	1	59	0	1	0	5	0	5.08	—	—	—	—	—	—	—

Season Team	League	REGULAR SEASON								PLAYOFFS						
		Gms.	Min	W	L	T	GA	SO	Avg.	Gms.	Min.	W	L	GA	SO	Avg.
95-96—Philadelphia	NHL	9	456	2	3	2	22	1	2.89	—	—	—	—	—	—	—
—Hershey	AHL	12	689	4	4	3	32	0	2.79	—	—	—	—	—	—	—
—Winnipeg	NHL	7	285	2	2	0	16	0	3.37	—	—	—	—	—	—	—
96-97—Philadelphia	AHL	36	1852	18	9	3	82	2	2.66	1	26	0	0	3	0	6.92
97-98—Canadian nat'l team	Int'l	41	2307	25	12	1	86	5	2.24	—	—	—	—	—	—	—
98-99—Anaheim	NHL	18	884	4	5	4	37	1	2.51	—	—	—	—	—	—	—
99-00—Anaheim	NHL	20	988	6	5	3	52	1	3.16	—	—	—	—	—	—	—
00-01—Anaheim	NHL	13	653	2	5	2	31	0	2.85	—	—	—	—	—	—	—
—Edmonton	NHL	8	348	1	4	0	21	0	3.62	—	—	—	—	—	—	—
NHL Totals (8 years)		205	10665	77	70	23	555	7	3.12	1	23	0	0	0	0	...

R ROY, ANDRE   RW   SENATORS

PERSONAL: Born February 8, 1975, in Port Chester, N.Y. ... 6-4/213. ... Shoots left. ... Full Name: Andre Christopher Roy. ... Name pronounced WAH.

TRANSACTIONS/CAREER NOTES: Selected by Boston Bruins in sixth round (fifth Bruins pick, 151st overall) of NHL entry draft (June 29, 1994). ... Signed as free agent by Ottawa Senators (March 19, 1999). ... Injured right knee (November 18, 1999); missed one game. ... Suffered back spasms (November 6, 2000); missed two games. ... Suffered from the flu (January 13, 2001); missed two games. ... Suspended two games by NHL for unsportsmanlike conduct (February 26, 2001). ... Strained groin (March 30, 2001); missed one game.

Season Team	League	REGULAR SEASON								PLAYOFFS				
		Gms.	G	A	Pts.	PIM	+/-	PP	SH	Gms.	G	A	Pts.	PIM
93-94—Beauport	QMJHL	33	6	7	13	125	...	...	...	—	—	—	—	—
—Chicoutimi	QMJHL	32	4	14	18	152	...	...	...	25	3	6	9	94
94-95—Chicoutimi	QMJHL	20	15	8	23	90	...	...	...	—	—	—	—	—
—Drummondville	QMJHL	34	18	13	31	233	...	...	...	4	2	0	2	34
95-96—Providence	AHL	58	7	8	15	167	...	...	...	1	0	0	0	10
—Boston	NHL	3	0	0	0	0	0	0	0	—	—	—	—	—
96-97—Providence	AHL	50	17	11	28	234	...	...	...	—	—	—	—	—
—Boston	NHL	10	0	2	2	12	-5	0	0	—	—	—	—	—
97-98—Providence	AHL	36	3	11	14	154	...	...	...	—	—	—	—	—
—Charlotte	ECHL	27	10	8	18	132	...	...	...	7	2	3	5	34
98-99—Fort Wayne	IHL	65	15	6	21	395	...	...	...	2	0	0	0	11
99-00—Ottawa	NHL	73	4	3	7	145	3	0	0	5	0	0	0	2
00-01—Ottawa	NHL	64	3	5	8	169	1	0	0	2	0	0	0	16
NHL Totals (4 years)		150	7	10	17	326	-1	0	0	7	0	0	0	18

ROY, PATRICK   G   AVALANCHE

PERSONAL: Born October 5, 1965, in Quebec City. ... 6-0/192. ... Catches left. ... Name pronounced WAH.

TRANSACTIONS/CAREER NOTES: Selected by Montreal Canadiens in third round (fourth Canadiens pick, 51st overall) of NHL entry draft (June 9, 1984). ... Suspended eight games by NHL for slashing (October 19, 1987). ... Sprained left knee ligaments (December 12, 1990); missed nine games. ... Tore left ankle ligaments (January 27, 1991); missed 14 games. ... Reinjured left ankle (March 16, 1991). ... Strained hip flexor (March 6, 1993). ... Suffered stiff neck (December 11, 1993); missed two games. ... Strained neck (December 22, 1993); missed four games. ... Traded by Canadiens with RW Mike Keane to Colorado Avalanche for G Jocelyn Thibault, LW Martin Rucinsky and RW Andrei Kovalenko (December 6, 1995). ... Sprained thumb (January 23, 1997); missed two games. ... Injured shoulder (March 26, 1997); missed two games. ... Partially dislocated shoulder (November 17, 1997); missed two games. ... Injured left knee (December 26, 1998); missed four games. ... Suffered back spasms (January 4, 1999); missed four games. ... Injured groin (February 21, 1999); missed two games. ... Injured neck (February 15, 2000); missed one game. ... Injured groin (February 18, 2000); missed two games. ... Suffered tendinitis in knee (March 20, 2001); missed one game.

HONORS: Won Conn Smythe Trophy (1985-86, 1992-93 and 2000-01). ... Named to NHL All-Rookie team (1985-86). ... Shared William M. Jennings Trophy with Brian Hayward (1986-87 through 1988-89). ... Named to NHL All-Star second team (1987-88 and 1990-91). ... Named to The Sporting News All-Star first team (1988-89, 1989-90 and 1991-92). ... Won Trico Goaltender Award (1988-89 and 1989-90). ... Named to NHL All-Star first team (1988-89, 1989-90 and 1991-92). ... Won Vezina Trophy (1988-89, 1989-90 and 1991-92). ... Played in NHL All-Star Game (1988, 1990-1994, 1997, 1998 and 2001). ... Named to The Sporting News All-Star second team (1990-91). ... Won William M. Jennings Trophy (1991-92).

RECORDS: Holds NHL career record for most wins by goaltender—484. ... Holds NHL career record for most 30-or-more win seasons by goaltender—11. ... Holds NHL career playoff records for most games played by goaltender—219; most wins by goaltender—137; most minutes played by goaltender —13,545; and most shutouts—19. ... Shares NHL single-season playoff record for most shutouts—4 (2000). ... Shares NHL single-season playoff records for most wins by goaltender—16 (1993, 1996 and 2000); and most consecutive wins by goaltender—11 (1993).

MISCELLANEOUS: Member of Stanley Cup championship team (1986, 1993, 1996 and 2001). ... Holds Colorado Avalanche franchise all-time records for most games played in by a goalie (352), wins (195), shutouts (23) and goals-against average (2.39). ... Stopped a penalty shot attempt (vs. Dan Daoust, January 1, 1986; vs. Ville Peltonen, March 5, 1996; vs. Jamie Baker, March 28, 1996; vs. Andrew Cassels, November 30, 1999). ... Allowed a penalty shot goal (vs. Michel Goulet, January 10, 1987; vs. Jock Callender, March 18, 1989; vs. Pierre Turgeon, October 17, 1990; vs. Kevin Miller, October 10, 1991; vs. Theoren Fleury, October 22, 1996; vs. Tom Chorske, March 7, 1998).

STATISTICAL NOTES: Led NHL in save percentage with .900 in 1987-88, .908 in 1988-89, .912 in 1989-90 and .914 in 1991-92.

Season Team	League	REGULAR SEASON								PLAYOFFS						
		Gms.	Min	W	L	T	GA	SO	Avg.	Gms.	Min.	W	L	GA	SO	Avg.
82-83—Granby	QMJHL	54	2808	13	35	1	293	0	6.26	—	—	—	—	—	—	—
83-84—Granby	QMJHL	61	3585	29	29	1	265	0	4.44	4	244	0	4	22	0	5.41
84-85—Granby	QMJHL	44	2463	16	25	1	228	0	5.55	—	—	—	—	—	—	—
—Montreal	NHL	1	20	1	0	0	0	0	...	—	—	—	—	—	—	—
—Sherbrooke	AHL	1	60	1	0	0	4	0	4.00	*13	*769	10	3	37	0	*2.89
85-86—Montreal	NHL	47	2651	23	18	3	148	1	3.35	20	1218	*15	5	39	†1	1.92
86-87—Montreal	NHL	46	2686	22	16	6	131	1	2.93	6	330	4	2	22	0	4.00
87-88—Montreal	NHL	45	2586	23	12	9	125	3	2.90	8	430	3	4	24	0	3.35
88-89—Montreal	NHL	48	2744	33	5	6	113	4	*2.47	19	1206	13	6	42	2	*2.09

Season Team	League	REGULAR SEASON								PLAYOFFS						
		Gms.	Min	W	L	T	GA	SO	Avg.	Gms.	Min.	W	L	GA	SO	Avg.
89-90—Montreal	NHL	54	3173	31	16	5	134	3	2.53	11	641	5	6	26	1	2.43
90-91—Montreal	NHL	48	2835	25	15	6	128	1	2.71	13	785	7	5	40	0	3.06
91-92—Montreal	NHL	67	3935	36	22	8	155	†5	*2.36	11	686	4	7	30	1	2.62
92-93—Montreal	NHL	62	3595	31	25	5	192	2	3.20	20	1293	*16	4	46	0	*2.13
93-94—Montreal	NHL	68	3867	35	17	11	161	†7	2.50	6	375	3	3	16	0	2.56
94-95—Montreal	NHL	†43	2566	17	20	6	127	1	2.97	—	—	—	—	—	—	—
95-96—Montreal	NHL	22	1260	12	9	1	62	1	2.95	—	—	—	—	—	—	—
—Colorado	NHL	39	2305	22	15	1	103	1	2.68	22	*1454	*16	6	*51	*3	2.10
96-97—Colorado	NHL	62	3698	*38	15	7	143	7	2.32	17	1034	10	7	38	3	2.21
97-98—Colorado	NHL	65	3835	31	19	13	153	4	2.39	7	430	3	4	18	0	2.51
—Can. Olympic team	Int'l	6	369	4	2	0	9	1	1.46	—	—	—	—	—	—	—
98-99—Colorado	NHL	61	3648	32	19	8	139	5	2.29	19	1173	11	†8	*52	1	2.66
99-00—Colorado	NHL	63	3704	32	21	8	141	2	2.28	17	1039	11	6	31	3	1.79
00-01—Colorado	NHL	62	3585	40	13	7	132	4	2.21	23	1451	*16	7	41	†4	*1.70
NHL Totals (17 years)		903	52693	484	277	110	2287	52	2.60	219	13545	137	80	516	19	2.29

ROZSIVAL, MICHAL D PENGUINS

PERSONAL: Born September 3, 1978, in Vlasim, Czechoslovakia. ... 6-1/208. ... Shoots right. ... Name pronounced RAH-sih-vahl.
TRANSACTIONS/CAREER NOTES: Selected by Pittsburgh Penguins in fourth round (fifth Penguins pick, 105th overall) of NHL entry draft (June 22, 1996). ... Strained hip flexor (March 21, 2000); missed two games.
HONORS: Named to Can.HL All-Star second team (1997-98). ... Won Bill Hunter Trophy (1997-98). ... Named to WHL (East) All-Star first team (1997-98).

Season Team	League	REGULAR SEASON								PLAYOFFS				
		Gms.	G	A	Pts.	PIM	+/-	PP	SH	Gms.	G	A	Pts.	PIM
94-95—Czech Rep.	Czech Rep.	31	8	13	21	...	...	...	...	—	—	—	—	—
95-96—Czech Rep.	Czech Rep.	36	3	4	7	...	...	...	...	—	—	—	—	—
96-97—Swift Current	WHL	63	8	31	39	80	...	...	...	10	0	6	6	15
97-98—Swift Current	WHL	71	14	55	69	122	...	...	...	12	0	5	5	33
98-99—Syracuse	AHL	49	3	22	25	72	...	...	...	—	—	—	—	—
99-00—Pittsburgh	NHL	75	4	17	21	48	11	1	0	2	0	0	0	4
00-01—Pittsburgh	NHL	30	1	4	5	26	3	0	0	—	—	—	—	—
—Wilkes-Barre/Scranton	AHL	29	8	8	16	32	...	...	...	21	3	*19	22	23
NHL Totals (2 years)		105	5	21	26	74	14	1	0	2	0	0	0	4

RUCCHIN, STEVE C MIGHTY DUCKS

PERSONAL: Born July 4, 1971, in Thunder Bay, Ont. ... 6-2/212. ... Shoots left. ... Full Name: Steven Andrew Rucchin. ... Name pronounced ROO-chihn.
TRANSACTIONS/CAREER NOTES: Selected by Mighty Ducks of Anaheim in first round (first Mighty Ducks pick, second overall) of NHL supplemental draft (June 28, 1994). ... Suffered from the flu (March 7, 1995); missed two games. ... Sprained left knee (November 27, 1995); missed 18 games. ... Strained groin (October 3, 1997); missed eight games. ... Strained left knee (April 9, 1998); missed two games. ... Injured groin (March 18, 1999); missed three games. ... Reinjured groin (March 31, 1999); missed seven games. ... Suffered infected left ankle (December 28, 1999); missed 11 games. ... Fractured hand (September 22, 2000); missed six games. ... Fractured nose and cheek bone (November 15, 2000) and underwent surgery; missed 10 games. ... Suffered from concussion (December 13, 2001); missed remainder of season.
HONORS: Named OUAA Player of the Year (1993-94). ... Named to CIAU All-Star first team (1993-94).

Season Team	League	REGULAR SEASON								PLAYOFFS				
		Gms.	G	A	Pts.	PIM	+/-	PP	SH	Gms.	G	A	Pts.	PIM
90-91—Univ. of W. Ontario	OUAA	34	13	16	29	14	...	...	...	—	—	—	—	—
91-92—Univ. of W. Ontario	OUAA	37	28	34	62	36	...	...	...	—	—	—	—	—
92-93—Univ. of W. Ontario	OUAA	34	22	26	48	16	...	...	...	—	—	—	—	—
93-94—Univ. of W. Ontario	OUAA	35	30	23	53	30	...	...	...	—	—	—	—	—
94-95—San Diego	IHL	41	11	15	26	14	...	...	...	—	—	—	—	—
—Anaheim	NHL	43	6	11	17	23	7	0	0	—	—	—	—	—
95-96—Anaheim	NHL	64	19	25	44	12	3	8	1	—	—	—	—	—
96-97—Anaheim	NHL	79	19	48	67	24	26	6	1	8	1	2	3	10
97-98—Anaheim	NHL	72	17	36	53	13	8	8	1	—	—	—	—	—
98-99—Anaheim	NHL	69	23	39	62	22	11	5	1	4	0	3	3	0
99-00—Anaheim	NHL	71	19	38	57	16	9	10	0	—	—	—	—	—
00-01—Anaheim	NHL	16	3	5	8	0	-5	2	0	—	—	—	—	—
NHL Totals (7 years)		414	106	202	308	110	59	39	4	12	1	5	6	10

RUCINSKI, MIKE D HURRICANES

PERSONAL: Born March 30, 1975, in Trenton, Mich. ... 5-11/188. ... Shoots left.
TRANSACTIONS/CAREER NOTES: Selected by Hartford Whalers in ninth round (eighth Whalers pick, 217th overall) of NHL entry draft (July 8, 1995). ... Whalers franchise moved to North Carolina and renamed Carolina Hurricanes for 1997-98 season; NHL approved move on June 25, 1997.

Season Team	League	REGULAR SEASON								PLAYOFFS				
		Gms.	G	A	Pts.	PIM	+/-	PP	SH	Gms.	G	A	Pts.	PIM
92-93—Det. Jr. Red Wings	OHL	66	6	13	19	59	...	...	...	15	0	4	4	12
93-94—Det. Jr. Red Wings	OHL	66	2	26	28	58	...	...	...	17	0	7	7	15
94-95—Det. Jr. Red Wings	OHL	64	9	18	27	61	...	...	...	21	3	3	6	8
95-96—Detroit	OHL	51	10	26	36	65	...	...	...	11	2	4	6	14

Season Team	League	REGULAR SEASON								PLAYOFFS				
		Gms.	G	A	Pts.	PIM	+/-	PP	SH	Gms.	G	A	Pts.	PIM
96-97—Springfield	AHL	6	0	1	1	0	...	...	...	—	—	—	—	—
—Richmond	ECHL	61	20	23	43	85	...	...	...	8	2	6	8	18
97-98—New Haven	AHL	65	5	17	22	50	...	...	...	1	0	0	0	0
—Carolina	NHL	9	0	1	1	2	0	0	0	—	—	—	—	—
—Cleveland	IHL	2	0	0	0	4	...	...	...	—	—	—	—	—
98-99—Carolina	NHL	15	0	1	1	8	1	0	0	—	—	—	—	—
—New Haven	AHL	23	2	6	8	27	...	...	...	—	—	—	—	—
99-00—Cincinnati	IHL	66	3	10	13	34	...	...	...	11	0	0	0	28
00-01—Cincinnati	IHL	79	1	22	23	46	...	...	...	5	0	0	0	2
—Carolina	NHL	2	0	0	0	0	0	0	0	—	—	—	—	—
NHL Totals (3 years)		26	0	2	2	10	1	0	0					

R

RUCINSKY, MARTIN   LW   CANADIENS

PERSONAL: Born March 11, 1971, in Most, Czechoslovakia. ... 6-1/205. ... Shoots left. ... Name pronounced roo-SHIHN-skee.

TRANSACTIONS/CAREER NOTES: Selected by Edmonton Oilers in first round (second Oilers pick, 20th overall) of NHL entry draft (June 22, 1991). ... Traded by Oilers to Quebec Nordiques for G Ron Tugnutt and LW Brad Zavisha (March 10, 1992). ... Suffered from the flu (February 28, 1993); missed one game. ... Bruised buttocks (December 3, 1994); missed one game. ... Sprained right wrist (January 11, 1994); missed one game. ... Fractured left cheekbone (January 30, 1994); missed four games. ... Suffered hairline fracture of right wrist (March 7, 1994); missed one game. ... Reinjured right wrist (March 21, 1994); missed six games. ... Reinjured right wrist (April 5, 1994); missed one game. ... Played in Europe during 1994-95 NHL lockout. ... Separated shoulder (February 25, 1995); missed 17 games. ... Reinjured shoulder (April 6, 1995); missed remainder of season. ... Nordiques franchise moved to Colorado and renamed Avalanche for 1995-96 season (June 21, 1995). ... Injured groin (November 28, 1995); missed one game. ... Traded by Avalanche with G Jocelyn Thibault and RW Andrei Kovalenko to Montreal Canadiens for G Patrick Roy and RW Mike Keane (December 6, 1995). ... Sprained right knee (April 6, 1996); missed two games. ... Injured hand (October 19, 1996); missed one game. ... Strained knee (November 25, 1996); missed one game. ... Separated shoulder (December 28, 1996); missed 10 games. ... Bruised foot (October 17, 1997); missed one game. ... Sprained ankle (April 4, 1998); missed three games. ... Injured shoulder (March 6, 1999); missed three games. ... Suffered concussion (November 16, 1999); missed one game. ... Suffered back spasms (March 25, 2000); missed one game. ... Sprained medial collateral ligament in knee (December 18, 2000); missed 21 games. ... Bruised left thigh (March 12, 2001); missed four games.

HONORS: Played in NHL All-Star Game (2000).

MISCELLANEOUS: Mermber of gold-medal-winning Czech Republic Olympic team (1998). ... Scored on a penalty shot (vs. Kevin Weekes, March 29, 2001). ... Failed to score on a penalty shot (vs. Corey Hirsch, January 2, 1999; vs. Jamie Storr, December 11, 1999; vs. Jean-Sebastien Aubin, February 28, 2001).

STATISTICAL PLATEAUS: Three-goal games: 1995-96 (1), 1996-97 (1). Total: 2.

Season Team	League	REGULAR SEASON								PLAYOFFS				
		Gms.	G	A	Pts.	PIM	+/-	PP	SH	Gms.	G	A	Pts.	PIM
88-89—CHZ Litvinov	Czech.	3	1	0	1	2	...	...	...	—	—	—	—	—
89-90—CHZ Litvinov	Czech.	47	12	6	18		...	...	...	—	—	—	—	—
90-91—CHZ Litvinov	Czech.	49	23	18	41	79	...	...	...	—	—	—	—	—
—Czechoslovakia Jr.	Czech.	7	9	5	14	2	...	...	...	—	—	—	—	—
91-92—Cape Breton	AHL	35	11	12	23	34	...	...	...	—	—	—	—	—
—Edmonton	NHL	2	0	0	0	0	-3	0	0	—	—	—	—	—
—Halifax	AHL	7	1	1	2	6	...	...	...	—	—	—	—	—
—Quebec	NHL	4	1	1	2	2	1	0	0	—	—	—	—	—
92-93—Quebec	NHL	77	18	30	48	51	16	4	0	6	1	1	2	4
93-94—Quebec	NHL	60	9	23	32	58	4	4	0	—	—	—	—	—
94-95—Chem. Litvinov	Czech Rep.	13	12	10	22	34	...	...	...	—	—	—	—	—
—Quebec	NHL	20	3	6	9	14	5	0	0	—	—	—	—	—
95-96—Vsetin	Czech Rep.	1	1	1	2	0	...	...	...	—	—	—	—	—
—Colorado	NHL	22	4	11	15	14	10	0	0	—	—	—	—	—
—Montreal	NHL	56	25	35	60	54	8	9	2	—	—	—	—	—
96-97—Montreal	NHL	70	28	27	55	62	1	6	3	5	0	0	0	4
97-98—Montreal	NHL	78	21	32	53	84	13	5	3	10	3	0	3	4
—Czech Rep. Oly. team..	Int'l	6	3	1	4	4	...	...	...	—	—	—	—	—
98-99—Montreal	NHL	73	17	17	34	50	-25	5	0	—	—	—	—	—
99-00—Montreal	NHL	80	25	24	49	70	1	7	1	—	—	—	—	—
00-01—Montreal	NHL	57	16	22	38	66	-5	5	1	—	—	—	—	—
NHL Totals (10 years)		599	167	228	395	525	26	45	10	21	4	1	5	12

RUDKOWSKY, CODY   G   BLUES

PERSONAL: Born July 21, 1978, in Willingdon, Alta. ... 6-1/200. ... Catches left.

TRANSACTIONS/CAREER NOTES: Signed as non-drafted free agent by St. Louis Blues (March 25, 1999).

HONORS: Won Del Wilson Trophy (1998-99). ... Won Four Broncos Memorial Trophy (1998-99). ... Won Can.HL Goaltender of the Year Award (1998-99). ... Named to WHL (West) All-Star first team (1998-99). ... Named to Can.HL All-Star first team (1998-99).

Season Team	League	REGULAR SEASON								PLAYOFFS						
		Gms.	Min	W	L	T	GA	SO	Avg.	Gms.	Min.	W	L	GA	SO	Avg.
95-96—Seattle	WHL	2	21	0	0	0	3	0	8.57	—	—	—	—	—	—	—
96-97—Seattle	WHL	40	2162	19	16	1	124	0	3.44	1	30	1	0	0	0	...
97-98—Seattle	WHL	53	2805	20	22	3	175	1	3.74	5	278	1	4	18	0	3.88
98-99—Seattle	WHL	64	3665	34	17	*10	177	*7	2.90	11	637	5	*6	31	1	2.92
99-00—Worcester	AHL	28	1405	9	7	6	75	0	3.20	—	—	—	—	—	—	—
—Peoria	ECHL	11	599	7	4	0	32	0	3.21	2	119	1	1	6	0	3.03
00-01—Worcester	AHL	25	1477	13	8	3	66	3	2.68	—	—	—	—	—	—	—

RUMBLE, DARREN D BLUES

PERSONAL: Born January 23, 1969, in Barrie, Ont. ... 6-1/200. ... Shoots left. ... Full Name: Darren William Rumble.
TRANSACTIONS/CAREER NOTES: Selected by Philadelphia Flyers in first round (first Flyers pick, 20th overall) of NHL entry draft (June 13, 1987). ... Stretched knee ligaments (November 27, 1988). ... Selected by Ottawa Senators in NHL expansion draft (June 18, 1992). ... Bruised thigh (November 29, 1993); missed four games. ... Injured thumb (March 5, 1994); missed one game. ... Signed as free agent by Flyers (July 31, 1995). ... Signed as free agent by St. Louis Blues (January 31, 2001). ... Injured hip (February 15, 2001); missed two games. ... Suspended two games by NHL for kneeing incident (February 28, 2001). ... Injured hip (March 10, 2001); missed one game.
HONORS: Named to AHL All-Star second team (1994-95). ... Won Eddie Shore Award (1996-97). ... Named to AHL All-Star first team (1996-97).

		REGULAR SEASON								PLAYOFFS				
Season Team	League	Gms.	G	A	Pts.	PIM	+/-	PP	SH	Gms.	G	A	Pts.	PIM
85-86—Barrie Jr. B	OHA	46	14	32	46	91	...	...	...	—	—	—	—	—
86-87—Kitchener	OHL	64	11	32	43	44	...	...	...	4	0	1	1	9
87-88—Kitchener	OHL	55	15	50	65	64	...	...	...	—	—	—	—	—
88-89—Kitchener	OHL	46	11	28	39	25	...	...	...	5	1	0	1	2
89-90—Hershey	AHL	57	2	13	15	31	...	...	...	—	—	—	—	—
90-91—Philadelphia	NHL	3	1	0	1	0	1	0	0	—	—	—	—	—
—Hershey	AHL	73	6	35	41	48	...	...	...	3	0	5	5	2
91-92—Hershey	AHL	79	12	54	66	118	...	...	...	6	0	3	3	2
92-93—Ottawa	NHL	69	3	13	16	61	-24	0	0	—	—	—	—	—
—New Haven	AHL	2	1	0	1	0	...	...	...	—	—	—	—	—
93-94—Ottawa	NHL	70	6	9	15	116	-50	0	0	—	—	—	—	—
—Prin. Edward Island	AHL	3	2	0	2	0	...	...	...	—	—	—	—	—
94-95—Prin. Edward Island	AHL	70	7	46	53	77	...	...	...	11	0	6	6	4
95-96—Philadelphia	NHL	5	0	0	0	4	0	0	0	—	—	—	—	—
—Hershey	AHL	58	13	37	50	83	...	...	...	5	0	0	0	6
96-97—Philadelphia	AHL	72	18	44	62	83	...	...	...	7	0	3	3	19
—Philadelphia	NHL	10	0	0	0	0	-2	0	0	—	—	—	—	—
97-98—San Antonio	IHL	46	7	22	29	47	...	...	...	—	—	—	—	—
98-99—Grand Rapids	IHL	53	6	22	28	44	...	...	...	—	—	—	—	—
—Utah	IHL	10	1	4	5	10	...	...	...	—	—	—	—	—
99-00—Grand Rapids	IHL	29	3	10	13	20	...	...	...	—	—	—	—	—
—Worcester	AHL	39	0	17	17	31	...	...	...	9	0	2	2	6
00-01—Worcester	AHL	53	6	24	30	65	...	...	...	8	0	1	1	10
—St. Louis	NHL	12	0	4	4	27	7	0	0	—	—	—	—	—
NHL Totals (6 years)		169	10	26	36	208	-68	0	0					

RUUTU, JARKKO RW CANUCKS

PERSONAL: Born August 23, 1975, in Vantaa, Finland. ... 6-2/194. ... Shoots left. ... Brother of Tuomo Ruutu, center/right wing, Chicago Blackhawks organization; brother of Mikko Ruutu, left wing, Ottawa Senators organization.
TRANSACTIONS/CAREER NOTES: Selected by Vancouver Canucks in third round (third Canucks pick, 68th overall) of NHL entry draft (June 27, 1998).

		REGULAR SEASON								PLAYOFFS				
Season Team	League	Gms.	G	A	Pts.	PIM	+/-	PP	SH	Gms.	G	A	Pts.	PIM
91-92—HIFK Helsinki	Finland Jr.	1	0	0	0	0	...	...	...	—	—	—	—	—
92-93—HIFK Helsinki	Finland Jr.	34	26	21	47	53	...	...	...	—	—	—	—	—
93-94—HIFK Helsinki	Finland Jr.	19	9	12	21	44	...	...	...	—	—	—	—	—
94-95—HIFK Helsinki	Finland Jr.	35	26	22	48	117	...	...	...	—	—	—	—	—
95-96—Michigan Tech	WCHA	39	12	10	22	96	...	...	...	—	—	—	—	—
96-97—HIFK Helsinki	Finland	48	11	10	21	155	...	...	...	—	—	—	—	—
97-98—HIFK Helsinki	Finland	37	10	10	20	87	...	...	...	8	7	4	11	10
98-99—HIFK Helsinki	Finland	25	10	4	14	136	...	...	...	9	0	2	2	43
99-00—Syracuse	AHL	65	26	32	58	164	...	...	...	4	3	1	4	8
—Vancouver	NHL	8	0	1	1	6	-1	0	0	—	—	—	—	—
00-01—Kansas City	IHL	46	11	18	29	111	...	...	...	—	—	—	—	—
—Vancouver	NHL	21	3	3	6	32	1	0	1	4	0	1	1	8
NHL Totals (2 years)		29	3	4	7	38	0	0	1	4	0	1	1	8

RYBIN, MAXIM RW MIGHTY DUCKS

PERSONAL: Born June 15, 1981, in Moscow, U.S.S.R. ... 5-9/176. ... Shoots right.
TRANSACTIONS/CAREER NOTES: Selected by Mighty Ducks of Anaheim in fifth round (fourth Mighty Ducks pick, 141st overall) of NHL entry draft (June 26, 1999).

		REGULAR SEASON								PLAYOFFS				
Season Team	League	Gms.	G	A	Pts.	PIM	+/-	PP	SH	Gms.	G	A	Pts.	PIM
96-97—Spartak Moscow	Russian	6	0	0	0	0	...	...	...	—	—	—	—	—
97-98—Spartak Moscow	Russian	5	0	0	0	2	...	...	...	—	—	—	—	—
—Spartak-2 Moscow	Rus. Div. III	25	13	5	18	26	...	...	...	—	—	—	—	—
98-99—Spartak Moscow	Russian	41	13	8	21	52	...	...	...	—	—	—	—	—
99-00—Sarnia	OHL	66	29	27	56	47	...	...	...	7	4	1	5	2
00-01—Sarnia	OHL	67	34	36	70	60	...	...	...	4	0	3	3	2

R

RYCROFT, MARK   RW   BLUES

PERSONAL: Born July 12, 1978, in Nanaimo, B.C. ... 5-11/197. ... Shoots right.
TRANSACTIONS/CAREER NOTES: Signed as non-drafted free agent by St. Louis Blues (May 15, 2000).

		REGULAR SEASON								PLAYOFFS				
Season Team	League	Gms.	G	A	Pts.	PIM	+/-	PP	SH	Gms.	G	A	Pts.	PIM
97-98—Univ. of Denver..........	WCHA	35	15	17	32	28	...	...	...	—	—	—	—	—
98-99—Univ. of Denver..........	WCHA	41	19	18	37	36	...	...	...	—	—	—	—	—
99-00—Univ. of Denver..........	WCHA	41	17	17	34	87	...	...	...	—	—	—	—	—
00-01—Worcester	AHL	71	24	26	50	68	...	...	...	11	2	5	7	4

SACCO, JOE   RW   CAPITALS

PERSONAL: Born February 4, 1969, in Medford, Mass. ... 6-1/190. ... Shoots left. ... Full Name: Joseph William Sacco. ... Brother of David Sacco, left winger with Toronto Maple Leafs (1993-94) and Mighty Ducks of Anaheim (1994-95 and 1995-96). ... Name pronounced SA-koh.
TRANSACTIONS/CAREER NOTES: Selected by Toronto Maple Leafs in fourth round (fourth Maple Leafs pick, 71st overall) of NHL entry draft (June 13, 1987). ... Selected by Mighty Ducks of Anaheim in NHL expansion draft (June 24, 1993). ... Bruised left thumb (February 5, 1995); missed seven games. ... Strained chest muscle (January 22, 1997); missed five games. ... Traded by Mighty Ducks with D J.J. Daigneault and C Mark Janssens to New York Islanders for C Travis Green, D Doug Houda and RW Tony Tuzzolino (February 6, 1998). ... Strained hip flexor (March 14, 1998); missed one game. ... Injured wrist (November 12, 1998); missed four games. ... Injured shoulder (April 10, 1999) and underwent surgery; missed final three games of season. ... Signed as free agent by Washington Capitals (July 27, 1999). ... Bruised leg (November 26, 1999); missed two games. ... Suffered from the flu (February 3, 2000); missed one game. ... Strained hip flexor (November 17, 2000); missed four games. ... Bruised shoulder (January 18, 2001); missed three games. ... Bruised shoulder (February 1, 2001); missed six games.
MISCELLANEOUS: Scored on a penalty shot (vs. Jocelyn Thibault, November 12, 1997; vs. Arturs Irbe, March 30, 2001).

		REGULAR SEASON								PLAYOFFS				
Season Team	League	Gms.	G	A	Pts.	PIM	+/-	PP	SH	Gms.	G	A	Pts.	PIM
85-86—Medford H.S.	Mass. H.S.	20	30	30	60	...	...	...	...	—	—	—	—	—
86-87—Medford H.S.	Mass. H.S.	21	22	32	54	...	...	...	...	—	—	—	—	—
87-88—Boston University	Hockey East	34	14	22	36	38	...	...	...	—	—	—	—	—
88-89—Boston University	Hockey East	33	21	19	40	66	...	...	...	—	—	—	—	—
89-90—Boston University	Hockey East	44	28	24	52	70	...	...	...	—	—	—	—	—
90-91—Newmarket	AHL	49	18	17	35	24	...	...	...	—	—	—	—	—
—Toronto	NHL	20	0	5	5	2	-5	0	0	—	—	—	—	—
91-92—U.S. national team	Int'l	50	11	26	37	51	...	...	...	—	—	—	—	—
—U.S. Olympic team ...	Int'l	8	0	2	2	0	...	...	...	—	—	—	—	—
—Toronto	NHL	17	7	4	11	4	8	0	0	—	—	—	—	—
—St. John's..................	AHL	—	—	—	—	—	...	...	...	1	1	1	2	0
92-93—Toronto	NHL	23	4	4	8	8	-4	0	0	—	—	—	—	—
—St. John's..................	AHL	37	14	16	30	45	...	...	...	7	6	4	10	2
93-94—Anaheim	NHL	84	19	18	37	61	-11	3	1	—	—	—	—	—
94-95—Anaheim	NHL	41	10	8	18	23	-8	2	0	—	—	—	—	—
95-96—Anaheim	NHL	76	13	14	27	40	1	1	2	—	—	—	—	—
96-97—Anaheim	NHL	77	12	17	29	35	1	1	1	11	2	0	2	2
97-98—Anaheim	NHL	55	8	11	19	24	-1	0	2	—	—	—	—	—
—New York Islanders.....	NHL	25	3	3	6	10	1	0	0	—	—	—	—	—
98-99—New York Islanders.....	NHL	73	3	0	3	45	-24	0	1	—	—	—	—	—
99-00—Washington	NHL	79	7	16	23	50	7	0	0	5	0	0	0	4
00-01—Washington	NHL	69	7	7	14	48	4	0	0	6	0	0	0	2
NHL Totals (11 years).........		639	93	107	200	350	-31	7	7	22	2	0	2	8

SAFRONOV, KIRILL   D   COYOTES

PERSONAL: Born February 26, 1981, in Leningrad, U.S.S.R. ... 6-2/196. ... Shoots left.
TRANSACTIONS/CAREER NOTES: Selected by Phoenix Coyotes in first round (second Coyotes pick, 19th overall) of NHL entry draft (June 26, 1999).
HONORS: Won Raymond Lagace Trophy (1999-2000).

		REGULAR SEASON								PLAYOFFS				
Season Team	League	Gms.	G	A	Pts.	PIM	+/-	PP	SH	Gms.	G	A	Pts.	PIM
96-97—SKA St. Petersburg.....	Russian	1	0	0	0	0	...	...	...	—	—	—	—	—
97-98—SKA St. Petersburg.....	Russian	9	0	1	1	4	...	...	...	—	—	—	—	—
—SKA-2 St. Petersburg .	Rus. Div. III	34	4	3	7	36	...	...	...	—	—	—	—	—
98-99—SKA St. Petersburg.....	Russian	35	1	1	2	26	...	...	...	—	—	—	—	—
99-00—Quebec	QMJHL	55	11	32	43	95	...	...	...	11	2	4	6	14
00-01—Springfield	AHL	66	5	13	18	77	...	...	...	—	—	—	—	—

SAKIC, JOE   C   AVALANCHE

PERSONAL: Born July 7, 1969, in Burnaby, B.C. ... 5-11/190. ... Shoots left. ... Full Name: Joseph Steve Sakic. ... Brother of Brian Sakic, left winger with Washington Capitals (1990-91 and 1991-92) and New York Rangers organizations (1992-93 through 1994-95). ... Name pronounced SAK-ihk.
TRANSACTIONS/CAREER NOTES: Selected by Quebec Nordiques in first round (second Nordiques pick, 15th overall) of NHL entry draft (June 13, 1987). ... Sprained right ankle (November 28, 1988). ... Developed bursitis in left ankle (January 21, 1992); missed three games. ... Suffered recurrence of bursitis in left ankle (January 30, 1992); missed eight games. ... Injured eye (January 2, 1993); missed six games. ... Nordiques franchise moved to Colorado and renamed Avalanche for 1995-96 season (June 21, 1995). ... Lacerated calf (January 4, 1997); missed 17 games. ... Injured knee (February 18, 1998); missed 18 games. ... Suspended one game and fined $1,000 by NHL for kneeing

incident (April 21, 1998). ... Sprained right shoulder (December 17, 1998); missed seven games. ... Injured rib cartilage (November 8, 1999); missed six games. ... Reinjured rib cartilage (November 26, 1999); missed 13 games. ... Suffered from the flu (January 18, 2000); missed one game. ... Injured groin (January 25, 2000); missed two games.

HONORS: Won WHL (East) Most Valuable Player Trophy (1986-87). ... Won WHL (East) Stewart (Butch) Paul Memorial Trophy (1986-87). ... Named to WHL All-Star second team (1986-87). ... Won Can.HL Player of the Year Award (1987-88). ... Won Four Broncos Memorial Trophy (1987-88). ... Shared Bob Clarke Trophy with Theoren Fleury (1987-88). ... Won WHL Player of the Year Award (1987-88). ... Named to WHL (East) All-Star first team (1987-88). ... Played in NHL All-Star Game (1990-1994, 1996, 1998, 2000 and 2001). ... Won Conn Smythe Trophy (1995-96). ... Named to play in NHL All-Star Game (1997); replaced by RW Teemu Selanne due to injury. ... Named to NHL All-Star first team (2000-01). ... Named to THE SPORTING NEWS All-Star first team (2000-01). ... Won Hart Memorial Trophy (2000-01). ... Won Lester B. Pearson Award (2000-01). ... Won Lady Byng Memorial Trophy (2000-01). ... Named NHL Player of the Year by THE SPORTING NEWS (2000-01).

RECORDS: Shares NHL single-season playoff record for most game-winning goals—6 (1996).

STATISTICAL PLATEAUS: Three-goal games: 1988-89 (2), 1989-90 (1), 1990-91 (1), 1996-97 (1), 1998-99 (1), 1999-00 (2), 2000-01 (2). Total: 10. ... Four-goal games: 1991-92 (1). ... Total hat tricks: 11.

MISCELLANEOUS: Member of Stanley Cup championship team (1996 and 2001). ... Captain of Quebec Nordiques (1990-91 through 1994-95). ... Captain of Colorado Avalanche (1995-96 through 2000-01). ... Holds Colorado Avalanche franchise all-time record for most goals (457), most assists (721), most points (1,178) and most games (934). ... Scored on a penalty shot (vs. Ken Wregget, December 9, 1989; vs. Trevor Kidd, January 14, 1996; vs. Tyler Moss, November 1, 1997; vs Roman Turek, May 12, 2001 (playoffs)).

STATISTICAL NOTES: Led NHL in game-winning goals with 12 (2000-01).

Season Team	League	REGULAR SEASON								PLAYOFFS				
		Gms.	G	A	Pts.	PIM	+/-	PP	SH	Gms.	G	A	Pts.	PIM
86-87—Swift Current	WHL	72	60	73	133	31	...	...	...	4	0	1	1	0
87-88—Swift Current	WHL	64	†78	82	†160	64	...	...	...	10	11	13	24	12
88-89—Quebec	NHL	70	23	39	62	24	-36	10	0	—	—	—	—	—
89-90—Quebec	NHL	80	39	63	102	27	-40	8	1	—	—	—	—	—
90-91—Quebec	NHL	80	48	61	109	24	-26	12	3	—	—	—	—	—
91-92—Quebec	NHL	69	29	65	94	20	5	6	3	—	—	—	—	—
92-93—Quebec	NHL	78	48	57	105	40	-3	20	2	6	3	3	6	2
93-94—Quebec	NHL	84	28	64	92	18	-8	10	1	—	—	—	—	—
94-95—Quebec	NHL	47	19	43	62	30	7	3	2	6	4	1	5	0
95-96—Colorado	NHL	82	51	69	120	44	14	17	6	22	*18	16	*34	14
96-97—Colorado	NHL	65	22	52	74	34	-10	10	2	17	8	17	25	14
97-98—Colorado	NHL	64	27	36	63	50	0	12	1	6	2	3	5	6
—Can. Olympic team	Int'l	4	1	2	3	4	...	...	...	—	—	—	—	—
98-99—Colorado	NHL	73	41	55	96	29	23	12	†5	19	6	13	19	8
99-00—Colorado	NHL	60	28	53	81	28	30	5	1	17	2	7	9	8
00-01—Colorado	NHL	82	54	64	118	30	45	19	3	21	*13	13	*26	6
NHL Totals (13 years)		934	457	721	1178	398	1	144	30	114	56	73	129	58

SALEI, RUSLAN — D — MIGHTY DUCKS

PERSONAL: Born November 2, 1974, in Minsk, U.S.S.R. ... 6-1/206. ... Shoots left. ... Name pronounced ROO-slahn suh-LAY.

TRANSACTIONS/CAREER NOTES: Selected by Mighty Ducks of Anaheim in first round (first Mighty Ducks pick, ninth overall) of NHL entry draft (June 22, 1996). ... Suffered charley horse (November 22, 1997); missed one game. ... Fractured bone in left foot (December 10, 1997); missed one game. ... Suspended two games and fined $1,000 by NHL for head-butting incident (February 4, 1998). ... Suspended five games and fined $1,000 by NHL for illegal hit in preseason game (October 9, 1998). ... Injured shoulder (March 17, 1999); missed two games. ... Suspended 10 games by NHL for checking from behind incident (October 5, 1999). ... Injured foot (October 20, 2000); missed two games. ... Reinjured foot (October 23, 2000); missed six games. ... Injured back (December 17, 2000); missed one game. ... Suffered from headaches (January 21, 2001); missed 23 games.

Season Team	League	REGULAR SEASON								PLAYOFFS				
		Gms.	G	A	Pts.	PIM	+/-	PP	SH	Gms.	G	A	Pts.	PIM
92-93—Tivali Minsk	CIS	9	1	0	1	10	...	...	...	—	—	—	—	—
93-94—Tivali Minsk	CIS	39	2	3	5	50	...	...	...	—	—	—	—	—
94-95—Tivali Minsk	CIS	51	4	2	6	44	...	...	...	—	—	—	—	—
95-96—Las Vegas	IHL	76	7	23	30	123	...	...	...	15	3	7	10	18
96-97—Anaheim	NHL	30	0	1	1	37	-8	0	0	—	—	—	—	—
—Baltimore	AHL	12	1	4	5	12	...	...	...	—	—	—	—	—
—Las Vegas	IHL	8	0	2	2	24	...	...	...	3	2	1	3	6
97-98—Anaheim	NHL	66	5	10	15	70	7	1	0	—	—	—	—	—
—Cincinnati	AHL	6	3	6	9	14	...	...	...	—	—	—	—	—
—Belarus Oly. team	Int'l	7	1	0	1	4	...	...	...	—	—	—	—	—
98-99—Anaheim	NHL	74	2	14	16	65	1	1	0	3	0	0	0	4
99-00—Anaheim	NHL	71	5	5	10	94	3	1	0	—	—	—	—	—
00-01—Anaheim	NHL	50	1	5	6	70	-14	0	0	—	—	—	—	—
NHL Totals (5 years)		291	13	35	48	336	-11	3	0	3	0	0	0	4

SALO, SAMI — D — SENATORS

PERSONAL: Born September 2, 1974, in Turku, Finland. ... 6-3/192. ... Shoots right.

TRANSACTIONS/CAREER NOTES: Selected by Ottawa Senators in ninth round (seventh Senators pick, 239th overall) of NHL entry draft (June 22, 1996). ... Strained groin (October 17, 1998); missed five games. ... Strained groin (November 28, 1998); missed six games. ... Bruised thigh (February 18, 1999); missed one game. ... Strained shoulder (April 14, 1999); missed two games. ... Bruised chest (October 2, 1999); missed one game. ... Fractured left wrist (October 30, 1999); missed 23 games. ... Reinjured left wrist (December 29, 1999); missed 19 games. ... Sprained medial collateral ligament in right knee (February 29, 2000); missed one game. ... Suffered from the flu (September 30, 2000); missed first two games of season. ... Injured left shoulder (November 16, 2000); missed six games. ... Reinjured left shoulder (December 9, 2000) and underwent surgery; missed 38 games. ... Bruised right foot (March 21, 2001); missed one game. ... Suffered concussion (March 26, 2001); missed one game. ... Injured right knee (April 1, 2001); missed final three games of regular season.

HONORS: Named to NHL All-Rookie team (1998-99).

STATISTICAL PLATEAUS: Three-goal games: 1998-99 (1).

Season Team	League	REGULAR SEASON								PLAYOFFS				
		Gms.	G	A	Pts.	PIM	+/-	PP	SH	Gms.	G	A	Pts.	PIM
94-95—TPS Turku	Finland	7	1	2	3	6	...	...	...	—	—	—	—	—
—Kiekko-67	Finland Div. 2	19	4	2	6	4				—	—	—	—	—
95-96—TPS Turku	Finland	47	7	14	21	32	...	...	...	11	1	3	4	8
96-97—TPS Turku	Finland	48	9	6	15	10	...	...	...	10	2	3	5	4
97-98—Jokerit Helsinki	Finland	35	3	5	8	10	...	...	...	8	0	1	1	2
98-99—Ottawa	NHL	61	7	12	19	24	20	2	0	4	0	0	0	0
—Detroit	IHL	5	0	2	2	0	...	...	...	—	—	—	—	—
99-00—Ottawa	NHL	37	6	8	14	2	6	3	0	6	1	1	2	0
00-01—Ottawa	NHL	31	2	16	18	10	9	1	0	4	0	0	0	0
NHL Totals (3 years)		129	15	36	51	36	35	6	0	14	1	1	2	0

SALO, TOMMY — G — OILERS

PERSONAL: Born February 1, 1971, in Surahammar, Sweden. ... 5-11/173. ... Catches left. ... Name pronounced SAH-loh.
TRANSACTIONS/CAREER NOTES: Selected by New York Islanders in fifth round (fifth Islanders pick, 118th overall) of NHL entry draft (June 26, 1993). ... Suffered from tonsillitis (February 8, 1997); missed one game. ... Fractured finger (December 20, 1998); missed six games. ... Traded by Islanders to Edmonton Oilers for LW Mats Lindgren and eighth-round pick (F Radek Martinek) in 1999 draft (March 20, 1999).
HONORS: Won James Gatchene Memorial Trophy (1994-95). ... Won James Norris Memorial Trophy (1994-95). ... Won Garry F. Longman Memorial Trophy (1994-95). ... Named to IHL All-Star first team (1994-95). ... Won N.R. (Bud) Poile Trophy (1995-96). ... Played in NHL All-Star Game (2000).
MISCELLANEOUS: Member of gold-medal-winning Swedish Olympic team (1994). ... Holds Edmonton Oilers all-time record for goals-against average (2.40). ... Stopped a penalty shot attempt (vs. Mike Sillinger, January 7, 2000). ... Allowed penalty shot goal (vs. Rob Zamuner, January 11, 1997).

Season Team	League	REGULAR SEASON								PLAYOFFS						
		Gms.	Min	W	L	T	GA	SO	Avg.	Gms.	Min.	W	L	GA	SO	Avg.
90-91—Vasteras	Sweden	2	100	...	...	...	11	0	6.60	—	—	—	—	—	—	—
91-92—Vasteras	Sweden							Did not play.								
92-93—Vasteras	Sweden	24	1431	...	...	...	59	2	2.47	—						
93-94—Vasteras	Sweden	32	1896	...	...	...	106	3	3.35	—						
—Swedish Oly. team	Int'l	6	370	...	...	...	13	1	2.11	—						
94-95—Denver	IHL	65	*3810	*45	14	‡4	165	†3	*2.60	8	390	7	0	20	0	3.08
—New York Islanders	NHL	6	358	1	5	0	18	0	3.02	—						
95-96—New York Islanders	NHL	10	523	1	7	1	35	0	4.02	—						
—Utah	IHL	45	2695	28	15	‡2	119	†4	2.65	22	1341	*15	7	51	*3	2.28
96-97—New York Islanders	NHL	58	3208	20	27	8	151	5	2.82	—						
97-98—New York Islanders	NHL	62	3461	23	29	5	152	4	2.64	—						
—Swedish Oly. team	Int'l	4	238	2	2	0	9	0	2.27	—						
98-99—New York Islanders	NHL	51	3018	17	26	7	132	5	2.62	—						
—Edmonton	NHL	13	700	8	2	2	27	0	2.31	4	296	0	4	11	0	2.23
99-00—Edmonton	NHL	70	4164	27	28	*13	162	2	2.33	5	297	1	4	14	0	2.83
00-01—Edmonton	NHL	73	4364	36	25	12	179	8	2.46	6	406	2	4	15	0	2.22
NHL Totals (7 years)		343	19796	133	149	48	856	24	2.59	15	999	3	12	40	0	2.40

SALVADOR, BRYCE — D — BLUES

PERSONAL: Born February 11, 1976, in Brandon, Man. ... 6-1/194. ... Shoots left. ... Full Name: Bryce Chad Salvador.
TRANSACTIONS/CAREER NOTES: Selected by Tampa Bay Lightning in sixth round (sixth Lightning pick, 138th overall) of NHL entry draft (June 29, 1994). ... Signed as free agent by St. Louis Blues (December 16, 1996). ... Strained hamstring (February 8, 2001); missed four games. ... Injured foot (March 6, 2001); missed one game. ... Injured wrist (March 20, 2001); missed one game.

Season Team	League	REGULAR SEASON								PLAYOFFS				
		Gms.	G	A	Pts.	PIM	+/-	PP	SH	Gms.	G	A	Pts.	PIM
92-93—Lethbridge	WHL	64	1	4	5	29	...	...	...	4	0	0	0	0
93-94—Lethbridge	WHL	61	4	14	18	36	...	...	...	9	0	1	1	2
94-95—Lethbridge	WHL	67	1	9	10	88	...	...	...	—	—	—	—	—
95-96—Lethbridge	WHL	56	4	12	16	75	...	...	...	3	0	1	1	2
96-97—Lethbridge	WHL	63	8	32	40	81	...	...	...	19	0	7	7	14
97-98—Worcester	AHL	46	2	8	10	74	...	...	...	11	0	1	1	45
98-99—Worcester	AHL	69	5	13	18	129	...	...	...	4	0	1	1	2
99-00—Worcester	AHL	55	0	13	13	53	...	...	...	9	0	1	1	2
00-01—St. Louis	NHL	75	2	8	10	69	-4	0	0	14	2	0	2	18
NHL Totals (1 year)		75	2	8	10	69	-4	0	0	14	2	0	2	18

SAMSONOV, SERGEI — LW — BRUINS

PERSONAL: Born October 27, 1978, in Moscow, U.S.S.R. ... 5-8/184. ... Shoots right. ... Name pronounced sam-SAH-nahf.
TRANSACTIONS/CAREER NOTES: Selected by Boston Bruins in first round (second Bruins pick, eighth overall) of NHL entry draft (June 21, 1997). ... Suffered from the flu (December 20, 1997); missed one game. ... Bruised thigh (February 12, 1998); missed one game. ... Suffered sinus infection (February 23, 1999); missed two games. ... Strained knee (January 4, 2000); missed five games.
HONORS: Won Garry F. Longman Memorial Trophy (1996-97). ... Named to IHL All-Rookie first team (1996-97). ... Named NHL Rookie of the Year by THE SPORTING NEWS (1997-98). ... Won Calder Memorial Trophy (1997-98). ... Named to NHL All-Rookie team (1997-98).
STATISTICAL PLATEAUS: Three-goal games: 1997-98 (1).

Season Team	League	Gms.	G	A	Pts.	PIM	+/-	PP	SH	Gms.	G	A	Pts.	PIM
94-95—CSKA Moscow	CIS	13	2	2	4	14	...	...	...	2	0	0	0	0
—CSKA Moscow	CIS Jrs.	50	110	72	182	...	...	...	...	—	—	—	—	—
95-96—CSKA Moscow	CIS	51	21	17	38	12	...	...	...	3	1	1	2	4
96-97—Detroit	IHL	73	29	35	64	18	...	...	...	19	8	4	12	12
97-98—Boston	NHL	81	22	25	47	8	9	7	0	6	2	5	7	0
98-99—Boston	NHL	79	25	26	51	18	-6	6	0	11	3	1	4	0
99-00—Boston	NHL	77	19	26	45	4	-6	6	0	—	—	—	—	—
00-01—Boston	NHL	82	29	46	75	18	6	3	0	—	—	—	—	—
NHL Totals (4 years)		319	95	123	218	48	3	22	0	17	5	6	11	0

SAMUELSSON, MIKAEL — C — RANGERS

PERSONAL: Born December 23, 1976, in Mariefred, Sweden. ... 6-1/195.

TRANSACTIONS/CAREER NOTES: Selected by San Jose Sharks in fifth round (seventh Sharks pick, 145th overall) of NHL entry draft (June 27, 1998). ... Traded by Sharks with D Christian Gosselin to New York Rangers for LW Adam Graves (June 24, 2001).

Season Team	League	Gms.	G	A	Pts.	PIM	+/-	PP	SH	Gms.	G	A	Pts.	PIM
94-95—Sodertalje	Sweden Jr.	30	8	6	14	12	...	...	...	—	—	—	—	—
95-96—Sodertalje	Sweden Dv. 2	18	5	1	6	0	...	...	...	4	0	0	0	0
—Sodertalje	Sweden Jr.	22	13	12	25	20	...	...	...	—	—	—	—	—
96-97—Sodertalje	Sweden	29	3	2	5	10	...	...	...	—	—	—	—	—
—Sodertalje	Sweden Jr.	2	2	1	3	...	...	...	...	—	—	—	—	—
97-98—Sodertalje	Sweden	31	8	8	16	47	...	...	...	—	—	—	—	—
98-99—Sodertalje	Sweden	12	7	9	16	20	...	...	...	—	—	—	—	—
—V. Frolunda HC Gote. ..	Sweden	27	0	5	5	10	...	...	...	—	—	—	—	—
99-00—Brynas Gavle	Sweden	40	4	3	7	76	...	...	...	11	7	2	9	6
00-01—Kentucky	AHL	66	32	46	78	58	...	...	...	3	1	0	1	0
—San Jose	NHL	4	0	0	0	0	0	0	0	—	—	—	—	—
NHL Totals (1 year)		4	0	0	0	0	0	0	0					

SANDERSON, GEOFF — LW — BLUE JACKETS

PERSONAL: Born February 1, 1972, in Hay River, Northwest Territories. ... 6-0/190. ... Shoots left.

TRANSACTIONS/CAREER NOTES: Selected by Hartford Whalers in second round (second Whalers pick, 36th overall) of NHL entry draft (June 16, 1990). ... Bruised shoulder (October 14, 1991); missed one game. ... Injured groin (November 13, 1991); missed three games. ... Bruised knee (December 7, 1991); missed five games. ... Suffered from the flu (February 1, 1994). ... Played in Europe during 1994-95 NHL lockout. ... Whalers franchise moved to North Carolina and renamed Carolina Hurricanes for 1997-98 season; NHL approved move on June 25, 1997. ... Traded by Hurricanes to Vancouver Canucks with D Enrico Ciccone and G Sean Burke for LW Martin Gelinas and G Kirk McLean (January 3, 1998). ... Injured shoulder (January 21, 1998); missed eight games. ... Traded by Canucks to Buffalo Sabres for LW Brad May and third-round pick (traded to Tampa Bay) in 1999 draft (February 4, 1998). ... Bruised hip (April 13, 1998); missed one game. ... Injured back (January 18, 1999); missed one game. ... Injured hip (February 19, 1999); missed one game. ... Injured knee (March 1, 2000); missed five games. ... Selected by Columbus Blue Jackets in NHL expansion draft (June 23, 2000). ... Fractured finger (February 25, 2001); missed one game. ... Sprained knee (March 14, 2001); missed 13 games.

HONORS: Played in NHL All-Star Game (1994 and 1997).

MISCELLANEOUS: Holds Columbus Blue Jackets all-time record for most goals (30) and most points (56).

STATISTICAL PLATEAUS: Three-goal games: 1992-93 (2), 1994-95 (1), 1995-96 (2), 1998-99 (1), 2000-01 (1). Total: 7.

Season Team	League	Gms.	G	A	Pts.	PIM	+/-	PP	SH	Gms.	G	A	Pts.	PIM
88-89—Swift Current	WHL	58	17	11	28	16	...	...	...	12	3	5	8	6
89-90—Swift Current	WHL	70	32	62	94	56	...	...	...	4	1	4	5	8
90-91—Swift Current	WHL	70	62	50	112	57	...	...	...	3	1	2	3	4
—Hartford	NHL	2	1	0	1	0	-2	0	0	3	0	0	0	0
—Springfield	AHL	—	—	—	—	—	...	...	...	1	0	0	0	2
91-92—Hartford	NHL	64	13	18	31	18	5	2	0	7	1	0	1	2
92-93—Hartford	NHL	82	46	43	89	28	-21	21	2	—	—	—	—	—
93-94—Hartford	NHL	82	41	26	67	42	-13	15	1	—	—	—	—	—
94-95—HPK Hameenlinna	Finland	12	6	4	10	24	...	...	...	—	—	—	—	—
—Hartford	NHL	46	18	14	32	24	-10	4	0	—	—	—	—	—
95-96—Hartford	NHL	81	34	31	65	40	0	6	0	—	—	—	—	—
96-97—Hartford	NHL	82	36	31	67	29	-9	12	1	—	—	—	—	—
97-98—Carolina	NHL	40	7	10	17	14	-4	2	0	—	—	—	—	—
—Vancouver	NHL	9	0	3	3	4	-1	0	0	—	—	—	—	—
—Buffalo	NHL	26	4	5	9	20	6	0	0	14	3	1	4	4
98-99—Buffalo	NHL	75	12	18	30	22	8	1	0	19	4	6	10	14
99-00—Buffalo	NHL	67	13	13	26	22	4	4	0	5	0	2	2	8
00-01—Columbus	NHL	68	30	26	56	46	4	9	0	—	—	—	—	—
NHL Totals (11 years)		724	255	238	493	309	-33	76	4	48	8	9	17	28

SAPRYKIN, OLEG — C/LW — FLAMES

PERSONAL: Born February 12, 1981, in Moscow, U.S.S.R. ... 6-0/187. ... Shoots left.

TRANSACTIONS/CAREER NOTES: Selected by Calgary Flames in first round (first Flames pick, 11th overall) of NHL entry draft (June 26, 1999). ... Suffered concussion (January 5, 2001); missed 11 games.

HONORS: Named to WHL (West) All-Star second team (1998-99 and 1999-2000).

Season Team	League	Gms.	G	A	Pts.	PIM	+/-	PP	SH	Gms.	G	A	Pts.	PIM
				REGULAR SEASON								PLAYOFFS		
97-98—CSKA Moscow	Russian	20	0	2	2	8	...	...	...	—	—	—	—	—
—HC CSKA	Rus. Div. II	15	0	3	3	6	...	...	...	—	—	—	—	—
98-99—Seattle	WHL	66	47	46	93	107	...	...	...	11	5	11	16	36
99-00—Calgary	NHL	4	0	1	1	2	-4	0	0	—	—	—	—	—
—Seattle	WHL	48	30	36	66	89	...	...	...	6	3	3	6	37
00-01—Calgary	NHL	59	9	14	23	43	4	2	0	—	—	—	—	—
NHL Totals (2 years)		63	9	15	24	45	0	2	0					

SARAULT, YVES — LW — PREDATORS

PERSONAL: Born December 23, 1972, in Valleyfield, Que. ... 6-1/183. ... Shoots left. ... Name pronounced EEV suh-ROH.

TRANSACTIONS/CAREER NOTES: Selected by Montreal Canadiens in third round (third Canadiens pick, 61st overall) of NHL entry draft (June 22, 1991). ... Traded by Canadiens with RW Craig Ferguson to Calgary Flames for eighth-round pick (D Petr Kubos) in 1997 draft (November 25, 1995). ... Signed as free agent by Colorado Avalanche (September 7, 1996). ... Signed as free agent by Ottawa Senators (July 28, 1998). ... Sprained wrist (October 29, 1998); missed 29 games. ... Suffered back spasms (February 26, 2000); missed two games. ... Signed as free agent by Atlanta Thrashers (July 20, 2000). ... Bruised shoulder (February 10, 2001); missed two games. ... Claimed on waivers by Nashville Predators (June 19, 2001).

HONORS: Named to QMJHL All-Star second team (1991-92).

Season Team	League	Gms.	G	A	Pts.	PIM	+/-	PP	SH	Gms.	G	A	Pts.	PIM
				REGULAR SEASON								PLAYOFFS		
89-90—Victoriaville	QMJHL	70	12	28	40	140	...	...	...	16	0	3	3	26
90-91—St. Jean	QMJHL	56	22	24	46	113	...	...	...	—	—	—	—	—
91-92—St. Jean	QMJHL	50	28	38	66	96	...	...	...	—	—	—	—	—
—Trois-Rivieres	QMJHL	18	16	14	30	10	...	...	...	15	10	10	20	18
92-93—Fredericton	AHL	59	14	17	31	41	...	...	...	3	0	1	1	2
—Wheeling	ECHL	2	1	3	4	0	...	...	...	—	—	—	—	—
93-94—Fredericton	AHL	60	13	14	27	72	...	...	...	—	—	—	—	—
94-95—Fredericton	AHL	69	24	21	45	96	...	...	...	13	2	1	3	33
—Montreal	NHL	8	0	1	1	0	-1	0	0	—	—	—	—	—
95-96—Montreal	NHL	14	0	0	0	4	-7	0	0	—	—	—	—	—
—Calgary	NHL	11	2	1	3	4	-2	0	0	—	—	—	—	—
—Saint John	AHL	26	10	12	22	34	...	...	...	16	6	2	8	33
96-97—Colorado	NHL	28	2	1	3	6	0	0	0	5	0	0	0	2
—Hershey	AHL	6	2	3	5	8	...	...	...	—	—	—	—	—
97-98—Hershey	AHL	63	23	36	59	43	...	...	...	7	1	2	3	14
—Colorado	NHL	2	1	0	1	0	1	0	0	—	—	—	—	—
98-99—Detroit	IHL	36	11	12	23	52	...	...	...	11	7	2	9	40
—Ottawa	NHL	11	0	1	1	4	1	0	0	—	—	—	—	—
99-00—Grand Rapids	IHL	62	17	26	43	77	...	...	...	17	7	4	11	32
—Ottawa	NHL	11	0	2	2	7	-3	0	0	—	—	—	—	—
00-01—Orlando	IHL	35	17	17	34	42	...	...	...	—	—	—	—	—
—Atlanta	NHL	20	5	4	9	26	-9	2	0	—	—	—	—	—
NHL Totals (7 years)		105	10	10	20	51	-20	2	0	5	0	0	0	2

SARICH, CORY — D — LIGHTNING

PERSONAL: Born August 16, 1978, in Saskatoon, Sask. ... 6-3/193. ... Shoots right. ... Name pronounced SAIRCH.

TRANSACTIONS/CAREER NOTES: Selected by Buffalo Sabres in second round (second Sabres pick, 27th overall) of NHL entry draft (June 22, 1996). ... Traded by Sabres with C Wayne Primeau, C/RW Brian Holzinger and third-round pick (RW Alexandre Kharitonov) in 2000 draft to Tampa Bay Lightning for C Chris Gratton and second-round pick (C Derek Roy) in 2001 draft (March 9, 2000).

HONORS: Named to WHL (West) All-Star second team (1997-98).

Season Team	League	Gms.	G	A	Pts.	PIM	+/-	PP	SH	Gms.	G	A	Pts.	PIM
				REGULAR SEASON								PLAYOFFS		
94-95—Saskatoon	WHL	6	0	0	0	4	...	...	...	3	0	1	1	0
95-96—Saskatoon	WHL	59	5	18	23	54	...	...	...	3	0	0	0	4
96-97—Saskatoon	WHL	58	6	27	33	158	...	...	...	—	—	—	—	—
97-98—Seattle	WHL	46	8	40	48	137	...	...	...	—	—	—	—	—
98-99—Rochester	AHL	77	3	26	29	82	...	...	...	20	2	4	6	14
—Buffalo	NHL	4	0	0	0	0	3	0	0	—	—	—	—	—
99-00—Buffalo	NHL	42	0	4	4	35	2	0	0	—	—	—	—	—
—Rochester	AHL	15	0	6	6	44	...	...	...	—	—	—	—	—
—Tampa Bay	NHL	17	0	2	2	42	-8	0	0	—	—	—	—	—
00-01—Tampa Bay	NHL	73	1	8	9	106	-25	0	0	—	—	—	—	—
—Detroit	IHL	3	0	2	2	2	...	...	...	—	—	—	—	—
NHL Totals (3 years)		136	1	14	15	183	-28	0	0					

SARNO, PETER — C — OILERS

PERSONAL: Born July 26, 1979, in Toronto. ... 5-11/185. ... Shoots left.

TRANSACTIONS/CAREER NOTES: Selected by Edmonton Oilers in sixth round (sixth Oilers pick, 141st overall) of NHL entry draft (June 21, 1997).

HONORS: Won Emms Family Award (1996-97). ... Named to OHL All-Rookie first team (1996-97). ... Won Eddie Powers Memorial Trophy (1997-98).

Season Team	League	Gms.	G	A	Pts.	PIM	+/-	PP	SH		Gms.	G	A	Pts.	PIM
		REGULAR SEASON									PLAYOFFS				
95-96—North York Flames	OPJHL	52	39	57	96	27	...	...	...		—	—	—	—	—
96-97—Windsor	OHL	66	20	63	83	59	...	...	...		5	0	3	3	6
97-98—Windsor	OHL	64	33	*88	*121	18	...	...	...		—	—	—	—	—
—Hamilton	AHL	8	1	1	2	2	...	...	...		—	—	—	—	—
98-99—Sarnia	OHL	68	37	*93	*130	49	...	...	...		6	1	7	8	2
99-00—Hamilton	AHL	67	10	36	46	31	...	...	...		—	—	—	—	—
00-01—Hamilton	AHL	79	19	46	65	64	...	...	...		—	—	—	—	—

SATAN, MIROSLAV   RW   SABRES

PERSONAL: Born October 22, 1974, in Topolcany, Czechoslovakia. ... 6-1/195. ... Shoots left. ... Name pronounced shuh-TAN.

TRANSACTIONS/CAREER NOTES: Selected by Edmonton Oilers in fifth round (sixth Oilers pick, 111th overall) of NHL entry draft (June 26, 1993). ... Suffered collapsed lung (October 1, 1995); missed two games. ... Separated right shoulder (January 13, 1996); missed four games. ... Suffered from the flu (March 9, 1997); missed one game. ... Traded by Oilers to Buffalo Sabres for D Craig Millar and LW Barrie Moore (March 18, 1997). ... Suffered from the flu (November 28, 1998); missed one game. ... Injured foot (April 25, 1999); missed nine playoff games.

HONORS: Played in NHL All-Star Game (2000).

MISCELLANEOUS: Scored on a penalty shot (vs. Damian Rhodes, October 9, 1999). ... Failed to score on a penalty shot (vs. Ken Wregget, December 28, 1999; vs. Kevin Weekes, March 4, 2000).

STATISTICAL NOTES: Led NHL in shooting percentage with 21.0 (1996-97).

STATISTICAL PLATEAUS: Three-goal games: 1996-97 (1), 1997-98 (1), 1999-00 (1). Total: 3.

Season Team	League	Gms.	G	A	Pts.	PIM	+/-	PP	SH		Gms.	G	A	Pts.	PIM
		REGULAR SEASON									PLAYOFFS				
91-92—VTJ Topolcany	Czech Dv.II	9	2	1	3	6	...	...	...		—	—	—	—	—
—VTJ Topolcany	Czech. Jrs.	31	30	22	52		...	...	...		—	—	—	—	—
92-93—Dukla Trencin	Czech.	38	11	6	17		...	...	...		—	—	—	—	—
93-94—Dukla Trencin	Slovakia	30	32	16	48	16	...	...	...		—	—	—	—	—
—Slovakian Oly. team	Int'l	8	9	0	9	0	...	...	...		—	—	—	—	—
94-95—Detroit	IHL	8	1	3	4	4	...	...	...		—	—	—	—	—
—San Diego	IHL	6	0	2	2	6	...	...	...		—	—	—	—	—
—Cape Breton	AHL	25	24	16	40	15	...	...	...		—	—	—	—	—
95-96—Edmonton	NHL	62	18	17	35	22	0	6	0		—	—	—	—	—
96-97—Edmonton	NHL	64	17	11	28	22	-4	5	0		—	—	—	—	—
—Buffalo	NHL	12	8	2	10	4	1	2	0		7	0	0	0	0
97-98—Buffalo	NHL	79	22	24	46	34	2	9	0		14	5	4	9	4
98-99—Buffalo	NHL	81	40	26	66	44	24	13	3		12	3	5	8	2
99-00—Dukla Trencin	Slovakia	3	2	8	10	2	...	...	...		—	—	—	—	—
—Buffalo	NHL	81	33	34	67	32	16	5	3		5	3	2	5	0
00-01—Buffalo	NHL	82	29	33	62	36	5	8	2		13	3	10	13	8
NHL Totals (6 years)		461	167	147	314	194	44	48	8		51	14	21	35	14

SAUVE, PHILIPPE   G   AVALANCHE

PERSONAL: Born February 27, 1980, in Buffalo. ... 6-0/175. ... Catches left.

TRANSACTIONS/CAREER NOTES: Selected by Colorado Avalanche in second round (sixth Avalanche pick, 38th overall) of NHL entry draft (June 27, 1998).

HONORS: Won Can.HL Humanitarian Award (1998-99).

Season Team	League	Gms.	Min	W	L	T	GA	SO	Avg.		Gms.	Min.	W	L	GA	SO	Avg.
		REGULAR SEASON									PLAYOFFS						
96-97—Rimouski	QMJHL	26	1332	11	9	2	84	0	3.78		1	14	0	0	3	0	12.86
97-98—Rimouski	QMJHL	40	2326	23	16	0	131	1	3.38		7	262	0	5	33	0	7.56
98-99—Rimouski	QMJHL	44	2401	16	19	4	155	0	3.87		11	595	6	4	30	†1	3.03
99-00—Drummondville	QMJHL	28	1526	12	12	2	106	0	4.17		—	—	—	—	—	—	—
—Hull	QMJHL	17	992	9	7	1	57	0	3.45		12	735	6	6	47	0	3.84
00-01—Hershey	AHL	42	2182	17	18	1	100	3	2.75		3	218	0	3	10	0	2.75

SAVAGE, ANDRE   C

PERSONAL: Born May 27, 1975, in Ottawa. ... 6-0/195. ... Shoots right. ... Full Name: Andre Ronald Savage. ... Name pronounced suh-VAHJ.

TRANSACTIONS/CAREER NOTES: Signed as non-drafted free agent by Boston Bruins (June 12, 1998). ... Bruised sternum (March 8, 2000); missed two games. ... Strained trapezius muscle (April 1, 2000); missed final four games of season. ... Dislocated shoulder (September 21, 2000) and underwent surgery; missed first 39 games of season.

HONORS: Named to WCHA All-Star first team (1997-98).

Season Team	League	Gms.	G	A	Pts.	PIM	+/-	PP	SH		Gms.	G	A	Pts.	PIM
		REGULAR SEASON									PLAYOFFS				
94-95—Michigan Tech	WCHA	39	7	17	24	56	...	...	...		—	—	—	—	—
95-96—Michigan Tech	WCHA	40	13	27	40	42	...	...	...		—	—	—	—	—
96-97—Michigan Tech	WCHA	37	18	20	38	34	...	...	...		—	—	—	—	—
97-98—Michigan Tech	WCHA	33	14	27	41	34	...	...	...		—	—	—	—	—
98-99—Providence	AHL	63	27	42	69	54	...	...	...		5	0	1	1	0
—Boston	NHL	6	1	0	1	0	2	0	0		—	—	—	—	—
99-00—Providence	AHL	30	15	17	32	22	...	...	...		14	6	7	13	22
—Boston	NHL	43	7	13	20	10	-8	2	0		—	—	—	—	—
00-01—Providence	AHL	35	13	15	28	47	...	...	...		17	3	4	7	18
—Boston	NHL	1	0	0	0	0	0	0	0		—	—	—	—	—
NHL Totals (3 years)		50	8	13	21	10	-6	2	0						

SAVAGE, BRIAN   RW   CANADIENS

PERSONAL: Born February 24, 1971, in Sudbury, Ont. ... 6-2/192. ... Shoots left.
TRANSACTIONS/CAREER NOTES: Selected by Montreal Canadiens in eighth round (11th Canadiens pick, 171st overall) of NHL entry draft (June 22, 1991). ... Bruised knee (February 4, 1995); missed 10 games. ... Bruised knee (April 5, 1995); missed one game. ... Suffered hip pointer (February 17, 1996); missed six games. ... Suffered from the flu (April 1, 1996); missed one game. ... Injured groin (October 26, 1996); missed one game. ... Fractured hand (October 1, 1997); missed seven games. ... Bruised thigh (November 26, 1997); missed one game. ... Fractured thumb (March 21, 1998); missed 10 games. ... Strained groin (November 4, 1998); missed one game. ... Reinjured groin (December 9, 1998); missed 11 games. ... Tore muscle in rib cage (January 21, 1999); missed 11 games. ... Fractured vertebrae in neck (November 20, 1999); missed 44 games. ... Fractured thumb (January 20, 2001); missed 20 games.
HONORS: Named to NCAA All-America (West) second team (1992-93). ... Named CCHA Player of the Year (1992-93). ... Named to CCHA All-Star first team (1992-93).
MISCELLANEOUS: Member of silver-medal-winning Canadian Olympic team (1994).
STATISTICAL PLATEAUS: Three-goal games: 1995-96 (1), 1996-97 (1), 1999-00 (2), 2000-01 (1). Total: 5. ... Four-goal games: 1997-98 (1). ... Total hat tricks: 6.

| | | REGULAR SEASON | | | | | | | | PLAYOFFS | | | | |
Season Team	League	Gms.	G	A	Pts.	PIM	+/-	PP	SH	Gms.	G	A	Pts.	PIM
89-90—Sudbury	OHA Mj. Jr.	32	45	40	85	61	...	...	...	—	—	—	—	—
90-91—Miami of Ohio	CCHA	28	5	6	11	26	...	...	...	—	—	—	—	—
91-92—Miami of Ohio	CCHA	40	24	16	40	43	...	...	...	—	—	—	—	—
92-93—Miami of Ohio	CCHA	38	37	21	58	44	...	...	...	—	—	—	—	—
—Canadian nat'l team	Int'l	9	3	0	3	12	...	...	...	—	—	—	—	—
93-94—Canadian nat'l team	Int'l	51	20	26	46	38	...	...	...	—	—	—	—	—
—Can. Olympic team	Int'l	8	2	2	4	6	...	...	...	—	—	—	—	—
—Fredericton	AHL	17	12	15	27	4	...	...	...	—	—	—	—	—
—Montreal	NHL	3	1	0	1	0	0	0	0	3	0	2	2	0
94-95—Montreal	NHL	37	12	7	19	27	5	0	0	—	—	—	—	—
95-96—Montreal	NHL	75	25	8	33	28	-8	4	0	6	0	2	2	2
96-97—Montreal	NHL	81	23	37	60	39	-14	5	0	5	1	1	2	0
97-98—Montreal	NHL	64	26	17	43	36	11	8	0	9	0	2	2	6
98-99—Montreal	NHL	54	16	10	26	20	-14	5	0	—	—	—	—	—
99-00—Montreal	NHL	38	17	12	29	19	-4	6	1	—	—	—	—	—
00-01—Montreal	NHL	62	21	24	45	26	-13	12	0	—	—	—	—	—
NHL Totals (8 years)		414	141	115	256	195	-37	40	1	23	1	7	8	8

SAVARD, MARC   C   FLAMES

PERSONAL: Born July 17, 1977, in Ottawa. ... 5-10/184. ... Shoots left. ... Name pronounced suh-VAHRD.
TRANSACTIONS/CAREER NOTES: Selected by New York Rangers in fourth round (third Rangers pick, 91st overall) of NHL entry draft (July 8, 1995). ... Traded by Rangers with first-round pick (C/LW Oleg Saprykin) in 1999 draft to Calgary Flames for rights to LW Jan Hlavac and first- (C Jamie Lundmark) and third-round (D Pat Aufiero) picks in 1999 draft (June 26, 1999). ... Suffered concussion (January 8, 2000); missed two games. ... Missed first two games of 2000-01 season due to contract dispute. ... Suffered concussion (December 31, 2000); missed three games.
HONORS: Won Can.HL Top Scorer Award (1994-95). ... Won Eddie Powers Memorial Trophy (1994-95). ... Named to OHL All-Star second team (1994-95).
STATISTICAL PLATEAUS: Four-goal games: 1999-00 (1).

| | | REGULAR SEASON | | | | | | | | PLAYOFFS | | | | |
Season Team	League	Gms.	G	A	Pts.	PIM	+/-	PP	SH	Gms.	G	A	Pts.	PIM
92-93—Metcalfe	Jr. B	31	46	53	99	26	...	...	...	—	—	—	—	—
93-94—Oshawa	OHL	61	18	39	57	24	...	...	...	5	4	3	7	8
94-95—Oshawa	OHL	66	43	96	*139	78	...	...	...	7	5	6	11	8
95-96—Oshawa	OHL	48	28	59	87	77	...	...	...	5	4	5	9	6
96-97—Oshawa	OHL	64	43	*87	*130	94	...	...	...	18	13	†24	*37	20
97-98—New York Rangers	NHL	28	1	5	6	4	-4	0	0	—	—	—	—	—
—Hartford	AHL	58	21	53	74	66	...	...	...	15	8	19	27	24
98-99—Hartford	AHL	9	3	10	13	16	...	...	...	7	1	12	13	16
—New York Rangers	NHL	70	9	36	45	38	-7	4	0	—	—	—	—	—
99-00—Calgary	NHL	78	22	31	53	56	-2	4	0	—	—	—	—	—
00-01—Calgary	NHL	77	23	42	65	46	-12	10	1	—	—	—	—	—
NHL Totals (4 years)		253	55	114	169	144	-25	18	1					

SAVIELS, ARGIS   D   AVALANCHE

PERSONAL: Born January 15, 1982, in Riga, U.S.S.R. ... 6-1/192. ... Shoots left.
TRANSACTIONS/CAREER NOTES: Selected by Colorado Avalanche in second round (fourth Avalanche pick, 63rd pick overall) of NHL entry draft (June 24, 2000).

| | | REGULAR SEASON | | | | | | | | PLAYOFFS | | | | |
Season Team	League	Gms.	G	A	Pts.	PIM	+/-	PP	SH	Gms.	G	A	Pts.	PIM
99-00—Owen Sound	OHL	65	7	25	32	56	...	...	...	—	—	—	—	—
00-01—Owen Sound	OHL	68	14	37	51	46	...	...	...	5	0	1	1	2
—Hershey	AHL	1	0	0	0	0	...	...	...	—	—	—	—	—

SAWYER, KEVIN — LW — MIGHTY DUCKS

PERSONAL: Born February 18, 1974, in Christina Lake, B.C. ... 6-2/205. ... Shoots left.
TRANSACTIONS/CAREER NOTES: Signed as non-drafted free agent by St. Louis Blues (February 16, 1995). ... Traded by Blues with D Steve Staios to Boston Bruins for RW Steve Leach (March 8, 1996). ... Signed as free agent by Dallas Stars (July 25, 1997). ... Signed as free agent by Blues (September 4, 1998). ... Signed as free agent by Phoenix Coyotes (August 15, 1999). ... Signed as free agent by Mighty Ducks of Anaheim (July 13, 2000).

Season Team	League	Gms.	G	A	Pts.	PIM	+/-	PP	SH	Gms.	G	A	Pts.	PIM
91-92—Kelowna	BCJHL	3	0	0	0	9	...	...	...	—	—	—	—	—
—Vernon	BCJHL	12	0	1	1	18	...	...	...	—	—	—	—	—
—Penticton	BCJHL	3	0	0	0	13	...	...	...	—	—	—	—	—
92-93—Spokane	WHL	62	4	3	7	274	...	...	...	—	—	—	—	—
93-94—Spokane	WHL	60	10	15	25	350	...	...	...	3	0	1	1	6
94-95—Spokane	WHL	54	7	9	16	365	...	...	...	11	2	0	2	58
—Peoria	IHL	—	—	—	—	—	...	...	...	2	0	0	0	12
95-96—Worcester	AHL	41	3	4	7	268	...	...	...	—	—	—	—	—
—St. Louis	NHL	6	0	0	0	23	-2	0	0	—	—	—	—	—
—Providence	AHL	4	0	0	0	29	...	...	...	4	0	1	1	9
—Boston	NHL	2	0	0	0	5	1	0	0	—	—	—	—	—
96-97—Providence	AHL	60	8	9	17	367	...	...	...	6	0	0	0	32
—Boston	NHL	2	0	0	0	0	0	0	0	—	—	—	—	—
97-98—Michigan	IHL	60	2	5	7	*398	...	...	...	3	0	0	0	23
98-99—Worcester	AHL	70	8	14	22	299	...	...	...	4	0	1	1	4
99-00—Phoenix	NHL	3	0	0	0	12	1	0	0	—	—	—	—	—
—Springfield	AHL	56	4	8	12	321	...	...	...	4	0	0	0	6
00-01—Cincinnati	AHL	41	2	12	14	211	...	...	...	—	—	—	—	—
—Anaheim	NHL	9	0	1	1	27	-1	0	0	—	—	—	—	—
NHL Totals (4 years)		22	0	1	1	67	-1	0	0					

S

SCATCHARD, DAVE — C — ISLANDERS

PERSONAL: Born February 20, 1976, in Hinton, Alta. ... 6-2/220. ... Shoots right. ... Name pronounced SKATCH-uhrd.
TRANSACTIONS/CAREER NOTES: Selected by Vancouver Canucks in second round (third Canucks pick, 42nd overall) of NHL entry draft (June 28, 1994). ... Suffered hip pointer (December 15, 1997); missed two games. ... Bruised ankle (October 13, 1999); missed five games. ... Traded by Canucks with G Kevin Weekes and RW Bill Muckalt to New York Islanders for G Felix Potvin, second-(traded to Atlanta) and third-round (C Thatcher Bell) picks in 2000 draft (December 19, 1999). ... Suffered concussion (March 22, 2000); missed final eight games of season. ... Strained neck (November 9, 2000); missed one game.
MISCELLANEOUS: Failed to score on a penalty shot (vs. Martin Brodeur, February 27, 2001).

Season Team	League	Gms.	G	A	Pts.	PIM	+/-	PP	SH	Gms.	G	A	Pts.	PIM
92-93—Kimberley	RMJHL	51	20	23	43	61	...	...	...	—	—	—	—	—
93-94—Portland	WHL	47	9	11	20	46	...	...	...	10	2	1	3	4
94-95—Portland	WHL	71	20	30	50	148	...	...	...	8	0	3	3	21
95-96—Portland	WHL	59	19	28	47	146	...	...	...	7	1	8	9	14
—Syracuse	AHL	1	0	0	0	0	...	...	...	15	2	5	7	29
96-97—Syracuse	AHL	26	8	7	15	65	...	...	...	—	—	—	—	—
97-98—Vancouver	NHL	76	13	11	24	165	-4	0	0	—	—	—	—	—
98-99—Vancouver	NHL	82	13	13	26	140	-12	0	2	—	—	—	—	—
99-00—Vancouver	NHL	21	0	4	4	24	-3	0	0	—	—	—	—	—
—New York Islanders	NHL	44	12	14	26	93	0	0	1	—	—	—	—	—
00-01—New York Islanders	NHL	81	21	24	45	114	-9	4	0	—	—	—	—	—
NHL Totals (4 years)		304	59	66	125	536	-28	4	3					

SCHAEFER, PETER — LW — CANUCKS

PERSONAL: Born July 12, 1977, in Yellow Grass, Sask. ... 5-11/195. ... Shoots left.
TRANSACTIONS/CAREER NOTES: Selected by Vancouver Canucks in third round (third Canucks pick, 66th overall) of NHL entry draft (July 8, 1995). ... Sprained shoulder (April 2, 1999); missed final six games of season. ... Suffered illness (November 20, 1999); missed one game. ... Injured knee (February 14, 2000); missed three games. ... Reinjured knee (February 23, 2000); missed four games. ... Suffered from the flu (April 2, 2000); missed one game.
HONORS: Named to WHL (East) All-Star first team (1995-96 and 1996-97). ... Won Four Broncos Memorial Trophy (1996-97). ... Named to Can.HL All-Star first team (1996-97).

Season Team	League	Gms.	G	A	Pts.	PIM	+/-	PP	SH	Gms.	G	A	Pts.	PIM
93-94—Brandon	WHL	2	1	0	1	0	...	...	...	—	—	—	—	—
94-95—Brandon	WHL	68	27	32	59	34	...	...	...	18	5	3	8	18
95-96—Brandon	WHL	69	47	61	108	53	...	...	...	19	10	13	23	5
96-97—Brandon	WHL	61	49	74	123	85	...	...	...	6	1	4	5	4
—Syracuse	AHL	5	0	3	3	0	...	...	...	3	1	3	4	14
97-98—Syracuse	AHL	73	19	44	63	41	...	...	...	5	2	1	3	2
98-99—Syracuse	AHL	41	10	19	29	66	...	...	...	—	—	—	—	—
—Vancouver	NHL	25	4	4	8	8	-1	1	0	—	—	—	—	—
99-00—Vancouver	NHL	71	16	15	31	20	0	2	2	—	—	—	—	—
—Syracuse	AHL	2	0	0	0	2	...	...	...	—	—	—	—	—
00-01—Vancouver	NHL	82	16	20	36	22	4	3	4	3	0	0	0	0
NHL Totals (3 years)		178	36	39	75	50	3	6	6	3	0	0	0	0

PERSONAL: Born April 18, 1979, in Angarsk, U.S.S.R. ... 6-1/204. ... Shoots left.
TRANSACTIONS/CAREER NOTES: Selected by Ottawa Senators in fourth round (fifth Senators pick, 101st overall) of NHL entry draft (June 27, 1998).

Season Team	League	REGULAR SEASON								PLAYOFFS				
		Gms.	G	A	Pts.	PIM	+/-	PP	SH	Gms.	G	A	Pts.	PIM
96-97—Yermak Angarsk	Rus. Div. III						Statistics unavailable.							
97-98—Torpedo-2 Yaroslavl	Rus. Div. II	47	15	9	24	34	...	...	...	—	—	—	—	—
—Torpedo Yaroslavl	Russian	4	0	0	0	0				—	—	—	—	—
98-99—Torpedo Yaroslavl	Russian	40	6	1	7	28	...	...	...	6	0	0	0	2
99-00—Grand Rapids	IHL	46	16	12	28	10	...	...	...	17	8	7	15	6
—Ottawa	NHL	13	2	5	7	2	4	1	0	1	0	0	0	0
00-01—Grand Rapids	IHL	43	10	14	24	10	...	...	...	7	4	4	8	0
—Ottawa	NHL	17	3	2	5	6	-1	0	0	—	—	—	—	—
NHL Totals (2 years)		30	5	7	12	8	3	1	0	1	0	0	0	0

PERSONAL: Born March 31, 1981, in Coronation, Alta. ... 6-5/202. ... Shoots right.
TRANSACTIONS/CAREER NOTES: Selected by Tampa Bay Lightning in third round (third Lightning pick, 75th overall) of NHL entry draft (June 26, 1999). ... Returned to draft pool by Lightning and selected by St. Louis Blues in sixth round (fifth Blues pick, 190th overall) of NHL entry draft (June 23, 2001).

Season Team	League	REGULAR SEASON								PLAYOFFS				
		Gms.	G	A	Pts.	PIM	+/-	PP	SH	Gms.	G	A	Pts.	PIM
97-98—Medicine Hat	WHL	25	0	1	1	69	...	...	...	—	—	—	—	—
98-99—Medicine Hat	WHL	69	3	10	13	252	...	...	...	—	—	—	—	—
99-00—Medicine Hat	WHL	71	1	9	10	281	...	...	...	—	—	—	—	—
00-01—Medicine Hat	WHL	62	3	10	13	279	...	...	...	—	—	—	—	—

PERSONAL: Born June 12, 1969, in New York. ... 5-10/192. ... Shoots left.
TRANSACTIONS/CAREER NOTES: Selected by Montreal Canadiens in third round (fourth Canadiens pick, 44th overall) of NHL entry draft (June 13, 1987). ... Bruised left shoulder (February 1990). ... Sprained left ankle (January 26, 1991); missed nine games. ... Sprained ankle (January 27, 1993); missed 24 games. ... Separated shoulder (April 18, 1993); missed seven playoff games. ... Injured ankle (December 6, 1993); missed two games. ... Underwent elbow surgery (March 29, 1994); missed five games. ... Suffered illness (February 27, 1995); missed one game. ... Traded by Canadiens with LW Kirk Muller and C Craig Darby to New York Islanders for D Vladimir Malakhov and C Pierre Turgeon (April 5, 1995). ... Bruised ribs (October 28, 1995); missed one game. ... Traded by Islanders with LW Wendel Clark and D D.J. Smith to Toronto Maple Leafs for LW Sean Haggerty, C Darby Hendrickson, D Kenny Jonsson and first-round pick (G Roberto Luongo) in 1997 draft (March 13, 1996). ... Suspended three games by NHL for elbowing incident (November 14, 1996). ... Strained groin (December 12, 1996); missed 27 games. ... Reinjured groin (February 12, 1997) and underwent surgery; and missed final 26 games of season. ... Suffered concussion and facial lacerations (December 2, 1997); missed two games. ... Bruised shoulder (January 6, 1998); missed two games. ... Strained upper abdominal muscle (February 2, 1998); missed one game. ... Strained groin (April 6, 1998); missed one game. ... Traded by Maple Leafs to New York Rangers for D Alexander Karpovtsev and fourth-round pick (LW Mirko Murovic) in 1999 draft (October 14, 1998). ... Suffered from the flu (January 27, 2000); missed one game. ... Suffered from the flu (March 26, 2000); missed one game. ... Selected by Columbus Blue Jackets in NHL expansion draft (June 23, 2000). ... Signed as free agent by Los Angeles Kings (August 13, 2000). ... Strained back (November 16, 2000); missed one game. ... Strained groin (February 23, 2001); missed eight games.
HONORS: Named to OHL All-Star first team (1987-88 and 1988-89). ... Played in NHL All-Star Game (1996).
MISCELLANEOUS: Member of Stanley Cup championship team (1993). ... Captain of New York Islanders (1995-March 13, 1996).

Season Team	League	REGULAR SEASON								PLAYOFFS				
		Gms.	G	A	Pts.	PIM	+/-	PP	SH	Gms.	G	A	Pts.	PIM
85-86—Mt. St. Charles H.S.	R.I.H.S.	19	3	27	30	...	...	...	...	—	—	—	—	—
86-87—Cornwall	OHL	63	7	29	36	75	...	...	...	5	0	0	0	22
87-88—Montreal	NHL	4	0	0	0	2	-2	0	0	—	—	—	—	—
—Cornwall	OHL	48	21	40	61	85	...	...	...	11	2	6	8	14
—Sherbrooke	AHL	—	—	—	—	—				3	0	3	3	12
88-89—Cornwall	OHL	59	16	57	73	96	...	...	...	18	7	20	27	30
89-90—Sherbrooke	AHL	28	6	13	19	20	...	...	...	—	—	—	—	—
—Montreal	NHL	44	7	14	21	25	2	5	0	9	1	3	4	31
90-91—Montreal	NHL	69	10	20	30	63	7	5	0	13	2	7	9	18
91-92—Montreal	NHL	78	8	24	32	72	10	2	0	10	1	4	5	6
92-93—Montreal	NHL	60	13	31	44	91	8	3	0	11	1	2	3	16
93-94—Montreal	NHL	75	20	32	52	62	15	11	0	1	0	0	0	0
94-95—Montreal	NHL	30	5	15	20	49	-3	2	0	—	—	—	—	—
—New York Islanders	NHL	13	3	6	9	30	-5	1	0	—	—	—	—	—
95-96—New York Islanders	NHL	65	11	36	47	93	-18	7	0	—	—	—	—	—
—Toronto	NHL	13	2	5	7	10	-2	0	0	6	0	4	4	8
96-97—Toronto	NHL	26	5	7	12	20	3	1	0	—	—	—	—	—
97-98—Toronto	NHL	76	11	26	37	44	-12	4	1	—	—	—	—	—
—U.S. Olympic team	Int'l	4	0	0	0	6	...	...	...	—	—	—	—	—
98-99—New York Rangers	NHL	75	10	24	34	71	-19	5	0	—	—	—	—	—
99-00—New York Rangers	NHL	80	10	20	30	78	-6	3	0	—	—	—	—	—
00-01—Los Angeles	NHL	73	16	35	51	56	0	7	1	13	0	9	9	10
NHL Totals (13 years)		781	131	295	426	766	-22	56	2	63	5	29	34	89

SCHULTZ, RAY — D — ISLANDERS

PERSONAL: Born November 14, 1976, in Red Deer, Alta. ... 6-2/200. ... Shoots left. ... Cousin of Rene Chapdelaine, defenseman with Los Angeles Kings (1990-91 through 1992-93).
TRANSACTIONS/CAREER NOTES: Selected by Ottawa Senators in eighth round (eighth Senators pick, 184th overall) of NHL entry draft (July 8, 1995). ... Signed as free agent by New York Islanders (June 17, 1997).

		REGULAR SEASON								PLAYOFFS				
Season Team	League	Gms.	G	A	Pts.	PIM	+/-	PP	SH	Gms.	G	A	Pts.	PIM
93-94—Tri-City	WHL	3	0	0	0	11	...	...	...	—	—	—	—	—
94-95—Tri-City	WHL	63	1	8	9	209	...	...	...	11	0	0	0	16
95-96—Calgary	WHL	66	3	17	20	282	...	...	...	—	—	—	—	—
96-97—Calgary	WHL	32	3	17	20	141	...	...	...	—	—	—	—	—
—Kelowna	WHL	23	3	11	14	63	...	...	...	6	0	2	2	12
97-98—Kentucky	AHL	51	2	4	6	179	...	...	...	1	0	0	0	25
—New York Islanders	NHL	13	0	1	1	45	3	0	0	—	—	—	—	—
98-99—Lowell	AHL	54	0	3	3	184	...	...	...	1	0	0	0	4
—New York Islanders	NHL	4	0	0	0	7	-2	0	0	—	—	—	—	—
99-00—Kansas City	IHL	65	5	5	10	208	...	...	...	—	—	—	—	—
—New York Islanders	NHL	9	0	1	1	30	1	0	0	—	—	—	—	—
00-01—Lowell	AHL	13	0	1	1	33	...	...	...	—	—	—	—	—
—Cleveland	IHL	44	3	5	8	127	...	...	...	3	1	0	1	16
—New York Islanders	NHL	13	0	2	2	40	-1	0	0	—	—	—	—	—
NHL Totals (4 years)		39	0	4	4	122	1	0	0					

SCOTT, TRAVIS — G — KINGS

PERSONAL: Born September 14, 1975, in Ottawa. ... 6-2/185. ... Catches left.
TRANSACTIONS/CAREER NOTES: Signed as non-drafted free agent by St. Louis Blues (December 30, 1996). ... Signed by Los Angeles Kings (February 18, 2000).
HONORS: Won ECHL Playoff MVP Award (1998-99).

		REGULAR SEASON								PLAYOFFS						
Season Team	League	Gms.	Min	W	L	T	GA	SO	Avg.	Gms.	Min.	W	L	GA	SO	Avg.
91-92—Smiths Falls-Nepean	Jr. A	22	1151	...	...	...	90	1	4.69	—	—	—	—	—	—	—
92-93—Nepean	COJHL	36	1968	...	...	...	133	0	4.05	—	—	—	—	—	—	—
93-94—Windsor	OHL	45	2312	20	18	0	158	1	4.10	4	240	0	4	16	0	4.00
94-95—Windsor	OHL	48	2644	26	14	3	147	*3	3.34	3	94	0	1	6	1	3.83
95-96—Oshawa	OHL	31	1763	15	9	4	78	†3	*2.65	5	315	1	4	23	0	4.38
96-97—Baton Rouge	ECHL	10	501	5	2	‡1	22	0	2.63	—	—	—	—	—	—	—
—Worcester	AHL	29	1482	14	10	1	75	1	3.04	—	—	—	—	—	—	—
97-98—Baton Rouge	ECHL	36	1949	14	11	‡6	96	1	2.96	—	—	—	—	—	—	—
98-99—Mississippi	ECHL	44	2337	22	12	‡5	112	1	2.88	†18	*1252	*14	4	42	3	2.01
99-00—Lowell	AHL	46	2595	15	23	3	126	3	2.91	1	60	0	1	2	0	2.00
00-01—Lowell	AHL	34	1977	16	15	1	83	2	2.52	4	209	1	2	7	1	2.01
—Los Angeles	NHL	1	25	0	0	0	3	0	7.20	—	—	—	—	—	—	—
NHL Totals (1 year)		1	25	0	0	0	3	0	7.20							

SEDIN, DANIEL — LW — CANUCKS

PERSONAL: Born September 26, 1980, in Ornskoldsvik, Sweden. ... 6-1/194. ... Shoots left. ... Twin brother of Henrik Sedin, center, Vancouver Canucks.
TRANSACTIONS/CAREER NOTES: Selected by Vancouver Canucks in first round (first Canucks pick, second overall) of NHL entry draft (June 26, 1999). ... Strained shoulder (November 30, 2000); missed four games. ... Injured back (March 25, 2001); missed two games. ... Reinjured back (April 2, 2001); missed one game.

		REGULAR SEASON								PLAYOFFS				
Season Team	League	Gms.	G	A	Pts.	PIM	+/-	PP	SH	Gms.	G	A	Pts.	PIM
96-97—MoDo Ornskoldsvik	Sweden Jr.	26	26	14	40		...	...	...	—	—	—	—	—
97-98—MoDo Ornskoldsvik	Sweden	45	4	8	12	26	...	...	...	9	0	0	0	2
—MoDo Ornskoldsvik	Sweden Jr.	4	3	3	6	4	...	...	...	—	—	—	—	—
98-99—MoDo Ornskoldsvik	Sweden	50	21	21	42	20	...	...	...	13	4	8	12	14
99-00—MoDo Ornskoldsvik	Sweden	50	19	26	45	28	...	...	...	13	†8	6	14	18
00-01—Vancouver	NHL	75	20	14	34	24	-3	10	0	4	1	2	3	0
NHL Totals (1 year)		75	20	14	34	24	-3	10	0	4	1	2	3	0

SEDIN, HENRIK — C — CANUCKS

PERSONAL: Born September 26, 1980, in Ornskoldsvik, Sweden. ... 6-2/196. ... Shoots left. ... Twin brother of Daniel Sedin, left winger, Vancouver Canucks.
TRANSACTIONS/CAREER NOTES: Selected by Vancouver Canucks in first round (second Canucks pick, third overall) of NHL entry draft (June 26, 1999).

		REGULAR SEASON								PLAYOFFS				
Season Team	League	Gms.	G	A	Pts.	PIM	+/-	PP	SH	Gms.	G	A	Pts.	PIM
96-97—MoDo Ornskoldsvik	Sweden Jr.	26	14	22	36		...	...	...	—	—	—	—	—
97-98—MoDo Ornskoldsvik	Sweden	39	1	4	5	8	...	...	...	7	0	0	0	0
—MoDo Ornskoldsvik	Sweden Jr.	8	4	7	11	6	...	...	...	—	—	—	—	—
98-99—MoDo Ornskoldsvik	Sweden	49	12	22	34	32	...	...	...	13	2	8	10	6
99-00—MoDo Ornskoldsvik	Sweden	50	9	38	47	22	...	...	...	13	5	9	14	2
00-01—Vancouver	NHL	82	9	20	29	38	-2	2	0	4	0	4	4	0
NHL Totals (1 year)		82	9	20	29	38	-2	2	0	4	0	4	4	0

SEKERAS, LUBOMIR　　　D　　　WILD

PERSONAL: Born November 18, 1968, in Trencin, Czechoslovakia. ... 6-0/176. ... Shoots left. ... Name pronounced SEH-kuhr-ahsh.
TRANSACTIONS/CAREER NOTES: Selected by Minnesota Wild in eighth round (eighth Wild pick, 232nd overall) of NHL entry draft (June 24, 2000). ... Bruised foot (January 10, 2001); missed one game. ... Suffered from the flu (April 4, 2001); missed one game.

		REGULAR SEASON								PLAYOFFS				
Season Team	League	Gms.	G	A	Pts.	PIM	+/-	PP	SH	Gms.	G	A	Pts.	PIM
88-89—Dukla Trencin..............	Czech.	16	2	5	7	22	...	...	...	11	0	4	4	0
89-90—Dukla Trencin..............	Czech.	44	6	8	14	...	...	...	...	9	0	2	2	...
90-91—Dukla Trencin..............	Czech.	52	6	16	22	...	...	...	...	6	0	1	1	...
91-92—Dukla Trencin..............	Czech.	30	2	6	8	32	...	...	...	13	1	1	2	0
92-93—Dukla Trencin..............	Czech.	40	5	19	24	48	...	...	...	11	4	9	13	0
93-94—Dukla Trencin..............	Slovakia	36	9	12	21	46	...	...	...	9	2	4	6	10
94-95—Dukla Trencin..............	Slovakia	36	11	11	22	24	...	...	...	9	2	7	9	8
95-96—Trinec..............	Czech	40	11	13	24	44	...	...	...	3	0	0	0	0
96-97—Trinec..............	Czech	52	14	21	35	56	...	...	...	4	1	0	1	2
97-98—Trinec..............	Czech	50	11	44	42	...	...	...	...	13	2	10	12	4
98-99—Trinec..............	Czech	50	8	15	23	38	...	...	...	10	2	6	8	0
99-00—Trinec..............	Czech	52	7	24	31	36	...	...	...	4	0	2	2	2
00-01—Minnesota..............	NHL	80	11	23	34	52	-8	4	0	—	—	—	—	—
NHL Totals (1 year)..............		80	11	23	34	52	-8	4	0	—	—	—	—	—

SELANNE, TEEMU　　　RW　　　SHARKS

PERSONAL: Born July 3, 1970, in Helsinki, Finland. ... 6-0/200. ... Shoots right. ... Name pronounced TAY-moo suh-LAH-nay. ... Nickname: The Finnish Flash.
TRANSACTIONS/CAREER NOTES: Selected by Winnipeg Jets in first round (first Jets pick, 10th overall) of NHL entry draft (June 11, 1988). ... Severed Achilles' tendon (January 26, 1994); missed 33 games. ... Played in Europe during 1994-95 NHL lockout. ... Suffered from patella tendonitis (February 28, 1995); missed one game. ... Suspended two games and fined $500 by NHL (March 28, 1995). ... Traded by Jets with C Marc Chouinard and fourth-round pick (traded to Toronto) in 1996 draft to Mighty Ducks of Anaheim for C Chad Kilger, D Oleg Tverdovsky and third-round pick (D Per-Anton Lundstrom) in 1996 draft (Frebraury 7, 1996). ... Strained abdominal muscle (March 23, 1997); missed four games. ... Strained abdominal muscle (February 7, 1998); missed five games. ... Strained groin (April 9, 1998); missed final four games of season. ... Strained thigh muscle (November 11,1998); missed six games. ... Reinjured thigh muscle (December 3, 1998); missed one game. ... Strained groin (November 14, 1999); missed three games. ... Strained groin (December 13, 2000); missed two games. ... Strained groin (December 22, 2000); missed two games. ... Injured knee (March 1, 2001) and underwent surgery; missed five games. ... Traded by Mighty Ducks to San Jose Sharks for LW Jeff Friesen, G Steve Shields and conditional pick in draft (March 5, 2001).
HONORS: Named to Finnish League All-Star team (1990-91 and 1991-92). ... Named NHL Rookie of the Year by THE SPORTING NEWS (1992-93). ... Won Calder Memorial Trophy (1992-93). ... Named to THE SPORTING NEWS All-Star first team (1992-93). ... Named to NHL All-Star first team (1992-93 and 1996-97). ... Named to NHL All-Rookie team (1992-93). ... Played in NHL All-Star Game (1993, 1994 and 1996-2000). ... Named to THE SPORTING NEWS All-Star team (1996-97 and 1997-98). ... Named All-Star Game Most Valuable Player (1998). ... Named to NHL All-Star second team (1997-98 and 1998-99). ... Won Maurice "Rocket" Richard Trophy (1998-99).
RECORDS: Holds NHL rookie-season records for most points—132; and goals—76 (1993).
STATISTICAL PLATEAUS: Three-goal games: 1992-93 (4), 1993-94 (2), 1995-96 (2), 1996-97 (1), 1997-98 (3), 1998-99 (1), 1999-00 (1), 2000-01 (2). Total: 16. ... Four-goal games: 1992-93 (1), 1995-96 (1). Total: 2. ... Total hat tricks: 18.
MISCELLANEOUS: Member of bronze-medal-winning Finnish Olympic team (1998). ... Captain of Mighty Ducks of Anaheim (October 1-December 10, 1997 and February 4, 1998 through remainder of season). ... Scored on a penalty shot (vs. Wendell Young, March 9, 1993). ... Failed to score on a penalty shot (vs. Trevor Kidd, February 6, 1995; vs. Jean-Sebastien Aubin, October 27, 1999).
STATISTICAL NOTES: Tied for NHL lead with three game-tying goals (1997-98).

		REGULAR SEASON								PLAYOFFS				
Season Team	League	Gms.	G	A	Pts.	PIM	+/-	PP	SH	Gms.	G	A	Pts.	PIM
87-88—Jokerit Helsinki	Finland Jr.	33	43	23	66	18	...	...	...	5	4	3	7	2
—Jokerit Helsinki	Finland	5	1	1	2	0	...	...	...	—	—	—	—	—
88-89—Jokerit Helsinki	Finland	34	35	33	68	12	...	...	...	5	7	3	10	4
89-90—Jokerit Helsinki	Finland	11	4	8	12	0	...	...	...	—	—	—	—	—
90-91—Jokerit Helsinki	Finland	42	*33	25	58	12	...	...	...	—	—	—	—	—
91-92—Fin. Olympic team	Int'l	8	7	4	11	...	...	...	...	—	—	—	—	—
—Jokerit Helsinki	Finland	44	39	23	62	20	...	...	...	—	—	—	—	—
92-93—Winnipeg	NHL	84	†76	56	132	45	8	24	0	6	4	2	6	2
93-94—Winnipeg	NHL	51	25	29	54	22	-23	11	0	—	—	—	—	—
94-95—Jokerit Helsinki	Finland	20	7	12	19	6	...	...	...	—	—	—	—	—
—Winnipeg	NHL	45	22	26	48	2	1	8	2	—	—	—	—	—
95-96—Winnipeg	NHL	51	24	48	72	18	3	6	1	—	—	—	—	—
—Anaheim	NHL	28	16	20	36	4	2	3	0	—	—	—	—	—
96-97—Anaheim	NHL	78	51	58	109	34	28	11	1	11	7	3	10	4
97-98—Anaheim	NHL	73	†52	34	86	30	12	10	1	—	—	—	—	—
—Fin. Olympic team	Int'l	5	4	6	10	8	...	...	...	—	—	—	—	—
98-99—Anaheim	NHL	75	*47	60	107	30	18	*25	0	4	2	2	4	2
99-00—Anaheim	NHL	79	33	52	85	12	6	8	0	—	—	—	—	—
00-01—Anaheim	NHL	61	26	33	59	36	-8	10	0	—	—	—	—	—
—San Jose	NHL	12	7	6	13	0	1	2	0	6	0	2	2	2
NHL Totals (9 years)..........		637	379	422	801	233	48	118	5	27	13	9	22	10

SELIVANOV, ALEX　　　RW

PERSONAL: Born March 23, 1971, in Moscow, U.S.S.R. ... 6-0/206. ... Shoots left. ... Full Name: Alexander Selivanov. ... Name pronounced sehl-ih-VAH-nahf.
TRANSACTIONS/CAREER NOTES: Selected by Philadelphia Flyers in sixth round (sixth Flyers pick, 140th overall) of NHL entry draft (June 29, 1994).

... Rights traded by Flyers to Tampa Bay Lightning for fourth-round pick (LW Radovan Somik) in 1995 draft (September 6, 1994). ... Sprained ankle (February 10, 1996); missed two games. ... Injured back (November 25, 1996); missed one game. ... Injured wrist (December 14, 1996); missed one game. ... Sprained knee (February 4, 1997); missed one game. ... Underwent knee surgery (February 25, 1997); missed eight games. ... Suffered a partial facial fracture (April 2, 1998); missed final eight games of season. ... Injured wrist (January 26, 1999); missed one game. ... Traded by Lightning to Edmonton Oilers for C/RW Alexandre Daigle (January 29, 1999). ... Signed as free agent by Columbus Blue Jackets (November 23, 2000). ... Sprained ankle (March 26, 2001); missed one game.

STATISTICAL PLATEAUS: Three-goal games: 1998-99 (1), 1999-00 (1). Total: 2. ... Four-goal games: 1999-00 (1). ... Total hat tricks: 3.

Season Team	League	REGULAR SEASON								PLAYOFFS				
		Gms.	G	A	Pts.	PIM	+/-	PP	SH	Gms.	G	A	Pts.	PIM
88-89—Spartak Moscow	USSR	1	0	0	0	0	...	...	...	—	—	—	—	—
89-90—Spartak Moscow	USSR	4	0	0	0	0	...	...	...	—	—	—	—	—
90-91—Spartak Moscow	USSR	21	3	1	4	6	...	...	...	—	—	—	—	—
91-92—Spartak Moscow	CIS	31	6	7	13	16	...	...	...	—	—	—	—	—
92-93—Spartak Moscow	CIS	42	12	19	31	16	...	...	...	3	2	0	2	2
93-94—Spartak Moscow	CIS	45	30	11	41	50	...	...	...	6	5	1	6	2
94-95—Atlanta	IHL	4	0	3	3	2	...	...	...	—	—	—	—	—
—Chicago	IHL	14	4	1	5	8	...	...	...	—	—	—	—	—
—Tampa Bay	NHL	43	10	6	16	14	-2	4	0	—	—	—	—	—
95-96—Tampa Bay	NHL	79	31	21	52	93	3	13	0	6	2	2	4	6
96-97—Tampa Bay	NHL	69	15	18	33	61	-3	3	0	—	—	—	—	—
97-98—Tampa Bay	NHL	70	16	19	35	85	-38	4	0	—	—	—	—	—
98-99—Cleveland	IHL	2	0	1	1	4	...	...	...	—	—	—	—	—
—Tampa Bay	NHL	43	6	13	19	18	-8	1	0	—	—	—	—	—
—Edmonton	NHL	29	8	6	14	24	0	1	0	2	0	1	1	2
99-00—Edmonton	NHL	67	27	20	47	46	2	10	0	5	0	0	0	8
00-01—Columbus	NHL	59	8	11	19	38	-11	5	0	—	—	—	—	—
NHL Totals (7 years)		459	121	114	235	379	-57	41	0	13	2	3	5	16

SELLARS, LUKE — D — THRASHERS

PERSONAL: Born May 21, 1981, in Toronto. ... 6-1/195. ... Shoots left.
TRANSACTIONS/CAREER NOTES: Selected by Atlanta Thrashers in second round (second Thrashers pick, 30th overall) of NHL entry draft (June 26, 1999).

Season Team	League	REGULAR SEASON								PLAYOFFS				
		Gms.	G	A	Pts.	PIM	+/-	PP	SH	Gms.	G	A	Pts.	PIM
97-98—Wexford	OHA Jr. A	40	7	30	37	170	...	...	...	—	—	—	—	—
98-99—Ottawa	OHL	56	4	19	23	87	...	...	...	—	—	—	—	—
99-00—Ottawa	OHL	56	8	34	42	147	...	...	...	11	4	6	10	28
00-01—Ottawa	OHL	59	9	21	30	136	...	...	...	18	4	10	14	47

SELMSER, SEAN — LW — BLUE JACKETS

PERSONAL: Born November 10, 1974, in Calgary. ... 6-1/180. ... Shoots left.
TRANSACTIONS/CAREER NOTES: Selected by Pittsburgh Penguins in seventh round (seventh Penguins pick, 182nd overall) of NHL entry draft (June 29, 1993). ... Signed as free agent by Columbus Blue Jackets (August 3, 2000).

Season Team	League	REGULAR SEASON								PLAYOFFS				
		Gms.	G	A	Pts.	PIM	+/-	PP	SH	Gms.	G	A	Pts.	PIM
92-93—Red Deer	WHL	70	13	27	40	216	...	...	...	4	0	0	0	10
93-94—Red Deer	WHL	71	25	25	50	201	...	...	...	4	1	0	1	14
94-95—Red Deer	WHL	33	11	17	28	65	...	...	...	—	—	—	—	—
95-96—Hampton Roads	ECHL	70	23	31	54	211	...	...	...	3	2	0	2	8
—Portland	AHL	6	4	1	5	28	...	...	...	5	2	3	5	11
96-97—Canadian nat'l team	Int'l	59	20	18	38	150	...	...	...	—	—	—	—	—
—Manitoba	IHL	4	0	2	2	12	...	...	...	—	—	—	—	—
97-98—Can. Nat'l "B" Team	Int'l	52	8	22	30	122	...	...	...	—	—	—	—	—
98-99—Fort Wayne	IHL	80	9	17	26	200	...	...	...	2	0	0	0	2
99-00—Hamilton	AHL	72	14	12	26	151	...	...	...	10	3	4	7	10
00-01—Syracuse	AHL	75	11	15	26	151	...	...	...	5	0	0	0	14
—Columbus	NHL	1	0	0	0	5	0	0	0	—	—	—	—	—
NHL Totals (1 year)		1	0	0	0	5	0	0	0					

SEMENOV, ALEXEI — D — OILERS

PERSONAL: Born April 10, 1981, in Murmansk, U.S.S.R. ... 6-6/210. ... Shoots left.
TRANSACTIONS/CAREER NOTES: Selected by Edmonton Oilers in second round (second Oilers pick, 36th overall) of NHL entry draft (June 26, 1999).
HONORS: Named to OHL All-Star first team (2000-01). ... Won Max Kaminsky Trophy (2000-01).

Season Team	League	REGULAR SEASON								PLAYOFFS				
		Gms.	G	A	Pts.	PIM	+/-	PP	SH	Gms.	G	A	Pts.	PIM
97-98—Krylja Sovetov-2 Mos.	Rus. Div. III	52	1	2	3	48	...	...	...	—	—	—	—	—
98-99—Sudbury	OHL	28	0	3	3	28	...	...	...	2	0	0	0	4
99-00—Sudbury	OHL	65	9	35	44	135	...	...	...	12	1	3	4	23
—Hamilton	AHL	—	—	—	—	—	...	...	...	3	0	0	0	0
00-01—Sudbury	OHL	65	21	42	63	106	...	...	...	12	4	13	17	17

PERSONAL: Born January 23, 1969, in Mimico, Ont. ... 6-3/215. ... Shoots right. ... Full Name: Brendan Frederick Shanahan.

TRANSACTIONS/CAREER NOTES: Selected by New Jersey Devils in first round (first Devils pick, second overall) of NHL entry draft (June 13, 1987). ... Fractured nose (December 1987). ... Suffered back spasms (March 1989). ... Suspended five games by NHL for stick-fighting (January 13, 1990). ... Suffered lower abdominal strain (February 1990). ... Suffered lacerations to lower right side of face and underwent surgery (January 8, 1991); missed five games. ... Signed as free agent by St. Louis Blues (July 25, 1991); D Scott Stevens awarded to Devils as compensation (September 3, 1991). ... Pulled groin (October 24, 1992); missed 12 games. ... Suspended six off-days and fined $500 by NHL for hitting another player in face with his stick (January 7, 1993). ... Suspended one game by NHL for high-sticking incident (February 23, 1993). ... Suffered viral infection (November 18, 1993); missed one game. ... Injured hamstring (March 22, 1994); missed two games. ... Played in Europe during 1994-95 NHL lockout. ... Suffered viral infection (January 20, 1995); missed three games. ... Fractured ankle (May 15, 1995); missed last two games of playoffs. ... Traded by Blues to Hartford Whalers for D Chris Pronger (July 27, 1995). ... Sprained wrist (November 11, 1995); missed eight games. ... Traded by Whalers with D Brian Glynn to Detroit Red Wings for C Keith Primeau, D Paul Coffey and first-round pick (traded to San Jose) in 1997 draft (October 9, 1996). ... Suspended one game and fined $1,000 by NHL for cross-checking incident (October 11, 1996). ... Strained groin (October 30, 1996); missed one game. ... Suffered stiff neck (October 12, 1997); missed four games. ... Suffered back spasms (April 15, 1998); missed final game of regular season and two playoff games. ... Suspended two games by NHL for stick-swinging incident (November 9, 1999).

HONORS: Played in NHL All-Star Game (1994 and 1996-2000). ... Named to NHL All-Star first team (1993-94 and 1999-2000).

MISCELLANEOUS: Member of Stanley Cup championship team (1997 and 1998). ... Captain of Hartford Whalers (1995-96). ... Failed to score on a penalty shot (vs. Grant Fuhr, December 27, 1992; vs. Trevor Kidd, November 5, 1997).

STATISTICAL PLATEAUS: Three-goal games: 1992-93 (1), 1993-94 (4), 1995-96 (1), 1996-97 (3), 1998-99 (2). Total: 11. ... Four-goal games: 2000-01 (1). ... Total hat tricks: 12.

		REGULAR SEASON							PLAYOFFS				
Season Team	League	Gms.	G	A	Pts.	PIM	+/-	PP	SH	Gms.	G	A	Pts.	PIM
84-85—Mississauga	MTHL	36	20	21	41	26	...	...	...	—	—	—	—	—
85-86—London	OHL	59	28	34	62	70	...	...	...	5	5	5	10	5
86-87—London	OHL	56	39	53	92	128	...	...	...	—	—	—	—	—
87-88—New Jersey	NHL	65	7	19	26	131	-20	2	0	12	2	1	3	44
88-89—New Jersey	NHL	68	22	28	50	115	2	9	0	—	—	—	—	—
89-90—New Jersey	NHL	73	30	42	72	137	15	8	0	6	3	3	6	20
90-91—New Jersey	NHL	75	29	37	66	141	4	7	0	7	3	5	8	12
91-92—St. Louis	NHL	80	33	36	69	171	-3	13	0	6	2	3	5	14
92-93—St. Louis	NHL	71	51	43	94	174	10	18	0	11	4	3	7	18
93-94—St. Louis	NHL	81	52	50	102	211	-9	15	*7	4	2	5	7	4
94-95—Dusseldorf	Germany	3	5	3	8	4	...	...	...	—	—	—	—	—
—St. Louis	NHL	45	20	21	41	136	7	6	2	5	4	5	9	14
95-96—Hartford	NHL	74	44	34	78	125	2	17	2	—	—	—	—	—
96-97—Hartford	NHL	2	1	0	1	0	1	0	1	—	—	—	—	—
—Detroit	NHL	79	46	41	87	131	31	†20	2	20	9	8	17	43
97-98—Detroit	NHL	75	28	29	57	154	6	15	1	20	5	4	9	22
—Can. Olympic team	Int'l	6	2	0	2	0	...	...	...	—	—	—	—	—
98-99—Detroit	NHL	81	31	27	58	123	2	5	0	10	3	7	10	6
99-00—Detroit	NHL	78	41	37	78	105	24	13	1	9	3	2	5	10
00-01—Detroit	NHL	81	31	45	76	81	9	15	1	2	2	2	4	0
NHL Totals (14 years)		1028	466	489	955	1935	81	163	17	112	42	48	90	207

PERSONAL: Born June 21, 1968, in Barrie, Ont. ... 6-2/208. ... Shoots left. ... Brother of Darrin Shannon, left winger with three NHL teams (1988-89 through 1997-98).

TRANSACTIONS/CAREER NOTES: Selected by Toronto Maple Leafs in second round (second Maple Leafs pick, 36th overall) of NHL entry draft (June 21, 1986). ... Fractured right leg and right thumb, bruised chest and suffered slipped disk in automobile accident (June 20, 1990). ... Signed as free agent with Winnipeg Jets (July 8, 1993). ... Traded by Jets with LW Michael Grosek to Buffalo Sabres for D Craig Muni (February 15, 1996). ... Injured right knee (April 10, 1996); missed one game. ... Bruised knee (December 29, 1997); missed four games. ... Selected by Atlanta Thrashers in NHL expansion draft (June 25, 1999). ... Traded by Thrashers with LW Jason Botterill to Calgary Flames for C Hnat Domenichelli and LW Dmitri Vlasenkov (February 11, 2000). ... Signed as free agent by Montreal Canadiens (September 19, 2000).

HONORS: Named to OHL All-Star second team (1986-87). ... Won Max Kaminsky Trophy (1987-88). ... Named to OHL All-Star first team (1987-88). ... Named to Memorial Cup All-Star team (1987-88).

		REGULAR SEASON							PLAYOFFS				
Season Team	League	Gms.	G	A	Pts.	PIM	+/-	PP	SH	Gms.	G	A	Pts.	PIM
84-85—Barrie Jr. B	OHA	39	5	23	28	50	...	...	...	16	5	6	11	22
85-86—Windsor	OHL	57	6	21	27	52	...	...	...	14	4	8	12	18
86-87—Windsor	OHL	64	23	27	50	83	...	...	...	14	4	8	12	18
87-88—Windsor	OHL	60	16	70	86	116	...	...	...	12	3	8	11	17
88-89—Toronto	NHL	14	1	3	4	6	5	0	0	—	—	—	—	—
—Newmarket	AHL	61	5	24	29	37	...	...	...	5	0	3	3	10
89-90—Newmarket	AHL	47	4	15	19	58	...	...	...	—	—	—	—	—
—Toronto	NHL	10	0	1	1	12	-10	0	0	—	—	—	—	—
90-91—Toronto	NHL	10	0	1	1	0	1	0	0	—	—	—	—	—
—Newmarket	AHL	47	2	14	16	51	...	...	...	—	—	—	—	—
91-92—Toronto	NHL	48	2	8	10	23	-17	1	0	—	—	—	—	—
92-93—Toronto	NHL	16	0	0	0	11	-5	0	0	—	—	—	—	—
—St. John's	AHL	7	1	1	2	4	...	...	...	—	—	—	—	—
93-94—Moncton	AHL	37	1	10	11	62	...	...	...	20	1	7	8	32
—Winnipeg	NHL	20	0	4	4	18	-6	0	0	—	—	—	—	—
94-95—Winnipeg	NHL	40	5	9	14	48	1	0	1	—	—	—	—	—
95-96—Winnipeg	NHL	48	2	7	9	72	5	0	0	—	—	—	—	—
—Buffalo	NHL	26	2	6	8	20	10	0	0	—	—	—	—	—
96-97—Buffalo	NHL	82	4	19	23	112	23	1	0	12	2	3	5	8
97-98—Buffalo	NHL	76	3	19	22	56	26	1	0	15	2	4	6	8

Season Team	League	REGULAR SEASON								PLAYOFFS				
		Gms.	G	A	Pts.	PIM	+/-	PP	SH	Gms.	G	A	Pts.	PIM
98-99—Buffalo	NHL	71	3	12	15	52	28	1	0	2	0	0	0	0
99-00—Atlanta	NHL	49	5	13	18	65	-14	1	0	—	—	—	—	—
—Calgary	NHL	27	1	8	9	22	-13	0	0	—	—	—	—	—
00-01—Montreal	NHL	7	0	1	1	6	-4	0	0	—	—	—	—	—
—Quebec	AHL	4	0	1	1	4	...	...	...	—	—	—	—	—
NHL Totals (13 years)		544	28	111	139	523	30	5	1	29	4	7	11	16

SHANTZ, JEFF C FLAMES

PERSONAL: Born October 10, 1973, in Edmonton. ... 6-0/195. ... Shoots right.

TRANSACTIONS/CAREER NOTES: Selected by Chicago Blackhawks in second round (second Blackhawks pick, 36th overall) of NHL entry draft (June 20, 1992). ... Bruised right shoulder (1993-94 season); missed six games. ... Suffered swollen eye (November 30, 1996); missed one game. ... Sprained knee (February 25, 1997); missed 10 games. ... Separated shoulder (January 4, 1998); missed six games. ... Tore anterior cruciate ligament in left knee (March 19, 1998); missed final 14 games of season. ... Traded by Blackhawks with C/LW Steve Dubinsky to Calgary Flames for D Jamie Allison, C/LW Marty McInnis and RW Erik Andersson (October 27, 1998). ... Suffered concussion (November 14, 1998); missed two games. ... Injured shoulder (March 25, 1999); missed four games. ... Bruised ribs (December 6, 1999); missed eight games. ... Injured knee (March 22, 2001); missed remainder of season.

HONORS: Named to WHL (East) All-Star first team (1992-93).

Season Team	League	REGULAR SEASON								PLAYOFFS				
		Gms.	G	A	Pts.	PIM	+/-	PP	SH	Gms.	G	A	Pts.	PIM
89-90—Regina	WHL	1	0	0	0	0	...	...	...	—	—	—	—	—
—Medicine Hat	AMHL	36	18	31	49	30	...	...	...	—	—	—	—	—
90-91—Regina	WHL	69	16	21	37	22	...	...	...	8	2	2	4	2
91-92—Regina	WHL	72	39	50	89	75	...	...	...	—	—	—	—	—
92-93—Regina	WHL	64	29	54	83	75	...	...	...	13	2	12	14	14
93-94—Chicago	NHL	52	3	13	16	30	-14	0	0	6	0	0	0	6
—Indianapolis	IHL	19	5	9	14	20	...	...	...	—	—	—	—	—
94-95—Indianapolis	IHL	32	9	15	24	20	...	...	...	—	—	—	—	—
—Chicago	NHL	45	6	12	18	33	11	0	2	16	3	1	4	2
95-96—Chicago	NHL	78	6	14	20	24	12	1	2	10	2	3	5	6
96-97—Chicago	NHL	69	9	21	30	28	11	0	1	6	0	4	4	6
97-98—Chicago	NHL	61	11	20	31	36	0	1	2	—	—	—	—	—
98-99—Chicago	NHL	7	1	0	1	4	-1	0	0	—	—	—	—	—
—Calgary	NHL	69	12	17	29	40	15	1	1	—	—	—	—	—
99-00—Calgary	NHL	74	13	18	31	30	-13	6	0	—	—	—	—	—
00-01—Calgary	NHL	73	5	15	20	58	-7	0	0	—	—	—	—	—
NHL Totals (8 years)		528	66	130	196	283	14	9	8	38	5	8	13	20

SHARIFIJANOV, VADIM RW CANUCKS

PERSONAL: Born December 23, 1975, in Ufa, U.S.S.R. ... 6-0/205. ... Shoots left. ... Name pronounced vah-DEEM shuh-RIH-fee-AH-nahf.

TRANSACTIONS/CAREER NOTES: Selected by New Jersey Devils in first round (first Devils pick, 25th overall) of NHL entry draft (June 28, 1994). ... Strained groin (October 10, 1998); missed one game. ... Suffered from the flu (January 18, 1999); missed one game. ... Traded by Devils with third-round pick (D Tim Branham) in 2000 draft to Vancouver Canucks for third-round pick (LW Max Birbraer) in 2000 draft (January 14, 2000). ... Injured hip (February 17, 2000); missed seven games.

Season Team	League	REGULAR SEASON								PLAYOFFS				
		Gms.	G	A	Pts.	PIM	+/-	PP	SH	Gms.	G	A	Pts.	PIM
92-93—Salavat Yulayev Ufa	CIS	37	6	4	10	16	...	...	...	2	1	0	1	0
93-94—Salavat Yulayev Ufa	CIS	46	10	6	16	36	...	...	...	5	3	0	3	4
94-95—CSKA Moscow	CIS	34	7	3	10	26	...	...	...	2	0	0	0	0
—Albany	AHL	1	1	1	2	0	...	...	...	9	3	3	6	10
95-96—Albany	AHL	69	14	28	42	28	...	...	...	—	—	—	—	—
96-97—Albany	AHL	70	14	27	41	89	...	...	...	10	3	3	6	6
—New Jersey	NHL	2	0	0	0	0	0	0	0	—	—	—	—	—
97-98—Albany	AHL	72	23	27	50	69	...	...	...	12	4	9	13	6
98-99—New Jersey	NHL	53	11	16	27	28	11	1	0	4	0	0	0	0
—Albany	AHL	2	1	1	2	0	...	...	...	—	—	—	—	—
99-00—New Jersey	NHL	20	3	4	7	8	-6	0	0	—	—	—	—	—
—Vancouver	NHL	17	2	1	3	14	-7	1	0	—	—	—	—	—
00-01—Kansas City	IHL	70	20	43	63	48	...	...	...	—	—	—	—	—
NHL Totals (3 years)		92	16	21	37	50	-2	2	0	4	0	0	0	0

SHEARER, ROB C

PERSONAL: Born October 19, 1976, in Kitchener, Ont. ... 5-10/190. ... Shoots right.

TRANSACTIONS/CAREER NOTES: Signed as non-drafted free agent by Colorado Avalanche (October 5, 1995).

Season Team	League	REGULAR SEASON								PLAYOFFS				
		Gms.	G	A	Pts.	PIM	+/-	PP	SH	Gms.	G	A	Pts.	PIM
94-95—Windsor	OHL	59	28	28	56	56	...	...	...	10	4	4	8	10
95-96—Windsor	OHL	63	40	53	93	74	...	...	...	7	6	3	9	8
96-97—Hershey	AHL	78	12	16	28	88	...	...	...	23	0	4	4	9
97-98—Hershey	AHL	79	30	30	60	44	...	...	...	7	0	5	5	6
98-99—Hershey	AHL	77	24	42	66	43	...	...	...	3	0	0	0	6
99-00—Hershey	AHL	70	21	46	67	55	...	...	...	14	1	7	8	10
00-01—Hershey	AHL	73	18	34	52	64	...	...	...	12	1	3	4	0
—Colorado	NHL	2	0	0	0	0	-2	0	0	—	—	—	—	—
NHL Totals (1 year)		2	0	0	0	0	-2	0	0	—	—	—	—	—

SHELLEY, JODY   LW   BLUE JACKETS

PERSONAL: Born February 6, 1976, in Yarmouth, Nova Scotia. ... 6-3/230. ... Shoots left.
TRANSACTIONS/CAREER NOTES: Signed as non-drafted free agent by Calgary Flames (September 1, 1998). ... Signed as free agent by Columbus Blue Jackets (February 1, 2001).

		REGULAR SEASON								PLAYOFFS				
Season Team	League	Gms.	G	A	Pts.	PIM	+/-	PP	SH	Gms.	G	A	Pts.	PIM
94-95—Halifax	QMJHL	72	10	12	22	194	...	...	...	7	0	1	1	12
95-96—Halifax	QMJHL	50	13	19	32	319	...	...	...	6	0	2	2	36
96-97—Halifax	QMJHL	58	25	19	44	448	...	...	...	17	6	6	12	123
97-98—Dalhousie University	AUAA	19	6	11	17	145	...	...	...	—	—	—	—	—
—Saint John	AHL	18	1	1	2	50	...	...	...	—	—	—	—	—
98-99—Saint John	AHL	8	0	0	0	46	...	...	...	—	—	—	—	—
—Johnstown	ECHL	52	12	17	29	†325	...	...	...	—	—	—	—	—
99-00—Johnstown	ECHL	36	9	17	26	256	...	...	...	—	—	—	—	—
—Saint John	AHL	22	1	4	5	93	...	...	...	3	0	0	0	2
00-01—Syracuse	AHL	69	1	7	8	*357	...	...	...	5	0	0	0	21
—Columbus	NHL	1	0	0	0	10	0	0	0	—	—	—	—	—
NHL Totals (1 year)		1	0	0	0	10	0	0	0					

SHIELDS, STEVE   G   MIGHTY DUCKS

PERSONAL: Born July 19, 1972, in Toronto. ... 6-3/215. ... Catches left.
TRANSACTIONS/CAREER NOTES: Selected by Buffalo Sabres in fifth round (fifth Sabres pick, 101st overall) of NHL entry draft (June 22, 1991). ... Traded by Sabres with fourth-round pick (RW Miroslav Zalesak) in 1998 draft to San Jose Sharks for G Kay Whitmore, second-round pick (RW Jaroslav Kristek) in 1998 draft and fifth-round pick (traded to Columbus) in 2000 draft (June 18, 1998). ... Sprained ankle (October 12, 2000); missed eight games. ... Traded by Sharks with LW Jeff Friesen and conditional pick in draft to Mighty Ducks of Anaheim for RW Teemu Selanne (March 5, 2001). ... Injured ligaments in left shoulder and underwent surgery (March 7, 2001); missed remainder of season.
HONORS: Named to NCCA All-America (West) second team (1992-93 and 1993-94). ... Named to CCHA All-Star first team (1992-93 and 1993-94).
MISCELLANEOUS: Stopped a penalty shot attempt (vs. Terry Yake, January 26, 1999; vs. Pierre Turgeon, December 30, 1999; vs. Robert Kron, November 3, 2000). ... Allowed penalty shot goal (vs. Eric Lindros, May 11, 1997 (playoffs)).

		REGULAR SEASON								PLAYOFFS						
Season Team	League	Gms.	Min	W	L	T	GA	SO	Avg.	Gms.	Min.	W	L	GA	SO	Avg.
90-91—Univ. of Michigan	CCHA	37	1963	26	6	3	106	0	3.24	—	—	—	—	—	—	—
91-92—Univ. of Michigan	CCHA	37	2091	27	7	2	98	1	2.81	—	—	—	—	—	—	—
92-93—Univ. of Michigan	CCHA	39	2027	30	6	2	75	...	2.22	—	—	—	—	—	—	—
93-94—Univ. of Michigan	CCHA	36	1961	28	6	1	87	2	2.66	—	—	—	—	—	—	—
94-95—South Carolina	ECHL	21	1158	11	5	‡2	52	2	2.69	3	144	0	2	11	0	4.58
—Rochester	AHL	13	673	3	8	0	53	0	4.73	1	20	0	0	3	0	9.00
95-96—Rochester	AHL	43	2356	20	17	2	140	1	3.57	*19	*1126	*15	3	47	1	2.50
—Buffalo	NHL	2	75	1	0	0	4	0	3.20	—	—	—	—	—	—	—
96-97—Rochester	AHL	23	1331	14	6	2	60	1	2.70	—	—	—	—	—	—	—
—Buffalo	NHL	13	789	3	8	2	39	0	2.97	10	570	4	6	26	1	2.74
97-98—Buffalo	NHL	16	785	3	6	4	37	0	2.83	—	—	—	—	—	—	—
—Rochester	AHL	1	59	0	1	0	3	0	3.05	—	—	—	—	—	—	—
98-99—San Jose	NHL	37	2162	15	11	8	80	4	2.22	1	60	0	1	6	0	6.00
99-00—San Jose	NHL	67	3797	27	30	8	162	4	2.56	12	696	5	7	36	0	3.10
00-01—San Jose	NHL	21	1135	6	8	5	47	2	2.48	—	—	—	—	—	—	—
NHL Totals (6 years)		156	8743	55	63	27	369	10	2.53	23	1326	9	14	68	1	3.08

SHVIDKI, DENIS   RW   PANTHERS

PERSONAL: Born November 21, 1980, in Kharkov, U.S.S.R. ... 6-0/205. ... Shoots left.
TRANSACTIONS/CAREER NOTES: Selected by Florida Panthers in first round (first Panthers pick, 12th overall) of NHL entry draft (June 26, 1999). ... Strained tendon in foot (February 28, 2001); missed three games.
HONORS: Named to OHL All-Star second team (1998-99).

		REGULAR SEASON								PLAYOFFS				
Season Team	League	Gms.	G	A	Pts.	PIM	+/-	PP	SH	Gms.	G	A	Pts.	PIM
96-97—Torpedo-Yaroslavl	Russian	17	3	2	5	6	...	...	...	—	—	—	—	—
97-98—Torpedo-Yaroslavl	Russian	15	1	1	2	2	...	...	...	—	—	—	—	—
—Torpedo-2 Yaroslavl	Rus. Div. II	32	20	13	33	20	...	...	...	—	—	—	—	—
98-99—Barrie	OHL	61	35	59	94	8	...	...	...	12	7	9	16	2
99-00—Barrie	OHL	61	41	65	106	55	...	...	...	9	3	1	4	2
00-01—Florida	NHL	43	6	10	16	16	6	0	0	—	—	—	—	—
—Louisville	AHL	34	15	11	26	20	...	...	...	—	—	—	—	—
NHL Totals (1 year)		43	6	10	16	16	6	0	0					

SILLINGER, MIKE   C   BLUE JACKETS

PERSONAL: Born June 29, 1971, in Regina, Sask. ... 5-11/191. ... Shoots right. ... Name pronounced SIHL-in-juhr.
TRANSACTIONS/CAREER NOTES: Selected by Detroit Red Wings in first round (first Red Wings pick, 11th overall) of NHL entry draft (June 17, 1989). ... Fractured rib in training camp (September 1990). ... Suffered from the flu (March 5, 1993); missed three games. ... Strained rotator cuff (October 9, 1993); missed four games. ... Played in Europe during 1994-95 NHL lockout. ... Injured eye (January 17, 1995); missed four games. ... Traded by Red Wings with D Jason York to Mighty Ducks of Anaheim for LW Stu Grimson, D Mark Ferner and sixth-round pick (LW Magnus Nilsson) in 1996 draft (April 4, 1995). ... Traded by Mighty Ducks to Vancouver Canucks for RW Roman Oksuita (March 15, 1996). ... Suffered concussion (March 26, 1997); missed two games. ... Traded by Canucks to Flyers for sixth-round pick (traded back to Philadelphia) in 1998 draft (February 5, 1998). ... Sprained left knee (October 22, 1998); missed one game. ... Traded by Flyers with C Chris Gratton to Tampa Bay Lightning for RW Mikael Renberg and C Daymond Langkow (December 12, 1998). ... Traded by Lightning to Florida

Panthers for C Ryan Johnson and LW Dwayne Hay (March 14, 2000). ... Fractured foot (November 8, 2000); missed 12 games. ... Strained groin (January 24, 2001); missed three games. ... Traded by Panthers to Ottawa Senators for third-round pick in 2002 draft and future considerations (March 13, 2001). ... Signed as free agent by Columbus Blue Jackets (July 5, 2001).
HONORS: Named to WHL All-Star second team (1989-90). ... Named to WHL (East) All-Star first team (1990-91).
MISCELLANEOUS: Scored on a penalty shot (vs. Mark Fitzpatrick, January 14, 1997). ... Failed to score on a penalty shot (vs. Tommy Salo, January 7, 2000).
STATISTICAL NOTES: Led NHL in shooting percentage with 21.9 (1997-98).

Season Team	League	REGULAR SEASON Gms.	G	A	Pts.	PIM	+/-	PP	SH	PLAYOFFS Gms.	G	A	Pts.	PIM
87-88—Regina	WHL	67	18	25	43	17	...	...	...	4	2	2	4	0
88-89—Regina	WHL	72	53	78	131	52	...	...	...	—	—	—	—	—
89-90—Regina	WHL	70	57	72	129	41	...	...	...	11	12	10	22	2
—Adirondack	AHL	—	—	—	—	—	...	...	...	1	0	0	0	0
90-91—Regina	WHL	57	50	66	116	42	...	...	...	8	6	9	15	4
—Detroit	NHL	3	0	1	1	0	-2	0	0	3	0	1	1	0
91-92—Adirondack	AHL	64	25	41	66	26	...	...	...	15	9	*19	*28	12
—Detroit	NHL	—	—	—	—	—	...	...	...	8	2	2	4	2
92-93—Detroit	NHL	51	4	17	21	16	0	0	0	—	—	—	—	—
—Adirondack	AHL	15	10	20	30	31	...	...	...	11	5	13	18	10
93-94—Detroit	NHL	62	8	21	29	10	2	0	1	—	—	—	—	—
94-95—Wien	Austria	13	13	14	27	10	...	...	...	—	—	—	—	—
—Detroit	NHL	13	2	6	8	2	3	0	0	—	—	—	—	—
—Anaheim	NHL	15	2	5	7	6	1	2	0	—	—	—	—	—
95-96—Anaheim	NHL	62	13	21	34	32	-20	7	0	—	—	—	—	—
—Vancouver	NHL	12	1	3	4	6	2	0	1	6	0	0	0	2
96-97—Vancouver	NHL	78	17	20	37	25	-3	3	3	—	—	—	—	—
97-98—Vancouver	NHL	48	10	9	19	34	-14	1	2	—	—	—	—	—
—Philadelphia	NHL	27	11	11	22	16	3	1	2	3	1	0	1	0
98-99—Philadelphia	NHL	25	0	3	3	8	-9	0	0	—	—	—	—	—
—Tampa Bay	NHL	54	8	2	10	28	-20	0	2	—	—	—	—	—
99-00—Tampa Bay	NHL	67	19	25	44	86	-29	6	3	—	—	—	—	—
—Florida	NHL	13	4	4	8	16	-1	2	0	4	2	1	3	2
00-01—Florida	NHL	55	13	21	34	44	-12	1	0	—	—	—	—	—
—Ottawa	NHL	13	3	4	7	4	1	0	0	4	0	0	0	2
NHL Totals (11 years)		598	115	173	288	333	-98	23	14	28	5	4	9	8

SIM, JON — LW — STARS

PERSONAL: Born September 29, 1977, in New Glasgow, Nova Scotia. ... 5-10/184. ... Shoots left. ... Full Name: Jonathan Sim.
TRANSACTIONS/CAREER NOTES: Selected by Dallas Stars in third round (second Stars pick, 70th overall) of NHL entry draft (June 22, 1996). ... Fractured shoulder blade (September 16, 2000); missed first six games of season.
HONORS: Named to OHL All-Star second team (1997-98).
MISCELLANEOUS: Member of Stanley Cup championship team (1999).

Season Team	League	REGULAR SEASON Gms.	G	A	Pts.	PIM	+/-	PP	SH	PLAYOFFS Gms.	G	A	Pts.	PIM
94-95—Laval	QMJHL	9	0	1	1	6	...	...	...	—	—	—	—	—
—Sarnia	OHL	25	9	12	21	19	...	...	...	4	3	2	5	2
95-96—Sarnia	OHL	63	56	46	102	130	...	...	...	10	8	7	15	26
96-97—Sarnia	OHL	64	†56	39	95	109	...	...	...	12	9	5	14	32
97-98—Sarnia	OHL	59	44	50	94	95	...	...	...	5	1	4	5	14
98-99—Michigan	IHL	68	24	27	51	91	...	...	...	5	3	1	4	18
—Dallas	NHL	7	1	0	1	12	1	0	0	4	0	0	0	0
99-00—Michigan	IHL	35	14	16	30	65	...	...	...	—	—	—	—	—
—Dallas	NHL	25	5	3	8	10	4	2	0	7	1	0	1	6
00-01—Dallas	NHL	15	0	3	3	6	-2	0	0	—	—	—	—	—
—Utah	IHL	39	16	13	29	44	...	...	...	—	—	—	—	—
NHL Totals (3 years)		47	6	6	12	28	3	2	0	11	1	0	1	6

SIMICEK, ROMAN — C — WILD

PERSONAL: Born November 4, 1971, in Ostrava, Czechoslovakia. ... 6-1/190. ... Shoots left.
TRANSACTIONS/CAREER NOTES: Selected by Pittsburgh Penguins in ninth round (ninth Penguins pick, 273rd overall) of NHL entry draft (June 24, 2000). ... Traded by Penguins to Minnesota Wild for LW Steve McKenna (January 14, 2001). ... Sprained right knee (February 24, 2001); missed three games. ... Sprained right knee (March 22, 2001); missed final seven games of season.

Season Team	League	REGULAR SEASON Gms.	G	A	Pts.	PIM	+/-	PP	SH	PLAYOFFS Gms.	G	A	Pts.	PIM
89-90—Vitkovice	Czech.	5	3	4	7	2	...	...	...	—	—	—	—	—
90-91—Vitkovice	Czech.	35	2	4	6	0	...	...	...	—	—	—	—	—
91-92—Vitkovice	Czech.	45	8	19	27	34	...	...	...	—	—	—	—	—
92-93—Vitkovice	Czech.	38	8	15	23	52	...	...	...	—	—	—	—	—
93-94—Vitkovice	Czech.	40	18	16	34	...	...	...	...	5	0	2	2	...
94-95—Vitkovice	Czech.	41	11	14	25	100	...	...	...	6	1	3	4	8
95-96—Vitkovice	Czech.	39	9	11	20	38	...	...	...	4	2	0	2	8
96-97—Vitkovice	Czech.	49	18	19	37	38	...	...	...	9	2	4	6	6
97-98—Vitkovice	Czech.	40	16	27	43	71	...	...	...	9	2	4	6	6
98-99—HPK Hameenlinna	Finland	49	24	27	51	75	...	...	...	—	—	—	—	—
99-00—HPK Hameenlinna	Finland	23	10	17	27	50	...	...	...	—	—	—	—	--
00-01—Pittsburgh	NHL	29	3	6	9	30	-5	1	0	—	—	—	—	—
—Minnesota	NHL	28	2	4	6	21	-4	2	0	—	—	—	—	—
NHL Totals (1 year)		57	5	10	15	51	-9	3	0	—	—	—	—	—

PERSONAL: Born January 30, 1972, in Wawa, Ont. ... 6-4/231. ... Shoots left.
TRANSACTIONS/CAREER NOTES: Selected by Philadelphia Flyers in second round (second Flyers pick, 25th overall) of NHL entry draft (June 16, 1990). ... Traded by Flyers with first-round pick (traded to Toronto) in 1994 draft to Quebec Nordiques (July 21, 1992) completing deal in which Flyers sent G Ron Hextall, C Mike Ricci, C Peter Forsberg, D Steve Duchesne, first-round pick (G Jocelyn Thibault) in 1993 draft and cash to Nordiques for C Eric Lindros (June 20, 1992). ... Suffered from the flu (March 13, 1993); missed one game. ... Injured back (December 1, 1993); missed 31 games. ... Injured back (February 16, 1994); missed one game. ... Injured back (March 6, 1994); missed one game. ... Injured back (March 18, 1994); missed remainder of season. ... Injured back (January 31, 1995); missed six games. ... Injured shoulder (March 22, 1995); missed 13 games. ... Nordiques franchise moved to Colorado and renamed Avalanche for 1995-96 season (June 21, 1995). ... Suffered back spasms (January 6, 1996); missed two games. ... Injured shoulder (February 5, 1996); missed four games. ... Traded by Avalanche with D Curtis Leschyshyn to Washington Capitals for RW Keith Jones and first- (D Scott Parker) and fourth-round (traded back to Washington) picks in 1998 draft (November 2, 1996). ... Injured arm (December 20, 1996); missed two games. ... Suffered back spasms (January 24, 1997); missed 17 games. ... Suffered back spasms (March 22, 1997); missed one game. ... Strained shoulder (March 29, 1997); missed six games. ... Suspended three games by NHL for alleged racial remarks (November 9, 1997). ... Bruised shoulder (October 25, 1997); missed five games. ... Reinjured shoulder (December 20, 1997) and underwent shoulder surgery; missed remainder of regular season. ... Strained shoulder (December 5, 1998) and underwent shoulder surgery; missed remainder of season. ... Strained neck (November 27, 1999); missed six games. ... Reinjured neck (December 21, 1999); missed one game. ... Suspended one playoff game by NHL for cross-checking incident (April 14, 2000). ... Missed first nine games of 2000-01 season due to contract dispute. ... Injured shoulder (March 1, 2001); missed five games. ... Reinjured shoulder (March 19, 2001); missed five games. ... Suspended two games by NHL for elbowing incident (April 6, 2001).
MISCELLANEOUS: Member of Stanley Cup championship team (1996).

			REGULAR SEASON								PLAYOFFS				
Season Team	League	Gms.	G	A	Pts.	PIM	+/-	PP	SH		Gms.	G	A	Pts.	PIM
87-88—Sault Ste. Marie	OHA	55	42	36	78	172	...	...	...		—	—	—	—	—
88-89—Ottawa	OHL	36	4	2	6	31	...	...	...		—	—	—	—	—
89-90—Ottawa	OHL	57	36	38	74	146	...	...	...		3	2	1	3	4
90-91—Ottawa	OHL	20	16	6	22	69	...	...	...		17	5	9	14	59
91-92—Ottawa	OHL	2	1	1	2	24	...	...	...		—	—	—	—	—
—Sault Ste. Marie	OHL	31	19	25	44	143	...	...	...		11	5	8	13	49
92-93—Halifax	AHL	36	12	6	18	131	...	...	...		—	—	—	—	—
—Quebec	NHL	16	1	1	2	67	-2	0	0		5	0	0	0	26
93-94—Quebec	NHL	37	4	4	8	132	-2	0	0		—	—	—	—	—
94-95—Quebec	NHL	29	3	9	12	106	14	0	0		6	1	1	2	19
95-96—Colorado	NHL	64	16	18	34	250	10	4	0		12	1	2	3	11
96-97—Washington	NHL	42	9	13	22	165	-1	3	0		—	—	—	—	—
97-98—Washington	NHL	28	7	10	17	38	-1	4	0		18	1	0	1	26
98-99—Washington	NHL	23	3	7	10	48	-4	0	0		—	—	—	—	—
99-00—Washington	NHL	75	29	20	49	146	11	7	0		4	2	0	2	24
00-01—Washington	NHL	60	10	10	20	109	-12	4	0		6	0	1	1	4
NHL Totals (9 years)		374	82	92	174	1061	13	22	0		51	5	4	9	110

PERSONAL: Born May 21, 1969, in Flin Flon, Man. ... 6-2/220. ... Shoots left. ... Full Name: Reid Philip Simpson.
TRANSACTIONS/CAREER NOTES: Selected by Philadelphia Flyers in fourth round (third Flyers pick, 72nd overall) of NHL entry draft (June 17, 1989). ... Signed as free agent by Minnesota North Stars (December 13, 1992). ... North Stars franchise moved from Minnesota to Dallas and renamed Stars for 1993-94 season. ... Traded by Stars with D Roy Mitchell to New Jersey Devils for future considerations (March 21, 1994). ... Bruised right shoulder (November 27, 1995); missed six games. ... Strained groin (September 9, 1996); missed first two games of season. ... Reinjured groin (October 16, 1996); underwent groin surgery (November 22, 1996) and missed 38 games. ... Injured hamstring (November 8, 1997); missed 13 games. ... Traded by Devils to Chicago Blackhawks for fourth-round pick (D Mikko Jokela) in 1998 draft and future considerations (January 8, 1998). ... Strained hip flexor (March 12, 1998); missed two games. ... Fractured hand (September 20, 1998); missed first eight games of season. ... Suspended two games and fined $1,000 by NHL for actions toward a spectator (November 14, 1998). ... Traded by Blackhawks with D Bryan Muir to Tampa Bay Lightning for C Michael Nylander (November 12, 1999). ... Fractured jaw (January 13, 2000); missed final 40 games of regular season. ... Signed as free agent by St. Louis Blues (August 24, 2000). ... Injured groin (November 21, 2000); missed five games. ... Injured groin (February 1, 2001); missed seven games.

			REGULAR SEASON								PLAYOFFS				
Season Team	League	Gms.	G	A	Pts.	PIM	+/-	PP	SH		Gms.	G	A	Pts.	PIM
85-86—Flin Flon	MJHL	40	20	21	41	200	...	...	...		—	—	—	—	—
—New Westminster	WHL	2	0	0	0	0	...	...	...		—	—	—	—	—
86-87—Prince Albert	WHL	47	3	8	11	105	...	...	...		—	—	—	—	—
87-88—Prince Albert	WHL	72	13	14	27	164	...	...	...		10	1	0	1	43
88-89—Prince Albert	WHL	59	26	29	55	264	...	...	...		4	2	1	3	30
89-90—Prince Albert	WHL	29	15	17	32	121	...	...	...		14	4	7	11	34
—Hershey	AHL	28	2	2	4	175	...	...	...		—	—	—	—	—
90-91—Hershey	AHL	54	9	15	24	183	...	...	...		1	0	0	0	0
91-92—Hershey	AHL	60	11	7	18	145	...	...	...		—	—	—	—	—
—Philadelphia	NHL	1	0	0	0	0	0	0	0		—	—	—	—	—
92-93—Kalamazoo	IHL	45	5	5	10	193	...	...	...		—	—	—	—	—
—Minnesota	NHL	1	0	0	0	5	0	0	0		—	—	—	—	—
93-94—Kalamazoo	IHL	5	0	0	0	16	...	...	...		—	—	—	—	—
—Albany	AHL	37	9	5	14	135	...	...	...		5	1	1	2	18
94-95—Albany	AHL	70	18	25	43	268	...	...	...		14	1	8	9	13
—New Jersey	NHL	9	0	0	0	27	-1	0	0		—	—	—	—	—
95-96—New Jersey	NHL	23	1	5	6	79	2	0	0		—	—	—	—	—
—Albany	AHL	6	1	3	4	17	...	...	...		—	—	—	—	—
96-97—Albany	AHL	3	0	0	0	10	...	...	...		—	—	—	—	—
—New Jersey	NHL	27	0	4	4	60	0	0	0		5	0	0	0	29
97-98—New Jersey	NHL	6	0	0	0	16	-2	0	0		—	—	—	—	—
—Chicago	NHL	38	3	2	5	102	-1	1	0		—	—	—	—	—

Season Team	League	REGULAR SEASON								PLAYOFFS				
		Gms.	G	A	Pts.	PIM	+/-	PP	SH	Gms.	G	A	Pts.	PIM
98-99—Chicago	NHL	53	5	4	9	145	2	1	0	—	—	—	—	—
99-00—Cleveland	IHL	12	2	2	4	56	...	...	...	—	—	—	—	—
—Tampa Bay	NHL	26	1	0	1	103	-3	0	0	—	—	—	—	—
00-01—St. Louis	NHL	38	2	1	3	96	-3	0	0	5	0	0	0	2
NHL Totals (9 years)		222	12	16	28	633	-6	2	0	10	0	0	0	31

SIMPSON, TODD — D — COYOTES

PERSONAL: Born May 28, 1973, in Edmonton. ... 6-3/215. ... Shoots left.

TRANSACTIONS/CAREER NOTES: Signed as non-drafted free agent by Calgary Flames (July 6, 1994). ... Injured knee (October 1, 1997) and underwent surgery; missed 10 games. ... Injured shoulder (November 15, 1997); missed four games. ... Suffered concussion (March 19, 1998); missed final 15 games of season. ... Suffered facial injury (March 13, 1999); missed nine games. ... Traded by Flames to Florida Panthers for LW Bill Lindsay (September 30, 1999). ... Fractured toe (October 9, 2000); missed five games. ... Suffered concussion (December 4, 2000); missed 40 games. ... Traded by Panthers to Phoenix Coyotes for second-round draft pick (traded to New Jersey) in 2001 draft (March 13, 2001).

MISCELLANEOUS: Captain of Calgary Flames (1997-98 and 1998-99).

Season Team	League	REGULAR SEASON								PLAYOFFS				
		Gms.	G	A	Pts.	PIM	+/-	PP	SH	Gms.	G	A	Pts.	PIM
91-92—Brown University	ECAC	14	1	3	4	18	...	...	...	—	—	—	—	—
92-93—Tri-City	WHL	69	5	18	23	196	...	...	...	4	0	0	0	13
93-94—Tri-City	WHL	12	2	3	5	32	...	...	...	—	—	—	—	—
—Saskatoon	WHL	51	7	19	26	175	...	...	...	16	1	5	6	42
94-95—Saint John	AHL	80	3	10	13	321	...	...	...	5	0	0	0	4
95-96—Calgary	NHL	6	0	0	0	32	0	0	0	—	—	—	—	—
—Saint John	AHL	66	4	13	17	277	...	...	...	16	2	3	5	32
96-97—Calgary	NHL	82	1	13	14	208	-14	0	0	—	—	—	—	—
97-98—Calgary	NHL	53	1	5	6	109	-10	0	0	—	—	—	—	—
98-99—Calgary	NHL	73	2	8	10	151	18	0	0	—	—	—	—	—
99-00—Florida	NHL	82	1	6	7	202	5	0	0	4	0	0	0	4
00-01—Florida	NHL	25	1	3	4	74	0	0	0	—	—	—	—	—
—Phoenix	NHL	13	0	1	1	12	-4	0	0	—	—	—	—	—
NHL Totals (6 years)		334	6	36	42	788	-5	0	0	4	0	0	0	4

SIVEK, MICHAL — C — PENGUINS

PERSONAL: Born January 21, 1981, in Nachod, Czechoslovakia. ... 6-3/209. ... Shoots left.

TRANSACTIONS/CAREER NOTES: Selected by Washington Capitals in second round (second Capitals pick, 29th overall) of NHL entry draft (June 26, 1999). ... Traded by Capitals with C Kris Beech, D Ross Lupaschuk and future considerations to Pittsburgh Penguins for RW Jaromir Jagu and D Frantisek Kucera (July 11, 2001).

Season Team	League	REGULAR SEASON								PLAYOFFS				
		Gms.	G	A	Pts.	PIM	+/-	PP	SH	Gms.	G	A	Pts.	PIM
96-97—Sparta Praha Jrs.	Czech Rep.	38	18	11	29	...	...	...	...	—	—	—	—	—
97-98—Sparta Praha	Czech Rep.	25	1	1	2	10	...	...	...	5	1	0	1	0
—Sparta Praha Jrs.	Czech Rep.	31	13	8	21	...	...	...	...	—	—	—	—	—
98-99—Sparta Praha	Czech Rep.	1	1	0	1	2	...	...	...	—	—	—	—	—
—Velvana Kladno	Czech Rep.	34	3	8	11	24	...	...	...	—	—	—	—	—
99-00—Prince Albert	WHL	53	23	37	60	65	...	...	...	6	1	4	5	10
00-01—Sparta Praha	Czech Rep.	32	6	7	13	28	...	...	...	13	4	2	6	8

SKALDE, JARROD — C — THRASHERS

PERSONAL: Born February 26, 1971, in Niagara Falls, Ont. ... 6-0/185. ... Shoots left. ... Name pronounced SKAHL-dee.

TRANSACTIONS/CAREER NOTES: Selected by New Jersey Devils in second round (third Devils pick, 26th overall) of NHL entry draft (June 17, 1989). ... Traded by Oshawa Generals to Belleville Bulls for RW Rob Pearson (November 18, 1990). ... Selected by Mighty Ducks of Anaheim in NHL expansion draft (June 24, 1993). ... Signed as free agent by Las Vegas Thunder (August 18, 1994). ... Signed as free agent by Mighty Ducks (May 31, 1995). ... Traded by Mighty Ducks to Calgary Flames for D Bobby Marshall (October 30, 1995). ... Signed as free agent by San Jose Sharks (August 13, 1997). ... Claimed on waivers by Dallas Stars (January 27, 1998). ... Claimed on waivers by Chicago Blackhawks (February 12, 1998). ... Claimed on waivers by Sharks (March 6, 1998). ... Signed as free agent by Atlanta Thrashers (July 21, 2000).

HONORS: Named to OHL All-Star second team (1990-91). ... Named to IHL All-Star first team (1999-2000).

Season Team	League	REGULAR SEASON								PLAYOFFS				
		Gms.	G	A	Pts.	PIM	+/-	PP	SH	Gms.	G	A	Pts.	PIM
86-87—Fort Erie Jr. B	OHA	41	27	34	61	36	...	...	...	—	—	—	—	—
87-88—Oshawa	OHL	60	12	16	28	24	...	...	...	7	2	1	3	2
88-89—Oshawa	OHL	65	38	38	76	36	...	...	...	6	1	5	6	2
89-90—Oshawa	OHL	62	40	52	92	66	...	...	...	17	10	7	17	6
90-91—New Jersey	NHL	1	0	1	1	0	0	0	0	—	—	—	—	—
—Utica	AHL	3	3	2	5	0	...	...	...	—	—	—	—	—
—Oshawa	OHL	15	8	14	22	14	...	...	...	—	—	—	—	—
—Belleville	OHL	40	30	52	82	21	...	...	...	6	9	6	15	10
91-92—Utica	AHL	62	20	20	40	56	...	...	...	4	3	1	4	8
—New Jersey	NHL	15	2	4	6	4	-1	0	0	—	—	—	—	—
92-93—Cincinnati	IHL	4	1	2	3	4	...	...	...	—	—	—	—	—
—Utica	AHL	59	21	39	60	76	...	...	...	5	0	2	2	19
—New Jersey	NHL	11	0	2	2	4	-3	0	0	—	—	—	—	—

Season Team	League	REGULAR SEASON								PLAYOFFS				
		Gms.	G	A	Pts.	PIM	+/-	PP	SH	Gms.	G	A	Pts.	PIM
93-94—San Diego	IHL	57	25	38	63	79	...	...	...	9	3	12	15	10
—Anaheim	NHL	20	5	4	9	10	-3	2	0	—	—	—	—	—
94-95—Las Vegas	IHL	74	34	41	75	103	...	...	...	9	2	4	6	8
95-96—Baltimore	AHL	11	2	6	8	55	...	...	...	—	—	—	—	—
—Saint John	AHL	68	27	40	67	98	...	...	...	16	4	9	13	6
—Calgary	NHL	1	0	0	0	0	0	0	0	—	—	—	—	—
96-97—Saint John	AHL	65	32	36	68	94	...	...	...	3	0	0	0	14
97-98—Kentucky	AHL	23	5	15	20	48	...	...	...	3	3	0	3	6
—San Jose	NHL	22	4	6	10	14	-2	0	0	—	—	—	—	—
—Chicago	NHL	7	0	1	1	4	0	0	0	—	—	—	—	—
—Indianapolis	IHL	2	0	2	2	0	...	...	...	—	—	—	—	—
—Dallas	NHL	1	0	0	0	0	0	0	0	—	—	—	—	—
98-99—San Jose	NHL	17	1	1	2	4	-6	0	0	—	—	—	—	—
—Kentucky	AHL	54	17	40	57	75	...	...	...	12	4	5	9	16
99-00—Utah	IHL	77	25	54	79	98	...	...	...	5	0	1	1	10
00-01—Atlanta	NHL	19	1	2	3	20	-8	0	0	—	—	—	—	—
—Orlando	IHL	60	14	40	54	56	...	...	...	15	3	6	9	20
NHL Totals (8 years)		114	13	21	34	60	-23	2	0					

SKOPINTSEV, ANDREI   D

PERSONAL: Born September 28, 1971, in Moscow, U.S.S.R. ... 6-0/185. ... Shoots right.
TRANSACTIONS/CAREER NOTES: Selected by Tampa Bay Lightning in sixth round (seventh Lightning pick, 153rd overall) of NHL entry draft (June 21, 1997). ... Strained abdominal muscle (November 29, 1998); missed 19 games. ... Injured shoulder (March 6, 1999); missed four games. ... Signed as free agent by Atlanta Thrashers (September 7, 2000). ... Strained muscle in abdomen (December 28, 2000); missed 16 games.

Season Team	League	REGULAR SEASON								PLAYOFFS				
		Gms.	G	A	Pts.	PIM	+/-	PP	SH	Gms.	G	A	Pts.	PIM
89-90—Krylja Sov. Moscow	USSR	20	0	0	0	10	...	...	...	—	—	—	—	—
90-91—Krylja Sov. Moscow	USSR	16	0	1	1	2	...	...	...	—	—	—	—	—
91-92—Krylja Sov. Moscow	CIS	36	1	1	2	14	...	...	...	—	—	—	—	—
92-93—Krylja Sov. Moscow	CIS	12	1	0	1	4	...	...	...	7	1	0	1	2
93-94—Krylja Sov. Moscow	CIS	43	4	8	12	14	...	...	...	3	1	0	1	0
94-95—Krylja Sov. Moscow	CIS	52	8	12	20	55	...	...	...	4	1	1	2	0
95-96—Augsburg	Germany	46	10	20	30	32	...	...	...	7	3	2	5	22
96-97—TPS Turku	Finland	46	3	6	9	80	...	...	...	10	1	1	2	4
97-98—TPS Turku	Finland	48	2	9	11	8	...	...	...	4	0	1	1	4
98-99—Cleveland	IHL	19	3	2	5	8	...	...	...	—	—	—	—	—
—Tampa Bay	NHL	19	1	1	2	10	1	0	0	—	—	—	—	—
99-00—Detroit	IHL	51	4	15	19	44	...	...	...	—	—	—	—	—
—Tampa Bay	NHL	4	0	0	0	6	-4	0	0	—	—	—	—	—
00-01—Orlando	IHL	25	0	6	6	22	...	...	...	—	—	—	—	—
—Atlanta	NHL	17	1	3	4	16	-7	0	0	—	—	—	—	—
NHL Totals (3 years)		40	2	4	6	32	-10	0	0					

SKOULA, MARTIN   D   AVALANCHE

PERSONAL: Born October 28, 1979, in Litvinov, Czechoslovakia. ... 6-3/218. ... Shoots left.
TRANSACTIONS/CAREER NOTES: Selected by Colorado Avalanche in first round (second Avalanche pick, 17th overall) of NHL entry draft (June 27, 1998). ... Injured shoulder (January 5, 2000); missed two games.
HONORS: Named to OHL All-Star second team (1998-99).
MISCELLANEOUS: Member of Stanley Cup championship team (2001).

Season Team	League	REGULAR SEASON								PLAYOFFS				
		Gms.	G	A	Pts.	PIM	+/-	PP	SH	Gms.	G	A	Pts.	PIM
95-96—Litvinov	Czech Jrs.	38	0	4	4	...	...	...	...	—	—	—	—	—
—Litvinov	Czech Rep.	—	—	—	—	—	...	...	...	1	0	0	0	0
96-97—Litvinov	Czech Jrs.	38	2	9	11	...	...	...	...	—	—	—	—	—
—Litvinov	Czech Rep.	1	0	0	0	0	...	...	...	—	—	—	—	—
97-98—Barrie	COJHL	66	8	36	44	36	...	...	...	6	1	3	4	4
98-99—Barrie	OHL	67	13	46	59	46	...	...	...	12	3	10	13	13
—Hershey	AHL	—	—	—	—	—	...	...	...	1	0	0	0	0
99-00—Colorado	NHL	80	3	13	16	20	5	2	0	17	0	2	2	4
00-01—Colorado	NHL	82	8	17	25	38	8	3	0	23	1	4	5	8
NHL Totals (2 years)		162	11	30	41	58	13	5	0	40	1	6	7	12

SKRASTINS, KARLIS   D   PREDATORS

PERSONAL: Born July 9, 1974, in Riga, U.S.S.R. ... 6-1/205. ... Shoots left.
TRANSACTIONS/CAREER NOTES: Selected by Nashville Predators in ninth round (eighth Predators pick, 230th overall) of 1998 NHL entry draft (June 27, 1998).

Season Team	League	REGULAR SEASON								PLAYOFFS				
		Gms.	G	A	Pts.	PIM	+/-	PP	SH	Gms.	G	A	Pts.	PIM
92-93—Riga Stars	CIS	40	3	5	8	16	...	...	...	2	0	0	0	0
93-94—Riga Stars	CIS	42	7	5	12	18	...	...	...	2	1	0	1	4
94-95—Riga Stars	CIS	52	4	14	18	69	...	...	...	—	—	—	—	—

Season Team	League	REGULAR SEASON								PLAYOFFS				
		Gms.	G	A	Pts.	PIM	+/-	PP	SH	Gms.	G	A	Pts.	PIM
95-96—TPS Turku	Finland	50	4	11	15	32	...	...	...	11	2	2	4	10
96-97—TPS Turku	Finland	50	2	8	10	20	...	...	...	—	—	—	—	—
97-98—TPS Turku	Finland	48	4	15	19	67	...	...	...	—	—	—	—	—
98-99—Milwaukee	IHL	75	8	36	44	47	...	...	...	2	0	1	1	2
—Nashville	NHL	2	0	1	1	0	0	0	0	—	—	—	—	—
99-00—Milwaukee	IHL	19	3	8	11	10	...	...	...	—	—	—	—	—
—Nashville	NHL	59	5	6	11	20	-7	1	0	—	—	—	—	—
00-01—Nashville	NHL	82	1	11	12	30	-12	0	0	—	—	—	—	—
NHL Totals (3 years)		143	6	18	24	50	-19	1	0					

SKRBEK, PAVEL — D — PREDATORS

PERSONAL: Born August 9, 1978, in Kladno, Czechoslovakia. ... 6-3/213. ... Shoots left.

TRANSACTIONS/CAREER NOTES: Selected by Pittsburgh Penguins in second round (second Penguins pick, 28th overall) of NHL entry draft (June 22, 1996). ... Traded by Penguins to Nashville Predators for D Bob Boughner (March 13, 2000). ... Suffered concussion (March 17, 2001); missed six games.

Season Team	League	REGULAR SEASON								PLAYOFFS				
		Gms.	G	A	Pts.	PIM	+/-	PP	SH	Gms.	G	A	Pts.	PIM
94-95—Poldi Kladno	Czech Rep.	29	7	6	13		...	...	...	—	—	—	—	—
95-96—HC Kladno	Czech Jrs.	29	10	12	22		...	...	...	—	—	—	—	—
—HC Kladno	Czech Rep.	13	0	1	1		...	...	...	5	0	0	0	...
96-97—Poldi Kladno	Czech Rep.	35	1	5	6	26	...	...	...	3	0	0	0	4
97-98—Poldi Kladno	Czech Rep.	47	4	10	14	126	...	...	...	—	—	—	—	—
98-99—Syracuse	AHL	64	6	16	22	38	...	...	...	—	—	—	—	—
—Pittsburgh	NHL	4	0	0	0	2	2	0	0	—	—	—	—	—
99-00—Wilkes-Barre/Scranton	AHL	51	7	16	23	50	...	...	...	—	—	—	—	—
—Milwaukee	IHL	6	0	0	0	0	...	...	...	—	—	—	—	—
00-01—Milwaukee	IHL	54	2	22	24	55	...	...	...	5	0	0	0	2
—Nashville	NHL	5	0	0	0	4	1	0	0	—	—	—	—	—
NHL Totals (2 years)		9	0	0	0	6	3	0	0					

SKROBOT, SERGEI — D — FLYERS

PERSONAL: Born March 9, 1980, in Most, Czechoslovakia. ... 6-3/191. ... Shoots right.

TRANSACTIONS/CAREER NOTES: Selected by Philadelphia Flyers in ninth round (13th Flyers pick, 258th overall) of NHL entry draft (June 27, 1998).

Season Team	League	REGULAR SEASON								PLAYOFFS				
		Gms.	G	A	Pts.	PIM	+/-	PP	SH	Gms.	G	A	Pts.	PIM
95-96—Dynamo Moscow	Russian Jr.	30	4	10	14	8	...	...	...	—	—	—	—	—
96-97—Dynamo-2 Moscow	Rus. Div. III	70	5	10	15	10	...	...	...	—	—	—	—	—
97-98—Dynamo-2 Moscow	Rus. Div. II	44	2	4	6	10	...	...	...	—	—	—	—	—
98-99—Tver	Rus. Div. II	11	2	3	5	0	...	...	...	—	—	—	—	—
99-00—Philadelphia	AHL	5	0	0	0	2	...	...	...	—	—	—	—	—
—Trenton	ECHL	58	4	17	21	24	...	...	...	14	3	5	8	6
00-01—Philadelphia	AHL	5	0	1	1	0	...	...	...	—	—	—	—	—
—Trenton	ECHL	65	7	18	25	48	...	...	...	13	2	3	5	5

SKUDRA, PETER — G — BRUINS

PERSONAL: Born April 24, 1973, in Riga, U.S.S.R. ... 6-1/189. ... Catches left. ... Name pronounced SKOO-druh.

TRANSACTIONS/CAREER NOTES: Signed as non-drafted free agent by Pittsburgh Penguins (September 25, 1997). ... Separated shoulder (September 8, 1998); missed first two games of season. ... Bruised lower left leg (November 3, 1998); missed 14 games. ... Injured ankle (November 6, 1999); missed three games. ... Suffered concussion (December 26, 1999); missed two games. ... Suffered from the flu (February 11, 2000); missed two games. ... Signed as free agent by Boston Bruins (October 3, 2000). ... Claimed on waivers by Buffalo Sabres (October 6, 2000). ... Claimed on waivers by Bruins (November 14, 2000).

MISCELLANEOUS: Stopped a penalty shot attempt (vs. Doug Gilmour, October 16, 1999).

Season Team	League	REGULAR SEASON								PLAYOFFS						
		Gms.	Min.	W	L	T	GA	SO	Avg.	Gms.	Min.	W	L	GA	SO	Avg.
92-93—Pardaugava Riga	CIS	27	1498	...	...	...	74	...	2.96	1	60	...	...	5	0	5.00
93-94—Pardaugava Riga	CIS	14	783	...	...	...	42	...	3.22	1	55	...	...	4	0	4.36
94-95—Greensboro	ECHL	33	1612	13	9	‡5	113	0	4.21	6	341	2	2	28	0	4.93
95-96—Erie	ECHL	12	681	3	8	‡1	47	0	4.14	—	—	—	—	—	—	—
—Johnstown	ECHL	30	1657	12	11	‡4	98	0	3.55	—	—	—	—	—	—	—
96-97—Johnstown	ECHL	4	200	2	1	‡1	11	0	3.30	—	—	—	—	—	—	—
—Hamilton	AHL	32	1615	8	16	2	101	0	3.75	—	—	—	—	—	—	—
97-98—Houston	IHL	9	499	5	3	‡1	23	0	2.77	—	—	—	—	—	—	—
—Pittsburgh	NHL	17	851	6	4	3	26	0	1.83	—	—	—	—	—	—	—
—Kansas City	IHL	13	776	10	3	0	37	0	2.86	8	513	4	4	20	1	*2.34
98-99—Pittsburgh	NHL	37	1914	15	11	5	89	3	2.79	—	—	—	—	—	—	—
99-00—Pittsburgh	NHL	20	922	5	7	3	48	1	3.12	1	20	0	0	1	0	3.00
00-01—Buffalo	NHL	1	0	0	0	0	0	0	...	—	—	—	—	—	—	—
—Rochester	AHL	2	120	2	0	0	5	0	2.50	—	—	—	—	—	—	—
—Boston	NHL	25	1116	6	12	1	62	0	3.33	—	—	—	—	—	—	—
—Providence	AHL	3	180	3	0	0	5	0	1.67	—	—	—	—	—	—	—
NHL Totals (4 years)		100	4803	32	34	12	225	4	2.81	1	20	0	0	1	0	3.00

S

SLANEY, JOHN   D   FLYERS

PERSONAL: Born February 7, 1972, in St. John's, Nfld. ... 6-0/185. ... Shoots left. ... Full Name: John G. Slaney.
TRANSACTIONS/CAREER NOTES: Selected by Washington Capitals in first round (first Capitals pick, ninth overall) of NHL entry draft (June 16, 1990). ... Sprained right ankle (March 9, 1994); missed six games. ... Traded by Capitals to Colorado Avalanche for third-round pick (C Shawn McNeil) in 1996 draft (July 12, 1995). ... Traded by Avalanche to Los Angeles Kings for sixth-round pick (RW Brian Willsie) in 1996 draft (December 28, 1995). ... Fractured right hand (March 6, 1996); missed 12 games. ... Suffered concussion (November 17, 1996); missed one game. ... Signed as free agent by Phoenix Coyotes (August 18, 1997). ... Bruised thigh (October 30, 1997); missed one game. ... Suffered from the flu (December 10, 1997); missed one game. ... Fractured thumb (January 24, 1998); missed seven games. ... Injured hamstring (April 18, 1998); missed one game. ... Selected by Nashville Predators in NHL expansion draft (June 26, 1998). ... Bruised thumb (January 28, 1999); missed two games. ... Sprained wrist (February 5, 1999); missed three games. ... Injured rib (March 28, 1999); missed final nine games of season. ... Signed as free agent by Pittsburgh Penguins (September 30, 1999). ... Traded by Penguins to Philadelphia Flyers for LW Kevin Stevens (January 14, 2001).
HONORS: Won Max Kaminsky Trophy (1989-90). ... Named to OHL All-Star first team (1989-90). ... Named to OHL All-Star second team (1990-91). ... Named to AHL All-Star first team (2000-01). ... Won Eddie Shore Plaque (2000-01).

Season Team	League	Gms.	G	A	Pts.	PIM	+/-	PP	SH	Gms.	G	A	Pts.	PIM
88-89—Cornwall	OHL	66	16	43	59	23	...	...	...	18	8	16	24	10
89-90—Cornwall	OHL	64	38	59	97	60	...	...	...	6	0	8	8	11
90-91—Cornwall	OHL	34	21	25	46	28	...	...	...	—	—	—	—	—
91-92—Cornwall	OHL	34	19	41	60	43	...	...	...	6	3	8	11	0
—Baltimore	AHL	6	2	4	6	0	...	...	...	—	—	—	—	—
92-93—Baltimore	AHL	79	20	46	66	60	...	...	...	7	0	7	7	8
93-94—Portland	AHL	29	14	13	27	17	...	...	...	—	—	—	—	—
—Washington	NHL	47	7	9	16	27	3	3	0	11	1	1	2	2
94-95—Washington	NHL	16	0	3	3	6	-3	0	0	—	—	—	—	—
—Portland	AHL	8	3	10	13	4	...	...	...	7	1	3	4	4
95-96—Colorado	NHL	7	0	3	3	4	2	0	0	—	—	—	—	—
—Cornwall	AHL	5	0	4	4	2	...	...	...	—	—	—	—	—
—Los Angeles	NHL	31	6	11	17	10	5	3	1	—	—	—	—	—
96-97—Los Angeles	NHL	32	3	11	14	4	-10	1	0	—	—	—	—	—
—Phoenix	IHL	35	9	25	34	8	...	...	...	—	—	—	—	—
97-98—Las Vegas	IHL	5	2	2	4	10	...	...	...	—	—	—	—	—
—Phoenix	NHL	55	3	14	17	24	-3	1	0	—	—	—	—	—
98-99—Nashville	NHL	46	2	12	14	14	-12	0	0	—	—	—	—	—
—Milwaukee	IHL	7	0	1	1	0	...	...	...	—	—	—	—	—
99-00—Pittsburgh	NHL	29	1	4	5	10	-10	1	0	2	1	0	1	2
—Wilkes-Barre/Scranton	AHL	49	30	30	60	25	...	...	...	—	—	—	—	—
00-01—Wilkes-Barre/Scranton	AHL	40	12	38	50	4	...	...	...	—	—	—	—	—
—Philadelphia	AHL	25	6	11	17	10	...	...	...	10	2	6	8	6
NHL Totals (7 years)		263	22	67	89	99	-28	9	1	13	2	1	3	4

SLEGR, JIRI   D   THRASHERS

PERSONAL: Born May 30, 1971, in Jihlava, Czechoslovakia. ... 6-0/206. ... Shoots left. ... Son of Jiri Bubla, defenseman with Vancouver Canucks (1981-82 through 1985-86). ... Name pronounced YIH-ree SLAY-guhr.
TRANSACTIONS/CAREER NOTES: Selected by Vancouver Canucks in second round (third Canucks pick, 23rd overall) of NHL entry draft (June 16, 1990). ... Played in Europe during 1994-95 NHL lockout. ... Traded by Canucks to Edmonton Oilers for RW Roman Oksiuta (April 7, 1995). ... Sprained ligaments in left knee (December 27, 1995); missed 19 games. ... Traded by Oilers to Pittsburgh Penguins for third-round pick (traded to New Jersey) in 1998 draft (August 12, 1997). ... Suffered hip pointer (November 14, 1997); missed four games. ... Suffered from the flu (December 16, 1997); missed one game. ... Injured shoulder (March 2, 1998); missed one game. ... Fractured hand (November 5, 1998); missed 13 games. ... Bruised knee (April 1, 1999); missed one game. ... Sprained ankle (October 8, 1999); missed five games. ... Suffered from the flu (November 20, 1999); missed one game. ... Sprained knee (November 26, 1999); missed two games. ... Traded by Penguins to Atlanta Thrashers for third-round pick (traded to Columbus) in 2001 draft (January 14, 2001). ... Strained groin (March 28, 2001); missed five games.
HONORS: Named to Czechoslovakian League All-Star team (1990-91).
MISCELLANEOUS: Member of gold-medal-winning Czech Republic Olympic team (1998).

Season Team	League	Gms.	G	A	Pts.	PIM	+/-	PP	SH	Gms.	G	A	Pts.	PIM
87-88—Litvinov	Czech Rep.	4	1	1	2	0	...	...	...	—	—	—	—	—
88-89—Litvinov	Czech.	8	0	0	0	0	...	...	...	—	—	—	—	—
89-90—Litvinov	Czech.	51	4	15	19	...	...	...	...	—	—	—	—	—
90-91—Litvinov	Czech.	39	10	33	43	26	...	...	...	—	—	—	—	—
91-92—Litvinov	Czech.	38	7	22	29	30	...	...	...	—	—	—	—	—
—Czech. Olympic Team	Int'l	8	1	1	2	...	...	...	...	—	—	—	—	—
92-93—Vancouver	NHL	41	4	22	26	109	16	2	0	5	0	3	3	4
—Hamilton	AHL	21	4	14	18	42	...	...	...	—	—	—	—	—
93-94—Vancouver	NHL	78	5	33	38	86	0	1	0	—	—	—	—	—
94-95—Chem. Litvinov	Czech Rep.	11	3	10	13	43	...	...	...	—	—	—	—	—
—Vancouver	NHL	19	1	5	6	32	0	0	0	—	—	—	—	—
—Edmonton	NHL	12	1	5	6	14	-5	1	0	—	—	—	—	—
95-96—Edmonton	NHL	57	4	13	17	74	-1	0	1	—	—	—	—	—
—Cape Breton	AHL	4	1	2	3	4	...	...	...	—	—	—	—	—
96-97—Chem. Litvinov	Czech Rep.	1	0	0	0	0	...	...	...	—	—	—	—	—
—Sodertalje SK	Sweden	30	4	14	18	62	...	...	...	—	—	—	—	—
97-98—Pittsburgh	NHL	73	5	12	17	109	10	1	1	6	0	4	4	2
—Czech Rep. Oly. team	Int'l	6	1	0	1	8	...	...	...	—	—	—	—	—
98-99—Pittsburgh	NHL	63	3	20	23	86	13	1	0	13	1	3	4	12
99-00—Pittsburgh	NHL	74	11	20	31	82	20	0	0	10	2	3	5	19
00-01—Pittsburgh	NHL	42	5	10	15	60	-9	0	1	—	—	—	—	—
—Atlanta	NHL	33	3	16	19	36	-1	2	0	—	—	—	—	—
NHL Totals (8 years)		492	42	156	198	688	43	8	3	34	3	13	16	37

SLOAN, BLAKE   RW   BLUE JACKETS

PERSONAL: Born July 27, 1975, in Park Ridge, Ill. ... 5-10/196. ... Shoots right.
TRANSACTIONS/CAREER NOTES: Signed as non-drafted free agent by Dallas Stars (March 10, 1999). ... Sprained ankle (February 21, 2000); missed 15 games. ... Claimed on waivers by Columbus Blue Jackets (March 13, 2001).
MISCELLANEOUS: Member of Stanley Cup championship team (1999). ... Played defense (1993-94 through 1998-99).

Season Team	League	REGULAR SEASON								PLAYOFFS				
		Gms.	G	A	Pts.	PIM	+/-	PP	SH	Gms.	G	A	Pts.	PIM
93-94—Univ. of Michigan	CCHA	38	2	4	6	48	...	...	...	—	—	—	—	—
94-95—Univ. of Michigan	CCHA	39	2	15	17	60	...	...	...	—	—	—	—	—
95-96—Univ. of Michigan	CCHA	41	6	24	30	57	...	...	...	—	—	—	—	—
96-97—Univ. of Michigan	CCHA	41	2	15	17	52	...	...	...	—	—	—	—	—
97-98—Houston	IHL	70	2	13	15	86	...	...	...	2	0	0	0	0
98-99—Houston	IHL	62	8	10	18	76	...	...	...	—	—	—	—	—
—Dallas	NHL	14	0	0	0	10	-1	0	0	19	0	2	2	8
99-00—Dallas	NHL	67	4	13	17	50	11	0	0	16	0	0	0	12
00-01—Dallas	NHL	33	2	2	4	4	-2	0	0	—	—	—	—	—
—Houston	IHL	20	7	4	11	18	...	...	...	—	—	—	—	—
—Columbus	NHL	14	1	0	1	13	-2	0	0	—	—	—	—	—
NHL Totals (3 years)		128	7	15	22	77	6	0	0	35	0	2	2	20

SMEHLIK, RICHARD   D   SABRES

S

PERSONAL: Born January 23, 1970, in Ostrava, Czechoslovakia. ... 6-3/222. ... Shoots left. ... Name pronounced SHMEHL-ihk.
TRANSACTIONS/CAREER NOTES: Selected by Buffalo Sabres in fifth round (third Sabres pick, 97th overall) of NHL entry draft (June 16, 1990). ... Injured hip (October 30, 1992); missed two games. ... Played in Europe during 1994-95 NHL lockout. ... Bruised shoulder (January 27, 1995); missed six games. ... Tore knee ligaments (August 10, 1995); missed entire 1995-96 season. ... Suffered tendonitis in knee (January 12, 1996); missed five games. ... Suffered sore knee (November 19, 1996); missed six games. ... Suffered sore knee (February 23, 1997); missed one game. ... Strained groin (March 30, 1997); missed three games. ... Injured wrist (February 4, 1998); missed two games. ... Bruised eye (February 25, 1998); missed seven games. ... Suspended one game and fined $1,000 by NHL for high-sticking incident (October 15, 1998). ... Bruised quadricep muscle (November 21, 1998); missed seven games. ... Injured rib (December 17, 1999); missed nine games. ... Suffered back spasms (February 17, 2000); missed three games. ... Strained groin (January 17, 2001); missed five games. ... Injured groin (February 22, 2001); missed 11 games. ... Injured ribs (March 14, 2001); missed 11 games.
MISCELLANEOUS: Member of gold-medal-winning Czech Republic Olympic team (1998).

Season Team	League	REGULAR SEASON								PLAYOFFS				
		Gms.	G	A	Pts.	PIM	+/-	PP	SH	Gms.	G	A	Pts.	PIM
88-89—Vitkovice	Czech.	38	2	5	7	12	...	...	...	—	—	—	—	—
89-90—Vitkovice	Czech.	43	4	3	7	...	...	...	...	—	—	—	—	—
90-91—Dukla Jihlava	Czech.	51	4	2	6	22	...	...	...	—	—	—	—	—
91-92—Vitkovice	Czech.	47	9	10	19	...	...	...	...	—	—	—	—	—
—Czech. Olympic Team	Int'l	8	0	1	1	2	...	...	...	—	—	—	—	—
92-93—Buffalo	NHL	80	4	27	31	59	9	0	0	8	0	4	4	2
93-94—Buffalo	NHL	84	14	27	41	69	22	3	3	7	0	2	2	10
94-95—HC Vitkovice	Czech Rep.	13	5	2	7	12	...	...	...	—	—	—	—	—
—Buffalo	NHL	39	4	7	11	46	5	0	1	5	0	0	0	2
95-96—Buffalo	NHL					Did not play.								
96-97—Buffalo	NHL	62	11	19	30	43	19	2	0	12	0	2	2	4
97-98—Buffalo	NHL	72	3	17	20	62	11	0	1	15	0	2	2	6
—Czech Rep. Oly. team	Int'l	6	0	1	1	4	...	...	...	—	—	—	—	—
98-99—Buffalo	NHL	72	3	11	14	44	-9	0	0	21	0	3	3	10
99-00—Buffalo	NHL	64	2	9	11	50	13	0	0	5	1	0	1	0
00-01—Buffalo	NHL	56	3	12	15	4	6	0	0	10	0	1	1	4
NHL Totals (9 years)		529	44	129	173	377	76	5	5	83	1	14	15	38

SMITH, BRANDON   D   SHARKS

PERSONAL: Born February 25, 1973, in Hazelton, B.C. ... 6-1/196. ... Shoots left. ... Full Name: Brandon Stuart Smith.
TRANSACTIONS/CAREER NOTES: Signed as non-drafted free agent by Detroit Red Wings (July 28, 1997). ... Signed as free agent by Boston Bruins (July 22, 1998). ... Separated shoulder (January 10, 2001); missed nine games. ... Signed as free agent by San Jose Sharks (July 23, 2001).
HONORS: Named to AHL All-Star first team (1998-99).

Season Team	League	REGULAR SEASON								PLAYOFFS				
		Gms.	G	A	Pts.	PIM	+/-	PP	SH	Gms.	G	A	Pts.	PIM
89-90—Portland	WHL	59	2	17	19	16	...	...	...	—	—	—	—	—
90-91—Portland	WHL	17	8	5	13	8	...	...	...	—	—	—	—	—
91-92—Portland	WHL	70	12	32	44	63	...	...	...	—	—	—	—	—
92-93—Portland	WHL	72	20	54	74	38	...	...	...	16	4	9	13	6
93-94—Portland	WHL	72	19	63	82	47	...	...	...	10	2	10	12	8
94-95—Dayton	ECHL	60	16	49	65	57	...	...	...	4	2	3	5	0
—Adirondack	AHL	14	1	2	3	7	...	...	...	3	0	0	0	2
95-96—Adirondack	AHL	48	4	13	17	22	...	...	...	3	0	1	1	2
96-97—Adirondack	AHL	80	8	26	34	30	...	...	...	4	0	0	0	0
97-98—Adirondack	AHL	64	9	27	36	26	...	...	...	1	0	1	1	0
98-99—Providence	AHL	72	16	46	62	32	...	...	...	19	1	9	10	12
—Boston	NHL	5	0	0	0	0	2	0	0	—	—	—	—	—
99-00—Providence	AHL	55	8	30	38	20	...	...	...	14	1	11	12	2
—Boston	NHL	22	2	4	6	10	-4	0	0	—	—	—	—	—
00-01—Providence	AHL	63	11	28	39	30	...	...	...	17	0	5	5	6
—Boston	NHL	3	1	0	1	0	-1	1	0	—	—	—	—	—
NHL Totals (3 years)		30	3	4	7	10	-3	1	0					

PERSONAL: Born May 13, 1977, in Windsor, Ont. ... 6-2/205. ... Shoots right. ... Full Name: Denis Smith.
TRANSACTIONS/CAREER NOTES: Selected by New York Islanders in second round (third Islanders pick, 41st overall) of NHL entry draft (July 8, 1995). ... Rights traded by Islanders with LW Wendel Clark and D Mathieu Schneider to Toronto Maple Leafs for LW Sean Haggerty, C Darby Hendrickson, D Kenny Jonsson and first-round pick (G Roberto Luongo) in 1997 draft (March 13, 1996).
HONORS: Named to OHL All-Star second team (1996-97).

		REGULAR SEASON								PLAYOFFS				
Season Team	League	Gms.	G	A	Pts.	PIM	+/-	PP	SH	Gms.	G	A	Pts.	PIM
92-93—Belle River	Jr. C	50	11	29	40	101	...	...	...	—	—	—	—	—
93-94—Windsor	Jr. B	51	8	34	42	267	...	...	...	—	—	—	—	—
94-95—Windsor	OHL	61	4	13	17	201	...	...	...	10	1	3	4	41
95-96—Windsor	OHL	64	14	45	59	260	...	...	...	7	1	7	8	23
96-97—Windsor	OHL	63	15	52	67	190	...	...	...	5	1	7	8	11
—Toronto	NHL	8	0	1	1	7	-5	0	0	—	—	—	—	—
—St. John's	AHL	—	—	—	—	—	...	...	...	1	0	0	0	0
97-98—St. John's	AHL	65	4	11	15	237	...	...	...	4	0	0	0	4
98-99—St. John's	AHL	79	7	28	35	216	...	...	...	5	0	1	1	0
99-00—St. John's	AHL	74	6	22	28	197	...	...	...	—	—	—	—	—
—Toronto	NHL	3	0	0	0	5	-1	0	0	—	—	—	—	—
00-01—St. John's	AHL	59	7	12	19	106	...	...	...	4	0	0	0	11
NHL Totals (2 years)		11	0	1	1	12	-6	0	0					

PERSONAL: Born October 19, 1976, in Fernie, B.C. ... 6-2/195. ... Shoots left.
TRANSACTIONS/CAREER NOTES: Selected by Colorado Avalanche in seventh round (seventh Avalanche pick, 181st overall) of NHL entry draft (July 8, 1995).

		REGULAR SEASON								PLAYOFFS				
Season Team	League	Gms.	G	A	Pts.	PIM	+/-	PP	SH	Gms.	G	A	Pts.	PIM
94-95—British Columbia	CWUAA	28	1	2	3	26	...	...	...	—	—	—	—	—
95-96—Tri-City	WHL	58	1	21	22	70	...	...	...	11	1	3	4	14
96-97—Tri-City	WHL	72	5	19	24	174	...	...	...	—	—	—	—	—
97-98—Hershey	AHL	50	1	2	3	71	...	...	...	6	0	0	0	4
98-99—Hershey	AHL	54	5	7	12	72	...	...	...	5	0	1	1	0
—Colorado	NHL	12	0	0	0	9	5	0	0	—	—	—	—	—
99-00—Hershey	AHL	49	7	15	22	56	...	...	...	—	—	—	—	—
—Colorado	NHL	3	0	0	0	0	2	0	0	—	—	—	—	—
00-01—Hershey	AHL	58	2	12	14	34	...	...	...	12	0	1	1	4
NHL Totals (2 years)		15	0	0	0	9	7	0	0					

PERSONAL: Born November 2, 1973, in Calgary. ... 6-3/208. ... Shoots right.
TRANSACTIONS/CAREER NOTES: Selected by New Jersey Devils in first round (first Devils pick, 18th overall) of NHL entry draft (June 20, 1992). ... Injured right knee (November 5, 1994); missed 37 games. ... Bruised hand (November 5, 1995); missed 15 games. ... Traded by Devils with C Steve Sullivan and C Alyn McCauley to Toronto Maple Leafs for C Doug Gilmour, D Dave Ellett and third-round pick (D Andre Lakos) in 1999 draft (February 25, 1997). ... Fractured toe (March 30, 1998); missed one game. ... Traded by Maple Leafs to Edmonton Oilers for fourth-round pick (D Jonathan Zion) in 1999 draft and second-round pick (C Kris Vernarsky) in 2000 (March 23, 1999). ... Bruised shoulder (February 23, 2000); missed one game.
HONORS: Named to Can.HL All-Rookie team (1991-92). ... Won Bill Hunter Trophy (1992-93). ... Named to Can.HL All-Star first team (1992-93). ... Named to WHL (East) All-Star first team (1992-93).

		REGULAR SEASON								PLAYOFFS				
Season Team	League	Gms.	G	A	Pts.	PIM	+/-	PP	SH	Gms.	G	A	Pts.	PIM
90-91—Calgary Canucks	AJHL	45	3	15	18	69	...	...	...	—	—	—	—	—
—Regina	WHL	2	0	0	0	7	...	...	...	—	—	—	—	—
91-92—Regina	WHL	62	9	29	38	168	...	...	...	—	—	—	—	—
92-93—Regina	WHL	64	14	52	66	175	...	...	...	13	4	8	12	39
—Utica	AHL	—	—	—	—	—	...	...	...	1	0	0	0	2
93-94—New Jersey	NHL	41	0	5	5	43	7	0	0	6	0	0	0	7
—Albany	AHL	20	6	3	9	31	...	...	...	—	—	—	—	—
94-95—Albany	AHL	7	0	2	2	15	...	...	...	11	2	2	4	19
—New Jersey	NHL	2	0	0	0	0	-3	0	0	—	—	—	—	—
95-96—New Jersey	NHL	64	2	1	3	86	5	0	0	—	—	—	—	—
96-97—New Jersey	NHL	57	1	2	3	38	-8	0	0	—	—	—	—	—
—Toronto	NHL	21	0	5	5	16	-4	0	0	—	—	—	—	—
97-98—Toronto	NHL	81	3	13	16	100	-5	0	0	—	—	—	—	—
98-99—Toronto	NHL	60	2	11	13	40	-9	0	0	—	—	—	—	—
—Edmonton	NHL	12	1	1	2	11	0	0	0	4	0	1	1	4
99-00—Edmonton	NHL	80	3	11	14	60	16	0	0	5	0	1	1	4
00-01—Edmonton	NHL	82	5	15	20	120	14	1	1	6	0	2	2	6
NHL Totals (8 years)		500	17	64	81	514	13	1	1	21	0	4	4	21

PERSONAL: Born October 24, 1977, in Eyebrow, Sask. ... 5-10/200. ... Shoots left.
TRANSACTIONS/CAREER NOTES: Selected by San Jose Sharks in ninth round (seventh Sharks pick, 219th overall) in NHL entry draft (June 21, 1997). ... Suffered concussion (November 5, 2000); missed seven games. ... Injured knee (February 26, 2001); missed three games.
HONORS: Named to WHL (East) All-Star second team (1997-98).

Season Team	League	REGULAR SEASON								PLAYOFFS				
		Gms.	G	A	Pts.	PIM	+/-	PP	SH	Gms.	G	A	Pts.	PIM
94-95—Lethbridge	WHL	49	3	4	7	25	...	...	...	—	—	—	—	—
95-96—Lethbridge	WHL	71	11	24	35	59	...	...	...	19	7	13	20	51
96-97—Lethbridge	WHL	62	19	38	57	125	...	...	...	19	7	13	20	51
97-98—Lethbridge	WHL	70	42	67	109	206	...	...	...	3	0	2	2	18
98-99—Kentucky	AHL	78	18	21	39	101	...	...	...	12	2	7	9	16
99-00—Kentucky	AHL	79	21	45	66	153	...	...	...	9	0	5	5	22
00-01—San Jose	NHL	42	2	2	4	51	2	0	0	—	—	—	—	—
—Kentucky	AHL	6	2	6	8	23	...	...	...	—	—	—	—	—
NHL Totals (1 year)		42	2	2	4	51	2	0	0					

SMITH, STEVE   D

PERSONAL: Born April 30, 1963, in Glasgow, Scotland. ... 6-4/215. ... Shoots left. ... Full Name: James Stephen Smith.

TRANSACTIONS/CAREER NOTES: Selected by Edmonton Oilers in sixth round (fifth Oilers pick, 111th overall) of NHL entry draft (June 10, 1981). ... Strained right shoulder (November 1, 1985). ... Pulled stomach muscle (February 1986). ... Separated left shoulder (September 20, 1988). ... Aggravated shoulder injury (October 1988). ... Dislocated left shoulder and tore cartilage (January 2, 1989). ... Underwent surgery to left shoulder (January 23, 1989); missed 45 games. ... Traded by Oilers to Chicago Blackhawks for D Dave Manson and third-round pick in either 1992 or 1993 draft; Oilers used third-round pick in 1992 draft to select RW Kirk Maltby (September 26, 1991). ... Pulled rib-cage muscle (December 31, 1991); missed three games. ... Strained back muscle (December 27, 1992); missed four games. ... Suspended four games and fined $500 by NHL for slashing (November 22, 1993). ... Fractured left leg (February 24, 1994); missed remainder of season. ... Suffered back spasms (October 5, 1995); missed 14 games. ... Suffered sore back (November 22, 1995); missed 11 games. ... Suffered sore back (January 2, 1996); missed 11 games. ... Suffered sore back (January 28, 1996); missed six games. ... Fractured left fibula (April 7, 1996); missed seven games. ... Injured nerve in leg (October 5, 1996); missed 10 games. ... Suffered sore back (November 17, 1996), missed three games. ... Suffered sore back (November 27, 1996); missed 13 games. ... Suffered sore back (December 31, 1996); missed 28 games. ... Announced retirement (August 14, 1997). ... Activated from retirement and signed by Calgary Flames (August 17, 1998). ... Injured ankle (March 13, 1999); missed seven games. ... Suffered laceration on neck (April 3, 1999); missed final six games of season. ... Suffered dislocated elbow (November 6, 1999); missed 22 games. ... Bruised spinal cord (January 8, 2000); missed final 40 games of season. ... Suffered concussion (November 8, 2000); missed 14 games. ... Announced retirement (December 7, 2000).

HONORS: Played in NHL All-Star Game (1991).

MISCELLANEOUS: Member of Stanley Cup championship team (1987, 1988 and 1990). ... Captain of Calgary Flames (1999-2000 and October 5-December 7, 2000).

Season Team	League	REGULAR SEASON								PLAYOFFS				
		Gms.	G	A	Pts.	PIM	+/-	PP	SH	Gms.	G	A	Pts.	PIM
80-81—London	OMJHL	62	4	12	16	141	...	...	...	—	—	—	—	—
81-82—London	OHL	58	10	36	46	207	...	...	...	4	1	2	3	13
82-83—London	OHL	50	6	35	41	133	...	...	...	3	1	0	1	10
—Moncton	AHL	2	0	0	0	0	...	...	...	—	—	—	—	—
83-84—Moncton	AHL	64	1	8	9	176	...	...	...	—	—	—	—	—
84-85—Nova Scotia	AHL	68	2	28	30	161	...	...	...	5	0	3	3	40
—Edmonton	NHL	2	0	0	0	2	-2	0	0	—	—	—	—	—
85-86—Nova Scotia	AHL	4	0	2	2	11	...	...	...	—	—	—	—	—
—Edmonton	NHL	55	4	20	24	166	30	1	0	6	0	1	1	14
86-87—Edmonton	NHL	62	7	15	22	165	11	2	0	15	1	3	4	45
87-88—Edmonton	NHL	79	12	43	55	286	40	5	0	19	1	11	12	55
88-89—Edmonton	NHL	35	3	19	22	97	5	0	0	7	2	2	4	20
89-90—Edmonton	NHL	75	7	34	41	171	6	3	0	22	5	10	15	37
90-91—Edmonton	NHL	77	13	41	54	193	14	4	0	18	1	2	3	45
91-92—Chicago	NHL	76	9	21	30	304	23	3	0	18	1	11	12	16
92-93—Chicago	NHL	78	10	47	57	214	12	7	1	4	0	0	0	10
93-94—Chicago	NHL	57	5	22	27	174	-5	1	0	—	—	—	—	—
94-95—Chicago	NHL	48	1	12	13	128	6	0	0	16	0	1	1	26
95-96—Chicago	NHL	37	0	9	9	71	12	0	0	6	0	0	0	16
96-97—Chicago	NHL	21	0	0	0	29	4	0	0	3	0	0	0	4
97-98—							Did not play.							
98-99—Calgary	NHL	69	1	14	15	80	3	0	0	—	—	—	—	—
99-00—Calgary	NHL	20	0	4	4	42	-13	0	0	—	—	—	—	—
00-01—Calgary	NHL	13	0	2	2	17	-2	0	0	—	—	—	—	—
NHL Totals (17 years)		804	72	303	375	2139	144	26	1	134	11	41	52	288

SMITH, WYATT   C   COYOTES

PERSONAL: Born February 13, 1977, in Thief River Falls, Minn. ... 5-11/200. ... Shoots left.

TRANSACTIONS/CAREER NOTES: Selected by Phoenix Coyotes in ninth-round (sixth Coyotes pick, 233rd overall) of NHL entry draft (June 21, 1997).

Season Team	League	REGULAR SEASON								PLAYOFFS				
		Gms.	G	A	Pts.	PIM	+/-	PP	SH	Gms.	G	A	Pts.	PIM
95-96—Univ. of Minnesota	WCHA	32	4	5	9	32	...	...	...	—	—	—	—	—
96-97—Univ. of Minnesota	WCHA	39	24	23	47	62	...	...	...	—	—	—	—	—
97-98—Univ. of Minnesota	WCHA	39	24	23	47	62	...	...	...	—	—	—	—	—
98-99—Univ. of Minnesota	WCHA	43	23	20	43	37	...	...	...	—	—	—	—	—
99-00—Springfield	AHL	60	14	26	40	26	...	...	...	5	2	3	5	13
—Phoenix	NHL	2	0	0	0	0	-2	0	0	—	—	—	—	—
00-01—Phoenix	NHL	42	3	7	10	13	7	0	1	—	—	—	—	—
—Springfield	AHL	18	5	7	12	11	...	...	...	—	—	—	—	—
NHL Totals (2 years)		44	3	7	10	13	5	0	1					

PERSONAL: Born December 27, 1971, in Toledo, Ohio. ... 6-1/208. ... Shoots right. ... Full Name: Bryan Anthony Smolinski.
TRANSACTIONS/CAREER NOTES: Selected by Boston Bruins in first round (first Bruins pick, 21st overall) of NHL entry draft (June 16, 1990) ... Injured knee (April 14, 1994); missed one game. ... Suffered charley horse (April 1995); missed four games. ... Traded by Bruins with RW Glen Murray to Pittsburgh Penguins for LW Kevin Stevens and C Shawn McEachern (August 2, 1995). ... Bruised knee (January 16, 1996) missed one game. ... Traded by Penguins to New York Islanders for D Darius Kasparaitis and C Andreas Johansson (November 17, 1996). ... Traded by Islanders with RW Zigmund Palffy, G Marcel Cousineau and fourth-round pick (C Daniel Johansson) in 1999 draft to Los Angeles Kings for C Olli Jokinen, LW Josh Green, D Mathieu Biron and first-round pick (LW Taylor Pyatt) in 1999 draft (June 20, 1999). ... Sprained knee (April 3, 1999); missed final three games of season. ... Suffered from back spasms (April 3, 2001); missed final two games of season.
HONORS: Named to CCHA All-Rookie team (1989-90). ... Named to NCAA All-America (West) first team (1992-93). ... Named to CCHA All Star first team (1992-93).
STATISTICAL PLATEAUS: Three-goal games: 1994-95 (1), 2000-01 (1). Total: 2.

		REGULAR SEASON								PLAYOFFS				
Season Team	League	Gms.	G	A	Pts.	PIM	+/-	PP	SH	Gms.	G	A	Pts.	PIM
87-88—Detroit Little Caesars ..	MNHL	80	43	77	120	...	...	...	...	—	—	—	—	—
88-89—Stratford Jr. B	OHA	46	32	62	94	132	...	...	...	—	—	—	—	—
89-90—Michigan State............	CCHA	39	10	17	27	45	...	...	...	—	—	—	—	—
90-91—Michigan State............	CCHA	35	9	12	21	24	...	...	...	—	—	—	—	—
91-92—Michigan State............	CCHA	44	30	35	65	59	...	...	...	—	—	—	—	—
92-93—Michigan State............	CCHA	40	31	37	68	93	...	...	...	—	—	—	—	—
—Boston	NHL	9	1	3	4	0	3	0	0	4	1	0	1	2
93-94—Boston	NHL	83	31	20	51	82	4	4	3	13	5	4	9	4
94-95—Boston	NHL	44	18	13	31	31	-3	6	0	5	0	1	1	4
95-96—Pittsburgh.................	NHL	81	24	40	64	69	6	8	2	18	5	4	9	10
96-97—Detroit....................	IHL	6	5	7	12	10	...	...	...	—	—	—	—	—
—New York Islanders.....	NHL	64	28	28	56	25	9	9	0	—	—	—	—	—
97-98—New York Islanders.....	NHL	81	13	30	43	34	-16	3	0	—	—	—	—	—
98-99—New York Islanders.....	NHL	82	16	24	40	49	-7	7	0	—	—	—	—	—
99-00—Los Angeles..............	NHL	79	20	36	56	48	2	2	0	4	0	0	0	2
00-01—Los Angeles..............	NHL	78	27	32	59	40	10	5	3	13	1	5	6	14
NHL Totals (9 years)..........		601	178	226	404	378	8	44	8	57	12	14	26	36

PERSONAL: Born February 16, 1979, in Martin, Czechoslovakia. ... 6-1/194. ... Shoots left. ... Name pronounced SMAIR-ehk.
TRANSACTIONS/CAREER NOTES: Selected by St. Louis Blues in third round (second Blues pick, 85th overall) of NHL entry draft (June 26 1999). ... Traded by Blues to New York Rangers for D Alexei Gusarov (March 5, 2001). ... Bruised ribs (March 10, 2001); missed two games

		REGULAR SEASON								PLAYOFFS				
Season Team	League	Gms.	G	A	Pts.	PIM	+/-	PP	SH	Gms.	G	A	Pts.	PIM
97-98—Martimex Martin Jrs...	Slov. Jr.	23	0	5	5	24	...	...	...	—	—	—	—	—
98-99—Des Moines	USHL	52	6	26	32	59	...	...	...	—	—	—	—	—
99-00—Worcester	AHL	64	5	19	24	26	...	...	...	2	0	0	0	4
—Peoria	ECHL	4	1	1	2	2	...	...	...	—	—	—	—	—
00-01—Worcester	AHL	50	2	7	9	71	...	...	...	—	—	—	—	—
—St. Louis	NHL	6	2	0	2	2	1	0	0	—	—	—	—	—
—New York Rangers......	NHL	14	0	3	3	12	1	0	0	—	—	—	—	—
—Hartford	AHL	—	—	—	—	—	—	—	—	5	0	2	2	2
NHL Totals (1 year)............		20	2	3	5	14	2	0	0					

PERSONAL: Born March 13, 1973, in Ottawa. ... 6-0/195. ... Shoots right. ... Name pronounced SMIHTH.
TRANSACTIONS/CAREER NOTES: Signed as non-drafted free agent by Florida Panthers (October 4, 1993). ... Traded by Panthers to Los Angeles Kings for third-round pick (D Vratislav Cech) in 1997 draft (November 28, 1996). ... Traded by Kings to New York Rangers for conditional draft pick (November 14, 1997). ... Signed as free agent by Nashville Predators (July 16, 1998). ... Traded by Predators to New York Rangers for future considerations (May 3, 1999).
HONORS: Named to AHL All-Star first team (1995-96 and 2000-01). ... Won John B. Sollenberger Trophy (1995-96). ... Won Les Cunningham Plaque (1995-96).

		REGULAR SEASON								PLAYOFFS				
Season Team	League	Gms.	G	A	Pts.	PIM	+/-	PP	SH	Gms.	G	A	Pts.	PIM
90-91—London	OHL	29	2	6	8	22	...	...	...	—	—	—	—	—
91-92—London	OHL	58	17	18	35	93	...	...	...	10	2	0	2	8
92-93—London	OHL	66	54	55	109	118	...	...	...	12	7	8	15	25
93-94—Cincinnati..................	IHL	30	7	3	10	54	...	...	...	—	—	—	—	—
—Birmingham...............	ECHL	29	26	30	56	38	...	...	...	10	8	8	16	19
94-95—Cincinnati..................	IHL	26	2	11	13	34	...	...	...	1	0	0	0	2
—Birmingham...............	ECHL	36	33	35	68	52	...	...	...	3	5	2	7	0
—Springfield	AHL	3	0	0	0	7	...	...	...	—	—	—	—	—
95-96—Carolina	AHL	68	*68	58	*126	80	...	...	...	—	—	—	—	—
—Florida	NHL	7	1	1	2	4	-3	1	0	—	—	—	—	—
96-97—Florida....................	NHL	8	1	0	1	2	-3	0	0	—	—	—	—	—
—Los Angeles..............	NHL	44	8	8	16	74	-7	0	0	—	—	—	—	—
—Phoenix....................	IHL	3	5	2	7	0	...	...	...	—	—	—	—	—
97-98—Los Angeles	NHL	9	1	3	4	4	-1	0	0	—	—	—	—	—
—Hartford	AHL	57	29	33	62	79	...	...	...	15	12	8	20	11
—New York Rangers......	NHL	1	0	0	0	0	0	0	0	—	—	—	—	—

Season Team	League	Gms.	G	A	Pts.	PIM	+/-	PP	SH	Gms.	G	A	Pts.	PIM
98-99—Milwaukee	IHL	34	11	16	27	21	...	...	...	—	—	—	—	—
—Nashville	NHL	3	0	0	0	6	-1	0	0	—	—	—	—	—
—Hartford	AHL	36	25	19	44	48	...	...	...	7	6	0	6	14
99-00—Hartford	AHL	80	39	37	76	62	...	...	...	23	13	10	23	8
00-01—Hartford	AHL	77	*50	29	79	110	...	...	...	5	2	3	5	8
—New York Rangers	NHL	4	1	0	1	4	0	0	0	—	—	—	—	—
NHL Totals (5 years)		76	12	12	24	94	-15	1	0					

SMYTH, RYAN — LW — OILERS

PERSONAL: Born February 21, 1976, in Banff, Alta. ... 6-1/195. ... Shoots left. ... Brother of Kevin Smyth, left winger with Hartford Whalers (1993-94 through 1995-96). ... Name pronounced SMIHTH.

TRANSACTIONS/CAREER NOTES: Selected by Edmonton Oilers in first round (second Oilers pick, sixth overall) of NHL entry draft (June 28, 1994). ... Tore medial collateral ligament in knee (January 20, 1998); missed 15 games. ... Bruised thigh (December 27, 1998); missed one game. ... Fractured jaw (March 10, 1999); missed seven games.

HONORS: Named to Can.HL All-Star first team (1994-95). ... Named to WHL (East) All-Star second team (1994-95).

STATISTICAL PLATEAUS: Three-goal games: 1996-97 (1), 1999-00 (1), 2000-01 (2). Total: 4.

Season Team	League	Gms.	G	A	Pts.	PIM	+/-	PP	SH	Gms.	G	A	Pts.	PIM
91-92—Moose Jaw	WHL	2	0	0	0	0	...	...	...	—	—	—	—	—
92-93—Moose Jaw	WHL	64	19	14	33	59	...	...	...	—	—	—	—	—
93-94—Moose Jaw	WHL	72	50	55	105	88	...	...	...	—	—	—	—	—
94-95—Moose Jaw	WHL	50	41	45	86	66	...	...	...	10	6	9	15	22
—Edmonton	NHL	3	0	0	0	0	-1	0	0	—	—	—	—	—
95-96—Edmonton	NHL	48	2	9	11	28	-10	1	0	—	—	—	—	—
—Cape Breton	AHL	9	6	5	11	4	...	...	...	—	—	—	—	—
96-97—Edmonton	NHL	82	39	22	61	76	-7	†20	0	12	5	5	10	12
97-98—Edmonton	NHL	65	20	13	33	44	-24	10	0	12	1	3	4	16
98-99—Edmonton	NHL	71	13	18	31	62	0	6	0	3	3	0	3	0
99-00—Edmonton	NHL	82	28	26	54	58	-2	11	0	5	1	0	1	6
00-01—Edmonton	NHL	82	31	39	70	58	10	11	0	6	3	4	7	4
NHL Totals (7 years)		433	133	127	260	326	-34	59	0	38	13	12	25	38

SNOW, GARTH — G — ISLANDERS

PERSONAL: Born July 28, 1969, in Wrentham, Mass. ... 6-3/210. ... Catches left.

TRANSACTIONS/CAREER NOTES: Selected by Quebec Nordiques in sixth round (sixth Nordiques pick, 114th overall) of NHL entry draft (June 13, 1987). ... Nordiques franchise moved to Colorado and renamed Avalanche for 1995-96 season (June 21, 1995). ... Rights traded by Avalanche to Philadelphia Flyers for third-(traded to Washington) and sixth-(G Kai Fischer) round picks in 1996 draft (July 12, 1995). ... Pulled groin (March 27, 1997); missed three games. ... Traded by Flyers to Vancouver Canucks for G Sean Burke (March 4, 1998). ... Strained hip flexor (March 18, 1998); missed three games. ... Strained hip flexor (October 31, 1998); missed two games. ... Injured finger (September 21, 1999); missed two games. ... Fractured finger (October 13, 1999); missed 15 games. ... Signed as free agent by Pittsburgh Penguins (October 10, 2000). ... Suspended two games by NHL for fighting incident (December 16, 2000). ... Strained groin (February 7, 2001); missed 25 games. ... Signed as free agent by New York Islanders (July 1, 2001).

HONORS: Named to NCAA All-Tournament team (1992-93). ... Named to Hockey East All-Star second team (1992-93).

MISCELLANEOUS: Stopped a penalty shot attempt (vs. Owen Nolan, December 26, 1998).

Season Team	League	Gms.	Min.	W	L	T	GA	SO	Avg.	Gms.	Min.	W	L	GA	SO	Avg.
88-89—Univ. of Maine	Hockey East	5	241	2	2	0	14	1	3.49	—	—	—	—	—	—	—
89-90—Univ. of Maine	Hockey East								Did not play.							
90-91—Univ. of Maine	Hockey East	25	1290	18	4	0	64	0	2.98	—	—	—	—	—	—	—
91-92—Univ. of Maine	Hockey East	31	1792	25	4	2	73	2	2.44	—	—	—	—	—	—	—
92-93—Univ. of Maine	Hockey East	23	1210	21	0	1	42	1	2.08	—	—	—	—	—	—	—
93-94—U.S. national team	Int'l	23	1324	13	5	3	71	1	3.22	—	—	—	—	—	—	—
—Quebec	NHL	5	279	3	2	0	16	0	3.44	—	—	—	—	—	—	—
—U.S. Olympic team	Int'l	5	299	1	2	2	17	0	3.41	—	—	—	—	—	—	—
—Cornwall	AHL	16	927	6	5	3	51	0	3.30	13	790	8	5	42	0	3.19
94-95—Cornwall	AHL	62	3558	*32	20	7	162	3	2.73	8	402	4	3	14	†2	*2.09
—Quebec	NHL	2	119	1	1	0	11	0	5.55	1	9	0	0	1	0	6.67
95-96—Philadelphia	NHL	26	1437	12	8	4	69	0	2.88	1	1	0	0	0	0	...
96-97—Philadelphia	NHL	35	1884	14	8	8	79	2	2.52	12	699	8	4	33	0	2.83
97-98—Philadelphia	NHL	29	1651	14	9	4	67	1	2.43	—	—	—	—	—	—	—
—Vancouver	NHL	12	504	3	6	0	26	0	3.10	—	—	—	—	—	—	—
98-99—Vancouver	NHL	65	3501	20	†31	8	†171	6	2.93	—	—	—	—	—	—	—
99-00—Vancouver	NHL	32	1712	10	15	7	76	0	2.66	—	—	—	—	—	—	—
00-01—Wilkes-Barre/Scranton	AHL	3	178	2	1	0	7	0	2.36	—	—	—	—	—	—	—
—Pittsburgh	NHL	35	2032	14	15	4	101	3	2.98	—	—	—	—	—	—	—
NHL Totals (8 years)		241	13119	91	95	31	616	12	2.82	14	709	8	4	34	0	2.88

SNYDER, DAN — C — THRASHERS

PERSONAL: Born February 23, 1978, in Elmira, Ont. ... 6-0/185. ... Shoots left.

TRANSACTIONS/CAREER NOTES: Signed as non-drafted free agent by Atlanta Thrashers (June 28, 1999).

Season Team	League	REGULAR SEASON Gms.	G	A	Pts.	PIM	+/-	PP	SH	PLAYOFFS Gms.	G	A	Pts.	PIM
95-96—Owen Sound	OHL	63	8	17	25	78	...	...	...	—	—	—	—	—
96-97—Owen Sound	OHL	57	17	29	46	96	...	...	...	4	2	3	5	8
97-98—Owen Sound	OHL	46	23	33	56	74	...	...	...	—	—	—	—	—
98-99—Owen Sound	OHL	64	27	67	94	110	...	...	...	16	8	5	13	30
99-00—Orlando	IHL	68	12	13	25	121	...	...	...	6	1	2	3	4
00-01—Orlando	IHL	78	13	30	43	127	...	...	...	16	7	3	10	20
—Atlanta	NHL	2	0	0	0	0	0	0	0	—	—	—	—	—
NHL Totals (1 year)		2	0	0	0	0	0	0	0					

SOMIK, RADOVAN — LW — FLYERS

PERSONAL: Born May 5, 1977, in Martin, Czechoslovakia. ... 6-2/194. ... Shoots right.
TRANSACTIONS/CAREER NOTES: Selected by Philadelphia Flyers in fourth round (third Flyers pick, 100th overall) of NHL entry draft (July 8, 1995).

Season Team	League	REGULAR SEASON Gms.	G	A	Pts.	PIM	+/-	PP	SH	PLAYOFFS Gms.	G	A	Pts.	PIM
93-94—Martimex ZTS Martin	Slovakia	1	0	0	0	0	...	...	...	—	—	—	—	—
94-95—Martimex ZTS Martin	Slovakia	28	4	0	4	31	...	...	...	3	1	0	1	2
95-96—Martimex ZTS Martin	Slovakia	25	3	6	9	8	...	...	...	9	1	0	1	...
96-97—Martimex ZTS Martin	Slovakia	35	3	5	8	...	...	...	...	3	0	0	0	0
97-98—Martimex ZTS Martin	Slovakia	26	6	9	15	10	...	...	...	3	0	0	0	0
98-99—Dukla Trencin	Slovakia	26	1	4	5	6	...	...	...	—	—	—	—	—
99-00—Martimex ZTS Martin	Slovakia	40	38	28	66	32	...	...	...	—	—	—	—	—
00-01—HC Continental Zlin	Czech Rep.	46	15	10	25	22	...	...	...	6	1	0	1	0

SONNENBERG, MARTIN — LW — PENGUINS

PERSONAL: Born January 23, 1978, in Wetaskiwin, Alta. ... 6-0/184. ... Shoots left.
TRANSACTIONS/CAREER NOTES: Signed as non-drafted free agent by Pittsburgh Penguins (October 9, 1998).

Season Team	League	REGULAR SEASON Gms.	G	A	Pts.	PIM	+/-	PP	SH	PLAYOFFS Gms.	G	A	Pts.	PIM
95-96—Saskatoon	WHL	58	8	7	15	24	...	...	...	3	0	0	0	2
96-97—Saskatoon	WHL	72	38	26	64	79	...	...	...	—	—	—	—	—
97-98—Saskatoon	WHL	72	40	52	92	87	...	...	...	6	1	3	4	9
98-99—Syracuse	AHL	37	16	9	25	31	...	...	...	—	—	—	—	—
—Pittsburgh	NHL	44	1	1	2	19	-2	0	0	7	0	0	0	0
99-00—Pittsburgh	NHL	14	1	2	3	0	0	1	0	—	—	—	—	—
—Wilkes-Barre/Scranton	AHL	62	20	33	53	109	...	...	...	—	—	—	—	—
00-01—Wilkes-Barre/Scranton	AHL	73	14	18	32	89	...	...	...	21	4	3	7	6
NHL Totals (2 years)		58	2	3	5	19	-2	1	0	7	0	0	0	0

SOPEL, BRENT — D — CANUCKS

PERSONAL: Born January 7, 1977, in Saskatoon, Sask. ... 6-1/205. ... Shoots right. ... Name pronounced SOH-puhl.
TRANSACTIONS/CAREER NOTES: Selected by Vancouver Canucks in sixth round (sixth Canucks pick, 144th overall) of NHL entry draft (July 8, 1995).

Season Team	League	REGULAR SEASON Gms.	G	A	Pts.	PIM	+/-	PP	SH	PLAYOFFS Gms.	G	A	Pts.	PIM
93-94—Saskatoon	WHL	11	2	2	4	2	...	...	...	—	—	—	—	—
94-95—Saskatoon	WHL	22	1	10	11	31	...	...	...	—	—	—	—	—
—Swift Current	WHL	41	4	19	23	50	...	...	...	3	0	3	3	0
95-96—Swift Current	WHL	71	13	48	61	87	...	...	...	6	1	2	3	4
—Syracuse	AHL	1	0	0	0	0	...	...	...	—	—	—	—	—
96-97—Swift Current	WHL	62	15	41	56	109	...	...	...	10	5	11	16	32
—Syracuse	AHL	2	0	0	0	0	...	...	...	3	0	0	0	0
97-98—Syracuse	AHL	76	10	33	43	70	...	...	...	5	0	7	7	12
98-99—Syracuse	AHL	53	10	21	31	59	...	...	...	—	—	—	—	—
—Vancouver	NHL	5	1	0	1	4	-1	1	0	—	—	—	—	—
99-00—Syracuse	AHL	50	6	25	31	67	...	...	...	4	0	2	2	8
—Vancouver	NHL	18	2	4	6	12	9	0	0	—	—	—	—	—
00-01—Vancouver	NHL	52	4	10	14	10	4	0	0	4	0	0	0	2
—Kansas City	IHL	4	0	1	1	0	...	...	...	—	—	—	—	—
NHL Totals (3 years)		75	7	14	21	26	12	1	0	4	0	0	0	2

SOURAY, SHELDON — D — CANADIENS

PERSONAL: Born July 13, 1976, in Elk Point, Alta. ... 6-4/230. ... Shoots left. ... Name pronounced SOOR-ay.
TRANSACTIONS/CAREER NOTES: Selected by New Jersey Devils in third round (third Devils pick, 71st overall) of NHL entry draft (June 29, 1994). ... Suffered head injury (September 27, 1997); missed five games. ... Bruised right wrist (October 17, 1997); missed four games. ... Suffered from the flu (December 18, 1997); missed one game. ... Suffered from the flu (January 30, 1998); missed one game. ... Traded by Devils with D Josh DeWolf and second-round pick (traded to Washington) in 2001 draft to Montreal Canadiens for D Vladimir Malakhov (March 1, 2000). ... Strained muscle in abdomen (September 23, 2000) and underwent surgery; missed first 29 games of season. ... Bruised ankle (February 10, 2001); missed one game.
HONORS: Named to WHL (West) All-Star second team (1995-96).

Season Team	League	REGULAR SEASON								PLAYOFFS				
		Gms.	G	A	Pts.	PIM	+/-	PP	SH	Gms.	G	A	Pts.	PIM
92-93—Fort Saskatchewan	AJHL	35	0	12	12	125	...	...	...	—	—	—	—	—
—Tri-City	WHL	2	0	0	0	0	...	...	...	—	—	—	—	—
93-94—Tri-City	WHL	42	3	6	9	122	...	...	...	—	—	—	—	—
94-95—Tri-City	WHL	40	2	24	26	140	...	...	...	—	—	—	—	—
—Prince George............	WHL	11	2	3	5	23	...	...	...	—	—	—	—	—
—Albany......................	AHL	7	0	2	2	8	...	...	...	—	—	—	—	—
95-96—Prince George............	WHL	32	9	18	27	91	...	...	...	—	—	—	—	—
—Kelowna......................	WHL	27	7	20	27	94	...	...	...	6	0	5	5	2
—Albany......................	AHL	6	0	2	2	12	...	...	...	4	0	1	1	4
96-97—Albany......................	AHL	70	2	11	13	160	...	...	...	16	2	3	5	47
97-98—New Jersey	NHL	60	3	7	10	85	18	0	0	3	0	1	1	2
—Albany......................	AHL	6	0	0	0	8	...	...	...	—	—	—	—	—
98-99—New Jersey	NHL	70	1	7	8	110	5	0	0	2	0	1	1	0
99-00—New Jersey	NHL	52	0	8	8	70	-6	0	0	—	—	—	—	—
—Montreal	NHL	19	3	0	3	44	7	0	0	—	—	—	—	—
00-01—Montreal	NHL	52	3	8	11	95	-11	0	0	—	—	—	—	—
NHL Totals (4 years)...........		253	10	30	40	404	13	0	0	5	0	2	2	2

SPACEK, JAROSLAV   D   BLACKHAWKS

PERSONAL: Born February 11, 1974, in Rokycany, Czechoslovakia. ... 5-11/198. ... Shoots left.
TRANSACTIONS/CAREER NOTES: Selected by Florida Panthers in fifth round (fifth Panthers pick, 117th overall) of NHL entry draft (June 27, 1998). ... Suffered from the flu (April 7, 1999); missed three games. ... Traded by Panthers to Chicago Blackhawks for D Anders Eriksson (November 6, 2000). ... Fractured left shoulder (January 14, 2001); missed 18 games.

Season Team	League	REGULAR SEASON								PLAYOFFS				
		Gms.	G	A	Pts.	PIM	+/-	PP	SH	Gms.	G	A	Pts.	PIM
92-93—Skoda Plzen................	Czech.	16	1	3	4	...	...	...	...	—	—	—	—	—
93-94—Skoda Plzen................	Czech Rep.	34	2	10	12	...	...	...	...	—	—	—	—	—
94-95—Interconex Plzen	Czech Rep.	38	4	8	12	14	...	...	...	3	1	0	1	2
95-96—ZKZ Plzen	Czech Rep.	40	3	10	13	42	...	...	...	3	0	1	1	4
96-97—ZKZ Plzen	Czech Rep.	52	9	29	38	44	...	...	...	—	—	—	—	—
97-98—Farjestad Karlstad	Sweden	45	10	16	26	63	...	...	...	12	2	5	7	14
98-99—Florida.....................	NHL	63	3	12	15	28	15	2	1	—	—	—	—	—
—New Haven	AHL	14	4	8	12	15	...	...	...	—	—	—	—	—
99-00—Florida.....................	NHL	82	10	26	36	53	7	4	0	4	0	0	0	0
00-01—Florida.....................	NHL	12	2	1	3	8	-4	1	0	—	—	—	—	—
—Chicago....................	NHL	50	5	18	23	20	7	2	0	—	—	—	—	—
NHL Totals (3 years)...........		207	20	57	77	109	25	9	1	4	0	0	0	0

SPANHEL, MARTIN   LW   BLUE JACKETS

PERSONAL: Born July 1, 1977, in Gottwaldov, Czechoslovakia. ... 6-2/202. ... Shoots left. ... Name pronounced spah-NEHL.
TRANSACTIONS/CAREER NOTES: Selected by Philadelphia Flyers in sixth round (fifth Flyers pick, 152nd overall) of NHL entry draft (July 8, 1995). ... Traded by Flyers with first (traded to Winnipeg)- and fourth-round (traded to Buffalo) picks in 1996 draft to San Jose Sharks for RW Pat Falloon (November 16, 1995). ... Signed as free agent by Columbus Blue Jackets (June 7, 2000).

Season Team	League	REGULAR SEASON								PLAYOFFS				
		Gms.	G	A	Pts.	PIM	+/-	PP	SH	Gms.	G	A	Pts.	PIM
94-95—ZPS Zlin Jrs................	Czech. Jrs.	33	25	16	41	...	...	...	...	—	—	—	—	—
—ZPS Zlin Jrs...............	Czech. Jrs.	33	25	16	41	...	...	...	...	—	—	—	—	—
—ZPS Zlin	Czech Rep.	1	0	0	0	...	...	...	...	—	—	—	—	—
95-96—Moose Jaw	WHL	61	4	12	16	33	...	...	...	—	—	—	—	—
—Lethbridge	WHL	6	1	0	1	0	...	...	...	—	—	—	—	—
96-97—ZPS Zlin	Czech Rep.	22	3	6	9	20	...	...	...	—	—	—	—	—
—ZPS Zlin Jrs...............	Czech. Jrs.	6	6	3	9	2	...	...	...	—	—	—	—	—
—Karlovy Vary	Czech. D-II	7	4	3	7	...	...	...	...	—	—	—	—	—
97-98—ZPS Zlin	Czech Rep.	40	7	9	16	70	...	...	...	—	—	—	—	—
98-99—HC Keramika Plzen	Czech Rep.	49	13	13	26	60	...	...	...	5	2	1	3	...
99-00—HC Keramika Plzen	Czech Rep.	52	21	27	48	86	...	...	...	7	1	4	5	12
00-01—Syracuse....................	AHL	67	11	13	24	75	...	...	...	2	0	0	0	8
—Columbus	NHL	6	1	0	1	2	-1	0	0	—	—	—	—	—
NHL Totals (1 year).............		6	1	0	1	2	-1	0	0					

ST. CROIX, CHRIS   D   FLAMES

PERSONAL: Born May 2, 1979, in Voorhees, N.J. ... 6-0/199. ... Shoots right.
TRANSACTIONS/CAREER NOTES: Selected by Calgary Flames in fourth round (seventh Flames pick, 92nd overall) of NHL entry draft (June 21, 1997). ... Traded by Flames to New York Rangers for D Burke Henry (June 24, 2001).

Season Team	League	REGULAR SEASON								PLAYOFFS				
		Gms.	G	A	Pts.	PIM	+/-	PP	SH	Gms.	G	A	Pts.	PIM
95-96—Kamloops	WHL	61	4	6	10	27	...	...	...	13	0	2	2	4
96-97—Kamloops	WHL	67	11	39	50	67	...	...	...	5	0	1	1	2
97-98—Kamloops	WHL	46	3	13	16	51	...	...	...	7	1	1	2	6
98-99—Kamloops	WHL	64	8	27	35	123	...	...	...	14	0	4	4	16
99-00—Saint John	AHL	75	5	16	21	51	...	...	...	3	0	1	1	2
00-01—Saint John	AHL	69	0	4	4	66	...	...	...	5	0	1	1	4

ST. JACQUES, BRUNO   D   FLYERS

PERSONAL: Born August 22, 1980, in Montreal. ... 6-2/204. ... Shoots left.
TRANSACTIONS/CAREER NOTES: Selected by Philadelphia Flyers in ninth round (12th Flyers pick, 253rd overall) of NHL entry draft (June 27, 1998).

Season Team	League	Gms.	G	A	Pts.	PIM	+/-	PP	SH	Gms.	G	A	Pts.	PIM
97-98—Baie-Comeau	QMJHL	63	13	29	42	253	...	...	...	—	—	—	—	—
98-99—Baie-Comeau	QMJHL	49	1	21	22	138	...	...	...	—	—	—	—	—
99-00—Baie-Comeau	QMJHL	60	8	28	36	120	...	...	...	—	—	—	—	—
—Philadelphia	AHL	3	0	1	1	0	...	...	...	1	0	0	0	0
00-01—Philadelphia	AHL	45	1	16	17	83	...	...	...	10	1	0	1	16

ST. LOUIS, MARTIN   RW   LIGHTNING

PERSONAL: Born September 8, 1971, in Laval, Que. ... 5-9/185. ... Shoots left.
TRANSACTIONS/CAREER NOTES: Signed as non-drafted free agent by Calgary Flames (February 18, 1998). ... Suffered concussion (March 15, 2000); missed two games. ... Signed as free agent by Tampa Bay Lightning (July 31, 2000).
HONORS: Named to NCAA All-America (East) first team (1994-95 through 1996-97). ... Named to ECAC All-Star first team (1994-95 through 1996-97).

Season Team	League	Gms.	G	A	Pts.	PIM	+/-	PP	SH	Gms.	G	A	Pts.	PIM
93-94—Vermont	ECAC	33	15	36	51	24	...	...	...	—	—	—	—	—
94-95—Vermont	ECAC	35	23	48	71	36	...	...	...	—	—	—	—	—
95-96—Vermont	ECAC	35	29	56	85	36	...	...	...	—	—	—	—	—
96-97—Vermont	ECAC	35	24	26	50	65	...	...	...	—	—	—	—	—
97-98—Cleveland	IHL	56	16	34	50	24	...	...	...	—	—	—	—	—
—Saint John	AHL	25	15	11	26	20	...	...	...	20	5	15	20	16
98-99—Calgary	NHL	13	1	1	2	10	-2	0	0	—	—	—	—	—
—Saint John	AHL	53	28	34	62	30	...	...	...	7	4	4	8	2
99-00—Saint John	AHL	17	15	11	26	14	...	...	...	—	—	—	—	—
—Calgary	NHL	56	3	15	18	22	-5	0	0	—	—	—	—	—
00-01—Tampa Bay	NHL	78	18	22	40	12	-4	3	3	—	—	—	—	—
NHL Totals (3 years)		147	22	38	60	44	-11	3	3					

STAIOS, STEVE   RW/D   OILERS

PERSONAL: Born July 28, 1973, in Hamilton, Ont. ... 6-1/200. ... Shoots right. ... Name pronounced STAY-ohz.
TRANSACTIONS/CAREER NOTES: Selected by St. Louis Blues in second round (first Blues pick, 27th overall) of NHL entry draft (June 22, 1991). ... Traded by Blues with LW Kevin Sawyer to Boston Bruins for RW Steve Leach (March 8, 1996). ... Strained groin (November 6, 1996); missed 13 games. ... Claimed on waivers by Vancouver Canucks (March 18, 1997). ... Injured knee (February 24, 1999); missed 16 games. ... Selected by Atlanta Thrashers in NHL expansion draft (June 25, 1999). ... Sprained medial collateral ligament in right knee (November 20, 1999); missed four games. ... Injured groin (December 30, 1999); missed 16 games. ... Reinjured groin (February 15, 2000); missed final 27 games of season. ... Traded by Thrashers to New Jersey Devils for ninth-round pick (C Simon Gamache) in 2000 draft (June 12, 2000). ... Traded by Devils to Thrashers for future considerations (July 10, 2000). ... Suffered concussion (November 27, 2000); missed five games. ... Bruised foot (December 22, 2000); missed two games. ... Strained hamstring (January 23, 2001); missed two games. ... Strained groin (February 7, 2001); missed three games. ... Signed as free agent by Edmonton Oilers (July 12, 2001).
MISCELLANEOUS: Captain of Atlanta Thrashers (2000-01).

Season Team	League	Gms.	G	A	Pts.	PIM	+/-	PP	SH	Gms.	G	A	Pts.	PIM
89-90—Hamilton Jr. B	OHA	40	9	27	36	66	...	...	...	—	—	—	—	—
90-91—Niagara Falls	OHL	66	17	29	46	115	...	...	...	12	2	3	5	10
91-92—Niagara Falls	OHL	65	11	42	53	122	...	...	...	17	7	8	15	27
92-93—Niagara Falls	OHL	12	4	14	18	30	...	...	...	—	—	—	—	—
—Sudbury	OHL	53	13	44	57	67	...	...	...	11	5	6	11	22
93-94—Peoria	IHL	38	3	9	12	42	...	...	...	—	—	—	—	—
94-95—Peoria	IHL	60	3	13	16	64	...	...	...	6	0	0	0	10
95-96—Peoria	IHL	6	0	1	1	14	...	...	...	—	—	—	—	—
—Worcester	AHL	57	1	11	12	114	...	...	...	—	—	—	—	—
—Providence	AHL	7	1	4	5	8	...	...	...	—	—	—	—	—
—Boston	NHL	12	0	0	0	4	-5	0	0	3	0	0	0	0
96-97—Boston	NHL	54	3	8	11	71	-26	0	0	—	—	—	—	—
—Vancouver	NHL	9	0	6	6	20	2	0	0	—	—	—	—	—
97-98—Vancouver	NHL	77	3	4	7	134	-3	0	0	—	—	—	—	—
98-99—Vancouver	NHL	57	0	2	2	54	-12	0	0	—	—	—	—	—
99-00—Atlanta	NHL	27	2	3	5	66	-5	0	0	—	—	—	—	—
00-01—Atlanta	NHL	70	9	13	22	137	-23	4	0	—	—	—	—	—
NHL Totals (6 years)		306	17	36	53	486	-72	4	0	3	0	0	0	0

STAPLETON, MIKE   C   CANUCKS

PERSONAL: Born May 5, 1966, in Sarnia, Ont. ... 5-10/185. ... Shoots right. ... Son of Pat Stapleton, defenseman with Boston Bruins (1961-62 and 1962-63), Chicago Blackhawks (1965-66 through 1972-73) and three WHA teams (1973-74 through 1977-78).
TRANSACTIONS/CAREER NOTES: Selected by Chicago Blackhawks in seventh round (seventh Blackhawks pick, 132nd overall) of NHL entry draft (June 9, 1984). ... Signed as free agent by Pittsburgh Penguins (September 4, 1992). ... Claimed on waivers by Edmonton Oilers (February 19, 1994). ... Signed as free agent by Winnipeg Jets (August 9, 1995). ... Suffered charley horse (October 12, 1995); missed one game.

... Fractured jaw (November 1, 1995); missed 16 games. ... Strained groin (March 27, 1996); missed five games. ... Jets franchise moved to Phoenix and renamed Coyotes for 1996-97 season; NHL approved move on January 18, 1996. ... Suffered eye abrasion (January 30, 1998); missed four games. ... Fractured foot (March 28, 1998); missed five games. ... Suffered from the flu (November 1, 1998); missed one game. ... Suffered charley horse (January 17, 1999); missed one game. ... Suffered facial lacerations (February 14, 1999); missed four games. ... Selected by Atlanta Thrashers in NHL expansion draft (June 25, 1999). ... Injured ribs (January 12, 2000); missed 13 games. ... Signed as free agent by New York Islanders (July 3, 2000). ... Traded by Islanders to Vancouver Canucks for ninth-round pick (traded to Washington) in 2001 draft (December 28, 2000).

Season Team	League	REGULAR SEASON								PLAYOFFS				
		Gms.	G	A	Pts.	PIM	+/-	PP	SH	Gms.	G	A	Pts.	PIM
82-83—Strathroy Jr. B	OHA	40	39	38	77	99	...	...	...	—	—	—	—	—
83-84—Cornwall	OHL	70	24	45	69	94	...	...	...	3	1	2	3	4
84-85—Cornwall	OHL	56	41	44	85	68	...	...	...	9	2	4	6	23
85-86—Cornwall	OHL	56	39	65	104	74	...	...	...	6	2	3	5	2
86-87—Canadian nat'l team	Int'l	21	2	4	6	4	...	...	...	—	—	—	—	—
—Chicago......................	NHL	39	3	6	9	6	-9	0	0	4	0	0	0	2
87-88—Saginaw	IHL	31	11	19	30	52	...	...	...	10	5	6	11	10
—Chicago......................	NHL	53	2	9	11	59	-10	0	0	—	—	—	—	—
88-89—Chicago...................	NHL	7	0	1	1	7	-1	0	0	—	—	—	—	—
—Saginaw....................	IHL	69	21	47	68	162	...	...	...	6	1	3	4	4
89-90—Arvika	Sweden	30	15	18	33	...				—	—	—	—	—
—Indianapolis	IHL	16	5	10	15	6	...	...	...	13	9	10	19	38
90-91—Indianapolis	NHL	7	0	1	1	2	0	0	0	—	—	—	—	—
—Indianapolis	IHL	75	29	52	81	76	...	...	...	7	1	4	5	0
91-92—Indianapolis	IHL	59	18	40	58	65	...	...	...	—	—	—	—	—
—Chicago......................	NHL	19	4	4	8	8	0	1	0	—	—	—	—	—
92-93—Pittsburgh..................	NHL	78	4	9	13	10	-8	0	1	4	0	0	0	0
93-94—Pittsburgh..................	NHL	58	7	4	11	18	-4	3	0	—	—	—	—	—
—Edmonton	NHL	23	5	9	14	28	-1	1	0	—	—	—	—	—
94-95—Edmonton	NHL	46	6	11	17	21	-12	3	0	—	—	—	—	—
95-96—Winnipeg	NHL	58	10	14	24	37	-4	3	1	6	0	0	0	21
96-97—Phoenix.....................	NHL	55	4	11	15	36	-4	2	0	7	0	0	0	14
97-98—Phoenix.....................	NHL	64	5	5	10	36	-4	1	1	6	0	0	0	2
98-99—Phoenix.....................	NHL	76	9	9	18	34	-6	0	2	7	1	0	1	0
99-00—Atlanta	NHL	62	10	12	22	30	-29	4	0	—	—	—	—	—
00-01—New York Islanders.....	NHL	34	1	4	5	2	-5	0	0	—	—	—	—	—
—Vancouver..................	NHL	18	1	2	3	8	-6	1	0	—	—	—	—	—
NHL Totals (14 years).........		697	71	111	182	342	-103	19	5	34	1	0	1	39

STEFAN, PATRIK   C   THRASHERS

PERSONAL: Born September 16, 1980, in Pribram, Czechoslovakia. ... 6-3/200. ... Shoots left.

TRANSACTIONS/CAREER NOTES: Selected by Atlanta Thrashers in first round (first Thrashers pick, first overall) of NHL entry draft (June 26, 1999). ... Suffered concussion (November 19, 1999); missed two games. ... Suffered back spasms (February 29, 2000); missed three games. ... Suffered from the flu (March 22, 2000); missed two games. ... Injured groin (September 26, 2000); missed first five games of season. ... Suffered from the flu (November 17, 2000); missed one game. ... Suffered concussion (November 22, 2000); missed three games. ... Suffered head injury (Deceber 29, 2000); missed one game. ... Strained groin (January 29, 2001); missed one game. ... Strained groin (February 7, 2001); missed three games. ... Suffered from the flu (February 23, 2001); missed one game.

Season Team	League	REGULAR SEASON								PLAYOFFS				
		Gms.	G	A	Pts.	PIM	+/-	PP	SH	Gms.	G	A	Pts.	PIM
96-97—Sparta Praha..............	Czech Rep.	5	0	1	1	2	...	...	...	7	1	0	1	0
97-98—Sparta Praha..............	Czech Rep.	27	2	6	8	16	...	...	...	—	—	—	—	—
—Long Beach................	IHL	25	5	15	20	10	...	...	...	10	1	1	2	2
98-99—Long Beach................	IHL	33	11	24	35	26	...	...	...	—	—	—	—	—
99-00—Atlanta	NHL	72	5	20	25	30	-20	1	0	—	—	—	—	—
00-01—Atlanta	NHL	66	10	21	31	22	-3	0	0	—	—	—	—	—
NHL Totals (2 years)...........		138	15	41	56	52	-23	1	0					

STEPHENS, CHARLIE   C/RW   AVALANCHE

PERSONAL: Born April 5, 1981, in Nilestown, Ont. ... 6-4/225. ... Shoots right.

TRANSACTIONS/CAREER NOTES: Selected by Washington Capitals in second round (third Capitals pick, 31st overall) of NHL entry draft (June 26, 1999). ... Returned to draft pool by Capitals and selected by Colorado Avalanche in sixth round (ninth Avalanche pick, 196th overall) of NHL entry draft (June 23, 2001).

Season Team	League	REGULAR SEASON								PLAYOFFS				
		Gms.	G	A	Pts.	PIM	+/-	PP	SH	Gms.	G	A	Pts.	PIM
97-98—Toronto St. Michael's..	OHL	58	9	21	30	38	...	...	...	—	—	—	—	—
98-99—Toronto St. Michael's..	OHL	7	2	4	6	8	...	...	...	—	—	—	—	—
—Guelph	OHL	61	24	28	52	72	...	...	...	11	3	5	8	19
99-00—Guelph	OHL	56	16	34	50	87	...	...	...	6	1	3	4	15
00-01—Guelph	OHL	67	38	38	76	53	...	...	...	4	0	2	2	2

STEVENS, KEVIN   LW   PENGUINS

PERSONAL: Born April 15, 1965, in Brockton, Mass. ... 6-3/230. ... Shoots left. ... Full Name: Kevin Michael Stevens.

TRANSACTIONS/CAREER NOTES: Selected by Los Angeles Kings in sixth round (sixth Kings pick, 108th overall) of NHL entry draft (June 8, 1983). ... Traded by Kings to Pittsburgh Penguins for LW Anders Hakansson (September 9, 1983). ... Injured left knee (November 5, 1992) and underwent surgery; missed nine games. ... Suspended one game by NHL (March 1993). ... Suffered from bronchitis (April 3, 1993); missed two games. ... Fractured left ankle (February 4, 1995); missed 21 games. ... Traded by Penguins with C Shawn McEachern to Boston Bruins for C Bryan Smolinski and RW Glen Murray (August 2, 1995). ... Traded by Bruins to Los Angeles Kings for RW Rick Tocchet (January 25, 1996).

... Fractured left fibula (February 29, 1996); missed 10 games. ... Suffered concussion (October 15, 1996); missed one game. ... Suffered back spasms (November 27, 1996); missed one game. ... Bruised ankle (February 20, 1997); missed seven games. ... Injured knee (April 9, 1997); missed two games. ... Traded by Kings to New York Rangers for LW Luc Robitaille (August 28, 1997). ... Strained groin (October 8, 1997); missed one game. ... Suffered from the flu (March 21, 1998); missed one game. ... Suffered from the flu (November 6, 1999); missed two games. ... Signed as free agent by Philadelphia Flyers (July 7, 2000). ... Strained quadriceps (November 3, 2000); missed three games. ... Traded by Flyers to Penguins for D John Slaney (January 14, 2001). ... Sprained knee (March 27, 2001); missed final six games of season.

HONORS: Named to NCAA All-America (East) second team (1986-87). ... Named to Hockey East All-Star first team (1986-87). ... Named to THE SPORTING NEWS All-Star second team (1990-91 and 1992-93). ... Named to NHL All-Star second team (1990-91 and 1992-93). ... Named to THE SPORTING NEWS All-Star first team (1991-92). ... Named to NHL All-Star first team (1991-92). ... Played in NHL All-Star Game (1991-1993).

MISCELLANEOUS: Member of Stanley Cup championship team (1991 and 1992). ... Failed to score on a penalty shot (vs. Nikolai Khabibulin, February 26, 1996; vs. Sean Burke, March 22, 1998).

STATISTICAL PLATEAUS: Three-goal games: 1989-90 (1), 1990-91 (1), 1991-92 (3), 1992-93 (2), 1993-94 (1), 1998-99 (1). Total: 9. ... Four-goal games: 1991-92 (1), 1992-93 (1). Total: 2. ... Total hat tricks: 11.

Season Team	League	REGULAR SEASON Gms.	G	A	Pts.	PIM	+/-	PP	SH	PLAYOFFS Gms.	G	A	Pts.	PIM
82-83—Silver Lake H.S.	Minn. H.S.	18	24	27	51	...	...	...	...	—	—	—	—	—
83-84—Boston College	ECAC	37	6	14	20	36	...	...	...	—	—	—	—	—
84-85—Boston College	Hockey East	40	13	23	36	36	...	...	...	—	—	—	—	—
85-86—Boston College	Hockey East	42	17	27	44	56	...	...	...	—	—	—	—	—
86-87—Boston College	Hockey East	39	*35	35	70	54	...	...	...	—	—	—	—	—
87-88—U.S. national team	Int'l	44	22	23	45	52	...	...	...	—	—	—	—	—
—U.S. Olympic team......	Int'l	5	1	3	4	2	...	...	...	—	—	—	—	—
—Pittsburgh..................	NHL	16	5	2	7	8	-6	2	0	—	—	—	—	—
88-89—Pittsburgh..................	NHL	24	12	3	15	19	-8	4	0	11	3	7	10	16
—Muskegon..................	IHL	45	24	41	65	113	...	...	...	—	—	—	—	—
89-90—Pittsburgh..................	NHL	76	29	41	70	171	-13	12	0	—	—	—	—	—
90-91—Pittsburgh..................	NHL	80	40	46	86	133	-1	18	0	24	*17	16	33	53
91-92—Pittsburgh..................	NHL	80	54	69	123	254	8	19	0	21	13	15	28	28
92-93—Pittsburgh..................	NHL	72	55	56	111	177	17	26	0	12	5	11	16	22
93-94—Pittsburgh..................	NHL	83	41	47	88	155	-24	21	0	6	1	1	2	10
94-95—Pittsburgh..................	NHL	27	15	12	27	51	0	6	0	12	4	7	11	21
95-96—Boston	NHL	41	10	13	23	49	1	3	0	—	—	—	—	—
—Los Angeles..................	NHL	20	3	10	13	22	-11	3	0	—	—	—	—	—
96-97—Los Angeles..................	NHL	69	14	20	34	96	-27	4	0	—	—	—	—	—
97-98—New York Rangers.....	NHL	80	14	27	41	130	-7	5	0	—	—	—	—	—
98-99—New York Rangers......	NHL	81	23	20	43	64	-10	8	0	—	—	—	—	—
99-00—New York Rangers......	NHL	38	3	5	8	43	-7	1	0	—	—	—	—	—
00-01—Philadelphia..................	NHL	23	2	7	9	18	-2	0	0	—	—	—	—	—
—Pittsburgh..................	NHL	32	8	15	23	55	-4	2	0	17	3	3	6	20
NHL Totals (14 years).........		842	328	393	721	1445	-94	134	0	103	46	60	106	170

STEVENS, SCOTT   D   DEVILS

PERSONAL: Born April 1, 1964, in Kitchener, Ont. ... 6-1/215. ... Shoots left. ... Brother of Mike Stevens, center/left winger with four NHL teams (1984-85 and 1987-88 through 1989-90).

TRANSACTIONS/CAREER NOTES: Selected by Washington Capitals in first round (first Capitals pick, fifth overall) of NHL entry draft (June 9, 1982). ... Bruised right knee (November 6, 1985); missed seven games. ... Fractured right index finger (December 14, 1986). ... Bruised shoulder (April 1988). ... Suffered from poison oak (November 1988). ... Fractured left foot (December 29, 1989); missed 17 games. ... Suspended three games by NHL for scratching (February 27, 1990). ... Bruised left shoulder (March 27, 1990). ... Dislocated left shoulder (May 3, 1990). ... Signed as free agent by St. Louis Blues (July 9, 1990); Blues owed Capitals two first-round draft picks among the top seven over next two years and $100,000 cash; upon failing to get a pick in the top seven in 1991, Blues forfeited their first-round pick in 1991 (LW Trevor Halverson), 1992 (D Sergei Gonchar), 1993 (D Brendan Witt), 1994 (traded to Toronto) and 1995 (LW Miikka Elomo) drafts to Capitals (July 9, 1990). ... Awarded to New Jersey Devils as compensation for Blues signing free agent RW/LW Brendan Shanahan (September 3, 1991). ... Strained right knee (February 20, 1992); missed 12 games. ... Suffered concussion (December 27, 1992); missed three games. ... Strained knee (November 19, 1993); missed one game. ... Suspended one game by NHL for highsticking incident (October 7, 1996). ... Suffered from the flu (December 23, 1996); missed one game. ... Suffered hip pointer (February 28, 1998); missed one game. ... Suffered from the flu (December 8, 1998); missed one game. ... Suffered back spasms (December 19, 1998); missed one game. ... Strained groin (March 15, 1999); missed five games. ... Suffered from the flu (January 8, 2000); missed two games. ... Suffered from the flu (March 24, 2000); missed one game.

HONORS: Named to NHL All-Rookie team (1982-83). ... Named to THE SPORTING NEWS All-Star second team (1987-88). ... Named to NHL All-Star first team (1987-88 and 1993-94). ... Named to NHL All-Star second team (1991-92, 1996-97 and 2000-01). ... Played in NHL All-Star Game (1985, 1989, 1991-1994 and 1996-2001). ... Named to THE SPORTING NEWS All-Star first team (1993-94). ... Won Conn Smythe Trophy (1999-2000).

MISCELLANEOUS: Member of Stanley Cup championship team (1995 and 2000). ... Captain of St. Louis Blues (1990-91). ... Captain of New Jersey Devils (1992-93 and 1995-96 through 2000-01).

Season Team	League	REGULAR SEASON Gms.	G	A	Pts.	PIM	+/-	PP	SH	PLAYOFFS Gms.	G	A	Pts.	PIM
80-81—Kitchener Jr. B	OHA	39	7	33	40	82	...	...	...	—	—	—	—	—
—Kitchener	OHL	1	0	0	0	0	...	...	...	—	—	—	—	—
81-82—Kitchener	OHL	68	6	36	42	158	...	...	...	15	1	10	11	71
82-83—Washington	NHL	77	9	16	25	195	15	0	0	4	1	0	1	26
83-84—Washington	NHL	78	13	32	45	201	26	7	0	8	1	8	9	21
84-85—Washington	NHL	80	21	44	65	221	19	16	0	5	0	1	1	20
85-86—Washington	NHL	73	15	38	53	165	0	3	0	9	3	8	11	12
86-87—Washington	NHL	77	10	51	61	283	13	2	0	7	0	5	5	19
87-88—Washington	NHL	80	12	60	72	184	14	5	1	13	1	11	12	46
88-89—Washington	NHL	80	7	61	68	225	1	6	0	6	1	4	5	11
89-90—Washington	NHL	56	11	29	40	154	1	7	0	15	2	7	9	25

Season Team	League	REGULAR SEASON								PLAYOFFS				
		Gms.	G	A	Pts.	PIM	+/-	PP	SH	Gms.	G	A	Pts.	PIM
90-91—St. Louis	NHL	78	5	44	49	150	23	1	0	13	0	3	3	36
91-92—New Jersey	NHL	68	17	42	59	124	24	7	1	7	2	1	3	29
92-93—New Jersey	NHL	81	12	45	57	120	14	8	0	5	2	2	4	10
93-94—New Jersey	NHL	83	18	60	78	112	*53	5	1	20	2	9	11	42
94-95—New Jersey	NHL	48	2	20	22	56	4	1	0	20	1	7	8	24
95-96—New Jersey	NHL	82	5	23	28	100	7	2	1	—	—	—	—	—
96-97—New Jersey	NHL	79	5	19	24	70	26	0	0	10	0	4	4	2
97-98—New Jersey	NHL	80	4	22	26	80	19	1	0	6	1	0	1	8
—Can. Olympic team	Int'l	6	0	0	0	2	...	...	...	—	—	—	—	—
98-99—New Jersey	NHL	75	5	22	27	64	29	0	0	7	2	1	3	10
99-00—New Jersey	NHL	78	8	21	29	103	30	0	1	23	3	8	11	6
00-01—New Jersey	NHL	81	9	22	31	71	40	3	0	25	1	7	8	37
NHL Totals (19 years)		1434	188	671	859	2678	358	74	5	203	23	86	109	384

STEVENSON, JEREMY   LW   PREDATORS

PERSONAL: Born July 28, 1974, in San Bernardino, Calif. ... 6-2/217. ... Shoots left. ... Full Name: Jeremy Joseph Stevenson.

TRANSACTIONS/CAREER NOTES: Selected by Winnipeg Jets in third round (third Jets pick, 60th overall) of NHL entry draft (June 20, 1992). ... Returned to draft pool by Jets and selected by Mighty Ducks of Anaheim in 11th round (10th Mighty Ducks pick, 262nd overall) of NHL entry draft (June 28, 1994). ... Fractured ankle (October 24, 1996); missed 33 games. ... Suffered concussion prior to 1997-98 season; missed first four games of season. ... Signed as free agent by Nashville Predators (September 25, 2000).

Season Team	League	REGULAR SEASON								PLAYOFFS				
		Gms.	G	A	Pts.	PIM	+/-	PP	SH	Gms.	G	A	Pts.	PIM
90-91—Cornwall	OHL	58	13	20	33	124	...	...	...	—	—	—	—	—
91-92—Cornwall	OHL	63	15	23	38	176	...	...	...	6	3	1	4	4
92-93—Newmarket	OHL	54	28	28	56	144	...	...	...	5	5	1	6	28
93-94—Newmarket	OHL	9	2	4	6	27	...	...	...	—	—	—	—	—
—Sault Ste. Marie	OHL	48	18	19	37	183	...	...	...	14	1	1	2	23
94-95—Greensboro	ECHL	43	14	13	27	231	...	...	...	17	6	11	17	64
95-96—Baltimore	AHL	60	11	10	21	295	...	...	...	12	4	2	6	23
—Anaheim	NHL	3	0	1	1	12	1	0	0	—	—	—	—	—
96-97—Baltimore	AHL	25	8	8	16	125	...	...	...	3	0	0	0	8
—Anaheim	NHL	5	0	0	0	14	-1	0	0	—	—	—	—	—
97-98—Anaheim	NHL	45	3	5	8	101	-4	0	0	—	—	—	—	—
—Cincinnati	AHL	10	5	0	5	34	...	...	...	—	—	—	—	—
98-99—Cincinnati	AHL	22	4	4	8	83	...	...	...	3	1	0	1	2
99-00—Cincinnati	AHL	41	11	14	25	100	...	...	...	—	—	—	—	—
—Anaheim	NHL	3	0	0	0	7	-1	0	0	—	—	—	—	—
00-01—Milwaukee	IHL	60	16	13	29	262	...	...	...	5	2	1	3	12
—Nashville	NHL	8	1	0	1	39	-1	0	0	—	—	—	—	—
NHL Totals (5 years)		64	4	6	10	173	-6	0	0					

STEVENSON, TURNER   RW   DEVILS

PERSONAL: Born May 18, 1972, in Port Alberni, B.C. ... 6-3/226. ... Shoots right.

TRANSACTIONS/CAREER NOTES: Selected by Montreal Canadiens in first round (first Canadiens pick, 12th overall) of NHL entry draft (June 16, 1990). ... Suffered from the flu (October 21, 1995); missed two games. ... Sprained knee (October 7, 1996); missed five games. ... Sprained knee (October 26, 1996); missed four games. ... Sprained knee (November 11, 1996); missed seven games. ... Sprained left shoulder (November 12, 1997); missed eight games. ... Tore cartilage in ribs (December 19, 1997); missed five games. ... Strained hamstring (April 15, 1998); missed three games. ... Suspended two games and fined $1,000 by NHL for elbowing incident (October 19, 1998). ... Suffered back spasms (December 29, 1998); missed one game. ... Sprained ankle (December 31, 1998); missed 10 games. ... Suffered back spasms (October 9, 1999); missed two games. ... Strained back (November 16, 1999); missed 13 games. ... Suffered from the flu (January 11, 2000); missed three games. ... Selected by Columbus Blue Jackets in NHL expansion draft (June 23, 2000). ... Traded by Blue Jackets to New Jersey Devils (June 23, 2000), completing deal in which Devils traded RW Krzysztof Oliwa to Blue Jackets for third-round pick (C/LW Brandon Nolan) in 2001 draft and future considerations (June 12, 2000). ... Sprained ankle (March 21, 2001); missed nine games.

HONORS: Named to Can.HL All-Star second team (1991-92). ... Named to Memorial Cup All-Star team (1991-92). ... Named to WHL (West) All-Star first team (1991-92).

Season Team	League	REGULAR SEASON								PLAYOFFS				
		Gms.	G	A	Pts.	PIM	+/-	PP	SH	Gms.	G	A	Pts.	PIM
88-89—Seattle	WHL	69	15	12	27	84	...	...	...	—	—	—	—	—
89-90—Seattle	WHL	62	29	32	61	276	...	...	...	13	3	2	5	35
90-91—Seattle	WHL	57	36	27	63	222	...	...	...	6	1	5	6	15
—Fredericton	AHL	—	—	—	—	—	...	...	...	4	0	0	0	5
91-92—Seattle	WHL	58	20	32	52	264	...	...	...	15	9	3	12	55
92-93—Fredericton	AHL	79	25	34	59	102	...	...	...	5	2	3	5	11
—Montreal	NHL	1	0	0	0	0	-1	0	0	—	—	—	—	—
93-94—Fredericton	AHL	66	19	28	47	155	...	...	...	—	—	—	—	—
—Montreal	NHL	2	0	0	0	2	-2	0	0	3	0	2	2	0
94-95—Fredericton	AHL	37	12	12	24	109	...	...	...	—	—	—	—	—
—Montreal	NHL	41	6	1	7	86	0	0	0	—	—	—	—	—
95-96—Montreal	NHL	80	9	16	25	167	-2	0	0	6	0	1	1	2
96-97—Montreal	NHL	65	8	13	21	97	-14	1	0	5	1	1	2	2
97-98—Montreal	NHL	63	4	6	10	110	-8	1	0	10	3	4	7	12
98-99—Montreal	NHL	69	10	17	27	88	6	0	0	—	—	—	—	—
99-00—Montreal	NHL	64	8	13	21	61	-1	0	0	—	—	—	—	—
00-01—New Jersey	NHL	69	8	18	26	97	11	2	0	23	1	3	4	20
NHL Totals (9 years)		454	53	84	137	708	-11	4	0	47	5	11	16	36

STEWART, CAM LW WILD

PERSONAL: Born September 18, 1971, in Kitchener, Ont. ... 5-11/196. ... Shoots left. ... Full Name: Cameron G. Stewart.
TRANSACTIONS/CAREER NOTES: Selected by Boston Bruins in third round (second Bruins pick, 63rd overall) of NHL entry draft (June 16, 1990). ... Fractured finger (November 13, 1993); missed seven games. ... Injured neck (January 11, 1997); missed two games. ... Suffered back spasms (January 20, 1997); missed six games. ... Signed as free agent by Florida Panthers (July 19, 1999). ... Suffered concussion (October 30, 1999); missed nine games. ... Bruised thigh (November 27, 1999); missed one game. ... Strained hip flexor (April 1, 2000); missed three games. ... Selected by Minnesota Wild in NHL expansion draft (June 23, 2000). ... Bruised back (November 12, 2000); missed 15 games. ... Bruised calf (March 28, 2001); missed five games.

			REGULAR SEASON							PLAYOFFS				
Season Team	League	Gms.	G	A	Pts.	PIM	+/-	PP	SH	Gms.	G	A	Pts.	PIM
88-89—Elmira Jr. B	OHA	43	38	50	88	138	...	...	...	—	—	—	—	—
89-90—Elmira Jr. B	OHA	46	44	95	139	172	...	...	...	—	—	—	—	—
90-91—Univ. of Michigan	CCHA	44	8	24	32	122	...	...	...	—	—	—	—	—
91-92—Univ. of Michigan	CCHA	44	13	15	28	106	...	...	...	—	—	—	—	—
92-93—Univ. of Michigan	CCHA	39	20	39	59	69	...	...	...	—	—	—	—	—
93-94—Boston	NHL	57	3	6	9	66	-6	0	0	8	0	3	3	7
—Providence	AHL	14	3	2	5	5	...	...	...	—	—	—	—	—
94-95—Boston	NHL	5	0	0	0	2	0	0	0	—	—	—	—	—
—Providence	AHL	31	13	11	24	38	...	...	...	9	2	5	7	0
95-96—Providence	AHL	54	17	25	42	39	...	...	...	—	—	—	—	—
—Boston	NHL	6	0	0	0	0	-2	0	0	5	1	0	1	2
96-97—Boston	NHL	15	0	1	1	4	-2	0	0	—	—	—	—	—
—Providence	AHL	18	4	3	7	37	...	...	...	—	—	—	—	—
—Cincinnati	IHL	7	3	2	5	8	...	...	...	1	0	0	0	0
97-98—Houston	IHL	63	18	27	45	51	...	...	...	4	0	1	1	18
98-99—Houston	IHL	61	36	26	62	75	...	...	...	19	10	5	15	26
99-00—Florida	NHL	65	9	7	16	30	-2	0	0	—	—	—	—	—
00-01—Minnesota	NHL	54	4	9	13	18	-3	0	1	—	—	—	—	—
NHL Totals (6 years)		202	16	23	39	120	-15	0	1	13	1	3	4	9

STILLMAN, CORY LW BLUES

PERSONAL: Born December 20, 1973, in Peterborough, Ont. ... 6-0/194. ... Shoots left. ... Second cousin of Cory Stillman, center, New York Islanders organization.
TRANSACTIONS/CAREER NOTES: Selected by Calgary Flames in first round (first Flames pick, sixth overall) of NHL entry draft (June 20, 1992). ... Suspended four games by AHL for incident involving on-ice official (March 29, 1995). ... Suffered from the flu (October 8, 1995); missed one game. ... Bruised knee (January 14, 1996); missed two games. ... Injured shoulder (December 16, 1996); missed five games. ... Bruised ribs (October 11, 1997); missed six games. ... Strained knee (December 27, 1998); missed five games. ... Injured shoulder (December 27, 1999); missed final 45 games of season. ... Injured shoulder (October 30, 2000); missed one game. ... Traded by Flames to St. Louis Blues for C Craig Conroy and seventh-round pick (LW David Moss) in 2001 draft (March 13, 2001).
HONORS: Won Emms Family Award (1990-91).
STATISTICAL PLATEAUS: Three-goal games: 1997-98 (1), 2000-01 (1). Total: 2.

			REGULAR SEASON							PLAYOFFS				
Season Team	League	Gms.	G	A	Pts.	PIM	+/-	PP	SH	Gms.	G	A	Pts.	PIM
89-90—Peterborough Jr. B	OHA	41	30	54	84	76	...	...	...	—	—	—	—	—
90-91—Windsor	OHL	64	31	70	101	31	...	...	...	11	3	6	9	8
91-92—Windsor	OHL	53	29	61	90	59	...	...	...	7	2	4	6	8
92-93—Peterborough	OHL	61	25	55	80	55	...	...	...	18	3	8	11	18
—Canadian nat'l team	Int'l	1	0	0	0	0	...	...	...	—	—	—	—	—
93-94—Saint John	AHL	79	35	48	83	52	...	...	...	7	2	4	6	16
94-95—Saint John	AHL	63	28	53	81	70	...	...	...	5	0	2	2	2
—Calgary	NHL	10	0	2	2	2	1	0	0	—	—	—	—	—
95-96—Calgary	NHL	74	16	19	35	41	-5	4	1	2	1	1	2	0
96-97—Calgary	NHL	58	6	20	26	14	-6	2	0	—	—	—	—	—
97-98—Calgary	NHL	72	27	22	49	40	-9	9	4	—	—	—	—	—
98-99—Calgary	NHL	76	27	30	57	38	7	9	3	—	—	—	—	—
99-00—Calgary	NHL	37	12	9	21	12	-9	6	0	—	—	—	—	—
00-01—Calgary	NHL	66	21	24	45	45	-6	7	0	—	—	—	—	—
—St. Louis	NHL	12	3	4	7	6	-2	3	0	15	3	5	8	8
NHL Totals (7 years)		405	112	130	242	198	-29	40	8	17	4	6	10	8

STOCK, P.J. C

PERSONAL: Born May 26, 1975, in Victoriaville, Que. ... 5-10/190. ... Shoots left.
TRANSACTIONS/CAREER NOTES: Signed as non-drafted free agent by New York Rangers (September 2, 1997). ... Signed as free agent by Montreal Canadiens (July 7, 2000). ... Traded by Canadiens with sixth-round pick (D Dennis Seidenberg) in 2001 draft to Philadelphia Flyers for LW Gino Odjick (December 7, 2000). ... Strained neck (April 7, 2001); missed final game of regular season.

			REGULAR SEASON							PLAYOFFS				
Season Team	League	Gms.	G	A	Pts.	PIM	+/-	PP	SH	Gms.	G	A	Pts.	PIM
94-95—Victoriaville	QMJHL	70	9	46	55	386	...	...	...	4	0	0	0	60
95-96—Victoriaville	QMJHL	67	19	43	62	432	...	...	...	12	5	4	9	79
96-97—St. Francis Xavier	CIAU	27	11	20	31	110	...	...	...	3	0	4	4	14
97-98—Hartford	AHL	41	8	8	16	202	...	...	...	11	1	3	4	79
—New York Rangers	NHL	38	2	3	5	114	4	0	0	—	—	—	—	—
98-99—New York Rangers	NHL	5	0	0	0	6	-1	0	0	—	—	—	—	—
—Hartford	AHL	55	4	14	18	250	...	...	...	6	0	1	1	35

Season Team	League	REGULAR SEASON								PLAYOFFS				
		Gms.	G	A	Pts.	PIM	+/-	PP	SH	Gms.	G	A	Pts.	PIM
99-00—Hartford	AHL	64	13	23	36	290	...	...	...	23	1	11	12	69
—New York Rangers	NHL	11	0	1	1	11	1	0	0	—	—	—	—	—
00-01—Montreal	NHL	20	1	2	3	32	-1	0	0	—	—	—	—	—
—Philadelphia	NHL	31	1	3	4	78	-2	0	0	2	0	0	0	0
—Philadelphia	AHL	9	1	2	3	37	...	...	...	—	—	—	—	—
NHL Totals (4 years)...........		105	4	9	13	241	1	0	0	2	0	0	0	0

STOREY, BEN D AVALANCHE

PERSONAL: Born June 22, 1977, in Ottawa. ... 6-2/180. ... Shoots left.
TRANSACTIONS/CAREER NOTES: Selected by Colorado Avalanche in fourth round (fourth Avalanche pick, 98th overall) of NHL entry draft (June 22, 1996).
HONORS: Named to ECAC All-Rookie team (1995-96).

Season Team	League	REGULAR SEASON								PLAYOFFS				
		Gms.	G	A	Pts.	PIM	+/-	PP	SH	Gms.	G	A	Pts.	PIM
94-95—Ottawa	Tier II Jr. A	51	6	33	39	83	...	...	...	—	—	—	—	—
—Canadian nat'l team	Int'l	2	0	1	1	2	...	...	...	—	—	—	—	—
95-96—Harvard University	ECAC	33	2	11	13	44	...	...	...	—	—	—	—	—
96-97—Harvard University	ECAC	25	0	6	6	40	...	...	...	—	—	—	—	—
97-98—Harvard University	ECAC	33	9	16	25	56	...	...	...	—	—	—	—	—
98-99—Harvard University	ECAC	23	4	11	15	30	...	...	...	—	—	—	—	—
—Hershey	AHL	5	0	0	0	0	...	...	...	—	—	—	—	—
99-00—Hershey	AHL	65	6	18	24	69	...	...	...	14	2	2	4	8
00-01—Hershey	AHL	58	2	12	14	71	...	...	...	4	1	3	4	2

STORR, JAMIE G KINGS

PERSONAL: Born December 28, 1975, in Brampton, Ont. ... 6-2/198. ... Catches left. ... Name pronounced STOHR.
TRANSACTIONS/CAREER NOTES: Selected by Los Angeles Kings in first round (first Kings pick, seventh overall) of NHL entry draft (June 28, 1994). ... Strained right groin (October 1, 1997); missed 12 games. ... Strained left groin (October 18, 1998); missed 16 games. ... Sprained ankle (April 2, 1999); missed final eight games of season. ... Strained right groin (November 23, 1999); missed one game. ... Suffered concussion (December 16, 1999); missed 10 games.
HONORS: Named to OHL All-Star first team (1993-94). ... Named to NHL All-Rookie team (1997-98).
MISCELLANEOUS: Holds Los Angeles Kings all-time record for goals-against average (2.58). ... Stopped a penalty shot attempt (vs. Todd White, February 26, 1999; vs. Martin Rucinsky, December 11, 1999).

Season Team	League	REGULAR SEASON							PLAYOFFS					
		Gms.	Min	W	L	T	GA	SO	Avg.	Gms.	Min.	W	L	GA	SO	Avg.
90-91—Brampton	Jr. B	24	1145	...	...	...	91	0	4.77	—	—	—	—	—	—	—
91-92—Owen Sound	OHL	34	1733	11	16	1	128	0	4.43	5	299	1	4	28	0	5.62
92-93—Owen Sound	OHL	41	2362	20	17	3	180	0	4.57	8	454	4	4	35	0	4.63
93-94—Owen Sound	OHL	35	2004	21	11	1	120	1	3.59	9	547	4	5	44	0	4.83
94-95—Owen Sound	OHL	17	977	5	9	2	64	0	3.93	—	—	—	—	—	—	—
—Los Angeles	NHL	5	263	1	3	1	17	0	3.88	—	—	—	—	—	—	—
—Windsor	OHL	4	241	3	1	0	8	1	1.99	10	520	6	3	34	1	3.92
95-96—Los Angeles	NHL	5	262	3	1	0	12	0	2.75	—	—	—	—	—	—	—
—Phoenix	IHL	48	2711	22	20	‡4	139	2	3.08	2	118	1	1	4	1	2.03
96-97—Phoenix	IHL	44	2441	16	22	‡4	147	0	3.61	—	—	—	—	—	—	—
—Los Angeles	NHL	5	265	2	1	1	11	0	2.49	—	—	—	—	—	—	—
97-98—Los Angeles	NHL	17	920	9	5	1	34	2	2.22	3	145	0	2	9	0	3.72
—Long Beach	IHL	11	629	7	2	‡1	31	0	2.96	—	—	—	—	—	—	—
98-99—Los Angeles	NHL	28	1525	12	12	2	61	4	2.40	—	—	—	—	—	—	—
99-00—Los Angeles	NHL	42	2206	18	15	5	93	1	2.53	1	36	0	1	2	0	3.33
00-01—Los Angeles	NHL	45	2498	19	18	6	114	4	2.74	—	—	—	—	—	—	—
NHL Totals (7 years).............		147	7939	64	55	16	342	11	2.58	4	181	0	3	11	0	3.65

STRAKA, MARTIN C PENGUINS

PERSONAL: Born September 3, 1972, in Plzen, Czechoslovakia. ... 5-9/176. ... Shoots left. ... Name pronounced STRAH-kuh.
TRANSACTIONS/CAREER NOTES: Selected by Pittsburgh Penguins in first round (first Penguins pick, 19th overall) of NHL entry draft (June 20, 1992). ... Played in Europe during 1994-95 NHL lockout. ... Suffered from the flu (February 14, 1995); missed four games. ... Traded by Penguins to Ottawa Senators for D Norm Maciver and C Troy Murray (April 7, 1995). ... Strained knee (April 19, 1995); missed remainder of season. ... Injured hamstring (November 11, 1995); missed one game. ... Traded by Senators with D Bryan Berard to New York Islanders for D Wade Redden and G Damian Rhodes (January 23, 1996). ... Claimed on waivers by Florida Panthers (March 15, 1996). ... Bruised buttocks (April 10, 1996); missed final two games of season. ... Strained groin (January 1, 1997); missed one game. ... Strained groin (January 8, 1997); missed two games. ... Strained groin (January 22, 1997); missed four games. ... Strained groin (March 5, 1997); missed nine games. ... Signed as free agent by Penguins (August 7, 1997). ... Fractured foot (December 29, 1997); missed seven games. ... Bruised shoulder (March 3, 1999); missed one game. ... Bruised shoulder (April 8, 1999); missed one game. ... Bruised knee (October 16, 1999); missed one game. ... Reinjured knee (October 27, 1999); missed two games. ... Bruised ribs (December 15, 1999); missed seven games. ... Bruised shin (April 5, 2000); missed one game.
HONORS: Named to Czechoslovakian League All-Star team (1991-92). ... Played in NHL All-Star Game (1999).
MISCELLANEOUS: Member of gold-medal-winning Czech Republic Olympic team (1998). ... Scored on a penalty shot (vs. Roman Turek, January 19, 2000; vs. Damian Rhodes, January 30, 2001). ... Failed to score on a penalty shot (vs. Jocelyn Thibault, March 16, 1995; vs. Damian Rhodes, April 3, 1996; vs. Evgeni Nabokov, November 1, 2000; vs. Byron Dafoe, January 9, 2001; vs. Dominik Hasek, May 2, 2001 (playoffs)).
STATISTICAL PLATEAUS: Three-goal games: 1993-94 (1), 1997-98 (1), 1998-99 (1), 2000-01 (1). Total: 4.

Season Team	League	REGULAR SEASON								PLAYOFFS				
		Gms.	G	A	Pts.	PIM	+/-	PP	SH	Gms.	G	A	Pts.	PIM
89-90—Skoda Plzen	Czech.	1	0	3	3	...	...	...	...	—	—	—	—	—
90-91—Skoda Plzen	Czech.	47	7	24	31	6	...	...	...	—	—	—	—	—
91-92—Skoda Plzen	Czech.	50	27	28	55	20	...	...	...	—	—	—	—	—
92-93—Pittsburgh	NHL	42	3	13	16	29	2	0	0	11	2	1	3	2
—Cleveland	IHL	4	4	3	7	0	...	...	...	—	—	—	—	—
93-94—Pittsburgh	NHL	84	30	34	64	24	24	2	0	6	1	0	1	2
94-95—Interconex Plzen	Czech Rep.	19	10	11	21	18	...	...	...	—	—	—	—	—
—Pittsburgh	NHL	31	4	12	16	16	0	0	0	—	—	—	—	—
—Ottawa	NHL	6	1	1	2	0	-1	0	0	—	—	—	—	—
95-96—Ottawa	NHL	43	9	16	25	29	-14	5	0	—	—	—	—	—
—New York Islanders	NHL	22	2	10	12	6	-6	0	0	—	—	—	—	—
—Florida	NHL	12	2	4	6	6	1	1	0	13	2	2	4	2
96-97—Florida	NHL	55	7	22	29	12	9	2	0	4	0	0	0	0
97-98—Pittsburgh	NHL	75	19	23	42	28	-1	4	3	6	2	0	2	2
—Czech Rep. Oly. team	Int'l	6	1	2	3	0	...	...	...	—	—	—	—	—
98-99—Pittsburgh	NHL	80	35	48	83	26	12	5	4	13	6	9	15	6
99-00—Pittsburgh	NHL	71	20	39	59	26	24	3	1	11	3	9	12	10
00-01—Pittsburgh	NHL	82	27	68	95	38	19	7	1	18	5	8	13	8
NHL Totals (9 years)		603	159	290	449	240	69	29	9	82	21	29	50	32

STRUDWICK, JASON   D   CANUCKS

PERSONAL: Born July 17, 1975, in Edmonton. ... 6-3/220. ... Shoots left. ... Name pronounced STRUHD-wihk.
TRANSACTIONS/CAREER NOTES: Selected by New York Islanders in third round (third Islanders pick, 63rd overall) of NHL entry draft (June 29, 1994). ... Traded by Islanders to Vancouver Canucks for LW Gino Odjick (March 23, 1998). ... Injured back (November 17, 1999); missed 10 games. ... Strained knee (February 24, 2001); missed 11 games.

Season Team	League	REGULAR SEASON								PLAYOFFS				
		Gms.	G	A	Pts.	PIM	+/-	PP	SH	Gms.	G	A	Pts.	PIM
93-94—Kamloops	WHL	61	6	8	14	118	...	...	...	19	0	4	4	24
94-95—Kamloops	WHL	72	3	11	14	183	...	...	...	21	1	1	2	39
95-96—Worcester	AHL	60	2	7	9	119	...	...	...	4	0	1	1	0
—New York Islanders	NHL	1	0	0	0	7	0	0	0	—	—	—	—	—
96-97—Kentucky	AHL	80	1	9	10	198	...	...	...	4	0	0	0	0
97-98—Kentucky	AHL	39	3	1	4	87	...	...	...	—	—	—	—	—
—New York Islanders	NHL	17	0	1	1	36	1	0	0	—	—	—	—	—
—Vancouver	NHL	11	0	1	1	29	-3	0	0	—	—	—	—	—
—Syracuse	AHL	—	—	—	—	—	...	...	...	3	0	0	0	6
98-99—Vancouver	NHL	65	0	3	3	114	-19	0	0	—	—	—	—	—
99-00—Vancouver	NHL	63	1	3	4	64	-13	0	0	—	—	—	—	—
00-01—Vancouver	NHL	60	1	4	5	64	16	0	0	2	0	0	0	0
NHL Totals (5 years)		217	2	12	14	314	-18	0	0	2	0	0	0	0

STUART, BRAD   D   SHARKS

PERSONAL: Born November 6, 1979, in Rocky Mountain House, Alta. ... 6-2/210. ... Shoots left.
TRANSACTIONS/CAREER NOTES: Selected by San Jose Sharks in first round (first Sharks pick, third overall) of NHL entry draft (June 27, 1998). ... Suspended two games by NHL for cross-checking incident (March 9, 2001).
HONORS: Named to WHL (East) All-Star second team (1997-98). ... Won Bill Hunter Trophy (1998-99). ... Won Can.HL Defenseman of the Year Award (1998-99). ... Named to WHL (East) All-Star first team (1998-99). ... Named to Can.HL All-Star first team (1998-99). ... Named to NHL All-Rookie team (1999-2000).

Season Team	League	REGULAR SEASON								PLAYOFFS				
		Gms.	G	A	Pts.	PIM	+/-	PP	SH	Gms.	G	A	Pts.	PIM
96-97—Regina	WHL	57	7	36	43	58	...	...	...	5	0	4	4	14
97-98—Regina	WHL	72	20	45	65	82	...	...	...	9	3	4	7	10
98-99—Regina	WHL	29	10	19	29	43	...	...	...	—	—	—	—	—
—Calgary	WHL	30	11	22	33	26	...	...	...	21	8	15	23	59
99-00—San Jose	NHL	82	10	26	36	32	3	5	1	12	1	0	1	6
00-01—San Jose	NHL	77	5	18	23	56	10	1	0	5	1	0	1	0
NHL Totals (2 years)		159	15	44	59	88	13	6	1	17	2	0	2	6

STUMPEL, JOZEF   C   KINGS

PERSONAL: Born July 20, 1972, in Nitra, Czechoslovakia. ... 6-3/216. ... Shoots right. ... Name pronounced JOH-sehf STUHM-puhl.
TRANSACTIONS/CAREER NOTES: Selected by Boston Bruins in second round (second Bruins pick, 40th overall) of NHL entry draft (June 22, 1991). ... Injured shoulder (December 1992); missed nine games. ... Injured knee (March 17, 1994); missed nine games. ... Played in Europe during 1994-95 NHL lockout. ... Injured knee (April 1995). ... Fractured cheek bone (February 27, 1996); missed three games. ... Suffered back spasms (January 4, 1997); missed one game. ... Suffered back spasms (February 1, 1997); missed three games. ... Traded by Bruins with RW Sandy Moger and fourth-round pick (traded to New Jersey) in 1998 draft to Los Angeles Kings for LW Dimitri Khristich and G Byron Dafoe (August 29, 1997). ... Suffered from the flu (February 7, 1998); missed one game. ... Bruised kidney (March 5, 1998); missed four games. ... Strained hip flexor and strained abdominal muscle (October 18, 1998); missed 10 games. ... Sprained right ankle (November 16, 1998); missed three games. ... Sprained right knee (April 8, 1999); missed final five games of season. ... Suffered hernia (November 3, 1999); missed 18 games. ... Bruised left knee (January 3, 2000); missed seven games. ... Missed first seven games of 2000-01 season due to contract dispute. ... Fractured toe (December 14, 2000); missed two games. ... Strained right hamstring (February 10, 2001); missed two games. ... Fractured rib (March 4, 2001); missed seven games.
STATISTICAL PLATEAUS: Three-goal games: 1995-96 (1), 1997-98 (1). Total: 2.

Season Team	League	REGULAR SEASON								PLAYOFFS				
		Gms.	G	A	Pts.	PIM	+/-	PP	SH	Gms.	G	A	Pts.	PIM
89-90—Nitra	Czech.	38	12	11	23	0	...	...	...	—	—	—	—	—
90-91—Nitra	Czech.	49	23	22	45	14	...	...	...	—	—	—	—	—
91-92—Boston	NHL	4	1	0	1	0	1	0	0	—	—	—	—	—
—Koln	Germany	33	19	18	37	35	...	...	...	—	—	—	—	—
92-93—Providence	AHL	56	31	61	92	26	...	...	...	6	4	4	8	0
—Boston	NHL	13	1	3	4	4	-3	0	0	—	—	—	—	—
93-94—Boston	NHL	59	8	15	23	14	4	0	0	13	1	7	8	4
—Providence	AHL	17	5	12	17	4	...	...	...	—	—	—	—	—
94-95—Koln	Germany	25	16	23	39	18	...	...	...	—	—	—	—	—
—Boston	NHL	44	5	13	18	8	4	1	0	5	0	0	0	0
95-96—Boston	NHL	76	18	36	54	14	-8	5	0	5	1	2	3	0
96-97—Boston	NHL	78	21	55	76	14	-22	6	0	—	—	—	—	—
97-98—Los Angeles	NHL	77	21	58	79	53	17	4	0	4	1	2	3	2
98-99—Los Angeles	NHL	64	13	21	34	10	-18	1	0	—	—	—	—	—
99-00—Los Angeles	NHL	57	17	41	58	10	23	3	0	4	0	4	4	8
00-01—Slovan Bratislava	Slovakia	9	2	4	6	16	...	...	...	—	—	—	—	—
—Los Angeles	NHL	63	16	39	55	14	20	9	0	13	3	5	8	10
NHL Totals (10 years)		535	121	281	402	141	18	29	0	44	6	20	26	24

STURM, MARCO   LW   SHARKS

S

PERSONAL: Born September 8, 1978, in Dingolfing, West Germany. ... 6-0/195. ... Shoots left.

TRANSACTIONS/CAREER NOTES: Selected by San Jose Sharks in first round (second Sharks pick, 21st overall) of NHL entry draft (June 22, 1996). ... Sprained wrist (April 1, 1998); missed six games. ... Injured foot (March 3, 1999); missed two games. ... Suffered concussion (December 2, 1999); missed four games.

HONORS: Played in NHL All-Star Game (1999).

STATISTICAL PLATEAUS: Three-goal games: 1998-99 (1).

Season Team	League	REGULAR SEASON								PLAYOFFS				
		Gms.	G	A	Pts.	PIM	+/-	PP	SH	Gms.	G	A	Pts.	PIM
95-96—Landshut	Germany	47	12	20	32	50	...	...	...	—	—	—	—	—
96-97—Landshut	Germany	46	16	27	43	40	...	...	...	7	1	4	5	6
97-98—San Jose	NHL	74	10	20	30	40	-2	2	0	2	0	0	0	0
—German Oly. team	Int'l	2	0	0	0	0	...	...	...	—	—	—	—	—
98-99—San Jose	NHL	78	16	22	38	52	7	3	2	6	2	2	4	4
99-00—San Jose	NHL	74	12	15	27	22	4	2	4	12	1	3	4	6
00-01—San Jose	NHL	81	14	18	32	28	9	2	3	6	0	2	2	0
NHL Totals (4 years)		307	52	75	127	142	18	9	9	26	3	7	10	10

SUCHY, RADOSLAV   D   COYOTES

PERSONAL: Born April 7, 1976, in Poprad, Czechoslovakia. ... 6-1/191. ... Shoots left.

TRANSACTIONS/CAREER NOTES: Signed as non-drafted free agent by Phoenix Coyotes (September 25, 1997).

HONORS: Won George Parsons Trophy (1996-97). ... Named to QMJHL All-Star second team (1996-97).

Season Team	League	REGULAR SEASON								PLAYOFFS				
		Gms.	G	A	Pts.	PIM	+/-	PP	SH	Gms.	G	A	Pts.	PIM
93-94—Poprad	Slovakia						Statistics unavailable.							
94-95—Sherbrooke	QMJHL	69	12	32	44	30	...	...	...	7	0	3	3	2
95-96—Sherbrooke	QMJHL	68	15	53	68	68	...	...	...	7	0	3	3	2
96-97—Sherbrooke	QMJHL	32	6	34	40	14	...	...	...	—	—	—	—	—
—Chicoutimi	QMJHL	28	5	24	29	24	...	...	...	19	6	15	21	12
97-98—Las Vegas	IHL	26	1	4	5	10	...	...	...	—	—	—	—	—
—Springfield	AHL	41	6	15	21	16	...	...	...	4	0	1	1	2
98-99—Springfield	AHL	69	4	32	36	10	...	...	...	3	0	1	1	0
99-00—Springfield	AHL	2	0	1	1	0	...	...	...	—	—	—	—	—
—Phoenix	NHL	60	0	6	6	16	2	0	0	5	0	1	1	0
00-01—Phoenix	NHL	72	0	10	10	22	1	0	0	—	—	—	—	—
NHL Totals (2 years)		132	0	16	16	38	3	0	0	5	0	1	1	0

SULLIVAN, MIKE   C   COYOTES

PERSONAL: Born February 28, 1968, in Marshfield, Mass. ... 6-2/201. ... Shoots left. ... Full Name: Michael Barry Sullivan.

TRANSACTIONS/CAREER NOTES: Selected by New York Rangers in fourth round (fourth Rangers pick, 69th overall) of NHL entry draft (June 13, 1987). ... Traded by Rangers with D Mark Tinordi, D Paul Jerrard, RW Brett Barnett and third-round pick (C Murray Garbutt) in 1989 draft to Minnesota North Stars for LW Igor Liba, C Brian Lawton and rights to LW Eric Bennett (October 11, 1988). ... Signed as free agent by San Jose Sharks (August 9, 1991). ... Sprained left knee (April 6, 1993); missed remainder of season. ... Claimed on waivers by Calgary Flames (January 6, 1994). ... Pulled groin (January 29, 1994); missed 13 games. ... Bruised knee (April 6, 1994); missed one game. ... Bruised left foot (March 17, 1995); missed two games. ... Sprained right ankle (April 13, 1995); missed final eight games of season. ... Suffered concussion (February 15, 1997); missed two games. ... Suffered back spasms (March 16, 1997); missed two games. ... Traded by Flames to Boston Bruins for seventh-round pick (RW Radek Duda) in 1998 draft (June 21, 1997). ... Injured wrist (February 4, 1998); missed two games. ... Selected by Nashville Predators in NHL expansion draft (June 26, 1998). ... Traded by Predators to Phoenix Coyotes for seventh-round pick (G Kyle Kettles) in 1999 draft (June 30, 1998). ... Fractured toe (December 17, 1998); missed three games. ... Fractured rib (January 11, 1999); missed 12 games. ... Separated shoulder (February 26, 1999); missed four games. ... Bruised ankle (January 12, 2000); missed three games. ... Strained muscle in abdomen (November 1, 2000); missed six games. ... Suffered concussion (January 23, 2001); missed three games.

Season Team	League	Gms.	G	A	Pts.	PIM	+/-	PP	SH	Gms.	G	A	Pts.	PIM
85-86—Boston College H.S.....	Mass. H.S.	22	26	33	59	...	...	...	...	—	—	—	—	—
86-87—Boston University	Hockey East	37	13	18	31	18	...	...	...	—	—	—	—	—
87-88—Boston University	Hockey East	30	18	22	40	30	...	...	...	—	—	—	—	—
88-89—Boston University	Hockey East	36	19	17	36	30	...	...	...	—	—	—	—	—
—Virginia	ECHL	2	0	0	0	0	...	...	...	—	—	—	—	—
89-90—Boston University	Hockey East	38	11	20	31	26	...	...	...	—	—	—	—	—
90-91—San Diego	IHL	74	12	23	35	27	...	...	...	—	—	—	—	—
91-92—Kansas City	IHL	10	2	8	10	8	...	...	...	—	—	—	—	—
—San Jose	NHL	64	8	11	19	15	-18	1	0	—	—	—	—	—
92-93—San Jose	NHL	81	6	8	14	30	-42	0	2	—	—	—	—	—
93-94—San Jose	NHL	26	2	2	4	4	-3	0	2	—	—	—	—	—
—Kansas City	IHL	6	3	3	6	0	...	...	...	—	—	—	—	—
—Saint John	AHL	5	2	0	2	4	...	...	...	—	—	—	—	—
—Calgary	NHL	19	2	3	5	6	2	0	0	7	1	1	2	8
94-95—Calgary	NHL	38	4	7	11	14	-2	0	0	7	3	5	8	2
95-96—Calgary	NHL	81	9	12	21	24	-6	0	1	4	0	0	0	0
96-97—Calgary	NHL	67	5	6	11	10	-11	0	3	—	—	—	—	—
—Adirondack	AHL	17	1	3	4	2	...	...	...	—	—	—	—	—
97-98—Boston	NHL	77	5	13	18	34	-1	0	0	6	0	1	1	2
98-99—Phoenix	NHL	63	2	4	6	24	-11	0	1	5	0	0	0	2
99-00—Phoenix	NHL	79	5	10	15	10	-4	0	2	5	0	1	1	0
00-01—Phoenix	NHL	72	5	4	9	16	-6	0	3	—	—	—	—	—
NHL Totals (10 years)		667	53	80	133	187	-102	1	14	34	4	8	12	14

S

SULLIVAN, STEVE — RW — BLACKHAWKS

PERSONAL: Born July 6, 1974, in Timmins, Ont. ... 5-9/160. ... Shoots right.
TRANSACTIONS/CAREER NOTES: Selected by New Jersey Devils in ninth round (10th Devils pick, 233rd overall) of NHL entry draft (June 29, 1994). ... Traded by Devils with D Jason Smith and C Alyn McCauley to Toronto Maple Leafs for C Doug Gilmour, D Dave Ellett and third-round pick (D Andre Lakos) in 1999 draft (February 25, 1997). ... Suffered from the flu (March 7, 1998); missed three games. ... Back spasms (May 11, 1999); missed one playoff game. ... Claimed on waivers by Chicago Blackhawks (October 23, 1999). ... Suffered from the flu (February 18, 2000); missed one game. ... Suffered from the flu (December 13, 2000); missed one game.
HONORS: Named to AHL All-Star first team (1995-96).
MISCELLANEOUS: Failed to score on a penalty shot (vs. Ron Tugnutt, March 6, 1999).
STATISTICAL PLATEAUS: Three-goal games: 2000-01 (1). ... Four-goal games: 1998-99 (1). ... Total hat tricks: 2.

Season Team	League	Gms.	G	A	Pts.	PIM	+/-	PP	SH	Gms.	G	A	Pts.	PIM
91-92—Timmins	OJHL	47	66	55	121	141	...	...	...	—	—	—	—	—
92-93—Sault Ste. Marie	OHL	62	36	27	63	44	...	...	...	16	3	8	11	18
93-94—Sault Ste. Marie	OHL	63	51	62	113	82	...	...	...	14	9	16	25	22
94-95—Albany	AHL	75	31	50	81	124	...	...	...	14	4	7	11	10
95-96—Albany	AHL	53	33	42	75	127	...	...	...	4	3	0	3	6
—New Jersey	NHL	16	5	4	9	8	3	2	0	—	—	—	—	—
96-97—Albany	AHL	15	8	7	15	16	...	...	...	—	—	—	—	—
—New Jersey	NHL	33	8	14	22	14	9	2	0	—	—	—	—	—
—Toronto	NHL	21	5	11	16	23	5	1	0	—	—	—	—	—
97-98—Toronto	NHL	63	10	18	28	40	-8	1	0	—	—	—	—	—
98-99—Toronto	NHL	63	20	20	40	28	12	4	0	13	3	3	6	14
99-00—Toronto	NHL	7	0	1	1	4	-1	0	0	—	—	—	—	—
—Chicago	NHL	73	22	42	64	52	20	2	1	—	—	—	—	—
00-01—Chicago	NHL	81	34	41	75	54	3	6	*8	—	—	—	—	—
NHL Totals (6 years)		357	104	151	255	223	43	18	9	13	3	3	6	14

SUNDIN, MATS — C — MAPLE LEAFS

PERSONAL: Born February 13, 1971, in Bromma, Sweden. ... 6-5/220. ... Shoots right. ... Full Name: Mats Johan Sundin. ... Name pronounced suhn-DEEN.
TRANSACTIONS/CAREER NOTES: Selected by Quebec Nordiques in first round (first Nordiques pick, first overall) of NHL entry draft (June 17, 1989). ... Separated right shoulder (January 2, 1993); missed three games. ... Suspended one game by NHL for second stick-related infraction (March 2, 1993). ... Traded by Nordiques with D Garth Butcher, LW Todd Warriner and first-round pick (traded to Washington Capitals) in 1994 draft to Toronto Maple Leafs for LW Wendel Clark, D Sylvain Lefebvre, RW Landon Wilson and first-round pick (D Jeffrey Kealty) in 1994 draft (June 28, 1994). ... Played in Europe during 1994-95 NHL lockout. ... Sprained shoulder (March 25, 1995); missed one game. ... Suffered slight tear of knee cartilage (October 24, 1995); missed four games. ... Fractured ankle (October 9, 1999); missed nine games.
HONORS: Named to Swedish League All-Star team (1990-91 and 1991-92). ... Played in NHL All-Star Game (1996-2001).
MISCELLANEOUS: Captain of Toronto Maple Leafs (1997-98 through 2000-01). ... Scored on a penalty shot (vs. Tom Draper, March 3, 1992; vs. Arturs Irbe, March 15, 1995; vs. Dominik Hasek, May 29, 1999 (playoffs)). ... Failed to score on a penalty shot (vs. Kelly Hrudey, February 2, 1993; vs. Andrei Trefilov, January 10, 1998; vs. John Vanbiesbrouck, April 22, 1999 (playoffs)).
STATISTICAL PLATEAUS: Three-goal games: 1990-91 (2), 1992-93 (1), 1996-97 (1), 1998-99 (1). Total: 5. ... Five-goal games: 1991-92 (1). ... Total hat tricks: 6.

Season Team	League	Gms.	G	A	Pts.	PIM	+/-	PP	SH	Gms.	G	A	Pts.	PIM
88-89—Nacka	Sweden	25	10	8	18	18	...	...	...	—	—	—	—	—
89-90—Djurgarden Stockholm	Sweden	34	10	8	18	16	...	...	...	8	7	0	7	4
90-91—Quebec	NHL	80	23	36	59	58	-24	4	0	—	—	—	—	—
91-92—Quebec	NHL	80	33	43	76	103	-19	8	2	—	—	—	—	—
92-93—Quebec	NHL	80	47	67	114	96	21	13	4	6	3	1	4	6

Season Team	League	REGULAR SEASON								PLAYOFFS				
		Gms.	G	A	Pts.	PIM	+/-	PP	SH	Gms.	G	A	Pts.	PIM
93-94—Quebec	NHL	84	32	53	85	60	1	6	2	—	—	—	—	—
94-95—Djurgarden Stockholm	Sweden	12	7	2	9	14	...	...	...	—	—	—	—	—
—Toronto	NHL	47	23	24	47	14	-5	9	0	7	5	4	9	4
95-96—Toronto	NHL	76	33	50	83	46	8	7	6	6	3	1	4	4
96-97—Toronto	NHL	82	41	53	94	59	6	7	4	—	—	—	—	—
97-98—Toronto	NHL	82	33	41	74	49	-3	9	1	—	—	—	—	—
—Swedish Oly. team	Int'l	4	3	0	3	4				—	—	—	—	—
98-99—Toronto	NHL	82	31	52	83	58	22	4	0	17	8	8	16	16
99-00—Toronto	NHL	73	32	41	73	46	16	10	2	12	3	5	8	10
00-01—Toronto	NHL	82	28	46	74	76	15	9	0	11	6	7	13	14
NHL Totals (11 years)		848	356	506	862	665	38	86	21	59	28	26	54	54

SUNDSTROM, NIKLAS   LW   SHARKS

S

PERSONAL: Born January 6, 1975, in Ornskoldsvik, Sweden. ... 6-0/195. ... Shoots left.
TRANSACTIONS/CAREER NOTES: Selected by New York Rangers in first round (first Rangers pick, eighth overall) of NHL entry draft (June 26, 1993). ... Fractured finger and sprained knee (December 5, 1997); missed 10 games. ... Traded by Rangers with G Dan Cloutier and first-(RW Nikita Alexeev) and third-round (traded to San Jose) picks in 2000 draft to Tampa Bay Lightning for first-round pick (RW Pavel Brendl) in 1999 draft (June 26, 1999). ... Traded by Lightning with third-round pick (traded to Chicago) in 2000 draft to San Jose Sharks for D Andrei Zyuzin, D Bill Houlder, LW Shawn Burr and C Steve Guolla (August 4, 1999).
STATISTICAL NOTES: Tied for NHL lead with three game-tying goals (1999-2000).

Season Team	League	REGULAR SEASON								PLAYOFFS				
		Gms.	G	A	Pts.	PIM	+/-	PP	SH	Gms.	G	A	Pts.	PIM
91-92—MoDo Ornskoldsvik	Sweden	9	1	3	4	0	...	...	...	—	—	—	—	—
92-93—MoDo Ornskoldsvik	Sweden	40	7	11	18	18	...	...	...	—	—	—	—	—
93-94—MoDo Ornskoldsvik	Sweden	37	7	12	19	28	...	...	...	11	4	3	7	2
94-95—MoDo Ornskoldsvik	Sweden	33	8	13	21	30	...	...	...	—	—	—	—	—
95-96—New York Rangers	NHL	82	9	12	21	14	2	1	1	11	4	3	7	4
96-97—New York Rangers	NHL	82	24	28	52	20	23	5	1	9	0	5	5	2
97-98—New York Rangers	NHL	70	19	28	47	24	0	4	0	—	—	—	—	—
—Swedish Oly. team	Int'l	4	1	1	2	2	...	...	...	—	—	—	—	—
98-99—New York Rangers	NHL	81	13	30	43	20	-2	1	2	—	—	—	—	—
99-00—San Jose	NHL	79	12	25	37	22	9	2	1	12	0	2	2	2
00-01—San Jose	NHL	82	10	39	49	28	10	4	1	6	0	3	3	2
NHL Totals (6 years)		476	87	162	249	128	42	17	6	38	4	13	17	10

SUSHINSKY, MAXIM   RW   WILD

PERSONAL: Born July 1, 1974, in Leningrad, U.S.S.R. ... 5-8/158. ... Shoots left.
TRANSACTIONS/CAREER NOTES: Selected by Minnesota Wild in fifth round (fourth Wild pick, 132nd overall) of NHL entry draft (June 24, 2000). ... Sprained wrist (November 8, 2000); missed four games.
MISCELLANEOUS: Failed to score on a penalty shot (vs. Felix Potvin, November 26, 2000).

Season Team	League	REGULAR SEASON								PLAYOFFS				
		Gms.	G	A	Pts.	PIM	+/-	PP	SH	Gms.	G	A	Pts.	PIM
91-92—St. Petersburg-2	CIS-3	20	14	1	15	38	...	...	...	—	—	—	—	—
—St. Petersburg	CIS-2	45	5	3	8	16	...	...	...	—	—	—	—	—
92-93—St. Petersburg	CIS	23	2	3	5	22	...	...	...	6	2	1	3	2
93-94—St. Petersburg	CIS	45	7	4	11	26	...	...	...	—	—	—	—	—
94-95—St. Petersburg	CIS	52	11	11	22	57	...	...	...	3	1	0	1	6
95-96—St. Petersburg	CIS	49	21	15	36	43	...	...	...	2	0	0	0	0
96-97—Avangard Omsk	Russian	39	20	16	36	24	...	...	...	5	3	1	4	0
97-98—Avangard Omsk	Russian	20	6	11	17	6	...	...	...	—	—	—	—	—
98-99—Avangard Omsk	Russian	41	16	15	31	46	...	...	...	8	2	5	7	6
99-00—Avangard Omsk	Russian	37	19	24	43	58	...	...	...	—	—	—	—	—
00-01—Avangard Omsk	Russian	12	5	3	8	14	...	...	...	13	*9	4	13	12
—Minnesota	NHL	30	7	4	11	29	-7	3	0	—	—	—	—	—
NHL Totals (1 year)		30	7	4	11	29	-7	3	0					

SUTER, GARY   D   SHARKS

PERSONAL: Born June 24, 1964, in Madison, Wis. ... 6-0/215. ... Shoots left. ... Full Name: Gary Lee Suter. ... Name pronounced SOO-tuhr.
TRANSACTIONS/CAREER NOTES: Selected by Calgary Flames in ninth round (ninth Flames pick, 180th overall) of NHL entry draft (June 9, 1984). ... Stretched knee ligament (December 1986). ... Suspended first four games of regular season and next six international games in which NHL participates for high-sticking during Canada Cup (September 4, 1987). ... Injured left knee (February 1988). ... Pulled hamstring (February 1989). ... Ruptured appendix (February 22, 1989); missed 16 games. ... Fractured jaw (April 11, 1989). ... Bruised knee (December 12, 1991); missed 10 games. ... Injured ribs (March 16, 1993); missed one game. ... Suffered from the flu (March 30, 1993); missed one game. ... Tore left knee ligaments (November 4, 1993); missed 33 games. ... Strained left leg muscle (January 24, 1994); missed 10 games. ... Traded by Flames with LW Paul Ranheim and C Ted Drury to Hartford Whalers for C Michael Nylander, D Zarley Zalapski and D James Patrick (March 10, 1994). ... Traded by Hartford with LW Randy Cunneyworth and third-round pick (traded to Vancouver) in 1995 draft to Chicago Blackhawks for D Frantisek Kucera and LW Jocelyn Lemieux (March 11, 1994). ... Fractured bone in ankle (May 25, 1995); missed four play-off games. ... Strained groin (December 14, 1997); missed five games. ... Suspended four games and fined $1,000 by NHL for cross-checking incident (February 3, 1998). ... Signed as free agent by San Jose Sharks (July 1, 1998). ... Injured elbow during offseason; missed first five games of season. ... Hyperextended elbow (October 24, 1998); missed remainder of season. ... Injured knee (February 23, 2000); missed six games. ... Injured ribs (October 18, 2000); missed three games. ... Injured knee (March 3, 2001); missed three games. ... Injured calf (March 29, 2001); missed final five games of season.

HONORS: Named USHL Top Defenseman (1982-83). ... Named to USHL All-Star first team (1982-83). ... Won Calder Memorial Trophy (1985-86). ... Named to NHL All-Rookie team (1985-86). ... Played in NHL All-Star Game (1986, 1988, 1989 and 1991). ... Named to THE SPORTING NEWS All-Star first team (1987-88). ... Named to NHL All-Star second team (1987-88). ... Named to THE SPORTING NEWS All-Star second team (1988-89). ... Named to play in NHL All-Star Game (1996); replaced by D Larry Murphy due to injury.
RECORDS: Shares NHL single-game record for most assists by a defenseman—6 (April 4, 1986).
MISCELLANEOUS: Member of Stanley Cup championship team (1989).

Season Team	League	REGULAR SEASON								PLAYOFFS				
		Gms.	G	A	Pts.	PIM	+/-	PP	SH	Gms.	G	A	Pts.	PIM
81-82—Dubuque	USHL	18	3	4	7	32	...	...	...	—	—	—	—	—
82-83—Dubuque	USHL	41	9	10	19	112	...	...	...	—	—	—	—	—
83-84—Univ. of Wisconsin	WCHA	35	4	18	22	68	...	...	...	—	—	—	—	—
84-85—Univ. of Wisconsin	WCHA	39	12	39	51	110	...	...	...	—	—	—	—	—
85-86—Calgary	NHL	80	18	50	68	141	11	9	0	10	2	8	10	8
86-87—Calgary	NHL	68	9	40	49	70	-10	4	0	6	0	3	3	10
87-88—Calgary	NHL	75	21	70	91	124	39	6	1	9	1	9	10	6
88-89—Calgary	NHL	63	13	49	62	78	26	8	0	5	0	3	3	10
89-90—Calgary	NHL	76	16	60	76	97	4	5	0	6	0	1	1	14
90-91—Calgary	NHL	79	12	58	70	102	26	6	0	7	1	6	7	12
91-92—Calgary	NHL	70	12	43	55	128	1	4	0	—	—	—	—	—
92-93—Calgary	NHL	81	23	58	81	112	-1	10	1	6	2	3	5	8
93-94—Calgary	NHL	25	4	9	13	20	-3	2	1	—	—	—	—	—
—Chicago	NHL	16	2	3	5	18	-9	2	0	6	3	2	5	6
94-95—Chicago	NHL	48	10	27	37	42	14	5	0	12	2	5	7	10
95-96—Chicago	NHL	82	20	47	67	80	3	12	2	10	3	3	6	8
96-97—Chicago	NHL	82	7	21	28	70	-4	3	0	6	1	4	5	8
97-98—Chicago	NHL	73	14	28	42	74	1	5	2	—	—	—	—	—
—U.S. Olympic team	Int'l	4	0	0	0	2	...	...	...	—	—	—	—	—
98-99—San Jose	NHL	1	0	0	0	0	0	0	0	—	—	—	—	—
99-00—San Jose	NHL	76	6	28	34	52	7	2	1	12	2	5	7	12
00-01—San Jose	NHL	68	10	24	34	84	8	4	0	1	0	0	0	0
NHL Totals (16 years)		1063	197	615	812	1292	113	87	8	96	17	52	69	112

SUTTER, RON   C

PERSONAL: Born December 2, 1963, in Viking, Alta. ... 6-0/185. ... Shoots right. ... Full Name: Ronald Sutter. ... Brother of Brian Sutter, head coach, Chicago Blackhawks and left winger with St. Louis Blues (1976-77 through 1987-88); brother of Brent Sutter, center with New York Islanders (1980-81 through 1991-92) Chicago Blackhawks (1991-92 through 1997-98); brother of Darryl Sutter, head coach, San Jose Sharks and left winger with Blackhawks (1979-80 through 1986-87); brother of Duane Sutter, head coach, Florida Panthers; right winger with Islanders (1979-80 through 1986-87) and Blackhawks (1987-88 through 1989-90); and twin brother of Rich Sutter, right winger with seven NHL teams (1982-83 through 1994-95).
TRANSACTIONS/CAREER NOTES: Selected by Philadelphia Flyers in first round (first Flyers pick, fourth overall) of NHL entry draft (June 9, 1982). ... Bruised ribs (March 1985). ... Suffered stress fracture in lower back (January 1987). ... Tore rib cartilage (March 1988). ... Fractured jaw (October 29, 1988). ... Pulled groin (March 1989). ... Traded by Flyers with D Murray Baron to St. Louis Blues for C Rod Brind'Amour and C Dan Quinn (September 22, 1991). ... Strained ligament in right knee (February 1, 1992); missed 10 games. ... Suffered abdominal pull (September 1992); missed first 18 games of season. ... Separated shoulder (March 30, 1993); missed remainder of season. ... Underwent abdominal surgery during off-season; missed nine games. ... Traded by Blues with C Bob Bassen and D Garth Butcher to Quebec Nordiques for D Steve Duchesne and RW Denis Chasse (January 23, 1994). ... Suffered sore neck (November 16, 1993); missed two games. ... Traded by Nordiques with first-round pick (RW Brett Lindros) in 1994 draft to New York Islanders for D Uwe Krupp and first-round pick (D Wade Belak) in 1994 draft (June 28, 1994). ... Sprained right ankle (February 7, 1995); missed 18 games. ... Signed as free agent by Boston Bruins (March 8, 1996). ... Signed as free agent by San Jose Sharks (October 12, 1996). ... Strained groin (November 10, 1997); missed eight games. ... Injured groin (December 2, 1997); missed eight games. ... Injured back (November 7, 1998); missed 12 games. ... Injured eye (February 15, 1999); missed four games. ... Suffered from the flu (November 27, 1999); missed two games. ... Released by Sharks (October 4, 2000). ... Signed as free agent by Calgary Flames (February 15, 2001). ... Injured foot (March 31, 2001); missed final four games of season.
MISCELLANEOUS: Captain of Philadelphia Flyers (1989-90 and 1990-91). ... Failed to score on a penalty shot (vs. Kelly Hrudey, November 18, 1984; vs. Grant Fuhr, May 28, 1985 (playoffs)).

Season Team	League	REGULAR SEASON								PLAYOFFS				
		Gms.	G	A	Pts.	PIM	+/-	PP	SH	Gms.	G	A	Pts.	PIM
79-80—Red Deer	AJHL	60	12	33	45	44	...	...	...	—	—	—	—	—
80-81—Lethbridge	WHL	72	13	32	45	152	...	...	...	9	2	5	7	29
81-82—Lethbridge	WHL	59	38	54	92	207	...	...	...	12	6	5	11	28
82-83—Lethbridge	WHL	58	35	48	83	98	...	...	...	20	*22	†19	*41	45
—Philadelphia	NHL	10	1	1	2	9	0	0	0	—	—	—	—	—
83-84—Philadelphia	NHL	79	19	32	51	101	4	5	3	3	0	0	0	22
84-85—Philadelphia	NHL	73	16	29	45	94	13	2	0	19	4	8	12	28
85-86—Philadelphia	NHL	75	18	42	60	159	26	0	0	5	0	2	2	10
86-87—Philadelphia	NHL	39	10	17	27	69	10	0	0	16	1	7	8	12
87-88—Philadelphia	NHL	69	8	25	33	146	-9	1	0	7	0	1	1	26
88-89—Philadelphia	NHL	55	26	22	48	80	25	4	1	19	1	9	10	51
89-90—Philadelphia	NHL	75	22	26	48	104	2	0	2	—	—	—	—	—
90-91—Philadelphia	NHL	80	17	28	45	92	2	2	0	—	—	—	—	—
91-92—St. Louis	NHL	68	19	27	46	91	9	5	4	6	1	3	4	8
92-93—St. Louis	NHL	59	12	15	27	99	-11	1	0	—	—	—	—	—
93-94—St. Louis	NHL	36	6	12	18	46	-1	1	0	—	—	—	—	—
—Quebec	NHL	37	9	13	22	44	3	4	0	—	—	—	—	—
94-95—New York Islanders	NHL	27	1	4	5	21	-8	0	0	—	—	—	—	—
95-96—Phoenix	IHL	25	6	13	19	28	...	...	...	—	—	—	—	—
—Boston	NHL	18	5	7	12	24	10	0	1	5	0	0	0	8
96-97—San Jose	NHL	78	5	7	12	65	-8	1	2	—	—	—	—	—
97-98—San Jose	NHL	57	2	7	9	22	-2	0	0	6	1	0	1	14
98-99—San Jose	NHL	59	3	6	9	40	-8	0	0	6	0	0	0	4
99-00—San Jose	NHL	78	5	6	11	34	-3	0	1	12	0	2	2	10
00-01—Calgary	NHL	21	1	3	4	12	4	0	0	—	—	—	—	—
NHL Totals (19 years)		1093	205	329	534	1352	58	29	14	104	8	32	40	193

PERSONAL: Born June 2, 1980, in Red Deer, Alta. ... 5-11/160. ... Shoots right. ... Son of Brian Sutter, head coach, Chicago Blackhawks and left winger with St. Louis Blues (1976-77 through 1987-88); nephew of Darryl Sutter, head coach, San Jose Sharks and left winger with Chicago Blackhawks (1979-80 through 1986-87); nephew of Brent Sutter, center with New York Islanders (1980-81 through 1991-92) and Blackhawks (1991-92 through 1997-98); nephew of Ron Sutter, center, San Jose Sharks; nephew of Rich Sutter, right winger with seven teams (1982-83 through 1994-95); nephew of Duane Sutter, head coach, Florida Panthers; right winger with Islanders (1979-80 through 1986-87) and Blackhawks (1987-88 through 1989-90).

TRANSACTIONS/CAREER NOTES: Selected by Calgary Flames in fourth round (fourth Flames pick, 102nd overall) of NHL entry draft (June 27, 1998).

Season Team	League	REGULAR SEASON								PLAYOFFS				
		Gms.	G	A	Pts.	PIM	+/-	PP	SH	Gms.	G	A	Pts.	PIM
96-97—Lethbridge	WHL	1	0	0	0	0	...	...	...	—	—	—	—	—
—Red Deer	AMHL	33	15	24	39	143	...	...	...	—	—	—	—	—
97-98—Lethbridge	WHL	69	11	9	20	146	...	...	...	4	0	0	0	4
98-99—Lethbridge	WHL	35	8	4	12	43	...	...	...	—	—	—	—	—
—Medicine Hat	WHL	23	9	5	14	38	...	...	...	—	—	—	—	—
99-00—Medicine Hat	WHL	29	1	7	8	43	...	...	...	—	—	—	—	—
—Calgary	WHL	6	0	1	1	8	...	...	...	—	—	—	—	—
00-01—Calgary	WHL	63	29	35	64	102	...	...	...	12	1	2	3	12
—Saint John	AHL	1	0	0	0	0	...	...	...	—	—	—	—	—

S

PERSONAL: Born March 10, 1975, in Kingston, Ont. ... 6-6/245. ... Full Name: Andy Cameron Sutton.

TRANSACTIONS/CAREER NOTES: Signed as non-drafted free agent by San Jose Sharks (March 20, 1998). ... Injured wrist (November 27, 1999); missed three games. ... Reinjured wrist (December 8, 1999); missed three games. ... Reinjured wrist (December 20, 1999); missed seven games. ... Reinjured wrist (January 12, 2000); missed 10 games. ... Traded by Sharks with seventh-round pick (RW/LW Peter Bartos) in 2000 draft and third round pick (traded to Atlanta) in 2001 draft to Minnesota Wild for eighth-round pick (traded to Calgary) in 2001 draft and future considerations (June 12, 2000). ... Bruised knee (November 8, 2000); missed two games. ... Dislocated shoulder (March 6, 2001); missed one game.

HONORS: Named to WCHA All-Star second team (1997-98).

Season Team	League	REGULAR SEASON								PLAYOFFS				
		Gms.	G	A	Pts.	PIM	+/-	PP	SH	Gms.	G	A	Pts.	PIM
94-95—Michigan Tech	WCHA	19	2	1	3	42	...	...	...	—	—	—	—	—
95-96—Michigan Tech	WCHA	32	2	2	4	38	...	...	...	—	—	—	—	—
96-97—Michigan Tech	WCHA	32	2	7	9	73	...	...	...	—	—	—	—	—
97-98—Michigan Tech	WCHA	38	16	24	40	97	...	...	...	—	—	—	—	—
—Kentucky	AHL	7	0	0	0	33	...	...	...	—	—	—	—	—
98-99—San Jose	NHL	31	0	3	3	65	-4	0	0	—	—	—	—	—
—Kentucky	AHL	21	5	10	15	53	...	...	...	5	0	0	0	23
99-00—San Jose	NHL	40	1	1	2	80	-5	0	0	—	—	—	—	—
—Kentucky	AHL	3	0	1	1	0	...	...	...	—	—	—	—	—
00-01—Minnesota	NHL	69	3	4	7	131	-11	2	0	—	—	—	—	—
NHL Totals (3 years)		140	4	8	12	276	-20	2	0	—	—	—	—	—

PERSONAL: Born November 5, 1969, in Edmonton. ... 6-1/205. ... Shoots left. ... Full Name: Kenneth Sutton.

TRANSACTIONS/CAREER NOTES: Selected by Buffalo Sabres in fifth round (fourth Sabres pick, 98th overall) of NHL entry draft (June 17, 1989). ... Separated shoulder (March 3, 1992); missed six games. ... Fractured ankle (September 15, 1992); missed first 19 games of season. ... Fractured finger (February 15, 1995); missed 10 games. ... Traded by Sabres to Edmonton Oilers for LW Scott Pearson (April 7, 1995). ... Traded by Oilers with D Igor Kravchuk to St. Louis Blues for D Donald Dufresne and D Jeff Norton (January 4, 1996). ... Traded by Blues with second-round pick (LW Brett Clouthier) in 1999 draft to New Jersey Devils for LW Mike Peluso and D Ricard Persson (November 26, 1996). ... Traded by Devils with RW John MacLean to San Jose Sharks for D Doug Bodger and LW Dody Wood (December 7, 1997). ... Traded by Sharks to Devils for fifth-round pick (RW Nicholas Dimitrakos) in 1999 draft (August 26, 1998). ... Claimed by Washington Capitals from Devils in NHL waiver draft (September 27, 1999). ... Traded by Capitals to Devils for future considerations (October 5, 1999). ... Signed as free agent by New York Islanders (July 5, 2001).

HONORS: Named to Memorial Cup All-Star team (1988-89). ... Named to AHL All-Star first team (1998-99). ... Won Eddie Shore Award (1998-99).

MISCELLANEOUS: Member of Stanley Cup championship team (2000).

Season Team	League	REGULAR SEASON								PLAYOFFS				
		Gms.	G	A	Pts.	PIM	+/-	PP	SH	Gms.	G	A	Pts.	PIM
87-88—Calgary Canucks	AJHL	53	13	43	56	228	...	...	...	—	—	—	—	—
88-89—Saskatoon	WHL	71	22	31	53	104	...	...	...	8	2	5	7	12
89-90—Rochester	AHL	57	5	14	19	83	...	...	...	11	1	6	7	15
90-91—Buffalo	NHL	15	3	6	9	13	2	2	0	6	0	1	1	2
—Rochester	AHL	62	7	24	31	65	...	...	...	3	1	1	2	14
91-92—Buffalo	NHL	64	2	18	20	71	5	0	0	7	0	2	2	4
92-93—Buffalo	NHL	63	8	14	22	30	-3	1	0	8	3	1	4	8
93-94—Buffalo	NHL	78	4	20	24	71	-6	1	0	4	0	0	0	2
94-95—Buffalo	NHL	12	1	2	3	30	-2	0	0	—	—	—	—	—
—Edmonton	NHL	12	3	1	4	12	-1	0	0	—	—	—	—	—
95-96—Edmonton	NHL	32	0	8	8	39	-12	0	0	—	—	—	—	—
—St. Louis	NHL	6	0	0	0	4	-1	0	0	1	0	0	0	0
—Worcester	AHL	32	4	16	20	60	...	...	...	4	0	2	2	21
96-97—Manitoba	IHL	20	3	10	13	48	...	...	...	—	—	—	—	—
—Albany	AHL	61	6	13	19	79	...	...	...	16	4	8	12	55

Season Team	League	Gms.	G	A	Pts.	PIM	+/-	PP	SH	Gms.	G	A	Pts.	PIM
97-98—Albany	AHL	10	0	7	7	15	...	...	...	—	—	—	—	—
—New Jersey	NHL	13	0	0	0	6	1	0	0	—	—	—	—	—
—San Jose	NHL	8	0	0	0	15	-4	0	0	—	—	—	—	—
98-99—Albany	AHL	75	13	42	55	118	...	...	...	5	0	2	2	12
—New Jersey	NHL	5	1	0	1	0	1	0	0	—	—	—	—	—
99-00—New Jersey	NHL	6	0	2	2	2	2	0	0	—	—	—	—	—
—Albany	AHL	57	5	16	21	129	...	...	...	—	—	—	—	—
00-01—New Jersey	NHL	53	1	7	8	37	9	0	0	6	0	0	0	13
NHL Totals (10 years)		367	23	78	101	330	-9	4	0	32	3	4	7	29

SVARTVADET, PER   LW   THRASHERS

PERSONAL: Born May 17, 1975, in Solleftea, Sweden. ... 6-1/190. ... Shoots left. ... Name pronounced PAIR SVAHRT-vuh-deht.
TRANSACTIONS/CAREER NOTES: Selected by Dallas Stars in sixth round (fifth Stars pick, 139th overall) of NHL entry draft (June 26, 1993). ... Traded by Stars to Atlanta Thrashers for sixth-round pick (RW Justin Cox) in 1999 draft (June 26, 1999). ... Fractured finger (October 16, 1999); missed one game. ... Sprained ankle (January 13, 2001); missed nine games.

Season Team	League	Gms.	G	A	Pts.	PIM	+/-	PP	SH	Gms.	G	A	Pts.	PIM
91-92—MoDo Hockey	Sweden Jrs.	30	17	19	36	36	...	...	...	—	—	—	—	—
92-93—MoDo Ornskoldsvik	Sweden	2	0	0	0	0	...	...	...	—	—	—	—	—
—MoDo Hockey	Sweden Jrs.	22	19	27	46	38	...	...	...	—	—	—	—	—
93-94—MoDo Ornskoldsvik	Sweden	36	2	1	3	4	...	...	...	11	0	0	0	6
94-95—MoDo Ornskoldsvik	Sweden	40	6	9	15	31	...	...	...	—	—	—	—	—
95-96—MoDo Ornskoldsvik	Sweden	40	9	14	23	26	...	...	...	8	2	3	5	0
96-97—MoDo Ornskoldsvik	Sweden	50	7	18	25	38	...	...	...	—	—	—	—	—
97-98—MoDo Ornskoldsvik	Sweden	46	6	12	18	28	...	...	...	7	3	2	5	2
98-99—MoDo Ornskoldsvik	Sweden	50	9	23	32	30	...	...	...	13	3	6	9	6
99-00—Atlanta	NHL	38	3	4	7	6	-8	0	0	—	—	—	—	—
—Orlando	IHL	27	4	6	10	10	...	...	...	5	0	1	1	0
00-01—Atlanta	NHL	69	10	11	21	20	-6	0	2	—	—	—	—	—
NHL Totals (2 years)		107	13	15	28	26	-14	0	2					

SVEHLA, ROBERT   D   PANTHERS

PERSONAL: Born January 2, 1969, in Martin, Czechoslovakia. ... 6-1/210. ... Shoots right. ... Name pronounced SVAY-luh.
TRANSACTIONS/CAREER NOTES: Selected by Calgary Flames in fourth round (fourth Flames pick, 78th overall) of NHL entry draft (June 20, 1992). ... Traded by Flames with D Magnus Svensson to Florida Panthers for third-round pick (LW Dmitri Vlasenkov) in 1996 draft and fourth-round pick (LW Ryan Ready) in 1997 draft (September 29, 1994). ... Sprained left rotator cuff (April 22, 1995); missed two games. ... Reinjured left rotator cuff (April 28, 1995); missed one game. ... Suffered back spasms (March 4, 1998); missed three games.
HONORS: Named Czechoslovakian League Player of the Year (1991-92). ... Named to Czechoslovakian League All-Star team (1991-92). ... Played in NHL All-Star Game (1997).
MISCELLANEOUS: Member of bronze-medal-winning Czechoslovakian Olympic team (1992). ... Holds Florida Panthers all-time record for most assists (207).

Season Team	League	Gms.	G	A	Pts.	PIM	+/-	PP	SH	Gms.	G	A	Pts.	PIM
89-90—Dukla Trencin	Czech.	29	4	3	7	...	...	...	...	—	—	—	—	—
90-91—Dukla Trencin	Czech.	58	16	9	25	...	...	...	...	—	—	—	—	—
91-92—Dukla Trencin	Czech.	51	23	28	51	0	...	...	...	—	—	—	—	—
—Czech. Olympic Team	Int'l	8	2	1	3	...	...	...	...	—	—	—	—	—
92-93—Malmo	Sweden	40	19	10	29	86	...	...	...	6	0	1	1	14
93-94—Malmo	Sweden	37	14	25	39	*127	...	...	...	10	5	1	6	23
—Slovakian Oly. team	Int'l	8	2	4	6	26	...	...	...	—	—	—	—	—
94-95—Malmo	Sweden	32	11	13	24	83	...	...	...	9	2	3	5	6
—Florida	NHL	5	1	1	2	0	3	1	0	—	—	—	—	—
95-96—Florida	NHL	81	8	49	57	94	-3	7	0	22	0	6	6	32
96-97—Florida	NHL	82	13	32	45	86	2	5	0	5	1	4	5	4
97-98—Florida	NHL	79	9	34	43	113	-3	3	0	—	—	—	—	—
—Slovakian Oly. team	Int'l	2	0	1	1	0	...	...	...	—	—	—	—	—
98-99—Florida	NHL	80	8	29	37	83	-13	4	0	—	—	—	—	—
99-00—Florida	NHL	82	9	40	49	64	23	3	0	4	0	1	1	4
00-01—Florida	NHL	82	6	22	28	76	-8	0	0	—	—	—	—	—
NHL Totals (7 years)		491	54	207	261	516	1	23	0	31	1	11	12	40

SVOBODA, JARSLAV   RW   HURRICANES

PERSONAL: Born June 1, 1980, in Cervenka, Czechoslovakia. ... 6-1/174.
TRANSACTIONS/CAREER NOTES: Selected by Carolina Hurricanes in eighth round (eighth Hurricanes pick, 208th overall) of NHL entry draft (June 21, 1997).

Season Team	League	Gms.	G	A	Pts.	PIM	+/-	PP	SH	Gms.	G	A	Pts.	PIM
97-98—Olomouc	Czech. Jrs.	43	15	18	33	0	...	...	...	—	—	—	—	—
98-99—Kootenay	WHL	54	26	33	59	46	...	...	...	7	2	2	4	11
99-00—Kootenay	WHL	56	23	43	66	97	...	...	...	21	*15	13	*28	51
00-01—Cincinnati	IHL	52	4	10	14	25	...	...	...	—	—	—	—	—

PERSONAL: Born February 14, 1966, in Most, Czechoslovakia. ... 6-2/198. ... Shoots left. ... Name pronounced svuh-BOH-duh.

TRANSACTIONS/CAREER NOTES: Selected by Montreal Canadiens in first round (first Canadiens pick, fifth overall) of NHL entry draft (June 9, 1984). ... Suffered back spasms (January 1988). ... Suffered hip pointer (March 1988). ... Sprained right wrist (November 21, 1988); missed five games. ... Injured back (March 1989). ... Separated shoulder (November 1989). ... Pulled groin (November 22, 1989). ... Reinjured groin (December 11, 1989); missed 15 games. ... Bruised left foot (March 11, 1990). ... Suffered stomach disorder (November 28, 1990); missed five games. ... Fractured left foot (January 15, 1991); missed 15 games. ... Injured mouth (December 14, 1991). ... Sprained ankle (February 17, 1992); missed seven games. ... Traded by Canadiens to Buffalo Sabres for D Kevin Haller (March 10, 1992). ... Bruised knee (October 28, 1992); missed four games. ... Tore ligament in right knee (January 17, 1993); missed remainder of season. ... Injured knee (October 12, 1993); missed three games. ... Suffered knee inflammation (October 16, 1993); missed seven games. ... Sprained left knee (March 17, 1994); missed 12 games. ... Played in Europe during 1994-95 NHL lockout. ... Separated shoulder (March 2, 1995); missed two games. ... Fractured jaw (March 16, 1995); missed one game. ... Traded by Sabres to Philadelphia Flyers for D Garry Galley (April 7, 1995). ... Strained neck (April 26, 1995); missed one game. ... Injured groin (October 31, 1995); missed one game. ... Suffered pinched nerve in neck (November 16, 1995); missed three games. ... Pulled hamstring (January 11, 1996); missed two games. ... Suffered concussion (February 2, 1996); missed one game. ... Strained shoulder (April 4, 1996); missed two games. ... Separated left shoulder (October 15, 1996); missed six games. ... Strained groin (December 31, 1996); missed four games. ... Suffered pinched nerve in neck (January 28, 1997); missed three games. ... Strained groin (March 13, 1997); missed two games. ... Fractured finger (October 1, 1997); missed 11 games. ... Strained neck (January 3, 1998); missed four games. ... Strained right elbow (March 5, 1998); missed four games. ... Bruised left thumb (March 24, 1998); missed seven games. ... Suffered hip flexor (October 31, 1998); missed three games. ... Sprained left knee (December 10, 1998); missed two games. ... Suffered from the flu (December 23, 1998); missed two games. ... Traded by Flyers to Tampa Bay Lightning for D Karl Dykhuis (December 28, 1998). ... Strained groin (January 29, 1999); missed five games. ... Reinjured groin (February 13, 1999); missed five games. ... Injured knee (March 24, 1999); missed two games. ... Injured shoulder (April 16, 1999); missed final game of season. ... Injured shoulder (January 5, 2000); missed one games. ... Injured shoulder (January 17, 2000); missed two games. ... Injured thumb (February 17, 2000); missed one game. ... Sprained thumb (March 1, 2000); missed two games. ... Strained muscle in abdomen (March 30, 2000); missed five games of season. ... Strained hip flexor October 27, 2000); missed one game. ... Strained back (November 3, 2000); missed four games. ... Suffered pinched nerve in neck (November 25, 2000); missed five games. ... Suffered concussion (December 14, 2000); missed final 52 games of season.

HONORS: Played in NHL All-Star Game (2000).

MISCELLANEOUS: Member of Stanley Cup championship team (1986). ... Member of gold-medal-winning Czech Republic Olympic team (1998).

			REGULAR SEASON							**PLAYOFFS**				
Season Team	League	Gms.	G	A	Pts.	PIM	+/-	PP	SH	Gms.	G	A	Pts.	PIM
82-83—Litvinov	Czech Rep.	4	0	0	0	2	...	...	...	—	—	—	—	—
83-84—Czechoslovakia Jr.	Czech.	40	15	21	36	14	...	...	...	—	—	—	—	—
84-85—Montreal	NHL	73	4	27	31	65	16	0	0	7	1	1	2	12
85-86—Montreal	NHL	73	1	18	19	93	24	0	0	8	0	0	0	21
86-87—Montreal	NHL	70	5	17	22	63	14	1	0	14	0	5	5	10
87-88—Montreal	NHL	69	7	22	29	149	46	2	0	10	0	5	5	12
88-89—Montreal	NHL	71	8	37	45	147	28	4	0	21	1	11	12	16
89-90—Montreal	NHL	60	5	31	36	98	20	2	0	10	0	5	5	2
90-91—Montreal	NHL	60	4	22	26	52	5	3	0	2	0	1	1	2
91-92—Montreal	NHL	58	5	16	21	94	9	1	0	—	—	—	—	—
—Buffalo	NHL	13	1	6	7	52	-8	0	0	7	1	4	5	6
92-93—Buffalo	NHL	40	2	24	26	59	3	1	0	—	—	—	—	—
93-94—Buffalo	NHL	60	2	14	16	89	11	1	0	3	0	0	0	4
94-95—Chem. Litvinov	Czech Rep.	8	2	0	2	40	...	...	...	—	—	—	—	—
—Buffalo	NHL	26	0	5	5	60	-5	0	0	—	—	—	—	—
—Philadelphia	NHL	11	0	3	3	10	0	0	0	14	0	4	4	8
95-96—Philadelphia	NHL	73	1	28	29	105	28	0	0	12	0	6	6	22
96-97—Philadelphia	NHL	67	2	12	14	94	10	1	0	16	1	2	3	16
97-98—Philadelphia	NHL	56	3	15	18	83	19	2	0	3	0	1	1	4
—Czech Rep. Oly. team	Int'l	6	1	1	2	39	...	...	...	—	—	—	—	—
98-99—Philadelphia	NHL	25	4	2	6	28	5	1	1	—	—	—	—	—
—Tampa Bay	NHL	34	1	16	17	53	-4	0	0	—	—	—	—	—
99-00—Tampa Bay	NHL	70	2	23	25	170	-11	2	0	—	—	—	—	—
00-01—Tampa Bay	NHL	19	1	3	4	41	-4	0	0	—	—	—	—	—
NHL Totals (17 years)		1028	58	341	399	1605	206	21	1	127	4	45	49	135

PERSONAL: Born June 20, 1980, in Jihlava, Czechoslovakia. ... 6-2/200. ... Shoots right.

TRANSACTIONS/CAREER NOTES: Selected by Toronto Maple Leafs in second round (second Maple Leafs pick, 35th overall) of NHL entry draft (June 27, 1998). ... Suffered injury (November 18, 2000); missed three games.

			REGULAR SEASON							**PLAYOFFS**				
Season Team	League	Gms.	G	A	Pts.	PIM	+/-	PP	SH	Gms.	G	A	Pts.	PIM
95-96—Jihlava	Czech Jrs.	38	4	12	16	50	...	...	...	—	—	—	—	—
96-97—Jihlava	Czech Jrs.	29	1	3	4	...	...	...	...	—	—	—	—	—
97-98—Dukla Jihlava	Czech Rep.	1	0	0	0	0	...	...	...	—	—	—	—	—
—Havlickuv Brod	Czech Rp. Dv.2	18	1	2	3	16	...	...	...	—	—	—	—	—
—Jihlava Jrs.	Czech Jrs.	12	0	2	2	...	...	...	...	—	—	—	—	—
98-99—Dukla Jihlava	Czech Rep.	40	1	5	6	28	...	...	...	—	—	—	—	—
99-00—Zelezarny Trinec	Czech Rep.	46	1	2	3	44	...	...	...	3	0	0	0	0
00-01—St. John's	AHL	38	7	7	14	48	...	...	...	4	0	0	0	4
—Toronto	NHL	18	1	2	3	10	-5	1	0	—	—	—	—	—
NHL Totals (1 year)		18	1	2	3	10	-5	1	0					

SWANSON, BRIAN   C   OILERS

PERSONAL: Born March 24, 1976, in Eagle River, Alaska. ... 5-10/185. ... Shoots left.
TRANSACTIONS/CAREER NOTES: Selected by San Jose Sharks in fifth round (fifth Sharks pick, 115th overall) of NHL entry draft (June 29, 1994). ... Traded by Sharks with D Jayson More and fourth-round pick (D Tomi Kallarsson) in 1997 draft to New York Rangers for D Marty McSorley (August 20, 1996). ... Signed as free agent by Edmonton Oilers (August 20, 1999).
HONORS: Named to WCHA All-Star second team (1995-96). ... Named WCHA Rookie of the Year (1995-96). ... Named to WCHA All-Rookie team (1995-96). ... Named to WCHA All-Star first team (1996-97 through 1998-99). ... Named to NCAA All-America (West) second team (1997-98). ... Named to NCAA All-America (West) first team (1998-99).

| | | REGULAR SEASON | | | | | | | | PLAYOFFS | | | | |
Season Team	League	Gms.	G	A	Pts.	PIM	+/-	PP	SH	Gms.	G	A	Pts.	PIM
93-94—Omaha	USHL	47	38	42	80	40	...	...	...	—	—	—	—	—
94-95—Portland	WHL	65	3	18	21	91	...	...	...	9	2	1	3	18
95-96—Colorado College	WCHA	40	26	33	59	24	...	...	...	—	—	—	—	—
96-97—Colorado College	WCHA	43	19	32	51	47	...	...	...	—	—	—	—	—
97-98—Colorado College	WCHA	42	18	*38	*56	26	...	...	...	—	—	—	—	—
98-99—Colorado College	WCHA	42	25	†41	66	28	...	...	...	—	—	—	—	—
—Hartford	AHL	4	0	0	0	4	...	...	...	—	—	—	—	—
99-00—Hamilton	AHL	69	19	40	59	18	...	...	...	10	2	5	7	6
00-01—Edmonton	NHL	16	1	1	2	6	-1	0	0	—	—	—	—	—
—Hamilton	AHL	49	18	29	47	20	...	...	...	—	—	—	—	—
NHL Totals (1 year)		16	1	1	2	6	-1	0	0					

S

SWEENEY, DON   D   BRUINS

PERSONAL: Born August 17, 1966, in St. Stephen, N.B. ... 5-10/184. ... Shoots left. ... Full Name: Donald Clark Sweeney.
TRANSACTIONS/CAREER NOTES: Selected by Boston Bruins in eighth round (eighth Bruins pick, 166th overall) of NHL entry draft (June 9, 1984). ... Bruised left heel (February 22, 1990). ... Injured knee (October 12, 1991); missed four games. ... Sprained knee (October 5, 1993); missed six games. ... Injured ribs (December 15, 1993); missed three games. ... Injured shoulder (October 17, 1995); missed three games. ... Injured shoulder (October 31, 1995); missed two games. ... Fractured shoulder (March 1, 1998); missed remainder of season. ... Suffered from the flu (January 13, 2000); missed one game. ... Underwent knee surgery (December 13, 2000); missed eight games. ... Injured knee (January 27, 2001); missed two games.
HONORS: Named to NCAA All-America (East) second team (1987-88). ... Named to ECAC All-Star first team (1987-88).

| | | REGULAR SEASON | | | | | | | | PLAYOFFS | | | | |
Season Team	League	Gms.	G	A	Pts.	PIM	+/-	PP	SH	Gms.	G	A	Pts.	PIM
83-84—St. Paul N.B. H.S.	N.B. H.S.	22	33	26	59	...	...	...	...	—	—	—	—	—
84-85—Harvard University	ECAC	29	3	7	10	30	...	...	...	—	—	—	—	—
85-86—Harvard University	ECAC	31	4	5	9	29	...	...	...	—	—	—	—	—
86-87—Harvard University	ECAC	34	7	14	21	22	...	...	...	—	—	—	—	—
87-88—Harvard University	ECAC	30	6	23	29	37	...	...	...	—	—	—	—	—
—Maine	AHL	—	—	—	—	—	...	...	...	6	1	3	4	0
88-89—Maine	AHL	42	8	17	25	24	...	...	...	—	—	—	—	—
—Boston	NHL	36	3	5	8	20	-4	0	0	—	—	—	—	—
89-90—Boston	NHL	58	3	5	8	58	11	0	0	21	1	5	6	18
—Maine	AHL	11	0	8	8	8	...	...	...	—	—	—	—	—
90-91—Boston	NHL	77	8	13	21	67	2	0	1	19	3	0	3	25
91-92—Boston	NHL	75	3	11	14	74	-9	0	0	15	0	0	0	10
92-93—Boston	NHL	84	7	27	34	68	34	0	1	4	0	0	0	4
93-94—Boston	NHL	75	6	15	21	50	29	1	2	12	2	1	3	4
94-95—Boston	NHL	47	3	19	22	24	6	1	0	5	0	0	0	4
95-96—Boston	NHL	77	4	24	28	42	-4	2	0	5	0	2	2	6
96-97—Boston	NHL	82	3	23	26	39	-5	0	0	—	—	—	—	—
97-98—Boston	NHL	59	1	15	16	24	12	0	0	—	—	—	—	—
98-99—Boston	NHL	81	2	10	12	64	14	0	0	11	3	0	3	6
99-00—Boston	NHL	81	1	13	14	48	-14	0	0	—	—	—	—	—
00-01—Boston	NHL	72	2	10	12	26	-1	1	0	—	—	—	—	—
NHL Totals (13 years)		904	46	190	236	604	69	5	4	92	9	8	17	77

SYDOR, DARRYL   D   STARS

PERSONAL: Born May 13, 1972, in Edmonton. ... 6-1/205. ... Shoots left. ... Full Name: Darryl Marion Sydor. ... Name pronounced sih-DOHR.
TRANSACTIONS/CAREER NOTES: Selected by Los Angeles Kings in first round (first Kings pick, seventh overall) of NHL entry draft (June 16, 1990). ... Bruised hip (November 27, 1992); missed two games. ... Sprained right shoulder (March 15, 1993); missed two games. ... Traded by Kings with seventh-round pick (G Eoin McInerney) in 1996 draft to Dallas Stars for RW Shane Churla and D Doug Zmolek (February 17, 1996). ... Sprained knee (February 21, 1999); missed three games. ... Reinjured knee (March 7, 1999); missed five games. ... Fractured eye socket (October 2, 1999); missed three games. ... Injured groin (October 20, 1999); missed three games. ... Injured neck (March 26, 2000); missed two games. ... Suffered from the flu (December 31, 2000); missed one game.
HONORS: Named to WHL (West) All-Star first team (1989-90 through 1991-92). ... Won Bill Hunter Trophy (1990-91). ... Named to Can.HL All-Star second team (1991-92) ... Played in NHL All-Star Game (1998 and 1999).
MISCELLANEOUS: Member of Stanley Cup championship team (1999).
STATISTICAL PLATEAUS: Three-goal games: 1997-98 (1).

| | | REGULAR SEASON | | | | | | | | PLAYOFFS | | | | |
Season Team	League	Gms.	G	A	Pts.	PIM	+/-	PP	SH	Gms.	G	A	Pts.	PIM
88-89—Kamloops	WHL	65	12	14	26	86	...	...	...	15	1	4	5	19
89-90—Kamloops	WHL	67	29	66	95	129	...	...	...	17	2	9	11	28
90-91—Kamloops	WHL	66	27	78	105	88	...	...	...	12	3	*22	25	10

Season Team	League	REGULAR SEASON								PLAYOFFS				
		Gms.	G	A	Pts.	PIM	+/-	PP	SH	Gms.	G	A	Pts.	PIM
91-92—Kamloops	WHL	29	9	39	48	43	...	...	...	17	3	15	18	18
—Los Angeles	NHL	18	1	5	6	22	-3	0	0	—	—	—	—	—
92-93—Los Angeles	NHL	80	6	23	29	63	-2	0	0	24	3	8	11	16
93-94—Los Angeles	NHL	84	8	27	35	94	-9	1	0	—	—	—	—	—
94-95—Los Angeles	NHL	48	4	19	23	36	-2	3	0	—	—	—	—	—
95-96—Los Angeles	NHL	58	1	11	12	34	-11	1	0	—	—	—	—	—
—Dallas	NHL	26	2	6	8	41	-1	1	0	—	—	—	—	—
96-97—Dallas	NHL	82	8	40	48	51	37	2	0	7	0	2	2	0
97-98—Dallas	NHL	79	11	35	46	51	17	4	1	17	0	5	5	14
98-99—Dallas	NHL	74	14	34	48	50	-1	9	0	23	3	9	12	16
99-00—Dallas	NHL	74	8	26	34	32	6	5	0	23	1	6	7	6
00-01—Dallas	NHL	81	10	37	47	34	5	8	0	10	1	3	4	0
NHL Totals (10 years)		704	73	263	336	508	36	34	1	104	8	33	41	52

SYKORA, MICHAL　　　D　　　FLYERS

PERSONAL: Born July 5, 1973, in Pardubice, Czechoslovakia. ... 6-5/225. ... Shoots left. ... Name pronounced sih-KOHR-uh.

TRANSACTIONS/CAREER NOTES: Selected by San Jose Sharks in sixth round (sixth Sharks pick, 123rd overall) of NHL entry draft (June 20, 1992). ... Strained knee (November 11, 1993); missed four games. ... Injured shoulder (February 24, 1995); missed remainder of season. ... Injured foot (February 17, 1996); missed one game. ... Traded by Sharks with G Chris Terreri and F Ulf Dahlen to Chicago Blackhawks for G Ed Belfour (January 25, 1997). ... Bruised left shoulder (March 10, 1997); missed three games. ... Suffered collapsed lung (March 15, 1998); missed remainder of season. ... Traded by Blackhawks to Tampa Bay Lightning for G Mark Fitzpatrick and fourth-round pick (traded to Montreal) in 1999 draft (July 17, 1998). ... Signed as free agent by Philadelphia Flyers (July 6, 2000). ... Strained lower back (November 14, 2000); missed nine games. ... Suffered laceration (December 10, 2000); missed two games. ... Injured hamstring (January 13, 2001); missed seven games.

HONORS: Named to Can.HL All-Star second team (1992-93). ... Named to WHL (West) All-Star first team (1992-93).

Season Team	League	REGULAR SEASON								PLAYOFFS				
		Gms.	G	A	Pts.	PIM	+/-	PP	SH	Gms.	G	A	Pts.	PIM
90-91—Pardubice	Czech.	2	0	0	0	0	...	...	...	—	—	—	—	—
91-92—Tacoma	WHL	61	13	23	36	66	...	...	...	4	0	2	2	2
92-93—Tacoma	WHL	70	23	50	73	73	...	...	...	7	4	8	12	2
93-94—San Jose	NHL	22	1	4	5	14	-4	0	0	—	—	—	—	—
—Kansas City	IHL	47	5	11	16	30	...	...	...	—	—	—	—	—
94-95—Kansas City	IHL	36	1	10	11	30	...	...	...	—	—	—	—	—
—San Jose	NHL	16	0	4	4	10	6	0	0	—	—	—	—	—
95-96—San Jose	NHL	79	4	16	20	54	-14	1	0	—	—	—	—	—
96-97—San Jose	NHL	35	2	5	7	59	0	1	0	—	—	—	—	—
—Chicago	NHL	28	1	9	10	10	4	0	0	1	0	0	0	0
97-98—Chicago	NHL	28	1	3	4	12	-10	0	0	—	—	—	—	—
—Indianapolis	IHL	6	0	0	0	4	...	...	...	—	—	—	—	—
98-99—Tampa Bay	NHL	10	1	2	3	0	-7	0	0	—	—	—	—	—
—Sparta Prague	Czech. Rep.	26	4	9	13	38	...	...	...	8	2	0	2	...
99-00—Sparta Praha	Czech. Rep.	48	11	14	25	89	...	...	...	9	5	3	8	8
00-01—Philadelphia	NHL	49	5	11	16	26	9	1	1	6	0	1	1	0
NHL Totals (7 years)		267	15	54	69	185	-16	3	1	7	0	1	1	0

SYKORA, PETR　　　RW　　　DEVILS

PERSONAL: Born November 19, 1976, in Plzen, Czechoslovakia. ... 6-0/190. ... Shoots left. ... Name pronounced sih-KOHR-uh.

TRANSACTIONS/CAREER NOTES: Selected by New Jersey Devils in first round (first Devils pick, 18th overall) of NHL entry draft (July 8, 1995). ... Injured back (February 21, 1996); missed two games. ... Injured groin (October 5, 1996); missed two games. ... Reinjured groin (November 9, 1996); missed four games. ... Reinjured groin (November 30, 1996); missed three games. ... Bruised shoulder (November 5, 1997); missed two games. ... Sprained left ankle (November 29, 1997); missed 20 games. ... Suffered from food poisoning (January 2, 1999); missed two games. ... Suffered from the flu (March 2, 2000); missed three games. ... Injured groin (October 26, 2000); missed three games. ... Reinjured groin (November 4, 2000); missed one game. ... Bruised shoulder (February 17, 2001); missed five games.

HONORS: Named to NHL All-Rookie team (1995-96).

MISCELLANEOUS: Member of Stanley Cup championship team (2000). ... Scored on a penalty shot (vs. Dwayne Roloson, January 6, 2000). ... Failed to score on a penalty shot (vs. Manny Fernandez, January 21, 2001).

Season Team	League	REGULAR SEASON								PLAYOFFS				
		Gms.	G	A	Pts.	PIM	+/-	PP	SH	Gms.	G	A	Pts.	PIM
91-92—Skoda Plzen	Czech.	30	50	50	100	...	...	...	...	—	—	—	—	—
92-93—Skoda Plzen	Czech.	19	12	5	17	...	...	...	...	—	—	—	—	—
93-94—Skoda Plzen	Czech. Rep.	37	10	16	26	...	...	...	...	4	0	1	1	...
—Cleveland	IHL	13	4	5	9	8	...	...	...	—	—	—	—	—
94-95—Detroit	IHL	29	12	17	29	16	...	...	...	—	—	—	—	—
95-96—Albany	AHL	5	4	1	5	0	...	...	...	—	—	—	—	—
—New Jersey	NHL	63	18	24	42	32	7	8	0	—	—	—	—	—
96-97—New Jersey	NHL	19	1	2	3	4	-8	0	0	2	0	0	0	2
—Albany	AHL	43	20	25	45	48	...	...	...	4	1	4	5	2
97-98—New Jersey	NHL	58	16	20	36	22	0	3	1	2	0	0	0	0
—Albany	AHL	2	4	1	5	0	...	...	...	—	—	—	—	—
98-99—New Jersey	NHL	80	29	43	72	22	16	15	0	7	3	3	6	4
99-00—New Jersey	NHL	79	25	43	68	26	24	5	1	23	9	8	17	10
00-01—New Jersey	NHL	73	35	46	81	32	36	9	2	25	10	12	22	12
NHL Totals (6 years)		372	124	178	302	138	75	40	4	59	22	23	45	28

SYKORA, PETR　　　　　C　　　　　PREDATORS

PERSONAL: Born December 21, 1978, in Pardubice, Czechoslovakia. ... 6-2/180. ... Shoots right.
TRANSACTIONS/CAREER NOTES: Selected by Detroit Red Wings in third round (second Red Wings pick, 76th overall) of NHL entry draft (June 21, 1997). ... Traded by Red Wings with third-round pick (traded to Edmonton) in 1999 draft and future considerations to Nashville Predators for RW Doug Brown (July 14, 1998).

Season Team	League	Gms.	G	A	Pts.	PIM	+/-	PP	SH	Gms.	G	A	Pts.	PIM
						REGULAR SEASON						**PLAYOFFS**		
94-95—HC Pardubice.............	Czech Jrs.	38	35	33	68	...	...	...	...	—	—	—	—	—
95-96—HC Pardubice.............	Czech Jrs.	26	13	9	22	...	...	...	...	—	—	—	—	—
96-97—Pojistovna Pardubice..	Czech Rep.	29	1	3	4	4	...	...	...	—	—	—	—	—
—Poji. Pardubice.............	Czech Jrs.	12	14	4	18	...	...	...	...	—	—	—	—	—
97-98—Pojistovna Pardubice..	Czech Rep.	39	4	5	9	8	...	...	...	3	0	0	0	0
98-99—Milwaukee..................	IHL	73	14	15	29	50	...	...	...	2	1	1	2	0
—Nashville....................	NHL	2	0	0	0	0	-1	0	0	—	—	—	—	—
99-00—Milwaukee..................	IHL	3	0	1	1	2	...	...	...	—	—	—	—	—
NHL Totals (1 year).............		2	0	0	0	0	-1	0	0					

SYLVESTER, DEAN　　　　　RW

PERSONAL: Born December 30, 1972, in Hanson, Mass. ... 6-2/210. ... Shoots right.
TRANSACTIONS/CAREER NOTES: Selected by San Jose Sharks in NHL supplemental draft (June 25, 1993). ... Signed as free agent by Buffalo Sabres (September 10, 1998). ... Traded by Sabres to Atlanta Thrashers for future considerations (June 25, 1999). ... Suffered back spasms (February 14, 2000); missed three games. ... Suffered back spasms (February 23, 2000); missed six games.
STATISTICAL PLATEAUS: Three-goal games: 1999-00 (1).

Season Team	League	Gms.	G	A	Pts.	PIM	+/-	PP	SH	Gms.	G	A	Pts.	PIM
						REGULAR SEASON						**PLAYOFFS**		
90-91—Boston College H.S.....	Mass. H.S.	18	19	13	32	...	...	...	...	—	—	—	—	—
91-92—Kent	Indep.	31	7	21	28	10	...	...	...	—	—	—	—	—
92-93—Kent	CCHA	38	33	20	53	28	...	...	...	—	—	—	—	—
93-94—Kent	CCHA	39	22	24	46	28	...	...	...	—	—	—	—	—
94-95—Michigan State...........	CCHA	40	15	15	30	38	...	...	...	—	—	—	—	—
95-96—Mobile.......................	ECHL	44	24	27	51	35	...	...	...	—	—	—	—	—
—Kansas City................	IHL	36	11	10	21	15	...	...	...	4	0	0	0	2
96-97—Kansas City................	IHL	77	23	22	45	47	...	...	...	3	1	1	2	0
97-98—Kansas City................	IHL	77	33	20	53	63	...	...	...	11	5	2	7	4
98-99—Rochester	AHL	76	35	30	65	46	...	...	...	18	†12	5	17	8
—Buffalo	NHL	1	0	0	0	0	-1	0	0	4	0	0	0	2
99-00—Orlando......................	IHL	16	4	3	7	43	...	...	...	—	—	—	—	—
—Atlanta	NHL	52	16	10	26	24	-14	1	0	—	—	—	—	—
00-01—Atlanta	NHL	43	5	6	11	8	-16	1	0	—	—	—	—	—
—Orlando......................	IHL	27	9	9	18	20	...	...	...	9	0	1	1	6
NHL Totals (3 years)............		96	21	16	37	32	-31	2	0	4	0	0	0	2

TALLAS, ROB　　　　　G

PERSONAL: Born March 20, 1973, in Edmonton. ... 6-0/163. ... Catches left. ... Name pronounced TAL-ihz.
TRANSACTIONS/CAREER NOTES: Signed as non-drafted free agent by Boston Bruins (September 13, 1995). ... Injured ankle (March 24, 1997); missed eight games. ... Strained hamstring (January 24, 1998); missed eight games. ... Lacerated finger (November 24, 1999); missed two games. ... Signed as free agent by Chicago Blackhawks (July 31, 2000).
MISCELLANEOUS: Stopped a penalty shot attempt (vs. Daymond Langkow, November 24, 1998). ... Allowed a penalty shot goal (vs. David Vyborny, October 15, 2000).

Season Team	League	Gms.	Min	W	L	T	GA	SO	Avg.	Gms.	Min.	W	L	GA	SO	Avg.
						REGULAR SEASON							**PLAYOFFS**			
91-92—Seattle.........................	WHL	14	708	4	7	0	52	0	4.41	—	—	—	—	—	—	—
92-93—Seattle.........................	WHL	52	3151	24	23	3	194	2	3.69	5	333	1	4	18	0	3.24
93-94—Seattle.........................	WHL	51	2849	23	21	3	188	0	3.96	9	567	5	4	40	0	4.23
94-95—Charlotte	ECHL	36	2011	21	9	‡3	114	0	3.40	—	—	—	—	—	—	—
—Providence.................	AHL	2	82	1	0	0	4	1	2.93	—	—	—	—	—	—	—
95-96—Boston	NHL	1	60	1	0	0	3	0	3.00	—	—	—	—	—	—	—
—Providence.................	AHL	37	2136	12	16	7	117	1	3.29	2	135	0	2	9	0	4.00
96-97—Providence.................	AHL	24	1423	9	14	1	83	0	3.50	—	—	—	—	—	—	—
—Boston	NHL	28	1244	8	12	1	69	1	3.33	—	—	—	—	—	—	—
97-98—Providence.................	AHL	10	575	1	8	1	39	0	4.07	—	—	—	—	—	—	—
—Boston	NHL	14	788	6	3	3	24	1	1.83	—	—	—	—	—	—	—
98-99—Boston	NHL	17	987	7	7	2	43	1	2.61	—	—	—	—	—	—	—
99-00—Boston	NHL	27	1363	4	13	4	72	0	3.17	—	—	—	—	—	—	—
00-01—Chicago	NHL	12	627	2	7	0	35	0	3.35	—	—	—	—	—	—	—
—Norfolk.......................	AHL	6	333	2	2	2	12	0	2.16	—	—	—	—	—	—	—
—Chicago.....................	IHL	3	87	0	1	0	6	0	4.14	—	—	—	—	—	—	—
NHL Totals (6 years).............		99	5069	28	42	10	246	3	2.91							

TALLINDER, HENRIK　　　　　D　　　　　SABRES

PERSONAL: Born January 10, 1979, in Stockholm, Sweden. ... 6-3/194. ... Shoots left.
TRANSACTIONS/CAREER NOTES: Selected by Buffalo Sabres in second round (second Sabres pick, 48th overall) of NHL entry draft (June 21, 1997).

Season Team	League	REGULAR SEASON								PLAYOFFS				
		Gms.	G	A	Pts.	PIM	+/-	PP	SH	Gms.	G	A	Pts.	PIM
95-96—AIK Solna...................	Sweden Jrs.	40	4	13	17	55				—	—	—	—	—
96-97—AIK Solna...................	Sweden Jrs.						Statistics unavailable.							
—AIK Solna...................	Sweden	1	0	0	0	0	...	...	...	—	—	—	—	—
97-98—AIK Solna...................	Sweden	34	0	0	0	26	...	...	...	—	—	—	—	—
98-99—AIK Solna...................	Sweden	36	0	0	0	30	...	...	...	—	—	—	—	—
99-00—AIK Solna...................	Sweden	50	0	2	2	59	...	...	...	—	—	—	—	—
00-01—TPS Turku..................	Finland	56	5	9	14	62	...	...	...	10	2	1	3	8

TAMER, CHRIS   D   THRASHERS

PERSONAL: Born November 17, 1970, in Dearborn, Mich. ... 6-2/208. ... Shoots left. ... Full Name: Chris Thomas Tamer. ... Name pronounced TAY-muhr.

TRANSACTIONS/CAREER NOTES: Selected by Pittsburgh Penguins in fourth round (third Penguins pick, 68th overall) of NHL entry draft (June 16, 1990). ... Injured shoulder (March 27, 1994); missed four games. ... Fractured ankle (May 6, 1995); missed eight playoff games. ... Pulled abdominal muscle (December 1995); missed five games. ... Sprained wrist (December 30, 1995); missed five games. ... Fractured jaw (January 17, 1996); missed two games. ... Pulled abdominal muscle (November 22, 1996); missed 20 games. ... Strained hip flexor (January 4, 1997); missed 13 games. ... Strained hip flexor (March 4, 1997); missed four games. ... Traded by Penguins with C Petr Nedved and C Sean Pronger to New York Rangers for RW Alexei Kovalev, C Harry York and future considerations (November 25, 1998). ... Selected by Atlanta Thrashers in NHL expansion draft (June 25, 1999). ... Sprained medial collateral ligament in knee (February 29, 2000); missed six games.

Season Team	League	REGULAR SEASON								PLAYOFFS				
		Gms.	G	A	Pts.	PIM	+/-	PP	SH	Gms.	G	A	Pts.	PIM
87-88—Redford......................	NAJHL	40	10	20	30	217	...	...	...	—	—	—	—	—
88-89—Redford......................	NAJHL	31	6	13	19	79	...	...	...	—	—	—	—	—
89-90—Univ. of Michigan......	CCHA	42	2	7	9	147	...	...	...	—	—	—	—	—
90-91—Univ. of Michigan......	CCHA	45	8	19	27	130	...	...	...	—	—	—	—	—
91-92—Univ. of Michigan......	CCHA	43	4	15	19	125	...	...	...	—	—	—	—	—
92-93—Univ. of Michigan......	CCHA	39	5	18	23	113	...	...	...	—	—	—	—	—
93-94—Cleveland	IHL	53	1	2	3	160	...	...	...	—	—	—	—	—
—Pittsburgh.................	NHL	12	0	0	0	9	3	0	0	5	0	0	0	2
94-95—Cleveland	IHL	48	4	10	14	204	...	...	...	—	—	—	—	—
—Pittsburgh.................	NHL	36	2	0	2	82	0	0	0	4	0	0	0	18
95-96—Pittsburgh.................	NHL	70	4	10	14	153	20	0	0	18	0	7	7	24
96-97—Pittsburgh.................	NHL	45	2	4	6	131	-25	0	1	4	0	0	0	4
97-98—Pittsburgh.................	NHL	79	0	7	7	181	4	0	0	6	0	1	1	4
98-99—Pittsburgh.................	NHL	11	0	0	0	32	-2	0	0	—	—	—	—	—
—New York Rangers......	NHL	52	1	5	6	92	-12	0	0	—	—	—	—	—
99-00—Atlanta	NHL	69	2	8	10	91	-32	0	0	—	—	—	—	—
00-01—Atlanta	NHL	82	4	13	17	128	-1	0	1	—	—	—	—	—
NHL Totals (8 years)...........		456	15	47	62	899	-45	0	2	37	0	8	8	52

TANABE, DAVID   D   HURRICANES

PERSONAL: Born July 19, 1980, in Minneapolis. ... 6-1/195. ... Shoots right. ... Full Name: David Michael Tanabe. ... Name pronounced tuh-nah-BEE.

TRANSACTIONS/CAREER NOTES: Selected by Carolina Hurricanes in first round (first Hurricanes pick, 16th overall) of NHL entry draft (June 26, 1999). ... Suffered concussion (October 18, 2000); missed five games. ... Suffered hip pointer (March 2, 2001); missed three games.

Season Team	League	REGULAR SEASON								PLAYOFFS				
		Gms.	G	A	Pts.	PIM	+/-	PP	SH	Gms.	G	A	Pts.	PIM
97-98—U.S. National..............	NAHL	73	8	21	29	96	...	...	...	—	—	—	—	—
98-99—Univ. of Wisconsin......	WCHA	35	10	12	22	44	...	...	...	—	—	—	—	—
99-00—Carolina	NHL	31	4	0	4	14	-4	3	0	—	—	—	—	—
—Cincinnati....................	IHL	32	0	13	13	14	...	...	...	11	1	4	5	6
00-01—Carolina	NHL	74	7	22	29	42	-9	5	0	6	2	0	2	12
NHL Totals (2 years)...........		105	11	22	33	56	-13	8	0	6	2	0	2	12

TANGUAY, ALEX   LW   AVALANCHE

PERSONAL: Born November 21, 1979, in Ste.-Justine, Que. ... 6-0/190. ... Shoots left. ... Name pronounced tan-GAY.

TRANSACTIONS/CAREER NOTES: Selected by Colorado Avalanche in first round (first Avalanche pick, 12th overall) of NHL entry draft (June 27, 1998). ... Strained neck (March 14, 2000); missed six games.

HONORS: Named to Can.HL All-Rookie team (1996-97). ... Named to QMJHL All-Rookie team (1996-97).

MISCELLANEOUS: Member of Stanley Cup championship team (2001). ... Failed to score on a penalty shot (vs. Ed Belfour, December 1, 2000).

Season Team	League	REGULAR SEASON								PLAYOFFS				
		Gms.	G	A	Pts.	PIM	+/-	PP	SH	Gms.	G	A	Pts.	PIM
96-97—Halifax.......................	QMJHL	70	27	41	68	50	...	...	...	12	4	8	12	8
97-98—Halifax.......................	QMJHL	51	47	38	85	32	...	...	...	5	7	6	13	4
98-99—Halifax.......................	QMJHL	31	27	34	61	30	...	...	...	5	1	2	3	2
—Hershey	AHL	5	1	2	3	2	...	...	...	5	0	2	2	0
99-00—Colorado	NHL	76	17	34	51	22	6	5	0	17	2	1	3	2
00-01—Colorado	NHL	82	27	50	77	37	35	7	1	23	6	15	21	8
NHL Totals (2 years)...........		158	44	84	128	59	41	12	1	40	8	16	24	10

T

TAPPER, BRAD   RW   THRASHERS

PERSONAL: Born April 28, 1978, in Scarborough, Ont. ... 6-0/175. ... Shoots right.
TRANSACTIONS/CAREER NOTES: Signed as non-drafted free agent by Atlanta Thrashers (April 11, 2000).
HONORS: Named to ECAC All-Star first team (1999-2000). ... Named to NCAA All-America (East) second team (1999-2000).

		REGULAR SEASON								PLAYOFFS				
Season Team	League	Gms.	G	A	Pts.	PIM	+/-	PP	SH	Gms.	G	A	Pts.	PIM
97-98—Rensselaer Poly. Inst..	ECAC	34	14	11	25	62	...	...	...	—	—	—	—	—
98-99—Rensselaer Poly. Inst..	ECAC	35	20	20	40	60	...	...	...	—	—	—	—	—
99-00—Rensselaer Poly. Inst..	ECAC	37	*31	20	51	81	...	...	...	—	—	—	—	—
00-01—Atlanta	NHL	16	2	3	5	6	1	0	0	—	—	—	—	—
—Orlando	IHL	45	7	9	16	39	...	...	...	2	0	0	0	2
NHL Totals (1 year)		16	2	3	5	6	1	0	0					

TARNSTROM, DICK   D   ISLANDERS

PERSONAL: Born January 20, 1975, in Sundbyberg, Sweden. ... 6-0/180. ... Shoots left.
TRANSACTIONS/CAREER NOTES: Selected by New York Islanders in 11th round (12th Islanders pick, 272nd overall) of NHL entry draft (June 29, 1994).

		REGULAR SEASON								PLAYOFFS				
Season Team	League	Gms.	G	A	Pts.	PIM	+/-	PP	SH	Gms.	G	A	Pts.	PIM
92-93—AIK	Sweden	3	0	0	0	0	...	...	...	—	—	—	—	—
93-94—AIK	Sweden	33	1	4	5		...	...	...	—	—	—	—	—
94-95—AIK	Sweden	37	8	4	12	26	...	...	...	—	—	—	—	—
95-96—AIK	Sweden	40	0	5	5	32	...	...	...	—	—	—	—	—
96-97—AIK	Sweden	49	5	3	8	38	...	...	...	7	0	1	1	6
97-98—AIK Solna	Sweden	45	2	12	14	30	...	...	...	—	—	—	—	—
98-99—AIK Solna	Sweden	47	9	14	23	36	...	...	...	—	—	—	—	—
99-00—AIK Solna	Sweden	42	7	15	22	20	...	...	...	—	—	—	—	—
00-01—AIK Solna	Sweden	50	10	18	28	28	...	...	...	5	0	0	0	8

TAYLOR, CHRIS   C   SABRES

PERSONAL: Born March 6, 1972, in Stratford, Ont. ... 6-0/189. ... Shoots left. ... Brother of Tim Taylor, center, Tampa Bay Lightning.
TRANSACTIONS/CAREER NOTES: Selected by New York Islanders in second round (second Islanders pick, 27th overall) of NHL entry draft (June 16, 1990). ... Signed as free agent by Los Angeles Kings (August 1, 1997). ... Signed as free agent by Boston Bruins (July 22, 1998). ... Signed as free agent by Buffalo Sabres (August 13, 1999).

		REGULAR SEASON								PLAYOFFS				
Season Team	League	Gms.	G	A	Pts.	PIM	+/-	PP	SH	Gms.	G	A	Pts.	PIM
88-89—London	OHL	62	7	16	23	52	...	...	...	15	0	2	2	15
89-90—London	OHL	66	45	60	105	60	...	...	...	6	3	2	5	6
90-91—London	OHL	65	50	78	128	50	...	...	...	7	4	8	12	6
91-92—London	OHL	66	48	74	122	57	...	...	...	10	8	16	24	9
92-93—Roanoke	ECHL	5	2	1	3	0	...	...	...	—	—	—	—	—
—Capital District	AHL	77	19	43	62	32	...	...	...	4	0	1	1	2
93-94—Raleigh	ECHL	2	0	0	0	0	...	...	...	—	—	—	—	—
—Salt Lake City	IHL	79	21	20	41	38	...	...	...	—	—	—	—	—
94-95—Denver	IHL	78	38	48	86	47	...	...	...	14	7	6	13	10
—Roanoke	ECHL	1	0	0	0	2	...	...	...	—	—	—	—	—
—New York Islanders	NHL	10	0	3	3	2	1	0	0	—	—	—	—	—
95-96—Utah	IHL	50	18	23	41	60	...	...	...	22	5	11	16	26
—New York Islanders	NHL	11	0	1	1	2	1	0	0	—	—	—	—	—
96-97—Utah	IHL	71	27	40	67	24	...	...	...	7	1	2	3	0
—New York Islanders	NHL	1	0	0	0	0	0	0	0	—	—	—	—	—
97-98—Utah	IHL	79	28	56	84	66	...	...	...	4	0	2	2	6
98-99—Boston	NHL	37	3	5	8	12	-3	0	1	—	—	—	—	—
—Providence	AHL	21	6	11	17	6	...	...	...	—	—	—	—	—
—Las Vegas	IHL	14	3	12	15	2	...	...	...	—	—	—	—	—
99-00—Rochester	AHL	49	21	28	49	21	...	...	...	—	—	—	—	—
—Buffalo	NHL	11	1	1	2	2	-2	0	0	2	0	0	0	2
00-01—Rochester	AHL	45	20	24	44	25	...	...	...	—	—	—	—	—
—Buffalo	NHL	14	0	2	2	6	1	0	0	—	—	—	—	—
NHL Totals (6 years)		84	4	12	16	24	-2	0	1	2	0	0	0	2

TAYLOR, TIM   C   LIGHTNING

PERSONAL: Born February 6, 1969, in Stratford, Ont. ... 6-1/188. ... Shoots left. ... Full Name: Tim Robertson Taylor. ... Brother of Chris Taylor, center, Buffalo Sabres.
TRANSACTIONS/CAREER NOTES: Selected by Washington Capitals in second round (second Capitals pick, 36th overall) of NHL entry draft (June 11, 1988). ... Traded by Capitals to Vancouver Canucks (January 29, 1993). ... Signed as free agent by Detroit Red Wings (July 28, 1993). ... Injured right shoulder (April 5, 1996); missed three games. ... Sprained shoulder (October 15, 1996); missed 16 games. ... Suffered from an illness (April 9, 1997); missed two games. ... Selected by Boston Bruins from Red Wings in NHL waiver draft (September 28, 1997). ... Injured ribs (March 21, 1998); missed one game. ... Injured hip (March 22, 1998); missed two games. ... Sprained ankle (October 14, 1998); missed 12 games. ... Reinjured ankle (November 13, 1998); missed six games. ... Reinjured ankle (December 10, 1998); missed 14 games. ... Strained groin (April 17, 1999); missed final game of season. ... Signed as free agent by New York Rangers (July 15, 1999). ... Suffered concussion (October 2, 1999); missed two games. ... Injured hand (October 20, 1999); missed one game. ... Injured

rib (November 24, 1999); missed one game. ... Suffered from the flu (February 13, 2000); missed two games. ... Injured shoulder (November 28, 2000); missed one game. ... Suffered abdominal muscle tear (December 31, 2000); missed remainder of season. ... Traded by Rangers to Tampa Bay Lightning for LW Nils Ekman and LW Kyle Freadrich (July 1, 2001).

HONORS: Won John B. Sollenberger Trophy (1993-94). ... Named to AHL All-Star first team (1993-94).

MISCELLANEOUS: Member of Stanley Cup championship team (1997). ... Scored on a penalty shot (vs. Jocelyn Thibault, April 15, 1998).

			REGULAR SEASON							PLAYOFFS				
Season Team	League	Gms.	G	A	Pts.	PIM	+/-	PP	SH	Gms.	G	A	Pts.	PIM
86-87—London	OHL	34	7	9	16	11	...	...	...	—	—	—	—	—
87-88—London	OHL	64	46	50	96	66	...	...	...	12	9	9	18	26
88-89—London	OHL	61	34	80	114	93	...	...	...	21	*21	25	*46	58
89-90—Baltimore	AHL	74	22	21	43	63	...	...	...	9	2	2	4	13
90-91—Baltimore	AHL	79	25	42	67	75	...	...	...	5	0	1	1	4
91-92—Baltimore	AHL	65	9	18	27	131	...	...	...	—	—	—	—	—
92-93—Baltimore	AHL	41	15	16	31	49	...	...	...	—	—	—	—	—
—Hamilton	AHL	36	15	22	37	37	...	...	...	—	—	—	—	—
93-94—Adirondack	AHL	79	36	*81	117	86	...	...	...	12	2	10	12	12
—Detroit	NHL	1	1	0	1	0	-1	0	0	—	—	—	—	—
94-95—Detroit	NHL	22	0	4	4	16	3	0	0	6	0	1	1	12
95-96—Detroit	NHL	72	11	14	25	39	11	1	1	18	0	4	4	4
96-97—Detroit	NHL	44	3	4	7	52	-6	0	1	2	0	0	0	0
97-98—Boston	NHL	79	20	11	31	57	-16	1	3	6	0	0	0	10
98-99—Boston	NHL	49	4	7	11	55	-10	0	0	12	0	3	3	8
99-00—New York Rangers	NHL	76	9	11	20	72	-4	0	0	—	—	—	—	—
00-01—New York Rangers	NHL	38	2	5	7	16	-6	0	0	—	—	—	—	—
NHL Totals (8 years)		381	50	56	106	307	-29	2	5	44	0	8	8	34

TELLQVIST, MIKAEL   G   MAPLE LEAFS

PERSONAL: Born September 19, 1979, in Sundbyberg, Sweden. ... 5-11/174.

TRANSACTIONS/CAREER NOTES: Selected by Toronto Maple Leafs in third round (third Maple Leafs pick, 70th overall) of NHL entry draft (June 24, 2000).

			REGULAR SEASON							PLAYOFFS					
Season Team	League	Gms.	Min	W	L	T	GA	SO	Avg.	Gms.	Min.	W	L	GA	SO	Avg.
98-99—Djurgarden Stockholm..	Sweden	3	124	...	...	...	8	0	3.87	4	240	...	...	11	0	2.75
99-00—Djurgarden Stockholm..	Sweden	30	1909	...	...	...	66	2	2.07	13	814	—	—	21	3	1.55
00-01—Djurgarden Stockholm..	Sweden	43	2622	...	...	...	91	†5	*2.08	*16	*1006	...	...	*45	†1	2.68

TENKRAT, PETR   RW   MIGHTY DUCKS

PERSONAL: Born May 31, 1977, in Kladno, Czechoslovakia. ... 6-1/185. ... Shoots right.

TRANSACTIONS/CAREER NOTES: Selected by Mighty Ducks of Anaheim in eighth round (sixth Mighty Ducks pick, 230th overall) of NHL entry draft (June 26, 1999).

			REGULAR SEASON							PLAYOFFS				
Season Team	League	Gms.	G	A	Pts.	PIM	+/-	PP	SH	Gms.	G	A	Pts.	PIM
94-95—Poldi Kladno	Czech Rep.	—	—	—	—	—	...	...	...	1	0	0	0	...
95-96—Poldi Kladno	Czech Rep.	18	0	3	3		...	...	...	3	0	0	0	...
96-97—Poldi Kladno	Czech Rep.	43	5	9	14	6	...	...	...	3	0	1	1	0
97-98—Poldi Kladno	Czech Rep.	52	9	10	19	24	...	...	...	—	—	—	—	—
98-99—Velvana Kladno	Czech Rep.	50	21	14	35	32	...	...	...	—	—	—	—	—
99-00—Ilves Tampere	Finland	53	35	14	49	75	...	...	...	3	1	1	2	14
00-01—Cincinnati	AHL	25	9	9	18	24	...	...	...	4	3	2	5	0
—Anaheim	NHL	46	5	9	14	16	-11	0	0	—	—	—	—	—
NHL Totals (1 year)		46	5	9	14	16	-11	0	0					

TERRERI, CHRIS   G

PERSONAL: Born November 15, 1964, in Providence, R.I. ... 5-9/170. ... Catches left. ... Full Name: Christopher Arnold Terreri. ... Name pronounced tuh-RAIR-ee.

TRANSACTIONS/CAREER NOTES: Selected by New Jersey Devils in fifth round (third Devils pick, 87th overall) of NHL entry draft (June 8, 1983). ... Strained knee (October 1986). ... Strained lower back (March 21, 1992); missed five games. ... Traded by Devils to San Jose Sharks for second-round pick (traded to Pittsburgh) in 1996 draft (November 14, 1995). ... Injured elbow (March 15, 1996); missed 12 games. ... Injured wrist (October 20, 1996); missed 12 games. ... Traded by Sharks with D Michal Sykora and RW Ulf Dahlen to Chicago Blackhawks for G Ed Belfour (January 25, 1997). ... Fractured finger (November 11, 1997); missed 20 games. ... Strained groin (January 1, 1998); missed 23 games. ... Traded by Blackhawks to Devils for second-round pick (D Stepan Mokhov) in 1999 draft (August 25, 1998). ... Suffered from the flu (January 14, 1999); missed two games. ... Selected by Minnesota Wild in NHL expansion draft (June 23, 2000). ... Traded by Wild to Devils with for D Brad Bombardir (June 23, 2000). ... Traded by Devils to New York Islanders for G John Vanbiesbrouck (March 12, 2001).

HONORS: Named NCAA Tournament Most Valuable Player (1984-85). ... Named Hockey East Player of the Year (1984-85). ... Named Hockey East Tournament Most Valuable Player (1984-85). ... Named to NCAA All-Tournament team (1984-85). ... Named to NCAA All-America (East) first team (1984-85). ... Named to Hockey East All-Star first team (1984-85). ... Named to NCAA All-America (East) second team (1985-86). ... Named to Hockey East All-Decade team (1994).

MISCELLANEOUS: Member of Stanley Cup championship team (1995 and 2000). ... Stopped a penalty shot attempt (vs. Mike Ricci, November 17, 1990; vs. Murray Craven, October 13, 1991; vs. Rob Zamuner, October 9, 1997). ... Allowed a penalty shot goal (vs. Mario Lemieux, December 31, 1988; vs. Bob Errey, January 5, 1991; vs. Ray Bourque, March 19, 1994).

Season Team	League	Gms.	Min	W	L	T	GA	SO	Avg.	Gms.	Min.	W	L	GA	SO	Avg.
82-83 —Providence College	ECAC	11	529	7	1	0	17	2	1.93	—	—	—	—	—	—	—
83-84 —Providence College	ECAC	10	391	4	2	0	20	0	3.07	—	—	—	—	—	—	—
84-85 —Providence College	Hockey East	41	2515	15	13	5	131	1	3.13	—	—	—	—	—	—	—
85-86 —Providence College	Hockey East	27	1540	6	16	0	96	0	3.74	—	—	—	—	—	—	—
86-87 —Maine	AHL	14	765	4	9	1	57	0	4.47	—	—	—	—	—	—	—
—New Jersey	NHL	7	286	0	3	1	21	0	4.41	—	—	—	—	—	—	—
87-88 —U.S. national team	Int'l	26	1430	17	7	2	81	0	3.40	—	—	—	—	—	—	—
—U.S. Olympic team	Int'l	3	128	1	1	0	14	0	6.56	—	—	—	—	—	—	—
—Utica...........................	AHL	7	399	5	1	0	18	0	2.71	—	—	—	—	—	—	—
88-89 —New Jersey	NHL	8	402	0	4	2	18	0	2.69	—	—	—	—	—	—	—
—Utica...........................	AHL	39	2314	20	15	3	132	0	3.42	2	80	0	1	6	0	4.50
89-90 —New Jersey	NHL	35	1931	15	12	3	110	0	3.42	4	238	2	2	13	0	3.28
90-91 —New Jersey	NHL	53	2970	24	21	7	144	1	2.91	7	428	3	4	21	0	2.94
91-92 —New Jersey	NHL	54	3186	22	22	10	169	1	3.18	7	386	3	3	23	0	3.58
92-93 —New Jersey	NHL	48	2672	19	21	3	151	2	3.39	4	219	1	3	17	0	4.66
93-94 —New Jersey	NHL	44	2340	20	11	4	106	2	2.72	4	200	3	0	9	0	2.70
94-95 —New Jersey	NHL	15	734	3	7	2	31	0	2.53	1	8	0	0	0	0	...
95-96 —New Jersey	NHL	4	210	3	0	0	9	0	2.57	—	—	—	—	—	—	—
—San Jose	NHL	46	2516	13	29	1	155	0	3.70	—	—	—	—	—	—	—
96-97 —San Jose	NHL	22	1200	6	10	3	55	0	2.75	—	—	—	—	—	—	—
—Chicago......................	NHL	7	429	4	1	2	19	0	2.66	2	44	0	0	3	0	4.09
97-98 —Chicago......................	NHL	21	1222	8	10	2	49	2	2.41	—	—	—	—	—	—	—
—Indianapolis	IHL	3	180	2	0	‡1	3	1	1.00	—	—	—	—	—	—	—
98-99 —New Jersey	NHL	12	726	8	3	1	30	1	2.48	—	—	—	—	—	—	—
99-00 —New Jersey	NHL	12	649	2	9	0	37	0	3.42	—	—	—	—	—	—	—
00-01 —New Jersey	NHL	10	453	2	5	1	21	0	2.78	—	—	—	—	—	—	—
—New York Islanders...	NHL	8	443	2	4	1	18	0	2.44	—	—	—	—	—	—	—
NHL Totals (14 years)...........		406	22369	151	172	43	1143	9	3.07	29	1523	12	12	86	0	3.39

TETARENKO, JOEY   D   PANTHERS

PERSONAL: Born March 3, 1978, in Prince Albert, Sask. ... 6-2/212. ... Shoots right.

TRANSACTIONS/CAREER NOTES: Selected by Florida Panthers in fourth round (fourth Panthers pick, 82nd overall) of NHL entry draft (June 22, 1996). ... Scratched cornea (March 21, 2001); missed one game.

			REGULAR SEASON							PLAYOFFS				
Season Team	League	Gms.	G	A	Pts.	PIM	+/-	PP	SH	Gms.	G	A	Pts.	PIM
94-95 —Portland	WHL	59	0	1	1	134	...	...	...	9	0	0	0	8
95-96 —Portland	WHL	71	4	11	15	190	...	...	...	7	0	1	1	17
96-97 —Portland	WHL	68	8	18	26	182	...	...	...	2	0	0	0	2
97-98 —Portland	WHL	49	2	12	14	148	...	...	...	16	0	2	2	30
98-99 —New Haven	AHL	65	4	10	14	154	...	...	...	—	—	—	—	—
99-00 —Louisville	AHL	57	3	11	14	136	...	...	...	4	0	0	0	2
00-01 —Florida......................	NHL	29	3	1	4	44	-1	0	0	—	—	—	—	—
NHL Totals (1 year).............		29	3	1	4	44	-1	0	0					

TEZIKOV, ALEXEI   D   MIGHTY DUCKS

PERSONAL: Born June 22, 1978, in Togliatti, U.S.S.R. ... 6-1/198. ... Shoots left. ... Name pronounced TEHS-ih-kahf.

TRANSACTIONS/CAREER NOTES: Selected by Buffalo Sabres in fifth round (seventh Sabres pick, 115th overall) of NHL entry draft (June 22, 1996). ... Traded by Sabres with future considerations to Washington Capitals for C Joe Juneau and third-round pick (LW Tim Preston) in 1999 draft (March 23, 1999). ... Suffered back spasms (November 11, 1999); missed three games. ... Suffered from the flu (March 9, 2000); missed two games. ... Traded by Capitals with fourth-round pick (D Brendan Rogers) in 2001 draft to Mighty Ducks of Anaheim for D Jason Marshall (March 13, 2001).

HONORS: Named to QMJHL All-Star second team (1997-98). ... Named to QMJHL All-Rookie Team (1997-98). ... Won Raymond Lagace Trophy (1997-98).

			REGULAR SEASON							PLAYOFFS				
Season Team	League	Gms.	G	A	Pts.	PIM	+/-	PP	SH	Gms.	G	A	Pts.	PIM
95-96 —Lada Togliatti	CIS	14	0	0	0	8	...	...	...	—	—	—	—	—
96-97 —Lada Togliatti	Russian	7	0	0	0	4	...	...	...	—	—	—	—	—
—Tor. Nichny Nov.	Russian	5	0	2	2	2	...	...	...	—	—	—	—	—
97-98 —Moncton	QMJHL	60	15	33	48	144	...	...	...	10	3	8	11	20
98-99 —Moncton	QMJHL	25	9	21	30	52	...	...	...	—	—	—	—	—
—Rochester	AHL	31	3	7	10	41	...	...	...	—	—	—	—	—
—Cincinnati..................	IHL	5	0	0	0	2	...	...	...	3	0	0	0	10
—Washington	NHL	5	0	0	0	0	-1	0	0	—	—	—	—	—
99-00 —Portland	AHL	53	6	9	15	70	...	...	...	—	—	—	—	—
—Washington	NHL	23	1	1	2	2	-2	1	0	—	—	—	—	—
00-01 —Portland	AHL	58	7	24	31	58	...	...	...	—	—	—	—	—
—Cincinnati..................	AHL	13	2	6	8	8	...	...	...	4	0	1	1	0
NHL Totals (2 years)...........		28	1	1	2	2	-3	1	0					

THEODORE, JOSE   G   CANADIENS

PERSONAL: Born September 13, 1976, in Laval, Que. ... 5-11/185. ... Catches right. ... Name pronounced JO-zhay TAY-uh-dohr.

TRANSACTIONS/CAREER NOTES: Selected by Montreal Canadiens in second round (second Canadiens pick, 44th overall) of NHL entry draft (June 28, 1994). ... Strained groin (March 29, 2000); missed three games.

HONORS: Named to QMJHL All-Star second team (1994-95 and 1995-96).
MISCELLANEOUS: Allowed a penalty shot goal (vs. Scott Niedermayer, November 11, 1998).
STATISTICAL NOTES: Tied for NHL lead with .919 save percentage (1999-2000).

			REGULAR SEASON								PLAYOFFS						
Season Team	League	Gms.	Min	W	L	T	GA	SO	Avg.	Gms.	Min.	W	L	GA	SO	Avg.
92-93 —St. Jean......................	QMJHL	34	1776	12	16	2	112	0	3.78	3	175	0	2	11	0	3.77
93-94 —St. Jean......................	QMJHL	57	3225	20	29	6	194	0	3.61	5	296	1	4	18	1	3.65
94-95 —Hull	QMJHL	58	3348	32	22	2	193	5	3.46	21	1263	15	6	59	1	2.80
—Fredericton..................	AHL	—	—	—	—	—	—	—	—	1	60	0	1	3	0	3.00
95-96 —Hull	QMJHL	48	2803	33	11	2	158	0	3.38	5	300	2	3	20	0	4.00
—Montreal.....................	NHL	1	9	0	0	0	1	0	6.67	—	—	—	—	—	—	—
96-97 —Fredericton..............	AHL	26	1469	12	12	0	87	0	3.55	—	—	—	—	—	—	—
—Montreal.....................	NHL	16	821	5	6	2	53	0	3.87	2	168	1	1	7	0	2.50
97-98 —Fredericton..............	AHL	53	3053	20	23	8	145	2	2.85	4	237	1	3	13	0	3.29
—Montreal.....................	NHL	—	—	—	—	—	—	—	—	3	120	0	1	1	0	.50
98-99 —Montreal...................	NHL	18	913	4	12	0	50	1	3.29	—	—	—	—	—	—	—
—Fredericton..............	AHL	27	1609	12	13	2	77	2	2.87	13	694	8	5	35	†1	3.03
99-00 —Montreal...................	NHL	30	1655	12	13	2	58	5	2.10	—	—	—	—	—	—	—
00-01 —Quebec.....................	AHL	3	180	3	0	0	9	0	3.00	—	—	—	—	—	—	—
—Montreal...................	NHL	59	3298	20	29	5	141	2	2.57	—	—	—	—	—	—	—
NHL Totals (6 years)............		124	6696	41	60	9	303	8	2.72	5	288	1	2	8	0	1.67

THERIEN, CHRIS   D   FLYERS

PERSONAL: Born December 14, 1971, in Ottawa. ... 6-4/230. ... Shoots left. ... Name pronounced TAIR-ee-uhn.
TRANSACTIONS/CAREER NOTES: Selected by Philadelphia Flyers in third round (seventh Flyers pick, 47th overall) of NHL entry draft (June 16, 1990). ... Suffered from the flu (November 3, 1997); missed one game. ... Sprained left knee (April 8, 1998); missed three games. ... Strained shoulder (October 9, 1998); missed first three games of season. ... Bruised left thigh (December 13, 1998); missed three games. ... Injured back (September 14, 2000). ... Injured back (October 17, 2000); missed eight games.
HONORS: Named to Hockey East All-Rookie Team (1990-91). ... Named to Hockey East All-Star second team (1992-93). ... Named to NHL All-Rookie team (1994-95).

			REGULAR SEASON							PLAYOFFS				
Season Team	League	Gms.	G	A	Pts.	PIM	+/-	PP	SH	Gms.	G	A	Pts.	PIM
89-90—Northwood School......	N.Y. H.S.	31	35	37	72	54	...	...	...	—	—	—	—	—
90-91—Providence College.....	Hockey East	36	4	18	22	36	...	...	...	—	—	—	—	—
91-92—Providence College.....	Hockey East	36	16	25	41	38	...	...	...	—	—	—	—	—
92-93—Providence College.....	Hockey East	33	8	11	19	52	...	...	...	—	—	—	—	—
—Canadian nat'l team	Int'l	8	1	4	5	8	...	...	...	—	—	—	—	—
93-94—Canadian nat'l team	Int'l	59	7	15	22	46	...	...	...	—	—	—	—	—
—Can. Olympic team	Int'l	4	0	0	0	4	...	...	...	—	—	—	—	—
—Hershey	AHL	6	0	0	0	2	...	...	...	—	—	—	—	—
94-95—Hershey	AHL	34	3	13	16	27	...	...	...	—	—	—	—	—
—Philadelphia	NHL	48	3	10	13	38	8	1	0	15	0	0	0	10
95-96—Philadelphia	NHL	82	6	17	23	89	16	3	0	12	0	0	0	18
96-97—Philadelphia	NHL	71	2	22	24	64	27	0	0	19	1	6	7	6
97-98—Philadelphia	NHL	78	3	16	19	80	5	1	0	5	0	1	1	4
98-99—Philadelphia	NHL	74	3	15	18	48	16	1	0	6	0	0	0	6
99-00—Philadelphia	NHL	80	4	9	13	66	11	1	0	18	0	1	1	12
00-01—Philadelphia	NHL	73	2	12	14	48	22	1	0	6	1	0	1	8
NHL Totals (7 years)............		506	23	101	124	433	105	8	0	81	2	8	10	64

THIBAULT, JOCELYN   G   BLACKHAWKS

PERSONAL: Born January 12, 1975, in Montreal. ... 5-11/170. ... Catches left. ... Name pronounced TEE-boh.
TRANSACTIONS/CAREER NOTES: Selected by Quebec Nordiques in first round (first Nordiques pick, 10th overall) of NHL entry draft (June 26, 1993). ... Sprained shoulder (March 28, 1995); missed 10 games. ... Nordiques franchise moved to Colorado and renamed Avalanche for 1995-96 season (June 21, 1995). ... Traded by Avalanche with LW Martin Rucinsky and RW Andrei Kovalenko to Montreal Canadiens for G Patrick Roy and RW Mike Keane (December 6, 1995). ... Bruised right hand (February 21, 1996); missed two games. ... Fractured finger (October 24, 1996); missed nine games. ... Suffered from the flu (February 3, 1997); missed two games. ... Bruised collarbone (January 8, 1998); missed one game. ... Traded by Canadiens with D Dave Manson and D Brad Brown to Chicago Blackhawks for G Jeff Hackett, D Eric Weinrich, D Alain Nasreddine and fourth-round pick (D Chris Dyment) in 1999 draft (November 16, 1998). ... Fractured finger (November 27, 1999); missed six games. ... Suffered from the flu (December 10, 2000); missed one game.
HONORS: Named to QMJHL All-Rookie team (1991-92). ... Won Can.HL Goaltender-of-the-Year Award (1992-93). ... Won Jacques Plante Trophy (1992-93). ... Won Michel Briere Trophy (1992-93). ... Won Marcel Robert Trophy (1992-93). ... Named to Can.HL All-Star first team (1992-93). ... Named to QMJHL All-Star first team (1992-93).
MISCELLANEOUS: Stopped a penalty shot attempt (vs. Tony Granato, November 25, 1993; vs. Martin Straka, March 16, 1995). ... Allowed a penalty shot goal (vs. Joe Sacco, November 12, 1997; vs. Tim Taylor, April 15, 1998).

			REGULAR SEASON							PLAYOFFS						
Season Team	League	Gms.	Min	W	L	T	GA	SO	Avg.	Gms.	Min.	W	L	GA	SO	Avg.
91-92—Trois-Rivieres...............	QMJHL	30	1497	14	7	1	77	0	3.09	3	110	1	1	4	0	2.18
92-93—Sherbrooke	QMJHL	56	3190	34	14	5	159	*3	*2.99	15	883	9	6	57	0	3.87
93-94—Quebec......................	NHL	29	1504	8	13	3	83	0	3.31	—	—	—	—	—	—	—
—Cornwall.....................	AHL	4	240	4	0	0	9	1	2.25	—	—	—	—	—	—	—
94-95—Sherbrooke	QMJHL	13	776	6	6	1	38	1	2.94	—	—	—	—	—	—	—
—Quebec.....................	NHL	18	898	12	2	2	35	1	2.34	3	148	1	2	8	0	3.24
95-96—Colorado	NHL	10	558	3	4	2	28	0	3.01	—	—	—	—	—	—	—
—Montreal...................	NHL	40	2334	23	13	3	110	3	2.83	6	311	2	4	18	0	3.47
96-97—Montreal...................	NHL	61	3397	22	24	11	164	1	2.90	3	179	0	3	13	0	4.36

Season Team	League	REGULAR SEASON								PLAYOFFS						
		Gms.	Min	W	L	T	GA	SO	Avg.	Gms.	Min.	W	L	GA	SO	Avg.
97-98—Montreal	NHL	47	2652	19	15	8	109	2	2.47	2	43	0	0	4	0	5.58
98-99—Montreal	NHL	10	529	3	4	2	23	1	2.61	—	—	—	—	—	—	—
—Chicago	NHL	52	3014	21	26	5	136	4	2.71	—	—	—	—	—	—	—
99-00—Chicago	NHL	60	3438	25	26	7	158	3	2.76	—	—	—	—	—	—	—
00-01—Chicago	NHL	66	3844	27	32	7	†180	6	2.81	—	—	—	—	—	—	—
NHL Totals (8 years)		393	22168	163	159	50	1026	21	2.78	14	681	3	9	43	0	3.79

THINEL, MARC-ANDRE   RW   CANADIENS

PERSONAL: Born March 24, 1981, in St. Jerome, Que. ... 5-11/158. ... Shoots left.
TRANSACTIONS/CAREER NOTES: Selected by Montreal Canadiens in fifth round (sixth Canadiens pick, 145th overall) of NHL entry draft (June 26, 1999).
HONORS: Named to QMJHL All-Star first team (1999-2000). ... Named to QMJHL All-Star second team (2000-01).

Season Team	League	REGULAR SEASON								PLAYOFFS				
		Gms.	G	A	Pts.	PIM	+/-	PP	SH	Gms.	G	A	Pts.	PIM
97-98—Victoriaville	QMJHL	58	7	10	17	20	...	...	...	6	0	3	3	4
98-99—Victoriaville	QMJHL	66	45	58	103	16	...	...	...	6	5	3	8	4
99-00—Victoriaville	QMJHL	71	59	73	132	55	...	...	...	6	5	6	11	18
00-01—Victoriaville	QMJHL	70	62	88	150	101	...	...	...	13	12	13	25	18

THOMAS, SCOTT   LW   KINGS

PERSONAL: Born January 18, 1970, in Buffalo. ... 6-2/200. ... Shoots right. ... Full Name: John Scott Thomas.
TRANSACTIONS/CAREER NOTES: Selected by Buffalo Sabres in third round (second Sabres pick, 56th overall) of NHL entry draft (June 17, 1989). ... Signed as free agent by Los Angeles Kings (August 26, 1999). ... Suffered concussion (March 19, 2001); missed four games.
HONORS: Named to ECAC All-Rookie team (1989-90). ... Named to IHL All-Star first team (1998-99).

Season Team	League	REGULAR SEASON								PLAYOFFS				
		Gms.	G	A	Pts.	PIM	+/-	PP	SH	Gms.	G	A	Pts.	PIM
87-88—Nichols School	N.Y. H.S.	16	23	39	62	82	...	...	...	—	—	—	—	—
88-89—Nichols School	N.Y. H.S.	...	38	52	90		...	...	...	—	—	—	—	—
89-90—Clarkson	ECAC	34	19	13	32	95	...	...	...	—	—	—	—	—
90-91—Clarkson	ECAC	40	28	14	42	90	...	...	...	—	—	—	—	—
91-92—Clarkson	ECAC	30	†25	21	46	62	...	...	...	—	—	—	—	—
—Rochester	AHL	—	—	—	—	—	...	...	...	9	0	1	1	17
92-93—Rochester	AHL	66	32	27	59	38	...	...	...	17	8	5	13	6
—Buffalo	NHL	7	1	1	2	15	2	0	0	—	—	—	—	—
93-94—Buffalo	NHL	32	2	2	4	8	-6	1	0	—	—	—	—	—
—Rochester	AHL	11	4	5	9	0	...	...	...	—	—	—	—	—
94-95—Rochester	AHL	55	21	25	46	115	...	...	...	5	4	0	4	4
95-96—Cincinnati	IHL	78	32	28	60	54	...	...	...	17	*13	2	15	4
96-97—Cincinnati	IHL	71	32	29	61	46	...	...	...	3	0	0	0	0
97-98—Detroit	IHL	44	11	16	27	18	...	...	...	—	—	—	—	—
—Manitoba	IHL	26	12	4	16	8	...	...	...	3	0	1	1	2
98-99—Manitoba	IHL	78	45	25	70	32	...	...	...	5	3	4	7	4
99-00—Long Beach	IHL	52	15	16	31	18	...	...	...	6	2	1	3	6
00-01—Manitoba	IHL	22	9	14	23	21	...	...	...	3	1	2	3	0
—Los Angeles	NHL	24	3	1	4	9	0	0	0	12	1	0	1	4
NHL Totals (3 years)		63	6	4	10	32	-4	1	0	12	1	0	1	4

THOMAS, STEVE   RW   BLACKHAWKS

PERSONAL: Born July 15, 1963, in Stockport, England. ... 5-10/185. ... Shoots left.
TRANSACTIONS/CAREER NOTES: Signed as non-drafted free agent by Toronto Maple Leafs (May 12, 1984). ... Fractured wrist during training camp (September 1984). ... Traded by Maple Leafs with RW Rick Vaive and D Bob McGill to Chicago Blackhawks for LW Al Secord and RW Ed Olczyk (September 3, 1987). ... Pulled stomach muscle (October 1987). ... Separated left shoulder (February 20, 1988) and underwent surgery. ... Pulled back muscle (October 18, 1988). ... Separated right shoulder (December 21, 1988). ... Underwent surgery to repair chronic shoulder separation problem (January 25, 1989). ... Strained knee ligaments during training camp (September 1990); missed first 11 games of season. ... Traded by Blackhawks with C Adam Creighton to New York Islanders for C Brent Sutter and RW Brad Lauer (October 25, 1991) ... Bruised ribs (March 10, 1992); missed one game. ... Bruised ribs (November 21, 1992); missed three games. ... Suffered neck muscle spasms (January 4, 1994); missed five games. ... Injured back and thumb (January 24, 1995); missed one game. ... Traded by Islanders to New Jersey Devils for RW Claude Lemieux (October 3, 1995). ... Injured head (February 1, 1996); missed one game. ... Suffered from the flu (October 24, 1996); missed two games. ... Strained ankle (November 30, 1996); missed 10 games. ... Strained knee (December 31, 1996) missed 12 games. ... Strained groin (October 23, 1997); missed 20 games. ... Bruised ribs (January 5, 1998); missed four games. ... Suffered back spasms (April 5, 1998); missed three games. ... Signed as free agent by Maple Leafs (July 12, 1998). ... Suffered back spasms (March 1, 1999); missed one game. ... Fractured toe (March 9, 1999); missed three games. ... Suffered injury (February 29, 2000); missed one game ... Lacerated hand (October 21, 2000); missed three games. ... Injured knee (november 30, 2000); missed 22 games. ... Signed as free agent by Blackhawks (July 18, 2001).
HONORS: Won Dudley (Red) Garrett Memorial Trophy (1984-85). ... Named to AHL All-Star first team (1984-85).
RECORDS: Holds NHL career record for most overtime goals—11.

Season Team	League	REGULAR SEASON								PLAYOFFS				
		Gms.	G	A	Pts.	PIM	+/-	PP	SH	Gms.	G	A	Pts.	PIM
81-82—Markham Tier II Jr. A.	OHA	48	68	57	125	113	...	...	...	—	—	—	—	—
82-83—Toronto	OHL	61	18	20	38	42	...	...	...	—	—	—	—	—
83-84—Toronto	OHL	70	51	54	105	77	...	...	...	—	—	—	—	—
84-85—Toronto	NHL	18	1	1	2	2	-13	0	0	—	—	—	—	—
—St. Catharines	AHL	64	42	48	90	56	...	...	...	—	—	—	—	—

Season Team	League	REGULAR SEASON Gms.	G	A	Pts.	PIM	+/-	PP	SH	PLAYOFFS Gms.	G	A	Pts.	PIM
85-86—St. Catharines	AHL	19	18	14	32	35	...	...	...	—	—	—	—	—
—Toronto	NHL	65	20	37	57	36	-15	5	0	10	6	8	14	9
86-87—Toronto	NHL	78	35	27	62	114	-3	3	0	13	2	3	5	13
87-88—Chicago	NHL	30	13	13	26	40	1	5	0	3	1	2	3	6
88-89—Chicago	NHL	45	21	19	40	69	-2	8	0	12	3	5	8	10
89-90—Chicago	NHL	76	40	30	70	91	-3	13	0	20	7	6	13	33
90-91—Chicago	NHL	69	19	35	54	129	8	2	0	6	1	2	3	15
91-92—Chicago	NHL	11	2	6	8	26	-3	0	0	—	—	—	—	—
—New York Islanders	NHL	71	28	42	70	71	11	3	0	—	—	—	—	—
92-93—New York Islanders	NHL	79	37	50	87	111	3	12	0	18	9	8	17	37
93-94—New York Islanders	NHL	78	42	33	75	139	-9	17	0	4	1	0	1	8
94-95—New York Islanders	NHL	47	11	15	26	60	-14	3	0	—	—	—	—	—
95-96—New Jersey	NHL	81	26	35	61	98	-2	6	0	—	—	—	—	—
96-97—New Jersey	NHL	57	15	19	34	46	9	1	0	10	1	1	2	18
97-98—New Jersey (March 28)	NHL	55	14	10	24	32	4	3	0	6	0	3	3	2
98-99—Toronto	NHL	78	28	45	73	33	26	11	0	17	6	3	9	12
99-00—Toronto	NHL	81	26	37	63	68	1	9	0	12	6	3	9	10
00-01—Toronto	NHL	57	8	26	34	46	0	1	0	11	6	3	9	4
NHL Totals (17 years)		1076	386	480	866	1211	-1	102	0	142	49	47	96	177

THOMPSON, ROCKY RW PANTHERS

PERSONAL: Born August 8, 1977, in Calgary. ... 6-2/205. ... Shoots right.
TRANSACTIONS/CAREER NOTES: Selected by Calgary Flames in third round (third Flames pick, 72nd overall) of NHL entry draft (July 8, 1995). ... Injured neck (February 3, 1998); missed two games. ... Suffered concussion (January 16, 1999); missed final 38 games of season. ... Traded by Flames to Florida Panthers for D Filip Kuba (March 16, 2000).

Season Team	League	REGULAR SEASON Gms.	G	A	Pts.	PIM	+/-	PP	SH	PLAYOFFS Gms.	G	A	Pts.	PIM
93-94—Medicine Hat	WHL	68	1	4	5	166	...	...	...	3	0	0	0	2
94-95—Medicine Hat	WHL	63	1	6	7	220	...	...	...	5	0	0	0	17
95-96—Medicine Hat	WHL	71	9	20	29	260	...	...	...	5	2	3	5	26
—Saint John	AHL	4	0	0	0	33	...	...	...	—	—	—	—	—
96-97—Medicine Hat	WHL	47	6	9	15	170	...	...	...	—	—	—	—	—
—Swift Current	WHL	22	3	5	8	90	...	...	...	10	1	2	3	22
97-98—Saint John	AHL	51	3	0	3	187	...	...	...	18	1	1	2	47
—Calgary	NHL	12	0	0	0	61	0	0	0	—	—	—	—	—
98-99—Saint John	AHL	27	2	2	4	108	...	...	...	—	—	—	—	—
—Calgary	NHL	3	0	0	0	25	0	0	0	—	—	—	—	—
99-00—Saint John	AHL	53	2	8	10	125	...	...	...	—	—	—	—	—
—Louisville	AHL	3	0	1	1	54	...	...	...	4	0	0	0	4
00-01—Louisville	AHL	55	3	5	8	193	...	...	...	—	—	—	—	—
—Florida	NHL	4	0	0	0	19	0	0	0	—	—	—	—	—
NHL Totals (3 years)		19	0	0	0	105	0	0	0					

THORNTON, JOE C BRUINS

PERSONAL: Born July 2, 1979, in London, Ont. ... 6-4/225. ... Shoots left. ... Cousin of Scott Thornton, left winger, San Jose Sharks.
TRANSACTIONS/CAREER NOTES: Selected by Boston Bruins in first round (first Bruins pick, first overall) of NHL entry draft (June 21, 1997). ... Suffered broken forearm prior to 1997-98 season; missed first three games. ... Injured ankle (December 13, 1997); missed 10 games. ... Suffered from viral infection (March 28, 1998); missed six games. ... Suffered chest injury (April 17, 1999); missed final game of regular season and one playoff game. ... Bruised knee (November 20, 1999); missed one game. ... Suffered charley horse (November 24, 2000); missed six games. ... Suspended two games by NHL for cross-checking incident (December 18, 2000). ... Suspended two games by NHL for cross-checking incident (February 6, 2001).
HONORS: Won Can.HL Rookie of the Year Award (1995-96). ... Won Emms Family Trophy (1995-96). ... Won Can.HL Top Prospect Award (1996-97). ... Named to Can.HL All-Star second team (1996-97). ... Named to OHL All-Star second team (1996-97).
STATISTICAL PLATEAUS: Three-goal games: 2000-01 (1).

Season Team	League	REGULAR SEASON Gms.	G	A	Pts.	PIM	+/-	PP	SH	PLAYOFFS Gms.	G	A	Pts.	PIM
94-95—St. Thomas	Jr. B	50	40	64	104	53	...	...	...	—	—	—	—	—
95-96—Sault Ste. Marie	OHL	66	30	46	76	51	...	...	...	4	1	1	2	11
96-97—Sault Ste. Marie	OHL	59	41	81	122	123	...	...	...	11	11	8	19	24
97-98—Boston	NHL	55	3	4	7	19	-6	0	0	6	0	0	0	9
98-99—Boston	NHL	81	16	25	41	69	3	7	0	11	3	6	9	4
99-00—Boston	NHL	81	23	37	60	82	-5	5	0	—	—	—	—	—
00-01—Boston	NHL	72	37	34	71	107	-4	19	1	—	—	—	—	—
NHL Totals (4 years)		289	79	100	179	277	-12	31	1	17	3	6	9	13

THORNTON, SCOTT LW SHARKS

PERSONAL: Born January 9, 1971, in London, Ont. ... 6-3/216. ... Shoots left. ... Full Name: Scott C. Thornton. ... Cousin of Joe Thornton, center, Boston Bruins.
TRANSACTIONS/CAREER NOTES: Selected by Toronto Maple Leafs in first round (first Maple Leafs pick, third overall) of NHL entry draft (June 17, 1989). ... Separated shoulder (January 24, 1991); missed eight games. ... Traded by Maple Leafs with LW Vincent Damphousse, D Luke Richardson, G Peter Ing and future considerations to Edmonton Oilers for G Grant Fuhr, RW/LW Glenn Anderson and LW Craig Berube (September 19, 1991). ... Suffered concussion (November 23, 1991); missed one game. ... Sprained ankle (October 6, 1993); missed 13 games.

... Suffered back spasms (November 21, 1993); missed one game. ... Suffered wrist contusion (April 14, 1994); missed one game. ... Suffered from Cytomegalo virus (January 9, 1996); missed three games. ... Traded by Oilers to Montreal Canadiens for RW Andrei Kovalenko (September 6, 1996). ... Bruised hand (December 28, 1996); missed three games. ... Suffered from the flu (February 10, 1997); missed one game. ... Underwent arthroscopic knee surgery (March 6, 1997); missed five games. ... Separated shoulder (January 3, 1998); missed two games. ... Injured neck (February 7, 1998); missed one game. ... Fractured rib (March 18, 1998); missed eight games. ... Injured shoulder (April 15, 1998); missed three games. ... Strained abdominal muscle (November 3, 1998) and underwent surgery; missed 31 games. ... Suffered from migraines (February 2, 1999); missed three games. ... Suffered back spasms (April 13, 1999); missed one game. ... Injured tricep (September 20, 1999); missed first two games of 1999-2000 season. ... Reinjured tricep (October 8, 1999); missed three games. ... Strained groin (December 12, 1999); missed one game. ... Traded by Canadiens to Dallas Stars for LW Juha Lind (January 22, 2000). ... Suffered from the flu (March 8, 2000); missed one game. ... Suspended for three games for by NHL for high-sticking incident (March 22, 2000). ... Signed as free agent by San Jose Sharks (July 1, 2000). ... Injured neck (January 4, 2001); missed three games. ... Injured neck (January 30, 2001); missed five games.

STATISTICAL PLATEAUS: Three-goal games: 2000-01 (1).

			REGULAR SEASON								PLAYOFFS				
Season Team	League	Gms.	G	A	Pts.	PIM	+/-	PP	SH		Gms.	G	A	Pts.	PIM
86-87—London Diamonds	OPJHL	31	10	7	17	10	...	...	...		—	—	—	—	—
87-88—Belleville	OHL	62	11	19	30	54	...	...	...		6	0	1	1	2
88-89—Belleville	OHL	59	28	34	62	103	...	...	...		5	1	1	2	6
89-90—Belleville	OHL	47	21	28	49	91	...	...	...		11	2	10	12	15
90-91—Belleville	OHL	3	2	1	3	2	...	...	...		6	0	7	7	14
—Newmarket	AHL	5	1	0	1	4	...	...	...		—	—	—	—	—
—Toronto	NHL	33	1	3	4	30	-15	0	0		—	—	—	—	—
91-92—Edmonton	NHL	15	0	1	1	43	-6	0	0		1	0	0	0	0
—Cape Breton..............	AHL	49	9	14	23	40	...	...	...		5	1	0	1	8
92-93—Cape Breton.............	AHL	58	23	27	50	102	...	...	...		16	1	2	3	35
—Edmonton	NHL	9	0	1	1	0	-4	0	0		—	—	—	—	—
93-94—Edmonton	NHL	61	4	7	11	104	-15	0	0		—	—	—	—	—
—Cape Breton..............	AHL	2	1	1	2	31	...	...	...		—	—	—	—	—
94-95—Edmonton	NHL	47	10	12	22	89	-4	0	1		—	—	—	—	—
95-96—Edmonton	NHL	77	9	9	18	149	-25	0	2		—	—	—	—	—
96-97—Montreal	NHL	73	10	10	20	128	-19	1	1		5	1	0	1	2
97-98—Montreal	NHL	67	6	9	15	158	0	1	0		9	0	2	2	10
98-99—Montreal	NHL	47	7	4	11	87	-2	1	0		—	—	—	—	—
99-00—Montreal	NHL	35	2	3	5	70	-7	0	0		—	—	—	—	—
—Dallas........................	NHL	30	6	3	9	38	-5	1	0		†23	2	7	9	28
00-01—San Jose..................	NHL	73	19	17	36	114	4	4	0		6	3	0	3	8
NHL Totals (11 years).........		567	74	79	153	1010	-98	8	4		44	6	9	15	48

TIBBETTS, BILLY   RW   PENGUINS

PERSONAL: Born October 14, 1974, in Boston. ... 6-2/215. ... Shoots right.
TRANSACTIONS/CAREER NOTES: Signed as non-drafted free agent by Pittsburgh Penguins (April 10, 2000). ... Suspended four games by NHL for fighting (January 29, 2001). ... Suspended one game by NHL for kneeing incident (February 21, 2001). ... Suffered from the flu (March 14, 2001); missed one game.

			REGULAR SEASON								PLAYOFFS				
Season Team	League	Gms.	G	A	Pts.	PIM	+/-	PP	SH		Gms.	G	A	Pts.	PIM
93-94—Tri-City	WHL	9	0	2	2	39	...	...	...		—	—	—	—	—
94-95—Birmingham................	ECHL	2	0	1	1	18	...	...	...		—	—	—	—	—
95-96—Johnstown.................	ECHL	58	37	31	68	300	...	...	...		—	—	—	—	—
96-97—							Did not play.								
97-98—							Did not play.								
98-99—							Did not play.								
99-00—							Did not play.								
00-01—Wilkes-Barre/Scranton	AHL	38	14	24	38	185	...	...	...		12	4	6	10	55
—Pittsburgh..................	NHL	29	1	2	3	79	-2	0	0		—	—	—	—	—
NHL Totals (1 year)............		29	1	2	3	79	-2	0	0						

TILEY, BRAD   D   FLYERS

PERSONAL: Born July 5, 1971, in Markdale, Ont. ... 6-1/185. ... Shoots left. ... Name pronounced TIGH-lee.
TRANSACTIONS/CAREER NOTES: Selected by Boston Bruins in fourth round (fourth Bruins pick, 84th overall) of NHL entry draft (June 22, 1991). ... Signed as free agent by New York Rangers (September 4, 1992). ... Traded by Rangers to Los Angeles Kings for 11th-round pick (LW Jamie Butt) in 1994 draft (January 28, 1994). ... Signed as free agent by Phoenix Coyotes (September 5, 1997). ... Signed as free agent by Philadelphia Flyers (July 14, 2000).
HONORS: Won Eddie Shore Plaque (1999-2000). ... Named to AHL All-Star first team (1999-2000).

			REGULAR SEASON								PLAYOFFS				
Season Team	League	Gms.	G	A	Pts.	PIM	+/-	PP	SH		Gms.	G	A	Pts.	PIM
87-88—Owen Sound Jr. B.......	OHA	40	19	25	44	68	...	...	...		—	—	—	—	—
88-89—Sault Ste. Marie	OHL	50	4	11	15	31	...	...	...		—	—	—	—	—
89-90—Sault Ste. Marie	OHL	66	9	32	41	47	...	...	...		—	—	—	—	—
90-91—Sault Ste. Marie	OHL	66	11	55	66	29	...	...	...		—	—	—	—	—
91-92—Maine	AHL	62	7	22	29	36	...	...	...		—	—	—	—	—
92-93—Binghamton	AHL	26	6	10	16	19	...	...	...		8	0	1	1	2
—Phoenix....................	IHL	46	11	27	38	35	...	...	...		—	—	—	—	—
93-94—Binghamton	AHL	29	6	10	16	6	...	...	...		—	—	—	—	—
—Phoenix....................	IHL	35	8	15	23	21	...	...	...		—	—	—	—	—
94-95—Detroit.......................	IHL	56	7	19	26	32	...	...	...		—	—	—	—	—
—Fort Wayne	IHL	14	1	6	7	2	...	...	...		3	1	2	3	0

Season Team	League	REGULAR SEASON								PLAYOFFS				
		Gms.	G	A	Pts.	PIM	+/-	PP	SH	Gms.	G	A	Pts.	PIM
95-96—Orlando	IHL	69	11	23	34	82	...	...	...	23	2	4	6	16
96-97—Phoenix	IHL	66	8	28	36	34	...	...	...	—	—	—	—	—
—Long Beach	IHL	3	1	0	1	2	...	...	...	—	—	—	—	—
97-98—Springfield	AHL	60	10	31	41	36	...	...	...	4	0	4	4	2
—Phoenix	NHL	1	0	0	0	0	1	0	0	—	—	—	—	—
98-99—Springfield	AHL	69	9	35	44	14	...	...	...	1	0	0	0	0
—Phoenix	NHL	8	0	0	0	0	-1	0	0	1	0	0	0	0
99-00—Springfield	AHL	80	14	54	68	51	...	...	...	5	0	4	4	2
00-01—Philadelphia	AHL	56	11	19	30	10	...	...	...	10	1	2	3	2
—Philadelphia	NHL	2	0	0	0	0	-1	0	0	—	—	—	—	—
NHL Totals (3 years)		11	0	0	0	0	-1	0	0	1	0	0	0	0

TIMANDER, MATTIAS · D · BLUE JACKETS

PERSONAL: Born April 16, 1974, in Solleftea, Sweden. ... 6-3/215. ... Shoots left. ... Name pronounced tih-MAN-duhr.
TRANSACTIONS/CAREER NOTES: Selected by Boston Bruins in seventh round (seventh Bruins pick, 208th overall) of NHL entry draft (June 21, 1992). ... Injured shoulder (November 26, 1996); missed four games. ... Injured finger (November 17, 1997); missed two games. ... Injured shoulder (March 2, 1999); missed two games. ... Reinjured shoulder (March 13, 1999); missed one game. ... Injured shoulder (November 22, 1999); missed 11 games. ... Selected by Columbus Blue Jackets in NHL expansion draft (June 23, 2000). ... Strained neck (December 16, 2000); missed five games. ... Suffered neck spasms (February 14, 2001); missed one game.

Season Team	League	REGULAR SEASON								PLAYOFFS				
		Gms.	G	A	Pts.	PIM	+/-	PP	SH	Gms.	G	A	Pts.	PIM
92-93—MoDo Ornskoldsvik	Sweden	1	0	0	0	0	...	...	...	—	—	—	—	—
93-94—MoDo Ornskoldsvik	Sweden	23	2	2	4	6	...	...	...	11	2	0	2	10
94-95—MoDo Ornskoldsvik	Sweden	39	8	9	17	24	...	...	...	—	—	—	—	—
95-96—MoDo Ornskoldsvik	Sweden	37	4	10	14	34	...	...	...	7	1	1	2	8
96-97—Boston	NHL	41	1	8	9	14	-9	0	0	—	—	—	—	—
—Providence	AHL	32	3	11	14	20	...	...	...	10	1	1	2	12
97-98—Boston	NHL	23	1	1	2	6	-9	0	0	—	—	—	—	—
—Providence	AHL	31	3	7	10	25	...	...	...	—	—	—	—	—
98-99—Providence	AHL	43	2	22	24	24	...	...	...	—	—	—	—	—
—Boston	NHL	22	0	6	6	10	4	0	0	4	1	1	2	2
99-00—Boston	NHL	60	0	8	8	22	-11	0	0	—	—	—	—	—
—Hershey	AHL	1	0	0	0	2	...	...	...	—	—	—	—	—
00-01—Columbus	NHL	76	2	9	11	24	-8	0	0	—	—	—	—	—
NHL Totals (5 years)		222	4	32	36	76	-33	0	0	4	1	1	2	2

TIMONEN, KIMMO · D · PREDATORS

PERSONAL: Born March 18, 1975, in Kuopio, Finland. ... 5-10/196. ... Shoots left. ... Brother of Jussi Timonen, defenseman, Philadelphia Flyers organization. ... Name pronounced KEE-moh TEE-muh-nehn.
TRANSACTIONS/CAREER NOTES: Selected by Los Angeles Kings in 10th round (11th Kings pick, 250th overall) of NHL entry draft (June 26, 1993). ... Rights traded by Kings with D Jan Vopat to Nashville Predators for future considerations (June 26, 1998). ... Lacerated lip (January 26, 1999); missed one game. ... Strained abdominal muscle (December 18, 1999); missed four games. ... Fractured wrist (January 11, 2000); missed 15 games. ... Fractured ankle (March 14, 2000); missed 12 games of season.
HONORS: Named to play in NHL All-Star Game (2000); missed game due to injury.
MISCELLANEOUS: Scored on a penalty shot (vs. Jeff Hackett, November 18, 1999).

Season Team	League	REGULAR SEASON								PLAYOFFS				
		Gms.	G	A	Pts.	PIM	+/-	PP	SH	Gms.	G	A	Pts.	PIM
91-92—KalPa Kuopio	Finland	5	0	0	0	0	...	...	...	—	—	—	—	—
92-93—KalPa Kuopio	Finland	33	0	2	2	4	...	...	...	—	—	—	—	—
93-94—KalPa Kuopio	Finland	46	6	7	13	55	...	...	...	—	—	—	—	—
94-95—TPS Turku	Finland	45	3	4	7	10	...	...	...	13	0	1	1	6
95-96—TPS Turku	Finland	48	3	21	24	22	...	...	...	9	1	2	3	12
96-97—TPS Turku	Finland	50	10	14	24	18	...	...	...	12	2	7	9	8
97-98—HIFK Helsinki	Finland	45	10	15	25	59	...	...	...	9	3	4	7	8
—Fin. Olympic team	Int'l	6	0	1	1	2	...	...	...	—	—	—	—	—
98-99—Milwaukee	IHL	29	2	13	15	22	...	...	...	—	—	—	—	—
—Nashville	NHL	50	4	8	12	30	-4	1	0	—	—	—	—	—
99-00—Nashville	NHL	51	8	25	33	26	-5	2	1	—	—	—	—	—
00-01—Nashville	NHL	82	12	13	25	50	-6	6	0	—	—	—	—	—
NHL Totals (3 years)		183	24	46	70	106	-15	9	1					

TITOV, GERMAN · C · MIGHTY DUCKS

PERSONAL: Born October 15, 1965, in Moscow, U.S.S.R. ... 6-1/201. ... Shoots left. ... Name pronounced GAIR-muhn TEE-tahf.
TRANSACTIONS/CAREER NOTES: Selected by Calgary Flames in 10th round (10th Flames pick, 252nd overall) of NHL entry draft (June 26, 1993). ... Fractured nose (December 31, 1993); missed four games. ... Bruised hand (February 18, 1994); missed two games. ... Bruised hand (April 2, 1994); missed one game. ... Played in Europe during 1994-95 NHL lockout. ... Pulled groin (March 28, 1995); missed eight games. ... Sore lower back (October 13, 1996); missed one game. ... Injured ankle (January 22, 1997); missed one game. ... Reinjured ankle (March , 1997); missed one game. ... Bruised hand (March 11, 1998); missed two games. ... Injured knee (April 7, 1998); missed final six games of season. ... Traded by Flames with C Todd Hlushko to Pittsburgh Penguins for G Ken Wregget and LW Dave Roche (June 17, 1998). ... Injured finger (November 19, 1998); missed one game. ... Bruised knee (November 25, 1998); missed two games. ... Strained hamstring (March 25, 1999); missed three games. ... Reinjured hamstring (April 5, 1999); missed three games. ... Strained groin and suffered from the flu (January 1, 2000); missed six games. ... Traded by Penguins to Edmonton Oilers for C Josef Beranek (March 14, 2000). ... Strained shoulder (March

25, 2000); missed five games. ... Signed as free agent by Mighty Ducks of Anaheim (July 1, 2000). ... Injured chest (October 20, 2000); missed three games. ... Bruised foot (November 11, 2000); missed one game. ... Suffered from headaches (November 24, 2000); missed three games. ... Bruised shoulder (February 11, 2001); missed four games.

MISCELLANEOUS: Member of silver-medal-winning Russian Olympic team (1998).

STATISTICAL PLATEAUS: Three-goal games: 1994-95 (1), 1996-97 (1). Total: 2.

| Season Team | League | REGULAR SEASON | | | | | | | | PLAYOFFS | | | | |
		Gms.	G	A	Pts.	PIM	+/-	PP	SH	Gms.	G	A	Pts.	PIM
82-83—Khimik	USSR	16	0	2	2	4	...	...	...					
83-84—Khimik	USSR				Did not play.									
84-85—Khimik	USSR				Did not play.									
85-86—Khimik	USSR				Did not play.									
86-87—Khimik	USSR	23	1	0	1	10	...	...	...	—	—	—	—	—
87-88—Khimik	USSR	39	6	5	11	10	...	...	...	—	—	—	—	—
88-89—Khimik	USSR	44	10	3	13	24	...	...	...	—	—	—	—	—
89-90—Khimik	USSR	44	6	14	20	19	...	...	...	—	—	—	—	—
90-91—Khimik	USSR	45	13	11	24	28	...	...	...	—	—	—	—	—
91-92—Khimik	CIS	42	18	13	31	35	...	...	...	—	—	—	—	—
92-93—TPS Turku	Finland	47	25	19	44	49	...	...	...	—	—	—	—	—
93-94—Calgary	NHL	76	27	18	45	28	20	8	3	7	2	1	3	4
94-95—TPS Turku	Finland	14	6	6	12	20	...	...	...	—	—	—	—	—
—Calgary	NHL	40	12	12	24	16	6	3	2	7	5	3	8	10
95-96—Calgary	NHL	82	28	39	67	24	9	13	2	4	0	2	2	0
96-97—Calgary	NHL	79	22	30	52	36	-12	12	0	—	—	—	—	—
97-98—Calgary	NHL	68	18	22	40	38	-1	6	1	—	—	—	—	—
—Russian Oly. team	Int'l	6	1	0	1	6	...	...	...	—	—	—	—	—
98-99—Pittsburgh	NHL	72	11	45	56	34	18	3	1	11	3	5	8	4
99-00—Pittsburgh	NHL	63	17	25	42	34	-3	4	2	—	—	—	—	—
—Edmonton	NHL	7	0	4	4	4	2	0	0	5	1	1	2	0
00-01—Anaheim	NHL	71	9	11	20	61	-21	1	0	—	—	—	—	—
NHL Totals (8 years)		558	144	206	350	275	18	50	11	34	11	12	23	18

TJARNQVIST, DANIEL   D   THRASHERS

PERSONAL: Born October 14, 1976, in Umea, Sweden. ... 6-2/180. ... Shoots left. ... Brother of Mathias Tjarnqvist, center, Dallas Stars organization. ... Name pronounced TAHRN-kuh-vihst.

TRANSACTIONS/CAREER NOTES: Selected by Florida Panthers in fourth round (fifth Panthers pick, 88th overall) of NHL entry draft (July 8, 1995). ... Traded by Panthers with D Gord Murphy, C Herbert Vasiljevs and sixth-round pick (traded to Dallas) in 1999 draft to Atlanta Thrashers for G Trevor Kidd (June 25, 1999).

| Season Team | League | REGULAR SEASON | | | | | | | | PLAYOFFS | | | | |
		Gms.	G	A	Pts.	PIM	+/-	PP	SH	Gms.	G	A	Pts.	PIM
94-95—Rogle Angelholm	Sweden	33	2	4	6	2	...	...	...	—	—	—	—	—
95-96—Rogle Angelholm	Sweden	22	1	7	8	6	...	...	...	—	—	—	—	—
96-97—Jokerit Helsinki	Finland	44	3	8	11	4	...	...	...	9	0	3	3	4
97-98—Djurgarden Stockholm	Sweden	40	5	9	14	12	...	...	...	15	1	1	2	2
98-99—Djurgarden Stockholm	Sweden	40	4	3	7	16	...	...	...	4	0	0	0	2
99-00—Djurgarden Stockholm	Sweden	42	3	16	19	8	...	...	...	5	0	0	0	2
00-01—Djurgarden Stockholm	Sweden	45	9	17	26	26	...	...	...	16	6	5	11	2

TKACHUK, KEITH   LW   BLUES

PERSONAL: Born March 28, 1972, in Melrose, Mass. ... 6-2/225. ... Shoots left. ... Full Name: Keith Matthew Tkachuk. ... Cousin of Tom Fitzgerald, right winger, Nashville Predators. ... Name pronounced kuh-CHUHK.

TRANSACTIONS/CAREER NOTES: Selected by Winnipeg Jets in first round (first Jets pick, 19th overall) of NHL entry draft (June 16, 1990). ... Lacerated forearm (November 12, 1993); missed one game. ... Strained groin (October 9, 1995); missed three games. ... Suffered concussion (November 26, 1995); missed one game. ... Suspended two games and fined $1,000 by NHL for stick-swinging incident (March 16, 1996). ... Jets franchise moved to Phoenix and renamed Coyotes for 1996-97 season; NHL approved move on January 18, 1996. ... Suffered from the flu (March 5, 1997); missed one game. ... Injured groin (March 2, 1998); missed two games. ... Suffered hairline fracture of rib (March 12, 1998); missed seven games. ... Injured groin (December 14, 1998); missed two games. ... Fractured ribs (December 20, 1998) missed eight games. ... Strained lower back (February 2, 1999); missed two games. ... Injured neck (December 4, 1999); missed three games. ... Suffered back spasms (December 26, 1999); missed four games. ... Sprained ankle (January 31, 2000); missed one game. ... Sprained ankle (February 12, 2000); missed 16 games. ... Suspended two games by NHL for high-sticking incident (March 24, 2000). ... Sprained ankle (March 29, 2000); missed final six games of regular season. ... Strained groin (October 12, 2000); missed one game. ... Suffered injury (October 30, 2000); missed one game. ... Suffered concussion (January 26, 2001); missed two games. ... Suffered injury (February 9, 2001) missed one game. ... Traded by Coyotes to St. Louis Blues for C Michal Handzus, RW Ladislav Nagy, C Jeff Taffe and first-round pick in 2002 draft (March 13, 2001).

HONORS: Named to Hockey East All-Rookie team (1990-91). ... Named to NHL All-Star second team (1994-95 and 1997-98). ... Named to THE SPORTING NEWS All-Star first team (1995-96). ... Played in NHL All-Star Game (1997-1999).

MISCELLANEOUS: Captain of Winnipeg Jets (1993-94 and 1994-95). ... Captain of Phoenix Coyotes (1996-97 through 2000-March 13, 2001). ... Holds Phoenix Coyotes franchise all-time record for penalty minutes (1,508). ... Scored on a penalty shot (vs. Jean-Sebastien Aubin, January 12, 2000). ... Failed to score on a penalty shot (vs. Bob Essensa, January 24, 1998).

STATISTICAL PLATEAUS: Three-goal games: 1993-94 (1), 1996-97 (1), 1997-98 (3), 1998-99 (1), 2000-01 (1). Total: 7. ... Four-goal games 1995-96 (1), 1996-97 (1). Total: 2. ... Total hat tricks: 9.

| Season Team | League | REGULAR SEASON | | | | | | | | PLAYOFFS | | | | |
		Gms.	G	A	Pts.	PIM	+/-	PP	SH	Gms.	G	A	Pts.	PIM
88-89—Malden Catholic H.S.	Mass. H.S.	21	30	16	46	...	...	...	...	—	—	—	—	—
89-90—Malden Catholic H.S.	Mass. H.S.	6	12	14	26	...	...	...	...	—	—	—	—	—
90-91—Boston University	Hockey East	36	17	23	40	70	...	...	...	—	—	—	—	—

Season Team	League	REGULAR SEASON								PLAYOFFS				
		Gms.	G	A	Pts.	PIM	+/-	PP	SH	Gms.	G	A	Pts.	PIM
91-92—U.S. national team	Int'l	45	10	10	20	141	...	...	...	—	—	—	—	—
—U.S. Olympic team	Int'l	8	1	1	2	12	...	...	...	—	—	—	—	—
—Winnipeg	NHL	17	3	5	8	28	0	2	0	7	3	0	3	30
92-93—Winnipeg	NHL	83	28	23	51	201	-13	12	0	6	4	0	4	14
93-94—Winnipeg	NHL	84	41	40	81	255	-12	22	3	—	—	—	—	—
94-95—Winnipeg	NHL	48	22	29	51	152	-4	7	2	—	—	—	—	—
95-96—Winnipeg	NHL	76	50	48	98	156	11	20	2	6	1	2	3	22
96-97—Phoenix	NHL	81	*52	34	86	228	-1	9	2	7	6	0	6	7
97-98—Phoenix	NHL	69	40	26	66	147	9	11	0	6	3	3	6	10
—U.S. Olympic team	Int'l	4	0	2	2	6	...	...	...	—	—	—	—	—
98-99—Phoenix	NHL	68	36	32	68	151	22	11	2	7	1	3	4	13
99-00—Phoenix	NHL	50	22	21	43	82	7	5	1	5	1	1	2	4
00-01—Phoenix	NHL	64	29	42	71	108	6	15	0	—	—	—	—	—
—St. Louis	NHL	12	6	2	8	14	-3	2	0	15	2	7	9	20
NHL Totals (10 years)		652	329	302	631	1522	22	116	12	59	21	16	37	120

TKACZUK, DANIEL   C   BLUES

PERSONAL: Born June 10, 1979, in Toronto. ... 6-1/197. ... Shoots left. ... Name pronounced kuh-CHOOK.

TRANSACTIONS/CAREER NOTES: Selected by Calgary Flames in first round (first Flames pick, sixth overall) of NHL entry draft (June 21, 1997). ... Suffered head injury (January 23, 2001); missed seven games. ... Traded by Flames with G Fred Brathwaite, RW Sergei Varlamov and ninth-round pick (C Grant Jacobsen) in 2001 draft to St. Louis Blues for G Roman Turek and fourth-round pick (F Egor Shastin) in 2001 draft (June 23, 2001).

HONORS: Named to OHL All-Star first team (1998-99). ... Named to Can.HL All-Star second team (1998-99).

Season Team	League	REGULAR SEASON								PLAYOFFS				
		Gms.	G	A	Pts.	PIM	+/-	PP	SH	Gms.	G	A	Pts.	PIM
95-96—Barrie	OHL	61	22	39	61	38	...	...	...	7	1	2	3	8
96-97—Barrie	OHL	62	45	48	93	49	...	...	...	9	7	2	9	2
97-98—Barrie	OHL	57	35	40	75	38	...	...	...	6	2	3	5	8
98-99—Barrie	OHL	58	43	62	105	58	...	...	...	12	7	8	15	10
99-00—Saint John	AHL	80	25	41	66	56	...	...	...	3	0	0	0	0
00-01—Saint John	AHL	50	15	21	36	48	...	...	...	14	10	9	19	4
—Calgary	NHL	19	4	7	11	14	1	1	0	—	—	—	—	—
NHL Totals (1 year)		19	4	7	11	14	1	1	0					

TOCCHET, RICK   RW   FLYERS

PERSONAL: Born April 9, 1964, in Scarborough, Ont. ... 6-0/210. ... Shoots right. ... Name pronounced TAH-kiht.

TRANSACTIONS/CAREER NOTES: Selected by Philadelphia Flyers in sixth round (fifth Flyers pick, 121st overall) of NHL entry draft (June 8, 1983). ... Bruised right knee (November 23, 1985); missed seven games. ... Separated left shoulder (February 1988). ... Suspended 10 games by NHL for injuring an opposing player during a fight (October 27, 1988). ... Hyperextended right knee (April 21, 1989). ... Suffered viral infection (November 1989). ... Tore tendon in left groin (January 26, 1991); missed five games. ... Reinjured groin (March 1991); missed five games. ... Sprained knee (November 29, 1991); missed five games. ... Bruised heel (January 18, 1991); missed 10 games. ... Traded by Flyers with G Ken Wregget, D Kjell Samuelsson and third-round pick (C Dave Roche) in 1993 draft to Pittsburgh Penguins for RW Mark Recchi, D Brian Benning and first-round pick (LW Jason Bowen) in 1992 draft (February 19, 1992). ... Fractured jaw (March 15, 1992); missed three games. ... Bruised left foot (October 1, 1992); missed two games. ... Bruised foot (February 8, 1993); missed one game. ... Bruised ribs (November 13, 1993); missed two games. ... Suffered back spasms (December 2, 1993); missed two games. ... Suffered back spasms (December 31, 1993); missed 12 games. ... Injured back (February 21, 1994); missed one game. ... Injured back (February 28, 1994); missed 10 games. ... Traded by Penguins with second-round pick (RW Pavel Rosa) in 1995 draft to Los Angeles Kings for LW Luc Robitaille (July 29, 1994). ... Strained lower back (April 1, 1995); missed five games. ... Suffered back spasms (April 17, 1995); missed six games. ... Suffered back spasms (May 3, 1995); missed one game. ... Traded by Kings to Boston Bruins for LW Kevin Stevens (January 25, 1996). ... Bruised shoulder (November 7, 1996); missed two games. ... Strained knee (November 26, 1996); missed 17 games. ... Traded by Bruins with C Adam Oates and G Bill Ranford to Washington Capitals for G Jim Carey, C Jason Allison, C Anson Carter and third-round pick (RW Lee Goren) in 1997 draft (March 1, 1997). ... Bruised foot (March 1, 1997); missed three games. ... Strained back (April 6, 1997); missed four games. ... Injured thumb (October 13, 1997); missed four games. ... Signed as free agent by Phoenix Coyotes (July 8, 1997). ... Suspended two games and fined $1,000 by NHL for injuring another player (January 23, 1998). ... Suspended five games by NHL for illegal check (January 30, 1998). ... Suspended two games and fined $1,000 by NHL for high-sticking incident (April 14, 1998). ... Traded by Coyotes to Flyers for RW Mikael Renberg (March 8, 2000). ... Bruised ankle (October 29, 2000); missed two games. ... Suffered from the flu (December 12, 2000); missed two games. ... Bruised hand (January 2, 2001); missed four games. ... Strained groin (February 22, 2001); missed six games. ... Strained lower back (April 3, 2001); missed final three games of season.

HONORS: Played in NHL All-Star Game (1989-1991 and 1993).

RECORDS: Shares NHL All-Star Game record for fastest goal from start of period—19 seconds (1993, second period).

STATISTICAL PLATEAUS: Three-goal games: 1987-88 (2), 1988-89 (2), 1989-90 (1), 1990-91 (1), 1991-92 (1), 1992-93 (2), 1994-95 (1), 1995-96 (1). Total: 12. ... Four-goal games: 1987-88 (1), 1989-90 (1). Total: 2. ... Total hat tricks: 14.

MISCELLANEOUS: Member of Stanley Cup championship team (1992). ... Captain of Philadelphia Flyers (1991-92). ... Holds Philadelphia Flyers all-time record for most penalty minutes (1,766). ... Failed to score on a penalty shot (vs. Craig Billington, January 6, 1987; vs. Geoff Sarjeant, March 18, 1996).

Season Team	League	REGULAR SEASON								PLAYOFFS				
		Gms.	G	A	Pts.	PIM	+/-	PP	SH	Gms.	G	A	Pts.	PIM
81-82—Sault Ste. Marie	OHL	59	7	15	22	184	...	...	...	11	1	1	2	28
82-83—Sault Ste. Marie	OHL	66	32	34	66	146	...	...	...	16	4	13	17	*67
83-84—Sault Ste. Marie	OHL	64	44	64	108	209	...	...	...	16	*22	14	†36	41
84-85—Philadelphia	NHL	75	14	25	39	181	6	0	0	19	3	4	7	72
85-86—Philadelphia	NHL	69	14	21	35	284	12	3	0	5	1	2	3	26
86-87—Philadelphia	NHL	69	21	26	47	288	16	1	1	26	11	10	21	72
87-88—Philadelphia	NHL	65	31	33	64	301	3	10	2	5	1	4	5	55
88-89—Philadelphia	NHL	66	45	36	81	183	-1	16	1	16	6	6	12	69
89-90—Philadelphia	NHL	75	37	59	96	196	4	15	1	—	—	—	—	—

Season Team	League	Gms.	G	A	Pts.	PIM	+/-	PP	SH	Gms.	G	A	Pts.	PIM
		REGULAR SEASON								**PLAYOFFS**				
90-91—Philadelphia	NHL	70	40	31	71	150	2	8	0	—	—	—	—	—
91-92—Philadelphia	NHL	42	13	16	29	102	3	4	0	—	—	—	—	—
—Pittsburgh	NHL	19	14	16	30	49	12	4	1	14	6	13	19	24
92-93—Pittsburgh	NHL	80	48	61	109	252	28	20	4	12	7	6	13	24
93-94—Pittsburgh	NHL	51	14	26	40	134	-15	5	1	6	2	3	5	20
94-95—Los Angeles	NHL	36	18	17	35	70	-8	7	1	—	—	—	—	—
95-96—Los Angeles	NHL	44	13	23	36	117	3	4	0	—	—	—	—	—
—Boston	NHL	27	16	8	24	64	7	6	0	5	4	0	4	21
96-97—Boston	NHL	40	16	14	30	67	-3	3	0	—	—	—	—	—
—Washington	NHL	13	5	5	10	31	0	1	0	—	—	—	—	—
97-98—Phoenix	NHL	68	26	19	45	157	1	8	0	6	6	2	8	25
98-99—Phoenix	NHL	81	26	30	56	147	5	6	1	7	0	3	3	8
99-00—Phoenix	NHL	64	12	17	29	67	-5	2	0	—	—	—	—	—
—Philadelphia	NHL	16	3	3	6	23	4	2	0	18	5	6	11	*49
00-01—Philadelphia	NHL	60	14	22	36	83	10	5	0	6	0	1	1	6
NHL Totals (17 years)		1130	440	508	948	2946	84	130	13	145	52	60	112	471

TOMS, JEFF   LW   RANGERS

PERSONAL: Born June 4, 1974, in Swift Current, Sask. ... 6-5/213. ... Shoots left.
TRANSACTIONS/CAREER NOTES: Selected by New Jersey Devils in ninth round (10th Devils pick, 210th overall) of NHL entry draft (June 26, 1993). ... Traded by Devils to Tampa Bay Lightning for fourth-round pick (traded to Calgary) in 1994 draft (May 31, 1994). ... Claimed on waivers by Washington Capitals (November 19, 1997). ... Sprained knee (December 12, 1997); missed 11 games. ... Strained abdominal muscle (January 7, 1999); missed 30 games. ... Signed as free agent by New York Islanders (July 27, 2000). ... Claimed on waivers by New York Rangers (January 13, 2001).

Season Team	League	Gms.	G	A	Pts.	PIM	+/-	PP	SH	Gms.	G	A	Pts.	PIM
		REGULAR SEASON								**PLAYOFFS**				
91-92—Sault Ste. Marie	OHL	36	9	5	14	0	...	...	...	16	0	1	1	2
92-93—Sault Ste. Marie	OHL	59	16	23	39	20	...	...	...	16	4	4	8	7
93-94—Sault Ste. Marie	OHL	64	52	45	97	19	...	...	...	14	11	4	15	2
94-95—Atlanta	IHL	40	7	8	15	10	...	...	...	4	0	0	0	4
95-96—Atlanta	IHL	68	16	18	34	18	...	...	...	1	0	0	0	0
—Tampa Bay	NHL	1	0	0	0	0	0	0	0	—	—	—	—	—
96-97—Adirondack	AHL	37	11	16	27	8	...	...	...	4	1	2	3	0
—Tampa Bay	NHL	34	2	8	10	10	2	0	0	—	—	—	—	—
97-98—Tampa Bay	NHL	13	1	2	3	7	-6	0	0	—	—	—	—	—
—Washington	NHL	33	3	4	7	8	-11	0	0	1	0	0	0	0
98-99—Portland	AHL	20	3	7	10	8	...	...	...	—	—	—	—	—
—Washington	NHL	21	1	5	6	2	0	0	0	—	—	—	—	—
99-00—Washington	NHL	20	1	2	3	4	-1	0	0	—	—	—	—	—
—Portland	AHL	33	16	21	37	16	...	...	...	4	1	1	2	2
00-01—New York Islanders	NHL	39	2	4	6	10	-7	0	0	—	—	—	—	—
—Springfield	AHL	5	6	5	11	0	...	...	...	—	—	—	—	—
—New York Rangers	NHL	15	1	1	2	0	-3	0	0	—	—	—	—	—
—Hartford	AHL	12	4	9	13	2	...	...	...	5	6	0	6	2
NHL Totals (6 years)		176	11	26	37	41	-26	0	0	1	0	0	0	0

TORRES, RAFFI   LW   ISLANDERS

PERSONAL: Born October 8, 1981, in Toronto. ... 6-0/207. ... Shoots left.
TRANSACTIONS/CAREER NOTES: Selected by New York Islanders in first round (second Islanders pick, fifth overall) of NHL entry draft (June 24, 2000).
HONORS: Named to OHL All-Star second team (1999-2000 and 2000-01).

Season Team	League	Gms.	G	A	Pts.	PIM	+/-	PP	SH	Gms.	G	A	Pts.	PIM
		REGULAR SEASON								**PLAYOFFS**				
97-98—Thornhill	Jr. A	46	17	16	33	90	...	...	...	—	—	—	—	—
98-99—Brampton	OHL	62	35	27	62	32	...	...	...	—	—	—	—	—
99-00—Brampton	OHL	68	43	48	91	40	...	...	...	6	5	2	7	23
00-01—Brampton	OHL	55	33	37	70	76	...	...	...	8	7	4	11	19

TOSKALA, VESA   G   SHARKS

PERSONAL: Born May 20, 1977, in Tampere, Finland. ... 5-9/172. ... Catches left.
TRANSACTIONS/CAREER NOTES: Selected by San Jose Sharks in fourth round (fourth Sharks pick, 90th overall) of NHL entry draft (July 8, 1995).

Season Team	League	Gms.	Min	W	L	T	GA	SO	Avg.	Gms.	Min.	W	L	GA	SO	Avg.
		REGULAR SEASON								**PLAYOFFS**						
93-94—Ilves	Finland Jrs.	2	...	...	...	...	...	...	...	—	—	—	—	—	—	—
94-95—Ilves	Finland Jrs.	17	956	...	...	...	36	...	2.26	—	—	—	—	—	—	—
95-96—Ilves Tampere	Finland	37	2073	...	...	...	109	1	3.15	2	78	...	...	11	0	8.46
—Koo Vee	Finland	2	119	...	...	...	5	...	2.52	—	—	—	—	—	—	—
—Ilves	Finland Jrs.	3	180	...	...	...	3	...	1.00	—	—	—	—	—	—	—
96-97—Ilves Tampere	Finland	40	2270	22	12	5	108	0	2.85	8	479	3	5	29	0	3.63
97-98—Ilves Tampere	Finland	48	2555	26	13	3	118	1	2.77	9	519	6	3	18	1	2.08
98-99—Ilves Tampere	Finland	33	1966	21	12	0	70	†5	2.14	4	248	1	3	14	...	3.39
99-00—Farjestad Karlstad	Sweden	44	2652	...	...	...	118	3	2.67	7	439	...	...	19	0	2.60
00-01—Kentucky	AHL	44	2466	22	13	5	114	2	2.77	3	197	0	3	8	0	2.44

TRAVERSE, PATRICK   D   CANADIENS

PERSONAL: Born March 14, 1974, in Montreal. ... 6-4/200. ... Shoots left.

TRANSACTIONS/CAREER NOTES: Selected by Ottawa Senators in third round (third Senators pick, 50th overall) of NHL entry draft (June 20, 1992). ... Suffered concussion (January 30, 1999); missed three games. ... Sprained shoulder (February 20, 1999); missed 13 games. ... Bruised right shoulder (February 17, 2000); missed seven games. ... Traded by Senators to Mighty Ducks of Anaheim for D Joel Kwiatkowski (June 12, 2000). ... Traded by Mighty Ducks with LW Andrei Nazarov to Boston Bruins for C Samuel Pahlsson (November 19, 2000). ... Traded by Bruins to Montreal Canadiens for D Eric Weinrich (February 21, 2001). ... Injured neck (April 5, 2001); missed final game of season.

		REGULAR SEASON								PLAYOFFS				
Season Team	League	Gms.	G	A	Pts.	PIM	+/-	PP	SH	Gms.	G	A	Pts.	PIM
91-92—Shawinigan	QMJHL	59	3	11	14	12	...	...	...	10	0	0	0	4
92-93—Shawinigan	QMJHL	53	5	24	29	24	...	...	...	—	—	—	—	—
—New Haven	AHL	2	0	0	0	2	...	...	...	—	—	—	—	—
—St. Jean	QMJHL	15	1	6	7	0	...	...	...	4	0	1	1	2
93-94—Prin. Edward Island	AHL	3	0	1	1	2	...	...	...	—	—	—	—	—
—St. Jean	QMJHL	66	15	37	52	30	...	...	...	5	0	4	4	4
94-95—Prin. Edward Island	AHL	70	5	13	18	19	...	...	...	7	0	2	2	0
95-96—Prin. Edward Island	AHL	55	4	21	25	32	...	...	...	5	1	2	3	2
—Ottawa	NHL	5	0	0	0	2	-1	0	0	—	—	—	—	—
96-97—Worcester	AHL	24	0	4	4	23	...	...	...	—	—	—	—	—
—Grand Rapids	IHL	10	2	1	3	10	...	...	...	2	0	1	1	2
97-98—Hershey	AHL	71	14	15	29	67	...	...	...	7	1	3	4	4
98-99—Ottawa	NHL	46	1	9	10	22	12	0	0	—	—	—	—	—
99-00—Ottawa	NHL	66	6	17	23	21	17	1	0	6	0	0	0	2
00-01—Anaheim	NHL	15	1	0	1	6	-6	0	0	—	—	—	—	—
—Boston	NHL	37	2	6	8	14	4	1	0	—	—	—	—	—
—Montreal	NHL	19	2	3	5	10	-8	0	0	—	—	—	—	—
NHL Totals (4 years)		188	12	35	47	75	18	2	0	6	0	0	0	2

TREBIL, DAN   D

PERSONAL: Born April 10, 1974, in Bloomington, Minn. ... 6-4/212. ... Shoots right. ... Full Name: Daniel Trebil. ... Name pronounced TREH-buhl.

TRANSACTIONS/CAREER NOTES: Selected by New Jersey Devils in sixth round (seventh Devils pick, 138th overall) of NHL entry draft (June 20, 1992). ... Signed as free agent by Mighty Ducks of Anaheim (May 30, 1996). ... Fractured right thumb (October 10, 1997); missed 16 games. ... Traded by Mighty Ducks to Pittsburgh Penguins for fifth-round pick (D Bill Cass) in 2000 draft (March 14, 2000). ... Signed as free agent by New York Islanders (July 28, 2000). ... Traded by Islanders to Penguins for ninth-round pick (F Roman Kuhtinov) in 2001 draft (November 14, 2000). ... Traded by Penguins to St. Louis Blues for D Marc Bergevin (December 28, 2000).

HONORS: Named to NCAA All-America (West) second team (1995-96). ... Named to WCHA All-Star second team (1995-96).

		REGULAR SEASON								PLAYOFFS				
Season Team	League	Gms.	G	A	Pts.	PIM	+/-	PP	SH	Gms.	G	A	Pts.	PIM
89-90—Thomas Jefferson	Minn. H.S.	22	3	6	9	10	...	...	...	—	—	—	—	—
90-91—Thomas Jefferson	Minn. H.S.	23	4	12	16	8	...	...	...	—	—	—	—	—
91-92—Thomas Jefferson	Minn. H.S.	28	7	26	33	6	...	...	...	—	—	—	—	—
92-93—Univ. of Minnesota	WCHA	36	2	11	13	16	...	...	...	—	—	—	—	—
93-94—Univ. of Minnesota	WCHA	42	1	21	22	24	...	...	...	—	—	—	—	—
94-95—Univ. of Minnesota	WCHA	44	10	33	43	10	...	...	...	—	—	—	—	—
95-96—Univ. of Minnesota	WCHA	42	11	35	46	36	...	...	...	—	—	—	—	—
96-97—Baltimore	AHL	49	4	20	24	38	...	...	...	—	—	—	—	—
—Anaheim	NHL	29	3	3	6	23	5	0	0	9	0	1	1	6
97-98—Anaheim	NHL	21	0	1	1	2	-8	0	0	—	—	—	—	—
—Cincinnati	AHL	32	5	15	20	21	...	...	...	—	—	—	—	—
98-99—Cincinnati	AHL	52	6	15	21	31	...	...	...	—	—	—	—	—
—Anaheim	NHL	6	0	0	0	0	-2	0	0	1	0	0	0	2
99-00—Cincinnati	AHL	52	7	21	28	48	...	...	...	—	—	—	—	—
—Pittsburgh	NHL	3	1	0	1	0	2	0	0	—	—	—	—	—
00-01—Chicago	IHL	6	0	2	2	4	...	...	...	—	—	—	—	—
—Pittsburgh	NHL	16	0	0	0	7	-1	0	0	—	—	—	—	—
—St. Louis	NHL	10	0	0	0	0	1	0	0	—	—	—	—	—
—Worcester	AHL	14	2	7	9	0	...	...	...	9	0	5	5	2
NHL Totals (5 years)		85	4	4	8	32	-3	0	0	10	0	1	1	8

TREMBLAY, YANNICK   D   THRASHERS

PERSONAL: Born November 15, 1975, in Pointe-aux-Trembles, Que. ... 6-2/200. ... Shoots right.

TRANSACTIONS/CAREER NOTES: Selected by Toronto Maple Leafs in sixth round (fourth Maple Leafs pick, 145th overall) of NHL entry draft (July 8, 1995). ... Selected by Atlanta Thrashers in NHL expansion draft (June 25, 1999). ... Strained groin (October 23, 1999); missed one game. ... Injured hip (December 8, 1999); missed one game. ... Strained hip flexor (February 7, 2000); missed one game. ... Suffered from the flu (April 8, 2000); missed two games. ... Suffered from the flu (December 11, 2000). ... Injured leg (December 19, 2000); missed three games. ... Reinjured leg (December 28, 2000); missed five games. ... Injured shoulder (February 10, 2001); missed remainder of season.

		REGULAR SEASON								PLAYOFFS				
Season Team	League	Gms.	G	A	Pts.	PIM	+/-	PP	SH	Gms.	G	A	Pts.	PIM
93-94—St. Thomas Univ.	AUAA	25	2	3	5	10	...	...	...	—	—	—	—	—
94-95—Beauport	QMJHL	70	10	32	42	22	...	...	...	17	6	8	14	6
95-96—Beauport	QMJHL	61	12	33	45	42	...	...	...	20	3	16	19	18
—St. John's	AHL	3	0	1	1	0	...	...	...	—	—	—	—	—
96-97—Sherbrooke	QMJHL	42	21	25	46	212	...	...	...	—	—	—	—	—
—St. John's	AHL	67	7	25	32	34	...	...	...	11	2	9	11	0
—Toronto	NHL	5	0	0	0	0	-4	0	0	—	—	—	—	—

Season Team	League	REGULAR SEASON Gms.	G	A	Pts.	PIM	+/-	PP	SH	PLAYOFFS Gms.	G	A	Pts.	PIM
97-98—St. John's...................	AHL	17	3	6	9	4	...	...	...	4	0	1	1	5
—Toronto	NHL	38	2	4	6	6	-6	1	0	—	—	—	—	—
98-99—Toronto	NHL	35	2	7	9	16	0	0	0	—	—	—	—	—
99-00—Atlanta	NHL	75	10	21	31	22	-42	4	1	—	—	—	—	—
00-01—Atlanta	NHL	46	4	8	12	30	-6	1	0	—	—	—	—	—
NHL Totals (5 years)...........		199	18	40	58	74	-58	6	1					

TREPANIER, PASCAL   D

PERSONAL: Born April 9, 1973, in Gaspe, Que. ... 6-0/210. ... Shoots right. ... Name pronounced TREH-puhn-yeh.
TRANSACTIONS/CAREER NOTES: Signed as non-drafted free agent by Colorado Avalanche (August 30, 1996). ... Selected by Mighty Ducks of Anaheim from Avalanche in NHL waiver draft (October 5, 1998). ... Bruised left leg (March 3, 1999); missed one game. ... Injured anterior cruciate ligament and meniscus in right knee (April 6, 1999) and underwent knee surgery; missed remainder of season. ... Suspended five games by NHL for elbowing incident (October 5, 1999). ... Suffered head injury (December 17, 1999); missed six games. ... Bruised left ankle (March 3, 2000); missed nine games.
HONORS: Named to AHL All-Star second team (1996-97).

Season Team	League	REGULAR SEASON Gms.	G	A	Pts.	PIM	+/-	PP	SH	PLAYOFFS Gms.	G	A	Pts.	PIM
90-91—Hull	QMJHL	46	3	3	6	56	...	...	...	4	0	2	2	7
91-92—Trois-Rivieres..............	QMJHL	53	4	18	22	125	...	...	...	15	3	5	8	21
92-93—Sherbrooke	QMJHL	59	15	33	48	130	...	...	...	15	5	7	12	36
93-94—Sherbrooke	QMJHL	48	16	41	57	67	...	...	...	12	1	8	9	14
94-95—Cornwall	AHL	4	0	0	0	9	...	...	...	—	—	—	—	—
—Dayton	ECHL	36	16	28	44	113	...	...	...	—	—	—	—	—
—Kalamazoo	IHL	14	1	2	3	47	...	...	...	—	—	—	—	—
95-96—Cornwall	AHL	70	13	20	33	142	...	...	...	8	1	2	3	24
96-97—Hershey	AHL	73	14	39	53	151	...	...	...	23	6	13	19	59
97-98—Colorado	NHL	15	0	1	1	18	-2	0	0	—	—	—	—	—
—Hershey	AHL	43	13	18	31	105	...	...	...	7	4	2	6	8
98-99—Anaheim	NHL	45	2	4	6	48	0	0	0	—	—	—	—	—
99-00—Anaheim	NHL	37	0	4	4	54	2	0	0	—	—	—	—	—
00-01—Anaheim	NHL	57	6	4	10	73	-12	3	0	—	—	—	—	—
NHL Totals (4 years)...........		154	8	13	21	193	-12	3	0					

TRNKA, PAVEL   D   MIGHTY DUCKS

PERSONAL: Born July 27, 1976, in Plzen, Czechoslovakia. ... 6-3/200. ... Shoots left. ... Name pronounced TRIHN-kuh.
TRANSACTIONS/CAREER NOTES: Selected by Mighty Ducks of Anaheim in fifth round (fifth Mighty Ducks pick, 106th overall) of NHL entry draft (June 29, 1994). ... Suffered concussion (January 12, 1998); missed one game. ... Strained groin (December 8, 1999); missed five games. ... Sprained ankle (March 17, 2000); missed final nine games of season. ... Sprained ankle (October 8, 2000); missed 17 games.

Season Team	League	REGULAR SEASON Gms.	G	A	Pts.	PIM	+/-	PP	SH	PLAYOFFS Gms.	G	A	Pts.	PIM
92-93—Skoda Plzen Jrs..........	Czech.					Statistics unavailable.								
93-94—Skoda Plzen	Czech Rep.	12	0	1	1	...	...	...		—	—	—	—	—
94-95—HC Kladno..................	Czech Rep.	28	0	5	5	...	...	...		—	—	—	—	—
—Interconex Plzen	Czech Rep.	6	0	0	0	...				—	—	—	—	—
95-96—Baltimore	AHL	69	2	6	8	44	...	...	...	6	0	0	0	2
96-97—Baltimore	AHL	69	6	14	20	86	...	...	...	3	0	0	0	2
97-98—Cincinnati	AHL	23	3	5	8	28	...	...	...	—	—	—	—	—
—Anaheim	NHL	48	3	4	7	40	-4	1	0	—	—	—	—	—
98-99—Anaheim	NHL	63	0	4	4	60	-6	0	0	4	0	1	1	2
99-00—Anaheim	NHL	57	2	15	17	34	12	0	0	—	—	—	—	—
00-01—Anaheim	NHL	59	1	7	8	42	-12	0	0	—	—	—	—	—
NHL Totals (4 years)...........		227	6	30	36	176	-10	1	0	4	0	1	1	2

TROSCHINSKY, ANDREI   C   BLUES

PERSONAL: Born February 14, 1978, in Ust-Kamenogorsk, U.S.S.R. ... 6-5/187. ... Shoots left.
TRANSACTIONS/CAREER NOTES: Selected by St. Louis Blues in sixth round (fifth Blues pick, 170th overall) of NHL entry draft (June 27, 1998).

Season Team	League	REGULAR SEASON Gms.	G	A	Pts.	PIM	+/-	PP	SH	PLAYOFFS Gms.	G	A	Pts.	PIM
95-96—Dynamo-2 Moscow	CIS Div. III					Statistics unavailable.								
96-97—Torpedo Ust-Kam.......	Rus. Div. II	9	1	1	2	8	...	...	...	—	—	—	—	—
97-98—Torpedo Ust-Kam.......	Rus. Div. II	47	10	16	26	34	...	...	...	—	—	—	—	—
99-00—Ust-Kamenogorsk.......	Russian	16	0	3	3	20	...	...	...	—	—	—	—	—
00-01—Worcester	AHL	78	17	28	45	32	...	...	...	11	2	2	4	2

TRUDEL, JEAN-GUY   RW   COYOTES

PERSONAL: Born October 18, 1975, in Cadillac, Que. ... 6-0/190. ... Shoots right.
TRANSACTIONS/CAREER NOTES: Signed as non-drafted free agent by Phoenix Coyotes (July 16, 1999).
HONORS: Named to ECHL All-Star first team (1997-98). ... Named to AHL All-Star second team (1999-2000). ... Named to AHL All-Star first team (2000-01).

Season Team	League	REGULAR SEASON								PLAYOFFS				
		Gms.	G	A	Pts.	PIM	+/-	PP	SH	Gms.	G	A	Pts.	PIM
94-95—Hull	QMJHL	54	29	42	71	76	...	...	...	19	4	13	17	25
95-96—Hull	QMJHL	70	50	71	121	96	...	...	...	17	11	18	29	8
96-97—Peoria	ECHL	37	25	29	54	47	...	...	...	9	9	10	19	22
—San Antonio	IHL	12	1	5	6	4	...	...	...	—	—	—	—	—
—Chicago.....................	IHL	6	1	2	3	2	...	...	...	—	—	—	—	—
97-98—Peoria	ECHL	62	39	74	113	147	...	...	...	3	0	0	0	2
98-99—Kansas City...............	IHL	76	24	25	49	66	...	...	...	3	1	0	1	0
99-00—Springfield	AHL	72	34	39	73	80	...	...	...	3	0	1	1	4
—Phoenix	NHL	1	0	0	0	0	-1	0	0	—	—	—	—	—
00-01—Springfield	AHL	80	34	65	99	89	...	...	...	—	—	—	—	—
NHL Totals (1 year).............		1	0	0	0	0	-1	0	0					

TSELIOS, NIKOS D HURRICANES

PERSONAL: Born January 20, 1979, in Oak Park, Ill. ... 6-4/187. ... Shoots left. ... Cousin of Chris Chelios, defenseman, Detroit Red Wings. ... Name pronounced NEE-kohz CHEL-yoz.

TRANSACTIONS/CAREER NOTES: Selected by Carolina Hurricanes in first round (first Hurricanes pick, 22nd overall) of NHL entry draft (June 21, 1997).

HONORS: Named to Can.HL All-Rookie team (1996-97). ... Named to OHL All-Rookie first team (1996-97).

Season Team	League	REGULAR SEASON								PLAYOFFS				
		Gms.	G	A	Pts.	PIM	+/-	PP	SH	Gms.	G	A	Pts.	PIM
95-96—Chicago.....................	MNHL	27	5	8	13	40	...	...	...	—	—	—	—	—
96-97—Belleville	OHL	64	9	37	46	61	...	...	...	—	—	—	—	—
97-98—Belleville	OHL	20	2	10	12	16	...	...	...	—	—	—	—	—
—Plymouth....................	OHL	41	8	20	28	27	...	...	...	15	1	8	9	27
98-99—Plymouth..................	OHL	60	21	39	60	60	...	...	...	11	4	10	14	8
99-00—Cincinnati..................	IHL	80	3	19	22	75	...	...	...	10	0	2	2	4
00-01—Cincinnati..................	IHL	79	7	18	25	98	...	...	...	5	0	3	3	0

TSYPLAKOV, VLADIMIR LW

PERSONAL: Born April 18, 1969, in Moscow, U.S.S.R. ... 6-1/210. ... Shoots left. ... Name pronounced SIHP-luh-kahf.

TRANSACTIONS/CAREER NOTES: Selected by Los Angeles Kings in third round (fourth Kings pick, 59th overall) of NHL entry draft (July 8, 1995). ... Underwent reconstructive surgery on right shoulder (December 14, 1995); missed 45 games. ... Strained abdominal muscle prior to 1995-96 season; missed first nine games of season. ... Strained groin (February 13, 1997); missed three games. ... Fractured right hand (November 11, 1997); missed two games. ... Sprained left knee (February 19, 1999); missed 12 games. ... Traded by Kings to Buffalo Sabres for eighth-round pick (RW Dan Welch) in 2000 draft (January 24, 2000). ... Suffered charley horse (December 7, 2000); missed two games. ... Injured ribs (February 19, 2001); missed two games.

Season Team	League	REGULAR SEASON								PLAYOFFS				
		Gms.	G	A	Pts.	PIM	+/-	PP	SH	Gms.	G	A	Pts.	PIM
88-89—Dynamo Minsk	USSR	19	6	1	7	4	...	...	...	—	—	—	—	—
89-90—Dynamo Minsk	USSR	47	11	6	17	20	...	...	...	—	—	—	—	—
90-91—Dynamo Minsk	USSR	28	6	5	11	14	...	...	...	—	—	—	—	—
91-92—Dynamo Minsk	CIS	29	10	9	19	16	...	...	...	—	—	—	—	—
92-93—Detroit......................	Col.HL	44	33	43	76	20	...	...	...	6	5	4	9	6
—Indianapolis...............	IHL	11	6	7	13	4	...	...	...	5	1	1	2	2
93-94—Fort Wayne	IHL	63	31	32	63	51	...	...	...	14	6	8	14	16
94-95—Fort Wayne	IHL	79	38	40	78	39	...	...	...	4	2	4	6	2
95-96—Las Vegas	IHL	9	5	6	11	4	...	...	...	—	—	—	—	—
—Los Angeles...............	NHL	23	5	5	10	4	1	0	0	—	—	—	—	—
96-97—Los Angeles...............	NHL	67	16	23	39	12	8	1	0	—	—	—	—	—
97-98—Los Angeles...............	NHL	73	18	34	52	18	15	2	0	4	0	1	1	8
—Belarus Oly. team.......	Int'l	5	1	1	2	2	...	...	...	—	—	—	—	—
98-99—Los Angeles...............	NHL	69	11	12	23	32	-7	0	2	—	—	—	—	—
99-00—Los Angeles...............	NHL	29	6	7	13	4	6	1	0	—	—	—	—	—
—Buffalo	NHL	34	6	13	19	10	17	0	0	5	0	1	1	4
00-01—Buffalo	NHL	36	7	7	14	10	2	0	0	9	1	0	1	4
NHL Totals (6 years)...........		331	69	101	170	90	42	4	2	18	1	2	3	16

TUCKER, DARCY C MAPLE LEAFS

PERSONAL: Born March 15, 1975, in Castor, Alta. ... 5-11/185. ... Shoots left.

TRANSACTIONS/CAREER NOTES: Selected by Montreal Canadiens in sixth round (eighth Canadiens pick, 151st overall) of NHL entry draft (June 26, 1993). ... Bruised knee (December 16, 1996); missed one game. ... Traded by Canadiens with RW Stephane Richer and D David Wilkie to Tampa Bay Lightning for C Patrick Poulin, RW Mick Vukota and D Igor Ulanov (January 15, 1998). ... Suspended two games by NHL for spearing incident (December 28, 1999). ... Traded by Lightning with fourth-round pick (RW Miguel Delisle) in 2000 draft to Toronto Maple Leafs for RW Mike Johnson, D Marek Posmyk and fifth-(RW Pavel Sedov) and sixth-round (D Aaron Gionet) picks in 2000 draft (February 9, 2000).

HONORS: Won Stafford Smythe Memorial Trophy (1993-94). ... Named to Can.HL All-Star first team (1993-94). ... Named to WHL (West) All-Star first team (1993-94 and 1994-95). ... Named to Memorial Cup All-Star team (1993-94 and 1994-95). ... Won Dudley (Red) Garrett Memorial Trophy (1995-96).

Season Team	League	REGULAR SEASON								PLAYOFFS				
		Gms.	G	A	Pts.	PIM	+/-	PP	SH	Gms.	G	A	Pts.	PIM
91-92—Kamloops	WHL	26	3	10	13	42	...	...	...	9	0	1	1	16
92-93—Kamloops	WHL	67	31	58	89	155	...	...	...	13	7	6	13	34
93-94—Kamloops	WHL	66	52	88	140	143	...	...	...	19	9	*18	*27	43
94-95—Kamloops	WHL	64	64	73	137	94	...	...	...	21	16	15	31	19
95-96—Fredericton	AHL	74	29	64	93	174	...	...	...	7	7	3	10	14
—Montreal	NHL	3	0	0	0	0	-1	0	0	—	—	—	—	—
96-97—Montreal	NHL	73	7	13	20	110	-5	1	0	4	0	0	0	0
97-98—Montreal	NHL	39	1	5	6	57	-6	0	0	—	—	—	—	—
—Tampa Bay	NHL	35	6	8	14	89	-8	1	1	—	—	—	—	—
98-99—Tampa Bay	NHL	82	21	22	43	176	-34	8	2	—	—	—	—	—
99-00—Tampa Bay	NHL	50	14	20	34	108	-15	1	0	—	—	—	—	—
—Toronto	NHL	27	7	10	17	55	3	0	2	12	4	2	6	15
00-01—Toronto	NHL	82	16	21	37	141	6	2	0	11	0	2	2	6
NHL Totals (6 years)		391	72	99	171	736	-60	13	5	27	4	4	8	21

TUGNUTT, RON   G   BLUE JACKETS

PERSONAL: Born October 22, 1967, in Scarborough, Ont. ... 5-11/160. ... Catches left. ... Full Name: Ronald Frederick Bradley Tugnutt.

TRANSACTIONS/CAREER NOTES: Selected by Quebec Nordiques in fourth round (fourth Nordiques pick, 81st overall) of NHL entry draft (June 21, 1986). ... Sprained ankle (March 1989). ... Sprained knee (January 13, 1990). ... Injured hamstring (January 29, 1991); missed 11 games. ... Traded by Nordiques with LW Brad Zavisha to Edmonton Oilers for LW Martin Rucinsky (March 10, 1992). ... Selected by Mighty Ducks of Anaheim in NHL expansion draft (June 24, 1993). ... Traded by Mighty Ducks to Montreal Canadiens for C Stephan Lebeau (February 20, 1994). ... Strained knee (January 28, 1995); missed five games. ... Signed as free agent by Washington Capitals (September 20, 1995). ... Signed as free agent by Ottawa Senators (July 17, 1996). ... Strained hip flexor (January 31, 1998); missed two games. ... Injured right knee (March 6, 1999); missed two games. ... Strained left knee prior to 1999-2000 season; missed two games. ... Reinjured left knee (November 28, 1999); missed two games. ... Suffered illness (January 28, 2000); missed three games. ... Traded by Senators with D Janne Laukkanen to Pittsburgh Penguins for G Tom Barrasso (March 14, 2000). ... Signed as free agent by Columbus Blue Jackets (July 4, 2000). ... Strained hip flexor (December 2, 2000); missed two games. ... Sprained thumb (December 29, 2000); missed five games.

HONORS: Won F.W. (Dinty) Moore Trophy (1984-85). ... Shared Dave Pinkney Trophy with Kay Whitmore (1985-86). ... Named to OHL All-Star first team (1986-87). ... Played in NHL All-Star Game (1999).

MISCELLANEOUS: Holds Columbus Blue Jackets all-time records for most games played (53), most wins (22), most shutouts (4) and goals-against average (2.44). ... Holds Ottawa Senators all-time records for wins (72), most shutouts (13) and goals-against average (2.32). ... Stopped penalty shot attempt (vs. Dave McLlwain, October 12, 1991; vs. Cam Neely, October 15, 1993; vs. Brett Harkins, March 22, 1997; vs. Steve Sullivan, March 6, 1999). ... Allowed penalty shot goal (vs. Benoit Hogue, February 16, 1993; vs. Jason Allison, March 24, 1999).

Season Team	League	REGULAR SEASON								PLAYOFFS						
		Gms.	Min	W	L	T	GA	SO	Avg.	Gms.	Min.	W	L	GA	SO	Avg.
84-85—Peterborough	OHL	18	938	7	4	2	59	0	3.77	—						
85-86—Peterborough	OHL	26	1543	18	7	0	74	1	2.88	3	133	2	0	6	0	2.71
86-87—Peterborough	OHL	31	1891	21	7	2	88	2	*2.79	6	374	3	3	21	1	3.37
87-88—Quebec	NHL	6	284	2	3	0	16	0	3.38	—						
—Fredericton	AHL	34	1962	20	9	4	118	1	3.61	4	204	1	2	11	0	3.24
88-89—Quebec	NHL	26	1367	10	10	3	82	0	3.60	—						
—Halifax	AHL	24	1368	14	7	2	79	1	3.46	—						
89-90—Quebec	NHL	35	1978	5	24	3	152	0	4.61	—						
—Halifax	AHL	6	366	1	5	0	23	0	3.77	—						
90-91—Halifax	AHL	2	100	0	1	0	8	0	4.80	—						
—Quebec	NHL	56	3144	12	†29	10	212	0	4.05	—						
91-92—Quebec	NHL	30	1583	6	17	3	106	1	4.02	—						
—Halifax	AHL	8	447	3	3	1	30	0	4.03	—						
—Edmonton	NHL	3	124	1	1	0	10	0	4.84	2	60	0	0	3	0	3.00
92-93—Edmonton	NHL	26	1338	9	12	2	93	0	4.17	—						
93-94—Anaheim	NHL	28	1520	10	15	1	76	1	3.00	—						
—Montreal	NHL	8	378	2	3	1	24	0	3.81	1	59	0	1	5	0	5.08
94-95—Montreal	NHL	7	346	1	3	1	18	0	3.12	—						
95-96—Portland	AHL	58	3067	21	23	6	171	2	3.35	13	781	7	6	36	1	2.77
96-97—Ottawa	NHL	37	1991	17	15	1	93	3	2.80	7	425	3	4	14	1	1.98
97-98—Ottawa	NHL	42	2236	15	14	8	84	3	2.25	2	74	0	1	6	0	4.86
98-99—Ottawa	NHL	43	2508	22	10	8	75	3	*1.79	2	118	0	2	6	0	3.05
99-00—Ottawa	NHL	44	2435	18	12	8	103	4	2.54	—						
—Pittsburgh	NHL	7	374	4	2	0	15	0	2.41	11	746	6	5	22	2	1.77
00-01—Columbus	NHL	53	3129	22	25	5	127	4	2.44	—						
NHL Totals (13 years)		451	24735	156	195	54	1286	19	3.12	25	1482	9	13	56	3	2.27

TUOMAINEN, MARKO   RW

PERSONAL: Born April 25, 1972, in Kuopio, Finland. ... 6-3/218. ... Shoots right. ... Name pronounced too-oh-MIGH-nehn.

TRANSACTIONS/CAREER NOTES: Selected by Edmonton Oilers in ninth round (10th Oilers pick, 205th overall) of NHL entry draft (June 20, 1992). ... Signed as free agent by Los Angeles Kings (June 1, 1999). ... Suffered eye injury (October 20, 1999); missed seven games.

HONORS: Named to ECAC All-Star first team (1992-93 and 1994-95). ... Named to NCAA All-America (East) second team (1994-95).

Season Team	League	REGULAR SEASON								PLAYOFFS				
		Gms.	G	A	Pts.	PIM	+/-	PP	SH	Gms.	G	A	Pts.	PIM
89-90—KalPa Kuopio	Finland	5	0	0	0	0	...	...	...	—				
90-91—KalPa Kuopio	Finland	30	2	1	3	2	...	...	...	8	0	0	0	6
91-92—Clarkson	ECAC	29	11	13	24	34	...	...	...	—				
92-93—Clarkson	ECAC	35	25	30	55	26	...	...	...	—				
93-94—Clarkson	ECAC	34	23	29	52	60	...	...	...	—				

Season Team	League	REGULAR SEASON								PLAYOFFS				
		Gms.	G	A	Pts.	PIM	+/-	PP	SH	Gms.	G	A	Pts.	PIM
94-95—Clarkson	ECAC	37	23	37	60	34	...	...	...	—	—	—	—	—
—Edmonton	NHL	4	0	0	0	0	0	0	0	—	—	—	—	—
95-96—Cape Breton	AHL	58	25	35	60	71	...	...	...	—	—	—	—	—
96-97—Hamilton	AHL	79	31	21	52	130	...	...	...	22	7	5	12	4
97-98—HIFK Helsinki	Finland	46	13	9	22	20	...	...	...	9	0	3	3	0
98-99—HIFK Helsinki	Finland	48	11	17	28	*173	...	...	...	11	1	3	4	*46
99-00—Los Angeles	NHL	63	9	8	17	80	-12	2	1	1	0	0	0	0
00-01—Lowell	AHL	59	28	39	67	73	...	...	...	4	3	3	6	10
—Los Angeles	NHL	11	0	1	1	4	1	0	0	—	—	—	—	—
NHL Totals (3 years)		78	9	9	18	84	-11	2	1	1	0	0	0	0

TURCO, MARTY   G   STARS

PERSONAL: Born August 13, 1975, in Sault Ste. Marie, Ont. ... 5-11/183. ... Catches left.
TRANSACTIONS/CAREER NOTES: Selected by Dallas Stars in fifth round (fourth Stars pick, 124th overall) of NHL entry draft (June 29, 1994).
HONORS: Named CCHA Rookie of the Year (1994-95). ... Named to NCAA All-Tournament team (1995-96 and 1997-98). ... Named to CCHA All-Star first team (1996-1997). ... Named NCAA All-America (West) first team (1996-97). ... Named NCAA Tournament Most Valuable Player (1997-98). ... Named to CCHA All-Star second team (1997-98). ... Won Garry F. Longman Memorial Trophy (1998-99).
STATISTICAL NOTES: Led NHL in save percentage with .925 in 2000-01.

Season Team	League	REGULAR SEASON								PLAYOFFS						
		Gms.	Min	W	L	T	GA	SO	Avg.	Gms.	Min.	W	L	GA	SO	Avg.
93-94—Cambridge Jr. B	OHA	34	1937	...	...	...	114	0	3.53	—	—	—	—	—	—	—
94-95—Univ. of Michigan	CCHA	37	2064	27	7	1	95	1	2.76	—	—	—	—	—	—	—
95-96—Univ. of Michigan	CCHA	42	2334	34	7	1	84	5	2.16	—	—	—	—	—	—	—
96-97—Univ. of Michigan	CCHA	41	2296	33	4	4	87	4	2.27	—	—	—	—	—	—	—
97-98—Univ. of Michigan	CCHA	*45	*2640	*33	10	1	95	3	2.16	—	—	—	—	—	—	—
98-99—Michigan	IHL	54	3127	24	17	‡10	136	1	2.61	5	300	2	3	14	0	2.80
99-00—Michigan	IHL	60	3399	28	*27	‡7	*139	*7	2.45	—	—	—	—	—	—	—
00-01—Dallas	NHL	26	1266	13	6	1	40	3	*1.90	—	—	—	—	—	—	—
NHL Totals (1 year)		26	1266	13	6	1	40	3	1.90							

TUREK, ROMAN   G   FLAMES

PERSONAL: Born May 21, 1970, in Pisek, Czechoslovakia. ... 6-3/200. ... Catches right. ... Name pronounced ROH-mahn TOOR-ihk.
TRANSACTIONS/CAREER NOTES: Selected by Minnesota North Stars in sixth round (sixth North Stars pick, 113th overall) of NHL entry draft (June 16, 1990). ... North Stars franchise moved from Minnesota to Dallas and renamed Stars for 1993-94 season. ... Strained groin (January 8, 1997); missed three games. ... Injured knee (March 31, 1997); missed seven games. ... Strained groin (November 15, 1997); missed 12 games. ... Strained groin (December 10, 1998); missed three games. ... Sprained knee (April 14, 1999); missed final three games of season. ... Traded by Stars to St. Louis Blues for second-round pick (D Dan Jancevski) in 1999 draft (June 20, 1999). ... Injured knee (February 6, 2001); missed one game. ... Traded by Blues with fourth-round pick (F Egor Shastin) in 2001 draft to Calgary Flames for G Fred Brathwaite, C Daniel Tkaczuk, RW Sergei Varlamov and ninth-round pick (C Grant Jacobsen) in 2001 draft (June 23, 2001).
HONORS: Shared William M. Jennings Trophy with Ed Belfour (1998-99). ... Played in NHL All-Star Game (2000). ... Named to THE SPORTING NEWS All-Star Team (1999-2000). ... Named to NHL All-Star second team (1999-2000). ... Won William M. Jennings Trophy (1999-2000).
MISCELLANEOUS: Member of Stanley Cup championship team (1999). ... Stopped a penalty shot attempt (vs. Jeff Friesen, December 30, 1999). ... Allowed a penalty shot goal (vs. Alexander Korolyuk, January 11, 2000; vs. Martin Straka, January 19, 2000; vs. Joe Sakic, May 12, 2001 (playoffs)). ... Holds St. Louis Blues all-time record for goals-against average (2.10).
STATISTICAL NOTES: Led NHL in winning percentage with .627 (1999-2000).

Season Team	League	REGULAR SEASON								PLAYOFFS						
		Gms.	Min	W	L	T	GA	SO	Avg.	Gms.	Min.	W	L	GA	SO	Avg.
90-91—Budejovice	Czech.	26	1244	...	...	...	98	0	4.73	—	—	—	—	—	—	—
91-92—Budejovice	Czech Dv.II	Did not play.														
92-93—Budejovice	Czech.	43	2555	...	...	...	121	...	2.84	—	—	—	—	—	—	—
93-94—Budejovice	Czech Rep.	44	2584	...	...	...	111	...	2.58	3	180	...	...	12	...	4.00
—Czech Rep. Oly. team	Int'l	2	120	2	0	0	4	2	2.00	—	—	—	—	—	—	—
94-95—Budejovice	Czech Rep.	44	2587	...	...	...	119	...	2.76	9	498	...	...	25	...	3.01
95-96—Nurnberg	Germany	48	2787	...	...	...	154	...	3.32	5	338	...	...	14	...	2.49
96-97—Michigan	IHL	29	1555	8	13	‡4	77	0	2.97	—	—	—	—	—	—	—
—Dallas	NHL	6	263	3	1	0	9	0	2.05	—	—	—	—	—	—	—
97-98—Dallas	NHL	23	1324	11	10	1	49	1	2.22	—	—	—	—	—	—	—
—Michigan	IHL	2	119	1	1	0	5	0	2.52	—	—	—	—	—	—	—
98-99—Dallas	NHL	26	1382	16	3	3	48	1	2.08	—	—	—	—	—	—	—
99-00—St. Louis	NHL	67	3960	42	15	9	129	*7	1.95	7	415	3	4	19	0	2.75
00-01—St. Louis	NHL	54	3232	24	18	10	123	6	2.28	14	908	9	5	31	0	2.05
NHL Totals (5 years)		176	10161	96	47	23	358	15	2.11	21	1323	12	9	50	0	2.27

TURGEON, PIERRE   C   STARS

PERSONAL: Born August 28, 1969, in Rouyn, Que. ... 6-1/199. ... Shoots left. ... Brother of Sylvain Turgeon, left winger with four NHL teams (1983-84 through 1994-95). ... Name pronounced TUHR-zhaw.
TRANSACTIONS/CAREER NOTES: Selected by Buffalo Sabres in first round (first Sabres pick, first overall) of NHL entry draft (June 13, 1987). ... Traded by Sabres with RW Benoit Hogue, D Uwe Krupp and C Dave McLlwain to New York Islanders for C Pat LaFontaine, LW Randy Wood, D Randy Hillier and future considerations; Sabres later received fourth-round pick (D Dean Melanson) in 1992 draft to complete deal (October 25, 1991). ... Injured right knee (January 3, 1992); missed three games. ... Separated shoulder (April 28, 1993); missed six playoff games. ... Suffered from tendinitis in right wrist (October 5, 1993); missed one game. ... Suffered from the flu (December 29, 1993); missed one game. ... Fractured cheekbone (January 26, 1994); missed 12 games. ... Traded by Islanders with D Vladimir Malakhov to Montreal Canadiens for

LW Kirk Muller, D Mathieu Schneider and C Craig Darby (April 5, 1995). ... Strained shoulder (November 8, 1995); missed two games. ... Bruised thigh (October 24, 1996); missed one game. ... Traded by Canadiens with C Craig Conroy and D Rory Fitzpatrick to St. Louis Blues for LW Shayne Corson, D Murray Baron and fifth-round pick (D Gennady Razin) in 1997 draft (October 29, 1996). ... Fractured right forearm (October 4, 1997); missed 22 games. ... Fractured hand (December 14, 1998); missed 14 games. ... Suffered back spasms (November 20, 1999); missed four games. ... Suffered from the flu (January 11, 2000); missed one game. ... Injured thumb (January 29, 2000); missed 24 games. ... Suffered concussion (January 11, 2001); missed three games. ... Signed as free agent by Dallas Stars (July 1, 2001).
HONORS: Won Michel Bergeron Trophy (1985-86). ... Won Michael Bossy Trophy (1986-87). ... Played in NHL All-Star Game (1990, 1993, 1994 and 1996). ... Won Lady Byng Memorial Trophy (1992-93). ... Named to play in NHL All-Star Game (2000); replaced by LW Ray Whitney due to injury.
MISCELLANEOUS: Captain of Montreal Canadiens (1995-96 through October 29, 1996). ... Scored on a penalty shot (vs. Patrick Roy, October 17, 1990; vs. Pat Jablonski, November 7, 1992). ... Failed to score on a penalty shot (vs. Steve Shields, December 30, 1999).
STATISTICAL PLATEAUS: Three-goal games: 1989-90 (1), 1990-91 (1), 1991-92 (2), 1992-93 (4), 1993-94 (2), 1994-95 (1), 1995-96 (1), 1998-99 (1), 1999-00 (1), 2000-01 (1). Total: 15.

			REGULAR SEASON								PLAYOFFS				
Season Team	League	Gms.	G	A	Pts.	PIM	+/-	PP	SH		Gms.	G	A	Pts.	PIM
85-86—Granby	QMJHL	69	47	67	114	31	...	...	...		—	—	—	—	—
86-87—Granby	QMJHL	58	69	85	154	8	...	...	...		7	9	6	15	15
87-88—Buffalo	NHL	76	14	28	42	34	-8	8	0		6	4	3	7	4
88-89—Buffalo	NHL	80	34	54	88	26	-2	19	0		5	3	5	8	2
89-90—Buffalo	NHL	80	40	66	106	29	10	17	1		6	2	4	6	2
90-91—Buffalo	NHL	78	32	47	79	26	14	13	2		6	3	1	4	6
91-92—Buffalo	NHL	8	2	6	8	4	-1	0	0		—	—	—	—	—
—New York Islanders	NHL	69	38	49	87	16	8	13	0		—	—	—	—	—
92-93—New York Islanders	NHL	83	58	74	132	26	-1	24	0		11	6	7	13	0
93-94—New York Islanders	NHL	69	38	56	94	18	14	10	4		4	0	1	1	0
94-95—New York Islanders	NHL	34	13	14	27	10	-12	3	2		—	—	—	—	—
—Montreal	NHL	15	11	9	20	4	12	2	0		—	—	—	—	—
95-96—Montreal	NHL	80	38	58	96	44	19	17	1		6	2	4	6	2
96-97—Montreal	NHL	9	1	10	11	2	4	0	0		—	—	—	—	—
—St. Louis	NHL	69	25	49	74	12	4	5	0		5	1	1	2	2
97-98—St. Louis	NHL	60	22	46	68	24	13	6	0		10	4	4	8	2
98-99—St. Louis	NHL	67	31	34	65	36	4	10	0		13	4	9	13	6
99-00—St. Louis	NHL	52	26	40	66	8	30	8	0		7	0	7	7	0
00-01—St. Louis	NHL	79	30	52	82	37	14	11	0		15	5	10	15	2
NHL Totals (14 years)		1008	453	692	1145	356	122	166	10		94	34	56	90	28

TUZZOLINO, TONY   RW   BRUINS

PERSONAL: Born October 9, 1975, in Buffalo. ... 6-2/202. ... Shoots right. ... Name pronounced TUZZ-oh-LEEN-oh.
TRANSACTIONS/CAREER NOTES: Selected by Quebec Nordiques in fifth round (seventh Nordiques pick, 113th overall) of NHL entry draft (June 29, 1994). ... Nordiques franchise moved to Colorado and renamed Avalanche for 1995-96 season (June 21, 1995). ... Signed as free agent by New York Islanders (April 23, 1997). ... Traded by Islanders with C Travis Green and D Doug Houda to Mighty Ducks of Anaheim for D J.J. Daigneault, C Mark Janssens and RW Joe Sacco (February 6, 1998). ... Signed as free agent by New York Rangers (October 5, 2000). ... Signed as free agent by Boston Bruins (July 23, 2001).

			REGULAR SEASON								PLAYOFFS				
Season Team	League	Gms.	G	A	Pts.	PIM	+/-	PP	SH		Gms.	G	A	Pts.	PIM
91-92—Niagara	NAJHL	45	19	27	46	82	...	...	...		—	—	—	—	—
92-93—Niagara	NAJHL	50	36	41	77	134	...	...	...		—	—	—	—	—
93-94—Michigan State	CCHA	38	4	3	7	50	...	...	...		—	—	—	—	—
94-95—Michigan State	CCHA	39	9	19	28	81	...	...	...		—	—	—	—	—
95-96—Michigan State	CCHA	41	12	17	29	120	...	...	...		—	—	—	—	—
96-97—Michigan State	CCHA	39	14	18	32	45	...	...	...		—	—	—	—	—
97-98—Kentucky	AHL	35	9	14	23	83	...	...	...		—	—	—	—	—
—Cincinnati	AHL	13	3	3	6	6	...	...	...		—	—	—	—	—
—Anaheim	NHL	1	0	0	0	2	-2	0	0		—	—	—	—	—
98-99—Cincinnati	AHL	50	4	10	14	55	...	...	...		—	—	—	—	—
—Cleveland	IHL	15	2	4	6	22	...	...	...		—	—	—	—	—
99-00—Cincinnati	AHL	15	0	3	3	8	...	...	...		—	—	—	—	—
—Huntington	ECHL	20	6	13	19	43	...	...	...		—	—	—	—	—
—Hartford	AHL	32	3	8	11	41	...	...	...		19	2	2	4	16
00-01—Hartford	AHL	47	12	23	35	136	...	...	...		5	0	2	2	6
—New York Rangers	NHL	6	0	0	0	5	-1	0	0		—	—	—	—	—
NHL Totals (2 years)		7	0	0	0	7	-3	0	0						

TVERDOVSKY, OLEG   D   MIGHTY DUCKS

PERSONAL: Born May 18, 1976, in Donetsk, U.S.S.R. ... 6-0/200. ... Shoots left. ... Name pronounced OH-lehg teh-vuhr-DAHV-skee.
TRANSACTIONS/CAREER NOTES: Selected by Mighty Ducks of Anaheim in first round (first Mighty Ducks pick, second overall) of NHL entry draft (June 28, 1994). ... Suffered from pink eye (March 15, 1995); missed two games. ... Traded by Mighty Ducks with C Chad Kilger and third-round pick (D Per-Anton Lundstrom) in 1996 draft to Winnipeg Jets for C Marc Chouinard, RW Teemu Selanne and fourth-round pick (traded to Toronto) in 1996 draft (February 7, 1996). ... Jets franchise moved to Phoenix and renamed Coyotes for 1996-97 season; NHL approved move on January 18, 1996. ... Pulled rib muscle (December 23, 1997); missed one game. ... Traded by Coyotes to Mighty Ducks for C Travis Green and first-round pick (C Scott Kelman) in 1999 draft (June 26, 1999).
HONORS: Played in NHL All-Star Game (1997).

Season Team	League	REGULAR SEASON								PLAYOFFS				
		Gms.	G	A	Pts.	PIM	+/-	PP	SH	Gms.	G	A	Pts.	PIM
92-93—Soviet Wings	CIS	21	0	1	1	6	...	...	...	6	0	0	0	...
93-94—Soviet Wings	CIS	46	4	10	14	22	...	...	...	3	1	0	1	2
94-95—Brandon	WHL	7	1	4	5	4	...	...	...	—	—	—	—	—
—Anaheim	NHL	36	3	9	12	14	-6	1	1	—	—	—	—	—
95-96—Anaheim	NHL	51	7	15	22	35	0	2	0	—	—	—	—	—
—Winnipeg	NHL	31	0	8	8	6	-7	0	0	6	0	1	1	0
96-97—Phoenix	NHL	82	10	45	55	30	-5	3	1	7	0	1	1	0
97-98—Hamilton	AHL	9	8	6	14	2	...	...	...	—	—	—	—	—
—Phoenix	NHL	46	7	12	19	12	1	4	0	6	0	7	7	0
98-99—Phoenix	NHL	82	7	18	25	32	11	2	0	6	0	2	2	6
99-00—Anaheim	NHL	82	15	36	51	30	5	5	0	—	—	—	—	—
00-01—Anaheim	NHL	82	14	39	53	32	-11	8	0	—	—	—	—	—
NHL Totals (7 years)		492	63	182	245	191	-12	25	2	25	0	11	11	6

ULANOV, IGOR   D   RANGERS

PERSONAL: Born October 1, 1969, in Kraskokamsk, U.S.S.R. ... 6-3/211. ... Shoots right. ... Name pronounced EE-gohr yoo-LAH-nahf.
TRANSACTIONS/CAREER NOTES: Selected by Winnipeg Jets in 10th round (eighth Jets pick, 203rd overall) of NHL entry draft (June 22, 1991). ... Suffered back spasms (March 7, 1992); missed five games. ... Fractured foot (March 16, 1995); missed 19 games. ... Traded by Jets with C Mike Eagles to Washington Capitals for third-round (traded to Dallas Stars) and fifth-round (G Brian Elder) picks in 1995 draft (April 7, 1995). ... Traded by Capitals to Chicago Blackhawks for third-round pick (G Dave Weninger) in 1996 draft (October 17, 1995). ... Traded by Blackhawks with LW Patrick Poulin and second-round pick (D Jeff Paul) in 1996 draft to Tampa Bay Lightning for D Enrico Ciccone (March 20, 1996). ... Injured ribs (October 5, 1996); missed three games. ... Strained groin (February 14, 1997); missed six games. ... Traded by Lightning with C Patrick Poulin and RW Mick Vukota to Montreal Canadiens for RW Stephane Richer, C Darcy Tucker and D David Wilkie (January 15, 1998). ... Tore ligaments in left knee (January 21, 1998); missed remainder of season. ... Fractured left foot (November 3, 1999); missed 13 games. ... Traded by Canadiens with D Alain Nasreddine to Edmonton Oilers for D Christian LaFlamme and D Mathieu Descoteaux (March 9, 2000). ... Bruised ankle (November 19, 2000); missed one game. ... Bruised right hand (December 2, 2000); missed two games. ... Suspended two games by NHL for cross-checking incident (December 14, 2000). ... Injured left eye (February 24, 2001); missed three games. ... Reinjured left eye (March 2, 2001); missed six games. ... Signed as free agent by New York Rangers (July 1, 2001).

Season Team	League	REGULAR SEASON								PLAYOFFS				
		Gms.	G	A	Pts.	PIM	+/-	PP	SH	Gms.	G	A	Pts.	PIM
90-91—Khimik	USSR	41	2	2	4	52	...	...	...	—	—	—	—	—
91-92—Khimik	CIS	27	1	4	5	24	...	...	...	—	—	—	—	—
—Winnipeg	NHL	27	2	9	11	67	5	0	0	7	0	0	0	39
—Moncton	AHL	3	0	1	1	16	...	...	...	—	—	—	—	—
92-93—Moncton	AHL	9	1	3	4	26	...	...	...	—	—	—	—	—
—Fort Wayne	IHL	3	0	1	1	29	...	...	...	—	—	—	—	—
—Winnipeg	NHL	56	2	14	16	124	6	0	0	4	0	0	0	4
93-94—Winnipeg	NHL	74	0	17	17	165	-11	0	0	—	—	—	—	—
94-95—Winnipeg	NHL	19	1	3	4	27	-2	0	0	—	—	—	—	—
—Washington	NHL	3	0	1	1	2	3	0	0	2	0	0	0	4
95-96—Indianapolis	IHL	1	0	0	0	0	...	...	...	—	—	—	—	—
—Chicago	NHL	53	1	8	9	92	12	0	0	—	—	—	—	—
—Tampa Bay	NHL	11	2	1	3	24	-1	0	0	5	0	0	0	15
96-97—Tampa Bay	NHL	59	1	7	8	108	2	0	0	—	—	—	—	—
97-98—Tampa Bay	NHL	45	2	7	9	85	-5	1	0	—	—	—	—	—
—Montreal	NHL	4	0	1	1	12	-2	0	0	10	1	4	5	12
98-99—Montreal	NHL	76	3	9	12	109	-3	0	0	—	—	—	—	—
99-00—Montreal	NHL	43	1	5	6	76	-11	0	0	—	—	—	—	—
—Edmonton	NHL	14	0	3	3	10	-3	0	0	5	0	0	0	6
00-01—Edmonton	NHL	67	3	20	23	90	15	1	0	6	0	0	0	4
NHL Totals (10 years)		551	18	105	123	991	5	2	0	39	1	4	5	84

ULMER, JEFF   RW   SENATORS

PERSONAL: Born April 27, 1977, in Wilcox, Sask. ... 5-11/190. ... Shoots right.
TRANSACTIONS/CAREER NOTES: Signed as non-drafted free agent by New York Rangers (July 27, 2000). ... Traded by Rangers with D Jason Doig to Ottawa Senators for D Sean Gagnon (June 29, 2001).

Season Team	League	REGULAR SEASON								PLAYOFFS				
		Gms.	G	A	Pts.	PIM	+/-	PP	SH	Gms.	G	A	Pts.	PIM
95-96—Univ. of North Dakota	WCHA	29	5	3	8	26	...	...	...	—	—	—	—	—
96-97—Univ. of North Dakota	WCHA	26	6	11	17	16	...	...	...	—	—	—	—	—
97-98—Univ. of North Dakota	WCHA	32	12	12	24	44	...	...	...	—	—	—	—	—
98-99—Univ. of North Dakota	WCHA	38	16	20	36	46	...	...	...	—	—	—	—	—
99-00—Canadian nat'l team	Int'l	48	14	25	39	20	...	...	...	—	—	—	—	—
—Houston	IHL	5	1	0	1	0	...	...	...	11	2	4	6	6
00-01—Hartford	AHL	48	11	14	25	34	...	...	...	—	—	—	—	—
—New York Rangers	NHL	21	3	0	3	8	-6	0	0	—	—	—	—	—
NHL Totals (1 year)		21	3	0	3	8	-6	0	0					

UPPER, DIMITRI   C   ISLANDERS

PERSONAL: Born August 27, 1978, in U.S.S.R. ... 6-0/176. ... Shoots right.
TRANSACTIONS/CAREER NOTES: Selected by New York Islanders in fifth round (fifth Islanders pick, 136th overall) of NHL entry draft (June 24, 2000).

Season Team	League	REGULAR SEASON								PLAYOFFS				
		Gms.	G	A	Pts.	PIM	+/-	PP	SH	Gms.	G	A	Pts.	PIM
98-99—Tor. Nichny Nov.	Russian	43	14	24	38	...	...	...	...	—	—	—	—	—
99-00—Tor. Nichny Nov.	Russian	36	14	6	20	50	...	...	...	—	—	—	—	—
00-01—Tor. Nichny Nov.	Russian	6	0	2	2	4	...	...	...	—	—	—	—	—
—Ak Bars Kazan.............	Russian	31	7	4	11	6	...	...	...	1	0	0	0	0

VAANANEN, OSSI   D   COYOTES

PERSONAL: Born August 18, 1980, in Vantaa, Finland. ... 6-3/200. ... Shoots left.

TRANSACTIONS/CAREER NOTES: Selected by Phoenix Coyotes in second round (second Coyotes pick, 43rd overall) of NHL entry draft (June 27, 1998).

Season Team	League	REGULAR SEASON								PLAYOFFS				
		Gms.	G	A	Pts.	PIM	+/-	PP	SH	Gms.	G	A	Pts.	PIM
95-96—Jokerit Helsinki	Finland Jr. B	2	0	0	0	0	...	...	...	—	—	—	—	—
96-97—Jokerit Helsinki	Finland Jr. B	17	1	2	3	43	...	...	...	—	—	—	—	—
97-98—Jokerit Helsinki	Finland Jr.	31	0	6	6	24	...	...	...	—	—	—	—	—
98-99—Jokerit Helsinki	Finland	48	0	1	1	42	...	...	...	3	0	1	1	2
99-00—Jokerit Helsinki	Finland	49	1	6	7	46	...	...	...	11	1	1	2	2
00-01—Phoenix......................	NHL	81	4	12	16	90	9	0	0	—	—	—	—	—
NHL Totals (1 year).............		81	4	12	16	90	9	0	0					

VALICEVIC, ROB   C

PERSONAL: Born January 6, 1971, in Detroit. ... 6-2/192. ... Shoots right. ... Full Name: Robert Valicevic.

TRANSACTIONS/CAREER NOTES: Selected by New York Islanders in sixth round (sixth Islanders pick, 114th overall) of NHL entry draft (June 22, 1991). ... Signed as free agent by Nashville Predators (June 8, 1998). ... Suffered concussion (January 31, 2000); missed two games. ... Injured right knee (November 6, 2000); missed three games. ... Underwent knee surgery (November 16, 2000); missed eight games. ... Injured knee (December 4, 2000); missed two games. ... Suffered concussion (March 10, 2001); missed three games.

STATISTICAL PLATEAUS: Three-goal games: 1999-00 (1).

Season Team	League	REGULAR SEASON								PLAYOFFS				
		Gms.	G	A	Pts.	PIM	+/-	PP	SH	Gms.	G	A	Pts.	PIM
90-91—Detroit......................	USHL	39	31	44	75	54	...	...	...	—	—	—	—	—
91-92—Lake Superior State	CCHA	32	8	4	12	12	...	...	...	—	—	—	—	—
92-93—Lake Superior State	CCHA	43	21	20	41	28	...	...	...	—	—	—	—	—
93-94—Lake Superior State	CCHA	45	18	20	38	46	...	...	...	—	—	—	—	—
94-95—Lake Superior State	CCHA	37	10	22	32	40	...	...	...	—	—	—	—	—
95-96—Louisiana	ECHL	60	42	20	62	85	...	...	...	5	2	3	5	8
—Springfield	AHL	2	0	0	0	2	...	...	...	—	—	—	—	—
96-97—Houston	IHL	58	11	12	23	42	...	...	...	12	1	3	4	11
—Louisiana	ECHL	8	7	2	9	21	...	...	...	—	—	—	—	—
97-98—Houston	IHL	72	29	28	57	47	...	...	...	4	2	0	2	2
98-99—Houston	IHL	57	16	33	49	62	...	...	...	19	7	10	17	8
—Nashville	NHL	19	4	2	6	2	4	0	0	—	—	—	—	—
99-00—Nashville	NHL	80	14	11	25	21	-11	2	1	—	—	—	—	—
00-01—Nashville	NHL	60	8	6	14	26	-2	1	0	—	—	—	—	—
NHL Totals (3 years)...........		159	26	19	45	49	-9	3	1					

VALK, GARRY   LW   MAPLE LEAFS

U
V

PERSONAL: Born November 27, 1967, in Edmonton. ... 6-1/200. ... Shoots left. ... Full Name: Garry P. Valk. ... Name pronounced VAHLK.

TRANSACTIONS/CAREER NOTES: Selected by Vancouver Canucks in sixth round (fifth Canucks pick, 108th overall) of NHL entry draft (June 13, 1987). ... Sprained thumb (November 24, 1991); missed one game. ... Sprained shoulder (January 21, 1992); missed eight games. ... Sprained knee (February 26, 1993); missed 12 games. ... Selected by Mighty Ducks of Anaheim in NHL waiver draft (October 3, 1993). ... Suffered concussion (December 5, 1993); missed one game. ... Suffered post-concussion syndrome (December 5, 1993); missed four games. ... Sprained left knee (January 16, 1995); missed 10 games. ... Injured right eye (December 7, 1995); missed one game. ... Injured ear (December 22, 1995); missed one game. ... Traded by Mighty Ducks to Pittsburgh Penguins for D J.J. Daigneault (February 21, 1997). ... Bruised ribs (March 16, 1997); missed five games. ... Injured knee (April 11, 1997); missed one game. ... Suffered charley horse (October 1, 1997); missed two games. ... Injured groin (October 24, 1997); missed three games. ... Strained abdomen (March 5, 1998); missed 13 games. ... Signed as free agent by Toronto Maple Leafs (October 6, 1998). ... Strained neck (November 25, 1998); missed two games. ... Strained muscle in abdomen (January 20, 1999); missed two games. ... Strained back (February 6, 1999); missed one game. ... Suffered injury (November 9, 1999); missed two games. ... Suffered injury (March 18, 2000); missed one game. ... Suffered injury (March 25, 2000); missed five games. ... Suffered injury (December 4, 2000); missed two games. ... Suffered injury (March 24, 2001); missed final six games of regular season.

STATISTICAL PLATEAUS: Three-goal games: 1995-96 (1).

Season Team	League	REGULAR SEASON								PLAYOFFS				
		Gms.	G	A	Pts.	PIM	+/-	PP	SH	Gms.	G	A	Pts.	PIM
85-86—Sherwood Park..........	AJHL	40	20	26	46	116	...	...	...	—	—	—	—	—
86-87—Sherwood Park..........	AJHL	59	42	44	86	204	...	...	...	—	—	—	—	—
87-88—Univ. of North Dakota .	WCHA	38	23	12	35	64	...	...	...	—	—	—	—	—
88-89—Univ. of North Dakota .	WCHA	40	14	17	31	71	...	...	...	—	—	—	—	—
89-90—Univ. of North Dakota .	WCHA	43	22	17	39	92	...	...	...	—	—	—	—	—
90-91—Vancouver..................	NHL	59	10	11	21	67	-23	1	0	5	0	0	0	20
—Milwaukee..............	IHL	10	12	4	16	13	...	...	...	3	0	0	0	2
91-92—Vancouver..................	NHL	65	8	17	25	56	3	2	1	4	0	0	0	5
92-93—Vancouver..................	NHL	48	6	7	13	77	6	0	0	7	0	1	1	12
—Hamilton	AHL	7	3	6	9	6	...	...	...	—	—	—	—	—
93-94—Anaheim	NHL	78	18	27	45	100	8	4	1	—	—	—	—	—

Season Team	League	REGULAR SEASON								PLAYOFFS				
		Gms.	G	A	Pts.	PIM	+/-	PP	SH	Gms.	G	A	Pts.	PIM
94-95—Anaheim	NHL	36	3	6	9	34	-4	0	0	—	—	—	—	—
95-96—Anaheim	NHL	79	12	12	24	125	8	1	1	—	—	—	—	—
96-97—Anaheim	NHL	53	7	7	14	53	-2	0	0	—	—	—	—	—
—Pittsburgh	NHL	17	3	4	7	25	-6	0	0	—	—	—	—	—
97-98—Pittsburgh	NHL	39	2	1	3	33	-3	0	0	—	—	—	—	—
98-99—Toronto	NHL	77	8	21	29	53	8	1	0	17	3	4	7	22
99-00—Toronto	NHL	73	10	14	24	44	-2	0	1	12	1	2	3	14
00-01—Toronto	NHL	74	8	18	26	46	4	1	0	5	1	0	1	2
NHL Totals (11 years)		698	95	145	240	713	-3	10	4	50	5	7	12	75

VALTONEN, TOMEK   LW   RED WINGS

PERSONAL: Born January 8, 1980, in Piotrkow Trybunalski, Poland. ... 6-1/198. ... Shoots left.
TRANSACTIONS/CAREER NOTES: Selected by Detroit Red Wings in second round (third Red Wings pick, 56th overall) of NHL entry draft (June 27, 1998).

Season Team	League	REGULAR SEASON								PLAYOFFS				
		Gms.	G	A	Pts.	PIM	+/-	PP	SH	Gms.	G	A	Pts.	PIM
95-96—Ilves Tampere	Finland Jr.	12	7	7	14	28	...	...	...	—	—	—	—	—
96-97—Ilves Tampere	Finland Jr.	27	10	9	19	82	...	...	...	3	0	1	1	6
97-98—Ilves Tampere	Finland	19	1	0	1	14	...	...	...	3	0	0	0	0
—Kiek.-Karhut Joensuu	Finland Div. 2	6	1	2	3	39	...	...	...	—	—	—	—	—
—Ilves Tampere	Finland Jr.	13	3	2	5	36	...	...	...	—	—	—	—	—
98-99—Plymouth	OHL	43	8	16	24	53	...	...	...	7	1	0	1	0
99-00—Jokerit	Finland	41	0	3	3	63	...	...	...	9	1	0	1	8
00-01—Jokerit	Finland	45	3	2	5	138	...	...	...	3	0	0	0	0

VAN ACKER, ERIC   D   BRUINS

PERSONAL: Born March 1, 1979, in St. Jean, Que. ... 6-5/220. ... Shoots left.
TRANSACTIONS/CAREER NOTES: Selected by Boston Bruins in ninth round (11th Bruins pick, 218th overall) of NHL entry draft (June 21, 1997).

Season Team	League	REGULAR SEASON								PLAYOFFS				
		Gms.	G	A	Pts.	PIM	+/-	PP	SH	Gms.	G	A	Pts.	PIM
96-97—Chicoutimi	QMJHL	69	1	5	6	141	...	...	...	16	0	0	0	4
97-98—Chicoutimi	QMJHL	49	1	5	6	136	...	...	...	6	0	0	0	14
98-99—Baie-Comeau	QMJHL	65	1	6	7	192	...	...	...	—	—	—	—	—
99-00—Greenville	ECHL	46	0	8	8	112	...	...	...	13	1	0	1	37
—Providence	AHL	4	0	0	0	2	...	...	...	—	—	—	—	—
00-01—Greenville	ECHL	59	1	2	3	149	...	...	...	—	—	—	—	—

VAN ALLEN, SHAUN   C   STARS

PERSONAL: Born August 29, 1967, in Calgary. ... 6-1/204. ... Shoots left. ... Full Name: Shaun Kelly Van Allen.
TRANSACTIONS/CAREER NOTES: Selected by Edmonton Oilers in fifth round (fifth Oilers pick, 105th overall) of NHL entry draft (June 13, 1987). ... Suffered concussion (January 9, 1993); missed 11 games. ... Signed as free agent by Mighty Ducks of Anaheim (July 22, 1993). ... Suffered back spasms (February 7, 1995); missed two games. ... Suffered from the flu (May 1, 1995); missed one game. ... Dislocated right thumb (November 15, 1995); missed 21 games. ... Suffered back spasms (February 7, 1996); missed four games. ... Traded by Mighty Ducks with D Jason York to Ottawa Senators for C Ted Drury and rights to D Marc Moro (October 1, 1996). ... Suffered back spasms (February 2, 1998); missed one game. ... Strained left knee (December 30, 1999); missed one game. ... Strained muscle in abdomen (January 12, 2000); missed five games. ... Signed as free agent by Dallas Stars (July 12, 2000). ... Suffered back spasms (October 10, 2000); missed five games.
HONORS: Named to AHL All-Star second team (1990-91). ... Won John B. Sollenberger Trophy (1991-92). ... Named to AHL All-Star first team (1991-92).
MISCELLANEOUS: Failed to score on a penalty shot (vs. Eric Fichaud, December 1, 1998).

V

Season Team	League	REGULAR SEASON								PLAYOFFS				
		Gms.	G	A	Pts.	PIM	+/-	PP	SH	Gms.	G	A	Pts.	PIM
84-85—Swift Current	SAJHL	61	12	20	32	136	...	...	...	—	—	—	—	—
85-86—Saskatoon	WHL	55	12	11	23	43	...	...	...	13	4	8	12	28
86-87—Saskatoon	WHL	72	38	59	97	116	...	...	...	11	4	6	10	24
87-88—Nova Scotia	AHL	19	4	10	14	17	...	...	...	4	1	1	2	4
—Milwaukee	IHL	40	14	28	42	34	...	...	...	—	—	—	—	—
88-89—Cape Breton	AHL	76	32	42	74	81	...	...	...	—	—	—	—	—
89-90—Cape Breton	AHL	61	25	44	69	83	...	...	...	4	0	2	2	8
90-91—Edmonton	NHL	2	0	0	0	0	0	0	0	—	—	—	—	—
—Cape Breton	AHL	76	25	75	100	182	...	...	...	4	0	1	1	8
91-92—Cape Breton	AHL	77	29	*84	*113	80	...	...	...	5	3	7	10	14
92-93—Cape Breton	AHL	43	14	62	76	68	...	...	...	15	8	9	17	18
—Edmonton	NHL	21	1	4	5	6	-2	0	0	—	—	—	—	—
93-94—Anaheim	NHL	80	8	25	33	64	0	2	2	—	—	—	—	—
94-95—Anaheim	NHL	45	8	21	29	32	-4	1	1	—	—	—	—	—
95-96—Anaheim	NHL	49	8	17	25	41	13	0	0	—	—	—	—	—
96-97—Ottawa	NHL	80	11	14	25	35	-8	1	1	7	0	1	1	4
97-98—Ottawa	NHL	80	4	15	19	48	4	0	0	11	0	1	1	10
98-99—Ottawa	NHL	79	6	11	17	30	3	0	1	4	0	0	0	0
99-00—Ottawa	NHL	75	9	19	28	37	20	0	2	6	0	1	1	9
00-01—Dallas	NHL	59	7	16	23	16	5	0	2	8	0	2	2	8
NHL Totals (10 years)		570	62	142	204	309	31	4	9	36	0	5	5	31

VAN HOOF, JEREMY D LIGHTNING

PERSONAL: Born August 12, 1981, in Lindsay, Ont. ... 6-3/200. ... Shoots left.
TRANSACTIONS/CAREER NOTES: Selected by Pittsburgh Penguins in second round (third Penguins pick, 57th overall) of NHL entry draft (June 26, 1999). ... Returned to draft pool by Penguins and selected by Tampa Bay Lightning in third round (ninth Lightning pick, 222nd overall) of NHL entry draft (June 23, 2001).

			REGULAR SEASON								PLAYOFFS				
Season Team	League	Gms.	G	A	Pts.	PIM	+/-	PP	SH		Gms.	G	A	Pts.	PIM
97-98—Lindsay	OPJHL	50	2	8	10	40	...	...	...		—	—	—	—	—
98-99—Ottawa	OHL	54	0	13	13	46	...	...	...		5	1	0	1	2
99-00—Ottawa	OHL	66	4	14	18	71	...	...	...		11	1	0	1	12
00-01—Ottawa	OHL	65	1	14	15	49	...	...	...		20	3	4	7	27

VAN IMPE, DARREN D BRUINS

PERSONAL: Born May 18, 1973, in Saskatoon, Sask. ... 6-1/205. ... Shoots left. ... Name pronounced VAN-IHMP.
TRANSACTIONS/CAREER NOTES: Selected by New York Islanders in seventh round (seventh Islanders pick, 170th overall) of NHL entry draft (June 26, 1993). ... Traded by Islanders to Mighty Ducks of Anaheim for ninth-round pick (LW Mike Broda) in 1995 draft (September 2, 1994). ... Claimed on waivers by Boston Bruins (November 26, 1997). ... Strained shoulder (January 7, 1998); missed one game. ... Hyperextended elbow (November 29, 1998); missed two games. ... Separated shoulder (February 9, 1999); missed 12 games. ... Sprained ankle (March 25, 1999); missed four games. ... Suffered concussion (April 4, 2000); missed final three games of season. ... Strained shoulder (October 29, 2000); missed two games. ... Sprained knee (December 1, 2000); missed five games. ... Injured shoulder (December 23, 2000); missed five games. ... Underwent shoulder surgery (January 10, 2001); missed remainder of season.
HONORS: Named to WHL (East) All-Star first team (1992-93 and 1993-94).

			REGULAR SEASON								PLAYOFFS				
Season Team	League	Gms.	G	A	Pts.	PIM	+/-	PP	SH		Gms.	G	A	Pts.	PIM
90-91—Prince Albert	WHL	70	15	45	60	57	...	...	...		3	1	1	2	2
91-92—Prince Albert	WHL	69	9	37	46	129	...	...	...		8	1	5	6	10
92-93—Red Deer	WHL	54	23	47	70	118	...	...	...		4	2	5	7	16
93-94—Red Deer	WHL	58	20	64	84	125	...	...	...		4	2	4	6	6
94-95—San Diego	IHL	76	6	17	23	74	...	...	...		5	0	0	0	0
—Anaheim	NHL	1	0	1	1	4	0	0	0		—	—	—	—	—
95-96—Baltimore	AHL	63	11	47	58	79	...	...	...		—	—	—	—	—
—Anaheim	NHL	16	1	2	3	14	8	0	0		—	—	—	—	—
96-97—Anaheim	NHL	74	4	19	23	90	3	2	0		9	0	2	2	16
97-98—Anaheim	NHL	19	1	3	4	4	-10	0	0		—	—	—	—	—
—Boston	NHL	50	2	8	10	36	4	2	0		6	2	1	3	0
98-99—Boston	NHL	60	5	15	20	66	-5	4	0		11	1	2	3	4
99-00—Boston	NHL	79	5	23	28	73	-19	4	0		—	—	—	—	—
00-01—Boston	NHL	31	3	10	13	41	-9	2	0		—	—	—	—	—
NHL Totals (7 years)		330	21	81	102	328	-28	14	0		26	3	5	8	20

VAN OENE, DARREN LW SABRES

PERSONAL: Born January 18, 1978, in Edmonton. ... 6-3/207. ... Shoots left. ... Name pronounced van OH-ihn.
TRANSACTIONS/CAREER NOTES: Selected by Buffalo Sabres in second round (third Sabres pick, 33rd overall) of NHL entry draft (June 22, 1996).

			REGULAR SEASON								PLAYOFFS				
Season Team	League	Gms.	G	A	Pts.	PIM	+/-	PP	SH		Gms.	G	A	Pts.	PIM
94-95—Brandon	WHL	59	5	13	18	108	...	...	...		18	1	1	2	34
95-96—Brandon	WHL	47	10	18	28	126	...	...	...		18	1	6	7	*78
96-97—Brandon	WHL	56	21	27	48	139	...	...	...		6	2	3	5	19
97-98—Brandon	WHL	51	23	24	47	161	...	...	...		17	6	7	13	51
98-99—Rochester	AHL	73	11	20	31	143	...	...	...		12	2	4	6	8
99-00—Rochester	AHL	80	20	18	38	153	...	...	...		21	1	3	4	24
00-01—Rochester	AHL	64	10	12	22	147	...	...	...		4	1	0	1	4

VAN RYN, MIKE D BLUES

PERSONAL: Born May 14, 1979, in London, Ont. ... 6-1/190. ... Shoots right.
TRANSACTIONS/CAREER NOTES: Selected by New Jersey Devils in first round (first Devils pick, 26th overall) of NHL entry draft (June 27, 1998). ... Signed as free agent by St. Louis Blues (June 30, 2000).
HONORS: Named to CCHA All-Rookie Team (1997-98).

			REGULAR SEASON								PLAYOFFS				
Season Team	League	Gms.	G	A	Pts.	PIM	+/-	PP	SH		Gms.	G	A	Pts.	PIM
95-96—London Jr. B	OHA	44	9	14	23	24	...	...	...		—	—	—	—	—
96-97—London Jr. B	OHA	46	14	31	45	32	...	...	...		—	—	—	—	—
97-98—University of Michigan	WCHA	25	4	14	18	36	...	...	...		—	—	—	—	—
98-99—University of Michigan	WCHA	37	10	13	23	52	...	...	...		—	—	—	—	—
99-00—Sarnia	OHL	61	6	35	41	34	...	...	...		7	0	5	5	4
00-01—St. Louis	NHL	1	0	0	0	0	-2	0	0		—	—	—	—	—
—Worcester	AHL	37	3	10	13	12	...	...	...		7	1	1	2	2
NHL Totals (1 year)		1	0	0	0	0	-2	0	0						

V

VANBIESBROUCK, JOHN   G

PERSONAL: Born September 4, 1963, in Detroit. ... 5-8/176. ... Catches left. ... Name pronounced van-BEES-bruk.

TRANSACTIONS/CAREER NOTES: Selected by New York Rangers in fourth round (fifth Rangers pick, 72nd overall) of NHL entry draft (June 10, 1981). ... Fractured jaw (October 1987). ... Severely lacerated wrist (June 1988). ... Underwent knee surgery (May 11, 1990). ... Suffered lower back spasms (February 25, 1992); missed 11 games. ... Pulled groin (November 2, 1992); missed four games. ... Traded by Rangers to Vancouver Canucks for future considerations (June 20, 1993); Rangers acquired D Doug Lidster to complete deal (June 25, 1993). ... Selected by Florida Panthers in NHL expansion draft (June 24, 1993). ... Lacerated hand (February 1, 1994); missed seven games. ... Signed as free agent by Philadelphia Flyers (July 7, 1998). ... Traded by Flyers to New York Islanders for fourth-round pick (traded to Nashville) in 2001 draft (June 25, 2000). ... Strained back (November 27, 2000); missed one game. ... Traded by Islanders to New Jersey Devils for G Chris Terreri (March 12, 2001). ... Announced retirement (June 10, 2001).

HONORS: Won F.W. (Dinty) Moore Trophy (1980-81). ... Shared Dave Pinkney Trophy with Marc D'Amour (1981-82). ... Named to OHL All-Star second team (1982-83). ... Shared Tommy Ivan Trophy with D Bruce Affleck (1983-84). ... Shared Terry Sawchuk Trophy with Ron Scott (1983-84). ... Named to CHL All-Star first team (1983-84). ... Won Vezina Trophy (1985-86). ... Named to THE SPORTING NEWS All-Star first team (1985-86 and 1993-94). ... Named to NHL All-Star first team (1985-86). ... Played in NHL All-Star Game (1994, 1996 and 1997). ... Named to NHL All-Star second team (1993-94).

MISCELLANEOUS: Holds Florida Panthers all-time records for most games played by goalie (268), most wins (106), most shutouts (13) and goals-against average (2.58). ... Holds Philadelphia Flyers all-time record for goals-against average (2.18). ... Stopped a penalty shot attempt (vs. Petr Klima, February 17, 1987; vs. Ray Bourque, November 11, 1988; vs. Pavel Bure, February 17, 1992; vs. Trent Klatt, October 1, 1997; vs. Mats Sundin, April 22, 1999 (playoffs); vs. Patrik Elias, December 1, 2000.) ... Allowed a penalty shot goal (vs. Pat Verbeek, March 27, 1988; vs. Keith Acton, March 25, 1990; vs. Mario Lemieux, April 11, 1997; vs. Derek King, February 7, 1998).

		REGULAR SEASON								PLAYOFFS						
Season Team	League	Gms.	Min	W	L	T	GA	SO	Avg.	Gms.	Min.	W	L	GA	SO	Avg.
80-81 —Sault Ste. Marie	OMJHL	56	2941	31	16	1	203	0	4.14	11	457	3	3	24	1	3.15
81-82 —Sault Ste. Marie	OHL	31	1686	12	12	2	102	0	3.63	7	276	1	4	20	0	4.35
—New York Rangers	NHL	1	60	1	0	0	1	0	1.00	—						
82-83 —Sault Ste. Marie	OHL	*62	3471	39	21	1	209	0	3.61	16	944	7	6	56	*1	3.56
83-84 —New York Rangers	NHL	3	180	2	1	0	10	0	3.33	1	1	0	0	0	0	—
—Tulsa	CHL	37	2153	20	13	2	124	*3	3.46	4	240	4	0	10	0	*2.50
84-85 —New York Rangers	NHL	42	2358	12	24	3	166	1	4.22	1	20	0	0	0	0	—
85-86 —New York Rangers	NHL	61	3326	31	21	5	184	3	3.32	16	899	8	8	49	*1	3.27
86-87 —New York Rangers	NHL	50	2656	18	20	5	161	0	3.64	4	195	1	3	11	1	3.38
87-88 —New York Rangers	NHL	56	3319	27	22	7	187	2	3.38	—						
88-89 —New York Rangers	NHL	56	3207	28	21	4	197	0	3.69	2	107	0	1	6	0	3.36
89-90 —New York Rangers	NHL	47	2734	19	19	7	154	1	3.38	6	298	2	3	15	0	3.02
90-91 —New York Rangers	NHL	40	2257	15	18	6	126	3	3.35	1	52	0	0	1	0	1.15
91-92 —New York Rangers	NHL	45	2526	27	13	3	120	2	2.85	7	368	2	5	23	0	3.75
92-93 —New York Rangers	NHL	48	2757	20	18	7	152	4	3.31	—						
93-94 —Florida	NHL	57	3440	21	25	11	145	1	2.53	—						
94-95 —Florida	NHL	37	2087	14	15	4	86	4	2.47	—						
95-96 —Florida	NHL	57	3178	26	20	7	142	2	2.68	22	1332	12	*10	50	1	2.25
96-97 —Florida	NHL	57	3347	27	19	10	128	2	2.29	5	328	1	4	13	1	2.38
97-98 —Florida	NHL	60	3451	18	29	11	165	4	2.87	—						
—U.S. Olympic team	Int'l	1	1	0	0	0	0	0	...	—						
98-99 —Philadelphia	NHL	62	3712	27	18	*15	135	6	2.18	6	369	2	4	9	1	1.46
99-00 —Philadelphia	NHL	50	2950	25	15	9	108	3	2.20	—						
00-01 —New York Islanders	NHL	44	2390	10	25	5	120	1	3.01	—						
—New Jersey	NHL	4	240	4	0	0	6	1	1.50	—						
NHL Totals (19 years)		877	50175	372	343	119	2493	40	2.98	71	3969	28	38	177	5	2.68

VANDENBUSSCHE, RYAN   RW   BLACKHAWKS

PERSONAL: Born February 28, 1973, in Simcoe, Ont. ... 6-0/200. ... Shoots right. ... Name pronounced VAN-dihn-bush.

TRANSACTIONS/CAREER NOTES: Selected by Toronto Maple Leafs in eighth round (173rd overall) of NHL entry draft (June 20, 1992). ... Signed as free agent by New York Rangers (August 22, 1995). ... Traded by Rangers to Chicago Blackhawks for D Ryan Risidore (March 24, 1998). ... Suspended one game by NHL for head-butting incident (March 28, 1999). ... Underwent elbow surgery prior to 1999-2000 season; missed first six games of season. ... Suffered sore back (December 3, 1999); missed five games. ... Lacerated left hand (March 3, 2000); missed 10 games.

		REGULAR SEASON							PLAYOFFS				
Season Team	League	Gms.	G	A	Pts.	PIM	+/-	PP	SH	Gms.	G	A	Pts.	PIM
90-91 —Cornwall	OHL	49	3	8	11	139	...	...	...	—				
91-92 —Cornwall	OHL	61	13	15	28	232	...	...	...	6	0	2	2	9
92-93 —Newmarket	OHL	30	15	12	27	161	...	...	...	—				
—Guelph	OHL	29	3	14	17	99	...	...	...	5	1	3	4	13
—St. John's	AHL	1	0	0	0	0	...	...	...	—				
93-94 —St. John's	AHL	44	4	10	14	124	...	...	...	—				
—Springfield	AHL	9	1	2	3	29	...	...	...	5	0	0	0	16
94-95 —St. John's	AHL	53	2	13	15	239	...	...	...	—				
95-96 —Binghamton	AHL	68	3	17	20	240	...	...	...	4	0	0	0	9
96-97 —Binghamton	AHL	38	8	11	19	133	...	...	...	—				
—New York Rangers	NHL	11	1	0	1	30	-2	0	0	—				
97-98 —New York Rangers	NHL	16	1	0	1	38	-2	0	0	—				
—Hartford	AHL	15	2	0	2	45	...	...	...	—				
—Chicago	NHL	4	0	1	1	5	0	0	0	—				
—Indianapolis	IHL	3	1	1	2	4	...	...	...	—				
98-99 —Indianapolis	IHL	34	3	10	13	130	...	...	...	—				
—Portland	AHL	37	4	1	5	119	...	...	...	—				
—Chicago	NHL	6	0	0	0	17	0	0	0	—				
99-00 —Chicago	NHL	52	0	1	1	143	-3	0	0	—				
00-01 —Chicago	NHL	64	2	5	7	146	-8	0	0	—				
NHL Totals (5 years)		153	4	7	11	379	-15	0	0					

V

VARADA, VACLAV — RW — SABRES

PERSONAL: Born April 26, 1976, in Vsetin, Czechoslovakia. ... 6-0/200. ... Shoots left. ... Name pronounced vuh-RAH-duh.
TRANSACTIONS/CAREER NOTES: Selected by San Jose Sharks in fourth round (fourth Sharks pick, 89th overall) of NHL entry draft (June 29, 1994). ... Traded by Sharks with LW Martin Spahnel and fourth-round pick (D Mike Martone) in 1996 draft to Buffalo Sabres for D Doug Bodger (November 16, 1995). ... Fractured left hand (February 2, 1997); missed 15 games. ... Sprained ankle (February 9, 1999); missed 10 games. ... Suffered ear injury (January 18, 2000); missed three games. ... Suffered concussion (February 25, 2001); missed six games.

Season Team	League	Gms.	G	A	Pts.	PIM	+/-	PP	SH	Gms.	G	A	Pts.	PIM
92-93—TJ Vitkovice	Czech.	1	0	0	0	...	...	...	...	—	—	—	—	—
93-94—HC Vitkovice	Czech Rep.	24	6	7	13	...	...	...	...	5	1	1	2	...
94-95—Tacoma	WHL	68	50	38	88	108	...	...	...	4	4	3	7	11
—Czech. Jr. nat'l team	Int'l	7	6	4	10	25	...	...	...	—	—	—	—	—
95-96—Kelowna	WHL	59	39	46	85	100	...	...	...	6	3	3	6	16
—Rochester	AHL	5	3	0	3	4	...	...	...	—	—	—	—	—
—Buffalo	NHL	1	0	0	0	0	0	0	0	—	—	—	—	—
—Czech. Jr. nat'l team	Int'l	6	5	1	6	8	...	...	...	—	—	—	—	—
96-97—Rochester	AHL	53	23	25	48	81	...	...	...	10	1	6	7	27
—Buffalo	NHL	5	0	0	0	2	0	0	0	—	—	—	—	—
97-98—Rochester	AHL	45	30	26	56	74	...	...	...	—	—	—	—	—
—Buffalo	NHL	27	5	6	11	15	0	0	0	15	3	4	7	18
98-99—Buffalo	NHL	72	7	24	31	61	11	1	0	21	5	4	9	14
99-00—HC Vitkovice	Czech Rep.	5	2	3	5	12	...	...	...	—	—	—	—	—
—Buffalo	NHL	76	10	27	37	62	12	0	0	5	0	0	0	8
00-01—Buffalo	NHL	75	10	21	31	81	-2	2	0	13	0	4	4	8
NHL Totals (6 years)		256	32	78	110	221	21	3	0	54	8	12	20	48

VARLAMOV, SERGEI — RW — BLUES

PERSONAL: Born July 21, 1978, in Kiev, U.S.S.R. ... 5-11/195. ... Shoots left. ... Name pronounced VAHR-luh-mahf.
TRANSACTIONS/CAREER NOTES: Signed as non-drafted free agent by Calgary Flames (September 18, 1996). ... Traded by Flames with G Fred Brathwaite, C Daniel Tkaczuk, and ninth-round pick (C Grant Jacobsen) in 2001 draft to St. Louis Blues for G Roman Turek and fourth-round pick (F Egor Shastin) in 2001 draft (June 23, 2001).
HONORS: Won Can.HL Player of the Year Award (1997-98). ... Named to Can.HL All-Star first team (1997-98). ... Won Bob Clarke Trophy (1997-98). ... Won Four Broncos Memorial Trophy (1997-98). ... Named to WHL (East) All-Star first team (1997-98).

Season Team	League	Gms.	G	A	Pts.	PIM	+/-	PP	SH	Gms.	G	A	Pts.	PIM
95-96—Swift Current	WHL	55	23	21	44	65	...	...	...	—	—	—	—	—
96-97—Swift Current	WHL	72	46	39	85	94	...	...	...	—	—	—	—	—
—Saint John	AHL	1	0	0	0	2	...	...	...	—	—	—	—	—
97-98—Swift Current	WHL	72	*66	53	*119	132	...	...	...	12	10	5	15	28
—Calgary	NHL	1	0	0	0	0	0	0	0	—	—	—	—	—
—Saint John	AHL	—	—	—	—	—	...	...	...	3	0	0	0	0
98-99—Saint John	AHL	76	24	33	57	66	...	...	...	7	0	4	4	8
99-00—Saint John	AHL	68	20	21	41	88	...	...	...	3	0	0	0	24
—Calgary	NHL	7	3	0	3	0	0	0	0	—	—	—	—	—
00-01—Saint John	AHL	55	21	30	51	56	...	...	...	19	*15	8	23	10
NHL Totals (2 years)		8	3	0	3	0	0	0	0					

VASICEK, JOSEF — C — HURRICANES

PERSONAL: Born September 12, 1980, in Havlickuv Brod, Czechoslovakia. ... 6-4/196. ... Shoots left.
TRANSACTIONS/CAREER NOTES: Selected by Carolina Hurricanes in fourth round (fourth Hurricanes pick, 91st overall) of NHL entry draft (June 27, 1998).

Season Team	League	Gms.	G	A	Pts.	PIM	+/-	PP	SH	Gms.	G	A	Pts.	PIM
95-96—Havlickuv Brod	Czech Jrs.	36	25	25	50	...	...	...	...	—	—	—	—	—
96-97—Slavia Praha Jrs.	Czech	37	20	40	60	...	...	...	...	—	—	—	—	—
97-98—Slavia Praha Jrs.	Czech	34	13	20	33	...	...	...	...	—	—	—	—	—
98-99—Sault Ste. Marie	OHL	66	21	35	56	30	...	...	...	5	3	0	3	10
99-00—Sault Ste. Marie	OHL	54	26	46	72	49	...	...	...	17	5	15	20	8
00-01—Carolina	NHL	76	8	13	21	53	-8	1	0	6	2	0	2	0
—Cincinnati	IHL	—	—	—	—	—	...	...	...	3	0	0	0	0
NHL Totals (1 year)		76	8	13	21	53	-8	1	0	6	2	0	2	0

VASILIEV, ALEXEI — D — PREDATORS

PERSONAL: Born September 1, 1977, in Yaroslavl, U.S.S.R. ... 6-1/192. ... Shoots left. ... Name pronounced vuh-SIHL-yehf.
TRANSACTIONS/CAREER NOTES: Selected by New York Rangers in fifth round (fourth Rangers pick, 110th overall) of NHL entry draft (July 8, 1995). ... Traded by Rangers to Nashville Predators for conditional pick in 2001 draft (September 25, 2000).

Season Team	League	Gms.	G	A	Pts.	PIM	+/-	PP	SH	Gms.	G	A	Pts.	PIM
93-94—Yaroslavl	CIS	2	0	1	1	4	...	...	...	—	—	—	—	—
94-95—Yaroslavl 2	CIS.2						Statistics unavailable.			—	—	—	—	—
95-96—Yaroslavl	CIS	40	4	7	11	4	...	...	...	—	—	—	—	—
96-97—Torpedo-Yaroslavl	Russian	44	2	8	10	10	...	...	...	9	1	1	2	8

Season Team	League	REGULAR SEASON								PLAYOFFS				
		Gms.	G	A	Pts.	PIM	+/-	PP	SH	Gms.	G	A	Pts.	PIM
97-98—Hartford	AHL					Did not play.								
98-99—Hartford	AHL	75	8	19	27	24	...	...	...	6	0	1	1	2
99-00—Hartford	AHL	75	10	28	38	20	...	...	...	15	3	1	4	2
—New York Rangers	NHL	1	0	0	0	2	-1	0	0	—	—	—	—	—
00-01—Milwaukee	IHL	69	6	12	18	20	...	...	...	4	0	0	0	2
NHL Totals (1 year)		1	0	0	0	2	-1	0	0					

VASILJEVS, HERBERT — C

PERSONAL: Born May 27, 1976, in Riga, U.S.S.R. ... 5-11/180. ... Shoots right.
TRANSACTIONS/CAREER NOTES: Signed as non-drafted free agent by Florida Panthers (October 3, 1997). ... Traded by Panthers with D Gord Murphy, D Daniel Tjarnqvist and sixth-round pick (traded to Dallas) in 1999 draft to Atlanta Thrashers for G Trevor Kidd (June 25, 1999).

Season Team	League	REGULAR SEASON								PLAYOFFS				
		Gms.	G	A	Pts.	PIM	+/-	PP	SH	Gms.	G	A	Pts.	PIM
94-95—Krefeld Pinguine	Germany	57	5	9	14	34	...	...	...	—	—	—	—	—
95-96—Guelph	OHL	65	34	33	67	63	...	...	...	16	6	13	19	6
96-97—Carolina	AHL	54	13	18	31	30	...	...	...	—	—	—	—	—
—Port Huron	Col.HL	3	3	2	5	4	...	...	...	—	—	—	—	—
—Knoxville	ECHL	3	1	1	2	0	...	...	...	—	—	—	—	—
97-98—New Haven	AHL	76	36	30	66	60	...	...	...	3	1	0	1	2
98-99—Kentucky	AHL	76	28	48	76	66	...	...	...	12	2	1	3	4
—Florida	NHL	5	0	0	0	2	-1	0	0	—	—	—	—	—
99-00—Orlando	IHL	73	25	35	60	60	...	...	...	6	2	2	4	6
—Atlanta	NHL	7	1	0	1	4	-3	0	0	—	—	—	—	—
00-01—Orlando	IHL	58	22	26	48	32	...	...	...	12	8	3	11	14
—Atlanta	NHL	21	4	5	9	14	-11	2	0	—	—	—	—	—
NHL Totals (3 years)		33	5	5	10	20	-15	2	0					

VAUCLAIR, JULIEN — D — SENATORS

PERSONAL: Born October 2, 1979, in Delemont, Switzerland. ... 6-0/200. ... Shoots left.
TRANSACTIONS/CAREER NOTES: Selected by Ottawa Senators in third round (fourth Senators pick, 74th overall) of NHL entry draft (June 27, 1998).

Season Team	League	REGULAR SEASON								PLAYOFFS				
		Gms.	G	A	Pts.	PIM	+/-	PP	SH	Gms.	G	A	Pts.	PIM
95-96—Ajoie	Switz. Div. 3	20	4	10	14	...	...	...	...	—	—	—	—	—
96-97—Ajoie	Switz. Div. 3	40	0	6	6	24	...	...	...	9	0	2	2	8
97-98—Lugano	Switzerland	36	1	2	3	12	...	...	...	7	0	0	0	25
98-99—Lugano	Switzerland	38	0	3	3	8	...	...	...	—	—	—	—	—
99-00—Lugano	Switzerland	45	3	3	6	16	...	...	...	14	0	0	0	0
00-01—Lugano	Switzerland	42	3	4	7	57	...	...	...	18	0	1	1	4

VERBEEK, PAT — RW

PERSONAL: Born May 24, 1964, in Sarnia, Ont. ... 5-9/192. ... Shoots right.
TRANSACTIONS/CAREER NOTES: Selected by New Jersey Devils in third round (third Devils pick, 43rd overall) of NHL entry draft (June 9, 1982). ... Suffered severed left thumb between knuckles in a corn-planting machine on his farm and underwent surgery to have thumb reconnected (May 15, 1985). ... Pulled side muscle (March 1987). ... Bruised chest (October 28, 1988). ... Traded by Devils to Hartford Whalers for LW Sylvain Turgeon (June 17, 1989). ... Missed first three games of 1991-92 season due to contract dispute. ... Traded by Whalers to New York Rangers for D Glen Featherstone, D Michael Stewart, first-round pick (G Jean-Sebastien Giguere) in 1995 draft and fourth-round pick (C Steve Wasylko) in 1996 draft (March 23, 1995). ... Injured knee (February 17, 1996); missed two games. ... Separated shoulder (March 1, 1996); missed nine games. ... Suffered back spasms (April 7, 1996); missed two games. ... Signed as free agent by Dallas Stars (July 3, 1996). ... Sprained knee (January 4, 1997); missed one game. ... Sprained knee (April 14, 1999); missed final three games of regular season and four playoff games. ... Suspended one playoff game by NHL for slashing incident (May 7, 1999). ... Signed as free agent by Detroit Red Wings (November 10, 1999).
HONORS: Won Emms Family Award (1981-82). ... Played in NHL All-Star Game (1991 and 1996).
MISCELLANEOUS: Member of Stanley Cup championship team (1999). ... Scored on a penalty shot (vs. John Vanbiesbrouck, March 27, 1988).
STATISTICAL NOTES: Only player in NHL history to lead team in goals scored and penalty minutes (1989-90 and 1990-91). ... Captain of Hartford Whalers (1992-93 through 1993-94).
STATISTICAL PLATEAUS: Three-goal games: 1985-86 (1), 1986-87 (1), 1987-88 (1), 1988-89 (1), 1992-93 (2), 1993-94 (2), 1995-96 (2), 1997-98 (1). Total: 11. ... Four-goal games: 1987-88 (1). ... Total hat tricks: 12.

Season Team	League	REGULAR SEASON								PLAYOFFS				
		Gms.	G	A	Pts.	PIM	+/-	PP	SH	Gms.	G	A	Pts.	PIM
79-80—Petrolia Jr. B.	OPJHL	41	17	24	41	85	...	...	...	—	—	—	—	—
80-81—Petrolia Jr. B.	OPJHL	42	44	44	88	155	...	...	...	—	—	—	—	—
81-82—Sudbury	OHL	66	37	51	88	180	...	...	...	—	—	—	—	—
82-83—Sudbury	OHL	61	40	67	107	184	...	...	...	—	—	—	—	—
—New Jersey	NHL	6	3	2	5	8	-2	0	0	—	—	—	—	—
83-84—New Jersey	NHL	79	20	27	47	158	-19	5	1	—	—	—	—	—
84-85—New Jersey	NHL	78	15	18	33	162	-24	5	1	—	—	—	—	—
85-86—New Jersey	NHL	76	25	28	53	79	-25	4	1	—	—	—	—	—
86-87—New Jersey	NHL	74	35	24	59	120	-23	17	0	—	—	—	—	—
87-88—New Jersey	NHL	73	46	31	77	227	29	13	0	20	4	8	12	51
88-89—New Jersey	NHL	77	26	21	47	189	-18	9	0	—	—	—	—	—

Season Team	League	Gms.	G	A	Pts.	PIM	+/-	PP	SH		Gms.	G	A	Pts.	PIM
89-90—Hartford	NHL	80	44	45	89	228	1	14	0		7	2	2	4	26
90-91—Hartford	NHL	80	43	39	82	246	0	15	0		6	3	2	5	40
91-92—Hartford	NHL	76	22	35	57	243	-16	10	0		7	0	2	2	12
92-93—Hartford	NHL	84	39	43	82	197	-7	16	0		—	—	—	—	—
93-94—Hartford	NHL	84	37	38	75	177	-15	15	1		—	—	—	—	—
94-95—Hartford	NHL	29	7	11	18	53	0	3	0		—	—	—	—	—
—New York Rangers	NHL	19	10	5	15	18	-2	4	0		10	4	6	10	20
95-96—New York Rangers	NHL	69	41	41	82	129	29	17	0		11	3	6	9	12
96-97—Dallas	NHL	81	17	36	53	128	3	5	0		7	1	3	4	16
97-98—Dallas	NHL	82	31	26	57	170	15	9	0		17	3	2	5	26
98-99—Dallas	NHL	78	17	17	34	133	11	8	0		18	3	4	7	14
99-00—Detroit	NHL	68	22	26	48	95	22	7	0		9	1	1	2	2
00-01—Detroit	NHL	67	15	15	30	73	0	7	0		5	2	0	2	6
NHL Totals (19 years)		1360	515	528	1043	2833	-41	183	4		117	26	36	62	225

VERMETTE, ANTOINE   C   SENATORS

PERSONAL: Born July 20, 1982, in St-Agapit, Que. ... 6-0/184. ... Shoots left.
TRANSACTIONS/CAREER NOTES: Selected by Ottawa Senators in second round (third Senators pick, 55th overall) of NHL entry draft (June 24, 2000).
HONORS: Won Mike Bossy Trophy (1999-2000).

Season Team	League	Gms.	G	A	Pts.	PIM	+/-	PP	SH		Gms.	G	A	Pts.	PIM
98-99—Quebec	QMJHL	57	9	17	26	32	...	...	...		13	0	0	0	2
99-00—Victoriaville	QMJHL	71	30	41	71	87	...	...	...		6	0	1	1	6
00-01—Victoriaville	QMJHL	71	57	62	119	102	...	...	...		9	4	6	10	14

VERNON, MIKE   G   FLAMES

PERSONAL: Born February 24, 1963, in Calgary. ... 5-9/180. ... Catches left.
TRANSACTIONS/CAREER NOTES: Selected by Calgary Flames in third round (second Flames pick, 56th overall) of NHL entry draft (June 10, 1981). ... Injured hip (March 2, 1988). ... Suffered back spasms (February 1989). ... Suffered back spasms (March 1990); missed 10 games. ... Suffered lacerated forehead (October 25, 1992); missed five games. ... Suffered from the flu (November 15, 1993); missed two games. ... Twisted knee (December 30, 1993); missed 14 games. ... Traded by Flames to Detroit Red Wings for D Steve Chiasson (June 29, 1994). ... Pulled groin (December 29, 1995); missed 12 games. ... Suffered from the flu (October 23, 1996); missed three games. ... Injured knee (March 12, 1997); missed three games. ... Traded by Red Wings to San Jose Sharks for second-round pick (D Maxim Linnik) in 1998 draft and second-round pick (traded to Tampa Bay) in 1999 draft (August 18, 1997). ... Injured groin (March 1, 1999); missed six games. ... Suffered from the flu (December 19, 1999); missed two games. ... Traded by Sharks with third-round pick (RW Sean O'Connor) in 2000 draft to Florida Panthers for RW Radek Dvorak (December 30, 1999). ... Selected by Minnesota Wild in NHL expansion draft (June 23, 2000). ... Traded by Wild to Flames for rights to C Dan Cavanaugh and eighth-round pick (LW Jake Riddle) in 2001 draft (June 23, 2000). ... Suffered concussion (December 22, 2000); missed two games.
HONORS: Won WHL Most Valuable Player Trophy (1981-82 and 1982-83). ... Won WHL Top Goaltender Trophy (1981-82 and 1982-83). ... Won WHL Player of the Year Award (1981-82). ... Named to WHL All-Star first team (1981-82 and 1982-83). ... Named to CHL All-Star second team (1983-84). ... Named to THE SPORTING NEWS All-Star second team (1988-89). ... Named to NHL All-Star second team (1988-89). ... Played in NHL All-Star Game (1988-1991 and 1993). ... Shared William M. Jennings Trophy with Chris Osgood (1995-96). ... Won Conn Smythe Trophy (1996-97).
RECORDS: Shares NHL single-season playoff record for most wins by a goaltender—16 (1989 and 1997).
MISCELLANEOUS: Member of Stanley Cup championship team (1989 and 1997). ... Holds Calgary Flames all-time records for games played by a goaltender (467) and wins (248). ... Holds San Jose Sharks all-time records for most shutouts (9) and lowest goals-against average (2.39). ... Stopped a penalty shot attempt (vs. Kirk Muller, March 14, 1989; vs. Jim Cummins, April 7, 1996; vs. Claude Lapointe, January 12, 2000). ... Allowed a penalty shot goal (vs. Stan Smyl, January 16, 1987; vs. Craig MacTavish, December 23, 1988; vs. Gino Odjick, October 19, 1991; vs. Paul Broten, January 16, 1992; vs. Pavel Bure, November 12, 1997).

Season Team	League	Gms.	Min	W	L	T	GA	SO	Avg.		Gms.	Min.	W	L	GA	SO	Avg.
80-81—Calgary	WHL	59	3154	33	17	1	198	1	3.77		22	1271	...	...	82	1	3.87
81-82—Calgary	WHL	42	2329	22	14	2	143	*3	*3.68		9	527	...	...	30	0	*3.42
—Oklahoma City	CHL	—	—	—	—	—	—	—	—		1	70	0	1	4	0	3.43
82-83—Calgary	WHL	50	2856	19	18	2	155	*3	*3.26		16	925	9	7	60	0	3.89
—Calgary	NHL	2	100	0	2	0	11	0	6.60		—	—	—	—	—	—	—
83-84—Calgary	NHL	1	11	0	1	0	4	0	21.82		—	—	—	—	—	—	—
—Colorado	CHL	*46	*2648	30	13	2	148	1	*3.35		6	347	2	4	21	0	3.63
84-85—Moncton	AHL	41	2050	10	20	4	134	0	3.92		—	—	—	—	—	—	—
85-86—Salt Lake City	IHL	10	601	6	4	0	34	1	3.39		—	—	—	—	—	—	—
—Moncton	AHL	6	374	3	1	2	21	0	3.37		—	—	—	—	—	—	—
—Calgary	NHL	18	921	9	3	3	52	1	3.39		*21	*1229	12	*9	*60	0	2.93
86-87—Calgary	NHL	54	2957	30	21	1	178	1	3.61		5	263	2	3	16	0	3.65
87-88—Calgary	NHL	64	3565	39	16	7	210	1	3.53		9	515	4	4	34	0	3.96
88-89—Calgary	NHL	52	2938	*37	6	5	130	0	2.65		*22	*1381	*16	5	*52	*3	2.26
89-90—Calgary	NHL	47	2795	23	14	9	146	0	3.13		6	342	2	3	19	0	3.33
90-91—Calgary	NHL	54	3121	31	19	3	172	1	3.31		7	427	3	4	21	0	2.95
91-92—Calgary	NHL	63	3640	24	30	9	217	0	3.58		—	—	—	—	—	—	—
92-93—Calgary	NHL	64	3732	29	26	9	203	2	3.26		4	150	1	1	15	0	6.00
93-94—Calgary	NHL	48	2798	26	17	5	131	3	2.81		7	466	3	4	23	0	2.96
94-95—Detroit	NHL	30	1807	19	6	4	76	1	2.52		18	1063	12	6	41	1	2.31
95-96—Detroit	NHL	32	1855	21	7	2	70	3	2.26		4	243	2	2	11	0	2.72
96-97—Detroit	NHL	33	1952	13	11	8	79	0	2.43		20	1229	16	4	36	1	1.76
97-98—San Jose	NHL	62	3564	30	22	8	146	5	2.46		6	348	2	4	14	1	2.41

Season Team	League	REGULAR SEASON								PLAYOFFS						
		Gms.	Min	W	L	T	GA	SO	Avg.	Gms.	Min.	W	L	GA	SO	Avg.
98-99—San Jose	NHL	49	2831	16	22	10	107	4	2.27	5	321	2	3	13	0	2.43
99-00—San Jose	NHL	15	772	6	5	1	32	0	2.49	—	—	—	—	—	—	—
—Florida	NHL	34	2019	18	13	2	83	1	2.47	4	237	0	4	12	0	3.04
00-01—Calgary	NHL	41	2246	12	23	5	121	3	3.23	—	—	—	—	—	—	—
NHL Totals (18 years)		763	43624	383	264	91	2168	26	2.98	138	8214	77	56	367	6	2.68

VIGIER, J.P.   RW   THRASHERS

PERSONAL: Born August 11, 1976, in Notre Dame de Lourdes, Man. ... 6-0/200. ... Shoots right.
TRANSACTIONS/CAREER NOTES: Signed as non-drafted free agent by Atlanta Thrashers (March 24, 2000).
HONORS: Named to CCHA All-Star second team (1998-99).

Season Team	League	REGULAR SEASON								PLAYOFFS				
		Gms.	G	A	Pts.	PIM	+/-	PP	SH	Gms.	G	A	Pts.	PIM
96-97—Northern Michigan	CCHA	36	10	14	24	54	...	...	...	—	—	—	—	—
97-98—Northern Michigan	CCHA	36	12	15	27	60	...	...	...	—	—	—	—	—
98-99—Northern Michigan	CCHA	42	21	18	39	80	...	...	...	—	—	—	—	—
99-00—Northern Michigan	CCHA	39	18	17	35	72	...	...	...	—	—	—	—	—
—Orlando	IHL	1	0	0	0	0	...	...	...	—	—	—	—	—
00-01—Orlando	IHL	78	23	17	40	66	...	...	...	16	6	6	12	14
—Atlanta	NHL	2	0	0	0	0	-2	0	0	—	—	—	—	—
NHL Totals (1 year)		2	0	0	0	0	-2	0	0					

VISHNEVSKI, VITALI   D   MIGHTY DUCKS

PERSONAL: Born March 18, 1980, in Kharkov, U.S.S.R. ... 6-2/190. ... Shoots left.
TRANSACTIONS/CAREER NOTES: Selected by Mighty Ducks of Anaheim in first round (first Mighty Ducks pick, fifth overall) of NHL entry draft (June 27, 1998). ... Suffered injury (April 5, 2000); missed final two games of season. ... Strained hip muscle (January 30, 2001); missed three games. ... Strained shoulder (March 16, 2001); missed three games.

Season Team	League	REGULAR SEASON								PLAYOFFS				
		Gms.	G	A	Pts.	PIM	+/-	PP	SH	Gms.	G	A	Pts.	PIM
95-96—Torpedo-2 Yaroslavl	CIS Div. II	40	4	4	8	20	...	...	...	—	—	—	—	—
96-97—Torpedo-2 Yaroslavl	Rus. Div. III	45	0	2	2	30	...	...	...	—	—	—	—	—
97-98—Torpedo-2 Yaroslavl	Rus. Div. II	47	8	9	17	164	...	...	...	—	—	—	—	—
98-99—Torpedo Yaroslavl	Russian	34	3	4	7	38	...	...	...	10	0	0	0	4
99-00—Cincinnati	AHL	35	1	3	4	45	...	...	...	—	—	—	—	—
—Anaheim	NHL	31	1	1	2	26	0	1	0	—	—	—	—	—
00-01—Anaheim	NHL	76	1	10	11	99	-1	0	0	—	—	—	—	—
NHL Totals (2 years)		107	2	11	13	125	-1	1	0					

VISNOVSKY, LUBOMIR   D   KINGS

PERSONAL: Born August 11, 1976, in Topolcany, Czechoslovakia. ... 5-10/172. ... Shoots left.
TRANSACTIONS/CAREER NOTES: Selected by Los Angeles Kings in fourth round (fourth Kings pick, 118th overall) of NHL entry draft (June 24, 2000). ... Suffered back spasms (December 3, 2000); missed one game.
HONORS: Named to NHL All-Rookie team (2000-01).

Season Team	League	REGULAR SEASON								PLAYOFFS				
		Gms.	G	A	Pts.	PIM	+/-	PP	SH	Gms.	G	A	Pts.	PIM
94-95—Bratislava	Slovakia	36	11	12	23	10	...	...	...	9	1	3	4	2
95-96—Bratislava	Slovakia	35	8	6	14	22	...	...	...	13	1	5	6	2
96-97—Bratislava	Slovakia	44	11	12	23	...	...	...	...	2	0	1	1	...
97-98—Bratislava	Slovakia	36	7	9	16	16	...	...	...	11	2	4	6	8
98-99—Bratislava	Slovakia	40	9	10	19	31	...	...	...	10	5	5	10	0
99-00—Bratislava	Slovakia	52	21	24	45	38	...	...	...	8	5	3	8	16
00-01—Los Angeles	NHL	81	7	32	39	36	16	3	0	8	0	0	0	0
NHL Totals (1 year)		81	7	32	39	36	16	3	0	8	0	0	0	0

VLASAK, TOMAS   C

PERSONAL: Born February 1, 1975, in Prague, Czechoslovakia. ... 5-10/161. ... Shoots right. ... Name pronounced VLA-sihk.
TRANSACTIONS/CAREER NOTES: Selected by Los Angeles Kings in fifth round (sixth Kings pick, 120th overall) of NHL entry draft (June 26, 1993). ... Released by Kings (December 5, 2000).

Season Team	League	REGULAR SEASON								PLAYOFFS				
		Gms.	G	A	Pts.	PIM	+/-	PP	SH	Gms.	G	A	Pts.	PIM
91-92—Slavia Praha	Czech Jrs.	69	49	43	92	24	...	...	...	—	—	—	—	—
92-93—Slavia Praha	Czech Dv.II	31	17	6	23	6	...	...	...	—	—	—	—	—
93-94—Litvinov	Czech Rep.	41	16	11	27	0	...	...	...	4	0	1	1	...
94-95—Litvinov	Czech Rep.	35	6	14	20	4	...	...	...	4	0	0	0	4
95-96—Litvinov	Czech Rep.	35	10	22	32	...	...	...	...	15	5	5	10	...
96-97—Litvinov	Czech Rep.	52	26	34	60	16	...	...	...	—	—	—	—	—
97-98—Chem. Litvinov	Czech Rep.	51	22	44	66	40	...	...	...	4	1	2	3	2
98-99—HPK Hameenlinna	Finland	54	28	29	57	36	...	...	...	8	2	*9	11	0
99-00—HPK Hameenlinna	Finland	48	24	39	63	63	...	...	...	8	3	4	7	6
00-01—Los Angeles	NHL	10	1	3	4	2	4	0	0	—	—	—	—	—
—Lowell	AHL	5	0	1	1	5	...	...	...	—	—	—	—	—
—HPK Hameenlinna	Finland	27	6	12	18	10	...	...	...	—	—	—	—	—
NHL Totals (1 year)		10	1	3	4	2	4	0	0					

V

VLASENKOV, DMITRI   LW   THRASHERS

PERSONAL: Born January 1, 1978, in Safonovo, U.S.S.R. ... 5-11/183. ... Shoots left.
TRANSACTIONS/CAREER NOTES: Selected by Calgary Flames in third round (fourth Flames pick, 73rd overall) of NHL entry draft (June 22, 1996). ... Traded by Flames with C Hnat Domenichelli to Atlanta Thrashers for D Darryl Shannon and LW Jason Botterill (February 11, 2000).

Season Team	League	REGULAR SEASON								PLAYOFFS				
		Gms.	G	A	Pts.	PIM	+/-	PP	SH	Gms.	G	A	Pts.	PIM
95-96—Torpedo Yaroslavl	CIS	17	1	1	2	4	...	...	...	—	—	—	—	—
96-97—Torpedo Yaroslavl	Russian	28	3	2	5	10	...	...	...	8	1	1	2	2
97-98—Torpedo Yaroslavl	Russian	44	10	3	13	12	...	...	...	—	—	—	—	—
98-99—Torpedo Yaroslavl	Russian	41	11	5	16	26	...	...	...	10	1	2	3	6
99-00—Torpedo Yaroslavl	Russian	38	15	20	35	10	...	...	...	10	3	4	7	6
00-01—Orlando	IHL	49	5	8	13	10	...	...	...	1	0	0	0	0

VOKOUN, TOMAS   G   PREDATORS

PERSONAL: Born July 2, 1976, in Karlovy Vary, Czechoslovakia. ... 6-3/183. ... Catches right. ... Name pronounced TOH-mahz voh-KOON.
TRANSACTIONS/CAREER NOTES: Selected by Montreal Canadiens in ninth round (11th Canadiens pick, 226th overall) of NHL entry draft (June 29, 1994). ... Selected by Nashville Predators in NHL expansion draft (June 26, 1998). ... Strained neck (January 19, 1999); missed one game. ... Suffered injury (March 31, 2000); missed final four games of season. ... Bruised foot (October 16, 2000); missed three games.
MISCELLANEOUS: Holds Nashville Predators all-time records for goals-against average (2.71). ... Stopped a penalty shot attempt (vs. Alex Zhamnov, March 22, 2001). ... Allowed a penalty shot goal (vs. Jeremy Roenick, March 17, 2000; vs. David Vyborny, March 19, 2001).

Season Team	League	REGULAR SEASON								PLAYOFFS						
		Gms.	Min	W	L	T	GA	SO	Avg.	Gms.	Min.	W	L	GA	SO	Avg.
93-94—Poldi Kladno	Czech Rep.	1	20	...	...	...	2	0	6.00	—	—	—	—	—	—	—
94-95—Poldi Kladno	Czech Rep.	26	1368	...	...	...	70	...	3.07	5	240	...	...	19	...	4.75
95-96—Wheeling	ECHL	35	1911	20	10	‡2	117	0	3.67	7	436	4	3	19	0	2.61
—Fredericton	AHL	—	—	—	—	—	—	—	—	1	59	0	1	4	0	4.07
96-97—Fredericton	AHL	47	2645	12	26	7	154	2	3.49	—	—	—	—	—	—	—
—Montreal	NHL	1	20	0	0	0	4	0	12.00	—	—	—	—	—	—	—
97-98—Fredericton	AHL	31	1735	13	13	2	90	0	3.11	—	—	—	—	—	—	—
98-99—Milwaukee	IHL	9	539	3	2	‡4	22	1	2.45	2	149	0	2	8	0	3.22
—Nashville	NHL	37	1954	12	18	4	96	1	2.95	—	—	—	—	—	—	—
99-00—Nashville	NHL	33	1879	9	20	1	87	1	2.78	—	—	—	—	—	—	—
—Milwaukee	IHL	7	364	6	2	0	17	0	2.80	—	—	—	—	—	—	—
00-01—Nashville	NHL	37	2088	13	17	5	85	2	2.44	—	—	—	—	—	—	—
NHL Totals (4 years)		108	5941	34	55	10	272	4	2.75							

VOLKOV, ALEXEY   G   KINGS

PERSONAL: Born March 15, 1980, in Yekaterinburg, U.S.S.R. ... 6-1/185. ... Catches left.
TRANSACTIONS/CAREER NOTES: Selected by Los Angeles Kings in third round (third Kings pick, 76th overall) of NHL entry draft (June 27, 1998).
HONORS: Won Raymond Lagace Trophy (1998-99).

Season Team	League	REGULAR SEASON								PLAYOFFS						
		Gms.	Min	W	L	T	GA	SO	Avg.	Gms.	Min.	W	L	GA	SO	Avg.
95-96—SKA-Avto-2 Yekat.	CIS Div. II	42	...	...	...	...	78	...	...	—	—	—	—	—	—	—
96-97—SKA Yekaterinburg	Rus. Div. III	34	...	...	...	...	66	...	...	—	—	—	—	—	—	—
—Krylja Sovetov Moscow	Russian Jr.	8	...	...	...	...	9	...	...	—	—	—	—	—	—	—
97-98—Krylja Sovetov-2 Mos.	Rus. Div. III	27	...	...	...	...	72	...	...	—	—	—	—	—	—	—
98-99—Halifax	QMJHL	39	2332	25	9	3	105	2	2.70	5	282	1	4	21	0	4.47
99-00—Halifax	QMJHL	40	2221	23	13	2	124	1	3.35	8	416	3	4	29	0	4.18
00-01—Lowell	AHL	5	202	1	1	0	16	0	4.75	—	—	—	—	—	—	—
—New Orleans	ECHL	29	1577	12	9	5	81	1	3.08	—	—	—	—	—	—	—

VON ARX, RETO   LW   BLACKHAWKS

PERSONAL: Born May 5, 1982, in Egerkingen, Switzerland ... 5-10/176. ... Shoots left.
TRANSACTIONS/CAREER NOTES: Selected by Chicago Blackhawks in ninth round (14th Blackhawks pick, 271st overall) of NHL entry draft (June 24, 2000). ... Strained groin (January 25, 2001); missed five games.

Season Team	League	REGULAR SEASON								PLAYOFFS				
		Gms.	G	A	Pts.	PIM	+/-	PP	SH	Gms.	G	A	Pts.	PIM
95-96—Davos	Switzerland	34	4	6	10	59	...	...	...	—	—	—	—	—
96-97—Davos	Switzerland	48	11	20	31	82	...	...	...	—	—	—	—	—
97-98—Davos	Switzerland	39	8	15	23	113	...	...	...	—	—	—	—	—
98-99—Davos	Switzerland	34	21	20	41	76	...	...	...	—	—	—	—	—
99-00—Davos	Switzerland	45	19	26	45	70	...	...	...	—	—	—	—	—
00-01—Chicago	NHL	19	3	1	4	4	-4	0	0	—	—	—	—	—
—Norfolk	AHL	49	16	26	42	28	...	...	...	9	1	2	3	8
NHL Totals (1 year)		19	3	1	4	4	-4	0	0					

VOROBIEV, PAVEL   RW   BLACKHAWKS

PERSONAL: Born May 5, 1982, in Karaganda, U.S.S.R. ... 6-0/183. ... Shoots left.
TRANSACTIONS/CAREER NOTES: Selected by Chicago Blackhawks in first round (second Blackhawks pick, 11th overall) of NHL entry draft (June 24, 2000).

V

Season Team	League	REGULAR SEASON								PLAYOFFS				
		Gms.	G	A	Pts.	PIM	+/-	PP	SH	Gms.	G	A	Pts.	PIM
98-99—Torpedo-2 Yaroslavl....	Rus. Div. II	17	0	1	1	0	...	...	...	—	—	—	—	—
99-00—Torpedo Yaroslavl	Russian	8	2	0	2	4	...	...	...	—	—	—	—	—
—Torpedo-2 Yaroslavl....	Rus. Div. II	40	19	15	34	8	...	...	...	—	—	—	—	—
00-01—Lokomotiv Yaroslavl ...	Russian	36	8	8	16	28	...	...	...	10	4	1	5	8

VRBATA, RADIM   RW   AVALANCHE

PERSONAL: Born June 13, 1981, in Mlada Boleslav, Czechoslovakia. ... 6-1/185. ... Shoots right. ... Name pronounced ra-DEEM vuhr-BA-tuh.
TRANSACTIONS/CAREER NOTES: Selected by Colorado Avalanche in eighth round (10th Avalanche pick, 212th overall) of NHL entry draft (June 26, 1999).

Season Team	League	REGULAR SEASON								PLAYOFFS				
		Gms.	G	A	Pts.	PIM	+/-	PP	SH	Gms.	G	A	Pts.	PIM
98-99—Hull..........................	QMJHL	64	22	38	60	16	...	...	...	23	6	13	19	6
99-00—Hull..........................	QMJHL	58	29	45	74	26	...	...	...	15	3	9	12	8
00-01—Shawinigan	QMJHL	55	56	64	120	67	...	...	...	10	4	7	11	4
—Hershey	AHL	—	—	—	—	—	...	...	...	1	0	1	1	2

VYBORNY, DAVID   C   BLUE JACKETS

PERSONAL: Born January 22, 1975, in Jihlava, Czechoslovakia. ... 5-10/183. ... Shoots left. ... Name pronounced vigh-BOHR-nee.
TRANSACTIONS/CAREER NOTES: Selected by Edmonton Oilers in second round (third Oilers pick, 33rd overall) of NHL entry draft (June 26, 1993). ... Signed as free agent by Columbus Blue Jackets (June 7, 2000). ... Strained hip flexor (February 20, 2001); missed one game. ... Strained groin (April 1, 2001); missed two games.
HONORS: Named Czechoslovakian League Rookie of the Year (1991-92).
MISCELLANEOUS: Scored on a penalty shot (vs. Robbie Tallas, October 15, 2000; vs. Tomas Vokoun, March 19, 2001).

Season Team	League	REGULAR SEASON								PLAYOFFS				
		Gms.	G	A	Pts.	PIM	+/-	PP	SH	Gms.	G	A	Pts.	PIM
90-91—Sparta Prague............	Czech.	3	0	0	0	0	...	...	...	—	—	—	—	—
91-92—Sparta Prague............	Czech.	32	6	9	15	2	...	...	...	—	—	—	—	—
92-93—Sparta Prague............	Czech.	52	20	24	44	...	...	...	...	—	—	—	—	—
93-94—Sparta Prague............	Czech Rep.	44	15	20	35	...	...	...	...	6	4	7	11	...
94-95—Cape Breton	AHL	76	23	38	61	30	...	...	...	—	—	—	—	—
95-96—Sparta Praha............	Czech Rep.	52	19	36	55	42	...	...	...	—	—	—	—	—
96-97—Sparta Praha............	Czech Rep.	47	20	29	49	14	...	...	...	—	—	—	—	—
97-98—MoDo Ornskoldsvik	Sweden	45	16	21	37	34	...	...	...	—	—	—	—	—
98-99—Sparta Praha............	Czech Rep.	52	24	†46	*70	22	...	...	...	8	1	3	4	...
99-00—Sparta Praha............	Czech Rep.	50	25	38	63	30	...	...	...	9	3	8	*11	4
00-01—Columbus	NHL	79	13	19	32	22	-9	5	0	—	—	—	—	—
NHL Totals (1 year)............		79	13	19	32	22	-9	5	0					

VYDARENY, RENE   D   CANUCKS

PERSONAL: Born May 6, 1981, in Bratislava, Czechoslovakia. ... 6-1/198. ... Shoots left. ... Name pronounced VEE-duh-RE-nee.
TRANSACTIONS/CAREER NOTES: Selected by Vancouver Canucks in third round (third Canucks pick, 69th overall) of NHL entry draft (June 26, 1999).

Season Team	League	REGULAR SEASON								PLAYOFFS				
		Gms.	G	A	Pts.	PIM	+/-	PP	SH	Gms.	G	A	Pts.	PIM
97-98—Bratislava..................	Slov. Jr.	50	5	14	19	74	...	...	...	—	—	—	—	—
98-99—Bratislava..................	Slov. Jr.	42	4	7	11	65	...	...	...	2	0	0	0	2
99-00—Rimouski	QMJHL	51	7	23	30	41	...	...	...	14	2	2	4	20
00-01—Kansas City................	IHL	39	0	1	1	25	...	...	...	—	—	—	—	—

VYSHEDKEVICH, SERGEI   D   MIGHTY DUCKS

PERSONAL: Born January 3, 1975, in Moscow, U.S.S.R. ... 6-0/195. ... Shoots left. ... Name pronounced vih-shuh-KEH-vihch.
TRANSACTIONS/CAREER NOTES: Selected by New Jersey Devils in third round (third Devils pick, 70th overall) of NHL entry draft (July 8, 1995). ... Traded by Devils to Atlanta Thrashers for future considerations (June 25, 1999). ... Bruised chest (October 25, 2000); missed five games. ... Traded by Thrashers with G Scott Langkow to Mighty Ducks of Anaheim for RW Ladislav Kohn (February 9, 2001).

Season Team	League	REGULAR SEASON								PLAYOFFS				
		Gms.	G	A	Pts.	PIM	+/-	PP	SH	Gms.	G	A	Pts.	PIM
93-94—Dynamo Moscow........	CIS	—	—	—	—	—	...	...	...	4	0	2	2	2
94-95—Dynamo Moscow........	CIS	49	6	7	13	67	...	...	...	14	2	0	2	12
95-96—Dynamo Moscow........	CIS	49	5	4	9	12	...	...	...	13	1	1	2	6
96-97—Albany......................	AHL	65	8	27	35	16	...	...	...	12	0	6	6	0
97-98—Albany......................	AHL	54	12	16	28	12	...	...	...	13	0	10	10	4
98-99—Albany......................	AHL	79	11	38	49	28	...	...	...	5	0	3	3	0
99-00—Orlando....................	IHL	69	11	24	35	32	...	...	...	6	3	3	6	8
—Atlanta	NHL	7	1	3	4	2	-3	1	0	—	—	—	—	—
00-01—Atlanta	NHL	23	1	2	3	14	-7	0	0	—	—	—	—	—
—Orlando....................	IHL	10	2	3	5	2	...	...	...	—	—	—	—	—
—Cincinnati..................	AHL	17	3	2	5	2	...	...	...	—	—	—	—	—
NHL Totals (2 years)...........		30	2	5	7	16	-10	1	0					

WALKER, MATT   D   BLUES

PERSONAL: Born April 7, 1980, in Beaverlodge, Alta. ... 6-2/212. ... Shoots right.
TRANSACTIONS/CAREER NOTES: Selected by St. Louis Blues in third round (third Blues pick, 83rd overall) of NHL entry draft (June 27, 1998).

		REGULAR SEASON							PLAYOFFS				
Season Team	League	Gms.	G	A	Pts.	PIM	+/-	PP	SH	Gms.	G	A	Pts.	PIM
97-98—Portland	WHL	64	2	13	15	124	...	...	...	16	0	0	0	21
98-99—Portland	WHL	64	1	10	11	151	...	...	...	—	—	—	—	—
99-00—Portland	WHL	38	2	7	9	97	...	...	...	—	—	—	—	—
—Kootenay	WHL	69	6	26	32	150	...	...	...	—	—	—	—	—
00-01—Worcester	AHL	61	4	8	12	131	...	...	...	11	0	0	0	6
—Peoria	ECHL	8	1	0	1	70	...	...	...	—	—	—	—	—

WALKER, SCOTT   RW   PREDATORS

PERSONAL: Born July 19, 1973, in Cambridge, Ont. ... 5-10/190. ... Shoots right.
TRANSACTIONS/CAREER NOTES: Selected by Vancouver Canucks in fifth round (fourth Canucks pick, 124th overall) of NHL entry draft (June 26, 1993). ... Strained abdominal muscle (October 12, 1996); missed eight games. ... Strained groin (December 13, 1996); missed six games. ... Fractured nasal bone (November 16, 1997); missed four games. ... Selected by Nashville Predators in NHL expansion draft (June 26, 1998). ... Separated shoulder (November 19, 1998); missed nine games. ... Suffered ear infection (January 26, 1999); missed two games. ... Suffered concussion (December 6, 1999); missed 10 games. ... Bruised foot (January 21, 2000); missed three games. ... Separated left shoulder (January 19, 2001); missed eight games.
HONORS: Named to OHL All-Star second team (1992-93).
STATISTICAL PLATEAUS: Three-goal games: 2000-01 (1).

		REGULAR SEASON							PLAYOFFS				
Season Team	League	Gms.	G	A	Pts.	PIM	+/-	PP	SH	Gms.	G	A	Pts.	PIM
89-90—Kitch.-Cambridge Jr.	OHA	33	7	27	34	91	...	...	...	—	—	—	—	—
90-91—Cambridge Jr. B	OHA	45	10	27	37	241	...	...	...	—	—	—	—	—
91-92—Owen Sound	OHL	53	7	31	38	128	...	...	...	5	0	7	7	8
92-93—Owen Sound	OHL	57	23	68	91	110	...	...	...	8	1	5	6	16
—Canadian nat'l team	Int'l	2	3	0	3	0	...	...	...	—	—	—	—	—
93-94—Hamilton	AHL	77	10	29	39	272	...	...	...	4	0	1	1	25
94-95—Syracuse	AHL	74	14	38	52	334	...	...	...	—	—	—	—	—
—Vancouver	NHL	11	0	1	1	33	0	0	0	—	—	—	—	—
95-96—Vancouver	NHL	63	4	8	12	137	-7	0	1	—	—	—	—	—
—Syracuse	AHL	15	3	12	15	52	...	...	...	16	9	8	17	39
96-97—Vancouver	NHL	64	3	15	18	132	2	0	0	—	—	—	—	—
97-98—Vancouver	NHL	59	3	10	13	164	-8	0	1	—	—	—	—	—
98-99—Nashville	NHL	71	15	25	40	103	0	0	1	—	—	—	—	—
99-00—Nashville	NHL	69	7	21	28	90	-16	0	1	—	—	—	—	—
00-01—Nashville	NHL	74	25	29	54	66	-2	9	3	—	—	—	—	—
NHL Totals (7 years)		411	57	109	166	725	-31	9	7					

WALLIN, JESSE   D   RED WINGS

PERSONAL: Born March 10, 1978, in Saskatoon, Sask. ... 6-2/190. ... Shoots left. ... Name pronounced WAH-lihn.
TRANSACTIONS/CAREER NOTES: Selected by Detroit Red Wings in first round (first Red Wings pick, 26th overall) of NHL entry draft (June 22, 1996).
HONORS: Won Can.HL Humanitarian of the Year Award (1996-97). ... Won WHL Humanitarian Award (1996-97).

		REGULAR SEASON							PLAYOFFS				
Season Team	League	Gms.	G	A	Pts.	PIM	+/-	PP	SH	Gms.	G	A	Pts.	PIM
94-95—Prince Albert	WHL	72	4	20	24	72	...	...	...	—	—	—	—	—
95-96—Red Deer	WHL	70	5	19	24	61	...	...	...	9	0	3	3	4
96-97—Red Deer	WHL	59	6	33	39	70	...	...	...	16	1	4	5	10
97-98—Red Deer	WHL	14	1	6	7	17	...	...	...	5	0	1	1	2
98-99—Adirondack	AHL	76	4	12	16	34	...	...	...	3	0	2	2	2
99-00—Cincinnati	AHL	75	3	14	17	61	...	...	...	—	—	—	—	—
—Detroit	NHL	1	0	0	0	0	-2	0	0	—	—	—	—	—
00-01—Cincinnati	AHL	76	2	15	17	50	...	...	...	4	0	1	1	4
—Detroit	NHL	1	0	0	0	2	0	0	0	—	—	—	—	—
NHL Totals (2 years)		2	0	0	0	2	-2	0	0					

WALLIN, NICLAS   D   HURRICANES

PERSONAL: Born February 20, 1975, in Sweden. ... 6-2/207. ... Shoots left.
TRANSACTIONS/CAREER NOTES: Selected by Carolina Hurricanes in fourth round (third Hurricanes pick, 97th overall) of NHL entry draft (June 24, 2000). ... Fractured wrist (October 5, 2000); missed six games. ... Strained shoulder (January 29, 2001); missed five games.

		REGULAR SEASON							PLAYOFFS				
Season Team	League	Gms.	G	A	Pts.	PIM	+/-	PP	SH	Gms.	G	A	Pts.	PIM
96-97—Brynas Gavle	Sweden	47	1	1	2	16	...	...	...	—	—	—	—	—
97-98—Brynas Gavle	Sweden	44	2	3	5	57	...	...	...	3	0	1	1	4
98-99—Brynas Gavle	Sweden	46	2	4	6	52	...	...	...	14	0	0	0	8
99-00—Brynas Gavle	Sweden	48	7	9	16	73	...	...	...	—	—	—	—	—
00-01—Carolina	NHL	37	2	3	5	21	-11	0	0	3	0	0	0	2
—Cincinnati	IHL	8	1	2	3	4	...	...	...	—	—	—	—	—
NHL Totals (1 year)		37	2	3	5	21	-11	0	0	3	0	0	0	2

W

PERSONAL: Born May 15, 1970, in Calgary. ... 5-10/185. ... Shoots right.
TRANSACTIONS/CAREER NOTES: Selected by Boston Bruins in third round (third Bruins pick, 57th overall) of NHL entry draft (June 17, 1989). ... Traded by Bruins with D Garry Galley and future considerations to Philadelphia Flyers for D Gord Murphy, RW Brian Dobbin and third-round pick (LW Sergei Zholtok) in 1992 draft (January 2, 1992). ... Signed as free agent by Calgary Flames (August 31, 1993). ... Strained hip (February 26, 1995); missed one game. ... Signed as free agent by Detroit Red Wings (August 11, 1995). ... Signed as free agent by Minnesota Wild (June 28, 2000).
HONORS: Won Jim Piggott Memorial Trophy (1988-89). ... Won WHL Player of the Year Award (1989-90). ... Named to WHL (East) All-Star first team (1989-90).
MISCELLANEOUS: Captain of Minnesota Wild (December 1-31, 2000). ... Failed to score on a penalty shot (vs. Tim Cheveldae, November 2, 1991). ... Shares Minnesota Wild all-time record for games played (82) and most goals (18).

Season Team	League	REGULAR SEASON								PLAYOFFS				
		Gms.	G	A	Pts.	PIM	+/-	PP	SH	Gms.	G	A	Pts.	PIM
87-88—Prince Albert	WHL	1	1	1	2	0	...	...	...	—	—	—	—	—
88-89—Lethbridge	WHL	63	29	75	104	32	...	...	...	8	1	5	6	6
89-90—Boston	NHL	2	1	1	2	0	-1	1	0	—	—	—	—	—
—Lethbridge	WHL	56	54	86	140	69	...	...	...	19	13	*24	†37	33
90-91—Maine	AHL	20	8	12	20	19	...	...	...	2	0	0	0	21
—Boston	NHL	56	8	8	16	32	-14	1	0	2	0	0	0	0
91-92—Boston	NHL	15	0	3	3	12	-3	0	0	—	—	—	—	—
—Maine	AHL	21	13	11	24	38	...	...	...	—	—	—	—	—
—Hershey	AHL	41	13	28	41	37	...	...	...	6	1	2	3	0
—Philadelphia	NHL	2	1	0	1	0	1	0	0	—	—	—	—	—
92-93—Hershey	AHL	78	35	45	80	106	...	...	...	—	—	—	—	—
93-94—Calgary	NHL	53	11	27	38	16	20	1	0	6	3	0	3	2
—Saint John	AHL	15	6	6	12	14	...	...	...	—	—	—	—	—
94-95—Calgary	NHL	39	6	12	18	11	7	4	0	1	0	0	0	0
95-96—Adirondack	AHL	38	20	35	55	58	...	...	...	—	—	—	—	—
—Detroit	NHL	2	0	0	0	0	0	0	0	—	—	—	—	—
96-97—Zug	Switzerland	41	24	22	46	67	...	...	...	—	—	—	—	—
97-98—Zug	Switzerland	38	18	34	52	32	...	...	...	20	16	12	28	18
98-99—Zug	Switzerland	42	22	27	49	75	...	...	...	10	3	9	12	2
99-00—Long Beach	IHL	6	4	3	7	8	...	...	...	—	—	—	—	—
—Lugano	Switzerland	13	7	11	18	14	...	...	...	5	3	4	7	4
00-01—Minnesota	NHL	82	18	12	30	37	-8	0	7	—	—	—	—	—
NHL Totals (7 years)		251	45	63	108	108	2	7	7	9	3	0	3	2

PERSONAL: Born January 17, 1973, in Windsor, Ont. ... 6-2/225. ... Shoots right. ... Full Name: Aaron Christian Ward.
TRANSACTIONS/CAREER NOTES: Selected by Winnipeg Jets in first round (first Jets pick, fifth overall) of NHL entry draft (June 22, 1991). ... Traded by Jets with fourth-round pick (D John Jakopin) in 1993 draft and future considerations to Detroit Red Wings for RW Paul Ysebaert (June 11, 1993); Red Wings acquired RW Alan Kerr to complete deal (June 18, 1993). ... Suffered bronchitis (December 22, 1996); missed three games. ... Suffered from the flu (October 26, 1997); missed two games. ... Bruised knee (November 26, 1997); missed one game. ... Fractured right foot (December 3, 1997); missed 19 games. ... Sprained shoulder (February 7, 1998); missed two games. ... Strained rotator cuff (November 21, 1998); missed two games. ... Injured ribs (October 22, 1999); missed seven games. ... Suffered injury (December 4, 1999); missed four games. ... Injured shoulder (January 22, 2000); missed final 35 games of regular season. ... Suffered from the flu (January 7, 2001); missed two games. ... Traded by Red Wings to Carolina Hurricanes for future second-round pick (July 9, 2001).
HONORS: Named to CCHA All-Rookie Team (1990-91).
MISCELLANEOUS: Member of Stanley Cup championship team (1997 and 1998).

Season Team	League	REGULAR SEASON								PLAYOFFS				
		Gms.	G	A	Pts.	PIM	+/-	PP	SH	Gms.	G	A	Pts.	PIM
88-89—Nepean	COJHL	56	2	17	19	44	...	...	...	—	—	—	—	—
89-90—Nepean	COJHL	52	6	33	39	85	...	...	...	—	—	—	—	—
90-91—Univ. of Michigan	CCHA	46	8	11	19	126	...	...	...	—	—	—	—	—
91-92—Univ. of Michigan	CCHA	42	7	12	19	64	...	...	...	—	—	—	—	—
92-93—Univ. of Michigan	CCHA	30	5	8	13	73	...	...	...	—	—	—	—	—
—Canadian nat'l team	Int'l	4	0	0	0	8	...	...	...	—	—	—	—	—
93-94—Detroit	NHL	5	1	0	1	4	2	0	0	—	—	—	—	—
—Adirondack	AHL	58	4	12	16	87	...	...	...	9	2	6	8	6
94-95—Adirondack	AHL	76	11	24	35	87	...	...	...	4	0	1	1	0
—Detroit	NHL	1	0	1	1	2	1	0	0	—	—	—	—	—
95-96—Adirondack	AHL	74	5	10	15	133	...	...	...	3	0	0	0	6
96-97—Detroit	NHL	49	2	5	7	52	-9	0	0	19	0	0	0	17
97-98—Detroit	NHL	52	5	5	10	47	-1	0	0	8	0	1	1	8
98-99—Detroit	NHL	60	3	8	11	52	-5	0	0	8	0	1	1	8
99-00—Detroit	NHL	36	1	3	4	24	-4	0	0	3	0	0	0	0
00-01—Detroit	NHL	73	4	5	9	57	-4	0	0	—	—	—	—	—
NHL Totals (7 years)		276	16	27	43	238	-20	0	0	30	0	1	1	25

PERSONAL: Born September 23, 1968, in Leduc, Alta. ... 6-0/200. ... Shoots right. ... Full Name: Dixon M. Ward Jr.
TRANSACTIONS/CAREER NOTES: Selected by Vancouver Canucks in seventh round (sixth Canucks pick, 128th overall) of NHL entry draft (June 11, 1988). ... Sprained ankle (March 14, 1993); missed four games. ... Suspended three games and fined $500 by NHL for checking from behind (October 15, 1993). ... Traded by Canucks to Los Angeles Kings for C Jimmy Carson (January 8, 1994). ... Traded by Kings with C Guy Leveque, RW Shayne Toporowski and C Kelly Fairchild to Toronto Maple Leafs for LW Eric Lacroix, D Chris Snell and fourth-round pick

(C Eric Belanger) in 1996 draft (October 3, 1994). ... Signed as free agent by Buffalo Sabres (August 24, 1995). ... Bruised sternum (April 10, 1999); missed two games. ... Injured neck (November 4, 1999); missed three games. ... Signed as free agent by Boston Bruins (November 3, 2000). ... Fractured foot (December 30, 2000); missed six games.
HONORS: Named to WCHA All-Star second team (1990-91 and 1991-92). ... Won Jack Butterfield Trophy (1995-96).
MISCELLANEOUS: Scored on a penalty shot (vs. Damian Rhodes, April 11, 1998).
STATISTICAL PLATEAUS: Three-goal games: 1998-99 (1).

				REGULAR SEASON						PLAYOFFS				
Season Team	League	Gms.	G	A	Pts.	PIM	+/-	PP	SH	Gms.	G	A	Pts.	PIM
86-87—Red Deer..................	AJHL	59	46	40	86	153	...	...	...	—	—	—	—	—
87-88—Red Deer..................	AJHL	51	60	71	131	167	...	...	...	—	—	—	—	—
88-89—Univ. of North Dakota .	WCHA	37	8	9	17	26	...	...	...	—	—	—	—	—
89-90—Univ. of North Dakota .	WCHA	45	35	34	69	44	...	...	...	—	—	—	—	—
90-91—Univ. of North Dakota .	WCHA	43	34	35	69	84	...	...	...	—	—	—	—	—
91-92—Univ. of North Dakota .	WCHA	38	33	31	64	90	...	...	...	—	—	—	—	—
92-93—Vancouver..................	NHL	70	22	30	52	82	34	4	1	9	2	3	5	0
93-94—Vancouver..................	NHL	33	6	1	7	37	-14	2	0	—	—	—	—	—
—Los Angeles..........	NHL	34	6	2	8	45	-8	2	0	—	—	—	—	—
94-95—Toronto..................	NHL	22	0	3	3	31	-4	0	0	—	—	—	—	—
—St. John's..........	AHL	6	3	3	6	19	...	...	...	—	—	—	—	—
—Detroit..........	IHL	7	3	6	9	7	...	...	...	5	3	0	3	7
95-96—Rochester..........	AHL	71	38	56	94	74	...	...	...	19	11	*24	*35	8
—Buffalo	NHL	8	2	2	4	6	1	0	0	—	—	—	—	—
96-97—Buffalo	NHL	79	13	32	45	36	17	1	2	12	2	3	5	6
97-98—Buffalo	NHL	71	10	13	23	42	9	0	2	15	3	8	11	6
98-99—Buffalo	NHL	78	20	24	44	44	10	2	1	21	7	5	12	32
99-00—Buffalo	NHL	71	11	9	20	41	1	1	2	5	0	1	1	2
00-01—Boston	NHL	63	5	13	18	65	-1	0	0	—	—	—	—	—
NHL Totals (9 years)..........		529	95	129	224	429	45	12	8	62	14	20	34	46

WARD, ED — RW — DEVILS

PERSONAL: Born November 10, 1969, in Edmonton. ... 6-3/220. ... Shoots right. ... Full Name: Edward John Ward.
TRANSACTIONS/CAREER NOTES: Selected by Quebec Nordiques in sixth round (seventh Nordiques pick, 108th overall) of NHL entry draft (June 11, 1988). ... Traded by Nordiques to Calgary Flames for D Francois Groleau (March 24, 1995). ... Bruised ribs (December 3, 1995); missed one game. ... Lacerated elbow (December 13, 1995); missed one game. ... Selected by Atlanta Thrashers in NHL expansion draft (June 25, 1999). ... Sprained ankle (February 15, 2000); missed nine games. ... Traded by Thrashers to Mighty Ducks of Anaheim for future considerations (March 14, 2000). ... Traded by Mighty Ducks to New Jersey Devils for seventh-round pick (C Tony Martensson) in 2001 draft (June 12, 2000).

				REGULAR SEASON						PLAYOFFS				
Season Team	League	Gms.	G	A	Pts.	PIM	+/-	PP	SH	Gms.	G	A	Pts.	PIM
86-87—Sherwood Park	AJHL	60	18	28	46	272	...	...	...	—	—	—	—	—
87-88—N. Michigan Univ.	WCHA	25	0	2	2	40	...	...	...	—	—	—	—	—
88-89—N. Michigan Univ.	WCHA	42	5	15	20	36	...	...	...	—	—	—	—	—
89-90—N. Michigan Univ.	WCHA	39	5	11	16	77	...	...	...	—	—	—	—	—
90-91—N. Michigan Univ.	WCHA	46	13	18	31	109	...	...	...	—	—	—	—	—
91-92—Halifax..........	AHL	51	7	11	18	65	...	...	...	—	—	—	—	—
—Greensboro............	ECHL	12	4	8	12	21	...	...	...	—	—	—	—	—
92-93—Halifax..........	AHL	70	13	19	32	56	...	...	...	—	—	—	—	—
93-94—Cornwall	AHL	60	12	30	42	65	...	...	...	12	1	3	4	14
—Quebec	NHL	7	1	0	1	5	0	0	0	—	—	—	—	—
94-95—Cornwall	AHL	56	10	14	24	118	...	...	...	—	—	—	—	—
—Saint John	AHL	11	4	5	9	20	...	...	...	5	1	0	1	10
—Calgary	NHL	2	1	1	2	2	-2	0	0	—	—	—	—	—
95-96—Saint John	AHL	12	1	2	3	45	...	...	...	16	4	4	8	27
—Calgary	NHL	41	3	5	8	44	-2	0	0	—	—	—	—	—
96-97—Saint John	AHL	1	0	0	0	0	...	...	...	—	—	—	—	—
—Detroit..........	IHL	31	7	6	13	45	...	...	...	—	—	—	—	—
—Calgary	NHL	40	5	8	13	49	-3	0	0	—	—	—	—	—
97-98—Calgary	NHL	64	4	5	9	122	-1	0	0	—	—	—	—	—
98-99—Calgary	NHL	68	3	5	8	67	-4	0	0	—	—	—	—	—
99-00—Atlanta	NHL	44	5	1	6	44	-5	0	2	—	—	—	—	—
—Anaheim	NHL	8	1	0	1	15	-2	0	0	—	—	—	—	—
00-01—New Jersey	NHL	4	0	1	1	6	2	0	0	—	—	—	—	—
—Albany..........	AHL	65	14	19	33	71	...	...	...	—	—	—	—	—
NHL Totals (8 years)..........		278	23	26	49	354	-17	0	2					

WARD, JASON — RW/C — CANADIENS

PERSONAL: Born January 16, 1979, in Chapleau, Ont. ... 6-2/193. ... Shoots right.
TRANSACTIONS/CAREER NOTES: Selected by Montreal Canadiens in first round (first Canadiens pick, 11th overall) of NHL entry draft (June 21, 1997). ... Fractured cheekbone (February 10, 2000); missed seven games. ... Injured knee (January 12, 2001); missed remainder of season.

				REGULAR SEASON						PLAYOFFS				
Season Team	League	Gms.	G	A	Pts.	PIM	+/-	PP	SH	Gms.	G	A	Pts.	PIM
94-95—Oshawa..................	Tier II Jr. A	47	30	31	61	75	...	...	...	—	—	—	—	—
95-96—Niagara Falls..............	OHL	64	15	35	50	139	...	...	...	10	6	4	10	23
96-97—Erie	OHL	58	25	39	64	137	...	...	...	5	1	2	3	2

W

Season Team	League	REGULAR SEASON Gms.	G	A	Pts.	PIM	+/-	PP	SH	PLAYOFFS Gms.	G	A	Pts.	PIM
97-98—Erie	OHL	21	7	9	16	42	...	...	...	—	—	—	—	—
—Windsor	OHL	26	19	27	46	34	...	...	...	—	—	—	—	—
—Fredericton	AHL	7	1	0	1	2	...	...	...	1	0	0	0	2
98-99—Windsor	OHL	12	8	11	19	25	...	...	...	—	—	—	—	—
—Plymouth	OHL	23	14	13	27	28	...	...	...	11	6	8	14	12
—Fredericton	AHL	—	—	—	—	—	...	...	...	10	4	2	6	22
99-00—Quebec	AHL	40	14	12	26	30	...	...	...	3	2	1	3	4
—Montreal	NHL	32	2	1	3	10	-1	1	0	—	—	—	—	—
00-01—Quebec	AHL	23	7	12	19	69	...	...	...	—	—	—	—	—
—Montreal	NHL	12	0	0	0	12	3	0	0	—	—	—	—	—
NHL Totals (2 years)		44	2	1	3	22	2	1	0					

WARD, LANCE   D   PANTHERS

PERSONAL: Born June 2, 1978, in Lloydminster, Alta. ... 6-3/215. ... Shoots left.
TRANSACTIONS/CAREER NOTES: Selected by New Jersey Devils in first round (first Devils pick, 10th overall) of NHL entry draft (June 22, 1996). ... Returned to draft pool by Devils and selected by Florida Panthers in third round (third Panthers pick, 63rd overall) of NHL entry draft (June 27, 1998). ... Injured back (February 28, 2001); missed 17 games.

Season Team	League	REGULAR SEASON Gms.	G	A	Pts.	PIM	+/-	PP	SH	PLAYOFFS Gms.	G	A	Pts.	PIM
93-94—Medicine Hat	WHL	68	1	4	5	166	...	...	...	3	0	0	0	2
94-95—Red Deer	WHL	28	0	0	0	57	...	...	...	—	—	—	—	—
95-96—Red Deer	WHL	72	4	13	17	127	...	...	...	10	0	4	4	10
96-97—Red Deer	WHL	70	5	34	39	229	...	...	...	16	0	3	3	36
97-98—Red Deer	WHL	71	8	25	33	233	...	...	...	5	0	0	0	16
98-99—Miami	ECHL	6	1	0	1	12	...	...	...	—	—	—	—	—
—Fort Wayne	IHL	13	0	2	2	28	...	...	...	—	—	—	—	—
—New Haven	AHL	43	2	5	7	51	...	...	...	—	—	—	—	—
99-00—Louisville	AHL	80	4	16	20	190	...	...	...	4	0	0	0	6
00-01—Louisville	AHL	35	3	2	5	78	...	...	...	—	—	—	—	—
—Florida	NHL	30	0	2	2	45	-3	0	0	—	—	—	—	—
NHL Totals (1 year)		30	0	2	2	45	-3	0	0					

WARRENER, RHETT   D   SABRES

PERSONAL: Born January 27, 1976, in Shaunavon, Sask. ... 6-1/210. ... Shoots right. ... Name pronounced REHT WAHR-uh-nuhr.
TRANSACTIONS/CAREER NOTES: Selected by Florida Panthers in second round (second Panthers pick, 27th overall) of NHL entry draft (June 28, 1994). ... Strained groin (October 20, 1996); missed four games. ... Reinjured groin (November 11, 1996); missed two games. ... Reinjured groin (December 22, 1996); missed 10 games. ... Strained groin (November 2, 1998); missed 12 games. ... Traded by Panthers with fifth-round pick (G Ryan Miller) in 1999 draft to Buffalo Sabres for D Mike Wilson (March 23, 1999). ... Injured shoulder (October 30, 1999); missed two games. ... Strained hip muscle (January 1, 2000); missed four games. ... Injured groin (February 21, 2000); missed eight games. ... Suffered concussion (November 17, 2000); missed five games.

Season Team	League	REGULAR SEASON Gms.	G	A	Pts.	PIM	+/-	PP	SH	PLAYOFFS Gms.	G	A	Pts.	PIM
91-92—Saskatoon	WHL	2	0	0	0	0	...	...	...	—	—	—	—	—
92-93—Saskatoon	WHL	68	2	17	19	100	...	...	...	9	0	0	0	14
93-94—Saskatoon	WHL	61	7	19	26	131	...	...	...	16	0	5	5	33
94-95—Saskatoon	WHL	66	13	26	39	137	...	...	...	10	0	3	3	6
95-96—Carolina	AHL	9	0	0	0	4	...	...	...	—	—	—	—	—
—Florida	NHL	28	0	3	3	46	4	0	0	21	0	3	3	10
96-97—Florida	NHL	62	4	9	13	88	20	1	0	5	0	0	0	0
97-98—Florida	NHL	79	0	4	4	99	-16	0	0	—	—	—	—	—
98-99—Florida	NHL	48	0	7	7	64	-1	0	0	—	—	—	—	—
—Buffalo	NHL	13	1	0	1	20	3	0	0	20	1	3	4	32
99-00—Buffalo	NHL	61	0	3	3	89	18	0	0	5	0	0	0	2
00-01—Buffalo	NHL	77	3	16	19	78	10	0	0	13	0	2	2	4
NHL Totals (6 years)		368	8	42	50	484	38	1	0	64	1	8	9	48

WARRINER, TODD   LW   COYOTES

PERSONAL: Born January 3, 1974, in Blenheim, Ont. ... 6-1/200. ... Shoots left. ... Name pronounced WAHR-ih-nuhr.
TRANSACTIONS/CAREER NOTES: Selected by Quebec Nordiques in first round (first Nordiques pick, fourth overall) of NHL entry draft (June 20, 1992). ... Traded by Nordiques with C Mats Sundin, D Garth Butcher and first-round pick (traded to Washington) in 1994 draft to Toronto Maple Leafs for LW Wendel Clark, D Sylvain Lefebvre, RW Landon Wilson and first-round pick (D Jeffrey Kealty) in 1994 draft (June 28, 1994). ... Suffered hip pointer (December 7, 1995); missed eight games. ... Injured hip flexor (October 3, 1996); missed one game. ... Injured hip flexor (November 19, 1996); missed four games. ... Suffered from the flu (April 2, 1997); missed one game. ... Sprained shoulder (October 15, 1997); missed three games. ... Bruised thigh (November 17, 1997); missed 27 games. ... Sprained knee (March 4, 1999); missed four games. ... Traded by Maple Leafs to Tampa Bay Lightning for third-round pick (G Mikael Tellqvist) in 2000 draft (November 29, 1999). ... Injured hip (January 15, 2000); missed two games. ... Strained groin (March 8, 2000); missed one game. ... Suffered from the flu (November 10, 2000); missed one game. ... Strained groin (March 4, 2000); missed two games. ... Strained medial collateral ligament in knee (March 8, 2001); missed final 14 games of season. ... Traded by Lightning to Phoenix Coyotes for C Yuha Ylonen (June 18, 2001).
HONORS: Won Can.HL Top Draft Prospect Award (1991-92). ... Won OHL Top Draft Prospect Award (1991-92). ... Named to Can.HL All-Star second team (1991-92). ... Named to OHL All-Star first team (1991-92).
MISCELLANEOUS: Member of silver-medal-winning Canadian Olympic team (1994).

W

Season Team	League	REGULAR SEASON								PLAYOFFS				
		Gms.	G	A	Pts.	PIM	+/-	PP	SH	Gms.	G	A	Pts.	PIM
88-89—Blenheim Jr. C	OHA	10	1	4	5	0	...	...	...	—	—	—	—	—
89-90—Chatham Jr. B	OHA	40	24	21	45	12	...	...	...	—	—	—	—	—
90-91—Windsor	OHL	57	36	28	64	26	...	...	...	11	5	6	11	12
91-92—Windsor	OHL	50	41	42	83	66	...	...	...	7	5	4	9	6
92-93—Windsor	OHL	23	13	21	34	29	...	...	...	—	—	—	—	—
—Kitchener	OHL	32	19	24	43	35	...	...	...	7	5	14	19	14
93-94—Canadian nat'l team	Int'l	50	11	20	31	33	...	...	...	—	—	—	—	—
—Can. Olympic team	Int'l	4	1	1	2	0	...	...	...	—	—	—	—	—
—Kitchener	OHL	—	—	—	—	—	...	...	...	1	0	1	1	0
—Cornwall	AHL	—	—	—	—	—	...	...	...	10	1	4	5	4
94-95—St. John's	AHL	46	8	10	18	22	...	...	...	4	1	0	1	2
—Toronto	NHL	5	0	0	0	0	-3	0	0	—	—	—	—	—
95-96—St. John's	AHL	11	5	6	11	16	...	...	...	—	—	—	—	—
—Toronto	NHL	57	7	8	15	26	-11	1	0	6	1	1	2	2
96-97—Toronto	NHL	75	12	21	33	41	-3	2	2	—	—	—	—	—
97-98—Toronto	NHL	45	5	8	13	20	5	0	0	—	—	—	—	—
98-99—Toronto	NHL	53	9	10	19	28	-6	1	0	9	0	0	0	2
99-00—Toronto	NHL	18	3	1	4	2	6	0	0	—	—	—	—	—
—Tampa Bay	NHL	55	11	13	24	34	-14	3	1	—	—	—	—	—
00-01—Tampa Bay	NHL	64	10	11	21	46	-13	3	2	—	—	—	—	—
NHL Totals (7 years)		372	57	72	129	197	-39	10	5	15	1	1	2	4

WASHBURN, STEVE   C

PERSONAL: Born April 10, 1975, in Ottawa. ... 6-2/198. ... Shoots left.
TRANSACTIONS/CAREER NOTES: Selected by Florida Panthers in third round (fifth Panthers pick, 78th overall) of NHL entry draft (June 26, 1993). ... Sprained knee (April 11, 1997); missed remainder of season. ... Separated right shoulder (October 28, 1997); missed nine games. ... Fractured finger (October 3, 1998); missed first five games of season. ... Tore right groin (November 7, 1998); missed 12 games. ... Strained groin (December 27, 1998); missed eight games. ... Claimed on waivers by Vancouver Canucks (February 18, 1999). ... Signed as free agent by Nashville Predators (August 10, 1999). ... Traded by Predators to Philadelphia Flyers for conditional pick in 2001 draft (November 16, 1999).

Season Team	League	REGULAR SEASON								PLAYOFFS				
		Gms.	G	A	Pts.	PIM	+/-	PP	SH	Gms.	G	A	Pts.	PIM
90-91—Gloucester	OPJHL	56	21	30	51	47	...	...	...	—	—	—	—	—
91-92—Ottawa	OHL	59	5	17	22	10	...	...	...	11	2	3	5	4
92-93—Ottawa	OHL	66	20	38	58	54	...	...	...	—	—	—	—	—
93-94—Ottawa	OHL	65	30	50	80	88	...	...	...	17	7	16	23	10
94-95—Ottawa	OHL	63	43	63	106	72	...	...	...	—	—	—	—	—
—Cincinnati	IHL	6	3	1	4	0	...	...	...	9	1	3	4	4
95-96—Carolina	AHL	78	29	54	83	45	...	...	...	—	—	—	—	—
—Florida	NHL	1	0	1	1	0	1	0	0	1	0	1	1	0
96-97—Carolina	AHL	60	23	40	63	66	...	...	...	—	—	—	—	—
—Florida	NHL	18	3	6	9	4	2	1	0	—	—	—	—	—
97-98—Florida	NHL	58	11	8	19	32	-6	4	0	—	—	—	—	—
—New Haven	AHL	6	3	5	8	4	...	...	...	3	2	0	2	15
98-99—Florida	NHL	4	0	0	0	4	-1	0	0	—	—	—	—	—
—New Haven	AHL	10	4	3	7	6	...	...	...	—	—	—	—	—
—Vancouver	NHL	8	0	0	0	2	0	0	0	—	—	—	—	—
—Syracuse	AHL	13	1	6	7	6	...	...	...	—	—	—	—	—
99-00—Milwaukee	IHL	12	0	4	4	16	...	...	...	—	—	—	—	—
—Philadelphia	AHL	61	19	52	71	93	...	...	...	5	0	2	2	8
—Philadelphia	NHL	1	0	0	0	0	0	0	0	—	—	—	—	—
00-01—Kloten	Switzerland	8	0	6	6	16	...	...	...	—	—	—	—	—
—Philadelphia	AHL	46	12	16	28	52	...	...	...	2	0	0	0	2
—Philadelphia	NHL	3	0	0	0	0	0	0	0	—	—	—	—	—
NHL Totals (6 years)		93	14	15	29	42	-4	5	0	1	0	1	1	0

WATT, MIKE   LW/C   FLYERS

PERSONAL: Born March 31, 1976, in Seaforth, Ont. ... 6-2/208. ... Shoots left.
TRANSACTIONS/CAREER NOTES: Selected by Edmonton Oilers in second round (third Oilers pick, 32nd overall) of NHL entry draft (June 28, 1994). ... Traded by Oilers to New York Islanders for G Eric Fichaud (June 18, 1998). ... Suffered charley horse (October 24, 1998); missed one game. ... Strained hand (November 6, 1999); missed three games. ... Claimed on waivers by Nashville Predators (May 23, 2000). ... Traded by Predators to Philadelphia Flyers for D Mikhail Chernov (May 24, 2001).

W

Season Team	League	REGULAR SEASON								PLAYOFFS				
		Gms.	G	A	Pts.	PIM	+/-	PP	SH	Gms.	G	A	Pts.	PIM
91-92—Stratford Jr. B	OHA	46	5	26	31	...	...	...	...	—	—	—	—	—
92-93—Stratford Jr. B	OHA	45	20	35	55	100	...	...	...	—	—	—	—	—
93-94—Stratford Jr. B	OHA	48	34	34	68	165	...	...	...	—	—	—	—	—
94-95—Michigan State	CCHA	39	12	6	18	64	...	...	...	—	—	—	—	—
95-96—Michigan State	CCHA	37	17	22	39	60	...	...	...	—	—	—	—	—
96-97—Michigan State	CCHA	39	24	17	41	109	...	...	...	—	—	—	—	—
97-98—Hamilton	AHL	63	24	25	49	65	...	...	...	9	2	2	4	8
—Edmonton	NHL	14	1	2	3	4	-4	0	0	—	—	—	—	—
98-99—New York Islanders	NHL	75	8	17	25	12	-2	0	0	—	—	—	—	—
99-00—New York Islanders	NHL	45	5	6	11	17	-8	0	1	—	—	—	—	—
—Lowell	AHL	16	6	11	17	6	...	...	...	7	1	1	2	4
00-01—Milwaukee	IHL	60	20	20	40	48	...	...	...	5	1	2	3	6
—Nashville	NHL	18	1	1	2	8	-2	0	0	—	—	—	—	—
NHL Totals (4 years)		152	15	26	41	41	-16	0	1	—	—	—	—	—

WEAVER, MIKE — D — THRASHERS

PERSONAL: Born May 2, 1978, in Bramalea, Ont. ... 5-9/185. ... Shoots right.
TRANSACTIONS/CAREER NOTES: Signed as non-drafted free agent by Atlanta Thrashers (June 15, 2000).
HONORS: Named to NCAA All-America (West) second team (1998-99 and 1999-2000). ... Named to CCHA All-Star first team (1998-99 and 1999-2000).

				REGULAR SEASON							PLAYOFFS				
Season Team	League	Gms.	G	A	Pts.	PIM	+/-	PP	SH		Gms.	G	A	Pts.	PIM
96-97—Michigan State	CCHA	39	0	7	7	46	...	...	...		—	—	—	—	—
97-98—Michigan State	CCHA	44	4	22	26	68	...	...	...		—	—	—	—	—
98-99—Michigan State	CCHA	42	1	6	7	54	...	...	...		—	—	—	—	—
99-00—Michigan State	CCHA	37	0	8	8	34	...	...	...		—	—	—	—	—
00-01—Orlando	IHL	68	0	8	8	34	...	...	...		16	0	2	2	8

WEBB, STEVE — RW — ISLANDERS

PERSONAL: Born April 30, 1975, in Peterborough, Ont. ... 6-0/208. ... Shoots right.
TRANSACTIONS/CAREER NOTES: Selected by Buffalo Sabres in seventh round (eighth Sabres pick, 176th overall) of NHL entry draft (June 29, 1994). ... Signed as free agent by New York Islanders (October 14, 1996). ... Injured lower back (October 27, 1999); missed one game. ... Injured back (November 4, 1999); missed four games. ... Suffered the flu (April 9, 2000); missed final game of season. ... Strained back (November 7, 2000); missed two games. ... Strained left knee (November 18, 2000); missed 11 games. ... Reinjured knee (December 12, 2000); missed 16 games. ... Reinjured knee (January 21, 2001); missed 22 games.

				REGULAR SEASON							PLAYOFFS				
Season Team	League	Gms.	G	A	Pts.	PIM	+/-	PP	SH		Gms.	G	A	Pts.	PIM
91-92—Peterborough	Jr. B	37	9	9	18	195	...	...	...		—	—	—	—	—
92-93—Windsor	OHL	63	14	25	39	181	...	...	...		—	—	—	—	—
93-94—Windsor	OHL	33	6	15	21	117	...	...	...		—	—	—	—	—
—Peterborough	OHL	2	0	1	1	9	...	...	...		—	—	—	—	—
94-95—Peterborough	OHL	42	8	16	24	109	...	...	...		11	3	3	6	22
95-96—Muskegon	Col.HL	58	18	24	42	263	...	...	...		5	1	2	3	22
—Detroit	IHL	4	0	0	0	24	...	...	...		—	—	—	—	—
96-97—Kentucky	AHL	25	6	6	12	103	...	...	...		2	0	0	0	19
—New York Islanders	NHL	41	1	4	5	144	-10	1	0		—	—	—	—	—
97-98—Kentucky	AHL	37	5	13	18	139	...	...	...		3	0	1	1	10
—New York Islanders	NHL	20	0	0	0	35	-2	0	0		—	—	—	—	—
98-99—Lowell	AHL	23	2	4	6	80	...	...	...		—	—	—	—	—
—New York Islanders	NHL	45	0	0	0	32	-10	0	0		—	—	—	—	—
99-00—New York Islanders	NHL	65	1	3	4	103	-4	0	0		—	—	—	—	—
00-01—New York Islanders	NHL	31	0	2	2	35	1	0	0		—	—	—	—	—
NHL Totals (5 years)		202	2	9	11	349	-25	1	0						

WEEKES, KEVIN — G — LIGHTNING

PERSONAL: Born April 4, 1975, in Toronto. ... 6-0/195. ... Catches left. ... Name pronounced WEEKS.
TRANSACTIONS/CAREER NOTES: Selected by Florida Panthers in second round (second Panthers pick, 41st overall) of NHL entry draft (June 26, 1993). ... Sprained right knee (March 19, 1998); missed remainder of season. ... Traded by Panthers with D Ed Jovanovski, C Dave Gagner, C Mike Brown and first-round pick (C Nathan Smith) in 2000 draft to Vancouver Canucks for RW Pavel Bure, D Bret Hedican, D Brad Ference and third-round pick (RW Robert Fried) in 2000 draft (January 17, 1999). ... Injured knee (October 28, 1999); missed three games. ... Traded by Canucks with C Dave Scatchard and RW Bill Muckalt to New York Islanders for G Felix Potvin, second-(traded to Atlanta) and third-round (C Thatcher Bell) picks in 2000 draft (December 19, 1999). ... Sore neck (April 9, 2000); missed final game of season. ... Traded by Islanders with D Kristian Kudroc and second-round pick (traded to Phoenix) in 2001 draft to Tampa Bay Lightning for first-(LW Raffi Torres), fourth-(RW/LW Vladimir Gorbunov) and seventh-round (D Ryan Caldwell) picks in 2000 draft (June 24, 2000). ... Injured knee (December 2, 2000); missed three games. ... Strained groin (January 7, 2001); missed three games. ... Strained groin (April 4, 2001); missed final three games of season.
MISCELLANEOUS: Stopped a penalty shot attempt (vs. Miroslav Satan, March 4, 2000). ... Allowed a penalty shot goal (vs. Paul Kariya, January 21, 1998; vs. Martin Rucinsky, March 29, 2001).

					REGULAR SEASON						PLAYOFFS					
Season Team	League	Gms.	Min.	W	L	T	GA	SO	Avg.		Gms.	Min.	W	L	GA	SO	Avg.
91-92—Toronto St. Mikes	OJHL	35	1575	...	...	...	68	4	2.59		—	—	—	—	—	—	—
—St. Michael's	Tier II Jr. A	2	127	...	...	...	11	0	5.20		—	—	—	—	—	—	—
92-93—Owen Sound	OHL	29	1645	9	12	5	143	0	5.22		1	26	0	0	5	0	11.54
93-94—Owen Sound	OHL	34	1974	13	19	1	158	0	4.80		—	—	—	—	—	—	—
94-95—Ottawa	OHL	41	2266	13	23	4	154	1	4.08		—	—	—	—	—	—	—
95-96—Carolina	AHL	60	3403	24	25	8	229	2	4.04		—	—	—	—	—	—	—
96-97—Carolina	AHL	51	2899	17	†28	4	172	1	3.56		—	—	—	—	—	—	—
97-98—Fort Wayne	IHL	12	719	9	2	‡1	34	1	2.84		—	—	—	—	—	—	—
—Florida	NHL	11	485	0	5	1	32	0	3.96		—	—	—	—	—	—	—
98-99—Detroit	IHL	33	1857	19	5	‡7	64	*4	*2.07		—	—	—	—	—	—	—
—Vancouver	NHL	11	532	0	8	1	34	0	3.83		—	—	—	—	—	—	—
99-00—Vancouver	NHL	20	987	6	7	4	47	1	2.86		—	—	—	—	—	—	—
—New York Islanders	NHL	36	2026	10	20	4	115	1	3.41		—	—	—	—	—	—	—
00-01—Tampa Bay	NHL	61	3378	20	*33	3	177	4	3.14		—	—	—	—	—	—	—
NHL Totals (4 years)		139	7408	36	73	13	405	6	3.28								

W

WEIGHT, DOUG   C   BLUES

PERSONAL: Born January 21, 1971, in Warren, Mich. ... 5-11/200. ... Shoots left. ... Full Name: Douglas D. Weight. ... Name pronounced WAYT.

TRANSACTIONS/CAREER NOTES: Selected by New York Rangers in second round (second Rangers pick, 34th overall) of NHL entry draft (June 16, 1990). ... Sprained elbow (October 14, 1991); missed three games. ... Damaged ligaments (January 11, 1991). ... Suspended four off-days and fined $500 by NHL for cross-checking (November 5, 1992). ... Traded by Rangers to Edmonton Oilers for LW Esa Tikkanen (March 17, 1993). ... Played in Europe during 1994-95 NHL lockout. ... Sprained ankle (February 15, 1997); missed one game. ... Injured ankle (February 21, 1997); missed one game. ... Sprained left shoulder (March 15, 1998); missed two games. ... Tore medial collateral ligament in right knee (October 28, 1998); missed 34 games. ... Fractured ribs (December 14, 1999); missed five games. ... Traded by Oilers with LW Michel Riesen to St. Louis Blues for C Marty Reasoner, C Jochen Hecht and D Jan Horacek (July 1, 2001).

HONORS: Named to CCHA All-Rookie team (1989-90). ... Named to NCAA All-America (West) second team (1990-91). ... Named to CCHA All-Star first team (1990-91). ... Played in NHL All-Star Game (1996, 1998 and 2001).

MISCELLANEOUS: Captain of Edmonton Oilers (1999-2000 and 2000-01). ... Scored on a penalty shot (vs. Mike Richter, October 8, 1997).

STATISTICAL PLATEAUS: Three-goal games: 1995-96 (1).

				REGULAR SEASON								PLAYOFFS			
Season Team	League	Gms.	G	A	Pts.	PIM	+/-	PP	SH		Gms.	G	A	Pts.	PIM
88-89—Bloomfield	NAJHL	34	26	53	79	105	...	...	...		—	—	—	—	—
89-90—Lake Superior State	CCHA	46	21	48	69	44	...	...	...		—	—	—	—	—
90-91—Lake Superior State	CCHA	42	29	46	75	86	...	...	...		—	—	—	—	—
—New York Rangers	NHL	—	—	—	—	—	...	...	...		1	0	0	0	0
91-92—New York Rangers	NHL	53	8	22	30	23	-3	0	0		7	2	2	4	0
—Binghamton	AHL	9	3	14	17	2	...	...	...		4	1	4	5	6
92-93—New York Rangers	NHL	65	15	25	40	55	4	3	0		—	—	—	—	—
—Edmonton	NHL	13	2	6	8	10	-2	0	0		—	—	—	—	—
93-94—Edmonton	NHL	84	24	50	74	47	-22	4	1		—	—	—	—	—
94-95—Rosenheim	Germany	8	2	3	5	18	...	...	...		—	—	—	—	—
—Edmonton	NHL	48	7	33	40	69	-17	1	0		—	—	—	—	—
95-96—Edmonton	NHL	82	25	79	104	95	-19	9	0		—	—	—	—	—
96-97—Edmonton	NHL	80	21	61	82	80	1	4	0		12	3	8	11	8
97-98—Edmonton	NHL	79	26	44	70	69	1	9	0		12	2	7	9	14
—U.S. Olympic team......	Int'l	4	0	2	2	2	...	...	...		—	—	—	—	—
98-99—Edmonton	NHL	43	6	31	37	12	-8	1	0		4	1	1	2	15
99-00—Edmonton	NHL	77	21	51	72	54	6	3	1		5	3	2	5	4
00-01—Edmonton	NHL	82	25	65	90	91	12	8	0		6	1	5	6	17
NHL Totals (11 years).........		706	180	467	647	605	-47	42	2		47	12	25	37	58

WEINHANDL, MATTIAS   RW   ISLANDERS

PERSONAL: Born June 1, 1980, in Ljungby, Sweden. ... 6-0/183. ... Shoots right.

TRANSACTIONS/CAREER NOTES: Selected by New York Islanders in third round (fifth Islanders pick, 78th overall) of NHL entry draft (June 26, 1999).

				REGULAR SEASON								PLAYOFFS			
Season Team	League	Gms.	G	A	Pts.	PIM	+/-	PP	SH		Gms.	G	A	Pts.	PIM
97-98—Troja-Ljungby..............	Sweden Dv. 2	29	4	2	6	10	...	...	...		—	—	—	—	—
98-99—Troja-Ljungby..............	Sweden Dv. 2	38	20	20	40	30	...	...	...		—	—	—	—	—
99-00—MoDo Ornskoldsvik	Sweden	32	15	9	24	6	...	...	...		13	5	3	8	8
00-01—MoDo Ornskoldsvik	Sweden	48	16	16	32	14	...	...	...		6	1	3	4	6

WEINRICH, ERIC   D   FLYERS

PERSONAL: Born December 19, 1966, in Roanoke, Va. ... 6-1/213. ... Shoots left. ... Full Name: Eric John Weinrich. ... Name pronounced WIGHN-rihch.

TRANSACTIONS/CAREER NOTES: Selected by New Jersey Devils in second round (third Devils pick, 32nd overall) of NHL entry draft (June 15, 1985). ... Traded by Devils with G Sean Burke to Hartford Whalers for RW Bobby Holik, second-round pick (LW Jay Pandolfo) in 1993 draft and future considerations (August 28, 1992). ... Suffered concussion (November 25, 1992); missed two games. ... Sprained knee (September 22, 1993); missed five games. ... Injured right knee (October 5, 1993); missed five games. ... Traded with LW Patrick Poulin by Whalers to the Chicago Blackhawks for RW Steve Larmer and D Bryan Marchment (November 2, 1993). ... Fractured jaw (February 24, 1994); missed 17 games. ... Cut eye (December 1, 1995); missed three games. ... Cut thigh (December 31, 1996); missed one game. ... Traded by Blackhawks with G Jeff Hackett, D Alain Nasreddine and fourth-round pick (D Chris Dyment) in 1999 draft to Montreal Canadiens for G Jocelyn Thibault, D Dave Manson and D Brad Brown (November 16, 1998). ... Fractured foot (March 22, 2000); missed five games. ... Traded by Canadiens to Boston Bruins for D Patrick Traverse (February 21, 2001). ... Signed as free agent by Philadelphia Flyers (July 5, 2001).

HONORS: Named to NCAA All-America (East) second team (1986-87). ... Named to Hockey East All-Star first team (1986-87). ... Won Eddie Shore Plaque (1989-90). ... Named to AHL All-Star first team (1989-90). ... Named to NHL All-Rookie team (1990-91).

MISCELLANEOUS: Captain of Montreal Canadiens (October 14-December 15, 2000).

				REGULAR SEASON								PLAYOFFS			
Season Team	League	Gms.	G	A	Pts.	PIM	+/-	PP	SH		Gms.	G	A	Pts.	PIM
83-84—North Yarmouth Acad.	Maine H.S.	17	23	33	56	...	...	...	...		—	—	—	—	—
84-85—North Yarmouth Acad.	Maine H.S.	20	6	21	27	...	...	...	...		—	—	—	—	—
85-86—Univ. of Maine	Hockey East	34	0	15	15	26	...	...	...		—	—	—	—	—
86-87—Univ. of Maine	Hockey East	41	12	32	44	59	...	...	...		—	—	—	—	—
87-88—Univ. of Maine	Hockey East	8	4	7	11	22	...	...	...		—	—	—	—	—
—U.S. national team	Int'l	39	3	9	12	24	...	...	...		—	—	—	—	—
—U.S. Olympic team......	Int'l	3	0	0	0	24	...	...	...		—	—	—	—	—
88-89—Utica	AHL	80	17	27	44	70	...	...	...		5	0	1	1	8
—New Jersey	NHL	2	0	0	0	0	-1	0	0		—	—	—	—	—
89-90—Utica	AHL	57	12	48	60	38	...	...	...		6	1	3	4	17
—New Jersey	NHL	19	2	7	9	11	1	1	0		—	—	—	—	—

W

eason Team	League	Gms.	G	A	Pts.	PIM	+/-	PP	SH	Gms.	G	A	Pts.	PIM
		REGULAR SEASON								**PLAYOFFS**				
0-91—New Jersey	NHL	76	4	34	38	48	10	1	0	7	1	2	3	6
1-92—New Jersey	NHL	76	7	25	32	55	10	5	0	7	0	2	2	4
2-93—Hartford	NHL	79	7	29	36	76	-11	0	2	—	—	—	—	—
3-94—Hartford	NHL	8	1	1	2	2	-5	1	0	—	—	—	—	—
—Chicago	NHL	54	3	23	26	31	6	1	0	6	0	2	2	6
4-95—Chicago	NHL	48	3	10	13	33	1	1	0	16	1	5	6	4
5-96—Chicago	NHL	77	5	10	15	65	14	0	0	10	1	4	5	10
6-97—Chicago	NHL	81	7	25	32	62	19	1	0	6	0	1	1	4
7-98—Chicago	NHL	82	2	21	23	106	10	0	0	—	—	—	—	—
8-99—Chicago	NHL	14	1	3	4	12	-13	0	0	—	—	—	—	—
—Montreal	NHL	66	6	12	18	77	-12	4	0	—	—	—	—	—
9-00—Montreal	NHL	77	4	25	29	39	4	2	0	—	—	—	—	—
0-01—Montreal	NHL	60	6	19	25	34	-1	2	0	—	—	—	—	—
—Boston	NHL	22	1	5	6	10	-8	1	0	—	—	—	—	—
NHL Totals (13 years)		841	59	249	308	661	24	20	2	58	4	19	23	51

WERENKA, BRAD   D   FLAMES

ERSONAL: Born February 12, 1969, in Two Hills, Alta. ... 6-1/218. ... Shoots left. ... Full Name: John Bradley Werenka. ... Name pronounced uh-REHN-kuh.

RANSACTIONS/CAREER NOTES: Selected by Edmonton Oilers as underage junior in second round (second Oilers pick, 42nd overall) of NHL ntry draft (June 13, 1987). ... Traded by Oilers to Quebec Nordiques for G Steve Passmore (March 21, 1994). ... Signed as free agent by hicago Blackhawks (August 10, 1995). ... Signed as free agent by Pittsburgh Penguins (July 31, 1997). ... Sprained ankle (October 17, 1997); iissed 10 games. ... Bruised shoulder (November 22, 1997); missed one game. ... Suspended one game by NHL for high-sticking incident March 28, 1999). ... Fractured orbital bone (December 26, 1999); missed two games. ... Traded by Penguins to Calgary Flames for LW Rene :orbet and G Tyler Moss (March 14, 2000). ... Suffered concussion (December 29, 2000); missed remainder of season.

IONORS: Named to NCAA All-America (West) first team (1990-91). ... Named to NCAA All-Tournament team (1990-91). ... Named to WCHA ll-Star first team (1990-91). ... Won Governors Trophy (1996-97). ... Named to IHL All-Star first team (1996-97).

IISCELLANEOUS: Member of silver-medal-winning Canadian Olympic team (1994).

eason Team	League	Gms.	G	A	Pts.	PIM	+/-	PP	SH	Gms.	G	A	Pts.	PIM
		REGULAR SEASON								**PLAYOFFS**				
5-86—Fort Saskatchewan	AJHL	29	12	23	35	24	...	...	...	—	—	—	—	—
6-87—N. Michigan Univ.	WCHA	30	4	4	8	35	...	...	...	—	—	—	—	—
7-88—N. Michigan Univ.	WCHA	34	7	23	30	26	...	...	...	—	—	—	—	—
8-89—N. Michigan Univ.	WCHA	28	7	13	20	16	...	...	...	—	—	—	—	—
9-90—N. Michigan Univ.	WCHA	8	2	5	7	8	...	...	...	—	—	—	—	—
0-91—N. Michigan Univ.	WCHA	47	20	43	63	36	...	...	...	—	—	—	—	—
1-92—Cape Breton	AHL	66	6	21	27	95	...	...	...	5	0	3	3	6
2-93—Canadian nat'l team	Int'l	18	3	7	10	10	...	...	...	—	—	—	—	—
—Edmonton	NHL	27	5	3	8	24	1	0	1	—	—	—	—	—
—Cape Breton	AHL	4	1	1	2	4	...	...	...	16	4	17	21	12
3-94—Cape Breton	AHL	25	6	17	23	19	...	...	...	—	—	—	—	—
—Edmonton	NHL	15	0	4	4	14	-1	0	0	—	—	—	—	—
—Can. Olympic team	Int'l	8	2	2	4	8	...	...	...	—	—	—	—	—
—Quebec	NHL	11	0	7	7	8	4	0	0	—	—	—	—	—
—Cornwall	AHL	—	—	—	—	—	...	...	...	12	2	10	12	36
4-95—Milwaukee	IHL	80	8	45	53	161	...	...	...	15	3	10	13	36
5-96—Indianapolis	IHL	73	15	42	57	85	...	...	...	5	1	3	4	8
—Chicago	NHL	9	0	0	0	8	-2	0	0	—	—	—	—	—
6-97—Indianapolis	IHL	82	20	56	76	83	...	...	...	4	1	4	5	6
7-98—Pittsburgh	NHL	71	3	15	18	46	15	2	0	6	1	0	1	8
8-99—Pittsburgh	NHL	81	6	18	24	93	17	1	0	13	1	1	2	6
9-00—Pittsburgh	NHL	61	3	8	11	69	15	0	0	—	—	—	—	—
—Calgary	NHL	12	1	1	2	21	-2	0	0	—	—	—	—	—
0-01—Calgary	NHL	33	1	4	5	16	-3	0	0	—	—	—	—	—
NHL Totals (7 years)		320	19	60	79	299	44	3	1	19	2	1	3	14

WESLEY, GLEN   D   HURRICANES

W

'ERSONAL: Born October 2, 1968, in Red Deer, Alta. ... 6-1/201. ... Shoots left. ... Brother of Blake Wesley, defenseman with four NHL teams 1979-80 through 1985-86).

'RANSACTIONS/CAREER NOTES: Selected by Boston Bruins in first round (first Bruins pick, third overall) of NHL entry draft (June 13, 1987). .. Sprained left knee (October 1988). ... Fractured foot (November 24, 1992); missed 14 games. ... Injured groin (February 1993); missed one ame. ... Injured groin (March 1993); missed three games. ... Injured groin (April 1993); missed two games. ... Injured kidney (March 3, 1994); iissed three games. ... Traded by Bruins to Hartford Whalers for first-round picks in 1995 (D Kyle McLaren), 1996 (D Johnathan Aitken) and 997 (C Sergei Samsonov) drafts (August 26, 1994). ... Bruised shin (November 4, 1995); missed two games. ... Injured groin (December '8, 1995); missed three games. ... Sprained knee (January 6, 1996); missed three games. ... Injured groin (January 17, 1996); missed four ames. ... Injured groin (January 25, 1996); missed three games. ... Strained hip flexor (November 4, 1996); missed one game. ... Fractured oot (November 16, 1996); missed 10 games. ... Suffered from the flu (February 5, 1997); missed one game. ... Whalers franchise moved to lorth Carolina and renamed Carolina Hurricanes for 1997-98 season; NHL approved move on June 25, 1997. ... Sprained ankle (March 24, 999); missed eight games. ... Strained groin (November 22, 1999); missed two games. ... Suffered eye injury (February 17, 2000); missed wo games. ... Fractured jaw (March 4, 2001); missed 11 games.

IONORS: Won WHL (West) Top Defenseman Trophy (1985-86 and 1986-87). ... Named to WHL (West) All-Star first team (1985-86 and 1986-7). ... Named to NHL All-Rookie team (1987-88). ... Played in NHL All-Star Game (1989).

IISCELLANEOUS: Captain of Hartford Whalers (1994-95).

STATISTICAL PLATEAUS: Three-goal games: 1993-94 (1).

Season Team	League	REGULAR SEASON Gms.	G	A	Pts.	PIM	+/-	PP	SH	PLAYOFFS Gms.	G	A	Pts.	PIM
83-84—Red Deer..................	AJHL	57	9	20	29	40	...	...	...	—	—	—	—	—
—Portland....................	WHL	3	1	2	3	0	...	...	...	—	—	—	—	—
84-85—Portland..................	WHL	67	16	52	68	76	...	...	...	6	1	6	7	8
85-86—Portland..................	WHL	69	16	75	91	96	...	...	...	15	3	11	14	29
86-87—Portland..................	WHL	63	16	46	62	72	...	...	...	20	8	18	26	27
87-88—Boston	NHL	79	7	30	37	69	21	1	2	23	6	8	14	22
88-89—Boston	NHL	77	19	35	54	61	23	8	1	10	0	2	2	4
89-90—Boston	NHL	78	9	27	36	48	6	5	0	21	2	6	8	36
90-91—Boston	NHL	80	11	32	43	78	0	5	1	19	2	9	11	19
91-92—Boston	NHL	78	9	37	46	54	-9	4	0	15	2	4	6	16
92-93—Boston	NHL	64	8	25	33	47	-2	4	1	4	0	0	0	0
93-94—Boston	NHL	81	14	44	58	64	1	6	1	13	3	3	6	12
94-95—Hartford	NHL	48	2	14	16	50	-6	1	0	—	—	—	—	—
95-96—Hartford	NHL	68	8	16	24	88	-9	6	0	—	—	—	—	—
96-97—Hartford	NHL	68	6	26	32	40	0	3	1	—	—	—	—	—
97-98—Carolina	NHL	82	6	19	25	36	7	1	0	—	—	—	—	—
98-99—Carolina	NHL	74	7	17	24	44	14	0	0	6	0	0	0	2
99-00—Carolina	NHL	78	7	15	22	38	-4	1	0	—	—	—	—	—
00-01—Carolina	NHL	71	5	16	21	42	-2	3	0	6	0	0	0	0
NHL Totals (14 years).........		**1026**	**118**	**353**	**471**	**759**	**40**	**48**	**7**	**117**	**15**	**32**	**47**	**111**

WESTLUND, TOMMY — RW — HURRICANES

PERSONAL: Born December 29, 1974, in Fors, Sweden. ... 6-0/202. ... Shoots right.
TRANSACTIONS/CAREER NOTES: Selected by Carolina Hurricanes in fourth round (fifth Hurricanes pick, 93rd overall) of NHL entry draft (June 27, 1998).

Season Team	League	REGULAR SEASON Gms.	G	A	Pts.	PIM	+/-	PP	SH	PLAYOFFS Gms.	G	A	Pts.	PIM
91-92—Avesta....................	Sweden Dv. 3	27	11	9	20	8	...	...	...	—	—	—	—	—
92-93—Avesta....................	Sweden Dv. 2	32	9	5	14	32	...	...	...	—	—	—	—	—
93-94—Avesta....................	Sweden Dv. 2	31	20	11	31	34	...	...	...	—	—	—	—	—
94-95—Avesta....................	Sweden Dv. 2	32	17	13	30	22	...	...	...	—	—	—	—	—
95-96—Brynas Gavle	Sweden	18	2	1	3	2	...	...	...	—	—	—	—	—
—Brynas Gavle	Sweden Dv. 2	18	10	10	20	4	...	...	...	8	1	0	1	4
96-97—Brynas Gavle	Sweden	50	21	13	34	16	...	...	...	3	0	1	1	0
97-98—Brynas Gavle	Sweden	46	29	9	38	45	...	...	...	3	0	1	1	0
98-99—New Haven	AHL	50	8	18	26	31	...	...	...	—	—	—	—	—
99-00—Carolina	NHL	81	4	8	12	19	-10	0	1	—	—	—	—	—
00-01—Carolina	NHL	79	5	3	8	23	-9	0	0	6	0	0	0	17
NHL Totals (2 years)...........		**160**	**9**	**11**	**20**	**42**	**-19**	**0**	**1**	**6**	**0**	**0**	**0**	**17**

WHITE, COLIN — D — DEVILS

PERSONAL: Born December 12, 1977, in New Glasgow, Nova Scotia. ... 6-4/210. ... Shoots left. ... Full Name: John Colin White.
TRANSACTIONS/CAREER NOTES: Selected by New Jersey Devils in second round (fifth Devils pick, 49th overall) of NHL entry draft (June 22, 1996). ... Suffered injury (January 28. 2000); missed two games. ... Suffered stiff neck (March 10, 2000); missed three games.
HONORS: Named to QMJHL All-Rookie team (1995-96). ... Named to NHL All-Rookie team (2000-01).
MISCELLANEOUS: Member of Stanley Cup championship team (2000).

Season Team	League	REGULAR SEASON Gms.	G	A	Pts.	PIM	+/-	PP	SH	PLAYOFFS Gms.	G	A	Pts.	PIM
94-95—Laval.........................	QMJHL	7	0	1	1	32	...	...	...	—	—	—	—	—
—Hull.............................	QMJHL	5	0	1	1	4	...	...	...	12	0	0	0	23
95-96—Hull.........................	QMJHL	62	2	8	10	303	...	...	...	18	0	4	4	42
96-97—Hull.........................	QMJHL	63	3	12	15	297	...	...	...	14	3	12	15	65
97-98—Albany......................	AHL	76	3	13	16	235	...	...	...	13	0	0	0	55
98-99—Albany......................	AHL	77	2	12	14	265	...	...	...	5	0	1	1	8
99-00—Albany......................	AHL	52	5	21	26	176	...	...	...	—	—	—	—	—
—New Jersey.................	NHL	21	2	1	3	40	3	0	0	23	1	5	6	18
00-01—New Jersey.................	NHL	82	1	19	20	155	32	0	0	25	0	3	3	42
NHL Totals (2 years)...........		**103**	**3**	**20**	**23**	**195**	**35**	**0**	**0**	**48**	**1**	**8**	**9**	**60**

W

WHITE, PETER — C — FLYERS

PERSONAL: Born March 15, 1969, in Montreal. ... 5-11/200. ... Shoots left. ... Full Name: Peter Toby White.
TRANSACTIONS/CAREER NOTES: Selected by Edmonton Oilers in fifth round (fourth Oilers pick, 92nd overall) of NHL entry draft (June 17, 1989). ... Traded by Oilers with fourth-round pick (RW Jason Sessa) in 1996 draft to Toronto Maple Leafs for LW Kent Manderville (December 4, 1995). ... Signed as free agent by Philadelphia Flyers (July 17, 1996).
HONORS: Named to CCHA All-Rookie team (1988-89). ... Named CCHA Playoff Most Valuable Player (1989-90). ... Won John B. Sellenberger Trophy (1994-95 and 1996-97). ... Named to AHL All-Star second team (1994-95, 1996-97 and 1997-98).

Season Team	League	REGULAR SEASON Gms.	G	A	Pts.	PIM	+/-	PP	SH	PLAYOFFS Gms.	G	A	Pts.	PIM
87-88—Pembroke	COJHL	56	90	136	226	32	...	...	...	—	—	—	—	—
88-89—Michigan State............	CCHA	46	20	33	53	17	...	...	...	—	—	—	—	—
89-90—Michigan State............	CCHA	45	22	40	62	6	...	...	...	—	—	—	—	—
90-91—Michigan State............	CCHA	37	7	31	38	28	...	...	...	—	—	—	—	—

Season Team	League	REGULAR SEASON								PLAYOFFS				
		Gms.	G	A	Pts.	PIM	+/-	PP	SH	Gms.	G	A	Pts.	PIM
91-92—Michigan State	CCHA	44	26	51	77	32	...	...	...	—	—	—	—	—
92-93—Cape Breton	AHL	64	12	28	40	10	...	...	...	16	3	3	6	12
93-94—Cape Breton	AHL	45	21	49	70	12	...	...	...	5	2	3	5	2
—Edmonton	NHL	26	3	5	8	2	1	0	0	—	—	—	—	—
94-95—Cape Breton	AHL	65	36	†69	*105	30	...	...	...	—	—	—	—	—
—Edmonton	NHL	9	2	4	6	0	1	2	0	—	—	—	—	—
95-96—Edmonton	NHL	26	5	3	8	0	-14	1	0	—	—	—	—	—
—Toronto	NHL	1	0	0	0	0	0	0	0	—	—	—	—	—
—St. John's	AHL	17	6	7	13	6	...	...	...	—	—	—	—	—
—Atlanta	IHL	36	21	20	41	4	...	...	...	3	0	3	3	2
96-97—Philadelphia	AHL	80	*44	61	*105	28	...	...	...	10	6	8	14	6
97-98—Philadelphia	AHL	80	27	*78	*105	28	...	...	...	20	9	9	18	6
98-99—Philadelphia	AHL	77	31	59	90	20	...	...	...	16	4	13	17	12
—Philadelphia	NHL	3	0	0	0	0	0	0	0	—	—	—	—	—
99-00—Philadelphia	AHL	62	20	41	61	38	...	...	...	—	—	—	—	—
—Philadelphia	NHL	21	1	5	6	6	1	0	0	16	0	2	2	0
00-01—Philadelphia	NHL	77	9	16	25	16	1	1	0	3	0	0	0	0
NHL Totals (6 years)		163	20	33	53	24	-10	4	0	19	0	2	2	0

WHITE, TODD   C   SENATORS

PERSONAL: Born May 21, 1975, in Kanata, Ont. ... 5-10/180. ... Shoots left.
TRANSACTIONS/CAREER NOTES: Signed as non-drafted free agent by Chicago Blackhawks (August 6, 1997). ... Suffered charley horse (October 4, 1997); missed one game. ... Bruised ribs prior to 1998-99 season; missed first six games of season. ... Traded by Blackhawks to Philadelphia Flyers for conditional pick in 2001 draft (January 26, 2000). ... Signed as free agent by Ottawa Senators (July 12, 2000).
HONORS: Named to ECAC All-Star second team (1995-96). ... Named to NCAA All-America (East) first team (1996-97). ... Named to ECAC All-Star first team (1996-97). ... Won Garry F. Longman Trophy (1997-98).
MISCELLANEOUS: Failed to score on a penalty shot (vs. Jamie Storr, Februaury 26, 1999).

Season Team	League	REGULAR SEASON								PLAYOFFS				
		Gms.	G	A	Pts.	PIM	+/-	PP	SH	Gms.	G	A	Pts.	PIM
93-94—Clarkson	ECAC	33	10	12	22	28	...	...	...	—	—	—	—	—
94-95—Clarkson	ECAC	34	13	16	29	44	...	...	...	—	—	—	—	—
95-96—Clarkson	ECAC	38	29	43	72	36	...	...	...	—	—	—	—	—
96-97—Clarkson	ECAC	37	38	36	74	22	...	...	...	—	—	—	—	—
97-98—Chicago	NHL	7	1	0	1	2	0	0	0	—	—	—	—	—
—Indianapolis	IHL	65	†46	36	82	28	...	...	...	5	2	3	5	4
98-99—Chicago	IHL	25	11	13	24	8	...	...	...	10	1	4	5	8
—Chicago	NHL	35	5	8	13	20	-1	2	0	—	—	—	—	—
99-00—Cleveland	IHL	42	21	30	51	32	...	...	...	—	—	—	—	—
—Chicago	NHL	1	0	0	0	0	0	0	0	—	—	—	—	—
—Philadelphia	AHL	32	19	24	43	12	...	...	...	5	2	1	3	8
—Philadelphia	NHL	3	1	0	1	0	-1	0	0	—	—	—	—	—
00-01—Grand Rapids	IHL	64	22	32	54	20	...	...	...	10	4	4	8	10
—Ottawa	NHL	16	4	1	5	4	5	0	0	2	0	0	0	0
NHL Totals (4 years)		62	11	9	20	26	3	2	0	2	0	0	0	0

WHITFIELD, TRENT   C   CAPITALS

PERSONAL: Born June 17, 1977, in Estevan, Sask. ... 5-11/199. ... Shoots left.
TRANSACTIONS/CAREER NOTES: Selected by Boston Bruins in fourth round (fifth Bruins pick, 100th overall) of NHL entry draft (June 22, 1996). ... Signed as free agent by Washington Capitals (September 1, 1998).
HONORS: Named to WHL (West) All-Star first team (1996-97). ... Named to WHL (West) All-Star second team (1997-98).

Season Team	League	REGULAR SEASON								PLAYOFFS				
		Gms.	G	A	Pts.	PIM	+/-	PP	SH	Gms.	G	A	Pts.	PIM
93-94—Spokane	WHL	5	1	1	2	0	...	...	...	—	—	—	—	—
94-95—Spokane	WHL	48	8	17	25	26	...	...	...	11	7	6	13	5
95-96—Spokane	WHL	72	33	51	84	75	...	...	...	18	8	10	18	10
96-97—Spokane	WHL	58	34	42	76	74	...	...	...	9	5	7	12	10
97-98—Spokane	WHL	65	38	44	82	97	...	...	...	18	9	10	19	15
98-99—Portland	AHL	50	10	8	18	20	...	...	...	—	—	—	—	—
—Hampton Roads	ECHL	19	13	12	25	12	...	...	...	4	2	0	2	14
99-00—Portland	AHL	79	18	35	53	52	...	...	...	3	1	1	2	2
—Washington	NHL	—	—	—	—	—	...	...	...	3	0	0	0	0
00-01—Portland	AHL	19	9	11	20	27	...	...	...	—	—	—	—	—
—Washington	NHL	61	2	4	6	35	3	0	0	5	0	0	0	2
NHL Totals (2 years)		61	2	4	6	35	3	0	0	8	0	0	0	2

W

WHITMORE, KAY   G   FLAMES

PERSONAL: Born April 10, 1967, in Sudbury, Ont. ... 5-11/180. ... Catches left.
TRANSACTIONS/CAREER NOTES: Selected by Hartford Whalers in second round (second Whalers pick, 26th overall) of NHL entry draft (June 5, 1985). ... Traded by Whalers to Vancouver Canucks for G Corrie D'Alessio and conditional pick in 1993 draft (October 1, 1992). ... Signed as free agent by San Jose Sharks (September 2, 1997). ... Traded by Sharks with second-round pick (RW Jaroslav Kristek) in 1998 draft and fifth-round pick (traded to Columbus) in 2000 draft to Buffalo Sabres for G Steve Shields and fourth-round pick (RW Miroslav Zalesak) in 1998 draft (June 19, 1998). ... Signed as free agent by New York Rangers (August 17, 1998). ... Signed as free agent by Boston Bruins (August 25, 1999).

... Traded by Bruins to Edmonton Oilers for D Mike Matteucci (December 29, 1999). ... Traded by Oilers to Bruins for future considerations (July 20, 2000). ... Signed as free agent by Calgary Flames (July 9, 2001).
HONORS: Shared Dave Pinkney Trophy with Ron Tugnutt (1985-86). ... Named to OHL All-Star first team (1985-86). ... Won Jack Butterfield Trophy (1990-91). ... Shared James Norris Trophy with Mike Buzak (1997-98).
MISCELLANEOUS: Stopped penalty shot attempt (vs. Randy Burridge, March 31, 1991). ... Allowed penalty shot goal (vs. Luc Robitaille, February 6, 1992).

			REGULAR SEASON								PLAYOFFS						
Season Team	League	Gms.	Min	W	L	T	GA	SO	Avg.	Gms.	Min.	W	L	GA	SO	Avg.
83-84—Peterborough	OHL	29	1471	17	8	0	110	0	4.49	—	—	—	—	—	—	—
84-85—Peterborough	OHL	*53	*3077	35	16	2	172	†2	3.35	*17	*1020	10	4	58	0	3.41
85-86—Peterborough	OHL	41	2467	27	12	2	114	†3	*2.77	14	837	8	5	40	0	2.87
86-87—Peterborough	OHL	36	2159	14	17	5	118	1	3.28	7	366	3	3	17	1	2.79
87-88—Binghamton	AHL	38	2137	17	15	4	121	3	3.40	2	118	0	2	10	0	5.08
88-89—Binghamton	AHL	*56	*3200	21	29	4	*241	1	4.52	—	—	—	—	—	—	—
—Hartford	NHL	3	180	2	1	0	10	0	3.33	2	135	0	2	10	0	4.44
89-90—Binghamton	AHL	24	1386	3	19	2	109	0	4.72	—	—	—	—	—	—	—
—Hartford	NHL	9	442	4	2	1	26	0	3.53	—	—	—	—	—	—	—
90-91—Hartford	NHL	18	850	3	9	3	52	0	3.67	—	—	—	—	—	—	—
—Springfield	AHL	33	1916	22	9	1	98	1	3.07	*15	*926	11	4	*37	0	*2.40
91-92—Hartford	NHL	45	2567	14	21	6	155	3	3.62	1	19	0	0	1	0	3.16
92-93—Vancouver	NHL	31	1817	19	8	4	94	1	3.10	—	—	—	—	—	—	—
93-94—Vancouver	NHL	32	1921	18	14	0	113	0	3.53	—	—	—	—	—	—	—
94-95—Vancouver	NHL	11	558	0	6	2	37	0	3.98	1	20	0	0	2	0	6.00
95-96—Los Angeles	IHL	30	1562	10	9	‡7	99	1	3.80	—	—	—	—	—	—	—
—Detroit	IHL	10	501	3	5	0	33	0	3.95	—	—	—	—	—	—	—
—Syracuse	AHL	11	662	6	4	1	37	0	3.35	—	—	—	—	—	—	—
96-97—Sodertalje	Sweden	25	1320	...	...	...	85	0	3.86	—	—	—	—	—	—	—
97-98—Long Beach	IHL	46	2516	28	12	‡3	109	3	2.60	14	839	9	5	43	0	3.08
98-99—Hartford	AHL	18	1080	8	8	2	47	0	2.61	—	—	—	—	—	—	—
—Milwaukee	IHL	23	1304	10	6	‡4	64	0	2.94	—	—	—	—	—	—	—
99-00—Providence	AHL	43	2393	17	19	3	127	1	3.18	1	59	0	1	2	0	2.03
00-01—Providence	AHL	26	1460	13	8	2	65	2	2.67	—	—	—	—	—	—	—
—Boston	NHL	5	203	1	2	0	18	0	5.32	—	—	—	—	—	—	—
NHL Totals (8 years)		154	8538	60	63	16	505	4	3.55	4	174	0	2	13	0	4.48

WHITNEY, RAY — LW — BLUE JACKETS

PERSONAL: Born May 8, 1972, in Fort Saskatchewan, Alta. ... 5-10/175. ... Shoots right.
TRANSACTIONS/CAREER NOTES: Selected by San Jose Sharks in second round (second Sharks pick, 23rd overall) of NHL entry draft (June 22, 1991). ... Sprained knee (October 30, 1993); missed 18 games. ... Suffered from the flu (December 15, 1993); missed one game. ... Injured ankle (February 20, 1995) and suffered eye infection (February 28, 1995); missed seven games. ... Suffered eye infection (March 21, 1995); missed one game. ... Suffered from the flu (April 9, 1995); missed one game. ... Injured groin (December 15, 1995); missed three games. ... Injured wrist (February 18, 1996); missed 17 games. ... Signed as free agent by Edmonton Oilers (October 1, 1997). ... Claimed on waivers by Florida Panthers (November 6, 1997). ... Strained groin (October 22, 1999); missed one game. ... Injured groin (November 10, 2000). ... Strained back (January 17, 2001); missed six games. ... Strained back (February 9, 2001); missed 28 games. ... Traded by Panthers with future considerations to Columbus Blue Jackets for C Kevyn Adams and fourth-round pick (RW Michael Woodford) in 2001 draft (March 13, 2001).
HONORS: Won Four Broncos Memorial Trophy (1990-91). ... Won Bob Clarke Trophy (1990-91). ... Won WHL (West) Player of the Year Award (1990-91). ... Won George Parsons Trophy (1990-91). ... Named to Memorial Cup All-Star team (1990-91). ... Named to WHL (West) All-Star first team (1990-91). ... Played in NHL All-Star Game (2000).
MISCELLANEOUS: Scored on a penalty shot (vs. Guy Hebert, March 21, 1999).

			REGULAR SEASON							PLAYOFFS				
Season Team	League	Gms.	G	A	Pts.	PIM	+/-	PP	SH	Gms.	G	A	Pts.	PIM
88-89—Spokane	WHL	71	17	33	50	16	...	...	...	—	—	—	—	—
89-90—Spokane	WHL	71	57	56	113	50	...	...	...	6	3	4	7	6
90-91—Spokane	WHL	72	67	118	*185	36	...	...	...	15	13	18	*31	12
91-92—San Diego	IHL	63	36	54	90	12	...	...	...	4	0	0	0	0
—San Jose	NHL	2	0	3	3	0	-1	0	0	—	—	—	—	—
—Koln	Germany	10	3	6	9	4	...	...	...	—	—	—	—	—
92-93—Kansas City	IHL	46	20	33	53	14	...	...	...	12	5	7	12	2
—San Jose	NHL	26	4	6	10	4	-14	1	0	—	—	—	—	—
93-94—San Jose	NHL	61	14	26	40	14	2	1	0	14	0	4	4	8
94-95—San Jose	NHL	39	13	12	25	14	-7	4	0	11	4	4	8	2
95-96—San Jose	NHL	60	17	24	41	16	-23	4	2	—	—	—	—	—
96-97—Kentucky	AHL	9	1	7	8	2	...	...	...	—	—	—	—	—
—Utah	IHL	43	13	35	48	34	...	...	...	7	3	1	4	6
—San Jose	NHL	12	0	2	2	4	-6	0	0	—	—	—	—	—
97-98—Edmonton	NHL	9	1	3	4	0	-1	0	0	—	—	—	—	—
—Florida	NHL	68	32	29	61	28	10	12	0	—	—	—	—	—
98-99—Florida	NHL	81	26	38	64	18	-3	7	0	—	—	—	—	—
99-00—Florida	NHL	81	29	42	71	35	16	5	0	4	1	0	1	4
00-01—Florida	NHL	43	10	21	31	28	-16	5	0	—	—	—	—	—
—Columbus	NHL	3	0	3	3	2	-1	0	0	—	—	—	—	—
NHL Totals (10 years)		485	146	209	355	163	-44	39	2	29	5	8	13	14

WIEMER, JASON — C — PANTHERS

PERSONAL: Born April 14, 1976, in Kimberley, B.C. ... 6-1/220. ... Shoots left. ... Name pronounced WEE-muhr.
TRANSACTIONS/CAREER NOTES: Selected by Tampa Bay Lightning in first round (first Lightning pick, eighth overall) of NHL entry draft (June 28, 1994). ... Suffered from the flu (March 2, 1995); missed one game. ... Injured jaw (November 3, 1995); missed one game. ... Injured back

April 12, 1996); missed one game. ... Broke bursa sac in elbow (November 30, 1996); missed 14 games. ... Traded by Lightning to Calgary Flames for RW Sandy McCarthy and third- (LW Brad Richards) and fifth-round (D Curtis Rich) picks in 1998 draft (March 24, 1998). ... Injured hand (March 30, 1999); missed three games. ... Injured knee prior to start of 1999-2000 season; missed first 10 games of season. ... Reinjured knee (October 28, 1999); missed three games. ... Suffered injury (March 31, 2000); missed final five games of season. ... Suffered concussion (December 31, 2000); missed 17 games. ... Traded by Flames with RW Valeri Bure to Florida Panthers for C Rob Niedermayer and second-round pick (G Andrei Medvedev) in 2001 draft (June 23, 2001).

STATISTICAL PLATEAUS: Three-goal games: 1995-96 (1).

		REGULAR SEASON								PLAYOFFS				
Season Team	League	Gms.	G	A	Pts.	PIM	+/-	PP	SH	Gms.	G	A	Pts.	PIM
91-92—Kimberley	RMJHL	45	34	33	67	211	...	...	...	—	—	—	—	—
—Portland.....................	WHL	2	0	1	1	0	...	...	...	—	—	—	—	—
92-93—Portland.................	WHL	68	18	34	52	159	...	...	...	16	7	3	10	27
93-94—Portland.................	WHL	72	45	51	96	236	...	...	...	10	4	4	8	32
94-95—Portland.................	WHL	16	10	14	24	63	...	...	...	—	—	—	—	—
—Tampa Bay	NHL	36	1	4	5	44	-2	0	0	—	—	—	—	—
95-96—Tampa Bay	NHL	66	9	9	18	81	-9	4	0	6	1	0	1	28
96-97—Tampa Bay	NHL	63	9	5	14	134	-13	2	0	—	—	—	—	—
—Adirondack	AHL	4	1	0	1	7	...	...	...	—	—	—	—	—
97-98—Tampa Bay	NHL	67	8	9	17	132	-9	2	0	—	—	—	—	—
—Calgary	NHL	12	4	1	5	28	-1	1	0	—	—	—	—	—
98-99—Calgary	NHL	78	8	13	21	177	-12	1	0	—	—	—	—	—
99-00—Calgary	NHL	64	11	11	22	120	-10	2	0	—	—	—	—	—
00-01—Calgary	NHL	65	10	5	15	177	-15	3	0	—	—	—	—	—
NHL Totals (7 years)............		451	60	57	117	893	-71	15	0	6	1	0	1	28

WILKIE, DAVID   D   RANGERS

PERSONAL: Born May 30, 1974, in Ellensburg, Wash. ... 6-2/210. ... Shoots right.

TRANSACTIONS/CAREER NOTES: Selected by Montreal Canadiens in first round (first Canadiens pick, 20th overall) of NHL entry draft (June 20, 1992). ... Injured right thigh (April 14, 1995); missed remainder of season. ... Injured groin (October 16, 1996); missed one game. ... Suffered concussion (February 1, 1997); missed four games. ... Traded by Canadiens with RW Stephane Richer and C Darcy Tucker to Tampa Bay Lightning for C Patrick Poulin, RW Mick Vukota and D Igor Ulanov (January 15, 1998). ... Suffered from the flu (February 4, 1998); missed one game. ... Suffered charley horse (October 30, 1998); missed one game. ... Injured finger (November 24, 1998); missed nine games. ... Strained groin (December 29, 1998); missed seven games. ... Signed as free agent by New York Rangers (September 29, 1999).

		REGULAR SEASON								PLAYOFFS				
Season Team	League	Gms.	G	A	Pts.	PIM	+/-	PP	SH	Gms.	G	A	Pts.	PIM
89-90—N.W. Americans Jr. B..	WCHL	41	21	27	48	59	...	...	...	—	—	—	—	—
90-91—Seattle.......................	WHL	25	1	1	2	22	...	...	...	—	—	—	—	—
91-92—Kamloops	WHL	71	12	28	40	153	...	...	...	16	6	5	11	19
92-93—Kamloops	WHL	53	11	26	37	109	...	...	...	6	4	2	6	2
93-94—Kamloops	WHL	27	11	18	29	18	...	...	...	—	—	—	—	—
—Regina	WHL	29	27	21	48	16	...	...	...	4	1	4	5	4
94-95—Fredericton	AHL	70	10	43	53	34	...	...	...	1	0	0	0	0
—Montreal	NHL	1	0	0	0	0	0	0	0	—	—	—	—	—
95-96—Fredericton	AHL	23	5	12	17	20	...	...	...	—	—	—	—	—
—Montreal	NHL	24	1	5	6	10	-10	1	0	6	1	2	3	12
96-97—Montreal	NHL	61	6	9	15	63	-9	3	0	2	0	0	0	2
97-98—Montreal	NHL	5	1	0	1	4	-1	0	0	—	—	—	—	—
—Tampa Bay	NHL	29	1	5	6	17	-21	0	0	—	—	—	—	—
98-99—Tampa Bay	NHL	46	1	7	8	69	-19	0	0	—	—	—	—	—
—Cleveland	IHL	2	0	2	2	0	...	...	...	—	—	—	—	—
99-00—Hartford	AHL	1	0	2	2	0	...	...	...	—	—	—	—	—
—Houston	IHL	57	4	24	28	71	...	...	...	11	1	8	9	10
00-01—Houston	IHL	49	8	11	19	29	...	...	...	7	1	1	2	4
—New York Rangers......	NHL	1	0	0	0	2	-2	0	0	—	—	—	—	—
NHL Totals (6 years)............		167	10	26	36	165	-62	4	0	8	1	2	3	14

WILLIAMS, JASON   C   RED WINGS

PERSONAL: Born August 11, 1980, in London, Ont. ... 5-11/185. ... Shoots right.
TRANSACTIONS/CAREER NOTES: Signed as non-drafted free agent by Detroit Red Wings (September 22, 2000).

		REGULAR SEASON								PLAYOFFS				
Season Team	League	Gms.	G	A	Pts.	PIM	+/-	PP	SH	Gms.	G	A	Pts.	PIM
96-97—Peterborough.............	OHL	60	4	8	12	8	...	...	...	10	1	0	1	2
97-98—Peterborough.............	OHL	55	8	27	35	31	...	...	...	4	0	1	1	2
98-99—Peterborough.............	OHL	68	26	48	74	42	...	...	...	5	1	2	3	2
99-00—Peterborough.............	OHL	66	36	37	73	64	...	...	...	5	2	1	3	2
00-01—Cincinnati....................	AHL	76	24	45	69	48	...	...	...	1	0	0	0	2
—Detroit......................	NHL	5	0	3	3	2	1	0	0	2	0	0	0	0
NHL Totals (1 year)............		5	0	3	3	2	1	0	0	2	0	0	0	0

W

WILLIAMS, JUSTIN   RW   FLYERS

PERSONAL: Born October 4, 1981, in Cobourg, Ont. ... 6-1/176. ... Shoots right.
TRANSACTIONS/CAREER NOTES: Selected by Philadelphia Flyers in first round (first Flyers pick, 28th overall) of NHL entry draft (June 24, 2000). ... Fractured hand (February 19, 2001); missed 12 games.

Season Team	League	Gms.	G	A	Pts.	PIM	+/-	PP	SH		Gms.	G	A	Pts.	PIM
97-98—Colborne	Jr. C	36	32	35	67	26	...	...	...		—	—	—	—	—
—Cobourg	Tier II Jr. A	17	0	3	3	5	...	...	...		—	—	—	—	—
98-99—Plymouth	OHL	47	4	8	12	28	...	...	...		7	1	2	3	0
99-00—Plymouth	OHL	68	37	46	83	46	...	...	...		23	*14	16	*30	10
00-01—Philadelphia	NHL	63	12	13	25	22	6	0	0		—	—	—	—	—
NHL Totals (1 year)		63	12	13	25	22	6	0	0						

WILLIS, SHANE   RW   HURRICANES

PERSONAL: Born June 13, 1977, in Edmonton. ... 6-0/176. ... Shoots right.

TRANSACTIONS/CAREER NOTES: Selected by Tampa Bay Lightning in third round (third Lightning pick, 56th overall) of NHL entry draft (July 8, 1995). ... Returned to draft pool by Lightning and selected by Carolina Hurricanes in fourth round (fourth Hurricanes pick, 88th overall) of NHL entry draft (June 21, 1997). ... Suffered back spasms (December 23, 2000); missed five games. ... Sprained ankle (March 1, 2001); missed four games.

HONORS: Named to Can.HL All-Rookie team (1994-95). ... Named to WHL (East) All-Star first team (1996-97 and 1997-98). ... Named to AHL All-Star first team (1998-99). ... Won Dudley (Red) Garrett Memorial Trophy (1998-99). ... Named to NHL All-Rookie team (2000-01).

STATISTICAL PLATEAUS: Three-goal games: 2000-01 (1).

Season Team	League	Gms.	G	A	Pts.	PIM	+/-	PP	SH		Gms.	G	A	Pts.	PIM
94-95—Prince Albert	WHL	65	24	19	43	38	...	...	...		13	3	4	7	6
95-96—Prince Albert	WHL	69	41	40	81	47	...	...	...		18	11	10	21	18
96-97—Prince Albert	WHL	41	34	22	56	63	...	...	...		—	—	—	—	—
—Lethbridge	WHL	26	22	17	39	24	...	...	...		19	13	11	24	20
97-98—New Haven	AHL	1	0	1	1	2	...	...	...		—	—	—	—	—
—Lethbridge	WHL	64	58	54	112	73	...	...	...		4	2	3	5	6
98-99—New Haven	AHL	73	31	50	81	49	...	...	...		—	—	—	—	—
—Carolina	NHL	7	0	0	0	0	-2	0	0		—	—	—	—	—
99-00—Cincinnati	IHL	80	35	25	60	64	...	...	...		11	5	3	8	8
—Carolina	NHL	2	0	0	0	0	-1	0	0		—	—	—	—	—
00-01—Carolina	NHL	73	20	24	44	45	-6	9	0		2	0	0	0	0
NHL Totals (3 years)		82	20	24	44	45	-9	9	0		2	0	0	0	0

WILM, CLARKE   C   FLAMES

PERSONAL: Born October 24, 1976, in Central Butte, Sask. ... 6-0/202. ... Shoots left. ... Name pronounced WIHLM.

TRANSACTIONS/CAREER NOTES: Selected by Calgary Flames in sixth round (fifth Flames pick, 150th overall) of NHL entry draft (July 8, 1995). ... Suffered concussion (November 27, 1998); missed two games.

Season Team	League	Gms.	G	A	Pts.	PIM	+/-	PP	SH		Gms.	G	A	Pts.	PIM
91-92—Saskatoon	WHL	—	—	—	—	—	...	...	...		1	0	0	0	0
92-93—Saskatoon	WHL	69	14	19	33	71	...	...	...		9	4	2	6	13
93-94—Saskatoon	WHL	70	18	32	50	181	...	...	...		16	0	9	9	19
94-95—Saskatoon	WHL	71	20	39	59	179	...	...	...		10	6	1	7	21
95-96—Saskatoon	WHL	72	49	61	110	83	...	...	...		4	1	1	2	4
96-97—Saint John	AHL	62	9	19	28	107	...	...	...		5	2	0	2	15
97-98—Saint John	AHL	68	13	26	39	112	...	...	...		21	5	9	14	8
98-99—Calgary	NHL	78	10	8	18	53	11	2	2		—	—	—	—	—
99-00—Calgary	NHL	78	10	12	22	67	-6	1	3		—	—	—	—	—
00-01—Calgary	NHL	81	7	8	15	69	-11	2	0		—	—	—	—	—
NHL Totals (3 years)		237	27	28	55	189	-6	5	5						

WILSON, LANDON   RW   COYOTES

PERSONAL: Born March 15, 1975, in St. Louis. ... 6-2/216. ... Shoots right. ... Son of Rick Wilson, defenseman with three NHL teams (1973-74 through 1976-77).

TRANSACTIONS/CAREER NOTES: Selected by Toronto Maple Leafs in first round (second Maple Leafs pick, 19th overall) of NHL entry draft (June 26, 1993). ... Traded by Maple Leafs with LW Wendel Clark, D Sylvain Lefebvre and first-round pick (D Jeffrey Kealty) in 1994 draft to Quebec Nordiques for C Mats Sundin, D Garth Butcher, LW Todd Warriner and first-round pick (traded to Washington Capitals) in 1994 draft (June 28, 1994). ... Nordiques franchise moved to Colorado and renamed Avalanche for 1995-96 season (June 21, 1995). ... Traded by Avalanche with D Anders Myrvold to Boston Bruins for first-round pick (D Robyn Regehr) in 1998 draft (November 22, 1996). ... Sprained shoulder (December 12, 1996); missed 10 games. ... Suffered charley horse (January 7, 1997); missed 12 games. ... Suffered concussion (March 9, 1999); missed two games. ... Strained abdominal muscle (April 15, 1999); missed one game. ... Strained shoulder (April 28, 1999); missed remainder of playoffs. ... Injured shoulder (November 4, 1999); missed seven games. ... Signed as free agent by Phoenix Coyotes (July 7, 2000). ... Suffered back spasms (November 19, 2000); missed one game. ... Strained knee (January 1, 2001); missed six games. ... Strained calf (March 13, 2001); missed five games.

HONORS: Named WCHA Rookie of the Year (1993-94). ... Named to WCHA All-Rookie team (1993-94). ... Named to AHL All-Star first team (1998-99).

MISCELLANEOUS: Failed to score on a penalty shot (vs. Curtis Joseph, March 17, 1999).

Season Team	League	Gms.	G	A	Pts.	PIM	+/-	PP	SH		Gms.	G	A	Pts.	PIM
92-93—Dubuque	USHL	43	29	36	65	284	...	...	...		—	—	—	—	—
93-94—Univ. of North Dakota	WCHA	35	18	15	33	147	...	...	...		—	—	—	—	—
94-95—Univ. of North Dakota	WCHA	31	7	16	23	141	...	...	...		—	—	—	—	—
—Cornwall	AHL	8	4	4	8	25	...	...	...		13	3	4	7	68

W

Season Team	League	REGULAR SEASON								PLAYOFFS				
		Gms.	G	A	Pts.	PIM	+/-	PP	SH	Gms.	G	A	Pts.	PIM
95-96—Cornwall	AHL	53	21	13	34	154	...	...	...	8	1	3	4	22
—Colorado	NHL	7	1	0	1	6	3	0	0	—	—	—	—	—
96-97—Colorado	NHL	9	1	2	3	23	1	0	0	—	—	—	—	—
—Boston	NHL	40	7	10	17	49	-6	0	0	—	—	—	—	—
—Providence	AHL	2	2	1	3	2	...	...	...	10	3	4	7	16
97-98—Boston	NHL	28	1	5	6	7	3	0	0	1	0	0	0	0
—Providence	AHL	42	18	10	28	146	...	...	...	—	—	—	—	—
98-99—Providence	AHL	48	31	22	53	89	...	...	...	11	7	1	8	19
—Boston	NHL	22	3	3	6	17	0	0	0	8	1	1	2	8
99-00—Boston	NHL	40	1	3	4	18	-6	0	0	—	—	—	—	—
—Providence	AHL	17	5	5	10	45	...	...	...	9	2	3	5	38
00-01—Phoenix	NHL	70	18	13	31	92	3	2	0	—	—	—	—	—
NHL Totals (6 years)		216	32	36	68	212	-2	2	0	9	1	1	2	8

WILSON, MIKE — D — PENGUINS

PERSONAL: Born February 26, 1975, in Brampton, Ont. ... 6-6/212. ... Shoots left.
TRANSACTIONS/CAREER NOTES: Selected by Vancouver Canucks in first round (first Canucks pick, 20th overall) of NHL entry draft (June 26, 1993). ... Traded by Canucks with RW Michael Peca and first-round pick (D Jay McKee) in 1995 draft to Buffalo Sabres for RW Alexander Mogilny and fifth-round pick (LW Todd Norman) in 1995 draft (July 8, 1995). ... Suffered concussion (January 26, 1996); missed two games. ... Bruised chest (November 13, 1997); missed one game. ... Suffered mild concussion (January 8, 1998); missed two games. ... Missed first 19 games of 1998-99 season due to contract dispute; played with Las Vegas of IHL. ... Traded by Sabres to Florida Panthers for D Rhett Warrener and fifth-round pick (G Ryan Miller) in 1999 draft (March 23, 1999). ... Suffered concussion (March 31, 1999); missed final nine games of season. ... Injured shoulder (October 22, 2000); missed 61 games. ... Signed as free agent by Pittsburgh Penguins (July 5, 2001).
HONORS: Named to Can.HL All-Rookie team (1992-93). ... Named to OHL All-Rookie team (1992-93).

Season Team	League	REGULAR SEASON								PLAYOFFS				
		Gms.	G	A	Pts.	PIM	+/-	PP	SH	Gms.	G	A	Pts.	PIM
91-92—Georgetown Jr. B	OHA	41	9	13	22	65	...	...	...	—	—	—	—	—
92-93—Sudbury	OHL	53	6	7	13	58	...	...	...	14	1	1	2	21
93-94—Sudbury	OHL	60	4	22	26	62	...	...	...	9	1	3	4	8
94-95—Sudbury	OHL	64	13	34	47	46	...	...	...	18	1	8	9	10
95-96—Rochester	AHL	15	0	5	5	38	...	...	...	—	—	—	—	—
—Buffalo	NHL	58	4	8	12	41	13	1	0	—	—	—	—	—
96-97—Buffalo	NHL	77	2	9	11	51	13	0	0	10	0	1	1	2
97-98—Buffalo	NHL	66	4	4	8	48	13	0	0	15	0	1	1	13
98-99—Las Vegas	IHL	6	3	1	4	6	...	...	...	—	—	—	—	—
—Buffalo	NHL	30	1	2	3	47	10	0	0	—	—	—	—	—
—Florida	NHL	4	0	0	0	0	2	0	0	—	—	—	—	—
99-00—Florida	NHL	60	4	16	20	35	10	0	0	4	0	0	0	0
00-01—Florida	NHL	19	0	1	1	25	-7	0	0	—	—	—	—	—
—Louisville	AHL	4	0	2	2	5	...	...	...	—	—	—	—	—
NHL Totals (6 years)		314	15	40	55	247	54	1	0	29	0	2	2	15

WITEHALL, JOHAN — RW

PERSONAL: Born January 7, 1972, in Goteborg, Sweden. ... 6-1/198. ... Shoots left.
TRANSACTIONS/CAREER NOTES: Selected by New York Rangers in eighth round (eighth Rangers pick, 207th overall) of NHL entry draft (June 27, 1998). ... Claimed on waivers by Montreal Canadiens (January 12, 2001).

Season Team	League	REGULAR SEASON								PLAYOFFS				
		Gms.	G	A	Pts.	PIM	+/-	PP	SH	Gms.	G	A	Pts.	PIM
97-98—Leksand	Sweden	42	12	4	16	34	...	...	...	2	0	0	0	2
98-99—Hartford	AHL	62	14	15	29	56	...	...	...	7	1	2	3	6
—New York Rangers	NHL	4	0	0	0	0	0	0	0	—	—	—	—	—
99-00—Hartford	AHL	73	17	24	41	65	...	...	...	17	6	7	13	10
—New York Rangers	NHL	9	1	1	2	2	0	0	0	—	—	—	—	—
00-01—Hartford	AHL	19	10	8	18	19	...	...	...	—	—	—	—	—
—New York Rangers	NHL	15	0	3	3	8	-5	0	0	—	—	—	—	—
—Montreal	NHL	26	1	1	2	6	0	0	0	—	—	—	—	—
—Quebec	AHL	1	0	0	0	0	...	...	...	9	3	5	8	6
NHL Totals (3 years)		54	2	5	7	16	-5	0	0					

WITT, BRENDAN — D — CAPITALS

PERSONAL: Born February 20, 1975, in Humboldt, Sask. ... 6-2/224. ... Shoots left.
TRANSACTIONS/CAREER NOTES: Selected by Washington Capitals in first round (first Capitals pick, 11th overall) of NHL entry draft (June 26, 1993). ... Missed entire 1994-95 season due to contract dispute. ... Fractured wrist (January 28, 1996); missed 34 games. ... Suffered from the flu (November 15, 1996); missed five games. ... Bruised shoulder (November 27, 1997); missed seven games. ... Suffered illness (January 6, 1998); missed three games. ... Injured wrist (April 6, 1998); missed final six games of regular season and five playoff games. ... Sprained knee (October 18, 1998); missed one game. ... Strained hip flexor (October 28, 1998); missed five games. ... Missed game for personal reasons (January 26, 1999). ... Sprained wrist (February 3, 1999); missed 15 games. ... Sprained knee (October 16, 1999); missed two games. ... Strained back (November 26, 1999); missed one game. ... Strained groin (March 11, 2000); missed one game. ... Injured thigh (March 25, 2000); missed one game. ... Injured left arm (October 17, 2000); missed one game. ... Suffered from the flu (December 16, 2000); missed three games. ... Separated shoulder (December 29, 2000); missed five games.
HONORS: Named to WHL (West) All-Star first team (1992-93 and 1993-94). ... Won Bill Hunter Trophy (1993-94). ... Named to Can.HL All-Star first team (1993-94).

W

Season Team	League	REGULAR SEASON								PLAYOFFS				
		Gms.	G	A	Pts.	PIM	+/-	PP	SH	Gms.	G	A	Pts.	PIM
90-91—Seattle	WHL	—	—	—	—	—	...	...	...	1	0	0	0	0
91-92—Seattle	WHL	67	3	9	12	212	...	...	...	15	1	1	2	84
92-93—Seattle	WHL	70	2	26	28	239	...	...	...	5	1	2	3	30
93-94—Seattle	WHL	56	8	31	39	235	...	...	...	9	3	8	11	23
94-95—					Did not play.									
95-96—Washington	NHL	48	2	3	5	85	-4	0	0	—	—	—	—	—
96-97—Washington	NHL	44	3	2	5	88	-20	0	0	—	—	—	—	—
—Portland	AHL	30	2	4	6	56	...	...	...	5	1	0	1	30
97-98—Washington	NHL	64	1	7	8	112	-11	0	0	16	1	0	1	14
98-99—Washington	NHL	54	2	5	7	87	-6	0	0	—	—	—	—	—
99-00—Washington	NHL	77	1	7	8	114	5	0	0	3	0	0	0	0
00-01—Washington	NHL	72	3	3	6	101	2	0	0	6	2	0	2	12
NHL Totals (7 years)		359	12	27	39	587	-34	0	0	25	3	0	3	26

WOOLLEY, JASON   D   SABRES

PERSONAL: Born July 27, 1969, in Toronto. ... 6-1/207. ... Shoots left. ... Full Name: Jason Douglas Woolley.

TRANSACTIONS/CAREER NOTES: Selected by Washington Capitals in third round (fourth Capitals pick, 61st overall) of NHL entry draft (June 17, 1989). ... Fractured wrist (October 12, 1992); missed 24 games. ... Tore abdominal muscle (January 2, 1994). ... Signed as free agent by Detroit Vipers (October 7, 1994). ... Contract sold by Vipers to Florida Panthers (February 14, 1995). ... Separated left shoulder (October 15, 1995); missed two games. ... Fractured left thumb (November 18, 1995); missed 13 games. ... Traded by Panthers with C Stu Barnes to Pittsburgh Penguins for C Chris Wells (November 19, 1996). ... Injured groin (November 22, 1996); missed one game. ... Strained groin (February 27, 1997); missed one game. ... Strained groin (March 4, 1997); missed two games. ... Bruised wrist (March 18, 1997); missed two games. ... Traded by Penguins to Buffalo Sabres for fifth-round pick (D Robert Scuderi) in 1998 draft (September 24, 1997). ... Fractured thumb (October 1, 1997); missed nine games. ... Suffered from the flu (February 15, 1999); missed one game. ... Strained groin (April 14, 1999); missed one game. ... Injured rib (November 12, 1999); missed four games. ... Suffered from the flu (March 4, 2000); missed two games. ... Injured groin (December 12, 2000); missed four games. ... Injured knee (February 25, 2001); missed two games.

HONORS: Named to CCHA All-Rookie team (1988-89). ... Named to NCAA All-America (West) first team (1990-91). ... Named to CCHA All-Star first team (1990-91).

MISCELLANEOUS: Member of silver-medal-winning Canadian Olympic team (1992).

Season Team	League	REGULAR SEASON								PLAYOFFS				
		Gms.	G	A	Pts.	PIM	+/-	PP	SH	Gms.	G	A	Pts.	PIM
87-88—St. Michael's Jr. B	ODHA	31	19	37	56	22	...	...	...	—	—	—	—	—
88-89—Michigan State	CCHA	47	12	25	37	26	...	...	...	—	—	—	—	—
89-90—Michigan State	CCHA	45	10	38	48	26	...	...	...	—	—	—	—	—
90-91—Michigan State	CCHA	40	15	44	59	24	...	...	...	—	—	—	—	—
91-92—Canadian nat'l team	Int'l	60	14	30	44	36	...	...	...	—	—	—	—	—
—Can. Olympic team	Int'l	8	0	5	5	4	...	...	...	—	—	—	—	—
—Baltimore	AHL	15	1	10	11	6	...	...	...	—	—	—	—	—
—Washington	NHL	1	0	0	0	0	1	0	0	—	—	—	—	—
92-93—Baltimore	AHL	29	14	27	41	22	...	...	...	1	0	2	2	0
—Washington	NHL	26	0	2	2	10	3	0	0	—	—	—	—	—
93-94—Portland	AHL	41	12	29	41	14	...	...	...	9	2	2	4	4
—Washington	NHL	10	1	2	3	4	2	0	0	4	1	0	1	4
94-95—Detroit	IHL	48	8	28	36	38	...	...	...	—	—	—	—	—
—Florida	NHL	34	4	9	13	18	-1	1	0	—	—	—	—	—
95-96—Florida	NHL	52	6	28	34	32	-9	3	0	13	2	6	8	14
96-97—Florida	NHL	3	0	0	0	2	1	0	0	—	—	—	—	—
—Pittsburgh	NHL	57	6	30	36	28	3	2	0	5	0	3	3	0
97-98—Buffalo	NHL	71	9	26	35	35	8	3	0	15	2	9	11	12
98-99—Buffalo	NHL	80	10	33	43	62	16	4	0	21	4	11	15	10
99-00—Buffalo	NHL	74	8	25	33	52	14	2	0	5	0	2	2	2
00-01—Buffalo	NHL	67	5	18	23	46	0	4	0	8	1	5	6	2
NHL Totals (10 years)		475	49	173	222	289	38	19	0	71	10	36	46	44

WORRELL, PETER   LW   PANTHERS

PERSONAL: Born August 18, 1977, in Pierrefonds, Que. ... 6-6/235. ... Shoots left. ... Name pronounced wuh-REHL.

TRANSACTIONS/CAREER NOTES: Selected by Florida Panthers in seventh round (seventh Panthers pick, 166th overall) of NHL entry draft (July 8, 1995). ... Suspended three games and fined $1,000 by NHL for elbowing incident (November 18, 1998). ... Sprained knee (September 21, 1999); missed nine games. ... Partially tore anterior collateral ligament in right knee (October 29, 1999); missed 12 games. ... Sprained knee (January 14, 2000); missed six games. ... Suffered head injury (March 19, 2000); missed six games. ... Strained back (March 2, 2001); missed one game. ... Injured shoulder (March 16, 2001); missed final 10 games of the season.

Season Team	League	REGULAR SEASON								PLAYOFFS				
		Gms.	G	A	Pts.	PIM	+/-	PP	SH	Gms.	G	A	Pts.	PIM
94-95—Hull	QMJHL	56	1	8	9	243	...	...	...	21	0	1	1	91
95-96—Hull	QMJHL	63	23	36	59	464	...	...	...	18	11	8	19	81
96-97—Hull	QMJHL	62	18	45	63	*495	...	...	...	14	3	13	16	83
97-98—New Haven	AHL	50	15	12	27	309	...	...	...	1	0	1	1	6
—Florida	NHL	19	0	0	0	153	-4	0	0	—	—	—	—	—
98-99—Florida	NHL	62	4	5	9	258	0	0	0	—	—	—	—	—
—New Haven	AHL	10	3	1	4	65	...	...	...	—	—	—	—	—
99-00—Florida	NHL	48	3	6	9	169	-7	2	0	4	1	0	1	8
00-01—Florida	NHL	71	3	7	10	248	-10	0	0	—	—	—	—	—
NHL Totals (4 years)		200	10	18	28	828	-21	2	0	4	1	0	1	8

W

PERSONAL: Born November 16, 1973, in Foxwarren, Man. ... 6-1/195. ... Shoots left. ... Name pronounced WAH-tehn.
TRANSACTIONS/CAREER NOTES: Selected by Vancouver Canucks in 10th round (11th Canucks pick, 237th overall) of NHL entry draft (June 20, 1992). ... Suffered blood clot in eye (May 17, 1995); missed six playoff games. ... Signed as free agent by Dallas Stars (July 7, 1999).
HONORS: Named to WHL (East) All-Star second team (1993-94).

Season Team	League	REGULAR SEASON								PLAYOFFS				
		Gms.	G	A	Pts.	PIM	+/-	PP	SH	Gms.	G	A	Pts.	PIM
89-90—Saskatoon	WHL	51	2	3	5	31	...	...	...	7	1	1	2	15
90-91—Saskatoon	WHL	45	4	11	15	37	...	...	...	—	—	—	—	—
91-92—Saskatoon	WHL	64	11	25	36	92	...	...	...	—	—	—	—	—
92-93—Saskatoon	WHL	71	15	51	66	90	...	...	...	9	6	5	11	18
93-94—Saskatoon	WHL	65	12	34	46	108	...	...	...	16	3	12	15	32
94-95—Syracuse	AHL	75	12	29	41	50	...	...	...	—	—	—	—	—
—Vancouver	NHL	1	0	0	0	0	1	0	0	5	0	0	0	4
95-96—Syracuse	AHL	80	10	35	45	96	...	...	...	15	1	12	13	20
96-97—Syracuse	AHL	27	2	8	10	25	...	...	...	2	0	0	0	4
—Vancouver	NHL	36	3	6	9	19	8	0	1	—	—	—	—	—
97-98—Vancouver	NHL	5	0	0	0	6	-2	0	0	—	—	—	—	—
—Syracuse	AHL	56	12	21	33	80	...	...	...	5	0	0	0	12
98-99—Syracuse	AHL	72	4	31	35	74	...	...	...	—	—	—	—	—
99-00—Michigan	IHL	70	3	7	10	72	...	...	...	—	—	—	—	—
00-01—Utah	IHL	63	2	2	4	64	...	...	...	—	—	—	—	—
—Dallas	NHL	1	0	0	0	0	0	0	0	—	—	—	—	—
NHL Totals (4 years)		43	3	6	9	25	7	0	1	5	0	0	0	4

PERSONAL: Born September 16, 1974, in Preston, Ont. ... 5-10/182. ... Shoots left.
TRANSACTIONS/CAREER NOTES: Selected by Los Angeles Kings in fourth round (third Kings pick, 94th overall) of NHL entry draft (June 26, 1993). ... Signed as free agent by Hartford Whalers (September 6, 1994). ... Signed as free agent by Mighty Ducks of Anaheim (October 17, 1996).
HONORS: Named to OHL All-Star second team (1992-93 and 1993-94).

Season Team	League	REGULAR SEASON								PLAYOFFS				
		Gms.	G	A	Pts.	PIM	+/-	PP	SH	Gms.	G	A	Pts.	PIM
89-90—Guelph	Jr. B	48	24	36	60	12	...	...	...	—	—	—	—	—
90-91—Kingston	Jr. B	32	27	28	55	85	...	...	...	—	—	—	—	—
91-92—Det. Jr. Red Wings	OHL	62	13	36	49	58	...	...	...	7	3	4	7	19
92-93—Det. Jr. Red Wings	OHL	63	57	88	145	91	...	...	...	15	4	11	15	20
93-94—Det. Jr. Red Wings	OHL	57	45	64	109	81	...	...	...	17	12	18	30	20
94-95—Springfield	AHL	61	16	15	31	118	...	...	...	—	—	—	—	—
—Richmond	ECHL	2	0	1	1	0	...	...	...	—	—	—	—	—
95-96—Detroit	IHL	1	0	0	0	0	...	...	...	—	—	—	—	—
—Knoxville	ECHL	50	21	35	56	257	...	...	...	8	4	11	15	32
96-97—Baltimore	AHL	72	23	36	59	97	...	...	...	3	1	1	2	0
97-98—Cincinnati	AHL	77	†42	58	100	151	...	...	...	—	—	—	—	—
—Anaheim	NHL	3	0	0	0	0	0	0	0	—	—	—	—	—
98-99—Cincinnati	AHL	73	27	43	70	102	...	...	...	3	1	2	3	8
99-00—Cincinnati	AHL	57	24	38	62	61	...	...	...	—	—	—	—	—
00-01—Cincinnati	AHL	70	20	47	67	103	...	...	...	4	4	2	6	2
—Anaheim	NHL	1	0	0	0	0	-1	0	0	—	—	—	—	—
NHL Totals (2 years)		4	0	0	0	0	-1	0	0					

PERSONAL: Born May 13, 1976, in Kitchener, Ont. ... 6-0/195. ... Shoots right.
TRANSACTIONS/CAREER NOTES: Selected by Dallas Stars in fourth round (third Stars pick, 98th overall) of NHL entry draft (June 29, 1994).
HONORS: Won Bobby Smith Trophy (1994-95).

Season Team	League	REGULAR SEASON								PLAYOFFS				
		Gms.	G	A	Pts.	PIM	+/-	PP	SH	Gms.	G	A	Pts.	PIM
91-92—Elmira Jr. B	OHA	44	17	11	28	46	...	...	...	—	—	—	—	—
92-93—Elmira Jr. B	OHA	47	22	32	54	52	...	...	...	—	—	—	—	—
93-94—Guelph	OHL	65	17	15	32	34	...	...	...	8	2	1	3	10
94-95—Guelph	OHL	65	43	39	82	36	...	...	...	14	6	8	14	6
95-96—Guelph	OHL	55	30	36	66	45	...	...	...	16	10	12	22	35
96-97—Michigan	IHL	60	6	8	14	34	...	...	...	1	0	0	0	0
97-98—Michigan	IHL	53	15	11	26	31	...	...	...	—	—	—	—	—
—Dallas	NHL	21	4	2	6	2	8	0	0	5	0	0	0	0
98-99—Dallas	NHL	11	0	0	0	0	-3	0	0	—	—	—	—	—
—Michigan	IHL	64	16	15	31	92	...	...	...	2	0	0	0	2
99-00—Michigan	IHL	49	12	4	16	64	...	...	...	—	—	—	—	—
—Dallas	NHL	23	1	4	5	16	4	0	0	—	—	—	—	—
00-01—Utah	IHL	74	25	27	52	126	...	...	...	—	—	—	—	—
—Dallas	NHL	2	1	0	1	0	-3	0	0	—	—	—	—	—
NHL Totals (4 years)		57	6	6	12	18	6	0	0	5	0	0	0	0

W

WRIGHT, TYLER   C   BLUE JACKETS

PERSONAL: Born April 6, 1973, in Canora, Sask. ... 5-11/187. ... Shoots right.
TRANSACTIONS/CAREER NOTES: Selected by Edmonton Oilers in first round (first Oilers pick, 12th overall) of NHL entry draft (June 22, 1991). ... Traded by Oilers to Pittsburgh Penguins for seventh-round pick (RW Brandon LaFrance) in 1996 draft (June 22, 1996). ... Bruised ribs (December 13, 1996); missed one game. ... Suffered back spasms (January 18, 2000); missed two games. ... Strained knee (April 3, 2000); missed two games. ... Selected by Columbus Blue Jackets in NHL expansion draft (June 23, 2000). ... Bruised ribs (December 23, 2000); missed five games. ... Suffered from the flu (February 21, 2001); missed one game.
STATISTICAL PLATEAUS: Three-goal games: 2000-01 (1).

		REGULAR SEASON								PLAYOFFS				
Season Team	League	Gms.	G	A	Pts.	PIM	+/-	PP	SH	Gms.	G	A	Pts.	PIM
89-90—Swift Current	WHL	67	14	18	32	119	...	...	...	4	0	0	0	12
90-91—Swift Current	WHL	66	41	51	92	157	...	...	...	3	0	0	0	6
91-92—Swift Current	WHL	63	36	46	82	295	...	...	...	8	2	5	7	16
92-93—Swift Current	WHL	37	24	41	65	76	...	...	...	17	9	17	26	49
—Edmonton	NHL	7	1	1	2	19	-4	0	0	—	—	—	—	—
93-94—Cape Breton	AHL	65	14	27	41	160	...	...	...	5	2	0	2	11
—Edmonton	NHL	5	0	0	0	4	-3	0	0	—	—	—	—	—
94-95—Cape Breton	AHL	70	16	15	31	184	...	...	...	—	—	—	—	—
—Edmonton	NHL	6	1	0	1	14	1	0	0	—	—	—	—	—
95-96—Edmonton	NHL	23	1	0	1	33	-7	0	0	—	—	—	—	—
—Cape Breton	AHL	31	6	12	18	158	...	...	...	—	—	—	—	—
96-97—Pittsburgh	NHL	45	2	2	4	70	-7	0	0	—	—	—	—	—
—Cleveland	IHL	10	4	3	7	34	...	...	...	14	4	2	6	44
97-98—Pittsburgh	NHL	82	3	4	7	112	-3	1	0	6	0	1	1	4
98-99—Pittsburgh	NHL	61	0	0	0	90	-2	0	0	13	0	0	0	19
99-00—Wilkes-Barre/Scranton	AHL	25	5	15	20	86	...	...	...	—	—	—	—	—
—Pittsburgh	NHL	50	12	10	22	45	4	0	0	11	3	1	4	17
00-01—Columbus	NHL	76	16	16	32	140	-9	4	1	—	—	—	—	—
NHL Totals (9 years)............		355	36	33	69	527	-30	5	1	30	3	2	5	40

YACHMENEV, VITALI   RW   PREDATORS

PERSONAL: Born January 8, 1975, in Chelyabinsk, U.S.S.R. ... 5-9/190. ... Shoots left. ... Name pronounced vee-TAL-ee YAHCH-mih-nehf.
TRANSACTIONS/CAREER NOTES: Selected by Los Angeles Kings in third round (third Kings pick, 59th overall) of NHL entry draft (June 29, 1994). ... Sprained left shoulder (October 4, 1996); missed eight games. ... Sprained ankle (December 27, 1996); missed seven games. ... Suffered from the flu (February 11, 1997); missed one game. ... Traded by Kings to Nashville Predators for future considerations (July 7, 1998). ... Partially dislocated shoulder (February 4, 1999); missed 10 games. ... Sprained wrist (November 3, 1999); missed three games. ... Reinjured wrist (November 13, 1999); missed seven games. ... Suffered concussion (March 12, 2000); missed four games. ... Strained back joint (December 17, 2000); missed four games.
HONORS: Named Can.HL Rookie of the Year (1993-94). ... Won Emms Family Award (1993-94). ... Named to Can.HL All-Rookie team (1993-94). ... Named to OHL All-Rookie team (1993-94). ... Won William Hanley Trophy (1994-95).
STATISTICAL PLATEAUS: Three-goal games: 1995-96 (1).

		REGULAR SEASON								PLAYOFFS				
Season Team	League	Gms.	G	A	Pts.	PIM	+/-	PP	SH	Gms.	G	A	Pts.	PIM
90-91—Traktor Chelyabinsk	USSR	80	88	60	148	72	...	...	...	—	—	—	—	—
91-92—Traktor Chelyabinsk	CIS	80	82	70	152	20	...	...	...	—	—	—	—	—
92-93—Mechel Chelyabinsk....	CIS Div. II	51	23	20	43	12	...	...	...	—	—	—	—	—
93-94—North Bay	OHL	66	*61	52	113	18	...	...	...	18	13	19	32	12
94-95—North Bay	OHL	59	53	52	105	8	...	...	...	6	1	8	9	2
—Phoenix..................	IHL	—	—	—	—	—	...	...	...	4	1	0	1	0
95-96—Los Angeles	NHL	80	19	34	53	16	-3	6	1	—	—	—	—	—
96-97—Los Angeles	NHL	65	10	22	32	10	-9	2	0	—	—	—	—	—
97-98—Los Angeles	NHL	4	0	1	1	4	1	0	0	—	—	—	—	—
—Long Beach..................	IHL	59	23	28	51	14	...	...	...	17	8	9	17	4
98-99—Milwaukee	IHL	16	7	6	13	0	...	...	...	—	—	—	—	—
—Nashville	NHL	55	7	10	17	10	-10	0	1	—	—	—	—	—
99-00—Nashville	NHL	68	16	16	32	12	5	1	1	—	—	—	—	—
00-01—Nashville	NHL	78	15	19	34	10	-5	4	1	—	—	—	—	—
NHL Totals (6 years)............		350	67	102	169	62	-21	13	4	—	—	—	—	—

YAKE, TERRY   C

PERSONAL: Born October 22, 1968, in New Westminster, B.C. ... 5-11/190. ... Shoots right.
TRANSACTIONS/CAREER NOTES: Selected by Hartford Whalers in fourth round (third Whalers pick, 81st overall) of NHL entry draft (June 13, 1987). ... Selected by Mighty Ducks of Anaheim in NHL expansion draft (June 24, 1993). ... Traded by Mighty Ducks to Toronto Maple Leafs for RW David Sacco (September 28, 1994). ... Signed as free agent by Buffalo Sabres (August 5, 1996). ... Signed as free agent by St. Louis Blues (August 12, 1997). ... Selected by Atlanta Thrashers in NHL expansion draft (June 25, 1999). ... Claimed by Blues from Thrashers in NHL waiver draft (September 27, 1999). ... Strained groin (November 17, 1999); missed nine games. ... Claimed on waivers by Washington Capitals (January 18, 2000).
MISCELLANEOUS: Failed to score on a penalty shot (vs. Steve Shields, January 26, 1999; vs. Sean Burke, November 18, 1999).
STATISTICAL PLATEAUS: Three-goal games: 1993-94 (1).

Season Team	League	REGULAR SEASON								PLAYOFFS				
		Gms.	G	A	Pts.	PIM	+/-	PP	SH	Gms.	G	A	Pts.	PIM
84-85—Brandon	WHL	11	1	1	2	0	...	...	...	—	—	—	—	—
85-86—Brandon	WHL	72	26	26	52	49	...	...	...	—	—	—	—	—
86-87—Brandon	WHL	71	44	58	102	64	...	...	...	—	—	—	—	—
87-88—Brandon	WHL	72	55	85	140	59	...	...	...	3	4	2	6	7
88-89—Hartford	NHL	2	0	0	0	0	1	0	0	—	—	—	—	—
—Binghamton	AHL	75	39	56	95	57	...	...	...	—	—	—	—	—
89-90—Hartford	NHL	2	0	1	1	0	-1	0	0	—	—	—	—	—
—Binghamton	AHL	77	13	42	55	37	...	...	...	—	—	—	—	—
90-91—Hartford	NHL	19	1	4	5	10	-3	0	0	6	1	1	2	16
—Springfield	AHL	60	35	42	77	56	...	...	...	15	9	9	18	10
91-92—Hartford	NHL	15	1	1	2	4	-2	0	0	—	—	—	—	—
—Springfield	AHL	53	21	34	55	63	...	...	...	8	3	4	7	2
92-93—Springfield	AHL	16	8	14	22	27	...	...	...	—	—	—	—	—
—Hartford	NHL	66	22	31	53	46	3	4	1	—	—	—	—	—
93-94—Anaheim	NHL	82	21	31	52	44	2	5	0	—	—	—	—	—
94-95—Toronto	NHL	19	3	2	5	2	1	1	0	—	—	—	—	—
—Denver	IHL	2	0	3	3	2	...	...	...	17	4	11	15	16
95-96—Milwaukee	IHL	70	32	56	88	70	...	...	...	5	3	6	9	4
96-97—Rochester	AHL	78	34	*67	101	77	...	...	...	10	8	8	16	2
97-98—St. Louis	NHL	65	10	15	25	38	1	3	1	10	2	1	3	6
98-99—Worcester	AHL	24	8	11	19	26	...	...	...	—	—	—	—	—
—St. Louis	NHL	60	9	18	27	34	-9	3	0	13	1	2	3	14
99-00—St. Louis	NHL	26	4	9	13	22	2	2	0	—	—	—	—	—
—Washington	NHL	35	6	5	11	12	2	1	0	3	0	0	0	0
00-01—Portland	AHL	55	11	38	49	47	...	...	...	3	0	1	1	12
—Washington	NHL	12	0	3	3	8	0	0	0	—	—	—	—	—
NHL Totals (11 years)		403	77	120	197	220	-3	19	2	32	4	4	8	36

YAKUBOV, MIKHAIL   C   BLACKHAWKS

PERSONAL: Born February 16, 1982, in Barnaul, U.S.S.R. ... 6-3/185. ... Shoots left.
TRANSACTIONS/CAREER NOTES: Selected by Chicago Blackhawks in first round (first Blackhawks pick, 10th overall) of NHL entry draft (June 24, 2000).

Season Team	League	REGULAR SEASON								PLAYOFFS				
		Gms.	G	A	Pts.	PIM	+/-	PP	SH	Gms.	G	A	Pts.	PIM
99-00—Lada Togliatti	Rus. Div. II	26	12	19	31	14	...	...	...	—	—	—	—	—
00-01—Lada Togliatti	Russian	25	0	0	0	4	...	...	...	4	0	0	0	0

YAKUSHIN, DMITRI   D   MAPLE LEAFS

PERSONAL: Born January 21, 1978, in Kharkov, Ukraine. ... 6-0/200. ... Shoots left.
TRANSACTIONS/CAREER NOTES: Selected by Toronto Maple Leafs in sixth round (ninth Maple Leafs pick, 140th overall) of NHL entry draft (June 22, 1996).

Season Team	League	REGULAR SEASON								PLAYOFFS				
		Gms.	G	A	Pts.	PIM	+/-	PP	SH	Gms.	G	A	Pts.	PIM
95-96—Pembroke	CJHL	31	8	5	13	62	...	...	...	—	—	—	—	—
96-97—Edmonton	WHL	63	3	14	17	103	...	...	...	—	—	—	—	—
97-98—Edmonton	WHL	29	1	10	11	41	...	...	...	—	—	—	—	—
—Regina	WHL	42	1	24	25	57	...	...	...	9	2	8	10	12
98-99—St. John's	AHL	71	2	6	8	65	...	...	...	4	0	0	0	0
99-00—St. John's	AHL	64	1	13	14	106	...	...	...	—	—	—	—	—
—Toronto	NHL	2	0	0	0	2	0	0	0	—	—	—	—	—
00-01—St. John's	AHL	45	2	0	2	61	...	...	...	1	0	0	0	0
NHL Totals (1 year)		2	0	0	0	2	0	0	0					

YASHIN, ALEXEI   C   ISLANDERS

PERSONAL: Born November 5, 1973, in Sverdlovsk, U.S.S.R. ... 6-3/225. ... Shoots right. ... Name pronounced uh-LEK-see YA-shihn.
TRANSACTIONS/CAREER NOTES: Selected by Ottawa Senators in first round (first Senators pick, second overall) of NHL entry draft (June 20, 1992). ... Suffered strep throat (December 4, 1993); missed one game. ... Missed entire 1999-2000 season due to contract dispute. ... Traded by Senators to New York Islanders for RW Bill Muckalt, D Zdeno Chara and first-round pick (C Jason Spezza) in 2001 draft (June 23, 2001).
HONORS: Named to CIS All-Star team (1992-93). ... Played in NHL All-Star Game (1994 and 1999). ... Named to THE SPORTING NEWS All-Star team (1998-99). ... Named to NHL All-Star second team (1998-99).
MISCELLANEOUS: Member of silver-medal-winning Russian Olympic team (1998). ... Captain of Ottawa Senators (1998-99). ... Holds Ottawa Senators all-time records for most games played (504), most goals (218), most assists (273) and most points (491).
STATISTICAL PLATEAUS: Three-goal games: 1993-94 (1), 1994-95 (1), 1995-96 (1), 1997-98 (1), 1998-99 (1), 2000-01 (1). Total: 6.

Season Team	League	REGULAR SEASON								PLAYOFFS				
		Gms.	G	A	Pts.	PIM	+/-	PP	SH	Gms.	G	A	Pts.	PIM
90-91—Avtomo. Sverdlovsk	USSR	26	2	1	3	10	...	...	...	—	—	—	—	—
91-92—Dynamo Moscow	CIS	35	7	5	12	19	...	...	...	—	—	—	—	—
92-93—Dynamo Moscow	CIS	27	10	12	22	18	...	...	...	10	7	3	10	18
93-94—Ottawa	NHL	83	30	49	79	22	-49	11	2	—	—	—	—	—
94-95—Las Vegas	IHL	24	15	20	35	32	...	...	...	—	—	—	—	—
—Ottawa	NHL	47	21	23	44	20	-20	11	0	—	—	—	—	—
95-96—Ottawa	NHL	46	15	24	39	28	-15	8	0	—	—	—	—	—

Season Team	League	REGULAR SEASON								PLAYOFFS				
		Gms.	G	A	Pts.	PIM	+/-	PP	SH	Gms.	G	A	Pts.	PIM
96-97—Ottawa	NHL	82	35	40	75	44	-7	10	0	7	1	5	6	2
97-98—Ottawa	NHL	82	33	39	72	24	6	5	0	11	5	3	8	8
—Russian Oly. team	Int'l	6	3	3	6	0	...	...	...	—	—	—	—	—
98-99—Ottawa	NHL	82	44	50	94	54	16	19	0	4	0	0	0	10
99-00—Ottawa	NHL								Did not play.					
00-01—Ottawa	NHL	82	40	48	88	30	10	13	2	4	0	1	1	0
NHL Totals (8 years)		504	218	273	491	222	-59	77	4	26	6	9	15	20

YELLE, STEPHANE   C   AVALANCHE

PERSONAL: Born May 9, 1974, in Ottawa. ... 6-1/190. ... Shoots left. ... Name pronounced YEHL.

TRANSACTIONS/CAREER NOTES: Selected by New Jersey Devils in eighth round (ninth Devils pick, 186th overall) of NHL entry draft (June 20, 1992). ... Traded by Devils with 11th-round pick (D Stephen Low) in 1994 draft to Quebec Nordiques for 11th-round pick (C Mike Hansen) in 1994 draft (June 1, 1994). ... Nordiques franchise moved to Colorado and renamed Avalanche for 1995-96 season (June 21, 1995). ... Pulled groin (February 15, 1996); missed nine games. ... Strained hip flexor (December 14, 1996); missed three games. ... Sprained right wrist (November 28, 1998); missed nine games. ... Sprained knee (May 3, 1999); missed nine playoff games. ... Injured sternum (January 25, 2000); missed two games. ... Strained hip flexor (March 7, 2000); missed one game. ... Injured ankle (October 25, 2000); missed one game. ... Strained groin (November 18, 2000); missed three games. ... Injured back (December 20, 2000); missed three games. ... Suffered herniated disk in back (December 27, 2000); missed 10 games. ... Injured knee (February 17, 2001); missed nine games. ... Sprained knee (March 24, 2001); missed six games.

MISCELLANEOUS: Member of Stanley Cup championship team (1996 and 2001).

Season Team	League	REGULAR SEASON								PLAYOFFS				
		Gms.	G	A	Pts.	PIM	+/-	PP	SH	Gms.	G	A	Pts.	PIM
91-92—Oshawa	OHL	55	12	14	26	20	...	...	...	7	2	0	2	1
92-93—Oshawa	OHL	66	24	50	74	20	...	...	...	10	2	4	6	4
93-94—Oshawa	OHL	66	35	69	104	22	...	...	...	5	1	7	8	2
94-95—Cornwall	AHL	40	18	15	33	22	...	...	...	13	7	7	14	8
95-96—Colorado	NHL	71	13	14	27	30	15	0	2	22	1	4	5	8
96-97—Colorado	NHL	79	9	17	26	38	1	0	1	12	1	6	7	2
97-98—Colorado	NHL	81	7	15	22	48	-10	1	1	7	1	0	1	12
98-99—Colorado	NHL	72	8	7	15	40	-8	1	0	10	0	1	1	6
99-00—Colorado	NHL	79	8	14	22		9	0	1	17	1	2	3	4
00-01—Colorado	NHL	50	4	10	14	20	-3	0	1	23	1	2	3	4
NHL Totals (6 years)		432	49	77	126	204	4	1	6	91	5	15	20	40

YEREMEYEV, VITALI   G   RANGERS

PERSONAL: Born September 23, 1975, in Ust-Kamenogorsk, U.S.S.R. ... 5-10/167.

TRANSACTIONS/CAREER NOTES: Selected by New York Rangers in ninth round (11th Rangers pick, 209th overall) of NHL entry draft (June 29, 1994).

Season Team	League	REGULAR SEASON								PLAYOFFS						
		Gms.	Min	W	L	T	GA	SO	Avg.	Gms.	Min.	W	L	GA	SO	Avg.
93-94—Ust-Kamenogorsk	CIS	19	1015	...	...	...	38	...	2.25	—						
94-95—CSKA Moscow	CIS	49	2733	...	...	...	97	...	2.13	2	120	...	...	8	...	4.00
95-96—CSKA Moscow	CIS	25	1339	...	...	...	37	...	1.66	3	179	...	...	7	...	2.35
96-97—HC CSKA Moscow	Russian	14	635	...	...	...	35	0	3.31	1	59	...	...	3	0	3.05
97-98—Torpedo Yaroslavl	Russian	17	979	...	...	...	19	3	1.16	—						
—Kazakhstan Oly. team	Int'l	7	292	1	4	1	28	0	5.75	—						
98-99—CSKA Moscow	Rus. Div. II	19		...	...	...	...	...	...	—						
99-00—Dynamo	Russian	26	1564	...	...	...	32	†7	*1.23	*17	*1039	...	...	22	*4	*1.27
00-01—Charlotte	ECHL	5	298	3	2	0	21	0	4.23	—						
—Hartford	AHL	36	1977	16	15	3	98	2	2.97	—						
—New York Rangers	NHL	4	212	0	4	0	16	0	4.53	—						
NHL Totals (1 year)		4	212	0	4	0	16	0	4.53							

YLONEN, JUHA   C   LIGHTNING

PERSONAL: Born February 13, 1972, in Helsinki, Finland. ... 6-1/189. ... Shoots left. ... Name pronounced YOO-hah u-LOH-nehn.

TRANSACTIONS/CAREER NOTES: Selected by Winnipeg Jets in fifth round (fifth Jets pick, 91st overall) of NHL entry draft (June 22, 1991). ... Jets franchise moved to Phoenix and renamed Coyotes for 1996-97 season; NHL approved move on January 18, 1996. ... Bruised foot (March 10, 1998); missed two games. ... Fractured leg (March 19, 1998); missed 14 games. ... Sprained knee (February 19, 1999); missed 14 games. ... Sprained knee (March 23, 1999); missed nine games. ... Suffered hip flexor (April 1, 2000); missed final four games of regular season. ... Bruised shoulder (September 18, 2000); missed first two games of season. ... Bruised shoulder (October 15, 2000); missed two games. ... Suffered from the flu (November 11, 2000); missed three games. ... Strained groin (December 5, 2000); missed three games. ... Strained groin (January 4, 2001); missed five games. ... Traded by Coyotes to Tampa Bay Lightning for LW Todd Warriner (June 18, 2001).

MISCELLANEOUS: Member of bronze-medal-winning Finnish Olympic team (1998).

Season Team	League	REGULAR SEASON								PLAYOFFS				
		Gms.	G	A	Pts.	PIM	+/-	PP	SH	Gms.	G	A	Pts.	PIM
90-91—Kiekko-Espoo	Finland Div. 2	40	12	21	33	4	...	...	...	—	—	—	—	—
91-92—HPK Hameenlinna	Finland	43	7	11	18	8	...	...	...	—	—	—	—	—
92-93—HPK Hameenlinna	Finland	48	8	18	26	22	...	...	...	12	3	5	8	2
93-94—Jokerit Helsinki	Finland	37	5	11	16	2	...	...	...	12	1	3	4	8
94-95—Jokerit Helsinki	Finland	50	13	15	28	10	...	...	...	11	3	2	5	0
95-96—Jokerit Helsinki	Finland	24	3	13	16	20	...	...	...	11	4	5	9	4

Y

Season Team	League	REGULAR SEASON Gms.	G	A	Pts.	PIM	+/-	PP	SH	PLAYOFFS Gms.	G	A	Pts.	PIM
96-97—Springfield	AHL	70	20	41	61	6	...	...	...	17	5	†16	21	4
—Phoenix	NHL	2	0	0	0	0	0	0	0	—	—	—	—	—
97-98—Phoenix	NHL	55	1	11	12	10	-3	0	1	—	—	—	—	—
—Fin. Olympic team	Int'l	6	0	0	0	8	...	...	...	—	—	—	—	—
98-99—Phoenix	NHL	59	6	17	23	20	18	2	0	2	0	2	2	2
99-00—Phoenix	NHL	76	6	23	29	12	-6	0	1	1	0	0	0	0
00-01—Phoenix	NHL	69	9	14	23	38	10	0	1	—	—	—	—	—
NHL Totals (5 years)		261	22	65	87	80	19	2	3	3	0	2	2	2

YORK, JASON D MIGHTY DUCKS

PERSONAL: Born May 20, 1970, in Nepean, Ont. ... 6-1/200. ... Shoots right.

TRANSACTIONS/CAREER NOTES: Selected by Detroit Red Wings in seventh round (sixth Red Wings pick, 129th overall) of NHL entry draft (June 16, 1990). ... Traded by Red Wings with C/RW Mike Sillinger to Mighty Ducks of Anaheim for LW Stu Grimson, D Mark Ferner and sixth-round pick (LW Magnus Nilsson) in 1996 draft (April 4, 1995). ... Sprained right ankle (December 1, 1995); missed two games. ... Traded by Mighty Ducks with C Shaun Van Allen to Ottawa Senators for C Ted Drury and rights to D Marc Moro (October 1, 1996). ... Strained groin (December 4, 1996); missed six games. ... Suffered concussion (January 3, 1998); missed four games. ... Injured right eye (April 13, 1998); missed three games. ... Strained shoulder (October 1, 1998); missed first two games of season. ... Strained groin (December 8, 1999); missed three games. ... Strained shoulder (October 27, 2000); missed one game. ... Suffered from the flu (January 16, 2001); missed one game. ... Fractured leg (February 8, 2001); missed six games. ... Signed as free agent by Mighty Ducks (July 3, 2001).

HONORS: Named to AHL All-Star first team (1993-94).

Season Team	League	REGULAR SEASON Gms.	G	A	Pts.	PIM	+/-	PP	SH	PLAYOFFS Gms.	G	A	Pts.	PIM
89-90—Windsor	OHL	39	9	30	39	38	...	...	...	—	—	—	—	—
—Kitchener	OHL	25	11	25	36	17	...	...	...	17	3	19	22	10
90-91—Windsor	OHL	66	13	80	93	40	...	...	...	11	3	10	13	12
91-92—Adirondack	AHL	49	4	20	24	32	...	...	...	5	0	1	1	0
92-93—Adirondack	AHL	77	15	40	55	86	...	...	...	11	0	3	3	18
—Detroit	NHL	2	0	0	0	0	0	0	0	—	—	—	—	—
93-94—Adirondack	AHL	74	10	56	66	98	...	...	...	12	3	11	14	22
—Detroit	NHL	7	1	2	3	2	0	0	0	—	—	—	—	—
94-95—Adirondack	AHL	5	1	3	4	4	...	...	...	—	—	—	—	—
—Detroit	NHL	10	1	2	3	2	0	0	0	—	—	—	—	—
—Anaheim	NHL	15	0	8	8	12	4	0	0	—	—	—	—	—
95-96—Anaheim	NHL	79	3	21	24	88	-7	0	0	—	—	—	—	—
96-97—Ottawa	NHL	75	4	17	21	67	-8	1	0	7	0	0	0	4
97-98—Ottawa	NHL	73	3	13	16	62	8	0	0	7	1	1	2	7
98-99—Ottawa	NHL	79	4	31	35	48	17	2	0	4	1	1	2	4
99-00—Ottawa	NHL	79	8	22	30	60	-3	1	0	6	0	2	2	2
00-01—Ottawa	NHL	74	6	16	22	72	7	3	0	4	0	0	0	4
NHL Totals (9 years)		493	30	132	162	413	18	7	0	28	2	4	6	21

YORK, MIKE C RANGERS

PERSONAL: Born January 3, 1978, in Pontiac, Mich. ... 5-10/185. ... Shoots right. ... Full Name: Michael York.

TRANSACTIONS/CAREER NOTES: Selected by New York Rangers in sixth round (seventh Rangers pick, 136th overall) of NHL entry draft (June 21, 1997). ... Bruised ribs (January 22, 2001); missed one game. ... Injured left shoulder (February 9, 2001); missed two games.

HONORS: Named to CCHA All-Rookie team (1995-96). ... Named to NCAA All-America (West) first team (1997-98 and 1998-99). ... Named CCHA Tournament Most Valuable Player (1997-98). ... Named to CCHA All-Star second team (1997-98). ... Named to CCHA All-Star first team (1998-99). ... Named to NHL All-Rookie team (1999-2000).

Season Team	League	REGULAR SEASON Gms.	G	A	Pts.	PIM	+/-	PP	SH	PLAYOFFS Gms.	G	A	Pts.	PIM
95-96—Michigan State	CCHA	39	12	27	39	20	...	...	...	—	—	—	—	—
96-97—Michigan State	CCHA	37	18	29	47	42	...	...	...	—	—	—	—	—
97-98—Michigan State	CCHA	40	27	34	61	38	...	...	...	—	—	—	—	—
98-99—Michigan State	CCHA	42	22	32	*54	41	...	...	...	—	—	—	—	—
—Hartford	AHL	3	2	2	4	0	...	...	...	6	3	1	4	0
99-00—New York Rangers	NHL	82	26	24	50	18	-17	8	0	—	—	—	—	—
00-01—New York Rangers	NHL	79	14	17	31	20	1	3	2	—	—	—	—	—
NHL Totals (2 years)		161	40	41	81	38	-16	11	2					

YOUNG, SCOTT RW BLUES

PERSONAL: Born October 1, 1967, in Clinton, Mass. ... 6-1/200. ... Shoots right. ... Full Name: Scott Allen Young.

TRANSACTIONS/CAREER NOTES: Selected by Hartford Whalers in first round (first Whalers pick, 11th overall) of NHL entry draft (June 21, 1986). ... Suffered lacerations above right eye (October 8, 1988). ... Lacerated face (February 18, 1990). ... Traded by Whalers to Pittsburgh Penguins for RW Rob Brown (December 21, 1990). ... Traded by Penguins to Quebec Nordiques for D Bryan Fogarty (March 10, 1992). ... Injured rib (February 14, 1993); missed one game. ... Bruised ribs (February 23, 1993); missed one game. ... Sprained right ankle (October 5, 1993); missed eight games. ... Played in Europe during 1994-95 NHL lockout. ... Nordiques franchise moved to Colorado and renamed Avalanche for 1995-96 season (June 21, 1995). ... Bruised right shoulder (December 23, 1996); missed five games. ... Traded by Avalanche to Mighty Ducks of Anaheim for third-round pick (traded to Florida) in 1998 draft (September 17, 1997). ... Bruised right foot (November 22, 1997); missed two games. ... Bruised right foot (November 29, 1997); missed five games. ... Suffered eye abrasion (March 9, 1998); missed two games. ... Signed as free agent by St. Louis Blues (July 16, 1998). ... Suffered sore back (February 8, 1999); missed one game. ... Injured back (January 28, 2000); missed three games. ... Separated shoulder (April 5, 2000); missed final two games of regular season. ... Injured shoulder (December 5, 2000); missed one game.

Y

Season Team	League	REGULAR SEASON								PLAYOFFS				
		Gms.	G	A	Pts.	PIM	+/-	PP	SH	Gms.	G	A	Pts.	PIM
84-85—St. Marks H.S.	Mass. H.S.	23	28	41	69	...	...	...	...	—	—	—	—	—
85-86—Boston University	Hockey East	38	16	13	29	31	...	...	...	—	—	—	—	—
86-87—Boston University	Hockey East	33	15	21	36	24	...	...	...	—	—	—	—	—
87-88—U.S. Olympic team......	Int'l	59	13	53	66	...	...	...	...	—	—	—	—	—
—Hartford	NHL	7	0	0	0	2	-6	0	0	4	1	0	1	0
88-89—Hartford	NHL	76	19	40	59	27	-21	6	0	4	2	0	2	4
89-90—Hartford	NHL	80	24	40	64	47	-24	10	2	7	2	0	2	2
90-91—Hartford	NHL	34	6	9	15	8	-9	3	1	—	—	—	—	—
—Pittsburgh	NHL	43	11	16	27	33	3	3	1	17	1	6	7	2
91-92—U.S. national team	Int'l	10	2	4	6	21	...	...	...	—	—	—	—	—
—U.S. Olympic team......	Int'l	8	2	1	3	2	...	...	...	—	—	—	—	—
—Bolzano	Italy	18	22	17	39	6	...	...	...	—	—	—	—	—
92-93—Quebec	NHL	82	30	30	60	20	5	9	6	6	4	1	5	0
93-94—Quebec	NHL	76	26	25	51	14	-4	6	1	—	—	—	—	—
94-95—Frankfurt	Germany	1	1	0	1	0	...	...	...	—	—	—	—	—
—Landshut...................	Germany	4	6	1	7	6	...	...	...	—	—	—	—	—
—Quebec	NHL	48	18	21	39	14	9	3	3	6	3	3	6	2
95-96—Colorado	NHL	81	21	39	60	50	2	7	0	22	3	12	15	10
96-97—Colorado	NHL	72	18	19	37	14	-5	7	0	17	4	2	6	14
97-98—Anaheim	NHL	73	13	20	33	22	-13	4	2	—	—	—	—	—
98-99—St. Louis	NHL	75	24	28	52	27	8	8	0	13	4	7	11	10
99-00—St. Louis	NHL	75	24	15	39	18	12	6	1	6	6	2	8	8
00-01—St. Louis	NHL	81	40	33	73	30	15	14	3	15	6	7	13	2
NHL Totals (13 years)........		903	274	335	609	326	-28	86	20	117	36	40	76	54

YTFELDT, DAVID D CANUCKS

PERSONAL: Born September 29, 1979, in Ornskoldsvik, Sweden. ... 6-0/187. ... Shoots left. ... Formerly known as David Jonsson.
TRANSACTIONS/CAREER NOTES: Selected by Vancouver Canucks in fifth round (sixth Canucks pick, 136th overall) of NHL entry draft (June 27, 1998).

Season Team	League	REGULAR SEASON								PLAYOFFS				
		Gms.	G	A	Pts.	PIM	+/-	PP	SH	Gms.	G	A	Pts.	PIM
96-97—Leksand	Sweden Jr.	25	3	5	8	...	...	...	...	—	—	—	—	—
97-98—Leksand	Sweden	10	0	0	0	2	...	...	...	—	—	—	—	—
—Leksand	Sweden Jr.	23	13	10	23	101	...	...	...	—	—	—	—	—
98-99—Leksand	Sweden	39	0	4	4	65	...	...	...	4	0	1	1	4
99-00—Leksand	Sweden	50	3	9	12	72	...	...	...	—	—	—	—	—
00-01—JyP Jyvaskyla	Finland	11	0	4	4	26	...	...	...	—	—	—	—	—
—Vastra Frolunda	Sweden	9	0	1	1	8	...	...	...	5	0	1	1	4

YUSHKEVICH, DMITRY D MAPLE LEAFS

PERSONAL: Born November 19, 1971, in Yaroslavl, U.S.S.R. ... 5-11/208. ... Shoots right. ... Name pronounced yoosh-KAY-vihch.
TRANSACTIONS/CAREER NOTES: Selected by Philadelphia Flyers in sixth round (sixth Flyers pick, 122nd overall) of NHL entry draft (June 22, 1991). ... Sprained wrist (January 28, 1993); missed two games. ... Strained groin (February 18, 1994); missed four games. ... Played in Europe during 1994-95 NHL lockout. ... Suffered from sore back (February 23, 1995); missed three games. ... Sprained left knee (April 16, 1995); missed five games. ... Traded by Flyers with second-round pick (G Francis Larivee) in 1996 draft to Toronto Maple Leafs for first-(RW Dainius Zubrus) and fourth-round (traded to Los Angeles) picks in 1996 draft and second-round pick (G Jean-Marc Pelletier) in 1997 draft (August 30, 1995). ... Sprained knee (October 26, 1995); missed eight games. ... Bruised knee (December 30, 1995); missed two games. ... Pulled hamstring (December 14, 1996); missed four games. ... Injured knee (March 22, 1997); missed two games. ... Fractured toe (October 15, 1997); missed six games. ... Sprained knee (December 31, 1997); missed two games. ... Strained groin (December 12, 1998); missed three games. ... Suffered injury (November 30, 2000); missed one game.
HONORS: Played in NHL All-Star Game (2000).
MISCELLANEOUS: Member of silver-medal-winning Russian Olympic team (1998).

Season Team	League	REGULAR SEASON								PLAYOFFS				
		Gms.	G	A	Pts.	PIM	+/-	PP	SH	Gms.	G	A	Pts.	PIM
88-89—Torpedo Yaroslavl	USSR	23	2	1	3	8	...	...	...	—	—	—	—	—
89-90—Torpedo Yaroslavl	USSR	41	2	3	5	39	...	...	...	—	—	—	—	—
90-91—Torpedo Yaroslavl	USSR	43	10	4	14	22	...	...	...	—	—	—	—	—
91-92—Dynamo Moscow........	CIS	41	6	7	13	14	...	...	...	—	—	—	—	—
—Unif. Olympic team......	Int'l	8	1	2	3	4	...	...	...	—	—	—	—	—
92-93—Philadelphia	NHL	82	5	27	32	71	12	1	0	—	—	—	—	—
93-94—Philadelphia	NHL	75	5	25	30	86	-8	1	0	—	—	—	—	—
94-95—Torpedo Yaroslavl	CIS	10	3	4	7	8	...	...	...	—	—	—	—	—
—Philadelphia	NHL	40	5	9	14	47	-4	3	1	15	1	5	6	12
95-96—Toronto	NHL	69	1	10	11	54	-14	1	0	4	0	0	0	0
96-97—Toronto	NHL	74	4	10	14	56	-24	1	1	—	—	—	—	—
97-98—Toronto	NHL	72	0	12	12	78	-13	0	0	—	—	—	—	—
—Russian Oly. team........	Int'l	6	0	0	0	2	...	...	...	—	—	—	—	—
98-99—Toronto	NHL	78	6	22	28	88	25	2	1	17	1	5	6	22
99-00—Toronto	NHL	77	3	24	27	55	2	2	1	12	1	1	2	4
00-01—Toronto	NHL	81	5	19	24	52	-2	1	0	11	0	4	4	12
NHL Totals (9 years)...........		648	34	158	192	587	-26	12	4	59	3	15	18	50

Y

YZERMAN, STEVE   C   RED WINGS

PERSONAL: Born May 9, 1965, in Cranbrook, B.C. ... 5-10/185. ... Shoots right. ... Name pronounced IGH-zuhr-muhn.

TRANSACTIONS/CAREER NOTES: Selected by Detroit Red Wings in first round (first Red Wings pick, fourth overall) of NHL entry draft (June 1983). ... Fractured collarbone (January 31, 1986). ... Injured ligaments of right knee (March 1, 1988) and underwent surgery. ... Injured right knee in playoff game (April 8, 1991). ... Suffered herniated disc (October 21, 1993); missed 26 games. ... Sprained knee (May 27, 1995); missed three playoff games. ... Suffered from the flu (March 17, 1996); missed one game. ... Bruised ankle (April 9, 1997); missed one game. ... Sprained medial collateral ligament in knee (January 28, 1998); missed three games. ... Strained groin (April 11, 1998); missed three games. ... Suffered lacerations to forehead and nose and fractured nose (January 21, 1999); missed one game. ... Sprained knee (March 29, 2000); missed final four games of regular season. ... Sprained knee (September 28, 2000); missed first two games of season. ... Underwent knee surgery (October 13, 2000); missed 23 games.

HONORS: Named NHL Rookie of the Year by THE SPORTING NEWS (1983-84). ... Named to NHL All-Rookie team (1983-84). ... Played in NHL All-Star Game (1984, 1988-1993, 1997 and 2000). ... Won Lester B. Pearson Award (1988-89). ... Won Conn Smythe Trophy (1997-98). ... Named to play in NHL All-Star Game (1999); replaced by LW Luc Robitaille due to injury. ... Named to THE SPORTING NEWS All-Star team (1999-2000). ... Named to NHL All-Star first team (1999-2000). ... Won Frank J. Selke Trophy (1999-2000).

MISCELLANEOUS: Member of Stanley Cup championship team (1997 and 1998). ... Captain of Detroit Red Wings (1986-87 through 2000-01). ... Scored on a penalty shot (vs. Bob Essensa, February 13, 1989; vs. Grant Fuhr, January 3, 1992; vs. Daren Puppa, January 29, 1992). ... Failed to score on a penalty shot (vs. Doug Keans, November 22, 1987; vs. Darcy Wakaluk, March 19, 1993; vs. Blaine Lacher, November , 1995). ... Became youngest player (18 years old) to play in NHL All-Star Game (January 31, 1984).

STATISTICAL PLATEAUS: Three-goal games: 1983-84 (1), 1984-85 (1), 1987-88 (2), 1988-89 (2), 1989-90 (2), 1990-91 (3), 1991-92 (3), 1992-93 (3). Total: 17. ... Four-goal games: 1989-90 (1). ... Total hat tricks: 18.

		REGULAR SEASON								PLAYOFFS				
Season Team	League	Gms.	G	A	Pts.	PIM	+/-	PP	SH	Gms.	G	A	Pts.	PIM
81-82—Peterborough	OHL	58	21	43	64	65	...	...	...	6	0	1	1	16
82-83—Peterborough	OHL	56	42	49	91	33	...	...	...	4	1	4	5	0
83-84—Detroit	NHL	80	39	48	87	33	-17	13	0	4	3	3	6	0
84-85—Detroit	NHL	80	30	59	89	58	-17	9	0	3	2	1	3	2
85-86—Detroit	NHL	51	14	28	42	16	-24	3	0	—	—	—	—	—
86-87—Detroit	NHL	80	31	59	90	43	-1	9	1	16	5	13	18	8
87-88—Detroit	NHL	64	50	52	102	44	30	10	6	3	1	3	4	6
88-89—Detroit	NHL	80	65	90	155	61	17	17	3	6	5	5	10	2
89-90—Detroit	NHL	79	62	65	127	79	-6	16	†7	—	—	—	—	—
90-91—Detroit	NHL	80	51	57	108	34	-2	12	6	7	3	3	6	4
91-92—Detroit	NHL	79	45	58	103	64	26	9	*8	11	3	5	8	12
92-93—Detroit	NHL	84	58	79	137	44	33	13	†7	7	4	3	7	4
93-94—Detroit	NHL	58	24	58	82	36	11	7	3	3	1	3	4	0
94-95—Detroit	NHL	47	12	26	38	40	6	4	0	15	4	8	12	0
95-96—Detroit	NHL	80	36	59	95	64	29	16	2	18	8	12	20	4
96-97—Detroit	NHL	81	22	63	85	78	22	8	0	20	7	6	13	4
97-98—Detroit	NHL	75	24	45	69	46	3	6	2	22	6	18	24	22
—Can. Olympic team	Int'l	6	1	1	2	10	...	...	...	—	—	—	—	—
98-99—Detroit	NHL	80	29	45	74	42	8	13	2	10	9	4	13	0
99-00—Detroit	NHL	78	35	44	79	34	28	15	2	8	0	4	4	0
00-01—Detroit	NHL	54	18	34	52	18	4	5	0	1	0	0	0	0
NHL Totals (18 years)		1310	645	969	1614	834	150	185	49	154	61	91	152	68

ZAINULLIN, RUSLAN   RW   COYOTES

PERSONAL: Born February 14, 1982, in Kazan, U.S.S.R. ... 6-2/202. ... Shoots left.

TRANSACTIONS/CAREER NOTES: Selected by Tampa Bay Lightning in second round (second Lightning pick, 34th pick overall) of NHL entry draft (June 24, 2000). ... Traded by Lightning with D Paul Mara, RW Mike Johnson and second-round pick (D Matthew Spiller) in 2001 draft to Phoenix Coyotes for G Nikolai Khabibulin and D Stan Neckar (March 5, 2001).

		REGULAR SEASON								PLAYOFFS				
Season Team	League	Gms.	G	A	Pts.	PIM	+/-	PP	SH	Gms.	G	A	Pts.	PIM
98-99—Ak Bars-2 Kazan	Rus. Div. II	36	13	8	21	22	...	...	...	—	—	—	—	—
99-00—Ak Bars Kazan	Russian	14	1	1	2	4	...	...	...	—	—	—	—	—
00-01—Ak Bars Kazan	Russian	29	1	3	4	14	...	...	...	1	0	0	0	0

ZALESAK, MIROSLAV   RW   SHARKS

PERSONAL: Born January 2, 1980, in Skalica, Czechoslovakia. ... 6-0/185. ... Shoots left.

TRANSACTIONS/CAREER NOTES: Selected by San Jose Sharks in fourth round (fifth Sharks pick, 104th overall) of NHL entry draft (June 27, 1998).

		REGULAR SEASON								PLAYOFFS				
Season Team	League	Gms.	G	A	Pts.	PIM	+/-	PP	SH	Gms.	G	A	Pts.	PIM
95-96—HC Nitra	Slovakia Jrs.	49	53	29	82	...	...	...	...	—	—	—	—	—
96-97—HC Nitra	Slovakia Jrs.	58	51	31	82	...	...	...	...	—	—	—	—	—
97-98—HC Nitra	Slovakia Jrs.	23	33	23	56	16	...	...	...	—	—	—	—	—
—Plastika Nitra	Slovakia	30	8	6	14	0	...	...	...	—	—	—	—	—
98-99—Plastika Nitra	Slovakia	15	4	3	7	10	...	...	...	—	—	—	—	—
—Drummondville	QMJHL	45	24	27	51	18	...	...	...	—	—	—	—	—
99-00—Drummondville	QMJHL	60	50	61	111	40	...	...	...	16	7	11	18	4
00-01—Kentucky	AHL	60	14	11	25	26	...	...	...	3	0	1	1	4

ZAMUNER, ROB   LW   BRUINS

PERSONAL: Born September 17, 1969, in Oakville, Ont. ... 6-3/203. ... Shoots left. ... Name pronounced ZAM-uh-nuhr.
TRANSACTIONS/CAREER NOTES: Selected by New York Rangers in third round (third Rangers pick, 45th overall) of NHL entry draft (June 17, 1989). ... Signed as free agent by Tampa Bay Lightning (July 14, 1992); Rangers awarded third-round pick in 1993 draft as compensation (July 23, 1992). ... Hyperextended elbow (March 19, 1995); missed five games. ... Sprained knee (October 4, 1995); missed 10 games. ... Suffered sore back (April 1, 1998); missed five games. ... Strained groin (October 30, 1998); missed three games. ... Strained groin (November 8, 1998); missed 18 games. ... Strained groin (February 26, 1999); missed three games. ... Traded by Lightning with second-round pick in 2002 draft to Ottawa Senators for C/LW Andreas Johansson to complete deal that allowed Tampa Bay to sign general manager Rick Dudley (June 30, 1999). ... Strained groin (October 28, 1999); missed five games. ... Sprained medial collateral ligament in left knee (December 23, 1999); missed 19 games. ... Strained groin (January 25, 2001); missed three games. ... Signed as free agent by Boston Bruins (July 6, 2001).
MISCELLANEOUS: Captain of Tampa Bay Lightning (1998-99). ... Holds Tampa Bay Lightning all-time record for most games played (475). ... Scored on a penalty shot (vs. Tommy Salo, January 11, 1997). ... Failed to score on a penalty shot (vs. Chris Terreri, October 9, 1997).
STATISTICAL PLATEAUS: Three-goal games: 1997-98 (1).

Season Team	League	REGULAR SEASON									PLAYOFFS				
		Gms.	G	A	Pts.	PIM	+/-	PP	SH		Gms.	G	A	Pts.	PIM
86-87—Guelph	OHL	62	6	15	21	8	...	...	...		—	—	—	—	—
87-88—Guelph	OHL	58	20	41	61	18	...	...	...		—	—	—	—	—
88-89—Guelph	OHL	66	46	65	111	38	...	...	...		7	5	5	10	9
89-90—Flint	IHL	77	44	35	79	32	...	...	...		4	1	0	1	6
90-91—Binghamton	AHL	80	25	58	83	50	...	...	...		9	7	6	13	35
91-92—Binghamton	AHL	61	19	53	72	42	...	...	...		11	8	9	17	8
—New York Rangers	NHL	9	1	2	3	2	0	0	0		—	—	—	—	—
92-93—Tampa Bay	NHL	84	15	28	43	74	-25	1	0		—	—	—	—	—
93-94—Tampa Bay	NHL	59	6	6	12	42	-9	0	0		—	—	—	—	—
94-95—Tampa Bay	NHL	43	9	6	15	24	-3	0	3		—	—	—	—	—
95-96—Tampa Bay	NHL	72	15	20	35	62	11	0	3		6	2	3	5	10
96-97—Tampa Bay	NHL	82	17	33	50	56	3	0	4		—	—	—	—	—
97-98—Tampa Bay	NHL	77	14	12	26	41	-31	0	3		—	—	—	—	—
—Can. Olympic team	Int'l	6	1	0	1	8	...	...	...		—	—	—	—	—
98-99—Ottawa	NHL	58	8	11	19	24	-15	1	1		—	—	—	—	—
99-00—Ottawa	NHL	57	9	12	21	32	-6	0	1		6	2	0	2	2
00-01—Ottawa	NHL	79	19	18	37	52	7	1	2		4	0	0	0	6
NHL Totals (10 years)		620	113	148	261	409	-68	3	17		16	4	3	7	18

ZEDNIK, RICHARD   RW   CANADIENS

PERSONAL: Born January 6, 1976, in Bystrica, Czechoslovakia. ... 6-0/199. ... Shoots left. ... Name pronounced ZEHD-nihk.
TRANSACTIONS/CAREER NOTES: Selected by Washington Capitals in 10th round (10th Capitals pick, 249th overall) of NHL entry draft (June 29, 1994). ... Suffered from the flu (November 6, 1996); missed two games. ... Suffered from the flu (December 12, 1997); missed one game. ... Suffered concussion (March 18, 1998); missed six games. ... Strained abdominal muscle (April 2, 1998); missed final eight games of regular season and four playoff games. ... Bruised shoulder (October 21, 1998); missed 10 games. ... Suspended four games and fined $1,000 by NHL for high-sticking incident (November 20, 1998). ... Strained groin (December 19, 1998); missed 19 games. ... Suffered concussion (February 23, 2000); missed 13 games. ... Suspended four games by NHL for cross-checking incident (October 19, 2000). ... Sprained foot (January 12, 2001); missed two games. ... Traded by Capitals with C Jan Bulis and first-round pick (C Alexander Perezhogin) in 2001 draft to Montreal Canadiens for C Trevor Linden, RW Dainius Zubrus and second-round pick (traded to Tampa Bay) in 2001 draft (March 13, 2001).
HONORS: Named to WHL (West) All-Star second team (1995-96).
MISCELLANEOUS: Failed to score on a penalty shot (vs. Mike Richter, November 11, 1999).
STATISTICAL NOTES: Tied for NHL lead in game-tying goals with three (1999-2000).
STATISTICAL PLATEAUS: Three-goal games: 2000-01 (1).

Season Team	League	REGULAR SEASON									PLAYOFFS				
		Gms.	G	A	Pts.	PIM	+/-	PP	SH		Gms.	G	A	Pts.	PIM
93-94—Banska Bystrica	Slovakia	25	3	6	9	...	...	...	...		—	—	—	—	—
94-95—Portland	WHL	65	35	51	86	89	...	...	...		9	5	5	10	20
95-96—Portland	WHL	61	44	37	81	154	...	...	...		7	8	4	12	23
—Portland	AHL	1	1	1	2	0	...	...	...		21	4	5	9	26
—Washington	NHL	1	0	0	0	0	0	0	0		—	—	—	—	—
96-97—Washington	NHL	11	2	1	3	4	-5	1	0		—	—	—	—	—
—Portland	AHL	56	15	20	35	70	...	...	...		5	1	0	1	6
97-98—Washington	NHL	65	17	9	26	28	-2	2	0		17	7	3	10	16
98-99—Washington	NHL	49	9	8	17	50	-6	1	0		—	—	—	—	—
99-00—Washington	NHL	69	19	16	35	54	6	1	0		5	0	0	0	5
00-01—Washington	NHL	62	16	19	35	61	-2	4	0		—	—	—	—	—
—Montreal	NHL	12	3	6	9	10	-2	1	0		—	—	—	—	—
NHL Totals (6 years)		269	66	59	125	207	-11	10	0		22	7	3	10	21

ZELEPUKIN, VALERI   LW   BLACKHAWKS

PERSONAL: Born September 17, 1968, in Voskresensk, U.S.S.R. ... 6-1/200. ... Shoots left. ... Name pronounced vuh-LAIR-ee zehl-ih-POO-kihn.
TRANSACTIONS/CAREER NOTES: Selected by New Jersey Devils in 11th round (13th Devils pick, 221st overall) of NHL entry draft (June 22, 1990). ... Bruised shoulder (January 22, 1993); missed five games. ... Bruised left shoulder (December 22, 1993); missed one game. ... Injured chest (April 14, 1994); missed one game. ... Injured eye (January 24, 1995); missed first 42 games of season. ... Bruised finger (April 26, 1995); missed one game. ... Injured eye (October 7, 1995); missed first two games of season. ... Injured calf (November 21, 1995); missed two games. ... Injured foot (February 18, 1996); missed one game. ... Bruised right knee (March 23, 1996); missed six games. ... Suffered from the flu (November 14, 1996); missed three games. ... Suffered infected elbow (January 2, 1997); missed four games. ... Traded by Devils with RW Bill Guerin to Edmonton Oilers for C Jason Arnott and D Bryan Muir (January 4, 1998). ... Traded by Oilers to Philadelphia Flyers for C Dan Lacroix (October 5, 1998). ... Strained right shoulder (November 1, 1998); missed one game. ... Reinjured right shoulder (November 7, 1998); missed three games. ... Reinjured right shoulder (November 17, 1998); missed one game. ... Strained lower back (November 18,

1999); missed one game. ... Bruised right ankle (March 18, 2000); missed four games. ... Signed as free agent by Chicago Blackhawks (July 18, 2000). ... Strained groin (December 27, 2000); missed nine games.

MISCELLANEOUS: Member of Stanley Cup championship team (1995). ... Member of silver-medal-winning Russian Olympic team (1998). ... Failed to score on a penalty shot (vs. Martin Brodeur, October 30, 1999).

			REGULAR SEASON								PLAYOFFS				
Season Team	League	Gms.	G	A	Pts.	PIM	+/-	PP	SH		Gms.	G	A	Pts.	PIM
84-85—Khimik	USSR	5	0	0	0	2	...	...	...		—	—	—	—	—
85-86—Khimik	USSR	33	2	2	4	10	...	...	...		—	—	—	—	—
86-87—Khimik	USSR	19	1	0	1	4	...	...	...		—	—	—	—	—
87-88—SKA Leningrad	USSR	18	18	6	24	...	...	...	...		—	—	—	—	—
—CSKA Moscow	USSR	19	3	1	4	8	...	...	...		—	—	—	—	—
88-89—CSKA Moscow	USSR	17	2	3	5	2	...	...	...		—	—	—	—	—
89-90—Khimik	USSR	46	17	14	31	26	...	...	...		—	—	—	—	—
90-91—Khimik	USSR	46	12	19	31	22	...	...	...		—	—	—	—	—
91-92—Utica	AHL	22	20	9	29	8	...	...	...		—	—	—	—	—
—New Jersey	NHL	44	13	18	31	28	11	3	0		4	1	1	2	2
92-93—New Jersey	NHL	78	23	41	64	70	19	5	1		5	0	2	2	0
93-94—New Jersey	NHL	82	26	31	57	70	36	8	0		20	5	2	7	14
94-95—New Jersey	NHL	4	1	2	3	6	3	0	0		18	1	2	3	12
95-96—New Jersey	NHL	61	6	9	15	107	-10	3	0		—	—	—	—	—
96-97—New Jersey	NHL	71	14	24	38	36	-10	3	0		8	3	2	5	2
97-98—New Jersey	NHL	35	2	8	10	32	0	0	0		—	—	—	—	—
—Edmonton	NHL	33	2	10	12	57	-2	0	0		8	1	2	3	2
—Russian Oly. team	Int'l	6	1	2	3	0	...	...	...		—	—	—	—	—
98-99—Philadelphia	NHL	74	16	9	25	48	0	0	0		4	1	0	1	4
99-00—Philadelphia	NHL	77	11	21	32	55	-3	2	0		18	1	2	3	12
00-01—Chicago	NHL	36	3	4	7	18	-14	0	2		—	—	—	—	—
—Norfolk	AHL	29	10	9	19	28	...	...	...		9	5	3	8	6
NHL Totals (10 years)		595	117	177	294	527	30	24	3		85	13	13	26	48

ZEPP, ROB   G   THRASHERS

PERSONAL: Born September 7, 1981, in Scarborough, Ont. ... 6-1/160. ... Catches left.

TRANSACTIONS/CAREER NOTES: Selected by Atlanta Thrashers in fourth round (fifth Thrashers pick, 99th overall) of NHL entry draft (June 26, 1999). ... Returned to draft pool by Thrashers and selected by Carolina Hurricanes in fourth round (fourth Hurricanes pick, 110th overall) of NHL entry draft (June 23, 2001).

HONORS: Won Can.HL Scholastic Player of the Year Award (1998-99). ... Shared Dave Pinkey Trophy with Robert Holsinger (1998-99). ... Shared Dave Pinkey Trophy with Bill Ruggiero (1999-2000). ... Shared Dave Pinkey Trophy with Paul Drew (2000-01). ... Named to OHL All-Star second team (1999-2000 and 2000-01).

			REGULAR SEASON								PLAYOFFS					
Season Team	League	Gms.	Min	W	L	T	GA	SO	Avg.		Gms.	Min.	W	L	GA	SO	Avg.
97-98—Newmarket	OJHL	3	181	...	...	...	13	0	4.31		—	—	—	—	—	—	—
98-99—Plymouth	OHL	31	1662	19	3	4	76	3	2.74		3	100	1	0	10	0	6.00
99-00—Plymouth	OHL	53	3005	*36	11	3	119	3	*2.38		†23	*1374	*15	†8	52	2	2.27
00-01—Plymouth	OHL	55	3246	*34	18	3	122	†4	*2.26		19	1139	14	5	*51	2	2.69

ZETTERBERG, HENRIK   C   RED WINGS

PERSONAL: Born October 9, 1980, in Njurunda, Sweden ... 5-11/180.

TRANSACTIONS/CAREER NOTES: Selected by Detroit Red Wings in seventh round (fourth Red Wings pick, 210th overall) of NHL entry draft (June 27, 1998).

			REGULAR SEASON								PLAYOFFS				
Season Team	League	Gms.	G	A	Pts.	PIM	+/-	PP	SH		Gms.	G	A	Pts.	PIM
97-98—Timra	Sweden Jr.	18	9	5	14	4	...	...	...		—	—	—	—	—
—Timra	Sweden Dv. 2	16	1	2	3	4	...	...	...		4	0	1	1	0
98-99—Timra	Sweden Dv. 2	37	15	13	28	2	...	...	...		4	2	1	3	2
99-00—Timra	Sweden Dv. 2	11	4	6	10	0	...	...	...		10	10	4	14	4
00-01—Timra	Sweden	47	15	31	46	24	...	...	...		—	—	—	—	—

ZETTLER, ROB   D   CAPITALS

PERSONAL: Born March 8, 1968, in Sept-Iles, Que. ... 6-3/197. ... Shoots left.

TRANSACTIONS/CAREER NOTES: Selected by Minnesota North Stars in fifth round (fifth North Stars pick, 55th overall) of NHL entry draft (June 21, 1986). ... Tore hip flexor (January 21, 1991); missed 11 games. ... Selected by San Jose Sharks in NHL dispersal draft (May 30, 1991). ... Strained back (October 20, 1992); missed three games. ... Injured groin (April 8, 1993); missed one game. ... Traded by Sharks to Philadelphia Flyers for C Viacheslav Butsayev (February 1, 1994). ... Traded by Flyers to Toronto Maple Leafs for fifth-round pick (G Per-Ragna Bergqvist) in 1996 draft (July 8, 1995). ... Suspended two games by NHL for checking from behind (January 4, 1996). ... Strained groin (April 3, 1997); missed three games. ... Dislocated thumb (November 11, 1997); missed three games. ... Selected by Nashville Predators in NHL expansion draft (June 26, 1998). ... Signed as free agent by Washington Capitals (September 7, 1999). ... Bruised shoulder (February 27, 2001); missed four games.

			REGULAR SEASON								PLAYOFFS				
Season Team	League	Gms.	G	A	Pts.	PIM	+/-	PP	SH		Gms.	G	A	Pts.	PIM
84-85—Sault Ste. Marie	OHL	60	2	14	16	37	...	...	...		—	—	—	—	—
85-86—Sault Ste. Marie	OHL	57	5	23	28	92	...	...	...		—	—	—	—	—
86-87—Sault Ste. Marie	OHL	64	13	22	35	89	...	...	...		4	0	0	0	0
87-88—Sault Ste. Marie	OHL	64	7	41	48	77	...	...	...		6	2	2	4	9
—Kalamazoo	IHL	2	0	1	1	0	...	...	...		7	0	2	2	2

					REGULAR SEASON						PLAYOFFS			
Season Team	League	Gms.	G	A	Pts.	PIM	+/-	PP	SH	Gms.	G	A	Pts.	PIM
88-89—Minnesota	NHL	2	0	0	0	0	1	0	0	—	—	—	—	—
—Kalamazoo	IHL	80	5	21	26	79	...	...	...	6	0	1	1	26
89-90—Minnesota	NHL	31	0	8	8	45	-7	0	0	—	—	—	—	—
—Kalamazoo	IHL	41	6	10	16	64	...	...	...	7	0	0	0	6
90-91—Kalamazoo	IHL	1	0	0	0	2	...	...	...	—	—	—	—	—
—Minnesota	NHL	47	1	4	5	119	-10	0	0	—	—	—	—	—
91-92—San Jose	NHL	74	1	8	9	99	-23	0	0	—	—	—	—	—
92-93—San Jose	NHL	80	0	7	7	150	-50	0	0	—	—	—	—	—
93-94—San Jose	NHL	42	0	3	3	65	-7	0	0	—	—	—	—	—
—Philadelphia	NHL	33	0	4	4	69	-19	0	0	—	—	—	—	—
94-95—Philadelphia	NHL	32	0	1	1	34	-3	0	0	1	0	0	0	2
95-96—Toronto	NHL	29	0	1	1	48	-1	0	0	2	0	0	0	0
96-97—Utah	IHL	30	0	10	10	60	...	...	...	—	—	—	—	—
—Toronto	NHL	48	2	12	14	51	8	0	0	—	—	—	—	—
97-98—Toronto	NHL	59	0	7	7	108	-8	0	0	—	—	—	—	—
98-99—Utah	IHL	77	2	16	18	136	...	...	...	—	—	—	—	—
—Nashville	NHL	2	0	0	0	2	-2	0	0	—	—	—	—	—
99-00—Portland	AHL	23	2	2	4	27	...	...	...	—	—	—	—	—
—Washington	NHL	12	0	2	2	19	-1	0	0	5	0	0	0	2
00-01—Portland	AHL	36	1	9	10	84	...	...	...	—	—	—	—	—
—Washington	NHL	29	0	4	4	55	0	0	0	6	0	0	0	0
NHL Totals (13 years)		520	4	61	65	864	-122	0	0	14	0	0	0	4

ZHAMNOV, ALEX — C — BLACKHAWKS

PERSONAL: Born October 1, 1970, in Moscow, U.S.S.R. ... 6-1/200. ... Shoots left. ... Name pronounced ZHAM-nahf.

TRANSACTIONS/CAREER NOTES: Selected by Winnipeg Jets in fourth round (fifth Jets pick, 77th overall) of NHL entry draft (June 16, 1990). ... Suffered hip flexor (November 2, 1992); missed two games. ... Suffered back spasms (January 27, 1993); missed one game. ... Suffered back spasms (February 3, 1993); missed one game. ... Suffered back spasms (February 12, 1993); missed 12 games. ... Suffered left quad contusion (October 26, 1993); missed three games. ... Sprained back (December 27, 1993); missed eight games. ... Suffered back spasms (March 19, 1994); missed remainder of season. ... Suffered stress fracture in leg (October 12, 1995); missed eight games. ... Suffered from the flu (January 5, 1996); missed one game. ... Bruised back (March 7, 1996); missed four games. ... Injured back (March 16, 1996); missed remainder of regular season. ... Jets franchise moved to Phoenix and renamed Coyotes for 1996-97 season; NHL approved move on January 18, 1996. ... Traded by Coyotes with RW Craig Mills and first-round pick (RW Ty Jones) in 1997 draft to Chicago Blackhawks for C Jeremy Roenick (August 16, 1996). ... Fractured toe (November 2, 1997); missed four games. ... Suffered concussion (November 29, 1997); missed one game. ... Suffered concussion (March 3, 1998); missed four games. ... Bruised back (April 4, 1998); missed one game. ... Fractured finger (April 15, 1998); missed two games. ... Bruised ankle (November 10, 1998); missed one game. ... Suffered from the flu (December 26, 1998); missed one game. ... Injured back (February 6, 1999); missed four games. ... Strained groin (November 7, 1999); missed three games. ... Strained hamstring (January 15, 2000); missed eight games. ... Fractured larynx (January 21, 2001); missed 18 games.

HONORS: Named to NHL All-Star second team (1994-95).

MISCELLANEOUS: Member of gold-medal-winning Unified Olympic team (1992). ... Member of silver-medal-winning Russian Olympic team (1998). ... Failed to score on a penalty shot (vs. Tomas Vokoun, March 22, 2001).

STATISTICAL PLATEAUS: Three-goal games: 1993-94 (2), 1994-95 (1), 1995-96 (1), 1996-97 (1). Total: 5. ... Five-goal games: 1994-95 (1). ... Total hat tricks: 6.

					REGULAR SEASON						PLAYOFFS			
Season Team	League	Gms.	G	A	Pts.	PIM	+/-	PP	SH	Gms.	G	A	Pts.	PIM
88-89—Dynamo Moscow	USSR	4	0	0	0	0	...	...	...	—	—	—	—	—
89-90—Dynamo Moscow	USSR	43	11	6	17	23	...	...	...	—	—	—	—	—
90-91—Dynamo Moscow	USSR	46	16	12	28	24	...	...	...	—	—	—	—	—
91-92—Dynamo Moscow	CIS	39	15	21	36	28	...	...	...	—	—	—	—	—
—Unif. Olympic team	Int'l	8	0	3	3	8	...	...	...	—	—	—	—	—
92-93—Winnipeg	NHL	68	25	47	72	58	7	6	1	6	0	2	2	2
93-94—Winnipeg	NHL	61	26	45	71	62	-20	7	0	—	—	—	—	—
94-95—Winnipeg	NHL	48	30	35	65	20	5	9	0	—	—	—	—	—
95-96—Winnipeg	NHL	58	22	37	59	65	-4	5	0	6	2	1	3	8
96-97—Chicago	NHL	74	20	42	62	56	18	6	1	—	—	—	—	—
97-98—Chicago	NHL	70	21	28	49	61	16	6	2	—	—	—	—	—
—Russian Oly. team	Int'l	6	2	1	3	2	...	...	...	—	—	—	—	—
98-99—Chicago	NHL	76	20	41	61	50	-10	8	1	—	—	—	—	—
99-00—Chicago	NHL	71	23	37	60	61	7	5	0	—	—	—	—	—
00-01—Chicago	NHL	63	13	36	49	40	-12	3	1	—	—	—	—	—
NHL Totals (9 years)		589	200	348	548	473	7	55	6	12	2	3	5	10

ZHITNIK, ALEXEI — D — SABRES

PERSONAL: Born October 10, 1972, in Kiev, U.S.S.R. ... 5-11/215. ... Shoots left. ... Name pronounced ZHIHT-nihk.

TRANSACTIONS/CAREER NOTES: Selected by Los Angeles Kings in fourth round (third Kings pick, 81st overall) of NHL entry draft (June 22, 1991). ... Suffered from the flu (January 12, 1993); missed five games. ... Suspended one game by NHL for cross-checking (November 30, 1993). ... Traded by Kings with D Charlie Huddy, G Robb Stauber and fifth-round pick (D Marian Menhart) in 1995 draft to Buffalo Sabres for G Grant Fuhr, D Philippe Boucher and D Denis Tsygurov (February 14, 1995). ... Fractured thumb (February 19, 1995); missed three games. ... Reinjured thumb (March 8, 1995); missed one game. ... Ruptured calf muscle (March 19, 1995); missed 11 games. ... Suspended two games and fined $1,000 by NHL for high-sticking incident (November 1, 1996). ... Missed first four games of 1997-98 season due to contract dispute. ... Bruised chest (November 29, 1998); missed one game. ... Suffered eye injury (October 17, 1999); missed one game. ... Fractured finger (March 8, 2000); missed six games. ... Suspended one playoff game by NHL for high-sticking incident (April 19, 2000). ... Suspended four games by NHL for high-sticking incident (October 18, 2000).

HONORS: Played in NHL All-Star Game (1999).

MISCELLANEOUS: Member of gold-medal-winning Unified Olympic team (1992). ... Member of silver-medal-winning Russian Olympic team (1998).

Season Team	League	REGULAR SEASON								PLAYOFFS				
		Gms.	G	A	Pts.	PIM	+/-	PP	SH	Gms.	G	A	Pts.	PIM
89-90—Sokol Kiev	USSR	31	3	4	7	16	...	...	...	—	—	—	—	—
90-91—Sokol Kiev	USSR	40	1	4	5	46	...	...	...	—	—	—	—	—
91-92—CSKA Moscow	CIS	36	2	7	9	48	...	...	...	—	—	—	—	—
—Unif. Olympic team	Int'l	8	1	0	1	0	...	...	...	—	—	—	—	—
92-93—Los Angeles	NHL	78	12	36	48	80	-3	5	0	24	3	9	12	26
93-94—Los Angeles	NHL	81	12	40	52	101	-11	11	0	—	—	—	—	—
94-95—Los Angeles	NHL	11	2	5	7	27	-3	2	0	—	—	—	—	—
—Buffalo	NHL	21	2	5	7	34	-3	1	0	5	0	1	1	14
95-96—Buffalo	NHL	80	6	30	36	58	-25	5	0	—	—	—	—	—
96-97—Buffalo	NHL	80	7	28	35	95	10	3	1	12	1	0	1	16
97-98—Buffalo	NHL	78	15	30	45	102	19	2	3	15	0	3	3	36
—Russian Oly. team	Int'l	6	0	2	2	2	...	...	...	—	—	—	—	—
98-99—Buffalo	NHL	81	7	26	33	96	-6	3	1	21	4	11	15	*52
99-00—Buffalo	NHL	74	2	11	13	95	-6	1	0	4	0	0	0	8
00-01—Buffalo	NHL	78	8	29	37	75	-3	5	0	13	1	6	7	12
NHL Totals (9 years)		662	73	240	313	763	-31	38	5	94	9	30	39	164

ZHOLTOK, SERGEI — C — WILD

PERSONAL: Born December 2, 1972, in Riga, U.S.S.R. ... 6-1/191. ... Shoots right. ... Name pronounced SAIR-gay ZOHL-tahk.
TRANSACTIONS/CAREER NOTES: Selected by Boston Bruins in third round (second Bruins pick, 56th overall) of NHL entry draft (June 20, 1992). ... Signed as free agent by Ottawa Senators (June 25, 1996). ... Signed as free agent by Montreal Canadiens (September 9, 1998). ... Sprained knee (November 30, 1998); missed one game. ... Bruised hip (April 6, 1999); missed three games. ... Injured shoulder prior to start of 1999-2000 season; missed first 11 games of season. ... Suffered injury (December 3, 1999); missed one game. ... Traded by Canadiens to Edmonton Oilers for C Chad Kilger (December 18, 2000). ... Traded by Oilers to Minnesota Wild for future considerations (June 29, 2001).

Season Team	League	REGULAR SEASON								PLAYOFFS				
		Gms.	G	A	Pts.	PIM	+/-	PP	SH	Gms.	G	A	Pts.	PIM
90-91—Dynamo Riga	USSR	39	4	0	4	16	...	...	...	—	—	—	—	—
91-92—HC Riga	CIS	27	6	3	9	6	...	...	...	—	—	—	—	—
92-93—Providence	AHL	64	31	35	66	57	...	...	...	6	3	5	8	4
—Boston	NHL	1	0	1	1	0	1	0	0	—	—	—	—	—
93-94—Providence	AHL	54	29	33	62	16	...	...	...	—	—	—	—	—
—Boston	NHL	24	2	1	3	2	-7	1	0	—	—	—	—	—
94-95—Providence	AHL	78	23	35	58	42	...	...	...	13	8	5	13	6
95-96—Las Vegas	IHL	82	51	50	101	30	...	...	...	15	7	13	20	6
96-97—Las Vegas	IHL	19	13	14	27	20	...	...	...	—	—	—	—	—
—Ottawa	NHL	57	12	16	28	19	2	5	0	7	1	1	2	0
97-98—Ottawa	NHL	78	10	13	23	16	-7	7	0	11	0	2	2	0
98-99—Montreal	NHL	70	7	15	22	6	-12	2	0	—	—	—	—	—
—Fredericton	AHL	7	3	4	7	0	...	...	...	—	—	—	—	—
99-00—Quebec	AHL	1	0	1	1	2	...	...	...	—	—	—	—	—
—Montreal	NHL	68	26	12	38	28	2	9	0	—	—	—	—	—
00-01—Montreal	NHL	32	1	10	11	8	-15	0	0	—	—	—	—	—
—Edmonton	NHL	37	4	16	20	22	8	1	0	3	0	0	0	0
NHL Totals (7 years)		367	62	84	146	101	-28	25	0	21	1	3	4	0

ZIEGLER, THOMAS — RW — LIGHTNING

PERSONAL: Born June 9, 1978, in Zurich, Switzerland. ... 5-11/174. ... Shoots left.
TRANSACTIONS/CAREER NOTES: Selected by Tampa Bay Lightning in ninth round (10th Lightning pick, 263rd overall) of NHL entry draft (June 24, 2000).

Season Team	League	REGULAR SEASON								PLAYOFFS				
		Gms.	G	A	Pts.	PIM	+/-	PP	SH	Gms.	G	A	Pts.	PIM
96-97—Zurich	Switzerland Jr.	34	19	11	30	...	...	...	...	—	—	—	—	—
—Zurich	Switz. Div. 2	11	0	1	1	2	...	...	...	—	—	—	—	—
97-98—Zurich	Switzerland	10	0	0	0	2	...	...	...	—	—	—	—	—
—Zurich	Switzerland Jr.	13	9	3	12	32	...	...	...	—	—	—	—	—
—Zurich	Switz. Div. 2	25	5	4	9	22	...	...	...	—	—	—	—	—
98-99—Ambri-Piotta	Switzerland	38	2	4	6	18	...	...	...	12	0	0	0	8
—Sierre	Switzerland	4	1	2	3	2	...	...	...	—	—	—	—	—
99-00—Ambri-Piotta	Switzerland	45	7	7	14	24	...	...	...	9	1	5	6	16
00-01—Detroit	IHL	67	8	19	27	40	...	...	...	—	—	—	—	—
—Tampa Bay	NHL	5	0	0	0	0	-2	0	0	—	—	—	—	—
NHL Totals (1 year)		5	0	0	0	0	-2	0	0					

ZION, JON — D — MAPLE LEAFS

PERSONAL: Born May 21, 1981, in Nepean, Ont. ... 6-0/187. ... Shoots left. ... Full Name: Jonathan Zion.
TRANSACTIONS/CAREER NOTES: Selected by Toronto Maple Leafs in fourth round (fourth Maple Leafs pick, 110th overall) of NHL entry draft (June 26, 1999).
HONORS: Named to OHL All-Rookie second team (1997-98). ... Named to OHL All-Star second team (2000-01). ... Named to Can.HL All-Star second team (2000-01).

Season Team	League	REGULAR SEASON								PLAYOFFS				
		Gms.	G	A	Pts.	PIM	+/-	PP	SH	Gms.	G	A	Pts.	PIM
97-98—Ottawa	OHL	53	4	19	23	20	...	...	...	13	3	12	15	2
98-99—Ottawa	OHL	60	8	33	41	10	...	...	...	9	2	3	5	8
99-00—Ottawa	OHL	66	7	52	59	16	...	...	...	11	3	10	13	8
00-01—Ottawa	OHL	59	22	51	73	38	...	...	...	20	3	*19	22	18

ZIZKA, TOMAS   D   KINGS

PERSONAL: Born October 10, 1979, in Sternberk, Czechoslovakia. ... 6-1/198. ... Shoots left.
TRANSACTIONS/CAREER NOTES: Selected by Los Angeles Kings in sixth round (sixth Kings pick, 163rd overall) of NHL entry draft (June 27, 1998).

Season Team	League	Gms.	G	A	Pts.	PIM	+/-	PP	SH	Gms.	G	A	Pts.	PIM
						REGULAR SEASON						PLAYOFFS		
94-95—ZPS Zlin	CzechRep.Jrs.	39	1	10	11	...	...	...	...	—	—	—	—	—
95-96—ZPS Zlin	CzechRep.Jrs.	47	2	8	10	...	...	...	...	—	—	—	—	—
96-97—ZPS Zlin	CzechRep.Jrs.	14	1	0	1	...	...	...	...	—	—	—	—	—
97-98—ZPS Zlin	Czech Rep.	33	0	3	3	2	...	...	...	—	—	—	—	—
—ZPS Zlin	CzechRep.Jrs.	11	3	4	7	...	...	...	...	—	—	—	—	—
98-99—ZPS Zlin	Czech Rep.	44	3	7	10	14	...	...	...	11	1	2	3	...
99-00—HC Barum Zlin	Czech Rep.	46	4	6	10	30	...	...	...	4	1	0	1	4
00-01—HC Continental Zlin	Czech Rep.	43	2	11	13	16	...	...	...	6	0	0	0	6

ZUBOV, SERGEI   D   STARS

PERSONAL: Born July 22, 1970, in Moscow, U.S.S.R. ... 6-1/200. ... Shoots right. ... Name pronounced SAIR-gay ZOO-bahf.
TRANSACTIONS/CAREER NOTES: Selected by New York Rangers in fifth round (sixth Rangers pick, 85th overall) of NHL entry draft (June 16, 1990). ... Suffered concussion (February 26, 1993); missed one game. ... Suffered from the flu (February 4, 1995); missed one game. ... Underwent wrist surgery (February 27, 1995); missed nine games. ... Traded by Rangers with C Petr Nedved to Pittsburgh Penguins for LW Luc Robitaille and D Ulf Samuelsson (August 31, 1995). ... Fractured finger (October 9, 1995); missed nine games. ... Reinjured finger (November 11, 1995); missed seven games. ... Bruised shoulder (March 31, 1996); missed one game. ... Traded by Penguins to Dallas Stars for D Kevin Hatcher (June 22, 1996). ... Suffered from the flu (November 20, 1996); missed one game. ... Suffered back spasms (January 24, 1997); missed two games. ... Sprained neck (March 4, 1998); missed nine games. ... Bruised wrist (April 14, 1999); missed one game. ... Sprained medial collateral ligament in knee (March 29, 2000); missed final five games of season. ... Bruised shoulder (January 6, 2001); missed two games.
HONORS: Played in NHL All-Star Game (1998-2000).
MISCELLANEOUS: Member of Stanley Cup championship team (1994 and 1999). ... Member of gold-medal-winning Unified Olympic team (1992).

Season Team	League	Gms.	G	A	Pts.	PIM	+/-	PP	SH	Gms.	G	A	Pts.	PIM
						REGULAR SEASON						PLAYOFFS		
88-89—CSKA Moscow	USSR	29	1	4	5	10	...	...	...	—	—	—	—	—
89-90—CSKA Moscow	USSR	48	6	2	8	16	...	...	...	—	—	—	—	—
90-91—CSKA Moscow	USSR	41	6	5	11	12	...	...	...	—	—	—	—	—
91-92—CSKA Moscow	CIS	36	4	7	11	6	...	...	...	—	—	—	—	—
—Unif. Olympic team	Int'l	8	0	1	1	0	...	...	...	—	—	—	—	—
92-93—CSKA Moscow	CIS	1	0	1	1	0	...	...	...	—	—	—	—	—
—Binghamton	AHL	30	7	29	36	14	...	...	...	11	5	5	10	2
—New York Rangers	NHL	49	8	23	31	4	-1	3	0	—	—	—	—	—
93-94—New York Rangers	NHL	78	12	77	89	39	20	9	0	22	5	14	19	0
—Binghamton	AHL	2	1	2	3	0	...	...	...	—	—	—	—	—
94-95—New York Rangers	NHL	38	10	26	36	18	-2	6	0	10	3	8	11	2
95-96—Pittsburgh	NHL	64	11	55	66	22	28	3	2	18	1	14	15	26
96-97—Dallas	NHL	78	13	30	43	24	19	1	0	7	0	3	3	2
97-98—Dallas	NHL	73	10	47	57	16	16	5	1	17	4	5	9	2
98-99—Dallas	NHL	81	10	41	51	20	9	5	0	23	1	12	13	4
99-00—Dallas	NHL	77	9	33	42	18	-2	3	1	18	2	7	9	6
00-01—Dallas	NHL	79	10	41	51	24	22	6	0	10	1	5	6	4
NHL Totals (9 years)		617	93	373	466	185	109	41	4	125	17	68	85	46

ZUBRUS, DAINIUS   RW   CAPITALS

PERSONAL: Born June 16, 1978, in Elektrenai, U.S.S.R. ... 6-4/224. ... Shoots left. ... Name pronounced DIGH-nuhz ZOO-bruhz.
TRANSACTIONS/CAREER NOTES: Selected by Philadelphia Flyers in first round (first Flyers pick, 15th overall) of NHL entry draft (June 22, 1996). ... Bruised right hand (October 8, 1997); missed two games. ... Reinjured right hand (October 15, 1997); missed five games. ... Suspended two games and fined $1,000 by NHL for slashing incident (April 2, 1998). ... Strained left hamstring (December 15, 1997); missed one game. ... Traded by Flyers with second-round pick (D Matt Carkner) in 1999 draft to Montreal Canadiens for RW Mark Recchi (March 10, 1999). ... Strained hip flexor (October 20, 1999); missed one game. ... Injured back (October 27, 1999); missed one game. ... Suffered back spasms (January 4, 2000); missed one game. ... Suffered concussion (February 27, 2000); missed six games. ... Injured ribcage (September 27, 2000); missed first two games of season. ... Suffered concussion (December 21, 2000); missed one game. ... Traded by Canadiens with C Trevor Linden and second-round pick (traded to Tampa Bay) in 2001 draft to Washington Capitals for F Jan Bulis, F Richard Zednik and first-round pick (C Alexander Perezhogin) in 2001 draft (March 13, 2001).
MISCELLANEOUS: Failed to score on a penalty shot (vs. Dominik Hasek, November 3, 2000).
STATISTICAL PLATEAUS: Three-goal games: 2000-01 (1).

Season Team	League	Gms.	G	A	Pts.	PIM	+/-	PP	SH	Gms.	G	A	Pts.	PIM
						REGULAR SEASON						PLAYOFFS		
95-96—Pembroke	CJHL	28	19	13	32	73	...	...	...	—	—	—	—	—
—Caledon	Jr. A	7	3	7	10	2	...	...	...	17	11	12	23	4
96-97—Philadelphia	NHL	68	8	13	21	22	3	1	0	19	5	4	9	12
97-98—Philadelphia	NHL	69	8	25	33	42	29	1	0	5	0	1	1	2
98-99—Philadelphia	NHL	63	3	5	8	25	-5	0	1	—	—	—	—	—
—Montreal	NHL	17	3	5	8	4	-3	0	0	—	—	—	—	—
99-00—Montreal	NHL	73	14	42	54	-1	3	0		—	—	—	—	—
00-01—Montreal	NHL	49	12	12	24	30	-7	3	0	—	—	—	—	—
—Washington	NHL	12	1	1	2	7	-4	1	0	6	0	0	0	2
NHL Totals (5 years)		351	49	89	138	184	12	9	1	30	5	5	10	16

ZULTEK, MATT   LW   FLYERS

PERSONAL: Born March 12, 1979, in Windsor, Ont. ... 6-3/218. ... Shoots left. ... Name pronounced ZOHL-tehk.
TRANSACTIONS/CAREER NOTES: Selected by Los Angeles Kings in first round (second Kings pick, 15th overall) of NHL entry draft (June 21, 1997). ... Returned to draft pool by Kings and selected by Boston Bruins in second round (second Bruins pick, 56th overall) of NHL entry draft (June 26, 1999). ... Traded by Bruins to Philadelphia Flyers for ninth-round pick (LW Marcel Rodman) in 2001 draft (February 13, 2001).
HONORS: Named to OHL All-Rookie second team (1996-97).

		REGULAR SEASON								PLAYOFFS				
Season Team	League	Gms.	G	A	Pts.	PIM	+/-	PP	SH	Gms.	G	A	Pts.	PIM
95-96—Caledon	Jr. A	50	19	14	33	40	...	...	...	—	—	—	—	—
96-97—Ottawa	OHL	63	27	13	40	76	...	...	...	21	7	6	13	27
97-98—Ottawa	OHL	62	28	28	56	156	...	...	...	13	6	12	18	20
98-99—Ottawa	OHL	56	33	33	66	71	...	...	...	9	6	2	8	4
99-00—Ottawa	OHL	28	9	6	15	34	...	...	...	11	3	5	8	12
00-01—Philadelphia	AHL	16	1	4	5	6	...	...	...	9	0	1	1	8

ZYUZIN, ANDREI   D   LIGHTNING

PERSONAL: Born January 21, 1978, in Ufa, U.S.S.R. ... 6-1/210. ... Shoots left. ... Name pronounced ZYOO-zihn.
TRANSACTIONS/CAREER NOTES: Selected by San Jose Sharks in first round (first Sharks pick, second overall) of NHL entry draft (June 22, 1996). ... Suspended two playoff games by NHL for slashing incident (April 19, 1999). ... Traded by Sharks with D Bill Houlder, LW Shawn Burr and C Steve Guolla to Tampa Bay Lightning for LW Niklas Sundstrom and third-round pick (traded to Chicago) in 2000 draft (August 4, 1999). ... Injured shoulder (October 28, 1999); missed five games. ... Injured shoulder (January 11, 2000); missed remainder of season. ... Suffered concussion (November 20, 2000); missed five games. ... Suffered concussion (December 1, 2000); missed five games. ... Injured shoulder (January 30, 2001); missed two games. ... Sprained ankle (March 15, 2001); missed one game. ... Suffered concussion (March 21, 2001); missed three games.

		REGULAR SEASON								PLAYOFFS				
Season Team	League	Gms.	G	A	Pts.	PIM	+/-	PP	SH	Gms.	G	A	Pts.	PIM
94-95—Salavat Yulayev Ufa	CIS	30	3	0	3	16	...	...	...	—	—	—	—	—
95-96—Salavat Yulayev Ufa	CIS	41	6	3	9	24	...	...	...	2	0	0	0	4
96-97—Salavet Yulayev Ufa	USSR	32	7	10	17	28	...	...	...	7	1	1	2	4
97-98—San Jose	NHL	56	6	7	13	66	8	2	0	6	1	0	1	14
—Kentucky	AHL	17	4	5	9	28	...	...	...	—	—	—	—	—
98-99—San Jose	NHL	25	3	1	4	38	5	2	0	—	—	—	—	—
—Kentucky	AHL	23	2	12	14	42	...	...	...	—	—	—	—	—
99-00—Tampa Bay	NHL	34	2	9	11	33	-11	0	0	—	—	—	—	—
00-01—Tampa Bay	NHL	64	4	16	20	76	-8	2	1	—	—	—	—	—
—Detroit	IHL	2	0	1	1	0	...	...	...	—	—	—	—	—
NHL Totals (4 years)		179	15	33	48	213	-6	6	1	6	1	0	1	14

2001 TOP DRAFT PICKS

ARMSTRONG, COLBY — RW — PENGUINS

PERSONAL: Born November 23, 1982, in Lloydminster, Sask. ... 6-1/180. ... Shoots right.
TRANSACTIONS/CAREER NOTES: Selected by Pittsburgh Penguins in first round (first Penguins pick, 21st overall) of NHL entry draft (June 23, 2001).

		REGULAR SEASON					PLAYOFFS				
Season Team	League	Gms.	G	A	Pts.	PIM	Gms.	G	A	Pts.	PIM
98-99—Red Deer	WHL	1	0	1	1	0	—	—	—	—	—
99-00—Red Deer	WHL	68	13	25	38	122	2	0	1	1	11
00-01—Red Deer	WHL	72	36	42	78	156	21	6	6	12	39

BACASHIHUA, JASON — G — STARS

PERSONAL: Born September 20, 1982, in Garden City, Mich. ... 5-11/167. ... Catches right.
TRANSACTIONS/CAREER NOTES: Selected by Dallas Stars in first round (first Stars pick, 26th overall) of NHL entry draft (June 23, 2001).

		REGULAR SEASON							PLAYOFFS						
Season Team	League	Gms.	Min	W	L	T	GA	SO	Avg.	Gms.	Min.	W	L	GA	SO	Avg.
00-01—Chicago	NAHL	39	2246	24	14	0	121	1	3.23	3	187	1	2	11	0	3.53

BEDNAR, JAROSLAV — C — KINGS

PERSONAL: Born November 8, 1976, in Prague, Czechoslovakia. ... 5-11/198. ... Shoots right.
TRANSACTIONS/CAREER NOTES: Selected by Los Angeles Kings in second round (third Kings pick, 51st overall) of NHL entry draft (June 23, 2001).

		REGULAR SEASON					PLAYOFFS				
Season Team	League	Gms.	G	A	Pts.	PIM	Gms.	G	A	Pts.	PIM
99-00—JyP Jyvaskyla	Finland	53	34	28	62	56	—	—	—	—	—
00-01—HIFK Helsinki	Finland	56	32	28	60	51	5	3	1	4	0

BLACKBURN, DAN — G — RANGERS

PERSONAL: Born May 20, 1983, in Montreal. ... 6-0/180. ... Catches left.
TRANSACTIONS/CAREER NOTES: Selected by New York Rangers in first round (first Rangers pick, 10th overall) of NHL entry draft (June 23, 2001).
HONORS: Won Jim Piggott Memorial Trophy (1999-2000). ... Named to WHL (East) All-Star second team (1999-2000). ... Won Can.HL Rookie of the Year Award (1999-2000). ... Named to WHL (East) All-Star first team (2000-01). ... Won Del Wilson Trophy (2000-01). ... Named to Can.HL All-Star first team (2000-01). ... Won Can.HL Goaltender of the Year Award (2000-01).

		REGULAR SEASON							PLAYOFFS						
Season Team	League	Gms.	Min	W	L	T	GA	SO	Avg.	Gms.	Min.	W	L	GA	SO	Avg.
99-00—Kootenay	WHL	51	3004	34	8	7	126	3	2.52	*21	*1272	*16	5	*43	2	2.03
00-01—Kootenay	WHL	50	2922	33	14	2	135	1	2.77	11	706	7	4	23	1	1.95

BUDAJ, PETER — G — AVALANCHE

PERSONAL: Born September 18, 1982, in Banska Bystrica, Czechoslovakia. ... 6-0/200. ... Catches left.
TRANSACTIONS/CAREER NOTES: Selected by Colorado Avalanche in second round (first Avalanche pick, 63rd overall) of NHL entry draft (June 23, 2001).

		REGULAR SEASON							PLAYOFFS						
Season Team	League	Gms.	Min	W	L	T	GA	SO	Avg.	Gms.	Min.	W	L	GA	SO	Avg.
00-01—Toronto St. Michael's	OHL	37	1996	17	12	3	95	3	2.86	11	621	6	4	26	1	2.51

CAMMALLERI, MIKE — C — KINGS

PERSONAL: Born June 8, 1982, in Richmond Hill, Ont. ... 5-8/175. ... Shoots left.
TRANSACTIONS/CAREER NOTES: Selected by Los Angeles Kings in second round (third Kings pick, 49th overall) of NHL entry draft (June 23, 2001).
HONORS: Named to CCHA All-Star first team (2000-01).

		REGULAR SEASON					PLAYOFFS				
Season Team	League	Gms.	G	A	Pts.	PIM	Gms.	G	A	Pts.	PIM
99-00—Univ. of Michigan	CCHA	39	13	13	26	32	—	—	—	—	—
00-01—Univ. of Michigan	CCHA	42	29	32	61	24	—	—	—	—	—

CARON, ED — LW — OILERS

PERSONAL: Born April 30, 1982, in Nashua, N.H. ... 6-2/214. ... Shoots left. ... Full Name: Edward Caron.
TRANSACTIONS/CAREER NOTES: Selected by Edmonton Oilers in second round (third Oilers pick, 52nd overall) of NHL entry draft (June 23, 2001).

Season Team	League	REGULAR SEASON					PLAYOFFS				
		Gms.	G	A	Pts.	PIM	Gms.	G	A	Pts.	PIM
99-00—Phillips-Exeter	USHS (East)	26	22	26	48	24	—	—	—	—	—
00-01—Phillips-Exeter	USHS (East)	17	30	20	50	42	—	—	—	—	—

CHISTOV, STANISLAV   C/RW   MIGHTY DUCKS

PERSONAL: Born April 17, 1983, in Cheljabinsk, U.S.S.R. ... 5-9/169. ... Shoots right.
TRANSACTIONS/CAREER NOTES: Selected by Mighty Ducks of Anaheim in first round (first Mighty Ducks pick, fifth overall) of NHL entry draft (June 23, 2001).

Season Team	League	REGULAR SEASON					PLAYOFFS				
		Gms.	G	A	Pts.	PIM	Gms.	G	A	Pts.	PIM
99-00—Avangard Omsk	Russian	3	1	0	1	2	—	—	—	—	—
00-01—Avangard Omsk	Russian	24	4	8	12	12	5	0	0	0	2

COLAIACOVO, CARLO   D   MAPLE LEAFS

PERSONAL: Born January 27, 1983, in Toronto. ... 6-1/184. ... Shoots left. ... Name pronounced KOH-lee-ah-kovo.
TRANSACTIONS/CAREER NOTES: Selected by Toronto Maple Leafs in first round (first Maple Leafs pick, 17th overall) of NHL entry draft (June 23, 2001).

Season Team	League	REGULAR SEASON					PLAYOFFS				
		Gms.	G	A	Pts.	PIM	Gms.	G	A	Pts.	PIM
99-00—Erie	OHL	52	4	18	22	12	13	2	4	6	9
00-01—Erie	OHL	62	12	27	39	59	14	4	7	11	16

FOSTER, ADRIAN   LW   DEVILS

PERSONAL: Born January 15, 1982, in Lethbridge, Alta. ... 6-1/200. ... Shoots left.
TRANSACTIONS/CAREER NOTES: Selected by New Jersey Devils in first round (first Devils pick, 28th overall) of NHL entry draft (June 23, 2001).

Season Team	League	REGULAR SEASON					PLAYOFFS				
		Gms.	G	A	Pts.	PIM	Gms.	G	A	Pts.	PIM
99-00—Saskatoon	WHL	7	1	2	3	6	—	—	—	—	—
00-01—Saskatoon	WHL	5	0	5	5	4	—	—	—	—	—

GLEASON, TIM   D   SENATORS

PERSONAL: Born January 29, 1983, in Southfield, Mich. ... 6-0/199. ... Shoots left.
TRANSACTIONS/CAREER NOTES: Selected by Ottawa Senators in first round (second Senators pick, 23rd overall) of NHL entry draft (June 23, 2001).

Season Team	League	REGULAR SEASON					PLAYOFFS				
		Gms.	G	A	Pts.	PIM	Gms.	G	A	Pts.	PIM
99-00—Windsor	OHL	55	5	13	18	101	12	2	4	6	14
00-01—Windsor	OHL	47	8	26	34	124	9	1	2	3	23

GOC, MARCEL   C   SHARKS

PERSONAL: Born August 24, 1983, in Calv, West Germany. ... 6-1/187. ... Shoots left. ... Brother of Sasha Goc, defenseman, New Jersey Devils.
TRANSACTIONS/CAREER NOTES: Selected by San Jose Sharks in first round (first Sharks pick, 20th overall) of NHL entry draft (June 23, 2001).

Season Team	League	REGULAR SEASON					PLAYOFFS				
		Gms.	G	A	Pts.	PIM	Gms.	G	A	Pts.	PIM
99-00—Schwenningen	Germany	62	1	4	5	6	—	—	—	—	—
00-01—Schwenningen	Germany	58	13	28	41	12	—	—	—	—	—

GRIGORENKO, IGOR   RW   RED WINGS

PERSONAL: Born April 9, 1983, in Samara, U.S.S.R. ... 5-11/183. ... Shoots right.
TRANSACTIONS/CAREER NOTES: Selected by Detroit Red Wings in second round (first Red Wings pick, 62nd overall) of NHL entry draft (June 23, 2001).

Season Team	League	REGULAR SEASON					PLAYOFFS				
		Gms.	G	A	Pts.	PIM	Gms.	G	A	Pts.	PIM
00-01—Lada Togliatti	Russian				Statistics unavailable.						

HAMHUIS, DAN   D   PREDATORS

PERSONAL: Born December 13, 1982, in Smithers, B.C. ... 6-0/195. ... Shoots left. ... Name pronounced HAM-hoos.
TRANSACTIONS/CAREER NOTES: Selected by Nashville Predators in first round (first Predators pick, 12th overall) of NHL entry draft (June 23, 2001).

Season Team	League	REGULAR SEASON					PLAYOFFS				
		Gms.	G	A	Pts.	PIM	Gms.	G	A	Pts.	PIM
98-99—Prince George	WHL	56	1	3	4	45	7	1	2	3	8
99-00—Prince George	WHL	70	10	23	33	140	13	2	3	5	35
00-01—Prince George	WHL	62	13	46	59	125	6	2	3	5	15

HEMSKY, ALES — RW — OILERS

PERSONAL: Born August 13, 1983, in Pardubice, Czechoslovakia. ... 6-0/170. ... Shoots right.
TRANSACTIONS/CAREER NOTES: Selected by Edmonton Oilers in first round (first Oilers pick, 13th overall) of NHL entry draft (June 23, 2001).
HONORS: Won Mike Bossy Trophy (2000-01).

Season Team	League	REGULAR SEASON					PLAYOFFS				
		Gms.	G	A	Pts.	PIM	Gms.	G	A	Pts.	PIM
99-00—Pardubice	Czech. Jrs.	52	24	50	74	90	—	—	—	—	—
—HC Pardubice	Czech Rep.	4	0	1	1	0	—	—	—	—	—
00-01—Hull	QMJHL	68	36	64	100	67	5	2	3	5	2

HOLMQVIST, ANDREAS — D — LIGHTNING

PERSONAL: Born July 23, 1981, in Stockholm, Sweden. ... 6-3/187. ... Shoots right.
TRANSACTIONS/CAREER NOTES: Selected by Tampa Bay Lightning in second round (third Lightning pick, 61st overall) of NHL entry draft (June 23, 2001).

Season Team	League	REGULAR SEASON					PLAYOFFS				
		Gms.	G	A	Pts.	PIM	Gms.	G	A	Pts.	PIM
00-01—Hammarby	Sweden Jr.	47	6	15	21	40	—	—	—	—	—

JACKMAN, TIM — RW — BLUE JACKETS

PERSONAL: Born November 14, 1981, in Minot, N.D. ... 6-2/190. ... Shoots right.
TRANSACTIONS/CAREER NOTES: Selected by Columbus Blue Jackets in second round (second Blue Jackets pick, 38th overall) of NHL entry draft (June 23, 2001).

Season Team	League	REGULAR SEASON					PLAYOFFS				
		Gms.	G	A	Pts.	PIM	Gms.	G	A	Pts.	PIM
99-00—Park Center	USHS (West)	19	34	22	56	...	—	—	—	—	—
00-01—Minnesota-Mankato	WCHA	35	11	14	25	82	—	—	—	—	—

KARLSSON, JENS — RW/LW — KINGS

PERSONAL: Born November 7, 1982, in Goteburg, Sweden. ... 6-3/200. ... Shoots right.
TRANSACTIONS/CAREER NOTES: Selected by Los Angeles Kings in first round (first Kings pick, 18th overall) of NHL entry draft (June 23, 2001).

Season Team	League	REGULAR SEASON					PLAYOFFS				
		Gms.	G	A	Pts.	PIM	Gms.	G	A	Pts.	PIM
00-01—Vastra Frolunda	Sweden	19	2	0	2	4	5	1	3	4	50

KEITH, MATT — RW — BLACKHAWKS

PERSONAL: Born April 11, 1983, in Edmonton. ... 6-1/190. ... Shoots right.
TRANSACTIONS/CAREER NOTES: Selected by Chicago Blackhawks in second round (third Blackhawks pick, 59th overall) of NHL entry draft (June 23, 2001).

Season Team	League	REGULAR SEASON					PLAYOFFS				
		Gms.	G	A	Pts.	PIM	Gms.	G	A	Pts.	PIM
98-99—Spokane	WHL	7	1	0	1	4	—	—	—	—	—
99-00—Spokane	WHL	39	1	3	4	37	15	1	2	3	11
00-01—Spokane	WHL	33	13	14	27	63	12	1	3	4	14

KNYAZEV, IGOR — D — HURRICANES

PERSONAL: Born January 27, 1983, in Elektrosal, U.S.S.R. ... 6-0/183. ... Shoots left.
TRANSACTIONS/CAREER NOTES: Selected by Carolina Hurricanes in first round (first Hurricanes pick, 15th overall) of NHL entry draft (June 23, 2001).

Season Team	League	REGULAR SEASON					PLAYOFFS				
		Gms.	G	A	Pts.	PIM	Gms.	G	A	Pts.	PIM
00-01—Spartak	Russian Div. 1	43	6	3	9	66	—	—	—	—	—

KOBASEW, CHUCK — RW — FLAMES

PERSONAL: Born April 17, 1982, in Osoyoos, B.C. ... 5-11/195. ... Shoots right.
TRANSACTIONS/CAREER NOTES: Selected by Calgary Flames in first round (first Flames pick, 14th overall) of NHL entry draft (June 23, 2001).
HONORS: Named to Hockey East All-Star second team (2000-01). ... Named to NCAA All-Tournament team (2000-01). ... Named NCAA Tournament Most Valuable Player (2000-01).

Season Team	League	REGULAR SEASON					PLAYOFFS				
		Gms.	G	A	Pts.	PIM	Gms.	G	A	Pts.	PIM
99-00—Penticton	BCHL	58	54	52	106	...	—	—	—	—	—
00-01—Boston College	Hockey East	43	27	22	49	38	—	—	—	—	—

KOIVU, MIKKO — C — WILD

PERSONAL: Born March 12, 1983, in Turku, Finland. ... 6-2/183. ... Shoots left. ... Brother of Saku Koivu, center, Montreal Canadiens.
TRANSACTIONS/CAREER NOTES: Selected by Minnesota Wild in first round (first Wild pick, sixth overall) of NHL entry draft (June 23, 2001).

Season Team	League	REGULAR SEASON					PLAYOFFS				
		Gms.	G	A	Pts.	PIM	Gms.	G	A	Pts.	PIM
99-00—TPS Turku	Finland Jr.	30	4	8	12	22	—	—	—	—	—
00-01—TPS Turku	Finland Jr.	30	11	38	49	34	—	—	—	—	—
—TPS Turku	Finland	21	0	1	1	2	—	—	—	—	—

KOMISAREK, MIKE — D — CANADIENS

PERSONAL: Born January 19, 1982, in Islip Terrace, N.Y. ... 6-4/225. ... Shoots right.
TRANSACTIONS/CAREER NOTES: Selected by Montreal Canadiens in first round (first Canadiens pick, seventh overall) of NHL entry draft (June 23, 2001).

Season Team	League	REGULAR SEASON					PLAYOFFS				
		Gms.	G	A	Pts.	PIM	Gms.	G	A	Pts.	PIM
99-00—U.S. National	USHL	51	5	8	13	124	—	—	—	—	—
00-01—Univ. of Michigan	CCHA	41	4	12	16	77	—	—	—	—	—

KOVALCHUK, ILYA — RW — THRASHERS

PERSONAL: Born April 15, 1983, in Tver, U.S.S.R. ... 6-2/207. ... Shoots right.
TRANSACTIONS/CAREER NOTES: Selected by Atlanta Thrashers in first round (first Thrashers pick, first overall) of NHL entry draft (June 23, 2001).

Season Team	League	REGULAR SEASON					PLAYOFFS				
		Gms.	G	A	Pts.	PIM	Gms.	G	A	Pts.	PIM
00-01—Spartak	Russian Div. 1	40	28	18	46	78	—	—	—	—	—

KRAJICEK, LUKAS — D — PANTHERS

PERSONAL: Born March 11, 1983, in Prostejov, Czechoslovakia. ... 6-1/183. ... Shoots left.
TRANSACTIONS/CAREER NOTES: Selected by Florida Panthers in first round (second Panthers pick, 24th overall) of NHL entry draft (June 23, 2001).

Season Team	League	REGULAR SEASON					PLAYOFFS				
		Gms.	G	A	Pts.	PIM	Gms.	G	A	Pts.	PIM
99-00—Detroit	NAHL	53	5	22	27	61	—	—	—	—	—
00-01—Peterborough	OHL	61	8	27	35	53	7	0	5	5	0

LECLAIRE, PASCAL — G — BLUE JACKETS

PERSONAL: Born November 7, 1982, in Repentigny, Que. ... 6-1/185. ... Catches left.
TRANSACTIONS/CAREER NOTES: Selected by Columbus Blue Jackets in first round (first Blue Jackets pick, eighth overall) of NHL entry draft (June 23, 2001).

Season Team	League	REGULAR SEASON							PLAYOFFS						
		Gms.	Min	W	L	T	GA	SO	Avg.	Gms.	Min.	W	L	GA	SO	Avg.
98-99—Halifax	QMJHL	33	1828	19	11	1	96	2	3.15	1	17	0	0	2	0	7.06
99-00—Halifax	QMJHL	31	1729	16	8	4	103	1	3.57	5	198	1	2	12	0	3.64
00-01—Halifax	QMJHL	33	2111	14	16	5	126	1	3.58	2	109	0	2	10	0	5.50

LYNCH, DOUG — D — OILERS

PERSONAL: Born April 4, 1983, in North Vancouver. ... 6-3/205. ... Shoots left.
TRANSACTIONS/CAREER NOTES: Selected by Edmonton Oilers in second round (second Oilers pick, 43rd overall) of NHL entry draft (June 23, 2001).

Season Team	League	REGULAR SEASON					PLAYOFFS				
		Gms.	G	A	Pts.	PIM	Gms.	G	A	Pts.	PIM
98-99—Red Deer	WHL	2	0	1	1	2	—	—	—	—	—
99-00—Red Deer	WHL	65	9	5	14	57	4	0	0	0	5
00-01—Red Deer	WHL	72	12	37	49	181	21	1	9	10	30

McCLEMENT, JAY — C — BLUES

PERSONAL: Born March 2, 1983, in Kingston, Ont. ... 6-1/193. ... Shoots left.
TRANSACTIONS/CAREER NOTES: Selected by St. Louis Blues in second round (first Blues pick, 57th overall) of NHL entry draft (June 23, 2001).

Season Team	League	REGULAR SEASON					PLAYOFFS				
		Gms.	G	A	Pts.	PIM	Gms.	G	A	Pts.	PIM
99-00—Brampton	OHL	63	13	16	29	34	6	0	4	4	8
00-01—Brampton	OHL	66	30	19	49	61	9	4	2	6	10

McLEOD, KIEL   C   BLUE JACKETS

PERSONAL: Born December 30, 1982, in Fort Saskatchewan, Alta. ... 6-5/211. ... Shoots right. ... Brother of Gavin McLeod, defenseman, Ottawa Senators organization.
TRANSACTIONS/CAREER NOTES: Selected by Columbus Blue Jackets in second round (third Blue Jackets pick, 53rd overall) of NHL entry draft (June 23, 2001).

Season Team	League	REGULAR SEASON					PLAYOFFS				
		Gms.	G	A	Pts.	PIM	Gms.	G	A	Pts.	PIM
98-99—Kelowna	WHL	55	12	15	27	48	6	0	1	1	2
99-00—Kelowna	WHL	59	17	13	30	100	5	2	1	3	2
00-01—Kelowna	WHL	65	38	28	66	94	4	4	1	5	8

MEDVEDEV, ANDREI   G   FLAMES

PERSONAL: Born April 1, 1983, in Moscow, U.S.S.R. ... 6-0/202. ... Catches left.
TRANSACTIONS/CAREER NOTES: Selected by Calgary Flames in second round (third Flames pick, 56th overall) of NHL entry draft (June 23, 2001).

Season Team	League	REGULAR SEASON							PLAYOFFS						
		Gms.	Min	W	L	T	GA	SO	Avg.	Gms.	Min.	W	L	GA	SO	Avg.
00-01—Spartak	Russian Div. 1	9	...	...	...	...	...	...	2.55	—	—	—	—	—	—	—

MILROY, DUNCAN   RW   CANADIENS

PERSONAL: Born February 8, 1983, in Edmonton. ... 6-0/180. ... Shoots right.
TRANSACTIONS/CAREER NOTES: Selected by Montreal Canadiens in second round (third Canadiens pick, 37th overall) of NHL entry draft (June 23, 2001).

Season Team	League	REGULAR SEASON					PLAYOFFS				
		Gms.	G	A	Pts.	PIM	Gms.	G	A	Pts.	PIM
98-99—Swift Current	WHL	3	0	0	0	0	—	—	—	—	—
99-00—Swift Current	WHL	68	15	15	30	20	12	3	5	8	12
00-01—Swift Current	WHL	68	38	54	92	51	19	9	12	21	6

MORRISONN, SHAONE   D   BRUINS

PERSONAL: Born December 23, 1982, in Vancouver. ... 6-3/182. ... Shoots left. ... Name pronounced Shane.
TRANSACTIONS/CAREER NOTES: Selected by Boston Bruins in first round (first Bruins pick, 19th overall) of NHL entry draft (June 23, 2001).

Season Team	League	REGULAR SEASON					PLAYOFFS				
		Gms.	G	A	Pts.	PIM	Gms.	G	A	Pts.	PIM
99-00—Kamloops	WHL	57	1	6	7	80	4	0	0	0	6
00-01—Kamloops	WHL	61	13	25	38	132	4	0	0	0	6

MUNRO, ADAM   G   BLACKHAWKS

PERSONAL: Born November 12, 1982, in Burlington, Ont. ... 6-1/187. ... Catches left.
TRANSACTIONS/CAREER NOTES: Selected by Chicago Blackhawks in first round (second Blackhawks pick, 29th overall) of NHL entry draft (June 23, 2001).

Season Team	League	REGULAR SEASON							PLAYOFFS						
		Gms.	Min	W	L	T	GA	SO	Avg.	Gms.	Min.	W	L	GA	SO	Avg.
99-00—Erie	OHL	22	948	8	7	1	48	1	3.04	1	5	0	0	1	0	12.00
00-01—Erie	OHL	41	2283	26	6	6	88	4	2.31	10	509	6	2	27	1	3.18

NOVOTNY, JIRI   C   SABRES

PERSONAL: Born August 12, 1983, in Pelhrimov, Czechoslovakia. ... 6-2/187. ... Shoots right.
TRANSACTIONS/CAREER NOTES: Selected by Buffalo Sabres in first round (first Sabres pick, 22nd overall) of NHL entry draft (June 23, 2001).

Season Team	League	REGULAR SEASON					PLAYOFFS				
		Gms.	G	A	Pts.	PIM	Gms.	G	A	Pts.	PIM
99-00—Budejovice	Czech. Jrs.	39	11	12	23	14	—	—	—	—	—
00-01—Budejovice	Czech. Jrs.	33	10	10	20	...	—	—	—	—	—
—HC Ceske Budejovice	Czech Rep.	19	0	4	4	2	—	—	—	—	—

PAETSCH, NATHAN   D   CAPITALS

PERSONAL: Born March 30, 1983, in Humboldt, Sask. ... 6-0/195. ... Shoots left.
TRANSACTIONS/CAREER NOTES: Selected by Washington Capitals in second round (first Capitals pick, 58th overall) of NHL entry draft (June 23, 2001).

Season Team	League	REGULAR SEASON					PLAYOFFS				
		Gms.	G	A	Pts.	PIM	Gms.	G	A	Pts.	PIM
98-99—Moose Jaw	WHL	2	0	0	0	0	—	—	—	—	—
99-00—Moose Jaw	WHL	68	9	35	44	48	4	0	1	1	0
00-01—Moose Jaw	WHL	70	8	54	62	118	4	1	2	3	6

PEREZHOGIN, ALEXANDER   C   CANADIENS

PERSONAL: Born August 10, 1983, in Ust-Kamenogorsk, U.S.S.R. ... 5-11/185. ... Shoots left.
TRANSACTIONS/CAREER NOTES: Selected by Montreal Canadiens in first round (second Canadiens pick, 25th overall) of NHL entry draft (June 23, 2001).

Season Team	League	Gms.	G	A	Pts.	PIM	Gms.	G	A	Pts.	PIM
		REGULAR SEASON					PLAYOFFS				
00-01—Avangard	Rus. Div. II				Statistics unavailable.						

PIHLMAN, THOMAS   LW   DEVILS

PERSONAL: Born November 13, 1982, in Espoo, Finland. ... 6-2/205. ... Shoots left.
TRANSACTIONS/CAREER NOTES: Selected by New Jersey Devils in second round (third Devils pick, 48th overall) of NHL entry draft (June 23, 2001).

Season Team	League	Gms.	G	A	Pts.	PIM	Gms.	G	A	Pts.	PIM
		REGULAR SEASON					PLAYOFFS				
00-01—JyP Jyvaskyla	Finland	47	3	6	9	59	—	—	—	—	—

PILAR, KAREL   D   MAPLE LEAFS

PERSONAL: Born December 23, 1977, in Prague, Czechoslovakia. ... 6-3/207. ... Shoots right.
TRANSACTIONS/CAREER NOTES: Selected by Toronto Maple Leafs in second round (second Maple Leafs pick, 39th overall) of NHL entry draft (June 23, 2001).

Season Team	League	Gms.	G	A	Pts.	PIM	Gms.	G	A	Pts.	PIM
		REGULAR SEASON					PLAYOFFS				
99-00—Litvinov	Czech Rep.	49	2	12	14	53	7	0	0	0	4
00-01—Litvinov	Czech Rep.	52	12	26	38	52	4	1	1	2	25

PODLESAK, MARTIN   C   COYOTES

PERSONAL: Born September 26, 1982, in Melnik, Czechoslovakia. ... 6-6/200. ... Shoots left.
TRANSACTIONS/CAREER NOTES: Selected by Phoenix Coyotes in second round (third Coyotes pick, 45th overall) of NHL entry draft (June 23, 2001).

Season Team	League	Gms.	G	A	Pts.	PIM	Gms.	G	A	Pts.	PIM
		REGULAR SEASON					PLAYOFFS				
99-00—Sparta Praha	Czech. Jrs.	35	12	9	21	...	—	—	—	—	—
00-01—Tri-City	WHL	39	13	13	26	36	—	—	—	—	—
—Lethbridge	WHL	21	8	6	14	23	3	1	1	2	2

POHANKA, IGOR   C   DEVILS

PERSONAL: Born July 5, 1983, in Plestany, Czechoslovakia. ... 6-3/185. ... Shoots left.
TRANSACTIONS/CAREER NOTES: Selected by New Jersey Devils in second round (second Devils pick, 44th overall) of NHL entry draft (June 23, 2001).

Season Team	League	Gms.	G	A	Pts.	PIM	Gms.	G	A	Pts.	PIM
		REGULAR SEASON					PLAYOFFS				
99-00—Bratislava	Slov. Jr.	32	12	18	30	29	—	—	—	—	—
00-01—Prince Albert	WHL	70	16	33	49	24	—	—	—	—	—

POLUSHIN, ALEXANDER   C/LW   LIGHTNING

PERSONAL: Born May 8, 1983, in Kirov, U.S.S.R. ... 6-3/198. ... Shoots left.
TRANSACTIONS/CAREER NOTES: Selected by Tampa Bay Lightning in second round (second Lightning pick, 47th overall) of NHL entry draft (June 23, 2001).

Season Team	League	Gms.	G	A	Pts.	PIM	Gms.	G	A	Pts.	PIM
		REGULAR SEASON					PLAYOFFS				
00-01—Tver	Russian Div. 1	38	10	5	15	10	—	—	—	—	—

POMINVILLE, JASON   RW   SABRES

PERSONAL: Born November 30, 1982, in Repentigny, Que. ... 5-11/174. ... Shoots right.
TRANSACTIONS/CAREER NOTES: Selected by Buffalo Sabres in second round (fourth Sabres pick, 55th overall) of NHL entry draft (June 23, 2001).

Season Team	League	Gms.	G	A	Pts.	PIM	Gms.	G	A	Pts.	PIM
		REGULAR SEASON					PLAYOFFS				
98-99—Shawinigan	QMJHL	2	0	0	0	0	—	—	—	—	—
99-00—Shawinigan	QMJHL	60	4	17	21	12	13	2	3	5	0
00-01—Shawinigan	QMJHL	71	46	61	107	24	10	6	6	12	0

2001 TOP DRAFT PICKS

POPOVIC, MARK   D   MIGHTY DUCKS

PERSONAL: Born October 11, 1982, in Stoney Creek, Ont. ... 6-1/194. ... Shoots left.
TRANSACTIONS/CAREER NOTES: Selected by Mighty Ducks of Anaheim in second round (second Mighty Ducks pick, 35th overall) of NHL entry draft (June 23, 2001).

		REGULAR SEASON					PLAYOFFS				
Season Team	League	Gms.	G	A	Pts.	PIM	Gms.	G	A	Pts.	PIM
98-99—Toronto St. Michael's	OHL	60	6	26	32	46	—	—	—	—	—
99-00—Toronto St. Michael's	OHL	68	11	29	40	68	—	—	—	—	—
00-01—Toronto St. Michael's	OHL	61	7	35	42	54	18	3	5	8	22

ROY, DEREK   C   SABRES

PERSONAL: Born May 4, 1983, in Ottawa. ... 5-8/187. ... Shoots left.
TRANSACTIONS/CAREER NOTES: Selected by Buffalo Sabres in second round (second Sabres pick, 32nd overall) of NHL entry draft (June 23, 2001).
HONORS: Won Emms Family Award (1999-2000).

		REGULAR SEASON					PLAYOFFS				
Season Team	League	Gms.	G	A	Pts.	PIM	Gms.	G	A	Pts.	PIM
99-00—Kitchener	OHL	66	34	53	87	44	5	4	1	5	6
00-01—Kitchener	OHL	65	42	39	81	114	—	—	—	—	—

RUUTU, TUOMO   C/RW   BLACKHAWKS

PERSONAL: Born February 16, 1983, in Vantaa, Finland. ... 6-2/196. ... Shoots left. ... Brother of Jarkko Ruutu, right wing, Vancouver Canucks; brother of Mikko Ruutu, left wing, Ottawa Senators organization.
TRANSACTIONS/CAREER NOTES: Selected by Chicago Blackhawks in first round (first Blackhawks pick, ninth overall) of NHL entry draft (June 23, 2001).

		REGULAR SEASON					PLAYOFFS				
Season Team	League	Gms.	G	A	Pts.	PIM	Gms.	G	A	Pts.	PIM
99-00—HIFK Helsinki	Finland Jr.	35	11	16	27	32	—	—	—	—	—
00-01—Jokerit	Finland	47	11	11	22	86	5	0	0	0	4

SHISKANOV, TIMOFEI   RW/LW   PREDATORS

PERSONAL: Born June 10, 1983, in Moscow, U.S.S.R. ... 6-0/183. ... Shoots right.
TRANSACTIONS/CAREER NOTES: Selected by Nashville Predators in second round (second Predators pick, 33rd overall) of NHL entry draft (June 23, 2001).

		REGULAR SEASON					PLAYOFFS				
Season Team	League	Gms.	G	A	Pts.	PIM	Gms.	G	A	Pts.	PIM
00-01—Spartak	Russian Jr.	13	0	0	0	0	—	—	—	—	—

SJOSTROM, FREDRIK   RW   COYOTES

PERSONAL: Born May 6, 1983, in Fargelanda, Sweden. ... 6-0/194. ... Shoots left.
TRANSACTIONS/CAREER NOTES: Selected by Phoenix Coyotes in first round (first Coyotes pick, 11th overall) of NHL entry draft (June 23, 2001).

		REGULAR SEASON					PLAYOFFS				
Season Team	League	Gms.	G	A	Pts.	PIM	Gms.	G	A	Pts.	PIM
99-00—MoDo Ornskoldsvik	Sweden Jr.	14	4	4	8	2	—	—	—	—	—
00-01—V. Frolunda Goteborg	Sweden Jr.	7	2	5	7	6	—	—	—	—	—
—Vastra Frolunda	Sweden	31	2	3	5	6	5	0	0	0	2

SLOVAK, TOMAS   D   PREDATORS

PERSONAL: Born April 5, 1983, in Kosice, Czechoslovakia. ... 6-1/191. ... Shoots right.
TRANSACTIONS/CAREER NOTES: Selected by Nashville Predators in second round (third Predators pick, 42nd overall) of NHL entry draft (June 23, 2001).

		REGULAR SEASON					PLAYOFFS				
Season Team	League	Gms.	G	A	Pts.	PIM	Gms.	G	A	Pts.	PIM
99-00—VSZ Kosice	Slovakia	2	0	0	0	0	—	—	—	—	—
00-01—HC Kosice	Slovakia	43	5	5	10	28	3	1	0	1	2

SPEZZA, JASON   C   SENATORS

PERSONAL: Born June 13, 1983, in Mississaugua, Ont. ... 6-2/214. ... Shoots right. ... Name pronounced speh-ZUH.
TRANSACTIONS/CAREER NOTES: Selected by Ottawa Senators in first round (first Senators pick, second overall) of NHL entry draft (June 23, 2001).
HONORS: Won Can.HL Top Draft Prospect Award (2000-01).

		REGULAR SEASON					PLAYOFFS				
Season Team	League	Gms.	G	A	Pts.	PIM	Gms.	G	A	Pts.	PIM
98-99—Brampton	OHL	67	22	49	71	18	—	—	—	—	—
99-00—Mississauga	OHL	52	24	37	61	33	—	—	—	—	—
00-01—Mississauga	OHL	15	7	23	30	11	—	—	—	—	—
—Windsor	OHL	41	36	50	86	32	9	4	5	9	10

SPILLER, MATTHEW — D — COYOTES

PERSONAL: Born February 7, 1983, in Daysland, Alta. ... 6-5/210. ... Shoots left.
TRANSACTIONS/CAREER NOTES: Selected by Phoenix Coyotes in second round (second Coyotes pick, 31st overall) of NHL entry draft (June 23, 2001).

		REGULAR SEASON					PLAYOFFS				
Season Team	League	Gms.	G	A	Pts.	PIM	Gms.	G	A	Pts.	PIM
99-00—Seattle	WHL	60	1	10	11	108	7	0	0	0	25
00-01—Seattle	WHL	71	4	7	11	174	9	1	0	1	22

STECKEL, DAVID — C — KINGS

PERSONAL: Born March 15, 1982, in Milwaukee. ... 6-5/200. ... Shoots left.
TRANSACTIONS/CAREER NOTES: Selected by Los Angeles Kings in first round (second Kings pick, 30th overall) of NHL entry draft (June 23, 2001).

		REGULAR SEASON					PLAYOFFS				
Season Team	League	Gms.	G	A	Pts.	PIM	Gms.	G	A	Pts.	PIM
99-00—U.S. National	USHL	52	13	13	26	94	—	—	—	—	—
00-01—Ohio State	CCHA	33	17	18	35	80	—	—	—	—	—

SVITOV, ALEXANDER — C — LIGHTNING

PERSONAL: Born November 3, 1982, in Omsk, U.S.S.R. ... 6-3/198. ... Shoots left.
TRANSACTIONS/CAREER NOTES: Selected by Tampa Bay Lightning in first round (first Lightning pick, third overall) of NHL entry draft (June 23, 2001).

		REGULAR SEASON					PLAYOFFS				
Season Team	League	Gms.	G	A	Pts.	PIM	Gms.	G	A	Pts.	PIM
99-00—Avangard Omsk	Russian	18	3	3	6	45	6	1	0	1	16
00-01—Avangard Omsk	Russian	39	8	6	14	115	14	2	1	3	34

TARATUKHIN, ANDREI — C — FLAMES

PERSONAL: Born February 22, 1983, in Omsk, U.S.S.R. ... 6-0/198. ... Shoots left.
TRANSACTIONS/CAREER NOTES: Selected by Calgary Flames in second round (second Flames pick, 41st overall) of NHL entry draft (June 23, 2001).

		REGULAR SEASON					PLAYOFFS				
Season Team	League	Gms.	G	A	Pts.	PIM	Gms.	G	A	Pts.	PIM
00-01—Avangard Omsk	Rus. Div. II				Statistics unavailable.						

THORBURN, CHRIS — C — SABRES

PERSONAL: Born May 3, 1983, in Sault Ste. Marie, Ont. ... 6-2/190. ... Shoots right.
TRANSACTIONS/CAREER NOTES: Selected by Buffalo Sabres in second round (second Sabres pick, 50th overall) of NHL entry draft (June 23, 2001).

		REGULAR SEASON					PLAYOFFS				
Season Team	League	Gms.	G	A	Pts.	PIM	Gms.	G	A	Pts.	PIM
99-00—North Bay	OHL	56	12	8	20	33	6	0	2	2	0
00-01—North Bay	OHL	66	22	32	54	64	4	0	1	1	9

TJUTIN, FEDOR — D — RANGERS

PERSONAL: Born July 19, 1983, in Izhevsk, U.S.S.R. ... 6-3/202. ... Shoots left.
TRANSACTIONS/CAREER NOTES: Selected by New York Rangers in second round (second Rangers pick, 40th overall) of NHL entry draft (June 23, 2001).

		REGULAR SEASON					PLAYOFFS				
Season Team	League	Gms.	G	A	Pts.	PIM	Gms.	G	A	Pts.	PIM
00-01—SKA St. Petersburg	Russian	34	2	4	6	20	—	—	—	—	—

UCHEVATOV, VICTOR — D — DEVILS

PERSONAL: Born February 10, 1983, in Angarsk, U.S.S.R. ... 6-4/205. ... Shoots left.
TRANSACTIONS/CAREER NOTES: Selected by New Jersey Devils in second round (fourth Devils pick, 60th overall) of NHL entry draft (June 23, 2001).

		REGULAR SEASON					PLAYOFFS				
Season Team	League	Gms.	G	A	Pts.	PIM	Gms.	G	A	Pts.	PIM
00-01—Torpedo Yaroslavl	Russian				Statistics unavailable.						

UMBERGER, R.J. — C — CANUCKS

PERSONAL: Born May 3, 1982, in Pittsburgh. ... 6-2/200. ... Shoots left.
TRANSACTIONS/CAREER NOTES: Selected by Vancouver Canucks in first round (first Canucks pick, 16th overall) of NHL entry draft (June 23, 2001).

		REGULAR SEASON					PLAYOFFS				
Season Team	League	Gms.	G	A	Pts.	PIM	Gms.	G	A	Pts.	PIM
99-00—U.S. National	USHL	57	33	35	68	20	—	—	—	—	—
00-01—Ohio State	CCHA	32	14	23	37	18	—	—	—	—	—

WANVIG, KYLE   RW   WILD

PERSONAL: Born January 29, 1981, in Calgary. ... 6-2/197. ... Shoots right.
TRANSACTIONS/CAREER NOTES: Selected by Boston Bruins in third round (third Bruins pick, 89th overall) of NHL entry draft (June 26, 1999). ... Returned to draft pool by Bruins and selected by Minnesota Wild in second round (second Wild pick, 36th overall) of NHL entry draft (June 23, 2001).
HONORS: Named to WHL (East) All-Star second team (2000-01). ... Named to Can.HL All-Star second team (2000-01).

		REGULAR SEASON					PLAYOFFS				
Season Team	League	Gms.	G	A	Pts.	PIM	Gms.	G	A	Pts.	PIM
97-98—Edmonton	WHL	62	17	12	29	69	—	—	—	—	—
98-99—Kootenay	WHL	71	12	20	32	119	7	1	3	4	18
99-00—Kootenay	WHL	6	2	2	4	12	—	—	—	—	—
—Red Deer	WHL	58	21	18	39	123	4	1	0	1	4
00-01—Red Deer	WHL	69	55	46	101	202	22	10	12	22	47

WATSON, GREG   C   PANTHERS

PERSONAL: Born March 2, 1983, in Eastend, Sask. ... 6-1/177. ... Shoots left.
TRANSACTIONS/CAREER NOTES: Selected by Florida Panthers in second round (third Panthers pick, 34th overall) of NHL entry draft (June 23, 2001).

		REGULAR SEASON					PLAYOFFS				
Season Team	League	Gms.	G	A	Pts.	PIM	Gms.	G	A	Pts.	PIM
98-99—Prince Albert	WHL	2	0	0	0	5	—	—	—	—	—
99-00—Prince Albert	WHL	67	10	5	15	63	6	0	2	2	2
00-01—Prince Albert	WHL	71	22	28	50	72	—	—	—	—	—

WEISS, STEPHEN   C   PANTHERS

PERSONAL: Born April 3, 1983, in Toronto. ... 5-11/178. ... Shoots left.
TRANSACTIONS/CAREER NOTES: Selected by Florida Panthers in first round (first Panthers pick, fourth overall) of NHL entry draft (June 23, 2001).

		REGULAR SEASON					PLAYOFFS				
Season Team	League	Gms.	G	A	Pts.	PIM	Gms.	G	A	Pts.	PIM
99-00—Plymouth	OHL	64	24	42	66	35	23	8	18	26	18
00-01—Plymouth	OHL	62	40	47	87	45	18	7	16	23	10

WELCH, NOAH   D   PENGUINS

PERSONAL: Born August 26, 1982, in Brighton, Mass. ... 6-3/212. ... Shoots left.
TRANSACTIONS/CAREER NOTES: Selected by Pittsburgh Penguins in second round (second Penguins pick, 54th overall) of NHL entry draft (June 23, 2001).

		REGULAR SEASON					PLAYOFFS				
Season Team	League	Gms.	G	A	Pts.	PIM	Gms.	G	A	Pts.	PIM
99-00—St. Sebastian's	USHS (East)	26	4	11	15	35	—	—	—	—	—
00-01—St. Sebastian's	USHS (East)	30	11	20	31	37	—	—	—	—	—

WOYWITKA, JEFF   D   FLYERS

PERSONAL: Born September 1, 1983, in Vermillion, Alta. ... 6-2/197. ... Shoots left.
TRANSACTIONS/CAREER NOTES: Selected by Philadelphia Flyers in first round (first Flyers pick, 27th overall) of NHL entry draft (June 23, 2001).

		REGULAR SEASON					PLAYOFFS				
Season Team	League	Gms.	G	A	Pts.	PIM	Gms.	G	A	Pts.	PIM
99-00—Red Deer	WHL	67	4	12	16	40	4	0	3	3	2
00-01—Red Deer	WHL	72	7	28	35	113	22	2	8	10	25

ZIGOMANIS, MIKE   C   HURRICANES

PERSONAL: Born January 17, 1981, in North York, Ont. ... 6-0/183. ... Shoots right. ... Full Name: Michael Zigomanis.
TRANSACTIONS/CAREER NOTES: Selected by Buffalo Sabres in second round (fourth Sabres pick, 64th overall) of NHL entry draft (June 22, 1999). ... Returned to draft pool by Sabres and selected by Carolina Hurricanes in second round (second Hurricanes pick, 46th overall) of NHL entry draft (June 23, 2001).
HONORS: Won William Hanley Trophy (1999-2000).

		REGULAR SEASON					PLAYOFFS				
Season Team	League	Gms.	G	A	Pts.	PIM	Gms.	G	A	Pts.	PIM
97-98—Kingston	OHL	62	23	51	74	30	12	1	6	7	2
98-99—Kingston	OHL	67	29	56	85	36	5	1	7	8	2
99-00—Kingston	OHL	59	40	54	94	49	5	0	4	4	0
00-01—Kingston	OHL	52	40	37	77	44	—	—	—	—	—

BARBER, BILL — FLYERS

PERSONAL: Born July 11, 1952, in Callander, Ont. ... Shot left.
TRANSACTIONS/CAREER NOTES: Selected by Philadelphia Flyers in first round (first Flyers pick, seventh overall) of 1972 NHL amateur draft.
HONORS: Named to NHL All-Star first team (1975-76). ... Played in NHL All-Star Game (1975, 1976, 1978, 1980, 1981 and 1982). ... Named to NHL All-Star second team (1978-79 and 1980-81).
MISCELLANEOUS: Member of Hockey Hall of Fame (1990). ... Member of Stanley Cup championship team (1973-74 and 1974-75). ... Captain of Philadelphia Flyers (1981-82 and 1982-83). ... Holds Philadelphia Flyers all-time record for most goals (420). ... Failed to score on a penalty shot (May 7, 1975, vs. Glenn Resch [playoffs]). ... Played left wing.
STATISTICAL PLATEAUS: Three-goal games: 1973-74 (1), 1975-76 (2), 1979-80 (1), 1980-81 (1), 1983-84 (1). Total: 6.

		REGULAR SEASON								PLAYOFFS				
Season Team	League	Gms.	G	A	Pts.	PIM	+/-	PP	SH	Gms.	G	A	Pts.	PIM
69-70—Kitchener	OHA	54	37	49	86	42	...	...	...	—	—	—	—	—
70-71—Kitchener	OHA	61	46	59	105	129	...	...	...	—	—	—	—	—
71-72—Kitchener	OHA	62	44	63	107	89	...	...	...	—	—	—	—	—
72-73—Philadelphia	NHL	69	30	34	64	46	10	7	0	11	3	2	5	22
—Richmond	AHL	11	9	5	14	4	...	...	...	—	—	—	—	—
73-74—Philadelphia	NHL	75	34	35	69	54	34	9	2	17	3	6	9	18
74-75—Philadelphia	NHL	79	34	37	71	66	46	8	5	17	6	9	15	8
75-76—Philadelphia	NHL	80	50	62	112	104	74	15	4	16	6	7	13	18
76-77—Philadelphia	NHL	73	20	35	55	62	32	3	0	10	1	4	5	2
77-78—Philadelphia	NHL	80	41	31	72	34	31	8	4	12	6	3	9	2
78-79—Philadelphia	NHL	79	34	46	80	22	19	10	6	8	3	4	7	10
79-80—Philadelphia	NHL	79	40	32	72	17	39	7	2	19	12	9	21	23
80-81—Philadelphia	NHL	80	43	42	85	69	6	16	2	12	11	5	16	0
81-82—Philadelphia	NHL	80	45	44	89	85	4	13	4	4	1	5	6	4
82-83—Philadelphia	NHL	66	27	33	60	28	17	5	2	3	1	1	2	2
83-84—Philadelphia	NHL	63	22	32	54	36	4	3	0	—	—	—	—	—
NHL Totals (12 years)		903	420	463	883	623	316	104	31	129	53	55	108	109

HEAD COACHING RECORD

BACKGROUND: Director of Pro Scouting, Philadelphia Flyers (1988-89 through 1995-96). ... Assistant coach, Flyers (1985-86 through 1987-88, January 1994 through 1994-95 and July 2000-December 10, 2000).
HONORS: Won Jack Adams Award (2000-01).
STATISTICAL PLATEAUS: Three-goal games: 1973-74 (1), 1975-76 (2), 1979-80 (1), 1980-81 (1), 1983-84 (1). Total: 6.

		REGULAR SEASON						PLAYOFFS		
Season Team	League	W	L	T	RT	Pct.	Finish	W	L	Pct.
84-85—Hershey	AHL	6	9	1	—	.406	6th/Southern Division	—	—	—
95-96—Hershey	AHL	22	19	7	—	.531	2nd/Southern Division	2	3	.400
96-97—Philadelphia	AHL	49	21	10	—	.675	1st/Mid-Atlantic Division	6	4	.600
97-98—Philadelphia	AHL	47	23	10	—	.650	1st/Mid-Atlantic Division	15	5	.750
98-99—Philadelphia	AHL	47	24	9	—	.644	1st/Mid-Atlantic Division	9	7	.563
99-00—Philadelphia	AHL	44	33	3	—	.569	3rd/Mid-Atlantic Division	2	3	.400
00-01—Philadelphia	NHL	31	16	7	0	.639	2nd/Atlantic Division	2	4	.333
NHL Totals (1 year)		31	16	7	0	.639	**NHL Totals (1 year)**	2	4	.333

NOTES:
95-96—Lost to Baltimore in conference quarterfinals in Calder Cup playoffs.
96-97—Defeated Baltimore in conference quarterfinals in Calder Cup playoffs; lost to Hershey in conference semifinals of Calder Cup playoffs.
97-98—Defeated Rochester in conference quarterfinals in Calder Cup playoffs; defeated Hershey in conference semifinals in Calder Cup playoffs; defeated Albany in conference finals of Calder Cup playoffs; defeated Saint John in Calder Cup finals.
98-99—Defeated Cincinnati in conference quarterfinals in Calder Cup playoffs; defeated Kentucky in conference semifinals in Calder Cup playoffs; lost to Rochester in conference finals in Calder Cup playoffs.
99-00—Lost to Hershey in conference quarterfinals in Calder Cup playoffs.
00-01—Replaced Craig Ramsay as head coach (December 10); lost to Buffalo in Eastern Conference quarterfinals.

BOWMAN, SCOTTY — RED WINGS

PERSONAL: Born September 18, 1933, in Montreal. ... Full Name: William Scott Bowman.
HONORS: Member of Hockey Hall of Fame (1991).

HEAD COACHING RECORD

BACKGROUND: Minor league hockey supervisor, Montreal Canadiens organization (1954-55 through 1956-57). ... Coach, Team Canada (1976 and 1981). ... Director of hockey operations/general manager, Buffalo Sabres (1979-80 through 1986-87). ... Director of player development, Pittsburgh Penguins (1990-91). ... Director of player personnel, Detroit Red Wings (1994-95 through 1996-97).
HONORS: Won Jack Adams Award (1976-77 and 1995-96). ... Named NHL Executive of the Year by THE SPORTING NEWS (1979-80). ... Named NHL Coach of the Year by THE SPORTING NEWS (1995-96 and 2000-01).
RECORDS: Holds NHL career regular-season records for wins—1,193; and winning percentage—.655. ... Holds NHL career playoff records for wins—207; and games—330.

		REGULAR SEASON						PLAYOFFS		
Season Team	League	W	L	T	RT	Pct.	Finish	W	L	Pct.
67-68—St. Louis	NHL	23	21	14	—	.517	3rd/Western Division	8	10	.444
68-69—St. Louis	NHL	37	25	14	—	.579	1st/Western Division	8	4	.667
69-70—St. Louis	NHL	37	27	12	—	.566	1st/Western Division	8	8	.500
70-71—St. Louis	NHL	13	10	5	—	.554	2nd/West Division	2	4	.333
71-72—Montreal	NHL	46	16	16	—	.692	3rd/Eastern Division	2	4	.333

Season Team	League	REGULAR SEASON						PLAYOFFS		
		W	L	T	RT	Pct.	Finish	W	L	Pct.
72-73—Montreal	NHL	52	10	16	—	.769	1st/East Division	12	5	.706
73-74—Montreal	NHL	45	24	9	—	.635	2nd/East Division	2	4	.333
74-75—Montreal	NHL	47	14	19	—	.706	1st/Adams Division	6	5	.545
75-76—Montreal	NHL	58	11	11	—	.794	1st/Adams Division	12	1	.923
76-77—Montreal	NHL	60	8	12	—	.825	1st/Adams Division	12	2	.857
77-78—Montreal	NHL	59	10	11	—	.806	1st/Adams Division	12	3	.800
78-79—Montreal	NHL	52	17	11	—	.719	1st/Adams Division	12	4	.750
79-80—Buffalo	NHL	47	17	16	—	.688	1st/Adams Division	9	5	.643
81-82—Buffalo	NHL	18	10	7	—	.614	3rd/Adams Division	1	3	.250
82-83—Buffalo	NHL	38	29	13	—	.556	3rd/Adams Division	6	4	.600
83-84—Buffalo	NHL	48	25	7	—	.644	2nd/Adams Division	0	3	.000
84-85—Buffalo	NHL	38	28	14	—	.563	3rd/Adams Division	2	3	.400
85-86—Buffalo	NHL	18	18	1	—	.500	5th/Adams Division	—	—	—
86-87—Buffalo	NHL	3	7	2	—	.333	5th/Adams Division	—	—	—
91-92—Pittsburgh	NHL	39	32	9	—	.544	3rd/Patrick Division	16	5	.762
92-93—Pittsburgh	NHL	56	21	7	—	.708	1st/Patrick Division	7	5	.583
93-94—Detroit	NHL	46	30	8	—	.595	1st/Central Division	3	4	.429
94-95—Detroit	NHL	33	11	4	—	.729	1st/Central Division	12	6	.667
95-96—Detroit	NHL	62	13	7	—	.799	1st/Central Division	10	9	.526
96-97—Detroit	NHL	38	26	18	—	.573	2nd/Central Division	16	4	.800
97-98—Detroit	NHL	44	23	15	—	.628	2nd/Central Division	16	6	.727
98-99—Detroit	NHL	39	31	7	—	.552	1st/Central Division	6	4	.600
99-00—Detroit	NHL	48	24	10	2	.646	2nd/Central Division	5	4	.556
00-01—Detroit	NHL	49	20	9	4	.686	1st/Central Division	2	4	.333
NHL Totals (29 years)		1193	558	304	6	.655	**NHL Totals (27 years)**	207	123	.627

NOTES:

67-68—Defeated Philadelphia in Western Division finals; defeated Minnesota in Stanley Cup semifinals; lost to Montreal in Stanley Cup finals.
68-69—Defeated Philadelphia in Stanley Cup quarterfinals; defeated Los Angeles in Stanley Cup semifinals; lost to Montreal in Stanley Cup finals.
69-70—Defeated Minnesota in Stanley Cup quarterfinals; defeated Pittsburgh in Stanley Cup semifinals; lost to Montreal in Stanley Cup finals.
70-71—Lost to Minnesota in Stanley Cup quarterfinals.
71-72—Lost to New York Rangers in Stanley Cup quarterfinals.
72-73—Defeated Buffalo in Stanley Cup quarterfinals; defeated Philadelphia in Stanley Cup semifinals; defeated Chicago in Stanley Cup finals.
73-74—Lost to New York Rangers in Stanley Cup quarterfinals.
74-75—Defeated Vancouver in Stanley Cup quarterfinals; lost to Buffalo in Stanley Cup semifinals.
75-76—Defeated Chicago in Stanley Cup quarterfinals; defeated New York Islanders in Stanley Cup semifinals; defeated Philadelphia in Stanley Cup finals.
76-77—Defeated St. Louis in Stanley Cup quarterfinals; defeated New York Islanders in Stanley Cup semifinals; defeated Boston in Stanley Cup finals.
77-78—Defeated Detroit in Stanley Cup quarterfinals; defeated Toronto in Stanley Cup semifinals; defeated Boston in Stanley Cup finals.
78-79—Defeated Toronto in Stanley Cup quarterfinals; defeated Boston in Stanley Cup semifinals; defeated New York Rangers in Stanley Cup finals.
79-80—Defeated Vancouver in Stanley Cup preliminary round; defeated Chicago in Stanley Cup quarterfinals; lost to New York Islanders in Stanley Cup semifinals.
81-82—Lost to Boston in Stanley Cup preliminary round.
82-83—Defeated Montreal in Adams Division semifinals; lost to Boston in Adams Division finals.
83-84—Lost to Quebec in Adams Division semifinals.
84-85—Lost to Quebec in Adams Division semifinals.
86-87—Replaced on interim basis by Craig Ramsay (November 1986).
91-92—Defeated Washington in Patrick Division semifinals; defeated New York Rangers in Patrick Division finals; defeated Boston in Wales Conference finals; defeated Chicago in Stanley Cup finals.
92-93—Defeated New Jersey in Patrick Division semifinals; lost to New York Islanders in Patrick Division finals.
93-94—Lost to San Jose in Western Conference quarterfinals.
94-95—Defeated Dallas in Western Conference quarterfinals; defeated San Jose in Western Conference semifinals; defeated Chicago in Western Conference finals; lost to New Jersey in Stanley Cup finals.
95-96—Defeated Winnipeg in Western Conference quarterfinals; defeated St. Louis in Western Conference semifinals; lost to Colorado in Western Conference finals.
96-97—Defeated St. Louis in Western Conference quarterfinals; defeated Anaheim in Western Conference semifinals; defeated Colorado in Western Conference finals; defeated Philadelphia in Stanley Cup finals.
97-98—Defeated Phoenix in Western Conference quarterfinals; defeated St. Louis in Western Conference semifinals; defeated Dallas in Western Conference finals; defeated Washington in Stanley Cup finals.
98-99—Missed first five games of season due to illness; defeated Anaheim in Western Conference quarterfinals; lost to Colorado in Western Conference semifinals.
99-00—Defeated Los Angeles in Western Conference quarterfinals; lost to Colorado in Western Conference semifinals.
00-01—Lost to Los Angeles in Western Conference quarterfinals.

CRAWFORD, MARC — CANUCKS

PERSONAL: Born February 13, 1961, in Belleville, Ont. ... Shot left. ... Full Name: Marc Joseph John Crawford. ... Brother of Bob Crawford, right winger with four NHL teams (1979-80 and 1981-82 through 1986-87).
TRANSACTIONS/CAREER NOTES: Selected by Vancouver Canucks in fourth round (third Canucks pick, 70th overall) of NHL entry draft (June 11, 1980). ... Suspended three games by NHL for leaving bench to fight (February 3, 1987).
MISCELLANEOUS: Played left wing.

Season Team	League	REGULAR SEASON								PLAYOFFS				
		Gms.	G	A	Pts.	PIM	+/-	PP	SH	Gms.	G	A	Pts.	PIM
79-80—Cornwall	OHL	54	27	36	63	127	...	...	...	18	8	20	28	48
80-81—Cornwall	OHL	63	42	57	99	242	...	...	...	19	20	15	35	27
81-82—Dallas	CHL	34	13	21	34	71	...	...	...	—	—	—	—	—
—Vancouver	NHL	40	4	8	12	29	0	0	0	14	1	0	1	11
82-83—Vancouver	NHL	41	4	5	9	28	-3	0	0	3	0	1	1	25
—Fredericton	AHL	30	15	9	24	59	...	...	...	9	1	3	4	10
83-84—Vancouver	NHL	19	0	1	1	9	0	0	0	—	—	—	—	—
—Fredericton	AHL	56	9	22	31	96	...	...	...	7	4	2	6	23
84-85—Vancouver	NHL	1	0	0	0	4	-4	0	0	—	—	—	—	—

Season Team	League	Gms.	G	A	Pts.	PIM	+/-	PP	SH	Gms.	G	A	Pts.	PIM
		REGULAR SEASON								**PLAYOFFS**				
85-86—Vancouver	NHL	54	11	14	25	92	-7	0	0	3	0	1	1	8
—Fredericton	AHL	26	10	14	24	55	...	...	...	—	—	—	—	—
86-87—Vancouver	NHL	21	0	3	3	67	-8	0	0	—	—	—	—	—
—Fredericton	AHL	25	8	11	19	21	...	...	...	—	—	—	—	—
87-88—Fredericton	AHL	43	5	13	18	90	...	...	...	2	0	0	0	14
88-89—Milwaukee	IHL	53	23	30	53	166	...	...	...	11	2	5	7	26
NHL Totals (6 years)		176	19	31	50	229	-22	0	0	20	1	2	3	44

HEAD COACHING RECORD

BACKGROUND: Player/assistant coach, Fredericton Express of AHL (1987-88). ... Nordiques franchise moved to Denver for 1995-96 season and renamed Colorado Avalanche. ... Hockey analyst, CBC television (1998-January 24, 1999).

HONORS: Won Louis A.R. Pieri Memorial Award (1992-93). ... Named NHL Coach of the Year by THE SPORTING NEWS (1994-95). ... Won Jack Adams Award (1994-95).

Season Team	League	W	L	T	RT	Pct.	Finish	W	L	Pct.
		REGULAR SEASON						**PLAYOFFS**		
89-90—Cornwall	OHL	24	38	4	—	.394	6th/Leyden Division	2	4	.333
90-91—Cornwall	OHL	23	42	1	—	.356	7th/Leyden Division	—	—	—
91-92—St. John's	AHL	39	29	12	—	.563	2nd/Atlantic Division	11	5	.688
92-93—St. John's	AHL	41	26	13	—	.594	1st/Atlantic Division	4	5	.444
93-94—St. John's	AHL	45	23	12	—	.638	1st/Atlantic Division	6	5	.545
94-95—Quebec	NHL	30	13	5	—	.677	1st/Northeast Division	2	4	.333
95-96—Colorado	NHL	47	25	10	—	.634	1st/Pacific Division	16	6	.727
96-97—Colorado	NHL	49	24	9	—	.652	1st/Pacific Division	10	7	.588
97-98—Colorado	NHL	39	26	17	—	.579	1st/Pacific Division	3	4	.429
98-99—Vancouver	NHL	8	23	6	—	.297	4th/Northwest Division	—	—	—
99-00—Vancouver	NHL	30	37	15	8	.457	3rd/Northwest Division	—	—	—
00-01—Vancouver	NHL	36	28	11	7	.553	3rd/Northwest Division	0	4	.000
NHL Totals (7 years)		239	176	73	15	.565	**NHL Totals (5 years)**	31	25	.554

NOTES:
89-90—Lost to Oshawa in Leyden Division quarterfinals.
91-92—Defeated Cape Breton in first round of Calder Cup playoffs; defeated Moncton in second round of Calder Cup playoffs; lost to Adirondack in Calder Cup finals.
92-93—Defeated Moncton in first round of Calder Cup playoffs; lost to Cape Breton in second round of Calder Cup playoffs.
93-94—Defeated Cape Breton in first round of Calder Cup playoffs; lost to Moncton in second round of Calder Cup playoffs.
94-95—Lost to New York Rangers in Eastern Conference quarterfinals.
95-96—Defeated Vancouver in Western Conference quarterfinals; defeated Chicago in Western Conference semifinals; defeated Detroit in Western Conference finals; defeated Florida in Stanley Cup finals.
96-97—Defeated Chicago in Western Conference quarterfinals; defeated Edmonton in Western Conference semifinals; lost to Detroit in Western Conference finals.
97-98—Lost to Edmonton in Western Conference quarterfinals.
98-99—Replaced Mike Keenan as head coach (January 24).
00-01—Lost to Colorado in Western Conference quarterfinals.

FRANCIS, BOBBY   COYOTES

PERSONAL: Born December 5, 1958, in North Battleford, Sask. ... Son of Emile Francis, goaltender with Chicago Blackhawks (1946-47 and 1947-48) and New York Rangers (1948-49 through 1951-52); and head coach with New York Rangers (1965-66 through 1974-75) and St. Louis Blues (1976-77, 1981-82 and 1982-83).
TRANSACTIONS/CAREER NOTES: Signed as non-drafted free agent by Calgary Flames (October 27, 1980). ... Traded by Flames to Detroit Red Wings for the rights to RW Yves Courteau (December 2, 1982).
HONORS: Named to CHL All-Star first team (1981-82). ... Won Ken McKenzie Trophy (1981-82). ... Won Tommy Ivan Trophy (1981-82).
MISCELLANEOUS: Played center.

Season Team	League	Gms.	G	A	Pts.	PIM	+/-	PP	SH	Gms.	G	A	Pts.	PIM
		REGULAR SEASON								**PLAYOFFS**				
72-73—Brooklyn	NYJHL	38	36	34	70	44	...	...	...	—	—	—	—	—
73-74—Brooklyn	NYJHL	41	41	53	94	63	...	...	...	12	17	11	28	24
74-75—Bronx	NYJHL	40	53	59	112	71	...	...	...	—	—	—	—	—
75-76—Beawick	NEJHL	40	62	74	136	61	...	...	...	—	—	—	—	—
76-77—Univ. of New Hamp.	Hockey East						Did not play.							
77-78—Univ. of New Hamp.	Hockey East	40	9	44	53	...	...	...	...	—	—	—	—	—
78-79—Univ. of New Hamp.	Hockey East	35	20	46	66	44	...	...	...	—	—	—	—	—
79-80—Univ. of New Hamp.	Hockey East	28	19	23	42	30	...	...	...	—	—	—	—	—
80-81—Birmingham	CHL	18	6	21	27	20	...	...	...	—	—	—	—	—
—Muskegon	IHL	27	16	17	33	33	...	...	...	—	—	—	—	—
81-82—Oklahoma City	CHL	80	48	66	114	76	...	...	...	4	1	2	3	11
82-83—Colorado	CHL	26	20	16	36	24	...	...	...	—	—	—	—	—
—Detroit	NHL	14	2	0	2	0	-1	0	0	—	—	—	—	—
—Adirondack	AHL	17	3	8	11	0	...	...	...	—	—	—	—	—
83-84—Colorado	CHL	68	32	50	82	53	...	...	...	1	0	1	1	0
84-85—Salt Lake City	IHL	53	24	16	40	36	...	...	...	6	1	1	2	0
85-86—Salt Lake City	IHL	82	32	44	76	163	...	...	...	5	0	4	4	10
86-87—Salt Lake City	IHL	82	29	69	98	86	...	...	...	17	9	8	17	13
NHL Totals (1 year)		14	2	0	2	0	-1	0	0					

HEAD COACHING RECORD

BACKGROUND: Assistant coach, Salt Lake City Golden Eagles of IHL (1986-87 through 1988-89). ... Assistant coach, Boston Bruins (1997-98 and 1998-99).

Season Team	League	REGULAR SEASON W	L	T	RT	Pct.	Finish	PLAYOFFS W	L	Pct.
89-90—Salt Lake City	IHL	37	36	9	—	.506	2nd/West Division	5	6	.455
90-91—Salt Lake City	IHL	50	28	5	—	.633	2nd/West Division	0	4	.000
91-92—Salt Lake City	IHL	33	40	9	—	.457	4th/West Division	1	4	.200
92-93—Salt Lake City	IHL	38	39	5	—	.494	2nd/Pacific Division	—	—	—
93-94—Saint John	AHL	37	33	10	—	.525	2nd/Atlantic Division	3	4	.429
94-95—Saint John	AHL	27	40	13	—	.419	4th/Atlantic Division	1	4	.200
95-96—Providence	AHL	30	40	10	—	.438	4th/Northern Division	1	3	.250
96-97—Providence	AHL	35	40	5	—	.469	4th/New England Division	4	6	.400
99-00—Phoenix	NHL	39	35	8	4	.524	3rd/Pacific Division	1	4	.200
00-01—Phoenix	NHL	35	27	17	3	.551	4th/Pacific Division	—	—	—
NHL Totals (2 years)		74	62	25	7	.537	NHL Totals (1 year)	1	4	.200

NOTES:
89-90—Defeated Milwaukee in quarterfinals of Turner Cup playoffs; lost to Indianapolis in semifinals of Turner Cup playoffs.
90-91—Lost to Phoenix in Turner Cup quarterfinals.
91-92—Lost to Kansas City in West Division quarterfinals.
93-94—Lost to Moncton in Atlantic Division semifinals.
94-95—Lost to Prince Edward Island in Atlantic Division semifinals.
95-96—Lost to Springfield in Eastern Conference quarterfinals.
96-97—Defeated Worcester in Southern Conference quarterfinals; lost to Springfield in Southern Conference semifinals.
99-00—Lost to Colorado in Western Conference quarterfinals.

FRASER, CURT — THRASHERS

PERSONAL: Born January 12, 1958, in Cincinnati. ... Shot left.
TRANSACTIONS/CAREER NOTES: Selected by Vancouver Canucks in second round of 1978 amateur draft. ... Traded by Canucks to Chicago Blackhawks for RW Tony Tanti (January 3, 1983). ... Tore knee ligaments (November 1983). ... Fractured bone in face (January 13, 1985). ... Sprained shoulder (December 14, 1985); missed 19 games. ... Bruised ribs (October 1987). ... Suffered from virus (November 1987). ... Traded by Blackhawks to Minnesota North Stars for LW Dirk Graham (January 4, 1988). ... Injured ribs (October 1988). ... Injured wrist (January 1989). ... Injured shoulder and underwent surgery (January 15, 1989). ... Missed most of 1989-90 season due to shoulder rehabilitation.
MISCELLANEOUS: Played left wing.

Season Team	League	REGULAR SEASON Gms.	G	A	Pts.	PIM	+/-	PP	SH	PLAYOFFS Gms.	G	A	Pts.	PIM
73-74—Kelowna	JR.ABCHL	52	32	32	64	85	...	...	...	—	—	—	—	—
74-75—Victoria	WCHL	68	17	32	49	105	...	...	...	—	—	—	—	—
75-76—Victoria	WCHL	71	43	64	107	167	...	...	...	—	—	—	—	—
76-77—Victoria	WCHL	60	34	41	75	82	...	...	...	4	4	2	6	4
77-78—Victoria	WCHL	66	48	44	92	256	...	...	...	13	10	7	17	28
78-79—Vancouver	NHL	78	16	19	35	116	-7	2	0	3	0	2	2	6
79-80—Vancouver	NHL	78	17	25	42	143	7	0	0	4	0	0	0	2
80-81—Vancouver	NHL	77	25	24	49	118	-19	7	0	3	1	0	1	2
81-82—Vancouver	NHL	79	28	39	67	175	2	11	0	17	3	7	10	98
82-83—Vancouver	NHL	36	6	7	13	99	-7	2	0	—	—	—	—	—
—Chicago	NHL	38	6	13	19	77	2	0	0	13	4	4	8	18
83-84—Chicago	NHL	29	5	12	17	26	9	1	0	5	0	0	0	14
84-85—Chicago	NHL	73	25	25	50	109	3	4	0	15	6	3	9	36
85-86—Chicago	NHL	61	29	39	68	84	11	7	0	3	0	1	1	12
86-87—Chicago	NHL	75	25	25	50	182	5	3	0	2	1	1	2	10
87-88—Chicago	NHL	27	4	6	10	57	-13	1	0	—	—	—	—	—
—Minnesota	NHL	10	1	1	2	20	-7	0	0	—	—	—	—	—
88-89—Minnesota	NHL	35	5	5	10	76	-15	1	0	—	—	—	—	—
89-90—Minnesota	NHL	8	1	0	1	22	-5	0	0	—	—	—	—	—
NHL Totals (12 years)		704	193	240	433	1304	-34	39	0	65	15	18	33	198

HEAD COACHING RECORD

BACKGROUND: Assistant coach, Milwaukee Admirals of IHL (1990-91 and 1991-92). ... Associate coach, Syracuse Crunch of AHL (1994-95).

Season Team	League	REGULAR SEASON W	L	T	RT	Pct.	Finish	PLAYOFFS W	L	Pct.
92-93—Milwaukee	IHL	49	23	10	—	.659	1st/Midwest Division	2	4	.333
93-94—Milwaukee	IHL	40	24	17	—	.599	2nd/Midwest Division	0	4	.000
95-96—Orlando	IHL	52	24	6	—	.671	1st/Central Division	11	12	.478
96-97—Orlando	IHL	53	24	5	—	.677	2nd/Northeast Division	4	6	.400
97-98—Orlando	IHL	42	30	10	—	.573	2nd/Northeast Division	9	8	.529
98-99—Orlando	IHL	45	33	4	—	.573	2nd/Northeast Division	10	7	.588
99-00—Atlanta	NHL	14	61	7	4	.213	5th/Southeast Division	—	—	—
00-01—Atlanta	NHL	23	45	12	2	.363	4th/Southeast Division	—	—	—
NHL Totals (2 years)		37	106	19	6	.287				

NOTES:
92-93—Lost to Kansas City in Western Conference quarterfinals.
93-94—Lost to Atlanta in Western Conference quarterfinals.
95-96—Defeated Fort Wayne in Eastern Conference quarterfinals; defeated Detroit in Eastern Conference semifinals; defeated Cincinnati in Eastern Conference finals; lost to Utah in Turner Cup Finals.
96-97—Defeated Grand Rapids in Eastern Conference quarterfinals; lost to Cleveland in Eastern Conference semifinals.
97-98—Defeated Indianapolis in Eastern Conference quarterfinals; defeated Cleveland in Eastern Conference semifinals; lost to Detroit in Eastern Conference finals.
98-99—Defeated Michigan in Eastern Conference semifinals; defeated Detroit in Eastern Conference finals; lost to Houston in Turner Cup finals.

PERSONAL: Born January 2, 1952, in Needham, Mass. ... Full Name: Robert Brian Ftorek.

TRANSACTIONS/CAREER NOTES: Signed as non-drafted free agent by Detroit Red Wings (October 1, 1972). ... Signed as free agent by Phoenix Roadrunners of World Hockey Association (1974). ... Sold to Cincinnati Stingers (May 30, 1977). ... Claimed by Quebec Nordiques in the World Hockey Association dispersal draft (June 1979). ... Traded by Nordiques with eighth-round pick (D Bryan Glynn) in 1982 draft to New York Rangers for LW Jere Gillis and RW Dean Talafous (December 1981); Nordiques acquired Pat Hickey due to Dean Talafous retirement. ... Announced retirement to become head coach of New Haven Nighthawks (July 1985).

HONORS: Named The Sporting News WHA Player of the Year (1978-79). ... Named Most Valuable Player in WHA (1976-77).

MISCELLANEOUS: Played center.

		REGULAR SEASON								PLAYOFFS				
Season Team	League	Gms.	G	A	Pts.	PIM	+/-	PP	SH	Gms.	G	A	Pts.	PIM
72-73—Virginia	AHL	55	17	42	59	36	...	...	...	5	2	2	4	4
—Detroit	NHL	3	0	0	0	0	0	0	0	—	—	—	—	—
73-74—Virginia	AHL	65	24	42	66	37	...	...	...	—	—	—	—	—
—Detroit	NHL	12	2	5	7	4	1	1	0	—	—	—	—	—
74-75—Tulsa	CHL	11	6	10	16	14	...	...	...	—	—	—	—	—
—Phoenix	WHA	53	31	37	68	29	...	...	...	5	2	5	7	2
75-76—Phoenix	WHA	80	41	72	113	109	...	...	...	5	1	3	4	2
76-77—Phoenix	WHA	80	46	71	117	86	...	...	...	—	—	—	—	—
77-78—Cincinnati	WHA	80	59	50	109	54	...	...	...	—	—	—	—	—
78-79—Cincinnati	WHA	80	39	77	116	87	...	...	...	3	3	2	5	6
79-80—Quebec	NHL	52	18	33	51	28	6	7	0	—	—	—	—	—
80-81—Quebec	NHL	78	24	49	73	104	-19	8	0	5	1	2	3	17
81-82—Quebec	NHL	19	1	8	9	4	-2	0	0	—	—	—	—	—
—New York Rangers	NHL	30	8	24	32	24	8	2	0	10	7	4	11	11
82-83—New York Rangers	NHL	61	12	19	31	41	11	1	0	4	1	0	1	0
83-84—New York Rangers	NHL	31	3	2	5	22	2	0	0	—	—	—	—	—
—Tulsa	CHL	25	11	11	22	10	...	...	...	9	4	5	9	2
84-85—New Haven	AHL	17	9	7	16	30	...	...	...	—	—	—	—	—
—New York Rangers	NHL	48	9	10	19	35	-7	0	1	—	—	—	—	—
85-86—New Haven	AHL	1	0	0	0	0	...	...	...	—	—	—	—	—
WHA Totals (5 years)		373	216	307	523	365	...	...	...	13	6	10	16	10
NHL Totals (8 years)		334	77	150	227	262	0	19	1	19	9	6	15	28

HEAD COACHING RECORD

BACKGROUND: Player/assistant coach, New Haven Nighthawks of AHL (1984-85). ... Assistant coach, Quebec Nordiques (1989-90 and 1990-91). ... Assistant coach, New Jersey Devils (1991-92, 1996-97 and 1997-98).

HONORS: Won Louis A. R. Pieri Memorial Award (1994-95 and 1995-96).

		REGULAR SEASON						PLAYOFFS		
Season Team	League	W	L	T	RT	Pct.	Finish	W	L	Pct.
85-86—New Haven	AHL	36	37	7	—	.494	4th/South Division	1	4	.200
86-87—New Haven	AHL	44	25	11	—	.619	3rd/South Division	3	4	.429
87-88—New Haven	AHL	16	8	3	—	.648	—			
—Los Angeles	NHL	23	25	4	—	.481	4th/Smythe Division	1	4	.200
88-89—Los Angeles	NHL	42	31	7	—	.569	2nd/Smythe Division	4	7	.364
89-90—Halifax	AHL	25	19	4	—	.563	—			
92-93—Utica	AHL	33	36	11	—	.481	3rd/Southern Division	1	4	.200
93-94—Albany	AHL	38	34	8	—	.525	3rd/Northern Division	1	4	.200
94-95—Albany	AHL	46	17	17	—	.681	1st/Northern Division	12	2	.857
95-96—Albany	AHL	54	19	17	—	.694	1st/Central Division	1	3	.250
98-99—New Jersey	NHL	47	24	11	—	.640	1st/Atlantic Division	3	4	.429
99-00—New Jersey	NHL	41	25	8	0	.608	—			
NHL Totals (4 years)		153	105	30	0	.583	**NHL Totals (3 years)**	8	15	.348

NOTES:

85-86—Lost to Hershey in quarterfinals of Calder Cup playoffs.

86-87—Lost to Binghamton in quarterfinals of Calder Cup playoffs.

87-88—Replaced Mike Murphy as head coach (December 9, 1987) with club in fifth place; lost to Calgary in Smythe Division semifinals in Stanley Cup playoffs.

88-89—Defeated Edmonton in Smythe Division semifinals of Stanley Cup playoffs; lost to Calgary in Smythe Division finals of Stanley Cup playoffs.

92-93—Lost to Rochester in quarterfinals of Calder Cup playoffs.

93-94—Lost to Portland in quarterfinals of Calder Cup playoffs.

94-95—Defeated Adirondack in division semifinals of Calder Cup playoffs; defeated Providence in division finals of Calder Cup playoffs; defeated Fredericton in Calder Cup finals.

95-96—Lost to Cornwall in conference quarterfinals of Calder Cup playoffs.

98-99—Lost to Pittsburgh in Eastern Conference quarterfinals.

99-00—Replaced as head coach by Larry Robinson with team in first place (March 23).

PERSONAL: Born January 22, 1967, in Mississauga, Ont. ... Shot left. ... Full Name: Gregory Scott Gilbert.

TRANSACTIONS/CAREER NOTES: Selected by New York Islanders in fourth round (fifth Islanders pick, 80th overall) of NHL entry draft (June 11, 1984). ... Stretched ligaments in left ankle (September 1984). ... Injured ligaments in knee and underwent surgery (February 27, 1985). ... Fractured jaw (October 11, 1986); missed 10 games. ... Bruised thigh (December 7, 1986). ... Bruised hip (February 1987). ... Separated right shoulder (March 1987). ... Bruised right knee (February 20, 1988). ... Injured left foot (April 1988). ... Suffered back spasms and injured left shoulder (February 1989). ... Traded by Islanders to Chicago Blackhawks for fifth-round pick (RW Steve Young) in 1989 draft (March 7, 1989). ... Fractured foot (March 1989). ... Strained abdominal muscle during practice (March 8, 1990). ... Bruised left shoulder (September 28, 1990); missed first eight games of season. ... Hyperextended left knee (April 1991). ... Pulled lateral muscle (November 13, 1991); missed two games. ... Fractured ankle (February 16, 1992). ... Strained left knee (April 4, 1992). ... Suffered from the flu (March 5, 1993); missed two games. ... Signed as free agent by New York Rangers (July 29, 1993). ... Suffered injury (January 14, 1994); missed two games. ... Sprained right knee (January 25, 1994); missed six games. ... Selected by St. Louis Blues in 1994-95 waiver draft for cash (January 18, 1995). ... Injured leg (March 12, 1995); missed one game. ... Reinjured leg (April 23, 1995); missed one game. ... Strained back (November 14, 1995); missed 59 games.

MISCELLANEOUS: Member of Stanley Cup championship teams (1982, 1983 and 1994).

						REGULAR SEASON							PLAYOFFS			
Season Team	League	Gms.	G	A	Pts.	PIM	+/-	PP	SH		Gms.	G	A	Pts.	PIM
79-80—Toronto	OMJHL	68	10	11	21	35	...	...	...		—	—	—	—	—
80-81—Toronto	OMJHL	64	30	37	67	73	...	...	...		5	2	6	8	16
81-82—Toronto	OHL	65	41	67	108	119	...	...	...		10	4	12	16	23
—New York Islanders	NHL	1	1	0	1	0	0	0	0		4	1	1	2	2
82-83—Indianapolis	CHL	24	11	16	27	23	...	...	...		—	—	—	—	—
—New York Islanders	NHL	45	8	11	19	30	1	0	0		10	1	0	1	14
83-84—New York Islanders	NHL	79	31	35	66	59	51	6	0		21	5	7	12	39
84-85—New York Islanders	NHL	58	13	25	38	36	-4	2	0		—	—	—	—	—
85-86—Springfield	AHL	2	0	0	0	2	...	...	...		—	—	—	—	—
—New York Islanders	NHL	60	9	19	28	82	5	1	0		2	0	0	0	9
86-87—New York Islanders	NHL	51	6	7	13	26	-12	0	0		10	2	2	4	6
87-88—New York Islanders	NHL	76	17	28	45	46	14	1	1		4	0	0	0	6
88-89—New York Islanders	NHL	55	8	13	21	45	1	0	0		—	—	—	—	—
—Chicago	NHL	4	0	0	0	0	1	0	0		15	1	5	6	20
89-90—Chicago	NHL	70	12	25	37	54	27	0	0		19	5	8	13	34
90-91—Chicago	NHL	72	10	15	25	58	6	1	0		5	0	1	1	2
91-92—Chicago	NHL	50	7	5	12	35	-4	0	0		10	1	3	4	16
92-93—Chicago	NHL	77	13	19	32	57	5	0	1		3	0	0	0	0
93-94—New York Rangers	NHL	76	4	11	15	29	-3	1	0		23	1	3	4	8
94-95—St. Louis	NHL	46	11	14	25	11	22	0	0		7	0	3	3	6
95-96—St. Louis	NHL	17	0	1	1	8	-1	0	0		—	—	—	—	—
NHL Totals (15 years)		**837**	**150**	**228**	**378**	**576**	**109**	**12**	**2**		**133**	**17**	**33**	**50**	**162**

HEAD COACHING RECORD

BACKGROUND: Assistant coach, Calgary Flames (2000-March 14, 2001).

HONORS: Won Louis A.R. Pieri Award (1996-97).

					REGULAR SEASON				PLAYOFFS		
Season Team	League	W	L	T	RT	Pct.	Finish		W	L	Pct.
96-97—Worcester	AHL	43	23	9	—	.633	1st/New England Division		2	3	.400
97-98—Worcester	AHL	34	31	9	—	.520	4th/New England Division		6	5	.545
98-99—Worcester	AHL	34	36	8	—	.487	4th/New England Division		1	3	.250
99-00—Worcester	AHL	34	31	11	4	.520	3rd/New England Division		4	5	.444
00-01—Calgary	NHL	4	8	2	0	.357	4th/Northwest Division		—	—	—
NHL Totals (1 year)		**4**	**8**	**2**	**0**	**.357**					

NOTES:

96-97—Lost to Providence in conference quarterfinals of Calder Cup playoffs.

97-98—Defeated Springfield in conference quarterfinals of Calder Cup playoffs; lost to Hartford in conference semifinals of Calder Cup playoffs.

98-99—Lost to Providence in conference quarterfinals of Calder Cup playoffs.

99-00—Defeated Portland in conference quarterfinals of Calder Cup playoffs; lost to Hartford in conference semifinals of Calder Cup playoffs.

00-01—Replaced Don Hay as head coach (March 14).

HARTLEY, BOB   AVALANCHE

PERSONAL: Born September 7, 1960, in Hawksbury, Ont. ... Full Name: Robert Hartley.

HEAD COACHING RECORD

					REGULAR SEASON				PLAYOFFS		
Season Team	League	W	L	T	RT	Pct.	Finish		W	L	Pct.
92-93—Laval	QMJHL	43	25	2	—	.629	1st/Robert Le Bel Division		12	1	.923
94-95—Cornwall	AHL	38	33	9	—	.531	2nd/Southern Division		8	6	.571
95-96—Cornwall	AHL	34	39	7	—	.469	4th/Central Division		3	5	.375
96-97—Hershey	AHL	43	22	10	—	.640	2nd/Mid-Atlantic Division		15	8	.652
97-98—Hershey	AHL	36	31	7	—	.534	2nd/Mid-Atlantic Division		3	4	.429
98-99—Colorado	NHL	44	28	10	—	.598	1st/ Northwest Division		11	8	.579
99-00—Colorado	NHL	42	29	11	1	.579	1st/Northwest Division		11	6	.647
00-01—Colorado	NHL	52	16	10	4	.731	1st/Northwest Division		16	7	.696
NHL Totals (3 years)		**138**	**73**	**31**	**5**	**.634**	**NHL Totals (3 years)**		**38**	**21**	**.644**

NOTES:

92-93—Defeated Verdun in quarterfinals of President Cup playoffs; defeated Drummondville in semifinals of President Cup playoffs; defeated Sherbrooke in finals of President Cup playoffs.

94-95—Defeated Hershey in division semifinals in Calder Cup playoffs; defeated Binghamton in division finals in Calder Cup playoffs; lost to Fredericton in league semifinals in Calder Cup playoffs.

95-96—Defeated Albany in conference quarterfinals in Calder Cup playoffs; lost to Rochester in conference finals in Calder Cup playoffs.

96-97—Defeated Kentucky in conference quarterfinals in Calder Cup playoffs; defeated Phliadelphia in conference semifinals in Calder Cup playoffs; defeated Springfield in conference finals in Calder Cup playoffs; defeated Hamilton in Calder Cup finals.

97-98—Defeated Kentucky in conference quarterfinals in Calder Cup playoffs; lost to Philadelphia in conference semifinals in Calder Cup playoffs.

98-99—Defeated San Jose in Western Conference quarterfinals; defeated Detroit in Western Conference semifinals; lost to Dallas in Western Conference finals.

99-00—Defeated Phoenix in Western Conference quarterfinals; defeated Detroit in Western Conference semifinals; lost to Dallas in Western Conference finals.

00-01—Defeated Vancouver in Western Conference quarterfinals; defeated Los Angeles in Western Conference semifinals; defeated St. Louis in Western Conference finals; defeated New Jersey in Stanley Cup finals.

PERSONAL: Born December 17, 1951, in Edmonton.
COLLEGE: University of Alberta.

HEAD COACHING RECORD

BACKGROUND: Assistant coach, Philadelphia Flyers (1990-91 through 1992-93).
HONORS: Won Can.HL Coach of the Year Award (1989-90). ... Named NHL Coach of the Year by THE SPORTING NEWS (1996-97).

				REGULAR SEASON						PLAYOFFS		
Season Team	League	W	L	T	RT	Pct.	Finish		W	L	Pct.
84-85—Kamloops	WHL	52	17	2	—	.746	1st/West Division		10	5	.667
85-86—Kamloops	WHL	49	19	4	—	.708	1st/West Division		14	2	.875
86-87—Kamloops	WHL	55	14	3	—	.785	1st/West Division		8	5	.615
87-88—Kamloops	WHL	45	26	1	—	.632	1st/West Division		12	6	.667
88-89—Kamloops	WHL	34	33	5	—	.507	3rd/West Division		8	8	.500
89-90—Kamloops	WHL	56	16	0	—	.778	1st/West Division		14	3	.824
93-94—Kalamazoo	IHL	48	26	7	—	.636	1st/Atlantic Division		1	4	.200
94-95—Kalamazoo	IHL	43	24	14	—	.617	2nd/Northern Division		10	6	.625
95-96—Michigan	IHL	19	10	11	—	.613	—		—	—	—
—Dallas	NHL	15	23	5	—	.407	6th/Central Division		—	—	—
96-97—Dallas	NHL	48	26	8	—	.634	1st/Central Division		2	4	.333
97-98—Dallas	NHL	49	22	11	—	.665	1st/Central Division		10	7	.588
98-99—Dallas	NHL	51	19	12	—	.695	1st/Pacific Division		16	7	.696
99-00—Dallas	NHL	43	29	10	6	.585	1st/Pacific Division		14	9	.609
00-01—Dallas	NHL	48	24	8	2	.650	1st/Pacific Division		4	6	.400
NHL Totals (6 years)		254	143	54	8	.623	**NHL Totals (5 years)**		46	33	.582

NOTES:
84-85—Defeated Portland in West Division semifinals; defeated New Westminster in West Division finals; lost to Prince Albert in WHL finals.
85-86—Defeated Seattle in West Division semifinals; defeated Portland in West Division finals; defeated Medicine Hat in WHL finals.
86-87—Defeated Victoria in West Division semifinals; lost to Portland in West Division finals.
87-88—Defeated New Westminster in West Division semifinals; defeated Spokane in West Division finals; lost to Medicine Hat in WHL finals.
88-89—Defeated Victoria in West Division semifinals; lost to Portland in West Division finals.
89-90—Defeated Spokane in West Division semifinals; defeated Seattle in West Division finals; defeated Lethbridge in WHL finals.
93-94—Lost to Cincinnati in Eastern Conference quarterfinals.
94-95—Defeated Chicago in Eastern Conference quarterfinals; defeated Cincinnati in Eastern Conference semifinals; lost to Kansas City in Eastern Conference finals.
95-96—Replaced Bob Gainey as head coach (January 8).
96-97—Lost to Edmonton in Western Conference quarterfinals.
97-98—Defeated San Jose in Western Conference quarterfinals; defeated Edmonton in Western Conference semifinals; lost to Detroit in Western Conference finals.
98-99—Defeated Edmonton in Western Conference quarterfinals; defeated St. Louis in Western Conference semifinals; defeated Colorado in Western Conference finals; defeated Buffalo in Stanley Cup finals.
99-00—Defeated Edmonton in Western Conference quarterfinals; defeated San Jose in Western Conference semifinals; defeated Colorado in Western Conference finals; lost to New Jersey in Stanley Cup finals.
00-01—Defeated Edmonton in Western Conference quarterfinals; lost to St. Louis in Western Conference semifinals.

PERSONAL: Born January 26, 1950, in Most, Czechoslovakia. ... Shot left.
TRANSACTIONS/CAREER NOTES: Rights traded by Winnipeg Jets to Vancouver Canucks for LW Brent Ashton and fourth-round pick (LW Tom Martin) in 1982 draft (July 15, 1981).
MISCELLANEOUS: Played center.

			REGULAR SEASON							PLAYOFFS				
Season Team	League	Gms.	G	A	Pts.	PIM	+/-	PP	SH	Gms.	G	A	Pts.	PIM
74-75—CHZ Litvinov	Czech.	...	36	42	78	...	...	...	...	—	—	—	—	—
75-76—CHZ Litvinov	Czech.					Statistics unavailable.								
76-77—CHZ Litvinov	Czech.					Statistics unavailable.								
77-78—CHZ Litvinov	Czech.					Statistics unavailable.								
78-79—Trencin-Litinov	Czech	...	17	20	37	...	...	...	...	13	4	8	12	...
79-80—CHZ Litvinov	Czech.					Statistics unavailable.								
80-81—CHZ Litvinov	Czech.	41	25	35	60	...	...	...	...	28	5	15	20	...
81-82—Vancouver	NHL	72	23	37	60	16	21	7	0	12	2	6	8	4
82-83—Vancouver	NHL	65	19	44	63	12	-3	8	0	4	1	4	5	4
NHL Totals (2 years)		137	42	81	123	28	18	15	0	16	3	10	13	8

HEAD COACHING RECORD

BACKGROUND: Head coach, Czechoslovakian National team. ... Head coach, Litvinov of Czecholslovakian League. ... Associate head coach, Pittsburgh Penguins (February 20, 2000-remainder of season).

				REGULAR SEASON						PLAYOFFS		
Season Team	League	W	L	T	RT	Pct.	Finish		W	L	Pct.
00-01—Pittsburgh	NHL	42	28	9	3	.589	3rd/Atlantic Division		9	9	.500
NHL Totals (1 year)		42	28	9	3	.589	**NHL Totals (1 year)**		9	9	.500

NOTES:
00-01—Defeated Washington in Eastern Conference quarterfinals; defeated Buffalo in Eastern Conference quarterfinals; lost to New Jersey in Eastern Conference finals.

KING, DAVE | BLUE JACKETS

PERSONAL: Born December 22, 1947, in North Battleford, Sask. ... Full Name: W. David King.
COLLEGE: University of Sasketchewan (degree in education, 1971).

HEAD COACHING RECORD

BACKGROUND: Head coach, University of Sasketchewan (1972-73 and 1978-79 through 1982-83). ... Head coach, Saskatoon Junior B Quakers (1973-74 through 1975-76). ... Vice-President/General Manager and head coach, Canadian National Teams (1983-84 through 1991-92). ... Consultant to Japanese Ice Hockey Federation and Nagano Olympic Games (1995-96 and 1996-97). ... Assistant coach, Montreal Canadiens (1997-98 and 1998-99). ... Director of European Scouting, Canadiens (1999-2000).
HONORS: Named CIAU Coach of the Year (1979-80).

Season Team	League	REGULAR SEASON W	L	T	RT	Pct.	Finish	PLAYOFFS W	L	Pct.
76-77—Saskatoon	WCHL	30	30	12	—	.500	2nd/Eastern Division	2	4	.333
77-78—Billings	WHL	32	31	9	—	.507	2nd/Central Division	7	5	.583
92-93—Calgary	NHL	43	30	11	—	.577	2nd/Smythe Division	2	4	.333
93-94—Calgary	NHL	42	29	13	—	.577	1st/Pacific Division	3	4	.429
94-95—Calgary	NHL	24	17	7	—	.573	1st/Pacific Division	3	4	.429
00-01—Columbus	NHL	28	39	9	6	.428	4th/Central Division	—	—	—
NHL Totals (4 years)		**137**	**115**	**40**	**6**	**.538**	**NHL Totals (3 years)**	**8**	**12**	**.400**

NOTES:
76-77—Lost to Lethbridge in first round of WCHL playoffs.
77-78—Defeated Medicine Hat in Central Division Final; eliminated Flin Flon in Round Robin League Semifinals; lost to New Westminster in League Finals.
92-93—Lost to Los Angeles in Smythe Division semifinals.
93-94—Lost to Vancouver in Western Conference quarterfinals.
94-95—Lost to San Jose in Western Conference quarterfinals.

LAVIOLETTE, PETER | ISLANDERS

PERSONAL: Born December 7, 1964, in Franklin, Mass. ... Shot left.
TRANSACTIONS/CAREER NOTES: Signed as non-drafted free agent by New York Rangers (August 12, 1987). ... Signed as free agent by Boston Bruins (September 8, 1992).
MISCELLANEOUS: Played defense.

Season Team	League	REGULAR SEASON Gms.	G	A	Pts.	PIM	+/-	PP	SH	PLAYOFFS Gms.	G	A	Pts.	PIM
85-86—Westfield State	NCAA	19	12	8	20	44	...	...	...	—	—	—	—	—
86-87—Indianapolis	IHL	72	10	20	30	146	...	...	...	5	0	2	2	12
87-88—U.S. national team	Int'l	56	3	22	25	...	...	...	...	—	—	—	—	—
—U.S. Olympic team	Int'l	5	0	2	2	4	...	...	...	—	—	—	—	—
—Colorado	IHL	19	2	5	7	27	...	...	...	9	3	5	8	7
88-89—Denver	IHL	57	6	19	25	120	...	...	...	3	0	0	0	4
—New York Rangers	NHL	12	0	0	0	6	2	0	0	—	—	—	—	—
89-90—Flint	IHL	62	6	18	24	82	...	...	...	4	0	0	0	4
90-91—Binghamton	AHL	65	12	24	36	72	...	...	...	10	2	7	9	30
91-92—Binghamton	AHL	50	4	10	14	50	...	...	...	11	2	7	9	9
92-93—Providence	AHL	74	13	42	55	64	...	...	...	6	0	4	4	10
93-94—U.S. national team	Int'l	56	10	25	35	63	...	...	...	—	—	—	—	—
—U.S. Olympic team	Int'l	8	1	0	1	6	...	...	...	—	—	—	—	—
—San Diego	IHL	17	3	4	7	20	...	...	...	9	3	0	3	6
94-95—Providence	AHL	65	7	23	30	84	...	...	...	13	2	8	10	17
95-96—Providence	AHL	72	9	17	26	53	...	...	...	4	1	1	2	8
96-97—Providence	AHL	41	6	8	14	40	...	...	...	—	—	—	—	—
NHL Totals (1 year)		**12**	**0**	**0**	**0**	**6**	**2**	**0**	**0**					

HEAD COACHING RECORD

BACKGROUND: Assistant coach, Boston Bruins (2000-01).
HONORS: Won Louis A. R. Pieri Memorial Trophy (1998-99).

Season Team	League	REGULAR SEASON W	L	T	RT	Pct.	Finish	PLAYOFFS W	L	Pct.
97-98—Wheeling	ECHL	37	24	9	—	.593	2nd/Northeast Division	8	7	.533
98-99—Providence	AHL	56	16	4	—	.763	1st/New England Division	15	4	.789
99-00—Providence	AHL	33	38	6	3	.468	5th/New England Division	10	4	.714

NOTES:
97-98—Defeated Dayton in preliminary round of playoffs; defeated Toledo in quarterfinals; lost to Hampton Roads in semifinals.
98-99—Defeated Worcester in conference quarterfinals of Calder Cup playoffs; defeated Hartford in conference semifinals of Calder Cup playoffs; defeated Fredericton in conference finals of Calder Cup playoffs; defeated Rochester in Calder Cup finals.
99-00—Defeated Quebec in conference quarterfinals of Calder Cup playoffs; defeated Lowell in conference semifinals of Calder Cup playoffs; lost to Hartford in conference finals of Calder Cup playoffs.

LEMAIRE, JACQUES | WILD

PERSONAL: Born September 7, 1945, in Ville LaSalle, Que. ... Full Name: Jacques Gerard Lemaire. ... Uncle of Manny Fernandez, goaltender, Minnesota Wild. ... Name pronounced luh-MAIR.
HONORS: Inducted into Hall of Fame (1984).
MISCELLANEOUS: Played center and left wing. ... Member of Stanley Cup championship teams (1968, 1969, 1971, 1973 and 1976-1979).
STATISTICAL PLATEAUS: Three-goal games: 1977-78 (1), 1978-79 (2). Total: 3.

Season Team	League	REGULAR SEASON								PLAYOFFS				
		Gms.	G	A	Pts.	PIM	+/-	PP	SH	Gms.	G	A	Pts.	PIM
62-63—Lachine	QJHL	42	41	63	104	...	...	...	...	—	—	—	—	—
63-64—Montreal Jr. Can.	OHA Jr. A	42	25	30	55	...	...	...	...	—	—	—	—	—
64-65—Montreal Jr. Can.	OHA Jr. A	56	25	47	72	...	...	...	...	—	—	—	—	—
—Quebec	AHL	1	0	0	0	0	...	...	...	—	—	—	—	—
65-66—Montreal Jr. Can.	OHA Jr. A	48	41	52	93	69	...	...	...	—	—	—	—	—
66-67—Houston	CPHL	69	19	30	49	19	...	...	...	6	0	1	1	0
67-68—Montreal	NHL	69	22	20	42	16	15	3	1	13	7	6	13	6
68-69—Montreal	NHL	75	29	34	63	29	31	5	0	14	4	2	6	6
69-70—Montreal	NHL	69	32	28	60	16	19	13	0	—	—	—	—	—
70-71—Montreal	NHL	78	28	28	56	18	0	6	0	20	9	10	19	17
71-72—Montreal	NHL	77	32	49	81	26	37	8	0	6	2	1	3	2
72-73—Montreal	NHL	77	44	51	95	16	59	9	0	17	7	13	20	2
73-74—Montreal	NHL	66	29	38	67	10	4	10	0	6	0	4	4	2
74-75—Montreal	NHL	80	36	56	92	20	25	12	0	11	5	7	12	4
75-76—Montreal	NHL	61	20	32	52	20	26	6	0	13	3	3	6	2
76-77—Montreal	NHL	75	34	41	75	22	70	5	2	14	7	12	19	6
77-78—Montreal	NHL	75	36	61	97	14	54	6	0	15	6	8	14	10
78-79—Montreal	NHL	50	24	31	55	10	9	6	1	16	11	12	23	6
NHL Totals (12 years)..........		**852**	**366**	**469**	**835**	**217**	**349**	**89**	**4**	**145**	**61**	**78**	**139**	**63**

HEAD COACHING RECORD

BACKGROUND: Assistant coach, University of Plattsburgh (1981-82). ... Assistant coach, Montreal Canadiens (October 1982-February 1983). ... Assistant to managing director/director of player personnel, Canadiens (1985-86 through 1987-88). ... Assistant to managing director of Verdun, Canadiens organization (1988-89). ... Assistant to managing director, Canadiens (1989-90 and 1990-91). ... Assistant to managing director of Fredericton, Canadiens organization (1991-92 and 1992-93). ... Served as interim coach of Montreal Canadiens while Jacques Demers was hospitalized with chest pains (March 10 and 11, 1993; team was 1-1 during that time). ... Consultant to General Manager, Canadiens (1998-99 and 1999-2000).

HONORS: Named NHL Coach of the Year by THE SPORTING NEWS (1993-94). ... Won Jack Adams Award (1993-94).

Season Team	League	REGULAR SEASON						PLAYOFFS		
		W	L	T	RT	Pct.	Finish	W	L	Pct.
79-80—Sierre	Swiss					Record unavailable.				
80-81—Sierre	Swiss					Record unavailable.				
82-83—Longueuil	QMJHL	37	29	4	—	.557	3rd/LeBel Division	8	7	.533
83-84—Montreal	NHL	7	10	0	—	.412	4th/Adams Division	9	6	.600
84-85—Montreal	NHL	41	27	12	—	.588	1st/Adams Division	6	6	.500
93-94—New Jersey	NHL	47	25	12	—	.631	2nd/Atlantic Division	11	9	.550
94-95—New Jersey	NHL	22	18	8	—	.542	2nd/Atlantic Division	16	4	.800
95-96—New Jersey	NHL	37	33	12	—	.524	5th/Atlantic Division	—	—	—
96-97—New Jersey	NHL	45	23	14	—	.634	1st/Atlantic Division	5	5	.500
97-98—New Jersey	NHL	48	23	11	—	.652	1st/Atlantic Division	2	4	.333
00-01—Minnesota	NHL	25	39	13	5	.409	5th/Northwest Division	—	—	—
NHL Totals (8 years)		**272**	**198**	**82**	**5**	**.567**	**NHL Totals (6 years)**	**49**	**34**	**.590**

NOTES:
82-83—Defeated Chicoutimi in President Cup quarterfinals; defeated Laval in President Cup semifinals; lost to Verdun in President Cup finals.
83-84—Defeated Boston in Adams Division semifinals; defeated Quebec in Adams Division finals; lost to New York Islanders in Wales Conference finals.
84-85—Defeated Boston in Adams Division semifinals; lost to Quebec in Adams Division finals.
93-94—Defeated Buffalo in Eastern Conference quarterfinals; defeated Boston in Eastern Conference semifinals; lost to New York Rangers in Eastern Conference finals.
94-95—Defeated Boston in Eastern Conference quarterfinals; defeated Pittsburgh in Eastern Conference semifinals; defeated Philadelphia in Eastern Conference finals; defeated Detroit in Stanley Cup finals.
96-97—Defeated Montreal in Eastern Conference quarterfinals; lost to New York Rangers in Eastern Conference semifinals.
97-98—Lost to Ottawa in Eastern Conference quarterfinals.

LOW, RON   RANGERS

PERSONAL: Born June 21, 1950, in Birtle, Man. ... Caught right. ... Full Name: Ron Albert Low. ... Name pronounced LOH.
TRANSACTIONS/CAREER NOTES: Selected by Toronto Maple Leafs in eighth round (eighth Maple Leafs pick, 103rd overall) of NHL amateur draft (June 11, 1970). ... Claimed by Washington Capitals from Maple Leafs in expansion draft (June 12, 1974). ... Signed as free agent by Detroit Red Wings (August 17, 1977). ... Claimed by Quebec Nordiques from Red Wings in expansion draft (June 13, 1979). ... Traded by Nordiques to Edmonton Oilers for C Ron Chipperfield (March 11, 1980). ... Traded by Oilers to New Jersey Devils with D Jim McTaggart for G Lindsay Middlebrook and C Paul Miller (February 19, 1983).
HONORS: Named to CHL All-Star second team (1973-74). ... Won Tommy Ivan Trophy (1978-79). ... Named to CHL All-Star first team (1978-79).
MISCELLANEOUS: Played goaltender.

Season Team	League	REGULAR SEASON								PLAYOFFS						
		Gms.	Min.	W	L	T	GA	SO	Avg.	Gms.	Min.	W	L	GA	SO	Avg.
70-71—Jacksonville	EHL	49	2940	...	...	...	293	1	5.98	—	—	—	—	—	—	—
—Tulsa	CHL	4	192	...	...	...	11	0	3.44	—	—	—	—	—	—	—
71-72—Richmond	AHL	1	60	...	...	...	2	0	2.00	—	—	—	—	—	—	—
—Tulsa	CHL	43	2428	...	...	...	135	1	3.34	8	474	...	...	15	1	1.90
72-73—Toronto	NHL	42	2343	12	24	4	152	1	3.89	—	—	—	—	—	—	—
73-74—Tulsa	CHL	56	3213	...	...	...	169	1	3.16	—	—	—	—	—	—	—
74-75—Washington...................	NHL	48	2588	8	36	2	235	1	5.45	—	—	—	—	—	—	—
75-76—Washington...................	NHL	43	2289	6	31	2	208	0	5.45	—	—	—	—	—	—	—
76-77—Washington...................	NHL	54	2918	16	27	5	188	0	3.87	—	—	—	—	—	—	—
77-78—Detroit.........................	NHL	32	1816	9	12	9	102	1	3.37	4	240	1	3	17	0	4.25
78-79—Kansas City	CHL	63	3795	...	...	...	244	0	3.86	4	237	...	...	15	...	3.80

NHL HEAD COACHES

Season Team	League	REGULAR SEASON Gms.	Min	W	L	T	GA	SO	Avg.	PLAYOFFS Gms.	Min.	W	L	GA	SO	Avg.
79-80—Syracuse	AHL	15	905	5	9	1	70	0	4.64	—	—	—	—	—	—	—
—Quebec	NHL	15	828	5	7	2	51	0	3.70	—	—	—	—	—	—	—
—Edmonton	NHL	11	650	8	2	1	37	0	3.42	3	212	0	3	12	...	3.40
80-81—Edmonton	NHL	24	1260	5	13	3	93	0	4.43	—	—	—	—	—	—	—
—Wichita	CHL	2	120	0	2	0	10	0	5.00	—	—	—	—	—	—	—
81-82—Edmonton	NHL	29	1554	17	7	1	100	0	3.86	—	—	—	—	—	—	—
82-83—Edmonton	NHL	3	104	0	1	0	10	0	5.77	—	—	—	—	—	—	—
—New Jersey	NHL	11	608	2	7	1	41	0	4.05	—	—	—	—	—	—	—
83-84—New Jersey	NHL	44	2218	8	25	4	161	0	4.36	—	—	—	—	—	—	—
84-85—New Jersey	NHL	26	1326	6	11	4	85	1	3.85	—	—	—	—	—	—	—
NHL Totals (11 years)		382	20502	102	203	38	1463	4	4.28	7	452	1	6	29	0	3.85

HEAD COACHING RECORD

BACKGROUND: Player/assistant coach, Nova Scotia Oilers (1985-86). ... Assistant coach, Nova Scotia Oilers (1986-87). ... Assistant coach, Edmonton Oilers (August 3, 1989 through 1994-95).

Season Team	League	REGULAR SEASON W	L	T	RT	Pct.	Finish	PLAYOFFS W	L	Pct.
87-88—Nova Scotia	AHL	35	36	9	—	.494	4th/Northern Division	—	—	—
88-89—Cape Breton	AHL	27	47	6	—	.375	7th/Northern Division	—	—	—
94-95—Edmonton	NHL	5	7	1	—	.423	5th/Pacific Division	—	—	—
95-96—Edmonton	NHL	30	44	8	—	.415	5th/Pacific Division	—	—	—
96-97—Edmonton	NHL	36	37	9	—	.494	3rd/Pacific Division	5	6	.455
97-98—Edmonton	NHL	35	37	10	—	.488	3rd/Pacific Division	5	7	.417
98-99—Edmonton	NHL	33	37	12	—	.476	2nd/Northwest Division	0	4	.000
99-00—Houston	IHL	44	29	9	—	.591	3rd/West Division	6	5	.545
00-01—New York Rangers	NHL	33	43	5	1	.438	4th/Atlantic Division	—	—	—
NHL Totals (6 years)		172	205	45	1	.461	NHL Totals (3 years)	10	17	.370

NOTES:
96-97—Defeated Dallas in Western Conference quarterfinals; lost to Colorado in Western Conferenece semifinals.
97-98—Defeated Colorado in Western Conference quarterfinals; lost to Dallas in Western Conference semifinals.
98-99—Lost to Dallas in Western Conference quarterfinals.
99-00—Defeated Utah in conference semifinals; lost to Chicago in conference finals.

MACTAVISH, CRAIG — OILERS

PERSONAL: Born August 15, 1958, in London, Ont. ... Shot left.
TRANSACTIONS/CAREER NOTES: Selected by Boston Bruins in ninth round (ninth Bruins pick, 153rd overall) of NHL amateur draft (June 15, 1978). ... Involved in automobile accident in which another driver was killed (January 25, 1984); pleaded guilty to vehicular homicide, driving while under the influence of alcohol and reckless driving and sentenced to a year in prison (May 1984); missed 1984-85 season. ... Signed as free agent by Edmonton Oilers (February 1, 1985). ... Strained lower back (January 1993); missed one game. ... Suffered concussion (March 10, 1993); missed one game. ... Strained wrist (October 18, 1993); missed one game. ... Reinjured wrist (December 7, 1993); missed one game. ... Suffered whiplash (December 15, 1993); missed four games. ... Bruised foot (December 30, 1993); missed one game. ... Traded by Oilers to New York Rangers for C Todd Marchant (March 21, 1994). ... Signed as free agent by Philadelphia Flyers (July 6, 1994). ... Injured foot (January 24, 1995); missed one game. ... Bruised foot (April 14, 1995); missed two games. ... Underwent knee surgery (September 25, 1995); missed first eight games of season. ... Traded by Flyers to St. Louis Blues for C Dale Hawerchuk (March 15, 1996). ... Announced retirement (April 29, 1997).
HONORS: Named ECAC Division II Rookie of the Year (1977-78). ... Named to ECAC Division II All-Star second team (1977-78). ... Named to NCAA All-America East (College Division) first team (1978-79). ... Named ECAC Division II Player of the Year (1978-79). ... Named to ECAC Division II All-Star first team (1978-79). ... Played in NHL All-Star Game (1996).
MISCELLANEOUS: Member of Stanley Cup championship teams (1987, 1988, 1990 and 1994). ... Captain of Edmonton Oilers (1992-93 and 1993-94). ... Scored on a penalty shot (vs. Mike Vernon, December 23, 1988).
STATISTICAL PLATEAUS: Three-goal games: 1985-86 (1), 1990-91 (1). Total: 2.

Season Team	League	REGULAR SEASON Gms.	G	A	Pts.	PIM	+/-	PP	SH	PLAYOFFS Gms.	G	A	Pts.	PIM
77-78—University of Lowell	ECAC-II	24	26	19	45	...	...	...	...	—	—	—	—	—
78-79—University of Lowell	ECAC-II	31	36	52	88	...	...	...	...	—	—	—	—	—
79-80—Binghamton	AHL	34	17	15	32	20	...	...	...	—	—	—	—	—
—Boston	NHL	46	11	17	28	8	...	0	0	10	2	3	5	7
80-81—Boston	NHL	24	3	5	8	13	-1	0	0	—	—	—	—	—
—Springfield	AHL	53	19	24	43	89	...	...	...	7	5	4	9	8
81-82—Erie	AHL	72	23	32	55	37	...	...	...	—	—	—	—	—
—Boston	NHL	2	0	1	1	0	...	...	...	—	—	—	—	—
82-83—Boston	NHL	75	10	20	30	18	15	0	0	17	3	1	4	18
83-84—Boston	NHL	70	20	23	43	35	9	7	0	1	0	0	0	0
84-85—Boston	NHL				Did not play.									
85-86—Edmonton	NHL	74	23	24	47	70	17	4	1	10	4	4	8	11
86-87—Edmonton	NHL	79	20	19	39	55	9	1	4	21	1	9	10	16
87-88—Edmonton	NHL	80	15	17	32	47	-3	0	3	19	0	1	1	31
88-89—Edmonton	NHL	80	21	31	52	55	10	2	4	7	0	1	1	8
89-90—Edmonton	NHL	80	21	22	43	89	13	1	6	22	2	6	8	29
90-91—Edmonton	NHL	80	17	15	32	76	-1	2	6	18	3	3	6	20
91-92—Edmonton	NHL	80	12	18	30	98	-1	0	2	16	3	0	3	28
92-93—Edmonton	NHL	82	10	20	30	110	-16	0	3	—	—	—	—	—
93-94—Edmonton	NHL	66	16	10	26	80	-20	0	0	—	—	—	—	—
—New York Rangers	NHL	12	4	2	6	11	6	1	0	23	1	4	5	22

Season Team	League	REGULAR SEASON								PLAYOFFS				
		Gms.	G	A	Pts.	PIM	+/-	PP	SH	Gms.	G	A	Pts.	PIM
94-95—Philadelphia	NHL	45	3	9	12	23	2	0	0	15	1	4	5	20
95-96—Philadelphia	NHL	55	5	8	13	62	-3	0	0	—	—	—	—	—
—St. Louis	NHL	13	0	1	1	8	-6	0	0	13	0	2	2	6
96-97—St. Louis	NHL	50	2	5	7	33	-12	0	0	1	0	0	0	2
NHL Totals (18 years)..........		1093	213	267	480	891	...	...	...	193	20	38	58	218

HEAD COACHING RECORD

BACKGROUND: Assistant coach, New York Rangers (1997-98 and 1998-99). ... Assistant coach, Edmonton Oilers (1999-2000).

Season Team	League	REGULAR SEASON						PLAYOFFS		
		W	L	T	RT	Pct.	Finish	W	L	Pct.
00-01—Edmonton	NHL	39	28	12	3	.570	2nd/Northwest Division	2	4	.333
NHL Totals (1 year)		39	28	12	3	.570	NHL Totals (1 year)........................	2	4	.333

NOTES:
00-01—Lost to Dallas in Western Conference quarterfinals.

MARTIN, JACQUES — SENATORS

PERSONAL: Born October 1, 1952, in Rockland, Ont.

HEAD COACHING RECORD

BACKGROUND: Assistant coach, Chicago Blackhawks (1988-89 through 1989-90). ... Assistant coach, Quebec Nordiques (1990-91 through 1992-93 and 1994-95). ... Assistant coach, Colorado Avalanche (1995 through January 24, 1996).
HONORS: Won Matt Leyden Trophy (1985-86). ... Named NHL Coach of the Year by THE SPORTING NEWS (1998-99). ... Won Jack Adams Award (1998-99).

Season Team	League	REGULAR SEASON						PLAYOFFS		
		W	L	T	RT	Pct.	Finish	W	L	Pct.
85-86—Guelph	OHL	41	23	2	—	.636	2nd/Emms Division	15	3	.833
86-87—St. Louis	NHL	32	33	15	—	.494	1st/Norris Division	2	4	.333
87-88—St. Louis	NHL	34	38	8	—	.475	2nd/Norris Division	5	5	.500
93-94—Cornwall	AHL	33	36	11	—	.481	T3rd/Southern Division	4	2	.667
95-96—Ottawa	NHL	10	24	4	—	.316	6th/Northeast Division	—	—	—
96-97—Ottawa	NHL	31	36	15	—	.470	T3rd/Northeast Division	3	4	.429
97-98—Ottawa	NHL	34	33	15	—	.506	5th/Northeast Division	5	6	.455
98-99—Ottawa	NHL	44	23	15	—	.628	1st/Northeast Division	0	4	.000
99-00—Ottawa	NHL	41	30	11	2	.567	2nd/Northeast Division	2	4	.333
00-01—Ottawa	NHL	48	21	9	4	.673	1st/Northeast Division	0	4	.000
NHL Totals (8 years)		274	238	92	6	.530	NHL Totals (7 years)........................	17	31	.354

NOTES:
85-86—Defeated Sudbury in OHL quarterfinals; defeated Windsor in OHL semifinals; defeated Belleville in J. Ross Robertson Cup finals.
86-87—Lost to Toronto in Norris Division semifinals.
87-88—Defeated Chicago in Norris Division semifinals; lost to Detroit in Norris Division finals.
93-94—Defeated Hamilton in quarterfinals of Calder Cup playoffs; defeated Hershey in division finals of Calder Cup playoffs; lost to Moncton in semifinals of Calder Cup playoffs.
95-96—Replaced Rick Bowness as head coach (January 24).
96-97—Lost to Buffalo in Eastern Conference quarterfinals.
97-98—Defeated New Jersey in Eastern Conference quarterfinals; lost to Washington in Eastern Conference semifinals.
98-99—Lost to Buffalo in Eastern Conference quarterfinals.
99-00—Lost to Toronto in Eastern Conference quarterfinals.
00-01—Lost to Toronto in Eastern Conference quarterfinals.

MAURICE, PAUL — HURRICANES

PERSONAL: Born January 30, 1967, in Sault Ste. Marie, Ont.

HEAD COACHING RECORD

BACKGROUND: Assistant coach, Hartford Whalers (June 9-November 6, 1995). ... Whalers franchise moved to North Carolina and renamed Carolina Hurricanes for 1997-98 season; NHL approved move on June 25, 1997.

Season Team	League	REGULAR SEASON						PLAYOFFS		
		W	L	T	RT	Pct.	Finish	W	L	Pct.
93-94—Detroit...................................	OHL	42	20	4	—	.667	1st/West Division	11	6	.647
94-95—Detroit...................................	OHL	44	18	4	—	.697	1st/West Division	16	5	.762
95-96—Hartford	NHL	29	33	8	—	.471	4th/Northeast Division	—	—	—
96-97—Hartford	NHL	32	39	11	—	.457	5th/Northeast Division	—	—	—
97-98—Carolina................................	NHL	33	41	8	—	.451	6th/Northeast Division	—	—	—
98-99—Carolina................................	NHL	34	30	18	—	.524	1st/Southeast Division	2	4	.333
99-00—Carolina................................	NHL	37	35	10	0	.512	3rd/Southeast Division	—	—	—
00-01—Carolina................................	NHL	38	32	9	3	.538	2nd/Southeast Division	2	4	.333
NHL Totals (6 years)		203	210	64	3	.493	NHL Totals (2 years)........................	4	8	.333

NOTES:
93-94—Defeated Owen Sound in quarterfinals of OHL playoffs; defeated Sault Ste. Marie in semifinals of OHL playoffs; lost to North Bay in OHL finals.
94-95—Defeated London in first round of OHL playoffs; defeated Peterborough in second round of OHL playoffs; defeated Sudbury in third round of OHL play-offs; defeated Guelph in J. Ross Robertson Cup finals.
95-96—Replaced Paul Homgren as head coach (November 6) with club in third place.
98-99—Lost to Boston in Eastern Conference quarterfinals.
00-01—Lost to New Jersey in Eastern Conference quarterfinals.

NHL HEAD COACHES

MURRAY, ANDY   KINGS

PERSONAL: Born March 3, 1951, in Gladstone, Man.
COLLEGE: Brandon (Man.) University (degree in political science/sociology, 1972); then University of Manitoba; then Simon Fraser University (B.C.); then University of North Dakota; then St. Thomas University, Miami (master's degree in sports management, 1986).

HEAD COACHING RECORD
BACKGROUND: Assistant coach, Brandon University (1973-74). ... Head coach, Brandon Travelers of Manitoba Junior A Hockey League (1974-75 through 1977-78). ... Head coach, Brandon University (1978-79 through 1980-81). ... Served as head coach for several of Switzerland Division-A teams (1981-82 through 1987-88). ... Assistant coach, Hershey Bears of AHL (1986-87 and 1987-88). ... Assistant coach, Philadelphia Flyers (1988-89 and 1989-90). ... Assistant coach, Minnesota North Stars (1990-91 and 1991-92). ... Head coach, Lugano of Swiss League (1991-92). ... Head coach, Eisbaren Berlin of German League (1992-93). ... Assistant coach, Winnipeg Jets (1993-94 and 1994-95). ... Head coach, Canadian national team (1996-97 and 1997-98). ... Head coach, Shattuck-St. Mary's (Fairbault, Minn.) HS (1998-99). ... General Manager, Koln of German League (1998-99).

		REGULAR SEASON						PLAYOFFS		
Season Team	League	W	L	T	RT	Pct.	Finish	W	L	Pct.
99-00—Los Angeles	NHL	39	31	12	4	.549	2nd/Pacific Division	0	4	.000
00-01—Los Angeles	NHL	38	28	13	3	.563	3rd/Pacific Division	7	6	.538
NHL Totals (2 years)		77	59	25	7	.556	**NHL Totals (2 years)**	7	10	.412

NOTES:
99-00—Lost to Detroit in Western Conference quarterfinals.
00-01—Defeated Detroit in Western Conference quarterfinals; lost to Colorado in Western Conference semifinals.

MURRAY, BRYAN   MIGHTY DUCKS

PERSONAL: Born December 5, 1942, in Shawville, Que. ... Full Name: Bryan Clarence Murray. ... Brother of Terry Murray, defenseman with four NHL teams (1972-73 through 1981-82) and head coach of three NHL teams (1989-90 through 1996-97 and 1998-99 through 2000-December 10, 2000).
HIGH SCHOOL: Shawville (Que.).
COLLEGE: McGill (Que.).

HEAD COACHING RECORD
BACKGROUND: General Manager, Detroit Red Wings (1990-91 through 1993-94). ... Vice President and General Manager, Florida Panthers (1994-95 through December 28, 2000).
HONORS: Named NHL Coach of the Year by THE SPORTING NEWS (1983-84). ... Won Jack Adams Award (1983-84). ... Named NHL Executive of the Year by THE SPORTING NEWS (1995-96).

		REGULAR SEASON						PLAYOFFS		
Season Team	League	W	L	T	RT	Pct.	Finish	W	L	Pct.
78-79—Regina	WHL	18	47	7	—	.299	4th/East Division	—	—	—
79-80—Regina	WHL	47	24	1	—	.660	1st/East Division	14	4	.778
80-81—Hershey	AHL	47	24	9	—	.644	1st/Southern Division	6	4	.600
81-82—Hershey	AHL	6	7	0	—	.462	—	—	—	—
—Washington	NHL	25	28	13	—	.477	5th/Patrick Division	—	—	—
82-83—Washington	NHL	38	25	16	—	.582	3rd/Patrick Division	1	3	.250
83-84—Washington	NHL	48	27	5	—	.631	2nd/Patrick Division	4	4	.500
84-85—Washington	NHL	46	25	9	—	.631	2nd/Patrick Division	2	3	.400
85-86—Washington	NHL	50	23	7	—	.669	2nd/Patrick Division	5	4	.556
86-87—Washington	NHL	38	32	10	—	.538	2nd/Patrick Division	3	4	.429
87-88—Washington	NHL	38	33	9	—	.531	2nd/Patrick Division	7	7	.500
88-89—Washington	NHL	41	29	10	—	.575	1st/Patrick Division	2	4	.333
89-90—Washington	NHL	18	24	4	—	.435	—	—	—	—
90-91—Detroit	NHL	34	38	8	—	.475	3rd/Norris Division	3	4	.429
91-92—Detroit	NHL	43	25	12	—	.613	1st/Norris Division	4	7	.364
92-93—Detroit	NHL	47	28	9	—	.613	2nd/Norris Division	3	4	.429
97-98—Florida	NHL	17	31	11	—	.381	6th/Atlantic Division	—	—	—
NHL Totals (13 years)		483	368	123	0	.559	**NHL Totals (10 years)**	34	44	.436

NOTES:
79-80—Defeated Lethbridge in East Division semifianls; eliminated Brandon in East Division round-robin series; defeated Medicine Hat in East Division finals; defeated Victoria in Monsignor Athol Murray Memorial Trophy finals.
80-81—Defeated New Haven in Calder Cup quarterfinals; lost to Adirondack in Calder Cup semifinals.
82-83—Lost to New York Islanders in Patrick Division semifinals.
83-84—Defeated Philadelphia in Patrick Division semifinals; lost to New York Islanders in Patrick Division finals.
84-85—Lost to New York Islanders in Patrick Division semifinals.
85-86—Defeated New York Islanders in Patrick Division semifinals; lost to to New York Rangers in Patrick Division finals.
86-87—Lost to New York Islanders in Patrick Division semifinals.
87-88—Defeated Philadelphia in Patrick Division semifinals; lost to New Jersey in in Patrick Division finals.
88-89—Lost to Philadelphia in Patrick Division semifinals.
89-90—Replaced as head coach by Terry Murray (January 15).
90-91—Lost to St. Louis in Norris Division semifinals.
91-92—Defeated Minnesota in Norris Division semifinals; lost to Chicago in Norris Division finals.
92-93—Lost to Toronto in Norris Division semifinals.
97-98—Replaced Doug Maclean as head coach on an interim basis (November 24).

QUENNEVILLE, JOEL — BLUES

PERSONAL: Born September 15, 1958, in Windsor, Ont. ... Shot left. ... Full Name: Joel Norman Quenneville.

TRANSACTIONS/CAREER NOTES: Selected by Toronto Maple Leafs in second round (first Maple Leafs pick, 21st overall) of NHL amateur draft (June 15, 1978). ... Traded by Maple Leafs with RW Lanny McDonald to Colorado Rockies for RW Wilf Paiement and LW Pat Hickey (December 1979). ... Injured ribcage (March 1980). ... Underwent surgery to repair torn ligaments in ring finger of left hand (March 1980). ... Sprained ankle, twisted knee and suffered facial lacerations (January 4, 1982). ... Rockies franchise moved to New Jersey and became the Devils (June 30, 1982). ... Traded by Devils with C Steve Tambellini to Calgary Flames for C Mel Bridgman and D Phil Russell (July 1983). ... Traded by Flames with D Richie Dunn to Hartford Whalers for D Mickey Volcan and third-round pick in 1984 draft (August 1983). ... Fractured right shoulder (December 18, 1986); missed 42 games. ... Separated left shoulder (January 19, 1989); missed nine games. ... Traded by Whalers to Washington Capitals for cash (October 3, 1990). ... Signed as free agent by Maple Leafs (July 30, 1991).

HONORS: Named to OMJHL All-Star second team (1977-78). ... Named to AHL All-Star second team (1991-92).

MISCELLANEOUS: Played defense.

Season Team	League	REGULAR SEASON								PLAYOFFS				
		Gms.	G	A	Pts.	PIM	+/-	PP	SH	Gms.	G	A	Pts.	PIM
75-76—Windsor	OHA Mj. Jr.	66	15	33	48	61	...	...	...	—	—	—	—	—
76-77—Windsor	OMJHL	65	19	59	78	169	...	...	...	9	6	5	11	112
77-78—Windsor	OMJHL	66	27	76	103	114	...	...	...	6	2	3	5	17
78-79—Toronto	NHL	61	2	9	11	60	7	0	0	6	0	1	1	4
—New Brunswick	AHL	16	1	10	11	10	...	...	...	—	—	—	—	—
79-80—Toronto	NHL	32	1	4	5	24	-2	1	0	—	—	—	—	—
—Colorado Rockies	NHL	35	5	7	12	26	-21	1	0	—	—	—	—	—
80-81—Colorado Rockies	NHL	71	10	24	34	86	-24	3	0	—	—	—	—	—
81-82—Colorado Rockies	NHL	64	5	10	15	55	-29	0	0	—	—	—	—	—
82-83—New Jersey	NHL	74	5	12	17	46	-13	0	1	—	—	—	—	—
83-84—Hartford	NHL	80	5	8	13	95	-11	0	2	—	—	—	—	—
84-85—Hartford	NHL	79	6	16	22	96	-15	0	0	—	—	—	—	—
85-86—Hartford	NHL	71	5	20	25	83	20	1	0	10	0	2	2	12
86-87—Hartford	NHL	37	3	7	10	24	8	0	1	6	0	0	0	0
87-88—Hartford	NHL	77	1	8	9	44	-13	0	0	6	0	2	2	2
88-89—Hartford	NHL	69	4	7	11	32	3	0	0	4	0	3	3	4
89-90—Hartford	NHL	44	1	4	5	34	9	0	0	—	—	—	—	—
90-91—Washington	NHL	9	1	0	1	0	-8	0	0	—	—	—	—	—
—Baltimore	AHL	59	6	13	19	58	...	...	...	6	1	1	2	6
91-92—St. John's	AHL	73	7	23	30	58	...	...	...	16	0	1	1	10
NHL Totals (13 years)		803	54	136	190	705	-89	6	4	32	0	8	8	22

HEAD COACHING RECORD

BACKGROUND: Player/coach, St. John's of the AHL (1991-92). ... Assistant coach, St. John's (1992-93). ... Assistant coach, Quebec Nordiques (1994-95). ... Quebec franchise moved to Denver and renamed Colorado Avalanche for 1995-96 season. ... Assistant coach, Colorado Avalanche (1995-96 through January 5, 1997).

HONORS: Named NHL Coach of the Year by THE SPORTING NEWS (1999-2000). ... Won Jack Adams Award (1999-2000).

Season Team	League	REGULAR SEASON						PLAYOFFS		
		W	L	T	RT	Pct.	Finish	W	L	Pct.
93-94—Springfield	AHL	29	38	13	—	.444	4th/Northern Division	2	4	.333
96-97—St. Louis	NHL	18	15	7	—	.538	4th/Central Division	2	4	.333
97-98—St. Louis	NHL	45	29	8	—	.598	3rd/Central Division	6	4	.600
98-99—St. Louis	NHL	37	32	13	—	.530	2nd/Central Division	6	7	.462
99-00—St. Louis	NHL	51	20	11	1	.689	1st/Central Division	3	4	.429
00-01—St. Louis	NHL	43	22	12	5	.636	2nd/Central Division	9	5	.643
NHL Totals (5 years)		194	118	51	6	.605	**NHL Totals (5 years)**	26	24	.520

NOTES:

93-94—Lost to Adirondack in division semifinals of Calder Cup playoffs.
96-97—Replaced Mike Keenan as coach (January 6); lost to Detroit in Western Conference quarterfinals.
97-98—Defeated Los Angeles in Western Conference quarterfinals; lost to Detroit in Western Conference semifinals.
98-99—Defeated Phoenix in Western Conference quarterfinals; lost to Dallas in Western Conference semifinals.
99-00—Lost to San Jose in Western Conference quarterfinals.
00-01—Defeated San Jose in Western Conference quarterfinals; defeated Dallas in Western Conference semifinals; lost to Colorado in Western Conference finals.

QUINN, PAT — MAPLE LEAFS

PERSONAL: Born January 29, 1943, in Hamilton, Ont. ... Shot left. ... Full Name: John Brian Patrick Quinn.

HIGH SCHOOL: Central (Hamilton, Ont.).

COLLEGE: UC San Diego, then Widener University (degree in law).

TRANSACTIONS/CAREER NOTES: Loaned by Detroit Red Wings to Tulsa Oilers for 1964-65 season. ... Fractured ankle (1965). ... Selected by Montreal Canadiens from Red Wings in intraleague draft (June 1966). ... Sold to Canadiens by St. Louis Blues (June 1967). ... Traded by Blues to Toronto Maple Leafs for rights to LW Dickie Moore (March 1968). ... Selected by Vancouver Canucks in NHL expansion draft (June 1970). ... Selected by Atlanta Flames in NHL expansion draft (June 1972). ... Fractured leg (1976).

MISCELLANEOUS: Captain of Atlanta Flames (1975-76 through 1976-77). ... Played defense.

Season Team	League	REGULAR SEASON								PLAYOFFS				
		Gms.	G	A	Pts.	PIM	+/-	PP	SH	Gms.	G	A	Pts.	PIM
58-59—Hamilton Jr. A	OHA	20	0	1	1	...	...	...	...	—	—	—	—	—
59-60—Hamilton Jr. A	OHA	27	0	1	1	...	...	...	...	—	—	—	—	—
60-61—Hamilton Jr. B	OHA					Statistics unavailable.				—	—	—	—	—
61-62—						Did not play.								
62-63—Edmonton	CAHL					Statistics unavailable.								
63-64—Knoxville	EHL	72	6	31	37	217	...	...	...	3	0	0	0	9

Season Team	League	REGULAR SEASON								PLAYOFFS				
		Gms.	G	A	Pts.	PIM	+/-	PP	SH	Gms.	G	A	Pts.	PIM
64-65—Tulsa	CPHL	70	3	32	35	202	...	...	...	—	—	—	—	—
65-66—Memphis	CPHL	67	2	16	18	135	...	...	...	—	—	—	—	—
66-67—Houston	CPHL	15	0	3	3	66	...	...	...	—	—	—	—	—
—Seattle	WHL	35	1	3	4	49	...	...	...	5	0	0	0	2
67-68—Tulsa	CPHL	51	3	15	18	178	...	...	...	11	1	4	5	19
68-69—Tulsa	CHL	17	0	6	6	25	...	...	...	—	—	—	—	—
—Toronto	NHL	40	2	7	9	95	10	0	0	4	0	0	0	13
69-70—Tulsa	CHL	2	0	1	1	6	...	...	...	—	—	—	—	—
—Toronto	NHL	59	0	5	5	88	-14	0	0	—	—	—	—	—
70-71—Vancouver	NHL	76	2	11	13	149	2	0	0	—	—	—	—	—
71-72—Vancouver	NHL	57	2	3	5	63	-28	0	0	—	—	—	—	—
72-73—Atlanta	NHL	78	2	18	20	113	2	0	1	—	—	—	—	—
73-74—Atlanta	NHL	77	5	27	32	94	15	0	0	4	0	0	0	6
74-75—Atlanta	NHL	80	2	19	21	156	12	0	0	—	—	—	—	—
75-76—Atlanta	NHL	80	2	11	13	134	5	0	1	2	0	1	1	2
76-77—Atlanta	NHL	59	1	12	13	58	-7	0	0	1	0	0	0	0
NHL Totals (10 years)		606	18	113	131	950	-3	0	2	11	0	1	1	21

HEAD COACHING RECORD

BACKGROUND: Assistant coach, Philadelphia Flyers (1977-78). ... Coach, Team Canada (1986). ... President/general manager, Vancouver Canucks (1987-88 through November 4, 1997). ... Assistant general manager, Team Canada (1996 and 1997).

HONORS: Named NHL Coach of the Year by The Sporting News (1979-80 and 1991-92). ... Won Jack Adams Award (1979-80 and 1991-92).

Season Team	League	REGULAR SEASON						PLAYOFFS		
		W	L	T	RT	Pct.	Finish	W	L	Pct.
78-79—Philadelphia	NHL	18	8	4	—	.667	2nd/Patrick Division	3	5	.375
79-80—Philadelphia	NHL	48	12	20	—	.725	1st/Patrick Division	13	6	.684
80-81—Philadelphia	NHL	41	24	15	—	.606	2nd/Patrick Division	6	6	.500
81-82—Philadelphia	NHL	34	29	9	—	.535	3rd/Patrick Division	—	—	—
84-85—Los Angeles	NHL	34	32	14	—	.513	4th/Smythe Division	0	3	.000
85-86—Los Angeles	NHL	23	49	8	—	.338	5th/Smythe Division	—	—	—
86-87—Los Angeles	NHL	18	20	4	—	.476	4th/Smythe Division	—	—	—
90-91—Vancouver	NHL	9	13	4	—	.423	4th/Smythe Division	2	4	.333
91-92—Vancouver	NHL	42	26	12	—	.600	1st/Smythe Division	6	7	.462
92-93—Vancouver	NHL	46	29	9	—	.601	1st/Smythe Division	6	6	.500
93-94—Vancouver	NHL	41	40	3	—	.506	2nd/Pacific Division	15	9	.625
95-96—Vancouver	NHL	3	3	0	—	.500	3rd/Pacific Division	2	4	.333
98-99—Toronto	NHL	45	30	7	—	.591	2nd/Northeast Division	9	8	.529
99-00—Toronto	NHL	45	30	7	3	.591	1st/Northeast Division	6	6	.500
00-01—Toronto	NHL	37	29	11	5	.552	3rd/Northeast Division	7	4	.636
NHL Totals (15 years)		484	374	127	8	.556	**NHL Totals (12 years)**	75	68	.524

NOTES:

78-79—Defeated Vancouver in Stanley Cup preliminary round; lost to New York Rangers in Stanley Cup quarterfinals.

79-80—Defeated Edmonton in Stanley Cup preliminary round; defeated New York Rangers in Stanley Cup quarterfinals; defeated Minnesota in Stanley Cup semifinals; lost to New York Islanders in Stanley Cup finals.

80-81—Defeated Quebec in Stanley Cup preliminary round; lost to Calgary in Stanley Cup quarterfinals.

84-85—Lost to Edmonton in Smythe Division semifinals.

90-91—Replaced Bob McCammon as head coach (January) with club in fifth place; lost to Los Angeles in Smythe Division semifinals.

91-92—Defeated Winnipeg in Smythe Division semifinals; lost to Edmonton in Smythe Division finals.

92-93—Defeated Winnipeg in Smythe Division semifinals; lost to Los Angeles in Smythe Division finals.

93-94—Defeated Calgary in Western Conference quarterfinals; defeated Dallas in Western Conference semifinals; defeated Toronto in Western Conference finals; lost to New York Rangers in Stanley Cup finals.

95-96—Replaced Rick Ley as head coach (March 28) with club in third place; lost to Colorado in Western Conference quarterfinals.

98-99—Defeated Philadelphia in Eastern Conference quarterfinals; defeated Pittsburgh in Eastern Conference semifinals; lost to Buffalo in Eastern Conference finals.

99-00—Defeated Ottawa in Eastern Conference quarterfinals; lost to New Jersey in Eastern Conference semifinals.

00-01—Defeated Ottawa in Eastern Conference quarterfinals; lost to New Jersey in Eastern Conference semifinals.

ROBINSON, LARRY — DEVILS

PERSONAL: Born June 2, 1951, in Winchester, Ont. ... Full Name: Larry Clark Robinson. ... Brother of Moe Robinson, defenseman with Montreal Canadiens (1979-80).

TRANSACTIONS/CAREER NOTES: Selected by Montreal Canadiens in second round (fourth Canadiens pick, 20th overall) of NHL amateur draft (June 10, 1971). ... Injured knee; missed part of 1978-79 season. ... Separated right shoulder (March 6, 1980). ... Injured groin (October 1980). ... Separated left shoulder (November 14, 1980). ... Fractured nose (January 8, 1981). ... Injured left shoulder (October 1982). ... Suffered skin infection behind right knee (October 1983). ... Hyperextended left elbow (March 1985). ... Strained ligaments in right ankle (March 9, 1987). ... Fractured right leg (August 1987). ... Sprained right wrist (December 1987). ... Hyperextended knee (May 23, 1989). ... Signed as free agent by Los Angeles Kings (July 26, 1989). ... Suffered food poisoning (March 1990). ... Injured eye (November 26, 1991); missed two games.

HONORS: Named to COJHL All-Star first team (1969-70). ... Played in NHL All-Star Game (1974, 1976-1978, 1980, 1982, 1986, 1988, 1989 and 1992). ... Won James Norris Memorial Trophy (1976-77 and 1979-80). ... Named to THE SPORTING NEWS All-Star first team (1976-77 through 1979-80). ... Named to NHL All-Star first team (1976-77, 1978-79 and 1979-80). ... Won Conn Smythe Trophy (1977-78). ... Named to NHL All-Star second team (1977-78, 1980-81 and 1985-86). ... Named to THE SPORTING NEWS All-Star second team (1980-81, 1981-82 and 1985-86).

RECORDS: Holds NHL career playoff record for most consecutive years in playoffs—20 (1972-73 through 1991-92).

STATISTICAL PLATEAUS: Three-goal games: 1985-86 (1).

MISCELLANEOUS: Member of Stanley Cup championship team (1973, 1976-1979 and 1986). ... Played defense.

Season Team	League	REGULAR SEASON								PLAYOFFS				
		Gms.	G	A	Pts.	PIM	+/-	PP	SH	Gms.	G	A	Pts.	PIM
68-69—Brockville.............	COJHL						Statistics unavailable.							
69-70—Brockville.............	COJHL	40	22	29	51	74	...	...	...	—	—	—	—	—
70-71—Kitchener..................	OHA Jr. A	61	12	39	51	65	...	...	...	—	—	—	—	—
71-72—Nova Scotia..............	AHL	74	10	14	24	54	...	...	...	15	2	10	12	31
72-73—Nova Scotia..............	AHL	38	6	33	39	33	...	...	...	—	—	—	—	—
—Montreal	NHL	36	2	4	6	20	3	0	0	11	1	4	5	9
73-74—Montreal	NHL	78	6	20	26	66	32	0	0	6	0	1	1	26
74-75—Montreal	NHL	80	14	47	61	76	61	1	0	11	0	4	4	27
75-76—Montreal	NHL	80	10	30	40	59	50	2	0	13	3	3	6	10
76-77—Montreal	NHL	77	19	66	85	45	*120	3	0	14	2	10	12	12
77-78—Montreal	NHL	80	13	52	65	39	71	3	2	15	4	17	21	6
78-79—Montreal	NHL	67	16	45	61	33	50	4	0	16	6	9	15	8
79-80—Montreal	NHL	72	14	61	75	39	38	6	0	10	0	4	4	2
80-81—Montreal	NHL	65	12	38	50	37	46	7	0	3	0	1	1	2
81-82—Montreal	NHL	71	12	47	59	41	57	5	1	5	0	1	1	8
82-83—Montreal	NHL	71	14	49	63	33	33	6	0	3	0	0	0	2
83-84—Montreal	NHL	74	9	34	43	39	4	4	0	15	0	5	5	22
84-85—Montreal	NHL	76	14	33	47	44	32	6	0	12	3	8	11	8
85-86—Montreal	NHL	78	19	63	82	39	29	10	0	20	0	13	13	22
86-87—Montreal	NHL	70	13	37	50	44	24	6	0	17	3	17	20	6
87-88—Montreal	NHL	53	6	34	40	30	26	2	0	11	1	4	5	4
88-89—Montreal	NHL	74	4	26	30	22	23	0	0	21	2	8	10	12
89-90—Los Angeles	NHL	64	7	32	39	34	7	1	0	10	2	3	5	10
90-91—Los Angeles	NHL	62	1	22	23	16	22	0	0	12	1	4	5	15
91-92—Los Angeles	NHL	56	3	10	13	37	1	0	0	2	0	0	0	0
NHL Totals (20 years)........		1384	208	750	958	793	729	66	3	227	28	116	144	211

HEAD COACHING RECORD

BACKGROUND: Assistant coach, New Jersey Devils (1993-94, 1994-95 and 1999-March 23, 2000).

Season Team	League	REGULAR SEASON						PLAYOFFS		
		W	L	T	RT	Pct.	Finish	W	L	Pct.
95-96—Los Angeles	NHL	24	40	18	—	.402	6th/Pacific Division	—	—	—
96-97—Los Angeles	NHL	28	43	11	—	.409	6th/Pacific Division	—	—	—
97-98—Los Angeles	NHL	38	33	11	—	.530	2nd/Pacific Division	0	4	.000
98-99—Los Angeles	NHL	32	45	5	—	.421	5th/Pacific Division	—	—	—
99-00—New Jersey	NHL	4	4	0	0	.500	2nd/Atlantic Division	16	7	.696
00-01—New Jersey	NHL	48	19	12	3	.684	1st/Atlantic Division	15	10	.600
NHL Totals (6 years)		174	184	57	3	.488	NHL Totals (3 years)	31	21	.596

NOTES:

97-98—Lost to St. Louis in Western Conference quarterfinals.

99-00—Replaced Robbie Ftorek as head coach (March 23); defeated Florida in Eastern Conference quarterfinals; defeated Toronto in Eastern Conference semifinals; defeated Philadelphia in Eastern Conference finals; defeated Dallas in Stanley Cup finals.

00-01—Defeated Carolina in Eastern Conference quarterfinals; defeated Toronto in Eastern Conference semifinals; defeated Pittsburgh in Eastern Conference semifinals; lost to Colorado in Stanley Cup finals.

RUFF, LINDY   SABRES

PERSONAL: Born February 17, 1960, in Warburg, Alta. ... Shot left. ... Full Name: Lindy Cameron Ruff.

TRANSACTIONS/CAREER NOTES: Selected by Buffalo Sabres in second round (second Sabres pick, 32nd overall) of NHL entry draft (August 9, 1979). ... Fractured ankle (December 1980). ... Fractured hand (March 1983). ... Injured shoulder (January 14, 1984). ... Separated shoulder (October 26, 1984). ... Fractured left clavicle (March 5, 1986). ... Sprained shoulder (November 1988). ... Traded by Sabres to New York Rangers for fifth-round pick (D Richard Smehlik) in 1990 draft (March 7, 1989). ... Fractured rib (January 23, 1990); missed seven games. ... Fractured nose (March 21, 1990). ... Bruised left thigh (April 1990). ... Signed as free agent by Sabres (September 1991).

HONORS: Named to IHL All-Star team (1992-93).

MISCELLANEOUS: Captain of Buffalo Sabres (1986-87 through 1988-89). ... Scored on a penalty shot (vs. Mario Brunetta, November 26, 1989). ... Played defense.

Season Team	League	REGULAR SEASON								PLAYOFFS				
		Gms.	G	A	Pts.	PIM	+/-	PP	SH	Gms.	G	A	Pts.	PIM
76-77—Taber..........................	AJHL	60	13	33	46	112	...	...	...	—	—	—	—	—
—Lethbridge	WCHL	2	0	2	2	0	...	...	...	—	—	—	—	—
77-78—Lethbridge	WCHL	66	9	24	33	219	...	...	...	8	2	8	10	4
78-79—Lethbridge	WHL	24	9	18	27	108	...	...	...	6	0	1	1	0
79-80—Buffalo	NHL	63	5	14	19	38	-2	1	0	8	1	1	2	19
80-81—Buffalo	NHL	65	8	18	26	121	3	1	0	6	3	1	4	23
81-82—Buffalo	NHL	79	16	32	48	194	1	3	0	4	0	0	0	28
82-83—Buffalo	NHL	60	12	17	29	130	14	2	0	10	4	2	6	47
83-84—Buffalo	NHL	58	14	31	45	101	15	3	0	3	1	0	1	9
84-85—Buffalo	NHL	39	13	11	24	45	-1	2	0	5	2	4	6	15
85-86—Buffalo	NHL	54	20	12	32	158	8	5	1	—	—	—	—	—
86-87—Buffalo	NHL	50	6	14	20	74	-12	0	0	—	—	—	—	—
87-88—Buffalo	NHL	77	2	23	25	179	-9	0	0	6	0	2	2	23
88-89—Buffalo	NHL	63	6	11	17	86	-17	0	0	—	—	—	—	—
—New York Rangers	NHL	13	0	5	5	31	-6	0	0	2	0	0	0	17
89-90—New York Rangers	NHL	56	3	6	9	80	-10	0	0	8	0	3	3	12
90-91—New York Rangers	NHL	14	0	1	1	27	-2	0	0	—	—	—	—	—
91-92—Rochester	AHL	62	10	24	34	110	...	...	...	13	0	4	4	16
92-93—San Diego	IHL	81	10	32	42	100	...	...	...	14	1	6	7	26
NHL Totals (12 years)..........		691	105	195	300	1264	-18	17	1	52	11	13	24	193

BACKGROUND: Assistant coach, Florida Panthers (1993-94 through 1996-97).

						REGULAR SEASON		PLAYOFFS		
Season Team	League	W	L	T	RT	Pct.	Finish	W	L	Pct.
97-98—Buffalo	NHL	36	29	17	—	.543	3rd/Northeast Division	10	5	.667
98-99—Buffalo	NHL	37	28	17	—	.555	3rd/Northeast Division	14	7	.667
99-00—Buffalo	NHL	35	36	11	4	.494	3rd/Northeast Division	1	4	.200
00-01—Buffalo	NHL	46	30	5	1	.599	2nd/Northeast Division	7	6	.538
NHL Totals (4 years)		154	123	50	5	.547	NHL Totals (4 years)	32	22	.593

NOTES:

97-98—Defeated Philadelphia in Eastern Conference quarterfinals; defeated Montreal in Eastern Conference semifinals; lost to Washington in Eastern Conference finals.

98-99—Defeated Ottawa in Eastern Conference quarterfinals; defeated Boston in Eastern Conference semifinals; defeated Toronto in Eastern Conference finals; lost to Dallas in Stanley Cup finals.

99-00—Lost to Philadelphia in Eastern Conference quarterfinals.

00-01—Defeated Philadelphia in Eastern Conference quarterfinals; lost to Pittsburgh in Eastern Conference semifinals.

SUTTER, BRIAN   BLACKHAWKS

PERSONAL: Born October 7, 1956, in Viking, Alta. ... Shot left. ... Full Name: Brian Louis Allen Sutter. ... Brother of Darryl Sutter, head coach, San Jose Sharks and left winger with Chicago Blackhawks (1979-80 through 1986-87); brother of Brent Sutter, center with New York Islanders (1980-81 through 1991-92) and Blackhawks (1991-92 through 1997-98); brother of Ron Sutter, center, Calgary Flames; brother of Rich Sutter, right winger with seven NHL teams (1982-83 through 1994-95); and brother of Duane Sutter, head coach, Florida Panthers; and right winger with New York Islanders (1979-80 through 1986-87) and Blackhawks (1987-88 through 89-90); father of Shaun Sutter, center Calgary Flames organization.

TRANSACTIONS/CAREER NOTES: Selected by St. Louis Blues from in second round (second Blues pick, 20th overall) of NHL amateur draft (June 1, 1976). ... Suffered hairline fracture of pelvis (November 3, 1983). ... Fractured left shoulder (January 16, 1986). ... Reinjured left shoulder (March 8, 1986). ... Damaged left shoulder muscle (November 1986). ... Sprained ankle (November 1987). ... Retired as player and signed as head coach of Blues (June 1988).

HONORS: Played in NHL All-Star Game (1982, 1983 and 1985).

MISCELLANEOUS: Captain of St. Louis Blues (1979-80). ... Holds St. Louis Blues record for most penalty minutes (1786). ... Played left wing.

				REGULAR SEASON						PLAYOFFS				
Season Team	League	Gms.	G	A	Pts.	PIM	+/-	PP	SH	Gms.	G	A	Pts.	PIM
72-73—Red Deer	AJHL	51	27	40	67	54	...	...	...	—	—	—	—	—
73-74—Red Deer	AJHL	59	42	54	96	139	...	...	...	—	—	—	—	—
74-75—Lethbridge	WCHL	53	34	47	81	134	...	...	...	6	0	1	1	39
75-76—Lethbridge	WCHL	72	36	56	92	233	...	...	...	7	3	4	7	45
76-77—Kansas City	CHL	38	15	23	38	47	...	...	...	—	—	—	—	—
—St. Louis	NHL	35	4	10	14	82	-38	4	0	4	1	0	1	14
77-78—St. Louis	NHL	78	9	13	22	123	-2	12	0	—	—	—	—	—
78-79—St. Louis	NHL	77	41	39	80	165	3	6	0	—	—	—	—	—
79-80—St. Louis	NHL	71	23	35	58	156	-8	0	0	3	0	0	0	4
80-81—St. Louis	NHL	78	35	34	69	232	12	17	0	11	6	3	9	77
81-82—St. Louis	NHL	74	39	36	75	239	-2	14	0	10	8	6	14	49
82-83—St. Louis	NHL	79	46	30	76	254	-1	11	0	4	2	1	3	10
83-84—St. Louis	NHL	76	32	51	83	162	-6	14	2	11	1	5	6	22
84-85—St. Louis	NHL	77	37	37	74	121	11	14	0	3	2	1	3	2
85-86—St. Louis	NHL	44	19	23	42	87	-12	8	0	9	1	2	3	22
86-87—St. Louis	NHL	14	3	3	6	18	-5	3	0	—	—	—	—	—
87-88—St. Louis	NHL	76	15	22	37	147	-16	4	1	10	0	3	3	49
NHL Totals (12 years)		779	303	333	636	1786	-64	107	3	65	21	21	42	249

HEAD COACHING RECORD

BACKGROUND: Assistant coach, Team Canada (1991).

HONORS: Won Jack Adams Trophy (1990-91).

						REGULAR SEASON		PLAYOFFS		
Season Team	League	W	L	T	RT	Pct.	Finish	W	L	Pct.
88-89—St. Louis	NHL	33	35	12	—	.488	2nd/Norris Division	5	5	.500
89-90—St. Louis	NHL	37	34	9	—	.519	2nd/Norris Division	7	5	.583
90-91—St. Louis	NHL	47	22	11	—	.656	2nd/Norris Division	6	7	.462
91-92—St. Louis	NHL	36	33	11	—	.519	3rd/Norris Division	2	4	.333
92-93—Boston	NHL	51	26	7	—	.649	1st/Adams Division	0	4	.000
93-94—Boston	NHL	42	29	13	—	.577	2nd/Northeast Division	6	7	.462
94-95—Boston	NHL	27	18	3	—	.594	3rd/Northeast Division	1	4	.200
97-98—Calgary	NHL	26	41	15	—	.409	5th/Pacific Division	—	—	—
98-99—Calgary	NHL	30	40	12	—	.439	3rd/Northwest Division	—	—	—
99-00—Calgary	NHL	31	41	10	5	.439	4th/Northwest Division	—	—	—
NHL Totals (10 years)		360	319	103	5	.526	NHL Totals (7 years)	27	36	.429

NOTES:

88-89—Defeated Minnesota in Norris Division semifinals; lost to Chicago in Norris Division finals.

89-90—Defeated Toronto in Norris Division semifinals; lost to Chicago in Norris Division finals.

90-91—Defeated Detroit in Norris Division semifinals; lost to Minnesota in Norris Division finals.

91-92—Lost to Chicago in Norris Division semifinals.

92-93—Lost to Buffalo in Adams Division semifinals.

93-94—Defeated Montreal in Eastern Conference quarterfinals; lost to New Jersey in Eastern Conference semifinals.

94-95—Lost to New Jersey in Eastern Conference quarterfinals.

SUTTER, DARRYL — SHARKS

PERSONAL: Born August 19, 1958, in Viking, Alta. ... Shot left. ... Brother of Brian Sutter, head coach, Chicago Blackhawks; and left winger with St. Louis Blues (1976-77 through 1987-88); brother of Duane Sutter, head coach, Florida Panthers; and right winger with New York Islanders (1979-80 through 1986-87) and Chicago Blackhawks (1987-88 through 1989-90); brother of Rich Sutter, right winger, with seven NHL teams (1982-83 through 1994-95); brother of Ron Sutter, center, Calgary Flames; brother of Brent Sutter, center with Islanders (1980-81 through 1991-92) and Blackhawks (1991-92 through 1997-98).

TRANSACTIONS/CAREER NOTES: Selected by Chicago Blackhawks in 11th round (11th Blackhawks pick, 179th overall) of NHL amateur draft (June 1978). ... Lacerated left elbow, developed infection and underwent surgery (November 27, 1981). ... Fractured nose (November 7, 1982). ... Fractured ribs (November 1983). ... Fracture left cheekbone and injured left eye (January 2, 1984). ... Underwent arthroscopic surgery to right knee (September 1984). ... Bruised ribs (October 1984). ... Fractured left ankle (December 26, 1984). ... Separated right shoulder and underwent surgery (November 13, 1985); missed 30 games. ... Injured knee (February 1987). ... Retired as player to become assistant coach of Blackhawks (June 1987).

HONORS: Named top rookie of Japan National League (1978-79). ... Won Dudley (Red) Garrett Memorial Trophy (1979-80). ... Named to AHL All-Star second team (1979-80).

MISCELLANEOUS: Captain of Chicago Blackhawks (1982-83 through 1986-87). ... Played left wing.

			REGULAR SEASON							PLAYOFFS				
Season Team	League	Gms.	G	A	Pts.	PIM	+/-	PP	SH	Gms.	G	A	Pts.	PIM
74-75—Red Deer	AJHL	60	16	20	36	43	...	...	...	—	—	—	—	—
75-76—Red Deer	AJHL	60	43	93	136	82	...	...	...	—	—	—	—	—
76-77—Red Deer	AJHL	56	55	78	133	131	...	...	...	—	—	—	—	—
—Lethbridge	WCHL	1	1	0	1	0	...	...	...	15	3	7	10	13
77-78—Lethbridge	WCHL	68	33	48	81	119	...	...	...	8	4	9	13	2
78-79—New Brunswick	AHL	19	7	6	13	6	...	...	...	5	1	2	3	0
—Iwakura	Japan	20	28	13	41	0	...	...	...	—	—	—	—	—
79-80—New Brunswick	AHL	69	35	31	66	69	...	...	...	12	6	6	12	8
—Chicago	NHL	8	2	0	2	2	1	0	0	7	3	1	4	2
80-81—Chicago	NHL	76	40	22	62	86	-1	14	0	3	3	1	4	2
81-82—Chicago	NHL	40	23	12	35	31	0	4	3	3	0	1	1	2
82-83—Chicago	NHL	80	31	30	61	53	18	10	0	13	4	6	10	8
83-84—Chicago	NHL	59	20	20	40	44	-18	8	0	5	1	1	2	0
84-85—Chicago	NHL	49	20	18	38	12	8	2	0	15	12	7	19	12
85-86—Chicago	NHL	50	17	10	27	44	-15	3	0	3	1	2	3	0
86-87—Chicago	NHL	44	8	6	14	16	-3	1	0	2	0	0	0	0
NHL Totals (8 years)		406	161	118	279	288	-10	42	3	51	24	19	43	26

HEAD COACHING RECORD

BACKGROUND: Assistant coach, Chicago Blackhawks (1987-88). ... Associate coach, Blackhawks (1991-92). ... Special assistant to general manager, Blackhawks (1995-96 and 1996-97).

HONORS: Won Commissioner's Trophy (1989-90).

		REGULAR SEASON						PLAYOFFS		
Season Team	League	W	L	T	RT	Pct.	Finish	W	L	Pct.
88-89—Saginaw	IHL	46	26	10	—	.622	2nd/East Division	2	4	.333
89-90—Indianapolis	IHL	53	21	8	—	.695	1st/West Division	12	2	.857
90-91—Indianapolis	IHL	48	29	5	—	.616	2nd/East Division	3	4	.429
92-93—Chicago	NHL	47	25	12	—	.631	1st/Norris Division	0	4	.000
93-94—Chicago	NHL	39	36	9	—	.518	5th/Central Division	2	4	.333
94-95—Chicago	NHL	24	19	5	—	.552	3rd/Central Division	9	7	.563
97-98—San Jose	NHL	34	38	10	—	.476	4th/Pacific Division	2	4	.333
98-99—San Jose	NHL	31	33	18	—	.488	3rd/Pacific Division	2	4	.333
99-00—San Jose	NHL	35	37	10	7	.488	4th/Pacific Division	5	7	.417
00-01—San Jose	NHL	40	27	12	3	.582	2nd/Pacific Division	2	4	.333
NHL Totals (7 years)		250	215	76	10	.532	**NHL Totals (7 years)**	22	34	.393

NOTES:

88-89—Lost to Fort Wayne in quarterfinals of Turner Cup playoffs.

89-90—Defeated Peoria in quarterfinals of Turner Cup playoffs; defeated Salt Lake City in semifinals of Turner Cup playoffs; defeated Muskegon in Turner Cup finals.

90-91—Lost to Fort Wayne in quarterfinals of Turner Cup playoffs.

92-93—Lost to St. Louis in Norris Division semifinals.

93-94—Lost to Toronto in Western Conference quarterfinals.

94-95—Defeated Toronto in Western Conference quarterfinals; defeated Vancouver in Western Conference semifinals; lost to Detroit in Western Conference finals.

97-98—Lost to Dallas in Western Conference quarterfinals.

98-99—Lost to Colorado in Western Conference quarterfinals.

99-00—Defeated St. Louis in Western Conference quarterfinals; lost to Dallas in Western Conference semifinals.

00-01—Lost to St. Louis in Western Conference quarterfinals.

SUTTER, DUANE — PANTHERS

PERSONAL: Born March 16, 1960, in Viking, Alta. ... Brother of Brian Sutter, head coach, Chicago Blackhawks; and left winger with St. Louis Blues (1976-77 through 1987-88); brother of Darryl Sutter, head coach, San Jose Sharks; and right winger with New York Islanders (1979-80 through 1986-87) and Chicago Blackhawks (1987-88 through 1989-90); brother of Rich Sutter, right winger, with seven NHL teams (1982-83 through 1994-95); brother of Ron Sutter, center, Calgary Flames; brother of Brent Sutter, center with Islanders (1980-81 through 1991-92) and Blackhawks (1991-92 through 1997-98).

TRANSACTIONS/CAREER NOTES: Selected by New York Islanders in first round (first Islanders pick, 17th overall) of 1979 NHL entry draft. ... Traded by Islanders to Chicago Blackhawks for second-round pick (LW Wayne Doucet) in 1988 draft (September 9, 1987).

MISCELLANEOUS: Member of Stanley Cup championship team (1980, 1981, 1982 and 1983). ... Played right wing.

Season Team	League	REGULAR SEASON Gms.	G	A	Pts.	PIM	+/-	PP	SH	PLAYOFFS Gms.	G	A	Pts.	PIM
76-77—Red Deer	AJHL	60	9	26	35	76	...	...	...	—	—	—	—	—
77-78—Red Deer	AJHL	59	47	53	100	218	...	...	...	—	—	—	—	—
78-79—Lethbridge	WHL	71	50	75	125	212	...	...	...	19	11	12	23	43
79-80—Lethbridge	WHL	21	18	16	34	74	...	...	...	—	—	—	—	—
—New York Islanders	NHL	56	15	9	24	55	5	0	0	21	3	7	10	74
80-81—New York Islanders	NHL	23	7	11	18	26	-8	1	0	12	3	1	4	10
81-82—New York Islanders	NHL	77	18	35	53	100	23	4	0	19	5	5	10	57
82-83—New York Islanders	NHL	75	13	19	32	118	8	1	0	20	9	21	30	43
83-84—New York Islanders	NHL	78	17	23	40	94	2	2	0	21	1	3	4	48
84-85—New York Islanders	NHL	78	17	24	41	174	-12	1	0	10	0	2	2	47
85-86—New York Islanders	NHL	80	20	33	53	157	15	4	0	3	0	0	0	16
86-87—New York Islanders	NHL	80	17	169	186	1	1	0	0	14	1	0	1	26
87-88—Chicago	NHL	37	7	9	16	70	2	3	0	5	0	0	0	21
88-89—Chicago	NHL	75	7	9	16	214	-11	0	0	16	3	1	4	15
89-90—Chicago	NHL	72	4	14	18	156	-2	0	0	20	1	1	2	48
NHL Totals (11 years)		731	142	355	497	1165	23	16	...	161	26	41	67	405

HEAD COACHING RECORD

BACKGROUND: Scout, Chicago Blackhawks (1990-91 and 1991-92). ... Assistant coach, Florida Panthers (1995-96 through 1997-98). ... Pro scout, Panthers (1998-99 through December 28, 2000).

Season Team	League	REGULAR SEASON W	L	T	RT	Pct.	Finish	PLAYOFFS W	L	Pct.
92-93—Indianapolis	IHL	34	39	9	—	.470	2nd/Central Division	1	4	.200
93-94—Indianapolis	IHL	28	46	7	—	.389	3rd/Central Division	—	—	—
94-95—Indianapolis	IHL	4	5	4	—	.462	—	—	—	—
00-01—Florida	NHL	16	20	6	4	.452	3rd/Southeast Division	—	—	—
NHL Totals (1 year)		16	20	6	4	.452				

NOTES:
92-93—Lost to Atlanta in Eastern Conference quarterfinals.
94-95—Replaced as head coach.
00-01—Replaced Terry Murray as head coach (December 28).

THERRIEN, MICHEL — CANADIENS

PERSONAL: Born November 4, 1963, in Montreal.

HEAD COACHING RECORD

Season Team	League	REGULAR SEASON W	L	T	RT	Pct.	Finish	PLAYOFFS W	L	Pct.
93-94—Laval	QMJHL	49	22	1	—	.688	1st/Robert LeBel Divsion	6	4	.600
94-95—Laval	QMJHL	48	22	2	—	.681	1st/Robert LeBel Division	5	5	.500
95-96—Granby	QMJHL	56	12	2	—	.814	1st/Robert LeBel Division	12	3	.800
96-97—Granby	QMJHL	44	20	6	—	.671	2nd/Robert LeBel Division	1	3	.250
97-98—Fredericton	AHL	33	32	10	—	.507	2nd/Atlantic Division	1	3	.250
98-99—Fredericton	AHL	33	36	6	—	.480	3rd/Atlantic Division	9	6	.600
99-00—Quebec	AHL	37	34	5	4	.520	1st/Atlantic Division	0	3	.000
00-01—Quebec	AHL	12	6	1	0	.658	—	—	—	—
—Montreal	NHL	23	27	6	6	.464	5th/Northeast Division	—	—	—
NHL Totals (1 year)		23	27	6	6	.464				

NOTES:
93-94—Defeated Beauport in President Cup semifinals; lost to Chicoutimi in President Cup finals.
94-95—Defeated Shawnigan in President Cup semifinals; lost to Hull in President Cup finals.
95-96—Defeated St. Hyacinthe in President Cup quarterfinals; defeated Chicoutimi in President Cup semifinals; defeated Beauport in President Cup finals.
96-97—Lost to Val d'Or in President Cup quarterfinals.
97-98—Lost to Portland in Calder Cup quarterfinals.
98-99—Defeated St. John's in quarterfinals of Calder Cup playoffs; defeated Saint John in division semifinals of Calder Cup playoffs; lost to Providence in conference finals of Calder Cup playoffs.
99-00—Lost to Providence in quarterfinals of Calder Cup playoffs.
00-01—Replaced Alain Vigneault as head coach (November 20).

TORTORELLA, JOHN — LIGHTNING

PERSONAL: Born in Boston.
HONORS: Named to ACHL All-Star second team (1985-86).

Season Team	League	REGULAR SEASON Gms.	G	A	Pts.	PIM	+/-	PP	SH	PLAYOFFS Gms.	G	A	Pts.	PIM
79-80—University of Maine	ECAC	31	14	22	36	71	...	...	...	—	—	—	—	—
82-83—Hampton Roads	ACHL	1	1	0	1	2	...	...	...	—	—	—	—	—
—Erie	ACHL	12	2	10	12	4	...	...	...	—	—	—	—	—
83-84—Virginia-Erie	ACHL	64	25	37	62	77	...	...	...	4	1	1	2	18
84-85—Virginia	ACHL	63	33	54	87	66	...	...	...	4	3	4	7	0
85-86—Virginia	ACHL	60	37	59	96	153	...	...	...	5	1	3	4	60

HEAD COACHING RECORD

BACKGROUND: General Manager, Virginia Lancers ACHL (1986-87 and 1987-88). ... Assistant coach, New Haven Nighthawks AHL (1988-89) ... Assistant coach, Buffalo Sabres (1989-90 through 1994-95). ... Assistant coach, Phoenix Coyotes (1997-98 and 1998-99). ... Assistant coach, New York Rangers (1999-March 28, 2000). ... Assistant coach, Tampa Bay Lightning (2000-January 6, 2001).
HONORS: Named ACHL Coach of the Year (1986-87). ... Named AAHL Coach of the Year (1987-88).

Season Team	League	W	L	T	RT	Pct.	Finish	W	L	Pct.
86-87—Virginia	ACHL	36	19	3	—	.647	1st overall	8	4	.667
87-88—Virginia	AAHL	37	5	1	—	.872	1st overall	3	5	.375
95-96—Rochester	AHL	37	38	5	—	.494	3rd/Central Division	15	4	.789
96-97—Rochester	AHL	40	30	9	—	.563	1st/Empire State Division	6	4	.600
99-00—New York Rangers	NHL	0	4	0	0	.000	4th/Atlantic Division	—	—	—
00-01—Tampa Bay	NHL	12	27	1	3	.313	5th/Southeast Division	—	—	—
NHL Totals (2 years)		12	31	1	3	.284				

NOTES:

86-87—Defeated Carolina in ACHL semifinals; defeated Mohawk Valley in ACHL finals.

87-88—Defeated Johnstown in round-robin series; lost to Carolina in AAHL finals.

95-96—Defeated Adirondack in conference quarterfinals of Calder Cup playoffs; defeated Cornwall in conference semifinals of Calder Cup playoffs; defeated Syracuse in conference finals of Calder Cup playoffs; defeated Portland in Calder Cup finals.

96-97—Defeated Syracuse in conference quarterfinals of Calder Cup playoffs; lost to Albany in conference semifinals of Calder Cup playoffs.

99-00—Replaced John Muckler as head coach on interim basis (March 28).

00-01—Replaced Steve Ludzik as head coach (January 6).

TROTZ, BARRY — PREDATORS

PERSONAL: Born July 15, 1962, in Winnipeg.

Season Team	League	Gms.	G	A	Pts.	PIM	+/-	PP	SH	Gms.	G	A	Pts.	PIM
79-80—Regina	WHL	41	4	8	12	42	...	...	...	—	—	—	—	—
80-81—Regina	WHL	62	4	13	17	115	...	...	...	—	—	—	—	—
81-82—Regina	WHL	50	6	28	34	155	...	...	...	20	1	7	8	79

HEAD COACHING RECORD

BACKGROUND: Player/assistant coach, University of Manitoba (1983-84). ... Head coach/general manager, Dauphin Kings junior team (1984-85 through 1986-87). ... Assistant coach, University of Manitoba (1987-88). ... Scout, Washington Capitals (1988-89 through 1990-91). ... Assistant coach, Baltimore Skipjacks of the AHL (1991-92). ... Scout, Nashville Predators (1997-98).

HONORS: Named AHL Coach of the Year (1993-94).

Season Team	League	W	L	T	RT	Pct.	Finish	W	L	Pct.
92-93—Baltimore	AHL	28	40	12	—	.425	4th/Southern Division	3	4	.429
93-94—Portland	AHL	43	27	10	—	.600	2nd/Northern Division	12	5	.706
94-95—Portland	AHL	46	22	12	—	.650	2nd/Northern Division	3	4	.429
95-96—Portland	AHL	32	38	10	—	.463	3rd/Northern Division	14	10	.583
96-97—Portland	AHL	37	26	10	—	.575	3rd/New England Division	2	3	.400
98-99—Nashville	NHL	28	47	7	—	.384	4th/Central Division	—	—	—
99-00—Nashville	NHL	28	47	7	7	.384	4th/Central Division	—	—	—
00-01—Nashville	NHL	34	36	9	3	.487	3rd/Central Division	—	—	—
NHL Totals (3 years)		90	130	23	10	.418				

NOTES:

92-93—Lost to Binghamton in the first round of Calder Cup playoffs.

93-94—Defeated Albany in Northern Division semifinals; defeated Adirondack in Northern Division finals; defeated Moncton in Calder Cup finals.

94-95—Lost to Providence in Northern Division semifinals.

95-96—Defeated Worcester in Eastern Conference quarterfinals; defeated Springfield in Eastern Conference semifinals; defeated Saint John in Eastern Conference finals; lost to Rochester in Calder Cup finals.

96-97—Lost to Springfield in Southern Conference quarterfinals.

WILSON, RON — CAPITALS

PERSONAL: Born May 28, 1955, in Windsor, Ont. ... Shot right. ... Full Name: Ronald Lawrence Wilson. ... Son of Larry Wilson, center with Detroit Red Wings (1949-50, 1951-52 and 1952-53) and Chicago Blackhawks (1953-54 through 1955-56) and coach with Red Wings (1976-77); and nephew of Johnny Wilson, left winger with four NHL teams (1949-50 through 1961-62) and coach with four NHL teams and two WHA teams (1969-70 through 1979-80).

TRANSACTIONS/CAREER NOTES: Selected by Toronto Maple Leafs in seventh round (seventh Maple Leafs pick, 132nd overall) in NHL entry draft (June 3, 1975). ... Loaned by Davos HC to Minnesota North Stars for remainder of NHL season and playoffs (March 1985). ... Loaned by Davos HC to Minnesota North Stars for remainder of NHL season and playoffs (March 1986). ... Traded by Davos HC to Minnesota North Stars for D Craig Levie (May 1986). ... Separated shoulder (March 9, 1987).

HONORS: Named to NCAA All-America (East) first team (1974-75 and 1975-76). ... Named to ECAC All-Star team (1973-74 through 1976-77). ... Named ECAC Player of the Year (1974-75).

MISCELLANEOUS: Played defense.

Season Team	League	Gms.	G	A	Pts.	PIM	+/-	PP	SH	Gms.	G	A	Pts.	PIM
73-74—Providence College	ECAC	26	16	22	38	...	...	...	...	—	—	—	—	—
74-75—Providence College	ECAC	27	26	61	87	12	...	...	...	—	—	—	—	—
—U.S. national team	Int'l	27	5	32	37	42	...	...	...	—	—	—	—	—
75-76—Providence College	ECAC	28	19	47	66	44	...	...	...	—	—	—	—	—
76-77—Providence College	ECAC	30	17	42	59	62	...	...	...	—	—	—	—	—
—Dallas	CHL	4	1	0	1	2	...	...	...	—	—	—	—	—
77-78—Dallas	CHL	67	31	38	69	18	...	...	...	—	—	—	—	—
—Toronto	NHL	13	2	1	3	0	-5	1	0	—	—	—	—	—
78-79—New Brunswick	AHL	31	11	20	31	13	...	...	...	—	—	—	—	—
—Toronto	NHL	46	5	12	17	4	-10	4	0	3	0	1	1	0

Season Team	League	REGULAR SEASON								PLAYOFFS				
		Gms.	G	A	Pts.	PIM	+/-	PP	SH	Gms.	G	A	Pts.	PIM
79-80—New Brunswick..........	AHL	43	20	43	63	10	...	...	...	—	—	—	—	—
—Toronto......................	NHL	5	0	2	2	0	-2	0	0	3	1	2	3	2
80-81—EHC Kloten	Switzerland	38	22	23	45	...	...	...	...	—	—	—	—	—
81-82—Davos HC..................	Switzerland	38	24	23	47	...	...	...	...	—	—	—	—	—
82-83—Davos HC..................	Switzerland	36	32	32	64	...	...	...	...	—	—	—	—	—
83-84—Davos HC..................	Switzerland	36	33	39	72	...	...	...	...	—	—	—	—	—
84-85—Davos HC..................	Switzerland	38	39	62	101	...	...	...	...	—	—	—	—	—
—Minnesota..................	NHL	13	4	8	12	2	-1	0	0	9	1	6	7	4
85-86—Davos HC..................	Switzerland	27	28	41	69	...	...	...	...	—	—	—	—	—
—Minnesota..................	NHL	11	1	3	4	8	-2	1	0	5	2	4	6	4
86-87—Minnesota..................	NHL	65	12	29	41	36	-9	6	0	—	—	—	—	—
87-88—Minnesota..................	NHL	24	2	12	14	16	-4	1	0	—	—	—	—	—
NHL Totals (7 years)...........		**177**	**26**	**67**	**93**	**66**	**-33**	**13**	**0**	**20**	**4**	**13**	**17**	**8**

HEAD COACHING RECORD

BACKGROUND: Assistant coach, Milwaukee Admirals of IHL (1989-90). ... Served as interim coach of Milwaukee while Ron Lapointe was hospitalized for cancer treatments (February and March 1990; team went 9-10). ... Assistant coach, Vancouver Canucks (1990-91 through 1992-93).

Season Team	League	REGULAR SEASON						PLAYOFFS		
		W	L	T	RT	Pct.	Finish	W	L	Pct.
93-94—Anaheim..............................	NHL	33	46	5	—	.423	4th/Pacific Division	—	—	—
94-95—Anaheim..............................	NHL	16	27	5	—	.385	6th/Pacific Division	—	—	—
95-96—Anaheim..............................	NHL	35	39	8	—	.476	4th/Pacific Division	—	—	—
96-97—Anaheim..............................	NHL	36	33	13	—	.518	2nd/Pacific Division	4	7	.364
97-98—Washington...........................	NHL	40	30	12	—	.561	3rd/Atlantic Division	12	9	.571
98-99—Washington...........................	NHL	31	45	6	—	.415	3rd/Southeast Division	—	—	—
99-00—Washington...........................	NHL	44	26	12	2	.610	1st/Southeast Division	1	4	.200
00-01—Washington...........................	NHL	41	27	10	4	.590	1st/Southeast Division	2	4	.333
NHL Totals (8 years)		**276**	**273**	**71**	**6**	**.502**	**NHL Totals (4 years)**......................	**19**	**24**	**.442**

NOTES:

96-97—Defeated Phoenix in Western Conference quarterfinals; lost to Detroit in Western Conference semifinals.

97-98—Defeated Boston in Eastern Conference quarterfinals; defeated Ottawa in Eastern Conference semifinals; defeated Buffalo in Eastern Conference finals; lost to Detroit in Stanley Cup finals.

99-00—Lost to Pittsburgh in Eastern Conference quarterfinals.

00-01—Lost to Pittsburgh in Eastern Conference quarterfinals.

NHL HEAD COACHES